AMERICAN
COST
OF
LIVING
SURVEY

AMERICAN
COST
OF
LIVING
SURVEY

*A Compilation of Price Data
for Nearly 600 Goods and
Services in 443 U.S. Cities
from More Than 70 Sources*

ARSEN J. DARNAY

HELEN S. FISHER

Gale Research Inc. • DETROIT • WASHINGTON, D.C. • LONDON

Arsen J. Darnay and Helen S. Fisher, *Editors*

Editorial Code & Data Inc. Staff

Marlita A. Reddy and Susan Turner, *Contributors*
Sherae R. Fowler, *Data Entry Associate*

Gale Research Inc. Staff

Donna Wood, *Senior Editor*

Mary Beth Trimper, *Production Director*
Shanna Heilveil, *Production Assistant*

Cynthia D. Baldwin, *Art Director*
Mark Howell, *Graphic Designer*

Copyright © 1994
Gale Research Inc.
835 Penobscot Building
Detroit, MI 48226-4094

ISBN 0-8103-6400-X
ISSN 1071-099X

Printed in the United States of America

Published simultaneously in the United Kingdom
by Gale Research International Limited
(An affiliated company of Gale Research Inc.)

The trademark **ITP** is used under license.

TABLE OF CONTENTS

STATE LISTING OF CITIES

INTRODUCTION

American Cost of Living Survey (*ACLS*) is a compilation of reported prices for nearly 600 products and services in 443 cities in the United States drawn from more than 70 sources, including federal and state statistical reports, city surveys, association databases, and the periodicals literature. The large number of items and communities covered ensures that cost of living data are now available to individuals, librarians, researchers, and analysts in a single, comprehensive, easy-to-use volume.

ACLS responds to a current need. Curiosity about the state of the economy is prevalent. At the national scale, economic indicators provide an insight into the general performance of the economy. But data at the local level are difficult to obtain; the Consumer Price Index (CPI) covers major cities but does not permit comparisons *between* cities and is unavailable for smaller communities. *ACLS* provides a convenient and current bridge between the relatively accessible "global" scale and the "local" scale where, after all, everybody lives.

ACLS is, thus, an excellent tool for those seeking cost of living information and those asked to supply it (librarians, counselors, employers, analysts, and others).

Uses of *ACLS* are many and varied. For example:

• People considering a move to another part of the United States can use the book to see how the move may affect their standard of living.

• Companies relocating employees can use *ACLS* to determine appropriate levels of compensation adjustment.

• Parents deciding the costs of education for their college-bound offspring can use *ACLS* to determine living costs in other areas.

- Individuals and organizations seeking adjustments in compensation — or organizations defending the levels of compensation they offer — can both use *ACLS* as a basis for analysis.

- Investors, market researchers, developers, and government agencies, similarly, will find well-organized data in *ACLS* to fill in the often missing information on local cost of living.

Making comparisons among locations can bring interesting differences to light. For example, the price of a bottle of 100 aspirins purchased in Abilene, Texas, is $4.89; the same product in Akron, Ohio, costs $4.74. A comparison of housing costs in the same two cities shows that the average rental rate for a one-bedroom apartment in Abilene is $310 per month; in Akron, $405. Obtaining information on such differences can aid the typical consumer in making decisions on where to live, where to look for employment, where to send children to college, and where to obtain medical care.

*   *   *

The remainder of this introduction presents a discussion of subjects covered, geographical coverage, periods of coverage, methodology of compilation, the consumer price index, arrangement and format, and sources.

<h2 align="center">SUBJECTS COVERED</h2>

ACLS contains nearly 69,000 entries for the average prices of nearly 600 items in 443 cities in the United States. For each community, if available, items are arranged under the following major topics:

Alcoholic Beverages	Funerals	Personal Services
Charity	Goods and Services	Restaurant Food
Child Care	Groceries	Taxes
Clothing	Health Care	Transportation
Communications	Household Goods	Travel
Construction	Housing	Utilities
Education	Insurance and Pensions	
Energy and Fuels	Legal Assistance	
Entertainment	Personal Goods	

Under each of these major topics, price information for more specific items within the broader topic is provided. A listing of these items, alphabetically arranged within each major topic, is provided in the *List of Items Covered* which appears on p. xxix.

Energy and Fuels. Energy substances — including natural gas, gasoline, and fuel oil — are placed under *Energy and Fuels*. The notable exception is electric power: all entries dealing with electric power have been placed under *Utilities* because, in general, people associate electric power with the "local utility."

The word *energy* is used in the heading because some of the data show costs of energy (usually in million BTUs) as reported by the U.S. Department of Energy and, thus, are somewhat outside the context of household energy costs. These data, typically reported at the regional level, provide the user with additional comparative values.

Utilities. Included under the heading of *Utilities* are electric power costs as well as costs associated with cable television, water, and similar services that are regulated or franchised. The chief exception is telephone service, which is classified under *Communications*.

Costs versus Expenditures. The majority of items shown are costs as they would be experienced by people buying the product or service. Some data shown are followed by the abbreviation *exp*. These indicate measured *levels of expenditure* on the item on a per capita basis or annual basis. In some cases — e.g., the per capita expenditures of state mental health agencies on mental health care — the values shown indicate an indirect cost to the consumer borne in the form of taxes rather than actual expenditures by each person in the city. In the example just given, the actual expenditure *per patient* may be substantially higher than the value shown.

Prices for Two or More Periods. In some cases prices for the same item were obtained for more than one period, sometimes from the same sources, sometimes from different sources. In these instances, both prices are shown, with the most recent period shown last. These data may be useful in tracking changes in price over a period of time.

ACCRA Indexes. For cities that are part of the ACCRA cost of living survey (discussed more fully below), the ACCRA composite index is shown as the first item; component indices are also shown under major topics.

The ACCRA indices measure the relative price levels for consumer goods and services in the areas that participate in the ACCRA survey. The average of all participating cities is defined as 100. For each community, the community's index is read as a percentage of the average of all places. The values are always on either side of 100, e.g., 95.6 or 105.2. A value less than 100 indicates an area where the price levels are *less* than the average of all places surveyed. A value greater than 100 indicates that price levels, on average, are *higher* than average prices of all places participating in the ACCRA survey.

GEOGRAPHIC COVERAGE

ACLS provides information on 443 cities. At least one city is covered in every state. For many cities, data are reported for metropolitan areas, e.g., Allentown-Bethlehem-Easton, PA, NJ. In this case, as in others, the cities listed second or third in order are also listed alphabetically in the *Table of Contents*. Thus, Bethlehem, PA and Easton, NJ can both be found separately in alphabetical order; page references, however, are to the Allentown-Bethlehem-Easton metropolitan area.

Geographical access to the data is provided, first, in the *Table of Contents*, where the cities are arranged in alphabetical order. Immediately following the *Table of Contents* is a *List of Cities by State*. Cities are listed alphabetically by state. Cost of living data for some items are only available at the state or regional level. The methods used to "allocate" such data to cities is described below under *Methodology of Compilation*.

Coverage of cities also varies depending on the data available. For most communities, many specific items are available. For others, reporting is more sparse. However, only communities in which data were available for most major categories are included in *ACLS*.

PERIODS OF COVERAGE

ACLS coverage extends from 1988 up to and including mid-1993. The majority of entries, however, are from the period 1990 to 1993. The dates reproduced with each entry refer either to the date of collection or, if not available from the source, the date of the source itself. To the extent possible, the time periods of data collection are reported in the *List of Sources* which concludes *ACLS*.

METHODOLOGY OF COMPILATION

Geographical Selection. The editors initially selected 300 metropolitan statistical areas (MSAs) for coverage using 1990 Census of Population data. All research and data acquisition efforts were then aimed at obtaining information for at least the targeted MSAs. One major source (ACCRA — discussed more fully below) provided data for many (but not all) of the targeted MSAs. ACCRA data were also available for cities that were not on the original target list. These cities were added to the list. Similarly, the number of communities covered grew as other sources came to light. The final list of communities was edited to conform to a single naming convention. Descriptive tags (such as "MSA," "Area," and others) were removed so that the database, once sorted, would not display variants of the same city name. The final result was a "master list" of cities to be included.

Data Acquisition. Data were obtained from a variety of sources using many methods. Data arrived on paper as well as on magnetic media. Mailings, telephone contacts, special arrangements, and literature searches were used to locate and to obtain data. Sources were classified by the geographical level of the data (city, metro area, state, region) and each item within each source was assigned to one of the major topics used.

Data Allocation. Some interesting data were obtainable only at the state level (e.g. vehicle registration costs, education costs) or at the Census region level (New England, Northwest, East South Central, etc.). If alternative sources for such categories could not be located, data were "allocated" to cities on the master list by using the state of each city and the known state composition of regions as a guide.

An obvious consequence of this method is that items marked as having a regional or a state-level source are not as accurate as items that have a city-level source. This is generally true except for those items where the price is controlled at the state level, e.g., motor vehicle registration rates or tuition at state educational facilities. In the case of many cities, data from regional/state as well as city-level sources are shown side-by-side permitting some judgement on the accuracy of the regional/state items.

Accuracy of Data. In all cases, data are reported exactly as obtained from the sources. The quality and accuracy of the data are obviously variable and depend on the methods used by the sources themselves. Data assigned from state or regional sources to cities were not changed in the process of allocation in any way.

COST OF LIVING VS. CONSUMER PRICE INDEX

ACLS does **not** report on the Consumer Price Index (CPI). A detailed listing of CPI data is available from another Gale title: *Economic Indicators Handbook.*

The difference between *cost of living* and the CPI is confusing for many people. For this reason, a brief outline of the differences is provided here.

The CPI measures price change from **one period to the next within the same city** (or in the Nation). A cost of living index measures differences in the price of goods and services **between cities within the same period**. To see how prices have changed in Chicago between 1989 and 1993, one would use the CPI. To see how Chicago compares with Dallas in cost of living, one would use a cost of living index or data such as those reported in *ACLS*.

ARRANGEMENT AND FORMAT

ACLS is arranged alphabetically by city. The city name and its state appear in boldface type at the head of a column of entries. The first item under each city name is usually the composite cost of living index attributed to that city by ACCRA.

Major topics covered are sorted alphabetically and appear in boldface print and initial caps, e.g., **Alcoholic Beverages**. Specific items covered within the major topic are arranged alphabetically.

The "Per" column typically contains a measurement, such as pound, month, or hour.

The "Value" column contains average prices represented in dollars or in fractions of dollars.

The "Date" column indicates the date on which that particular price was charged for that item, or in some cases, the date of the source material consulted. In some cases, there are two prices or price ranges given for a particular item; these reflect different dates from different source materials which included some of the same products, or the difference in price between a brand-name product and a generic product.

The "Ref." (for Reference) column contains numbers to be used when consulting the *List of Sources* section of *ACLS*. Each reference number is followed by a letter representing the geographical level for which data were reported in the source materials: s = State, r = Region, c = City or Metropolitan area.

A list of abbreviations used in *ACLS* is provided below (page xxvii).

SOURCES

General. More than 70 sources were used to compile *ACLS*. These included newspapers, magazines, government reports and publications, and surveys or other reports compiled by independent governmental agencies.

In addition to governmental sources, *ACLS* cites significant databases that are copyrighted and are included by special arrangement with the originators or publishers. Some of these sources are mentioned in the acknowledgments below. One source, ACCRA, represents what might well be described as the spine of the *ACLS* database by providing a large number of items for a large number of cities.

ACCRA. A large database was obtained by a special arrangement with ACCRA, the association of applied community researchers (formerly the American Chambers of Commerce Research Association). ACCRA is an affiliate of the American Chamber of Commerce Executives and the American Economic Development Council. ACCRA produces the *ACCRA Cost of Living Index* in cooperation with chambers of commerce or analogous organizations in 300 urban areas. Participation in the survey is voluntary and communities covered also change from one reporting period to the next.

In addition to price information, ACCRA provides a weighted *cost of living index* for the city as a whole ("composite index") and for components of expenditure (e.g., "grocery items," "utilities," etc.). These indexes are also included in *ACLS*. The user should note that these indexes are specifically built to reflect "differentials for a midmanagement standard of living." The use of ACCRA indexes, therefore, should not be applied indiscriminately to other groupings, e.g., "clerical workers" or "all urban consumers".

All sources are cited by number in each entry of *ACLS* in the column headed by the abbreviation "Ref." The reference numbers can be used as a guide to the sources shown in the *List of Sources* at the end of *ACLS*. A given source may be cited more than once if several different issues of the same source were used. This applies especially to periodicals.

Source entries include comments and notes that are useful for further interpretation of the data. Wherever possible, the address and telephone number of the publisher, association, or agency have been provided as a convenience for further research.

ACKNOWLEDGMENTS

A compilation like *ACLS* would not be possible without the help of numerous people who provided information, took time to discuss the availability of data, made useful referrals, and otherwise lent the editors a helping hand.

Furthermore, each source—whether containing many entries or just a few that filled a gap—was valued and appreciated.

The editors, therefore, would like to thank all those who made a contribution. Without intending to slight any contributor, we would like to acknowledge the unusual efforts on our behalf of the following persons/organizations:

● ACCRA

● American Public Transit Association

- Bellcore, Inc.

- Mark Alan Chesner for permission to use information from his report, "Group Comprehensive Major Medical Net Claim Cost Relationships by Area"

- The Council of State Governments

- Health Insurance Association of America (HIAA)

- National Association of Insurance Commissioners

- National Association of Realtors

- National Association of Regulatory Utility Commissioners (NARUC)

- National Funeral Directors Association

- *Sales & Marketing Management*

- *Supermarket Business*

COMMENTS AND SUGGESTIONS

Comments on *ACLS* and suggestions for improvement of its usefulness, format, and coverage are always welcome. Although every effort is made to maintain accuracy, errors may occasionally occur; the editors would be grateful if these are called to their attention. Please contact:

Editors
American Cost of Living Survey
Gale Research, Inc.
835 Penobscot Building
Detroit, Michigan 48226-4094
Phone: (313) 961-2926 or (800) 347- GALE
Fax: (313) 961-6815

ABBREVIATIONS

The following abbreviations are used throughout *American Cost of Living Survey*.

<	less than	KWh	Kilowatt hour
4Q	Fourth Quarter	lb	pound
BTU	British Thermal Unit	mg	milligram
c	city, metro	mi	mile
CPI	Consumer Price Index	mil	million
cu ft	cubic foot	min	minute
doz	dozen	misc	miscellaneous
ex	except, excluding	ml	milliliter
exp	expenditures	oz	ounce
ft	foot	pk	pack
FTC	Federal Trade Commission	priv	private
gal	gallon	r	region
gov't	government	s	state
in	inch	sq ft	square foot
inc	including	yr	year

LIST OF ITEMS COVERED

This listing shows all categories of items contained in *American Cost of Living Survey*. Items are arranged in alphabetical order under topic headings as they appear in the body of the book.

Composite ACCRA index

Alcoholic Beverages

Alcoholic beverages, exp
Beer, Miller Lite or Budweiser, 12-oz containers
Liquor, J & B Scotch
Wine, Gallo Chablis blanc, 1.5 liter

Charity

Cash contributions

Child Care

Child care, on-site
Child care fee, average, center
Child care fee, average, nonregulated family day care
Child care fee, average, regulated family day care

Clothing

Clothes, females, exp
Clothes, infants, exp
Clothes, males, exp
Jeans, man's denim
Shirt, man's dress shirt
Undervest, boy's size 10-14, cotton

Communications

Long-distance telephone service, day, initial minute, 0-100 miles
Long-distance telephone service, day, additional minute, 0-100 miles
Long-distance telephone service, evenings/weekends, 0-100 mi, initial minute
Long-distance telephone service, evenings/weekends, 0-100 mi, additional minute
Newspaper subscription, daily and Sunday home delivery, large-city
Postage and stationery, exp

Telephone, exp
Telephone, flat rate
Telephone, residential, private line, rotary, unlimited calling
Telephone bill, family of four

Construction

Plywood, post-Hurricane Andrew
Plywood, pre-Hurricane Andrew

Education

Board, 4-yr private college/university
Board, 4-yr public college/university
Cooking lessons
Education, exp
Expenditures, local gov't, public elementary/secondary
Room, 4-year private college/university
Room, 4-year public college/university
Tuition, 2-year priv college/university
Tuition, 2-year public college/university
Tuition, 4-year private college/university
Tuition, 4-year public college/university, in-state

Energy and Fuels

Coal
Energy
Energy, combined forms, 1,800 sq ft heating area
Energy, exc electricity, 1,800 sq ft heating area
Energy exp/householder, 1-family unit
Energy exp/householder, less than 1,000 sq ft heating area
Energy exp/householder, 1,000-1,999 sq ft heating area
Energy exp/householder, 2,000 + sq ft heating area
Energy exp/householder, mobile home
Energy exp/householder, multifamily

Fuel oil #2
Fuel oil, other fuel, exp
Gas, cooking, 10 therms
Gas, cooking, 30 therms
Gas, cooking, 50 therms
Gas, cooking, winter, 10 therms
Gas, cooking, winter, 30 therms
Gas, cooking, winter, 50 therms
Gas, heating, winter, 100 therms
Gas, heating, winter, average use
Gas, natural
Gas, piped
Gasoline, all types
Gasoline, leaded regular
Gasoline, motor
Gasoline, regular unleaded, taxes included,
  cash, self-service
Gasoline, unleaded premium
Gasoline, unleaded premium 93 octane
Gasoline, unleaded regular

Entertainment

Bowling, evening rate
Dinner entree, restaurant
Entertainment exp
Fees and admissions
Football game expenditures, pro
Miniature golf admission
Monopoly game, Parker Brothers', No. 9
Movie
Pets, toys, playground equipment, exp
Reading, exp
Ski-lift price
Supplies, equipment, services, exp
Tennis balls, yellow, Wilson or Penn, 3
Waterpark admission

Funerals

Casket, 18-gauge steel, velvet interior
Cosmetology, hair care, etc.
Embalming
Facility use for ceremony
Hearse, local
Limousine, local
Remains to funeral home, transfer
Service charge, professional
Vault, concrete, non-metallic liner

Viewing facilities, use

Goods and Services

Goods and services
Goods and services, misc.
Miscellaneous goods and services, ACCRA
  Index
Police protection expense

Groceries

Aluminum foil, Reynolds
Apples, Red Delicious
Average annual expenditures
Babyfood, strained vegetables, lowest price
Bacon
Bacon, Oscar Mayer
Bakery products, exp
Bananas
Bananas, brand name
Barbecue sauce
Barbecue sauce, Hunt's
Beans, Green Giant, canned
Beef, exp
Beef, ground chuck steak, 80% lean
Beef, ground chuck steak, USDA choice
Beef, stew, boneless
Beverages, nonalcoholic, exp
Bologna, all beef or mixed
Bologna, Oscar Mayer
Bread, French
Bread, Mrs. Baird's white
Bread, Pepperidge Farm white
Bread, Sunbeam white
Bread, white
Bread, white, pan
Bread, whole wheat, pan
Bread, Wonder
Butter
Butter, Land O'Lakes, light salt
Butter, private label
Cabbage
Cake, Entenmann's French Crumb
Cake, Entenmann's Louisiana Crunch
Candy, M&Ms
Carrots, short trimmed and topped
Cat food, dry
Cat food, Meow Mix

Cat food, Purina Cat Chow
Celery
Cereal, Cheerios
Cereal, Corn Flakes
Cereal, Fruit Loops
Cereal, Kellogg's Corn Flakes
Cereal, Nabisco Shredded Wheat
Cereal, Quaker Oats Instant 10-pk
Cereal, Rice Krispies
Cereals and bakery products, exp
Cereals and baking products, exp
Cereals and cereal products, exp
Cheese, American
Cheese, Cheddar
Cheese, Kraft American singles
Cheese, Kraft grated Parmesan
Cherries
Chicken, fresh, whole
Chicken, fryer, whole
Chicken, Perdue
Chicken breast, bone-in
Chicken fryer breasts
Chicken legs, bone-in
Chuck roast, graded and ungraded, ex USDA
  prime and choice
Chuck roast, USDA choice, bone-in
Chuck roast, USDA choice, boneless
Cigarettes, Marlboro
Cigarettes, Winston
Coffee, 100% ground roast, 13.1-20 oz can
Coffee, 100% ground roast, all sizes
Coffee, Maxwell House
Coffee, Maxwell House auto grind
Coffee, Maxwell House regular grind
Coffee, vacuum-packed
Cookies, chocolate chip
Cookies, Nabisco Oreos
Corn, frozen
Corn Flakes, Kellogg's or Post Toasties
Corn on the cob
Crackers, Premium saltines
Crackers, soda, salted
Cucumbers
Dairy product purchases
Dairy products, exp
Dairy products, miscellaneous, exp
Diapers, Pampers disposable

Dog food, Purina Dog Chow
Eggs
Eggs, exp
Eggs, Grade A large
Eggs, Grade AA large
Eggs, private label, large, white
Eggs, private label, white
Fats and oils, exp
Fish and seafood, exp
Flour, white, all purpose
Food, exp
Food eaten at home, exp
Food eaten away from home, exp
Food prepared on out-of-town trips, exp
Food purchased away from home, exp
Foods, miscellaneous, exp
Frankfurters, all meat or all beef
Frankfurters, Deckerumbo
Frankfurters, Hebrew National
Frankfurters, Kahn's
Frankfurters, Oscar Mayer
Frankfurters, Oscar Mayer Jumbo
Frozen dinner, Healthy Choice chicken Par-
  mesan
Frozen dinner, Stouffer's Lean Cuisine glazed
  chicken
Fruits, fresh, exp
Fruits, processed, exp
Fruits and vegetables, exp
Grapefruit
Grapes, Thompson Seedless
Green beans, Green Giant, canned
Groceries, ACCRA Index
Ground beef, 100% beef
Ground beef, lean and extra lean
Ground beef or hamburger
Ground chuck, 100% beef
Ham, boneless, excluding canned
Ham, canned
Ham, canned, 3 or 5 lbs.
Ham, Krakus canned
Ham, picnic, shoulder, bone-in, smoked
Ham, rump or steak half, bone-in, smoked
Honey, jar
Honey, squeeze bear
Ice cream, prepackaged, bulk, regular
Jelly, Welch's grape

Ketchup, Heinz
Lamb and mutton, bone-in
Lasagna, Stouffer's
Laundry detergent, Tide Ultra
Lemons
Lettuce
Lettuce, iceberg
Margarine
Margarine, Blue Bonnet
Margarine, Blue Bonnet or Parkay cubes
Margarine, Fleishmann's
Margarine, Parkay sticks
Margarine, soft, tubs
Margarine, stick
Mayonnaise, Hellmann's
Meats, miscellaneous, exp
Meats, poultry, fish and eggs, exp
Milk
Milk, fresh, low fat
Milk, fresh, whole, fortified
Milk, private label, whole
Milk, whole
Milk and cream, fresh, exp
Muffins, Bay's English
Muffins, Thomas English
Onions, dry yellow
Orange juice, frozen
Orange juice, Minute Maid frozen
Orange juice, Tropicana
Oranges
Oranges, navel
Oranges, Valencia
Peaches
Peanut butter, creamy, all sizes
Peanut butter, Peter Pan creamy
Peanut butter, Skippy
Peanut butter, Skippy, creamy
Pears, Anjou
Peas, Bird's Eye frozen
Peas, Green Giant frozen
Peas, Green Giant, canned
Peas Sweet, Del Monte or Green Giant
Pizza, Ellio's cheese
Pizza, Ellio's frozen
Pizza, Ellio's frozen cheese
Pizza, Jeno's frozen cheese
Pizza, Jeno's frozen pepperoni

Pizza, Totino's cheese
Pork, exp
Pork chops, center cut, bone-in
Potato chips
Potatoes
Potatoes, white
Potatoes, white or red
Poultry, exp
Rib roast, USDA choice, bone-in
Rice, white, long grain, uncooked
Round roast, graded & ungraded, ex USDA
　prime & choice
Round roast, USDA choice, boneless
Sausage, bulk or link
Sausage, fresh, loose
Sausage, Jimmy Dean
Sausage, Jimmy Dean, 100% pork
Sausage, Jimmy Dean, bulk or link
Short ribs, bone-in
Shortening, vegetable oil blends
Shortening, vegetable, Crisco
Snacks, Doritos corn chips
Snacks, Doritos nacho cheese corn chips
Snacks, Doritos toasted corn chips
Snacks, Lays potato chips
Snacks, potato chips
Soft drink, Coca Cola
Soft drink, Cola, nondiet, cans, 72 oz 6 pk
Soft drink, Diet Coca Cola
Soft drink, Diet Pepsi
Soft drink, Pepsi
Spaghetti
Spaghetti, Creamette
Spaghetti, Luxury
Spaghetti, Mueller's
Spaghetti and macaroni
Spaghetti sauce
Spaghetti sauce, Prego
Spaghetti sauce, Ragu
Spaghetti sauce w/mushrooms, Prego
Spaghetti sauce w/mushrooms, Ragu
Steak, rib eye, USDA choice, boneless
Steak, round, graded & ungraded, ex USDA
　prime & choice
Steak, round, USDA choice, boneless
Steak, sirloin
Steak, sirloin, graded & ungraded, ex USDA

prime & choice
Steak, sirloin, USDA choice, bone-in
Steak, sirloin, USDA choice, boneless
Steak, T-bone
Steak, T-bone, USDA choice, bone-in
Strawberries, dry pint
Sugar
Sugar, cane or beet
Sugar, Imperial granulated
Sugar, regular granulated
Sugar, white
Sugar, white, 33-80 oz pk
Sugar and other sweets, exp
Tea, Lipton
Tea, Lipton tea bags
Tobacco products, exp
Tomato soup, Campbell's
Tomatoes, canned, whole
Tomatoes, field grown
Tomatoes, Hunt's or Del Monte
Tuna, Bumble Bee
Tuna, Chicken of the Sea chunk light
Tuna, chunk, light
Turkey, frozen, whole
Vegetables, fresh, exp
Vegetables, processed, exp
Yogurt, Columbo
Yogurt, natural, fruit flavored

Health Care

Analgesic, Advil
Analgesic, Aspirin, Bayer, 325 mg tablets
Appendectomy
Appendectomy, physician fee
Cardizem 60 mg tablets
Cector 250 mg tablets
Childbirth, cesarean
Childbirth, cesarean, hospital
Childbirth, cesarean, physician's fee
Childbirth, normal, hospital
Childbirth, normal, physician's fee
Cholecystectomy
Coronary bypass surgery, triple
Dentist's fee, adult teeth cleaning and periodic
  oral exam
Doctor's fee, routine exam, established patient
Drugs, exp

Gallbladder removal, physician fee
Health care, ACCRA Index
Health care, exp
Health care spending, state
Health insurance, exp
Health maintenance organization coverage,
  employee
Hernia repair, physician fee
Hospital care, semiprivate room
Hysterectomy
Indemnity plan medical coverage, employee
Insurance coverage, traditional, employee
Lumpectomy
Medical insurance premium, per employee,
  small group comprehensive
Medical plan per employee
Medical services, exp
Medical supplies, exp
Mental health care, exp
Mental health care, exp, state mental health
  agency
Mental health care, hospital psychiatric ser-
  vices, non-Federal, exp
Mental health care, mental health organization,
  multiservice, exp
Mental health care, psychiatric hospitals,
  private, exp
Mental health care, psychiatric out-patient
  clinics, freestanding, exp
Mental health care, psychiatric partial-care or-
  ganizations, freestanding, exp
Mental health care, state and county mental
  hospitals, exp
Mental health care, VA medical centers, exp
Mevacor 20 mg tablets
Nursing home, semi-private room, average
Oophorectomy
Physician fee, family practice, first-visit
Physician fee, family practice, revisit
Physician fee, general practice, first-visit
Physician fee, general practice, revisit
Physician fee, general surgeon, first-visit
Physician fee, general surgeon, revisit
Physician fee, internal medicine, first-visit
Physician fee, internal medicine, revisit
Physician fee, median, neurosurgeon, first-visit
Physician fee, median, nonsurgical specialist,

first-visit

Physician fee, median, orthopedic surgeon, first-visit

Physician fee, median, plastic surgeon, first-visit

Physician fee, median, surgical specialist, first-visit

Physician fee, median, thoracic surgeon, first-visit

Physician fee, neurosurgeon, revisit

Physician fee, nonsurgical specialist, revisit

Physician fee, obstetrics/gynecology, first-visit

Physician fee, obstetrics/gynecology, revisit

Physician fee, orthopedic surgeon, revisit

Physician fee, pediatrician, first-visit

Physician fee, pediatrician, revisit

Physician fee, plastic surgeon, revisit

Physician fee, surgical specialist, revisit

Physician fee, thoracic surgeon, revisit

Preferred provider organization medical coverage, employee

Prescription drug co-pay, Medicaid

Prostatectomy, retro-pubic

Prozac 20 mg tablets

Salpingo-oophorectomy

Substance abuse, hospital ancillary charge

Substance abuse, hospital physician charge

Substance abuse, hospital room and board

Tagamet 300 mg tablets

Vasectomy

Xanax 0.25 mg tablets

Zantac 160 mg tablets

Household Goods

Aluminum foil, Reynolds

Appliance repair, home, service call, washing machine

Appliances, major, exp

Appliances, small, exp

Appliances, small, misc. housewares, exp

Cat litter, Tidy Cat 3

Dishwashing detergent, Cascade

Equipment, misc., exp

Floor coverings, exp

Furnishings and equipment, exp

Furniture, exp

Gifts, exp

Household equipment, misc., exp

Household products, misc., exp

Household textiles, exp

Housekeeping supplies, exp

Laundry and cleaning supplies, exp

Laundry detergent, Tide liquid

Laundry detergent, Tide powder

Laundry detergent, Tide Ultra

Laundry detergent, Tide Ultra, Bold, or Cheer

Laundry supplies, Bounce fabric softener

Paper towels

Paper towels, Bounty

Pet products, cat litter

Plastic wrap

Plastic wrap, Glad Cling

Plastic wrap, Saran

Textiles, exp

Tissues, facial, Kleenex brand

Toilet tissue, Charmin

TVs, radios, sound equipment, exp

Housing

Dwellings, exp

Home, median price

House, 1,800 sq ft, 8,000 sq ft lot, new, urban, utilities

House payment, principal and interest, 25% down payment

Household expenses, misc.

Household operations, exp

Housing, ACCRA Index

Housing, exp

Lodging, exp

Maintenance, repairs, insurance, and other, exp

Mortgage interest, exp

Mortgage rate, incl. points & origination fee, 30-year fixed or adjustable rate

Rent, apartment, 1 bedroom - 1 bath

Rent, apartment, 2 bedrooms - 1 bath

Rent, apartment, 2 bedrooms - 1-1/2 to 2 baths, unfurnished, 950 sq ft, water

Rent, apartment, 2 bedrooms - 2 baths

Rent, apartment, 3 bedrooms - 2 baths

Rent, house

Rent, median

Rent, townhouse

Rental unit, 1 bedroom

Rental unit, 2 bedroom

Rental unit, 3 bedroom
Rental unit, 4 bedroom
Rental unit, apartment, 1 bedroom
Rental unit, apartment, 2 bedrooms
Rental unit, efficiency
Rental unit, house, 3-4 bedrooms and garage
Rented dwellings, exp
Residential home, new
Residential home, resale
Shelter, exp

Insurance and Pensions

Auto insurance
Auto insurance, private passenger
Insurance, life and other personal, exp
Insurance and pensions, personal, exp
Pensions and social security, exp
Vehicle insurance

Legal Assistance

Living trust, 77-year-old, $80,000 estate
Living trust, married couple with $150,000 home
  and $50,000 in stocks
Will
Will and probate, $80,000 estate
Will and probate, 77-year-old, $80,000 estate

Personal Goods

Deodorant, Ban
Deodorant, Secret Solid
Diapers, disposable
Feminine hygiene product, Kotex
Feminine hygiene product, Stayfree
Gifts, exp
Jewelry & watches, exp
Mouthwash, Listerine
Mouthwash, Scope
Products and services, exp
Razor blades, Gillette Trac II
Razors, Gillette Good News Disposables
Razors, Gillette Trac II
Shampoo, Alberto VO5
Shampoo, Pert Plus
Shave cream, Barbasol
Toothpaste
Toothpaste, Crest
Toothpaste, Crest gel

Toothpaste, Crest or Colgate

Personal Services

Dry cleaning, man's 2-piece suit
Haircare, woman's shampoo, trim and blow-dry
Haircut, man's barbershop, no styling
Services, exp

Restaurant Food

Chicken, fried, thigh and drumstick
Hamburger with cheese
Pizza, Pizza Hut or Pizza Inn, cheese, thin crust

Taxes

Property tax, exp
Tax, cigarette
Tax, gasoline
Taxes, hotel room
Taxes, sales
Taxes, state

Transportation

Auto rental, average
Auto rental, midsize car
Automobile fixed costs, midsize
Automobile operating cost, midsize
Bus fare
Bus fare, children (up to age 5), suburban net-
  work
Bus fare, park and ride, suburban network
Bus fare, regular, suburban network
Bus fare, seniors and disabled (off peak times),
  suburban network
Bus fare, up to 10 miles
Bus fare, youth (16-18), suburban network
Cable car fare
Commuter train fare (automated guideway)
Commuter train fare (inclined plane)
Driver's license fee
Ferry boat fare
Limo fare, airport-city, average
Public transit, exp
Railway fare, commuter
Railway fare, heavy rail
Railway fare, light rail
Taxi fare, airport-city, average
Tire balance, computer or spin balance, front

Transportation, ACCRA Index
Trolley fare
Vehicle expenses, misc.
Vehicle finance charges
Vehicle maintenance
Vehicle registration
Vehicle registration and license plate
Vehicle rental and license

Travel

Breakfast
Business travel
Dinner
Lodging
Lunch
Travel, business

Utilities

Cable-television, basic service
Cable-television, expanded service

Cable-television service
Cable-television service, more than one provider
Cable-television service, with no competition
Electricity
Electricity, all electric, 1,800 sq ft living area
  new home
Electricity, exp
Electricity, partial electric and other energy,
  1,800 sq ft living area new home
Electricity, residential
Electricity, winter, 250 KWh
Electricity, winter, 500 KWh
Electricity, winter, 750 KWh
Electricity, winter, 1000 KWh
Utilities, ACCRA Index
Utilities, fuels, public services, exp
Water, other public service, exp
Water, public services, exp

AMERICAN
COST
OF
LIVING
SURVEY

Abilene, TX

Item	Per	Value	Date	Ref.
Composite ACCRA index		95.20	4Q 92	4c
Alcoholic Beverages				
Beer, Miller Lite or Budweiser, 12-oz containers	6 pack	3.86	4Q 92	4c
Liquor, J & B Scotch	750 ml	18.60	4Q 92	4c
Wine, Gallo Chablis blanc, 1.5 liter	bottle	4.31	4Q 92	4c
Child Care				
Child care fee, average, center	hour	1.29	90	65r
Child care fee, average, nonregulated family day care	hour	0.89	90	65r
Child care fee, average, regulated family day care	hour	1.32	90	65r
Clothing				
Jeans, man's denim		23.98	4Q 92	4c
Shirt, man's dress shirt		23.80	4Q 92	4c
Undervest, boy's size 10-14, cotton	3	4.73	4Q 92	4c
Communications				
Long-distance telephone service, day, initial minute, 0-100 miles	min	0.10-0.46	91	12s
Long-distance telephone service, day, additional minute, 0-100 miles	min	0.06-0.45	91	12s
Newspaper subscription, daily and Sunday home delivery, large-city	month	11.95	4Q 92	4c
Telephone, flat rate	month	8.80	91	11c
Telephone bill, family of four	month	15.89	4Q 92	4c
Education				
Board, 4-yr private college/university	year	1883	91	22s
Board, 4-yr public college/university	year	1605	91	22s
Expenditures, local gov't, public elementary/secondary	pupil	4593	92	20s
Room, 4-year private college/university	year	1620	91	22s
Room, 4-year public college/university	year	1532	91	22s
Tuition, 2-year private college/university	year	4394	91	22s
Tuition, 2-year public college/university	year	495	91	22s
Tuition, 4-year private college/university	year	6497	91	22s
Tuition, 4-year public college/university, in-state	year	986	91	22s
Energy and Fuels				
Coal	mil Btu	1.44	90	64s
Energy	mil Btu	6.48	90	64s
Energy, combined forms, 1,800 sq ft heating area	month	118.08	4Q 92	4c
Energy, exc electricity, 1,800 sq ft heating area	month	29.66	4Q 92	4c
Energy exp/householder, 1-family unit	year	471	90	28r
Energy exp/householder, <1,000 sq ft heating area	year	384	90	28r
Energy exp/householder, 1,000-1,999 sq ft heating area	year	421	90	28r
Energy exp/householder, 2,000+ sq ft heating area	year	625	90	28r
Energy exp/householder, mobile home	year	271	90	28r
Energy exp/householder, multifamily	year	355	90	28r
Gas, natural	mil Btu	2.47	90	64s
Gas, natural	000 cu ft	5.71	91	46s
Gas, natural, exp	year	388	91	46s
Gasoline, motor	gal	1.12	4Q 92	4c
Gasoline, unleaded regular	mil Btu	9.16	90	64s

Item	Per	Value	Date	Ref.
Entertainment				
Bowling, evening rate	game	2.64	4Q 92	4c
Miniature golf admission	adult	6.18	92	1r
Miniature golf admission	child	5.14	92	1r
Monopoly game, Parker Brothers', No. 9		9.98	4Q 92	4c
Movie	admission	5.00	4Q 92	4c
Tennis balls, yellow, Wilson or Penn, 3	can	2.91	4Q 92	4c
Waterpark admission	adult	11.00	92	1r
Waterpark admission	child	8.55	92	1r
Funerals				
Casket, 18-gauge steel, velvet interior		2274.41	91	24r
Cosmetology, hair care, etc.		74.62	91	24r
Embalming		229.94	91	24r
Facility use for ceremony		176.61	91	24r
Hearse, local		116.34	91	24r
Limousine, local		72.68	91	24r
Remains to funeral home, transfer		87.72	91	24r
Service charge, professional		712.53	91	24r
Vault, concrete, non-metallic liner		750.55	91	24r
Viewing facilities, use		155.31	91	24r
Goods and Services				
ACCRA Index, Miscellaneous Goods and Services		99.60	4Q 92	4c
Groceries				
ACCRA Index, Groceries		91.30	4Q 92	4c
Apples, Red Delicious	lb	0.79	4/93	16r
Babyfood, strained vegetables, lowest price	4-4.5 oz jar	0.24	4Q 92	4c
Bacon	lb	1.75	4/93	16r
Bananas	lb	0.33	4Q 92	4c
Bananas	lb	0.42	4/93	16r
Beef, stew, boneless	lb	2.61	4/93	16r
Bologna, all beef or mixed	lb	2.24	4/93	16r
Bread, white	24 oz	0.63	4Q 92	4c
Bread, white, pan	lb	0.64	4/93	16r
Bread, whole wheat, pan	lb	0.96	4/93	16r
Cabbage	lb	0.37	4/93	16r
Carrots, short trimmed and topped	lb	0.47	4/93	16r
Celery	lb	0.64	4/93	16r
Cheese, American	lb	2.98	4/93	16r
Cheese, Cheddar	lb	3.28	4/93	16r
Cheese, Kraft grated Parmesan	8-oz canister	3.36	4Q 92	4c
Chicken, fresh, whole	lb	0.77	4/93	16r
Chicken, fryer, whole	lb	0.53	4Q 92	4c
Chicken breast, bone-in	lb	1.92	4/93	16r
Chicken legs, bone-in	lb	1.06	4/93	16r
Chuck roast, graded and ungraded, ex USDA prime and choice	lb	2.40	4/93	16r
Chuck roast, USDA choice, bone-in	lb	2.19	4/93	16r
Chuck roast, USDA choice, boneless	lb	2.38	4/93	16r
Cigarettes, Winston	carton	19.15	4Q 92	4c
Coffee, 100% ground roast, all sizes	lb	2.48	4/93	16r
Coffee, vacuum-packed	13-oz can	1.80	4Q 92	4c
Corn, frozen	10 oz	0.58	4Q 92	4c
Corn Flakes, Kellogg's or Post Toasties	18 oz	1.95	4Q 92	4c
Crackers, soda, salted	lb	1.15	4/93	16r
Eggs, Grade A large	doz	0.81	4Q 92	4c
Eggs, Grade A large	doz	0.96	4/93	16r
Flour, white, all purpose	lb	0.24	4/93	16r

Values are in dollars or fractions of dollars. In the column headed *Ref*, references are shown to sources. Each reference is followed by a letter. These refer to the geographical level for which data were reported: s = State, r = Region, and c = City or metro. The abbreviation *ex* is used to mean *except* or *excluding*; *exp* stands for expenditures. For other abbreviations and further explanations, please see the Introduction.

Abilene, TX - continued

Item	Per	Value	Date	Ref.
Groceries				
Frankfurters, all meat or all beef	lb	2.01	4/93	16r
Grapefruit	lb	0.44	4/93	16r
Grapes, Thompson Seedless	lb	1.40	4/93	16r
Ground beef, 100% beef	lb	1.58	4/93	16r
Ground beef, lean and extra lean	lb	2.09	4/93	16r
Ground beef or hamburger	lb	1.16	4Q 92	4c
Ground chuck, 100% beef	lb	1.98	4/93	16r
Ham, boneless, excluding canned	lb	2.89	4/93	16r
Ham, picnic, shoulder, bone-in, smoked	lb	1.02	4/93	16r
Ham, rump or steak half, bone-in, smoked	lb	1.48	4/93	16r
Honey, jar	8 oz	0.73-1.19	92	5r
Honey, jar	lb	1.10-1.79	92	5r
Honey, squeeze bear	12-oz	1.19-1.50	92	5r
Ice cream, prepackaged, bulk, regular	1/2 gal	2.41	4/93	16r
Lemons	lb	1.05	4/93	16r
Lettuce, iceberg	head	0.93	4Q 92	4c
Lettuce, iceberg	lb	0.81	4/93	16r
Margarine, Blue Bonnet or Parkay cubes	lb	0.52	4Q 92	4c
Margarine, stick	lb	0.88	4/93	16r
Milk, whole	1/2 gal	1.22	4Q 92	4c
Orange juice, Minute Maid frozen	12-oz can	1.29	4Q 92	4c
Oranges, navel	lb	0.55	4/93	16r
Peaches	29-oz can	1.39	4Q 92	4c
Pears, Anjou	lb	0.92	4/93	16r
Peas Sweet, Del Monte or Green Giant	15-17 oz can	0.62	4Q 92	4c
Pork chops, center cut, bone-in	lb	3.13	4/93	16r
Potato chips	16 oz	2.94	4/93	16r
Potatoes, white	lb	0.43	4/93	16r
Potatoes, white or red	10-lb sack	2.47	4Q 92	4c
Rib roast, USDA choice, bone-in	lb	4.63	4/93	16r
Rice, white, long grain, uncooked	lb	0.45	4/93	16r
Round roast, graded & ungraded, ex USDA prime & choice	lb	3.03	4/93	16r
Round roast, USDA choice, boneless	lb	3.09	4/93	16r
Sausage, fresh, loose	lb	2.08	4/93	16r
Sausage, Jimmy Dean, 100% pork	lb	2.44	4Q 92	4c
Short ribs, bone-in	lb	2.66	4/93	16r
Shortening, vegetable oil blends	lb	0.69	4/93	16r
Shortening, vegetable, Crisco	3-lb can	1.97	4Q 92	4c
Soft drink, Coca Cola	2 liter	1.33	4Q 92	4c
Spaghetti and macaroni	lb	0.81	4/93	16r
Steak, rib eye, USDA choice, boneless	lb	6.24	4/93	16r
Steak, round, graded & ungraded, ex USDA prime & choice	lb	3.31	4/93	16r
Steak, round, USDA choice, boneless	lb	3.34	4/93	16r
Steak, sirloin, graded & ungraded, ex USDA prime & choice	lb	4.19	4/93	16r
Steak, sirloin, USDA choice, boneless	lb	4.46	4/93	16r
Steak, T-bone	lb	4.75	4Q 92	4c
Steak, T-bone, USDA choice, bone-in	lb	5.25	4/93	16r
Strawberries, dry pint	12 oz	0.92	4/93	16r
Sugar, cane or beet	4 lb	1.78	4Q 92	4c
Sugar, white	lb	0.39	4/93	16r
Sugar, white, 33-80 oz pk	lb	0.38	4/93	16r
Tomatoes, field grown	lb	0.88	4/93	16r
Tomatoes, Hunt's or Del Monte	14.5-oz can	0.70	4Q 92	4c
Tuna, chunk, light	6.125-6.5 oz can	0.53	4Q 92	4c
Tuna, chunk, light	lb	1.79	4/93	16r
Turkey, frozen, whole	lb	1.04	4/93	16r
Yogurt, natural, fruit flavored	1/2 pint	0.57	4/93	16r
Health Care				
ACCRA Index, Health Care		90.70	4Q 92	4c
Analgesic, Aspirin, Bayer, 325 mg tablets	100	4.89	4Q 92	4c

Item	Per	Value	Date	Ref.
Health Care - continued				
Childbirth, cesarean, hospital		5034	91	62r
Childbirth, cesarean, physician's fee		2053	91	62r
Childbirth, normal, hospital		2712	91	62r
Childbirth, normal, physician's fee		1492	91	62r
Dentist's fee, adult teeth cleaning and periodic oral exam	visit	44.40	4Q 92	4c
Doctor's fee, routine exam, established patient	visit	27.02	4Q 92	4c
Health care spending, state	capita	2192	3/93	84s
Hospital care, semiprivate room	day	268.00	90	27c
Hospital care, semiprivate room	day	356.50	4Q 92	4c
Medical insurance premium, per employee, small group comprehensive	month	335.80	10/91	25c
Mental health care, exp	capita	20.37-28.83	90	38s
Mental health care, exp, state mental health agency	capita	22.72	90	38s
Mental health care, hospital psychiatric services, non-Federal, exp	capita	7.95	88	38s
Mental health care, mental health organization, multiservice, exp	capita	12.05	88	38s
Mental health care, psychiatric hospitals, private, exp	capita	37.78	88	38s
Mental health care, psychiatric out-patient clinics, freestanding, exp	capita	0.43	88	38s
Mental health care, state and county mental hospitals, exp	capita	12.54	88	38s
Mental health care, VA medical centers, exp	capita	5.35	88	38s
Physician fee, family practice, first-visit		75.00	91	62r
Physician fee, family practice, revisit		34.00	91	62r
Physician fee, general practice, first-visit		61.00	91	62r
Physician fee, general practice, revisit		32.00	91	62r
Physician fee, general surgeon, first-visit		64.00	91	62r
Physician fee, general surgeon, revisit		40.00	91	62r
Physician fee, internal medicine, first-visit		98.00	91	62r
Physician fee, internal medicine, revisit		40.00	91	62r
Physician fee, median, neurosurgeon, first-visit		130.00	91	62r
Physician fee, median, nonsurgical specialist, first-visit		95.00	91	62r
Physician fee, median, orthopedic surgeon, first-visit		91.00	91	62r
Physician fee, median, plastic surgeon, first-visit		66.00	91	62r
Physician fee, median, surgical specialist, first-visit		62.00	91	62r
Physician fee, neurosurgeon, revisit		50.00	91	62r
Physician fee, nonsurgical specialist, revisit		40.00	91	62r
Physician fee, obstetrics/gynecology, first-visit		64.00	91	62r
Physician fee, obstetrics/gynecology, revisit		41.00	91	62r
Physician fee, orthopedic surgeon, revisit		40.00	91	62r
Physician fee, pediatrician, first-visit		49.00	91	62r
Physician fee, pediatrician, revisit		33.00	91	62r
Physician fee, plastic surgeon, revisit		43.00	91	62r
Physician fee, surgical specialist, revisit		37.00	91	62r
Substance abuse, hospital ancillary charge	incident	3750	90	70s
Substance abuse, hospital physician charge	incident	1080	90	70s
Substance abuse, hospital room and board	incident	5320	90	70s
Household Goods				
Appliance repair, home, service call, washing machine	min labor charge	30.70	4Q 92	4c
Laundry detergent, Tide Ultra, Bold, or Cheer	42 oz	2.91	4Q 92	4c
Tissues, facial, Kleenex brand	175-count box	1.04	4Q 92	4c

Values are in dollars or fractions of dollars. In the column headed *Ref*, references are shown as sources. Each reference is followed by a letter. These refer to the geographical level for which data were reported: s=State, r=Region, and c=City or metro. The abbreviation *ex* is used to mean *except* or *excluding*; *exp* stands for expenditures. For other abbreviations and further explanations, please see the Introduction.

Abilene, TX - continued

Item	Per	Value	Date	Ref.
Housing				
ACCRA Index, Housing		86.60	4Q 92	4c
House, 1,800 sq ft, 8,000 sq ft lot, new, urban	total	95000	4Q 92	4c
House payment, principal and interest, 25% down payment	month	528	4Q 92	4c
Mortgage rate, incl. points & origination fee, 30-year fixed or adjustable rate	per-cent	8.11	4Q 92	4c
Rent, apartment, 2 bedrooms - 1-1/2 to 2 baths, unfurnished, 950 sq ft, water	month	438	4Q 92	4c
Rental unit, 1 bedroom	month	310	93	23c
Rental unit, 2 bedroom	month	365	93	23c
Rental unit, 3 bedroom	month	456	93	23c
Rental unit, 4 bedroom	month	511	93	23c
Rental unit, efficiency	month	256	93	23c
Insurance and Pensions				
Auto insurance, private passenger	year	709.79	91	63s
Personal Goods				
Shampoo, Alberto VO5	15 oz	0.99	4Q 92	4c
Toothpaste, Crest or Colgate	6-7 oz	1.91	4Q 92	4c
Personal Services				
Dry cleaning, man's 2-piece suit		5.27	4Q 92	4c
Haircare, woman's shampoo, trim and blow-dry		18.60	4Q 92	4c
Haircut, man's barbershop, no styling		6.79	4Q 92	4c
Restaurant Food				
Chicken, fried, thigh and drumstick		1.96	4Q 92	4c
Hamburger with cheese	1/4 lb	1.85	4Q 92	4c
Pizza, Pizza Hut or Pizza Inn, cheese, thin crust	12-13 in	8.54	4Q 92	4c
Taxes				
Tax, cigarette	pack	41	91	77s
Tax, gasoline	gal	20	91	77s
Taxes, state	capita	923	91	77s
Transportation				
ACCRA Index, Transportation		101.60	4Q 92	4c
Driver's license fee		16.00	12/90	43s
Tire balance, computer or spin balance, front	wheel	6.79	4Q 92	4c
Travel				
Business travel	day	193.00	4/93	89r
Utilities				
ACCRA Index, Utilities		105.50	4Q 92	4c
Electricity	mil Btu	17.09	90	64s
Electricity, partial electric and other energy, 1,800 sq ft living area new home	month	88.42	4Q 92	4c
Electricity, residential	KWh	5.92	2/93	94s
Electricity, winter, 250 KWh	month	23.70	92	55c
Electricity, winter, 500 KWh	month	40.89	92	55c
Electricity, winter, 750 KWh	month	58.09	92	55c
Electricity, winter, 1000 KWh	month	75.29	92	55c

Akron, OH

Item	Per	Value	Date	Ref.
Composite ACCRA index		94.10	4Q 92	4c
Alcoholic Beverages				
Beer, Miller Lite or Budweiser, 12-oz containers	6 pack	3.99	4Q 92	4c
Liquor, J & B Scotch	750 ml	18.25	4Q 92	4c
Wine, Gallo Chablis blanc, 1.5 liter	bottle	5.51	4Q 92	4c
Child Care				
Child care fee, average, center	hour	1.63	90	65r
Child care fee, average, nonregulated family day care	hour	1.83	90	65r
Child care fee, average, regulated family day care	hour	1.42	90	65r

Akron, OH - continued

Item	Per	Value	Date	Ref.
Clothing				
Jeans, man's denim		24.39	4Q 92	4c
Shirt, man's dress shirt		20.99	4Q 92	4c
Undervest, boy's size 10-14, cotton	3	4.15	4Q 92	4c
Communications				
Long-distance telephone service, day, initial minute, 0-100 miles	min	0.26-0.43	91	12s
Long-distance telephone service, day, additional minute, 0-100 miles	min	0.14-0.24	91	12s
Long-distance telephone service, evenings/weekends, 0-100 mi, initial minute	min	0.11-0.17	91	12s
Long-distance telephone service, evenings/weekends, 0-100 mi, additional minute	min	0.06-0.10	91	12s
Newspaper subscription, daily and Sunday home delivery, large-city	month	10.87	4Q 92	4c
Telephone bill, family of four	month	22.45	4Q 92	4c
Education				
Board, 4-yr private college/university	year	1872	91	22s
Board, 4-yr public college/university	year	1742	91	22s
Expenditures, local gov't, public elementary/secondary	pupil	5451	92	20s
Room, 4-year private college/university	year	1695	91	22s
Room, 4-year public college/university	year	2259	91	22s
Tuition, 2-year private college/university	year	6093	91	22s
Tuition, 2-year public college/university	year	1768	91	22s
Tuition, 4-year private college/university	year	8729	91	22s
Tuition, 4-year public college/university, in-state	year	2622	91	22s
Energy and Fuels				
Coal	mil Btu	1.54	90	64s
Energy	mil Btu	8.32	90	64s
Energy, combined forms, 1,800 sq ft heating area	month	126.11	4Q 92	4c
Energy, exc electricity, 1,800 sq ft heating area	month	41.88	4Q 92	4c
Energy exp/householder, 1-family unit	year	471	90	28r
Energy exp/householder, <1,000 sq ft heating area	year	430	90	28r
Energy exp/householder, 1,000-1,999 sq ft heating area	year	481	90	28r
Energy exp/householder, 2,000+ sq ft heating area	year	473	90	28r
Energy exp/householder, mobile home	year	430	90	28r
Energy exp/householder, multifamily	year	461	90	28r
Gas, natural	mil Btu	4.54	90	64s
Gas, natural	000 cu ft	5.28	91	46s
Gas, natural, exp	year	606	91	46s
Gasoline, motor	gal	1.05	4Q 92	4c
Gasoline, unleaded regular	mil Btu	9.35	90	64s
Entertainment				
Bowling, evening rate	game	1.90	4Q 92	4c
Miniature golf admission	adult	6.18	92	1r
Miniature golf admission	child	5.14	92	1r
Monopoly game, Parker Brothers', No. 9		10.59	4Q 92	4c
Movie	admission	6.00	4Q 92	4c
Tennis balls, yellow, Wilson or Penn, 3	can	2.40	4Q 92	4c
Waterpark admission	adult	11.00	92	1r
Waterpark admission	child	8.55	92	1r
Funerals				
Casket, 18-gauge steel, velvet interior		1926.72	91	24r
Cosmetology, hair care, etc.		97.64	91	24r
Embalming		249.14	91	24r
Facility use for ceremony		208.59	91	24r
Hearse, local		130.12	91	24r
Limousine, local		104.66	91	24r
Remains to funeral home, transfer		93.61	91	24r
Service charge, professional		724.62	91	24r
Vault, concrete, non-metallic liner		734.53	91	24r

Values are in dollars or fractions of dollars. In the column headed *Ref*, references are shown to sources. Each reference is followed by a letter. These refer to the geographical level for which data were reported: s = State, r = Region, and c = City or metro. The abbreviation *ex* is used to mean *except* or *excluding*; *exp* stands for expenditures. For other abbreviations and further explanations, please see the Introduction.

Akron, OH - continued

Item	Per	Value	Date	Ref.
Funerals				
Viewing facilities, use		236.06	91	24r
Goods and Services				
ACCRA Index, Miscellaneous Goods and Services		93.10	4Q 92	4c
Groceries				
ACCRA Index, Groceries		95.90	4Q 92	4c
Apples, Red Delicious	lb	0.77	4/93	16r
Babyfood, strained vegetables, lowest price	4-4.5 oz jar	0.30	4Q 92	4c
Bacon	lb	1.85	4/93	16r
Bananas	lb	0.46	4Q 92	4c
Bananas	lb	0.46	4/93	16r
Beef, stew, boneless	lb	2.53	4/93	16r
Bologna, all beef or mixed	lb	2.19	4/93	16r
Bread, white	24 oz	0.57	4Q 92	4c
Bread, white, pan	lb	0.78	4/93	16r
Butter	lb	1.50	4/93	16r
Cabbage	lb	0.40	4/93	16r
Carrots, short trimmed and topped	lb	0.45	4/93	16r
Cheese, Cheddar	lb	3.47	4/93	16r
Cheese, Kraft grated Parmesan	8-oz canister	2.80	4Q 92	4c
Chicken, fresh, whole	lb	0.84	4/93	16r
Chicken, fryer, whole	lb	0.87	4Q 92	4c
Chicken breast, bone-in	lb	1.94	4/93	16r
Chicken legs, bone-in	lb	1.02	4/93	16r
Chuck roast, graded and ungraded, ex USDA prime and choice	lb	2.43	4/93	16r
Chuck roast, USDA choice, bone-in	lb	2.11	4/93	16r
Chuck roast, USDA choice, boneless	lb	2.44	4/93	16r
Cigarettes, Winston	carton	16.54	4Q 92	4c
Coffee, 100% ground roast, all sizes	lb	2.47	4/93	16r
Coffee, vacuum-packed	13-oz can	2.31	4Q 92	4c
Cookies, chocolate chip	lb	2.73	4/93	16r
Corn, frozen	10 oz	0.67	4Q 92	4c
Corn Flakes, Kellogg's or Post Toasties	18 oz	1.95	4Q 92	4c
Eggs, Grade A large	doz	0.72	4Q 92	4c
Eggs, Grade A large	doz	0.93	4/93	16r
Flour, white, all purpose	lb	0.21	4/93	16r
Grapefruit	lb	0.45	4/93	16r
Grapes, Thompson Seedless	lb	1.46	4/93	16r
Ground beef, 100% beef	lb	1.63	4/93	16r
Ground beef, lean and extra lean	lb	2.08	4/93	16r
Ground beef or hamburger	lb	1.40	4Q 92	4c
Ground chuck, 100% beef	lb	1.94	4/93	16r
Ham, boneless, excluding canned	lb	2.21	4/93	16r
Honey, jar	8 oz	0.97-1.25	92	5r
Honey, jar	lb	1.25-2.25	92	5r
Honey, squeeze bear	12-oz	1.25-1.99	92	5r
Ice cream, prepackaged, bulk, regular	1/2 gal	2.41	4/93	16r
Lemons	lb	0.82	4/93	16r
Lettuce, iceberg	head	0.93	4Q 92	4c
Lettuce, iceberg	lb	0.83	4/93	16r
Margarine, Blue Bonnet or Parkay cubes	lb	0.58	4Q 92	4c
Margarine, stick	lb	0.77	4/93	16r
Milk, whole	1/2 gal	1.25	4Q 92	4c
Orange juice, Minute Maid frozen	12-oz can	1.42	4Q 92	4c
Oranges, navel	lb	0.50	4/93	16r
Peaches	29-oz can	1.35	4Q 92	4c
Peanut butter, creamy, all sizes	lb	1.82	4/93	16r
Pears, Anjou	lb	0.85	4/93	16r
Peas Sweet, Del Monte or Green Giant	15-17 oz can	0.59	4Q 92	4c
Pork chops, center cut, bone-in	lb	3.17	4/93	16r
Potato chips	16 oz	2.68	4/93	16r
Potatoes, white	lb	0.26	4/93	16r

Akron, OH - continued

Item	Per	Value	Date	Ref.
Groceries - continued				
Potatoes, white or red	10-lb sack	1.55	4Q 92	4c
Round roast, graded & ungraded, ex USDA prime & choice	lb	2.88	4/93	16r
Round roast, USDA choice, boneless	lb	2.96	4/93	16r
Sausage, Jimmy Dean, 100% pork	lb	2.59	4Q 92	4c
Shortening, vegetable oil blends	lb	0.79	4/93	16r
Shortening, vegetable, Crisco	3-lb can	2.26	4Q 92	4c
Soft drink, Coca Cola	2 liter	0.99	4Q 92	4c
Spaghetti and macaroni	lb	0.76	4/93	16r
Steak, rib eye, USDA choice, boneless	lb	6.29	4/93	16r
Steak, round, USDA choice, boneless	lb	3.24	4/93	16r
Steak, sirloin, graded & ungraded, ex USDA prime & choice	lb	4.00	4/93	16r
Steak, sirloin, USDA choice, bone-in	lb	3.57	4/93	16r
Steak, sirloin, USDA choice, boneless	lb	4.17	4/93	16r
Steak, T-bone	lb	5.51	4Q 92	4c
Steak, T-bone, USDA choice, bone-in	lb	5.60	4/93	16r
Strawberries, dry pint	12 oz	0.90	4/93	16r
Sugar, cane or beet	4 lb	1.38	4Q 92	4c
Sugar, white	lb	0.36	4/93	16r
Sugar, white, 33-80 oz pk	lb	0.35	4/93	16r
Tomatoes, field grown	lb	0.99	4/93	16r
Tomatoes, Hunt's or Del Monte	14.5-oz can	0.70	4Q 92	4c
Tuna, chunk, light	6.125-6.5 oz can	0.64	4Q 92	4c
Tuna, chunk, light	lb	1.76	4/93	16r
Turkey, frozen, whole	lb	0.91	4/93	16r
Health Care				
ACCRA Index, Health Care		93.90	4Q 92	4c
Analgesic, Aspirin, Bayer, 325 mg tablets	100	4.74	4Q 92	4c
Childbirth, cesarean, hospital		4688	91	62r
Childbirth, cesarean, physician's fee		2053	91	62r
Childbirth, normal, hospital		2657	91	62r
Childbirth, normal, physician's fee		1492	91	62r
Dentist's fee, adult teeth cleaning and periodic oral exam	visit	44.00	4Q 92	4c
Doctor's fee, routine exam, established patient	visit	30.90	4Q 92	4c
Hospital care, semiprivate room	day	289.96	90	27c
Hospital care, semiprivate room	day	358.80	4Q 92	4c
Medical insurance premium, per employee, small group comprehensive	month	328.50	10/91	25c
Medical plan per employee	year	3443	91	45r
Mental health care, exp	capita	37.60-53.67	90	38s
Mental health care, exp, state mental health agency	capita	40.93	90	38s
Mental health care, hospital psychiatric services, non-Federal, exp	capita	15.03	88	38s
Mental health care, mental health organization, multiservice, exp	capita	14.46	88	38s
Mental health care, psychiatric hospitals, private, exp	capita	7.93	88	38s
Mental health care, psychiatric out-patient clinics, freestanding, exp	capita	2.93	88	38s
Mental health care, psychiatric partial-care organizations, freestanding, exp	capita	0.32	88	38s
Mental health care, state and county mental hospitals, exp	capita	23.79	88	38s
Mental health care, VA medical centers, exp	capita	7.76	88	38s
Physician fee, family practice, first-visit		76.00	91	62r
Physician fee, family practice, revisit		33.00	91	62r
Physician fee, general practice, first-visit		61.00	91	62r
Physician fee, general practice, revisit		31.00	91	62r
Physician fee, general surgeon, first-visit		65.00	91	62r
Physician fee, general surgeon, revisit		35.00	91	62r
Physician fee, internal medicine, first-visit		91.00	91	62r
Physician fee, internal medicine, revisit		40.00	91	62r

Values are in dollars or fractions of dollars. In the column headed *Ref*, references are shown to sources. Each reference is followed by a letter. These refer to the geographical level for which data were reported: s=State, r=Region, and c=City or metro. The abbreviation *ex* is used to mean *except* or *excluding*; *exp* stands for expenditures. For other abbreviations and further explanations, please see the Introduction.

Akron, OH - continued

Item	Per	Value	Date	Ref.
Health Care				
Physician fee, median, neurosurgeon, first-visit		106.00	91	62r
Physician fee, median, nonsurgical specialist, first-visit		90.00	91	62r
Physician fee, median, orthopedic surgeon, first-visit		83.00	91	62r
Physician fee, median, surgical specialist, first-visit		61.00	91	62r
Physician fee, neurosurgeon, revisit		41.00	91	62r
Physician fee, nonsurgical specialist, revisit		40.00	91	62r
Physician fee, obstetrics/gynecology, first-visit		61.00	91	62r
Physician fee, obstetrics/gynecology, revisit		40.00	91	62r
Physician fee, orthopedic surgeon, revisit		41.00	91	62r
Physician fee, pediatrician, first-visit		46.00	91	62r
Physician fee, pediatrician, revisit		33.00	91	62r
Physician fee, surgical specialist, revisit		36.00	91	62r
Substance abuse, hospital ancillary charge	incident	940	90	70s
Substance abuse, hospital physician charge	incident	380	90	70s
Substance abuse, hospital room and board	incident	5410	90	70s
Household Goods				
Appliance repair, home, service call, washing machine	min labor charge	24.69	4Q 92	4c
Laundry detergent, Tide Ultra, Bold, or Cheer	42 oz	2.89	4Q 92	4c
Tissues, facial, Kleenex brand	175-count box	1.11	4Q 92	4c
Housing				
ACCRA Index, Housing		86.20	4Q 92	4c
Home, median price	unit	79.30		26c
House, 1,800 sq ft, 8,000 sq ft lot, new, urban	total	93200	4Q 92	4c
House payment, principal and interest, 25% down payment	month	521	4Q 92	4c
Mortgage rate, incl. points & origination fee, 30-year fixed or adjustable rate	percent	8.17	4Q 92	4c
Rent, apartment, 2 bedrooms - 1-1/2 to 2 baths, unfurnished, 950 sq ft, water	month	445	4Q 92	4c
Rental unit, 1 bedroom	month	405	93	23c
Rental unit, 2 bedroom	month	480	93	23c
Rental unit, 3 bedroom	month	600	93	23c
Rental unit, 4 bedroom	month	671	93	23c
Rental unit, efficiency	month	333	93	23c
Insurance and Pensions				
Auto insurance, private passenger	year	547.38	91	63s
Personal Goods				
Shampoo, Alberto VO5	15 oz	1.28	4Q 92	4c
Toothpaste, Crest or Colgate	6-7 oz	1.90	4Q 92	4c
Personal Services				
Dry cleaning, man's 2-piece suit		4.07	4Q 92	4c
Haircare, woman's shampoo, trim and blow-dry		13.59	4Q 92	4c
Haircut, man's barbershop, no styling		8.20	4Q 92	4c
Restaurant Food				
Chicken, fried, thigh and drumstick		2.11	4Q 92	4c
Hamburger with cheese	1/4 lb	1.79	4Q 92	4c
Pizza, Pizza Hut or Pizza Inn, cheese, thin crust	12-13 in	8.00	4Q 92	4c
Taxes				
Tax, cigarette	pack	18	91	77s
Tax, gasoline	gal	21	91	77s
Taxes, state	capita	1056	91	77s

Akron, OH - continued

Item	Per	Value	Date	Ref.
Transportation				
ACCRA Index, Transportation		98.50	4Q 92	4c
Auto rental, average	day	55.00	6/91	60c
Bus fare	one-way	0.65	3/93	2c
Bus fare, up to 10 miles	one-way	0.65	4Q 92	4c
Driver's license fee		5.00	12/90	43s
Limo fare, airport-city, average	day	8.25	6/91	60c
Taxi fare, airport-city, average	day	32.00	6/91	60c
Tire balance, computer or spin balance, front	wheel	7.09	4Q 92	4c
Travel				
Breakfast	day	5.14	6/91	60c
Dinner	day	17.63	6/91	60c
Lodging	day	84.00	91	60c
Lunch	day	7.42	6/91	60c
Utilities				
ACCRA Index, Utilities		115.50	4Q 92	4c
Electricity	mil Btu	17.33	90	64s
Electricity, partial electric and other energy, 1,800 sq ft living area new home	month	84.23	4Q 92	4c
Electricity, winter, 250 KWh	month	31.95	92	55c
Electricity, winter, 500 KWh	month	59.86	92	55c
Electricity, winter, 750 KWh	month	87.76	92	55c
Electricity, winter, 1000 KWh	month	115.68	92	55c

Albany, GA

Item	Per	Value	Date	Ref.
Child Care				
Child care fee, average, center	hour	1.29	90	65r
Child care fee, average, nonregulated family day care	hour	0.89	90	65r
Child care fee, average, regulated family day care	hour	1.32	90	65r
Communications				
Long-distance telephone service, day, initial minute, 0-100 miles	min	0.16-0.26	91	12s
Long-distance telephone service, day, additional minute, 0-100 miles	min	0.08-0.23	91	12s
Long-distance telephone service, evenings/weekends, 0-100 mi, initial minute	min	0.06-0.13	91	12s
Long-distance telephone service, evenings/weekends, 0-100 mi, additional minute	min	0.04-0.12	91	12s
Education				
Board, 4-yr private college/university	year	1801	91	22s
Board, 4-yr public college/university	year	1501	91	22s
Expenditures, local gov't, public elementary/secondary	pupil	4747	92	20s
Room, 4-year private college/university	year	2139	91	22s
Room, 4-year public college/university	year	1192	91	22s
Tuition, 2-year private college/university	year	4457	91	22s
Tuition, 2-year public college/university	year	946	91	22s
Tuition, 4-year private college/university	year	7542	91	22s
Tuition, 4-year public college/university, in-state	year	1680	91	22s
Energy and Fuels				
Coal	mil Btu	1.79	90	64s
Energy	mil Btu	8.88	90	64s
Energy exp/householder, 1-family unit	year	487	90	28r
Energy exp/householder, <1,000 sq ft heating area	year	393	90	28r
Energy exp/householder, 1,000-1,999 sq ft heating area	year	442	90	28r
Energy exp/householder, 2,000+ sq ft heating area	year	577	90	28r
Energy exp/householder, mobile home	year	366	90	28r
Energy exp/householder, multifamily	year	382	90	28r
Gas, natural	mil Btu	4.80	90	64s

Values are in dollars or fractions of dollars. In the column headed *Ref*, references are shown to sources. Each reference is followed by a letter. These refer to the geographical level for which data were reported: s=State, r=Region, and c=City or metro. The abbreviation *ex* is used to mean *except* or *excluding*; *exp* stands for expenditures. For other abbreviations and further explanations, please see the Introduction.

Albany, GA - continued

Item	Per	Value	Date	Ref.
Energy and Fuels				
Gas, natural	000 cu ft	6.70	91	46s
Gas, natural, exp	year	475	91	46s
Gasoline, unleaded regular	mil Btu	8.24	90	64s
Entertainment				
Miniature golf admission	adult	6.18	92	1r
Miniature golf admission	child	5.14	92	1r
Waterpark admission	adult	11.00	92	1r
Waterpark admission	child	8.55	92	1r
Funerals				
Casket, 18-gauge steel, velvet interior		2029.08	91	24r
Cosmetology, hair care, etc.		75.10	91	24r
Embalming		249.24	91	24r
Facility use for ceremony		162.27	91	24r
Hearse, local		114.04	91	24r
Limousine, local		88.57	91	24r
Remains to funeral home, transfer		92.61	91	24r
Service charge, professional		682.42	91	24r
Vault, concrete, non-metallic liner		798.70	91	24r
Viewing facilities, use		163.86	91	24r
Groceries				
Apples, Red Delicious	lb	0.79	4/93	16r
Bacon	lb	1.75	4/93	16r
Bananas	lb	0.42	4/93	16r
Beef, stew, boneless	lb	2.61	4/93	16r
Bologna, all beef or mixed	lb	2.24	4/93	16r
Bread, white, pan	lb	0.64	4/93	16r
Bread, whole wheat, pan	lb	0.96	4/93	16r
Cabbage	lb	0.37	4/93	16r
Carrots, short trimmed and topped	lb	0.47	4/93	16r
Celery	lb	0.64	4/93	16r
Cheese, American	lb	2.98	4/93	16r
Cheese, Cheddar	lb	3.28	4/93	16r
Chicken, fresh, whole	lb	0.77	4/93	16r
Chicken breast, bone-in	lb	1.92	4/93	16r
Chicken legs, bone-in	lb	1.06	4/93	16r
Chuck roast, graded and ungraded, ex USDA prime and choice	lb	2.40	4/93	16r
Chuck roast, USDA choice, bone-in	lb	2.19	4/93	16r
Chuck roast, USDA choice, boneless	lb	2.38	4/93	16r
Coffee, 100% ground roast, all sizes	lb	2.48	4/93	16r
Crackers, soda, salted	lb	1.15	4/93	16r
Eggs, Grade A large	doz	0.96	4/93	16r
Flour, white, all purpose	lb	0.24	4/93	16r
Frankfurters, all meat or all beef	lb	2.01	4/93	16r
Grapefruit	lb	0.44	4/93	16r
Grapes, Thompson Seedless	lb	1.40	4/93	16r
Ground beef, 100% beef	lb	1.58	4/93	16r
Ground beef, lean and extra lean	lb	2.09	4/93	16r
Ground chuck, 100% beef	lb	1.98	4/93	16r
Ham, boneless, excluding canned	lb	2.89	4/93	16r
Ham, picnic, shoulder, bone-in, smoked	lb	1.02	4/93	16r
Ham, rump or steak half, bone-in, smoked	lb	1.48	4/93	16r
Ice cream, prepackaged, bulk, regular	1/2 gal	2.41	4/93	16r
Lemons	lb	1.05	4/93	16r
Lettuce, iceberg	lb	0.81	4/93	16r
Margarine, stick	lb	0.88	4/93	16r
Oranges, navel	lb	0.55	4/93	16r
Pears, Anjou	lb	0.92	4/93	16r
Pork chops, center cut, bone-in	lb	3.13	4/93	16r
Potato chips	16 oz	2.94	4/93	16r
Potatoes, white	lb	0.43	4/93	16r
Rib roast, USDA choice, bone-in	lb	4.63	4/93	16r
Rice, white, long grain, uncooked	lb	0.45	4/93	16r
Round roast, graded & ungraded, ex USDA prime & choice	lb	3.03	4/93	16r
Round roast, USDA choice, boneless	lb	3.09	4/93	16r
Sausage, fresh, loose	lb	2.08	4/93	16r
Short ribs, bone-in	lb	2.66	4/93	16r
Shortening, vegetable oil blends	lb	0.69	4/93	16r
Spaghetti and macaroni	lb	0.81	4/93	16r

Albany, GA - continued

Item	Per	Value	Date	Ref.
Groceries - continued				
Steak, rib eye, USDA choice, boneless	lb	6.24	4/93	16r
Steak, round, graded & ungraded, ex USDA prime & choice	lb	3.31	4/93	16r
Steak, round, USDA choice, boneless	lb	3.34	4/93	16r
Steak, sirloin, graded & ungraded, ex USDA prime & choice	lb	4.19	4/93	16r
Steak, sirloin, USDA choice, boneless	lb	4.46	4/93	16r
Steak, T-bone, USDA choice, bone-in	lb	5.25	4/93	16r
Strawberries, dry pint	12 oz	0.92	4/93	16r
Sugar, white	lb	0.39	4/93	16r
Sugar, white, 33-80 oz pk	lb	0.38	4/93	16r
Tomatoes, field grown	lb	0.88	4/93	16r
Tuna, chunk, light	lb	1.79	4/93	16r
Turkey, frozen, whole	lb	1.04	4/93	16r
Yogurt, natural, fruit flavored	1/2 pint	0.57	4/93	16r
Health Care				
Childbirth, cesarean, hospital		5034	91	62r
Childbirth, cesarean, physician's fee		2053	91	62r
Childbirth, normal, hospital		2712	91	62r
Childbirth, normal, physician's fee		1492	91	62r
Medical plan per employee	year	3495	91	45r
Mental health care, exp	capita	37.60-53.67	90	38s
Mental health care, exp, state mental health agency	capita	50.98	90	38s
Mental health care, hospital psychiatric services, non-Federal, exp	capita	9.66	88	38s
Mental health care, mental health organization, multiservice, exp	capita	16.40	88	38s
Mental health care, psychiatric hospitals, private, exp	capita	26.36	88	38s
Mental health care, psychiatric out-patient clinics, freestanding, exp	capita	0.13	88	38s
Mental health care, state and county mental hospitals, exp	capita	38.94	88	38s
Mental health care, VA medical centers, exp	capita	3.91	88	38s
Physician fee, family practice, first-visit		75.00	91	62r
Physician fee, family practice, revisit		34.00	91	62r
Physician fee, general practice, first-visit		61.00	91	62r
Physician fee, general practice, revisit		32.00	91	62r
Physician fee, general surgeon, first-visit		64.00	91	62r
Physician fee, general surgeon, revisit		40.00	91	62r
Physician fee, internal medicine, first-visit		98.00	91	62r
Physician fee, internal medicine, revisit		40.00	91	62r
Physician fee, median, neurosurgeon, first-visit		130.00	91	62r
Physician fee, median, nonsurgical specialist, first-visit		95.00	91	62r
Physician fee, median, orthopedic surgeon, first-visit		91.00	91	62r
Physician fee, median, plastic surgeon, first-visit		66.00	91	62r
Physician fee, median, surgical specialist, first-visit		62.00	91	62r
Physician fee, neurosurgeon, revisit		50.00	91	62r
Physician fee, nonsurgical specialist, revisit		40.00	91	62r
Physician fee, obstetrics/gynecology, first-visit		64.00	91	62r
Physician fee, obstetrics/gynecology, revisit		41.00	91	62r
Physician fee, orthopedic surgeon, revisit		40.00	91	62r
Physician fee, pediatrician, first-visit		49.00	91	62r
Physician fee, pediatrician, revisit		33.00	91	62r
Physician fee, plastic surgeon, revisit		43.00	91	62r
Physician fee, surgical specialist, revisit		37.00	91	62r
Substance abuse, hospital ancillary charge	incident	1800	90	70s
Substance abuse, hospital physician charge	incident	890	90	70s
Substance abuse, hospital room and board	incident	5560	90	70s

Values are in dollars or fractions of dollars. In the column headed *Ref*, references are shown to sources. Each reference is followed by a letter. These refer to the geographical level for which data were reported: s=State, r=Region, and c=City or metro. The abbreviation *ex* is used to mean *except* or *excluding*; *exp* stands for expenditures. For other abbreviations and further explanations, please see the Introduction.

Albany, GA - continued

Item	Per	Value	Date	Ref.
Insurance and Pensions				
Auto insurance, private passenger	year	651.31	91	63s
Taxes				
Tax, cigarette	pack	12	91	77s
Tax, gasoline	gal	7.50	91	77s
Taxes, state	capita	1080	91	77s
Transportation				
Driver's license fee		4.50	12/90	43s
Travel				
Business travel	day	193.00	4/93	89r
Utilities				
Electricity	mil Btu	19.25	90	64s

Albany-Schenectady-Troy, NY

Item	Per	Value	Date	Ref.
Composite ACCRA index		112.60	4Q 92	4c
Alcoholic Beverages				
Beer, Miller Lite or Budweiser, 12-oz containers	6 pack	4.37	4Q 92	4c
Liquor, J & B Scotch	750 ml	18.07	4Q 92	4c
Wine, Gallo Chablis blanc, 1.5 liter	bottle	6.19	4Q 92	4c
Child Care				
Child care fee, average, center	hour	2.18	90	65r
Child care fee, average, nonregulated family day care	hour	1.83	90	65r
Child care fee, average, regulated family day care	hour	2.02	90	65r
Clothing				
Jeans, man's denim		31.99	4Q 92	4c
Shirt, man's dress shirt		23.80	4Q 92	4c
Undervest, boy's size 10-14, cotton	3	4.71	4Q 92	4c
Communications				
Newspaper subscription, daily and Sunday home delivery, large-city	month	12.17	4Q 92	4c
Telephone bill, family of four	month	34.67	4Q 92	4c
Construction				
Plywood, post-Hurricane Andrew	4x8 sheet	10.69	92	13c
Plywood, pre-Hurricane Andrew	4x8 sheet	8.19	92	13c
Education				
Board, 4-yr private college/university	year	2451	91	22s
Board, 4-yr public college/university	year	1725	91	22s
Expenditures, local gov't, public elementary/secondary	pupil	8603	92	20s
Room, 4-year private college/university	year	2652	91	22s
Room, 4-year public college/university	year	2183	91	22s
Tuition, 2-year private college/university	year	5926	91	22s
Tuition, 2-year public college/university	year	1419	91	22s
Tuition, 4-year private college/university	year	10340	91	22s
Tuition, 4-year public college/university, in-state	year	1587	91	22s
Energy and Fuels				
Coal	mil Btu	1.66	90	64s
Energy	mil Btu	10.68	90	64s
Energy, combined forms, 1,800 sq ft heating area	month	145.84	4Q 92	4c
Energy, exc electricity, 1,800 sq ft heating area	month	63.28	4Q 92	4c
Energy exp/householder, 1-family unit	year	588	90	28r
Energy exp/householder, <1,000 sq ft heating area	year	477	90	28r
Energy exp/householder, 1,000-1,999 sq ft heating area	year	517	90	28r
Energy exp/householder, 2,000+ sq ft heating area	year	630	90	28r
Energy exp/householder, mobile home	year	412	90	28r

Item	Per	Value	Date	Ref.
Energy and Fuels - continued				
Energy exp/householder, multifamily	year	498	90	28r
Gas, natural	mil Btu	5.25	90	64s
Gas, natural	000 cu ft	7.35	91	46s
Gas, natural, exp	year	557	91	46s
Gasoline, motor	gal	1.19	4Q 92	4c
Gasoline, unleaded premium	gal	61.65-73.00	12/92	31c
Gasoline, unleaded regular	mil Btu	8.83	90	64s
Entertainment				
Bowling, evening rate	game	2.36	4Q 92	4c
Monopoly game, Parker Brothers', No. 9		11.37	4Q 92	4c
Movie	admission	6.75	4Q 92	4c
Tennis balls, yellow, Wilson or Penn, 3	can	2.41	4Q 92	4c
Funerals				
Casket, 18-gauge steel, velvet interior		1811.58	91	24r
Cosmetology, hair care, etc.		111.08	91	24r
Embalming		329.42	91	24r
Facility use for ceremony		201.29	91	24r
Hearse, local		135.27	91	24r
Limousine, local		127.24	91	24r
Remains to funeral home, transfer		103.98	91	24r
Service charge, professional		724.98	91	24r
Vault, concrete, non-metallic liner		766.71	91	24r
Viewing facilities, use		260.60	91	24r
Goods and Services				
ACCRA Index, Miscellaneous Goods and Services		107.90	4Q 92	4c
Groceries				
ACCRA Index, Groceries		113.90	4Q 92	4c
Apples, Red Delicious	lb	0.85	4/93	16r
Babyfood, strained vegetables, lowest price	4-4.5 oz jar	0.34	4Q 92	4c
Bacon	lb	2.12	4/93	16r
Bananas	lb	0.55	4Q 92	4c
Bananas	lb	0.54	4/93	16r
Bread, white	24 oz	0.99	4Q 92	4c
Bread, white, pan	lb	0.81	4/93	16r
Butter	lb	2.02	4/93	16r
Carrots, short trimmed and topped	lb	0.51	4/93	16r
Cheese, Kraft grated Parmesan	8-oz canister	3.17	4Q 92	4c
Chicken, fresh, whole	lb	1.04	4/93	16r
Chicken, fryer, whole	lb	1.08	4Q 92	4c
Chicken breast, bone-in	lb	2.21	4/93	16r
Chicken legs, bone-in	lb	1.16	4/93	16r
Chuck roast, USDA choice, boneless	lb	2.82	4/93	16r
Cigarettes, Winston	carton	20.61	4Q 92	4c
Coffee, 100% ground roast, all sizes	lb	2.66	4/93	16r
Coffee, vacuum-packed	13-oz can	2.35	4Q 92	4c
Corn, frozen	10 oz	0.65	4Q 92	4c
Corn Flakes, Kellogg's or Post Toasties	18 oz	2.23	4Q 92	4c
Cucumbers	lb	0.85	4/93	16r
Eggs, Grade A large	doz	1.19	4Q 92	4c
Eggs, Grade A large	doz	1.15	4/93	16r
Grapefruit	lb	0.45	4/93	16r
Grapes, Thompson Seedless	lb	1.52	4/93	16r
Ground beef, lean and extra lean	lb	2.36	4/93	16r
Ground beef or hamburger	lb	1.76	4Q 92	4c
Ground chuck, 100% beef	lb	2.02	4/93	16r
Honey, jar	8 oz	0.96-1.75	92	5r
Honey, jar	lb	1.50-3.00	92	5r
Honey, squeeze bear	12-oz	1.50-1.99	92	5r
Ice cream, prepackaged, bulk, regular	1/2 gal	2.80	4/93	16r
Lemons	lb	0.96	4/93	16r
Lettuce, iceberg	head	0.99	4Q 92	4c
Lettuce, iceberg	lb	0.95	4/93	16r

Values are in dollars or fractions of dollars. In the column headed *Ref*, references are shown to sources. Each reference is followed by a letter. These refer to the geographical level for which data were reported: s = State, r = Region, and c = City or metro. The abbreviation *ex* is used to mean *except* or *excluding*; *exp* stands for expenditures. For other abbreviations and further explanations, please see the Introduction.

Albany-Schenectady-Troy, NY - continued

Item	Per	Value	Date	Ref.
Groceries				
Margarine, Blue Bonnet or Parkay cubes	lb	0.63	4Q 92	4c
Margarine, stick	lb	0.81	4/93	16r
Milk, fresh, whole, fortified	1/2 gal	1.30	4/93	16r
Milk, whole	1/2 gal	1.25	4Q 92	4c
Orange juice, Minute Maid frozen	12-oz can	1.43	4Q 92	4c
Oranges, navel	lb	0.56	4/93	16r
Peaches	29-oz can	1.59	4Q 92	4c
Peanut butter, creamy, all sizes	lb	1.88	4/93	16r
Peas Sweet, Del Monte or Green Giant	15-17 oz can	0.45	4Q 92	4c
Pork chops, center cut, bone-in	lb	3.34	4/93	16r
Potato chips	16 oz	2.88	4/93	16r
Potatoes, white	lb	0.37	4/93	16r
Potatoes, white or red	10-lb sack	1.93	4Q 92	4c
Rib roast, USDA choice, bone-in	lb	4.94	4/93	16r
Round roast, USDA choice, boneless	lb	3.17	4/93	16r
Sausage, Jimmy Dean, 100% pork	lb	2.89	4Q 92	4c
Shortening, vegetable oil blends	lb	0.98	4/93	16r
Shortening, vegetable, Crisco	3-lb can	2.67	4Q 92	4c
Soft drink, Coca Cola	2 liter	1.24	4Q 92	4c
Spaghetti and macaroni	lb	0.82	4/93	16r
Steak, round, graded & ungraded, ex USDA prime & choice	lb	4.04	4/93	16r
Steak, round, USDA choice, boneless	lb	3.90	4/93	16r
Steak, sirloin, USDA choice, boneless	lb	4.97	4/93	16r
Steak, T-bone	lb	5.79	4Q 92	4c
Strawberries, dry pint	12 oz	0.90	4/93	16r
Sugar, cane or beet	4 lb	1.85	4Q 92	4c
Sugar, white	lb	0.50	4/93	16r
Sugar, white, 33-80 oz pk	lb	0.41	4/93	16r
Tomatoes, field grown	lb	1.23	4/93	16r
Tomatoes, Hunt's or Del Monte	14.5-oz can	0.77	4Q 92	4c
Tuna, chunk, light	6.125-6.5 oz can	0.77	4Q 92	4c
Tuna, chunk, light	lb	2.22	4/93	16r
Turkey, frozen, whole	lb	1.04	4/93	16r
Health Care				
ACCRA Index, Health Care		100.60	4Q 92	4c
Analgesic, Aspirin, Bayer, 325 mg tablets	100	5.44	4Q 92	4c
Childbirth, cesarean, hospital		5826	91	62r
Childbirth, cesarean, physician's fee		2053	91	62r
Childbirth, normal, hospital		2964	91	62r
Childbirth, normal, physician's fee		1492	91	62r
Dentist's fee, adult teeth cleaning and periodic oral exam	visit	45.40	4Q 92	4c
Doctor's fee, routine exam, established patient	visit	41.00	4Q 92	4c
Hospital care, semiprivate room	day	257.68	90	27c
Hospital care, semiprivate room	day	262.60	4Q 92	4c
Medical insurance premium, per employee, small group comprehensive	month	295.65	10/91	25c
Medical plan per employee	year	3942	91	45r
Mental health care, exp	capita	53.68-118.35	90	38s
Mental health care, exp, state mental health agency	capita	118.34	90	38s
Mental health care, hospital psychiatric services, non-Federal, exp	capita	29.77	88	38s
Mental health care, mental health organization, multiservice, exp	capita	20.03	88	38s
Mental health care, psychiatric hospitals, private, exp	capita	8.37	88	38s
Mental health care, psychiatric out-patient clinics, freestanding, exp	capita	7.96	88	38s
Mental health care, psychiatric partial-care organizations, freestanding, exp	capita	1.24	88	38s

Albany-Schenectady-Troy, NY - continued

Item	Per	Value	Date	Ref.
Health Care - continued				
Mental health care, state and county mental hospitals, exp	capita	89.52	88	38s
Mental health care, VA medical centers, exp	capita	7.12	88	38s
Prescription drug co-pay, Medicaid	month	23.00	91	21s
Substance abuse, hospital ancillary charge	incident	1040	90	70s
Substance abuse, hospital physician charge	incident	360	90	70s
Substance abuse, hospital room and board	incident	6330	90	70s
Household Goods				
Appliance repair, home, service call, washing machine	min labor charge	35.97	4Q 92	4c
Laundry detergent, Tide Ultra, Bold, or Cheer	42 oz	3.37	4Q 92	4c
Tissues, facial, Kleenex brand	175-count box	1.19	4Q 92	4c
Housing				
ACCRA Index, Housing		112.70	4Q 92	4c
Home, median price	unit	111.40		26c
House, 1,800 sq ft, 8,000 sq ft lot, new, urban	total	119272	4Q 92	4c
House payment, principal and interest, 25% down payment	month	659	4Q 92	4c
Mortgage rate, incl. points & origination fee, 30-year fixed or adjustable rate	percent	8.05	4Q 92	4c
Rent, apartment, 2 bedrooms - 1-1/2 to 2 baths, unfurnished, 950 sq ft, water	month	633	4Q 92	4c
Rental unit, 1 bedroom	month	463	93	23c
Rental unit, 2 bedroom	month	547	93	23c
Rental unit, 3 bedroom	month	689	93	23c
Rental unit, 4 bedroom	month	766	93	23c
Rental unit, efficiency	month	385	93	23c
Insurance and Pensions				
Auto insurance, private passenger	year	840.89	91	63s
Personal Goods				
Shampoo, Alberto VO5	15 oz	1.63	4Q 92	4c
Toothpaste, Crest or Colgate	6-7 oz	2.25	4Q 92	4c
Personal Services				
Dry cleaning, man's 2-piece suit		5.95	4Q 92	4c
Haircare, woman's shampoo, trim and blow-dry		22.10	4Q 92	4c
Haircut, man's barbershop, no styling		9.00	4Q 92	4c
Restaurant Food				
Chicken, fried, thigh and drumstick		2.03	4Q 92	4c
Hamburger with cheese	1/4 lb	1.87	4Q 92	4c
Pizza, Pizza Hut or Pizza Inn, cheese, thin crust	12-13 in	8.19	4Q 92	4c
Taxes				
Tax, cigarette	pack	39	91	77s
Tax, gasoline	gal	8	91	77s
Taxes, state	capita	1567	91	77s
Transportation				
ACCRA Index, Transportation		110.50	4Q 92	4c
Auto rental, average	day	51.50	6/91	60c
Bus fare	one-way	0.75	3/93	2c
Driver's license fee		17.50	12/90	43s
Limo fare, airport-city, average	day	13.00	6/91	60c
Taxi fare, airport-city, average	day	13.00	6/91	60c
Tire balance, computer or spin balance, front	wheel	7.46	4Q 92	4c
Vehicle registration and license plate	2 years	27.50-149.50	93	67s

Values are in dollars or fractions of dollars. In the column headed *Ref*, references are shown to sources. Each reference is followed by a letter. These refer to the geographical level for which data were reported: s = State, r = Region, and c = City or metro. The abbreviation *ex* is used to mean *except* or *excluding*; *exp* stands for *expenditures*. For other abbreviations and further explanations, please see the Introduction.

Albany-Schenectady-Troy, NY - continued

Item	Per	Value	Date	Ref.
Travel				
Breakfast	day	4.56	6/91	60c
Business travel	day	165.00	4/93	89r
Dinner	day	17.45	6/91	60c
Lodging	day	103.17	91	60c
Lunch	day	6.44	6/91	60c
Utilities				
ACCRA Index, Utilities		138.00	4Q 92	4c
Electricity	mil Btu	27.51	90	64s
Electricity, partial electric and other energy, 1,800 sq ft living area new home	month	82.56	4Q 92	4c

Albuquerque, NM

Item	Per	Value	Date	Ref.
Composite ACCRA index		99.60	4Q 92	4c
Alcoholic Beverages				
Beer, Miller Lite or Budweiser, 12-oz containers	6 pack	3.81	4Q 92	4c
Liquor, J & B Scotch	750 ml	14.94	4Q 92	4c
Wine, Gallo Chablis blanc, 1.5 liter	bottle	4.78	4Q 92	4c
Child Care				
Child care fee, average, center	hour	1.71	90	65r
Child care fee, average, nonregulated family day care	hour	1.32	90	65r
Child care fee, average, regulated family day care	hour	1.86	90	65r
Clothing				
Jeans, man's denim		30.78	4Q 92	4c
Shirt, man's dress shirt		20.93	4Q 92	4c
Undervest, boy's size 10-14, cotton	3	3.83	4Q 92	4c
Communications				
Long-distance telephone service, day, initial minute, 0-100 miles	min	0.19-0.32	91	12s
Long-distance telephone service, day, additional minute, 0-100 miles	min	0.11-0.24	91	12s
Long-distance telephone service, evenings/weekends, 0-100 mi, initial minute	min	0.11-0.20	91	12s
Long-distance telephone service, evenings/weekends, 0-100 mi, additional minute	min	0.07-0.14	91	12s
Newspaper subscription, daily and Sunday home delivery, large-city	month	9.50	4Q 92	4c
Telephone, flat rate	month	14.55	91	11c
Telephone bill, family of four	month	20.86	4Q 92	4c
Education				
Board, 4-yr private college/university	year	1890	91	22s
Board, 4-yr public college/university	year	1527	91	22s
Expenditures, local gov't, public elementary/secondary	pupil	4524	92	20s
Room, 4-year private college/university	year	1468	91	22s
Room, 4-year public college/university	year	1321	91	22s
Tuition, 2-year private college/university	year	3594	91	22s
Tuition, 2-year public college/university	year	536	91	22s
Tuition, 4-year private college/university	year	8187	91	22s
Tuition, 4-year public college/university, in-state	year	1409	91	22s
Energy and Fuels				
Coal	mil Btu	1.32	90	64s
Energy	mil Btu	9.22	90	64s
Energy, combined forms, 1,800 sq ft heating area	month	109.11	4Q 92	4c
Energy, exc electricity, 1,800 sq ft heating area	month	43.33	4Q 92	4c
Energy exp/householder, 1-family unit	year	372	90	28r
Energy exp/householder, <1,000 sq ft heating area	year	335	90	28r
Energy exp/householder, 1,000-1,999 sq ft heating area	year	365	90	28r
Energy exp/householder, 2,000+ sq ft heating area	year	411	90	28r

Albuquerque, NM - continued

Item	Per	Value	Date	Ref.
Energy and Fuels - continued				
Energy exp/householder, mobile home	year	305	90	28r
Energy exp/householder, multifamily	year	372	90	28r
Gas, cooking, winter, 10 therms	month	12.40	92	56c
Gas, cooking, winter, 30 therms	month	19.11	92	56c
Gas, cooking, winter, 50 therms	month	25.92	92	56c
Gas, heating, winter, 100 therms	month	42.77	92	56c
Gas, natural	mil Btu	3.84	90	64s
Gas, natural	000 cu ft	5.40	91	46s
Gas, natural, exp	year	424	91	46s
Gasoline, motor	gal	1.18	4Q 92	4c
Gasoline, unleaded regular	mil Btu	9.23	90	64s
Entertainment				
Bowling, evening rate	game	1.88	4Q 92	4c
Miniature golf admission	adult	6.18	92	1r
Miniature golf admission	child	5.14	92	1r
Monopoly game, Parker Brothers', No. 9		10.98	4Q 92	4c
Movie	admission	5.90	4Q 92	4c
Tennis balls, yellow, Wilson or Penn, 3	can	2.32	4Q 92	4c
Waterpark admission	adult	11.00	92	1r
Waterpark admission	child	8.55	92	1r
Funerals				
Casket, 18-gauge steel, velvet interior		1929.04	91	24r
Cosmetology, hair care, etc.		88.52	91	24r
Embalming		249.33	91	24r
Facility use for ceremony		182.75	91	24r
Hearse, local		110.04	91	24r
Limousine, local		66.67	91	24r
Remains to funeral home, transfer		84.58	91	24r
Service charge, professional		593.00	91	24r
Vault, concrete, non-metallic liner		647.38	91	24r
Viewing facilities, use		99.87	91	24r
Goods and Services				
ACCRA Index, Miscellaneous Goods and Services		95.20	4Q 92	4c
Groceries				
ACCRA Index, Groceries		93.70	4Q 92	4c
Apples, Red Delicious	lb	0.80	4/93	16r
Babyfood, strained vegetables, lowest price	4-4.5 oz jar	0.25	4Q 92	4c
Bacon	lb	1.79	4/93	16r
Bananas	lb	0.38	4Q 92	4c
Bananas	lb	0.53	4/93	16r
Bologna, all beef or mixed	lb	2.67	4/93	16r
Bread, white	24 oz	0.61	4Q 92	4c
Bread, white, pan	lb	0.81	4/93	16r
Carrots, short trimmed and topped	lb	0.39	4/93	16r
Cheese, Kraft grated Parmesan	8-oz canister	3.55	4Q 92	4c
Chicken, fresh, whole	lb	0.94	4/93	16r
Chicken, fryer, whole	lb	0.60	4Q 92	4c
Chicken breast, bone-in	lb	2.19	4/93	16r
Chuck roast, graded and ungraded, ex USDA prime and choice	lb	2.26	4/93	16r
Cigarettes, Winston	carton	15.90	4Q 92	4c
Coffee, 100% ground roast, all sizes	lb	2.33	4/93	16r
Coffee, vacuum-packed	13-oz can	2.01	4Q 92	4c
Corn, frozen	10 oz	0.79	4Q 92	4c
Corn Flakes, Kellogg's or Post Toasties	18 oz	1.89	4Q 92	4c
Eggs, Grade A large	doz	0.86	4Q 92	4c
Eggs, Grade AA large	doz	1.18	4/93	16r
Flour, white, all purpose	lb	0.22	4/93	16r
Grapefruit	lb	0.52	4/93	16r
Grapes, Thompson Seedless	lb	1.50	4/93	16r
Ground beef, 100% beef	lb	1.44	4/93	16r
Ground beef, lean and extra lean	lb	2.34	4/93	16r
Ground beef or hamburger	lb	1.21	4Q 92	4c

Values are in dollars or fractions of dollars. In the column headed *Ref*, references are shown to sources. Each reference is followed by a letter. These refer to the geographical level for which data were reported: s = State, r = Region, and c = City or metro. The abbreviation *ex* is used to mean *except* or *excluding*; *exp* stands for expenditures. For other abbreviations and further explanations, please see the Introduction.

Albuquerque, NM - continued

Item	Per	Value	Date	Ref.
Groceries				
Ham, boneless, excluding canned	lb	2.56	4/93	16r
Honey, jar	8 oz	0.89-1.00	92	5r
Honey, jar	lb	1.35-1.97	92	5r
Honey, squeeze bear	12-oz	1.19-1.50	92	5r
Ice cream, prepackaged, bulk, regular	1/2 gal	2.40	4/93	16r
Lemons	lb	0.81	4/93	16r
Lettuce, iceberg	head	0.83	4Q 92	4c
Lettuce, iceberg	lb	0.84	4/93	16r
Margarine, Blue Bonnet or Parkay cubes	lb	0.59	4Q 92	4c
Margarine, stick	lb	0.81	4/93	16r
Milk, whole	1/2 gal	1.54	4Q 92	4c
Orange juice, Minute Maid frozen	12-oz can	1.29	4Q 92	4c
Oranges, navel	lb	0.48	4/93	16r
Peaches	29-oz can	1.42	4Q 92	4c
Peas Sweet, Del Monte or Green Giant	15-17 oz can	0.54	4Q 92	4c
Pork chops, center cut, bone-in	lb	3.25	4/93	16r
Potato chips	16 oz	2.89	4/93	16r
Potatoes, white	lb	0.38	4/93	16r
Potatoes, white or red	10-lb sack	1.95	4Q 92	4c
Round roast, graded & ungraded, ex USDA prime & choice	lb	3.00	4/93	16r
Round roast, USDA choice, boneless	lb	3.16	4/93	16r
Sausage, Jimmy Dean, 100% pork	lb	2.22	4Q 92	4c
Shortening, vegetable oil blends	lb	0.86	4/93	16r
Shortening, vegetable, Crisco	3-lb can	2.05	4Q 92	4c
Soft drink, Coca Cola	2 liter	1.34	4Q 92	4c
Spaghetti and macaroni	lb	0.84	4/93	16r
Steak, round, graded & ungraded, ex USDA prime & choice	lb	3.34	4/93	16r
Steak, round, USDA choice, boneless	lb	3.24	4/93	16r
Steak, sirloin, graded & ungraded, ex USDA prime & choice	lb	3.75	4/93	16r
Steak, sirloin, USDA choice, boneless	lb	4.49	4/93	16r
Steak, T-bone	lb	4.85	4Q 92	4c
Sugar, cane or beet	4 lb	1.73	4Q 92	4c
Sugar, white	lb	0.41	4/93	16r
Sugar, white, 33-80 oz pk	lb	0.38	4/93	16r
Tomatoes, field grown	lb	1.01	4/93	16r
Tomatoes, Hunt's or Del Monte	14.5-oz can	0.66	4Q 92	4c
Tuna, chunk, light	6.125-6.5 oz can	0.64	4Q 92	4c
Turkey, frozen, whole	lb	1.04	4/93	16r
Health Care				
ACCRA Index, Health Care		113.90	4Q 92	4c
Analgesic, Aspirin, Bayer, 325 mg tablets	100	4.99	4Q 92	4c
Childbirth, cesarean, hospital		5533	91	62r
Childbirth, cesarean, physician's fee		2053	91	62r
Childbirth, normal, hospital		2745	91	62r
Childbirth, normal, physician's fee		1492	91	62r
Dentist's fee, adult teeth cleaning and periodic oral exam	visit	56.80	4Q 92	4c
Doctor's fee, routine exam, established patient	visit	43.40	4Q 92	4c
Hospital care, semiprivate room	day	250.00	90	27c
Hospital care, semiprivate room	day	322.00	4Q 92	4c
Medical insurance premium, per employee, small group comprehensive	month	332.15	10/91	25c
Medical plan per employee	year	3218	91	45r
Mental health care, exp	capita	20.37-28.83	90	38s
Mental health care, exp, state mental health agency	capita	22.88	90	38s
Mental health care, hospital psychiatric services, non-Federal, exp	capita	7.77	88	38s

Albuquerque, NM - continued

Item	Per	Value	Date	Ref.
Health Care - continued				
Mental health care, mental health organization, multiservice, exp	capita	16.77	88	38s
Mental health care, psychiatric hospitals, private, exp	capita	32.81	88	38s
Mental health care, psychiatric out-patient clinics, freestanding, exp	capita	2.18	88	38s
Mental health care, psychiatric partial-care organizations, freestanding, exp	capita	1.80	88	38s
Mental health care, state and county mental hospitals, exp	capita	20.94	88	38s
Mental health care, VA medical centers, exp	capita	2.32	88	38s
Physician fee, family practice, first-visit		111.00	91	62r
Physician fee, family practice, revisit		45.00	91	62r
Physician fee, general practice, first-visit		100.00	91	62r
Physician fee, general practice, revisit		40.00	91	62r
Physician fee, internal medicine, first-visit		137.00	91	62r
Physician fee, internal medicine, revisit		48.00	91	62r
Physician fee, median, neurosurgeon, first-visit		157.00	91	62r
Physician fee, median, nonsurgical specialist, first-visit		131.00	91	62r
Physician fee, median, orthopedic surgeon, first-visit		124.00	91	62r
Physician fee, median, plastic surgeon, first-visit		88.00	91	62r
Physician fee, median, surgical specialist, first-visit		100.00	91	62r
Physician fee, neurosurgeon, revisit		51.00	91	62r
Physician fee, nonsurgical specialist, revisit		47.00	91	62r
Physician fee, obstetrics/gynecology, first-visit		95.00	91	62r
Physician fee, obstetrics/gynecology, revisit		50.00	91	62r
Physician fee, orthopedic surgeon, revisit		51.00	91	62r
Physician fee, pediatrician, first-visit		81.00	91	62r
Physician fee, pediatrician, revisit		42.00	91	62r
Physician fee, plastic surgeon, revisit		48.00	91	62r
Physician fee, surgical specialist, revisit		49.00	91	62r
Substance abuse, hospital ancillary charge	incident	2630	90	70s
Substance abuse, hospital physician charge	incident	840	90	70s
Substance abuse, hospital room and board	incident	6500	90	70s
Household Goods				
Appliance repair, home, service call, washing machine	min labor charge	27.96	4Q 92	4c
Laundry detergent, Tide Ultra, Bold, or Cheer	42 oz	3.14	4Q 92	4c
Tissues, facial, Kleenex brand	175-count box	1.25	4Q 92	4c
Housing				
ACCRA Index, Housing		104.20	4Q 92	4c
Home, median price	unit	92.00		26c
House, 1,800 sq ft, 8,000 sq ft lot, new, urban	total	114512	4Q 92	4c
House payment, principal and interest, 25% down payment	month	628	4Q 92	4c
Mortgage rate, incl. points & origination fee, 30-year fixed or adjustable rate	percent	7.96	4Q 92	4c
Rent, apartment, 2 bedrooms - 1-1/2 to 2 baths, unfurnished, 950 sq ft, water	month	544	4Q 92	4c
Rental unit, 1 bedroom	month	479	93	23c
Rental unit, 2 bedroom	month	562	93	23c
Rental unit, 3 bedroom	month	704	93	23c
Rental unit, 4 bedroom	month	789	93	23c
Rental unit, efficiency	month	393	93	23c
Insurance and Pensions				
Auto insurance, private passenger	year	628.37	91	63s

Values are in dollars or fractions of dollars. In the column headed *Ref*, references are shown to sources. Each reference is followed by a letter. These refer to the geographical level for which data were reported: s=State, r=Region, and c=City or metro. The abbreviation *ex* is used to mean *except* or *excluding*; *exp* stands for expenditures. For other abbreviations and further explanations, please see the Introduction.

Albuquerque, NM - continued

Item	Per	Value	Date	Ref.
Personal Goods				
Shampoo, Alberto VO5	15 oz	1.35	4Q 92	4c
Toothpaste, Crest or Colgate	6-7 oz	1.97	4Q 92	4c
Personal Services				
Dry cleaning, man's 2-piece suit		5.90	4Q 92	4c
Haircare, woman's shampoo, trim and blow-dry		20.99	4Q 92	4c
Haircut, man's barbershop, no styling		7.00	4Q 92	4c
Restaurant Food				
Chicken, fried, thigh and drumstick		1.76	4Q 92	4c
Hamburger with cheese	1/4 lb	1.95	4Q 92	4c
Pizza, Pizza Hut or Pizza Inn, cheese, thin crust	12-13 in	7.67	4Q 92	4c
Taxes				
Tax, cigarette	pack	15	91	77s
Tax, gasoline	gal	16	91	77s
Taxes, state	capita	1347	91	77s
Transportation				
ACCRA Index, Transportation		101.20	4Q 92	4c
Auto rental, average	day	42.50	6/91	60c
Bus fare	one-way	0.75	3/93	2c
Bus fare, up to 10 miles	one-way	0.75	4Q 92	4c
Driver's license fee		10.00	12/90	43s
Limo fare, airport-city, average	day	10.00	6/91	60c
Taxi fare, airport-city, average	day	10.00	6/91	60c
Tire balance, computer or spin balance, front	wheel	6.57	4Q 92	4c
Travel				
Breakfast	day	6.59	6/91	60c
Business travel	day	178.00	4/93	89r
Dinner	day	17.28	6/91	60c
Lodging	day	79.50	91	60c
Lunch	day	10.86	6/91	60c
Utilities				
ACCRA Index, Utilities		100.70	4Q 92	4c
Electricity	mil Btu	20.99	90	64s
Electricity, partial electric and other energy, 1,800 sq ft living area new home	month	65.78	4Q 92	4c
Electricity, residential	KWh	9.58	2/93	94s
Electricity, winter, 250 KWh	month	24.73	92	55c
Electricity, winter, 500 KWh	month	48.09	92	55c
Electricity, winter, 750 KWh	month	71.46	92	55c
Electricity, winter, 1000 KWh	month	94.82	92	55c

Alexandria, LA

Item	Per	Value	Date	Ref.
Child Care				
Child care fee, average, center	hour	1.29	90	65r
Child care fee, average, nonregulated family day care	hour	0.89	90	65r
Child care fee, average, regulated family day care	hour	1.32	90	65r
Communications				
Long-distance telephone service, day, initial minute, 0-100 miles	min	0.14-0.41	91	12s
Long-distance telephone service, day, additional minute, 0-100 miles	min	0.09-0.29	91	12s
Long-distance telephone service, evenings/weekends, 0-100 mi, initial minute	min	0.06-0.16	91	12s
Long-distance telephone service, evenings/weekends, 0-100 mi, additional minute	min	0.04-0.12	91	12s
Education				
Board, 4-yr private college/university	year	2125	91	22s
Board, 4-yr public college/university	year	1453	91	22s
Expenditures, local gov't, public elementary/secondary	pupil	4299	92	20s

Alexandria, LA - continued

Item	Per	Value	Date	Ref.
Education - continued				
Room, 4-year private college/university	year	2216	91	22s
Room, 4-year public college/university	year	1323	91	22s
Tuition, 2-year private college/university	year	5671	91	22s
Tuition, 2-year public college/university	year	852	91	22s
Tuition, 4-year private college/university	year	9783	91	22s
Tuition, 4-year public college/university, in-state	year	1791	91	22s
Energy and Fuels				
Coal	mil Btu	1.68	90	64s
Energy	mil Btu	6.05	90	64s
Energy exp/householder, 1-family unit	year	471	90	28r
Energy exp/householder, <1,000 sq ft heating area	year	384	90	28r
Energy exp/householder, 1,000-1,999 sq ft heating area	year	421	90	28r
Energy exp/householder, 2,000+ sq ft heating area	year	625	90	28r
Energy exp/householder, mobile home	year	271	90	28r
Energy exp/householder, multifamily	year	355	90	28r
Gas, natural	mil Btu	2.11	90	64s
Gas, natural	000 cu ft	5.77	91	46s
Gas, natural, exp	year	336	91	46s
Gasoline, unleaded regular	mil Btu	9.47	90	64s
Entertainment				
Miniature golf admission	adult	6.18	92	1r
Miniature golf admission	child	5.14	92	1r
Waterpark admission	adult	11.00	92	1r
Waterpark admission	child	8.55	92	1r
Funerals				
Casket, 18-gauge steel, velvet interior		2274.41	91	24r
Cosmetology, hair care, etc.		74.62	91	24r
Embalming		229.94	91	24r
Facility use for ceremony		176.61	91	24r
Hearse, local		116.34	91	24r
Limousine, local		72.68	91	24r
Remains to funeral home, transfer		87.72	91	24r
Service charge, professional		712.53	91	24r
Vault, concrete, non-metallic liner		750.55	91	24r
Viewing facilities, use		155.31	91	24r
Groceries				
Apples, Red Delicious	lb	0.79	4/93	16r
Bacon	lb	1.75	4/93	16r
Bananas	lb	0.42	4/93	16r
Beef, stew, boneless	lb	2.61	4/93	16r
Bologna, all beef or mixed	lb	2.24	4/93	16r
Bread, white, pan	lb	0.64	4/93	16r
Bread, whole wheat, pan	lb	0.96	4/93	16r
Cabbage	lb	0.37	4/93	16r
Carrots, short trimmed and topped	lb	0.47	4/93	16r
Celery	lb	0.64	4/93	16r
Cheese, American	lb	2.98	4/93	16r
Cheese, Cheddar	lb	3.28	4/93	16r
Chicken, fresh, whole	lb	0.77	4/93	16r
Chicken breast, bone-in	lb	1.92	4/93	16r
Chicken legs, bone-in	lb	1.06	4/93	16r
Chuck roast, graded and ungraded, ex USDA prime and choice	lb	2.40	4/93	16r
Chuck roast, USDA choice, bone-in	lb	2.19	4/93	16r
Chuck roast, USDA choice, boneless	lb	2.38	4/93	16r
Coffee, 100% ground roast, all sizes	lb	2.48	4/93	16r
Crackers, soda, salted	lb	1.15	4/93	16r
Eggs, Grade A large	doz	0.96	4/93	16r
Flour, white, all purpose	lb	0.24	4/93	16r
Frankfurters, all meat or all beef	lb	2.01	4/93	16r
Grapefruit	lb	0.44	4/93	16r
Grapes, Thompson Seedless	lb	1.40	4/93	16r
Ground beef, 100% beef	lb	1.58	4/93	16r
Ground beef, lean and extra lean	lb	2.09	4/93	16r
Ground chuck, 100% beef	lb	1.98	4/93	16r

Values are in dollars or fractions of dollars. In the column headed *Ref*, references are shown to sources. Each reference is followed by a letter. These refer to the geographical level for which data were reported: s = State, r = Region, and c = City or metro. The abbreviation *ex* is used to mean *except* or *excluding*; *exp* stands for expenditures. For other abbreviations and further explanations, please see the Introduction.

Alexandria, LA - continued

Item	Per	Value	Date	Ref.
Groceries				
Ham, boneless, excluding canned	lb	2.89	4/93	16r
Ham, picnic, shoulder, bone-in, smoked	lb	1.02	4/93	16r
Ham, rump or steak half, bone-in, smoked	lb	1.48	4/93	16r
Honey, jar	8 oz	0.73-1.19	92	5r
Honey, jar	lb	1.10-1.79	92	5r
Honey, squeeze bear	12-oz	1.19-1.50	92	5r
Ice cream, prepackaged, bulk, regular	1/2 gal	2.41	4/93	16r
Lemons	lb	1.05	4/93	16r
Lettuce, iceberg	lb	0.81	4/93	16r
Margarine, stick	lb	0.88	4/93	16r
Oranges, navel	lb	0.55	4/93	16r
Pears, Anjou	lb	0.92	4/93	16r
Pork chops, center cut, bone-in	lb	3.13	4/93	16r
Potato chips	16 oz	2.94	4/93	16r
Potatoes, white	lb	0.43	4/93	16r
Rib roast, USDA choice, bone-in	lb	4.63	4/93	16r
Rice, white, long grain, uncooked	lb	0.45	4/93	16r
Round roast, graded & ungraded, ex USDA prime & choice	lb	3.03	4/93	16r
Round roast, USDA choice, boneless	lb	3.09	4/93	16r
Sausage, fresh, loose	lb	2.08	4/93	16r
Short ribs, bone-in	lb	2.66	4/93	16r
Shortening, vegetable oil blends	lb	0.69	4/93	16r
Spaghetti and macaroni	lb	0.81	4/93	16r
Steak, rib eye, USDA choice, boneless	lb	6.24	4/93	16r
Steak, round, graded & ungraded, ex USDA prime & choice	lb	3.31	4/93	16r
Steak, round, USDA choice, boneless	lb	3.34	4/93	16r
Steak, sirloin, graded & ungraded, ex USDA prime & choice	lb	4.19	4/93	16r
Steak, sirloin, USDA choice, boneless	lb	4.46	4/93	16r
Steak, T-bone, USDA choice, bone-in	lb	5.25	4/93	16r
Strawberries, dry pint	12 oz	0.92	4/93	16r
Sugar, white	lb	0.39	4/93	16r
Sugar, white, 33-80 oz pk	lb	0.38	4/93	16r
Tomatoes, field grown	lb	0.88	4/93	16r
Tuna, chunk, light	lb	1.79	4/93	16r
Turkey, frozen, whole	lb	1.04	4/93	16r
Yogurt, natural, fruit flavored	1/2 pint	0.57	4/93	16r
Health Care				
Childbirth, cesarean, hospital		5034	91	62r
Childbirth, cesarean, physician's fee		2053	91	62r
Childbirth, normal, hospital		2712	91	62r
Childbirth, normal, physician's fee		1492	91	62r
Mental health care, exp	capita	20.37-28.83	90	38s
Mental health care, exp, state mental health agency	capita	28.44	90	38s
Mental health care, hospital psychiatric services, non-Federal, exp	capita	8.19	88	38s
Mental health care, mental health organization, multiservice, exp	capita	0.49	88	38s
Mental health care, psychiatric hospitals, private, exp	capita	43.54	88	38s
Mental health care, psychiatric out-patient clinics, freestanding, exp	capita	4.11	88	38s
Mental health care, state and county mental hospitals, exp	capita	18.74	88	38s
Mental health care, VA medical centers, exp	capita	2.60	88	38s
Physician fee, family practice, first-visit		75.00	91	62r
Physician fee, family practice, revisit		34.00	91	62r
Physician fee, general practice, first-visit		61.00	91	62r
Physician fee, general practice, revisit		32.00	91	62r
Physician fee, general surgeon, first-visit		64.00	91	62r
Physician fee, general surgeon, revisit		40.00	91	62r
Physician fee, internal medicine, first-visit		98.00	91	62r
Physician fee, internal medicine, revisit		40.00	91	62r
Physician fee, median, neurosurgeon, first-visit		130.00	91	62r
Physician fee, median, nonsurgical specialist, first-visit		95.00	91	62r

Alexandria, LA - continued

Item	Per	Value	Date	Ref.
Health Care - continued				
Physician fee, median, orthopedic surgeon, first-visit		91.00	91	62r
Physician fee, median, plastic surgeon, first-visit		66.00	91	62r
Physician fee, median, surgical specialist, first-visit		62.00	91	62r
Physician fee, neurosurgeon, revisit		50.00	91	62r
Physician fee, nonsurgical specialist, revisit		40.00	91	62r
Physician fee, obstetrics/gynecology, first-visit		64.00	91	62r
Physician fee, obstetrics/gynecology, revisit		41.00	91	62r
Physician fee, orthopedic surgeon, revisit		40.00	91	62r
Physician fee, pediatrician, first-visit		49.00	91	62r
Physician fee, pediatrician, revisit		33.00	91	62r
Physician fee, plastic surgeon, revisit		43.00	91	62r
Physician fee, surgical specialist, revisit		37.00	91	62r
Substance abuse, hospital ancillary charge	incident	2600	90	70s
Substance abuse, hospital physician charge	incident	840	90	70s
Substance abuse, hospital room and board	incident	6410	90	70s
Insurance and Pensions				
Auto insurance, private passenger	year	778.70	91	63s
Taxes				
Tax, cigarette	pack	20	91	77s
Tax, gasoline	gal	20	91	77s
Taxes, state	capita	1013	91	77s
Transportation				
Driver's license fee		18.00	12/90	43s
Travel				
Business travel	day	193.00	4/93	89r
Utilities				
Electricity	mil Btu	17.77	90	64s

Allentown-Bethlehem-Easton, PA, NJ

Item	Per	Value	Date	Ref.
Composite ACCRA index		108.80	4Q 92	4c
Alcoholic Beverages				
Beer, Miller Lite or Budweiser, 12-oz containers	6 pack	5.42	4Q 92	4c
Liquor, J & B Scotch	750 ml	16.39	4Q 92	4c
Wine, Gallo Chablis blanc, 1.5 liter	bottle	5.79	4Q 92	4c
Child Care				
Child care fee, average, center	hour	2.18	90	65r
Child care fee, average, nonregulated family day care	hour	1.83	90	65r
Child care fee, average, regulated family day care	hour	2.02	90	65r
Clothing				
Jeans, man's denim		29.99	4Q 92	4c
Shirt, man's dress shirt		26.00	4Q 92	4c
Undervest, boy's size 10-14, cotton	3	4.69	4Q 92	4c
Communications				
Long-distance telephone service, day, initial minute, 0-100 miles	min	0.15-0.29	91	12s
Long-distance telephone service, day, additional minute, 0-100 miles	min	0.06-0.22	91	12s
Long-distance telephone service, evenings/weekends, 0-100 mi, initial minute	min	0.06-0.14	91	12s
Long-distance telephone service, evenings/weekends, 0-100 mi, additional minute	min	0.03-0.11	91	12s
Newspaper subscription, daily and Sunday home delivery, large-city	month	12.83	4Q 92	4c
Telephone, residential, private line, rotary, unlimited calling	month	15.07	10/91	78c
Telephone bill, family of four	month	16.29	4Q 92	4c

Values are in dollars or fractions of dollars. In the column headed *Ref*, references are shown to sources. Each reference is followed by a letter. These refer to the geographical level for which data were reported: s = State, r = Region, and c = City or metro. The abbreviation *ex* is used to mean *except* or *excluding*; *exp* stands for expenditures. For other abbreviations and further explanations, please see the Introduction.

Allentown-Bethlehem-Easton, PA, NJ - continued

Item	Per	Value	Date	Ref.
Education				
Board, 4-yr private college/university	year	2019	91	22s
Board, 4-yr public college/university	year	1656	91	22s
Expenditures, local gov't, public elementary/secondary	pupil	6980	92	20s
Room, 4-year private college/university	year	2179	91	22s
Room, 4-year public college/university	year	1719	91	22s
Tuition, 2-year private college/university	year	6314	91	22s
Tuition, 2-year public college/university	year	1505	91	22s
Tuition, 4-year private college/university	year	9848	91	22s
Tuition, 4-year public college/university, in-state	year	3401	91	22s
Energy and Fuels				
Coal	mil Btu	1.57	90	64s
Energy	mil Btu	8.63	90	64s
Energy, combined forms, 1,800 sq ft heating area	month	134.59	4Q 92	4c
Energy exp/householder, 1-family unit	year	588	90	28r
Energy exp/householder, <1,000 sq ft heating area	year	477	90	28r
Energy exp/householder, 1,000-1,999 sq ft heating area	year	517	90	28r
Energy exp/householder, 2,000+ sq ft heating area	year	630	90	28r
Energy exp/householder, mobile home	year	412	90	28r
Energy exp/householder, multifamily	year	498	90	28r
Gas, cooking, winter, 10 therms	month	12.36	92	56c
Gas, cooking, winter, 30 therms	month	24.71	92	56c
Gas, cooking, winter, 50 therms	month	37.06	92	56c
Gas, heating, winter, 100 therms	month	55.75	92	56c
Gas, heating, winter, average use	month	87.11	92	56c
Gas, natural	mil Btu	5.24	90	64s
Gas, natural	000 cu ft	6.76	91	46s
Gas, natural, exp	year	703	91	46s
Gasoline, motor	gal	1.14	4Q 92	4c
Gasoline, unleaded regular	mil Btu	9.35	90	64s
Entertainment				
Bowling, evening rate	game	2.19	4Q 92	4c
Monopoly game, Parker Brothers', No. 9		11.24	4Q 92	4c
Movie	admission	5.12	4Q 92	4c
Tennis balls, yellow, Wilson or Penn, 3	can	2.89	4Q 92	4c
Funerals				
Casket, 18-gauge steel, velvet interior		1811.58	91	24r
Cosmetology, hair care, etc.		111.08	91	24r
Embalming		329.42	91	24r
Facility use for ceremony		201.29	91	24r
Hearse, local		135.27	91	24r
Limousine, local		127.24	91	24r
Remains to funeral home, transfer		103.98	91	24r
Service charge, professional		724.98	91	24r
Vault, concrete, non-metallic liner		766.71	91	24r
Viewing facilities, use		260.60	91	24r
Goods and Services				
ACCRA Index, Miscellaneous Goods and Services		109.10	4Q 92	4c
Groceries				
ACCRA Index, Groceries		111.90	4Q 92	4c
Apples, Red Delicious	lb	0.85	4/93	16r
Babyfood, strained vegetables, lowest price	4-4.5 oz jar	0.38	4Q 92	4c
Bacon	lb	2.12	4/93	16r
Bananas	lb	0.54	4Q 92	4c
Bananas	lb	0.54	4/93	16r
Bread, white	24 oz	1.00	4Q 92	4c
Bread, white, pan	lb	0.81	4/93	16r
Butter	lb	2.02	4/93	16r
Carrots, short trimmed and topped	lb	0.51	4/93	16r

Allentown-Bethlehem-Easton, PA, NJ - continued

Item	Per	Value	Date	Ref.
Groceries - continued				
Cheese, Kraft grated Parmesan	8-oz canister	3.39	4Q 92	4c
Chicken, fresh, whole	lb	1.04	4/93	16r
Chicken, fryer, whole	lb	0.93	4Q 92	4c
Chicken breast, bone-in	lb	2.21	4/93	16r
Chicken legs, bone-in	lb	1.16	4/93	16r
Chuck roast, USDA choice, boneless	lb	2.82	4/93	16r
Cigarettes, Winston	carton	17.98	4Q 92	4c
Coffee, 100% ground roast, all sizes	lb	2.66	4/93	16r
Coffee, vacuum-packed	13-oz can	2.22	4Q 92	4c
Corn, frozen	10 oz	0.64	4Q 92	4c
Corn Flakes, Kellogg's or Post Toasties	18 oz	2.09	4Q 92	4c
Cucumbers	lb	0.85	4/93	16r
Eggs, Grade A large	doz	0.84	4Q 92	4c
Eggs, Grade A large	doz	1.15	4/93	16r
Grapefruit	lb	0.45	4/93	16r
Grapes, Thompson Seedless	lb	1.52	4/93	16r
Ground beef, lean and extra lean	lb	2.36	4/93	16r
Ground beef or hamburger	lb	1.60	4Q 92	4c
Ground chuck, 100% beef	lb	2.02	4/93	16r
Honey, jar	8 oz	0.96-1.75	92	5r
Honey, jar	lb	1.50-3.00	92	5r
Honey, squeeze bear	12-oz	1.50-1.99	92	5r
Ice cream, prepackaged, bulk, regular	1/2 gal	2.80	4/93	16r
Lemons	lb	0.96	4/93	16r
Lettuce, iceberg	head	1.19	4Q 92	4c
Lettuce, iceberg	lb	0.95	4/93	16r
Margarine, Blue Bonnet or Parkay cubes	lb	0.75	4Q 92	4c
Margarine, stick	lb	0.81	4/93	16r
Milk, fresh, whole, fortified	1/2 gal	1.30	4/93	16r
Milk, whole	1/2 gal	1.23	4Q 92	4c
Orange juice, Minute Maid frozen	12-oz can	1.81	4Q 92	4c
Oranges, navel	lb	0.56	4/93	16r
Peaches	29-oz can	1.45	4Q 92	4c
Peanut butter, creamy, all sizes	lb	1.88	4/93	16r
Peas Sweet, Del Monte or Green Giant	15-17 oz can	0.62	4Q 92	4c
Pork chops, center cut, bone-in	lb	3.34	4/93	16r
Potato chips	16 oz	2.88	4/93	16r
Potatoes, white	lb	0.37	4/93	16r
Potatoes, white or red	10-lb sack	2.36	4Q 92	4c
Rib roast, USDA choice, bone-in	lb	4.94	4/93	16r
Round roast, USDA choice, boneless	lb	3.17	4/93	16r
Sausage, Jimmy Dean, 100% pork	lb	2.86	4Q 92	4c
Shortening, vegetable oil blends	lb	0.98	4/93	16r
Shortening, vegetable, Crisco	3-lb can	2.64	4Q 92	4c
Soft drink, Coca Cola	2 liter	1.21	4Q 92	4c
Spaghetti and macaroni	lb	0.82	4/93	16r
Steak, round, graded & ungraded, ex USDA prime & choice	lb	4.04	4/93	16r
Steak, round, USDA choice, boneless	lb	3.90	4/93	16r
Steak, sirloin, USDA choice, boneless	lb	4.97	4/93	16r
Steak, T-bone	lb	5.67	4Q 92	4c
Strawberries, dry pint	12 oz	0.90	4/93	16r
Sugar, cane or beet	4 lb	1.91	4Q 92	4c
Sugar, white	lb	0.50	4/93	16r
Sugar, white, 33-80 oz pk	lb	0.41	4/93	16r
Tomatoes, field grown	lb	1.23	4/93	16r
Tomatoes, Hunt's or Del Monte	14.5-oz can	0.77	4Q 92	4c
Tuna, chunk, light	6.125-6.5 oz can	0.74	4Q 92	4c
Tuna, chunk, light	lb	2.22	4/93	16r
Turkey, frozen, whole	lb	1.04	4/93	16r

Values are in dollars or fractions of dollars. In the column headed *Ref*, references are shown to sources. Each reference is followed by a letter. These refer to the geographical level for which data were reported: s = State, r = Region, and c = City or metro. The abbreviation *ex* is used to mean *except* or *excluding*; *exp* stands for expenditures. For other abbreviations and further explanations, please see the Introduction.

Allentown-Bethlehem-Easton, PA, NJ - continued

Item	Per	Value	Date	Ref.
Health Care				
ACCRA Index, Health Care		103.60	4Q 92	4c
Analgesic, Aspirin, Bayer, 325 mg tablets	100	5.52	4Q 92	4c
Childbirth, cesarean, hospital		5826	91	62r
Childbirth, cesarean, physician's fee		2053	91	62r
Childbirth, normal, hospital		2964	91	62r
Childbirth, normal, physician's fee		1492	91	62r
Dentist's fee, adult teeth cleaning and periodic oral exam	visit	54.00	4Q 92	4c
Doctor's fee, routine exam, established patient	visit	30.61	4Q 92	4c
Hospital care, semiprivate room	day	329.00	90	27c
Hospital care, semiprivate room	day	371.33	4Q 92	4c
Medical insurance premium, per employee, small group comprehensive	month	328.50	10/91	25c
Medical plan per employee	year	3942	91	45r
Mental health care, exp	capita	53.68-118.35	90	38s
Mental health care, exp, state mental health agency	capita	56.85	90	38s
Mental health care, hospital psychiatric services, non-Federal, exp	capita	22.11	88	38s
Mental health care, mental health organization, multiservice, exp	capita	21.01	88	38s
Mental health care, psychiatric hospitals, private, exp	capita	26.48	88	38s
Mental health care, psychiatric out-patient clinics, freestanding, exp	capita	4.17	88	38s
Mental health care, psychiatric partial-care organizations, freestanding, exp	capita	0.94	88	38s
Mental health care, state and county mental hospitals, exp	capita	37.11	88	38s
Mental health care, VA medical centers, exp	capita	9.77	88	38s
Prescription drug co-pay, Medicaid	month	6.00	91	21s
Substance abuse, hospital ancillary charge	inci-dent	720	90	70s
Substance abuse, hospital physician charge	inci-dent	210	90	70s
Substance abuse, hospital room and board	inci-dent	5400	90	70s
Household Goods				
Appliance repair, home, service call, washing machine	min labor charge	37.00	4Q 92	4c
Laundry detergent, Tide Ultra, Bold, or Cheer	42 oz	3.23	4Q 92	4c
Tissues, facial, Kleenex brand	175-count box	1.26	4Q 92	4c
Housing				
ACCRA Index, Housing		107.90	4Q 92	4c
House, 1,800 sq ft, 8,000 sq ft lot, new, urban	total	119650	4Q 92	4c
House payment, principal and interest, 25% down payment	month	664	4Q 92	4c
Mortgage rate, incl. points & origination fee, 30-year fixed or adjustable rate	per-cent	8.09	4Q 92	4c
Rent, apartment, 2 bedrooms - 1-1/2 to 2 baths, unfurnished, 950 sq ft, water	month	530	4Q 92	4c
Rental unit, 1 bedroom	month	462	93	23c
Rental unit, 2 bedroom	month	540	93	23c
Rental unit, 3 bedroom	month	681	93	23c
Rental unit, 4 bedroom	month	759	93	23c
Rental unit, efficiency	month	380	93	23c
Insurance and Pensions				
Auto insurance, private passenger	year	683.57	91	63c
Personal Goods				
Shampoo, Alberto VO5	15 oz	1.59	4Q 92	4c
Toothpaste, Crest or Colgate	6-7 oz	2.45	4Q 92	4c

Allentown-Bethlehem-Easton, PA, NJ - continued

Item	Per	Value	Date	Ref.
Personal Services				
Dry cleaning, man's 2-piece suit		6.60	4Q 92	4c
Haircare, woman's shampoo, trim and blow-dry		22.67	4Q 92	4c
Haircut, man's barbershop, no styling		9.50	4Q 92	4c
Restaurant Food				
Chicken, fried, thigh and drumstick		2.38	4Q 92	4c
Hamburger with cheese	1/4 lb	1.88	4Q 92	4c
Pizza, Pizza Hut or Pizza Inn, cheese, thin crust	12-13 in	7.69	4Q 92	4c
Taxes				
Tax, cigarette	pack	31	91	77s
Tax, gasoline	gal	12	91	77s
Taxes, state	capita	1089	91	77s
Transportation				
ACCRA Index, Transportation		99.80	4Q 92	4c
Auto rental, average	day	54.95	6/91	60c
Bus fare	one-way	1.00	3/93	2c
Bus fare, up to 10 miles	one-way	1.00	4Q 92	4c
Driver's license fee		22.00	12/90	43s
Limo fare, airport-city, average	day	8.50	6/91	60c
Taxi fare, airport-city, average	day	26.00	6/91	60c
Tire balance, computer or spin balance, front	wheel	6.20	4Q 92	4c
Travel				
Breakfast	day	6.58	6/91	60c
Business travel	day	165.00	4/93	89r
Dinner	day	27.40	6/91	60c
Lodging	day	81.38	91	60c
Lunch	day	10.90	6/91	60c
Utilities				
ACCRA Index, Utilities		119.30	4Q 92	4c
Electricity	mil Btu	22.46	90	64s
Electricity, all electric, 1,800 sq ft living area new home	month	134.59	4Q 92	4c

Altoona, PA

Item	Per	Value	Date	Ref.
Child Care				
Child care fee, average, center	hour	2.18	90	65r
Child care fee, average, nonregulated family day care	hour	1.83	90	65r
Child care fee, average, regulated family day care	hour	2.02	90	65r
Communications				
Long-distance telephone service, day, initial minute, 0-100 miles	min	0.15-0.29	91	12s
Long-distance telephone service, day, additional minute, 0-100 miles	min	0.06-0.22	91	12s
Long-distance telephone service, evenings/weekends, 0-100 mi, initial minute	min	0.06-0.14	91	12s
Long-distance telephone service, evenings/weekends, 0-100 mi, additional minute	min	0.03-0.11	91	12s
Education				
Board, 4-yr private college/university	year	2019	91	22s
Board, 4-yr public college/university	year	1656	91	22s
Expenditures, local gov't, public elementary/secondary	pupil	6980	92	20s
Room, 4-year private college/university	year	2179	91	22s
Room, 4-year public college/university	year	1719	91	22s
Tuition, 2-year private college/university	year	6314	91	22s
Tuition, 2-year public college/university	year	1505	91	22s
Tuition, 4-year private college/university	year	9848	91	22s
Tuition, 4-year public college/university, in-state	year	3401	91	22s

Values are in dollars or fractions of dollars. In the column headed *Ref*, references are shown to sources. Each reference is followed by a letter. These refer to the geographical level for which data were reported: s=State, r=Region, and c=City or metro. The abbreviation *ex* is used to mean *except* or *excluding*; *exp* stands for expenditures. For other abbreviations and further explanations, please see the Introduction.

Altoona, PA - continued

Energy and Fuels

Item	Per	Value	Date	Ref.
Coal	mil Btu	1.57	90	64s
Energy	mil Btu	8.63	90	64s
Energy exp/householder, 1-family unit	year	588	90	28r
Energy exp/householder, <1,000 sq ft heating area	year	477	90	28r
Energy exp/householder, 1,000-1,999 sq ft heating area	year	517	90	28r
Energy exp/householder, 2,000+ sq ft heating area	year	630	90	28r
Energy exp/householder, mobile home	year	412	90	28r
Energy exp/householder, multifamily	year	498	90	28r
Gas, natural	mil Btu	5.24	90	64s
Gas, natural	000 cu ft	6.76	91	46s
Gas, natural, exp	year	703	91	46s
Gasoline, unleaded regular	mil Btu	9.35	90	64s

Funerals

Item	Per	Value	Date	Ref.
Casket, 18-gauge steel, velvet interior		1811.58	91	24r
Cosmetology, hair care, etc.		111.08	91	24r
Embalming		329.42	91	24r
Facility use for ceremony		201.29	91	24r
Hearse, local		135.27	91	24r
Limousine, local		127.24	91	24r
Remains to funeral home, transfer		103.98	91	24r
Service charge, professional		724.98	91	24r
Vault, concrete, non-metallic liner		766.71	91	24r
Viewing facilities, use		260.60	91	24r

Groceries

Item	Per	Value	Date	Ref.
Apples, Red Delicious	lb	0.85	4/93	16r
Bacon	lb	2.12	4/93	16r
Bananas	lb	0.54	4/93	16r
Bread, white, pan	lb	0.81	4/93	16r
Butter	lb	2.02	4/93	16r
Carrots, short trimmed and topped	lb	0.51	4/93	16r
Chicken, fresh, whole	lb	1.04	4/93	16r
Chicken breast, bone-in	lb	2.21	4/93	16r
Chicken legs, bone-in	lb	1.16	4/93	16r
Chuck roast, USDA choice, boneless	lb	2.82	4/93	16r
Coffee, 100% ground roast, all sizes	lb	2.66	4/93	16r
Cucumbers	lb	0.85	4/93	16r
Eggs, Grade A large	doz	1.15	4/93	16r
Grapefruit	lb	0.45	4/93	16r
Grapes, Thompson Seedless	lb	1.52	4/93	16r
Ground beef, lean and extra lean	lb	2.36	4/93	16r
Ground chuck, 100% beef	lb	2.02	4/93	16r
Honey, jar	8 oz	0.96-1.75	92	5r
Honey, jar	lb	1.50-3.00	92	5r
Honey, squeeze bear	12-oz	1.50-1.99	92	5r
Ice cream, prepackaged, bulk, regular	1/2 gal	2.80	4/93	16r
Lemons	lb	0.96	4/93	16r
Lettuce, iceberg	lb	0.95	4/93	16r
Margarine, stick	lb	0.81	4/93	16r
Milk, fresh, whole, fortified	1/2 gal	1.30	4/93	16r
Oranges, navel	lb	0.56	4/93	16r
Peanut butter, creamy, all sizes	lb	1.88	4/93	16r
Pork chops, center cut, bone-in	lb	3.34	4/93	16r
Potato chips	16 oz	2.88	4/93	16r
Potatoes, white	lb	0.37	4/93	16r
Rib roast, USDA choice, bone-in	lb	4.94	4/93	16r
Round roast, USDA choice, boneless	lb	3.17	4/93	16r
Shortening, vegetable oil blends	lb	0.98	4/93	16r
Spaghetti and macaroni	lb	0.82	4/93	16r
Steak, round, graded & ungraded, ex USDA prime & choice	lb	4.04	4/93	16r
Steak, round, USDA choice, boneless	lb	3.90	4/93	16r
Steak, sirloin, USDA choice, boneless	lb	4.97	4/93	16r
Strawberries, dry pint	12 oz	0.90	4/93	16r
Sugar, white	lb	0.50	4/93	16r
Sugar, white, 33-80 oz pk	lb	0.41	4/93	16r
Tomatoes, field grown	lb	1.23	4/93	16r
Tuna, chunk, light	lb	2.22	4/93	16r

Altoona, PA - continued

Groceries - continued

Item	Per	Value	Date	Ref.
Turkey, frozen, whole	lb	1.04	4/93	16r

Health Care

Item	Per	Value	Date	Ref.
Childbirth, cesarean, hospital		5826	91	62r
Childbirth, cesarean, physician's fee		2053	91	62r
Childbirth, normal, hospital		2964	91	62r
Childbirth, normal, physician's fee		1492	91	62r
Medical plan per employee	year	3942	91	45r
Mental health care, exp	capita	53.68-118.35	90	38s
Mental health care, exp, state mental health agency	capita	56.85	90	38s
Mental health care, hospital psychiatric services, non-Federal, exp	capita	22.11	88	38s
Mental health care, mental health organization, multiservice, exp	capita	21.01	88	38s
Mental health care, psychiatric hospitals, private, exp	capita	26.48	88	38s
Mental health care, psychiatric out-patient clinics, freestanding, exp	capita	4.17	88	38s
Mental health care, psychiatric partial-care organizations, freestanding, exp	capita	0.94	88	38s
Mental health care, state and county mental hospitals, exp	capita	37.11	88	38s
Mental health care, VA medical centers, exp	capita	9.77	88	38s
Prescription drug co-pay, Medicaid	month	6.00	91	21s
Substance abuse, hospital ancillary charge	incident	720	90	70s
Substance abuse, hospital physician charge	incident	210	90	70s
Substance abuse, hospital room and board	incident	5400	90	70s

Insurance and Pensions

Item	Per	Value	Date	Ref.
Auto insurance, private passenger	year	683.57	91	63s

Taxes

Item	Per	Value	Date	Ref.
Tax, cigarette	pack	31	91	77s
Tax, gasoline	gal	12	91	77s
Taxes, state	capita	1089	91	77s

Transportation

Item	Per	Value	Date	Ref.
Driver's license fee		22.00	12/90	43s

Travel

Item	Per	Value	Date	Ref.
Business travel	day	165.00	4/93	89r

Utilities

Item	Per	Value	Date	Ref.
Electricity	mil Btu	22.46	90	64s

Amarillo, TX

Item	Per	Value	Date	Ref.
Composite ACCRA index		87.90	4Q 92	4c

Alcoholic Beverages

Item	Per	Value	Date	Ref.
Beer, Miller Lite or Budweiser, 12-oz containers	6 pack	3.89	4Q 92	4c
Liquor, J & B Scotch	750 ml	17.75	4Q 92	4c
Wine, Gallo Chablis blanc, 1.5 liter	bottle	5.45	4Q 92	4c

Child Care

Item	Per	Value	Date	Ref.
Child care fee, average, center	hour	1.29	90	65r
Child care fee, average, nonregulated family day care	hour	0.89	90	65r
Child care fee, average, regulated family day care	hour	1.32	90	65r

Clothing

Item	Per	Value	Date	Ref.
Jeans, man's denim		25.19	4Q 92	4c
Shirt, man's dress shirt		21.20	4Q 92	4c
Undervest, boy's size 10-14, cotton	3	3.74	4Q 92	4c

Communications

Item	Per	Value	Date	Ref.
Long-distance telephone service, day, initial minute, 0-100 miles	min	0.10-0.46	91	12s

Values are in dollars or fractions of dollars. In the column headed *Ref*, references are shown to sources. Each reference is followed by a letter. These refer to the geographical level for which data were reported: s=State, r=Region, and c=City or metro. The abbreviation *ex* is used to mean *except* or *excluding*; *exp* stands for expenditures. For other abbreviations and further explanations, please see the Introduction.

Amarillo, TX - continued

Item	Per	Value	Date	Ref.
Communications				
Long-distance telephone service, day, additional minute, 0-100 miles	min	0.06-0.45	91	12s
Newspaper subscription, daily and Sunday home delivery, large-city	month	8.28	4Q 92	4c
Telephone, flat rate	month	9.10	91	11c
Telephone bill, family of four	month	15.13	4Q 92	4c
Education				
Board, 4-yr private college/university	year	1883	91	22s
Board, 4-yr public college/university	year	1605	91	22s
Expenditures, local gov't, public elementary/secondary	pupil	4593	92	20s
Room, 4-year private college/university	year	1620	91	22s
Room, 4-year public college/university	year	1532	91	22s
Tuition, 2-year private college/university	year	4394	91	22s
Tuition, 2-year public college/university	year	495	91	22s
Tuition, 4-year private college/university	year	6497	91	22s
Tuition, 4-year public college/university, in-state	year	986	91	22s
Energy and Fuels				
Coal	mil Btu	1.44	90	64s
Energy	mil Btu	6.48	90	64s
Energy, combined forms, 1,800 sq ft heating area	month	81.91	4Q 92	4c
Energy, exc electricity, 1,800 sq ft heating area	month	30.51	4Q 92	4c
Energy exp/householder, 1-family unit	year	471	90	28r
Energy exp/householder, <1,000 sq ft heating area	year	384	90	28r
Energy exp/householder, 1,000-1,999 sq ft heating area	year	421	90	28r
Energy exp/householder, 2,000+ sq ft heating area	year	625	90	28r
Energy exp/householder, mobile home	year	271	90	28r
Energy exp/householder, multifamily	year	355	90	28r
Gas, cooking, winter, 10 therms	month	6.76	92	56c
Gas, cooking, winter, 30 therms	month	14.38	92	56c
Gas, cooking, winter, 50 therms	month	21.24	92	56c
Gas, heating, winter, 100 therms	month	38.41	92	56c
Gas, heating, winter, average use	month	226.69	92	56c
Gas, natural	mil Btu	2.47	90	64s
Gas, natural	000 cu ft	5.71	91	46s
Gas, natural, exp	year	388	91	46s
Gasoline, motor	gal	1.13	4Q 92	4c
Gasoline, unleaded regular	mil Btu	9.16	90	64s
Entertainment				
Bowling, evening rate	game	1.90	4Q 92	4c
Miniature golf admission	adult	6.18	92	1r
Miniature golf admission	child	5.14	92	1r
Monopoly game, Parker Brothers', No. 9		9.76	4Q 92	4c
Movie	admission	5.50	4Q 92	4c
Tennis balls, yellow, Wilson or Penn, 3	can	2.05	4Q 92	4c
Waterpark admission	adult	11.00	92	1r
Waterpark admission	child	8.55	92	1r
Funerals				
Casket, 18-gauge steel, velvet interior		2274.41	91	24r
Cosmetology, hair care, etc.		74.62	91	24r
Embalming		229.94	91	24r
Facility use for ceremony		176.61	91	24r
Hearse, local		116.34	91	24r
Limousine, local		72.68	91	24r
Remains to funeral home, transfer		87.72	91	24r
Service charge, professional		712.53	91	24r
Vault, concrete, non-metallic liner		750.55	91	24r
Viewing facilities, use		155.31	91	24r
Goods and Services				
ACCRA Index, Miscellaneous Goods and Services		94.80	4Q 92	4c

Amarillo, TX - continued

Item	Per	Value	Date	Ref.
Groceries				
ACCRA Index, Groceries		99.90	4Q 92	4c
Apples, Red Delicious	lb	0.79	4/93	16r
Babyfood, strained vegetables, lowest price	4-4.5 oz jar	0.34	4Q 92	4c
Bacon	lb	1.75	4/93	16r
Bananas	lb	0.45	4Q 92	4c
Bananas	lb	0.42	4/93	16r
Beef, stew, boneless	lb	2.61	4/93	16r
Bologna, all beef or mixed	lb	2.24	4/93	16r
Bread, white	24 oz	0.75	4Q 92	4c
Bread, white, pan	lb	0.64	4/93	16r
Bread, whole wheat, pan	lb	0.96	4/93	16r
Cabbage	lb	0.37	4/93	16r
Carrots, short trimmed and topped	lb	0.47	4/93	16r
Celery	lb	0.64	4/93	16r
Cheese, American	lb	2.98	4/93	16r
Cheese, Cheddar	lb	3.28	4/93	16r
Cheese, Kraft grated Parmesan	8-oz canister	3.74	4Q 92	4c
Chicken, fresh, whole	lb	0.77	4/93	16r
Chicken, fryer, whole	lb	0.67	4Q 92	4c
Chicken breast, bone-in	lb	1.92	4/93	16r
Chicken legs, bone-in	lb	1.06	4/93	16r
Chuck roast, graded and ungraded, ex USDA prime and choice	lb	2.40	4/93	16r
Chuck roast, USDA choice, bone-in	lb	2.19	4/93	16r
Chuck roast, USDA choice, boneless	lb	2.38	4/93	16r
Cigarettes, Winston	carton	18.77	4Q 92	4c
Coffee, 100% ground roast, all sizes	lb	2.48	4/93	16r
Coffee, vacuum-packed	13-oz can	1.81	4Q 92	4c
Corn, frozen	10 oz	0.63	4Q 92	4c
Corn Flakes, Kellogg's or Post Toasties	18 oz	2.18	4Q 92	4c
Crackers, soda, salted	lb	1.15	4/93	16r
Eggs, Grade A large	doz	0.91	4Q 92	4c
Eggs, Grade A large	doz	0.96	4/93	16r
Flour, white, all purpose	lb	0.24	4/93	16r
Frankfurters, all meat or all beef	lb	2.01	4/93	16r
Grapefruit	lb	0.44	4/93	16r
Grapes, Thompson Seedless	lb	1.40	4/93	16r
Ground beef, 100% beef	lb	1.58	4/93	16r
Ground beef, lean and extra lean	lb	2.09	4/93	16r
Ground beef or hamburger	lb	1.35	4Q 92	4c
Ground chuck, 100% beef	lb	1.98	4/93	16r
Ham, boneless, excluding canned	lb	2.89	4/93	16r
Ham, picnic, shoulder, bone-in, smoked	lb	1.02	4/93	16r
Ham, rump or steak half, bone-in, smoked	lb	1.48	4/93	16r
Honey, jar	8 oz	0.73-1.19	92	5r
Honey, jar	lb	1.10-1.79	92	5r
Honey, squeeze bear	12-oz	1.19-1.50	92	5r
Ice cream, prepackaged, bulk, regular	1/2 gal	2.41	4/93	16r
Lemons	lb	1.05	4/93	16r
Lettuce, iceberg	head	1.03	4Q 92	4c
Lettuce, iceberg	lb	0.81	4/93	16r
Margarine, Blue Bonnet or Parkay cubes	lb	0.63	4Q 92	4c
Margarine, stick	lb	0.88	4/93	16r
Milk, whole	1/2 gal	1.48	4Q 92	4c
Orange juice, Minute Maid frozen	12-oz can	1.48	4Q 92	4c
Oranges, navel	lb	0.55	4/93	16r
Peaches	29-oz can	1.41	4Q 92	4c
Pears, Anjou	lb	0.92	4/93	16r
Peas Sweet, Del Monte or Green Giant	15-17 oz can	0.59	4Q 92	4c
Pork chops, center cut, bone-in	lb	3.13	4/93	16r
Potato chips	16 oz	2.94	4/93	16r
Potatoes, white	lb	0.43	4/93	16r
Potatoes, white or red	10-lb sack	1.93	4Q 92	4c
Rib roast, USDA choice, bone-in	lb	4.63	4/93	16r

Values are in dollars or fractions of dollars. In the column headed *Ref*, references are shown to sources. Each reference is followed by a letter. These refer to the geographical level for which data were reported: s=State, r=Region, and c=City or metro. The abbreviation *ex* is used to mean *except* or *excluding*; *exp* stands for expenditures. For other abbreviations and further explanations, please see the Introduction.

Amarillo, TX - continued

Item	Per	Value	Date	Ref.
Groceries				
Rice, white, long grain, uncooked	lb	0.45	4/93	16r
Round roast, graded & ungraded, ex USDA prime & choice	lb	3.03	4/93	16r
Round roast, USDA choice, boneless	lb	3.09	4/93	16r
Sausage, fresh, loose	lb	2.08	4/93	16r
Sausage, Jimmy Dean, 100% pork	lb	2.44	4Q 92	4c
Short ribs, bone-in	lb	2.66	4/93	16r
Shortening, vegetable oil blends	lb	0.69	4/93	16r
Shortening, vegetable, Crisco	3-lb can	2.21	4Q 92	4c
Soft drink, Coca Cola	2 liter	1.39	4Q 92	4c
Spaghetti and macaroni	lb	0.81	4/93	16r
Steak, rib eye, USDA choice, boneless	lb	6.24	4/93	16r
Steak, round, graded & ungraded, ex USDA prime & choice	lb	3.31	4/93	16r
Steak, round, USDA choice, boneless	lb	3.34	4/93	16r
Steak, sirloin, graded & ungraded, ex USDA prime & choice	lb	4.19	4/93	16r
Steak, sirloin, USDA choice, boneless	lb	4.46	4/93	16r
Steak, T-bone	lb	4.67	4Q 92	4c
Steak, T-bone, USDA choice, bone-in	lb	5.25	4/93	16r
Strawberries, dry pint	12 oz	0.92	4/93	16r
Sugar, cane or beet	4 lb	1.49	4Q 92	4c
Sugar, white	lb	0.39	4/93	16r
Sugar, white, 33-80 oz pk	lb	0.38	4/93	16r
Tomatoes, field grown	lb	0.88	4/93	16r
Tomatoes, Hunt's or Del Monte	14.5-oz can	0.67	4Q 92	4c
Tuna, chunk, light	6.125-6.5 oz can	0.67	4Q 92	4c
Tuna, chunk, light	lb	1.79	4/93	16r
Turkey, frozen, whole	lb	1.04	4/93	16r
Yogurt, natural, fruit flavored	1/2 pint	0.57	4/93	16r
Health Care				
ACCRA Index, Health Care		84.00	4Q 92	4c
Analgesic, Aspirin, Bayer, 325 mg tablets	100	4.12	4Q 92	4c
Childbirth, cesarean, hospital		5034	91	62r
Childbirth, cesarean, physician's fee		2053	91	62r
Childbirth, normal, hospital		2712	91	62r
Childbirth, normal, physician's fee		1492	91	62r
Dentist's fee, adult teeth cleaning and periodic oral exam	visit	32.80	4Q 92	4c
Doctor's fee, routine exam, established patient	visit	35.75	4Q 92	4c
Health care spending, state	capita	2192	3/93	84s
Hospital care, semiprivate room	day	199.71	90	27c
Hospital care, semiprivate room	day	277.25	4Q 92	4c
Medical insurance premium, per employee, small group comprehensive	month	335.80	10/91	25c
Mental health care, exp	capita	20.37-28.83	90	38s
Mental health care, exp, state mental health agency	capita	22.72	90	38s
Mental health care, hospital psychiatric services, non-Federal, exp	capita	7.95	88	38s
Mental health care, mental health organization, multiservice, exp	capita	12.05	88	38s
Mental health care, psychiatric hospitals, private, exp	capita	37.78	88	38s
Mental health care, psychiatric out-patient clinics, freestanding, exp	capita	0.43	88	38s
Mental health care, state and county mental hospitals, exp	capita	12.54	88	38s
Mental health care, VA medical centers, exp	capita	5.35	88	38s
Physician fee, family practice, first-visit		75.00	91	62r
Physician fee, family practice, revisit		34.00	91	62r
Physician fee, general practice, first-visit		61.00	91	62r
Physician fee, general practice, revisit		32.00	91	62r
Physician fee, general surgeon, first-visit		64.00	91	62r
Physician fee, general surgeon, revisit		40.00	91	62r

Amarillo, TX - continued

Item	Per	Value	Date	Ref.
Health Care - continued				
Physician fee, internal medicine, first-visit		98.00	91	62r
Physician fee, internal medicine, revisit		40.00	91	62r
Physician fee, median, neurosurgeon, first-visit		130.00	91	62r
Physician fee, median, nonsurgical specialist, first-visit		95.00	91	62r
Physician fee, median, orthopedic surgeon, first-visit		91.00	91	62r
Physician fee, median, plastic surgeon, first-visit		66.00	91	62r
Physician fee, median, surgical specialist, first-visit		62.00	91	62r
Physician fee, neurosurgeon, revisit		50.00	91	62r
Physician fee, nonsurgical specialist, revisit		40.00	91	62r
Physician fee, obstetrics/gynecology, first-visit		64.00	91	62r
Physician fee, obstetrics/gynecology, revisit		41.00	91	62r
Physician fee, orthopedic surgeon, revisit		40.00	91	62r
Physician fee, pediatrician, first-visit		49.00	91	62r
Physician fee, pediatrician, revisit		33.00	91	62r
Physician fee, plastic surgeon, revisit		43.00	91	62r
Physician fee, surgical specialist, revisit		37.00	91	62r
Substance abuse, hospital ancillary charge	incident	3750	90	70s
Substance abuse, hospital physician charge	incident	1080	90	70s
Substance abuse, hospital room and board	incident	5320	90	70s
Household Goods				
Appliance repair, home, service call, washing machine	min labor charge	33.80	4Q 92	4c
Laundry detergent, Tide Ultra, Bold, or Cheer	42 oz	3.07	4Q 92	4c
Tissues, facial, Kleenex brand	175-count box	1.11	4Q 92	4c
Housing				
ACCRA Index, Housing		75.60	4Q 92	4c
Home, median price	unit	58.10		26c
House, 1,800 sq ft, 8,000 sq ft lot, new, urban	total	83267	4Q 92	4c
House payment, principal and interest, 25% down payment	month	459	4Q 92	4c
Mortgage rate, incl. points & origination fee, 30-year fixed or adjustable rate	percent	8.02	4Q 92	4c
Rent, apartment, 2 bedrooms - 1-1/2 to 2 baths, unfurnished, 950 sq ft, water	month	386	4Q 92	4c
Rental unit, 1 bedroom	month	359	93	23c
Rental unit, 2 bedroom	month	424	93	23c
Rental unit, 3 bedroom	month	530	93	23c
Rental unit, 4 bedroom	month	594	93	23c
Rental unit, efficiency	month	296	93	23c
Insurance and Pensions				
Auto insurance, private passenger	year	709.79	91	63s
Personal Goods				
Shampoo, Alberto VO5	15 oz	0.86	4Q 92	4c
Toothpaste, Crest or Colgate	6-7 oz	1.61	4Q 92	4c
Personal Services				
Dry cleaning, man's 2-piece suit		5.63	4Q 92	4c
Haircare, woman's shampoo, trim and blow-dry		21.80	4Q 92	4c
Haircut, man's barbershop, no styling		7.40	4Q 92	4c
Restaurant Food				
Chicken, fried, thigh and drumstick		1.99	4Q 92	4c
Hamburger with cheese	1/4 lb	1.89	4Q 92	4c
Pizza, Pizza Hut or Pizza Inn, cheese, thin crust	12-13 in	9.64	4Q 92	4c

Values are in dollars or fractions of dollars. In the column headed *Ref*, references are shown to sources. Each reference is followed by a letter. These refer to the geographical level for which data were reported: s=State, r=Region, and c=City or metro. The abbreviation *ex* is used to mean *except* or *excluding*; *exp* stands for expenditures. For other abbreviations and further explanations, please see the Introduction.

Amarillo, TX - continued

Item	Per	Value	Date	Ref.
Taxes				
Tax, cigarette	pack	41	91	77s
Tax, gasoline	gal	20	91	77s
Taxes, state	capita	923	91	77s
Transportation				
ACCRA Index, Transportation		96.00	4Q 92	4c
Driver's license fee		16.00	12/90	43s
Tire balance, computer or spin balance, front	wheel	6.00	4Q 92	4c
Travel				
Business travel	day	193.00	4/93	89r
Utilities				
ACCRA Index, Utilities		75.30	4Q 92	4c
Electricity	mil Btu	17.09	90	64s
Electricity, partial electric and other energy, 1,800 sq ft living area new home	month	51.40	4Q 92	4c
Electricity, residential	KWh	5.92	2/93	94s
Electricity, winter, 250 KWh	month	19.64	92	55c
Electricity, winter, 500 KWh	month	34.63	92	55c
Electricity, winter, 750 KWh	month	49.61	92	55c
Electricity, winter, 1000 KWh	month	64.60	92	55c

Americus, GA

Item	Per	Value	Date	Ref.
Composite ACCRA index		96.40	4Q 92	4c
Alcoholic Beverages				
Beer, Miller Lite or Budweiser, 12-oz containers	6 pack	4.35	4Q 92	4c
Liquor, J & B Scotch	750 ml	16.29	4Q 92	4c
Wine, Gallo Chablis blanc, 1.5 liter	bottle	6.73	4Q 92	4c
Clothing				
Jeans, man's denim		31.59	4Q 92	4c
Shirt, man's dress shirt		25.50	4Q 92	4c
Undervest, boy's size 10-14, cotton	3	5.00	4Q 92	4c
Communications				
Newspaper subscription, daily and Sunday home delivery, large-city	month	14.26	4Q 92	4c
Telephone, flat rate	month	11.55	91	11c
Telephone bill, family of four	month	17.23	4Q 92	4c
Energy and Fuels				
Energy, combined forms, 1,800 sq ft heating area	month	136.34	4Q 92	4c
Gasoline, motor	gal	1.01	4Q 92	4c
Entertainment				
Bowling, evening rate	game	2.20	4Q 92	4c
Monopoly game, Parker Brothers', No. 9		11.48	4Q 92	4c
Movie	admission	3.00	4Q 92	4c
Tennis balls, yellow, Wilson or Penn, 3	can	2.86	4Q 92	4c
Goods and Services				
ACCRA Index, Miscellaneous Goods and Services		101.60	4Q 92	4c
Groceries				
ACCRA Index, Groceries		97.20	4Q 92	4c
Babyfood, strained vegetables, lowest price	4-4.5 oz jar	0.31	4Q 92	4c
Bananas	lb	0.43	4Q 92	4c
Bread, white	24 oz	0.76	4Q 92	4c
Cheese, Kraft grated Parmesan	8-oz canister	3.11	4Q 92	4c
Chicken, fryer, whole	lb	0.58	4Q 92	4c
Cigarettes, Winston	carton	15.57	4Q 92	4c
Coffee, vacuum-packed	13-oz can	1.98	4Q 92	4c
Corn, frozen	10 oz	0.69	4Q 92	4c
Corn Flakes, Kellogg's or Post Toasties	18 oz	1.73	4Q 92	4c

Americus, GA - continued

Item	Per	Value	Date	Ref.
Groceries - continued				
Eggs, Grade A large	doz	0.84	4Q 92	4c
Ground beef or hamburger	lb	1.66	4Q 92	4c
Lettuce, iceberg	head	0.99	4Q 92	4c
Margarine, Blue Bonnet or Parkay cubes	lb	0.56	4Q 92	4c
Milk, whole	1/2 gal	1.66	4Q 92	4c
Orange juice, Minute Maid frozen	12-oz can	1.51	4Q 92	4c
Peaches	29-oz can	1.24	4Q 92	4c
Peas Sweet, Del Monte or Green Giant	15-17 oz can	0.53	4Q 92	4c
Potatoes, white or red	10-lb sack	2.86	4Q 92	4c
Sausage, Jimmy Dean, 100% pork	lb	2.16	4Q 92	4c
Shortening, vegetable, Crisco	3-lb can	2.22	4Q 92	4c
Soft drink, Coca Cola	2 liter	1.00	4Q 92	4c
Steak, T-bone	lb	4.66	4Q 92	4c
Sugar, cane or beet	4 lb	1.73	4Q 92	4c
Tomatoes, Hunt's or Del Monte	14.5-oz can	0.57	4Q 92	4c
Tuna, chunk, light	6.125-6.5 oz can	0.60	4Q 92	4c
Health Care				
ACCRA Index, Health Care		89.90	4Q 92	4c
Analgesic, Aspirin, Bayer, 325 mg tablets	100	5.00	4Q 92	4c
Dentist's fee, adult teeth cleaning and periodic oral exam	visit	36.20	4Q 92	4c
Doctor's fee, routine exam, established patient	visit	41.25	4Q 92	4c
Hospital care, semiprivate room	day	210.00	4Q 92	4c
Household Goods				
Appliance repair, home, service call, washing machine	min labor charge	34.98	4Q 92	4c
Laundry detergent, Tide Ultra, Bold, or Cheer	42 oz	3.06	4Q 92	4c
Tissues, facial, Kleenex brand	175-count box	1.11	4Q 92	4c
Housing				
ACCRA Index, Housing		81.50	4Q 92	4c
House, 1,800 sq ft, 8,000 sq ft lot, new, urban	total	90807	4Q 92	4c
House payment, principal and interest, 25% down payment	month	518	4Q 92	4c
Mortgage rate, incl. points & origination fee, 30-year fixed or adjustable rate	percent	8.38	4Q 92	4c
Rent, apartment, 2 bedrooms - 1-1/2 to 2 baths, unfurnished, 950 sq ft, water	month	363	4Q 92	4c
Personal Goods				
Shampoo, Alberto VO5	15 oz	1.19	4Q 92	4c
Toothpaste, Crest or Colgate	6-7 oz	2.24	4Q 92	4c
Personal Services				
Dry cleaning, man's 2-piece suit		5.00	4Q 92	4c
Haircare, woman's shampoo, trim and blow-dry		14.83	4Q 92	4c
Haircut, man's barbershop, no styling		7.80	4Q 92	4c
Restaurant Food				
Chicken, fried, thigh and drumstick		1.68	4Q 92	4c
Hamburger with cheese	1/4 lb	1.69	4Q 92	4c
Pizza, Pizza Hut or Pizza Inn, cheese, thin crust	12-13 in	7.99	4Q 92	4c
Transportation				
ACCRA Index, Transportation		99.80	4Q 92	4c
Tire balance, computer or spin balance, front	wheel	7.17	4Q 92	4c

Values are in dollars or fractions of dollars. In the column headed *Ref*, references are shown to sources. Each reference is followed by a letter. These refer to the geographical level for which data were reported: s=State, r=Region, and c=City or metro. The abbreviation *ex* is used to mean *except* or *excluding*; *exp* stands for expenditures. For other abbreviations and further explanations, please see the Introduction.

Americus, GA - continued

Item	Per	Value	Date	Ref.
Utilities				
ACCRA Index, Utilities		121.20	4Q 92	4c
Electricity, all electric, 1,800 sq ft living area new home	month	136.34	4Q 92	4c

Ames, IA

Item	Per	Value	Date	Ref.
Composite ACCRA index		99.20	4Q 92	4c
Alcoholic Beverages				
Beer, Miller Lite or Budweiser, 12-oz containers	6 pack	3.79	4Q 92	4c
Liquor, J & B Scotch	750 ml	18.69	4Q 92	4c
Wine, Gallo Chablis blanc, 1.5 liter	bottle	5.49	4Q 92	4c
Clothing				
Jeans, man's denim		29.99	4Q 92	4c
Shirt, man's dress shirt		25.37	4Q 92	4c
Undervest, boy's size 10-14, cotton	3	3.41	4Q 92	4c
Communications				
Newspaper subscription, daily and Sunday home delivery, large-city	month	14.13	4Q 92	4c
Telephone, flat rate	month	13.95	91	11c
Telephone bill, family of four	month	18.48	4Q 92	4c
Energy and Fuels				
Energy, combined forms, 1,800 sq ft heating area	month	106.10	4Q 92	4c
Energy, exc electricity, 1,800 sq ft heating area	month	46.36	4Q 92	4c
Gas, cooking, 10 therms	month	9.48	92	56c
Gas, cooking, 30 therms	month	19.95	92	56c
Gas, cooking, 50 therms	month	28.26	92	56c
Gas, heating, winter, 100 therms	month	49.01	92	56c
Gas, heating, winter, average use	month	87.62	92	56c
Gasoline, motor	gal	1.15	4Q 92	4c
Entertainment				
Bowling, evening rate	game	1.73	4Q 92	4c
Monopoly game, Parker Brothers', No. 9		9.98	4Q 92	4c
Movie	admission	4.50	4Q 92	4c
Tennis balls, yellow, Wilson or Penn, 3	can	1.96	4Q 92	4c
Goods and Services				
ACCRA Index, Miscellaneous Goods and Services		95.40	4Q 92	4c
Groceries				
ACCRA Index, Groceries		90.80	4Q 92	4c
Babyfood, strained vegetables, lowest price	4-4.5 oz jar	0.28	4Q 92	4c
Bananas	lb	0.49	4Q 92	4c
Bread, white	24 oz	0.54	4Q 92	4c
Cheese, Kraft grated Parmesan	8-oz canister	2.91	4Q 92	4c
Chicken, fryer, whole	lb	0.69	4Q 92	4c
Cigarettes, Winston	carton	18.42	4Q 92	4c
Coffee, vacuum-packed	13-oz can	1.90	4Q 92	4c
Corn, frozen	10 oz	0.64	4Q 92	4c
Corn Flakes, Kellogg's or Post Toasties	18 oz	1.81	4Q 92	4c
Eggs, Grade A large	doz	0.65	4Q 92	4c
Ground beef or hamburger	lb	1.19	4Q 92	4c
Lettuce, iceberg	head	0.85	4Q 92	4c
Margarine, Blue Bonnet or Parkay cubes	lb	0.53	4Q 92	4c
Milk, whole	1/2 gal	1.20	4Q 92	4c
Orange juice, Minute Maid frozen	12-oz can	1.30	4Q 92	4c
Peaches	29-oz can	1.28	4Q 92	4c
Peas Sweet, Del Monte or Green Giant	15-17 oz can	0.51	4Q 92	4c

Ames, IA - continued

Item	Per	Value	Date	Ref.
Groceries - continued				
Potatoes, white or red	10-lb sack	1.59	4Q 92	4c
Sausage, Jimmy Dean, 100% pork	lb	2.40	4Q 92	4c
Shortening, vegetable, Crisco	3-lb can	1.76	4Q 92	4c
Soft drink, Coca Cola	2 liter	1.15	4Q 92	4c
Steak, T-bone	lb	4.62	4Q 92	4c
Sugar, cane or beet	4 lb	1.59	4Q 92	4c
Tomatoes, Hunt's or Del Monte	14.5-oz can	0.57	4Q 92	4c
Tuna, chunk, light	6.125-6.5 oz can	0.56	4Q 92	4c
Health Care				
ACCRA Index, Health Care		98.80	4Q 92	4c
Analgesic, Aspirin, Bayer, 325 mg tablets	100	3.91	4Q 92	4c
Dentist's fee, adult teeth cleaning and periodic oral exam	visit	46.33	4Q 92	4c
Doctor's fee, routine exam, established patient	visit	40.00	4Q 92	4c
Hospital care, semiprivate room	day	295.00	4Q 92	4c
Household Goods				
Appliance repair, home, service call, washing machine	min labor charge	28.73	4Q 92	4c
Laundry detergent, Tide Ultra, Bold, or Cheer	42 oz	3.59	4Q 92	4c
Tissues, facial, Kleenex brand	175-count box	1.15	4Q 92	4c
Housing				
ACCRA Index, Housing		106.10	4Q 92	4c
House, 1,800 sq ft, 8,000 sq ft lot, new, urban	total	115667	4Q 92	4c
House payment, principal and interest, 25% down payment	month	654	4Q 92	4c
Mortgage rate, incl. points & origination fee, 30-year fixed or adjustable rate	percent	8.29	4Q 92	4c
Rent, apartment, 2 bedrooms - 1-1/2 to 2 baths, unfurnished, 950 sq ft, water	month	519	4Q 92	4c
Personal Goods				
Shampoo, Alberto VO5	15 oz	1.22	4Q 92	4c
Toothpaste, Crest or Colgate	6-7 oz	1.55	4Q 92	4c
Personal Services				
Dry cleaning, man's 2-piece suit		6.25	4Q 92	4c
Haircare, woman's shampoo, trim and blow-dry		14.17	4Q 92	4c
Haircut, man's barbershop, no styling		8.67	4Q 92	4c
Restaurant Food				
Chicken, fried, thigh and drumstick		2.00	4Q 92	4c
Hamburger with cheese	1/4 lb	1.95	4Q 92	4c
Pizza, Pizza Hut or Pizza Inn, cheese, thin crust	12-13 in	8.39	4Q 92	4c
Transportation				
ACCRA Index, Transportation		106.70	4Q 92	4c
Bus fare	one-way	0.75	3/93	2c
Tire balance, computer or spin balance, front	wheel	7.25	4Q 92	4c
Utilities				
ACCRA Index, Utilities		97.00	4Q 92	4c
Electricity, partial electric and other energy, 1,800 sq ft living area new home	month	59.74	4Q 92	4c

---

Values are in dollars or fractions of dollars. In the column headed *Ref*, references are shown to sources. Each reference is followed by a letter. These refer to the geographical level for which data were reported: s = State, r = Region, and c = City or metro. The abbreviation *ex* is used to mean *except* or *excluding*; *exp* stands for expenditures. For other abbreviations and further explanations, please see the Introduction.

Anaheim-Santa Ana, CA

Item	Per	Value	Date	Ref.
Child Care				
Child care fee, average, center	hour	1.71	90	65r
Child care fee, average, nonregulated family day care	hour	1.32	90	65r
Child care fee, average, regulated family day care	hour	1.86	90	65r
Communications				
Long-distance telephone service, day, initial minute, 0-100 miles	min	0.17-0.40	91	12s
Long-distance telephone service, day, additional minute, 0-100 miles	min	0.07-0.31	91	12s
Long-distance telephone service, evenings/ weekends, 0-100 mi, initial minute	min	0.07-0.16	91	12s
Long-distance telephone service, evenings/ weekends, 0-100 mi, additional minute	min	0.03-0.12	91	12s
Telephone, flat rate	month	8.35	91	11c
Telephone, residential, private line, rotary, unlimited calling	month	12.28	10/91	78c
Education				
Board, 4-yr private college/university	year	2515	91	22s
Board, 4-yr public college/university	year	2268	91	22s
Expenditures, local gov't, public elementary/secondary	pupil	4866	92	20s
Room, 4-year private college/university	year	2622	91	22s
Room, 4-year public college/university	year	2406	91	22s
Tuition, 2-year private college/university	year	7942	91	22s
Tuition, 2-year public college/university	year	114	91	22s
Tuition, 4-year private college/university	year	10863	91	22s
Tuition, 4-year public college/university, in-state	year	1220	91	22s
Energy and Fuels				
Coal	mil Btu	2.01	90	64s
Energy	mil Btu	9.08	90	64s
Energy exp/householder, 1-family unit	year	362	90	28r
Energy exp/householder, <1,000 sq ft heating area	year	254	90	28r
Energy exp/householder, 1,000-1,999 sq ft heating area	year	358	90	28r
Energy exp/householder, 2,000+ sq ft heating area	year	467	90	28r
Energy exp/householder, mobile home	year	390	90	28r
Energy exp/householder, multifamily	year	252	90	28r
Gas, natural	mil Btu	4.31	90	64s
Gas, natural	000 cu ft	6.27	91	46s
Gas, natural, exp	year	369	91	46s
Gasoline, unleaded regular	mil Btu	8.57	90	64s
Entertainment				
Miniature golf admission	adult	6.18	92	1r
Miniature golf admission	child	5.14	92	1r
Waterpark admission	adult	11.00	92	1r
Waterpark admission	child	8.55	92	1r
Funerals				
Casket, 18-gauge steel, velvet interior		1781.09	91	24r
Cosmetology, hair care, etc.		84.64	91	24r
Embalming		207.41	91	24r
Facility use for ceremony		205.76	91	24r
Hearse, local		105.14	91	24r
Limousine, local		83.21	91	24r
Remains to funeral home, transfer		113.82	91	24r
Service charge, professional		626.33	91	24r
Vault, concrete, non-metallic liner		599.54	91	24r
Viewing facilities, use		85.81	91	24r
Groceries				
Apples, Red Delicious	lb	0.80	4/93	16r
Bacon	lb	1.79	4/93	16r
Bananas	lb	0.53	4/93	16r
Bologna, all beef or mixed	lb	2.67	4/93	16r
Bread, white, pan	lb	0.81	4/93	16r

Anaheim-Santa Ana, CA - continued

Item	Per	Value	Date	Ref.
Groceries - continued				
Carrots, short trimmed and topped	lb	0.39	4/93	16r
Chicken, fresh, whole	lb	0.94	4/93	16r
Chicken breast, bone-in	lb	2.19	4/93	16r
Chuck roast, graded and ungraded, ex USDA prime and choice	lb	2.26	4/93	16r
Coffee, 100% ground roast, all sizes	lb	2.33	4/93	16r
Eggs, Grade AA large	doz	1.18	4/93	16r
Flour, white, all purpose	lb	0.22	4/93	16r
Grapefruit	lb	0.52	4/93	16r
Grapes, Thompson Seedless	lb	1.50	4/93	16r
Ground beef, 100% beef	lb	1.44	4/93	16r
Ground beef, lean and extra lean	lb	2.34	4/93	16r
Ham, boneless, excluding canned	lb	2.56	4/93	16r
Honey, jar	8 oz	0.89-1.00	92	5r
Honey, jar	lb	1.35-1.97	92	5r
Honey, squeeze bear	12-oz	1.19-1.50	92	5r
Ice cream, prepackaged, bulk, regular	1/2 gal	2.40	4/93	16r
Lemons	lb	0.81	4/93	16r
Lettuce, iceberg	lb	0.84	4/93	16r
Margarine, stick	lb	0.81	4/93	16r
Oranges, navel	lb	0.48	4/93	16r
Pork chops, center cut, bone-in	lb	3.25	4/93	16r
Potato chips	16 oz	2.89	4/93	16r
Potatoes, white	lb	0.38	4/93	16r
Round roast, graded & ungraded, ex USDA prime & choice	lb	3.00	4/93	16r
Round roast, USDA choice, boneless	lb	3.16	4/93	16r
Shortening, vegetable oil blends	lb	0.86	4/93	16r
Spaghetti and macaroni	lb	0.84	4/93	16r
Steak, round, graded & ungraded, ex USDA prime & choice	lb	3.34	4/93	16r
Steak, round, USDA choice, boneless	lb	3.24	4/93	16r
Steak, sirloin, graded & ungraded, ex USDA prime & choice	lb	3.75	4/93	16r
Steak, sirloin, USDA choice, boneless	lb	4.49	4/93	16r
Sugar, white	lb	0.41	4/93	16r
Sugar, white, 33-80 oz pk	lb	0.38	4/93	16r
Tomatoes, field grown	lb	1.01	4/93	16r
Turkey, frozen, whole	lb	1.04	4/93	16r
Health Care				
Cardizem 60 mg tablets	30	24.04	92	49s
Cector 250 mg tablets	15	35.87	92	49s
Childbirth, cesarean, hospital		5533	91	62r
Childbirth, cesarean, physician's fee		2053	91	62r
Childbirth, normal, hospital		2745	91	62r
Childbirth, normal, physician's fee		1492	91	62r
Health care spending, state	capita	2894	3/93	84s
Hospital care, semiprivate room	day	499.00	90	27c
Medical insurance premium, per employee, small group comprehensive	month	529.25	10/91	25c
Medical plan per employee	year	3421	91	45r
Mental health care, exp	capita	37.60-53.67	90	38s
Mental health care, exp, state mental health agency	capita	42.32	90	38s
Mental health care, hospital psychiatric services, non-Federal, exp	capita	10.64	88	38s
Mental health care, mental health organization, multiservice, exp	capita	28.56	88	38s
Mental health care, psychiatric hospitals, private, exp	capita	18.60	88	38s
Mental health care, psychiatric out-patient clinics, freestanding, exp	capita	2.28	88	38s
Mental health care, psychiatric partial-care organizations, freestanding, exp	capita	0.24	88	38s
Mental health care, state and county mental hospitals, exp	capita	13.60	88	38s
Mental health care, VA medical centers, exp	capita	2.33	88	38s
Mevacor 20 mg tablets	30	67.62	92	49s
Physician fee, family practice, first-visit		111.00	91	62r
Physician fee, family practice, revisit		45.00	91	62r
Physician fee, general practice, first-visit		100.00	91	62r

Values are in dollars or fractions of dollars. In the column headed *Ref*, references are shown to sources. Each reference is followed by a letter. These refer to the geographical level for which data were reported: s=State, r=Region, and c=City or metro. The abbreviation *ex* is used to mean *except* or *excluding*; *exp* stands for expenditures. For other abbreviations and further explanations, please see the Introduction.

Anaheim-Santa Ana, CA - continued

Item	Per	Value	Date	Ref.
Health Care				
Physician fee, general practice, revisit		40.00	91	62r
Physician fee, internal medicine, first-visit		137.00	91	62r
Physician fee, internal medicine, revisit		48.00	91	62r
Physician fee, median, neurosurgeon, first-visit		157.00	91	62r
Physician fee, median, nonsurgical specialist, first-visit		131.00	91	62r
Physician fee, median, orthopedic surgeon, first-visit		124.00	91	62r
Physician fee, median, plastic surgeon, first-visit		88.00	91	62r
Physician fee, median, surgical specialist, first-visit		100.00	91	62r
Physician fee, neurosurgeon, revisit		51.00	91	62r
Physician fee, nonsurgical specialist, revisit		47.00	91	62r
Physician fee, obstetrics/gynecology, first-visit		95.00	91	62r
Physician fee, obstetrics/gynecology, revisit		50.00	91	62r
Physician fee, orthopedic surgeon, revisit		51.00	91	62r
Physician fee, pediatrician, first-visit		81.00	91	62r
Physician fee, pediatrician, revisit		42.00	91	62r
Physician fee, plastic surgeon, revisit		48.00	91	62r
Physician fee, surgical specialist, revisit		49.00	91	62r
Prozac 20 mg tablets	14	33.22	92	49s
Substance abuse, hospital ancillary charge	incident	1760	90	70s
Substance abuse, hospital physician charge	incident	750	90	70s
Substance abuse, hospital room and board	incident	6390	90	70s
Tagamet 300 mg tablets	100	77.08	92	49s
Xanax 0.25 mg tablets	90	64.08	92	49s
Zantac 160 mg tablets	60	92.31	92	49s
Housing				
Home, median price	unit	234.90		26c
Home, median price	unit	131,200	92	58s
House, median price	unit	0.00	92	8c
Rent, house	month	693.00	92	8c
Rental unit, 1 bedroom	month	751	93	23c
Rental unit, 2 bedroom	month	883	93	23c
Rental unit, 3 bedroom	month	1104	93	23c
Rental unit, 4 bedroom	month	1236	93	23c
Rental unit, efficiency	month	618	93	23c
Insurance and Pensions				
Auto insurance, private passenger	year	904.37	91	63s
Taxes				
Tax, cigarette	pack	35	91	77s
Tax, gasoline	gal	16	91	77s
Taxes, state	capita	1477	91	77s
Transportation				
Auto rental, average	day	48.50	6/91	60c
Driver's license fee		10.00	12/90	43s
Limo fare, airport-city, average	day	10.00	6/91	60c
Taxi fare, airport-city, average	day	24.50	6/91	60c
Travel				
Breakfast	day	6.23	6/91	60c
Business travel	day	178.00	4/93	89r
Dinner	day	18.10	6/91	60c
Lodging	day	112.10	91	60c
Lunch	day	11.03	6/91	60c
Utilities				
Electricity	mil Btu	25.98	90	64s

Anchorage, AK

Item	Per	Value	Date	Ref.
Composite ACCRA index		133.80	4Q 92	4c
Alcoholic Beverages				
Beer, Miller Lite or Budweiser, 12-oz containers	6 pack	4.98	4Q 92	4c
Liquor, J & B Scotch	750 ml	21.81	4Q 92	4c
Wine, Gallo Chablis blanc, 1.5 liter	bottle	4.99	4Q 92	4c
Child Care				
Child care fee, average, center	hour	1.71	90	65r
Child care fee, average, nonregulated family day care	hour	1.32	90	65r
Child care fee, average, regulated family day care	hour	1.86	90	65r
Clothing				
Jeans, man's denim		30.17	4Q 92	4c
Shirt, man's dress shirt		26.00	4Q 92	4c
Undervest, boy's size 10-14, cotton	3	5.17	4Q 92	4c
Communications				
Newspaper subscription, daily and Sunday home delivery, large-city	month	9.50	4Q 92	4c
Telephone, residential, private line, rotary, unlimited calling	month	8.14	10/91	78c
Telephone bill, family of four	month	14.45	4Q 92	4c
Education				
Board, 4-yr private college/university	year	1373	91	22s
Board, 4-yr public college/university	year	1632	91	22s
Expenditures, local gov't, public elementary/secondary	pupil	8188	92	20s
Room, 4-year private college/university	year	1221	91	22s
Room, 4-year public college/university	year	1558	91	22s
Tuition, 2-year private college/university	year	10400	91	22s
Tuition, 4-year private college/university	year	5842	91	22s
Tuition, 4-year public college/university, in-state	year	1382	91	22s
Energy and Fuels				
Coal	mil Btu	3.67	90	64s
Energy	mil Btu	7.03	90	64s
Energy, combined forms, 1,800 sq ft heating area	month	112.60	4Q 92	4c
Energy, exc electricity, 1,800 sq ft heating area	month	46.18	4Q 92	4c
Energy exp/householder, 1-family unit	year	362	90	28r
Energy exp/householder, <1,000 sq ft heating area	year	254	90	28r
Energy exp/householder, 1,000-1,999 sq ft heating area	year	358	90	28r
Energy exp/householder, 2,000+ sq ft heating area	year	467	90	28r
Energy exp/householder, mobile home	year	390	90	28r
Energy exp/householder, multifamily	year	252	90	28r
Gas, cooking, 10 therms	month	8.04	92	56c
Gas, cooking, 30 therms	month	15.12	92	56c
Gas, cooking, 50 therms	month	22.21	92	56c
Gas, heating, winter, 100 therms	month	39.92	92	56c
Gas, heating, winter, average use	month	96.59	92	56c
Gas, natural	mil Btu	1.96	90	64s
Gas, natural	000 cu ft	4.18	91	46s
Gas, natural, exp	year	781	91	46s
Gasoline, motor	gal	1.16	4Q 92	4c
Gasoline, unleaded regular	mil Btu	10.03	90	64s
Entertainment				
Bowling, evening rate	game	2.80	4Q 92	4c
Miniature golf admission	adult	6.18	92	1r
Miniature golf admission	child	5.14	92	1r
Monopoly game, Parker Brothers', No. 9		16.19	4Q 92	4c
Movie	admission	6.81	4Q 92	4c
Tennis balls, yellow, Wilson or Penn, 3	can	4.34	4Q 92	4c
Waterpark admission	adult	11.00	92	1r

Values are in dollars or fractions of dollars. In the column headed *Ref*, references are shown to sources. Each reference is followed by a letter. These refer to the geographical level for which data were reported: s = State, r = Region, and c = City or metro. The abbreviation *ex* is used to mean *except* or *excluding*; *exp* stands for expenditures. For other abbreviations and further explanations, please see the Introduction.

Anchorage, AK - continued

Item	Per	Value	Date	Ref.
Entertainment				
Waterpark admission	child	8.55	92	1r
Funerals				
Casket, 18-gauge steel, velvet interior		1781.09	91	24r
Cosmetology, hair care, etc.		84.64	91	24r
Embalming		207.41	91	24r
Facility use for ceremony		205.76	91	24r
Hearse, local		105.14	91	24r
Limousine, local		83.21	91	24r
Remains to funeral home, transfer		113.82	91	24r
Service charge, professional		626.33	91	24r
Vault, concrete, non-metallic liner		599.54	91	24r
Viewing facilities, use		85.81	91	24r
Goods and Services				
ACCRA Index, Miscellaneous Goods and Services		127.50	4Q 92	4c
Goods and services	year	18067	92	36c
Goods and services, misc.	year	18067	92	37c
Groceries				
ACCRA Index, Groceries		139.00	4Q 92	4c
Apples, Red Delicious	lb	0.80	4/93	16r
Babyfood, strained vegetables, lowest price	4-4.5 oz jar	0.43	4Q 92	4c
Bacon	lb	1.79	4/93	16r
Bananas	lb	0.89	4Q 92	4c
Bananas	lb	0.53	4/93	16r
Bologna, all beef or mixed	lb	2.67	4/93	16r
Bread, white	24 oz	1.11	4Q 92	4c
Bread, white, pan	lb	0.81	4/93	16r
Carrots, short trimmed and topped	lb	0.39	4/93	16r
Cheese, Kraft grated Parmesan	8-oz canis-ter	3.42	4Q 92	4c
Chicken, fresh, whole	lb	0.94	4/93	16r
Chicken, fryer, whole	lb	1.40	4Q 92	4c
Chicken breast, bone-in	lb	2.19	4/93	16r
Chuck roast, graded and ungraded, ex USDA prime and choice	lb	2.26	4/93	16r
Cigarettes, Winston	carton	20.79	4Q 92	4c
Coffee, 100% ground roast, all sizes	lb	2.33	4/93	16r
Coffee, vacuum-packed	13-oz can	2.43	4Q 92	4c
Corn, frozen	10 oz	0.73	4Q 92	4c
Corn Flakes, Kellogg's or Post Toasties	18 oz	2.46	4Q 92	4c
Eggs, Grade A large	doz	1.72	4Q 92	4c
Eggs, Grade AA large	doz	1.18	4/93	16r
Flour, white, all purpose	lb	0.22	4/93	16r
Grapefruit	lb	0.52	4/93	16r
Grapes, Thompson Seedless	lb	1.50	4/93	16r
Ground beef, 100% beef	lb	1.44	4/93	16r
Ground beef, lean and extra lean	lb	2.34	4/93	16r
Ground beef or hamburger	lb	1.74	4Q 92	4c
Ham, boneless, excluding canned	lb	2.56	4/93	16r
Honey, jar	8 oz	0.89-1.00	92	5r
Honey, jar	lb	1.35-1.97	92	5r
Honey, squeeze bear	12-oz	1.19-1.50	92	5r
Ice cream, prepackaged, bulk, regular	1/2 gal	2.40	4/93	16r
Lemons	lb	0.81	4/93	16r
Lettuce, iceberg	head	1.52	4Q 92	4c
Lettuce, iceberg	lb	0.84	4/93	16r
Margarine, Blue Bonnet or Parkay cubes	lb	0.89	4Q 92	4c
Margarine, stick	lb	0.81	4/93	16r
Milk, whole	1/2 gal	2.06	4Q 92	4c
Orange juice, Minute Maid frozen	12-oz can	1.62	4Q 92	4c
Oranges, navel	lb	0.48	4/93	16r
Peaches	29-oz can	1.63	4Q 92	4c
Peas Sweet, Del Monte or Green Giant	15-17 oz can	0.74	4Q 92	4c
Pork chops, center cut, bone-in	lb	3.25	4/93	16r
Potato chips	16 oz	2.89	4/93	16r

Anchorage, AK - continued

Item	Per	Value	Date	Ref.
Groceries - continued				
Potatoes, white	lb	0.38	4/93	16r
Potatoes, white or red	10-lb sack	3.49	4Q 92	4c
Round roast, graded & ungraded, ex USDA prime & choice	lb	3.00	4/93	16r
Round roast, USDA choice, boneless	lb	3.16	4/93	16r
Sausage, Jimmy Dean, 100% pork	lb	3.25	4Q 92	4c
Shortening, vegetable oil blends	lb	0.86	4/93	16r
Shortening, vegetable, Crisco	3-lb can	2.47	4Q 92	4c
Soft drink, Coca Cola	2 liter	2.33	4Q 92	4c
Spaghetti and macaroni	lb	0.84	4/93	16r
Steak, round, graded & ungraded, ex USDA prime & choice	lb	3.34	4/93	16r
Steak, round, USDA choice, boneless	lb	3.24	4/93	16r
Steak, sirloin, graded & ungraded, ex USDA prime & choice	lb	3.75	4/93	16r
Steak, sirloin, USDA choice, boneless	lb	4.49	4/93	16r
Steak, T-bone	lb	5.99	4Q 92	4c
Sugar, cane or beet	4 lb	1.91	4Q 92	4c
Sugar, white	lb	0.41	4/93	16r
Sugar, white, 33-80 oz pk	lb	0.38	4/93	16r
Tomatoes, field grown	lb	1.01	4/93	16r
Tomatoes, Hunt's or Del Monte	14.5-oz can	0.75	4Q 92	4c
Tuna, chunk, light	6.125-6.5 oz can	0.89	4Q 92	4c
Turkey, frozen, whole	lb	1.04	4/93	16r
Health Care				
ACCRA Index, Health Care		185.70	4Q 92	4c
Analgesic, Aspirin, Bayer, 325 mg tablets	100	5.25	4Q 92	4c
Childbirth, cesarean, hospital		5533	91	62r
Childbirth, cesarean, physician's fee		2053	91	62r
Childbirth, normal, hospital		2745	91	62r
Childbirth, normal, physician's fee		1492	91	62r
Dentist's fee, adult teeth cleaning and periodic oral exam	visit	97.60	4Q 92	4c
Doctor's fee, routine exam, established patient	visit	73.00	4Q 92	4c
Hospital care, semiprivate room	day	362.12	90	27c
Hospital care, semiprivate room	day	532.50	4Q 92	4c
Medical insurance premium, per employee, small group comprehensive	month	441.65	10/91	25c
Medical plan per employee	year	3421	91	45r
Mental health care, exp	capita	53.68-118.35	90	38s
Mental health care, exp, state mental health agency	capita	72.24	90	38s
Mental health care, hospital psychiatric services, non-Federal, exp	capita	4.61	88	38s
Mental health care, mental health organization, multiservice, exp	capita	20.26	88	38s
Mental health care, psychiatric hospitals, private, exp	capita	15.53	88	38s
Mental health care, psychiatric out-patient clinics, freestanding, exp	capita	10.43	88	38s
Mental health care, state and county mental hospitals, exp	capita	27.47	88	38s
Physician fee, family practice, first-visit		111.00	91	62r
Physician fee, family practice, revisit		45.00	91	62r
Physician fee, general practice, first-visit		100.00	91	62r
Physician fee, general practice, revisit		40.00	91	62r
Physician fee, internal medicine, first-visit		137.00	91	62r
Physician fee, internal medicine, revisit		48.00	91	62r
Physician fee, median, neurosurgeon, first-visit		157.00	91	62r
Physician fee, median, nonsurgical specialist, first-visit		131.00	91	62r
Physician fee, median, orthopedic surgeon, first-visit		124.00	91	62r

Values are in dollars or fractions of dollars. In the column headed *Ref*, references are shown to sources. Each reference is followed by a letter. These refer to the geographical level for which data were reported: s=State, r=Region, and c=City or metro. The abbreviation *ex* is used to mean *except* or *excluding*; *exp* stands for expenditures. For other abbreviations and further explanations, please see the Introduction.

Anchorage, AK - continued

Item	Per	Value	Date	Ref.
Health Care				
Physician fee, median, plastic surgeon, first-visit		88.00	91	62r
Physician fee, median, surgical specialist, first-visit		100.00	91	62r
Physician fee, neurosurgeon, revisit		51.00	91	62r
Physician fee, nonsurgical specialist, revisit		47.00	91	62r
Physician fee, obstetrics/gynecology, first-visit		95.00	91	62r
Physician fee, obstetrics/gynecology, revisit		50.00	91	62r
Physician fee, orthopedic surgeon, revisit		51.00	91	62r
Physician fee, pediatrician, first-visit		81.00	91	62r
Physician fee, pediatrician, revisit		42.00	91	62r
Physician fee, plastic surgeon, revisit		48.00	91	62r
Physician fee, surgical specialist, revisit		49.00	91	62r
Household Goods				
Appliance repair, home, service call, washing machine	min labor charge	42.58	4Q 92	4c
Laundry detergent, Tide Ultra, Bold, or Cheer	42 oz	5.50	4Q 92	4c
Tissues, facial, Kleenex brand	175-count box	1.64	4Q 92	4c
Housing				
ACCRA Index, Housing		145.70	4Q 92	4c
House, 1,800 sq ft, 8,000 sq ft lot, new, urban	total	159246	4Q 92	4c
House payment, principal and interest, 25% down payment	month	891	4Q 92	4c
Mortgage rate, incl. points & origination fee, 30-year fixed or adjustable rate	percent	8.16	4Q 92	4c
Rent, apartment, 2 bedrooms - 1-1/2 to 2 baths, unfurnished, 950 sq ft, water	month	729	4Q 92	4c
Rental unit, 1 bedroom	month	558	93	23c
Rental unit, 2 bedroom	month	656	93	23c
Rental unit, 3 bedroom	month	820	93	23c
Rental unit, 4 bedroom	month	918	93	23c
Rental unit, apartment, 1 bedroom	month	425.00-550.00	92	9c
Rental unit, apartment, 2 bedrooms	month	0.00	92	9c
Rental unit, efficiency	month	459	93	23c
Insurance and Pensions				
Auto insurance, private passenger	year	810.11	91	63s
Personal Goods				
Shampoo, Alberto VO5	15 oz	1.39	4Q 92	4c
Toothpaste, Crest or Colgate	6-7 oz	1.99	4Q 92	4c
Personal Services				
Dry cleaning, man's 2-piece suit		8.70	4Q 92	4c
Haircare, woman's shampoo, trim and blow-dry		29.14	4Q 92	4c
Haircut, man's barbershop, no styling		12.43	4Q 92	4c
Restaurant Food				
Chicken, fried, thigh and drumstick		2.90	4Q 92	4c
Hamburger with cheese	1/4 lb	2.45	4Q 92	4c
Pizza, Pizza Hut or Pizza Inn, cheese, thin crust	12-13 in	9.99	4Q 92	4c
Taxes				
Tax, cigarette	pack	29	91	77s
Tax, gasoline	gal	8	91	77s
Taxes, sales	year	0	92	37c
Taxes, state	capita	3172	91	77s
Transportation				
ACCRA Index, Transportation		120.00	4Q 92	4c
Bus fare	one-way	1.00	3/93	2c
Bus fare, up to 10 miles	one-way	1.00	4Q 92	4c
Driver's license fee		10.00	12/90	43s

Anchorage, AK - continued

Item	Per	Value	Date	Ref.
Transportation - continued				
Tire balance, computer or spin balance, front	wheel	9.00	4Q 92	4c
Travel				
Business travel	day	178.00	4/93	89r
Utilities				
ACCRA Index, Utilities		100.20	4Q 92	4c
Electricity	mil Btu	27.80	90	64s
Electricity, partial electric and other energy, 1,800 sq ft living area new home	month	66.42	4Q 92	4c

Anderson, IN

Item	Per	Value	Date	Ref.
Composite ACCRA index		95.60	4Q 92	4c
Alcoholic Beverages				
Beer, Miller Lite or Budweiser, 12-oz containers	6 pack	3.49	4Q 92	4c
Liquor, J & B Scotch	750 ml	15.51	4Q 92	4c
Wine, Gallo Chablis blanc, 1.5 liter	bottle	4.95	4Q 92	4c
Child Care				
Child care fee, average, center	hour	1.63	90	65r
Child care fee, average, nonregulated family day care	hour	1.83	90	65r
Child care fee, average, regulated family day care	hour	1.42	90	65r
Clothing				
Jeans, man's denim		28.23	4Q 92	4c
Shirt, man's dress shirt		19.13	4Q 92	4c
Undervest, boy's size 10-14, cotton	3	3.95	4Q 92	4c
Communications				
Long-distance telephone service, day, initial minute, 0-100 miles	min	0.18-0.45	91	12s
Long-distance telephone service, day, additional minute, 0-100 miles	min	0.10-0.30	91	12s
Long-distance telephone service, evenings/weekends, 0-100 mi, initial minute	min	0.08-0.19	91	12s
Long-distance telephone service, evenings/weekends, 0-100 mi, additional minute	min	0.04-0.13	91	12s
Newspaper subscription, daily and Sunday home delivery, large-city	month	10.87	4Q 92	4c
Telephone, flat rate	month	11.11	91	11c
Telephone bill, family of four	month	19.39	4Q 92	4c
Education				
Board, 4-yr private college/university	year	1714	91	22s
Board, 4-yr public college/university	year	1829	91	22s
Expenditures, local gov't, public elementary/secondary	pupil	5545	92	20s
Room, 4-year private college/university	year	1512	91	22s
Room, 4-year public college/university	year	1435	91	22s
Tuition, 2-year private college/university	year	6756	91	22s
Tuition, 2-year public college/university	year	1423	91	22s
Tuition, 4-year private college/university	year	8451	91	22s
Tuition, 4-year public college/university, in-state	year	2067	91	22s
Energy and Fuels				
Coal	mil Btu	1.46	90	64s
Energy	mil Btu	6.77	90	64s
Energy, combined forms, 1,800 sq ft heating area	month	108.21	4Q 92	4c
Energy, exc electricity, 1,800 sq ft heating area	month	51.90	4Q 92	4c
Energy exp/householder, 1-family unit	year	471	90	28r
Energy exp/householder, <1,000 sq ft heating area	year	430	90	28r
Energy exp/householder, 1,000-1,999 sq ft heating area	year	481	90	28r
Energy exp/householder, 2,000+ sq ft heating area	year	473	90	28r

Values are in dollars or fractions of dollars. In the column headed *Ref*, references are shown to sources. Each reference is followed by a letter. These refer to the geographical level for which data were reported: s=State, r=Region, and c=City or metro. The abbreviation *ex* is used to mean *except* or *excluding*; *exp* stands for expenditures. For other abbreviations and further explanations, please see the Introduction.

Anderson, IN - continued

Item	Per	Value	Date	Ref.
Energy and Fuels				
Energy exp/householder, mobile home	year	430	90	28r
Energy exp/householder, multifamily	year	461	90	28r
Gas, natural	mil Btu	4.27	90	64s
Gas, natural	000 cu ft	5.46	91	46s
Gas, natural, exp	year	588	91	46s
Gasoline, motor	gal	1.10	4Q 92	4c
Gasoline, unleaded regular	mil Btu	8.74	90	64s
Entertainment				
Bowling, evening rate	game	1.80	4Q 92	4c
Miniature golf admission	adult	6.18	92	1r
Miniature golf admission	child	5.14	92	1r
Monopoly game, Parker Brothers', No. 9		10.57	4Q 92	4c
Movie	admission	5.08	4Q 92	4c
Tennis balls, yellow, Wilson or Penn, 3	can	1.90	4Q 92	4c
Waterpark admission	adult	11.00	92	1r
Waterpark admission	child	8.55	92	1r
Funerals				
Casket, 18-gauge steel, velvet interior		1926.72	91	24r
Cosmetology, hair care, etc.		97.64	91	24r
Embalming		249.14	91	24r
Facility use for ceremony		208.59	91	24r
Hearse, local		130.12	91	24r
Limousine, local		104.66	91	24r
Remains to funeral home, transfer		93.61	91	24r
Service charge, professional		724.62	91	24r
Vault, concrete, non-metallic liner		734.53	91	24r
Viewing facilities, use		236.06	91	24r
Goods and Services				
ACCRA Index, Miscellaneous Goods and Services		91.90	4Q 92	4c
Groceries				
ACCRA Index, Groceries		97.30	4Q 92	4c
Apples, Red Delicious	lb	0.77	4/93	16r
Babyfood, strained vegetables, lowest price	4-4.5 oz jar	0.33	4Q 92	4c
Bacon	lb	1.85	4/93	16r
Bananas	lb	0.31	4Q 92	4c
Bananas	lb	0.46	4/93	16r
Beef, stew, boneless	lb	2.53	4/93	16r
Bologna, all beef or mixed	lb	2.19	4/93	16r
Bread, white	24 oz	0.67	4Q 92	4c
Bread, white, pan	lb	0.78	4/93	16r
Butter	lb	1.50	4/93	16r
Cabbage	lb	0.40	4/93	16r
Carrots, short trimmed and topped	lb	0.45	4/93	16r
Cheese, Cheddar	lb	3.47	4/93	16r
Cheese, Kraft grated Parmesan	8-oz canister	3.22	4Q 92	4c
Chicken, fresh, whole	lb	0.84	4/93	16r
Chicken, fryer, whole	lb	0.75	4Q 92	4c
Chicken breast, bone-in	lb	1.94	4/93	16r
Chicken legs, bone-in	lb	1.02	4/93	16r
Chuck roast, graded and ungraded, ex USDA prime and choice	lb	2.43	4/93	16r
Chuck roast, USDA choice, bone-in	lb	2.11	4/93	16r
Chuck roast, USDA choice, boneless	lb	2.44	4/93	16r
Cigarettes, Winston	carton	16.45	4Q 92	4c
Coffee, 100% ground roast, all sizes	lb	2.47	4/93	16r
Coffee, vacuum-packed	13-oz can	2.12	4Q 92	4c
Cookies, chocolate chip	lb	2.73	4/93	16r
Corn, frozen	10 oz	0.79	4Q 92	4c
Corn Flakes, Kellogg's or Post Toasties	18 oz	1.91	4Q 92	4c
Eggs, Grade A large	doz	0.69	4Q 92	4c
Eggs, Grade A large	doz	0.93	4/93	16r
Flour, white, all purpose	lb	0.21	4/93	16r
Grapefruit	lb	0.45	4/93	16r

Anderson, IN - continued

Item	Per	Value	Date	Ref.
Groceries - continued				
Grapes, Thompson Seedless	lb	1.46	4/93	16r
Ground beef, 100% beef	lb	1.63	4/93	16r
Ground beef, lean and extra lean	lb	2.08	4/93	16r
Ground beef or hamburger	lb	1.43	4Q 92	4c
Ground chuck, 100% beef	lb	1.94	4/93	16r
Ham, boneless, excluding canned	lb	2.21	4/93	16r
Honey, jar	8 oz	0.97-1.25	92	5r
Honey, jar	lb	1.25-2.25	92	5r
Honey, squeeze bear	12-oz	1.25-1.99	92	5r
Ice cream, prepackaged, bulk, regular	1/2 gal	2.41	4/93	16r
Lemons	lb	0.82	4/93	16r
Lettuce, iceberg	head	0.95	4Q 92	4c
Lettuce, iceberg	lb	0.83	4/93	16r
Margarine, Blue Bonnet or Parkay cubes	lb	0.63	4Q 92	4c
Margarine, stick	lb	0.77	4/93	16r
Milk, whole	1/2 gal	1.38	4Q 92	4c
Orange juice, Minute Maid frozen	12-oz can	1.46	4Q 92	4c
Oranges, navel	lb	0.50	4/93	16r
Peaches	29-oz can	1.36	4Q 92	4c
Peanut butter, creamy, all sizes	lb	1.82	4/93	16r
Pears, Anjou	lb	0.85	4/93	16r
Peas Sweet, Del Monte or Green Giant	15-17 oz can	0.52	4Q 92	4c
Pork chops, center cut, bone-in	lb	3.17	4/93	16r
Potato chips	16 oz	2.68	4/93	16r
Potatoes, white	lb	0.26	4/93	16r
Potatoes, white or red	10-lb sack	1.85	4Q 92	4c
Round roast, graded & ungraded, ex USDA prime & choice	lb	2.88	4/93	16r
Round roast, USDA choice, boneless	lb	2.96	4/93	16r
Sausage, Jimmy Dean, 100% pork	lb	2.83	4Q 92	4c
Shortening, vegetable oil blends	lb	0.79	4/93	16r
Shortening, vegetable, Crisco	3-lb can	2.29	4Q 92	4c
Soft drink, Coca Cola	2 liter	1.21	4Q 92	4c
Spaghetti and macaroni	lb	0.76	4/93	16r
Steak, rib eye, USDA choice, boneless	lb	6.29	4/93	16r
Steak, round, USDA choice, boneless	lb	3.24	4/93	16r
Steak, sirloin, graded & ungraded, ex USDA prime & choice	lb	4.00	4/93	16r
Steak, sirloin, USDA choice, bone-in	lb	3.57	4/93	16r
Steak, sirloin, USDA choice, boneless	lb	4.17	4/93	16r
Steak, T-bone	lb	4.10	4Q 92	4c
Steak, T-bone, USDA choice, bone-in	lb	5.60	4/93	16r
Strawberries, dry pint	12 oz	0.90	4/93	16r
Sugar, cane or beet	4 lb	1.35	4Q 92	4c
Sugar, white	lb	0.36	4/93	16r
Sugar, white, 33-80 oz pk	lb	0.35	4/93	16r
Tomatoes, field grown	lb	0.99	4/93	16r
Tomatoes, Hunt's or Del Monte	14.5-oz can	0.82	4Q 92	4c
Tuna, chunk, light	6.125-6.5 oz can	0.74	4Q 92	4c
Tuna, chunk, light	lb	1.76	4/93	16r
Turkey, frozen, whole	lb	0.91	4/93	16r
Health Care				
ACCRA Index, Health Care		93.80	4Q 92	4c
Analgesic, Aspirin, Bayer, 325 mg tablets	100	5.21	4Q 92	4c
Childbirth, cesarean, hospital		4688	91	62r
Childbirth, cesarean, physician's fee		2053	91	62r
Childbirth, normal, hospital		2657	91	62r
Childbirth, normal, physician's fee		1492	91	62r
Dentist's fee, adult teeth cleaning and periodic oral exam	visit	47.58	4Q 92	4c
Doctor's fee, routine exam, established patient	visit	31.50	4Q 92	4c
Hospital care, semiprivate room	day	282.50	4Q 92	4c

Values are in dollars or fractions of dollars. In the column headed *Ref*, references are shown to sources. Each reference is followed by a letter. These refer to the geographical level for which data were reported: s=State, r=Region, and c=City or metro. The abbreviation *ex* is used to mean *except* or *excluding*; *exp* stands for expenditures. For other abbreviations and further explanations, please see the Introduction.

Anderson, IN - continued

Item	Per	Value	Date	Ref.
Health Care				
Medical insurance premium, per employee, small group comprehensive	month	302.95	10/91	25c
Medical plan per employee	year	3443	91	45r
Mental health care, exp	capita	37.60-53.67	90	38s
Mental health care, exp, state mental health agency	capita	47.05	90	38s
Mental health care, hospital psychiatric services, non-Federal, exp	capita	22.14	88	38s
Mental health care, mental health organization, multiservice, exp	capita	10.33	88	38s
Mental health care, psychiatric hospitals, private, exp	capita	20.10	88	38s
Mental health care, state and county mental hospitals, exp	capita	24.00	88	38s
Mental health care, VA medical centers, exp	capita	3.20	88	38s
Physician fee, family practice, first-visit		76.00	91	62r
Physician fee, family practice, revisit		33.00	91	62r
Physician fee, general practice, first-visit		61.00	91	62r
Physician fee, general practice, revisit		31.00	91	62r
Physician fee, general surgeon, first-visit		65.00	91	62r
Physician fee, general surgeon, revisit		35.00	91	62r
Physician fee, internal medicine, first-visit		91.00	91	62r
Physician fee, internal medicine, revisit		40.00	91	62r
Physician fee, median, neurosurgeon, first-visit		106.00	91	62r
Physician fee, median, nonsurgical specialist, first-visit		90.00	91	62r
Physician fee, median, orthopedic surgeon, first-visit		83.00	91	62r
Physician fee, median, surgical specialist, first-visit		61.00	91	62r
Physician fee, neurosurgeon, revisit		41.00	91	62r
Physician fee, nonsurgical specialist, revisit		40.00	91	62r
Physician fee, obstetrics/gynecology, first-visit		61.00	91	62r
Physician fee, obstetrics/gynecology, revisit		40.00	91	62r
Physician fee, orthopedic surgeon, revisit		41.00	91	62r
Physician fee, pediatrician, first-visit		46.00	91	62r
Physician fee, pediatrician, revisit		33.00	91	62r
Physician fee, surgical specialist, revisit		36.00	91	62r
Substance abuse, hospital ancillary charge	incident	1230	90	70s
Substance abuse, hospital physician charge	incident	410	90	70s
Substance abuse, hospital room and board	incident	5510	90	70s
Household Goods				
Appliance repair, home, service call, washing machine	min labor charge	30.80	4Q 92	4c
Laundry detergent, Tide Ultra, Bold, or Cheer	42 oz	3.55	4Q 92	4c
Tissues, facial, Kleenex brand	175-count box	1.19	4Q 92	4c
Housing				
ACCRA Index, Housing		96.00	4Q 92	4c
House, 1,800 sq ft, 8,000 sq ft lot, new, urban	total	108450	4Q 92	4c
House payment, principal and interest, 25% down payment	month	609	4Q 92	4c
Mortgage rate, incl. points & origination fee, 30-year fixed or adjustable rate	percent	8.21	4Q 92	4c
Rent, apartment, 2 bedrooms - 1-1/2 to 2 baths, unfurnished, 950 sq ft, water	month	430	4Q 92	4c
Rental unit, 1 bedroom	month	346	93	23c
Rental unit, 2 bedroom	month	406	93	23c
Rental unit, 3 bedroom	month	510	93	23c
Rental unit, 4 bedroom	month	573	93	23c
Rental unit, efficiency	month	284	93	23c

Anderson, IN - continued

Item	Per	Value	Date	Ref.
Insurance and Pensions				
Auto insurance, private passenger	year	548.99	91	63s
Personal Goods				
Shampoo, Alberto VO5	15 oz	1.34	4Q 92	4c
Toothpaste, Crest or Colgate	6-7 oz	2.32	4Q 92	4c
Personal Services				
Dry cleaning, man's 2-piece suit		5.13	4Q 92	4c
Haircare, woman's shampoo, trim and blow-dry		17.40	4Q 92	4c
Haircut, man's barbershop, no styling		6.10	4Q 92	4c
Restaurant Food				
Chicken, fried, thigh and drumstick		2.25	4Q 92	4c
Hamburger with cheese	1/4 lb	1.69	4Q 92	4c
Pizza, Pizza Hut or Pizza Inn, cheese, thin crust	12-13 in	7.50	4Q 92	4c
Taxes				
Tax, cigarette	pack	15.50	91	77s
Tax, gasoline	gal	15	91	77s
Taxes, state	capita	1102	91	77s
Transportation				
ACCRA Index, Transportation		102.40	4Q 92	4c
Driver's license fee		6.00	12/90	43s
Tire balance, computer or spin balance, front	wheel	7.00	4Q 92	4c
Utilities				
ACCRA Index, Utilities		99.20	4Q 92	4c
Electricity	mil Btu	15.75	90	64s
Electricity, partial electric and other energy, 1,800 sq ft living area new home	month	56.31	4Q 92	4c

Anderson, SC

Item	Per	Value	Date	Ref.
Composite ACCRA index		96.60	4Q 92	4c
Alcoholic Beverages				
Beer, Miller Lite or Budweiser, 12-oz containers	6 pack	3.84	4Q 92	4c
Liquor, J & B Scotch	750 ml	16.51	4Q 92	4c
Wine, Gallo Chablis blanc, 1.5 liter	bottle	4.99	4Q 92	4c
Child Care				
Child care fee, average, center	hour	1.29	90	65r
Child care fee, average, nonregulated family day care	hour	0.89	90	65r
Child care fee, average, regulated family day care	hour	1.32	90	65r
Clothing				
Jeans, man's denim		31.66	4Q 92	4c
Shirt, man's dress shirt		25.00	4Q 92	4c
Undervest, boy's size 10-14, cotton	3	4.56	4Q 92	4c
Communications				
Long-distance telephone service, day, initial minute, 0-100 miles	min	0.24-0.52	91	12s
Long-distance telephone service, day, additional minute, 0-100 miles	min	0.13-0.35	91	12s
Long-distance telephone service, evenings/weekends, 0-100 mi, initial minute	min	0.12-0.26	91	12s
Long-distance telephone service, evenings/weekends, 0-100 mi, additional minute	min	0.07-0.16	91	12s
Newspaper subscription, daily and Sunday home delivery, large-city	month	9.95	4Q 92	4c
Telephone, flat rate	month	15.55	91	11c
Telephone bill, family of four	month	24.65	4Q 92	4c
Education				
Board, 4-yr private college/university	year	1468	91	22s
Board, 4-yr public college/university	year	1632	91	22s
Expenditures, local gov't, public elementary/secondary	pupil	4312	92	20s
Room, 4-year private college/university	year	1393	91	22s

Values are in dollars or fractions of dollars. In the column headed *Ref*, references are shown to sources. Each reference is followed by a letter. These refer to the geographical level for which data were reported: s = State, r = Region, and c = City or metro. The abbreviation *ex* is used to mean *except* or *excluding*; *exp* stands for expenditures. For other abbreviations and further explanations, please see the Introduction.

Anderson, SC - continued

Item	Per	Value	Date	Ref.
Education				
Room, 4-year public college/university	year	1492	91	22s
Tuition, 2-year private college/university	year	5110	91	22s
Tuition, 2-year public college/university	year	813	91	22s
Tuition, 4-year private college/university	year	6434	91	22s
Tuition, 4-year public college/university, in-state	year	2317	91	22s
Energy and Fuels				
Coal	mil Btu	1.73	90	64s
Energy	mil Btu	8.93	90	64s
Energy, combined forms, 1,800 sq ft heating area	month	119.35	4Q 92	4c
Energy exp/householder, 1-family unit	year	487	90	28r
Energy exp/householder, <1,000 sq ft heating area	year	393	90	28r
Energy exp/householder, 1,000-1,999 sq ft heating area	year	442	90	28r
Energy exp/householder, 2,000+ sq ft heating area	year	577	90	28r
Energy exp/householder, mobile home	year	366	90	28r
Energy exp/householder, multifamily	year	382	90	28r
Gas, natural	mil Btu	4.01	90	64s
Gas, natural	000 cu ft	6.98	91	46s
Gas, natural, exp	year	397	91	46s
Gasoline, motor	gal	1.02	4Q 92	4c
Gasoline, unleaded regular	mil Btu	8.80	90	64s
Entertainment				
Bowling, evening rate	game	2.25	4Q 92	4c
Miniature golf admission	adult	6.18	92	1r
Miniature golf admission	child	5.14	92	1r
Monopoly game, Parker Brothers', No. 9		10.65	4Q 92	4c
Movie	admission	5.50	4Q 92	4c
Tennis balls, yellow, Wilson or Penn, 3	can	2.09	4Q 92	4c
Waterpark admission	adult	11.00	92	1r
Waterpark admission	child	8.55	92	1r
Funerals				
Casket, 18-gauge steel, velvet interior		2029.08	91	24r
Cosmetology, hair care, etc.		75.10	91	24r
Embalming		249.24	91	24r
Facility use for ceremony		162.27	91	24r
Hearse, local		114.04	91	24r
Limousine, local		88.57	91	24r
Remains to funeral home, transfer		92.61	91	24r
Service charge, professional		682.42	91	24r
Vault, concrete, non-metallic liner		798.70	91	24r
Viewing facilities, use		163.86	91	24r
Goods and Services				
ACCRA Index, Miscellaneous Goods and Services		100.60	4Q 92	4c
Groceries				
ACCRA Index, Groceries		94.80	4Q 92	4c
Apples, Red Delicious	lb	0.79	4/93	16r
Babyfood, strained vegetables, lowest price	4-4.5 oz jar	0.33	4Q 92	4c
Bacon	lb	1.75	4/93	16r
Bananas	lb	0.49	4Q 92	4c
Bananas	lb	0.42	4/93	16r
Beef, stew, boneless	lb	2.61	4/93	16r
Bologna, all beef or mixed	lb	2.24	4/93	16r
Bread, white	24 oz	0.56	4Q 92	4c
Bread, white, pan	lb	0.64	4/93	16r
Bread, whole wheat, pan	lb	0.96	4/93	16r
Cabbage	lb	0.37	4/93	16r
Carrots, short trimmed and topped	lb	0.47	4/93	16r
Celery	lb	0.64	4/93	16r
Cheese, American	lb	2.98	4/93	16r
Cheese, Cheddar	lb	3.28	4/93	16r

Anderson, SC - continued

Item	Per	Value	Date	Ref.
Groceries - continued				
Cheese, Kraft grated Parmesan	8-oz canister	3.28	4Q 92	4c
Chicken, fresh, whole	lb	0.77	4/93	16r
Chicken, fryer, whole	lb	0.75	4Q 92	4c
Chicken breast, bone-in	lb	1.92	4/93	16r
Chicken legs, bone-in	lb	1.06	4/93	16r
Chuck roast, graded and ungraded, ex USDA prime and choice	lb	2.40	4/93	16r
Chuck roast, USDA choice, bone-in	lb	2.19	4/93	16r
Chuck roast, USDA choice, boneless	lb	2.38	4/93	16r
Cigarettes, Winston	carton	15.39	4Q 92	4c
Coffee, 100% ground roast, all sizes	lb	2.48	4/93	16r
Coffee, vacuum-packed	13-oz can	1.95	4Q 92	4c
Corn, frozen	10 oz	0.52	4Q 92	4c
Corn Flakes, Kellogg's or Post Toasties	18 oz	1.54	4Q 92	4c
Crackers, soda, salted	lb	1.15	4/93	16r
Eggs, Grade A large	doz	0.88	4Q 92	4c
Eggs, Grade A large	doz	0.96	4/93	16r
Flour, white, all purpose	lb	0.24	4/93	16r
Frankfurters, all meat or all beef	lb	2.01	4/93	16r
Grapefruit	lb	0.44	4/93	16r
Grapes, Thompson Seedless	lb	1.40	4/93	16r
Ground beef, 100% beef	lb	1.58	4/93	16r
Ground beef, lean and extra lean	lb	2.09	4/93	16r
Ground beef or hamburger	lb	1.73	4Q 92	4c
Ground chuck, 100% beef	lb	1.98	4/93	16r
Ham, boneless, excluding canned	lb	2.89	4/93	16r
Ham, picnic, shoulder, bone-in, smoked	lb	1.02	4/93	16r
Ham, rump or steak half, bone-in, smoked	lb	1.48	4/93	16r
Ice cream, prepackaged, bulk, regular	1/2 gal	2.41	4/93	16r
Lemons	lb	1.05	4/93	16r
Lettuce, iceberg	head	0.99	4Q 92	4c
Lettuce, iceberg	lb	0.81	4/93	16r
Margarine, Blue Bonnet or Parkay cubes	lb	0.49	4Q 92	4c
Margarine, stick	lb	0.88	4/93	16r
Milk, whole	1/2 gal	1.45	4Q 92	4c
Orange juice, Minute Maid frozen	12-oz can	1.30	4Q 92	4c
Oranges, navel	lb	0.55	4/93	16r
Peaches	29-oz can	1.30	4Q 92	4c
Pears, Anjou	lb	0.92	4/93	16r
Peas Sweet, Del Monte or Green Giant	15-17 oz can	0.51	4Q 92	4c
Pork chops, center cut, bone-in	lb	3.13	4/93	16r
Potato chips	16 oz	2.94	4/93	16r
Potatoes, white	lb	0.43	4/93	16r
Potatoes, white or red	10-lb sack	1.83	4Q 92	4c
Rib roast, USDA choice, bone-in	lb	4.63	4/93	16r
Rice, white, long grain, uncooked	lb	0.45	4/93	16r
Round roast, graded & ungraded, ex USDA prime & choice	lb	3.03	4/93	16r
Round roast, USDA choice, boneless	lb	3.09	4/93	16r
Sausage, fresh, loose	lb	2.08	4/93	16r
Sausage, Jimmy Dean, 100% pork	lb	2.39	4Q 92	4c
Short ribs, bone-in	lb	2.66	4/93	16r
Shortening, vegetable oil blends	lb	0.69	4/93	16r
Shortening, vegetable, Crisco	3-lb can	1.99	4Q 92	4c
Soft drink, Coca Cola	2 liter	1.15	4Q 92	4c
Spaghetti and macaroni	lb	0.81	4/93	16r
Steak, rib eye, USDA choice, boneless	lb	6.24	4/93	16r
Steak, round, graded & ungraded, ex USDA prime & choice	lb	3.31	4/93	16r
Steak, round, USDA choice, boneless	lb	3.34	4/93	16r
Steak, sirloin, graded & ungraded, ex USDA prime & choice	lb	4.19	4/93	16r
Steak, sirloin, USDA choice, boneless	lb	4.46	4/93	16r
Steak, T-bone	lb	5.40	4Q 92	4c

Values are in dollars or fractions of dollars. In the column headed *Ref*, references are shown to sources. Each reference is followed by a letter. These refer to the geographical level for which data were reported: s=State, r=Region, and c=City or metro. The abbreviation *ex* is used to mean *except* or *excluding*; *exp* stands for expenditures. For other abbreviations and further explanations, please see the Introduction.

Anderson, SC - continued

Item	Per	Value	Date	Ref.
Groceries				
Steak, T-bone, USDA choice, bone-in	lb	5.25	4/93	16r
Strawberries, dry pint	12 oz	0.92	4/93	16r
Sugar, cane or beet	4 lb	1.41	4Q 92	4c
Sugar, white	lb	0.39	4/93	16r
Sugar, white, 33-80 oz pk	lb	0.38	4/93	16r
Tomatoes, field grown	lb	0.88	4/93	16r
Tomatoes, Hunt's or Del Monte	14.5-oz can	0.50	4Q 92	4c
Tuna, chunk, light	6.125-6.5 oz can	0.55	4Q 92	4c
Tuna, chunk, light	lb	1.79	4/93	16r
Turkey, frozen, whole	lb	1.04	4/93	16r
Yogurt, natural, fruit flavored	1/2 pint	0.57	4/93	16r
Health Care				
ACCRA Index, Health Care		82.90	4Q 92	4c
Analgesic, Aspirin, Bayer, 325 mg tablets	100	4.70	4Q 92	4c
Childbirth, cesarean, hospital		5034	91	62r
Childbirth, cesarean, physician's fee		2053	91	62r
Childbirth, normal, hospital		2712	91	62r
Childbirth, normal, physician's fee		1492	91	62r
Dentist's fee, adult teeth cleaning and periodic oral exam	visit	36.50	4Q 92	4c
Doctor's fee, routine exam, established patient	visit	32.38	4Q 92	4c
Health care spending, state	capita	1689	3/93	84s
Hospital care, semiprivate room	day	243.00	4Q 92	4c
Medical insurance premium, per employee, small group comprehensive	month	281.05	10/91	25c
Medical plan per employee	year	3495	91	45r
Mental health care, exp	capita	37.60-53.67	90	38s
Mental health care, exp, state mental health agency	capita	51.12	90	38s
Mental health care, hospital psychiatric services, non-Federal, exp	capita	10.67	88	38s
Mental health care, mental health organization, multiservice, exp	capita	11.38	88	38s
Mental health care, psychiatric hospitals, private, exp	capita	9.21	88	38s
Mental health care, psychiatric out-patient clinics, freestanding, exp	capita	0.68	88	38s
Mental health care, state and county mental hospitals, exp	capita	25.02	88	38s
Mental health care, VA medical centers, exp	capita	0.62	88	38s
Physician fee, family practice, first-visit		75.00	91	62r
Physician fee, family practice, revisit		34.00	91	62r
Physician fee, general practice, first-visit		61.00	91	62r
Physician fee, general practice, revisit		32.00	91	62r
Physician fee, general surgeon, first-visit		64.00	91	62r
Physician fee, general surgeon, revisit		40.00	91	62r
Physician fee, internal medicine, first-visit		98.00	91	62r
Physician fee, internal medicine, revisit		40.00	91	62r
Physician fee, median, neurosurgeon, first-visit		130.00	91	62r
Physician fee, median, nonsurgical specialist, first-visit		95.00	91	62r
Physician fee, median, orthopedic surgeon, first-visit		91.00	91	62r
Physician fee, median, plastic surgeon, first-visit		66.00	91	62r
Physician fee, median, surgical specialist, first-visit		62.00	91	62r
Physician fee, neurosurgeon, revisit		50.00	91	62r
Physician fee, nonsurgical specialist, revisit		40.00	91	62r
Physician fee, obstetrics/gynecology, first-visit		64.00	91	62r
Physician fee, obstetrics/gynecology, revisit		41.00	91	62r
Physician fee, orthopedic surgeon, revisit		40.00	91	62r
Physician fee, pediatrician, first-visit		49.00	91	62r
Physician fee, pediatrician, revisit		33.00	91	62r

Anderson, SC - continued

Item	Per	Value	Date	Ref.
Health Care - continued				
Physician fee, plastic surgeon, revisit		43.00	91	62r
Physician fee, surgical specialist, revisit		37.00	91	62r
Substance abuse, hospital ancillary charge	incident	1250	90	70s
Substance abuse, hospital physician charge	incident	250	90	70s
Substance abuse, hospital room and board	incident	6100	90	70s
Household Goods				
Appliance repair, home, service call, washing machine	min labor charge	33.59	4Q 92	4c
Laundry detergent, Tide Ultra, Bold, or Cheer	42 oz	3.09	4Q 92	4c
Tissues, facial, Kleenex brand	175-count box	1.05	4Q 92	4c
Housing				
ACCRA Index, Housing		91.90	4Q 92	4c
House, 1,800 sq ft, 8,000 sq ft lot, new, urban	total	102388	4Q 92	4c
House payment, principal and interest, 25% down payment	month	575	4Q 92	4c
Mortgage rate, incl. points & origination fee, 30-year fixed or adjustable rate	percent	8.22	4Q 92	4c
Rent, apartment, 2 bedrooms - 1-1/2 to 2 baths, unfurnished, 950 sq ft, water	month	429	4Q 92	4c
Rental unit, 1 bedroom	month	315	93	23c
Rental unit, 2 bedroom	month	371	93	23c
Rental unit, 3 bedroom	month	466	93	23c
Rental unit, 4 bedroom	month	521	93	23c
Rental unit, efficiency	month	260	93	23c
Insurance and Pensions				
Auto insurance, private passenger	year	605.26	91	63s
Personal Goods				
Shampoo, Alberto VO5	15 oz	0.99	4Q 92	4c
Toothpaste, Crest or Colgate	6-7 oz	1.88	4Q 92	4c
Personal Services				
Dry cleaning, man's 2-piece suit		5.96	4Q 92	4c
Haircare, woman's shampoo, trim and blow-dry		15.30	4Q 92	4c
Haircut, man's barbershop, no styling		8.55	4Q 92	4c
Restaurant Food				
Chicken, fried, thigh and drumstick		1.99	4Q 92	4c
Hamburger with cheese	1/4 lb	1.85	4Q 92	4c
Pizza, Pizza Hut or Pizza Inn, cheese, thin crust	12-13 in	7.97	4Q 92	4c
Taxes				
Tax, cigarette	pack	7	91	77s
Tax, gasoline	gal	16	91	77s
Taxes, state	capita	1105	91	77s
Transportation				
ACCRA Index, Transportation		92.00	4Q 92	4c
Driver's license fee		10.00	12/90	43s
Tire balance, computer or spin balance, front	wheel	6.11	4Q 92	4c
Travel				
Business travel	day	193.00	4/93	89r
Utilities				
ACCRA Index, Utilities		111.00	4Q 92	4c
Electricity	mil Btu	16.39	90	64s
Electricity, all electric, 1,800 sq ft living area new home	month	119.35	4Q 92	4c

Values are in dollars or fractions of dollars. In the column headed *Ref*, references are shown to sources. Each reference is followed by a letter. These refer to the geographical level for which data were reported: s=State, r=Region, and c=City or metro. The abbreviation *ex* is used to mean *except* or *excluding*; *exp* stands for expenditures. For other abbreviations and further explanations, please see the Introduction.

Ann Arbor, MI

Item	Per	Value	Date	Ref.
Child Care				
Child care fee, average, center	hour	1.63	90	65r
Child care fee, average, nonregulated family day care	hour	1.83	90	65r
Child care fee, average, regulated family day care	hour	1.42	90	65r
Communications				
Long-distance telephone service, day, initial minute, 0-100 miles	min	0.14-0.36	91	12s
Long-distance telephone service, day, additional minute, 0-100 miles	min	0.14-0.36	91	12s
Long-distance telephone service, evenings/ weekends, 0-100 mi, initial minute	min	0.07-0.19	91	12s
Long-distance telephone service, evenings/ weekends, 0-100 mi, additional minute	min	0.04-0.14	91	12s
Education				
Board, 4-yr private college/university	year	1698	91	22s
Board, 4-yr public college/university	year	1962	91	22s
Expenditures, local gov't, public elementary/secondary	pupil	5671	92	20s
Room, 4-year private college/university	year	1440	91	22s
Room, 4-year public college/university	year	1687	91	22s
Tuition, 2-year private college/university	year	4749	91	22s
Tuition, 2-year public college/university	year	1124	91	22s
Tuition, 4-year private college/university	year	6885	91	22s
Tuition, 4-year public college/university, in-state	year	2635	91	22s
Energy and Fuels				
Coal	mil Btu	1.63	90	64s
Energy	mil Btu	8.17	90	64s
Energy exp/householder, 1-family unit	year	471	90	28r
Energy exp/householder, <1,000 sq ft heating area	year	430	90	28r
Energy exp/householder, 1,000-1,999 sq ft heating area	year	481	90	28r
Energy exp/householder, 2,000+ sq ft heating area	year	473	90	28r
Energy exp/householder, mobile home	year	430	90	28r
Energy exp/householder, multifamily	year	461	90	28r
Gas, natural	mil Btu	4.36	90	64s
Gas, natural	000 cu ft	5.07	91	46s
Gas, natural, exp	year	655	91	46s
Gasoline, unleaded regular	mil Btu	8.78	90	64s
Entertainment				
Miniature golf admission	adult	6.18	92	1r
Miniature golf admission	child	5.14	92	1r
Waterpark admission	adult	11.00	92	1r
Waterpark admission	child	8.55	92	1r
Funerals				
Casket, 18-gauge steel, velvet interior		1926.72	91	24r
Cosmetology, hair care, etc.		97.64	91	24r
Embalming		249.14	91	24r
Facility use for ceremony		208.59	91	24r
Hearse, local		130.12	91	24r
Limousine, local		104.66	91	24r
Remains to funeral home, transfer		93.61	91	24r
Service charge, professional		724.62	91	24r
Vault, concrete, non-metallic liner		734.53	91	24r
Viewing facilities, use		236.06	91	24r
Groceries				
Apples, Red Delicious	lb	0.77	4/93	16r
Bacon	lb	1.85	4/93	16r
Bananas	lb	0.46	4/93	16r
Beef, stew, boneless	lb	2.53	4/93	16r
Bologna, all beef or mixed	lb	2.19	4/93	16r
Bread, white, pan	lb	0.78	4/93	16r
Butter	lb	1.50	4/93	16r
Cabbage	lb	0.40	4/93	16r

Ann Arbor, MI - continued

Item	Per	Value	Date	Ref.
Groceries - continued				
Carrots, short trimmed and topped	lb	0.45	4/93	16r
Cheese, Cheddar	lb	3.47	4/93	16r
Chicken, fresh, whole	lb	0.84	4/93	16r
Chicken breast, bone-in	lb	1.94	4/93	16r
Chicken legs, bone-in	lb	1.02	4/93	16r
Chuck roast, graded and ungraded, ex USDA prime and choice	lb	2.43	4/93	16r
Chuck roast, USDA choice, bone-in	lb	2.11	4/93	16r
Chuck roast, USDA choice, boneless	lb	2.44	4/93	16r
Coffee, 100% ground roast, all sizes	lb	2.47	4/93	16r
Cookies, chocolate chip	lb	2.73	4/93	16r
Eggs, Grade A large	doz	0.93	4/93	16r
Flour, white, all purpose	lb	0.21	4/93	16r
Grapefruit	lb	0.45	4/93	16r
Grapes, Thompson Seedless	lb	1.46	4/93	16r
Ground beef, 100% beef	lb	1.63	4/93	16r
Ground beef, lean and extra lean	lb	2.08	4/93	16r
Ground chuck, 100% beef	lb	1.94	4/93	16r
Ham, boneless, excluding canned	lb	2.21	4/93	16r
Honey, jar	8 oz	0.97-1.25	92	5r
Honey, jar	lb	1.25-2.25	92	5r
Honey, squeeze bear	12-oz	1.25-1.99	92	5r
Ice cream, prepackaged, bulk, regular	1/2 gal	2.41	4/93	16r
Lemons	lb	0.82	4/93	16r
Lettuce, iceberg	lb	0.83	4/93	16r
Margarine, stick	lb	0.77	4/93	16r
Oranges, navel	lb	0.50	4/93	16r
Peanut butter, creamy, all sizes	lb	1.82	4/93	16r
Pears, Anjou	lb	0.85	4/93	16r
Pork chops, center cut, bone-in	lb	3.17	4/93	16r
Potato chips	16 oz	2.68	4/93	16r
Potatoes, white	lb	0.26	4/93	16r
Round roast, graded & ungraded, ex USDA prime & choice	lb	2.88	4/93	16r
Round roast, USDA choice, boneless	lb	2.96	4/93	16r
Shortening, vegetable oil blends	lb	0.79	4/93	16r
Spaghetti and macaroni	lb	0.76	4/93	16r
Steak, rib eye, USDA choice, boneless	lb	6.29	4/93	16r
Steak, round, USDA choice, boneless	lb	3.24	4/93	16r
Steak, sirloin, graded & ungraded, ex USDA prime & choice	lb	4.00	4/93	16r
Steak, sirloin, USDA choice, bone-in	lb	3.57	4/93	16r
Steak, sirloin, USDA choice, boneless	lb	4.17	4/93	16r
Steak, T-bone, USDA choice, bone-in	lb	5.60	4/93	16r
Strawberries, dry pint	12 oz	0.90	4/93	16r
Sugar, white	lb	0.36	4/93	16r
Sugar, white, 33-80 oz pk	lb	0.35	4/93	16r
Tomatoes, field grown	lb	0.99	4/93	16r
Tuna, chunk, light	lb	1.76	4/93	16r
Turkey, frozen, whole	lb	0.91	4/93	16r
Health Care				
Childbirth, cesarean, hospital		4688	91	62r
Childbirth, cesarean, physician's fee		2053	91	62r
Childbirth, normal, hospital		2657	91	62r
Childbirth, normal, physician's fee		1492	91	62r
Medical plan per employee	year	3443	91	45r
Mental health care, exp	capita	53.68-118.35	90	38s
Mental health care, exp, state mental health agency	capita	73.73	90	38s
Mental health care, hospital psychiatric services, non-Federal, exp	capita	22.52	88	38s
Mental health care, mental health organization, multiservice, exp	capita	42.68	88	38s
Mental health care, psychiatric hospitals, private, exp	capita	10.80	88	38s
Mental health care, psychiatric out-patient clinics, freestanding, exp	capita	3.47	88	38s
Mental health care, psychiatric partial-care organizations, freestanding, exp	capita	0.73	88	38s
Mental health care, state and county mental hospitals, exp	capita	36.77	88	38s

Values are in dollars or fractions of dollars. In the column headed *Ref*, references are shown to sources. Each reference is followed by a letter. These refer to the geographical level for which data were reported: s=State, r=Region, and c=City or metro. The abbreviation *ex* is used to mean *except* or *excluding*; *exp* stands for expenditures. For other abbreviations and further explanations, please see the Introduction.

Ann Arbor, MI - continued

Item	Per	Value	Date	Ref.
Health Care				
Mental health care, VA medical centers, exp	capita	4.03	88	38s
Physician fee, family practice, first-visit		76.00	91	62r
Physician fee, family practice, revisit		33.00	91	62r
Physician fee, general practice, first-visit		61.00	91	62r
Physician fee, general practice, revisit		31.00	91	62r
Physician fee, general surgeon, first-visit		65.00	91	62r
Physician fee, general surgeon, revisit		35.00	91	62r
Physician fee, internal medicine, first-visit		91.00	91	62r
Physician fee, internal medicine, revisit		40.00	91	62r
Physician fee, median, neurosurgeon, first-visit		106.00	91	62r
Physician fee, median, nonsurgical specialist, first-visit		90.00	91	62r
Physician fee, median, orthopedic surgeon, first-visit		83.00	91	62r
Physician fee, median, surgical specialist, first-visit		61.00	91	62r
Physician fee, neurosurgeon, revisit		41.00	91	62r
Physician fee, nonsurgical specialist, revisit		40.00	91	62r
Physician fee, obstetrics/gynecology, first-visit		61.00	91	62r
Physician fee, obstetrics/gynecology, revisit		40.00	91	62r
Physician fee, orthopedic surgeon, revisit		41.00	91	62r
Physician fee, pediatrician, first visit		46.00	91	62r
Physician fee, pediatrician, revisit		33.00	91	62r
Physician fee, surgical specialist, revisit		36.00	91	62r
Substance abuse, hospital ancillary charge	incident	1480	90	70s
Substance abuse, hospital physician charge	incident	250	90	70s
Substance abuse, hospital room and board	incident	4070	90	70s
Insurance and Pensions				
Auto insurance, private passenger	year	716.78	91	63s
Taxes				
Tax, cigarette	pack	25	91	77s
Tax, gasoline	gal	15	91	77s
Taxes, state	capita	1185	91	77s
Transportation				
Driver's license fee		12.00	12/90	43s
Vehicle registration and license plate	year	14.00-200.00	93	40s
Utilities				
Electricity	mil Btu	20.85	90	64s

Anniston, AL

Item	Per	Value	Date	Ref.
Child Care				
Child care fee, average, center	hour	1.29	90	65r
Child care fee, average, nonregulated family day care	hour	0.89	90	65r
Child care fee, average, regulated family day care	hour	1.32	90	65r
Communications				
Long-distance telephone service, day, initial minute, 0-100 miles	min	0.11-0.36	91	12s
Long-distance telephone service, day, additional minute, 0-100 miles	min	0.09-0.26	91	12s
Long-distance telephone service, evenings/weekends, 0-100 mi, initial minute	min	0.04-0.14	91	12s
Long-distance telephone service, evenings/weekends, 0-100 mi, additional minute	min	0.04-0.10	91	12s
Education				
Board, 4-yr private college/university	year	1795	91	22s
Board, 4-yr public college/university	year	1469	91	22s
Expenditures, local gov't, public elementary/secondary	pupil	3675	92	20s
Room, 4-year private college/university	year	1340	91	22s

Anniston, AL - continued

Item	Per	Value	Date	Ref.
Education - continued				
Room, 4-year public college/university	year	1295	91	22s
Tuition, 2-year private college/university	year	4148	91	22s
Tuition, 2-year public college/university	year	689	91	22s
Tuition, 4-year private college/university	year	5942	91	22s
Tuition, 4-year public college/university, in-state	year	1593	91	22s
Energy and Fuels				
Coal	mil Btu	1.83	90	64s
Energy	mil Btu	7.92	90	64s
Energy exp/householder, 1-family unit	year	403	90	28r
Energy exp/householder, <1,000 sq ft heating area	year	342	90	28r
Energy exp/householder, 1,000-1,999 sq ft heating area	year	388	90	28r
Energy exp/householder, 2,000+ sq ft heating area	year	434	90	28r
Energy exp/householder, mobile home	year	320	90	28r
Energy exp/householder, multifamily	year	338	90	28r
Gas, natural	mil Btu	4.07	90	64s
Gas, natural	000 cu ft	7.05	91	46s
Gas, natural, exp	year	461	91	46s
Gasoline, unleaded regular	mil Btu	8.96	90	64s
Entertainment				
Miniature golf admission	adult	6.18	92	1r
Miniature golf admission	child	5.14	92	1r
Waterpark admission	adult	11.00	92	1r
Waterpark admission	child	8.55	92	1r
Funerals				
Casket, 18-gauge steel, velvet interior		2329.05	91	24r
Cosmetology, hair care, etc.		72.78	91	24r
Embalming		240.71	91	24r
Facility use for ceremony		181.67	91	24r
Hearse, local		106.25	91	24r
Limousine, local		70.92	91	24r
Remains to funeral home, transfer		96.30	91	24r
Service charge, professional		687.09	91	24r
Vault, concrete, non-metallic liner		732.09	91	24r
Viewing facilities, use		190.30	91	24r
Groceries				
Apples, Red Delicious	lb	0.79	4/93	16r
Bacon	lb	1.75	4/93	16r
Bananas	lb	0.42	4/93	16r
Beef, stew, boneless	lb	2.61	4/93	16r
Bologna, all beef or mixed	lb	2.24	4/93	16r
Bread, white, pan	lb	0.64	4/93	16r
Bread, whole wheat, pan	lb	0.96	4/93	16r
Cabbage	lb	0.37	4/93	16r
Carrots, short trimmed and topped	lb	0.47	4/93	16r
Celery	lb	0.64	4/93	16r
Cheese, American	lb	2.98	4/93	16r
Cheese, Cheddar	lb	3.28	4/93	16r
Chicken, fresh, whole	lb	0.77	4/93	16r
Chicken breast, bone-in	lb	1.92	4/93	16r
Chicken legs, bone-in	lb	1.06	4/93	16r
Chuck roast, graded and ungraded, ex USDA prime and choice	lb	2.40	4/93	16r
Chuck roast, USDA choice, bone-in	lb	2.19	4/93	16r
Chuck roast, USDA choice, boneless	lb	2.38	4/93	16r
Coffee, 100% ground roast, all sizes	lb	2.48	4/93	16r
Crackers, soda, salted	lb	1.15	4/93	16r
Eggs, Grade A large	doz	0.96	4/93	16r
Flour, white, all purpose	lb	0.24	4/93	16r
Frankfurters, all meat or all beef	lb	2.01	4/93	16r
Grapefruit	lb	0.44	4/93	16r
Grapes, Thompson Seedless	lb	1.40	4/93	16r
Ground beef, 100% beef	lb	1.58	4/93	16r
Ground beef, lean and extra lean	lb	2.09	4/93	16r
Ground chuck, 100% beef	lb	1.98	4/93	16r
Ham, boneless, excluding canned	lb	2.89	4/93	16r

Values are in dollars or fractions of dollars. In the column headed *Ref*, references are shown to sources. Each reference is followed by a letter. These refer to the geographical level for which data were reported: s=State, r=Region, and c=City or metro. The abbreviation *ex* is used to mean *except* or *excluding*; *exp* stands for expenditures. For other abbreviations and further explanations, please see the Introduction.

Anniston, AL - continued

Item	Per	Value	Date	Ref.
Groceries				
Ham, picnic, shoulder, bone-in, smoked	lb	1.02	4/93	16r
Ham, rump or steak half, bone-in, smoked	lb	1.48	4/93	16r
Honey, jar	8 oz	0.89-1.09	92	5r
Honey, jar	lb	1.39-2.25	92	5r
Honey, squeeze bear	12-oz	1.00-1.50	92	5r
Ice cream, prepackaged, bulk, regular	1/2 gal	2.41	4/93	16r
Lemons	lb	1.05	4/93	16r
Lettuce, iceberg	lb	0.81	4/93	16r
Margarine, stick	lb	0.88	4/93	16r
Oranges, navel	lb	0.55	4/93	16r
Pears, Anjou	lb	0.92	4/93	16r
Pork chops, center cut, bone-in	lb	3.13	4/93	16r
Potato chips	16 oz	2.94	4/93	16r
Potatoes, white	lb	0.43	4/93	16r
Rib roast, USDA choice, bone-in	lb	4.63	4/93	16r
Rice, white, long grain, uncooked	lb	0.45	4/93	16r
Round roast, graded & ungraded, ex USDA prime & choice	lb	3.03	4/93	16r
Round roast, USDA choice, boneless	lb	3.09	4/93	16r
Sausage, fresh, loose	lb	2.08	4/93	16r
Short ribs, bone-in	lb	2.66	4/93	16r
Shortening, vegetable oil blends	lb	0.69	4/93	16r
Spaghetti and macaroni	lb	0.81	4/93	16r
Steak, rib eye, USDA choice, boneless	lb	6.24	4/93	16r
Steak, round, graded & ungraded, ex USDA prime & choice	lb	3.31	4/93	16r
Steak, round, USDA choice, boneless	lb	3.34	4/93	16r
Steak, sirloin, graded & ungraded, ex USDA prime & choice	lb	4.19	4/93	16r
Steak, sirloin, USDA choice, boneless	lb	4.46	4/93	16r
Steak, T-bone, USDA choice, bone-in	lb	5.25	4/93	16r
Strawberries, dry pint	12 oz	0.92	4/93	16r
Sugar, white	lb	0.39	4/93	16r
Sugar, white, 33-80 oz pk	lb	0.38	4/93	16r
Tomatoes, field grown	lb	0.88	4/93	16r
Tuna, chunk, light	lb	1.79	4/93	16r
Turkey, frozen, whole	lb	1.04	4/93	16r
Yogurt, natural, fruit flavored	1/2 pint	0.57	4/93	16r
Health Care				
Childbirth, cesarean, hospital		5034	91	62r
Childbirth, cesarean, physician's fee		2053	91	62r
Childbirth, normal, hospital		2712	91	62r
Childbirth, normal, physician's fee		1492	91	62r
Mental health care, exp	capita	37.60-53.67	90	38s
Mental health care, exp, state mental health agency	capita	38.35	90	38s
Mental health care, hospital psychiatric services, non-Federal, exp	capita	13.58	88	38s
Mental health care, mental health organization, multiservice, exp	capita	12.40	88	38s
Mental health care, psychiatric hospitals, private, exp	capita	9.49	88	38s
Mental health care, state and county mental hospitals, exp	capita	22.15	88	38s
Mental health care, VA medical centers, exp	capita	10.94	88	38s
Physician fee, family practice, first-visit		75.00	91	62r
Physician fee, family practice, revisit		34.00	91	62r
Physician fee, general practice, first-visit		61.00	91	62r
Physician fee, general practice, revisit		32.00	91	62r
Physician fee, general surgeon, first-visit		64.00	91	62r
Physician fee, general surgeon, revisit		40.00	91	62r
Physician fee, internal medicine, first-visit		98.00	91	62r
Physician fee, internal medicine, revisit		40.00	91	62r
Physician fee, median, neurosurgeon, first-visit		130.00	91	62r
Physician fee, median, nonsurgical specialist, first-visit		95.00	91	62r
Physician fee, median, orthopedic surgeon, first-visit		91.00	91	62r

Anniston, AL - continued

Item	Per	Value	Date	Ref.
Health Care - continued				
Physician fee, median, plastic surgeon, first-visit		66.00	91	62r
Physician fee, median, surgical specialist, first-visit		62.00	91	62r
Physician fee, neurosurgeon, revisit		50.00	91	62r
Physician fee, nonsurgical specialist, revisit		40.00	91	62r
Physician fee, obstetrics/gynecology, first-visit		64.00	91	62r
Physician fee, obstetrics/gynecology, revisit		41.00	91	62r
Physician fee, orthopedic surgeon, revisit		40.00	91	62r
Physician fee, pediatrician, first-visit		49.00	91	62r
Physician fee, pediatrician, revisit		33.00	91	62r
Physician fee, plastic surgeon, revisit		43.00	91	62r
Physician fee, surgical specialist, revisit		37.00	91	62r
Substance abuse, hospital ancillary charge	inci-dent	1390	90	70s
Substance abuse, hospital physician charge	inci-dent	520	90	70s
Substance abuse, hospital room and board	inci-dent	5830	90	70s
Insurance and Pensions				
Auto insurance, private passenger	year	562.59	91	63s
Taxes				
Tax, cigarette	pack	16.50	91	77s
Tax, gasoline	gal	16	91	77s
Taxes, state	capita	964	91	77s
Transportation				
Driver's license fee		15.00	12/90	43s
Travel				
Business travel	day	193.00	4/93	89r
Utilities				
Electricity	mil Btu	16.46	90	64s

Appleton-Neenah, WI

Item	Per	Value	Date	Ref.
Composite ACCRA index		97.10	4Q 92	4c
Alcoholic Beverages				
Beer, Miller Lite or Budweiser, 12-oz containers	6 pack	3.51	4Q 92	4c
Liquor, J & B Scotch	750 ml	13.34	4Q 92	4c
Wine, Gallo Chablis blanc, 1.5 liter	bottle	3.96	4Q 92	4c
Child Care				
Child care fee, average, center	hour	1.63	90	65r
Child care fee, average, nonregulated family day care	hour	1.83	90	65r
Child care fee, average, regulated family day care	hour	1.42	90	65r
Clothing				
Jeans, man's denim		29.99	4Q 92	4c
Shirt, man's dress shirt		22.97	4Q 92	4c
Undervest, boy's size 10-14, cotton	3	3.58	4Q 92	4c
Communications				
Long-distance telephone service, day, initial minute, 0-100 miles	min	0.15-0.29	91	12s
Long-distance telephone service, day, additional minute, 0-100 miles	min	0.10-0.27	91	12s
Newspaper subscription, daily and Sunday home delivery, large-city	month	13.00	4Q 92	4c
Telephone, flat rate	month	6.00	91	11c
Telephone bill, family of four	month	16.39	4Q 92	4c
Education				
Board, 4-yr private college/university	year	1533	91	22s
Board, 4-yr public college/university	year	1404	91	22s
Expenditures, local gov't, public elementary/secondary	pupil	5972	92	20s
Room, 4-year private college/university	year	1256	91	22s

Values are in dollars or fractions of dollars. In the column headed *Ref*, references are shown to sources. Each reference is followed by a letter. These refer to the geographical level for which data were reported: s=State, r=Region, and c=City or metro. The abbreviation *ex* is used to mean *except* or *excluding*; *exp* stands for expenditures. For other abbreviations and further explanations, please see the Introduction.

Appleton-Neenah, WI - continued

Item	Per	Value	Date	Ref.
Education				
Room, 4-year public college/university	year	1416	91	22s
Tuition, 2-year private college/university	year	4768	91	22s
Tuition, 2-year public college/university	year	1234	91	22s
Tuition, 4-year private college/university	year	8237	91	22s
Tuition, 4-year public college/university, in-state	year	1951	91	22s
Energy and Fuels				
Coal	mil Btu	1.41	90	64s
Energy	mil Btu	8.27	90	64s
Energy, combined forms, 1,800 sq ft heating area	month	103.84	4Q 92	4c
Energy, exc electricity, 1,800 sq ft heating area	month	62.04	4Q 92	4c
Energy exp/householder, 1-family unit	year	471	90	28r
Energy exp/householder, <1,000 sq ft heating area	year	430	90	28r
Energy exp/householder, 1,000-1,999 sq ft heating area	year	481	90	28r
Energy exp/householder, 2,000+ sq ft heating area	year	473	90	28r
Energy exp/householder, mobile home	year	430	90	28r
Energy exp/householder, multifamily	year	461	90	28r
Gas, natural	mil Btu	4.56	90	64s
Gas, natural	000 cu ft	5.61	91	46s
Gas, natural, exp	year	605	91	46s
Gasoline, motor	gal	1.14	4Q 92	4c
Gasoline, unleaded regular	mil Btu	9.38	90	64s
Entertainment				
Bowling, evening rate	game	1.75	4Q 92	4c
Miniature golf admission	adult	6.18	92	1r
Miniature golf admission	child	5.14	92	1r
Monopoly game, Parker Brothers', No. 9		11.66	4Q 92	4c
Movie	admission	5.67	4Q 92	4c
Tennis balls, yellow, Wilson or Penn, 3	can	2.20	4Q 92	4c
Waterpark admission	adult	11.00	92	1r
Waterpark admission	child	8.55	92	1r
Funerals				
Casket, 18-gauge steel, velvet interior		1926.72	91	24r
Cosmetology, hair care, etc.		97.64	91	24r
Embalming		249.14	91	24r
Facility use for ceremony		208.59	91	24r
Hearse, local		130.12	91	24r
Limousine, local		104.66	91	24r
Remains to funeral home, transfer		93.61	91	24r
Service charge, professional		724.62	91	24r
Vault, concrete, non-metallic liner		734.53	91	24r
Viewing facilities, use		236.06	91	24r
Goods and Services				
ACCRA Index, Miscellaneous Goods and Services		97.00	4Q 92	4c
Groceries				
ACCRA Index, Groceries		96.30	4Q 92	4c
Apples, Red Delicious	lb	0.77	4/93	16r
Babyfood, strained vegetables, lowest price	4-4.5 oz jar	0.38	4Q 92	4c
Bacon	lb	1.85	4/93	16r
Bananas	lb	0.40	4Q 92	4c
Bananas	lb	0.46	4/93	16r
Beef, stew, boneless	lb	2.53	4/93	16r
Bologna, all beef or mixed	lb	2.19	4/93	16r
Bread, white	24 oz	0.48	4Q 92	4c
Bread, white, pan	lb	0.78	4/93	16r
Butter	lb	1.50	4/93	16r
Cabbage	lb	0.40	4/93	16r
Carrots, short trimmed and topped	lb	0.45	4/93	16r
Cheese, Cheddar	lb	3.47	4/93	16r

Appleton-Neenah, WI - continued

Item	Per	Value	Date	Ref.
Groceries - continued				
Cheese, Kraft grated Parmesan	8-oz canister	2.89	4Q 92	4c
Chicken, fresh, whole	lb	0.84	4/93	16r
Chicken, fryer, whole	lb	0.82	4Q 92	4c
Chicken breast, bone-in	lb	1.94	4/93	16r
Chicken legs, bone-in	lb	1.02	4/93	16r
Chuck roast, graded and ungraded, ex USDA prime and choice	lb	2.43	4/93	16r
Chuck roast, USDA choice, bone-in	lb	2.11	4/93	16r
Chuck roast, USDA choice, boneless	lb	2.44	4/93	16r
Cigarettes, Winston	carton	18.72	4Q 92	4c
Coffee, 100% ground roast, all sizes	lb	2.47	4/93	16r
Coffee, vacuum-packed	13-oz can	1.95	4Q 92	4c
Cookies, chocolate chip	lb	2.73	4/93	16r
Corn, frozen	10 oz	0.63	4Q 92	4c
Corn Flakes, Kellogg's or Post Toasties	18 oz	1.89	4Q 92	4c
Eggs, Grade A large	doz	0.73	4Q 92	4c
Eggs, Grade A large	doz	0.93	4/93	16r
Flour, white, all purpose	lb	0.21	4/93	16r
Grapefruit	lb	0.45	4/93	16r
Grapes, Thompson Seedless	lb	1.46	4/93	16r
Ground beef, 100% beef	lb	1.63	4/93	16r
Ground beef, lean and extra lean	lb	2.08	4/93	16r
Ground beef or hamburger	lb	1.77	4Q 92	4c
Ground chuck, 100% beef	lb	1.94	4/93	16r
Ham, boneless, excluding canned	lb	2.21	4/93	16r
Honey, jar	8 oz	0.97-1.25	92	5r
Honey, jar	lb	1.25-2.25	92	5r
Honey, squeeze bear	12-oz	1.25-1.99	92	5r
Ice cream, prepackaged, bulk, regular	1/2 gal	2.41	4/93	16r
Lemons	lb	0.82	4/93	16r
Lettuce, iceberg	head	0.84	4Q 92	4c
Lettuce, iceberg	lb	0.83	4/93	16r
Margarine, Blue Bonnet or Parkay cubes	lb	0.50	4Q 92	4c
Margarine, stick	lb	0.77	4/93	16r
Milk, whole	1/2 gal	1.33	4Q 92	4c
Orange juice, Minute Maid frozen	12-oz can	1.27	4Q 92	4c
Oranges, navel	lb	0.50	4/93	16r
Peaches	29-oz can	1.39	4Q 92	4c
Peanut butter, creamy, all sizes	lb	1.82	4/93	16r
Pears, Anjou	lb	0.85	4/93	16r
Peas Sweet, Del Monte or Green Giant	15-17 oz can	0.51	4Q 92	4c
Pork chops, center cut, bone-in	lb	3.17	4/93	16r
Potato chips	16 oz	2.68	4/93	16r
Potatoes, white	lb	0.26	4/93	16r
Potatoes, white or red	10-lb sack	1.75	4Q 92	4c
Round roast, graded & ungraded, ex USDA prime & choice	lb	2.88	4/93	16r
Round roast, USDA choice, boneless	lb	2.96	4/93	16r
Sausage, Jimmy Dean, 100% pork	lb	2.50	4Q 92	4c
Shortening, vegetable oil blends	lb	0.79	4/93	16r
Shortening, vegetable, Crisco	3-lb can	2.25	4Q 92	4c
Soft drink, Coca Cola	2 liter	0.97	4Q 92	4c
Spaghetti and macaroni	lb	0.76	4/93	16r
Steak, rib eye, USDA choice, boneless	lb	6.29	4/93	16r
Steak, round, USDA choice, boneless	lb	3.24	4/93	16r
Steak, sirloin, graded & ungraded, ex USDA prime & choice	lb	4.00	4/93	16r
Steak, sirloin, USDA choice, bone-in	lb	3.57	4/93	16r
Steak, sirloin, USDA choice, boneless	lb	4.17	4/93	16r
Steak, T-bone	lb	4.93	4Q 92	4c
Steak, T-bone, USDA choice, bone-in	lb	5.60	4/93	16r
Strawberries, dry pint	12 oz	0.90	4/93	16r
Sugar, cane or beet	4 lb	1.45	4Q 92	4c
Sugar, white	lb	0.36	4/93	16r

Values are in dollars or fractions of dollars. In the column headed *Ref*, references are shown to sources. Each reference is followed by a letter. These refer to the geographical level for which data were reported: s = State, r = Region, and c = City or metro. The abbreviation *ex* is used to mean *except* or *excluding*; *exp* stands for *expenditures*. For other abbreviations and further explanations, please see the Introduction.

Appleton-Neenah, WI - continued

Item	Per	Value	Date	Ref.
Groceries				
Sugar, white, 33-80 oz pk	lb	0.35	4/93	16r
Tomatoes, field grown	lb	0.99	4/93	16r
Tomatoes, Hunt's or Del Monte	14.5-oz can	0.72	4Q 92	4c
Tuna, chunk, light	6.125-6.5 oz can	0.69	4Q 92	4c
Tuna, chunk, light	lb	1.76	4/93	16r
Turkey, frozen, whole	lb	0.91	4/93	16r
Health Care				
ACCRA Index, Health Care		92.80	4Q 92	4c
Analgesic, Aspirin, Bayer, 325 mg tablets	100	4.75	4Q 92	4c
Childbirth, cesarean, hospital		4688	91	62r
Childbirth, cesarean, physician's fee		2053	91	62r
Childbirth, normal, hospital		2657	91	62r
Childbirth, normal, physician's fee		1492	91	62r
Dentist's fee, adult teeth cleaning and periodic oral exam	visit	43.66	4Q 92	4c
Doctor's fee, routine exam, established patient	visit	39.00	4Q 92	4c
Hospital care, semiprivate room	day	209.00	4Q 92	4c
Medical insurance premium, per employee, small group comprehensive	month	266.45	10/91	25c
Medical plan per employee	year	3443	91	45r
Mental health care, exp	capita	28.84-37.59	90	38s
Mental health care, exp, state mental health agency	capita	36.62	90	38s
Mental health care, hospital psychiatric services, non-Federal, exp	capita	13.05	88	38s
Mental health care, mental health organization, multiservice, exp	capita	10.93	88	38s
Mental health care, psychiatric hospitals, private, exp	capita	8.71	88	38s
Mental health care, psychiatric out-patient clinics, freestanding, exp	capita	5.33	88	38s
Mental health care, psychiatric partial-care organizations, freestanding, exp	capita	0.20	88	38s
Mental health care, state and county mental hospitals, exp	capita	28.29	88	38s
Mental health care, VA medical centers, exp	capita	7.57	88	38s
Physician fee, family practice, first-visit		76.00	91	62r
Physician fee, family practice, revisit		33.00	91	62r
Physician fee, general practice, first-visit		61.00	91	62r
Physician fee, general practice, revisit		31.00	91	62r
Physician fee, general surgeon, first-visit		65.00	91	62r
Physician fee, general surgeon, revisit		35.00	91	62r
Physician fee, internal medicine, first-visit		91.00	91	62r
Physician fee, internal medicine, revisit		40.00	91	62r
Physician fee, median, neurosurgeon, first-visit		106.00	91	62r
Physician fee, median, nonsurgical specialist, first-visit		90.00	91	62r
Physician fee, median, orthopedic surgeon, first-visit		83.00	91	62r
Physician fee, median, surgical specialist, first-visit		61.00	91	62r
Physician fee, neurosurgeon, revisit		41.00	91	62r
Physician fee, nonsurgical specialist, revisit		40.00	91	62r
Physician fee, obstetrics/gynecology, first-visit		61.00	91	62r
Physician fee, obstetrics/gynecology, revisit		40.00	91	62r
Physician fee, orthopedic surgeon, revisit		41.00	91	62r
Physician fee, pediatrician, first-visit		46.00	91	62r
Physician fee, pediatrician, revisit		33.00	91	62r
Physician fee, surgical specialist, revisit		36.00	91	62r
Substance abuse, hospital ancillary charge	incident	960	90	70s
Substance abuse, hospital physician charge	incident	470	90	70s
Substance abuse, hospital room and board	incident	3980	90	70s

Appleton-Neenah, WI - continued

Item	Per	Value	Date	Ref.
Household Goods				
Appliance repair, home, service call, washing machine	min labor charge	29.63	4Q 92	4c
Laundry detergent, Tide Ultra, Bold, or Cheer	42 oz	3.03	4Q 92	4c
Tissues, facial, Kleenex brand	175-count box	1.08	4Q 92	4c
Housing				
ACCRA Index, Housing		100.50	4Q 92	4c
Home, median price	unit	71.00		26c
House, 1,800 sq ft, 8,000 sq ft lot, new, urban	total	112933	4Q 92	4c
House payment, principal and interest, 25% down payment	month	639	4Q 92	4c
Mortgage rate, incl. points & origination fee, 30-year fixed or adjustable rate	percent	8.29	4Q 92	4c
Rent, apartment, 2 bedrooms - 1-1/2 to 2 baths, unfurnished, 950 sq ft, water	month	446	4Q 92	4c
Rental unit, 1 bedroom	month	365	93	23c
Rental unit, 2 bedroom	month	432	93	23c
Rental unit, 3 bedroom	month	539	93	23c
Rental unit, 4 bedroom	month	603	93	23c
Rental unit, efficiency	month	300	93	23c
Insurance and Pensions				
Auto insurance, private passenger	year	510.11	91	63s
Personal Goods				
Shampoo, Alberto VO5	15 oz	1.04	4Q 92	4c
Toothpaste, Crest or Colgate	6-7 oz	1.61	4Q 92	4c
Personal Services				
Dry cleaning, man's 2-piece suit		7.27	4Q 92	4c
Haircare, woman's shampoo, trim and blow-dry		18.33	4Q 92	4c
Haircut, man's barbershop, no styling		7.50	4Q 92	4c
Restaurant Food				
Chicken, fried, thigh and drumstick		2.12	4Q 92	4c
Hamburger with cheese	1/4 lb	1.77	4Q 92	4c
Pizza, Pizza Hut or Pizza Inn, cheese, thin crust	12-13 in	9.35	4Q 92	4c
Taxes				
Tax, cigarette	pack	38	91	77s
Tax, gasoline	gal	22.20	91	77s
Taxes, state	capita	1416	91	77s
Transportation				
ACCRA Index, Transportation		93.70	4Q 92	4c
Driver's license fee		9.00	12/90	43s
Tire balance, computer or spin balance, front	wheel	5.64	4Q 92	4c
Utilities				
ACCRA Index, Utilities		94.00	4Q 92	4c
Electricity	mil Btu	15.77	90	64s
Electricity, partial electric and other energy, 1,800 sq ft living area new home	month	41.80	4Q 92	4c

Ardmore, OK

Item	Per	Value	Date	Ref.
Composite ACCRA index		88.70	4Q 92	4c
Alcoholic Beverages				
Beer, Miller Lite or Budweiser, 12-oz containers	6 pack	4.37	4Q 92	4c
Liquor, J & B Scotch	750 ml	16.06	4Q 92	4c
Wine, Gallo Chablis blanc, 1.5 liter	bottle	5.74	4Q 92	4c
Clothing				
Jeans, man's denim		27.96	4Q 92	4c
Shirt, man's dress shirt		18.50	4Q 92	4c
Undervest, boy's size 10-14, cotton	3	3.56	4Q 92	4c

Values are in dollars or fractions of dollars. In the column headed *Ref*, references are shown to sources. Each reference is followed by a letter. These refer to the geographical level for which data were reported: s=State, r=Region, and c=City or metro. The abbreviation *ex* is used to mean *except* or *excluding*; *exp* stands for expenditures. For other abbreviations and further explanations, please see the Introduction.

Ardmore, OK - continued

Item	Per	Value	Date	Ref.
Communications				
Newspaper subscription, daily and Sunday home delivery, large-city	month	12.85	4Q 92	4c
Telephone, flat rate	month	10.87	91	11c
Telephone bill, family of four	month	17.88	4Q 92	4c
Energy and Fuels				
Energy, combined forms, 1,800 sq ft heating area	month	107.65	4Q 92	4c
Gasoline, motor	gal	1.09	4Q 92	4c
Entertainment				
Bowling, evening rate	game	1.80	4Q 92	4c
Monopoly game, Parker Brothers', No. 9		9.92	4Q 92	4c
Movie	admission	5.00	4Q 92	4c
Tennis balls, yellow, Wilson or Penn, 3	can	2.31	4Q 92	4c
Goods and Services				
ACCRA Index, Miscellaneous Goods and Services		92.30	4Q 92	4c
Groceries				
ACCRA Index, Groceries		98.40	4Q 92	4c
Babyfood, strained vegetables, lowest price	4-4.5 oz jar	0.28	4Q 92	4c
Bananas	lb	0.42	4Q 92	4c
Bread, white	24 oz	0.70	4Q 92	4c
Cheese, Kraft grated Parmesan	8-oz canister	3.37	4Q 92	4c
Chicken, fryer, whole	lb	0.69	4Q 92	4c
Cigarettes, Winston	carton	16.51	4Q 92	4c
Coffee, vacuum-packed	13-oz can	1.96	4Q 92	4c
Corn, frozen	10 oz	0.54	4Q 92	4c
Corn Flakes, Kellogg's or Post Toasties	18 oz	1.72	4Q 92	4c
Eggs, Grade A large	doz	0.86	4Q 92	4c
Ground beef or hamburger	lb	1.65	4Q 92	4c
Lettuce, iceberg	head	1.02	4Q 92	4c
Margarine, Blue Bonnet or Parkay cubes	lb	0.54	4Q 92	4c
Milk, whole	1/2 gal	1.37	4Q 92	4c
Orange juice, Minute Maid frozen	12-oz can	1.42	4Q 92	4c
Peaches	29-oz can	1.16	4Q 92	4c
Peas Sweet, Del Monte or Green Giant	15-17 oz can	0.62	4Q 92	4c
Potatoes, white or red	10-lb sack	2.29	4Q 92	4c
Sausage, Jimmy Dean, 100% pork	lb	2.22	4Q 92	4c
Shortening, vegetable, Crisco	3-lb can	2.27	4Q 92	4c
Soft drink, Coca Cola	2 liter	1.14	4Q 92	4c
Steak, T-bone	lb	4.85	4Q 92	4c
Sugar, cane or beet	4 lb	1.74	4Q 92	4c
Tomatoes, Hunt's or Del Monte	14.5-oz can	0.71	4Q 92	4c
Tuna, chunk, light	6.125-6.5 oz can	0.84	4Q 92	4c
Health Care				
ACCRA Index, Health Care		97.00	4Q 92	4c
Analgesic, Aspirin, Bayer, 325 mg tablets	100	4.60	4Q 92	4c
Dentist's fee, adult teeth cleaning and periodic oral exam	visit	47.00	4Q 92	4c
Doctor's fee, routine exam, established patient	visit	41.00	4Q 92	4c
Hospital care, semiprivate room	day	215.00	90	27c
Hospital care, semiprivate room	day	210.00	4Q 92	4c
Household Goods				
Appliance repair, home, service call, washing machine	min labor charge	30.00	4Q 92	4c

Ardmore, OK - continued

Item	Per	Value	Date	Ref.
Household Goods - continued				
Laundry detergent, Tide Ultra, Bold, or Cheer	42 oz	3.55	4Q 92	4c
Tissues, facial, Kleenex brand	175-count box	1.14	4Q 92	4c
Housing				
ACCRA Index, Housing		73.10	4Q 92	4c
House, 1,800 sq ft, 8,000 sq ft lot, new, urban	total	77557	4Q 92	4c
House payment, principal and interest, 25% down payment	month	444	4Q 92	4c
Mortgage rate, incl. points & origination fee, 30-year fixed or adjustable rate	percent	8.43	4Q 92	4c
Rent, apartment, 2 bedrooms - 1-1/2 to 2 baths, unfurnished, 950 sq ft, water	month	372	4Q 92	4c
Personal Goods				
Shampoo, Alberto VO5	15 oz	1.08	4Q 92	4c
Toothpaste, Crest or Colgate	6-7 oz	1.85	4Q 92	4c
Personal Services				
Dry cleaning, man's 2-piece suit		7.00	4Q 92	4c
Haircare, woman's shampoo, trim and blow-dry		13.50	4Q 92	4c
Haircut, man's barbershop, no styling		5.00	4Q 92	4c
Restaurant Food				
Chicken, fried, thigh and drumstick		1.94	4Q 92	4c
Hamburger with cheese	1/4 lb	1.80	4Q 92	4c
Pizza, Pizza Hut or Pizza Inn, cheese, thin crust	12-13 in	8.60	4Q 92	4c
Transportation				
ACCRA Index, Transportation		94.30	4Q 92	4c
Tire balance, computer or spin balance, front	wheel	6.00	4Q 92	4c
Utilities				
ACCRA Index, Utilities		97.90	4Q 92	4c
Electricity, all electric, 1,800 sq ft living area new home	month	107.65	4Q 92	4c

Asheville, NC

Item	Per	Value	Date	Ref.
Child Care				
Child care fee, average, center	hour	1.29	90	65r
Child care fee, average, nonregulated family day care	hour	0.89	90	65r
Child care fee, average, regulated family day care	hour	1.32	90	65r
Communications				
Long-distance telephone service, day, initial minute, 0-100 miles	min	0.10-0.33	91	12s
Long-distance telephone service, day, additional minute, 0-100 miles	min	0.10-0.33	91	12s
Long-distance telephone service, evenings/weekends, 0-100 mi, initial minute	min	0.08-0.24	91	12s
Long-distance telephone service, evenings/weekends, 0-100 mi, additional minute	min	0.05-0.17	91	12s
Education				
Board, 4-yr private college/university	year	1768	91	22s
Board, 4-yr public college/university	year	1568	91	22s
Expenditures, local gov't, public elementary/secondary	pupil	5078	92	20s
Room, 4-year private college/university	year	1467	91	22s
Room, 4-year public college/university	year	1386	91	22s
Tuition, 2-year private college/university	year	4964	91	22s
Tuition, 2-year public college/university	year	334	91	22s
Tuition, 4-year private college/university	year	7826	91	22s
Tuition, 4-year public college/university, in-state	year	1112	91	22s

Values are in dollars or fractions of dollars. In the column headed *Ref*, references are shown to sources. Each reference is followed by a letter. These refer to the geographical level for which data were reported: s=State, r=Region, and c=City or metro. The abbreviation *ex* is used to mean *except* or *excluding*; *exp* stands for *expenditures*. For other abbreviations and further explanations, please see the Introduction.

Asheville, NC - continued

Item	Per	Value	Date	Ref.
Energy and Fuels				
Coal	mil Btu	1.79	90	64s
Energy	mil Btu	10.06	90	64s
Energy exp/householder, 1-family unit	year	487	90	28r
Energy exp/householder, <1,000 sq ft heating area	year	393	90	28r
Energy exp/householder, 1,000-1,999 sq ft heating area	year	442	90	28r
Energy exp/householder, 2,000+ sq ft heating area	year	577	90	28r
Energy exp/householder, mobile home	year	366	90	28r
Energy exp/householder, multifamily	year	382	90	28r
Gas, natural	mil Btu	4.19	90	64s
Gas, natural	000 cu ft	6.24	91	46s
Gas, natural, exp	year	439	91	46s
Gasoline, unleaded regular	mil Btu	9.44	90	64s
Entertainment				
Miniature golf admission	adult	6.18	92	1r
Miniature golf admission	child	5.14	92	1r
Waterpark admission	adult	11.00	92	1r
Waterpark admission	child	8.55	92	1r
Funerals				
Casket, 18-gauge steel, velvet interior		2029.08	91	24r
Cosmetology, hair care, etc.		75.10	91	24r
Embalming		249.24	91	24r
Facility use for ceremony		162.27	91	24r
Hearse, local		114.04	91	24r
Limousine, local		88.57	91	24r
Remains to funeral home, transfer		92.61	91	24r
Service charge, professional		682.42	91	24r
Vault, concrete, non-metallic liner		798.70	91	24r
Viewing facilities, use		163.86	91	24r
Groceries				
Apples, Red Delicious	lb	0.79	4/93	16r
Bacon	lb	1.75	4/93	16r
Bananas	lb	0.42	4/93	16r
Beef, stew, boneless	lb	2.61	4/93	16r
Bologna, all beef or mixed	lb	2.24	4/93	16r
Bread, white, pan	lb	0.64	4/93	16r
Bread, whole wheat, pan	lb	0.96	4/93	16r
Cabbage	lb	0.37	4/93	16r
Carrots, short trimmed and topped	lb	0.47	4/93	16r
Celery	lb	0.64	4/93	16r
Cheese, American	lb	2.98	4/93	16r
Cheese, Cheddar	lb	3.28	4/93	16r
Chicken, fresh, whole	lb	0.77	4/93	16r
Chicken breast, bone-in	lb	1.92	4/93	16r
Chicken legs, bone-in	lb	1.06	4/93	16r
Chuck roast, graded and ungraded, ex USDA prime and choice	lb	2.40	4/93	16r
Chuck roast, USDA choice, bone-in	lb	2.19	4/93	16r
Chuck roast, USDA choice, boneless	lb	2.38	4/93	16r
Coffee, 100% ground roast, all sizes	lb	2.48	4/93	16r
Crackers, soda, salted	lb	1.15	4/93	16r
Eggs, Grade A large	doz	0.96	4/93	16r
Flour, white, all purpose	lb	0.24	4/93	16r
Frankfurters, all meat or all beef	lb	2.01	4/93	16r
Grapefruit	lb	0.44	4/93	16r
Grapes, Thompson Seedless	lb	1.40	4/93	16r
Ground beef, 100% beef	lb	1.58	4/93	16r
Ground beef, lean and extra lean	lb	2.09	4/93	16r
Ground chuck, 100% beef	lb	1.98	4/93	16r
Ham, boneless, excluding canned	lb	2.89	4/93	16r
Ham, picnic, shoulder, bone-in, smoked	lb	1.02	4/93	16r
Ham, rump or steak half, bone-in, smoked	lb	1.48	4/93	16r
Ice cream, prepackaged, bulk, regular	1/2 gal	2.41	4/93	16r
Lemons	lb	1.05	4/93	16r
Lettuce, iceberg	lb	0.81	4/93	16r
Margarine, stick	lb	0.88	4/93	16r
Oranges, navel	lb	0.55	4/93	16r
Pears, Anjou	lb	0.92	4/93	16r

Asheville, NC - continued

Item	Per	Value	Date	Ref.
Groceries - continued				
Pork chops, center cut, bone-in	lb	3.13	4/93	16r
Potato chips	16 oz	2.94	4/93	16r
Potatoes, white	lb	0.43	4/93	16r
Rib roast, USDA choice, bone-in	lb	4.63	4/93	16r
Rice, white, long grain, uncooked	lb	0.45	4/93	16r
Round roast, graded & ungraded, ex USDA prime & choice	lb	3.03	4/93	16r
Round roast, USDA choice, boneless	lb	3.09	4/93	16r
Sausage, fresh, loose	lb	2.08	4/93	16r
Short ribs, bone-in	lb	2.66	4/93	16r
Shortening, vegetable oil blends	lb	0.69	4/93	16r
Spaghetti and macaroni	lb	0.81	4/93	16r
Steak, rib eye, USDA choice, boneless	lb	6.24	4/93	16r
Steak, round, graded & ungraded, ex USDA prime & choice	lb	3.31	4/93	16r
Steak, round, USDA choice, boneless	lb	3.34	4/93	16r
Steak, sirloin, graded & ungraded, ex USDA prime & choice	lb	4.19	4/93	16r
Steak, sirloin, USDA choice, boneless	lb	4.46	4/93	16r
Steak, T-bone, USDA choice, bone-in	lb	5.25	4/93	16r
Strawberries, dry pint	12 oz	0.92	4/93	16r
Sugar, white	lb	0.39	4/93	16r
Sugar, white, 33-80 oz pk	lb	0.38	4/93	16r
Tomatoes, field grown	lb	0.88	4/93	16r
Tuna, chunk, light	lb	1.79	4/93	16r
Turkey, frozen, whole	lb	1.04	4/93	16r
Yogurt, natural, fruit flavored	1/2 pint	0.57	4/93	16r
Health Care				
Childbirth, cesarean, hospital		5034	91	62r
Childbirth, cesarean, physician's fee		2053	91	62r
Childbirth, normal, hospital		2712	91	62r
Childbirth, normal, physician's fee		1492	91	62r
Medical plan per employee	year	3495	91	45r
Mental health care, exp	capita	37.60-53.67	90	38s
Mental health care, exp, state mental health agency	capita	45.66	90	38s
Mental health care, hospital psychiatric services, non-Federal, exp	capita	12.05	88	38s
Mental health care, mental health organization, multiservice, exp	capita	29.54	88	38s
Mental health care, psychiatric hospitals, private, exp	capita	15.07	88	38s
Mental health care, psychiatric out-patient clinics, freestanding, exp	capita	0.11	88	38s
Mental health care, state and county mental hospitals, exp	capita	26.36	88	38s
Mental health care, VA medical centers, exp	capita	2.23	88	38s
Physician fee, family practice, first-visit		75.00	91	62r
Physician fee, family practice, revisit		34.00	91	62r
Physician fee, general practice, first-visit		61.00	91	62r
Physician fee, general practice, revisit		32.00	91	62r
Physician fee, general surgeon, first-visit		64.00	91	62r
Physician fee, general surgeon, revisit		40.00	91	62r
Physician fee, internal medicine, first-visit		98.00	91	62r
Physician fee, internal medicine, revisit		40.00	91	62r
Physician fee, median, neurosurgeon, first-visit		130.00	91	62r
Physician fee, median, nonsurgical specialist, first-visit		95.00	91	62r
Physician fee, median, orthopedic surgeon, first-visit		91.00	91	62r
Physician fee, median, plastic surgeon, first-visit		66.00	91	62r
Physician fee, median, surgical specialist, first-visit		62.00	91	62r
Physician fee, neurosurgeon, revisit		50.00	91	62r
Physician fee, nonsurgical specialist, revisit		40.00	91	62r
Physician fee, obstetrics/gynecology, first-visit		64.00	91	62r
Physician fee, obstetrics/gynecology, revisit		41.00	91	62r

Values are in dollars or fractions of dollars. In the column headed *Ref*, references are shown to sources. Each reference is followed by a letter. These refer to the geographical level for which data were reported: s=State, r=Region, and c=City or metro. The abbreviation *ex* is used to mean *except* or *excluding*; *exp* stands for expenditures. For other abbreviations and further explanations, please see the Introduction.

Asheville, NC - continued

Item	Per	Value	Date	Ref.
Health Care				
Physician fee, orthopedic surgeon, revisit		40.00	91	62r
Physician fee, pediatrician, first-visit		49.00	91	62r
Physician fee, pediatrician, revisit		33.00	91	62r
Physician fee, plastic surgeon, revisit		43.00	91	62r
Physician fee, surgical specialist, revisit		37.00	91	62r
Substance abuse, hospital ancillary charge	inci-dent	1090	90	70s
Substance abuse, hospital physician charge	inci-dent	460	90	70s
Substance abuse, hospital room and board	inci-dent	4880	90	70s
Insurance and Pensions				
Auto insurance, private passenger	year	522.39	91	63s
Taxes				
Tax, cigarette	pack	5	91	77s
Tax, gasoline	gal	21.90	91	77s
Taxes, state	capita	1165	91	77s
Transportation				
Driver's license fee		15.00	12/90	43s
Vehicle registration and license plate	year	35.00	93	50s
Travel				
Business travel	day	193.00	4/93	89r
Utilities				
Electricity	mil Btu	18.74	90	64s

Athens, GA

Item	Per	Value	Date	Ref.
Composite ACCRA index		98.70	4Q 92	4c
Alcoholic Beverages				
Beer, Miller Lite or Budweiser, 12-oz containers	6 pack	4.24	4Q 92	4c
Liquor, J & B Scotch	750 ml	16.99	4Q 92	4c
Wine, Gallo Chablis blanc, 1.5 liter	bottle	6.25	4Q 92	4c
Child Care				
Child care fee, average, center	hour	1.29	90	65r
Child care fee, average, nonregulated family day care	hour	0.89	90	65r
Child care fee, average, regulated family day care	hour	1.32	90	65r
Clothing				
Jeans, man's denim		28.50	4Q 92	4c
Shirt, man's dress shirt		26.08	4Q 92	4c
Undervest, boy's size 10-14, cotton	3	4.26	4Q 92	4c
Communications				
Long-distance telephone service, day, initial minute, 0-100 miles	min	0.16-0.26	91	12s
Long-distance telephone service, day, additional minute, 0-100 miles	min	0.08-0.23	91	12s
Long-distance telephone service, evenings/weekends, 0-100 mi, initial minute	min	0.06-0.13	91	12s
Long-distance telephone service, evenings/weekends, 0-100 mi, additional minute	min	0.04-0.12	91	12s
Newspaper subscription, daily and Sunday home delivery, large-city	month	12.09	4Q 92	4c
Telephone, flat rate	month	13.35	91	11c
Telephone bill, family of four	month	21.11	4Q 92	4c
Education				
Board, 4-yr private college/university	year	1801	91	22s
Board, 4-yr public college/university	year	1501	91	22s
Expenditures, local gov't, public elementary/secondary	pupil	4747	92	20s
Room, 4-year private college/university	year	2139	91	22s
Room, 4-year public college/university	year	1192	91	22s
Tuition, 2-year private college/university	year	4457	91	22s
Tuition, 2-year public college/university	year	946	91	22s
Tuition, 4-year private college/university	year	7542	91	22s

Athens, GA - continued

Item	Per	Value	Date	Ref.
Education - continued				
Tuition, 4-year public college/university, in-state	year	1680	91	22s
Energy and Fuels				
Coal	mil Btu	1.79	90	64s
Energy	mil Btu	8.88	90	64s
Energy, combined forms, 1,800 sq ft heating area	month	125.18	4Q 92	4c
Energy, exc electricity, 1,800 sq ft heating area	month	51.20	4Q 92	4c
Energy exp/householder, 1-family unit	year	487	90	28r
Energy exp/householder, <1,000 sq ft heating area	year	393	90	28r
Energy exp/householder, 1,000-1,999 sq ft heating area	year	442	90	28r
Energy exp/householder, 2,000+ sq ft heating area	year	577	90	28r
Energy exp/householder, mobile home	year	366	90	28r
Energy exp/householder, multifamily	year	382	90	28r
Gas, natural	mil Btu	4.80	90	64s
Gas, natural	000 cu ft	6.70	91	46s
Gas, natural, exp	year	475	91	46s
Gasoline, motor	gal	1.02	4Q 92	4c
Gasoline, unleaded regular	mil Btu	8.24	90	64s
Entertainment				
Bowling, evening rate	game	2.50	4Q 92	4c
Miniature golf admission	adult	6.18	92	1r
Miniature golf admission	child	5.14	92	1r
Monopoly game, Parker Brothers', No. 9		11.98	4Q 92	4c
Movie	admission	6.00	4Q 92	4c
Tennis balls, yellow, Wilson or Penn, 3	can	2.78	4Q 92	4c
Waterpark admission	adult	11.00	92	1r
Waterpark admission	child	8.55	92	1r
Funerals				
Casket, 18-gauge steel, velvet interior		2029.08	91	24r
Cosmetology, hair care, etc.		75.10	91	24r
Embalming		249.24	91	24r
Facility use for ceremony		162.27	91	24r
Hearse, local		114.04	91	24r
Limousine, local		88.57	91	24r
Remains to funeral home, transfer		92.61	91	24r
Service charge, professional		682.42	91	24r
Vault, concrete, non-metallic liner		798.70	91	24r
Viewing facilities, use		163.86	91	24r
Goods and Services				
ACCRA Index, Miscellaneous Goods and Services		104.00	4Q 92	4c
Groceries				
ACCRA Index, Groceries		95.80	4Q 92	4c
Apples, Red Delicious	lb	0.79	4/93	16r
Babyfood, strained vegetables, lowest price	4-4.5 oz jar	0.35	4Q 92	4c
Bacon	lb	1.75	4/93	16r
Bananas	lb	0.40	4Q 92	4c
Bananas	lb	0.42	4/93	16r
Beef, stew, boneless	lb	2.61	4/93	16r
Bologna, all beef or mixed	lb	2.24	4/93	16r
Bread, white	24 oz	0.89	4Q 92	4c
Bread, white, pan	lb	0.64	4/93	16r
Bread, whole wheat, pan	lb	0.96	4/93	16r
Cabbage	lb	0.37	4/93	16r
Carrots, short trimmed and topped	lb	0.47	4/93	16r
Celery	lb	0.64	4/93	16r
Cheese, American	lb	2.98	4/93	16r
Cheese, Cheddar	lb	3.28	4/93	16r
Cheese, Kraft grated Parmesan	8-oz canister	3.28	4Q 92	4c

Values are in dollars or fractions of dollars. In the column headed *Ref*, references are shown to sources. Each reference is followed by a letter. These refer to the geographical level for which data were reported: s=State, r=Region, and c=City or metro. The abbreviation *ex* is used to mean *except* or *excluding*; *exp* stands for expenditures. For other abbreviations and further explanations, please see the Introduction.

Athens, GA - continued

Item	Per	Value	Date	Ref.
Groceries				
Chicken, fresh, whole	lb	0.77	4/93	16r
Chicken, fryer, whole	lb	0.67	4Q 92	4c
Chicken breast, bone-in	lb	1.92	4/93	16r
Chicken legs, bone-in	lb	1.06	4/93	16r
Chuck roast, graded and ungraded, ex USDA prime and choice	lb	2.40	4/93	16r
Chuck roast, USDA choice, bone-in	lb	2.19	4/93	16r
Chuck roast, USDA choice, boneless	lb	2.38	4/93	16r
Cigarettes, Winston	carton	15.96	4Q 92	4c
Coffee, 100% ground roast, all sizes	lb	2.48	4/93	16r
Coffee, vacuum-packed	13-oz can	1.84	4Q 92	4c
Corn, frozen	10 oz	0.53	4Q 92	4c
Corn Flakes, Kellogg's or Post Toasties	18 oz	1.76	4Q 92	4c
Crackers, soda, salted	lb	1.15	4/93	16r
Eggs, Grade A large	doz	0.88	4Q 92	4c
Eggs, Grade A large	doz	0.96	4/93	16r
Flour, white, all purpose	lb	0.24	4/93	16r
Frankfurters, all meat or all beef	lb	2.01	4/93	16r
Grapefruit	lb	0.44	4/93	16r
Grapes, Thompson Seedless	lb	1.40	4/93	16r
Ground beef, 100% beef	lb	1.58	4/93	16r
Ground beef, lean and extra lean	lb	2.09	4/93	16r
Ground beef or hamburger	lb	1.47	4Q 92	4c
Ground chuck, 100% beef	lb	1.98	4/93	16r
Ham, boneless, excluding canned	lb	2.89	4/93	16r
Ham, picnic, shoulder, bone-in, smoked	lb	1.02	4/93	16r
Ham, rump or steak half, bone-in, smoked	lb	1.48	4/93	16r
Ice cream, prepackaged, bulk, regular	1/2 gal	2.41	4/93	16r
Lemons	lb	1.05	4/93	16r
Lettuce, iceberg	head	0.92	4Q 92	4c
Lettuce, iceberg	lb	0.81	4/93	16r
Margarine, Blue Bonnet or Parkay cubes	lb	0.54	4Q 92	4c
Margarine, stick	lb	0.88	4/93	16r
Milk, whole	1/2 gal	1.36	4Q 92	4c
Orange juice, Minute Maid frozen	12-oz can	1.25	4Q 92	4c
Oranges, navel	lb	0.55	4/93	16r
Peaches	29-oz can	1.22	4Q 92	4c
Pears, Anjou	lb	0.92	4/93	16r
Peas Sweet, Del Monte or Green Giant	15-17 oz can	0.58	4Q 92	4c
Pork chops, center cut, bone-in	lb	3.13	4/93	16r
Potato chips	16 oz	2.94	4/93	16r
Potatoes, white	lb	0.43	4/93	16r
Potatoes, white or red	10-lb sack	1.96	4Q 92	4c
Rib roast, USDA choice, bone-in	lb	4.63	4/93	16r
Rice, white, long grain, uncooked	lb	0.45	4/93	16r
Round roast, graded & ungraded, ex USDA prime & choice	lb	3.03	4/93	16r
Round roast, USDA choice, boneless	lb	3.09	4/93	16r
Sausage, fresh, loose	lb	2.08	4/93	16r
Sausage, Jimmy Dean, 100% pork	lb	2.20	4Q 92	4c
Short ribs, bone-in	lb	2.66	4/93	16r
Shortening, vegetable oil blends	lb	0.69	4/93	16r
Shortening, vegetable, Crisco	3-lb can	1.99	4Q 92	4c
Soft drink, Coca Cola	2 liter	1.10	4Q 92	4c
Spaghetti and macaroni	lb	0.81	4/93	16r
Steak, rib eye, USDA choice, boneless	lb	6.24	4/93	16r
Steak, round, graded & ungraded, ex USDA prime & choice	lb	3.31	4/93	16r
Steak, round, USDA choice, boneless	lb	3.34	4/93	16r
Steak, sirloin, graded & ungraded, ex USDA prime & choice	lb	4.19	4/93	16r
Steak, sirloin, USDA choice, boneless	lb	4.46	4/93	16r
Steak, T-bone	lb	5.39	4Q 92	4c
Steak, T-bone, USDA choice, bone-in	lb	5.25	4/93	16r
Strawberries, dry pint	12 oz	0.92	4/93	16r
Sugar, cane or beet	4 lb	1.43	4Q 92	4c

Athens, GA - continued

Item	Per	Value	Date	Ref.
Groceries - continued				
Sugar, white	lb	0.39	4/93	16r
Sugar, white, 33-80 oz pk	lb	0.38	4/93	16r
Tomatoes, field grown	lb	0.88	4/93	16r
Tomatoes, Hunt's or Del Monte	14.5-oz can	0.62	4Q 92	4c
Tuna, chunk, light	6.125-6.5 oz can	0.54	4Q 92	4c
Tuna, chunk, light	lb	1.79	4/93	16r
Turkey, frozen, whole	lb	1.04	4/93	16r
Yogurt, natural, fruit flavored	1/2 pint	0.57	4/93	16r
Health Care				
ACCRA Index, Health Care		86.40	4Q 92	4c
Analgesic, Aspirin, Bayer, 325 mg tablets	100	5.05	4Q 92	4c
Childbirth, cesarean, hospital		5034	91	62r
Childbirth, cesarean, physician's fee		2053	91	62r
Childbirth, normal, hospital		2712	91	62r
Childbirth, normal, physician's fee		1492	91	62r
Dentist's fee, adult teeth cleaning and periodic oral exam	visit	36.50	4Q 92	4c
Doctor's fee, routine exam, established patient	visit	32.30	4Q 92	4c
Hospital care, semiprivate room	day	202.20	90	27c
Hospital care, semiprivate room	day	292.50	4Q 92	4c
Medical insurance premium, per employee, small group comprehensive	month	317.55	10/91	25c
Medical plan per employee	year	3495	91	45r
Mental health care, exp	capita	37.60-53.67	90	38s
Mental health care, exp, state mental health agency	capita	50.98	90	38s
Mental health care, hospital psychiatric services, non-Federal, exp	capita	9.66	88	38s
Mental health care, mental health organization, multiservice, exp	capita	16.40	88	38s
Mental health care, psychiatric hospitals, private, exp	capita	26.36	88	38s
Mental health care, psychiatric out-patient clinics, freestanding, exp	capita	0.13	88	38s
Mental health care, state and county mental hospitals, exp	capita	38.94	88	38s
Mental health care, VA medical centers, exp	capita	3.91	88	38s
Physician fee, family practice, first-visit		75.00	91	62r
Physician fee, family practice, revisit		34.00	91	62r
Physician fee, general practice, first-visit		61.00	91	62r
Physician fee, general practice, revisit		32.00	91	62r
Physician fee, general surgeon, first-visit		64.00	91	62r
Physician fee, general surgeon, revisit		40.00	91	62r
Physician fee, internal medicine, first-visit		98.00	91	62r
Physician fee, internal medicine, revisit		40.00	91	62r
Physician fee, median, neurosurgeon, first-visit		130.00	91	62r
Physician fee, median, nonsurgical specialist, first-visit		95.00	91	62r
Physician fee, median, orthopedic surgeon, first-visit		91.00	91	62r
Physician fee, median, plastic surgeon, first-visit		66.00	91	62r
Physician fee, median, surgical specialist, first-visit		62.00	91	62r
Physician fee, neurosurgeon, revisit		50.00	91	62r
Physician fee, nonsurgical specialist, revisit		40.00	91	62r
Physician fee, obstetrics/gynecology, first-visit		64.00	91	62r
Physician fee, obstetrics/gynecology, revisit		41.00	91	62r
Physician fee, orthopedic surgeon, revisit		40.00	91	62r
Physician fee, pediatrician, first-visit		49.00	91	62r
Physician fee, pediatrician, revisit		33.00	91	62r
Physician fee, plastic surgeon, revisit		43.00	91	62r
Physician fee, surgical specialist, revisit		37.00	91	62r

Values are in dollars or fractions of dollars. In the column headed *Ref*, references are shown to sources. Each reference is followed by a letter. These refer to the geographical level for which data were reported: s=State, r=Region, and c=City or metro. The abbreviation *ex* is used to mean *except* or *excluding*; *exp* stands for expenditures. For other abbreviations and further explanations, please see the Introduction.

Athens, GA - continued

Item	Per	Value	Date	Ref.
Health Care				
Substance abuse, hospital ancillary charge	incident	1800	90	70s
Substance abuse, hospital physician charge	incident	890	90	70s
Substance abuse, hospital room and board	incident	5560	90	70s
Household Goods				
Appliance repair, home, service call, washing machine	min labor charge	34.98	4Q 92	4c
Laundry detergent, Tide Ultra, Bold, or Cheer	42 oz	3.12	4Q 92	4c
Tissues, facial, Kleenex brand	175-count box	1.03	4Q 92	4c
Housing				
ACCRA Index, Housing		93.40	4Q 92	4c
House, 1,800 sq ft, 8,000 sq ft lot, new, urban	total	100467	4Q 92	4c
House payment, principal and interest, 25% down payment	month	545	4Q 92	4c
Mortgage rate, incl. points & origination fee, 30-year fixed or adjustable rate	percent	7.85	4Q 92	4c
Rent, apartment, 2 bedrooms - 1-1/2 to 2 baths, unfurnished, 950 sq ft, water	month	528	4Q 92	4c
Rental unit, 1 bedroom	month	360	93	23c
Rental unit, 2 bedroom	month	424	93	23c
Rental unit, 3 bedroom	month	531	93	23c
Rental unit, 4 bedroom	month	595	93	23c
Rental unit, efficiency	month	296	93	23c
Insurance and Pensions				
Auto insurance, private passenger	year	651.31	91	63s
Personal Goods				
Shampoo, Alberto VO5	15 oz	1.07	4Q 92	4c
Toothpaste, Crest or Colgate	6-7 oz	2.02	4Q 92	4c
Personal Services				
Dry cleaning, man's 2-piece suit		5.77	4Q 92	4c
Haircare, woman's shampoo, trim and blow-dry		17.56	4Q 92	4c
Haircut, man's barbershop, no styling		6.67	4Q 92	4c
Restaurant Food				
Chicken, fried, thigh and drumstick		1.98	4Q 92	4c
Hamburger with cheese	1/4 lb	1.89	4Q 92	4c
Pizza, Pizza Hut or Pizza Inn, cheese, thin crust	12-13 in	7.79	4Q 92	4c
Taxes				
Tax, cigarette	pack	12	91	77s
Tax, gasoline	gal	7.50	91	77s
Taxes, state	capita	1080	91	77s
Transportation				
ACCRA Index, Transportation		91.10	4Q 92	4c
Bus fare	one-way	0.75	3/93	2c
Driver's license fee		4.50	12/90	43s
Tire balance, computer or spin balance, front	wheel	5.99	4Q 92	4c
Travel				
Business travel	day	193.00	4/93	89r
Utilities				
ACCRA Index, Utilities		114.00	4Q 92	4c
Electricity	mil Btu	19.25	90	64s
Electricity, partial electric and other energy, 1,800 sq ft living area new home	month	73.98	4Q 92	4c

Atlanta, GA

Item	Per	Value	Date	Ref.
Composite ACCRA index		99.50	4Q 92	4c
Alcoholic Beverages				
Beer, Miller Lite or Budweiser, 12-oz containers	6 pack	4.18	4Q 92	4c
Liquor, J & B Scotch	750 ml	14.69	4Q 92	4c
Wine, Gallo Chablis blanc, 1.5 liter	bottle	5.81	4Q 92	4c
Child Care				
Child care fee, average, center	hour	1.29	90	65r
Child care fee, average, nonregulated family day care	hour	0.89	90	65r
Child care fee, average, regulated family day care	hour	1.32	90	65r
Clothing				
Jeans, man's denim		25.39	4Q 92	4c
Shirt, man's dress shirt		21.80	4Q 92	4c
Undervest, boy's size 10-14, cotton	3	3.16	4Q 92	4c
Communications				
Long-distance telephone service, day, initial minute, 0-100 miles	min	0.16-0.26	91	12s
Long-distance telephone service, day, additional minute, 0-100 miles	min	0.08-0.23	91	12s
Long-distance telephone service, evenings/weekends, 0-100 mi, initial minute	min	0.06-0.13	91	12s
Long-distance telephone service, evenings/weekends, 0-100 mi, additional minute	min	0.04-0.12	91	12s
Newspaper subscription, daily and Sunday home delivery, large-city	month	10.01	4Q 92	4c
Telephone, flat rate	month	15.90	91	11c
Telephone, residential, private line, rotary, unlimited calling	month	23.51	10/91	78c
Telephone bill, family of four	month	20.84	4Q 92	4c
Construction				
Plywood, post-Hurricane Andrew	4x8 sheet	10.99	92	13c
Plywood, pre-Hurricane Andrew	4x8 sheet	7.99	92	13c
Education				
Board, 4-yr private college/university	year	1801	91	22s
Board, 4-yr public college/university	year	1501	91	22s
Expenditures, local gov't, public elementary/secondary	pupil	4747	92	20s
Room, 4-year private college/university	year	2139	91	22s
Room, 4-year public college/university	year	1192	91	22s
Tuition, 2-year private college/university	year	4457	91	22s
Tuition, 2-year public college/university	year	946	91	22s
Tuition, 4-year private college/university	year	7542	91	22s
Tuition, 4-year public college/university, in-state	year	1680	91	22s
Energy and Fuels				
Coal	mil Btu	1.79	90	64s
Energy	mil Btu	8.88	90	64s
Energy, combined forms, 1,800 sq ft heating area	month	122.90	4Q 92	4c
Energy, exc electricity, 1,800 sq ft heating area	month	50.36	4Q 92	4c
Energy exp/householder, 1-family unit	year	487	90	28r
Energy exp/householder, <1,000 sq ft heating area	year	393	90	28r
Energy exp/householder, 1,000-1,999 sq ft heating area	year	442	90	28r
Energy exp/householder, 2,000+ sq ft heating area	year	577	90	28r
Energy exp/householder, mobile home	year	366	90	28r
Energy exp/householder, multifamily	year	382	90	28r
Gas, cooking, 10 therms	month	11.99	92	56c
Gas, cooking, 30 therms	month	23.32	92	56c
Gas, cooking, 50 therms	month	33.48	92	56c
Gas, heating, winter, 100 therms	month	59.48	92	56c
Gas, heating, winter, average use	month	45.66	92	56c

Values are in dollars or fractions of dollars. In the column headed *Ref*, references are shown to sources. Each reference is followed by a letter. These refer to the geographical level for which data were reported: s = State, r = Region, and c = City or metro. The abbreviation *ex* is used to mean *except* or *excluding*; *exp* stands for expenditures. For other abbreviations and further explanations, please see the Introduction.

Atlanta, GA - continued

Item	Per	Value	Date	Ref.
Energy and Fuels				
Gas, natural	mil Btu	4.80	90	64s
Gas, natural	000 cu ft	6.70	91	46s
Gas, natural, exp	year	475	91	46s
Gasoline, motor	gal	1.01	4Q 92	4c
Gasoline, unleaded regular	mil Btu	8.24	90	64s
Entertainment				
Bowling, evening rate	game	2.29	4Q 92	4c
Dinner entree, restaurant		44.00-56.00	92	83c
Miniature golf admission	adult	6.18	92	1r
Miniature golf admission	child	5.14	92	1r
Monopoly game, Parker Brothers', No. 9		10.76	4Q 92	4c
Movie	admission	6.20	4Q 92	4c
Tennis balls, yellow, Wilson or Penn, 3	can	1.93	4Q 92	4c
Waterpark admission	adult	11.00	92	1r
Waterpark admission	child	8.55	92	1r
Funerals				
Casket, 18-gauge steel, velvet interior		2029.08	91	24r
Cosmetology, hair care, etc.		75.10	91	24r
Embalming		249.24	91	24r
Facility use for ceremony		162.27	91	24r
Hearse, local		114.04	91	24r
Limousine, local		88.57	91	24r
Remains to funeral home, transfer		92.61	91	24r
Service charge, professional		682.42	91	24r
Vault, concrete, non-metallic liner		798.70	91	24r
Viewing facilities, use		163.86	91	24r
Goods and Services				
ACCRA Index, Miscellaneous Goods and Services		92.30	4Q 92	4c
Goods and services	year	16383	92	36c
Goods and services, misc.	year	16383	92	37c
Groceries				
ACCRA Index, Groceries		98.90	4Q 92	4c
Apples, Red Delicious	lb	0.79	4/93	16r
Babyfood, strained vegetables, lowest price	4-4.5 oz jar	0.31	4Q 92	4c
Bacon	lb	1.75	4/93	16r
Bakery products, exp	year	173	89	15c
Bananas	lb	0.40	4Q 92	4c
Bananas	lb	0.42	4/93	16r
Beef, exp	year	201	89	15c
Beef, stew, boneless	lb	2.61	4/93	16r
Bologna, all beef or mixed	lb	2.24	4/93	16r
Bread, white	24 oz	0.90	4Q 92	4c
Bread, white, pan	lb	0.64	4/93	16r
Bread, whole wheat, pan	lb	0.96	4/93	16r
Cabbage	lb	0.37	4/93	16r
Carrots, short trimmed and topped	lb	0.47	4/93	16r
Celery	lb	0.64	4/93	16r
Cereals and bakery products, exp	year	286	89	15c
Cereals and cereal products, exp	year	113	89	15c
Cheese, American	lb	2.98	4/93	16r
Cheese, Cheddar	lb	3.28	4/93	16r
Cheese, Kraft grated Parmesan	8-oz canister	2.85	4Q 92	4c
Chicken, fresh, whole	lb	0.77	4/93	16r
Chicken, fryer, whole	lb	0.70	4Q 92	4c
Chicken breast, bone-in	lb	1.92	4/93	16r
Chicken legs, bone-in	lb	1.06	4/93	16r
Chuck roast, graded and ungraded, ex USDA prime and choice	lb	2.40	4/93	16r
Chuck roast, USDA choice, bone-in	lb	2.19	4/93	16r
Chuck roast, USDA choice, boneless	lb	2.38	4/93	16r
Cigarettes, Winston	carton	16.45	4Q 92	4c
Coffee, 100% ground roast, all sizes	lb	2.48	4/93	16r

Atlanta, GA - continued

Item	Per	Value	Date	Ref.
Groceries - continued				
Coffee, vacuum-packed	13-oz can	2.23	4Q 92	4c
Corn, frozen	10 oz	0.64	4Q 92	4c
Corn Flakes, Kellogg's or Post Toasties	18 oz	1.71	4Q 92	4c
Crackers, soda, salted	lb	1.15	4/93	16r
Dairy products, exp	year	243	89	15c
Dairy products, miscellaneous, exp	year	120	89	15c
Eggs, exp	year	27	89	15c
Eggs, Grade A large	doz	0.78	4Q 92	4c
Eggs, Grade A large	doz	0.96	4/93	16r
Fish and seafood, exp	year	71	89	15c
Flour, white, all purpose	lb	0.24	4/93	16r
Food, exp	year	3658	89	15c
Food eaten at home, exp	year	2031	89	15c
Frankfurters, all meat or all beef	lb	2.01	4/93	16r
Fruits, fresh, exp	year	121	89	15c
Fruits, processed, exp	year	82	89	15c
Fruits and vegetables, exp	year	395	89	15c
Grapefruit	lb	0.44	4/93	16r
Grapes, Thompson Seedless	lb	1.40	4/93	16r
Ground beef, 100% beef	lb	1.58	4/93	16r
Ground beef, lean and extra lean	lb	2.09	4/93	16r
Ground beef or hamburger	lb	1.61	4Q 92	4c
Ground chuck, 100% beef	lb	1.98	4/93	16r
Ham, boneless, excluding canned	lb	2.89	4/93	16r
Ham, picnic, shoulder, bone-in, smoked	lb	1.02	4/93	16r
Ham, rump or steak half, bone-in, smoked	lb	1.48	4/93	16r
Ice cream, prepackaged, bulk, regular	1/2 gal	2.41	4/93	16r
Lemons	lb	1.05	4/93	16r
Lettuce, iceberg	head	1.00	4Q 92	4c
Lettuce, iceberg	lb	0.81	4/93	16r
Margarine, Blue Bonnet or Parkay cubes	lb	0.56	4Q 92	4c
Margarine, stick	lb	0.88	4/93	16r
Meats, poultry, fish and eggs, exp	year	546	89	15c
Milk, whole	1/2 gal	1.43	4Q 92	4c
Milk and cream, fresh, exp	year	123	89	15c
Orange juice, Minute Maid frozen	12-oz can	1.31	4Q 92	4c
Oranges, navel	lb	0.55	4/93	16r
Peaches	29-oz can	1.42	4Q 92	4c
Pears, Anjou	lb	0.92	4/93	16r
Peas Sweet, Del Monte or Green Giant	15-17 oz can	0.59	4Q 92	4c
Pork, exp	year	99	89	15c
Pork chops, center cut, bone-in	lb	3.13	4/93	16r
Potato chips	16 oz	2.94	4/93	16r
Potatoes, white	lb	0.43	4/93	16r
Potatoes, white or red	10-lb sack	2.10	4Q 92	4c
Poultry, exp	year	94	89	15c
Rib roast, USDA choice, bone-in	lb	4.63	4/93	16r
Rice, white, long grain, uncooked	lb	0.45	4/93	16r
Round roast, graded & ungraded, ex USDA prime & choice	lb	3.03	4/93	16r
Round roast, USDA choice, boneless	lb	3.09	4/93	16r
Sausage, fresh, loose	lb	2.08	4/93	16r
Sausage, Jimmy Dean, 100% pork	lb	2.29	4Q 92	4c
Short ribs, bone-in	lb	2.66	4/93	16r
Shortening, vegetable oil blends	lb	0.69	4/93	16r
Shortening, vegetable, Crisco	3-lb can	2.04	4Q 92	4c
Soft drink, Coca Cola	2 liter	1.09	4Q 92	4c
Spaghetti and macaroni	lb	0.81	4/93	16r
Steak, rib eye, USDA choice, boneless	lb	6.24	4/93	16r
Steak, round, graded & ungraded, ex USDA prime & choice	lb	3.31	4/93	16r
Steak, round, USDA choice, boneless	lb	3.34	4/93	16r
Steak, sirloin, graded & ungraded, ex USDA prime & choice	lb	4.19	4/93	16r
Steak, sirloin, USDA choice, boneless	lb	4.46	4/93	16r
Steak, T-bone	lb	5.53	4Q 92	4c

Values are in dollars or fractions of dollars. In the column headed *Ref*, references are shown to sources. Each reference is followed by a letter. These refer to the geographical level for which data were reported: s=State, r=Region, and c=City or metro. The abbreviation *ex* is used to mean *except* or *excluding*; *exp* stands for expenditures. For other abbreviations and further explanations, please see the Introduction.

Atlanta, GA - continued

Item	Per	Value	Date	Ref.
Groceries				
Steak, T-bone, USDA choice, bone-in	lb	5.25	4/93	16r
Strawberries, dry pint	12 oz	0.92	4/93	16r
Sugar, cane or beet	4 lb	1.44	4Q 92	4c
Sugar, white	lb	0.39	4/93	16r
Sugar, white, 33-80 oz pk	lb	0.38	4/93	16r
Tomatoes, field grown	lb	0.88	4/93	16r
Tomatoes, Hunt's or Del Monte	14.5-oz can	0.58	4Q 92	4c
Tuna, chunk, light	6.125-6.5 oz can	0.59	4Q 92	4c
Tuna, chunk, light	lb	1.79	4/93	16r
Turkey, frozen, whole	lb	1.04	4/93	16r
Vegetables, fresh, exp	year	134	89	15c
Vegetables, processed, exp	year	57	89	15c
Yogurt, natural, fruit flavored	1/2 pint	0.57	4/93	16r
Health Care				
ACCRA Index, Health Care		132.70	4Q 92	4c
Analgesic, Aspirin, Bayer, 325 mg tablets	100	4.41	4Q 92	4c
Appendectomy		958	91	62c
Appendectomy, physician fee	average	977.00	2/93	93c
Childbirth, cesarean		2408	91	62c
Childbirth, cesarean, hospital		5034	91	62r
Childbirth, cesarean, physician's fee		2053	91	62r
Childbirth, normal, hospital		2712	91	62r
Childbirth, normal, physician's fee		1492	91	62r
Cholecystectomy		1498	91	62c
Coronary bypass surgery, triple		4656	91	62c
Dentist's fee, adult teeth cleaning and periodic oral exam	visit	61.00	4Q 92	4c
Doctor's fee, routine exam, established patient	visit	64.00	4Q 92	4c
Health maintenance organization coverage, employee	year	3311	93	39c
Health maintenance organization medical coverage, employee	year	3311	92	42c
Hospital care, semiprivate room	day	204.59	90	27c
Hospital care, semiprivate room	day	273.40	4Q 92	4c
Hysterectomy		2176	91	62c
Indemnity plan medical coverage, employee	year	3729	92	42c
Insurance coverage, traditional, employee	year	3729	93	39c
Lumpectomy		570	91	62c
Medical insurance premium, per employee, small group comprehensive	month	386.90	10/91	25c
Medical plan per employee	year	3495	91	45r
Mental health care, exp	capita	37.60-53.67	90	38s
Mental health care, exp, state mental health agency	capita	50.98	90	38s
Mental health care, hospital psychiatric services, non-Federal, exp	capita	9.66	88	38s
Mental health care, mental health organization, multiservice, exp	capita	16.40	88	38s
Mental health care, psychiatric hospitals, private, exp	capita	26.36	88	38s
Mental health care, psychiatric out-patient clinics, freestanding, exp	capita	0.13	88	38s
Mental health care, state and county mental hospitals, exp	capita	38.94	88	38s
Mental health care, VA medical centers, exp	capita	3.91	88	38s
Oophorectomy		1349	91	62c
Physician fee, family practice, first-visit		75.00	91	62r
Physician fee, family practice, revisit		34.00	91	62r
Physician fee, general practice, first-visit		61.00	91	62r
Physician fee, general practice, revisit		32.00	91	62r
Physician fee, general surgeon, first-visit		64.00	91	62r
Physician fee, general surgeon, revisit		40.00	91	62r
Physician fee, internal medicine, first-visit		98.00	91	62r
Physician fee, internal medicine, revisit		40.00	91	62r

Atlanta, GA - continued

Item	Per	Value	Date	Ref.
Health Care - continued				
Physician fee, median, neurosurgeon, first-visit		130.00	91	62r
Physician fee, median, nonsurgical specialist, first-visit		95.00	91	62r
Physician fee, median, orthopedic surgeon, first-visit		91.00	91	62r
Physician fee, median, plastic surgeon, first-visit		66.00	91	62r
Physician fee, median, surgical specialist, first-visit		62.00	91	62r
Physician fee, neurosurgeon, revisit		50.00	91	62r
Physician fee, nonsurgical specialist, revisit		40.00	91	62r
Physician fee, obstetrics/gynecology, first-visit		64.00	91	62r
Physician fee, obstetrics/gynecology, revisit		41.00	91	62r
Physician fee, orthopedic surgeon, revisit		40.00	91	62r
Physician fee, pediatrician, first-visit		49.00	91	62r
Physician fee, pediatrician, revisit		33.00	91	62r
Physician fee, plastic surgeon, revisit		43.00	91	62r
Physician fee, surgical specialist, revisit		37.00	91	62r
Preferred provider organization medical coverage, employee	year	3363	92	42c
Prostatectomy, retro-pubic		2256	91	62c
Salpingo-oophorectomy		1314	91	62c
Substance abuse, hospital ancillary charge	incident	1800	90	70s
Substance abuse, hospital physician charge	incident	890	90	70s
Substance abuse, hospital room and board	incident	5560	90	70s
Vasectomy		395	91	62c
Household Goods				
Appliance repair, home, service call, washing machine	min labor charge	24.80	4Q 92	4c
Laundry detergent, Tide Ultra, Bold, or Cheer	42 oz	3.30	4Q 92	4c
Tissues, facial, Kleenex brand	175-count box	0.98	4Q 92	4c
Housing				
ACCRA Index, Housing		98.90	4Q 92	4c
House, 1,800 sq ft, 8,000 sq ft lot, new, urban	total	106160	4Q 92	4c
House payment, principal and interest, 25% down payment	month	580	4Q 92	4c
Mortgage rate, incl. points & origination fee, 30-year fixed or adjustable rate	percent	7.92	4Q 92	4c
Rent, apartment, 2 bedrooms - 1-1/2 to 2 baths, unfurnished, 950 sq ft, water	month	552	4Q 92	4c
Rental unit, 1 bedroom	month	492	93	23c
Rental unit, 2 bedroom	month	580	93	23c
Rental unit, 3 bedroom	month	725	93	23c
Rental unit, 4 bedroom	month	813	93	23c
Rental unit, efficiency	month	405	93	23c
Insurance and Pensions				
Auto insurance, private passenger	year	651.31	91	63s
Personal Goods				
Shampoo, Alberto VO5	15 oz	1.23	4Q 92	4c
Toothpaste, Crest or Colgate	6-7 oz	1.82	4Q 92	4c
Personal Services				
Dry cleaning, man's 2-piece suit		5.55	4Q 92	4c
Haircare, woman's shampoo, trim and blow-dry		18.20	4Q 92	4c
Haircut, man's barbershop, no styling		8.00	4Q 92	4c
Restaurant Food				
Chicken, fried, thigh and drumstick		1.93	4Q 92	4c
Hamburger with cheese	1/4 lb	1.93	4Q 92	4c

Values are in dollars or fractions of dollars. In the column headed *Ref*, references are shown to sources. Each reference is followed by a letter. These refer to the geographical level for which data were reported: s = State, r = Region, and c = City or metro. The abbreviation *ex* is used to mean *except* or *excluding*; *exp* stands for expenditures. For other abbreviations and further explanations, please see the Introduction.

Atlanta, GA - continued

Item	Per	Value	Date	Ref.
Restaurant Food				
Pizza, Pizza Hut or Pizza Inn, cheese, thin crust	12-13 in	7.77	4Q 92	4c
Taxes				
Tax, cigarette	pack	12	91	77s
Tax, gasoline	gal	7.50	91	77s
Taxes, hotel room	day	7.62	92	33c
Taxes, sales	year	1058	92	37c
Taxes, state	capita	1080	91	77s
Transportation				
ACCRA Index, Transportation		99.10	4Q 92	4c
Auto rental, average	day	53.00	6/91	60c
Bus fare	one-way	1.25	3/93	2c
Bus fare, up to 10 miles	one-way	1.14	4Q 92	4c
Driver's license fee		4.50	12/90	43s
Limo fare, airport-city, average	day	7.00	6/91	60c
Railway fare, heavy rail	one-way	1.25	3/93	2c
Taxi fare, airport-city, average	day	15.00	6/91	60c
Tire balance, computer or spin balance, front	wheel	6.60	4Q 92	4c
Travel				
Breakfast	day	7.48	6/91	60c
Business travel	day	158.00	92	86c
Business travel	day	193.00	4/93	89r
Dinner	day	33.95	6/91	60c
Dinner	day	24.20	92	85c
Lodging	day	123.09	91	60c
Lodging	day	115.00	92	85c
Lunch	day	10.72	6/91	60c
Travel, business	day	197.21	93	88c
Utilities				
ACCRA Index, Utilities		112.10	4Q 92	4c
Cable-television service, with no competition	month	20.95	92	81c
Electricity	mil Btu	19.25	90	64s
Electricity, partial electric and other energy, 1,800 sq ft living area new home	month	72.63	4Q 92	4c
Electricity, winter, 250 KWh	month	22.82	92	55c
Electricity, winter, 500 KWh	month	38.14	92	55c
Electricity, winter, 750 KWh	month	52.76	92	55c
Electricity, winter, 1000 KWh	month	66.39	92	55c

Atlantic City, NJ

Item	Per	Value	Date	Ref.
Child Care				
Child care fee, average, center	hour	2.18	90	65r
Child care fee, average, nonregulated family day care	hour	1.83	90	65r
Child care fee, average, regulated family day care	hour	2.02	90	65r
Communications				
Long-distance telephone service, day, initial minute, 0-100 miles	min	0.09-0.42	91	12s
Long-distance telephone service, day, additional minute, 0-100 miles	min	0.03-0.12	91	12s
Telephone, flat rate	month	7.45	91	11c
Education				
Board, 4-yr private college/university	year	2883	91	22s
Board, 4-yr public college/university	year	1647	91	22s
Expenditures, local gov't, public elementary/secondary	pupil	9940	92	20s
Room, 4-year private college/university	year	2440	91	22s
Room, 4-year public college/university	year	2415	91	22s
Tuition, 2-year private college/university	year	5874	91	22s
Tuition, 2-year public college/university	year	1235	91	22s
Tuition, 4-year private college/university	year	10281	91	22s

Atlantic City, NJ - continued

Item	Per	Value	Date	Ref.
Education - continued				
Tuition, 4-year public college/university, in-state	year	2860	91	22s
Energy and Fuels				
Coal	mil Btu	1.79	90	64s
Energy	mil Btu	9.32	90	64s
Energy exp/householder, 1-family unit	year	588	90	28r
Energy exp/householder, <1,000 sq ft heating area	year	477	90	28r
Energy exp/householder, 1,000-1,999 sq ft heating area	year	517	90	28r
Energy exp/householder, 2,000+ sq ft heating area	year	630	90	28r
Energy exp/householder, mobile home	year	412	90	28r
Energy exp/householder, multifamily	year	498	90	28r
Gas, cooking, winter, 10 therms	month	11.64	92	56c
Gas, cooking, winter, 30 therms	month	22.82	92	56c
Gas, cooking, winter, 50 therms	month	32.28	92	56c
Gas, heating, winter, 100 therms	month	55.21	92	56c
Gas, heating, winter, average use	month	79.49	92	56c
Gas, natural	mil Btu	5.05	90	64s
Gas, natural	000 cu ft	6.73	91	46s
Gas, natural, exp	year	593	91	46s
Gasoline, unleaded regular	mil Btu	9.03	90	64s
Funerals				
Casket, 18-gauge steel, velvet interior		1811.58	91	24r
Cosmetology, hair care, etc.		111.08	91	24r
Embalming		329.42	91	24r
Facility use for ceremony		201.29	91	24r
Hearse, local		135.27	91	24r
Limousine, local		127.24	91	24r
Remains to funeral home, transfer		103.98	91	24r
Service charge, professional		724.98	91	24r
Vault, concrete, non-metallic liner		766.71	91	24r
Viewing facilities, use		260.60	91	24r
Groceries				
Apples, Red Delicious	lb	0.85	4/93	16r
Bacon	lb	2.12	4/93	16r
Bananas	lb	0.54	4/93	16r
Bread, white, pan	lb	0.81	4/93	16r
Butter	lb	2.02	4/93	16r
Carrots, short trimmed and topped	lb	0.51	4/93	16r
Chicken, fresh, whole	lb	1.04	4/93	16r
Chicken breast, bone-in	lb	2.21	4/93	16r
Chicken legs, bone-in	lb	1.16	4/93	16r
Chuck roast, USDA choice, boneless	lb	2.82	4/93	16r
Coffee, 100% ground roast, all sizes	lb	2.66	4/93	16r
Cucumbers	lb	0.85	4/93	16r
Eggs, Grade A large	doz	1.15	4/93	16r
Grapefruit	lb	0.45	4/93	16r
Grapes, Thompson Seedless	lb	1.52	4/93	16r
Ground beef, lean and extra lean	lb	2.36	4/93	16r
Ground chuck, 100% beef	lb	2.02	4/93	16r
Honey, jar	8 oz	0.96-1.75	92	5r
Honey, jar	lb	1.50-3.00	92	5r
Honey, squeeze bear	12-oz	1.50-1.99	92	5r
Ice cream, prepackaged, bulk, regular	1/2 gal	2.80	4/93	16r
Lemons	lb	0.96	4/93	16r
Lettuce, iceberg	lb	0.95	4/93	16r
Margarine, stick	lb	0.81	4/93	16r
Milk, fresh, whole, fortified	1/2 gal	1.30	4/93	16r
Oranges, navel	lb	0.56	4/93	16r
Peanut butter, creamy, all sizes	lb	1.88	4/93	16r
Pork chops, center cut, bone-in	lb	3.34	4/93	16r
Potato chips	16 oz	2.88	4/93	16r
Potatoes, white	lb	0.37	4/93	16r
Rib roast, USDA choice, bone-in	lb	4.94	4/93	16r
Round roast, USDA choice, boneless	lb	3.17	4/93	16r
Shortening, vegetable oil blends	lb	0.98	4/93	16r
Spaghetti and macaroni	lb	0.82	4/93	16r

Values are in dollars or fractions of dollars. In the column headed *Ref*, references are shown to sources. Each reference is followed by a letter. These refer to the geographical level for which data were reported: s=State, r=Region, and c=City or metro. The abbreviation *ex* is used to mean *except* or *excluding*; *exp* stands for expenditures. For other abbreviations and further explanations, please see the Introduction.

Atlantic City, NJ - continued

Item	Per	Value	Date	Ref.
Groceries				
Steak, round, graded & ungraded, ex USDA prime & choice	lb	4.04	4/93	16r
Steak, round, USDA choice, boneless	lb	3.90	4/93	16r
Steak, sirloin, USDA choice, boneless	lb	4.97	4/93	16r
Strawberries, dry pint	12 oz	0.90	4/93	16r
Sugar, white	lb	0.50	4/93	16r
Sugar, white, 33-80 oz pk	lb	0.41	4/93	16r
Tomatoes, field grown	lb	1.23	4/93	16r
Tuna, chunk, light	lb	2.22	4/93	16r
Turkey, frozen, whole	lb	1.04	4/93	16r
Health Care				
Childbirth, cesarean, hospital		5826	91	62r
Childbirth, cesarean, physician's fee		2053	91	62r
Childbirth, normal, hospital		2964	91	62r
Childbirth, normal, physician's fee		1492	91	62r
Medical insurance premium, per employee, small group comprehensive	month	349.45	10/91	25c
Medical plan per employee	year	3942	91	45r
Mental health care, exp	capita	28.84-37.59	90	38s
Mental health care, exp, state mental health agency	capita	57.16	90	38s
Mental health care, hospital psychiatric services, non-Federal, exp	capita	16.04	88	38s
Mental health care, mental health organization, multiservice, exp	capita	11.14	88	38s
Mental health care, psychiatric hospitals, private, exp	capita	17.85	88	38s
Mental health care, psychiatric out-patient clinics, freestanding, exp	capita	1.56	88	38s
Mental health care, psychiatric partial-care organizations, freestanding, exp	capita	0.66	88	38s
Mental health care, state and county mental hospitals, exp	capita	36.80	88	38s
Mental health care, VA medical centers, exp	capita	5.61	88	38s
Prescription drug co-pay, Medicaid	month	5.00	91	21s
Substance abuse, hospital ancillary charge	incident	780	90	70s
Substance abuse, hospital physician charge	incident	550	90	70s
Substance abuse, hospital room and board	incident	6300	90	70s
Housing				
Home, median price	unit	109.10		26c
Rental unit, 1 bedroom	month	552	93	23c
Rental unit, 2 bedroom	month	647	93	23c
Rental unit, 3 bedroom	month	808	93	23c
Rental unit, 4 bedroom	month	909	93	23c
Rental unit, efficiency	month	451	93	23c
Insurance and Pensions				
Auto insurance, private passenger	year	1081.45	91	63s
Taxes				
Tax, cigarette	pack	40	91	77s
Tax, gasoline	gal	10.50	91	77s
Taxes, state	capita	1501	91	77s
Transportation				
Auto rental, average	day	41.25	6/91	60c
Bus fare	one-way	1.00	3/93	2c
Driver's license fee		16.00-17.50	12/90	43s
Limo fare, airport-city, average	day	7.00	6/91	60c
Railway fare, commuter	one-way	0.85	3/93	2c
Taxi fare, airport-city, average	day	25.00	6/91	60c
Vehicle registration and license plate	year	32.90-93.90	93	44s

Atlantic City, NJ - continued

Item	Per	Value	Date	Ref.
Travel				
Business travel	day	165.00	4/93	89r
Lodging	day	153.36	91	60c
Utilities				
Electricity	mil Btu	26.63	90	64s

Augusta, GA, SC

Item	Per	Value	Date	Ref.
Composite ACCRA index		100.50	4Q 92	4c
Alcoholic Beverages				
Beer, Miller Lite or Budweiser, 12-oz containers	6 pack	3.96	4Q 92	4c
Liquor, J & B Scotch	750 ml	17.47	4Q 92	4c
Wine, Gallo Chablis blanc, 1.5 liter	bottle	5.31	4Q 92	4c
Child Care				
Child care fee, average, center	hour	1.29	90	65r
Child care fee, average, nonregulated family day care	hour	0.89	90	65r
Child care fee, average, regulated family day care	hour	1.32	90	65r
Clothing				
Jeans, man's denim		34.39	4Q 92	4c
Shirt, man's dress shirt		24.99	4Q 92	4c
Undervest, boy's size 10-14, cotton	3	5.39	4Q 92	4c
Communications				
Long-distance telephone service, day, initial minute, 0-100 miles	min	0.16-0.26	91	12s
Long-distance telephone service, day, additional minute, 0-100 miles	min	0.08-0.23	91	12s
Long-distance telephone service, evenings/weekends, 0-100 mi, initial minute	min	0.06-0.13	91	12s
Long-distance telephone service, evenings/weekends, 0-100 mi, additional minute	min	0.04-0.12	91	12s
Newspaper subscription, daily and Sunday home delivery, large-city	month	9.50	4Q 92	4c
Telephone, flat rate	month	13.55	91	11c
Telephone bill, family of four	month	21.71	4Q 92	4c
Education				
Board, 4-yr private college/university	year	1801	91	22s
Board, 4-yr public college/university	year	1501	91	22s
Expenditures, local gov't, public elementary/secondary	pupil	4747	92	20s
Room, 4-year private college/university	year	2139	91	22s
Room, 4-year public college/university	year	1192	91	22s
Tuition, 2-year private college/university	year	4457	91	22s
Tuition, 2-year public college/university	year	946	91	22s
Tuition, 4-year private college/university	year	7542	91	22s
Tuition, 4-year public college/university, in-state	year	1680	91	22s
Energy and Fuels				
Coal	mil Btu	1.79	90	64s
Energy	mil Btu	8.88	90	64s
Energy, combined forms, 1,800 sq ft heating area	month	124.88	4Q 92	4c
Energy, exc electricity, 1,800 sq ft heating area	month	48.39	4Q 92	4c
Energy exp/householder, 1-family unit	year	487	90	28r
Energy exp/householder, <1,000 sq ft heating area	year	393	90	28r
Energy exp/householder, 1,000-1,999 sq ft heating area	year	442	90	28r
Energy exp/householder, 2,000+ sq ft heating area	year	577	90	28r
Energy exp/householder, mobile home	year	366	90	28r
Energy exp/householder, multifamily	year	382	90	28r
Gas, natural	mil Btu	4.80	90	64s
Gas, natural	000 cu ft	6.70	91	46s
Gas, natural, exp	year	475	91	46s

Values are in dollars or fractions of dollars. In the column headed *Ref*, references are shown to sources. Each reference is followed by a letter. These refer to the geographical level for which data were reported: s = State, r = Region, and c = City or metro. The abbreviation *ex* is used to mean *except* or *excluding*; *exp* stands for expenditures. For other abbreviations and further explanations, please see the Introduction.

Augusta, GA, SC - continued

Item	Per	Value	Date	Ref.
Energy and Fuels				
Gasoline, motor	gal	0.96	4Q 92	4c
Gasoline, unleaded regular	mil Btu	8.24	90	64s
Entertainment				
Bowling, evening rate	game	2.41	4Q 92	4c
Miniature golf admission	adult	6.18	92	1r
Miniature golf admission	child	5.14	92	1r
Monopoly game, Parker Brothers', No. 9		9.93	4Q 92	4c
Movie	admission	5.45	4Q 92	4c
Tennis balls, yellow, Wilson or Penn, 3	can	2.21	4Q 92	4c
Waterpark admission	adult	11.00	92	1r
Waterpark admission	child	8.55	92	1r
Funerals				
Casket, 18-gauge steel, velvet interior		2029.08	91	24r
Cosmetology, hair care, etc.		75.10	91	24r
Embalming		249.24	91	24r
Facility use for ceremony		162.27	91	24r
Hearse, local		114.04	91	24r
Limousine, local		88.57	91	24r
Remains to funeral home, transfer		92.61	91	24r
Service charge, professional		682.42	91	24r
Vault, concrete, non-metallic liner		798.70	91	24r
Viewing facilities, use		163.86	91	24r
Goods and Services				
ACCRA Index, Miscellaneous Goods and Services		101.60	4Q 92	4c
Groceries				
ACCRA Index, Groceries		91.70	4Q 92	4c
Apples, Red Delicious	lb	0.79	4/93	16r
Babyfood, strained vegetables, lowest price	4-4.5 oz jar	0.31	4Q 92	4c
Bacon	lb	1.75	4/93	16r
Bananas	lb	0.45	4Q 92	4c
Bananas	lb	0.42	4/93	16r
Beef, stew, boneless	lb	2.61	4/93	16r
Bologna, all beef or mixed	lb	2.24	4/93	16r
Bread, white	24 oz	0.63	4Q 92	4c
Bread, white, pan	lb	0.64	4/93	16r
Bread, whole wheat, pan	lb	0.96	4/93	16r
Cabbage	lb	0.37	4/93	16r
Carrots, short trimmed and topped	lb	0.47	4/93	16r
Celery	lb	0.64	4/93	16r
Cheese, American	lb	2.98	4/93	16r
Cheese, Cheddar	lb	3.28	4/93	16r
Cheese, Kraft grated Parmesan	8-oz canister	3.19	4Q 92	4c
Chicken, fresh, whole	lb	0.77	4/93	16r
Chicken, fryer, whole	lb	0.69	4Q 92	4c
Chicken breast, bone-in	lb	1.92	4/93	16r
Chicken legs, bone-in	lb	1.06	4/93	16r
Chuck roast, graded and ungraded, ex USDA prime and choice	lb	2.40	4/93	16r
Chuck roast, USDA choice, bone-in	lb	2.19	4/93	16r
Chuck roast, USDA choice, boneless	lb	2.38	4/93	16r
Cigarettes, Winston	carton	15.56	4Q 92	4c
Coffee, 100% ground roast, all sizes	lb	2.48	4/93	16r
Coffee, vacuum-packed	13-oz can	1.83	4Q 92	4c
Corn, frozen	10 oz	0.56	4Q 92	4c
Corn Flakes, Kellogg's or Post Toasties	18 oz	1.60	4Q 92	4c
Crackers, soda, salted	lb	1.15	4/93	16r
Eggs, Grade A large	doz	0.79	4Q 92	4c
Eggs, Grade A large	doz	0.96	4/93	16r
Flour, white, all purpose	lb	0.24	4/93	16r
Frankfurters, all meat or all beef	lb	2.01	4/93	16r
Grapefruit	lb	0.44	4/93	16r
Grapes, Thompson Seedless	lb	1.40	4/93	16r
Ground beef, 100% beef	lb	1.58	4/93	16r
Ground beef, lean and extra lean	lb	2.09	4/93	16r

Augusta, GA, SC - continued

Item	Per	Value	Date	Ref.
Groceries - continued				
Ground beef or hamburger	lb	1.48	4Q 92	4c
Ground chuck, 100% beef	lb	1.98	4/93	16r
Ham, boneless, excluding canned	lb	2.89	4/93	16r
Ham, picnic, shoulder, bone-in, smoked	lb	1.02	4/93	16r
Ham, rump or steak half, bone-in, smoked	lb	1.48	4/93	16r
Ice cream, prepackaged, bulk, regular	1/2 gal	2.41	4/93	16r
Lemons	lb	1.05	4/93	16r
Lettuce, iceberg	head	0.99	4Q 92	4c
Lettuce, iceberg	lb	0.81	4/93	16r
Margarine, Blue Bonnet or Parkay cubes	lb	0.49	4Q 92	4c
Margarine, stick	lb	0.88	4/93	16r
Milk, whole	1/2 gal	1.36	4Q 92	4c
Orange juice, Minute Maid frozen	12-oz can	1.16	4Q 92	4c
Oranges, navel	lb	0.55	4/93	16r
Peaches	29-oz can	1.19	4Q 92	4c
Pears, Anjou	lb	0.92	4/93	16r
Peas Sweet, Del Monte or Green Giant	15-17 oz can	0.49	4Q 92	4c
Pork chops, center cut, bone-in	lb	3.13	4/93	16r
Potato chips	16 oz	2.94	4/93	16r
Potatoes, white	lb	0.43	4/93	16r
Potatoes, white or red	10-lb sack	2.37	4Q 92	4c
Rib roast, USDA choice, bone-in	lb	4.63	4/93	16r
Rice, white, long grain, uncooked	lb	0.45	4/93	16r
Round roast, graded & ungraded, ex USDA prime & choice	lb	3.03	4/93	16r
Round roast, USDA choice, boneless	lb	3.09	4/93	16r
Sausage, fresh, loose	lb	2.08	4/93	16r
Sausage, Jimmy Dean, 100% pork	lb	1.95	4Q 92	4c
Short ribs, bone-in	lb	2.66	4/93	16r
Shortening, vegetable oil blends	lb	0.69	4/93	16r
Shortening, vegetable, Crisco	3-lb can	2.01	4Q 92	4c
Soft drink, Coca Cola	2 liter	1.26	4Q 92	4c
Spaghetti and macaroni	lb	0.81	4/93	16r
Steak, rib eye, USDA choice, boneless	lb	6.24	4/93	16r
Steak, round, graded & ungraded, ex USDA prime & choice	lb	3.31	4/93	16r
Steak, round, USDA choice, boneless	lb	3.34	4/93	16r
Steak, sirloin, graded & ungraded, ex USDA prime & choice	lb	4.19	4/93	16r
Steak, sirloin, USDA choice, boneless	lb	4.46	4/93	16r
Steak, T-bone	lb	5.48	4Q 92	4c
Steak, T-bone, USDA choice, bone-in	lb	5.25	4/93	16r
Strawberries, dry pint	12 oz	0.92	4/93	16r
Sugar, cane or beet	4 lb	1.42	4Q 92	4c
Sugar, white	lb	0.39	4/93	16r
Sugar, white, 33-80 oz pk	lb	0.38	4/93	16r
Tomatoes, field grown	lb	0.88	4/93	16r
Tomatoes, Hunt's or Del Monte	14.5-oz can	0.53	4Q 92	4c
Tuna, chunk, light	6.125-6.5 oz can	0.52	4Q 92	4c
Tuna, chunk, light	lb	1.79	4/93	16r
Turkey, frozen, whole	lb	1.04	4/93	16r
Yogurt, natural, fruit flavored	1/2 pint	0.57	4/93	16r
Health Care				
ACCRA Index, Health Care		90.50	4Q 92	4c
Analgesic, Aspirin, Bayer, 325 mg tablets	100	5.38	4Q 92	4c
Childbirth, cesarean, hospital		5034	91	62r
Childbirth, cesarean, physician's fee		2053	91	62r
Childbirth, normal, hospital		2712	91	62r
Childbirth, normal, physician's fee		1492	91	62r
Dentist's fee, adult teeth cleaning and periodic oral exam	visit	42.00	4Q 92	4c
Doctor's fee, routine exam, established patient	visit	33.06	4Q 92	4c

Values are in dollars or fractions of dollars. In the column headed *Ref*, references are shown to sources. Each reference is followed by a letter. These refer to the geographical level for which data were reported: s=State, r=Region, and c=City or metro. The abbreviation *ex* is used to mean *except* or *excluding*; *exp* stands for *expenditures*. For other abbreviations and further explanations, please see the Introduction.

42

Augusta, GA, SC - continued

Item	Per	Value	Date	Ref.
Health Care				
Hospital care, semiprivate room	day	231.09	90	27c
Hospital care, semiprivate room	day	265.00	4Q 92	4c
Medical insurance premium, per employee, small group comprehensive	month	332.15	10/91	25c
Medical plan per employee	year	3495	91	45r
Mental health care, exp	capita	37.60-53.67	90	38s
Mental health care, exp, state mental health agency	capita	50.98	90	38s
Mental health care, hospital psychiatric services, non-Federal, exp	capita	9.66	88	38s
Mental health care, mental health organization, multiservice, exp	capita	16.40	88	38s
Mental health care, psychiatric hospitals, private, exp	capita	26.36	88	38s
Mental health care, psychiatric out-patient clinics, freestanding, exp	capita	0.13	88	38s
Mental health care, state and county mental hospitals, exp	capita	38.94	88	38s
Mental health care, VA medical centers, exp	capita	3.91	88	38s
Physician fee, family practice, first-visit		75.00	91	62r
Physician fee, family practice, revisit		34.00	91	62r
Physician fee, general practice, first-visit		61.00	91	62r
Physician fee, general practice, revisit		32.00	91	62r
Physician fee, general surgeon, first-visit		64.00	91	62r
Physician fee, general surgeon, revisit		40.00	91	62r
Physician fee, internal medicine, first-visit		98.00	91	62r
Physician fee, internal medicine, revisit		40.00	91	62r
Physician fee, median, neurosurgeon, first-visit		130.00	91	62r
Physician fee, median, nonsurgical specialist, first-visit		95.00	91	62r
Physician fee, median, orthopedic surgeon, first-visit		91.00	91	62r
Physician fee, median, plastic surgeon, first-visit		66.00	91	62r
Physician fee, median, surgical specialist, first-visit		62.00	91	62r
Physician fee, neurosurgeon, revisit		50.00	91	62r
Physician fee, nonsurgical specialist, revisit		40.00	91	62r
Physician fee, obstetrics/gynecology, first-visit		64.00	91	62r
Physician fee, obstetrics/gynecology, revisit		41.00	91	62r
Physician fee, orthopedic surgeon, revisit		40.00	91	62r
Physician fee, pediatrician, first-visit		49.00	91	62r
Physician fee, pediatrician, revisit		33.00	91	62r
Physician fee, plastic surgeon, revisit		43.00	91	62r
Physician fee, surgical specialist, revisit		37.00	91	62r
Substance abuse, hospital ancillary charge	incident	1800	90	70s
Substance abuse, hospital physician charge	incident	890	90	70s
Substance abuse, hospital room and board	incident	5560	90	70s
Household Goods				
Appliance repair, home, service call, washing machine	min labor charge	26.00	4Q 92	4c
Laundry detergent, Tide Ultra, Bold, or Cheer	42 oz	3.01	4Q 92	4c
Tissues, facial, Kleenex brand	175-count box	0.95	4Q 92	4c
Housing				
ACCRA Index, Housing		100.90	4Q 92	4c
House, 1,800 sq ft, 8,000 sq ft lot, new, urban	total	118750	4Q 92	4c
House payment, principal and interest, 25% down payment	month	657	4Q 92	4c
Mortgage rate, incl. points & origination fee, 30-year fixed or adjustable rate	percent	8.05	4Q 92	4c

Augusta, GA, SC - continued

Item	Per	Value	Date	Ref.
Housing - continued				
Rent, apartment, 2 bedrooms - 1-1/2 to 2 baths, unfurnished, 950 sq ft, water	month	413	4Q 92	4c
Rental unit, 1 bedroom	month	365	93	23c
Rental unit, 2 bedroom	month	424	93	23c
Rental unit, 3 bedroom	month	531	93	23c
Rental unit, 4 bedroom	month	595	93	23c
Rental unit, efficiency	month	301	93	23c
Insurance and Pensions				
Auto insurance, private passenger	year	651.31	91	63s
Personal Goods				
Shampoo, Alberto VO5	15 oz	0.99	4Q 92	4c
Toothpaste, Crest or Colgate	6-7 oz	1.86	4Q 92	4c
Personal Services				
Dry cleaning, man's 2-piece suit		4.85	4Q 92	4c
Haircare, woman's shampoo, trim and blow-dry		19.30	4Q 92	4c
Haircut, man's barbershop, no styling		7.40	4Q 92	4c
Restaurant Food				
Chicken, fried, thigh and drumstick		1.91	4Q 92	4c
Hamburger with cheese	1/4 lb	1.89	4Q 92	4c
Pizza, Pizza Hut or Pizza Inn, cheese, thin crust	12-13 in	7.99	4Q 92	4c
Taxes				
Tax, cigarette	pack	12	91	77s
Tax, gasoline	gal	7.50	91	77s
Taxes, state	capita	1080	91	77s
Transportation				
ACCRA Index, Transportation		99.50	4Q 92	4c
Bus fare	one-way	0.75	3/93	2c
Driver's license fee		4.50	12/90	43s
Tire balance, computer or spin balance, front	wheel	7.39	4Q 92	4c
Travel				
Business travel	day	193.00	4/93	89r
Utilities				
ACCRA Index, Utilities		114.10	4Q 92	4c
Electricity	mil Btu	19.25	90	64s
Electricity, partial electric and other energy, 1,800 sq ft living area new home	month	76.49	4Q 92	4c

Aurora-Elgin, IL

Item	Per	Value	Date	Ref.
Child Care				
Child care fee, average, center	hour	1.63	90	65r
Child care fee, average, nonregulated family day care	hour	1.83	90	65r
Child care fee, average, regulated family day care	hour	1.42	90	65r
Communications				
Long-distance telephone service, day, initial minute, 0-100 miles	min	0.10-0.34	91	12s
Long-distance telephone service, day, additional minute, 0-100 miles	min	0.04-0.16	91	12s
Long-distance telephone service, evenings/weekends, 0-100 mi, initial minute	min	0.06-0.20	91	12s
Long-distance telephone service, evenings/weekends, 0-100 mi, additional minute	min	0.02-0.10	91	12s
Education				
Board, 4-yr private college/university	year	1797	91	22s
Board, 4-yr public college/university	year	1857	91	22s
Expenditures, local gov't, public elementary/secondary	pupil	5248	92	20s
Room, 4-year private college/university	year	2095	91	22s
Room, 4-year public college/university	year	1454	91	22s
Tuition, 2-year private college/university	year	5279	91	22s

Values are in dollars or fractions of dollars. In the column headed *Ref*, references are shown to sources. Each reference is followed by a letter. These refer to the geographical level for which data were reported: s = State, r = Region, and c = City or metro. The abbreviation *ex* is used to mean *except* or *excluding*; *exp* stands for *expenditures*. For other abbreviations and further explanations, please see the Introduction.

Aurora-Elgin, IL - continued

Item	Per	Value	Date	Ref.
Education				
Tuition, 2-year public college/university	year	906	91	22s
Tuition, 4-year private college/university	year	8853	91	22s
Tuition, 4-year public college/university, in-state	year	2465	91	22s
Energy and Fuels				
Coal	mil Btu	1.72	90	64s
Energy	mil Btu	8.74	90	64s
Energy exp/householder, 1-family unit	year	471	90	28r
Energy exp/householder, <1,000 sq ft heating area	year	430	90	28r
Energy exp/householder, 1,000-1,999 sq ft heating area	year	481	90	28r
Energy exp/householder, 2,000+ sq ft heating area	year	473	90	28r
Energy exp/householder, mobile home	year	430	90	28r
Energy exp/householder, multifamily	year	461	90	28r
Gas, natural	mil Btu	4.57	90	64s
Gas, natural	000 cu ft	4.95	91	46s
Gas, natural, exp	year	696	91	46s
Gasoline, unleaded regular	mil Btu	9.35	90	64s
Entertainment				
Miniature golf admission	adult	6.18	92	1r
Miniature golf admission	child	5.14	92	1r
Waterpark admission	adult	11.00	92	1r
Waterpark admission	child	8.55	92	1r
Funerals				
Casket, 18-gauge steel, velvet interior		1926.72	91	24r
Cosmetology, hair care, etc.		97.64	91	24r
Embalming		249.14	91	24r
Facility use for ceremony		208.59	91	24r
Hearse, local		130.12	91	24r
Limousine, local		104.66	91	24r
Remains to funeral home, transfer		93.61	91	24r
Service charge, professional		724.62	91	24r
Vault, concrete, non-metallic liner		734.53	91	24r
Viewing facilities, use		236.06	91	24r
Groceries				
Apples, Red Delicious	lb	0.77	4/93	16r
Bacon	lb	1.85	4/93	16r
Bananas	lb	0.46	4/93	16r
Beef, stew, boneless	lb	2.53	4/93	16r
Bologna, all beef or mixed	lb	2.19	4/93	16r
Bread, white, pan	lb	0.78	4/93	16r
Butter	lb	1.50	4/93	16r
Cabbage	lb	0.40	4/93	16r
Carrots, short trimmed and topped	lb	0.45	4/93	16r
Cheese, Cheddar	lb	3.47	4/93	16r
Chicken, fresh, whole	lb	0.84	4/93	16r
Chicken breast, bone-in	lb	1.94	4/93	16r
Chicken legs, bone-in	lb	1.02	4/93	16r
Chuck roast, graded and ungraded, ex USDA prime and choice	lb	2.43	4/93	16r
Chuck roast, USDA choice, bone-in	lb	2.11	4/93	16r
Chuck roast, USDA choice, boneless	lb	2.44	4/93	16r
Coffee, 100% ground roast, all sizes	lb	2.47	4/93	16r
Cookies, chocolate chip	lb	2.73	4/93	16r
Eggs, Grade A large	doz	0.93	4/93	16r
Flour, white, all purpose	lb	0.21	4/93	16r
Grapefruit	lb	0.45	4/93	16r
Grapes, Thompson Seedless	lb	1.46	4/93	16r
Ground beef, 100% beef	lb	1.63	4/93	16r
Ground beef, lean and extra lean	lb	2.08	4/93	16r
Ground chuck, 100% beef	lb	1.94	4/93	16r
Ham, boneless, excluding canned	lb	2.21	4/93	16r
Honey, jar	8 oz	0.97-1.25	92	5r
Honey, jar	lb	1.25-2.25	92	5r
Honey, squeeze bear	12-oz	1.25-1.99	92	5r
Ice cream, prepackaged, bulk, regular	1/2 gal	2.41	4/93	16r
Lemons	lb	0.82	4/93	16r

Aurora-Elgin, IL - continued

Item	Per	Value	Date	Ref.
Groceries - continued				
Lettuce, iceberg	lb	0.83	4/93	16r
Margarine, stick	lb	0.77	4/93	16r
Oranges, navel	lb	0.50	4/93	16r
Peanut butter, creamy, all sizes	lb	1.82	4/93	16r
Pears, Anjou	lb	0.85	4/93	16r
Pork chops, center cut, bone-in	lb	3.17	4/93	16r
Potato chips	16 oz	2.68	4/93	16r
Potatoes, white	lb	0.26	4/93	16r
Round roast, graded & ungraded, ex USDA prime & choice	lb	2.88	4/93	16r
Round roast, USDA choice, boneless	lb	2.96	4/93	16r
Shortening, vegetable oil blends	lb	0.79	4/93	16r
Spaghetti and macaroni	lb	0.76	4/93	16r
Steak, rib eye, USDA choice, boneless	lb	6.29	4/93	16r
Steak, round, USDA choice, boneless	lb	3.24	4/93	16r
Steak, sirloin, graded & ungraded, ex USDA prime & choice	lb	4.00	4/93	16r
Steak, sirloin, USDA choice, bone-in	lb	3.57	4/93	16r
Steak, sirloin, USDA choice, boneless	lb	4.17	4/93	16r
Steak, T-bone, USDA choice, bone-in	lb	5.60	4/93	16r
Strawberries, dry pint	12 oz	0.90	4/93	16r
Sugar, white	lb	0.36	4/93	16r
Sugar, white, 33-80 oz pk	lb	0.35	4/93	16r
Tomatoes, field grown	lb	0.99	4/93	16r
Tuna, chunk, light	lb	1.76	4/93	16r
Turkey, frozen, whole	lb	0.91	4/93	16r
Health Care				
Childbirth, cesarean, hospital		4688	91	62r
Childbirth, cesarean, physician's fee		2053	91	62r
Childbirth, normal, hospital		2657	91	62r
Childbirth, normal, physician's fee		1492	91	62r
Medical plan per employee	year	3443	91	45r
Mental health care, exp	capita	28.84-37.59	90	38s
Mental health care, exp, state mental health agency	capita	34.43	90	38s
Mental health care, hospital psychiatric services, non-Federal, exp	capita	18.46	88	38s
Mental health care, mental health organization, multiservice, exp	capita	11.97	88	38s
Mental health care, psychiatric hospitals, private, exp	capita	7.84	88	38s
Mental health care, psychiatric out-patient clinics, freestanding, exp	capita	3.21	88	38s
Mental health care, psychiatric partial-care organizations, freestanding, exp	capita	0.51	88	38s
Mental health care, state and county mental hospitals, exp	capita	18.11	88	38s
Mental health care, VA medical centers, exp	capita	3.69	88	38s
Physician fee, family practice, first-visit		76.00	91	62r
Physician fee, family practice, revisit		33.00	91	62r
Physician fee, general practice, first-visit		61.00	91	62r
Physician fee, general practice, revisit		31.00	91	62r
Physician fee, general surgeon, first-visit		65.00	91	62r
Physician fee, general surgeon, revisit		35.00	91	62r
Physician fee, internal medicine, first-visit		91.00	91	62r
Physician fee, internal medicine, revisit		40.00	91	62r
Physician fee, median, neurosurgeon, first-visit		106.00	91	62r
Physician fee, median, nonsurgical specialist, first-visit		90.00	91	62r
Physician fee, median, orthopedic surgeon, first-visit		83.00	91	62r
Physician fee, median, surgical specialist, first-visit		61.00	91	62r
Physician fee, neurosurgeon, revisit		41.00	91	62r
Physician fee, nonsurgical specialist, revisit		40.00	91	62r
Physician fee, obstetrics/gynecology, first-visit		61.00	91	62r
Physician fee, obstetrics/gynecology, revisit		40.00	91	62r
Physician fee, orthopedic surgeon, revisit		41.00	91	62r
Physician fee, pediatrician, first-visit		46.00	91	62r

Values are in dollars or fractions of dollars. In the column headed *Ref*, references are shown to sources. Each reference is followed by a letter. These refer to the geographical level for which data were reported: s=State, r=Region, and c=City or metro. The abbreviation *ex* is used to mean *except* or *excluding*; *exp* stands for expenditures. For other abbreviations and further explanations, please see the Introduction.

Aurora-Elgin, IL - continued

Item	Per	Value	Date	Ref.
Health Care				
Physician fee, pediatrician, revisit		33.00	91	62r
Physician fee, surgical specialist, revisit		36.00	91	62r
Prescription drug co-pay, Medicaid	month	25.00	91	21s
Substance abuse, hospital ancillary charge	incident	1310	90	70s
Substance abuse, hospital physician charge	incident	540	90	70s
Substance abuse, hospital room and board	incident	6150	90	70s
Insurance and Pensions				
Auto insurance, private passenger	year	621.37	91	63s
Taxes				
Tax, cigarette	pack	30	91	77s
Tax, gasoline	gal	19	91	77s
Taxes, state	capita	1151	91	77s
Transportation				
Driver's license fee		10.00	12/90	43s
Vehicle registration and license plate	multi-year	48.00	93	52s
Utilities				
Electricity	mil Btu	22.02	90	64s

Austin, TX

Item	Per	Value	Date	Ref.
Child Care				
Child care fee, average, center	hour	1.29	90	65r
Child care fee, average, nonregulated family day care	hour	0.89	90	65r
Child care fee, average, regulated family day care	hour	1.32	90	65r
Communications				
Long-distance telephone service, day, initial minute, 0-100 miles	min	0.10-0.46	91	12s
Long-distance telephone service, day, additional minute, 0-100 miles	min	0.06-0.45	91	12s
Education				
Board, 4-yr private college/university	year	1883	91	22s
Board, 4-yr public college/university	year	1605	91	22s
Expenditures, local gov't, public elementary/secondary	pupil	4593	92	20s
Room, 4-year private college/university	year	1620	91	22s
Room, 4-year public college/university	year	1532	91	22s
Tuition, 2-year private college/university	year	4394	91	22s
Tuition, 2-year public college/university	year	495	91	22s
Tuition, 4-year private college/university	year	6497	91	22s
Tuition, 4-year public college/university, in-state	year	986	91	22s
Energy and Fuels				
Coal	mil Btu	1.44	90	64s
Energy	mil Btu	6.48	90	64s
Energy exp/householder, 1-family unit	year	471	90	28r
Energy exp/householder, <1,000 sq ft heating area	year	384	90	28r
Energy exp/householder, 1,000-1,999 sq ft heating area	year	421	90	28r
Energy exp/householder, 2,000+ sq ft heating area	year	625	90	28r
Energy exp/householder, mobile home	year	271	90	28r
Energy exp/householder, multifamily	year	355	90	28r
Gas, natural	mil Btu	2.47	90	64s
Gas, natural	000 cu ft	5.71	91	46s
Gas, natural, exp	year	388	91	46s
Gasoline, unleaded regular	mil Btu	9.16	90	64s
Entertainment				
Miniature golf admission	adult	6.18	92	1r
Miniature golf admission	child	5.14	92	1r

Austin, TX - continued

Item	Per	Value	Date	Ref.
Entertainment - continued				
Waterpark admission	adult	11.00	92	1r
Waterpark admission	child	8.55	92	1r
Funerals				
Casket, 18-gauge steel, velvet interior		2274.41	91	24r
Cosmetology, hair care, etc.		74.62	91	24r
Embalming		229.94	91	24r
Facility use for ceremony		176.61	91	24r
Hearse, local		116.34	91	24r
Limousine, local		72.68	91	24r
Remains to funeral home, transfer		87.72	91	24r
Service charge, professional		712.53	91	24r
Vault, concrete, non-metallic liner		750.55	91	24r
Viewing facilities, use		155.31	91	24r
Groceries				
Apples, Red Delicious	lb	0.79	4/93	16r
Bacon	lb	1.75	4/93	16r
Bananas	lb	0.42	4/93	16r
Beef, stew, boneless	lb	2.61	4/93	16r
Bologna, all beef or mixed	lb	2.24	4/93	16r
Bread, white, pan	lb	0.64	4/93	16r
Bread, whole wheat, pan	lb	0.96	4/93	16r
Cabbage	lb	0.37	4/93	16r
Carrots, short trimmed and topped	lb	0.47	4/93	16r
Celery	lb	0.64	4/93	16r
Cheese, American	lb	2.98	4/93	16r
Cheese, Cheddar	lb	3.28	4/93	16r
Chicken, fresh, whole	lb	0.77	4/93	16r
Chicken breast, bone-in	lb	1.92	4/93	16r
Chicken legs, bone-in	lb	1.06	4/93	16r
Chuck roast, graded and ungraded, ex USDA prime and choice	lb	2.40	4/93	16r
Chuck roast, USDA choice, bone-in	lb	2.19	4/93	16r
Chuck roast, USDA choice, boneless	lb	2.38	4/93	16r
Coffee, 100% ground roast, all sizes	lb	2.48	4/93	16r
Crackers, soda, salted	lb	1.15	4/93	16r
Eggs, Grade A large	doz	0.96	4/93	16r
Flour, white, all purpose	lb	0.24	4/93	16r
Frankfurters, all meat or all beef	lb	2.01	4/93	16r
Grapefruit	lb	0.44	4/93	16r
Grapes, Thompson Seedless	lb	1.40	4/93	16r
Ground beef, 100% beef	lb	1.58	4/93	16r
Ground beef, lean and extra lean	lb	2.09	4/93	16r
Ground chuck, 100% beef	lb	1.98	4/93	16r
Ham, boneless, excluding canned	lb	2.89	4/93	16r
Ham, picnic, shoulder, bone-in, smoked	lb	1.02	4/93	16r
Ham, rump or steak half, bone-in, smoked	lb	1.48	4/93	16r
Honey, jar	8 oz	0.73-1.19	92	5r
Honey, jar	lb	1.10-1.79	92	5r
Honey, squeeze bear	12-oz	1.19-1.50	92	5r
Ice cream, prepackaged, bulk, regular	1/2 gal	2.41	4/93	16r
Lemons	lb	1.05	4/93	16r
Lettuce, iceberg	lb	0.81	4/93	16r
Margarine, stick	lb	0.88	4/93	16r
Oranges, navel	lb	0.55	4/93	16r
Pears, Anjou	lb	0.92	4/93	16r
Pork chops, center cut, bone-in	lb	3.13	4/93	16r
Potato chips	16 oz	2.94	4/93	16r
Potatoes, white	lb	0.43	4/93	16r
Rib roast, USDA choice, bone-in	lb	4.63	4/93	16r
Rice, white, long grain, uncooked	lb	0.45	4/93	16r
Round roast, graded & ungraded, ex USDA prime & choice	lb	3.03	4/93	16r
Round roast, USDA choice, boneless	lb	3.09	4/93	16r
Sausage, fresh, loose	lb	2.08	4/93	16r
Short ribs, bone-in	lb	2.66	4/93	16r
Shortening, vegetable oil blends	lb	0.69	4/93	16r
Spaghetti and macaroni	lb	0.81	4/93	16r
Steak, rib eye, USDA choice, boneless	lb	6.24	4/93	16r
Steak, round, graded & ungraded, ex USDA prime & choice	lb	3.31	4/93	16r
Steak, round, USDA choice, boneless	lb	3.34	4/93	16r

Values are in dollars or fractions of dollars. In the column headed *Ref*, references are shown to sources. Each reference is followed by a letter. These refer to the geographical level for which data were reported: s=State, r=Region, and c=City or metro. The abbreviation *ex* is used to mean *except* or *excluding*; *exp* stands for expenditures. For other abbreviations and further explanations, please see the Introduction.

Austin, TX - continued

Item	Per	Value	Date	Ref.
Groceries				
Steak, sirloin, graded & ungraded, ex USDA prime & choice	lb	4.19	4/93	16r
Steak, sirloin, USDA choice, boneless	lb	4.46	4/93	16r
Steak, T-bone, USDA choice, bone-in	lb	5.25	4/93	16r
Strawberries, dry pint	12 oz	0.92	4/93	16r
Sugar, white	lb	0.39	4/93	16r
Sugar, white, 33-80 oz pk	lb	0.38	4/93	16r
Tomatoes, field grown	lb	0.88	4/93	16r
Tuna, chunk, light	lb	1.79	4/93	16r
Turkey, frozen, whole	lb	1.04	4/93	16r
Yogurt, natural, fruit flavored	1/2 pint	0.57	4/93	16r
Health Care				
Childbirth, cesarean, hospital		5034	91	62r
Childbirth, cesarean, physician's fee		2053	91	62r
Childbirth, normal, hospital		2712	91	62r
Childbirth, normal, physician's fee		1492	91	62r
Health care spending, state	capita	2192	3/93	84s
Mental health care, exp	capita	20.37-28.83	90	38s
Mental health care, exp, state mental health agency	capita	22.72	90	38s
Mental health care, hospital psychiatric services, non-Federal, exp	capita	7.95	88	38s
Mental health care, mental health organization, multiservice, exp	capita	12.05	88	38s
Mental health care, psychiatric hospitals, private, exp	capita	37.78	88	38s
Mental health care, psychiatric out-patient clinics, freestanding, exp	capita	0.43	88	38s
Mental health care, state and county mental hospitals, exp	capita	12.54	88	38s
Mental health care, VA medical centers, exp	capita	5.35	88	38s
Physician fee, family practice, first-visit		75.00	91	62r
Physician fee, family practice, revisit		34.00	91	62r
Physician fee, general practice, first-visit		61.00	91	62r
Physician fee, general practice, revisit		32.00	91	62r
Physician fee, general surgeon, first-visit		64.00	91	62r
Physician fee, general surgeon, revisit		40.00	91	62r
Physician fee, internal medicine, first-visit		98.00	91	62r
Physician fee, internal medicine, revisit		40.00	91	62r
Physician fee, median, neurosurgeon, first-visit		130.00	91	62r
Physician fee, median, nonsurgical specialist, first-visit		95.00	91	62r
Physician fee, median, orthopedic surgeon, first-visit		91.00	91	62r
Physician fee, median, plastic surgeon, first-visit		66.00	91	62r
Physician fee, median, surgical specialist, first-visit		62.00	91	62r
Physician fee, neurosurgeon, revisit		50.00	91	62r
Physician fee, nonsurgical specialist, revisit		40.00	91	62r
Physician fee, obstetrics/gynecology, first-visit		64.00	91	62r
Physician fee, obstetrics/gynecology, revisit		41.00	91	62r
Physician fee, orthopedic surgeon, revisit		40.00	91	62r
Physician fee, pediatrician, first-visit		49.00	91	62r
Physician fee, pediatrician, revisit		33.00	91	62r
Physician fee, plastic surgeon, revisit		43.00	91	62r
Physician fee, surgical specialist, revisit		37.00	91	62r
Substance abuse, hospital ancillary charge	incident	3750	90	70s
Substance abuse, hospital physician charge	incident	1080	90	70s
Substance abuse, hospital room and board	incident	5320	90	70s
Insurance and Pensions				
Auto insurance, private passenger	year	709.79	91	63s

Austin, TX - continued

Item	Per	Value	Date	Ref.
Taxes				
Tax, cigarette	pack	41	91	77s
Tax, gasoline	gal	20	91	77s
Taxes, state	capita	923	91	77s
Transportation				
Driver's license fee		16.00	12/90	43s
Travel				
Business travel	day	193.00	4/93	89r
Utilities				
Electricity	mil Btu	17.09	90	64s
Electricity, residential	KWh	5.92	2/93	94s

Bainbridge, GA

Item	Per	Value	Date	Ref.
Composite ACCRA index		91.50	4Q 92	4c
Alcoholic Beverages				
Beer, Miller Lite or Budweiser, 12-oz containers	6 pack	4.35	4Q 92	4c
Liquor, J & B Scotch	750 ml	15.67	4Q 92	4c
Wine, Gallo Chablis blanc, 1.5 liter	bottle	6.07	4Q 92	4c
Clothing				
Jeans, man's denim		24.64	4Q 92	4c
Shirt, man's dress shirt		20.87	4Q 92	4c
Undervest, boy's size 10-14, cotton	3	4.77	4Q 92	4c
Communications				
Newspaper subscription, daily and Sunday home delivery, large-city	month	12.64	4Q 92	4c
Telephone, flat rate	month	11.55	91	11c
Telephone bill, family of four	month	17.36	4Q 92	4c
Energy and Fuels				
Energy, combined forms, 1,800 sq ft heating area	month	124.70	4Q 92	4c
Gasoline, motor	gal	1.01	4Q 92	4c
Entertainment				
Bowling, evening rate	game	1.50	4Q 92	4c
Monopoly game, Parker Brothers', No. 9		11.41	4Q 92	4c
Movie	admission	5.50	4Q 92	4c
Tennis balls, yellow, Wilson or Penn, 3	can	2.71	4Q 92	4c
Goods and Services				
ACCRA Index, Miscellaneous Goods and Services		96.80	4Q 92	4c
Groceries				
ACCRA Index, Groceries		92.70	4Q 92	4c
Babyfood, strained vegetables, lowest price	4-4.5 oz jar	0.31	4Q 92	4c
Bananas	lb	0.42	4Q 92	4c
Bread, white	24 oz	0.74	4Q 92	4c
Cheese, Kraft grated Parmesan	8-oz canister	3.19	4Q 92	4c
Chicken, fryer, whole	lb	0.76	4Q 92	4c
Cigarettes, Winston	carton	16.03	4Q 92	4c
Coffee, vacuum-packed	13-oz can	1.89	4Q 92	4c
Corn, frozen	10 oz	0.55	4Q 92	4c
Corn Flakes, Kellogg's or Post Toasties	18 oz	1.66	4Q 92	4c
Eggs, Grade A large	doz	0.86	4Q 92	4c
Ground beef or hamburger	lb	1.42	4Q 92	4c
Lettuce, iceberg	head	0.99	4Q 92	4c
Margarine, Blue Bonnet or Parkay cubes	lb	0.51	4Q 92	4c
Milk, whole	1/2 gal	1.44	4Q 92	4c
Orange juice, Minute Maid frozen	12-oz can	1.36	4Q 92	4c
Peaches	29-oz can	1.30	4Q 92	4c

Values are in dollars or fractions of dollars. In the column headed *Ref*, references are shown to sources. Each reference is followed by a letter. These refer to the geographical level for which data were reported: s = State, r = Region, and c = City or metro. The abbreviation *ex* is used to mean *except* or *excluding*; *exp* stands for *expenditures*. For other abbreviations and further explanations, please see the Introduction.

Bainbridge, GA - continued

Item	Per	Value	Date	Ref.
Groceries				
Peas Sweet, Del Monte or Green Giant	15-17 oz can	0.53	4Q 92	4c
Potatoes, white or red	10-lb sack	1.89	4Q 92	4c
Sausage, Jimmy Dean, 100% pork	lb	2.08	4Q 92	4c
Shortening, vegetable, Crisco	3-lb can	2.17	4Q 92	4c
Soft drink, Coca Cola	2 liter	0.91	4Q 92	4c
Steak, T-bone	lb	4.51	4Q 92	4c
Sugar, cane or beet	4 lb	1.52	4Q 92	4c
Tomatoes, Hunt's or Del Monte	14.5-oz can	0.53	4Q 92	4c
Tuna, chunk, light	6.125-6.5 oz can	0.54	4Q 92	4c
Health Care				
ACCRA Index, Health Care		89.60	4Q 92	4c
Analgesic, Aspirin, Bayer, 325 mg tablets	100	4.88	4Q 92	4c
Dentist's fee, adult teeth cleaning and periodic oral exam	visit	46.80	4Q 92	4c
Doctor's fee, routine exam, established patient	visit	34.87	4Q 92	4c
Hospital care, semiprivate room	day	175.00	4Q 92	4c
Household Goods				
Appliance repair, home, service call, washing machine	min labor charge	25.25	4Q 92	4c
Laundry detergent, Tide Ultra, Bold, or Cheer	42 oz	2.72	4Q 92	4c
Tissues, facial, Kleenex brand	175-count box	1.08	4Q 92	4c
Housing				
ACCRA Index, Housing		81.20	4Q 92	4c
House, 1,800 sq ft, 8,000 sq ft lot, new, urban	total	88750	4Q 92	4c
House payment, principal and interest, 25% down payment	month	492	4Q 92	4c
Mortgage rate, incl. points & origination fee, 30-year fixed or adjustable rate	percent	8.07	4Q 92	4c
Rent, apartment, 2 bedrooms - 1-1/2 to 2 baths, unfurnished, 950 sq ft, water	month	416	4Q 92	4c
Personal Goods				
Shampoo, Alberto VO5	15 oz	1.18	4Q 92	4c
Toothpaste, Crest or Colgate	6-7 oz	1.93	4Q 92	4c
Personal Services				
Dry cleaning, man's 2-piece suit		5.35	4Q 92	4c
Haircare, woman's shampoo, trim and blow-dry		17.75	4Q 92	4c
Haircut, man's barbershop, no styling		8.50	4Q 92	4c
Restaurant Food				
Chicken, fried, thigh and drumstick		2.18	4Q 92	4c
Hamburger with cheese	1/4 lb	2.01	4Q 92	4c
Pizza, Pizza Hut or Pizza Inn, cheese, thin crust	12-13 in	7.49	4Q 92	4c
Transportation				
ACCRA Index, Transportation		83.20	4Q 92	4c
Tire balance, computer or spin balance, front	wheel	5.00	4Q 92	4c
Utilities				
ACCRA Index, Utilities		111.70	4Q 92	4c
Electricity, all electric, 1,800 sq ft living area new home	month	124.70	4Q 92	4c

Bakersfield, CA

Item	Per	Value	Date	Ref.
Composite ACCRA index		114.00	4Q 92	4c
Alcoholic Beverages				
Beer, Miller Lite or Budweiser, 12-oz containers	6 pack	3.69	4Q 92	4c
Liquor, J & B Scotch	750 ml	15.27	4Q 92	4c
Wine, Gallo Chablis blanc, 1.5 liter	bottle	3.78	4Q 92	4c
Child Care				
Child care fee, average, center	hour	1.71	90	65r
Child care fee, average, nonregulated family day care	hour	1.32	90	65r
Child care fee, average, regulated family day care	hour	1.86	90	65r
Clothing				
Jeans, man's denim		33.59	4Q 92	4c
Shirt, man's dress shirt		25.60	4Q 92	4c
Undervest, boy's size 10-14, cotton	3	6.92	4Q 92	4c
Communications				
Long-distance telephone service, day, initial minute, 0-100 miles	min	0.17-0.40	91	12s
Long-distance telephone service, day, additional minute, 0-100 miles	min	0.07-0.31	91	12s
Long-distance telephone service, evenings/weekends, 0-100 mi, initial minute	min	0.07-0.16	91	12s
Long-distance telephone service, evenings/weekends, 0-100 mi, additional minute	min	0.03-0.12	91	12s
Newspaper subscription, daily and Sunday home delivery, large-city	month	9.50	4Q 92	4c
Telephone, flat rate	month	8.35	91	11c
Telephone, residential, private line, rotary, unlimited calling	month	12.28	10/91	78c
Telephone bill, family of four	month	12.45	4Q 92	4c
Education				
Board, 4-yr private college/university	year	2515	91	22s
Board, 4-yr public college/university	year	2268	91	22s
Expenditures, local gov't, public elementary/secondary	pupil	4866	92	20s
Room, 4-year private college/university	year	2622	91	22s
Room, 4-year public college/university	year	2406	91	22s
Tuition, 2-year private college/university	year	7942	91	22s
Tuition, 2-year public college/university	year	114	91	22s
Tuition, 4-year private college/university	year	10863	91	22s
Tuition, 4-year public college/university, in-state	year	1220	91	22s
Energy and Fuels				
Coal	mil Btu	2.01	90	64s
Energy	mil Btu	9.08	90	64s
Energy, combined forms, 1,800 sq ft heating area	month	133.75	4Q 92	4c
Energy, exc electricity, 1,800 sq ft heating area	month	22.81	4Q 92	4c
Energy exp/householder, 1-family unit	year	362	90	28r
Energy exp/householder, <1,000 sq ft heating area	year	254	90	28r
Energy exp/householder, 1,000-1,999 sq ft heating area	year	358	90	28r
Energy exp/householder, 2,000+ sq ft heating area	year	467	90	28r
Energy exp/householder, mobile home	year	390	90	28r
Energy exp/householder, multifamily	year	252	90	28r
Gas, natural	mil Btu	4.31	90	64s
Gas, natural	000 cu ft	6.27	91	46s
Gas, natural, exp	year	369	91	46s
Gasoline, motor	gal	1.26	4Q 92	4c
Gasoline, unleaded regular	mil Btu	8.57	90	64s
Entertainment				
Bowling, evening rate	game	2.00	4Q 92	4c
Miniature golf admission	adult	6.18	92	1r
Miniature golf admission	child	5.14	92	1r

Values are in dollars or fractions of dollars. In the column headed *Ref*, references are shown to sources. Each reference is followed by a letter. These refer to the geographical level for which data were reported: s = State, r = Region, and c = City or metro. The abbreviation *ex* is used to mean *except* or *excluding*; *exp* stands for expenditures. For other abbreviations and further explanations, please see the Introduction.

Bakersfield, CA - continued

Item	Per	Value	Date	Ref.
Entertainment				
Monopoly game, Parker Brothers', No. 9		11.99	4Q 92	4c
Movie	admission	6.00	4Q 92	4c
Tennis balls, yellow, Wilson or Penn, 3	can	2.59	4Q 92	4c
Waterpark admission	adult	11.00	92	1r
Waterpark admission	child	8.55	92	1r
Funerals				
Casket, 18-gauge steel, velvet interior		1781.09	91	24r
Cosmetology, hair care, etc.		84.64	91	24r
Embalming		207.41	91	24r
Facility use for ceremony		205.76	91	24r
Hearse, local		105.14	91	24r
Limousine, local		83.21	91	24r
Remains to funeral home, transfer		113.82	91	24r
Service charge, professional		626.33	91	24r
Vault, concrete, non-metallic liner		599.54	91	24r
Viewing facilities, use		85.81	91	24r
Goods and Services				
ACCRA Index, Miscellaneous Goods and Services		113.70	4Q 92	4c
Groceries				
ACCRA Index, Groceries		109.20	4Q 92	4c
Apples, Red Delicious	lb	0.80	4/93	16r
Babyfood, strained vegetables, lowest price	4-4.5 oz jar	0.36	4Q 92	4c
Bacon	lb	1.79	4/93	16r
Bananas	lb	0.53	4Q 92	4c
Bananas	lb	0.53	4/93	16r
Bologna, all beef or mixed	lb	2.67	4/93	16r
Bread, white	24 oz	0.96	4Q 92	4c
Bread, white, pan	lb	0.81	4/93	16r
Carrots, short trimmed and topped	lb	0.39	4/93	16r
Cheese, Kraft grated Parmesan	8-oz canister	3.37	4Q 92	4c
Chicken, fresh, whole	lb	0.94	4/93	16r
Chicken, fryer, whole	lb	0.91	4Q 92	4c
Chicken breast, bone-in	lb	2.19	4/93	16r
Chuck roast, graded and ungraded, ex USDA prime and choice	lb	2.26	4/93	16r
Cigarettes, Winston	carton	20.75	4Q 92	4c
Coffee, 100% ground roast, all sizes	lb	2.33	4/93	16r
Coffee, vacuum-packed	13-oz can	2.09	4Q 92	4c
Corn, frozen	10 oz	0.68	4Q 92	4c
Corn Flakes, Kellogg's or Post Toasties	18 oz	2.00	4Q 92	4c
Eggs, Grade A large	doz	1.45	4Q 92	4c
Eggs, Grade AA large	doz	1.18	4/93	16r
Flour, white, all purpose	lb	0.22	4/93	16r
Grapefruit	lb	0.52	4/93	16r
Grapes, Thompson Seedless	lb	1.50	4/93	16r
Ground beef, 100% beef	lb	1.44	4/93	16r
Ground beef, lean and extra lean	lb	2.34	4/93	16r
Ground beef or hamburger	lb	1.51	4Q 92	4c
Ham, boneless, excluding canned	lb	2.56	4/93	16r
Honey, jar	8 oz	0.89-1.00	92	5r
Honey, jar	lb	1.35-1.97	92	5r
Honey, squeeze bear	12-oz	1.19-1.50	92	5r
Ice cream, prepackaged, bulk, regular	1/2 gal	2.40	4/93	16r
Lemons	lb	0.81	4/93	16r
Lettuce, iceberg	head	0.73	4Q 92	4c
Lettuce, iceberg	lb	0.84	4/93	16r
Margarine, Blue Bonnet or Parkay cubes	lb	0.86	4Q 92	4c
Margarine, stick	lb	0.81	4/93	16r
Milk, whole	1/2 gal	1.41	4Q 92	4c
Orange juice, Minute Maid frozen	12-oz can	1.30	4Q 92	4c
Oranges, navel	lb	0.48	4/93	16r
Peaches	29-oz can	1.22	4Q 92	4c

Bakersfield, CA - continued

Item	Per	Value	Date	Ref.
Groceries - continued				
Peas Sweet, Del Monte or Green Giant	15-17 oz can	0.67	4Q 92	4c
Pork chops, center cut, bone-in	lb	3.25	4/93	16r
Potato chips	16 oz	2.89	4/93	16r
Potatoes, white	lb	0.38	4/93	16r
Potatoes, white or red	10-lb sack	1.93	4Q 92	4c
Round roast, graded & ungraded, ex USDA prime & choice	lb	3.00	4/93	16r
Round roast, USDA choice, boneless	lb	3.16	4/93	16r
Sausage, Jimmy Dean, 100% pork	lb	2.68	4Q 92	4c
Shortening, vegetable oil blends	lb	0.86	4/93	16r
Shortening, vegetable, Crisco	3-lb can	2.57	4Q 92	4c
Soft drink, Coca Cola	2 liter	1.19	4Q 92	4c
Spaghetti and macaroni	lb	0.84	4/93	16r
Steak, round, graded & ungraded, ex USDA prime & choice	lb	3.34	4/93	16r
Steak, round, USDA choice, boneless	lb	3.24	4/93	16r
Steak, sirloin, graded & ungraded, ex USDA prime & choice	lb	3.75	4/93	16r
Steak, sirloin, USDA choice, boneless	lb	4.49	4/93	16r
Steak, T-bone	lb	5.05	4Q 92	4c
Sugar, cane or beet	4 lb	1.55	4Q 92	4c
Sugar, white	lb	0.41	4/93	16r
Sugar, white, 33-80 oz pk	lb	0.38	4/93	16r
Tomatoes, field grown	lb	1.01	4/93	16r
Tomatoes, Hunt's or Del Monte	14.5-oz can	0.77	4Q 92	4c
Tuna, chunk, light	6.125-6.5 oz can	0.65	4Q 92	4c
Turkey, frozen, whole	lb	1.04	4/93	16r
Health Care				
ACCRA Index, Health Care		124.30	4Q 92	4c
Analgesic, Aspirin, Bayer, 325 mg tablets	100	6.11	4Q 92	4c
Cardizem 60 mg tablets	30	24.04	92	49s
Cector 250 mg tablets	15	35.87	92	49s
Childbirth, cesarean, hospital		5533	91	62r
Childbirth, cesarean, physician's fee		2053	91	62r
Childbirth, normal, hospital		2745	91	62r
Childbirth, normal, physician's fee		1492	91	62r
Dentist's fee, adult teeth cleaning and periodic oral exam	visit	64.00	4Q 92	4c
Doctor's fee, routine exam, established patient	visit	37.40	4Q 92	4c
Health care spending, state	capita	2894	3/93	84s
Hospital care, semiprivate room	day	347.57	90	27c
Hospital care, semiprivate room	day	463.75	4Q 92	4c
Medical insurance premium, per employee, small group comprehensive	month	416.10	10/91	25c
Medical plan per employee	year	3421	91	45r
Mental health care, exp	capita	37.60-53.67	90	38s
Mental health care, exp, state mental health agency	capita	42.32	90	38s
Mental health care, hospital psychiatric services, non-Federal, exp	capita	10.64	88	38s
Mental health care, mental health organization, multiservice, exp	capita	28.56	88	38s
Mental health care, psychiatric hospitals, private, exp	capita	18.60	88	38s
Mental health care, psychiatric out-patient clinics, freestanding, exp	capita	2.28	88	38s
Mental health care, psychiatric partial-care organizations, freestanding, exp	capita	0.24	88	38s
Mental health care, state and county mental hospitals, exp	capita	13.60	88	38s
Mental health care, VA medical centers, exp	capita	2.33	88	38s
Mevacor 20 mg tablets	30	67.62	92	49s
Physician fee, family practice, first-visit		111.00	91	62r
Physician fee, family practice, revisit		45.00	91	62r

Values are in dollars or fractions of dollars. In the column headed *Ref*, references are shown to sources. Each reference is followed by a letter. These refer to the geographical level for which data were reported: s = State, r = Region, and c = City or metro. The abbreviation *ex* is used to mean *except* or *excluding*; *exp* stands for *expenditures*. For other abbreviations and further explanations, please see the Introduction.

Bakersfield, CA - continued

Item	Per	Value	Date	Ref.
Health Care				
Physician fee, general practice, first-visit		100.00	91	62r
Physician fee, general practice, revisit		40.00	91	62r
Physician fee, internal medicine, first-visit		137.00	91	62r
Physician fee, internal medicine, revisit		48.00	91	62r
Physician fee, median, neurosurgeon, first-visit		157.00	91	62r
Physician fee, median, nonsurgical specialist, first-visit		131.00	91	62r
Physician fee, median, orthopedic surgeon, first-visit		124.00	91	62r
Physician fee, median, plastic surgeon, first-visit		88.00	91	62r
Physician fee, median, surgical specialist, first-visit		100.00	91	62r
Physician fee, neurosurgeon, revisit		51.00	91	62r
Physician fee, nonsurgical specialist, revisit		47.00	91	62r
Physician fee, obstetrics/gynecology, first-visit		95.00	91	62r
Physician fee, obstetrics/gynecology, revisit		50.00	91	62r
Physician fee, orthopedic surgeon, revisit		51.00	91	62r
Physician fee, pediatrician, first-visit		81.00	91	62r
Physician fee, pediatrician, revisit		42.00	91	62r
Physician fee, plastic surgeon, revisit		48.00	91	62r
Physician fee, surgical specialist, revisit		49.00	91	62r
Prozac 20 mg tablets	14	33.22	92	49s
Substance abuse, hospital ancillary charge	incident	1760	90	70s
Substance abuse, hospital physician charge	incident	750	90	70s
Substance abuse, hospital room and board	incident	6390	90	70s
Tagamet 300 mg tablets	100	77.08	92	49s
Xanax 0.25 mg tablets	90	64.08	92	49s
Zantac 160 mg tablets	60	92.31	92	49s
Household Goods				
Appliance repair, home, service call, washing machine	min labor charge	37.20	4Q 92	4c
Laundry detergent, Tide Ultra, Bold, or Cheer	42 oz	4.20	4Q 92	4c
Tissues, facial, Kleenex brand	175-count box	1.09	4Q 92	4c
Housing				
ACCRA Index, Housing		114.70	4Q 92	4c
Home, median price	unit	131,200	92	58s
House, 1,800 sq ft, 8,000 sq ft lot, new, urban	total	125722	4Q 92	4c
House payment, principal and interest, 25% down payment	month	699	4Q 92	4c
Mortgage rate, incl. points & origination fee, 30-year fixed or adjustable rate	per-cent	8.11	4Q 92	4c
Rent, apartment, 2 bedrooms - 1-1/2 to 2 baths, unfurnished, 950 sq ft, water	month	579	4Q 92	4c
Rental unit, 1 bedroom	month	525	93	23c
Rental unit, 2 bedroom	month	618	93	23c
Rental unit, 3 bedroom	month	772	93	23c
Rental unit, 4 bedroom	month	866	93	23c
Rental unit, efficiency	month	432	93	23c
Insurance and Pensions				
Auto insurance, private passenger	year	904.37	91	63s
Personal Goods				
Shampoo, Alberto VO5	15 oz	1.11	4Q 92	4c
Toothpaste, Crest or Colgate	6-7 oz	2.28	4Q 92	4c
Personal Services				
Dry cleaning, man's 2-piece suit		7.93	4Q 92	4c
Haircare, woman's shampoo, trim and blow-dry		21.40	4Q 92	4c
Haircut, man's barbershop, no styling		8.00	4Q 92	4c

Bakersfield, CA - continued

Item	Per	Value	Date	Ref.
Restaurant Food				
Chicken, fried, thigh and drumstick		1.99	4Q 92	4c
Hamburger with cheese	1/4 lb	1.82	4Q 92	4c
Pizza, Pizza Hut or Pizza Inn, cheese, thin crust	12-13 in	11.29	4Q 92	4c
Taxes				
Tax, cigarette	pack	35	91	77s
Tax, gasoline	gal	16	91	77s
Taxes, state	capita	1477	91	77s
Transportation				
ACCRA Index, Transportation		111.50	4Q 92	4c
Bus fare	one-way	0.50	3/93	2c
Bus fare, up to 10 miles	one-way	0.50	4Q 92	4c
Driver's license fee		10.00	12/90	43s
Tire balance, computer or spin balance, front	wheel	7.99	4Q 92	4c
Travel				
Business travel	day	178.00	4/93	89r
Utilities				
ACCRA Index, Utilities		116.60	4Q 92	4c
Electricity	mil Btu	25.98	90	64s
Electricity, partial electric and other energy, 1,800 sq ft living area new home	month	110.94	4Q 92	4c

Baltimore, MD

Item	Per	Value	Date	Ref.
Communications				
Long-distance telephone service, day, initial minute, 0-100 miles	min	0.25-0.54	91	12s
Long-distance telephone service, day, additional minute, 0-100 miles	min	0.10-0.37	91	12s
Long-distance telephone service, evenings/weekends, 0-100 mi, initial minute	min	0.10-0.22	91	12s
Long-distance telephone service, evenings/weekends, 0-100 mi, additional minute	min	0.04-0.15	91	12s
Telephone, flat rate	month	16.15	91	11c
Telephone, residential, private line, rotary, unlimited calling	month	23.29	10/91	78c
Education				
Board, 4-yr private college/university	year	2490	91	22s
Board, 4-yr public college/university	year	2139	91	22s
Expenditures, local gov't, public elementary/secondary	pupil	6314	92	20s
Room, 4-year private college/university	year	2610	91	22s
Room, 4-year public college/university	year	2365	91	22s
Tuition, 2-year private college/university	year	6101	91	22s
Tuition, 2-year public college/university	year	1244	91	22s
Tuition, 4-year private college/university	year	10698	91	22s
Tuition, 4-year public college/university, in-state	year	2287	91	22s
Energy and Fuels				
Coal	mil Btu	1.62	90	64s
Energy	mil Btu	9.40	90	64s
Energy exp/householder, 1-family unit	year	487	90	28r
Energy exp/householder, <1,000 sq ft heating area	year	393	90	28r
Energy exp/householder, 1,000-1,999 sq ft heating area	year	442	90	28r
Energy exp/householder, 2,000+ sq ft heating area	year	577	90	28r
Energy exp/householder, mobile home	year	366	90	28r
Energy exp/householder, multifamily	year	382	90	28r
Fuel oil #2	gal	1.01	4/93	16c
Gas, cooking, 10 therms	month	12.44	92	56c
Gas, cooking, 30 therms	month	22.31	92	56c
Gas, cooking, 50 therms	month	32.19	92	56c
Gas, heating, winter, 100 therms	month	56.86	92	56c

Values are in dollars or fractions of dollars. In the column headed *Ref*, references are shown to sources. Each reference is followed by a letter. These refer to the geographical level for which data were reported: s=State, r=Region, and c=City or metro. The abbreviation *ex* is used to mean *except* or *excluding*; *exp* stands for expenditures. For other abbreviations and further explanations, please see the Introduction.

Baltimore, MD - continued

Item	Per	Value	Date	Ref.
Energy and Fuels				
Gas, heating, winter, average use	month	13.52	92	56c
Gas, natural	mil Btu	5.07	90	64s
Gas, natural	000 cu ft	6.16	91	46s
Gas, natural, exp	year	545	91	46s
Gas, piped	100 therms	61.67	4/93	16c
Gas, piped	40 therms	29.16	4/93	16c
Gas, piped	therm	0.69	4/93	16c
Gasoline, all types	gal	1.18	4/93	16c
Gasoline, regular unleaded, taxes included, cash, self-service	gal	1.28	4/93	16c
Gasoline, unleaded premium	gal	62.75-69.50	12/92	31c
Gasoline, unleaded premium 93 octane	gal	1.10	4/93	16c
Gasoline, unleaded regular	mil Btu	9.88	90	64s
Entertainment				
Miniature golf admission	adult	6.18	92	1r
Miniature golf admission	child	5.14	92	1r
Waterpark admission	adult	11.00	92	1r
Waterpark admission	child	8.55	92	1r
Funerals				
Casket, 18-gauge steel, velvet interior		2029.08	91	24r
Cosmetology, hair care, etc.		75.10	91	24r
Embalming		249.24	91	24r
Facility use for ceremony		162.27	91	24r
Hearse, local		114.04	91	24r
Limousine, local		88.57	91	24r
Remains to funeral home, transfer		92.61	91	24r
Service charge, professional		682.42	91	24r
Vault, concrete, non-metallic liner		798.70	91	24r
Viewing facilities, use		163.86	91	24r
Goods and Services				
Police protection expense	resident	228.00	92	18c
Groceries				
Bakery products, exp	year	217	89	15c
Beef, exp	year	253	89	15c
Cereals and bakery products, exp	year	343	89	15c
Cereals and cereal products, exp	year	126	89	15c
Dairy products, exp	year	300	89	15c
Dairy products, miscellaneous, exp	year	175	89	15c
Eggs, exp	year	33	89	15c
Fish and seafood, exp	year	118	89	15c
Food, exp	year	4560	89	15c
Food eaten at home, exp	year	2575	89	15c
Fruits, fresh, exp	year	120	89	15c
Fruits, processed, exp	year	95	89	15c
Fruits and vegetables, exp	year	397	89	15c
Meats, poultry, fish and eggs, exp	year	794	89	15c
Milk and cream, fresh, exp	year	126	89	15c
Pork, exp	year	147	89	15c
Poultry, exp	year	142	89	15c
Vegetables, fresh, exp	year	111	89	15c
Vegetables, processed, exp	year	72	89	15c
Health Care				
Hospital care, semiprivate room	day	364.37	90	27c
Medical insurance premium, per employee, small group comprehensive	month	379.60	10/91	25c
Medical plan per employee	year	3495	91	45r
Mental health care, exp	capita	53.68-118.35	90	38s
Mental health care, exp, state mental health agency	capita	61.28	90	38s
Mental health care, hospital psychiatric services, non-Federal, exp	capita	10.31	88	38s
Mental health care, mental health organization, multiservice, exp	capita	10.94	88	38s

Baltimore, MD - continued

Item	Per	Value	Date	Ref.
Health Care - continued				
Mental health care, psychiatric hospitals, private, exp	capita	15.34	88	38s
Mental health care, psychiatric out-patient clinics, freestanding, exp	capita	7.16	88	38s
Mental health care, psychiatric partial-care organizations, freestanding, exp	capita	0.36	88	38s
Mental health care, state and county mental hospitals, exp	capita	38.11	88	38s
Mental health care, VA medical centers, exp	capita	4.16	88	38s
Prescription drug co-pay, Medicaid	month	5.00	91	21s
Substance abuse, hospital ancillary charge	incident	770	90	70s
Substance abuse, hospital physician charge	incident	300	90	70s
Substance abuse, hospital room and board	incident	4470	90	70s
Housing				
Home, median price	unit	113.40		26c
Rental unit, 1 bedroom	month	504	93	23c
Rental unit, 2 bedroom	month	593	93	23c
Rental unit, 3 bedroom	month	742	93	23c
Rental unit, 4 bedroom	month	831	93	23c
Rental unit, efficiency	month	414	93	23c
Insurance and Pensions				
Auto insurance, private passenger	year	744.88	91	63s
Taxes				
Tax, cigarette	pack	36	91	77s
Tax, gasoline	gal	23.50	91	77s
Taxes, state	capita	1317	91	77s
Transportation				
Auto fixed costs, midsize		4088	91	60c
Auto operating cost, midsize		1508	91	60c
Auto rental, average	day	42.75	6/91	60c
Bus fare	one-way	1.25	3/93	2c
Driver's license fee		6.00	12/90	43s
Limo fare, airport-city, average	day	5.00	6/91	60c
Railway fare, commuter	one-way	2.75	3/93	2c
Railway fare, heavy rail	one-way	1.25	3/93	2c
Railway fare, light rail	one-way	1.25	93	2c
Taxi fare, airport-city, average	day	13.00	6/91	60c
Travel				
Breakfast	day	7.58	6/91	60c
Dinner	day	23.06	6/91	60c
Lodging	day	135.00	91	60c
Lunch	day	10.32	6/91	60c
Travel, business	day	186.30	93	88c
Utilities				
Electricity	500 KWh	45.81	4/93	16c
Electricity	KWh	0.08	4/93	16c
Electricity	mil Btu	18.47	90	64s
Electricity, winter, 250 KWh	month	25.63	92	55c
Electricity, winter, 500 KWh	month	47.76	92	55c
Electricity, winter, 750 KWh	month	65.26	92	55c
Electricity, winter, 1000 KWh	month	82.77	92	55c

Bangor, ME

Item	Per	Value	Date	Ref.
Child Care				
Child care fee, average, center	hour	2.18	90	65r
Child care fee, average, nonregulated family day care	hour	1.83	90	65r
Child care fee, average, regulated family day care	hour	2.02	90	65r

Values are in dollars or fractions of dollars. In the column headed *Ref*, references are shown to sources. Each reference is followed by a letter. These refer to the geographical level for which data were reported: s=State, r=Region, and c=City or metro. The abbreviation *ex* is used to mean *except* or *excluding*; *exp* stands for expenditures. For other abbreviations and further explanations, please see the Introduction.

Bangor, ME - continued

Item	Per	Value	Date	Ref.
Communications				
Long-distance telephone service, day, initial minute, 0-100 miles	min	0.19-0.64	91	12s
Long-distance telephone service, day, additional minute, 0-100 miles	min	0.15-0.40	91	12s
Long-distance telephone service, evenings/weekends, 0-100 mi, initial minute	min	0.08-0.26	91	12s
Long-distance telephone service, evenings/weekends, 0-100 mi, additional minute	min	0.80-0.16	91	12s
Telephone, flat rate	month	12.46	91	11c
Education				
Board, 4-yr private college/university	year	2441	91	22s
Board, 4-yr public college/university	year	1855	91	22s
Expenditures, local gov't, public elementary/secondary	pupil	5969	92	20s
Room, 4-year private college/university	year	2344	91	22s
Room, 4-year public college/university	year	1886	91	22s
Tuition, 2-year private college/university	year	3899	91	22s
Tuition, 2-year public college/university	year	1497	91	22s
Tuition, 4-year private college/university	year	10928	91	22s
Tuition, 4-year public college/university, in-state	year	2263	91	22s
Energy and Fuels				
Coal	mil Btu	2.72	90	64s
Energy	mil Btu	9.54	90	64s
Energy exp/householder, 1-family unit	year	588	90	28r
Energy exp/householder, <1,000 sq ft heating area	year	477	90	28r
Energy exp/householder, 1,000-1,999 sq ft heating area	year	517	90	28r
Energy exp/householder, 2,000+ sq ft heating area	year	630	90	28r
Energy exp/householder, mobile home	year	412	90	28r
Energy exp/householder, multifamily	year	498	90	28r
Gas, natural	mil Btu	6.05	90	64s
Gas, natural	000 cu ft	6.86	91	46s
Gas, natural, exp	year	399	91	46s
Gasoline, unleaded regular	mil Btu	9.74	90	64s
Entertainment				
Miniature golf admission	adult	6.18	92	1r
Miniature golf admission	child	5.14	92	1r
Waterpark admission	adult	11.00	92	1r
Waterpark admission	child	8.55	92	1r
Funerals				
Casket, 18-gauge steel, velvet interior		1853.42	91	24r
Cosmetology, hair care, etc.		98.33	91	24r
Embalming		273.94	91	24r
Facility use for ceremony		196.06	91	24r
Hearse, local		145.67	91	24r
Limousine, local		131.07	91	24r
Remains to funeral home, transfer		135.24	91	24r
Service charge, professional		843.16	91	24r
Vault, concrete, non-metallic liner		709.14	91	24r
Viewing facilities, use		229.85	91	24r
Groceries				
Apples, Red Delicious	lb	0.85	4/93	16r
Bacon	lb	2.12	4/93	16r
Bananas	lb	0.54	4/93	16r
Bread, white, pan	lb	0.81	4/93	16r
Butter	lb	2.02	4/93	16r
Carrots, short trimmed and topped	lb	0.51	4/93	16r
Chicken, fresh, whole	lb	1.04	4/93	16r
Chicken breast, bone-in	lb	2.21	4/93	16r
Chicken legs, bone-in	lb	1.16	4/93	16r
Chuck roast, USDA choice, boneless	lb	2.82	4/93	16r
Coffee, 100% ground roast, all sizes	lb	2.66	4/93	16r
Cucumbers	lb	0.85	4/93	16r
Eggs, Grade A large	doz	1.15	4/93	16r
Grapefruit	lb	0.45	4/93	16r

Bangor, ME - continued

Item	Per	Value	Date	Ref.
Groceries - continued				
Grapes, Thompson Seedless	lb	1.52	4/93	16r
Ground beef, lean and extra lean	lb	2.36	4/93	16r
Ground chuck, 100% beef	lb	2.02	4/93	16r
Honey, jar	8 oz	0.96-1.75	92	5r
Honey, jar	lb	1.50-3.00	92	5r
Honey, squeeze bear	12-oz	1.50-1.99	92	5r
Ice cream, prepackaged, bulk, regular	1/2 gal	2.80	4/93	16r
Lemons	lb	0.96	4/93	16r
Lettuce, iceberg	lb	0.95	4/93	16r
Margarine, stick	lb	0.81	4/93	16r
Milk, fresh, whole, fortified	1/2 gal	1.30	4/93	16r
Oranges, navel	lb	0.56	4/93	16r
Peanut butter, creamy, all sizes	lb	1.88	4/93	16r
Pork chops, center cut, bone-in	lb	3.34	4/93	16r
Potato chips	16 oz	2.88	4/93	16r
Potatoes, white	lb	0.37	4/93	16r
Rib roast, USDA choice, bone-in	lb	4.94	4/93	16r
Round roast, USDA choice, boneless	lb	3.17	4/93	16r
Shortening, vegetable oil blends	lb	0.98	4/93	16r
Spaghetti and macaroni	lb	0.82	4/93	16r
Steak, round, graded & ungraded, ex USDA prime & choice	lb	4.04	4/93	16r
Steak, round, USDA choice, boneless	lb	3.90	4/93	16r
Steak, sirloin, USDA choice, boneless	lb	4.97	4/93	16r
Strawberries, dry pint	12 oz	0.90	4/93	16r
Sugar, white	lb	0.50	4/93	16r
Sugar, white, 33-80 oz pk	lb	0.41	4/93	16r
Tomatoes, field grown	lb	1.23	4/93	16r
Tuna, chunk, light	lb	2.22	4/93	16r
Turkey, frozen, whole	lb	1.04	4/93	16r
Health Care				
Childbirth, cesarean, hospital		5826	91	62r
Childbirth, cesarean, physician's fee		2053	91	62r
Childbirth, normal, hospital		2964	91	62r
Childbirth, normal, physician's fee		1492	91	62r
Hospital care, semiprivate room	day	314.65	90	27c
Medical insurance premium, per employee, small group comprehensive	month	299.30	10/91	25c
Medical plan per employee	year	3958	91	45r
Mental health care, exp	capita	53.68-118.35	90	38s
Mental health care, exp, state mental health agency	capita	67.29	90	38s
Mental health care, hospital psychiatric services, non-Federal, exp	capita	16.12	88	38s
Mental health care, mental health organization, multiservice, exp	capita	17.98	88	38s
Mental health care, psychiatric hospitals, private, exp	capita	7.97	88	38s
Mental health care, psychiatric out-patient clinics, freestanding, exp	capita	1.60	88	38s
Mental health care, psychiatric partial-care organizations, freestanding, exp	capita	0.38	88	38s
Mental health care, state and county mental hospitals, exp	capita	29.80	88	38s
Mental health care, VA medical centers, exp	capita	8.16	88	38s
Prescription drug co-pay, Medicaid	month	3.00-5.00	91	21s
Substance abuse, hospital ancillary charge	incident	840	90	70s
Substance abuse, hospital physician charge	incident	170	90	70s
Substance abuse, hospital room and board	incident	4720	90	70s
Housing				
Rental unit, 1 bedroom	month	448	93	23c
Rental unit, 2 bedroom	month	528	93	23c
Rental unit, 3 bedroom	month	662	93	23c
Rental unit, 4 bedroom	month	742	93	23c
Rental unit, efficiency	month	369	93	23c

Values are in dollars or fractions of dollars. In the column headed *Ref*, references are shown to sources. Each reference is followed by a letter. These refer to the geographical level for which data were reported: s=State, r=Region, and c=City or metro. The abbreviation *ex* is used to mean *except* or *excluding*; *exp* stands for expenditures. For other abbreviations and further explanations, please see the Introduction.

Bangor, ME - continued

Item	Per	Value	Date	Ref.
Insurance and Pensions				
Auto insurance, private passenger	year	558.21	91	63s
Taxes				
Tax, cigarette	pack	37	91	77s
Tax, gasoline	gal	19	91	77s
Taxes, state	capita	1262	91	77s
Transportation				
Driver's license fee		18.00	12/90	43s
Vehicle registration and license plate	year	22.00	93	61s
Travel				
Business travel	day	165.00	4/93	89r
Utilities				
Electricity	mil Btu	22.42	90	64s
Electricity, winter, 250 KWh	month	29.66	92	55c
Electricity, winter, 500 KWh	month	59.32	92	55c
Electricity, winter, 750 KWh	month	88.98	92	55c
Electricity, winter, 1000 KWh	month	118.64	92	55c

Bartlesville, OK

Item	Per	Value	Date	Ref.
Composite ACCRA index		93.20	4Q 92	4c
Alcoholic Beverages				
Beer, Miller Lite or Budweiser, 12-oz containers	6 pack	3.88	4Q 92	4c
Liquor, J & B Scotch	750 ml	14.30	4Q 92	4c
Wine, Gallo Chablis blanc, 1.5 liter	bottle	4.73	4Q 92	4c
Clothing				
Jeans, man's denim		25.33	4Q 92	4c
Shirt, man's dress shirt		23.25	4Q 92	4c
Undervest, boy's size 10-14, cotton	3	4.03	4Q 92	4c
Communications				
Newspaper subscription, daily and Sunday home delivery, large-city	month	8.25	4Q 92	4c
Telephone, flat rate	month	11.32	91	11c
Telephone bill, family of four	month	18.33	4Q 92	4c
Energy and Fuels				
Energy, combined forms, 1,800 sq ft heating area	month	93.18	4Q 92	4c
Energy, exc electricity, 1,800 sq ft heating area	month	30.67	4Q 92	4c
Gas, cooking, winter, 10 therms	month	12.71	92	56c
Gas, cooking, winter, 30 therms	month	20.83	92	56c
Gas, cooking, winter, 50 therms	month	28.94	92	56c
Gas, heating, winter, 100 therms	month	49.23	92	56c
Gas, heating, winter, average use	month	63.16	92	56c
Gasoline, motor	gal	1.10	4Q 92	4c
Entertainment				
Bowling, evening rate	game	2.10	4Q 92	4c
Monopoly game, Parker Brothers', No. 9		9.97	4Q 92	4c
Movie	admission	5.00	4Q 92	4c
Tennis balls, yellow, Wilson or Penn, 3	can	1.91	4Q 92	4c
Goods and Services				
ACCRA Index, Miscellaneous Goods and Services		95.60	4Q 92	4c
Groceries				
ACCRA Index, Groceries		99.60	4Q 92	4c
Babyfood, strained vegetables, lowest price	4-4.5 oz jar	0.32	4Q 92	4c
Bananas	lb	0.47	4Q 92	4c
Bread, white	24 oz	0.60	4Q 92	4c
Cheese, Kraft grated Parmesan	8-oz canister	3.56	4Q 92	4c
Chicken, fryer, whole	lb	0.78	4Q 92	4c
Cigarettes, Winston	carton	17.38	4Q 92	4c

Bartlesville, OK - continued

Item	Per	Value	Date	Ref.
Groceries - continued				
Coffee, vacuum-packed	13-oz can	1.90	4Q 92	4c
Corn, frozen	10 oz	0.56	4Q 92	4c
Corn Flakes, Kellogg's or Post Toasties	18 oz	2.12	4Q 92	4c
Eggs, Grade A large	doz	0.86	4Q 92	4c
Ground beef or hamburger	lb	1.58	4Q 92	4c
Lettuce, iceberg	head	0.94	4Q 92	4c
Margarine, Blue Bonnet or Parkay cubes	lb	0.61	4Q 92	4c
Milk, whole	1/2 gal	1.34	4Q 92	4c
Orange juice, Minute Maid frozen	12-oz can	1.41	4Q 92	4c
Peaches	29-oz can	1.47	4Q 92	4c
Peas Sweet, Del Monte or Green Giant	15-17 oz can	0.57	4Q 92	4c
Potatoes, white or red	10-lb sack	2.54	4Q 92	4c
Sausage, Jimmy Dean, 100% pork	lb	2.48	4Q 92	4c
Shortening, vegetable, Crisco	3-lb can	2.16	4Q 92	4c
Soft drink, Coca Cola	2 liter	1.21	4Q 92	4c
Steak, T-bone	lb	5.04	4Q 92	4c
Sugar, cane or beet	4 lb	1.64	4Q 92	4c
Tomatoes, Hunt's or Del Monte	14.5-oz can	0.67	4Q 92	4c
Tuna, chunk, light	6.125-6.5 oz can	0.68	4Q 92	4c
Health Care				
ACCRA Index, Health Care		95.60	4Q 92	4c
Analgesic, Aspirin, Bayer, 325 mg tablets	100	5.34	4Q 92	4c
Dentist's fee, adult teeth cleaning and periodic oral exam	visit	44.67	4Q 92	4c
Doctor's fee, routine exam, established patient	visit	35.59	4Q 92	4c
Hospital care, semiprivate room	day	279.00	4Q 92	4c
Household Goods				
Appliance repair, home, service call, washing machine	min labor charge	33.32	4Q 92	4c
Laundry detergent, Tide Ultra, Bold, or Cheer	42 oz	3.16	4Q 92	4c
Tissues, facial, Kleenex brand	175-count box	1.18	4Q 92	4c
Housing				
ACCRA Index, Housing		87.60	4Q 92	4c
House, 1,800 sq ft, 8,000 sq ft lot, new, urban	total	96250	4Q 92	4c
House payment, principal and interest, 25% down payment	month	537	4Q 92	4c
Mortgage rate, incl. points & origination fee, 30-year fixed or adjustable rate	percent	8.15	4Q 92	4c
Rent, apartment, 2 bedrooms - 1-1/2 to 2 baths, unfurnished, 950 sq ft, water	month	436	4Q 92	4c
Personal Goods				
Shampoo, Alberto VO5	15 oz	1.31	4Q 92	4c
Toothpaste, Crest or Colgate	6-7 oz	2.01	4Q 92	4c
Personal Services				
Dry cleaning, man's 2-piece suit		6.31	4Q 92	4c
Haircare, woman's shampoo, trim and blow-dry		16.17	4Q 92	4c
Haircut, man's barbershop, no styling		7.00	4Q 92	4c
Restaurant Food				
Chicken, fried, thigh and drumstick		2.59	4Q 92	4c
Hamburger with cheese	1/4 lb	1.79	4Q 92	4c
Pizza, Pizza Hut or Pizza Inn, cheese, thin crust	12-13 in	7.99	4Q 92	4c

Values are in dollars or fractions of dollars. In the column headed *Ref*, references are shown to sources. Each reference is followed by a letter. These refer to the geographical level for which data were reported: s=State, r=Region, and c=City or metro. The abbreviation *ex* is used to mean *except* or *excluding*; *exp* stands for *expenditures*. For other abbreviations and further explanations, please see the Introduction.

Bartlesville, OK - continued

Item	Per	Value	Date	Ref.
Transportation				
ACCRA Index, Transportation		97.50	4Q 92	4c
Tire balance, computer or spin balance, front	wheel	6.36	4Q 92	4c
Utilities				
ACCRA Index, Utilities		86.20	4Q 92	4c
Electricity, partial electric and other energy, 1,800 sq ft living area new home	month	62.51	4Q 92	4c

Baton Rouge, LA

Item	Per	Value	Date	Ref.
Composite ACCRA index		99.00	4Q 92	4c
Alcoholic Beverages				
Beer, Miller Lite or Budweiser, 12-oz containers	6 pack	3.69	4Q 92	4c
Liquor, J & B Scotch	750 ml	13.79	4Q 92	4c
Wine, Gallo Chablis blanc, 1.5 liter	bottle	4.29	4Q 92	4c
Child Care				
Child care fee, average, center	hour	1.29	90	65r
Child care fee, average, nonregulated family day care	hour	0.89	90	65r
Child care fee, average, regulated family day care	hour	1.32	90	65r
Clothing				
Jeans, man's denim		26.40	4Q 92	4c
Shirt, man's dress shirt		25.30	4Q 92	4c
Undervest, boy's size 10-14, cotton	3	5.32	4Q 92	4c
Communications				
Long-distance telephone service, day, initial minute, 0-100 miles	min	0.14-0.41	91	12s
Long-distance telephone service, day, additional minute, 0-100 miles	min	0.09-0.29	91	12s
Long-distance telephone service, evenings/weekends, 0-100 mi, initial minute	min	0.06-0.16	91	12s
Long-distance telephone service, evenings/weekends, 0-100 mi, additional minute	min	0.04-0.12	91	12s
Newspaper subscription, daily and Sunday home delivery, large-city	month	9.65	4Q 92	4c
Telephone, flat rate	month	13.69	91	11c
Telephone, residential, private line, rotary, unlimited calling	month	20.86	10/91	78c
Telephone bill, family of four	month	22.46	4Q 92	4c
Education				
Board, 4-yr private college/university	year	2125	91	22s
Board, 4-yr public college/university	year	1453	91	22s
Expenditures, local gov't, public elementary/secondary	pupil	4299	92	20s
Room, 4-year private college/university	year	2216	91	22s
Room, 4-year public college/university	year	1323	91	22s
Tuition, 2-year private college/university	year	5671	91	22s
Tuition, 2-year public college/university	year	852	91	22s
Tuition, 4-year private college/university	year	9783	91	22s
Tuition, 4-year public college/university, in-state	year	1791	91	22s
Energy and Fuels				
Coal	mil Btu	1.68	90	64s
Energy	mil Btu	6.05	90	64s
Energy, combined forms, 1,800 sq ft heating area	month	132.21	4Q 92	4c
Energy, exc electricity, 1,800 sq ft heating area	month	17.26	4Q 92	4c
Energy exp/householder, 1-family unit	year	471	90	28r
Energy exp/householder, <1,000 sq ft heating area	year	384	90	28r
Energy exp/householder, 1,000-1,999 sq ft heating area	year	421	90	28r
Energy exp/householder, 2,000+ sq ft heating area	year	625	90	28r
Energy exp/householder, mobile home	year	271	90	28r

Baton Rouge, LA - continued

Item	Per	Value	Date	Ref.
Energy and Fuels - continued				
Energy exp/householder, multifamily	year	355	90	28r
Gas, cooking, 10 therms	month	7.53	92	56c
Gas, cooking, 30 therms	month	14.07	92	56c
Gas, cooking, 50 therms	month	21.99	92	56c
Gas, heating, winter, 100 therms	month	41.78	92	56c
Gas, heating, winter, average use	month	40.99	92	56c
Gas, natural	mil Btu	2.11	90	64s
Gas, natural	000 cu ft	5.77	91	46s
Gas, natural, exp	year	336	91	46s
Gasoline, motor	gal	1.12	4Q 92	4c
Gasoline, unleaded regular	mil Btu	9.47	90	64s
Entertainment				
Bowling, evening rate	game	2.32	4Q 92	4c
Miniature golf admission	adult	6.18	92	1r
Miniature golf admission	child	5.14	92	1r
Monopoly game, Parker Brothers', No. 9		13.78	4Q 92	4c
Movie	admission	6.00	4Q 92	4c
Tennis balls, yellow, Wilson or Penn, 3	can	2.21	4Q 92	4c
Waterpark admission	adult	11.00	92	1r
Waterpark admission	child	8.55	92	1r
Funerals				
Casket, 18-gauge steel, velvet interior		2274.41	91	24r
Cosmetology, hair care, etc.		74.62	91	24r
Embalming		229.94	91	24r
Facility use for ceremony		176.61	91	24r
Hearse, local		116.34	91	24r
Limousine, local		72.68	91	24r
Remains to funeral home, transfer		87.72	91	24r
Service charge, professional		712.53	91	24r
Vault, concrete, non-metallic liner		750.55	91	24r
Viewing facilities, use		155.31	91	24r
Goods and Services				
ACCRA Index, Miscellaneous Goods and Services		101.90	4Q 92	4c
Groceries				
ACCRA Index, Groceries		97.40	4Q 92	4c
Apples, Red Delicious	lb	0.79	4/93	16r
Babyfood, strained vegetables, lowest price	4-4.5 oz jar	0.27	4Q 92	4c
Bacon	lb	1.75	4/93	16r
Bananas	lb	0.48	4Q 92	4c
Bananas	lb	0.42	4/93	16r
Beef, stew, boneless	lb	2.61	4/93	16r
Bologna, all beef or mixed	lb	2.24	4/93	16r
Bread, white	24 oz	0.54	4Q 92	4c
Bread, white, pan	lb	0.64	4/93	16r
Bread, whole wheat, pan	lb	0.96	4/93	16r
Cabbage	lb	0.37	4/93	16r
Carrots, short trimmed and topped	lb	0.47	4/93	16r
Celery	lb	0.64	4/93	16r
Cheese, American	lb	2.98	4/93	16r
Cheese, Cheddar	lb	3.28	4/93	16r
Cheese, Kraft grated Parmesan	8-oz canister	3.46	4Q 92	4c
Chicken, fresh, whole	lb	0.77	4/93	16r
Chicken, fryer, whole	lb	0.62	4Q 92	4c
Chicken breast, bone-in	lb	1.92	4/93	16r
Chicken legs, bone-in	lb	1.06	4/93	16r
Chuck roast, graded and ungraded, ex USDA prime and choice	lb	2.40	4/93	16r
Chuck roast, USDA choice, bone-in	lb	2.19	4/93	16r
Chuck roast, USDA choice, boneless	lb	2.38	4/93	16r
Cigarettes, Winston	carton	17.11	4Q 92	4c
Coffee, 100% ground roast, all sizes	lb	2.48	4/93	16r
Coffee, vacuum-packed	13-oz can	2.03	4Q 92	4c
Corn, frozen	10 oz	0.59	4Q 92	4c

Values are in dollars or fractions of dollars. In the column headed *Ref*, references are shown to sources. Each reference is followed by a letter. These refer to the geographical level for which data were reported: s=State, r=Region, and c=City or metro. The abbreviation *ex* is used to mean *except* or *excluding*; *exp* stands for expenditures. For other abbreviations and further explanations, please see the Introduction.

Baton Rouge, LA - continued

Item	Per	Value	Date	Ref.
Groceries				
Corn Flakes, Kellogg's or Post Toasties	18 oz	1.92	4Q 92	4c
Crackers, soda, salted	lb	1.15	4/93	16r
Eggs, Grade A large	doz	0.92	4Q 92	4c
Eggs, Grade A large	doz	0.96	4/93	16r
Flour, white, all purpose	lb	0.24	4/93	16r
Frankfurters, all meat or all beef	lb	2.01	4/93	16r
Grapefruit	lb	0.44	4/93	16r
Grapes, Thompson Seedless	lb	1.40	4/93	16r
Ground beef, 100% beef	lb	1.58	4/93	16r
Ground beef, lean and extra lean	lb	2.09	4/93	16r
Ground beef or hamburger	lb	1.39	4Q 92	4c
Ground chuck, 100% beef	lb	1.98	4/93	16r
Ham, boneless, excluding canned	lb	2.89	4/93	16r
Ham, picnic, shoulder, bone-in, smoked	lb	1.02	4/93	16r
Ham, rump or steak half, bone-in, smoked	lb	1.48	4/93	16r
Honey, jar	8 oz	0.73-1.19	92	5r
Honey, jar	lb	1.10-1.79	92	5r
Honey, squeeze bear	12-oz	1.19-1.50	92	5r
Ice cream, prepackaged, bulk, regular	1/2 gal	2.41	4/93	16r
Lemons	lb	1.05	4/93	16r
Lettuce, iceberg	head	0.77	4Q 92	4c
Lettuce, iceberg	lb	0.81	4/93	16r
Margarine, Blue Bonnet or Parkay cubes	lb	0.64	4Q 92	4c
Margarine, stick	lb	0.88	4/93	16r
Milk, whole	1/2 gal	1.43	4Q 92	4c
Orange juice, Minute Maid frozen	12-oz can	1.33	4Q 92	4c
Oranges, navel	lb	0.55	4/93	16r
Peaches	29-oz can	1.43	4Q 92	4c
Pears, Anjou	lb	0.92	4/93	16r
Peas Sweet, Del Monte or Green Giant	15-17 oz can	0.63	4Q 92	4c
Pork chops, center cut, bone-in	lb	3.13	4/93	16r
Potato chips	16 oz	2.94	4/93	16r
Potatoes, white	lb	0.43	4/93	16r
Potatoes, white or red	10-lb sack	2.40	4Q 92	4c
Rib roast, USDA choice, bone-in	lb	4.63	4/93	16r
Rice, white, long grain, uncooked	lb	0.45	4/93	16r
Round roast, graded & ungraded, ex USDA prime & choice	lb	3.03	4/93	16r
Round roast, USDA choice, boneless	lb	3.09	4/93	16r
Sausage, fresh, loose	lb	2.08	4/93	16r
Sausage, Jimmy Dean, 100% pork	lb	2.50	4Q 92	4c
Short ribs, bone-in	lb	2.66	4/93	16r
Shortening, vegetable oil blends	lb	0.69	4/93	16r
Shortening, vegetable, Crisco	3-lb can	2.06	4Q 92	4c
Soft drink, Coca Cola	2 liter	1.17	4Q 92	4c
Spaghetti and macaroni	lb	0.81	4/93	16r
Steak, rib eye, USDA choice, boneless	lb	6.24	4/93	16r
Steak, round, graded & ungraded, ex USDA prime & choice	lb	3.31	4/93	16r
Steak, round, USDA choice, boneless	lb	3.34	4/93	16r
Steak, sirloin, graded & ungraded, ex USDA prime & choice	lb	4.19	4/93	16r
Steak, sirloin, USDA choice, boneless	lb	4.46	4/93	16r
Steak, T-bone	lb	5.52	4Q 92	4c
Steak, T-bone, USDA choice, bone-in	lb	5.25	4/93	16r
Strawberries, dry pint	12 oz	0.92	4/93	16r
Sugar, cane or beet	4 lb	1.69	4Q 92	4c
Sugar, white	lb	0.39	4/93	16r
Sugar, white, 33-80 oz pk	lb	0.38	4/93	16r
Tomatoes, field grown	lb	0.88	4/93	16r
Tomatoes, Hunt's or Del Monte	14.5-oz can	0.74	4Q 92	4c
Tuna, chunk, light	6.125-6.5 oz can	0.59	4Q 92	4c
Tuna, chunk, light	lb	1.79	4/93	16r
Turkey, frozen, whole	lb	1.04	4/93	16r

Item	Per	Value	Date	Ref.
Groceries - continued				
Yogurt, natural, fruit flavored	1/2 pint	0.57	4/93	16r
Health Care				
ACCRA Index, Health Care		98.20	4Q 92	4c
Analgesic, Aspirin, Bayer, 325 mg tablets	100	4.10	4Q 92	4c
Childbirth, cesarean, hospital		5034	91	62r
Childbirth, cesarean, physician's fee		2053	91	62r
Childbirth, normal, hospital		2712	91	62r
Childbirth, normal, physician's fee		1492	91	62r
Dentist's fee, adult teeth cleaning and periodic oral exam	visit	47.60	4Q 92	4c
Doctor's fee, routine exam, established patient	visit	37.00	4Q 92	4c
Hospital care, semiprivate room	day	199.43	90	27c
Hospital care, semiprivate room	day	310.00	4Q 92	4c
Medical insurance premium, per employee, small group comprehensive	month	372.30	10/91	25c
Mental health care, exp	capita	20.37-28.83	90	38s
Mental health care, exp, state mental health agency	capita	28.44	90	38s
Mental health care, hospital psychiatric services, non-Federal, exp	capita	8.19	88	38s
Mental health care, mental health organization, multiservice, exp	capita	0.49	88	38s
Mental health care, psychiatric hospitals, private, exp	capita	43.54	88	38s
Mental health care, psychiatric out-patient clinics, freestanding, exp	capita	4.11	88	38s
Mental health care, state and county mental hospitals, exp	capita	18.74	88	38s
Mental health care, VA medical centers, exp	capita	2.60	88	38s
Physician fee, family practice, first-visit		75.00	91	62r
Physician fee, family practice, revisit		34.00	91	62r
Physician fee, general practice, first-visit		61.00	91	62r
Physician fee, general practice, revisit		32.00	91	62r
Physician fee, general surgeon, first-visit		64.00	91	62r
Physician fee, general surgeon, revisit		40.00	91	62r
Physician fee, internal medicine, first-visit		98.00	91	62r
Physician fee, internal medicine, revisit		40.00	91	62r
Physician fee, median, neurosurgeon, first-visit		130.00	91	62r
Physician fee, median, nonsurgical specialist, first-visit		95.00	91	62r
Physician fee, median, orthopedic surgeon, first-visit		91.00	91	62r
Physician fee, median, plastic surgeon, first-visit		66.00	91	62r
Physician fee, median, surgical specialist, first-visit		62.00	91	62r
Physician fee, neurosurgeon, revisit		50.00	91	62r
Physician fee, nonsurgical specialist, revisit		40.00	91	62r
Physician fee, obstetrics/gynecology, first-visit		64.00	91	62r
Physician fee, obstetrics/gynecology, revisit		41.00	91	62r
Physician fee, orthopedic surgeon, revisit		40.00	91	62r
Physician fee, pediatrician, first-visit		49.00	91	62r
Physician fee, pediatrician, revisit		33.00	91	62r
Physician fee, plastic surgeon, revisit		43.00	91	62r
Physician fee, surgical specialist, revisit		37.00	91	62r
Substance abuse, hospital ancillary charge	incident	2600	90	70s
Substance abuse, hospital physician charge	incident	840	90	70s
Substance abuse, hospital room and board	incident	6410	90	70s
Household Goods				
Appliance repair, home, service call, washing machine	min labor charge	27.99	4Q 92	4c

Values are in dollars or fractions of dollars. In the column headed *Ref*, references are shown to sources. Each reference is followed by a letter. These refer to the geographical level for which data were reported: s=State, r=Region, and c=City or metro. The abbreviation *ex* is used to mean *except* or *excluding*; *exp* stands for expenditures. For other abbreviations and further explanations, please see the Introduction.

Baton Rouge, LA - continued

Item	Per	Value	Date	Ref.
Household Goods				
Laundry detergent, Tide Ultra, Bold, or Cheer	42 oz	3.80	4Q 92	4c
Tissues, facial, Kleenex brand	175-count box	1.25	4Q 92	4c
Housing				
ACCRA Index, Housing		88.30	4Q 92	4c
Home, median price	unit	73.60		26c
House, 1,800 sq ft, 8,000 sq ft lot, new, urban	total	95333	4Q 92	4c
House payment, principal and interest, 25% down payment	month	535	4Q 92	4c
Mortgage rate, incl. points & origination fee, 30-year fixed or adjustable rate	percent	8.21	4Q 92	4c
Rent, apartment, 2 bedrooms - 1-1/2 to 2 baths, unfurnished, 950 sq ft, water	month	454	4Q 92	4c
Rental unit, 1 bedroom	month	428	93	23c
Rental unit, 2 bedroom	month	504	93	23c
Rental unit, 3 bedroom	month	630	93	23c
Rental unit, 4 bedroom	month	707	93	23c
Rental unit, efficiency	month	353	93	23c
Insurance and Pensions				
Auto insurance, private passenger	year	778.70	91	63s
Personal Goods				
Shampoo, Alberto VO5	15 oz	1.15	4Q 92	4c
Toothpaste, Crest or Colgate	6-7 oz	2.00	4Q 92	4c
Personal Services				
Dry cleaning, man's 2-piece suit		6.32	4Q 92	4c
Haircare, woman's shampoo, trim and blow-dry		21.40	4Q 92	4c
Haircut, man's barbershop, no styling		9.09	4Q 92	4c
Restaurant Food				
Chicken, fried, thigh and drumstick		1.89	4Q 92	4c
Hamburger with cheese	1/4 lb	1.89	4Q 92	4c
Pizza, Pizza Hut or Pizza Inn, cheese, thin crust	12-13 in	7.49	4Q 92	4c
Taxes				
Tax, cigarette	pack	20	91	77s
Tax, gasoline	gal	20	91	77s
Taxes, state	capita	1013	91	77s
Transportation				
ACCRA Index, Transportation		101.60	4Q 92	4c
Bus fare, up to 10 miles	one-way	0.75	4Q 92	4c
Driver's license fee		18.00	12/90	43s
Tire balance, computer or spin balance, front	wheel	6.99	4Q 92	4c
Travel				
Business travel	day	193.00	4/93	89r
Utilities				
ACCRA Index, Utilities		120.50	4Q 92	4c
Electricity	mil Btu	17.77	90	64s
Electricity, partial electric and other energy, 1,800 sq ft living area new home	month	114.95	4Q 92	4c
Electricity, winter, 250 KWh	month	25.60	92	55c
Electricity, winter, 500 KWh	month	45.21	92	55c
Electricity, winter, 750 KWh	month	64.81	92	55c
Electricity, winter, 1000 KWh	month	84.41	92	55c

Battle Creek, MI

Item	Per	Value	Date	Ref.
Child Care				
Child care fee, average, center	hour	1.63	90	65r
Child care fee, average, nonregulated family day care	hour	1.83	90	65r

Battle Creek, MI - continued

Item	Per	Value	Date	Ref.
Child Care - continued				
Child care fee, average, regulated family day care	hour	1.42	90	65r
Communications				
Long-distance telephone service, day, initial minute, 0-100 miles	min	0.14-0.36	91	12s
Long-distance telephone service, day, additional minute, 0-100 miles	min	0.14-0.36	91	12s
Long-distance telephone service, evenings/weekends, 0-100 mi, initial minute	min	0.07-0.19	91	12s
Long-distance telephone service, evenings/weekends, 0-100 mi, additional minute	min	0.04-0.14	91	12s
Education				
Board, 4-yr private college/university	year	1698	91	22s
Board, 4-yr public college/university	year	1962	91	22s
Expenditures, local gov't, public elementary/secondary	pupil	5671	92	20s
Room, 4-year private college/university	year	1440	91	22s
Room, 4-year public college/university	year	1687	91	22s
Tuition, 2-year private college/university	year	4749	91	22s
Tuition, 2-year public college/university	year	1124	91	22s
Tuition, 4-year private college/university	year	6885	91	22s
Tuition, 4-year public college/university, in-state	year	2635	91	22s
Energy and Fuels				
Coal	mil Btu	1.63	90	64s
Energy	mil Btu	8.17	90	64s
Energy exp/householder, 1-family unit	year	471	90	28r
Energy exp/householder, <1,000 sq ft heating area	year	430	90	28r
Energy exp/householder, 1,000-1,999 sq ft heating area	year	481	90	28r
Energy exp/householder, 2,000+ sq ft heating area	year	473	90	28r
Energy exp/householder, mobile home	year	430	90	28r
Energy exp/householder, multifamily	year	461	90	28r
Gas, natural	mil Btu	4.36	90	64s
Gas, natural	000 cu ft	5.07	91	46s
Gas, natural, exp	year	655	91	46s
Gasoline, unleaded regular	mil Btu	8.78	90	64s
Entertainment				
Miniature golf admission	adult	6.18	92	1r
Miniature golf admission	child	5.14	92	1r
Waterpark admission	adult	11.00	92	1r
Waterpark admission	child	8.55	92	1r
Funerals				
Casket, 18-gauge steel, velvet interior		1926.72	91	24r
Cosmetology, hair care, etc.		97.64	91	24r
Embalming		249.14	91	24r
Facility use for ceremony		208.59	91	24r
Hearse, local		130.12	91	24r
Limousine, local		104.66	91	24r
Remains to funeral home, transfer		93.61	91	24r
Service charge, professional		724.62	91	24r
Vault, concrete, non-metallic liner		734.53	91	24r
Viewing facilities, use		236.06	91	24r
Groceries				
Apples, Red Delicious	lb	0.77	4/93	16r
Bacon	lb	1.85	4/93	16r
Bananas	lb	0.46	4/93	16r
Beef, stew, boneless	lb	2.53	4/93	16r
Bologna, all beef or mixed	lb	2.19	4/93	16r
Bread, white, pan	lb	0.78	4/93	16r
Butter	lb	1.50	4/93	16r
Cabbage	lb	0.40	4/93	16r
Carrots, short trimmed and topped	lb	0.45	4/93	16r
Cheese, Cheddar	lb	3.47	4/93	16r
Chicken, fresh, whole	lb	0.84	4/93	16r
Chicken breast, bone-in	lb	1.94	4/93	16r

Values are in dollars or fractions of dollars. In the column headed *Ref*, references are shown to sources. Each reference is followed by a letter. These refer to the geographical level for which data were reported: s = State, r = Region, and c = City or metro. The abbreviation *ex* is used to mean *except* or *excluding*; *exp* stands for expenditures. For other abbreviations and further explanations, please see the Introduction.

Battle Creek, MI - continued

Item	Per	Value	Date	Ref.
Groceries				
Chicken legs, bone-in	lb	1.02	4/93	16r
Chuck roast, graded and ungraded, ex USDA prime and choice	lb	2.43	4/93	16r
Chuck roast, USDA choice, bone-in	lb	2.11	4/93	16r
Chuck roast, USDA choice, boneless	lb	2.44	4/93	16r
Coffee, 100% ground roast, all sizes	lb	2.47	4/93	16r
Cookies, chocolate chip	lb	2.73	4/93	16r
Eggs, Grade A large	doz	0.93	4/93	16r
Flour, white, all purpose	lb	0.21	4/93	16r
Grapefruit	lb	0.45	4/93	16r
Grapes, Thompson Seedless	lb	1.46	4/93	16r
Ground beef, 100% beef	lb	1.63	4/93	16r
Ground beef, lean and extra lean	lb	2.08	4/93	16r
Ground chuck, 100% beef	lb	1.94	4/93	16r
Ham, boneless, excluding canned	lb	2.21	4/93	16r
Honey, jar	8 oz	0.97-1.25	92	5r
Honey, jar	lb	1.25-2.25	92	5r
Honey, squeeze bear	12-oz	1.25-1.99	92	5r
Ice cream, prepackaged, bulk, regular	1/2 gal	2.41	4/93	16r
Lemons	lb	0.82	4/93	16r
Lettuce, iceberg	lb	0.83	4/93	16r
Margarine, stick	lb	0.77	4/93	16r
Oranges, navel	lb	0.50	4/93	16r
Peanut butter, creamy, all sizes	lb	1.82	4/93	16r
Pears, Anjou	lb	0.85	4/93	16r
Pork chops, center cut, bone-in	lb	3.17	4/93	16r
Potato chips	16 oz	2.68	4/93	16r
Potatoes, white	lb	0.26	4/93	16r
Round roast, graded & ungraded, ex USDA prime & choice	lb	2.88	4/93	16r
Round roast, USDA choice, boneless	lb	2.96	4/93	16r
Shortening, vegetable oil blends	lb	0.79	4/93	16r
Spaghetti and macaroni	lb	0.76	4/93	16r
Steak, rib eye, USDA choice, boneless	lb	6.29	4/93	16r
Steak, round, USDA choice, boneless	lb	3.24	4/93	16r
Steak, sirloin, graded & ungraded, ex USDA prime & choice	lb	4.00	4/93	16r
Steak, sirloin, USDA choice, bone-in	lb	3.57	4/93	16r
Steak, sirloin, USDA choice, boneless	lb	4.17	4/93	16r
Steak, T-bone, USDA choice, bone-in	lb	5.60	4/93	16r
Strawberries, dry pint	12 oz	0.90	4/93	16r
Sugar, white	lb	0.36	4/93	16r
Sugar, white, 33-80 oz pk	lb	0.35	4/93	16r
Tomatoes, field grown	lb	0.99	4/93	16r
Tuna, chunk, light	lb	1.76	4/93	16r
Turkey, frozen, whole	lb	0.91	4/93	16r
Health Care				
Childbirth, cesarean, hospital		4688	91	62r
Childbirth, cesarean, physician's fee		2053	91	62r
Childbirth, normal, hospital		2657	91	62r
Childbirth, normal, physician's fee		1492	91	62r
Medical plan per employee	year	3443	91	45r
Mental health care, exp	capita	53.68-118.35	90	38s
Mental health care, exp, state mental health agency	capita	73.73	90	38s
Mental health care, hospital psychiatric services, non-Federal, exp	capita	22.52	88	38s
Mental health care, mental health organization, multiservice, exp	capita	42.68	88	38s
Mental health care, psychiatric hospitals, private, exp	capita	10.80	88	38s
Mental health care, psychiatric out-patient clinics, freestanding, exp	capita	3.47	88	38s
Mental health care, psychiatric partial-care organizations, freestanding, exp	capita	0.73	88	38s
Mental health care, state and county mental hospitals, exp	capita	36.77	88	38s
Mental health care, VA medical centers, exp	capita	4.03	88	38s
Physician fee, family practice, first-visit		76.00	91	62r
Physician fee, family practice, revisit		33.00	91	62r
Physician fee, general practice, first-visit		61.00	91	62r

Battle Creek, MI - continued

Item	Per	Value	Date	Ref.
Health Care - continued				
Physician fee, general practice, revisit		31.00	91	62r
Physician fee, general surgeon, first-visit		65.00	91	62r
Physician fee, general surgeon, revisit		35.00	91	62r
Physician fee, internal medicine, first-visit		91.00	91	62r
Physician fee, internal medicine, revisit		40.00	91	62r
Physician fee, median, neurosurgeon, first-visit		106.00	91	62r
Physician fee, median, nonsurgical specialist, first-visit		90.00	91	62r
Physician fee, median, orthopedic surgeon, first-visit		83.00	91	62r
Physician fee, median, surgical specialist, first-visit		61.00	91	62r
Physician fee, neurosurgeon, revisit		41.00	91	62r
Physician fee, nonsurgical specialist, revisit		40.00	91	62r
Physician fee, obstetrics/gynecology, first-visit		61.00	91	62r
Physician fee, obstetrics/gynecology, revisit		40.00	91	62r
Physician fee, orthopedic surgeon, revisit		41.00	91	62r
Physician fee, pediatrician, first-visit		46.00	91	62r
Physician fee, pediatrician, revisit		33.00	91	62r
Physician fee, surgical specialist, revisit		36.00	91	62r
Substance abuse, hospital ancillary charge	incident	1480	90	70s
Substance abuse, hospital physician charge	incident	250	90	70s
Substance abuse, hospital room and board	incident	4070	90	70s
Insurance and Pensions				
Auto insurance, private passenger	year	716.78	91	63s
Taxes				
Tax, cigarette	pack	25	91	77s
Tax, gasoline	gal	15	91	77s
Taxes, state	capita	1185	91	77s
Transportation				
Driver's license fee		12.00	12/90	43s
Vehicle registration and license plate	year	14.00-200.00	93	40s
Utilities				
Electricity	mil Btu	20.85	90	64s

Beaumont-Port Arthur, TX

Item	Per	Value	Date	Ref.
Composite ACCRA index		95.30	4Q 92	4c
Alcoholic Beverages				
Beer, Miller Lite or Budweiser, 12-oz containers	6 pack	3.78	4Q 92	4c
Liquor, J & B Scotch	750 ml	16.11	4Q 92	4c
Wine, Gallo Chablis blanc, 1.5 liter	bottle	4.91	4Q 92	4c
Child Care				
Child care fee, average, center	hour	1.29	90	65r
Child care fee, average, nonregulated family day care	hour	0.89	90	65r
Child care fee, average, regulated family day care	hour	1.32	90	65r
Clothing				
Jeans, man's denim		22.20	4Q 92	4c
Shirt, man's dress shirt		27.20	4Q 92	4c
Undervest, boy's size 10-14, cotton	3	6.15	4Q 92	4c
Communications				
Long-distance telephone service, day, initial minute, 0-100 miles	min	0.10-0.46	91	12s
Long-distance telephone service, day, additional minute, 0-100 miles	min	0.06-0.45	91	12s
Newspaper subscription, daily and Sunday home delivery, large-city	month	8.00	4Q 92	4c
Telephone, flat rate	month	9.10	91	11c

Values are in dollars or fractions of dollars. In the column headed *Ref*, references are shown to sources. Each reference is followed by a letter. These refer to the geographical level for which data were reported: s=State, r=Region, and c=City or metro. The abbreviation *ex* is used to mean *except* or *excluding*; *exp* stands for expenditures. For other abbreviations and further explanations, please see the Introduction.

Beaumont-Port Arthur, TX - continued

Item	Per	Value	Date	Ref.
Communications				
Telephone bill, family of four	month	16.36	4Q 92	4c
Education				
Board, 4-yr private college/university	year	1883	91	22s
Board, 4-yr public college/university	year	1605	91	22s
Expenditures, local gov't, public elementary/secondary	pupil	4593	92	20s
Room, 4-year private college/university	year	1620	91	22s
Room, 4-year public college/university	year	1532	91	22s
Tuition, 2-year private college/university	year	4394	91	22s
Tuition, 2-year public college/university	year	495	91	22s
Tuition, 4-year private college/university	year	6497	91	22s
Tuition, 4-year public college/university, in-state	year	986	91	22s
Energy and Fuels				
Coal	mil Btu	1.44	90	64s
Energy	mil Btu	6.48	90	64s
Energy, combined forms, 1,800 sq ft heating area	month	115.73	4Q 92	4c
Energy, exc electricity, 1,800 sq ft heating area	month	32.10	4Q 92	4c
Energy exp/householder, 1-family unit	year	471	90	28r
Energy exp/householder, <1,000 sq ft heating area	year	384	90	28r
Energy exp/householder, 1,000-1,999 sq ft heating area	year	421	90	28r
Energy exp/householder, 2,000+ sq ft heating area	year	625	90	28r
Energy exp/householder, mobile home	year	271	90	28r
Energy exp/householder, multifamily	year	355	90	28r
Gas, natural	mil Btu	2.47	90	64s
Gas, natural	000 cu ft	5.71	91	46s
Gas, natural, exp	year	388	91	46s
Gasoline, motor	gal	1.13	4Q 92	4c
Gasoline, unleaded regular	mil Btu	9.16	90	64s
Entertainment				
Bowling, evening rate	game	2.25	4Q 92	4c
Miniature golf admission	adult	6.18	92	1r
Miniature golf admission	child	5.14	92	1r
Monopoly game, Parker Brothers', No. 9		12.39	4Q 92	4c
Movie	admission	5.37	4Q 92	4c
Tennis balls, yellow, Wilson or Penn, 3	can	2.07	4Q 92	4c
Waterpark admission	adult	11.00	92	1r
Waterpark admission	child	8.55	92	1r
Funerals				
Casket, 18-gauge steel, velvet interior		2274.41	91	24r
Cosmetology, hair care, etc.		74.62	91	24r
Embalming		229.94	91	24r
Facility use for ceremony		176.61	91	24r
Hearse, local		116.34	91	24r
Limousine, local		72.68	91	24r
Remains to funeral home, transfer		87.72	91	24r
Service charge, professional		712.53	91	24r
Vault, concrete, non-metallic liner		750.55	91	24r
Viewing facilities, use		155.31	91	24r
Goods and Services				
ACCRA Index, Miscellaneous Goods and Services		101.10	4Q 92	4c
Groceries				
ACCRA Index, Groceries		98.80	4Q 92	4c
Apples, Red Delicious	lb	0.79	4/93	16r
Babyfood, strained vegetables, lowest price	4-4.5 oz jar	0.23	4Q 92	4c
Bacon	lb	1.75	4/93	16r
Bananas	lb	0.45	4Q 92	4c
Bananas	lb	0.42	4/93	16r
Beef, stew, boneless	lb	2.61	4/93	16r
Bologna, all beef or mixed	lb	2.24	4/93	16r

Beaumont-Port Arthur, TX - continued

Item	Per	Value	Date	Ref.
Groceries - continued				
Bread, white	24 oz	0.61	4Q 92	4c
Bread, white, pan	lb	0.64	4/93	16r
Bread, whole wheat, pan	lb	0.96	4/93	16r
Cabbage	lb	0.37	4/93	16r
Carrots, short trimmed and topped	lb	0.47	4/93	16r
Celery	lb	0.64	4/93	16r
Cheese, American	lb	2.98	4/93	16r
Cheese, Cheddar	lb	3.28	4/93	16r
Cheese, Kraft grated Parmesan	8-oz canister	3.33	4Q 92	4c
Chicken, fresh, whole	lb	0.77	4/93	16r
Chicken, fryer, whole	lb	0.66	4Q 92	4c
Chicken breast, bone-in	lb	1.92	4/93	16r
Chicken legs, bone-in	lb	1.06	4/93	16r
Chuck roast, graded and ungraded, ex USDA prime and choice	lb	2.40	4/93	16r
Chuck roast, USDA choice, bone-in	lb	2.19	4/93	16r
Chuck roast, USDA choice, boneless	lb	2.38	4/93	16r
Cigarettes, Winston	carton	20.01	4Q 92	4c
Coffee, 100% ground roast, all sizes	lb	2.48	4/93	16r
Coffee, vacuum-packed	13-oz can	2.01	4Q 92	4c
Corn, frozen	10 oz	0.53	4Q 92	4c
Corn Flakes, Kellogg's or Post Toasties	18 oz	1.86	4Q 92	4c
Crackers, soda, salted	lb	1.15	4/93	16r
Eggs, Grade A large	doz	0.85	4Q 92	4c
Eggs, Grade A large	doz	0.96	4/93	16r
Flour, white, all purpose	lb	0.24	4/93	16r
Frankfurters, all meat or all beef	lb	2.01	4/93	16r
Grapefruit	lb	0.44	4/93	16r
Grapes, Thompson Seedless	lb	1.40	4/93	16r
Ground beef, 100% beef	lb	1.58	4/93	16r
Ground beef, lean and extra lean	lb	2.09	4/93	16r
Ground beef or hamburger	lb	1.85	4Q 92	4c
Ground chuck, 100% beef	lb	1.98	4/93	16r
Ham, boneless, excluding canned	lb	2.89	4/93	16r
Ham, picnic, shoulder, bone-in, smoked	lb	1.02	4/93	16r
Ham, rump or steak half, bone-in, smoked	lb	1.48	4/93	16r
Honey, jar	8 oz	0.73-1.19	92	5r
Honey, jar	lb	1.10-1.79	92	5r
Honey, squeeze bear	12-oz	1.19-1.50	92	5r
Ice cream, prepackaged, bulk, regular	1/2 gal	2.41	4/93	16r
Lemons	lb	1.05	4/93	16r
Lettuce, iceberg	head	0.91	4Q 92	4c
Lettuce, iceberg	lb	0.81	4/93	16r
Margarine, Blue Bonnet or Parkay cubes	lb	0.56	4Q 92	4c
Margarine, stick	lb	0.88	4/93	16r
Milk, whole	1/2 gal	1.30	4Q 92	4c
Orange juice, Minute Maid frozen	12-oz can	1.32	4Q 92	4c
Oranges, navel	lb	0.55	4/93	16r
Peaches	29-oz can	1.29	4Q 92	4c
Pears, Anjou	lb	0.92	4/93	16r
Peas Sweet, Del Monte or Green Giant	15-17 oz can	0.53	4Q 92	4c
Pork chops, center cut, bone-in	lb	3.13	4/93	16r
Potato chips	16 oz	2.94	4/93	16r
Potatoes, white	lb	0.43	4/93	16r
Potatoes, white or red	10-lb sack	1.57	4Q 92	4c
Rib roast, USDA choice, bone-in	lb	4.63	4/93	16r
Rice, white, long grain, uncooked	lb	0.45	4/93	16r
Round roast, graded & ungraded, ex USDA prime & choice	lb	3.03	4/93	16r
Round roast, USDA choice, boneless	lb	3.09	4/93	16r
Sausage, fresh, loose	lb	2.08	4/93	16r
Sausage, Jimmy Dean, 100% pork	lb	2.41	4Q 92	4c
Short ribs, bone-in	lb	2.66	4/93	16r
Shortening, vegetable oil blends	lb	0.69	4/93	16r

Values are in dollars or fractions of dollars. In the column headed *Ref*, references are shown to sources. Each reference is followed by a letter. These refer to the geographical level for which data were reported: s = State, r = Region, and c = City or metro. The abbreviation *ex* is used to mean *except* or *excluding*; *exp* stands for expenditures. For other abbreviations and further explanations, please see the Introduction.

Beaumont-Port Arthur, TX - continued

Item	Per	Value	Date	Ref.
Groceries				
Shortening, vegetable, Crisco	3-lb can	2.10	4Q 92	4c
Soft drink, Coca Cola	2 liter	1.22	4Q 92	4c
Spaghetti and macaroni	lb	0.81	4/93	16r
Steak, rib eye, USDA choice, boneless	lb	6.24	4/93	16r
Steak, round, graded & ungraded, ex USDA prime & choice	lb	3.31	4/93	16r
Steak, round, USDA choice, boneless	lb	3.34	4/93	16r
Steak, sirloin, graded & ungraded, ex USDA prime & choice	lb	4.19	4/93	16r
Steak, sirloin, USDA choice, boneless	lb	4.46	4/93	16r
Steak, T-bone	lb	5.57	4Q 92	4c
Steak, T-bone, USDA choice, bone-in	lb	5.25	4/93	16r
Strawberries, dry pint	12 oz	0.92	4/93	16r
Sugar, cane or beet	4 lb	1.33	4Q 92	4c
Sugar, white	lb	0.39	4/93	16r
Sugar, white, 33-80 oz pk	lb	0.38	4/93	16r
Tomatoes, field grown	lb	0.88	4/93	16r
Tomatoes, Hunt's or Del Monte	14.5-oz can	0.74	4Q 92	4c
Tuna, chunk, light	6.125-6.5 oz can	0.67	4Q 92	4c
Tuna, chunk, light	lb	1.79	4/93	16r
Turkey, frozen, whole	lb	1.04	4/93	16r
Yogurt, natural, fruit flavored	1/2 pint	0.57	4/93	16r
Health Care				
ACCRA Index, Health Care		90.40	4Q 92	4c
Analgesic, Aspirin, Bayer, 325 mg tablets	100	5.62	4Q 92	4c
Childbirth, cesarean, hospital		5034	91	62r
Childbirth, cesarean, physician's fee		2053	91	62r
Childbirth, normal, hospital		2712	91	62r
Childbirth, normal, physician's fee		1492	91	62r
Dentist's fee, adult teeth cleaning and periodic oral exam	visit	39.40	4Q 92	4c
Doctor's fee, routine exam, established patient	visit	37.00	4Q 92	4c
Health care spending, state	capita	2192	3/93	84s
Hospital care, semiprivate room	day	222.92	90	27c
Hospital care, semiprivate room	day	223.33	4Q 92	4c
Medical insurance premium, per employee, small group comprehensive	month	405.15	10/91	25c
Mental health care, exp	capita	20.37-28.83	90	38s
Mental health care, exp, state mental health agency	capita	22.72	90	38s
Mental health care, hospital psychiatric services, non-Federal, exp	capita	7.95	88	38s
Mental health care, mental health organization, multiservice, exp	capita	12.05	88	38s
Mental health care, psychiatric hospitals, private, exp	capita	37.78	88	38s
Mental health care, psychiatric out-patient clinics, freestanding, exp	capita	0.43	88	38s
Mental health care, state and county mental hospitals, exp	capita	12.54	88	38s
Mental health care, VA medical centers, exp	capita	5.35	88	38s
Physician fee, family practice, first-visit		75.00	91	62r
Physician fee, family practice, revisit		34.00	91	62r
Physician fee, general practice, first-visit		61.00	91	62r
Physician fee, general practice, revisit		32.00	91	62r
Physician fee, general surgeon, first-visit		64.00	91	62r
Physician fee, general surgeon, revisit		40.00	91	62r
Physician fee, internal medicine, first-visit		98.00	91	62r
Physician fee, internal medicine, revisit		40.00	91	62r
Physician fee, median, neurosurgeon, first-visit		130.00	91	62r
Physician fee, median, nonsurgical specialist, first-visit		95.00	91	62r
Physician fee, median, orthopedic surgeon, first-visit		91.00	91	62r

Beaumont-Port Arthur, TX - continued

Item	Per	Value	Date	Ref.
Health Care - continued				
Physician fee, median, plastic surgeon, first-visit		66.00	91	62r
Physician fee, median, surgical specialist, first-visit		62.00	91	62r
Physician fee, neurosurgeon, revisit		50.00	91	62r
Physician fee, nonsurgical specialist, revisit		40.00	91	62r
Physician fee, obstetrics/gynecology, first-visit		64.00	91	62r
Physician fee, obstetrics/gynecology, revisit		41.00	91	62r
Physician fee, orthopedic surgeon, revisit		40.00	91	62r
Physician fee, pediatrician, first-visit		49.00	91	62r
Physician fee, pediatrician, revisit		33.00	91	62r
Physician fee, plastic surgeon, revisit		43.00	91	62r
Physician fee, surgical specialist, revisit		37.00	91	62r
Substance abuse, hospital ancillary charge	incident	3750	90	70s
Substance abuse, hospital physician charge	incident	1080	90	70s
Substance abuse, hospital room and board	incident	5320	90	70s
Household Goods				
Appliance repair, home, service call, washing machine	min labor charge	32.40	4Q 92	4c
Laundry detergent, Tide Ultra, Bold, or Cheer	42 oz	3.52	4Q 92	4c
Tissues, facial, Kleenex brand	175-count box	1.17	4Q 92	4c
Housing				
ACCRA Index, Housing		79.50	4Q 92	4c
Home, median price	unit	61.50		26c
House, 1,800 sq ft, 8,000 sq ft lot, new, urban	total	81100	4Q 92	4c
House payment, principal and interest, 25% down payment	month	457	4Q 92	4c
Mortgage rate, incl. points & origination fee, 30-year fixed or adjustable rate	percent	8.24	4Q 92	4c
Rent, apartment, 2 bedrooms - 1-1/2 to 2 baths, unfurnished, 950 sq ft, water	month	466	4Q 92	4c
Rental unit, 1 bedroom	month	414	93	23c
Rental unit, 2 bedroom	month	489	93	23c
Rental unit, 3 bedroom	month	611	93	23c
Rental unit, 4 bedroom	month	683	93	23c
Rental unit, efficiency	month	342	93	23c
Insurance and Pensions				
Auto insurance, private passenger	year	709.79	91	63s
Personal Goods				
Shampoo, Alberto VO5	15 oz	1.15	4Q 92	4c
Toothpaste, Crest or Colgate	6-7 oz	2.31	4Q 92	4c
Personal Services				
Dry cleaning, man's 2-piece suit		5.26	4Q 92	4c
Haircare, woman's shampoo, trim and blow-dry		17.20	4Q 92	4c
Haircut, man's barbershop, no styling		9.40	4Q 92	4c
Restaurant Food				
Chicken, fried, thigh and drumstick		1.44	4Q 92	4c
Hamburger with cheese	1/4 lb	1.94	4Q 92	4c
Pizza, Pizza Hut or Pizza Inn, cheese, thin crust	12-13 in	8.35	4Q 92	4c
Taxes				
Tax, cigarette	pack	41	91	77s
Tax, gasoline	gal	20	91	77s
Taxes, state	capita	923	91	77s
Transportation				
ACCRA Index, Transportation		109.50	4Q 92	4c
Driver's license fee		16.00	12/90	43s

Values are in dollars or fractions of dollars. In the column headed *Ref*, references are shown to sources. Each reference is followed by a letter. These refer to the geographical level for which data were reported: s = State, r = Region, and c = City or metro. The abbreviation *ex* is used to mean *except* or *excluding*; *exp* stands for expenditures. For other abbreviations and further explanations, please see the Introduction.

Beaumont-Port Arthur, TX - continued

Item	Per	Value	Date	Ref.
Transportation				
Tire balance, computer or spin balance, front	wheel	7.75	4Q 92	4c
Travel				
Business travel	day	193.00	4/93	89r
Utilities				
ACCRA Index, Utilities		103.80	4Q 92	4c
Electricity	mil Btu	17.09	90	64s
Electricity, partial electric and other energy, 1,800 sq ft living area new home	month	83.63	4Q 92	4c
Electricity, residential	KWh	5.92	2/93	94s
Electricity, winter, 250 KWh	month	25.83	92	55c
Electricity, winter, 500 KWh	month	45.41	92	55c
Electricity, winter, 750 KWh	month	65.00	92	55c
Electricity, winter, 1000 KWh	month	84.58	92	55c

Bellingham, WA

Item	Per	Value	Date	Ref.
Composite ACCRA index		105.00	4Q 92	4c
Alcoholic Beverages				
Beer, Miller Lite or Budweiser, 12-oz containers	6 pack	3.21	4Q 92	4c
Liquor, J & B Scotch	750 ml	17.95	4Q 92	4c
Wine, Gallo Chablis blanc, 1.5 liter	bottle	4.90	4Q 92	4c
Child Care				
Child care fee, average, center	hour	1.71	90	65r
Child care fee, average, nonregulated family day care	hour	1.32	90	65r
Child care fee, average, regulated family day care	hour	1.86	90	65r
Clothing				
Jeans, man's denim		31.39	4Q 92	4c
Shirt, man's dress shirt		24.93	4Q 92	4c
Undervest, boy's size 10-14, cotton	3	4.86	4Q 92	4c
Communications				
Long-distance telephone service, day, initial minute, 0-100 miles	min	0.15-0.37	91	12s
Long-distance telephone service, day, additional minute, 0-100 miles	min	0.01-0.03	91	12s
Long-distance telephone service, evenings/weekends, 0-100 mi, initial minute	min	0.05-0.19	91	12s
Long-distance telephone service, evenings/weekends, 0-100 mi, additional minute	min	0.00-0.01	91	12s
Newspaper subscription, daily and Sunday home delivery, large-city	month	10.25	4Q 92	4c
Telephone, flat rate	month	9.75	91	11c
Telephone bill, family of four	month	14.96	4Q 92	4c
Education				
Board, 4-yr private college/university	year	1811	91	22s
Board, 4-yr public college/university	year	1539	91	22s
Expenditures, local gov't, public elementary/secondary	pupil	5317	92	20s
Room, 4-year private college/university	year	1885	91	22s
Room, 4-year public college/university	year	1698	91	22s
Tuition, 2-year private college/university	year	6743	91	22s
Tuition, 2-year public college/university	year	844	91	22s
Tuition, 4-year private college/university	year	9463	91	22s
Tuition, 4-year public college/university, in-state	year	1823	91	22s
Energy and Fuels				
Energy	mil Btu	7.39	90	64s
Energy, combined forms, 1,800 sq ft heating area	month	63.66	4Q 92	4c
Energy, exc electricity, 1,800 sq ft heating area	month	32.60	4Q 92	4c
Energy exp/householder, 1-family unit	year	362	90	28r
Energy exp/householder, <1,000 sq ft heating area	year	254	90	28r

Bellingham, WA - continued

Item	Per	Value	Date	Ref.
Energy and Fuels - continued				
Energy exp/householder, 1,000-1,999 sq ft heating area	year	358	90	28r
Energy exp/householder, 2,000+ sq ft heating area	year	467	90	28r
Energy exp/householder, mobile home	year	390	90	28r
Energy exp/householder, multifamily	year	252	90	28r
Gas, cooking, winter, 10 therms	month	6.19	92	56c
Gas, cooking, winter, 30 therms	month	15.57	92	56c
Gas, cooking, winter, 50 therms	month	24.95	92	56c
Gas, heating, winter, 100 therms	month	45.91	92	56c
Gas, heating, winter, average use	month	40.53	92	56c
Gas, natural	mil Btu	3.60	90	64s
Gas, natural	000 cu ft	4.68	91	46s
Gas, natural, exp	year	440	91	46s
Gasoline, motor	gal	1.26	4Q 92	4c
Gasoline, unleaded regular	mil Btu	9.45	90	64s
Entertainment				
Bowling, evening rate	game	2.24	4Q 92	4c
Miniature golf admission	adult	6.18	92	1r
Miniature golf admission	child	5.14	92	1r
Monopoly game, Parker Brothers', No. 9		10.58	4Q 92	4c
Movie	admission	5.50	4Q 92	4c
Tennis balls, yellow, Wilson or Penn, 3	can	2.41	4Q 92	4c
Waterpark admission	adult	11.00	92	1r
Waterpark admission	child	8.55	92	1r
Funerals				
Casket, 18-gauge steel, velvet interior		1781.09	91	24r
Cosmetology, hair care, etc.		84.64	91	24r
Embalming		207.41	91	24r
Facility use for ceremony		205.76	91	24r
Hearse, local		105.14	91	24r
Limousine, local		83.21	91	24r
Remains to funeral home, transfer		113.82	91	24r
Service charge, professional		626.33	91	24r
Vault, concrete, non-metallic liner		599.54	91	24r
Viewing facilities, use		85.81	91	24r
Goods and Services				
ACCRA Index, Miscellaneous Goods and Services		106.30	4Q 92	4c
Groceries				
ACCRA Index, Groceries		98.90	4Q 92	4c
Apples, Red Delicious	lb	0.80	4/93	16r
Babyfood, strained vegetables, lowest price	4-4.5 oz jar	0.27	4Q 92	4c
Bacon	lb	1.79	4/93	16r
Bananas	lb	0.38	4Q 92	4c
Bananas	lb	0.53	4/93	16r
Bologna, all beef or mixed	lb	2.67	4/93	16r
Bread, white	24 oz	0.56	4Q 92	4c
Bread, white, pan	lb	0.81	4/93	16r
Carrots, short trimmed and topped	lb	0.39	4/93	16r
Cheese, Kraft grated Parmesan	8-oz canister	3.53	4Q 92	4c
Chicken, fresh, whole	lb	0.94	4/93	16r
Chicken, fryer, whole	lb	0.88	4Q 92	4c
Chicken breast, bone-in	lb	2.19	4/93	16r
Chuck roast, graded and ungraded, ex USDA prime and choice	lb	2.26	4/93	16r
Cigarettes, Winston	carton	20.20	4Q 92	4c
Coffee, 100% ground roast, all sizes	lb	2.33	4/93	16r
Coffee, vacuum-packed	13-oz can	2.09	4Q 92	4c
Corn, frozen	10 oz	0.66	4Q 92	4c
Corn Flakes, Kellogg's or Post Toasties	18 oz	1.97	4Q 92	4c
Eggs, Grade A large	doz	0.88	4Q 92	4c
Eggs, Grade AA large	doz	1.18	4/93	16r
Flour, white, all purpose	lb	0.22	4/93	16r

Values are in dollars or fractions of dollars. In the column headed *Ref*, references are shown to sources. Each reference is followed by a letter. These refer to the geographical level for which data were reported: s=State, r=Region, and c=City or metro. The abbreviation *ex* is used to mean *except* or *excluding*; *exp* stands for expenditures. For other abbreviations and further explanations, please see the Introduction.

Bellingham, WA - continued

Item	Per	Value	Date	Ref.
Groceries				
Grapefruit	lb	0.52	4/93	16r
Grapes, Thompson Seedless	lb	1.50	4/93	16r
Ground beef, 100% beef	lb	1.44	4/93	16r
Ground beef, lean and extra lean	lb	2.34	4/93	16r
Ground beef or hamburger	lb	1.60	4Q 92	4c
Ham, boneless, excluding canned	lb	2.56	4/93	16r
Honey, jar	8 oz	0.89-1.00	92	5r
Honey, jar	lb	1.35-1.97	92	5r
Honey, squeeze bear	12-oz	1.19-1.50	92	5r
Ice cream, prepackaged, bulk, regular	1/2 gal	2.40	4/93	16r
Lemons	lb	0.81	4/93	16r
Lettuce, iceberg	head	0.86	4Q 92	4c
Lettuce, iceberg	lb	0.84	4/93	16r
Margarine, Blue Bonnet or Parkay cubes	lb	0.46	4Q 92	4c
Margarine, stick	lb	0.81	4/93	16r
Milk, whole	1/2 gal	1.41	4Q 92	4c
Orange juice, Minute Maid frozen	12-oz can	1.07	4Q 92	4c
Oranges, navel	lb	0.48	4/93	16r
Peaches	29-oz can	1.49	4Q 92	4c
Peas Sweet, Del Monte or Green Giant	15-17 oz can	0.66	4Q 92	4c
Pork chops, center cut, bone-in	lb	3.25	4/93	16r
Potato chips	16 oz	2.89	4/93	16r
Potatoes, white	lb	0.38	4/93	16r
Potatoes, white or red	10-lb sack	1.48	4Q 92	4c
Round roast, graded & ungraded, ex USDA prime & choice	lb	3.00	4/93	16r
Round roast, USDA choice, boneless	lb	3.16	4/93	16r
Sausage, Jimmy Dean, 100% pork	lb	3.15	4Q 92	4c
Shortening, vegetable oil blends	lb	0.86	4/93	16r
Shortening, vegetable, Crisco	3-lb can	1.39	4Q 92	4c
Soft drink, Coca Cola	2 liter	1.22	4Q 92	4c
Spaghetti and macaroni	lb	0.84	4/93	16r
Steak, round, graded & ungraded, ex USDA prime & choice	lb	3.34	4/93	16r
Steak, round, USDA choice, boneless	lb	3.24	4/93	16r
Steak, sirloin, graded & ungraded, ex USDA prime & choice	lb	3.75	4/93	16r
Steak, sirloin, USDA choice, boneless	lb	4.49	4/93	16r
Steak, T-bone	lb	4.99	4Q 92	4c
Sugar, cane or beet	4 lb	1.22	4Q 92	4c
Sugar, white	lb	0.41	4/93	16r
Sugar, white, 33-80 oz pk	lb	0.38	4/93	16r
Tomatoes, field grown	lb	1.01	4/93	16r
Tomatoes, Hunt's or Del Monte	14.5-oz can	0.58	4Q 92	4c
Tuna, chunk, light	6.125-6.5 oz can	0.54	4Q 92	4c
Turkey, frozen, whole	lb	1.04	4/93	16r
Health Care				
ACCRA Index, Health Care		141.10	4Q 92	4c
Analgesic, Aspirin, Bayer, 325 mg tablets	100	4.93	4Q 92	4c
Childbirth, cesarean, hospital		5533	91	62r
Childbirth, cesarean, physician's fee		2053	91	62r
Childbirth, normal, hospital		2745	91	62r
Childbirth, normal, physician's fee		1492	91	62r
Dentist's fee, adult teeth cleaning and periodic oral exam	visit	74.80	4Q 92	4c
Doctor's fee, routine exam, established patient	visit	47.90	4Q 92	4c
Hospital care, semiprivate room	day	485.00	4Q 92	4c
Medical insurance premium, per employee, small group comprehensive	month	292.00	10/91	25c
Medical plan per employee	year	3421	91	45r
Mental health care, exp	capita	37.60-53.67	90	38s
Physician fee, family practice, first-visit		111.00	91	62r

Bellingham, WA - continued

Item	Per	Value	Date	Ref.
Health Care - continued				
Physician fee, family practice, revisit		45.00	91	62r
Physician fee, general practice, first-visit		100.00	91	62r
Physician fee, general practice, revisit		40.00	91	62r
Physician fee, internal medicine, first-visit		137.00	91	62r
Physician fee, internal medicine, revisit		48.00	91	62r
Physician fee, median, neurosurgeon, first-visit		157.00	91	62r
Physician fee, median, nonsurgical specialist, first-visit		131.00	91	62r
Physician fee, median, orthopedic surgeon, first-visit		124.00	91	62r
Physician fee, median, plastic surgeon, first-visit		88.00	91	62r
Physician fee, median, surgical specialist, first-visit		100.00	91	62r
Physician fee, neurosurgeon, revisit		51.00	91	62r
Physician fee, nonsurgical specialist, revisit		47.00	91	62r
Physician fee, obstetrics/gynecology, first-visit		95.00	91	62r
Physician fee, obstetrics/gynecology, revisit		50.00	91	62r
Physician fee, orthopedic surgeon, revisit		51.00	91	62r
Physician fee, pediatrician, first-visit		81.00	91	62r
Physician fee, pediatrician, revisit		42.00	91	62r
Physician fee, plastic surgeon, revisit		48.00	91	62r
Physician fee, surgical specialist, revisit		49.00	91	62r
Substance abuse, hospital ancillary charge	incident	1360	90	70s
Substance abuse, hospital physician charge	incident	150	90	70s
Substance abuse, hospital room and board	incident	4200	90	70s
Household Goods				
Appliance repair, home, service call, washing machine	min labor charge	34.16	4Q 92	4c
Laundry detergent, Tide Ultra, Bold, or Cheer	42 oz	3.60	4Q 92	4c
Tissues, facial, Kleenex brand	175-count box	1.33	4Q 92	4c
Housing				
ACCRA Index, Housing		116.90	4Q 92	4c
House, 1,800 sq ft, 8,000 sq ft lot, new, urban	total	129500	4Q 92	4c
House payment, principal and interest, 25% down payment	month	719	4Q 92	4c
Mortgage rate, incl. points & origination fee, 30-year fixed or adjustable rate	percent	8.10	4Q 92	4c
Rent, apartment, 2 bedrooms - 1-1/2 to 2 baths, unfurnished, 950 sq ft, water	month	575	4Q 92	4c
Rental unit, 1 bedroom	month	526	93	23c
Rental unit, 2 bedroom	month	619	93	23c
Rental unit, 3 bedroom	month	792	93	23c
Rental unit, 4 bedroom	month	870	93	23c
Rental unit, efficiency	month	431	93	23c
Insurance and Pensions				
Auto insurance, private passenger	year	627.71	91	63s
Personal Goods				
Shampoo, Alberto VO5	15 oz	1.20	4Q 92	4c
Toothpaste, Crest or Colgate	6-7 oz	2.01	4Q 92	4c
Personal Services				
Dry cleaning, man's 2-piece suit		7.01	4Q 92	4c
Haircare, woman's shampoo, trim and blow-dry		19.19	4Q 92	4c
Haircut, man's barbershop, no styling		9.50	4Q 92	4c
Restaurant Food				
Chicken, fried, thigh and drumstick		2.29	4Q 92	4c
Hamburger with cheese	1/4 lb	1.95	4Q 92	4c

Values are in dollars or fractions of dollars. In the column headed *Ref*, references are shown to sources. Each reference is followed by a letter. These refer to the geographical level for which data were reported: s=State, r=Region, and c=City or metro. The abbreviation *ex* is used to mean *except* or *excluding*; *exp* stands for *expenditures*. For other abbreviations and further explanations, please see the Introduction.

Bellingham, WA - continued

Item	Per	Value	Date	Ref.
Restaurant Food				
Pizza, Pizza Hut or Pizza Inn, cheese, thin crust	12-13 in	9.66	4Q 92	4c
Taxes				
Tax, cigarette	pack	34	91	77s
Tax, gasoline	gal	23	91	77s
Taxes, state	capita	1592	91	77s
Transportation				
ACCRA Index, Transportation		97.10	4Q 92	4c
Bus fare	one-way	0.25	3/93	2c
Bus fare, up to 10 miles	one-way	0.25	4Q 92	4c
Driver's license fee		14.00	12/90	43s
Tire balance, computer or spin balance, front	wheel	6.34	4Q 92	4c
Travel				
Business travel	day	178.00	4/93	89r
Utilities				
ACCRA Index, Utilities		60.20	4Q 92	4c
Electricity	mil Btu	10.03	90	64s
Electricity, partial electric and other energy, 1,800 sq ft living area new home	month	31.06	4Q 92	4c

Benton Harbor-Saint Joseph, MI

Item	Per	Value	Date	Ref.
Composite ACCRA index		105.70	4Q 92	4c
Alcoholic Beverages				
Beer, Miller Lite or Budweiser, 12-oz containers	6 pack	3.73	4Q 92	4c
Liquor, J & B Scotch	750 ml	17.51	4Q 92	4c
Wine, Gallo Chablis blanc, 1.5 liter	bottle	5.71	4Q 92	4c
Child Care				
Child care fee, average, center	hour	1.63	90	65r
Child care fee, average, nonregulated family day care	hour	1.83	90	65r
Child care fee, average, regulated family day care	hour	1.42	90	65r
Clothing				
Jeans, man's denim		33.99	4Q 92	4c
Shirt, man's dress shirt		22.00	4Q 92	4c
Undervest, boy's size 10-14, cotton	3	4.62	4Q 92	4c
Communications				
Long-distance telephone service, day, initial minute, 0-100 miles	min	0.14-0.36	91	12s
Long-distance telephone service, day, additional minute, 0-100 miles	min	0.14-0.36	91	12s
Long-distance telephone service, evenings/weekends, 0-100 mi, initial minute	min	0.07-0.19	91	12s
Long-distance telephone service, evenings/weekends, 0-100 mi, additional minute	min	0.04-0.14	91	12s
Newspaper subscription, daily and Sunday home delivery, large-city	month	7.80	4Q 92	4c
Telephone, flat rate	month	9.40	91	11c
Telephone bill, family of four	month	21.50	4Q 92	4c
Education				
Board, 4-yr private college/university	year	1698	91	22s
Board, 4-yr public college/university	year	1962	91	22s
Expenditures, local gov't, public elementary/secondary	pupil	5671	92	20s
Room, 4-year private college/university	year	1440	91	22s
Room, 4-year public college/university	year	1687	91	22s
Tuition, 2-year private college/university	year	4749	91	22s
Tuition, 2-year public college/university	year	1124	91	22s
Tuition, 4-year private college/university	year	6885	91	22s
Tuition, 4-year public college/university, in-state	year	2635	91	22s

Item	Per	Value	Date	Ref.
Energy and Fuels				
Coal	mil Btu	1.63	90	64s
Energy	mil Btu	8.17	90	64s
Energy, combined forms, 1,800 sq ft heating area	month	93.67	4Q 92	4c
Energy, exc electricity, 1,800 sq ft heating area	month	47.02	4Q 92	4c
Energy exp/householder, 1-family unit	year	471	90	28r
Energy exp/householder, <1,000 sq ft heating area	year	430	90	28r
Energy exp/householder, 1,000-1,999 sq ft heating area	year	481	90	28r
Energy exp/householder, 2,000+ sq ft heating area	year	473	90	28r
Energy exp/householder, mobile home	year	430	90	28r
Energy exp/householder, multifamily	year	461	90	28r
Gas, natural	mil Btu	4.36	90	64s
Gas, natural	000 cu ft	5.07	91	46s
Gas, natural, exp	year	655	91	46s
Gasoline, motor	gal	1.10	4Q 92	4c
Gasoline, unleaded regular	mil Btu	8.78	90	64s
Entertainment				
Bowling, evening rate	game	1.85	4Q 92	4c
Miniature golf admission	adult	6.18	92	1r
Miniature golf admission	child	5.14	92	1r
Monopoly game, Parker Brothers', No. 9		13.89	4Q 92	4c
Movie	admission	5.50	4Q 92	4c
Tennis balls, yellow, Wilson or Penn, 3	can	3.02	4Q 92	4c
Waterpark admission	adult	11.00	92	1r
Waterpark admission	child	8.55	92	1r
Funerals				
Casket, 18-gauge steel, velvet interior		1926.72	91	24r
Cosmetology, hair care, etc.		97.64	91	24r
Embalming		249.14	91	24r
Facility use for ceremony		208.59	91	24r
Hearse, local		130.12	91	24r
Limousine, local		104.66	91	24r
Remains to funeral home, transfer		93.61	91	24r
Service charge, professional		724.62	91	24r
Vault, concrete, non-metallic liner		734.53	91	24r
Viewing facilities, use		236.06	91	24r
Goods and Services				
ACCRA Index, Miscellaneous Goods and Services		104.30	4Q 92	4c
Groceries				
ACCRA Index, Groceries		111.20	4Q 92	4c
Apples, Red Delicious	lb	0.77	4/93	16r
Babyfood, strained vegetables, lowest price	4-4.5 oz jar	0.41	4Q 92	4c
Bacon	lb	1.85	4/93	16r
Bananas	lb	0.45	4Q 92	4c
Bananas	lb	0.46	4/93	16r
Beef, stew, boneless	lb	2.53	4/93	16r
Bologna, all beef or mixed	lb	2.19	4/93	16r
Bread, white	24 oz	0.91	4Q 92	4c
Bread, white, pan	lb	0.78	4/93	16r
Butter	lb	1.50	4/93	16r
Cabbage	lb	0.40	4/93	16r
Carrots, short trimmed and topped	lb	0.45	4/93	16r
Cheese, Cheddar	lb	3.47	4/93	16r
Cheese, Kraft grated Parmesan	8-oz canister	3.45	4Q 92	4c
Chicken, fresh, whole	lb	0.84	4/93	16r
Chicken, fryer, whole	lb	0.79	4Q 92	4c
Chicken breast, bone-in	lb	1.94	4/93	16r
Chicken legs, bone-in	lb	1.02	4/93	16r
Chuck roast, graded and ungraded, ex USDA prime and choice	lb	2.43	4/93	16r

Values are in dollars or fractions of dollars. In the column headed *Ref*, references are shown to sources. Each reference is followed by a letter. These refer to the geographical level for which data were reported: s=State, r=Region, and c=City or metro. The abbreviation *ex* is used to mean *except* or *excluding*; *exp* stands for expenditures. For other abbreviations and further explanations, please see the Introduction.

Benton Harbor-Saint Joseph, MI - continued

Item	Per	Value	Date	Ref.
Groceries				
Chuck roast, USDA choice, bone-in	lb	2.11	4/93	16r
Chuck roast, USDA choice, boneless	lb	2.44	4/93	16r
Cigarettes, Winston	carton	17.86	4Q 92	4c
Coffee, 100% ground roast, all sizes	lb	2.47	4/93	16r
Coffee, vacuum-packed	13-oz can	2.01	4Q 92	4c
Cookies, chocolate chip	lb	2.73	4/93	16r
Corn, frozen	10 oz	0.70	4Q 92	4c
Corn Flakes, Kellogg's or Post Toasties	18 oz	2.19	4Q 92	4c
Eggs, Grade A large	doz	0.81	4Q 92	4c
Eggs, Grade A large	doz	0.93	4/93	16r
Flour, white, all purpose	lb	0.21	4/93	16r
Grapefruit	lb	0.45	4/93	16r
Grapes, Thompson Seedless	lb	1.46	4/93	16r
Ground beef, 100% beef	lb	1.63	4/93	16r
Ground beef, lean and extra lean	lb	2.08	4/93	16r
Ground beef or hamburger	lb	1.89	4Q 92	4c
Ground chuck, 100% beef	lb	1.94	4/93	16r
Ham, boneless, excluding canned	lb	2.21	4/93	16r
Honey, jar	8 oz	0.97-1.25	92	5r
Honey, jar	lb	1.25-2.25	92	5r
Honey, squeeze bear	12-oz	1.25-1.99	92	5r
Ice cream, prepackaged, bulk, regular	1/2 gal	2.41	4/93	16r
Lemons	lb	0.82	4/93	16r
Lettuce, iceberg	head	1.03	4Q 92	4c
Lettuce, iceberg	lb	0.83	4/93	16r
Margarine, Blue Bonnet or Parkay cubes	lb	0.85	4Q 92	4c
Margarine, stick	lb	0.77	4/93	16r
Milk, whole	1/2 gal	1.60	4Q 92	4c
Orange juice, Minute Maid frozen	12-oz can	1.56	4Q 92	4c
Oranges, navel	lb	0.50	4/93	16r
Peaches	29-oz can	1.53	4Q 92	4c
Peanut butter, creamy, all sizes	lb	1.82	4/93	16r
Pears, Anjou	lb	0.85	4/93	16r
Peas Sweet, Del Monte or Green Giant	15-17 oz can	0.67	4Q 92	4c
Pork chops, center cut, bone-in	lb	3.17	4/93	16r
Potato chips	16 oz	2.68	4/93	16r
Potatoes, white	lb	0.26	4/93	16r
Potatoes, white or red	10-lb sack	2.03	4Q 92	4c
Round roast, graded & ungraded, ex USDA prime & choice	lb	2.88	4/93	16r
Round roast, USDA choice, boneless	lb	2.96	4/93	16r
Sausage, Jimmy Dean, 100% pork	lb	2.75	4Q 92	4c
Shortening, vegetable oil blends	lb	0.79	4/93	16r
Shortening, vegetable, Crisco	3-lb can	2.52	4Q 92	4c
Soft drink, Coca Cola	2 liter	1.27	4Q 92	4c
Spaghetti and macaroni	lb	0.76	4/93	16r
Steak, rib eye, USDA choice, boneless	lb	6.29	4/93	16r
Steak, round, USDA choice, boneless	lb	3.24	4/93	16r
Steak, sirloin, graded & ungraded, ex USDA prime & choice	lb	4.00	4/93	16r
Steak, sirloin, USDA choice, bone-in	lb	3.57	4/93	16r
Steak, sirloin, USDA choice, boneless	lb	4.17	4/93	16r
Steak, T-bone	lb	5.33	4Q 92	4c
Steak, T-bone, USDA choice, bone-in	lb	5.60	4/93	16r
Strawberries, dry pint	12 oz	0.90	4/93	16r
Sugar, cane or beet	4 lb	1.39	4Q 92	4c
Sugar, white	lb	0.36	4/93	16r
Sugar, white, 33-80 oz pk	lb	0.35	4/93	16r
Tomatoes, field grown	lb	0.99	4/93	16r
Tomatoes, Hunt's or Del Monte	14.5-oz can	0.76	4Q 92	4c
Tuna, chunk, light	6.125-6.5 oz can	0.75	4Q 92	4c
Tuna, chunk, light	lb	1.76	4/93	16r
Turkey, frozen, whole	lb	0.91	4/93	16r

Benton Harbor-Saint Joseph, MI - continued

Item	Per	Value	Date	Ref.
Health Care				
ACCRA Index, Health Care		96.80	4Q 92	4c
Analgesic, Aspirin, Bayer, 325 mg tablets	100	5.07	4Q 92	4c
Childbirth, cesarean, hospital		4688	91	62r
Childbirth, cesarean, physician's fee		2053	91	62r
Childbirth, normal, hospital		2657	91	62r
Childbirth, normal, physician's fee		1492	91	62r
Dentist's fee, adult teeth cleaning and periodic oral exam	visit	46.67	4Q 92	4c
Doctor's fee, routine exam, established patient	visit	33.00	4Q 92	4c
Hospital care, semiprivate room	day	326.00	4Q 92	4c
Medical insurance premium, per employee, small group comprehensive	month	317.55	10/91	25c
Medical plan per employee	year	3443	91	45r
Mental health care, exp	capita	53.68-118.35	90	38s
Mental health care, exp, state mental health agency	capita	73.73	90	38s
Mental health care, hospital psychiatric services, non-Federal, exp	capita	22.52	88	38s
Mental health care, mental health organization, multiservice, exp	capita	42.68	88	38s
Mental health care, psychiatric hospitals, private, exp	capita	10.80	88	38s
Mental health care, psychiatric out-patient clinics, freestanding, exp	capita	3.47	88	38s
Mental health care, psychiatric partial-care organizations, freestanding, exp	capita	0.73	88	38s
Mental health care, state and county mental hospitals, exp	capita	36.77	88	38s
Mental health care, VA medical centers, exp	capita	4.03	88	38s
Physician fee, family practice, first-visit		76.00	91	62r
Physician fee, family practice, revisit		33.00	91	62r
Physician fee, general practice, first-visit		61.00	91	62r
Physician fee, general practice, revisit		31.00	91	62r
Physician fee, general surgeon, first-visit		65.00	91	62r
Physician fee, general surgeon, revisit		35.00	91	62r
Physician fee, internal medicine, first-visit		91.00	91	62r
Physician fee, internal medicine, revisit		40.00	91	62r
Physician fee, median, neurosurgeon, first-visit		106.00	91	62r
Physician fee, median, nonsurgical specialist, first-visit		90.00	91	62r
Physician fee, median, orthopedic surgeon, first-visit		83.00	91	62r
Physician fee, median, surgical specialist, first-visit		61.00	91	62r
Physician fee, neurosurgeon, revisit		41.00	91	62r
Physician fee, nonsurgical specialist, revisit		40.00	91	62r
Physician fee, obstetrics/gynecology, first-visit		61.00	91	62r
Physician fee, obstetrics/gynecology, revisit		40.00	91	62r
Physician fee, orthopedic surgeon, revisit		41.00	91	62r
Physician fee, pediatrician, first-visit		46.00	91	62r
Physician fee, pediatrician, revisit		33.00	91	62r
Physician fee, surgical specialist, revisit		36.00	91	62r
Substance abuse, hospital ancillary charge	incident	1480	90	70s
Substance abuse, hospital physician charge	incident	250	90	70s
Substance abuse, hospital room and board	incident	4070	90	70s
Household Goods				
Appliance repair, home, service call, washing machine	min labor charge	40.98	4Q 92	4c
Laundry detergent, Tide Ultra, Bold, or Cheer	42 oz	4.19	4Q 92	4c
Tissues, facial, Kleenex brand	175-count box	1.17	4Q 92	4c

Values are in dollars or fractions of dollars. In the column headed *Ref*, references are shown as sources. Each reference is followed by a letter. These refer to the geographical level for which data were reported: s=State, r=Region, and c=City or metro. The abbreviation *ex* is used to mean *except* or *excluding*; *exp* stands for expenditures. For other abbreviations and further explanations, please see the Introduction.

Benton Harbor-Saint Joseph, MI - continued

Item	Per	Value	Date	Ref.
Housing				
ACCRA Index, Housing		115.50	4Q 92	4c
House, 1,800 sq ft, 8,000 sq ft lot, new, urban	total	133200	4Q 92	4c
House payment, principal and interest, 25% down payment	month	747	4Q 92	4c
Mortgage rate, incl. points & origination fee, 30-year fixed or adjustable rate	per-cent	8.20	4Q 92	4c
Rent, apartment, 2 bedrooms - 1-1/2 to 2 baths, unfurnished, 950 sq ft, water	month	484	4Q 92	4c
Rental unit, 1 bedroom	month	402	93	23c
Rental unit, 2 bedroom	month	471	93	23c
Rental unit, 3 bedroom	month	591	93	23c
Rental unit, 4 bedroom	month	602	93	23c
Rental unit, efficiency	month	330	93	23c
Insurance and Pensions				
Auto insurance, private passenger	year	716.78	91	63s
Personal Goods				
Shampoo, Alberto VO5	15 oz	1.08	4Q 92	4c
Toothpaste, Crest or Colgate	6-7 oz	1.93	4Q 92	4c
Personal Services				
Dry cleaning, man's 2-piece suit		6.42	4Q 92	4c
Haircare, woman's shampoo, trim and blow-dry		15.40	4Q 92	4c
Haircut, man's barbershop, no styling		6.50	4Q 92	4c
Restaurant Food				
Chicken, fried, thigh and drumstick		1.98	4Q 92	4c
Hamburger with cheese	1/4 lb	1.97	4Q 92	4c
Pizza, Pizza Hut or Pizza Inn, cheese, thin crust	12-13 in	7.99	4Q 92	4c
Taxes				
Tax, cigarette	pack	25	91	77s
Tax, gasoline	gal	15	91	77s
Taxes, state	capita	1185	91	77s
Transportation				
ACCRA Index, Transportation		95.70	4Q 92	4c
Driver's license fee		12.00	12/90	43s
Tire balance, computer or spin balance, front	wheel	6.12	4Q 92	4c
Vehicle registration and license plate	year	14.00-200.00	93	40s
Utilities				
ACCRA Index, Utilities		88.30	4Q 92	4c
Electricity	mil Btu	20.85	90	64s
Electricity, partial electric and other energy, 1,800 sq ft living area new home	month	46.65	4Q 92	4c

Bergen-Passaic, NJ

Item	Per	Value	Date	Ref.
Child Care				
Child care fee, average, center	hour	2.18	90	65r
Child care fee, average, nonregulated family day care	hour	1.83	90	65r
Child care fee, average, regulated family day care	hour	2.02	90	65r
Communications				
Long-distance telephone service, day, initial minute, 0-100 miles	min	0.09-0.42	91	12s
Long-distance telephone service, day, additional minute, 0-100 miles	min	0.03-0.12	91	12s
Education				
Board, 4-yr private college/university	year	2883	91	22s
Board, 4-yr public college/university	year	1647	91	22s
Expenditures, local gov't, public elementary/secondary	pupil	9940	92	20s
Room, 4-year private college/university	year	2440	91	22s
Room, 4-year public college/university	year	2415	91	22s

Bergen-Passaic, NJ - continued

Item	Per	Value	Date	Ref.
Education - continued				
Tuition, 2-year private college/university	year	5874	91	22s
Tuition, 2-year public college/university	year	1235	91	22s
Tuition, 4-year private college/university	year	10281	91	22s
Tuition, 4-year public college/university, in-state	year	2860	91	22s
Energy and Fuels				
Coal	mil Btu	1.79	90	64s
Energy	mil Btu	9.32	90	64s
Energy exp/householder, 1-family unit	year	588	90	28r
Energy exp/householder, <1,000 sq ft heating area	year	477	90	28r
Energy exp/householder, 1,000-1,999 sq ft heating area	year	517	90	28r
Energy exp/householder, 2,000+ sq ft heating area	year	630	90	28r
Energy exp/householder, mobile home	year	412	90	28r
Energy exp/householder, multifamily	year	498	90	28r
Gas, natural	mil Btu	5.05	90	64s
Gas, natural	000 cu ft	6.73	91	46s
Gas, natural, exp	year	593	91	46s
Gasoline, unleaded regular	mil Btu	9.03	90	64s
Funerals				
Casket, 18-gauge steel, velvet interior		1811.58	91	24r
Cosmetology, hair care, etc.		111.08	91	24r
Embalming		329.42	91	24r
Facility use for ceremony		201.29	91	24r
Hearse, local		135.27	91	24r
Limousine, local		127.24	91	24r
Remains to funeral home, transfer		103.98	91	24r
Service charge, professional		724.98	91	24r
Vault, concrete, non-metallic liner		766.71	91	24r
Viewing facilities, use		260.60	91	24r
Groceries				
Apples, Red Delicious	lb	0.85	4/93	16r
Bacon	lb	2.12	4/93	16r
Bananas	lb	0.54	4/93	16r
Bread, white, pan	lb	0.81	4/93	16r
Butter	lb	2.02	4/93	16r
Carrots, short trimmed and topped	lb	0.51	4/93	16r
Chicken, fresh, whole	lb	1.04	4/93	16r
Chicken breast, bone-in	lb	2.21	4/93	16r
Chicken legs, bone-in	lb	1.16	4/93	16r
Chuck roast, USDA choice, boneless	lb	2.82	4/93	16r
Coffee, 100% ground roast, all sizes	lb	2.66	4/93	16r
Cucumbers	lb	0.85	4/93	16r
Eggs, Grade A large	doz	1.15	4/93	16r
Grapefruit	lb	0.45	4/93	16r
Grapes, Thompson Seedless	lb	1.52	4/93	16r
Ground beef, lean and extra lean	lb	2.36	4/93	16r
Ground chuck, 100% beef	lb	2.02	4/93	16r
Honey, jar	8 oz	0.96-1.75	92	5r
Honey, jar	lb	1.50-3.00	92	5r
Honey, squeeze bear	12-oz	1.50-1.99	92	5r
Ice cream, prepackaged, bulk, regular	1/2 gal	2.80	4/93	16r
Lemons	lb	0.96	4/93	16r
Lettuce, iceberg	lb	0.95	4/93	16r
Margarine, stick	lb	0.81	4/93	16r
Milk, fresh, whole, fortified	1/2 gal	1.30	4/93	16r
Oranges, navel	lb	0.56	4/93	16r
Peanut butter, creamy, all sizes	lb	1.88	4/93	16r
Pork chops, center cut, bone-in	lb	3.34	4/93	16r
Potato chips	16 oz	2.88	4/93	16r
Potatoes, white	lb	0.37	4/93	16r
Rib roast, USDA choice, bone-in	lb	4.94	4/93	16r
Round roast, USDA choice, boneless	lb	3.17	4/93	16r
Shortening, vegetable oil blends	lb	0.98	4/93	16r
Spaghetti and macaroni	lb	0.82	4/93	16r
Steak, round, graded & ungraded, ex USDA prime & choice	lb	4.04	4/93	16r
Steak, round, USDA choice, boneless	lb	3.90	4/93	16r

Values are in dollars or fractions of dollars. In the column headed *Ref*, references are shown to sources. Each reference is followed by a letter. These refer to the geographical level for which data were reported: s=State, r=Region, and c=City or metro. The abbreviation *ex* is used to mean *except* or *excluding*; *exp* stands for expenditures. For other abbreviations and further explanations, please see the Introduction.

Bergen-Passaic, NJ - continued

Item	Per	Value	Date	Ref.
Groceries				
Steak, sirloin, USDA choice, boneless	lb	4.97	4/93	16r
Strawberries, dry pint	12 oz	0.90	4/93	16r
Sugar, white	lb	0.50	4/93	16r
Sugar, white, 33-80 oz pk	lb	0.41	4/93	16r
Tomatoes, field grown	lb	1.23	4/93	16r
Tuna, chunk, light	lb	2.22	4/93	16r
Turkey, frozen, whole	lb	1.04	4/93	16r
Health Care				
Childbirth, cesarean, hospital		5826	91	62r
Childbirth, cesarean, physician's fee		2053	91	62r
Childbirth, normal, hospital		2964	91	62r
Childbirth, normal, physician's fee		1492	91	62r
Medical plan per employee	year	3942	91	45r
Mental health care, exp	capita	28.84-37.59	90	38s
Mental health care, exp, state mental health agency	capita	57.16	90	38s
Mental health care, hospital psychiatric services, non-Federal, exp	capita	16.04	88	38s
Mental health care, mental health organization, multiservice, exp	capita	11.14	88	38s
Mental health care, psychiatric hospitals, private, exp	capita	17.85	88	38s
Mental health care, psychiatric out-patient clinics, freestanding, exp	capita	1.56	88	38s
Mental health care, psychiatric partial-care organizations, freestanding, exp	capita	0.66	88	38s
Mental health care, state and county mental hospitals, exp	capita	36.80	88	38s
Mental health care, VA medical centers, exp	capita	5.61	88	38s
Prescription drug co-pay, Medicaid	month	5.00	91	21s
Substance abuse, hospital ancillary charge	incident	780	90	70s
Substance abuse, hospital physician charge	incident	550	90	70s
Substance abuse, hospital room and board	incident	6300	90	70s
Insurance and Pensions				
Auto insurance, private passenger	year	1081.45	91	63s
Taxes				
Tax, cigarette	pack	40	91	77s
Tax, gasoline	gal	10.50	91	77s
Taxes, state	capita	1501	91	77s
Transportation				
Driver's license fee		16.00-17.50	12/90	43s
Vehicle registration and license plate	year	32.90-93.90	93	44s
Travel				
Business travel	day	165.00	4/93	89r
Utilities				
Electricity	mil Btu	26.63	90	64s

Billings, MT

Item	Per	Value	Date	Ref.
Composite ACCRA index		103.80	4Q 92	4c
Alcoholic Beverages				
Beer, Miller Lite or Budweiser, 12-oz containers	6 pack	4.10	4Q 92	4c
Liquor, J & B Scotch	750 ml	18.10	4Q 92	4c
Wine, Gallo Chablis blanc, 1.5 liter	bottle	5.55	4Q 92	4c
Child Care				
Child care fee, average, center	hour	1.71	90	65r
Child care fee, average, nonregulated family day care	hour	1.32	90	65r
Child care fee, average, regulated family day care	hour	1.86	90	65r

Billings, MT - continued

Item	Per	Value	Date	Ref.
Clothing				
Jeans, man's denim		28.79	4Q 92	4c
Shirt, man's dress shirt		20.59	4Q 92	4c
Undervest, boy's size 10-14, cotton	3	5.85	4Q 92	4c
Communications				
Long-distance telephone service, day, initial minute, 0-100 miles	min	0.13-0.36	91	12s
Long-distance telephone service, day, additional minute, 0-100 miles	min	0.04-0.27	91	12s
Long-distance telephone service, evenings/weekends, 0-100 mi, initial minute	min	0.08-0.22	91	12s
Long-distance telephone service, evenings/weekends, 0-100 mi, additional minute	min	0.02-0.16	91	12s
Newspaper subscription, daily and Sunday home delivery, large-city	month	16.30	4Q 92	4c
Telephone, flat rate	month	13.84	91	11c
Telephone bill, family of four	month	19.25	4Q 92	4c
Education				
Board, 4-yr private college/university	year	1831	91	22s
Board, 4-yr public college/university	year	2200	91	22s
Expenditures, local gov't, public elementary/secondary	pupil	5271	92	20s
Room, 4-year private college/university	year	1209	91	22s
Room, 4-year public college/university	year	1427	91	22s
Tuition, 2-year private college/university	year	1140	91	22s
Tuition, 2-year public college/university	year	964	91	22s
Tuition, 4-year private college/university	year	5565	91	22s
Tuition, 4-year public college/university, in-state	year	1553	91	22s
Energy and Fuels				
Coal	mil Btu	0.70	90	64s
Energy	mil Btu	7.87	90	64s
Energy, combined forms, 1,800 sq ft heating area	month	86.68	4Q 92	4c
Energy, exc electricity, 1,800 sq ft heating area	month	42.05	4Q 92	4c
Energy exp/householder, 1-family unit	year	372	90	28r
Energy exp/householder, <1,000 sq ft heating area	year	335	90	28r
Energy exp/householder, 1,000-1,999 sq ft heating area	year	365	90	28r
Energy exp/householder, 2,000+ sq ft heating area	year	411	90	28r
Energy exp/householder, mobile home	year	305	90	28r
Energy exp/householder, multifamily	year	372	90	28r
Gas, cooking, 10 therms	month	8.41	92	56c
Gas, cooking, 30 therms	month	11.74	92	56c
Gas, cooking, 50 therms	month	24.06	92	56c
Gas, heating, winter, 100 therms	month	43.62	92	56c
Gas, heating, winter, average use	month	54.77	92	56c
Gas, natural	mil Btu	4.16	90	64s
Gas, natural	000 cu ft	4.52	91	46s
Gas, natural, exp	year	468	91	46s
Gasoline, motor	gal	1.30	4Q 92	4c
Gasoline, unleaded regular	mil Btu	9.56	90	64s
Entertainment				
Bowling, evening rate	game	1.57	4Q 92	4c
Miniature golf admission	adult	6.18	92	1r
Miniature golf admission	child	5.14	92	1r
Monopoly game, Parker Brothers', No. 9		10.59	4Q 92	4c
Movie	admission	5.25	4Q 92	4c
Tennis balls, yellow, Wilson or Penn, 3	can	2.42	4Q 92	4c
Waterpark admission	adult	11.00	92	1r
Waterpark admission	child	8.55	92	1r
Funerals				
Casket, 18-gauge steel, velvet interior		1929.04	91	24r
Cosmetology, hair care, etc.		88.52	91	24r
Embalming		249.33	91	24r

Values are in dollars or fractions of dollars. In the column headed *Ref*, references are shown to sources. Each reference is followed by a letter. These refer to the geographical level for which data were reported: s=State, r=Region, and c=City or metro. The abbreviation *ex* is used to mean *except* or *excluding*; *exp* stands for expenditures. For other abbreviations and further explanations, please see the Introduction.

Billings, MT - continued

Item	Per	Value	Date	Ref.
Funerals				
Facility use for ceremony		182.75	91	24r
Hearse, local		110.04	91	24r
Limousine, local		66.67	91	24r
Remains to funeral home, transfer		84.58	91	24r
Service charge, professional		593.00	91	24r
Vault, concrete, non-metallic liner		647.38	91	24r
Viewing facilities, use		99.87	91	24r
Goods and Services				
ACCRA Index, Miscellaneous Goods and Services		103.60	4Q 92	4c
Goods and services	year	15476	92	36c
Goods and services, misc.	year	15476	92	37c
Groceries				
ACCRA Index, Groceries		104.20	4Q 92	4c
Apples, Red Delicious	lb	0.80	4/93	16r
Babyfood, strained vegetables, lowest price	4-4.5 oz jar	0.25	4Q 92	4c
Bacon	lb	1.79	4/93	16r
Bananas	lb	0.31	4Q 92	4c
Bananas	lb	0.53	4/93	16r
Bologna, all beef or mixed	lb	2.67	4/93	16r
Bread, white	24 oz	0.94	4Q 92	4c
Bread, white, pan	lb	0.81	4/93	16r
Carrots, short trimmed and topped	lb	0.39	4/93	16r
Cheese, Kraft grated Parmesan	8-oz canister	3.53	4Q 92	4c
Chicken, fresh, whole	lb	0.94	4/93	16r
Chicken, fryer, whole	lb	0.63	4Q 92	4c
Chicken breast, bone-in	lb	2.19	4/93	16r
Chuck roast, graded and ungraded, ex USDA prime and choice	lb	2.26	4/93	16r
Cigarettes, Winston	carton	17.82	4Q 92	4c
Coffee, 100% ground roast, all sizes	lb	2.33	4/93	16r
Coffee, vacuum-packed	13-oz can	2.09	4Q 92	4c
Corn, frozen	10 oz	0.69	4Q 92	4c
Corn Flakes, Kellogg's or Post Toasties	18 oz	2.06	4Q 92	4c
Eggs, Grade A large	doz	0.88	4Q 92	4c
Eggs, Grade AA large	doz	1.18	4/93	16r
Flour, white, all purpose	lb	0.22	4/93	16r
Grapefruit	lb	0.52	4/93	16r
Grapes, Thompson Seedless	lb	1.50	4/93	16r
Ground beef, 100% beef	lb	1.44	4/93	16r
Ground beef, lean and extra lean	lb	2.34	4/93	16r
Ground beef or hamburger	lb	1.61	4Q 92	4c
Ham, boneless, excluding canned	lb	2.56	4/93	16r
Honey, jar	8 oz	0.89-1.00	92	5r
Honey, jar	lb	1.35-1.97	92	5r
Honey, squeeze bear	12-oz	1.19-1.50	92	5r
Ice cream, prepackaged, bulk, regular	1/2 gal	2.40	4/93	16r
Lemons	lb	0.81	4/93	16r
Lettuce, iceberg	head	1.16	4Q 92	4c
Lettuce, iceberg	lb	0.84	4/93	16r
Margarine, Blue Bonnet or Parkay cubes	lb	0.64	4Q 92	4c
Margarine, stick	lb	0.81	4/93	16r
Milk, whole	1/2 gal	1.45	4Q 92	4c
Orange juice, Minute Maid frozen	12-oz can	1.30	4Q 92	4c
Oranges, navel	lb	0.48	4/93	16r
Peaches	29-oz can	1.44	4Q 92	4c
Peas Sweet, Del Monte or Green Giant	15-17 oz can	0.66	4Q 92	4c
Pork chops, center cut, bone-in	lb	3.25	4/93	16r
Potato chips	16 oz	2.89	4/93	16r
Potatoes, white	lb	0.38	4/93	16r
Potatoes, white or red	10-lb sack	2.09	4Q 92	4c
Round roast, graded & ungraded, ex USDA prime & choice	lb	3.00	4/93	16r

Billings, MT - continued

Item	Per	Value	Date	Ref.
Groceries - continued				
Round roast, USDA choice, boneless	lb	3.16	4/93	16r
Sausage, Jimmy Dean, 100% pork	lb	3.43	4Q 92	4c
Shortening, vegetable oil blends	lb	0.86	4/93	16r
Shortening, vegetable, Crisco	3-lb can	2.27	4Q 92	4c
Soft drink, Coca Cola	2 liter	1.42	4Q 92	4c
Spaghetti and macaroni	lb	0.84	4/93	16r
Steak, round, graded & ungraded, ex USDA prime & choice	lb	3.34	4/93	16r
Steak, round, USDA choice, boneless	lb	3.24	4/93	16r
Steak, sirloin, graded & ungraded, ex USDA prime & choice	lb	3.75	4/93	16r
Steak, sirloin, USDA choice, boneless	lb	4.49	4/93	16r
Steak, T-bone	lb	4.48	4Q 92	4c
Sugar, cane or beet	4 lb	1.31	4Q 92	4c
Sugar, white	lb	0.41	4/93	16r
Sugar, white, 33-80 oz pk	lb	0.38	4/93	16r
Tomatoes, field grown	lb	1.01	4/93	16r
Tomatoes, Hunt's or Del Monte	14.5-oz can	0.66	4Q 92	4c
Tuna, chunk, light	6.125-6.5 oz can	0.70	4Q 92	4c
Turkey, frozen, whole	lb	1.04	4/93	16r
Health Care				
ACCRA Index, Health Care		104.20	4Q 92	4c
Analgesic, Aspirin, Bayer, 325 mg tablets	100	5.40	4Q 92	4c
Childbirth, cesarean, hospital		5533	91	62r
Childbirth, cesarean, physician's fee		2053	91	62r
Childbirth, normal, hospital		2745	91	62r
Childbirth, normal, physician's fee		1492	91	62r
Dentist's fee, adult teeth cleaning and periodic oral exam	visit	47.00	4Q 92	4c
Doctor's fee, routine exam, established patient	visit	37.80	4Q 92	4c
Hospital care, semiprivate room	day	275.66	90	27c
Hospital care, semiprivate room	day	359.00	4Q 92	4c
Medical insurance premium, per employee, small group comprehensive	month	313.90	10/91	25c
Medical plan per employee	year	3218	91	45r
Mental health care, exp	capita	20.37-28.83	90	38s
Mental health care, exp, state mental health agency	capita	28.42	90	38s
Mental health care, hospital psychiatric services, non-Federal, exp	capita	16.46	88	38s
Mental health care, mental health organization, multiservice, exp	capita	15.10	88	38s
Mental health care, psychiatric hospitals, private, exp	capita	17.28	88	38s
Mental health care, state and county mental hospitals, exp	capita	27.18	88	38s
Physician fee, family practice, first-visit		111.00	91	62r
Physician fee, family practice, revisit		45.00	91	62r
Physician fee, general practice, first-visit		100.00	91	62r
Physician fee, general practice, revisit		40.00	91	62r
Physician fee, internal medicine, first-visit		137.00	91	62r
Physician fee, internal medicine, revisit		48.00	91	62r
Physician fee, median, neurosurgeon, first-visit		157.00	91	62r
Physician fee, median, nonsurgical specialist, first-visit		131.00	91	62r
Physician fee, median, orthopedic surgeon, first-visit		124.00	91	62r
Physician fee, median, plastic surgeon, first-visit		88.00	91	62r
Physician fee, median, surgical specialist, first-visit		100.00	91	62r
Physician fee, neurosurgeon, revisit		51.00	91	62r
Physician fee, nonsurgical specialist, revisit		47.00	91	62r
Physician fee, obstetrics/gynecology, first-visit		95.00	91	62r

Values are in dollars or fractions of dollars. In the column headed *Ref*, references are shown to sources. Each reference is followed by a letter. These refer to the geographical level for which data were reported: s = State, r = Region, and c = City or metro. The abbreviation *ex* is used to mean *except* or *excluding*; *exp* stands for expenditures. For other abbreviations and further explanations, please see the Introduction.

Billings, MT - continued

Item	Per	Value	Date	Ref.
Health Care				
Physician fee, obstetrics/gynecology, revisit		50.00	91	62r
Physician fee, orthopedic surgeon, revisit		51.00	91	62r
Physician fee, pediatrician, first-visit		81.00	91	62r
Physician fee, pediatrician, revisit		42.00	91	62r
Physician fee, plastic surgeon, revisit		48.00	91	62r
Physician fee, surgical specialist, revisit		49.00	91	62r
Substance abuse, hospital ancillary charge	incident	320	90	70s
Substance abuse, hospital physician charge	incident	210	90	70s
Substance abuse, hospital room and board	incident	5290	90	70s
Household Goods				
Appliance repair, home, service call, washing machine	min labor charge	31.59	4Q 92	4c
Laundry detergent, Tide Ultra, Bold, or Cheer	42 oz	3.69	4Q 92	4c
Tissues, facial, Kleenex brand	175-count box	1.24	4Q 92	4c
Housing				
ACCRA Index, Housing		109.50	4Q 92	4c
House, 1,800 sq ft, 8,000 sq ft lot, new, urban	total	133750	4Q 92	4c
House payment, principal and interest, 25% down payment	month	756	4Q 92	4c
Mortgage rate, incl. points & origination fee, 30-year fixed or adjustable rate	percent	8.28	4Q 92	4c
Rent, apartment, 2 bedrooms - 1-1/2 to 2 baths, unfurnished, 950 sq ft, water	month	350	4Q 92	4c
Rental unit, 1 bedroom	month	467	93	23c
Rental unit, 2 bedroom	month	550	93	23c
Rental unit, 3 bedroom	month	688	93	23c
Rental unit, 4 bedroom	month	771	93	23c
Rental unit, efficiency	month	384	93	23c
Insurance and Pensions				
Auto insurance, private passenger	year	475.81	91	63s
Personal Goods				
Shampoo, Alberto VO5	15 oz	1.58	4Q 92	4c
Toothpaste, Crest or Colgate	6-7 oz	2.35	4Q 92	4c
Personal Services				
Dry cleaning, man's 2-piece suit		7.01	4Q 92	4c
Haircare, woman's shampoo, trim and blow-dry		16.80	4Q 92	4c
Haircut, man's barbershop, no styling		7.80	4Q 92	4c
Restaurant Food				
Chicken, fried, thigh and drumstick		2.14	4Q 92	4c
Hamburger with cheese	1/4 lb	1.85	4Q 92	4c
Pizza, Pizza Hut or Pizza Inn, cheese, thin crust	12-13 in	8.39	4Q 92	4c
Taxes				
Tax, cigarette	pack	19.26	91	77s
Tax, gasoline	gal	20	91	77s
Taxes, sales	year	0	92	37c
Taxes, state	capita	1011	91	77s
Transportation				
ACCRA Index, Transportation		108.10	4Q 92	4c
Driver's license fee		16.00-24.00	12/90	43s
Tire balance, computer or spin balance, front	wheel	6.60	4Q 92	4c
Travel				
Business travel	day	178.00	4/93	89r
Utilities				
ACCRA Index, Utilities		81.30	4Q 92	4c
Electricity	mil Btu	11.67	90	64s

Billings, MT - continued

Item	Per	Value	Date	Ref.
Utilities - continued				
Electricity, partial electric and other energy, 1,800 sq ft living area new home	month	44.63	4Q 92	4c
Electricity, winter, 250 KWh	month	21.29	92	55c
Electricity, winter, 500 KWh	month	39.13	92	55c
Electricity, winter, 750 KWh	month	56.97	92	55c
Electricity, winter, 1000 KWh	month	74.81	92	55c

Biloxi, MS

Item	Per	Value	Date	Ref.
Child Care				
Child care fee, average, center	hour	1.29	90	65r
Child care fee, average, nonregulated family day care	hour	0.89	90	65r
Child care fee, average, regulated family day care	hour	1.32	90	65r
Communications				
Long-distance telephone service, day, initial minute, 0-100 miles	min	0.19-0.47	91	12s
Long-distance telephone service, day, additional minute, 0-100 miles	min	0.11-0.34	91	12s
Long-distance telephone service, evenings/weekends, 0-100 mi, initial minute	min	0.06-0.19	91	12s
Long-distance telephone service, evenings/weekends, 0-100 mi, additional minute	min	0.04-0.14	91	12s
Education				
Board, 4-yr private college/university	year	1312	91	22s
Board, 4-yr public college/university	year	1924	91	22s
Expenditures, local gov't, public elementary/secondary	pupil	3344	92	20s
Room, 4-year private college/university	year	1002	91	22s
Room, 4-year public college/university	year	1154	91	22s
Tuition, 2-year private college/university	year	3721	91	22s
Tuition, 2-year public college/university	year	722	91	22s
Tuition, 4-year private college/university	year	5238	91	22s
Tuition, 4-year public college/university, in-state	year	1927	91	22s
Energy and Fuels				
Coal	mil Btu	1.65	90	64s
Energy	mil Btu	8.31	90	64s
Energy exp/householder, 1-family unit	year	403	90	28r
Energy exp/householder, <1,000 sq ft heating area	year	342	90	28r
Energy exp/householder, 1,000-1,999 sq ft heating area	year	388	90	28r
Energy exp/householder, 2,000+ sq ft heating area	year	434	90	28r
Energy exp/householder, mobile home	year	320	90	28r
Energy exp/householder, multifamily	year	338	90	28r
Gas, natural	mil Btu	2.75	90	64s
Gas, natural	000 cu ft	5.21	91	46s
Gas, natural, exp	year	348	91	46s
Gasoline, unleaded regular	mil Btu	9.21	90	64s
Entertainment				
Miniature golf admission	adult	6.18	92	1r
Miniature golf admission	child	5.14	92	1r
Waterpark admission	adult	11.00	92	1r
Waterpark admission	child	8.55	92	1r
Funerals				
Casket, 18-gauge steel, velvet interior		2329.05	91	24r
Cosmetology, hair care, etc.		72.78	91	24r
Embalming		240.71	91	24r
Facility use for ceremony		181.67	91	24r
Hearse, local		106.25	91	24r
Limousine, local		70.92	91	24r
Remains to funeral home, transfer		96.30	91	24r
Service charge, professional		687.09	91	24r
Vault, concrete, non-metallic liner		732.09	91	24r

Values are in dollars or fractions of dollars. In the column headed *Ref*, references are shown to sources. Each reference is followed by a letter. These refer to the geographical level for which data were reported: s=State, r=Region, and c=City or metro. The abbreviation *ex* is used to mean *except* or *excluding*; *exp* stands for expenditures. For other abbreviations and further explanations, please see the Introduction.

Biloxi, MS - continued

Item	Per	Value	Date	Ref.
Funerals				
Viewing facilities, use		190.30	91	24r
Groceries				
Apples, Red Delicious	lb	0.79	4/93	16r
Bacon	lb	1.75	4/93	16r
Bananas	lb	0.42	4/93	16r
Beef, stew, boneless	lb	2.61	4/93	16r
Bologna, all beef or mixed	lb	2.24	4/93	16r
Bread, white, pan	lb	0.64	4/93	16r
Bread, whole wheat, pan	lb	0.96	4/93	16r
Cabbage	lb	0.37	4/93	16r
Carrots, short trimmed and topped	lb	0.47	4/93	16r
Celery	lb	0.64	4/93	16r
Cheese, American	lb	2.98	4/93	16r
Cheese, Cheddar	lb	3.28	4/93	16r
Chicken, fresh, whole	lb	0.77	4/93	16r
Chicken breast, bone-in	lb	1.92	4/93	16r
Chicken legs, bone-in	lb	1.06	4/93	16r
Chuck roast, graded and ungraded, ex USDA prime and choice	lb	2.40	4/93	16r
Chuck roast, USDA choice, bone-in	lb	2.19	4/93	16r
Chuck roast, USDA choice, boneless	lb	2.38	4/93	16r
Coffee, 100% ground roast, all sizes	lb	2.48	4/93	16r
Crackers, soda, salted	lb	1.15	4/93	16r
Eggs, Grade A large	doz	0.96	4/93	16r
Flour, white, all purpose	lb	0.24	4/93	16r
Frankfurters, all meat or all beef	lb	2.01	4/93	16r
Grapefruit	lb	0.44	4/93	16r
Grapes, Thompson Seedless	lb	1.40	4/93	16r
Ground beef, 100% beef	lb	1.58	4/93	16r
Ground beef, lean and extra lean	lb	2.09	4/93	16r
Ground chuck, 100% beef	lb	1.98	4/93	16r
Ham, boneless, excluding canned	lb	2.89	4/93	16r
Ham, picnic, shoulder, bone-in, smoked	lb	1.02	4/93	16r
Ham, rump or steak half, bone-in, smoked	lb	1.48	4/93	16r
Honey, jar	8 oz	0.89-1.09	92	5r
Honey, jar	lb	1.39-2.25	92	5r
Honey, squeeze bear	12-oz	1.00-1.50	92	5r
Ice cream, prepackaged, bulk, regular	1/2 gal	2.41	4/93	16r
Lemons	lb	1.05	4/93	16r
Lettuce, iceberg	lb	0.81	4/93	16r
Margarine, stick	lb	0.88	4/93	16r
Oranges, navel	lb	0.55	4/93	16r
Pears, Anjou	lb	0.92	4/93	16r
Pork chops, center cut, bone-in	lb	3.13	4/93	16r
Potato chips	16 oz	2.94	4/93	16r
Potatoes, white	lb	0.43	4/93	16r
Rib roast, USDA choice, bone-in	lb	4.63	4/93	16r
Rice, white, long grain, uncooked	lb	0.45	4/93	16r
Round roast, graded & ungraded, ex USDA prime & choice	lb	3.03	4/93	16r
Round roast, USDA choice, boneless	lb	3.09	4/93	16r
Sausage, fresh, loose	lb	2.08	4/93	16r
Short ribs, bone-in	lb	2.66	4/93	16r
Shortening, vegetable oil blends	lb	0.69	4/93	16r
Spaghetti and macaroni	lb	0.81	4/93	16r
Steak, rib eye, USDA choice, boneless	lb	6.24	4/93	16r
Steak, round, graded & ungraded, ex USDA prime & choice	lb	3.31	4/93	16r
Steak, round, USDA choice, boneless	lb	3.34	4/93	16r
Steak, sirloin, graded & ungraded, ex USDA prime & choice	lb	4.19	4/93	16r
Steak, sirloin, USDA choice, boneless	lb	4.46	4/93	16r
Steak, T-bone, USDA choice, bone-in	lb	5.25	4/93	16r
Strawberries, dry pint	12 oz	0.92	4/93	16r
Sugar, white	lb	0.39	4/93	16r
Sugar, white, 33-80 oz pk	lb	0.38	4/93	16r
Tomatoes, field grown	lb	0.88	4/93	16r
Tuna, chunk, light	lb	1.79	4/93	16r
Turkey, frozen, whole	lb	1.04	4/93	16r
Yogurt, natural, fruit flavored	1/2 pint	0.57	4/93	16r

Item	Per	Value	Date	Ref.
Health Care				
Childbirth, cesarean, hospital		5034	91	62r
Childbirth, cesarean, physician's fee		2053	91	62r
Childbirth, normal, hospital		2712	91	62r
Childbirth, normal, physician's fee		1492	91	62r
Mental health care, exp	capita	28.84-37.59	90	38s
Mental health care, exp, state mental health agency	capita	33.71	90	38s
Mental health care, hospital psychiatric services, non-Federal, exp	capita	5.17	88	38s
Mental health care, mental health organization, multiservice, exp	capita	8.65	88	38s
Mental health care, psychiatric hospitals, private, exp	capita	6.85	88	38s
Mental health care, state and county mental hospitals, exp	capita	20.41	88	38s
Mental health care, VA medical centers, exp	capita	7.21	88	38s
Physician fee, family practice, first-visit		75.00	91	62r
Physician fee, family practice, revisit		34.00	91	62r
Physician fee, general practice, first-visit		61.00	91	62r
Physician fee, general practice, revisit		32.00	91	62r
Physician fee, general surgeon, first-visit		64.00	91	62r
Physician fee, general surgeon, revisit		40.00	91	62r
Physician fee, internal medicine, first-visit		98.00	91	62r
Physician fee, internal medicine, revisit		40.00	91	62r
Physician fee, median, neurosurgeon, first-visit		130.00	91	62r
Physician fee, median, nonsurgical specialist, first-visit		95.00	91	62r
Physician fee, median, orthopedic surgeon, first-visit		91.00	91	62r
Physician fee, median, plastic surgeon, first-visit		66.00	91	62r
Physician fee, median, surgical specialist, first-visit		62.00	91	62r
Physician fee, neurosurgeon, revisit		50.00	91	62r
Physician fee, nonsurgical specialist, revisit		40.00	91	62r
Physician fee, obstetrics/gynecology, first-visit		64.00	91	62r
Physician fee, obstetrics/gynecology, revisit		41.00	91	62r
Physician fee, orthopedic surgeon, revisit		40.00	91	62r
Physician fee, pediatrician, first-visit		49.00	91	62r
Physician fee, pediatrician, revisit		33.00	91	62r
Physician fee, plastic surgeon, revisit		43.00	91	62r
Physician fee, surgical specialist, revisit		37.00	91	62r
Substance abuse, hospital ancillary charge	incident	1760	90	70s
Substance abuse, hospital physician charge	incident	540	90	70s
Substance abuse, hospital room and board	incident	4060	90	70s
Insurance and Pensions				
Auto insurance, private passenger	year	576.42	91	63s
Taxes				
Tax, cigarette	pack	18	91	77s
Tax, gasoline	gal	18	91	77s
Taxes, state	capita	949	91	77s
Transportation				
Driver's license fee		13.00	12/90	43s
Travel				
Business travel	day	193.00	4/93	89r
Utilities				
Electricity	mil Btu	18.05	90	64s

Values are in dollars or fractions of dollars. In the column headed *Ref*, references are shown to sources. Each reference is followed by a letter. These refer to the geographical level for which data were reported: s = State, r = Region, and c = City or metro. The abbreviation *ex* is used to mean *except* or *excluding*; *exp* stands for expenditures. For other abbreviations and further explanations, please see the Introduction.

Binghamton, NY

Item	Per	Value	Date	Ref.
Composite ACCRA index		100.70	4Q 92	4c
Alcoholic Beverages				
Beer, Miller Lite or Budweiser, 12-oz containers	6 pack	3.86	4Q 92	4c
Liquor, J & B Scotch	750 ml	17.29	4Q 92	4c
Wine, Gallo Chablis blanc, 1.5 liter	bottle	5.79	4Q 92	4c
Child Care				
Child care fee, average, center	hour	2.18	90	65r
Child care fee, average, nonregulated family day care	hour	1.83	90	65r
Child care fee, average, regulated family day care	hour	2.02	90	65r
Clothing				
Jeans, man's denim		31.56	4Q 92	4c
Shirt, man's dress shirt		24.60	4Q 92	4c
Undervest, boy's size 10-14, cotton	3	4.07	4Q 92	4c
Communications				
Newspaper subscription, daily and Sunday home delivery, large-city	month	13.26	4Q 92	4c
Telephone, residential, private line, rotary, unlimited calling	month	24.18	10/91	78c
Telephone bill, family of four	month	25.73	4Q 92	4c
Education				
Board, 4-yr private college/university	year	2451	91	22s
Board, 4-yr public college/university	year	1725	91	22s
Expenditures, local gov't, public elementary/secondary	pupil	8603	92	20s
Room, 4-year private college/university	year	2652	91	22s
Room, 4-year public college/university	year	2183	91	22s
Tuition, 2-year private college/university	year	5926	91	22s
Tuition, 2-year public college/university	year	1419	91	22s
Tuition, 4-year private college/university	year	10340	91	22s
Tuition, 4-year public college/university, in-state	year	1587	91	22s
Energy and Fuels				
Coal	mil Btu	1.66	90	64s
Energy	mil Btu	10.68	90	64s
Energy, combined forms, 1,800 sq ft heating area	month	125.09	4Q 92	4c
Energy, exc electricity, 1,800 sq ft heating area	month	58.31	4Q 92	4c
Energy exp/householder, 1-family unit	year	588	90	28r
Energy exp/householder, <1,000 sq ft heating area	year	477	90	28r
Energy exp/householder, 1,000-1,999 sq ft heating area	year	517	90	28r
Energy exp/householder, 2,000+ sq ft heating area	year	630	90	28r
Energy exp/householder, mobile home	year	412	90	28r
Energy exp/householder, multifamily	year	498	90	28r
Gas, natural	mil Btu	5.25	90	64s
Gas, natural	000 cu ft	7.35	91	46s
Gas, natural, exp	year	557	91	46s
Gasoline, motor	gal	1.20	4Q 92	4c
Gasoline, unleaded regular	mil Btu	8.83	90	64s
Entertainment				
Bowling, evening rate	game	2.18	4Q 92	4c
Monopoly game, Parker Brothers', No. 9		11.99	4Q 92	4c
Movie	admission	6.00	4Q 92	4c
Tennis balls, yellow, Wilson or Penn, 3	can	2.43	4Q 92	4c
Funerals				
Casket, 18-gauge steel, velvet interior		1811.58	91	24r
Cosmetology, hair care, etc.		111.08	91	24r
Embalming		329.42	91	24r
Facility use for ceremony		201.29	91	24r
Hearse, local		135.27	91	24r
Limousine, local		127.24	91	24r

Binghamton, NY - continued

Item	Per	Value	Date	Ref.
Funerals - continued				
Remains to funeral home, transfer		103.98	91	24r
Service charge, professional		724.98	91	24r
Vault, concrete, non-metallic liner		766.71	91	24r
Viewing facilities, use		260.60	91	24r
Goods and Services				
ACCRA Index, Miscellaneous Goods and Services		101.90	4Q 92	4c
Groceries				
ACCRA Index, Groceries		100.30	4Q 92	4c
Apples, Red Delicious	lb	0.85	4/93	16r
Babyfood, strained vegetables, lowest price	4-4.5 oz jar	0.30	4Q 92	4c
Bacon	lb	2.12	4/93	16r
Bananas	lb	0.41	4Q 92	4c
Bananas	lb	0.54	4/93	16r
Bread, white	24 oz	0.65	4Q 92	4c
Bread, white, pan	lb	0.81	4/93	16r
Butter	lb	2.02	4/93	16r
Carrots, short trimmed and topped	lb	0.51	4/93	16r
Cheese, Kraft grated Parmesan	8-oz canister	2.85	4Q 92	4c
Chicken, fresh, whole	lb	1.04	4/93	16r
Chicken, fryer, whole	lb	0.43	4Q 92	4c
Chicken breast, bone-in	lb	2.21	4/93	16r
Chicken legs, bone-in	lb	1.16	4/93	16r
Chuck roast, USDA choice, boneless	lb	2.82	4/93	16r
Cigarettes, Winston	carton	19.54	4Q 92	4c
Coffee, 100% ground roast, all sizes	lb	2.66	4/93	16r
Coffee, vacuum-packed	13-oz can	2.01	4Q 92	4c
Corn, frozen	10 oz	0.70	4Q 92	4c
Corn Flakes, Kellogg's or Post Toasties	18 oz	1.88	4Q 92	4c
Cucumbers	lb	0.85	4/93	16r
Eggs, Grade A large	doz	0.80	4Q 92	4c
Eggs, Grade A large	doz	1.15	4/93	16r
Grapefruit	lb	0.45	4/93	16r
Grapes, Thompson Seedless	lb	1.52	4/93	16r
Ground beef, lean and extra lean	lb	2.36	4/93	16r
Ground beef or hamburger	lb	1.68	4Q 92	4c
Ground chuck, 100% beef	lb	2.02	4/93	16r
Honey, jar	8 oz	0.96-1.75	92	5r
Honey, jar	lb	1.50-3.00	92	5r
Honey, squeeze bear	12-oz	1.50-1.99	92	5r
Ice cream, prepackaged, bulk, regular	1/2 gal	2.80	4/93	16r
Lemons	lb	0.96	4/93	16r
Lettuce, iceberg	head	0.97	4Q 92	4c
Lettuce, iceberg	lb	0.95	4/93	16r
Margarine, Blue Bonnet or Parkay cubes	lb	0.53	4Q 92	4c
Margarine, stick	lb	0.81	4/93	16r
Milk, fresh, whole, fortified	1/2 gal	1.30	4/93	16r
Milk, whole	1/2 gal	1.23	4Q 92	4c
Orange juice, Minute Maid frozen	12-oz can	1.30	4Q 92	4c
Oranges, navel	lb	0.56	4/93	16r
Peaches	29-oz can	1.41	4Q 92	4c
Peanut butter, creamy, all sizes	lb	1.88	4/93	16r
Peas Sweet, Del Monte or Green Giant	15-17 oz can	0.51	4Q 92	4c
Pork chops, center cut, bone-in	lb	3.34	4/93	16r
Potato chips	16 oz	2.88	4/93	16r
Potatoes, white	lb	0.37	4/93	16r
Potatoes, white or red	10-lb sack	1.33	4Q 92	4c
Rib roast, USDA choice, bone-in	lb	4.94	4/93	16r
Round roast, USDA choice, boneless	lb	3.17	4/93	16r
Sausage, Jimmy Dean, 100% pork	lb	3.21	4Q 92	4c
Shortening, vegetable oil blends	lb	0.98	4/93	16r
Shortening, vegetable, Crisco	3-lb can	2.35	4Q 92	4c

Values are in dollars or fractions of dollars. In the column headed *Ref*, references are shown to sources. Each reference is followed by a letter. These refer to the geographical level for which data were reported: s = State, r = Region, and c = City or metro. The abbreviation *ex* is used to mean *except* or *excluding*; *exp* stands for expenditures. For other abbreviations and further explanations, please see the Introduction.

Binghamton, NY - continued

Item	Per	Value	Date	Ref.
Groceries				
Soft drink, Coca Cola	2 liter	1.38	4Q 92	4c
Spaghetti and macaroni	lb	0.82	4/93	16r
Steak, round, graded & ungraded, ex USDA prime & choice	lb	4.04	4/93	16r
Steak, round, USDA choice, boneless	lb	3.90	4/93	16r
Steak, sirloin, USDA choice, boneless	lb	4.97	4/93	16r
Steak, T-bone	lb	5.92	4Q 92	4c
Strawberries, dry pint	12 oz	0.90	4/93	16r
Sugar, cane or beet	4 lb	1.66	4Q 92	4c
Sugar, white	lb	0.50	4/93	16r
Sugar, white, 33-80 oz pk	lb	0.41	4/93	16r
Tomatoes, field grown	lb	1.23	4/93	16r
Tomatoes, Hunt's or Del Monte	14.5-oz can	0.65	4Q 92	4c
Tuna, chunk, light	6.125-6.5 oz can	0.66	4Q 92	4c
Tuna, chunk, light	lb	2.22	4/93	16r
Turkey, frozen, whole	lb	1.04	4/93	16r
Health Care				
ACCRA Index, Health Care		92.60	4Q 92	4c
Analgesic, Aspirin, Bayer, 325 mg tablets	100	5.17	4Q 92	4c
Childbirth, cesarean, hospital		5826	91	62r
Childbirth, cesarean, physician's fee		2053	91	62r
Childbirth, normal, hospital		2964	91	62r
Childbirth, normal, physician's fee		1492	91	62r
Dentist's fee, adult teeth cleaning and periodic oral exam	visit	43.20	4Q 92	4c
Doctor's fee, routine exam, established patient	visit	38.00	4Q 92	4c
Hospital care, semiprivate room	day	328.81	90	27c
Hospital care, semiprivate room	day	212.67	4Q 92	4c
Medical insurance premium, per employee, small group comprehensive	month	299.30	10/91	25c
Medical plan per employee	year	3942	91	45r
Mental health care, exp	capita	53.68-118.35	90	38s
Mental health care, exp, state mental health agency	capita	118.34	90	38s
Mental health care, hospital psychiatric services, non-Federal, exp	capita	29.77	88	38s
Mental health care, mental health organization, multiservice, exp	capita	20.03	88	38s
Mental health care, psychiatric hospitals, private, exp	capita	8.37	88	38s
Mental health care, psychiatric out-patient clinics, freestanding, exp	capita	7.96	88	38s
Mental health care, psychiatric partial-care organizations, freestanding, exp	capita	1.24	88	38s
Mental health care, state and county mental hospitals, exp	capita	89.52	88	38s
Mental health care, VA medical centers, exp	capita	7.12	88	38s
Prescription drug co-pay, Medicaid	month	23.00	91	21s
Substance abuse, hospital ancillary charge	incident	1040	90	70s
Substance abuse, hospital physician charge	incident	360	90	70s
Substance abuse, hospital room and board	incident	6330	90	70s
Household Goods				
Appliance repair, home, service call, washing machine	min labor charge	29.57	4Q 92	4c
Laundry detergent, Tide Ultra, Bold, or Cheer	42 oz	3.99	4Q 92	4c
Tissues, facial, Kleenex brand	175-count box	1.09	4Q 92	4c
Housing				
ACCRA Index, Housing		93.50	4Q 92	4c

Binghamton, NY - continued

Item	Per	Value	Date	Ref.
Housing - continued				
House, 1,800 sq ft, 8,000 sq ft lot, new, urban	total	101925	4Q 92	4c
House payment, principal and interest, 25% down payment	month	576	4Q 92	4c
Mortgage rate, incl. points & origination fee, 30-year fixed or adjustable rate	percent	8.28	4Q 92	4c
Rent, apartment, 2 bedrooms - 1-1/2 to 2 baths, unfurnished, 950 sq ft, water	month	458	4Q 92	4c
Rental unit, 1 bedroom	month	418	93	23c
Rental unit, 2 bedroom	month	494	93	23c
Rental unit, 3 bedroom	month	611	93	23c
Rental unit, 4 bedroom	month	687	93	23c
Rental unit, efficiency	month	346	93	23c
Insurance and Pensions				
Auto insurance, private passenger	year	840.89	91	63s
Personal Goods				
Shampoo, Alberto VO5	15 oz	1.33	4Q 92	4c
Toothpaste, Crest or Colgate	6-7 oz	1.94	4Q 92	4c
Personal Services				
Dry cleaning, man's 2-piece suit		6.30	4Q 92	4c
Haircare, woman's shampoo, trim and blow-dry		14.67	4Q 92	4c
Haircut, man's barbershop, no styling		6.30	4Q 92	4c
Restaurant Food				
Chicken, fried, thigh and drumstick		2.38	4Q 92	4c
Hamburger with cheese	1/4 lb	1.94	4Q 92	4c
Pizza, Pizza Hut or Pizza Inn, cheese, thin crust	12-13 in	7.49	4Q 92	4c
Taxes				
Tax, cigarette	pack	39	91	77s
Tax, gasoline	gal	8	91	77s
Taxes, state	capita	1567	91	77s
Transportation				
ACCRA Index, Transportation		107.60	4Q 92	4c
Driver's license fee		17.50	12/90	43s
Tire balance, computer or spin balance, front	wheel	7.09	4Q 92	4c
Vehicle registration and license plate	2 years	27.50-149.50	93	67s
Travel				
Business travel	day	165.00	4/93	89r
Utilities				
ACCRA Index, Utilities		116.30	4Q 92	4c
Electricity	mil Btu	27.51	90	64s
Electricity, partial electric and other energy, 1,800 sq ft living area new home	month	66.78	4Q 92	4c
Electricity, winter, 250 KWh	month	31.29	92	55c
Electricity, winter, 500 KWh	month	56.78	92	55c
Electricity, winter, 750 KWh	month	82.27	92	55c
Electricity, winter, 1000 KWh	month	107.77	92	55c

Birmingham, AL

Item	Per	Value	Date	Ref.
Composite ACCRA index		102.60	4Q 92	4c
Alcoholic Beverages				
Beer, Miller Lite or Budweiser, 12-oz containers	6 pack	3.99	4Q 92	4c
Liquor, J & B Scotch	750 ml	19.99	4Q 92	4c
Wine, Gallo Chablis blanc, 1.5 liter	bottle	5.62	4Q 92	4c
Child Care				
Child care fee, average, center	hour	1.29	90	65r
Child care fee, average, nonregulated family day care	hour	0.89	90	65r
Child care fee, average, regulated family day care	hour	1.32	90	65r

Values are in dollars or fractions of dollars. In the column headed *Ref*, references are shown to sources. Each reference is followed by a letter. These refer to the geographical level for which data were reported: s = State, r = Region, and c = City or metro. The abbreviation *ex* is used to mean *except* or *excluding*; *exp* stands for expenditures. For other abbreviations and further explanations, please see the Introduction.

Birmingham, AL - continued

Item	Per	Value	Date	Ref.
Clothing				
Jeans, man's denim		37.15	4Q 92	4c
Shirt, man's dress shirt		24.38	4Q 92	4c
Undervest, boy's size 10-14, cotton	3	3.49	4Q 92	4c
Communications				
Long-distance telephone service, day, initial minute, 0-100 miles	min	0.11-0.36	91	12s
Long-distance telephone service, day, additional minute, 0-100 miles	min	0.09-0.26	91	12s
Long-distance telephone service, evenings/weekends, 0-100 mi, initial minute	min	0.04-0.14	91	12s
Long-distance telephone service, evenings/weekends, 0-100 mi, additional minute	min	0.04-0.10	91	12s
Newspaper subscription, daily and Sunday home delivery, large-city	month	9.95	4Q 92	4c
Telephone, flat rate	month	19.61	91	11c
Telephone bill, family of four	month	26.13	4Q 92	4c
Education				
Board, 4-yr private college/university	year	1795	91	22s
Board, 4-yr public college/university	year	1469	91	22s
Expenditures, local gov't, public elementary/secondary	pupil	3675	92	20s
Room, 4-year private college/university	year	1340	91	22s
Room, 4-year public college/university	year	1295	91	22s
Tuition, 2-year private college/university	year	4148	91	22s
Tuition, 2-year public college/university	year	689	91	22s
Tuition, 4-year private college/university	year	5942	91	22s
Tuition, 4-year public college/university, in-state	year	1593	91	22s
Energy and Fuels				
Coal	mil Btu	1.83	90	64s
Energy	mil Btu	7.92	90	64s
Energy, combined forms, 1,800 sq ft heating area	month	128.76	4Q 92	4c
Energy, exc electricity, 1,800 sq ft heating area	month	42.92	4Q 92	4c
Energy exp/householder, 1-family unit	year	403	90	28r
Energy exp/householder, <1,000 sq ft heating area	year	342	90	28r
Energy exp/householder, 1,000-1,999 sq ft heating area	year	388	90	28r
Energy exp/householder, 2,000+ sq ft heating area	year	434	90	28r
Energy exp/householder, mobile home	year	320	90	28r
Energy exp/householder, multifamily	year	338	90	28r
Gas, cooking, 10 therms	month	13.89	92	56c
Gas, cooking, 30 therms	month	25.74	92	56c
Gas, cooking, 50 therms	month	37.59	92	56c
Gas, heating, winter, 100 therms	month	63.12	92	56c
Gas, heating, winter, average use	month	83.74	92	56c
Gas, natural	mil Btu	4.07	90	64s
Gas, natural	000 cu ft	7.05	91	46s
Gas, natural, exp	year	461	91	46s
Gasoline, motor	gal	1.11	4Q 92	4c
Gasoline, unleaded regular	mil Btu	8.96	90	64s
Entertainment				
Bowling, evening rate	game	2.19	4Q 92	4c
Miniature golf admission	adult	6.18	92	1r
Miniature golf admission	child	5.14	92	1r
Monopoly game, Parker Brothers', No. 9		11.65	4Q 92	4c
Movie	admission	5.50	4Q 92	4c
Tennis balls, yellow, Wilson or Penn, 3	can	2.22	4Q 92	4c
Waterpark admission	adult	11.00	92	1r
Waterpark admission	child	8.55	92	1r
Funerals				
Casket, 18-gauge steel, velvet interior		2329.05	91	24r
Cosmetology, hair care, etc.		72.78	91	24r
Embalming		240.71	91	24r

Birmingham, AL - continued

Item	Per	Value	Date	Ref.
Funerals - continued				
Facility use for ceremony		181.67	91	24r
Hearse, local		106.25	91	24r
Limousine, local		70.92	91	24r
Remains to funeral home, transfer		96.30	91	24r
Service charge, professional		687.09	91	24r
Vault, concrete, non-metallic liner		732.09	91	24r
Viewing facilities, use		190.30	91	24r
Goods and Services				
ACCRA Index, Miscellaneous Goods and Services		101.40	4Q 92	4c
Groceries				
ACCRA Index, Groceries		96.50	4Q 92	4c
Apples, Red Delicious	lb	0.79	4/93	16r
Babyfood, strained vegetables, lowest price	4-4.5 oz jar	0.29	4Q 92	4c
Bacon	lb	1.75	4/93	16r
Bananas	lb	0.43	4Q 92	4c
Bananas	lb	0.42	4/93	16r
Beef, stew, boneless	lb	2.61	4/93	16r
Bologna, all beef or mixed	lb	2.24	4/93	16r
Bread, white	24 oz	0.70	4Q 92	4c
Bread, white, pan	lb	0.64	4/93	16r
Bread, whole wheat, pan	lb	0.96	4/93	16r
Cabbage	lb	0.37	4/93	16r
Carrots, short trimmed and topped	lb	0.47	4/93	16r
Celery	lb	0.64	4/93	16r
Cheese, American	lb	2.98	4/93	16r
Cheese, Cheddar	lb	3.28	4/93	16r
Cheese, Kraft grated Parmesan	8-oz canister	3.18	4Q 92	4c
Chicken, fresh, whole	lb	0.77	4/93	16r
Chicken, fryer, whole	lb	0.72	4Q 92	4c
Chicken breast, bone-in	lb	1.92	4/93	16r
Chicken legs, bone-in	lb	1.06	4/93	16r
Chuck roast, graded and ungraded, ex USDA prime and choice	lb	2.40	4/93	16r
Chuck roast, USDA choice, bone-in	lb	2.19	4/93	16r
Chuck roast, USDA choice, boneless	lb	2.38	4/93	16r
Cigarettes, Winston	carton	16.19	4Q 92	4c
Coffee, 100% ground roast, all sizes	lb	2.48	4/93	16r
Coffee, vacuum-packed	13-oz can	2.02	4Q 92	4c
Corn, frozen	10 oz	0.56	4Q 92	4c
Corn Flakes, Kellogg's or Post Toasties	18 oz	1.60	4Q 92	4c
Crackers, soda, salted	lb	1.15	4/93	16r
Eggs, Grade A large	doz	0.76	4Q 92	4c
Eggs, Grade A large	doz	0.96	4/93	16r
Flour, white, all purpose	lb	0.24	4/93	16r
Frankfurters, all meat or all beef	lb	2.01	4/93	16r
Grapefruit	lb	0.44	4/93	16r
Grapes, Thompson Seedless	lb	1.40	4/93	16r
Ground beef, 100% beef	lb	1.58	4/93	16r
Ground beef, lean and extra lean	lb	2.09	4/93	16r
Ground beef or hamburger	lb	1.72	4Q 92	4c
Ground chuck, 100% beef	lb	1.98	4/93	16r
Ham, boneless, excluding canned	lb	2.89	4/93	16r
Ham, picnic, shoulder, bone-in, smoked	lb	1.02	4/93	16r
Ham, rump or steak half, bone-in, smoked	lb	1.48	4/93	16r
Honey, jar	8 oz	0.89-1.09	92	5r
Honey, jar	lb	1.39-2.25	92	5r
Honey, squeeze bear	12-oz	1.00-1.50	92	5r
Ice cream, prepackaged, bulk, regular	1/2 gal	2.41	4/93	16r
Lemons	lb	1.05	4/93	16r
Lettuce, iceberg	head	1.07	4Q 92	4c
Lettuce, iceberg	lb	0.81	4/93	16r
Margarine, Blue Bonnet or Parkay cubes	lb	0.50	4Q 92	4c
Margarine, stick	lb	0.88	4/93	16r
Milk, whole	1/2 gal	1.45	4Q 92	4c
Orange juice, Minute Maid frozen	12-oz can	1.31	4Q 92	4c

Values are in dollars or fractions of dollars. In the column headed *Ref*, references are shown to sources. Each reference is followed by a letter. These refer to the geographical level for which data were reported: s=State, r=Region, and c=City or metro. The abbreviation *ex* is used to mean *except* or *excluding*; *exp* stands for *expenditures*. For other abbreviations and further explanations, please see the Introduction.

Birmingham, AL - continued

Item	Per	Value	Date	Ref.
Groceries				
Oranges, navel	lb	0.55	4/93	16r
Peaches	29-oz can	1.27	4Q 92	4c
Pears, Anjou	lb	0.92	4/93	16r
Peas Sweet, Del Monte or Green Giant	15-17 oz can	0.54	4Q 92	4c
Pork chops, center cut, bone-in	lb	3.13	4/93	16r
Potato chips	16 oz	2.94	4/93	16r
Potatoes, white	lb	0.43	4/93	16r
Potatoes, white or red	10-lb sack	2.84	4Q 92	4c
Rib roast, USDA choice, bone-in	lb	4.63	4/93	16r
Rice, white, long grain, uncooked	lb	0.45	4/93	16r
Round roast, graded & ungraded, ex USDA prime & choice	lb	3.03	4/93	16r
Round roast, USDA choice, boneless	lb	3.09	4/93	16r
Sausage, fresh, loose	lb	2.08	4/93	16r
Sausage, Jimmy Dean, 100% pork	lb	2.21	4Q 92	4c
Short ribs, bone-in	lb	2.66	4/93	16r
Shortening, vegetable oil blends	lb	0.69	4/93	16r
Shortening, vegetable, Crisco	3-lb can	2.19	4Q 92	4c
Soft drink, Coca Cola	2 liter	1.38	4Q 92	4c
Spaghetti and macaroni	lb	0.81	4/93	16r
Steak, rib eye, USDA choice, boneless	lb	6.24	4/93	16r
Steak, round, graded & ungraded, ex USDA prime & choice	lb	3.31	4/93	16r
Steak, round, USDA choice, boneless	lb	3.34	4/93	16r
Steak, sirloin, graded & ungraded, ex USDA prime & choice	lb	4.19	4/93	16r
Steak, sirloin, USDA choice, boneless	lb	4.46	4/93	16r
Steak, T-bone	lb	5.37	4Q 92	4c
Steak, T-bone, USDA choice, bone-in	lb	5.25	4/93	16r
Strawberries, dry pint	12 oz	0.92	4/93	16r
Sugar, cane or beet	4 lb	1.33	4Q 92	4c
Sugar, white	lb	0.39	4/93	16r
Sugar, white, 33-80 oz pk	lb	0.38	4/93	16r
Tomatoes, field grown	lb	0.88	4/93	16r
Tomatoes, Hunt's or Del Monte	14.5-oz can	0.57	4Q 92	4c
Tuna, chunk, light	6.125-6.5 oz can	0.51	4Q 92	4c
Tuna, chunk, light	lb	1.79	4/93	16r
Turkey, frozen, whole	lb	1.04	4/93	16r
Yogurt, natural, fruit flavored	1/2 pint	0.57	4/93	16r
Health Care				
ACCRA Index, Health Care		103.80	4Q 92	4c
Analgesic, Aspirin, Bayer, 325 mg tablets	100	3.94	4Q 92	4c
Childbirth, cesarean, hospital		5034	91	62r
Childbirth, cesarean, physician's fee		2053	91	62r
Childbirth, normal, hospital		2712	91	62r
Childbirth, normal, physician's fee		1492	91	62r
Dentist's fee, adult teeth cleaning and periodic oral exam	visit	45.17	4Q 92	4c
Doctor's fee, routine exam, established patient	visit	43.00	4Q 92	4c
Hospital care, semiprivate room	day	143.85	90	27c
Hospital care, semiprivate room	day	347.00	4Q 92	4c
Medical insurance premium, per employee, small group comprehensive	month	386.90	10/91	25c
Mental health care, exp	capita	37.60-53.67	90	38s
Mental health care, exp, state mental health agency	capita	38.35	90	38s
Mental health care, hospital psychiatric services, non-Federal, exp	capita	13.58	88	38s
Mental health care, mental health organization, multiservice, exp	capita	12.40	88	38s
Mental health care, psychiatric hospitals, private, exp	capita	9.49	88	38s

Birmingham, AL - continued

Item	Per	Value	Date	Ref.
Health Care - continued				
Mental health care, state and county mental hospitals, exp	capita	22.15	88	38s
Mental health care, VA medical centers, exp	capita	10.94	88	38s
Physician fee, family practice, first-visit		75.00	91	62r
Physician fee, family practice, revisit		34.00	91	62r
Physician fee, general practice, first-visit		61.00	91	62r
Physician fee, general practice, revisit		32.00	91	62r
Physician fee, general surgeon, first-visit		64.00	91	62r
Physician fee, general surgeon, revisit		40.00	91	62r
Physician fee, internal medicine, first-visit		98.00	91	62r
Physician fee, internal medicine, revisit		40.00	91	62r
Physician fee, median, neurosurgeon, first-visit		130.00	91	62r
Physician fee, median, nonsurgical specialist, first-visit		95.00	91	62r
Physician fee, median, orthopedic surgeon, first-visit		91.00	91	62r
Physician fee, median, plastic surgeon, first-visit		66.00	91	62r
Physician fee, median, surgical specialist, first-visit		62.00	91	62r
Physician fee, neurosurgeon, revisit		50.00	91	62r
Physician fee, nonsurgical specialist, revisit		40.00	91	62r
Physician fee, obstetrics/gynecology, first-visit		64.00	91	62r
Physician fee, obstetrics/gynecology, revisit		41.00	91	62r
Physician fee, orthopedic surgeon, revisit		40.00	91	62r
Physician fee, pediatrician, first-visit		49.00	91	62r
Physician fee, pediatrician, revisit		33.00	91	62r
Physician fee, plastic surgeon, revisit		43.00	91	62r
Physician fee, surgical specialist, revisit		37.00	91	62r
Substance abuse, hospital ancillary charge	incident	1390	90	70s
Substance abuse, hospital physician charge	incident	520	90	70s
Substance abuse, hospital room and board	incident	5830	90	70s
Household Goods				
Appliance repair, home, service call, washing machine	min labor charge	31.39	4Q 92	4c
Laundry detergent, Tide Ultra, Bold, or Cheer	42 oz	2.73	4Q 92	4c
Tissues, facial, Kleenex brand	175-count box	1.03	4Q 92	4c
Housing				
ACCRA Index, Housing		102.20	4Q 92	4c
Home, median price	unit	90.90		26c
House, 1,800 sq ft, 8,000 sq ft lot, new, urban	total	116391	4Q 92	4c
House payment, principal and interest, 25% down payment	month	644	4Q 92	4c
Mortgage rate, incl. points & origination fee, 30-year fixed or adjustable rate	percent	8.06	4Q 92	4c
Rent, apartment, 2 bedrooms - 1-1/2 to 2 baths, unfurnished, 950 sq ft, water	month	468	4Q 92	4c
Rental unit, 1 bedroom	month	365	93	23c
Rental unit, 2 bedroom	month	428	93	23c
Rental unit, 3 bedroom	month	535	93	23c
Rental unit, 4 bedroom	month	599	93	23c
Rental unit, efficiency	month	299	93	23c
Insurance and Pensions				
Auto insurance, private passenger	year	562.59	91	63s
Personal Goods				
Shampoo, Alberto VO5	15 oz	0.92	4Q 92	4c
Toothpaste, Crest or Colgate	6-7 oz	1.81	4Q 92	4c
Personal Services				
Dry cleaning, man's 2-piece suit		6.05	4Q 92	4c

Values are in dollars or fractions of dollars. In the column headed *Ref*, references are shown to sources. Each reference is followed by a letter. These refer to the geographical level for which data were reported: s=State, r=Region, and c=City or metro. The abbreviation *ex* is used to mean *except* or *excluding*; *exp* stands for expenditures. For other abbreviations and further explanations, please see the Introduction.

Birmingham, AL - continued

Item	Per	Value	Date	Ref.
Personal Services				
Haircare, woman's shampoo, trim and blow-dry		18.17	4Q 92	4c
Haircut, man's barbershop, no styling		8.17	4Q 92	4c
Restaurant Food				
Chicken, fried, thigh and drumstick		2.09	4Q 92	4c
Hamburger with cheese	1/4 lb	1.84	4Q 92	4c
Pizza, Pizza Hut or Pizza Inn, cheese, thin crust	12-13 in	8.79	4Q 92	4c
Taxes				
Tax, cigarette	pack	16.50	91	77s
Tax, gasoline	gal	16	91	77s
Taxes, state	capita	964	91	77s
Transportation				
ACCRA Index, Transportation		99.60	4Q 92	4c
Auto fixed costs, midsize		3432	91	60c
Auto operating cost, midsize		1350	91	60c
Auto rental, average	day	57.00	6/91	60c
Bus fare	one-way	0.80	3/93	2c
Bus fare, up to 10 miles	one-way	1.00	4Q 92	4c
Driver's license fee		15.00	12/90	43s
Taxi fare, airport-city, average	day	8.50	6/91	60c
Tire balance, computer or spin balance, front	wheel	6.33	4Q 92	4c
Travel				
Breakfast	day	6.27	6/91	60c
Business travel	day	193.00	4/93	89r
Dinner	day	18.66	6/91	60c
Lodging	day	74.00	91	60c
Lunch	day	7.93	6/91	60c
Utilities				
ACCRA Index, Utilities		119.60	4Q 92	4c
Electricity	mil Btu	16.46	90	64s
Electricity, partial electric and other energy, 1,800 sq ft living area new home	month	85.84	4Q 92	4c
Electricity, winter, 250 KWh	month	24.54	92	55c
Electricity, winter, 500 KWh	month	41.85	92	55c
Electricity, winter, 750 KWh	month	59.15	92	55c
Electricity, winter, 1000 KWh	month	73.38	92	55c

Bismarck, ND

Item	Per	Value	Date	Ref.
Child Care				
Child care fee, average, center	hour	1.63	90	65r
Child care fee, average, nonregulated family day care	hour	1.83	90	65r
Child care fee, average, regulated family day care	hour	1.42	90	65r
Communications				
Long-distance telephone service, day, initial minute, 0-100 miles	min	0.24-0.51	91	12s
Long-distance telephone service, day, additional minute, 0-100 miles	min	0.10-0.35	91	12s
Long-distance telephone service, evenings/weekends, 0-100 mi, initial minute	min	0.14-0.31	91	12s
Long-distance telephone service, evenings/weekends, 0-100 mi, additional minute	min	0.06-0.21	91	12s
Education				
Board, 4-yr private college/university	year	1422	91	22s
Board, 4-yr public college/university	year	1618	91	22s
Expenditures, local gov't, public elementary/secondary	pupil	8755	92	20s
Room, 4-year private college/university	year	1049	91	22s
Room, 4-year public college/university	year	790	91	22s
Tuition, 2-year public college/university	year	1584	91	22s
Tuition, 4-year private college/university	year	5389	91	22s

Bismarck, ND - continued

Item	Per	Value	Date	Ref.
Education - continued				
Tuition, 4-year public college/university, in-state	year	1930	91	22s
Energy and Fuels				
Coal	mil Btu	1.18	90	64s
Energy	mil Btu	6.64	90	64s
Energy exp/householder, 1-family unit	year	473	90	28r
Energy exp/householder, <1,000 sq ft heating area	year	429	90	28r
Energy exp/householder, 1,000-1,999 sq ft heating area	year	442	90	28r
Energy exp/householder, 2,000+ sq ft heating area	year	498	90	28r
Energy exp/householder, mobile home	year	442	90	28r
Energy exp/householder, multifamily	year	407	90	28r
Gas, natural	mil Btu	4.12	90	64s
Gas, natural	000 cu ft	4.82	91	46s
Gas, natural, exp	year	568	91	46s
Gasoline, unleaded regular	mil Btu	9.87	90	64s
Entertainment				
Miniature golf admission	adult	6.18	92	1r
Miniature golf admission	child	5.14	92	1r
Waterpark admission	adult	11.00	92	1r
Waterpark admission	child	8.55	92	1r
Funerals				
Casket, 18-gauge steel, velvet interior		1952.97	91	24r
Cosmetology, hair care, etc.		90.03	91	24r
Embalming		251.75	91	24r
Facility use for ceremony		180.75	91	24r
Hearse, local		117.51	91	24r
Limousine, local		71.86	91	24r
Remains to funeral home, transfer		81.14	91	24r
Service charge, professional		740.03	91	24r
Vault, concrete, non-metallic liner		801.47	91	24r
Viewing facilities, use		169.33	91	24r
Groceries				
Apples, Red Delicious	lb	0.77	4/93	16r
Bacon	lb	1.85	4/93	16r
Bananas	lb	0.46	4/93	16r
Beef, stew, boneless	lb	2.53	4/93	16r
Bologna, all beef or mixed	lb	2.19	4/93	16r
Bread, white, pan	lb	0.78	4/93	16r
Butter	lb	1.50	4/93	16r
Cabbage	lb	0.40	4/93	16r
Carrots, short trimmed and topped	lb	0.45	4/93	16r
Cheese, Cheddar	lb	3.47	4/93	16r
Chicken, fresh, whole	lb	0.84	4/93	16r
Chicken breast, bone-in	lb	1.94	4/93	16r
Chicken legs, bone-in	lb	1.02	4/93	16r
Chuck roast, graded and ungraded, ex USDA prime and choice	lb	2.43	4/93	16r
Chuck roast, USDA choice, bone-in	lb	2.11	4/93	16r
Chuck roast, USDA choice, boneless	lb	2.44	4/93	16r
Coffee, 100% ground roast, all sizes	lb	2.47	4/93	16r
Cookies, chocolate chip	lb	2.73	4/93	16r
Eggs, Grade A large	doz	0.93	4/93	16r
Flour, white, all purpose	lb	0.21	4/93	16r
Grapefruit	lb	0.45	4/93	16r
Grapes, Thompson Seedless	lb	1.46	4/93	16r
Ground beef, 100% beef	lb	1.63	4/93	16r
Ground beef, lean and extra lean	lb	2.08	4/93	16r
Ground chuck, 100% beef	lb	1.94	4/93	16r
Ham, boneless, excluding canned	lb	2.21	4/93	16r
Ice cream, prepackaged, bulk, regular	1/2 gal	2.41	4/93	16r
Lemons	lb	0.82	4/93	16r
Lettuce, iceberg	lb	0.83	4/93	16r
Margarine, stick	lb	0.77	4/93	16r
Oranges, navel	lb	0.50	4/93	16r
Peanut butter, creamy, all sizes	lb	1.82	4/93	16r
Pears, Anjou	lb	0.85	4/93	16r

Values are in dollars or fractions of dollars. In the column headed *Ref*, references are shown to sources. Each reference is followed by a letter. These refer to the geographical level for which data were reported: s = State, r = Region, and c = City or metro. The abbreviation *ex* is used to mean *except* or *excluding*; *exp* stands for *expenditures*. For other abbreviations and further explanations, please see the Introduction.

Bismarck, ND - continued

Item	Per	Value	Date	Ref.
Groceries				
Pork chops, center cut, bone-in	lb	3.17	4/93	16r
Potato chips	16 oz	2.68	4/93	16r
Potatoes, white	lb	0.26	4/93	16r
Round roast, graded & ungraded, ex USDA prime & choice	lb	2.88	4/93	16r
Round roast, USDA choice, boneless	lb	2.96	4/93	16r
Shortening, vegetable oil blends	lb	0.79	4/93	16r
Spaghetti and macaroni	lb	0.76	4/93	16r
Steak, rib eye, USDA choice, boneless	lb	6.29	4/93	16r
Steak, round, USDA choice, boneless	lb	3.24	4/93	16r
Steak, sirloin, graded & ungraded, ex USDA prime & choice	lb	4.00	4/93	16r
Steak, sirloin, USDA choice, bone-in	lb	3.57	4/93	16r
Steak, sirloin, USDA choice, boneless	lb	4.17	4/93	16r
Steak, T-bone, USDA choice, bone-in	lb	5.60	4/93	16r
Strawberries, dry pint	12 oz	0.90	4/93	16r
Sugar, white	lb	0.36	4/93	16r
Sugar, white, 33-80 oz pk	lb	0.35	4/93	16r
Tomatoes, field grown	lb	0.99	4/93	16r
Tuna, chunk, light	lb	1.76	4/93	16r
Turkey, frozen, whole	lb	0.91	4/93	16r
Health Care				
Childbirth, cesarean, hospital		4688	91	62r
Childbirth, cesarean, physician's fee		2053	91	62r
Childbirth, normal, hospital		2657	91	62r
Childbirth, normal, physician's fee		1492	91	62r
Medical plan per employee	year	3443	91	45r
Mental health care, exp	capita	28.84-37.59	90	38s
Mental health care, exp, state mental health agency	capita	40.24	90	38s
Mental health care, hospital psychiatric services, non-Federal, exp	capita	18.67	88	38s
Mental health care, mental health organization, multiservice, exp	capita	27.50	88	38s
Mental health care, state and county mental hospitals, exp	capita	32.62	88	38s
Physician fee, family practice, first-visit		76.00	91	62r
Physician fee, family practice, revisit		33.00	91	62r
Physician fee, general practice, first-visit		61.00	91	62r
Physician fee, general practice, revisit		31.00	91	62r
Physician fee, general surgeon, first-visit		65.00	91	62r
Physician fee, general surgeon, revisit		35.00	91	62r
Physician fee, internal medicine, first-visit		91.00	91	62r
Physician fee, internal medicine, revisit		40.00	91	62r
Physician fee, median, neurosurgeon, first-visit		106.00	91	62r
Physician fee, median, nonsurgical specialist, first-visit		90.00	91	62r
Physician fee, median, orthopedic surgeon, first-visit		83.00	91	62r
Physician fee, median, surgical specialist, first-visit		61.00	91	62r
Physician fee, neurosurgeon, revisit		41.00	91	62r
Physician fee, nonsurgical specialist, revisit		40.00	91	62r
Physician fee, obstetrics/gynecology, first-visit		61.00	91	62r
Physician fee, obstetrics/gynecology, revisit		40.00	91	62r
Physician fee, orthopedic surgeon, revisit		41.00	91	62r
Physician fee, pediatrician, first-visit		46.00	91	62r
Physician fee, pediatrician, revisit		33.00	91	62r
Physician fee, surgical specialist, revisit		36.00	91	62r
Insurance and Pensions				
Auto insurance, private passenger	year	413.64	91	63s
Taxes				
Tax, cigarette	pack	29	91	77s
Tax, gasoline	gal	17	91	77s
Taxes, state	capita	1189	91	77s

Bismarck, ND - continued

Item	Per	Value	Date	Ref.
Transportation				
Driver's license fee		10.00	12/90	43s
Vehicle registration and license plate	year	26.00-251.00	92	51s
Utilities				
Electricity	mil Btu	16.86	90	64s

Bloomington, IN

Item	Per	Value	Date	Ref.
Composite ACCRA index		102.50	4Q 92	4c
Alcoholic Beverages				
Beer, Miller Lite or Budweiser, 12-oz containers	6 pack	3.73	4Q 92	4c
Liquor, J & B Scotch	750 ml	15.35	4Q 92	4c
Wine, Gallo Chablis blanc, 1.5 liter	bottle	4.65	4Q 92	4c
Child Care				
Child care fee, average, center	hour	1.63	90	65r
Child care fee, average, nonregulated family day care	hour	1.83	90	65r
Child care fee, average, regulated family day care	hour	1.42	90	65r
Clothing				
Jeans, man's denim		32.99	4Q 92	4c
Shirt, man's dress shirt		26.12	4Q 92	4c
Undervest, boy's size 10-14, cotton	3	4.07	4Q 92	4c
Communications				
Long-distance telephone service, day, initial minute, 0-100 miles	min	0.18-0.45	91	12s
Long-distance telephone service, day, additional minute, 0-100 miles	min	0.10-0.30	91	12s
Long-distance telephone service, evenings/weekends, 0-100 mi, initial minute	min	0.08-0.19	91	12s
Long-distance telephone service, evenings/weekends, 0-100 mi, additional minute	min	0.04-0.13	91	12s
Newspaper subscription, daily and Sunday home delivery, large-city	month	9.95	4Q 92	4c
Telephone, flat rate	month	9.85	91	11c
Telephone bill, family of four	month	21.14	4Q 92	4c
Education				
Board, 4-yr private college/university	year	1714	91	22s
Board, 4-yr public college/university	year	1829	91	22s
Expenditures, local gov't, public elementary/secondary	pupil	5545	92	20s
Room, 4-year private college/university	year	1512	91	22s
Room, 4-year public college/university	year	1435	91	22s
Tuition, 2-year private college/university	year	6756	91	22s
Tuition, 2-year public college/university	year	1423	91	22s
Tuition, 4-year private college/university	year	8451	91	22s
Tuition, 4-year public college/university, in-state	year	2067	91	22s
Energy and Fuels				
Coal	mil Btu	1.46	90	64s
Energy	mil Btu	6.77	90	64s
Energy, combined forms, 1,800 sq ft heating area	month	105.56	4Q 92	4c
Energy, exc electricity, 1,800 sq ft heating area	month	47.75	4Q 92	4c
Energy exp/householder, 1-family unit	year	471	90	28r
Energy exp/householder, <1,000 sq ft heating area	year	430	90	28r
Energy exp/householder, 1,000-1,999 sq ft heating area	year	481	90	28r
Energy exp/householder, 2,000+ sq ft heating area	year	473	90	28r
Energy exp/householder, mobile home	year	430	90	28r
Energy exp/householder, multifamily	year	461	90	28r
Gas, natural	mil Btu	4.27	90	64s
Gas, natural	000 cu ft	5.46	91	46s

Values are in dollars or fractions of dollars. In the column headed *Ref*, references are shown to sources. Each reference is followed by a letter. These refer to the geographical level for which data were reported: s = State, r = Region, and c = City or metro. The abbreviation *ex* is used to mean *except* or *excluding*; *exp* stands for expenditures. For other abbreviations and further explanations, please see the Introduction.

Bloomington, IN - continued

Item	Per	Value	Date	Ref.
Energy and Fuels				
Gas, natural, exp	year	588	91	46s
Gasoline, motor	gal	1.08	4Q 92	4c
Gasoline, unleaded regular	mil Btu	8.74	90	64s
Entertainment				
Bowling, evening rate	game	2.00	4Q 92	4c
Miniature golf admission	adult	6.18	92	1r
Miniature golf admission	chlld	5.14	92	1r
Monopoly game, Parker Brothers', No. 9		11.04	4Q 92	4c
Movie	admission	5.00	4Q 92	4c
Tennis balls, yellow, Wilson or Penn, 3	can	3.04	4Q 92	4c
Waterpark admission	adult	11.00	92	1r
Waterpark admission	child	8.55	92	1r
Funerals				
Casket, 18-gauge steel, velvet interior		1926.72	91	24r
Cosmetology, hair care, etc.		97.64	91	24r
Embalming		249.14	91	24r
Facility use for ceremony		208.59	91	24r
Hearse, local		130.12	91	24r
Limousine, local		104.66	91	24r
Remains to funeral home, transfer		93.61	91	24r
Service charge, professional		724.62	91	24r
Vault, concrete, non-metallic liner		734.53	91	24r
Viewing facilities, use		236.06	91	24r
Goods and Services				
ACCRA Index, Miscellaneous Goods and Services		103.20	4Q 92	4c
Groceries				
ACCRA Index, Groceries		104.70	4Q 92	4c
Apples, Red Delicious	lb	0.77	4/93	16r
Babyfood, strained vegetables, lowest price	4-4.5 oz jar	0.37	4Q 92	4c
Bacon	lb	1.85	4/93	16r
Bananas	lb	0.55	4Q 92	4c
Bananas	lb	0.46	4/93	16r
Beef, stew, boneless	lb	2.53	4/93	16r
Bologna, all beef or mixed	lb	2.19	4/93	16r
Bread, white	24 oz	0.58	4Q 92	4c
Bread, white, pan	lb	0.78	4/93	16r
Butter	lb	1.50	4/93	16r
Cabbage	lb	0.40	4/93	16r
Carrots, short trimmed and topped	lb	0.45	4/93	16r
Cheese, Cheddar	lb	3.47	4/93	16r
Cheese, Kraft grated Parmesan	8-oz canister	3.43	4Q 92	4c
Chicken, fresh, whole	lb	0.84	4/93	16r
Chicken, fryer, whole	lb	0.79	4Q 92	4c
Chicken breast, bone-in	lb	1.94	4/93	16r
Chicken legs, bone-in	lb	1.02	4/93	16r
Chuck roast, graded and ungraded, ex USDA prime and choice	lb	2.43	4/93	16r
Chuck roast, USDA choice, bone-in	lb	2.11	4/93	16r
Chuck roast, USDA choice, boneless	lb	2.44	4/93	16r
Cigarettes, Winston	carton	16.81	4Q 92	4c
Coffee, 100% ground roast, all sizes	lb	2.47	4/93	16r
Coffee, vacuum-packed	13-oz can	2.25	4Q 92	4c
Cookies, chocolate chip	lb	2.73	4/93	16r
Corn, frozen	10 oz	0.75	4Q 92	4c
Corn Flakes, Kellogg's or Post Toasties	18 oz	2.13	4Q 92	4c
Eggs, Grade A large	doz	0.79	4Q 92	4c
Eggs, Grade A large	doz	0.93	4/93	16r
Flour, white, all purpose	lb	0.21	4/93	16r
Grapefruit	lb	0.45	4/93	16r
Grapes, Thompson Seedless	lb	1.46	4/93	16r
Ground beef, 100% beef	lb	1.63	4/93	16r
Ground beef, lean and extra lean	lb	2.08	4/93	16r
Ground beef or hamburger	lb	1.65	4Q 92	4c
Ground chuck, 100% beef	lb	1.94	4/93	16r

Bloomington, IN - continued

Item	Per	Value	Date	Ref.
Groceries - continued				
Ham, boneless, excluding canned	lb	2.21	4/93	16r
Honey, jar	8 oz	0.97-1.25	92	5r
Honey, jar	lb	1.25-2.25	92	5r
Honey, squeeze bear	12-oz	1.25-1.99	92	5r
Ice cream, prepackaged, bulk, regular	1/2 gal	2.41	4/93	16r
Lemons	lb	0.82	4/93	16r
Lettuce, iceberg	head	0.91	4Q 92	4c
Lettuce, iceberg	lb	0.83	4/93	16r
Margarine, Blue Bonnet or Parkay cubes	lb	0.77	4Q 92	4c
Margarine, stick	lb	0.77	4/93	16r
Milk, whole	1/2 gal	1.55	4Q 92	4c
Orange juice, Minute Maid frozen	12-oz can	1.57	4Q 92	4c
Oranges, navel	lb	0.50	4/93	16r
Peaches	29-oz can	1.40	4Q 92	4c
Peanut butter, creamy, all sizes	lb	1.82	4/93	16r
Pears, Anjou	lb	0.85	4/93	16r
Peas Sweet, Del Monte or Green Giant	15-17 oz can	0.67	4Q 92	4c
Pork chops, center cut, bone-in	lb	3.17	4/93	16r
Potato chips	16 oz	2.68	4/93	16r
Potatoes, white	lb	0.26	4/93	16r
Potatoes, white or red	10-lb sack	2.03	4Q 92	4c
Round roast, graded & ungraded, ex USDA prime & choice	lb	2.88	4/93	16r
Round roast, USDA choice, boneless	lb	2.96	4/93	16r
Sausage, Jimmy Dean, 100% pork	lb	2.75	4Q 92	4c
Shortening, vegetable oil blends	lb	0.79	4/93	16r
Shortening, vegetable, Crisco	3-lb can	2.58	4Q 92	4c
Soft drink, Coca Cola	2 liter	1.23	4Q 92	4c
Spaghetti and macaroni	lb	0.76	4/93	16r
Steak, rib eye, USDA choice, boneless	lb	6.29	4/93	16r
Steak, round, USDA choice, boneless	lb	3.24	4/93	16r
Steak, sirloin, graded & ungraded, ex USDA prime & choice	lb	4.00	4/93	16r
Steak, sirloin, USDA choice, bone-in	lb	3.57	4/93	16r
Steak, sirloin, USDA choice, boneless	lb	4.17	4/93	16r
Steak, T-bone	lb	5.01	4Q 92	4c
Steak, T-bone, USDA choice, bone-in	lb	5.60	4/93	16r
Strawberries, dry pint	12 oz	0.90	4/93	16r
Sugar, cane or beet	4 lb	1.49	4Q 92	4c
Sugar, white	lb	0.36	4/93	16r
Sugar, white, 33-80 oz pk	lb	0.35	4/93	16r
Tomatoes, field grown	lb	0.99	4/93	16r
Tomatoes, Hunt's or Del Monte	14.5-oz can	0.85	4Q 92	4c
Tuna, chunk, light	6.125-6.5 oz can	0.69	4Q 92	4c
Tuna, chunk, light	lb	1.76	4/93	16r
Turkey, frozen, whole	lb	0.91	4/93	16r
Health Care				
ACCRA Index, Health Care		97.20	4Q 92	4c
Analgesic, Aspirin, Bayer, 325 mg tablets	100	5.72	4Q 92	4c
Childbirth, cesarean, hospital		4688	91	62r
Childbirth, cesarean, physician's fee		2053	91	62r
Childbirth, normal, hospital		2657	91	62r
Childbirth, normal, physician's fee		1492	91	62r
Dentist's fee, adult teeth cleaning and periodic oral exam	visit	41.60	4Q 92	4c
Doctor's fee, routine exam, established patient	visit	31.60	4Q 92	4c
Hospital care, semiprivate room	day	336.00	90	27c
Hospital care, semiprivate room	day	399.00	4Q 92	4c
Medical insurance premium, per employee, small group comprehensive	month	267.40	10/91	25c
Medical plan per employee	year	3443	91	45r
Mental health care, exp	capita	37.60-53.67	90	38s

Values are in dollars or fractions of dollars. In the column headed *Ref*, references are shown to sources. Each reference is followed by a letter. These refer to the geographical level for which data were reported: s=State, r=Region, and c=City or metro. The abbreviation *ex* is used to mean *except* or *excluding*; *exp* stands for expenditures. For other abbreviations and further explanations, please see the Introduction.

Bloomington, IN - continued

Item	Per	Value	Date	Ref.
Health Care				
Mental health care, exp, state mental health agency	capita	47.05	90	38s
Mental health care, hospital psychiatric services, non-Federal, exp	capita	22.14	88	38s
Mental health care, mental health organization, multiservice, exp	capita	10.33	88	38s
Mental health care, psychiatric hospitals, private, exp	capita	20.10	88	38s
Mental health care, state and county mental hospitals, exp	capita	24.00	88	38s
Mental health care, VA medical centers, exp	capita	3.20	88	38s
Physician fee, family practice, first-visit		76.00	91	62r
Physician fee, family practice, revisit		33.00	91	62r
Physician fee, general practice, first-visit		61.00	91	62r
Physician fee, general practice, revisit		31.00	91	62r
Physician fee, general surgeon, first-visit		65.00	91	62r
Physician fee, general surgeon, revisit		35.00	91	62r
Physician fee, internal medicine, first-visit		91.00	91	62r
Physician fee, internal medicine, revisit		40.00	91	62r
Physician fee, median, neurosurgeon, first-visit		106.00	91	62r
Physician fee, median, nonsurgical specialist, first-visit		90.00	91	62r
Physician fee, median, orthopedic surgeon, first-visit		83.00	91	62r
Physician fee, median, surgical specialist, first-visit		61.00	91	62r
Physician fee, neurosurgeon, revisit		41.00	91	62r
Physician fee, nonsurgical specialist, revisit		40.00	91	62r
Physician fee, obstetrics/gynecology, first-visit		61.00	91	62r
Physician fee, obstetrics/gynecology, revisit		40.00	91	62r
Physician fee, orthopedic surgeon, revisit		41.00	91	62r
Physician fee, pediatrician, first-visit		46.00	91	62r
Physician fee, pediatrician, revisit		33.00	91	62r
Physician fee, surgical specialist, revisit		36.00	91	62r
Substance abuse, hospital ancillary charge	incident	1230	90	70s
Substance abuse, hospital physician charge	incident	410	90	70s
Substance abuse, hospital room and board	incident	5510	90	70s
Household Goods				
Appliance repair, home, service call, washing machine	min labor charge	36.59	4Q 92	4c
Laundry detergent, Tide Ultra, Bold, or Cheer	42 oz	3.97	4Q 92	4c
Tissues, facial, Kleenex brand	175-count box	1.17	4Q 92	4c
Housing				
ACCRA Index, Housing		106.10	4Q 92	4c
House, 1,800 sq ft, 8,000 sq ft lot, new, urban	total	117324	4Q 92	4c
House payment, principal and interest, 25% down payment	month	665	4Q 92	4c
Mortgage rate, incl. points & origination fee, 30-year fixed or adjustable rate	percent	8.32	4Q 92	4c
Rent, apartment, 2 bedrooms - 1-1/2 to 2 baths, unfurnished, 950 sq ft, water	month	493	4Q 92	4c
Rental unit, 1 bedroom	month	373	93	23c
Rental unit, 2 bedroom	month	440	93	23c
Rental unit, 3 bedroom	month	551	93	23c
Rental unit, 4 bedroom	month	617	93	23c
Rental unit, efficiency	month	307	93	23c
Insurance and Pensions				
Auto insurance, private passenger	year	548.99	91	63s

Bloomington, IN - continued

Item	Per	Value	Date	Ref.
Personal Goods				
Shampoo, Alberto VO5	15 oz	1.50	4Q 92	4c
Toothpaste, Crest or Colgate	6-7 oz	2.27	4Q 92	4c
Personal Services				
Dry cleaning, man's 2-piece suit		5.80	4Q 92	4c
Haircare, woman's shampoo, trim and blow-dry		16.60	4Q 92	4c
Haircut, man's barbershop, no styling		7.15	4Q 92	4c
Restaurant Food				
Chicken, fried, thigh and drumstick		2.08	4Q 92	4c
Hamburger with cheese	1/4 lb	1.79	4Q 92	4c
Pizza, Pizza Hut or Pizza Inn, cheese, thin crust	12-13 in	8.81	4Q 92	4c
Taxes				
Tax, cigarette	pack	15.50	91	77s
Tax, gasoline	gal	15	91	77s
Taxes, state	capita	1102	91	77s
Transportation				
ACCRA Index, Transportation		93.80	4Q 92	4c
Bus fare	one-way	0.50	3/93	2c
Driver's license fee		6.00	12/90	43s
Tire balance, computer or spin balance, front	wheel	6.00	4Q 92	4c
Utilities				
ACCRA Index, Utilities		97.90	4Q 92	4c
Electricity	mil Btu	15.75	90	64s
Electricity, partial electric and other energy, 1,800 sq ft living area new home	month	57.81	4Q 92	4c

Bloomington-Normal, IL

Item	Per	Value	Date	Ref.
Composite ACCRA index		104.40	4Q 92	4c
Alcoholic Beverages				
Beer, Miller Lite or Budweiser, 12-oz containers	6 pack	3.81	4Q 92	4c
Liquor, J & B Scotch	750 ml	14.43	4Q 92	4c
Wine, Gallo Chablis blanc, 1.5 liter	bottle	4.57	4Q 92	4c
Child Care				
Child care fee, average, center	hour	1.63	90	65r
Child care fee, average, nonregulated family day care	hour	1.83	90	65r
Child care fee, average, regulated family day care	hour	1.42	90	65r
Clothing				
Jeans, man's denim		33.99	4Q 92	4c
Shirt, man's dress shirt		30.70	4Q 92	4c
Undervest, boy's size 10-14, cotton	3	4.37	4Q 92	4c
Communications				
Long-distance telephone service, day, initial minute, 0-100 miles	min	0.10-0.34	91	12s
Long-distance telephone service, day, additional minute, 0-100 miles	min	0.04-0.16	91	12s
Long-distance telephone service, evenings/weekends, 0-100 mi, initial minute	min	0.06-0.20	91	12s
Long-distance telephone service, evenings/weekends, 0-100 mi, additional minute	min	0.02-0.10	91	12s
Newspaper subscription, daily and Sunday home delivery, large-city	month	11.96	4Q 92	4c
Telephone bill, family of four	month	21.09	4Q 92	4c
Education				
Board, 4-yr private college/university	year	1797	91	22s
Board, 4-yr public college/university	year	1857	91	22s
Expenditures, local gov't, public elementary/secondary	pupil	5248	92	20s
Room, 4-year private college/university	year	2095	91	22s
Room, 4-year public college/university	year	1454	91	22s

Values are in dollars or fractions of dollars. In the column headed *Ref*, references are shown to sources. Each reference is followed by a letter. These refer to the geographical level for which data were reported: s=State, r=Region, and c=City or metro. The abbreviation *ex* is used to mean *except* or *excluding*; *exp* stands for expenditures. For other abbreviations and further explanations, please see the Introduction.

Bloomington-Normal, IL - continued

Item	Per	Value	Date	Ref.
Education				
Tuition, 2-year private college/university	year	5279	91	22s
Tuition, 2-year public college/university	year	906	91	22s
Tuition, 4-year private college/university	year	8853	91	22s
Tuition, 4-year public college/university, in-state	year	2465	91	22s
Energy and Fuels				
Coal	mil Btu	1.72	90	64s
Energy	mil Btu	8.74	90	64s
Energy, combined forms, 1,800 sq ft heating area	month	133.71	4Q 92	4c
Energy, exc electricity, 1,800 sq ft heating area	month	46.30	4Q 92	4c
Energy exp/householder, 1-family unit	year	471	90	28r
Energy exp/householder, <1,000 sq ft heating area	year	430	90	28r
Energy exp/householder, 1,000-1,999 sq ft heating area	year	481	90	28r
Energy exp/householder, 2,000+ sq ft heating area	year	473	90	28r
Energy exp/householder, mobile home	year	430	90	28r
Energy exp/householder, multifamily	year	461	90	28r
Gas, natural	mil Btu	4.57	90	64s
Gas, natural	000 cu ft	4.95	91	46s
Gas, natural, exp	year	696	91	46s
Gasoline, motor	gal	1.15	4Q 92	4c
Gasoline, unleaded regular	mil Btu	9.35	90	64s
Entertainment				
Bowling, evening rate	game	2.27	4Q 92	4c
Miniature golf admission	adult	6.18	92	1r
Miniature golf admission	child	5.14	92	1r
Monopoly game, Parker Brothers', No. 9		11.64	4Q 92	4c
Movie	admission	5.00	4Q 92	4c
Tennis balls, yellow, Wilson or Penn, 3	can	2.68	4Q 92	4c
Waterpark admission	adult	11.00	92	1r
Waterpark admission	child	8.55	92	1r
Funerals				
Casket, 18-gauge steel, velvet interior		1926.72	91	24r
Cosmetology, hair care, etc.		97.64	91	24r
Embalming		249.14	91	24r
Facility use for ceremony		208.59	91	24r
Hearse, local		130.12	91	24r
Limousine, local		104.66	91	24r
Remains to funeral home, transfer		93.61	91	24r
Service charge, professional		724.62	91	24r
Vault, concrete, non-metallic liner		734.53	91	24r
Viewing facilities, use		236.06	91	24r
Goods and Services				
ACCRA Index, Miscellaneous Goods and Services		106.80	4Q 92	4c
Groceries				
ACCRA Index, Groceries		100.50	4Q 92	4c
Apples, Red Delicious	lb	0.77	4/93	16r
Babyfood, strained vegetables, lowest price	4-4.5 oz jar	0.31	4Q 92	4c
Bacon	lb	1.85	4/93	16r
Bananas	lb	0.49	4Q 92	4c
Bananas	lb	0.46	4/93	16r
Beef, stew, boneless	lb	2.53	4/93	16r
Bologna, all beef or mixed	lb	2.19	4/93	16r
Bread, white	24 oz	0.67	4Q 92	4c
Bread, white, pan	lb	0.78	4/93	16r
Butter	lb	1.50	4/93	16r
Cabbage	lb	0.40	4/93	16r
Carrots, short trimmed and topped	lb	0.45	4/93	16r
Cheese, Cheddar	lb	3.47	4/93	16r

Bloomington-Normal, IL - continued

Item	Per	Value	Date	Ref.
Groceries - continued				
Cheese, Kraft grated Parmesan	8-oz canister	3.12	4Q 92	4c
Chicken, fresh, whole	lb	0.84	4/93	16r
Chicken, fryer, whole	lb	0.59	4Q 92	4c
Chicken breast, bone-in	lb	1.94	4/93	16r
Chicken legs, bone-in	lb	1.02	4/93	16r
Chuck roast, graded and ungraded, ex USDA prime and choice	lb	2.43	4/93	16r
Chuck roast, USDA choice, bone-in	lb	2.11	4/93	16r
Chuck roast, USDA choice, boneless	lb	2.44	4/93	16r
Cigarettes, Winston	carton	18.06	4Q 92	4c
Coffee, 100% ground roast, all sizes	lb	2.47	4/93	16r
Coffee, vacuum-packed	13-oz can	2.19	4Q 92	4c
Cookies, chocolate chip	lb	2.73	4/93	16r
Corn, frozen	10 oz	0.68	4Q 92	4c
Corn Flakes, Kellogg's or Post Toasties	18 oz	1.79	4Q 92	4c
Eggs, Grade A large	doz	0.79	4Q 92	4c
Eggs, Grade A large	doz	0.93	4/93	16r
Flour, white, all purpose	lb	0.21	4/93	16r
Grapefruit	lb	0.45	4/93	16r
Grapes, Thompson Seedless	lb	1.46	4/93	16r
Ground beef, 100% beef	lb	1.63	4/93	16r
Ground beef, lean and extra lean	lb	2.08	4/93	16r
Ground beef or hamburger	lb	1.69	4Q 92	4c
Ground chuck, 100% beef	lb	1.94	4/93	16r
Ham, boneless, excluding canned	lb	2.21	4/93	16r
Honey, jar	8 oz	0.97-1.25	92	5r
Honey, jar	lb	1.25-2.25	92	5r
Honey, squeeze bear	12-oz	1.25-1.99	92	5r
Ice cream, prepackaged, bulk, regular	1/2 gal	2.41	4/93	16r
Lemons	lb	0.82	4/93	16r
Lettuce, iceberg	head	0.90	4Q 92	4c
Lettuce, iceberg	lb	0.83	4/93	16r
Margarine, Blue Bonnet or Parkay cubes	lb	0.58	4Q 92	4c
Margarine, stick	lb	0.77	4/93	16r
Milk, whole	1/2 gal	1.47	4Q 92	4c
Orange juice, Minute Maid frozen	12-oz can	1.44	4Q 92	4c
Oranges, navel	lb	0.50	4/93	16r
Peaches	29-oz can	1.37	4Q 92	4c
Peanut butter, creamy, all sizes	lb	1.82	4/93	16r
Pears, Anjou	lb	0.85	4/93	16r
Peas Sweet, Del Monte or Green Giant	15-17 oz can	0.66	4Q 92	4c
Pork chops, center cut, bone-in	lb	3.17	4/93	16r
Potato chips	16 oz	2.68	4/93	16r
Potatoes, white	lb	0.26	4/93	16r
Potatoes, white or red	10-lb sack	2.77	4Q 92	4c
Round roast, graded & ungraded, ex USDA prime & choice	lb	2.88	4/93	16r
Round roast, USDA choice, boneless	lb	2.96	4/93	16r
Sausage, Jimmy Dean, 100% pork	lb	2.76	4Q 92	4c
Shortening, vegetable oil blends	lb	0.79	4/93	16r
Shortening, vegetable, Crisco	3-lb can	2.10	4Q 92	4c
Soft drink, Coca Cola	2 liter	1.10	4Q 92	4c
Spaghetti and macaroni	lb	0.76	4/93	16r
Steak, rib eye, USDA choice, boneless	lb	6.29	4/93	16r
Steak, round, USDA choice, boneless	lb	3.24	4/93	16r
Steak, sirloin, graded & ungraded, ex USDA prime & choice	lb	4.00	4/93	16r
Steak, sirloin, USDA choice, bone-in	lb	3.57	4/93	16r
Steak, sirloin, USDA choice, boneless	lb	4.17	4/93	16r
Steak, T-bone	lb	5.11	4Q 92	4c
Steak, T-bone, USDA choice, bone-in	lb	5.60	4/93	16r
Strawberries, dry pint	12 oz	0.90	4/93	16r
Sugar, cane or beet	4 lb	1.34	4Q 92	4c
Sugar, white	lb	0.36	4/93	16r

Values are in dollars or fractions of dollars. In the column headed *Ref*, references are shown to sources. Each reference is followed by a letter. These refer to the geographical level for which data were reported: s=State, r=Region, and c=City or metro. The abbreviation *ex* is used to mean *except* or *excluding*; *exp* stands for expenditures. For other abbreviations and further explanations, please see the Introduction.

Bloomington-Normal, IL - continued

Item	Per	Value	Date	Ref.
Groceries				
Sugar, white, 33-80 oz pk	lb	0.35	4/93	16r
Tomatoes, field grown	lb	0.99	4/93	16r
Tomatoes, Hunt's or Del Monte	14.5-oz can	0.73	4Q 92	4c
Tuna, chunk, light	6.125-6.5 oz can	0.64	4Q 92	4c
Tuna, chunk, light	lb	1.76	4/93	16r
Turkey, frozen, whole	lb	0.91	4/93	16r
Health Care				
ACCRA Index, Health Care		92.10	4Q 92	4c
Analgesic, Aspirin, Bayer, 325 mg tablets	100	4.42	4Q 92	4c
Childbirth, cesarean, hospital		4688	91	62r
Childbirth, cesarean, physician's fee		2053	91	62r
Childbirth, normal, hospital		2657	91	62r
Childbirth, normal, physician's fee		1492	91	62r
Dentist's fee, adult teeth cleaning and periodic oral exam	visit	44.00	4Q 92	4c
Doctor's fee, routine exam, established patient	visit	34.00	4Q 92	4c
Hospital care, semiprivate room	day	206.50	90	27c
Hospital care, semiprivate room	day	288.00	4Q 92	4c
Medical insurance premium, per employee, small group comprehensive	month	310.25	10/91	25c
Medical plan per employee	year	3443	91	45r
Mental health care, exp	capita	28.84-37.59	90	38s
Mental health care, exp, state mental health agency	capita	34.43	90	38s
Mental health care, hospital psychiatric services, non-Federal, exp	capita	18.46	88	38s
Mental health care, mental health organization, multiservice, exp	capita	11.97	88	38s
Mental health care, psychiatric hospitals, private, exp	capita	7.84	88	38s
Mental health care, psychiatric out-patient clinics, freestanding, exp	capita	3.21	88	38s
Mental health care, psychiatric partial-care organizations, freestanding, exp	capita	0.51	88	38s
Mental health care, state and county mental hospitals, exp	capita	18.11	88	38s
Mental health care, VA medical centers, exp	capita	3.69	88	38s
Physician fee, family practice, first-visit		76.00	91	62r
Physician fee, family practice, revisit		33.00	91	62r
Physician fee, general practice, first-visit		61.00	91	62r
Physician fee, general practice, revisit		31.00	91	62r
Physician fee, general surgeon, first-visit		65.00	91	62r
Physician fee, general surgeon, revisit		35.00	91	62r
Physician fee, internal medicine, first-visit		91.00	91	62r
Physician fee, internal medicine, revisit		40.00	91	62r
Physician fee, median, neurosurgeon, first-visit		106.00	91	62r
Physician fee, median, nonsurgical specialist, first-visit		90.00	91	62r
Physician fee, median, orthopedic surgeon, first-visit		83.00	91	62r
Physician fee, median, surgical specialist, first-visit		61.00	91	62r
Physician fee, neurosurgeon, revisit		41.00	91	62r
Physician fee, nonsurgical specialist, revisit		40.00	91	62r
Physician fee, obstetrics/gynecology, first-visit		61.00	91	62r
Physician fee, obstetrics/gynecology, revisit		40.00	91	62r
Physician fee, orthopedic surgeon, revisit		41.00	91	62r
Physician fee, pediatrician, first-visit		46.00	91	62r
Physician fee, pediatrician, revisit		33.00	91	62r
Physician fee, surgical specialist, revisit		36.00	91	62r
Prescription drug co-pay, Medicaid	month	25.00	91	21s
Substance abuse, hospital ancillary charge	incident	1310	90	70s
Substance abuse, hospital physician charge	incident	540	90	70s

Bloomington-Normal, IL - continued

Item	Per	Value	Date	Ref.
Health Care - continued				
Substance abuse, hospital room and board	incident	6150	90	70s
Household Goods				
Appliance repair, home, service call, washing machine	min labor charge	35.19	4Q 92	4c
Laundry detergent, Tide Ultra, Bold, or Cheer	42 oz	3.45	4Q 92	4c
Tissues, facial, Kleenex brand	175-count box	1.15	4Q 92	4c
Housing				
ACCRA Index, Housing		100.80	4Q 92	4c
House, 1,800 sq ft, 8,000 sq ft lot, new, urban	total	102835	4Q 92	4c
House payment, principal and interest, 25% down payment	month	575	4Q 92	4c
Mortgage rate, incl. points & origination fee, 30-year fixed or adjustable rate	percent	8.18	4Q 92	4c
Rent, apartment, 2 bedrooms - 1-1/2 to 2 baths, unfurnished, 950 sq ft, water	month	601	4Q 92	4c
Rental unit, 1 bedroom	month	419	93	23c
Rental unit, 2 bedroom	month	491	93	23c
Rental unit, 3 bedroom	month	614	93	23c
Rental unit, 4 bedroom	month	688	93	23c
Rental unit, efficiency	month	343	93	23c
Insurance and Pensions				
Auto insurance, private passenger	year	621.37	91	63s
Personal Goods				
Shampoo, Alberto VO5	15 oz	1.22	4Q 92	4c
Toothpaste, Crest or Colgate	6-7 oz	1.85	4Q 92	4c
Personal Services				
Dry cleaning, man's 2-piece suit		5.98	4Q 92	4c
Haircare, woman's shampoo, trim and blow-dry		22.80	4Q 92	4c
Haircut, man's barbershop, no styling		7.70	4Q 92	4c
Restaurant Food				
Chicken, fried, thigh and drumstick		2.18	4Q 92	4c
Hamburger with cheese	1/4 lb	1.86	4Q 92	4c
Pizza, Pizza Hut or Pizza Inn, cheese, thin crust	12-13 in	7.79	4Q 92	4c
Taxes				
Tax, cigarette	pack	30	91	77s
Tax, gasoline	gal	19	91	77s
Taxes, state	capita	1151	91	77s
Transportation				
ACCRA Index, Transportation		102.40	4Q 92	4c
Driver's license fee		10.00	12/90	43s
Tire balance, computer or spin balance, front	wheel	6.69	4Q 92	4c
Vehicle registration and license plate	multi-year	48.00	93	52s
Utilities				
ACCRA Index, Utilities		121.10	4Q 92	4c
Electricity	mil Btu	22.02	90	64s
Electricity, partial electric and other energy, 1,800 sq ft living area new home	month	87.41	4Q 92	4c

Blythe, CA

Item	Per	Value	Date	Ref.
Composite ACCRA index		105.70	4Q 92	4c
Alcoholic Beverages				
Beer, Miller Lite or Budweiser, 12-oz containers	6 pack	4.20	4Q 92	4c
Liquor, J & B Scotch	750 ml	16.64	4Q 92	4c
Wine, Gallo Chablis blanc, 1.5 liter	bottle	4.55	4Q 92	4c

Values are in dollars or fractions of dollars. In the column headed *Ref*, references are shown to sources. Each reference is followed by a letter. These refer to the geographical level for which data were reported: s=State, r=Region, and c=City or metro. The abbreviation *ex* is used to mean *except* or *excluding*; *exp* stands for expenditures. For other abbreviations and further explanations, please see the Introduction.

Blythe, CA - continued

Item	Per	Value	Date	Ref.
Clothing				
Jeans, man's denim		30.23	4Q 92	4c
Shirt, man's dress shirt		17.50	4Q 92	4c
Undervest, boy's size 10-14, cotton	3	4.35	4Q 92	4c
Communications				
Newspaper subscription, daily and Sunday home delivery, large-city	month	8.10	4Q 92	4c
Telephone bill, family of four	month	19.21	4Q 92	4c
Energy and Fuels				
Energy, combined forms, 1,800 sq ft heating area	month	112.22	4Q 92	4c
Energy, exc electricity, 1,800 sq ft heating area	month	24.60	4Q 92	4c
Gasoline, motor	gal	1.44	4Q 92	4c
Entertainment				
Bowling, evening rate	game	1.75	4Q 92	4c
Monopoly game, Parker Brothers', No. 9		12.43	4Q 92	4c
Movie	admis-sion	4.00	4Q 92	4c
Tennis balls, yellow, Wilson or Penn, 3	can	2.62	4Q 92	4c
Goods and Services				
ACCRA Index, Miscellaneous Goods and Services		98.60	4Q 92	4c
Groceries				
ACCRA Index, Groceries		107.60	4Q 92	4c
Babyfood, strained vegetables, lowest price	4-4.5 oz jar	0.32	4Q 92	4c
Bananas	lb	0.46	4Q 92	4c
Bread, white	24 oz	0.87	4Q 92	4c
Cheese, Kraft grated Parmesan	8-oz canis-ter	3.27	4Q 92	4c
Chicken, fryer, whole	lb	0.84	4Q 92	4c
Cigarettes, Winston	carton	20.92	4Q 92	4c
Coffee, vacuum-packed	13-oz can	2.04	4Q 92	4c
Corn, frozen	10 oz	0.54	4Q 92	4c
Corn Flakes, Kellogg's or Post Toasties	18 oz	1.57	4Q 92	4c
Eggs, Grade A large	doz	1.93	4Q 92	4c
Ground beef or hamburger	lb	1.39	4Q 92	4c
Lettuce, iceberg	head	0.82	4Q 92	4c
Margarine, Blue Bonnet or Parkay cubes	lb	0.77	4Q 92	4c
Milk, whole	1/2 gal	1.44	4Q 92	4c
Orange juice, Minute Maid frozen	12-oz can	1.69	4Q 92	4c
Peaches	29-oz can	1.27	4Q 92	4c
Peas Sweet, Del Monte or Green Giant	15-17 oz can	0.65	4Q 92	4c
Potatoes, white or red	10-lb sack	1.74	4Q 92	4c
Sausage, Jimmy Dean, 100% pork	lb	2.66	4Q 92	4c
Shortening, vegetable, Crisco	3-lb can	2.40	4Q 92	4c
Soft drink, Coca Cola	2 liter	1.14	4Q 92	4c
Steak, T-bone	lb	5.19	4Q 92	4c
Sugar, cane or beet	4 lb	1.92	4Q 92	4c
Tomatoes, Hunt's or Del Monte	14.5-oz can	0.78	4Q 92	4c
Tuna, chunk, light	6.125-6.5 oz can	0.58	4Q 92	4c
Health Care				
ACCRA Index, Health Care		129.20	4Q 92	4c
Analgesic, Aspirin, Bayer, 325 mg tablets	100	5.62	4Q 92	4c
Dentist's fee, adult teeth cleaning and periodic oral exam	visit	66.25	4Q 92	4c
Doctor's fee, routine exam, established patient	visit	46.67	4Q 92	4c
Hospital care, semiprivate room	day	385.00	4Q 92	4c

Blythe, CA - continued

Item	Per	Value	Date	Ref.
Household Goods				
Appliance repair, home, service call, washing machine	min labor charge	41.50	4Q 92	4c
Laundry detergent, Tide Ultra, Bold, or Cheer	42 oz	4.26	4Q 92	4c
Tissues, facial, Kleenex brand	175-count box	1.22	4Q 92	4c
Housing				
ACCRA Index, Housing		108.60	4Q 92	4c
House, 1,800 sq ft, 8,000 sq ft lot, new, urban	total	126000	4Q 92	4c
House payment, principal and interest, 25% down payment	month	710	4Q 92	4c
Mortgage rate, incl. points & origination fee, 30-year fixed or adjustable rate	per-cent	8.25	4Q 92	4c
Rent, apartment, 2 bedrooms - 1-1/2 to 2 baths, unfurnished, 950 sq ft, water	month	438	4Q 92	4c
Personal Goods				
Shampoo, Alberto VO5	15 oz	1.46	4Q 92	4c
Toothpaste, Crest or Colgate	6-7 oz	2.09	4Q 92	4c
Personal Services				
Dry cleaning, man's 2-piece suit		6.00	4Q 92	4c
Haircare, woman's shampoo, trim and blow-dry		20.40	4Q 92	4c
Haircut, man's barbershop, no styling		6.67	4Q 92	4c
Restaurant Food				
Chicken, fried, thigh and drumstick		1.99	4Q 92	4c
Hamburger with cheese	1/4 lb	2.05	4Q 92	4c
Pizza, Pizza Hut or Pizza Inn, cheese, thin crust	12-13 in	8.49	4Q 92	4c
Transportation				
ACCRA Index, Transportation		111.10	4Q 92	4c
Tire balance, computer or spin balance, front	wheel	6.17	4Q 92	4c
Utilities				
ACCRA Index, Utilities		102.40	4Q 92	4c
Electricity, partial electric and other energy, 1,800 sq ft living area new home	month	87.62	4Q 92	4c

Boca Raton, FL

Item	Per	Value	Date	Ref.
Composite ACCRA index		111.20	4Q 92	4c
Alcoholic Beverages				
Beer, Miller Lite or Budweiser, 12-oz containers	6 pack	3.45	4Q 92	4c
Liquor, J & B Scotch	750 ml	16.71	4Q 92	4c
Wine, Gallo Chablis blanc, 1.5 liter	bottle	5.00	4Q 92	4c
Clothing				
Jeans, man's denim		30.39	4Q 92	4c
Shirt, man's dress shirt		17.06	4Q 92	4c
Undervest, boy's size 10-14, cotton	3	4.52	4Q 92	4c
Communications				
Newspaper subscription, daily and Sunday home delivery, large-city	month	10.66	4Q 92	4c
Telephone, flat rate	month	10.05	91	11c
Telephone bill, family of four	month	15.90	4Q 92	4c
Energy and Fuels				
Energy, combined forms, 1,800 sq ft heating area	month	137.44	4Q 92	4c
Gasoline, motor	gal	1.12	4Q 92	4c
Entertainment				
Bowling, evening rate	game	2.57	4Q 92	4c
Dinner entree, restaurant		18.00-32.00	92	83c
Monopoly game, Parker Brothers', No. 9		12.69	4Q 92	4c

Values are in dollars or fractions of dollars. In the column headed *Ref*, references are shown to sources. Each reference is followed by a letter. These refer to the geographical level for which data were reported: s=State, r=Region, and c=City or metro. The abbreviation *ex* is used to mean *except* or *excluding*; *exp* stands for expenditures. For other abbreviations and further explanations, please see the Introduction.

Boca Raton, FL - continued

Item	Per	Value	Date	Ref.
Entertainment				
Movie	admission	5.60	4Q 92	4c
Tennis balls, yellow, Wilson or Penn, 3	can	2.39	4Q 92	4c
Goods and Services				
ACCRA Index, Miscellaneous Goods and Services		104.70	4Q 92	4c
Groceries				
ACCRA Index, Groceries		94.80	4Q 92	4c
Babyfood, strained vegetables, lowest price	4-4.5 oz jar	0.33	4Q 92	4c
Bananas	lb	0.30	4Q 92	4c
Bread, white	24 oz	0.46	4Q 92	4c
Cheese, Kraft grated Parmesan	8-oz canister	3.02	4Q 92	4c
Chicken, fryer, whole	lb	0.81	4Q 92	4c
Cigarettes, Winston	carton	19.04	4Q 92	4c
Coffee, vacuum-packed	13-oz can	1.81	4Q 92	4c
Corn, frozen	10 oz	0.54	4Q 92	4c
Corn Flakes, Kellogg's or Post Toasties	18 oz	1.62	4Q 92	4c
Eggs, Grade A large	doz	0.80	4Q 92	4c
Ground beef or hamburger	lb	1.61	4Q 92	4c
Lettuce, iceberg	head	0.95	4Q 92	4c
Margarine, Blue Bonnet or Parkay cubes	lb	0.52	4Q 92	4c
Milk, whole	1/2 gal	1.59	4Q 92	4c
Orange juice, Minute Maid frozen	12-oz can	1.09	4Q 92	4c
Peaches	29-oz can	1.33	4Q 92	4c
Peas Sweet, Del Monte or Green Giant	15-17 oz can	0.58	4Q 92	4c
Potatoes, white or red	10-lb sack	2.03	4Q 92	4c
Sausage, Jimmy Dean, 100% pork	lb	2.32	4Q 92	4c
Shortening, vegetable, Crisco	3-lb can	2.49	4Q 92	4c
Soft drink, Coca Cola	2 liter	1.02	4Q 92	4c
Steak, T-bone	lb	5.31	4Q 92	4c
Sugar, cane or beet	4 lb	1.77	4Q 92	4c
Tomatoes, Hunt's or Del Monte	14.5-oz can	0.56	4Q 92	4c
Tuna, chunk, light	6.125-6.5 oz can	0.51	4Q 92	4c
Health Care				
ACCRA Index, Health Care		94.40	4Q 92	4c
Analgesic, Aspirin, Bayer, 325 mg tablets	100	3.37	4Q 92	4c
Dentist's fee, adult teeth cleaning and periodic oral exam	visit	50.50	4Q 92	4c
Doctor's fee, routine exam, established patient	visit	33.00	4Q 92	4c
Hospital care, semiprivate room	day	299.20	4Q 92	4c
Household Goods				
Appliance repair, home, service call, washing machine	min labor charge	35.97	4Q 92	4c
Laundry detergent, Tide Ultra, Bold, or Cheer	42 oz	2.85	4Q 92	4c
Tissues, facial, Kleenex brand	175-count box	1.17	4Q 92	4c
Housing				
ACCRA Index, Housing		126.70	4Q 92	4c
House, 1,800 sq ft, 8,000 sq ft lot, new, urban	total	136120	4Q 92	4c
House payment, principal and interest, 25% down payment	month	756	4Q 92	4c

Boca Raton, FL - continued

Item	Per	Value	Date	Ref.
Housing - continued				
Mortgage rate, incl. points & origination fee, 30-year fixed or adjustable rate	percent	8.10	4Q 92	4c
Rent, apartment, 2 bedrooms - 1-1/2 to 2 baths, unfurnished, 950 sq ft, water	month	678	4Q 92	4c
Personal Goods				
Shampoo, Alberto VO5	15 oz	0.99	4Q 92	4c
Toothpaste, Crest or Colgate	6-7 oz	1.56	4Q 92	4c
Personal Services				
Dry cleaning, man's 2-piece suit		7.33	4Q 92	4c
Haircare, woman's shampoo, trim and blow-dry		26.50	4Q 92	4c
Haircut, man's barbershop, no styling		13.40	4Q 92	4c
Restaurant Food				
Chicken, fried, thigh and drumstick		2.32	4Q 92	4c
Hamburger with cheese	1/4 lb	1.92	4Q 92	4c
Pizza, Pizza Hut or Pizza Inn, cheese, thin crust	12-13 in	7.99	4Q 92	4c
Transportation				
ACCRA Index, Transportation		110.90	4Q 92	4c
Tire balance, computer or spin balance, front	wheel	7.97	4Q 92	4c
Utilities				
ACCRA Index, Utilities		121.50	4Q 92	4c
Electricity, all electric, 1,800 sq ft living area new home	month	137.44	4Q 92	4c

Boise, ID

Item	Per	Value	Date	Ref.
Composite ACCRA index		104.60	4Q 92	4c
Alcoholic Beverages				
Beer, Miller Lite or Budweiser, 12-oz containers	6 pack	3.78	4Q 92	4c
Liquor, J & B Scotch	750 ml	17.95	4Q 92	4c
Wine, Gallo Chablis blanc, 1.5 liter	bottle	4.97	4Q 92	4c
Child Care				
Child care fee, average, center	hour	1.71	90	65r
Child care fee, average, nonregulated family day care	hour	1.32	90	65r
Child care fee, average, regulated family day care	hour	1.86	90	65r
Clothing				
Jeans, man's denim		32.59	4Q 92	4c
Shirt, man's dress shirt		24.35	4Q 92	4c
Undervest, boy's size 10-14, cotton	3	5.11	4Q 92	4c
Communications				
Long-distance telephone service, day, initial minute, 0-100 miles	min	0.15-0.51	91	12s
Long-distance telephone service, day, additional minute, 0-100 miles	min	0.07-0.40	91	12s
Long-distance telephone service, evenings/weekends, 0-100 mi, initial minute	min	0.08-0.25	91	12s
Long-distance telephone service, evenings/weekends, 0-100 mi, additional minute	min	0.03-0.19	91	12s
Newspaper subscription, daily and Sunday home delivery, large-city	month	13.04	4Q 92	4c
Telephone, flat rate	month	12.03	91	11c
Telephone bill, family of four	month	16.74	4Q 92	4c
Education				
Board, 4-yr private college/university	year	2583	91	22s
Board, 4-yr public college/university	year	2072	91	22s
Expenditures, local gov't, public elementary/secondary	pupil	3280	92	20s
Room, 4-year private college/university	year	959	91	22s
Room, 4-year public college/university	year	1026	91	22s
Tuition, 2-year private college/university	year	1609	91	22s
Tuition, 2-year public college/university	year	802	91	22s

Values are in dollars or fractions of dollars. In the column headed *Ref*, references are shown to sources. Each reference is followed by a letter. These refer to the geographical level for which data were reported: s=State, r=Region, and c=City or metro. The abbreviation *ex* is used to mean *except* or *excluding*; *exp* stands for expenditures. For other abbreviations and further explanations, please see the Introduction.

Boise, ID - continued

Item	Per	Value	Date	Ref.
Education				
Tuition, 4-year private college/university	year	7203	91	22s
Tuition, 4-year public college/university, in-state	year	1189	91	22s
Energy and Fuels				
Coal	mil Btu	1.76	90	64s
Energy	mil Btu	7.81	90	64s
Energy, combined forms, 1,800 sq ft heating area	month	77.04	4Q 92	4c
Energy, exc electricity, 1,800 sq ft heating area	month	36.98	4Q 92	4c
Energy exp/householder, 1-family unit	year	372	90	28r
Energy exp/householder, <1,000 sq ft heating area	year	335	90	28r
Energy exp/householder, 1,000-1,999 sq ft heating area	year	365	90	28r
Energy exp/householder, 2,000+ sq ft heating area	year	411	90	28r
Energy exp/householder, mobile home	year	305	90	28r
Energy exp/householder, multifamily	year	372	90	28r
Gas, cooking, 10 therms	month	11.15	92	56c
Gas, cooking, 30 therms	month	20.45	92	56c
Gas, cooking, 50 therms	month	29.75	92	56c
Gas, heating, winter, 100 therms	month	47.78	92	56c
Gas, heating, winter, average use	month	68.41	92	56c
Gas, natural	mil Btu	3.43	90	64s
Gas, natural	000 cu ft	5.19	91	46s
Gas, natural, exp	year	420	91	46s
Gasoline, motor	gal	1.24	4Q 92	4c
Gasoline, unleaded regular	mil Btu	9.15	90	64s
Entertainment				
Bowling, evening rate	game	1.76	4Q 92	4c
Miniature golf admission	adult	6.18	92	1r
Miniature golf admission	child	5.14	92	1r
Monopoly game, Parker Brothers', No. 9		10.39	4Q 92	4c
Movie	admission	5.50	4Q 92	4c
Tennis balls, yellow, Wilson or Penn, 3	can	2.93	4Q 92	4c
Waterpark admission	adult	11.00	92	1r
Waterpark admission	child	8.55	92	1r
Funerals				
Casket, 18-gauge steel, velvet interior		1929.04	91	24r
Cosmetology, hair care, etc.		88.52	91	24r
Embalming		249.33	91	24r
Facility use for ceremony		182.75	91	24r
Hearse, local		110.04	91	24r
Limousine, local		66.67	91	24r
Remains to funeral home, transfer		84.58	91	24r
Service charge, professional		593.00	91	24r
Vault, concrete, non-metallic liner		647.38	91	24r
Viewing facilities, use		99.87	91	24r
Goods and Services				
ACCRA Index, Miscellaneous Goods and Services		105.40	4Q 92	4c
Groceries				
ACCRA Index, Groceries		99.00	4Q 92	4c
Apples, Red Delicious	lb	0.80	4/93	16r
Babyfood, strained vegetables, lowest price	4-4.5 oz jar	0.27	4Q 92	4c
Bacon	lb	1.79	4/93	16r
Bananas	lb	0.33	4Q 92	4c
Bananas	lb	0.53	4/93	16r
Bologna, all beef or mixed	lb	2.67	4/93	16r
Bread, white	24 oz	0.76	4Q 92	4c
Bread, white, pan	lb	0.81	4/93	16r
Carrots, short trimmed and topped	lb	0.39	4/93	16r
Cheese, Kraft grated Parmesan	8-oz canister	3.67	4Q 92	4c

Boise, ID - continued

Item	Per	Value	Date	Ref.
Groceries - continued				
Chicken, fresh, whole	lb	0.94	4/93	16r
Chicken, fryer, whole	lb	0.86	4Q 92	4c
Chicken breast, bone-in	lb	2.19	4/93	16r
Chuck roast, graded and ungraded, ex USDA prime and choice	lb	2.26	4/93	16r
Cigarettes, Winston	carton	16.91	4Q 92	4c
Coffee, 100% ground roast, all sizes	lb	2.33	4/93	16r
Coffee, vacuum-packed	13-oz can	2.28	4Q 92	4c
Corn, frozen	10 oz	0.61	4Q 92	4c
Corn Flakes, Kellogg's or Post Toasties	18 oz	1.87	4Q 92	4c
Eggs, Grade A large	doz	0.85	4Q 92	4c
Eggs, Grade AA large	doz	1.18	4/93	16r
Flour, white, all purpose	lb	0.22	4/93	16r
Grapefruit	lb	0.52	4/93	16r
Grapes, Thompson Seedless	lb	1.50	4/93	16r
Ground beef, 100% beef	lb	1.44	4/93	16r
Ground beef, lean and extra lean	lb	2.34	4/93	16r
Ground beef or hamburger	lb	1.38	4Q 92	4c
Ham, boneless, excluding canned	lb	2.56	4/93	16r
Honey, jar	8 oz	0.99-1.19	92	5r
Honey, jar	lb	1.35-1.97	92	5r
Honey, squeeze bear	12-oz	1.00-1.89	92	5r
Ice cream, prepackaged, bulk, regular	1/2 gal	2.40	4/93	16r
Lemons	lb	0.81	4/93	16r
Lettuce, iceberg	head	0.80	4Q 92	4c
Lettuce, iceberg	lb	0.84	4/93	16r
Margarine, Blue Bonnet or Parkay cubes	lb	0.59	4Q 92	4c
Margarine, stick	lb	0.81	4/93	16r
Milk, whole	1/2 gal	1.45	4Q 92	4c
Orange juice, Minute Maid frozen	12-oz can	1.29	4Q 92	4c
Oranges, navel	lb	0.48	4/93	16r
Peaches	29-oz can	1.27	4Q 92	4c
Peas Sweet, Del Monte or Green Giant	15-17 oz can	0.60	4Q 92	4c
Pork chops, center cut, bone-in	lb	3.25	4/93	16r
Potato chips	16 oz	2.89	4/93	16r
Potatoes, white	lb	0.38	4/93	16r
Potatoes, white or red	10-lb sack	1.63	4Q 92	4c
Round roast, graded & ungraded, ex USDA prime & choice	lb	3.00	4/93	16r
Round roast, USDA choice, boneless	lb	3.16	4/93	16r
Sausage, Jimmy Dean, 100% pork	lb	3.01	4Q 92	4c
Shortening, vegetable oil blends	lb	0.86	4/93	16r
Shortening, vegetable, Crisco	3-lb can	2.22	4Q 92	4c
Soft drink, Coca Cola	2 liter	1.15	4Q 92	4c
Spaghetti and macaroni	lb	0.84	4/93	16r
Steak, round, graded & ungraded, ex USDA prime & choice	lb	3.34	4/93	16r
Steak, round, USDA choice, boneless	lb	3.24	4/93	16r
Steak, sirloin, graded & ungraded, ex USDA prime & choice	lb	3.75	4/93	16r
Steak, sirloin, USDA choice, boneless	lb	4.49	4/93	16r
Steak, T-bone	lb	4.10	4Q 92	4c
Sugar, cane or beet	4 lb	1.48	4Q 92	4c
Sugar, white	lb	0.41	4/93	16r
Sugar, white, 33-80 oz pk	lb	0.38	4/93	16r
Tomatoes, field grown	lb	1.01	4/93	16r
Tomatoes, Hunt's or Del Monte	14.5-oz can	0.68	4Q 92	4c
Tuna, chunk, light	6.125-6.5 oz can	0.73	4Q 92	4c
Turkey, frozen, whole	lb	1.04	4/93	16r
Health Care				
ACCRA Index, Health Care		111.70	4Q 92	4c
Analgesic, Aspirin, Bayer, 325 mg tablets	100	4.69	4Q 92	4c
Childbirth, cesarean, hospital		5533	91	62r

Values are in dollars or fractions of dollars. In the column headed *Ref*, references are shown to sources. Each reference is followed by a letter. These refer to the geographical level for which data were reported: s=State, r=Region, and c=City or metro. The abbreviation *ex* is used to mean *except* or *excluding*; *exp* stands for expenditures. For other abbreviations and further explanations, please see the Introduction.

Boise, ID - continued

Item	Per	Value	Date	Ref.
Health Care				
Childbirth, cesarean, physician's fee		2053	91	62r
Childbirth, normal, hospital		2745	91	62r
Childbirth, normal, physician's fee		1492	91	62r
Dentist's fee, adult teeth cleaning and periodic oral exam	visit	56.40	4Q 92	4c
Doctor's fee, routine exam, established patient	visit	40.40	4Q 92	4c
Hospital care, semiprivate room	day	329.00	90	27c
Hospital care, semiprivate room	day	350.50	4Q 92	4c
Medical insurance premium, per employee, small group comprehensive	month	292.00	10/91	25c
Medical plan per employee	year	3218	91	45r
Mental health care, exp	capita	20.37-28.83	90	38s
Mental health care, exp, state mental health agency	capita	20.37	90	38s
Mental health care, hospital psychiatric services, non-Federal, exp	capita	7.65	88	38s
Mental health care, mental health organization, multiservice, exp	capita	5.74	88	38s
Mental health care, psychiatric hospitals, private, exp	capita	15.07	88	38s
Mental health care, psychiatric out-patient clinics, freestanding, exp	capita	0.79	88	38s
Mental health care, state and county mental hospitals, exp	capita	9.13	88	38s
Mental health care, VA medical centers, exp	capita	1.52	88	38s
Physician fee, family practice, first-visit		111.00	91	62r
Physician fee, family practice, revisit		45.00	91	62r
Physician fee, general practice, first-visit		100.00	91	62r
Physician fee, general practice, revisit		40.00	91	62r
Physician fee, internal medicine, first-visit		137.00	91	62r
Physician fee, internal medicine, revisit		48.00	91	62r
Physician fee, median, neurosurgeon, first-visit		157.00	91	62r
Physician fee, median, nonsurgical specialist, first-visit		131.00	91	62r
Physician fee, median, orthopedic surgeon, first-visit		124.00	91	62r
Physician fee, median, plastic surgeon, first-visit		88.00	91	62r
Physician fee, median, surgical specialist, first-visit		100.00	91	62r
Physician fee, neurosurgeon, revisit		51.00	91	62r
Physician fee, nonsurgical specialist, revisit		47.00	91	62r
Physician fee, obstetrics/gynecology, first-visit		95.00	91	62r
Physician fee, obstetrics/gynecology, revisit		50.00	91	62r
Physician fee, orthopedic surgeon, revisit		51.00	91	62r
Physician fee, pediatrician, first-visit		81.00	91	62r
Physician fee, pediatrician, revisit		42.00	91	62r
Physician fee, plastic surgeon, revisit		48.00	91	62r
Physician fee, surgical specialist, revisit		49.00	91	62r
Household Goods				
Appliance repair, home, service call, washing machine	min labor charge	32.60	4Q 92	4c
Laundry detergent, Tide Ultra, Bold, or Cheer	42 oz	4.10	4Q 92	4c
Tissues, facial, Kleenex brand	175-count box	1.11	4Q 92	4c
Housing				
ACCRA Index, Housing		117.30	4Q 92	4c
Home, median price	unit	82.50		26c
House, 1,800 sq ft, 8,000 sq ft lot, new, urban	total	123672	4Q 92	4c
House payment, principal and interest, 25% down payment	month	690	4Q 92	4c
Mortgage rate, incl. points & origination fee, 30-year fixed or adjustable rate	per-cent	8.14	4Q 92	4c

Boise, ID - continued

Item	Per	Value	Date	Ref.
Housing - continued				
Rent, apartment, 2 bedrooms - 1-1/2 to 2 baths, unfurnished, 950 sq ft, water	month	652	4Q 92	4c
Rental unit, 1 bedroom	month	503	93	23c
Rental unit, 2 bedroom	month	594	93	23c
Rental unit, 3 bedroom	month	742	93	23c
Rental unit, 4 bedroom	month	832	93	23c
Rental unit, efficiency	month	414	93	23c
Insurance and Pensions				
Auto insurance, private passenger	year	472.71	91	63s
Personal Goods				
Shampoo, Alberto VO5	15 oz	1.40	4Q 92	4c
Toothpaste, Crest or Colgate	6-7 oz	2.08	4Q 92	4c
Personal Services				
Dry cleaning, man's 2-piece suit		6.13	4Q 92	4c
Haircare, woman's shampoo, trim and blow-dry		20.80	4Q 92	4c
Haircut, man's barbershop, no styling		7.45	4Q 92	4c
Restaurant Food				
Chicken, fried, thigh and drumstick		1.99	4Q 92	4c
Hamburger with cheese	1/4 lb	1.89	4Q 92	4c
Pizza, Pizza Hut or Pizza Inn, cheese, thin crust	12-13 in	8.95	4Q 92	4c
Taxes				
Tax, cigarette	pack	18	91	77s
Tax, gasoline	gal	22	91	77s
Taxes, state	capita	1159	91	77s
Transportation				
ACCRA Index, Transportation		98.90	4Q 92	4c
Auto rental, average	day	41.25	6/91	60c
Bus fare, up to 10 miles	one-way	0.75	4Q 92	4c
Driver's license fee		19.50	12/90	43s
Taxi fare, airport-city, average	day	8.00	6/91	60c
Tire balance, computer or spin balance, front	wheel	5.90	4Q 92	4c
Vehicle registration and license plate	year	1.34-39.52	93	29s
Travel				
Business travel	day	178.00	4/93	89r
Lodging	day	79.10	91	60c
Utilities				
ACCRA Index, Utilities		72.10	4Q 92	4c
Electricity	mil Btu	11.15	90	64s
Electricity, partial electric and other energy, 1,800 sq ft living area new home	month	40.06	4Q 92	4c
Electricity, winter, 250 KWh	month	11.75	92	55c
Electricity, winter, 500 KWh	month	23.51	92	55c
Electricity, winter, 750 KWh	month	35.26	92	55c
Electricity, winter, 1000 KWh	month	47.02	92	55c

Boston, MA

Item	Per	Value	Date	Ref.
Composite ACCRA index		139.70	4Q 92	4c
Alcoholic Beverages				
Beer, Miller Lite or Budweiser, 12-oz containers	6 pack	5.08	4Q 92	4c
Liquor, J & B Scotch	750 ml	17.19	4Q 92	4c
Wine, Gallo Chablis blanc, 1.5 liter	bottle	5.49	4Q 92	4c
Child Care				
Child care, on-site	year	6344	93	17c
Child care fee, average, center	hour	2.18	90	65r
Child care fee, average, nonregulated family day care	hour	1.83	90	65r
Child care fee, average, regulated family day care	hour	2.02	90	65r

Values are in dollars or fractions of dollars. In the column headed *Ref*, references are shown to sources. Each reference is followed by a letter. These refer to the geographical level for which data were reported: s=State, r=Region, and c=City or metro. The abbreviation *ex* is used to mean *except* or *excluding*; *exp* stands for expenditures. For other abbreviations and further explanations, please see the Introduction.

Boston, MA - continued

Item	Per	Value	Date	Ref.
Clothing				
Jeans, man's denim		35.99	4Q 92	4c
Shirt, man's dress shirt		19.99	4Q 92	4c
Undervest, boy's size 10-14, cotton	3	5.93	4Q 92	4c
Communications				
Long-distance telephone service, day, initial minute, 0-100 miles	min	0.18-0.31	91	12s
Long-distance telephone service, day, additional minute, 0-100 miles	min	0.08-0.13	91	12s
Long-distance telephone service, evenings/weekends, 0-100 mi, initial minute	min	0.67-0.12	91	12s
Long-distance telephone service, evenings/weekends, 0-100 mi, additional minute	min	0.04-0.05	91	12s
Newspaper subscription, daily and Sunday home delivery, large-city	month	17.39	4Q 92	4c
Telephone, exp	year	548	89	15c
Telephone, residential, private line, rotary, unlimited calling	month	17.91	10/91	78c
Telephone bill, family of four	month	18.66	4Q 92	4c
Construction				
Plywood, post-Hurricane Andrew	4x8 sheet	10.69	92	13c
Plywood, pre-Hurricane Andrew	4x8 sheet	8.49	92	13c
Education				
Board, 4-yr private college/university	year	2698	91	22s
Board, 4-yr public college/university	year	1741	91	22s
Expenditures, local gov't, public elementary/secondary	pupil	6687	92	20s
Room, 4-year private college/university	year	2945	91	22s
Room, 4-year public college/university	year	2144	91	22s
Tuition, 2-year private college/university	year	7750	91	22s
Tuition, 2-year public college/university	year	1528	91	22s
Tuition, 4-year private college/university	year	12446	91	22s
Tuition, 4-year public college/university, in-state	year	2580	91	22s
Energy and Fuels				
Coal	mil Btu	1.77	90	64s
Energy	mil Btu	10.57	90	64s
Energy, combined forms, 1,800 sq ft heating area	month	164.96	4Q 92	4c
Energy, exc electricity, 1,800 sq ft heating area	month	39.99	4Q 92	4c
Energy exp/householder, 1-family unit	year	588	90	28r
Energy exp/householder, <1,000 sq ft heating area	year	477	90	28r
Energy exp/householder, 1,000-1,999 sq ft heating area	year	517	90	28r
Energy exp/householder, 2,000+ sq ft heating area	year	630	90	28r
Energy exp/householder, mobile home	year	412	90	28r
Energy exp/householder, multifamily	year	498	90	28r
Fuel oil #2	gal	0.98	4/93	16c
Fuel oil, other fuel, exp	year	334	89	15c
Gas, cooking, 10 therms	month	15.75	92	56c
Gas, cooking, 30 therms	month	33.74	92	56c
Gas, cooking, 50 therms	month	45.44	92	56c
Gas, heating, winter, 100 therms	month	82.80	92	56c
Gas, heating, winter, average use	month	174.87	92	56c
Gas, natural	mil Btu	5.55	90	64s
Gas, natural	000 cu ft	8.11	91	46s
Gas, natural, exp	year	262	89	15c
Gas, natural, exp	year	741	91	46s
Gas, piped	100 therms	84.73	4/93	16c
Gas, piped	40 therms	37.09	4/93	16c
Gas, piped	therm	0.85	4/93	16c
Gasoline, all types	gal	1.19	4/93	16c
Gasoline, motor	gal	1.16	4Q 92	4c

Boston, MA - continued

Item	Per	Value	Date	Ref.
Energy and Fuels - continued				
Gasoline, regular unleaded, taxes included, cash, self-service	gal	1.35	4/93	16c
Gasoline, unleaded premium	gal	61.25-74.10	12/92	31c
Gasoline, unleaded premium 93 octane	gal	1.11	4/93	16c
Gasoline, unleaded regular	mil Btu	9.53	90	64s
Entertainment				
Bowling, evening rate	game	1.82	4Q 92	4c
Dinner entree, restaurant		26.00-38.00	92	83c
Miniature golf admission	adult	6.18	92	1r
Miniature golf admission	child	5.14	92	1r
Monopoly game, Parker Brothers', No. 9		17.58	4Q 92	4c
Movie	admission	6.75	4Q 92	4c
Tennis balls, yellow, Wilson or Penn, 3	can	2.63	4Q 92	4c
Waterpark admission	adult	11.00	92	1r
Waterpark admission	child	8.55	92	1r
Funerals				
Casket, 18-gauge steel, velvet interior		1853.42	91	24r
Cosmetology, hair care, etc.		98.33	91	24r
Embalming		273.94	91	24r
Facility use for ceremony		196.06	91	24r
Hearse, local		145.67	91	24r
Limousine, local		131.07	91	24r
Remains to funeral home, transfer		135.24	91	24r
Service charge, professional		843.16	91	24r
Vault, concrete, non-metallic liner		709.14	91	24r
Viewing facilities, use		229.85	91	24r
Goods and Services				
ACCRA Index, Miscellaneous Goods and Services		116.00	4Q 92	4c
Police protection expense	resident	209.00	92	18c
Groceries				
ACCRA Index, Groceries		115.00	4Q 92	4c
Apples, Red Delicious	lb	0.85	4/93	16r
Babyfood, strained vegetables, lowest price	4-4.5 oz jar	0.37	4Q 92	4c
Bacon	lb	2.12	4/93	16r
Bakery products, exp	year	193	89	15c
Bananas	lb	0.57	4Q 92	4c
Bananas	lb	0.54	4/93	16r
Beef, exp	year	195	89	15c
Beverages, nonalcoholic, exp	year	190	89	15c
Bread, white	24 oz	0.71	4Q 92	4c
Bread, white, pan	lb	0.81	4/93	16r
Butter	lb	2.02	4/93	16r
Carrots, short trimmed and topped	lb	0.51	4/93	16r
Cereals and baking products, exp	year	279	89	15c
Cereals and cereal products, exp	year	86	89	15c
Cheese, Kraft grated Parmesan	8-oz canister	3.31	4Q 92	4c
Chicken, fresh, whole	lb	1.04	4/93	16r
Chicken, fryer, whole	lb	0.89	4Q 92	4c
Chicken breast, bone-in	lb	2.21	4/93	16r
Chicken legs, bone-in	lb	1.16	4/93	16r
Chuck roast, USDA choice, boneless	lb	2.82	4/93	16r
Cigarettes, Winston	carton	18.87	4Q 92	4c
Coffee, 100% ground roast, all sizes	lb	2.66	4/93	16r
Coffee, vacuum-packed	13-oz can	2.49	4Q 92	4c
Corn, frozen	10 oz	0.59	4Q 92	4c
Corn Flakes, Kellogg's or Post Toasties	18 oz	2.20	4Q 92	4c
Cucumbers	lb	0.85	4/93	16r
Dairy product purchases	year	246	89	15c
Dairy products, miscellaneous, exp	year	118	89	15c
Eggs, exp	year	28	89	15c
Eggs, Grade A large	doz	1.25	4Q 92	4c

Values are in dollars or fractions of dollars. In the column headed *Ref*, references are shown to sources. Each reference is followed by a letter. These refer to the geographical level for which data were reported: s=State, r=Region, and c=City or metro. The abbreviation *ex* is used to mean *except* or *excluding*; *exp* stands for expenditures. For other abbreviations and further explanations, please see the Introduction.

Boston, MA - continued

Item	Per	Value	Date	Ref.
Groceries				
Eggs, Grade A large	doz	1.15	4/93	16r
Fats and oils, exp	year	31	89	15c
Fish and seafood, exp	year	91	89	15c
Food, exp	year	4024	89	15c
Food eaten at home, exp	year	499	89	15c
Food eaten at home, exp	year	1972	89	15c
Food purchased away from home, exp	year	2052	89	15c
Foods, miscellaneous, exp	year	176	89	15c
Fruits, fresh, exp	year	110	89	15c
Fruits, processed, exp	year	75	89	15c
Fruits and vegetables, exp	year	335	89	15c
Grapefruit	lb	0.45	4/93	16r
Grapes, Thompson Seedless	lb	1.52	4/93	16r
Ground beef, lean and extra lean	lb	2.36	4/93	16r
Ground beef or hamburger	lb	1.55	4Q 92	4c
Ground chuck, 100% beef	lb	2.02	4/93	16r
Honey, jar	8 oz	0.96-1.75	92	5r
Honey, jar	lb	1.50-3.00	92	5r
Honey, squeeze bear	12-oz	1.50-1.99	92	5r
Ice cream, prepackaged, bulk, regular	1/2 gal	2.80	4/93	16r
Lemons	lb	0.96	4/93	16r
Lettuce, iceberg	head	1.15	4Q 92	4c
Lettuce, iceberg	lb	0.95	4/93	16r
Margarine, Blue Bonnet or Parkay cubes	lb	0.73	4Q 92	4c
Margarine, stick	lb	0.81	4/93	16r
Meats, miscellaneous, exp	year	75	89	15c
Meats, poultry, fish and eggs, exp	year	614	89	15c
Milk, fresh, whole, fortified	1/2 gal	1.30	4/93	16r
Milk, whole	1/2 gal	1.52	4Q 92	4c
Milk and cream, fresh, exp	year	128	89	15c
Orange juice, Minute Maid frozen	12-oz can	1.39	4Q 92	4c
Oranges, navel	lb	0.56	4/93	16r
Peaches	29-oz can	1.69	4Q 92	4c
Peanut butter, creamy, all sizes	lb	1.88	4/93	16r
Peas Sweet, Del Monte or Green Giant	15-17 oz can	0.55	4Q 92	4c
Pork, exp	year	80	89	15c
Pork chops, center cut, bone-in	lb	3.34	4/93	16r
Potato chips	16 oz	2.88	4/93	16r
Potatoes, white	lb	0.37	4/93	16r
Potatoes, white or red	10-lb sack	1.51	4Q 92	4c
Poultry, exp	year	144	89	15c
Rib roast, USDA choice, bone-in	lb	4.94	4/93	16r
Round roast, USDA choice, boneless	lb	3.17	4/93	16r
Sausage, Jimmy Dean, 100% pork	lb	3.40	4Q 92	4c
Shortening, vegetable oil blends	lb	0.98	4/93	16r
Shortening, vegetable, Crisco	3-lb can	2.91	4Q 92	4c
Soft drink, Coca Cola	2 liter	1.15	4Q 92	4c
Spaghetti and macaroni	lb	0.82	4/93	16r
Steak, round, graded & ungraded, ex USDA prime & choice	lb	4.04	4/93	16r
Steak, round, USDA choice, boneless	lb	3.90	4/93	16r
Steak, sirloin, USDA choice, boneless	lb	4.97	4/93	16r
Steak, T-bone	lb	6.69	4Q 92	4c
Strawberries, dry pint	12 oz	0.90	4/93	16r
Sugar, cane or beet	4 lb	2.07	4Q 92	4c
Sugar, white	lb	0.50	4/93	16r
Sugar, white, 33-80 oz pk	lb	0.41	4/93	16r
Sugar and other sweets, exp	year	60	89	15c
Tomatoes, field grown	lb	1.23	4/93	16r
Tomatoes, Hunt's or Del Monte	14.5-oz can	0.60	4Q 92	4c
Tuna, chunk, light	6.125-6.5 oz can	0.95	4Q 92	4c
Tuna, chunk, light	lb	2.22	4/93	16r
Turkey, frozen, whole	lb	1.04	4/93	16r
Vegetables, fresh, exp	year	115	89	15c

Boston, MA - continued

Item	Per	Value	Date	Ref.
Groceries - continued				
Vegetables, processed, exp	year	35	89	15c
Health Care				
ACCRA Index, Health Care		136.80	4Q 92	4c
Analgesic, Aspirin, Bayer, 325 mg tablets	100	5.77	4Q 92	4c
Childbirth, cesarean, hospital		5826	91	62r
Childbirth, cesarean, physician's fee		2053	91	62r
Childbirth, normal, hospital		2964	91	62r
Childbirth, normal, physician's fee		1492	91	62r
Dentist's fee, adult teeth cleaning and periodic oral exam	visit	58.20	4Q 92	4c
Doctor's fee, routine exam, established patient	visit	54.00	4Q 92	4c
Health care spending, state	capita	3031	3/93	84s
Hospital care, semiprivate room	day	449.71	90	27c
Hospital care, semiprivate room	day	495.60	4Q 92	4c
Medical insurance premium, per employee, small group comprehensive	month	416.10	10/91	25c
Medical plan per employee	year	3958	91	45r
Mental health care, exp	capita	53.68-118.35	90	38s
Mental health care, exp, state mental health agency	capita	83.91	90	38s
Mental health care, hospital psychiatric services, non-Federal, exp	capita	22.67	88	38s
Mental health care, mental health organization, multiservice, exp	capita	36.07	88	38s
Mental health care, psychiatric hospitals, private, exp	capita	38.65	88	38s
Mental health care, psychiatric out-patient clinics, freestanding, exp	capita	4.41	88	38s
Mental health care, psychiatric partial-care organizations, freestanding, exp	capita	0.92	88	38s
Mental health care, state and county mental hospitals, exp	capita	30.59	88	38s
Mental health care, VA medical centers, exp	capita	21.14	88	38s
Substance abuse, hospital ancillary charge	incident	1310	90	70s
Substance abuse, hospital physician charge	incident	460	90	70s
Substance abuse, hospital room and board	incident	3450	90	70s
Household Goods				
Appliance repair, home, service call, washing machine	min labor charge	38.69	4Q 92	4c
Appliances, major, exp	year	189	89	15c
Appliances, small, misc. housewares, exp	year	84	89	15c
Floor coverings, exp	year	89	89	15c
Household equipment, misc., exp	year	353	89	15c
Laundry detergent, Tide Ultra, Bold, or Cheer	42 oz	4.23	4Q 92	4c
Tissues, facial, Kleenex brand	175-count box	1.13	4Q 92	4c
Housing				
ACCRA Index, Housing		186.30	4Q 92	4c
Home, median price	unit	173.10		26c
House, 1,800 sq ft, 8,000 sq ft lot, new, urban	total	219812	4Q 92	4c
House payment, principal and interest, 25% down payment	month	1226	4Q 92	4c
Mortgage rate, incl. points & origination fee, 30-year fixed or adjustable rate	percent	8.15	4Q 92	4c
Rent, apartment, 2 bedrooms - 1-1/2 to 2 baths, unfurnished, 950 sq ft, water	month	731	4Q 92	4c
Insurance and Pensions				
Auto insurance, private passenger	year	912.83	91	63s
Personal Goods				
Shampoo, Alberto VO5	15 oz	1.59	4Q 92	4c

Values are in dollars or fractions of dollars. In the column headed *Ref*, references are shown to sources. Each reference is followed by a letter. These refer to the geographical level for which data were reported: s = State, r = Region, and c = City or metro. The abbreviation *ex* is used to mean *except* or *excluding*; *exp* stands for expenditures. For other abbreviations and further explanations, please see the Introduction.

Boston, MA - continued

Item	Per	Value	Date	Ref.
Personal Goods				
Toothpaste, Crest or Colgate	6-7 oz	2.33	4Q 92	4c
Personal Services				
Dry cleaning, man's 2-piece suit		6.80	4Q 92	4c
Haircare, woman's shampoo, trim and blow-dry		20.40	4Q 92	4c
Haircut, man's barbershop, no styling		8.70	4Q 92	4c
Restaurant Food				
Chicken, fried, thigh and drumstick		2.65	4Q 92	4c
Hamburger with cheese	1/4 lb	1.99	4Q 92	4c
Pizza, Pizza Hut or Pizza Inn, cheese, thin crust	12-13 in	7.87	4Q 92	4c
Taxes				
Tax, cigarette	pack	26	91	77s
Tax, gasoline	gal	21	91	77s
Taxes, hotel room	day	8.50	92	33c
Taxes, state	capita	1615	91	77s
Transportation				
ACCRA Index, Transportation		120.40	4Q 92	4c
Auto fixed costs, midsize		4538	91	60c
Auto operating cost, midsize		1493	91	60c
Auto rental, average	day	42.50	6/91	60c
Auto rental, midsize car	day	41.97	92	91c
Bus fare	one-way	0.60	3/93	2c
Bus fare, up to 10 miles	one-way	2.00	4Q 92	4c
Driver's license fee		35.00	12/90	43s
Ferry boat fare	one-way	4.00	3/93	2c
Limo fare, airport-city, average	day	7.00	6/91	60c
Railway fare, commuter	one-way	0.85	3/93	2c
Railway fare, heavy rail	one-way	0.85	3/93	2c
Railway fare, light rail	one-way	0.85	93	2c
Taxi fare, airport-city, average	day	10.00	6/91	60c
Tire balance, computer or spin balance, front	wheel	7.39	4Q 92	4c
Trolley fare	one-way	0.60	3/93	2c
Travel				
Breakfast	day	6.21	6/91	60c
Business travel	day	197.00	92	86c
Business travel	day	165.00	4/93	89r
Dinner	day	25.86	6/91	60c
Dinner	day	24.85	92	85c
Lodging	day	163.88	91	60c
Lodging	day	153.00	92	85c
Lunch	day	10.95	6/91	60c
Travel, business	day	237.73	92	82c
Travel, business	day	234.67	93	88c
Utilities				
ACCRA Index, Utilities		145.60	4Q 92	4c
Cable-television service, with no competition	month	15.95	92	81c
Electricity	500 KWh	52.78	4/93	16c
Electricity	KWh	0.10	4/93	16c
Electricity	mil Btu	25.93	90	64s
Electricity, exp	year	555	89	15c
Electricity, partial electric and other energy, 1,800 sq ft living area new home	month	124.97	4Q 92	4c
Electricity, winter, 250 KWh	month	28.17	92	55c
Electricity, winter, 500 KWh	month	50.53	92	55c
Electricity, winter, 750 KWh	month	72.91	92	55c
Electricity, winter, 1000 KWh	month	95.27	92	55c
Utilities, fuels, public services, exp	year	1793	89	15c
Water, other public service, exp	year	93	89	15c

Boulder, CO

Item	Per	Value	Date	Ref.
Composite ACCRA index		120.40	4Q 92	4c
Alcoholic Beverages				
Beer, Miller Lite or Budweiser, 12-oz containers	6 pack	4.08	4Q 92	4c
Liquor, J & B Scotch	750 ml	16.15	4Q 92	4c
Wine, Gallo Chablis blanc, 1.5 liter	bottle	5.09	4Q 92	4c
Child Care				
Child care fee, average, center	hour	1.71	90	65r
Child care fee, average, nonregulated family day care	hour	1.32	90	65r
Child care fee, average, regulated family day care	hour	1.86	90	65r
Clothing				
Jeans, man's denim		24.79	4Q 92	4c
Shirt, man's dress shirt		24.00	4Q 92	4c
Undervest, boy's size 10-14, cotton	3	6.59	4Q 92	4c
Communications				
Long-distance telephone service, day, initial minute, 0-100 miles	min	0.11-0.35	91	12s
Long-distance telephone service, day, additional minute, 0-100 miles	min	0.13-0.27	91	12s
Long-distance telephone service, evenings/weekends, 0-100 mi, initial minute	min	0.08-0.17	91	12s
Long-distance telephone service, evenings/weekends, 0-100 mi, additional minute	min	0.06-0.14	91	12s
Newspaper subscription, daily and Sunday home delivery, large-city	month	8.61	4Q 92	4c
Telephone, flat rate	month	14.22	91	11c
Telephone, residential, private line, rotary, unlimited calling	month	20.71	10/91	78c
Telephone bill, family of four	month	17.72	4Q 92	4c
Education				
Board, 4-yr private college/university	year	2162	91	22s
Board, 4-yr public college/university	year	1747	91	22s
Expenditures, local gov't, public elementary/secondary	pupil	5259	92	20s
Room, 4-year private college/university	year	1984	91	22s
Room, 4-year public college/university	year	1546	91	22s
Tuition, 2-year private college/university	year	6731	91	22s
Tuition, 2-year public college/university	year	943	91	22s
Tuition, 4-year private college/university	year	9516	91	22s
Tuition, 4-year public college/university, in-state	year	1919	91	22s
Energy and Fuels				
Coal	mil Btu	1.07	90	64s
Energy	mil Btu	8.14	90	64s
Energy, combined forms, 1,800 sq ft heating area	month	99.16	4Q 92	4c
Energy, exc electricity, 1,800 sq ft heating area	month	40.84	4Q 92	4c
Energy exp/householder, 1-family unit	year	372	90	28r
Energy exp/householder, <1,000 sq ft heating area	year	335	90	28r
Energy exp/householder, 1,000-1,999 sq ft heating area	year	365	90	28r
Energy exp/householder, 2,000+ sq ft heating area	year	411	90	28r
Energy exp/householder, mobile home	year	305	90	28r
Energy exp/householder, multifamily	year	372	90	28r
Gas, natural	mil Btu	3.92	90	64s
Gas, natural	000 cu ft	4.59	91	46s
Gas, natural, exp	year	446	91	46s
Gasoline, motor	gal	1.25	4Q 92	4c
Gasoline, unleaded regular	mil Btu	9.29	90	64s
Entertainment				
Bowling, evening rate	game	2.00	4Q 92	4c
Miniature golf admission	adult	6.18	92	1r
Miniature golf admission	child	5.14	92	1r

Values are in dollars or fractions of dollars. In the column headed *Ref*, references are shown as sources. Each reference is followed by a letter. These refer to the geographical level for which data were reported: s=State, r=Region, and c=City or metro. The abbreviation *ex* is used to mean *except* or *excluding*; *exp* stands for expenditures. For other abbreviations and further explanations, please see the Introduction.

Boulder, CO - continued

Item	Per	Value	Date	Ref.
Entertainment				
Monopoly game, Parker Brothers', No. 9		10.58	4Q 92	4c
Movie	admission	6.25	4Q 92	4c
Tennis balls, yellow, Wilson or Penn, 3	can	2.89	4Q 92	4c
Waterpark admission	adult	11.00	92	1r
Waterpark admission	child	8.55	92	1r
Funerals				
Casket, 18-gauge steel, velvet interior		1929.04	91	24r
Cosmetology, hair care, etc.		88.52	91	24r
Embalming		249.33	91	24r
Facility use for ceremony		182.75	91	24r
Hearse, local		110.04	91	24r
Limousine, local		66.67	91	24r
Remains to funeral home, transfer		84.58	91	24r
Service charge, professional		593.00	91	24r
Vault, concrete, non-metallic liner		647.38	91	24r
Viewing facilities, use		99.87	91	24r
Goods and Services				
ACCRA Index, Miscellaneous Goods and Services		106.90	4Q 92	4c
Groceries				
ACCRA Index, Groceries		105.80	4Q 92	4c
Apples, Red Delicious	lb	0.80	4/93	16r
Babyfood, strained vegetables, lowest price	4-4.5 oz jar	0.32	4Q 92	4c
Bacon	lb	1.79	4/93	16r
Bananas	lb	0.55	4Q 92	4c
Bananas	lb	0.53	4/93	16r
Bologna, all beef or mixed	lb	2.67	4/93	16r
Bread, white	24 oz	0.68	4Q 92	4c
Bread, white, pan	lb	0.81	4/93	16r
Carrots, short trimmed and topped	lb	0.39	4/93	16r
Cheese, Kraft grated Parmesan	8-oz canister	3.06	4Q 92	4c
Chicken, fresh, whole	lb	0.94	4/93	16r
Chicken, fryer, whole	lb	0.99	4Q 92	4c
Chicken breast, bone-in	lb	2.19	4/93	16r
Chuck roast, graded and ungraded, ex USDA prime and choice	lb	2.26	4/93	16r
Cigarettes, Winston	carton	16.78	4Q 92	4c
Coffee, 100% ground roast, all sizes	lb	2.33	4/93	16r
Coffee, vacuum-packed	13-oz can	2.14	4Q 92	4c
Corn, frozen	10 oz	0.67	4Q 92	4c
Corn Flakes, Kellogg's or Post Toasties	18 oz	1.91	4Q 92	4c
Eggs, Grade A large	doz	0.74	4Q 92	4c
Eggs, Grade AA large	doz	1.18	4/93	16r
Flour, white, all purpose	lb	0.22	4/93	16r
Grapefruit	lb	0.52	4/93	16r
Grapes, Thompson Seedless	lb	1.50	4/93	16r
Ground beef, 100% beef	lb	1.44	4/93	16r
Ground beef, lean and extra lean	lb	2.34	4/93	16r
Ground beef or hamburger	lb	1.54	4Q 92	4c
Ham, boneless, excluding canned	lb	2.56	4/93	16r
Honey, jar	8 oz	0.99-1.19	92	5r
Honey, jar	lb	1.49-2.25	92	5r
Honey, squeeze bear	12-oz	1.00-1.89	92	5r
Ice cream, prepackaged, bulk, regular	1/2 gal	2.40	4/93	16r
Lemons	lb	0.81	4/93	16r
Lettuce, iceberg	head	0.93	4Q 92	4c
Lettuce, iceberg	lb	0.84	4/93	16r
Margarine, Blue Bonnet or Parkay cubes	lb	0.77	4Q 92	4c
Margarine, stick	lb	0.81	4/93	16r
Milk, whole	1/2 gal	1.58	4Q 92	4c
Orange juice, Minute Maid frozen	12-oz can	1.34	4Q 92	4c
Oranges, navel	lb	0.48	4/93	16r
Peaches	29-oz can	1.64	4Q 92	4c

Boulder, CO - continued

Item	Per	Value	Date	Ref.
Groceries - continued				
Peas Sweet, Del Monte or Green Giant	15-17 oz can	0.72	4Q 92	4c
Pork chops, center cut, bone-in	lb	3.25	4/93	16r
Potato chips	16 oz	2.89	4/93	16r
Potatoes, white	lb	0.38	4/93	16r
Potatoes, white or red	10-lb sack	2.33	4Q 92	4c
Round roast, graded & ungraded, ex USDA prime & choice	lb	3.00	4/93	16r
Round roast, USDA choice, boneless	lb	3.16	4/93	16r
Sausage, Jimmy Dean, 100% pork	lb	3.56	4Q 92	4c
Shortening, vegetable oil blends	lb	0.86	4/93	16r
Shortening, vegetable, Crisco	3-lb can	2.33	4Q 92	4c
Soft drink, Coca Cola	2 liter	1.17	4Q 92	4c
Spaghetti and macaroni	lb	0.84	4/93	16r
Steak, round, graded & ungraded, ex USDA prime & choice	lb	3.34	4/93	16r
Steak, round, USDA choice, boneless	lb	3.24	4/93	16r
Steak, sirloin, graded & ungraded, ex USDA prime & choice	lb	3.75	4/93	16r
Steak, sirloin, USDA choice, boneless	lb	4.49	4/93	16r
Steak, T-bone	lb	4.55	4Q 92	4c
Sugar, cane or beet	4 lb	1.36	4Q 92	4c
Sugar, white	lb	0.41	4/93	16r
Sugar, white, 33-80 oz pk	lb	0.38	4/93	16r
Tomatoes, field grown	lb	1.01	4/93	16r
Tomatoes, Hunt's or Del Monte	14.5-oz can	0.72	4Q 92	4c
Tuna, chunk, light	6.125-6.5 oz can	0.74	4Q 92	4c
Turkey, frozen, whole	lb	1.04	4/93	16r
Health Care				
ACCRA Index, Health Care		122.70	4Q 92	4c
Analgesic, Aspirin, Bayer, 325 mg tablets	100	5.69	4Q 92	4c
Childbirth, cesarean, hospital		5533	91	62r
Childbirth, cesarean, physician's fee		2053	91	62r
Childbirth, normal, hospital		2745	91	62r
Childbirth, normal, physician's fee		1492	91	62r
Dentist's fee, adult teeth cleaning and periodic oral exam	visit	58.00	4Q 92	4c
Doctor's fee, routine exam, established patient	visit	44.60	4Q 92	4c
Hospital care, semiprivate room	day	410.00	90	27c
Hospital care, semiprivate room	day	412.00	4Q 92	4c
Medical insurance premium, per employee, small group comprehensive	month	332.15	10/91	25c
Medical plan per employee	year	3218	91	45r
Mental health care, exp	capita	28.84-37.59	90	38s
Mental health care, exp, state mental health agency	capita	33.55	90	38s
Mental health care, hospital psychiatric services, non-Federal, exp	capita	11.38	88	38s
Mental health care, mental health organization, multiservice, exp	capita	21.76	88	38s
Mental health care, psychiatric hospitals, private, exp	capita	14.39	88	38s
Mental health care, psychiatric out-patient clinics, freestanding, exp	capita	0.11	88	38s
Mental health care, state and county mental hospitals, exp	capita	19.03	88	38s
Mental health care, VA medical centers, exp	capita	3.80	88	38s
Physician fee, family practice, first-visit		111.00	91	62r
Physician fee, family practice, revisit		45.00	91	62r
Physician fee, general practice, first-visit		100.00	91	62r
Physician fee, general practice, revisit		40.00	91	62r
Physician fee, internal medicine, first-visit		137.00	91	62r
Physician fee, internal medicine, revisit		48.00	91	62r
Physician fee, median, neurosurgeon, first-visit		157.00	91	62r

Values are in dollars or fractions of dollars. In the column headed *Ref*, references are shown to sources. Each reference is followed by a letter. These refer to the geographical level for which data were reported: s = State, r = Region, and c = City or metro. The abbreviation *ex* is used to mean *except* or *excluding*; *exp* stands for expenditures. For other abbreviations and further explanations, please see the Introduction.

Boulder, CO - continued

Item	Per	Value	Date	Ref.
Health Care				
Physician fee, median, nonsurgical specialist, first-visit		131.00	91	62r
Physician fee, median, orthopedic surgeon, first-visit		124.00	91	62r
Physician fee, median, plastic surgeon, first-visit		88.00	91	62r
Physician fee, median, surgical specialist, first-visit		100.00	91	62r
Physician fee, neurosurgeon, revisit		51.00	91	62r
Physician fee, nonsurgical specialist, revisit		47.00	91	62r
Physician fee, obstetrics/gynecology, first-visit		95.00	91	62r
Physician fee, obstetrics/gynecology, revisit		50.00	91	62r
Physician fee, orthopedic surgeon, revisit		51.00	91	62r
Physician fee, pediatrician, first-visit		81.00	91	62r
Physician fee, pediatrician, revisit		42.00	91	62r
Physician fee, plastic surgeon, revisit		48.00	91	62r
Physician fee, surgical specialist, revisit		49.00	91	62r
Substance abuse, hospital ancillary charge	incident	1040	90	70s
Substance abuse, hospital physician charge	incident	380	90	70s
Substance abuse, hospital room and board	incident	4880	90	70s
Household Goods				
Appliance repair, home, service call, washing machine	min labor charge	30.30	4Q 92	4c
Laundry detergent, Tide Ultra, Bold, or Cheer	42 oz	3.55	4Q 92	4c
Tissues, facial, Kleenex brand	175-count box	1.03	4Q 92	4c
Housing				
ACCRA Index, Housing		157.20	4Q 92	4c
House, 1,800 sq ft, 8,000 sq ft lot, new, urban	total	178700	4Q 92	4c
House payment, principal and interest, 25% down payment	month	997	4Q 92	4c
Mortgage rate, incl. points & origination fee, 30-year fixed or adjustable rate	percent	8.14	4Q 92	4c
Rent, apartment, 2 bedrooms - 1-1/2 to 2 baths, unfurnished, 950 sq ft, water	month	705	4Q 92	4c
Rental unit, 1 bedroom	month	511	93	23c
Rental unit, 2 bedroom	month	601	93	23c
Rental unit, 3 bedroom	month	752	93	23c
Rental unit, 4 bedroom	month	841	93	23c
Rental unit, efficiency	month	421	93	23c
Insurance and Pensions				
Auto insurance, private passenger	year	684.81	91	63s
Personal Goods				
Shampoo, Alberto VO5	15 oz	1.23	4Q 92	4c
Toothpaste, Crest or Colgate	6-7 oz	2.10	4Q 92	4c
Personal Services				
Dry cleaning, man's 2-piece suit		7.54	4Q 92	4c
Haircare, woman's shampoo, trim and blow-dry		21.40	4Q 92	4c
Haircut, man's barbershop, no styling		10.19	4Q 92	4c
Restaurant Food				
Chicken, fried, thigh and drumstick		1.99	4Q 92	4c
Hamburger with cheese	1/4 lb	1.99	4Q 92	4c
Pizza, Pizza Hut or Pizza Inn, cheese, thin crust	12-13 in	7.69	4Q 92	4c
Taxes				
Tax, cigarette	pack	20	91	77s
Tax, gasoline	gal	22	91	77s
Taxes, state	capita	951	91	77s

Boulder, CO - continued

Item	Per	Value	Date	Ref.
Transportation				
ACCRA Index, Transportation		108.90	4Q 92	4c
Bus fare	one-way	0.60	3/93	2c
Bus fare, up to 10 miles	one-way	1.00	4Q 92	4c
Driver's license fee		15.00	12/90	43s
Tire balance, computer or spin balance, front	wheel	6.90	4Q 92	4c
Travel				
Business travel	day	178.00	4/93	89r
Utilities				
ACCRA Index, Utilities		90.80	4Q 92	4c
Electricity	mil Btu	17.31	90	64s
Electricity, partial electric and other energy, 1,800 sq ft living area new home	month	58.32	4Q 92	4c
Electricity, residential	KWh	7.70	2/93	94s

Bowling Green, KY

Item	Per	Value	Date	Ref.
Composite ACCRA index		91.30	4Q 92	4c
Alcoholic Beverages				
Beer, Miller Lite or Budweiser, 12-oz containers	6 pack	4.52	4Q 92	4c
Liquor, J & B Scotch	750 ml	16.53	4Q 92	4c
Wine, Gallo Chablis blanc, 1.5 liter	bottle	5.54	4Q 92	4c
Clothing				
Jeans, man's denim		24.99	4Q 92	4c
Shirt, man's dress shirt		27.16	4Q 92	4c
Undervest, boy's size 10-14, cotton	3	3.00	4Q 92	4c
Communications				
Newspaper subscription, daily and Sunday home delivery, large-city	month	14.67	4Q 92	4c
Telephone, flat rate	month	12.69	91	11c
Telephone bill, family of four	month	19.83	4Q 92	4c
Energy and Fuels				
Energy, combined forms, 1,800 sq ft heating area	month	95.18	4Q 92	4c
Energy, exc electricity, 1,800 sq ft heating area	month	37.14	4Q 92	4c
Gasoline, motor	gal	1.02	4Q 92	4c
Entertainment				
Bowling, evening rate	game	2.10	4Q 92	4c
Monopoly game, Parker Brothers', No. 9		10.14	4Q 92	4c
Movie	admission	5.00	4Q 92	4c
Tennis balls, yellow, Wilson or Penn, 3	can	2.31	4Q 92	4c
Goods and Services				
ACCRA Index, Miscellaneous Goods and Services		95.50	4Q 92	4c
Groceries				
ACCRA Index, Groceries		98.50	4Q 92	4c
Babyfood, strained vegetables, lowest price	4-4.5 oz jar	0.33	4Q 92	4c
Bananas	lb	0.42	4Q 92	4c
Bread, white	24 oz	0.89	4Q 92	4c
Cheese, Kraft grated Parmesan	8-oz canister	3.16	4Q 92	4c
Chicken, fryer, whole	lb	0.75	4Q 92	4c
Cigarettes, Winston	carton	15.52	4Q 92	4c
Coffee, vacuum-packed	13-oz can	1.99	4Q 92	4c
Corn, frozen	10 oz	0.90	4Q 92	4c
Corn Flakes, Kellogg's or Post Toasties	18 oz	1.79	4Q 92	4c
Eggs, Grade A large	doz	0.76	4Q 92	4c
Ground beef or hamburger	lb	1.55	4Q 92	4c
Lettuce, iceberg	head	1.22	4Q 92	4c

Values are in dollars or fractions of dollars. In the column headed *Ref*, references are shown to sources. Each reference is followed by a letter. These refer to the geographical level for which data were reported: s=State, r=Region, and c=City or metro. The abbreviation *ex* is used to mean *except* or *excluding*; *exp* stands for expenditures. For other abbreviations and further explanations, please see the Introduction.

Bowling Green, KY - continued

Item	Per	Value	Date	Ref.
Groceries				
Margarine, Blue Bonnet or Parkay cubes	lb	0.49	4Q 92	4c
Milk, whole	1/2 gal	1.43	4Q 92	4c
Orange juice, Minute Maid frozen	12-oz can	1.21	4Q 92	4c
Peaches	29-oz can	1.26	4Q 92	4c
Peas Sweet, Del Monte or Green Giant	15-17 oz can	0.62	4Q 92	4c
Potatoes, white or red	10-lb sack	2.35	4Q 92	4c
Sausage, Jimmy Dean, 100% pork	lb	2.29	4Q 92	4c
Shortening, vegetable, Crisco	3-lb can	1.99	4Q 92	4c
Soft drink, Coca Cola	2 liter	1.19	4Q 92	4c
Steak, T-bone	lb	5.15	4Q 92	4c
Sugar, cane or beet	4 lb	1.39	4Q 92	4c
Tomatoes, Hunt's or Del Monte	14.5-oz can	0.77	4Q 92	4c
Tuna, chunk, light	6.125-6.5 oz can	0.55	4Q 92	4c
Health Care				
ACCRA Index, Health Care		94.60	4Q 92	4c
Analgesic, Aspirin, Bayer, 325 mg tablets	100	3.72	4Q 92	4c
Dentist's fee, adult teeth cleaning and periodic oral exam	visit	50.33	4Q 92	4c
Doctor's fee, routine exam, established patient	visit	32.67	4Q 92	4c
Hospital care, semiprivate room	day	169.00	90	27c
Hospital care, semiprivate room	day	297.00	4Q 92	4c
Household Goods				
Appliance repair, home, service call, washing machine	min labor charge	26.50	4Q 92	4c
Laundry detergent, Tide Ultra, Bold, or Cheer	42 oz	2.99	4Q 92	4c
Tissues, facial, Kleenex brand	175-count box	1.12	4Q 92	4c
Housing				
ACCRA Index, Housing		83.10	4Q 92	4c
House, 1,800 sq ft, 8,000 sq ft lot, new, urban	total	93667	4Q 92	4c
House payment, principal and interest, 25% down payment	month	527	4Q 92	4c
Mortgage rate, incl. points & origination fee, 30-year fixed or adjustable rate	percent	8.24	4Q 92	4c
Rent, apartment, 2 bedrooms - 1-1/2 to 2 baths, unfurnished, 950 sq ft, water	month	373	4Q 92	4c
Personal Goods				
Shampoo, Alberto VO5	15 oz	1.22	4Q 92	4c
Toothpaste, Crest or Colgate	6-7 oz	2.09	4Q 92	4c
Personal Services				
Dry cleaning, man's 2-piece suit		5.12	4Q 92	4c
Haircare, woman's shampoo, trim and blow-dry		20.67	4Q 92	4c
Haircut, man's barbershop, no styling		6.33	4Q 92	4c
Restaurant Food				
Chicken, fried, thigh and drumstick		2.28	4Q 92	4c
Hamburger with cheese	1/4 lb	1.82	4Q 92	4c
Pizza, Pizza Hut or Pizza Inn, cheese, thin crust	12-13 in	7.99	4Q 92	4c
Transportation				
ACCRA Index, Transportation		91.20	4Q 92	4c
Tire balance, computer or spin balance, front	wheel	6.00	4Q 92	4c

Bowling Green, KY - continued

Item	Per	Value	Date	Ref.
Utilities				
ACCRA Index, Utilities		88.60	4Q 92	4c
Electricity, partial electric and other energy, 1,800 sq ft living area new home	month	58.04	4Q 92	4c

Bozeman, MT

Item	Per	Value	Date	Ref.
Composite ACCRA index		104.90	4Q 92	4c
Alcoholic Beverages				
Beer, Miller Lite or Budweiser, 12-oz containers	6 pack	4.26	4Q 92	4c
Liquor, J & B Scotch	750 ml	18.10	4Q 92	4c
Wine, Gallo Chablis blanc, 1.5 liter	bottle	5.24	4Q 92	4c
Clothing				
Jeans, man's denim		25.79	4Q 92	4c
Shirt, man's dress shirt		24.50	4Q 92	4c
Undervest, boy's size 10-14, cotton	3	5.11	4Q 92	4c
Communications				
Newspaper subscription, daily and Sunday home delivery, large-city	month	13.04	4Q 92	4c
Telephone, flat rate	month	13.84	91	11c
Telephone bill, family of four	month	19.25	4Q 92	4c
Energy and Fuels				
Energy, combined forms, 1,800 sq ft heating area	month	96.34	4Q 92	4c
Energy, exc electricity, 1,800 sq ft heating area	month	50.34	4Q 92	4c
Gasoline, motor	gal	1.30	4Q 92	4c
Entertainment				
Bowling, evening rate	game	1.50	4Q 92	4c
Monopoly game, Parker Brothers', No. 9		12.15	4Q 92	4c
Movie	admission	5.00	4Q 92	4c
Tennis balls, yellow, Wilson or Penn, 3	can	3.03	4Q 92	4c
Goods and Services				
ACCRA Index, Miscellaneous Goods and Services		104.10	4Q 92	4c
Groceries				
ACCRA Index, Groceries		106.00	4Q 92	4c
Babyfood, strained vegetables, lowest price	4-4.5 oz jar	0.31	4Q 92	4c
Bananas	lb	0.44	4Q 92	4c
Bread, white	24 oz	0.59	4Q 92	4c
Cheese, Kraft grated Parmesan	8-oz canister	3.66	4Q 92	4c
Chicken, fryer, whole	lb	0.81	4Q 92	4c
Cigarettes, Winston	carton	17.72	4Q 92	4c
Coffee, vacuum-packed	13-oz can	2.24	4Q 92	4c
Corn, frozen	10 oz	0.66	4Q 92	4c
Corn Flakes, Kellogg's or Post Toasties	18 oz	2.15	4Q 92	4c
Eggs, Grade A large	doz	0.86	4Q 92	4c
Ground beef or hamburger	lb	1.59	4Q 92	4c
Lettuce, iceberg	head	0.99	4Q 92	4c
Margarine, Blue Bonnet or Parkay cubes	lb	0.82	4Q 92	4c
Milk, whole	1/2 gal	1.47	4Q 92	4c
Orange juice, Minute Maid frozen	12-oz can	1.60	4Q 92	4c
Peaches	29-oz can	1.45	4Q 92	4c
Peas Sweet, Del Monte or Green Giant	15-17 oz can	0.67	4Q 92	4c
Potatoes, white or red	10-lb sack	1.69	4Q 92	4c
Sausage, Jimmy Dean, 100% pork	lb	3.28	4Q 92	4c
Shortening, vegetable, Crisco	3-lb can	2.36	4Q 92	4c
Soft drink, Coca Cola	2 liter	1.54	4Q 92	4c

Values are in dollars or fractions of dollars. In the column headed *Ref*, references are shown to sources. Each reference is followed by a letter. These refer to the geographical level for which data were reported: s=State, r=Region, and c=City or metro. The abbreviation *ex* is used to mean *except* or *excluding*; *exp* stands for expenditures. For other abbreviations and further explanations, please see the Introduction.

87

Bozeman, MT - continued

Item	Per	Value	Date	Ref.
Groceries				
Steak, T-bone	lb	4.71	4Q 92	4c
Sugar, cane or beet	4 lb	1.48	4Q 92	4c
Tomatoes, Hunt's or Del Monte	14.5-oz can	0.65	4Q 92	4c
Tuna, chunk, light	6.125-6.5 oz can	0.78	4Q 92	4c
Health Care				
ACCRA Index, Health Care		100.40	4Q 92	4c
Analgesic, Aspirin, Bayer, 325 mg tablets	100	5.57	4Q 92	4c
Dentist's fee, adult teeth cleaning and periodic oral exam	visit	51.12	4Q 92	4c
Doctor's fee, routine exam, established patient	visit	35.44	4Q 92	4c
Hospital care, semiprivate room	day	270.00	4Q 92	4c
Household Goods				
Appliance repair, home, service call, washing machine	min labor charge	32.19	4Q 92	4c
Laundry detergent, Tide Ultra, Bold, or Cheer	42 oz	4.20	4Q 92	4c
Tissues, facial, Kleenex brand	175-count box	1.20	4Q 92	4c
Housing				
ACCRA Index, Housing		106.90	4Q 92	4c
House, 1,800 sq ft, 8,000 sq ft lot, new, urban	total	116975	4Q 92	4c
House payment, principal and interest, 25% down payment	month	664	4Q 92	4c
Mortgage rate, incl. points & origination fee, 30-year fixed or adjustable rate	percent	8.32	4Q 92	4c
Rent, apartment, 2 bedrooms - 1-1/2 to 2 baths, unfurnished, 950 sq ft, water	month	512	4Q 92	4c
Personal Goods				
Shampoo, Alberto VO5	15 oz	1.60	4Q 92	4c
Toothpaste, Crest or Colgate	6-7 oz	2.34	4Q 92	4c
Personal Services				
Dry cleaning, man's 2-piece suit		6.61	4Q 92	4c
Haircare, woman's shampoo, trim and blow-dry		17.31	4Q 92	4c
Haircut, man's barbershop, no styling		8.29	4Q 92	4c
Restaurant Food				
Chicken, fried, thigh and drumstick		2.30	4Q 92	4c
Hamburger with cheese	1/4 lb	1.95	4Q 92	4c
Pizza, Pizza Hut or Pizza Inn, cheese, thin crust	12-13 in	8.39	4Q 92	4c
Transportation				
ACCRA Index, Transportation		116.50	4Q 92	4c
Tire balance, computer or spin balance, front	wheel	7.68	4Q 92	4c
Utilities				
ACCRA Index, Utilities		89.30	4Q 92	4c
Electricity, partial electric and other energy, 1,800 sq ft living area new home	month	46.00	4Q 92	4c

Bradenton, FL

Item	Per	Value	Date	Ref.
Child Care				
Child care fee, average, center	hour	1.29	90	65r
Child care fee, average, nonregulated family day care	hour	0.89	90	65r
Child care fee, average, regulated family day care	hour	1.32	90	65r

Bradenton, FL - continued

Item	Per	Value	Date	Ref.
Communications				
Long-distance telephone service, day, initial minute, 0-100 miles	min	0.15-0.20	91	12s
Long-distance telephone service, day, additional minute, 0-100 miles	min	0.08-0.20	91	12s
Long-distance telephone service, evenings/weekends, 0-100 mi, initial minute	min	0.09-0.12	91	12s
Long-distance telephone service, evenings/weekends, 0-100 mi, additional minute	min	0.05-0.12	91	12s
Education				
Board, 4-yr private college/university	year	1924	91	22s
Board, 4-yr public college/university	year	1955	91	22s
Expenditures, local gov't, public elementary/secondary	pupil	5235	92	20s
Room, 4-year private college/university	year	1904	91	22s
Room, 4-year public college/university	year	1510	91	22s
Tuition, 2-year private college/university	year	4751	91	22s
Tuition, 2-year public college/university	year	788	91	22s
Tuition, 4-year private college/university	year	7992	91	22s
Tuition, 4-year public college/university, in-state	year	1337	91	22s
Energy and Fuels				
Coal	mil Btu	1.85	90	64s
Energy	mil Btu	10.58	90	64s
Energy exp/householder, 1-family unit	year	487	90	28r
Energy exp/householder, <1,000 sq ft heating area	year	393	90	28r
Energy exp/householder, 1,000-1,999 sq ft heating area	year	442	90	28r
Energy exp/householder, 2,000+ sq ft heating area	year	577	90	28r
Energy exp/householder, mobile home	year	366	90	28r
Energy exp/householder, multifamily	year	382	90	28r
Gas, natural	mil Btu	3.21	90	64s
Gas, natural	000 cu ft	8.98	91	46s
Gas, natural, exp	year	248	91	46s
Gasoline, unleaded regular	mil Btu	8.85	90	64s
Entertainment				
Miniature golf admission	adult	6.18	92	1r
Miniature golf admission	child	5.14	92	1r
Waterpark admission	adult	11.00	92	1r
Waterpark admission	child	8.55	92	1r
Funerals				
Casket, 18-gauge steel, velvet interior		2029.08	91	24r
Cosmetology, hair care, etc.		75.10	91	24r
Embalming		249.24	91	24r
Facility use for ceremony		162.27	91	24r
Hearse, local		114.04	91	24r
Limousine, local		88.57	91	24r
Remains to funeral home, transfer		92.61	91	24r
Service charge, professional		682.42	91	24r
Vault, concrete, non-metallic liner		798.70	91	24r
Viewing facilities, use		163.86	91	24r
Groceries				
Apples, Red Delicious	lb	0.79	4/93	16r
Bacon	lb	1.75	4/93	16r
Bananas	lb	0.42	4/93	16r
Beef, stew, boneless	lb	2.61	4/93	16r
Bologna, all beef or mixed	lb	2.24	4/93	16r
Bread, white, pan	lb	0.64	4/93	16r
Bread, whole wheat, pan	lb	0.96	4/93	16r
Cabbage	lb	0.37	4/93	16r
Carrots, short trimmed and topped	lb	0.47	4/93	16r
Celery	lb	0.64	4/93	16r
Cheese, American	lb	2.98	4/93	16r
Cheese, Cheddar	lb	3.28	4/93	16r
Chicken, fresh, whole	lb	0.77	4/93	16r
Chicken breast, bone-in	lb	1.92	4/93	16r
Chicken legs, bone-in	lb	1.06	4/93	16r

Values are in dollars or fractions of dollars. In the column headed *Ref*, references are shown to sources. Each reference is followed by a letter. These refer to the geographical level for which data were reported: s=State, r=Region, and c=City or metro. The abbreviation *ex* is used to mean *except* or *excluding*; *exp* stands for expenditures. For other abbreviations and further explanations, please see the Introduction.

Bradenton, FL - continued

Item	Per	Value	Date	Ref.
Groceries				
Chuck roast, graded and ungraded, ex USDA prime and choice	lb	2.40	4/93	16r
Chuck roast, USDA choice, bone-in	lb	2.19	4/93	16r
Chuck roast, USDA choice, boneless	lb	2.38	4/93	16r
Coffee, 100% ground roast, all sizes	lb	2.48	4/93	16r
Crackers, soda, salted	lb	1.15	4/93	16r
Eggs, Grade A large	doz	0.96	4/93	16r
Flour, white, all purpose	lb	0.24	4/93	16r
Frankfurters, all meat or all beef	lb	2.01	4/93	16r
Grapefruit	lb	0.44	4/93	16r
Grapes, Thompson Seedless	lb	1.40	4/93	16r
Ground beef, 100% beef	lb	1.58	4/93	16r
Ground beef, lean and extra lean	lb	2.09	4/93	16r
Ground chuck, 100% beef	lb	1.98	4/93	16r
Ham, boneless, excluding canned	lb	2.89	4/93	16r
Ham, picnic, shoulder, bone-in, smoked	lb	1.02	4/93	16r
Ham, rump or steak half, bone-in, smoked	lb	1.48	4/93	16r
Ice cream, prepackaged, bulk, regular	1/2 gal	2.41	4/93	16r
Lemons	lb	1.05	4/93	16r
Lettuce, iceberg	lb	0.81	4/93	16r
Margarine, stick	lb	0.88	4/93	16r
Oranges, navel	lb	0.55	4/93	16r
Pears, Anjou	lb	0.92	4/93	16r
Pork chops, center cut, bone-in	lb	3.13	4/93	16r
Potato chips	16 oz	2.94	4/93	16r
Potatoes, white	lb	0.43	4/93	16r
Rib roast, USDA choice, bone-in	lb	4.63	4/93	16r
Rice, white, long grain, uncooked	lb	0.45	4/93	16r
Round roast, graded & ungraded, ex USDA prime & choice	lb	3.03	4/93	16r
Round roast, USDA choice, boneless	lb	3.09	4/93	16r
Sausage, fresh, loose	lb	2.08	4/93	16r
Short ribs, bone-in	lb	2.66	4/93	16r
Shortening, vegetable oil blends	lb	0.69	4/93	16r
Spaghetti and macaroni	lb	0.81	4/93	16r
Steak, rib eye, USDA choice, boneless	lb	6.24	4/93	16r
Steak, round, graded & ungraded, ex USDA prime & choice	lb	3.31	4/93	16r
Steak, round, USDA choice, boneless	lb	3.34	4/93	16r
Steak, sirloin, graded & ungraded, ex USDA prime & choice	lb	4.19	4/93	16r
Steak, sirloin, USDA choice, boneless	lb	4.46	4/93	16r
Steak, T-bone, USDA choice, bone-in	lb	5.25	4/93	16r
Strawberries, dry pint	12 oz	0.92	4/93	16r
Sugar, white	lb	0.39	4/93	16r
Sugar, white, 33-80 oz pk	lb	0.38	4/93	16r
Tomatoes, field grown	lb	0.88	4/93	16r
Tuna, chunk, light	lb	1.79	4/93	16r
Turkey, frozen, whole	lb	1.04	4/93	16r
Yogurt, natural, fruit flavored	1/2 pint	0.57	4/93	16r
Health Care				
Childbirth, cesarean, hospital		5034	91	62r
Childbirth, cesarean, physician's fee		2053	91	62r
Childbirth, normal, hospital		2712	91	62r
Childbirth, normal, physician's fee		1492	91	62r
Medical plan per employee	year	3495	91	45r
Mental health care, exp	capita	28.84-37.59	90	38s
Mental health care, exp, state mental health agency	capita	37.49	90	38s
Mental health care, hospital psychiatric services, non-Federal, exp	capita	9.11	88	38s
Mental health care, mental health organization, multiservice, exp	capita	16.21	88	38s
Mental health care, psychiatric hospitals, private, exp	capita	22.26	88	38s
Mental health care, psychiatric out-patient clinics, freestanding, exp	capita	0.89	88	38s
Mental health care, psychiatric partial-care organizations, freestanding, exp	capita	0.41	88	38s

Bradenton, FL - continued

Item	Per	Value	Date	Ref.
Health Care - continued				
Mental health care, state and county mental hospitals, exp	capita	16.25	88	38s
Mental health care, VA medical centers, exp	capita	1.69	88	38s
Physician fee, family practice, first-visit		75.00	91	62r
Physician fee, family practice, revisit		34.00	91	62r
Physician fee, general practice, first-visit		61.00	91	62r
Physician fee, general practice, revisit		32.00	91	62r
Physician fee, general surgeon, first-visit		64.00	91	62r
Physician fee, general surgeon, revisit		40.00	91	62r
Physician fee, internal medicine, first-visit		98.00	91	62r
Physician fee, internal medicine, revisit		40.00	91	62r
Physician fee, median, neurosurgeon, first-visit		130.00	91	62r
Physician fee, median, nonsurgical specialist, first-visit		95.00	91	62r
Physician fee, median, orthopedic surgeon, first-visit		91.00	91	62r
Physician fee, median, plastic surgeon, first-visit		66.00	91	62r
Physician fee, median, surgical specialist, first-visit		62.00	91	62r
Physician fee, neurosurgeon, revisit		50.00	91	62r
Physician fee, nonsurgical specialist, revisit		40.00	91	62r
Physician fee, obstetrics/gynecology, first-visit		64.00	91	62r
Physician fee, obstetrics/gynecology, revisit		41.00	91	62r
Physician fee, orthopedic surgeon, revisit		40.00	91	62r
Physician fee, pediatrician, first-visit		49.00	91	62r
Physician fee, pediatrician, revisit		33.00	91	62r
Physician fee, plastic surgeon, revisit		43.00	91	62r
Physician fee, surgical specialist, revisit		37.00	91	62r
Substance abuse, hospital ancillary charge	incident	1390	90	70s
Substance abuse, hospital physician charge	incident	770	90	70s
Substance abuse, hospital room and board	incident	5600	90	70s
Insurance and Pensions				
Auto insurance, private passenger	year	727.60	91	63s
Taxes				
Tax, cigarette	pack	33.90	91	77s
Tax, gasoline	gal	11.60	91	77s
Taxes, state	capita	1037	91	77s
Transportation				
Driver's license fee		15.00	12/90	43s
Travel				
Business travel	day	193.00	4/93	89r
Utilities				
Electricity	mil Btu	20.62	90	64s

Brazoria, TX

Item	Per	Value	Date	Ref.
Child Care				
Child care fee, average, center	hour	1.29	90	65r
Child care fee, average, nonregulated family day care	hour	0.89	90	65r
Child care fee, average, regulated family day care	hour	1.32	90	65r
Communications				
Long-distance telephone service, day, initial minute, 0-100 miles	min	0.10-0.46	91	12s
Long-distance telephone service, day, additional minute, 0-100 miles	min	0.06-0.45	91	12s
Education				
Board, 4-yr private college/university	year	1883	91	22s
Board, 4-yr public college/university	year	1605	91	22s

Values are in dollars or fractions of dollars. In the column headed *Ref*, references are shown to sources. Each reference is followed by a letter. These refer to the geographical level for which data were reported: s=State, r=Region, and c=City or metro. The abbreviation *ex* is used to mean *except* or *excluding*; *exp* stands for expenditures. For other abbreviations and further explanations, please see the Introduction.

Brazoria, TX - continued

Item	Per	Value	Date	Ref.
Education				
Expenditures, local gov't, public elementary/secondary	pupil	4593	92	20s
Room, 4-year private college/university	year	1620	91	22s
Room, 4-year public college/university	year	1532	91	22s
Tuition, 2-year private college/university	year	4394	91	22s
Tuition, 2-year public college/university	year	495	91	22s
Tuition, 4-year private college/university	year	6497	91	22s
Tuition, 4-year public college/university, in-state	year	986	91	22s
Energy and Fuels				
Coal	mil Btu	1.44	90	64s
Energy	mil Btu	6.48	90	64s
Energy exp/householder, 1-family unit	year	471	90	28r
Energy exp/householder, <1,000 sq ft heating area	year	384	90	28r
Energy exp/householder, 1,000-1,999 sq ft heating area	year	421	90	28r
Energy exp/householder, 2,000+ sq ft heating area	year	625	90	28r
Energy exp/householder, mobile home	year	271	90	28r
Energy exp/householder, multifamily	year	355	90	28r
Gas, natural	mil Btu	2.47	90	64s
Gas, natural	000 cu ft	5.71	91	46s
Gas, natural, exp	year	388	91	46s
Gasoline, unleaded regular	mil Btu	9.16	90	64s
Entertainment				
Miniature golf admission	adult	6.18	92	1r
Miniature golf admission	child	5.14	92	1r
Waterpark admission	adult	11.00	92	1r
Waterpark admission	child	8.55	92	1r
Funerals				
Casket, 18-gauge steel, velvet interior		2274.41	91	24r
Cosmetology, hair care, etc.		74.62	91	24r
Embalming		229.94	91	24r
Facility use for ceremony		176.61	91	24r
Hearse, local		116.34	91	24r
Limousine, local		72.68	91	24r
Remains to funeral home, transfer		87.72	91	24r
Service charge, professional		712.53	91	24r
Vault, concrete, non-metallic liner		750.55	91	24r
Viewing facilities, use		155.31	91	24r
Groceries				
Apples, Red Delicious	lb	0.79	4/93	16r
Bacon	lb	1.75	4/93	16r
Bananas	lb	0.42	4/93	16r
Beef, stew, boneless	lb	2.61	4/93	16r
Bologna, all beef or mixed	lb	2.24	4/93	16r
Bread, white, pan	lb	0.64	4/93	16r
Bread, whole wheat, pan	lb	0.96	4/93	16r
Cabbage	lb	0.37	4/93	16r
Carrots, short trimmed and topped	lb	0.47	4/93	16r
Celery	lb	0.64	4/93	16r
Cheese, American	lb	2.98	4/93	16r
Cheese, Cheddar	lb	3.28	4/93	16r
Chicken, fresh, whole	lb	0.77	4/93	16r
Chicken breast, bone-in	lb	1.92	4/93	16r
Chicken legs, bone-in	lb	1.06	4/93	16r
Chuck roast, graded and ungraded, ex USDA prime and choice	lb	2.40	4/93	16r
Chuck roast, USDA choice, bone-in	lb	2.19	4/93	16r
Chuck roast, USDA choice, boneless	lb	2.38	4/93	16r
Coffee, 100% ground roast, all sizes	lb	2.48	4/93	16r
Crackers, soda, salted	lb	1.15	4/93	16r
Eggs, Grade A large	doz	0.96	4/93	16r
Flour, white, all purpose	lb	0.24	4/93	16r
Frankfurters, all meat or all beef	lb	2.01	4/93	16r
Grapefruit	lb	0.44	4/93	16r
Grapes, Thompson Seedless	lb	1.40	4/93	16r
Ground beef, 100% beef	lb	1.58	4/93	16r

Brazoria, TX - continued

Item	Per	Value	Date	Ref.
Groceries - continued				
Ground beef, lean and extra lean	lb	2.09	4/93	16r
Ground chuck, 100% beef	lb	1.98	4/93	16r
Ham, boneless, excluding canned	lb	2.89	4/93	16r
Ham, picnic, shoulder, bone-in, smoked	lb	1.02	4/93	16r
Ham, rump or steak half, bone-in, smoked	lb	1.48	4/93	16r
Honey, jar	8 oz	0.73-1.19	92	5r
Honey, jar	lb	1.10-1.79	92	5r
Honey, squeeze bear	12-oz	1.19-1.50	92	5r
Ice cream, prepackaged, bulk, regular	1/2 gal	2.41	4/93	16r
Lemons	lb	1.05	4/93	16r
Lettuce, iceberg	lb	0.81	4/93	16r
Margarine, stick	lb	0.88	4/93	16r
Oranges, navel	lb	0.55	4/93	16r
Pears, Anjou	lb	0.92	4/93	16r
Pork chops, center cut, bone-in	lb	3.13	4/93	16r
Potato chips	16 oz	2.94	4/93	16r
Potatoes, white	lb	0.43	4/93	16r
Rib roast, USDA choice, bone-in	lb	4.63	4/93	16r
Rice, white, long grain, uncooked	lb	0.45	4/93	16r
Round roast, graded & ungraded, ex USDA prime & choice	lb	3.03	4/93	16r
Round roast, USDA choice, boneless	lb	3.09	4/93	16r
Sausage, fresh, loose	lb	2.08	4/93	16r
Short ribs, bone-in	lb	2.66	4/93	16r
Shortening, vegetable oil blends	lb	0.69	4/93	16r
Spaghetti and macaroni	lb	0.81	4/93	16r
Steak, rib eye, USDA choice, boneless	lb	6.24	4/93	16r
Steak, round, graded & ungraded, ex USDA prime & choice	lb	3.31	4/93	16r
Steak, round, USDA choice, boneless	lb	3.34	4/93	16r
Steak, sirloin, graded & ungraded, ex USDA prime & choice	lb	4.19	4/93	16r
Steak, sirloin, USDA choice, boneless	lb	4.46	4/93	16r
Steak, T-bone, USDA choice, bone-in	lb	5.25	4/93	16r
Strawberries, dry pint	12 oz	0.92	4/93	16r
Sugar, white	lb	0.39	4/93	16r
Sugar, white, 33-80 oz pk	lb	0.38	4/93	16r
Tomatoes, field grown	lb	0.88	4/93	16r
Tuna, chunk, light	lb	1.79	4/93	16r
Turkey, frozen, whole	lb	1.04	4/93	16r
Yogurt, natural, fruit flavored	1/2 pint	0.57	4/93	16r
Health Care				
Childbirth, cesarean, hospital		5034	91	62r
Childbirth, cesarean, physician's fee		2053	91	62r
Childbirth, normal, hospital		2712	91	62r
Childbirth, normal, physician's fee		1492	91	62r
Health care spending, state	capita	2192	3/93	84s
Mental health care, exp	capita	20.37-28.83	90	38s
Mental health care, exp, state mental health agency	capita	22.72	90	38s
Mental health care, hospital psychiatric services, non-Federal, exp	capita	7.95	88	38s
Mental health care, mental health organization, multiservice, exp	capita	12.05	88	38s
Mental health care, psychiatric hospitals, private, exp	capita	37.78	88	38s
Mental health care, psychiatric out-patient clinics, freestanding, exp	capita	0.43	88	38s
Mental health care, state and county mental hospitals, exp	capita	12.54	88	38s
Mental health care, VA medical centers, exp	capita	5.35	88	38s
Physician fee, family practice, first-visit		75.00	91	62r
Physician fee, family practice, revisit		34.00	91	62r
Physician fee, general practice, first-visit		61.00	91	62r
Physician fee, general practice, revisit		32.00	91	62r
Physician fee, general surgeon, first-visit		64.00	91	62r
Physician fee, general surgeon, revisit		40.00	91	62r
Physician fee, internal medicine, first-visit		98.00	91	62r
Physician fee, internal medicine, revisit		40.00	91	62r

Values are in dollars or fractions of dollars. In the column headed *Ref*, references are shown to sources. Each reference is followed by a letter. These refer to the geographical level for which data were reported: s=State, r=Region, and c=City or metro. The abbreviation *ex* is used to mean *except* or *excluding*; *exp* stands for expenditures. For other abbreviations and further explanations, please see the Introduction.

Brazoria, TX - continued

Item	Per	Value	Date	Ref.
Health Care				
Physician fee, median, neurosurgeon, first-visit		130.00	91	62r
Physician fee, median, nonsurgical specialist, first-visit		95.00	91	62r
Physician fee, median, orthopedic surgeon, first-visit		91.00	91	62r
Physician fee, median, plastic surgeon, first-visit		66.00	91	62r
Physician fee, median, surgical specialist, first-visit		62.00	91	62r
Physician fee, neurosurgeon, revisit		50.00	91	62r
Physician fee, nonsurgical specialist, revisit		40.00	91	62r
Physician fee, obstetrics/gynecology, first-visit		64.00	91	62r
Physician fee, obstetrics/gynecology, revisit		41.00	91	62r
Physician fee, orthopedic surgeon, revisit		40.00	91	62r
Physician fee, pediatrician, first-visit		49.00	91	62r
Physician fee, pediatrician, revisit		33.00	91	62r
Physician fee, plastic surgeon, revisit		43.00	91	62r
Physician fee, surgical specialist, revisit		37.00	91	62r
Substance abuse, hospital ancillary charge	incident	3750	90	70s
Substance abuse, hospital physician charge	incident	1080	90	70s
Substance abuse, hospital room and board	incident	5320	90	70s
Insurance and Pensions				
Auto insurance, private passenger	year	709.79	91	63s
Taxes				
Tax, cigarette	pack	41	91	77s
Tax, gasoline	gal	20	91	77s
Taxes, state	capita	923	91	77s
Transportation				
Driver's license fee		16.00	12/90	43s
Travel				
Business travel	day	193.00	4/93	89r
Utilities				
Electricity	mil Btu	17.09	90	64s
Electricity, residential	KWh	5.92	2/93	94s

Bremerton, WA

Item	Per	Value	Date	Ref.
Child Care				
Child care fee, average, center	hour	1.71	90	65r
Child care fee, average, nonregulated family day care	hour	1.32	90	65r
Child care fee, average, regulated family day care	hour	1.86	90	65r
Communications				
Long-distance telephone service, day, initial minute, 0-100 miles	min	0.15-0.37	91	12s
Long-distance telephone service, day, additional minute, 0-100 miles	min	0.01-0.03	91	12s
Long-distance telephone service, evenings/weekends, 0-100 mi, initial minute	min	0.05-0.19	91	12s
Long-distance telephone service, evenings/weekends, 0-100 mi, additional minute	min	0.00-0.01	91	12s
Education				
Board, 4-yr private college/university	year	1811	91	22s
Board, 4-yr public college/university	year	1539	91	22s
Expenditures, local gov't, public elementary/secondary	pupil	5317	92	20s
Room, 4-year private college/university	year	1885	91	22s
Room, 4-year public college/university	year	1698	91	22s
Tuition, 2-year private college/university	year	6743	91	22s
Tuition, 2-year public college/university	year	844	91	22s
Tuition, 4-year private college/university	year	9463	91	22s

Bremerton, WA - continued

Item	Per	Value	Date	Ref.
Education - continued				
Tuition, 4-year public college/university, in-state	year	1823	91	22s
Energy and Fuels				
Energy	mil Btu	7.39	90	64s
Energy exp/householder, 1-family unit	year	362	90	28r
Energy exp/householder, <1,000 sq ft heating area	year	254	90	28r
Energy exp/householder, 1,000-1,999 sq ft heating area	year	358	90	28r
Energy exp/householder, 2,000+ sq ft heating area	year	467	90	28r
Energy exp/householder, mobile home	year	390	90	28r
Energy exp/householder, multifamily	year	252	90	28r
Gas, natural	mil Btu	3.60	90	64s
Gas, natural	000 cu ft	4.68	91	46s
Gas, natural, exp	year	440	91	46s
Gasoline, unleaded regular	mil Btu	9.45	90	64s
Entertainment				
Miniature golf admission	adult	6.18	92	1r
Miniature golf admission	child	5.14	92	1r
Waterpark admission	adult	11.00	92	1r
Waterpark admission	child	8.55	92	1r
Funerals				
Casket, 18-gauge steel, velvet interior		1781.09	91	24r
Cosmetology, hair care, etc.		84.64	91	24r
Embalming		207.41	91	24r
Facility use for ceremony		205.76	91	24r
Hearse, local		105.14	91	24r
Limousine, local		83.21	91	24r
Remains to funeral home, transfer		113.82	91	24r
Service charge, professional		626.33	91	24r
Vault, concrete, non-metallic liner		599.54	91	24r
Viewing facilities, use		85.81	91	24r
Groceries				
Apples, Red Delicious	lb	0.80	4/93	16r
Bacon	lb	1.79	4/93	16r
Bananas	lb	0.53	4/93	16r
Bologna, all beef or mixed	lb	2.67	4/93	16r
Bread, white, pan	lb	0.81	4/93	16r
Carrots, short trimmed and topped	lb	0.39	4/93	16r
Chicken, fresh, whole	lb	0.94	4/93	16r
Chicken breast, bone-in	lb	2.19	4/93	16r
Chuck roast, graded and ungraded, ex USDA prime and choice	lb	2.26	4/93	16r
Coffee, 100% ground roast, all sizes	lb	2.33	4/93	16r
Eggs, Grade AA large	doz	1.18	4/93	16r
Flour, white, all purpose	lb	0.22	4/93	16r
Grapefruit	lb	0.52	4/93	16r
Grapes, Thompson Seedless	lb	1.50	4/93	16r
Ground beef, 100% beef	lb	1.44	4/93	16r
Ground beef, lean and extra lean	lb	2.34	4/93	16r
Ham, boneless, excluding canned	lb	2.56	4/93	16r
Honey, jar	8 oz	0.89-1.00	92	5r
Honey, jar	lb	1.35-1.97	92	5r
Honey, squeeze bear	12-oz	1.19-1.50	92	5r
Ice cream, prepackaged, bulk, regular	1/2 gal	2.40	4/93	16r
Lemons	lb	0.81	4/93	16r
Lettuce, iceberg	lb	0.84	4/93	16r
Margarine, stick	lb	0.81	4/93	16r
Oranges, navel	lb	0.48	4/93	16r
Pork chops, center cut, bone-in	lb	3.25	4/93	16r
Potato chips	16 oz	2.89	4/93	16r
Potatoes, white	lb	0.38	4/93	16r
Round roast, graded & ungraded, ex USDA prime & choice	lb	3.00	4/93	16r
Round roast, USDA choice, boneless	lb	3.16	4/93	16r
Shortening, vegetable oil blends	lb	0.86	4/93	16r
Spaghetti and macaroni	lb	0.84	4/93	16r

Values are in dollars or fractions of dollars. In the column headed *Ref*, references are shown to sources. Each reference is followed by a letter. These refer to the geographical level for which data were reported: s=State, r=Region, and c=City or metro. The abbreviation *ex* is used to mean *except* or *excluding*; *exp* stands for expenditures. For other abbreviations and further explanations, please see the Introduction.

Bremerton, WA - continued

Item	Per	Value	Date	Ref.
Groceries				
Steak, round, graded & ungraded, ex USDA prime & choice	lb	3.34	4/93	16r
Steak, round, USDA choice, boneless	lb	3.24	4/93	16r
Steak, sirloin, graded & ungraded, ex USDA prime & choice	lb	3.75	4/93	16r
Steak, sirloin, USDA choice, boneless	lb	4.49	4/93	16r
Sugar, white	lb	0.41	4/93	16r
Sugar, white, 33-80 oz pk	lb	0.38	4/93	16r
Tomatoes, field grown	lb	1.01	4/93	16r
Turkey, frozen, whole	lb	1.04	4/93	16r
Health Care				
Childbirth, cesarean, hospital		5533	91	62r
Childbirth, cesarean, physician's fee		2053	91	62r
Childbirth, normal, hospital		2745	91	62r
Childbirth, normal, physician's fee		1492	91	62r
Medical plan per employee	year	3421	91	45r
Mental health care, exp	capita	37.60-53.67	90	38s
Physician fee, family practice, first-visit		111.00	91	62r
Physician fee, family practice, revisit		45.00	91	62r
Physician fee, general practice, first-visit		100.00	91	62r
Physician fee, general practice, revisit		40.00	91	62r
Physician fee, internal medicine, first-visit		137.00	91	62r
Physician fee, internal medicine, revisit		48.00	91	62r
Physician fee, median, neurosurgeon, first-visit		157.00	91	62r
Physician fee, median, nonsurgical specialist, first-visit		131.00	91	62r
Physician fee, median, orthopedic surgeon, first-visit		124.00	91	62r
Physician fee, median, plastic surgeon, first-visit		88.00	91	62r
Physician fee, median, surgical specialist, first-visit		100.00	91	62r
Physician fee, neurosurgeon, revisit		51.00	91	62r
Physician fee, nonsurgical specialist, revisit		47.00	91	62r
Physician fee, obstetrics/gynecology, first-visit		95.00	91	62r
Physician fee, obstetrics/gynecology, revisit		50.00	91	62r
Physician fee, orthopedic surgeon, revisit		51.00	91	62r
Physician fee, pediatrician, first-visit		81.00	91	62r
Physician fee, pediatrician, revisit		42.00	91	62r
Physician fee, plastic surgeon, revisit		48.00	91	62r
Physician fee, surgical specialist, revisit		49.00	91	62r
Substance abuse, hospital ancillary charge	incident	1360	90	70s
Substance abuse, hospital physician charge	incident	150	90	70s
Substance abuse, hospital room and board	incident	4200	90	70s
Insurance and Pensions				
Auto insurance, private passenger	year	627.71	91	63s
Taxes				
Tax, cigarette	pack	34	91	77s
Tax, gasoline	gal	23	91	77s
Taxes, state	capita	1592	91	77s
Transportation				
Driver's license fee		14.00	12/90	43s
Travel				
Business travel	day	178.00	4/93	89r
Utilities				
Electricity	mil Btu	10.03	90	64s

Bridgeport, CT

Item	Per	Value	Date	Ref.
Child Care				
Child care fee, average, center	hour	2.18	90	65r
Child care fee, average, nonregulated family day care	hour	1.83	90	65r
Child care fee, average, regulated family day care	hour	2.02	90	65r
Communications				
Long-distance telephone service, day, initial minute, 0-100 miles	min	0.18-0.45	91	12s
Long-distance telephone service, day, additional minute, 0-100 miles	min	0.10-0.26	91	12s
Long-distance telephone service, evenings/weekends, 0-100 mi, initial minute	min	0.07-0.18	91	12s
Long-distance telephone service, evenings/weekends, 0-100 mi, additional minute	min	0.04-0.10	91	12s
Telephone, flat rate	month	12.79	91	11c
Education				
Board, 4-yr private college/university	year	2182	91	22s
Board, 4-yr public college/university	year	1750	91	22s
Expenditures, local gov't, public elementary/secondary	pupil	8308	92	20s
Room, 4-year private college/university	year	2703	91	22s
Room, 4-year public college/university	year	1913	91	22s
Tuition, 2-year private college/university	year	8586	91	22s
Tuition, 2-year public college/university	year	972	91	22s
Tuition, 4-year private college/university	year	12315	91	22s
Tuition, 4-year public college/university, in-state	year	2313	91	22s
Energy and Fuels				
Coal	mil Btu	2.15	90	64s
Energy	mil Btu	11.62	90	64s
Energy exp/householder, 1-family unit	year	588	90	28r
Energy exp/householder, <1,000 sq ft heating area	year	477	90	28r
Energy exp/householder, 1,000-1,999 sq ft heating area	year	517	90	28r
Energy exp/householder, 2,000+ sq ft heating area	year	630	90	28r
Energy exp/householder, mobile home	year	412	90	28r
Energy exp/householder, multifamily	year	498	90	28r
Gas, cooking, 10 therms	month	16.40	92	56c
Gas, cooking, 30 therms	month	34.59	92	56c
Gas, cooking, 50 therms	month	52.79	92	56c
Gas, heating, winter, 100 therms	month	98.28	92	56c
Gas, heating, winter, average use	month	183.47	92	56c
Gas, natural	mil Btu	6.40	90	64s
Gas, natural	000 cu ft	8.74	91	46s
Gas, natural, exp	year	756	91	46s
Gasoline, unleaded regular	mil Btu	10.06	90	64s
Entertainment				
Miniature golf admission	adult	6.18	92	1r
Miniature golf admission	child	5.14	92	1r
Waterpark admission	adult	11.00	92	1r
Waterpark admission	child	8.55	92	1r
Funerals				
Casket, 18-gauge steel, velvet interior		1853.42	91	24r
Cosmetology, hair care, etc.		98.33	91	24r
Embalming		273.94	91	24r
Facility use for ceremony		196.06	91	24r
Hearse, local		145.67	91	24r
Limousine, local		131.07	91	24r
Remains to funeral home, transfer		135.24	91	24r
Service charge, professional		843.16	91	24r
Vault, concrete, non-metallic liner		709.14	91	24r
Viewing facilities, use		229.85	91	24r
Groceries				
Apples, Red Delicious	lb	0.85	4/93	16r
Bacon	lb	2.12	4/93	16r

Values are in dollars or fractions of dollars. In the column headed *Ref*, references are shown to sources. Each reference is followed by a letter. These refer to the geographical level for which data were reported: s=State, r=Region, and c=City or metro. The abbreviation *ex* is used to mean *except* or *excluding*; *exp* stands for expenditures. For other abbreviations and further explanations, please see the Introduction.

Bridgeport, CT - continued

Item	Per	Value	Date	Ref.
Groceries				
Bananas	lb	0.54	4/93	16r
Bread, white, pan	lb	0.81	4/93	16r
Butter	lb	2.02	4/93	16r
Carrots, short trimmed and topped	lb	0.51	4/93	16r
Chicken, fresh, whole	lb	1.04	4/93	16r
Chicken breast, bone-in	lb	2.21	4/93	16r
Chicken legs, bone-in	lb	1.16	4/93	16r
Chuck roast, USDA choice, boneless	lb	2.82	4/93	16r
Coffee, 100% ground roast, all sizes	lb	2.66	4/93	16r
Cucumbers	lb	0.85	4/93	16r
Eggs, Grade A large	doz	1.15	4/93	16r
Grapefruit	lb	0.45	4/93	16r
Grapes, Thompson Seedless	lb	1.52	4/93	16r
Ground beef, lean and extra lean	lb	2.36	4/93	16r
Ground chuck, 100% beef	lb	2.02	4/93	16r
Honey, jar	8 oz	0.96-1.75	92	5r
Honey, jar	lb	1.50-3.00	92	5r
Honey, squeeze bear	12-oz	1.50-1.99	92	5r
Ice cream, prepackaged, bulk, regular	1/2 gal	2.80	4/93	16r
Lemons	lb	0.96	4/93	16r
Lettuce, iceberg	lb	0.95	4/93	16r
Margarine, stick	lb	0.81	4/93	16r
Milk, fresh, whole, fortified	1/2 gal	1.30	4/93	16r
Oranges, navel	lb	0.56	4/93	16r
Peanut butter, creamy, all sizes	lb	1.88	4/93	16r
Pork chops, center cut, bone-in	lb	3.34	4/93	16r
Potato chips	16 oz	2.88	4/93	16r
Potatoes, white	lb	0.37	4/93	16r
Rib roast, USDA choice, bone-in	lb	4.94	4/93	16r
Round roast, USDA choice, boneless	lb	3.17	4/93	16r
Shortening, vegetable oil blends	lb	0.98	4/93	16r
Spaghetti and macaroni	lb	0.82	4/93	16r
Steak, round, graded & ungraded, ex USDA prime & choice	lb	4.04	4/93	16r
Steak, round, USDA choice, boneless	lb	3.90	4/93	16r
Steak, sirloin, USDA choice, boneless	lb	4.97	4/93	16r
Strawberries, dry pint	12 oz	0.90	4/93	16r
Sugar, white	lb	0.50	4/93	16r
Sugar, white, 33-80 oz pk	lb	0.41	4/93	16r
Tomatoes, field grown	lb	1.23	4/93	16r
Tuna, chunk, light	lb	2.22	4/93	16r
Turkey, frozen, whole	lb	1.04	4/93	16r
Health Care				
Childbirth, cesarean, hospital		5826	91	62r
Childbirth, cesarean, physician's fee		2053	91	62r
Childbirth, normal, hospital		2964	91	62r
Childbirth, normal, physician's fee		1492	91	62r
Hospital care, semiprivate room	day	491.74	90	27c
Medical plan per employee	year	3958	91	45r
Mental health care, exp	capita	53.68-118.35	90	38s
Mental health care, exp, state mental health agency	capita	72.81	90	38s
Mental health care, hospital psychiatric services, non-Federal, exp	capita	19.30	88	38s
Mental health care, mental health organization, multiservice, exp	capita	19.14	88	38s
Mental health care, psychiatric hospitals, private, exp	capita	35.86	88	38s
Mental health care, psychiatric out-patient clinics, freestanding, exp	capita	5.83	88	38s
Mental health care, psychiatric partial-care organizations, freestanding, exp	capita	0.15	88	38s
Mental health care, state and county mental hospitals, exp	capita	51.85	88	38s
Mental health care, VA medical centers, exp	capita	1.74	88	38s
Prescription drug co-pay, Medicaid	month	10.00	91	21s
Substance abuse, hospital ancillary charge	inci-dent	1200	90	70s
Substance abuse, hospital physician charge	inci-dent	270	90	70s

Bridgeport, CT - continued

Item	Per	Value	Date	Ref.
Health Care - continued				
Substance abuse, hospital room and board	inci-dent	4420	90	70s
Housing				
Rental unit, 1 bedroom	month	619	93	23c
Rental unit, 2 bedroom	month	731	93	23c
Rental unit, 3 bedroom	month	912	93	23c
Rental unit, 4 bedroom	month	1024	93	23c
Rental unit, efficiency	month	510	93	23c
Insurance and Pensions				
Auto insurance, private passenger	year	928.10	91	63s
Taxes				
Tax, cigarette	pack	45	91	77s
Tax, gasoline	gal	26	91	77s
Taxes, state	capita	1514	91	77s
Transportation				
Auto rental, average	day	43.72	6/91	60c
Bus fare	one-way	0.85	3/93	2c
Driver's license fee		31.00	12/90	43s
Limo fare, airport-city, average	day	10.00	6/91	60c
Taxi fare, airport-city, average	day	10.00	6/91	60c
Travel				
Breakfast	day	5.50	6/91	60c
Business travel	day	165.00	4/93	89r
Dinner	day	19.05	6/91	60c
Lodging	day	132.67	91	60c
Lunch	day	11.06	6/91	60c
Utilities				
Electricity	mil Btu	26.83	90	64s
Electricity, winter, 250 KWh	month	34.96	92	55c
Electricity, winter, 500 KWh	month	62.43	92	55c
Electricity, winter, 750 KWh	month	89.89	92	55c
Electricity, winter, 1000 KWh	month	117.36	92	55c

Bristol, CT

Item	Per	Value	Date	Ref.
Child Care				
Child care fee, average, center	hour	2.18	90	65r
Child care fee, average, nonregulated family day care	hour	1.83	90	65r
Child care fee, average, regulated family day care	hour	2.02	90	65r
Communications				
Long-distance telephone service, day, initial minute, 0-100 miles	min	0.18-0.45	91	12s
Long-distance telephone service, day, additional minute, 0-100 miles	min	0.10-0.26	91	12s
Long-distance telephone service, evenings/weekends, 0-100 mi, initial minute	min	0.07-0.18	91	12s
Long-distance telephone service, evenings/weekends, 0-100 mi, additional minute	min	0.04-0.10	91	12s
Education				
Board, 4-yr private college/university	year	2182	91	22s
Board, 4-yr public college/university	year	1750	91	22s
Expenditures, local gov't, public elementary/secondary	pupil	8308	92	20s
Room, 4-year private college/university	year	2703	91	22s
Room, 4-year public college/university	year	1913	91	22s
Tuition, 2-year private college/university	year	8586	91	22s
Tuition, 2-year public college/university	year	972	91	22s
Tuition, 4-year private college/university	year	12315	91	22s
Tuition, 4-year public college/university, in-state	year	2313	91	22s
Energy and Fuels				
Coal	mil Btu	2.15	90	64s
Energy	mil Btu	11.62	90	64s

Values are in dollars or fractions of dollars. In the column headed *Ref*, references are shown to sources. Each reference is followed by a letter. These refer to the geographical level for which data were reported: s = State, r = Region, and c = City or metro. The abbreviation *ex* is used to mean *except* or *excluding*; *exp* stands for expenditures. For other abbreviations and further explanations, please see the Introduction.

Bristol, CT - continued

Item	Per	Value	Date	Ref.
Energy and Fuels				
Energy exp/householder, 1-family unit	year	588	90	28r
Energy exp/householder, <1,000 sq ft heating area	year	477	90	28r
Energy exp/householder, 1,000-1,999 sq ft heating area	year	517	90	28r
Energy exp/householder, 2,000+ sq ft heating area	year	630	90	28r
Energy exp/householder, mobile home	year	412	90	28r
Energy exp/householder, multifamily	year	498	90	28r
Gas, natural	mil Btu	6.40	90	64s
Gas, natural	000 cu ft	8.74	91	46s
Gas, natural, exp	year	756	91	46s
Gasoline, unleaded regular	mil Btu	10.06	90	64s
Entertainment				
Miniature golf admission	adult	6.18	92	1r
Miniature golf admission	child	5.14	92	1r
Waterpark admission	adult	11.00	92	1r
Waterpark admission	child	8.55	92	1r
Funerals				
Casket, 18-gauge steel, velvet interior		1853.42	91	24r
Cosmetology, hair care, etc.		98.33	91	24r
Embalming		273.94	91	24r
Facility use for ceremony		196.06	91	24r
Hearse, local		145.67	91	24r
Limousine, local		131.07	91	24r
Remains to funeral home, transfer		135.24	91	24r
Service charge, professional		843.16	91	24r
Vault, concrete, non-metallic liner		709.14	91	24r
Viewing facilities, use		229.85	91	24r
Groceries				
Apples, Red Delicious	lb	0.85	4/93	16r
Bacon	lb	2.12	4/93	16r
Bananas	lb	0.54	4/93	16r
Bread, white, pan	lb	0.81	4/93	16r
Butter	lb	2.02	4/93	16r
Carrots, short trimmed and topped	lb	0.51	4/93	16r
Chicken, fresh, whole	lb	1.04	4/93	16r
Chicken breast, bone-in	lb	2.21	4/93	16r
Chicken legs, bone-in	lb	1.16	4/93	16r
Chuck roast, USDA choice, boneless	lb	2.82	4/93	16r
Coffee, 100% ground roast, all sizes	lb	2.66	4/93	16r
Cucumbers	lb	0.85	4/93	16r
Eggs, Grade A large	doz	1.15	4/93	16r
Grapefruit	lb	0.45	4/93	16r
Grapes, Thompson Seedless	lb	1.52	4/93	16r
Ground beef, lean and extra lean	lb	2.36	4/93	16r
Ground chuck, 100% beef	lb	2.02	4/93	16r
Honey, jar	8 oz	0.96-1.75	92	5r
Honey, jar	lb	1.50-3.00	92	5r
Honey, squeeze bear	12-oz	1.50-1.99	92	5r
Ice cream, prepackaged, bulk, regular	1/2 gal	2.80	4/93	16r
Lemons	lb	0.96	4/93	16r
Lettuce, iceberg	lb	0.95	4/93	16r
Margarine, stick	lb	0.81	4/93	16r
Milk, fresh, whole, fortified	1/2 gal	1.30	4/93	16r
Oranges, navel	lb	0.56	4/93	16r
Peanut butter, creamy, all sizes	lb	1.88	4/93	16r
Pork chops, center cut, bone-in	lb	3.34	4/93	16r
Potato chips	16 oz	2.88	4/93	16r
Potatoes, white	lb	0.37	4/93	16r
Rib roast, USDA choice, bone-in	lb	4.94	4/93	16r
Round roast, USDA choice, boneless	lb	3.17	4/93	16r
Shortening, vegetable oil blends	lb	0.98	4/93	16r
Spaghetti and macaroni	lb	0.82	4/93	16r
Steak, round, graded & ungraded, ex USDA prime & choice	lb	4.04	4/93	16r
Steak, round, USDA choice, boneless	lb	3.90	4/93	16r
Steak, sirloin, USDA choice, boneless	lb	4.97	4/93	16r
Strawberries, dry pint	12 oz	0.90	4/93	16r
Sugar, white	lb	0.50	4/93	16r

Bristol, CT - continued

Item	Per	Value	Date	Ref.
Groceries - continued				
Sugar, white, 33-80 oz pk	lb	0.41	4/93	16r
Tomatoes, field grown	lb	1.23	4/93	16r
Tuna, chunk, light	lb	2.22	4/93	16r
Turkey, frozen, whole	lb	1.04	4/93	16r
Health Care				
Childbirth, cesarean, hospital		5826	91	62r
Childbirth, cesarean, physician's fee		2053	91	62r
Childbirth, normal, hospital		2964	91	62r
Childbirth, normal, physician's fee		1492	91	62r
Medical plan per employee	year	3958	91	45r
Mental health care, exp	capita	53.68-118.35	90	38s
Mental health care, exp, state mental health agency	capita	72.81	90	38s
Mental health care, hospital psychiatric services, non-Federal, exp	capita	19.30	88	38s
Mental health care, mental health organization, multiservice, exp	capita	19.14	88	38s
Mental health care, psychiatric hospitals, private, exp	capita	35.86	88	38s
Mental health care, psychiatric out-patient clinics, freestanding, exp	capita	5.83	88	38s
Mental health care, psychiatric partial-care organizations, freestanding, exp	capita	0.15	88	38s
Mental health care, state and county mental hospitals, exp	capita	51.85	88	38s
Mental health care, VA medical centers, exp	capita	1.74	88	38s
Prescription drug co-pay, Medicaid	month	10.00	91	21s
Substance abuse, hospital ancillary charge	incident	1200	90	70s
Substance abuse, hospital physician charge	incident	270	90	70s
Substance abuse, hospital room and board	incident	4420	90	70s
Insurance and Pensions				
Auto insurance, private passenger	year	928.10	91	63s
Taxes				
Tax, cigarette	pack	45	91	77s
Tax, gasoline	gal	26	91	77s
Taxes, state	capita	1514	91	77s
Transportation				
Driver's license fee		31.00	12/90	43s
Travel				
Business travel	day	165.00	4/93	89r
Utilities				
Electricity	mil Btu	26.83	90	64s

Brockton, MA

Item	Per	Value	Date	Ref.
Child Care				
Child care fee, average, center	hour	2.18	90	65r
Child care fee, average, nonregulated family day care	hour	1.83	90	65r
Child care fee, average, regulated family day care	hour	2.02	90	65r
Communications				
Long-distance telephone service, day, initial minute, 0-100 miles	min	0.18-0.31	91	12s
Long-distance telephone service, day, additional minute, 0-100 miles	min	0.08-0.13	91	12s
Long-distance telephone service, evenings/weekends, 0-100 mi, initial minute	min	0.67-0.12	91	12s
Long-distance telephone service, evenings/weekends, 0-100 mi, additional minute	min	0.04-0.05	91	12s
Education				
Board, 4-yr private college/university	year	2698	91	22s
Board, 4-yr public college/university	year	1741	91	22s

Values are in dollars or fractions of dollars. In the column headed *Ref*, references are shown to sources. Each reference is followed by a letter. These refer to the geographical level for which data were reported: s = State, r = Region, and c = City or metro. The abbreviation *ex* is used to mean *except* or *excluding*; *exp* stands for expenditures. For other abbreviations and further explanations, please see the Introduction.

Brockton, MA - continued

Item	Per	Value	Date	Ref.
Education				
Expenditures, local gov't, public elementary/secondary	pupil	6687	92	20s
Room, 4-year private college/university	year	2945	91	22s
Room, 4-year public college/university	year	2144	91	22s
Tuition, 2-year private college/university	year	7750	91	22s
Tuition, 2-year public college/university	year	1528	91	22s
Tuition, 4-year private college/university	year	12446	91	22s
Tuition, 4-year public college/university, in-state	year	2580	91	22s
Energy and Fuels				
Coal	mil Btu	1.77	90	64s
Energy	mil Btu	10.57	90	64s
Energy exp/householder, 1-family unit	year	588	90	28r
Energy exp/householder, <1,000 sq ft heating area	year	477	90	28r
Energy exp/householder, 1,000-1,999 sq ft heating area	year	517	90	28r
Energy exp/householder, 2,000+ sq ft heating area	year	630	90	28r
Energy exp/householder, mobile home	year	412	90	28r
Energy exp/householder, multifamily	year	498	90	28r
Gas, natural	mil Btu	5.55	90	64s
Gas, natural	000 cu ft	8.11	91	46s
Gas, natural, exp	year	741	91	46s
Gasoline, unleaded regular	mil Btu	9.53	90	64s
Entertainment				
Miniature golf admission	adult	6.18	92	1r
Miniature golf admission	child	5.14	92	1r
Waterpark admission	adult	11.00	92	1r
Waterpark admission	child	8.55	92	1r
Funerals				
Casket, 18-gauge steel, velvet interior		1853.42	91	24r
Cosmetology, hair care, etc.		98.33	91	24r
Embalming		273.94	91	24r
Facility use for ceremony		196.06	91	24r
Hearse, local		145.67	91	24r
Limousine, local		131.07	91	24r
Remains to funeral home, transfer		135.24	91	24r
Service charge, professional		843.16	91	24r
Vault, concrete, non-metallic liner		709.14	91	24r
Viewing facilities, use		229.85	91	24r
Groceries				
Apples, Red Delicious	lb	0.85	4/93	16r
Bacon	lb	2.12	4/93	16r
Bananas	lb	0.54	4/93	16r
Bread, white, pan	lb	0.81	4/93	16r
Butter	lb	2.02	4/93	16r
Carrots, short trimmed and topped	lb	0.51	4/93	16r
Chicken, fresh, whole	lb	1.04	4/93	16r
Chicken breast, bone-in	lb	2.21	4/93	16r
Chicken legs, bone-in	lb	1.16	4/93	16r
Chuck roast, USDA choice, boneless	lb	2.82	4/93	16r
Coffee, 100% ground roast, all sizes	lb	2.66	4/93	16r
Cucumbers	lb	0.85	4/93	16r
Eggs, Grade A large	doz	1.15	4/93	16r
Grapefruit	lb	0.45	4/93	16r
Grapes, Thompson Seedless	lb	1.52	4/93	16r
Ground beef, lean and extra lean	lb	2.36	4/93	16r
Ground chuck, 100% beef	lb	2.02	4/93	16r
Honey, jar	8 oz	0.96-1.75	92	5r
Honey, jar	lb	1.50-3.00	92	5r
Honey, squeeze bear	12-oz	1.50-1.99	92	5r
Ice cream, prepackaged, bulk, regular	1/2 gal	2.80	4/93	16r
Lemons	lb	0.96	4/93	16r
Lettuce, iceberg	lb	0.95	4/93	16r
Margarine, stick	lb	0.81	4/93	16r
Milk, fresh, whole, fortified	1/2 gal	1.30	4/93	16r
Oranges, navel	lb	0.56	4/93	16r
Peanut butter, creamy, all sizes	lb	1.88	4/93	16r

Brockton, MA - continued

Item	Per	Value	Date	Ref.
Groceries - continued				
Pork chops, center cut, bone-in	lb	3.34	4/93	16r
Potato chips	16 oz	2.88	4/93	16r
Potatoes, white	lb	0.37	4/93	16r
Rib roast, USDA choice, bone-in	lb	4.94	4/93	16r
Round roast, USDA choice, boneless	lb	3.17	4/93	16r
Shortening, vegetable oil blends	lb	0.98	4/93	16r
Spaghetti and macaroni	lb	0.82	4/93	16r
Steak, round, graded & ungraded, ex USDA prime & choice	lb	4.04	4/93	16r
Steak, round, USDA choice, boneless	lb	3.90	4/93	16r
Steak, sirloin, USDA choice, boneless	lb	4.97	4/93	16r
Strawberries, dry pint	12 oz	0.90	4/93	16r
Sugar, white	lb	0.50	4/93	16r
Sugar, white, 33-80 oz pk	lb	0.41	4/93	16r
Tomatoes, field grown	lb	1.23	4/93	16r
Tuna, chunk, light	lb	2.22	4/93	16r
Turkey, frozen, whole	lb	1.04	4/93	16r
Health Care				
Childbirth, cesarean, hospital		5826	91	62r
Childbirth, cesarean, physician's fee		2053	91	62r
Childbirth, normal, hospital		2964	91	62r
Childbirth, normal, physician's fee		1492	91	62r
Health care spending, state	capita	3031	3/93	84s
Medical plan per employee	year	3958	91	45r
Mental health care, exp	capita	53.68-118.35	90	38s
Mental health care, exp, state mental health agency	capita	83.91	90	38s
Mental health care, hospital psychiatric services, non-Federal, exp	capita	22.67	88	38s
Mental health care, mental health organization, multiservice, exp	capita	36.07	88	38s
Mental health care, psychiatric hospitals, private, exp	capita	38.65	88	38s
Mental health care, psychiatric out-patient clinics, freestanding, exp	capita	4.41	88	38s
Mental health care, psychiatric partial-care organizations, freestanding, exp	capita	0.92	88	38s
Mental health care, state and county mental hospitals, exp	capita	30.59	88	38s
Mental health care, VA medical centers, exp	capita	21.14	88	38s
Substance abuse, hospital ancillary charge	incident	1310	90	70s
Substance abuse, hospital physician charge	incident	460	90	70s
Substance abuse, hospital room and board	incident	3450	90	70s
Insurance and Pensions				
Auto insurance, private passenger	year	912.83	91	63s
Taxes				
Tax, cigarette	pack	26	91	77s
Tax, gasoline	gal	21	91	77s
Taxes, state	capita	1615	91	77s
Transportation				
Driver's license fee		35.00	12/90	43s
Travel				
Business travel	day	165.00	4/93	89r
Utilities				
Electricity	mil Btu	25.93	90	64s

Brownsville-Harlingen, TX

Item	Per	Value	Date	Ref.
Child Care				
Child care fee, average, center	hour	1.29	90	65r
Child care fee, average, nonregulated family day care	hour	0.89	90	65r
Child care fee, average, regulated family day care	hour	1.32	90	65r

Values are in dollars or fractions of dollars. In the column headed *Ref*, references are shown to sources. Each reference is followed by a letter. These refer to the geographical level for which data were reported: s = State, r = Region, and c = City or metro. The abbreviation *ex* is used to mean *except* or *excluding*; *exp* stands for expenditures. For other abbreviations and further explanations, please see the Introduction.

Brownsville-Harlingen, TX - continued

Item	Per	Value	Date	Ref.
Communications				
Long-distance telephone service, day, initial minute, 0-100 miles	min	0.10-0.46	91	12s
Long-distance telephone service, day, additional minute, 0-100 miles	min	0.06-0.45	91	12s
Education				
Board, 4-yr private college/university	year	1883	91	22s
Board, 4-yr public college/university	year	1605	91	22s
Expenditures, local gov't, public elementary/secondary	pupil	4593	92	20s
Room, 4-year private college/university	year	1620	91	22s
Room, 4-year public college/university	year	1532	91	22s
Tuition, 2-year private college/university	year	4394	91	22s
Tuition, 2-year public college/university	year	495	91	22s
Tuition, 4-year private college/university	year	6497	91	22s
Tuition, 4-year public college/university, in-state	year	986	91	22s
Energy and Fuels				
Coal	mil Btu	1.44	90	64s
Energy	mil Btu	6.48	90	64s
Energy exp/householder, 1-family unit	year	471	90	28r
Energy exp/householder, <1,000 sq ft heating area	year	384	90	28r
Energy exp/householder, 1,000-1,999 sq ft heating area	year	421	90	28r
Energy exp/householder, 2,000+ sq ft heating area	year	625	90	28r
Energy exp/householder, mobile home	year	271	90	28r
Energy exp/householder, multifamily	year	355	90	28r
Gas, natural	mil Btu	2.47	90	64s
Gas, natural	000 cu ft	5.71	91	46s
Gas, natural, exp	year	388	91	46s
Gasoline, unleaded regular	mil Btu	9.16	90	64s
Entertainment				
Miniature golf admission	adult	6.18	92	1r
Miniature golf admission	child	5.14	92	1r
Waterpark admission	adult	11.00	92	1r
Waterpark admission	child	8.55	92	1r
Funerals				
Casket, 18-gauge steel, velvet interior		2274.41	91	24r
Cosmetology, hair care, etc.		74.62	91	24r
Embalming		229.94	91	24r
Facility use for ceremony		176.61	91	24r
Hearse, local		116.34	91	24r
Limousine, local		72.68	91	24r
Remains to funeral home, transfer		87.72	91	24r
Service charge, professional		712.53	91	24r
Vault, concrete, non-metallic liner		750.55	91	24r
Viewing facilities, use		155.31	91	24r
Groceries				
Apples, Red Delicious	lb	0.79	4/93	16r
Bacon	lb	1.75	4/93	16r
Bananas	lb	0.42	4/93	16r
Beef, stew, boneless	lb	2.61	4/93	16r
Bologna, all beef or mixed	lb	2.24	4/93	16r
Bread, white, pan	lb	0.64	4/93	16r
Bread, whole wheat, pan	lb	0.96	4/93	16r
Cabbage	lb	0.37	4/93	16r
Carrots, short trimmed and topped	lb	0.47	4/93	16r
Celery	lb	0.64	4/93	16r
Cheese, American	lb	2.98	4/93	16r
Cheese, Cheddar	lb	3.28	4/93	16r
Chicken, fresh, whole	lb	0.77	4/93	16r
Chicken breast, bone-in	lb	1.92	4/93	16r
Chicken legs, bone-in	lb	1.06	4/93	16r
Chuck roast, graded and ungraded, ex USDA prime and choice	lb	2.40	4/93	16r
Chuck roast, USDA choice, bone-in	lb	2.19	4/93	16r
Chuck roast, USDA choice, boneless	lb	2.38	4/93	16r

Brownsville-Harlingen, TX - continued

Item	Per	Value	Date	Ref.
Groceries - continued				
Coffee, 100% ground roast, all sizes	lb	2.48	4/93	16r
Crackers, soda, salted	lb	1.15	4/93	16r
Eggs, Grade A large	doz	0.96	4/93	16r
Flour, white, all purpose	lb	0.24	4/93	16r
Frankfurters, all meat or all beef	lb	2.01	4/93	16r
Grapefruit	lb	0.44	4/93	16r
Grapes, Thompson Seedless	lb	1.40	4/93	16r
Ground beef, 100% beef	lb	1.58	4/93	16r
Ground beef, lean and extra lean	lb	2.09	4/93	16r
Ground chuck, 100% beef	lb	1.98	4/93	16r
Ham, boneless, excluding canned	lb	2.89	4/93	16r
Ham, picnic, shoulder, bone-in, smoked	lb	1.02	4/93	16r
Ham, rump or steak half, bone-in, smoked	lb	1.48	4/93	16r
Honey, jar	8 oz	0.73-1.19	92	5r
Honey, jar	lb	1.10-1.79	92	5r
Honey, squeeze bear	12-oz	1.19-1.50	92	5r
Ice cream, prepackaged, bulk, regular	1/2 gal	2.41	4/93	16r
Lemons	lb	1.05	4/93	16r
Lettuce, iceberg	lb	0.81	4/93	16r
Margarine, stick	lb	0.88	4/93	16r
Oranges, navel	lb	0.55	4/93	16r
Pears, Anjou	lb	0.92	4/93	16r
Pork chops, center cut, bone-in	lb	3.13	4/93	16r
Potato chips	16 oz	2.94	4/93	16r
Potatoes, white	lb	0.43	4/93	16r
Rib roast, USDA choice, bone-in	lb	4.63	4/93	16r
Rice, white, long grain, uncooked	lb	0.45	4/93	16r
Round roast, graded & ungraded, ex USDA prime & choice	lb	3.03	4/93	16r
Round roast, USDA choice, boneless	lb	3.09	4/93	16r
Sausage, fresh, loose	lb	2.08	4/93	16r
Short ribs, bone-in	lb	2.66	4/93	16r
Shortening, vegetable oil blends	lb	0.69	4/93	16r
Spaghetti and macaroni	lb	0.81	4/93	16r
Steak, rib eye, USDA choice, boneless	lb	6.24	4/93	16r
Steak, round, graded & ungraded, ex USDA prime & choice	lb	3.31	4/93	16r
Steak, round, USDA choice, boneless	lb	3.34	4/93	16r
Steak, sirloin, graded & ungraded, ex USDA prime & choice	lb	4.19	4/93	16r
Steak, sirloin, USDA choice, boneless	lb	4.46	4/93	16r
Steak, T-bone, USDA choice, bone-in	lb	5.25	4/93	16r
Strawberries, dry pint	12 oz	0.92	4/93	16r
Sugar, white	lb	0.39	4/93	16r
Sugar, white, 33-80 oz pk	lb	0.38	4/93	16r
Tomatoes, field grown	lb	0.88	4/93	16r
Tuna, chunk, light	lb	1.79	4/93	16r
Turkey, frozen, whole	lb	1.04	4/93	16r
Yogurt, natural, fruit flavored	1/2 pint	0.57	4/93	16r
Health Care				
Childbirth, cesarean, hospital		5034	91	62r
Childbirth, cesarean, physician's fee		2053	91	62r
Childbirth, normal, hospital		2712	91	62r
Childbirth, normal, physician's fee		1492	91	62r
Health care spending, state	capita	2192	3/93	84s
Mental health care, exp	capita	20.37-28.83	90	38s
Mental health care, exp, state mental health agency	capita	22.72	90	38s
Mental health care, hospital psychiatric services, non-Federal, exp	capita	7.95	88	38s
Mental health care, mental health organization, multiservice, exp	capita	12.05	88	38s
Mental health care, psychiatric hospitals, private, exp	capita	37.78	88	38s
Mental health care, psychiatric out-patient clinics, freestanding, exp	capita	0.43	88	38s
Mental health care, state and county mental hospitals, exp	capita	12.54	88	38s
Mental health care, VA medical centers, exp	capita	5.35	88	38s
Physician fee, family practice, first-visit		75.00	91	62r

Values are in dollars or fractions of dollars. In the column headed *Ref*, references are shown to sources. Each reference is followed by a letter. These refer to the geographical level for which data were reported: s = State, r = Region, and c = City or metro. The abbreviation *ex* is used to mean *except* or *excluding*; *exp* stands for expenditures. For other abbreviations and further explanations, please see the Introduction.

Brownsville-Harlingen, TX - continued

Item	Per	Value	Date	Ref.
Health Care				
Physician fee, family practice, revisit		34.00	91	62r
Physician fee, general practice, first-visit		61.00	91	62r
Physician fee, general practice, revisit		32.00	91	62r
Physician fee, general surgeon, first-visit		64.00	91	62r
Physician fee, general surgeon, revisit		40.00	91	62r
Physician fee, internal medicine, first-visit		98.00	91	62r
Physician fee, internal medicine, revisit		40.00	91	62r
Physician fee, median, neurosurgeon, first-visit		130.00	91	62r
Physician fee, median, nonsurgical specialist, first-visit		95.00	91	62r
Physician fee, median, orthopedic surgeon, first-visit		91.00	91	62r
Physician fee, median, plastic surgeon, first-visit		66.00	91	62r
Physician fee, median, surgical specialist, first-visit		62.00	91	62r
Physician fee, neurosurgeon, revisit		50.00	91	62r
Physician fee, nonsurgical specialist, revisit		40.00	91	62r
Physician fee, obstetrics/gynecology, first-visit		64.00	91	62r
Physician fee, obstetrics/gynecology, revisit		41.00	91	62r
Physician fee, orthopedic surgeon, revisit		40.00	91	62r
Physician fee, pediatrician, first-visit		49.00	91	62r
Physician fee, pediatrician, revisit		33.00	91	62r
Physician fee, plastic surgeon, revisit		43.00	91	62r
Physician fee, surgical specialist, revisit		37.00	91	62r
Substance abuse, hospital ancillary charge	incident	3750	90	70s
Substance abuse, hospital physician charge	incident	1080	90	70s
Substance abuse, hospital room and board	incident	5320	90	70s
Insurance and Pensions				
Auto insurance, private passenger	year	709.79	91	63s
Taxes				
Tax, cigarette	pack	41	91	77s
Tax, gasoline	gal	20	91	77s
Taxes, state	capita	923	91	77s
Transportation				
Driver's license fee		16.00	12/90	43s
Travel				
Business travel	day	193.00	4/93	89r
Utilities				
Electricity	mil Btu	17.09	90	64s
Electricity, residential	KWh	5.92	2/93	94s

Bryan-College Station, TX

Item	Per	Value	Date	Ref.
Child Care				
Child care fee, average, center	hour	1.29	90	65r
Child care fee, average, nonregulated family day care	hour	0.89	90	65r
Child care fee, average, regulated family day care	hour	1.32	90	65r
Communications				
Long-distance telephone service, day, initial minute, 0-100 miles	min	0.10-0.46	91	12s
Long-distance telephone service, day, additional minute, 0-100 miles	min	0.06-0.45	91	12s
Education				
Board, 4-yr private college/university	year	1883	91	22s
Board, 4-yr public college/university	year	1605	91	22s
Expenditures, local gov't, public elementary/secondary	pupil	4593	92	20s
Room, 4-year private college/university	year	1620	91	22s
Room, 4-year public college/university	year	1532	91	22s

Bryan-College Station, TX - continued

Item	Per	Value	Date	Ref.
Education - continued				
Tuition, 2-year private college/university	year	4394	91	22s
Tuition, 2-year public college/university	year	495	91	22s
Tuition, 4-year private college/university	year	6497	91	22s
Tuition, 4-year public college/university, in-state	year	986	91	22s
Energy and Fuels				
Coal	mil Btu	1.44	90	64s
Energy	mil Btu	6.48	90	64s
Energy exp/householder, 1-family unit	year	471	90	28r
Energy exp/householder, <1,000 sq ft heating area	year	384	90	28r
Energy exp/householder, 1,000-1,999 sq ft heating area	year	421	90	28r
Energy exp/householder, 2,000+ sq ft heating area	year	625	90	28r
Energy exp/householder, mobile home	year	271	90	28r
Energy exp/householder, multifamily	year	355	90	28r
Gas, natural	mil Btu	2.47	90	64s
Gas, natural	000 cu ft	5.71	91	46s
Gas, natural, exp	year	388	91	46s
Gasoline, unleaded regular	mil Btu	9.16	90	64s
Entertainment				
Miniature golf admission	adult	6.18	92	1r
Miniature golf admission	child	5.14	92	1r
Waterpark admission	adult	11.00	92	1r
Waterpark admission	child	8.55	92	1r
Funerals				
Casket, 18-gauge steel, velvet interior		2274.41	91	24r
Cosmetology, hair care, etc.		74.62	91	24r
Embalming		229.94	91	24r
Facility use for ceremony		176.61	91	24r
Hearse, local		116.34	91	24r
Limousine, local		72.68	91	24r
Remains to funeral home, transfer		87.72	91	24r
Service charge, professional		712.53	91	24r
Vault, concrete, non-metallic liner		750.55	91	24r
Viewing facilities, use		155.31	91	24r
Groceries				
Apples, Red Delicious	lb	0.79	4/93	16r
Bacon	lb	1.75	4/93	16r
Bananas	lb	0.42	4/93	16r
Beef, stew, boneless	lb	2.61	4/93	16r
Bologna, all beef or mixed	lb	2.24	4/93	16r
Bread, white, pan	lb	0.64	4/93	16r
Bread, whole wheat, pan	lb	0.96	4/93	16r
Cabbage	lb	0.37	4/93	16r
Carrots, short trimmed and topped	lb	0.47	4/93	16r
Celery	lb	0.64	4/93	16r
Cheese, American	lb	2.98	4/93	16r
Cheese, Cheddar	lb	3.28	4/93	16r
Chicken, fresh, whole	lb	0.77	4/93	16r
Chicken breast, bone-in	lb	1.92	4/93	16r
Chicken legs, bone-in	lb	1.06	4/93	16r
Chuck roast, graded and ungraded, ex USDA prime and choice	lb	2.40	4/93	16r
Chuck roast, USDA choice, bone-in	lb	2.19	4/93	16r
Chuck roast, USDA choice, boneless	lb	2.38	4/93	16r
Coffee, 100% ground roast, all sizes	lb	2.48	4/93	16r
Crackers, soda, salted	lb	1.15	4/93	16r
Eggs, Grade A large	doz	0.96	4/93	16r
Flour, white, all purpose	lb	0.24	4/93	16r
Frankfurters, all meat or all beef	lb	2.01	4/93	16r
Grapefruit	lb	0.44	4/93	16r
Grapes, Thompson Seedless	lb	1.40	4/93	16r
Ground beef, 100% beef	lb	1.58	4/93	16r
Ground beef, lean and extra lean	lb	2.09	4/93	16r
Ground chuck, 100% beef	lb	1.98	4/93	16r
Ham, boneless, excluding canned	lb	2.89	4/93	16r
Ham, picnic, shoulder, bone-in, smoked	lb	1.02	4/93	16r

Values are in dollars or fractions of dollars. In the column headed *Ref*, references are shown to sources. Each reference is followed by a letter. These refer to the geographical level for which data were reported: s=State, r=Region, and c=City or metro. The abbreviation *ex* is used to mean *except* or *excluding*; *exp* stands for expenditures. For other abbreviations and further explanations, please see the Introduction.

Bryan-College Station, TX - continued

Item	Per	Value	Date	Ref.
Groceries				
Ham, rump or steak half, bone-in, smoked	lb	1.48	4/93	16r
Honey, jar	8 oz	0.73-1.19	92	5r
Honey, jar	lb	1.10-1.79	92	5r
Honey, squeeze bear	12-oz	1.19-1.50	92	5r
Ice cream, prepackaged, bulk, regular	1/2 gal	2.41	4/93	16r
Lemons	lb	1.05	4/93	16r
Lettuce, iceberg	lb	0.81	4/93	16r
Margarine, stick	lb	0.88	4/93	16r
Oranges, navel	lb	0.55	4/93	16r
Pears, Anjou	lb	0.92	4/93	16r
Pork chops, center cut, bone-in	lb	3.13	4/93	16r
Potato chips	16 oz	2.94	4/93	16r
Potatoes, white	lb	0.43	4/93	16r
Rib roast, USDA choice, bone-in	lb	4.63	4/93	16r
Rice, white, long grain, uncooked	lb	0.45	4/93	16r
Round roast, graded & ungraded, ex USDA prime & choice	lb	3.03	4/93	16r
Round roast, USDA choice, boneless	lb	3.09	4/93	16r
Sausage, fresh, loose	lb	2.08	4/93	16r
Short ribs, bone-in	lb	2.66	4/93	16r
Shortening, vegetable oil blends	lb	0.69	4/93	16r
Spaghetti and macaroni	lb	0.81	4/93	16r
Steak, rib eye, USDA choice, boneless	lb	6.24	4/93	16r
Steak, round, graded & ungraded, ex USDA prime & choice	lb	3.31	4/93	16r
Steak, round, USDA choice, boneless	lb	3.34	4/93	16r
Steak, sirloin, graded & ungraded, ex USDA prime & choice	lb	4.19	4/93	16r
Steak, sirloin, USDA choice, boneless	lb	4.46	4/93	16r
Steak, T-bone, USDA choice, bone-in	lb	5.25	4/93	16r
Strawberries, dry pint	12 oz	0.92	4/93	16r
Sugar, white	lb	0.39	4/93	16r
Sugar, white, 33-80 oz pk	lb	0.38	4/93	16r
Tomatoes, field grown	lb	0.88	4/93	16r
Tuna, chunk, light	lb	1.79	4/93	16r
Turkey, frozen, whole	lb	1.04	4/93	16r
Yogurt, natural, fruit flavored	1/2 pint	0.57	4/93	16r
Health Care				
Childbirth, cesarean, hospital		5034	91	62r
Childbirth, cesarean, physician's fee		2053	91	62r
Childbirth, normal, hospital		2712	91	62r
Childbirth, normal, physician's fee		1492	91	62r
Health care spending, state	capita	2192	3/93	84s
Mental health care, exp	capita	20.37-28.83	90	38s
Mental health care, exp, state mental health agency	capita	22.72	90	38s
Mental health care, hospital psychiatric services, non-Federal, exp	capita	7.95	88	38s
Mental health care, mental health organization, multiservice, exp	capita	12.05	88	38s
Mental health care, psychiatric hospitals, private, exp	capita	37.78	88	38s
Mental health care, psychiatric out-patient clinics, freestanding, exp	capita	0.43	88	38s
Mental health care, state and county mental hospitals, exp	capita	12.54	88	38s
Mental health care, VA medical centers, exp	capita	5.35	88	38s
Physician fee, family practice, first-visit		75.00	91	62r
Physician fee, family practice, revisit		34.00	91	62r
Physician fee, general practice, first-visit		61.00	91	62r
Physician fee, general practice, revisit		32.00	91	62r
Physician fee, general surgeon, first-visit		64.00	91	62r
Physician fee, general surgeon, revisit		40.00	91	62r
Physician fee, internal medicine, first-visit		98.00	91	62r
Physician fee, internal medicine, revisit		40.00	91	62r
Physician fee, median, neurosurgeon, first-visit		130.00	91	62r
Physician fee, median, nonsurgical specialist, first-visit		95.00	91	62r

Bryan-College Station, TX - continued

Item	Per	Value	Date	Ref.
Health Care - continued				
Physician fee, median, orthopedic surgeon, first-visit		91.00	91	62r
Physician fee, median, plastic surgeon, first-visit		66.00	91	62r
Physician fee, median, surgical specialist, first-visit		62.00	91	62r
Physician fee, neurosurgeon, revisit		50.00	91	62r
Physician fee, nonsurgical specialist, revisit		40.00	91	62r
Physician fee, obstetrics/gynecology, first-visit		64.00	91	62r
Physician fee, obstetrics/gynecology, revisit		41.00	91	62r
Physician fee, orthopedic surgeon, revisit		40.00	91	62r
Physician fee, pediatrician, first-visit		49.00	91	62r
Physician fee, pediatrician, revisit		33.00	91	62r
Physician fee, plastic surgeon, revisit		43.00	91	62r
Physician fee, surgical specialist, revisit		37.00	91	62r
Substance abuse, hospital ancillary charge	incident	3750	90	70s
Substance abuse, hospital physician charge	incident	1080	90	70s
Substance abuse, hospital room and board	incident	5320	90	70s
Insurance and Pensions				
Auto insurance, private passenger	year	709.79	91	63s
Taxes				
Tax, cigarette	pack	41	91	77s
Tax, gasoline	gal	20	91	77s
Taxes, state	capita	923	91	77s
Transportation				
Driver's license fee		16.00	12/90	43s
Travel				
Business travel	day	193.00	4/93	89r
Utilities				
Electricity	mil Btu	17.09	90	64s
Electricity, residential	KWh	5.92	2/93	94s

Buffalo, NY

Item	Per	Value	Date	Ref.
Child Care				
Child care fee, average, center	hour	2.18	90	65r
Child care fee, average, nonregulated family day care	hour	1.83	90	65r
Child care fee, average, regulated family day care	hour	2.02	90	65r
Communications				
Telephone, exp	year	486	89	15c
Telephone, residential, private line, rotary, unlimited calling	month	31.65	10/91	78c
Education				
Board, 4-yr private college/university	year	2451	91	22s
Board, 4-yr public college/university	year	1725	91	22s
Expenditures, local gov't, public elementary/secondary	pupil	8603	92	20s
Room, 4-year private college/university	year	2652	91	22s
Room, 4-year public college/university	year	2183	91	22s
Tuition, 2-year private college/university	year	5926	91	22s
Tuition, 2-year public college/university	year	1419	91	22s
Tuition, 4-year private college/university	year	10340	91	22s
Tuition, 4-year public college/university, in-state	year	1587	91	22s
Energy and Fuels				
Coal	mil Btu	1.66	90	64s
Energy	mil Btu	10.68	90	64s
Energy exp/householder, 1-family unit	year	588	90	28r
Energy exp/householder, <1,000 sq ft heating area	year	477	90	28r

Values are in dollars or fractions of dollars. In the column headed *Ref*, references are shown to sources. Each reference is followed by a letter. These refer to the geographical level for which data were reported: s=State, r=Region, and c=City or metro. The abbreviation *ex* is used to mean *except* or *excluding*; *exp* stands for expenditures. For other abbreviations and further explanations, please see the Introduction.

Buffalo, NY - continued

Item	Per	Value	Date	Ref.
Energy and Fuels				
Energy exp/householder, 1,000-1,999 sq ft heating area	year	517	90	28r
Energy exp/householder, 2,000+ sq ft heating area	year	630	90	28r
Energy exp/householder, mobile home	year	412	90	28r
Energy exp/householder, multifamily	year	498	90	28r
Fuel oil, other fuel, exp	year	25	89	15c
Gas, cooking, winter, 10 therms	month	15.72	92	56c
Gas, cooking, winter, 30 therms	month	26.31	92	56c
Gas, cooking, winter, 50 therms	month	36.90	92	56c
Gas, heating, winter, 100 therms	month	61.89	92	56c
Gas, heating, winter, average use	month	161.84	92	56c
Gas, natural	mil Btu	5.25	90	64s
Gas, natural	000 cu ft	7.35	91	46s
Gas, natural, exp	year	600	89	15c
Gas, natural, exp	year	557	91	46s
Gasoline, unleaded regular	mil Btu	8.83	90	64s
Funerals				
Casket, 18-gauge steel, velvet interior		1811.58	91	24r
Cosmetology, hair care, etc.		111.08	91	24r
Embalming		329.42	91	24r
Facility use for ceremony		201.29	91	24r
Hearse, local		135.27	91	24r
Limousine, local		127.24	91	24r
Remains to funeral home, transfer		103.98	91	24r
Service charge, professional		724.98	91	24r
Vault, concrete, non-metallic liner		766.71	91	24r
Viewing facilities, use		260.60	91	24r
Groceries				
Apples, Red Delicious	lb	0.85	4/93	16r
Bacon	lb	2.12	4/93	16r
Bakery products, exp	year	281	89	15c
Bananas	lb	0.54	4/93	16r
Beef, exp	year	242	89	15c
Beverages, nonalcoholic, exp	year	237	89	15c
Bread, white, pan	lb	0.81	4/93	16r
Butter	lb	2.02	4/93	16r
Carrots, short trimmed and topped	lb	0.51	4/93	16r
Cereals and baking products, exp	year	452	89	15c
Cereals and cereal products, exp	year	171	89	15c
Chicken, fresh, whole	lb	1.04	4/93	16r
Chicken breast, bone-in	lb	2.21	4/93	16r
Chicken legs, bone-in	lb	1.16	4/93	16r
Chuck roast, USDA choice, boneless	lb	2.82	4/93	16r
Coffee, 100% ground roast, all sizes	lb	2.66	4/93	16r
Cucumbers	lb	0.85	4/93	16r
Dairy product purchases	year	412	89	15c
Dairy products, miscellaneous, exp	year	220	89	15c
Eggs, exp	year	41	89	15c
Eggs, Grade A large	doz	1.15	4/93	16r
Fats and oils, exp	year	67	89	15c
Fish and seafood, exp	year	66	89	15c
Food, exp	year	4310	89	15c
Food eaten at home, exp	year	803	89	15c
Food eaten at home, exp	year	2911	89	15c
Food purchased away from home, exp	year	1399	89	15c
Foods, miscellaneous, exp	year	368	89	15c
Fruits, fresh, exp	year	171	89	15c
Fruits, processed, exp	year	115	89	15c
Fruits and vegetables, exp	year	540	89	15c
Grapefruit	lb	0.45	4/93	16r
Grapes, Thompson Seedless	lb	1.52	4/93	16r
Ground beef, lean and extra lean	lb	2.36	4/93	16r
Ground chuck, 100% beef	lb	2.02	4/93	16r
Honey, jar	8 oz	0.96-1.75	92	5r
Honey, jar	lb	1.50-3.00	92	5r
Honey, squeeze bear	12-oz	1.50-1.99	92	5r
Ice cream, prepackaged, bulk, regular	1/2 gal	2.80	4/93	16r
Lemons	lb	0.96	4/93	16r
Lettuce, iceberg	lb	0.95	4/93	16r

Buffalo, NY - continued

Item	Per	Value	Date	Ref.
Groceries - continued				
Margarine, stick	lb	0.81	4/93	16r
Meats, miscellaneous, exp	year	115	89	15c
Meats, poultry, fish and eggs, exp	year	704	89	15c
Milk, fresh, whole, fortified	1/2 gal	1.30	4/93	16r
Milk and cream, fresh, exp	year	192	89	15c
Oranges, navel	lb	0.56	4/93	16r
Peanut butter, creamy, all sizes	lb	1.88	4/93	16r
Pork, exp	year	133	89	15c
Pork chops, center cut, bone-in	lb	3.34	4/93	16r
Potato chips	16 oz	2.88	4/93	16r
Potatoes, white	lb	0.37	4/93	16r
Poultry, exp	year	107	89	15c
Rib roast, USDA choice, bone-in	lb	4.94	4/93	16r
Round roast, USDA choice, boneless	lb	3.17	4/93	16r
Shortening, vegetable oil blends	lb	0.98	4/93	16r
Spaghetti and macaroni	lb	0.82	4/93	16r
Steak, round, graded & ungraded, ex USDA prime & choice	lb	4.04	4/93	16r
Steak, round, USDA choice, boneless	lb	3.90	4/93	16r
Steak, sirloin, USDA choice, boneless	lb	4.97	4/93	16r
Strawberries, dry pint	12 oz	0.90	4/93	16r
Sugar, white	lb	0.50	4/93	16r
Sugar, white, 33-80 oz pk	lb	0.41	4/93	16r
Sugar and other sweets, exp	year	113	89	15c
Tomatoes, field grown	lb	1.23	4/93	16r
Tuna, chunk, light	lb	2.22	4/93	16r
Turkey, frozen, whole	lb	1.04	4/93	16r
Vegetables, fresh, exp	year	172	89	15c
Vegetables, processed, exp	year	83	89	15c
Health Care				
Childbirth, cesarean, hospital		5826	91	62r
Childbirth, cesarean, physician's fee		2053	91	62r
Childbirth, normal, hospital		2964	91	62r
Childbirth, normal, physician's fee		1492	91	62r
Hospital care, semiprivate room	day	209.07	90	27c
Medical insurance premium, per employee, small group comprehensive	month	273.75	10/91	25c
Medical plan per employee	year	3942	91	45r
Mental health care, exp	capita	53.68-118.35	90	38s
Mental health care, exp, state mental health agency	capita	118.34	90	38s
Mental health care, hospital psychiatric services, non-Federal, exp	capita	29.77	88	38s
Mental health care, mental health organization, multiservice, exp	capita	20.03	88	38s
Mental health care, psychiatric hospitals, private, exp	capita	8.37	88	38s
Mental health care, psychiatric out-patient clinics, freestanding, exp	capita	7.96	88	38s
Mental health care, psychiatric partial-care organizations, freestanding, exp	capita	1.24	88	38s
Mental health care, state and county mental hospitals, exp	capita	89.52	88	38s
Mental health care, VA medical centers, exp	capita	7.12	88	38s
Prescription drug co-pay, Medicaid	month	23.00	91	21s
Substance abuse, hospital ancillary charge	incident	1040	90	70s
Substance abuse, hospital physician charge	incident	360	90	70s
Substance abuse, hospital room and board	incident	6330	90	70s
Household Goods				
Appliances, major, exp	year	111	89	15c
Appliances, small, misc. housewares, exp	year	28	89	15c
Floor coverings, exp	year	24	89	15c
Household equipment, misc., exp	year	285	89	15c
Housing				
Home, median price	unit	81.70		26c
Rental unit, 1 bedroom	month	401	93	23c
Rental unit, 2 bedroom	month	471	93	23c

Values are in dollars or fractions of dollars. In the column headed *Ref*, references are shown to sources. Each reference is followed by a letter. These refer to the geographical level for which data were reported: s = State, r = Region, and c = City or metro. The abbreviation *ex* is used to mean *except* or *excluding*; *exp* stands for expenditures. For other abbreviations and further explanations, please see the Introduction.

Buffalo, NY - continued

Item	Per	Value	Date	Ref.
Housing				
Rental unit, 3 bedroom	month	590	93	23c
Rental unit, 4 bedroom	month	660	93	23c
Rental unit, efficiency	month	329	93	23c
Insurance and Pensions				
Auto insurance, private passenger	year	840.89	91	63s
Taxes				
Tax, cigarette	pack	39	91	77s
Tax, gasoline	gal	8	91	77s
Taxes, state	capita	1567	91	77s
Transportation				
Auto rental, average	day	44.00	6/91	60c
Bus fare	one-way	1.10	3/93	2c
Driver's license fee		17.50	12/90	43s
Limo fare, airport-city, average	day	5.00	6/91	60c
Railway fare, light rail	one-way	1.10	93	2c
Taxi fare, airport-city, average	day	14.00	6/91	60c
Vehicle registration and license plate	2 years	27.50-149.50	93	67s
Travel				
Breakfast	day	9.04	6/91	60c
Business travel	day	165.00	4/93	89r
Dinner	day	21.96	6/91	60c
Lodging	day	116.83	91	60c
Lunch	day	12.41	6/91	60c
Utilities				
Electricity	mil Btu	27.51	90	64s
Electricity, exp	year	521	89	15c
Electricity, winter, 250 KWh	month	29.51	92	55c
Electricity, winter, 500 KWh	month	52.32	92	55c
Electricity, winter, 750 KWh	month	75.14	92	55c
Electricity, winter, 1000 KWh	month	97.95	92	55c
Utilities, fuels, public services, exp	year	1747	89	15c
Water, other public service, exp	year	115	89	15c

Burlington, NC

Item	Per	Value	Date	Ref.
Composite ACCRA index		95.70	4Q 92	4c
Alcoholic Beverages				
Beer, Miller Lite or Budweiser, 12-oz containers	6 pack	3.51	4Q 92	4c
Liquor, J & B Scotch	750 ml	17.65	4Q 92	4c
Wine, Gallo Chablis blanc, 1.5 liter	bottle	4.19	4Q 92	4c
Child Care				
Child care fee, average, center	hour	1.29	90	65r
Child care fee, average, nonregulated family day care	hour	0.89	90	65r
Child care fee, average, regulated family day care	hour	1.32	90	65r
Clothing				
Jeans, man's denim		30.46	4Q 92	4c
Shirt, man's dress shirt		23.25	4Q 92	4c
Undervest, boy's size 10-14, cotton	3	3.15	4Q 92	4c
Communications				
Long-distance telephone service, day, initial minute, 0-100 miles	min	0.10-0.33	91	12s
Long-distance telephone service, day, additional minute, 0-100 miles	min	0.10-0.33	91	12s
Long-distance telephone service, evenings/weekends, 0-100 mi, initial minute	min	0.08-0.24	91	12s
Long-distance telephone service, evenings/weekends, 0-100 mi, additional minute	min	0.05-0.17	91	12s
Newspaper subscription, daily and Sunday home delivery, large-city	month	8.70	4Q 92	4c
Telephone, flat rate	month	11.34	91	11c
Telephone bill, family of four	month	16.64	4Q 92	4c

Burlington, NC - continued

Item	Per	Value	Date	Ref.
Education				
Board, 4-yr private college/university	year	1768	91	22s
Board, 4-yr public college/university	year	1568	91	22s
Expenditures, local gov't, public elementary/secondary	pupil	5078	92	20s
Room, 4-year private college/university	year	1467	91	22s
Room, 4-year public college/university	year	1386	91	22s
Tuition, 2-year private college/university	year	4964	91	22s
Tuition, 2-year public college/university	year	334	91	22s
Tuition, 4-year private college/university	year	7826	91	22s
Tuition, 4-year public college/university, in-state	year	1112	91	22s
Energy and Fuels				
Coal	mil Btu	1.79	90	64s
Energy	mil Btu	10.06	90	64s
Energy, combined forms, 1,800 sq ft heating area	month	119.32	4Q 92	4c
Energy exp/householder, 1-family unit	year	487	90	28r
Energy exp/householder, <1,000 sq ft heating area	year	393	90	28r
Energy exp/householder, 1,000-1,999 sq ft heating area	year	442	90	28r
Energy exp/householder, 2,000+ sq ft heating area	year	577	90	28r
Energy exp/householder, mobile home	year	366	90	28r
Energy exp/householder, multifamily	year	382	90	28r
Gas, natural	mil Btu	4.19	90	64s
Gas, natural	000 cu ft	6.24	91	46s
Gas, natural, exp	year	439	91	46s
Gasoline, motor	gal	1.09	4Q 92	4c
Gasoline, unleaded regular	mil Btu	9.44	90	64s
Entertainment				
Bowling, evening rate	game	2.25	4Q 92	4c
Miniature golf admission	adult	6.18	92	1r
Miniature golf admission	child	5.14	92	1r
Monopoly game, Parker Brothers', No. 9		10.23	4Q 92	4c
Movie	admission	4.50	4Q 92	4c
Tennis balls, yellow, Wilson or Penn, 3	can	2.06	4Q 92	4c
Waterpark admission	adult	11.00	92	1r
Waterpark admission	child	8.55	92	1r
Funerals				
Casket, 18-gauge steel, velvet interior		2029.08	91	24r
Cosmetology, hair care, etc.		75.10	91	24r
Embalming		249.24	91	24r
Facility use for ceremony		162.27	91	24r
Hearse, local		114.04	91	24r
Limousine, local		88.57	91	24r
Remains to funeral home, transfer		92.61	91	24r
Service charge, professional		682.42	91	24r
Vault, concrete, non-metallic liner		798.70	91	24r
Viewing facilities, use		163.86	91	24r
Goods and Services				
ACCRA Index, Miscellaneous Goods and Services		94.10	4Q 92	4c
Groceries				
ACCRA Index, Groceries		89.70	4Q 92	4c
Apples, Red Delicious	lb	0.79	4/93	16r
Babyfood, strained vegetables, lowest price	4-4.5 oz jar	0.31	4Q 92	4c
Bacon	lb	1.75	4/93	16r
Bananas	lb	0.49	4Q 92	4c
Bananas	lb	0.42	4/93	16r
Beef, stew, boneless	lb	2.61	4/93	16r
Bologna, all beef or mixed	lb	2.24	4/93	16r
Bread, white	24 oz	0.65	4Q 92	4c
Bread, white, pan	lb	0.64	4/93	16r
Bread, whole wheat, pan	lb	0.96	4/93	16r
Cabbage	lb	0.37	4/93	16r

Values are in dollars or fractions of dollars. In the column headed *Ref*, references are shown to sources. Each reference is followed by a letter. These refer to the geographical level for which data were reported: s=State, r=Region, and c=City or metro. The abbreviation *ex* is used to mean *except* or *excluding*; *exp* stands for expenditures. For other abbreviations and further explanations, please see the Introduction.

Burlington, NC - continued

Item	Per	Value	Date	Ref.
Groceries				
Carrots, short trimmed and topped	lb	0.47	4/93	16r
Celery	lb	0.64	4/93	16r
Cheese, American	lb	2.98	4/93	16r
Cheese, Cheddar	lb	3.28	4/93	16r
Cheese, Kraft grated Parmesan	8-oz canister	3.22	4Q 92	4c
Chicken, fresh, whole	lb	0.77	4/93	16r
Chicken, fryer, whole	lb	0.73	4Q 92	4c
Chicken breast, bone-in	lb	1.92	4/93	16r
Chicken legs, bone-in	lb	1.06	4/93	16r
Chuck roast, graded and ungraded, ex USDA prime and choice	lb	2.40	4/93	16r
Chuck roast, USDA choice, bone-in	lb	2.19	4/93	16r
Chuck roast, USDA choice, boneless	lb	2.38	4/93	16r
Cigarettes, Winston	carton	15.19	4Q 92	4c
Coffee, 100% ground roast, all sizes	lb	2.48	4/93	16r
Coffee, vacuum-packed	13-oz can	1.77	4Q 92	4c
Corn, frozen	10 oz	0.50	4Q 92	4c
Corn Flakes, Kellogg's or Post Toasties	18 oz	1.77	4Q 92	4c
Crackers, soda, salted	lb	1.15	4/93	16r
Eggs, Grade A large	doz	0.90	4Q 92	4c
Eggs, Grade A large	doz	0.96	4/93	16r
Flour, white, all purpose	lb	0.24	4/93	16r
Frankfurters, all meat or all beef	lb	2.01	4/93	16r
Grapefruit	lb	0.44	4/93	16r
Grapes, Thompson Seedless	lb	1.40	4/93	16r
Ground beef, 100% beef	lb	1.58	4/93	16r
Ground beef, lean and extra lean	lb	2.09	4/93	16r
Ground beef or hamburger	lb	1.05	4Q 92	4c
Ground chuck, 100% beef	lb	1.98	4/93	16r
Ham, boneless, excluding canned	lb	2.89	4/93	16r
Ham, picnic, shoulder, bone-in, smoked	lb	1.02	4/93	16r
Ham, rump or steak half, bone-in, smoked	lb	1.48	4/93	16r
Ice cream, prepackaged, bulk, regular	1/2 gal	2.41	4/93	16r
Lemons	lb	1.05	4/93	16r
Lettuce, iceberg	head	0.89	4Q 92	4c
Lettuce, iceberg	lb	0.81	4/93	16r
Margarine, Blue Bonnet or Parkay cubes	lb	0.45	4Q 92	4c
Margarine, stick	lb	0.88	4/93	16r
Milk, whole	1/2 gal	1.37	4Q 92	4c
Orange juice, Minute Maid frozen	12-oz can	1.22	4Q 92	4c
Oranges, navel	lb	0.55	4/93	16r
Peaches	29-oz can	1.30	4Q 92	4c
Pears, Anjou	lb	0.92	4/93	16r
Peas Sweet, Del Monte or Green Giant	15-17 oz can	0.44	4Q 92	4c
Pork chops, center cut, bone-in	lb	3.13	4/93	16r
Potato chips	16 oz	2.94	4/93	16r
Potatoes, white	lb	0.43	4/93	16r
Potatoes, white or red	10-lb sack	2.09	4Q 92	4c
Rib roast, USDA choice, bone-in	lb	4.63	4/93	16r
Rice, white, long grain, uncooked	lb	0.45	4/93	16r
Round roast, graded & ungraded, ex USDA prime & choice	lb	3.03	4/93	16r
Round roast, USDA choice, boneless	lb	3.09	4/93	16r
Sausage, fresh, loose	lb	2.08	4/93	16r
Sausage, Jimmy Dean, 100% pork	lb	1.80	4Q 92	4c
Short ribs, bone-in	lb	2.66	4/93	16r
Shortening, vegetable oil blends	lb	0.69	4/93	16r
Shortening, vegetable, Crisco	3-lb can	1.99	4Q 92	4c
Soft drink, Coca Cola	2 liter	1.19	4Q 92	4c
Spaghetti and macaroni	lb	0.81	4/93	16r
Steak, rib eye, USDA choice, boneless	lb	6.24	4/93	16r
Steak, round, graded & ungraded, ex USDA prime & choice	lb	3.31	4/93	16r
Steak, round, USDA choice, boneless	lb	3.34	4/93	16r

Burlington, NC - continued

Item	Per	Value	Date	Ref.
Groceries - continued				
Steak, sirloin, graded & ungraded, ex USDA prime & choice	lb	4.19	4/93	16r
Steak, sirloin, USDA choice, boneless	lb	4.46	4/93	16r
Steak, T-bone	lb	5.53	4Q 92	4c
Steak, T-bone, USDA choice, bone-in	lb	5.25	4/93	16r
Strawberries, dry pint	12 oz	0.92	4/93	16r
Sugar, cane or beet	4 lb	1.41	4Q 92	4c
Sugar, white	lb	0.39	4/93	16r
Sugar, white, 33-80 oz pk	lb	0.38	4/93	16r
Tomatoes, field grown	lb	0.88	4/93	16r
Tomatoes, Hunt's or Del Monte	14.5-oz can	0.60	4Q 92	4c
Tuna, chunk, light	6.125-6.5 oz can	0.55	4Q 92	4c
Tuna, chunk, light	lb	1.79	4/93	16r
Turkey, frozen, whole	lb	1.04	4/93	16r
Yogurt, natural, fruit flavored	1/2 pint	0.57	4/93	16r
Health Care				
ACCRA Index, Health Care		92.60	4Q 92	4c
Analgesic, Aspirin, Bayer, 325 mg tablets	100	4.00	4Q 92	4c
Childbirth, cesarean, hospital		5034	91	62r
Childbirth, cesarean, physician's fee		2053	91	62r
Childbirth, normal, hospital		2712	91	62r
Childbirth, normal, physician's fee		1492	91	62r
Dentist's fee, adult teeth cleaning and periodic oral exam	visit	43.80	4Q 92	4c
Doctor's fee, routine exam, established patient	visit	32.80	4Q 92	4c
Hospital care, semiprivate room	day	336.00	4Q 92	4c
Medical insurance premium, per employee, small group comprehensive	month	273.75	10/91	25c
Medical plan per employee	year	3495	91	45r
Mental health care, exp	capita	37.60-53.67	90	38s
Mental health care, exp, state mental health agency	capita	45.66	90	38s
Mental health care, hospital psychiatric services, non-Federal, exp	capita	12.05	88	38s
Mental health care, mental health organization, multiservice, exp	capita	29.54	88	38s
Mental health care, psychiatric hospitals, private, exp	capita	15.07	88	38s
Mental health care, psychiatric out-patient clinics, freestanding, exp	capita	0.11	88	38s
Mental health care, state and county mental hospitals, exp	capita	26.36	88	38s
Mental health care, VA medical centers, exp	capita	2.23	88	38s
Physician fee, family practice, first-visit		75.00	91	62r
Physician fee, family practice, revisit		34.00	91	62r
Physician fee, general practice, first-visit		61.00	91	62r
Physician fee, general practice, revisit		32.00	91	62r
Physician fee, general surgeon, first-visit		64.00	91	62r
Physician fee, general surgeon, revisit		40.00	91	62r
Physician fee, internal medicine, first-visit		98.00	91	62r
Physician fee, internal medicine, revisit		40.00	91	62r
Physician fee, median, neurosurgeon, first-visit		130.00	91	62r
Physician fee, median, nonsurgical specialist, first-visit		95.00	91	62r
Physician fee, median, orthopedic surgeon, first-visit		91.00	91	62r
Physician fee, median, plastic surgeon, first-visit		66.00	91	62r
Physician fee, median, surgical specialist, first-visit		62.00	91	62r
Physician fee, neurosurgeon, revisit		50.00	91	62r
Physician fee, nonsurgical specialist, revisit		40.00	91	62r
Physician fee, obstetrics/gynecology, first-visit		64.00	91	62r
Physician fee, obstetrics/gynecology, revisit		41.00	91	62r

Values are in dollars or fractions of dollars. In the column headed *Ref*, references are shown to sources. Each reference is followed by a letter. These refer to the geographical level for which data were reported: s=State, r=Region, and c=City or metro. The abbreviation *ex* is used to mean *except* or *excluding*; *exp* stands for *expenditures*. For other abbreviations and further explanations, please see the Introduction.

Burlington, NC - continued

Item	Per	Value	Date	Ref.
Health Care				
Physician fee, orthopedic surgeon, revisit		40.00	91	62r
Physician fee, pediatrician, first-visit		49.00	91	62r
Physician fee, pediatrician, revisit		33.00	91	62r
Physician fee, plastic surgeon, revisit		43.00	91	62r
Physician fee, surgical specialist, revisit		37.00	91	62r
Substance abuse, hospital ancillary charge	incident	1090	90	70s
Substance abuse, hospital physician charge	incident	460	90	70s
Substance abuse, hospital room and board	incident	4880	90	70s
Household Goods				
Appliance repair, home, service call, washing machine	min labor charge	38.50	4Q 92	4c
Laundry detergent, Tide Ultra, Bold, or Cheer	42 oz	2.94	4Q 92	4c
Tissues, facial, Kleenex brand	175-count box	0.95	4Q 92	4c
Housing				
ACCRA Index, Housing		100.60	4Q 92	4c
House, 1,800 sq ft, 8,000 sq ft lot, new, urban	total	115525	4Q 92	4c
House payment, principal and interest, 25% down payment	month	640	4Q 92	4c
Mortgage rate, incl. points & origination fee, 30-year fixed or adjustable rate	percent	8.07	4Q 92	4c
Rent, apartment, 2 bedrooms - 1-1/2 to 2 baths, unfurnished, 950 sq ft, water	month	447	4Q 92	4c
Rental unit, 1 bedroom	month	421	93	23c
Rental unit, 2 bedroom	month	497	93	23c
Rental unit, 3 bedroom	month	621	93	23c
Rental unit, 4 bedroom	month	697	93	23c
Rental unit, efficiency	month	347	93	23c
Insurance and Pensions				
Auto insurance, private passenger	year	522.39	91	63s
Personal Goods				
Shampoo, Alberto VO5	15 oz	0.96	4Q 92	4c
Toothpaste, Crest or Colgate	6-7 oz	1.64	4Q 92	4c
Personal Services				
Dry cleaning, man's 2-piece suit		5.51	4Q 92	4c
Haircare, woman's shampoo, trim and blow-dry		17.60	4Q 92	4c
Haircut, man's barbershop, no styling		5.60	4Q 92	4c
Restaurant Food				
Chicken, fried, thigh and drumstick		2.19	4Q 92	4c
Hamburger with cheese	1/4 lb	1.81	4Q 92	4c
Pizza, Pizza Hut or Pizza Inn, cheese, thin crust	12-13 in	7.49	4Q 92	4c
Taxes				
Tax, cigarette	pack	5	91	77s
Tax, gasoline	gal	21.90	91	77s
Taxes, state	capita	1165	91	77s
Transportation				
ACCRA Index, Transportation		86.70	4Q 92	4c
Driver's license fee		15.00	12/90	43s
Tire balance, computer or spin balance, front	wheel	5.00	4Q 92	4c
Vehicle registration and license plate	year	35.00	93	50s
Travel				
Business travel	day	193.00	4/93	89r
Utilities				
ACCRA Index, Utilities		106.90	4Q 92	4c
Electricity	mil Btu	18.74	90	64s
Electricity, all electric, 1,800 sq ft living area new home	month	119.32	4Q 92	4c

Burlington, VT

Item	Per	Value	Date	Ref.
Child Care				
Child care fee, average, center	hour	2.18	90	65r
Child care fee, average, nonregulated family day care	hour	1.83	90	65r
Child care fee, average, regulated family day care	hour	2.02	90	65r
Communications				
Long-distance telephone service, day, initial minute, 0-100 miles	min	0.29-0.63	91	12s
Long-distance telephone service, day, additional minute, 0-100 miles	min	0.15-0.31	91	12s
Long-distance telephone service, evenings/weekends, 0-100 mi, initial minute	min	0.12-0.27	91	12s
Long-distance telephone service, evenings/weekends, 0-100 mi, additional minute	min	0.06-0.13	91	12s
Telephone, flat rate	month	18.55	91	11c
Education				
Board, 4-yr private college/university	year	2188	91	22s
Board, 4-yr public college/university	year	1588	91	22s
Expenditures, local gov't, public elementary/secondary	pupil	6045	92	20s
Room, 4-year private college/university	year	2310	91	22s
Room, 4-year public college/university	year	2479	91	22s
Tuition, 2-year private college/university	year	6768	91	22s
Tuition, 2-year public college/university	year	2424	91	22s
Tuition, 4-year private college/university	year	10649	91	22s
Tuition, 4-year public college/university, in-state	year	4092	91	22s
Energy and Fuels				
Coal	mil Btu	3.73	90	64s
Energy	mil Btu	11.64	90	64s
Energy exp/householder, 1-family unit	year	588	90	28r
Energy exp/householder, <1,000 sq ft heating area	year	477	90	28r
Energy exp/householder, 1,000-1,999 sq ft heating area	year	517	90	28r
Energy exp/householder, 2,000+ sq ft heating area	year	630	90	28r
Energy exp/householder, mobile home	year	412	90	28r
Energy exp/householder, multifamily	year	498	90	28r
Gas, cooking, winter, 10 therms	month	10.12	92	56c
Gas, cooking, winter, 30 therms	month	29.35	92	56c
Gas, cooking, winter, 50 therms	month	35.29	92	56c
Gas, heating, winter, 100 therms	month	65.14	92	56c
Gas, heating, winter, average use	month	141.14	92	56c
Gas, natural	mil Btu	4.65	90	64s
Gas, natural	000 cu ft	6.23	91	46s
Gas, natural, exp	year	691	91	46s
Gasoline, unleaded regular	mil Btu	9.66	90	64s
Entertainment				
Miniature golf admission	adult	6.18	92	1r
Miniature golf admission	child	5.14	92	1r
Waterpark admission	adult	11.00	92	1r
Waterpark admission	child	8.55	92	1r
Funerals				
Casket, 18-gauge steel, velvet interior		1853.42	91	24r
Cosmetology, hair care, etc.		98.33	91	24r
Embalming		273.94	91	24r
Facility use for ceremony		196.06	91	24r
Hearse, local		145.67	91	24r
Limousine, local		131.07	91	24r
Remains to funeral home, transfer		135.24	91	24r
Service charge, professional		843.16	91	24r
Vault, concrete, non-metallic liner		709.14	91	24r
Viewing facilities, use		229.85	91	24r
Groceries				
Apples, Red Delicious	lb	0.85	4/93	16r
Bacon	lb	2.12	4/93	16r

Values are in dollars or fractions of dollars. In the column headed *Ref*, references are shown to sources. Each reference is followed by a letter. These refer to the geographical level for which data were reported: s = State, r = Region, and c = City or metro. The abbreviation *ex* is used to mean *except* or *excluding*; *exp* stands for expenditures. For other abbreviations and further explanations, please see the Introduction.

Burlington, VT - continued

Item	Per	Value	Date	Ref.
Groceries				
Bananas	lb	0.54	4/93	16r
Bread, white, pan	lb	0.81	4/93	16r
Butter	lb	2.02	4/93	16r
Carrots, short trimmed and topped	lb	0.51	4/93	16r
Chicken, fresh, whole	lb	1.04	4/93	16r
Chicken breast, bone-in	lb	2.21	4/93	16r
Chicken legs, bone-in	lb	1.16	4/93	16r
Chuck roast, USDA choice, boneless	lb	2.82	4/93	16r
Coffee, 100% ground roast, all sizes	lb	2.66	4/93	16r
Cucumbers	lb	0.85	4/93	16r
Eggs, Grade A large	doz	1.15	4/93	16r
Grapefruit	lb	0.45	4/93	16r
Grapes, Thompson Seedless	lb	1.52	4/93	16r
Ground beef, lean and extra lean	lb	2.36	4/93	16r
Ground chuck, 100% beef	lb	2.02	4/93	16r
Honey, jar	8 oz	0.96-1.75	92	5r
Honey, jar	lb	1.50-3.00	92	5r
Honey, squeeze bear	12-oz	1.50-1.99	92	5r
Ice cream, prepackaged, bulk, regular	1/2 gal	2.80	4/93	16r
Lemons	lb	0.96	4/93	16r
Lettuce, iceberg	lb	0.95	4/93	16r
Margarine, stick	lb	0.81	4/93	16r
Milk, fresh, whole, fortified	1/2 gal	1.30	4/93	16r
Oranges, navel	lb	0.56	4/93	16r
Peanut butter, creamy, all sizes	lb	1.88	4/93	16r
Pork chops, center cut, bone-in	lb	3.34	4/93	16r
Potato chips	16 oz	2.88	4/93	16r
Potatoes, white	lb	0.37	4/93	16r
Rib roast, USDA choice, bone-in	lb	4.94	4/93	16r
Round roast, USDA choice, boneless	lb	3.17	4/93	16r
Shortening, vegetable oil blends	lb	0.98	4/93	16r
Spaghetti and macaroni	lb	0.82	4/93	16r
Steak, round, graded & ungraded, ex USDA prime & choice	lb	4.04	4/93	16r
Steak, round, USDA choice, boneless	lb	3.90	4/93	16r
Steak, sirloin, USDA choice, boneless	lb	4.97	4/93	16r
Strawberries, dry pint	12 oz	0.90	4/93	16r
Sugar, white	lb	0.50	4/93	16r
Sugar, white, 33-80 oz pk	lb	0.41	4/93	16r
Tomatoes, field grown	lb	1.23	4/93	16r
Tuna, chunk, light	lb	2.22	4/93	16r
Turkey, frozen, whole	lb	1.04	4/93	16r
Health Care				
Childbirth, cesarean, hospital		5826	91	62r
Childbirth, cesarean, physician's fee		2053	91	62r
Childbirth, normal, hospital		2964	91	62r
Childbirth, normal, physician's fee		1492	91	62r
Hospital care, semiprivate room	day	372.69	90	27c
Medical insurance premium, per employee, small group comprehensive	month	267.40	10/91	25c
Medical plan per employee	year	3958	91	45r
Mental health care, exp	capita	53.68-118.35	90	38s
Mental health care, exp, state mental health agency	capita	53.77	90	38s
Mental health care, hospital psychiatric services, non-Federal, exp	capita	21.71	88	38s
Mental health care, mental health organization, multiservice, exp	capita	62.84	88	38s
Mental health care, psychiatric hospitals, private, exp	capita	55.07	88	38s
Mental health care, state and county mental hospitals, exp	capita	19.93	88	38s
Mental health care, VA medical centers, exp	capita	1.54	88	38s
Substance abuse, hospital ancillary charge	incident	1020	90	70s
Substance abuse, hospital physician charge	incident	80	90	70s
Substance abuse, hospital room and board	incident	7700	90	70s

Burlington, VT - continued

Item	Per	Value	Date	Ref.
Housing				
Rental unit, 1 bedroom	month	583	93	23c
Rental unit, 2 bedroom	month	684	93	23c
Rental unit, 3 bedroom	month	856	93	23c
Rental unit, 4 bedroom	month	960	93	23c
Rental unit, efficiency	month	479	93	23c
Insurance and Pensions				
Auto insurance, private passenger	year	554.28	91	63s
Taxes				
Tax, cigarette	pack	20	91	77s
Tax, gasoline	gal	15	91	77s
Taxes, state	capita	1206	91	77s
Transportation				
Auto rental, average	day	45.00	6/91	60c
Bus fare	one-way	0.75	3/93	2c
Driver's license fee		12.00-20.00	12/90	43s
Taxi fare, airport-city, average	day	6.50	6/91	60c
Vehicle registration and license plate	year	42.00	93	68s
Travel				
Business travel	day	165.00	4/93	89r
Lodging	day	96.50	91	60c
Utilities				
Electricity	mil Btu	24.24	90	64s

Canton, OH

Item	Per	Value	Date	Ref.
Composite ACCRA index		98.50	4Q 92	4c
Alcoholic Beverages				
Beer, Miller Lite or Budweiser, 12-oz containers	6 pack	3.99	4Q 92	4c
Liquor, J & B Scotch	750 ml	18.20	4Q 92	4c
Wine, Gallo Chablis blanc, 1.5 liter	bottle	4.69	4Q 92	4c
Child Care				
Child care fee, average, center	hour	1.63	90	65r
Child care fee, average, nonregulated family day care	hour	1.83	90	65r
Child care fee, average, regulated family day care	hour	1.42	90	65r
Clothing				
Jeans, man's denim		26.57	4Q 92	4c
Shirt, man's dress shirt		25.40	4Q 92	4c
Undervest, boy's size 10-14, cotton	3	4.03	4Q 92	4c
Communications				
Long-distance telephone service, day, initial minute, 0-100 miles	min	0.26-0.43	91	12s
Long-distance telephone service, day, additional minute, 0-100 miles	min	0.14-0.24	91	12s
Long-distance telephone service, evenings/weekends, 0-100 mi, initial minute	min	0.11-0.17	91	12s
Long-distance telephone service, evenings/weekends, 0-100 mi, additional minute	min	0.06-0.10	91	12s
Newspaper subscription, daily and Sunday home delivery, large-city	month	10.65	4Q 92	4c
Telephone, residential, private line, rotary, unlimited calling	month	19.44	10/91	78c
Telephone bill, family of four	month	21.86	4Q 92	4c
Education				
Board, 4-yr private college/university	year	1872	91	22s
Board, 4-yr public college/university	year	1742	91	22s
Expenditures, local gov't, public elementary/secondary	pupil	5451	92	20s
Room, 4-year private college/university	year	1695	91	22s
Room, 4-year public college/university	year	2259	91	22s
Tuition, 2-year private college/university	year	6093	91	22s
Tuition, 2-year public college/university	year	1768	91	22s

Values are in dollars or fractions of dollars. In the column headed *Ref*, references are shown to sources. Each reference is followed by a letter. These refer to the geographical level for which data were reported: s=State, r=Region, and c=City or metro. The abbreviation *ex* is used to mean *except* or *excluding*; *exp* stands for expenditures. For other abbreviations and further explanations, please see the Introduction.

Canton, OH - continued

Item	Per	Value	Date	Ref.
Education				
Tuition, 4-year private college/university	year	8729	91	22s
Tuition, 4-year public college/university, in-state	year	2622	91	22s
Energy and Fuels				
Coal	mil Btu	1.54	90	64s
Energy	mil Btu	8.32	90	64s
Energy, combined forms, 1,800 sq ft heating area	month	110.76	4Q 92	4c
Energy, exc electricity, 1,800 sq ft heating area	month	41.04	4Q 92	4c
Energy exp/householder, 1-family unit	year	471	90	28r
Energy exp/householder, <1,000 sq ft heating area	year	430	90	28r
Energy exp/householder, 1,000-1,999 sq ft heating area	year	481	90	28r
Energy exp/householder, 2,000+ sq ft heating area	year	473	90	28r
Energy exp/householder, mobile home	year	430	90	28r
Energy exp/householder, multifamily	year	461	90	28r
Gas, natural	mil Btu	4.54	90	64s
Gas, natural	000 cu ft	5.28	91	46s
Gas, natural, exp	year	606	91	46s
Gasoline, motor	gal	1.08	4Q 92	4c
Gasoline, unleaded regular	mil Btu	9.35	90	64s
Entertainment				
Bowling, evening rate	game	1.69	4Q 92	4c
Miniature golf admission	adult	6.18	92	1r
Miniature golf admission	child	5.14	92	1r
Monopoly game, Parker Brothers', No. 9		11.58	4Q 92	4c
Movie	admission	5.75	4Q 92	4c
Tennis balls, yellow, Wilson or Penn, 3	can	2.74	4Q 92	4c
Waterpark admission	adult	11.00	92	1r
Waterpark admission	child	8.55	92	1r
Funerals				
Casket, 18-gauge steel, velvet interior		1926.72	91	24r
Cosmetology, hair care, etc.		97.64	91	24r
Embalming		249.14	91	24r
Facility use for ceremony		208.59	91	24r
Hearse, local		130.12	91	24r
Limousine, local		104.66	91	24r
Remains to funeral home, transfer		93.61	91	24r
Service charge, professional		724.62	91	24r
Vault, concrete, non-metallic liner		734.53	91	24r
Viewing facilities, use		236.06	91	24r
Goods and Services				
ACCRA Index, Miscellaneous Goods and Services		98.40	4Q 92	4c
Groceries				
ACCRA Index, Groceries		92.00	4Q 92	4c
Apples, Red Delicious	lb	0.77	4/93	16r
Babyfood, strained vegetables, lowest price	4-4.5 oz jar	0.29	4Q 92	4c
Bacon	lb	1.85	4/93	16r
Bananas	lb	0.39	4Q 92	4c
Bananas	lb	0.46	4/93	16r
Beef, stew, boneless	lb	2.53	4/93	16r
Bologna, all beef or mixed	lb	2.19	4/93	16r
Bread, white	24 oz	0.55	4Q 92	4c
Bread, white, pan	lb	0.78	4/93	16r
Butter	lb	1.50	4/93	16r
Cabbage	lb	0.40	4/93	16r
Carrots, short trimmed and topped	lb	0.45	4/93	16r
Cheese, Cheddar	lb	3.47	4/93	16r
Cheese, Kraft grated Parmesan	8-oz canister	2.90	4Q 92	4c
Chicken, fresh, whole	lb	0.84	4/93	16r

Canton, OH - continued

Item	Per	Value	Date	Ref.
Groceries - continued				
Chicken, fryer, whole	lb	0.79	4Q 92	4c
Chicken breast, bone-in	lb	1.94	4/93	16r
Chicken legs, bone-in	lb	1.02	4/93	16r
Chuck roast, graded and ungraded, ex USDA prime and choice	lb	2.43	4/93	16r
Chuck roast, USDA choice, bone-in	lb	2.11	4/93	16r
Chuck roast, USDA choice, boneless	lb	2.44	4/93	16r
Cigarettes, Winston	carton	16.24	4Q 92	4c
Coffee, 100% ground roast, all sizes	lb	2.47	4/93	16r
Coffee, vacuum-packed	13-oz can	2.11	4Q 92	4c
Cookies, chocolate chip	lb	2.73	4/93	16r
Corn, frozen	10 oz	0.68	4Q 92	4c
Corn Flakes, Kellogg's or Post Toasties	18 oz	1.89	4Q 92	4c
Eggs, Grade A large	doz	0.74	4Q 92	4c
Eggs, Grade A large	doz	0.93	4/93	16r
Flour, white, all purpose	lb	0.21	4/93	16r
Grapefruit	lb	0.45	4/93	16r
Grapes, Thompson Seedless	lb	1.46	4/93	16r
Ground beef, 100% beef	lb	1.63	4/93	16r
Ground beef, lean and extra lean	lb	2.08	4/93	16r
Ground beef or hamburger	lb	1.22	4Q 92	4c
Ground chuck, 100% beef	lb	1.94	4/93	16r
Ham, boneless, excluding canned	lb	2.21	4/93	16r
Honey, jar	8 oz	0.97-1.25	92	5r
Honey, jar	lb	1.25-2.25	92	5r
Honey, squeeze bear	12-oz	1.25-1.99	92	5r
Ice cream, prepackaged, bulk, regular	1/2 gal	2.41	4/93	16r
Lemons	lb	0.82	4/93	16r
Lettuce, iceberg	head	0.87	4Q 92	4c
Lettuce, iceberg	lb	0.83	4/93	16r
Margarine, Blue Bonnet or Parkay cubes	lb	0.51	4Q 92	4c
Margarine, stick	lb	0.77	4/93	16r
Milk, whole	1/2 gal	1.17	4Q 92	4c
Orange juice, Minute Maid frozen	12-oz can	1.31	4Q 92	4c
Oranges, navel	lb	0.50	4/93	16r
Peaches	29-oz can	1.26	4Q 92	4c
Peanut butter, creamy, all sizes	lb	1.82	4/93	16r
Pears, Anjou	lb	0.85	4/93	16r
Peas Sweet, Del Monte or Green Giant	15-17 oz can	0.60	4Q 92	4c
Pork chops, center cut, bone-in	lb	3.17	4/93	16r
Potato chips	16 oz	2.68	4/93	16r
Potatoes, white	lb	0.26	4/93	16r
Potatoes, white or red	10-lb sack	1.61	4Q 92	4c
Round roast, graded & ungraded, ex USDA prime & choice	lb	2.88	4/93	16r
Round roast, USDA choice, boneless	lb	2.96	4/93	16r
Sausage, Jimmy Dean, 100% pork	lb	2.49	4Q 92	4c
Shortening, vegetable oil blends	lb	0.79	4/93	16r
Shortening, vegetable, Crisco	3-lb can	2.14	4Q 92	4c
Soft drink, Coca Cola	2 liter	1.01	4Q 92	4c
Spaghetti and macaroni	lb	0.76	4/93	16r
Steak, rib eye, USDA choice, boneless	lb	6.29	4/93	16r
Steak, round, USDA choice, boneless	lb	3.24	4/93	16r
Steak, sirloin, graded & ungraded, ex USDA prime & choice	lb	4.00	4/93	16r
Steak, sirloin, USDA choice, bone-in	lb	3.57	4/93	16r
Steak, sirloin, USDA choice, boneless	lb	4.17	4/93	16r
Steak, T-bone	lb	5.87	4Q 92	4c
Steak, T-bone, USDA choice, bone-in	lb	5.60	4/93	16r
Strawberries, dry pint	12 oz	0.90	4/93	16r
Sugar, cane or beet	4 lb	1.29	4Q 92	4c
Sugar, white	lb	0.36	4/93	16r
Sugar, white, 33-80 oz pk	lb	0.35	4/93	16r
Tomatoes, field grown	lb	0.99	4/93	16r
Tomatoes, Hunt's or Del Monte	14.5-oz can	0.62	4Q 92	4c

Values are in dollars or fractions of dollars. In the column headed *Ref*, references are shown to sources. Each reference is followed by a letter. These refer to the geographical level for which data were reported: s = State, r = Region, and c = City or metro. The abbreviation *ex* is used to mean *except* or *excluding*; *exp* stands for expenditures. For other abbreviations and further explanations, please see the Introduction.

Canton, OH - continued

Item	Per	Value	Date	Ref.
Groceries				
Tuna, chunk, light	6.125-6.5 oz can	0.58	4Q 92	4c
Tuna, chunk, light	lb	1.76	4/93	16r
Turkey, frozen, whole	lb	0.91	4/93	16r
Health Care				
ACCRA Index, Health Care		87.50	4Q 92	4c
Analgesic, Aspirin, Bayer, 325 mg tablets	100	5.06	4Q 92	4c
Childbirth, cesarean, hospital		4688	91	62r
Childbirth, cesarean, physician's fee		2053	91	62r
Childbirth, normal, hospital		2657	91	62r
Childbirth, normal, physician's fee		1492	91	62r
Dentist's fee, adult teeth cleaning and periodic oral exam	visit	42.20	4Q 92	4c
Doctor's fee, routine exam, established patient	visit	33.80	4Q 92	4c
Hospital care, semiprivate room	day	181.76	90	27c
Hospital care, semiprivate room	day	210.80	4Q 92	4c
Medical insurance premium, per employee, small group comprehensive	month	306.60	10/91	25c
Medical plan per employee	year	3443	91	45r
Mental health care, exp	capita	37.60-53.67	90	38s
Mental health care, exp, state mental health agency	capita	40.93	90	38s
Mental health care, hospital psychiatric services, non-Federal, exp	capita	15.03	88	38s
Mental health care, mental health organization, multiservice, exp	capita	14.46	88	38s
Mental health care, psychiatric hospitals, private, exp	capita	7.93	88	38s
Mental health care, psychiatric out-patient clinics, freestanding, exp	capita	2.93	88	38s
Mental health care, psychiatric partial-care organizations, freestanding, exp	capita	0.32	88	38s
Mental health care, state and county mental hospitals, exp	capita	23.79	88	38s
Mental health care, VA medical centers, exp	capita	7.76	88	38s
Physician fee, family practice, first-visit		76.00	91	62r
Physician fee, family practice, revisit		33.00	91	62r
Physician fee, general practice, first-visit		61.00	91	62r
Physician fee, general practice, revisit		31.00	91	62r
Physician fee, general surgeon, first-visit		65.00	91	62r
Physician fee, general surgeon, revisit		35.00	91	62r
Physician fee, internal medicine, first-visit		91.00	91	62r
Physician fee, internal medicine, revisit		40.00	91	62r
Physician fee, median, neurosurgeon, first-visit		106.00	91	62r
Physician fee, median, nonsurgical specialist, first-visit		90.00	91	62r
Physician fee, median, orthopedic surgeon, first-visit		83.00	91	62r
Physician fee, median, surgical specialist, first-visit		61.00	91	62r
Physician fee, neurosurgeon, revisit		41.00	91	62r
Physician fee, nonsurgical specialist, revisit		40.00	91	62r
Physician fee, obstetrics/gynecology, first-visit		61.00	91	62r
Physician fee, obstetrics/gynecology, revisit		40.00	91	62r
Physician fee, orthopedic surgeon, revisit		41.00	91	62r
Physician fee, pediatrician, first-visit		46.00	91	62r
Physician fee, pediatrician, revisit		33.00	91	62r
Physician fee, surgical specialist, revisit		36.00	91	62r
Substance abuse, hospital ancillary charge	incident	940	90	70s
Substance abuse, hospital physician charge	incident	380	90	70s
Substance abuse, hospital room and board	incident	5410	90	70s

Canton, OH - continued

Item	Per	Value	Date	Ref.
Household Goods				
Appliance repair, home, service call, washing machine	min labor charge	34.60	4Q 92	4c
Laundry detergent, Tide Ultra, Bold, or Cheer	42 oz	3.55	4Q 92	4c
Tissues, facial, Kleenex brand	175-count box	1.01	4Q 92	4c
Housing				
ACCRA Index, Housing		100.60	4Q 92	4c
Home, median price	unit	71.10		26c
House, 1,800 sq ft, 8,000 sq ft lot, new, urban	total	115833	4Q 92	4c
House payment, principal and interest, 25% down payment	month	661	4Q 92	4c
Mortgage rate, incl. points & origination fee, 30-year fixed or adjustable rate	percent	8.38	4Q 92	4c
Rent, apartment, 2 bedrooms - 1-1/2 to 2 baths, unfurnished, 950 sq ft, water	month	397	4Q 92	4c
Rental unit, 1 bedroom	month	348	93	23c
Rental unit, 2 bedroom	month	410	93	23c
Rental unit, 3 bedroom	month	513	93	23c
Rental unit, 4 bedroom	month	578	93	23c
Rental unit, efficiency	month	287	93	23c
Insurance and Pensions				
Auto insurance, private passenger	year	547.38	91	63s
Personal Goods				
Shampoo, Alberto VO5	15 oz	1.17	4Q 92	4c
Toothpaste, Crest or Colgate	6-7 oz	1.83	4Q 92	4c
Personal Services				
Dry cleaning, man's 2-piece suit		5.86	4Q 92	4c
Haircare, woman's shampoo, trim and blow-dry		16.10	4Q 92	4c
Haircut, man's barbershop, no styling		6.80	4Q 92	4c
Restaurant Food				
Chicken, fried, thigh and drumstick		1.94	4Q 92	4c
Hamburger with cheese	1/4 lb	1.79	4Q 92	4c
Pizza, Pizza Hut or Pizza Inn, cheese, thin crust	12-13 in	8.00	4Q 92	4c
Taxes				
Tax, cigarette	pack	18	91	77s
Tax, gasoline	gal	21	91	77s
Taxes, state	capita	1056	91	77s
Transportation				
ACCRA Index, Transportation		103.10	4Q 92	4c
Bus fare	one-way	0.70	3/93	2c
Driver's license fee		5.00	12/90	43s
Tire balance, computer or spin balance, front	wheel	7.20	4Q 92	4c
Utilities				
ACCRA Index, Utilities		102.50	4Q 92	4c
Electricity	mil Btu	17.33	90	64s
Electricity, partial electric and other energy, 1,800 sq ft living area new home	month	69.72	4Q 92	4c
Electricity, winter, 250 KWh	month	19.78	92	55c
Electricity, winter, 500 KWh	month	36.29	92	55c
Electricity, winter, 750 KWh	month	53.82	92	55c
Electricity, winter, 1000 KWh	month	66.19	92	55c

Carlsbad, NM

Item	Per	Value	Date	Ref.
Composite ACCRA index		88.80	4Q 92	4c
Alcoholic Beverages				
Beer, Miller Lite or Budweiser, 12-oz containers	6 pack	3.52	4Q 92	4c

Values are in dollars or fractions of dollars. In the column headed *Ref*, references are shown as sources. Each reference is followed by a letter. These refer to the geographical level for which data were reported: s = State, r = Region, and c = City or metro. The abbreviation *ex* is used to mean *except* or *excluding*; *exp* stands for expenditures. For other abbreviations and further explanations, please see the Introduction.

Carlsbad, NM - continued

Item	Per	Value	Date	Ref.
Alcoholic Beverages				
Liquor, J & B Scotch	750 ml	16.32	4Q 92	4c
Wine, Gallo Chablis blanc, 1.5 liter	bottle	4.76	4Q 92	4c
Clothing				
Jeans, man's denim		26.91	4Q 92	4c
Shirt, man's dress shirt		22.99	4Q 92	4c
Undervest, boy's size 10-14, cotton	3	3.03	4Q 92	4c
Communications				
Newspaper subscription, daily and Sunday home delivery, large-city	month	8.25	4Q 92	4c
Telephone bill, family of four	month	20.74	4Q 92	4c
Energy and Fuels				
Energy, combined forms, 1,800 sq ft heating area	month	69.96	4Q 92	4c
Gasoline, motor	gal	1.14	4Q 92	4c
Entertainment				
Bowling, evening rate	game	1.90	4Q 92	4c
Monopoly game, Parker Brothers', No. 9		11.64	4Q 92	4c
Movie	admission	4.50	4Q 92	4c
Tennis balls, yellow, Wilson or Penn, 3	can	2.55	4Q 92	4c
Goods and Services				
ACCRA Index, Miscellaneous Goods and Services		90.50	4Q 92	4c
Groceries				
ACCRA Index, Groceries		95.20	4Q 92	4c
Babyfood, strained vegetables, lowest price	4-4.5 oz jar	0.30	4Q 92	4c
Bananas	lb	0.41	4Q 92	4c
Bread, white	24 oz	0.68	4Q 92	4c
Cheese, Kraft grated Parmesan	8-oz canister	3.28	4Q 92	4c
Chicken, fryer, whole	lb	0.64	4Q 92	4c
Cigarettes, Winston	carton	16.43	4Q 92	4c
Coffee, vacuum-packed	13-oz can	1.99	4Q 92	4c
Corn, frozen	10 oz	0.73	4Q 92	4c
Corn Flakes, Kellogg's or Post Toasties	18 oz	2.17	4Q 92	4c
Eggs, Grade A large	doz	0.89	4Q 92	4c
Ground beef or hamburger	lb	1.19	4Q 92	4c
Lettuce, iceberg	head	1.02	4Q 92	4c
Margarine, Blue Bonnet or Parkay cubes	lb	0.79	4Q 92	4c
Milk, whole	1/2 gal	1.19	4Q 92	4c
Orange juice, Minute Maid frozen	12-oz can	1.29	4Q 92	4c
Peaches	29-oz can	1.56	4Q 92	4c
Peas Sweet, Del Monte or Green Giant	15-17 oz can	0.56	4Q 92	4c
Potatoes, white or red	10-lb sack	2.26	4Q 92	4c
Sausage, Jimmy Dean, 100% pork	lb	2.05	4Q 92	4c
Shortening, vegetable, Crisco	3-lb can	2.14	4Q 92	4c
Soft drink, Coca Cola	2 liter	1.46	4Q 92	4c
Steak, T-bone	lb	4.76	4Q 92	4c
Sugar, cane or beet	4 lb	1.57	4Q 92	4c
Tomatoes, Hunt's or Del Monte	14.5-oz can	0.71	4Q 92	4c
Tuna, chunk, light	6.125-6.5 oz can	0.64	4Q 92	4c
Health Care				
ACCRA Index, Health Care		96.90	4Q 92	4c
Analgesic, Aspirin, Bayer, 325 mg tablets	100	4.22	4Q 92	4c
Dentist's fee, adult teeth cleaning and periodic oral exam	visit	55.50	4Q 92	4c

Carlsbad, NM - continued

Item	Per	Value	Date	Ref.
Health Care - continued				
Doctor's fee, routine exam, established patient	visit	31.04	4Q 92	4c
Hospital care, semiprivate room	day	277.00	4Q 92	4c
Household Goods				
Appliance repair, home, service call, washing machine	min labor charge	29.17	4Q 92	4c
Laundry detergent, Tide Ultra, Bold, or Cheer	42 oz	3.27	4Q 92	4c
Tissues, facial, Kleenex brand	175-count box	1.14	4Q 92	4c
Housing				
ACCRA Index, Housing		84.80	4Q 92	4c
House, 1,800 sq ft, 8,000 sq ft lot, new, urban	total	98171	4Q 92	4c
House payment, principal and interest, 25% down payment	month	549	4Q 92	4c
Mortgage rate, incl. points & origination fee, 30-year fixed or adjustable rate	percent	8.16	4Q 92	4c
Rent, apartment, 2 bedrooms - 1-1/2 to 2 baths, unfurnished, 950 sq ft, water	month	354	4Q 92	4c
Personal Goods				
Shampoo, Alberto VO5	15 oz	1.08	4Q 92	4c
Toothpaste, Crest or Colgate	6-7 oz	1.85	4Q 92	4c
Personal Services				
Dry cleaning, man's 2-piece suit		5.08	4Q 92	4c
Haircare, woman's shampoo, trim and blow-dry		15.33	4Q 92	4c
Haircut, man's barbershop, no styling		6.17	4Q 92	
Restaurant Food				
Chicken, fried, thigh and drumstick		1.90	4Q 92	4c
Hamburger with cheese	1/4 lb	1.89	4Q 92	4c
Pizza, Pizza Hut or Pizza Inn, cheese, thin crust	12-13 in	8.05	4Q 92	4c
Transportation				
ACCRA Index, Transportation		100.20	4Q 92	4c
Tire balance, computer or spin balance, front	wheel	6.50	4Q 92	4c
Utilities				
ACCRA Index, Utilities		68.30	4Q 92	4c
Electricity, all electric, 1,800 sq ft living area new home	month	69.92	4Q 92	4c

Carrollton, GA

Item	Per	Value	Date	Ref.
Composite ACCRA index		93.70	4Q 92	4c
Alcoholic Beverages				
Beer, Miller Lite or Budweiser, 12-oz containers	6 pack	4.11	4Q 92	4c
Liquor, J & B Scotch	750 ml	17.99	4Q 92	4c
Wine, Gallo Chablis blanc, 1.5 liter	bottle	4.99	4Q 92	4c
Clothing				
Jeans, man's denim		26.99	4Q 92	4c
Shirt, man's dress shirt		23.50	4Q 92	4c
Undervest, boy's size 10-14, cotton	3	4.06	4Q 92	4c
Communications				
Newspaper subscription, daily and Sunday home delivery, large-city	month	12.09	4Q 92	4c
Telephone, flat rate	month	13.00	91	11c
Telephone bill, family of four	month	18.98	4Q 92	4c
Energy and Fuels				
Energy, combined forms, 1,800 sq ft heating area	month	120.94	4Q 92	4c
Energy, exc electricity, 1,800 sq ft heating area	month	43.86	4Q 92	4c

Values are in dollars or fractions of dollars. In the column headed *Ref*, references are shown to sources. Each reference is followed by a letter. These refer to the geographical level for which data were reported: s = State, r = Region, and c = City or metro. The abbreviation *ex* is used to mean *except* or *excluding*; *exp* stands for expenditures. For other abbreviations and further explanations, please see the Introduction.

Carrollton, GA - continued

Item	Per	Value	Date	Ref.
Energy and Fuels				
Gasoline, motor	gal	0.98	4Q 92	4c
Entertainment				
Bowling, evening rate	game	2.25	4Q 92	4c
Monopoly game, Parker Brothers', No. 9		10.98	4Q 92	4c
Movie	admission	5.50	4Q 92	4c
Tennis balls, yellow, Wilson or Penn, 3	can	2.31	4Q 92	4c
Goods and Services				
ACCRA Index, Miscellaneous Goods and Services		97.20	4Q 92	4c
Groceries				
ACCRA Index, Groceries		93.50	4Q 92	4c
Babyfood, strained vegetables, lowest price	4-4.5 oz jar	0.30	4Q 92	4c
Bananas	lb	0.43	4Q 92	4c
Bread, white	24 oz	0.71	4Q 92	4c
Cheese, Kraft grated Parmesan	8-oz canister	2.73	4Q 92	4c
Chicken, fryer, whole	lb	0.65	4Q 92	4c
Cigarettes, Winston	carton	15.93	4Q 92	4c
Coffee, vacuum-packed	13-oz can	1.73	4Q 92	4c
Corn, frozen	10 oz	0.54	4Q 92	4c
Corn Flakes, Kellogg's or Post Toasties	18 oz	1.64	4Q 92	4c
Eggs, Grade A large	doz	0.70	4Q 92	4c
Ground beef or hamburger	lb	1.67	4Q 92	4c
Lettuce, iceberg	head	0.87	4Q 92	4c
Margarine, Blue Bonnet or Parkay cubes	lb	0.49	4Q 92	4c
Milk, whole	1/2 gal	1.40	4Q 92	4c
Orange juice, Minute Maid frozen	12-oz can	1.20	4Q 92	4c
Peaches	29-oz can	1.30	4Q 92	4c
Peas Sweet, Del Monte or Green Giant	15-17 oz can	0.47	4Q 92	4c
Potatoes, white or red	10-lb sack	2.36	4Q 92	4c
Sausage, Jimmy Dean, 100% pork	lb	2.16	4Q 92	4c
Shortening, vegetable, Crisco	3-lb can	2.02	4Q 92	4c
Soft drink, Coca Cola	2 liter	1.12	4Q 92	4c
Steak, T-bone	lb	5.79	4Q 92	4c
Sugar, cane or beet	4 lb	1.40	4Q 92	4c
Tomatoes, Hunt's or Del Monte	14.5-oz can	0.50	4Q 92	4c
Tuna, chunk, light	6.125-6.5 oz can	0.56	4Q 92	4c
Health Care				
ACCRA Index, Health Care		89.90	4Q 92	4c
Analgesic, Aspirin, Bayer, 325 mg tablets	100	4.55	4Q 92	4c
Dentist's fee, adult teeth cleaning and periodic oral exam	visit	44.80	4Q 92	4c
Doctor's fee, routine exam, established patient	visit	33.60	4Q 92	4c
Hospital care, semiprivate room	day	240.50	4Q 92	4c
Household Goods				
Appliance repair, home, service call, washing machine	min labor charge	31.67	4Q 92	4c
Laundry detergent, Tide Ultra, Bold, or Cheer	42 oz	2.84	4Q 92	4c
Tissues, facial, Kleenex brand	175-count box	0.97	4Q 92	4c
Housing				
ACCRA Index, Housing		86.10	4Q 92	4c

Carrollton, GA - continued

Item	Per	Value	Date	Ref.
Housing - continued				
House, 1,800 sq ft, 8,000 sq ft lot, new, urban	total	97250	4Q 92	4c
House payment, principal and interest, 25% down payment	month	542	4Q 92	4c
Mortgage rate, incl. points & origination fee, 30-year fixed or adjustable rate	percent	8.13	4Q 92	4c
Rent, apartment, 2 bedrooms - 1-1/2 to 2 baths, unfurnished, 950 sq ft, water	month	395	4Q 92	4c
Personal Goods				
Shampoo, Alberto VO5	15 oz	0.95	4Q 92	4c
Toothpaste, Crest or Colgate	6-7 oz	1.77	4Q 92	4c
Personal Services				
Dry cleaning, man's 2-piece suit		6.55	4Q 92	4c
Haircare, woman's shampoo, trim and blow-dry		16.25	4Q 92	4c
Haircut, man's barbershop, no styling		5.67	4Q 92	4c
Restaurant Food				
Chicken, fried, thigh and drumstick		1.99	4Q 92	4c
Hamburger with cheese	1/4 lb	1.81	4Q 92	4c
Pizza, Pizza Hut or Pizza Inn, cheese, thin crust	12-13 in	7.79	4Q 92	4c
Transportation				
ACCRA Index, Transportation		90.40	4Q 92	4c
Tire balance, computer or spin balance, front	wheel	6.12	4Q 92	4c
Utilities				
ACCRA Index, Utilities		109.40	4Q 92	4c
Electricity, partial electric and other energy, 1,800 sq ft living area new home	month	77.08	4Q 92	4c

Carson City, NV

Item	Per	Value	Date	Ref.
Composite ACCRA index		109.90	4Q 92	4c
Alcoholic Beverages				
Beer, Miller Lite or Budweiser, 12-oz containers	6 pack	3.97	4Q 92	4c
Liquor, J & B Scotch	750 ml	16.09	4Q 92	4c
Wine, Gallo Chablis blanc, 1.5 liter	bottle	3.94	4Q 92	4c
Clothing				
Jeans, man's denim		34.74	4Q 92	4c
Shirt, man's dress shirt		20.75	4Q 92	4c
Undervest, boy's size 10-14, cotton	3	5.27	4Q 92	4c
Communications				
Newspaper subscription, daily and Sunday home delivery, large-city	month	8.59	4Q 92	4c
Telephone bill, family of four	month	14.69	4Q 92	4c
Energy and Fuels				
Energy, combined forms, 1,800 sq ft heating area	month	101.33	4Q 92	4c
Energy, exc electricity, 1,800 sq ft heating area	month	49.44	4Q 92	4c
Gasoline, motor	gal	1.24	4Q 92	4c
Entertainment				
Bowling, evening rate	game	2.10	4Q 92	4c
Monopoly game, Parker Brothers', No. 9		9.99	4Q 92	4c
Movie	admission	5.50	4Q 92	4c
Tennis balls, yellow, Wilson or Penn, 3	can	2.79	4Q 92	4c
Goods and Services				
ACCRA Index, Miscellaneous Goods and Services		105.30	4Q 92	4c
Groceries				
ACCRA Index, Groceries		102.00	4Q 92	4c
Babyfood, strained vegetables, lowest price	4-4.5 oz jar	0.36	4Q 92	4c

Values are in dollars or fractions of dollars. In the column headed *Ref*, references are shown to sources. Each reference is followed by a letter. These refer to the geographical level for which data were reported: s = State, r = Region, and c = City or metro. The abbreviation *ex* is used to mean *except* or *excluding*; *exp* stands for *expenditures*. For other abbreviations and further explanations, please see the Introduction.

Carson City, NV - continued

Item	Per	Value	Date	Ref.
Groceries				
Bananas	lb	0.44	4Q 92	4c
Bread, white	24 oz	0.77	4Q 92	4c
Cheese, Kraft grated Parmesan	8-oz canister	3.55	4Q 92	4c
Chicken, fryer, whole	lb	0.83	4Q 92	4c
Cigarettes, Winston	carton	19.14	4Q 92	4c
Coffee, vacuum-packed	13-oz can	2.23	4Q 92	4c
Corn, frozen	10 oz	0.61	4Q 92	4c
Corn Flakes, Kellogg's or Post Toasties	18 oz	1.91	4Q 92	4c
Eggs, Grade A large	doz	0.81	4Q 92	4c
Ground beef or hamburger	lb	1.52	4Q 92	4c
Lettuce, iceberg	head	0.75	4Q 92	4c
Margarine, Blue Bonnet or Parkay cubes	lb	0.60	4Q 92	4c
Milk, whole	1/2 gal	1.26	4Q 92	4c
Orange juice, Minute Maid frozen	12-oz can	1.59	4Q 92	4c
Peaches	29-oz can	1.23	4Q 92	4c
Peas Sweet, Del Monte or Green Giant	15-17 oz can	0.62	4Q 92	4c
Potatoes, white or red	10-lb sack	1.61	4Q 92	4c
Sausage, Jimmy Dean, 100% pork	lb	3.08	4Q 92	4c
Shortening, vegetable, Crisco	3-lb can	2.53	4Q 92	4c
Soft drink, Coca Cola	2 liter	1.30	4Q 92	4c
Steak, T-bone	lb	4.72	4Q 92	4c
Sugar, cane or beet	4 lb	1.36	4Q 92	4c
Tomatoes, Hunt's or Del Monte	14.5-oz can	0.69	4Q 92	4c
Tuna, chunk, light	6.125-6.5 oz can	0.62	4Q 92	4c
Health Care				
ACCRA Index, Health Care		129.60	4Q 92	4c
Analgesic, Aspirin, Bayer, 325 mg tablets	100	5.27	4Q 92	4c
Dentist's fee, adult teeth cleaning and periodic oral exam	visit	77.80	4Q 92	4c
Doctor's fee, routine exam, established patient	visit	40.80	4Q 92	4c
Hospital care, semiprivate room	day	350.00	4Q 92	4c
Household Goods				
Appliance repair, home, service call, washing machine	min labor charge	30.00	4Q 92	4c
Laundry detergent, Tide Ultra, Bold, or Cheer	42 oz	3.11	4Q 92	4c
Tissues, facial, Kleenex brand	175-count box	1.15	4Q 92	4c
Housing				
ACCRA Index, Housing		121.70	4Q 92	4c
House, 1,800 sq ft, 8,000 sq ft lot, new, urban	total	137204	4Q 92	4c
House payment, principal and interest, 25% down payment	month	767	4Q 92	4c
Mortgage rate, incl. points & origination fee, 30-year fixed or adjustable rate	percent	8.16	4Q 92	4c
Rent, apartment, 2 bedrooms - 1-1/2 to 2 baths, unfurnished, 950 sq ft, water	month	557	4Q 92	4c
Personal Goods				
Shampoo, Alberto VO5	15 oz	1.49	4Q 92	4c
Toothpaste, Crest or Colgate	6-7 oz	2.18	4Q 92	4c
Personal Services				
Dry cleaning, man's 2-piece suit		7.45	4Q 92	4c
Haircare, woman's shampoo, trim and blow-dry		19.60	4Q 92	4c

Carson City, NV - continued

Item	Per	Value	Date	Ref.
Personal Services - continued				
Haircut, man's barbershop, no styling		11.00	4Q 92	4c
Restaurant Food				
Chicken, fried, thigh and drumstick		2.20	4Q 92	4c
Hamburger with cheese	1/4 lb	1.84	4Q 92	4c
Pizza, Pizza Hut or Pizza Inn, cheese, thin crust	12-13 in	8.75	4Q 92	4c
Transportation				
ACCRA Index, Transportation		110.20	4Q 92	4c
Tire balance, computer or spin balance, front	wheel	7.20	4Q 92	4c
Utilities				
ACCRA Index, Utilities		91.10	4Q 92	4c
Electricity, partial electric and other energy, 1,800 sq ft living area new home	month	51.89	4Q 92	4c

Cartersville, GA

Item	Per	Value	Date	Ref.
Composite ACCRA index		93.30	4Q 92	4c
Alcoholic Beverages				
Beer, Miller Lite or Budweiser, 12-oz containers	6 pack	4.11	4Q 92	4c
Liquor, J & B Scotch	750 ml	17.74	4Q 92	4c
Wine, Gallo Chablis blanc, 1.5 liter	bottle	5.56	4Q 92	4c
Clothing				
Jeans, man's denim		35.50	4Q 92	4c
Shirt, man's dress shirt		24.33	4Q 92	4c
Undervest, boy's size 10-14, cotton	3	3.12	4Q 92	4c
Communications				
Newspaper subscription, daily and Sunday home delivery, large-city	month	11.93	4Q 92	4c
Telephone, flat rate	month	12.25	91	11c
Telephone bill, family of four	month	18.62	4Q 92	4c
Energy and Fuels				
Energy, combined forms, 1,800 sq ft heating area	month	107.55	4Q 92	4c
Energy, exc electricity, 1,800 sq ft heating area	month	38.68	4Q 92	4c
Gasoline, motor	gal	1.02	4Q 92	4c
Entertainment				
Bowling, evening rate	game	2.00	4Q 92	4c
Monopoly game, Parker Brothers', No. 9		9.97	4Q 92	4c
Movie	admission	5.75	4Q 92	4c
Tennis balls, yellow, Wilson or Penn, 3	can	1.92	4Q 92	4c
Goods and Services				
ACCRA Index, Miscellaneous Goods and Services		97.30	4Q 92	4c
Groceries				
ACCRA Index, Groceries		95.40	4Q 92	4c
Babyfood, strained vegetables, lowest price	4-4.5 oz jar	0.31	4Q 92	4c
Bananas	lb	0.46	4Q 92	4c
Bread, white	24 oz	0.69	4Q 92	4c
Cheese, Kraft grated Parmesan	8-oz canister	3.05	4Q 92	4c
Chicken, fryer, whole	lb	0.65	4Q 92	4c
Cigarettes, Winston	carton	16.26	4Q 92	4c
Coffee, vacuum-packed	13-oz can	1.68	4Q 92	4c
Corn, frozen	10 oz	0.50	4Q 92	4c
Corn Flakes, Kellogg's or Post Toasties	18 oz	1.68	4Q 92	4c
Eggs, Grade A large	doz	0.84	4Q 92	4c
Ground beef or hamburger	lb	1.82	4Q 92	4c
Lettuce, iceberg	head	0.99	4Q 92	4c
Margarine, Blue Bonnet or Parkay cubes	lb	0.55	4Q 92	4c

Values are in dollars or fractions of dollars. In the column headed *Ref*, references are shown to sources. Each reference is followed by a letter. These refer to the geographical level for which data were reported: s=State, r=Region, and c=City or metro. The abbreviation *ex* is used to mean *except* or *excluding*; *exp* stands for expenditures. For other abbreviations and further explanations, please see the Introduction.

Cartersville, GA - continued

Item	Per	Value	Date	Ref.
Groceries				
Milk, whole	1/2 gal	1.45	4Q 92	4c
Orange juice, Minute Maid frozen	12-oz can	1.19	4Q 92	4c
Peaches	29-oz can	1.36	4Q 92	4c
Peas Sweet, Del Monte or Green Giant	15-17 oz can	0.49	4Q 92	4c
Potatoes, white or red	10-lb sack	1.92	4Q 92	4c
Sausage, Jimmy Dean, 100% pork	lb	2.09	4Q 92	4c
Shortening, vegetable, Crisco	3-lb can	2.02	4Q 92	4c
Soft drink, Coca Cola	2 liter	1.15	4Q 92	4c
Steak, T-bone	lb	5.89	4Q 92	4c
Sugar, cane or beet	4 lb	1.38	4Q 92	4c
Tomatoes, Hunt's or Del Monte	14.5-oz can	0.50	4Q 92	4c
Tuna, chunk, light	6.125-6.5 oz can	0.57	4Q 92	4c
Health Care				
ACCRA Index, Health Care		88.00	4Q 92	4c
Analgesic, Aspirin, Bayer, 325 mg tablets	100	4.49	4Q 92	4c
Dentist's fee, adult teeth cleaning and periodic oral exam	visit	44.00	4Q 92	4c
Doctor's fee, routine exam, established patient	visit	33.00	4Q 92	4c
Hospital care, semiprivate room	day	230.00	4Q 92	4c
Household Goods				
Appliance repair, home, service call, washing machine	min labor charge	34.48	4Q 92	4c
Laundry detergent, Tide Ultra, Bold, or Cheer	42 oz	2.78	4Q 92	4c
Tissues, facial, Kleenex brand	175-count box	0.94	4Q 92	4c
Housing				
ACCRA Index, Housing		90.20	4Q 92	4c
House, 1,800 sq ft, 8,000 sq ft lot, new, urban	total	95900	4Q 92	4c
House payment, principal and interest, 25% down payment	month	532	4Q 92	4c
Mortgage rate, incl. points & origination fee, 30-year fixed or adjustable rate	percent	8.09	4Q 92	4c
Rent, apartment, 2 bedrooms - 1-1/2 to 2 baths, unfurnished, 950 sq ft, water	month	497	4Q 92	4c
Personal Goods				
Shampoo, Alberto VO5	15 oz	0.98	4Q 92	4c
Toothpaste, Crest or Colgate	6-7 oz	1.72	4Q 92	4c
Personal Services				
Dry cleaning, man's 2-piece suit		3.75	4Q 92	4c
Haircare, woman's shampoo, trim and blow-dry		19.00	4Q 92	4c
Haircut, man's barbershop, no styling		8.00	4Q 92	4c
Restaurant Food				
Chicken, fried, thigh and drumstick		1.99	4Q 92	4c
Hamburger with cheese	1/4 lb	1.89	4Q 92	4c
Pizza, Pizza Hut or Pizza Inn, cheese, thin crust	12-13 in	7.79	4Q 92	4c
Transportation				
ACCRA Index, Transportation		83.70	4Q 92	4c
Tire balance, computer or spin balance, front	wheel	5.00	4Q 92	4c
Utilities				
ACCRA Index, Utilities		98.20	4Q 92	4c
Electricity, partial electric and other energy, 1,800 sq ft living area new home	month	68.87	4Q 92	4c

Casper, WY

Item	Per	Value	Date	Ref.
Composite ACCRA index		99.40	4Q 92	4c
Alcoholic Beverages				
Beer, Miller Lite or Budweiser, 12-oz containers	6 pack	4.65	4Q 92	4c
Liquor, J & B Scotch	750 ml	17.03	4Q 92	4c
Wine, Gallo Chablis blanc, 1.5 liter	bottle	5.46	4Q 92	4c
Child Care				
Child care fee, average, center	hour	1.71	90	65r
Child care fee, average, nonregulated family day care	hour	1.32	90	65r
Child care fee, average, regulated family day care	hour	1.86	90	65r
Clothing				
Jeans, man's denim		29.66	4Q 92	4c
Shirt, man's dress shirt		25.00	4Q 92	4c
Undervest, boy's size 10-14, cotton	3	4.41	4Q 92	4c
Communications				
Long-distance telephone service, day, initial minute, 0-100 miles	min	0.19-0.43	91	12s
Long-distance telephone service, day, additional minute, 0-100 miles	min	0.09-0.29	91	12s
Long-distance telephone service, evenings/weekends, 0-100 mi, initial minute	min	0.10-0.24	91	12s
Long-distance telephone service, evenings/weekends, 0-100 mi, additional minute	min	0.05-0.16	91	12s
Newspaper subscription, daily and Sunday home delivery, large-city	month	11.09	4Q 92	4c
Telephone, flat rate	month	11.96	91	11c
Telephone bill, family of four	month	18.76	4Q 92	4c
Education				
Board, 4-yr public college/university	year	1767	91	22s
Expenditures, local gov't, public elementary/secondary	pupil	5355	92	20s
Room, 4-year public college/university	year	1312	91	22s
Tuition, 2-year private college/university	year	7500	91	22s
Tuition, 2-year public college/university	year	662	91	22s
Tuition, 4-year public college/university, in-state	year	1148	91	22s
Energy and Fuels				
Coal	mil Btu	0.86	90	64s
Energy	mil Btu	6.46	90	64s
Energy, combined forms, 1,800 sq ft heating area	month	76.74	4Q 92	4c
Energy, exc electricity, 1,800 sq ft heating area	month	40.97	4Q 92	4c
Energy exp/householder, 1-family unit	year	372	90	28r
Energy exp/householder, <1,000 sq ft heating area	year	335	90	28r
Energy exp/householder, 1,000-1,999 sq ft heating area	year	365	90	28r
Energy exp/householder, 2,000+ sq ft heating area	year	411	90	28r
Energy exp/householder, mobile home	year	305	90	28r
Energy exp/householder, multifamily	year	372	90	28r
Gas, cooking, winter, 10 therms	month	4.55	92	56c
Gas, cooking, winter, 30 therms	month	13.65	92	56c
Gas, cooking, winter, 50 therms	month	22.76	92	56c
Gas, heating, winter, 100 therms	month	45.52	92	56c
Gas, heating, winter, average use	month	91.03	92	56c
Gas, natural	mil Btu	3.57	90	64s
Gas, natural	000 cu ft	4.74	91	46s
Gas, natural, exp	year	501	91	46s
Gasoline, motor	gal	1.20	4Q 92	4c
Gasoline, unleaded regular	mil Btu	8.66	90	64s
Entertainment				
Bowling, evening rate	game	1.60	4Q 92	4c
Miniature golf admission	adult	6.18	92	1r
Miniature golf admission	child	5.14	92	1r

Values are in dollars or fractions of dollars. In the column headed *Ref*, references are shown to sources. Each reference is followed by a letter. These refer to the geographical level for which data were reported: s=State, r=Region, and c=City or metro. The abbreviation *ex* is used to mean *except* or *excluding*; *exp* stands for expenditures. For other abbreviations and further explanations, please see the Introduction.

Casper, WY - continued

Item	Per	Value	Date	Ref.
Entertainment				
Monopoly game, Parker Brothers', No. 9		9.99	4Q 92	4c
Movie	admission	4.75	4Q 92	4c
Tennis balls, yellow, Wilson or Penn, 3	can	1.93	4Q 92	4c
Waterpark admission	adult	11.00	92	1r
Waterpark admission	child	8.55	92	1r
Funerals				
Casket, 18-gauge steel, velvet interior		1929.04	91	24r
Cosmetology, hair care, etc.		88.52	91	24r
Embalming		249.33	91	24r
Facility use for ceremony		182.75	91	24r
Hearse, local		110.04	91	24r
Limousine, local		66.67	91	24r
Remains to funeral home, transfer		84.58	91	24r
Service charge, professional		593.00	91	24r
Vault, concrete, non-metallic liner		647.38	91	24r
Viewing facilities, use		99.87	91	24r
Goods and Services				
ACCRA Index, Miscellaneous Goods and Services		98.50	4Q 92	4c
Groceries				
ACCRA Index, Groceries		109.00	4Q 92	4c
Apples, Red Delicious	lb	0.80	4/93	16r
Babyfood, strained vegetables, lowest price	4-4.5 oz jar	0.30	4Q 92	4c
Bacon	lb	1.79	4/93	16r
Bananas	lb	0.59	4Q 92	4c
Bananas	lb	0.53	4/93	16r
Bologna, all beef or mixed	lb	2.67	4/93	16r
Bread, white	24 oz	0.70	4Q 92	4c
Bread, white, pan	lb	0.81	4/93	16r
Carrots, short trimmed and topped	lb	0.39	4/93	16r
Cheese, Kraft grated Parmesan	8-oz canister	3.46	4Q 92	4c
Chicken, fresh, whole	lb	0.94	4/93	16r
Chicken, fryer, whole	lb	0.64	4Q 92	4c
Chicken breast, bone-in	lb	2.19	4/93	16r
Chuck roast, graded and ungraded, ex USDA prime and choice	lb	2.26	4/93	16r
Cigarettes, Winston	carton	17.04	4Q 92	4c
Coffee, 100% ground roast, all sizes	lb	2.33	4/93	16r
Coffee, vacuum-packed	13-oz can	2.54	4Q 92	4c
Corn, frozen	10 oz	0.89	4Q 92	4c
Corn Flakes, Kellogg's or Post Toasties	18 oz	2.16	4Q 92	4c
Eggs, Grade A large	doz	0.90	4Q 92	4c
Eggs, Grade AA large	doz	1.18	4/93	16r
Flour, white, all purpose	lb	0.22	4/93	16r
Grapefruit	lb	0.52	4/93	16r
Grapes, Thompson Seedless	lb	1.50	4/93	16r
Ground beef, 100% beef	lb	1.44	4/93	16r
Ground beef, lean and extra lean	lb	2.34	4/93	16r
Ground beef or hamburger	lb	1.36	4Q 92	4c
Ham, boneless, excluding canned	lb	2.56	4/93	16r
Honey, jar	8 oz	0.99-1.19	92	5r
Honey, jar	lb	1.49-2.25	92	5r
Honey, squeeze bear	12-oz	1.19-1.50	92	5r
Ice cream, prepackaged, bulk, regular	1/2 gal	2.40	4/93	16r
Lemons	lb	0.81	4/93	16r
Lettuce, iceberg	head	0.92	4Q 92	4c
Lettuce, iceberg	lb	0.84	4/93	16r
Margarine, Blue Bonnet or Parkay cubes	lb	0.75	4Q 92	4c
Margarine, stick	lb	0.81	4/93	16r
Milk, whole	1/2 gal	1.64	4Q 92	4c
Orange juice, Minute Maid frozen	12-oz can	1.59	4Q 92	4c
Oranges, navel	lb	0.48	4/93	16r
Peaches	29-oz can	1.43	4Q 92	4c

Item	Per	Value	Date	Ref.
Groceries - continued				
Peas Sweet, Del Monte or Green Giant	15-17 oz can	0.72	4Q 92	4c
Pork chops, center cut, bone-in	lb	3.25	4/93	16r
Potato chips	16 oz	2.89	4/93	16r
Potatoes, white	lb	0.38	4/93	16r
Potatoes, white or red	10-lb sack	2.29	4Q 92	4c
Round roast, graded & ungraded, ex USDA prime & choice	lb	3.00	4/93	16r
Round roast, USDA choice, boneless	lb	3.16	4/93	16r
Sausage, Jimmy Dean, 100% pork	lb	3.41	4Q 92	4c
Shortening, vegetable oil blends	lb	0.86	4/93	16r
Shortening, vegetable, Crisco	3-lb can	2.26	4Q 92	4c
Soft drink, Coca Cola	2 liter	1.89	4Q 92	4c
Spaghetti and macaroni	lb	0.84	4/93	16r
Steak, round, graded & ungraded, ex USDA prime & choice	lb	3.34	4/93	16r
Steak, round, USDA choice, boneless	lb	3.24	4/93	16r
Steak, sirloin, graded & ungraded, ex USDA prime & choice	lb	3.75	4/93	16r
Steak, sirloin, USDA choice, boneless	lb	4.49	4/93	16r
Steak, T-bone	lb	4.46	4Q 92	4c
Sugar, cane or beet	4 lb	1.83	4Q 92	4c
Sugar, white	lb	0.41	4/93	16r
Sugar, white, 33-80 oz pk	lb	0.38	4/93	16r
Tomatoes, field grown	lb	1.01	4/93	16r
Tomatoes, Hunt's or Del Monte	14.5-oz can	0.73	4Q 92	4c
Tuna, chunk, light	6.125-6.5 oz can	0.88	4Q 92	4c
Turkey, frozen, whole	lb	1.04	4/93	16r
Health Care				
ACCRA Index, Health Care		102.10	4Q 92	4c
Analgesic, Aspirin, Bayer, 325 mg tablets	100	5.19	4Q 92	4c
Childbirth, cesarean, hospital		5533	91	62r
Childbirth, cesarean, physician's fee		2053	91	62r
Childbirth, normal, hospital		2745	91	62r
Childbirth, normal, physician's fee		1492	91	62r
Dentist's fee, adult teeth cleaning and periodic oral exam	visit	45.33	4Q 92	4c
Doctor's fee, routine exam, established patient	visit	35.00	4Q 92	4c
Hospital care, semiprivate room	day	400.00	4Q 92	4c
Medical insurance premium, per employee, small group comprehensive	month	284.70	10/91	25c
Medical plan per employee	year	3218	91	45r
Mental health care, exp	capita	28.84-37.59	90	38s
Mental health care, exp, state mental health agency	capita	34.62	90	38s
Mental health care, hospital psychiatric services, non-Federal, exp	capita	3.06	88	38s
Mental health care, mental health organization, multiservice, exp	capita	9.72	88	38s
Mental health care, psychiatric hospitals, private, exp	capita	24.34	88	38s
Mental health care, psychiatric out-patient clinics, freestanding, exp	capita	9.27	88	38s
Mental health care, state and county mental hospitals, exp	capita	25.55	88	38s
Mental health care, VA medical centers, exp	capita	39.92	88	38s
Physician fee, family practice, first-visit		111.00	91	62r
Physician fee, family practice, revisit		45.00	91	62r
Physician fee, general practice, first-visit		100.00	91	62r
Physician fee, general practice, revisit		40.00	91	62r
Physician fee, internal medicine, first-visit		137.00	91	62r
Physician fee, internal medicine, revisit		48.00	91	62r
Physician fee, median, neurosurgeon, first-visit		157.00	91	62r

Values are in dollars or fractions of dollars. In the column headed *Ref*, references are shown to sources. Each reference is followed by a letter. These refer to the geographical level for which data were reported: s = State, r = Region, and c = City or metro. The abbreviation *ex* is used to mean *except* or *excluding*; *exp* stands for *expenditures*. For other abbreviations and further explanations, please see the Introduction.

Casper, WY - continued

Item	Per	Value	Date	Ref.
Health Care				
Physician fee, median, nonsurgical specialist, first-visit		131.00	91	62r
Physician fee, median, orthopedic surgeon, first-visit		124.00	91	62r
Physician fee, median, plastic surgeon, first-visit		88.00	91	62r
Physician fee, median, surgical specialist, first-visit		100.00	91	62r
Physician fee, neurosurgeon, revisit		51.00	91	62r
Physician fee, nonsurgical specialist, revisit		47.00	91	62r
Physician fee, obstetrics/gynecology, first-visit		95.00	91	62r
Physician fee, obstetrics/gynecology, revisit		50.00	91	62r
Physician fee, orthopedic surgeon, revisit		51.00	91	62r
Physician fee, pediatrician, first-visit		81.00	91	62r
Physician fee, pediatrician, revisit		42.00	91	62r
Physician fee, plastic surgeon, revisit		48.00	91	62r
Physician fee, surgical specialist, revisit		49.00	91	62r
Household Goods				
Appliance repair, home, service call, washing machine	min labor charge	33.00	4Q 92	4c
Laundry detergent, Tide Ultra, Bold, or Cheer	42 oz	4.08	4Q 92	4c
Tissues, facial, Kleenex brand	175-count box	1.25	4Q 92	4c
Housing				
ACCRA Index, Housing		104.40	4Q 92	4c
House, 1,800 sq ft, 8,000 sq ft lot, new, urban	total	130000	4Q 92	4c
House payment, principal and interest, 25% down payment	month	727	4Q 92	4c
Mortgage rate, incl. points & origination fee, 30-year fixed or adjustable rate	per-cent	8.17	4Q 92	4c
Rent, apartment, 2 bedrooms - 1-1/2 to 2 baths, unfurnished, 950 sq ft, water	month	317	4Q 92	4c
Rental unit, 1 bedroom	month	551	93	23c
Rental unit, 2 bedroom	month	647	93	23c
Rental unit, 3 bedroom	month	812	93	23c
Rental unit, 4 bedroom	month	910	93	23c
Rental unit, efficiency	month	454	93	23c
Insurance and Pensions				
Auto insurance, private passenger	year	450.33	91	63s
Personal Goods				
Shampoo, Alberto VO5	15 oz	1.59	4Q 92	4c
Toothpaste, Crest or Colgate	6-7 oz	2.16	4Q 92	4c
Personal Services				
Dry cleaning, man's 2-piece suit		6.01	4Q 92	4c
Haircare, woman's shampoo, trim and blow-dry		18.33	4Q 92	4c
Haircut, man's barbershop, no styling		6.83	4Q 92	4c
Restaurant Food				
Chicken, fried, thigh and drumstick		2.10	4Q 92	4c
Hamburger with cheese	1/4 lb	1.89	4Q 92	4c
Pizza, Pizza Hut or Pizza Inn, cheese, thin crust	12-13 in	7.99	4Q 92	4c
Taxes				
Tax, cigarette	pack	12	91	77s
Tax, gasoline	gal	9	91	77s
Taxes, state	capita	1385	91	77s
Transportation				
ACCRA Index, Transportation		99.00	4Q 92	4c
Driver's license fee		5.00	12/90	43s
Tire balance, computer or spin balance, front	wheel	5.98	4Q 92	4c

Casper, WY - continued

Item	Per	Value	Date	Ref.
Travel				
Business travel	day	178.00	4/93	89r
Utilities				
ACCRA Index, Utilities		72.90	4Q 92	4c
Electricity	mil Btu	12.37	90	64s
Electricity, partial electric and other energy, 1,800 sq ft living area new home	month	35.77	4Q 92	4c
Electricity, winter, 250 KWh	month	15.03	92	55c
Electricity, winter, 500 KWh	month	30.03	92	55c
Electricity, winter, 750 KWh	month	41.93	92	55c
Electricity, winter, 1000 KWh	month	54.56	92	55c

Cedar City, UT

Item	Per	Value	Date	Ref.
Composite ACCRA index		91.20	4Q 92	4c
Alcoholic Beverages				
Beer, Miller Lite or Budweiser, 12-oz containers	6 pack	4.09	4Q 92	4c
Liquor, J & B Scotch	750 ml	19.25	4Q 92	4c
Wine, Gallo Chablis blanc, 1.5 liter	bottle	4.95	4Q 92	4c
Clothing				
Jeans, man's denim		32.64	4Q 92	4c
Shirt, man's dress shirt		24.00	4Q 92	4c
Undervest, boy's size 10-14, cotton	3	4.08	4Q 92	4c
Communications				
Newspaper subscription, daily and Sunday home delivery, large-city	month	10.00	4Q 92	4c
Telephone, flat rate	month	7.98	91	11c
Telephone bill, family of four	month	13.52	4Q 92	4c
Energy and Fuels				
Energy, combined forms, 1,800 sq ft heating area	month	92.89	4Q 92	4c
Energy, exc electricity, 1,800 sq ft heating area	month	43.47	4Q 92	4c
Gasoline, motor	gal	1.23	4Q 92	4c
Entertainment				
Bowling, evening rate	game	1.75	4Q 92	4c
Monopoly game, Parker Brothers', No. 9		10.44	4Q 92	4c
Movie	admission	4.50	4Q 92	4c
Tennis balls, yellow, Wilson or Penn, 3	can	2.15	4Q 92	4c
Goods and Services				
ACCRA Index, Miscellaneous Goods and Services		96.00	4Q 92	4c
Groceries				
ACCRA Index, Groceries		103.40	4Q 92	4c
Babyfood, strained vegetables, lowest price	4-4.5 oz jar	0.39	4Q 92	4c
Bananas	lb	0.43	4Q 92	4c
Bread, white	24 oz	0.71	4Q 92	4c
Cheese, Kraft grated Parmesan	8-oz canister	3.89	4Q 92	4c
Chicken, fryer, whole	lb	0.94	4Q 92	4c
Cigarettes, Winston	carton	18.89	4Q 92	4c
Coffee, vacuum-packed	13-oz can	2.48	4Q 92	4c
Corn, frozen	10 oz	0.61	4Q 92	4c
Corn Flakes, Kellogg's or Post Toasties	18 oz	2.06	4Q 92	4c
Eggs, Grade A large	doz	0.85	4Q 92	4c
Ground beef or hamburger	lb	1.35	4Q 92	4c
Lettuce, iceberg	head	0.66	4Q 92	4c
Margarine, Blue Bonnet or Parkay cubes	lb	0.62	4Q 92	4c
Milk, whole	1/2 gal	1.44	4Q 92	4c
Orange juice, Minute Maid frozen	12-oz can	1.36	4Q 92	4c
Peaches	29-oz can	1.33	4Q 92	4c

Values are in dollars or fractions of dollars. In the column headed *Ref*, references are shown to sources. Each reference is followed by a letter. These refer to the geographical level for which data were reported: s = State, r = Region, and c = City or metro. The abbreviation *ex* is used to mean *except* or *excluding*; *exp* stands for *expenditures*. For other abbreviations and further explanations, please see the Introduction.

Cedar City, UT - continued

Item	Per	Value	Date	Ref.
Groceries				
Peas Sweet, Del Monte or Green Giant	15-17 oz can	0.60	4Q 92	4c
Potatoes, white or red	10-lb sack	1.39	4Q 92	4c
Sausage, Jimmy Dean, 100% pork	lb	3.10	4Q 92	4c
Shortening, vegetable, Crisco	3-lb can	2.65	4Q 92	4c
Soft drink, Coca Cola	2 liter	1.19	4Q 92	4c
Steak, T-bone	lb	4.19	4Q 92	4c
Sugar, cane or beet	4 lb	1.61	4Q 92	4c
Tomatoes, Hunt's or Del Monte	14.5-oz can	0.74	4Q 92	4c
Tuna, chunk, light	6.125-6.5 oz can	0.74	4Q 92	4c
Health Care				
ACCRA Index, Health Care		86.80	4Q 92	4c
Analgesic, Aspirin, Bayer, 325 mg tablets	100	5.59	4Q 92	4c
Dentist's fee, adult teeth cleaning and periodic oral exam	visit	45.20	4Q 92	4c
Doctor's fee, routine exam, established patient	visit	24.40	4Q 92	4c
Hospital care, semiprivate room	day	293.80	4Q 92	4c
Household Goods				
Appliance repair, home, service call, washing machine	min labor charge	25.98	4Q 92	4c
Laundry detergent, Tide Ultra, Bold, or Cheer	42 oz	3.52	4Q 92	4c
Tissues, facial, Kleenex brand	175-count box	1.22	4Q 92	4c
Housing				
ACCRA Index, Housing		80.30	4Q 92	4c
House, 1,800 sq ft, 8,000 sq ft lot, new, urban	total	92000	4Q 92	4c
House payment, principal and interest, 25% down payment	month	511	4Q 92	4c
Mortgage rate, incl. points & origination fee, 30-year fixed or adjustable rate	per-cent	8.09	4Q 92	4c
Rent, apartment, 2 bedrooms - 1-1/2 to 2 baths, unfurnished, 950 sq ft, water	month	356	4Q 92	4c
Personal Goods				
Shampoo, Alberto VO5	15 oz	1.36	4Q 92	4c
Toothpaste, Crest or Colgate	6-7 oz	2.34	4Q 92	4c
Personal Services				
Dry cleaning, man's 2-piece suit		6.62	4Q 92	4c
Haircare, woman's shampoo, trim and blow-dry		14.33	4Q 92	4c
Haircut, man's barbershop, no styling		6.17	4Q 92	4c
Restaurant Food				
Chicken, fried, thigh and drumstick		1.95	4Q 92	4c
Hamburger with cheese	1/4 lb	1.99	4Q 92	4c
Pizza, Pizza Hut or Pizza Inn, cheese, thin crust	12-13 in	7.99	4Q 92	4c
Transportation				
ACCRA Index, Transportation		98.20	4Q 92	4c
Tire balance, computer or spin balance, front	wheel	5.70	4Q 92	4c
Utilities				
ACCRA Index, Utilities		83.50	4Q 92	4c
Electricity, partial electric and other energy, 1,800 sq ft living area new home	month	49.42	4Q 92	4c

Cedar Rapids, IA

Item	Per	Value	Date	Ref.
Composite ACCRA index		99.20	4Q 92	4c
Alcoholic Beverages				
Beer, Miller Lite or Budweiser, 12-oz containers	6 pack	3.44	4Q 92	4c
Liquor, J & B Scotch	750 ml	17.27	4Q 92	4c
Wine, Gallo Chablis blanc, 1.5 liter	bottle	5.07	4Q 92	4c
Child Care				
Child care fee, average, center	hour	1.63	90	65r
Child care fee, average, nonregulated family day care	hour	1.83	90	65r
Child care fee, average, regulated family day care	hour	1.42	90	65r
Clothing				
Jeans, man's denim		28.99	4Q 92	4c
Shirt, man's dress shirt		24.80	4Q 92	4c
Undervest, boy's size 10-14, cotton	3	3.94	4Q 92	4c
Communications				
Long-distance telephone service, day, initial minute, 0-100 miles	min	0.21-0.41	91	12s
Long-distance telephone service, day, additional minute, 0-100 miles	min	0.11-0.30	91	12s
Long-distance telephone service, evenings/weekends, 0-100 mi, initial minute	min	0.11-0.20	91	12s
Long-distance telephone service, evenings/weekends, 0-100 mi, additional minute	min	0.06-0.15	91	12s
Newspaper subscription, daily and Sunday home delivery, large-city	month	13.00	4Q 92	4c
Telephone, flat rate	month	14.45	91	11c
Telephone bill, family of four	month	24.57	4Q 92	4c
Education				
Board, 4-yr private college/university	year	1703	91	22s
Board, 4-yr public college/university	year	1183	91	22s
Expenditures, local gov't, public elementary/secondary	pupil	5026	92	20s
Room, 4-year private college/university	year	1392	91	22s
Room, 4-year public college/university	year	1188	91	22s
Tuition, 2-year private college/university	year	5119	91	22s
Tuition, 2-year public college/university	year	1298	91	22s
Tuition, 4-year private college/university	year	8703	91	22s
Tuition, 4-year public college/university, in-state	year	1880	91	22s
Energy and Fuels				
Coal	mil Btu	1.16	90	64s
Energy	mil Btu	7.71	90	64s
Energy, combined forms, 1,800 sq ft heating area	month	104.12	4Q 92	4c
Energy, exc electricity, 1,800 sq ft heating area	month	35.42	4Q 92	4c
Energy exp/householder, 1-family unit	year	473	90	28r
Energy exp/householder, <1,000 sq ft heating area	year	429	90	28r
Energy exp/householder, 1,000-1,999 sq ft heating area	year	442	90	28r
Energy exp/householder, 2,000+ sq ft heating area	year	498	90	28r
Energy exp/householder, mobile home	year	442	90	28r
Energy exp/householder, multifamily	year	407	90	28r
Gas, cooking, 10 therms	month	7.66	92	56c
Gas, cooking, 30 therms	month	14.17	92	56c
Gas, cooking, 50 therms	month	20.70	92	56c
Gas, heating, winter, 100 therms	month	35.14	92	56c
Gas, heating, winter, average use	month	62.02	92	56c
Gas, natural	mil Btu	3.81	90	64s
Gas, natural	000 cu ft	4.81	91	46s
Gas, natural, exp	year	530	91	46s
Gasoline, motor	gal	1.15	4Q 92	4c
Gasoline, unleaded regular	mil Btu	9.38	90	64s

Values are in dollars or fractions of dollars. In the column headed *Ref*, references are shown to sources. Each reference is followed by a letter. These refer to the geographical level for which data were reported: s = State, r = Region, and c = City or metro. The abbreviation *ex* is used to mean *except* or *excluding*; *exp* stands for expenditures. For other abbreviations and further explanations, please see the Introduction.

Cedar Rapids, IA - continued

Item	Per	Value	Date	Ref.
Entertainment				
Bowling, evening rate	game	1.79	4Q 92	4c
Miniature golf admission	adult	6.18	92	1r
Miniature golf admission	child	5.14	92	1r
Monopoly game, Parker Brothers', No. 9		10.98	4Q 92	4c
Movie	admission	5.25	4Q 92	4c
Tennis balls, yellow, Wilson or Penn, 3	can	2.33	4Q 92	4c
Waterpark admission	adult	11.00	92	1r
Waterpark admission	child	8.55	92	1r
Funerals				
Casket, 18-gauge steel, velvet interior		1952.97	91	24r
Cosmetology, hair care, etc.		90.03	91	24r
Embalming		251.75	91	24r
Facility use for ceremony		180.75	91	24r
Hearse, local		117.51	91	24r
Limousine, local		71.86	91	24r
Remains to funeral home, transfer		81.14	91	24r
Service charge, professional		740.03	91	24r
Vault, concrete, non-metallic liner		801.47	91	24r
Viewing facilities, use		169.33	91	24r
Goods and Services				
ACCRA Index, Miscellaneous Goods and Services		99.90	4Q 92	4c
Groceries				
ACCRA Index, Groceries		94.70	4Q 92	4c
Apples, Red Delicious	lb	0.77	4/93	16r
Babyfood, strained vegetables, lowest price	4-4.5 oz jar	0.35	4Q 92	4c
Bacon	lb	1.85	4/93	16r
Bananas	lb	0.47	4Q 92	4c
Bananas	lb	0.46	4/93	16r
Beef, stew, boneless	lb	2.53	4/93	16r
Bologna, all beef or mixed	lb	2.19	4/93	16r
Bread, white	24 oz	0.57	4Q 92	4c
Bread, white, pan	lb	0.78	4/93	16r
Butter	lb	1.50	4/93	16r
Cabbage	lb	0.40	4/93	16r
Carrots, short trimmed and topped	lb	0.45	4/93	16r
Cheese, Cheddar	lb	3.47	4/93	16r
Cheese, Kraft grated Parmesan	8-oz canister	3.34	4Q 92	4c
Chicken, fresh, whole	lb	0.84	4/93	16r
Chicken, fryer, whole	lb	0.68	4Q 92	4c
Chicken breast, bone-in	lb	1.94	4/93	16r
Chicken legs, bone-in	lb	1.02	4/93	16r
Chuck roast, graded and ungraded, ex USDA prime and choice	lb	2.43	4/93	16r
Chuck roast, USDA choice, bone-in	lb	2.11	4/93	16r
Chuck roast, USDA choice, boneless	lb	2.44	4/93	16r
Cigarettes, Winston	carton	17.94	4Q 92	4c
Coffee, 100% ground roast, all sizes	lb	2.47	4/93	16r
Coffee, vacuum-packed	13-oz can	1.83	4Q 92	4c
Cookies, chocolate chip	lb	2.73	4/93	16r
Corn, frozen	10 oz	0.65	4Q 92	4c
Corn Flakes, Kellogg's or Post Toasties	18 oz	1.80	4Q 92	4c
Eggs, Grade A large	doz	0.72	4Q 92	4c
Eggs, Grade A large	doz	0.93	4/93	16r
Flour, white, all purpose	lb	0.21	4/93	16r
Grapefruit	lb	0.45	4/93	16r
Grapes, Thompson Seedless	lb	1.46	4/93	16r
Ground beef, 100% beef	lb	1.63	4/93	16r
Ground beef, lean and extra lean	lb	2.08	4/93	16r
Ground beef or hamburger	lb	1.28	4Q 92	4c
Ground chuck, 100% beef	lb	1.94	4/93	16r
Ham, boneless, excluding canned	lb	2.21	4/93	16r
Ice cream, prepackaged, bulk, regular	1/2 gal	2.41	4/93	16r
Lemons	lb	0.82	4/93	16r
Lettuce, iceberg	head	0.95	4Q 92	4c
Lettuce, iceberg	lb	0.83	4/93	16r

Cedar Rapids, IA - continued

Item	Per	Value	Date	Ref.
Groceries - continued				
Margarine, Blue Bonnet or Parkay cubes	lb	0.57	4Q 92	4c
Margarine, stick	lb	0.77	4/93	16r
Milk, whole	1/2 gal	1.21	4Q 92	4c
Orange juice, Minute Maid frozen	12-oz can	1.55	4Q 92	4c
Oranges, navel	lb	0.50	4/93	16r
Peaches	29-oz can	1.32	4Q 92	4c
Peanut butter, creamy, all sizes	lb	1.82	4/93	16r
Pears, Anjou	lb	0.85	4/93	16r
Peas Sweet, Del Monte or Green Giant	15-17 oz can	0.60	4Q 92	4c
Pork chops, center cut, bone-in	lb	3.17	4/93	16r
Potato chips	16 oz	2.68	4/93	16r
Potatoes, white	lb	0.26	4/93	16r
Potatoes, white or red	10-lb sack	2.09	4Q 92	4c
Round roast, graded & ungraded, ex USDA prime & choice	lb	2.88	4/93	16r
Round roast, USDA choice, boneless	lb	2.96	4/93	16r
Sausage, Jimmy Dean, 100% pork	lb	2.42	4Q 92	4c
Shortening, vegetable oil blends	lb	0.79	4/93	16r
Shortening, vegetable, Crisco	3-lb can	2.09	4Q 92	4c
Soft drink, Coca Cola	2 liter	1.40	4Q 92	4c
Spaghetti and macaroni	lb	0.76	4/93	16r
Steak, rib eye, USDA choice, boneless	lb	6.29	4/93	16r
Steak, round, USDA choice, boneless	lb	3.24	4/93	16r
Steak, sirloin, graded & ungraded, ex USDA prime & choice	lb	4.00	4/93	16r
Steak, sirloin, USDA choice, bone-in	lb	3.57	4/93	16r
Steak, sirloin, USDA choice, boneless	lb	4.17	4/93	16r
Steak, T-bone	lb	5.01	4Q 92	4c
Steak, T-bone, USDA choice, bone-in	lb	5.60	4/93	16r
Strawberries, dry pint	12 oz	0.90	4/93	16r
Sugar, cane or beet	4 lb	1.60	4Q 92	4c
Sugar, white	lb	0.36	4/93	16r
Sugar, white, 33-80 oz pk	lb	0.35	4/93	16r
Tomatoes, field grown	lb	0.99	4/93	16r
Tomatoes, Hunt's or Del Monte	14.5-oz can	0.68	4Q 92	4c
Tuna, chunk, light	6.125-6.5 oz can	0.55	4Q 92	4c
Tuna, chunk, light	lb	1.76	4/93	16r
Turkey, frozen, whole	lb	0.91	4/93	16r
Health Care				
ACCRA Index, Health Care		93.20	4Q 92	4c
Analgesic, Aspirin, Bayer, 325 mg tablets	100	5.10	4Q 92	4c
Childbirth, cesarean, hospital		4688	91	62r
Childbirth, cesarean, physician's fee		2053	91	62r
Childbirth, normal, hospital		2657	91	62r
Childbirth, normal, physician's fee		1492	91	62r
Dentist's fee, adult teeth cleaning and periodic oral exam	visit	47.60	4Q 92	4c
Doctor's fee, routine exam, established patient	visit	29.70	4Q 92	4c
Health care spending, state	capita	2351	3/93	84s
Hospital care, semiprivate room	day	217.66	90	27c
Hospital care, semiprivate room	day	305.50	4Q 92	4c
Medical insurance premium, per employee, small group comprehensive	month	267.40	10/91	25c
Medical plan per employee	year	3443	91	45r
Mental health care, exp	capita	20.37-28.83	90	38s
Mental health care, exp, state mental health agency	capita	17.07	90	38s
Mental health care, hospital psychiatric services, non-Federal, exp	capita	23.51	88	38s
Mental health care, mental health organization, multiservice, exp	capita	7.66	88	38s

Values are in dollars or fractions of dollars. In the column headed *Ref*, references are shown to sources. Each reference is followed by a letter. These refer to the geographical level for which data were reported: s=State, r=Region, and c=City or metro. The abbreviation *ex* is used to mean *except* or *excluding*; *exp* stands for expenditures. For other abbreviations and further explanations, please see the Introduction.

Cedar Rapids, IA - continued

Item	Per	Value	Date	Ref.
Health Care				
Mental health care, psychiatric hospitals, private, exp	capita	2.86	88	38s
Mental health care, psychiatric out-patient clinics, freestanding, exp	capita	3.02	88	38s
Mental health care, state and county mental hospitals, exp	capita	14.54	88	38s
Mental health care, VA medical centers, exp	capita	13.98	88	38s
Physician fee, family practice, first-visit		76.00	91	62r
Physician fee, family practice, revisit		33.00	91	62r
Physician fee, general practice, first-visit		61.00	91	62r
Physician fee, general practice, revisit		31.00	91	62r
Physician fee, general surgeon, first-visit		65.00	91	62r
Physician fee, general surgeon, revisit		35.00	91	62r
Physician fee, internal medicine, first-visit		91.00	91	62r
Physician fee, internal medicine, revisit		40.00	91	62r
Physician fee, median, neurosurgeon, first-visit		106.00	91	62r
Physician fee, median, nonsurgical specialist, first-visit		90.00	91	62r
Physician fee, median, orthopedic surgeon, first-visit		83.00	91	62r
Physician fee, median, surgical specialist, first-visit		61.00	91	62r
Physician fee, neurosurgeon, revisit		41.00	91	62r
Physician fee, nonsurgical specialist, revisit		40.00	91	62r
Physician fee, obstetrics/gynecology, first-visit		61.00	91	62r
Physician fee, obstetrics/gynecology, revisit		40.00	91	62r
Physician fee, orthopedic surgeon, revisit		41.00	91	62r
Physician fee, pediatrician, first-visit		46.00	91	62r
Physician fee, pediatrician, revisit		33.00	91	62r
Physician fee, surgical specialist, revisit		36.00	91	62r
Substance abuse, hospital ancillary charge	incident	950	90	70s
Substance abuse, hospital physician charge	incident	250	90	70s
Substance abuse, hospital room and board	incident	3110	90	70s
Household Goods				
Appliance repair, home, service call, washing machine	min labor charge	32.46	4Q 92	4c
Laundry detergent, Tide Ultra, Bold, or Cheer	42 oz	2.94	4Q 92	4c
Tissues, facial, Kleenex brand	175-count box	1.12	4Q 92	4c
Housing				
ACCRA Index, Housing		104.80	4Q 92	4c
Home, median price	unit	71.90		26c
House, 1,800 sq ft, 8,000 sq ft lot, new, urban	total	118838	4Q 92	4c
House payment, principal and interest, 25% down payment	month	676	4Q 92	4c
Mortgage rate, incl. points & origination fee, 30-year fixed or adjustable rate	percent	8.36	4Q 92	4c
Rent, apartment, 2 bedrooms - 1-1/2 to 2 baths, unfurnished, 950 sq ft, water	month	444	4Q 92	4c
Rental unit, 1 bedroom	month	433	93	23c
Rental unit, 2 bedroom	month	510	93	23c
Rental unit, 3 bedroom	month	640	93	23c
Rental unit, 4 bedroom	month	719	93	23c
Rental unit, efficiency	month	359	93	23c
Insurance and Pensions				
Auto insurance, private passenger	year	422.46	91	63s
Personal Goods				
Shampoo, Alberto VO5	15 oz	1.38	4Q 92	4c
Toothpaste, Crest or Colgate	6-7 oz	1.77	4Q 92	4c

Cedar Rapids, IA - continued

Item	Per	Value	Date	Ref.
Personal Services				
Dry cleaning, man's 2-piece suit		6.99	4Q 92	4c
Haircare, woman's shampoo, trim and blow-dry		18.49	4Q 92	4c
Haircut, man's barbershop, no styling		7.50	4Q 92	4c
Restaurant Food				
Chicken, fried, thigh and drumstick		2.30	4Q 92	4c
Hamburger with cheese	1/4 lb	1.89	4Q 92	4c
Pizza, Pizza Hut or Pizza Inn, cheese, thin crust	12-13 in	7.95	4Q 92	4c
Taxes				
Tax, cigarette	pack	36	91	77s
Tax, gasoline	gal	20	91	77s
Taxes, state	capita	1233	91	77s
Transportation				
ACCRA Index, Transportation		90.50	4Q 92	4c
Driver's license fee		16.00	12/90	43s
Tire balance, computer or spin balance, front	wheel	5.20	4Q 92	4c
Utilities				
ACCRA Index, Utilities		98.50	4Q 92	4c
Electricity	mil Btu	17.37	90	64s
Electricity, partial electric and other energy, 1,800 sq ft living area new home	month	68.70	4Q 92	4c
Electricity, winter, 250 KWh	month	33.05	92	55c
Electricity, winter, 250 KWh	month	33.18	2/93	30c
Electricity, winter, 500 KWh	month	52.86	92	55c
Electricity, winter, 500 KWh	month	53.11	2/93	30c
Electricity, winter, 750 KWh	month	69.83	92	55c
Electricity, winter, 750 KWh	month	70.21	2/93	30c
Electricity, winter, 1000 KWh	month	86.81	92	55c
Electricity, winter, 1000 KWh	month	87.31	2/93	30c

Centralia, IL

Item	Per	Value	Date	Ref.
Composite ACCRA index		99.30	4Q 92	4c
Alcoholic Beverages				
Beer, Miller Lite or Budweiser, 12-oz containers	6 pack	3.95	4Q 92	4c
Liquor, J & B Scotch	750 ml	16.32	4Q 92	4c
Wine, Gallo Chablis blanc, 1.5 liter	bottle	5.32	4Q 92	4c
Clothing				
Jeans, man's denim		37.64	4Q 92	4c
Shirt, man's dress shirt		24.00	4Q 92	4c
Undervest, boy's size 10-14, cotton	3	3.31	4Q 92	4c
Communications				
Newspaper subscription, daily and Sunday home delivery, large-city	month	14.05	4Q 92	4c
Telephone bill, family of four	month	21.99	4Q 92	4c
Energy and Fuels				
Energy, combined forms, 1,800 sq ft heating area	month	132.72	4Q 92	4c
Energy, exc electricity, 1,800 sq ft heating area	month	42.00	4Q 92	4c
Gasoline, motor	gal	1.14	4Q 92	4c
Entertainment				
Bowling, evening rate	game	1.75	4Q 92	4c
Monopoly game, Parker Brothers', No. 9		9.63	4Q 92	4c
Movie	admission	5.75	4Q 92	4c
Tennis balls, yellow, Wilson or Penn, 3	can	1.98	4Q 92	4c
Goods and Services				
ACCRA Index, Miscellaneous Goods and Services		99.90	4Q 92	4c
Groceries				
ACCRA Index, Groceries		104.80	4Q 92	4c

Values are in dollars or fractions of dollars. In the column headed *Ref*, references are shown to sources. Each reference is followed by a letter. These refer to the geographical level for which data were reported: s = State, r = Region, and c = City or metro. The abbreviation *ex* is used to mean *except* or *excluding*; *exp* stands for expenditures. For other abbreviations and further explanations, please see the Introduction.

Centralia, IL - continued

Item	Per	Value	Date	Ref.
Groceries				
Babyfood, strained vegetables, lowest price	4-4.5 oz jar	0.30	4Q 92	4c
Bananas	lb	0.52	4Q 92	4c
Bread, white	24 oz	0.67	4Q 92	4c
Cheese, Kraft grated Parmesan	8-oz canister	3.58	4Q 92	4c
Chicken, fryer, whole	lb	0.75	4Q 92	4c
Cigarettes, Winston	carton	17.87	4Q 92	4c
Coffee, vacuum-packed	13-oz can	2.32	4Q 92	4c
Corn, frozen	10 oz	0.72	4Q 92	4c
Corn Flakes, Kellogg's or Post Toasties	18 oz	2.00	4Q 92	4c
Eggs, Grade A large	doz	0.88	4Q 92	4c
Ground beef or hamburger	lb	1.65	4Q 92	4c
Lettuce, iceberg	head	0.86	4Q 92	4c
Margarine, Blue Bonnet or Parkay cubes	lb	0.77	4Q 92	4c
Milk, whole	1/2 gal	1.56	4Q 92	4c
Orange juice, Minute Maid frozen	12-oz can	1.58	4Q 92	4c
Peaches	29-oz can	1.48	4Q 92	4c
Peas Sweet, Del Monte or Green Giant	15-17 oz can	0.71	4Q 92	4c
Potatoes, white or red	10-lb sack	2.26	4Q 92	4c
Sausage, Jimmy Dean, 100% pork	lb	2.39	4Q 92	4c
Shortening, vegetable, Crisco	3-lb can	2.12	4Q 92	4c
Soft drink, Coca Cola	2 liter	1.22	4Q 92	4c
Steak, T-bone	lb	5.42	4Q 92	4c
Sugar, cane or beet	4 lb	1.25	4Q 92	4c
Tomatoes, Hunt's or Del Monte	14.5-oz can	0.74	4Q 92	4c
Tuna, chunk, light	6.125-6.5 oz can	0.76	4Q 92	4c
Health Care				
ACCRA Index, Health Care		86.10	4Q 92	4c
Analgesic, Aspirin, Bayer, 325 mg tablets	100	5.26	4Q 92	4c
Dentist's fee, adult teeth cleaning and periodic oral exam	visit	37.50	4Q 92	4c
Doctor's fee, routine exam, established patient	visit	30.32	4Q 92	4c
Hospital care, semiprivate room	day	256.70	90	27c
Hospital care, semiprivate room	day	298.00	4Q 92	4c
Household Goods				
Appliance repair, home, service call, washing machine	min labor charge	35.36	4Q 92	4c
Laundry detergent, Tide Ultra, Bold, or Cheer	42 oz	4.12	4Q 92	4c
Tissues, facial, Kleenex brand	175-count box	1.17	4Q 92	4c
Housing				
ACCRA Index, Housing		91.90	4Q 92	4c
House, 1,800 sq ft, 8,000 sq ft lot, new, urban	total	101500	4Q 92	4c
House payment, principal and interest, 25% down payment	month	581	4Q 92	4c
Mortgage rate, incl. points & origination fee, 30-year fixed or adjustable rate	percent	8.43	4Q 92	4c
Rent, apartment, 2 bedrooms - 1-1/2 to 2 baths, unfurnished, 950 sq ft, water	month	415	4Q 92	4c
Personal Goods				
Shampoo, Alberto VO5	15 oz	1.39	4Q 92	4c
Toothpaste, Crest or Colgate	6-7 oz	2.29	4Q 92	4c

Centralia, IL - continued

Item	Per	Value	Date	Ref.
Personal Services				
Dry cleaning, man's 2-piece suit		4.72	4Q 92	4c
Haircare, woman's shampoo, trim and blow-dry		14.67	4Q 92	4c
Haircut, man's barbershop, no styling		7.50	4Q 92	4c
Restaurant Food				
Chicken, fried, thigh and drumstick		2.29	4Q 92	4c
Hamburger with cheese	1/4 lb	1.89	4Q 92	4c
Pizza, Pizza Hut or Pizza Inn, cheese, thin crust	12-13 in	7.99	4Q 92	4c
Transportation				
ACCRA Index, Transportation		97.70	4Q 92	4c
Tire balance, computer or spin balance, front	wheel	6.16	4Q 92	4c
Utilities				
ACCRA Index, Utilities		120.70	4Q 92	4c
Electricity, partial electric and other energy, 1,800 sq ft living area new home	month	90.72	4Q 92	4c

Champaign-Urbana, IL

Item	Per	Value	Date	Ref.
Alcoholic Beverages				
Beer, Miller Lite or Budweiser, 12-oz containers	6 pack	3.70	4Q 92	4c
Liquor, J & B Scotch	750 ml	13.99	4Q 92	4c
Wine, Gallo Chablis blanc, 1.5 liter	bottle	3.99	4Q 92	4c
Child Care				
Child care fee, average, center	hour	1.63	90	65r
Child care fee, average, nonregulated family day care	hour	1.83	90	65r
Child care fee, average, regulated family day care	hour	1.42	90	65r
Clothing				
Jeans, man's denim		30.99	4Q 92	4c
Shirt, man's dress shirt		26.00	4Q 92	4c
Undervest, boy's size 10-14, cotton	3	3.59	4Q 92	4c
Communications				
Long-distance telephone service, day, initial minute, 0-100 miles	min	0.10-0.34	91	12s
Long-distance telephone service, day, additional minute, 0-100 miles	min	0.04-0.16	91	12s
Long-distance telephone service, evenings/weekends, 0-100 mi, initial minute	min	0.06-0.20	91	12s
Long-distance telephone service, evenings/weekends, 0-100 mi, additional minute	min	0.02-0.10	91	12s
Newspaper subscription, daily and Sunday home delivery, large-city	month	11.52	4Q 92	4c
Telephone bill, family of four	month	21.69	4Q 92	4c
Education				
Board, 4-yr private college/university	year	1797	91	22s
Board, 4-yr public college/university	year	1857	91	22s
Expenditures, local gov't, public elementary/secondary	pupil	5248	92	20s
Room, 4-year private college/university	year	2095	91	22s
Room, 4-year public college/university	year	1454	91	22s
Tuition, 2-year private college/university	year	5279	91	22s
Tuition, 2-year public college/university	year	906	91	22s
Tuition, 4-year private college/university	year	8853	91	22s
Tuition, 4-year public college/university, in-state	year	2465	91	22s
Energy and Fuels				
Coal	mil Btu	1.72	90	64s
Energy	mil Btu	8.74	90	64s
Energy, combined forms, 1,800 sq ft heating area	month	122.42	4Q 92	4c
Energy, exc electricity, 1,800 sq ft heating area	month	41.52	4Q 92	4c
Energy exp/householder, 1-family unit	year	471	90	28r

Values are in dollars or fractions of dollars. In the column headed *Ref*, references are shown to sources. Each reference is followed by a letter. These refer to the geographical level for which data were reported: s=State, r=Region, and c=City or metro. The abbreviation *ex* is used to mean *except* or *excluding*; *exp* stands for expenditures. For other abbreviations and further explanations, please see the Introduction.

Champaign-Urbana, IL - continued

Item	Per	Value	Date	Ref.
Energy and Fuels				
Energy exp/householder, <1,000 sq ft heating area	year	430	90	28r
Energy exp/householder, 1,000-1,999 sq ft heating area	year	481	90	28r
Energy exp/householder, 2,000+ sq ft heating area	year	473	90	28r
Energy exp/householder, mobile home	year	430	90	28r
Energy exp/householder, multifamily	year	461	90	28r
Gas, natural	mil Btu	4.57	90	64s
Gas, natural	000 cu ft	4.95	91	46s
Gas, natural, exp	year	696	91	46s
Gasoline, motor	gal	1.16	4Q 92	4c
Gasoline, unleaded regular	mil Btu	9.35	90	64s
Entertainment				
Bowling, evening rate	game	2.20	4Q 92	4c
Miniature golf admission	adult	6.18	92	1r
Miniature golf admission	child	5.14	92	1r
Monopoly game, Parker Brothers', No. 9		11.98	4Q 92	4c
Movie	admission	5.33	4Q 92	4c
Tennis balls, yellow, Wilson or Penn, 3	can	2.03	4Q 92	4c
Waterpark admission	adult	11.00	92	1r
Waterpark admission	child	8.55	92	1r
Funerals				
Casket, 18-gauge steel, velvet interior		1926.72	91	24r
Cosmetology, hair care, etc.		97.64	91	24r
Embalming		249.14	91	24r
Facility use for ceremony		208.59	91	24r
Hearse, local		130.12	91	24r
Limousine, local		104.66	91	24r
Remains to funeral home, transfer		93.61	91	24r
Service charge, professional		724.62	91	24r
Vault, concrete, non-metallic liner		734.53	91	24r
Viewing facilities, use		236.06	91	24r
Groceries				
Apples, Red Delicious	lb	0.77	4/93	16r
Babyfood, strained vegetables, lowest price	4-4.5 oz jar	0.34	4Q 92	4c
Bacon	lb	1.85	4/93	16r
Bananas	lb	0.40	4Q 92	4c
Bananas	lb	0.46	4/93	16r
Beef, stew, boneless	lb	2.53	4/93	16r
Bologna, all beef or mixed	lb	2.19	4/93	16r
Bread, white	24 oz	0.77	4Q 92	4c
Bread, white, pan	lb	0.78	4/93	16r
Butter	lb	1.50	4/93	16r
Cabbage	lb	0.40	4/93	16r
Carrots, short trimmed and topped	lb	0.45	4/93	16r
Cheese, Cheddar	lb	3.47	4/93	16r
Cheese, Kraft grated Parmesan	8-oz canister	3.18	4Q 92	4c
Chicken, fresh, whole	lb	0.84	4/93	16r
Chicken, fryer, whole	lb	0.66	4Q 92	4c
Chicken breast, bone-in	lb	1.94	4/93	16r
Chicken legs, bone-in	lb	1.02	4/93	16r
Chuck roast, graded and ungraded, ex USDA prime and choice	lb	2.43	4/93	16r
Chuck roast, USDA choice, bone-in	lb	2.11	4/93	16r
Chuck roast, USDA choice, boneless	lb	2.44	4/93	16r
Cigarettes, Winston	carton	17.99	4Q 92	4c
Coffee, 100% ground roast, all sizes	lb	2.47	4/93	16r
Coffee, vacuum-packed	13-oz can	2.00	4Q 92	4c
Cookies, chocolate chip	lb	2.73	4/93	16r
Corn, frozen	10 oz	0.71	4Q 92	4c
Corn Flakes, Kellogg's or Post Toasties	18 oz	1.92	4Q 92	4c
Eggs, Grade A large	doz	0.82	4Q 92	4c
Eggs, Grade A large	doz	0.93	4/93	16r
Flour, white, all purpose	lb	0.21	4/93	16r

Item	Per	Value	Date	Ref.
Groceries - continued				
Grapefruit	lb	0.45	4/93	16r
Grapes, Thompson Seedless	lb	1.46	4/93	16r
Ground beef, 100% beef	lb	1.63	4/93	16r
Ground beef, lean and extra lean	lb	2.08	4/93	16r
Ground beef or hamburger	lb	1.31	4Q 92	4c
Ground chuck, 100% beef	lb	1.94	4/93	16r
Ham, boneless, excluding canned	lb	2.21	4/93	16r
Honey, jar	8 oz	0.97-1.25	92	5r
Honey, jar	lb	1.25-2.25	92	5r
Honey, squeeze bear	12-oz	1.25-1.99	92	5r
Ice cream, prepackaged, bulk, regular	1/2 gal	2.41	4/93	16r
Lemons	lb	0.82	4/93	16r
Lettuce, iceberg	head	1.02	4Q 92	4c
Lettuce, iceberg	lb	0.83	4/93	16r
Margarine, Blue Bonnet or Parkay cubes	lb	0.68	4Q 92	4c
Margarine, stick	lb	0.77	4/93	16r
Milk, whole	1/2 gal	1.52	4Q 92	4c
Orange juice, Minute Maid frozen	12-oz can	1.18	4Q 92	4c
Oranges, navel	lb	0.50	4/93	16r
Peaches	29-oz can	1.43	4Q 92	4c
Peanut butter, creamy, all sizes	lb	1.82	4/93	16r
Pears, Anjou	lb	0.85	4/93	16r
Peas Sweet, Del Monte or Green Giant	15-17 oz can	0.60	4Q 92	4c
Pork chops, center cut, bone-in	lb	3.17	4/93	16r
Potato chips	16 oz	2.68	4/93	16r
Potatoes, white	lb	0.26	4/93	16r
Potatoes, white or red	10-lb sack	2.25	4Q 92	4c
Round roast, graded & ungraded, ex USDA prime & choice	lb	2.88	4/93	16r
Round roast, USDA choice, boneless	lb	2.96	4/93	16r
Sausage, Jimmy Dean, 100% pork	lb	2.59	4Q 92	4c
Shortening, vegetable oil blends	lb	0.79	4/93	16r
Shortening, vegetable, Crisco	3-lb can	2.34	4Q 92	4c
Soft drink, Coca Cola	2 liter	1.21	4Q 92	4c
Spaghetti and macaroni	lb	0.76	4/93	16r
Steak, rib eye, USDA choice, boneless	lb	6.29	4/93	16r
Steak, round, USDA choice, boneless	lb	3.24	4/93	16r
Steak, sirloin, graded & ungraded, ex USDA prime & choice	lb	4.00	4/93	16r
Steak, sirloin, USDA choice, bone-in	lb	3.57	4/93	16r
Steak, sirloin, USDA choice, boneless	lb	4.17	4/93	16r
Steak, T-bone	lb	5.37	4Q 92	4c
Steak, T-bone, USDA choice, bone-in	lb	5.60	4/93	16r
Strawberries, dry pint	12 oz	0.90	4/93	16r
Sugar, cane or beet	4 lb	1.35	4Q 92	4c
Sugar, white	lb	0.36	4/93	16r
Sugar, white, 33-80 oz pk	lb	0.35	4/93	16r
Tomatoes, field grown	lb	0.99	4/93	16r
Tomatoes, Hunt's or Del Monte	14.5-oz can	0.74	4Q 92	4c
Tuna, chunk, light	6.125-6.5 oz can	0.61	4Q 92	4c
Tuna, chunk, light	lb	1.76	4/93	16r
Turkey, frozen, whole	lb	0.91	4/93	16r
Health Care				
Analgesic, Aspirin, Bayer, 325 mg tablets	100	5.75	4Q 92	4c
Childbirth, cesarean, hospital		4688	91	62r
Childbirth, cesarean, physician's fee		2053	91	62r
Childbirth, normal, hospital		2657	91	62r
Childbirth, normal, physician's fee		1492	91	62r
Dentist's fee, adult teeth cleaning and periodic oral exam	visit	51.00	4Q 92	4c
Doctor's fee, routine exam, established patient	visit	34.06	4Q 92	4c
Hospital care, semiprivate room	day	283.90	90	27c
Hospital care, semiprivate room	day	393.00	4Q 92	4c

Values are in dollars or fractions of dollars. In the column headed *Ref*, references are shown to sources. Each reference is followed by a letter. These refer to the geographical level for which data were reported: s=State, r=Region, and c=City or metro. The abbreviation *ex* is used to mean *except* or *excluding*; *exp* stands for expenditures. For other abbreviations and further explanations, please see the Introduction.

Champaign-Urbana, IL - continued

Item	Per	Value	Date	Ref.
Health Care				
Medical insurance premium, per employee, small group comprehensive	month	313.90	10/91	25c
Medical plan per employee	year	3443	91	45r
Mental health care, exp	capita	28.84-37.59	90	38s
Mental health care, exp, state mental health agency	capita	34.43	90	38s
Mental health care, hospital psychiatric services, non-Federal, exp	capita	18.46	88	38s
Mental health care, mental health organization, multiservice, exp	capita	11.97	88	38s
Mental health care, psychiatric hospitals, private, exp	capita	7.84	88	38s
Mental health care, psychiatric out-patient clinics, freestanding, exp	capita	3.21	88	38s
Mental health care, psychiatric partial-care organizations, freestanding, exp	capita	0.51	88	38s
Mental health care, state and county mental hospitals, exp	capita	18.11	88	38s
Mental health care, VA medical centers, exp	capita	3.69	88	38s
Physician fee, family practice, first-visit		76.00	91	62r
Physician fee, family practice, revisit		33.00	91	62r
Physician fee, general practice, first-visit		61.00	91	62r
Physician fee, general practice, revisit		31.00	91	62r
Physician fee, general surgeon, first-visit		65.00	91	62r
Physician fee, general surgeon, revisit		35.00	91	62r
Physician fee, internal medicine, first-visit		91.00	91	62r
Physician fee, internal medicine, revisit		40.00	91	62r
Physician fee, median, neurosurgeon, first-visit		106.00	91	62r
Physician fee, median, nonsurgical specialist, first-visit		90.00	91	62r
Physician fee, median, orthopedic surgeon, first-visit		83.00	91	62r
Physician fee, median, surgical specialist, first-visit		61.00	91	62r
Physician fee, neurosurgeon, revisit		41.00	91	62r
Physician fee, nonsurgical specialist, revisit		40.00	91	62r
Physician fee, obstetrics/gynecology, first-visit		61.00	91	62r
Physician fee, obstetrics/gynecology, revisit		40.00	91	62r
Physician fee, orthopedic surgeon, revisit		41.00	91	62r
Physician fee, pediatrician, first-visit		46.00	91	62r
Physician fee, pediatrician, revisit		33.00	91	62r
Physician fee, surgical specialist, revisit		36.00	91	62r
Prescription drug co-pay, Medicaid	month	25.00	91	21s
Substance abuse, hospital ancillary charge	incident	1310	90	70s
Substance abuse, hospital physician charge	incident	540	90	70s
Substance abuse, hospital room and board	incident	6150	90	70s
Household Goods				
Appliance repair, home, service call, washing machine	min labor charge	30.12	4Q 92	4c
Laundry detergent, Tide Ultra, Bold, or Cheer	42 oz	3.77	4Q 92	4c
Tissues, facial, Kleenex brand	175-count box	1.02	4Q 92	4c
Housing				
Home, median price	unit	66.60		26c
House, 1,800 sq ft, 8,000 sq ft lot, new, urban	total	105955	4Q 92	4c
House payment, principal and interest, 25% down payment	month	596	4Q 92	4c
Mortgage rate, incl. points & origination fee, 30-year fixed or adjustable rate	percent	8.23	4Q 92	4c
Rent, apartment, 2 bedrooms - 1-1/2 to 2 baths, unfurnished, 950 sq ft, water	month	480	4Q 92	4c

Champaign-Urbana, IL - continued

Item	Per	Value	Date	Ref.
Housing - continued				
Rental unit, 1 bedroom	month	403	93	23c
Rental unit, 2 bedroom	month	476	93	23c
Rental unit, 3 bedroom	month	598	93	23c
Rental unit, 4 bedroom	month	668	93	23c
Rental unit, efficiency	month	332	93	23c
Insurance and Pensions				
Auto insurance, private passenger	year	621.37	91	63s
Personal Goods				
Shampoo, Alberto VO5	15 oz	1.51	4Q 92	4c
Toothpaste, Crest or Colgate	6-7 oz	2.04	4Q 92	4c
Personal Services				
Dry cleaning, man's 2-piece suit		7.11	4Q 92	4c
Haircare, woman's shampoo, trim and blow-dry		20.04	4Q 92	4c
Haircut, man's barbershop, no styling		9.50	4Q 92	4c
Restaurant Food				
Chicken, fried, thigh and drumstick		1.98	4Q 92	4c
Hamburger with cheese	1/4 lb	1.75	4Q 92	4c
Pizza, Pizza Hut or Pizza Inn, cheese, thin crust	12-13 in	7.79	4Q 92	4c
Taxes				
Tax, cigarette	pack	30	91	77s
Tax, gasoline	gal	19	91	77s
Taxes, state	capita	1151	91	77s
Transportation				
Bus fare	one-way	0.75	3/93	2c
Bus fare, up to 10 miles	one-way	0.75	4Q 92	4c
Driver's license fee		10.00	12/90	43s
Tire balance, computer or spin balance, front	wheel	6.62	4Q 92	4c
Vehicle registration and license plate	multi-year	48.00	93	52s
Utilities				
Electricity	mil Btu	22.02	90	64s
Electricity, partial electric and other energy, 1,800 sq ft living area new home	month	80.90	4Q 92	4c

Chapel Hill, NC

Item	Per	Value	Date	Ref.
Alcoholic Beverages				
Beer, Miller Lite or Budweiser, 12-oz containers	6 pack	3.73	4Q 92	4c
Liquor, J & B Scotch	750 ml	17.65	4Q 92	4c
Wine, Gallo Chablis blanc, 1.5 liter	bottle	5.32	4Q 92	4c
Clothing				
Jeans, man's denim		37.00	4Q 92	4c
Shirt, man's dress shirt		22.50	4Q 92	4c
Undervest, boy's size 10-14, cotton	3	5.42	4Q 92	4c
Communications				
Newspaper subscription, daily and Sunday home delivery, large-city	month	11.00	4Q 92	4c
Telephone bill, family of four	month	18.33	4Q 92	4c
Energy and Fuels				
Energy, combined forms, 1,800 sq ft heating area	month	119.35	4Q 92	4c
Gasoline, motor	gal	1.12	4Q 92	4c
Entertainment				
Bowling, evening rate	game	0.89	4Q 92	4c
Monopoly game, Parker Brothers', No. 9		11.99	4Q 92	4c
Movie	admission	5.00	4Q 92	4c
Tennis balls, yellow, Wilson or Penn, 3	can	2.60	4Q 92	4c

Values are in dollars or fractions of dollars. In the column headed *Ref*, references are shown to sources. Each reference is followed by a letter. These refer to the geographical level for which data were reported: s = State, r = Region, and c = City or metro. The abbreviation *ex* is used to mean *except* or *excluding*; *exp* stands for expenditures. For other abbreviations and further explanations, please see the Introduction.

Chapel Hill, NC - continued

Item	Per	Value	Date	Ref.
Groceries				
Babyfood, strained vegetables, lowest price	4-4.5 oz jar	0.32	4Q 92	4c
Bananas	lb	0.48	4Q 92	4c
Bread, white	24 oz	0.54	4Q 92	4c
Cheese, Kraft grated Parmesan	8-oz canister	3.26	4Q 92	4c
Chicken, fryer, whole	lb	0.72	4Q 92	4c
Cigarettes, Winston	carton	14.58	4Q 92	4c
Coffee, vacuum-packed	13-oz can	1.90	4Q 92	4c
Corn, frozen	10 oz	0.71	4Q 92	4c
Corn Flakes, Kellogg's or Post Toasties	18 oz	1.79	4Q 92	4c
Eggs, Grade A large	doz	0.83	4Q 92	4c
Ground beef or hamburger	lb	1.28	4Q 92	4c
Lettuce, iceberg	head	0.96	4Q 92	4c
Margarine, Blue Bonnet or Parkay cubes	lb	0.50	4Q 92	4c
Milk, whole	1/2 gal	1.56	4Q 92	4c
Orange juice, Minute Maid frozen	12-oz can	1.30	4Q 92	4c
Peaches	29-oz can	1.35	4Q 92	4c
Peas Sweet, Del Monte or Green Giant	15-17 oz can	0.62	4Q 92	4c
Potatoes, white or red	10-lb sack	1.99	4Q 92	4c
Sausage, Jimmy Dean, 100% pork	lb	2.09	4Q 92	4c
Shortening, vegetable, Crisco	3-lb can	1.99	4Q 92	4c
Soft drink, Coca Cola	2 liter	1.15	4Q 92	4c
Steak, T-bone	lb	5.99	4Q 92	4c
Sugar, cane or beet	4 lb	1.51	4Q 92	4c
Tomatoes, Hunt's or Del Monte	14.5-oz can	0.55	4Q 92	4c
Tuna, chunk, light	6.125-6.5 oz can	0.69	4Q 92	4c
Health Care				
Analgesic, Aspirin, Bayer, 325 mg tablets	100	5.90	4Q 92	4c
Dentist's fee, adult teeth cleaning and periodic oral exam	visit	58.67	4Q 92	4c
Doctor's fee, routine exam, established patient	visit	32.67	4Q 92	4c
Hospital care, semiprivate room	day	385.00	4Q 92	4c
Household Goods				
Appliance repair, home, service call, washing machine	min labor charge	35.00	4Q 92	4c
Laundry detergent, Tide Ultra, Bold, or Cheer	42 oz	2.58	4Q 92	4c
Tissues, facial, Kleenex brand	175-count box	0.98	4Q 92	4c
Housing				
House, 1,800 sq ft, 8,000 sq ft lot, new, urban	total	126333	4Q 92	4c
House payment, principal and interest, 25% down payment	month	694	4Q 92	4c
Mortgage rate, incl. points & origination fee, 30-year fixed or adjustable rate	percent	7.98	4Q 92	4c
Rent, apartment, 2 bedrooms - 1-1/2 to 2 baths, unfurnished, 950 sq ft, water	month	527	4Q 92	4c
Personal Goods				
Shampoo, Alberto VO5	15 oz	1.26	4Q 92	4c
Toothpaste, Crest or Colgate	6-7 oz	1.99	4Q 92	4c
Personal Services				
Dry cleaning, man's 2-piece suit		6.72	4Q 92	4c
Haircare, woman's shampoo, trim and blow-dry		21.75	4Q 92	4c

Chapel Hill, NC - continued

Item	Per	Value	Date	Ref.
Personal Services - continued				
Haircut, man's barbershop, no styling		9.20	4Q 92	4c
Restaurant Food				
Chicken, fried, thigh and drumstick		1.89	4Q 92	4c
Hamburger with cheese	1/4 lb	1.89	4Q 92	4c
Pizza, Pizza Hut or Pizza Inn, cheese, thin crust	12-13 in	7.74	4Q 92	4c
Transportation				
Bus fare, up to 10 miles	one-way	0.60	4Q 92	4c
Tire balance, computer or spin balance, front	wheel	6.33	4Q 92	4c
Utilities				
Electricity, all electric, 1,800 sq ft living area new home	month	119.35	4Q 92	4c

Charleston, SC

Item	Per	Value	Date	Ref.
Alcoholic Beverages				
Beer, Miller Lite or Budweiser, 12-oz containers	6 pack	4.03	4Q 92	4c
Liquor, J & B Scotch	750 ml	15.75	4Q 92	4c
Wine, Gallo Chablis blanc, 1.5 liter	bottle	5.09	4Q 92	4c
Child Care				
Child care fee, average, center	hour	1.29	90	65r
Child care fee, average, nonregulated family day care	hour	0.89	90	65r
Child care fee, average, regulated family day care	hour	1.32	90	65r
Clothing				
Jeans, man's denim		29.17	4Q 92	4c
Shirt, man's dress shirt		24.00	4Q 92	4c
Undervest, boy's size 10-14, cotton	3	5.63	4Q 92	4c
Communications				
Long-distance telephone service, day, initial minute, 0-100 miles	min	0.24-0.52	91	12s
Long-distance telephone service, day, additional minute, 0-100 miles	min	0.13-0.35	91	12s
Long-distance telephone service, evenings/weekends, 0-100 mi, initial minute	min	0.12-0.26	91	12s
Long-distance telephone service, evenings/weekends, 0-100 mi, additional minute	min	0.07-0.16	91	12s
Newspaper subscription, daily and Sunday home delivery, large-city	month	8.95	4Q 92	4c
Telephone, flat rate	month	16.90	91	11c
Telephone bill, family of four	month	25.96	4Q 92	4c
Education				
Board, 4-yr private college/university	year	1468	91	22s
Board, 4-yr public college/university	year	1632	91	22s
Expenditures, local gov't, public elementary/secondary	pupil	4312	92	20s
Room, 4-year private college/university	year	1393	91	22s
Room, 4-year public college/university	year	1492	91	22s
Tuition, 2-year private college/university	year	5110	91	22s
Tuition, 2-year public college/university	year	813	91	22s
Tuition, 4-year private college/university	year	6434	91	22s
Tuition, 4-year public college/university, in-state	year	2317	91	22s
Energy and Fuels				
Coal	mil Btu	1.73	90	64s
Energy	mil Btu	8.93	90	64s
Energy, combined forms, 1,800 sq ft heating area	month	100.89	4Q 92	4c
Energy exp/householder, 1-family unit	year	487	90	28r
Energy exp/householder, <1,000 sq ft heating area	year	393	90	28r
Energy exp/householder, 1,000-1,999 sq ft heating area	year	442	90	28r

Values are in dollars or fractions of dollars. In the column headed *Ref*, references are shown to sources. Each reference is followed by a letter. These refer to the geographical level for which data were reported: s = State, r = Region, and c = City or metro. The abbreviation *ex* is used to mean *except* or *excluding*; *exp* stands for expenditures. For other abbreviations and further explanations, please see the Introduction.

Charleston, SC - continued

Item	Per	Value	Date	Ref.
Energy and Fuels				
Energy exp/householder, 2,000+ sq ft heating area	year	577	90	28r
Energy exp/householder, mobile home	year	366	90	28r
Energy exp/householder, multifamily	year	382	90	28r
Gas, natural	mil Btu	4.01	90	64s
Gas, natural	000 cu ft	6.98	91	46s
Gas, natural, exp	year	397	91	46s
Gasoline, motor	gal	1.05	4Q 92	4c
Gasoline, unleaded regular	mil Btu	8.80	90	64s
Entertainment				
Bowling, evening rate	game	2.32	4Q 92	4c
Miniature golf admission	adult	6.18	92	1r
Miniature golf admission	child	5.14	92	1r
Monopoly game, Parker Brothers', No. 9		11.98	4Q 92	4c
Movie	admission	5.65	4Q 92	4c
Tennis balls, yellow, Wilson or Penn, 3	can	2.42	4Q 92	4c
Waterpark admission	adult	11.00	92	1r
Waterpark admission	child	8.55	92	1r
Funerals				
Casket, 18-gauge steel, velvet interior		2029.08	91	24r
Cosmetology, hair care, etc.		75.10	91	24r
Embalming		249.24	91	24r
Facility use for ceremony		162.27	91	24r
Hearse, local		114.04	91	24r
Limousine, local		88.57	91	24r
Remains to funeral home, transfer		92.61	91	24r
Service charge, professional		682.42	91	24r
Vault, concrete, non-metallic liner		798.70	91	24r
Viewing facilities, use		163.86	91	24r
Groceries				
Apples, Red Delicious	lb	0.79	4/93	16r
Babyfood, strained vegetables, lowest price	4-4.5 oz jar	0.33	4Q 92	4c
Bacon	lb	1.75	4/93	16r
Bananas	lb	0.49	4Q 92	4c
Bananas	lb	0.42	4/93	16r
Beef, stew, boneless	lb	2.61	4/93	16r
Bologna, all beef or mixed	lb	2.24	4/93	16r
Bread, white	24 oz	0.67	4Q 92	4c
Bread, white, pan	lb	0.64	4/93	16r
Bread, whole wheat, pan	lb	0.96	4/93	16r
Cabbage	lb	0.37	4/93	16r
Carrots, short trimmed and topped	lb	0.47	4/93	16r
Celery	lb	0.64	4/93	16r
Cheese, American	lb	2.98	4/93	16r
Cheese, Cheddar	lb	3.28	4/93	16r
Cheese, Kraft grated Parmesan	8-oz canister	2.83	4Q 92	4c
Chicken, fresh, whole	lb	0.77	4/93	16r
Chicken, fryer, whole	lb	0.82	4Q 92	4c
Chicken breast, bone-in	lb	1.92	4/93	16r
Chicken legs, bone-in	lb	1.06	4/93	16r
Chuck roast, graded and ungraded, ex USDA prime and choice	lb	2.40	4/93	16r
Chuck roast, USDA choice, bone-in	lb	2.19	4/93	16r
Chuck roast, USDA choice, boneless	lb	2.38	4/93	16r
Cigarettes, Winston	carton	15.47	4Q 92	4c
Coffee, 100% ground roast, all sizes	lb	2.48	4/93	16r
Coffee, vacuum-packed	13-oz can	1.77	4Q 92	4c
Corn, frozen	10 oz	0.55	4Q 92	4c
Corn Flakes, Kellogg's or Post Toasties	18 oz	1.77	4Q 92	4c
Crackers, soda, salted	lb	1.15	4/93	16r
Eggs, Grade A large	doz	0.90	4Q 92	4c
Eggs, Grade A large	doz	0.96	4/93	16r
Flour, white, all purpose	lb	0.24	4/93	16r
Frankfurters, all meat or all beef	lb	2.01	4/93	16r
Grapefruit	lb	0.44	4/93	16r

Charleston, SC - continued

Item	Per	Value	Date	Ref.
Groceries - continued				
Grapes, Thompson Seedless	lb	1.40	4/93	16r
Ground beef, 100% beef	lb	1.58	4/93	16r
Ground beef, lean and extra lean	lb	2.09	4/93	16r
Ground beef or hamburger	lb	1.65	4Q 92	4c
Ground chuck, 100% beef	lb	1.98	4/93	16r
Ham, boneless, excluding canned	lb	2.89	4/93	16r
Ham, picnic, shoulder, bone-in, smoked	lb	1.02	4/93	16r
Ham, rump or steak half, bone-in, smoked	lb	1.48	4/93	16r
Ice cream, prepackaged, bulk, regular	1/2 gal	2.41	4/93	16r
Lemons	lb	1.05	4/93	16r
Lettuce, iceberg	head	0.91	4Q 92	4c
Lettuce, iceberg	lb	0.81	4/93	16r
Margarine, Blue Bonnet or Parkay cubes	lb	0.51	4Q 92	4c
Margarine, stick	lb	0.88	4/93	16r
Milk, whole	1/2 gal	1.41	4Q 92	4c
Orange juice, Minute Maid frozen	12-oz can	1.28	4Q 92	4c
Oranges, navel	lb	0.55	4/93	16r
Peaches	29-oz can	1.37	4Q 92	4c
Pears, Anjou	lb	0.92	4/93	16r
Peas Sweet, Del Monte or Green Giant	15-17 oz can	0.50	4Q 92	4c
Pork chops, center cut, bone-in	lb	3.13	4/93	16r
Potato chips	16 oz	2.94	4/93	16r
Potatoes, white	lb	0.43	4/93	16r
Potatoes, white or red	10-lb sack	1.99	4Q 92	4c
Rib roast, USDA choice, bone-in	lb	4.63	4/93	16r
Rice, white, long grain, uncooked	lb	0.45	4/93	16r
Round roast, graded & ungraded, ex USDA prime & choice	lb	3.03	4/93	16r
Round roast, USDA choice, boneless	lb	3.09	4/93	16r
Sausage, fresh, loose	lb	2.08	4/93	16r
Sausage, Jimmy Dean, 100% pork	lb	2.17	4Q 92	4c
Short ribs, bone-in	lb	2.66	4/93	16r
Shortening, vegetable oil blends	lb	0.69	4/93	16r
Shortening, vegetable, Crisco	3-lb can	1.99	4Q 92	4c
Soft drink, Coca Cola	2 liter	1.10	4Q 92	4c
Spaghetti and macaroni	lb	0.81	4/93	16r
Steak, rib eye, USDA choice, boneless	lb	6.24	4/93	16r
Steak, round, graded & ungraded, ex USDA prime & choice	lb	3.31	4/93	16r
Steak, round, USDA choice, boneless	lb	3.34	4/93	16r
Steak, sirloin, graded & ungraded, ex USDA prime & choice	lb	4.19	4/93	16r
Steak, sirloin, USDA choice, boneless	lb	4.46	4/93	16r
Steak, T-bone	lb	5.19	4Q 92	4c
Steak, T-bone, USDA choice, bone-in	lb	5.25	4/93	16r
Strawberries, dry pint	12 oz	0.92	4/93	16r
Sugar, cane or beet	4 lb	1.44	4Q 92	4c
Sugar, white	lb	0.39	4/93	16r
Sugar, white, 33-80 oz pk	lb	0.38	4/93	16r
Tomatoes, field grown	lb	0.88	4/93	16r
Tomatoes, Hunt's or Del Monte	14.5-oz can	0.54	4Q 92	4c
Tuna, chunk, light	6.125-6.5 oz can	0.56	4Q 92	4c
Tuna, chunk, light	lb	1.79	4/93	16r
Turkey, frozen, whole	lb	1.04	4/93	16r
Yogurt, natural, fruit flavored	1/2 pint	0.57	4/93	16r
Health Care				
Analgesic, Aspirin, Bayer, 325 mg tablets	100	5.99	4Q 92	4c
Childbirth, cesarean, hospital		5034	91	62r
Childbirth, cesarean, physician's fee		2053	91	62r
Childbirth, normal, hospital		2712	91	62r
Childbirth, normal, physician's fee		1492	91	62r
Dentist's fee, adult teeth cleaning and periodic oral exam	visit	47.28	4Q 92	4c

Values are in dollars or fractions of dollars. In the column headed *Ref*, references are shown to sources. Each reference is followed by a letter. These refer to the geographical level for which data were reported: s = State, r = Region, and c = City or metro. The abbreviation *ex* is used to mean *except* or *excluding*; *exp* stands for *expenditures*. For other abbreviations and further explanations, please see the Introduction.

Charleston, SC - continued

Item	Per	Value	Date	Ref.
Health Care				
Doctor's fee, routine exam, established patient	visit	37.60	4Q 92	4c
Health care spending, state	capita	1689	3/93	84s
Hospital care, semiprivate room	day	208.11	90	27c
Hospital care, semiprivate room	day	264.50	4Q 92	4c
Medical insurance premium, per employee, small group comprehensive	month	299.30	10/91	25c
Medical plan per employee	year	3495	91	45r
Mental health care, exp	capita	37.60-53.67	90	38s
Mental health care, exp, state mental health agency	capita	51.12	90	38s
Mental health care, hospital psychiatric services, non-Federal, exp	capita	10.67	88	38s
Mental health care, mental health organization, multiservice, exp	capita	11.38	88	38s
Mental health care, psychiatric hospitals, private, exp	capita	9.21	88	38s
Mental health care, psychiatric out-patient clinics, freestanding, exp	capita	0.68	88	38s
Mental health care, state and county mental hospitals, exp	capita	25.02	88	38s
Mental health care, VA medical centers, exp	capita	0.62	88	38s
Physician fee, family practice, first-visit		75.00	91	62r
Physician fee, family practice, revisit		34.00	91	62r
Physician fee, general practice, first-visit		61.00	91	62r
Physician fee, general practice, revisit		32.00	91	62r
Physician fee, general surgeon, first-visit		64.00	91	62r
Physician fee, general surgeon, revisit		40.00	91	62r
Physician fee, internal medicine, first-visit		98.00	91	62r
Physician fee, internal medicine, revisit		40.00	91	62r
Physician fee, median, neurosurgeon, first-visit		130.00	91	62r
Physician fee, median, nonsurgical specialist, first-visit		95.00	91	62r
Physician fee, median, orthopedic surgeon, first-visit		91.00	91	62r
Physician fee, median, plastic surgeon, first-visit		66.00	91	62r
Physician fee, median, surgical specialist, first-visit		62.00	91	62r
Physician fee, neurosurgeon, revisit		50.00	91	62r
Physician fee, nonsurgical specialist, revisit		40.00	91	62r
Physician fee, obstetrics/gynecology, first-visit		64.00	91	62r
Physician fee, obstetrics/gynecology, revisit		41.00	91	62r
Physician fee, orthopedic surgeon, revisit		40.00	91	62r
Physician fee, pediatrician, first-visit		49.00	91	62r
Physician fee, pediatrician, revisit		33.00	91	62r
Physician fee, plastic surgeon, revisit		43.00	91	62r
Physician fee, surgical specialist, revisit		37.00	91	62r
Substance abuse, hospital ancillary charge	incident	1250	90	70s
Substance abuse, hospital physician charge	incident	250	90	70s
Substance abuse, hospital room and board	incident	6100	90	70s
Household Goods				
Appliance repair, home, service call, washing machine	min labor charge	38.59	4Q 92	4c
Laundry detergent, Tide Ultra, Bold, or Cheer	42 oz	3.19	4Q 92	4c
Tissues, facial, Kleenex brand	175-count box	1.05	4Q 92	4c
Housing				
Home, median price	unit	82.30		26c
House, 1,800 sq ft, 8,000 sq ft lot, new, urban	total	109968	4Q 92	4c

Charleston, SC - continued

Item	Per	Value	Date	Ref.
Housing - continued				
House payment, principal and interest, 25% down payment	month	604	4Q 92	4c
Mortgage rate, incl. points & origination fee, 30-year fixed or adjustable rate	percent	7.97	4Q 92	4c
Rent, apartment, 2 bedrooms - 1-1/2 to 2 baths, unfurnished, 950 sq ft, water	month	540	4Q 92	4c
Rental unit, 1 bedroom	month	391	93	23c
Rental unit, 2 bedroom	month	462	93	23c
Rental unit, 3 bedroom	month	575	93	23c
Rental unit, 4 bedroom	month	647	93	23c
Rental unit, efficiency	month	320	93	23c
Insurance and Pensions				
Auto insurance, private passenger	year	605.26	91	63s
Personal Goods				
Shampoo, Alberto VO5	15 oz	0.99	4Q 92	4c
Toothpaste, Crest or Colgate	6-7 oz	2.11	4Q 92	4c
Personal Services				
Dry cleaning, man's 2-piece suit		6.08	4Q 92	4c
Haircare, woman's shampoo, trim and blow-dry		25.60	4Q 92	4c
Haircut, man's barbershop, no styling		8.17	4Q 92	4c
Restaurant Food				
Chicken, fried, thigh and drumstick		1.95	4Q 92	4c
Hamburger with cheese	1/4 lb	1.89	4Q 92	4c
Pizza, Pizza Hut or Pizza Inn, cheese, thin crust	12-13 in	7.79	4Q 92	4c
Taxes				
Tax, cigarette	pack	7	91	77s
Tax, gasoline	gal	16	91	77s
Taxes, state	capita	1105	91	77s
Transportation				
Auto rental, average	day	33.40	6/91	60c
Bus fare	one-way	0.75	3/93	2c
Bus fare, up to 10 miles	one-way	0.50	4Q 92	4c
Driver's license fee		10.00	12/90	43s
Limo fare, airport-city, average	day	7.00	6/91	60c
Taxi fare, airport-city, average	day	15.00	6/91	60c
Tire balance, computer or spin balance, front	wheel	6.06	4Q 92	4c
Travel				
Breakfast	day	4.11	6/91	60c
Business travel	day	193.00	4/93	89r
Dinner	day	22.65	6/91	60c
Lodging	day	119.13	91	60c
Lunch	day	11.55	6/91	60c
Utilities				
Electricity	mil Btu	16.39	90	64s
Electricity, all electric, 1,800 sq ft living area new home	month	100.89	4Q 92	4c

Charleston, WV

Item	Per	Value	Date	Ref.
Composite ACCRA index		104.20	4Q 92	4c
Alcoholic Beverages				
Beer, Miller Lite or Budweiser, 12-oz containers	6 pack	4.17	4Q 92	4c
Liquor, J & B Scotch	750 ml	16.13	4Q 92	4c
Wine, Gallo Chablis blanc, 1.5 liter	bottle	5.71	4Q 92	4c
Child Care				
Child care fee, average, center	hour	1.29	90	65r
Child care fee, average, nonregulated family day care	hour	0.89	90	65r
Child care fee, average, regulated family day care	hour	1.32	90	65r

Values are in dollars or fractions of dollars. In the column headed *Ref*, references are shown to sources. Each reference is followed by a letter. These refer to the geographical level for which data were reported: s = State, r = Region, and c = City or metro. The abbreviation *ex* is used to mean *except* or *excluding*; *exp* stands for *expenditures*. For other abbreviations and further explanations, please see the Introduction.

Charleston, WV - continued

Item	Per	Value	Date	Ref.
Clothing				
Jeans, man's denim		34.99	4Q 92	4c
Shirt, man's dress shirt		26.59	4Q 92	4c
Undervest, boy's size 10-14, cotton	3	3.31	4Q 92	4c
Communications				
Long-distance telephone service, day, initial minute, 0-100 miles	min	0.26-0.70	91	12s
Long-distance telephone service, day, additional minute, 0-100 miles	min	0.13-0.45	91	12s
Long-distance telephone service, evenings/weekends, 0-100 mi, initial minute	min	0.10-0.28	91	12s
Long-distance telephone service, evenings/weekends, 0-100 mi, additional minute	min	0.05-0.18	91	12s
Newspaper subscription, daily and Sunday home delivery, large-city	month	8.70	4Q 92	4c
Telephone, flat rate	month	60.00	91	11c
Telephone bill, family of four	month	29.93	4Q 92	4c
Education				
Board, 4-yr private college/university	year	1664	91	22s
Board, 4-yr public college/university	year	1723	91	22s
Expenditures, local gov't, public elementary/secondary	pupil	5401	92	20s
Room, 4-year private college/university	year	1401	91	22s
Room, 4-year public college/university	year	1556	91	22s
Tuition, 2-year private college/university	year	2767	91	22s
Tuition, 2-year public college/university	year	930	91	22s
Tuition, 4-year private college/university	year	8751	91	22s
Tuition, 4-year public college/university, in-state	year	1543	91	22s
Energy and Fuels				
Coal	mil Btu	1.47	90	64s
Energy	mil Btu	6.77	90	64s
Energy, combined forms, 1,800 sq ft heating area	month	103.58	4Q 92	4c
Energy exp/householder, 1-family unit	year	487	90	28r
Energy exp/householder, <1,000 sq ft heating area	year	393	90	28r
Energy exp/householder, 1,000-1,999 sq ft heating area	year	442	90	28r
Energy exp/householder, 2,000+ sq ft heating area	year	577	90	28r
Energy exp/householder, mobile home	year	366	90	28r
Energy exp/householder, multifamily	year	382	90	28r
Gas, cooking, winter, 10 therms	month	10.38	92	56c
Gas, cooking, winter, 30 therms	month	21.14	92	56c
Gas, cooking, winter, 50 therms	month	31.90	92	56c
Gas, heating, winter, 100 therms	month	58.80	92	56c
Gas, heating, winter, average use	month	96.46	92	56c
Gas, natural	mil Btu	4.40	90	64s
Gas, natural	000 cu ft	6.50	91	46s
Gas, natural, exp	year	605	91	46s
Gasoline, motor	gal	1.17	4Q 92	4c
Gasoline, unleaded regular	mil Btu	9.96	90	64s
Entertainment				
Bowling, evening rate	game	1.90	4Q 92	4c
Miniature golf admission	adult	6.18	92	1r
Miniature golf admission	child	5.14	92	1r
Monopoly game, Parker Brothers', No. 9		10.17	4Q 92	4c
Movie	admission	5.50	4Q 92	4c
Tennis balls, yellow, Wilson or Penn, 3	can	2.55	4Q 92	4c
Waterpark admission	adult	11.00	92	1r
Waterpark admission	child	8.55	92	1r
Funerals				
Casket, 18-gauge steel, velvet interior		2029.08	91	24r
Cosmetology, hair care, etc.		75.10	91	24r
Embalming		249.24	91	24r
Facility use for ceremony		162.27	91	24r
Hearse, local		114.04	91	24r

Charleston, WV - continued

Item	Per	Value	Date	Ref.
Funerals - continued				
Limousine, local		88.57	91	24r
Remains to funeral home, transfer		92.61	91	24r
Service charge, professional		682.42	91	24r
Vault, concrete, non-metallic liner		798.70	91	24r
Viewing facilities, use		163.86	91	24r
Goods and Services				
ACCRA Index, Miscellaneous Goods and Services		100.20	4Q 92	4c
Groceries				
ACCRA Index, Groceries		95.80	4Q 92	4c
Apples, Red Delicious	lb	0.79	4/93	16r
Babyfood, strained vegetables, lowest price	4-4.5 oz jar	0.24	4Q 92	4c
Bacon	lb	1.75	4/93	16r
Bananas	lb	0.40	4Q 92	4c
Bananas	lb	0.42	4/93	16r
Beef, stew, boneless	lb	2.61	4/93	16r
Bologna, all beef or mixed	lb	2.24	4/93	16r
Bread, white	24 oz	0.55	4Q 92	4c
Bread, white, pan	lb	0.64	4/93	16r
Bread, whole wheat, pan	lb	0.96	4/93	16r
Cabbage	lb	0.37	4/93	16r
Carrots, short trimmed and topped	lb	0.47	4/93	16r
Celery	lb	0.64	4/93	16r
Cheese, American	lb	2.98	4/93	16r
Cheese, Cheddar	lb	3.28	4/93	16r
Cheese, Kraft grated Parmesan	8-oz canister	3.23	4Q 92	4c
Chicken, fresh, whole	lb	0.77	4/93	16r
Chicken, fryer, whole	lb	0.89	4Q 92	4c
Chicken breast, bone-in	lb	1.92	4/93	16r
Chicken legs, bone-in	lb	1.06	4/93	16r
Chuck roast, graded and ungraded, ex USDA prime and choice	lb	2.40	4/93	16r
Chuck roast, USDA choice, bone-in	lb	2.19	4/93	16r
Chuck roast, USDA choice, boneless	lb	2.38	4/93	16r
Cigarettes, Winston	carton	17.75	4Q 92	4c
Coffee, 100% ground roast, all sizes	lb	2.48	4/93	16r
Coffee, vacuum-packed	13-oz can	2.11	4Q 92	4c
Corn, frozen	10 oz	0.64	4Q 92	4c
Corn Flakes, Kellogg's or Post Toasties	18 oz	2.13	4Q 92	4c
Crackers, soda, salted	lb	1.15	4/93	16r
Eggs, Grade A large	doz	0.83	4Q 92	4c
Eggs, Grade A large	doz	0.96	4/93	16r
Flour, white, all purpose	lb	0.24	4/93	16r
Frankfurters, all meat or all beef	lb	2.01	4/93	16r
Grapefruit	lb	0.44	4/93	16r
Grapes, Thompson Seedless	lb	1.40	4/93	16r
Ground beef, 100% beef	lb	1.58	4/93	16r
Ground beef, lean and extra lean	lb	2.09	4/93	16r
Ground beef or hamburger	lb	1.75	4Q 92	4c
Ground chuck, 100% beef	lb	1.98	4/93	16r
Ham, boneless, excluding canned	lb	2.89	4/93	16r
Ham, picnic, shoulder, bone-in, smoked	lb	1.02	4/93	16r
Ham, rump or steak half, bone-in, smoked	lb	1.48	4/93	16r
Ice cream, prepackaged, bulk, regular	1/2 gal	2.41	4/93	16r
Lemons	lb	1.05	4/93	16r
Lettuce, iceberg	head	0.75	4Q 92	4c
Lettuce, iceberg	lb	0.81	4/93	16r
Margarine, Blue Bonnet or Parkay cubes	lb	0.53	4Q 92	4c
Margarine, stick	lb	0.88	4/93	16r
Milk, whole	1/2 gal	1.42	4Q 92	4c
Orange juice, Minute Maid frozen	12-oz can	1.11	4Q 92	4c
Oranges, navel	lb	0.55	4/93	16r
Peaches	29-oz can	1.47	4Q 92	4c
Pears, Anjou	lb	0.92	4/93	16r

Values are in dollars or fractions of dollars. In the column headed *Ref*, references are shown to sources. Each reference is followed by a letter. These refer to the geographical level for which data were reported: s = State, r = Region, and c = City or metro. The abbreviation *ex* is used to mean *except* or *excluding*; *exp* stands for expenditures. For other abbreviations and further explanations, please see the Introduction.

Charleston, WV - continued

Item	Per	Value	Date	Ref.
Groceries				
Peas Sweet, Del Monte or Green Giant	15-17 oz can	0.55	4Q 92	4c
Pork chops, center cut, bone-in	lb	3.13	4/93	16r
Potato chips	16 oz	2.94	4/93	16r
Potatoes, white	lb	0.43	4/93	16r
Potatoes, white or red	10-lb sack	1.57	4Q 92	4c
Rib roast, USDA choice, bone-in	lb	4.63	4/93	16r
Rice, white, long grain, uncooked	lb	0.45	4/93	16r
Round roast, graded & ungraded, ex USDA prime & choice	lb	3.03	4/93	16r
Round roast, USDA choice, boneless	lb	3.09	4/93	16r
Sausage, fresh, loose	lb	2.08	4/93	16r
Sausage, Jimmy Dean, 100% pork	lb	1.75	4Q 92	4c
Short ribs, bone-in	lb	2.66	4/93	16r
Shortening, vegetable oil blends	lb	0.69	4/93	16r
Shortening, vegetable, Crisco	3-lb can	2.07	4Q 92	4c
Soft drink, Coca Cola	2 liter	1.11	4Q 92	4c
Spaghetti and macaroni	lb	0.81	4/93	16r
Steak, rib eye, USDA choice, boneless	lb	6.24	4/93	16r
Steak, round, graded & ungraded, ex USDA prime & choice	lb	3.31	4/93	16r
Steak, round, USDA choice, boneless	lb	3.34	4/93	16r
Steak, sirloin, graded & ungraded, ex USDA prime & choice	lb	4.19	4/93	16r
Steak, sirloin, USDA choice, boneless	lb	4.46	4/93	16r
Steak, T-bone	lb	6.05	4Q 92	4c
Steak, T-bone, USDA choice, bone-in	lb	5.25	4/93	16r
Strawberries, dry pint	12 oz	0.92	4/93	16r
Sugar, cane or beet	4 lb	1.18	4Q 92	4c
Sugar, white	lb	0.39	4/93	16r
Sugar, white, 33-80 oz pk	lb	0.38	4/93	16r
Tomatoes, field grown	lb	0.88	4/93	16r
Tomatoes, Hunt's or Del Monte	14.5-oz can	0.71	4Q 92	4c
Tuna, chunk, light	6.125-6.5 oz can	0.62	4Q 92	4c
Tuna, chunk, light	lb	1.79	4/93	16r
Turkey, frozen, whole	lb	1.04	4/93	16r
Yogurt, natural, fruit flavored	1/2 pint	0.57	4/93	16r
Health Care				
ACCRA Index, Health Care		99.90	4Q 92	4c
Analgesic, Aspirin, Bayer, 325 mg tablets	100	5.77	4Q 92	4c
Childbirth, cesarean, hospital		5034	91	62r
Childbirth, cesarean, physician's fee		2053	91	62r
Childbirth, normal, hospital		2712	91	62r
Childbirth, normal, physician's fee		1492	91	62r
Dentist's fee, adult teeth cleaning and periodic oral exam	visit	45.20	4Q 92	4c
Doctor's fee, routine exam, established patient	visit	39.00	4Q 92	4c
Hospital care, semiprivate room	day	250.49	90	27c
Hospital care, semiprivate room	day	273.00	4Q 92	4c
Medical insurance premium, per employee, small group comprehensive	month	346.75	10/91	25c
Medical plan per employee	year	3495	91	45r
Mental health care, exp	capita	20.37-28.83	90	38s
Mental health care, exp, state mental health agency	capita	23.72	90	38s
Mental health care, hospital psychiatric services, non-Federal, exp	capita	9.26	88	38s
Mental health care, mental health organization, multiservice, exp	capita	26.55	88	38s
Mental health care, psychiatric hospitals, private, exp	capita	5.67	88	38s
Mental health care, psychiatric out-patient clinics, freestanding, exp	capita	1.30	88	38s

Charleston, WV - continued

Item	Per	Value	Date	Ref.
Health Care - continued				
Mental health care, state and county mental hospitals, exp	capita	11.86	88	38s
Mental health care, VA medical centers, exp	capita	0.70	88	38s
Physician fee, family practice, first-visit		75.00	91	62r
Physician fee, family practice, revisit		34.00	91	62r
Physician fee, general practice, first-visit		61.00	91	62r
Physician fee, general practice, revisit		32.00	91	62r
Physician fee, general surgeon, first-visit		64.00	91	62r
Physician fee, general surgeon, revisit		40.00	91	62r
Physician fee, internal medicine, first-visit		98.00	91	62r
Physician fee, internal medicine, revisit		40.00	91	62r
Physician fee, median, neurosurgeon, first-visit		130.00	91	62r
Physician fee, median, nonsurgical specialist, first-visit		95.00	91	62r
Physician fee, median, orthopedic surgeon, first-visit		91.00	91	62r
Physician fee, median, plastic surgeon, first-visit		66.00	91	62r
Physician fee, median, surgical specialist, first-visit		62.00	91	62r
Physician fee, neurosurgeon, revisit		50.00	91	62r
Physician fee, nonsurgical specialist, revisit		40.00	91	62r
Physician fee, obstetrics/gynecology, first-visit		64.00	91	62r
Physician fee, obstetrics/gynecology, revisit		41.00	91	62r
Physician fee, orthopedic surgeon, revisit		40.00	91	62r
Physician fee, pediatrician, first-visit		49.00	91	62r
Physician fee, pediatrician, revisit		33.00	91	62r
Physician fee, plastic surgeon, revisit		43.00	91	62r
Physician fee, surgical specialist, revisit		37.00	91	62r
Substance abuse, hospital ancillary charge	incident	1900	90	70s
Substance abuse, hospital physician charge	incident	1270	90	70s
Substance abuse, hospital room and board	incident	4590	90	70s
Household Goods				
Appliance repair, home, service call, washing machine	min labor charge	36.07	4Q 92	4c
Laundry detergent, Tide Ultra, Bold, or Cheer	42 oz	3.35	4Q 92	4c
Tissues, facial, Kleenex brand	175-count box	1.05	4Q 92	4c
Housing				
ACCRA Index, Housing		114.20	4Q 92	4c
Home, median price	unit	70.30		26c
House, 1,800 sq ft, 8,000 sq ft lot, new, urban	total	126000	4Q 92	4c
House payment, principal and interest, 25% down payment	month	707	4Q 92	4c
Mortgage rate, incl. points & origination fee, 30-year fixed or adjustable rate	percent	8.21	4Q 92	4c
Rent, apartment, 2 bedrooms - 1-1/2 to 2 baths, unfurnished, 950 sq ft, water	month	551	4Q 92	4c
Rental unit, 1 bedroom	month	473	93	23c
Rental unit, 2 bedroom	month	558	93	23c
Rental unit, 3 bedroom	month	698	93	23c
Rental unit, 4 bedroom	month	782	93	23c
Rental unit, efficiency	month	389	93	23c
Insurance and Pensions				
Auto insurance, private passenger	year	621.65	91	63s
Personal Goods				
Shampoo, Alberto VO5	15 oz	1.47	4Q 92	4c
Toothpaste, Crest or Colgate	6-7 oz	1.97	4Q 92	4c
Personal Services				
Dry cleaning, man's 2-piece suit		6.05	4Q 92	4c

Values are in dollars or fractions of dollars. In the column headed *Ref*, references are shown to sources. Each reference is followed by a letter. These refer to the geographical level for which data were reported: s=State, r=Region, and c=City or metro. The abbreviation *ex* is used to mean *except* or *excluding*; *exp* stands for expenditures. For other abbreviations and further explanations, please see the Introduction.

Charleston, WV - continued

Item	Per	Value	Date	Ref.
Personal Services				
Haircare, woman's shampoo, trim and blow-dry		20.40	4Q 92	4c
Haircut, man's barbershop, no styling		6.20	4Q 92	4c
Restaurant Food				
Chicken, fried, thigh and drumstick		1.98	4Q 92	4c
Hamburger with cheese	1/4 lb	1.77	4Q 92	4c
Pizza, Pizza Hut or Pizza Inn, cheese, thin crust	12-13 in	7.49	4Q 92	4c
Taxes				
Tax, cigarette	pack	17	91	77s
Tax, gasoline	gal	15.50	91	77s
Taxes, state	capita	1293	91	77s
Transportation				
ACCRA Index, Transportation		106.40	4Q 92	4c
Bus fare, up to 10 miles	one-way	1.25	4Q 92	4c
Driver's license fee		10.00	12/90	43s
Tire balance, computer or spin balance, front	wheel	6.56	4Q 92	4c
Vehicle registration and license plate	year	26.50-37.50	93	69s
Travel				
Business travel	day	193.00	4/93	89r
Utilities				
ACCRA Index, Utilities		100.80	4Q 92	4c
Electricity	mil Btu	13.90	90	64s
Electricity, all electric, 1,800 sq ft living area new home	month	103.58	4Q 92	4c
Electricity, winter, 250 KWh	month	21.89	92	55s
Electricity, winter, 500 KWh	month	38.44	92	55s
Electricity, winter, 750 KWh	month	53.70	92	55s
Electricity, winter, 1000 KWh	month	68.96	92	55s

Charlotte, NC

Item	Per	Value	Date	Ref.
Composite ACCRA index		100.30	4Q 92	4c
Alcoholic Beverages				
Beer, Miller Lite or Budweiser, 12-oz containers	6 pack	4.13	4Q 92	4c
Liquor, J & B Scotch	750 ml	17.65	4Q 92	4c
Wine, Gallo Chablis blanc, 1.5 liter	bottle	4.37	4Q 92	4c
Child Care				
Child care fee, average, center	hour	1.29	90	65r
Child care fee, average, nonregulated family day care	hour	0.89	90	65r
Child care fee, average, regulated family day care	hour	1.32	90	65r
Clothing				
Jeans, man's denim		31.59	4Q 92	4c
Shirt, man's dress shirt		24.40	4Q 92	4c
Undervest, boy's size 10-14, cotton	3	4.32	4Q 92	4c
Communications				
Long-distance telephone service, day, initial minute, 0-100 miles	min	0.10-0.33	91	12s
Long-distance telephone service, day, additional minute, 0-100 miles	min	0.10-0.33	91	12s
Long-distance telephone service, evenings/weekends, 0-100 mi, initial minute	min	0.08-0.24	91	12s
Long-distance telephone service, evenings/weekends, 0-100 mi, additional minute	min	0.05-0.17	91	12s
Newspaper subscription, daily and Sunday home delivery, large-city	month	10.83	4Q 92	4c
Telephone bill, family of four	month	18.10	4Q 92	4c
Education				
Board, 4-yr private college/university	year	1768	91	22s
Board, 4-yr public college/university	year	1568	91	22s

Charlotte, NC - continued

Item	Per	Value	Date	Ref.
Education - continued				
Expenditures, local gov't, public elementary/secondary	pupil	5078	92	20s
Room, 4-year private college/university	year	1467	91	22s
Room, 4-year public college/university	year	1386	91	22s
Tuition, 2-year private college/university	year	4964	91	22s
Tuition, 2-year public college/university	year	334	91	22s
Tuition, 4-year private college/university	year	7826	91	22s
Tuition, 4-year public college/university, in-state	year	1112	91	22s
Energy and Fuels				
Coal	mil Btu	1.79	90	64s
Energy	mil Btu	10.06	90	64s
Energy, combined forms, 1,800 sq ft heating area	month	119.35	4Q 92	4c
Energy exp/householder, 1-family unit	year	487	90	28r
Energy exp/householder, <1,000 sq ft heating area	year	393	90	28r
Energy exp/householder, 1,000-1,999 sq ft heating area	year	442	90	28r
Energy exp/householder, 2,000+ sq ft heating area	year	577	90	28r
Energy exp/householder, mobile home	year	366	90	28r
Energy exp/householder, multifamily	year	382	90	28r
Gas, cooking, winter, 10 therms	month	11.31	92	56c
Gas, cooking, winter, 30 therms	month	19.93	92	56c
Gas, cooking, winter, 50 therms	month	28.55	92	56c
Gas, heating, winter, 100 therms	month	53.09	92	56c
Gas, heating, winter, average use	month	64.30	92	56c
Gas, natural	mil Btu	4.19	90	64s
Gas, natural	000 cu ft	6.24	91	46s
Gas, natural, exp	year	439	91	46s
Gasoline, motor	gal	1.09	4Q 92	4c
Gasoline, unleaded regular	mil Btu	9.44	90	64s
Entertainment				
Bowling, evening rate	game	2.30	4Q 92	4c
Miniature golf admission	adult	6.18	92	1r
Miniature golf admission	child	5.14	92	1r
Monopoly game, Parker Brothers', No. 9		10.18	4Q 92	4c
Movie	admission	5.65	4Q 92	4c
Tennis balls, yellow, Wilson or Penn, 3	can	1.90	4Q 92	4c
Waterpark admission	adult	11.00	92	1r
Waterpark admission	child	8.55	92	1r
Funerals				
Casket, 18-gauge steel, velvet interior		2029.08	91	24r
Cosmetology, hair care, etc.		75.10	91	24r
Embalming		249.24	91	24r
Facility use for ceremony		162.27	91	24r
Hearse, local		114.04	91	24r
Limousine, local		88.57	91	24r
Remains to funeral home, transfer		92.61	91	24r
Service charge, professional		682.42	91	24r
Vault, concrete, non-metallic liner		798.70	91	24r
Viewing facilities, use		163.86	91	24r
Goods and Services				
ACCRA Index, Miscellaneous Goods and Services		99.90	4Q 92	4c
Groceries				
ACCRA Index, Groceries		94.60	4Q 92	4c
Apples, Red Delicious	lb	0.79	4/93	16r
Babyfood, strained vegetables, lowest price	4-4.5 oz jar	0.31	4Q 92	4c
Bacon	lb	1.75	4/93	16r
Bacon, Oscar Mayer	lb	2.83	2/92	73c
Bananas	lb	0.49	4Q 92	4c
Bananas	lb	0.42	4/93	16r
Bananas, brand name	lb	0.59	2/92	73c

Values are in dollars or fractions of dollars. In the column headed *Ref*, references are shown to sources. Each reference is followed by a letter. These refer to the geographical level for which data were reported: s = State, r = Region, and c = City or metro. The abbreviation *ex* is used to mean *except* or *excluding*; *exp* stands for expenditures. For other abbreviations and further explanations, please see the Introduction.

Charlotte, NC - continued

Item	Per	Value	Date	Ref.
Groceries				
Beans, Green Giant, canned	14 1/2 oz	0.48	2/92	73c
Beef, ground chuck steak, USDA choice	lb	2.12	2/92	73c
Beef, stew, boneless	lb	2.61	4/93	16r
Bologna, all beef or mixed	lb	2.24	4/93	16r
Bologna, Oscar Mayer	8 oz	1.78	2/92	73c
Bread, Sunbeam white	20 oz	1.16	2/92	73c
Bread, white	24 oz	0.74	4Q 92	4c
Bread, white, pan	lb	0.64	4/93	16r
Bread, whole wheat, pan	lb	0.96	4/93	16r
Butter, Land O'Lakes, light salt	lb	1.67	2/92	73c
Butter, private label	lb	1.38	2/92	73c
Cabbage	lb	0.37	4/93	16r
Carrots, short trimmed and topped	lb	0.47	4/93	16r
Celery	lb	0.64	4/93	16r
Cereal, Kellogg's Corn Flakes	18 oz	1.69	2/92	73c
Cereal, Rice Krispies	10 oz	2.41	2/92	73c
Cheese, American	lb	2.98	4/93	16r
Cheese, Cheddar	lb	3.28	4/93	16r
Cheese, Kraft American singles	16 oz	2.78	2/92	73c
Cheese, Kraft grated Parmesan	8-oz canister	3.07	4Q 92	4c
Chicken, fresh, whole	lb	0.77	4/93	16r
Chicken, fryer, whole	lb	0.77	4Q 92	4c
Chicken breast, bone-in	lb	1.92	4/93	16r
Chicken fryer breasts	lb	2.23	2/92	73c
Chicken legs, bone-in	lb	1.06	4/93	16r
Chuck roast, graded and ungraded, ex USDA prime and choice	lb	2.40	4/93	16r
Chuck roast, USDA choice, bone-in	lb	2.19	4/93	16r
Chuck roast, USDA choice, boneless	lb	2.38	4/93	16r
Cigarettes, Winston	carton	15.08	4Q 92	4c
Coffee, 100% ground roast, all sizes	lb	2.48	4/93	16r
Coffee, Maxwell House regular grind	13 oz	1.89	2/92	73c
Coffee, vacuum-packed	13-oz can	1.75	4Q 92	4c
Cookies, Nabisco Oreos	20 oz	3.03	2/92	73c
Corn, frozen	10 oz	0.50	4Q 92	4c
Corn Flakes, Kellogg's or Post Toasties	18 oz	1.73	4Q 92	4c
Crackers, soda, salted	lb	1.15	4/93	16r
Eggs, Grade A large	doz	0.85	4Q 92	4c
Eggs, Grade A large	doz	0.96	4/93	16r
Eggs, private label, large, white	doz	0.85	2/92	73c
Flour, white, all purpose	lb	0.24	4/93	16r
Frankfurters, all meat or all beef	lb	2.01	4/93	16r
Frozen dinner, Stouffer's Lean Cuisine glazed chicken		2.31	2/92	73c
Grapefruit	lb	0.44	4/93	16r
Grapes, Thompson Seedless	lb	1.40	4/93	16r
Ground beef, 100% beef	lb	1.58	4/93	16r
Ground beef, lean and extra lean	lb	2.09	4/93	16r
Ground beef or hamburger	lb	1.57	4Q 92	4c
Ground chuck, 100% beef	lb	1.98	4/93	16r
Ham, boneless, excluding canned	lb	2.89	4/93	16r
Ham, picnic, shoulder, bone-in, smoked	lb	1.02	4/93	16r
Ham, rump or steak half, bone-in, smoked	lb	1.48	4/93	16r
Ice cream, prepackaged, bulk, regular	1/2 gal	2.41	4/93	16r
Jelly, Welch's grape	32 oz	1.37	2/92	73c
Ketchup, Heinz	14 oz	0.96	2/92	73c
Lemons	lb	1.05	4/93	16r
Lettuce, iceberg	head	0.81	2/92	73c
Lettuce, iceberg	head	0.99	4Q 92	4c
Lettuce, iceberg	lb	0.81	4/93	16r
Margarine, Blue Bonnet or Parkay cubes	lb	0.47	4Q 92	4c
Margarine, Parkay sticks	lb	0.54	2/92	73c
Margarine, stick	lb	0.88	4/93	16r
Mayonnaise, Hellmann's	quart	2.29	2/92	73c
Milk, private label, whole	gal	2.49	2/92	73c
Milk, whole	1/2 gal	1.39	4Q 92	4c
Muffins, Thomas English	6	1.73	2/92	73c
Orange juice, Minute Maid frozen	12 oz	1.39	2/92	73c

Charlotte, NC - continued

Item	Per	Value	Date	Ref.
Groceries - continued				
Orange juice, Minute Maid frozen	12-oz can	1.18	4Q 92	4c
Oranges, navel	lb	0.55	4/93	16r
Peaches	29-oz can	1.29	4Q 92	4c
Peanut butter, Peter Pan creamy	18 oz	1.89	2/92	73c
Pears, Anjou	lb	0.92	4/93	16r
Peas, Bird's Eye frozen	10 oz	1.02	2/92	73c
Peas, Green Giant frozen	16 oz	1.59	2/92	73c
Peas Sweet, Del Monte or Green Giant	15-17 oz can	0.43	4Q 92	4c
Pizza, Jeno's frozen pepperoni	7.4 oz	1.02	2/92	73c
Pork chops, center cut, bone-in	lb	3.13	4/93	16r
Potato chips	16 oz	2.94	4/93	16r
Potatoes, white	lb	0.43	4/93	16r
Potatoes, white or red	10-lb sack	1.85	4Q 92	4c
Rib roast, USDA choice, bone-in	lb	4.63	4/93	16r
Rice, white, long grain, uncooked	lb	0.45	4/93	16r
Round roast, graded & ungraded, ex USDA prime & choice	lb	3.03	4/93	16r
Round roast, USDA choice, boneless	lb	3.09	4/93	16r
Sausage, fresh, loose	lb	2.08	4/93	16r
Sausage, Jimmy Dean	12 oz	2.32	2/92	73c
Sausage, Jimmy Dean, 100% pork	lb	2.20	4Q 92	4c
Short ribs, bone-in	lb	2.66	4/93	16r
Shortening, vegetable oil blends	lb	0.69	4/93	16r
Shortening, vegetable, Crisco	3-lb can	1.99	4Q 92	4c
Snacks, Doritos nacho cheese corn chips	9.5 oz	1.95	2/92	73c
Soft drink, Coca Cola	2 liter	1.33	2/92	73c
Soft drink, Coca Cola	2 liter	1.11	4Q 92	4c
Soft drink, Diet Coca Cola	2 liter	1.33	2/92	73c
Soft drink, Diet Pepsi	2 liter	1.27	2/92	73c
Soft drink, Pepsi	2 liter	1.11	2/92	73c
Spaghetti, Mueller's	16 oz	0.67	2/92	73c
Spaghetti and macaroni	lb	0.81	4/93	16r
Spaghetti sauce, Ragu	14 oz	1.17	2/92	73c
Steak, rib eye, USDA choice, boneless	lb	6.24	4/93	16r
Steak, round, graded & ungraded, ex USDA prime & choice	lb	3.31	4/93	16r
Steak, round, USDA choice, boneless	lb	3.34	4/93	16r
Steak, sirloin, graded & ungraded, ex USDA prime & choice	lb	4.19	4/93	16r
Steak, sirloin, USDA choice, boneless	lb	4.46	4/93	16r
Steak, T-bone	lb	5.67	4Q 92	4c
Steak, T-bone, USDA choice, bone-in	lb	5.25	4/93	16r
Strawberries, dry pint	12 oz	0.92	4/93	16r
Sugar, cane or beet	4 lb	1.39	4Q 92	4c
Sugar, regular granulated	5 lb	1.99	2/92	73c
Sugar, white	lb	0.39	4/93	16r
Sugar, white, 33-80 oz pk	lb	0.38	4/93	16r
Tea, Lipton tea bags	100	2.89	2/92	73c
Tomato soup, Campbell's	10 3/4 oz	0.39	2/92	73c
Tomatoes, field grown	lb	0.88	4/93	16r
Tomatoes, Hunt's or Del Monte	14.5-oz can	0.53	4Q 92	4c
Tuna, Chicken of the Sea chunk light	6.5 oz	0.59	2/92	73c
Tuna, chunk, light	6.125-6.5 oz can	0.54	4Q 92	4c
Tuna, chunk, light	lb	1.79	4/93	16r
Turkey, frozen, whole	lb	1.04	4/93	16r
Yogurt, natural, fruit flavored	1/2 pint	0.57	4/93	16r
Health Care				
ACCRA Index, Health Care		117.80	4Q 92	4c
Analgesic, Aspirin, Bayer, 325 mg tablets	100	4.71	4Q 92	4c
Childbirth, cesarean, hospital		5034	91	62r
Childbirth, cesarean, physician's fee		2053	91	62r
Childbirth, normal, hospital		2712	91	62r

Values are in dollars or fractions of dollars. In the column headed *Ref*, references are shown to sources. Each reference is followed by a letter. These refer to the geographical level for which data were reported: s = State, r = Region, and c = City or metro. The abbreviation *ex* is used to mean *except* or *excluding*; *exp* stands for expenditures. For other abbreviations and further explanations, please see the Introduction.

Charlotte, NC - continued

Item	Per	Value	Date	Ref.
Health Care				
Childbirth, normal, physician's fee		1492	91	62r
Dentist's fee, adult teeth cleaning and periodic oral exam	visit	51.80	4Q 92	4c
Doctor's fee, routine exam, established patient	visit	53.80	4Q 92	4c
Hospital care, semiprivate room	day	193.83	90	27c
Hospital care, semiprivate room	day	293.67	4Q 92	4c
Medical insurance premium, per employee, small group comprehensive	month	281.05	10/91	25c
Medical plan per employee	year	3495	91	45r
Mental health care, exp	capita	37.60-53.67	90	38s
Mental health care, exp, state mental health agency	capita	45.66	90	38s
Mental health care, hospital psychiatric services, non-Federal, exp	capita	12.05	88	38s
Mental health care, mental health organization, multiservice, exp	capita	29.54	88	38s
Mental health care, psychiatric hospitals, private, exp	capita	15.07	88	38s
Mental health care, psychiatric out-patient clinics, freestanding, exp	capita	0.11	88	38s
Mental health care, state and county mental hospitals, exp	capita	26.36	88	38s
Mental health care, VA medical centers, exp	capita	2.23	88	38s
Physician fee, family practice, first-visit		75.00	91	62r
Physician fee, family practice, revisit		34.00	91	62r
Physician fee, general practice, first-visit		61.00	91	62r
Physician fee, general practice, revisit		32.00	91	62r
Physician fee, general surgeon, first-visit		64.00	91	62r
Physician fee, general surgeon, revisit		40.00	91	62r
Physician fee, internal medicine, first-visit		98.00	91	62r
Physician fee, internal medicine, revisit		40.00	91	62r
Physician fee, median, neurosurgeon, first-visit		130.00	91	62r
Physician fee, median, nonsurgical specialist, first-visit		95.00	91	62r
Physician fee, median, orthopedic surgeon, first-visit		91.00	91	62r
Physician fee, median, plastic surgeon, first-visit		66.00	91	62r
Physician fee, median, surgical specialist, first-visit		62.00	91	62r
Physician fee, neurosurgeon, revisit		50.00	91	62r
Physician fee, nonsurgical specialist, revisit		40.00	91	62r
Physician fee, obstetrics/gynecology, first-visit		64.00	91	62r
Physician fee, obstetrics/gynecology, revisit		41.00	91	62r
Physician fee, orthopedic surgeon, revisit		40.00	91	62r
Physician fee, pediatrician, first-visit		49.00	91	62r
Physician fee, pediatrician, revisit		33.00	91	62r
Physician fee, plastic surgeon, revisit		43.00	91	62r
Physician fee, surgical specialist, revisit		37.00	91	62r
Substance abuse, hospital ancillary charge	incident	1090	90	70s
Substance abuse, hospital physician charge	incident	460	90	70s
Substance abuse, hospital room and board	incident	4880	90	70s
Household Goods				
Laundry detergent, Tide Ultra	42 oz	2.98	2/92	73c
Appliance repair, home, service call, washing machine	min labor charge	34.60	4Q 92	4c
Laundry detergent, Tide Ultra, Bold, or Cheer	42 oz	3.31	4Q 92	4c
Paper towels, Bounty	60 ft	0.79	2/92	73c
Plastic wrap, Saran	50 ft	1.42	2/92	73c
Tissues, facial, Kleenex brand	175-count box	0.95	4Q 92	4c

Charlotte, NC - continued

Item	Per	Value	Date	Ref.
Housing				
ACCRA Index, Housing		99.40	4Q 92	4c
Home, median price	unit	102.20		26c
House, 1,800 sq ft, 8,000 sq ft lot, new, urban	total	115200	4Q 92	4c
House payment, principal and interest, 25% down payment	month	645	4Q 92	4c
Mortgage rate, incl. points & origination fee, 30-year fixed or adjustable rate	percent	8.18	4Q 92	4c
Rent, apartment, 2 bedrooms - 1-1/2 to 2 baths, unfurnished, 950 sq ft, water	month	412	4Q 92	4c
Rental unit, 1 bedroom	month	385	93	23c
Rental unit, 2 bedroom	month	453	93	23c
Rental unit, 3 bedroom	month	566	93	23c
Rental unit, 4 bedroom	month	633	93	23c
Rental unit, efficiency	month	319	93	23c
Insurance and Pensions				
Auto insurance, private passenger	year	522.39	91	63s
Personal Goods				
Feminine hygiene product, Stayfree	24	2.76	2/92	73c
Shampoo, Alberto VO5	15 oz	1.14	4Q 92	4c
Shave cream, Barbasol	11 oz	1.11	2/92	73c
Toothpaste, Crest gel	6.4 oz	1.99	2/92	73c
Toothpaste, Crest or Colgate	6-7 oz	1.78	4Q 92	4c
Personal Services				
Dry cleaning, man's 2-piece suit		5.80	4Q 92	4c
Haircare, woman's shampoo, trim and blow-dry		20.80	4Q 92	4c
Haircut, man's barbershop, no styling		7.39	4Q 92	4c
Restaurant Food				
Chicken, fried, thigh and drumstick		1.99	4Q 92	4c
Hamburger with cheese	1/4 lb	1.83	4Q 92	4c
Pizza, Pizza Hut or Pizza Inn, cheese, thin crust	12-13 in	7.49	4Q 92	4c
Taxes				
Tax, cigarette	pack	5	91	77s
Tax, gasoline	gal	21.90	91	77s
Taxes, state	capita	1165	91	77s
Transportation				
ACCRA Index, Transportation		96.30	4Q 92	4c
Auto rental, average	day	52.00	6/91	60c
Bus fare	one-way	0.80	3/93	2c
Bus fare, up to 10 miles	one-way	0.80	4Q 92	4c
Driver's license fee		15.00	12/90	43s
Limo fare, airport-city, average	day	4.00	6/91	60c
Taxi fare, airport-city, average	day	11.00	6/91	60c
Tire balance, computer or spin balance, front	wheel	6.30	4Q 92	4c
Vehicle registration and license plate	year	35.00	93	50s
Travel				
Breakfast	day	8.11	6/91	60c
Business travel	day	193.00	4/93	89r
Dinner	day	22.76	6/91	60c
Lodging	day	108.27	91	60c
Lunch	day	11.23	6/91	60c
Utilities				
ACCRA Index, Utilities		107.70	4Q 92	4c
Electricity	mil Btu	18.74	90	64s
Electricity, all electric, 1,800 sq ft living area new home	month	119.35	4Q 92	4c
Electricity, winter, 250 KWh	month	24.23	92	55c
Electricity, winter, 500 KWh	month	41.66	92	55c
Electricity, winter, 750 KWh	month	59.81	92	55c
Electricity, winter, 1000 KWh	month	77.95	92	55c

Values are in dollars or fractions of dollars. In the column headed *Ref*, references are shown to sources. Each reference is followed by a letter. These refer to the geographical level for which data were reported: s = State, r = Region, and c = City or metro. The abbreviation *ex* is used to mean *except* or *excluding*; *exp* stands for expenditures. For other abbreviations and further explanations, please see the Introduction.

Charlottesville, VA

Item	Per	Value	Date	Ref.
Child Care				
Child care fee, average, center	hour	1.29	90	65r
Child care fee, average, nonregulated family day care	hour	0.89	90	65r
Child care fee, average, regulated family day care	hour	1.32	90	65r
Communications				
Long-distance telephone service, day, initial minute, 0-100 miles	min	0.21 0.35	91	12s
Long-distance telephone service, day, additional minute, 0-100 miles	min	0.12-0.21	91	12s
Long-distance telephone service, evenings/weekends, 0-100 mi, initial minute	min	0.08-0.14	91	12s
Long-distance telephone service, evenings/weekends, 0-100 mi, additional minute	min	0.05-0.08	91	12s
Education				
Board, 4-yr private college/university	year	1804	91	22s
Board, 4-yr public college/university	year	1688	91	22s
Expenditures, local gov't, public elementary/secondary	pupil	5487	92	20s
Room, 4-year private college/university	year	1659	91	22s
Room, 4-year public college/university	year	1916	91	22s
Tuition, 2-year private college/university	year	4852	91	22s
Tuition, 2-year public college/university	year	867	91	22s
Tuition, 4-year private college/university	year	7621	91	22s
Tuition, 4-year public college/university, in-state	year	2691	91	22s
Energy and Fuels				
Coal	mil Btu	1.60	90	64s
Energy	mil Btu	8.89	90	64s
Energy exp/householder, 1-family unit	year	487	90	28r
Energy exp/householder, <1,000 sq ft heating area	year	393	90	28r
Energy exp/householder, 1,000-1,999 sq ft heating area	year	442	90	28r
Energy exp/householder, 2,000+ sq ft heating area	year	577	90	28r
Energy exp/householder, mobile home	year	366	90	28r
Energy exp/householder, multifamily	year	382	90	28r
Gas, natural	mil Btu	4.67	90	64s
Gas, natural	000 cu ft	6.80	91	46s
Gas, natural, exp	year	566	91	46s
Gasoline, unleaded regular	mil Btu	9.46	90	64s
Entertainment				
Miniature golf admission	adult	6.18	92	1r
Miniature golf admission	child	5.14	92	1r
Waterpark admission	adult	11.00	92	1r
Waterpark admission	child	8.55	92	1r
Funerals				
Casket, 18-gauge steel, velvet interior		2029.08	91	24r
Cosmetology, hair care, etc.		75.10	91	24r
Embalming		249.24	91	24r
Facility use for ceremony		162.27	91	24r
Hearse, local		114.04	91	24r
Limousine, local		88.57	91	24r
Remains to funeral home, transfer		92.61	91	24r
Service charge, professional		682.42	91	24r
Vault, concrete, non-metallic liner		798.70	91	24r
Viewing facilities, use		163.86	91	24r
Groceries				
Apples, Red Delicious	lb	0.79	4/93	16r
Bacon	lb	1.75	4/93	16r
Bananas	lb	0.42	4/93	16r
Beef, stew, boneless	lb	2.61	4/93	16r
Bologna, all beef or mixed	lb	2.24	4/93	16r
Bread, white, pan	lb	0.64	4/93	16r
Bread, whole wheat, pan	lb	0.96	4/93	16r
Cabbage	lb	0.37	4/93	16r

Charlottesville, VA - continued

Item	Per	Value	Date	Ref.
Groceries - continued				
Carrots, short trimmed and topped	lb	0.47	4/93	16r
Celery	lb	0.64	4/93	16r
Cheese, American	lb	2.98	4/93	16r
Cheese, Cheddar	lb	3.28	4/93	16r
Chicken, fresh, whole	lb	0.77	4/93	16r
Chicken breast, bone-in	lb	1.92	4/93	16r
Chicken legs, bone-in	lb	1.06	4/93	16r
Chuck roast, graded and ungraded, ex USDA prime and choice	lb	2.40	4/93	16r
Chuck roast, USDA choice, bone-in	lb	2.19	4/93	16r
Chuck roast, USDA choice, boneless	lb	2.38	4/93	16r
Coffee, 100% ground roast, all sizes	lb	2.48	4/93	16r
Crackers, soda, salted	lb	1.15	4/93	16r
Eggs, Grade A large	doz	0.96	4/93	16r
Flour, white, all purpose	lb	0.24	4/93	16r
Frankfurters, all meat or all beef	lb	2.01	4/93	16r
Grapefruit	lb	0.44	4/93	16r
Grapes, Thompson Seedless	lb	1.40	4/93	16r
Ground beef, 100% beef	lb	1.58	4/93	16r
Ground beef, lean and extra lean	lb	2.09	4/93	16r
Ground chuck, 100% beef	lb	1.98	4/93	16r
Ham, boneless, excluding canned	lb	2.89	4/93	16r
Ham, picnic, shoulder, bone-in, smoked	lb	1.02	4/93	16r
Ham, rump or steak half, bone-in, smoked	lb	1.48	4/93	16r
Ice cream, prepackaged, bulk, regular	1/2 gal	2.41	4/93	16r
Lemons	lb	1.05	4/93	16r
Lettuce, iceberg	lb	0.81	4/93	16r
Margarine, stick	lb	0.88	4/93	16r
Oranges, navel	lb	0.55	4/93	16r
Pears, Anjou	lb	0.92	4/93	16r
Pork chops, center cut, bone-in	lb	3.13	4/93	16r
Potato chips	16 oz	2.94	4/93	16r
Potatoes, white	lb	0.43	4/93	16r
Rib roast, USDA choice, bone-in	lb	4.63	4/93	16r
Rice, white, long grain, uncooked	lb	0.45	4/93	16r
Round roast, graded & ungraded, ex USDA prime & choice	lb	3.03	4/93	16r
Round roast, USDA choice, boneless	lb	3.09	4/93	16r
Sausage, fresh, loose	lb	2.08	4/93	16r
Short ribs, bone-in	lb	2.66	4/93	16r
Shortening, vegetable oil blends	lb	0.69	4/93	16r
Spaghetti and macaroni	lb	0.81	4/93	16r
Steak, rib eye, USDA choice, boneless	lb	6.24	4/93	16r
Steak, round, graded & ungraded, ex USDA prime & choice	lb	3.31	4/93	16r
Steak, round, USDA choice, boneless	lb	3.34	4/93	16r
Steak, sirloin, graded & ungraded, ex USDA prime & choice	lb	4.19	4/93	16r
Steak, sirloin, USDA choice, boneless	lb	4.46	4/93	16r
Steak, T-bone, USDA choice, bone-in	lb	5.25	4/93	16r
Strawberries, dry pint	12 oz	0.92	4/93	16r
Sugar, white	lb	0.39	4/93	16r
Sugar, white, 33-80 oz pk	lb	0.38	4/93	16r
Tomatoes, field grown	lb	0.88	4/93	16r
Tuna, chunk, light	lb	1.79	4/93	16r
Turkey, frozen, whole	lb	1.04	4/93	16r
Yogurt, natural, fruit flavored	1/2 pint	0.57	4/93	16r
Health Care				
Childbirth, cesarean, hospital		5034	91	62r
Childbirth, cesarean, physician's fee		2053	91	62r
Childbirth, normal, hospital		2712	91	62r
Childbirth, normal, physician's fee		1492	91	62r
Medical plan per employee	year	3495	91	45r
Mental health care, exp	capita	37.60-53.67	90	38s
Mental health care, exp, state mental health agency	capita	44.54	90	38s
Mental health care, hospital psychiatric services, non-Federal, exp	capita	9.90	88	38s
Mental health care, mental health organization, multiservice, exp	capita	17.29	88	38s

Values are in dollars or fractions of dollars. In the column headed *Ref*, references are shown to sources. Each reference is followed by a letter. These refer to the geographical level for which data were reported: s=State, r=Region, and c=City or metro. The abbreviation *ex* is used to mean *except* or *excluding; exp* stands for expenditures. For other abbreviations and further explanations, please see the Introduction.

Charlottesville, VA - continued

Item	Per	Value	Date	Ref.
Health Care				
Mental health care, psychiatric hospitals, private, exp	capita	32.58	88	38s
Mental health care, psychiatric out-patient clinics, freestanding, exp	capita	0.93	88	38s
Mental health care, psychiatric partial-care organizations, freestanding, exp	capita	0.25	88	38s
Mental health care, state and county mental hospitals, exp	capita	28.61	88	38s
Mental health care, VA medical centers, exp	capita	3.95	88	38s
Physician fee, family practice, first-visit		75.00	91	62r
Physician fee, family practice, revisit		34.00	91	62r
Physician fee, general practice, first-visit		61.00	91	62r
Physician fee, general practice, revisit		32.00	91	62r
Physician fee, general surgeon, first-visit		64.00	91	62r
Physician fee, general surgeon, revisit		40.00	91	62r
Physician fee, internal medicine, first-visit		98.00	91	62r
Physician fee, internal medicine, revisit		40.00	91	62r
Physician fee, median, neurosurgeon, first-visit		130.00	91	62r
Physician fee, median, nonsurgical specialist, first-visit		95.00	91	62r
Physician fee, median, orthopedic surgeon, first-visit		91.00	91	62r
Physician fee, median, plastic surgeon, first-visit		66.00	91	62r
Physician fee, median, surgical specialist, first-visit		62.00	91	62r
Physician fee, neurosurgeon, revisit		50.00	91	62r
Physician fee, nonsurgical specialist, revisit		40.00	91	62r
Physician fee, obstetrics/gynecology, first-visit		64.00	91	62r
Physician fee, obstetrics/gynecology, revisit		41.00	91	62r
Physician fee, orthopedic surgeon, revisit		40.00	91	62r
Physician fee, pediatrician, first-visit		49.00	91	62r
Physician fee, pediatrician, revisit		33.00	91	62r
Physician fee, plastic surgeon, revisit		43.00	91	62r
Physician fee, surgical specialist, revisit		37.00	91	62r
Substance abuse, hospital ancillary charge	incident	1220	90	70s
Substance abuse, hospital physician charge	incident	590	90	70s
Substance abuse, hospital room and board	incident	6280	90	70s
Insurance and Pensions				
Auto insurance, private passenger	year	559.45	91	63s
Taxes				
Tax, cigarette	pack	2.50	91	77s
Tax, gasoline	gal	17.50	91	77s
Taxes, state	capita	1090	91	77s
Transportation				
Driver's license fee		12.00	12/90	43s
Vehicle registration and license plate	year	26.50-37.50	93	90s
Travel				
Business travel	day	193.00	4/93	89r
Utilities				
Electricity	mil Btu	17.70	90	64s

Chattanooga, TN

Item	Per	Value	Date	Ref.
Composite ACCRA index		92.10	4Q 92	4c
Alcoholic Beverages				
Beer, Miller Lite or Budweiser, 12-oz containers	6 pack	4.00	4Q 92	4c
Liquor, J & B Scotch	750 ml	17.53	4Q 92	4c
Wine, Gallo Chablis blanc, 1.5 liter	bottle	5.41	4Q 92	4c

Chattanooga, TN - continued

Item	Per	Value	Date	Ref.
Child Care				
Child care fee, average, center	hour	1.29	90	65r
Child care fee, average, nonregulated family day care	hour	0.89	90	65r
Child care fee, average, regulated family day care	hour	1.32	90	65r
Clothing				
Jeans, man's denim		31.78	4Q 92	4c
Shirt, man's dress shirt		23.53	4Q 92	4c
Undervest, boy's size 10-14, cotton	3	3.60	4Q 92	4c
Communications				
Long-distance telephone service, day, initial minute, 0-100 miles	min	0.10-0.22	91	12s
Long-distance telephone service, day, additional minute, 0-100 miles	min	0.10-0.22	91	12s
Long-distance telephone service, evenings/weekends, 0-100 mi, initial minute	min	0.05-0.10	91	12s
Long-distance telephone service, evenings/weekends, 0-100 mi, additional minute	min	0.05-0.10	91	12s
Newspaper subscription, daily and Sunday home delivery, large-city	month	11.05	4Q 92	4c
Telephone, flat rate	month	11.85	91	11c
Telephone bill, family of four	month	20.38	4Q 92	4c
Education				
Board, 4-yr private college/university	year	1845	91	22s
Board, 4-yr public college/university	year	1499	91	22s
Expenditures, local gov't, public elementary/secondary	pupil	3736	92	20s
Room, 4-year private college/university	year	1679	91	22s
Room, 4-year public college/university	year	1339	91	22s
Tuition, 2-year private college/university	year	4203	91	22s
Tuition, 2-year public college/university	year	848	91	22s
Tuition, 4-year private college/university	year	6889	91	22s
Tuition, 4-year public college/university, in-state	year	1518	91	22s
Energy and Fuels				
Coal	mil Btu	1.35	90	64s
Energy	mil Btu	8.61	90	64s
Energy, combined forms, 1,800 sq ft heating area	month	101.18	4Q 92	4c
Energy, exc electricity, 1,800 sq ft heating area	month	36.40	4Q 92	4c
Energy exp/householder, 1-family unit	year	403	90	28r
Energy exp/householder, <1,000 sq ft heating area	year	342	90	28r
Energy exp/householder, 1,000-1,999 sq ft heating area	year	388	90	28r
Energy exp/householder, 2,000+ sq ft heating area	year	434	90	28r
Energy exp/householder, mobile home	year	320	90	28r
Energy exp/householder, multifamily	year	338	90	28r
Gas, cooking, winter, 10 therms	month	11.93	92	56c
Gas, cooking, winter, 30 therms	month	21.80	92	56c
Gas, cooking, winter, 50 therms	month	31.67	92	56c
Gas, heating, winter, 100 therms	month	56.34	92	56c
Gas, natural	mil Btu	3.98	90	64s
Gas, natural	000 cu ft	5.19	91	46s
Gas, natural, exp	year	388	91	46s
Gasoline, motor	gal	1.07	4Q 92	4c
Gasoline, unleaded regular	mil Btu	9.40	90	64s
Entertainment				
Bowling, evening rate	game	2.20	4Q 92	4c
Miniature golf admission	adult	6.18	92	1r
Miniature golf admission	child	5.14	92	1r
Monopoly game, Parker Brothers', No. 9		9.88	4Q 92	4c
Movie	admission	5.20	4Q 92	4c
Tennis balls, yellow, Wilson or Penn, 3	can	2.12	4Q 92	4c
Waterpark admission	adult	11.00	92	1r

Values are in dollars or fractions of dollars. In the column headed *Ref*, references are shown to sources. Each reference is followed by a letter. These refer to the geographical level for which data were reported: s=State, r=Region, and c=City or metro. The abbreviation *ex* is used to mean *except* or *excluding*; *exp* stands for expenditures. For other abbreviations and further explanations, please see the Introduction.

Chattanooga, TN - continued

Item	Per	Value	Date	Ref.
Entertainment				
Waterpark admission	child	8.55	92	1r
Funerals				
Casket, 18-gauge steel, velvet interior		2329.05	91	24r
Cosmetology, hair care, etc.		72.78	91	24r
Embalming		240.71	91	24r
Facility use for ceremony		181.67	91	24r
Hearse, local		106.25	91	24r
Limousine, local		70.92	91	24r
Remains to funeral home, transfer		96.30	91	24r
Service charge, professional		687.09	91	24r
Vault, concrete, non-metallic liner		732.09	91	24r
Viewing facilities, use		190.30	91	24r
Goods and Services				
ACCRA Index, Miscellaneous Goods and Services		96.10	4Q 92	4c
Groceries				
ACCRA Index, Groceries		94.10	4Q 92	4c
Apples, Red Delicious	lb	0.79	4/93	16r
Babyfood, strained vegetables, lowest price	4-4.5 oz jar	0.30	4Q 92	4c
Bacon	lb	1.75	4/93	16r
Bananas	lb	0.29	4Q 92	4c
Bananas	lb	0.42	4/93	16r
Beef, stew, boneless	lb	2.61	4/93	16r
Bologna, all beef or mixed	lb	2.24	4/93	16r
Bread, white	24 oz	0.65	4Q 92	4c
Bread, white, pan	lb	0.64	4/93	16r
Bread, whole wheat, pan	lb	0.96	4/93	16r
Cabbage	lb	0.37	4/93	16r
Carrots, short trimmed and topped	lb	0.47	4/93	16r
Celery	lb	0.64	4/93	16r
Cheese, American	lb	2.98	4/93	16r
Cheese, Cheddar	lb	3.28	4/93	16r
Cheese, Kraft grated Parmesan	8-oz canister	3.27	4Q 92	4c
Chicken, fresh, whole	lb	0.77	4/93	16r
Chicken, fryer, whole	lb	0.61	4Q 92	4c
Chicken breast, bone-in	lb	1.92	4/93	16r
Chicken legs, bone-in	lb	1.06	4/93	16r
Chuck roast, graded and ungraded, ex USDA prime and choice	lb	2.40	4/93	16r
Chuck roast, USDA choice, bone-in	lb	2.19	4/93	16r
Chuck roast, USDA choice, boneless	lb	2.38	4/93	16r
Cigarettes, Winston	carton	16.47	4Q 92	4c
Coffee, 100% ground roast, all sizes	lb	2.48	4/93	16r
Coffee, vacuum-packed	13-oz can	1.73	4Q 92	4c
Corn, frozen	10 oz	0.52	4Q 92	4c
Corn Flakes, Kellogg's or Post Toasties	18 oz	1.67	4Q 92	4c
Crackers, soda, salted	lb	1.15	4/93	16r
Eggs, Grade A large	doz	0.81	4Q 92	4c
Eggs, Grade A large	doz	0.96	4/93	16r
Flour, white, all purpose	lb	0.24	4/93	16r
Frankfurters, all meat or all beef	lb	2.01	4/93	16r
Grapefruit	lb	0.44	4/93	16r
Grapes, Thompson Seedless	lb	1.40	4/93	16r
Ground beef, 100% beef	lb	1.58	4/93	16r
Ground beef, lean and extra lean	lb	2.09	4/93	16r
Ground beef or hamburger	lb	1.74	4Q 92	4c
Ground chuck, 100% beef	lb	1.98	4/93	16r
Ham, boneless, excluding canned	lb	2.89	4/93	16r
Ham, picnic, shoulder, bone-in, smoked	lb	1.02	4/93	16r
Ham, rump or steak half, bone-in, smoked	lb	1.48	4/93	16r
Honey, jar	8 oz	0.89-1.09	92	5r
Honey, jar	lb	1.39-2.25	92	5r
Honey, squeeze bear	12-oz	1.00-1.50	92	5r
Ice cream, prepackaged, bulk, regular	1/2 gal	2.41	4/93	16r
Lemons	lb	1.05	4/93	16r
Lettuce, iceberg	head	0.99	4Q 92	4c
Lettuce, iceberg	lb	0.81	4/93	16r

Chattanooga, TN - continued

Item	Per	Value	Date	Ref.
Groceries - continued				
Margarine, Blue Bonnet or Parkay cubes	lb	0.47	4Q 92	4c
Margarine, stick	lb	0.88	4/93	16r
Milk, whole	1/2 gal	1.29	4Q 92	4c
Orange juice, Minute Maid frozen	12-oz can	1.22	4Q 92	4c
Oranges, navel	lb	0.55	4/93	16r
Peaches	29-oz can	1.27	4Q 92	4c
Pears, Anjou	lb	0.92	4/93	16r
Peas Sweet, Del Monte or Green Giant	15-17 oz can	0.57	4Q 92	4c
Pork chops, center cut, bone-in	lb	3.13	4/93	16r
Potato chips	16 oz	2.94	4/93	16r
Potatoes, white	lb	0.43	4/93	16r
Potatoes, white or red	10-lb sack	2.80	4Q 92	4c
Rib roast, USDA choice, bone-in	lb	4.63	4/93	16r
Rice, white, long grain, uncooked	lb	0.45	4/93	16r
Round roast, graded & ungraded, ex USDA prime & choice	lb	3.03	4/93	16r
Round roast, USDA choice, boneless	lb	3.09	4/93	16r
Sausage, fresh, loose	lb	2.08	4/93	16r
Sausage, Jimmy Dean, 100% pork	lb	2.49	4Q 92	4c
Short ribs, bone-in	lb	2.66	4/93	16r
Shortening, vegetable oil blends	lb	0.69	4/93	16r
Shortening, vegetable, Crisco	3-lb can	1.99	4Q 92	4c
Soft drink, Coca Cola	2 liter	1.23	4Q 92	4c
Spaghetti and macaroni	lb	0.81	4/93	16r
Steak, rib eye, USDA choice, boneless	lb	6.24	4/93	16r
Steak, round, graded & ungraded, ex USDA prime & choice	lb	3.31	4/93	16r
Steak, round, USDA choice, boneless	lb	3.34	4/93	16r
Steak, sirloin, graded & ungraded, ex USDA prime & choice	lb	4.19	4/93	16r
Steak, sirloin, USDA choice, boneless	lb	4.46	4/93	16r
Steak, T-bone	lb	5.57	4Q 92	4c
Steak, T-bone, USDA choice, bone-in	lb	5.25	4/93	16r
Strawberries, dry pint	12 oz	0.92	4/93	16r
Sugar, cane or beet	4 lb	1.46	4Q 92	4c
Sugar, white	lb	0.39	4/93	16r
Sugar, white, 33-80 oz pk	lb	0.38	4/93	16r
Tomatoes, field grown	lb	0.88	4/93	16r
Tomatoes, Hunt's or Del Monte	14.5-oz can	0.49	4Q 92	4c
Tuna, chunk, light	6.125-6.5 oz can	0.55	4Q 92	4c
Tuna, chunk, light	lb	1.79	4/93	16r
Turkey, frozen, whole	lb	1.04	4/93	16r
Yogurt, natural, fruit flavored	1/2 pint	0.57	4/93	16r
Health Care				
ACCRA Index, Health Care		89.30	4Q 92	4c
Analgesic, Aspirin, Bayer, 325 mg tablets	100	5.64	4Q 92	4c
Childbirth, cesarean, hospital		5034	91	62r
Childbirth, cesarean, physician's fee		2053	91	62r
Childbirth, normal, hospital		2712	91	62r
Childbirth, normal, physician's fee		1492	91	62r
Dentist's fee, adult teeth cleaning and periodic oral exam	visit	41.80	4Q 92	4c
Doctor's fee, routine exam, established patient	visit	31.40	4Q 92	4c
Hospital care, semiprivate room	day	200.00	90	27c
Hospital care, semiprivate room	day	264.80	4Q 92	4c
Medical insurance premium, per employee, small group comprehensive	month	335.80	10/91	25c
Mental health care, exp	capita	20.37-28.83	90	38s
Mental health care, exp, state mental health agency	capita	28.84	90	38s

Values are in dollars or fractions of dollars. In the column headed *Ref*, references are shown to sources. Each reference is followed by a letter. These refer to the geographical level for which data were reported: s = State, r = Region, and c = City or metro. The abbreviation *ex* is used to mean *except* or *excluding*; *exp* stands for expenditures. For other abbreviations and further explanations, please see the Introduction.

Chattanooga, TN - continued

Item	Per	Value	Date	Ref.
Health Care				
Mental health care, hospital psychiatric services, non-Federal, exp	capita	13.48	88	38s
Mental health care, mental health organization, multiservice, exp	capita	11.35	88	38s
Mental health care, psychiatric hospitals, private, exp	capita	22.28	88	38s
Mental health care, psychiatric out-patient clinics, freestanding, exp	capita	2.58	88	38s
Mental health care, psychiatric partial-care organizations, freestanding, exp	capita	0.25	88	38s
Mental health care, state and county mental hospitals, exp	capita	20.05	88	38s
Mental health care, VA medical centers, exp	capita	4.98	88	38s
Physician fee, family practice, first-visit		75.00	91	62r
Physician fee, family practice, revisit		34.00	91	62r
Physician fee, general practice, first-visit		61.00	91	62r
Physician fee, general practice, revisit		32.00	91	62r
Physician fee, general surgeon, first-visit		64.00	91	62r
Physician fee, general surgeon, revisit		40.00	91	62r
Physician fee, internal medicine, first-visit		98.00	91	62r
Physician fee, internal medicine, revisit		40.00	91	62r
Physician fee, median, neurosurgeon, first-visit		130.00	91	62r
Physician fee, median, nonsurgical specialist, first-visit		95.00	91	62r
Physician fee, median, orthopedic surgeon, first-visit		91.00	91	62r
Physician fee, median, plastic surgeon, first-visit		66.00	91	62r
Physician fee, median, surgical specialist, first-visit		62.00	91	62r
Physician fee, neurosurgeon, revisit		50.00	91	62r
Physician fee, nonsurgical specialist, revisit		40.00	91	62r
Physician fee, obstetrics/gynecology, first-visit		64.00	91	62r
Physician fee, obstetrics/gynecology, revisit		41.00	91	62r
Physician fee, orthopedic surgeon, revisit		40.00	91	62r
Physician fee, pediatrician, first-visit		49.00	91	62r
Physician fee, pediatrician, revisit		33.00	91	62r
Physician fee, plastic surgeon, revisit		43.00	91	62r
Physician fee, surgical specialist, revisit		37.00	91	62r
Substance abuse, hospital ancillary charge	incident	1330	90	70s
Substance abuse, hospital physician charge	Incident	580	90	70s
Substance abuse, hospital room and board	incident	5180	90	70s
Household Goods				
Appliance repair, home, service call, washing machine	min labor charge	29.49	4Q 92	4c
Laundry detergent, Tide Ultra, Bold, or Cheer	42 oz	2.74	4Q 92	4c
Tissues, facial, Kleenex brand	175-count box	1.08	4Q 92	4c
Housing				
ACCRA Index, Housing		88.00	4Q 92	4c
Home, median price	unit	73.00		26c
House, 1,800 sq ft, 8,000 sq ft lot, new, urban	total	89774	4Q 92	4c
House payment, principal and interest, 25% down payment	month	502	4Q 92	4c
Mortgage rate, incl. points & origination fee, 30-year fixed or adjustable rate	percent	8.16	4Q 92	4c
Rent, apartment, 2 bedrooms - 1-1/2 to 2 baths, unfurnished, 950 sq ft, water	month	524	4Q 92	4c
Rental unit, 1 bedroom	month	390	93	23c
Rental unit, 2 bedroom	month	460	93	23c
Rental unit, 3 bedroom	month	575	93	23c
Rental unit, 4 bedroom	month	647	93	23c

Chattanooga, TN - continued

Item	Per	Value	Date	Ref.
Housing - continued				
Rental unit, efficiency	month	320	93	23c
Insurance and Pensions				
Auto insurance, private passenger	year	554.60	91	63s
Personal Goods				
Shampoo, Alberto VO5	15 oz	1.05	4Q 92	4c
Toothpaste, Crest or Colgate	6-7 oz	2.17	4Q 92	4c
Personal Services				
Dry cleaning, man's 2-piece suit		5.13	4Q 92	4c
Haircare, woman's shampoo, trim and blow-dry		18.39	4Q 92	4c
Haircut, man's barbershop, no styling		7.20	4Q 92	4c
Restaurant Food				
Chicken, fried, thigh and drumstick		1.99	4Q 92	4c
Hamburger with cheese	1/4 lb	1.75	4Q 92	4c
Pizza, Pizza Hut or Pizza Inn, cheese, thin crust	12-13 in	7.99	4Q 92	4c
Taxes				
Tax, cigarette	pack	13	91	77s
Tax, gasoline	gal	22.40	91	77s
Taxes, state	capita	870	91	77s
Transportation				
ACCRA Index, Transportation		87.10	4Q 92	4c
Bus fare	one-way	0.75	3/93	2c
Bus fare, up to 10 miles	one-way	0.75	4Q 92	4c
Commuter train fare (inclined plane)	one-way	6.00	3/93	2c
Driver's license fee		14.00-16.00	12/90	43s
Tire balance, computer or spin balance, front	wheel	5.20	4Q 92	4c
Travel				
Business travel	day	193.00	4/93	89r
Utilities				
ACCRA Index, Utilities		93.90	4Q 92	4c
Electricity	mil Btu	15.59	90	64s
Electricity, partial electric and other energy, 1,800 sq ft living area new home	month	64.78	4Q 92	4c

Cheyenne, WY

Item	Per	Value	Date	Ref.
Composite ACCRA index		96.60	4Q 92	4c
Alcoholic Beverages				
Beer, Miller Lite or Budweiser, 12-oz containers	6 pack	4.26	4Q 92	4c
Liquor, J & B Scotch	750 ml	17.04	4Q 92	4c
Wine, Gallo Chablis blanc, 1.5 liter	bottle	5.45	4Q 92	4c
Child Care				
Child care fee, average, center	hour	1.71	90	65r
Child care fee, average, nonregulated family day care	hour	1.32	90	65r
Child care fee, average, regulated family day care	hour	1.86	90	65r
Clothing				
Jeans, man's denim		30.19	4Q 92	4c
Shirt, man's dress shirt		18.99	4Q 92	4c
Undervest, boy's size 10-14, cotton	3	3.49	4Q 92	4c
Communications				
Long-distance telephone service, day, initial minute, 0-100 miles	min	0.19-0.43	91	12s
Long-distance telephone service, day, additional minute, 0-100 miles	min	0.09-0.29	91	12s
Long-distance telephone service, evenings/weekends, 0-100 mi, initial minute	min	0.10-0.24	91	12s

Values are in dollars or fractions of dollars. In the column headed *Ref*, references are shown to sources. Each reference is followed by a letter. These refer to the geographical level for which data were reported: s = State, r = Region, and c = City or metro. The abbreviation *ex* is used to mean *except* or *excluding*; *exp* stands for expenditures. For other abbreviations and further explanations, please see the Introduction.

Cheyenne, WY - continued

Item	Per	Value	Date	Ref.
Communications				
Long-distance telephone service, evenings/ weekends, 0-100 mi, additional minute	min	0.05-0.16	91	12s
Newspaper subscription, daily and Sunday home delivery, large-city	month	6.00	4Q 92	4c
Telephone, flat rate	month	11.96	91	11c
Telephone bill, family of four	month	22.35	4Q 92	4c
Education				
Board, 4-yr public college/university	year	1767	91	22s
Expenditures, local gov't, public elementary/secondary	pupil	5355	92	20s
Room, 4-year public college/university	year	1312	91	22s
Tuition, 2-year private college/university	year	7500	91	22s
Tuition, 2-year public college/university	year	662	91	22s
Tuition, 4-year public college/university, in-state	year	1148	91	22s
Energy and Fuels				
Coal	mil Btu	0.86	90	64s
Energy	mil Btu	6.46	90	64s
Energy, combined forms, 1,800 sq ft heating area	month	84.98	4Q 92	4c
Energy, exc electricity, 1,800 sq ft heating area	month	29.35	4Q 92	4c
Energy exp/householder, 1-family unit	year	372	90	28r
Energy exp/householder, <1,000 sq ft heating area	year	335	90	28r
Energy exp/householder, 1,000-1,999 sq ft heating area	year	365	90	28r
Energy exp/householder, 2,000+ sq ft heating area	year	411	90	28r
Energy exp/householder, mobile home	year	305	90	28r
Energy exp/householder, multifamily	year	372	90	28r
Gas, cooking, winter, 10 therms	month	10.09	92	56c
Gas, cooking, winter, 30 therms	month	15.48	92	56c
Gas, cooking, winter, 50 therms	month	20.86	92	56c
Gas, heating, winter, 100 therms	month	34.32	92	56c
Gas, heating, winter, average use	month	53.84	92	56c
Gas, natural	mil Btu	3.57	90	64s
Gas, natural	000 cu ft	4.74	91	46s
Gas, natural, exp	year	501	91	46s
Gasoline, motor	gal	1.20	4Q 92	4c
Gasoline, unleaded regular	mil Btu	8.66	90	64s
Entertainment				
Bowling, evening rate	game	1.92	4Q 92	4c
Miniature golf admission	adult	6.18	92	1r
Miniature golf admission	child	5.14	92	1r
Monopoly game, Parker Brothers', No. 9		10.88	4Q 92	4c
Movie	admission	4.75	4Q 92	4c
Tennis balls, yellow, Wilson or Penn, 3	can	2.88	4Q 92	4c
Waterpark admission	adult	11.00	92	1r
Waterpark admission	child	8.55	92	1r
Funerals				
Casket, 18-gauge steel, velvet interior		1929.04	91	24r
Cosmetology, hair care, etc.		88.52	91	24r
Embalming		249.33	91	24r
Facility use for ceremony		182.75	91	24r
Hearse, local		110.04	91	24r
Limousine, local		66.67	91	24r
Remains to funeral home, transfer		84.58	91	24r
Service charge, professional		593.00	91	24r
Vault, concrete, non-metallic liner		647.38	91	24r
Viewing facilities, use		99.87	91	24r
Goods and Services				
ACCRA Index, Miscellaneous Goods and Services		97.40	4Q 92	4c
Groceries				
ACCRA Index, Groceries		100.90	4Q 92	4c
Apples, Red Delicious	lb	0.80	4/93	16r

Cheyenne, WY - continued

Item	Per	Value	Date	Ref.
Groceries - continued				
Babyfood, strained vegetables, lowest price	4-4.5 oz jar	0.33	4Q 92	4c
Bacon	lb	1.79	4/93	16r
Bananas	lb	0.50	4Q 92	4c
Bananas	lb	0.53	4/93	16r
Bologna, all beef or mixed	lb	2.67	4/93	16r
Bread, white	24 oz	0.79	4Q 92	4c
Bread, white, pan	lb	0.81	4/93	16r
Carrots, short trimmed and topped	lb	0.39	4/93	16r
Cheese, Kraft grated Parmesan	8-oz canister	3.32	4Q 92	4c
Chicken, fresh, whole	lb	0.94	4/93	16r
Chicken, fryer, whole	lb	0.70	4Q 92	4c
Chicken breast, bone-in	lb	2.19	4/93	16r
Chuck roast, graded and ungraded, ex USDA prime and choice	lb	2.26	4/93	16r
Cigarettes, Winston	carton	16.15	4Q 92	4c
Coffee, 100% ground roast, all sizes	lb	2.33	4/93	16r
Coffee, vacuum-packed	13-oz can	2.44	4Q 92	4c
Corn, frozen	10 oz	0.75	4Q 92	4c
Corn Flakes, Kellogg's or Post Toasties	18 oz	1.98	4Q 92	4c
Eggs, Grade A large	doz	0.86	4Q 92	4c
Eggs, Grade AA large	doz	1.18	4/93	16r
Flour, white, all purpose	lb	0.22	4/93	16r
Grapefruit	lb	0.52	4/93	16r
Grapes, Thompson Seedless	lb	1.50	4/93	16r
Ground beef, 100% beef	lb	1.44	4/93	16r
Ground beef, lean and extra lean	lb	2.34	4/93	16r
Ground beef or hamburger	lb	1.11	4Q 92	4c
Ham, boneless, excluding canned	lb	2.56	4/93	16r
Honey, jar	8 oz	0.99-1.19	92	5r
Honey, jar	lb	1.35-1.97	92	5r
Honey, squeeze bear	12-oz	1.00-1.89	92	5r
Ice cream, prepackaged, bulk, regular	1/2 gal	2.40	4/93	16r
Lemons	lb	0.81	4/93	16r
Lettuce, iceberg	head	0.95	4Q 92	4c
Lettuce, iceberg	lb	0.84	4/93	16r
Margarine, Blue Bonnet or Parkay cubes	lb	0.72	4Q 92	4c
Margarine, stick	lb	0.81	4/93	16r
Milk, whole	1/2 gal	1.43	4Q 92	4c
Orange juice, Minute Maid frozen	12-oz can	1.50	4Q 92	4c
Oranges, navel	lb	0.48	4/93	16r
Peaches	29-oz can	1.48	4Q 92	4c
Peas Sweet, Del Monte or Green Giant	15-17 oz can	0.66	4Q 92	4c
Pork chops, center cut, bone-in	lb	3.25	4/93	16r
Potato chips	16 oz	2.89	4/93	16r
Potatoes, white	lb	0.38	4/93	16r
Potatoes, white or red	10-lb sack	2.29	4Q 92	4c
Round roast, graded & ungraded, ex USDA prime & choice	lb	3.00	4/93	16r
Round roast, USDA choice, boneless	lb	3.16	4/93	16r
Sausage, Jimmy Dean, 100% pork	lb	2.65	4Q 92	4c
Shortening, vegetable oil blends	lb	0.86	4/93	16r
Shortening, vegetable, Crisco	3-lb can	2.07	4Q 92	4c
Soft drink, Coca Cola	2 liter	1.51	4Q 92	4c
Spaghetti and macaroni	lb	0.84	4/93	16r
Steak, round, graded & ungraded, ex USDA prime & choice	lb	3.34	4/93	16r
Steak, round, USDA choice, boneless	lb	3.24	4/93	16r
Steak, sirloin, graded & ungraded, ex USDA prime & choice	lb	3.75	4/93	16r
Steak, sirloin, USDA choice, boneless	lb	4.49	4/93	16r
Steak, T-bone	lb	4.47	4Q 92	4c
Sugar, cane or beet	4 lb	1.38	4Q 92	4c
Sugar, white	lb	0.41	4/93	16r

Values are in dollars or fractions of dollars. In the column headed *Ref*, references are shown to sources. Each reference is followed by a letter. These refer to the geographical level for which data were reported: s=State, r=Region, and c=City or metro. The abbreviation *ex* is used to mean *except* or *excluding*; *exp* stands for expenditures. For other abbreviations and further explanations, please see the Introduction.

Cheyenne, WY - continued

Item	Per	Value	Date	Ref.
Groceries				
Sugar, white, 33-80 oz pk	lb	0.38	4/93	16r
Tomatoes, field grown	lb	1.01	4/93	16r
Tomatoes, Hunt's or Del Monte	14.5-oz can	0.75	4Q 92	4c
Tuna, chunk, light	6.125-6.5 oz can	0.70	4Q 92	4c
Turkey, frozen, whole	lb	1.04	4/93	16r
Health Care				
ACCRA Index, Health Care		95.30	4Q 92	4c
Analgesic, Aspirin, Bayer, 325 mg tablets	100	4.36	4Q 92	4c
Childbirth, cesarean, hospital		5533	91	62r
Childbirth, cesarean, physician's fee		2053	91	62r
Childbirth, normal, hospital		2745	91	62r
Childbirth, normal, physician's fee		1492	91	62r
Dentist's fee, adult teeth cleaning and periodic oral exam	visit	46.80	4Q 92	4c
Doctor's fee, routine exam, established patient	visit	33.50	4Q 92	4c
Hospital care, semiprivate room	day	318.50	4Q 92	4c
Medical insurance premium, per employee, small group comprehensive	month	284.70	10/91	25c
Medical plan per employee	year	3218	91	45r
Mental health care, exp	capita	28.84-37.59	90	38s
Mental health care, exp, state mental health agency	capita	34.62	90	38s
Mental health care, hospital psychiatric services, non-Federal, exp	capita	3.06	88	38s
Mental health care, mental health organization, multiservice, exp	capita	9.72	88	38s
Mental health care, psychiatric hospitals, private, exp	capita	24.34	88	38s
Mental health care, psychiatric out-patient clinics, freestanding, exp	capita	9.27	88	38s
Mental health care, state and county mental hospitals, exp	capita	25.55	88	38s
Mental health care, VA medical centers, exp	capita	39.92	88	38s
Physician fee, family practice, first-visit		111.00	91	62r
Physician fee, family practice, revisit		45.00	91	62r
Physician fee, general practice, first-visit		100.00	91	62r
Physician fee, general practice, revisit		40.00	91	62r
Physician fee, internal medicine, first-visit		137.00	91	62r
Physician fee, internal medicine, revisit		48.00	91	62r
Physician fee, median, neurosurgeon, first-visit		157.00	91	62r
Physician fee, median, nonsurgical specialist, first-visit		131.00	91	62r
Physician fee, median, orthopedic surgeon, first-visit		124.00	91	62r
Physician fee, median, plastic surgeon, first-visit		88.00	91	62r
Physician fee, median, surgical specialist, first-visit		100.00	91	62r
Physician fee, neurosurgeon, revisit		51.00	91	62r
Physician fee, nonsurgical specialist, revisit		47.00	91	62r
Physician fee, obstetrics/gynecology, first-visit		95.00	91	62r
Physician fee, obstetrics/gynecology, revisit		50.00	91	62r
Physician fee, orthopedic surgeon, revisit		51.00	91	62r
Physician fee, pediatrician, first-visit		81.00	91	62r
Physician fee, pediatrician, revisit		42.00	91	62r
Physician fee, plastic surgeon, revisit		48.00	91	62r
Physician fee, surgical specialist, revisit		49.00	91	62r
Household Goods				
Appliance repair, home, service call, washing machine	min labor charge	36.57	4Q 92	4c
Laundry detergent, Tide Ultra, Bold, or Cheer	42 oz	3.80	4Q 92	4c

Cheyenne, WY - continued

Item	Per	Value	Date	Ref.
Household Goods - continued				
Tissues, facial, Kleenex brand	175-count box	1.18	4Q 92	4c
Housing				
ACCRA Index, Housing		95.50	4Q 92	4c
House, 1,800 sq ft, 8,000 sq ft lot, new, urban	total	98500	4Q 92	4c
House payment, principal and interest, 25% down payment	month	553	4Q 92	4c
Mortgage rate, incl. points & origination fee, 30-year fixed or adjustable rate	percent	8.21	4Q 92	4c
Rent, apartment, 2 bedrooms - 1-1/2 to 2 baths, unfurnished, 950 sq ft, water	month	550	4Q 92	4c
Insurance and Pensions				
Auto insurance, private passenger	year	450.33	91	63s
Personal Goods				
Shampoo, Alberto VO5	15 oz	1.07	4Q 92	4c
Toothpaste, Crest or Colgate	6-7 oz	1.82	4Q 92	4c
Personal Services				
Dry cleaning, man's 2-piece suit		6.00	4Q 92	4c
Haircare, woman's shampoo, trim and blow-dry		19.00	4Q 92	4c
Haircut, man's barbershop, no styling		9.00	4Q 92	4c
Restaurant Food				
Chicken, fried, thigh and drumstick		2.10	4Q 92	4c
Hamburger with cheese	1/4 lb	1.89	4Q 92	4c
Pizza, Pizza Hut or Pizza Inn, cheese, thin crust	12-13 in	9.05	4Q 92	4c
Taxes				
Tax, cigarette	pack	12	91	77s
Tax, gasoline	gal	9	91	77s
Taxes, state	capita	1385	91	77s
Transportation				
ACCRA Index, Transportation		105.60	4Q 92	4c
Driver's license fee		5.00	12/90	43s
Tire balance, computer or spin balance, front	wheel	6.80	4Q 92	4c
Travel				
Business travel	day	178.00	4/93	89r
Utilities				
ACCRA Index, Utilities		81.50	4Q 92	4c
Electricity	mil Btu	12.37	90	64s
Electricity, partial electric and other energy, 1,800 sq ft living area new home	month	55.63	4Q 92	4c
Electricity, winter, 250 KWh	month	15.60	92	55c
Electricity, winter, 500 KWh	month	31.20	92	55c
Electricity, winter, 750 KWh	month	43.58	92	55c
Electricity, winter, 1000 KWh	month	56.70	92	55c

Chicago, IL

Item	Per	Value	Date	Ref.
Alcoholic Beverages				
Alcoholic beverages, exp	year	389	89	15c
Charity				
Cash contributions	year	872	89	15c
Child Care				
Child care, on-site	year	4732	93	17c
Child care fee, average, center	hour	1.63	90	65r
Child care fee, average, nonregulated family day care	hour	1.83	90	65r
Child care fee, average, regulated family day care	hour	1.42	90	65r

Values are in dollars or fractions of dollars. In the column headed *Ref*, references are shown to sources. Each reference is followed by a letter. These refer to the geographical level for which data were reported: s = State, r = Region, and c = City or metro. The abbreviation *ex* is used to mean *except* or *excluding*; *exp* stands for *expenditures*. For other abbreviations and further explanations, please see the Introduction.

Chicago, IL - continued

Item	Per	Value	Date	Ref.
Communications				
Long-distance telephone service, day, initial minute, 0-100 miles	min	0.10-0.34	91	12s
Long-distance telephone service, day, additional minute, 0-100 miles	min	0.04-0.16	91	12s
Long-distance telephone service, evenings/weekends, 0-100 mi, initial minute	min	0.06-0.20	91	12s
Long-distance telephone service, evenings/weekends, 0-100 mi, additional minute	min	0.02-0.10	91	12s
Postage and stationery, exp	year	206	89	15c
Telephone, exp	year	559	89	15c
Telephone, residential, private line, rotary, unlimited calling	month	17.23	10/91	78c
Education				
Board, 4-yr private college/university	year	1797	91	22s
Board, 4-yr public college/university	year	1857	91	22s
Education, exp	year	493	89	15c
Expenditures, local gov't, public elementary/secondary	pupil	5248	92	20s
Room, 4-year private college/university	year	2095	91	22s
Room, 4-year public college/university	year	1454	91	22s
Tuition, 2-year private college/university	year	5279	91	22s
Tuition, 2-year public college/university	year	906	91	22s
Tuition, 4-year private college/university	year	8853	91	22s
Tuition, 4-year public college/university, in-state	year	2465	91	22s
Energy and Fuels				
Coal	mil Btu	1.72	90	64s
Energy	mil Btu	8.74	90	64s
Energy exp/householder, 1-family unit	year	471	90	28r
Energy exp/householder, <1,000 sq ft heating area	year	430	90	28r
Energy exp/householder, 1,000-1,999 sq ft heating area	year	481	90	28r
Energy exp/householder, 2,000+ sq ft heating area	year	473	90	28r
Energy exp/householder, mobile home	year	430	90	28r
Energy exp/householder, multifamily	year	461	90	28r
Fuel oil #2	gal	1.08	4/93	16c
Fuel oil, other fuel, exp	year	13	89	15c
Gas, cooking, 10 therms	month	12.09	92	56c
Gas, cooking, 30 therms	month	22.28	92	56c
Gas, cooking, 50 therms	month	32.47	92	56c
Gas, heating, winter, 100 therms	month	56.95	92	56c
Gas, heating, winter, average use	month	130.97	92	56c
Gas, natural	mil Btu	4.57	90	64s
Gas, natural	000 cu ft	4.95	91	46s
Gas, natural, exp	year	491	89	15c
Gas, natural, exp	year	696	91	46s
Gas, piped	100 therms	65.22	4/93	16c
Gas, piped	40 therms	33.96	4/93	16c
Gas, piped	therm	0.50	4/93	16c
Gasoline, all types	gal	1.23	4/93	16c
Gasoline, regular unleaded, taxes included, cash, self-service	gal	1.35	4/93	16c
Gasoline, unleaded premium 93 octane	gal	1.17	4/93	16c
Gasoline, unleaded regular	mil Btu	9.35	90	64s
Entertainment				
Dinner entree, restaurant		19.25-29.95	92	83c
Entertainment exp	year	1345	89	15c
Fees and admissions	year	498	89	15c
Miniature golf admission	adult	6.18	92	1r
Miniature golf admission	child	5.14	92	1r
Pets, toys, playground equipment, exp	year	247	89	15c
Reading, exp	year	185	89	15c
Supplies, equipment, services, exp	year	207	89	15c
Waterpark admission	adult	11.00	92	1r
Waterpark admission	child	8.55	92	1r

Chicago, IL - continued

Item	Per	Value	Date	Ref.
Funerals				
Casket, 18-gauge steel, velvet interior		1926.72	91	24r
Cosmetology, hair care, etc.		97.64	91	24r
Embalming		249.14	91	24r
Facility use for ceremony		208.59	91	24r
Hearse, local		130.12	91	24r
Limousine, local		104.66	91	24r
Remains to funeral home, transfer		93.61	91	24r
Service charge, professional		724.62	91	24r
Vault, concrete, non-metallic liner		734.53	91	24r
Viewing facilities, use		236.06	91	24r
Goods and Services				
Police protection expense	resident	266.00	92	18c
Groceries				
Apples, Red Delicious	lb	0.77	4/93	16r
Bacon	lb	1.85	4/93	16r
Bakery products, exp	year	248	89	15c
Bananas	lb	0.46	4/93	16r
Beef, exp	year	250	89	15c
Beef, stew, boneless	lb	2.53	4/93	16r
Beverages, nonalcoholic, exp	year	231	89	15c
Bologna, all beef or mixed	lb	2.19	4/93	16r
Bread, white, pan	lb	0.78	4/93	16r
Butter	lb	1.50	4/93	16r
Cabbage	lb	0.40	4/93	16r
Carrots, short trimmed and topped	lb	0.45	4/93	16r
Cereals and bakery products, exp	year	366	89	15c
Cereals and cereal products, exp	year	118	89	15c
Cheese, Cheddar	lb	3.47	4/93	16r
Chicken, fresh, whole	lb	0.84	4/93	16r
Chicken breast, bone-in	lb	1.94	4/93	16r
Chicken legs, bone-in	lb	1.02	4/93	16r
Chuck roast, graded and ungraded, ex USDA prime and choice	lb	2.43	4/93	16r
Chuck roast, USDA choice, bone-in	lb	2.11	4/93	16r
Chuck roast, USDA choice, boneless	lb	2.44	4/93	16r
Coffee, 100% ground roast, all sizes	lb	2.47	4/93	16r
Cookies, chocolate chip	lb	2.73	4/93	16r
Dairy products, exp	year	294	89	15c
Dairy products, miscellaneous, exp	year	157	89	15c
Eggs, exp	year	28	89	15c
Eggs, Grade A large	doz	0.93	4/93	16r
Fats and oils, exp	year	60	89	15c
Fish and seafood, exp	year	71	89	15c
Flour, white, all purpose	lb	0.21	4/93	16r
Food, exp	year	4692	89	15c
Food eaten at home, exp	year	2545	89	15c
Food eaten away from home, exp	year	2148	89	15c
Food prepared on out-of-town trips, exp	year	28	89	15c
Foods, miscellaneous, exp	year	352	89	15c
Fruits, fresh, exp	year	134	89	15c
Fruits, processed, exp	year	96	89	15c
Fruits and vegetables, exp	year	440	89	15c
Grapefruit	lb	0.45	4/93	16r
Grapes, Thompson Seedless	lb	1.46	4/93	16r
Ground beef, 100% beef	lb	1.63	4/93	16r
Ground beef, lean and extra lean	lb	2.08	4/93	16r
Ground chuck, 100% beef	lb	1.94	4/93	16r
Ham, boneless, excluding canned	lb	2.21	4/93	16r
Honey, jar	8 oz	0.97-1.25	92	5r
Honey, jar	lb	1.25-2.25	92	5r
Honey, squeeze bear	12-oz	1.25-1.99	92	5r
Ice cream, prepackaged, bulk, regular	1/2 gal	2.41	4/93	16r
Lemons	lb	0.82	4/93	16r
Lettuce, iceberg	lb	0.83	4/93	16r
Margarine, stick	lb	0.77	4/93	16r
Meats, miscellaneous, exp	year	106	89	15c
Meats, poultry, fish and eggs, exp	year	675	89	15c
Milk and cream, fresh, exp	year	137	89	15c
Oranges, navel	lb	0.50	4/93	16r
Peanut butter, creamy, all sizes	lb	1.82	4/93	16r

Values are in dollars or fractions of dollars. In the column headed *Ref*, references are shown to sources. Each reference is followed by a letter. These refer to the geographical level for which data were reported: s = State, r = Region, and c = City or metro. The abbreviation *ex* is used to mean *except* or *excluding*; *exp* stands for expenditures. For other abbreviations and further explanations, please see the Introduction.

Chicago, IL - continued

Item	Per	Value	Date	Ref.
Groceries				
Pears, Anjou	lb	0.85	4/93	16r
Pork, exp	year	139	89	15c
Pork chops, center cut, bone-in	lb	3.17	4/93	16r
Potato chips	16 oz	2.68	4/93	16r
Potatoes, white	lb	0.26	4/93	16r
Poultry, exp	year	81	89	15c
Round roast, graded & ungraded, ex USDA prime & choice	lb	2.88	4/93	16r
Round roast, USDA choice, boneless	lb	2.96	4/93	16r
Shortening, vegetable oil blends	lb	0.79	4/93	16r
Spaghetti and macaroni	lb	0.76	4/93	16r
Steak, rib eye, USDA choice, boneless	lb	6.29	4/93	16r
Steak, round, USDA choice, boneless	lb	3.24	4/93	16r
Steak, sirloin, graded & ungraded, ex USDA prime & choice	lb	4.00	4/93	16r
Steak, sirloin, USDA choice, bone-in	lb	3.57	4/93	16r
Steak, sirloin, USDA choice, boneless	lb	4.17	4/93	16r
Steak, T-bone, USDA choice, bone-in	lb	5.60	4/93	16r
Strawberries, dry pint	12 oz	0.90	4/93	16r
Sugar, white	lb	0.36	4/93	16r
Sugar, white, 33-80 oz pk	lb	0.35	4/93	16r
Sugar and other sweets, exp	year	99	89	15c
Tobacco products, exp	year	328	89	15c
Tomatoes, field grown	lb	0.99	4/93	16r
Tuna, chunk, light	lb	1.76	4/93	16r
Turkey, frozen, whole	lb	0.91	4/93	16r
Vegetables, fresh, exp	year	135	89	15c
Vegetables, processed, exp	year	75	89	15c
Health Care				
Appendectomy		1126	91	62c
Childbirth, cesarean		2337	91	62c
Childbirth, cesarean, hospital		4688	91	62r
Childbirth, cesarean, physician's fee		2053	91	62r
Childbirth, normal, hospital		2657	91	62r
Childbirth, normal, physician's fee		1492	91	62r
Cholecystectomy		1740	91	62c
Coronary bypass surgery, triple		5902	91	62c
Drugs, exp	year	202	89	15c
Health care, exp	year	1321	89	15c
Health insurance, exp	year	443	89	15c
Health maintenance organization coverage, employee	year	3088	93	39c
Health maintenance organization medical coverage, employee	year	3088	92	42c
Hospital care, semiprivate room	day	418.17	90	27c
Hysterectomy		2516	91	62c
Indemnity plan medical coverage, employee	year	4245	92	42c
Insurance coverage, traditional, employee	year	4245	93	39c
Lumpectomy		612	91	62c
Medical insurance premium, per employee, small group comprehensive	month	427.05	10/91	25c
Medical plan per employee	year	3443	91	45r
Medical services, exp	year	557	89	15c
Medical supplies, exp	year	119	89	15c
Mental health care, exp	capita	28.84-37.59	90	38s
Mental health care, exp, state mental health agency	capita	34.43	90	38s
Mental health care, hospital psychiatric services, non-Federal, exp	capita	18.46	88	38s
Mental health care, mental health organization, multiservice, exp	capita	11.97	88	38s
Mental health care, psychiatric hospitals, private, exp	capita	7.84	88	38s
Mental health care, psychiatric out-patient clinics, freestanding, exp	capita	3.21	88	38s
Mental health care, psychiatric partial-care organizations, freestanding, exp	capita	0.51	88	38s
Mental health care, state and county mental hospitals, exp	capita	18.11	88	38s
Mental health care, VA medical centers, exp	capita	3.69	88	38s
Oophorectomy		1616	91	62c

Chicago, IL - continued

Item	Per	Value	Date	Ref.
Health Care - continued				
Physician fee, family practice, first-visit		76.00	91	62r
Physician fee, family practice, revisit		33.00	91	62r
Physician fee, general practice, first-visit		61.00	91	62r
Physician fee, general practice, revisit		31.00	91	62r
Physician fee, general surgeon, first-visit		65.00	91	62r
Physician fee, general surgeon, revisit		35.00	91	62r
Physician fee, internal medicine, first-visit		91.00	91	62r
Physician fee, internal medicine, revisit		40.00	91	62r
Physician fee, median, neurosurgeon, first-visit		106.00	91	62r
Physician fee, median, nonsurgical specialist, first-visit		90.00	91	62r
Physician fee, median, orthopedic surgeon, first-visit		83.00	91	62r
Physician fee, median, surgical specialist, first-visit		61.00	91	62r
Physician fee, neurosurgeon, revisit		41.00	91	62r
Physician fee, nonsurgical specialist, revisit		40.00	91	62r
Physician fee, obstetrics/gynecology, first-visit		61.00	91	62r
Physician fee, obstetrics/gynecology, revisit		40.00	91	62r
Physician fee, orthopedic surgeon, revisit		41.00	91	62r
Physician fee, pediatrician, first-visit		46.00	91	62r
Physician fee, pediatrician, revisit		33.00	91	62r
Physician fee, surgical specialist, revisit		36.00	91	62r
Preferred provider organization medical coverage, employee	year	3684	92	42c
Prescription drug co-pay, Medicaid	month	25.00	91	21s
Prostatectomy, retro-pubic		1829	91	62c
Salpingo-oophorectomy		1589	91	62c
Substance abuse, hospital ancillary charge	incident	1310	90	70s
Substance abuse, hospital physician charge	incident	540	90	70s
Substance abuse, hospital room and board	incident	6150	90	70s
Vasectomy		451	91	62c
Household Goods				
Appliances, major, exp	year	142	89	15c
Appliances, small, exp	year	86	89	15c
Equipment, misc., exp	year	484	89	15c
Floor coverings, exp	year	72	89	15c
Furnishings and equipment, exp	year	1420	89	15c
Furniture, exp	year	473	89	15c
Household products, misc., exp	year	168	89	15c
Household textiles, exp	year	163	89	15c
Housekeeping supplies, exp	year	505	89	15c
Laundry and cleaning supplies, exp	year	130	89	15c
TVs, radios, sound equipment, exp	year	393	89	15c
Housing				
Dwellings, exp	year	3712	89	15c
Home, median price	unit	135.90		26c
Household expenses, misc.	year	239	89	15c
Household operations, exp	year	457	89	15c
Housing, exp	year	10310	89	15c
Lodging, exp	year	654	89	15c
Maintenance, repairs, insurance, and other, exp	year	507	89	15c
Mortgage interest, exp	year	2223	89	15c
Rental unit, 1 bedroom	month	591	93	23c
Rental unit, 2 bedroom	month	692	93	23c
Rental unit, 3 bedroom	month	870	93	23c
Rental unit, 4 bedroom	month	974	93	23c
Rental unit, efficiency	month	480	93	23c
Rented dwellings, exp	year	1649	89	15c
Shelter, exp	year	6014	89	15c
Insurance and Pensions				
Auto insurance, private passenger	year	621.37	91	63s
Insurance, life and other personal, exp	year	324	89	15c
Insurance and pensions, personal, exp	year	2933	89	15c
Pensions and social security, exp	year	2608	89	15c

Values are in dollars or fractions of dollars. In the column headed *Ref*, references are shown to sources. Each reference is followed by a letter. These refer to the geographical level for which data were reported: s = State, r = Region, and c = City or metro. The abbreviation *ex* is used to mean *except* or *excluding*; *exp* stands for expenditures. For other abbreviations and further explanations, please see the Introduction.

Chicago, IL - continued

Item	Per	Value	Date	Ref.
Insurance and Pensions				
Vehicle insurance	year	527	89	15c
Personal Goods				
Products and services, exp	year	498	89	15c
Personal Services				
Services, exp	year	218	89	15c
Taxes				
Property tax, exp	year	982	89	15c
Tax, cigarette	pack	30	91	77s
Tax, gasoline	gal	19	91	77s
Taxes, hotel room	day	11.36	92	33c
Taxes, state	capita	1151	91	77s
Transportation				
Auto fixed costs, midsize		4032	91	60c
Auto operating cost, midsize		1665	91	60c
Auto rental, average	day	54.75	6/91	60c
Auto rental, midsize car	day	47.72	92	91c
Bus fare	one-way	1.25	3/93	2c
Driver's license fee		10.00	12/90	43s
Limo fare, airport-city, average	day	12.00	6/91	60c
Public transit, exp	year	510	89	15c
Railway fare, commuter	one-way	1.85	3/93	2c
Railway fare, heavy rail	one-way	1.50	3/93	2c
Taxi fare, airport-city, average	day	24.00	6/91	60c
Vehicle expenses, misc.	year	1662	89	15c
Vehicle finance charges	year	318	89	15c
Vehicle maintenance	year	599	89	15c
Vehicle registration and license plate	multi-year	48.00	93	52s
Vehicle rental and license	year	218	89	15c
Travel				
Breakfast	day	7.47	6/91	60c
Business travel	day	215.00	92	86c
Dinner	day	26.33	6/91	60c
Dinner	day	25.65	92	85c
Lodging	day	143.41	91	60c
Lodging	day	168.00	92	85c
Lunch	day	9.75	6/91	60c
Travel, business	day	236.78	92	82c
Travel, business	day	219.18	93	88c
Utilities				
Electricity	500 KWh	58.98	4/93	16c
Electricity	KWh	0.11	4/93	16c
Electricity	mil Btu	22.02	90	64s
Electricity, exp	year	691	89	15c
Electricity, winter, 250 KWh	month	33.66	92	55c
Electricity, winter, 500 KWh	month	54.53	92	55c
Electricity, winter, 750 KWh	month	69.81	92	55c
Electricity, winter, 1000 KWh	month	85.09	92	55c
Utilities, fuels, public services, exp	year	1915	89	15c
Water, public services, exp	year	161	89	15c

Chico, CA

Item	Per	Value	Date	Ref.
Child Care				
Child care fee, average, center	hour	1.71	90	65r
Child care fee, average, nonregulated family day care	hour	1.32	90	65r
Child care fee, average, regulated family day care	hour	1.86	90	65r
Communications				
Long-distance telephone service, day, initial minute, 0-100 miles	min	0.17-0.40	91	12s

Chico, CA - continued

Item	Per	Value	Date	Ref.
Communications - continued				
Long-distance telephone service, day, additional minute, 0-100 miles	min	0.07-0.31	91	12s
Long-distance telephone service, evenings/weekends, 0-100 mi, initial minute	min	0.07-0.16	91	12s
Long-distance telephone service, evenings/weekends, 0-100 mi, additional minute	min	0.03-0.12	91	12s
Education				
Board, 4-yr private college/university	year	2515	91	22s
Board, 4-yr public college/university	year	2268	91	22s
Expenditures, local gov't, public elementary/secondary	pupil	4866	92	20s
Room, 4-year private college/university	year	2622	91	22s
Room, 4-year public college/university	year	2406	91	22s
Tuition, 2-year private college/university	year	7942	91	22s
Tuition, 2-year public college/university	year	114	91	22s
Tuition, 4-year private college/university	year	10863	91	22s
Tuition, 4-year public college/university, in-state	year	1220	91	22s
Energy and Fuels				
Coal	mil Btu	2.01	90	64s
Energy	mil Btu	9.08	90	64s
Energy exp/householder, 1-family unit	year	362	90	28r
Energy exp/householder, <1,000 sq ft heating area	year	254	90	28r
Energy exp/householder, 1,000-1,999 sq ft heating area	year	358	90	28r
Energy exp/householder, 2,000+ sq ft heating area	year	467	90	28r
Energy exp/householder, mobile home	year	390	90	28r
Energy exp/householder, multifamily	year	252	90	28r
Gas, natural	mil Btu	4.31	90	64s
Gas, natural	000 cu ft	6.27	91	46s
Gas, natural, exp	year	369	91	46s
Gasoline, unleaded regular	mil Btu	8.57	90	64s
Entertainment				
Miniature golf admission	adult	6.18	92	1r
Miniature golf admission	child	5.14	92	1r
Waterpark admission	adult	11.00	92	1r
Waterpark admission	child	8.55	92	1r
Funerals				
Casket, 18-gauge steel, velvet interior		1781.09	91	24r
Cosmetology, hair care, etc.		84.64	91	24r
Embalming		207.41	91	24r
Facility use for ceremony		205.76	91	24r
Hearse, local		105.14	91	24r
Limousine, local		83.21	91	24r
Remains to funeral home, transfer		113.82	91	24r
Service charge, professional		626.33	91	24r
Vault, concrete, non-metallic liner		599.54	91	24r
Viewing facilities, use		85.81	91	24r
Groceries				
Apples, Red Delicious	lb	0.80	4/93	16r
Bacon	lb	1.79	4/93	16r
Bananas	lb	0.53	4/93	16r
Bologna, all beef or mixed	lb	2.67	4/93	16r
Bread, white, pan	lb	0.81	4/93	16r
Carrots, short trimmed and topped	lb	0.39	4/93	16r
Chicken, fresh, whole	lb	0.94	4/93	16r
Chicken breast, bone-in	lb	2.19	4/93	16r
Chuck roast, graded and ungraded, ex USDA prime and choice	lb	2.26	4/93	16r
Coffee, 100% ground roast, all sizes	lb	2.33	4/93	16r
Eggs, Grade AA large	doz	1.18	4/93	16r
Flour, white, all purpose	lb	0.22	4/93	16r
Grapefruit	lb	0.52	4/93	16r
Grapes, Thompson Seedless	lb	1.50	4/93	16r
Ground beef, 100% beef	lb	1.44	4/93	16r
Ground beef, lean and extra lean	lb	2.34	4/93	16r

Values are in dollars or fractions of dollars. In the column headed *Ref*, references are shown to sources. Each reference is followed by a letter. These refer to the geographical level for which data were reported: s = State, r = Region, and c = City or metro. The abbreviation *ex* is used to mean *except* or *excluding*; *exp* stands for expenditures. For other abbreviations and further explanations, please see the Introduction.

Chico, CA - continued

Item	Per	Value	Date	Ref.
Groceries				
Ham, boneless, excluding canned	lb	2.56	4/93	16r
Honey, jar	8 oz	0.89-1.00	92	5r
Honey, jar	lb	1.35-1.97	92	5r
Honey, squeeze bear	12-oz	1.19-1.50	92	5r
Ice cream, prepackaged, bulk, regular	1/2 gal	2.40	4/93	16r
Lemons	lb	0.81	4/93	16r
Lettuce, iceberg	lb	0.84	4/93	16r
Margarine, stick	lb	0.81	4/93	16r
Oranges, navel	lb	0.48	4/93	16r
Pork chops, center cut, bone-in	lb	3.25	4/93	16r
Potato chips	16 oz	2.89	4/93	16r
Potatoes, white	lb	0.38	4/93	16r
Round roast, graded & ungraded, ex USDA prime & choice	lb	3.00	4/93	16r
Round roast, USDA choice, boneless	lb	3.16	4/93	16r
Shortening, vegetable oil blends	lb	0.86	4/93	16r
Spaghetti and macaroni	lb	0.84	4/93	16r
Steak, round, graded & ungraded, ex USDA prime & choice	lb	3.34	4/93	16r
Steak, round, USDA choice, boneless	lb	3.24	4/93	16r
Steak, sirloin, graded & ungraded, ex USDA prime & choice	lb	3.75	4/93	16r
Steak, sirloin, USDA choice, boneless	lb	4.49	4/93	16r
Sugar, white	lb	0.41	4/93	16r
Sugar, white, 33-80 oz pk	lb	0.38	4/93	16r
Tomatoes, field grown	lb	1.01	4/93	16r
Turkey, frozen, whole	lb	1.04	4/93	16r
Health Care				
Cardizem 60 mg tablets	30	24.04	92	49s
Cector 250 mg tablets	15	35.87	92	49s
Childbirth, cesarean, hospital		5533	91	62r
Childbirth, cesarean, physician's fee		2053	91	62r
Childbirth, normal, hospital		2745	91	62r
Childbirth, normal, physician's fee		1492	91	62r
Health care spending, state	capita	2894	3/93	84s
Medical plan per employee	year	3421	91	45s
Mental health care, exp	capita	37.60-53.67	90	38s
Mental health care, exp, state mental health agency	capita	42.32	90	38s
Mental health care, hospital psychiatric services, non-Federal, exp	capita	10.64	88	38s
Mental health care, mental health organization, multiservice, exp	capita	28.56	88	38s
Mental health care, psychiatric hospitals, private, exp	capita	18.60	88	38s
Mental health care, psychiatric out-patient clinics, freestanding, exp	capita	2.28	88	38s
Mental health care, psychiatric partial-care organizations, freestanding, exp	capita	0.24	88	38s
Mental health care, state and county mental hospitals, exp	capita	13.60	88	38s
Mental health care, VA medical centers, exp	capita	2.33	88	38s
Mevacor 20 mg tablets	30	67.62	92	49s
Physician fee, family practice, first-visit		111.00	91	62r
Physician fee, family practice, revisit		45.00	91	62r
Physician fee, general practice, first-visit		100.00	91	62r
Physician fee, general practice, revisit		40.00	91	62r
Physician fee, internal medicine, first-visit		137.00	91	62r
Physician fee, internal medicine, revisit		48.00	91	62r
Physician fee, median, neurosurgeon, first-visit		157.00	91	62r
Physician fee, median, nonsurgical specialist, first-visit		131.00	91	62r
Physician fee, median, orthopedic surgeon, first-visit		124.00	91	62r
Physician fee, median, plastic surgeon, first-visit		88.00	91	62r
Physician fee, median, surgical specialist, first-visit		100.00	91	62r
Physician fee, neurosurgeon, revisit		51.00	91	62r
Physician fee, nonsurgical specialist, revisit		47.00	91	62r

Chico, CA - continued

Item	Per	Value	Date	Ref.
Health Care - continued				
Physician fee, obstetrics/gynecology, first-visit		95.00	91	62r
Physician fee, obstetrics/gynecology, revisit		50.00	91	62r
Physician fee, orthopedic surgeon, revisit		51.00	91	62r
Physician fee, pediatrician, first-visit		81.00	91	62r
Physician fee, pediatrician, revisit		42.00	91	62r
Physician fee, plastic surgeon, revisit		48.00	91	62r
Physician fee, surgical specialist, revisit		49.00	91	62r
Prozac 20 mg tablets	14	33.22	92	49s
Substance abuse, hospital ancillary charge	incident	1760	90	70s
Substance abuse, hospital physician charge	incident	750	90	70s
Substance abuse, hospital room and board	incident	6390	90	70s
Tagamet 300 mg tablets	100	77.08	92	49s
Xanax 0.25 mg tablets	90	64.08	92	49s
Zantac 160 mg tablets	60	92.31	92	49s
Housing				
Home, median price	unit	131,200	92	58s
Insurance and Pensions				
Auto insurance, private passenger	year	904.37	91	63s
Taxes				
Tax, cigarette	pack	35	91	77s
Tax, gasoline	gal	16	91	77s
Taxes, state	capita	1477	91	77s
Transportation				
Driver's license fee		10.00	12/90	43s
Travel				
Business travel	day	178.00	4/93	89r
Utilities				
Electricity	mil Btu	25.98	90	64s

Cincinnati, OH

Item	Per	Value	Date	Ref.
Composite ACCRA index		104.90	4Q 92	4c
Alcoholic Beverages				
Alcoholic beverages, exp	year	280	89	15c
Beer, Miller Lite or Budweiser, 12-oz containers	6 pack	3.90	4Q 92	4c
Liquor, J & B Scotch	750 ml	18.20	4Q 92	4c
Wine, Gallo Chablis blanc, 1.5 liter	bottle	5.49	4Q 92	4c
Charity				
Cash contributions	year	452	89	15c
Child Care				
Child care fee, average, center	hour	1.63	90	65r
Child care fee, average, nonregulated family day care	hour	1.83	90	65r
Child care fee, average, regulated family day care	hour	1.42	90	65r
Clothing				
Jeans, man's denim		32.19	4Q 92	4c
Shirt, man's dress shirt		28.00	4Q 92	4c
Undervest, boy's size 10-14, cotton	3	5.49	4Q 92	4c
Communications				
Long-distance telephone service, day, initial minute, 0-100 miles	min	0.26-0.43	91	12s
Long-distance telephone service, day, additional minute, 0-100 miles	min	0.14-0.24	91	12s
Long-distance telephone service, evenings/weekends, 0-100 mi, initial minute	min	0.11-0.17	91	12s
Long-distance telephone service, evenings/weekends, 0-100 mi, additional minute	min	0.06-0.10	91	12s
Newspaper subscription, daily and Sunday home delivery, large-city	month	14.25	4Q 92	4c
Postage and stationery, exp	year	88	89	15c

Values are in dollars or fractions of dollars. In the column headed *Ref*, references are shown to sources. Each reference is followed by a letter. These refer to the geographical level for which data were reported: s = State, r = Region, and c = City or metro. The abbreviation *ex* is used to mean *except* or *excluding*; *exp* stands for expenditures. For other abbreviations and further explanations, please see the Introduction.

Cincinnati, OH - continued

Item	Per	Value	Date	Ref.
Communications				
Telephone, exp	year	497	89	15c
Telephone, flat rate	month	10.04-14.54	91	11c
Telephone, residential, private line, rotary, unlimited calling	month	19.12	10/91	78c
Telephone bill, family of four	month	20.30	4Q 92	4c
Education				
Board, 4-yr private college/university	year	1872	91	22s
Board, 4-yr public college/university	year	1742	91	22s
Education, exp	year	455	89	15c
Expenditures, local gov't, public elementary/secondary	pupil	5451	92	20s
Room, 4-year private college/university	year	1695	91	22s
Room, 4-year public college/university	year	2259	91	22s
Tuition, 2-year private college/university	year	6093	91	22s
Tuition, 2-year public college/university	year	1768	91	22s
Tuition, 4-year private college/university	year	8729	91	22s
Tuition, 4-year public college/university, in-state	year	2622	91	22s
Energy and Fuels				
Coal	mil Btu	1.54	90	64s
Energy	mil Btu	8.32	90	64s
Energy, combined forms, 1,800 sq ft heating area	month	108.68	4Q 92	4c
Energy, exc electricity, 1,800 sq ft heating area	month	32.07	4Q 92	4c
Energy exp/householder, 1-family unit	year	471	90	28r
Energy exp/householder, <1,000 sq ft heating area	year	430	90	28r
Energy exp/householder, 1,000-1,999 sq ft heating area	year	481	90	28r
Energy exp/householder, 2,000+ sq ft heating area	year	473	90	28r
Energy exp/householder, mobile home	year	430	90	28r
Energy exp/householder, multifamily	year	461	90	28r
Fuel oil, other fuel, exp	year	81	89	15c
Gas, cooking, winter, 10 therms	month	10.19	92	56c
Gas, cooking, winter, 30 therms	month	19.96	92	56c
Gas, cooking, winter, 50 therms	month	29.74	92	56c
Gas, heating, winter, 100 therms	month	54.18	92	56c
Gas, heating, winter, average use	month	110.88	92	56c
Gas, natural	mil Btu	4.54	90	64s
Gas, natural	000 cu ft	5.28	91	46s
Gas, natural, exp	year	155	89	15c
Gas, natural, exp	year	606	91	46s
Gasoline, motor	gal	1.15	4Q 92	4c
Gasoline, unleaded regular	mil Btu	9.35	90	64s
Entertainment				
Bowling, evening rate	game	2.02	4Q 92	4c
Dinner entree, restaurant		19.00-29.00	92	83c
Entertainment exp	year	1422	89	15c
Fees and admissions	year	432	89	15c
Miniature golf admission	adult	6.18	92	1r
Miniature golf admission	child	5.14	92	1r
Monopoly game, Parker Brothers', No. 9		12.79	4Q 92	4c
Movie	admission	6.50	4Q 92	4c
Pets, toys, playground equipment, exp	year	250	89	15c
Reading, exp	year	189	89	15c
Supplies, equipment, services, exp	year	296	89	15c
Tennis balls, yellow, Wilson or Penn, 3	can	2.60	4Q 92	4c
Waterpark admission	adult	11.00	92	1r
Waterpark admission	child	8.55	92	1r
Funerals				
Casket, 18-gauge steel, velvet interior		1926.72	91	24r
Cosmetology, hair care, etc.		97.64	91	24r
Embalming		249.14	91	24r
Facility use for ceremony		208.59	91	24r

Cincinnati, OH - continued

Item	Per	Value	Date	Ref.
Funerals - continued				
Hearse, local		130.12	91	24r
Limousine, local		104.66	91	24r
Remains to funeral home, transfer		93.61	91	24r
Service charge, professional		724.62	91	24r
Vault, concrete, non-metallic liner		734.53	91	24r
Viewing facilities, use		236.06	91	24r
Goods and Services				
ACCRA Index, Miscellaneous Goods and Services		108.20	4Q 92	4c
Groceries				
ACCRA Index, Groceries		90.80	4Q 92	4c
Apples, Red Delicious	lb	0.77	4/93	16r
Babyfood, strained vegetables, lowest price	4-4.5 oz jar	0.30	4Q 92	4c
Bacon	lb	1.85	4/93	16r
Bakery products, exp	year	252	89	15c
Bananas	lb	0.39	4Q 92	4c
Bananas	lb	0.46	4/93	16r
Beef, exp	year	269	89	15c
Beef, stew, boneless	lb	2.53	4/93	16r
Beverages, nonalcoholic, exp	year	252	89	15c
Bologna, all beef or mixed	lb	2.19	4/93	16r
Bread, white	24 oz	0.44	4Q 92	4c
Bread, white, pan	lb	0.78	4/93	16r
Butter	lb	1.50	4/93	16r
Cabbage	lb	0.40	4/93	16r
Carrots, short trimmed and topped	lb	0.45	4/93	16r
Cereals and bakery products, exp	year	371	89	15c
Cereals and cereal products, exp	year	119	89	15c
Cheese, Cheddar	lb	3.47	4/93	16r
Cheese, Kraft grated Parmesan	8-oz canister	2.95	4Q 92	4c
Chicken, fresh, whole	lb	0.84	4/93	16r
Chicken, fryer, whole	lb	0.73	4Q 92	4c
Chicken breast, bone-in	lb	1.94	4/93	16r
Chicken legs, bone-in	lb	1.02	4/93	16r
Chuck roast, graded and ungraded, ex USDA prime and choice	lb	2.43	4/93	16r
Chuck roast, USDA choice, bone-in	lb	2.11	4/93	16r
Chuck roast, USDA choice, boneless	lb	2.44	4/93	16r
Cigarettes, Winston	carton	16.24	4Q 92	4c
Coffee, 100% ground roast, all sizes	lb	2.47	4/93	16r
Coffee, vacuum-packed	13-oz can	2.19	4Q 92	4c
Cookies, chocolate chip	lb	2.73	4/93	16r
Corn, frozen	10 oz	0.53	4Q 92	4c
Corn Flakes, Kellogg's or Post Toasties	18 oz	1.73	4Q 92	4c
Dairy products, exp	year	310	89	15c
Dairy products, miscellaneous, exp	year	180	89	15c
Eggs, exp	year	25	89	15c
Eggs, Grade A large	doz	0.76	4Q 92	4c
Eggs, Grade A large	doz	0.93	4/93	16r
Fats and oils, exp	year	62	89	15c
Fish and seafood, exp	year	65	89	15c
Flour, white, all purpose	lb	0.21	4/93	16r
Food, exp	year	4560	89	15c
Food eaten at home, exp	year	2585	89	15c
Food eaten away from home, exp	year	1975	89	15c
Food prepared on out-of-town trips, exp	year	19	89	15c
Foods, miscellaneous, exp	year	393	89	15c
Fruits, fresh, exp	year	123	89	15c
Fruits, processed, exp	year	87	89	15c
Fruits and vegetables, exp	year	389	89	15c
Grapefruit	lb	0.45	4/93	16r
Grapes, Thompson Seedless	lb	1.46	4/93	16r
Ground beef, 100% beef	lb	1.63	4/93	16r
Ground beef, lean and extra lean	lb	2.08	4/93	16r
Ground beef or hamburger	lb	1.35	4Q 92	4c
Ground chuck, 100% beef	lb	1.94	4/93	16r
Ham, boneless, excluding canned	lb	2.21	4/93	16r

Values are in dollars or fractions of dollars. In the column headed *Ref*, references are shown to sources. Each reference is followed by a letter. These refer to the geographical level for which data were reported: s=State, r=Region, and c=City or metro. The abbreviation *ex* is used to mean *except* or *excluding*; *exp* stands for expenditures. For other abbreviations and further explanations, please see the Introduction.

Cincinnati, OH - continued

Item	Per	Value	Date	Ref.
Groceries				
Honey, jar	8 oz	0.97-1.25	92	5r
Honey, jar	lb	1.25-2.25	92	5r
Honey, squeeze bear	12-oz	1.25-1.99	92	5r
Ice cream, prepackaged, bulk, regular	1/2 gal	2.41	4/93	16r
Lemons	lb	0.82	4/93	16r
Lettuce, iceberg	head	0.59	4Q 92	4c
Lettuce, iceberg	lb	0.83	4/93	16r
Margarine, Blue Bonnet or Parkay cubes	lb	0.53	4Q 92	4c
Margarine, stick	lb	0.77	4/93	16r
Meats, miscellaneous, exp	year	109	89	15c
Meats, poultry, fish and eggs, exp	year	676	89	15c
Milk, whole	1/2 gal	1.35	4Q 92	4c
Milk and cream, fresh, exp	year	130	89	15c
Orange juice, Minute Maid frozen	12-oz can	1.07	4Q 92	4c
Oranges, navel	lb	0.50	4/93	16r
Peaches	29-oz can	1.61	4Q 92	4c
Peanut butter, creamy, all sizes	lb	1.82	4/93	16r
Pears, Anjou	lb	0.85	4/93	16r
Peas Sweet, Del Monte or Green Giant	15-17 oz can	0.49	4Q 92	4c
Pork, exp	year	131	89	15c
Pork chops, center cut, bone-in	lb	3.17	4/93	16r
Potato chips	16 oz	2.68	4/93	16r
Potatoes, white	lb	0.26	4/93	16r
Potatoes, white or red	10-lb sack	2.39	4Q 92	4c
Poultry, exp	year	77	89	15c
Round roast, graded & ungraded, ex USDA prime & choice	lb	2.88	4/93	16r
Round roast, USDA choice, boneless	lb	2.96	4/93	16r
Sausage, Jimmy Dean, 100% pork	lb	2.55	4Q 92	4c
Shortening, vegetable oil blends	lb	0.79	4/93	16r
Shortening, vegetable, Crisco	3-lb can	2.29	4Q 92	4c
Soft drink, Coca Cola	2 liter	0.95	4Q 92	4c
Spaghetti and macaroni	lb	0.76	4/93	16r
Steak, rib eye, USDA choice, boneless	lb	6.29	4/93	16r
Steak, round, USDA choice, boneless	lb	3.24	4/93	16r
Steak, sirloin, graded & ungraded, ex USDA prime & choice	lb	4.00	4/93	16r
Steak, sirloin, USDA choice, bone-in	lb	3.57	4/93	16r
Steak, sirloin, USDA choice, boneless	lb	4.17	4/93	16r
Steak, T-bone	lb	5.59	4Q 92	4c
Steak, T-bone, USDA choice, bone-in	lb	5.60	4/93	16r
Strawberries, dry pint	12 oz	0.90	4/93	16r
Sugar, cane or beet	4 lb	1.47	4Q 92	4c
Sugar, white	lb	0.36	4/93	16r
Sugar, white, 33-80 oz pk	lb	0.35	4/93	16r
Sugar and other sweets, exp	year	113	89	15c
Tobacco products, exp	year	291	89	15c
Tomatoes, field grown	lb	0.99	4/93	16r
Tomatoes, Hunt's or Del Monte	14.5-oz can	0.75	4Q 92	4c
Tuna, chunk, light	6.125-6.5 oz can	0.48	4Q 92	4c
Tuna, chunk, light	lb	1.76	4/93	16r
Turkey, frozen, whole	lb	0.91	4/93	16r
Vegetables, fresh, exp	year	116	89	15c
Vegetables, processed, exp	year	63	89	15c
Health Care				
ACCRA Index, Health Care		93.50	4Q 92	4c
Analgesic, Aspirin, Bayer, 325 mg tablets	100	3.92	4Q 92	4c
Childbirth, cesarean, hospital		4688	91	62r
Childbirth, cesarean, physician's fee		2053	91	62r
Childbirth, normal, hospital		2657	91	62r
Childbirth, normal, physician's fee		1492	91	62r
Dentist's fee, adult teeth cleaning and periodic oral exam	visit	42.20	4Q 92	4c

Cincinnati, OH - continued

Item	Per	Value	Date	Ref.
Health Care - continued				
Doctor's fee, routine exam, established patient	visit	34.60	4Q 92	4c
Drugs, exp	year	262	89	15c
Health care, exp	year	1242	89	15c
Health insurance, exp	year	508	89	15c
Hernia repair, physician fee	average	923.00	2/93	93c
Hospital care, semiprivate room	day	263.80	90	27c
Hospital care, semiprivate room	day	346.25	4Q 92	4c
Medical insurance premium, per employee, small group comprehensive	month	317.55	10/91	25c
Medical plan per employee	year	3443	91	45r
Medical services, exp	year	411	89	15c
Medical supplies, exp	year	61	89	15c
Mental health care, exp	capita	37.60-53.67	90	38s
Mental health care, exp, state mental health agency	capita	40.93	90	38s
Mental health care, hospital psychiatric services, non-Federal, exp	capita	15.03	88	38s
Mental health care, mental health organization, multiservice, exp	capita	14.46	88	38s
Mental health care, psychiatric hospitals, private, exp	capita	7.93	88	38s
Mental health care, psychiatric out-patient clinics, freestanding, exp	capita	2.93	88	38s
Mental health care, psychiatric partial-care organizations, freestanding, exp	capita	0.32	88	38s
Mental health care, state and county mental hospitals, exp	capita	23.79	88	38s
Mental health care, VA medical centers, exp	capita	7.76	88	38s
Physician fee, family practice, first-visit		76.00	91	62r
Physician fee, family practice, revisit		33.00	91	62r
Physician fee, general practice, first-visit		61.00	91	62r
Physician fee, general practice, revisit		31.00	91	62r
Physician fee, general surgeon, first-visit		65.00	91	62r
Physician fee, general surgeon, revisit		35.00	91	62r
Physician fee, internal medicine, first-visit		91.00	91	62r
Physician fee, internal medicine, revisit		40.00	91	62r
Physician fee, median, neurosurgeon, first-visit		106.00	91	62r
Physician fee, median, nonsurgical specialist, first-visit		90.00	91	62r
Physician fee, median, orthopedic surgeon, first-visit		83.00	91	62r
Physician fee, median, surgical specialist, first-visit		61.00	91	62r
Physician fee, neurosurgeon, revisit		41.00	91	62r
Physician fee, nonsurgical specialist, revisit		40.00	91	62r
Physician fee, obstetrics/gynecology, first-visit		61.00	91	62r
Physician fee, obstetrics/gynecology, revisit		40.00	91	62r
Physician fee, orthopedic surgeon, revisit		41.00	91	62r
Physician fee, pediatrician, first-visit		46.00	91	62r
Physician fee, pediatrician, revisit		33.00	91	62r
Physician fee, surgical specialist, revisit		36.00	91	62r
Substance abuse, hospital ancillary charge	incident	940	90	70s
Substance abuse, hospital physician charge	incident	380	90	70s
Substance abuse, hospital room and board	incident	5410	90	70s
Household Goods				
Appliance repair, home, service call, washing machine	min labor charge	34.30	4Q 92	4c
Appliances, major, exp	year	150	89	15c
Appliances, small, exp	year	56	89	15c
Equipment, misc., exp	year	473	89	15c
Floor coverings, exp	year	175	89	15c
Furnishings and equipment, exp	year	1298	89	15c
Furniture, exp	year	304	89	15c

Values are in dollars or fractions of dollars. In the column headed *Ref*, references are shown to sources. Each reference is followed by a letter. These refer to the geographical level for which data were reported: s=State, r=Region, and c=City or metro. The abbreviation *ex* is used to mean *except* or *excluding*; *exp* stands for expenditures. For other abbreviations and further explanations, please see the Introduction.

Cincinnati, OH - continued

Item	Per	Value	Date	Ref.
Household Goods				
Household products, misc., exp	year	201	89	15c
Household textiles, exp	year	140	89	15c
Housekeeping supplies, exp	year	406	89	15c
Laundry and cleaning supplies, exp	year	117	89	15c
Laundry detergent, Tide Ultra, Bold, or Cheer	42 oz	2.99	4Q 92	4c
Tissues, facial, Kleenex brand	175-count box	0.95	4Q 92	4c
TVs, radios, sound equipment, exp	year	444	89	15c
Housing				
ACCRA Index, Housing		110.10	4Q 92	4c
Dwellings, exp	year	2691	89	15c
Home, median price	unit	88.60		26c
House, 1,800 sq ft, 8,000 sq ft lot, new, urban	total	120385	4Q 92	4c
House payment, principal and interest, 25% down payment	month	665	4Q 92	4c
Household expenses, misc.	year	211	89	15c
Household operations, exp	year	457	89	15c
Housing, exp	year	8224	89	15c
Lodging, exp	year	370	89	15c
Maintenance, repairs, insurance, and other, exp	year	508	89	15c
Mortgage interest, exp	year	1735	89	15c
Mortgage rate, incl. points & origination fee, 30-year fixed or adjustable rate	percent	8.05	4Q 92	4c
Rent, apartment, 2 bedrooms - 1-1/2 to 2 baths, unfurnished, 950 sq ft, water	month	570	4Q 92	4c
Rental unit, 1 bedroom	month	415	93	23c
Rental unit, 2 bedroom	month	489	93	23c
Rental unit, 3 bedroom	month	611	93	23c
Rental unit, 4 bedroom	month	684	93	23c
Rental unit, efficiency	month	342	93	23c
Rented dwellings, exp	year	1200	89	15c
Shelter, exp	year	4262	89	15c
Insurance and Pensions				
Auto insurance, private passenger	year	547.38	91	63s
Insurance, life and other personal, exp	year	301	89	15c
Insurance and pensions, personal, exp	year	2091	89	15c
Pensions and social security, exp	year	1790	89	15c
Vehicle insurance	year	551	89	15c
Personal Goods				
Products and services, exp	year	310	89	15c
Shampoo, Alberto VO5	15 oz	0.99	4Q 92	4c
Toothpaste, Crest or Colgate	6-7 oz	1.41	4Q 92	4c
Personal Services				
Dry cleaning, man's 2-piece suit		7.00	4Q 92	4c
Haircare, woman's shampoo, trim and blow-dry		19.20	4Q 92	4c
Haircut, man's barbershop, no styling		6.60	4Q 92	4c
Services, exp	year	246	89	15c
Restaurant Food				
Chicken, fried, thigh and drumstick		1.98	4Q 92	4c
Hamburger with cheese	1/4 lb	1.75	4Q 92	4c
Pizza, Pizza Hut or Pizza Inn, cheese, thin crust	12-13 in	7.59	4Q 92	4c
Taxes				
Property tax, exp	year	442	89	15c
Tax, cigarette	pack	18	91	77s
Tax, gasoline	gal	21	91	77s
Taxes, state	capita	1056	91	77s
Transportation				
ACCRA Index, Transportation		107.10	4Q 92	4c
Auto rental, average	day	46.25	6/91	60c
Bus fare	one-way	0.75	3/93	2c

Cincinnati, OH - continued

Item	Per	Value	Date	Ref.
Transportation - continued				
Bus fare, up to 10 miles	one-way	0.65	4Q 92	4c
Driver's license fee		5.00	12/90	43s
Limo fare, airport-city, average	day	8.00	6/91	60c
Public transit, exp	year	184	89	15c
Taxi fare, airport-city, average	day	18.00	6/91	60c
Tire balance, computer or spin balance, front	wheel	7.79	4Q 92	4c
Vehicle expenses, misc.	year	1818	89	15c
Vehicle finance charges	year	389	89	15c
Vehicle maintenance	year	563	89	15c
Vehicle rental and license	year	315	89	15c
Travel				
Breakfast	day	6.79	6/91	60c
Dinner	day	21.35	6/91	60c
Lodging	day	105.56	91	60c
Lunch	day	11.93	6/91	60c
Utilities				
ACCRA Index, Utilities		100.00	4Q 92	4c
Electricity	mil Btu	17.33	90	64s
Electricity, exp	year	898	89	15c
Electricity, partial electric and other energy, 1,800 sq ft living area new home	month	76.61	4Q 92	4c
Electricity, winter, 250 KWh	month	19.69	92	55c
Electricity, winter, 500 KWh	month	36.00	92	55c
Electricity, winter, 750 KWh	month	52.47	92	55c
Electricity, winter, 1000 KWh	month	68.80	92	55c
Utilities, fuels, public services, exp	year	1802	89	15c
Water, public services, exp	year	170	89	15c

Clarksville, TN

Item	Per	Value	Date	Ref.
Composite ACCRA index		91.40	4Q 92	4c
Alcoholic Beverages				
Beer, Miller Lite or Budweiser, 12-oz containers	6 pack	4.08	4Q 92	4c
Liquor, J & B Scotch	750 ml	18.91	4Q 92	4c
Wine, Gallo Chablis blanc, 1.5 liter	bottle	5.62	4Q 92	4c
Child Care				
Child care fee, average, center	hour	1.29	90	65r
Child care fee, average, nonregulated family day care	hour	0.89	90	65r
Child care fee, average, regulated family day care	hour	1.32	90	65r
Clothing				
Jeans, man's denim		26.18	4Q 92	4c
Shirt, man's dress shirt		23.99	4Q 92	4c
Undervest, boy's size 10-14, cotton	3	4.99	4Q 92	4c
Communications				
Long-distance telephone service, day, initial minute, 0-100 miles	min	0.10-0.22	91	12s
Long-distance telephone service, day, additional minute, 0-100 miles	min	0.10-0.22	91	12s
Long-distance telephone service, evenings/weekends, 0-100 mi, initial minute	min	0.05-0.10	91	12s
Long-distance telephone service, evenings/weekends, 0-100 mi, additional minute	min	0.05-0.10	91	12s
Newspaper subscription, daily and Sunday home delivery, large-city	month	13.04	4Q 92	4c
Telephone, flat rate	month	9.05	91	11c
Telephone bill, family of four	month	16.21	4Q 92	4c
Education				
Board, 4-yr private college/university	year	1845	91	22s
Board, 4-yr public college/university	year	1499	91	22s
Expenditures, local gov't, public elementary/secondary	pupil	3736	92	20s
Room, 4-year private college/university	year	1679	91	22s
Room, 4-year public college/university	year	1339	91	22s

Values are in dollars or fractions of dollars. In the column headed *Ref*, references are shown to sources. Each reference is followed by a letter. These refer to the geographical level for which data were reported: s = State, r = Region, and c = City or metro. The abbreviation *ex* is used to mean *except* or *excluding*; *exp* stands for *expenditures*. For other abbreviations and further explanations, please see the Introduction.

Clarksville, TN - continued

Item	Per	Value	Date	Ref.
Education				
Tuition, 2-year private college/university	year	4203	91	22s
Tuition, 2-year public college/university	year	848	91	22s
Tuition, 4-year private college/university	year	6889	91	22s
Tuition, 4-year public college/university, in-state	year	1518	91	22s
Energy and Fuels				
Coal	mil Btu	1.35	90	64s
Energy	mil Btu	8.61	90	64s
Energy, combined forms, 1,800 sq ft heating area	month	103.66	4Q 92	4c
Energy exp/householder, 1-family unit	year	403	90	28r
Energy exp/householder, <1,000 sq ft heating area	year	342	90	28r
Energy exp/householder, 1,000-1,999 sq ft heating area	year	388	90	28r
Energy exp/householder, 2,000+ sq ft heating area	year	434	90	28r
Energy exp/householder, mobile home	year	320	90	28r
Energy exp/householder, multifamily	year	338	90	28r
Gas, natural	mil Btu	3.98	90	64s
Gas, natural	000 cu ft	5.19	91	46s
Gas, natural, exp	year	388	91	46s
Gasoline, motor	gal	1.09	4Q 92	4c
Gasoline, unleaded regular	mil Btu	9.40	90	64s
Entertainment				
Bowling, evening rate	game	2.60	4Q 92	4c
Miniature golf admission	adult	6.18	92	1r
Miniature golf admission	child	5.14	92	1r
Monopoly game, Parker Brothers', No. 9		9.22	4Q 92	4c
Movie	admission	5.00	4Q 92	4c
Tennis balls, yellow, Wilson or Penn, 3	can	1.92	4Q 92	4c
Waterpark admission	adult	11.00	92	1r
Waterpark admission	child	8.55	92	1r
Funerals				
Casket, 18-gauge steel, velvet interior		2329.05	91	24r
Cosmetology, hair care, etc.		72.78	91	24r
Embalming		240.71	91	24r
Facility use for ceremony		181.67	91	24r
Hearse, local		106.25	91	24r
Limousine, local		70.92	91	24r
Remains to funeral home, transfer		96.30	91	24r
Service charge, professional		687.09	91	24r
Vault, concrete, non-metallic liner		732.09	91	24r
Viewing facilities, use		190.30	91	24r
Goods and Services				
ACCRA Index, Miscellaneous Goods and Services		97.20	4Q 92	4c
Groceries				
ACCRA Index, Groceries		95.20	4Q 92	4c
Apples, Red Delicious	lb	0.79	4/93	16r
Babyfood, strained vegetables, lowest price	4-4.5 oz jar	0.31	4Q 92	4c
Bacon	lb	1.75	4/93	16r
Bananas	lb	0.41	4Q 92	4c
Bananas	lb	0.42	4/93	16r
Beef, stew, boneless	lb	2.61	4/93	16r
Bologna, all beef or mixed	lb	2.24	4/93	16r
Bread, white	24 oz	0.89	4Q 92	4c
Bread, white, pan	lb	0.64	4/93	16r
Bread, whole wheat, pan	lb	0.96	4/93	16r
Cabbage	lb	0.37	4/93	16r
Carrots, short trimmed and topped	lb	0.47	4/93	16r
Celery	lb	0.64	4/93	16r
Cheese, American	lb	2.98	4/93	16r
Cheese, Cheddar	lb	3.28	4/93	16r

Clarksville, TN - continued

Item	Per	Value	Date	Ref.
Groceries - continued				
Cheese, Kraft grated Parmesan	8-oz canister	3.14	4Q 92	4c
Chicken, fresh, whole	lb	0.77	4/93	16r
Chicken, fryer, whole	lb	0.70	4Q 92	4c
Chicken breast, bone-in	lb	1.92	4/93	16r
Chicken legs, bone-in	lb	1.06	4/93	16r
Chuck roast, graded and ungraded, ex USDA prime and choice	lb	2.40	4/93	16r
Chuck roast, USDA choice, bone-in	lb	2.19	4/93	16r
Chuck roast, USDA choice, boneless	lb	2.38	4/93	16r
Cigarettes, Winston	carton	16.27	4Q 92	4c
Coffee, 100% ground roast, all sizes	lb	2.48	4/93	16r
Coffee, vacuum-packed	13-oz can	1.76	4Q 92	4c
Corn, frozen	10 oz	0.55	4Q 92	4c
Corn Flakes, Kellogg's or Post Toasties	18 oz	1.76	4Q 92	4c
Crackers, soda, salted	lb	1.15	4/93	16r
Eggs, Grade A large	doz	0.79	4Q 92	4c
Eggs, Grade A large	doz	0.96	4/93	16r
Flour, white, all purpose	lb	0.24	4/93	16r
Frankfurters, all meat or all beef	lb	2.01	4/93	16r
Grapefruit	lb	0.44	4/93	16r
Grapes, Thompson Seedless	lb	1.40	4/93	16r
Ground beef, 100% beef	lb	1.58	4/93	16r
Ground beef, lean and extra lean	lb	2.09	4/93	16r
Ground beef or hamburger	lb	1.42	4Q 92	4c
Ground chuck, 100% beef	lb	1.98	4/93	16r
Ham, boneless, excluding canned	lb	2.89	4/93	16r
Ham, picnic, shoulder, bone-in, smoked	lb	1.02	4/93	16r
Ham, rump or steak half, bone-in, smoked	lb	1.48	4/93	16r
Honey, jar	8 oz	0.89-1.09	92	5r
Honey, jar	lb	1.39-2.25	92	5r
Honey, squeeze bear	12-oz	1.00-1.50	92	5r
Ice cream, prepackaged, bulk, regular	1/2 gal	2.41	4/93	16r
Lemons	lb	1.05	4/93	16r
Lettuce, iceberg	head	0.99	4Q 92	4c
Lettuce, iceberg	lb	0.81	4/93	16r
Margarine, Blue Bonnet or Parkay cubes	lb	0.52	4Q 92	4c
Margarine, stick	lb	0.88	4/93	16r
Milk, whole	1/2 gal	1.33	4Q 92	4c
Orange juice, Minute Maid frozen	12-oz can	1.26	4Q 92	4c
Oranges, navel	lb	0.55	4/93	16r
Peaches	29-oz can	1.37	4Q 92	4c
Pears, Anjou	lb	0.92	4/93	16r
Peas Sweet, Del Monte or Green Giant	15-17 oz can	0.56	4Q 92	4c
Pork chops, center cut, bone-in	lb	3.13	4/93	16r
Potato chips	16 oz	2.94	4/93	16r
Potatoes, white	lb	0.43	4/93	16r
Potatoes, white or red	10-lb sack	2.04	4Q 92	4c
Rib roast, USDA choice, bone-in	lb	4.63	4/93	16r
Rice, white, long grain, uncooked	lb	0.45	4/93	16r
Round roast, graded & ungraded, ex USDA prime & choice	lb	3.03	4/93	16r
Round roast, USDA choice, boneless	lb	3.09	4/93	16r
Sausage, fresh, loose	lb	2.08	4/93	16r
Sausage, Jimmy Dean, 100% pork	lb	2.18	4Q 92	4c
Short ribs, bone-in	lb	2.66	4/93	16r
Shortening, vegetable oil blends	lb	0.69	4/93	16r
Shortening, vegetable, Crisco	3-lb can	2.10	4Q 92	4c
Soft drink, Coca Cola	2 liter	1.13	4Q 92	4c
Spaghetti and macaroni	lb	0.81	4/93	16r
Steak, rib eye, USDA choice, boneless	lb	6.24	4/93	16r
Steak, round, graded & ungraded, ex USDA prime & choice	lb	3.31	4/93	16r
Steak, round, USDA choice, boneless	lb	3.34	4/93	16r

Values are in dollars or fractions of dollars. In the column headed *Ref*, references are shown to sources. Each reference is followed by a letter. These refer to the geographical level for which data were reported: s=State, r=Region, and c=City or metro. The abbreviation *ex* is used to mean *except* or *excluding*; *exp* stands for expenditures. For other abbreviations and further explanations, please see the Introduction.

Clarksville, TN - continued

Item	Per	Value	Date	Ref.
Groceries				
Steak, sirloin, graded & ungraded, ex USDA prime & choice	lb	4.19	4/93	16r
Steak, sirloin, USDA choice, boneless	lb	4.46	4/93	16r
Steak, T-bone	lb	5.09	4Q 92	4c
Steak, T-bone, USDA choice, bone-in	lb	5.25	4/93	16r
Strawberries, dry pint	12 oz	0.92	4/93	16r
Sugar, cane or beet	4 lb	1.48	4Q 92	4c
Sugar, white	lb	0.39	4/93	16r
Sugar, white, 33-80 oz pk	lb	0.38	4/93	16r
Tomatoes, field grown	lb	0.88	4/93	16r
Tomatoes, Hunt's or Del Monte	14.5-oz can	0.62	4Q 92	4c
Tuna, chunk, light	6.125-6.5 oz can	0.58	4Q 92	4c
Tuna, chunk, light	lb	1.79	4/93	16r
Turkey, frozen, whole	lb	1.04	4/93	16r
Yogurt, natural, fruit flavored	1/2 pint	0.57	4/93	16r
Health Care				
ACCRA Index, Health Care		81.20	4Q 92	4c
Analgesic, Aspirin, Bayer, 325 mg tablets	100	4.91	4Q 92	4c
Childbirth, cesarean, hospital		5034	91	62r
Childbirth, cesarean, physician's fee		2053	91	62r
Childbirth, normal, hospital		2712	91	62r
Childbirth, normal, physician's fee		1492	91	62r
Dentist's fee, adult teeth cleaning and periodic oral exam	visit	38.40	4Q 92	4c
Doctor's fee, routine exam, established patient	visit	30.20	4Q 92	4c
Hospital care, semiprivate room	day	216.00	4Q 92	4c
Medical insurance premium, per employee, small group comprehensive	month	324.85	10/91	25c
Mental health care, exp	capita	20.37-28.83	90	38s
Mental health care, exp, state mental health agency	capita	28.84	90	38s
Mental health care, hospital psychiatric services, non-Federal, exp	capita	13.48	88	38s
Mental health care, mental health organization, multiservice, exp	capita	11.35	88	38s
Mental health care, psychiatric hospitals, private, exp	capita	22.28	88	38s
Mental health care, psychiatric out-patient clinics, freestanding, exp	capita	2.58	88	38s
Mental health care, psychiatric partial-care organizations, freestanding, exp	capita	0.25	88	38s
Mental health care, state and county mental hospitals, exp	capita	20.05	88	38s
Mental health care, VA medical centers, exp	capita	4.98	88	38s
Physician fee, family practice, first-visit		75.00	91	62r
Physician fee, family practice, revisit		34.00	91	62r
Physician fee, general practice, first-visit		61.00	91	62r
Physician fee, general practice, revisit		32.00	91	62r
Physician fee, general surgeon, first-visit		64.00	91	62r
Physician fee, general surgeon, revisit		40.00	91	62r
Physician fee, internal medicine, first-visit		98.00	91	62r
Physician fee, internal medicine, revisit		40.00	91	62r
Physician fee, median, neurosurgeon, first-visit		130.00	91	62r
Physician fee, median, nonsurgical specialist, first-visit		95.00	91	62r
Physician fee, median, orthopedic surgeon, first-visit		91.00	91	62r
Physician fee, median, plastic surgeon, first-visit		66.00	91	62r
Physician fee, median, surgical specialist, first-visit		62.00	91	62r
Physician fee, neurosurgeon, revisit		50.00	91	62r
Physician fee, nonsurgical specialist, revisit		40.00	91	62r
Physician fee, obstetrics/gynecology, first-visit		64.00	91	62r

Clarksville, TN - continued

Item	Per	Value	Date	Ref.
Health Care - continued				
Physician fee, obstetrics/gynecology, revisit		41.00	91	62r
Physician fee, orthopedic surgeon, revisit		40.00	91	62r
Physician fee, pediatrician, first-visit		49.00	91	62r
Physician fee, pediatrician, revisit		33.00	91	62r
Physician fee, plastic surgeon, revisit		43.00	91	62r
Physician fee, surgical specialist, revisit		37.00	91	62r
Substance abuse, hospital ancillary charge	incident	1330	90	70s
Substance abuse, hospital physician charge	incident	580	90	70s
Substance abuse, hospital room and board	incident	5180	90	70s
Household Goods				
Appliance repair, home, service call, washing machine	min labor charge	23.88	4Q 92	4c
Laundry detergent, Tide Ultra, Bold, or Cheer	42 oz	2.60	4Q 92	4c
Tissues, facial, Kleenex brand	175-count box	1.12	4Q 92	4c
Housing				
ACCRA Index, Housing		81.90	4Q 92	4c
House, 1,800 sq ft, 8,000 sq ft lot, new, urban	total	93390	4Q 92	4c
House payment, principal and interest, 25% down payment	month	515	4Q 92	4c
Mortgage rate, incl. points & origination fee, 30-year fixed or adjustable rate	percent	8.02	4Q 92	4c
Rent, apartment, 2 bedrooms - 1-1/2 to 2 baths, unfurnished, 950 sq ft, water	month	378	4Q 92	4c
Rental unit, 1 bedroom	month	374	93	23c
Rental unit, 2 bedroom	month	468	93	23c
Rental unit, 3 bedroom	month	569	93	23c
Rental unit, 4 bedroom	month	632	93	23c
Rental unit, efficiency	month	297	93	23c
Insurance and Pensions				
Auto insurance, private passenger	year	554.60	91	63s
Personal Goods				
Shampoo, Alberto VO5	15 oz	1.30	4Q 92	4c
Toothpaste, Crest or Colgate	6-7 oz	2.00	4Q 92	4c
Personal Services				
Dry cleaning, man's 2-piece suit		5.11	4Q 92	4c
Haircare, woman's shampoo, trim and blow-dry		18.00	4Q 92	4c
Haircut, man's barbershop, no styling		5.50	4Q 92	4c
Restaurant Food				
Chicken, fried, thigh and drumstick		2.08	4Q 92	4c
Hamburger with cheese	1/4 lb	1.87	4Q 92	4c
Pizza, Pizza Hut or Pizza Inn, cheese, thin crust	12-13 in	7.89	4Q 92	4c
Taxes				
Tax, cigarette	pack	13	91	77s
Tax, gasoline	gal	22.40	91	77s
Taxes, state	capita	870	91	77s
Transportation				
ACCRA Index, Transportation		95.80	4Q 92	4c
Bus fare	one-way	0.75	3/93	2c
Driver's license fee		14.00-16.00	12/90	43s
Tire balance, computer or spin balance, front	wheel	6.20	4Q 92	4c
Travel				
Business travel	day	193.00	4/93	89r

Values are in dollars or fractions of dollars. In the column headed *Ref*, references are shown to sources. Each reference is followed by a letter. These refer to the geographical level for which data were reported: s = State, r = Region, and c = City or metro. The abbreviation *ex* is used to mean *except* or *excluding*; *exp* stands for expenditures. For other abbreviations and further explanations, please see the Introduction.

Clarksville, TN - continued

Item	Per	Value	Date	Ref.
Utilities				
ACCRA Index, Utilities		93.80	4Q 92	4c
Electricity	mil Btu	15.59	90	64s
Electricity, all electric, 1,800 sq ft living area new home	month	103.66	4Q 92	4c

Cleveland, OH

Item	Per	Value	Date	Ref.
Composite ACCRA index		111.00	4Q 92	4c
Alcoholic Beverages				
Alcoholic beverages, exp	year	286	89	15c
Beer, Miller Lite or Budweiser, 12-oz containers	6 pack	3.98	4Q 92	4c
Liquor, J & B Scotch	750 ml	18.05	4Q 92	4c
Wine, Gallo Chablis blanc, 1.5 liter	bottle	5.49	4Q 92	4c
Charity				
Cash contributions	year	846	89	15c
Child Care				
Child care fee, average, center	hour	1.63	90	65r
Child care fee, average, nonregulated family day care	hour	1.83	90	65r
Child care fee, average, regulated family day care	hour	1.42	90	65r
Clothing				
Jeans, man's denim		28.71	4Q 92	4c
Shirt, man's dress shirt		22.85	4Q 92	4c
Undervest, boy's size 10-14, cotton	3	4.09	4Q 92	4c
Communications				
Long-distance telephone service, day, initial minute, 0-100 miles	min	0.26-0.43	91	12s
Long-distance telephone service, day, additional minute, 0-100 miles	min	0.14-0.24	91	12s
Long-distance telephone service, evenings/weekends, 0-100 mi, initial minute	min	0.11-0.17	91	12s
Long-distance telephone service, evenings/weekends, 0-100 mi, additional minute	min	0.06-0.10	91	12s
Newspaper subscription, daily and Sunday home delivery, large-city	month	10.87	4Q 92	4c
Postage and stationery, exp	year	131	89	15c
Telephone, exp	year	490	89	15c
Telephone, residential, private line, rotary, unlimited calling	month	19.44	10/91	78c
Telephone bill, family of four	month	24.90	4Q 92	4c
Education				
Board, 4-yr private college/university	year	1872	91	22s
Board, 4-yr public college/university	year	1742	91	22s
Education, exp	year	532	89	15c
Expenditures, local gov't, public elementary/secondary	pupil	5451	92	20s
Room, 4-year private college/university	year	1695	91	22s
Room, 4-year public college/university	year	2259	91	22s
Tuition, 2-year private college/university	year	6093	91	22s
Tuition, 2-year public college/university	year	1768	91	22s
Tuition, 4-year private college/university	year	8729	91	22s
Tuition, 4-year public college/university, in-state	year	2622	91	22s
Energy and Fuels				
Coal	mil Btu	1.54	90	64s
Energy	mil Btu	8.32	90	64s
Energy, combined forms, 1,800 sq ft heating area	month	142.40	4Q 92	4c
Energy, exc electricity, 1,800 sq ft heating area	month	55.20	4Q 92	4c
Energy exp/householder, 1-family unit	year	471	90	28r
Energy exp/householder, <1,000 sq ft heating area	year	430	90	28r
Energy exp/householder, 1,000-1,999 sq ft heating area	year	481	90	28r

Cleveland, OH - continued

Item	Per	Value	Date	Ref.
Energy and Fuels - continued				
Energy exp/householder, 2,000+ sq ft heating area	year	473	90	28r
Energy exp/householder, mobile home	year	430	90	28r
Energy exp/householder, multifamily	year	461	90	28r
Fuel oil, other fuel, exp	year	64	89	15c
Gas, cooking, winter, 10 therms	month	8.70	92	56c
Gas, cooking, winter, 30 therms	month	17.54	92	56c
Gas, cooking, winter, 50 therms	month	26.38	92	56c
Gas, heating, winter, 100 therms	month	48.48	92	56c
Gas, heating, winter, average use	month	130.69	92	56c
Gas, natural	mil Btu	4.54	90	64s
Gas, natural	000 cu ft	5.28	91	46s
Gas, natural, exp	year	464	89	15c
Gas, natural, exp	year	606	91	46s
Gas, piped	100 therms	47.75	4/93	16c
Gas, piped	40 therms	23.05	4/93	16c
Gas, piped	therm	0.47	4/93	16c
Gasoline, all types	gal	1.21	4/93	16c
Gasoline, motor	gal	1.15	4Q 92	4c
Gasoline, regular unleaded, taxes included, cash, self-service	gal	1.31	4/93	16c
Gasoline, unleaded premium 93 octane	gal	1.17	4/93	16c
Gasoline, unleaded regular	mil Btu	9.35	90	64s
Entertainment				
Bowling, evening rate	game	1.56	4Q 92	4c
Entertainment exp	year	1469	89	15c
Fees and admissions	year	446	89	15c
Miniature golf admission	adult	6.18	92	1r
Miniature golf admission	child	5.14	92	1r
Monopoly game, Parker Brothers', No. 9		11.13	4Q 92	4c
Movie	admission	6.04	4Q 92	4c
Pets, toys, playground equipment, exp	year	289	89	15c
Reading, exp	year	175	89	15c
Supplies, equipment, services, exp	year	239	89	15c
Tennis balls, yellow, Wilson or Penn, 3	can	2.79	4Q 92	4c
Waterpark admission	adult	11.00	92	1r
Waterpark admission	child	8.55	92	1r
Funerals				
Casket, 18-gauge steel, velvet interior		1926.72	91	24r
Cosmetology, hair care, etc.		97.64	91	24r
Embalming		249.14	91	24r
Facility use for ceremony		208.59	91	24r
Hearse, local		130.12	91	24r
Limousine, local		104.66	91	24r
Remains to funeral home, transfer		93.61	91	24r
Service charge, professional		724.62	91	24r
Vault, concrete, non-metallic liner		734.53	91	24r
Viewing facilities, use		236.06	91	24r
Goods and Services				
ACCRA Index, Miscellaneous Goods and Services		101.60	4Q 92	4c
Police protection expense	resident	197.00	92	18c
Groceries				
ACCRA Index, Groceries		103.90	4Q 92	4c
Apples, Red Delicious	lb	0.77	4/93	16r
Babyfood, strained vegetables, lowest price	4-4.5 oz jar	0.34	4Q 92	4c
Bacon	lb	1.85	4/93	16r
Bakery products, exp	year	227	89	15c
Bananas	lb	0.46	4Q 92	4c
Bananas	lb	0.46	4/93	16r
Beef, exp	year	216	89	15c
Beef, stew, boneless	lb	2.53	4/93	16r
Beverages, nonalcoholic, exp	year	195	89	15c
Bologna, all beef or mixed	lb	2.19	4/93	16r

Values are in dollars or fractions of dollars. In the column headed *Ref*, references are shown to sources. Each reference is followed by a letter. These refer to the geographical level for which data were reported: s=State, r=Region, and c=City or metro. The abbreviation *ex* is used to mean *except* or *excluding*; *exp* stands for *expenditures*. For other abbreviations and further explanations, please see the Introduction.

Cleveland, OH - continued

Item	Per	Value	Date	Ref.
Groceries				
Bread, white	24 oz	0.96	4Q 92	4c
Bread, white, pan	lb	0.78	4/93	16r
Butter	lb	1.50	4/93	16r
Cabbage	lb	0.40	4/93	16r
Carrots, short trimmed and topped	lb	0.45	4/93	16r
Cereals and bakery products, exp	year	333	89	15c
Cereals and cereal products, exp	year	106	89	15c
Cheese, Cheddar	lb	3.47	4/93	16r
Cheese, Kraft grated Parmesan	8-oz canister	2.64	4Q 92	4c
Chicken, fresh, whole	lb	0.84	4/93	16r
Chicken, fryer, whole	lb	1.07	4Q 92	4c
Chicken breast, bone-in	lb	1.94	4/93	16r
Chicken legs, bone-in	lb	1.02	4/93	16r
Chuck roast, graded and ungraded, ex USDA prime and choice	lb	2.43	4/93	16r
Chuck roast, USDA choice, bone-in	lb	2.11	4/93	16r
Chuck roast, USDA choice, boneless	lb	2.44	4/93	16r
Cigarettes, Winston	carton	17.21	4Q 92	4c
Coffee, 100% ground roast, all sizes	lb	2.47	4/93	16r
Coffee, vacuum-packed	13-oz can	2.48	4Q 92	4c
Cookies, chocolate chip	lb	2.73	4/93	16r
Corn, frozen	10 oz	0.63	4Q 92	4c
Corn Flakes, Kellogg's or Post Toasties	18 oz	1.78	4Q 92	4c
Dairy products, exp	year	270	89	15c
Dairy products, miscellaneous, exp	year	140	89	15c
Eggs, exp	year	17	89	15c
Eggs, Grade A large	doz	0.70	4Q 92	4c
Eggs, Grade A large	doz	0.93	4/93	16r
Fats and oils, exp	year	57	89	15c
Fish and seafood, exp	year	49	89	15c
Flour, white, all purpose	lb	0.21	4/93	16r
Food, exp	year	4080	89	15c
Food eaten at home, exp	year	2232	89	15c
Food eaten away from home, exp	year	1849	89	15c
Food prepared on out-of-town trips, exp	year	19	89	15c
Foods, miscellaneous, exp	year	257	89	15c
Fruits, fresh, exp	year	101	89	15c
Fruits, processed, exp	year	89	89	15c
Fruits and vegetables, exp	year	356	89	15c
Grapefruit	lb	0.45	4/93	16r
Grapes, Thompson Seedless	lb	1.46	4/93	16r
Ground beef, 100% beef	lb	1.63	4/93	16r
Ground beef, lean and extra lean	lb	2.08	4/93	16r
Ground beef or hamburger	lb	1.63	4Q 92	4c
Ground chuck, 100% beef	lb	1.94	4/93	16r
Ham, boneless, excluding canned	lb	2.21	4/93	16r
Honey, jar	8 oz	0.97-1.25	92	5r
Honey, jar	lb	1.25-2.25	92	5r
Honey, squeeze bear	12-oz	1.25-1.99	92	5r
Ice cream, prepackaged, bulk, regular	1/2 gal	2.41	4/93	16r
Lemons	lb	0.82	4/93	16r
Lettuce, iceberg	head	1.07	4Q 92	4c
Lettuce, iceberg	lb	0.83	4/93	16r
Margarine, Blue Bonnet or Parkay cubes	lb	0.54	4Q 92	4c
Margarine, stick	lb	0.77	4/93	16r
Meats, miscellaneous, exp	year	111	89	15c
Meats, poultry, fish and eggs, exp	year	655	89	15c
Milk, whole	1/2 gal	1.27	4Q 92	4c
Milk and cream, fresh, exp	year	129	89	15c
Orange juice, Minute Maid frozen	12-oz can	1.39	4Q 92	4c
Oranges, navel	lb	0.50	4/93	16r
Peaches	29-oz can	1.32	4Q 92	4c
Peanut butter, creamy, all sizes	lb	1.82	4/93	16r
Pears, Anjou	lb	0.85	4/93	16r
Peas Sweet, Del Monte or Green Giant	15-17 oz can	0.55	4Q 92	4c
Pork, exp	year	137	89	15c

Cleveland, OH - continued

Item	Per	Value	Date	Ref.
Groceries - continued				
Pork chops, center cut, bone-in	lb	3.17	4/93	16r
Potato chips	16 oz	2.68	4/93	16r
Potatoes, white	lb	0.26	4/93	16r
Potatoes, white or red	10-lb sack	1.53	4Q 92	4c
Poultry, exp	year	106	89	15c
Round roast, graded & ungraded, ex USDA prime & choice	lb	2.88	4/93	16r
Round roast, USDA choice, boneless	lb	2.96	4/93	16r
Sausage, Jimmy Dean, 100% pork	lb	2.51	4Q 92	4c
Shortening, vegetable oil blends	lb	0.79	4/93	16r
Shortening, vegetable, Crisco	3-lb can	2.36	4Q 92	4c
Soft drink, Coca Cola	2 liter	0.93	4Q 92	4c
Spaghetti and macaroni	lb	0.76	4/93	16r
Steak, rib eye, USDA choice, boneless	lb	6.29	4/93	16r
Steak, round, USDA choice, boneless	lb	3.24	4/93	16r
Steak, sirloin, graded & ungraded, ex USDA prime & choice	lb	4.00	4/93	16r
Steak, sirloin, USDA choice, bone-in	lb	3.57	4/93	16r
Steak, sirloin, USDA choice, boneless	lb	4.17	4/93	16r
Steak, T-bone	lb	5.30	4Q 92	4c
Steak, T-bone, USDA choice, bone-in	lb	5.60	4/93	16r
Strawberries, dry pint	12 oz	0.90	4/93	16r
Sugar, cane or beet	4 lb	1.37	4Q 92	4c
Sugar, white	lb	0.36	4/93	16r
Sugar, white, 33-80 oz pk	lb	0.35	4/93	16r
Sugar and other sweets, exp	year	90	89	15c
Tobacco products, exp	year	304	89	15c
Tomatoes, field grown	lb	0.99	4/93	16r
Tomatoes, Hunt's or Del Monte	14.5-oz can	0.81	4Q 92	4c
Tuna, chunk, light	6.125-6.5 oz can	0.66	4Q 92	4c
Tuna, chunk, light	lb	1.76	4/93	16r
Turkey, frozen, whole	lb	0.91	4/93	16r
Vegetables, fresh, exp	year	107	89	15c
Vegetables, processed, exp	year	60	89	15c
Health Care				
ACCRA Index, Health Care		110.60	4Q 92	4c
Analgesic, Aspirin, Bayer, 325 mg tablets	100	5.27	4Q 92	4c
Childbirth, cesarean, hospital		4688	91	62r
Childbirth, cesarean, physician's fee		2053	91	62r
Childbirth, normal, hospital		2657	91	62r
Childbirth, normal, physician's fee		1492	91	62r
Dentist's fee, adult teeth cleaning and periodic oral exam	visit	50.00	4Q 92	4c
Doctor's fee, routine exam, established patient	visit	34.43	4Q 92	4c
Drugs, exp	year	218	89	15c
Health care, exp	year	1305	89	15c
Health insurance, exp	year	429	89	15c
Health maintenance organization coverage, employee	year	3727	93	39c
Health maintenance organization medical coverage, employee	year	3727	92	42c
Hospital care, semiprivate room	day	434.02	90	27c
Hospital care, semiprivate room	day	493.33	4Q 92	4c
Indemnity plan medical coverage, employee	year	4027	92	42c
Insurance coverage, traditional, employee	year	4027	93	39c
Medical insurance premium, per employee, small group comprehensive	month	394.20	10/91	25c
Medical plan per employee	year	3443	91	45r
Medical services, exp	year	550	89	15c
Medical supplies, exp	year	108	89	15c
Mental health care, exp	capita	37.60-53.67	90	38s
Mental health care, exp, state mental health agency	capita	40.93	90	38s
Mental health care, hospital psychiatric services, non-Federal, exp	capita	15.03	88	38s

Values are in dollars or fractions of dollars. In the column headed *Ref*, references are shown to sources. Each reference is followed by a letter. These refer to the geographical level for which data were reported: s=State, r=Region, and c=City or metro. The abbreviation *ex* is used to mean *except* or *excluding*; *exp* stands for expenditures. For other abbreviations and further explanations, please see the Introduction.

Cleveland, OH - continued

Item	Per	Value	Date	Ref.
Health Care				
Mental health care, mental health organization, multiservice, exp	capita	14.46	88	38s
Mental health care, psychiatric hospitals, private, exp	capita	7.93	88	38s
Mental health care, psychiatric out-patient clinics, freestanding, exp	capita	2.93	88	38s
Mental health care, psychiatric partial-care organizations, freestanding, exp	capita	0.32	88	38s
Mental health care, state and county mental hospitals, exp	capita	23.79	88	38s
Mental health care, VA medical centers, exp	capita	7.76	88	38s
Physician fee, family practice, first-visit		76.00	91	62r
Physician fee, family practice, revisit		33.00	91	62r
Physician fee, general practice, first-visit		61.00	91	62r
Physician fee, general practice, revisit		31.00	91	62r
Physician fee, general surgeon, first-visit		65.00	91	62r
Physician fee, general surgeon, revisit		35.00	91	62r
Physician fee, internal medicine, first-visit		91.00	91	62r
Physician fee, internal medicine, revisit		40.00	91	62r
Physician fee, median, neurosurgeon, first-visit		106.00	91	62r
Physician fee, median, nonsurgical specialist, first-visit		90.00	91	62r
Physician fee, median, orthopedic surgeon, first-visit		83.00	91	62r
Physician fee, median, surgical specialist, first-visit		61.00	91	62r
Physician fee, neurosurgeon, revisit		41.00	91	62r
Physician fee, nonsurgical specialist, revisit		40.00	91	62r
Physician fee, obstetrics/gynecology, first-visit		61.00	91	62r
Physician fee, obstetrics/gynecology, revisit		40.00	91	62r
Physician fee, orthopedic surgeon, revisit		41.00	91	62r
Physician fee, pediatrician, first-visit		46.00	91	62r
Physician fee, pediatrician, revisit		33.00	91	62r
Physician fee, surgical specialist, revisit		36.00	91	62r
Preferred provider organization medical coverage, employee	year	3459	92	42c
Substance abuse, hospital ancillary charge	incident	940	90	70s
Substance abuse, hospital physician charge	incident	380	90	70s
Substance abuse, hospital room and board	incident	5410	90	70s
Household Goods				
Appliance repair, home, service call, washing machine	min labor charge	31.68	4Q 92	4c
Appliances, major, exp	year	183	89	15c
Appliances, small, exp	year	98	89	15c
Equipment, misc., exp	year	565	89	15c
Floor coverings, exp	year	33	89	15c
Furnishings and equipment, exp	year	1411	89	15c
Furniture, exp	year	385	89	15c
Household products, misc., exp	year	163	89	15c
Household textiles, exp	year	147	89	15c
Housekeeping supplies, exp	year	414	89	15c
Laundry and cleaning supplies, exp	year	120	89	15c
Laundry detergent, Tide Ultra, Bold, or Cheer	42 oz	3.88	4Q 92	4c
Tissues, facial, Kleenex brand	175-count box	1.10	4Q 92	4c
TVs, radios, sound equipment, exp	year	495	89	15c
Housing				
ACCRA Index, Housing		119.70	4Q 92	4c
Dwellings, exp	year	2048	89	15c
Home, median price	unit	90.70		26c
House, 1,800 sq ft, 8,000 sq ft lot, new, urban	total	127926	4Q 92	4c

Cleveland, OH - continued

Item	Per	Value	Date	Ref.
Housing - continued				
House payment, principal and interest, 25% down payment	month	729	4Q 92	4c
Household expenses, misc.	year	217	89	15c
Household operations, exp	year	447	89	15c
Housing, exp	year	7726	89	15c
Lodging, exp	year	318	89	15c
Maintenance, repairs, insurance, and other, exp	year	406	89	15c
Mortgage interest, exp	year	1199	89	15c
Mortgage rate, incl. points & origination fee, 30-year fixed or adjustable rate	percent	8.38	4Q 92	4c
Rent, apartment, 2 bedrooms - 1-1/2 to 2 baths, unfurnished, 950 sq ft, water	month	607	4Q 92	4c
Rental unit, 1 bedroom	month	429	93	23c
Rental unit, 2 bedroom	month	505	93	23c
Rental unit, 3 bedroom	month	632	93	23c
Rental unit, 4 bedroom	month	707	93	23c
Rental unit, efficiency	month	353	93	23c
Rented dwellings, exp	year	1228	89	15c
Shelter, exp	year	3593	89	15c
Insurance and Pensions				
Auto insurance, private passenger	year	547.38	91	63s
Insurance, life and other personal, exp	year	291	89	15c
Insurance and pensions, personal, exp	year	2264	89	15c
Pensions and social security, exp	year	1973	89	15c
Vehicle insurance	year	633	89	15c
Personal Goods				
Products and services, exp	year	379	89	15c
Shampoo, Alberto VO5	15 oz	1.35	4Q 92	4c
Toothpaste, Crest or Colgate	6-7 oz	2.21	4Q 92	4c
Personal Services				
Dry cleaning, man's 2-piece suit		6.60	4Q 92	4c
Haircare, woman's shampoo, trim and blow-dry		24.42	4Q 92	4c
Haircut, man's barbershop, no styling		9.43	4Q 92	4c
Services, exp	year	230	89	15c
Restaurant Food				
Chicken, fried, thigh and drumstick		2.24	4Q 92	4c
Hamburger with cheese	1/4 lb	1.81	4Q 92	4c
Pizza, Pizza Hut or Pizza Inn, cheese, thin crust	12-13 in	7.84	4Q 92	4c
Taxes				
Property tax, exp	year	442	89	15c
Tax, cigarette	pack	18	91	77s
Tax, gasoline	gal	21	91	77s
Taxes, state	capita	1056	91	77s
Transportation				
ACCRA Index, Transportation		111.20	4Q 92	4c
Auto rental, average	day	50.75	6/91	60c
Bus fare	one-way	0.75	3/93	2c
Bus fare, up to 10 miles	one-way	1.25	4Q 92	4c
Driver's license fee		5.00	12/90	43s
Limo fare, airport-city, average	day	10.50	6/91	60c
Public transit, exp	year	237	89	15c
Railway fare, heavy rail	one-way	1.50	3/93	2c
Railway fare, light rail	one-way	1.50	93	2c
Taxi fare, airport-city, average	day	16.50	6/91	60c
Tire balance, computer or spin balance, front	wheel	7.39	4Q 92	4c
Vehicle expenses, misc.	year	1966	89	15c
Vehicle finance charges	year	371	89	15c
Vehicle maintenance	year	694	89	15c
Vehicle rental and license	year	269	89	15c

Values are in dollars or fractions of dollars. In the column headed Ref, references are shown to sources. Each reference is followed by a letter. These refer to the geographical level for which data were reported: s=State, r=Region, and c=City or metro. The abbreviation ex is used to mean except or excluding; exp stands for expenditures. For other abbreviations and further explanations, please see the Introduction.

Cleveland, OH - continued

Item	Per	Value	Date	Ref.
Travel				
Breakfast	day	5.14	6/91	60c
Dinner	day	24.70	6/91	60c
Lodging	day	106.69	91	60c
Lunch	day	9.81	6/91	60c
Travel, business	day	192.51	93	88c
Utilities				
ACCRA Index, Utilities		130.20	4Q 92	4c
Electricity	500 KWh	56.75	4/93	16c
Electricity	KWh	0.11	4/93	16c
Electricity	mil Btu	17.33	90	64s
Electricity, exp	year	668	89	15c
Electricity, partial electric and other energy, 1,800 sq ft living area new home	month	87.20	4Q 92	4c
Electricity, winter, 250 KWh	month	28.38	92	55c
Electricity, winter, 500 KWh	month	56.74	92	55c
Electricity, winter, 750 KWh	month	83.58	92	55c
Electricity, winter, 1000 KWh	month	110.40	92	55c
Utilities, fuels, public services, exp	year	1860	89	15c
Water, public services, exp	year	175	89	15c

Cleveland, TN

Item	Per	Value	Date	Ref.
Composite ACCRA index		91.00	4Q 92	4c
Alcoholic Beverages				
Beer, Miller Lite or Budweiser, 12-oz containers	6 pack	4.06	4Q 92	4c
Liquor, J & B Scotch	750 ml	17.53	4Q 92	4c
Wine, Gallo Chablis blanc, 1.5 liter	bottle	5.41	4Q 92	4c
Clothing				
Jeans, man's denim		32.87	4Q 92	4c
Shirt, man's dress shirt		20.80	4Q 92	4c
Undervest, boy's size 10-14, cotton	3	3.14	4Q 92	4c
Communications				
Newspaper subscription, daily and Sunday home delivery, large-city	month	11.09	4Q 92	4c
Telephone bill, family of four	month	18.67	4Q 92	4c
Energy and Fuels				
Energy, combined forms, 1,800 sq ft heating area	month	101.18	4Q 92	4c
Energy, exc electricity, 1,800 sq ft heating area	month	36.40	4Q 92	4c
Gasoline, motor	gal	1.00	4Q 92	4c
Entertainment				
Bowling, evening rate	game	1.78	4Q 92	4c
Monopoly game, Parker Brothers', No. 9		8.46	4Q 92	4c
Movie	admission	4.83	4Q 92	4c
Tennis balls, yellow, Wilson or Penn, 3	can	1.91	4Q 92	4c
Goods and Services				
ACCRA Index, Miscellaneous Goods and Services		92.20	4Q 92	4c
Groceries				
ACCRA Index, Groceries		91.10	4Q 92	4c
Babyfood, strained vegetables, lowest price	4-4.5 oz jar	0.30	4Q 92	4c
Bananas	lb	0.34	4Q 92	4c
Bread, white	24 oz	0.68	4Q 92	4c
Cheese, Kraft grated Parmesan	8-oz canister	3.26	4Q 92	4c
Chicken, fryer, whole	lb	0.61	4Q 92	4c
Cigarettes, Winston	carton	16.41	4Q 92	4c
Coffee, vacuum-packed	13-oz can	1.76	4Q 92	4c
Corn, frozen	10 oz	0.58	4Q 92	4c
Corn Flakes, Kellogg's or Post Toasties	18 oz	1.66	4Q 92	4c

Cleveland, TN - continued

Item	Per	Value	Date	Ref.
Groceries - continued				
Eggs, Grade A large	doz	0.80	4Q 92	4c
Ground beef or hamburger	lb	1.04	4Q 92	4c
Lettuce, iceberg	head	0.91	4Q 92	4c
Margarine, Blue Bonnet or Parkay cubes	lb	0.47	4Q 92	4c
Milk, whole	1/2 gal	1.30	4Q 92	4c
Orange juice, Minute Maid frozen	12-oz can	1.14	4Q 92	4c
Peaches	29-oz can	1.36	4Q 92	4c
Peas Sweet, Del Monte or Green Giant	15-17 oz can	0.48	4Q 92	4c
Potatoes, white or red	10-lb sack	2.51	4Q 92	4c
Sausage, Jimmy Dean, 100% pork	lb	2.31	4Q 92	4c
Shortening, vegetable, Crisco	3-lb can	2.04	4Q 92	4c
Soft drink, Coca Cola	2 liter	0.98	4Q 92	4c
Steak, T-bone	lb	5.66	4Q 92	4c
Sugar, cane or beet	4 lb	1.40	4Q 92	4c
Tomatoes, Hunt's or Del Monte	14.5-oz can	0.53	4Q 92	4c
Tuna, chunk, light	6.125-6.5 oz can	0.79	4Q 92	4c
Health Care				
ACCRA Index, Health Care		86.10	4Q 92	4c
Analgesic, Aspirin, Bayer, 325 mg tablets	100	4.04	4Q 92	4c
Dentist's fee, adult teeth cleaning and periodic oral exam	visit	47.75	4Q 92	4c
Doctor's fee, routine exam, established patient	visit	31.00	4Q 92	4c
Hospital care, semiprivate room	day	198.75	4Q 92	4c
Household Goods				
Appliance repair, home, service call, washing machine	min labor charge	35.71	4Q 92	4c
Laundry detergent, Tide Ultra, Bold, or Cheer	42 oz	2.73	4Q 92	4c
Tissues, facial, Kleenex brand	175-count box	1.08	4Q 92	4c
Housing				
ACCRA Index, Housing		90.30	4Q 92	4c
House, 1,800 sq ft, 8,000 sq ft lot, new, urban	total	101840	4Q 92	4c
House payment, principal and interest, 25% down payment	month	567	4Q 92	4c
Mortgage rate, incl. points & origination fee, 30-year fixed or adjustable rate	percent	8.13	4Q 92	4c
Rent, apartment, 2 bedrooms - 1-1/2 to 2 baths, unfurnished, 950 sq ft, water	month	417	4Q 92	4c
Personal Goods				
Shampoo, Alberto VO5	15 oz	0.97	4Q 92	4c
Toothpaste, Crest or Colgate	6-7 oz	1.71	4Q 92	4c
Personal Services				
Dry cleaning, man's 2-piece suit		4.88	4Q 92	4c
Haircare, woman's shampoo, trim and blow-dry		16.20	4Q 92	4c
Haircut, man's barbershop, no styling		5.98	4Q 92	4c
Restaurant Food				
Chicken, fried, thigh and drumstick		1.98	4Q 92	4c
Hamburger with cheese	1/4 lb	1.89	4Q 92	4c
Pizza, Pizza Hut or Pizza Inn, cheese, thin crust	12-13 in	7.74	4Q 92	4c
Transportation				
ACCRA Index, Transportation		88.80	4Q 92	4c
Tire balance, computer or spin balance, front	wheel	5.80	4Q 92	4c

Values are in dollars or fractions of dollars. In the column headed *Ref*, references are shown to sources. Each reference is followed by a letter. These refer to the geographical level for which data were reported: s = State, r = Region, and c = City or metro. The abbreviation *ex* is used to mean *except* or *excluding*; *exp* stands for *expenditures*. For other abbreviations and further explanations, please see the Introduction.

Cleveland, TN - continued

Item	Per	Value	Date	Ref.
Utilities				
ACCRA Index, Utilities		93.00	4Q 92	4c
Electricity, partial electric and other energy, 1,800 sq ft living area new home	month	64.78	4Q 92	4c

Clovis-Portales, NM

Item	Per	Value	Date	Ref.
Composite ACCRA index		95.10	4Q 92	4c
Alcoholic Beverages				
Beer, Miller Lite or Budweiser, 12-oz containers	6 pack	3.49	4Q 92	4c
Liquor, J & B Scotch	750 ml	15.04	4Q 92	4c
Wine, Gallo Chablis blanc, 1.5 liter	bottle	4.66	4Q 92	4c
Clothing				
Jeans, man's denim		30.49	4Q 92	4c
Shirt, man's dress shirt		22.33	4Q 92	4c
Undervest, boy's size 10-14, cotton	3	4.04	4Q 92	4c
Communications				
Newspaper subscription, daily and Sunday home delivery, large-city	month	8.75	4Q 92	4c
Telephone bill, family of four	month	17.42	4Q 92	4c
Energy and Fuels				
Energy, combined forms, 1,800 sq ft heating area	month	106.73	4Q 92	4c
Gasoline, motor	gal	1.20	4Q 92	4c
Entertainment				
Bowling, evening rate	game	1.95	4Q 92	4c
Monopoly game, Parker Brothers', No. 9		12.70	4Q 92	4c
Movie	admission	4.67	4Q 92	4c
Tennis balls, yellow, Wilson or Penn, 3	can	2.70	4Q 92	4c
Goods and Services				
ACCRA Index, Miscellaneous Goods and Services		98.90	4Q 92	4c
Groceries				
ACCRA Index, Groceries		95.90	4Q 92	4c
Babyfood, strained vegetables, lowest price	4-4.5 oz jar	0.29	4Q 92	4c
Bananas	lb	0.35	4Q 92	4c
Bread, white	24 oz	0.69	4Q 92	4c
Cheese, Kraft grated Parmesan	8-oz canister	3.86	4Q 92	4c
Chicken, fryer, whole	lb	0.66	4Q 92	4c
Cigarettes, Winston	carton	16.26	4Q 92	4c
Coffee, vacuum-packed	13-oz can	1.91	4Q 92	4c
Corn, frozen	10 oz	0.77	4Q 92	4c
Corn Flakes, Kellogg's or Post Toasties	18 oz	2.15	4Q 92	4c
Eggs, Grade A large	doz	0.80	4Q 92	4c
Ground beef or hamburger	lb	1.16	4Q 92	4c
Lettuce, iceberg	head	0.96	4Q 92	4c
Margarine, Blue Bonnet or Parkay cubes	lb	0.74	4Q 92	4c
Milk, whole	1/2 gal	1.43	4Q 92	4c
Orange juice, Minute Maid frozen	12-oz can	1.41	4Q 92	4c
Peaches	29-oz can	1.45	4Q 92	4c
Peas Sweet, Del Monte or Green Giant	15-17 oz can	0.66	4Q 92	4c
Potatoes, white or red	10-lb sack	1.97	4Q 92	4c
Sausage, Jimmy Dean, 100% pork	lb	2.11	4Q 92	4c
Shortening, vegetable, Crisco	3-lb can	2.14	4Q 92	4c
Soft drink, Coca Cola	2 liter	1.39	4Q 92	4c
Steak, T-bone	lb	4.76	4Q 92	4c
Sugar, cane or beet	4 lb	1.45	4Q 92	4c

Clovis-Portales, NM - continued

Item	Per	Value	Date	Ref.
Groceries - continued				
Tomatoes, Hunt's or Del Monte	14.5-oz can	0.76	4Q 92	4c
Tuna, chunk, light	6.125-6.5 oz can	0.69	4Q 92	4c
Health Care				
ACCRA Index, Health Care		90.20	4Q 92	4c
Analgesic, Aspirin, Bayer, 325 mg tablets	100	6.26	4Q 92	4c
Dentist's fee, adult teeth cleaning and periodic oral exam	visit	44.25	4Q 92	4c
Doctor's fee, routine exam, established patient	visit	30.98	4Q 92	4c
Hospital care, semiprivate room	day	230.00	4Q 92	4c
Household Goods				
Appliance repair, home, service call, washing machine	min labor charge	30.61	4Q 92	4c
Laundry detergent, Tide Ultra, Bold, or Cheer	42 oz	3.06	4Q 92	4c
Tissues, facial, Kleenex brand	175-count box	1.24	4Q 92	4c
Housing				
ACCRA Index, Housing		89.20	4Q 92	4c
House, 1,800 sq ft, 8,000 sq ft lot, new, urban	total	89350	4Q 92	4c
House payment, principal and interest, 25% down payment	month	497	4Q 92	4c
Mortgage rate, incl. points & origination fee, 30-year fixed or adjustable rate	percent	8.11	4Q 92	4c
Rent, apartment, 2 bedrooms - 1-1/2 to 2 baths, unfurnished, 950 sq ft, water	month	560	4Q 92	4c
Personal Goods				
Shampoo, Alberto VO5	15 oz	1.44	4Q 92	4c
Toothpaste, Crest or Colgate	6-7 oz	2.36	4Q 92	4c
Personal Services				
Dry cleaning, man's 2-piece suit		5.19	4Q 92	4c
Haircare, woman's shampoo, trim and blow-dry		17.86	4Q 92	4c
Haircut, man's barbershop, no styling		8.10	4Q 92	4c
Restaurant Food				
Chicken, fried, thigh and drumstick		2.34	4Q 92	4c
Hamburger with cheese	1/4 lb	1.85	4Q 92	4c
Pizza, Pizza Hut or Pizza Inn, cheese, thin crust	12-13 in	8.90	4Q 92	4c
Transportation				
ACCRA Index, Transportation		97.80	4Q 92	4c
Tire balance, computer or spin balance, front	wheel	5.83	4Q 92	4c
Utilities				
ACCRA Index, Utilities		96.90	4Q 92	4c
Electricity, all electric, 1,800 sq ft living area new home	month	106.73	4Q 92	4c

Colorado Springs, CO

Item	Per	Value	Date	Ref.
Composite ACCRA index		94.40	4Q 92	4c
Alcoholic Beverages				
Beer, Miller Lite or Budweiser, 12-oz containers	6 pack	3.59	4Q 92	4c
Liquor, J & B Scotch	750 ml	15.24	4Q 92	4c
Wine, Gallo Chablis blanc, 1.5 liter	bottle	4.25	4Q 92	4c
Child Care				
Child care fee, average, center	hour	1.71	90	65r
Child care fee, average, nonregulated family day care	hour	1.32	90	65r

Values are in dollars or fractions of dollars. In the column headed *Ref*, references are shown to sources. Each reference is followed by a letter. These refer to the geographical level for which data were reported: s=State, r=Region, and c=City or metro. The abbreviation *ex* is used to mean *except* or *excluding*; *exp* stands for expenditures. For other abbreviations and further explanations, please see the Introduction.

Colorado Springs, CO - continued

Item	Per	Value	Date	Ref.
Child Care				
Child care fee, average, regulated family day care	hour	1.86	90	65r
Clothing				
Jeans, man's denim		19.80	4Q 92	4c
Shirt, man's dress shirt		21.80	4Q 92	4c
Undervest, boy's size 10-14, cotton	3	5.03	4Q 92	4c
Communications				
Long-distance telephone service, day, initial minute, 0-100 miles	min	0.11-0.35	91	12s
Long-distance telephone service, day, additional minute, 0-100 miles	min	0.13-0.27	91	12s
Long-distance telephone service, evenings/weekends, 0-100 mi, initial minute	min	0.08-0.17	91	12s
Long-distance telephone service, evenings/weekends, 0-100 mi, additional minute	min	0.06-0.14	91	12s
Newspaper subscription, daily and Sunday home delivery, large-city	month	7.50	4Q 92	4c
Telephone, flat rate	month	14.22	91	11c
Telephone, residential, private line, rotary, unlimited calling	month	16.73	10/91	78c
Telephone bill, family of four	month	16.77	4Q 92	4c
Education				
Board, 4-yr private college/university	year	2162	91	22s
Board, 4-yr public college/university	year	1747	91	22s
Expenditures, local gov't, public elementary/secondary	pupil	5259	92	20s
Room, 4-year private college/university	year	1984	91	22s
Room, 4-year public college/university	year	1546	91	22s
Tuition, 2-year private college/university	year	6731	91	22s
Tuition, 2-year public college/university	year	943	91	22s
Tuition, 4-year private college/university	year	9516	91	22s
Tuition, 4-year public college/university, in-state	year	1919	91	22s
Energy and Fuels				
Coal	mil Btu	1.07	90	64s
Energy	mil Btu	8.14	90	64s
Energy, combined forms, 1,800 sq ft heating area	month	78.21	4Q 92	4c
Energy, exc electricity, 1,800 sq ft heating area	month	35.58	4Q 92	4c
Energy exp/householder, 1-family unit	year	372	90	28r
Energy exp/householder, <1,000 sq ft heating area	year	335	90	28r
Energy exp/householder, 1,000-1,999 sq ft heating area	year	365	90	28r
Energy exp/householder, 2,000+ sq ft heating area	year	411	90	28r
Energy exp/householder, mobile home	year	305	90	28r
Energy exp/householder, multifamily	year	372	90	28r
Gas, natural	mil Btu	3.92	90	64s
Gas, natural	000 cu ft	4.59	91	46s
Gas, natural, exp	year	446	91	46s
Gasoline, motor	gal	1.28	4Q 92	4c
Gasoline, unleaded regular	mil Btu	9.29	90	64s
Entertainment				
Bowling, evening rate	game	1.88	4Q 92	4c
Miniature golf admission	adult	6.18	92	1r
Miniature golf admission	child	5.14	92	1r
Monopoly game, Parker Brothers', No. 9		12.19	4Q 92	4c
Movie	admission	5.50	4Q 92	4c
Tennis balls, yellow, Wilson or Penn, 3	can	2.89	4Q 92	4c
Waterpark admission	adult	11.00	92	1r
Waterpark admission	child	8.55	92	1r
Funerals				
Casket, 18-gauge steel, velvet interior		1929.04	91	24r
Cosmetology, hair care, etc.		88.52	91	24r
Embalming		249.33	91	24r

Item	Per	Value	Date	Ref.
Funerals - continued				
Facility use for ceremony		182.75	91	24r
Hearse, local		110.04	91	24r
Limousine, local		66.67	91	24r
Remains to funeral home, transfer		84.58	91	24r
Service charge, professional		593.00	91	24r
Vault, concrete, non-metallic liner		647.38	91	24r
Viewing facilities, use		99.87	91	24r
Goods and Services				
ACCRA Index, Miscellaneous Goods and Services		94.20	4Q 92	4c
Groceries				
ACCRA Index, Groceries		103.80	4Q 92	4c
Apples, Red Delicious	lb	0.80	4/93	16r
Babyfood, strained vegetables, lowest price	4-4.5 oz jar	0.33	4Q 92	4c
Bacon	lb	1.79	4/93	16r
Bananas	lb	0.51	4Q 92	4c
Bananas	lb	0.53	4/93	16r
Bologna, all beef or mixed	lb	2.67	4/93	16r
Bread, white	24 oz	0.79	4Q 92	4c
Bread, white, pan	lb	0.81	4/93	16r
Carrots, short trimmed and topped	lb	0.39	4/93	16r
Cheese, Kraft grated Parmesan	8-oz canister	3.18	4Q 92	4c
Chicken, fresh, whole	lb	0.94	4/93	16r
Chicken, fryer, whole	lb	0.65	4Q 92	4c
Chicken breast, bone-in	lb	2.19	4/93	16r
Chuck roast, graded and ungraded, ex USDA prime and choice	lb	2.26	4/93	16r
Cigarettes, Winston	carton	15.32	4Q 92	4c
Coffee, 100% ground roast, all sizes	lb	2.33	4/93	16r
Coffee, vacuum-packed	13-oz can	2.41	4Q 92	4c
Corn, frozen	10 oz	0.66	4Q 92	4c
Corn Flakes, Kellogg's or Post Toasties	18 oz	1.97	4Q 92	4c
Eggs, Grade A large	doz	0.97	4Q 92	4c
Eggs, Grade AA large	doz	1.18	4/93	16r
Flour, white, all purpose	lb	0.22	4/93	16r
Grapefruit	lb	0.52	4/93	16r
Grapes, Thompson Seedless	lb	1.50	4/93	16r
Ground beef, 100% beef	lb	1.44	4/93	16r
Ground beef, lean and extra lean	lb	2.34	4/93	16r
Ground beef or hamburger	lb	1.93	4Q 92	4c
Ham, boneless, excluding canned	lb	2.56	4/93	16r
Honey, jar	8 oz	0.99-1.19	92	5r
Honey, jar	lb	1.49-2.25	92	5r
Honey, squeeze bear	12-oz	1.00-1.89	92	5r
Ice cream, prepackaged, bulk, regular	1/2 gal	2.40	4/93	16r
Lemons	lb	0.81	4/93	16r
Lettuce, iceberg	head	0.87	4Q 92	4c
Lettuce, iceberg	lb	0.84	4/93	16r
Margarine, Blue Bonnet or Parkay cubes	lb	0.61	4Q 92	4c
Margarine, stick	lb	0.81	4/93	16r
Milk, whole	1/2 gal	1.39	4Q 92	4c
Orange juice, Minute Maid frozen	12-oz can	1.47	4Q 92	4c
Oranges, navel	lb	0.48	4/93	16r
Peaches	29-oz can	1.31	4Q 92	4c
Peas Sweet, Del Monte or Green Giant	15-17 oz can	0.69	4Q 92	4c
Pork chops, center cut, bone-in	lb	3.25	4/93	16r
Potato chips	16 oz	2.89	4/93	16r
Potatoes, white	lb	0.38	4/93	16r
Potatoes, white or red	10-lb sack	1.65	4Q 92	4c
Round roast, graded & ungraded, ex USDA prime & choice	lb	3.00	4/93	16r
Round roast, USDA choice, boneless	lb	3.16	4/93	16r
Sausage, Jimmy Dean, 100% pork	lb	3.40	4Q 92	4c

Values are in dollars or fractions of dollars. In the column headed *Ref*, references are shown to sources. Each reference is followed by a letter. These refer to the geographical level for which data were reported: s=State, r=Region, and c=City or metro. The abbreviation *ex* is used to mean *except* or *excluding*; *exp* stands for expenditures. For other abbreviations and further explanations, please see the Introduction.

Colorado Springs, CO - continued

Item	Per	Value	Date	Ref.
Groceries				
Shortening, vegetable oil blends	lb	0.86	4/93	16r
Shortening, vegetable, Crisco	3-lb can	2.33	4Q 92	4c
Soft drink, Coca Cola	2 liter	1.00	4Q 92	4c
Spaghetti and macaroni	lb	0.84	4/93	16r
Steak, round, graded & ungraded, ex USDA prime & choice	lb	3.34	4/93	16r
Steak, round, USDA choice, boneless	lb	3.24	4/93	16r
Steak, sirloin, graded & ungraded, ex USDA prime & choice	lb	3.75	4/93	16r
Steak, sirloin, USDA choice, boneless	lb	4.49	4/93	16r
Steak, T-bone	lb	4.63	4Q 92	4c
Sugar, cane or beet	4 lb	1.59	4Q 92	4c
Sugar, white	lb	0.41	4/93	16r
Sugar, white, 33-80 oz pk	lb	0.38	4/93	16r
Tomatoes, field grown	lb	1.01	4/93	16r
Tomatoes, Hunt's or Del Monte	14.5-oz can	0.75	4Q 92	4c
Tuna, chunk, light	6.125-6.5 oz can	0.69	4Q 92	4c
Turkey, frozen, whole	lb	1.04	4/93	16r
Health Care				
ACCRA Index, Health Care		95.40	4Q 92	4c
Analgesic, Aspirin, Bayer, 325 mg tablets	100	4.89	4Q 92	4c
Childbirth, cesarean, hospital		5533	91	62r
Childbirth, cesarean, physician's fee		2053	91	62r
Childbirth, normal, hospital		2745	91	62r
Childbirth, normal, physician's fee		1492	91	62r
Dentist's fee, adult teeth cleaning and periodic oral exam	visit	33.40	4Q 92	4c
Doctor's fee, routine exam, established patient	visit	33.80	4Q 92	4c
Hospital care, semiprivate room	day	308.00	90	27c
Hospital care, semiprivate room	day	471.25	4Q 92	4c
Medical insurance premium, per employee, small group comprehensive	month	313.90	10/91	25c
Medical plan per employee	year	3218	91	45r
Mental health care, exp	capita	28.84-37.59	90	38s
Mental health care, exp, state mental health agency	capita	33.55	90	38s
Mental health care, hospital psychiatric services, non-Federal, exp	capita	11.38	88	38s
Mental health care, mental health organization, multiservice, exp	capita	21.76	88	38s
Mental health care, psychiatric hospitals, private, exp	capita	14.39	88	38s
Mental health care, psychiatric out-patient clinics, freestanding, exp	capita	0.11	88	38s
Mental health care, state and county mental hospitals, exp	capita	19.03	88	38s
Mental health care, VA medical centers, exp	capita	3.80	88	38s
Physician fee, family practice, first-visit		111.00	91	62r
Physician fee, family practice, revisit		45.00	91	62r
Physician fee, general practice, first-visit		100.00	91	62r
Physician fee, general practice, revisit		40.00	91	62r
Physician fee, internal medicine, first-visit		137.00	91	62r
Physician fee, internal medicine, revisit		48.00	91	62r
Physician fee, median, neurosurgeon, first-visit		157.00	91	62r
Physician fee, median, nonsurgical specialist, first-visit		131.00	91	62r
Physician fee, median, orthopedic surgeon, first-visit		124.00	91	62r
Physician fee, median, plastic surgeon, first-visit		88.00	91	62r
Physician fee, median, surgical specialist, first-visit		100.00	91	62r
Physician fee, neurosurgeon, revisit		51.00	91	62r
Physician fee, nonsurgical specialist, revisit		47.00	91	62r

Colorado Springs, CO - continued

Item	Per	Value	Date	Ref.
Health Care - continued				
Physician fee, obstetrics/gynecology, first-visit		95.00	91	62r
Physician fee, obstetrics/gynecology, revisit		50.00	91	62r
Physician fee, orthopedic surgeon, revisit		51.00	91	62r
Physician fee, pediatrician, first-visit		81.00	91	62r
Physician fee, pediatrician, revisit		42.00	91	62r
Physician fee, plastic surgeon, revisit		48.00	91	62r
Physician fee, surgical specialist, revisit		49.00	91	62r
Substance abuse, hospital ancillary charge	incident	1040	90	70s
Substance abuse, hospital physician charge	incident	380	90	70s
Substance abuse, hospital room and board	incident	4880	90	70s
Household Goods				
Appliance repair, home, service call, washing machine	min labor charge	24.80	4Q 92	4c
Laundry detergent, Tide Ultra, Bold, or Cheer	42 oz	3.99	4Q 92	4c
Tissues, facial, Kleenex brand	175-count box	0.97	4Q 92	4c
Housing				
ACCRA Index, Housing		94.80	4Q 92	4c
House, 1,800 sq ft, 8,000 sq ft lot, new, urban	total	111250	4Q 92	4c
House payment, principal and interest, 25% down payment	month	627	4Q 92	4c
Mortgage rate, incl. points & origination fee, 30-year fixed or adjustable rate	percent	8.25	4Q 92	4c
Rent, apartment, 2 bedrooms - 1-1/2 to 2 baths, unfurnished, 950 sq ft, water	month	365	4Q 92	4c
Rental unit, 1 bedroom	month	428	93	23c
Rental unit, 2 bedroom	month	504	93	23c
Rental unit, 3 bedroom	month	632	93	23c
Rental unit, 4 bedroom	month	708	93	23c
Rental unit, efficiency	month	353	93	23c
Residential home, new	average	140,456	91	14c
Residential home, resale	average	83,656	91	14c
Insurance and Pensions				
Auto insurance, private passenger	year	684.81	91	63s
Personal Goods				
Shampoo, Alberto VO5	15 oz	1.47	4Q 92	4c
Toothpaste, Crest or Colgate	6-7 oz	1.83	4Q 92	4c
Personal Services				
Dry cleaning, man's 2-piece suit		4.75	4Q 92	4c
Haircare, woman's shampoo, trim and blow-dry		17.70	4Q 92	4c
Haircut, man's barbershop, no styling		7.55	4Q 92	4c
Restaurant Food				
Chicken, fried, thigh and drumstick		1.98	4Q 92	4c
Hamburger with cheese	1/4 lb	1.89	4Q 92	4c
Pizza, Pizza Hut or Pizza Inn, cheese, thin crust	12-13 in	8.32	4Q 92	4c
Taxes				
Tax, cigarette	pack	20	91	77s
Tax, gasoline	gal	22	91	77s
Taxes, state	capita	951	91	77s
Transportation				
ACCRA Index, Transportation		100.60	4Q 92	4c
Auto rental, average	day	31.96	6/91	60c
Driver's license fee		15.00	12/90	43s
Taxi fare, airport-city, average	day	10.00	6/91	60c
Tire balance, computer or spin balance, front	wheel	5.70	4Q 92	4c

Values are in dollars or fractions of dollars. In the column headed *Ref*, references are shown to sources. Each reference is followed by a letter. These refer to the geographical level for which data were reported: s = State, r = Region, and c = City or metro. The abbreviation *ex* is used to mean *except* or *excluding*; *exp* stands for expenditures. For other abbreviations and further explanations, please see the Introduction.

Colorado Springs, CO - continued

Item	Per	Value	Date	Ref.
Travel				
Business travel	day	178.00	4/93	89r
Lodging	day	91.25	91	60c
Utilities				
ACCRA Index, Utilities		73.10	4Q 92	4c
Electricity	mil Btu	17.31	90	64s
Electricity, partial electric and other energy, 1,800 sq ft living area new home	month	42.63	4Q 92	4c
Electricity, residential	KWh	7.70	2/93	94s

Columbia, MO

Item	Per	Value	Date	Ref.
Composite ACCRA index		92.60	4Q 92	4c
Alcoholic Beverages				
Beer, Miller Lite or Budweiser, 12-oz containers	6 pack	3.73	4Q 92	4c
Liquor, J & B Scotch	750 ml	15.60	4Q 92	4c
Wine, Gallo Chablis blanc, 1.5 liter	bottle	4.97	4Q 92	4c
Child Care				
Child care fee, average, center	hour	1.63	90	65r
Child care fee, average, nonregulated family day care	hour	1.83	90	65r
Child care fee, average, regulated family day care	hour	1.42	90	65r
Clothing				
Jeans, man's denim		25.11	4Q 92	4c
Shirt, man's dress shirt		23.00	4Q 92	4c
Undervest, boy's size 10-14, cotton	3	3.57	4Q 92	4c
Communications				
Long-distance telephone service, day, initial minute, 0-100 miles	min	0.10-0.46	91	12s
Long-distance telephone service, day, additional minute, 0-100 miles	min	0.06-0.29	91	12s
Newspaper subscription, daily and Sunday home delivery, large-city	month	8.65	4Q 92	4c
Telephone bill, family of four	month	12.57	4Q 92	4c
Education				
Board, 4-yr private college/university	year	1789	91	22s
Board, 4-yr public college/university	year	1162	91	22s
Expenditures, local gov't, public elementary/secondary	pupil	4537	92	20s
Room, 4-year private college/university	year	1817	91	22s
Room, 4-year public college/university	year	1450	91	22s
Tuition, 2-year private college/university	year	5208	91	22s
Tuition, 2-year public college/university	year	891	91	22s
Tuition, 4-year private college/university	year	7487	91	22s
Tuition, 4-year public college/university, in-state	year	1733	91	22s
Energy and Fuels				
Coal	mil Btu	1.35	90	64s
Energy	mil Btu	8.91	90	64s
Energy, combined forms, 1,800 sq ft heating area	month	81.17	4Q 92	4c
Energy, exc electricity, 1,800 sq ft heating area	month	34.00	4Q 92	4c
Energy exp/householder, 1-family unit	year	473	90	28r
Energy exp/householder, <1,000 sq ft heating area	year	429	90	28r
Energy exp/householder, 1,000-1,999 sq ft heating area	year	442	90	28r
Energy exp/householder, 2,000+ sq ft heating area	year	498	90	28r
Energy exp/householder, mobile home	year	442	90	28r
Energy exp/householder, multifamily	year	407	90	28r
Gas, natural	mil Btu	4.69	90	64s
Gas, natural	000 cu ft	5.14	91	46s
Gas, natural, exp	year	512	91	46s
Gasoline, motor	gal	1.05	4Q 92	4c

Columbia, MO - continued

Item	Per	Value	Date	Ref.
Energy and Fuels - continued				
Gasoline, unleaded regular	mil Btu	8.61	90	64s
Entertainment				
Bowling, evening rate	game	1.83	4Q 92	4c
Miniature golf admission	adult	6.18	92	1r
Miniature golf admission	child	5.14	92	1r
Monopoly game, Parker Brothers', No. 9		12.62	4Q 92	4c
Movie	admission	4.81	4Q 92	4c
Tennis balls, yellow, Wilson or Penn, 3	can	2.82	4Q 92	4c
Waterpark admission	adult	11.00	92	1r
Waterpark admission	child	8.55	92	1r
Funerals				
Casket, 18-gauge steel, velvet interior		1952.97	91	24r
Cosmetology, hair care, etc.		90.03	91	24r
Embalming		251.75	91	24r
Facility use for ceremony		180.75	91	24r
Hearse, local		117.51	91	24r
Limousine, local		71.86	91	24r
Remains to funeral home, transfer		81.14	91	24r
Service charge, professional		740.03	91	24r
Vault, concrete, non-metallic liner		801.47	91	24r
Viewing facilities, use		169.33	91	24r
Goods and Services				
ACCRA Index, Miscellaneous Goods and Services		96.50	4Q 92	4c
Groceries				
ACCRA Index, Groceries		96.40	4Q 92	4c
Apples, Red Delicious	lb	0.77	4/93	16r
Babyfood, strained vegetables, lowest price	4-4.5 oz jar	0.23	4Q 92	4c
Bacon	lb	1.85	4/93	16r
Bananas	lb	0.47	4Q 92	4c
Bananas	lb	0.46	4/93	16r
Beef, stew, boneless	lb	2.53	4/93	16r
Bologna, all beef or mixed	lb	2.19	4/93	16r
Bread, white	24 oz	0.75	4Q 92	4c
Bread, white, pan	lb	0.78	4/93	16r
Butter	lb	1.50	4/93	16r
Cabbage	lb	0.40	4/93	16r
Carrots, short trimmed and topped	lb	0.45	4/93	16r
Cheese, Cheddar	lb	3.47	4/93	16r
Cheese, Kraft grated Parmesan	8-oz canister	3.15	4Q 92	4c
Chicken, fresh, whole	lb	0.84	4/93	16r
Chicken, fryer, whole	lb	0.70	4Q 92	4c
Chicken breast, bone-in	lb	1.94	4/93	16r
Chicken legs, bone-in	lb	1.02	4/93	16r
Chuck roast, graded and ungraded, ex USDA prime and choice	lb	2.43	4/93	16r
Chuck roast, USDA choice, bone-in	lb	2.11	4/93	16r
Chuck roast, USDA choice, boneless	lb	2.44	4/93	16r
Cigarettes, Winston	carton	17.67	4Q 92	4c
Coffee, 100% ground roast, all sizes	lb	2.47	4/93	16r
Coffee, vacuum-packed	13-oz can	1.92	4Q 92	4c
Cookies, chocolate chip	lb	2.73	4/93	16r
Corn, frozen	10 oz	0.62	4Q 92	4c
Corn Flakes, Kellogg's or Post Toasties	18 oz	1.77	4Q 92	4c
Eggs, Grade A large	doz	0.61	4Q 92	4c
Eggs, Grade A large	doz	0.93	4/93	16r
Flour, white, all purpose	lb	0.21	4/93	16r
Grapefruit	lb	0.45	4/93	16r
Grapes, Thompson Seedless	lb	1.46	4/93	16r
Ground beef, 100% beef	lb	1.63	4/93	16r
Ground beef, lean and extra lean	lb	2.08	4/93	16r
Ground beef or hamburger	lb	1.32	4Q 92	4c
Ground chuck, 100% beef	lb	1.94	4/93	16r
Ham, boneless, excluding canned	lb	2.21	4/93	16r
Ice cream, prepackaged, bulk, regular	1/2 gal	2.41	4/93	16r

Values are in dollars or fractions of dollars. In the column headed *Ref*, references are shown to sources. Each reference is followed by a letter. These refer to the geographical level for which data were reported: s=State, r=Region, and c=City or metro. The abbreviation *ex* is used to mean *except* or *excluding*; *exp* stands for expenditures. For other abbreviations and further explanations, please see the Introduction.

Columbia, MO - continued

Item	Per	Value	Date	Ref.
Groceries				
Lemons	lb	0.82	4/93	16r
Lettuce, iceberg	head	0.91	4Q 92	4c
Lettuce, iceberg	lb	0.83	4/93	16r
Margarine, Blue Bonnet or Parkay cubes	lb	0.54	4Q 92	4c
Margarine, stick	lb	0.77	4/93	16r
Milk, whole	1/2 gal	1.30	4Q 92	4c
Orange juice, Minute Maid frozen	12-oz can	1.48	4Q 92	4c
Oranges, navel	lb	0.50	4/93	16r
Peaches	29-oz can	1.30	4Q 92	4c
Peanut butter, creamy, all sizes	lb	1.82	4/93	16r
Pears, Anjou	lb	0.85	4/93	16r
Peas Sweet, Del Monte or Green Giant	15-17 oz can	0.57	4Q 92	4c
Pork chops, center cut, bone-in	lb	3.17	4/93	16r
Potato chips	16 oz	2.68	4/93	16r
Potatoes, white	lb	0.26	4/93	16r
Potatoes, white or red	10-lb sack	2.29	4Q 92	4c
Round roast, graded & ungraded, ex USDA prime & choice	lb	2.88	4/93	16r
Round roast, USDA choice, boneless	lb	2.96	4/93	16r
Sausage, Jimmy Dean, 100% pork	lb	2.65	4Q 92	4c
Shortening, vegetable oil blends	lb	0.79	4/93	16r
Shortening, vegetable, Crisco	3-lb can	2.41	4Q 92	4c
Soft drink, Coca Cola	2 liter	1.13	4Q 92	4c
Spaghetti and macaroni	lb	0.76	4/93	16r
Steak, rib eye, USDA choice, boneless	lb	6.29	4/93	16r
Steak, round, USDA choice, boneless	lb	3.24	4/93	16r
Steak, sirloin, graded & ungraded, ex USDA prime & choice	lb	4.00	4/93	16r
Steak, sirloin, USDA choice, bone-in	lb	3.57	4/93	16r
Steak, sirloin, USDA choice, boneless	lb	4.17	4/93	16r
Steak, T-bone	lb	5.38	4Q 92	4c
Steak, T-bone, USDA choice, bone-in	lb	5.60	4/93	16r
Strawberries, dry pint	12 oz	0.90	4/93	16r
Sugar, cane or beet	4 lb	1.42	4Q 92	4c
Sugar, white	lb	0.36	4/93	16r
Sugar, white, 33-80 oz pk	lb	0.35	4/93	16r
Tomatoes, field grown	lb	0.99	4/93	16r
Tomatoes, Hunt's or Del Monte	14.5-oz can	0.77	4Q 92	4c
Tuna, chunk, light	6.125-6.5 oz can	0.61	4Q 92	4c
Tuna, chunk, light	lb	1.76	4/93	16r
Turkey, frozen, whole	lb	0.91	4/93	16r
Health Care				
ACCRA Index, Health Care		105.60	4Q 92	4c
Analgesic, Aspirin, Bayer, 325 mg tablets	100	4.38	4Q 92	4c
Childbirth, cesarean, hospital		4688	91	62r
Childbirth, cesarean, physician's fee		2053	91	62r
Childbirth, normal, hospital		2657	91	62r
Childbirth, normal, physician's fee		1492	91	62r
Dentist's fee, adult teeth cleaning and periodic oral exam	visit	46.78	4Q 92	4c
Doctor's fee, routine exam, established patient	visit	41.50	4Q 92	4c
Hospital care, semiprivate room	day	269.00	90	27c
Hospital care, semiprivate room	day	364.00	4Q 92	4c
Medical insurance premium, per employee, small group comprehensive	month	302.95	10/91	25c
Medical plan per employee	year	3443	91	45r
Mental health care, exp	capita	37.60-53.67	90	38s
Mental health care, exp, state mental health agency	capita	35.47	90	38s
Mental health care, hospital psychiatric services, non-Federal, exp	capita	22.53	88	38s

Columbia, MO - continued

Item	Per	Value	Date	Ref.
Health Care - continued				
Mental health care, mental health organization, multiservice, exp	capita	6.98	88	38s
Mental health care, psychiatric hospitals, private, exp	capita	5.96	88	38s
Mental health care, psychiatric out-patient clinics, freestanding, exp	capita	0.79	88	38s
Mental health care, state and county mental hospitals, exp	capita	33.35	88	38s
Mental health care, VA medical centers, exp	capita	3.33	88	38s
Physician fee, family practice, first-visit		76.00	91	62r
Physician fee, family practice, revisit		33.00	91	62r
Physician fee, general practice, first-visit		61.00	91	62r
Physician fee, general practice, revisit		31.00	91	62r
Physician fee, general surgeon, first-visit		65.00	91	62r
Physician fee, general surgeon, revisit		35.00	91	62r
Physician fee, internal medicine, first-visit		91.00	91	62r
Physician fee, internal medicine, revisit		40.00	91	62r
Physician fee, median, neurosurgeon, first-visit		106.00	91	62r
Physician fee, median, nonsurgical specialist, first-visit		90.00	91	62r
Physician fee, median, orthopedic surgeon, first-visit		83.00	91	62r
Physician fee, median, surgical specialist, first-visit		61.00	91	62r
Physician fee, neurosurgeon, revisit		41.00	91	62r
Physician fee, nonsurgical specialist, revisit		40.00	91	62r
Physician fee, obstetrics/gynecology, first-visit		61.00	91	62r
Physician fee, obstetrics/gynecology, revisit		40.00	91	62r
Physician fee, orthopedic surgeon, revisit		41.00	91	62r
Physician fee, pediatrician, first-visit		46.00	91	62r
Physician fee, pediatrician, revisit		33.00	91	62r
Physician fee, surgical specialist, revisit		36.00	91	62r
Substance abuse, hospital ancillary charge	incident	1380	90	70s
Substance abuse, hospital physician charge	incident	560	90	70s
Substance abuse, hospital room and board	incident	5670	90	70s
Household Goods				
Appliance repair, home, service call, washing machine	min labor charge	32.23	4Q 92	4c
Laundry detergent, Tide Ultra, Bold, or Cheer	42 oz	2.89	4Q 92	4c
Tissues, facial, Kleenex brand	175-count box	1.13	4Q 92	4c
Housing				
ACCRA Index, Housing		87.50	4Q 92	4c
House, 1,800 sq ft, 8,000 sq ft lot, new, urban	total	97160	4Q 92	4c
House payment, principal and interest, 25% down payment	month	543	4Q 92	4c
Mortgage rate, incl. points & origination fee, 30-year fixed or adjustable rate	percent	8.16	4Q 92	4c
Rent, apartment, 2 bedrooms - 1-1/2 to 2 baths, unfurnished, 950 sq ft, water	month	419	4Q 92	4c
Rental unit, 1 bedroom	month	353	93	23c
Rental unit, 2 bedroom	month	416	93	23c
Rental unit, 3 bedroom	month	520	93	23c
Rental unit, 4 bedroom	month	583	93	23c
Rental unit, efficiency	month	291	93	23c
Insurance and Pensions				
Auto insurance, private passenger	year	551.85	91	63s
Personal Goods				
Shampoo, Alberto VO5	15 oz	1.32	4Q 92	4c
Toothpaste, Crest or Colgate	6-7 oz	1.73	4Q 92	4c

Values are in dollars or fractions of dollars. In the column headed *Ref*, references are shown to sources. Each reference is followed by a letter. These refer to the geographical level for which data were reported: s = State, r = Region, and c = City or metro. The abbreviation *ex* is used to mean *except* or *excluding*; *exp* stands for expenditures. For other abbreviations and further explanations, please see the Introduction.

Columbia, MO - continued

Item	Per	Value	Date	Ref.
Personal Services				
Dry cleaning, man's 2-piece suit		5.63	4Q 92	4c
Haircare, woman's shampoo, trim and blow-dry		21.75	4Q 92	4c
Haircut, man's barbershop, no styling		7.90	4Q 92	4c
Restaurant Food				
Chicken, fried, thigh and drumstick		2.19	4Q 92	4c
Hamburger with cheese	1/4 lb	1.82	4Q 92	4c
Pizza, Pizza Hut or Pizza Inn, cheese, thin crust	12-13 in	8.60	4Q 92	4c
Taxes				
Tax, cigarette	pack	13	91	77s
Tax, gasoline	gal	13	91	77s
Taxes, state	capita	969	91	77s
Transportation				
ACCRA Index, Transportation		98.60	4Q 92	4c
Driver's license fee		7.50	12/90	43s
Tire balance, computer or spin balance, front	wheel	6.80	4Q 92	4c
Vehicle registration and license plate	year	1.65-51.15	93	41s
Utilities				
ACCRA Index, Utilities		73.40	4Q 92	4c
Electricity	mil Btu	18.94	90	64s
Electricity, partial electric and other energy, 1,800 sq ft living area new home	month	47.17	4Q 92	4c

Columbia, SC

Item	Per	Value	Date	Ref.
Composite ACCRA index		97.70	4Q 92	4c
Alcoholic Beverages				
Beer, Miller Lite or Budweiser, 12-oz containers	6 pack	3.40	4Q 92	4c
Liquor, J & B Scotch	750 ml	17.58	4Q 92	4c
Wine, Gallo Chablis blanc, 1.5 liter	bottle	5.63	4Q 92	4c
Child Care				
Child care fee, average, center	hour	1.29	90	65r
Child care fee, average, nonregulated family day care	hour	0.89	90	65r
Child care fee, average, regulated family day care	hour	1.32	90	65r
Clothing				
Jeans, man's denim		24.35	4Q 92	4c
Shirt, man's dress shirt		23.40	4Q 92	4c
Undervest, boy's size 10-14, cotton	3	3.85	4Q 92	4c
Communications				
Long-distance telephone service, day, initial minute, 0-100 miles	min	0.24-0.52	91	12s
Long-distance telephone service, day, additional minute, 0-100 miles	min	0.13-0.35	91	12s
Long-distance telephone service, evenings/weekends, 0-100 mi, initial minute	min	0.12-0.26	91	12s
Long-distance telephone service, evenings/weekends, 0-100 mi, additional minute	min	0.07-0.16	91	12s
Newspaper subscription, daily and Sunday home delivery, large-city	month	11.27	4Q 92	4c
Telephone, flat rate	month	16.90	91	11c
Telephone bill, family of four	month	23.05	4Q 92	4c
Education				
Board, 4-yr private college/university	year	1468	91	22s
Board, 4-yr public college/university	year	1632	91	22s
Expenditures, local gov't, public elementary/secondary	pupil	4312	92	20s
Room, 4-year private college/university	year	1393	91	22s
Room, 4-year public college/university	year	1492	91	22s
Tuition, 2-year private college/university	year	5110	91	22s
Tuition, 2-year public college/university	year	813	91	22s
Tuition, 4-year private college/university	year	6434	91	22s

Columbia, SC - continued

Item	Per	Value	Date	Ref.
Education - continued				
Tuition, 4-year public college/university, in-state	year	2317	91	22s
Energy and Fuels				
Coal	mil Btu	1.73	90	64s
Energy	mil Btu	8.93	90	64s
Energy, combined forms, 1,800 sq ft heating area	month	109.10	4Q 92	4c
Energy exp/householder, 1-family unit	year	487	90	28r
Energy exp/householder, <1,000 sq ft heating area	year	393	90	28r
Energy exp/householder, 1,000-1,999 sq ft heating area	year	442	90	28r
Energy exp/householder, 2,000+ sq ft heating area	year	577	90	28r
Energy exp/householder, mobile home	year	366	90	28r
Energy exp/householder, multifamily	year	382	90	28r
Gas, cooking, winter, 10 therms	month	9.02	92	56c
Gas, cooking, winter, 30 therms	month	21.40	92	56c
Gas, cooking, winter, 50 therms	month	34.75	92	56c
Gas, heating, winter, 100 therms	month	68.14	92	56c
Gas, heating, winter, average use	month	74.81	92	56c
Gas, natural	mil Btu	4.01	90	64s
Gas, natural	000 cu ft	6.98	91	46s
Gas, natural, exp	year	397	91	46s
Gasoline, motor	gal	1.03	4Q 92	4c
Gasoline, unleaded regular	mil Btu	8.80	90	64s
Entertainment				
Bowling, evening rate	game	2.41	4Q 92	4c
Miniature golf admission	adult	6.18	92	1r
Miniature golf admission	child	5.14	92	1r
Monopoly game, Parker Brothers', No. 9		10.32	4Q 92	4c
Movie	admission	5.50	4Q 92	4c
Tennis balls, yellow, Wilson or Penn, 3	can	2.67	4Q 92	4c
Waterpark admission	adult	11.00	92	1r
Waterpark admission	child	8.55	92	1r
Funerals				
Casket, 18-gauge steel, velvet interior		2029.08	91	24r
Cosmetology, hair care, etc.		75.10	91	24r
Embalming		249.24	91	24r
Facility use for ceremony		162.27	91	24r
Hearse, local		114.04	91	24r
Limousine, local		88.57	91	24r
Remains to funeral home, transfer		92.61	91	24r
Service charge, professional		682.42	91	24r
Vault, concrete, non-metallic liner		798.70	91	24r
Viewing facilities, use		163.86	91	24r
Goods and Services				
ACCRA Index, Miscellaneous Goods and Services		95.80	4Q 92	4c
Goods and services	year	14886	92	36c
Groceries				
ACCRA Index, Groceries		94.10	4Q 92	4c
Apples, Red Delicious	lb	0.79	4/93	16r
Babyfood, strained vegetables, lowest price	4-4.5 oz jar	0.32	4Q 92	4c
Bacon	lb	1.75	4/93	16r
Bananas	lb	0.42	4Q 92	4c
Bananas	lb	0.42	4/93	16r
Beef, stew, boneless	lb	2.61	4/93	16r
Bologna, all beef or mixed	lb	2.24	4/93	16r
Bread, white	24 oz	0.56	4Q 92	4c
Bread, white, pan	lb	0.64	4/93	16r
Bread, whole wheat, pan	lb	0.96	4/93	16r
Cabbage	lb	0.37	4/93	16r
Carrots, short trimmed and topped	lb	0.47	4/93	16r
Celery	lb	0.64	4/93	16r
Cheese, American	lb	2.98	4/93	16r

Values are in dollars or fractions of dollars. In the column headed *Ref*, references are shown to sources. Each reference is followed by a letter. These refer to the geographical level for which data were reported: s=State, r=Region, and c=City or metro. The abbreviation *ex* is used to mean *except* or *excluding*; *exp* stands for expenditures. For other abbreviations and further explanations, please see the Introduction.

Columbia, SC - continued

Item	Per	Value	Date	Ref.
Groceries				
Cheese, Cheddar	lb	3.28	4/93	16r
Cheese, Kraft grated Parmesan	8-oz canister	3.17	4Q 92	4c
Chicken, fresh, whole	lb	0.77	4/93	16r
Chicken, fryer, whole	lb	0.82	4Q 92	4c
Chicken breast, bone-in	lb	1.92	4/93	16r
Chicken legs, bone-in	lb	1.06	4/93	16r
Chuck roast, graded and ungraded, ex USDA prime and choice	lb	2.40	4/93	16r
Chuck roast, USDA choice, bone-in	lb	2.19	4/93	16r
Chuck roast, USDA choice, boneless	lb	2.38	4/93	16r
Cigarettes, Winston	carton	15.41	4Q 92	4c
Coffee, 100% ground roast, all sizes	lb	2.48	4/93	16r
Coffee, vacuum-packed	13-oz can	1.87	4Q 92	4c
Corn, frozen	10 oz	0.64	4Q 92	4c
Corn Flakes, Kellogg's or Post Toasties	18 oz	1.81	4Q 92	4c
Crackers, soda, salted	lb	1.15	4/93	16r
Eggs, Grade A large	doz	0.79	4Q 92	4c
Eggs, Grade A large	doz	0.96	4/93	16r
Flour, white, all purpose	lb	0.24	4/93	16r
Frankfurters, all meat or all beef	lb	2.01	4/93	16r
Grapefruit	lb	0.44	4/93	16r
Grapes, Thompson Seedless	lb	1.40	4/93	16r
Ground beef, 100% beef	lb	1.58	4/93	16r
Ground beef, lean and extra lean	lb	2.09	4/93	16r
Ground beef or hamburger	lb	1.65	4Q 92	4c
Ground chuck, 100% beef	lb	1.98	4/93	16r
Ham, boneless, excluding canned	lb	2.89	4/93	16r
Ham, picnic, shoulder, bone-in, smoked	lb	1.02	4/93	. 16r
Ham, rump or steak half, bone-in, smoked	lb	1.48	4/93	16r
Ice cream, prepackaged, bulk, regular	1/2 gal	2.41	4/93	16r
Lemons	lb	1.05	4/93	16r
Lettuce, iceberg	head	0.99	4Q 92	4c
Lettuce, iceberg	lb	0.81	4/93	16r
Margarine, Blue Bonnet or Parkay cubes	lb	0.47	4Q 92	4c
Margarine, stick	lb	0.88	4/93	16r
Milk, whole	1/2 gal	1.41	4Q 92	4c
Orange juice, Minute Maid frozen	12-oz can	1.33	4Q 92	4c
Oranges, navel	lb	0.55	4/93	16r
Peaches	29-oz can	1.25	4Q 92	4c
Pears, Anjou	lb	0.92	4/93	16r
Peas Sweet, Del Monte or Green Giant	15-17 oz can	0.60	4Q 92	4c
Pork chops, center cut, bone-in	lb	3.13	4/93	16r
Potato chips	16 oz	2.94	4/93	16r
Potatoes, white	lb	0.43	4/93	16r
Potatoes, white or red	10-lb sack	1.95	4Q 92	4c
Rib roast, USDA choice, bone-in	lb	4.63	4/93	16r
Rice, white, long grain, uncooked	lb	0.45	4/93	16r
Round roast, graded & ungraded, ex USDA prime & choice	lb	3.03	4/93	16r
Round roast, USDA choice, boneless	lb	3.09	4/93	16r
Sausage, fresh, loose	lb	2.08	4/93	16r
Sausage, Jimmy Dean, 100% pork	lb	2.21	4Q 92	4c
Short ribs, bone-in	lb	2.66	4/93	16r
Shortening, vegetable oil blends	lb	0.69	4/93	16r
Shortening, vegetable, Crisco	3-lb can	2.04	4Q 92	4c
Soft drink, Coca Cola	2 liter	1.13	4Q 92	4c
Spaghetti and macaroni	lb	0.81	4/93	16r
Steak, rib eye, USDA choice, boneless	lb	6.24	4/93	16r
Steak, round, graded & ungraded, ex USDA prime & choice	lb	3.31	4/93	16r
Steak, round, USDA choice, boneless	lb	3.34	4/93	16r
Steak, sirloin, graded & ungraded, ex USDA prime & choice	lb	4.19	4/93	16r
Steak, sirloin, USDA choice, boneless	lb	4.46	4/93	16r

Columbia, SC - continued

Item	Per	Value	Date	Ref.
Groceries - continued				
Steak, T-bone	lb	4.91	4Q 92	4c
Steak, T-bone, USDA choice, bone-in	lb	5.25	4/93	16r
Strawberries, dry pint	12 oz	0.92	4/93	16r
Sugar, cane or beet	4 lb	1.50	4Q 92	4c
Sugar, white	lb	0.39	4/93	16r
Sugar, white, 33-80 oz pk	lb	0.38	4/93	16r
Tomatoes, field grown	lb	0.88	4/93	16r
Tomatoes, Hunt's or Del Monte	14.5-oz can	0.53	4Q 92	4c
Tuna, chunk, light	6.125-6.5 oz can	0.61	4Q 92	4c
Tuna, chunk, light	lb	1.79	4/93	16r
Turkey, frozen, whole	lb	1.04	4/93	16r
Yogurt, natural, fruit flavored	1/2 pint	0.57	4/93	16r
Health Care				
ACCRA Index, Health Care		105.30	4Q 92	4c
Analgesic, Aspirin, Bayer, 325 mg tablets	100	5.37	4Q 92	4c
Childbirth, cesarean, hospital		5034	91	62r
Childbirth, cesarean, physician's fee		2053	91	62r
Childbirth, normal, hospital		2712	91	62r
Childbirth, normal, physician's fee		1492	91	62r
Dentist's fee, adult teeth cleaning and periodic oral exam	visit	53.20	4Q 92	4c
Doctor's fee, routine exam, established patient	visit	35.33	4Q 92	4c
Health care spending, state	capita	1689	3/93	84s
Hospital care, semiprivate room	day	229.00	90	27c
Hospital care, semiprivate room	day	337.67	4Q 92	4c
Medical insurance premium, per employee, small group comprehensive	month	292.00	10/91	25c
Medical plan per employee	year	3495	91	45r
Mental health care, exp	capita	37.60-53.67	90	38s
Mental health care, exp, state mental health agency	capita	51.12	90	38s
Mental health care, hospital psychiatric services, non-Federal, exp	capita	10.67	88	38s
Mental health care, mental health organization, multiservice, exp	capita	11.38	88	38s
Mental health care, psychiatric hospitals, private, exp	capita	9.21	88	38s
Mental health care, psychiatric out-patient clinics, freestanding, exp	capita	0.68	88	38s
Mental health care, state and county mental hospitals, exp	capita	25.02	88	38s
Mental health care, VA medical centers, exp	capita	0.62	88	38s
Physician fee, family practice, first-visit		75.00	91	62r
Physician fee, family practice, revisit		34.00	91	62r
Physician fee, general practice, first-visit		61.00	91	62r
Physician fee, general practice, revisit		32.00	91	62r
Physician fee, general surgeon, first-visit		64.00	91	62r
Physician fee, general surgeon, revisit		40.00	91	62r
Physician fee, internal medicine, first-visit		98.00	91	62r
Physician fee, internal medicine, revisit		40.00	91	62r
Physician fee, median, neurosurgeon, first-visit		130.00	91	62r
Physician fee, median, nonsurgical specialist, first-visit		95.00	91	62r
Physician fee, median, orthopedic surgeon, first-visit		91.00	91	62r
Physician fee, median, plastic surgeon, first-visit		66.00	91	62r
Physician fee, median, surgical specialist, first-visit		62.00	91	62r
Physician fee, neurosurgeon, revisit		50.00	91	62r
Physician fee, nonsurgical specialist, revisit		40.00	91	62r
Physician fee, obstetrics/gynecology, first-visit		64.00	91	62r
Physician fee, obstetrics/gynecology, revisit		41.00	91	62r
Physician fee, orthopedic surgeon, revisit		40.00	91	62r

Values are in dollars or fractions of dollars. In the column headed *Ref*, references are shown to sources. Each reference is followed by a letter. These refer to the geographical level for which data were reported: s=State, r=Region, and c=City or metro. The abbreviation *ex* is used to mean *except* or *excluding*; *exp* stands for expenditures. For other abbreviations and further explanations, please see the Introduction.

Columbia, SC - continued

Item	Per	Value	Date	Ref.
Health Care				
Physician fee, pediatrician, first-visit		49.00	91	62r
Physician fee, pediatrician, revisit		33.00	91	62r
Physician fee, plastic surgeon, revisit		43.00	91	62r
Physician fee, surgical specialist, revisit		37.00	91	62r
Substance abuse, hospital ancillary charge	incident	1250	90	70s
Substance abuse, hospital physician charge	incident	250	90	70s
Substance abuse, hospital room and board	incident	6100	90	70s
Household Goods				
Appliance repair, home, service call, washing machine	min labor charge	31.30	4Q 92	4c
Laundry detergent, Tide Ultra, Bold, or Cheer	42 oz	3.25	4Q 92	4c
Tissues, facial, Kleenex brand	175-count box	1.03	4Q 92	4c
Housing				
ACCRA Index, Housing		104.20	4Q 92	4c
House, 1,800 sq ft, 8,000 sq ft lot, new, urban	total	112110	4Q 92	4c
House payment, principal and interest, 25% down payment	month	629	4Q 92	4c
Mortgage rate, incl. points & origination fee, 30-year fixed or adjustable rate	percent	8.20	4Q 92	4c
Rent, apartment, 2 bedrooms - 1-1/2 to 2 baths, unfurnished, 950 sq ft, water	month	541	4Q 92	4c
Rental unit, 1 bedroom	month	396	93	23c
Rental unit, 2 bedroom	month	467	93	23c
Rental unit, 3 bedroom	month	584	93	23c
Rental unit, 4 bedroom	month	653	93	23c
Rental unit, efficiency	month	325	93	23c
Insurance and Pensions				
Auto insurance, private passenger	year	605.26	91	63s
Personal Goods				
Shampoo, Alberto VO5	15 oz	0.99	4Q 92	4c
Toothpaste, Crest or Colgate	6-7 oz	1.97	4Q 92	4c
Personal Services				
Dry cleaning, man's 2-piece suit		5.85	4Q 92	4c
Haircare, woman's shampoo, trim and blow-dry		14.39	4Q 92	4c
Haircut, man's barbershop, no styling		7.90	4Q 92	4c
Restaurant Food				
Chicken, fried, thigh and drumstick		1.78	4Q 92	4c
Hamburger with cheese	1/4 lb	1.82	4Q 92	4c
Pizza, Pizza Hut or Pizza Inn, cheese, thin crust	12-13 in	7.55	4Q 92	4c
Taxes				
Tax, cigarette	pack	7	91	77s
Tax, gasoline	gal	16	91	77s
Taxes, state	capita	1105	91	77s
Transportation				
ACCRA Index, Transportation		83.70	4Q 92	4c
Auto rental, average	day	42.25	6/91	60c
Driver's license fee		10.00	12/90	43s
Limo fare, airport-city, average	day	11.00	6/91	60c
Taxi fare, airport-city, average	day	22.50	6/91	60c
Tire balance, computer or spin balance, front	wheel	4.99	4Q 92	4c
Travel				
Breakfast	day	7.35	6/91	60c
Business travel	day	193.00	4/93	89r
Dinner	day	22.47	6/91	60c
Lodging	day	74.43	91	60c
Lunch	day	10.00	6/91	60c

Columbia, SC - continued

Item	Per	Value	Date	Ref.
Utilities				
ACCRA Index, Utilities		101.80	4Q 92	4c
Electricity	mil Btu	16.39	90	64s
Electricity, all electric, 1,800 sq ft living area new home	month	109.10	4Q 92	4c
Electricity, winter, 250 KWh	month	21.99	92	55c
Electricity, winter, 500 KWh	month	37.98	92	55c
Electricity, winter, 750 KWh	month	53.96	92	55c
Electricity, winter, 1000 KWh	month	69.37	92	55c

Columbus, OH

Item	Per	Value	Date	Ref.
Child Care				
Child care fee, average, center	hour	1.63	90	65r
Child care fee, average, nonregulated family day care	hour	1.83	90	65r
Child care fee, average, regulated family day care	hour	1.42	90	65r
Communications				
Long-distance telephone service, day, initial minute, 0-100 miles	min	0.26-0.43	91	12s
Long-distance telephone service, day, additional minute, 0-100 miles	min	0.14-0.24	91	12s
Long-distance telephone service, evenings/weekends, 0-100 mi, initial minute	min	0.11-0.17	91	12s
Long-distance telephone service, evenings/weekends, 0-100 mi, additional minute	min	0.06-0.10	91	12s
Telephone, residential, private line, rotary, unlimited calling	month	19.44	10/91	78c
Education				
Board, 4-yr private college/university	year	1872	91	22s
Board, 4-yr public college/university	year	1742	91	22s
Expenditures, local gov't, public elementary/secondary	pupil	5451	92	20s
Room, 4-year private college/university	year	1695	91	22s
Room, 4-year public college/university	year	2259	91	22s
Tuition, 2-year private college/university	year	6093	91	22s
Tuition, 2-year public college/university	year	1768	91	22s
Tuition, 4-year private college/university	year	8729	91	22s
Tuition, 4-year public college/university, in-state	year	2622	91	22s
Energy and Fuels				
Coal	mil Btu	1.54	90	64s
Energy	mil Btu	8.32	90	64s
Energy exp/householder, 1-family unit	year	471	90	28r
Energy exp/householder, <1,000 sq ft heating area	year	430	90	28r
Energy exp/householder, 1,000-1,999 sq ft heating area	year	481	90	28r
Energy exp/householder, 2,000+ sq ft heating area	year	473	90	28r
Energy exp/householder, mobile home	year	430	90	28r
Energy exp/householder, multifamily	year	461	90	28r
Gas, cooking, winter, 10 therms	month	11.37	92	56c
Gas, cooking, winter, 30 therms	month	21.12	92	56c
Gas, cooking, winter, 50 therms	month	30.86	92	56c
Gas, heating, winter, 100 therms	month	55.22	92	56c
Gas, heating, winter, average use	month	84.81	92	56c
Gas, natural	mil Btu	4.54	90	64s
Gas, natural	000 cu ft	5.28	91	46s
Gas, natural, exp	year	606	91	46s
Gasoline, unleaded regular	mil Btu	9.35	90	64s
Entertainment				
Miniature golf admission	adult	6.18	92	1r
Miniature golf admission	child	5.14	92	1r
Waterpark admission	adult	11.00	92	1r
Waterpark admission	child	8.55	92	1r

Values are in dollars or fractions of dollars. In the column headed *Ref*, references are shown to sources. Each reference is followed by a letter. These refer to the geographical level for which data were reported: s=State, r=Region, and c=City or metro. The abbreviation *ex* is used to mean *except* or *excluding*; *exp* stands for expenditures. For other abbreviations and further explanations, please see the Introduction.

Columbus, OH - continued

Item	Per	Value	Date	Ref.
Funerals				
Casket, 18-gauge steel, velvet interior		1926.72	91	24r
Cosmetology, hair care, etc.		97.64	91	24r
Embalming		249.14	91	24r
Facility use for ceremony		208.59	91	24r
Hearse, local		130.12	91	24r
Limousine, local		104.66	91	24r
Remains to funeral home, transfer		93.61	91	24r
Service charge, professional		724.62	91	24r
Vault, concrete, non-metallic liner		734.53	91	24r
Viewing facilities, use		236.06	91	24r
Groceries				
Apples, Red Delicious	lb	0.77	4/93	16r
Bacon	lb	1.85	4/93	16r
Bananas	lb	0.46	4/93	16r
Beef, stew, boneless	lb	2.53	4/93	16r
Bologna, all beef or mixed	lb	2.19	4/93	16r
Bread, white, pan	lb	0.78	4/93	16r
Butter	lb	1.50	4/93	16r
Cabbage	lb	0.40	4/93	16r
Carrots, short trimmed and topped	lb	0.45	4/93	16r
Cheese, Cheddar	lb	3.47	4/93	16r
Chicken, fresh, whole	lb	0.84	4/93	16r
Chicken breast, bone-in	lb	1.94	4/93	16r
Chicken legs, bone-in	lb	1.02	4/93	16r
Chuck roast, graded and ungraded, ex USDA prime and choice	lb	2.43	4/93	16r
Chuck roast, USDA choice, bone-in	lb	2.11	4/93	16r
Chuck roast, USDA choice, boneless	lb	2.44	4/93	16r
Coffee, 100% ground roast, all sizes	lb	2.47	4/93	16r
Cookies, chocolate chip	lb	2.73	4/93	16r
Eggs, Grade A large	doz	0.93	4/93	16r
Flour, white, all purpose	lb	0.21	4/93	16r
Grapefruit	lb	0.45	4/93	16r
Grapes, Thompson Seedless	lb	1.46	4/93	16r
Ground beef, 100% beef	lb	1.63	4/93	16r
Ground beef, lean and extra lean	lb	2.08	4/93	16r
Ground chuck, 100% beef	lb	1.94	4/93	16r
Ham, boneless, excluding canned	lb	2.21	4/93	16r
Honey, jar	8 oz	0.97-1.25	92	5r
Honey, jar	lb	1.25-2.25	92	5r
Honey, squeeze bear	12-oz	1.25-1.99	92	5r
Ice cream, prepackaged, bulk, regular	1/2 gal	2.41	4/93	16r
Lemons	lb	0.82	4/93	16r
Lettuce, iceberg	lb	0.83	4/93	16r
Margarine, stick	lb	0.77	4/93	16r
Oranges, navel	lb	0.50	4/93	16r
Peanut butter, creamy, all sizes	lb	1.82	4/93	16r
Pears, Anjou	lb	0.85	4/93	16r
Pork chops, center cut, bone-in	lb	3.17	4/93	16r
Potato chips	16 oz	2.68	4/93	16r
Potatoes, white	lb	0.26	4/93	16r
Round roast, graded & ungraded, ex USDA prime & choice	lb	2.88	4/93	16r
Round roast, USDA choice, boneless	lb	2.96	4/93	16r
Shortening, vegetable oil blends	lb	0.79	4/93	16r
Spaghetti and macaroni	lb	0.76	4/93	16r
Steak, rib eye, USDA choice, boneless	lb	6.29	4/93	16r
Steak, round, USDA choice, boneless	lb	3.24	4/93	16r
Steak, sirloin, graded & ungraded, ex USDA prime & choice	lb	4.00	4/93	16r
Steak, sirloin, USDA choice, bone-in	lb	3.57	4/93	16r
Steak, sirloin, USDA choice, boneless	lb	4.17	4/93	16r
Steak, T-bone, USDA choice, bone-in	lb	5.60	4/93	16r
Strawberries, dry pint	12 oz	0.90	4/93	16r
Sugar, white	lb	0.36	4/93	16r
Sugar, white, 33-80 oz pk	lb	0.35	4/93	16r
Tomatoes, field grown	lb	0.99	4/93	16r
Tuna, chunk, light	lb	1.76	4/93	16r
Turkey, frozen, whole	lb	0.91	4/93	16r

Columbus, OH - continued

Item	Per	Value	Date	Ref.
Health Care				
Childbirth, cesarean, hospital		4688	91	62r
Childbirth, cesarean, physician's fee		2053	91	62r
Childbirth, normal, hospital		2657	91	62r
Childbirth, normal, physician's fee		1492	91	62r
Hospital care, semiprivate room	day	268.40	90	27c
Medical insurance premium, per employee, small group comprehensive	month	306.60	10/91	25c
Medical plan per employee	year	3443	91	45r
Mental health care, exp	capita	37.60-53.67	90	38s
Mental health care, exp, state mental health agency	capita	40.93	90	38s
Mental health care, hospital psychiatric services, non-Federal, exp	capita	15.03	88	38s
Mental health care, mental health organization, multiservice, exp	capita	14.46	88	38s
Mental health care, psychiatric hospitals, private, exp	capita	7.93	88	38s
Mental health care, psychiatric out-patient clinics, freestanding, exp	capita	2.93	88	38s
Mental health care, psychiatric partial-care organizations, freestanding, exp	capita	0.32	88	38s
Mental health care, state and county mental hospitals, exp	capita	23.79	88	38s
Mental health care, VA medical centers, exp	capita	7.76	88	38s
Physician fee, family practice, first-visit		76.00	91	62r
Physician fee, family practice, revisit		33.00	91	62r
Physician fee, general practice, first-visit		61.00	91	62r
Physician fee, general practice, revisit		31.00	91	62r
Physician fee, general surgeon, first-visit		65.00	91	62r
Physician fee, general surgeon, revisit		35.00	91	62r
Physician fee, internal medicine, first-visit		91.00	91	62r
Physician fee, internal medicine, revisit		40.00	91	62r
Physician fee, median, neurosurgeon, first-visit		106.00	91	62r
Physician fee, median, nonsurgical specialist, first-visit		90.00	91	62r
Physician fee, median, orthopedic surgeon, first-visit		83.00	91	62r
Physician fee, median, surgical specialist, first-visit		61.00	91	62r
Physician fee, neurosurgeon, revisit		41.00	91	62r
Physician fee, nonsurgical specialist, revisit		40.00	91	62r
Physician fee, obstetrics/gynecology, first-visit		61.00	91	62r
Physician fee, obstetrics/gynecology, revisit		40.00	91	62r
Physician fee, orthopedic surgeon, revisit		41.00	91	62r
Physician fee, pediatrician, first-visit		46.00	91	62r
Physician fee, pediatrician, revisit		33.00	91	62r
Physician fee, surgical specialist, revisit		36.00	91	62r
Substance abuse, hospital ancillary charge	incident	940	90	70s
Substance abuse, hospital physician charge	incident	380	90	70s
Substance abuse, hospital room and board	incident	5410	90	70s
Housing				
Home, median price	unit	91.00		26c
Rental unit, 1 bedroom	month	393	93	23c
Rental unit, 2 bedroom	month	468	93	23c
Rental unit, 3 bedroom	month	584	93	23c
Rental unit, 4 bedroom	month	657	93	23c
Rental unit, efficiency	month	327	93	23c
Insurance and Pensions				
Auto insurance, private passenger	year	547.38	91	63s
Taxes				
Tax, cigarette	pack	18	91	77s
Tax, gasoline	gal	21	91	77s
Taxes, state	capita	1056	91	77s

Values are in dollars or fractions of dollars. In the column headed *Ref*, references are shown to sources. Each reference is followed by a letter. These refer to the geographical level for which data were reported: s = State, r = Region, and c = City or metro. The abbreviation *ex* is used to mean *except* or *excluding*; *exp* stands for expenditures. For other abbreviations and further explanations, please see the Introduction.

Columbus, OH - continued

Item	Per	Value	Date	Ref.
Transportation				
Auto rental, average	day	44.75	6/91	60c
Bus fare	one-way	1.00	3/93	2c
Driver's license fee		5.00	12/90	43s
Limo fare, airport-city, average	day	5.25	6/91	60c
Taxi fare, airport-city, average	day	12.00	6/91	60c
Travel				
Breakfast	day	6.68	6/91	60c
Dinner	day	21.57	6/91	60c
Lodging	day	97.50	91	60c
Lunch	day	7.70	6/91	60c
Utilities				
Electricity	mil Btu	17.33	90	64s
Electricity, winter, 250 KWh	month	21.08	92	55c
Electricity, winter, 500 KWh	month	38.67	92	55c
Electricity, winter, 750 KWh	month	56.26	92	55c
Electricity, winter, 1000 KWh	month	65.96	92	55c

Corpus Christi, TX

Item	Per	Value	Date	Ref.
Composite ACCRA index		92.80	4Q 92	4c
Alcoholic Beverages				
Beer, Miller Lite or Budweiser, 12-oz containers	6 pack	3.84	4Q 92	4c
Liquor, J & B Scotch	750 ml	16.99	4Q 92	4c
Wine, Gallo Chablis blanc, 1.5 liter	bottle	4.42	4Q 92	4c
Child Care				
Child care fee, average, center	hour	1.29	90	65r
Child care fee, average, nonregulated family day care	hour	0.69	00	65r
Child care fee, average, regulated family day care	hour	1.32	90	65r
Clothing				
Jeans, man's denim		24.58	4Q 92	4c
Shirt, man's dress shirt		25.36	4Q 92	4c
Undervest, boy's size 10-14, cotton	3	4.13	4Q 92	4c
Communications				
Long-distance telephone service, day, initial minute, 0-100 miles	min	0.10-0.46	91	12s
Long-distance telephone service, day, additional minute, 0-100 miles	min	0.06-0.45	91	12s
Newspaper subscription, daily and Sunday home delivery, large-city	month	10.04	4Q 92	4c
Telephone, flat rate	month	9.10	91	11c
Telephone, residential, private line, rotary, unlimited calling	month	15.01	10/91	78c
Telephone bill, family of four	month	17.82	4Q 92	4c
Education				
Board, 4-yr private college/university	year	1883	91	22s
Board, 4-yr public college/university	year	1605	91	22s
Expenditures, local gov't, public elementary/secondary	pupil	4593	92	20s
Room, 4-year private college/university	year	1620	91	22s
Room, 4-year public college/university	year	1532	91	22s
Tuition, 2-year private college/university	year	4394	91	22s
Tuition, 2-year public college/university	year	495	91	22s
Tuition, 4-year private college/university	year	6497	91	22s
Tuition, 4-year public college/university, in-state	year	986	91	22s
Energy and Fuels				
Coal	mil Btu	1.44	90	64s
Energy	mil Btu	6.48	90	64s
Energy, combined forms, 1,800 sq ft heating area	month	123.38	4Q 92	4c
Energy, exc electricity, 1,800 sq ft heating area	month	23.44	4Q 92	4c
Energy exp/householder, 1-family unit	year	471	90	28r

Corpus Christi, TX - continued

Item	Per	Value	Date	Ref.
Energy and Fuels - continued				
Energy exp/householder, <1,000 sq ft heating area	year	384	90	28r
Energy exp/householder, 1,000-1,999 sq ft heating area	year	421	90	28r
Energy exp/householder, 2,000+ sq ft heating area	year	625	90	28r
Energy exp/householder, mobile home	year	271	90	28r
Energy exp/householder, multifamily	year	355	90	28r
Gas, natural	mil Btu	2.47	90	64s
Gas, natural	000 cu ft	5.71	91	46s
Gas, natural, exp	year	388	91	46s
Gasoline, motor	gal	1.13	4Q 92	4c
Gasoline, unleaded regular	mil Btu	9.16	90	64s
Entertainment				
Bowling, evening rate	game	2.50	4Q 92	4c
Miniature golf admission	adult	6.18	92	1r
Miniature golf admission	child	5.14	92	1r
Monopoly game, Parker Brothers', No. 9		11.47	4Q 92	4c
Movie	admission	5.50	4Q 92	4c
Tennis balls, yellow, Wilson or Penn, 3	can	2.57	4Q 92	4c
Waterpark admission	adult	11.00	92	1r
Waterpark admission	child	8.55	92	1r
Funerals				
Casket, 18-gauge steel, velvet interior		2274.41	91	24r
Cosmetology, hair care, etc.		74.62	91	24r
Embalming		229.94	91	24r
Facility use for ceremony		176.61	91	24r
Hearse, local		116.34	91	24r
Limousine, local		72.68	91	24r
Remains to funeral home, transfer		87.72	91	24r
Service charge, professional		712.53	91	24r
Vault, concrete, non-metallic liner		750.55	91	24r
Viewing facilities, use		155.31	91	24r
Goods and Services				
ACCRA Index, Miscellaneous Goods and Services		99.90	4Q 92	4c
Groceries				
ACCRA Index, Groceries		93.10	4Q 92	4c
Apples, Red Delicious	lb	0.79	4/93	16r
Babyfood, strained vegetables, lowest price	4-4.5 oz jar	0.23	4Q 92	4c
Bacon	lb	1.75	4/93	16r
Bananas	lb	0.45	4Q 92	4c
Bananas	lb	0.42	4/93	16r
Beef, stew, boneless	lb	2.61	4/93	16r
Bologna, all beef or mixed	lb	2.24	4/93	16r
Bread, white	24 oz	0.57	4Q 92	4c
Bread, white, pan	lb	0.64	4/93	16r
Bread, whole wheat, pan	lb	0.96	4/93	16r
Cabbage	lb	0.37	4/93	16r
Carrots, short trimmed and topped	lb	0.47	4/93	16r
Celery	lb	0.64	4/93	16r
Cheese, American	lb	2.98	4/93	16r
Cheese, Cheddar	lb	3.28	4/93	16r
Cheese, Kraft grated Parmesan	8-oz canister	3.31	4Q 92	4c
Chicken, fresh, whole	lb	0.77	4/93	16r
Chicken, fryer, whole	lb	0.43	4Q 92	4c
Chicken breast, bone-in	lb	1.92	4/93	16r
Chicken legs, bone-in	lb	1.06	4/93	16r
Chuck roast, graded and ungraded, ex USDA prime and choice	lb	2.40	4/93	16r
Chuck roast, USDA choice, bone-in	lb	2.19	4/93	16r
Chuck roast, USDA choice, boneless	lb	2.38	4/93	16r
Cigarettes, Winston	carton	19.49	4Q 92	4c
Coffee, 100% ground roast, all sizes	lb	2.48	4/93	16r

Values are in dollars or fractions of dollars. In the column headed *Ref*, references are shown to sources. Each reference is followed by a letter. These refer to the geographical level for which data were reported: s = State, r = Region, and c = City or metro. The abbreviation *ex* is used to mean *except* or *excluding*; *exp* stands for expenditures. For other abbreviations and further explanations, please see the Introduction.

Corpus Christi, TX - continued

Item	Per	Value	Date	Ref.
Groceries				
Coffee, vacuum-packed	13-oz can	1.92	4Q 92	4c
Corn, frozen	10 oz	0.60	4Q 92	4c
Corn Flakes, Kellogg's or Post Toasties	18 oz	1.79	4Q 92	4c
Crackers, soda, salted	lb	1.15	4/93	16r
Eggs, Grade A large	doz	0.92	4Q 92	4c
Eggs, Grade A large	doz	0.96	4/93	16r
Flour, white, all purpose	lb	0.24	4/93	16r
Frankfurters, all meat or all beef	lb	2.01	4/93	16r
Grapefruit	lb	0.44	4/93	16r
Grapes, Thompson Seedless	lb	1.40	4/93	16r
Ground beef, 100% beef	lb	1.58	4/93	16r
Ground beef, lean and extra lean	lb	2.09	4/93	16r
Ground beef or hamburger	lb	1.39	4Q 92	4c
Ground chuck, 100% beef	lb	1.98	4/93	16r
Ham, boneless, excluding canned	lb	2.89	4/93	16r
Ham, picnic, shoulder, bone-in, smoked	lb	1.02	4/93	16r
Ham, rump or steak half, bone-in, smoked	lb	1.48	4/93	16r
Honey, jar	8 oz	0.73-1.19	92	5r
Honey, jar	lb	1.10-1.79	92	5r
Honey, squeeze bear	12-oz	1.19-1.50	92	5r
Ice cream, prepackaged, bulk, regular	1/2 gal	2.41	4/93	16r
Lemons	lb	1.05	4/93	16r
Lettuce, iceberg	head	0.80	4Q 92	4c
Lettuce, iceberg	lb	0.81	4/93	16r
Margarine, Blue Bonnet or Parkay cubes	lb	0.48	4Q 92	4c
Margarine, stick	lb	0.88	4/93	16r
Milk, whole	1/2 gal	1.28	4Q 92	4c
Orange juice, Minute Maid frozen	12-oz can	1.25	4Q 92	4c
Oranges, navel	lb	0.55	4/93	16r
Peaches	29-oz can	1.33	4Q 92	4c
Pears, Anjou	lb	0.92	4/93	16r
Peas Sweet, Del Monte or Green Giant	15-17 oz can	0.52	4Q 92	4c
Pork chops, center cut, bone-in	lb	3.13	4/93	16r
Potato chips	16 oz	2.94	4/93	16r
Potatoes, white	lb	0.43	4/93	16r
Potatoes, white or red	10-lb sack	2.59	4Q 92	4c
Rib roast, USDA choice, bone-in	lb	4.63	4/93	16r
Rice, white, long grain, uncooked	lb	0.45	4/93	16r
Round roast, graded & ungraded, ex USDA prime & choice	lb	3.03	4/93	16r
Round roast, USDA choice, boneless	lb	3.09	4/93	16r
Sausage, fresh, loose	lb	2.08	4/93	16r
Sausage, Jimmy Dean, 100% pork	lb	2.39	4Q 92	4c
Short ribs, bone-in	lb	2.66	4/93	16r
Shortening, vegetable oil blends	lb	0.69	4/93	16r
Shortening, vegetable, Crisco	3-lb can	1.97	4Q 92	4c
Soft drink, Coca Cola	2 liter	1.89	4Q 92	4c
Spaghetti and macaroni	lb	0.81	4/93	16r
Steak, rib eye, USDA choice, boneless	lb	6.24	4/93	16r
Steak, round, graded & ungraded, ex USDA prime & choice	lb	3.31	4/93	16r
Steak, round, USDA choice, boneless	lb	3.34	4/93	16r
Steak, sirloin, graded & ungraded, ex USDA prime & choice	lb	4.19	4/93	16r
Steak, sirloin, USDA choice, boneless	lb	4.46	4/93	16r
Steak, T-bone	lb	5.21	4Q 92	4c
Steak, T-bone, USDA choice, bone-in	lb	5.25	4/93	16r
Strawberries, dry pint	12 oz	0.92	4/93	16r
Sugar, cane or beet	4 lb	1.50	4Q 92	4c
Sugar, white	lb	0.39	4/93	16r
Sugar, white, 33-80 oz pk	lb	0.38	4/93	16r
Tomatoes, field grown	lb	0.88	4/93	16r
Tomatoes, Hunt's or Del Monte	14.5-oz can	0.61	4Q 92	4c

Corpus Christi, TX - continued

Item	Per	Value	Date	Ref.
Groceries - continued				
Tuna, chunk, light	6.125-6.5 oz can	0.48	4Q 92	4c
Tuna, chunk, light	lb	1.79	4/93	16r
Turkey, frozen, whole	lb	1.04	4/93	16r
Yogurt, natural, fruit flavored	1/2 pint	0.57	4/93	16r
Health Care				
ACCRA Index, Health Care		90.40	4Q 92	4c
Analgesic, Aspirin, Bayer, 325 mg tablets	100	4.79	4Q 92	4c
Childbirth, cesarean, hospital		5034	91	62r
Childbirth, cesarean, physician's fee		2053	91	62r
Childbirth, normal, hospital		2712	91	62r
Childbirth, normal, physician's fee		1492	91	62r
Dentist's fee, adult teeth cleaning and periodic oral exam	visit	38.90	4Q 92	4c
Doctor's fee, routine exam, established patient	visit	36.00	4Q 92	4c
Health care spending, state	capita	2192	3/93	84s
Hospital care, semiprivate room	day	250.00	90	27c
Hospital care, semiprivate room	day	279.00	4Q 92	4c
Medical insurance premium, per employee, small group comprehensive	month	343.10	10/91	25c
Mental health care, exp	capita	20.37-28.83	90	38s
Mental health care, exp, state mental health agency	capita	22.72	90	38s
Mental health care, hospital psychiatric services, non-Federal, exp	capita	7.95	88	38s
Mental health care, mental health organization, multiservice, exp	capita	12.05	88	38s
Mental health care, psychiatric hospitals, private, exp	capita	37.78	88	38s
Mental health care, psychiatric out-patient clinics, freestanding, exp	capita	0.43	88	38s
Mental health care, state and county mental hospitals, exp	capita	12.54	88	38s
Mental health care, VA medical centers, exp	capita	5.35	88	38s
Physician fee, family practice, first-visit		75.00	91	62r
Physician fee, family practice, revisit		34.00	91	62r
Physician fee, general practice, first-visit		61.00	91	62r
Physician fee, general practice, revisit		32.00	91	62r
Physician fee, general surgeon, first-visit		64.00	91	62r
Physician fee, general surgeon, revisit		40.00	91	62r
Physician fee, internal medicine, first-visit		98.00	91	62r
Physician fee, internal medicine, revisit		40.00	91	62r
Physician fee, median, neurosurgeon, first-visit		130.00	91	62r
Physician fee, median, nonsurgical specialist, first-visit		95.00	91	62r
Physician fee, median, orthopedic surgeon, first-visit		91.00	91	62r
Physician fee, median, plastic surgeon, first-visit		66.00	91	62r
Physician fee, median, surgical specialist, first-visit		62.00	91	62r
Physician fee, neurosurgeon, revisit		50.00	91	62r
Physician fee, nonsurgical specialist, revisit		40.00	91	62r
Physician fee, obstetrics/gynecology, first-visit		64.00	91	62r
Physician fee, obstetrics/gynecology, revisit		41.00	91	62r
Physician fee, orthopedic surgeon, revisit		40.00	91	62r
Physician fee, pediatrician, first-visit		49.00	91	62r
Physician fee, pediatrician, revisit		33.00	91	62r
Physician fee, plastic surgeon, revisit		43.00	91	62r
Physician fee, surgical specialist, revisit		37.00	91	62r
Substance abuse, hospital ancillary charge	incident	3750	90	70s
Substance abuse, hospital physician charge	incident	1080	90	70s
Substance abuse, hospital room and board	incident	5320	90	70s

Values are in dollars or fractions of dollars. In the column headed *Ref*, references are shown to sources. Each reference is followed by a letter. These refer to the geographical level for which data were reported: s = State, r = Region, and c = City or metro. The abbreviation *ex* is used to mean *except* or *excluding*; *exp* stands for expenditures. For other abbreviations and further explanations, please see the Introduction.

Corpus Christi, TX - continued

Item	Per	Value	Date	Ref.
Household Goods				
Appliance repair, home, service call, washing machine	min labor charge	34.17	4Q 92	4c
Laundry detergent, Tide Ultra, Bold, or Cheer	42 oz	2.89	4Q 92	4c
Tissues, facial, Kleenex brand	175-count box	1.03	4Q 92	4c
Housing				
ACCRA Index, Housing		81.80	4Q 92	4c
Home, median price	unit	67.50		26c
House, 1,800 sq ft, 8,000 sq ft lot, new, urban	total	86240	4Q 92	4c
House payment, principal and interest, 25% down payment	month	479	4Q 92	4c
Mortgage rate, incl. points & origination fee, 30-year fixed or adjustable rate	percent	8.11	4Q 92	4c
Rent, apartment, 2 bedrooms - 1-1/2 to 2 baths, unfurnished, 950 sq ft, water	month	458	4Q 92	4c
Rental unit, 1 bedroom	month	423	93	23c
Rental unit, 2 bedroom	month	499	93	23c
Rental unit, 3 bedroom	month	625	93	23c
Rental unit, 4 bedroom	month	701	93	23c
Rental unit, efficiency	month	349	93	23c
Insurance and Pensions				
Auto insurance, private passenger	year	709.79	91	63s
Personal Goods				
Shampoo, Alberto VO5	15 oz	0.91	4Q 92	4c
Toothpaste, Crest or Colgate	6-7 oz	1.77	4Q 92	4c
Personal Services				
Dry cleaning, man's 2-piece suit		6.33	4Q 92	4c
Haircare, woman's shampoo, trim and blow-dry		20.15	4Q 92	4c
Haircut, man's barbershop, no styling		7.37	4Q 92	4c
Restaurant Food				
Chicken, fried, thigh and drumstick		1.99	4Q 92	4c
Hamburger with cheese	1/4 lb	1.90	4Q 92	4c
Pizza, Pizza Hut or Pizza Inn, cheese, thin crust	12-13 in	7.99	4Q 92	4c
Taxes				
Tax, cigarette	pack	41	91	77s
Tax, gasoline	gal	20	91	77s
Taxes, state	capita	923	91	77s
Transportation				
ACCRA Index, Transportation		83.00	4Q 92	4c
Bus fare	one-way	0.50	3/93	2c
Bus fare, up to 10 miles	one-way	0.25	4Q 92	4c
Driver's license fee		16.00	12/90	43s
Tire balance, computer or spin balance, front	wheel	5.07	4Q 92	4c
Travel				
Business travel	day	193.00	4/93	89r
Utilities				
ACCRA Index, Utilities		110.90	4Q 92	4c
Electricity	mil Btu	17.09	90	64s
Electricity, partial electric and other energy, 1,800 sq ft living area new home	month	99.94	4Q 92	4c
Electricity, residential	KWh	5.92	2/93	94s
Electricity, winter, 250 KWh	month	25.16	92	55c
Electricity, winter, 500 KWh	month	43.02	92	55c
Electricity, winter, 750 KWh	month	60.90	92	55c
Electricity, winter, 1000 KWh	month	78.77	92	55c

Cumberland, MD

Item	Per	Value	Date	Ref.
Composite ACCRA index		99.80	4Q 92	4c
Alcoholic Beverages				
Beer, Miller Lite or Budweiser, 12-oz containers	6 pack	4.19	4Q 92	4c
Liquor, J & B Scotch	750 ml	15.03	4Q 92	4c
Wine, Gallo Chablis blanc, 1.5 liter	bottle	5.40	4Q 92	4c
Clothing				
Jeans, man's denim		34.99	4Q 92	4c
Shirt, man's dress shirt		20.49	4Q 92	4c
Undervest, boy's size 10-14, cotton	3	4.01	4Q 92	4c
Communications				
Long-distance telephone service, day, initial minute, 0-100 miles	min	0.25-0.54	91	12s
Long-distance telephone service, day, additional minute, 0-100 miles	min	0.10-0.37	91	12s
Long-distance telephone service, evenings/weekends, 0-100 mi, initial minute	min	0.10-0.22	91	12s
Long-distance telephone service, evenings/weekends, 0-100 mi, additional minute	min	0.04-0.15	91	12s
Newspaper subscription, daily and Sunday home delivery, large-city	month	9.75	4Q 92	4c
Telephone, flat rate	month	14.88	91	11c
Telephone bill, family of four	month	26.83	4Q 92	4c
Education				
Board, 4-yr private college/university	year	2490	91	22s
Board, 4-yr public college/university	year	2139	91	22s
Expenditures, local gov't, public elementary/secondary	pupil	6314	92	20s
Room, 4-year private college/university	year	2610	91	22s
Room, 4-year public college/university	year	2365	91	22s
Tuition, 2-year private college/university	year	6101	91	22s
Tuition, 2-year public college/university	year	1244	91	22s
Tuition, 4-year private college/university	year	10698	91	22s
Tuition, 4-year public college/university, in-state	year	2287	91	22s
Energy and Fuels				
Coal	mil Btu	1.62	90	64s
Energy	mil Btu	9.40	90	64s
Energy, combined forms, 1,800 sq ft heating area	month	127.98	4Q 92	4c
Energy exp/householder, 1-family unit	year	487	90	28r
Energy exp/householder, <1,000 sq ft heating area	year	393	90	28r
Energy exp/householder, 1,000-1,999 sq ft heating area	year	442	90	28r
Energy exp/householder, 2,000+ sq ft heating area	year	577	90	28r
Energy exp/householder, mobile home	year	366	90	28r
Energy exp/householder, multifamily	year	382	90	28r
Gas, natural	mil Btu	5.07	90	64s
Gas, natural	000 cu ft	6.16	91	46s
Gas, natural, exp	year	545	91	46s
Gasoline, motor	gal	1.19	4Q 92	4c
Gasoline, unleaded regular	mil Btu	9.88	90	64s
Entertainment				
Bowling, evening rate	game	1.91	4Q 92	4c
Miniature golf admission	adult	6.18	92	1r
Miniature golf admission	child	5.14	92	1r
Monopoly game, Parker Brothers', No. 9		11.17	4Q 92	4c
Movie	admission	4.50	4Q 92	4c
Tennis balls, yellow, Wilson or Penn, 3	can	2.87	4Q 92	4c
Waterpark admission	adult	11.00	92	1r
Waterpark admission	child	8.55	92	1r
Funerals				
Casket, 18-gauge steel, velvet interior		2029.08	91	24r
Cosmetology, hair care, etc.		75.10	91	24r
Embalming		249.24	91	24r

Values are in dollars or fractions of dollars. In the column headed *Ref*, references are shown to sources. Each reference is followed by a letter. These refer to the geographical level for which data were reported: s = State, r = Region, and c = City or metro. The abbreviation *ex* is used to mean *except* or *excluding*; *exp* stands for expenditures. For other abbreviations and further explanations, please see the Introduction.

Cumberland, MD - continued

Item	Per	Value	Date	Ref.
Funerals				
Facility use for ceremony		162.27	91	24r
Hearse, local		114.04	91	24r
Limousine, local		88.57	91	24r
Remains to funeral home, transfer		92.61	91	24r
Service charge, professional		682.42	91	24r
Vault, concrete, non-metallic liner		798.70	91	24r
Viewing facilities, use		163.86	91	24r
Goods and Services				
ACCRA Index, Miscellaneous Goods and Services		96.10	4Q 92	4c
Groceries				
ACCRA Index, Groceries		102.90	4Q 92	4c
Babyfood, strained vegetables, lowest price	4-4.5 oz jar	0.34	4Q 92	4c
Bananas	lb	0.39	4Q 92	4c
Bread, white	24 oz	0.69	4Q 92	4c
Cheese, Kraft grated Parmesan	8-oz canister	2.72	4Q 92	4c
Chicken, fryer, whole	lb	0.93	4Q 92	4c
Cigarettes, Winston	carton	18.90	4Q 92	4c
Coffee, vacuum-packed	13-oz can	2.36	4Q 92	4c
Corn, frozen	10 oz	0.73	4Q 92	4c
Corn Flakes, Kellogg's or Post Toasties	18 oz	1.90	4Q 92	4c
Eggs, Grade A large	doz	0.84	4Q 92	4c
Ground beef or hamburger	lb	1.65	4Q 92	4c
Lettuce, iceberg	head	0.81	4Q 92	4c
Margarine, Blue Bonnet or Parkay cubes	lb	0.83	4Q 92	4c
Milk, whole	1/2 gal	1.15	4Q 92	4c
Orange juice, Minute Maid frozen	12-oz can	1.72	4Q 92	4c
Peaches	29-oz can	1.32	4Q 92	4c
Peas Sweet, Del Monte or Green Giant	15-17 oz can	0.60	4Q 92	4c
Potatoes, white or red	10-lb sack	1.79	4Q 92	4c
Sausage, Jimmy Dean, 100% pork	lb	2.27	4Q 92	4c
Shortening, vegetable, Crisco	3-lb can	2.37	4Q 92	4c
Soft drink, Coca Cola	2 liter	1.29	4Q 92	4c
Steak, T-bone	lb	5.42	4Q 92	4c
Sugar, cane or beet	4 lb	1.56	4Q 92	4c
Tomatoes, Hunt's or Del Monte	14.5-oz can	0.70	4Q 92	4c
Tuna, chunk, light	6.125-6.5 oz can	0.67	4Q 92	4c
Health Care				
ACCRA Index, Health Care		91.20	4Q 92	4c
Analgesic, Aspirin, Bayer, 325 mg tablets	100	5.60	4Q 92	4c
Dentist's fee, adult teeth cleaning and periodic oral exam	visit	38.40	4Q 92	4c
Doctor's fee, routine exam, established patient	visit	36.40	4Q 92	4c
Hospital care, semiprivate room	day	235.50	90	27c
Hospital care, semiprivate room	day	261.75	4Q 92	4c
Medical insurance premium, per employee, small group comprehensive	month	292.00	10/91	25c
Medical plan per employee	year	3495	91	45r
Mental health care, exp	capita	53.68-118.35	90	38s
Mental health care, exp, state mental health agency	capita	61.28	90	38s
Mental health care, hospital psychiatric services, non-Federal, exp	capita	10.31	88	38s
Mental health care, mental health organization, multiservice, exp	capita	10.94	88	38s
Mental health care, psychiatric hospitals, private, exp	capita	15.34	88	38s

Cumberland, MD - continued

Item	Per	Value	Date	Ref.
Health Care - continued				
Mental health care, psychiatric out-patient clinics, freestanding, exp	capita	7.16	88	38s
Mental health care, psychiatric partial-care organizations, freestanding, exp	capita	0.36	88	38s
Mental health care, state and county mental hospitals, exp	capita	38.11	88	38s
Mental health care, VA medical centers, exp	capita	4.16	88	38s
Prescription drug co-pay, Medicaid	month	5.00	91	21s
Substance abuse, hospital ancillary charge	incident	770	90	70s
Substance abuse, hospital physician charge	incident	300	90	70s
Substance abuse, hospital room and board	incident	4470	90	70s
Household Goods				
Appliance repair, home, service call, washing machine	min labor charge	23.40	4Q 92	4c
Laundry detergent, Tide Ultra, Bold, or Cheer	42 oz	4.10	4Q 92	4c
Tissues, facial, Kleenex brand	175-count box	1.10	4Q 92	4c
Housing				
ACCRA Index, Housing		103.00	4Q 92	4c
House, 1,800 sq ft, 8,000 sq ft lot, new, urban	total	123100	4Q 92	4c
House payment, principal and interest, 25% down payment	month	684	4Q 92	4c
Mortgage rate, incl. points & origination fee, 30-year fixed or adjustable rate	percent	8.11	4Q 92	4c
Rent, apartment, 2 bedrooms - 1-1/2 to 2 baths, unfurnished, 950 sq ft, water	month	391	4Q 92	4c
Rental unit, 1 bedroom	month	350	93	23c
Rental unit, 2 bedroom	month	411	93	23c
Rental unit, 3 bedroom	month	507	93	23c
Rental unit, 4 bedroom	month	566	93	23c
Rental unit, efficiency	month	294	93	23c
Insurance and Pensions				
Auto insurance, private passenger	year	744.88	91	63s
Personal Goods				
Shampoo, Alberto VO5	15 oz	1.41	4Q 92	4c
Toothpaste, Crest or Colgate	6-7 oz	2.29	4Q 92	4c
Personal Services				
Dry cleaning, man's 2-piece suit		5.65	4Q 92	4c
Haircare, woman's shampoo, trim and blow-dry		13.60	4Q 92	4c
Haircut, man's barbershop, no styling		4.70	4Q 92	4c
Restaurant Food				
Chicken, fried, thigh and drumstick		2.25	4Q 92	4c
Hamburger with cheese	1/4 lb	1.79	4Q 92	4c
Pizza, Pizza Hut or Pizza Inn, cheese, thin crust	12-13 in	8.79	4Q 92	4c
Taxes				
Tax, cigarette	pack	36	91	77s
Tax, gasoline	gal	23.50	91	77s
Taxes, state	capita	1317	91	77s
Transportation				
ACCRA Index, Transportation		86.40	4Q 92	4c
Driver's license fee		6.00	12/90	43s
Tire balance, computer or spin balance, front	wheel	4.40	4Q 92	4c
Utilities				
ACCRA Index, Utilities		119.30	4Q 92	4c
Electricity	mil Btu	18.47	90	64s
Electricity, all electric, 1,800 sq ft living area new home	month	127.98	4Q 92	4c

Values are in dollars or fractions of dollars. In the column headed *Ref*, references are shown to sources. Each reference is followed by a letter. These refer to the geographical level for which data were reported: s=State, r=Region, and c=City or metro. The abbreviation ex is used to mean *except* or *excluding*; exp stands for *expenditures*. For other abbreviations and further explanations, please see the Introduction.

Dallas-Fort Worth, TX

Item	Per	Value	Date	Ref.
Composite ACCRA index		103.50	4Q 92	4c
Alcoholic Beverages				
Beer, Miller Lite or Budweiser, 12-oz containers	6 pack	4.44	4Q 92	4c
Liquor, J & B Scotch	750 ml	18.24	4Q 92	4c
Wine, Gallo Chablis blanc, 1.5 liter	bottle	4.59	4Q 92	4c
Child Care				
Child care fee, average, center	hour	1.29	90	65r
Child care fee, average, nonregulated family day care	hour	0.89	90	65r
Child care fee, average, regulated family day care	hour	1.32	90	65r
Clothing				
Jeans, man's denim		31.12	4Q 92	4c
Shirt, man's dress shirt		23.16	4Q 92	4c
Undervest, boy's size 10-14, cotton	3	4.77	4Q 92	4c
Communications				
Long-distance telephone service, day, initial minute, 0-100 miles	min	0.10-0.46	91	12s
Long-distance telephone service, day, additional minute, 0-100 miles	min	0.06-0.45	91	12s
Newspaper subscription, daily and Sunday home delivery, large-city	month	9.50	4Q 92	4c
Telephone, flat rate	month	10.40	91	11c
Telephone, residential, private line, rotary, unlimited calling	month	17.19	10/91	78c
Telephone bill, family of four	month	19.46	4Q 92	4c
Education				
Board, 4 yr private college/university	year	1883	91	22s
Board, 4-yr public college/university	year	1605	91	22s
Expenditures, local gov't, public elementary/secondary	pupil	4593	92	20s
Room, 4-year private college/university	year	1620	91	22s
Room, 4-year public college/university	year	1532	91	22s
Tuition, 2-year private college/university	year	4394	91	22s
Tuition, 2-year public college/university	year	495	91	22s
Tuition, 4-year private college/university	year	6497	91	22s
Tuition, 4-year public college/university, in-state	year	986	91	22s
Energy and Fuels				
Coal	mil Btu	1.44	90	64s
Energy	mil Btu	6.48	90	64s
Energy, combined forms, 1,800 sq ft heating area	month	131.37	4Q 92	4c
Energy, exc electricity, 1,800 sq ft heating area	month	35.57	4Q 92	4c
Energy exp/householder, 1-family unit	year	471	90	28r
Energy exp/householder, <1,000 sq ft heating area	year	384	90	28r
Energy exp/householder, 1,000-1,999 sq ft heating area	year	421	90	28r
Energy exp/householder, 2,000+ sq ft heating area	year	625	90	28r
Energy exp/householder, mobile home	year	271	90	28r
Energy exp/householder, multifamily	year	355	90	28r
Gas, cooking, winter, 10 therms	month	10.46	92	56c
Gas, cooking, winter, 30 therms	month	20.39	92	56c
Gas, cooking, winter, 50 therms	month	30.32	92	56c
Gas, heating, winter, 100 therms	month	55.14	92	56c
Gas, heating, winter, average use	month	75.50	92	56c
Gas, natural	mil Btu	2.47	90	64s
Gas, natural	000 cu ft	5.71	91	46s
Gas, natural, exp	year	388	91	46s
Gas, piped	100 therms	56.21	4/93	16c
Gas, piped	40 therms	26.07	4/93	16c
Gas, piped	therm	0.72	4/93	16c
Gasoline, all types	gal	1.12	4/93	16c

Dallas-Fort Worth, TX - continued

Item	Per	Value	Date	Ref.
Energy and Fuels - continued				
Gasoline, motor	gal	1.09	4Q 92	4c
Gasoline, regular unleaded, taxes included, cash, self-service	gal	1.24	4/93	16c
Gasoline, unleaded premium 93 octane	gal	1.04	4/93	16c
Gasoline, unleaded regular	mil Btu	9.16	90	64s
Entertainment				
Bowling, evening rate	game	2.51	4Q 92	4c
Dinner entree, restaurant		23.33-33.66	92	83c
Football game expenditures, pro		184.33	91	80c
Miniature golf admission	adult	6.18	92	1r
Miniature golf admission	child	5.14	92	1r
Monopoly game, Parker Brothers', No. 9		10.88	4Q 92	4c
Movie	admission	5.88	4Q 92	4c
Tennis balls, yellow, Wilson or Penn, 3	can	2.60	4Q 92	4c
Waterpark admission	adult	11.00	92	1r
Waterpark admission	child	8.55	92	1r
Funerals				
Casket, 18-gauge steel, velvet interior		2274.41	91	24r
Cosmetology, hair care, etc.		74.62	91	24r
Embalming		229.94	91	24r
Facility use for ceremony		176.61	91	24r
Hearse, local		116.34	91	24r
Limousine, local		72.68	91	24r
Remains to funeral home, transfer		87.72	91	24r
Service charge, professional		712.53	91	24r
Vault, concrete, non-metallic liner		750.55	91	24r
Viewing facilities, use		155.31	91	24r
Goods and Services				
ACCRA Index, Miscellaneous Goods and Services		104.00	4Q 92	4c
Groceries				
ACCRA Index, Groceries		96.20	4Q 92	4c
Apples, Red Delicious	lb	0.79	4/93	16r
Babyfood, strained vegetables, lowest price	4-4.5 oz jar	0.27	4Q 92	4c
Bacon	lb	1.75	4/93	16r
Bacon, Oscar Mayer	lb	2.42	5/92	76c
Bakery products, exp	year	182	89	15c
Bananas	lb	0.35	5/92	76c
Bananas	lb	0.37	4Q 92	4c
Bananas	lb	0.42	4/93	16r
Beef, exp	year	216	89	15c
Beef, stew, boneless	lb	2.61	4/93	16r
Bologna, all beef or mixed	lb	2.24	4/93	16r
Bologna, Oscar Mayer	8 oz	1.56	5/92	76c
Bread, Mrs. Baird's white	lb	0.94	5/92	76c
Bread, Pepperidge Farm white	lb	1.73	5/92	76c
Bread, white	24 oz	0.63	4Q 92	4c
Bread, white, pan	lb	0.64	4/93	16r
Bread, whole wheat, pan	lb	0.96	4/93	16r
Butter, Land O'Lakes, light salt	lb	1.61	5/92	76c
Butter, private label	lb	1.44	5/92	76c
Cabbage	lb	0.37	4/93	16r
Cake, Entenmann's French Crumb		3.33	5/92	76c
Carrots, short trimmed and topped	lb	0.47	4/93	16r
Celery	lb	0.64	4/93	16r
Cereal, Fruit Loops	15 oz	3.19	5/92	76c
Cereal, Kellogg's Corn Flakes	18 oz	1.85	5/92	76c
Cereal, Rice Krispies	13 oz	2.34	5/92	76c
Cereals and bakery products, exp	year	285	89	15c
Cereals and cereal products, exp	year	103	89	15c
Cheese, American	lb	2.98	4/93	16r
Cheese, Cheddar	lb	3.28	4/93	16r
Cheese, Kraft American singles	16 oz	3.48	5/92	76c
Cheese, Kraft grated Parmesan	8-oz canister	3.48	4Q 92	4c
Chicken, fresh, whole	lb	0.77	4/93	16r

Values are in dollars or fractions of dollars. In the column headed *Ref*, references are shown to sources. Each reference is followed by a letter. These refer to the geographical level for which data were reported: s = State, r = Region, and c = City or metro. The abbreviation *ex* is used to mean *except* or *excluding*; *exp* stands for expenditures. For other abbreviations and further explanations, please see the Introduction.

Dallas-Fort Worth, TX - continued

Item	Per	Value	Date	Ref.
Groceries				
Chicken, fryer, whole	lb	0.65	4Q 92	4c
Chicken breast, bone-in	lb	1.92	4/93	16r
Chicken fryer breasts	lb	1.93	5/92	76c
Chicken legs, bone-in	lb	1.06	4/93	16r
Chuck roast, graded and ungraded, ex USDA prime and choice	lb	2.40	4/93	16r
Chuck roast, USDA choice, bone-in	lb	2.19	4/93	16r
Chuck roast, USDA choice, boneless	lb	2.38	4/93	16r
Cigarettes, Winston	carton	19.50	4Q 92	4c
Coffee, 100% ground roast, all sizes	lb	2.48	4/93	16r
Coffee, Maxwell House auto grind	13 oz	2.27	5/92	76c
Coffee, vacuum-packed	13-oz can	1.87	4Q 92	4c
Cookies, Nabisco Oreos	20 oz	2.72	5/92	76c
Corn, frozen	10 oz	0.63	4Q 92	4c
Corn Flakes, Kellogg's or Post Toasties	18 oz	2.07	4Q 92	4c
Crackers, soda, salted	lb	1.15	4/93	16r
Dairy products, exp	year	275	89	15c
Dairy products, miscellaneous, exp	year	147	89	15c
Eggs, exp	year	30	89	15c
Eggs, Grade A large	doz	0.90	4Q 92	4c
Eggs, Grade A large	doz	0.96	4/93	16r
Eggs, private label, white	doz	0.66	5/92	76c
Fish and seafood, exp	year	64	89	15c
Flour, white, all purpose	lb	0.24	4/93	16r
Food, exp	year	4318	89	15c
Food eaten at home, exp	year	2281	89	15c
Frankfurters, all meat or all beef	lb	2.01	4/93	16r
Frankfurters, Oscar Mayer	lb	2.16	5/92	76c
Frozen dinner, Stouffer's Lean Cuisine glazed chicken		2.40	5/92	76c
Fruits, fresh, exp	year	113	89	15c
Fruits, processed, exp	year	68	89	15c
Fruits and vegetables, exp	year	385	89	15c
Grapefruit	lb	0.44	4/93	16r
Grapes, Thompson Seedless	lb	1.40	4/93	16r
Green beans, Green Giant, canned	14.5 oz	0.57	5/92	76c
Ground beef, 100% beef	lb	1.58	4/93	16r
Ground beef, lean and extra lean	lb	2.09	4/93	16r
Ground beef or hamburger	lb	1.25	4Q 92	4c
Ground chuck, 100% beef	lb	1.98	4/93	16r
Ham, boneless, excluding canned	lb	2.89	4/93	16r
Ham, picnic, shoulder, bone-in, smoked	lb	1.02	4/93	16r
Ham, rump or steak half, bone-in, smoked	lb	1.48	4/93	16r
Honey, jar	8 oz	0.73-1.19	92	5r
Honey, jar	lb	1.10-1.79	92	5r
Honey, squeeze bear	12-oz	1.19-1.50	92	5r
Ice cream, prepackaged, bulk, regular	1/2 gal	2.41	4/93	16r
Jelly, Welch's grape	32 oz	1.81	5/92	76c
Ketchup, Heinz	14 oz	1.02	5/92	76c
Laundry detergent, Tide Ultra	42 oz	3.61	5/92	76c
Lemons	lb	1.05	4/93	16r
Lettuce	head	0.71	5/92	76c
Lettuce, iceberg	head	0.87	4Q 92	4c
Lettuce, iceberg	lb	0.81	4/93	16r
Margarine, Blue Bonnet or Parkay cubes	lb	0.56	4Q 92	4c
Margarine, Parkay sticks	lb	0.50	5/92	76c
Margarine, stick	lb	0.88	4/93	16r
Mayonnaise, Hellmann's	quart	2.24	5/92	76c
Meats, poultry, fish and eggs, exp	year	597	89	15c
Milk, private label, whole	gal	1.75	5/92	76c
Milk, whole	1/2 gal	1.39	4Q 92	4c
Milk and cream, fresh, exp	year	128	89	15c
Orange juice, Minute Maid frozen	12 oz	1.39	5/92	76c
Orange juice, Minute Maid frozen	12-oz can	1.22	4Q 92	4c
Oranges	4 lb	2.33	5/92	76c
Oranges, navel	lb	0.55	4/93	16r
Peaches	29-oz can	1.51	4Q 92	4c
Peanut butter, Skippy, creamy	18 oz	2.39	5/92	76c
Pears, Anjou	lb	0.92	4/93	16r

Dallas-Fort Worth, TX - continued

Item	Per	Value	Date	Ref.
Groceries - continued				
Peas Sweet, Del Monte or Green Giant	15-17 oz can	0.60	4Q 92	4c
Pizza, Totino's cheese	10 oz	1.29	5/92	76c
Pork, exp	year	116	89	15c
Pork chops, center cut, bone-in	lb	3.13	4/93	16r
Potato chips	16 oz	2.94	4/93	16r
Potatoes, white	lb	0.43	4/93	16r
Potatoes, white or red	10-lb sack	2.24	4Q 92	4c
Poultry, exp	year	89	89	15c
Rib roast, USDA choice, bone-in	lb	4.63	4/93	16r
Rice, white, long grain, uncooked	lb	0.45	4/93	16r
Round roast, graded & ungraded, ex USDA prime & choice	lb	3.03	4/93	16r
Round roast, USDA choice, boneless	lb	3.09	4/93	16r
Sausage, fresh, loose	lb	2.08	4/93	16r
Sausage, Jimmy Dean	16 oz	2.43	5/92	76c
Sausage, Jimmy Dean, 100% pork	lb	2.43	4Q 92	4c
Short ribs, bone-in	lb	2.66	4/93	16r
Shortening, vegetable oil blends	lb	0.69	4/93	16r
Shortening, vegetable, Crisco	3-lb can	2.24	4Q 92	4c
Snacks, Doritos toasted corn chips	15 oz	2.69	5/92	76c
Soft drink, Coca Cola	2 liter	1.22	5/92	76c
Soft drink, Coca Cola	2 liter	1.16	4Q 92	4c
Soft drink, Diet Coca Cola	2 liter	1.22	5/92	76c
Soft drink, Diet Pepsi	2 liter	0.83	5/92	76c
Soft drink, Pepsi	2 liter	0.83	5/92	76c
Spaghetti, Creamette	16 oz	0.96	5/92	76c
Spaghetti and macaroni	lb	0.81	4/93	16r
Spaghetti sauce, Prego	30 oz	1.86	5/92	76c
Spaghetti sauce, Ragu	14 oz	1.29	5/92	76c
Steak, rib eye, USDA choice, boneless	lb	6.24	4/93	16r
Steak, round, graded & ungraded, ex USDA prime & choice	lb	3.31	4/93	16r
Steak, round, USDA choice, boneless	lb	3.34	4/93	16r
Steak, sirloin, graded & ungraded, ex USDA prime & choice	lb	4.19	4/93	16r
Steak, sirloin, USDA choice, boneless	lb	4.46	4/93	16r
Steak, T-bone	lb	5.34	4Q 92	4c
Steak, T-bone, USDA choice, bone-in	lb	5.25	4/93	16r
Strawberries, dry pint	12 oz	0.92	4/93	16r
Sugar, cane or beet	4 lb	1.51	4Q 92	4c
Sugar, Imperial granulated	5 lb	1.91	5/92	76c
Sugar, white	lb	0.39	4/93	16r
Sugar, white, 33-80 oz pk	lb	0.38	4/93	16r
Tea, Lipton tea bags	100	3.04	5/92	76c
Tomato soup, Campbell's	10 3/4 oz	0.40	5/92	76c
Tomatoes, field grown	lb	0.88	4/93	16r
Tomatoes, Hunt's or Del Monte	14.5-oz can	0.70	4Q 92	4c
Tuna, Chicken of the Sea chunk light	6.5 oz	0.63	5/92	76c
Tuna, chunk, light	6.125-6.5 oz can	0.64	4Q 92	4c
Tuna, chunk, light	lb	1.79	4/93	16r
Turkey, frozen, whole	lb	1.04	4/93	16r
Vegetables, fresh, exp	year	131	89	15c
Vegetables, processed, exp	year	73	89	15c
Yogurt, natural, fruit flavored	1/2 pint	0.57	4/93	16r
Health Care				
ACCRA Index, Health Care		114.70	4Q 92	4c
Analgesic, Aspirin, Bayer, 325 mg tablets	100	5.54	4Q 92	4c
Appendectomy		938	91	62c
Childbirth, cesarean		1982	91	62c
Childbirth, cesarean, hospital		5034	91	62r
Childbirth, cesarean, physician's fee		2053	91	62r
Childbirth, normal, hospital		2712	91	62r
Childbirth, normal, physician's fee		1492	91	62r
Cholecystectomy		1506	91	62c

Values are in dollars or fractions of dollars. In the column headed *Ref*, references are shown to sources. Each reference is followed by a letter. These refer to the geographical level for which data were reported: s = State, r = Region, and c = City or metro. The abbreviation *ex* is used to mean *except* or *excluding*; *exp* stands for expenditures. For other abbreviations and further explanations, please see the Introduction.

Dallas-Fort Worth, TX - continued

Item	Per	Value	Date	Ref.
Health Care				
Coronary bypass surgery, triple		2461	91	62c
Dentist's fee, adult teeth cleaning and periodic oral exam	visit	53.33	4Q 92	4c
Doctor's fee, routine exam, established patient	visit	43.89	4Q 92	4c
Health care spending, state	capita	2192	3/93	84s
Health maintenance organization coverage, employee	year	3330	93	39c
Health maintenance organization medical coverage, employee	year	3330	92	42c
Hospital care, semiprivate room	day	286.03	90	27c
Hospital care, semiprivate room	day	352.10	4Q 92	4c
Hysterectomy		1905	91	62c
Indemnity plan medical coverage, employee	year	3917	92	42c
Insurance coverage, traditional, employee	year	3917	93	39c
Lumpectomy		581	91	62c
Medical insurance premium, per employee, small group comprehensive	month	390.55	10/91	25c
Mental health care, exp	capita	20.37- 28.83	90	38s
Mental health care, exp, state mental health agency	capita	22.72	90	38s
Mental health care, hospital psychiatric services, non-Federal, exp	capita	7.95	88	38s
Mental health care, mental health organization, multiservice, exp	capita	12.05	88	38s
Mental health care, psychiatric hospitals, private, exp	capita	37.78	88	38s
Mental health care, psychiatric out-patient clinics, freestanding, exp	capita	0.43	88	38s
Mental health care, state and county mental hospitals, exp	capita	12.54	88	38s
Mental health care, VA medical centers, exp	capita	5.35	88	38s
Oophorectomy		1131	91	62c
Physician fee, family practice, first-visit		75.00	91	62r
Physician fee, family practice, revisit		34.00	91	62r
Physician fee, general practice, first-visit		61.00	91	62r
Physician fee, general practice, revisit		32.00	91	62r
Physician fee, general surgeon, first-visit		64.00	91	62r
Physician fee, general surgeon, revisit		40.00	91	62r
Physician fee, internal medicine, first-visit		98.00	91	62r
Physician fee, internal medicine, revisit		40.00	91	62r
Physician fee, median, neurosurgeon, first-visit		130.00	91	62r
Physician fee, median, nonsurgical specialist, first-visit		95.00	91	62r
Physician fee, median, orthopedic surgeon, first-visit		91.00	91	62r
Physician fee, median, plastic surgeon, first-visit		66.00	91	62r
Physician fee, median, surgical specialist, first-visit		62.00	91	62r
Physician fee, neurosurgeon, revisit		50.00	91	62r
Physician fee, nonsurgical specialist, revisit		40.00	91	62r
Physician fee, obstetrics/gynecology, first-visit		64.00	91	62r
Physician fee, obstetrics/gynecology, revisit		41.00	91	62r
Physician fee, orthopedic surgeon, revisit		40.00	91	62r
Physician fee, pediatrician, first-visit		49.00	91	62r
Physician fee, pediatrician, revisit		33.00	91	62r
Physician fee, plastic surgeon, revisit		43.00	91	62r
Physician fee, surgical specialist, revisit		37.00	91	62r
Preferred provider organization medical coverage, employee	year	3837	92	42c
Prostatectomy, retro-pubic		1447	91	62c
Salpingo-oophorectomy		1263	91	62c
Substance abuse, hospital ancillary charge	incident	3750	90	70s
Substance abuse, hospital physician charge	incident	1080	90	70s
Substance abuse, hospital room and board	incident	5320	90	70s

Dallas-Fort Worth, TX - continued

Item	Per	Value	Date	Ref.
Health Care - continued				
Vasectomy		367	91	62c
Household Goods				
Appliance repair, home, service call, washing machine	min labor charge	30.96	4Q 92	4c
Laundry detergent, Tide Ultra, Bold, or Cheer	42 oz	3.38	4Q 92	4c
Paper towels, Bounty	60 ft	0.83	5/92	76c
Plastic wrap, Saran	50 ft	1.61	5/92	76c
Tissues, facial, Kleenex brand	175-count box	1.09	4Q 92	4c
Housing				
ACCRA Index, Housing		98.10	4Q 92	4c
Home, median price	unit	91.30		26c
House, 1,800 sq ft, 8,000 sq ft lot, new, urban	total	102594	4Q 92	4c
House payment, principal and interest, 25% down payment	month	560	4Q 92	4c
Mortgage rate, incl. points & origination fee, 30-year fixed or adjustable rate	percent	7.92	4Q 92	4c
Rent, apartment, 2 bedrooms - 1-1/2 to 2 baths, unfurnished, 950 sq ft, water	month	584	4Q 92	4c
Rental unit, 1 bedroom	month	485	93	23c
Rental unit, 2 bedroom	month	571	93	23c
Rental unit, 3 bedroom	month	713	93	23c
Rental unit, 4 bedroom	month	798	93	23c
Rental unit, efficiency	month	398	93	23c
Insurance and Pensions				
Auto insurance, private passenger	year	709.79	91	63s
Personal Goods				
Feminine hygiene product, Stayfree	24	2.83	5/92	76c
Shampoo, Alberto VO5	15 oz	1.18	4Q 92	4c
Shave cream, Barbasol	11 oz	1.19	5/92	76c
Toothpaste, Crest gel	6.4 oz	1.96	5/92	76c
Toothpaste, Crest or Colgate	6-7 oz	2.04	4Q 92	4c
Personal Services				
Dry cleaning, man's 2-piece suit		6.41	4Q 92	4c
Haircare, woman's shampoo, trim and blow-dry		25.30	4Q 92	4c
Haircut, man's barbershop, no styling		8.94	4Q 92	4c
Restaurant Food				
Chicken, fried, thigh and drumstick		1.83	4Q 92	4c
Hamburger with cheese	1/4 lb	1.88	4Q 92	4c
Pizza, Pizza Hut or Pizza Inn, cheese, thin crust	12-13 in	7.96	4Q 92	4c
Taxes				
Tax, cigarette	pack	41	91	77s
Tax, gasoline	gal	20	91	77s
Taxes, hotel room	day	8.16	92	33c
Taxes, state	capita	923	91	77s
Transportation				
ACCRA Index, Transportation		107.10	4Q 92	4c
Bus fare	one-way	0.75	3/93	2c
Bus fare, up to 10 miles	one-way	1.25	4Q 92	4c
Driver's license fee		16.00	12/90	43s
Tire balance, computer or spin balance, front	wheel	7.12	4Q 92	4c
Travel				
Breakfast	day	6.47	6/91	60c
Business travel	day	193.00	4/93	89r
Dinner	day	25.75	6/91	60c
Lodging	day	122.46	91	60c
Lunch	day	11.12	6/91	60c
Travel, business	day	210.24	93	88c

Values are in dollars or fractions of dollars. In the column headed *Ref*, references are shown to sources. Each reference is followed by a letter. These refer to the geographical level for which data were reported: s=State, r=Region, and c=City or metro. The abbreviation *ex* is used to mean *except* or *excluding*; *exp* stands for expenditures. For other abbreviations and further explanations, please see the Introduction.

Dallas-Fort Worth, TX - continued

Item	Per	Value	Date	Ref.
Utilities				
ACCRA Index, Utilities		118.30	4Q 92	4c
Electricity	500 KWh	43.59	4/93	16c
Electricity	KWh	0.06	4/93	16c
Electricity	mil Btu	17.09	90	64s
Electricity, partial electric and other energy, 1,800 sq ft living area new home	month	95.80	4Q 92	4c
Electricity, residential	KWh	5.92	2/93	94s
Electricity, winter, 250 KWh	month	24.64	92	55c
Electricity, winter, 500 KWh	month	43.28	92	55c
Electricity, winter, 750 KWh	month	57.64	92	55c
Electricity, winter, 1000 KWh	month	69.15	92	55c

Dalton, GA

Item	Per	Value	Date	Ref.
Composite ACCRA index		90.50	4Q 92	4c
Alcoholic Beverages				
Beer, Miller Lite or Budweiser, 12-oz containers	6 pack	4.29	4Q 92	4c
Liquor, J & B Scotch	750 ml	18.89	4Q 92	4c
Wine, Gallo Chablis blanc, 1.5 liter	bottle	6.03	4Q 92	4c
Clothing				
Jeans, man's denim		32.96	4Q 92	4c
Shirt, man's dress shirt		25.33	4Q 92	4c
Undervest, boy's size 10-14, cotton	3	4.07	4Q 92	4c
Communications				
Newspaper subscription, daily and Sunday home delivery, large-city	month	8.45	4Q 92	4c
Telephone bill, family of four	month	22.41	4Q 92	4c
Energy and Fuels				
Energy, combined forms, 1,800 sq ft heating area	month	75.86	4Q 92	4c
Gasoline, motor	gal	1.09	4Q 92	4c
Entertainment				
Bowling, evening rate	game	1.85	4Q 92	4c
Monopoly game, Parker Brothers', No. 9		10.31	4Q 92	4c
Movie	admission	5.00	4Q 92	4c
Tennis balls, yellow, Wilson or Penn, 3	can	2.41	4Q 92	4c
Goods and Services				
ACCRA Index, Miscellaneous Goods and Services		97.10	4Q 92	4c
Groceries				
ACCRA Index, Groceries		92.80	4Q 92	4c
Babyfood, strained vegetables, lowest price	4-4.5 oz jar	0.29	4Q 92	4c
Bananas	lb	0.34	4Q 92	4c
Bread, white	24 oz	0.57	4Q 92	4c
Cheese, Kraft grated Parmesan	8-oz canister	2.85	4Q 92	4c
Chicken, fryer, whole	lb	0.59	4Q 92	4c
Cigarettes, Winston	carton	16.43	4Q 92	4c
Coffee, vacuum-packed	13-oz can	1.61	4Q 92	4c
Corn, frozen	10 oz	0.53	4Q 92	4c
Corn Flakes, Kellogg's or Post Toasties	18 oz	1.76	4Q 92	4c
Eggs, Grade A large	doz	0.81	4Q 92	4c
Ground beef or hamburger	lb	1.78	4Q 92	4c
Lettuce, iceberg	head	0.99	4Q 92	4c
Margarine, Blue Bonnet or Parkay cubes	lb	0.45	4Q 92	4c
Milk, whole	1/2 gal	1.51	4Q 92	4c
Orange juice, Minute Maid frozen	12-oz can	1.16	4Q 92	4c
Peaches	29-oz can	1.30	4Q 92	4c
Peas Sweet, Del Monte or Green Giant	15-17 oz can	0.59	4Q 92	4c

Dalton, GA - continued

Item	Per	Value	Date	Ref.
Groceries - continued				
Potatoes, white or red	10-lb sack	2.21	4Q 92	4c
Sausage, Jimmy Dean, 100% pork	lb	2.25	4Q 92	4c
Shortening, vegetable, Crisco	3-lb can	2.02	4Q 92	4c
Soft drink, Coca Cola	2 liter	1.05	4Q 92	4c
Steak, T-bone	lb	5.95	4Q 92	4c
Sugar, cane or beet	4 lb	1.33	4Q 92	4c
Tomatoes, Hunt's or Del Monte	14.5-oz can	0.50	4Q 92	4c
Tuna, chunk, light	6.125-6.5 oz can	0.57	4Q 92	4c
Health Care				
ACCRA Index, Health Care		87.90	4Q 92	4c
Analgesic, Aspirin, Bayer, 325 mg tablets	100	4.38	4Q 92	4c
Dentist's fee, adult teeth cleaning and periodic oral exam	visit	38.75	4Q 92	4c
Doctor's fee, routine exam, established patient	visit	35.00	4Q 92	4c
Hospital care, semiprivate room	day	270.00	4Q 92	4c
Household Goods				
Appliance repair, home, service call, washing machine	min labor charge	27.83	4Q 92	4c
Laundry detergent, Tide Ultra, Bold, or Cheer	42 oz	2.86	4Q 92	4c
Tissues, facial, Kleenex brand	175-count box	0.99	4Q 92	4c
Housing				
ACCRA Index, Housing		86.50	4Q 92	4c
House, 1,800 sq ft, 8,000 sq ft lot, new, urban	total	95000	4Q 92	4c
House payment, principal and interest, 25% down payment	month	533	4Q 92	4c
Mortgage rate, incl. points & origination fee, 30-year fixed or adjustable rate	percent	8.20	4Q 92	4c
Rent, apartment, 2 bedrooms - 1-1/2 to 2 baths, unfurnished, 950 sq ft, water	month	423	4Q 92	4c
Personal Goods				
Shampoo, Alberto VO5	15 oz	1.05	4Q 92	4c
Toothpaste, Crest or Colgate	6-7 oz	1.52	4Q 92	4c
Personal Services				
Dry cleaning, man's 2-piece suit		4.69	4Q 92	4c
Haircare, woman's shampoo, trim and blow-dry		20.00	4Q 92	4c
Haircut, man's barbershop, no styling		6.67	4Q 92	4c
Restaurant Food				
Chicken, fried, thigh and drumstick		1.99	4Q 92	4c
Hamburger with cheese	1/4 lb	1.81	4Q 92	4c
Pizza, Pizza Hut or Pizza Inn, cheese, thin crust	12-13 in	7.99	4Q 92	4c
Transportation				
ACCRA Index, Transportation		91.90	4Q 92	4c
Tire balance, computer or spin balance, front	wheel	5.67	4Q 92	4c
Utilities				
ACCRA Index, Utilities		74.00	4Q 92	4c
Electricity, all electric, 1,800 sq ft living area new home	month	75.86	4Q 92	4c

Values are in dollars or fractions of dollars. In the column headed *Ref*, references are shown to sources. Each reference is followed by a letter. These refer to the geographical level for which data were reported: s = State, r = Region, and c = City or metro. The abbreviation *ex* is used to mean *except* or *excluding*; *exp* stands for expenditures. For other abbreviations and further explanations, please see the Introduction.

Danbury, CT

Item	Per	Value	Date	Ref.
Child Care				
Child care fee, average, center	hour	2.18	90	65r
Child care fee, average, nonregulated family day care	hour	1.83	90	65r
Child care fee, average, regulated family day care	hour	2.02	90	65r
Communications				
Long-distance telephone service, day, initial minute, 0-100 miles	min	0.18-0.45	91	12s
Long-distance telephone service, day, additional minute, 0-100 miles	min	0.10-0.26	91	12s
Long-distance telephone service, evenings/weekends, 0-100 mi, initial minute	min	0.07-0.18	91	12s
Long-distance telephone service, evenings/weekends, 0-100 mi, additional minute	min	0.04-0.10	91	12s
Education				
Board, 4-yr private college/university	year	2182	91	22s
Board, 4-yr public college/university	year	1750	91	22s
Expenditures, local gov't, public elementary/secondary	pupil	8308	92	20s
Room, 4-year private college/university	year	2703	91	22s
Room, 4-year public college/university	year	1913	91	22s
Tuition, 2-year private college/university	year	8586	91	22s
Tuition, 2-year public college/university	year	972	91	22s
Tuition, 4-year private college/university	year	12315	91	22s
Tuition, 4-year public college/university, in-state	year	2313	91	22s
Energy and Fuels				
Coal	mil Btu	2.15	90	64s
Energy	mil Btu	11.62	90	64s
Energy exp/householder, 1-family unit	year	588	90	28r
Energy exp/householder, <1,000 sq ft heating area	year	477	90	28r
Energy exp/householder, 1,000-1,999 sq ft heating area	year	517	90	28r
Energy exp/householder, 2,000+ sq ft heating area	year	630	90	28r
Energy exp/householder, mobile home	year	412	90	28r
Energy exp/householder, multifamily	year	498	90	28r
Gas, natural	mil Btu	6.40	90	64s
Gas, natural	000 cu ft	8.74	91	46s
Gas, natural, exp	year	756	91	46s
Gasoline, unleaded regular	mil Btu	10.06	90	64s
Entertainment				
Miniature golf admission	adult	6.18	92	1r
Miniature golf admission	child	5.14	92	1r
Waterpark admission	adult	11.00	92	1r
Waterpark admission	child	8.55	92	1r
Funerals				
Casket, 18-gauge steel, velvet interior		1853.42	91	24r
Cosmetology, hair care, etc.		98.33	91	24r
Embalming		273.94	91	24r
Facility use for ceremony		196.06	91	24r
Hearse, local		145.67	91	24r
Limousine, local		131.07	91	24r
Remains to funeral home, transfer		135.24	91	24r
Service charge, professional		843.16	91	24r
Vault, concrete, non-metallic liner		709.14	91	24r
Viewing facilities, use		229.85	91	24r
Groceries				
Apples, Red Delicious	lb	0.85	4/93	16r
Bacon	lb	2.12	4/93	16r
Bananas	lb	0.54	4/93	16r
Bread, white, pan	lb	0.81	4/93	16r
Butter	lb	2.02	4/93	16r
Carrots, short trimmed and topped	lb	0.51	4/93	16r
Chicken, fresh, whole	lb	1.04	4/93	16r
Chicken breast, bone-in	lb	2.21	4/93	16r

Danbury, CT - continued

Item	Per	Value	Date	Ref.
Groceries - continued				
Chicken legs, bone-in	lb	1.16	4/93	16r
Chuck roast, USDA choice, boneless	lb	2.82	4/93	16r
Coffee, 100% ground roast, all sizes	lb	2.66	4/93	16r
Cucumbers	lb	0.85	4/93	16r
Eggs, Grade A large	doz	1.15	4/93	16r
Grapefruit	lb	0.45	4/93	16r
Grapes, Thompson Seedless	lb	1.52	4/93	16r
Ground beef, lean and extra lean	lb	2.36	4/93	16r
Ground chuck, 100% beef	lb	2.02	4/93	16r
Honey, jar	8 oz	0.96-1.75	92	5r
Honey, jar	lb	1.50-3.00	92	5r
Honey, squeeze bear	12-oz	1.50-1.99	92	5r
Ice cream, prepackaged, bulk, regular	1/2 gal	2.80	4/93	16r
Lemons	lb	0.96	4/93	16r
Lettuce, iceberg	lb	0.95	4/93	16r
Margarine, stick	lb	0.81	4/93	16r
Milk, fresh, whole, fortified	1/2 gal	1.30	4/93	16r
Oranges, navel	lb	0.56	4/93	16r
Peanut butter, creamy, all sizes	lb	1.88	4/93	16r
Pork chops, center cut, bone-in	lb	3.34	4/93	16r
Potato chips	16 oz	2.88	4/93	16r
Potatoes, white	lb	0.37	4/93	16r
Rib roast, USDA choice, bone-in	lb	4.94	4/93	16r
Round roast, USDA choice, boneless	lb	3.17	4/93	16r
Shortening, vegetable oil blends	lb	0.98	4/93	16r
Spaghetti and macaroni	lb	0.82	4/93	16r
Steak, round, graded & ungraded, ex USDA prime & choice	lb	4.04	4/93	16r
Steak, round, USDA choice, boneless	lb	3.90	4/93	16r
Steak, sirloin, USDA choice, boneless	lb	4.97	4/93	16r
Strawberries, dry pint	12 oz	0.90	4/93	16r
Sugar, white	lb	0.50	4/93	16r
Sugar, white, 33-80 oz pk	lb	0.41	4/93	16r
Tomatoes, field grown	lb	1.23	4/93	16r
Tuna, chunk, light	lb	2.22	4/93	16r
Turkey, frozen, whole	lb	1.04	4/93	16r
Health Care				
Childbirth, cesarean, hospital		5826	91	62r
Childbirth, cesarean, physician's fee		2053	91	62r
Childbirth, normal, hospital		2964	91	62r
Childbirth, normal, physician's fee		1492	91	62r
Medical plan per employee	year	3958	91	45r
Mental health care, exp	capita	53.68-118.35	90	38s
Mental health care, exp, state mental health agency	capita	72.81	90	38s
Mental health care, hospital psychiatric services, non-Federal, exp	capita	19.30	88	38s
Mental health care, mental health organization, multiservice, exp	capita	19.14	88	38s
Mental health care, psychiatric hospitals, private, exp	capita	35.86	88	38s
Mental health care, psychiatric out-patient clinics, freestanding, exp	capita	5.83	88	38s
Mental health care, psychiatric partial-care organizations, freestanding, exp	capita	0.15	88	38s
Mental health care, state and county mental hospitals, exp	capita	51.85	88	38s
Mental health care, VA medical centers, exp	capita	1.74	88	38s
Prescription drug co-pay, Medicaid	month	10.00	91	21s
Substance abuse, hospital ancillary charge	incident	1200	90	70s
Substance abuse, hospital physician charge	incident	270	90	70s
Substance abuse, hospital room and board	incident	4420	90	70s
Insurance and Pensions				
Auto insurance, private passenger	year	928.10	91	63s
Taxes				
Tax, cigarette	pack	45	91	77s
Tax, gasoline	gal	26	91	77s

Values are in dollars or fractions of dollars. In the column headed *Ref*, references are shown to sources. Each reference is followed by a letter. These refer to the geographical level for which data were reported: s=State, r=Region, and c=City or metro. The abbreviation *ex* is used to mean *except* or *excluding*; *exp* stands for *expenditures*. For other abbreviations and further explanations, please see the Introduction.

Danbury, CT - continued

Item	Per	Value	Date	Ref.
Taxes				
Taxes, state	capita	1514	91	77s
Transportation				
Driver's license fee		31.00	12/90	43s
Travel				
Business travel	day	165.00	4/93	89r
Utilities				
Electricity	mil Btu	26.83	90	64s

Danville, IL

Item	Per	Value	Date	Ref.
Composite ACCRA index		102.20	4Q 92	4c
Alcoholic Beverages				
Beer, Miller Lite or Budweiser, 12-oz containers	6 pack	3.70	4Q 92	4c
Liquor, J & B Scotch	750 ml	14.96	4Q 92	4c
Wine, Gallo Chablis blanc, 1.5 liter	bottle	5.15	4Q 92	4c
Clothing				
Jeans, man's denim		34.98	4Q 92	4c
Shirt, man's dress shirt		16.80	4Q 92	4c
Undervest, boy's size 10-14, cotton	3	5.21	4Q 92	4c
Communications				
Newspaper subscription, daily and Sunday home delivery, large-city	month	11.30	4Q 92	4c
Telephone bill, family of four	month	20.19	4Q 92	4c
Energy and Fuels				
Energy, combined forms, 1,800 sq ft heating area	month	122.42	4Q 92	4c
Energy, exc electricity, 1,800 sq ft heating area	month	41.52	4Q 92	4c
Gasoline, motor	gal	1.14	4Q 92	4c
Entertainment				
Bowling, evening rate	game	1.60	4Q 92	4c
Monopoly game, Parker Brothers', No. 9		12.49	4Q 92	4c
Movie	admission	4.50	4Q 92	4c
Tennis balls, yellow, Wilson or Penn, 3	can	2.06	4Q 92	4c
Goods and Services				
ACCRA Index, Miscellaneous Goods and Services		96.80	4Q 92	4c
Groceries				
ACCRA Index, Groceries		99.90	4Q 92	4c
Babyfood, strained vegetables, lowest price	4-4.5 oz jar	0.35	4Q 92	4c
Bananas	lb	0.39	4Q 92	4c
Bread, white	24 oz	0.56	4Q 92	4c
Cheese, Kraft grated Parmesan	8-oz canister	3.37	4Q 92	4c
Chicken, fryer, whole	lb	0.66	4Q 92	4c
Cigarettes, Winston	carton	19.14	4Q 92	4c
Coffee, vacuum-packed	13-oz can	1.91	4Q 92	4c
Corn, frozen	10 oz	0.68	4Q 92	4c
Corn Flakes, Kellogg's or Post Toasties	18 oz	2.04	4Q 92	4c
Eggs, Grade A large	doz	0.79	4Q 92	4c
Ground beef or hamburger	lb	1.57	4Q 92	4c
Lettuce, iceberg	head	0.99	4Q 92	4c
Margarine, Blue Bonnet or Parkay cubes	lb	0.60	4Q 92	4c
Milk, whole	1/2 gal	1.69	4Q 92	4c
Orange juice, Minute Maid frozen	12-oz can	1.36	4Q 92	4c
Peaches	29-oz can	1.43	4Q 92	4c
Peas Sweet, Del Monte or Green Giant	15-17 oz can	0.63	4Q 92	4c

Danville, IL - continued

Item	Per	Value	Date	Ref.
Groceries - continued				
Potatoes, white or red	10-lb sack	1.59	4Q 92	4c
Sausage, Jimmy Dean, 100% pork	lb	2.55	4Q 92	4c
Shortening, vegetable, Crisco	3-lb can	2.35	4Q 92	4c
Soft drink, Coca Cola	2 liter	1.29	4Q 92	4c
Steak, T-bone	lb	4.83	4Q 92	4c
Sugar, cane or beet	4 lb	1.55	4Q 92	4c
Tomatoes, Hunt's or Del Monte	14.5-oz can	0.77	4Q 92	4c
Tuna, chunk, light	6.125-6.5 oz can	0.64	4Q 92	4c
Health Care				
ACCRA Index, Health Care		99.10	4Q 92	4c
Analgesic, Aspirin, Bayer, 325 mg tablets	100	4.79	4Q 92	4c
Dentist's fee, adult teeth cleaning and periodic oral exam	visit	41.50	4Q 92	4c
Doctor's fee, routine exam, established patient	visit	36.75	4Q 92	4c
Hospital care, semiprivate room	day	385.00	4Q 92	4c
Household Goods				
Appliance repair, home, service call, washing machine	min labor charge	30.50	4Q 92	4c
Laundry detergent, Tide Ultra, Bold, or Cheer	42 oz	3.86	4Q 92	4c
Tissues, facial, Kleenex brand	175-count box	1.12	4Q 92	4c
Housing				
ACCRA Index, Housing		105.30	4Q 92	4c
House, 1,800 sq ft, 8,000 sq ft lot, new, urban	total	120000	4Q 92	4c
House payment, principal and interest, 25% down payment	month	686	4Q 92	4c
Mortgage rate, incl. points & origination fee, 30-year fixed or adjustable rate	percent	8.40	4Q 92	4c
Rent, apartment, 2 bedrooms - 1-1/2 to 2 baths, unfurnished, 950 sq ft, water	month	430	4Q 92	4c
Personal Goods				
Shampoo, Alberto VO5	15 oz	1.04	4Q 92	4c
Toothpaste, Crest or Colgate	6-7 oz	2.02	4Q 92	4c
Personal Services				
Dry cleaning, man's 2-piece suit		5.28	4Q 92	4c
Haircare, woman's shampoo, trim and blow-dry		14.80	4Q 92	4c
Haircut, man's barbershop, no styling		6.60	4Q 92	4c
Restaurant Food				
Chicken, fried, thigh and drumstick		2.18	4Q 92	4c
Hamburger with cheese	1/4 lb	2.00	4Q 92	4c
Pizza, Pizza Hut or Pizza Inn, cheese, thin crust	12-13 in	7.94	4Q 92	4c
Transportation				
ACCRA Index, Transportation		109.10	4Q 92	4c
Tire balance, computer or spin balance, front	wheel	7.62	4Q 92	4c
Utilities				
ACCRA Index, Utilities		111.30	4Q 92	4c
Electricity, partial electric and other energy, 1,800 sq ft living area new home	month	80.90	4Q 92	4c

Values are in dollars or fractions of dollars. In the column headed *Ref*, references are shown to sources. Each reference is followed by a letter. These refer to the geographical level for which data were reported: s = State, r = Region, and c = City or metro. The abbreviation *ex* is used to mean *except* or *excluding*; *exp* stands for *expenditures*. For other abbreviations and further explanations, please see the Introduction.

Danville, VA

Item	Per	Value	Date	Ref.
Child Care				
Child care fee, average, center	hour	1.29	90	65r
Child care fee, average, nonregulated family day care	hour	0.89	90	65r
Child care fee, average, regulated family day care	hour	1.32	90	65r
Communications				
Long-distance telephone service, day, initial minute, 0-100 miles	min	0.21-0.35	91	12s
Long-distance telephone service, day, additional minute, 0-100 miles	min	0.12-0.21	91	12s
Long-distance telephone service, evenings/weekends, 0-100 mi, initial minute	min	0.08-0.14	91	12s
Long-distance telephone service, evenings/weekends, 0-100 mi, additional minute	min	0.05-0.08	91	12s
Education				
Board, 4-yr private college/university	year	1804	91	22s
Board, 4-yr public college/university	year	1688	91	22s
Expenditures, local gov't, public elementary/secondary	pupil	5487	92	20s
Room, 4-year private college/university	year	1659	91	22s
Room, 4-year public college/university	year	1916	91	22s
Tuition, 2-year private college/university	year	4852	91	22s
Tuition, 2-year public college/university	year	867	91	22s
Tuition, 4-year private college/university	year	7621	91	22s
Tuition, 4-year public college/university, in-state	year	2691	91	22s
Energy and Fuels				
Coal	mil Btu	1.60	90	64s
Energy	mil Btu	8.89	90	64s
Energy exp/householder, 1-family unit	year	487	90	28r
Energy exp/householder, <1,000 sq ft heating area	year	393	90	28r
Energy exp/householder, 1,000-1,999 sq ft heating area	year	442	90	28r
Energy exp/householder, 2,000+ sq ft heating area	year	577	90	28r
Energy exp/householder, mobile home	year	366	90	28r
Energy exp/householder, multifamily	year	382	90	28r
Gas, natural	mil Btu	4.67	90	64s
Gas, natural	000 cu ft	6.80	91	46s
Gas, natural, exp	year	566	91	46s
Gasoline, unleaded regular	mil Btu	9.46	90	64s
Entertainment				
Miniature golf admission	adult	6.18	92	1r
Miniature golf admission	child	5.14	92	1r
Waterpark admission	adult	11.00	92	1r
Waterpark admission	child	8.55	92	1r
Funerals				
Casket, 18-gauge steel, velvet interior		2029.08	91	24r
Cosmetology, hair care, etc.		75.10	91	24r
Embalming		249.24	91	24r
Facility use for ceremony		162.27	91	24r
Hearse, local		114.04	91	24r
Limousine, local		88.57	91	24r
Remains to funeral home, transfer		92.61	91	24r
Service charge, professional		682.42	91	24r
Vault, concrete, non-metallic liner		798.70	91	24r
Viewing facilities, use		163.86	91	24r
Groceries				
Apples, Red Delicious	lb	0.79	4/93	16r
Bacon	lb	1.75	4/93	16r
Bananas	lb	0.42	4/93	16r
Beef, stew, boneless	lb	2.61	4/93	16r
Bologna, all beef or mixed	lb	2.24	4/93	16r
Bread, white, pan	lb	0.64	4/93	16r
Bread, whole wheat, pan	lb	0.96	4/93	16r
Cabbage	lb	0.37	4/93	16r

Item	Per	Value	Date	Ref.
Groceries - continued				
Carrots, short trimmed and topped	lb	0.47	4/93	16r
Celery	lb	0.64	4/93	16r
Cheese, American	lb	2.98	4/93	16r
Cheese, Cheddar	lb	3.28	4/93	16r
Chicken, fresh, whole	lb	0.77	4/93	16r
Chicken breast, bone-in	lb	1.92	4/93	16r
Chicken legs, bone-in	lb	1.06	4/93	16r
Chuck roast, graded and ungraded, ex USDA prime and choice	lb	2.40	4/93	16r
Chuck roast, USDA choice, bone-in	lb	2.19	4/93	16r
Chuck roast, USDA choice, boneless	lb	2.38	4/93	16r
Coffee, 100% ground roast, all sizes	lb	2.48	4/93	16r
Crackers, soda, salted	lb	1.15	4/93	16r
Eggs, Grade A large	doz	0.96	4/93	16r
Flour, white, all purpose	lb	0.24	4/93	16r
Frankfurters, all meat or all beef	lb	2.01	4/93	16r
Grapefruit	lb	0.44	4/93	16r
Grapes, Thompson Seedless	lb	1.40	4/93	16r
Ground beef, 100% beef	lb	1.58	4/93	16r
Ground beef, lean and extra lean	lb	2.09	4/93	16r
Ground chuck, 100% beef	lb	1.98	4/93	16r
Ham, boneless, excluding canned	lb	2.89	4/93	16r
Ham, picnic, shoulder, bone-in, smoked	lb	1.02	4/93	16r
Ham, rump or steak half, bone-in, smoked	lb	1.48	4/93	16r
Ice cream, prepackaged, bulk, regular	1/2 gal	2.41	4/93	16r
Lemons	lb	1.05	4/93	16r
Lettuce, iceberg	lb	0.81	4/93	16r
Margarine, stick	lb	0.88	4/93	16r
Oranges, navel	lb	0.55	4/93	16r
Pears, Anjou	lb	0.92	4/93	16r
Pork chops, center cut, bone-in	lb	3.13	4/93	16r
Potato chips	16 oz	2.94	4/93	16r
Potatoes, white	lb	0.43	4/93	16r
Rib roast, USDA choice, bone-in	lb	4.63	4/93	16r
Rice, white, long grain, uncooked	lb	0.45	4/93	16r
Round roast, graded & ungraded, ex USDA prime & choice	lb	3.03	4/93	16r
Round roast, USDA choice, boneless	lb	3.09	4/93	16r
Sausage, fresh, loose	lb	2.08	4/93	16r
Short ribs, bone-in	lb	2.66	4/93	16r
Shortening, vegetable oil blends	lb	0.69	4/93	16r
Spaghetti and macaroni	lb	0.81	4/93	16r
Steak, rib eye, USDA choice, boneless	lb	6.24	4/93	16r
Steak, round, graded & ungraded, ex USDA prime & choice	lb	3.31	4/93	16r
Steak, round, USDA choice, boneless	lb	3.34	4/93	16r
Steak, sirloin, graded & ungraded, ex USDA prime & choice	lb	4.19	4/93	16r
Steak, sirloin, USDA choice, boneless	lb	4.46	4/93	16r
Steak, T-bone, USDA choice, bone-in	lb	5.25	4/93	16r
Strawberries, dry pint	12 oz	0.92	4/93	16r
Sugar, white	lb	0.39	4/93	16r
Sugar, white, 33-80 oz pk	lb	0.38	4/93	16r
Tomatoes, field grown	lb	0.88	4/93	16r
Tuna, chunk, light	lb	1.79	4/93	16r
Turkey, frozen, whole	lb	1.04	4/93	16r
Yogurt, natural, fruit flavored	1/2 pint	0.57	4/93	16r
Health Care				
Childbirth, cesarean, hospital		5034	91	62r
Childbirth, cesarean, physician's fee		2053	91	62r
Childbirth, normal, hospital		2712	91	62r
Childbirth, normal, physician's fee		1492	91	62r
Medical plan per employee	year	3495	91	45r
Mental health care, exp	capita	37.60-53.67	90	38s
Mental health care, exp, state mental health agency	capita	44.54	90	38s
Mental health care, hospital psychiatric services, non-Federal, exp	capita	9.90	88	38s
Mental health care, mental health organization, multiservice, exp	capita	17.29	88	38s

Values are in dollars or fractions of dollars. In the column headed *Ref*, references are shown to sources. Each reference is followed by a letter. These refer to the geographical level for which data were reported: s=State, r=Region, and c=City or metro. The abbreviation *ex* is used to mean *except* or *excluding*; *exp* stands for expenditures. For other abbreviations and further explanations, please see the Introduction.

Danville, VA - continued

Item	Per	Value	Date	Ref.
Health Care				
Mental health care, psychiatric hospitals, private, exp	capita	32.58	88	38s
Mental health care, psychiatric out-patient clinics, freestanding, exp	capita	0.93	88	38s
Mental health care, psychiatric partial-care organizations, freestanding, exp	capita	0.25	88	38s
Mental health care, state and county mental hospitals, exp	capita	28.61	88	38s
Mental health care, VA medical centers, exp	capita	3.95	88	38s
Physician fee, family practice, first-visit		75.00	91	62r
Physician fee, family practice, revisit		34.00	91	62r
Physician fee, general practice, first-visit		61.00	91	62r
Physician fee, general practice, revisit		32.00	91	62r
Physician fee, general surgeon, first-visit		64.00	91	62r
Physician fee, general surgeon, revisit		40.00	91	62r
Physician fee, internal medicine, first-visit		98.00	91	62r
Physician fee, internal medicine, revisit		40.00	91	62r
Physician fee, median, neurosurgeon, first-visit		130.00	91	62r
Physician fee, median, nonsurgical specialist, first-visit		95.00	91	62r
Physician fee, median, orthopedic surgeon, first-visit		91.00	91	62r
Physician fee, median, plastic surgeon, first-visit		66.00	91	62r
Physician fee, median, surgical specialist, first-visit		62.00	91	62r
Physician fee, neurosurgeon, revisit		50.00	91	62r
Physician fee, nonsurgical specialist, revisit		40.00	91	62r
Physician fee, obstetrics/gynecology, first-visit		64.00	91	62r
Physician fee, obstetrics/gynecology, revisit		41.00	91	62r
Physician fee, orthopedic surgeon, revisit		40.00	91	62r
Physician fee, pediatrician, first-visit		49.00	91	62r
Physician fee, pediatrician, revisit		33.00	91	62r
Physician fee, plastic surgeon, revisit		43.00	91	62r
Physician fee, surgical specialist, revisit		37.00	91	62r
Substance abuse, hospital ancillary charge	incident	1220	90	70s
Substance abuse, hospital physician charge	incident	590	90	70s
Substance abuse, hospital room and board	incident	6280	90	70s
Insurance and Pensions				
Auto insurance, private passenger	year	559.45	91	63s
Taxes				
Tax, cigarette	pack	2.50	91	77s
Tax, gasoline	gal	17.50	91	77s
Taxes, state	capita	1090	91	77s
Transportation				
Driver's license fee		12.00	12/90	43s
Vehicle registration and license plate	year	26.50-37.50	93	90s
Travel				
Business travel	day	193.00	4/93	89r
Utilities				
Electricity	mil Btu	17.70	90	64s

Dare County, NC

Item	Per	Value	Date	Ref.
Composite ACCRA index		108.80	4Q 92	4c
Alcoholic Beverages				
Beer, Miller Lite or Budweiser, 12-oz containers	6 pack	3.72	4Q 92	4c
Liquor, J & B Scotch	750 ml	17.65	4Q 92	4c
Wine, Gallo Chablis blanc, 1.5 liter	bottle	4.99	4Q 92	4c

Dare County, NC - continued

Item	Per	Value	Date	Ref.
Clothing				
Jeans, man's denim		28.95	4Q 92	4c
Shirt, man's dress shirt		26.00	4Q 92	4c
Undervest, boy's size 10-14, cotton	3	4.83	4Q 92	4c
Communications				
Newspaper subscription, daily and Sunday home delivery, large-city	month	10.00	4Q 92	4c
Telephone bill, family of four	month	16.69	4Q 92	4c
Energy and Fuels				
Energy, combined forms, 1,800 sq ft heating area	month	117.36	4Q 92	4c
Gasoline, motor	gal	1.17	4Q 92	4c
Entertainment				
Bowling, evening rate	game	2.50	4Q 92	4c
Monopoly game, Parker Brothers', No. 9		13.24	4Q 92	4c
Movie	admission	5.00	4Q 92	4c
Tennis balls, yellow, Wilson or Penn, 3	can	2.23	4Q 92	4c
Goods and Services				
ACCRA Index, Miscellaneous Goods and Services		109.00	4Q 92	4c
Groceries				
ACCRA Index, Groceries		98.30	4Q 92	4c
Babyfood, strained vegetables, lowest price	4-4.5 oz jar	0.33	4Q 92	4c
Bananas	lb	0.52	4Q 92	4c
Bread, white	24 oz	0.68	4Q 92	4c
Cheese, Kraft grated Parmesan	8-oz canister	3.44	4Q 92	4c
Chicken, fryer, whole	lb	0.82	4Q 92	4c
Cigarettes, Winston	carton	15.23	4Q 92	4c
Coffee, vacuum-packed	13-oz can	2.11	4Q 92	4c
Corn, frozen	10 oz	0.55	4Q 92	4c
Corn Flakes, Kellogg's or Post Toasties	18 oz	1.94	4Q 92	4c
Eggs, Grade A large	doz	0.94	4Q 92	4c
Ground beef or hamburger	lb	1.48	4Q 92	4c
Lettuce, iceberg	head	0.99	4Q 92	4c
Margarine, Blue Bonnet or Parkay cubes	lb	0.64	4Q 92	4c
Milk, whole	1/2 gal	1.42	4Q 92	4c
Orange juice, Minute Maid frozen	12-oz can	1.44	4Q 92	4c
Peaches	29-oz can	1.36	4Q 92	4c
Peas Sweet, Del Monte or Green Giant	15-17 oz can	0.57	4Q 92	4c
Potatoes, white or red	10-lb sack	2.26	4Q 92	4c
Sausage, Jimmy Dean, 100% pork	lb	2.05	4Q 92	4c
Shortening, vegetable, Crisco	3-lb can	2.16	4Q 92	4c
Soft drink, Coca Cola	2 liter	0.96	4Q 92	4c
Steak, T-bone	lb	5.76	4Q 92	4c
Sugar, cane or beet	4 lb	1.52	4Q 92	4c
Tomatoes, Hunt's or Del Monte	14.5-oz can	0.57	4Q 92	4c
Tuna, chunk, light	6.125-6.5 oz can	0.60	4Q 92	4c
Health Care				
ACCRA Index, Health Care		95.10	4Q 92	4c
Analgesic, Aspirin, Bayer, 325 mg tablets	100	5.14	4Q 92	4c
Dentist's fee, adult teeth cleaning and periodic oral exam	visit	43.75	4Q 92	4c
Doctor's fee, routine exam, established patient	visit	37.33	4Q 92	4c
Hospital care, semiprivate room	day	261.00	4Q 92	4c

Values are in dollars or fractions of dollars. In the column headed *Ref*, references are shown to sources. Each reference is followed by a letter. These refer to the geographical level for which data were reported: s=State, r=Region, and c=City or metro. The abbreviation *ex* is used to mean *except* or *excluding*; *exp* stands for expenditures. For other abbreviations and further explanations, please see the Introduction.

Dare County, NC - continued

Item	Per	Value	Date	Ref.
Household Goods				
Appliance repair, home, service call, washing machine	min labor charge	45.79	4Q 92	4c
Laundry detergent, Tide Ultra, Bold, or Cheer	42 oz	3.19	4Q 92	4c
Tissues, facial, Kleenex brand	175-count box	1.08	4Q 92	4c
Housing				
ACCRA Index, Housing		119.90	4Q 92	4c
House, 1,800 sq ft, 8,000 sq ft lot, new, urban	total	133400	4Q 92	4c
House payment, principal and interest, 25% down payment	month	745	4Q 92	4c
Mortgage rate, incl. points & origination fee, 30-year fixed or adjustable rate	percent	8.16	4Q 92	4c
Personal Goods				
Shampoo, Alberto VO5	15 oz	1.85	4Q 92	4c
Toothpaste, Crest or Colgate	6-7 oz	1.76	4Q 92	4c
Personal Services				
Dry cleaning, man's 2-piece suit		5.80	4Q 92	4c
Haircare, woman's shampoo, trim and blow-dry		21.00	4Q 92	4c
Haircut, man's barbershop, no styling		10.30	4Q 92	4c
Restaurant Food				
Chicken, fried, thigh and drumstick		2.52	4Q 92	4c
Hamburger with cheese	1/4 lb	1.90	4Q 92	4c
Pizza, Pizza Hut or Pizza Inn, cheese, thin crust	12-13 in	7.75	4Q 92	4c
Transportation				
ACCRA Index, Transportation		100.70	4Q 92	4c
Tire balance, computer or spin balance, front	wheel	6.38	4Q 92	4c
Utilities				
ACCRA Index, Utilities		105.30	4Q 92	4c
Electricity, all electric, 1,800 sq ft living area new home	month	117.36	4Q 92	4c

Davenport, IA

Item	Per	Value	Date	Ref.
Child Care				
Child care fee, average, center	hour	1.63	90	65r
Child care fee, average, nonregulated family day care	hour	1.83	90	65r
Child care fee, average, regulated family day care	hour	1.42	90	65r
Communications				
Long-distance telephone service, day, initial minute, 0-100 miles	min	0.21-0.41	91	12s
Long-distance telephone service, day, additional minute, 0-100 miles	min	0.11-0.30	91	12s
Long-distance telephone service, evenings/weekends, 0-100 mi, initial minute	min	0.11-0.20	91	12s
Long-distance telephone service, evenings/weekends, 0-100 mi, additional minute	min	0.06-0.15	91	12s
Telephone, flat rate	month	15.95	91	11c
Education				
Board, 4-yr private college/university	year	1703	91	22s
Board, 4-yr public college/university	year	1183	91	22s
Expenditures, local gov't, public elementary/secondary	pupil	5026	92	20s
Room, 4-year private college/university	year	1392	91	22s
Room, 4-year public college/university	year	1188	91	22s

Item	Per	Value	Date	Ref.
Education - continued				
Tuition, 2-year private college/university	year	5119	91	22s
Tuition, 2-year public college/university	year	1298	91	22s
Tuition, 4-year private college/university	year	8703	91	22s
Tuition, 4-year public college/university, in-state	year	1880	91	22s
Energy and Fuels				
Coal	mil Btu	1.16	90	64s
Energy	mil Btu	7.71	90	64s
Energy exp/householder, 1-family unit	year	473	90	28r
Energy exp/householder, <1,000 sq ft heating area	year	429	90	28r
Energy exp/householder, 1,000-1,999 sq ft heating area	year	442	90	28r
Energy exp/householder, 2,000+ sq ft heating area	year	498	90	28r
Energy exp/householder, mobile home	year	442	90	28r
Energy exp/householder, multifamily	year	407	90	28r
Gas, natural	mil Btu	3.81	90	64s
Gas, natural	000 cu ft	4.81	91	46s
Gas, natural, exp	year	530	91	46s
Gasoline, unleaded regular	mil Btu	9.38	90	64s
Entertainment				
Miniature golf admission	adult	6.18	92	1r
Miniature golf admission	child	5.14	92	1r
Waterpark admission	adult	11.00	92	1r
Waterpark admission	child	8.55	92	1r
Funerals				
Casket, 18-gauge steel, velvet interior		1952.97	91	24r
Cosmetology, hair care, etc.		90.03	91	24r
Embalming		251.75	91	24r
Facility use for ceremony		180.75	91	24r
Hearse, local		117.51	91	24r
Limousine, local		71.86	91	24r
Remains to funeral home, transfer		81.14	91	24r
Service charge, professional		740.03	91	24r
Vault, concrete, non-metallic liner		801.47	91	24r
Viewing facilities, use		169.33	91	24r
Groceries				
Apples, Red Delicious	lb	0.77	4/93	16r
Bacon	lb	1.85	4/93	16r
Bananas	lb	0.46	4/93	16r
Beef, stew, boneless	lb	2.53	4/93	16r
Bologna, all beef or mixed	lb	2.19	4/93	16r
Bread, white, pan	lb	0.78	4/93	16r
Butter	lb	1.50	4/93	16r
Cabbage	lb	0.40	4/93	16r
Carrots, short trimmed and topped	lb	0.45	4/93	16r
Cheese, Cheddar	lb	3.47	4/93	16r
Chicken, fresh, whole	lb	0.84	4/93	16r
Chicken breast, bone-in	lb	1.94	4/93	16r
Chicken legs, bone-in	lb	1.02	4/93	16r
Chuck roast, graded and ungraded, ex USDA prime and choice	lb	2.43	4/93	16r
Chuck roast, USDA choice, bone-in	lb	2.11	4/93	16r
Chuck roast, USDA choice, boneless	lb	2.44	4/93	16r
Coffee, 100% ground roast, all sizes	lb	2.47	4/93	16r
Cookies, chocolate chip	lb	2.73	4/93	16r
Eggs, Grade A large	doz	0.93	4/93	16r
Flour, white, all purpose	lb	0.21	4/93	16r
Grapefruit	lb	0.45	4/93	16r
Grapes, Thompson Seedless	lb	1.46	4/93	16r
Ground beef, 100% beef	lb	1.63	4/93	16r
Ground beef, lean and extra lean	lb	2.08	4/93	16r
Ground chuck, 100% beef	lb	1.94	4/93	16r
Ham, boneless, excluding canned	lb	2.21	4/93	16r

Values are in dollars or fractions of dollars. In the column headed *Ref*, references are shown to sources. Each reference is followed by a letter. These refer to the geographical level for which data were reported: s = State, r = Region, and c = City or metro. The abbreviation *ex* is used to mean *except* or *excluding*; *exp* stands for expenditures. For other abbreviations and further explanations, please see the Introduction.

Davenport, IA - continued

Item	Per	Value	Date	Ref.
Groceries				
Ice cream, prepackaged, bulk, regular	1/2 gal	2.41	4/93	16r
Lemons	lb	0.82	4/93	16r
Lettuce, iceberg	lb	0.83	4/93	16r
Margarine, stick	lb	0.77	4/93	16r
Oranges, navel	lb	0.50	4/93	16r
Peanut butter, creamy, all sizes	lb	1.82	4/93	16r
Pears, Anjou	lb	0.85	4/93	16r
Pork chops, center cut, bone-in	lb	3.17	4/93	16r
Potato chips	16 oz	2.68	4/93	16r
Potatoes, white	lb	0.26	4/93	16r
Round roast, graded & ungraded, ex USDA prime & choice	lb	2.88	4/93	16r
Round roast, USDA choice, boneless	lb	2.96	4/93	16r
Shortening, vegetable oil blends	lb	0.79	4/93	16r
Spaghetti and macaroni	lb	0.76	4/93	16r
Steak, rib eye, USDA choice, boneless	lb	6.29	4/93	16r
Steak, round, USDA choice, boneless	lb	3.24	4/93	16r
Steak, sirloin, graded & ungraded, ex USDA prime & choice	lb	4.00	4/93	16r
Steak, sirloin, USDA choice, bone-in	lb	3.57	4/93	16r
Steak, sirloin, USDA choice, boneless	lb	4.17	4/93	16r
Steak, T-bone, USDA choice, bone-in	lb	5.60	4/93	16r
Strawberries, dry pint	12 oz	0.90	4/93	16r
Sugar, white	lb	0.36	4/93	16r
Sugar, white, 33-80 oz pk	lb	0.35	4/93	16r
Tomatoes, field grown	lb	0.99	4/93	16r
Tuna, chunk, light	lb	1.76	4/93	16r
Turkey, frozen, whole	lb	0.91	4/93	16r
Health Care				
Childbirth, cesarean, hospital		4688	91	62r
Childbirth, cesarean, physician's fee		2053	91	62r
Childbirth, normal, hospital		2657	91	62r
Childbirth, normal, physician's fee		1492	91	62r
Health care spending, state	capita	2351	3/93	84s
Hospital care, semiprivate room	day	202.35	90	27c
Medical insurance premium, per employee, small group comprehensive	month	288.35	10/91	25c
Medical plan per employee	year	3443	91	45r
Mental health care, exp	capita	20.37-28.83	90	38s
Mental health care, exp, state mental health agency	capita	17.07	90	38s
Mental health care, hospital psychiatric services, non-Federal, exp	capita	23.51	88	38s
Mental health care, mental health organization, multiservice, exp	capita	7.66	88	38s
Mental health care, psychiatric hospitals, private, exp	capita	2.86	88	38s
Mental health care, psychiatric out-patient clinics, freestanding, exp	capita	3.02	88	38s
Mental health care, state and county mental hospitals, exp	capita	14.54	88	38s
Mental health care, VA medical centers, exp	capita	13.98	88	38s
Physician fee, family practice, first-visit		76.00	91	62r
Physician fee, family practice, revisit		33.00	91	62r
Physician fee, general practice, first-visit		61.00	91	62r
Physician fee, general practice, revisit		31.00	91	62r
Physician fee, general surgeon, first-visit		65.00	91	62r
Physician fee, general surgeon, revisit		35.00	91	62r
Physician fee, internal medicine, first-visit		91.00	91	62r
Physician fee, internal medicine, revisit		40.00	91	62r
Physician fee, median, neurosurgeon, first-visit		106.00	91	62r
Physician fee, median, nonsurgical specialist, first-visit		90.00	91	62r
Physician fee, median, orthopedic surgeon, first-visit		83.00	91	62r
Physician fee, median, surgical specialist, first-visit		61.00	91	62r
Physician fee, neurosurgeon, revisit		41.00	91	62r
Physician fee, nonsurgical specialist, revisit		40.00	91	62r

Davenport, IA - continued

Item	Per	Value	Date	Ref.
Health Care - continued				
Physician fee, obstetrics/gynecology, first-visit		61.00	91	62r
Physician fee, obstetrics/gynecology, revisit		40.00	91	62r
Physician fee, orthopedic surgeon, revisit		41.00	91	62r
Physician fee, pediatrician, first-visit		46.00	91	62r
Physician fee, pediatrician, revisit		33.00	91	62r
Physician fee, surgical specialist, revisit		36.00	91	62r
Substance abuse, hospital ancillary charge	incident	950	90	70s
Substance abuse, hospital physician charge	incident	250	90	70s
Substance abuse, hospital room and board	incident	3110	90	70s
Housing				
Rental unit, 1 bedroom	month	448	93	23c
Rental unit, 2 bedroom	month	528	93	23c
Rental unit, 3 bedroom	month	659	93	23c
Rental unit, 4 bedroom	month	738	93	23c
Rental unit, efficiency	month	368	93	23c
Insurance and Pensions				
Auto insurance, private passenger	year	422.46	91	63s
Taxes				
Tax, cigarette	pack	36	91	77s
Tax, gasoline	gal	20	91	77s
Taxes, state	capita	1233	91	77s
Transportation				
Driver's license fee		16.00	12/90	43s
Utilities				
Electricity	mil Btu	17.37	90	64s
Electricity, winter, 250 KWh	month	24.28	92	55c
Electricity, winter, 250 KWh	month	24.63	2/93	30c
Electricity, winter, 500 KWh	month	43.56	92	55c
Electricity, winter, 500 KWh	month	44.25	2/93	30c
Electricity, winter, 750 KWh	month	59.36	92	55c
Electricity, winter, 750 KWh	month	63.87	2/93	30c
Electricity, winter, 1000 KWh	month	69.80	92	55c
Electricity, winter, 1000 KWh	month	75.41	2/93	30c

Davenport, IL

Item	Per	Value	Date	Ref.
Child Care				
Child care fee, average, center	hour	1.63	90	65r
Child care fee, average, nonregulated family day care	hour	1.83	90	65r
Child care fee, average, regulated family day care	hour	1.42	90	65r
Communications				
Long-distance telephone service, day, initial minute, 0-100 miles	min	0.10-0.34	91	12s
Long-distance telephone service, day, additional minute, 0-100 miles	min	0.04-0.16	91	12s
Long-distance telephone service, evenings/weekends, 0-100 mi, initial minute	min	0.06-0.20	91	12s
Long-distance telephone service, evenings/weekends, 0-100 mi, additional minute	min	0.02-0.10	91	12s
Education				
Board, 4-yr private college/university	year	1797	91	22s
Board, 4-yr public college/university	year	1857	91	22s
Expenditures, local gov't, public elementary/secondary	pupil	5248	92	20s
Room, 4-year private college/university	year	2095	91	22s
Room, 4-year public college/university	year	1454	91	22s
Tuition, 2-year private college/university	year	5279	91	22s
Tuition, 2-year public college/university	year	906	91	22s
Tuition, 4-year private college/university	year	8853	91	22s
Tuition, 4-year public college/university, in-state	year	2465	91	22s

Values are in dollars or fractions of dollars. In the column headed *Ref*, references are shown to sources. Each reference is followed by a letter. These refer to the geographical level for which data were reported: s=State, r=Region, and c=City or metro. The abbreviation *ex* is used to mean *except* or *excluding*; *exp* stands for expenditures. For other abbreviations and further explanations, please see the Introduction.

Davenport, IL - continued

Item	Per	Value	Date	Ref.
Energy and Fuels				
Coal	mil Btu	1.72	90	64s
Energy	mil Btu	8.74	90	64s
Energy exp/householder, 1-family unit	year	471	90	28r
Energy exp/householder, <1,000 sq ft heating area	year	430	90	28r
Energy exp/householder, 1,000-1,999 sq ft heating area	year	481	90	28r
Energy exp/householder, 2,000+ sq ft heating area	year	473	90	28r
Energy exp/householder, mobile home	year	430	90	28r
Energy exp/householder, multifamily	year	461	90	28r
Gas, natural	mil Btu	4.57	90	64s
Gas, natural	000 cu ft	4.95	91	46s
Gas, natural, exp	year	696	91	46s
Gasoline, unleaded regular	mil Btu	9.35	90	64s
Entertainment				
Miniature golf admission	adult	6.18	92	1r
Miniature golf admission	child	5.14	92	1r
Waterpark admission	adult	11.00	92	1r
Waterpark admission	child	8.55	92	1r
Funerals				
Casket, 18-gauge steel, velvet interior		1926.72	91	24r
Cosmetology, hair care, etc.		97.64	91	24r
Embalming		249.14	91	24r
Facility use for ceremony		208.59	91	24r
Hearse, local		130.12	91	24r
Limousine, local		104.66	91	24r
Remains to funeral home, transfer		93.61	91	24r
Service charge, professional		724.62	91	24r
Vault, concrete, non-metallic liner		734.53	91	24r
Viewing facilities, use		236.06	91	24r
Groceries				
Apples, Red Delicious	lb	0.77	4/93	16r
Bacon	lb	1.85	4/93	16r
Bananas	lb	0.46	4/93	16r
Beef, stew, boneless	lb	2.53	4/93	16r
Bologna, all beef or mixed	lb	2.19	4/93	16r
Bread, white, pan	lb	0.78	4/93	16r
Butter	lb	1.50	4/93	16r
Cabbage	lb	0.40	4/93	16r
Carrots, short trimmed and topped	lb	0.45	4/93	16r
Cheese, Cheddar	lb	3.47	4/93	16r
Chicken, fresh, whole	lb	0.84	4/93	16r
Chicken breast, bone-in	lb	1.94	4/93	16r
Chicken legs, bone-in	lb	1.02	4/93	16r
Chuck roast, graded and ungraded, ex USDA prime and choice	lb	2.43	4/93	16r
Chuck roast, USDA choice, bone-in	lb	2.11	4/93	16r
Chuck roast, USDA choice, boneless	lb	2.44	4/93	16r
Coffee, 100% ground roast, all sizes	lb	2.47	4/93	16r
Cookies, chocolate chip	lb	2.73	4/93	16r
Eggs, Grade A large	doz	0.93	4/93	16r
Flour, white, all purpose	lb	0.21	4/93	16r
Grapefruit	lb	0.45	4/93	16r
Grapes, Thompson Seedless	lb	1.46	4/93	16r
Ground beef, 100% beef	lb	1.63	4/93	16r
Ground beef, lean and extra lean	lb	2.08	4/93	16r
Ground chuck, 100% beef	lb	1.94	4/93	16r
Ham, boneless, excluding canned	lb	2.21	4/93	16r
Honey, jar	8 oz	0.97-1.25	92	5r
Honey, jar	lb	1.25-2.25	92	5r
Honey, squeeze bear	12-oz	1.25-1.99	92	5r
Ice cream, prepackaged, bulk, regular	1/2 gal	2.41	4/93	16r
Lemons	lb	0.82	4/93	16r
Lettuce, iceberg	lb	0.83	4/93	16r
Margarine, stick	lb	0.77	4/93	16r
Oranges, navel	lb	0.50	4/93	16r
Peanut butter, creamy, all sizes	lb	1.82	4/93	16r
Pears, Anjou	lb	0.85	4/93	16r
Pork chops, center cut, bone-in	lb	3.17	4/93	16r

Davenport, IL - continued

Item	Per	Value	Date	Ref.
Groceries - continued				
Potato chips	16 oz	2.68	4/93	16r
Potatoes, white	lb	0.26	4/93	16r
Round roast, graded & ungraded, ex USDA prime & choice	lb	2.88	4/93	16r
Round roast, USDA choice, boneless	lb	2.96	4/93	16r
Shortening, vegetable oil blends	lb	0.79	4/93	16r
Spaghetti and macaroni	lb	0.76	4/93	16r
Steak, rib eye, USDA choice, boneless	lb	6.29	4/93	16r
Steak, round, USDA choice, boneless	lb	3.24	4/93	16r
Steak, sirloin, graded & ungraded, ex USDA prime & choice	lb	4.00	4/93	16r
Steak, sirloin, USDA choice, bone-in	lb	3.57	4/93	16r
Steak, sirloin, USDA choice, boneless	lb	4.17	4/93	16r
Steak, T-bone, USDA choice, bone-in	lb	5.60	4/93	16r
Strawberries, dry pint	12 oz	0.90	4/93	16r
Sugar, white	lb	0.36	4/93	16r
Sugar, white, 33-80 oz pk	lb	0.35	4/93	16r
Tomatoes, field grown	lb	0.99	4/93	16r
Tuna, chunk, light	lb	1.76	4/93	16r
Turkey, frozen, whole	lb	0.91	4/93	16r
Health Care				
Childbirth, cesarean, hospital		4688	91	62r
Childbirth, cesarean, physician's fee		2053	91	62r
Childbirth, normal, hospital		2657	91	62r
Childbirth, normal, physician's fee		1492	91	62r
Medical plan per employee	year	3443	91	45r
Mental health care, exp	capita	28.84-37.59	90	38s
Mental health care, exp, state mental health agency	capita	34.43	90	38s
Mental health care, hospital psychiatric services, non-Federal, exp	capita	18.46	88	38s
Mental health care, mental health organization, multiservice, exp	capita	11.97	88	38s
Mental health care, psychiatric hospitals, private, exp	capita	7.84	88	38s
Mental health care, psychiatric out-patient clinics, freestanding, exp	capita	3.21	88	38s
Mental health care, psychiatric partial-care organizations, freestanding, exp	capita	0.51	88	38s
Mental health care, state and county mental hospitals, exp	capita	18.11	88	38s
Mental health care, VA medical centers, exp	capita	3.69	88	38s
Physician fee, family practice, first-visit		76.00	91	62r
Physician fee, family practice, revisit		33.00	91	62r
Physician fee, general practice, first-visit		61.00	91	62r
Physician fee, general practice, revisit		31.00	91	62r
Physician fee, general surgeon, first-visit		65.00	91	62r
Physician fee, general surgeon, revisit		35.00	91	62r
Physician fee, internal medicine, first-visit		91.00	91	62r
Physician fee, internal medicine, revisit		40.00	91	62r
Physician fee, median, neurosurgeon, first-visit		106.00	91	62r
Physician fee, median, nonsurgical specialist, first-visit		90.00	91	62r
Physician fee, median, orthopedic surgeon, first-visit		83.00	91	62r
Physician fee, median, surgical specialist, first-visit		61.00	91	62r
Physician fee, neurosurgeon, revisit		41.00	91	62r
Physician fee, nonsurgical specialist, revisit		40.00	91	62r
Physician fee, obstetrics/gynecology, first-visit		61.00	91	62r
Physician fee, obstetrics/gynecology, revisit		40.00	91	62r
Physician fee, orthopedic surgeon, revisit		41.00	91	62r
Physician fee, pediatrician, first-visit		46.00	91	62r
Physician fee, pediatrician, revisit		33.00	91	62r
Physician fee, surgical specialist, revisit		36.00	91	62r
Prescription drug co-pay, Medicaid	month	25.00	91	21s
Substance abuse, hospital ancillary charge	incident	1310	90	70s

Values are in dollars or fractions of dollars. In the column headed *Ref*, references are shown to sources. Each reference is followed by a letter. These refer to the geographical level for which data were reported: s = State, r = Region, and c = City or metro. The abbreviation *ex* is used to mean *except* or *excluding*; *exp* stands for expenditures. For other abbreviations and further explanations, please see the Introduction.

Davenport, IL - continued

Item	Per	Value	Date	Ref.
Health Care				
Substance abuse, hospital physician charge	incident	540	90	70s
Substance abuse, hospital room and board	incident	6150	90	70s
Insurance and Pensions				
Auto insurance, private passenger	year	621.37	91	63s
Taxes				
Tax, cigarette	pack	30	91	77s
Tax, gasoline	gal	19	91	77s
Taxes, state	capita	1151	91	77s
Transportation				
Driver's license fee		10.00	12/90	43s
Vehicle registration and license plate	multi-year	48.00	93	52s
Utilities				
Electricity	mil Btu	22.02	90	64s

Dayton, OH

Item	Per	Value	Date	Ref.
Child Care				
Child care fee, average, center	hour	1.63	90	65r
Child care fee, average, nonregulated family day care	hour	1.83	90	65r
Child care fee, average, regulated family day care	hour	1.42	90	65r
Communications				
Long-distance telephone service, day, initial minute, 0-100 miles	min	0.26-0.43	91	12s
Long-distance telephone service, day, additional minute, 0-100 miles	min	0.14-0.24	91	12s
Long-distance telephone service, evenings/weekends, 0-100 mi, initial minute	min	0.11-0.17	91	12s
Long-distance telephone service, evenings/weekends, 0-100 mi, additional minute	min	0.06-0.10	91	12s
Education				
Board, 4-yr private college/university	year	1872	91	22s
Board, 4-yr public college/university	year	1742	91	22s
Expenditures, local gov't, public elementary/secondary	pupil	5451	92	20s
Room, 4-year private college/university	year	1695	91	22s
Room, 4-year public college/university	year	2259	91	22s
Tuition, 2-year private college/university	year	6093	91	22s
Tuition, 2-year public college/university	year	1768	91	22s
Tuition, 4-year private college/university	year	8729	91	22s
Tuition, 4-year public college/university, in-state	year	2622	91	22s
Energy and Fuels				
Coal	mil Btu	1.54	90	64s
Energy	mil Btu	8.32	90	64s
Energy exp/householder, 1-family unit	year	471	90	28r
Energy exp/householder, <1,000 sq ft heating area	year	430	90	28r
Energy exp/householder, 1,000-1,999 sq ft heating area	year	481	90	28r
Energy exp/householder, 2,000+ sq ft heating area	year	473	90	28r
Energy exp/householder, mobile home	year	430	90	28r
Energy exp/householder, multifamily	year	461	90	28r
Gas, natural	mil Btu	4.54	90	64s
Gas, natural	000 cu ft	5.28	91	46s
Gas, natural, exp	year	606	91	46s
Gasoline, unleaded regular	mil Btu	9.35	90	64s
Entertainment				
Miniature golf admission	adult	6.18	92	1r
Miniature golf admission	child	5.14	92	1r
Waterpark admission	adult	11.00	92	1r

Dayton, OH - continued

Item	Per	Value	Date	Ref.
Entertainment - continued				
Waterpark admission	child	8.55	92	1r
Funerals				
Casket, 18-gauge steel, velvet interior		1926.72	91	24r
Cosmetology, hair care, etc.		97.64	91	24r
Embalming		249.14	91	24r
Facility use for ceremony		208.59	91	24r
Hearse, local		130.12	91	24r
Limousine, local		104.66	91	24r
Remains to funeral home, transfer		93.61	91	24r
Service charge, professional		724.62	91	24r
Vault, concrete, non-metallic liner		734.53	91	24r
Viewing facilities, use		236.06	91	24r
Groceries				
Apples, Red Delicious	lb	0.77	4/93	16r
Bacon	lb	1.85	4/93	16r
Bananas	lb	0.46	4/93	16r
Beef, stew, boneless	lb	2.53	4/93	16r
Bologna, all beef or mixed	lb	2.19	4/93	16r
Bread, white, pan	lb	0.78	4/93	16r
Butter	lb	1.50	4/93	16r
Cabbage	lb	0.40	4/93	16r
Carrots, short trimmed and topped	lb	0.45	4/93	16r
Cheese, Cheddar	lb	3.47	4/93	16r
Chicken, fresh, whole	lb	0.84	4/93	16r
Chicken breast, bone-in	lb	1.94	4/93	16r
Chicken legs, bone-in	lb	1.02	4/93	16r
Chuck roast, graded and ungraded, ex USDA prime and choice	lb	2.43	4/93	16r
Chuck roast, USDA choice, bone-in	lb	2.11	4/93	16r
Chuck roast, USDA choice, boneless	lb	2.44	4/93	16r
Coffee, 100% ground roast, all sizes	lb	2.47	4/93	16r
Cookies, chocolate chip	lb	2.73	4/93	16r
Eggs, Grade A large	doz	0.93	4/93	16r
Flour, white, all purpose	lb	0.21	4/93	16r
Grapefruit	lb	0.45	4/93	16r
Grapes, Thompson Seedless	lb	1.46	4/93	16r
Ground beef, 100% beef	lb	1.63	4/93	16r
Ground beef, lean and extra lean	lb	2.08	4/93	16r
Ground chuck, 100% beef	lb	1.94	4/93	16r
Ham, boneless, excluding canned	lb	2.21	4/93	16r
Honey, jar	8 oz	0.97-1.25	92	5r
Honey, jar	lb	1.25-2.25	92	5r
Honey, squeeze bear	12-oz	1.25-1.99	92	5r
Ice cream, prepackaged, bulk, regular	1/2 gal	2.41	4/93	16r
Lemons	lb	0.82	4/93	16r
Lettuce, iceberg	lb	0.83	4/93	16r
Margarine, stick	lb	0.77	4/93	16r
Oranges, navel	lb	0.50	4/93	16r
Peanut butter, creamy, all sizes	lb	1.82	4/93	16r
Pears, Anjou	lb	0.85	4/93	16r
Pork chops, center cut, bone-in	lb	3.17	4/93	16r
Potato chips	16 oz	2.68	4/93	16r
Potatoes, white	lb	0.26	4/93	16r
Round roast, graded & ungraded, ex USDA prime & choice	lb	2.88	4/93	16r
Round roast, USDA choice, boneless	lb	2.96	4/93	16r
Shortening, vegetable oil blends	lb	0.79	4/93	16r
Spaghetti and macaroni	lb	0.76	4/93	16r
Steak, rib eye, USDA choice, boneless	lb	6.29	4/93	16r
Steak, round, USDA choice, boneless	lb	3.24	4/93	16r
Steak, sirloin, graded & ungraded, ex USDA prime & choice	lb	4.00	4/93	16r
Steak, sirloin, USDA choice, bone-in	lb	3.57	4/93	16r
Steak, sirloin, USDA choice, boneless	lb	4.17	4/93	16r
Steak, T-bone, USDA choice, bone-in	lb	5.60	4/93	16r
Strawberries, dry pint	12 oz	0.90	4/93	16r
Sugar, white	lb	0.36	4/93	16r
Sugar, white, 33-80 oz pk	lb	0.35	4/93	16r
Tomatoes, field grown	lb	0.99	4/93	16r
Tuna, chunk, light	lb	1.76	4/93	16r
Turkey, frozen, whole	lb	0.91	4/93	16r

Values are in dollars or fractions of dollars. In the column headed *Ref*, references are shown to sources. Each reference is followed by a letter. These refer to the geographical level for which data were reported: s=State, r=Region, and c=City or metro. The abbreviation *ex* is used to mean *except* or *excluding*; *exp* stands for expenditures. For other abbreviations and further explanations, please see the Introduction.

Dayton, OH - continued

Item	Per	Value	Date	Ref.
Health Care				
Childbirth, cesarean, hospital		4688	91	62r
Childbirth, cesarean, physician's fee		2053	91	62r
Childbirth, normal, hospital		2657	91	62r
Childbirth, normal, physician's fee		1492	91	62r
Medical plan per employee	year	3443	91	45r
Mental health care, exp	capita	37.60-53.67	90	38s
Mental health care, exp, state mental health agency	capita	40.93	90	38s
Mental health care, hospital psychiatric services, non-Federal, exp	capita	15.03	88	38s
Mental health care, mental health organization, multiservice, exp	capita	14.46	88	38s
Mental health care, psychiatric hospitals, private, exp	capita	7.93	88	38s
Mental health care, psychiatric out-patient clinics, freestanding, exp	capita	2.93	88	38s
Mental health care, psychiatric partial-care organizations, freestanding, exp	capita	0.32	88	38s
Mental health care, state and county mental hospitals, exp	capita	23.79	88	38s
Mental health care, VA medical centers, exp	capita	7.76	88	38s
Physician fee, family practice, first-visit		76.00	91	62r
Physician fee, family practice, revisit		33.00	91	62r
Physician fee, general practice, first-visit		61.00	91	62r
Physician fee, general practice, revisit		31.00	91	62r
Physician fee, general surgeon, first-visit		65.00	91	62r
Physician fee, general surgeon, revisit		35.00	91	62r
Physician fee, internal medicine, first-visit		91.00	91	62r
Physician fee, internal medicine, revisit		40.00	91	62r
Physician fee, median, neurosurgeon, first-visit		106.00	91	62r
Physician fee, median, nonsurgical specialist, first-visit		90.00	91	62r
Physician fee, median, orthopedic surgeon, first-visit		83.00	91	62r
Physician fee, median, surgical specialist, first-visit		61.00	91	62r
Physician fee, neurosurgeon, revisit		41.00	91	62r
Physician fee, nonsurgical specialist, revisit		40.00	91	62r
Physician fee, obstetrics/gynecology, first-visit		61.00	91	62r
Physician fee, obstetrics/gynecology, revisit		40.00	91	62r
Physician fee, orthopedic surgeon, revisit		41.00	91	62r
Physician fee, pediatrician, first-visit		46.00	91	62r
Physician fee, pediatrician, revisit		33.00	91	62r
Physician fee, surgical specialist, revisit		36.00	91	62r
Substance abuse, hospital ancillary charge	incident	940	90	70s
Substance abuse, hospital physician charge	incident	380	90	70s
Substance abuse, hospital room and board	incident	5410	90	70s
Insurance and Pensions				
Auto insurance, private passenger	year	547.38	91	63s
Taxes				
Tax, cigarette	pack	18	91	77s
Tax, gasoline	gal	21	91	77s
Taxes, state	capita	1056	91	77s
Transportation				
Driver's license fee		5.00	12/90	43s
Utilities				
Electricity	mil Btu	17.33	90	64s

Daytona Beach, FL

Item	Per	Value	Date	Ref.
Child Care				
Child care fee, average, center	hour	1.29	90	65r
Child care fee, average, nonregulated family day care	hour	0.89	90	65r
Child care fee, average, regulated family day care	hour	1.32	90	65r
Communications				
Long-distance telephone service, day, initial minute, 0-100 miles	min	0.15-0.20	91	12s
Long-distance telephone service, day, additional minute, 0-100 miles	min	0.08-0.20	91	12s
Long-distance telephone service, evenings/weekends, 0-100 mi, initial minute	min	0.09-0.12	91	12s
Long-distance telephone service, evenings/weekends, 0-100 mi, additional minute	min	0.05-0.12	91	12s
Education				
Board, 4-yr private college/university	year	1924	91	22s
Board, 4-yr public college/university	year	1955	91	22s
Expenditures, local gov't, public elementary/secondary	pupil	5235	92	20s
Room, 4-year private college/university	year	1904	91	22s
Room, 4-year public college/university	year	1510	91	22s
Tuition, 2-year private college/university	year	4751	91	22s
Tuition, 2-year public college/university	year	788	91	22s
Tuition, 4-year private college/university	year	7992	91	22s
Tuition, 4-year public college/university, in-state	year	1337	91	22s
Energy and Fuels				
Coal	mil Btu	1.85	90	64s
Energy	mil Btu	10.58	90	64s
Energy exp/householder, 1-family unit	year	487	90	28r
Energy exp/householder, <1,000 sq ft heating area	year	393	90	28r
Energy exp/householder, 1,000-1,999 sq ft heating area	year	442	90	28r
Energy exp/householder, 2,000+ sq ft heating area	year	577	90	28r
Energy exp/householder, mobile home	year	366	90	28r
Energy exp/householder, multifamily	year	382	90	28r
Gas, natural	mil Btu	3.21	90	64s
Gas, natural	000 cu ft	8.98	91	46s
Gas, natural, exp	year	248	91	46s
Gasoline, unleaded regular	mil Btu	8.85	90	64s
Entertainment				
Miniature golf admission	adult	6.18	92	1r
Miniature golf admission	child	5.14	92	1r
Waterpark admission	adult	11.00	92	1r
Waterpark admission	child	8.55	92	1r
Funerals				
Casket, 18-gauge steel, velvet interior		2029.08	91	24r
Cosmetology, hair care, etc.		75.10	91	24r
Embalming		249.24	91	24r
Facility use for ceremony		162.27	91	24r
Hearse, local		114.04	91	24r
Limousine, local		88.57	91	24r
Remains to funeral home, transfer		92.61	91	24r
Service charge, professional		682.42	91	24r
Vault, concrete, non-metallic liner		798.70	91	24r
Viewing facilities, use		163.86	91	24r
Groceries				
Apples, Red Delicious	lb	0.79	4/93	16r
Bacon	lb	1.75	4/93	16r
Bananas	lb	0.42	4/93	16r
Beef, stew, boneless	lb	2.61	4/93	16r
Bologna, all beef or mixed	lb	2.24	4/93	16r
Bread, white, pan	lb	0.64	4/93	16r
Bread, whole wheat, pan	lb	0.96	4/93	16r
Cabbage	lb	0.37	4/93	16r

Values are in dollars or fractions of dollars. In the column headed *Ref*, references are shown to sources. Each reference is followed by a letter. These refer to the geographical level for which data were reported: s=State, r=Region, and c=City or metro. The abbreviation *ex* is used to mean *except* or *excluding*; *exp* stands for expenditures. For other abbreviations and further explanations, please see the Introduction.

Daytona Beach, FL - continued

Item	Per	Value	Date	Ref.
Groceries				
Carrots, short trimmed and topped	lb	0.47	4/93	16r
Celery	lb	0.64	4/93	16r
Cheese, American	lb	2.98	4/93	16r
Cheese, Cheddar	lb	3.28	4/93	16r
Chicken, fresh, whole	lb	0.77	4/93	16r
Chicken breast, bone-in	lb	1.92	4/93	16r
Chicken legs, bone-in	lb	1.06	4/93	16r
Chuck roast, graded and ungraded, ex USDA prime and choice	lb	2.40	4/93	16r
Chuck roast, USDA choice, bone-in	lb	2.19	4/93	16r
Chuck roast, USDA choice, boneless	lb	2.38	4/93	16r
Coffee, 100% ground roast, all sizes	lb	2.48	4/93	16r
Crackers, soda, salted	lb	1.15	4/93	16r
Eggs, Grade A large	doz	0.96	4/93	16r
Flour, white, all purpose	lb	0.24	4/93	16r
Frankfurters, all meat or all beef	lb	2.01	4/93	16r
Grapefruit	lb	0.44	4/93	16r
Grapes, Thompson Seedless	lb	1.40	4/93	16r
Ground beef, 100% beef	lb	1.58	4/93	16r
Ground beef, lean and extra lean	lb	2.09	4/93	16r
Ground chuck, 100% beef	lb	1.98	4/93	16r
Ham, boneless, excluding canned	lb	2.89	4/93	16r
Ham, picnic, shoulder, bone-in, smoked	lb	1.02	4/93	16r
Ham, rump or steak half, bone-in, smoked	lb	1.48	4/93	16r
Ice cream, prepackaged, bulk, regular	1/2 gal	2.41	4/93	16r
Lemons	lb	1.05	4/93	16r
Lettuce, iceberg	lb	0.81	4/93	16r
Margarine, stick	lb	0.88	4/93	16r
Oranges, navel	lb	0.55	4/93	16r
Pears, Anjou	lb	0.92	4/93	16r
Pork chops, center cut, bone-in	lb	3.13	4/93	16r
Potato chips	16 oz	2.94	4/93	16r
Potatoes, white	lb	0.43	4/93	16r
Rib roast, USDA choice, bone-in	lb	4.63	4/93	16r
Rice, white, long grain, uncooked	lb	0.45	4/93	16r
Round roast, graded & ungraded, ex USDA prime & choice	lb	3.03	4/93	16r
Round roast, USDA choice, boneless	lb	3.09	4/93	16r
Sausage, fresh, loose	lb	2.08	4/93	16r
Short ribs, bone-in	lb	2.66	4/93	16r
Shortening, vegetable oil blends	lb	0.69	4/93	16r
Spaghetti and macaroni	lb	0.81	4/93	16r
Steak, rib eye, USDA choice, boneless	lb	6.24	4/93	16r
Steak, round, graded & ungraded, ex USDA prime & choice	lb	3.31	4/93	16r
Steak, round, USDA choice, boneless	lb	3.34	4/93	16r
Steak, sirloin, graded & ungraded, ex USDA prime & choice	lb	4.19	4/93	16r
Steak, sirloin, USDA choice, boneless	lb	4.46	4/93	16r
Steak, T-bone, USDA choice, bone-in	lb	5.25	4/93	16r
Strawberries, dry pint	12 oz	0.92	4/93	16r
Sugar, white	lb	0.39	4/93	16r
Sugar, white, 33-80 oz pk	lb	0.38	4/93	16r
Tomatoes, field grown	lb	0.88	4/93	16r
Tuna, chunk, light	lb	1.79	4/93	16r
Turkey, frozen, whole	lb	1.04	4/93	16r
Yogurt, natural, fruit flavored	1/2 pint	0.57	4/93	16r
Health Care				
Childbirth, cesarean, hospital		5034	91	62r
Childbirth, cesarean, physician's fee		2053	91	62r
Childbirth, normal, hospital		2712	91	62r
Childbirth, normal, physician's fee		1492	91	62r
Medical plan per employee	year	3495	91	45r
Mental health care, exp	capita	28.84-37.59	90	38s
Mental health care, exp, state mental health agency	capita	37.49	90	38s
Mental health care, hospital psychiatric services, non-Federal, exp	capita	9.11	88	38s
Mental health care, mental health organization, multiservice, exp	capita	16.21	88	38s

Daytona Beach, FL - continued

Item	Per	Value	Date	Ref.
Health Care - continued				
Mental health care, psychiatric hospitals, private, exp	capita	22.26	88	38s
Mental health care, psychiatric out-patient clinics, freestanding, exp	capita	0.89	88	38s
Mental health care, psychiatric partial-care organizations, freestanding, exp	capita	0.41	88	38s
Mental health care, state and county mental hospitals, exp	capita	16.25	88	38s
Mental health care, VA medical centers, exp	capita	1.69	88	38s
Physician fee, family practice, first-visit		75.00	91	62r
Physician fee, family practice, revisit		34.00	91	62r
Physician fee, general practice, first-visit		61.00	91	62r
Physician fee, general practice, revisit		32.00	91	62r
Physician fee, general surgeon, first-visit		64.00	91	62r
Physician fee, general surgeon, revisit		40.00	91	62r
Physician fee, internal medicine, first-visit		98.00	91	62r
Physician fee, internal medicine, revisit		40.00	91	62r
Physician fee, median, neurosurgeon, first-visit		130.00	91	62r
Physician fee, median, nonsurgical specialist, first-visit		95.00	91	62r
Physician fee, median, orthopedic surgeon, first-visit		91.00	91	62r
Physician fee, median, plastic surgeon, first-visit		66.00	91	62r
Physician fee, median, surgical specialist, first-visit		62.00	91	62r
Physician fee, neurosurgeon, revisit		50.00	91	62r
Physician fee, nonsurgical specialist, revisit		40.00	91	62r
Physician fee, obstetrics/gynecology, first-visit		64.00	91	62r
Physician fee, obstetrics/gynecology, revisit		41.00	91	62r
Physician fee, orthopedic surgeon, revisit		40.00	91	62r
Physician fee, pediatrician, first-visit		49.00	91	62r
Physician fee, pediatrician, revisit		33.00	91	62r
Physician fee, plastic surgeon, revisit		43.00	91	62r
Physician fee, surgical specialist, revisit		37.00	91	62r
Substance abuse, hospital ancillary charge	incident	1390	90	70s
Substance abuse, hospital physician charge	incident	770	90	70s
Substance abuse, hospital room and board	incident	5600	90	70s
Insurance and Pensions				
Auto insurance, private passenger	year	727.60	91	63s
Taxes				
Tax, cigarette	pack	33.90	91	77s
Tax, gasoline	gal	11.60	91	77s
Taxes, state	capita	1037	91	77s
Transportation				
Driver's license fee		15.00	12/90	43s
Travel				
Business travel	day	193.00	4/93	89r
Utilities				
Electricity	mil Btu	20.62	90	64s

DeKalb, IL

Item	Per	Value	Date	Ref.
Alcoholic Beverages				
Beer, Miller Lite or Budweiser, 12-oz containers	6 pack	3.12	4Q 92	4c
Liquor, J & B Scotch	750 ml	14.62	4Q 92	4c
Wine, Gallo Chablis blanc, 1.5 liter	bottle	4.69	4Q 92	4c
Clothing				
Jeans, man's denim		28.65	4Q 92	4c
Shirt, man's dress shirt		26.46	4Q 92	4c
Undervest, boy's size 10-14, cotton	3	3.87	4Q 92	4c

Values are in dollars or fractions of dollars. In the column headed *Ref*, references are shown to sources. Each reference is followed by a letter. These refer to the geographical level for which data were reported: s=State, r=Region, and c=City or metro. The abbreviation *ex* is used to mean *except* or *excluding*; *exp* stands for expenditures. For other abbreviations and further explanations, please see the Introduction.

DeKalb, IL - continued

Item	Per	Value	Date	Ref.
Communications				
Newspaper subscription, daily and Sunday home delivery, large-city	month	15.22	4Q 92	4c
Telephone bill, family of four	month	34.65	4Q 92	4c
Energy and Fuels				
Energy, combined forms, 1,800 sq ft heating area	month	129.39	4Q 92	4c
Energy, exc electricity, 1,800 sq ft heating area	month	40.85	4Q 92	4c
Gasoline, motor	gal	1.12	4Q 92	4c
Entertainment				
Bowling, evening rate	game	1.85	4Q 92	4c
Monopoly game, Parker Brothers', No. 9		9.83	4Q 92	4c
Movie	admission	4.25	4Q 92	4c
Tennis balls, yellow, Wilson or Penn, 3	can	1.84	4Q 92	4c
Groceries				
Babyfood, strained vegetables, lowest price	4-4.5 oz jar	0.38	4Q 92	4c
Bananas	lb	0.58	4Q 92	4c
Bread, white	24 oz	0.77	4Q 92	4c
Cheese, Kraft grated Parmesan	8-oz canister	3.19	4Q 92	4c
Chicken, fryer, whole	lb	0.66	4Q 92	4c
Cigarettes, Winston	carton	18.24	4Q 92	4c
Coffee, vacuum-packed	13-oz can	2.26	4Q 92	4c
Corn, frozen	10 oz	0.69	4Q 92	4c
Corn Flakes, Kellogg's or Post Toasties	18 oz	1.74	4Q 92	4c
Eggs, Grade A large	doz	0.71	4Q 92	4c
Ground beef or hamburger	lb	1.69	4Q 92	4c
Lettuce, iceberg	head	0.81	4Q 92	4c
Margarine, Blue Bonnet or Parkay cubes	lb	0.68	4Q 92	4c
Milk, whole	1/2 gal	1.56	4Q 92	4c
Orange juice, Minute Maid frozen	12-oz can	1.53	4Q 92	4c
Peaches	29-oz can	1.43	4Q 92	4c
Peas Sweet, Del Monte or Green Giant	15-17 oz can	0.71	4Q 92	4c
Potatoes, white or red	10-lb sack	3.09	4Q 92	4c
Sausage, Jimmy Dean, 100% pork	lb	2.74	4Q 92	4c
Shortening, vegetable, Crisco	3-lb can	2.32	4Q 92	4c
Soft drink, Coca Cola	2 liter	0.96	4Q 92	4c
Steak, T-bone	lb	4.36	4Q 92	4c
Sugar, cane or beet	4 lb	1.35	4Q 92	4c
Tomatoes, Hunt's or Del Monte	14.5-oz can	0.81	4Q 92	4c
Tuna, chunk, light	6.125-6.5 oz can	0.59	4Q 92	4c
Health Care				
Analgesic, Aspirin, Bayer, 325 mg tablets	100	4.10	4Q 92	4c
Dentist's fee, adult teeth cleaning and periodic oral exam	visit	40.00	4Q 92	4c
Doctor's fee, routine exam, established patient	visit	41.25	4Q 92	4c
Hospital care, semiprivate room	day	299.00	4Q 92	4c
Household Goods				
Appliance repair, home, service call, washing machine	min labor charge	37.33	4Q 92	4c
Laundry detergent, Tide Ultra, Bold, or Cheer	42 oz	3.86	4Q 92	4c
Tissues, facial, Kleenex brand	175-count box	1.09	4Q 92	4c

DeKalb, IL - continued

Item	Per	Value	Date	Ref.
Housing				
House, 1,800 sq ft, 8,000 sq ft lot, new, urban	total	124850	4Q 92	4c
House payment, principal and interest, 25% down payment	month	679	4Q 92	4c
Mortgage rate, incl. points & origination fee, 30-year fixed or adjustable rate	percent	7.88	4Q 92	4c
Rent, apartment, 2 bedrooms - 1-1/2 to 2 baths, unfurnished, 950 sq ft, water	month	525	4Q 92	4c
Personal Goods				
Shampoo, Alberto VO5	15 oz	1.16	4Q 92	4c
Toothpaste, Crest or Colgate	6-7 oz	2.08	4Q 92	4c
Personal Services				
Dry cleaning, man's 2-piece suit		5.08	4Q 92	4c
Haircare, woman's shampoo, trim and blow-dry		19.25	4Q 92	4c
Haircut, man's barbershop, no styling		7.70	4Q 92	4c
Restaurant Food				
Chicken, fried, thigh and drumstick		2.38	4Q 92	4c
Hamburger with cheese	1/4 lb	1.75	4Q 92	4c
Pizza, Pizza Hut or Pizza Inn, cheese, thin crust	12-13 in	7.59	4Q 92	4c
Transportation				
Tire balance, computer or spin balance, front	wheel	5.20	4Q 92	4c
Utilities				
Electricity, partial electric and other energy, 1,800 sq ft living area new home	month	88.54	4Q 92	4c

Decatur, IL

Item	Per	Value	Date	Ref.
Composite ACCRA index		94.40	4Q 92	4c
Alcoholic Beverages				
Beer, Miller Lite or Budweiser, 12-oz containers	6 pack	3.85	4Q 92	4c
Liquor, J & B Scotch	750 ml	14.74	4Q 92	4c
Wine, Gallo Chablis blanc, 1.5 liter	bottle	4.56	4Q 92	4c
Child Care				
Child care fee, average, center	hour	1.63	90	65r
Child care fee, average, nonregulated family day care	hour	1.83	90	65r
Child care fee, average, regulated family day care	hour	1.42	90	65r
Clothing				
Jeans, man's denim		34.99	4Q 92	4c
Shirt, man's dress shirt		24.87	4Q 92	4c
Undervest, boy's size 10-14, cotton	3	3.72	4Q 92	4c
Communications				
Long-distance telephone service, day, initial minute, 0-100 miles	min	0.10-0.34	91	12s
Long-distance telephone service, day, additional minute, 0-100 miles	min	0.04-0.16	91	12s
Long-distance telephone service, evenings/weekends, 0-100 mi, initial minute	min	0.06-0.20	91	12s
Long-distance telephone service, evenings/weekends, 0-100 mi, additional minute	min	0.02-0.10	91	12s
Newspaper subscription, daily and Sunday home delivery, large-city	month	12.50	4Q 92	4c
Telephone, residential, private line, rotary, unlimited calling	month	19.46	10/91	78c
Telephone bill, family of four	month	17.32	4Q 92	4c
Education				
Board, 4-yr private college/university	year	1797	91	22s
Board, 4-yr public college/university	year	1857	91	22s
Expenditures, local gov't, public elementary/secondary	pupil	5248	92	20s
Room, 4-year private college/university	year	2095	91	22s

Values are in dollars or fractions of dollars. In the column headed *Ref*, references are shown to sources. Each reference is followed by a letter. These refer to the geographical level for which data were reported: s=State, r=Region, and c=City or metro. The abbreviation *ex* is used to mean *except* or *excluding*; *exp* stands for expenditures. For other abbreviations and further explanations, please see the Introduction.

Decatur, IL - continued

Item	Per	Value	Date	Ref.
Education				
Room, 4-year public college/university	year	1454	91	22s
Tuition, 2-year private college/university	year	5279	91	22s
Tuition, 2-year public college/university	year	906	91	22s
Tuition, 4-year private college/university	year	8853	91	22s
Tuition, 4-year public college/university, in-state	year	2465	91	22s
Energy and Fuels				
Coal	mil Btu	1.72	90	64s
Energy	mil Btu	8.74	90	64s
Energy, combined forms, 1,800 sq ft heating area	month	122.42	4Q 92	4c
Energy, exc electricity, 1,800 sq ft heating area	month	41.52	4Q 92	4c
Energy exp/householder, 1-family unit	year	471	90	28r
Energy exp/householder, <1,000 sq ft heating area	year	430	90	28r
Energy exp/householder, 1,000-1,999 sq ft heating area	year	481	90	28r
Energy exp/householder, 2,000+ sq ft heating area	year	473	90	28r
Energy exp/householder, mobile home	year	430	90	28r
Energy exp/householder, multifamily	year	461	90	28r
Gas, cooking, 10 therms	month	13.06	92	56c
Gas, cooking, 30 therms	month	22.18	92	56c
Gas, cooking, 50 therms	month	31.31	92	56c
Gas, heating, winter, 100 therms	month	53.24	92	56c
Gas, heating, winter, average use	month	116.01	92	56c
Gas, natural	mil Btu	4.57	90	64s
Gas, natural	000 cu ft	4.95	91	46s
Gas, natural, exp	year	696	91	46s
Gasoline, motor	gal	1.08	4Q 92	4c
Gasoline, unleaded regular	mil Btu	9.35	90	64s
Entertainment				
Bowling, evening rate	game	1.73	4Q 92	4c
Miniature golf admission	adult	6.18	92	1r
Miniature golf admission	child	5.14	92	1r
Monopoly game, Parker Brothers', No. 9		11.65	4Q 92	4c
Movie	admission	4.50	4Q 92	4c
Tennis balls, yellow, Wilson or Penn, 3	can	2.58	4Q 92	4c
Waterpark admission	adult	11.00	92	1r
Waterpark admission	child	8.55	92	1r
Funerals				
Casket, 18-gauge steel, velvet interior		1926.72	91	24r
Cosmetology, hair care, etc.		97.64	91	24r
Embalming		249.14	91	24r
Facility use for ceremony		208.59	91	24r
Hearse, local		130.12	91	24r
Limousine, local		104.66	91	24r
Remains to funeral home, transfer		93.61	91	24r
Service charge, professional		724.62	91	24r
Vault, concrete, non-metallic liner		734.53	91	24r
Viewing facilities, use		236.06	91	24r
Goods and Services				
ACCRA Index, Miscellaneous Goods and Services		98.70	4Q 92	4c
Groceries				
ACCRA Index, Groceries		97.60	4Q 92	4c
Apples, Red Delicious	lb	0.77	4/93	16r
Babyfood, strained vegetables, lowest price	4-4.5 oz jar	0.29	4Q 92	4c
Bacon	lb	1.85	4/93	16r
Bananas	lb	0.42	4Q 92	4c
Bananas	lb	0.46	4/93	16r
Beef, stew, boneless	lb	2.53	4/93	16r
Bologna, all beef or mixed	lb	2.19	4/93	16r
Bread, white	24 oz	0.69	4Q 92	4c
Bread, white, pan	lb	0.78	4/93	16r

Decatur, IL - continued

Item	Per	Value	Date	Ref.
Groceries - continued				
Butter	lb	1.50	4/93	16r
Cabbage	lb	0.40	4/93	16r
Carrots, short trimmed and topped	lb	0.45	4/93	16r
Cheese, Cheddar	lb	3.47	4/93	16r
Cheese, Kraft grated Parmesan	8-oz canister	3.32	4Q 92	4c
Chicken, fresh, whole	lb	0.84	4/93	16r
Chicken, fryer, whole	lb	0.49	4Q 92	4c
Chicken breast, bone-in	lb	1.94	4/93	16r
Chicken legs, bone-in	lb	1.02	4/93	16r
Chuck roast, graded and ungraded, ex USDA prime and choice	lb	2.43	4/93	16r
Chuck roast, USDA choice, bone-in	lb	2.11	4/93	16r
Chuck roast, USDA choice, boneless	lb	2.44	4/93	16r
Cigarettes, Winston	carton	18.85	4Q 92	4c
Coffee, 100% ground roast, all sizes	lb	2.47	4/93	16r
Coffee, vacuum-packed	13-oz can	2.20	4Q 92	4c
Cookies, chocolate chip	lb	2.73	4/93	16r
Corn, frozen	10 oz	0.63	4Q 92	4c
Corn Flakes, Kellogg's or Post Toasties	18 oz	1.84	4Q 92	4c
Eggs, Grade A large	doz	0.76	4Q 92	4c
Eggs, Grade A large	doz	0.93	4/93	16r
Flour, white, all purpose	lb	0.21	4/93	16r
Grapefruit	lb	0.45	4/93	16r
Grapes, Thompson Seedless	lb	1.46	4/93	16r
Ground beef, 100% beef	lb	1.63	4/93	16r
Ground beef, lean and extra lean	lb	2.08	4/93	16r
Ground beef or hamburger	lb	1.49	4Q 92	4c
Ground chuck, 100% beef	lb	1.94	4/93	16r
Ham, boneless, excluding canned	lb	2.21	4/93	16r
Honey, jar	8 oz	0.97-1.25	92	5r
Honey, jar	lb	1.25-2.25	92	5r
Honey, squeeze bear	12-oz	1.25-1.99	92	5r
Ice cream, prepackaged, bulk, regular	1/2 gal	2.41	4/93	16r
Lemons	lb	0.82	4/93	16r
Lettuce, iceberg	head	0.86	4Q 92	4c
Lettuce, iceberg	lb	0.83	4/93	16r
Margarine, Blue Bonnet or Parkay cubes	lb	0.67	4Q 92	4c
Margarine, stick	lb	0.77	4/93	16r
Milk, whole	1/2 gal	1.46	4Q 92	4c
Orange juice, Minute Maid frozen	12-oz can	1.64	4Q 92	4c
Oranges, navel	lb	0.50	4/93	16r
Peaches	29-oz can	1.44	4Q 92	4c
Peanut butter, creamy, all sizes	lb	1.82	4/93	16r
Pears, Anjou	lb	0.85	4/93	16r
Peas Sweet, Del Monte or Green Giant	15-17 oz can	0.66	4Q 92	4c
Pork chops, center cut, bone-in	lb	3.17	4/93	16r
Potato chips	16 oz	2.68	4/93	16r
Potatoes, white	lb	0.26	4/93	16r
Potatoes, white or red	10-lb sack	1.79	4Q 92	4c
Round roast, graded & ungraded, ex USDA prime & choice	lb	2.88	4/93	16r
Round roast, USDA choice, boneless	lb	2.96	4/93	16r
Sausage, Jimmy Dean, 100% pork	lb	2.36	4Q 92	4c
Shortening, vegetable oil blends	lb	0.79	4/93	16r
Shortening, vegetable, Crisco	3-lb can	2.14	4Q 92	4c
Soft drink, Coca Cola	2 liter	1.09	4Q 92	4c
Spaghetti and macaroni	lb	0.76	4/93	16r
Steak, rib eye, USDA choice, boneless	lb	6.29	4/93	16r
Steak, round, USDA choice, boneless	lb	3.24	4/93	16r
Steak, sirloin, graded & ungraded, ex USDA prime & choice	lb	4.00	4/93	16r
Steak, sirloin, USDA choice, bone-in	lb	3.57	4/93	16r
Steak, sirloin, USDA choice, boneless	lb	4.17	4/93	16r
Steak, T-bone	lb	5.12	4Q 92	4c

Values are in dollars or fractions of dollars. In the column headed *Ref*, references are shown to sources. Each reference is followed by a letter. These refer to the geographical level for which data were reported: s=State, r=Region, and c=City or metro. The abbreviation *ex* is used to mean *except* or *excluding*; *exp* stands for expenditures. For other abbreviations and further explanations, please see the Introduction.

Decatur, IL - continued

Item	Per	Value	Date	Ref.
Groceries				
Steak, T-bone, USDA choice, bone-in	lb	5.60	4/93	16r
Strawberries, dry pint	12 oz	0.90	4/93	16r
Sugar, cane or beet	4 lb	1.25	4Q 92	4c
Sugar, white	lb	0.36	4/93	16r
Sugar, white, 33-80 oz pk	lb	0.35	4/93	16r
Tomatoes, field grown	lb	0.99	4/93	16r
Tomatoes, Hunt's or Del Monte	14.5-oz can	0.84	4Q 92	4c
Tuna, chunk, light	6.125-6.5 oz can	0.61	4Q 92	4c
Tuna, chunk, light	lb	1.76	4/93	16r
Turkey, frozen, whole	lb	0.91	4/93	16r
Health Care				
ACCRA Index, Health Care		87.90	4Q 92	4c
Analgesic, Aspirin, Bayer, 325 mg tablets	100	4.22	4Q 92	4c
Childbirth, cesarean, hospital		4688	91	62r
Childbirth, cesarean, physician's fee		2053	91	62r
Childbirth, normal, hospital		2657	91	62r
Childbirth, normal, physician's fee		1492	91	62r
Dentist's fee, adult teeth cleaning and periodic oral exam	visit	39.86	4Q 92	4c
Doctor's fee, routine exam, established patient	visit	33.67	4Q 92	4c
Hospital care, semiprivate room	day	284.00	4Q 92	4c
Medical insurance premium, per employee, small group comprehensive	month	313.90	10/91	25c
Medical plan per employee	year	3443	91	45r
Mental health care, exp	capita	28.84-37.59	90	38s
Mental health care, exp, state mental health agency	capita	34.43	90	38s
Mental health care, hospital psychiatric services, non-Federal, exp	capita	18.46	88	38s
Mental health care, mental health organization, multiservice, exp	capita	11.97	88	38s
Mental health care, psychiatric hospitals, private, exp	capita	7.84	88	38s
Mental health care, psychiatric out-patient clinics, freestanding, exp	capita	3.21	88	38s
Mental health care, psychiatric partial-care organizations, freestanding, exp	capita	0.51	88	38s
Mental health care, state and county mental hospitals, exp	capita	18.11	88	38s
Mental health care, VA medical centers, exp	capita	3.69	88	38s
Physician fee, family practice, first-visit		76.00	91	62r
Physician fee, family practice, revisit		33.00	91	62r
Physician fee, general practice, first-visit		61.00	91	62r
Physician fee, general practice, revisit		31.00	91	62r
Physician fee, general surgeon, first-visit		65.00	91	62r
Physician fee, general surgeon, revisit		35.00	91	62r
Physician fee, internal medicine, first-visit		91.00	91	62r
Physician fee, internal medicine, revisit		40.00	91	62r
Physician fee, median, neurosurgeon, first-visit		106.00	91	62r
Physician fee, median, nonsurgical specialist, first-visit		90.00	91	62r
Physician fee, median, orthopedic surgeon, first-visit		83.00	91	62r
Physician fee, median, surgical specialist, first-visit		61.00	91	62r
Physician fee, neurosurgeon, revisit		41.00	91	62r
Physician fee, nonsurgical specialist, revisit		40.00	91	62r
Physician fee, obstetrics/gynecology, first-visit		61.00	91	62r
Physician fee, obstetrics/gynecology, revisit		40.00	91	62r
Physician fee, orthopedic surgeon, revisit		41.00	91	62r
Physician fee, pediatrician, first-visit		46.00	91	62r
Physician fee, pediatrician, revisit		33.00	91	62r
Physician fee, surgical specialist, revisit		36.00	91	62r
Prescription drug co-pay, Medicaid	month	25.00	91	21s

Decatur, IL - continued

Item	Per	Value	Date	Ref.
Health Care - continued				
Substance abuse, hospital ancillary charge	incident	1310	90	70s
Substance abuse, hospital physician charge	incident	540	90	70s
Substance abuse, hospital room and board	incident	6150	90	70s
Household Goods				
Appliance repair, home, service call, washing machine	min labor charge	34.50	4Q 92	4c
Laundry detergent, Tide Ultra, Bold, or Cheer	42 oz	4.10	4Q 92	4c
Tissues, facial, Kleenex brand	175-count box	1.01	4Q 92	4c
Housing				
ACCRA Index, Housing		82.80	4Q 92	4c
House, 1,800 sq ft, 8,000 sq ft lot, new, urban	total	86000	4Q 92	4c
House payment, principal and interest, 25% down payment	month	489	4Q 92	4c
Mortgage rate, incl. points & origination fee, 30-year fixed or adjustable rate	percent	8.35	4Q 92	4c
Rent, apartment, 2 bedrooms - 1-1/2 to 2 baths, unfurnished, 950 sq ft, water	month	455	4Q 92	4c
Rental unit, 1 bedroom	month	403	93	23c
Rental unit, 2 bedroom	month	476	93	23c
Rental unit, 3 bedroom	month	598	93	23c
Rental unit, 4 bedroom	month	668	93	23c
Rental unit, efficiency	month	332	93	23c
Insurance and Pensions				
Auto insurance, private passenger	year	621.37	91	63s
Personal Goods				
Shampoo, Alberto VO5	15 oz	1.06	4Q 92	4c
Toothpaste, Crest or Colgate	6-7 oz	1.25	4Q 92	4c
Personal Services				
Dry cleaning, man's 2-piece suit		6.25	4Q 92	4c
Haircare, woman's shampoo, trim and blow-dry		15.50	4Q 92	4c
Haircut, man's barbershop, no styling		7.75	4Q 92	4c
Restaurant Food				
Chicken, fried, thigh and drumstick		2.18	4Q 92	4c
Hamburger with cheese	1/4 lb	1.69	4Q 92	4c
Pizza, Pizza Hut or Pizza Inn, cheese, thin crust	12-13 in	7.79	4Q 92	4c
Taxes				
Tax, cigarette	pack	30	91	77s
Tax, gasoline	gal	19	91	77s
Taxes, state	capita	1151	91	77s
Transportation				
ACCRA Index, Transportation		96.90	4Q 92	4c
Bus fare	one-way	0.50	3/93	2c
Driver's license fee		10.00	12/90	43s
Tire balance, computer or spin balance, front	wheel	6.40	4Q 92	4c
Vehicle registration and license plate	multi-year	48.00	93	52s
Utilities				
ACCRA Index, Utilities		109.80	4Q 92	4c
Electricity	mil Btu	22.02	90	64s
Electricity, partial electric and other energy, 1,800 sq ft living area new home	month	80.90	4Q 92	4c
Electricity, winter, 250 KWh	month	32.52	92	55c
Electricity, winter, 500 KWh	month	50.55	92	55c
Electricity, winter, 750 KWh	month	68.07	92	55c
Electricity, winter, 1000 KWh	month	85.59	92	55c

Values are in dollars or fractions of dollars. In the column headed *Ref*, references are shown to sources. Each reference is followed by a letter. These refer to the geographical level for which data were reported: s=State, r=Region, and c=City or metro. The abbreviation *ex* is used to mean *except* or *excluding*; *exp* stands for expenditures. For other abbreviations and further explanations, please see the Introduction.

Decatur-Hartselle, AL

Item	Per	Value	Date	Ref.
Composite ACCRA index		90.80	4Q 92	4c
Alcoholic Beverages				
Beer, Miller Lite or Budweiser, 12-oz containers	6 pack	4.41	4Q 92	4c
Liquor, J & B Scotch	750 ml	19.99	4Q 92	4c
Wine, Gallo Chablis blanc, 1.5 liter	bottle	6.31	4Q 92	4c
Child Care				
Child care fee, average, center	hour	1.29	90	65r
Child care fee, average, nonregulated family day care	hour	0.89	90	65r
Child care fee, average, regulated family day care	hour	1.32	90	65r
Clothing				
Jeans, man's denim		31.59	4Q 92	4c
Shirt, man's dress shirt		22.12	4Q 92	4c
Undervest, boy's size 10-14, cotton	3	3.33	4Q 92	4c
Communications				
Long-distance telephone service, day, initial minute, 0-100 miles	min	0.11-0.36	91	12s
Long-distance telephone service, day, additional minute, 0-100 miles	min	0.09-0.26	91	12s
Long-distance telephone service, evenings/weekends, 0-100 mi, initial minute	min	0.04-0.14	91	12s
Long-distance telephone service, evenings/weekends, 0-100 mi, additional minute	min	0.04-0.10	91	12s
Newspaper subscription, daily and Sunday home delivery, large-city	month	8.00	4Q 92	4c
Telephone bill, family of four	month	24.34	4Q 92	4c
Education				
Board, 4-yr private college/university	year	1795	91	22s
Board, 4-yr public college/university	year	1469	91	22s
Expenditures, local gov't, public elementary/secondary	pupil	3675	92	20s
Room, 4-year private college/university	year	1340	91	22s
Room, 4-year public college/university	year	1295	91	22s
Tuition, 2-year private college/university	year	4148	91	22s
Tuition, 2-year public college/university	year	689	91	22s
Tuition, 4-year private college/university	year	5942	91	22s
Tuition, 4-year public college/university, in-state	year	1593	91	22s
Energy and Fuels				
Coal	mil Btu	1.83	90	64s
Energy	mil Btu	7.92	90	64s
Energy, combined forms, 1,800 sq ft heating area	month	93.67	4Q 92	4c
Energy exp/householder, 1-family unit	year	403	90	28r
Energy exp/householder, <1,000 sq ft heating area	year	342	90	28r
Energy exp/householder, 1,000-1,999 sq ft heating area	year	388	90	28r
Energy exp/householder, 2,000+ sq ft heating area	year	434	90	28r
Energy exp/householder, mobile home	year	320	90	28r
Energy exp/householder, multifamily	year	338	90	28r
Gas, natural	mil Btu	4.07	90	64s
Gas, natural	000 cu ft	7.05	91	46s
Gas, natural, exp	year	461	91	46s
Gasoline, motor	gal	1.16	4Q 92	4c
Gasoline, unleaded regular	mil Btu	8.96	90	64s
Entertainment				
Bowling, evening rate	game	2.13	4Q 92	4c
Miniature golf admission	adult	6.18	92	1r
Miniature golf admission	child	5.14	92	1r
Monopoly game, Parker Brothers', No. 9		10.13	4Q 92	4c
Movie	admission	5.00	4Q 92	4c
Tennis balls, yellow, Wilson or Penn, 3	can	2.16	4Q 92	4c
Waterpark admission	adult	11.00	92	1r

Decatur-Hartselle, AL - continued

Item	Per	Value	Date	Ref.
Entertainment - continued				
Waterpark admission	child	8.55	92	1r
Funerals				
Casket, 18-gauge steel, velvet interior		2329.05	91	24r
Cosmetology, hair care, etc.		72.78	91	24r
Embalming		240.71	91	24r
Facility use for ceremony		181.67	91	24r
Hearse, local		106.25	91	24r
Limousine, local		70.92	91	24r
Remains to funeral home, transfer		96.30	91	24r
Service charge, professional		687.09	91	24r
Vault, concrete, non-metallic liner		732.09	91	24r
Viewing facilities, use		190.30	91	24r
Goods and Services				
ACCRA Index, Miscellaneous Goods and Services		94.60	4Q 92	4c
Groceries				
ACCRA Index, Groceries		93.20	4Q 92	4c
Apples, Red Delicious	lb	0.79	4/93	16r
Babyfood, strained vegetables, lowest price	4-4.5 oz jar	0.27	4Q 92	4c
Bacon	lb	1.75	4/93	16r
Bananas	lb	0.41	4Q 92	4c
Bananas	lb	0.42	4/93	16r
Beef, stew, boneless	lb	2.61	4/93	16r
Bologna, all beef or mixed	lb	2.24	4/93	16r
Bread, white	24 oz	0.70	4Q 92	4c
Bread, white, pan	lb	0.64	4/93	16r
Bread, whole wheat, pan	lb	0.96	4/93	16r
Cabbage	lb	0.37	4/93	16r
Carrots, short trimmed and topped	lb	0.47	4/93	16r
Celery	lb	0.64	4/93	16r
Cheese, American	lb	2.98	4/93	16r
Cheese, Cheddar	lb	3.28	4/93	16r
Cheese, Kraft grated Parmesan	8-oz canister	2.96	4Q 92	4c
Chicken, fresh, whole	lb	0.77	4/93	16r
Chicken, fryer, whole	lb	0.63	4Q 92	4c
Chicken breast, bone-in	lb	1.92	4/93	16r
Chicken legs, bone-in	lb	1.06	4/93	16r
Chuck roast, graded and ungraded, ex USDA prime and choice	lb	2.40	4/93	16r
Chuck roast, USDA choice, bone-in	lb	2.19	4/93	16r
Chuck roast, USDA choice, boneless	lb	2.38	4/93	16r
Cigarettes, Winston	carton	16.17	4Q 92	4c
Coffee, 100% ground roast, all sizes	lb	2.48	4/93	16r
Coffee, vacuum-packed	13-oz can	1.99	4Q 92	4c
Corn, frozen	10 oz	0.67	4Q 92	4c
Corn Flakes, Kellogg's or Post Toasties	18 oz	1.72	4Q 92	4c
Crackers, soda, salted	lb	1.15	4/93	16r
Eggs, Grade A large	doz	0.81	4Q 92	4c
Eggs, Grade A large	doz	0.96	4/93	16r
Flour, white, all purpose	lb	0.24	4/93	16r
Frankfurters, all meat or all beef	lb	2.01	4/93	16r
Grapefruit	lb	0.44	4/93	16r
Grapes, Thompson Seedless	lb	1.40	4/93	16r
Ground beef, 100% beef	lb	1.58	4/93	16r
Ground beef, lean and extra lean	lb	2.09	4/93	16r
Ground beef or hamburger	lb	1.47	4Q 92	4c
Ground chuck, 100% beef	lb	1.98	4/93	16r
Ham, boneless, excluding canned	lb	2.89	4/93	16r
Ham, picnic, shoulder, bone-in, smoked	lb	1.02	4/93	16r
Ham, rump or steak half, bone-in, smoked	lb	1.48	4/93	16r
Honey, jar	8 oz	0.89-1.09	92	5r
Honey, jar	lb	1.39-2.25	92	5r
Honey, squeeze bear	12-oz	1.00-1.50	92	5r
Ice cream, prepackaged, bulk, regular	1/2 gal	2.41	4/93	16r
Lemons	lb	1.05	4/93	16r
Lettuce, iceberg	head	0.91	4Q 92	4c
Lettuce, iceberg	lb	0.81	4/93	16r

Values are in dollars or fractions of dollars. In the column headed *Ref*, references are shown to sources. Each reference is followed by a letter. These refer to the geographical level for which data were reported: s=State, r=Region, and c=City or metro. The abbreviation *ex* is used to mean *except* or *excluding*; *exp* stands for *expenditures*. For other abbreviations and further explanations, please see the Introduction.

Decatur-Hartselle, AL - continued

Item	Per	Value	Date	Ref.
Groceries				
Margarine, Blue Bonnet or Parkay cubes	lb	0.49	4Q 92	4c
Margarine, stick	lb	0.88	4/93	16r
Milk, whole	1/2 gal	1.41	4Q 92	4c
Orange juice, Minute Maid frozen	12-oz can	1.17	4Q 92	4c
Oranges, navel	lb	0.55	4/93	16r
Peaches	29-oz can	1.21	4Q 92	4c
Pears, Anjou	lb	0.92	4/93	16r
Peas Sweet, Del Monte or Green Giant	15-17 oz can	0.54	4Q 92	4c
Pork chops, center cut, bone-in	lb	3.13	4/93	16r
Potato chips	16 oz	2.94	4/93	16r
Potatoes, white	lb	0.43	4/93	16r
Potatoes, white or red	10-lb sack	2.71	4Q 92	4c
Rib roast, USDA choice, bone-in	lb	4.63	4/93	16r
Rice, white, long grain, uncooked	lb	0.45	4/93	16r
Round roast, graded & ungraded, ex USDA prime & choice	lb	3.03	4/93	16r
Round roast, USDA choice, boneless	lb	3.09	4/93	16r
Sausage, fresh, loose	lb	2.08	4/93	16r
Sausage, Jimmy Dean, 100% pork	lb	2.21	4Q 92	4c
Short ribs, bone-in	lb	2.66	4/93	16r
Shortening, vegetable oil blends	lb	0.69	4/93	16r
Shortening, vegetable, Crisco	3-lb can	1.97	4Q 92	4c
Soft drink, Coca Cola	2 liter	1.12	4Q 92	4c
Spaghetti and macaroni	lb	0.81	4/93	16r
Steak, rib eye, USDA choice, boneless	lb	6.24	4/93	16r
Steak, round, graded & ungraded, ex USDA prime & choice	lb	3.31	4/93	16r
Steak, round, USDA choice, boneless	lb	3.34	4/93	16r
Steak, sirloin, graded & ungraded, ex USDA prime & choice	lb	4.19	4/93	16r
Steak, sirloin, USDA choice, boneless	lb	4.46	4/93	16r
Steak, T-bone	lb	5.35	4Q 92	4c
Steak, T-bone, USDA choice, bone-in	lb	5.25	4/93	16r
Strawberries, dry pint	12 oz	0.92	4/93	16r
Sugar, cane or beet	4 lb	1.53	4Q 92	4c
Sugar, white	lb	0.39	4/93	16r
Sugar, white, 33-80 oz pk	lb	0.38	4/93	16r
Tomatoes, field grown	lb	0.88	4/93	16r
Tomatoes, Hunt's or Del Monte	14.5-oz can	0.48	4Q 92	4c
Tuna, chunk, light	6.125-6.5 oz can	0.59	4Q 92	4c
Tuna, chunk, light	lb	1.79	4/93	16r
Turkey, frozen, whole	lb	1.04	4/93	16r
Yogurt, natural, fruit flavored	1/2 pint	0.57	4/93	16r
Health Care				
ACCRA Index, Health Care		88.60	4Q 92	4c
Analgesic, Aspirin, Bayer, 325 mg tablets	100	4.27	4Q 92	4c
Childbirth, cesarean, hospital		5034	91	62r
Childbirth, cesarean, physician's fee		2053	91	62r
Childbirth, normal, hospital		2712	91	62r
Childbirth, normal, physician's fee		1492	91	62r
Dentist's fee, adult teeth cleaning and periodic oral exam	visit	40.80	4Q 92	4c
Doctor's fee, routine exam, established patient	visit	36.20	4Q 92	4c
Hospital care, semiprivate room	day	238.33	4Q 92	4c
Mental health care, exp	capita	37.60-53.67	90	38s
Mental health care, exp, state mental health agency	capita	38.35	90	38s
Mental health care, hospital psychiatric services, non-Federal, exp	capita	13.58	88	38s
Mental health care, mental health organization, multiservice, exp	capita	12.40	88	38s

Decatur-Hartselle, AL - continued

Item	Per	Value	Date	Ref.
Health Care - continued				
Mental health care, psychiatric hospitals, private, exp	capita	9.49	88	38s
Mental health care, state and county mental hospitals, exp	capita	22.15	88	38s
Mental health care, VA medical centers, exp	capita	10.94	88	38s
Physician fee, family practice, first-visit		75.00	91	62r
Physician fee, family practice, revisit		34.00	91	62r
Physician fee, general practice, first-visit		61.00	91	62r
Physician fee, general practice, revisit		32.00	91	62r
Physician fee, general surgeon, first-visit		64.00	91	62r
Physician fee, general surgeon, revisit		40.00	91	62r
Physician fee, internal medicine, first-visit		98.00	91	62r
Physician fee, internal medicine, revisit		40.00	91	62r
Physician fee, median, neurosurgeon, first-visit		130.00	91	62r
Physician fee, median, nonsurgical specialist, first-visit		95.00	91	62r
Physician fee, median, orthopedic surgeon, first-visit		91.00	91	62r
Physician fee, median, plastic surgeon, first-visit		66.00	91	62r
Physician fee, median, surgical specialist, first-visit		62.00	91	62r
Physician fee, neurosurgeon, revisit		50.00	91	62r
Physician fee, nonsurgical specialist, revisit		40.00	91	62r
Physician fee, obstetrics/gynecology, first-visit		64.00	91	62r
Physician fee, obstetrics/gynecology, revisit		41.00	91	62r
Physician fee, orthopedic surgeon, revisit		40.00	91	62r
Physician fee, pediatrician, first-visit		49.00	91	62r
Physician fee, pediatrician, revisit		33.00	91	62r
Physician fee, plastic surgeon, revisit		43.00	91	62r
Physician fee, surgical specialist, revisit		37.00	91	62r
Substance abuse, hospital ancillary charge	incident	1390	90	70s
Substance abuse, hospital physician charge	incident	520	90	70s
Substance abuse, hospital room and board	incident	5830	90	70s
Household Goods				
Appliance repair, home, service call, washing machine	min labor charge	30.99	4Q 92	4c
Laundry detergent, Tide Ultra, Bold, or Cheer	42 oz	2.87	4Q 92	4c
Tissues, facial, Kleenex brand	175-count box	1.02	4Q 92	4c
Housing				
ACCRA Index, Housing		82.10	4Q 92	4c
House, 1,800 sq ft, 8,000 sq ft lot, new, urban	total	92333	4Q 92	4c
House payment, principal and interest, 25% down payment	month	515	4Q 92	4c
Mortgage rate, incl. points & origination fee, 30-year fixed or adjustable rate	percent	8.14	4Q 92	4c
Rent, apartment, 2 bedrooms - 1-1/2 to 2 baths, unfurnished, 950 sq ft, water	month	382	4Q 92	4c
Insurance and Pensions				
Auto insurance, private passenger	year	562.59	91	63s
Personal Goods				
Shampoo, Alberto VO5	15 oz	1.23	4Q 92	4c
Toothpaste, Crest or Colgate	6-7 oz	1.73	4Q 92	4c
Personal Services				
Dry cleaning, man's 2-piece suit		5.60	4Q 92	4c
Haircare, woman's shampoo, trim and blow-dry		18.10	4Q 92	4c
Haircut, man's barbershop, no styling		6.40	4Q 92	4c

Values are in dollars or fractions of dollars. In the column headed *Ref*, references are shown to sources. Each reference is followed by a letter. These refer to the geographical level for which data were reported: s=State, r=Region, and c=City or metro. The abbreviation *ex* is used to mean *except* or *excluding*; *exp* stands for expenditures. For other abbreviations and further explanations, please see the Introduction.

Decatur-Hartselle, AL - continued

Item	Per	Value	Date	Ref.
Restaurant Food				
Chicken, fried, thigh and drumstick		1.79	4Q 92	4c
Hamburger with cheese	1/4 lb	1.85	4Q 92	4c
Pizza, Pizza Hut or Pizza Inn, cheese, thin crust	12-13 in	7.99	4Q 92	4c
Taxes				
Tax, cigarette	pack	16.50	91	77s
Tax, gasoline	gal	16	91	77s
Taxes, state	capita	964	91	77s
Transportation				
ACCRA Index, Transportation		100.50	4Q 92	4c
Driver's license fee		15.00	12/90	43s
Tire balance, computer or spin balance, front	wheel	6.40	4Q 92	4c
Travel				
Business travel	day	193.00	4/93	89r
Utilities				
ACCRA Index, Utilities		89.70	4Q 92	4c
Electricity	mil Btu	16.46	90	64s
Electricity, all electric, 1,800 sq ft living area new home	month	93.67	4Q 92	4c

Denver, CO

Item	Per	Value	Date	Ref.
Composite ACCRA index		104.80	4Q 92	4c
Alcoholic Beverages				
Beer, Miller Lite or Budweiser, 12-oz containers	6 pack	3.71	4Q 92	4c
Liquor, J & B Scotch	750 ml	17.21	4Q 92	4c
Wine, Gallo Chablis blanc, 1.5 liter	bottle	4.49	4Q 92	4c
Child Care				
Child care fee, average, center	hour	1.71	90	65r
Child care fee, average, nonregulated family day care	hour	1.32	90	65r
Child care fee, average, regulated family day care	hour	1.86	90	65r
Clothing				
Jeans, man's denim		29.32	4Q 92	4c
Shirt, man's dress shirt		22.00	4Q 92	4c
Undervest, boy's size 10-14, cotton	3	5.92	4Q 92	4c
Communications				
Long-distance telephone service, day, initial minute, 0-100 miles	min	0.11-0.35	91	12s
Long-distance telephone service, day, additional minute, 0-100 miles	min	0.13-0.27	91	12s
Long-distance telephone service, evenings/weekends, 0-100 mi, initial minute	min	0.08-0.17	91	12s
Long-distance telephone service, evenings/weekends, 0-100 mi, additional minute	min	0.06-0.14	91	12s
Newspaper subscription, daily and Sunday home delivery, large-city	month	7.80	4Q 92	4c
Telephone, flat rate	month	14.22	91	11c
Telephone, residential, private line, rotary, unlimited calling	month	20.90	10/91	78c
Telephone bill, family of four	month	19.70	4Q 92	4c
Education				
Board, 4-yr private college/university	year	2162	91	22s
Board, 4-yr public college/university	year	1747	91	22s
Expenditures, local gov't, public elementary/secondary	pupil	5259	92	20s
Room, 4-year private college/university	year	1984	91	22s
Room, 4-year public college/university	year	1546	91	22s
Tuition, 2-year private college/university	year	6731	91	22s
Tuition, 2-year public college/university	year	943	91	22s
Tuition, 4-year private college/university	year	9516	91	22s
Tuition, 4-year public college/university, in-state	year	1919	91	22s

Denver, CO - continued

Item	Per	Value	Date	Ref.
Energy and Fuels				
Coal	mil Btu	1.07	90	64s
Energy	mil Btu	8.14	90	64s
Energy, combined forms, 1,800 sq ft heating area	month	99.16	4Q 92	4c
Energy, exc electricity, 1,800 sq ft heating area	month	40.84	4Q 92	4c
Energy exp/householder, 1-family unit	year	372	90	28r
Energy exp/householder, <1,000 sq ft heating area	year	335	90	28r
Energy exp/householder, 1,000-1,999 sq ft heating area	year	365	90	28r
Energy exp/householder, 2,000+ sq ft heating area	year	411	90	28r
Energy exp/householder, mobile home	year	305	90	28r
Energy exp/householder, multifamily	year	372	90	28r
Gas, cooking, 10 therms	month	9.10	92	56c
Gas, cooking, 30 therms	month	16.90	92	56c
Gas, cooking, 50 therms	month	24.71	92	56c
Gas, heating, winter, 100 therms	month	44.20	92	56c
Gas, heating, winter, average use	month	57.53	92	56c
Gas, natural	mil Btu	3.92	90	64s
Gas, natural	000 cu ft	4.59	91	46s
Gas, natural, exp	year	446	91	46s
Gasoline, motor	gal	1.19	4Q 92	4c
Gasoline, unleaded regular	mil Btu	9.29	90	64s
Entertainment				
Bowling, evening rate	game	1.40	4Q 92	4c
Miniature golf admission	adult	6.18	92	1r
Miniature golf admission	child	5.14	92	1r
Monopoly game, Parker Brothers', No. 9		9.99	4Q 92	4c
Movie	admission	5.91	4Q 92	4c
Tennis balls, yellow, Wilson or Penn, 3	can	2.51	4Q 92	4c
Waterpark admission	adult	11.00	92	1r
Waterpark admission	child	8.55	92	1r
Funerals				
Casket, 18-gauge steel, velvet interior		1929.04	91	24r
Cosmetology, hair care, etc.		88.52	91	24r
Embalming		249.33	91	24r
Facility use for ceremony		182.75	91	24r
Hearse, local		110.04	91	24r
Limousine, local		66.67	91	24r
Remains to funeral home, transfer		84.58	91	24r
Service charge, professional		593.00	91	24r
Vault, concrete, non-metallic liner		647.38	91	24r
Viewing facilities, use		99.87	91	24r
Goods and Services				
ACCRA Index, Miscellaneous Goods and Services		99.60	4Q 92	4c
Groceries				
ACCRA Index, Groceries		99.80	4Q 92	4c
Apples, Red Delicious	lb	0.80	4/93	16r
Babyfood, strained vegetables, lowest price	4-4.5 oz jar	0.32	4Q 92	4c
Bacon	lb	1.79	4/93	16r
Bananas	lb	0.53	4Q 92	4c
Bananas	lb	0.53	4/93	16r
Bologna, all beef or mixed	lb	2.67	4/93	16r
Bread, white	24 oz	0.58	4Q 92	4c
Bread, white, pan	lb	0.81	4/93	16r
Carrots, short trimmed and topped	lb	0.39	4/93	16r
Cheese, Kraft grated Parmesan	8-oz canister	3.04	4Q 92	4c
Chicken, fresh, whole	lb	0.94	4/93	16r
Chicken, fryer, whole	lb	0.63	4Q 92	4c
Chicken breast, bone-in	lb	2.19	4/93	16r
Chuck roast, graded and ungraded, ex USDA prime and choice	lb	2.26	4/93	16r

Values are in dollars or fractions of dollars. In the column headed *Ref*, references are shown to sources. Each reference is followed by a letter. These refer to the geographical level for which data were reported: s = State, r = Region, and c = City or metro. The abbreviation *ex* is used to mean *except* or *excluding*; *exp* stands for expenditures. For other abbreviations and further explanations, please see the Introduction.

Denver, CO - continued

Item	Per	Value	Date	Ref.
Groceries				
Cigarettes, Winston	carton	16.78	4Q 92	4c
Coffee, 100% ground roast, all sizes	lb	2.33	4/93	16r
Coffee, vacuum-packed	13-oz can	2.11	4Q 92	4c
Corn, frozen	10 oz	0.67	4Q 92	4c
Corn Flakes, Kellogg's or Post Toasties	18 oz	1.91	4Q 92	4c
Eggs, Grade A large	doz	0.74	4Q 92	4c
Eggs, Grade AA large	doz	1.18	4/93	16r
Flour, white, all purpose	lb	0.22	4/93	16r
Grapefruit	lb	0.52	4/93	16r
Grapes, Thompson Seedless	lb	1.50	4/93	16r
Ground beef, 100% beef	lb	1.44	4/93	16r
Ground beef, lean and extra lean	lb	2.34	4/93	16r
Ground beef or hamburger	lb	1.60	4Q 92	4c
Ham, boneless, excluding canned	lb	2.56	4/93	16r
Honey, jar	8 oz	0.89-1.00	92	5r
Honey, jar	lb	1.49-2.25	92	5r
Honey, squeeze bear	12-oz	1.00-1.89	92	5r
Ice cream, prepackaged, bulk, regular	1/2 gal	2.40	4/93	16r
Lemons	lb	0.81	4/93	16r
Lettuce, iceberg	head	1.11	4Q 92	4c
Lettuce, iceberg	lb	0.84	4/93	16r
Margarine, Blue Bonnet or Parkay cubes	lb	0.49	4Q 92	4c
Margarine, stick	lb	0.81	4/93	16r
Milk, whole	1/2 gal	1.49	4Q 92	4c
Orange juice, Minute Maid frozen	12-oz can	1.41	4Q 92	4c
Oranges, navel	lb	0.48	4/93	16r
Peaches	29-oz can	1.55	4Q 92	4c
Peas Sweet, Del Monte or Green Giant	15-17 oz can	0.73	4Q 92	4c
Pork chops, center cut, bone-in	lb	3.25	4/93	16r
Potato chips	16 oz	2.89	4/93	16r
Potatoes, white	lb	0.38	4/93	16r
Potatoes, white or red	10-lb sack	2.34	4Q 92	4c
Round roast, graded & ungraded, ex USDA prime & choice	lb	3.00	4/93	16r
Round roast, USDA choice, boneless	lb	3.16	4/93	16r
Sausage, Jimmy Dean, 100% pork	lb	3.40	4Q 92	4c
Shortening, vegetable oil blends	lb	0.86	4/93	16r
Shortening, vegetable, Crisco	3-lb can	2.35	4Q 92	4c
Soft drink, Coca Cola	2 liter	1.09	4Q 92	4c
Spaghetti and macaroni	lb	0.84	4/93	16r
Steak, round, graded & ungraded, ex USDA prime & choice	lb	3.34	4/93	16r
Steak, round, USDA choice, boneless	lb	3.24	4/93	16r
Steak, sirloin, graded & ungraded, ex USDA prime & choice	lb	3.75	4/93	16r
Steak, sirloin, USDA choice, boneless	lb	4.49	4/93	16r
Steak, T-bone	lb	4.73	4Q 92	4c
Sugar, cane or beet	4 lb	1.31	4Q 92	4c
Sugar, white	lb	0.41	4/93	16r
Sugar, white, 33-80 oz pk	lb	0.38	4/93	16r
Tomatoes, field grown	lb	1.01	4/93	16r
Tomatoes, Hunt's or Del Monte	14.5-oz can	0.69	4Q 92	4c
Tuna, chunk, light	6.125-6.5 oz can	0.72	4Q 92	4c
Turkey, frozen, whole	lb	1.04	4/93	16r
Health Care				
ACCRA Index, Health Care		126.50	4Q 92	4c
Analgesic, Aspirin, Bayer, 325 mg tablets	100	5.06	4Q 92	4c
Appendectomy		885	91	62c
Childbirth, cesarean		2203	91	62c
Childbirth, cesarean, hospital		5533	91	62r
Childbirth, cesarean, physician's fee		2053	91	62r
Childbirth, normal, hospital		2745	91	62r
Childbirth, normal, physician's fee		1492	91	62r

Denver, CO - continued

Item	Per	Value	Date	Ref.
Health Care - continued				
Cholecystectomy		1509	91	62c
Coronary bypass surgery, triple		4499	91	62c
Dentist's fee, adult teeth cleaning and periodic oral exam	visit	57.22	4Q 92	4c
Doctor's fee, routine exam, established patient	visit	50.17	4Q 92	4c
Hospital care, semiprivate room	day	344.15	90	27c
Hospital care, semiprivate room	day	419.90	4Q 92	4c
Hysterectomy		1707	91	62c
Lumpectomy		463	91	62c
Medical insurance premium, per employee, small group comprehensive	month	346.75	10/91	25c
Medical plan per employee	year	3218	91	45r
Mental health care, exp	capita	28.84-37.59	90	38s
Mental health care, exp, state mental health agency	capita	33.55	90	38s
Mental health care, hospital psychiatric services, non-Federal, exp	capita	11.38	88	38s
Mental health care, mental health organization, multiservice, exp	capita	21.76	88	38s
Mental health care, psychiatric hospitals, private, exp	capita	14.39	88	38s
Mental health care, psychiatric out-patient clinics, freestanding, exp	capita	0.11	88	38s
Mental health care, state and county mental hospitals, exp	capita	19.03	88	38s
Mental health care, VA medical centers, exp	capita	3.80	88	38s
Oophorectomy		917	91	62c
Physician fee, family practice, first-visit		111.00	91	62r
Physician fee, family practice, revisit		45.00	91	62r
Physician fee, general practice, first-visit		100.00	91	62r
Physician fee, general practice, revisit		40.00	91	62r
Physician fee, internal medicine, first-visit		137.00	91	62r
Physician fee, internal medicine, revisit		48.00	91	62r
Physician fee, median, neurosurgeon, first-visit		157.00	91	62r
Physician fee, median, nonsurgical specialist, first-visit		131.00	91	62r
Physician fee, median, orthopedic surgeon, first-visit		124.00	91	62r
Physician fee, median, plastic surgeon, first-visit		88.00	91	62r
Physician fee, median, surgical specialist, first-visit		100.00	91	62r
Physician fee, neurosurgeon, revisit		51.00	91	62r
Physician fee, nonsurgical specialist, revisit		47.00	91	62r
Physician fee, obstetrics/gynecology, first-visit		95.00	91	62r
Physician fee, obstetrics/gynecology, revisit		50.00	91	62r
Physician fee, orthopedic surgeon, revisit		51.00	91	62r
Physician fee, pediatrician, first-visit		81.00	91	62r
Physician fee, pediatrician, revisit		42.00	91	62r
Physician fee, plastic surgeon, revisit		48.00	91	62r
Physician fee, surgical specialist, revisit		49.00	91	62r
Prostatectomy, retro-pubic		1533	91	62c
Salpingo-oophorectomy		925	91	62c
Substance abuse, hospital ancillary charge	incident	1040	90	70s
Substance abuse, hospital physician charge	incident	380	90	70s
Substance abuse, hospital room and board	incident	4880	90	70s
Vasectomy		347	91	62c
Household Goods				
Appliance repair, home, service call, washing machine	min labor charge	27.34	4Q 92	4c
Laundry detergent, Tide Ultra, Bold, or Cheer	42 oz	2.98	4Q 92	4c

Values are in dollars or fractions of dollars. In the column headed *Ref*, references are shown to sources. Each reference is followed by a letter. These refer to the geographical level for which data were reported: s=State, r=Region, and c=City or metro. The abbreviation *ex* is used to mean *except* or *excluding*; *exp* stands for expenditures. For other abbreviations and further explanations, please see the Introduction.

Denver, CO - continued

Item	Per	Value	Date	Ref.
Household Goods				
Tissues, facial, Kleenex brand	175-count box	1.00	4Q 92	4c
Housing				
ACCRA Index, Housing		112.40	4Q 92	4c
Home, median price	unit	95.80		26c
House, 1,800 sq ft, 8,000 sq ft lot, new, urban	total	123279	4Q 92	4c
House payment, principal and interest, 25% down payment	month	672	4Q 92	4c
Mortgage rate, incl. points & origination fee, 30-year fixed or adjustable rate	per-cent	7.90	4Q 92	4c
Rent, apartment, 2 bedrooms - 1-1/2 to 2 baths, unfurnished, 950 sq ft, water	month	599	4Q 92	4c
Rental unit, 1 bedroom	month	443	93	23c
Rental unit, 2 bedroom	month	522	93	23c
Rental unit, 3 bedroom	month	652	93	23c
Rental unit, 4 bedroom	month	730	93	23c
Rental unit, efficiency	month	365	93	23c
Insurance and Pensions				
Auto insurance, private passenger	year	684.81	91	63s
Personal Goods				
Shampoo, Alberto VO5	15 oz	1.24	4Q 92	4c
Toothpaste, Crest or Colgate	6-7 oz	2.06	4Q 92	4c
Personal Services				
Dry cleaning, man's 2-piece suit		6.35	4Q 92	4c
Haircare, woman's shampoo, trim and blow-dry		20.19	4Q 92	4c
Haircut, man's barbershop, no styling		7.58	4Q 92	4c
Restaurant Food				
Chicken, fried, thigh and drumstick		1.92	4Q 92	4c
Hamburger with cheese	1/4 lb	2.00	4Q 92	4c
Pizza, Pizza Hut or Pizza Inn, cheese, thin crust	12-13 in	7.69	4Q 92	4c
Taxes				
Tax, cigarette	pack	20	91	77s
Tax, gasoline	gal	22	91	77s
Taxes, state	capita	951	91	77s
Transportation				
ACCRA Index, Transportation		109.00	4Q 92	4c
Auto rental, average	day	42.75	6/91	60c
Bus fare	one-way	0.50	3/93	2c
Bus fare, up to 10 miles	one-way	1.25	4Q 92	4c
Driver's license fee		15.00	12/90	43s
Limo fare, airport-city, average	day	5.00	6/91	60c
Taxi fare, airport-city, average	day	11.00	6/91	60c
Tire balance, computer or spin balance, front	wheel	6.83	4Q 92	4c
Travel				
Breakfast	day	6.99	6/91	60c
Business travel	day	144.00	92	86c
Business travel	day	178.00	4/93	89r
Dinner	day	20.81	6/91	60c
Dinner	day	23.15	92	85c
Lodging	day	119.75	91	60c
Lodging	day	103.00	92	85c
Lunch	day	9.95	6/91	60c
Utilities				
ACCRA Index, Utilities		91.90	4Q 92	4c
Electricity	mil Btu	17.31	90	64s
Electricity, partial electric and other energy, 1,800 sq ft living area new home	month	58.32	4Q 92	4c
Electricity, residential	KWh	7.70	2/93	94s
Electricity, winter, 250 KWh	month	20.09	92	55c
Electricity, winter, 500 KWh	month	35.11	92	55c

Denver, CO - continued

Item	Per	Value	Date	Ref.
Utilities - continued				
Electricity, winter, 750 KWh	month	50.13	92	55c
Electricity, winter, 1000 KWh	month	65.14	92	55c

Des Moines, IA

Item	Per	Value	Date	Ref.
Child Care				
Child care fee, average, center	hour	1.63	90	65r
Child care fee, average, nonregulated family day care	hour	1.83	90	65r
Child care fee, average, regulated family day care	hour	1.42	90	65r
Communications				
Long-distance telephone service, day, initial minute, 0-100 miles	min	0.21-0.41	91	12s
Long-distance telephone service, day, additional minute, 0-100 miles	min	0.11-0.30	91	12s
Long-distance telephone service, evenings/weekends, 0-100 mi, initial minute	min	0.11-0.20	91	12s
Long-distance telephone service, evenings/weekends, 0-100 mi, additional minute	min	0.06-0.15	91	12s
Telephone, flat rate	month	15.95	91	11c
Education				
Board, 4-yr private college/university	year	1703	91	22s
Board, 4-yr public college/university	year	1183	91	22s
Expenditures, local gov't, public elementary/secondary	pupil	5026	92	20s
Room, 4-year private college/university	year	1392	91	22s
Room, 4-year public college/university	year	1188	91	22s
Tuition, 2-year private college/university	year	5119	91	22s
Tuition, 2-year public college/university	year	1298	91	22s
Tuition, 4-year private college/university	year	8703	91	22s
Tuition, 4-year public college/university, in-state	year	1880	91	22s
Energy and Fuels				
Coal	mil Btu	1.16	90	64s
Energy	mil Btu	7.71	90	64s
Energy exp/householder, 1-family unit	year	473	90	28r
Energy exp/householder, <1,000 sq ft heating area	year	429	90	28r
Energy exp/householder, 1,000-1,999 sq ft heating area	year	442	90	28r
Energy exp/householder, 2,000+ sq ft heating area	year	498	90	28r
Energy exp/householder, mobile home	year	442	90	28r
Energy exp/householder, multifamily	year	407	90	28r
Gas, cooking, 10 therms	month	13.25	92	56c
Gas, cooking, 30 therms	month	21.30	92	56c
Gas, cooking, 50 therms	month	29.35	92	56c
Gas, heating, winter, 100 therms	month	49.45	92	56c
Gas, heating, winter, average use	month	86.85	92	56c
Gas, natural	mil Btu	3.81	90	64s
Gas, natural	000 cu ft	4.81	91	46s
Gas, natural, exp	year	530	91	46s
Gasoline, unleaded regular	mil Btu	9.38	90	64s
Entertainment				
Miniature golf admission	adult	6.18	92	1r
Miniature golf admission	child	5.14	92	1r
Waterpark admission	adult	11.00	92	1r
Waterpark admission	child	8.55	92	1r
Funerals				
Casket, 18-gauge steel, velvet interior		1952.97	91	24r
Cosmetology, hair care, etc.		90.03	91	24r
Embalming		251.75	91	24r
Facility use for ceremony		180.75	91	24r
Hearse, local		117.51	91	24r
Limousine, local		71.86	91	24r
Remains to funeral home, transfer		81.14	91	24r

Values are in dollars or fractions of dollars. In the column headed *Ref*, references are shown to sources. Each reference is followed by a letter. These refer to the geographical level for which data were reported: s = State, r = Region, and c = City or metro. The abbreviation *ex* is used to mean *except* or *excluding*; *exp* stands for expenditures. For other abbreviations and further explanations, please see the Introduction.

Des Moines, IA - continued

Item	Per	Value	Date	Ref.
Funerals				
Service charge, professional		740.03	91	24r
Vault, concrete, non-metallic liner		801.47	91	24r
Viewing facilities, use		169.33	91	24r
Groceries				
Apples, Red Delicious	lb	0.77	4/93	16r
Bacon	lb	1.85	4/93	16r
Bananas	lb	0.46	4/93	16r
Beef, stew, boneless	lb	2.53	4/93	16r
Bologna, all beef or mixed	lb	2.19	4/93	16r
Bread, white, pan	lb	0.78	4/93	16r
Butter	lb	1.50	4/93	16r
Cabbage	lb	0.40	4/93	16r
Carrots, short trimmed and topped	lb	0.45	4/93	16r
Cheese, Cheddar	lb	3.47	4/93	16r
Chicken, fresh, whole	lb	0.84	4/93	16r
Chicken breast, bone-in	lb	1.94	4/93	16r
Chicken legs, bone-in	lb	1.02	4/93	16r
Chuck roast, graded and ungraded, ex USDA prime and choice	lb	2.43	4/93	16r
Chuck roast, USDA choice, bone-in	lb	2.11	4/93	16r
Chuck roast, USDA choice, boneless	lb	2.44	4/93	16r
Coffee, 100% ground roast, all sizes	lb	2.47	4/93	16r
Cookies, chocolate chip	lb	2.73	4/93	16r
Eggs, Grade A large	doz	0.93	4/93	16r
Flour, white, all purpose	lb	0.21	4/93	16r
Grapefruit	lb	0.45	4/93	16r
Grapes, Thompson Seedless	lb	1.46	4/93	16r
Ground beef, 100% beef	lb	1.63	4/93	16r
Ground beef, lean and extra lean	lb	2.08	4/93	16r
Ground chuck, 100% beef	lb	1.94	4/93	16r
Ham, boneless, excluding canned	lb	2.21	4/93	16r
Ice cream, prepackaged, bulk, regular	1/2 gal	2.41	4/93	16r
Lemons	lb	0.82	4/93	16r
Lettuce, iceberg	lb	0.83	4/93	16r
Margarine, stick	lb	0.77	4/93	16r
Oranges, navel	lb	0.50	4/93	16r
Peanut butter, creamy, all sizes	lb	1.82	4/93	16r
Pears, Anjou	lb	0.85	4/93	16r
Pork chops, center cut, bone-in	lb	3.17	4/93	16r
Potato chips	16 oz	2.68	4/93	16r
Potatoes, white	lb	0.26	4/93	16r
Round roast, graded & ungraded, ex USDA prime & choice	lb	2.88	4/93	16r
Round roast, USDA choice, boneless	lb	2.96	4/93	16r
Shortening, vegetable oil blends	lb	0.79	4/93	16r
Spaghetti and macaroni	lb	0.76	4/93	16r
Steak, rib eye, USDA choice, boneless	lb	6.29	4/93	16r
Steak, round, USDA choice, boneless	lb	3.24	4/93	16r
Steak, sirloin, graded & ungraded, ex USDA prime & choice	lb	4.00	4/93	16r
Steak, sirloin, USDA choice, bone-in	lb	3.57	4/93	16r
Steak, sirloin, USDA choice, boneless	lb	4.17	4/93	16r
Steak, T-bone, USDA choice, bone-in	lb	5.60	4/93	16r
Strawberries, dry pint	12 oz	0.90	4/93	16r
Sugar, white	lb	0.36	4/93	16r
Sugar, white, 33-80 oz pk	lb	0.35	4/93	16r
Tomatoes, field grown	lb	0.99	4/93	16r
Tuna, chunk, light	lb	1.76	4/93	16r
Turkey, frozen, whole	lb	0.91	4/93	16r
Health Care				
Childbirth, cesarean, hospital		4688	91	62r
Childbirth, cesarean, physician's fee		2053	91	62r
Childbirth, normal, hospital		2657	91	62r
Childbirth, normal, physician's fee		1492	91	62r
Health care spending, state	capita	2351	3/93	84s
Hospital care, semiprivate room	day	269.13	90	27c
Medical insurance premium, per employee, small group comprehensive	month	306.60	10/91	25c
Medical plan per employee	year	3443	91	45r
Mental health care, exp	capita	20.37-28.83	90	38s

Des Moines, IA - continued

Item	Per	Value	Date	Ref.
Health Care - continued				
Mental health care, exp, state mental health agency	capita	17.07	90	38s
Mental health care, hospital psychiatric services, non-Federal, exp	capita	23.51	88	38s
Mental health care, mental health organization, multiservice, exp	capita	7.66	88	38s
Mental health care, psychiatric hospitals, private, exp	capita	2.86	88	38s
Mental health care, psychiatric out-patient clinics, freestanding, exp	capita	3.02	88	38s
Mental health care, state and county mental hospitals, exp	capita	14.54	88	38s
Mental health care, VA medical centers, exp	capita	13.98	88	38s
Physician fee, family practice, first-visit		76.00	91	62r
Physician fee, family practice, revisit		33.00	91	62r
Physician fee, general practice, first-visit		61.00	91	62r
Physician fee, general practice, revisit		31.00	91	62r
Physician fee, general surgeon, first-visit		65.00	91	62r
Physician fee, general surgeon, revisit		35.00	91	62r
Physician fee, internal medicine, first-visit		91.00	91	62r
Physician fee, internal medicine, revisit		40.00	91	62r
Physician fee, median, neurosurgeon, first-visit		106.00	91	62r
Physician fee, median, nonsurgical specialist, first-visit		90.00	91	62r
Physician fee, median, orthopedic surgeon, first-visit		83.00	91	62r
Physician fee, median, surgical specialist, first-visit		61.00	91	62r
Physician fee, neurosurgeon, revisit		41.00	91	62r
Physician fee, nonsurgical specialist, revisit		40.00	91	62r
Physician fee, obstetrics/gynecology, first-visit		61.00	91	62r
Physician fee, obstetrics/gynecology, revisit		40.00	91	62r
Physician fee, orthopedic surgeon, revisit		41.00	91	62r
Physician fee, pediatrician, first-visit		46.00	91	62r
Physician fee, pediatrician, revisit		33.00	91	62r
Physician fee, surgical specialist, revisit		36.00	91	62r
Substance abuse, hospital ancillary charge	incident	950	90	70s
Substance abuse, hospital physician charge	incident	250	90	70s
Substance abuse, hospital room and board	incident	3110	90	70s
Housing				
Home, median price	unit	73.00		26c
Rental unit, 1 bedroom	month	432	93	23c
Rental unit, 2 bedroom	month	509	93	23c
Rental unit, 3 bedroom	month	639	93	23c
Rental unit, 4 bedroom	month	716	93	23c
Rental unit, efficiency	month	355	93	23c
Insurance and Pensions				
Auto insurance, private passenger	year	422.46	91	63s
Taxes				
Tax, cigarette	pack	36	91	77s
Tax, gasoline	gal	20	91	77s
Taxes, state	capita	1233	91	77s
Transportation				
Auto fixed costs, midsize		3439	91	60c
Auto operating cost, midsize		1403	91	60c
Auto rental, average	day	46.25	6/91	60c
Bus fare	one-way	0.75	3/93	2c
Driver's license fee		16.00	12/90	43s
Taxi fare, airport-city, average	day	10.00	6/91	60c
Travel				
Breakfast	day	6.65	6/91	60c
Dinner	day	16.14	6/91	60c
Lodging	day	73.00	91	60c

Values are in dollars or fractions of dollars. In the column headed *Ref*, references are shown to sources. Each reference is followed by a letter. These refer to the geographical level for which data were reported: s=State, r=Region, and c=City or metro. The abbreviation *ex* is used to mean *except* or *excluding*; *exp* stands for expenditures. For other abbreviations and further explanations, please see the Introduction.

Des Moines, IA - continued

Item	Per	Value	Date	Ref.
Travel				
Lunch	day	7.02	6/91	60c
Utilities				
Cable-television service, with no competition	month	24.95	92	81c
Electricity	mil Btu	17.37	90	64s
Electricity, winter, 250 KWh	month	29.04	92	55c
Electricity, winter, 250 KWh	month	29.12	2/93	30c
Electricity, winter, 500 KWh	month	48.18	92	55c
Electricity, winter, 500 KWh	month	48.33	2/93	30c
Electricity, winter, 750 KWh	month	67.32	92	55c
Electricity, winter, 750 KWh	month	67.55	2/93	30c
Electricity, winter, 1000 KWh	month	86.46	92	55c
Electricity, winter, 1000 KWh	month	86.76	2/93	30c

Detroit-Ann Arbor, MI

Item	Per	Value	Date	Ref.
Alcoholic Beverages				
Alcoholic beverages, exp	year	314	89	15c
Charity				
Cash contributions	year	442	89	15c
Child Care				
Child care, on-site	year	3900	93	17c
Child care fee, average, center	hour	1.63	90	65r
Child care fee, average, nonregulated family day care	hour	1.83	90	65r
Child care fee, average, regulated family day care	hour	1.42	90	65r
Communications				
Long-distance telephone service, day, initial minute, 0-100 miles	min	0.14-0.36	91	12s
Long-distance telephone service, day, additional minute, 0-100 miles	min	0.14-0.36	91	12s
Long-distance telephone service, evenings/weekends, 0-100 mi, initial minute	min	0.07-0.19	91	12s
Long-distance telephone service, evenings/weekends, 0-100 mi, additional minute	min	0.04-0.14	91	12s
Postage and stationery, exp	year	173	89	15c
Telephone, exp	year	664	89	15c
Telephone, flat rate	month	11.95	91	11c
Telephone, residential, private line, rotary, unlimited calling	month	16.30	10/91	78c
Education				
Board, 4-yr private college/university	year	1698	91	22s
Board, 4-yr public college/university	year	1962	91	22s
Education, exp	year	348	89	15c
Expenditures, local gov't, public elementary/secondary	pupil	5671	92	20s
Room, 4-year private college/university	year	1440	91	22s
Room, 4-year public college/university	year	1687	91	22s
Tuition, 2-year private college/university	year	4749	91	22s
Tuition, 2-year public college/university	year	1124	91	22s
Tuition, 4-year private college/university	year	6885	91	22s
Tuition, 4-year public college/university, in-state	year	2635	91	22s
Energy and Fuels				
Coal	mil Btu	1.63	90	64s
Energy	mil Btu	8.17	90	64s
Energy exp/householder, 1-family unit	year	471	90	28r
Energy exp/householder, <1,000 sq ft heating area	year	430	90	28r
Energy exp/householder, 1,000-1,999 sq ft heating area	year	481	90	28r
Energy exp/householder, 2,000+ sq ft heating area	year	473	90	28r
Energy exp/householder, mobile home	year	430	90	28r
Energy exp/householder, multifamily	year	461	90	28r
Fuel oil #2	gal	0.97	4/93	16c
Fuel oil, other fuel, exp	year	48	89	15c
Gas, cooking, 10 therms	month	11.93	92	56c

Detroit-Ann Arbor, MI - continued

Item	Per	Value	Date	Ref.
Energy and Fuels - continued				
Gas, cooking, 30 therms	month	20.78	92	56c
Gas, cooking, 50 therms	month	29.63	92	56c
Gas, heating, winter, 100 therms	month	51.76	92	56c
Gas, heating, winter, average use	month	100.47	92	56c
Gas, natural	mil Btu	4.36	90	64s
Gas, natural	000 cu ft	5.07	91	46s
Gas, natural, exp	year	568	89	15c
Gas, natural, exp	year	655	91	46s
Gas, piped	100 therms	49.22	4/93	16c
Gas, piped	40 therms	23.57	4/93	16c
Gas, piped	therm	0.48	4/93	16c
Gasoline, all types	gal	1.09	4/93	16c
Gasoline, regular unleaded, taxes included, cash, self-service	gal	1.24	4/93	16c
Gasoline, unleaded premium 93 octane	gal	1.06	4/93	16c
Gasoline, unleaded regular	mil Btu	8.78	90	64s
Entertainment				
Entertainment exp	year	1228	89	15c
Fees and admissions	year	346	89	15c
Football game expenditures, pro		125.17	91	80c
Miniature golf admission	adult	6.18	92	1r
Miniature golf admission	child	5.14	92	1r
Pets, toys, playground equipment, exp	year	192	89	15c
Reading, exp	year	166	89	15c
Supplies, equipment, services, exp	year	222	89	15c
Waterpark admission	adult	11.00	92	1r
Waterpark admission	child	8.55	92	1r
Funerals				
Casket, 18-gauge steel, velvet interior		1926.72	91	24r
Cosmetology, hair care, etc.		97.64	91	24r
Embalming		249.14	91	24r
Facility use for ceremony		208.59	91	24r
Hearse, local		130.12	91	24r
Limousine, local		104.66	91	24r
Remains to funeral home, transfer		93.61	91	24r
Service charge, professional		724.62	91	24r
Vault, concrete, non-metallic liner		734.53	91	24r
Viewing facilities, use		236.06	91	24r
Goods and Services				
Police protection expense	resident	318.00	92	18c
Groceries				
Apples, Red Delicious	lb	0.77	4/93	16r
Bacon	lb	1.85	4/93	16r
Bakery products, exp	year	185	89	15c
Bananas	lb	0.46	4/93	16r
Beef, exp	year	152	89	15c
Beef, stew, boneless	lb	2.53	4/93	16r
Beverages, nonalcoholic, exp	year	158	89	15c
Bologna, all beef or mixed	lb	2.19	4/93	16r
Bread, white, pan	lb	0.78	4/93	16r
Butter	lb	1.50	4/93	16r
Cabbage	lb	0.40	4/93	16r
Carrots, short trimmed and topped	lb	0.45	4/93	16r
Cereals and bakery products, exp	year	292	89	15c
Cereals and cereal products, exp	year	107	89	15c
Cheese, Cheddar	lb	3.47	4/93	16r
Chicken, fresh, whole	lb	0.84	4/93	16r
Chicken breast, bone-in	lb	1.94	4/93	16r
Chicken legs, bone-in	lb	1.02	4/93	16r
Chuck roast, graded and ungraded, ex USDA prime and choice	lb	2.43	4/93	16r
Chuck roast, USDA choice, bone-in	lb	2.11	4/93	16r
Chuck roast, USDA choice, boneless	lb	2.44	4/93	16r
Coffee, 100% ground roast, all sizes	lb	2.47	4/93	16r
Cookies, chocolate chip	lb	2.73	4/93	16r
Dairy products, exp	year	239	89	15c

Values are in dollars or fractions of dollars. In the column headed *Ref*, references are shown to sources. Each reference is followed by a letter. These refer to the geographical level for which data were reported: s = State, r = Region, and c = City or metro. The abbreviation *ex* is used to mean *except* or *excluding*; *exp* stands for *expenditures*. For other abbreviations and further explanations, please see the Introduction.

Detroit-Ann Arbor, MI - continued

Item	Per	Value	Date	Ref.
Groceries				
Dairy products, miscellaneous, exp	year	119	89	15c
Eggs, exp	year	22	89	15c
Eggs, Grade A large	doz	0.93	4/93	16r
Fats and oils, exp	year	47	89	15c
Fish and seafood, exp	year	77	89	15c
Flour, white, all purpose	lb	0.21	4/93	16r
Food, exp	year	3682	89	15c
Food eaten at home, exp	year	2004	89	15c
Food eaten away from home, exp	year	1678	89	15c
Food prepared on out-of-town trips, exp	year	47	89	15c
Foods, miscellaneous, exp	year	238	89	15c
Fruits, fresh, exp	year	134	89	15c
Fruits, processed, exp	year	84	89	15c
Fruits and vegetables, exp	year	375	89	15c
Grapefruit	lb	0.45	4/93	16r
Grapes, Thompson Seedless	lb	1.46	4/93	16r
Ground beef, 100% beef	lb	1.63	4/93	16r
Ground beef, lean and extra lean	lb	2.08	4/93	16r
Ground chuck, 100% beef	lb	1.94	4/93	16r
Ham, boneless, excluding canned	lb	2.21	4/93	16r
Honey, jar	8 oz	0.97-1.25	92	5r
Honey, jar	lb	1.25-2.25	92	5r
Honey, squeeze bear	12-oz	1.25-1.99	92	5r
Ice cream, prepackaged, bulk, regular	1/2 gal	2.41	4/93	16r
Lemons	lb	0.82	4/93	16r
Lettuce, iceberg	lb	0.83	4/93	16r
Margarine, stick	lb	0.77	4/93	16r
Meats, miscellaneous, exp	year	105	89	15c
Meats, poultry, fish and eggs, exp	year	552	89	15c
Milk and cream, fresh, exp	year	119	89	15c
Oranges, navel	lb	0.50	4/93	16r
Peanut butter, creamy, all sizes	lb	1.82	4/93	16r
Pears, Anjou	lb	0.85	4/93	16r
Pork, exp	year	104	89	15c
Pork chops, center cut, bone-in	lb	3.17	4/93	16r
Potato chips	16 oz	2.68	4/93	16r
Potatoes, white	lb	0.26	4/93	16r
Poultry, exp	year	93	89	15c
Round roast, graded & ungraded, ex USDA prime & choice	lb	2.88	4/93	16r
Round roast, USDA choice, boneless	lb	2.96	4/93	16r
Shortening, vegetable oil blends	lb	0.79	4/93	16r
Spaghetti and macaroni	lb	0.76	4/93	16r
Steak, rib eye, USDA choice, boneless	lb	6.29	4/93	16r
Steak, round, USDA choice, boneless	lb	3.24	4/93	16r
Steak, sirloin, graded & ungraded, ex USDA prime & choice	lb	4.00	4/93	16r
Steak, sirloin, USDA choice, bone-in	lb	3.57	4/93	16r
Steak, sirloin, USDA choice, boneless	lb	4.17	4/93	16r
Steak, T-bone, USDA choice, bone-in	lb	5.60	4/93	16r
Strawberries, dry pint	12 oz	0.90	4/93	16r
Sugar, white	lb	0.36	4/93	16r
Sugar, white, 33-80 oz pk	lb	0.35	4/93	16r
Sugar and other sweets, exp	year	56	89	15c
Tobacco products, exp	year	304	89	15c
Tomatoes, field grown	lb	0.99	4/93	16r
Tuna, chunk, light	lb	1.76	4/93	16r
Turkey, frozen, whole	lb	0.91	4/93	16r
Vegetables, fresh, exp	year	113	89	15c
Vegetables, processed, exp	year	45	89	15c
Health Care				
Childbirth, cesarean, hospital		4688	91	62r
Childbirth, cesarean, physician's fee		2053	91	62r
Childbirth, normal, hospital		2657	91	62r
Childbirth, normal, physician's fee		1492	91	62r
Drugs, exp	year	199	89	15c
Health care, exp	year	1216	89	15c
Health insurance, exp	year	405	89	15c
Hospital care, semiprivate room	day	409.59	90	27c
Medical insurance premium, per employee, small group comprehensive	month	430.70	10/91	25c
Medical plan per employee	year	3443	91	45r

Detroit-Ann Arbor, MI - continued

Item	Per	Value	Date	Ref.
Health Care - continued				
Medical services, exp	year	551	89	15c
Medical supplies, exp	year	61	89	15c
Mental health care, exp	capita	53.68-118.35	90	38s
Mental health care, exp, state mental health agency	capita	73.73	90	38s
Mental health care, hospital psychiatric services, non-Federal, exp	capita	22.52	88	38s
Mental health care, mental health organization, multiservice, exp	capita	42.68	88	38s
Mental health care, psychiatric hospitals, private, exp	capita	10.80	88	38s
Mental health care, psychiatric out-patient clinics, freestanding, exp	capita	3.47	88	38s
Mental health care, psychiatric partial-care organizations, freestanding, exp	capita	0.73	88	38s
Mental health care, state and county mental hospitals, exp	capita	36.77	88	38s
Mental health care, VA medical centers, exp	capita	4.03	88	38s
Physician fee, family practice, first-visit		76.00	91	62r
Physician fee, family practice, revisit		33.00	91	62r
Physician fee, general practice, first-visit		61.00	91	62r
Physician fee, general practice, revisit		31.00	91	62r
Physician fee, general surgeon, first-visit		65.00	91	62r
Physician fee, general surgeon, revisit		35.00	91	62r
Physician fee, internal medicine, first-visit		91.00	91	62r
Physician fee, internal medicine, revisit		40.00	91	62r
Physician fee, median, neurosurgeon, first-visit		106.00	91	62r
Physician fee, median, nonsurgical specialist, first-visit		90.00	91	62r
Physician fee, median, orthopedic surgeon, first-visit		83.00	91	62r
Physician fee, median, surgical specialist, first-visit		61.00	91	62r
Physician fee, neurosurgeon, revisit		41.00	91	62r
Physician fee, nonsurgical specialist, revisit		40.00	91	62r
Physician fee, obstetrics/gynecology, first-visit		61.00	91	62r
Physician fee, obstetrics/gynecology, revisit		40.00	91	62r
Physician fee, orthopedic surgeon, revisit		41.00	91	62r
Physician fee, pediatrician, first-visit		46.00	91	62r
Physician fee, pediatrician, revisit		33.00	91	62r
Physician fee, surgical specialist, revisit		36.00	91	62r
Substance abuse, hospital ancillary charge	incident	1480	90	70s
Substance abuse, hospital physician charge	incident	250	90	70s
Substance abuse, hospital room and board	incident	4070	90	70s
Household Goods				
Appliances, major, exp	year	170	89	15c
Appliances, small, exp	year	62	89	15c
Equipment, misc., exp	year	434	89	15c
Floor coverings, exp	year	69	89	15c
Furnishings and equipment, exp	year	1187	89	15c
Furniture, exp	year	365	89	15c
Household products, misc., exp	year	123	89	15c
Household textiles, exp	year	88	89	15c
Housekeeping supplies, exp	year	397	89	15c
Laundry and cleaning supplies, exp	year	101	89	15c
TVs, radios, sound equipment, exp	year	468	89	15c
Housing				
Dwellings, exp	year	3423	89	15c
Home, median price	unit	81.30		26c
Household expenses, misc.	year	207	89	15c
Household operations, exp	year	305	89	15c
Housing, exp	year	9224	89	15c
Lodging, exp	year	541	89	15c
Maintenance, repairs, insurance, and other, exp	year	664	89	15c

Values are in dollars or fractions of dollars. In the column headed *Ref*, references are shown to sources. Each reference is followed by a letter. These refer to the geographical level for which data were reported: s = State, r = Region, and c = City or metro. The abbreviation *ex* is used to mean *except* or *excluding*; *exp* stands for expenditures. For other abbreviations and further explanations, please see the Introduction.

Detroit-Ann Arbor, MI - continued

Item	Per	Value	Date	Ref.
Housing				
Mortgage interest, exp	year	1495	89	15c
Rental unit, 1 bedroom	month	528	93	23c
Rental unit, 2 bedroom	month	522	93	23c
Rental unit, 3 bedroom	month	653	93	23c
Rental unit, 4 bedroom	month	872	93	23c
Rental unit, efficiency	month	365	93	23c
Rented dwellings, exp	year	1331	89	15c
Shelter, exp	year	5295	89	15c
Insurance and Pensions				
Auto insurance, private passenger	year	716.78	91	63s
Insurance, life and other personal, exp	year	255	89	15c
Insurance and pensions, personal, exp	year	2327	89	15c
Pensions and social security, exp	year	2072	89	15c
Vehicle insurance	year	744	89	15c
Personal Goods				
Products and services, exp	year	378	89	15c
Personal Services				
Services, exp	year	98	89	15c
Taxes				
Property tax, exp	year	1264	89	15c
Tax, cigarette	pack	25	91	77s
Tax, gasoline	gal	15	91	77s
Taxes, state	capita	1185	91	77s
Transportation				
Auto rental, average	day	58.00	6/91	60c
Bus fare	one-way	1.00	3/93	2c
Bus fare, children (up to age 5), suburban network	one-way	0.00	4/93	19c
Bus fare, park and ride, suburban network	one-way	2.00	4/93	19c
Bus fare, regular, suburban network	one-way	1.50	4/93	19c
Bus fare, seniors and disabled (off peak times), suburban network	one-way	0.75	4/93	19c
Bus fare, youth (16-18), suburban network	one-way	1.00	4/93	19c
Driver's license fee		12.00	12/90	43s
Limo fare, airport-city, average	day	12.00	6/91	60c
Public transit, exp	year	318	89	15c
Taxi fare, airport-city, average	day	28.00	6/91	60c
Vehicle expenses, misc.	year	1907	89	15c
Vehicle finance charges	year	400	89	15c
Vehicle maintenance	year	535	89	15c
Vehicle registration and license plate	year	14.00-200.00	93	40s
Vehicle rental and license	year	229	89	15c
Travel				
Breakfast	day	6.67	6/91	60c
Dinner	day	22.82	6/91	60c
Lodging	day	103.69	91	60c
Lunch	day	10.38	6/91	60c
Travel, business	day	190.70	93	88c
Utilities				
Electricity	500 KWh	49.55	4/93	16c
Electricity	KWh	0.10	4/93	16c
Electricity	mil Btu	20.85	90	64s
Electricity, exp	year	619	89	15c
Electricity, winter, 250 KWh	month	24.37	92	55c
Electricity, winter, 500 KWh	month	48.74	92	55c
Electricity, winter, 750 KWh	month	76.75	92	55c
Electricity, winter, 1000 KWh	month	104.92	92	55c
Utilities, fuels, public services, exp	year	2041	89	15c
Water, public services, exp	year	142	89	15c

Dothan, AL

Item	Per	Value	Date	Ref.
Composite ACCRA index		88.30	4Q 92	4c
Alcoholic Beverages				
Beer, Miller Lite or Budweiser, 12-oz containers	6 pack	4.27	4Q 92	4c
Liquor, J & B Scotch	750 ml	19.99	4Q 92	4c
Wine, Gallo Chablis blanc, 1.5 liter	bottle	6.37	4Q 92	4c
Child Care				
Child care fee, average, center	hour	1.29	90	65r
Child care fee, average, nonregulated family day care	hour	0.89	90	65r
Child care fee, average, regulated family day care	hour	1.32	90	65r
Clothing				
Jeans, man's denim		22.75	4Q 92	4c
Shirt, man's dress shirt		17.79	4Q 92	4c
Undervest, boy's size 10-14, cotton	3	3.20	4Q 92	4c
Communications				
Long-distance telephone service, day, initial minute, 0-100 miles	min	0.11-0.36	91	12s
Long-distance telephone service, day, additional minute, 0-100 miles	min	0.09-0.26	91	12s
Long-distance telephone service, evenings/weekends, 0-100 mi, initial minute	min	0.04-0.14	91	12s
Long-distance telephone service, evenings/weekends, 0-100 mi, additional minute	min	0.04-0.10	91	12s
Newspaper subscription, daily and Sunday home delivery, large-city	month	9.30	4Q 92	4c
Telephone bill, family of four	month	20.25	4Q 92	4c
Education				
Board, 4-yr private college/university	year	1795	91	22s
Board, 4-yr public college/university	year	1469	91	22s
Expenditures, local gov't, public elementary/secondary	pupil	3675	92	20s
Room, 4-year private college/university	year	1340	91	22s
Room, 4-year public college/university	year	1295	91	22s
Tuition, 2-year private college/university	year	4148	91	22s
Tuition, 2-year public college/university	year	689	91	22s
Tuition, 4-year private college/university	year	5942	91	22s
Tuition, 4-year public college/university, in-state	year	1593	91	22s
Energy and Fuels				
Coal	mil Btu	1.83	90	64s
Energy	mil Btu	7.92	90	64s
Energy, combined forms, 1,800 sq ft heating area	month	105.66	4Q 92	4c
Energy exp/householder, 1-family unit	year	403	90	28r
Energy exp/householder, <1,000 sq ft heating area	year	342	90	28r
Energy exp/householder, 1,000-1,999 sq ft heating area	year	388	90	28r
Energy exp/householder, 2,000+ sq ft heating area	year	434	90	28r
Energy exp/householder, mobile home	year	320	90	28r
Energy exp/householder, multifamily	year	338	90	28r
Gas, natural	mil Btu	4.07	90	64s
Gas, natural	000 cu ft	7.05	91	46s
Gas, natural, exp	year	461	91	46s
Gasoline, motor	gal	1.15	4Q 92	4c
Gasoline, unleaded regular	mil Btu	8.96	90	64s
Entertainment				
Bowling, evening rate	game	1.77	4Q 92	4c
Miniature golf admission	adult	6.18	92	1r
Miniature golf admission	child	5.14	92	1r
Monopoly game, Parker Brothers', No. 9		10.38	4Q 92	4c
Movie	admission	5.00	4Q 92	4c
Tennis balls, yellow, Wilson or Penn, 3	can	2.23	4Q 92	4c
Waterpark admission	adult	11.00	92	1r

Values are in dollars or fractions of dollars. In the column headed *Ref*, references are shown to sources. Each reference is followed by a letter. These refer to the geographical level for which data were reported: s=State, r=Region, and c=City or metro. The abbreviation *ex* is used to mean *except* or *excluding*; *exp* stands for expenditures. For other abbreviations and further explanations, please see the Introduction.

Dothan, AL - continued

Item	Per	Value	Date	Ref.
Entertainment				
Waterpark admission	child	8.55	92	1r
Funerals				
Casket, 18-gauge steel, velvet interior		2329.05	91	24r
Cosmetology, hair care, etc.		72.78	91	24r
Embalming		240.71	91	24r
Facility use for ceremony		181.67	91	24r
Hearse, local		106.25	91	24r
Limousine, local		70.92	91	24r
Remains to funeral home, transfer		96.30	91	24r
Service charge, professional		687.09	91	24r
Vault, concrete, non-metallic liner		732.09	91	24r
Viewing facilities, use		190.30	91	24r
Goods and Services				
ACCRA Index, Miscellaneous Goods and Services		83.60	4Q 92	4c
Groceries				
ACCRA Index, Groceries		99.10	4Q 92	4c
Apples, Red Delicious	lb	0.79	4/93	16r
Babyfood, strained vegetables, lowest price	4-4.5 oz jar	0.25	4Q 92	4c
Bacon	lb	1.75	4/93	16r
Bananas	lb	0.43	4Q 92	4c
Bananas	lb	0.42	4/93	16r
Beef, stew, boneless	lb	2.61	4/93	16r
Bologna, all beef or mixed	lb	2.24	4/93	16r
Bread, white	24 oz	0.74	4Q 92	4c
Bread, white, pan	lb	0.64	4/93	16r
Bread, whole wheat, pan	lb	0.96	4/93	16r
Cabbage	lb	0.37	4/93	16r
Carrots, short trimmed and topped	lb	0.47	4/93	16r
Celery	lb	0.64	4/93	16r
Cheese, American	lb	2.98	4/93	16r
Cheese, Cheddar	lb	3.28	4/93	16r
Cheese, Kraft grated Parmesan	8-oz canister	3.27	4Q 92	4c
Chicken, fresh, whole	lb	0.77	4/93	16r
Chicken, fryer, whole	lb	0.68	4Q 92	4c
Chicken breast, bone-in	lb	1.92	4/93	16r
Chicken legs, bone-in	lb	1.06	4/93	16r
Chuck roast, graded and ungraded, ex USDA prime and choice	lb	2.40	4/93	16r
Chuck roast, USDA choice, bone-in	lb	2.19	4/93	16r
Chuck roast, USDA choice, boneless	lb	2.38	4/93	16r
Cigarettes, Winston	carton	16.76	4Q 92	4c
Coffee, 100% ground roast, all sizes	lb	2.48	4/93	16r
Coffee, vacuum-packed	13-oz can	2.06	4Q 92	4c
Corn, frozen	10 oz	0.53	4Q 92	4c
Corn Flakes, Kellogg's or Post Toasties	18 oz	1.70	4Q 92	4c
Crackers, soda, salted	lb	1.15	4/93	16r
Eggs, Grade A large	doz	0.76	4Q 92	4c
Eggs, Grade A large	doz	0.96	4/93	16r
Flour, white, all purpose	lb	0.24	4/93	16r
Frankfurters, all meat or all beef	lb	2.01	4/93	16r
Grapefruit	lb	0.44	4/93	16r
Grapes, Thompson Seedless	lb	1.40	4/93	16r
Ground beef, 100% beef	lb	1.58	4/93	16r
Ground beef, lean and extra lean	lb	2.09	4/93	16r
Ground beef or hamburger	lb	1.70	4Q 92	4c
Ground chuck, 100% beef	lb	1.98	4/93	16r
Ham, boneless, excluding canned	lb	2.89	4/93	16r
Ham, picnic, shoulder, bone-in, smoked	lb	1.02	4/93	16r
Ham, rump or steak half, bone-in, smoked	lb	1.48	4/93	16r
Honey, jar	8 oz	0.89-1.09	92	5r
Honey, jar	lb	1.39-2.25	92	5r
Honey, squeeze bear	12-oz	1.00-1.50	92	5r
Ice cream, prepackaged, bulk, regular	1/2 gal	2.41	4/93	16r
Lemons	lb	1.05	4/93	16r
Lettuce, iceberg	head	0.99	4Q 92	4c
Lettuce, iceberg	lb	0.81	4/93	16r

Dothan, AL - continued

Item	Per	Value	Date	Ref.
Groceries - continued				
Margarine, Blue Bonnet or Parkay cubes	lb	0.44	4Q 92	4c
Margarine, stick	lb	0.88	4/93	16r
Milk, whole	1/2 gal	1.41	4Q 92	4c
Orange juice, Minute Maid frozen	12-oz can	1.38	4Q 92	4c
Oranges, navel	lb	0.55	4/93	16r
Peaches	29-oz can	1.44	4Q 92	4c
Pears, Anjou	lb	0.92	4/93	16r
Peas Sweet, Del Monte or Green Giant	15-17 oz can	0.50	4Q 92	4c
Pork chops, center cut, bone-in	lb	3.13	4/93	16r
Potato chips	16 oz	2.94	4/93	16r
Potatoes, white	lb	0.43	4/93	16r
Potatoes, white or red	10-lb sack	3.01	4Q 92	4c
Rib roast, USDA choice, bone-in	lb	4.63	4/93	16r
Rice, white, long grain, uncooked	lb	0.45	4/93	16r
Round roast, graded & ungraded, ex USDA prime & choice	lb	3.03	4/93	16r
Round roast, USDA choice, boneless	lb	3.09	4/93	16r
Sausage, fresh, loose	lb	2.08	4/93	16r
Sausage, Jimmy Dean, 100% pork	lb	2.38	4Q 92	4c
Short ribs, bone-in	lb	2.66	4/93	16r
Shortening, vegetable oil blends	lb	0.69	4/93	16r
Shortening, vegetable, Crisco	3-lb can	2.19	4Q 92	4c
Soft drink, Coca Cola	2 liter	1.42	4Q 92	4c
Spaghetti and macaroni	lb	0.81	4/93	16r
Steak, rib eye, USDA choice, boneless	lb	6.24	4/93	16r
Steak, round, graded & ungraded, ex USDA prime & choice	lb	3.31	4/93	16r
Steak, round, USDA choice, boneless	lb	3.34	4/93	16r
Steak, sirloin, graded & ungraded, ex USDA prime & choice	lb	4.19	4/93	16r
Steak, sirloin, USDA choice, boneless	lb	4.46	4/93	16r
Steak, T-bone	lb	6.35	4Q 92	4c
Steak, T-bone, USDA choice, bone-in	lb	5.25	4/93	16r
Strawberries, dry pint	12 oz	0.92	4/93	16r
Sugar, cane or beet	4 lb	1.40	4Q 92	4c
Sugar, white	lb	0.39	4/93	16r
Sugar, white, 33-80 oz pk	lb	0.38	4/93	16r
Tomatoes, field grown	lb	0.88	4/93	16r
Tomatoes, Hunt's or Del Monte	14.5-oz can	0.55	4Q 92	4c
Tuna, chunk, light	6.125-6.5 oz can	0.51	4Q 92	4c
Tuna, chunk, light	lb	1.79	4/93	16r
Turkey, frozen, whole	lb	1.04	4/93	16r
Yogurt, natural, fruit flavored	1/2 pint	0.57	4/93	16r
Health Care				
ACCRA Index, Health Care		79.10	4Q 92	4c
Analgesic, Aspirin, Bayer, 325 mg tablets	100	4.21	4Q 92	4c
Childbirth, cesarean, hospital		5034	91	62r
Childbirth, cesarean, physician's fee		2053	91	62r
Childbirth, normal, hospital		2712	91	62r
Childbirth, normal, physician's fee		1492	91	62r
Dentist's fee, adult teeth cleaning and periodic oral exam	visit	29.40	4Q 92	4c
Doctor's fee, routine exam, established patient	visit	36.40	4Q 92	4c
Hospital care, semiprivate room	day	165.00	90	27c
Hospital care, semiprivate room	day	223.00	4Q 92	4c
Medical insurance premium, per employee, small group comprehensive	month	321.20	10/91	25c
Mental health care, exp	capita	37.60-53.67	90	38s
Mental health care, exp, state mental health agency	capita	38.35	90	38s

Values are in dollars or fractions of dollars. In the column headed *Ref*, references are shown to sources. Each reference is followed by a letter. These refer to the geographical level for which data were reported: s = State, r = Region, and c = City or metro. The abbreviation *ex* is used to mean *except* or *excluding*; *exp* stands for expenditures. For other abbreviations and further explanations, please see the Introduction.

Dothan, AL - continued

Item	Per	Value	Date	Ref.
Health Care				
Mental health care, hospital psychiatric services, non-Federal, exp	capita	13.58	88	38s
Mental health care, mental health organization, multiservice, exp	capita	12.40	88	38s
Mental health care, psychiatric hospitals, private, exp	capita	9.49	88	38s
Mental health care, state and county mental hospitals, exp	capita	22.15	88	38s
Mental health care, VA medical centers, exp	capita	10.94	88	38s
Physician fee, family practice, first-visit		75.00	91	62r
Physician fee, family practice, revisit		34.00	91	62r
Physician fee, general practice, first-visit		61.00	91	62r
Physician fee, general practice, revisit		32.00	91	62r
Physician fee, general surgeon, first-visit		64.00	91	62r
Physician fee, general surgeon, revisit		40.00	91	62r
Physician fee, internal medicine, first-visit		98.00	91	62r
Physician fee, internal medicine, revisit		40.00	91	62r
Physician fee, median, neurosurgeon, first-visit		130.00	91	62r
Physician fee, median, nonsurgical specialist, first-visit		95.00	91	62r
Physician fee, median, orthopedic surgeon, first-visit		91.00	91	62r
Physician fee, median, plastic surgeon, first-visit		66.00	91	62r
Physician fee, median, surgical specialist, first-visit		62.00	91	62r
Physician fee, neurosurgeon, revisit		50.00	91	62r
Physician fee, nonsurgical specialist, revisit		40.00	91	62r
Physician fee, obstetrics/gynecology, first-visit		64.00	91	62r
Physician fee, obstetrics/gynecology, revisit		41.00	91	62r
Physician fee, orthopedic surgeon, revisit		40.00	91	62r
Physician fee, pediatrician, first-visit		49.00	91	62r
Physician fee, pediatrician, revisit		33.00	91	62r
Physician fee, plastic surgeon, revisit		43.00	91	62r
Physician fee, surgical specialist, revisit		37.00	91	62r
Substance abuse, hospital ancillary charge	incident	1390	90	70s
Substance abuse, hospital physician charge	incident	520	90	70s
Substance abuse, hospital room and board	incident	5830	90	70s
Household Goods				
Appliance repair, home, service call, washing machine	min labor charge	28.39	4Q 92	4c
Laundry detergent, Tide Ultra, Bold, or Cheer	42 oz	2.84	4Q 92	4c
Tissues, facial, Kleenex brand	175-count box	1.09	4Q 92	4c
Housing				
ACCRA Index, Housing		83.20	4Q 92	4c
House, 1,800 sq ft, 8,000 sq ft lot, new, urban	total	96000	4Q 92	4c
House payment, principal and interest, 25% down payment	month	538	4Q 92	4c
Mortgage rate, incl. points & origination fee, 30-year fixed or adjustable rate	percent	8.18	4Q 92	4c
Rent, apartment, 2 bedrooms - 1-1/2 to 2 baths, unfurnished, 950 sq ft, water	month	350	4Q 92	4c
Rental unit, 1 bedroom	month	365	93	23c
Rental unit, 2 bedroom	month	429	93	23c
Rental unit, 3 bedroom	month	537	93	23c
Rental unit, 4 bedroom	month	601	93	23c
Rental unit, efficiency	month	301	93	23c
Insurance and Pensions				
Auto insurance, private passenger	year	562.59	91	63s

Dothan, AL - continued

Item	Per	Value	Date	Ref.
Personal Goods				
Shampoo, Alberto VO5	15 oz	0.99	4Q 92	4c
Toothpaste, Crest or Colgate	6-7 oz	1.53	4Q 92	4c
Personal Services				
Dry cleaning, man's 2-piece suit		4.95	4Q 92	4c
Haircare, woman's shampoo, trim and blow-dry		18.20	4Q 92	4c
Haircut, man's barbershop, no styling		6.10	4Q 92	4c
Restaurant Food				
Chicken, fried, thigh and drumstick		1.86	4Q 92	4c
Hamburger with cheese	1/4 lb	0.99	4Q 92	4c
Pizza, Pizza Hut or Pizza Inn, cheese, thin crust	12-13 in	6.59	4Q 92	4c
Taxes				
Tax, cigarette	pack	16.50	91	77s
Tax, gasoline	gal	16	91	77s
Taxes, state	capita	964	91	77s
Transportation				
ACCRA Index, Transportation		100.90	4Q 92	4c
Driver's license fee		15.00	12/90	43s
Tire balance, computer or spin balance, front	wheel	6.50	4Q 92	4c
Travel				
Business travel	day	193.00	4/93	89r
Utilities				
ACCRA Index, Utilities		97.50	4Q 92	4c
Electricity	mil Btu	16.46	90	64s
Electricity, all electric, 1,800 sq ft living area new home	month	105.66	4Q 92	4c

Douglas, GA

Item	Per	Value	Date	Ref.
Composite ACCRA index		92.60	4Q 92	4c
Alcoholic Beverages				
Beer, Miller Lite or Budweiser, 12-oz containers	6 pack	4.60	4Q 92	4c
Liquor, J & B Scotch	750 ml	20.06	4Q 92	4c
Wine, Gallo Chablis blanc, 1.5 liter	bottle	5.41	4Q 92	4c
Clothing				
Jeans, man's denim		38.24	4Q 92	4c
Shirt, man's dress shirt		27.50	4Q 92	4c
Undervest, boy's size 10-14, cotton	3	4.43	4Q 92	4c
Communications				
Newspaper subscription, daily and Sunday home delivery, large-city	month	9.75	4Q 92	4c
Telephone bill, family of four	month	20.49	4Q 92	4c
Energy and Fuels				
Energy, combined forms, 1,800 sq ft heating area	month	116.88	4Q 92	4c
Gasoline, motor	gal	1.07	4Q 92	4c
Entertainment				
Bowling, evening rate	game	1.85	4Q 92	4c
Monopoly game, Parker Brothers', No. 9		9.82	4Q 92	4c
Movie	admission	5.00	4Q 92	4c
Tennis balls, yellow, Wilson or Penn, 3	can	2.72	4Q 92	4c
Goods and Services				
ACCRA Index, Miscellaneous Goods and Services		102.80	4Q 92	4c
Groceries				
ACCRA Index, Groceries		99.40	4Q 92	4c
Babyfood, strained vegetables, lowest price	4-4.5 oz jar	0.32	4Q 92	4c
Bananas	lb	0.44	4Q 92	4c
Bread, white	24 oz	0.77	4Q 92	4c

Values are in dollars or fractions of dollars. In the column headed *Ref*, references are shown to sources. Each reference is followed by a letter. These refer to the geographical level for which data were reported: s = State, r = Region, and c = City or metro. The abbreviation *ex* is used to mean *except* or *excluding*; *exp* stands for expenditures. For other abbreviations and further explanations, please see the Introduction.

Douglas, GA - continued

Item	Per	Value	Date	Ref.
Groceries				
Cheese, Kraft grated Parmesan	8-oz canister	3.36	4Q 92	4c
Chicken, fryer, whole	lb	0.68	4Q 92	4c
Cigarettes, Winston	carton	16.66	4Q 92	4c
Coffee, vacuum-packed	13-oz can	1.99	4Q 92	4c
Corn, frozen	10 oz	0.57	4Q 92	4c
Corn Flakes, Kellogg's or Post Toasties	18 oz	1.82	4Q 92	4c
Eggs, Grade A large	doz	0.86	4Q 92	4c
Ground beef or hamburger	lb	1.79	4Q 92	4c
Lettuce, iceberg	head	0.99	4Q 92	4c
Margarine, Blue Bonnet or Parkay cubes	lb	0.61	4Q 92	4c
Milk, whole	1/2 gal	1.49	4Q 92	4c
Orange juice, Minute Maid frozen	12-oz can	1.42	4Q 92	4c
Peaches	29-oz can	1.29	4Q 92	4c
Peas Sweet, Del Monte or Green Giant	15-17 oz can	0.60	4Q 92	4c
Potatoes, white or red	10-lb sack	2.76	4Q 92	4c
Sausage, Jimmy Dean, 100% pork	lb	2.22	4Q 92	4c
Shortening, vegetable, Crisco	3-lb can	2.16	4Q 92	4c
Soft drink, Coca Cola	2 liter	1.12	4Q 92	4c
Steak, T-bone	lb	4.85	4Q 92	4c
Sugar, cane or beet	4 lb	1.48	4Q 92	4c
Tomatoes, Hunt's or Del Monte	14.5-oz can	0.56	4Q 92	4c
Tuna, chunk, light	6.125-6.5 oz can	0.57	4Q 92	4c
Health Care				
ACCRA Index, Health Care		84.10	4Q 92	4c
Analgesic, Aspirin, Bayer, 325 mg tablets	100	4.75	4Q 92	4c
Dentist's fee, adult teeth cleaning and periodic oral exam	visit	47.00	4Q 92	4c
Doctor's fee, routine exam, established patient	visit	29.40	4Q 92	4c
Hospital care, semiprivate room	day	173.00	4Q 92	4c
Household Goods				
Appliance repair, home, service call, washing machine	min labor charge	32.49	4Q 92	4c
Laundry detergent, Tide Ultra, Bold, or Cheer	42 oz	3.19	4Q 92	4c
Tissues, facial, Kleenex brand	175-count box	1.16	4Q 92	4c
Housing				
ACCRA Index, Housing		73.20	4Q 92	4c
House, 1,800 sq ft, 8,000 sq ft lot, new, urban	total	83500	4Q 92	4c
House payment, principal and interest, 25% down payment	month	461	4Q 92	4c
Mortgage rate, incl. points & origination fee, 30-year fixed or adjustable rate	percent	8.04	4Q 92	4c
Rent, apartment, 2 bedrooms - 1-1/2 to 2 baths, unfurnished, 950 sq ft, water	month	335	4Q 92	4c
Personal Goods				
Shampoo, Alberto VO5	15 oz	1.14	4Q 92	4c
Toothpaste, Crest or Colgate	6-7 oz	1.99	4Q 92	4c
Personal Services				
Dry cleaning, man's 2-piece suit		5.22	4Q 92	4c
Haircare, woman's shampoo, trim and blow-dry		14.25	4Q 92	4c
Haircut, man's barbershop, no styling		5.50	4Q 92	4c

Douglas, GA - continued

Item	Per	Value	Date	Ref.
Restaurant Food				
Chicken, fried, thigh and drumstick		2.09	4Q 92	4c
Hamburger with cheese	1/4 lb	1.81	4Q 92	4c
Pizza, Pizza Hut or Pizza Inn, cheese, thin crust	12-13 in	7.99	4Q 92	4c
Transportation				
ACCRA Index, Transportation		93.40	4Q 92	4c
Tire balance, computer or spin balance, front	wheel	6.00	4Q 92	4c
Utilities				
ACCRA Index, Utilities		106.90	4Q 92	4c
Electricity, all electric, 1,800 sq ft living area new home	month	116.88	4Q 92	4c

Dover, DE

Item	Per	Value	Date	Ref.
Composite ACCRA index		106.80	4Q 92	4c
Alcoholic Beverages				
Beer, Miller Lite or Budweiser, 12-oz containers	6 pack	4.15	4Q 92	4c
Liquor, J & B Scotch	750 ml	16.50	4Q 92	4c
Wine, Gallo Chablis blanc, 1.5 liter	bottle	5.84	4Q 92	4c
Clothing				
Jeans, man's denim		35.16	4Q 92	4c
Shirt, man's dress shirt		24.47	4Q 92	4c
Undervest, boy's size 10-14, cotton	3	4.12	4Q 92	4c
Communications				
Newspaper subscription, daily and Sunday home delivery, large-city	month	9.78	4Q 92	4c
Telephone, flat rate	month	1.60	91	11c
Telephone bill, family of four	month	14.61	4Q 92	4c
Energy and Fuels				
Energy, combined forms, 1,800 sq ft heating area	month	109.90	4Q 92	4c
Energy, exc electricity, 1,800 sq ft heating area	month	48.41	4Q 92	4c
Gasoline, motor	gal	1.09	4Q 92	4c
Entertainment				
Bowling, evening rate	game	2.30	4Q 92	4c
Monopoly game, Parker Brothers', No. 9		11.90	4Q 92	4c
Movie	admission	6.00	4Q 92	4c
Tennis balls, yellow, Wilson or Penn, 3	can	2.43	4Q 92	4c
Goods and Services				
ACCRA Index, Miscellaneous Goods and Services		105.90	4Q 92	4c
Groceries				
ACCRA Index, Groceries		108.40	4Q 92	4c
Babyfood, strained vegetables, lowest price	4-4.5 oz jar	0.37	4Q 92	4c
Bananas	lb	0.44	4Q 92	4c
Bread, white	24 oz	0.81	4Q 92	4c
Cheese, Kraft grated Parmesan	8-oz canister	3.79	4Q 92	4c
Chicken, fryer, whole	lb	0.81	4Q 92	4c
Cigarettes, Winston	carton	17.61	4Q 92	4c
Coffee, vacuum-packed	13-oz can	2.16	4Q 92	4c
Corn, frozen	10 oz	0.66	4Q 92	4c
Corn Flakes, Kellogg's or Post Toasties	18 oz	1.88	4Q 92	4c
Eggs, Grade A large	doz	0.81	4Q 92	4c
Ground beef or hamburger	lb	1.66	4Q 92	4c
Lettuce, iceberg	head	1.11	4Q 92	4c
Margarine, Blue Bonnet or Parkay cubes	lb	0.78	4Q 92	4c
Milk, whole	1/2 gal	1.28	4Q 92	4c
Orange juice, Minute Maid frozen	12-oz can	1.61	4Q 92	4c

Values are in dollars or fractions of dollars. In the column headed *Ref*, references are shown to sources. Each reference is followed by a letter. These refer to the geographical level for which data were reported: s=State, r=Region, and c=City or metro. The abbreviation *ex* is used to mean *except* or *excluding*; *exp* stands for expenditures. For other abbreviations and further explanations, please see the Introduction.

Dover, DE - continued

Item	Per	Value	Date	Ref.
Groceries				
Peaches	29-oz can	1.43	4Q 92	4c
Peas Sweet, Del Monte or Green Giant	15-17 oz can	0.61	4Q 92	4c
Potatoes, white or red	10-lb sack	2.25	4Q 92	4c
Sausage, Jimmy Dean, 100% pork	lb	3.45	4Q 92	4c
Shortening, vegetable, Crisco	3-lb can	2.77	4Q 92	4c
Soft drink, Coca Cola	2 liter	0.86	4Q 92	4c
Steak, T-bone	lb	5.66	4Q 92	4c
Sugar, cane or beet	4 lb	1.96	4Q 92	4c
Tomatoes, Hunt's or Del Monte	14.5-oz can	0.82	4Q 92	4c
Tuna, chunk, light	6.125-6.5 oz can	0.75	4Q 92	4c
Health Care				
ACCRA Index, Health Care		105.00	4Q 92	4c
Analgesic, Aspirin, Bayer, 325 mg tablets	100	5.12	4Q 92	4c
Dentist's fee, adult teeth cleaning and periodic oral exam	visit	53.00	4Q 92	4c
Doctor's fee, routine exam, established patient	visit	32.40	4Q 92	4c
Hospital care, semiprivate room	day	395.00	4Q 92	4c
Household Goods				
Appliance repair, home, service call, washing machine	min labor charge	38.50	4Q 92	4c
Laundry detergent, Tide Ultra, Bold, or Cheer	42 oz	3.24	4Q 92	4c
Tissues, facial, Kleenex brand	175-count box	1.10	4Q 92	4c
Housing				
ACCRA Index, Housing		112.90	4Q 92	4c
House, 1,800 sq ft, 8,000 sq ft lot, new, urban	total	125300	4Q 92	4c
House payment, principal and interest, 25% down payment	month	702	4Q 92	4c
Mortgage rate, incl. points & origination fee, 30-year fixed or adjustable rate	percent	8.20	4Q 92	4c
Rent, apartment, 2 bedrooms - 1-1/2 to 2 baths, unfurnished, 950 sq ft, water	month	538	4Q 92	4c
Personal Goods				
Shampoo, Alberto VO5	15 oz	1.21	4Q 92	4c
Toothpaste, Crest or Colgate	6-7 oz	2.32	4Q 92	4c
Personal Services				
Dry cleaning, man's 2-piece suit		6.62	4Q 92	4c
Haircare, woman's shampoo, trim and blow-dry		18.55	4Q 92	4c
Haircut, man's barbershop, no styling		6.65	4Q 92	4c
Restaurant Food				
Chicken, fried, thigh and drumstick		1.99	4Q 92	4c
Hamburger with cheese	1/4 lb	1.88	4Q 92	4c
Pizza, Pizza Hut or Pizza Inn, cheese, thin crust	12-13 in	8.99	4Q 92	4c
Transportation				
ACCRA Index, Transportation		99.60	4Q 92	4c
Bus fare	one-way	0.75	3/93	2c
Tire balance, computer or spin balance, front	wheel	6.67	4Q 92	4c
Utilities				
ACCRA Index, Utilities		98.10	4Q 92	4c
Electricity, partial electric and other energy, 1,800 sq ft living area new home	month	61.49	4Q 92	4c

Dubuque, IA

Item	Per	Value	Date	Ref.
Composite ACCRA index		99.60	4Q 92	4c
Alcoholic Beverages				
Beer, Miller Lite or Budweiser, 12-oz containers	6 pack	3.63	4Q 92	4c
Liquor, J & B Scotch	750 ml	17.58	4Q 92	4c
Wine, Gallo Chablis blanc, 1.5 liter	bottle	4.85	4Q 92	4c
Child Care				
Child care fee, average, center	hour	1.63	90	65r
Child care fee, average, nonregulated family day care	hour	1.83	90	65r
Child care fee, average, regulated family day care	hour	1.42	90	65r
Clothing				
Jeans, man's denim		32.99	4Q 92	4c
Shirt, man's dress shirt		24.50	4Q 92	4c
Undervest, boy's size 10-14, cotton	3	3.35	4Q 92	4c
Communications				
Long-distance telephone service, day, initial minute, 0-100 miles	min	0.21-0.41	91	12s
Long-distance telephone service, day, additional minute, 0-100 miles	min	0.11-0.30	91	12s
Long-distance telephone service, evenings/weekends, 0-100 mi, initial minute	min	0.11-0.20	91	12s
Long-distance telephone service, evenings/weekends, 0-100 mi, additional minute	min	0.06-0.15	91	12s
Newspaper subscription, daily and Sunday home delivery, large-city	month	11.96	4Q 92	4c
Telephone, flat rate	month	14.45	91	11c
Telephone bill, family of four	month	20.75	4Q 92	4c
Education				
Board, 4-yr private college/university	year	1703	91	22s
Board, 4-yr public college/university	year	1183	91	22s
Expenditures, local gov't, public elementary/secondary	pupil	5026	92	20s
Room, 4-year private college/university	year	1392	91	22s
Room, 4-year public college/university	year	1188	91	22s
Tuition, 2-year private college/university	year	5119	91	22s
Tuition, 2-year public college/university	year	1298	91	22s
Tuition, 4-year private college/university	year	8703	91	22s
Tuition, 4-year public college/university, in-state	year	1880	91	22s
Energy and Fuels				
Coal	mil Btu	1.16	90	64s
Energy	mil Btu	7.71	90	64s
Energy, combined forms, 1,800 sq ft heating area	month	90.88	4Q 92	4c
Energy, exc electricity, 1,800 sq ft heating area	month	39.12	4Q 92	4c
Energy exp/householder, 1-family unit	year	473	90	28r
Energy exp/householder, <1,000 sq ft heating area	year	429	90	28r
Energy exp/householder, 1,000-1,999 sq ft heating area	year	442	90	28r
Energy exp/householder, 2,000+ sq ft heating area	year	498	90	28r
Energy exp/householder, mobile home	year	442	90	28r
Energy exp/householder, multifamily	year	407	90	28r
Gas, natural	mil Btu	3.81	90	64s
Gas, natural	000 cu ft	4.81	91	46s
Gas, natural, exp	year	530	91	46s
Gasoline, motor	gal	1.20	4Q 92	4c
Gasoline, unleaded regular	mil Btu	9.38	90	64s
Entertainment				
Bowling, evening rate	game	1.50	4Q 92	4c
Miniature golf admission	adult	6.18	92	1r
Miniature golf admission	child	5.14	92	1r
Monopoly game, Parker Brothers', No. 9		10.19	4Q 92	4c

Values are in dollars or fractions of dollars. In the column headed *Ref*, references are shown to sources. Each reference is followed by a letter. These refer to the geographical level for which data were reported: s = State, r = Region, and c = City or metro. The abbreviation *ex* is used to mean *except* or *excluding*; *exp* stands for expenditures. For other abbreviations and further explanations, please see the Introduction.

Dubuque, IA - continued

Item	Per	Value	Date	Ref.
Entertainment				
Movie	admission	5.00	4Q 92	4c
Tennis balls, yellow, Wilson or Penn, 3	can	1.99	4Q 92	4c
Waterpark admission	adult	11.00	92	1r
Waterpark admission	child	8.55	92	1r
Funerals				
Casket, 18-gauge steel, velvet interior		1952.97	91	24r
Cosmetology, hair care, etc.		90.03	91	24r
Embalming		251.75	91	24r
Facility use for ceremony		180.75	91	24r
Hearse, local		117.51	91	24r
Limousine, local		71.86	91	24r
Remains to funeral home, transfer		81.14	91	24r
Service charge, professional		740.03	91	24r
Vault, concrete, non-metallic liner		801.47	91	24r
Viewing facilities, use		169.33	91	24r
Goods and Services				
ACCRA Index, Miscellaneous Goods and Services		96.30	4Q 92	4c
Groceries				
ACCRA Index, Groceries		103.20	4Q 92	4c
Apples, Red Delicious	lb	0.77	4/93	16r
Babyfood, strained vegetables, lowest price	4-4.5 oz jar	0.31	4Q 92	4c
Bacon	lb	1.85	4/93	16r
Bananas	lb	0.43	4Q 92	4c
Bananas	lb	0.46	4/93	16r
Beef, stew, boneless	lb	2.53	4/93	16r
Bologna, all beef or mixed	lb	2.19	4/93	16r
Bread, white	24 oz	0.85	4Q 92	4c
Bread, white, pan	lb	0.78	4/93	16r
Butter	lb	1.50	4/93	16r
Cabbage	lb	0.40	4/93	16r
Carrots, short trimmed and topped	lb	0.45	4/93	16r
Cheese, Cheddar	lb	3.47	4/93	16r
Cheese, Kraft grated Parmesan	8-oz canister	3.01	4Q 92	4c
Chicken, fresh, whole	lb	0.84	4/93	16r
Chicken, fryer, whole	lb	0.79	4Q 92	4c
Chicken breast, bone-in	lb	1.94	4/93	16r
Chicken legs, bone-in	lb	1.02	4/93	16r
Chuck roast, graded and ungraded, ex USDA prime and choice	lb	2.43	4/93	16r
Chuck roast, USDA choice, bone-in	lb	2.11	4/93	16r
Chuck roast, USDA choice, boneless	lb	2.44	4/93	16r
Cigarettes, Winston	carton	18.03	4Q 92	4c
Coffee, 100% ground roast, all sizes	lb	2.47	4/93	16r
Coffee, vacuum-packed	13-oz can	2.02	4Q 92	4c
Cookies, chocolate chip	lb	2.73	4/93	16r
Corn, frozen	10 oz	0.67	4Q 92	4c
Corn Flakes, Kellogg's or Post Toasties	18 oz	1.93	4Q 92	4c
Eggs, Grade A large	doz	0.72	4Q 92	4c
Eggs, Grade A large	doz	0.93	4/93	16r
Flour, white, all purpose	lb	0.21	4/93	16r
Grapefruit	lb	0.45	4/93	16r
Grapes, Thompson Seedless	lb	1.46	4/93	16r
Ground beef, 100% beef	lb	1.63	4/93	16r
Ground beef, lean and extra lean	lb	2.08	4/93	16r
Ground beef or hamburger	lb	1.45	4Q 92	4c
Ground chuck, 100% beef	lb	1.94	4/93	16r
Ham, boneless, excluding canned	lb	2.21	4/93	16r
Ice cream, prepackaged, bulk, regular	1/2 gal	2.41	4/93	16r
Lemons	lb	0.82	4/93	16r
Lettuce, iceberg	head	0.98	4Q 92	4c
Lettuce, iceberg	lb	0.83	4/93	16r
Margarine, Blue Bonnet or Parkay cubes	lb	0.59	4Q 92	4c
Margarine, stick	lb	0.77	4/93	16r
Milk, whole	1/2 gal	1.31	4Q 92	4c

Dubuque, IA - continued

Item	Per	Value	Date	Ref.
Groceries - continued				
Orange juice, Minute Maid frozen	12-oz can	1.44	4Q 92	4c
Oranges, navel	lb	0.50	4/93	16r
Peaches	29-oz can	1.44	4Q 92	4c
Peanut butter, creamy, all sizes	lb	1.82	4/93	16r
Pears, Anjou	lb	0.85	4/93	16r
Peas Sweet, Del Monte or Green Giant	15-17 oz can	0.61	4Q 92	4c
Pork chops, center cut, bone-in	lb	3.17	4/93	16r
Potato chips	16 oz	2.68	4/93	16r
Potatoes, white	lb	0.26	4/93	16r
Potatoes, white or red	10-lb sack	2.97	4Q 92	4c
Round roast, graded & ungraded, ex USDA prime & choice	lb	2.88	4/93	16r
Round roast, USDA choice, boneless	lb	2.96	4/93	16r
Sausage, Jimmy Dean, 100% pork	lb	3.19	4Q 92	4c
Shortening, vegetable oil blends	lb	0.79	4/93	16r
Shortening, vegetable, Crisco	3-lb can	2.36	4Q 92	4c
Soft drink, Coca Cola	2 liter	1.13	4Q 92	4c
Spaghetti and macaroni	lb	0.76	4/93	16r
Steak, rib eye, USDA choice, boneless	lb	6.29	4/93	16r
Steak, round, USDA choice, boneless	lb	3.24	4/93	16r
Steak, sirloin, graded & ungraded, ex USDA prime & choice	lb	4.00	4/93	16r
Steak, sirloin, USDA choice, bone-in	lb	3.57	4/93	16r
Steak, sirloin, USDA choice, boneless	lb	4.17	4/93	16r
Steak, T-bone	lb	4.97	4Q 92	4c
Steak, T-bone, USDA choice, bone-in	lb	5.60	4/93	16r
Strawberries, dry pint	12 oz	0.90	4/93	16r
Sugar, cane or beet	4 lb	1.59	4Q 92	4c
Sugar, white	lb	0.36	4/93	16r
Sugar, white, 33-80 oz pk	lb	0.35	4/93	16r
Tomatoes, field grown	lb	0.99	4/93	16r
Tomatoes, Hunt's or Del Monte	14.5-oz can	0.79	4Q 92	4c
Tuna, chunk, light	6.125-6.5 oz can	0.60	4Q 92	4c
Tuna, chunk, light	lb	1.76	4/93	16r
Turkey, frozen, whole	lb	0.91	4/93	16r
Health Care				
ACCRA Index, Health Care		99.00	4Q 92	4c
Analgesic, Aspirin, Bayer, 325 mg tablets	100	5.04	4Q 92	4c
Childbirth, cesarean, hospital		4688	91	62r
Childbirth, cesarean, physician's fee		2053	91	62r
Childbirth, normal, hospital		2657	91	62r
Childbirth, normal, physician's fee		1492	91	62r
Dentist's fee, adult teeth cleaning and periodic oral exam	visit	42.40	4Q 92	4c
Doctor's fee, routine exam, established patient	visit	44.00	4Q 92	4c
Health care spending, state	capita	2351	3/93	84s
Hospital care, semiprivate room	day	223.74	90	27c
Hospital care, semiprivate room	day	240.00	4Q 92	4c
Medical insurance premium, per employee, small group comprehensive	month	281.05	10/91	25c
Medical plan per employee	year	3443	91	45r
Mental health care, exp	capita	20.37-28.83	90	38s
Mental health care, exp, state mental health agency	capita	17.07	90	38s
Mental health care, hospital psychiatric services, non-Federal, exp	capita	23.51	88	38s
Mental health care, mental health organization, multiservice, exp	capita	7.66	88	38s
Mental health care, psychiatric hospitals, private, exp	capita	2.86	88	38s
Mental health care, psychiatric out-patient clinics, freestanding, exp	capita	3.02	88	38s

Values are in dollars or fractions of dollars. In the column headed *Ref*, references are shown to sources. Each reference is followed by a letter. These refer to the geographical level for which data were reported: s = State, r = Region, and c = City or metro. The abbreviation *ex* is used to mean *except* or *excluding*; *exp* stands for expenditures. For other abbreviations and further explanations, please see the Introduction.

Dubuque, IA - continued

Item	Per	Value	Date	Ref.
Health Care				
Mental health care, state and county mental hospitals, exp	capita	14.54	88	38s
Mental health care, VA medical centers, exp	capita	13.98	88	38s
Physician fee, family practice, first-visit		76.00	91	62r
Physician fee, family practice, revisit		33.00	91	62r
Physician fee, general practice, first-visit		61.00	91	62r
Physician fee, general practice, revisit		31.00	91	62r
Physician fee, general surgeon, first-visit		65.00	91	62r
Physician fee, general surgeon, revisit		35.00	91	62r
Physician fee, internal medicine, first-visit		91.00	91	62r
Physician fee, internal medicine, revisit		40.00	91	62r
Physician fee, median, neurosurgeon, first-visit		106.00	91	62r
Physician fee, median, nonsurgical specialist, first-visit		90.00	91	62r
Physician fee, median, orthopedic surgeon, first-visit		83.00	91	62r
Physician fee, median, surgical specialist, first-visit		61.00	91	62r
Physician fee, neurosurgeon, revisit		41.00	91	62r
Physician fee, nonsurgical specialist, revisit		40.00	91	62r
Physician fee, obstetrics/gynecology, first-visit		61.00	91	62r
Physician fee, obstetrics/gynecology, revisit		40.00	91	62r
Physician fee, orthopedic surgeon, revisit		41.00	91	62r
Physician fee, pediatrician, first-visit		46.00	91	62r
Physician fee, pediatrician, revisit		33.00	91	62r
Physician fee, surgical specialist, revisit		36.00	91	62r
Substance abuse, hospital ancillary charge	incident	950	90	70s
Substance abuse, hospital physician charge	incident	250	90	70s
Substance abuse, hospital room and board	incident	3110	90	70s
Household Goods				
Appliance repair, home, service call, washing machine	min labor charge	35.00	4Q 92	4c
Laundry detergent, Tide Ultra, Bold, or Cheer	42 oz	3.67	4Q 92	4c
Tissues, facial, Kleenex brand	175-count box	1.17	4Q 92	4c
Housing				
ACCRA Index, Housing		106.20	4Q 92	4c
House, 1,800 sq ft, 8,000 sq ft lot, new, urban	total	116250	4Q 92	4c
House payment, principal and interest, 25% down payment	month	649	4Q 92	4c
Mortgage rate, incl. points & origination fee, 30-year fixed or adjustable rate	percent	8.16	4Q 92	4c
Rent, apartment, 2 bedrooms - 1-1/2 to 2 baths, unfurnished, 950 sq ft, water	month	533	4Q 92	4c
Rental unit, 1 bedroom	month	400	93	23c
Rental unit, 2 bedroom	month	472	93	23c
Rental unit, 3 bedroom	month	592	93	23c
Rental unit, 4 bedroom	month	662	93	23c
Rental unit, efficiency	month	331	93	23c
Insurance and Pensions				
Auto insurance, private passenger	year	422.46	91	63s
Personal Goods				
Shampoo, Alberto VO5	15 oz	1.18	4Q 92	4c
Toothpaste, Crest or Colgate	6-7 oz	1.70	4Q 92	4c
Personal Services				
Dry cleaning, man's 2-piece suit		5.94	4Q 92	4c
Haircare, woman's shampoo, trim and blow-dry		13.64	4Q 92	4c
Haircut, man's barbershop, no styling		7.65	4Q 92	4c

Dubuque, IA - continued

Item	Per	Value	Date	Ref.
Restaurant Food				
Chicken, fried, thigh and drumstick		2.25	4Q 92	4c
Hamburger with cheese	1/4 lb	1.95	4Q 92	4c
Pizza, Pizza Hut or Pizza Inn, cheese, thin crust	12-13 in	7.69	4Q 92	4c
Taxes				
Tax, cigarette	pack	36	91	77s
Tax, gasoline	gal	20	91	77s
Taxes, state	capita	1233	91	77s
Transportation				
ACCRA Index, Transportation		100.50	4Q 92	4c
Bus fare, up to 10 miles	one-way	0.80	4Q 92	4c
Driver's license fee		16.00	12/90	43s
Tire balance, computer or spin balance, front	wheel	6.29	4Q 92	4c
Utilities				
ACCRA Index, Utilities		85.60	4Q 92	4c
Electricity	mil Btu	17.37	90	64s
Electricity, partial electric and other energy, 1,800 sq ft living area new home	month	51.76	4Q 92	4c
Electricity, winter, 250 KWh	month	18.97	92	55c
Electricity, winter, 250 KWh	month	20.16	2/93	30c
Electricity, winter, 500 KWh	month	34.61	92	55c
Electricity, winter, 500 KWh	month	34.92	2/93	30c
Electricity, winter, 750 KWh	month	49.05	92	55c
Electricity, winter, 750 KWh	month	47.01	2/93	30c
Electricity, winter, 1000 KWh	month	62.67	92	55c
Electricity, winter, 1000 KWh	month	39.10	2/93	30c

Duluth, MN

Item	Per	Value	Date	Ref.
Child Care				
Child care fee, average, center	hour	1.63	90	65r
Child care fee, average, nonregulated family day care	hour	1.83	90	65r
Child care fee, average, regulated family day care	hour	1.42	90	65r
Communications				
Long-distance telephone service, day, initial minute, 0-100 miles	min	0.14-0.52	91	12s
Long-distance telephone service, day, additional minute, 0-100 miles	min	0.05-0.35	91	12s
Long-distance telephone service, evenings/weekends, 0-100 mi, initial minute	min	0.08-0.31	91	12s
Long-distance telephone service, evenings/weekends, 0-100 mi, additional minute	min	0.03-0.21	91	12s
Telephone, flat rate	month	14.61	91	11c
Education				
Board, 4-yr private college/university	year	1718	91	22s
Board, 4-yr public college/university	year	1321	91	22s
Expenditures, local gov't, public elementary/secondary	pupil	5500	92	20s
Room, 4-year private college/university	year	1587	91	22s
Room, 4-year public college/university	year	1344	91	22s
Tuition, 2-year private college/university	year	7664	91	22s
Tuition, 2-year public college/university	year	1578	91	22s
Tuition, 4-year private college/university	year	9507	91	22s
Tuition, 4-year public college/university, in-state	year	2216	91	22s
Energy and Fuels				
Coal	mil Btu	1.32	90	64s
Energy	mil Btu	8.17	90	64s
Energy exp/householder, 1-family unit	year	473	90	28r
Energy exp/householder, <1,000 sq ft heating area	year	429	90	28r
Energy exp/householder, 1,000-1,999 sq ft heating area	year	442	90	28r

Values are in dollars or fractions of dollars. In the column headed *Ref*, references are shown to sources. Each reference is followed by a letter. These refer to the geographical level for which data were reported: s=State, r=Region, and c=City or metro. The abbreviation *ex* is used to mean *except* or *excluding*; *exp* stands for expenditures. For other abbreviations and further explanations, please see the Introduction.

Duluth, MN - continued

Item	Per	Value	Date	Ref.
Energy and Fuels				
Energy exp/householder, 2,000+ sq ft heating area	year	498	90	28r
Energy exp/householder, mobile home	year	442	90	28r
Energy exp/householder, multifamily	year	407	90	28r
Gas, natural	mil Btu	3.87	90	64s
Gas, natural	000 cu ft	4.52	91	46s
Gas, natural, exp	year	545	91	46s
Gasoline, unleaded regular	mil Btu	9.56	90	64s
Entertainment				
Miniature golf admission	adult	6.18	92	1r
Miniature golf admission	child	5.14	92	1r
Waterpark admission	adult	11.00	92	1r
Waterpark admission	child	8.55	92	1r
Funerals				
Casket, 18-gauge steel, velvet interior		1952.97	91	24r
Cosmetology, hair care, etc.		90.03	91	24r
Embalming		251.75	91	24r
Facility use for ceremony		180.75	91	24r
Hearse, local		117.51	91	24r
Limousine, local		71.86	91	24r
Remains to funeral home, transfer		81.14	91	24r
Service charge, professional		740.03	91	24r
Vault, concrete, non-metallic liner		801.47	91	24r
Viewing facilities, use		169.33	91	24r
Groceries				
Apples, Red Delicious	lb	0.77	4/93	16r
Bacon	lb	1.85	4/93	16r
Bananas	lb	0.46	4/93	16r
Beef, stew, boneless	lb	2.53	4/93	16r
Bologna, all beef or mixed	lb	2.19	4/93	16r
Bread, white, pan	lb	0.78	4/93	16r
Butter	lb	1.50	4/93	16r
Cabbage	lb	0.40	4/93	16r
Carrots, short trimmed and topped	lb	0.45	4/93	16r
Cheese, Cheddar	lb	3.47	4/93	16r
Chicken, fresh, whole	lb	0.84	4/93	16r
Chicken breast, bone-in	lb	1.94	4/93	16r
Chicken legs, bone-in	lb	1.02	4/93	16r
Chuck roast, graded and ungraded, ex USDA prime and choice	lb	2.43	4/93	16r
Chuck roast, USDA choice, bone-in	lb	2.11	4/93	16r
Chuck roast, USDA choice, boneless	lb	2.44	4/93	16r
Coffee, 100% ground roast, all sizes	lb	2.47	4/93	16r
Cookies, chocolate chip	lb	2.73	4/93	16r
Eggs, Grade A large	doz	0.93	4/93	16r
Flour, white, all purpose	lb	0.21	4/93	16r
Grapefruit	lb	0.45	4/93	16r
Grapes, Thompson Seedless	lb	1.46	4/93	16r
Ground beef, 100% beef	lb	1.63	4/93	16r
Ground beef, lean and extra lean	lb	2.08	4/93	16r
Ground chuck, 100% beef	lb	1.94	4/93	16r
Ham, boneless, excluding canned	lb	2.21	4/93	16r
Ice cream, prepackaged, bulk, regular	1/2 gal	2.41	4/93	16r
Lemons	lb	0.82	4/93	16r
Lettuce, iceberg	lb	0.83	4/93	16r
Margarine, stick	lb	0.77	4/93	16r
Oranges, navel	lb	0.50	4/93	16r
Peanut butter, creamy, all sizes	lb	1.82	4/93	16r
Pears, Anjou	lb	0.85	4/93	16r
Pork chops, center cut, bone-in	lb	3.17	4/93	16r
Potato chips	16 oz	2.68	4/93	16r
Potatoes, white	lb	0.26	4/93	16r
Round roast, graded & ungraded, ex USDA prime & choice	lb	2.88	4/93	16r
Round roast, USDA choice, boneless	lb	2.96	4/93	16r
Shortening, vegetable oil blends	lb	0.79	4/93	16r
Spaghetti and macaroni	lb	0.76	4/93	16r
Steak, rib eye, USDA choice, boneless	lb	6.29	4/93	16r
Steak, round, USDA choice, boneless	lb	3.24	4/93	16r

Duluth, MN - continued

Item	Per	Value	Date	Ref.
Groceries - continued				
Steak, sirloin, graded & ungraded, ex USDA prime & choice	lb	4.00	4/93	16r
Steak, sirloin, USDA choice, bone-in	lb	3.57	4/93	16r
Steak, sirloin, USDA choice, boneless	lb	4.17	4/93	16r
Steak, T-bone, USDA choice, bone-in	lb	5.60	4/93	16r
Strawberries, dry pint	12 oz	0.90	4/93	16r
Sugar, white	lb	0.36	4/93	16r
Sugar, white, 33-80 oz pk	lb	0.35	4/93	16r
Tomatoes, field grown	lb	0.99	4/93	16r
Tuna, chunk, light	lb	1.76	4/93	16r
Turkey, frozen, whole	lb	0.91	4/93	16r
Health Care				
Childbirth, cesarean, hospital		4688	91	62r
Childbirth, cesarean, physician's fee		2053	91	62r
Childbirth, normal, hospital		2657	91	62r
Childbirth, normal, physician's fee		1492	91	62r
Hospital care, semiprivate room	day	238.36	90	27c
Medical insurance premium, per employee, small group comprehensive	month	267.40	10/91	25c
Medical plan per employee	year	3443	91	45r
Mental health care, exp	capita	20.37-28.83	90	38s
Mental health care, exp, state mental health agency	capita	53.67	90	38s
Mental health care, hospital psychiatric services, non-Federal, exp	capita	18.62	88	38s
Mental health care, mental health organization, multiservice, exp	capita	9.59	88	38s
Mental health care, psychiatric hospitals, private, exp	capita	2.70	88	38s
Mental health care, psychiatric out-patient clinics, freestanding, exp	capita	8.41	88	38s
Mental health care, state and county mental hospitals, exp	capita	27.18	88	38s
Mental health care, VA medical centers, exp	capita	7.88	88	38s
Physician fee, family practice, first-visit		76.00	91	62r
Physician fee, family practice, revisit		33.00	91	62r
Physician fee, general practice, first-visit		61.00	91	62r
Physician fee, general practice, revisit		31.00	91	62r
Physician fee, general surgeon, first-visit		65.00	91	62r
Physician fee, general surgeon, revisit		35.00	91	62r
Physician fee, internal medicine, first-visit		91.00	91	62r
Physician fee, internal medicine, revisit		40.00	91	62r
Physician fee, median, neurosurgeon, first-visit		106.00	91	62r
Physician fee, median, nonsurgical specialist, first-visit		90.00	91	62r
Physician fee, median, orthopedic surgeon, first-visit		83.00	91	62r
Physician fee, median, surgical specialist, first-visit		61.00	91	62r
Physician fee, neurosurgeon, revisit		41.00	91	62r
Physician fee, nonsurgical specialist, revisit		40.00	91	62r
Physician fee, obstetrics/gynecology, first-visit		61.00	91	62r
Physician fee, obstetrics/gynecology, revisit		40.00	91	62r
Physician fee, orthopedic surgeon, revisit		41.00	91	62r
Physician fee, pediatrician, first-visit		46.00	91	62r
Physician fee, pediatrician, revisit		33.00	91	62r
Physician fee, surgical specialist, revisit		36.00	91	62r
Substance abuse, hospital ancillary charge	incident	670	90	70s
Substance abuse, hospital physician charge	incident	310	90	70s
Substance abuse, hospital room and board	incident	3800	90	70s
Housing				
Rental unit, 1 bedroom	month	395	93	23c
Rental unit, 2 bedroom	month	466	93	23c
Rental unit, 3 bedroom	month	585	93	23c
Rental unit, 4 bedroom	month	657	93	23c

Values are in dollars or fractions of dollars. In the column headed *Ref*, references are shown to sources. Each reference is followed by a letter. These refer to the geographical level for which data were reported: s=State, r=Region, and c=City or metro. The abbreviation *ex* is used to mean *except* or *excluding*; *exp* stands for expenditures. For other abbreviations and further explanations, please see the Introduction.

Duluth, MN - continued

Item	Per	Value	Date	Ref.
Housing				
Rental unit, efficiency	month	331	93	23c
Insurance and Pensions				
Auto insurance, private passenger	year	584.92	91	63s
Taxes				
Tax, cigarette	pack	48	91	77s
Tax, gasoline	gal	20	91	77s
Taxes, state	capita	1591	91	77s
Transportation				
Bus fare	one-way	0.50	3/93	2c
Driver's license fee		15.00	12/90	43s
Vehicle registration and license plate	year	10.00	93	66s
Utilities				
Electricity	mil Btu	15.68	90	64s
Electricity, winter, 250 KWh	month	13.46	92	55c
Electricity, winter, 500 KWh	month	27.32	92	55c
Electricity, winter, 750 KWh	month	42.36	92	55c
Electricity, winter, 1000 KWh	month	56.10	92	55c

Dyersburg, TN

Item	Per	Value	Date	Ref.
Composite ACCRA index		92.80	4Q 92	4c
Alcoholic Beverages				
Beer, Miller Lite or Budweiser, 12-oz containers	6 pack	4.06	4Q 92	4c
Liquor, J & B Scotch	750 ml	19.35	4Q 92	4c
Wine, Gallo Chablis blanc, 1.5 liter	bottle	7.62	4Q 92	4c
Clothing				
Jeans, man's denim		32.73	4Q 92	4c
Shirt, man's dress shirt		28.00	4Q 92	4c
Undervest, boy's size 10-14, cotton	3	3.88	4Q 92	4c
Communications				
Newspaper subscription, daily and Sunday home delivery, large-city	month	15.16	4Q 92	4c
Telephone, flat rate	month	8.50	91	11c
Telephone bill, family of four	month	15.63	4Q 92	4c
Energy and Fuels				
Energy, combined forms, 1,800 sq ft heating area	month	94.81	4Q 92	4c
Energy, exc electricity, 1,800 sq ft heating area	month	26.05	4Q 92	4c
Gasoline, motor	gal	1.18	4Q 92	4c
Entertainment				
Bowling, evening rate	game	2.00	4Q 92	4c
Monopoly game, Parker Brothers', No. 9		13.99	4Q 92	4c
Movie	admission	5.00	4Q 92	4c
Tennis balls, yellow, Wilson or Penn, 3	can	2.34	4Q 92	4c
Goods and Services				
ACCRA Index, Miscellaneous Goods and Services		101.00	4Q 92	4c
Groceries				
ACCRA Index, Groceries		97.30	4Q 92	4c
Babyfood, strained vegetables, lowest price	4-4.5 oz jar	0.33	4Q 92	4c
Bananas	lb	0.42	4Q 92	4c
Bread, white	24 oz	0.70	4Q 92	4c
Cheese, Kraft grated Parmesan	8-oz canister	3.61	4Q 92	4c
Chicken, fryer, whole	lb	0.68	4Q 92	4c
Cigarettes, Winston	carton	16.88	4Q 92	4c
Coffee, vacuum-packed	13-oz can	1.95	4Q 92	4c
Corn, frozen	10 oz	0.85	4Q 92	4c
Corn Flakes, Kellogg's or Post Toasties	18 oz	2.08	4Q 92	4c

Dyersburg, TN - continued

Item	Per	Value	Date	Ref.
Groceries - continued				
Eggs, Grade A large	doz	0.75	4Q 92	4c
Ground beef or hamburger	lb	1.36	4Q 92	4c
Lettuce, iceberg	head	0.82	4Q 92	4c
Margarine, Blue Bonnet or Parkay cubes	lb	0.52	4Q 92	4c
Milk, whole	1/2 gal	1.48	4Q 92	4c
Orange juice, Minute Maid frozen	12-oz can	1.58	4Q 92	4c
Peaches	29-oz can	1.27	4Q 92	4c
Peas Sweet, Del Monte or Green Giant	15-17 oz can	0.55	4Q 92	4c
Potatoes, white or red	10-lb sack	2.04	4Q 92	4c
Sausage, Jimmy Dean, 100% pork	lb	2.55	4Q 92	4c
Shortening, vegetable, Crisco	3-lb can	2.45	4Q 92	4c
Soft drink, Coca Cola	2 liter	0.89	4Q 92	4c
Steak, T-bone	lb	4.96	4Q 92	4c
Sugar, cane or beet	4 lb	1.46	4Q 92	4c
Tomatoes, Hunt's or Del Monte	14.5-oz can	0.71	4Q 92	4c
Tuna, chunk, light	6.125-6.5 oz can	0.64	4Q 92	4c
Health Care				
ACCRA Index, Health Care		86.70	4Q 92	4c
Analgesic, Aspirin, Bayer, 325 mg tablets	100	5.39	4Q 92	4c
Dentist's fee, adult teeth cleaning and periodic oral exam	visit	37.29	4Q 92	4c
Doctor's fee, routine exam, established patient	visit	37.00	4Q 92	4c
Hospital care, semiprivate room	day	195.00	4Q 92	4c
Household Goods				
Appliance repair, home, service call, washing machine	min labor charge	25.99	4Q 92	4c
Laundry detergent, Tide Ultra, Bold, or Cheer	42 oz	3.12	4Q 92	4c
Tissues, facial, Kleenex brand	175-count box	1.22	4Q 92	4c
Housing				
ACCRA Index, Housing		81.70	4Q 92	4c
House, 1,800 sq ft, 8,000 sq ft lot, new, urban	total	89854	4Q 92	4c
House payment, principal and interest, 25% down payment	month	498	4Q 92	4c
Mortgage rate, incl. points & origination fee, 30-year fixed or adjustable rate	per-cent	8.08	4Q 92	4c
Rent, apartment, 2 bedrooms - 1-1/2 to 2 baths, unfurnished, 950 sq ft, water	month	413	4Q 92	4c
Personal Goods				
Shampoo, Alberto VO5	15 oz	1.33	4Q 92	4c
Toothpaste, Crest or Colgate	6-7 oz	2.14	4Q 92	4c
Personal Services				
Dry cleaning, man's 2-piece suit		5.70	4Q 92	4c
Haircare, woman's shampoo, trim and blow-dry		14.83	4Q 92	4c
Haircut, man's barbershop, no styling		6.20	4Q 92	4c
Restaurant Food				
Chicken, fried, thigh and drumstick		1.85	4Q 92	4c
Hamburger with cheese	1/4 lb	1.79	4Q 92	4c
Pizza, Pizza Hut or Pizza Inn, cheese, thin crust	12-13 in	7.95	4Q 92	4c
Transportation				
ACCRA Index, Transportation		98.40	4Q 92	4c
Tire balance, computer or spin balance, front	wheel	6.00	4Q 92	4c

Values are in dollars or fractions of dollars. In the column headed *Ref*, references are shown to sources. Each reference is followed by a letter. These refer to the geographical level for which data were reported: s=State, r=Region, and c=City or metro. The abbreviation *ex* is used to mean *except* or *excluding*; *exp* stands for *expenditures*. For other abbreviations and further explanations, please see the Introduction.

Dyersburg, TN - continued

Item	Per	Value	Date	Ref.
Utilities				
ACCRA Index, Utilities		86.20	4Q 92	4c
Electricity, partial electric and other energy, 1,800 sq ft living area new home	month	68.76	4Q 92	4c

Eau Claire, WI

Item	Per	Value	Date	Ref.
Composite ACCRA index		96.30	4Q 92	4c
Alcoholic Beverages				
Beer, Miller Lite or Budweiser, 12-oz containers	6 pack	3.46	4Q 92	4c
Liquor, J & B Scotch	750 ml	16.10	4Q 92	4c
Wine, Gallo Chablis blanc, 1.5 liter	bottle	4.79	4Q 92	4c
Child Care				
Child care fee, average, center	hour	1.63	90	65r
Child care fee, average, nonregulated family day care	hour	1.83	90	65r
Child care fee, average, regulated family day care	hour	1.42	90	65r
Clothing				
Jeans, man's denim		35.66	4Q 92	4c
Shirt, man's dress shirt		27.00	4Q 92	4c
Undervest, boy's size 10-14, cotton	3	2.67	4Q 92	4c
Communications				
Long-distance telephone service, day, initial minute, 0-100 miles	min	0.15-0.29	91	12s
Long-distance telephone service, day, additional minute, 0-100 miles	min	0.10-0.27	91	12s
Newspaper subscription, daily and Sunday home delivery, large-city	month	9.57	4Q 92	4c
Telephone, flat rate	month	6.00	91	11c
Telephone bill, family of four	month	16.31	4Q 92	4c
Education				
Board, 4-yr private college/university	year	1533	91	22s
Board, 4-yr public college/university	year	1404	91	22s
Expenditures, local gov't, public elementary/secondary	pupil	5972	92	20s
Room, 4-year private college/university	year	1256	91	22s
Room, 4-year public college/university	year	1416	91	22s
Tuition, 2-year private college/university	year	4768	91	22s
Tuition, 2-year public college/university	year	1234	91	22s
Tuition, 4-year private college/university	year	8237	91	22s
Tuition, 4-year public college/university, in-state	year	1951	91	22s
Energy and Fuels				
Coal	mil Btu	1.41	90	64s
Energy	mil Btu	8.27	90	64s
Energy, combined forms, 1,800 sq ft heating area	month	102.73	4Q 92	4c
Energy, exc electricity, 1,800 sq ft heating area	month	57.86	4Q 92	4c
Energy exp/householder, 1-family unit	year	471	90	28r
Energy exp/householder, <1,000 sq ft heating area	year	430	90	28r
Energy exp/householder, 1,000-1,999 sq ft heating area	year	481	90	28r
Energy exp/householder, 2,000+ sq ft heating area	year	473	90	28r
Energy exp/householder, mobile home	year	430	90	28r
Energy exp/householder, multifamily	year	461	90	28r
Gas, cooking, winter, 10 therms	month	8.56	92	56c
Gas, cooking, winter, 30 therms	month	18.68	92	56c
Gas, cooking, winter, 50 therms	month	28.80	92	56c
Gas, heating, winter, 100 therms	month	54.10	92	56c
Gas, heating, winter, average use	month	79.04	92	56c
Gas, natural	mil Btu	4.56	90	64s

Eau Claire, WI - continued

Item	Per	Value	Date	Ref.
Energy and Fuels - continued				
Gas, natural	000 cu ft	5.61	91	46s
Gas, natural, exp	year	605	91	46s
Gasoline, motor	gal	1.18	4Q 92	4c
Gasoline, unleaded regular	mil Btu	9.38	90	64s
Entertainment				
Bowling, evening rate	game	1.90	4Q 92	4c
Miniature golf admission	adult	6.18	92	1r
Miniature golf admission	child	5.14	92	1r
Monopoly game, Parker Brothers', No. 9		8.77	4Q 92	4c
Movie	admission	5.00	4Q 92	4c
Tennis balls, yellow, Wilson or Penn, 3	can	2.36	4Q 92	4c
Waterpark admission	adult	11.00	92	1r
Waterpark admission	child	8.55	92	1r
Funerals				
Casket, 18-gauge steel, velvet interior		1926.72	91	24r
Cosmetology, hair care, etc.		97.64	91	24r
Embalming		249.14	91	24r
Facility use for ceremony		208.59	91	24r
Hearse, local		130.12	91	24r
Limousine, local		104.66	91	24r
Remains to funeral home, transfer		93.61	91	24r
Service charge, professional		724.62	91	24r
Vault, concrete, non-metallic liner		734.53	91	24r
Viewing facilities, use		236.06	91	24r
Goods and Services				
ACCRA Index, Miscellaneous Goods and Services		96.30	4Q 92	4c
Groceries				
ACCRA Index, Groceries		102.90	4Q 92	4c
Apples, Red Delicious	lb	0.77	4/93	16r
Babyfood, strained vegetables, lowest price	4-4.5 oz jar	0.35	4Q 92	4c
Bacon	lb	1.85	4/93	16r
Bananas	lb	0.34	4Q 92	4c
Bananas	lb	0.46	4/93	16r
Beef, stew, boneless	lb	2.53	4/93	16r
Bologna, all beef or mixed	lb	2.19	4/93	16r
Bread, white	24 oz	0.93	4Q 92	4c
Bread, white, pan	lb	0.78	4/93	16r
Butter	lb	1.50	4/93	16r
Cabbage	lb	0.40	4/93	16r
Carrots, short trimmed and topped	lb	0.45	4/93	16r
Cheese, Cheddar	lb	3.47	4/93	16r
Cheese, Kraft grated Parmesan	8-oz canister	3.12	4Q 92	4c
Chicken, fresh, whole	lb	0.84	4/93	16r
Chicken, fryer, whole	lb	0.91	4Q 92	4c
Chicken breast, bone-in	lb	1.94	4/93	16r
Chicken legs, bone-in	lb	1.02	4/93	16r
Chuck roast, graded and ungraded, ex USDA prime and choice	lb	2.43	4/93	16r
Chuck roast, USDA choice, bone-in	lb	2.11	4/93	16r
Chuck roast, USDA choice, boneless	lb	2.44	4/93	16r
Cigarettes, Winston	carton	18.70	4Q 92	4c
Coffee, 100% ground roast, all sizes	lb	2.47	4/93	16r
Coffee, vacuum-packed	13-oz can	1.92	4Q 92	4c
Cookies, chocolate chip	lb	2.73	4/93	16r
Corn, frozen	10 oz	0.68	4Q 92	4c
Corn Flakes, Kellogg's or Post Toasties	18 oz	1.90	4Q 92	4c
Eggs, Grade A large	doz	0.79	4Q 92	4c
Eggs, Grade A large	doz	0.93	4/93	16r
Flour, white, all purpose	lb	0.21	4/93	16r

Eau Claire, WI - continued

Item	Per	Value	Date	Ref.
Groceries				
Grapefruit	lb	0.45	4/93	16r
Grapes, Thompson Seedless	lb	1.46	4/93	16r
Ground beef, 100% beef	lb	1.63	4/93	16r
Ground beef, lean and extra lean	lb	2.08	4/93	16r
Ground beef or hamburger	lb	1.65	4Q 92	4c
Ground chuck, 100% beef	lb	1.94	4/93	16r
Ham, boneless, excluding canned	lb	2.21	4/93	16r
Honey, jar	8 oz	0.97-1.25	92	5r
Honey, jar	lb	1.25-2.25	92	5r
Honey, squeeze bear	12-oz	1.25-1.99	92	5r
Ice cream, prepackaged, bulk, regular	1/2 gal	2.41	4/93	16r
Lemons	lb	0.82	4/93	16r
Lettuce, iceberg	head	0.89	4Q 92	4c
Lettuce, iceberg	lb	0.83	4/93	16r
Margarine, Blue Bonnet or Parkay cubes	lb	0.52	4Q 92	4c
Margarine, stick	lb	0.77	4/93	16r
Milk, whole	1/2 gal	1.46	4Q 92	4c
Orange juice, Minute Maid frozen	12-oz can	1.32	4Q 92	4c
Oranges, navel	lb	0.50	4/93	16r
Peaches	29-oz can	1.37	4Q 92	4c
Peanut butter, creamy, all sizes	lb	1.82	4/93	16r
Pears, Anjou	lb	0.85	4/93	16r
Peas Sweet, Del Monte or Green Giant	15-17 oz can	0.59	4Q 92	4c
Pork chops, center cut, bone-in	lb	3.17	4/93	16r
Potato chips	16 oz	2.68	4/93	16r
Potatoes, white	lb	0.26	4/93	16r
Potatoes, white or red	10-lb sack	2.57	4Q 92	4c
Round roast, graded & ungraded, ex USDA prime & choice	lb	2.88	4/93	16r
Round roast, USDA choice, boneless	lb	2.96	4/93	16r
Sausage, Jimmy Dean, 100% pork	lb	2.63	4Q 92	4c
Shortening, vegetable oil blends	lb	0.79	4/93	16r
Shortening, vegetable, Crisco	3-lb can	2.48	4Q 92	4c
Soft drink, Coca Cola	2 liter	1.07	4Q 92	4c
Spaghetti and macaroni	lb	0.76	4/93	16r
Steak, rib eye, USDA choice, boneless	lb	6.29	4/93	16r
Steak, round, USDA choice, boneless	lb	3.24	4/93	16r
Steak, sirloin, graded & ungraded, ex USDA prime & choice	lb	4.00	4/93	16r
Steak, sirloin, USDA choice, bone-in	lb	3.57	4/93	16r
Steak, sirloin, USDA choice, boneless	lb	4.17	4/93	16r
Steak, T-bone	lb	5.39	4Q 92	4c
Steak, T-bone, USDA choice, bone-in	lb	5.60	4/93	16r
Strawberries, dry pint	12 oz	0.90	4/93	16r
Sugar, cane or beet	4 lb	1.28	4Q 92	4c
Sugar, white	lb	0.36	4/93	16r
Sugar, white, 33-80 oz pk	lb	0.35	4/93	16r
Tomatoes, field grown	lb	0.99	4/93	16r
Tomatoes, Hunt's or Del Monte	14.5-oz can	0.67	4Q 92	4c
Tuna, chunk, light	6.125-6.5 oz can	0.56	4Q 92	4c
Tuna, chunk, light	lb	1.76	4/93	16r
Turkey, frozen, whole	lb	0.91	4/93	16r
Health Care				
ACCRA Index, Health Care		103.00	4Q 92	4c
Analgesic, Aspirin, Bayer, 325 mg tablets	100	5.85	4Q 92	4c
Childbirth, cesarean, hospital		4688	91	62r
Childbirth, cesarean, physician's fee		2053	91	62r
Childbirth, normal, hospital		2657	91	62r
Childbirth, normal, physician's fee		1492	91	62r
Dentist's fee, adult teeth cleaning and periodic oral exam	visit	42.50	4Q 92	4c
Doctor's fee, routine exam, established patient	visit	45.60	4Q 92	4c
Hospital care, semiprivate room	day	203.92	90	27c

Eau Claire, WI - continued

Item	Per	Value	Date	Ref.
Health Care - continued				
Hospital care, semiprivate room	day	250.00	4Q 92	4c
Medical insurance premium, per employee, small group comprehensive	month	270.10	10/91	25c
Medical plan per employee	year	3443	91	45r
Mental health care, exp	capita	28.84-37.59	90	38s
Mental health care, exp, state mental health agency	capita	36.62	90	38s
Mental health care, hospital psychiatric services, non-Federal, exp	capita	13.05	88	38s
Mental health care, mental health organization, multiservice, exp	capita	10.93	88	38s
Mental health care, psychiatric hospitals, private, exp	capita	8.71	88	38s
Mental health care, psychiatric out-patient clinics, freestanding, exp	capita	5.33	88	38s
Mental health care, psychiatric partial-care organizations, freestanding, exp	capita	0.20	88	38s
Mental health care, state and county mental hospitals, exp	capita	28.29	88	38s
Mental health care, VA medical centers, exp	capita	7.57	88	38s
Physician fee, family practice, first-visit		76.00	91	62r
Physician fee, family practice, revisit		33.00	91	62r
Physician fee, general practice, first-visit		61.00	91	62r
Physician fee, general practice, revisit		31.00	91	62r
Physician fee, general surgeon, first-visit		65.00	91	62r
Physician fee, general surgeon, revisit		35.00	91	62r
Physician fee, internal medicine, first-visit		91.00	91	62r
Physician fee, internal medicine, revisit		40.00	91	62r
Physician fee, median, neurosurgeon, first-visit		106.00	91	62r
Physician fee, median, nonsurgical specialist, first-visit		90.00	91	62r
Physician fee, median, orthopedic surgeon, first-visit		83.00	91	62r
Physician fee, median, surgical specialist, first-visit		61.00	91	62r
Physician fee, neurosurgeon, revisit		41.00	91	62r
Physician fee, nonsurgical specialist, revisit		40.00	91	62r
Physician fee, obstetrics/gynecology, first-visit		61.00	91	62r
Physician fee, obstetrics/gynecology, revisit		40.00	91	62r
Physician fee, orthopedic surgeon, revisit		41.00	91	62r
Physician fee, pediatrician, first-visit		46.00	91	62r
Physician fee, pediatrician, revisit		33.00	91	62r
Physician fee, surgical specialist, revisit		36.00	91	62r
Substance abuse, hospital ancillary charge	incident	960	90	70s
Substance abuse, hospital physician charge	incident	470	90	70s
Substance abuse, hospital room and board	incident	3980	90	70s
Household Goods				
Appliance repair, home, service call, washing machine	min labor charge	26.21	4Q 92	4c
Laundry detergent, Tide Ultra, Bold, or Cheer	42 oz	3.13	4Q 92	4c
Tissues, facial, Kleenex brand	175-count box	1.08	4Q 92	4c
Housing				
ACCRA Index, Housing		93.60	4Q 92	4c
House, 1,800 sq ft, 8,000 sq ft lot, new, urban	total	96000	4Q 92	4c
House payment, principal and interest, 25% down payment	month	538	4Q 92	4c
Mortgage rate, incl. points & origination fee, 30-year fixed or adjustable rate	percent	8.19	4Q 92	4c
Rent, apartment, 2 bedrooms - 1-1/2 to 2 baths, unfurnished, 950 sq ft, water	month	548	4Q 92	4c

Values are in dollars or fractions of dollars. In the column headed *Ref*, references are shown to sources. Each reference is followed by a letter. These refer to the geographical level for which data were reported: s = State, r = Region, and c = City or metro. The abbreviation *ex* is used to mean *except* or *excluding*; *exp* stands for expenditures. For other abbreviations and further explanations, please see the Introduction.

Eau Claire, WI - continued

Item	Per	Value	Date	Ref.
Housing				
Rental unit, 1 bedroom	month	363	93	23c
Rental unit, 2 bedroom	month	429	93	23c
Rental unit, 3 bedroom	month	534	93	23c
Rental unit, 4 bedroom	month	599	93	23c
Rental unit, efficiency	month	297	93	23c
Insurance and Pensions				
Auto insurance, private passenger	year	510.11	91	63s
Personal Goods				
Shampoo, Alberto VO5	15 oz	1.22	4Q 92	4c
Toothpaste, Crest or Colgate	6-7 oz	2.15	4Q 92	4c
Personal Services				
Dry cleaning, man's 2-piece suit		6.33	4Q 92	4c
Haircare, woman's shampoo, trim and blow-dry		15.38	4Q 92	4c
Haircut, man's barbershop, no styling		8.19	4Q 92	4c
Restaurant Food				
Chicken, fried, thigh and drumstick		2.23	4Q 92	4c
Hamburger with cheese	1/4 lb	1.75	4Q 92	4c
Pizza, Pizza Hut or Pizza Inn, cheese, thin crust	12-13 in	8.99	4Q 92	4c
Taxes				
Tax, cigarette	pack	38	91	77s
Tax, gasoline	gal	22.20	91	77s
Taxes, state	capita	1416	91	77s
Transportation				
ACCRA Index, Transportation		95.30	4Q 92	4c
Bus fare, up to 10 miles	one-way	0.60	4Q 92	4c
Driver's license fee		9.00	12/90	43s
Tire balance, computer or spin balance, front	wheel	6.00	4Q 92	4c
Utilities				
ACCRA Index, Utilities		93.10	4Q 92	4c
Electricity	mil Btu	15.77	90	64s
Electricity, partial electric and other energy, 1,800 sq ft living area new home	month	44.87	4Q 92	4c
Electricity, winter, 250 KWh	month	19.89	92	55c
Electricity, winter, 500 KWh	month	36.29	92	55c
Electricity, winter, 750 KWh	month	52.68	92	55c
Electricity, winter, 1000 KWh	month	69.07	92	55c

El Paso, TX

Item	Per	Value	Date	Ref.
Composite ACCRA index		97.50	4Q 92	4c
Alcoholic Beverages				
Beer, Miller Lite or Budweiser, 12-oz containers	6 pack	3.87	4Q 92	4c
Liquor, J & B Scotch	750 ml	18.15	4Q 92	4c
Wine, Gallo Chablis blanc, 1.5 liter	bottle	4.49	4Q 92	4c
Child Care				
Child care fee, average, center	hour	1.29	90	65r
Child care fee, average, nonregulated family day care	hour	0.89	90	65r
Child care fee, average, regulated family day care	hour	1.32	90	65r
Clothing				
Jeans, man's denim		23.99	4Q 92	4c
Shirt, man's dress shirt		24.00	4Q 92	4c
Undervest, boy's size 10-14, cotton	3	4.25	4Q 92	4c
Communications				
Long-distance telephone service, day, initial minute, 0-100 miles	min	0.10-0.46	91	12s
Long-distance telephone service, day, additional minute, 0-100 miles	min	0.06-0.45	91	12s
Newspaper subscription, daily and Sunday home delivery, large-city	month	10.50	4Q 92	4c

El Paso, TX - continued

Item	Per	Value	Date	Ref.
Communications - continued				
Telephone, flat rate	month	9.35	91	11c
Telephone bill, family of four	month	16.53	4Q 92	4c
Education				
Board, 4-yr private college/university	year	1883	91	22s
Board, 4-yr public college/university	year	1605	91	22s
Expenditures, local gov't, public elementary/secondary	pupil	4593	92	20s
Room, 4-year private college/university	year	1620	91	22s
Room, 4-year public college/university	year	1532	91	22s
Tuition, 2-year private college/university	year	4394	91	22s
Tuition, 2-year public college/university	year	495	91	22s
Tuition, 4-year private college/university	year	6497	91	22s
Tuition, 4-year public college/university, in-state	year	986	91	22s
Energy and Fuels				
Coal	mil Btu	1.44	90	64s
Energy	mil Btu	6.48	90	64s
Energy, combined forms, 1,800 sq ft heating area	month	100.02	4Q 92	4c
Energy, exc electricity, 1,800 sq ft heating area	month	22.99	4Q 92	4c
Energy exp/householder, 1-family unit	year	471	90	28r
Energy exp/householder, <1,000 sq ft heating area	year	384	90	28r
Energy exp/householder, 1,000-1,999 sq ft heating area	year	421	90	28r
Energy exp/householder, 2,000+ sq ft heating area	year	625	90	28r
Energy exp/householder, mobile home	year	271	90	28r
Energy exp/householder, multifamily	year	355	90	28r
Gas, cooking, winter, 10 therms	month	7.45	92	56c
Gas, cooking, winter, 30 therms	month	12.38	92	56c
Gas, cooking, winter, 50 therms	month	17.22	92	56c
Gas, heating, winter, 100 therms	month	29.43	92	56c
Gas, heating, winter, average use	month	36.98	92	56c
Gas, natural	mil Btu	2.47	90	64s
Gas, natural	000 cu ft	5.71	91	46s
Gas, natural, exp	year	388	91	46s
Gasoline, motor	gal	1.20	4Q 92	4c
Gasoline, unleaded regular	mil Btu	9.16	90	64s
Entertainment				
Bowling, evening rate	game	1.87	4Q 92	4c
Miniature golf admission	adult	6.18	92	1r
Miniature golf admission	child	5.14	92	1r
Monopoly game, Parker Brothers', No. 9		12.99	4Q 92	4c
Movie	admission	6.00	4Q 92	4c
Tennis balls, yellow, Wilson or Penn, 3	can	3.03	4Q 92	4c
Waterpark admission	adult	11.00	92	1r
Waterpark admission	child	8.55	92	1r
Funerals				
Casket, 18-gauge steel, velvet interior		2274.41	91	24r
Cosmetology, hair care, etc.		74.62	91	24r
Embalming		229.94	91	24r
Facility use for ceremony		176.61	91	24r
Hearse, local		116.34	91	24r
Limousine, local		72.68	91	24r
Remains to funeral home, transfer		87.72	91	24r
Service charge, professional		712.53	91	24r
Vault, concrete, non-metallic liner		750.55	91	24r
Viewing facilities, use		155.31	91	24r
Goods and Services				
ACCRA Index, Miscellaneous Goods and Services		101.70	4Q 92	4c
Groceries				
ACCRA Index, Groceries		93.60	4Q 92	4c
Apples, Red Delicious	lb	0.79	4/93	16r

Values are in dollars or fractions of dollars. In the column headed *Ref*, references are shown to sources. Each reference is followed by a letter. These refer to the geographical level for which data were reported: s=State, r=Region, and c=City or metro. The abbreviation *ex* is used to mean *except* or *excluding*; *exp* stands for expenditures. For other abbreviations and further explanations, please see the Introduction.

El Paso, TX - continued

Item	Per	Value	Date	Ref.
Groceries				
Babyfood, strained vegetables, lowest price	4-4.5 oz jar	0.25	4Q 92	4c
Bacon	lb	1.75	4/93	16r
Bananas	lb	0.44	4Q 92	4c
Bananas	lb	0.42	4/93	16r
Beef, stew, boneless	lb	2.61	4/93	16r
Bologna, all beef or mixed	lb	2.24	4/93	16r
Bread, white	24 oz	0.57	4Q 92	4c
Bread, white, pan	lb	0.64	4/93	16r
Bread, whole wheat, pan	lb	0.96	4/93	16r
Cabbage	lb	0.37	4/93	16r
Carrots, short trimmed and topped	lb	0.47	4/93	16r
Celery	lb	0.64	4/93	16r
Cheese, American	lb	2.98	4/93	16r
Cheese, Cheddar	lb	3.28	4/93	16r
Cheese, Kraft grated Parmesan	8-oz canis-ter	3.46	4Q 92	4c
Chicken, fresh, whole	lb	0.77	4/93	16r
Chicken, fryer, whole	lb	0.56	4Q 92	4c
Chicken breast, bone-in	lb	1.92	4/93	16r
Chicken legs, bone-in	lb	1.06	4/93	16r
Chuck roast, graded and ungraded, ex USDA prime and choice	lb	2.40	4/93	16r
Chuck roast, USDA choice, bone-in	lb	2.19	4/93	16r
Chuck roast, USDA choice, boneless	lb	2.38	4/93	16r
Cigarettes, Winston	carton	18.60	4Q 92	4c
Coffee, 100% ground roast, all sizes	lb	2.48	4/93	16r
Coffee, vacuum-packed	13-oz can	1.82	4Q 92	4c
Corn, frozen	10 oz	0.71	4Q 92	4c
Corn Flakes, Kellogg's or Post Toasties	18 oz	1.97	4Q 92	4c
Crackers, soda, salted	lb	1.15	4/93	16r
Eggs, Grade A large	doz	0.88	4Q 92	4c
Eggs, Grade A large	doz	0.96	4/93	16r
Flour, white, all purpose	lb	0.24	4/93	16r
Frankfurters, all meat or all beef	lb	2.01	4/93	16r
Grapefruit	lb	0.44	4/93	16r
Grapes, Thompson Seedless	lb	1.40	4/93	16r
Ground beef, 100% beef	lb	1.58	4/93	16r
Ground beef, lean and extra lean	lb	2.09	4/93	16r
Ground beef or hamburger	lb	1.23	4Q 92	4c
Ground chuck, 100% beef	lb	1.98	4/93	16r
Ham, boneless, excluding canned	lb	2.89	4/93	16r
Ham, picnic, shoulder, bone-in, smoked	lb	1.02	4/93	16r
Ham, rump or steak half, bone-in, smoked	lb	1.48	4/93	16r
Honey, jar	8 oz	0.73-1.19	92	5r
Honey, jar	lb	1.10-1.79	92	5r
Honey, squeeze bear	12-oz	1.19-1.50	92	5r
Ice cream, prepackaged, bulk, regular	1/2 gal	2.41	4/93	16r
Lemons	lb	1.05	4/93	16r
Lettuce, iceberg	head	0.95	4Q 92	4c
Lettuce, iceberg	lb	0.81	4/93	16r
Margarine, Blue Bonnet or Parkay cubes	lb	0.72	4Q 92	4c
Margarine, stick	lb	0.88	4/93	16r
Milk, whole	1/2 gal	1.57	4Q 92	4c
Orange juice, Minute Maid frozen	12-oz can	1.22	4Q 92	4c
Oranges, navel	lb	0.55	4/93	16r
Peaches	29-oz can	1.42	4Q 92	4c
Pears, Anjou	lb	0.92	4/93	16r
Peas Sweet, Del Monte or Green Giant	15-17 oz can	0.50	4Q 92	4c
Pork chops, center cut, bone-in	lb	3.13	4/93	16r
Potato chips	16 oz	2.94	4/93	16r
Potatoes, white	lb	0.43	4/93	16r
Potatoes, white or red	10-lb sack	1.13	4Q 92	4c
Rib roast, USDA choice, bone-in	lb	4.63	4/93	16r
Rice, white, long grain, uncooked	lb	0.45	4/93	16r

El Paso, TX - continued

Item	Per	Value	Date	Ref.
Groceries - continued				
Round roast, graded & ungraded, ex USDA prime & choice	lb	3.03	4/93	16r
Round roast, USDA choice, boneless	lb	3.09	4/93	16r
Sausage, fresh, loose	lb	2.08	4/93	16r
Sausage, Jimmy Dean, 100% pork	lb	2.25	4Q 92	4c
Short ribs, bone-in	lb	2.66	4/93	16r
Shortening, vegetable oil blends	lb	0.69	4/93	16r
Shortening, vegetable, Crisco	3-lb can	1.95	4Q 92	4c
Soft drink, Coca Cola	2 liter	1.28	4Q 92	4c
Spaghetti and macaroni	lb	0.81	4/93	16r
Steak, rib eye, USDA choice, boneless	lb	6.24	4/93	16r
Steak, round, graded & ungraded, ex USDA prime & choice	lb	3.31	4/93	16r
Steak, round, USDA choice, boneless	lb	3.34	4/93	16r
Steak, sirloin, graded & ungraded, ex USDA prime & choice	lb	4.19	4/93	16r
Steak, sirloin, USDA choice, boneless	lb	4.46	4/93	16r
Steak, T-bone	lb	4.81	4Q 92	4c
Steak, T-bone, USDA choice, bone-in	lb	5.25	4/93	16r
Strawberries, dry pint	12 oz	0.92	4/93	16r
Sugar, cane or beet	4 lb	1.58	4Q 92	4c
Sugar, white	lb	0.39	4/93	16r
Sugar, white, 33-80 oz pk	lb	0.38	4/93	16r
Tomatoes, field grown	lb	0.88	4/93	16r
Tomatoes, Hunt's or Del Monte	14.5-oz can	0.68	4Q 92	4c
Tuna, chunk, light	6.125-6.5 oz can	0.64	4Q 92	4c
Tuna, chunk, light	lb	1.79	4/93	16r
Turkey, frozen, whole	lb	1.04	4/93	16r
Yogurt, natural, fruit flavored	1/2 pint	0.57	4/93	16r
Health Care				
ACCRA Index, Health Care		93.40	4Q 92	4c
Analgesic, Aspirin, Bayer, 325 mg tablets	100	4.67	4Q 92	4c
Childbirth, cesarean, hospital		5034	91	62r
Childbirth, cesarean, physician's fee		2053	91	62r
Childbirth, normal, hospital		2712	91	62r
Childbirth, normal, physician's fee		1492	91	62r
Dentist's fee, adult teeth cleaning and periodic oral exam	visit	37.80	4Q 92	4c
Doctor's fee, routine exam, established patient	visit	39.80	4Q 92	4c
Health care spending, state	capita	2192	3/93	84s
Hospital care, semiprivate room	day	188.76	90	27c
Hospital care, semiprivate room	day	288.00	4Q 92	4c
Medical insurance premium, per employee, small group comprehensive	month	324.85	10/91	25c
Mental health care, exp	capita	20.37-28.83	90	38s
Mental health care, exp, state mental health agency	capita	22.72	90	38s
Mental health care, hospital psychiatric services, non-Federal, exp	capita	7.95	88	38s
Mental health care, mental health organization, multiservice, exp	capita	12.05	88	38s
Mental health care, psychiatric hospitals, private, exp	capita	37.78	88	38s
Mental health care, psychiatric out-patient clinics, freestanding, exp	capita	0.43	88	38s
Mental health care, state and county mental hospitals, exp	capita	12.54	88	38s
Mental health care, VA medical centers, exp	capita	5.35	88	38s
Physician fee, family practice, first-visit		75.00	91	62r
Physician fee, family practice, revisit		34.00	91	62r
Physician fee, general practice, first-visit		61.00	91	62r
Physician fee, general practice, revisit		32.00	91	62r
Physician fee, general surgeon, first-visit		64.00	91	62r
Physician fee, general surgeon, revisit		40.00	91	62r
Physician fee, internal medicine, first-visit		98.00	91	62r

Values are in dollars or fractions of dollars. In the column headed *Ref*, references are shown to sources. Each reference is followed by a letter. These refer to the geographical level for which data were reported: s=State, r=Region, and c=City or metro. The abbreviation *ex* is used to mean *except* or *excluding*; *exp* stands for expenditures. For other abbreviations and further explanations, please see the Introduction.

El Paso, TX - continued

Item	Per	Value	Date	Ref.
Health Care				
Physician fee, internal medicine, revisit		40.00	91	62r
Physician fee, median, neurosurgeon, first-visit		130.00	91	62r
Physician fee, median, nonsurgical specialist, first-visit		95.00	91	62r
Physician fee, median, orthopedic surgeon, first-visit		91.00	91	62r
Physician fee, median, plastic surgeon, first-visit		66.00	91	62r
Physician fee, median, surgical specialist, first-visit		62.00	91	62r
Physician fee, neurosurgeon, revisit		50.00	91	62r
Physician fee, nonsurgical specialist, revisit		40.00	91	62r
Physician fee, obstetrics/gynecology, first-visit		64.00	91	62r
Physician fee, obstetrics/gynecology, revisit		41.00	91	62r
Physician fee, orthopedic surgeon, revisit		40.00	91	62r
Physician fee, pediatrician, first-visit		49.00	91	62r
Physician fee, pediatrician, revisit		33.00	91	62r
Physician fee, plastic surgeon, revisit		43.00	91	62r
Physician fee, surgical specialist, revisit		37.00	91	62r
Substance abuse, hospital ancillary charge	incident	3750	90	70s
Substance abuse, hospital physician charge	incident	1080	90	70s
Substance abuse, hospital room and board	incident	5320	90	70s
Household Goods				
Appliance repair, home, service call, washing machine	min labor charge	36.98	4Q 92	4c
Laundry detergent, Tide Ultra, Bold, or Cheer	42 oz	2.97	4Q 92	4c
Tissues, facial, Kleenex brand	175-count box	1.16	4Q 92	4c
Housing				
ACCRA Index, Housing		92.70	4Q 92	4c
Home, median price	unit	67.50		26c
House, 1,800 sq ft, 8,000 sq ft lot, new, urban	total	98855	4Q 92	4c
House payment, principal and interest, 25% down payment	month	542	4Q 92	4c
Mortgage rate, incl. points & origination fee, 30-year fixed or adjustable rate	percent	7.96	4Q 92	4c
Rent, apartment, 2 bedrooms - 1-1/2 to 2 baths, unfurnished, 950 sq ft, water	month	522	4Q 92	4c
Rental unit, 1 bedroom	month	394	93	23c
Rental unit, 2 bedroom	month	463	93	23c
Rental unit, 3 bedroom	month	579	93	23c
Rental unit, 4 bedroom	month	648	93	23c
Rental unit, efficiency	month	324	93	23c
Insurance and Pensions				
Auto insurance, private passenger	year	709.79	91	63s
Personal Goods				
Shampoo, Alberto VO5	15 oz	1.23	4Q 92	4c
Toothpaste, Crest or Colgate	6-7 oz	2.05	4Q 92	4c
Personal Services				
Dry cleaning, man's 2-piece suit		5.95	4Q 92	4c
Haircare, woman's shampoo, trim and blow-dry		26.00	4Q 92	4c
Haircut, man's barbershop, no styling		5.60	4Q 92	4c
Restaurant Food				
Chicken, fried, thigh and drumstick		2.23	4Q 92	4c
Hamburger with cheese	1/4 lb	1.78	4Q 92	4c
Pizza, Pizza Hut or Pizza Inn, cheese, thin crust	12-13 in	7.82	4Q 92	4c

El Paso, TX - continued

Item	Per	Value	Date	Ref.
Taxes				
Tax, cigarette	pack	41	91	77s
Tax, gasoline	gal	20	91	77s
Taxes, state	capita	923	91	77s
Transportation				
ACCRA Index, Transportation		109.70	4Q 92	4c
Auto rental, average	day	46.75	6/91	60c
Bus fare	one-way	0.75	3/93	2c
Bus fare, up to 10 miles	one-way	0.75	4Q 92	4c
Driver's license fee		16.00	12/90	43s
Limo fare, airport-city, average	day	9.00	6/91	60c
Taxi fare, airport-city, average	day	14.00	6/91	60c
Tire balance, computer or spin balance, front	wheel	7.70	4Q 92	4c
Travel				
Breakfast	day	6.59	6/91	60c
Business travel	day	193.00	4/93	89r
Dinner	day	20.35	6/91	60c
Lodging	day	109.17	91	60c
Lunch	day	10.52	6/91	60c
Utilities				
ACCRA Index, Utilities		90.90	4Q 92	4c
Electricity	mil Btu	17.09	90	64s
Electricity, partial electric and other energy, 1,800 sq ft living area new home	month	77.03	4Q 92	4c
Electricity, residential	KWh	5.92	2/93	94s
Electricity, winter, 250 KWh	month	27.75	92	55c
Electricity, winter, 500 KWh	month	50.99	92	55c
Electricity, winter, 750 KWh	month	74.23	92	55c
Electricity, winter, 1000 KWh	month	97.47	92	55c

Elkhart-Goshen, IN

Item	Per	Value	Date	Ref.
Child Care				
Child care fee, average, center	hour	1.63	90	65r
Child care fee, average, nonregulated family day care	hour	1.83	90	65r
Child care fee, average, regulated family day care	hour	1.42	90	65r
Communications				
Long-distance telephone service, day, initial minute, 0-100 miles	min	0.18-0.45	91	12s
Long-distance telephone service, day, additional minute, 0-100 miles	min	0.10-0.30	91	12s
Long-distance telephone service, evenings/weekends, 0-100 mi, initial minute	min	0.08-0.19	91	12s
Long-distance telephone service, evenings/weekends, 0-100 mi, additional minute	min	0.04-0.13	91	12s
Education				
Board, 4-yr private college/university	year	1714	91	22s
Board, 4-yr public college/university	year	1829	91	22s
Expenditures, local gov't, public elementary/secondary	pupil	5545	92	20s
Room, 4-year private college/university	year	1512	91	22s
Room, 4-year public college/university	year	1435	91	22s
Tuition, 2-year private college/university	year	6756	91	22s
Tuition, 2-year public college/university	year	1423	91	22s
Tuition, 4-year private college/university	year	8451	91	22s
Tuition, 4-year public college/university, in-state	year	2067	91	22s
Energy and Fuels				
Coal	mil Btu	1.46	90	64s
Energy	mil Btu	6.77	90	64s
Energy exp/householder, 1-family unit	year	471	90	28r
Energy exp/householder, <1,000 sq ft heating area	year	430	90	28r

Values are in dollars or fractions of dollars. In the column headed *Ref*, references are shown to sources. Each reference is followed by a letter. These refer to the geographical level for which data were reported: s=State, r=Region, and c=City or metro. The abbreviation *ex* is used to mean *except* or *excluding*; *exp* stands for expenditures. For other abbreviations and further explanations, please see the Introduction.

Elkhart-Goshen, IN - continued

Item	Per	Value	Date	Ref.
Energy and Fuels				
Energy exp/householder, 1,000-1,999 sq ft heating area	year	481	90	28r
Energy exp/householder, 2,000+ sq ft heating area	year	473	90	28r
Energy exp/householder, mobile home	year	430	90	28r
Energy exp/householder, multifamily	year	461	90	28r
Gas, natural	mil Btu	4.27	90	64s
Gas, natural	000 cu ft	5.46	91	46s
Gas, natural, exp	year	588	91	46s
Gasoline, unleaded regular	mil Btu	8.74	90	64s
Entertainment				
Miniature golf admission	adult	6.18	92	1r
Miniature golf admission	child	5.14	92	1r
Waterpark admission	adult	11.00	92	1r
Waterpark admission	child	8.55	92	1r
Funerals				
Casket, 18-gauge steel, velvet interior		1926.72	91	24r
Cosmetology, hair care, etc.		97.64	91	24r
Embalming		249.14	91	24r
Facility use for ceremony		208.59	91	24r
Hearse, local		130.12	91	24r
Limousine, local		104.66	91	24r
Remains to funeral home, transfer		93.61	91	24r
Service charge, professional		724.62	91	24r
Vault, concrete, non-metallic liner		734.53	91	24r
Viewing facilities, use		236.06	91	24r
Groceries				
Apples, Red Delicious	lb	0.77	4/93	16r
Bacon	lb	1.85	4/93	16r
Bananas	lb	0.46	4/93	16r
Beef, stew, boneless	lb	2.53	4/93	16r
Bologna, all beef or mixed	lb	2.19	4/93	16r
Bread, white, pan	lb	0.78	4/93	16r
Butter	lb	1.50	4/93	16r
Cabbage	lb	0.40	4/93	16r
Carrots, short trimmed and topped	lb	0.45	4/93	16r
Cheese, Cheddar	lb	3.47	4/93	16r
Chicken, fresh, whole	lb	0.84	4/93	16r
Chicken breast, bone-in	lb	1.94	4/93	16r
Chicken legs, bone-in	lb	1.02	4/93	16r
Chuck roast, graded and ungraded, ex USDA prime and choice	lb	2.43	4/93	16r
Chuck roast, USDA choice, bone-in	lb	2.11	4/93	16r
Chuck roast, USDA choice, boneless	lb	2.44	4/93	16r
Coffee, 100% ground roast, all sizes	lb	2.47	4/93	16r
Cookies, chocolate chip	lb	2.73	4/93	16r
Eggs, Grade A large	doz	0.93	4/93	16r
Flour, white, all purpose	lb	0.21	4/93	16r
Grapefruit	lb	0.45	4/93	16r
Grapes, Thompson Seedless	lb	1.46	4/93	16r
Ground beef, 100% beef	lb	1.63	4/93	16r
Ground beef, lean and extra lean	lb	2.08	4/93	16r
Ground chuck, 100% beef	lb	1.94	4/93	16r
Ham, boneless, excluding canned	lb	2.21	4/93	16r
Honey, jar	8 oz	0.97-1.25	92	5r
Honey, jar	lb	1.25-2.25	92	5r
Honey, squeeze bear	12-oz	1.25-1.99	92	5r
Ice cream, prepackaged, bulk, regular	1/2 gal	2.41	4/93	16r
Lemons	lb	0.82	4/93	16r
Lettuce, iceberg	lb	0.83	4/93	16r
Margarine, stick	lb	0.77	4/93	16r
Oranges, navel	lb	0.50	4/93	16r
Peanut butter, creamy, all sizes	lb	1.82	4/93	16r
Pears, Anjou	lb	0.85	4/93	16r
Pork chops, center cut, bone-in	lb	3.17	4/93	16r
Potato chips	16 oz	2.68	4/93	16r
Potatoes, white	lb	0.26	4/93	16r
Round roast, graded & ungraded, ex USDA prime & choice	lb	2.88	4/93	16r
Round roast, USDA choice, boneless	lb	2.96	4/93	16r

Elkhart-Goshen, IN - continued

Item	Per	Value	Date	Ref.
Groceries - continued				
Shortening, vegetable oil blends	lb	0.79	4/93	16r
Spaghetti and macaroni	lb	0.76	4/93	16r
Steak, rib eye, USDA choice, boneless	lb	6.29	4/93	16r
Steak, round, USDA choice, boneless	lb	3.24	4/93	16r
Steak, sirloin, graded & ungraded, ex USDA prime & choice	lb	4.00	4/93	16r
Steak, sirloin, USDA choice, bone-in	lb	3.57	4/93	16r
Steak, sirloin, USDA choice, boneless	lb	4.17	4/93	16r
Steak, T-bone, USDA choice, bone-in	lb	5.60	4/93	16r
Strawberries, dry pint	12 oz	0.90	4/93	16r
Sugar, white	lb	0.36	4/93	16r
Sugar, white, 33-80 oz pk	lb	0.35	4/93	16r
Tomatoes, field grown	lb	0.99	4/93	16r
Tuna, chunk, light	lb	1.76	4/93	16r
Turkey, frozen, whole	lb	0.91	4/93	16r
Health Care				
Childbirth, cesarean, hospital		4688	91	62r
Childbirth, cesarean, physician's fee		2053	91	62r
Childbirth, normal, hospital		2657	91	62r
Childbirth, normal, physician's fee		1492	91	62r
Medical plan per employee	year	3443	91	45r
Mental health care, exp	capita	37.60-53.67	90	38s
Mental health care, exp, state mental health agency	capita	47.05	90	38s
Mental health care, hospital psychiatric services, non-Federal, exp	capita	22.14	88	38s
Mental health care, mental health organization, multiservice, exp	capita	10.33	88	38s
Mental health care, psychiatric hospitals, private, exp	capita	20.10	88	38s
Mental health care, state and county mental hospitals, exp	capita	24.00	88	38s
Mental health care, VA medical centers, exp	capita	3.20	88	38s
Physician fee, family practice, first-visit		76.00	91	62r
Physician fee, family practice, revisit		33.00	91	62r
Physician fee, general practice, first-visit		61.00	91	62r
Physician fee, general practice, revisit		31.00	91	62r
Physician fee, general surgeon, first-visit		65.00	91	62r
Physician fee, general surgeon, revisit		35.00	91	62r
Physician fee, internal medicine, first-visit		91.00	91	62r
Physician fee, internal medicine, revisit		40.00	91	62r
Physician fee, median, neurosurgeon, first-visit		106.00	91	62r
Physician fee, median, nonsurgical specialist, first-visit		90.00	91	62r
Physician fee, median, orthopedic surgeon, first-visit		83.00	91	62r
Physician fee, median, surgical specialist, first-visit		61.00	91	62r
Physician fee, neurosurgeon, revisit		41.00	91	62r
Physician fee, nonsurgical specialist, revisit		40.00	91	62r
Physician fee, obstetrics/gynecology, first-visit		61.00	91	62r
Physician fee, obstetrics/gynecology, revisit		40.00	91	62r
Physician fee, orthopedic surgeon, revisit		41.00	91	62r
Physician fee, pediatrician, first-visit		46.00	91	62r
Physician fee, pediatrician, revisit		33.00	91	62r
Physician fee, surgical specialist, revisit		36.00	91	62r
Substance abuse, hospital ancillary charge	incident	1230	90	70s
Substance abuse, hospital physician charge	incident	410	90	70s
Substance abuse, hospital room and board	incident	5510	90	70s
Insurance and Pensions				
Auto insurance, private passenger	year	548.99	91	63s
Taxes				
Tax, cigarette	pack	15.50	91	77s
Tax, gasoline	gal	15	91	77s
Taxes, state	capita	1102	91	77s

Values are in dollars or fractions of dollars. In the column headed *Ref*, references are shown to sources. Each reference is followed by a letter. These refer to the geographical level for which data were reported: s=State, r=Region, and c=City or metro. The abbreviation *ex* is used to mean *except* or *excluding*; *exp* stands for expenditures. For other abbreviations and further explanations, please see the Introduction.

Elkhart-Goshen, IN - continued

Item	Per	Value	Date	Ref.
Transportation				
Driver's license fee		6.00	12/90	43s
Utilities				
Electricity	mil Btu	15.75	90	64s

Elmira, NY

Item	Per	Value	Date	Ref.
Child Care				
Child care fee, average, center	hour	2.18	90	65r
Child care fee, average, nonregulated family day care	hour	1.83	90	65r
Child care fee, average, regulated family day care	hour	2.02	90	65r
Education				
Board, 4-yr private college/university	year	2451	91	22s
Board, 4-yr public college/university	year	1725	91	22s
Expenditures, local gov't, public elementary/secondary	pupil	8603	92	20s
Room, 4-year private college/university	year	2652	91	22s
Room, 4-year public college/university	year	2183	91	22s
Tuition, 2-year private college/university	year	5926	91	22s
Tuition, 2-year public college/university	year	1419	91	22s
Tuition, 4-year private college/university	year	10340	91	22s
Tuition, 4-year public college/university, in-state	year	1587	91	22s
Energy and Fuels				
Coal	mil Btu	1.66	90	64s
Energy	mil Btu	10.68	90	64s
Energy exp/householder, 1-family unit	year	588	90	28r
Energy exp/householder, <1,000 sq ft heating area	year	477	90	28r
Energy exp/householder, 1,000-1,999 sq ft heating area	year	517	90	28r
Energy exp/householder, 2,000+ sq ft heating area	year	630	90	28r
Energy exp/householder, mobile home	year	412	90	28r
Energy exp/householder, multifamily	year	498	90	28r
Gas, natural	mil Btu	5.25	90	64s
Gas, natural	000 cu ft	7.35	91	46s
Gas, natural, exp	year	557	91	46s
Gasoline, unleaded regular	mil Btu	8.83	90	64s
Funerals				
Casket, 18-gauge steel, velvet interior		1811.58	91	24r
Cosmetology, hair care, etc.		111.08	91	24r
Embalming		329.42	91	24r
Facility use for ceremony		201.29	91	24r
Hearse, local		135.27	91	24r
Limousine, local		127.24	91	24r
Remains to funeral home, transfer		103.98	91	24r
Service charge, professional		724.98	91	24r
Vault, concrete, non-metallic liner		766.71	91	24r
Viewing facilities, use		260.60	91	24r
Groceries				
Apples, Red Delicious	lb	0.85	4/93	16r
Bacon	lb	2.12	4/93	16r
Bananas	lb	0.54	4/93	16r
Bread, white, pan	lb	0.81	4/93	16r
Butter	lb	2.02	4/93	16r
Carrots, short trimmed and topped	lb	0.51	4/93	16r
Chicken, fresh, whole	lb	1.04	4/93	16r
Chicken breast, bone-in	lb	2.21	4/93	16r
Chicken legs, bone-in	lb	1.16	4/93	16r
Chuck roast, USDA choice, boneless	lb	2.82	4/93	16r
Coffee, 100% ground roast, all sizes	lb	2.66	4/93	16r
Cucumbers	lb	0.85	4/93	16r
Eggs, Grade A large	doz	1.15	4/93	16r
Grapefruit	lb	0.45	4/93	16r
Grapes, Thompson Seedless	lb	1.52	4/93	16r

Elmira, NY - continued

Item	Per	Value	Date	Ref.
Groceries - continued				
Ground beef, lean and extra lean	lb	2.36	4/93	16r
Ground chuck, 100% beef	lb	2.02	4/93	16r
Honey, jar	8 oz	0.96-1.75	92	5r
Honey, jar	lb	1.50-3.00	92	5r
Honey, squeeze bear	12-oz	1.50-1.99	92	5r
Ice cream, prepackaged, bulk, regular	1/2 gal	2.80	4/93	16r
Lemons	lb	0.96	4/93	16r
Lettuce, iceberg	lb	0.95	4/93	16r
Margarine, stick	lb	0.81	4/93	16r
Milk, fresh, whole, fortified	1/2 gal	1.30	4/93	16r
Oranges, navel	lb	0.56	4/93	16r
Peanut butter, creamy, all sizes	lb	1.88	4/93	16r
Pork chops, center cut, bone-in	lb	3.34	4/93	16r
Potato chips	16 oz	2.88	4/93	16r
Potatoes, white	lb	0.37	4/93	16r
Rib roast, USDA choice, bone-in	lb	4.94	4/93	16r
Round roast, USDA choice, boneless	lb	3.17	4/93	16r
Shortening, vegetable oil blends	lb	0.98	4/93	16r
Spaghetti and macaroni	lb	0.82	4/93	16r
Steak, round, graded & ungraded, ex USDA prime & choice	lb	4.04	4/93	16r
Steak, round, USDA choice, boneless	lb	3.90	4/93	16r
Steak, sirloin, USDA choice, boneless	lb	4.97	4/93	16r
Strawberries, dry pint	12 oz	0.90	4/93	16r
Sugar, white	lb	0.50	4/93	16r
Sugar, white, 33-80 oz pk	lb	0.41	4/93	16r
Tomatoes, field grown	lb	1.23	4/93	16r
Tuna, chunk, light	lb	2.22	4/93	16r
Turkey, frozen, whole	lb	1.04	4/93	16r
Health Care				
Childbirth, cesarean, hospital		5826	91	62r
Childbirth, cesarean, physician's fee		2053	91	62r
Childbirth, normal, hospital		2964	91	62r
Childbirth, normal, physician's fee		1492	91	62r
Medical plan per employee	year	3942	91	45r
Mental health care, exp	capita	53.68-118.35	90	38s
Mental health care, exp, state mental health agency	capita	118.34	90	38s
Mental health care, hospital psychiatric services, non-Federal, exp	capita	29.77	88	38s
Mental health care, mental health organization, multiservice, exp	capita	20.03	88	38s
Mental health care, psychiatric hospitals, private, exp	capita	8.37	88	38s
Mental health care, psychiatric out-patient clinics, freestanding, exp	capita	7.96	88	38s
Mental health care, psychiatric partial-care organizations, freestanding, exp	capita	1.24	88	38s
Mental health care, state and county mental hospitals, exp	capita	89.52	88	38s
Mental health care, VA medical centers, exp	capita	7.12	88	38s
Prescription drug co-pay, Medicaid	month	23.00	91	21s
Substance abuse, hospital ancillary charge	incident	1040	90	70s
Substance abuse, hospital physician charge	incident	360	90	70s
Substance abuse, hospital room and board	incident	6330	90	70s
Insurance and Pensions				
Auto insurance, private passenger	year	840.89	91	63s
Taxes				
Tax, cigarette	pack	39	91	77s
Tax, gasoline	gal	8	91	77s
Taxes, state	capita	1567	91	77s
Transportation				
Driver's license fee		17.50	12/90	43s
Vehicle registration and license plate	2 years	27.50-149.50	93	67s

Values are in dollars or fractions of dollars. In the column headed *Ref*, references are shown to sources. Each reference is followed by a letter. These refer to the geographical level for which data were reported: s=State, r=Region, and c=City or metro. The abbreviation *ex* is used to mean *except* or *excluding*; *exp* stands for expenditures. For other abbreviations and further explanations, please see the Introduction.

Elmira, NY - continued

Item	Per	Value	Date	Ref.
Travel				
Business travel	day	165.00	4/93	89r
Utilities				
Electricity	mil Btu	27.51	90	64s

Enid, OK

Item	Per	Value	Date	Ref.
Child Care				
Child care fee, average, center	hour	1.29	90	65r
Child care fee, average, nonregulated family day care	hour	0.89	90	65r
Child care fee, average, regulated family day care	hour	1.32	90	65r
Communications				
Long-distance telephone service, day, initial minute, 0-100 miles	min	0.12-0.45	91	12s
Long-distance telephone service, day, additional minute, 0-100 miles	min	0.07-0.39	91	12s
Education				
Board, 4-yr private college/university	year	1664	91	22s
Board, 4-yr public college/university	year	1368	91	22s
Expenditures, local gov't, public elementary/secondary	pupil	3901	92	20s
Room, 4-year private college/university	year	1384	91	22s
Room, 4-year public college/university	year	1119	91	22s
Tuition, 2-year private college/university	year	5732	91	22s
Tuition, 2-year public college/university	year	864	91	22s
Tuition, 4-year private college/university	year	5852	91	22s
Tuition, 4-year public college/university, in-state	year	1340	91	22s
Energy and Fuels				
Coal	mil Btu	1.40	90	64s
Energy	mil Btu	7.46	90	64s
Energy exp/householder, 1-family unit	year	471	90	28r
Energy exp/householder, <1,000 sq ft heating area	year	384	90	28r
Energy exp/householder, 1,000-1,999 sq ft heating area	year	421	90	28r
Energy exp/householder, 2,000+ sq ft heating area	year	625	90	28r
Energy exp/householder, mobile home	year	271	90	28r
Energy exp/householder, multifamily	year	355	90	28r
Gas, natural	mil Btu	2.80	90	64s
Gas, natural	000 cu ft	4.72	91	46s
Gas, natural, exp	year	396	91	46s
Gasoline, unleaded regular	mil Btu	9.00	90	64s
Entertainment				
Miniature golf admission	adult	6.18	92	1r
Miniature golf admission	child	5.14	92	1r
Waterpark admission	adult	11.00	92	1r
Waterpark admission	child	8.55	92	1r
Funerals				
Casket, 18-gauge steel, velvet interior		2274.41	91	24r
Cosmetology, hair care, etc.		74.62	91	24r
Embalming		229.94	91	24r
Facility use for ceremony		176.61	91	24r
Hearse, local		116.34	91	24r
Limousine, local		72.68	91	24r
Remains to funeral home, transfer		87.72	91	24r
Service charge, professional		712.53	91	24r
Vault, concrete, non-metallic liner		750.55	91	24r
Viewing facilities, use		155.31	91	24r
Groceries				
Apples, Red Delicious	lb	0.79	4/93	16r
Bacon	lb	1.75	4/93	16r
Bananas	lb	0.42	4/93	16r
Beef, stew, boneless	lb	2.61	4/93	16r

Enid, OK - continued

Item	Per	Value	Date	Ref.
Groceries - continued				
Bologna, all beef or mixed	lb	2.24	4/93	16r
Bread, white, pan	lb	0.64	4/93	16r
Bread, whole wheat, pan	lb	0.96	4/93	16r
Cabbage	lb	0.37	4/93	16r
Carrots, short trimmed and topped	lb	0.47	4/93	16r
Celery	lb	0.64	4/93	16r
Cheese, American	lb	2.98	4/93	16r
Cheese, Cheddar	lb	3.28	4/93	16r
Chicken, fresh, whole	lb	0.77	4/93	16r
Chicken breast, bone-in	lb	1.92	4/93	16r
Chicken legs, bone-in	lb	1.06	4/93	16r
Chuck roast, graded and ungraded, ex USDA prime and choice	lb	2.40	4/93	16r
Chuck roast, USDA choice, bone-in	lb	2.19	4/93	16r
Chuck roast, USDA choice, boneless	lb	2.38	4/93	16r
Coffee, 100% ground roast, all sizes	lb	2.48	4/93	16r
Crackers, soda, salted	lb	1.15	4/93	16r
Eggs, Grade A large	doz	0.96	4/93	16r
Flour, white, all purpose	lb	0.24	4/93	16r
Frankfurters, all meat or all beef	lb	2.01	4/93	16r
Grapefruit	lb	0.44	4/93	16r
Grapes, Thompson Seedless	lb	1.40	4/93	16r
Ground beef, 100% beef	lb	1.58	4/93	16r
Ground beef, lean and extra lean	lb	2.09	4/93	16r
Ground chuck, 100% beef	lb	1.98	4/93	16r
Ham, boneless, excluding canned	lb	2.89	4/93	16r
Ham, picnic, shoulder, bone-in, smoked	lb	1.02	4/93	16r
Ham, rump or steak half, bone-in, smoked	lb	1.48	4/93	16r
Honey, jar	8 oz	0.73-1.19	92	5r
Honey, jar	lb	1.10-1.79	92	5r
Honey, squeeze bear	12-oz	1.19-1.50	92	5r
Ice cream, prepackaged, bulk, regular	1/2 gal	2.41	4/93	16r
Lemons	lb	1.05	4/93	16r
Lettuce, iceberg	lb	0.81	4/93	16r
Margarine, stick	lb	0.88	4/93	16r
Oranges, navel	lb	0.55	4/93	16r
Pears, Anjou	lb	0.92	4/93	16r
Pork chops, center cut, bone-in	lb	3.13	4/93	16r
Potato chips	16 oz	2.94	4/93	16r
Potatoes, white	lb	0.43	4/93	16r
Rib roast, USDA choice, bone-in	lb	4.63	4/93	16r
Rice, white, long grain, uncooked	lb	0.45	4/93	16r
Round roast, graded & ungraded, ex USDA prime & choice	lb	3.03	4/93	16r
Round roast, USDA choice, boneless	lb	3.09	4/93	16r
Sausage, fresh, loose	lb	2.08	4/93	16r
Short ribs, bone-in	lb	2.66	4/93	16r
Shortening, vegetable oil blends	lb	0.69	4/93	16r
Spaghetti and macaroni	lb	0.81	4/93	16r
Steak, rib eye, USDA choice, boneless	lb	6.24	4/93	16r
Steak, round, graded & ungraded, ex USDA prime & choice	lb	3.31	4/93	16r
Steak, round, USDA choice, boneless	lb	3.34	4/93	16r
Steak, sirloin, graded & ungraded, ex USDA prime & choice	lb	4.19	4/93	16r
Steak, sirloin, USDA choice, boneless	lb	4.46	4/93	16r
Steak, T-bone, USDA choice, bone-in	lb	5.25	4/93	16r
Strawberries, dry pint	12 oz	0.92	4/93	16r
Sugar, white	lb	0.39	4/93	16r
Sugar, white, 33-80 oz pk	lb	0.38	4/93	16r
Tomatoes, field grown	lb	0.88	4/93	16r
Tuna, chunk, light	lb	1.79	4/93	16r
Turkey, frozen, whole	lb	1.04	4/93	16r
Yogurt, natural, fruit flavored	1/2 pint	0.57	4/93	16r
Health Care				
Childbirth, cesarean, hospital		5034	91	62r
Childbirth, cesarean, physician's fee		2053	91	62r
Childbirth, normal, hospital		2712	91	62r
Childbirth, normal, physician's fee		1492	91	62r
Mental health care, exp	capita	28.84-37.59	90	38s

Values are in dollars or fractions of dollars. In the column headed *Ref*, references are shown to sources. Each reference is followed by a letter. These refer to the geographical level for which data were reported: s=State, r=Region, and c=City or metro. The abbreviation *ex* is used to mean *except* or *excluding*; *exp* stands for expenditures. For other abbreviations and further explanations, please see the Introduction.

Enid, OK - continued

Item	Per	Value	Date	Ref.
Health Care				
Mental health care, exp, state mental health agency	capita	35.92	90	38s
Mental health care, hospital psychiatric services, non-Federal, exp	capita	11.62	88	38s
Mental health care, mental health organization, multiservice, exp	capita	13.80	88	38s
Mental health care, psychiatric hospitals, private, exp	capita	21.32	88	38s
Mental health care, psychiatric out-patient clinics, freestanding, exp	capita	3.63	88	38s
Mental health care, psychiatric partial-care organizations, freestanding, exp	capita	0.04	88	38s
Mental health care, state and county mental hospitals, exp	capita	20.87	88	38s
Mental health care, VA medical centers, exp	capita	0.46	88	38s
Physician fee, family practice, first-visit		75.00	91	62r
Physician fee, family practice, revisit		34.00	91	62r
Physician fee, general practice, first-visit		61.00	91	62r
Physician fee, general practice, revisit		32.00	91	62r
Physician fee, general surgeon, first-visit		64.00	91	62r
Physician fee, general surgeon, revisit		40.00	91	62r
Physician fee, internal medicine, first-visit		98.00	91	62r
Physician fee, internal medicine, revisit		40.00	91	62r
Physician fee, median, neurosurgeon, first-visit		130.00	91	62r
Physician fee, median, nonsurgical specialist, first-visit		95.00	91	62r
Physician fee, median, orthopedic surgeon, first-visit		91.00	91	62r
Physician fee, median, plastic surgeon, first-visit		66.00	91	62r
Physician fee, median, surgical specialist, first-visit		62.00	91	62r
Physician fee, neurosurgeon, revisit		50.00	91	62r
Physician fee, nonsurgical specialist, revisit		40.00	91	62r
Physician fee, obstetrics/gynecology, first-visit		64.00	91	62r
Physician fee, obstetrics/gynecology, revisit		41.00	91	62r
Physician fee, orthopedic surgeon, revisit		40.00	91	62r
Physician fee, pediatrician, first-visit		49.00	91	62r
Physician fee, pediatrician, revisit		33.00	91	62r
Physician fee, plastic surgeon, revisit		43.00	91	62r
Physician fee, surgical specialist, revisit		37.00	91	62r
Substance abuse, hospital ancillary charge	incident	1220	90	70s
Substance abuse, hospital physician charge	incident	160	90	70s
Substance abuse, hospital room and board	incident	5490	90	70s
Insurance and Pensions				
Auto insurance, private passenger	year	554.09	91	63s
Taxes				
Tax, cigarette	pack	23	91	77s
Tax, gasoline	gal	17	91	77s
Taxes, state	capita	1216	91	77s
Transportation				
Driver's license fee		7.00-14.00	12/90	43s
Travel				
Business travel	day	193.00	4/93	89r
Utilities				
Electricity	mil Btu	16.08	90	64s
Electricity, residential	KWh	6.24	2/93	94s

Erie, PA

Item	Per	Value	Date	Ref.
Composite ACCRA index		109.20	4Q 92	4c
Alcoholic Beverages				
Beer, Miller Lite or Budweiser, 12-oz containers	6 pack	4.67	4Q 92	4c
Liquor, J & B Scotch	750 ml	16.39	4Q 92	4c
Wine, Gallo Chablis blanc, 1.5 liter	bottle	5.79	4Q 92	4c
Child Care				
Child care fee, average, center	hour	2.18	90	65r
Child care fee, average, nonregulated family day care	hour	1.83	90	65r
Child care fee, average, regulated family day care	hour	2.02	90	65r
Clothing				
Jeans, man's denim		35.24	4Q 92	4c
Shirt, man's dress shirt		23.50	4Q 92	4c
Undervest, boy's size 10-14, cotton	3	5.99	4Q 92	4c
Communications				
Long-distance telephone service, day, initial minute, 0-100 miles	min	0.15-0.29	91	12s
Long-distance telephone service, day, additional minute, 0-100 miles	min	0.06-0.22	91	12s
Long-distance telephone service, evenings/weekends, 0-100 mi, initial minute	min	0.06-0.14	91	12s
Long-distance telephone service, evenings/weekends, 0-100 mi, additional minute	min	0.03-0.11	91	12s
Newspaper subscription, daily and Sunday home delivery, large-city	month	11.96	4Q 92	4c
Telephone bill, family of four	month	21.88	4Q 92	4c
Education				
Board, 4-yr private college/university	year	2019	91	22s
Board, 4-yr public college/university	year	1656	91	22s
Expenditures, local gov't, public elementary/secondary	pupil	6980	92	20s
Room, 4-year private college/university	year	2179	91	22s
Room, 4-year public college/university	year	1719	91	22s
Tuition, 2-year private college/university	year	6314	91	22s
Tuition, 2-year public college/university	year	1505	91	22s
Tuition, 4-year private college/university	year	9848	91	22s
Tuition, 4-year public college/university, in-state	year	3401	91	22s
Energy and Fuels				
Coal	mil Btu	1.57	90	64s
Energy	mil Btu	8.63	90	64s
Energy, combined forms, 1,800 sq ft heating area	month	111.99	4Q 92	4c
Energy, exc electricity, 1,800 sq ft heating area	month	62.16	4Q 92	4c
Energy exp/householder, 1-family unit	year	588	90	28r
Energy exp/householder, <1,000 sq ft heating area	year	477	90	28r
Energy exp/householder, 1,000-1,999 sq ft heating area	year	517	90	28r
Energy exp/householder, 2,000+ sq ft heating area	year	630	90	28r
Energy exp/householder, mobile home	year	412	90	28r
Energy exp/householder, multifamily	year	498	90	28r
Gas, cooking, winter, 10 therms	month	16.21	92	56c
Gas, cooking, winter, 30 therms	month	25.24	92	56c
Gas, cooking, winter, 50 therms	month	34.28	92	56c
Gas, heating, winter, 100 therms	month	56.41	92	56c
Gas, heating, winter, average use	month	105.12	92	56c
Gas, natural	mil Btu	5.24	90	64s
Gas, natural	000 cu ft	6.76	91	46s
Gas, natural, exp	year	703	91	46s
Gasoline, motor	gal	1.26	4Q 92	4c
Gasoline, unleaded regular	mil Btu	9.35	90	64s
Entertainment				
Bowling, evening rate	game	1.61	4Q 92	4c

Values are in dollars or fractions of dollars. In the column headed *Ref*, references are shown to sources. Each reference is followed by a letter. These refer to the geographical level for which data were reported: s = State, r = Region, and c = City or metro. The abbreviation *ex* is used to mean *except* or *excluding*; *exp* stands for expenditures. For other abbreviations and further explanations, please see the Introduction.

Erie, PA - continued

Item	Per	Value	Date	Ref.
Entertainment				
Monopoly game, Parker Brothers', No. 9		9.98	4Q 92	4c
Movie	admis-sion	5.50	4Q 92	4c
Tennis balls, yellow, Wilson or Penn, 3	can	2.79	4Q 92	4c
Funerals				
Casket, 18-gauge steel, velvet interior		1811.58	91	24r
Cosmetology, hair care, etc.		111.08	91	24r
Embalming		329.42	91	24r
Facility use for ceremony		201.29	91	24r
Hearse, local		135.27	91	24r
Limousine, local		127.24	91	24r
Remains to funeral home, transfer		103.98	91	24r
Service charge, professional		724.98	91	24r
Vault, concrete, non-metallic liner		766.71	91	24r
Viewing facilities, use		260.60	91	24r
Goods and Services				
ACCRA Index, Miscellaneous Goods and Services		108.80	4Q 92	4c
Goods and services	year	15227	92	36c
Groceries				
ACCRA Index, Groceries		94.30	4Q 92	4c
Apples, Red Delicious	lb	0.85	4/93	16r
Babyfood, strained vegetables, lowest price	4-4.5 oz jar	0.21	4Q 92	4c
Bacon	lb	2.12	4/93	16r
Bananas	lb	0.40	4Q 92	4c
Bananas	lb	0.54	4/93	16r
Bread, white	24 oz	0.63	4Q 92	4c
Bread, white, pan	lb	0.81	4/93	16r
Butter	lb	2.02	4/93	16r
Carrots, short trimmed and topped	lb	0.51	4/93	16r
Cheese, Kraft grated Parmesan	8-oz canis-ter	3.16	4Q 92	4c
Chicken, fresh, whole	lb	1.04	4/93	16r
Chicken, fryer, whole	lb	0.77	4Q 92	4c
Chicken breast, bone-in	lb	2.21	4/93	16r
Chicken legs, bone-in	lb	1.16	4/93	16r
Chuck roast, USDA choice, boneless	lb	2.82	4/93	16r
Cigarettes, Winston	carton	18.02	4Q 92	4c
Coffee, 100% ground roast, all sizes	lb	2.66	4/93	16r
Coffee, vacuum-packed	13-oz can	2.47	4Q 92	4c
Corn, frozen	10 oz	0.63	4Q 92	4c
Corn Flakes, Kellogg's or Post Toasties	18 oz	1.70	4Q 92	4c
Cucumbers	lb	0.85	4/93	16r
Eggs, Grade A large	doz	0.75	4Q 92	4c
Eggs, Grade A large	doz	1.15	4/93	16r
Grapefruit	lb	0.45	4/93	16r
Grapes, Thompson Seedless	lb	1.52	4/93	16r
Ground beef, lean and extra lean	lb	2.36	4/93	16r
Ground beef or hamburger	lb	1.20	4Q 92	4c
Ground chuck, 100% beef	lb	2.02	4/93	16r
Honey, jar	8 oz	0.96-1.75	92	5r
Honey, jar	lb	1.50-3.00	92	5r
Honey, squeeze bear	12-oz	1.50-1.99	92	5r
Ice cream, prepackaged, bulk, regular	1/2 gal	2.80	4/93	16r
Lemons	lb	0.96	4/93	16r
Lettuce, iceberg	head	0.96	4Q 92	4c
Lettuce, iceberg	lb	0.95	4/93	16r
Margarine, Blue Bonnet or Parkay cubes	lb	0.48	4Q 92	4c
Margarine, stick	lb	0.81	4/93	16r
Milk, fresh, whole, fortified	1/2 gal	1.30	4/93	16r
Milk, whole	1/2 gal	1.26	4Q 92	4c
Orange juice, Minute Maid frozen	12-oz can	1.27	4Q 92	4c
Oranges, navel	lb	0.56	4/93	16r
Peaches	29-oz can	1.39	4Q 92	4c
Peanut butter, creamy, all sizes	lb	1.88	4/93	16r

Erie, PA - continued

Item	Per	Value	Date	Ref.
Groceries - continued				
Peas Sweet, Del Monte or Green Giant	15-17 oz can	0.64	4Q 92	4c
Pork chops, center cut, bone-in	lb	3.34	4/93	16r
Potato chips	16 oz	2.88	4/93	16r
Potatoes, white	lb	0.37	4/93	16r
Potatoes, white or red	10-lb sack	1.48	4Q 92	4c
Rib roast, USDA choice, bone-in	lb	4.94	4/93	16r
Round roast, USDA choice, boneless	lb	3.17	4/93	16r
Sausage, Jimmy Dean, 100% pork	lb	2.50	4Q 92	4c
Shortening, vegetable oil blends	lb	0.98	4/93	16r
Shortening, vegetable, Crisco	3-lb can	1.99	4Q 92	4c
Soft drink, Coca Cola	2 liter	1.01	4Q 92	4c
Spaghetti and macaroni	lb	0.82	4/93	16r
Steak, round, graded & ungraded, ex USDA prime & choice	lb	4.04	4/93	16r
Steak, round, USDA choice, boneless	lb	3.90	4/93	16r
Steak, sirloin, USDA choice, boneless	lb	4.97	4/93	16r
Steak, T-bone	lb	5.66	4Q 92	4c
Strawberries, dry pint	12 oz	0.90	4/93	16r
Sugar, cane or beet	4 lb	1.30	4Q 92	4c
Sugar, white	lb	0.50	4/93	16r
Sugar, white, 33-80 oz pk	lb	0.41	4/93	16r
Tomatoes, field grown	lb	1.23	4/93	16r
Tomatoes, Hunt's or Del Monte	14.5-oz can	0.84	4Q 92	4c
Tuna, chunk, light	6.125-6.5 oz can	0.60	4Q 92	4c
Tuna, chunk, light	lb	2.22	4/93	16r
Turkey, frozen, whole	lb	1.04	4/93	16r
Health Care				
ACCRA Index, Health Care		104.80	4Q 92	4c
Analgesic, Aspirin, Bayer, 325 mg tablets	100	5.30	4Q 92	4c
Childbirth, cesarean, hospital		5826	91	62r
Childbirth, cesarean, physician's fee		2053	91	62r
Childbirth, normal, hospital		2964	91	62r
Childbirth, normal, physician's fee		1492	91	62r
Dentist's fee, adult teeth cleaning and periodic oral exam	visit	46.00	4Q 92	4c
Doctor's fee, routine exam, established patient	visit	35.25	4Q 92	4c
Hospital care, semiprivate room	day	313.01	90	27c
Hospital care, semiprivate room	day	429.00	4Q 92	4c
Medical insurance premium, per employee, small group comprehensive	month	328.50	10/91	25c
Medical plan per employee	year	3942	91	45r
Mental health care, exp	capita	53.68-118.35	90	38s
Mental health care, exp, state mental health agency	capita	56.85	90	38s
Mental health care, hospital psychiatric services, non-Federal, exp	capita	22.11	88	38s
Mental health care, mental health organization, multiservice, exp	capita	21.01	88	38s
Mental health care, psychiatric hospitals, private, exp	capita	26.48	88	38s
Mental health care, psychiatric out-patient clinics, freestanding, exp	capita	4.17	88	38s
Mental health care, psychiatric partial-care organizations, freestanding, exp	capita	0.94	88	38s
Mental health care, state and county mental hospitals, exp	capita	37.11	88	38s
Mental health care, VA medical centers, exp	capita	9.77	88	38s
Prescription drug co-pay, Medicaid	month	6.00	91	21s
Substance abuse, hospital ancillary charge	inci-dent	720	90	70s
Substance abuse, hospital physician charge	inci-dent	210	90	70s
Substance abuse, hospital room and board	inci-dent	5400	90	70s

Values are in dollars or fractions of dollars. In the column headed *Ref*, references are shown to sources. Each reference is followed by a letter. These refer to the geographical level for which data were reported: s = State, r = Region, and c = City or metro. The abbreviation *ex* is used to mean *except* or *excluding*; *exp* stands for *expenditures*. For other abbreviations and further explanations, please see the Introduction.

Erie, PA - continued

Item	Per	Value	Date	Ref.
Household Goods				
Appliance repair, home, service call, washing machine	min labor charge	33.28	4Q 92	4c
Laundry detergent, Tide Ultra, Bold, or Cheer	42 oz	3.80	4Q 92	4c
Tissues, facial, Kleenex brand	175-count box	1.07	4Q 92	4c
Housing				
ACCRA Index, Housing		121.30	4Q 92	4c
House, 1,800 sq ft, 8,000 sq ft lot, new, urban	total	139500	4Q 92	4c
House payment, principal and interest, 25% down payment	month	782	4Q 92	4c
Mortgage rate, incl. points & origination fee, 30-year fixed or adjustable rate	percent	8.19	4Q 92	4c
Rent, apartment, 2 bedrooms - 1-1/2 to 2 baths, unfurnished, 950 sq ft, water	month	515.	4Q 92	4c
Rental unit, 1 bedroom	month	473	93	23c
Rental unit, 2 bedroom	month	556	93	23c
Rental unit, 3 bedroom	month	698	93	23c
Rental unit, 4 bedroom	month	781	93	23c
Rental unit, efficiency	month	383	93	23c
Insurance and Pensions				
Auto insurance, private passenger	year	683.57	91	63s
Personal Goods				
Shampoo, Alberto VO5	15 oz	1.38	4Q 92	4c
Toothpaste, Crest or Colgate	6-7 oz	2.04	4Q 92	4c
Personal Services				
Dry cleaning, man's 2-piece suit		7.37	4Q 92	4c
Haircare, woman's shampoo, trim and blow-dry		16.75	4Q 92	4c
Haircut, man's barbershop, no styling		6.88	4Q 92	4c
Restaurant Food				
Chicken, fried, thigh and drumstick		2.57	4Q 92	4c
Hamburger with cheese	1/4 lb	1.79	4Q 92	4c
Pizza, Pizza Hut or Pizza Inn, cheese, thin crust	12-13 in	8.69	4Q 92	4c
Taxes				
Tax, cigarette	pack	31	91	77s
Tax, gasoline	gal	12	91	77s
Taxes, state	capita	1089	91	77s
Transportation				
ACCRA Index, Transportation		103.40	4Q 92	4c
Bus fare	one-way	0.75	3/93	2c
Bus fare, up to 10 miles	one-way	0.75	4Q 92	4c
Driver's license fee		22.00	12/90	43s
Tire balance, computer or spin balance, front	wheel	6.44	4Q 92	4c
Travel				
Business travel	day	165.00	4/93	89r
Utilities				
ACCRA Index, Utilities		103.60	4Q 92	4c
Electricity	mil Btu	22.46	90	64s
Electricity, partial electric and other energy, 1,800 sq ft living area new home	month	49.83	4Q 92	4c
Electricity, winter, 250 KWh	month	25.31	92	55c
Electricity, winter, 500 KWh	month	43.67	92	55c
Electricity, winter, 750 KWh	month	62.05	92	55c
Electricity, winter, 1000 KWh	month	74.91	92	55c

Eugene, OR

Item	Per	Value	Date	Ref.
Alcoholic Beverages				
Beer, Miller Lite or Budweiser, 12-oz containers	6 pack	3.81	4Q 92	4c
Liquor, J & B Scotch	750 ml	20.05	4Q 92	4c
Wine, Gallo Chablis blanc, 1.5 liter	bottle	4.61	4Q 92	4c
Child Care				
Child care fee, average, center	hour	1.71	90	65r
Child care fee, average, nonregulated family day care	hour	1.32	90	65r
Child care fee, average, regulated family day care	hour	1.86	90	65r
Clothing				
Jeans, man's denim		26.99	4Q 92	4c
Shirt, man's dress shirt		26.00	4Q 92	4c
Undervest, boy's size 10-14, cotton	3	4.49	4Q 92	4c
Communications				
Long-distance telephone service, day, initial minute, 0-100 miles	min	0.13-0.26	91	12s
Long-distance telephone service, day, additional minute, 0-100 miles	min	0.10-0.21	91	12s
Long-distance telephone service, evenings/weekends, 0-100 mi, initial minute	min	0.07-0.13	91	12s
Long-distance telephone service, evenings/weekends, 0-100 mi, additional minute	min	0.04-0.07	91	12s
Newspaper subscription, daily and Sunday home delivery, large-city	month	9.78	4Q 92	4c
Telephone, flat rate	month	13.68	91	11c
Telephone bill, family of four	month	17.46	4Q 92	4c
Education				
Board, 4-yr private college/university	year	2004	91	22s
Board, 4-yr public college/university	year	1954	91	22s
Expenditures, local gov't, public elementary/secondary	pupil	5463	92	20s
Room, 4-year private college/university	year	1621	91	22s
Room, 4-year public college/university	year	1329	91	22s
Tuition, 2-year private college/university	year	7570	91	22s
Tuition, 2-year public college/university	year	794	91	22s
Tuition, 4-year private college/university	year	9606	91	22s
Tuition, 4-year public college/university, in-state	year	1906	91	22s
Energy and Fuels				
Coal	mil Btu	1.22	90	64s
Energy	mil Btu	8.39	90	64s
Energy, combined forms, 1,800 sq ft heating area	month	72.96	4Q 92	4c
Energy exp/householder, 1-family unit	year	362	90	28r
Energy exp/householder, <1,000 sq ft heating area	year	254	90	28r
Energy exp/householder, 1,000-1,999 sq ft heating area	year	358	90	28r
Energy exp/householder, 2,000+ sq ft heating area	year	467	90	28r
Energy exp/householder, mobile home	year	390	90	28r
Energy exp/householder, multifamily	year	252	90	28r
Gas, natural	mil Btu	4.28	90	64s
Gas, natural	000 cu ft	6.13	91	46s
Gas, natural, exp	year	429	91	46s
Gasoline, motor	gal	1.27	4Q 92	4c
Gasoline, unleaded regular	mil Btu	9.45	90	64s
Entertainment				
Bowling, evening rate	game	1.76	4Q 92	4c
Miniature golf admission	adult	6.18	92	1r
Miniature golf admission	child	5.14	92	1r
Monopoly game, Parker Brothers', No. 9		10.69	4Q 92	4c
Movie	admission	5.12	4Q 92	4c
Tennis balls, yellow, Wilson or Penn, 3	can	2.39	4Q 92	4c
Waterpark admission	adult	11.00	92	1r

Values are in dollars or fractions of dollars. In the column headed *Ref*, references are shown to sources. Each reference is followed by a letter. These refer to the geographical level for which data were reported: s=State, r=Region, and c=City or metro. The abbreviation *ex* is used to mean *except* or *excluding*; *exp* stands for expenditures. For other abbreviations and further explanations, please see the Introduction.

Eugene, OR - continued

Item	Per	Value	Date	Ref.
Entertainment				
Waterpark admission	child	8.55	92	1r
Funerals				
Casket, 18-gauge steel, velvet interior		1781.09	91	24r
Cosmetology, hair care, etc.		84.64	91	24r
Embalming		207.41	91	24r
Facility use for ceremony		205.76	91	24r
Hearse, local		105.14	91	24r
Limousine, local		83.21	91	24r
Remains to funeral home, transfer		113.82	91	24r
Service charge, professional		626.33	91	24r
Vault, concrete, non-metallic liner		599.54	91	24r
Viewing facilities, use		85.81	91	24r
Groceries				
Apples, Red Delicious	lb	0.80	4/93	16r
Babyfood, strained vegetables, lowest price	4-4.5 oz jar	0.24	4Q 92	4c
Bacon	lb	1.79	4/93	16r
Bananas	lb	0.44	4Q 92	4c
Bananas	lb	0.53	4/93	16r
Bologna, all beef or mixed	lb	2.67	4/93	16r
Bread, white	24 oz	0.44	4Q 92	4c
Bread, white, pan	lb	0.81	4/93	16r
Carrots, short trimmed and topped	lb	0.39	4/93	16r
Cheese, Kraft grated Parmesan	8-oz canister	3.36	4Q 92	4c
Chicken, fresh, whole	lb	0.94	4/93	16r
Chicken, fryer, whole	lb	0.78	4Q 92	4c
Chicken breast, bone-in	lb	2.19	4/93	16r
Chuck roast, graded and ungraded, ex USDA prime and choice	lb	2.26	4/93	16r
Cigarettes, Winston	carton	17.67	4Q 92	4c
Coffee, 100% ground roast, all sizes	lb	2.33	4/93	16r
Coffee, vacuum-packed	13-oz can	2.52	4Q 92	4c
Corn, frozen	10 oz	0.63	4Q 92	4c
Corn Flakes, Kellogg's or Post Toasties	18 oz	2.00	4Q 92	4c
Eggs, Grade A large	doz	0.84	4Q 92	4c
Eggs, Grade AA large	doz	1.18	4/93	16r
Flour, white, all purpose	lb	0.22	4/93	16r
Grapefruit	lb	0.52	4/93	16r
Grapes, Thompson Seedless	lb	1.50	4/93	16r
Ground beef, 100% beef	lb	1.44	4/93	16r
Ground beef, lean and extra lean	lb	2.34	4/93	16r
Ground beef or hamburger	lb	1.59	4Q 92	4c
Ham, boneless, excluding canned	lb	2.56	4/93	16r
Honey, jar	8 oz	0.89-1.00	92	5r
Honey, jar	lb	1.35-1.97	92	5r
Honey, squeeze bear	12-oz	1.19-1.50	92	5r
Ice cream, prepackaged, bulk, regular	1/2 gal	2.40	4/93	16r
Lemons	lb	0.81	4/93	16r
Lettuce, iceberg	head	0.80	4Q 92	4c
Lettuce, iceberg	lb	0.84	4/93	16r
Margarine, Blue Bonnet or Parkay cubes	lb	0.49	4Q 92	4c
Margarine, stick	lb	0.81	4/93	16r
Milk, whole	1/2 gal	1.20	4Q 92	4c
Orange juice, Minute Maid frozen	12-oz can	1.10	4Q 92	4c
Oranges, navel	lb	0.48	4/93	16r
Peaches	29-oz can	1.59	4Q 92	4c
Peas Sweet, Del Monte or Green Giant	15-17 oz can	0.72	4Q 92	4c
Pork chops, center cut, bone-in	lb	3.25	4/93	16r
Potato chips	16 oz	2.89	4/93	16r
Potatoes, white	lb	0.38	4/93	16r
Potatoes, white or red	10-lb sack	1.23	4Q 92	4c
Round roast, graded & ungraded, ex USDA prime & choice	lb	3.00	4/93	16r
Round roast, USDA choice, boneless	lb	3.16	4/93	16r

Eugene, OR - continued

Item	Per	Value	Date	Ref.
Groceries - continued				
Sausage, Jimmy Dean, 100% pork	lb	3.45	4Q 92	4c
Shortening, vegetable oil blends	lb	0.86	4/93	16r
Shortening, vegetable, Crisco	3-lb can	2.03	4Q 92	4c
Soft drink, Coca Cola	2 liter	1.41	4Q 92	4c
Spaghetti and macaroni	lb	0.84	4/93	16r
Steak, round, graded & ungraded, ex USDA prime & choice	lb	3.34	4/93	16r
Steak, round, USDA choice, boneless	lb	3.24	4/93	16r
Steak, sirloin, graded & ungraded, ex USDA prime & choice	lb	3.75	4/93	16r
Steak, sirloin, USDA choice, boneless	lb	4.49	4/93	16r
Steak, T-bone	lb	4.76	4Q 92	4c
Sugar, cane or beet	4 lb	1.13	4Q 92	4c
Sugar, white	lb	0.41	4/93	16r
Sugar, white, 33-80 oz pk	lb	0.38	4/93	16r
Tomatoes, field grown	lb	1.01	4/93	16r
Tomatoes, Hunt's or Del Monte	14.5-oz can	0.76	4Q 92	4c
Tuna, chunk, light	6.125-6.5 oz can	0.76	4Q 92	4c
Turkey, frozen, whole	lb	1.04	4/93	16r
Health Care				
Analgesic, Aspirin, Bayer, 325 mg tablets	100	4.60	4Q 92	4c
Childbirth, cesarean, hospital		5533	91	62r
Childbirth, cesarean, physician's fee		2053	91	62r
Childbirth, normal, hospital		2745	91	62r
Childbirth, normal, physician's fee		1492	91	62r
Dentist's fee, adult teeth cleaning and periodic oral exam	visit	46.00	4Q 92	4c
Doctor's fee, routine exam, established patient	visit	47.25	4Q 92	4c
Hospital care, semiprivate room	day	252.00	90	27c
Hospital care, semiprivate room	day	318.50	4Q 92	4c
Medical insurance premium, per employee, small group comprehensive	month	281.05	10/91	25c
Medical plan per employee	year	3421	91	45r
Mental health care, exp, state mental health agency	capita	40.68	90	38s
Mental health care, hospital psychiatric services, non-Federal, exp	capita	9.91	88	38s
Mental health care, mental health organization, multiservice, exp	capita	25.94	88	38s
Mental health care, psychiatric hospitals, private, exp	capita	1.48	88	38s
Mental health care, psychiatric out-patient clinics, freestanding, exp	capita	3.50	88	38s
Mental health care, psychiatric partial-care organizations, freestanding, exp	capita	0.58	88	38s
Mental health care, state and county mental hospitals, exp	capita	18.67	88	38s
Mental health care, VA medical centers, exp	capita	2.53	88	38s
Physician fee, family practice, first-visit		111.00	91	62r
Physician fee, family practice, revisit		45.00	91	62r
Physician fee, general practice, first-visit		100.00	91	62r
Physician fee, general practice, revisit		40.00	91	62r
Physician fee, internal medicine, first-visit		137.00	91	62r
Physician fee, internal medicine, revisit		48.00	91	62r
Physician fee, median, neurosurgeon, first-visit		157.00	91	62r
Physician fee, median, nonsurgical specialist, first-visit		131.00	91	62r
Physician fee, median, orthopedic surgeon, first-visit		124.00	91	62r
Physician fee, median, plastic surgeon, first-visit		88.00	91	62r
Physician fee, median, surgical specialist, first-visit		100.00	91	62r
Physician fee, neurosurgeon, revisit		51.00	91	62r
Physician fee, nonsurgical specialist, revisit		47.00	91	62r

Values are in dollars or fractions of dollars. In the column headed *Ref*, references are shown to sources. Each reference is followed by a letter. These refer to the geographical level for which data were reported: s = State, r = Region, and c = City or metro. The abbreviation *ex* is used to mean *except* or *excluding*; *exp* stands for expenditures. For other abbreviations and further explanations, please see the Introduction.

Eugene, OR - continued

Item	Per	Value	Date	Ref.
Health Care				
Physician fee, obstetrics/gynecology, first-visit		95.00	91	62r
Physician fee, obstetrics/gynecology, revisit		50.00	91	62r
Physician fee, orthopedic surgeon, revisit		51.00	91	62r
Physician fee, pediatrician, first-visit		81.00	91	62r
Physician fee, pediatrician, revisit		42.00	91	62r
Physician fee, plastic surgeon, revisit		48.00	91	62r
Physician fee, surgical specialist, revisit		49.00	91	62r
Substance abuse, hospital ancillary charge	incident	710	90	70s
Substance abuse, hospital physician charge	incident	70	90	70s
Substance abuse, hospital room and board	incident	3330	90	70s
Household Goods				
Appliance repair, home, service call, washing machine	min labor charge	29.72	4Q 92	4c
Laundry detergent, Tide Ultra, Bold, or Cheer	42 oz	3.71	4Q 92	4c
Tissues, facial, Kleenex brand	175-count box	1.41	4Q 92	4c
Housing				
Home, median price	unit	79.90		26c
House, 1,800 sq ft, 8,000 sq ft lot, new, urban	total	151470	4Q 92	4c
House payment, principal and interest, 25% down payment	month	834	4Q 92	4c
Mortgage rate, incl. points & origination fee, 30-year fixed or adjustable rate	percent	8.00	4Q 92	4c
Rent, apartment, 2 bedrooms - 1-1/2 to 2 baths, unfurnished, 950 sq ft, water	month	568	4Q 92	4c
Rental unit, 1 bedroom	month	516	93	23c
Rental unit, 2 bedroom	month	608	93	23c
Rental unit, 3 bedroom	month	760	93	23c
Rental unit, 4 bedroom	month	851	93	23c
Rental unit, efficiency	month	424	93	23c
Insurance and Pensions				
Auto insurance, private passenger	year	598.04	91	63s
Personal Goods				
Shampoo, Alberto VO5	15 oz	1.34	4Q 92	4c
Toothpaste, Crest or Colgate	6-7 oz	1.85	4Q 92	4c
Personal Services				
Dry cleaning, man's 2-piece suit		7.80	4Q 92	4c
Haircare, woman's shampoo, trim and blow-dry		19.20	4Q 92	4c
Haircut, man's barbershop, no styling		8.59	4Q 92	4c
Restaurant Food				
Chicken, fried, thigh and drumstick		2.29	4Q 92	4c
Hamburger with cheese	1/4 lb	1.95	4Q 92	4c
Pizza, Pizza Hut or Pizza Inn, cheese, thin crust	12-13 in	9.30	4Q 92	4c
Taxes				
Tax, cigarette	pack	28	91	77s
Tax, gasoline	gal	22	91	77s
Taxes, state	capita	1037	91	77s
Transportation				
Bus fare, up to 10 miles	one-way	0.75	4Q 92	4c
Driver's license fee		15.00	12/90	43s
Tire balance, computer or spin balance, front	wheel	6.90	4Q 92	4c
Vehicle registration and license plate	year	32.50	93	53s
Travel				
Business travel	day	178.00	4/93	89r

Eugene, OR - continued

Item	Per	Value	Date	Ref.
Utilities				
Electricity	mil Btu	12.25	90	64s
Electricity, all electric, 1,800 sq ft living area new home	month	72.96	4Q 92	4c

Evansville, IN

Item	Per	Value	Date	Ref.
Composite ACCRA index		91.90	4Q 92	4c
Alcoholic Beverages				
Beer, Miller Lite or Budweiser, 12-oz containers	6 pack	3.66	4Q 92	4c
Liquor, J & B Scotch	750 ml	17.15	4Q 92	4c
Wine, Gallo Chablis blanc, 1.5 liter	bottle	5.13	4Q 92	4c
Child Care				
Child care fee, average, center	hour	1.63	90	65r
Child care fee, average, nonregulated family day care	hour	1.83	90	65r
Child care fee, average, regulated family day care	hour	1.42	90	65r
Clothing				
Jeans, man's denim		30.18	4Q 92	4c
Shirt, man's dress shirt		19.39	4Q 92	4c
Undervest, boy's size 10-14, cotton	3	3.00	4Q 92	4c
Communications				
Long-distance telephone service, day, initial minute, 0-100 miles	min	0.18-0.45	91	12s
Long-distance telephone service, day, additional minute, 0-100 miles	min	0.10-0.30	91	12s
Long-distance telephone service, evenings/weekends, 0-100 mi, initial minute	min	0.08-0.19	91	12s
Long-distance telephone service, evenings/weekends, 0-100 mi, additional minute	min	0.04-0.13	91	12s
Newspaper subscription, daily and Sunday home delivery, large-city	month	13.25	4Q 92	4c
Telephone, flat rate	month	11.11	91	11c
Telephone bill, family of four	month	24.29	4Q 92	4c
Education				
Board, 4-yr private college/university	year	1714	91	22s
Board, 4-yr public college/university	year	1829	91	22s
Expenditures, local gov't, public elementary/secondary	pupil	5545	92	20s
Room, 4-year private college/university	year	1512	91	22s
Room, 4-year public college/university	year	1435	91	22s
Tuition, 2-year private college/university	year	6756	91	22s
Tuition, 2-year public college/university	year	1423	91	22s
Tuition, 4-year private college/university	year	8451	91	22s
Tuition, 4-year public college/university, in-state	year	2067	91	22s
Energy and Fuels				
Coal	mil Btu	1.46	90	64s
Energy	mil Btu	6.77	90	64s
Energy, combined forms, 1,800 sq ft heating area	month	91.37	4Q 92	4c
Energy, exc electricity, 1,800 sq ft heating area	month	24.46	4Q 92	4c
Energy exp/householder, 1-family unit	year	471	90	28r
Energy exp/householder, <1,000 sq ft heating area	year	430	90	28r
Energy exp/householder, 1,000-1,999 sq ft heating area	year	481	90	28r
Energy exp/householder, 2,000+ sq ft heating area	year	473	90	28r
Energy exp/householder, mobile home	year	430	90	28r
Energy exp/householder, multifamily	year	461	90	28r
Gas, cooking, 10 therms	month	5.86	92	56c
Gas, cooking, 30 therms	month	12.18	92	56c
Gas, cooking, 50 therms	month	18.52	92	56c
Gas, heating, winter, 100 therms	month	33.64	92	56c
Gas, heating, winter, average use	month	55.13	92	56c

Values are in dollars or fractions of dollars. In the column headed *Ref*, references are shown to sources. Each reference is followed by a letter. These refer to the geographical level for which data were reported: s=State, r=Region, and c=City or metro. The abbreviation *ex* is used to mean *except* or *excluding*; *exp* stands for expenditures. For other abbreviations and further explanations, please see the Introduction.

Evansville, IN - continued

Item	Per	Value	Date	Ref.
Energy and Fuels				
Gas, natural	mil Btu	4.27	90	64s
Gas, natural	000 cu ft	5.46	91	46s
Gas, natural, exp	year	588	91	46s
Gasoline, motor	gal	1.07	4Q 92	4c
Gasoline, unleaded regular	mil Btu	8.74	90	64s
Entertainment				
Bowling, evening rate	game	1.72	4Q 92	4c
Miniature golf admission	adult	6.18	92	1r
Miniature golf admission	child	5.14	92	1r
Monopoly game, Parker Brothers', No. 9		10.34	4Q 92	4c
Movie	admission	4.88	4Q 92	4c
Tennis balls, yellow, Wilson or Penn, 3	can	1.98	4Q 92	4c
Waterpark admission	adult	11.00	92	1r
Waterpark admission	child	8.55	92	1r
Funerals				
Casket, 18-gauge steel, velvet interior		1926.72	91	24r
Cosmetology, hair care, etc.		97.64	91	24r
Embalming		249.14	91	24r
Facility use for ceremony		208.59	91	24r
Hearse, local		130.12	91	24r
Limousine, local		104.66	91	24r
Remains to funeral home, transfer		93.61	91	24r
Service charge, professional		724.62	91	24r
Vault, concrete, non-metallic liner		734.53	91	24r
Viewing facilities, use		236.06	91	24r
Goods and Services				
ACCRA Index, Miscellaneous Goods and Services		91.60	4Q 92	4c
Groceries				
ACCRA Index, Groceries		99.10	4Q 92	4c
Apples, Red Delicious	lb	0.77	4/93	16r
Babyfood, strained vegetables, lowest price	4-4.5 oz jar	0.28	4Q 92	4c
Bacon	lb	1.85	4/93	16r
Bananas	lb	0.27	4Q 92	4c
Bananas	lb	0.46	4/93	16r
Beef, stew, boneless	lb	2.53	4/93	16r
Bologna, all beef or mixed	lb	2.19	4/93	16r
Bread, white	24 oz	0.99	4Q 92	4c
Bread, white, pan	lb	0.78	4/93	16r
Butter	lb	1.50	4/93	16r
Cabbage	lb	0.40	4/93	16r
Carrots, short trimmed and topped	lb	0.45	4/93	16r
Cheese, Cheddar	lb	3.47	4/93	16r
Cheese, Kraft grated Parmesan	8-oz canister	2.91	4Q 92	4c
Chicken, fresh, whole	lb	0.84	4/93	16r
Chicken, fryer, whole	lb	0.76	4Q 92	4c
Chicken breast, bone-in	lb	1.94	4/93	16r
Chicken legs, bone-in	lb	1.02	4/93	16r
Chuck roast, graded and ungraded, ex USDA prime and choice	lb	2.43	4/93	16r
Chuck roast, USDA choice, bone-in	lb	2.11	4/93	16r
Chuck roast, USDA choice, boneless	lb	2.44	4/93	16r
Cigarettes, Winston	carton	16.91	4Q 92	4c
Coffee, 100% ground roast, all sizes	lb	2.47	4/93	16r
Coffee, vacuum-packed	13-oz can	1.84	4Q 92	4c
Cookies, chocolate chip	lb	2.73	4/93	16r
Corn, frozen	10 oz	0.75	4Q 92	4c
Corn Flakes, Kellogg's or Post Toasties	18 oz	1.98	4Q 92	4c
Eggs, Grade A large	doz	0.78	4Q 92	4c
Eggs, Grade A large	doz	0.93	4/93	16r
Flour, white, all purpose	lb	0.21	4/93	16r
Grapefruit	lb	0.45	4/93	16r
Grapes, Thompson Seedless	lb	1.46	4/93	16r
Ground beef, 100% beef	lb	1.63	4/93	16r

Evansville, IN - continued

Item	Per	Value	Date	Ref.
Groceries - continued				
Ground beef, lean and extra lean	lb	2.08	4/93	16r
Ground beef or hamburger	lb	1.40	4Q 92	4c
Ground chuck, 100% beef	lb	1.94	4/93	16r
Ham, boneless, excluding canned	lb	2.21	4/93	16r
Honey, jar	8 oz	0.97-1.25	92	5r
Honey, jar	lb	1.25-2.25	92	5r
Honey, squeeze bear	12-oz	1.25-1.99	92	5r
Ice cream, prepackaged, bulk, regular	1/2 gal	2.41	4/93	16r
Lemons	lb	0.82	4/93	16r
Lettuce, iceberg	head	0.97	4Q 92	4c
Lettuce, iceberg	lb	0.83	4/93	16r
Margarine, Blue Bonnet or Parkay cubes	lb	0.57	4Q 92	4c
Margarine, stick	lb	0.77	4/93	16r
Milk, whole	1/2 gal	1.59	4Q 92	4c
Orange juice, Minute Maid frozen	12-oz can	1.27	4Q 92	4c
Oranges, navel	lb	0.50	4/93	16r
Peaches	29-oz can	1.29	4Q 92	4c
Peanut butter, creamy, all sizes	lb	1.82	4/93	16r
Pears, Anjou	lb	0.85	4/93	16r
Peas Sweet, Del Monte or Green Giant	15-17 oz can	0.64	4Q 92	4c
Pork chops, center cut, bone-in	lb	3.17	4/93	16r
Potato chips	16 oz	2.68	4/93	16r
Potatoes, white	lb	0.26	4/93	16r
Potatoes, white or red	10-lb sack	1.99	4Q 92	4c
Round roast, graded & ungraded, ex USDA prime & choice	lb	2.88	4/93	16r
Round roast, USDA choice, boneless	lb	2.96	4/93	16r
Sausage, Jimmy Dean, 100% pork	lb	2.36	4Q 92	4c
Shortening, vegetable oil blends	lb	0.79	4/93	16r
Shortening, vegetable, Crisco	3-lb can	2.30	4Q 92	4c
Soft drink, Coca Cola	2 liter	1.04	4Q 92	4c
Spaghetti and macaroni	lb	0.76	4/93	16r
Steak, rib eye, USDA choice, boneless	lb	6.29	4/93	16r
Steak, round, USDA choice, boneless	lb	3.24	4/93	16r
Steak, sirloin, graded & ungraded, ex USDA prime & choice	lb	4.00	4/93	16r
Steak, sirloin, USDA choice, bone-in	lb	3.57	4/93	16r
Steak, sirloin, USDA choice, boneless	lb	4.17	4/93	16r
Steak, T-bone	lb	5.39	4Q 92	4c
Steak, T-bone, USDA choice, bone-in	lb	5.60	4/93	16r
Strawberries, dry pint	12 oz	0.90	4/93	16r
Sugar, cane or beet	4 lb	1.26	4Q 92	4c
Sugar, white	lb	0.36	4/93	16r
Sugar, white, 33-80 oz pk	lb	0.35	4/93	16r
Tomatoes, field grown	lb	0.99	4/93	16r
Tomatoes, Hunt's or Del Monte	14.5-oz can	0.71	4Q 92	4c
Tuna, chunk, light	6.125-6.5 oz can	0.67	4Q 92	4c
Tuna, chunk, light	lb	1.76	4/93	16r
Turkey, frozen, whole	lb	0.91	4/93	16r
Health Care				
ACCRA Index, Health Care		85.20	4Q 92	4c
Analgesic, Aspirin, Bayer, 325 mg tablets	100	3.37	4Q 92	4c
Childbirth, cesarean, hospital		4688	91	62r
Childbirth, cesarean, physician's fee		2053	91	62r
Childbirth, normal, hospital		2657	91	62r
Childbirth, normal, physician's fee		1492	91	62r
Dentist's fee, adult teeth cleaning and periodic oral exam	visit	35.38	4Q 92	4c
Doctor's fee, routine exam, established patient	visit	32.58	4Q 92	4c
Hospital care, semiprivate room	day	274.15	90	27c
Hospital care, semiprivate room	day	347.33	4Q 92	4c
Medical insurance premium, per employee, small group comprehensive	month	306.60	10/91	25c

Values are in dollars or fractions of dollars. In the column headed *Ref*, references are shown to sources. Each reference is followed by a letter. These refer to the geographical level for which data were reported: s = State, r = Region, and c = City or metro. The abbreviation *ex* is used to mean *except* or *excluding*; *exp* stands for expenditures. For other abbreviations and further explanations, please see the Introduction.

Evansville, IN - continued

Item	Per	Value	Date	Ref.
Health Care				
Medical plan per employee	year	3443	91	45r
Mental health care, exp	capita	37.60-53.67	90	38s
Mental health care, exp, state mental health agency	capita	47.05	90	38s
Mental health care, hospital psychiatric services, non-Federal, exp	capita	22.14	88	38s
Mental health care, mental health organization, multiservice, exp	capita	10.33	88	38s
Mental health care, psychiatric hospitals, private, exp	capita	20.10	88	38s
Mental health care, state and county mental hospitals, exp	capita	24.00	88	38s
Mental health care, VA medical centers, exp	capita	3.20	88	38s
Physician fee, family practice, first-visit		76.00	91	62r
Physician fee, family practice, revisit		33.00	91	62r
Physician fee, general practice, first-visit		61.00	91	62r
Physician fee, general practice, revisit		31.00	91	62r
Physician fee, general surgeon, first-visit		65.00	91	62r
Physician fee, general surgeon, revisit		35.00	91	62r
Physician fee, internal medicine, first-visit		91.00	91	62r
Physician fee, internal medicine, revisit		40.00	91	62r
Physician fee, median, neurosurgeon, first-visit		106.00	91	62r
Physician fee, median, nonsurgical specialist, first-visit		90.00	91	62r
Physician fee, median, orthopedic surgeon, first-visit		83.00	91	62r
Physician fee, median, surgical specialist, first-visit		61.00	91	62r
Physician fee, neurosurgeon, revisit		41.00	91	62r
Physician fee, nonsurgical specialist, revisit		40.00	91	62r
Physician fee, obstetrics/gynecology, first-visit		61.00	91	62r
Physician fee, obstetrics/gynecology, revisit		40.00	91	62r
Physician fee, orthopedic surgeon, revisit		41.00	91	62r
Physician fee, pediatrician, first-visit		46.00	91	62r
Physician fee, pediatrician, revisit		33.00	91	62r
Physician fee, surgical specialist, revisit		36.00	91	62r
Substance abuse, hospital ancillary charge	incident	1230	90	70s
Substance abuse, hospital physician charge	incident	410	90	70s
Substance abuse, hospital room and board	incident	5510	90	70s
Household Goods				
Appliance repair, home, service call, washing machine	min labor charge	29.89	4Q 92	4c
Laundry detergent, Tide Ultra, Bold, or Cheer	42 oz	3.00	4Q 92	4c
Tissues, facial, Kleenex brand	175-count box	1.17	4Q 92	4c
Housing				
ACCRA Index, Housing		90.30	4Q 92	4c
House, 1,800 sq ft, 8,000 sq ft lot, new, urban	total	101700	4Q 92	4c
House payment, principal and interest, 25% down payment	month	571	4Q 92	4c
Mortgage rate, incl. points & origination fee, 30-year fixed or adjustable rate	percent	8.22	4Q 92	4c
Rent, apartment, 2 bedrooms - 1-1/2 to 2 baths, unfurnished, 950 sq ft, water	month	409	4Q 92	4c
Rental unit, 1 bedroom	month	376	93	23c
Rental unit, 2 bedroom	month	441	93	23c
Rental unit, 3 bedroom	month	553	93	23c
Rental unit, 4 bedroom	month	619	93	23c
Rental unit, efficiency	month	315	93	23c

Evansville, IN - continued

Item	Per	Value	Date	Ref.
Insurance and Pensions				
Auto insurance, private passenger	year	548.99	91	63s
Personal Goods				
Shampoo, Alberto VO5	15 oz	0.94	4Q 92	4c
Toothpaste, Crest or Colgate	6-7 oz	1.18	4Q 92	4c
Personal Services				
Dry cleaning, man's 2-piece suit		6.56	4Q 92	4c
Haircare, woman's shampoo, trim and blow-dry		18.50	4Q 92	4c
Haircut, man's barbershop, no styling		6.25	4Q 92	4c
Restaurant Food				
Chicken, fried, thigh and drumstick		2.29	4Q 92	4c
Hamburger with cheese	1/4 lb	1.87	4Q 92	4c
Pizza, Pizza Hut or Pizza Inn, cheese, thin crust	12-13 in	7.69	4Q 92	4c
Taxes				
Tax, cigarette	pack	15.50	91	77s
Tax, gasoline	gal	15	91	77s
Taxes, state	capita	1102	91	77s
Transportation				
ACCRA Index, Transportation		94.70	4Q 92	4c
Driver's license fee		6.00	12/90	43s
Tire balance, computer or spin balance, front	wheel	6.14	4Q 92	4c
Utilities				
ACCRA Index, Utilities		87.80	4Q 92	4c
Electricity	mil Btu	15.75	90	64s
Electricity, partial electric and other energy, 1,800 sq ft living area new home	month	66.91	4Q 92	4c
Electricity, winter, 250 KWh	month	22.37	92	55c
Electricity, winter, 500 KWh	month	38.07	92	55c
Electricity, winter, 750 KWh	month	53.77	92	55c
Electricity, winter, 1000 KWh	month	69.47	92	55c

Fairbanks, AK

Item	Per	Value	Date	Ref.
Composite ACCRA index		131.70	4Q 92	4c
Alcoholic Beverages				
Beer, Miller Lite or Budweiser, 12-oz containers	6 pack	5.14	4Q 92	4c
Liquor, J & B Scotch	750 ml	20.32	4Q 92	4c
Wine, Gallo Chablis blanc, 1.5 liter	bottle	5.87	4Q 92	4c
Clothing				
Jeans, man's denim		36.50	4Q 92	4c
Shirt, man's dress shirt		23.58	4Q 92	4c
Undervest, boy's size 10-14, cotton	3	4.94	4Q 92	4c
Communications				
Newspaper subscription, daily and Sunday home delivery, large-city	month	13.76	4Q 92	4c
Telephone bill, family of four	month	13.68	4Q 92	4c
Energy and Fuels				
Energy, combined forms, 1,800 sq ft heating area	month	163.09	4Q 92	4c
Energy, exc electricity, 1,800 sq ft heating area	month	96.00	4Q 92	4c
Gasoline, motor	gal	1.22	4Q 92	4c
Entertainment				
Bowling, evening rate	game	3.00	4Q 92	4c
Monopoly game, Parker Brothers', No. 9		15.49	4Q 92	4c
Movie	admission	6.75	4Q 92	4c
Tennis balls, yellow, Wilson or Penn, 3	can	3.71	4Q 92	4c
Goods and Services				
ACCRA Index, Miscellaneous Goods and Services		130.00	4Q 92	4c

Values are in dollars or fractions of dollars. In the column headed *Ref*, references are shown to sources. Each reference is followed by a letter. These refer to the geographical level for which data were reported: s=State, r=Region, and c=City or metro. The abbreviation *ex* is used to mean *except* or *excluding*; *exp* stands for expenditures. For other abbreviations and further explanations, please see the Introduction.

Fairbanks, AK - continued

Item	Per	Value	Date	Ref.
Groceries				
ACCRA Index, Groceries		126.20	4Q 92	4c
Babyfood, strained vegetables, lowest price	4-4.5 oz jar	0.39	4Q 92	4c
Bananas	lb	0.76	4Q 92	4c
Bread, white	24 oz	1.09	4Q 92	4c
Cheese, Kraft grated Parmesan	8-oz canister	2.99	4Q 92	4c
Chicken, fryer, whole	lb	1.27	4Q 92	4c
Cigarettes, Winston	carton	18.26	4Q 92	4c
Coffee, vacuum-packed	13-oz can	2.45	4Q 92	4c
Corn, frozen	10 oz	0.83	4Q 92	4c
Corn Flakes, Kellogg's or Post Toasties	18 oz	1.98	4Q 92	4c
Eggs, Grade A large	doz	1.58	4Q 92	4c
Ground beef or hamburger	lb	1.67	4Q 92	4c
Lettuce, iceberg	head	1.28	4Q 92	4c
Margarine, Blue Bonnet or Parkay cubes	lb	0.65	4Q 92	4c
Milk, whole	1/2 gal	1.81	4Q 92	4c
Orange juice, Minute Maid frozen	12-oz can	1.26	4Q 92	4c
Peaches	29-oz can	1.59	4Q 92	4c
Peas Sweet, Del Monte or Green Giant	15-17 oz can	0.70	4Q 92	4c
Potatoes, white or red	10-lb sack	3.26	4Q 92	4c
Sausage, Jimmy Dean, 100% pork	lb	3.34	4Q 92	4c
Shortening, vegetable, Crisco	3-lb can	2.38	4Q 92	4c
Soft drink, Coca Cola	2 liter	2.35	4Q 92	4c
Steak, T-bone	lb	5.45	4Q 92	4c
Sugar, cane or beet	4 lb	1.66	4Q 92	4c
Tomatoes, Hunt's or Del Monte	14.5-oz can	0.80	4Q 92	4c
Tuna, chunk, light	6.125-6.5 oz can	0.72	4Q 92	4c
Health Care				
ACCRA Index, Health Care		191.70	4Q 92	4c
Analgesic, Aspirin, Bayer, 325 mg tablets	100	5.64	4Q 92	4c
Dentist's fee, adult teeth cleaning and periodic oral exam	visit	120.17	4Q 92	4c
Doctor's fee, routine exam, established patient	visit	68.50	4Q 92	4c
Hospital care, semiprivate room	day	430.50	90	27c
Hospital care, semiprivate room	day	398.00	4Q 92	4c
Household Goods				
Appliance repair, home, service call, washing machine	min labor charge	48.15	4Q 92	4c
Laundry detergent, Tide Ultra, Bold, or Cheer	42 oz	4.53	4Q 92	4c
Tissues, facial, Kleenex brand	175-count box	1.33	4Q 92	4c
Housing				
ACCRA Index, Housing		129.70	4Q 92	4c
House, 1,800 sq ft, 8,000 sq ft lot, new, urban	total	138750	4Q 92	4c
House payment, principal and interest, 25% down payment	month	775	4Q 92	4c
Mortgage rate, incl. points & origination fee, 30-year fixed or adjustable rate	percent	8.16	4Q 92	4c
Rent, apartment, 2 bedrooms - 1-1/2 to 2 baths, unfurnished, 950 sq ft, water	month	692	4Q 92	4c
Personal Goods				
Shampoo, Alberto VO5	15 oz	1.64	4Q 92	4c
Toothpaste, Crest or Colgate	6-7 oz	2.19	4Q 92	4c

Fairbanks, AK - continued

Item	Per	Value	Date	Ref.
Personal Services				
Dry cleaning, man's 2-piece suit		9.30	4Q 92	4c
Haircare, woman's shampoo, trim and blow-dry		23.20	4Q 92	4c
Haircut, man's barbershop, no styling		12.89	4Q 92	4c
Restaurant Food				
Chicken, fried, thigh and drumstick		3.18	4Q 92	4c
Hamburger with cheese	1/4 lb	2.30	4Q 92	4c
Pizza, Pizza Hut or Pizza Inn, cheese, thin crust	12-13 in	9.99	4Q 92	4c
Transportation				
ACCRA Index, Transportation		111.40	4Q 92	4c
Bus fare	one-way	1.50	3/93	2c
Tire balance, computer or spin balance, front	wheel	7.49	4Q 92	4c
Utilities				
ACCRA Index, Utilities		141.50	4Q 92	4c
Electricity, partial electric and other energy, 1,800 sq ft living area new home	month	67.09	4Q 92	4c

Fairfield, CT

Item	Per	Value	Date	Ref.
Groceries				
Bacon	lb	1.75	12/91	72c
Bananas	lb	0.53	12/91	72c
Barbecue sauce, Hunt's	oz	0.07	12/91	72c
Bread, Wonder	22 oz	1.43	12/91	72c
Butter	8 oz	0.98	12/91	72c
Candy, M&Ms	lb	2.61	12/91	72c
Cat food, dry	lb	0.88	12/91	72c
Cereal, Cheerios	oz	0.19	12/91	72c
Cereal, Corn Flakes	oz	0.09	12/91	72c
Cheese, American	lb	2.84	12/91	72c
Cheese, Cheddar	lb	2.82	12/91	72c
Chicken, Perdue	lb	1.30	12/91	72c
Cigarettes, Marlboro	carton	19.68	12/91	72c
Coffee, Maxwell House	oz	0.15	12/91	72c
Cookies, Nabisco Oreos	oz	0.13	12/91	72c
Corn, frozen	oz	0.09	12/91	72c
Diapers, Pampers disposable	1	0.22	12/91	72c
Dog food, Purina Dog Chow	lb	0.42	12/91	72c
Eggs	1	0.09	12/91	72c
Frankfurters, Hebrew National	oz	0.19	12/91	72c
Ham, Krakus canned	lb	4.16	12/91	72c
Jelly, Welch's grape	oz	0.06	12/91	72c
Ketchup, Heinz	oz	0.06	12/91	72c
Lasagna, Stouffer's	oz	0.16	12/91	72c
Lettuce	head	0.99	12/91	72c
Margarine, Fleishmann's	lb	1.60	12/91	72c
Mayonnaise, Hellmann's	48 oz	3.53	12/91	72c
Milk	1/2 gal	1.26	12/91	72c
Muffins, Thomas English	48 oz	2.82	12/91	72c
Orange juice, frozen	oz	0.07	12/91	72c
Orange juice, Tropicana	oz	0.04	12/91	72c
Peanut butter, Skippy	oz	0.14	12/91	72c
Peas, Green Giant, canned	15 oz	0.68	12/91	72c
Pizza, Ellio's frozen	24 oz	3.20	12/91	72c
Potatoes	lb	0.33	12/91	72c
Sausage, bulk or link	oz	0.18	12/91	72c
Snacks, Doritos corn chips	oz	0.17	12/91	72c
Snacks, Lays potato chips	oz	0.19	12/91	72c
Soft drink, Diet Coca Cola	2 liter	1.16	12/91	72c
Soft drink, Pepsi	2 liter	1.12	12/91	72c
Spaghetti	lb	0.57	12/91	72c
Spaghetti sauce, Ragu	oz	0.06	12/91	72c
Steak, sirloin	lb	4.53	12/91	72c
Sugar	5 lb	2.00	12/91	72c
Tea, Lipton	bag	0.04	12/91	72c
Tomato soup, Campbell's	oz	0.04	12/91	72c

Values are in dollars or fractions of dollars. In the column headed *Ref*, references are shown to sources. Each reference is followed by a letter. These refer to the geographical level for which data were reported: s = State, r = Region, and c = City or metro. The abbreviation *ex* is used to mean *except* or *excluding*; *exp* stands for expenditures. For other abbreviations and further explanations, please see the Introduction.

Fairfield, CT - continued

Item	Per	Value	Date	Ref.
Groceries				
Tuna, Bumble Bee	6 1/8 oz	1.22	12/91	72c
Health Care				
Analgesic, Advil	tablet	0.11	12/91	72c
Household Goods				
Aluminum foil, Reynolds	100 ft	2.60	12/91	72c
Cat litter, Tidy Cat 3	lb	0.18	12/91	72c
Dishwashing detergent, Cascade	oz	0.05	12/91	72c
Laundry detergent, Tide liquid	gal	5.97	12/91	72c
Laundry detergent, Tide powder	oz	0.06	12/91	72c
Laundry supplies, Bounce fabric softener	sheet	0.06	12/91	72c
Paper towels	68.7 ft	0.62	12/91	72c
Toilet tissue, Charmin	roll	0.30	12/91	72c
Personal Goods				
Deodorant, Secret Solid	2.7 oz	3.52	12/91	72c
Feminine hygiene product, Stayfree	24	2.66	12/93	72c
Mouthwash, Listerine	oz	0.19	12/91	72c
Mouthwash, Scope	oz	0.20	12/91	72c
Razors, Gillette Trac II		0.62	12/91	72c
Shampoo, Pert Plus	oz	0.19	12/91	72c
Toothpaste, Crest	oz	0.33	12/93	72c

Fall River, MA

Item	Per	Value	Date	Ref.
Child Care				
Child care fee, average, center	hour	2.18	90	65r
Child care fee, average, nonregulated family day care	hour	1.83	90	65r
Child care fee, average, regulated family day care	hour	2.02	90	65r
Communications				
Long-distance telephone service, day, initial minute, 0-100 miles	min	0.18-0.31	91	12s
Long-distance telephone service, day, additional minute, 0-100 miles	min	0.08-0.13	91	12s
Long-distance telephone service, evenings/ weekends, 0-100 mi, initial minute	min	0.67-0.12	91	12s
Long-distance telephone service, evenings/ weekends, 0-100 mi, additional minute	min	0.04-0.05	91	12s
Education				
Board, 4-yr private college/university	year	2698	91	22s
Board, 4-yr public college/university	year	1741	91	22s
Expenditures, local gov't, public elementary/secondary	pupil	6687	92	20s
Room, 4-year private college/university	year	2945	91	22s
Room, 4-year public college/university	year	2144	91	22s
Tuition, 2-year private college/university	year	7750	91	22s
Tuition, 2-year public college/university	year	1528	91	22s
Tuition, 4-year private college/university	year	12446	91	22s
Tuition, 4-year public college/university, in-state	year	2580	91	22s
Energy and Fuels				
Coal	mil Btu	1.77	90	64s
Energy	mil Btu	10.57	90	64s
Energy exp/householder, 1-family unit	year	588	90	28r
Energy exp/householder, <1,000 sq ft heating area	year	477	90	28r
Energy exp/householder, 1,000-1,999 sq ft heating area	year	517	90	28r
Energy exp/householder, 2,000+ sq ft heating area	year	630	90	28r
Energy exp/householder, mobile home	year	412	90	28r
Energy exp/householder, multifamily	year	498	90	28r
Gas, natural	mil Btu	5.55	90	64s
Gas, natural	000 cu ft	8.11	91	46s
Gas, natural, exp	year	741	91	46s
Gasoline, unleaded regular	mil Btu	9.53	90	64s

Fall River, MA - continued

Item	Per	Value	Date	Ref.
Entertainment				
Miniature golf admission	adult	6.18	92	1r
Miniature golf admission	child	5.14	92	1r
Waterpark admission	adult	11.00	92	1r
Waterpark admission	child	8.55	92	1r
Funerals				
Casket, 18-gauge steel, velvet interior		1853.42	91	24r
Cosmetology, hair care, etc.		98.33	91	24r
Embalming		273.94	91	24r
Facility use for ceremony		196.06	91	24r
Hearse, local		145.67	91	24r
Limousine, local		131.07	91	24r
Remains to funeral home, transfer		135.24	91	24r
Service charge, professional		843.16	91	24r
Vault, concrete, non-metallic liner		709.14	91	24r
Viewing facilities, use		229.85	91	24r
Groceries				
Apples, Red Delicious	lb	0.85	4/93	16r
Bacon	lb	2.12	4/93	16r
Bananas	lb	0.54	4/93	16r
Bread, white, pan	lb	0.81	4/93	16r
Butter	lb	2.02	4/93	16r
Carrots, short trimmed and topped	lb	0.51	4/93	16r
Chicken, fresh, whole	lb	1.04	4/93	16r
Chicken breast, bone-in	lb	2.21	4/93	16r
Chicken legs, bone-in	lb	1.16	4/93	16r
Chuck roast, USDA choice, boneless	lb	2.82	4/93	16r
Coffee, 100% ground roast, all sizes	lb	2.66	4/93	16r
Cucumbers	lb	0.85	4/93	16r
Eggs, Grade A large	doz	1.15	4/93	16r
Grapefruit	lb	0.45	4/93	16r
Grapes, Thompson Seedless	lb	1.52	4/93	16r
Ground beef, lean and extra lean	lb	2.36	4/93	16r
Ground chuck, 100% beef	lb	2.02	4/93	16r
Honey, jar	8 oz	0.96-1.75	92	5r
Honey, jar	lb	1.50-3.00	92	5r
Honey, squeeze bear	12-oz	1.50-1.99	92	5r
Ice cream, prepackaged, bulk, regular	1/2 gal	2.80	4/93	16r
Lemons	lb	0.96	4/93	16r
Lettuce, iceberg	lb	0.95	4/93	16r
Margarine, stick	lb	0.81	4/93	16r
Milk, fresh, whole, fortified	1/2 gal	1.30	4/93	16r
Oranges, navel	lb	0.56	4/93	16r
Peanut butter, creamy, all sizes	lb	1.88	4/93	16r
Pork chops, center cut, bone-in	lb	3.34	4/93	16r
Potato chips	16 oz	2.88	4/93	16r
Potatoes, white	lb	0.37	4/93	16r
Rib roast, USDA choice, bone-in	lb	4.94	4/93	16r
Round roast, USDA choice, boneless	lb	3.17	4/93	16r
Shortening, vegetable oil blends	lb	0.98	4/93	16r
Spaghetti and macaroni	lb	0.82	4/93	16r
Steak, round, graded & ungraded, ex USDA prime & choice	lb	4.04	4/93	16r
Steak, round, USDA choice, boneless	lb	3.90	4/93	16r
Steak, sirloin, USDA choice, boneless	lb	4.97	4/93	16r
Strawberries, dry pint	12 oz	0.90	4/93	16r
Sugar, white	lb	0.50	4/93	16r
Sugar, white, 33-80 oz pk	lb	0.41	4/93	16r
Tomatoes, field grown	lb	1.23	4/93	16r
Tuna, chunk, light	lb	2.22	4/93	16r
Turkey, frozen, whole	lb	1.04	4/93	16r
Health Care				
Childbirth, cesarean, hospital		5826	91	62r
Childbirth, cesarean, physician's fee		2053	91	62r
Childbirth, normal, hospital		2964	91	62r
Childbirth, normal, physician's fee		1492	91	62r
Health care spending, state	capita	3031	3/93	84s
Medical plan per employee	year	3958	91	45r
Mental health care, exp	capita	53.68-118.35	90	38s
Mental health care, exp, state mental health agency	capita	83.91	90	38s

Values are in dollars or fractions of dollars. In the column headed *Ref*, references are shown to sources. Each reference is followed by a letter. These refer to the geographical level for which data were reported: s=State, r=Region, and c=City or metro. The abbreviation *ex* is used to mean *except* or *excluding*; *exp* stands for expenditures. For other abbreviations and further explanations, please see the Introduction.

Fall River, MA - continued

Item	Per	Value	Date	Ref.
Health Care				
Mental health care, hospital psychiatric services, non-Federal, exp	capita	22.67	88	38s
Mental health care, mental health organization, multiservice, exp	capita	36.07	88	38s
Mental health care, psychiatric hospitals, private, exp	capita	38.65	88	38s
Mental health care, psychiatric out-patient clinics, freestanding, exp	capita	4.41	88	38s
Mental health care, psychiatric partial-care organizations, freestanding, exp	capita	0.92	88	38s
Mental health care, state and county mental hospitals, exp	capita	30.59	88	38s
Mental health care, VA medical centers, exp	capita	21.14	88	38s
Substance abuse, hospital ancillary charge	incident	1310	90	70s
Substance abuse, hospital physician charge	incident	460	90	70s
Substance abuse, hospital room and board	incident	3450	90	70s
Insurance and Pensions				
Auto insurance, private passenger	year	912.83	91	63s
Taxes				
Tax, cigarette	pack	26	91	77s
Tax, gasoline	gal	21	91	77s
Taxes, state	capita	1615	91	77s
Transportation				
Driver's license fee		35.00	12/90	43s
Travel				
Business travel	day	165.00	4/93	89r
Utilities				
Electricity	mil Btu	25.93	90	64s

Fargo-Moorhead, ND, MN

Item	Per	Value	Date	Ref.
Composite ACCRA index		102.80	4Q 92	4c
Alcoholic Beverages				
Beer, Miller Lite or Budweiser, 12-oz containers	6 pack	3.95	4Q 92	4c
Liquor, J & B Scotch	750 ml	17.20	4Q 92	4c
Wine, Gallo Chablis blanc, 1.5 liter	bottle	5.49	4Q 92	4c
Child Care				
Child care fee, average, center	hour	1.63	90	65r
Child care fee, average, nonregulated family day care	hour	1.83	90	65r
Child care fee, average, regulated family day care	hour	1.42	90	65r
Clothing				
Jeans, man's denim		27.32	4Q 92	4c
Shirt, man's dress shirt		27.71	4Q 92	4c
Undervest, boy's size 10-14, cotton	3	4.29	4Q 92	4c
Communications				
Long-distance telephone service, day, initial minute, 0-100 miles	min	0.24-0.51	91	12s
Long-distance telephone service, day, additional minute, 0-100 miles	min	0.10-0.35	91	12s
Long-distance telephone service, evenings/weekends, 0-100 mi, initial minute	min	0.14-0.31	91	12s
Long-distance telephone service, evenings/weekends, 0-100 mi, additional minute	min	0.06-0.21	91	12s
Newspaper subscription, daily and Sunday home delivery, large-city	month	13.14	4Q 92	4c
Telephone, flat rate	month	13.00	91	11c
Telephone bill, family of four	month	19.49	4Q 92	4c
Education				
Board, 4-yr private college/university	year	1422	91	22s
Board, 4-yr public college/university	year	1618	91	22s

Fargo-Moorhead, ND, MN - continued

Item	Per	Value	Date	Ref.
Education - continued				
Expenditures, local gov't, public elementary/secondary	pupil	8755	92	20s
Room, 4-year private college/university	year	1049	91	22s
Room, 4-year public college/university	year	790	91	22s
Tuition, 2-year public college/university	year	1584	91	22s
Tuition, 4-year private college/university	year	5389	91	22s
Tuition, 4-year public college/university, in-state	year	1930	91	22s
Energy and Fuels				
Coal	mil Btu	1.18	90	64s
Energy	mil Btu	6.64	90	64s
Energy, combined forms, 1,800 sq ft heating area	month	96.24	4Q 92	4c
Energy exp/householder, 1-family unit	year	473	90	28r
Energy exp/householder, <1,000 sq ft heating area	year	429	90	28r
Energy exp/householder, 1,000-1,999 sq ft heating area	year	442	90	28r
Energy exp/householder, 2,000+ sq ft heating area	year	498	90	28r
Energy exp/householder, mobile home	year	442	90	28r
Energy exp/householder, multifamily	year	407	90	28r
Gas, cooking, winter, 10 therms	month	9.15	92	56c
Gas, cooking, winter, 30 therms	month	17.44	92	56c
Gas, cooking, winter, 50 therms	month	25.77	92	56c
Gas, heating, winter, 100 therms	month	43.02	92	56c
Gas, heating, winter, average use	month	83.13	92	56c
Gas, natural	mil Btu	4.12	90	64s
Gas, natural	000 cu ft	4.82	91	46s
Gas, natural, exp	year	568	91	46s
Gasoline, motor	gal	1.20	4Q 92	4c
Gasoline, unleaded regular	mil Btu	9.87	90	64s
Entertainment				
Bowling, evening rate	game	1.53	4Q 92	4c
Miniature golf admission	adult	6.18	92	1r
Miniature golf admission	child	5.14	92	1r
Monopoly game, Parker Brothers', No. 9		11.33	4Q 92	4c
Movie	admission	5.00	4Q 92	4c
Tennis balls, yellow, Wilson or Penn, 3	can	2.33	4Q 92	4c
Waterpark admission	adult	11.00	92	1r
Waterpark admission	child	8.55	92	1r
Funerals				
Casket, 18-gauge steel, velvet interior		1952.97	91	24r
Cosmetology, hair care, etc.		90.03	91	24r
Embalming		251.75	91	24r
Facility use for ceremony		180.75	91	24r
Hearse, local		117.51	91	24r
Limousine, local		71.86	91	24r
Remains to funeral home, transfer		81.14	91	24r
Service charge, professional		740.03	91	24r
Vault, concrete, non-metallic liner		801.47	91	24r
Viewing facilities, use		169.33	91	24r
Goods and Services				
ACCRA Index, Miscellaneous Goods and Services		98.10	4Q 92	4c
Goods and services	year	15170	92	36c
Groceries				
ACCRA Index, Groceries		103.50	4Q 92	4c
Apples, Red Delicious	lb	0.77	4/93	16r
Babyfood, strained vegetables, lowest price	4-4.5 oz jar	0.30	4Q 92	4c
Bacon	lb	1.85	4/93	16r
Bananas	lb	0.44	4Q 92	4c
Bananas	lb	0.46	4/93	16r
Beef, stew, boneless	lb	2.53	4/93	16r
Bologna, all beef or mixed	lb	2.19	4/93	16r
Bread, white	24 oz	0.96	4Q 92	4c

Values are in dollars or fractions of dollars. In the column headed *Ref*, references are shown to sources. Each reference is followed by a letter. These refer to the geographical level for which data were reported: s=State, r=Region, and c=City or metro. The abbreviation *ex* is used to mean *except* or *excluding*; *exp* stands for expenditures. For other abbreviations and further explanations, please see the Introduction.

Fargo-Moorhead, ND, MN - continued

Item	Per	Value	Date	Ref.
Groceries				
Bread, white, pan	lb	0.78	4/93	16r
Butter	lb	1.50	4/93	16r
Cabbage	lb	0.40	4/93	16r
Carrots, short trimmed and topped	lb	0.45	4/93	16r
Cheese, Cheddar	lb	3.47	4/93	16r
Cheese, Kraft grated Parmesan	8-oz canister	2.77	4Q 92	4c
Chicken, fresh, whole	lb	0.84	4/93	16r
Chicken, fryer, whole	lb	0.88	4Q 92	4c
Chicken breast, bone-in	lb	1.94	4/93	16r
Chicken legs, bone-in	lb	1.02	4/93	16r
Chuck roast, graded and ungraded, ex USDA prime and choice	lb	2.43	4/93	16r
Chuck roast, USDA choice, bone-in	lb	2.11	4/93	16r
Chuck roast, USDA choice, boneless	lb	2.44	4/93	16r
Cigarettes, Winston	carton	18.73	4Q 92	4c
Coffee, 100% ground roast, all sizes	lb	2.47	4/93	16r
Coffee, vacuum-packed	13-oz can	2.01	4Q 92	4c
Cookies, chocolate chip	lb	2.73	4/93	16r
Corn, frozen	10 oz	0.72	4Q 92	4c
Corn Flakes, Kellogg's or Post Toasties	18 oz	2.12	4Q 92	4c
Eggs, Grade A large	doz	0.78	4Q 92	4c
Eggs, Grade A large	doz	0.93	4/93	16r
Flour, white, all purpose	lb	0.21	4/93	16r
Grapefruit	lb	0.45	4/93	16r
Grapes, Thompson Seedless	lb	1.46	4/93	16r
Ground beef, 100% beef	lb	1.63	4/93	16r
Ground beef, lean and extra lean	lb	2.08	4/93	16r
Ground beef or hamburger	lb	1.34	4Q 92	4c
Ground chuck, 100% beef	lb	1.94	4/03	16r
Ham, boneless, excluding canned	lb	2.21	4/93	16r
Ice cream, prepackaged, bulk, regular	1/2 gal	2.41	4/93	16r
Lemons	lb	0.82	4/93	16r
Lettuce, iceberg	head	0.98	4Q 92	4c
Lettuce, iceberg	lb	0.83	4/93	16r
Margarine, Blue Bonnet or Parkay cubes	lb	0.47	4Q 92	4c
Margarine, stick	lb	0.77	4/93	16r
Milk, whole	1/2 gal	1.49	4Q 92	4c
Orange juice, Minute Maid frozen	12-oz can	1.44	4Q 92	4c
Oranges, navel	lb	0.50	4/93	16r
Peaches	29-oz can	1.40	4Q 92	4c
Peanut butter, creamy, all sizes	lb	1.82	4/93	16r
Pears, Anjou	lb	0.85	4/93	16r
Peas Sweet, Del Monte or Green Giant	15-17 oz can	0.65	4Q 92	4c
Pork chops, center cut, bone-in	lb	3.17	4/93	16r
Potato chips	16 oz	2.68	4/93	16r
Potatoes, white	lb	0.26	4/93	16r
Potatoes, white or red	10-lb sack	1.92	4Q 92	4c
Round roast, graded & ungraded, ex USDA prime & choice	lb	2.88	4/93	16r
Round roast, USDA choice, boneless	lb	2.96	4/93	16r
Sausage, Jimmy Dean, 100% pork	lb	2.80	4Q 92	4c
Shortening, vegetable oil blends	lb	0.79	4/93	16r
Shortening, vegetable, Crisco	3-lb can	2.30	4Q 92	4c
Soft drink, Coca Cola	2 liter	1.42	4Q 92	4c
Spaghetti and macaroni	lb	0.76	4/93	16r
Steak, rib eye, USDA choice, boneless	lb	6.29	4/93	16r
Steak, round, USDA choice, boneless	lb	3.24	4/93	16r
Steak, sirloin, graded & ungraded, ex USDA prime & choice	lb	4.00	4/93	16r
Steak, sirloin, USDA choice, bone-in	lb	3.57	4/93	16r
Steak, sirloin, USDA choice, boneless	lb	4.17	4/93	16r
Steak, T-bone	lb	4.72	4Q 92	4c
Steak, T-bone, USDA choice, bone-in	lb	5.60	4/93	16r
Strawberries, dry pint	12 oz	0.90	4/93	16r

Fargo-Moorhead, ND, MN - continued

Item	Per	Value	Date	Ref.
Groceries - continued				
Sugar, cane or beet	4 lb	1.50	4Q 92	4c
Sugar, white	lb	0.36	4/93	16r
Sugar, white, 33-80 oz pk	lb	0.35	4/93	16r
Tomatoes, field grown	lb	0.99	4/93	16r
Tomatoes, Hunt's or Del Monte	14.5-oz can	0.73	4Q 92	4c
Tuna, chunk, light	6.125-6.5 oz can	0.62	4Q 92	4c
Tuna, chunk, light	lb	1.76	4/93	16r
Turkey, frozen, whole	lb	0.91	4/93	16r
Health Care				
ACCRA Index, Health Care		98.40	4Q 92	4c
Analgesic, Aspirin, Bayer, 325 mg tablets	100	4.93	4Q 92	4c
Childbirth, cesarean, hospital		4688	91	62r
Childbirth, cesarean, physician's fee		2053	91	62r
Childbirth, normal, hospital		2657	91	62r
Childbirth, normal, physician's fee		1492	91	62r
Dentist's fee, adult teeth cleaning and periodic oral exam	visit	41.50	4Q 92	4c
Doctor's fee, routine exam, established patient	visit	41.03	4Q 92	4c
Hospital care, semiprivate room	day	235.43	90	27c
Hospital care, semiprivate room	day	294.67	4Q 92	4c
Medical insurance premium, per employee, small group comprehensive	month	306.60	10/91	25c
Medical plan per employee	year	3443	91	45r
Mental health care, exp	capita	28.84-37.59	90	38s
Mental health care, exp, state mental health agency	capita	40.24	90	38s
Mental health care, hospital psychiatric services, non-Federal, exp	capita	18.67	88	38s
Mental health care, mental health organization, multiservice, exp	capita	27.50	88	38s
Mental health care, state and county mental hospitals, exp	capita	32.62	88	38s
Physician fee, family practice, first-visit		76.00	91	62r
Physician fee, family practice, revisit		33.00	91	62r
Physician fee, general practice, first-visit		61.00	91	62r
Physician fee, general practice, revisit		31.00	91	62r
Physician fee, general surgeon, first-visit		65.00	91	62r
Physician fee, general surgeon, revisit		35.00	91	62r
Physician fee, internal medicine, first-visit		91.00	91	62r
Physician fee, internal medicine, revisit		40.00	91	62r
Physician fee, median, neurosurgeon, first-visit		106.00	91	62r
Physician fee, median, nonsurgical specialist, first-visit		90.00	91	62r
Physician fee, median, orthopedic surgeon, first-visit		83.00	91	62r
Physician fee, median, surgical specialist, first-visit		61.00	91	62r
Physician fee, neurosurgeon, revisit		41.00	91	62r
Physician fee, nonsurgical specialist, revisit		40.00	91	62r
Physician fee, obstetrics/gynecology, first-visit		61.00	91	62r
Physician fee, obstetrics/gynecology, revisit		40.00	91	62r
Physician fee, orthopedic surgeon, revisit		41.00	91	62r
Physician fee, pediatrician, first-visit		46.00	91	62r
Physician fee, pediatrician, revisit		33.00	91	62r
Physician fee, surgical specialist, revisit		36.00	91	62r
Household Goods				
Appliance repair, home, service call, washing machine	min labor charge	27.04	4Q 92	4c
Laundry detergent, Tide Ultra, Bold, or Cheer	42 oz	3.67	4Q 92	4c
Tissues, facial, Kleenex brand	175-count box	1.17	4Q 92	4c

Values are in dollars or fractions of dollars. In the column headed *Ref*, references are shown to sources. Each reference is followed by a letter. These refer to the geographical level for which data were reported: s=State, r=Region, and c=City or metro. The abbreviation *ex* is used to mean *except* or *excluding*; *exp* stands for expenditures. For other abbreviations and further explanations, please see the Introduction.

Fargo-Moorhead, ND, MN - continued

Item	Per	Value	Date	Ref.
Housing				
ACCRA Index, Housing		114.90	4Q 92	4c
Home, median price	unit	70.70		26c
House, 1,800 sq ft, 8,000 sq ft lot, new, urban	total	134200	4Q 92	4c
House payment, principal and interest, 25% down payment	month	748	4Q 92	4c
Mortgage rate, incl. points & origination fee, 30-year fixed or adjustable rate	per-cent	8.13	4Q 92	4c
Rent, apartment, 2 bedrooms - 1-1/2 to 2 baths, unfurnished, 950 sq ft, water	month	471	4Q 92	4c
Rental unit, 1 bedroom	month	407	93	23c
Rental unit, 2 bedroom	month	478	93	23c
Rental unit, 3 bedroom	month	600	93	23c
Rental unit, 4 bedroom	month	672	93	23c
Rental unit, efficiency	month	335	93	23c
Insurance and Pensions				
Auto insurance, private passenger	year	413.64	91	63s
Personal Goods				
Shampoo, Alberto VO5	15 oz	1.37	4Q 92	4c
Toothpaste, Crest or Colgate	6-7 oz	1.86	4Q 92	4c
Personal Services				
Dry cleaning, man's 2-piece suit		6.16	4Q 92	4c
Haircare, woman's shampoo, trim and blow-dry		16.25	4Q 92	4c
Haircut, man's barbershop, no styling		8.90	4Q 92	4c
Restaurant Food				
Chicken, fried, thigh and drumstick		1.99	4Q 92	4c
Hamburger with cheese	1/4 lb	1.89	4Q 92	4c
Pizza, Pizza Hut or Pizza Inn, cheese, thin crust	12-13 in	7.49	4Q 92	4c
Taxes				
Tax, cigarette	pack	29	91	77s
Tax, gasoline	gal	17	91	77s
Taxes, state	capita	1189	91	77s
Transportation				
ACCRA Index, Transportation		99.30	4Q 92	4c
Driver's license fee		10.00	12/90	43s
Tire balance, computer or spin balance, front	wheel	6.02	4Q 92	4c
Vehicle registration and license plate	year	26.00-251.00	92	51s
Utilities				
ACCRA Index, Utilities		89.30	4Q 92	4c
Electricity	mil Btu	16.86	90	64s
Electricity, all electric, 1,800 sq ft living area new home	month	96.24	4Q 92	4c
Electricity, winter, 250 KWh	month	16.47	92	55c
Electricity, winter, 500 KWh	month	28.94	92	55c
Electricity, winter, 750 KWh	month	41.40	92	55c
Electricity, winter, 1000 KWh	month	53.87	92	55c

Farmington, NM

Item	Per	Value	Date	Ref.
Composite ACCRA index		95.20	4Q 92	4c
Alcoholic Beverages				
Beer, Miller Lite or Budweiser, 12-oz containers	6 pack	3.57	4Q 92	4c
Liquor, J & B Scotch	750 ml	16.57	4Q 92	4c
Wine, Gallo Chablis blanc, 1.5 liter	bottle	4.97	4Q 92	4c
Clothing				
Jeans, man's denim		26.79	4Q 92	4c
Shirt, man's dress shirt		25.50	4Q 92	4c
Undervest, boy's size 10-14, cotton	3	4.24	4Q 92	4c
Communications				
Newspaper subscription, daily and Sunday home delivery, large-city	month	9.50	4Q 92	4c

Farmington, NM - continued

Item	Per	Value	Date	Ref.
Communications - continued				
Telephone bill, family of four	month	19.94	4Q 92	4c
Energy and Fuels				
Energy, combined forms, 1,800 sq ft heating area	month	95.58	4Q 92	4c
Energy, exc electricity, 1,800 sq ft heating area	month	35.67	4Q 92	4c
Gasoline, motor	gal	1.24	4Q 92	4c
Entertainment				
Bowling, evening rate	game	1.50	4Q 92	4c
Monopoly game, Parker Brothers', No. 9		10.95	4Q 92	4c
Movie	admis-sion	5.00	4Q 92	4c
Tennis balls, yellow, Wilson or Penn, 3	can	2.26	4Q 92	4c
Goods and Services				
ACCRA Index, Miscellaneous Goods and Services		97.60	4Q 92	4c
Groceries				
ACCRA Index, Groceries		94.40	4Q 92	4c
Babyfood, strained vegetables, lowest price	4-4.5 oz jar	0.28	4Q 92	4c
Bananas	lb	0.40	4Q 92	4c
Bread, white	24 oz	0.56	4Q 92	4c
Cheese, Kraft grated Parmesan	8-oz canis-ter	3.43	4Q 92	4c
Chicken, fryer, whole	lb	0.55	4Q 92	4c
Cigarettes, Winston	carton	15.50	4Q 92	4c
Coffee, vacuum-packed	13-oz can	2.21	4Q 92	4c
Corn, frozen	10 oz	0.70	4Q 92	4c
Corn Flakes, Kellogg's or Post Toasties	18 oz	1.95	4Q 92	4c
Eggs, Grade A large	doz	0.84	4Q 92	4c
Ground beef or hamburger	lb	1.43	4Q 92	4c
Lettuce, iceberg	head	0.90	4Q 92	4c
Margarine, Blue Bonnet or Parkay cubes	lb	0.61	4Q 92	4c
Milk, whole	1/2 gal	1.35	4Q 92	4c
Orange juice, Minute Maid frozen	12-oz can	1.48	4Q 92	4c
Peaches	29-oz can	1.56	4Q 92	4c
Peas Sweet, Del Monte or Green Giant	15-17 oz can	0.55	4Q 92	4c
Potatoes, white or red	10-lb sack	2.34	4Q 92	4c
Sausage, Jimmy Dean, 100% pork	lb	2.62	4Q 92	4c
Shortening, vegetable, Crisco	3-lb can	2.13	4Q 92	4c
Soft drink, Coca Cola	2 liter	1.29	4Q 92	4c
Steak, T-bone	lb	4.55	4Q 92	4c
Sugar, cane or beet	4 lb	1.32	4Q 92	4c
Tomatoes, Hunt's or Del Monte	14.5-oz can	0.69	4Q 92	4c
Tuna, chunk, light	6.125-6.5 oz can	0.69	4Q 92	4c
Health Care				
ACCRA Index, Health Care		93.20	4Q 92	4c
Analgesic, Aspirin, Bayer, 325 mg tablets	100	4.95	4Q 92	4c
Dentist's fee, adult teeth cleaning and periodic oral exam	visit	48.75	4Q 92	4c
Doctor's fee, routine exam, established patient	visit	31.52	4Q 92	4c
Hospital care, semiprivate room	day	265.00	4Q 92	4c
Household Goods				
Appliance repair, home, service call, washing machine	min labor charge	31.91	4Q 92	4c
Laundry detergent, Tide Ultra, Bold, or Cheer	42 oz	3.13	4Q 92	4c

Values are in dollars or fractions of dollars. In the column headed *Ref*, references are shown to sources. Each reference is followed by a letter. These refer to the geographical level for which data were reported: s=State, r=Region, and c=City or metro. The abbreviation *ex* is used to mean *except* or *excluding*; *exp* stands for *expenditures*. For other abbreviations and further explanations, please see the Introduction.

Farmington, NM - continued

Item	Per	Value	Date	Ref.
Household Goods				
Tissues, facial, Kleenex brand	175-count box	1.10	4Q 92	4c
Housing				
ACCRA Index, Housing		92.80	4Q 92	4c
House, 1,800 sq ft, 8,000 sq ft lot, new, urban	total	104250	4Q 92	4c
House payment, principal and interest, 25% down payment	month	580	4Q 92	4c
Mortgage rate, incl. points & origination fee, 30-year fixed or adjustable rate	percent	8.12	4Q 92	4c
Rent, apartment, 2 bedrooms - 1-1/2 to 2 baths, unfurnished, 950 sq ft, water	month	435	4Q 92	4c
Personal Goods				
Shampoo, Alberto VO5	15 oz	1.45	4Q 92	4c
Toothpaste, Crest or Colgate	6-7 oz	2.03	4Q 92	4c
Personal Services				
Dry cleaning, man's 2-piece suit		5.65	4Q 92	4c
Haircare, woman's shampoo, trim and blow-dry		16.00	4Q 92	4c
Haircut, man's barbershop, no styling		6.88	4Q 92	4c
Restaurant Food				
Chicken, fried, thigh and drumstick		2.27	4Q 92	4c
Hamburger with cheese	1/4 lb	2.09	4Q 92	4c
Pizza, Pizza Hut or Pizza Inn, cheese, thin crust	12-13 in	8.56	4Q 92	4c
Transportation				
ACCRA Index, Transportation		100.70	4Q 92	4c
Tire balance, computer or spin balance, front	wheel	6.00	4Q 92	4c
Utilities				
ACCRA Index, Utilities		89.00	4Q 92	4c
Electricity, partial electric and other energy, 1,800 sq ft living area new home	month	59.91	4Q 92	4c

Fayetteville, AR

Item	Per	Value	Date	Ref.
Composite ACCRA index		90.60	4Q 92	4c
Alcoholic Beverages				
Beer, Miller Lite or Budweiser, 12-oz containers	6 pack	4.12	4Q 92	4c
Liquor, J & B Scotch	750 ml	17.79	4Q 92	4c
Wine, Gallo Chablis blanc, 1.5 liter	bottle	5.82	4Q 92	4c
Child Care				
Child care fee, average, center	hour	1.29	90	65r
Child care fee, average, nonregulated family day care	hour	0.89	90	65r
Child care fee, average, regulated family day care	hour	1.32	90	65r
Clothing				
Jeans, man's denim		27.99	4Q 92	4c
Shirt, man's dress shirt		25.50	4Q 92	4c
Undervest, boy's size 10-14, cotton	3	4.14	4Q 92	4c
Communications				
Long-distance telephone service, day, initial minute, 0-100 miles	min	0.10-0.42	91	12s
Long-distance telephone service, day, additional minute, 0-100 miles	min	0.08-0.34	91	12s
Long-distance telephone service, evenings/weekends, 0-100 mi, initial minute	min	0.06-0.23	91	12s
Long-distance telephone service, evenings/weekends, 0-100 mi, additional minute	min	0.04-0.19	91	12s
Newspaper subscription, daily and Sunday home delivery, large-city	month	6.50	4Q 92	4c
Telephone, flat rate	month	13.91	91	11c
Telephone bill, family of four	month	22.74	4Q 92	4c

Fayetteville, AR - continued

Item	Per	Value	Date	Ref.
Education				
Board, 4-yr private college/university	year	1651	91	22s
Board, 4-yr public college/university	year	1253	91	22s
Expenditures, local gov't, public elementary/secondary	pupil	3770	92	20s
Room, 4-year private college/university	year	1111	91	22s
Room, 4-year public college/university	year	1173	91	22s
Tuition, 2-year private college/university	year	2482	91	22s
Tuition, 2-year public college/university	year	648	91	22s
Tuition, 4-year private college/university	year	4464	91	22s
Tuition, 4-year public college/university, in-state	year	1418	91	22s
Energy and Fuels				
Coal	mil Btu	1.62	90	64s
Energy	mil Btu	8.81	90	64s
Energy, combined forms, 1,800 sq ft heating area	month	91.61	4Q 92	4c
Energy, exc electricity, 1,800 sq ft heating area	month	37.55	4Q 92	4c
Energy exp/householder, 1-family unit	year	471	90	28r
Energy exp/householder, <1,000 sq ft heating area	year	384	90	28r
Energy exp/householder, 1,000-1,999 sq ft heating area	year	421	90	28r
Energy exp/householder, 2,000+ sq ft heating area	year	625	90	28r
Energy exp/householder, mobile home	year	271	90	28r
Energy exp/householder, multifamily	year	355	90	28r
Gas, cooking, 10 therms	month	10.72	92	56c
Gas, cooking, 30 therms	month	20.17	92	56c
Gas, cooking, 50 therms	month	27.98	92	56c
Gas, heating, winter, 100 therms	month	47.52	92	56c
Gas, heating, winter, average use	month	51.04	92	56c
Gas, natural	mil Btu	3.27	90	64s
Gas, natural	000 cu ft	4.98	91	46s
Gas, natural, exp	year	408	91	46s
Gasoline, motor	gal	1.19	4Q 92	4c
Gasoline, unleaded regular	mil Btu	8.86	90	64s
Entertainment				
Bowling, evening rate	game	1.85	4Q 92	4c
Miniature golf admission	adult	6.18	92	1r
Miniature golf admission	child	5.14	92	1r
Monopoly game, Parker Brothers', No. 9		9.99	4Q 92	4c
Movie	admission	5.50	4Q 92	4c
Tennis balls, yellow, Wilson or Penn, 3	can	1.93	4Q 92	4c
Waterpark admission	adult	11.00	92	1r
Waterpark admission	child	8.55	92	1r
Funerals				
Casket, 18-gauge steel, velvet interior		2274.41	91	24r
Cosmetology, hair care, etc.		74.62	91	24r
Embalming		229.94	91	24r
Facility use for ceremony		176.61	91	24r
Hearse, local		116.34	91	24r
Limousine, local		72.68	91	24r
Remains to funeral home, transfer		87.72	91	24r
Service charge, professional		712.53	91	24r
Vault, concrete, non-metallic liner		750.55	91	24r
Viewing facilities, use		155.31	91	24r
Goods and Services				
ACCRA Index, Miscellaneous Goods and Services		98.40	4Q 92	4c
Groceries				
ACCRA Index, Groceries		93.50	4Q 92	4c
Apples, Red Delicious	lb	0.79	4/93	16r
Babyfood, strained vegetables, lowest price	4-4.5 oz jar	0.30	4Q 92	4c
Bacon	lb	1.75	4/93	16r
Bananas	lb	0.43	4Q 92	4c

Values are in dollars or fractions of dollars. In the column headed *Ref*, references are shown to sources. Each reference is followed by a letter. These refer to the geographical level for which data were reported: s=State, r=Region, and c=City or metro. The abbreviation *ex* is used to mean *except* or *excluding*; *exp* stands for expenditures. For other abbreviations and further explanations, please see the Introduction.

Fayetteville, AR - continued

Item	Per	Value	Date	Ref.
Groceries				
Bananas	lb	0.42	4/93	16r
Beef, stew, boneless	lb	2.61	4/93	16r
Bologna, all beef or mixed	lb	2.24	4/93	16r
Bread, white	24 oz	0.59	4Q 92	4c
Bread, white, pan	lb	0.64	4/93	16r
Bread, whole wheat, pan	lb	0.96	4/93	16r
Cabbage	lb	0.37	4/93	16r
Carrots, short trimmed and topped	lb	0.47	4/93	16r
Celery	lb	0.64	4/93	16r
Cheese, American	lb	2.98	4/93	16r
Cheese, Cheddar	lb	3.28	4/93	16r
Cheese, Kraft grated Parmesan	8-oz canister	3.38	4Q 92	4c
Chicken, fresh, whole	lb	0.77	4/93	16r
Chicken, fryer, whole	lb	0.70	4Q 92	4c
Chicken breast, bone-in	lb	1.92	4/93	16r
Chicken legs, bone-in	lb	1.06	4/93	16r
Chuck roast, graded and ungraded, ex USDA prime and choice	lb	2.40	4/93	16r
Chuck roast, USDA choice, bone-in	lb	2.19	4/93	16r
Chuck roast, USDA choice, boneless	lb	2.38	4/93	16r
Cigarettes, Winston	carton	17.49	4Q 92	4c
Coffee, 100% ground roast, all sizes	lb	2.48	4/93	16r
Coffee, vacuum-packed	13-oz can	1.97	4Q 92	4c
Corn, frozen	10 oz	0.65	4Q 92	4c
Corn Flakes, Kellogg's or Post Toasties	18 oz	1.95	4Q 92	4c
Crackers, soda, salted	lb	1.15	4/93	16r
Eggs, Grade A large	doz	0.65	4Q 92	4c
Eggs, Grade A large	doz	0.96	4/93	16r
Flour, white, all purpose	lb	0.24	4/93	16r
Frankfurters, all meat or all beef	lb	2.01	4/93	16r
Grapefruit	lb	0.44	4/93	16r
Grapes, Thompson Seedless	lb	1.40	4/93	16r
Ground beef, 100% beef	lb	1.58	4/93	16r
Ground beef, lean and extra lean	lb	2.09	4/93	16r
Ground beef or hamburger	lb	1.15	4Q 92	4c
Ground chuck, 100% beef	lb	1.98	4/93	16r
Ham, boneless, excluding canned	lb	2.89	4/93	16r
Ham, picnic, shoulder, bone-in, smoked	lb	1.02	4/93	16r
Ham, rump or steak half, bone-in, smoked	lb	1.48	4/93	16r
Honey, jar	8 oz	0.73-1.19	92	5r
Honey, jar	lb	1.10-1.79	92	5r
Honey, squeeze bear	12-oz	1.19-1.50	92	5r
Ice cream, prepackaged, bulk, regular	1/2 gal	2.41	4/93	16r
Lemons	lb	1.05	4/93	16r
Lettuce, iceberg	head	0.85	4Q 92	4c
Lettuce, iceberg	lb	0.81	4/93	16r
Margarine, Blue Bonnet or Parkay cubes	lb	0.50	4Q 92	4c
Margarine, stick	lb	0.88	4/93	16r
Milk, whole	1/2 gal	1.34	4Q 92	4c
Orange juice, Minute Maid frozen	12-oz can	1.62	4Q 92	4c
Oranges, navel	lb	0.55	4/93	16r
Peaches	29-oz can	1.23	4Q 92	4c
Pears, Anjou	lb	0.92	4/93	16r
Peas Sweet, Del Monte or Green Giant	15-17 oz can	0.44	4Q 92	4c
Pork chops, center cut, bone-in	lb	3.13	4/93	16r
Potato chips	16 oz	2.94	4/93	16r
Potatoes, white	lb	0.43	4/93	16r
Potatoes, white or red	10-lb sack	1.97	4Q 92	4c
Rib roast, USDA choice, bone-in	lb	4.63	4/93	16r
Rice, white, long grain, uncooked	lb	0.45	4/93	16r
Round roast, graded & ungraded, ex USDA prime & choice	lb	3.03	4/93	16r
Round roast, USDA choice, boneless	lb	3.09	4/93	16r
Sausage, fresh, loose	lb	2.08	4/93	16r
Sausage, Jimmy Dean, 100% pork	lb	2.60	4Q 92	4c

Fayetteville, AR - continued

Item	Per	Value	Date	Ref.
Groceries - continued				
Short ribs, bone-in	lb	2.66	4/93	16r
Shortening, vegetable oil blends	lb	0.69	4/93	16r
Shortening, vegetable, Crisco	3-lb can	2.01	4Q 92	4c
Soft drink, Coca Cola	2 liter	1.00	4Q 92	4c
Spaghetti and macaroni	lb	0.81	4/93	16r
Steak, rib eye, USDA choice, boneless	lb	6.24	4/93	16r
Steak, round, graded & ungraded, ex USDA prime & choice	lb	3.31	4/93	16r
Steak, round, USDA choice, boneless	lb	3.34	4/93	16r
Steak, sirloin, graded & ungraded, ex USDA prime & choice	lb	4.19	4/93	16r
Steak, sirloin, USDA choice, boneless	lb	4.46	4/93	16r
Steak, T-bone	lb	5.17	4Q 92	4c
Steak, T-bone, USDA choice, bone-in	lb	5.25	4/93	16r
Strawberries, dry pint	12 oz	0.92	4/93	16r
Sugar, cane or beet	4 lb	1.09	4Q 92	4c
Sugar, white	lb	0.39	4/93	16r
Sugar, white, 33-80 oz pk	lb	0.38	4/93	16r
Tomatoes, field grown	lb	0.88	4/93	16r
Tomatoes, Hunt's or Del Monte	14.5-oz can	0.69	4Q 92	4c
Tuna, chunk, light	6.125-6.5 oz can	0.58	4Q 92	4c
Tuna, chunk, light	lb	1.79	4/93	16r
Turkey, frozen, whole	lb	1.04	4/93	16r
Yogurt, natural, fruit flavored	1/2 pint	0.57	4/93	16r
Health Care				
ACCRA Index, Health Care		84.20	4Q 92	4c
Analgesic, Aspirin, Bayer, 325 mg tablets	100	5.62	4Q 92	4c
Childbirth, cesarean, hospital		5034	91	62r
Childbirth, cesarean, physician's fee		2053	91	62r
Childbirth, normal, hospital		2712	91	62r
Childbirth, normal, physician's fee		1492	91	62r
Dentist's fee, adult teeth cleaning and periodic oral exam	visit	35.40	4Q 92	4c
Doctor's fee, routine exam, established patient	visit	36.00	4Q 92	4c
Health care spending, state	capita	1944	3/93	84s
Hospital care, semiprivate room	day	148.58	90	27c
Hospital care, semiprivate room	day	185.00	4Q 92	4c
Medical insurance premium, per employee, small group comprehensive	month	288.35	10/91	25c
Mental health care, exp	capita	20.37-28.83	90	38s
Mental health care, exp, state mental health agency	capita	25.92	90	38s
Mental health care, hospital psychiatric services, non-Federal, exp	capita	5.26	88	38s
Mental health care, mental health organization, multiservice, exp	capita	15.69	88	38s
Mental health care, psychiatric hospitals, private, exp	capita	15.15	88	38s
Mental health care, psychiatric out-patient clinics, freestanding, exp	capita	0.46	88	38s
Mental health care, state and county mental hospitals, exp	capita	6.78	88	38s
Mental health care, VA medical centers, exp	capita	7.18	88	38s
Physician fee, family practice, first-visit		75.00	91	62r
Physician fee, family practice, revisit		34.00	91	62r
Physician fee, general practice, first-visit		61.00	91	62r
Physician fee, general practice, revisit		32.00	91	62r
Physician fee, general surgeon, first-visit		64.00	91	62r
Physician fee, general surgeon, revisit		40.00	91	62r
Physician fee, internal medicine, first-visit		98.00	91	62r
Physician fee, internal medicine, revisit		40.00	91	62r
Physician fee, median, neurosurgeon, first-visit		130.00	91	62r
Physician fee, median, nonsurgical specialist, first-visit		95.00	91	62r

Values are in dollars or fractions of dollars. In the column headed *Ref*, references are shown to sources. Each reference is followed by a letter. These refer to the geographical level for which data were reported: s=State, r=Region, and c=City or metro. The abbreviation *ex* is used to mean *except* or *excluding*; *exp* stands for expenditures. For other abbreviations and further explanations, please see the Introduction.

Fayetteville, AR - continued

Item	Per	Value	Date	Ref.
Health Care				
Physician fee, median, orthopedic surgeon, first-visit		91.00	91	62r
Physician fee, median, plastic surgeon, first-visit		66.00	91	62r
Physician fee, median, surgical specialist, first-visit		62.00	91	62r
Physician fee, neurosurgeon, revisit		50.00	91	62r
Physician fee, nonsurgical specialist, revisit		40.00	91	62r
Physician fee, obstetrics/gynecology, first-visit		64.00	91	62r
Physician fee, obstetrics/gynecology, revisit		41.00	91	62r
Physician fee, orthopedic surgeon, revisit		40.00	91	62r
Physician fee, pediatrician, first-visit		49.00	91	62r
Physician fee, pediatrician, revisit		33.00	91	62r
Physician fee, plastic surgeon, revisit		43.00	91	62r
Physician fee, surgical specialist, revisit		37.00	91	62r
Substance abuse, hospital ancillary charge	incident	1680	90	70s
Substance abuse, hospital physician charge	incident	450	90	70s
Substance abuse, hospital room and board	incident	4490	90	70s
Household Goods				
Appliance repair, home, service call, washing machine	min labor charge	30.90	4Q 92	4c
Laundry detergent, Tide Ultra, Bold, or Cheer	42 oz	3.87	4Q 92	4c
Tissues, facial, Kleenex brand	175-count box	1.16	4Q 92	4c
Housing				
ACCRA Index, Housing		80.60	4Q 92	4c
House, 1,800 sq ft, 8,000 sq ft lot, new, urban	total	88550	4Q 92	4c
House payment, principal and interest, 25% down payment	month	503	4Q 92	4c
Mortgage rate, incl. points & origination fee, 30-year fixed or adjustable rate	percent	8.33	4Q 92	4c
Rent, apartment, 2 bedrooms - 1-1/2 to 2 baths, unfurnished, 950 sq ft, water	month	380	4Q 92	4c
Rental unit, 1 bedroom	month	344	93	23c
Rental unit, 2 bedroom	month	406	93	23c
Rental unit, 3 bedroom	month	506	93	23c
Rental unit, 4 bedroom	month	568	93	23c
Rental unit, efficiency	month	284	93	23c
Insurance and Pensions				
Auto insurance, private passenger	year	501.00	91	63s
Personal Goods				
Shampoo, Alberto VO5	15 oz	1.40	4Q 92	4c
Toothpaste, Crest or Colgate	6-7 oz	2.03	4Q 92	4c
Personal Services				
Dry cleaning, man's 2-piece suit		5.90	4Q 92	4c
Haircare, woman's shampoo, trim and blow-dry		20.50	4Q 92	4c
Haircut, man's barbershop, no styling		8.00	4Q 92	4c
Restaurant Food				
Chicken, fried, thigh and drumstick		2.48	4Q 92	4c
Hamburger with cheese	1/4 lb	1.87	4Q 92	4c
Pizza, Pizza Hut or Pizza Inn, cheese, thin crust	12-13 in	7.74	4Q 92	4c
Taxes				
Tax, cigarette	pack	22	91	77s
Tax, gasoline	gal	18.50	91	77s
Taxes, state	capita	997	91	77s
Transportation				
ACCRA Index, Transportation		94.00	4Q 92	4c
Driver's license fee		14.25	12/90	43s

Fayetteville, AR - continued

Item	Per	Value	Date	Ref.
Transportation - continued				
Tire balance, computer or spin balance, front	wheel	5.40	4Q 92	4c
Vehicle registration and license plate	year	17.00-30.00	93	10s
Travel				
Business travel	day	193.00	4/93	89r
Utilities				
ACCRA Index, Utilities		87.20	4Q 92	4c
Electricity	mil Btu	19.78	90	64s
Electricity, partial electric and other energy, 1,800 sq ft living area new home	month	54.06	4Q 92	4c
Electricity, winter, 250 KWh	month	21.60	92	55c
Electricity, winter, 500 KWh	month	36.11	92	55c
Electricity, winter, 750 KWh	month	50.62	92	55c
Electricity, winter, 1000 KWh	month	65.13	92	55c

Fayetteville, NC

Item	Per	Value	Date	Ref.
Composite ACCRA index		98.20	4Q 92	4c
Alcoholic Beverages				
Beer, Miller Lite or Budweiser, 12-oz containers	6 pack	3.70	4Q 92	4c
Liquor, J & B Scotch	750 ml	17.65	4Q 92	4c
Wine, Gallo Chablis blanc, 1.5 liter	bottle	4.52	4Q 92	4c
Child Care				
Child care fee, average, center	hour	1.29	90	65r
Child care fee, average, nonregulated family day care	hour	0.89	90	65r
Child care fee, average, regulated family day care	hour	1.32	90	65r
Clothing				
Jeans, man's denim		31.99	4Q 92	4c
Shirt, man's dress shirt		30.33	4Q 92	4c
Undervest, boy's size 10-14, cotton	3	4.74	4Q 92	4c
Communications				
Long-distance telephone service, day, initial minute, 0-100 miles	min	0.10-0.33	91	12s
Long-distance telephone service, day, additional minute, 0-100 miles	min	0.10-0.33	91	12s
Long-distance telephone service, evenings/weekends, 0-100 mi, initial minute	min	0.08-0.24	91	12s
Long-distance telephone service, evenings/weekends, 0-100 mi, additional minute	min	0.05-0.17	91	12s
Newspaper subscription, daily and Sunday home delivery, large-city	month	9.25	4Q 92	4c
Telephone bill, family of four	month	18.16	4Q 92	4c
Education				
Board, 4-yr private college/university	year	1768	91	22s
Board, 4-yr public college/university	year	1568	91	22s
Expenditures, local gov't, public elementary/secondary	pupil	5078	92	20s
Room, 4-year private college/university	year	1467	91	22s
Room, 4-year public college/university	year	1386	91	22s
Tuition, 2-year private college/university	year	4964	91	22s
Tuition, 2-year public college/university	year	334	91	22s
Tuition, 4-year private college/university	year	7826	91	22s
Tuition, 4-year public college/university, in-state	year	1112	91	22s
Energy and Fuels				
Coal	mil Btu	1.79	90	64s
Energy	mil Btu	10.06	90	64s
Energy, combined forms, 1,800 sq ft heating area	month	126.88	4Q 92	4c
Energy exp/householder, 1-family unit	year	487	90	28r
Energy exp/householder, <1,000 sq ft heating area	year	393	90	28r

Values are in dollars or fractions of dollars. In the column headed *Ref*, references are shown to sources. Each reference is followed by a letter. These refer to the geographical level for which data were reported: s=State, r=Region, and c=City or metro. The abbreviation *ex* is used to mean *except* or *excluding*; *exp* stands for expenditures. For other abbreviations and further explanations, please see the Introduction.

Fayetteville, NC - continued

Item	Per	Value	Date	Ref.
Energy and Fuels				
Energy exp/householder, 1,000-1,999 sq ft heating area	year	442	90	28r
Energy exp/householder, 2,000+ sq ft heating area	year	577	90	28r
Energy exp/householder, mobile home	year	366	90	28r
Energy exp/householder, multifamily	year	382	90	28r
Gas, cooking, winter, 10 therms	month	11.04	92	56c
Gas, cooking, winter, 30 therms	month	18.93	92	56c
Gas, cooking, winter, 50 therms	month	26.82	92	56c
Gas, heating, winter, 100 therms	month	50.45	92	56c
Gas, heating, winter, average use	month	53.88	92	56c
Gas, natural	mil Btu	4.19	90	64s
Gas, natural	000 cu ft	6.24	91	46s
Gas, natural, exp	year	439	91	46s
Gasoline, motor	gal	1.10	4Q 92	4c
Gasoline, unleaded regular	mil Btu	9.44	90	64s
Entertainment				
Bowling, evening rate	game	2.44	4Q 92	4c
Miniature golf admission	adult	6.18	92	1r
Miniature golf admission	child	5.14	92	1r
Monopoly game, Parker Brothers', No. 9		9.64	4Q 92	4c
Movie	admission	5.62	4Q 92	4c
Tennis balls, yellow, Wilson or Penn, 3	can	2.20	4Q 92	4c
Waterpark admission	adult	11.00	92	1r
Waterpark admission	child	8.55	92	1r
Funerals				
Casket, 18-gauge steel, velvet interior		2029.08	91	24r
Cosmetology, hair care, etc.		75.10	91	24r
Embalming		249.24	91	24r
Facility use for ceremony		162.27	91	24r
Hearse, local		114.04	91	24r
Limousine, local		88.57	91	24r
Remains to funeral home, transfer		92.61	91	24r
Service charge, professional		682.42	91	24r
Vault, concrete, non-metallic liner		798.70	91	24r
Viewing facilities, use		163.86	91	24r
Goods and Services				
ACCRA Index, Miscellaneous Goods and Services		102.90	4Q 92	4c
Goods and services	year	14813	92	36c
Goods and services, misc.	year	14813	92	37c
Groceries				
ACCRA Index, Groceries		95.30	4Q 92	4c
Apples, Red Delicious	lb	0.79	4/93	16r
Babyfood, strained vegetables, lowest price	4-4.5 oz jar	0.32	4Q 92	4c
Bacon	lb	1.75	4/93	16r
Bananas	lb	0.46	4Q 92	4c
Bananas	lb	0.42	4/93	16r
Beef, stew, boneless	lb	2.61	4/93	16r
Bologna, all beef or mixed	lb	2.24	4/93	16r
Bread, white	24 oz	0.68	4Q 92	4c
Bread, white, pan	lb	0.64	4/93	16r
Bread, whole wheat, pan	lb	0.96	4/93	16r
Cabbage	lb	0.37	4/93	16r
Carrots, short trimmed and topped	lb	0.47	4/93	16r
Celery	lb	0.64	4/93	16r
Cheese, American	lb	2.98	4/93	16r
Cheese, Cheddar	lb	3.28	4/93	16r
Cheese, Kraft grated Parmesan	8-oz canister	3.16	4Q 92	4c
Chicken, fresh, whole	lb	0.77	4/93	16r
Chicken, fryer, whole	lb	0.77	4Q 92	4c
Chicken breast, bone-in	lb	1.92	4/93	16r
Chicken legs, bone-in	lb	1.06	4/93	16r
Chuck roast, graded and ungraded, ex USDA prime and choice	lb	2.40	4/93	16r

Fayetteville, NC - continued

Item	Per	Value	Date	Ref.
Groceries - continued				
Chuck roast, USDA choice, bone-in	lb	2.19	4/93	16r
Chuck roast, USDA choice, boneless	lb	2.38	4/93	16r
Cigarettes, Winston	carton	15.25	4Q 92	4c
Coffee, 100% ground roast, all sizes	lb	2.48	4/93	16r
Coffee, vacuum-packed	13-oz can	1.67	4Q 92	4c
Corn, frozen	10 oz	0.50	4Q 92	4c
Corn Flakes, Kellogg's or Post Toasties	18 oz	1.55	4Q 92	4c
Crackers, soda, salted	lb	1.15	4/93	16r
Eggs, Grade A large	doz	0.83	4Q 92	4c
Eggs, Grade A large	doz	0.96	4/93	16r
Flour, white, all purpose	lb	0.24	4/93	16r
Frankfurters, all meat or all beef	lb	2.01	4/93	16r
Grapefruit	lb	0.44	4/93	16r
Grapes, Thompson Seedless	lb	1.40	4/93	16r
Ground beef, 100% beef	lb	1.58	4/93	16r
Ground beef, lean and extra lean	lb	2.09	4/93	16r
Ground beef or hamburger	lb	1.79	4Q 92	4c
Ground chuck, 100% beef	lb	1.98	4/93	16r
Ham, boneless, excluding canned	lb	2.89	4/93	16r
Ham, picnic, shoulder, bone-in, smoked	lb	1.02	4/93	16r
Ham, rump or steak half, bone-in, smoked	lb	1.48	4/93	16r
Ice cream, prepackaged, bulk, regular	1/2 gal	2.41	4/93	16r
Lemons	lb	1.05	4/93	16r
Lettuce, iceberg	head	0.81	4Q 92	4c
Lettuce, iceberg	lb	0.81	4/93	16r
Margarine, Blue Bonnet or Parkay cubes	lb	0.45	4Q 92	4c
Margarine, stick	lb	0.88	4/93	16r
Milk, whole	1/2 gal	1.37	4Q 92	4c
Orange juice, Minute Maid frozen	12-oz can	1.19	4Q 92	4c
Oranges, navel	lb	0.55	4/93	16r
Peaches	29-oz can	1.29	4Q 92	4c
Pears, Anjou	lb	0.92	4/93	16r
Peas Sweet, Del Monte or Green Giant	15-17 oz can	0.46	4Q 92	4c
Pork chops, center cut, bone-in	lb	3.13	4/93	16r
Potato chips	16 oz	2.94	4/93	16r
Potatoes, white	lb	0.43	4/93	16r
Potatoes, white or red	10-lb sack	1.93	4Q 92	4c
Rib roast, USDA choice, bone-in	lb	4.63	4/93	16r
Rice, white, long grain, uncooked	lb	0.45	4/93	16r
Round roast, graded & ungraded, ex USDA prime & choice	lb	3.03	4/93	16r
Round roast, USDA choice, boneless	lb	3.09	4/93	16r
Sausage, fresh, loose	lb	2.08	4/93	16r
Sausage, Jimmy Dean, 100% pork	lb	2.14	4Q 92	4c
Short ribs, bone-in	lb	2.66	4/93	16r
Shortening, vegetable oil blends	lb	0.69	4/93	16r
Shortening, vegetable, Crisco	3-lb can	1.97	4Q 92	4c
Soft drink, Coca Cola	2 liter	1.32	4Q 92	4c
Spaghetti and macaroni	lb	0.81	4/93	16r
Steak, rib eye, USDA choice, boneless	lb	6.24	4/93	16r
Steak, round, graded & ungraded, ex USDA prime & choice	lb	3.31	4/93	16r
Steak, round, USDA choice, boneless	lb	3.34	4/93	16r
Steak, sirloin, graded & ungraded, ex USDA prime & choice	lb	4.19	4/93	16r
Steak, sirloin, USDA choice, boneless	lb	4.46	4/93	16r
Steak, T-bone	lb	5.67	4Q 92	4c
Steak, T-bone, USDA choice, bone-in	lb	5.25	4/93	16r
Strawberries, dry pint	12 oz	0.92	4/93	16r
Sugar, cane or beet	4 lb	1.42	4Q 92	4c
Sugar, white	lb	0.39	4/93	16r
Sugar, white, 33-80 oz pk	lb	0.38	4/93	16r
Tomatoes, field grown	lb	0.88	4/93	16r
Tomatoes, Hunt's or Del Monte	14.5-oz can	0.70	4Q 92	4c

Values are in dollars or fractions of dollars. In the column headed *Ref*, references are shown to sources. Each reference is followed by a letter. These refer to the geographical level for which data were reported: s=State, r=Region, and c=City or metro. The abbreviation *ex* is used to mean *except* or *excluding*; *exp* stands for expenditures. For other abbreviations and further explanations, please see the Introduction.

Fayetteville, NC - continued

Item	Per	Value	Date	Ref.
Groceries				
Tuna, chunk, light	6.125-6.5 oz can	0.51	4Q 92	4c
Tuna, chunk, light	lb	1.79	4/93	16r
Turkey, frozen, whole	lb	1.04	4/93	16r
Yogurt, natural, fruit flavored	1/2 pint	0.57	4/93	16r
Health Care				
ACCRA Index, Health Care		102.30	4Q 92	4c
Analgesic, Aspirin, Bayer, 325 mg tablets	100	5.52	4Q 92	4c
Childbirth, cesarean, hospital		5034	91	62r
Childbirth, cesarean, physician's fee		2053	91	62r
Childbirth, normal, hospital		2712	91	62r
Childbirth, normal, physician's fee		1492	91	62r
Dentist's fee, adult teeth cleaning and periodic oral exam	visit	45.00	4Q 92	4c
Doctor's fee, routine exam, established patient	visit	37.67	4Q 92	4c
Hospital care, semiprivate room	day	249.60	90	27c
Hospital care, semiprivate room	day	350.00	4Q 92	4c
Medical plan per employee	year	3495	91	45r
Mental health care, exp	capita	37.60-53.67	90	38s
Mental health care, exp, state mental health agency	capita	45.66	90	38s
Mental health care, hospital psychiatric services, non-Federal, exp	capita	12.05	88	38s
Mental health care, mental health organization, multiservice, exp	capita	29.54	88	38s
Mental health care, psychiatric hospitals, private, exp	capita	15.07	88	38s
Mental health care, psychiatric out-patient clinics, freestanding, exp	capita	0.11	88	38s
Mental health care, state and county mental hospitals, exp	capita	26.36	88	38s
Mental health care, VA medical centers, exp	capita	2.23	88	38s
Physician fee, family practice, first-visit		75.00	91	62r
Physician fee, family practice, revisit		34.00	91	62r
Physician fee, general practice, first-visit		61.00	91	62r
Physician fee, general practice, revisit		32.00	91	62r
Physician fee, general surgeon, first-visit		64.00	91	62r
Physician fee, general surgeon, revisit		40.00	91	62r
Physician fee, internal medicine, first-visit		98.00	91	62r
Physician fee, internal medicine, revisit		40.00	91	62r
Physician fee, median, neurosurgeon, first-visit		130.00	91	62r
Physician fee, median, nonsurgical specialist, first-visit		95.00	91	62r
Physician fee, median, orthopedic surgeon, first-visit		91.00	91	62r
Physician fee, median, plastic surgeon, first-visit		66.00	91	62r
Physician fee, median, surgical specialist, first-visit		62.00	91	62r
Physician fee, neurosurgeon, revisit		50.00	91	62r
Physician fee, nonsurgical specialist, revisit		40.00	91	62r
Physician fee, obstetrics/gynecology, first-visit		64.00	91	62r
Physician fee, obstetrics/gynecology, revisit		41.00	91	62r
Physician fee, orthopedic surgeon, revisit		40.00	91	62r
Physician fee, pediatrician, first-visit		49.00	91	62r
Physician fee, pediatrician, revisit		33.00	91	62r
Physician fee, plastic surgeon, revisit		43.00	91	62r
Physician fee, surgical specialist, revisit		37.00	91	62r
Substance abuse, hospital ancillary charge	incident	1090	90	70s
Substance abuse, hospital physician charge	incident	460	90	70s
Substance abuse, hospital room and board	incident	4880	90	70s

Fayetteville, NC - continued

Item	Per	Value	Date	Ref.
Household Goods				
Appliance repair, home, service call, washing machine	min labor charge	29.98	4Q 92	4c
Laundry detergent, Tide Ultra, Bold, or Cheer	42 oz	3.45	4Q 92	4c
Tissues, facial, Kleenex brand	175-count box	1.02	4Q 92	4c
Housing				
ACCRA Index, Housing		88.20	4Q 92	4c
House, 1,800 sq ft, 8,000 sq ft lot, new, urban	total	97200	4Q 92	4c
House payment, principal and interest, 25% down payment	month	543	4Q 92	4c
Mortgage rate, incl. points & origination fee, 30-year fixed or adjustable rate	per-cent	8.16	4Q 92	4c
Rent, apartment, 2 bedrooms - 1-1/2 to 2 baths, unfurnished, 950 sq ft, water	month	434	4Q 92	4c
Rental unit, 1 bedroom	month	414	93	23c
Rental unit, 2 bedroom	month	432	93	23c
Rental unit, 3 bedroom	month	559	93	23c
Rental unit, 4 bedroom	month	684	93	23c
Rental unit, efficiency	month	294	93	23c
Insurance and Pensions				
Auto insurance, private passenger	year	522.39	91	63s
Personal Goods				
Shampoo, Alberto VO5	15 oz	1.11	4Q 92	4c
Toothpaste, Crest or Colgate	6-7 oz	1.92	4Q 92	4c
Personal Services				
Dry cleaning, man's 2-piece suit		6.35	4Q 92	4c
Haircare, woman's shampoo, trim and blow-dry		19.00	4Q 92	4c
Haircut, man's barbershop, no styling		6.25	4Q 92	4c
Restaurant Food				
Chicken, fried, thigh and drumstick		2.00	4Q 92	4c
Hamburger with cheese	1/4 lb	1.90	4Q 92	4c
Pizza, Pizza Hut or Pizza Inn, cheese, thin crust	12-13 in	7.64	4Q 92	4c
Taxes				
Tax, cigarette	pack	5	91	77s
Tax, gasoline	gal	21.90	91	77s
Taxes, sales	year	950	92	37c
Taxes, state	capita	1165	91	77s
Transportation				
ACCRA Index, Transportation		97.50	4Q 92	4c
Driver's license fee		15.00	12/90	43s
Tire balance, computer or spin balance, front	wheel	6.38	4Q 92	4c
Vehicle registration and license plate	year	35.00	93	50s
Travel				
Business travel	day	193.00	4/93	89r
Utilities				
ACCRA Index, Utilities		113.90	4Q 92	4c
Electricity	mil Btu	18.74	90	64s
Electricity, all electric, 1,800 sq ft living area new home	month	126.88	4Q 92	4c

Findlay, OH

Item	Per	Value	Date	Ref.
Composite ACCRA index		102.50	4Q 92	4c
Alcoholic Beverages				
Beer, Miller Lite or Budweiser, 12-oz containers	6 pack	3.92	4Q 92	4c
Liquor, J & B Scotch	750 ml	18.20	4Q 92	4c
Wine, Gallo Chablis blanc, 1.5 liter	bottle	5.66	4Q 92	4c

Values are in dollars or fractions of dollars. In the column headed *Ref*, references are shown to sources. Each reference is followed by a letter. These refer to the geographical level for which data were reported: s=State, r=Region, and c=City or metro. The abbreviation *ex* is used to mean *except* or *excluding*; *exp* stands for *expenditures*. For other abbreviations and further explanations, please see the Introduction.

Findlay, OH - continued

Item	Per	Value	Date	Ref.
Clothing				
Jeans, man's denim		36.49	4Q 92	4c
Shirt, man's dress shirt		29.15	4Q 92	4c
Undervest, boy's size 10-14, cotton	3	4.04	4Q 92	4c
Communications				
Newspaper subscription, daily and Sunday home delivery, large-city	month	8.91	4Q 92	4c
Telephone bill, family of four	month	21.62	4Q 92	4c
Energy and Fuels				
Energy, combined forms, 1,800 sq ft heating area	month	114.70	4Q 92	4c
Energy, exc electricity, 1,800 sq ft heating area	month	58.14	4Q 92	4c
Gasoline, motor	gal	1.14	4Q 92	4c
Entertainment				
Bowling, evening rate	game	2.22	4Q 92	4c
Monopoly game, Parker Brothers', No. 9		11.23	4Q 92	4c
Movie	admission	5.50	4Q 92	4c
Tennis balls, yellow, Wilson or Penn, 3	can	2.38	4Q 92	4c
Goods and Services				
ACCRA Index, Miscellaneous Goods and Services		104.30	4Q 92	4c
Groceries				
ACCRA Index, Groceries		106.40	4Q 92	4c
Babyfood, strained vegetables, lowest price	4-4.5 oz jar	0.44	4Q 92	4c
Bananas	lb	0.41	4Q 92	4c
Bread, white	24 oz	0.74	4Q 92	4c
Cheese, Kraft grated Parmesan	8-oz canister	3.34	4Q 92	4c
Chicken, fryer, whole	lb	0.87	4Q 92	4c
Cigarettes, Winston	carton	16.60	4Q 92	4c
Coffee, vacuum-packed	13-oz can	2.24	4Q 92	4c
Corn, frozen	10 oz	0.81	4Q 92	4c
Corn Flakes, Kellogg's or Post Toasties	18 oz	2.09	4Q 92	4c
Eggs, Grade A large	doz	0.79	4Q 92	4c
Ground beef or hamburger	lb	1.51	4Q 92	4c
Lettuce, iceberg	head	0.99	4Q 92	4c
Margarine, Blue Bonnet or Parkay cubes	lb	0.64	4Q 92	4c
Milk, whole	1/2 gal	1.40	4Q 92	4c
Orange juice, Minute Maid frozen	12-oz can	1.58	4Q 92	4c
Peaches	29-oz can	1.53	4Q 92	4c
Peas Sweet, Del Monte or Green Giant	15-17 oz can	0.75	4Q 92	4c
Potatoes, white or red	10-lb sack	1.66	4Q 92	4c
Sausage, Jimmy Dean, 100% pork	lb	2.66	4Q 92	4c
Shortening, vegetable, Crisco	3-lb can	2.61	4Q 92	4c
Soft drink, Coca Cola	2 liter	1.22	4Q 92	4c
Steak, T-bone	lb	5.76	4Q 92	4c
Sugar, cane or beet	4 lb	1.61	4Q 92	4c
Tomatoes, Hunt's or Del Monte	14.5-oz can	0.77	4Q 92	4c
Tuna, chunk, light	6.125-6.5 oz can	0.72	4Q 92	4c
Health Care				
ACCRA Index, Health Care		93.50	4Q 92	4c
Analgesic, Aspirin, Bayer, 325 mg tablets	100	4.53	4Q 92	4c
Dentist's fee, adult teeth cleaning and periodic oral exam	visit	46.25	4Q 92	4c
Doctor's fee, routine exam, established patient	visit	34.25	4Q 92	4c
Hospital care, semiprivate room	day	275.00	4Q 92	4c

Findlay, OH - continued

Item	Per	Value	Date	Ref.
Household Goods				
Appliance repair, home, service call, washing machine	min labor charge	37.21	4Q 92	4c
Laundry detergent, Tide Ultra, Bold, or Cheer	42 oz	4.81	4Q 92	4c
Tissues, facial, Kleenex brand	175-count box	1.05	4Q 92	4c
Housing				
ACCRA Index, Housing		99.60	4Q 92	4c
House, 1,800 sq ft, 8,000 sq ft lot, new, urban	total	108750	4Q 92	4c
House payment, principal and interest, 25% down payment	month	620	4Q 92	4c
Mortgage rate, incl. points & origination fee, 30-year fixed or adjustable rate	percent	8.38	4Q 92	4c
Rent, apartment, 2 bedrooms - 1-1/2 to 2 baths, unfurnished, 950 sq ft, water	month	474	4Q 92	4c
Personal Goods				
Shampoo, Alberto VO5	15 oz	1.04	4Q 92	4c
Toothpaste, Crest or Colgate	6-7 oz	1.84	4Q 92	4c
Personal Services				
Dry cleaning, man's 2-piece suit		6.75	4Q 92	4c
Haircare, woman's shampoo, trim and blow-dry		16.25	4Q 92	4c
Haircut, man's barbershop, no styling		7.38	4Q 92	4c
Restaurant Food				
Chicken, fried, thigh and drumstick		1.94	4Q 92	4c
Hamburger with cheese	1/4 lb	1.80	4Q 92	4c
Pizza, Pizza Hut or Pizza Inn, cheese, thin crust	12-13 in	7.25	4Q 92	4c
Transportation				
ACCRA Index, Transportation		101.30	4Q 92	4c
Tire balance, computer or spin balance, front	wheel	6.62	4Q 92	4c
Utilities				
ACCRA Index, Utilities		105.70	4Q 92	4c
Electricity, partial electric and other energy, 1,800 sq ft living area new home	month	56.56	4Q 92	4c

Fitchburg-Leominster, MA

Item	Per	Value	Date	Ref.
Child Care				
Child care fee, average, center	hour	2.18	90	65r
Child care fee, average, nonregulated family day care	hour	1.83	90	65r
Child care fee, average, regulated family day care	hour	2.02	90	65r
Communications				
Long-distance telephone service, day, initial minute, 0-100 miles	min	0.18-0.31	91	12s
Long-distance telephone service, day, additional minute, 0-100 miles	min	0.08-0.13	91	12s
Long-distance telephone service, evenings/weekends, 0-100 mi, initial minute	min	0.67-0.12	91	12s
Long-distance telephone service, evenings/weekends, 0-100 mi, additional minute	min	0.04-0.05	91	12s
Education				
Board, 4-yr private college/university	year	2698	91	22s
Board, 4-yr public college/university	year	1741	91	22s
Expenditures, local gov't, public elementary/secondary	pupil	6687	92	20s
Room, 4-year private college/university	year	2945	91	22s
Room, 4-year public college/university	year	2144	91	22s
Tuition, 2-year private college/university	year	7750	91	22s
Tuition, 2-year public college/university	year	1528	91	22s
Tuition, 4-year private college/university	year	12446	91	22s

Values are in dollars or fractions of dollars. In the column headed *Ref*, references are shown to sources. Each reference is followed by a letter. These refer to the geographical level for which data were reported: s=State, r=Region, and c=City or metro. The abbreviation *ex* is used to mean *except* or *excluding*; *exp* stands for expenditures. For other abbreviations and further explanations, please see the Introduction.

Fitchburg-Leominster, MA - continued

Item	Per	Value	Date	Ref.
Education				
Tuition, 4-year public college/university, in-state	year	2580	91	22s
Energy and Fuels				
Coal	mil Btu	1.77	90	64s
Energy	mil Btu	10.57	90	64s
Energy exp/householder, 1-family unit	year	588	90	28r
Energy exp/householder, <1,000 sq ft heating area	year	477	90	28r
Energy exp/householder, 1,000-1,999 sq ft heating area	year	517	90	28r
Energy exp/householder, 2,000+ sq ft heating area	year	630	90	28r
Energy exp/householder, mobile home	year	412	90	28r
Energy exp/householder, multifamily	year	498	90	28r
Gas, natural	mil Btu	5.55	90	64s
Gas, natural	000 cu ft	8.11	91	46s
Gas, natural, exp	year	741	91	46s
Gasoline, unleaded regular	mil Btu	9.53	90	64s
Entertainment				
Miniature golf admission	adult	6.18	92	1r
Miniature golf admission	child	5.14	92	1r
Waterpark admission	adult	11.00	92	1r
Waterpark admission	child	8.55	92	1r
Funerals				
Casket, 18-gauge steel, velvet interior		1853.42	91	24r
Cosmetology, hair care, etc.		98.33	91	24r
Embalming		273.94	91	24r
Facility use for ceremony		196.06	91	24r
Hearse, local		145.67	91	24r
Limousine, local		131.07	91	24r
Remains to funeral home, transfer		135.24	91	24r
Service charge, professional		843.16	91	24r
Vault, concrete, non-metallic liner		709.14	91	24r
Viewing facilities, use		229.85	91	24r
Groceries				
Apples, Red Delicious	lb	0.85	4/93	16r
Bacon	lb	2.12	4/93	16r
Bananas	lb	0.54	4/93	16r
Bread, white, pan	lb	0.81	4/93	16r
Butter	lb	2.02	4/93	16r
Carrots, short trimmed and topped	lb	0.51	4/93	16r
Chicken, fresh, whole	lb	1.04	4/93	16r
Chicken breast, bone-in	lb	2.21	4/93	16r
Chicken legs, bone-in	lb	1.16	4/93	16r
Chuck roast, USDA choice, boneless	lb	2.82	4/93	16r
Coffee, 100% ground roast, all sizes	lb	2.66	4/93	16r
Cucumbers	lb	0.85	4/93	16r
Eggs, Grade A large	doz	1.15	4/93	16r
Grapefruit	lb	0.45	4/93	16r
Grapes, Thompson Seedless	lb	1.52	4/93	16r
Ground beef, lean and extra lean	lb	2.36	4/93	16r
Ground chuck, 100% beef	lb	2.02	4/93	16r
Honey, jar	8 oz	0.96-1.75	92	5r
Honey, jar	lb	1.50-3.00	92	5r
Honey, squeeze bear	12-oz	1.50-1.99	92	5r
Ice cream, prepackaged, bulk, regular	1/2 gal	2.80	4/93	16r
Lemons	lb	0.96	4/93	16r
Lettuce, iceberg	lb	0.95	4/93	16r
Margarine, stick	lb	0.81	4/93	16r
Milk, fresh, whole, fortified	1/2 gal	1.30	4/93	16r
Oranges, navel	lb	0.56	4/93	16r
Peanut butter, creamy, all sizes	lb	1.88	4/93	16r
Pork chops, center cut, bone-in	lb	3.34	4/93	16r
Potato chips	16 oz	2.88	4/93	16r
Potatoes, white	lb	0.37	4/93	16r
Rib roast, USDA choice, bone-in	lb	4.94	4/93	16r
Round roast, USDA choice, boneless	lb	3.17	4/93	16r
Shortening, vegetable oil blends	lb	0.98	4/93	16r
Spaghetti and macaroni	lb	0.82	4/93	16r

Fitchburg-Leominster, MA - continued

Item	Per	Value	Date	Ref.
Groceries - continued				
Steak, round, graded & ungraded, ex USDA prime & choice	lb	4.04	4/93	16r
Steak, round, USDA choice, boneless	lb	3.90	4/93	16r
Steak, sirloin, USDA choice, boneless	lb	4.97	4/93	16r
Strawberries, dry pint	12 oz	0.90	4/93	16r
Sugar, white	lb	0.50	4/93	16r
Sugar, white, 33-80 oz pk	lb	0.41	4/93	16r
Tomatoes, field grown	lb	1.23	4/93	16r
Tuna, chunk, light	lb	2.22	4/93	16r
Turkey, frozen, whole	lb	1.04	4/93	16r
Health Care				
Childbirth, cesarean, hospital		5826	91	62r
Childbirth, cesarean, physician's fee		2053	91	62r
Childbirth, normal, hospital		2964	91	62r
Childbirth, normal, physician's fee		1492	91	62r
Health care spending, state	capita	3031	3/93	84s
Medical plan per employee	year	3958	91	45r
Mental health care, exp	capita	53.68-118.35	90	38s
Mental health care, exp, state mental health agency	capita	83.91	90	38s
Mental health care, hospital psychiatric services, non-Federal, exp	capita	22.67	88	38s
Mental health care, mental health organization, multiservice, exp	capita	36.07	88	38s
Mental health care, psychiatric hospitals, private, exp	capita	38.65	88	38s
Mental health care, psychiatric out-patient clinics, freestanding, exp	capita	4.41	88	38s
Mental health care, psychiatric partial-care organizations, freestanding, exp	capita	0.92	88	38s
Mental health care, state and county mental hospitals, exp	capita	30.59	88	38s
Mental health care, VA medical centers, exp	capita	21.14	88	38s
Substance abuse, hospital ancillary charge	incident	1310	90	70s
Substance abuse, hospital physician charge	incident	460	90	70s
Substance abuse, hospital room and board	incident	3450	90	70s
Insurance and Pensions				
Auto insurance, private passenger	year	912.83	91	63s
Taxes				
Tax, cigarette	pack	26	91	77s
Tax, gasoline	gal	21	91	77s
Taxes, state	capita	1615	91	77s
Transportation				
Driver's license fee		35.00	12/90	43s
Travel				
Business travel	day	165.00	4/93	89r
Utilities				
Electricity	mil Btu	25.93	90	64s

Flagstaff, AZ

Item	Per	Value	Date	Ref.
Composite ACCRA index		102.20	4Q 92	4c
Alcoholic Beverages				
Beer, Miller Lite or Budweiser, 12-oz containers	6 pack	3.67	4Q 92	4c
Liquor, J & B Scotch	750 ml	15.42	4Q 92	4c
Wine, Gallo Chablis blanc, 1.5 liter	bottle	4.17	4Q 92	4c
Clothing				
Jeans, man's denim		24.74	4Q 92	4c
Shirt, man's dress shirt		22.86	4Q 92	4c
Undervest, boy's size 10-14, cotton	3	4.52	4Q 92	4c

Values are in dollars or fractions of dollars. In the column headed *Ref*, references are shown to sources. Each reference is followed by a letter. These refer to the geographical level for which data were reported: s=State, r=Region, and c=City or metro. The abbreviation *ex* is used to mean *except* or *excluding*; *exp* stands for expenditures. For other abbreviations and further explanations, please see the Introduction.

Flagstaff, AZ - continued

Item	Per	Value	Date	Ref.
Communications				
Newspaper subscription, daily and Sunday home delivery, large-city	month	8.00	4Q 92	4c
Telephone, flat rate	month	12.40	91	11c
Telephone bill, family of four	month	18.14	4Q 92	4c
Energy and Fuels				
Energy, combined forms, 1,800 sq ft heating area	month	99.30	4Q 92	4c
Energy, exc electricity, 1,800 sq ft heating area	month	41.51	4Q 92	4c
Gas, cooking, 10 therms	month	8.53	92	56c
Gas, cooking, 30 therms	month	16.60	92	56c
Gas, cooking, 50 therms	month	24.66	92	56c
Gas, heating, winter, 100 therms	month	44.81	92	56c
Gasoline, motor	gal	1.26	4Q 92	4c
Entertainment				
Bowling, evening rate	game	1.85	4Q 92	4c
Monopoly game, Parker Brothers', No. 9		12.18	4Q 92	4c
Movie	admission	5.00	4Q 92	4c
Tennis balls, yellow, Wilson or Penn, 3	can	2.29	4Q 92	4c
Goods and Services				
ACCRA Index, Miscellaneous Goods and Services		99.40	4Q 92	4c
Groceries				
ACCRA Index, Groceries		94.40	4Q 92	4c
Babyfood, strained vegetables, lowest price	4-4.5 oz jar	0.33	4Q 92	4c
Bananas	lb	0.25	4Q 92	4c
Bread, white	24 oz	0.49	4Q 92	4c
Cheese, Kraft grated Parmesan	8-oz canister	3.18	4Q 92	4c
Chicken, fryer, whole	lb	0.55	4Q 92	4c
Cigarettes, Winston	carton	17.07	4Q 92	4c
Coffee, vacuum-packed	13-oz can	1.78	4Q 92	4c
Corn, frozen	10 oz	0.63	4Q 92	4c
Corn Flakes, Kellogg's or Post Toasties	18 oz	2.25	4Q 92	4c
Eggs, Grade A large	doz	0.82	4Q 92	4c
Ground beef or hamburger	lb	1.36	4Q 92	4c
Lettuce, iceberg	head	0.92	4Q 92	4c
Margarine, Blue Bonnet or Parkay cubes	lb	0.77	4Q 92	4c
Milk, whole	1/2 gal	1.47	4Q 92	4c
Orange juice, Minute Maid frozen	12-oz can	1.26	4Q 92	4c
Peaches	29-oz can	1.44	4Q 92	4c
Peas Sweet, Del Monte or Green Giant	15-17 oz can	0.65	4Q 92	4c
Potatoes, white or red	10-lb sack	2.02	4Q 92	4c
Sausage, Jimmy Dean, 100% pork	lb	3.03	4Q 92	4c
Shortening, vegetable, Crisco	3-lb can	2.27	4Q 92	4c
Soft drink, Coca Cola	2 liter	1.32	4Q 92	4c
Steak, T-bone	lb	4.59	4Q 92	4c
Sugar, cane or beet	4 lb	1.41	4Q 92	4c
Tomatoes, Hunt's or Del Monte	14.5-oz can	0.71	4Q 92	4c
Tuna, chunk, light	6.125-6.5 oz can	0.49	4Q 92	4c
Health Care				
ACCRA Index, Health Care		107.90	4Q 92	4c
Analgesic, Aspirin, Bayer, 325 mg tablets	100	5.70	4Q 92	4c
Dentist's fee, adult teeth cleaning and periodic oral exam	visit	54.80	4Q 92	4c
Doctor's fee, routine exam, established patient	visit	38.33	4Q 92	4c

Flagstaff, AZ - continued

Item	Per	Value	Date	Ref.
Health Care - continued				
Hospital care, semiprivate room	day	192.08	90	27c
Hospital care, semiprivate room	day	300.00	4Q 92	4c
Household Goods				
Appliance repair, home, service call, washing machine	min labor charge	35.00	4Q 92	4c
Laundry detergent, Tide Ultra, Bold, or Cheer	42 oz	3.14	4Q 92	4c
Tissues, facial, Kleenex brand	175-count box	1.30	4Q 92	4c
Housing				
ACCRA Index, Housing		107.90	4Q 92	4c
House, 1,800 sq ft, 8,000 sq ft lot, new, urban	total	116400	4Q 92	4c
House payment, principal and interest, 25% down payment	month	642	4Q 92	4c
Mortgage rate, incl. points & origination fee, 30-year fixed or adjustable rate	percent	8.02	4Q 92	4c
Rent, apartment, 2 bedrooms - 1-1/2 to 2 baths, unfurnished, 950 sq ft, water	month	583	4Q 92	4c
Personal Goods				
Shampoo, Alberto VO5	15 oz	1.25	4Q 92	4c
Toothpaste, Crest or Colgate	6-7 oz	2.27	4Q 92	4c
Personal Services				
Dry cleaning, man's 2-piece suit		7.37	4Q 92	4c
Haircare, woman's shampoo, trim and blow-dry		17.20	4Q 92	4c
Haircut, man's barbershop, no styling		8.50	4Q 92	4c
Restaurant Food				
Chicken, fried, thigh and drumstick		2.08	4Q 92	4c
Hamburger with cheese	1/4 lb	1.95	4Q 92	4c
Pizza, Pizza Hut or Pizza Inn, cheese, thin crust	12-13 in	9.58	4Q 92	4c
Transportation				
ACCRA Index, Transportation		113.50	4Q 92	4c
Tire balance, computer or spin balance, front	wheel	7.50	4Q 92	4c
Utilities				
ACCRA Index, Utilities		91.20	4Q 92	4c
Electricity, partial electric and other energy, 1,800 sq ft living area new home	month	57.79	4Q 92	4c

Flint, MI

Item	Per	Value	Date	Ref.
Child Care				
Child care fee, average, center	hour	1.63	90	65r
Child care fee, average, nonregulated family day care	hour	1.83	90	65r
Child care fee, average, regulated family day care	hour	1.42	90	65r
Communications				
Long-distance telephone service, day, initial minute, 0-100 miles	min	0.14-0.36	91	12s
Long-distance telephone service, day, additional minute, 0-100 miles	min	0.14-0.36	91	12s
Long-distance telephone service, evenings/weekends, 0-100 mi, initial minute	min	0.07-0.19	91	12s
Long-distance telephone service, evenings/weekends, 0-100 mi, additional minute	min	0.04-0.14	91	12s
Education				
Board, 4-yr private college/university	year	1698	91	22s
Board, 4-yr public college/university	year	1962	91	22s
Expenditures, local gov't, public elementary/secondary	pupil	5671	92	20s
Room, 4-year private college/university	year	1440	91	22s

Values are in dollars or fractions of dollars. In the column headed *Ref*, references are shown to sources. Each reference is followed by a letter. These refer to the geographical level for which data were reported: s = State, r = Region, and c = City or metro. The abbreviation *ex* is used to mean *except* or *excluding*; *exp* stands for expenditures. For other abbreviations and further explanations, please see the Introduction.

Flint, MI - continued

Item	Per	Value	Date	Ref.
Education				
Room, 4-year public college/university	year	1687	91	22s
Tuition, 2-year private college/university	year	4749	91	22s
Tuition, 2-year public college/university	year	1124	91	22s
Tuition, 4-year private college/university	year	6885	91	22s
Tuition, 4-year public college/university, in-state	year	2635	91	22s
Energy and Fuels				
Coal	mil Btu	1.63	90	64s
Energy	mil Btu	8.17	90	64s
Energy exp/householder, 1-family unit	year	471	90	28r
Energy exp/householder, <1,000 sq ft heating area	year	430	90	28r
Energy exp/householder, 1,000-1,999 sq ft heating area	year	481	90	28r
Energy exp/householder, 2,000+ sq ft heating area	year	473	90	28r
Energy exp/householder, mobile home	year	430	90	28r
Energy exp/householder, multifamily	year	461	90	28r
Gas, natural	mil Btu	4.36	90	64s
Gas, natural	000 cu ft	5.07	91	46s
Gas, natural, exp	year	655	91	46s
Gasoline, unleaded regular	mil Btu	8.78	90	64s
Entertainment				
Miniature golf admission	adult	6.18	92	1r
Miniature golf admission	child	5.14	92	1r
Waterpark admission	adult	11.00	92	1r
Waterpark admission	child	8.55	92	1r
Funerals				
Casket, 18-gauge steel, velvet interior		1926.72	91	24r
Cosmetology, hair care, etc.		97.64	91	24r
Embalming		249.14	91	24r
Facility use for ceremony		208.59	91	24r
Hearse, local		130.12	91	24r
Limousine, local		104.66	91	24r
Remains to funeral home, transfer		93.61	91	24r
Service charge, professional		724.62	91	24r
Vault, concrete, non-metallic liner		734.53	91	24r
Viewing facilities, use		236.06	91	24r
Groceries				
Apples, Red Delicious	lb	0.77	4/93	16r
Bacon	lb	1.85	4/93	16r
Bananas	lb	0.46	4/93	16r
Beef, stew, boneless	lb	2.53	4/93	16r
Bologna, all beef or mixed	lb	2.19	4/93	16r
Bread, white, pan	lb	0.78	4/93	16r
Butter	lb	1.50	4/93	16r
Cabbage	lb	0.40	4/93	16r
Carrots, short trimmed and topped	lb	0.45	4/93	16r
Cheese, Cheddar	lb	3.47	4/93	16r
Chicken, fresh, whole	lb	0.84	4/93	16r
Chicken breast, bone-in	lb	1.94	4/93	16r
Chicken legs, bone-in	lb	1.02	4/93	16r
Chuck roast, graded and ungraded, ex USDA prime and choice	lb	2.43	4/93	16r
Chuck roast, USDA choice, bone-in	lb	2.11	4/93	16r
Chuck roast, USDA choice, boneless	lb	2.44	4/93	16r
Coffee, 100% ground roast, all sizes	lb	2.47	4/93	16r
Cookies, chocolate chip	lb	2.73	4/93	16r
Eggs, Grade A large	doz	0.93	4/93	16r
Flour, white, all purpose	lb	0.21	4/93	16r
Grapefruit	lb	0.45	4/93	16r
Grapes, Thompson Seedless	lb	1.46	4/93	16r
Ground beef, 100% beef	lb	1.63	4/93	16r
Ground beef, lean and extra lean	lb	2.08	4/93	16r
Ground chuck, 100% beef	lb	1.94	4/93	16r
Ham, boneless, excluding canned	lb	2.21	4/93	16r
Honey, jar	8 oz	0.97-1.25	92	5r
Honey, jar	lb	1.25-2.25	92	5r
Honey, squeeze bear	12-oz	1.25-1.99	92	5r

Flint, MI - continued

Item	Per	Value	Date	Ref.
Groceries - continued				
Ice cream, prepackaged, bulk, regular	1/2 gal	2.41	4/93	16r
Lemons	lb	0.82	4/93	16r
Lettuce, iceberg	lb	0.83	4/93	16r
Margarine, stick	lb	0.77	4/93	16r
Oranges, navel	lb	0.50	4/93	16r
Peanut butter, creamy, all sizes	lb	1.82	4/93	16r
Pears, Anjou	lb	0.85	4/93	16r
Pork chops, center cut, bone-in	lb	3.17	4/93	16r
Potato chips	16 oz	2.68	4/93	16r
Potatoes, white	lb	0.26	4/93	16r
Round roast, graded & ungraded, ex USDA prime & choice	lb	2.88	4/93	16r
Round roast, USDA choice, boneless	lb	2.96	4/93	16r
Shortening, vegetable oil blends	lb	0.79	4/93	16r
Spaghetti and macaroni	lb	0.76	4/93	16r
Steak, rib eye, USDA choice, boneless	lb	6.29	4/93	16r
Steak, round, USDA choice, boneless	lb	3.24	4/93	16r
Steak, sirloin, graded & ungraded, ex USDA prime & choice	lb	4.00	4/93	16r
Steak, sirloin, USDA choice, bone-in	lb	3.57	4/93	16r
Steak, sirloin, USDA choice, boneless	lb	4.17	4/93	16r
Steak, T-bone, USDA choice, bone-in	lb	5.60	4/93	16r
Strawberries, dry pint	12 oz	0.90	4/93	16r
Sugar, white	lb	0.36	4/93	16r
Sugar, white, 33-80 oz pk	lb	0.35	4/93	16r
Tomatoes, field grown	lb	0.99	4/93	16r
Tuna, chunk, light	lb	1.76	4/93	16r
Turkey, frozen, whole	lb	0.91	4/93	16r
Health Care				
Childbirth, cesarean, hospital		4688	91	62r
Childbirth, cesarean, physician's fee		2053	91	62r
Childbirth, normal, hospital		2657	91	62r
Childbirth, normal, physician's fee		1492	91	62r
Medical plan per employee	year	3443	91	45r
Mental health care, exp	capita	53.68-118.35	90	38s
Mental health care, exp, state mental health agency	capita	73.73	90	38s
Mental health care, hospital psychiatric services, non-Federal, exp	capita	22.52	88	38s
Mental health care, mental health organization, multiservice, exp	capita	42.68	88	38s
Mental health care, psychiatric hospitals, private, exp	capita	10.80	88	38s
Mental health care, psychiatric out-patient clinics, freestanding, exp	capita	3.47	88	38s
Mental health care, psychiatric partial-care organizations, freestanding, exp	capita	0.73	88	38s
Mental health care, state and county mental hospitals, exp	capita	36.77	88	38s
Mental health care, VA medical centers, exp	capita	4.03	88	38s
Physician fee, family practice, first-visit		76.00	91	62r
Physician fee, family practice, revisit		33.00	91	62r
Physician fee, general practice, first-visit		61.00	91	62r
Physician fee, general practice, revisit		31.00	91	62r
Physician fee, general surgeon, first-visit		65.00	91	62r
Physician fee, general surgeon, revisit		35.00	91	62r
Physician fee, internal medicine, first-visit		91.00	91	62r
Physician fee, internal medicine, revisit		40.00	91	62r
Physician fee, median, neurosurgeon, first-visit		106.00	91	62r
Physician fee, median, nonsurgical specialist, first-visit		90.00	91	62r
Physician fee, median, orthopedic surgeon, first-visit		83.00	91	62r
Physician fee, median, surgical specialist, first-visit		61.00	91	62r
Physician fee, neurosurgeon, revisit		41.00	91	62r
Physician fee, nonsurgical specialist, revisit		40.00	91	62r
Physician fee, obstetrics/gynecology, first-visit		61.00	91	62r
Physician fee, obstetrics/gynecology, revisit		40.00	91	62r

Values are in dollars or fractions of dollars. In the column headed *Ref*, references are shown to sources. Each reference is followed by a letter. These refer to the geographical level for which data were reported: s=State, r=Region, and c=City or metro. The abbreviation *ex* is used to mean *except* or *excluding*; *exp* stands for expenditures. For other abbreviations and further explanations, please see the Introduction.

Flint, MI - continued

Item	Per	Value	Date	Ref.
Health Care				
Physician fee, orthopedic surgeon, revisit		41.00	91	62r
Physician fee, pediatrician, first-visit		46.00	91	62r
Physician fee, pediatrician, revisit		33.00	91	62r
Physician fee, surgical specialist, revisit		36.00	91	62r
Substance abuse, hospital ancillary charge	incident	1480	90	70s
Substance abuse, hospital physician charge	incident	250	90	70s
Substance abuse, hospital room and board	incident	4070	90	70s
Insurance and Pensions				
Auto insurance, private passenger	year	716.78	91	63s
Taxes				
Tax, cigarette	pack	25	91	77s
Tax, gasoline	gal	15	91	77s
Taxes, state	capita	1185	91	77s
Transportation				
Driver's license fee		12.00	12/90	43s
Vehicle registration and license plate	year	14.00-200.00	93	40s
Utilities				
Electricity	mil Btu	20.85	90	64s

Florence, AL

Item	Per	Value	Date	Ref.
Composite ACCRA index		95.10	4Q 92	4c
Alcoholic Beverages				
Beer, Miller Lite or Budweiser, 12-oz containers	6 pack	4.05	4Q 92	4c
Liquor, J & B Scotch	750 ml	19.99	4Q 92	4c
Wine, Gallo Chablis blanc, 1.5 liter	bottle	5.25	4Q 92	4c
Child Care				
Child care fee, average, center	hour	1.29	90	65r
Child care fee, average, nonregulated family day care	hour	0.89	90	65r
Child care fee, average, regulated family day care	hour	1.32	90	65r
Clothing				
Jeans, man's denim		27.99	4Q 92	4c
Shirt, man's dress shirt		28.00	4Q 92	4c
Undervest, boy's size 10-14, cotton	3	3.44	4Q 92	4c
Communications				
Long-distance telephone service, day, initial minute, 0-100 miles	min	0.11-0.36	91	12s
Long-distance telephone service, day, additional minute, 0-100 miles	min	0.09-0.26	91	12s
Long-distance telephone service, evenings/weekends, 0-100 mi, initial minute	min	0.04-0.14	91	12s
Long-distance telephone service, evenings/weekends, 0-100 mi, additional minute	min	0.04-0.10	91	12s
Newspaper subscription, daily and Sunday home delivery, large-city	month	9.25	4Q 92	4c
Telephone, flat rate	month	16.56	91	11c
Telephone bill, family of four	month	24.77	4Q 92	4c
Education				
Board, 4-yr private college/university	year	1795	91	22s
Board, 4-yr public college/university	year	1469	91	22s
Expenditures, local gov't, public elementary/secondary	pupil	3675	92	20s
Room, 4-year private college/university	year	1340	91	22s
Room, 4-year public college/university	year	1295	91	22s
Tuition, 2-year private college/university	year	4148	91	22s
Tuition, 2-year public college/university	year	689	91	22s
Tuition, 4-year private college/university	year	5942	91	22s
Tuition, 4-year public college/university, in-state	year	1593	91	22s

Florence, AL - continued

Item	Per	Value	Date	Ref.
Energy and Fuels				
Coal	mil Btu	1.83	90	64s
Energy	mil Btu	7.92	90	64s
Energy, combined forms, 1,800 sq ft heating area	month	132.76	4Q 92	4c
Energy, exc electricity, 1,800 sq ft heating area	month	34.72	4Q 92	4c
Energy exp/householder, 1-family unit	year	403	90	28r
Energy exp/householder, <1,000 sq ft heating area	year	342	90	28r
Energy exp/householder, 1,000-1,999 sq ft heating area	year	388	90	28r
Energy exp/householder, 2,000+ sq ft heating area	year	434	90	28r
Energy exp/householder, mobile home	year	320	90	28r
Energy exp/householder, multifamily	year	338	90	28r
Gas, natural	mil Btu	4.07	90	64s
Gas, natural	000 cu ft	7.05	91	46s
Gas, natural, exp	year	461	91	46s
Gasoline, motor	gal	1.07	4Q 92	4c
Gasoline, unleaded regular	mil Btu	8.96	90	64s
Entertainment				
Bowling, evening rate	game	1.85	4Q 92	4c
Miniature golf admission	adult	6.18	92	1r
Miniature golf admission	child	5.14	92	1r
Monopoly game, Parker Brothers', No. 9		9.97	4Q 92	4c
Movie	admission	5.00	4Q 92	4c
Tennis balls, yellow, Wilson or Penn, 3	can	1.97	4Q 92	4c
Waterpark admission	adult	11.00	92	1r
Waterpark admission	child	8.55	92	1r
Funerals				
Casket, 18-gauge steel, velvet interior		2329.05	91	24r
Cosmetology, hair care, etc.		72.78	91	24r
Embalming		240.71	91	24r
Facility use for ceremony		181.67	91	24r
Hearse, local		106.25	91	24r
Limousine, local		70.92	91	24r
Remains to funeral home, transfer		96.30	91	24r
Service charge, professional		687.09	91	24r
Vault, concrete, non-metallic liner		732.09	91	24r
Viewing facilities, use		190.30	91	24r
Goods and Services				
ACCRA Index, Miscellaneous Goods and Services		96.60	4Q 92	4c
Groceries				
ACCRA Index, Groceries		93.00	4Q 92	4c
Apples, Red Delicious	lb	0.79	4/93	16r
Babyfood, strained vegetables, lowest price	4-4.5 oz jar	0.26	4Q 92	4c
Bacon	lb	1.75	4/93	16r
Bananas	lb	0.42	4Q 92	4c
Bananas	lb	0.42	4/93	16r
Beef, stew, boneless	lb	2.61	4/93	16r
Bologna, all beef or mixed	lb	2.24	4/93	16r
Bread, white	24 oz	0.56	4Q 92	4c
Bread, white, pan	lb	0.64	4/93	16r
Bread, whole wheat, pan	lb	0.96	4/93	16r
Cabbage	lb	0.37	4/93	16r
Carrots, short trimmed and topped	lb	0.47	4/93	16r
Celery	lb	0.64	4/93	16r
Cheese, American	lb	2.98	4/93	16r
Cheese, Cheddar	lb	3.28	4/93	16r
Cheese, Kraft grated Parmesan	8-oz canister	3.03	4Q 92	4c
Chicken, fresh, whole	lb	0.77	4/93	16r
Chicken, fryer, whole	lb	0.63	4Q 92	4c
Chicken breast, bone-in	lb	1.92	4/93	16r
Chicken legs, bone-in	lb	1.06	4/93	16r

Values are in dollars or fractions of dollars. In the column headed *Ref*, references are shown to sources. Each reference is followed by a letter. These refer to the geographical level for which data were reported: s = State, r = Region, and c = City or metro. The abbreviation *ex* is used to mean *except* or *excluding*; *exp* stands for expenditures. For other abbreviations and further explanations, please see the Introduction.

Florence, AL - continued

Item	Per	Value	Date	Ref.
Groceries				
Chuck roast, graded and ungraded, ex USDA prime and choice	lb	2.40	4/93	16r
Chuck roast, USDA choice, bone-in	lb	2.19	4/93	16r
Chuck roast, USDA choice, boneless	lb	2.38	4/93	16r
Cigarettes, Winston	carton	16.30	4Q 92	4c
Coffee, 100% ground roast, all sizes	lb	2.48	4/93	16r
Coffee, vacuum-packed	13-oz can	1.90	4Q 92	4c
Corn, frozen	10 oz	0.57	4Q 92	4c
Corn Flakes, Kellogg's or Post Toasties	18 oz	1.68	4Q 92	4c
Crackers, soda, salted	lb	1.15	4/93	16r
Eggs, Grade A large	doz	0.75	4Q 92	4c
Eggs, Grade A large	doz	0.96	4/93	16r
Flour, white, all purpose	lb	0.24	4/93	16r
Frankfurters, all meat or all beef	lb	2.01	4/93	16r
Grapefruit	lb	0.44	4/93	16r
Grapes, Thompson Seedless	lb	1.40	4/93	16r
Ground beef, 100% beef	lb	1.58	4/93	16r
Ground beef, lean and extra lean	lb	2.09	4/93	16r
Ground beef or hamburger	lb	1.58	4Q 92	4c
Ground chuck, 100% beef	lb	1.98	4/93	16r
Ham, boneless, excluding canned	lb	2.89	4/93	16r
Ham, picnic, shoulder, bone-in, smoked	lb	1.02	4/93	16r
Ham, rump or steak half, bone-in, smoked	lb	1.48	4/93	16r
Honey, jar	8 oz	0.89-1.09	92	5r
Honey, jar	lb	1.39-2.25	92	5r
Honey, squeeze bear	12-oz	1.00-1.50	92	5r
Ice cream, prepackaged, bulk, regular	1/2 gal	2.41	4/93	16r
Lemons	lb	1.05	4/93	16r
Lettuce, iceberg	head	1.02	4Q 92	4c
Lettuce, iceberg	lb	0.81	4/93	16r
Margarine, Blue Bonnet or Parkay cubes	lb	0.48	4Q 92	4c
Margarine, stick	lb	0.88	4/93	16r
Milk, whole	1/2 gal	1.33	4Q 92	4c
Orange juice, Minute Maid frozen	12-oz can	1.25	4Q 92	4c
Oranges, navel	lb	0.55	4/93	16r
Peaches	29-oz can	1.22	4Q 92	4c
Pears, Anjou	lb	0.92	4/93	16r
Peas Sweet, Del Monte or Green Giant	15-17 oz can	0.53	4Q 92	4c
Pork chops, center cut, bone-in	lb	3.13	4/93	16r
Potato chips	16 oz	2.94	4/93	16r
Potatoes, white	lb	0.43	4/93	16r
Potatoes, white or red	10-lb sack	2.98	4Q 92	4c
Rib roast, USDA choice, bone-in	lb	4.63	4/93	16r
Rice, white, long grain, uncooked	lb	0.45	4/93	16r
Round roast, graded & ungraded, ex USDA prime & choice	lb	3.03	4/93	16r
Round roast, USDA choice, boneless	lb	3.09	4/93	16r
Sausage, fresh, loose	lb	2.08	4/93	16r
Sausage, Jimmy Dean, 100% pork	lb	2.17	4Q 92	4c
Short ribs, bone-in	lb	2.66	4/93	16r
Shortening, vegetable oil blends	lb	0.69	4/93	16r
Shortening, vegetable, Crisco	3-lb can	1.97	4Q 92	4c
Soft drink, Coca Cola	2 liter	1.59	4Q 92	4c
Spaghetti and macaroni	lb	0.81	4/93	16r
Steak, rib eye, USDA choice, boneless	lb	6.24	4/93	16r
Steak, round, graded & ungraded, ex USDA prime & choice	lb	3.31	4/93	16r
Steak, round, USDA choice, boneless	lb	3.34	4/93	16r
Steak, sirloin, graded & ungraded, ex USDA prime & choice	lb	4.19	4/93	16r
Steak, sirloin, USDA choice, boneless	lb	4.46	4/93	16r
Steak, T-bone	lb	5.37	4Q 92	4c
Steak, T-bone, USDA choice, bone-in	lb	5.25	4/93	16r
Strawberries, dry pint	12 oz	0.92	4/93	16r
Sugar, cane or beet	4 lb	1.30	4Q 92	4c
Sugar, white	lb	0.39	4/93	16r

Florence, AL - continued

Item	Per	Value	Date	Ref.
Groceries - continued				
Sugar, white, 33-80 oz pk	lb	0.38	4/93	16r
Tomatoes, field grown	lb	0.88	4/93	16r
Tomatoes, Hunt's or Del Monte	14.5-oz can	0.61	4Q 92	4c
Tuna, chunk, light	6.125-6.5 oz can	0.54	4Q 92	4c
Tuna, chunk, light	lb	1.79	4/93	16r
Turkey, frozen, whole	lb	1.04	4/93	16r
Yogurt, natural, fruit flavored	1/2 pint	0.57	4/93	16r
Health Care				
ACCRA Index, Health Care		100.50	4Q 92	4c
Analgesic, Aspirin, Bayer, 325 mg tablets	100	4.33	4Q 92	4c
Childbirth, cesarean, hospital		5034	91	62r
Childbirth, cesarean, physician's fee		2053	91	62r
Childbirth, normal, hospital		2712	91	62r
Childbirth, normal, physician's fee		1492	91	62r
Dentist's fee, adult teeth cleaning and periodic oral exam	visit	44.40	4Q 92	4c
Doctor's fee, routine exam, established patient	visit	45.00	4Q 92	4c
Hospital care, semiprivate room	day	250.50	4Q 92	4c
Medical insurance premium, per employee, small group comprehensive	month	321.20	10/91	25c
Mental health care, exp	capita	37.60-53.67	90	38s
Mental health care, exp, state mental health agency	capita	38.35	90	38s
Mental health care, hospital psychiatric services, non-Federal, exp	capita	13.58	88	38s
Mental health care, mental health organization, multiservice, exp	capita	12.40	88	38s
Mental health care, psychiatric hospitals, private, exp	capita	9.49	88	38s
Mental health care, state and county mental hospitals, exp	capita	22.15	88	38s
Mental health care, VA medical centers, exp	capita	10.94	88	38s
Physician fee, family practice, first-visit		75.00	91	62r
Physician fee, family practice, revisit		34.00	91	62r
Physician fee, general practice, first-visit		61.00	91	62r
Physician fee, general practice, revisit		32.00	91	62r
Physician fee, general surgeon, first-visit		64.00	91	62r
Physician fee, general surgeon, revisit		40.00	91	62r
Physician fee, internal medicine, first-visit		98.00	91	62r
Physician fee, internal medicine, revisit		40.00	91	62r
Physician fee, median, neurosurgeon, first-visit		130.00	91	62r
Physician fee, median, nonsurgical specialist, first-visit		95.00	91	62r
Physician fee, median, orthopedic surgeon, first-visit		91.00	91	62r
Physician fee, median, plastic surgeon, first-visit		66.00	91	62r
Physician fee, median, surgical specialist, first-visit		62.00	91	62r
Physician fee, neurosurgeon, revisit		50.00	91	62r
Physician fee, nonsurgical specialist, revisit		40.00	91	62r
Physician fee, obstetrics/gynecology, first-visit		64.00	91	62r
Physician fee, obstetrics/gynecology, revisit		41.00	91	62r
Physician fee, orthopedic surgeon, revisit		40.00	91	62r
Physician fee, pediatrician, first-visit		49.00	91	62r
Physician fee, pediatrician, revisit		33.00	91	62r
Physician fee, plastic surgeon, revisit		43.00	91	62r
Physician fee, surgical specialist, revisit		37.00	91	62r
Substance abuse, hospital ancillary charge	incident	1390	90	70s
Substance abuse, hospital physician charge	incident	520	90	70s
Substance abuse, hospital room and board	incident	5830	90	70s

Values are in dollars or fractions of dollars. In the column headed *Ref*, references are shown to sources. Each reference is followed by a letter. These refer to the geographical level for which data were reported: s=State, r=Region, and c=City or metro. The abbreviation *ex* is used to mean *except* or *excluding*; *exp* stands for expenditures. For other abbreviations and further explanations, please see the Introduction.

Florence, AL - continued

Item	Per	Value	Date	Ref.
Household Goods				
Appliance repair, home, service call, washing machine	min labor charge	35.88	4Q 92	4c
Laundry detergent, Tide Ultra, Bold, or Cheer	42 oz	2.88	4Q 92	4c
Tissues, facial, Kleenex brand	175-count box	1.08	4Q 92	4c
Housing				
ACCRA Index, Housing		84.30	4Q 92	4c
House, 1,800 sq ft, 8,000 sq ft lot, new, urban	total	93325	4Q 92	4c
House payment, principal and interest, 25% down payment	month	523	4Q 92	4c
Mortgage rate, incl. points & origination fee, 30-year fixed or adjustable rate	percent	8.20	4Q 92	4c
Rent, apartment, 2 bedrooms - 1-1/2 to 2 baths, unfurnished, 950 sq ft, water	month	403	4Q 92	4c
Rental unit, 1 bedroom	month	332	93	23c
Rental unit, 2 bedroom	month	392	93	23c
Rental unit, 3 bedroom	month	488	93	23c
Rental unit, 4 bedroom	month	545	93	23c
Rental unit, efficiency	month	271	93	23c
Insurance and Pensions				
Auto insurance, private passenger	year	562.59	91	63s
Personal Goods				
Shampoo, Alberto VO5	15 oz	0.97	4Q 92	4c
Toothpaste, Crest or Colgate	6-7 oz	1.69	4Q 92	4c
Personal Services				
Dry cleaning, man's 2-piece suit		5.54	4Q 92	4c
Haircare, woman's shampoo, trim and blow-dry		16.80	4Q 92	4c
Haircut, man's barbershop, no styling		8.50	4Q 92	4c
Restaurant Food				
Chicken, fried, thigh and drumstick		1.79	4Q 92	4c
Hamburger with cheese	1/4 lb	1.99	4Q 92	4c
Pizza, Pizza Hut or Pizza Inn, cheese, thin crust	12-13 in	7.99	4Q 92	4c
Taxes				
Tax, cigarette	pack	16.50	91	77s
Tax, gasoline	gal	16	91	77s
Taxes, state	capita	964	91	77s
Transportation				
ACCRA Index, Transportation		95.90	4Q 92	4c
Driver's license fee		15.00	12/90	43s
Tire balance, computer or spin balance, front	wheel	6.29	4Q 92	4c
Travel				
Business travel	day	193.00	4/93	89r
Utilities				
ACCRA Index, Utilities		122.20	4Q 92	4c
Electricity	mil Btu	16.46	90	64s
Electricity, partial electric and other energy, 1,800 sq ft living area new home	month	98.04	4Q 92	4c

Florence, SC

Item	Per	Value	Date	Ref.
Composite ACCRA index		91.40	4Q 92	4c
Alcoholic Beverages				
Beer, Miller Lite or Budweiser, 12-oz containers	6 pack	3.97	4Q 92	4c
Liquor, J & B Scotch	750 ml	14.16	4Q 92	4c
Wine, Gallo Chablis blanc, 1.5 liter	bottle	5.09	4Q 92	4c
Child Care				
Child care fee, average, center	hour	1.29	90	65r

Florence, SC - continued

Item	Per	Value	Date	Ref.
Child Care - continued				
Child care fee, average, nonregulated family day care	hour	0.89	90	65r
Child care fee, average, regulated family day care	hour	1.32	90	65r
Clothing				
Jeans, man's denim		31.40	4Q 92	4c
Shirt, man's dress shirt		21.00	4Q 92	4c
Undervest, boy's size 10-14, cotton	3	3.15	4Q 92	4c
Communications				
Long-distance telephone service, day, initial minute, 0-100 miles	min	0.24-0.52	91	12s
Long-distance telephone service, day, additional minute, 0-100 miles	min	0.13-0.35	91	12s
Long-distance telephone service, evenings/weekends, 0-100 mi, initial minute	min	0.12-0.26	91	12s
Long-distance telephone service, evenings/weekends, 0-100 mi, additional minute	min	0.07-0.16	91	12s
Newspaper subscription, daily and Sunday home delivery, large-city	month	8.90	4Q 92	4c
Telephone, flat rate	month	16.00	91	11c
Telephone bill, family of four	month	21.85	4Q 92	4c
Education				
Board, 4-yr private college/university	year	1468	91	22s
Board, 4-yr public college/university	year	1632	91	22s
Expenditures, local gov't, public elementary/secondary	pupil	4312	92	20s
Room, 4-year private college/university	year	1393	91	22s
Room, 4-year public college/university	year	1492	91	22s
Tuition, 2-year private college/university	year	5110	91	22s
Tuition, 2-year public college/university	year	813	91	22s
Tuition, 4-year private college/university	year	6434	91	22s
Tuition, 4-year public college/university, in-state	year	2317	91	22s
Energy and Fuels				
Coal	mil Btu	1.73	90	64s
Energy	mil Btu	8.93	90	64s
Energy, combined forms, 1,800 sq ft heating area	month	111.75	4Q 92	4c
Energy exp/householder, 1-family unit	year	487	90	28r
Energy exp/householder, <1,000 sq ft heating area	year	393	90	28r
Energy exp/householder, 1,000-1,999 sq ft heating area	year	442	90	28r
Energy exp/householder, 2,000+ sq ft heating area	year	577	90	28r
Energy exp/householder, mobile home	year	366	90	28r
Energy exp/householder, multifamily	year	382	90	28r
Gas, natural	mil Btu	4.01	90	64s
Gas, natural	000 cu ft	6.98	91	46s
Gas, natural, exp	year	397	91	46s
Gasoline, motor	gal	1.01	4Q 92	4c
Gasoline, unleaded regular	mil Btu	8.80	90	64s
Entertainment				
Bowling, evening rate	game	2.25	4Q 92	4c
Miniature golf admission	adult	6.18	92	1r
Miniature golf admission	child	5.14	92	1r
Monopoly game, Parker Brothers', No. 9		12.89	4Q 92	4c
Movie	admission	5.00	4Q 92	4c
Tennis balls, yellow, Wilson or Penn, 3	can	1.99	4Q 92	4c
Waterpark admission	adult	11.00	92	1r
Waterpark admission	child	8.55	92	1r
Funerals				
Casket, 18-gauge steel, velvet interior		2029.08	91	24r
Cosmetology, hair care, etc.		75.10	91	24r
Embalming		249.24	91	24r
Facility use for ceremony		162.27	91	24r
Hearse, local		114.04	91	24r

Values are in dollars or fractions of dollars. In the column headed *Ref*, references are shown to sources. Each reference is followed by a letter. These refer to the geographical level for which data were reported: s = State, r = Region, and c = City or metro. The abbreviation *ex* is used to mean *except* or *excluding*; *exp* stands for expenditures. For other abbreviations and further explanations, please see the Introduction.

Florence, SC - continued

Item	Per	Value	Date	Ref.
Funerals				
Limousine, local		88.57	91	24r
Remains to funeral home, transfer		92.61	91	24r
Service charge, professional		682.42	91	24r
Vault, concrete, non-metallic liner		798.70	91	24r
Viewing facilities, use		163.86	91	24r
Goods and Services				
ACCRA Index, Miscellaneous Goods and Services		94.50	4Q 92	4c
Groceries				
ACCRA Index, Groceries		94.60	4Q 92	4c
Apples, Red Delicious	lb	0.79	4/93	16r
Babyfood, strained vegetables, lowest price	4-4.5 oz jar	0.33	4Q 92	4c
Bacon	lb	1.75	4/93	16r
Bananas	lb	0.51	4Q 92	4c
Bananas	lb	0.42	4/93	16r
Beef, stew, boneless	lb	2.61	4/93	16r
Bologna, all beef or mixed	lb	2.24	4/93	16r
Bread, white	24 oz	0.59	4Q 92	4c
Bread, white, pan	lb	0.64	4/93	16r
Bread, whole wheat, pan	lb	0.96	4/93	16r
Cabbage	lb	0.37	4/93	16r
Carrots, short trimmed and topped	lb	0.47	4/93	16r
Celery	lb	0.64	4/93	16r
Cheese, American	lb	2.98	4/93	16r
Cheese, Cheddar	lb	3.28	4/93	16r
Cheese, Kraft grated Parmesan	8-oz canister	3.15	4Q 92	4c
Chicken, fresh, whole	lb	0.77	4/93	16r
Chicken, fryer, whole	lb	0.64	4Q 92	4c
Chicken breast, bone-in	lb	1.92	4/93	16r
Chicken legs, bone-in	lb	1.06	4/93	16r
Chuck roast, graded and ungraded, ex USDA prime and choice	lb	2.40	4/93	16r
Chuck roast, USDA choice, bone-in	lb	2.19	4/93	16r
Chuck roast, USDA choice, boneless	lb	2.38	4/93	16r
Cigarettes, Winston	carton	15.05	4Q 92	4c
Coffee, 100% ground roast, all sizes	lb	2.48	4/93	16r
Coffee, vacuum-packed	13-oz can	2.13	4Q 92	4c
Corn, frozen	10 oz	0.52	4Q 92	4c
Corn Flakes, Kellogg's or Post Toasties	18 oz	1.79	4Q 92	4c
Crackers, soda, salted	lb	1.15	4/93	16r
Eggs, Grade A large	doz	0.84	4Q 92	4c
Eggs, Grade A large	doz	0.96	4/93	16r
Flour, white, all purpose	lb	0.24	4/93	16r
Frankfurters, all meat or all beef	lb	2.01	4/93	16r
Grapefruit	lb	0.44	4/93	16r
Grapes, Thompson Seedless	lb	1.40	4/93	16r
Ground beef, 100% beef	lb	1.58	4/93	16r
Ground beef, lean and extra lean	lb	2.09	4/93	16r
Ground beef or hamburger	lb	1.85	4Q 92	4c
Ground chuck, 100% beef	lb	1.98	4/93	16r
Ham, boneless, excluding canned	lb	2.89	4/93	16r
Ham, picnic, shoulder, bone-in, smoked	lb	1.02	4/93	16r
Ham, rump or steak half, bone-in, smoked	lb	1.48	4/93	16r
Ice cream, prepackaged, bulk, regular	1/2 gal	2.41	4/93	16r
Lemons	lb	1.05	4/93	16r
Lettuce, iceberg	head	0.89	4Q 92	4c
Lettuce, iceberg	lb	0.81	4/93	16r
Margarine, Blue Bonnet or Parkay cubes	lb	0.45	4Q 92	4c
Margarine, stick	lb	0.88	4/93	16r
Milk, whole	1/2 gal	1.27	4Q 92	4c
Orange juice, Minute Maid frozen	12-oz can	1.21	4Q 92	4c
Oranges, navel	lb	0.55	4/93	16r
Peaches	29-oz can	1.29	4Q 92	4c
Pears, Anjou	lb	0.92	4/93	16r

Florence, SC - continued

Item	Per	Value	Date	Ref.
Groceries - continued				
Peas Sweet, Del Monte or Green Giant	15-17 oz can	0.51	4Q 92	4c
Pork chops, center cut, bone-in	lb	3.13	4/93	16r
Potato chips	16 oz	2.94	4/93	16r
Potatoes, white	lb	0.43	4/93	16r
Potatoes, white or red	10-lb sack	2.07	4Q 92	4c
Rib roast, USDA choice, bone-in	lb	4.63	4/93	16r
Rice, white, long grain, uncooked	lb	0.45	4/93	16r
Round roast, graded & ungraded, ex USDA prime & choice	lb	3.03	4/93	16r
Round roast, USDA choice, boneless	lb	3.09	4/93	16r
Sausage, fresh, loose	lb	2.08	4/93	16r
Sausage, Jimmy Dean, 100% pork	lb	2.11	4Q 92	4c
Short ribs, bone-in	lb	2.66	4/93	16r
Shortening, vegetable oil blends	lb	0.69	4/93	16r
Shortening, vegetable, Crisco	3-lb can	2.11	4Q 92	4c
Soft drink, Coca Cola	2 liter	1.11	4Q 92	4c
Spaghetti and macaroni	lb	0.81	4/93	16r
Steak, rib eye, USDA choice, boneless	lb	6.24	4/93	16r
Steak, round, graded & ungraded, ex USDA prime & choice	lb	3.31	4/93	16r
Steak, round, USDA choice, boneless	lb	3.34	4/93	16r
Steak, sirloin, graded & ungraded, ex USDA prime & choice	lb	4.19	4/93	16r
Steak, sirloin, USDA choice, boneless	lb	4.46	4/93	16r
Steak, T-bone	lb	5.85	4Q 92	4c
Steak, T-bone, USDA choice, bone-in	lb	5.25	4/93	16r
Strawberries, dry pint	12 oz	0.92	4/93	16r
Sugar, cane or beet	4 lb	1.55	4Q 92	4c
Sugar, white	lb	0.39	4/93	16r
Sugar, white, 33-80 oz pk	lb	0.38	4/93	16r
Tomatoes, field grown	lb	0.88	4/93	16r
Tomatoes, Hunt's or Del Monte	14.5-oz can	0.46	4Q 92	4c
Tuna, chunk, light	6.125-6.5 oz can	0.55	4Q 92	4c
Tuna, chunk, light	lb	1.79	4/93	16r
Turkey, frozen, whole	lb	1.04	4/93	16r
Yogurt, natural, fruit flavored	1/2 pint	0.57	4/93	16r
Health Care				
ACCRA Index, Health Care		83.90	4Q 92	4c
Analgesic, Aspirin, Bayer, 325 mg tablets	100	4.75	4Q 92	4c
Childbirth, cesarean, hospital		5034	91	62r
Childbirth, cesarean, physician's fee		2053	91	62r
Childbirth, normal, hospital		2712	91	62r
Childbirth, normal, physician's fee		1492	91	62r
Dentist's fee, adult teeth cleaning and periodic oral exam	visit	37.00	4Q 92	4c
Doctor's fee, routine exam, established patient	visit	31.40	4Q 92	4c
Health care spending, state	capita	1689	3/93	84s
Hospital care, semiprivate room	day	195.00	90	27c
Hospital care, semiprivate room	day	267.67	4Q 92	4c
Medical insurance premium, per employee, small group comprehensive	month	292.00	10/91	25c
Medical plan per employee	year	3495	91	45r
Mental health care, exp	capita	37.60-53.67	90	38s
Mental health care, exp, state mental health agency	capita	51.12	90	38s
Mental health care, hospital psychiatric services, non-Federal, exp	capita	10.67	88	38s
Mental health care, mental health organization, multiservice, exp	capita	11.38	88	38s
Mental health care, psychiatric hospitals, private, exp	capita	9.21	88	38s
Mental health care, psychiatric out-patient clinics, freestanding, exp	capita	0.68	88	38s

Values are in dollars or fractions of dollars. In the column headed *Ref*, references are shown to sources. Each reference is followed by a letter. These refer to the geographical level for which data were reported: s=State, r=Region, and c=City or metro. The abbreviation *ex* is used to mean *except* or *excluding*; *exp* stands for expenditures. For other abbreviations and further explanations, please see the Introduction.

Florence, SC - continued

Item	Per	Value	Date	Ref.
Health Care				
Mental health care, state and county mental hospitals, exp	capita	25.02	88	38s
Mental health care, VA medical centers, exp	capita	0.62	88	38s
Physician fee, family practice, first-visit		75.00	91	62r
Physician fee, family practice, revisit		34.00	91	62r
Physician fee, general practice, first-visit		61.00	91	62r
Physician fee, general practice, revisit		32.00	91	62r
Physician fee, general surgeon, first-visit		64.00	91	62r
Physician fee, general surgeon, revisit		40.00	91	62r
Physician fee, internal medicine, first-visit		98.00	91	62r
Physician fee, internal medicine, revisit		40.00	91	62r
Physician fee, median, neurosurgeon, first-visit		130.00	91	62r
Physician fee, median, nonsurgical specialist, first-visit		95.00	91	62r
Physician fee, median, orthopedic surgeon, first-visit		91.00	91	62r
Physician fee, median, plastic surgeon, first-visit		66.00	91	62r
Physician fee, median, surgical specialist, first-visit		62.00	91	62r
Physician fee, neurosurgeon, revisit		50.00	91	62r
Physician fee, nonsurgical specialist, revisit		40.00	91	62r
Physician fee, obstetrics/gynecology, first-visit		64.00	91	62r
Physician fee, obstetrics/gynecology, revisit		41.00	91	62r
Physician fee, orthopedic surgeon, revisit		40.00	91	62r
Physician fee, pediatrician, first-visit		49.00	91	62r
Physician fee, pediatrician, revisit		33.00	91	62r
Physician fee, plastic surgeon, revisit		43.00	91	62r
Physician fee, surgical specialist, revisit		37.00	91	62r
Substance abuse, hospital ancillary charge	incident	1250	90	70s
Substance abuse, hospital physician charge	incident	250	90	70s
Substance abuse, hospital room and board	incident	6100	90	70s
Household Goods				
Appliance repair, home, service call, washing machine	min labor charge	34.20	4Q 92	4c
Laundry detergent, Tide Ultra, Bold, or Cheer	42 oz	3.09	4Q 92	4c
Tissues, facial, Kleenex brand	175-count box	1.01	4Q 92	4c
Housing				
ACCRA Index, Housing		85.50	4Q 92	4c
House, 1,800 sq ft, 8,000 sq ft lot, new, urban	total	94175	4Q 92	4c
House payment, principal and interest, 25% down payment	month	538	4Q 92	4c
Mortgage rate, incl. points & origination fee, 30-year fixed or adjustable rate	percent	8.40	4Q 92	4c
Rent, apartment, 2 bedrooms - 1-1/2 to 2 baths, unfurnished, 950 sq ft, water	month	394	4Q 92	4c
Rental unit, 1 bedroom	month	319	93	23c
Rental unit, 2 bedroom	month	378	93	23c
Rental unit, 3 bedroom	month	472	93	23c
Rental unit, 4 bedroom	month	530	93	23c
Rental unit, efficiency	month	263	93	23c
Insurance and Pensions				
Auto insurance, private passenger	year	605.26	91	63s
Personal Goods				
Shampoo, Alberto VO5	15 oz	1.03	4Q 92	4c
Toothpaste, Crest or Colgate	6-7 oz	1.79	4Q 92	4c
Personal Services				
Dry cleaning, man's 2-piece suit		5.20	4Q 92	4c

Florence, SC - continued

Item	Per	Value	Date	Ref.
Personal Services - continued				
Haircare, woman's shampoo, trim and blow-dry		18.00	4Q 92	4c
Haircut, man's barbershop, no styling		6.00	4Q 92	4c
Restaurant Food				
Chicken, fried, thigh and drumstick		2.10	4Q 92	4c
Hamburger with cheese	1/4 lb	1.99	4Q 92	4c
Pizza, Pizza Hut or Pizza Inn, cheese, thin crust	12-13 in	7.74	4Q 92	4c
Taxes				
Tax, cigarette	pack	7	91	77s
Tax, gasoline	gal	16	91	77s
Taxes, state	capita	1105	91	77s
Transportation				
ACCRA Index, Transportation		86.20	4Q 92	4c
Driver's license fee		10.00	12/90	43s
Tire balance, computer or spin balance, front	wheel	5.40	4Q 92	4c
Travel				
Business travel	day	193.00	4/93	89r
Utilities				
ACCRA Index, Utilities		103.30	4Q 92	4c
Electricity	mil Btu	16.39	90	64s
Electricity, all electric, 1,800 sq ft living area new home	month	111.75	4Q 92	4c
Electricity, winter, 250 KWh	month	26.06	92	55c
Electricity, winter, 500 KWh	month	45.62	92	55c
Electricity, winter, 750 KWh	month	65.18	92	55c
Electricity, winter, 1000 KWh	month	84.74	92	55c

Fond du Lac, WI

Item	Per	Value	Date	Ref.
Composite ACCRA index		98.00	4Q 92	4c
Alcoholic Beverages				
Beer, Miller Lite or Budweiser, 12-oz containers	6 pack	3.38	4Q 92	4c
Liquor, J & B Scotch	750 ml	15.19	4Q 92	4c
Wine, Gallo Chablis blanc, 1.5 liter	bottle	4.47	4Q 92	4c
Clothing				
Jeans, man's denim		31.59	4Q 92	4c
Shirt, man's dress shirt		22.50	4Q 92	4c
Undervest, boy's size 10-14, cotton	3	3.40	4Q 92	4c
Communications				
Newspaper subscription, daily and Sunday home delivery, large-city	month	11.96	4Q 92	4c
Telephone bill, family of four	month	16.31	4Q 92	4c
Energy and Fuels				
Energy, combined forms, 1,800 sq ft heating area	month	98.74	4Q 92	4c
Energy, exc electricity, 1,800 sq ft heating area	month	57.37	4Q 92	4c
Gasoline, motor	gal	1.16	4Q 92	4c
Entertainment				
Bowling, evening rate	game	1.43	4Q 92	4c
Monopoly game, Parker Brothers', No. 9		11.40	4Q 92	4c
Movie	admission	5.50	4Q 92	4c
Tennis balls, yellow, Wilson or Penn, 3	can	2.37	4Q 92	4c
Goods and Services				
ACCRA Index, Miscellaneous Goods and Services		92.80	4Q 92	4c
Groceries				
ACCRA Index, Groceries		101.80	4Q 92	4c
Babyfood, strained vegetables, lowest price	4-4.5 oz jar	0.39	4Q 92	4c
Bananas	lb	0.44	4Q 92	4c

Values are in dollars or fractions of dollars. In the column headed *Ref*, references are shown to sources. Each reference is followed by a letter. These refer to the geographical level for which data were reported: s=State, r=Region, and c=City or metro. The abbreviation *ex* is used to mean *except* or *excluding*; *exp* stands for expenditures. For other abbreviations and further explanations, please see the Introduction.

Fond du Lac, WI - continued

Item	Per	Value	Date	Ref.
Groceries				
Bread, white	24 oz	0.66	4Q 92	4c
Cheese, Kraft grated Parmesan	8-oz canister	3.13	4Q 92	4c
Chicken, fryer, whole	lb	0.93	4Q 92	4c
Cigarettes, Winston	carton	19.37	4Q 92	4c
Coffee, vacuum-packed	13-oz can	1.90	4Q 92	4c
Corn, frozen	10 oz	0.67	4Q 92	4c
Corn Flakes, Kellogg's or Post Toasties	18 oz	2.01	4Q 92	4c
Eggs, Grade A large	doz	0.76	4Q 92	4c
Ground beef or hamburger	lb	1.72	4Q 92	4c
Lettuce, iceberg	head	0.99	4Q 92	4c
Margarine, Blue Bonnet or Parkay cubes	lb	0.54	4Q 92	4c
Milk, whole	1/2 gal	1.52	4Q 92	4c
Orange juice, Minute Maid frozen	12-oz can	1.19	4Q 92	4c
Peaches	29-oz can	1.45	4Q 92	4c
Peas Sweet, Del Monte or Green Giant	15-17 oz can	0.56	4Q 92	4c
Potatoes, white or red	10-lb sack	1.66	4Q 92	4c
Sausage, Jimmy Dean, 100% pork	lb	2.58	4Q 92	4c
Shortening, vegetable, Crisco	3-lb can	2.44	4Q 92	4c
Soft drink, Coca Cola	2 liter	0.99	4Q 92	4c
Steak, T-bone	lb	4.97	4Q 92	4c
Sugar, cane or beet	4 lb	1.65	4Q 92	4c
Tomatoes, Hunt's or Del Monte	14.5-oz can	0.85	4Q 92	4c
Tuna, chunk, light	6.125-6.5 oz can	0.57	4Q 92	4c
Health Care				
ACCRA Index, Health Care		90.00	4Q 92	4c
Analgesic, Aspirin, Bayer, 325 mg tablets	100	4.00	4Q 92	4c
Dentist's fee, adult teeth cleaning and periodic oral exam	visit	43.50	4Q 92	4c
Doctor's fee, routine exam, established patient	visit	32.50	4Q 92	4c
Hospital care, semiprivate room	day	300.00	4Q 92	4c
Household Goods				
Appliance repair, home, service call, washing machine	min labor charge	22.45	4Q 92	4c
Laundry detergent, Tide Ultra, Bold, or Cheer	42 oz	3.25	4Q 92	4c
Tissues, facial, Kleenex brand	175-count box	1.14	4Q 92	4c
Housing				
ACCRA Index, Housing		107.00	4Q 92	4c
House, 1,800 sq ft, 8,000 sq ft lot, new, urban	total	122500	4Q 92	4c
House payment, principal and interest, 25% down payment	month	687	4Q 92	4c
Mortgage rate, incl. points & origination fee, 30-year fixed or adjustable rate	percent	8.20	4Q 92	4c
Rent, apartment, 2 bedrooms - 1-1/2 to 2 baths, unfurnished, 950 sq ft, water	month	460	4Q 92	4c
Personal Goods				
Shampoo, Alberto VO5	15 oz	1.04	4Q 92	4c
Toothpaste, Crest or Colgate	6-7 oz	1.27	4Q 92	4c
Personal Services				
Dry cleaning, man's 2-piece suit		7.31	4Q 92	4c
Haircare, woman's shampoo, trim and blow-dry		15.81	4Q 92	4c
Haircut, man's barbershop, no styling		8.18	4Q 92	4c

Fond du Lac, WI - continued

Item	Per	Value	Date	Ref.
Restaurant Food				
Chicken, fried, thigh and drumstick		1.78	4Q 92	4c
Hamburger with cheese	1/4 lb	1.77	4Q 92	4c
Pizza, Pizza Hut or Pizza Inn, cheese, thin crust	12-13 in	8.91	4Q 92	4c
Transportation				
ACCRA Index, Transportation		97.90	4Q 92	4c
Bus fare	one-way	0.60	3/93	2c
Bus fare, up to 10 miles	one-way	0.60	4Q 92	4c
Tire balance, computer or spin balance, front	wheel	6.48	4Q 92	4c
Utilities				
ACCRA Index, Utilities		89.80	4Q 92	4c
Electricity, partial electric and other energy, 1,800 sq ft living area new home	month	41.37	4Q 92	4c

Fort Collins, CO

Item	Per	Value	Date	Ref.
Composite ACCRA index		102.70	4Q 92	4c
Alcoholic Beverages				
Beer, Miller Lite or Budweiser, 12-oz containers	6 pack	4.05	4Q 92	4c
Liquor, J & B Scotch	750 ml	16.95	4Q 92	4c
Wine, Gallo Chablis blanc, 1.5 liter	bottle	4.69	4Q 92	4c
Child Care				
Child care fee, average, center	hour	1.71	90	65r
Child care fee, average, nonregulated family day care	hour	1.32	90	65r
Child care fee, average, regulated family day care	hour	1.86	90	65r
Clothing				
Jeans, man's denim		36.80	4Q 92	4c
Shirt, man's dress shirt		19.80	4Q 92	4c
Undervest, boy's size 10-14, cotton	3	5.75	4Q 92	4c
Communications				
Long-distance telephone service, day, initial minute, 0-100 miles	min	0.11-0.35	91	12s
Long-distance telephone service, day, additional minute, 0-100 miles	min	0.13-0.27	91	12s
Long-distance telephone service, evenings/weekends, 0-100 mi, initial minute	min	0.08-0.17	91	12s
Long-distance telephone service, evenings/weekends, 0-100 mi, additional minute	min	0.06-0.14	91	12s
Newspaper subscription, daily and Sunday home delivery, large-city	month	8.70	4Q 92	4c
Telephone, flat rate	month	14.22	91	11c
Telephone bill, family of four	month	20.21	4Q 92	4c
Education				
Board, 4-yr private college/university	year	2162	91	22s
Board, 4-yr public college/university	year	1747	91	22s
Expenditures, local gov't, public elementary/secondary	pupil	5259	92	20s
Room, 4-year private college/university	year	1984	91	22s
Room, 4-year public college/university	year	1546	91	22s
Tuition, 2-year private college/university	year	6731	91	22s
Tuition, 2-year public college/university	year	943	91	22s
Tuition, 4-year private college/university	year	9516	91	22s
Tuition, 4-year public college/university, in-state	year	1919	91	22s
Energy and Fuels				
Coal	mil Btu	1.07	90	64s
Energy	mil Btu	8.14	90	64s
Energy, combined forms, 1,800 sq ft heating area	month	72.45	4Q 92	4c
Energy, exc electricity, 1,800 sq ft heating area	month	31.55	4Q 92	4c

Values are in dollars or fractions of dollars. In the column headed *Ref*, references are shown to sources. Each reference is followed by a letter. These refer to the geographical level for which data were reported: s=State, r=Region, and c=City or metro. The abbreviation *ex* is used to mean *except* or *excluding*; *exp* stands for expenditures. For other abbreviations and further explanations, please see the Introduction.

Fort Collins, CO - continued

Item	Per	Value	Date	Ref.
Energy and Fuels				
Energy exp/householder, 1-family unit	year	372	90	28r
Energy exp/householder, <1,000 sq ft heating area	year	335	90	28r
Energy exp/householder, 1,000-1,999 sq ft heating area	year	365	90	28r
Energy exp/householder, 2,000+ sq ft heating area	year	411	90	28r
Energy exp/householder, mobile home	year	305	90	28r
Energy exp/householder, multifamily	year	372	90	28r
Gas, natural	mil Btu	3.92	90	64s
Gas, natural	000 cu ft	4.59	91	46s
Gas, natural, exp	year	446	91	46s
Gasoline, motor	gal	1.23	4Q 92	4c
Gasoline, unleaded regular	mil Btu	9.29	90	64s
Entertainment				
Bowling, evening rate	game	2.12	4Q 92	4c
Miniature golf admission	adult	6.18	92	1r
Miniature golf admission	child	5.14	92	1r
Monopoly game, Parker Brothers', No. 9		11.99	4Q 92	4c
Movie	admission	6.33	4Q 92	4c
Tennis balls, yellow, Wilson or Penn, 3	can	2.99	4Q 92	4c
Waterpark admission	adult	11.00	92	1r
Waterpark admission	child	8.55	92	1r
Funerals				
Casket, 18-gauge steel, velvet interior		1929.04	91	24r
Cosmetology, hair care, etc.		88.52	91	24r
Embalming		249.33	91	24r
Facility use for ceremony		182.75	91	24r
Hearse, local		110.04	91	24r
Limousine, local		66.67	91	24r
Remains to funeral home, transfer		84.58	91	24r
Service charge, professional		593.00	91	24r
Vault, concrete, non-metallic liner		647.38	91	24r
Viewing facilities, use		99.87	91	24r
Goods and Services				
ACCRA Index, Miscellaneous Goods and Services		103.40	4Q 92	4c
Groceries				
ACCRA Index, Groceries		104.40	4Q 92	4c
Apples, Red Delicious	lb	0.80	4/93	16r
Babyfood, strained vegetables, lowest price	4-4.5 oz jar	0.33	4Q 92	4c
Bacon	lb	1.79	4/93	16r
Bananas	lb	0.57	4Q 92	4c
Bananas	lb	0.53	4/93	16r
Bologna, all beef or mixed	lb	2.67	4/93	16r
Bread, white	24 oz	0.78	4Q 92	4c
Bread, white, pan	lb	0.81	4/93	16r
Carrots, short trimmed and topped	lb	0.39	4/93	16r
Cheese, Kraft grated Parmesan	8-oz canister	3.06	4Q 92	4c
Chicken, fresh, whole	lb	0.94	4/93	16r
Chicken, fryer, whole	lb	0.59	4Q 92	4c
Chicken breast, bone-in	lb	2.19	4/93	16r
Chuck roast, graded and ungraded, ex USDA prime and choice	lb	2.26	4/93	16r
Cigarettes, Winston	carton	16.84	4Q 92	4c
Coffee, 100% ground roast, all sizes	lb	2.33	4/93	16r
Coffee, vacuum-packed	13-oz can	2.14	4Q 92	4c
Corn, frozen	10 oz	0.69	4Q 92	4c
Corn Flakes, Kellogg's or Post Toasties	18 oz	1.92	4Q 92	4c
Eggs, Grade A large	doz	0.76	4Q 92	4c
Eggs, Grade AA large	doz	1.18	4/93	16r
Flour, white, all purpose	lb	0.22	4/93	16r
Grapefruit	lb	0.52	4/93	16r
Grapes, Thompson Seedless	lb	1.50	4/93	16r

Fort Collins, CO - continued

Item	Per	Value	Date	Ref.
Groceries - continued				
Ground beef, 100% beef	lb	1.44	4/93	16r
Ground beef, lean and extra lean	lb	2.34	4/93	16r
Ground beef or hamburger	lb	1.45	4Q 92	4c
Ham, boneless, excluding canned	lb	2.56	4/93	16r
Honey, jar	8 oz	0.99-1.19	92	5r
Honey, jar	lb	1.35-1.97	92	5r
Honey, squeeze bear	12-oz	1.00-1.89	92	5r
Ice cream, prepackaged, bulk, regular	1/2 gal	2.40	4/93	16r
Lemons	lb	0.81	4/93	16r
Lettuce, iceberg	head	0.92	4Q 92	4c
Lettuce, iceberg	lb	0.84	4/93	16r
Margarine, Blue Bonnet or Parkay cubes	lb	0.78	4Q 92	4c
Margarine, stick	lb	0.81	4/93	16r
Milk, whole	1/2 gal	1.68	4Q 92	4c
Orange juice, Minute Maid frozen	12-oz can	1.42	4Q 92	4c
Oranges, navel	lb	0.48	4/93	16r
Peaches	29-oz can	1.60	4Q 92	4c
Peas Sweet, Del Monte or Green Giant	15-17 oz can	0.75	4Q 92	4c
Pork chops, center cut, bone-in	lb	3.25	4/93	16r
Potato chips	16 oz	2.89	4/93	16r
Potatoes, white	lb	0.38	4/93	16r
Potatoes, white or red	10-lb sack	2.31	4Q 92	4c
Round roast, graded & ungraded, ex USDA prime & choice	lb	3.00	4/93	16r
Round roast, USDA choice, boneless	lb	3.16	4/93	16r
Sausage, Jimmy Dean, 100% pork	lb	3.57	4Q 92	4c
Shortening, vegetable oil blends	lb	0.86	4/93	16r
Shortening, vegetable, Crisco	3-lb can	2.33	4Q 92	4c
Soft drink, Coca Cola	2 liter	1.03	4Q 92	4c
Spaghetti and macaroni	lb	0.84	4/93	16r
Steak, round, graded & ungraded, ex USDA prime & choice	lb	3.34	4/93	16r
Steak, round, USDA choice, boneless	lb	3.24	4/93	16r
Steak, sirloin, graded & ungraded, ex USDA prime & choice	lb	3.75	4/93	16r
Steak, sirloin, USDA choice, boneless	lb	4.49	4/93	16r
Steak, T-bone	lb	4.81	4Q 92	4c
Sugar, cane or beet	4 lb	1.37	4Q 92	4c
Sugar, white	lb	0.41	4/93	16r
Sugar, white, 33-80 oz pk	lb	0.38	4/93	16r
Tomatoes, field grown	lb	1.01	4/93	16r
Tomatoes, Hunt's or Del Monte	14.5-oz can	0.73	4Q 92	4c
Tuna, chunk, light	6.125-6.5 oz can	0.79	4Q 92	4c
Turkey, frozen, whole	lb	1.04	4/93	16r
Health Care				
ACCRA Index, Health Care		112.80	4Q 92	4c
Analgesic, Aspirin, Bayer, 325 mg tablets	100	5.22	4Q 92	4c
Childbirth, cesarean, hospital		5533	91	62r
Childbirth, cesarean, physician's fee		2053	91	62r
Childbirth, normal, hospital		2745	91	62r
Childbirth, normal, physician's fee		1492	91	62r
Dentist's fee, adult teeth cleaning and periodic oral exam	visit	48.40	4Q 92	4c
Doctor's fee, routine exam, established patient	visit	44.00	4Q 92	4c
Hospital care, semiprivate room	day	395.00	4Q 92	4c
Medical insurance premium, per employee, small group comprehensive	month	306.60	10/91	25c
Medical plan per employee	year	3218	91	45r
Mental health care, exp	capita	28.84-37.59	90	38s
Mental health care, exp, state mental health agency	capita	33.55	90	38s

Values are in dollars or fractions of dollars. In the column headed *Ref*, references are shown to sources. Each reference is followed by a letter. These refer to the geographical level for which data were reported: s=State, r=Region, and c=City or metro. The abbreviation *ex* is used to mean *except* or *excluding*; *exp* stands for expenditures. For other abbreviations and further explanations, please see the Introduction.

Fort Collins, CO - continued

Item	Per	Value	Date	Ref.
Health Care				
Mental health care, hospital psychiatric services, non-Federal, exp	capita	11.38	88	38s
Mental health care, mental health organization, multiservice, exp	capita	21.76	88	38s
Mental health care, psychiatric hospitals, private, exp	capita	14.39	88	38s
Mental health care, psychiatric out-patient clinics, freestanding, exp	capita	0.11	88	38s
Mental health care, state and county mental hospitals, exp	capita	19.03	88	38s
Mental health care, VA medical centers, exp	capita	3.80	88	38s
Physician fee, family practice, first-visit		111.00	91	62r
Physician fee, family practice, revisit		45.00	91	62r
Physician fee, general practice, first-visit		100.00	91	62r
Physician fee, general practice, revisit		40.00	91	62r
Physician fee, internal medicine, first-visit		137.00	91	62r
Physician fee, internal medicine, revisit		48.00	91	62r
Physician fee, median, neurosurgeon, first-visit		157.00	91	62r
Physician fee, median, nonsurgical specialist, first-visit		131.00	91	62r
Physician fee, median, orthopedic surgeon, first-visit		124.00	91	62r
Physician fee, median, plastic surgeon, first-visit		88.00	91	62r
Physician fee, median, surgical specialist, first-visit		100.00	91	62r
Physician fee, neurosurgeon, revisit		51.00	91	62r
Physician fee, nonsurgical specialist, revisit		47.00	91	62r
Physician fee, obstetrics/gynecology, first-visit		95.00	91	62r
Physician fee, obstetrics/gynecology, revisit		50.00	91	62r
Physician fee, orthopedic surgeon, revisit		51.00	91	62r
Physician fee, pediatrician, first-visit		81.00	91	62r
Physician fee, pediatrician, revisit		42.00	91	62r
Physician fee, plastic surgeon, revisit		48.00	91	62r
Physician fee, surgical specialist, revisit		49.00	91	62r
Substance abuse, hospital ancillary charge	incident	1040	90	70s
Substance abuse, hospital physician charge	incident	380	90	70s
Substance abuse, hospital room and board	incident	4880	90	70s
Household Goods				
Appliance repair, home, service call, washing machine	min labor charge	23.00	4Q 92	4c
Laundry detergent, Tide Ultra, Bold, or Cheer	42 oz	2.99	4Q 92	4c
Tissues, facial, Kleenex brand	175-count box	1.03	4Q 92	4c
Housing				
ACCRA Index, Housing		109.60	4Q 92	4c
House, 1,800 sq ft, 8,000 sq ft lot, new, urban	total	123784	4Q 92	4c
House payment, principal and interest, 25% down payment	month	688	4Q 92	4c
Mortgage rate, incl. points & origination fee, 30-year fixed or adjustable rate	percent	8.10	4Q 92	4c
Rent, apartment, 2 bedrooms - 1-1/2 to 2 baths, unfurnished, 950 sq ft, water	month	509	4Q 92	4c
Rental unit, 1 bedroom	month	494	93	23c
Rental unit, 2 bedroom	month	581	93	23c
Rental unit, 3 bedroom	month	726	93	23c
Rental unit, 4 bedroom	month	815	93	23c
Rental unit, efficiency	month	406	93	23c
Insurance and Pensions				
Auto insurance, private passenger	year	684.81	91	63s

Fort Collins, CO - continued

Item	Per	Value	Date	Ref.
Personal Goods				
Shampoo, Alberto VO5	15 oz	1.26	4Q 92	4c
Toothpaste, Crest or Colgate	6-7 oz	2.04	4Q 92	4c
Personal Services				
Dry cleaning, man's 2-piece suit		5.79	4Q 92	4c
Haircare, woman's shampoo, trim and blow-dry		15.79	4Q 92	4c
Haircut, man's barbershop, no styling		7.85	4Q 92	4c
Restaurant Food				
Chicken, fried, thigh and drumstick		1.95	4Q 92	4c
Hamburger with cheese	1/4 lb	1.95	4Q 92	4c
Pizza, Pizza Hut or Pizza Inn, cheese, thin crust	12-13 in	7.69	4Q 92	4c
Taxes				
Tax, cigarette	pack	20	91	77s
Tax, gasoline	gal	22	91	77s
Taxes, state	capita	951	91	77s
Transportation				
ACCRA Index, Transportation		103.40	4Q 92	4c
Bus fare	one-way	0.55	3/93	2c
Driver's license fee		15.00	12/90	43s
Tire balance, computer or spin balance, front	wheel	6.40	4Q 92	4c
Travel				
Business travel	day	178.00	4/93	89r
Utilities				
ACCRA Index, Utilities		70.10	4Q 92	4c
Electricity	mil Btu	17.31	90	64s
Electricity, partial electric and other energy, 1,800 sq ft living area new home	month	40.90	4Q 92	4c
Electricity, residential	KWh	7.70	2/93	94s

Fort Dodge, IA

Item	Per	Value	Date	Ref.
Composite ACCRA index		98.90	4Q 92	4c
Alcoholic Beverages				
Beer, Miller Lite or Budweiser, 12-oz containers	6 pack	3.75	4Q 92	4c
Liquor, J & B Scotch	750 ml	18.75	4Q 92	4c
Wine, Gallo Chablis blanc, 1.5 liter	bottle	5.08	4Q 92	4c
Clothing				
Jeans, man's denim		31.66	4Q 92	4c
Shirt, man's dress shirt		25.50	4Q 92	4c
Undervest, boy's size 10-14, cotton	3	3.23	4Q 92	4c
Communications				
Newspaper subscription, daily and Sunday home delivery, large-city	month	8.70	4Q 92	4c
Telephone, residential, private line, rotary, unlimited calling	month	12.90	10/91	78c
Telephone bill, family of four	month	13.97	4Q 92	4c
Energy and Fuels				
Energy, combined forms, 1,800 sq ft heating area	month	119.59	4Q 92	4c
Energy, exc electricity, 1,800 sq ft heating area	month	54.49	4Q 92	4c
Gasoline, motor	gal	1.18	4Q 92	4c
Entertainment				
Bowling, evening rate	game	1.95	4Q 92	4c
Monopoly game, Parker Brothers', No. 9		9.98	4Q 92	4c
Movie	admission	4.50	4Q 92	4c
Tennis balls, yellow, Wilson or Penn, 3	can	1.92	4Q 92	4c
Goods and Services				
ACCRA Index, Miscellaneous Goods and Services		93.80	4Q 92	4c

Values are in dollars or fractions of dollars. In the column headed *Ref*, references are shown to sources. Each reference is followed by a letter. These refer to the geographical level for which data were reported: s=State, r=Region, and c=City or metro. The abbreviation *ex* is used to mean *except* or *excluding*; *exp* stands for expenditures. For other abbreviations and further explanations, please see the Introduction.

Fort Dodge, IA - continued

Item	Per	Value	Date	Ref.
Groceries				
ACCRA Index, Groceries		97.00	4Q 92	4c
Babyfood, strained vegetables, lowest price	4-4.5 oz jar	0.35	4Q 92	4c
Bananas	lb	0.49	4Q 92	4c
Bread, white	24 oz	0.70	4Q 92	4c
Cheese, Kraft grated Parmesan	8-oz canister	3.39	4Q 92	4c
Chicken, fryer, whole	lb	0.79	4Q 92	4c
Cigarettes, Winston	carton	18.59	4Q 92	4c
Coffee, vacuum-packed	13-oz can	1.90	4Q 92	4c
Corn, frozen	10 oz	0.66	4Q 92	4c
Corn Flakes, Kellogg's or Post Toasties	18 oz	1.95	4Q 92	4c
Eggs, Grade A large	doz	0.68	4Q 92	4c
Ground beef or hamburger	lb	1.28	4Q 92	4c
Lettuce, iceberg	head	0.86	4Q 92	4c
Margarine, Blue Bonnet or Parkay cubes	lb	0.54	4Q 92	4c
Milk, whole	1/2 gal	1.22	4Q 92	4c
Orange juice, Minute Maid frozen	12-oz can	1.54	4Q 92	4c
Peaches	29-oz can	1.40	4Q 92	4c
Peas Sweet, Del Monte or Green Giant	15-17 oz can	0.41	4Q 92	4c
Potatoes, white or red	10-lb sack	2.06	4Q 92	4c
Sausage, Jimmy Dean, 100% pork	lb	2.31	4Q 92	4c
Shortening, vegetable, Crisco	3-lb can	2.05	4Q 92	4c
Soft drink, Coca Cola	2 liter	1.31	4Q 92	4c
Steak, T-bone	lb	4.99	4Q 92	4c
Sugar, cane or beet	4 lb	1.58	4Q 92	4c
Tomatoes, Hunt's or Del Monte	14.5-oz can	0.69	4Q 92	4c
Tuna, chunk, light	6.125-6.5 oz can	0.49	4Q 92	4c
Health Care				
ACCRA Index, Health Care		86.70	4Q 92	4c
Analgesic, Aspirin, Bayer, 325 mg tablets	100	5.39	4Q 92	4c
Dentist's fee, adult teeth cleaning and periodic oral exam	visit	37.00	4Q 92	4c
Doctor's fee, routine exam, established patient	visit	29.43	4Q 92	4c
Hospital care, semiprivate room	day	160.00	90	27c
Hospital care, semiprivate room	day	325.00	4Q 92	4c
Household Goods				
Appliance repair, home, service call, washing machine	min labor charge	29.33	4Q 92	4c
Laundry detergent, Tide Ultra, Bold, or Cheer	42 oz	3.86	4Q 92	4c
Tissues, facial, Kleenex brand	175-count box	1.09	4Q 92	4c
Housing				
ACCRA Index, Housing		102.30	4Q 92	4c
House, 1,800 sq ft, 8,000 sq ft lot, new, urban	total	117000	4Q 92	4c
House payment, principal and interest, 25% down payment	month	659	4Q 92	4c
Mortgage rate, incl. points & origination fee, 30-year fixed or adjustable rate	percent	8.25	4Q 92	4c
Rent, apartment, 2 bedrooms - 1-1/2 to 2 baths, unfurnished, 950 sq ft, water	month	435	4Q 92	4c
Personal Goods				
Shampoo, Alberto VO5	15 oz	1.08	4Q 92	4c
Toothpaste, Crest or Colgate	6-7 oz	1.95	4Q 92	4c

Fort Dodge, IA - continued

Item	Per	Value	Date	Ref.
Personal Services				
Dry cleaning, man's 2-piece suit		6.48	4Q 92	4c
Haircare, woman's shampoo, trim and blow-dry		16.00	4Q 92	4c
Haircut, man's barbershop, no styling		7.67	4Q 92	4c
Restaurant Food				
Chicken, fried, thigh and drumstick		1.90	4Q 92	4c
Hamburger with cheese	1/4 lb	1.87	4Q 92	4c
Pizza, Pizza Hut or Pizza Inn, cheese, thin crust	12-13 in	7.79	4Q 92	4c
Transportation				
ACCRA Index, Transportation		109.70	4Q 92	4c
Tire balance, computer or spin balance, front	wheel	7.50	4Q 92	4c
Utilities				
ACCRA Index, Utilities		105.80	4Q 92	4c
Electricity, partial electric and other energy, 1,800 sq ft living area new home	month	65.10	4Q 92	4c

Fort Lauderdale-Hollywood-Pompano Beach, FL

Item	Per	Value	Date	Ref.
Child Care				
Child care fee, average, center	hour	1.29	90	65r
Child care fee, average, nonregulated family day care	hour	0.89	90	65r
Child care fee, average, regulated family day care	hour	1.32	90	65r
Communications				
Long-distance telephone service, day, initial minute, 0-100 miles	min	0.15-0.20	91	12s
Long-distance telephone service, day, additional minute, 0-100 miles	min	0.08-0.20	91	12s
Long-distance telephone service, evenings/weekends, 0-100 mi, initial minute	min	0.09-0.12	91	12s
Long-distance telephone service, evenings/weekends, 0-100 mi, additional minute	min	0.05-0.12	91	12s
Telephone, flat rate	month	10.65	91	11c
Education				
Board, 4-yr private college/university	year	1924	91	22s
Board, 4-yr public college/university	year	1955	91	22s
Expenditures, local gov't, public elementary/secondary	pupil	5235	92	20s
Room, 4-year private college/university	year	1904	91	22s
Room, 4-year public college/university	year	1510	91	22s
Tuition, 2-year private college/university	year	4751	91	22s
Tuition, 2-year public college/university	year	788	91	22s
Tuition, 4-year private college/university	year	7992	91	22s
Tuition, 4-year public college/university, in-state	year	1337	91	22s
Energy and Fuels				
Coal	mil Btu	1.85	90	64s
Energy	mil Btu	10.58	90	64s
Energy exp/householder, 1-family unit	year	487	90	28r
Energy exp/householder, <1,000 sq ft heating area	year	393	90	28r
Energy exp/householder, 1,000-1,999 sq ft heating area	year	442	90	28r
Energy exp/householder, 2,000+ sq ft heating area	year	577	90	28r
Energy exp/householder, mobile home	year	366	90	28r
Energy exp/householder, multifamily	year	382	90	28r
Gas, natural	mil Btu	3.21	90	64s
Gas, natural	000 cu ft	8.98	91	46s
Gas, natural, exp	year	248	91	46s
Gasoline, unleaded regular	mil Btu	8.85	90	64s

Values are in dollars or fractions of dollars. In the column headed *Ref*, references are shown to sources. Each reference is followed by a letter. These refer to the geographical level for which data were reported: s = State, r = Region, and c = City or metro. The abbreviation *ex* is used to mean *except* or *excluding*; *exp* stands for expenditures. For other abbreviations and further explanations, please see the Introduction.

Fort Lauderdale-Hollywood-Pompano Beach, FL - continued

Item	Per	Value	Date	Ref.
Entertainment				
Miniature golf admission	adult	6.18	92	1r
Miniature golf admission	child	5.14	92	1r
Waterpark admission	adult	11.00	92	1r
Waterpark admission	child	8.55	92	1r
Funerals				
Casket, 18-gauge steel, velvet interior		2029.08	91	24r
Cosmetology, hair care, etc.		75.10	91	24r
Embalming		249.24	91	24r
Facility use for ceremony		162.27	91	24r
Hearse, local		114.04	91	24r
Limousine, local		88.57	91	24r
Remains to funeral home, transfer		92.61	91	24r
Service charge, professional		682.42	91	24r
Vault, concrete, non-metallic liner		798.70	91	24r
Viewing facilities, use		163.86	91	24r
Groceries				
Apples, Red Delicious	lb	0.79	4/93	16r
Bacon	lb	1.75	4/93	16r
Bananas	lb	0.42	4/93	16r
Beef, stew, boneless	lb	2.61	4/93	16r
Bologna, all beef or mixed	lb	2.24	4/93	16r
Bread, white, pan	lb	0.64	4/93	16r
Bread, whole wheat, pan	lb	0.96	4/93	16r
Cabbage	lb	0.37	4/93	16r
Carrots, short trimmed and topped	lb	0.47	4/93	16r
Celery	lb	0.64	4/93	16r
Cheese, American	lb	2.98	4/93	16r
Cheese, Cheddar	lb	3.28	4/93	16r
Chicken, fresh, whole	lb	0.77	4/93	16r
Chicken breast, bone-in	lb	1.92	4/93	16r
Chicken legs, bone-in	lb	1.06	4/03	16r
Chuck roast, graded and ungraded, ex USDA prime and choice	lb	2.40	4/93	16r
Chuck roast, USDA choice, bone-in	lb	2.19	4/93	16r
Chuck roast, USDA choice, boneless	lb	2.38	4/93	16r
Coffee, 100% ground roast, all sizes	lb	2.48	4/93	16r
Crackers, soda, salted	lb	1.15	4/93	16r
Eggs, Grade A large	doz	0.96	4/93	16r
Flour, white, all purpose	lb	0.24	4/93	16r
Frankfurters, all meat or all beef	lb	2.01	4/93	16r
Grapefruit	lb	0.44	4/93	16r
Grapes, Thompson Seedless	lb	1.40	4/93	16r
Ground beef, 100% beef	lb	1.58	4/93	16r
Ground beef, lean and extra lean	lb	2.09	4/93	16r
Ground chuck, 100% beef	lb	1.98	4/93	16r
Ham, boneless, excluding canned	lb	2.89	4/93	16r
Ham, picnic, shoulder, bone-in, smoked	lb	1.02	4/93	16r
Ham, rump or steak half, bone-in, smoked	lb	1.48	4/93	16r
Ice cream, prepackaged, bulk, regular	1/2 gal	2.41	4/93	16r
Lemons	lb	1.05	4/93	16r
Lettuce, iceberg	lb	0.81	4/93	16r
Margarine, stick	lb	0.88	4/93	16r
Oranges, navel	lb	0.55	4/93	16r
Pears, Anjou	lb	0.92	4/93	16r
Pork chops, center cut, bone-in	lb	3.13	4/93	16r
Potato chips	16 oz	2.94	4/93	16r
Potatoes, white	lb	0.43	4/93	16r
Rib roast, USDA choice, bone-in	lb	4.63	4/93	16r
Rice, white, long grain, uncooked	lb	0.45	4/93	16r
Round roast, graded & ungraded, ex USDA prime & choice	lb	3.03	4/93	16r
Round roast, USDA choice, boneless	lb	3.09	4/93	16r
Sausage, fresh, loose	lb	2.08	4/93	16r
Short ribs, bone-in	lb	2.66	4/93	16r
Shortening, vegetable oil blends	lb	0.69	4/93	16r
Spaghetti and macaroni	lb	0.81	4/93	16r
Steak, rib eye, USDA choice, boneless	lb	6.24	4/93	16r
Steak, round, graded & ungraded, ex USDA prime & choice	lb	3.31	4/93	16r
Steak, round, USDA choice, boneless	lb	3.34	4/93	16r

Fort Lauderdale-Hollywood-Pompano Beach, FL - continued

Item	Per	Value	Date	Ref.
Groceries - continued				
Steak, sirloin, graded & ungraded, ex USDA prime & choice	lb	4.19	4/93	16r
Steak, sirloin, USDA choice, boneless	lb	4.46	4/93	16r
Steak, T-bone, USDA choice, bone-in	lb	5.25	4/93	16r
Strawberries, dry pint	12 oz	0.92	4/93	16r
Sugar, white	lb	0.39	4/93	16r
Sugar, white, 33-80 oz pk	lb	0.38	4/93	16r
Tomatoes, field grown	lb	0.88	4/93	16r
Tuna, chunk, light	lb	1.79	4/93	16r
Turkey, frozen, whole	lb	1.04	4/93	16r
Yogurt, natural, fruit flavored	1/2 pint	0.57	4/93	16r
Health Care				
Childbirth, cesarean, hospital		5034	91	62r
Childbirth, cesarean, physician's fee		2053	91	62r
Childbirth, normal, hospital		2712	91	62r
Childbirth, normal, physician's fee		1492	91	62r
Hospital care, semiprivate room	day	236.27	90	27c
Medical insurance premium, per employee, small group comprehensive	month	536.55	10/91	25c
Medical plan per employee	year	3495	91	45r
Mental health care, exp	capita	28.84-37.59	90	38s
Mental health care, exp, state mental health agency	capita	37.49	90	38s
Mental health care, hospital psychiatric services, non-Federal, exp	capita	9.11	88	38s
Mental health care, mental health organization, multiservice, exp	capita	16.21	88	38s
Mental health care, psychiatric hospitals, private, exp	capita	22.26	88	38s
Mental health care, psychiatric out-patient clinics, freestanding, exp	capita	0.89	88	38s
Mental health care, psychiatric partial-care organizations, freestanding, exp	capita	0.41	88	38s
Mental health care, state and county mental hospitals, exp	capita	16.25	88	38s
Mental health care, VA medical centers, exp	capita	1.69	88	38s
Physician fee, family practice, first-visit		75.00	91	62r
Physician fee, family practice, revisit		34.00	91	62r
Physician fee, general practice, first-visit		61.00	91	62r
Physician fee, general practice, revisit		32.00	91	62r
Physician fee, general surgeon, first-visit		64.00	91	62r
Physician fee, general surgeon, revisit		40.00	91	62r
Physician fee, internal medicine, first-visit		98.00	91	62r
Physician fee, internal medicine, revisit		40.00	91	62r
Physician fee, median, neurosurgeon, first-visit		130.00	91	62r
Physician fee, median, nonsurgical specialist, first-visit		95.00	91	62r
Physician fee, median, orthopedic surgeon, first-visit		91.00	91	62r
Physician fee, median, plastic surgeon, first-visit		66.00	91	62r
Physician fee, median, surgical specialist, first-visit		62.00	91	62r
Physician fee, neurosurgeon, revisit		50.00	91	62r
Physician fee, nonsurgical specialist, revisit		40.00	91	62r
Physician fee, obstetrics/gynecology, first-visit		64.00	91	62r
Physician fee, obstetrics/gynecology, revisit		41.00	91	62r
Physician fee, orthopedic surgeon, revisit		40.00	91	62r
Physician fee, pediatrician, first-visit		49.00	91	62r
Physician fee, pediatrician, revisit		33.00	91	62r
Physician fee, plastic surgeon, revisit		43.00	91	62r
Physician fee, surgical specialist, revisit		37.00	91	62r
Substance abuse, hospital ancillary charge	incident	1390	90	70s
Substance abuse, hospital physician charge	incident	770	90	70s
Substance abuse, hospital room and board	incident	5600	90	70s

Values are in dollars or fractions of dollars. In the column headed *Ref*, references are shown to sources. Each reference is followed by a letter. These refer to the geographical level for which data were reported: s = State, r = Region, and c = City or metro. The abbreviation *ex* is used to mean *except* or *excluding*; *exp* stands for expenditures. For other abbreviations and further explanations, please see the Introduction.

Fort Lauderdale-Hollywood-Pompano Beach, FL - continued

Item	Per	Value	Date	Ref.
Housing				
Home, median price	unit	99.10		26c
Rental unit, 1 bedroom	month	573	93	23c
Rental unit, 2 bedroom	month	674	93	23c
Rental unit, 3 bedroom	month	843	93	23c
Rental unit, 4 bedroom	month	944	93	23c
Rental unit, efficiency	month	472	93	23c
Insurance and Pensions				
Auto insurance, private passenger	year	727.60	91	63s
Taxes				
Tax, cigarette	pack	33.90	91	77s
Tax, gasoline	gal	11.60	91	77s
Taxes, state	capita	1037	91	77s
Transportation				
Auto rental, average	day	38.25	6/91	60c
Bus fare	one-way	0.85	3/93	2c
Driver's license fee		15.00	12/90	43s
Limo fare, airport-city, average	day	9.00	6/91	60c
Taxi fare, airport-city, average	day	8.00	6/91	60c
Travel				
Breakfast	day	4.79	6/91	60c
Business travel	day	193.00	4/93	89r
Dinner	day	19.51	6/91	60c
Lodging	day	147.91	91	60c
Lunch	day	9.19	6/91	60c
Utilities				
Electricity	mil Btu	20.62	90	64s

Fort Myers-Cape Coral, FL

Item	Per	Value	Date	Ref.
Child Care				
Child care fee, average, center	hour	1.29	90	65r
Child care fee, average, nonregulated family day care	hour	0.89	90	65r
Child care fee, average, regulated family day care	hour	1.32	90	65r
Communications				
Long-distance telephone service, day, initial minute, 0-100 miles	min	0.15-0.20	91	12s
Long-distance telephone service, day, additional minute, 0-100 miles	min	0.08-0.20	91	12s
Long-distance telephone service, evenings/weekends, 0-100 mi, initial minute	min	0.09-0.12	91	12s
Long-distance telephone service, evenings/weekends, 0-100 mi, additional minute	min	0.05-0.12	91	12s
Education				
Board, 4-yr private college/university	year	1924	91	22s
Board, 4-yr public college/university	year	1955	91	22s
Expenditures, local gov't, public elementary/secondary	pupil	5235	92	20s
Room, 4-year private college/university	year	1904	91	22s
Room, 4-year public college/university	year	1510	91	22s
Tuition, 2-year private college/university	year	4751	91	22s
Tuition, 2-year public college/university	year	788	91	22s
Tuition, 4-year private college/university	year	7992	91	22s
Tuition, 4-year public college/university, in-state	year	1337	91	22s
Energy and Fuels				
Coal	mil Btu	1.85	90	64s
Energy	mil Btu	10.58	90	64s
Energy exp/householder, 1-family unit	year	487	90	28r
Energy exp/householder, <1,000 sq ft heating area	year	393	90	28r
Energy exp/householder, 1,000-1,999 sq ft heating area	year	442	90	28r
Energy exp/householder, 2,000+ sq ft heating area	year	577	90	28r

Fort Myers-Cape Coral, FL - continued

Item	Per	Value	Date	Ref.
Energy and Fuels - continued				
Energy exp/householder, mobile home	year	366	90	28r
Energy exp/householder, multifamily	year	382	90	28r
Gas, natural	mil Btu	3.21	90	64s
Gas, natural	000 cu ft	8.98	91	46s
Gas, natural, exp	year	248	91	46s
Gasoline, unleaded regular	mil Btu	8.85	90	64s
Entertainment				
Miniature golf admission	adult	6.18	92	1r
Miniature golf admission	child	5.14	92	1r
Waterpark admission	adult	11.00	92	1r
Waterpark admission	child	8.55	92	1r
Funerals				
Casket, 18-gauge steel, velvet interior		2029.08	91	24r
Cosmetology, hair care, etc.		75.10	91	24r
Embalming		249.24	91	24r
Facility use for ceremony		162.27	91	24r
Hearse, local		114.04	91	24r
Limousine, local		88.57	91	24r
Remains to funeral home, transfer		92.61	91	24r
Service charge, professional		682.42	91	24r
Vault, concrete, non-metallic liner		798.70	91	24r
Viewing facilities, use		163.86	91	24r
Groceries				
Apples, Red Delicious	lb	0.79	4/93	16r
Bacon	lb	1.75	4/93	16r
Bananas	lb	0.42	4/93	16r
Beef, stew, boneless	lb	2.61	4/93	16r
Bologna, all beef or mixed	lb	2.24	4/93	16r
Bread, white, pan	lb	0.64	4/93	16r
Bread, whole wheat, pan	lb	0.96	4/93	16r
Cabbage	lb	0.37	4/93	16r
Carrots, short trimmed and topped	lb	0.47	4/93	16r
Celery	lb	0.64	4/93	16r
Cheese, American	lb	2.98	4/93	16r
Cheese, Cheddar	lb	3.28	4/93	16r
Chicken, fresh, whole	lb	0.77	4/93	16r
Chicken breast, bone-in	lb	1.92	4/93	16r
Chicken legs, bone-in	lb	1.06	4/93	16r
Chuck roast, graded and ungraded, ex USDA prime and choice	lb	2.40	4/93	16r
Chuck roast, USDA choice, bone-in	lb	2.19	4/93	16r
Chuck roast, USDA choice, boneless	lb	2.38	4/93	16r
Coffee, 100% ground roast, all sizes	lb	2.48	4/93	16r
Crackers, soda, salted	lb	1.15	4/93	16r
Eggs, Grade A large	doz	0.96	4/93	16r
Flour, white, all purpose	lb	0.24	4/93	16r
Frankfurters, all meat or all beef	lb	2.01	4/93	16r
Grapefruit	lb	0.44	4/93	16r
Grapes, Thompson Seedless	lb	1.40	4/93	16r
Ground beef, 100% beef	lb	1.58	4/93	16r
Ground beef, lean and extra lean	lb	2.09	4/93	16r
Ground chuck, 100% beef	lb	1.98	4/93	16r
Ham, boneless, excluding canned	lb	2.89	4/93	16r
Ham, picnic, shoulder, bone-in, smoked	lb	1.02	4/93	16r
Ham, rump or steak half, bone-in, smoked	lb	1.48	4/93	16r
Ice cream, prepackaged, bulk, regular	1/2 gal	2.41	4/93	16r
Lemons	lb	1.05	4/93	16r
Lettuce, iceberg	lb	0.81	4/93	16r
Margarine, stick	lb	0.88	4/93	16r
Oranges, navel	lb	0.55	4/93	16r
Pears, Anjou	lb	0.92	4/93	16r
Pork chops, center cut, bone-in	lb	3.13	4/93	16r
Potato chips	16 oz	2.94	4/93	16r
Potatoes, white	lb	0.43	4/93	16r
Rib roast, USDA choice, bone-in	lb	4.63	4/93	16r
Rice, white, long grain, uncooked	lb	0.45	4/93	16r
Round roast, graded & ungraded, ex USDA prime & choice	lb	3.03	4/93	16r
Round roast, USDA choice, boneless	lb	3.09	4/93	16r
Sausage, fresh, loose	lb	2.08	4/93	16r

Values are in dollars or fractions of dollars. In the column headed *Ref*, references are shown to sources. Each reference is followed by a letter. These refer to the geographical level for which data were reported: s = State, r = Region, and c = City or metro. The abbreviation *ex* is used to mean *except* or *excluding*; *exp* stands for expenditures. For other abbreviations and further explanations, please see the Introduction.

Fort Myers-Cape Coral, FL - continued

Item	Per	Value	Date	Ref.
Groceries				
Short ribs, bone-in	lb	2.66	4/93	16r
Shortening, vegetable oil blends	lb	0.69	4/93	16r
Spaghetti and macaroni	lb	0.81	4/93	16r
Steak, rib eye, USDA choice, boneless	lb	6.24	4/93	16r
Steak, round, graded & ungraded, ex USDA prime & choice	lb	3.31	4/93	16r
Steak, round, USDA choice, boneless	lb	3.34	4/93	16r
Steak, sirloin, graded & ungraded, ex USDA prime & choice	lb	4.19	4/93	16r
Steak, sirloin, USDA choice, boneless	lb	4.46	4/93	16r
Steak, T-bone, USDA choice, bone-in	lb	5.25	4/93	16r
Strawberries, dry pint	12 oz	0.92	4/93	16r
Sugar, white	lb	0.39	4/93	16r
Sugar, white, 33-80 oz pk	lb	0.38	4/93	16r
Tomatoes, field grown	lb	0.88	4/93	16r
Tuna, chunk, light	lb	1.79	4/93	16r
Turkey, frozen, whole	lb	1.04	4/93	16r
Yogurt, natural, fruit flavored	1/2 pint	0.57	4/93	16r
Health Care				
Childbirth, cesarean, hospital		5034	91	62r
Childbirth, cesarean, physician's fee		2053	91	62r
Childbirth, normal, hospital		2712	91	62r
Childbirth, normal, physician's fee		1492	91	62r
Medical plan per employee	year	3495	91	45r
Mental health care, exp	capita	28.84-37.59	90	38s
Mental health care, exp, state mental health agency	capita	37.49	90	38s
Mental health care, hospital psychiatric services, non-Federal, exp	capita	9.11	88	38s
Mental health care, mental health organization, multiservice, exp	capita	10.21	88	38s
Mental health care, psychiatric hospitals, private, exp	capita	22.26	88	38s
Mental health care, psychiatric out-patient clinics, freestanding, exp	capita	0.89	88	38s
Mental health care, psychiatric partial-care organizations, freestanding, exp	capita	0.41	88	38s
Mental health care, state and county mental hospitals, exp	capita	16.25	88	38s
Mental health care, VA medical centers, exp	capita	1.69	88	38s
Physician fee, family practice, first-visit		75.00	91	62r
Physician fee, family practice, revisit		34.00	91	62r
Physician fee, general practice, first-visit		61.00	91	62r
Physician fee, general practice, revisit		32.00	91	62r
Physician fee, general surgeon, first-visit		64.00	91	62r
Physician fee, general surgeon, revisit		40.00	91	62r
Physician fee, internal medicine, first-visit		98.00	91	62r
Physician fee, internal medicine, revisit		40.00	91	62r
Physician fee, median, neurosurgeon, first-visit		130.00	91	62r
Physician fee, median, nonsurgical specialist, first-visit		95.00	91	62r
Physician fee, median, orthopedic surgeon, first-visit		91.00	91	62r
Physician fee, median, plastic surgeon, first-visit		66.00	91	62r
Physician fee, median, surgical specialist, first-visit		62.00	91	62r
Physician fee, neurosurgeon, revisit		50.00	91	62r
Physician fee, nonsurgical specialist, revisit		40.00	91	62r
Physician fee, obstetrics/gynecology, first-visit		64.00	91	62r
Physician fee, obstetrics/gynecology, revisit		41.00	91	62r
Physician fee, orthopedic surgeon, revisit		40.00	91	62r
Physician fee, pediatrician, first-visit		49.00	91	62r
Physician fee, pediatrician, revisit		33.00	91	62r
Physician fee, plastic surgeon, revisit		43.00	91	62r
Physician fee, surgical specialist, revisit		37.00	91	62r
Substance abuse, hospital ancillary charge	incident	1390	90	70s

Fort Myers-Cape Coral, FL - continued

Item	Per	Value	Date	Ref.
Health Care - continued				
Substance abuse, hospital physician charge	incident	770	90	70s
Substance abuse, hospital room and board	incident	5600	90	70s
Insurance and Pensions				
Auto insurance, private passenger	year	727.60	91	63s
Taxes				
Tax, cigarette	pack	33.90	91	77s
Tax, gasoline	gal	11.60	91	77s
Taxes, state	capita	1037	91	77s
Transportation				
Driver's license fee		15.00	12/90	43s
Travel				
Business travel	day	193.00	4/93	89r
Utilities				
Electricity	mil Btu	20.62	90	64s

Fort Pierce, FL

Item	Per	Value	Date	Ref.
Child Care				
Child care fee, average, center	hour	1.29	90	65r
Child care fee, average, nonregulated family day care	hour	0.89	90	65r
Child care fee, average, regulated family day care	hour	1.32	90	65r
Communications				
Long-distance telephone service, day, initial minute, 0-100 miles	min	0.15-0.20	91	12s
Long-distance telephone service, day, additional minute, 0-100 miles	min	0.08-0.20	91	12s
Long-distance telephone service, evenings/weekends, 0-100 mi, initial minute	min	0.09-0.12	91	12s
Long-distance telephone service, evenings/weekends, 0-100 mi, additional minute	min	0.05-0.12	91	12s
Education				
Board, 4-yr private college/university	year	1924	91	22s
Board, 4-yr public college/university	year	1955	91	22s
Expenditures, local gov't, public elementary/secondary	pupil	5235	92	20s
Room, 4-year private college/university	year	1904	91	22s
Room, 4-year public college/university	year	1510	91	22s
Tuition, 2-year private college/university	year	4751	91	22s
Tuition, 2-year public college/university	year	788	91	22s
Tuition, 4-year private college/university	year	7992	91	22s
Tuition, 4-year public college/university, in-state	year	1337	91	22s
Energy and Fuels				
Coal	mil Btu	1.85	90	64s
Energy	mil Btu	10.58	90	64s
Energy exp/householder, 1-family unit	year	487	90	28r
Energy exp/householder, <1,000 sq ft heating area	year	393	90	28r
Energy exp/householder, 1,000-1,999 sq ft heating area	year	442	90	28r
Energy exp/householder, 2,000+ sq ft heating area	year	577	90	28r
Energy exp/householder, mobile home	year	366	90	28r
Energy exp/householder, multifamily	year	382	90	28r
Gas, natural	mil Btu	3.21	90	64s
Gas, natural	000 cu ft	8.98	91	46s
Gas, natural, exp	year	248	91	46s
Gasoline, unleaded regular	mil Btu	8.85	90	64s
Entertainment				
Miniature golf admission	adult	6.18	92	1r
Miniature golf admission	child	5.14	92	1r

Values are in dollars or fractions of dollars. In the column headed *Ref*, references are shown to sources. Each reference is followed by a letter. These refer to the geographical level for which data were reported: s=State, r=Region, and c=City or metro. The abbreviation *ex* is used to mean *except* or *excluding*; *exp* stands for expenditures. For other abbreviations and further explanations, please see the Introduction.

Fort Pierce, FL - continued

Item	Per	Value	Date	Ref.
Entertainment				
Waterpark admission	adult	11.00	92	1r
Waterpark admission	child	8.55	92	1r
Funerals				
Casket, 18-gauge steel, velvet interior		2029.08	91	24r
Cosmetology, hair care, etc.		75.10	91	24r
Embalming		249.24	91	24r
Facility use for ceremony		162.27	91	24r
Hearse, local		114.04	91	24r
Limousine, local		88.57	91	24r
Remains to funeral home, transfer		92.61	91	24r
Service charge, professional		682.42	91	24r
Vault, concrete, non-metallic liner		798.70	91	24r
Viewing facilities, use		163.86	91	24r
Groceries				
Apples, Red Delicious	lb	0.79	4/93	16r
Bacon	lb	1.75	4/93	16r
Bananas	lb	0.42	4/93	16r
Beef, stew, boneless	lb	2.61	4/93	16r
Bologna, all beef or mixed	lb	2.24	4/93	16r
Bread, white, pan	lb	0.64	4/93	16r
Bread, whole wheat, pan	lb	0.96	4/93	16r
Cabbage	lb	0.37	4/93	16r
Carrots, short trimmed and topped	lb	0.47	4/93	16r
Celery	lb	0.64	4/93	16r
Cheese, American	lb	2.98	4/93	16r
Cheese, Cheddar	lb	3.28	4/93	16r
Chicken, fresh, whole	lb	0.77	4/93	16r
Chicken breast, bone-in	lb	1.92	4/93	16r
Chicken legs, bone-in	lb	1.06	4/93	16r
Chuck roast, graded and ungraded, ex USDA prime and choice	lb	2.40	4/93	16r
Chuck roast, USDA choice, bone-in	lb	2.19	4/93	16r
Chuck roast, USDA choice, boneless	lb	2.38	4/93	16r
Coffee, 100% ground roast, all sizes	lb	2.48	4/93	16r
Crackers, soda, salted	lb	1.15	4/93	16r
Eggs, Grade A large	doz	0.96	4/93	16r
Flour, white, all purpose	lb	0.24	4/93	16r
Frankfurters, all meat or all beef	lb	2.01	4/93	16r
Grapefruit	lb	0.44	4/93	16r
Grapes, Thompson Seedless	lb	1.40	4/93	16r
Ground beef, 100% beef	lb	1.58	4/93	16r
Ground beef, lean and extra lean	lb	2.09	4/93	16r
Ground chuck, 100% beef	lb	1.98	4/93	16r
Ham, boneless, excluding canned	lb	2.89	4/93	16r
Ham, picnic, shoulder, bone-in, smoked	lb	1.02	4/93	16r
Ham, rump or steak half, bone-in, smoked	lb	1.48	4/93	16r
Ice cream, prepackaged, bulk, regular	1/2 gal	2.41	4/93	16r
Lemons	lb	1.05	4/93	16r
Lettuce, iceberg	lb	0.81	4/93	16r
Margarine, stick	lb	0.88	4/93	16r
Oranges, navel	lb	0.55	4/93	16r
Pears, Anjou	lb	0.92	4/93	16r
Pork chops, center cut, bone-in	lb	3.13	4/93	16r
Potato chips	16 oz	2.94	4/93	16r
Potatoes, white	lb	0.43	4/93	16r
Rib roast, USDA choice, bone-in	lb	4.63	4/93	16r
Rice, white, long grain, uncooked	lb	0.45	4/93	16r
Round roast, graded & ungraded, ex USDA prime & choice	lb	3.03	4/93	16r
Round roast, USDA choice, boneless	lb	3.09	4/93	16r
Sausage, fresh, loose	lb	2.08	4/93	16r
Short ribs, bone-in	lb	2.66	4/93	16r
Shortening, vegetable oil blends	lb	0.69	4/93	16r
Spaghetti and macaroni	lb	0.81	4/93	16r
Steak, rib eye, USDA choice, boneless	lb	6.24	4/93	16r
Steak, round, graded & ungraded, ex USDA prime & choice	lb	3.31	4/93	16r
Steak, round, USDA choice, boneless	lb	3.34	4/93	16r
Steak, sirloin, graded & ungraded, ex USDA prime & choice	lb	4.19	4/93	16r
Steak, sirloin, USDA choice, boneless	lb	4.46	4/93	16r

Fort Pierce, FL - continued

Item	Per	Value	Date	Ref.
Groceries - continued				
Steak, T-bone, USDA choice, bone-in	lb	5.25	4/93	16r
Strawberries, dry pint	12 oz	0.92	4/93	16r
Sugar, white	lb	0.39	4/93	16r
Sugar, white, 33-80 oz pk	lb	0.38	4/93	16r
Tomatoes, field grown	lb	0.88	4/93	16r
Tuna, chunk, light	lb	1.79	4/93	16r
Turkey, frozen, whole	lb	1.04	4/93	16r
Yogurt, natural, fruit flavored	1/2 pint	0.57	4/93	16r
Health Care				
Childbirth, cesarean, hospital		5034	91	62r
Childbirth, cesarean, physician's fee		2053	91	62r
Childbirth, normal, hospital		2712	91	62r
Childbirth, normal, physician's fee		1492	91	62r
Medical plan per employee	year	3495	91	45r
Mental health care, exp	capita	28.84-37.59	90	38s
Mental health care, exp, state mental health agency	capita	37.49	90	38s
Mental health care, hospital psychiatric services, non-Federal, exp	capita	9.11	88	38s
Mental health care, mental health organization, multiservice, exp	capita	16.21	88	38s
Mental health care, psychiatric hospitals, private, exp	capita	22.26	88	38s
Mental health care, psychiatric out-patient clinics, freestanding, exp	capita	0.89	88	38s
Mental health care, psychiatric partial-care organizations, freestanding, exp	capita	0.41	88	38s
Mental health care, state and county mental hospitals, exp	capita	16.25	88	38s
Mental health care, VA medical centers, exp	capita	1.69	88	38s
Physician fee, family practice, first-visit		75.00	91	62r
Physician fee, family practice, revisit		34.00	91	62r
Physician fee, general practice, first-visit		61.00	91	62r
Physician fee, general practice, revisit		32.00	91	62r
Physician fee, general surgeon, first-visit		64.00	91	62r
Physician fee, general surgeon, revisit		40.00	91	62r
Physician fee, internal medicine, first-visit		98.00	91	62r
Physician fee, internal medicine, revisit		40.00	91	62r
Physician fee, median, neurosurgeon, first-visit		130.00	91	62r
Physician fee, median, nonsurgical specialist, first-visit		95.00	91	62r
Physician fee, median, orthopedic surgeon, first-visit		91.00	91	62r
Physician fee, median, plastic surgeon, first-visit		66.00	91	62r
Physician fee, median, surgical specialist, first-visit		62.00	91	62r
Physician fee, neurosurgeon, revisit		50.00	91	62r
Physician fee, nonsurgical specialist, revisit		40.00	91	62r
Physician fee, obstetrics/gynecology, first-visit		64.00	91	62r
Physician fee, obstetrics/gynecology, revisit		41.00	91	62r
Physician fee, orthopedic surgeon, revisit		40.00	91	62r
Physician fee, pediatrician, first-visit		49.00	91	62r
Physician fee, pediatrician, revisit		33.00	91	62r
Physician fee, plastic surgeon, revisit		43.00	91	62r
Physician fee, surgical specialist, revisit		37.00	91	62r
Substance abuse, hospital ancillary charge	incident	1390	90	70s
Substance abuse, hospital physician charge	incident	770	90	70s
Substance abuse, hospital room and board	incident	5600	90	70s
Insurance and Pensions				
Auto insurance, private passenger	year	727.60	91	63s
Taxes				
Tax, cigarette	pack	33.90	91	77s
Tax, gasoline	gal	11.60	91	77s

Values are in dollars or fractions of dollars. In the column headed *Ref*, references are shown to sources. Each reference is followed by a letter. These refer to the geographical level for which data were reported: s = State, r = Region, and c = City or metro. The abbreviation *ex* is used to mean *except* or *excluding*; *exp* stands for *expenditures*. For other abbreviations and further explanations, please see the Introduction.

Fort Pierce, FL - continued

Item	Per	Value	Date	Ref.
Taxes				
Taxes, state	capita	1037	91	77s
Transportation				
Driver's license fee		15.00	12/90	43s
Travel				
Business travel	day	193.00	4/93	89r
Utilities				
Electricity	mil Btu	20.62	90	64s

Fort Smith, AR

Item	Per	Value	Date	Ref.
Composite ACCRA index		90.30	4Q 92	4c
Alcoholic Beverages				
Beer, Miller Lite or Budweiser, 12-oz containers	6 pack	4.41	4Q 92	4c
Liquor, J & B Scotch	750 ml	17.51	4Q 92	4c
Wine, Gallo Chablis blanc, 1.5 liter	bottle	6.45	4Q 92	4c
Child Care				
Child care fee, average, center	hour	1.29	90	65r
Child care fee, average, nonregulated family day care	hour	0.89	90	65r
Child care fee, average, regulated family day care	hour	1.32	90	65r
Clothing				
Jeans, man's denim		28.67	4Q 92	4c
Shirt, man's dress shirt		25.00	4Q 92	4c
Undervest, boy's size 10-14, cotton	3	3.30	4Q 92	4c
Communications				
Long-distance telephone service, day, initial minute, 0-100 miles	min	0.10-0.42	91	12s
Long-distance telephone service, day, additional minute, 0-100 miles	min	0.08-0.34	91	12s
Long-distance telephone service, evenings/ weekends, 0-100 mi, initial minute	min	0.06-0.23	91	12s
Long-distance telephone service, evenings/ weekends, 0-100 mi, additional minute	min	0.04-0.19	91	12s
Newspaper subscription, daily and Sunday home delivery, large-city	month	7.00	4Q 92	4c
Telephone, flat rate	month	13.91	91	11c
Telephone bill, family of four	month	22.30	4Q 92	4c
Education				
Board, 4-yr private college/university	year	1651	91	22s
Board, 4-yr public college/university	year	1253	91	22s
Expenditures, local gov't, public elementary/secondary	pupil	3770	92	20s
Room, 4-year private college/university	year	1111	91	22s
Room, 4-year public college/university	year	1173	91	22s
Tuition, 2-year private college/university	year	2482	91	22s
Tuition, 2-year public college/university	year	648	91	22s
Tuition, 4-year private college/university	year	4464	91	22s
Tuition, 4-year public college/university, in-state	year	1418	91	22s
Energy and Fuels				
Coal	mil Btu	1.62	90	64s
Energy	mil Btu	8.81	90	64s
Energy, combined forms, 1,800 sq ft heating area	month	113.41	4Q 92	4c
Energy, exc electricity, 1,800 sq ft heating area	month	33.21	4Q 92	4c
Energy exp/householder, 1-family unit	year	471	90	28r
Energy exp/householder, <1,000 sq ft heating area	year	384	90	28r
Energy exp/householder, 1,000-1,999 sq ft heating area	year	421	90	28r
Energy exp/householder, 2,000+ sq ft heating area	year	625	90	28r
Energy exp/householder, mobile home	year	271	90	28r
Energy exp/householder, multifamily	year	355	90	28r

Fort Smith, AR - continued

Item	Per	Value	Date	Ref.
Energy and Fuels - continued				
Gas, cooking, 10 therms	month	9.64	92	56c
Gas, cooking, 30 therms	month	14.93	92	56c
Gas, cooking, 50 therms	month	20.22	92	56c
Gas, heating, winter, 100 therms	month	33.44	92	56c
Gas, heating, winter, average use	month	44.02	92	56c
Gas, natural	mil Btu	3.27	90	64s
Gas, natural	000 cu ft	4.98	91	46s
Gas, natural, exp	year	408	91	46s
Gasoline, motor	gal	1.09	4Q 92	4c
Gasoline, unleaded regular	mil Btu	8.86	90	64s
Entertainment				
Bowling, evening rate	game	2.10	4Q 92	4c
Miniature golf admission	adult	6.18	92	1r
Miniature golf admission	child	5.14	92	1r
Monopoly game, Parker Brothers', No. 9		10.30	4Q 92	4c
Movie	admission	5.00	4Q 92	4c
Tennis balls, yellow, Wilson or Penn, 3	can	2.00	4Q 92	4c
Waterpark admission	adult	11.00	92	1r
Waterpark admission	child	8.55	92	1r
Funerals				
Casket, 18-gauge steel, velvet interior		2274.41	91	24r
Cosmetology, hair care, etc.		74.62	91	24r
Embalming		229.94	91	24r
Facility use for ceremony		176.61	91	24r
Hearse, local		116.34	91	24r
Limousine, local		72.68	91	24r
Remains to funeral home, transfer		87.72	91	24r
Service charge, professional		712.53	91	24r
Vault, concrete, non metallic liner		750.55	91	24r
Viewing facilities, use		155.31	91	24r
Goods and Services				
ACCRA Index, Miscellaneous Goods and Services		98.00	4Q 92	4c
Groceries				
ACCRA Index, Groceries		94.70	4Q 92	4c
Apples, Red Delicious	lb	0.79	4/93	16r
Babyfood, strained vegetables, lowest price	4-4.5 oz jar	0.30	4Q 92	4c
Bacon	lb	1.75	4/93	16r
Bananas	lb	0.51	4Q 92	4c
Bananas	lb	0.42	4/93	16r
Beef, stew, boneless	lb	2.61	4/93	16r
Bologna, all beef or mixed	lb	2.24	4/93	16r
Bread, white	24 oz	0.69	4Q 92	4c
Bread, white, pan	lb	0.64	4/93	16r
Bread, whole wheat, pan	lb	0.96	4/93	16r
Cabbage	lb	0.37	4/93	16r
Carrots, short trimmed and topped	lb	0.47	4/93	16r
Celery	lb	0.64	4/93	16r
Cheese, American	lb	2.98	4/93	16r
Cheese, Cheddar	lb	3.28	4/93	16r
Cheese, Kraft grated Parmesan	8-oz canister	3.50	4Q 92	4c
Chicken, fresh, whole	lb	0.77	4/93	16r
Chicken, fryer, whole	lb	0.71	4Q 92	4c
Chicken breast, bone-in	lb	1.92	4/93	16r
Chicken legs, bone-in	lb	1.06	4/93	16r
Chuck roast, graded and ungraded, ex USDA prime and choice	lb	2.40	4/93	16r
Chuck roast, USDA choice, bone-in	lb	2.19	4/93	16r
Chuck roast, USDA choice, boneless	lb	2.38	4/93	16r
Cigarettes, Winston	carton	17.29	4Q 92	4c
Coffee, 100% ground roast, all sizes	lb	2.48	4/93	16r
Coffee, vacuum-packed	13-oz can	1.95	4Q 92	4c
Corn, frozen	10 oz	0.74	4Q 92	4c
Corn Flakes, Kellogg's or Post Toasties	18 oz	1.65	4Q 92	4c

Values are in dollars or fractions of dollars. In the column headed *Ref*, references are shown to sources. Each reference is followed by a letter. These refer to the geographical level for which data were reported: s=State, r=Region, and c=City or metro. The abbreviation *ex* is used to mean *except* or *excluding*; *exp* stands for expenditures. For other abbreviations and further explanations, please see the Introduction.

Fort Smith, AR - continued

Item	Per	Value	Date	Ref.
Groceries				
Crackers, soda, salted	lb	1.15	4/93	16r
Eggs, Grade A large	doz	0.76	4Q 92	4c
Eggs, Grade A large	doz	0.96	4/93	16r
Flour, white, all purpose	lb	0.24	4/93	16r
Frankfurters, all meat or all beef	lb	2.01	4/93	16r
Grapefruit	lb	0.44	4/93	16r
Grapes, Thompson Seedless	lb	1.40	4/93	16r
Ground beef, 100% beef	lb	1.58	4/93	16r
Ground beef, lean and extra lean	lb	2.09	4/93	16r
Ground beef or hamburger	lb	1.41	4Q 92	4c
Ground chuck, 100% beef	lb	1.98	4/93	16r
Ham, boneless, excluding canned	lb	2.89	4/93	16r
Ham, picnic, shoulder, bone-in, smoked	lb	1.02	4/93	16r
Ham, rump or steak half, bone-in, smoked	lb	1.48	4/93	16r
Honey, jar	8 oz	0.73-1.19	92	5r
Honey, jar	lb	1.10-1.79	92	5r
Honey, squeeze bear	12-oz	1.19-1.50	92	5r
Ice cream, prepackaged, bulk, regular	1/2 gal	2.41	4/93	16r
Lemons	lb	1.05	4/93	16r
Lettuce, iceberg	head	0.73	4Q 92	4c
Lettuce, iceberg	lb	0.81	4/93	16r
Margarine, Blue Bonnet or Parkay cubes	lb	0.48	4Q 92	4c
Margarine, stick	lb	0.88	4/93	16r
Milk, whole	1/2 gal	1.34	4Q 92	4c
Orange juice, Minute Maid frozen	12-oz can	1.13	4Q 92	4c
Oranges, navel	lb	0.55	4/93	16r
Peaches	29-oz can	1.33	4Q 92	4c
Pears, Anjou	lb	0.92	4/93	16r
Peas Sweet, Del Monte or Green Giant	15-17 oz can	0.56	4Q 92	4c
Pork chops, center cut, bone-in	lb	3.13	4/93	16r
Potato chips	16 oz	2.94	4/93	16r
Potatoes, white	lb	0.43	4/93	16r
Potatoes, white or red	10-lb sack	2.42	4Q 92	4c
Rib roast, USDA choice, bone-in	lb	4.63	4/93	16r
Rice, white, long grain, uncooked	lb	0.45	4/93	16r
Round roast, graded & ungraded, ex USDA prime & choice	lb	3.03	4/93	16r
Round roast, USDA choice, boneless	lb	3.09	4/93	16r
Sausage, fresh, loose	lb	2.08	4/93	16r
Sausage, Jimmy Dean, 100% pork	lb	2.28	4Q 92	4c
Short ribs, bone-in	lb	2.66	4/93	16r
Shortening, vegetable oil blends	lb	0.69	4/93	16r
Shortening, vegetable, Crisco	3-lb can	2.15	4Q 92	4c
Soft drink, Coca Cola	2 liter	1.00	4Q 92	4c
Spaghetti and macaroni	lb	0.81	4/93	16r
Steak, rib eye, USDA choice, boneless	lb	6.24	4/93	16r
Steak, round, graded & ungraded, ex USDA prime & choice	lb	3.31	4/93	16r
Steak, round, USDA choice, boneless	lb	3.34	4/93	16r
Steak, sirloin, graded & ungraded, ex USDA prime & choice	lb	4.19	4/93	16r
Steak, sirloin, USDA choice, boneless	lb	4.46	4/93	16r
Steak, T-bone	lb	5.35	4Q 92	4c
Steak, T-bone, USDA choice, bone-in	lb	5.25	4/93	16r
Strawberries, dry pint	12 oz	0.92	4/93	16r
Sugar, cane or beet	4 lb	1.40	4Q 92	4c
Sugar, white	lb	0.39	4/93	16r
Sugar, white, 33-80 oz pk	lb	0.38	4/93	16r
Tomatoes, field grown	lb	0.88	4/93	16r
Tomatoes, Hunt's or Del Monte	14.5-oz can	0.74	4Q 92	4c
Tuna, chunk, light	6.125-6.5 oz can	0.58	4Q 92	4c
Tuna, chunk, light	lb	1.79	4/93	16r
Turkey, frozen, whole	lb	1.04	4/93	16r

Fort Smith, AR - continued

Item	Per	Value	Date	Ref.
Groceries - continued				
Yogurt, natural, fruit flavored	1/2 pint	0.57	4/93	16r
Health Care				
ACCRA Index, Health Care		93.10	4Q 92	4c
Analgesic, Aspirin, Bayer, 325 mg tablets	100	5.40	4Q 92	4c
Childbirth, cesarean, hospital		5034	91	62r
Childbirth, cesarean, physician's fee		2053	91	62r
Childbirth, normal, hospital		2712	91	62r
Childbirth, normal, physician's fee		1492	91	62r
Dentist's fee, adult teeth cleaning and periodic oral exam	visit	46.20	4Q 92	4c
Doctor's fee, routine exam, established patient	visit	37.00	4Q 92	4c
Health care spending, state	capita	1944	3/93	84s
Hospital care, semiprivate room	day	160.00	90	27c
Hospital care, semiprivate room	day	188.50	4Q 92	4c
Medical insurance premium, per employee, small group comprehensive	month	299.30	10/91	25c
Mental health care, exp	capita	20.37-28.83	90	38s
Mental health care, exp, state mental health agency	capita	25.92	90	38s
Mental health care, hospital psychiatric services, non-Federal, exp	capita	5.26	88	38s
Mental health care, mental health organization, multiservice, exp	capita	15.69	88	38s
Mental health care, psychiatric hospitals, private, exp	capita	15.15	88	38s
Mental health care, psychiatric out-patient clinics, freestanding, exp	capita	0.46	88	38s
Mental health care, state and county mental hospitals, exp	capita	6.78	88	38s
Mental health care, VA medical centers, exp	capita	7.18	88	38s
Physician fee, family practice, first-visit		75.00	91	62r
Physician fee, family practice, revisit		34.00	91	62r
Physician fee, general practice, first-visit		61.00	91	62r
Physician fee, general practice, revisit		32.00	91	62r
Physician fee, general surgeon, first-visit		64.00	91	62r
Physician fee, general surgeon, revisit		40.00	91	62r
Physician fee, internal medicine, first-visit		98.00	91	62r
Physician fee, internal medicine, revisit		40.00	91	62r
Physician fee, median, neurosurgeon, first-visit		130.00	91	62r
Physician fee, median, nonsurgical specialist, first-visit		95.00	91	62r
Physician fee, median, orthopedic surgeon, first-visit		91.00	91	62r
Physician fee, median, plastic surgeon, first-visit		66.00	91	62r
Physician fee, median, surgical specialist, first-visit		62.00	91	62r
Physician fee, neurosurgeon, revisit		50.00	91	62r
Physician fee, nonsurgical specialist, revisit		40.00	91	62r
Physician fee, obstetrics/gynecology, first-visit		64.00	91	62r
Physician fee, obstetrics/gynecology, revisit		41.00	91	62r
Physician fee, orthopedic surgeon, revisit		40.00	91	62r
Physician fee, pediatrician, first-visit		49.00	91	62r
Physician fee, pediatrician, revisit		33.00	91	62r
Physician fee, plastic surgeon, revisit		43.00	91	62r
Physician fee, surgical specialist, revisit		37.00	91	62r
Substance abuse, hospital ancillary charge	incident	1680	90	70s
Substance abuse, hospital physician charge	incident	450	90	70s
Substance abuse, hospital room and board	incident	4490	90	70s
Household Goods				
Appliance repair, home, service call, washing machine	min labor charge	35.08	4Q 92	4c

Values are in dollars or fractions of dollars. In the column headed *Ref*, references are shown to sources. Each reference is followed by a letter. These refer to the geographical level for which data were reported: s = State, r = Region, and c = City or metro. The abbreviation *ex* is used to mean *except* or *excluding*; *exp* stands for expenditures. For other abbreviations and further explanations, please see the Introduction.

Fort Smith, AR - continued

Item	Per	Value	Date	Ref.
Household Goods				
Laundry detergent, Tide Ultra, Bold, or Cheer	42 oz	2.94	4Q 92	4c
Tissues, facial, Kleenex brand	175-count box	1.05	4Q 92	4c
Housing				
ACCRA Index, Housing		72.30	4Q 92	4c
House, 1,800 sq ft, 8,000 sq ft lot, new, urban	total	79200	4Q 92	4c
House payment, principal and interest, 25% down payment	month	440	4Q 92	4c
Mortgage rate, incl. points & origination fee, 30-year fixed or adjustable rate	percent	8.11	4Q 92	4c
Rent, apartment, 2 bedrooms - 1-1/2 to 2 baths, unfurnished, 950 sq ft, water	month	367	4Q 92	4c
Rental unit, 1 bedroom	month	333	93	23c
Rental unit, 2 bedroom	month	393	93	23c
Rental unit, 3 bedroom	month	494	93	23c
Rental unit, 4 bedroom	month	553	93	23c
Rental unit, efficiency	month	273	93	23c
Insurance and Pensions				
Auto insurance, private passenger	year	501.00	91	63s
Personal Goods				
Shampoo, Alberto VO5	15 oz	1.48	4Q 92	4c
Toothpaste, Crest or Colgate	6-7 oz	2.40	4Q 92	4c
Personal Services				
Dry cleaning, man's 2-piece suit		5.19	4Q 92	4c
Haircare, woman's shampoo, trim and blow-dry		18.40	4Q 92	4c
Haircut, man's barbershop, no styling		7.80	4Q 92	4c
Restaurant Food				
Chicken, fried, thigh and drumstick		2.39	4Q 92	4c
Hamburger with cheese	1/4 lb	1.79	4Q 92	4c
Pizza, Pizza Hut or Pizza Inn, cheese, thin crust	12-13 in	8.68	4Q 92	4c
Taxes				
Tax, cigarette	pack	22	91	77s
Tax, gasoline	gal	18.50	91	77s
Taxes, state	capita	997	91	77s
Transportation				
ACCRA Index, Transportation		93.70	4Q 92	4c
Driver's license fee		14.25	12/90	43s
Tire balance, computer or spin balance, front	wheel	5.90	4Q 92	4c
Vehicle registration and license plate	year	17.00-30.00	93	10s
Travel				
Business travel	day	193.00	4/93	89r
Utilities				
ACCRA Index, Utilities		104.90	4Q 92	4c
Electricity	mil Btu	19.78	90	64s
Electricity, partial electric and other energy, 1,800 sq ft living area new home	month	80.20	4Q 92	4c
Electricity, winter, 250 KWh	month	19.41	92	55c
Electricity, winter, 500 KWh	month	32.87	92	55c
Electricity, winter, 750 KWh	month	46.33	92	55c
Electricity, winter, 1000 KWh	month	59.80	92	55c

Fort Walton Beach, FL

Item	Per	Value	Date	Ref.
Child Care				
Child care fee, average, center	hour	1.29	90	65r
Child care fee, average, nonregulated family day care	hour	0.89	90	65r
Child care fee, average, regulated family day care	hour	1.32	90	65r

Fort Walton Beach, FL - continued

Item	Per	Value	Date	Ref.
Communications				
Long-distance telephone service, day, initial minute, 0-100 miles	min	0.15-0.20	91	12s
Long-distance telephone service, day, additional minute, 0-100 miles	min	0.08-0.20	91	12s
Long-distance telephone service, evenings/weekends, 0-100 mi, initial minute	min	0.09-0.12	91	12s
Long-distance telephone service, evenings/weekends, 0-100 mi, additional minute	min	0.05-0.12	91	12s
Education				
Board, 4-yr private college/university	year	1924	91	22s
Board, 4-yr public college/university	year	1955	91	22s
Expenditures, local gov't, public elementary/secondary	pupil	5235	92	20s
Room, 4-year private college/university	year	1904	91	22s
Room, 4-year public college/university	year	1510	91	22s
Tuition, 2-year private college/university	year	4751	91	22s
Tuition, 2-year public college/university	year	788	91	22s
Tuition, 4-year private college/university	year	7992	91	22s
Tuition, 4-year public college/university, in-state	year	1337	91	22s
Energy and Fuels				
Coal	mil Btu	1.85	90	64s
Energy	mil Btu	10.58	90	64s
Energy exp/householder, 1-family unit	year	487	90	28r
Energy exp/householder, <1,000 sq ft heating area	year	393	90	28r
Energy exp/householder, 1,000-1,999 sq ft heating area	year	442	90	28r
Energy exp/householder, 2,000+ sq ft heating area	year	577	90	28r
Energy exp/householder, mobile home	year	366	90	28r
Energy exp/householder, multifamily	year	382	90	28r
Gas, natural	mil Btu	3.21	90	64s
Gas, natural	000 cu ft	8.98	91	46s
Gas, natural, exp	year	248	91	46s
Gasoline, unleaded regular	mil Btu	8.85	90	64s
Entertainment				
Miniature golf admission	adult	6.18	92	1r
Miniature golf admission	child	5.14	92	1r
Waterpark admission	adult	11.00	92	1r
Waterpark admission	child	8.55	92	1r
Funerals				
Casket, 18-gauge steel, velvet interior		2029.08	91	24r
Cosmetology, hair care, etc.		75.10	91	24r
Embalming		249.24	91	24r
Facility use for ceremony		162.27	91	24r
Hearse, local		114.04	91	24r
Limousine, local		88.57	91	24r
Remains to funeral home, transfer		92.61	91	24r
Service charge, professional		682.42	91	24r
Vault, concrete, non-metallic liner		798.70	91	24r
Viewing facilities, use		163.86	91	24r
Groceries				
Apples, Red Delicious	lb	0.79	4/93	16r
Bacon	lb	1.75	4/93	16r
Bananas	lb	0.42	4/93	16r
Beef, stew, boneless	lb	2.61	4/93	16r
Bologna, all beef or mixed	lb	2.24	4/93	16r
Bread, white, pan	lb	0.64	4/93	16r
Bread, whole wheat, pan	lb	0.96	4/93	16r
Cabbage	lb	0.37	4/93	16r
Carrots, short trimmed and topped	lb	0.47	4/93	16r
Celery	lb	0.64	4/93	16r
Cheese, American	lb	2.98	4/93	16r
Cheese, Cheddar	lb	3.28	4/93	16r
Chicken, fresh, whole	lb	0.77	4/93	16r
Chicken breast, bone-in	lb	1.92	4/93	16r
Chicken legs, bone-in	lb	1.06	4/93	16r

Values are in dollars or fractions of dollars. In the column headed *Ref*, references are shown to sources. Each reference is followed by a letter. These refer to the geographical level for which data were reported: s=State, r=Region, and c=City or metro. The abbreviation *ex* is used to mean *except* or *excluding*; *exp* stands for expenditures. For other abbreviations and further explanations, please see the Introduction.

Fort Walton Beach, FL - continued

Item	Per	Value	Date	Ref.
Groceries				
Chuck roast, graded and ungraded, ex USDA prime and choice	lb	2.40	4/93	16r
Chuck roast, USDA choice, bone-in	lb	2.19	4/93	16r
Chuck roast, USDA choice, boneless	lb	2.38	4/93	16r
Coffee, 100% ground roast, all sizes	lb	2.48	4/93	16r
Crackers, soda, salted	lb	1.15	4/93	16r
Eggs, Grade A large	doz	0.96	4/93	16r
Flour, white, all purpose	lb	0.24	4/93	16r
Frankfurters, all meat or all beef	lb	2.01	4/93	16r
Grapefruit	lb	0.44	4/93	16r
Grapes, Thompson Seedless	lb	1.40	4/93	16r
Ground beef, 100% beef	lb	1.58	4/93	16r
Ground beef, lean and extra lean	lb	2.09	4/93	16r
Ground chuck, 100% beef	lb	1.98	4/93	16r
Ham, boneless, excluding canned	lb	2.89	4/93	16r
Ham, picnic, shoulder, bone-in, smoked	lb	1.02	4/93	16r
Ham, rump or steak half, bone-in, smoked	lb	1.48	4/93	16r
Ice cream, prepackaged, bulk, regular	1/2 gal	2.41	4/93	16r
Lemons	lb	1.05	4/93	16r
Lettuce, iceberg	lb	0.81	4/93	16r
Margarine, stick	lb	0.88	4/93	16r
Oranges, navel	lb	0.55	4/93	16r
Pears, Anjou	lb	0.92	4/93	16r
Pork chops, center cut, bone-in	lb	3.13	4/93	16r
Potato chips	16 oz	2.94	4/93	16r
Potatoes, white	lb	0.43	4/93	16r
Rib roast, USDA choice, bone-in	lb	4.63	4/93	16r
Rice, white, long grain, uncooked	lb	0.45	4/93	16r
Round roast, graded & ungraded, ex USDA prime & choice	lb	3.03	4/93	16r
Round roast, USDA choice, boneless	lb	3.09	4/93	16r
Sausage, fresh, loose	lb	2.08	4/93	16r
Short ribs, bone-in	lb	2.66	4/93	16r
Shortening, vegetable oil blends	lb	0.69	4/93	16r
Spaghetti and macaroni	lb	0.81	4/93	16r
Steak, rib eye, USDA choice, boneless	lb	6.24	4/93	16r
Steak, round, graded & ungraded, ex USDA prime & choice	lb	3.31	4/93	16r
Steak, round, USDA choice, boneless	lb	3.34	4/93	16r
Steak, sirloin, graded & ungraded, ex USDA prime & choice	lb	4.19	4/93	16r
Steak, sirloin, USDA choice, boneless	lb	4.46	4/93	16r
Steak, T-bone, USDA choice, bone-in	lb	5.25	4/93	16r
Strawberries, dry pint	12 oz	0.92	4/93	16r
Sugar, white	lb	0.39	4/93	16r
Sugar, white, 33-80 oz pk	lb	0.38	4/93	16r
Tomatoes, field grown	lb	0.88	4/93	16r
Tuna, chunk, light	lb	1.79	4/93	16r
Turkey, frozen, whole	lb	1.04	4/93	16r
Yogurt, natural, fruit flavored	1/2 pint	0.57	4/93	16r
Health Care				
Childbirth, cesarean, hospital		5034	91	62r
Childbirth, cesarean, physician's fee		2053	91	62r
Childbirth, normal, hospital		2712	91	62r
Childbirth, normal, physician's fee		1492	91	62r
Medical plan per employee	year	3495	91	45r
Mental health care, exp	capita	28.84-37.59	90	38s
Mental health care, exp, state mental health agency	capita	37.49	90	38s
Mental health care, hospital psychiatric services, non-Federal, exp	capita	9.11	88	38s
Mental health care, mental health organization, multiservice, exp	capita	16.21	88	38s
Mental health care, psychiatric hospitals, private, exp	capita	22.26	88	38s
Mental health care, psychiatric out-patient clinics, freestanding, exp	capita	0.89	88	38s
Mental health care, psychiatric partial-care organizations, freestanding, exp	capita	0.41	88	38s

Fort Walton Beach, FL - continued

Item	Per	Value	Date	Ref.
Health Care - continued				
Mental health care, state and county mental hospitals, exp	capita	16.25	88	38s
Mental health care, VA medical centers, exp	capita	1.69	88	38s
Physician fee, family practice, first-visit		75.00	91	62r
Physician fee, family practice, revisit		34.00	91	62r
Physician fee, general practice, first-visit		61.00	91	62r
Physician fee, general practice, revisit		32.00	91	62r
Physician fee, general surgeon, first-visit		64.00	91	62r
Physician fee, general surgeon, revisit		40.00	91	62r
Physician fee, internal medicine, first-visit		98.00	91	62r
Physician fee, internal medicine, revisit		40.00	91	62r
Physician fee, median, neurosurgeon, first-visit		130.00	91	62r
Physician fee, median, nonsurgical specialist, first-visit		95.00	91	62r
Physician fee, median, orthopedic surgeon, first-visit		91.00	91	62r
Physician fee, median, plastic surgeon, first-visit		66.00	91	62r
Physician fee, median, surgical specialist, first-visit		62.00	91	62r
Physician fee, neurosurgeon, revisit		50.00	91	62r
Physician fee, nonsurgical specialist, revisit		40.00	91	62r
Physician fee, obstetrics/gynecology, first-visit		64.00	91	62r
Physician fee, obstetrics/gynecology, revisit		41.00	91	62r
Physician fee, orthopedic surgeon, revisit		40.00	91	62r
Physician fee, pediatrician, first-visit		49.00	91	62r
Physician fee, pediatrician, revisit		33.00	91	62r
Physician fee, plastic surgeon, revisit		43.00	91	62r
Physician fee, surgical specialist, revisit		37.00	91	62r
Substance abuse, hospital ancillary charge	incident	1390	90	70s
Substance abuse, hospital physician charge	incident	770	90	70s
Substance abuse, hospital room and board	incident	5600	90	70s
Insurance and Pensions				
Auto insurance, private passenger	year	727.60	91	63s
Taxes				
Tax, cigarette	pack	33.90	91	77s
Tax, gasoline	gal	11.60	91	77s
Taxes, state	capita	1037	91	77s
Transportation				
Driver's license fee		15.00	12/90	43s
Travel				
Business travel	day	193.00	4/93	89r
Utilities				
Electricity	mil Btu	20.62	90	64s

Fort Wayne, IN

Item	Per	Value	Date	Ref.
Composite ACCRA index		90.00	4Q 92	4c
Alcoholic Beverages				
Beer, Miller Lite or Budweiser, 12-oz containers	6 pack	3.54	4Q 92	4c
Liquor, J & B Scotch	750 ml	14.55	4Q 92	4c
Wine, Gallo Chablis blanc, 1.5 liter	bottle	3.34	4Q 92	4c
Child Care				
Child care fee, average, center	hour	1.63	90	65r
Child care fee, average, nonregulated family day care	hour	1.83	90	65r
Child care fee, average, regulated family day care	hour	1.42	90	65r
Clothing				
Jeans, man's denim		27.59	4Q 92	4c
Shirt, man's dress shirt		15.79	4Q 92	4c

Values are in dollars or fractions of dollars. In the column headed *Ref*, references are shown to sources. Each reference is followed by a letter. These refer to the geographical level for which data were reported: s = State, r = Region, and c = City or metro. The abbreviation *ex* is used to mean *except* or *excluding*; *exp* stands for expenditures. For other abbreviations and further explanations, please see the Introduction.

Fort Wayne, IN - continued

Item	Per	Value	Date	Ref.
Clothing				
Undervest, boy's size 10-14, cotton	3	2.88	4Q 92	4c
Communications				
Long-distance telephone service, day, initial minute, 0-100 miles	min	0.18-0.45	91	12s
Long-distance telephone service, day, additional minute, 0-100 miles	min	0.10-0.30	91	12s
Long-distance telephone service, evenings/ weekends, 0-100 mi, initial minute	min	0.08-0.19	91	12s
Long-distance telephone service, evenings/ weekends, 0-100 mi, additional minute	min	0.04-0.13	91	12s
Newspaper subscription, daily and Sunday home delivery, large-city	month	13.04	4Q 92	4c
Telephone bill, family of four	month	20.21	4Q 92	4c
Education				
Board, 4-yr private college/university	year	1714	91	22s
Board, 4-yr public college/university	year	1829	91	22s
Expenditures, local gov't, public elementary/secondary	pupil	5545	92	20s
Room, 4-year private college/university	year	1512	91	22s
Room, 4-year public college/university	year	1435	91	22s
Tuition, 2-year private college/university	year	6756	91	22s
Tuition, 2-year public college/university	year	1423	91	22s
Tuition, 4-year private college/university	year	8451	91	22s
Tuition, 4-year public college/university, in-state	year	2067	91	22s
Energy and Fuels				
Coal	mil Btu	1.46	90	64s
Energy	mil Btu	6.77	90	64s
Energy, combined forms, 1,800 sq ft heating area	month	111.16	4Q 92	4c
Energy, exc electricity, 1,800 sq ft heating area	month	49.81	4Q 92	4c
Energy exp/householder, 1-family unit	year	471	90	28r
Energy exp/householder, <1,000 sq ft heating area	year	430	90	28r
Energy exp/householder, 1,000-1,999 sq ft heating area	year	481	90	28r
Energy exp/householder, 2,000+ sq ft heating area	year	473	90	28r
Energy exp/householder, mobile home	year	430	90	28r
Energy exp/householder, multifamily	year	461	90	28r
Gas, natural	mil Btu	4.27	90	64s
Gas, natural	000 cu ft	5.46	91	46s
Gas, natural, exp	year	588	91	46s
Gasoline, motor	gal	1.08	4Q 92	4c
Gasoline, unleaded regular	mil Btu	8.74	90	64s
Entertainment				
Bowling, evening rate	game	1.82	4Q 92	4c
Miniature golf admission	adult	6.18	92	1r
Miniature golf admission	child	5.14	92	1r
Monopoly game, Parker Brothers', No. 9		9.97	4Q 92	4c
Movie	admission	5.20	4Q 92	4c
Tennis balls, yellow, Wilson or Penn, 3	can	1.95	4Q 92	4c
Waterpark admission	adult	11.00	92	1r
Waterpark admission	child	8.55	92	1r
Funerals				
Casket, 18-gauge steel, velvet interior		1926.72	91	24r
Cosmetology, hair care, etc.		97.64	91	24r
Embalming		249.14	91	24r
Facility use for ceremony		208.59	91	24r
Hearse, local		130.12	91	24r
Limousine, local		104.66	91	24r
Remains to funeral home, transfer		93.61	91	24r
Service charge, professional		724.62	91	24r
Vault, concrete, non-metallic liner		734.53	91	24r
Viewing facilities, use		236.06	91	24r

Fort Wayne, IN - continued

Item	Per	Value	Date	Ref.
Goods and Services				
ACCRA Index, Miscellaneous Goods and Services		85.60	4Q 92	4c
Groceries				
ACCRA Index, Groceries		93.30	4Q 92	4c
Apples, Red Delicious	lb	0.77	4/93	16r
Babyfood, strained vegetables, lowest price	4-4.5 oz jar	0.33	4Q 92	4c
Bacon	lb	1.85	4/93	16r
Bananas	lb	0.43	4Q 92	4c
Bananas	lb	0.46	4/93	16r
Beef, stew, boneless	lb	2.53	4/93	16r
Bologna, all beef or mixed	lb	2.19	4/93	16r
Bread, white	24 oz	0.49	4Q 92	4c
Bread, white, pan	lb	0.78	4/93	16r
Butter	lb	1.50	4/93	16r
Cabbage	lb	0.40	4/93	16r
Carrots, short trimmed and topped	lb	0.45	4/93	16r
Cheese, Cheddar	lb	3.47	4/93	16r
Cheese, Kraft grated Parmesan	8-oz canister	2.96	4Q 92	4c
Chicken, fresh, whole	lb	0.84	4/93	16r
Chicken, fryer, whole	lb	0.65	4Q 92	4c
Chicken breast, bone-in	lb	1.94	4/93	16r
Chicken legs, bone-in	lb	1.02	4/93	16r
Chuck roast, graded and ungraded, ex USDA prime and choice	lb	2.43	4/93	16r
Chuck roast, USDA choice, bone-in	lb	2.11	4/93	16r
Chuck roast, USDA choice, boneless	lb	2.44	4/93	16r
Cigarettes, Winston	carton	16.22	4Q 92	4c
Coffee, 100% ground roast, all sizes	lb	2.47	4/93	16r
Coffee, vacuum-packed	13-oz can	2.07	4Q 92	4c
Cookies, chocolate chip	lb	2.73	4/93	16r
Corn, frozen	10 oz	0.70	4Q 92	4c
Corn Flakes, Kellogg's or Post Toasties	18 oz	1.99	4Q 92	4c
Eggs, Grade A large	doz	0.67	4Q 92	4c
Eggs, Grade A large	doz	0.93	4/93	16r
Flour, white, all purpose	lb	0.21	4/93	16r
Grapefruit	lb	0.45	4/93	16r
Grapes, Thompson Seedless	lb	1.46	4/93	16r
Ground beef, 100% beef	lb	1.63	4/93	16r
Ground beef, lean and extra lean	lb	2.08	4/93	16r
Ground beef or hamburger	lb	1.34	4Q 92	4c
Ground chuck, 100% beef	lb	1.94	4/93	16r
Ham, boneless, excluding canned	lb	2.21	4/93	16r
Honey, jar	8 oz	0.97-1.25	92	5r
Honey, jar	lb	1.25-2.25	92	5r
Honey, squeeze bear	12-oz	1.25-1.99	92	5r
Ice cream, prepackaged, bulk, regular	1/2 gal	2.41	4/93	16r
Lemons	lb	0.82	4/93	16r
Lettuce, iceberg	head	0.81	4Q 92	4c
Lettuce, iceberg	lb	0.83	4/93	16r
Margarine, Blue Bonnet or Parkay cubes	lb	0.63	4Q 92	4c
Margarine, stick	lb	0.77	4/93	16r
Milk, whole	1/2 gal	1.22	4Q 92	4c
Orange juice, Minute Maid frozen	12-oz can	1.53	4Q 92	4c
Oranges, navel	lb	0.50	4/93	16r
Peaches	29-oz can	1.18	4Q 92	4c
Peanut butter, creamy, all sizes	lb	1.82	4/93	16r
Pears, Anjou	lb	0.85	4/93	16r
Peas Sweet, Del Monte or Green Giant	15-17 oz can	0.61	4Q 92	4c
Pork chops, center cut, bone-in	lb	3.17	4/93	16r
Potato chips	16 oz	2.68	4/93	16r
Potatoes, white	lb	0.26	4/93	16r
Potatoes, white or red	10-lb sack	1.25	4Q 92	4c
Round roast, graded & ungraded, ex USDA prime & choice	lb	2.88	4/93	16r

Values are in dollars or fractions of dollars. In the column headed *Ref*, references are shown to sources. Each reference is followed by a letter. These refer to the geographical level for which data were reported: s=State, r=Region, and c=City or metro. The abbreviation *ex* is used to mean *except* or *excluding*; *exp* stands for expenditures. For other abbreviations and further explanations, please see the Introduction.

238

Fort Wayne, IN - continued

Item	Per	Value	Date	Ref.
Groceries				
Round roast, USDA choice, boneless	lb	2.96	4/93	16r
Sausage, Jimmy Dean, 100% pork	lb	2.97	4Q 92	4c
Shortening, vegetable oil blends	lb	0.79	4/93	16r
Shortening, vegetable, Crisco	3-lb can	2.17	4Q 92	4c
Soft drink, Coca Cola	2 liter	1.21	4Q 92	4c
Spaghetti and macaroni	lb	0.76	4/93	16r
Steak, rib eye, USDA choice, boneless	lb	6.29	4/93	16r
Steak, round, USDA choice, boneless	lb	3.24	4/93	16r
Steak, sirloin, graded & ungraded, ex USDA prime & choice	lb	4.00	4/93	16r
Steak, sirloin, USDA choice, bone-in	lb	3.57	4/93	16r
Steak, sirloin, USDA choice, boneless	lb	4.17	4/93	16r
Steak, T-bone	lb	5.15	4Q 92	4c
Steak, T-bone, USDA choice, bone-in	lb	5.60	4/93	16r
Strawberries, dry pint	12 oz	0.90	4/93	16r
Sugar, cane or beet	4 lb	1.30	4Q 92	4c
Sugar, white	lb	0.36	4/93	16r
Sugar, white, 33-80 oz pk	lb	0.35	4/93	16r
Tomatoes, field grown	lb	0.99	4/93	16r
Tomatoes, Hunt's or Del Monte	14.5-oz can	0.68	4Q 92	4c
Tuna, chunk, light	6.125-6.5 oz can	0.57	4Q 92	4c
Tuna, chunk, light	lb	1.76	4/93	16r
Turkey, frozen, whole	lb	0.91	4/93	16r
Health Care				
ACCRA Index, Health Care		81.70	4Q 92	4c
Analgesic, Aspirin, Bayer, 325 mg tablets	100	3.85	4Q 92	4c
Childbirth, cesarean, hospital		4688	91	62r
Childbirth, cesarean, physician's fee		2053	91	62r
Childbirth, normal, hospital		2657	91	62r
Childbirth, normal, physician's fee		1492	91	62r
Dentist's fee, adult teeth cleaning and periodic oral exam	visit	37.20	4Q 92	4c
Doctor's fee, routine exam, established patient	visit	29.40	4Q 92	4c
Hospital care, semiprivate room	day	242.98	90	27c
Hospital care, semiprivate room	day	295.33	4Q 92	4c
Medical insurance premium, per employee, small group comprehensive	month	292.00	10/91	25c
Medical plan per employee	year	3443	91	45r
Mental health care, exp	capita	37.60-53.67	90	38s
Mental health care, exp, state mental health agency	capita	47.05	90	38s
Mental health care, hospital psychiatric services, non-Federal, exp	capita	22.14	88	38s
Mental health care, mental health organization, multiservice, exp	capita	10.33	88	38s
Mental health care, psychiatric hospitals, private, exp	capita	20.10	88	38s
Mental health care, state and county mental hospitals, exp	capita	24.00	88	38s
Mental health care, VA medical centers, exp	capita	3.20	88	38s
Physician fee, family practice, first-visit		76.00	91	62r
Physician fee, family practice, revisit		33.00	91	62r
Physician fee, general practice, first-visit		61.00	91	62r
Physician fee, general practice, revisit		31.00	91	62r
Physician fee, general surgeon, first-visit		65.00	91	62r
Physician fee, general surgeon, revisit		35.00	91	62r
Physician fee, internal medicine, first-visit		91.00	91	62r
Physician fee, internal medicine, revisit		40.00	91	62r
Physician fee, median, neurosurgeon, first-visit		106.00	91	62r
Physician fee, median, nonsurgical specialist, first-visit		90.00	91	62r
Physician fee, median, orthopedic surgeon, first-visit		83.00	91	62r
Physician fee, median, surgical specialist, first-visit		61.00	91	62r

Fort Wayne, IN - continued

Item	Per	Value	Date	Ref.
Health Care - continued				
Physician fee, neurosurgeon, revisit		41.00	91	62r
Physician fee, nonsurgical specialist, revisit		40.00	91	62r
Physician fee, obstetrics/gynecology, first-visit		61.00	91	62r
Physician fee, obstetrics/gynecology, revisit		40.00	91	62r
Physician fee, orthopedic surgeon, revisit		41.00	91	62r
Physician fee, pediatrician, first-visit		46.00	91	62r
Physician fee, pediatrician, revisit		33.00	91	62r
Physician fee, surgical specialist, revisit		36.00	91	62r
Substance abuse, hospital ancillary charge	incident	1230	90	70s
Substance abuse, hospital physician charge	incident	410	90	70s
Substance abuse, hospital room and board	incident	5510	90	70s
Household Goods				
Appliance repair, home, service call, washing machine	min labor charge	26.97	4Q 92	4c
Laundry detergent, Tide Ultra, Bold, or Cheer	42 oz	3.07	4Q 92	4c
Tissues, facial, Kleenex brand	175-count box	1.21	4Q 92	4c
Housing				
ACCRA Index, Housing		89.90	4Q 92	4c
House, 1,800 sq ft, 8,000 sq ft lot, new, urban	total	96060	4Q 92	4c
House payment, principal and interest, 25% down payment	month	545	4Q 92	4c
Mortgage rate, incl. points & origination fee, 30-year fixed or adjustable rate	percent	8.33	4Q 92	4c
Rent, apartment, 2 bedrooms - 1-1/2 to 2 baths, unfurnished, 950 sq ft, water	month	461	4Q 92	4c
Rental unit, 1 bedroom	month	381	93	23c
Rental unit, 2 bedroom	month	444	93	23c
Rental unit, 3 bedroom	month	557	93	23c
Rental unit, 4 bedroom	month	619	93	23c
Rental unit, efficiency	month	315	93	23c
Insurance and Pensions				
Auto insurance, private passenger	year	548.99	91	63s
Personal Goods				
Shampoo, Alberto VO5	15 oz	0.94	4Q 92	4c
Toothpaste, Crest or Colgate	6-7 oz	1.20	4Q 92	4c
Personal Services				
Dry cleaning, man's 2-piece suit		6.07	4Q 92	4c
Haircare, woman's shampoo, trim and blow-dry		17.70	4Q 92	4c
Haircut, man's barbershop, no styling		7.65	4Q 92	4c
Restaurant Food				
Chicken, fried, thigh and drumstick		2.19	4Q 92	4c
Hamburger with cheese	1/4 lb	1.72	4Q 92	4c
Pizza, Pizza Hut or Pizza Inn, cheese, thin crust	12-13 in	6.35	4Q 92	4c
Taxes				
Tax, cigarette	pack	15.50	91	77s
Tax, gasoline	gal	15	91	77s
Taxes, state	capita	1102	91	77s
Transportation				
ACCRA Index, Transportation		95.20	4Q 92	4c
Bus fare	one-way	1.00	3/93	2c
Bus fare, up to 10 miles	one-way	1.00	4Q 92	4c
Driver's license fee		6.00	12/90	43s
Tire balance, computer or spin balance, front	wheel	5.90	4Q 92	4c

Values are in dollars or fractions of dollars. In the column headed *Ref*, references are shown to sources. Each reference is followed by a letter. These refer to the geographical level for which data were reported: s=State, r=Region, and c=City or metro. The abbreviation *ex* is used to mean *except* or *excluding*; *exp* stands for expenditures. For other abbreviations and further explanations, please see the Introduction.

Fort Wayne, IN - continued

Item	Per	Value	Date	Ref.
Utilities				
ACCRA Index, Utilities		102.00	4Q 92	4c
Electricity	mil Btu	15.75	90	64s
Electricity, partial electric and other energy, 1,800 sq ft living area new home	month	61.35	4Q 92	4c
Electricity, winter, 250 KWh	month	23.45	92	55c
Electricity, winter, 500 KWh	month	38.12	92	55c
Electricity, winter, 750 KWh	month	51.50	92	55c
Electricity, winter, 1000 KWh	month	64.88	92	55c

Fort Worth, TX

Item	Per	Value	Date	Ref.
Composite ACCRA index		98.20	4Q 92	4c
Alcoholic Beverages				
Beer, Miller Lite or Budweiser, 12-oz containers	6 pack	3.87	4Q 92	4c
Liquor, J & B Scotch	750 ml	17.25	4Q 92	4c
Wine, Gallo Chablis blanc, 1.5 liter	bottle	4.71	4Q 92	4c
Child Care				
Child care fee, average, center	hour	1.29	90	65r
Child care fee, average, nonregulated family day care	hour	0.89	90	65r
Child care fee, average, regulated family day care	hour	1.32	90	65r
Clothing				
Jeans, man's denim		28.59	4Q 92	4c
Shirt, man's dress shirt		22.70	4Q 92	4c
Undervest, boy's size 10-14, cotton	3	4.85	4Q 92	4c
Communications				
Long-distance telephone service, day, initial minute, 0-100 miles	min	0.10-0.46	91	12s
Long-distance telephone service, day, additional minute, 0-100 miles	min	0.06-0.45	91	12s
Newspaper subscription, daily and Sunday home delivery, large-city	month	10.95	4Q 92	4c
Telephone, flat rate	month	9.85	91	11c
Telephone, residential, private line, rotary, unlimited calling	month	15.60	10/91	78c
Telephone bill, family of four	month	16.62	4Q 92	4c
Education				
Board, 4-yr private college/university	year	1883	91	22s
Board, 4-yr public college/university	year	1605	91	22s
Expenditures, local gov't, public elementary/secondary	pupil	4593	92	20s
Room, 4-year private college/university	year	1620	91	22s
Room, 4-year public college/university	year	1532	91	22s
Tuition, 2-year private college/university	year	4394	91	22s
Tuition, 2-year public college/university	year	495	91	22s
Tuition, 4-year private college/university	year	6497	91	22s
Tuition, 4-year public college/university, in-state	year	986	91	22s
Energy and Fuels				
Coal	mil Btu	1.44	90	64s
Energy	mil Btu	6.48	90	64s
Energy, combined forms, 1,800 sq ft heating area	month	120.76	4Q 92	4c
Energy exp/householder, 1-family unit	year	471	90	28r
Energy exp/householder, <1,000 sq ft heating area	year	384	90	28r
Energy exp/householder, 1,000-1,999 sq ft heating area	year	421	90	28r
Energy exp/householder, 2,000+ sq ft heating area	year	625	90	28r
Energy exp/householder, mobile home	year	271	90	28r
Energy exp/householder, multifamily	year	355	90	28r
Gas, natural	mil Btu	2.47	90	64s
Gas, natural	000 cu ft	5.71	91	46s
Gas, natural, exp	year	388	91	46s

Fort Worth, TX - continued

Item	Per	Value	Date	Ref.
Energy and Fuels - continued				
Gasoline, motor	gal	1.11	4Q 92	4c
Gasoline, unleaded regular	mil Btu	9.16	90	64s
Entertainment				
Bowling, evening rate	game	2.56	4Q 92	4c
Miniature golf admission	adult	6.18	92	1r
Miniature golf admission	child	5.14	92	1r
Monopoly game, Parker Brothers', No. 9		10.59	4Q 92	4c
Movie	admission	5.95	4Q 92	4c
Tennis balls, yellow, Wilson or Penn, 3	can	1.93	4Q 92	4c
Waterpark admission	adult	11.00	92	1r
Waterpark admission	child	8.55	92	1r
Funerals				
Casket, 18-gauge steel, velvet interior		2274.41	91	24r
Cosmetology, hair care, etc.		74.62	91	24r
Embalming		229.94	91	24r
Facility use for ceremony		176.61	91	24r
Hearse, local		116.34	91	24r
Limousine, local		72.68	91	24r
Remains to funeral home, transfer		87.72	91	24r
Service charge, professional		712.53	91	24r
Vault, concrete, non-metallic liner		750.55	91	24r
Viewing facilities, use		155.31	91	24r
Goods and Services				
ACCRA Index, Miscellaneous Goods and Services		99.70	4Q 92	4c
Groceries				
ACCRA Index, Groceries		103.70	4Q 92	4c
Apples, Red Delicious	lb	0.79	4/93	16r
Babyfood, strained vegetables, lowest price	4-4.5 oz jar	0.30	4Q 92	4c
Bacon	lb	1.75	4/93	16r
Bananas	lb	0.33	4Q 92	4c
Bananas	lb	0.42	4/93	16r
Beef, stew, boneless	lb	2.61	4/93	16r
Bologna, all beef or mixed	lb	2.24	4/93	16r
Bread, white	24 oz	0.73	4Q 92	4c
Bread, white, pan	lb	0.64	4/93	16r
Bread, whole wheat, pan	lb	0.96	4/93	16r
Cabbage	lb	0.37	4/93	16r
Carrots, short trimmed and topped	lb	0.47	4/93	16r
Celery	lb	0.64	4/93	16r
Cheese, American	lb	2.98	4/93	16r
Cheese, Cheddar	lb	3.28	4/93	16r
Cheese, Kraft grated Parmesan	8-oz canister	3.43	4Q 92	4c
Chicken, fresh, whole	lb	0.77	4/93	16r
Chicken, fryer, whole	lb	1.03	4Q 92	4c
Chicken breast, bone-in	lb	1.92	4/93	16r
Chicken legs, bone-in	lb	1.06	4/93	16r
Chuck roast, graded and ungraded, ex USDA prime and choice	lb	2.40	4/93	16r
Chuck roast, USDA choice, bone-in	lb	2.19	4/93	16r
Chuck roast, USDA choice, boneless	lb	2.38	4/93	16r
Cigarettes, Winston	carton	19.38	4Q 92	4c
Coffee, 100% ground roast, all sizes	lb	2.48	4/93	16r
Coffee, vacuum-packed	13-oz can	2.01	4Q 92	4c
Corn, frozen	10 oz	0.75	4Q 92	4c
Corn Flakes, Kellogg's or Post Toasties	18 oz	2.15	4Q 92	4c
Crackers, soda, salted	lb	1.15	4/93	16r
Eggs, Grade A large	doz	0.89	4Q 92	4c
Eggs, Grade A large	doz	0.96	4/93	16r
Flour, white, all purpose	lb	0.24	4/93	16r
Frankfurters, all meat or all beef	lb	2.01	4/93	16r
Grapefruit	lb	0.44	4/93	16r
Grapes, Thompson Seedless	lb	1.40	4/93	16r
Ground beef, 100% beef	lb	1.58	4/93	16r
Ground beef, lean and extra lean	lb	2.09	4/93	16r

Values are in dollars or fractions of dollars. In the column headed *Ref*, references are shown to sources. Each reference is followed by a letter. These refer to the geographical level for which data were reported: s = State, r = Region, and c = City or metro. The abbreviation *ex* is used to mean *except* or *excluding*; *exp* stands for expenditures. For other abbreviations and further explanations, please see the Introduction.

Fort Worth, TX - continued

Item	Per	Value	Date	Ref.
Groceries				
Ground beef or hamburger	lb	1.42	4Q 92	4c
Ground chuck, 100% beef	lb	1.98	4/93	16r
Ham, boneless, excluding canned	lb	2.89	4/93	16r
Ham, picnic, shoulder, bone-in, smoked	lb	1.02	4/93	16r
Ham, rump or steak half, bone-in, smoked	lb	1.48	4/93	16r
Honey, jar	8 oz	0.73-1.19	92	5r
Honey, jar	lb	1.10-1.79	92	5r
Honey, squeeze bear	12-oz	1.19-1.50	92	5r
Ice cream, prepackaged, bulk, regular	1/2 gal	2.41	4/93	16r
Lemons	lb	1.05	4/93	16r
Lettuce, iceberg	head	0.99	4Q 92	4c
Lettuce, iceberg	lb	0.81	4/93	16r
Margarine, Blue Bonnet or Parkay cubes	lb	0.55	4Q 92	4c
Margarine, stick	lb	0.88	4/93	16r
Milk, whole	1/2 gal	1.39	4Q 92	4c
Orange juice, Minute Maid frozen	12-oz can	1.36	4Q 92	4c
Oranges, navel	lb	0.55	4/93	16r
Peaches	29-oz can	1.47	4Q 92	4c
Pears, Anjou	lb	0.92	4/93	16r
Peas Sweet, Del Monte or Green Giant	15-17 oz can	0.61	4Q 92	4c
Pork chops, center cut, bone-in	lb	3.13	4/93	16r
Potato chips	16 oz	2.94	4/93	16r
Potatoes, white	lb	0.43	4/93	16r
Potatoes, white or red	10-lb sack	2.29	4Q 92	4c
Rib roast, USDA choice, bone-in	lb	4.63	4/93	16r
Rice, white, long grain, uncooked	lb	0.45	4/93	16r
Round roast, graded & ungraded, ex USDA prime & choice	lb	3.03	4/93	16r
Round roast, USDA choice, boneless	lb	3.09	4/93	16r
Sausage, fresh, loose	lb	2.08	4/93	16r
Sausage, Jimmy Dean, 100% pork	lb	2.57	4Q 92	4c
Short ribs, bone-in	lb	2.66	4/93	16r
Shortening, vegetable oil blends	lb	0.69	4/93	16r
Shortening, vegetable, Crisco	3-lb can	2.18	4Q 92	4c
Soft drink, Coca Cola	2 liter	1.26	4Q 92	4c
Spaghetti and macaroni	lb	0.81	4/93	16r
Steak, rib eye, USDA choice, boneless	lb	6.24	4/93	16r
Steak, round, graded & ungraded, ex USDA prime & choice	lb	3.31	4/93	16r
Steak, round, USDA choice, boneless	lb	3.34	4/93	16r
Steak, sirloin, graded & ungraded, ex USDA prime & choice	lb	4.19	4/93	16r
Steak, sirloin, USDA choice, boneless	lb	4.46	4/93	16r
Steak, T-bone	lb	6.28	4Q 92	4c
Steak, T-bone, USDA choice, bone-in	lb	5.25	4/93	16r
Strawberries, dry pint	12 oz	0.92	4/93	16r
Sugar, cane or beet	4 lb	1.53	4Q 92	4c
Sugar, white	lb	0.39	4/93	16r
Sugar, white, 33-80 oz pk	lb	0.38	4/93	16r
Tomatoes, field grown	lb	0.88	4/93	16r
Tomatoes, Hunt's or Del Monte	14.5-oz can	0.72	4Q 92	4c
Tuna, chunk, light	6.125-6.5 oz can	0.59	4Q 92	4c
Tuna, chunk, light	lb	1.79	4/93	16r
Turkey, frozen, whole	lb	1.04	4/93	16r
Yogurt, natural, fruit flavored	1/2 pint	0.57	4/93	16r
Health Care				
ACCRA Index, Health Care		107.90	4Q 92	4c
Analgesic, Aspirin, Bayer, 325 mg tablets	100	4.24	4Q 92	4c
Childbirth, cesarean, hospital		5034	91	62r
Childbirth, cesarean, physician's fee		2053	91	62r
Childbirth, normal, hospital		2712	91	62r
Childbirth, normal, physician's fee		1492	91	62r

Fort Worth, TX - continued

Item	Per	Value	Date	Ref.
Health Care - continued				
Dentist's fee, adult teeth cleaning and periodic oral exam	visit	53.40	4Q 92	4c
Doctor's fee, routine exam, established patient	visit	41.60	4Q 92	4c
Health care spending, state	capita	2192	3/93	84s
Hospital care, semiprivate room	day	241.88	90	27c
Hospital care, semiprivate room	day	321.20	4Q 92	4c
Medical insurance premium, per employee, small group comprehensive	month	372.30	10/91	25c
Mental health care, exp	capita	20.37-28.83	90	38s
Mental health care, exp, state mental health agency	capita	22.72	90	38s
Mental health care, hospital psychiatric services, non-Federal, exp	capita	7.95	88	38s
Mental health care, mental health organization, multiservice, exp	capita	12.05	88	38s
Mental health care, psychiatric hospitals, private, exp	capita	37.78	88	38s
Mental health care, psychiatric out-patient clinics, freestanding, exp	capita	0.43	88	38s
Mental health care, state and county mental hospitals, exp	capita	12.54	88	38s
Mental health care, VA medical centers, exp	capita	5.35	88	38s
Physician fee, family practice, first-visit		75.00	91	62r
Physician fee, family practice, revisit		34.00	91	62r
Physician fee, general practice, first-visit		61.00	91	62r
Physician fee, general practice, revisit		32.00	91	62r
Physician fee, general surgeon, first-visit		64.00	91	62r
Physician fee, general surgeon, revisit		40.00	91	62r
Physician fee, internal medicine, first-visit		98.00	91	62r
Physician fee, internal medicine, revisit		40.00	91	62r
Physician fee, median, neurosurgeon, first-visit		130.00	91	62r
Physician fee, median, nonsurgical specialist, first-visit		95.00	91	62r
Physician fee, median, orthopedic surgeon, first-visit		91.00	91	62r
Physician fee, median, plastic surgeon, first-visit		66.00	91	62r
Physician fee, median, surgical specialist, first-visit		62.00	91	62r
Physician fee, neurosurgeon, revisit		50.00	91	62r
Physician fee, nonsurgical specialist, revisit		40.00	91	62r
Physician fee, obstetrics/gynecology, first-visit		64.00	91	62r
Physician fee, obstetrics/gynecology, revisit		41.00	91	62r
Physician fee, orthopedic surgeon, revisit		40.00	91	62r
Physician fee, pediatrician, first-visit		49.00	91	62r
Physician fee, pediatrician, revisit		33.00	91	62r
Physician fee, plastic surgeon, revisit		43.00	91	62r
Physician fee, surgical specialist, revisit		37.00	91	62r
Substance abuse, hospital ancillary charge	incident	3750	90	70s
Substance abuse, hospital physician charge	incident	1080	90	70s
Substance abuse, hospital room and board	incident	5320	90	70s
Household Goods				
Appliance repair, home, service call, washing machine	min labor charge	33.26	4Q 92	4c
Laundry detergent, Tide Ultra, Bold, or Cheer	42 oz	3.71	4Q 92	4c
Tissues, facial, Kleenex brand	175-count box	1.06	4Q 92	4c
Housing				
ACCRA Index, Housing		86.80	4Q 92	4c
Home, median price	unit	80.20		26c

Values are in dollars or fractions of dollars. In the column headed *Ref*, references are shown to sources. Each reference is followed by a letter. These refer to the geographical level for which data were reported: s=State, r=Region, and c=City or metro. The abbreviation *ex* is used to mean *except* or *excluding*; *exp* stands for expenditures. For other abbreviations and further explanations, please see the Introduction.

Fort Worth, TX - continued

Item	Per	Value	Date	Ref.
Housing				
House, 1,800 sq ft, 8,000 sq ft lot, new, urban	total	87600	4Q 92	4c
House payment, principal and interest, 25% down payment	month	482	4Q 92	4c
Mortgage rate, incl. points & origination fee, 30-year fixed or adjustable rate	percent	8.00	4Q 92	4c
Rent, apartment, 2 bedrooms - 1-1/2 to 2 baths, unfurnished, 950 sq ft, water	month	548	4Q 92	4c
Rental unit, 1 bedroom	month	451	93	23c
Rental unit, 2 bedroom	month	532	93	23c
Rental unit, 3 bedroom	month	665	93	23c
Rental unit, 4 bedroom	month	745	93	23c
Rental unit, efficiency	month	371	93	23c
Insurance and Pensions				
Auto insurance, private passenger	year	709.79	91	63s
Personal Goods				
Shampoo, Alberto VO5	15 oz	0.94	4Q 92	4c
Toothpaste, Crest or Colgate	6-7 oz	1.62	4Q 92	4c
Personal Services				
Dry cleaning, man's 2-piece suit		6.03	4Q 92	4c
Haircare, woman's shampoo, trim and blow-dry		13.54	4Q 92	4c
Haircut, man's barbershop, no styling		7.99	4Q 92	4c
Restaurant Food				
Chicken, fried, thigh and drumstick		1.99	4Q 92	4c
Hamburger with cheese	1/4 lb	1.89	4Q 92	4c
Pizza, Pizza Hut or Pizza Inn, cheese, thin crust	12-13 in	7.89	4Q 92	4c
Taxes				
Tax, cigarette	pack	41	91	77s
Tax, gasoline	gal	20	91	77s
Taxes, state	capita	923	91	77s
Transportation				
ACCRA Index, Transportation		103.90	4Q 92	4c
Auto rental, average	day	46.75	6/91	60c
Bus fare, up to 10 miles	one-way	0.75	4Q 92	4c
Driver's license fee		16.00	12/90	43s
Limo fare, airport-city, average	day	7.00	6/91	60c
Taxi fare, airport-city, average	day	22.00	6/91	60c
Tire balance, computer or spin balance, front	wheel	7.38	4Q 92	4c
Travel				
Breakfast	day	5.96	6/91	60c
Business travel	day	193.00	4/93	89r
Dinner	day	19.57	6/91	60c
Lodging	day	95.42	91	60c
Lunch	day	9.37	6/91	60c
Utilities				
ACCRA Index, Utilities		108.10	4Q 92	4c
Electricity	mil Btu	17.09	90	64s
Electricity, all electric, 1,800 sq ft living area new home	month	120.76	4Q 92	4c
Electricity, residential	KWh	5.92	2/93	94s

Framingham-Natick, MA

Item	Per	Value	Date	Ref.
Composite ACCRA index		138.00	4Q 92	4c
Alcoholic Beverages				
Beer, Miller Lite or Budweiser, 12-oz containers	6 pack	4.77	4Q 92	4c
Liquor, J & B Scotch	750 ml	16.69	4Q 92	4c
Wine, Gallo Chablis blanc, 1.5 liter	bottle	4.92	4Q 92	4c
Clothing				
Jeans, man's denim		35.98	4Q 92	4c
Shirt, man's dress shirt		21.59	4Q 92	4c

Framingham-Natick, MA - continued

Item	Per	Value	Date	Ref.
Clothing - continued				
Undervest, boy's size 10-14, cotton	3	6.58	4Q 92	4c
Communications				
Newspaper subscription, daily and Sunday home delivery, large-city	month	17.39	4Q 92	4c
Telephone, flat rate	month	11.67-14.18	91	11c
Telephone bill, family of four	month	18.09	4Q 92	4c
Energy and Fuels				
Energy, combined forms, 1,800 sq ft heating area	month	167.98	4Q 92	4c
Energy, exc electricity, 1,800 sq ft heating area	month	91.58	4Q 92	4c
Gasoline, motor	gal	1.23	4Q 92	4c
Entertainment				
Bowling, evening rate	game	2.12	4Q 92	4c
Monopoly game, Parker Brothers', No. 9		12.55	4Q 92	4c
Movie	admission	6.75	4Q 92	4c
Tennis balls, yellow, Wilson or Penn, 3	can	2.56	4Q 92	4c
Goods and Services				
ACCRA Index, Miscellaneous Goods and Services		116.10	4Q 92	4c
Groceries				
ACCRA Index, Groceries		109.60	4Q 92	4c
Babyfood, strained vegetables, lowest price	4-4.5 oz jar	0.38	4Q 92	4c
Bananas	lb	0.59	4Q 92	4c
Bread, white	24 oz	0.97	4Q 92	4c
Cheese, Kraft grated Parmesan	8-oz canister	3.17	4Q 92	4c
Chicken, fryer, whole	lb	0.99	4Q 92	4c
Cigarettes, Winston	carton	18.36	4Q 92	4c
Coffee, vacuum-packed	13-oz can	2.19	4Q 92	4c
Corn, frozen	10 oz	0.59	4Q 92	4c
Corn Flakes, Kellogg's or Post Toasties	18 oz	2.08	4Q 92	4c
Eggs, Grade A large	doz	0.89	4Q 92	4c
Ground beef or hamburger	lb	1.37	4Q 92	4c
Lettuce, iceberg	head	0.99	4Q 92	4c
Margarine, Blue Bonnet or Parkay cubes	lb	0.67	4Q 92	4c
Milk, whole	1/2 gal	1.29	4Q 92	4c
Orange juice, Minute Maid frozen	12-oz can	1.21	4Q 92	4c
Peaches	29-oz can	1.56	4Q 92	4c
Peas Sweet, Del Monte or Green Giant	15-17 oz can	0.53	4Q 92	4c
Potatoes, white or red	10-lb sack	1.61	4Q 92	4c
Sausage, Jimmy Dean, 100% pork	lb	3.56	4Q 92	4c
Shortening, vegetable, Crisco	3-lb can	2.86	4Q 92	4c
Soft drink, Coca Cola	2 liter	1.19	4Q 92	4c
Steak, T-bone	lb	4.99	4Q 92	4c
Sugar, cane or beet	4 lb	1.74	4Q 92	4c
Tomatoes, Hunt's or Del Monte	14.5-oz can	0.61	4Q 92	4c
Tuna, chunk, light	6.125-6.5 oz can	0.80	4Q 92	4c
Health Care				
ACCRA Index, Health Care		143.70	4Q 92	4c
Analgesic, Aspirin, Bayer, 325 mg tablets	100	5.64	4Q 92	4c
Dentist's fee, adult teeth cleaning and periodic oral exam	visit	66.25	4Q 92	4c
Doctor's fee, routine exam, established patient	visit	50.00	4Q 92	4c
Hospital care, semiprivate room	day	387.60	90	27c

Values are in dollars or fractions of dollars. In the column headed *Ref*, references are shown to sources. Each reference is followed by a letter. These refer to the geographical level for which data were reported: s = State, r = Region, and c = City or metro. The abbreviation *ex* is used to mean *except* or *excluding*; *exp* stands for *expenditures*. For other abbreviations and further explanations, please see the Introduction.

Framingham-Natick, MA - continued

Item	Per	Value	Date	Ref.
Health Care				
Hospital care, semiprivate room	day	581.50	4Q 92	4c
Household Goods				
Appliance repair, home, service call, washing machine	min labor charge	37.48	4Q 92	4c
Laundry detergent, Tide Ultra, Bold, or Cheer	42 oz	3.36	4Q 92	4c
Tissues, facial, Kleenex brand	175-count box	1.19	4Q 92	4c
Housing				
ACCRA Index, Housing		178.00	4Q 92	4c
House, 1,800 sq ft, 8,000 sq ft lot, new, urban	total	204323	4Q 92	4c
House payment, principal and interest, 25% down payment	month	1131	4Q 92	4c
Mortgage rate, incl. points & origination fee, 30-year fixed or adjustable rate	percent	8.06	4Q 92	4c
Rent, apartment, 2 bedrooms - 1-1/2 to 2 baths, unfurnished, 950 sq ft, water	month	794	4Q 92	4c
Personal Goods				
Shampoo, Alberto VO5	15 oz	1.52	4Q 92	4c
Toothpaste, Crest or Colgate	6-7 oz	2.29	4Q 92	4c
Personal Services				
Dry cleaning, man's 2-piece suit		6.71	4Q 92	4c
Haircare, woman's shampoo, trim and blow-dry		19.75	4Q 92	4c
Haircut, man's barbershop, no styling		8.24	4Q 92	4c
Restaurant Food				
Chicken, fried, thigh and drumstick		2.68	4Q 92	4c
Hamburger with cheese	1/4 lb	2.01	4Q 92	4c
Pizza, Pizza Hut or Pizza Inn, cheese, thin crust	12-13 in	7.69	4Q 92	4c
Transportation				
ACCRA Index, Transportation		128.40	4Q 92	4c
Tire balance, computer or spin balance, front	wheel	9.60	4Q 92	4c
Utilities				
ACCRA Index, Utilities		147.80	4Q 92	4c
Electricity, partial electric and other energy, 1,800 sq ft living area new home	month	76.40	4Q 92	4c

Freeport, IL

Item	Per	Value	Date	Ref.
Composite ACCRA index		102.30	4Q 92	4c
Alcoholic Beverages				
Beer, Miller Lite or Budweiser, 12-oz containers	6 pack	3.82	4Q 92	4c
Liquor, J & B Scotch	750 ml	13.16	4Q 92	4c
Wine, Gallo Chablis blanc, 1.5 liter	bottle	4.29	4Q 92	4c
Clothing				
Jeans, man's denim		38.33	4Q 92	4c
Shirt, man's dress shirt		22.67	4Q 92	4c
Undervest, boy's size 10-14, cotton	3	4.56	4Q 92	4c
Communications				
Newspaper subscription, daily and Sunday home delivery, large-city	month	9.10	4Q 92	4c
Telephone bill, family of four	month	28.54	4Q 92	4c
Energy and Fuels				
Energy, combined forms, 1,800 sq ft heating area	month	139.35	4Q 92	4c
Energy, exc electricity, 1,800 sq ft heating area	month	53.98	4Q 92	4c
Gasoline, motor	gal	1.27	4Q 92	4c

Freeport, IL - continued

Item	Per	Value	Date	Ref.
Entertainment				
Bowling, evening rate	game	1.50	4Q 92	4c
Monopoly game, Parker Brothers', No. 9		10.32	4Q 92	4c
Movie	admission	3.50	4Q 92	4c
Tennis balls, yellow, Wilson or Penn, 3	can	3.22	4Q 92	4c
Goods and Services				
ACCRA Index, Miscellaneous Goods and Services		100.60	4Q 92	4c
Groceries				
ACCRA Index, Groceries		109.50	4Q 92	4c
Babyfood, strained vegetables, lowest price	4-4.5 oz jar	0.37	4Q 92	4c
Bananas	lb	0.46	4Q 92	4c
Bread, white	24 oz	1.38	4Q 92	4c
Cheese, Kraft grated Parmesan	8-oz canister	3.27	4Q 92	4c
Chicken, fryer, whole	lb	0.84	4Q 92	4c
Cigarettes, Winston	carton	18.10	4Q 92	4c
Coffee, vacuum-packed	13-oz can	2.08	4Q 92	4c
Corn, frozen	10 oz	0.67	4Q 92	4c
Corn Flakes, Kellogg's or Post Toasties	18 oz	2.26	4Q 92	4c
Eggs, Grade A large	doz	0.72	4Q 92	4c
Ground beef or hamburger	lb	1.47	4Q 92	4c
Lettuce, iceberg	head	0.89	4Q 92	4c
Margarine, Blue Bonnet or Parkay cubes	lb	0.69	4Q 92	4c
Milk, whole	1/2 gal	1.54	4Q 92	4c
Orange juice, Minute Maid frozen	12-oz can	1.39	4Q 92	4c
Peaches	29-oz can	1.49	4Q 92	4c
Peas Sweet, Del Monte or Green Giant	15-17 oz can	0.59	4Q 92	4c
Potatoes, white or red	10-lb sack	1.99	4Q 92	4c
Sausage, Jimmy Dean, 100% pork	lb	2.45	4Q 92	4c
Shortening, vegetable, Crisco	3-lb can	2.24	4Q 92	4c
Soft drink, Coca Cola	2 liter	1.36	4Q 92	4c
Steak, T-bone	lb	4.89	4Q 92	4c
Sugar, cane or beet	4 lb	1.40	4Q 92	4c
Tomatoes, Hunt's or Del Monte	14.5-oz can	0.73	4Q 92	4c
Tuna, chunk, light	6.125-6.5 oz can	0.67	4Q 92	4c
Health Care				
ACCRA Index, Health Care		89.80	4Q 92	4c
Analgesic, Aspirin, Bayer, 325 mg tablets	100	5.21	4Q 92	4c
Dentist's fee, adult teeth cleaning and periodic oral exam	visit	40.00	4Q 92	4c
Doctor's fee, routine exam, established patient	visit	37.00	4Q 92	4c
Hospital care, semiprivate room	day	220.00	4Q 92	4c
Household Goods				
Appliance repair, home, service call, washing machine	min labor charge	40.33	4Q 92	4c
Laundry detergent, Tide Ultra, Bold, or Cheer	42 oz	3.70	4Q 92	4c
Tissues, facial, Kleenex brand	175-count box	1.11	4Q 92	4c
Housing				
ACCRA Index, Housing		92.80	4Q 92	4c
House, 1,800 sq ft, 8,000 sq ft lot, new, urban	total	104333	4Q 92	4c

Values are in dollars or fractions of dollars. In the column headed *Ref*, references are shown to sources. Each reference is followed by a letter. These refer to the geographical level for which data were reported: s = State, r = Region, and c = City or metro. The abbreviation *ex* is used to mean *except* or *excluding*; *exp* stands for *expenditures*. For other abbreviations and further explanations, please see the Introduction.

Freeport, IL - continued

Item	Per	Value	Date	Ref.
Housing				
House payment, principal and interest, 25% down payment	month	594	4Q 92	4c
Mortgage rate, incl. points & origination fee, 30-year fixed or adjustable rate	percent	8.36	4Q 92	4c
Rent, apartment, 2 bedrooms - 1-1/2 to 2 baths, unfurnished, 950 sq ft, water	month	403	4Q 92	4c
Personal Goods				
Shampoo, Alberto VO5	15 oz	1.48	4Q 92	4c
Toothpaste, Crest or Colgate	6-7 oz	2.25	4Q 92	4c
Personal Services				
Dry cleaning, man's 2-piece suit		5.08	4Q 92	4c
Haircare, woman's shampoo, trim and blow-dry		14.00	4Q 92	4c
Haircut, man's barbershop, no styling		7.33	4Q 92	4c
Restaurant Food				
Chicken, fried, thigh and drumstick		1.99	4Q 92	4c
Hamburger with cheese	1/4 lb	1.81	4Q 92	4c
Pizza, Pizza Hut or Pizza Inn, cheese, thin crust	12-13 in	7.85	4Q 92	4c
Transportation				
ACCRA Index, Transportation		107.20	4Q 92	4c
Tire balance, computer or spin balance, front	wheel	6.67	4Q 92	4c
Utilities				
ACCRA Index, Utilities		129.50	4Q 92	4c
Electricity, partial electric and other energy, 1,800 sq ft living area new home	month	85.37	4Q 92	4c

Fresno, CA

Item	Per	Value	Date	Ref.
Child Care				
Child care fee, average, center	hour	1.71	90	65r
Child care fee, average, nonregulated family day care	hour	1.32	90	65r
Child care fee, average, regulated family day care	hour	1.86	90	65r
Communications				
Long-distance telephone service, day, initial minute, 0-100 miles	min	0.17-0.40	91	12s
Long-distance telephone service, day, additional minute, 0-100 miles	min	0.07-0.31	91	12s
Long-distance telephone service, evenings/weekends, 0-100 mi, initial minute	min	0.07-0.16	91	12s
Long-distance telephone service, evenings/weekends, 0-100 mi, additional minute	min	0.03-0.12	91	12s
Telephone, residential, private line, rotary, unlimited calling	month	12.28	10/91	78c
Education				
Board, 4-yr private college/university	year	2515	91	22s
Board, 4-yr public college/university	year	2268	91	22s
Expenditures, local gov't, public elementary/secondary	pupil	4866	92	20s
Room, 4-year private college/university	year	2622	91	22s
Room, 4-year public college/university	year	2406	91	22s
Tuition, 2-year private college/university	year	7942	91	22s
Tuition, 2-year public college/university	year	114	91	22s
Tuition, 4-year private college/university	year	10863	91	22s
Tuition, 4-year public college/university, in-state	year	1220	91	22s
Energy and Fuels				
Coal	mil Btu	2.01	90	64s
Energy	mil Btu	9.08	90	64s
Energy exp/householder, 1-family unit	year	362	90	28r
Energy exp/householder, <1,000 sq ft heating area	year	254	90	28r
Energy exp/householder, 1,000-1,999 sq ft heating area	year	358	90	28r

Fresno, CA - continued

Item	Per	Value	Date	Ref.
Energy and Fuels - continued				
Energy exp/householder, 2,000+ sq ft heating area	year	467	90	28r
Energy exp/householder, mobile home	year	390	90	28r
Energy exp/householder, multifamily	year	252	90	28r
Gas, natural	mil Btu	4.31	90	64s
Gas, natural	000 cu ft	6.27	91	46s
Gas, natural, exp	year	369	91	46s
Gasoline, unleaded regular	mil Btu	8.57	90	64s
Entertainment				
Miniature golf admission	adult	6.18	92	1r
Miniature golf admission	child	5.14	92	1r
Waterpark admission	adult	11.00	92	1r
Waterpark admission	child	8.55	92	1r
Funerals				
Casket, 18-gauge steel, velvet interior		1781.09	91	24r
Cosmetology, hair care, etc.		84.64	91	24r
Embalming		207.41	91	24r
Facility use for ceremony		205.76	91	24r
Hearse, local		105.14	91	24r
Limousine, local		83.21	91	24r
Remains to funeral home, transfer		113.82	91	24r
Service charge, professional		626.33	91	24r
Vault, concrete, non-metallic liner		599.54	91	24r
Viewing facilities, use		85.81	91	24r
Groceries				
Apples, Red Delicious	lb	0.80	4/93	16r
Bacon	lb	1.79	4/93	16r
Bananas	lb	0.53	4/93	16r
Bologna, all beef or mixed	lb	2.67	4/93	16r
Bread, white, pan	lb	0.81	4/93	16r
Carrots, short trimmed and topped	lb	0.39	4/93	16r
Chicken, fresh, whole	lb	0.94	4/93	16r
Chicken breast, bone-in	lb	2.19	4/93	16r
Chuck roast, graded and ungraded, ex USDA prime and choice	lb	2.26	4/93	16r
Coffee, 100% ground roast, all sizes	lb	2.33	4/93	16r
Eggs, Grade AA large	doz	1.18	4/93	16r
Flour, white, all purpose	lb	0.22	4/93	16r
Grapefruit	lb	0.52	4/93	16r
Grapes, Thompson Seedless	lb	1.50	4/93	16r
Ground beef, 100% beef	lb	1.44	4/93	16r
Ground beef, lean and extra lean	lb	2.34	4/93	16r
Ham, boneless, excluding canned	lb	2.56	4/93	16r
Honey, jar	8 oz	0.89-1.00	92	5r
Honey, jar	lb	1.35-1.97	92	5r
Honey, squeeze bear	12-oz	1.19-1.50	92	5r
Ice cream, prepackaged, bulk, regular	1/2 gal	2.40	4/93	16r
Lemons	lb	0.81	4/93	16r
Lettuce, iceberg	lb	0.84	4/93	16r
Margarine, stick	lb	0.81	4/93	16r
Oranges, navel	lb	0.48	4/93	16r
Pork chops, center cut, bone-in	lb	3.25	4/93	16r
Potato chips	16 oz	2.89	4/93	16r
Potatoes, white	lb	0.38	4/93	16r
Round roast, graded & ungraded, ex USDA prime & choice	lb	3.00	4/93	16r
Round roast, USDA choice, boneless	lb	3.16	4/93	16r
Shortening, vegetable oil blends	lb	0.86	4/93	16r
Spaghetti and macaroni	lb	0.84	4/93	16r
Steak, round, graded & ungraded, ex USDA prime & choice	lb	3.34	4/93	16r
Steak, round, USDA choice, boneless	lb	3.24	4/93	16r
Steak, sirloin, graded & ungraded, ex USDA prime & choice	lb	3.75	4/93	16r
Steak, sirloin, USDA choice, boneless	lb	4.49	4/93	16r
Sugar, white	lb	0.41	4/93	16r
Sugar, white, 33-80 oz pk	lb	0.38	4/93	16r
Tomatoes, field grown	lb	1.01	4/93	16r
Turkey, frozen, whole	lb	1.04	4/93	16r

Values are in dollars or fractions of dollars. In the column headed *Ref*, references are shown to sources. Each reference is followed by a letter. These refer to the geographical level for which data were reported: s=State, r=Region, and c=City or metro. The abbreviation *ex* is used to mean *except* or *excluding*; *exp* stands for expenditures. For other abbreviations and further explanations, please see the Introduction.

Fresno, CA - continued

Item	Per	Value	Date	Ref.
Health Care				
Cardizem 60 mg tablets	30	24.04	92	49s
Cector 250 mg tablets	15	35.87	92	49s
Childbirth, cesarean, hospital		5533	91	62r
Childbirth, cesarean, physician's fee		2053	91	62r
Childbirth, normal, hospital		2745	91	62r
Childbirth, normal, physician's fee		1492	91	62r
Health care spending, state	capita	2894	3/93	84s
Hospital care, semiprivate room	day	330.00	90	27c
Medical insurance premium, per employee, small group comprehensive	month	394.20	10/91	25c
Medical plan per employee	year	3421	91	45r
Mental health care, exp	capita	37.60-53.67	90	38s
Mental health care, exp, state mental health agency	capita	42.32	90	38s
Mental health care, hospital psychiatric services, non-Federal, exp	capita	10.64	88	38s
Mental health care, mental health organization, multiservice, exp	capita	28.56	88	38s
Mental health care, psychiatric hospitals, private, exp	capita	18.60	88	38s
Mental health care, psychiatric out-patient clinics, freestanding, exp	capita	2.28	88	38s
Mental health care, psychiatric partial-care organizations, freestanding, exp	capita	0.24	88	38s
Mental health care, state and county mental hospitals, exp	capita	13.60	88	38s
Mental health care, VA medical centers, exp	capita	2.33	88	38s
Mevacor 20 mg tablets	30	67.62	92	49s
Physician fee, family practice, first-visit		111.00	91	62r
Physician fee, family practice, revisit		45.00	91	62r
Physician fee, general practice, first-visit		100.00	91	62r
Physician fee, general practice, revisit		40.00	91	62r
Physician fee, internal medicine, first-visit		137.00	91	62r
Physician fee, internal medicine, revisit		48.00	91	62r
Physician fee, median, neurosurgeon, first-visit		157.00	91	62r
Physician fee, median, nonsurgical specialist, first-visit		131.00	91	62r
Physician fee, median, orthopedic surgeon, first-visit		124.00	91	62r
Physician fee, median, plastic surgeon, first-visit		88.00	91	62r
Physician fee, median, surgical specialist, first-visit		100.00	91	62r
Physician fee, neurosurgeon, revisit		51.00	91	62r
Physician fee, nonsurgical specialist, revisit		47.00	91	62r
Physician fee, obstetrics/gynecology, first-visit		95.00	91	62r
Physician fee, obstetrics/gynecology, revisit		50.00	91	62r
Physician fee, orthopedic surgeon, revisit		51.00	91	62r
Physician fee, pediatrician, first-visit		81.00	91	62r
Physician fee, pediatrician, revisit		42.00	91	62r
Physician fee, plastic surgeon, revisit		48.00	91	62r
Physician fee, surgical specialist, revisit		49.00	91	62r
Prozac 20 mg tablets	14	33.22	92	49s
Substance abuse, hospital ancillary charge	incident	1760	90	70s
Substance abuse, hospital physician charge	incident	750	90	70s
Substance abuse, hospital room and board	incident	6390	90	70s
Tagamet 300 mg tablets	100	77.08	92	49s
Xanax 0.25 mg tablets	90	64.08	92	49s
Zantac 160 mg tablets	60	92.31	92	49s
Housing				
Home, median price	unit	131,200	92	58s
Rental unit, 1 bedroom	month	479	93	23c
Rental unit, 2 bedroom	month	565	93	23c
Rental unit, 3 bedroom	month	705	93	23c
Rental unit, 4 bedroom	month	791	93	23c
Rental unit, efficiency	month	394	93	23c

Fresno, CA - continued

Item	Per	Value	Date	Ref.
Insurance and Pensions				
Auto insurance, private passenger	year	904.37	91	63s
Taxes				
Tax, cigarette	pack	35	91	77s
Tax, gasoline	gal	16	91	77s
Taxes, state	capita	1477	91	77s
Transportation				
Auto rental, average	day	33.67	6/91	60c
Bus fare	one-way	0.75	3/93	2c
Driver's license fee		10.00	12/90	43s
Taxi fare, airport-city, average	day	12.50	6/91	60c
Travel				
Breakfast	day	7.67	6/91	60c
Business travel	day	178.00	4/93	89r
Dinner	day	19.30	6/91	60c
Lodging	day	80.83	91	60c
Lunch	day	10.63	6/91	60c
Utilities				
Electricity	mil Btu	25.98	90	64s

Gadsden, AL

Item	Per	Value	Date	Ref.
Composite ACCRA index		90.10	4Q 92	4c
Alcoholic Beverages				
Beer, Miller Lite or Budweiser, 12-oz containers	6 pack	4.39	4Q 92	4c
Liquor, J & B Scotch	750 ml	19.99	4Q 92	4c
Wine, Gallo Chablis blanc, 1.5 liter	bottle	5.49	4Q 92	4c
Child Care				
Child care fee, average, center	hour	1.29	90	65r
Child care fee, average, nonregulated family day care	hour	0.89	90	65r
Child care fee, average, regulated family day care	hour	1.32	90	65r
Clothing				
Jeans, man's denim		32.59	4Q 92	4c
Shirt, man's dress shirt		25.50	4Q 92	4c
Undervest, boy's size 10-14, cotton	3	3.45	4Q 92	4c
Communications				
Long-distance telephone service, day, initial minute, 0-100 miles	min	0.11-0.36	91	12s
Long-distance telephone service, day, additional minute, 0-100 miles	min	0.09-0.26	91	12s
Long-distance telephone service, evenings/weekends, 0-100 mi, initial minute	min	0.04-0.14	91	12s
Long-distance telephone service, evenings/weekends, 0-100 mi, additional minute	min	0.04-0.10	91	12s
Newspaper subscription, daily and Sunday home delivery, large-city	month	8.41	4Q 92	4c
Telephone, flat rate	month	16.21	91	11c
Telephone bill, family of four	month	19.55	4Q 92	4c
Education				
Board, 4-yr private college/university	year	1795	91	22s
Board, 4-yr public college/university	year	1469	91	22s
Expenditures, local gov't, public elementary/secondary	pupil	3675	92	20s
Room, 4-year private college/university	year	1340	91	22s
Room, 4-year public college/university	year	1295	91	22s
Tuition, 2-year private college/university	year	4148	91	22s
Tuition, 2-year public college/university	year	689	91	22s
Tuition, 4-year private college/university	year	5942	91	22s
Tuition, 4-year public college/university, in-state	year	1593	91	22s
Energy and Fuels				
Coal	mil Btu	1.83	90	64s
Energy	mil Btu	7.92	90	64s

Values are in dollars or fractions of dollars. In the column headed *Ref*, references are shown to sources. Each reference is followed by a letter. These refer to the geographical level for which data were reported: s=State, r=Region, and c=City or metro. The abbreviation *ex* is used to mean *except* or *excluding*; *exp* stands for expenditures. For other abbreviations and further explanations, please see the Introduction.

Gadsden, AL - continued

Item	Per	Value	Date	Ref.
Energy and Fuels				
Energy, combined forms, 1,800 sq ft heating area	month	123.23	4Q 92	4c
Energy, exc electricity, 1,800 sq ft heating area	month	42.93	4Q 92	4c
Energy exp/householder, 1-family unit	year	403	90	28r
Energy exp/householder, <1,000 sq ft heating area	year	342	90	28r
Energy exp/householder, 1,000-1,999 sq ft heating area	year	388	90	28r
Energy exp/householder, 2,000+ sq ft heating area	year	434	90	28r
Energy exp/householder, mobile home	year	320	90	28r
Energy exp/householder, multifamily	year	338	90	28r
Gas, natural	mil Btu	4.07	90	64s
Gas, natural	000 cu ft	7.05	91	46s
Gas, natural, exp	year	461	91	46s
Gasoline, motor	gal	1.13	4Q 92	4c
Gasoline, unleaded regular	mil Btu	8.96	90	64s
Entertainment				
Bowling, evening rate	game	2.00	4Q 92	4c
Miniature golf admission	adult	6.18	92	1r
Miniature golf admission	child	5.14	92	1r
Monopoly game, Parker Brothers', No. 9		9.96	4Q 92	4c
Movie	admission	5.00	4Q 92	4c
Tennis balls, yellow, Wilson or Penn, 3	can	1.97	4Q 92	4c
Waterpark admission	adult	11.00	92	1r
Waterpark admission	child	8.55	92	1r
Funerals				
Casket, 18-gauge steel, velvet interior		2329.05	91	24r
Cosmetology, hair care, etc.		72.78	91	24r
Embalming		240.71	91	24r
Facility use for ceremony		181.67	91	24r
Hearse, local		106.25	91	24r
Limousine, local		70.92	91	24r
Remains to funeral home, transfer		96.30	91	24r
Service charge, professional		687.09	91	24r
Vault, concrete, non-metallic liner		732.09	91	24r
Viewing facilities, use		190.30	91	24r
Goods and Services				
ACCRA Index, Miscellaneous Goods and Services		94.60	4Q 92	4c
Groceries				
ACCRA Index, Groceries		95.50	4Q 92	4c
Apples, Red Delicious	lb	0.79	4/93	16r
Babyfood, strained vegetables, lowest price	4-4.5 oz jar	0.31	4Q 92	4c
Bacon	lb	1.75	4/93	16r
Bananas	lb	0.35	4Q 92	4c
Bananas	lb	0.42	4/93	16r
Beef, stew, boneless	lb	2.61	4/93	16r
Bologna, all beef or mixed	lb	2.24	4/93	16r
Bread, white	24 oz	0.66	4Q 92	4c
Bread, white, pan	lb	0.64	4/93	16r
Bread, whole wheat, pan	lb	0.96	4/93	16r
Cabbage	lb	0.37	4/93	16r
Carrots, short trimmed and topped	lb	0.47	4/93	16r
Celery	lb	0.64	4/93	16r
Cheese, American	lb	2.98	4/93	16r
Cheese, Cheddar	lb	3.28	4/93	16r
Cheese, Kraft grated Parmesan	8-oz canister	3.23	4Q 92	4c
Chicken, fresh, whole	lb	0.77	4/93	16r
Chicken, fryer, whole	lb	0.85	4Q 92	4c
Chicken breast, bone-in	lb	1.92	4/93	16r
Chicken legs, bone-in	lb	1.06	4/93	16r
Chuck roast, graded and ungraded, ex USDA prime and choice	lb	2.40	4/93	16r

Gadsden, AL - continued

Item	Per	Value	Date	Ref.
Groceries - continued				
Chuck roast, USDA choice, bone-in	lb	2.19	4/93	16r
Chuck roast, USDA choice, boneless	lb	2.38	4/93	16r
Cigarettes, Winston	carton	16.54	4Q 92	4c
Coffee, 100% ground roast, all sizes	lb	2.48	4/93	16r
Coffee, vacuum-packed	13-oz can	1.86	4Q 92	4c
Corn, frozen	10 oz	0.81	4Q 92	4c
Corn Flakes, Kellogg's or Post Toasties	18 oz	1.67	4Q 92	4c
Crackers, soda, salted	lb	1.15	4/93	16r
Eggs, Grade A large	doz	0.70	4Q 92	4c
Eggs, Grade A large	doz	0.96	4/93	16r
Flour, white, all purpose	lb	0.24	4/93	16r
Frankfurters, all meat or all beef	lb	2.01	4/93	16r
Grapefruit	lb	0.44	4/93	16r
Grapes, Thompson Seedless	lb	1.40	4/93	16r
Ground beef, 100% beef	lb	1.58	4/93	16r
Ground beef, lean and extra lean	lb	2.09	4/93	16r
Ground beef or hamburger	lb	1.69	4Q 92	4c
Ground chuck, 100% beef	lb	1.98	4/93	16r
Ham, boneless, excluding canned	lb	2.89	4/93	16r
Ham, picnic, shoulder, bone-in, smoked	lb	1.02	4/93	16r
Ham, rump or steak half, bone-in, smoked	lb	1.48	4/93	16r
Honey, jar	8 oz	0.89-1.09	92	5r
Honey, jar	lb	1.39-2.25	92	5r
Honey, squeeze bear	12-oz	1.00-1.50	92	5r
Ice cream, prepackaged, bulk, regular	1/2 gal	2.41	4/93	16r
Lemons	lb	1.05	4/93	16r
Lettuce, iceberg	head	0.87	4Q 92	4c
Lettuce, iceberg	lb	0.81	4/93	16r
Margarine, Blue Bonnet or Parkay cubes	lb	0.65	4Q 92	4c
Margarine, stick	lb	0.88	4/93	16r
Milk, whole	1/2 gal	1.54	4Q 92	4c
Orange juice, Minute Maid frozen	12-oz can	1.26	4Q 92	4c
Oranges, navel	lb	0.55	4/93	16r
Peaches	29-oz can	1.58	4Q 92	4c
Pears, Anjou	lb	0.92	4/93	16r
Peas Sweet, Del Monte or Green Giant	15-17 oz can	0.68	4Q 92	4c
Pork chops, center cut, bone-in	lb	3.13	4/93	16r
Potato chips	16 oz	2.94	4/93	16r
Potatoes, white	lb	0.43	4/93	16r
Potatoes, white or red	10-lb sack	1.95	4Q 92	4c
Rib roast, USDA choice, bone-in	lb	4.63	4/93	16r
Rice, white, long grain, uncooked	lb	0.45	4/93	16r
Round roast, graded & ungraded, ex USDA prime & choice	lb	3.03	4/93	16r
Round roast, USDA choice, boneless	lb	3.09	4/93	16r
Sausage, fresh, loose	lb	2.08	4/93	16r
Sausage, Jimmy Dean, 100% pork	lb	2.23	4Q 92	4c
Short ribs, bone-in	lb	2.66	4/93	16r
Shortening, vegetable oil blends	lb	0.69	4/93	16r
Shortening, vegetable, Crisco	3-lb can	2.22	4Q 92	4c
Soft drink, Coca Cola	2 liter	0.99	4Q 92	4c
Spaghetti and macaroni	lb	0.81	4/93	16r
Steak, rib eye, USDA choice, boneless	lb	6.24	4/93	16r
Steak, round, graded & ungraded, ex USDA prime & choice	lb	3.31	4/93	16r
Steak, round, USDA choice, boneless	lb	3.34	4/93	16r
Steak, sirloin, graded & ungraded, ex USDA prime & choice	lb	4.19	4/93	16r
Steak, sirloin, USDA choice, boneless	lb	4.46	4/93	16r
Steak, T-bone	lb	4.15	4Q 92	4c
Steak, T-bone, USDA choice, bone-in	lb	5.25	4/93	16r
Strawberries, dry pint	12 oz	0.92	4/93	16r
Sugar, cane or beet	4 lb	1.22	4Q 92	4c
Sugar, white	lb	0.39	4/93	16r
Sugar, white, 33-80 oz pk	lb	0.38	4/93	16r
Tomatoes, field grown	lb	0.88	4/93	16r

Values are in dollars or fractions of dollars. In the column headed *Ref*, references are shown to sources. Each reference is followed by a letter. These refer to the geographical level for which data were reported: s=State, r=Region, and c=City or metro. The abbreviation *ex* is used to mean *except* or *excluding*; *exp* stands for expenditures. For other abbreviations and further explanations, please see the Introduction.

Gadsden, AL - continued

Item	Per	Value	Date	Ref.
Groceries				
Tomatoes, Hunt's or Del Monte	14.5-oz can	0.78	4Q 92	4c
Tuna, chunk, light	6.125-6.5 oz can	0.54	4Q 92	4c
Tuna, chunk, light	lb	1.79	4/93	16r
Turkey, frozen, whole	lb	1.04	4/93	16r
Yogurt, natural, fruit flavored	1/2 pint	0.57	4/93	16r
Health Care				
ACCRA Index, Health Care		93.60	4Q 92	4c
Analgesic, Aspirin, Bayer, 325 mg tablets	100	3.55	4Q 92	4c
Childbirth, cesarean, hospital		5034	91	62r
Childbirth, cesarean, physician's fee		2053	91	62r
Childbirth, normal, hospital		2712	91	62r
Childbirth, normal, physician's fee		1492	91	62r
Dentist's fee, adult teeth cleaning and periodic oral exam	visit	42.33	4Q 92	4c
Doctor's fee, routine exam, established patient	visit	35.00	4Q 92	4c
Hospital care, semiprivate room	day	244.39	90	27c
Hospital care, semiprivate room	day	355.00	4Q 92	4c
Medical insurance premium, per employee, small group comprehensive	month	321.20	10/91	25c
Mental health care, exp	capita	37.60-53.67	90	38s
Mental health care, exp, state mental health agency	capita	38.35	90	38s
Mental health care, hospital psychiatric services, non-Federal, exp	capita	13.58	88	38s
Mental health care, mental health organization, multiservice, exp	capita	12.40	88	38s
Mental health care, psychiatric hospitals, private, exp	capita	9.49	88	38s
Mental health care, state and county mental hospitals, exp	capita	22.15	88	38s
Mental health care, VA medical centers, exp	capita	10.94	88	38s
Physician fee, family practice, first-visit		75.00	91	62r
Physician fee, family practice, revisit		34.00	91	62r
Physician fee, general practice, first-visit		61.00	91	62r
Physician fee, general practice, revisit		32.00	91	62r
Physician fee, general surgeon, first-visit		64.00	91	62r
Physician fee, general surgeon, revisit		40.00	91	62r
Physician fee, internal medicine, first-visit		98.00	91	62r
Physician fee, internal medicine, revisit		40.00	91	62r
Physician fee, median, neurosurgeon, first-visit		130.00	91	62r
Physician fee, median, nonsurgical specialist, first-visit		95.00	91	62r
Physician fee, median, orthopedic surgeon, first-visit		91.00	91	62r
Physician fee, median, plastic surgeon, first-visit		66.00	91	62r
Physician fee, median, surgical specialist, first-visit		62.00	91	62r
Physician fee, neurosurgeon, revisit		50.00	91	62r
Physician fee, nonsurgical specialist, revisit		40.00	91	62r
Physician fee, obstetrics/gynecology, first-visit		64.00	91	62r
Physician fee, obstetrics/gynecology, revisit		41.00	91	62r
Physician fee, orthopedic surgeon, revisit		40.00	91	62r
Physician fee, pediatrician, first-visit		49.00	91	62r
Physician fee, pediatrician, revisit		33.00	91	62r
Physician fee, plastic surgeon, revisit		43.00	91	62r
Physician fee, surgical specialist, revisit		37.00	91	62r
Substance abuse, hospital ancillary charge	incident	1390	90	70s
Substance abuse, hospital physician charge	incident	520	90	70s
Substance abuse, hospital room and board	incident	5830	90	70s

Gadsden, AL - continued

Item	Per	Value	Date	Ref.
Household Goods				
Appliance repair, home, service call, washing machine	min labor charge	29.00	4Q 92	4c
Laundry detergent, Tide Ultra, Bold, or Cheer	42 oz	3.86	4Q 92	4c
Tissues, facial, Kleenex brand	175-count box	0.92	4Q 92	4c
Housing				
ACCRA Index, Housing		73.50	4Q 92	4c
House, 1,800 sq ft, 8,000 sq ft lot, new, urban	total	84600	4Q 92	4c
House payment, principal and interest, 25% down payment	month	469	4Q 92	4c
Mortgage rate, incl. points & origination fee, 30-year fixed or adjustable rate	percent	8.08	4Q 92	4c
Rent, apartment, 2 bedrooms - 1-1/2 to 2 baths, unfurnished, 950 sq ft, water	month	322	4Q 92	4c
Rental unit, 1 bedroom	month	288	93	23c
Rental unit, 2 bedroom	month	341	93	23c
Rental unit, 3 bedroom	month	426	93	23c
Rental unit, 4 bedroom	month	477	93	23c
Rental unit, efficiency	month	235	93	23c
Insurance and Pensions				
Auto insurance, private passenger	year	562.59	91	63s
Personal Goods				
Shampoo, Alberto VO5	15 oz	1.20	4Q 92	4c
Toothpaste, Crest or Colgate	6-7 oz	1.61	4Q 92	4c
Personal Services				
Dry cleaning, man's 2-piece suit		4.31	4Q 92	4c
Haircare, woman's shampoo, trim and blow-dry		15.17	4Q 92	4c
Haircut, man's barbershop, no styling		5.67	4Q 92	4c
Restaurant Food				
Chicken, fried, thigh and drumstick		1.91	4Q 92	4c
Hamburger with cheese	1/4 lb	1.99	4Q 92	4c
Pizza, Pizza Hut or Pizza Inn, cheese, thin crust	12-13 in	8.79	4Q 92	4c
Taxes				
Tax, cigarette	pack	16.50	91	77s
Tax, gasoline	gal	16	91	77s
Taxes, state	capita	964	91	77s
Transportation				
ACCRA Index, Transportation		91.50	4Q 92	4c
Driver's license fee		15.00	12/90	43s
Tire balance, computer or spin balance, front	wheel	5.40	4Q 92	4c
Travel				
Business travel	day	193.00	4/93	89r
Utilities				
ACCRA Index, Utilities		111.60	4Q 92	4c
Electricity	mil Btu	16.46	90	64s
Electricity, partial electric and other energy, 1,800 sq ft living area new home	month	80.30	4Q 92	4c

Gainesville, FL

Item	Per	Value	Date	Ref.
Child Care				
Child care fee, average, center	hour	1.29	90	65r
Child care fee, average, nonregulated family day care	hour	0.89	90	65r
Child care fee, average, regulated family day care	hour	1.32	90	65r
Communications				
Long-distance telephone service, day, initial minute, 0-100 miles	min	0.15-0.20	91	12s

Values are in dollars or fractions of dollars. In the column headed *Ref*, references are shown to sources. Each reference is followed by a letter. These refer to the geographical level for which data were reported: s = State, r = Region, and c = City or metro. The abbreviation *ex* is used to mean *except* or *excluding*; *exp* stands for expenditures. For other abbreviations and further explanations, please see the Introduction.

Gainesville, FL - continued

Item	Per	Value	Date	Ref.
Communications				
Long-distance telephone service, day, additional minute, 0-100 miles	min	0.08-0.20	91	12s
Long-distance telephone service, evenings/weekends, 0-100 mi, initial minute	min	0.09-0.12	91	12s
Long-distance telephone service, evenings/weekends, 0-100 mi, additional minute	min	0.05-0.12	91	12s
Education				
Board, 4-yr private college/university	year	1924	91	22s
Board, 4-yr public college/university	year	1955	91	22s
Expenditures, local gov't, public elementary/secondary	pupil	5235	92	20s
Room, 4-year private college/university	year	1904	91	22s
Room, 4-year public college/university	year	1510	91	22s
Tuition, 2-year private college/university	year	4751	91	22s
Tuition, 2-year public college/university	year	788	91	22s
Tuition, 4-year private college/university	year	7992	91	22s
Tuition, 4-year public college/university, in-state	year	1337	91	22s
Energy and Fuels				
Coal	mil Btu	1.85	90	64s
Energy	mil Btu	10.58	90	64s
Energy exp/householder, 1-family unit	year	487	90	28r
Energy exp/householder, <1,000 sq ft heating area	year	393	90	28r
Energy exp/householder, 1,000-1,999 sq ft heating area	year	442	90	28r
Energy exp/householder, 2,000+ sq ft heating area	year	577	90	28r
Energy exp/householder, mobile home	year	366	90	28r
Energy exp/householder, multifamily	year	382	90	28r
Gas, natural	mil Btu	3.21	90	64s
Gas, natural	000 cu ft	8.98	91	46s
Gas, natural, exp	year	248	91	46s
Gasoline, unleaded regular	mil Btu	8.85	90	64s
Entertainment				
Miniature golf admission	adult	6.18	92	1r
Miniature golf admission	child	5.14	92	1r
Waterpark admission	adult	11.00	92	1r
Waterpark admission	child	8.55	92	1r
Funerals				
Casket, 18-gauge steel, velvet interior		2029.08	91	24r
Cosmetology, hair care, etc.		75.10	91	24r
Embalming		249.24	91	24r
Facility use for ceremony		162.27	91	24r
Hearse, local		114.04	91	24r
Limousine, local		88.57	91	24r
Remains to funeral home, transfer		92.61	91	24r
Service charge, professional		682.42	91	24r
Vault, concrete, non-metallic liner		798.70	91	24r
Viewing facilities, use		163.86	91	24r
Groceries				
Apples, Red Delicious	lb	0.79	4/93	16r
Bacon	lb	1.75	4/93	16r
Bananas	lb	0.42	4/93	16r
Beef, stew, boneless	lb	2.61	4/93	16r
Bologna, all beef or mixed	lb	2.24	4/93	16r
Bread, white, pan	lb	0.64	4/93	16r
Bread, whole wheat, pan	lb	0.96	4/93	16r
Cabbage	lb	0.37	4/93	16r
Carrots, short trimmed and topped	lb	0.47	4/93	16r
Celery	lb	0.64	4/93	16r
Cheese, American	lb	2.98	4/93	16r
Cheese, Cheddar	lb	3.28	4/93	16r
Chicken, fresh, whole	lb	0.77	4/93	16r
Chicken breast, bone-in	lb	1.92	4/93	16r
Chicken legs, bone-in	lb	1.06	4/93	16r
Chuck roast, graded and ungraded, ex USDA prime and choice	lb	2.40	4/93	16r

Gainesville, FL - continued

Item	Per	Value	Date	Ref.
Groceries - continued				
Chuck roast, USDA choice, bone-in	lb	2.19	4/93	16r
Chuck roast, USDA choice, boneless	lb	2.38	4/93	16r
Coffee, 100% ground roast, all sizes	lb	2.48	4/93	16r
Crackers, soda, salted	lb	1.15	4/93	16r
Eggs, Grade A large	doz	0.96	4/93	16r
Flour, white, all purpose	lb	0.24	4/93	16r
Frankfurters, all meat or all beef	lb	2.01	4/93	16r
Grapefruit	lb	0.44	4/93	16r
Grapes, Thompson Seedless	lb	1.40	4/93	16r
Ground beef, 100% beef	lb	1.58	4/93	16r
Ground beef, lean and extra lean	lb	2.09	4/93	16r
Ground chuck, 100% beef	lb	1.98	4/93	16r
Ham, boneless, excluding canned	lb	2.89	4/93	16r
Ham, picnic, shoulder, bone-in, smoked	lb	1.02	4/93	16r
Ham, rump or steak half, bone-in, smoked	lb	1.48	4/93	16r
Ice cream, prepackaged, bulk, regular	1/2 gal	2.41	4/93	16r
Lemons	lb	1.05	4/93	16r
Lettuce, iceberg	lb	0.81	4/93	16r
Margarine, stick	lb	0.88	4/93	16r
Oranges, navel	lb	0.55	4/93	16r
Pears, Anjou	lb	0.92	4/93	16r
Pork chops, center cut, bone-in	lb	3.13	4/93	16r
Potato chips	16 oz	2.94	4/93	16r
Potatoes, white	lb	0.43	4/93	16r
Rib roast, USDA choice, bone-in	lb	4.63	4/93	16r
Rice, white, long grain, uncooked	lb	0.45	4/93	16r
Round roast, graded & ungraded, ex USDA prime & choice	lb	3.03	4/93	16r
Round roast, USDA choice, boneless	lb	3.09	4/93	16r
Sausage, fresh, loose	lb	2.08	4/93	16r
Short ribs, bone-in	lb	2.66	4/93	16r
Shortening, vegetable oil blends	lb	0.69	4/93	10r
Spaghetti and macaroni	lb	0.81	4/93	16r
Steak, rib eye, USDA choice, boneless	lb	6.24	4/93	16r
Steak, round, graded & ungraded, ex USDA prime & choice	lb	3.31	4/93	16r
Steak, round, USDA choice, boneless	lb	3.34	4/93	16r
Steak, sirloin, graded & ungraded, ex USDA prime & choice	lb	4.19	4/93	16r
Steak, sirloin, USDA choice, boneless	lb	4.46	4/93	16r
Steak, T-bone, USDA choice, bone-in	lb	5.25	4/93	16r
Strawberries, dry pint	12 oz	0.92	4/93	16r
Sugar, white	lb	0.39	4/93	16r
Sugar, white, 33-80 oz pk	lb	0.38	4/93	16r
Tomatoes, field grown	lb	0.88	4/93	16r
Tuna, chunk, light	lb	1.79	4/93	16r
Turkey, frozen, whole	lb	1.04	4/93	16r
Yogurt, natural, fruit flavored	1/2 pint	0.57	4/93	16r
Health Care				
Childbirth, cesarean, hospital		5034	91	62r
Childbirth, cesarean, physician's fee		2053	91	62r
Childbirth, normal, hospital		2712	91	62r
Childbirth, normal, physician's fee		1492	91	62r
Medical plan per employee	year	3495	91	45r
Mental health care, exp	capita	28.84-37.59	90	38s
Mental health care, exp, state mental health agency	capita	37.49	90	38s
Mental health care, hospital psychiatric services, non-Federal, exp	capita	9.11	88	38s
Mental health care, mental health organization, multiservice, exp	capita	16.21	88	38s
Mental health care, psychiatric hospitals, private, exp	capita	22.26	88	38s
Mental health care, psychiatric out-patient clinics, freestanding, exp	capita	0.89	88	38s
Mental health care, psychiatric partial-care organizations, freestanding, exp	capita	0.41	88	38s
Mental health care, state and county mental hospitals, exp	capita	16.25	88	38s
Mental health care, VA medical centers, exp	capita	1.69	88	38s

Values are in dollars or fractions of dollars. In the column headed *Ref*, references are shown to sources. Each reference is followed by a letter. These refer to the geographical level for which data were reported: s=State, r=Region, and c=City or metro. The abbreviation *ex* is used to mean *except* or *excluding*; *exp* stands for expenditures. For other abbreviations and further explanations, please see the Introduction.

Gainesville, FL - continued

Item	Per	Value	Date	Ref.
Health Care				
Physician fee, family practice, first-visit		75.00	91	62r
Physician fee, family practice, revisit		34.00	91	62r
Physician fee, general practice, first-visit		61.00	91	62r
Physician fee, general practice, revisit		32.00	91	62r
Physician fee, general surgeon, first-visit		64.00	91	62r
Physician fee, general surgeon, revisit		40.00	91	62r
Physician fee, internal medicine, first-visit		98.00	91	62r
Physician fee, internal medicine, revisit		40.00	91	62r
Physician fee, median, neurosurgeon, first-visit		130.00	91	62r
Physician fee, median, nonsurgical specialist, first-visit		95.00	91	62r
Physician fee, median, orthopedic surgeon, first-visit		91.00	91	62r
Physician fee, median, plastic surgeon, first-visit		66.00	91	62r
Physician fee, median, surgical specialist, first-visit		62.00	91	62r
Physician fee, neurosurgeon, revisit		50.00	91	62r
Physician fee, nonsurgical specialist, revisit		40.00	91	62r
Physician fee, obstetrics/gynecology, first-visit		64.00	91	62r
Physician fee, obstetrics/gynecology, revisit		41.00	91	62r
Physician fee, orthopedic surgeon, revisit		40.00	91	62r
Physician fee, pediatrician, first-visit		49.00	91	62r
Physician fee, pediatrician, revisit		33.00	91	62r
Physician fee, plastic surgeon, revisit		43.00	91	62r
Physician fee, surgical specialist, revisit		37.00	91	62r
Substance abuse, hospital ancillary charge	incident	1390	90	70s
Substance abuse, hospital physician charge	incident	770	90	70s
Substance abuse, hospital room and board	incident	5600	90	70s
Insurance and Pensions				
Auto insurance, private passenger	year	727.60	91	63s
Taxes				
Tax, cigarette	pack	33.90	91	77s
Tax, gasoline	gal	11.60	91	77s
Taxes, state	capita	1037	91	77s
Transportation				
Driver's license fee		15.00	12/90	43s
Travel				
Business travel	day	193.00	4/93	89r
Utilities				
Electricity	mil Btu	20.62	90	64s

Galveston-Texas City, TX

Item	Per	Value	Date	Ref.
Child Care				
Child care fee, average, center	hour	1.29	90	65r
Child care fee, average, nonregulated family day care	hour	0.89	90	65r
Child care fee, average, regulated family day care	hour	1.32	90	65r
Communications				
Long-distance telephone service, day, initial minute, 0-100 miles	min	0.10-0.46	91	12s
Long-distance telephone service, day, additional minute, 0-100 miles	min	0.06-0.45	91	12s
Education				
Board, 4-yr private college/university	year	1883	91	22s
Board, 4-yr public college/university	year	1605	91	22s
Expenditures, local gov't, public elementary/secondary	pupil	4593	92	20s
Room, 4-year private college/university	year	1620	91	22s
Room, 4-year public college/university	year	1532	91	22s

Galveston-Texas City, TX - continued

Item	Per	Value	Date	Ref.
Education - continued				
Tuition, 2-year private college/university	year	4394	91	22s
Tuition, 2-year public college/university	year	495	91	22s
Tuition, 4-year private college/university	year	6497	91	22s
Tuition, 4-year public college/university, in-state	year	986	91	22s
Energy and Fuels				
Coal	mil Btu	1.44	90	64s
Energy	mil Btu	6.48	90	64s
Energy exp/householder, 1-family unit	year	471	90	28r
Energy exp/householder, <1,000 sq ft heating area	year	384	90	28r
Energy exp/householder, 1,000-1,999 sq ft heating area	year	421	90	28r
Energy exp/householder, 2,000+ sq ft heating area	year	625	90	28r
Energy exp/householder, mobile home	year	271	90	28r
Energy exp/householder, multifamily	year	355	90	28r
Gas, natural	mil Btu	2.47	90	64s
Gas, natural	000 cu ft	5.71	91	46s
Gas, natural, exp	year	388	91	46s
Gasoline, unleaded regular	mil Btu	9.16	90	64s
Entertainment				
Miniature golf admission	adult	6.18	92	1r
Miniature golf admission	child	5.14	92	1r
Waterpark admission	adult	11.00	92	1r
Waterpark admission	child	8.55	92	1r
Funerals				
Casket, 18-gauge steel, velvet interior		2274.41	91	24r
Cosmetology, hair care, etc.		74.62	91	24r
Embalming		229.94	91	24r
Facility use for ceremony		176.61	91	24r
Hearse, local		116.34	91	24r
Limousine, local		72.68	91	24r
Remains to funeral home, transfer		87.72	91	24r
Service charge, professional		712.53	91	24r
Vault, concrete, non-metallic liner		750.55	91	24r
Viewing facilities, use		155.31	91	24r
Groceries				
Apples, Red Delicious	lb	0.79	4/93	16r
Bacon	lb	1.75	4/93	16r
Bananas	lb	0.42	4/93	16r
Beef, stew, boneless	lb	2.61	4/93	16r
Bologna, all beef or mixed	lb	2.24	4/93	16r
Bread, white, pan	lb	0.64	4/93	16r
Bread, whole wheat, pan	lb	0.96	4/93	16r
Cabbage	lb	0.37	4/93	16r
Carrots, short trimmed and topped	lb	0.47	4/93	16r
Celery	lb	0.64	4/93	16r
Cheese, American	lb	2.98	4/93	16r
Cheese, Cheddar	lb	3.28	4/93	16r
Chicken, fresh, whole	lb	0.77	4/93	16r
Chicken breast, bone-in	lb	1.92	4/93	16r
Chicken legs, bone-in	lb	1.06	4/93	16r
Chuck roast, graded and ungraded, ex USDA prime and choice	lb	2.40	4/93	16r
Chuck roast, USDA choice, bone-in	lb	2.19	4/93	16r
Chuck roast, USDA choice, boneless	lb	2.38	4/93	16r
Coffee, 100% ground roast, all sizes	lb	2.48	4/93	16r
Crackers, soda, salted	lb	1.15	4/93	16r
Eggs, Grade A large	doz	0.96	4/93	16r
Flour, white, all purpose	lb	0.24	4/93	16r
Frankfurters, all meat or all beef	lb	2.01	4/93	16r
Grapefruit	lb	0.44	4/93	16r
Grapes, Thompson Seedless	lb	1.40	4/93	16r
Ground beef, 100% beef	lb	1.58	4/93	16r
Ground beef, lean and extra lean	lb	2.09	4/93	16r
Ground chuck, 100% beef	lb	1.98	4/93	16r
Ham, boneless, excluding canned	lb	2.89	4/93	16r
Ham, picnic, shoulder, bone-in, smoked	lb	1.02	4/93	16r

Values are in dollars or fractions of dollars. In the column headed *Ref*, references are shown to sources. Each reference is followed by a letter. These refer to the geographical level for which data were reported: s=State, r=Region, and c=City or metro. The abbreviation *ex* is used to mean *except* or *excluding*; *exp* stands for expenditures. For other abbreviations and further explanations, please see the Introduction.

Galveston-Texas City, TX - continued

Item	Per	Value	Date	Ref.
Groceries				
Ham, rump or steak half, bone-in, smoked	lb	1.48	4/93	16r
Honey, jar	8 oz	0.73-1.19	92	5r
Honey, jar	lb	1.10-1.79	92	5r
Honey, squeeze bear	12-oz	1.19-1.50	92	5r
Ice cream, prepackaged, bulk, regular	1/2 gal	2.41	4/93	16r
Lemons	lb	1.05	4/93	16r
Lettuce, iceberg	lb	0.81	4/93	16r
Margarine, stick	lb	0.88	4/93	16r
Oranges, navel	lb	0.55	4/93	16r
Pears, Anjou	lb	0.92	4/93	16r
Pork chops, center cut, bone-in	lb	3.13	4/93	16r
Potato chips	16 oz	2.94	4/93	16r
Potatoes, white	lb	0.43	4/93	16r
Rib roast, USDA choice, bone-in	lb	4.63	4/93	16r
Rice, white, long grain, uncooked	lb	0.45	4/93	16r
Round roast, graded & ungraded, ex USDA prime & choice	lb	3.03	4/93	16r
Round roast, USDA choice, boneless	lb	3.09	4/93	16r
Sausage, fresh, loose	lb	2.08	4/93	16r
Short ribs, bone-in	lb	2.66	4/93	16r
Shortening, vegetable oil blends	lb	0.69	4/93	16r
Spaghetti and macaroni	lb	0.81	4/93	16r
Steak, rib eye, USDA choice, boneless	lb	6.24	4/93	16r
Steak, round, graded & ungraded, ex USDA prime & choice	lb	3.31	4/93	16r
Steak, round, USDA choice, boneless	lb	3.34	4/93	16r
Steak, sirloin, graded & ungraded, ex USDA prime & choice	lb	4.19	4/93	16r
Steak, sirloin, USDA choice, boneless	lb	4.46	4/93	16r
Steak, T-bone, USDA choice, bone-in	lb	5.25	4/93	16r
Strawberries, dry pint	12 oz	0.92	4/93	16r
Sugar, white	lb	0.39	4/93	16r
Sugar, white, 33-80 oz pk	lb	0.38	4/93	16r
Tomatoes, field grown	lb	0.88	4/93	16r
Tuna, chunk, light	lb	1.79	4/93	16r
Turkey, frozen, whole	lb	1.04	4/93	16r
Yogurt, natural, fruit flavored	1/2 pint	0.57	4/93	16r
Health Care				
Childbirth, cesarean, hospital		5034	91	62r
Childbirth, cesarean, physician's fee		2053	91	62r
Childbirth, normal, hospital		2712	91	62r
Childbirth, normal, physician's fee		1492	91	62r
Health care spending, state	capita	2192	3/93	84s
Mental health care, exp	capita	20.37-28.83	90	38s
Mental health care, exp, state mental health agency	capita	22.72	90	38s
Mental health care, hospital psychiatric services, non-Federal, exp	capita	7.95	88	38s
Mental health care, mental health organization, multiservice, exp	capita	12.05	88	38s
Mental health care, psychiatric hospitals, private, exp	capita	37.78	88	38s
Mental health care, psychiatric out-patient clinics, freestanding, exp	capita	0.43	88	38s
Mental health care, state and county mental hospitals, exp	capita	12.54	88	38s
Mental health care, VA medical centers, exp	capita	5.35	88	38s
Physician fee, family practice, first-visit		75.00	91	62r
Physician fee, family practice, revisit		34.00	91	62r
Physician fee, general practice, first-visit		61.00	91	62r
Physician fee, general practice, revisit		32.00	91	62r
Physician fee, general surgeon, first-visit		64.00	91	62r
Physician fee, general surgeon, revisit		40.00	91	62r
Physician fee, internal medicine, first-visit		98.00	91	62r
Physician fee, internal medicine, revisit		40.00	91	62r
Physician fee, median, neurosurgeon, first-visit		130.00	91	62r
Physician fee, median, nonsurgical specialist, first-visit		95.00	91	62r

Galveston-Texas City, TX - continued

Item	Per	Value	Date	Ref.
Health Care - continued				
Physician fee, median, orthopedic surgeon, first-visit		91.00	91	62r
Physician fee, median, plastic surgeon, first-visit		66.00	91	62r
Physician fee, median, surgical specialist, first-visit		62.00	91	62r
Physician fee, neurosurgeon, revisit		50.00	91	62r
Physician fee, nonsurgical specialist, revisit		40.00	91	62r
Physician fee, obstetrics/gynecology, first-visit		64.00	91	62r
Physician fee, obstetrics/gynecology, revisit		41.00	91	62r
Physician fee, orthopedic surgeon, revisit		40.00	91	62r
Physician fee, pediatrician, first-visit		49.00	91	62r
Physician fee, pediatrician, revisit		33.00	91	62r
Physician fee, plastic surgeon, revisit		43.00	91	62r
Physician fee, surgical specialist, revisit		37.00	91	62r
Substance abuse, hospital ancillary charge	incident	3750	90	70s
Substance abuse, hospital physician charge	incident	1080	90	70s
Substance abuse, hospital room and board	incident	5320	90	70s
Insurance and Pensions				
Auto insurance, private passenger	year	709.79	91	63s
Taxes				
Tax, cigarette	pack	41	91	77s
Tax, gasoline	gal	20	91	77s
Taxes, state	capita	923	91	77s
Transportation				
Driver's license fee		16.00	12/90	43s
Travel				
Business travel	day	193.00	4/93	89r
Utilities				
Electricity	mil Btu	17.09	90	64s
Electricity, residential	KWh	5.92	2/93	94s

Gary-Hammond, IN

Item	Per	Value	Date	Ref.
Child Care				
Child care fee, average, center	hour	1.63	90	65r
Child care fee, average, nonregulated family day care	hour	1.83	90	65r
Child care fee, average, regulated family day care	hour	1.42	90	65r
Communications				
Long-distance telephone service, day, initial minute, 0-100 miles	min	0.18-0.45	91	12s
Long-distance telephone service, day, additional minute, 0-100 miles	min	0.10-0.30	91	12s
Long-distance telephone service, evenings/weekends, 0-100 mi, initial minute	min	0.08-0.19	91	12s
Long-distance telephone service, evenings/weekends, 0-100 mi, additional minute	min	0.04-0.13	91	12s
Education				
Board, 4-yr private college/university	year	1714	91	22s
Board, 4-yr public college/university	year	1829	91	22s
Expenditures, local gov't, public elementary/secondary	pupil	5545	92	20s
Room, 4-year private college/university	year	1512	91	22s
Room, 4-year public college/university	year	1435	91	22s
Tuition, 2-year private college/university	year	6756	91	22s
Tuition, 2-year public college/university	year	1423	91	22s
Tuition, 4-year private college/university	year	8451	91	22s
Tuition, 4-year public college/university, in-state	year	2067	91	22s

Values are in dollars or fractions of dollars. In the column headed *Ref*, references are shown to sources. Each reference is followed by a letter. These refer to the geographical level for which data were reported: s=State, r=Region, and c=City or metro. The abbreviation *ex* is used to mean *except* or *excluding*; *exp* stands for expenditures. For other abbreviations and further explanations, please see the Introduction.

Gary-Hammond, IN - continued

Item	Per	Value	Date	Ref.
Energy and Fuels				
Coal	mil Btu	1.46	90	64s
Energy	mil Btu	6.77	90	64s
Energy exp/householder, 1-family unit	year	471	90	28r
Energy exp/householder, <1,000 sq ft heating area	year	430	90	28r
Energy exp/householder, 1,000-1,999 sq ft heating area	year	481	90	28r
Energy exp/householder, 2,000+ sq ft heating area	year	473	90	28r
Energy exp/householder, mobile home	year	430	90	28r
Energy exp/householder, multifamily	year	461	90	28r
Gas, natural	mil Btu	4.27	90	64s
Gas, natural	000 cu ft	5.46	91	46s
Gas, natural, exp	year	588	91	46s
Gasoline, unleaded regular	mil Btu	8.74	90	64s
Entertainment				
Miniature golf admission	adult	6.18	92	1r
Miniature golf admission	child	5.14	92	1r
Waterpark admission	adult	11.00	92	1r
Waterpark admission	child	8.55	92	1r
Funerals				
Casket, 18-gauge steel, velvet interior		1926.72	91	24r
Cosmetology, hair care, etc.		97.64	91	24r
Embalming		249.14	91	24r
Facility use for ceremony		208.59	91	24r
Hearse, local		130.12	91	24r
Limousine, local		104.66	91	24r
Remains to funeral home, transfer		93.61	91	24r
Service charge, professional		724.62	91	24r
Vault, concrete, non-metallic liner		734.53	91	24r
Viewing facilities, use		236.06	91	24r
Groceries				
Apples, Red Delicious	lb	0.77	4/93	16r
Bacon	lb	1.85	4/93	16r
Bananas	lb	0.46	4/93	16r
Beef, stew, boneless	lb	2.53	4/93	16r
Bologna, all beef or mixed	lb	2.19	4/93	16r
Bread, white, pan	lb	0.78	4/93	16r
Butter	lb	1.50	4/93	16r
Cabbage	lb	0.40	4/93	16r
Carrots, short trimmed and topped	lb	0.45	4/93	16r
Cheese, Cheddar	lb	3.47	4/93	16r
Chicken, fresh, whole	lb	0.84	4/93	16r
Chicken breast, bone-in	lb	1.94	4/93	16r
Chicken legs, bone-in	lb	1.02	4/93	16r
Chuck roast, graded and ungraded, ex USDA prime and choice	lb	2.43	4/93	16r
Chuck roast, USDA choice, bone-in	lb	2.11	4/93	16r
Chuck roast, USDA choice, boneless	lb	2.44	4/93	16r
Coffee, 100% ground roast, all sizes	lb	2.47	4/93	16r
Cookies, chocolate chip	lb	2.73	4/93	16r
Eggs, Grade A large	doz	0.93	4/93	16r
Flour, white, all purpose	lb	0.21	4/93	16r
Grapefruit	lb	0.45	4/93	16r
Grapes, Thompson Seedless	lb	1.46	4/93	16r
Ground beef, 100% beef	lb	1.63	4/93	16r
Ground beef, lean and extra lean	lb	2.08	4/93	16r
Ground chuck, 100% beef	lb	1.94	4/93	16r
Ham, boneless, excluding canned	lb	2.21	4/93	16r
Honey, jar	8 oz	0.97-1.25	92	5r
Honey, jar	lb	1.25-2.25	92	5r
Honey, squeeze bear	12-oz	1.25-1.99	92	5r
Ice cream, prepackaged, bulk, regular	1/2 gal	2.41	4/93	16r
Lemons	lb	0.82	4/93	16r
Lettuce, iceberg	lb	0.83	4/93	16r
Margarine, stick	lb	0.77	4/93	16r
Oranges, navel	lb	0.50	4/93	16r
Peanut butter, creamy, all sizes	lb	1.82	4/93	16r
Pears, Anjou	lb	0.85	4/93	16r
Pork chops, center cut, bone-in	lb	3.17	4/93	16r

Gary-Hammond, IN - continued

Item	Per	Value	Date	Ref.
Groceries - continued				
Potato chips	16 oz	2.68	4/93	16r
Potatoes, white	lb	0.26	4/93	16r
Round roast, graded & ungraded, ex USDA prime & choice	lb	2.88	4/93	16r
Round roast, USDA choice, boneless	lb	2.96	4/93	16r
Shortening, vegetable oil blends	lb	0.79	4/93	16r
Spaghetti and macaroni	lb	0.76	4/93	16r
Steak, rib eye, USDA choice, boneless	lb	6.29	4/93	16r
Steak, round, USDA choice, boneless	lb	3.24	4/93	16r
Steak, sirloin, graded & ungraded, ex USDA prime & choice	lb	4.00	4/93	16r
Steak, sirloin, USDA choice, bone-in	lb	3.57	4/93	16r
Steak, sirloin, USDA choice, boneless	lb	4.17	4/93	16r
Steak, T-bone, USDA choice, bone-in	lb	5.60	4/93	16r
Strawberries, dry pint	12 oz	0.90	4/93	16r
Sugar, white	lb	0.36	4/93	16r
Sugar, white, 33-80 oz pk	lb	0.35	4/93	16r
Tomatoes, field grown	lb	0.99	4/93	16r
Tuna, chunk, light	lb	1.76	4/93	16r
Turkey, frozen, whole	lb	0.91	4/93	16r
Health Care				
Childbirth, cesarean, hospital		4688	91	62r
Childbirth, cesarean, physician's fee		2053	91	62r
Childbirth, normal, hospital		2657	91	62r
Childbirth, normal, physician's fee		1492	91	62r
Medical plan per employee	year	3443	91	45r
Mental health care, exp	capita	37.60-53.67	90	38s
Mental health care, exp, state mental health agency	capita	47.05	90	38s
Mental health care, hospital psychiatric services, non-Federal, exp	capita	22.14	88	38s
Mental health care, mental health organization, multiservice, exp	capita	10.33	88	38s
Mental health care, psychiatric hospitals, private, exp	capita	20.10	88	38s
Mental health care, state and county mental hospitals, exp	capita	24.00	88	38s
Mental health care, VA medical centers, exp	capita	3.20	88	38s
Physician fee, family practice, first-visit		76.00	91	62r
Physician fee, family practice, revisit		33.00	91	62r
Physician fee, general practice, first-visit		61.00	91	62r
Physician fee, general practice, revisit		31.00	91	62r
Physician fee, general surgeon, first-visit		65.00	91	62r
Physician fee, general surgeon, revisit		35.00	91	62r
Physician fee, internal medicine, first-visit		91.00	91	62r
Physician fee, internal medicine, revisit		40.00	91	62r
Physician fee, median, neurosurgeon, first-visit		106.00	91	62r
Physician fee, median, nonsurgical specialist, first-visit		90.00	91	62r
Physician fee, median, orthopedic surgeon, first-visit		83.00	91	62r
Physician fee, median, surgical specialist, first-visit		61.00	91	62r
Physician fee, neurosurgeon, revisit		41.00	91	62r
Physician fee, nonsurgical specialist, revisit		40.00	91	62r
Physician fee, obstetrics/gynecology, first-visit		61.00	91	62r
Physician fee, obstetrics/gynecology, revisit		40.00	91	62r
Physician fee, orthopedic surgeon, revisit		41.00	91	62r
Physician fee, pediatrician, first-visit		46.00	91	62r
Physician fee, pediatrician, revisit		33.00	91	62r
Physician fee, surgical specialist, revisit		36.00	91	62r
Substance abuse, hospital ancillary charge	incident	1230	90	70s
Substance abuse, hospital physician charge	incident	410	90	70s
Substance abuse, hospital room and board	incident	5510	90	70s

Values are in dollars or fractions of dollars. In the column headed *Ref*, references are shown to sources. Each reference is followed by a letter. These refer to the geographical level for which data were reported: s = State, r = Region, and c = City or metro. The abbreviation *ex* is used to mean *except* or *excluding*; *exp* stands for expenditures. For other abbreviations and further explanations, please see the Introduction.

Gary-Hammond, IN - continued

Item	Per	Value	Date	Ref.
Insurance and Pensions				
Auto insurance, private passenger	year	548.99	91	63s
Taxes				
Tax, cigarette	pack	15.50	91	77s
Tax, gasoline	gal	15	91	77s
Taxes, state	capita	1102	91	77s
Transportation				
Driver's license fee		6.00	12/90	43s
Utilities				
Electricity	mil Btu	15.75	90	64s

Gastonia, NC

Item	Per	Value	Date	Ref.
Composite ACCRA index		90.70	4Q 92	4c
Alcoholic Beverages				
Beer, Miller Lite or Budweiser, 12-oz containers	6 pack	3.71	4Q 92	4c
Liquor, J & B Scotch	750 ml	17.65	4Q 92	4c
Wine, Gallo Chablis blanc, 1.5 liter	bottle	4.43	4Q 92	4c
Clothing				
Jeans, man's denim		22.33	4Q 92	4c
Shirt, man's dress shirt		20.33	4Q 92	4c
Undervest, boy's size 10-14, cotton	3	2.78	4Q 92	4c
Communications				
Newspaper subscription, daily and Sunday home delivery, large-city	month	9.75	4Q 92	4c
Telephone, flat rate	month	11.66	91	11c
Telephone bill, family of four	month	17.19	4Q 92	4c
Energy and Fuels				
Energy, combined forms, 1,800 sq ft heating area	month	119.35	4Q 92	4c
Gasoline, motor	gal	1.13	4Q 92	4c
Entertainment				
Bowling, evening rate	game	2.24	4Q 92	4c
Monopoly game, Parker Brothers', No. 9		9.98	4Q 92	4c
Movie	admission	5.00	4Q 92	4c
Tennis balls, yellow, Wilson or Penn, 3	can	1.95	4Q 92	4c
Goods and Services				
ACCRA Index, Miscellaneous Goods and Services		87.00	4Q 92	4c
Groceries				
ACCRA Index, Groceries		94.80	4Q 92	4c
Babyfood, strained vegetables, lowest price	4-4.5 oz jar	0.32	4Q 92	4c
Bananas	lb	0.49	4Q 92	4c
Bread, white	24 oz	0.65	4Q 92	4c
Cheese, Kraft grated Parmesan	8-oz canister	3.16	4Q 92	4c
Chicken, fryer, whole	lb	0.71	4Q 92	4c
Cigarettes, Winston	carton	15.21	4Q 92	4c
Coffee, vacuum-packed	13-oz can	1.71	4Q 92	4c
Corn, frozen	10 oz	0.56	4Q 92	4c
Corn Flakes, Kellogg's or Post Toasties	18 oz	1.77	4Q 92	4c
Eggs, Grade A large	doz	0.90	4Q 92	4c
Ground beef or hamburger	lb	1.73	4Q 92	4c
Lettuce, iceberg	head	0.91	4Q 92	4c
Margarine, Blue Bonnet or Parkay cubes	lb	0.47	4Q 92	4c
Milk, whole	1/2 gal	1.39	4Q 92	4c
Orange juice, Minute Maid frozen	12-oz can	1.20	4Q 92	4c
Peaches	29-oz can	1.33	4Q 92	4c
Peas Sweet, Del Monte or Green Giant	15-17 oz can	0.49	4Q 92	4c

Gastonia, NC - continued

Item	Per	Value	Date	Ref.
Groceries - continued				
Potatoes, white or red	10-lb sack	1.86	4Q 92	4c
Sausage, Jimmy Dean, 100% pork	lb	2.28	4Q 92	4c
Shortening, vegetable, Crisco	3-lb can	2.01	4Q 92	4c
Soft drink, Coca Cola	2 liter	1.23	4Q 92	4c
Steak, T-bone	lb	5.69	4Q 92	4c
Sugar, cane or beet	4 lb	1.43	4Q 92	4c
Tomatoes, Hunt's or Del Monte	14.5-oz can	0.51	4Q 92	4c
Tuna, chunk, light	6.125-6.5 oz can	0.56	4Q 92	4c
Health Care				
ACCRA Index, Health Care		83.60	4Q 92	4c
Analgesic, Aspirin, Bayer, 325 mg tablets	100	5.23	4Q 92	4c
Dentist's fee, adult teeth cleaning and periodic oral exam	visit	39.00	4Q 92	4c
Doctor's fee, routine exam, established patient	visit	28.67	4Q 92	4c
Hospital care, semiprivate room	day	263.00	4Q 92	4c
Household Goods				
Appliance repair, home, service call, washing machine	min labor charge	28.33	4Q 92	4c
Laundry detergent, Tide Ultra, Bold, or Cheer	42 oz	2.68	4Q 92	4c
Tissues, facial, Kleenex brand	175-count box	0.99	4Q 92	4c
Housing				
ACCRA Index, Housing		88.60	4Q 92	4c
House, 1,800 sq ft, 8,000 sq ft lot, new, urban	total	99620	4Q 92	4c
House payment, principal and interest, 25% down payment	month	552	4Q 92	4c
Mortgage rate, incl. points & origination fee, 30-year fixed or adjustable rate	per-cent	8.07	4Q 92	4c
Rent, apartment, 2 bedrooms - 1-1/2 to 2 baths, unfurnished, 950 sq ft, water	month	420	4Q 92	4c
Personal Goods				
Shampoo, Alberto VO5	15 oz	0.97	4Q 92	4c
Toothpaste, Crest or Colgate	6-7 oz	1.89	4Q 92	4c
Personal Services				
Dry cleaning, man's 2-piece suit		5.92	4Q 92	4c
Haircare, woman's shampoo, trim and blow-dry		13.62	4Q 92	4c
Haircut, man's barbershop, no styling		5.75	4Q 92	4c
Restaurant Food				
Chicken, fried, thigh and drumstick		2.20	4Q 92	4c
Hamburger with cheese	1/4 lb	1.81	4Q 92	4c
Pizza, Pizza Hut or Pizza Inn, cheese, thin crust	12-13 in	7.49	4Q 92	4c
Transportation				
ACCRA Index, Transportation		93.30	4Q 92	4c
Tire balance, computer or spin balance, front	wheel	5.65	4Q 92	4c
Utilities				
ACCRA Index, Utilities		107.20	4Q 92	4c
Electricity, all electric, 1,800 sq ft living area new home	month	119.35	4Q 92	4c

Values are in dollars or fractions of dollars. In the column headed *Ref*, references are shown to sources. Each reference is followed by a letter. These refer to the geographical level for which data were reported: s=State, r=Region, and c=City or metro. The abbreviation *ex* is used to mean *except* or *excluding*; *exp* stands for expenditures. For other abbreviations and further explanations, please see the Introduction.

Georgetown, TX

Item	Per	Value	Date	Ref.
Composite ACCRA index		97.50	4Q 92	4c
Alcoholic Beverages				
Beer, Miller Lite or Budweiser, 12-oz containers	6 pack	3.84	4Q 92	4c
Liquor, J & B Scotch	750 ml	17.92	4Q 92	4c
Wine, Gallo Chablis blanc, 1.5 liter	bottle	5.84	4Q 92	4c
Clothing				
Jeans, man's denim		24.48	4Q 92	4c
Shirt, man's dress shirt		24.95	4Q 92	4c
Undervest, boy's size 10-14, cotton	3	3.75	4Q 92	4c
Communications				
Newspaper subscription, daily and Sunday home delivery, large-city	month	11.99	4Q 92	4c
Telephone bill, family of four	month	24.67	4Q 92	4c
Energy and Fuels				
Energy, combined forms, 1,800 sq ft heating area	month	107.49	4Q 92	4c
Energy, exc electricity, 1,800 sq ft heating area	month	27.00	4Q 92	4c
Gasoline, motor	gal	1.14	4Q 92	4c
Entertainment				
Bowling, evening rate	game	2.30	4Q 92	4c
Monopoly game, Parker Brothers', No. 9		10.96	4Q 92	4c
Movie	admission	5.50	4Q 92	4c
Tennis balls, yellow, Wilson or Penn, 3	can	2.68	4Q 92	4c
Goods and Services				
ACCRA Index, Miscellaneous Goods and Services		99.10	4Q 92	4c
Groceries				
ACCRA Index, Groceries		101.90	4Q 92	4c
Babyfood, strained vegetables, lowest price	4-4.5 oz jar	0.30	4Q 92	4c
Bananas	lb	0.42	4Q 92	4c
Bread, white	24 oz	0.59	4Q 92	4c
Cheese, Kraft grated Parmesan	8-oz canister	3.37	4Q 92	4c
Chicken, fryer, whole	lb	0.72	4Q 92	4c
Cigarettes, Winston	carton	19.44	4Q 92	4c
Coffee, vacuum-packed	13-oz can	2.03	4Q 92	4c
Corn, frozen	10 oz	0.56	4Q 92	4c
Corn Flakes, Kellogg's or Post Toasties	18 oz	1.98	4Q 92	4c
Eggs, Grade A large	doz	0.86	4Q 92	4c
Ground beef or hamburger	lb	1.79	4Q 92	4c
Lettuce, iceberg	head	0.92	4Q 92	4c
Margarine, Blue Bonnet or Parkay cubes	lb	0.68	4Q 92	4c
Milk, whole	1/2 gal	1.31	4Q 92	4c
Orange juice, Minute Maid frozen	12-oz can	1.37	4Q 92	4c
Peaches	29-oz can	1.42	4Q 92	4c
Peas Sweet, Del Monte or Green Giant	15-17 oz can	0.57	4Q 92	4c
Potatoes, white or red	10-lb sack	2.97	4Q 92	4c
Sausage, Jimmy Dean, 100% pork	lb	2.64	4Q 92	4c
Shortening, vegetable, Crisco	3-lb can	2.18	4Q 92	4c
Soft drink, Coca Cola	2 liter	1.44	4Q 92	4c
Steak, T-bone	lb	4.92	4Q 92	4c
Sugar, cane or beet	4 lb	1.54	4Q 92	4c
Tomatoes, Hunt's or Del Monte	14.5-oz can	0.68	4Q 92	4c
Tuna, chunk, light	6.125-6.5 oz can	0.70	4Q 92	4c

Georgetown, TX - continued

Item	Per	Value	Date	Ref.
Health Care				
ACCRA Index, Health Care		103.80	4Q 92	4c
Analgesic, Aspirin, Bayer, 325 mg tablets	100	5.09	4Q 92	4c
Dentist's fee, adult teeth cleaning and periodic oral exam	visit	43.33	4Q 92	4c
Doctor's fee, routine exam, established patient	visit	46.33	4Q 92	4c
Hospital care, semiprivate room	day	270.00	4Q 92	4c
Household Goods				
Appliance repair, home, service call, washing machine	min labor charge	34.95	4Q 92	4c
Laundry detergent, Tide Ultra, Bold, or Cheer	42 oz	3.70	4Q 92	4c
Tissues, facial, Kleenex brand	175-count box	1.08	4Q 92	4c
Housing				
ACCRA Index, Housing		88.70	4Q 92	4c
House, 1,800 sq ft, 8,000 sq ft lot, new, urban	total	99163	4Q 92	4c
House payment, principal and interest, 25% down payment	month	542	4Q 92	4c
Mortgage rate, incl. points & origination fee, 30-year fixed or adjustable rate	percent	7.94	4Q 92	4c
Rent, apartment, 2 bedrooms - 1-1/2 to 2 baths, unfurnished, 950 sq ft, water	month	445	4Q 92	4c
Personal Goods				
Shampoo, Alberto VO5	15 oz	1.26	4Q 92	4c
Toothpaste, Crest or Colgate	6-7 oz	2.04	4Q 92	4c
Personal Services				
Dry cleaning, man's 2-piece suit		5.50	4Q 92	4c
Haircare, woman's shampoo, trim and blow-dry		18.50	4Q 92	4c
Haircut, man's barbershop, no styling		5.50	4Q 92	4c
Restaurant Food				
Chicken, fried, thigh and drumstick		2.09	4Q 92	4c
Hamburger with cheese	1/4 lb	1.89	4Q 92	4c
Pizza, Pizza Hut or Pizza Inn, cheese, thin crust	12-13 in	7.99	4Q 92	4c
Transportation				
ACCRA Index, Transportation		104.20	4Q 92	4c
Tire balance, computer or spin balance, front	wheel	7.00	4Q 92	4c
Utilities				
ACCRA Index, Utilities		101.30	4Q 92	4c
Electricity, partial electric and other energy, 1,800 sq ft living area new home	month	80.49	4Q 92	4c

Gillette, WY

Item	Per	Value	Date	Ref.
Composite ACCRA index		100.60	4Q 92	4c
Alcoholic Beverages				
Beer, Miller Lite or Budweiser, 12-oz containers	6 pack	5.13	4Q 92	4c
Liquor, J & B Scotch	750 ml	18.52	4Q 92	4c
Wine, Gallo Chablis blanc, 1.5 liter	bottle	6.07	4Q 92	4c
Clothing				
Jeans, man's denim		23.97	4Q 92	4c
Shirt, man's dress shirt		23.49	4Q 92	4c
Undervest, boy's size 10-14, cotton	3	3.53	4Q 92	4c
Communications				
Newspaper subscription, daily and Sunday home delivery, large-city	month	11.05	4Q 92	4c
Telephone, flat rate	month	11.22	91	11c
Telephone bill, family of four	month	20.82	4Q 92	4c

Values are in dollars or fractions of dollars. In the column headed *Ref*, references are shown to sources. Each reference is followed by a letter. These refer to the geographical level for which data were reported: s=State, r=Region, and c=City or metro. The abbreviation *ex* is used to mean *except* or *excluding*; *exp* stands for expenditures. For other abbreviations and further explanations, please see the Introduction.

253

Gillette, WY - continued

Item	Per	Value	Date	Ref.
Energy and Fuels				
Energy, combined forms, 1,800 sq ft heating area	month	117.15	4Q 92	4c
Gasoline, motor	gal	1.20	4Q 92	4c
Entertainment				
Bowling, evening rate	game	1.85	4Q 92	4c
Monopoly game, Parker Brothers', No. 9		11.91	4Q 92	4c
Movie	admission	5.00	4Q 92	4c
Tennis balls, yellow, Wilson or Penn, 3	can	2.28	4Q 92	4c
Goods and Services				
ACCRA Index, Miscellaneous Goods and Services		97.90	4Q 92	4c
Groceries				
ACCRA Index, Groceries		100.90	4Q 92	4c
Babyfood, strained vegetables, lowest price	4-4.5 oz jar	0.34	4Q 92	4c
Bananas	lb	0.42	4Q 92	4c
Bread, white	24 oz	0.96	4Q 92	4c
Cheese, Kraft grated Parmesan	8-oz canister	3.61	4Q 92	4c
Chicken, fryer, whole	lb	0.70	4Q 92	4c
Cigarettes, Winston	carton	15.57	4Q 92	4c
Coffee, vacuum-packed	13-oz can	2.35	4Q 92	4c
Corn, frozen	10 oz	0.66	4Q 92	4c
Corn Flakes, Kellogg's or Post Toasties	18 oz	2.08	4Q 92	4c
Eggs, Grade A large	doz	0.71·	4Q 92	4c
Ground beef or hamburger	lb	1.12	4Q 92	4c
Lettuce, iceberg	head	1.03	4Q 92	4c
Margarine, Blue Bonnet or Parkay cubes	lb	0.56	4Q 92	4c
Milk, whole	1/2 gal	1.61	4Q 92	4c
Orange juice, Minute Maid frozen	12-oz can	1.45	4Q 92	4c
Peaches	29-oz can	1.53	4Q 92	4c
Peas Sweet, Del Monte or Green Giant	15-17 oz can	0.60	4Q 92	4c
Potatoes, white or red	10-lb sack	2.44	4Q 92	4c
Sausage, Jimmy Dean, 100% pork	lb	2.35	4Q 92	4c
Shortening, vegetable, Crisco	3-lb can	2.97	4Q 92	4c
Soft drink, Coca Cola	2 liter	1.04	4Q 92	4c
Steak, T-bone	lb	4.66	4Q 92	4c
Sugar, cane or beet	4 lb	1.46	4Q 92	4c
Tomatoes, Hunt's or Del Monte	14.5-oz can	0.67	4Q 92	4c
Tuna, chunk, light	6.125-6.5 oz can	0.71	4Q 92	4c
Health Care				
ACCRA Index, Health Care		93.60	4Q 92	4c
Analgesic, Aspirin, Bayer, 325 mg tablets	100	3.08	4Q 92	4c
Dentist's fee, adult teeth cleaning and periodic oral exam	visit	49.60	4Q 92	4c
Doctor's fee, routine exam, established patient	visit	33.60	4Q 92	4c
Hospital care, semiprivate room	day	300.00	4Q 92	4c
Household Goods				
Appliance repair, home, service call, washing machine	min labor charge	35.20	4Q 92	4c
Laundry detergent, Tide Ultra, Bold, or Cheer	42 oz	3.35	4Q 92	4c
Tissues, facial, Kleenex brand	175-count box	1.16	4Q 92	4c

Gillette, WY - continued

Item	Per	Value	Date	Ref.
Housing				
ACCRA Index, Housing		103.60	4Q 92	4c
House, 1,800 sq ft, 8,000 sq ft lot, new, urban	total	126500	4Q 92	4c
House payment, principal and interest, 25% down payment	month	707	4Q 92	4c
Mortgage rate, incl. points & origination fee, 30-year fixed or adjustable rate	percent	8.17	4Q 92	4c
Rent, apartment, 2 bedrooms - 1-1/2 to 2 baths, unfurnished, 950 sq ft, water	month	349	4Q 92	4c
Personal Goods				
Shampoo, Alberto VO5	15 oz	1.16	4Q 92	4c
Toothpaste, Crest or Colgate	6-7 oz	1.60	4Q 92	4c
Personal Services				
Dry cleaning, man's 2-piece suit		5.33	4Q 92	4c
Haircare, woman's shampoo, trim and blow-dry		14.25	4Q 92	4c
Haircut, man's barbershop, no styling		7.70	4Q 92	4c
Restaurant Food				
Chicken, fried, thigh and drumstick		2.68	4Q 92	4c
Hamburger with cheese	1/4 lb	1.95	4Q 92	4c
Pizza, Pizza Hut or Pizza Inn, cheese, thin crust	12-13 in	8.39	4Q 92	4c
Transportation				
ACCRA Index, Transportation		98.30	4Q 92	4c
Tire balance, computer or spin balance, front	wheel	5.90	4Q 92	4c
Utilities				
ACCRA Index, Utilities		107.30	4Q 92	4c
Electricity, all electric, 1,800 sq ft living area new home	month	117.15	4Q 92	4c

Glens Falls, NY

Item	Per	Value	Date	Ref.
Alcoholic Beverages				
Beer, Miller Lite or Budweiser, 12-oz containers	6 pack	4.57	4Q 92	4c
Liquor, J & B Scotch	750 ml	18.61	4Q 92	4c
Wine, Gallo Chablis blanc, 1.5 liter	bottle	6.55	4Q 92	4c
Child Care				
Child care fee, average, center	hour	2.18	90	65r
Child care fee, average, nonregulated family day care	hour	1.83	90	65r
Child care fee, average, regulated family day care	hour	2.02	90	65r
Clothing				
Jeans, man's denim		38.00	4Q 92	4c
Shirt, man's dress shirt		25.19	4Q 92	4c
Undervest, boy's size 10-14, cotton	3	4.67	4Q 92	4c
Communications				
Newspaper subscription, daily and Sunday home delivery, large-city	month	11.52	4Q 92	4c
Telephone bill, family of four	month	24.99	4Q 92	4c
Education				
Board, 4-yr private college/university	year	2451	91	22s
Board, 4-yr public college/university	year	1725	91	22s
Expenditures, local gov't, public elementary/secondary	pupil	8603	92	20s
Room, 4-year private college/university	year	2652	91	22s
Room, 4-year public college/university	year	2183	91	22s
Tuition, 2-year private college/university	year	5926	91	22s
Tuition, 2-year public college/university	year	1419	91	22s
Tuition, 4-year private college/university	year	10340	91	22s
Tuition, 4-year public college/university, in-state	year	1587	91	22s

Values are in dollars or fractions of dollars. In the column headed *Ref*, references are shown to sources. Each reference is followed by a letter. These refer to the geographical level for which data were reported: s=State, r=Region, and c=City or metro. The abbreviation *ex* is used to mean *except* or *excluding*; *exp* stands for expenditures. For other abbreviations and further explanations, please see the Introduction.

Glens Falls, NY - continued

Item	Per	Value	Date	Ref.
Energy and Fuels				
Coal	mil Btu	1.66	90	64s
Energy	mil Btu	10.68	90	64s
Energy, combined forms, 1,800 sq ft heating area	month	144.49	4Q 92	4c
Energy, exc electricity, 1,800 sq ft heating area	month	81.05	4Q 92	4c
Energy exp/householder, 1-family unit	year	588	90	28r
Energy exp/householder, <1,000 sq ft heating area	year	477	90	28r
Energy exp/householder, 1,000-1,999 sq ft heating area	year	517	90	28r
Energy exp/householder, 2,000+ sq ft heating area	year	630	90	28r
Energy exp/householder, mobile home	year	412	90	28r
Energy exp/householder, multifamily	year	498	90	28r
Gas, natural	mil Btu	5.25	90	64s
Gas, natural	000 cu ft	7.35	91	46s
Gas, natural, exp	year	557	91	46s
Gasoline, motor	gal	1.19	4Q 92	4c
Gasoline, unleaded regular	mil Btu	8.83	90	64s
Entertainment				
Bowling, evening rate	game	1.75	4Q 92	4c
Monopoly game, Parker Brothers', No. 9		10.94	4Q 92	4c
Movie	admission	5.25	4Q 92	4c
Tennis balls, yellow, Wilson or Penn, 3	can	2.03	4Q 92	4c
Funerals				
Casket, 18-gauge steel, velvet interior		1811.58	91	24r
Cosmetology, hair care, etc.		111.08	91	24r
Embalming		329.42	91	24r
Facility use for ceremony		201.29	91	24r
Hearse, local		135.27	91	24r
Limousine, local		127.24	91	24r
Remains to funeral home, transfer		103.98	91	24r
Service charge, professional		724.98	91	24r
Vault, concrete, non-metallic liner		766.71	91	24r
Viewing facilities, use		260.60	91	24r
Groceries				
Apples, Red Delicious	lb	0.85	4/93	16r
Babyfood, strained vegetables, lowest price	4-4.5 oz jar	0.34	4Q 92	4c
Bacon	lb	2.12	4/93	16r
Bananas	lb	0.59	4Q 92	4c
Bananas	lb	0.54	4/93	16r
Bread, white	24 oz	0.78	4Q 92	4c
Bread, white, pan	lb	0.81	4/93	16r
Butter	lb	2.02	4/93	16r
Carrots, short trimmed and topped	lb	0.51	4/93	16r
Cheese, Kraft grated Parmesan	8-oz canister	3.15	4Q 92	4c
Chicken, fresh, whole	lb	1.04	4/93	16r
Chicken, fryer, whole	lb	1.15	4Q 92	4c
Chicken breast, bone-in	lb	2.21	4/93	16r
Chicken legs, bone-in	lb	1.16	4/93	16r
Chuck roast, USDA choice, boneless	lb	2.82	4/93	16r
Cigarettes, Winston	carton	20.11	4Q 92	4c
Coffee, 100% ground roast, all sizes	lb	2.66	4/93	16r
Coffee, vacuum-packed	13-oz can	2.22	4Q 92	4c
Corn, frozen	10 oz	0.62	4Q 92	4c
Corn Flakes, Kellogg's or Post Toasties	18 oz	2.19	4Q 92	4c
Cucumbers	lb	0.85	4/93	16r
Eggs, Grade A large	doz	0.93	4Q 92	4c
Eggs, Grade A large	doz	1.15	4/93	16r
Grapefruit	lb	0.45	4/93	16r
Grapes, Thompson Seedless	lb	1.52	4/93	16r
Ground beef, lean and extra lean	lb	2.36	4/93	16r
Ground beef or hamburger	lb	1.80	4Q 92	4c
Ground chuck, 100% beef	lb	2.02	4/93	16r

Glens Falls, NY - continued

Item	Per	Value	Date	Ref.
Groceries - continued				
Honey, jar	8 oz	0.96-1.75	92	5r
Honey, jar	lb	1.50-3.00	92	5r
Honey, squeeze bear	12-oz	1.50-1.99	92	5r
Ice cream, prepackaged, bulk, regular	1/2 gal	2.80	4/93	16r
Lemons	lb	0.96	4/93	16r
Lettuce, iceberg	head	0.99	4Q 92	4c
Lettuce, iceberg	lb	0.95	4/93	16r
Margarine, Blue Bonnet or Parkay cubes	lb	0.67	4Q 92	4c
Margarine, stick	lb	0.81	4/93	16r
Milk, fresh, whole, fortified	1/2 gal	1.30	4/93	16r
Milk, whole	1/2 gal	1.26	4Q 92	4c
Orange juice, Minute Maid frozen	12-oz can	1.41	4Q 92	4c
Oranges, navel	lb	0.56	4/93	16r
Peaches	29-oz can	1.69	4Q 92	4c
Peanut butter, creamy, all sizes	lb	1.88	4/93	16r
Peas Sweet, Del Monte or Green Giant	15-17 oz can	0.67	4Q 92	4c
Pork chops, center cut, bone-in	lb	3.34	4/93	16r
Potato chips	16 oz	2.88	4/93	16r
Potatoes, white	lb	0.37	4/93	16r
Potatoes, white or red	10-lb sack	2.17	4Q 92	4c
Rib roast, USDA choice, bone-in	lb	4.94	4/93	16r
Round roast, USDA choice, boneless	lb	3.17	4/93	16r
Sausage, Jimmy Dean, 100% pork	lb	3.24	4Q 92	4c
Shortening, vegetable oil blends	lb	0.98	4/93	16r
Shortening, vegetable, Crisco	3-lb can	2.80	4Q 92	4c
Soft drink, Coca Cola	2 liter	1.24	4Q 92	4c
Spaghetti and macaroni	lb	0.82	4/93	16r
Steak, round, graded & ungraded, ex USDA prime & choice	lb	4.04	4/93	16r
Steak, round, USDA choice, boneless	lb	3.90	4/93	16r
Steak, sirloin, USDA choice, boneless	lb	4.97	4/93	16r
Steak, T-bone	lb	6.01	4Q 92	4c
Strawberries, dry pint	12 oz	0.90	4/93	16r
Sugar, cane or beet	4 lb	1.82	4Q 92	4c
Sugar, white	lb	0.50	4/93	16r
Sugar, white, 33-80 oz pk	lb	0.41	4/93	16r
Tomatoes, field grown	lb	1.23	4/93	16r
Tomatoes, Hunt's or Del Monte	14.5-oz can	0.81	4Q 92	4c
Tuna, chunk, light	6.125-6.5 oz can	0.81	4Q 92	4c
Tuna, chunk, light	lb	2.22	4/93	16r
Turkey, frozen, whole	lb	1.04	4/93	16r
Health Care				
Analgesic, Aspirin, Bayer, 325 mg tablets	100	5.29	4Q 92	4c
Childbirth, cesarean, hospital		5826	91	62r
Childbirth, cesarean, physician's fee		2053	91	62r
Childbirth, normal, hospital		2964	91	62r
Childbirth, normal, physician's fee		1492	91	62r
Dentist's fee, adult teeth cleaning and periodic oral exam	visit	62.00	4Q 92	4c
Doctor's fee, routine exam, established patient	visit	51.00	4Q 92	4c
Hospital care, semiprivate room	day	240.00	90	27c
Hospital care, semiprivate room	day	228.00	4Q 92	4c
Medical insurance premium, per employee, small group comprehensive	month	266.45	10/91	25c
Medical plan per employee	year	3942	91	45r
Mental health care, exp	capita	53.68-118.35	90	38s
Mental health care, exp, state mental health agency	capita	118.34	90	38s
Mental health care, hospital psychiatric services, non-Federal, exp	capita	29.77	88	38s
Mental health care, mental health organization, multiservice, exp	capita	20.03	88	38s

Values are in dollars or fractions of dollars. In the column headed *Ref*, references are shown to sources. Each reference is followed by a letter. These refer to the geographical level for which data were reported: s=State, r=Region, and c=City or metro. The abbreviation *ex* is used to mean *except* or *excluding*; *exp* stands for expenditures. For other abbreviations and further explanations, please see the Introduction.

Glens Falls, NY - continued

Item	Per	Value	Date	Ref.
Health Care				
Mental health care, psychiatric hospitals, private, exp	capita	8.37	88	38s
Mental health care, psychiatric out-patient clinics, freestanding, exp	capita	7.96	88	38s
Mental health care, psychiatric partial-care organizations, freestanding, exp	capita	1.24	88	38s
Mental health care, state and county mental hospitals, exp	capita	89.52	88	38s
Mental health care, VA medical centers, exp	capita	7.12	88	38s
Prescription drug co-pay, Medicaid	month	23.00	91	21s
Substance abuse, hospital ancillary charge	incident	1040	90	70s
Substance abuse, hospital physician charge	incident	360	90	70s
Substance abuse, hospital room and board	incident	6330	90	70s
Household Goods				
Appliance repair, home, service call, washing machine	min labor charge	34.39	4Q 92	4c
Laundry detergent, Tide Ultra, Bold, or Cheer	42 oz	3.91	4Q 92	4c
Tissues, facial, Kleenex brand	175-count box	1.19	4Q 92	4c
Housing				
House, 1,800 sq ft, 8,000 sq ft lot, new, urban	total	100750	4Q 92	4c
House payment, principal and interest, 25% down payment	month	577	4Q 92	4c
Mortgage rate, incl. points & origination fee, 30-year fixed or adjustable rate	percent	8.42	4Q 92	4c
Rent, apartment, 2 bedrooms - 1-1/2 to 2 baths, unfurnished, 950 sq ft, water	month	507	4Q 92	4c
Rental unit, 1 bedroom	month	442	93	23c
Rental unit, 2 bedroom	month	520	93	23c
Rental unit, 3 bedroom	month	649	93	23c
Rental unit, 4 bedroom	month	730	93	23c
Rental unit, efficiency	month	363	93	23c
Insurance and Pensions				
Auto insurance, private passenger	year	840.89	91	63s
Personal Goods				
Shampoo, Alberto VO5	15 oz	1.25	4Q 92	4c
Toothpaste, Crest or Colgate	6-7 oz	2.01	4Q 92	4c
Personal Services				
Dry cleaning, man's 2-piece suit		6.24	4Q 92	4c
Haircare, woman's shampoo, trim and blow-dry		20.30	4Q 92	4c
Haircut, man's barbershop, no styling		7.90	4Q 92	4c
Restaurant Food				
Chicken, fried, thigh and drumstick		2.29	4Q 92	4c
Hamburger with cheese	1/4 lb	2.02	4Q 92	4c
Pizza, Pizza Hut or Pizza Inn, cheese, thin crust	12-13 in	7.99	4Q 92	4c
Taxes				
Tax, cigarette	pack	39	91	77s
Tax, gasoline	gal	8	91	77s
Taxes, state	capita	1567	91	77s
Transportation				
Driver's license fee		17.50	12/90	43s
Tire balance, computer or spin balance, front	wheel	6.60	4Q 92	4c
Vehicle registration and license plate	2 years	27.50-149.50	93	67s
Travel				
Business travel	day	165.00	4/93	89r

Glens Falls, NY - continued

Item	Per	Value	Date	Ref.
Utilities				
Electricity	mil Btu	27.51	90	64s
Electricity, partial electric and other energy, 1,800 sq ft living area new home	month	63.44	4Q 92	4c

Goldsboro, NC

Item	Per	Value	Date	Ref.
Composite ACCRA index		98.00	4Q 92	4c
Alcoholic Beverages				
Beer, Miller Lite or Budweiser, 12-oz containers	6 pack	4.12	4Q 92	4c
Liquor, J & B Scotch	750 ml	17.65	4Q 92	4c
Wine, Gallo Chablis blanc, 1.5 liter	bottle	4.74	4Q 92	4c
Clothing				
Jeans, man's denim		35.66	4Q 92	4c
Shirt, man's dress shirt		23.33	4Q 92	4c
Undervest, boy's size 10-14, cotton	3	4.84	4Q 92	4c
Communications				
Newspaper subscription, daily and Sunday home delivery, large-city	month	11.96	4Q 92	4c
Telephone, flat rate	month	11.03	91	11c
Telephone bill, family of four	month	15.14	4Q 92	4c
Energy and Fuels				
Energy, combined forms, 1,800 sq ft heating area	month	127.12	4Q 92	4c
Gasoline, motor	gal	1.10	4Q 92	4c
Entertainment				
Bowling, evening rate	game	1.49	4Q 92	4c
Monopoly game, Parker Brothers', No. 9		11.45	4Q 92	4c
Movie	admission	5.00	4Q 92	4c
Tennis balls, yellow, Wilson or Penn, 3	can	2.12	4Q 92	4c
Goods and Services				
ACCRA Index, Miscellaneous Goods and Services		100.40	4Q 92	4c
Groceries				
ACCRA Index, Groceries		98.80	4Q 92	4c
Babyfood, strained vegetables, lowest price	4-4.5 oz jar	0.32	4Q 92	4c
Bananas	lb	0.44	4Q 92	4c
Bread, white	24 oz	0.86	4Q 92	4c
Cheese, Kraft grated Parmesan	8-oz canister	3.36	4Q 92	4c
Chicken, fryer, whole	lb	0.87	4Q 92	4c
Cigarettes, Winston	carton	15.20	4Q 92	4c
Coffee, vacuum-packed	13-oz can	1.86	4Q 92	4c
Corn, frozen	10 oz	0.67	4Q 92	4c
Corn Flakes, Kellogg's or Post Toasties	18 oz	1.80	4Q 92	4c
Eggs, Grade A large	doz	0.76	4Q 92	4c
Ground beef or hamburger	lb	1.51	4Q 92	4c
Lettuce, iceberg	head	1.01	4Q 92	4c
Margarine, Blue Bonnet or Parkay cubes	lb	0.52	4Q 92	4c
Milk, whole	1/2 gal	1.41	4Q 92	4c
Orange juice, Minute Maid frozen	12-oz can	1.35	4Q 92	4c
Peaches	29-oz can	1.39	4Q 92	4c
Peas Sweet, Del Monte or Green Giant	15-17 oz can	0.52	4Q 92	4c
Potatoes, white or red	10-lb sack	2.21	4Q 92	4c
Sausage, Jimmy Dean, 100% pork	lb	2.27	4Q 92	4c
Shortening, vegetable, Crisco	3-lb can	2.04	4Q 92	4c
Soft drink, Coca Cola	2 liter	1.05	4Q 92	4c
Steak, T-bone	lb	5.21	4Q 92	4c
Sugar, cane or beet	4 lb	1.69	4Q 92	4c

Values are in dollars or fractions of dollars. In the column headed *Ref*, references are shown to sources. Each reference is followed by a letter. These refer to the geographical level for which data were reported: s=State, r=Region, and c=City or metro. The abbreviation *ex* is used to mean *except* or *excluding*; *exp* stands for expenditures. For other abbreviations and further explanations, please see the Introduction.

Goldsboro, NC - continued

Item	Per	Value	Date	Ref.
Groceries				
Tomatoes, Hunt's or Del Monte	14.5-oz can	0.59	4Q 92	4c
Tuna, chunk, light	6.125-6.5 oz can	0.56	4Q 92	4c
Health Care				
ACCRA Index, Health Care		92.30	4Q 92	4c
Analgesic, Aspirin, Bayer, 325 mg tablets	100	4.47	4Q 92	4c
Dentist's fee, adult teeth cleaning and periodic oral exam	visit	44.71	4Q 92	4c
Doctor's fee, routine exam, established patient	visit	33.80	4Q 92	4c
Hospital care, semiprivate room	day	284.00	4Q 92	4c
Household Goods				
Appliance repair, home, service call, washing machine	min labor charge	32.80	4Q 92	4c
Laundry detergent, Tide Ultra, Bold, or Cheer	42 oz	3.51	4Q 92	4c
Tissues, facial, Kleenex brand	175-count box	1.13	4Q 92	4c
Housing				
ACCRA Index, Housing		92.00	4Q 92	4c
House, 1,800 sq ft, 8,000 sq ft lot, new, urban	total	104000	4Q 92	4c
House payment, principal and interest, 25% down payment	month	584	4Q 92	4c
Mortgage rate, incl. points & origination fee, 30-year fixed or adjustable rate	per-cent	8.21	4Q 92	4c
Rent, apartment, 2 bedrooms - 1-1/2 to 2 baths, unfurnished, 950 sq ft, water	month	412	4Q 92	4c
Personal Goods				
Shampoo, Alberto VO5	15 oz	1.31	4Q 92	4c
Toothpaste, Crest or Colgate	6-7 oz	2.05	4Q 92	4c
Personal Services				
Dry cleaning, man's 2-piece suit		5.73	4Q 92	4c
Haircare, woman's shampoo, trim and blow-dry		15.00	4Q 92	4c
Haircut, man's barbershop, no styling		6.56	4Q 92	4c
Restaurant Food				
Chicken, fried, thigh and drumstick		2.26	4Q 92	4c
Hamburger with cheese	1/4 lb	1.85	4Q 92	4c
Pizza, Pizza Hut or Pizza Inn, cheese, thin crust	12-13 in	7.62	4Q 92	4c
Transportation				
ACCRA Index, Transportation		94.70	4Q 92	4c
Tire balance, computer or spin balance, front	wheel	6.00	4Q 92	4c
Utilities				
ACCRA Index, Utilities		112.60	4Q 92	4c
Electricity, all electric, 1,800 sq ft living area new home	month	127.12	4Q 92	4c

Grand Forks, ND

Item	Per	Value	Date	Ref.
Child Care				
Child care fee, average, center	hour	1.63	90	65r
Child care fee, average, nonregulated family day care	hour	1.83	90	65r
Child care fee, average, regulated family day care	hour	1.42	90	65r
Communications				
Long-distance telephone service, day, initial minute, 0-100 miles	min	0.24-0.51	91	12s

Grand Forks, ND - continued

Item	Per	Value	Date	Ref.
Communications - continued				
Long-distance telephone service, day, additional minute, 0-100 miles	min	0.10-0.35	91	12s
Long-distance telephone service, evenings/weekends, 0-100 mi, initial minute	min	0.14-0.31	91	12s
Long-distance telephone service, evenings/weekends, 0-100 mi, additional minute	min	0.06-0.21	91	12s
Education				
Board, 4-yr private college/university	year	1422	91	22s
Board, 4-yr public college/university	year	1618	91	22s
Expenditures, local gov't, public elementary/secondary	pupil	8755	92	20s
Room, 4-year private college/university	year	1049	91	22s
Room, 4-year public college/university	year	790	91	22s
Tuition, 2-year public college/university	year	1584	91	22s
Tuition, 4-year private college/university	year	5389	91	22s
Tuition, 4-year public college/university, in-state	year	1930	91	22s
Energy and Fuels				
Coal	mil Btu	1.18	90	64s
Energy	mil Btu	6.64	90	64s
Energy exp/householder, 1-family unit	year	473	90	28r
Energy exp/householder, <1,000 sq ft heating area	year	429	90	28r
Energy exp/householder, 1,000-1,999 sq ft heating area	year	442	90	28r
Energy exp/householder, 2,000+ sq ft heating area	year	498	90	28r
Energy exp/householder, mobile home	year	442	90	28r
Energy exp/householder, multifamily	year	407	90	28r
Gas, natural	mil Btu	4.12	90	64s
Gas, natural	000 cu ft	4.82	91	46s
Gas, natural, exp	year	568	91	46s
Gasoline, unleaded regular	mil Btu	9.87	90	64s
Entertainment				
Miniature golf admission	adult	6.18	92	1r
Miniature golf admission	child	5.14	92	1r
Waterpark admission	adult	11.00	92	1r
Waterpark admission	child	8.55	92	1r
Funerals				
Casket, 18-gauge steel, velvet interior		1952.97	91	24r
Cosmetology, hair care, etc.		90.03	91	24r
Embalming		251.75	91	24r
Facility use for ceremony		180.75	91	24r
Hearse, local		117.51	91	24r
Limousine, local		71.86	91	24r
Remains to funeral home, transfer		81.14	91	24r
Service charge, professional		740.03	91	24r
Vault, concrete, non-metallic liner		801.47	91	24r
Viewing facilities, use		169.33	91	24r
Groceries				
Apples, Red Delicious	lb	0.77	4/93	16r
Bacon	lb	1.85	4/93	16r
Bananas	lb	0.46	4/93	16r
Beef, stew, boneless	lb	2.53	4/93	16r
Bologna, all beef or mixed	lb	2.19	4/93	16r
Bread, white, pan	lb	0.78	4/93	16r
Butter	lb	1.50	4/93	16r
Cabbage	lb	0.40	4/93	16r
Carrots, short trimmed and topped	lb	0.45	4/93	16r
Cheese, Cheddar	lb	3.47	4/93	16r
Chicken, fresh, whole	lb	0.84	4/93	16r
Chicken breast, bone-in	lb	1.94	4/93	16r
Chicken legs, bone-in	lb	1.02	4/93	16r
Chuck roast, graded and ungraded, ex USDA prime and choice	lb	2.43	4/93	16r
Chuck roast, USDA choice, bone-in	lb	2.11	4/93	16r
Chuck roast, USDA choice, boneless	lb	2.44	4/93	16r
Coffee, 100% ground roast, all sizes	lb	2.47	4/93	16r

Values are in dollars or fractions of dollars. In the column headed *Ref*, references are shown to sources. Each reference is followed by a letter. These refer to the geographical level for which data were reported: s=State, r=Region, and c=City or metro. The abbreviation *ex* is used to mean *except* or *excluding*; *exp* stands for expenditures. For other abbreviations and further explanations, please see the Introduction.

Grand Forks, ND - continued

Item	Per	Value	Date	Ref.
Groceries				
Cookies, chocolate chip	lb	2.73	4/93	16r
Eggs, Grade A large	doz	0.93	4/93	16r
Flour, white, all purpose	lb	0.21	4/93	16r
Grapefruit	lb	0.45	4/93	16r
Grapes, Thompson Seedless	lb	1.46	4/93	16r
Ground beef, 100% beef	lb	1.63	4/93	16r
Ground beef, lean and extra lean	lb	2.08	4/93	16r
Ground chuck, 100% beef	lb	1.94	4/93	16r
Ham, boneless, excluding canned	lb	2.21	4/93	16r
Ice cream, prepackaged, bulk, regular	1/2 gal	2.41	4/93	16r
Lemons	lb	0.82	4/93	16r
Lettuce, iceberg	lb	0.83	4/93	16r
Margarine, stick	lb	0.77	4/93	16r
Oranges, navel	lb	0.50	4/93	16r
Peanut butter, creamy, all sizes	lb	1.82	4/93	16r
Pears, Anjou	lb	0.85	4/93	16r
Pork chops, center cut, bone-in	lb	3.17	4/93	16r
Potato chips	16 oz	2.68	4/93	16r
Potatoes, white	lb	0.26	4/93	16r
Round roast, graded & ungraded, ex USDA prime & choice	lb	2.88	4/93	16r
Round roast, USDA choice, boneless	lb	2.96	4/93	16r
Shortening, vegetable oil blends	lb	0.79	4/93	16r
Spaghetti and macaroni	lb	0.76	4/93	16r
Steak, rib eye, USDA choice, boneless	lb	6.29	4/93	16r
Steak, round, USDA choice, boneless	lb	3.24	4/93	16r
Steak, sirloin, graded & ungraded, ex USDA prime & choice	lb	4.00	4/93	16r
Steak, sirloin, USDA choice, bone-in	lb	3.57	4/93	16r
Steak, sirloin, USDA choice, boneless	lb	4.17	4/93	16r
Steak, T-bone, USDA choice, bone-in	lb	5.60	4/93	16r
Strawberries, dry pint	12 oz	0.90	4/93	16r
Sugar, white	lb	0.36	4/93	16r
Sugar, white, 33-80 oz pk	lb	0.35	4/93	16r
Tomatoes, field grown	lb	0.99	4/93	16r
Tuna, chunk, light	lb	1.76	4/93	16r
Turkey, frozen, whole	lb	0.91	4/93	16r
Health Care				
Childbirth, cesarean, hospital		4688	91	62r
Childbirth, cesarean, physician's fee		2053	91	62r
Childbirth, normal, hospital		2657	91	62r
Childbirth, normal, physician's fee		1492	91	62r
Medical plan per employee	year	3443	91	45r
Mental health care, exp	capita	28.84-37.59	90	38s
Mental health care, exp, state mental health agency	capita	40.24	90	38s
Mental health care, hospital psychiatric services, non-Federal, exp	capita	18.67	88	38s
Mental health care, mental health organization, multiservice, exp	capita	27.50	88	38s
Mental health care, state and county mental hospitals, exp	capita	32.62	88	38s
Physician fee, family practice, first-visit		76.00	91	62r
Physician fee, family practice, revisit		33.00	91	62r
Physician fee, general practice, first-visit		61.00	91	62r
Physician fee, general practice, revisit		31.00	91	62r
Physician fee, general surgeon, first-visit		65.00	91	62r
Physician fee, general surgeon, revisit		35.00	91	62r
Physician fee, internal medicine, first-visit		91.00	91	62r
Physician fee, internal medicine, revisit		40.00	91	62r
Physician fee, median, neurosurgeon, first-visit		106.00	91	62r
Physician fee, median, nonsurgical specialist, first-visit		90.00	91	62r
Physician fee, median, orthopedic surgeon, first-visit		83.00	91	62r
Physician fee, median, surgical specialist, first-visit		61.00	91	62r
Physician fee, neurosurgeon, revisit		41.00	91	62r
Physician fee, nonsurgical specialist, revisit		40.00	91	62r

Grand Forks, ND - continued

Item	Per	Value	Date	Ref.
Health Care - continued				
Physician fee, obstetrics/gynecology, first-visit		61.00	91	62r
Physician fee, obstetrics/gynecology, revisit		40.00	91	62r
Physician fee, orthopedic surgeon, revisit		41.00	91	62r
Physician fee, pediatrician, first-visit		46.00	91	62r
Physician fee, pediatrician, revisit		33.00	91	62r
Physician fee, surgical specialist, revisit		36.00	91	62r
Insurance and Pensions				
Auto insurance, private passenger	year	413.64	91	63s
Taxes				
Tax, cigarette	pack	29	91	77s
Tax, gasoline	gal	17	91	77s
Taxes, state	capita	1189	91	77s
Transportation				
Driver's license fee		10.00	12/90	43s
Vehicle registration and license plate	year	26.00-251.00	92	51s
Utilities				
Electricity	mil Btu	16.86	90	64s

Grand Island, NE

Item	Per	Value	Date	Ref.
Composite ACCRA index		89.60	4Q 92	4c
Alcoholic Beverages				
Beer, Miller Lite or Budweiser, 12-oz containers	6 pack	3.88	4Q 92	4c
Liquor, J & B Scotch	750 ml	17.78	4Q 92	4c
Wine, Gallo Chablis blanc, 1.5 liter	bottle	5.33	4Q 92	4c
Clothing				
Jeans, man's denim		25.80	4Q 92	4c
Shirt, man's dress shirt		25.40	4Q 92	4c
Undervest, boy's size 10-14, cotton	3	3.28	4Q 92	4c
Communications				
Newspaper subscription, daily and Sunday home delivery, large-city	month	7.00	4Q 92	4c
Telephone, flat rate	month	14.90	91	11c
Telephone, residential, private line, rotary, unlimited calling	month	21.81	10/91	78c
Telephone bill, family of four	month	21.40	4Q 92	4c
Energy and Fuels				
Energy, combined forms, 1,800 sq ft heating area	month	87.75	4Q 92	4c
Energy, exc electricity, 1,800 sq ft heating area	month	39.29	4Q 92	4c
Gasoline, motor	gal	1.14	4Q 92	4c
Entertainment				
Bowling, evening rate	game	1.95	4Q 92	4c
Monopoly game, Parker Brothers', No. 9		10.74	4Q 92	4c
Movie	admission	5.00	4Q 92	4c
Tennis balls, yellow, Wilson or Penn, 3	can	2.34	4Q 92	4c
Goods and Services				
ACCRA Index, Miscellaneous Goods and Services		92.20	4Q 92	4c
Groceries				
ACCRA Index, Groceries		101.20	4Q 92	4c
Babyfood, strained vegetables, lowest price	4-4.5 oz jar	0.33	4Q 92	4c
Bananas	lb	0.44	4Q 92	4c
Bread, white	24 oz	0.87	4Q 92	4c
Cheese, Kraft grated Parmesan	8-oz canister	3.18	4Q 92	4c
Chicken, fryer, whole	lb	0.76	4Q 92	4c
Cigarettes, Winston	carton	17.74	4Q 92	4c

Values are in dollars or fractions of dollars. In the column headed *Ref*, references are shown to sources. Each reference is followed by a letter. These refer to the geographical level for which data were reported: s=State, r=Region, and c=City or metro. The abbreviation *ex* is used to mean *except* or *excluding*; *exp* stands for expenditures. For other abbreviations and further explanations, please see the Introduction.

Grand Island, NE - continued

Item	Per	Value	Date	Ref.
Groceries				
Coffee, vacuum-packed	13-oz can	1.94	4Q 92	4c
Corn, frozen	10 oz	0.65	4Q 92	4c
Corn Flakes, Kellogg's or Post Toasties	18 oz	1.81	4Q 92	4c
Eggs, Grade A large	doz	0.66	4Q 92	4c
Ground beef or hamburger	lb	1.32	4Q 92	4c
Lettuce, iceberg	head	0.93	4Q 92	4c
Margarine, Blue Bonnet or Parkay cubes	lb	0.55	4Q 92	4c
Milk, whole	1/2 gal	1.41	4Q 92	4c
Orange juice, Minute Maid frozen	12-oz can	1.46	4Q 92	4c
Peaches	29-oz can	1.34	4Q 92	4c
Peas Sweet, Del Monte or Green Giant	15-17 oz can	0.58	4Q 92	4c
Potatoes, white or red	10-lb sack	1.59	4Q 92	4c
Sausage, Jimmy Dean, 100% pork	lb	3.05	4Q 92	4c
Shortening, vegetable, Crisco	3-lb can	2.25	4Q 92	4c
Soft drink, Coca Cola	2 liter	1.35	4Q 92	4c
Steak, T-bone	lb	4.99	4Q 92	4c
Sugar, cane or beet	4 lb	1.58	4Q 92	4c
Tomatoes, Hunt's or Del Monte	14.5-oz can	0.78	4Q 92	4c
Tuna, chunk, light	6.125-6.5 oz can	0.66	4Q 92	4c
Health Care				
ACCRA Index, Health Care		75.60	4Q 92	4c
Analgesic, Aspirin, Bayer, 325 mg tablets	100	3.59	4Q 92	4c
Dentist's fee, adult teeth cleaning and periodic oral exam	visit	39.80	4Q 92	4c
Doctor's fee, routine exam, established patient	visit	25.40	4Q 92	4c
Hospital care, semiprivate room	day	186.61	90	27c
Hospital care, semiprivate room	day	232.00	4Q 92	4c
Household Goods				
Appliance repair, home, service call, washing machine	min labor charge	27.19	4Q 92	4c
Laundry detergent, Tide Ultra, Bold, or Cheer	42 oz	3.67	4Q 92	4c
Tissues, facial, Kleenex brand	175-count box	1.04	4Q 92	4c
Housing				
ACCRA Index, Housing		83.80	4Q 92	4c
House, 1,800 sq ft, 8,000 sq ft lot, new, urban	total	95200	4Q 92	4c
House payment, principal and interest, 25% down payment	month	537	4Q 92	4c
Mortgage rate, incl. points & origination fee, 30-year fixed or adjustable rate	percent	8.27	4Q 92	4c
Rent, apartment, 2 bedrooms - 1-1/2 to 2 baths, unfurnished, 950 sq ft, water	month	362	4Q 92	4c
Personal Goods				
Shampoo, Alberto VO5	15 oz	1.30	4Q 92	4c
Toothpaste, Crest or Colgate	6-7 oz	1.49	4Q 92	4c
Personal Services				
Dry cleaning, man's 2-piece suit		6.43	4Q 92	4c
Haircare, woman's shampoo, trim and blow-dry		16.20	4Q 92	4c
Haircut, man's barbershop, no styling		8.55	4Q 92	4c
Restaurant Food				
Chicken, fried, thigh and drumstick		1.80	4Q 92	4c
Hamburger with cheese	1/4 lb	1.80	4Q 92	4c
Pizza, Pizza Hut or Pizza Inn, cheese, thin crust	12-13 in	7.49	4Q 92	4c

Grand Island, NE - continued

Item	Per	Value	Date	Ref.
Transportation				
ACCRA Index, Transportation		93.90	4Q 92	4c
Tire balance, computer or spin balance, front	wheel	5.69	4Q 92	4c
Utilities				
ACCRA Index, Utilities		83.30	4Q 92	4c
Electricity, partial electric and other energy, 1,800 sq ft living area new home	month	48.46	4Q 92	4c

Grand Junction, CO

Item	Per	Value	Date	Ref.
Composite ACCRA index		93.50	4Q 92	4c
Alcoholic Beverages				
Beer, Miller Lite or Budweiser, 12-oz containers	6 pack	4.18	4Q 92	4c
Liquor, J & B Scotch	750 ml	18.07	4Q 92	4c
Wine, Gallo Chablis blanc, 1.5 liter	bottle	4.39	4Q 92	4c
Clothing				
Jeans, man's denim		27.74	4Q 92	4c
Shirt, man's dress shirt		22.50	4Q 92	4c
Undervest, boy's size 10-14, cotton	3	4.27	4Q 92	4c
Communications				
Newspaper subscription, daily and Sunday home delivery, large-city	month	9.75	4Q 92	4c
Telephone, flat rate	month	14.22	91	11c
Telephone bill, family of four	month	20.58	4Q 92	4c
Energy and Fuels				
Energy, combined forms, 1,800 sq ft heating area	month	83.32	4Q 92	4c
Energy, exc electricity, 1,800 sq ft heating area	month	33.88	4Q 92	4c
Gasoline, motor	gal	1.30	4Q 92	4c
Entertainment				
Bowling, evening rate	game	1.90	4Q 92	4c
Monopoly game, Parker Brothers', No. 9		12.37	4Q 92	4c
Movie	admission	5.08	4Q 92	4c
Tennis balls, yellow, Wilson or Penn, 3	can	2.61	4Q 92	4c
Goods and Services				
ACCRA Index, Miscellaneous Goods and Services		97.60	4Q 92	4c
Groceries				
ACCRA Index, Groceries		108.40	4Q 92	4c
Babyfood, strained vegetables, lowest price	4-4.5 oz jar	0.37	4Q 92	4c
Bananas	lb	0.56	4Q 92	4c
Bread, white	24 oz	0.66	4Q 92	4c
Cheese, Kraft grated Parmesan	8-oz canister	3.31	4Q 92	4c
Chicken, fryer, whole	lb	0.69	4Q 92	4c
Cigarettes, Winston	carton	17.14	4Q 92	4c
Coffee, vacuum-packed	13-oz can	2.39	4Q 92	4c
Corn, frozen	10 oz	0.79	4Q 92	4c
Corn Flakes, Kellogg's or Post Toasties	18 oz	2.02	4Q 92	4c
Eggs, Grade A large	doz	0.79	4Q 92	4c
Ground beef or hamburger	lb	1.52	4Q 92	4c
Lettuce, iceberg	head	0.92	4Q 92	4c
Margarine, Blue Bonnet or Parkay cubes	lb	0.68	4Q 92	4c
Milk, whole	1/2 gal	1.65	4Q 92	4c
Orange juice, Minute Maid frozen	12-oz can	1.46	4Q 92	4c
Peaches	29-oz can	1.50	4Q 92	4c
Peas Sweet, Del Monte or Green Giant	15-17 oz can	0.74	4Q 92	4c

Values are in dollars or fractions of dollars. In the column headed *Ref*, references are shown to sources. Each reference is followed by a letter. These refer to the geographical level for which data were reported: s = State, r = Region, and c = City or metro. The abbreviation *ex* is used to mean *except* or *excluding*; *exp* stands for expenditures. For other abbreviations and further explanations, please see the Introduction.

259

Grand Junction, CO - continued

Item	Per	Value	Date	Ref.
Groceries				
Potatoes, white or red	10-lb sack	2.49	4Q 92	4c
Sausage, Jimmy Dean, 100% pork	lb	3.41	4Q 92	4c
Shortening, vegetable, Crisco	3-lb can	2.73	4Q 92	4c
Soft drink, Coca Cola	2 liter	1.49	4Q 92	4c
Steak, T-bone	lb	4.52	4Q 92	4c
Sugar, cane or beet	4 lb	1.57	4Q 92	4c
Tomatoes, Hunt's or Del Monte	14.5-oz can	0.81	4Q 92	4c
Tuna, chunk, light	6.125-6.5 oz can	0.93	4Q 92	4c
Health Care				
ACCRA Index, Health Care		97.10	4Q 92	4c
Analgesic, Aspirin, Bayer, 325 mg tablets	100	4.25	4Q 92	4c
Dentist's fee, adult teeth cleaning and periodic oral exam	visit	49.50	4Q 92	4c
Doctor's fee, routine exam, established patient	visit	31.86	4Q 92	4c
Hospital care, semiprivate room	day	345.50	4Q 92	4c
Household Goods				
Appliance repair, home, service call, washing machine	min labor charge	28.33	4Q 92	4c
Laundry detergent, Tide Ultra, Bold, or Cheer	42 oz	4.14	4Q 92	4c
Tissues, facial, Kleenex brand	175-count box	1.10	4Q 92	4c
Housing				
ACCRA Index, Housing		81.30	4Q 92	4c
House, 1,800 sq ft, 8,000 sq ft lot, new, urban	total	90917	4Q 92	4c
House payment, principal and interest, 25% down payment	month	505	4Q 92	4c
Mortgage rate, incl. points & origination fee, 30-year fixed or adjustable rate	per-cent	8.10	4Q 92	4c
Personal Goods				
Shampoo, Alberto VO5	15 oz	1.35	4Q 92	4c
Toothpaste, Crest or Colgate	6-7 oz	1.85	4Q 92	4c
Personal Services				
Dry cleaning, man's 2-piece suit		5.61	4Q 92	4c
Haircare, woman's shampoo, trim and blow-dry		14.64	4Q 92	4c
Haircut, man's barbershop, no styling		6.33	4Q 92	4c
Restaurant Food				
Chicken, fried, thigh and drumstick		2.20	4Q 92	4c
Hamburger with cheese	1/4 lb	1.99	4Q 92	4c
Pizza, Pizza Hut or Pizza Inn, cheese, thin crust	12-13 in	8.93	4Q 92	4c
Transportation				
ACCRA Index, Transportation		104.60	4Q 92	4c
Tire balance, computer or spin balance, front	wheel	6.12	4Q 92	4c
Utilities				
ACCRA Index, Utilities		79.30	4Q 92	4c
Electricity, partial electric and other energy, 1,800 sq ft living area new home	month	49.44	4Q 92	4c

Grand Rapids, MI

Item	Per	Value	Date	Ref.
Composite ACCRA index		111.40	4Q 92	4c
Alcoholic Beverages				
Beer, Miller Lite or Budweiser, 12-oz containers	6 pack	3.89	4Q 92	4c

Grand Rapids, MI - continued

Item	Per	Value	Date	Ref.
Alcoholic Beverages - continued				
Liquor, J & B Scotch	750 ml	17.51	4Q 92	4c
Wine, Gallo Chablis blanc, 1.5 liter	bottle	6.13	4Q 92	4c
Child Care				
Child care fee, average, center	hour	1.63	90	65r
Child care fee, average, nonregulated family day care	hour	1.83	90	65r
Child care fee, average, regulated family day care	hour	1.42	90	65r
Clothing				
Jeans, man's denim		38.99	4Q 92	4c
Shirt, man's dress shirt		27.60	4Q 92	4c
Undervest, boy's size 10-14, cotton	3	4.26	4Q 92	4c
Communications				
Long-distance telephone service, day, initial minute, 0-100 miles	min	0.14-0.36	91	12s
Long-distance telephone service, day, additional minute, 0-100 miles	min	0.14-0.36	91	12s
Long-distance telephone service, evenings/weekends, 0-100 mi, initial minute	min	0.07-0.19	91	12s
Long-distance telephone service, evenings/weekends, 0-100 mi, additional minute	min	0.04-0.14	91	12s
Newspaper subscription, daily and Sunday home delivery, large-city	month	10.00	4Q 92	4c
Telephone, flat rate	month	10.93	91	11c
Telephone, residential, private line, rotary, unlimited calling	month	14.44	10/91	78c
Telephone bill, family of four	month	17.18	4Q 92	4c
Education				
Board, 4-yr private college/university	year	1698	91	22s
Board, 4-yr public college/university	year	1962	91	22s
Expenditures, local gov't, public elementary/secondary	pupil	5671	92	20s
Room, 4-year private college/university	year	1440	91	22s
Room, 4-year public college/university	year	1687	91	22s
Tuition, 2-year private college/university	year	4749	91	22s
Tuition, 2-year public college/university	year	1124	91	22s
Tuition, 4-year private college/university	year	6885	91	22s
Tuition, 4-year public college/university, in-state	year	2635	91	22s
Energy and Fuels				
Coal	mil Btu	1.63	90	64s
Energy	mil Btu	8.17	90	64s
Energy, combined forms, 1,800 sq ft heating area	month	104.57	4Q 92	4c
Energy, exc electricity, 1,800 sq ft heating area	month	58.94	4Q 92	4c
Energy exp/householder, 1-family unit	year	471	90	28r
Energy exp/householder, <1,000 sq ft heating area	year	430	90	28r
Energy exp/householder, 1,000-1,999 sq ft heating area	year	481	90	28r
Energy exp/householder, 2,000+ sq ft heating area	year	473	90	28r
Energy exp/householder, mobile home	year	430	90	28r
Energy exp/householder, multifamily	year	461	90	28r
Gas, natural	mil Btu	4.36	90	64s
Gas, natural	000 cu ft	5.07	91	46s
Gas, natural, exp	year	655	91	46s
Gasoline, motor	gal	1.13	4Q 92	4c
Gasoline, unleaded regular	mil Btu	8.78	90	64s
Entertainment				
Bowling, evening rate	game	1.96	4Q 92	4c
Miniature golf admission	adult	6.18	92	1r
Miniature golf admission	child	5.14	92	1r
Monopoly game, Parker Brothers', No. 9		9.99	4Q 92	4c
Movie	admission	5.58	4Q 92	4c
Tennis balls, yellow, Wilson or Penn, 3	can	2.40	4Q 92	4c

Values are in dollars or fractions of dollars. In the column headed *Ref*, references are shown to sources. Each reference is followed by a letter. These refer to the geographical level for which data were reported: s=State, r=Region, and c=City or metro. The abbreviation *ex* is used to mean *except* or *excluding*; *exp* stands for expenditures. For other abbreviations and further explanations, please see the Introduction.

Grand Rapids, MI - continued

Item	Per	Value	Date	Ref.
Entertainment				
Waterpark admission	adult	11.00	92	1r
Waterpark admission	child	8.55	92	1r
Funerals				
Casket, 18-gauge steel, velvet interior		1926.72	91	24r
Cosmetology, hair care, etc.		97.64	91	24r
Embalming		249.14	91	24r
Facility use for ceremony		208.59	91	24r
Hearse, local		130.12	91	24r
Limousine, local		104.66	91	24r
Remains to funeral home, transfer		93.61	91	24r
Service charge, professional		724.62	91	24r
Vault, concrete, non-metallic liner		734.53	91	24r
Viewing facilities, use		236.06	91	24r
Goods and Services				
ACCRA Index, Miscellaneous Goods and Services		105.10	4Q 92	4c
Groceries				
ACCRA Index, Groceries		105.50	4Q 92	4c
Apples, Red Delicious	lb	0.77	4/93	16r
Babyfood, strained vegetables, lowest price	4-4.5 oz jar	0.39	4Q 92	4c
Bacon	lb	1.85	4/93	16r
Bananas	lb	0.38	4Q 92	4c
Bananas	lb	0.46	4/93	16r
Beef, stew, boneless	lb	2.53	4/93	16r
Bologna, all beef or mixed	lb	2.19	4/93	16r
Bread, white	24 oz	0.91	4Q 92	4c
Bread, white, pan	lb	0.78	4/93	16r
Butter	lb	1.50	4/93	16r
Cabbage	lb	0.40	4/93	16r
Carrots, short trimmed and topped	lb	0.45	4/93	16r
Cheese, Cheddar	lb	3.47	4/93	16r
Cheese, Kraft grated Parmesan	8-oz canister	3.41	4Q 92	4c
Chicken, fresh, whole	lb	0.84	4/93	16r
Chicken, fryer, whole	lb	0.89	4Q 92	4c
Chicken breast, bone-in	lb	1.94	4/93	16r
Chicken legs, bone-in	lb	1.02	4/93	16r
Chuck roast, graded and ungraded, ex USDA prime and choice	lb	2.43	4/93	16r
Chuck roast, USDA choice, bone-in	lb	2.11	4/93	16r
Chuck roast, USDA choice, boneless	lb	2.44	4/93	16r
Cigarettes, Winston	carton	16.99	4Q 92	4c
Coffee, 100% ground roast, all sizes	lb	2.47	4/93	16r
Coffee, vacuum-packed	13-oz can	1.95	4Q 92	4c
Cookies, chocolate chip	lb	2.73	4/93	16r
Corn, frozen	10 oz	0.69	4Q 92	4c
Corn Flakes, Kellogg's or Post Toasties	18 oz	2.11	4Q 92	4c
Eggs, Grade A large	doz	0.79	4Q 92	4c
Eggs, Grade A large	doz	0.93	4/93	16r
Flour, white, all purpose	lb	0.21	4/93	16r
Grapefruit	lb	0.45	4/93	16r
Grapes, Thompson Seedless	lb	1.46	4/93	16r
Ground beef, 100% beef	lb	1.63	4/93	16r
Ground beef, lean and extra lean	lb	2.08	4/93	16r
Ground beef or hamburger	lb	1.27	4Q 92	4c
Ground chuck, 100% beef	lb	1.94	4/93	16r
Ham, boneless, excluding canned	lb	2.21	4/93	16r
Honey, jar	8 oz	0.97-1.25	92	5r
Honey, jar	lb	1.25-2.25	92	5r
Honey, squeeze bear	12-oz	1.25-1.99	92	5r
Ice cream, prepackaged, bulk, regular	1/2 gal	2.41	4/93	16r
Lemons	lb	0.82	4/93	16r
Lettuce, iceberg	head	0.99	4Q 92	4c
Lettuce, iceberg	lb	0.83	4/93	16r
Margarine, Blue Bonnet or Parkay cubes	lb	0.73	4Q 92	4c
Margarine, stick	lb	0.77	4/93	16r
Milk, whole	1/2 gal	1.49	4Q 92	4c

Grand Rapids, MI - continued

Item	Per	Value	Date	Ref.
Groceries - continued				
Orange juice, Minute Maid frozen	12-oz can	1.39	4Q 92	4c
Oranges, navel	lb	0.50	4/93	16r
Peaches	29-oz can	1.40	4Q 92	4c
Peanut butter, creamy, all sizes	lb	1.82	4/93	16r
Pears, Anjou	lb	0.85	4/93	16r
Peas Sweet, Del Monte or Green Giant	15-17 oz can	0.52	4Q 92	4c
Pork chops, center cut, bone-in	lb	3.17	4/93	16r
Potato chips	16 oz	2.68	4/93	16r
Potatoes, white	lb	0.26	4/93	16r
Potatoes, white or red	10-lb sack	1.65	4Q 92	4c
Round roast, graded & ungraded, ex USDA prime & choice	lb	2.88	4/93	16r
Round roast, USDA choice, boneless	lb	2.96	4/93	16r
Sausage, Jimmy Dean, 100% pork	lb	2.73	4Q 92	4c
Shortening, vegetable oil blends	lb	0.79	4/93	16r
Shortening, vegetable, Crisco	3-lb can	2.59	4Q 92	4c
Soft drink, Coca Cola	2 liter	1.37	4Q 92	4c
Spaghetti and macaroni	lb	0.76	4/93	16r
Steak, rib eye, USDA choice, boneless	lb	6.29	4/93	16r
Steak, round, USDA choice, boneless	lb	3.24	4/93	16r
Steak, sirloin, graded & ungraded, ex USDA prime & choice	lb	4.00	4/93	16r
Steak, sirloin, USDA choice, bone-in	lb	3.57	4/93	16r
Steak, sirloin, USDA choice, boneless	lb	4.17	4/93	16r
Steak, T-bone	lb	5.25	4Q 92	4c
Steak, T-bone, USDA choice, bone-in	lb	5.60	4/93	16r
Strawberries, dry pint	12 oz	0.90	4/93	16r
Sugar, cane or beet	4 lb	1.59	4Q 92	4c
Sugar, white	lb	0.36	4/93	16r
Sugar, white, 33-80 oz pk	lb	0.35	4/93	16r
Tomatoes, field grown	lb	0.99	4/93	16r
Tomatoes, Hunt's or Del Monte	14.5-oz can	0.73	4Q 92	4c
Tuna, chunk, light	6.125-6.5 oz can	0.79	4Q 92	4c
Tuna, chunk, light	lb	1.76	4/93	16r
Turkey, frozen, whole	lb	0.91	4/93	16r
Health Care				
ACCRA Index, Health Care		96.00	4Q 92	4c
Analgesic, Aspirin, Bayer, 325 mg tablets	100	4.69	4Q 92	4c
Childbirth, cesarean, hospital		4688	91	62r
Childbirth, cesarean, physician's fee		2053	91	62r
Childbirth, normal, hospital		2657	91	62r
Childbirth, normal, physician's fee		1492	91	62r
Dentist's fee, adult teeth cleaning and periodic oral exam	visit	42.20	4Q 92	4c
Doctor's fee, routine exam, established patient	visit	35.40	4Q 92	4c
Hospital care, semiprivate room	day	264.65	90	27c
Hospital care, semiprivate room	day	346.20	4Q 92	4c
Medical insurance premium, per employee, small group comprehensive	month	302.95	10/91	25c
Medical plan per employee	year	3443	91	45r
Mental health care, exp	capita	53.68-118.35	90	38s
Mental health care, exp, state mental health agency	capita	73.73	90	38s
Mental health care, hospital psychiatric services, non-Federal, exp	capita	22.52	88	38s
Mental health care, mental health organization, multiservice, exp	capita	42.68	88	38s
Mental health care, psychiatric hospitals, private, exp	capita	10.80	88	38s
Mental health care, psychiatric out-patient clinics, freestanding, exp	capita	3.47	88	38s

Values are in dollars or fractions of dollars. In the column headed *Ref*, references are shown to sources. Each reference is followed by a letter. These refer to the geographical level for which data were reported: s = State, r = Region, and c = City or metro. The abbreviation *ex* is used to mean *except* or *excluding*; *exp* stands for expenditures. For other abbreviations and further explanations, please see the Introduction.

261

Grand Rapids, MI - continued

Item	Per	Value	Date	Ref.
Health Care				
Mental health care, psychiatric partial-care organizations, freestanding, exp	capita	0.73	88	38s
Mental health care, state and county mental hospitals, exp	capita	36.77	88	38s
Mental health care, VA medical centers, exp	capita	4.03	88	38s
Physician fee, family practice, first-visit		76.00	91	62r
Physician fee, family practice, revisit		33.00	91	62r
Physician fee, general practice, first-visit		61.00	91	62r
Physician fee, general practice, revisit		31.00	91	62r
Physician fee, general surgeon, first-visit		65.00	91	62r
Physician fee, general surgeon, revisit		35.00	91	62r
Physician fee, internal medicine, first-visit		91.00	91	62r
Physician fee, internal medicine, revisit		40.00	91	62r
Physician fee, median, neurosurgeon, first-visit		106.00	91	62r
Physician fee, median, nonsurgical specialist, first-visit		90.00	91	62r
Physician fee, median, orthopedic surgeon, first-visit		83.00	91	62r
Physician fee, median, surgical specialist, first-visit		61.00	91	62r
Physician fee, neurosurgeon, revisit		41.00	91	62r
Physician fee, nonsurgical specialist, revisit		40.00	91	62r
Physician fee, obstetrics/gynecology, first-visit		61.00	91	62r
Physician fee, obstetrics/gynecology, revisit		40.00	91	62r
Physician fee, orthopedic surgeon, revisit		41.00	91	62r
Physician fee, pediatrician, first-visit		46.00	91	62r
Physician fee, pediatrician, revisit		33.00	91	62r
Physician fee, surgical specialist, revisit		36.00	91	62r
Substance abuse, hospital ancillary charge	incident	1480	90	70s
Substance abuse, hospital physician charge	incident	250	90	70s
Substance abuse, hospital room and board	incident	4070	90	70s
Household Goods				
Appliance repair, home, service call, washing machine	min labor charge	33.48	4Q 92	4c
Laundry detergent, Tide Ultra, Bold, or Cheer	42 oz	4.05	4Q 92	4c
Tissues, facial, Kleenex brand	175-count box	1.17	4Q 92	4c
Housing				
ACCRA Index, Housing		132.80	4Q 92	4c
Home, median price	unit	73.10		26c
House, 1,800 sq ft, 8,000 sq ft lot, new, urban	total	155975	4Q 92	4c
House payment, principal and interest, 25% down payment	month	879	4Q 92	4c
Mortgage rate, incl. points & origination fee, 30-year fixed or adjustable rate	percent	8.25	4Q 92	4c
Rent, apartment, 2 bedrooms - 1-1/2 to 2 baths, unfurnished, 950 sq ft, water	month	510	4Q 92	4c
Rental unit, 1 bedroom	month	431	93	23c
Rental unit, 2 bedroom	month	505	93	23c
Rental unit, 3 bedroom	month	631	93	23c
Rental unit, 4 bedroom	month	713	93	23c
Rental unit, efficiency	month	351	93	23c
Insurance and Pensions				
Auto insurance, private passenger	year	716.78	91	63s
Personal Goods				
Shampoo, Alberto VO5	15 oz	0.99	4Q 92	4c
Toothpaste, Crest or Colgate	6-7 oz	1.87	4Q 92	4c
Personal Services				
Dry cleaning, man's 2-piece suit		6.43	4Q 92	4c

Grand Rapids, MI - continued

Item	Per	Value	Date	Ref.
Personal Services - continued				
Haircare, woman's shampoo, trim and blow-dry		20.20	4Q 92	4c
Haircut, man's barbershop, no styling		8.30	4Q 92	4c
Restaurant Food				
Chicken, fried, thigh and drumstick		2.19	4Q 92	4c
Hamburger with cheese	1/4 lb	1.70	4Q 92	4c
Pizza, Pizza Hut or Pizza Inn, cheese, thin crust	12-13 in	7.99	4Q 92	4c
Taxes				
Tax, cigarette	pack	25	91	77s
Tax, gasoline	gal	15	91	77s
Taxes, state	capita	1185	91	77s
Transportation				
ACCRA Index, Transportation		103.90	4Q 92	4c
Auto rental, average	day	48.00	6/91	60c
Bus fare	one-way	0.90	3/93	2c
Driver's license fee		12.00	12/90	43s
Taxi fare, airport-city, average	day	20.00	6/91	60c
Tire balance, computer or spin balance, front	wheel	7.00	4Q 92	4c
Vehicle registration and license plate	year	14.00-200.00	93	40s
Travel				
Breakfast	day	7.70	6/91	60c
Dinner	day	19.23	6/91	60c
Lodging	day	91.06	91	60c
Lunch	day	11.52	6/91	60c
Utilities				
ACCRA Index, Utilities		95.00	4Q 92	4c
Electricity	mil Btu	20.85	90	64s
Electricity, partial electric and other energy, 1,800 sq ft living area new home	month	45.63	4Q 92	4c
Electricity, winter, 250 KWh	month	17.07	92	55c
Electricity, winter, 500 KWh	month	34.14	92	55c
Electricity, winter, 750 KWh	month	51.22	92	55c
Electricity, winter, 1000 KWh	month	68.29	92	55c

Great Falls, MT

Item	Per	Value	Date	Ref.
Composite ACCRA index		97.70	4Q 92	4c
Alcoholic Beverages				
Beer, Miller Lite or Budweiser, 12-oz containers	6 pack	4.27	4Q 92	4c
Liquor, J & B Scotch	750 ml	18.10	4Q 92	4c
Wine, Gallo Chablis blanc, 1.5 liter	bottle	5.28	4Q 92	4c
Child Care				
Child care fee, average, center	hour	1.71	90	65r
Child care fee, average, nonregulated family day care	hour	1.32	90	65r
Child care fee, average, regulated family day care	hour	1.86	90	65r
Clothing				
Jeans, man's denim		25.49	4Q 92	4c
Shirt, man's dress shirt		24.24	4Q 92	4c
Undervest, boy's size 10-14, cotton	3	4.81	4Q 92	4c
Communications				
Long-distance telephone service, day, initial minute, 0-100 miles	min	0.13-0.36	91	12s
Long-distance telephone service, day, additional minute, 0-100 miles	min	0.04-0.27	91	12s
Long-distance telephone service, evenings/weekends, 0-100 mi, initial minute	min	0.08-0.22	91	12s
Long-distance telephone service, evenings/weekends, 0-100 mi, additional minute	min	0.02-0.16	91	12s
Newspaper subscription, daily and Sunday home delivery, large-city	month	12.17	4Q 92	4c

Values are in dollars or fractions of dollars. In the column headed *Ref*, references are shown to sources. Each reference is followed by a letter. These refer to the geographical level for which data were reported: s = State, r = Region, and c = City or metro. The abbreviation *ex* is used to mean *except* or *excluding*; *exp* stands for expenditures. For other abbreviations and further explanations, please see the Introduction.

Great Falls, MT - continued

Item	Per	Value	Date	Ref.
Communications				
Telephone, flat rate	month	13.84	91	11c
Telephone bill, family of four	month	20.78	4Q 92	4c
Education				
Board, 4-yr private college/university	year	1831	91	22s
Board, 4-yr public college/university	year	2200	91	22s
Expenditures, local gov't, public elementary/secondary	pupil	5271	92	20s
Room, 4-year private college/university	year	1209	91	22s
Room, 4-year public college/university	year	1427	91	22s
Tuition, 2-year private college/university	year	1140	91	22s
Tuition, 2-year public college/university	year	964	91	22s
Tuition, 4-year private college/university	year	5565	91	22s
Tuition, 4-year public college/university, in-state	year	1553	91	22s
Energy and Fuels				
Coal	mil Btu	0.70	90	64s
Energy	mil Btu	7.87	90	64s
Energy, combined forms, 1,800 sq ft heating area	month	100.41	4Q 92	4c
Energy, exc electricity, 1,800 sq ft heating area	month	49.99	4Q 92	4c
Energy exp/householder, 1-family unit	year	372	90	28r
Energy exp/householder, <1,000 sq ft heating area	year	335	90	28r
Energy exp/householder, 1,000-1,999 sq ft heating area	year	365	90	28r
Energy exp/householder, 2,000+ sq ft heating area	year	411	90	28r
Energy exp/householder, mobile home	year	305	90	28r
Energy exp/householder, multifamily	year	372	90	28r
Gas, cooking, 10 therms	month	6.94	92	56c
Gas, cooking, 30 therms	month	14.94	92	56c
Gas, cooking, 50 therms	month	22.90	92	56c
Gas, heating, winter, 100 therms	month	41.47	92	56c
Gas, heating, winter, average use	month	46.58	92	56c
Gas, natural	mil Btu	4.16	90	64s
Gas, natural	000 cu ft	4.52	91	46s
Gas, natural, exp	year	468	91	46s
Gasoline, motor	gal	1.27	4Q 92	4c
Gasoline, unleaded regular	mil Btu	9.56	90	64s
Entertainment				
Bowling, evening rate	game	1.70	4Q 92	4c
Miniature golf admission	adult	6.18	92	1r
Miniature golf admission	child	5.14	92	1r
Monopoly game, Parker Brothers', No. 9		10.11	4Q 92	4c
Movie	admission	5.00	4Q 92	4c
Tennis balls, yellow, Wilson or Penn, 3	can	2.49	4Q 92	4c
Waterpark admission	adult	11.00	92	1r
Waterpark admission	child	8.55	92	1r
Funerals				
Casket, 18-gauge steel, velvet interior		1929.04	91	24r
Cosmetology, hair care, etc.		88.52	91	24r
Embalming		249.33	91	24r
Facility use for ceremony		182.75	91	24r
Hearse, local		110.04	91	24r
Limousine, local		66.67	91	24r
Remains to funeral home, transfer		84.58	91	24r
Service charge, professional		593.00	91	24r
Vault, concrete, non-metallic liner		647.38	91	24r
Viewing facilities, use		99.87	91	24r
Goods and Services				
ACCRA Index, Miscellaneous Goods and Services		100.70	4Q 92	4c
Groceries				
ACCRA Index, Groceries		107.50	4Q 92	4c
Apples, Red Delicious	lb	0.80	4/93	16r

Great Falls, MT - continued

Item	Per	Value	Date	Ref.
Groceries - continued				
Babyfood, strained vegetables, lowest price	4-4.5 oz jar	0.27	4Q 92	4c
Bacon	lb	1.79	4/93	16r
Bananas	lb	0.33	4Q 92	4c
Bananas	lb	0.53	4/93	16r
Bologna, all beef or mixed	lb	2.67	4/93	16r
Bread, white	24 oz	1.04	4Q 92	4c
Bread, white, pan	lb	0.81	4/93	16r
Carrots, short trimmed and topped	lb	0.39	4/93	16r
Cheese, Kraft grated Parmesan	8-oz canister	3.58	4Q 92	4c
Chicken, fresh, whole	lb	0.94	4/93	16r
Chicken, fryer, whole	lb	0.76	4Q 92	4c
Chicken breast, bone-in	lb	2.19	4/93	16r
Chuck roast, graded and ungraded, ex USDA prime and choice	lb	2.26	4/93	16r
Cigarettes, Winston	carton	17.88	4Q 92	4c
Coffee, 100% ground roast, all sizes	lb	2.33	4/93	16r
Coffee, vacuum-packed	13-oz can	2.42	4Q 92	4c
Corn, frozen	10 oz	0.60	4Q 92	4c
Corn Flakes, Kellogg's or Post Toasties	18 oz	1.84	4Q 92	4c
Eggs, Grade A large	doz	0.82	4Q 92	4c
Eggs, Grade AA large	doz	1.18	4/93	16r
Flour, white, all purpose	lb	0.22	4/93	16r
Grapefruit	lb	0.52	4/93	16r
Grapes, Thompson Seedless	lb	1.50	4/93	16r
Ground beef, 100% beef	lb	1.44	4/93	16r
Ground beef, lean and extra lean	lb	2.34	4/93	16r
Ground beef or hamburger	lb	1.71	4Q 92	4c
Ham, boneless, excluding canned	lb	2.56	4/93	16r
Honey, jar	8 oz	0.99-1.19	92	5r
Honey, jar	lb	1.49-2.25	92	5r
Honey, squeeze bear	12-oz	1.19-1.50	92	5r
Ice cream, prepackaged, bulk, regular	1/2 gal	2.40	4/93	16r
Lemons	lb	0.81	4/93	16r
Lettuce, iceberg	head	1.01	4Q 92	4c
Lettuce, iceberg	lb	0.84	4/93	16r
Margarine, Blue Bonnet or Parkay cubes	lb	0.77	4Q 92	4c
Margarine, stick	lb	0.81	4/93	16r
Milk, whole	1/2 gal	1.47	4Q 92	4c
Orange juice, Minute Maid frozen	12-oz can	1.36	4Q 92	4c
Oranges, navel	lb	0.48	4/93	16r
Peaches	29-oz can	1.43	4Q 92	4c
Peas Sweet, Del Monte or Green Giant	15-17 oz can	0.65	4Q 92	4c
Pork chops, center cut, bone-in	lb	3.25	4/93	16r
Potato chips	16 oz	2.89	4/93	16r
Potatoes, white	lb	0.38	4/93	16r
Potatoes, white or red	10-lb sack	2.11	4Q 92	4c
Round roast, graded & ungraded, ex USDA prime & choice	lb	3.00	4/93	16r
Round roast, USDA choice, boneless	lb	3.16	4/93	16r
Sausage, Jimmy Dean, 100% pork	lb	3.57	4Q 92	4c
Shortening, vegetable oil blends	lb	0.86	4/93	16r
Shortening, vegetable, Crisco	3-lb can	2.20	4Q 92	4c
Soft drink, Coca Cola	2 liter	1.23	4Q 92	4c
Spaghetti and macaroni	lb	0.84	4/93	16r
Steak, round, graded & ungraded, ex USDA prime & choice	lb	3.34	4/93	16r
Steak, round, USDA choice, boneless	lb	3.24	4/93	16r
Steak, sirloin, graded & ungraded, ex USDA prime & choice	lb	3.75	4/93	16r
Steak, sirloin, USDA choice, boneless	lb	4.49	4/93	16r
Steak, T-bone	lb	4.24	4Q 92	4c
Sugar, cane or beet	4 lb	1.30	4Q 92	4c
Sugar, white	lb	0.41	4/93	16r

Values are in dollars or fractions of dollars. In the column headed *Ref*, references are shown to sources. Each reference is followed by a letter. These refer to the geographical level for which data were reported: s=State, r=Region, and c=City or metro. The abbreviation *ex* is used to mean *except* or *excluding*; *exp* stands for expenditures. For other abbreviations and further explanations, please see the Introduction.

Great Falls, MT - continued

Item	Per	Value	Date	Ref.
Groceries				
Sugar, white, 33-80 oz pk	lb	0.38	4/93	16r
Tomatoes, field grown	lb	1.01	4/93	16r
Tomatoes, Hunt's or Del Monte	14.5-oz can	0.62	4Q 92	4c
Tuna, chunk, light	6.125-6.5 oz can	0.73	4Q 92	4c
Turkey, frozen, whole	lb	1.04	4/93	16r
Health Care				
ACCRA Index, Health Care		105.20	4Q 92	4c
Analgesic, Aspirin, Bayer, 325 mg tablets	100	5.86	4Q 92	4c
Childbirth, cesarean, hospital		5533	91	62r
Childbirth, cesarean, physician's fee		2053	91	62r
Childbirth, normal, hospital		2745	91	62r
Childbirth, normal, physician's fee		1492	91	62r
Dentist's fee, adult teeth cleaning and periodic oral exam	visit	55.50	4Q 92	4c
Doctor's fee, routine exam, established patient	visit	33.60	4Q 92	4c
Hospital care, semiprivate room	day	257.05	90	27c
Hospital care, semiprivate room	day	315.00	4Q 92	4c
Medical insurance premium, per employee, small group comprehensive	month	317.55	10/91	25c
Medical plan per employee	year	3218	91	45r
Mental health care, exp	capita	20.37-28.83	90	38s
Mental health care, exp, state mental health agency	capita	28.42	90	38s
Mental health care, hospital psychiatric services, non-Federal, exp	capita	16.46	88	38s
Mental health care, mental health organization, multiservice, exp	capita	15.10	88	38s
Mental health care, psychiatric hospitals, private, exp	capita	17.28	88	38s
Mental health care, state and county mental hospitals, exp	capita	27.18	88	38s
Physician fee, family practice, first-visit		111.00	91	62r
Physician fee, family practice, revisit		45.00	91	62r
Physician fee, general practice, first-visit		100.00	91	62r
Physician fee, general practice, revisit		40.00	91	62r
Physician fee, internal medicine, first-visit		137.00	91	62r
Physician fee, internal medicine, revisit		48.00	91	62r
Physician fee, median, neurosurgeon, first-visit		157.00	91	62r
Physician fee, median, nonsurgical specialist, first-visit		131.00	91	62r
Physician fee, median, orthopedic surgeon, first-visit		124.00	91	62r
Physician fee, median, plastic surgeon, first-visit		88.00	91	62r
Physician fee, median, surgical specialist, first-visit		100.00	91	62r
Physician fee, neurosurgeon, revisit		51.00	91	62r
Physician fee, nonsurgical specialist, revisit		47.00	91	62r
Physician fee, obstetrics/gynecology, first-visit		95.00	91	62r
Physician fee, obstetrics/gynecology, revisit		50.00	91	62r
Physician fee, orthopedic surgeon, revisit		51.00	91	62r
Physician fee, pediatrician, first-visit		81.00	91	62r
Physician fee, pediatrician, revisit		42.00	91	62r
Physician fee, plastic surgeon, revisit		48.00	91	62r
Physician fee, surgical specialist, revisit		49.00	91	62r
Substance abuse, hospital ancillary charge	incident	320	90	70s
Substance abuse, hospital physician charge	incident	210	90	70s
Substance abuse, hospital room and board	incident	5290	90	70s

Great Falls, MT - continued

Item	Per	Value	Date	Ref.
Household Goods				
Appliance repair, home, service call, washing machine	min labor charge	35.50	4Q 92	4c
Laundry detergent, Tide Ultra, Bold, or Cheer	42 oz	3.93	4Q 92	4c
Tissues, facial, Kleenex brand	175-count box	1.19	4Q 92	4c
Housing				
ACCRA Index, Housing		86.30	4Q 92	4c
House, 1,800 sq ft, 8,000 sq ft lot, new, urban	total	98900	4Q 92	4c
House payment, principal and interest, 25% down payment	month	563	4Q 92	4c
Mortgage rate, incl. points & origination fee, 30-year fixed or adjustable rate	percent	8.36	4Q 92	4c
Rent, apartment, 2 bedrooms - 1-1/2 to 2 baths, unfurnished, 950 sq ft, water	month	351	4Q 92	4c
Rental unit, 1 bedroom	month	412	93	23c
Rental unit, 2 bedroom	month	487	93	23c
Rental unit, 3 bedroom	month	610	93	23c
Rental unit, 4 bedroom	month	683	93	23c
Rental unit, efficiency	month	340	93	23c
Insurance and Pensions				
Auto insurance, private passenger	year	475.81	91	63s
Personal Goods				
Shampoo, Alberto VO5	15 oz	1.53	4Q 92	4c
Toothpaste, Crest or Colgate	6-7 oz	2.24	4Q 92	4c
Personal Services				
Dry cleaning, man's 2-piece suit		6.06	4Q 92	4c
Haircare, woman's shampoo, trim and blow-dry		14.12	4Q 92	4c
Haircut, man's barbershop, no styling		8.75	4Q 92	4c
Restaurant Food				
Chicken, fried, thigh and drumstick		2.10	4Q 92	4c
Hamburger with cheese	1/4 lb	1.80	4Q 92	4c
Pizza, Pizza Hut or Pizza Inn, cheese, thin crust	12-13 in	8.70	4Q 92	4c
Taxes				
Tax, cigarette	pack	19.26	91	77s
Tax, gasoline	gal	20	91	77s
Taxes, state	capita	1011	91	77s
Transportation				
ACCRA Index, Transportation		106.20	4Q 92	4c
Driver's license fee		16.00-24.00	12/90	43s
Tire balance, computer or spin balance, front	wheel	6.50	4Q 92	4c
Travel				
Business travel	day	178.00	4/93	89r
Utilities				
ACCRA Index, Utilities		93.40	4Q 92	4c
Electricity	mil Btu	11.67	90	64s
Electricity, partial electric and other energy, 1,800 sq ft living area new home	month	50.42	4Q 92	4c

Greeley, CO

Item	Per	Value	Date	Ref.
Composite ACCRA index		91.80	4Q 92	4c
Alcoholic Beverages				
Beer, Miller Lite or Budweiser, 12-oz containers	6 pack	3.77	4Q 92	4c
Liquor, J & B Scotch	750 ml	18.44	4Q 92	4c
Wine, Gallo Chablis blanc, 1.5 liter	bottle	5.19	4Q 92	4c

Values are in dollars or fractions of dollars. In the column headed *Ref*, references are shown to sources. Each reference is followed by a letter. These refer to the geographical level for which data were reported: s=State, r=Region, and c=City or metro. The abbreviation *ex* is used to mean *except* or *excluding*; *exp* stands for expenditures. For other abbreviations and further explanations, please see the Introduction.

Greeley, CO - continued

Item	Per	Value	Date	Ref.
Child Care				
Child care fee, average, center	hour	1.71	90	65r
Child care fee, average, nonregulated family day care	hour	1.32	90	65r
Child care fee, average, regulated family day care	hour	1.86	90	65r
Clothing				
Jeans, man's denim		28.18	4Q 92	4c
Shirt, man's dress shirt		22.80	4Q 92	4c
Undervest, boy's size 10-14, cotton	3	4.15	4Q 92	4c
Communications				
Long-distance telephone service, day, initial minute, 0-100 miles	min	0.11-0.35	91	12s
Long-distance telephone service, day, additional minute, 0-100 miles	min	0.13-0.27	91	12s
Long-distance telephone service, evenings/weekends, 0-100 mi, initial minute	min	0.08-0.17	91	12s
Long-distance telephone service, evenings/weekends, 0-100 mi, additional minute	min	0.06-0.14	91	12s
Newspaper subscription, daily and Sunday home delivery, large-city	month	7.50	4Q 92	4c
Telephone, flat rate	month	14.22	91	11c
Telephone bill, family of four	month	15.70	4Q 92	4c
Education				
Board, 4-yr private college/university	year	2162	91	22s
Board, 4-yr public college/university	year	1747	91	22s
Expenditures, local gov't, public elementary/secondary	pupil	5259	92	20s
Room, 4-year private college/university	year	1984	91	22s
Room, 4-year public college/university	year	1546	91	22s
Tuition, 2-year private college/university	year	6731	91	22s
Tuition, 2-year public college/university	year	943	91	22s
Tuition, 4-year private college/university	year	9516	91	22s
Tuition, 4-year public college/university, in-state	year	1919	91	22s
Energy and Fuels				
Coal	mil Btu	1.07	90	64s
Energy	mil Btu	8.14	90	64s
Energy, combined forms, 1,800 sq ft heating area	month	109.93	4Q 92	4c
Energy, exc electricity, 1,800 sq ft heating area	month	64.33	4Q 92	4c
Energy exp/householder, 1-family unit	year	372	90	28r
Energy exp/householder, <1,000 sq ft heating area	year	335	90	28r
Energy exp/householder, 1,000-1,999 sq ft heating area	year	365	90	28r
Energy exp/householder, 2,000+ sq ft heating area	year	411	90	28r
Energy exp/householder, mobile home	year	305	90	28r
Energy exp/householder, multifamily	year	372	90	28r
Gas, cooking, 10 therms	month	9.20	92	56c
Gas, cooking, 30 therms	month	16.80	92	56c
Gas, cooking, 50 therms	month	24.40	92	56c
Gas, heating, winter, 100 therms	month	43.40	92	56c
Gas, heating, winter, average use	month	68.10	92	56c
Gas, natural	mil Btu	3.92	90	64s
Gas, natural	000 cu ft	4.59	91	46s
Gas, natural, exp	year	446	91	46s
Gasoline, motor	gal	1.17	4Q 92	4c
Gasoline, unleaded regular	mil Btu	9.29	90	64s
Entertainment				
Bowling, evening rate	game	1.90	4Q 92	4c
Miniature golf admission	adult	6.18	92	1r
Miniature golf admission	child	5.14	92	1r
Monopoly game, Parker Brothers', No. 9		13.83	4Q 92	4c
Movie	admission	5.00	4Q 92	4c
Tennis balls, yellow, Wilson or Penn, 3	can	3.21	4Q 92	4c

Greeley, CO - continued

Item	Per	Value	Date	Ref.
Entertainment - continued				
Waterpark admission	adult	11.00	92	1r
Waterpark admission	child	8.55	92	1r
Funerals				
Casket, 18-gauge steel, velvet interior		1929.04	91	24r
Cosmetology, hair care, etc.		88.52	91	24r
Embalming		249.33	91	24r
Facility use for ceremony		182.75	91	24r
Hearse, local		110.04	91	24r
Limousine, local		66.67	91	24r
Remains to funeral home, transfer		84.58	91	24r
Service charge, professional		593.00	91	24r
Vault, concrete, non-metallic liner		647.38	91	24r
Viewing facilities, use		99.87	91	24r
Goods and Services				
ACCRA Index, Miscellaneous Goods and Services		98.60	4Q 92	4c
Groceries				
ACCRA Index, Groceries		101.00	4Q 92	4c
Apples, Red Delicious	lb	0.80	4/93	16r
Babyfood, strained vegetables, lowest price	4-4.5 oz jar	0.34	4Q 92	4c
Bacon	lb	1.79	4/93	16r
Bananas	lb	0.54	4Q 92	4c
Bananas	lb	0.53	4/93	16r
Bologna, all beef or mixed	lb	2.67	4/93	16r
Bread, white	24 oz	0.65	4Q 92	4c
Bread, white, pan	lb	0.81	4/93	16r
Carrots, short trimmed and topped	lb	0.39	4/93	16r
Cheese, Kraft grated Parmesan	8-oz canister	2.83	4Q 92	4c
Chicken, fresh, whole	lb	0.94	4/93	16r
Chicken, fryer, whole	lb	0.69	4Q 92	4c
Chicken breast, bone-in	lb	2.19	4/93	16r
Chuck roast, graded and ungraded, ex USDA prime and choice	lb	2.26	4/93	16r
Cigarettes, Winston	carton	16.72	4Q 92	4c
Coffee, 100% ground roast, all sizes	lb	2.33	4/93	16r
Coffee, vacuum-packed	13-oz can	1.94	4Q 92	4c
Corn, frozen	10 oz	0.75	4Q 92	4c
Corn Flakes, Kellogg's or Post Toasties	18 oz	1.90	4Q 92	4c
Eggs, Grade A large	doz	0.82	4Q 92	4c
Eggs, Grade AA large	doz	1.18	4/93	16r
Flour, white, all purpose	lb	0.22	4/93	16r
Grapefruit	lb	0.52	4/93	16r
Grapes, Thompson Seedless	lb	1.50	4/93	16r
Ground beef, 100% beef	lb	1.44	4/93	16r
Ground beef, lean and extra lean	lb	2.34	4/93	16r
Ground beef or hamburger	lb	1.31	4Q 92	4c
Ham, boneless, excluding canned	lb	2.56	4/93	16r
Honey, jar	8 oz	0.99-1.19	92	5r
Honey, jar	lb	1.49-2.25	92	5r
Honey, squeeze bear	12-oz	1.19-1.50	92	5r
Ice cream, prepackaged, bulk, regular	1/2 gal	2.40	4/93	16r
Lemons	lb	0.81	4/93	16r
Lettuce, iceberg	head	1.08	4Q 92	4c
Lettuce, iceberg	lb	0.84	4/93	16r
Margarine, Blue Bonnet or Parkay cubes	lb	0.70	4Q 92	4c
Margarine, stick	lb	0.81	4/93	16r
Milk, whole	1/2 gal	1.48	4Q 92	4c
Orange juice, Minute Maid frozen	12-oz can	1.47	4Q 92	4c
Oranges, navel	lb	0.48	4/93	16r
Peaches	29-oz can	1.51	4Q 92	4c
Peas Sweet, Del Monte or Green Giant	15-17 oz can	0.67	4Q 92	4c
Pork chops, center cut, bone-in	lb	3.25	4/93	16r
Potato chips	16 oz	2.89	4/93	16r
Potatoes, white	lb	0.38	4/93	16r

Values are in dollars or fractions of dollars. In the column headed *Ref*, references are shown to sources. Each reference is followed by a letter. These refer to the geographical level for which data were reported: s=State, r=Region, and c=City or metro. The abbreviation *ex* is used to mean *except* or *excluding*; *exp* stands for expenditures. For other abbreviations and further explanations, please see the Introduction.

Greeley, CO - continued

Item	Per	Value	Date	Ref.
Groceries				
Potatoes, white or red	10-lb sack	2.21	4Q 92	4c
Round roast, graded & ungraded, ex USDA prime & choice	lb	3.00	4/93	16r
Round roast, USDA choice, boneless	lb	3.16	4/93	16r
Sausage, Jimmy Dean, 100% pork	lb	3.39	4Q 92	4c
Shortening, vegetable oil blends	lb	0.86	4/93	16r
Shortening, vegetable, Crisco	3-lb can	2.34	4Q 92	4c
Soft drink, Coca Cola	2 liter	1.03	4Q 92	4c
Spaghetti and macaroni	lb	0.84	4/93	16r
Steak, round, graded & ungraded, ex USDA prime & choice	lb	3.34	4/93	16r
Steak, round, USDA choice, boneless	lb	3.24	4/93	16r
Steak, sirloin, graded & ungraded, ex USDA prime & choice	lb	3.75	4/93	16r
Steak, sirloin, USDA choice, boneless	lb	4.49	4/93	16r
Steak, T-bone	lb	4.59	4Q 92	4c
Sugar, cane or beet	4 lb	1.22	4Q 92	4c
Sugar, white	lb	0.41	4/93	16r
Sugar, white, 33-80 oz pk	lb	0.38	4/93	16r
Tomatoes, field grown	lb	1.01	4/93	16r
Tomatoes, Hunt's or Del Monte	14.5-oz can	0.76	4Q 92	4c
Tuna, chunk, light	6.125-6.5 oz can	0.84	4Q 92	4c
Turkey, frozen, whole	lb	1.04	4/93	16r
Health Care				
ACCRA Index, Health Care		106.10	4Q 92	4c
Analgesic, Aspirin, Bayer, 325 mg tablets	100	4.72	4Q 92	4c
Childbirth, cesarean, hospital		5533	91	62r
Childbirth, cesarean, physician's fee		2053	91	62r
Childbirth, normal, hospital		2745	91	62r
Childbirth, normal, physician's fee		1492	91	62r
Dentist's fee, adult teeth cleaning and periodic oral exam	visit	44.40	4Q 92	4c
Doctor's fee, routine exam, established patient	visit	36.10	4Q 92	4c
Hospital care, semiprivate room	day	482.00	4Q 92	4c
Medical insurance premium, per employee, small group comprehensive	month	302.95	10/91	25c
Medical plan per employee	year	3218	91	45r
Mental health care, exp	capita	28.84-37.59	90	38s
Mental health care, exp, state mental health agency	capita	33.55	90	38s
Mental health care, hospital psychiatric services, non-Federal, exp	capita	11.38	88	38s
Mental health care, mental health organization, multiservice, exp	capita	21.76	88	38s
Mental health care, psychiatric hospitals, private, exp	capita	14.39	88	38s
Mental health care, psychiatric out-patient clinics, freestanding, exp	capita	0.11	88	38s
Mental health care, state and county mental hospitals, exp	capita	19.03	88	38s
Mental health care, VA medical centers, exp	capita	3.80	88	38s
Physician fee, family practice, first-visit		111.00	91	62r
Physician fee, family practice, revisit		45.00	91	62r
Physician fee, general practice, first-visit		100.00	91	62r
Physician fee, general practice, revisit		40.00	91	62r
Physician fee, internal medicine, first-visit		137.00	91	62r
Physician fee, internal medicine, revisit		48.00	91	62r
Physician fee, median, neurosurgeon, first-visit		157.00	91	62r
Physician fee, median, nonsurgical specialist, first-visit		131.00	91	62r
Physician fee, median, orthopedic surgeon, first-visit		124.00	91	62r
Physician fee, median, plastic surgeon, first-visit		88.00	91	62r

Greeley, CO - continued

Item	Per	Value	Date	Ref.
Health Care - continued				
Physician fee, median, surgical specialist, first-visit		100.00	91	62r
Physician fee, neurosurgeon, revisit		51.00	91	62r
Physician fee, nonsurgical specialist, revisit		47.00	91	62r
Physician fee, obstetrics/gynecology, first-visit		95.00	91	62r
Physician fee, obstetrics/gynecology, revisit		50.00	91	62r
Physician fee, orthopedic surgeon, revisit		51.00	91	62r
Physician fee, pediatrician, first-visit		81.00	91	62r
Physician fee, pediatrician, revisit		42.00	91	62r
Physician fee, plastic surgeon, revisit		48.00	91	62r
Physician fee, surgical specialist, revisit		49.00	91	62r
Substance abuse, hospital ancillary charge	incident	1040	90	70s
Substance abuse, hospital physician charge	incident	380	90	70s
Substance abuse, hospital room and board	incident	4880	90	70s
Household Goods				
Appliance repair, home, service call, washing machine	min labor charge	25.79	4Q 92	4c
Laundry detergent, Tide Ultra, Bold, or Cheer	42 oz	3.65	4Q 92	4c
Tissues, facial, Kleenex brand	175-count box	1.01	4Q 92	4c
Housing				
ACCRA Index, Housing		73.40	4Q 92	4c
House, 1,800 sq ft, 8,000 sq ft lot, new, urban	total	80164	4Q 92	4c
House payment, principal and interest, 25% down payment	month	449	4Q 92	4c
Mortgage rate, incl. points & origination fee, 30-year fixed or adjustable rate	percent	8.19	4Q 92	4c
Rent, apartment, 2 bedrooms - 1-1/2 to 2 baths, unfurnished, 950 sq ft, water	month	367	4Q 92	4c
Rental unit, 1 bedroom	month	426	93	23c
Rental unit, 2 bedroom	month	501	93	23c
Rental unit, 3 bedroom	month	630	93	23c
Rental unit, 4 bedroom	month	705	93	23c
Rental unit, efficiency	month	352	93	23c
Insurance and Pensions				
Auto insurance, private passenger	year	684.81	91	63s
Personal Goods				
Shampoo, Alberto VO5	15 oz	1.27	4Q 92	4c
Toothpaste, Crest or Colgate	6-7 oz	1.87	4Q 92	4c
Personal Services				
Dry cleaning, man's 2-piece suit		7.34	4Q 92	4c
Haircare, woman's shampoo, trim and blow-dry		15.60	4Q 92	4c
Haircut, man's barbershop, no styling		7.37	4Q 92	4c
Restaurant Food				
Chicken, fried, thigh and drumstick		2.10	4Q 92	4c
Hamburger with cheese	1/4 lb	1.95	4Q 92	4c
Pizza, Pizza Hut or Pizza Inn, cheese, thin crust	12-13 in	7.69	4Q 92	4c
Taxes				
Tax, cigarette	pack	20	91	77s
Tax, gasoline	gal	22	91	77s
Taxes, state	capita	951	91	77s
Transportation				
ACCRA Index, Transportation		93.80	4Q 92	4c
Bus fare, up to 10 miles	one-way	0.50	4Q 92	4c
Driver's license fee		15.00	12/90	43s
Tire balance, computer or spin balance, front	wheel	6.00	4Q 92	4c

Values are in dollars or fractions of dollars. In the column headed *Ref*, references are shown to sources. Each reference is followed by a letter. These refer to the geographical level for which data were reported: s = State, r = Region, and c = City or metro. The abbreviation *ex* is used to mean *except* or *excluding*; *exp* stands for expenditures. For other abbreviations and further explanations, please see the Introduction.

Greeley, CO - continued

Item	Per	Value	Date	Ref.
Travel				
Business travel	day	178.00	4/93	89r
Utilities				
ACCRA Index, Utilities		98.70	4Q 92	4c
Electricity	mil Btu	17.31	90	64s
Electricity, partial electric and other energy, 1,800 sq ft living area new home	month	45.60	4Q 92	4c
Electricity, residential	KWh	7.70	2/93	94s

Green Bay, WI

Item	Per	Value	Date	Ref.
Composite ACCRA index		97.80	4Q 92	4c
Alcoholic Beverages				
Beer, Miller Lite or Budweiser, 12-oz containers	6 pack	3.43	4Q 92	4c
Liquor, J & B Scotch	750 ml	16.51	4Q 92	4c
Wine, Gallo Chablis blanc, 1.5 liter	bottle	4.87	4Q 92	4c
Child Care				
Child care fee, average, center	hour	1.63	90	65r
Child care fee, average, nonregulated family day care	hour	1.83	90	65r
Child care fee, average, regulated family day care	hour	1.42	90	65r
Clothing				
Jeans, man's denim		34.19	4Q 92	4c
Shirt, man's dress shirt		25.20	4Q 92	4c
Undervest, boy's size 10-14, cotton	3	3.64	4Q 92	4c
Communications				
Long-distance telephone service, day, initial minute, 0-100 miles	min	0.15-0.29	91	12s
Long-distance telephone service, day, additional minute, 0-100 miles	min	0.10-0.27	91	12s
Newspaper subscription, daily and Sunday home delivery, large-city	month	14.13	4Q 92	4c
Telephone, flat rate	month	6.00	91	11c
Telephone bill, family of four	month	16.54	4Q 92	4c
Education				
Board, 4-yr private college/university	year	1533	91	22s
Board, 4-yr public college/university	year	1404	91	22s
Expenditures, local gov't, public elementary/secondary	pupil	5972	92	20s
Room, 4-year private college/university	year	1256	91	22s
Room, 4-year public college/university	year	1416	91	22s
Tuition, 2-year private college/university	year	4768	91	22s
Tuition, 2-year public college/university	year	1234	91	22s
Tuition, 4-year private college/university	year	8237	91	22s
Tuition, 4-year public college/university, in-state	year	1951	91	22s
Energy and Fuels				
Coal	mil Btu	1.41	90	64s
Energy	mil Btu	8.27	90	64s
Energy, combined forms, 1,800 sq ft heating area	month	93.86	4Q 92	4c
Energy, exc electricity, 1,800 sq ft heating area	month	53.28	4Q 92	4c
Energy exp/householder, 1-family unit	year	471	90	28r
Energy exp/householder, <1,000 sq ft heating area	year	430	90	28r
Energy exp/householder, 1,000-1,999 sq ft heating area	year	481	90	28r
Energy exp/householder, 2,000+ sq ft heating area	year	473	90	28r
Energy exp/householder, mobile home	year	430	90	28r
Energy exp/householder, multifamily	year	461	90	28r
Gas, cooking, winter, 10 therms	month	8.48	92	56c
Gas, cooking, winter, 30 therms	month	18.44	92	56c
Gas, cooking, winter, 50 therms	month	28.40	92	56c
Gas, heating, winter, 100 therms	month	53.29	92	56c
Gas, heating, winter, average use	month	95.11	92	56c

Green Bay, WI - continued

Item	Per	Value	Date	Ref.
Energy and Fuels - continued				
Gas, natural	mil Btu	4.56	90	64s
Gas, natural	000 cu ft	5.61	91	46s
Gas, natural, exp	year	605	91	46s
Gasoline, motor	gal	1.17	4Q 92	4c
Gasoline, unleaded regular	mil Btu	9.38	90	64s
Entertainment				
Bowling, evening rate	game	1.32	4Q 92	4c
Miniature golf admission	adult	6.18	92	1r
Miniature golf admission	child	5.14	92	1r
Monopoly game, Parker Brothers', No. 9		10.98	4Q 92	4c
Movie	admission	5.75	4Q 92	4c
Tennis balls, yellow, Wilson or Penn, 3	can	1.96	4Q 92	4c
Waterpark admission	adult	11.00	92	1r
Waterpark admission	child	8.55	92	1r
Funerals				
Casket, 18-gauge steel, velvet interior		1926.72	91	24r
Cosmetology, hair care, etc.		97.64	91	24r
Embalming		249.14	91	24r
Facility use for ceremony		208.59	91	24r
Hearse, local		130.12	91	24r
Limousine, local		104.66	91	24r
Remains to funeral home, transfer		93.61	91	24r
Service charge, professional		724.62	91	24r
Vault, concrete, non-metallic liner		734.53	91	24r
Viewing facilities, use		236.06	91	24r
Goods and Services				
ACCRA Index, Miscellaneous Goods and Services		98.30	4Q 92	4c
Groceries				
ACCRA Index, Groceries		96.40	4Q 92	4c
Apples, Red Delicious	lb	0.77	4/93	16r
Babyfood, strained vegetables, lowest price	4-4.5 oz jar	0.37	4Q 92	4c
Bacon	lb	1.85	4/93	16r
Bananas	lb	0.39	4Q 92	4c
Bananas	lb	0.46	4/93	16r
Beef, stew, boneless	lb	2.53	4/93	16r
Bologna, all beef or mixed	lb	2.19	4/93	16r
Bread, white	24 oz	0.63	4Q 92	4c
Bread, white, pan	lb	0.78	4/93	16r
Butter	lb	1.50	4/93	16r
Cabbage	lb	0.40	4/93	16r
Carrots, short trimmed and topped	lb	0.45	4/93	16r
Cheese, Cheddar	lb	3.47	4/93	16r
Cheese, Kraft grated Parmesan	8-oz canister	2.84	4Q 92	4c
Chicken, fresh, whole	lb	0.84	4/93	16r
Chicken, fryer, whole	lb	0.81	4Q 92	4c
Chicken breast, bone-in	lb	1.94	4/93	16r
Chicken legs, bone-in	lb	1.02	4/93	16r
Chuck roast, graded and ungraded, ex USDA prime and choice	lb	2.43	4/93	16r
Chuck roast, USDA choice, bone-in	lb	2.11	4/93	16r
Chuck roast, USDA choice, boneless	lb	2.44	4/93	16r
Cigarettes, Winston	carton	18.84	4Q 92	4c
Coffee, 100% ground roast, all sizes	lb	2.47	4/93	16r
Coffee, vacuum-packed	13-oz can	1.83	4Q 92	4c
Cookies, chocolate chip	lb	2.73	4/93	16r
Corn, frozen	10 oz	0.63	4Q 92	4c
Corn Flakes, Kellogg's or Post Toasties	18 oz	1.86	4Q 92	4c
Eggs, Grade A large	doz	0.73	4Q 92	4c
Eggs, Grade A large	doz	0.93	4/93	16r
Flour, white, all purpose	lb	0.21	4/93	16r
Grapefruit	lb	0.45	4/93	16r
Grapes, Thompson Seedless	lb	1.46	4/93	16r
Ground beef, 100% beef	lb	1.63	4/93	16r

Values are in dollars or fractions of dollars. In the column headed *Ref*, references are shown to sources. Each reference is followed by a letter. These refer to the geographical level for which data were reported: s=State, r=Region, and c=City or metro. The abbreviation *ex* is used to mean *except* or *excluding*; *exp* stands for expenditures. For other abbreviations and further explanations, please see the Introduction.

Green Bay, WI - continued

Item	Per	Value	Date	Ref.
Groceries				
Ground beef, lean and extra lean	lb	2.08	4/93	16r
Ground beef or hamburger	lb	1.55	4Q 92	4c
Ground chuck, 100% beef	lb	1.94	4/93	16r
Ham, boneless, excluding canned	lb	2.21	4/93	16r
Honey, jar	8 oz	0.97-1.25	92	5r
Honey, jar	lb	1.25-2.25	92	5r
Honey, squeeze bear	12-oz	1.25-1.99	92	5r
Ice cream, prepackaged, bulk, regular	1/2 gal	2.41	4/93	16r
Lemons	lb	0.82	4/93	16r
Lettuce, iceberg	head	0.97	4Q 92	4c
Lettuce, iceberg	lb	0.83	4/93	16r
Margarine, Blue Bonnet or Parkay cubes	lb	0.59	4Q 92	4c
Margarine, stick	lb	0.77	4/93	16r
Milk, whole	1/2 gal	1.30	4Q 92	4c
Orange juice, Minute Maid frozen	12-oz can	1.30	4Q 92	4c
Oranges, navel	lb	0.50	4/93	16r
Peaches	29-oz can	1.37	4Q 92	4c
Peanut butter, creamy, all sizes	lb	1.82	4/93	16r
Pears, Anjou	lb	0.85	4/93	16r
Peas Sweet, Del Monte or Green Giant	15-17 oz can	0.55	4Q 92	4c
Pork chops, center cut, bone-in	lb	3.17	4/93	16r
Potato chips	16 oz	2.68	4/93	16r
Potatoes, white	lb	0.26	4/93	16r
Potatoes, white or red	10-lb sack	1.88	4Q 92	4c
Round roast, graded & ungraded, ex USDA prime & choice	lb	2.88	4/93	16r
Round roast, USDA choice, boneless	lb	2.96	4/93	16r
Sausage, Jimmy Dean, 100% pork	lb	2.56	4Q 92	4c
Shortening, vegetable oil blends	lb	0.79	4/93	16r
Shortening, vegetable, Crisco	3-lb can	2.41	4Q 92	4c
Soft drink, Coca Cola	2 liter	0.99	4Q 92	4c
Spaghetti and macaroni	lb	0.76	4/93	16r
Steak, rib eye, USDA choice, boneless	lb	6.29	4/93	16r
Steak, round, USDA choice, boneless	lb	3.24	4/93	16r
Steak, sirloin, graded & ungraded, ex USDA prime & choice	lb	4.00	4/93	16r
Steak, sirloin, USDA choice, bone-in	lb	3.57	4/93	16r
Steak, sirloin, USDA choice, boneless	lb	4.17	4/93	16r
Steak, T-bone	lb	4.99	4Q 92	4c
Steak, T-bone, USDA choice, bone-in	lb	5.60	4/93	16r
Strawberries, dry pint	12 oz	0.90	4/93	16r
Sugar, cane or beet	4 lb	1.48	4Q 92	4c
Sugar, white	lb	0.36	4/93	16r
Sugar, white, 33-80 oz pk	lb	0.35	4/93	16r
Tomatoes, field grown	lb	0.99	4/93	16r
Tomatoes, Hunt's or Del Monte	14.5-oz can	0.70	4Q 92	4c
Tuna, chunk, light	6.125-6.5 oz can	0.61	4Q 92	4c
Tuna, chunk, light	lb	1.76	4/93	16r
Turkey, frozen, whole	lb	0.91	4/93	16r
Health Care				
ACCRA Index, Health Care		96.40	4Q 92	4c
Analgesic, Aspirin, Bayer, 325 mg tablets	100	4.12	4Q 92	4c
Childbirth, cesarean, hospital		4688	91	62r
Childbirth, cesarean, physician's fee		2053	91	62r
Childbirth, normal, hospital		2657	91	62r
Childbirth, normal, physician's fee		1492	91	62r
Dentist's fee, adult teeth cleaning and periodic oral exam	visit	46.80	4Q 92	4c
Doctor's fee, routine exam, established patient	visit	37.25	4Q 92	4c
Hospital care, semiprivate room	day	199.99	90	27c
Hospital care, semiprivate room	day	283.33	4Q 92	4c
Medical insurance premium, per employee, small group comprehensive	month	266.45	10/91	25c

Green Bay, WI - continued

Item	Per	Value	Date	Ref.
Health Care - continued				
Medical plan per employee	year	3443	91	45r
Mental health care, exp	capita	28.84-37.59	90	38s
Mental health care, exp, state mental health agency	capita	36.62	90	38s
Mental health care, hospital psychiatric services, non-Federal, exp	capita	13.05	88	38s
Mental health care, mental health organization, multiservice, exp	capita	10.93	88	38s
Mental health care, psychiatric hospitals, private, exp	capita	8.71	88	38s
Mental health care, psychiatric out-patient clinics, freestanding, exp	capita	5.33	88	38s
Mental health care, psychiatric partial-care organizations, freestanding, exp	capita	0.20	88	38s
Mental health care, state and county mental hospitals, exp	capita	28.29	88	38s
Mental health care, VA medical centers, exp	capita	7.57	88	38s
Physician fee, family practice, first-visit		76.00	91	62r
Physician fee, family practice, revisit		33.00	91	62r
Physician fee, general practice, first-visit		61.00	91	62r
Physician fee, general practice, revisit		31.00	91	62r
Physician fee, general surgeon, first-visit		65.00	91	62r
Physician fee, general surgeon, revisit		35.00	91	62r
Physician fee, internal medicine, first-visit		91.00	91	62r
Physician fee, internal medicine, revisit		40.00	91	62r
Physician fee, median, neurosurgeon, first-visit		106.00	91	62r
Physician fee, median, nonsurgical specialist, first-visit		90.00	91	62r
Physician fee, median, orthopedic surgeon, first visit		83.00	91	62r
Physician fee, median, surgical specialist, first-visit		61.00	91	62r
Physician fee, neurosurgeon, revisit		41.00	91	62r
Physician fee, nonsurgical specialist, revisit		40.00	91	62r
Physician fee, obstetrics/gynecology, first-visit		61.00	91	62r
Physician fee, obstetrics/gynecology, revisit		40.00	91	62r
Physician fee, orthopedic surgeon, revisit		41.00	91	62r
Physician fee, pediatrician, first-visit		46.00	91	62r
Physician fee, pediatrician, revisit		33.00	91	62r
Physician fee, surgical specialist, revisit		36.00	91	62r
Substance abuse, hospital ancillary charge	incident	960	90	70s
Substance abuse, hospital physician charge	incident	470	90	70s
Substance abuse, hospital room and board	incident	3980	90	70s
Household Goods				
Appliance repair, home, service call, washing machine	min labor charge	31.06	4Q 92	4c
Laundry detergent, Tide Ultra, Bold, or Cheer	42 oz	2.93	4Q 92	4c
Tissues, facial, Kleenex brand	175-count box	0.93	4Q 92	4c
Housing				
ACCRA Index, Housing		101.90	4Q 92	4c
Home, median price	unit	72.90		26c
House, 1,800 sq ft, 8,000 sq ft lot, new, urban	total	110420	4Q 92	4c
House payment, principal and interest, 25% down payment	month	622	4Q 92	4c
Mortgage rate, incl. points & origination fee, 30-year fixed or adjustable rate	per-cent	8.25	4Q 92	4c
Rent, apartment, 2 bedrooms - 1-1/2 to 2 baths, unfurnished, 950 sq ft, water	month	512	4Q 92	4c
Rental unit, 1 bedroom	month	365	93	23c
Rental unit, 2 bedroom	month	434	93	23c

Values are in dollars or fractions of dollars. In the column headed *Ref*, references are shown to sources. Each reference is followed by a letter. These refer to the geographical level for which data were reported: s=State, r=Region, and c=City or metro. The abbreviation *ex* is used to mean *except* or *excluding*; *exp* stands for expenditures. For other abbreviations and further explanations, please see the Introduction.

Green Bay, WI - continued

Item	Per	Value	Date	Ref.
Housing				
Rental unit, 3 bedroom	month	539	93	23c
Rental unit, 4 bedroom	month	603	93	23c
Rental unit, efficiency	month	300	93	23c
Insurance and Pensions				
Auto insurance, private passenger	year	510.11	91	63s
Personal Goods				
Shampoo, Alberto VO5	15 oz	0.90	4Q 92	4c
Toothpaste, Crest or Colgate	6-7 oz	1.48	4Q 92	4c
Personal Services				
Dry cleaning, man's 2-piece suit		6.45	4Q 92	4c
Haircare, woman's shampoo, trim and blow-dry		17.50	4Q 92	4c
Haircut, man's barbershop, no styling		7.44	4Q 92	4c
Restaurant Food				
Chicken, fried, thigh and drumstick		2.18	4Q 92	4c
Hamburger with cheese	1/4 lb	1.83	4Q 92	4c
Pizza, Pizza Hut or Pizza Inn, cheese, thin crust	12-13 in	8.91	4Q 92	4c
Taxes				
Tax, cigarette	pack	38	91	77s
Tax, gasoline	gal	22.20	91	77s
Taxes, state	capita	1416	91	77s
Transportation				
ACCRA Index, Transportation		97.70	4Q 92	4c
Bus fare, up to 10 miles	one-way	0.60	4Q 92	4c
Driver's license fee		9.00	12/90	43s
Tire balance, computer or spin balance, front	wheel	6.39	4Q 92	4c
Utilities				
ACCRA Index, Utilities		85.90	4Q 92	4c
Electricity	mil Btu	15.77	90	64s
Electricity, partial electric and other energy, 1,800 sq ft living area new home	month	40.58	4Q 92	4c
Electricity, winter, 250 KWh	month	19.20	92	55c
Electricity, winter, 500 KWh	month	34.80	92	55c
Electricity, winter, 750 KWh	month	50.40	92	55c
Electricity, winter, 1000 KWh	month	66.00	92	55c

Greensboro, NC

Item	Per	Value	Date	Ref.
Composite ACCRA index		94.00	4Q 92	4c
Alcoholic Beverages				
Beer, Miller Lite or Budweiser, 12-oz containers	6 pack	3.55	4Q 92	4c
Liquor, J & B Scotch	750 ml	17.65	4Q 92	4c
Wine, Gallo Chablis blanc, 1.5 liter	bottle	4.47	4Q 92	4c
Child Care				
Child care fee, average, center	hour	1.29	90	65r
Child care fee, average, nonregulated family day care	hour	0.89	90	65r
Child care fee, average, regulated family day care	hour	1.32	90	65r
Clothing				
Jeans, man's denim		26.60	4Q 92	4c
Shirt, man's dress shirt		24.40	4Q 92	4c
Undervest, boy's size 10-14, cotton	3	3.48	4Q 92	4c
Communications				
Long-distance telephone service, day, initial minute, 0-100 miles	min	0.10-0.33	91	12s
Long-distance telephone service, day, additional minute, 0-100 miles	min	0.10-0.33	91	12s
Long-distance telephone service, evenings/weekends, 0-100 mi, initial minute	min	0.08-0.24	91	12s
Long-distance telephone service, evenings/weekends, 0-100 mi, additional minute	min	0.05-0.17	91	12s

Greensboro, NC - continued

Item	Per	Value	Date	Ref.
Communications - continued				
Newspaper subscription, daily and Sunday home delivery, large-city	month	8.70	4Q 92	4c
Telephone, flat rate	month	12.19	91	11c
Telephone bill, family of four	month	19.55	4Q 92	4c
Education				
Board, 4-yr private college/university	year	1768	91	22s
Board, 4-yr public college/university	year	1568	91	22s
Expenditures, local gov't, public elementary/secondary	pupil	5078	92	20s
Room, 4-year private college/university	year	1467	91	22s
Room, 4-year public college/university	year	1386	91	22s
Tuition, 2-year private college/university	year	4964	91	22s
Tuition, 2-year public college/university	year	334	91	22s
Tuition, 4-year private college/university	year	7826	91	22s
Tuition, 4-year public college/university, in-state	year	1112	91	22s
Energy and Fuels				
Coal	mil Btu	1.79	90	64s
Energy	mil Btu	10.06	90	64s
Energy, combined forms, 1,800 sq ft heating area	month	119.35	4Q 92	4c
Energy exp/householder, 1-family unit	year	487	90	28r
Energy exp/householder, <1,000 sq ft heating area	year	393	90	28r
Energy exp/householder, 1,000-1,999 sq ft heating area	year	442	90	28r
Energy exp/householder, 2,000+ sq ft heating area	year	577	90	28r
Energy exp/householder, mobile home	year	366	90	28r
Energy exp/householder, multifamily	year	382	90	28r
Gas, natural	mil Btu	4.19	90	64s
Gas, natural	000 cu ft	6.24	91	46s
Gas, natural, exp	year	439	91	46s
Gasoline, motor	gal	1.08	4Q 92	4c
Gasoline, unleaded regular	mil Btu	9.44	90	64s
Entertainment				
Bowling, evening rate	game	2.47	4Q 92	4c
Miniature golf admission	adult	6.18	92	1r
Miniature golf admission	child	5.14	92	1r
Monopoly game, Parker Brothers', No. 9		10.35	4Q 92	4c
Movie	admission	5.17	4Q 92	4c
Tennis balls, yellow, Wilson or Penn, 3	can	2.07	4Q 92	4c
Waterpark admission	adult	11.00	92	1r
Waterpark admission	child	8.55	92	1r
Funerals				
Casket, 18-gauge steel, velvet interior		2029.08	91	24r
Cosmetology, hair care, etc.		75.10	91	24r
Embalming		249.24	91	24r
Facility use for ceremony		162.27	91	24r
Hearse, local		114.04	91	24r
Limousine, local		88.57	91	24r
Remains to funeral home, transfer		92.61	91	24r
Service charge, professional		682.42	91	24r
Vault, concrete, non-metallic liner		798.70	91	24r
Viewing facilities, use		163.86	91	24r
Goods and Services				
ACCRA Index, Miscellaneous Goods and Services		95.10	4Q 92	4c
Groceries				
ACCRA Index, Groceries		90.30	4Q 92	4c
Apples, Red Delicious	lb	0.79	4/93	16r
Babyfood, strained vegetables, lowest price	4-4.5 oz jar	0.27	4Q 92	4c
Bacon	lb	1.75	4/93	16r
Bananas	lb	0.53	4Q 92	4c
Bananas	lb	0.42	4/93	16r
Beef, stew, boneless	lb	2.61	4/93	16r

Values are in dollars or fractions of dollars. In the column headed *Ref*, references are shown to sources. Each reference is followed by a letter. These refer to the geographical level for which data were reported: s = State, r = Region, and c = City or metro. The abbreviation *ex* is used to mean *except* or *excluding*; *exp* stands for expenditures. For other abbreviations and further explanations, please see the Introduction.

Greensboro, NC - continued

Item	Per	Value	Date	Ref.
Groceries				
Bologna, all beef or mixed	lb	2.24	4/93	16r
Bread, white	24 oz	0.55	4Q 92	4c
Bread, white, pan	lb	0.64	4/93	16r
Bread, whole wheat, pan	lb	0.96	4/93	16r
Cabbage	lb	0.37	4/93	16r
Carrots, short trimmed and topped	lb	0.47	4/93	16r
Celery	lb	0.64	4/93	16r
Cheese, American	lb	2.98	4/93	16r
Cheese, Cheddar	lb	3.28	4/93	16r
Cheese, Kraft grated Parmesan	8-oz canister	3.09	4Q 92	4c
Chicken, fresh, whole	lb	0.77	4/93	16r
Chicken, fryer, whole	lb	0.65	4Q 92	4c
Chicken breast, bone-in	lb	1.92	4/93	16r
Chicken legs, bone in	lb	1.06	4/93	16r
Chuck roast, graded and ungraded, ex USDA prime and choice	lb	2.40	4/93	16r
Chuck roast, USDA choice, bone-in	lb	2.19	4/93	16r
Chuck roast, USDA choice, boneless	lb	2.38	4/93	16r
Cigarettes, Winston	carton	13.98	4Q 92	4c
Coffee, 100% ground roast, all sizes	lb	2.48	4/93	16r
Coffee, vacuum-packed	13-oz can	2.15	4Q 92	4c
Corn, frozen	10 oz	0.51	4Q 92	4c
Corn Flakes, Kellogg's or Post Toasties	18 oz	1.85	4Q 92	4c
Crackers, soda, salted	lb	1.15	4/93	16r
Eggs, Grade A large	doz	0.77	4Q 92	4c
Eggs, Grade A large	doz	0.96	4/93	16r
Flour, white, all purpose	lb	0.24	4/93	16r
Frankfurters, all meat or all beef	lb	2.01	4/93	16r
Grapefruit	lb	0.44	4/93	16r
Grapes, Thompson Seedless	lb	1.40	4/93	16r
Ground beef, 100% beef	lb	1.58	4/93	16r
Ground beef, lean and extra lean	lb	2.09	4/93	16r
Ground beef or hamburger	lb	1.29	4Q 92	4c
Ground chuck, 100% beef	lb	1.98	4/93	16r
Ham, boneless, excluding canned	lb	2.89	4/93	16r
Ham, picnic, shoulder, bone-in, smoked	lb	1.02	4/93	16r
Ham, rump or steak half, bone-in, smoked	lb	1.48	4/93	16r
Ice cream, prepackaged, bulk, regular	1/2 gal	2.41	4/93	16r
Lemons	lb	1.05	4/93	16r
Lettuce, iceberg	head	0.93	4Q 92	4c
Lettuce, iceberg	lb	0.81	4/93	16r
Margarine, Blue Bonnet or Parkay cubes	lb	0.55	4Q 92	4c
Margarine, stick	lb	0.88	4/93	16r
Milk, whole	1/2 gal	1.39	4Q 92	4c
Orange juice, Minute Maid frozen	12-oz can	1.32	4Q 92	4c
Oranges, navel	lb	0.55	4/93	16r
Peaches	29-oz can	1.33	4Q 92	4c
Pears, Anjou	lb	0.92	4/93	16r
Peas Sweet, Del Monte or Green Giant	15-17 oz can	0.52	4Q 92	4c
Pork chops, center cut, bone-in	lb	3.13	4/93	16r
Potato chips	16 oz	2.94	4/93	16r
Potatoes, white	lb	0.43	4/93	16r
Potatoes, white or red	10-lb sack	1.35	4Q 92	4c
Rib roast, USDA choice, bone-in	lb	4.63	4/93	16r
Rice, white, long grain, uncooked	lb	0.45	4/93	16r
Round roast, graded & ungraded, ex USDA prime & choice	lb	3.03	4/93	16r
Round roast, USDA choice, boneless	lb	3.09	4/93	16r
Sausage, fresh, loose	lb	2.08	4/93	16r
Sausage, Jimmy Dean, 100% pork	lb	1.99	4Q 92	4c
Short ribs, bone-in	lb	2.66	4/93	16r
Shortening, vegetable oil blends	lb	0.69	4/93	16r
Shortening, vegetable, Crisco	3-lb can	1.99	4Q 92	4c
Soft drink, Coca Cola	2 liter	1.05	4Q 92	4c

Greensboro, NC - continued

Item	Per	Value	Date	Ref.
Groceries - continued				
Spaghetti and macaroni	lb	0.81	4/93	16r
Steak, rib eye, USDA choice, boneless	lb	6.24	4/93	16r
Steak, round, graded & ungraded, ex USDA prime & choice	lb	3.31	4/93	16r
Steak, round, USDA choice, boneless	lb	3.34	4/93	16r
Steak, sirloin, graded & ungraded, ex USDA prime & choice	lb	4.19	4/93	16r
Steak, sirloin, USDA choice, boneless	lb	4.46	4/93	16r
Steak, T-bone	lb	5.33	4Q 92	4c
Steak, T-bone, USDA choice, bone-in	lb	5.25	4/93	16r
Strawberries, dry pint	12 oz	0.92	4/93	16r
Sugar, cane or beet	4 lb	1.69	4Q 92	4c
Sugar, white	lb	0.39	4/93	16r
Sugar, white, 33-80 oz pk	lb	0.38	4/93	16r
Tomatoes, field grown	lb	0.88	4/93	16r
Tomatoes, Hunt's or Del Monte	14.5-oz can	0.52	4Q 92	4c
Tuna, chunk, light	6.125-6.5 oz can	0.63	4Q 92	4c
Tuna, chunk, light	lb	1.79	4/93	16r
Turkey, frozen, whole	lb	1.04	4/93	16r
Yogurt, natural, fruit flavored	1/2 pint	0.57	4/93	16r
Health Care				
ACCRA Index, Health Care		82.80	4Q 92	4c
Analgesic, Aspirin, Bayer, 325 mg tablets	100	4.26	4Q 92	4c
Childbirth, cesarean, hospital		5034	91	62r
Childbirth, cesarean, physician's fee		2053	91	62r
Childbirth, normal, hospital		2712	91	62r
Childbirth, normal, physician's fee		1492	91	62r
Dentist's fee, adult teeth cleaning and periodic oral exam	visit	37.57	4Q 92	4c
Doctor's fee, routine exam, established patient	visit	34.71	4Q 92	4c
Hospital care, semiprivate room	day	229.27	90	27c
Hospital care, semiprivate room	day	205.00	4Q 92	4c
Medical insurance premium, per employee, small group comprehensive	month	267.40	10/91	25c
Medical plan per employee	year	3495	91	45r
Mental health care, exp	capita	37.60-53.67	90	38s
Mental health care, exp, state mental health agency	capita	45.66	90	38s
Mental health care, hospital psychiatric services, non-Federal, exp	capita	12.05	88	38s
Mental health care, mental health organization, multiservice, exp	capita	29.54	88	38s
Mental health care, psychiatric hospitals, private, exp	capita	15.07	88	38s
Mental health care, psychiatric out-patient clinics, freestanding, exp	capita	0.11	88	38s
Mental health care, state and county mental hospitals, exp	capita	26.36	88	38s
Mental health care, VA medical centers, exp	capita	2.23	88	38s
Physician fee, family practice, first-visit		75.00	91	62r
Physician fee, family practice, revisit		34.00	91	62r
Physician fee, general practice, first-visit		61.00	91	62r
Physician fee, general practice, revisit		32.00	91	62r
Physician fee, general surgeon, first-visit		64.00	91	62r
Physician fee, general surgeon, revisit		40.00	91	62r
Physician fee, internal medicine, first-visit		98.00	91	62r
Physician fee, internal medicine, revisit		40.00	91	62r
Physician fee, median, neurosurgeon, first-visit		130.00	91	62r
Physician fee, median, nonsurgical specialist, first-visit		95.00	91	62r
Physician fee, median, orthopedic surgeon, first-visit		91.00	91	62r
Physician fee, median, plastic surgeon, first-visit		66.00	91	62r

Values are in dollars or fractions of dollars. In the column headed *Ref*, references are shown to sources. Each reference is followed by a letter. These refer to the geographical level for which data were reported: s=State, r=Region, and c=City or metro. The abbreviation *ex* is used to mean *except* or *excluding*; *exp* stands for expenditures. For other abbreviations and further explanations, please see the Introduction.

Greensboro, NC - continued

Item	Per	Value	Date	Ref.
Health Care				
Physician fee, median, surgical specialist, first-visit		62.00	91	62r
Physician fee, neurosurgeon, revisit		50.00	91	62r
Physician fee, nonsurgical specialist, revisit		40.00	91	62r
Physician fee, obstetrics/gynecology, first-visit		64.00	91	62r
Physician fee, obstetrics/gynecology, revisit		41.00	91	62r
Physician fee, orthopedic surgeon, revisit		40.00	91	62r
Physician fee, pediatrician, first-visit		49.00	91	62r
Physician fee, pediatrician, revisit		33.00	91	62r
Physician fee, plastic surgeon, revisit		43.00	91	62r
Physician fee, surgical specialist, revisit		37.00	91	62r
Substance abuse, hospital ancillary charge	incident	1090	90	70s
Substance abuse, hospital physician charge	incident	460	90	70s
Substance abuse, hospital room and board	incident	4880	90	70s
Household Goods				
Appliance repair, home, service call, washing machine	min labor charge	37.60	4Q 92	4c
Laundry detergent, Tide Ultra, Bold, or Cheer	42 oz	2.77	4Q 92	4c
Tissues, facial, Kleenex brand	175-count box	1.09	4Q 92	4c
Housing				
ACCRA Index, Housing		92.80	4Q 92	4c
Home, median price	unit	88.40		26c
House, 1,800 sq ft, 8,000 sq ft lot, new, urban	total	107983	4Q 92	4c
House payment, principal and interest, 25% down payment	month	592	4Q 92	4c
Mortgage rate, incl. points & origination fee, 30-year fixed or adjustable rate	percent	7.96	4Q 92	4c
Rent, apartment, 2 bedrooms - 1-1/2 to 2 baths, unfurnished, 950 sq ft, water	month	409	4Q 92	4c
Rental unit, 1 bedroom	month	366	93	23c
Rental unit, 2 bedroom	month	428	93	23c
Rental unit, 3 bedroom	month	538	93	23c
Rental unit, 4 bedroom	month	603	93	23c
Rental unit, efficiency	month	299	93	23c
Insurance and Pensions				
Auto insurance, private passenger	year	522.39	91	63s
Personal Goods				
Shampoo, Alberto VO5	15 oz	1.02	4Q 92	4c
Toothpaste, Crest or Colgate	6-7 oz	1.33	4Q 92	4c
Personal Services				
Dry cleaning, man's 2-piece suit		5.85	4Q 92	4c
Haircare, woman's shampoo, trim and blow-dry		16.40	4Q 92	4c
Haircut, man's barbershop, no styling		7.00	4Q 92	4c
Restaurant Food				
Chicken, fried, thigh and drumstick		1.94	4Q 92	4c
Hamburger with cheese	1/4 lb	1.81	4Q 92	4c
Pizza, Pizza Hut or Pizza Inn, cheese, thin crust	12-13 in	7.59	4Q 92	4c
Taxes				
Tax, cigarette	pack	5	91	77s
Tax, gasoline	gal	21.90	91	77s
Taxes, state	capita	1165	91	77s
Transportation				
ACCRA Index, Transportation		91.10	4Q 92	4c
Auto rental, average	day	33.70	6/91	60c
Driver's license fee		15.00	12/90	43s
Limo fare, airport-city, average	day	7.50	6/91	60c
Taxi fare, airport-city, average	day	14.00	6/91	60c

Greensboro, NC - continued

Item	Per	Value	Date	Ref.
Transportation - continued				
Tire balance, computer or spin balance, front	wheel	5.67	4Q 92	4c
Vehicle registration and license plate	year	35.00	93	50s
Travel				
Breakfast	day	5.92	6/91	60c
Business travel	day	193.00	4/93	89r
Dinner	day	17.35	6/91	60c
Lodging	day	102.29	91	60c
Lunch	day	8.33	6/91	60c
Utilities				
ACCRA Index, Utilities		108.40	4Q 92	4c
Electricity	mil Btu	18.74	90	64s
Electricity, all electric, 1,800 sq ft living area new home	month	119.35	4Q 92	4c

Greenville, NC

Item	Per	Value	Date	Ref.
Composite ACCRA index		96.00	4Q 92	4c
Alcoholic Beverages				
Beer, Miller Lite or Budweiser, 12-oz containers	6 pack	3.73	4Q 92	4c
Liquor, J & B Scotch	750 ml	17.65	4Q 92	4c
Wine, Gallo Chablis blanc, 1.5 liter	bottle	4.77	4Q 92	4c
Clothing				
Jeans, man's denim		31.47	4Q 92	4c
Shirt, man's dress shirt		23.50	4Q 92	4c
Undervest, boy's size 10-14, cotton	3	3.66	4Q 92	4c
Communications				
Newspaper subscription, daily and Sunday home delivery, large-city	month	8.00	4Q 92	4c
Telephone bill, family of four	month	17.51	4Q 92	4c
Energy and Fuels				
Energy, combined forms, 1,800 sq ft heating area	month	129.34	4Q 92	4c
Gasoline, motor	gal	1.09	4Q 92	4c
Entertainment				
Bowling, evening rate	game	2.65	4Q 92	4c
Monopoly game, Parker Brothers', No. 9		8.97	4Q 92	4c
Movie	admission	5.00	4Q 92	4c
Tennis balls, yellow, Wilson or Penn, 3	can	2.30	4Q 92	4c
Goods and Services				
ACCRA Index, Miscellaneous Goods and Services		98.30	4Q 92	4c
Groceries				
ACCRA Index, Groceries		91.60	4Q 92	4c
Babyfood, strained vegetables, lowest price	4-4.5 oz jar	0.32	4Q 92	4c
Bananas	lb	0.45	4Q 92	4c
Bread, white	24 oz	0.64	4Q 92	4c
Cheese, Kraft grated Parmesan	8-oz canister	3.23	4Q 92	4c
Chicken, fryer, whole	lb	0.78	4Q 92	4c
Cigarettes, Winston	carton	15.36	4Q 92	4c
Coffee, vacuum-packed	13-oz can	1.92	4Q 92	4c
Corn, frozen	10 oz	0.56	4Q 92	4c
Corn Flakes, Kellogg's or Post Toasties	18 oz	1.84	4Q 92	4c
Eggs, Grade A large	doz	0.88	4Q 92	4c
Ground beef or hamburger	lb	1.25	4Q 92	4c
Lettuce, iceberg	head	0.83	4Q 92	4c
Margarine, Blue Bonnet or Parkay cubes	lb	0.48	4Q 92	4c
Milk, whole	1/2 gal	1.39	4Q 92	4c
Orange juice, Minute Maid frozen	12-oz can	1.28	4Q 92	4c

Values are in dollars or fractions of dollars. In the column headed *Ref*, references are shown to sources. Each reference is followed by a letter. These refer to the geographical level for which data were reported: s=State, r=Region, and c=City or metro. The abbreviation *ex* is used to mean *except* or *excluding*; *exp* stands for *expenditures*. For other abbreviations and further explanations, please see the Introduction.

Greenville, NC - continued

Item	Per	Value	Date	Ref.
Groceries				
Peaches	29-oz can	1.31	4Q 92	4c
Peas Sweet, Del Monte or Green Giant	15-17 oz can	0.50	4Q 92	4c
Potatoes, white or red	10-lb sack	2.07	4Q 92	4c
Sausage, Jimmy Dean, 100% pork	lb	2.07	4Q 92	4c
Shortening, vegetable, Crisco	3-lb can	2.02	4Q 92	4c
Soft drink, Coca Cola	2 liter	1.03	4Q 92	4c
Steak, T-bone	lb	5.29	4Q 92	4c
Sugar, cane or beet	4 lb	1.43	4Q 92	4c
Tomatoes, Hunt's or Del Monte	14.5-oz can	0.56	4Q 92	4c
Tuna, chunk, light	6.125-6.5 oz can	0.54	4Q 92	4c
Health Care				
ACCRA Index, Health Care		100.90	4Q 92	4c
Analgesic, Aspirin, Bayer, 325 mg tablets	100	5.41	4Q 92	4c
Dentist's fee, adult teeth cleaning and periodic oral exam	visit	50.50	4Q 92	4c
Doctor's fee, routine exam, established patient	visit	35.40	4Q 92	4c
Hospital care, semiprivate room	day	295.00	4Q 92	4c
Household Goods				
Appliance repair, home, service call, washing machine	min labor charge	35.10	4Q 92	4c
Laundry detergent, Tide Ultra, Bold, or Cheer	42 oz	2.81	4Q 92	4c
Tissues, facial, Kleenex brand	175-count box	1.02	4Q 92	4c
Housing				
ACCRA Index, Housing		90.60	4Q 92	4c
House, 1,800 sq ft, 8,000 sq ft lot, new, urban	total	102000	4Q 92	4c
House, payment, principal and interest, 25% down payment	month	567	4Q 92	4c
Mortgage rate, incl. points & origination fee, 30-year fixed or adjustable rate	percent	8.11	4Q 92	4c
Rent, apartment, 2 bedrooms - 1-1/2 to 2 baths, unfurnished, 950 sq ft, water	month	423	4Q 92	4c
Personal Goods				
Shampoo, Alberto VO5	15 oz	1.27	4Q 92	4c
Toothpaste, Crest or Colgate	6-7 oz	2.00	4Q 92	4c
Personal Services				
Dry cleaning, man's 2-piece suit		6.55	4Q 92	4c
Haircare, woman's shampoo, trim and blow-dry		18.00	4Q 92	4c
Haircut, man's barbershop, no styling		8.40	4Q 92	4c
Restaurant Food				
Chicken, fried, thigh and drumstick		1.49	4Q 92	4c
Hamburger with cheese	1/4 lb	2.00	4Q 92	4c
Pizza, Pizza Hut or Pizza Inn, cheese, thin crust	12-13 in	8.22	4Q 92	4c
Transportation				
ACCRA Index, Transportation		89.10	4Q 92	4c
Tire balance, computer or spin balance, front	wheel	5.30	4Q 92	4c
Utilities				
ACCRA Index, Utilities		115.60	4Q 92	4c
Electricity, all electric, 1,800 sq ft living area new home	month	129.34	4Q 92	4c

Greenville, SC

Item	Per	Value	Date	Ref.
Composite ACCRA index		99.50	4Q 92	4c
Alcoholic Beverages				
Beer, Miller Lite or Budweiser, 12-oz containers	6 pack	3.85	4Q 92	4c
Liquor, J & B Scotch	750 ml	15.27	4Q 92	4c
Wine, Gallo Chablis blanc, 1.5 liter	bottle	4.82	4Q 92	4c
Child Care				
Child care fee, average, center	hour	1.29	90	65r
Child care fee, average, nonregulated family day care	hour	0.89	90	65r
Child care fee, average, regulated family day care	hour	1.32	90	65r
Clothing				
Jeans, man's denim		33.74	4Q 92	4c
Shirt, man's dress shirt		24.50	4Q 92	4c
Undervest, boy's size 10-14, cotton	3	4.11	4Q 92	4c
Communications				
Long-distance telephone service, day, initial minute, 0-100 miles	min	0.24-0.52	91	12s
Long-distance telephone service, day, additional minute, 0-100 miles	min	0.13-0.35	91	12s
Long-distance telephone service, evenings/weekends, 0-100 mi, initial minute	min	0.12-0.26	91	12s
Long-distance telephone service, evenings/weekends, 0-100 mi, additional minute	min	0.07-0.16	91	12s
Newspaper subscription, daily and Sunday home delivery, large-city	month	11.41	4Q 92	4c
Telephone, flat rate	month	16.90	91	11c
Telephone bill, family of four	month	25.61	4Q 92	4c
Education				
Board, 4-yr private college/university	year	1468	91	22s
Board, 4-yr public college/university	year	1632	91	22s
Expenditures, local gov't, public elementary/secondary	pupil	4312	92	20s
Room, 4-year private college/university	year	1393	91	22s
Room, 4-year public college/university	year	1492	91	22s
Tuition, 2-year private college/university	year	5110	91	22s
Tuition, 2-year public college/university	year	813	91	22s
Tuition, 4-year private college/university	year	6434	91	22s
Tuition, 4-year public college/university, in-state	year	2317	91	22s
Energy and Fuels				
Coal	mil Btu	1.73	90	64s
Energy	mil Btu	8.93	90	64s
Energy, combined forms, 1,800 sq ft heating area	month	117.15	4Q 92	4c
Energy exp/householder, 1-family unit	year	487	90	28r
Energy exp/householder, <1,000 sq ft heating area	year	393	90	28r
Energy exp/householder, 1,000-1,999 sq ft heating area	year	442	90	28r
Energy exp/householder, 2,000+ sq ft heating area	year	577	90	28r
Energy exp/householder, mobile home	year	366	90	28r
Energy exp/householder, multifamily	year	382	90	28r
Gas, cooking, winter, 10 therms	month	8.85	92	56c
Gas, cooking, winter, 30 therms	month	20.56	92	56c
Gas, cooking, winter, 50 therms	month	32.26	92	56c
Gas, heating, winter, 100 therms	month	64.40	92	56c
Gas, heating, winter, average use	month	76.07	92	56c
Gas, natural	mil Btu	4.01	90	64s
Gas, natural	000 cu ft	6.98	91	46s
Gas, natural, exp	year	397	91	46s
Gasoline, motor	gal	1.02	4Q 92	4c
Gasoline, unleaded regular	mil Btu	8.80	90	64s
Entertainment				
Bowling, evening rate	game	2.08	4Q 92	4c
Miniature golf admission	adult	6.18	92	1r

Values are in dollars or fractions of dollars. In the column headed *Ref*, references are shown to sources. Each reference is followed by a letter. These refer to the geographical level for which data were reported: s = State, r = Region, and c = City or metro. The abbreviation *ex* is used to mean *except* or *excluding*; *exp* stands for expenditures. For other abbreviations and further explanations, please see the Introduction.

Greenville, SC - continued

Item	Per	Value	Date	Ref.
Entertainment				
Miniature golf admission	child	5.14	92	1r
Monopoly game, Parker Brothers', No. 9		11.09	4Q 92	4c
Movie	admission	5.50	4Q 92	4c
Tennis balls, yellow, Wilson or Penn, 3	can	2.21	4Q 92	4c
Waterpark admission	adult	11.00	92	1r
Waterpark admission	child	8.55	92	1r
Funerals				
Casket, 18-gauge steel, velvet interior		2029.08	91	24r
Cosmetology, hair care, etc.		75.10	91	24r
Embalming		249.24	91	24r
Facility use for ceremony		162.27	91	24r
Hearse, local		114.04	91	24r
Limousine, local		88.57	91	24r
Remains to funeral home, transfer		92.61	91	24r
Service charge, professional		682.42	91	24r
Vault, concrete, non-metallic liner		798.70	91	24r
Viewing facilities, use		163.86	91	24r
Goods and Services				
ACCRA Index, Miscellaneous Goods and Services		101.50	4Q 92	4c
Groceries				
ACCRA Index, Groceries		96.90	4Q 92	4c
Apples, Red Delicious	lb	0.79	4/93	16r
Babyfood, strained vegetables, lowest price	4-4.5 oz jar	0.32	4Q 92	4c
Bacon	lb	1.75	4/93	16r
Bananas	lb	0.51	4Q 92	4c
Bananas	lb	0.42	4/93	16r
Beef, stew, boneless	lb	2.61	4/93	16r
Bologna, all beef or mixed	lb	2.24	4/93	16r
Bread, white	24 oz	0.64	4Q 92	4c
Bread, white, pan	lb	0.64	4/93	16r
Bread, whole wheat, pan	lb	0.96	4/93	16r
Cabbage	lb	0.37	4/93	16r
Carrots, short trimmed and topped	lb	0.47	4/93	16r
Celery	lb	0.64	4/93	16r
Cheese, American	lb	2.98	4/93	16r
Cheese, Cheddar	lb	3.28	4/93	16r
Cheese, Kraft grated Parmesan	8-oz canister	3.26	4Q 92	4c
Chicken, fresh, whole	lb	0.77	4/93	16r
Chicken, fryer, whole	lb	0.81	4Q 92	4c
Chicken breast, bone-in	lb	1.92	4/93	16r
Chicken legs, bone-in	lb	1.06	4/93	16r
Chuck roast, graded and ungraded, ex USDA prime and choice	lb	2.40	4/93	16r
Chuck roast, USDA choice, bone-in	lb	2.19	4/93	16r
Chuck roast, USDA choice, boneless	lb	2.38	4/93	16r
Cigarettes, Winston	carton	15.40	4Q 92	4c
Coffee, 100% ground roast, all sizes	lb	2.48	4/93	16r
Coffee, vacuum-packed	13-oz can	1.69	4Q 92	4c
Corn, frozen	10 oz	0.51	4Q 92	4c
Corn Flakes, Kellogg's or Post Toasties	18 oz	1.70	4Q 92	4c
Crackers, soda, salted	lb	1.15	4/93	16r
Eggs, Grade A large	doz	0.88	4Q 92	4c
Eggs, Grade A large	doz	0.96	4/93	16r
Flour, white, all purpose	lb	0.24	4/93	16r
Frankfurters, all meat or all beef	lb	2.01	4/93	16r
Grapefruit	lb	0.44	4/93	16r
Grapes, Thompson Seedless	lb	1.40	4/93	16r
Ground beef, 100% beef	lb	1.58	4/93	16r
Ground beef, lean and extra lean	lb	2.09	4/93	16r
Ground beef or hamburger	lb	1.83	4Q 92	4c
Ground chuck, 100% beef	lb	1.98	4/93	16r
Ham, boneless, excluding canned	lb	2.89	4/93	16r
Ham, picnic, shoulder, bone-in, smoked	lb	1.02	4/93	16r
Ham, rump or steak half, bone-in, smoked	lb	1.48	4/93	16r
Ice cream, prepackaged, bulk, regular	1/2 gal	2.41	4/93	16r

Greenville, SC - continued

Item	Per	Value	Date	Ref.
Groceries - continued				
Lemons	lb	1.05	4/93	16r
Lettuce, iceberg	head	0.91	4Q 92	4c
Lettuce, iceberg	lb	0.81	4/93	16r
Margarine, Blue Bonnet or Parkay cubes	lb	0.51	4Q 92	4c
Margarine, stick	lb	0.88	4/93	16r
Milk, whole	1/2 gal	1.55	4Q 92	4c
Orange juice, Minute Maid frozen	12-oz can	1.13	4Q 92	4c
Oranges, navel	lb	0.55	4/93	16r
Peaches	29-oz can	1.30	4Q 92	4c
Pears, Anjou	lb	0.92	4/93	16r
Peas Sweet, Del Monte or Green Giant	15-17 oz can	0.46	4Q 92	4c
Pork chops, center cut, bone-in	lb	3.13	4/93	16r
Potato chips	16 oz	2.94	4/93	16r
Potatoes, white	lb	0.43	4/93	16r
Potatoes, white or red	10-lb sack	2.61	4Q 92	4c
Rib roast, USDA choice, bone-in	lb	4.63	4/93	16r
Rice, white, long grain, uncooked	lb	0.45	4/93	16r
Round roast, graded & ungraded, ex USDA prime & choice	lb	3.03	4/93	16r
Round roast, USDA choice, boneless	lb	3.09	4/93	16r
Sausage, fresh, loose	lb	2.08	4/93	16r
Sausage, Jimmy Dean, 100% pork	lb	2.33	4Q 92	4c
Short ribs, bone-in	lb	2.66	4/93	16r
Shortening, vegetable oil blends	lb	0.69	4/93	16r
Shortening, vegetable, Crisco	3-lb can	1.99	4Q 92	4c
Soft drink, Coca Cola	2 liter	0.94	4Q 92	4c
Spaghetti and macaroni	lb	0.81	4/93	16r
Steak, rib eye, USDA choice, boneless	lb	6.24	4/93	16r
Steak, round, graded & ungraded, ex USDA prime & choice	lb	3.31	4/93	16r
Steak, round, USDA choice, boneless	lb	3.34	4/93	16r
Steak, sirloin, graded & ungraded, ex USDA prime & choice	lb	4.19	4/93	16r
Steak, sirloin, USDA choice, boneless	lb	4.46	4/93	16r
Steak, T-bone	lb	5.46	4Q 92	4c
Steak, T-bone, USDA choice, bone-in	lb	5.25	4/93	16r
Strawberries, dry pint	12 oz	0.92	4/93	16r
Sugar, cane or beet	4 lb	1.42	4Q 92	4c
Sugar, white	lb	0.39	4/93	16r
Sugar, white, 33-80 oz pk	lb	0.38	4/93	16r
Tomatoes, field grown	lb	0.88	4/93	16r
Tomatoes, Hunt's or Del Monte	14.5-oz can	0.48	4Q 92	4c
Tuna, chunk, light	6.125-6.5 oz can	0.55	4Q 92	4c
Tuna, chunk, light	lb	1.79	4/93	16r
Turkey, frozen, whole	lb	1.04	4/93	16r
Yogurt, natural, fruit flavored	1/2 pint	0.57	4/93	16r
Health Care				
ACCRA Index, Health Care		92.00	4Q 92	4c
Analgesic, Aspirin, Bayer, 325 mg tablets	100	5.28	4Q 92	4c
Childbirth, cesarean, hospital		5034	91	62r
Childbirth, cesarean, physician's fee		2053	91	62r
Childbirth, normal, hospital		2712	91	62r
Childbirth, normal, physician's fee		1492	91	62r
Dentist's fee, adult teeth cleaning and periodic oral exam	visit	47.75	4Q 92	4c
Doctor's fee, routine exam, established patient	visit	33.00	4Q 92	4c
Gallbladder removal, physician fee	average	1180.00	2/93	93c
Health care spending, state	capita	1689	3/93	84s
Hospital care, semiprivate room	day	207.22	90	27c
Hospital care, semiprivate room	day	220.20	4Q 92	4c

Values are in dollars or fractions of dollars. In the column headed *Ref*, references are shown to sources. Each reference is followed by a letter. These refer to the geographical level for which data were reported: s = State, r = Region, and c = City or metro. The abbreviation *ex* is used to mean *except* or *excluding*; *exp* stands for *expenditures*. For other abbreviations and further explanations, please see the Introduction.

Greenville, SC - continued

Item	Per	Value	Date	Ref.
Health Care				
Medical insurance premium, per employee, small group comprehensive	month	267.40	10/91	25c
Medical plan per employee	year	3495	91	45r
Mental health care, exp	capita	37.60-53.67	90	38s
Mental health care, exp, state mental health agency	capita	51.12	90	38s
Mental health care, hospital psychiatric services, non-Federal, exp	capita	10.67	88	38s
Mental health care, mental health organization, multiservice, exp	capita	11.38	88	38s
Mental health care, psychiatric hospitals, private, exp	capita	9.21	88	38s
Mental health care, psychiatric out-patient clinics, freestanding, exp	capita	0.68	88	38s
Mental health care, state and county mental hospitals, exp	capita	25.02	88	38s
Mental health care, VA medical centers, exp	capita	0.62	88	38s
Physician fee, family practice, first-visit		75.00	91	62r
Physician fee, family practice, revisit		34.00	91	62r
Physician fee, general practice, first-visit		61.00	91	62r
Physician fee, general practice, revisit		32.00	91	62r
Physician fee, general surgeon, first-visit		64.00	91	62r
Physician fee, general surgeon, revisit		40.00	91	62r
Physician fee, internal medicine, first-visit		98.00	91	62r
Physician fee, internal medicine, revisit		40.00	91	62r
Physician fee, median, neurosurgeon, first-visit		130.00	91	62r
Physician fee, median, nonsurgical specialist, first-visit		95.00	91	62r
Physician fee, median, orthopedic surgeon, first-visit		91.00	91	62r
Physician fee, median, plastic surgeon, first-visit		66.00	91	62r
Physician fee, median, surgical specialist, first-visit		62.00	91	62r
Physician fee, neurosurgeon, revisit		50.00	91	62r
Physician fee, nonsurgical specialist, revisit		40.00	91	62r
Physician fee, obstetrics/gynecology, first-visit		64.00	91	62r
Physician fee, obstetrics/gynecology, revisit		41.00	91	62r
Physician fee, orthopedic surgeon, revisit		40.00	91	62r
Physician fee, pediatrician, first-visit		49.00	91	62r
Physician fee, pediatrician, revisit		33.00	91	62r
Physician fee, plastic surgeon, revisit		43.00	91	62r
Physician fee, surgical specialist, revisit		37.00	91	62r
Substance abuse, hospital ancillary charge	incident	1250	90	70s
Substance abuse, hospital physician charge	incident	250	90	70s
Substance abuse, hospital room and board	incident	6100	90	70s
Household Goods				
Appliance repair, home, service call, washing machine	min labor charge	32.20	4Q 92	4c
Laundry detergent, Tide Ultra, Bold, or Cheer	42 oz	3.29	4Q 92	4c
Tissues, facial, Kleenex brand	175-count box	1.00	4Q 92	4c
Housing				
ACCRA Index, Housing		100.60	4Q 92	4c
Home, median price	unit	82.90		26c
House, 1,800 sq ft, 8,000 sq ft lot, new, urban	total	110587	4Q 92	4c
House payment, principal and interest, 25% down payment	month	617	4Q 92	4c
Mortgage rate, incl. points & origination fee, 30-year fixed or adjustable rate	percent	8.14	4Q 92	4c

Greenville, SC - continued

Item	Per	Value	Date	Ref.
Housing - continued				
Rent, apartment, 2 bedrooms - 1-1/2 to 2 baths, unfurnished, 950 sq ft, water	month	500	4Q 92	4c
Rental unit, 1 bedroom	month	345	93	23c
Rental unit, 2 bedroom	month	408	93	23c
Rental unit, 3 bedroom	month	508	93	23c
Rental unit, 4 bedroom	month	571	93	23c
Rental unit, efficiency	month	283	93	23c
Insurance and Pensions				
Auto insurance, private passenger	year	605.26	91	63s
Personal Goods				
Shampoo, Alberto VO5	15 oz	0.98	4Q 92	4c
Toothpaste, Crest or Colgate	6-7 oz	1.89	4Q 92	4c
Personal Services				
Dry cleaning, man's 2-piece suit		6.28	4Q 92	4c
Haircare, woman's shampoo, trim and blow-dry		19.38	4Q 92	4c
Haircut, man's barbershop, no styling		10.00	4Q 92	4c
Restaurant Food				
Chicken, fried, thigh and drumstick		2.09	4Q 92	4c
Hamburger with cheese	1/4 lb	1.85	4Q 92	4c
Pizza, Pizza Hut or Pizza Inn, cheese, thin crust	12-13 in	7.99	4Q 92	4c
Taxes				
Tax, cigarette	pack	7	91	77s
Tax, gasoline	gal	16	91	77s
Taxes, state	capita	1105	91	77s
Transportation				
ACCRA Index, Transportation		87.20	4Q 92	4c
Auto rental, average	day	45.25	6/91	60c
Bus fare	one-way	0.85	3/93	2c
Driver's license fee		10.00	12/90	43s
Limo fare, airport-city, average	day	14.00	6/91	60c
Taxi fare, airport-city, average	day	15.00	6/91	60c
Tire balance, computer or spin balance, front	wheel	5.50	4Q 92	4c
Travel				
Breakfast	day	7.70	6/91	60c
Business travel	day	193.00	4/93	89r
Dinner	day	25.73	6/91	60c
Lodging	day	79.43	91	60c
Lunch	day	11.06	6/91	60c
Utilities				
ACCRA Index, Utilities		109.70	4Q 92	4c
Electricity	mil Btu	16.39	90	64s
Electricity, all electric, 1,800 sq ft living area new home	month	117.15	4Q 92	4c
Electricity, winter, 250 KWh	month	23.64	92	55c
Electricity, winter, 500 KWh	month	41.12	92	55c
Electricity, winter, 750 KWh	month	58.60	92	55c
Electricity, winter, 1000 KWh	month	76.08	92	55c

Gunnison, CO

Item	Per	Value	Date	Ref.
Composite ACCRA index		100.10	4Q 92	4c
Alcoholic Beverages				
Beer, Miller Lite or Budweiser, 12-oz containers	6 pack	4.33	4Q 92	4c
Liquor, J & B Scotch	750 ml	15.32	4Q 92	4c
Wine, Gallo Chablis blanc, 1.5 liter	bottle	5.22	4Q 92	4c
Clothing				
Jeans, man's denim		27.16	4Q 92	4c
Shirt, man's dress shirt		19.00	4Q 92	4c
Undervest, boy's size 10-14, cotton	3	5.98	4Q 92	4c

Values are in dollars or fractions of dollars. In the column headed *Ref*, references are shown to sources. Each reference is followed by a letter. These refer to the geographical level for which data were reported: s=State, r=Region, and c=City or metro. The abbreviation *ex* is used to mean *except* or *excluding*; *exp* stands for expenditures. For other abbreviations and further explanations, please see the Introduction.

Gunnison, CO - continued

Item	Per	Value	Date	Ref.
Communications				
Newspaper subscription, daily and Sunday home delivery, large-city	month	8.00	4Q 92	4c
Telephone, flat rate	month	14.22	91	11c
Telephone bill, family of four	month	20.69	4Q 92	4c
Energy and Fuels				
Energy, combined forms, 1,800 sq ft heating area	month	131.42	4Q 92	4c
Energy, exc electricity, 1,800 sq ft heating area	month	53.46	4Q 92	4c
Gasoline, motor	gal	1.37	4Q 92	4c
Entertainment				
Bowling, evening rate	game	1.75	4Q 92	4c
Monopoly game, Parker Brothers', No. 9		10.48	4Q 92	4c
Movie	admission	4.75	4Q 92	4c
Tennis balls, yellow, Wilson or Penn, 3	can	2.52	4Q 92	4c
Goods and Services				
ACCRA Index, Miscellaneous Goods and Services		97.20	4Q 92	4c
Groceries				
ACCRA Index, Groceries		116.00	4Q 92	4c
Babyfood, strained vegetables, lowest price	4-4.5 oz jar	0.45	4Q 92	4c
Bananas	lb	0.59	4Q 92	4c
Bread, white	24 oz	0.82	4Q 92	4c
Cheese, Kraft grated Parmesan	8-oz canister	3.24	4Q 92	4c
Chicken, fryer, whole	lb	0.68	4Q 92	4c
Cigarettes, Winston	carton	15.84	4Q 92	4c
Coffee, vacuum-packed	13-oz can	2.37	4Q 92	4c
Corn, frozen	10 oz	0.92	4Q 92	4c
Corn Flakes, Kellogg's or Post Toasties	18 oz	2.56	4Q 92	4c
Eggs, Grade A large	doz	1.12	4Q 92	4c
Ground beef or hamburger	lb	1.58	4Q 92	4c
Lettuce, iceberg	head	0.79	4Q 92	4c
Margarine, Blue Bonnet or Parkay cubes	lb	0.77	4Q 92	4c
Milk, whole	1/2 gal	1.57	4Q 92	4c
Orange juice, Minute Maid frozen	12-oz can	1.58	4Q 92	4c
Peaches	29-oz can	1.70	4Q 92	4c
Peas Sweet, Del Monte or Green Giant	15-17 oz can	0.72	4Q 92	4c
Potatoes, white or red	10-lb sack	2.54	4Q 92	4c
Sausage, Jimmy Dean, 100% pork	lb	3.72	4Q 92	4c
Shortening, vegetable, Crisco	3-lb can	3.16	4Q 92	4c
Soft drink, Coca Cola	2 liter	1.94	4Q 92	4c
Steak, T-bone	lb	4.48	4Q 92	4c
Sugar, cane or beet	4 lb	1.99	4Q 92	4c
Tomatoes, Hunt's or Del Monte	14.5-oz can	0.83	4Q 92	4c
Tuna, chunk, light	6.125-6.5 oz can	1.04	4Q 92	4c
Health Care				
ACCRA Index, Health Care		90.40	4Q 92	4c
Analgesic, Aspirin, Bayer, 325 mg tablets	100	4.73	4Q 92	4c
Dentist's fee, adult teeth cleaning and periodic oral exam	visit	41.20	4Q 92	4c
Doctor's fee, routine exam, established patient	visit	33.00	4Q 92	4c
Hospital care, semiprivate room	day	300.00	4Q 92	4c

Gunnison, CO - continued

Item	Per	Value	Date	Ref.
Household Goods				
Appliance repair, home, service call, washing machine	min labor charge	20.50	4Q 92	4c
Laundry detergent, Tide Ultra, Bold, or Cheer	42 oz	3.95	4Q 92	4c
Tissues, facial, Kleenex brand	175-count box	1.10	4Q 92	4c
Housing				
ACCRA Index, Housing		89.30	4Q 92	4c
House, 1,800 sq ft, 8,000 sq ft lot, new, urban	total	98333	4Q 92	4c
House payment, principal and interest, 25% down payment	month	581	4Q 92	4c
Mortgage rate, incl. points & origination fee, 30-year fixed or adjustable rate	percent	8.77	4Q 92	4c
Rent, apartment, 2 bedrooms - 1-1/2 to 2 baths, unfurnished, 950 sq ft, water	month	367	4Q 92	4c
Personal Goods				
Shampoo, Alberto VO5	15 oz	1.41	4Q 92	4c
Toothpaste, Crest or Colgate	6-7 oz	2.22	4Q 92	4c
Personal Services				
Dry cleaning, man's 2-piece suit		8.42	4Q 92	4c
Haircare, woman's shampoo, trim and blow-dry		15.33	4Q 92	4c
Haircut, man's barbershop, no styling		6.50	4Q 92	4c
Restaurant Food				
Chicken, fried, thigh and drumstick		2.00	4Q 92	4c
Hamburger with cheese	1/4 lb	1.99	4Q 92	4c
Pizza, Pizza Hut or Pizza Inn, cheese, thin crust	12-13 in	8.19	4Q 92	4c
Transportation				
ACCRA Index, Transportation		107.90	4Q 92	4c
Tire balance, computer or spin balance, front	wheel	6.17	4Q 92	4c
Utilities				
ACCRA Index, Utilities		119.00	4Q 92	4c
Electricity, partial electric and other energy, 1,800 sq ft living area new home	month	77.96	4Q 92	4c

Hagerstown, MD

Item	Per	Value	Date	Ref.
Composite ACCRA index		100.80	4Q 92	4c
Alcoholic Beverages				
Beer, Miller Lite or Budweiser, 12-oz containers	6 pack	4.34	4Q 92	4c
Liquor, J & B Scotch	750 ml	15.53	4Q 92	4c
Wine, Gallo Chablis blanc, 1.5 liter	bottle	5.58	4Q 92	4c
Clothing				
Jeans, man's denim		33.35	4Q 92	4c
Shirt, man's dress shirt		25.19	4Q 92	4c
Undervest, boy's size 10-14, cotton	3	3.10	4Q 92	4c
Communications				
Long-distance telephone service, day, initial minute, 0-100 miles	min	0.25-0.54	91	12s
Long-distance telephone service, day, additional minute, 0-100 miles	min	0.10-0.37	91	12s
Long-distance telephone service, evenings/weekends, 0-100 mi, initial minute	min	0.10-0.22	91	12s
Long-distance telephone service, evenings/weekends, 0-100 mi, additional minute	min	0.04-0.15	91	12s
Newspaper subscription, daily and Sunday home delivery, large-city	month	9.25	4Q 92	4c
Telephone, flat rate	month	14.88	91	11c
Telephone bill, family of four	month	20.75	4Q 92	4c

Values are in dollars or fractions of dollars. In the column headed *Ref*, references are shown to sources. Each reference is followed by a letter. These refer to the geographical level for which data were reported: s = State, r = Region, and c = City or metro. The abbreviation *ex* is used to mean *except* or *excluding*; *exp* stands for *expenditures*. For other abbreviations and further explanations, please see the Introduction.

Hagerstown, MD - continued

Item	Per	Value	Date	Ref.
Education				
Board, 4-yr private college/university	year	2490	91	22s
Board, 4-yr public college/university	year	2139	91	22s
Expenditures, local gov't, public elementary/secondary	pupil	6314	92	20s
Room, 4-year private college/university	year	2610	91	22s
Room, 4-year public college/university	year	2365	91	22s
Tuition, 2-year private college/university	year	6101	91	22s
Tuition, 2-year public college/university	year	1244	91	22s
Tuition, 4-year private college/university	year	10698	91	22s
Tuition, 4-year public college/university, in-state	year	2287	91	22s
Energy and Fuels				
Coal	mil Btu	1.62	90	64s
Energy	mil Btu	9.40	90	64s
Energy, combined forms, 1,800 sq ft heating area	month	102.70	4Q 92	4c
Energy, exc electricity, 1,800 sq ft heating area	month	50.30	4Q 92	4c
Energy exp/householder, 1-family unit	year	487	90	28r
Energy exp/householder, <1,000 sq ft heating area	year	393	90	28r
Energy exp/householder, 1,000-1,999 sq ft heating area	year	442	90	28r
Energy exp/householder, 2,000+ sq ft heating area	year	577	90	28r
Energy exp/householder, mobile home	year	366	90	28r
Energy exp/householder, multifamily	year	382	90	28r
Gas, natural	mil Btu	5.07	90	64s
Gas, natural	000 cu ft	6.16	91	46s
Gas, natural, exp	year	545	91	46s
Gasoline, motor	gal	1.15	4Q 92	4c
Gasoline, unleaded regular	mil Btu	9.88	90	64s
Entertainment				
Bowling, evening rate	game	2.05	4Q 92	4c
Miniature golf admission	adult	6.18	92	1r
Miniature golf admission	child	5.14	92	1r
Monopoly game, Parker Brothers', No. 9		11.45	4Q 92	4c
Movie	admission	5.50	4Q 92	4c
Tennis balls, yellow, Wilson or Penn, 3	can	2.27	4Q 92	4c
Waterpark admission	adult	11.00	92	1r
Waterpark admission	child	8.55	92	1r
Funerals				
Casket, 18-gauge steel, velvet interior		2029.08	91	24r
Cosmetology, hair care, etc.		75.10	91	24r
Embalming		249.24	91	24r
Facility use for ceremony		162.27	91	24r
Hearse, local		114.04	91	24r
Limousine, local		88.57	91	24r
Remains to funeral home, transfer		92.61	91	24r
Service charge, professional		682.42	91	24r
Vault, concrete, non-metallic liner		798.70	91	24r
Viewing facilities, use		163.86	91	24r
Goods and Services				
ACCRA Index, Miscellaneous Goods and Services		98.80	4Q 92	4c
Groceries				
ACCRA Index, Groceries		91.60	4Q 92	4c
Babyfood, strained vegetables, lowest price	4-4.5 oz jar	0.31	4Q 92	4c
Bananas	lb	0.41	4Q 92	4c
Bread, white	24 oz	0.65	4Q 92	4c
Cheese, Kraft grated Parmesan	8-oz canister	3.10	4Q 92	4c
Chicken, fryer, whole	lb	0.65	4Q 92	4c
Cigarettes, Winston	carton	18.48	4Q 92	4c

Hagerstown, MD - continued

Item	Per	Value	Date	Ref.
Groceries - continued				
Coffee, vacuum-packed	13-oz can	1.84	4Q 92	4c
Corn, frozen	10 oz	0.54	4Q 92	4c
Corn Flakes, Kellogg's or Post Toasties	18 oz	1.88	4Q 92	4c
Eggs, Grade A large	doz	0.79	4Q 92	4c
Ground beef or hamburger	lb	1.35	4Q 92	4c
Lettuce, iceberg	head	0.88	4Q 92	4c
Margarine, Blue Bonnet or Parkay cubes	lb	0.64	4Q 92	4c
Milk, whole	1/2 gal	1.03	4Q 92	4c
Orange juice, Minute Maid frozen	12-oz can	1.26	4Q 92	4c
Peaches	29-oz can	1.18	4Q 92	4c
Peas Sweet, Del Monte or Green Giant	15-17 oz can	0.48	4Q 92	4c
Potatoes, white or red	10-lb sack	1.39	4Q 92	4c
Sausage, Jimmy Dean, 100% pork	lb	2.36	4Q 92	4c
Shortening, vegetable, Crisco	3-lb can	2.19	4Q 92	4c
Soft drink, Coca Cola	2 liter	1.05	4Q 92	4c
Steak, T-bone	lb	4.93	4Q 92	4c
Sugar, cane or beet	4 lb	1.40	4Q 92	4c
Tomatoes, Hunt's or Del Monte	14.5-oz can	0.69	4Q 92	4c
Tuna, chunk, light	6.125-6.5 oz can	0.57	4Q 92	4c
Health Care				
ACCRA Index, Health Care		99.80	4Q 92	4c
Analgesic, Aspirin, Bayer, 325 mg tablets	100	5.13	4Q 92	4c
Dentist's fee, adult teeth cleaning and periodic oral exam	visit	45.57	4Q 92	4c
Doctor's fee, routine exam, established patient	visit	37.30	4Q 92	4c
Hospital care, semiprivate room	day	320.00	4Q 92	4c
Medical insurance premium, per employee, small group comprehensive	month	317.55	10/91	25c
Medical plan per employee	year	3495	91	45r
Mental health care, exp	capita	53.68-118.35	90	38s
Mental health care, exp, state mental health agency	capita	61.28	90	38s
Mental health care, hospital psychiatric services, non-Federal, exp	capita	10.31	88	38s
Mental health care, mental health organization, multiservice, exp	capita	10.94	88	38s
Mental health care, psychiatric hospitals, private, exp	capita	15.34	88	38s
Mental health care, psychiatric out-patient clinics, freestanding, exp	capita	7.16	88	38s
Mental health care, psychiatric partial-care organizations, freestanding, exp	capita	0.36	88	38s
Mental health care, state and county mental hospitals, exp	capita	38.11	88	38s
Mental health care, VA medical centers, exp	capita	4.16	88	38s
Prescription drug co-pay, Medicaid	month	5.00	91	21s
Substance abuse, hospital ancillary charge	incident	770	90	70s
Substance abuse, hospital physician charge	incident	300	90	70s
Substance abuse, hospital room and board	incident	4470	90	70s
Household Goods				
Appliance repair, home, service call, washing machine	min labor charge	35.82	4Q 92	4c
Laundry detergent, Tide Ultra, Bold, or Cheer	42 oz	3.19	4Q 92	4c

Values are in dollars or fractions of dollars. In the column headed *Ref*, references are shown to sources. Each reference is followed by a letter. These refer to the geographical level for which data were reported: s=State, r=Region, and c=City or metro. The abbreviation *ex* is used to mean *except* or *excluding*; *exp* stands for *expenditures*. For other abbreviations and further explanations, please see the Introduction.

Hagerstown, MD - continued

Item	Per	Value	Date	Ref.
Household Goods				
Tissues, facial, Kleenex brand	175-count box	1.10	4Q 92	4c
Housing				
ACCRA Index, Housing		111.80	4Q 92	4c
House, 1,800 sq ft, 8,000 sq ft lot, new, urban	total	130031	4Q 92	4c
House payment, principal and interest, 25% down payment	month	720	4Q 92	4c
Mortgage rate, incl. points & origination fee, 30-year fixed or adjustable rate	percent	8.06	4Q 92	4c
Rent, apartment, 2 bedrooms - 1-1/2 to 2 baths, unfurnished, 950 sq ft, water	month	476	4Q 92	4c
Rental unit, 1 bedroom	month	400	93	23c
Rental unit, 2 bedroom	month	472	93	23c
Rental unit, 3 bedroom	month	591	93	23c
Rental unit, 4 bedroom	month	660	93	23c
Rental unit, efficiency	month	329	93	23c
Insurance and Pensions				
Auto insurance, private passenger	year	744.88	91	63s
Personal Goods				
Shampoo, Alberto VO5	15 oz	1.13	4Q 92	4c
Toothpaste, Crest or Colgate	6-7 oz	1.92	4Q 92	4c
Personal Services				
Dry cleaning, man's 2-piece suit		5.83	4Q 92	4c
Haircare, woman's shampoo, trim and blow-dry		16.20	4Q 92	4c
Haircut, man's barbershop, no styling		4.58	4Q 92	4c
Restaurant Food				
Chicken, fried, thigh and drumstick		2.33	4Q 92	4c
Hamburger with cheese	1/4 lb	1.73	4Q 92	4c
Pizza, Pizza Hut or Pizza Inn, cheese, thin crust	12-13 in	8.79	4Q 92	4c
Taxes				
Tax, cigarette	pack	36	91	77s
Tax, gasoline	gal	23.50	91	77s
Taxes, state	capita	1317	91	77s
Transportation				
ACCRA Index, Transportation		94.90	4Q 92	4c
Driver's license fee		6.00	12/90	43s
Tire balance, computer or spin balance, front	wheel	5.72	4Q 92	4c
Utilities				
ACCRA Index, Utilities		95.30	4Q 92	4c
Electricity	mil Btu	18.47	90	64s
Electricity, partial electric and other energy, 1,800 sq ft living area new home	month	52.40	4Q 92	4c

Hamilton, OH

Item	Per	Value	Date	Ref.
Child Care				
Child care fee, average, center	hour	1.63	90	65r
Child care fee, average, nonregulated family day care	hour	1.83	90	65r
Child care fee, average, regulated family day care	hour	1.42	90	65r
Communications				
Long-distance telephone service, day, initial minute, 0-100 miles	min	0.26-0.43	91	12s
Long-distance telephone service, day, additional minute, 0-100 miles	min	0.14-0.24	91	12s
Long-distance telephone service, evenings/weekends, 0-100 mi, initial minute	min	0.11-0.17	91	12s
Long-distance telephone service, evenings/weekends, 0-100 mi, additional minute	min	0.06-0.10	91	12s

Hamilton, OH - continued

Item	Per	Value	Date	Ref.
Education				
Board, 4-yr private college/university	year	1872	91	22s
Board, 4-yr public college/university	year	1742	91	22s
Expenditures, local gov't, public elementary/secondary	pupil	5451	92	20s
Room, 4-year private college/university	year	1695	91	22s
Room, 4-year public college/university	year	2259	91	22s
Tuition, 2-year private college/university	year	6093	91	22s
Tuition, 2-year public college/university	year	1768	91	22s
Tuition, 4-year private college/university	year	8729	91	22s
Tuition, 4-year public college/university, in-state	year	2622	91	22s
Energy and Fuels				
Coal	mil Btu	1.54	90	64s
Energy	mil Btu	8.32	90	64s
Energy exp/householder, 1-family unit	year	471	90	28r
Energy exp/householder, <1,000 sq ft heating area	year	430	90	28r
Energy exp/householder, 1,000-1,999 sq ft heating area	year	481	90	28r
Energy exp/householder, 2,000+ sq ft heating area	year	473	90	28r
Energy exp/householder, mobile home	year	430	90	28r
Energy exp/householder, multifamily	year	461	90	28r
Gas, natural	mil Btu	4.54	90	64s
Gas, natural	000 cu ft	5.28	91	46s
Gas, natural, exp	year	606	91	46s
Gasoline, unleaded regular	mil Btu	9.35	90	64s
Entertainment				
Miniature golf admission	adult	6.18	92	1r
Miniature golf admission	child	5.14	92	1r
Waterpark admission	adult	11.00	92	1r
Waterpark admission	child	8.55	92	1r
Funerals				
Casket, 18-gauge steel, velvet interior		1926.72	91	24r
Cosmetology, hair care, etc.		97.64	91	24r
Embalming		249.14	91	24r
Facility use for ceremony		208.59	91	24r
Hearse, local		130.12	91	24r
Limousine, local		104.66	91	24r
Remains to funeral home, transfer		93.61	91	24r
Service charge, professional		724.62	91	24r
Vault, concrete, non-metallic liner		734.53	91	24r
Viewing facilities, use		236.06	91	24r
Groceries				
Apples, Red Delicious	lb	0.77	4/93	16r
Bacon	lb	1.85	4/93	16r
Bananas	lb	0.46	4/93	16r
Beef, stew, boneless	lb	2.53	4/93	16r
Bologna, all beef or mixed	lb	2.19	4/93	16r
Bread, white, pan	lb	0.78	4/93	16r
Butter	lb	1.50	4/93	16r
Cabbage	lb	0.40	4/93	16r
Carrots, short trimmed and topped	lb	0.45	4/93	16r
Cheese, Cheddar	lb	3.47	4/93	16r
Chicken, fresh, whole	lb	0.84	4/93	16r
Chicken breast, bone-in	lb	1.94	4/93	16r
Chicken legs, bone-in	lb	1.02	4/93	16r
Chuck roast, graded and ungraded, ex USDA prime and choice	lb	2.43	4/93	16r
Chuck roast, USDA choice, bone-in	lb	2.11	4/93	16r
Chuck roast, USDA choice, boneless	lb	2.44	4/93	16r
Coffee, 100% ground roast, all sizes	lb	2.47	4/93	16r
Cookies, chocolate chip	lb	2.73	4/93	16r
Eggs, Grade A large	doz	0.93	4/93	16r
Flour, white, all purpose	lb	0.21	4/93	16r
Grapefruit	lb	0.45	4/93	16r
Grapes, Thompson Seedless	lb	1.46	4/93	16r
Ground beef, 100% beef	lb	1.63	4/93	16r
Ground beef, lean and extra lean	lb	2.08	4/93	16r

Values are in dollars or fractions of dollars. In the column headed *Ref*, references are shown to sources. Each reference is followed by a letter. These refer to the geographical level for which data were reported: s = State, r = Region, and c = City or metro. The abbreviation *ex* is used to mean *except* or *excluding*; *exp* stands for *expenditures*. For other abbreviations and further explanations, please see the Introduction.

Hamilton, OH - continued

Item	Per	Value	Date	Ref.
Groceries				
Ground chuck, 100% beef	lb	1.94	4/93	16r
Ham, boneless, excluding canned	lb	2.21	4/93	16r
Honey, jar	8 oz	0.97-1.25	92	5r
Honey, jar	lb	1.25-2.25	92	5r
Honey, squeeze bear	12-oz	1.25-1.99	92	5r
Ice cream, prepackaged, bulk, regular	1/2 gal	2.41	4/93	16r
Lemons	lb	0.82	4/93	16r
Lettuce, iceberg	lb	0.83	4/93	16r
Margarine, stick	lb	0.77	4/93	16r
Oranges, navel	lb	0.50	4/93	16r
Peanut butter, creamy, all sizes	lb	1.82	4/93	16r
Pears, Anjou	lb	0.85	4/93	16r
Pork chops, center cut, bone-in	lb	3.17	4/93	16r
Potato chips	16 oz	2.68	4/93	16r
Potatoes, white	lb	0.26	4/93	16r
Round roast, graded & ungraded, ex USDA prime & choice	lb	2.88	4/93	16r
Round roast, USDA choice, boneless	lb	2.96	4/93	16r
Shortening, vegetable oil blends	lb	0.79	4/93	16r
Spaghetti and macaroni	lb	0.76	4/93	16r
Steak, rib eye, USDA choice, boneless	lb	6.29	4/93	16r
Steak, round, USDA choice, boneless	lb	3.24	4/93	16r
Steak, sirloin, graded & ungraded, ex USDA prime & choice	lb	4.00	4/93	16r
Steak, sirloin, USDA choice, bone-in	lb	3.57	4/93	16r
Steak, sirloin, USDA choice, boneless	lb	4.17	4/93	16r
Steak, T-bone, USDA choice, bone-in	lb	5.60	4/93	16r
Strawberries, dry pint	12 oz	0.90	4/93	16r
Sugar, white	lb	0.36	4/93	16r
Sugar, white, 33-80 oz pk	lb	0.35	4/93	16r
Tomatoes, field grown	lb	0.99	4/93	16r
Tuna, chunk, light	lb	1.76	4/93	16r
Turkey, frozen, whole	lb	0.91	4/93	16r
Health Care				
Childbirth, cesarean, hospital		4688	91	62r
Childbirth, cesarean, physician's fee		2053	91	62r
Childbirth, normal, hospital		2657	91	62r
Childbirth, normal, physician's fee		1492	91	62r
Medical plan per employee	year	3443	91	45r
Mental health care, exp	capita	37.60-53.67	90	38s
Mental health care, exp, state mental health agency	capita	40.93	90	38s
Mental health care, hospital psychiatric services, non-Federal, exp	capita	15.03	88	38s
Mental health care, mental health organization, multiservice, exp	capita	14.46	88	38s
Mental health care, psychiatric hospitals, private, exp	capita	7.93	88	38s
Mental health care, psychiatric out-patient clinics, freestanding, exp	capita	2.93	88	38s
Mental health care, psychiatric partial-care organizations, freestanding, exp	capita	0.32	88	38s
Mental health care, state and county mental hospitals, exp	capita	23.79	88	38s
Mental health care, VA medical centers, exp	capita	7.76	88	38s
Physician fee, family practice, first-visit		76.00	91	62r
Physician fee, family practice, revisit		33.00	91	62r
Physician fee, general practice, first-visit		61.00	91	62r
Physician fee, general practice, revisit		31.00	91	62r
Physician fee, general surgeon, first-visit		65.00	91	62r
Physician fee, general surgeon, revisit		35.00	91	62r
Physician fee, internal medicine, first-visit		91.00	91	62r
Physician fee, internal medicine, revisit		40.00	91	62r
Physician fee, median, neurosurgeon, first-visit		106.00	91	62r

Hamilton, OH - continued

Item	Per	Value	Date	Ref.
Health Care - continued				
Physician fee, median, nonsurgical specialist, first-visit		90.00	91	62r
Physician fee, median, orthopedic surgeon, first-visit		83.00	91	62r
Physician fee, median, surgical specialist, first-visit		61.00	91	62r
Physician fee, neurosurgeon, revisit		41.00	91	62r
Physician fee, nonsurgical specialist, revisit		40.00	91	62r
Physician fee, obstetrics/gynecology, first-visit		61.00	91	62r
Physician fee, obstetrics/gynecology, revisit		40.00	91	62r
Physician fee, orthopedic surgeon, revisit		41.00	91	62r
Physician fee, pediatrician, first-visit		46.00	91	62r
Physician fee, pediatrician, revisit		33.00	91	62r
Physician fee, surgical specialist, revisit		36.00	91	62r
Substance abuse, hospital ancillary charge	incident	940	90	70s
Substance abuse, hospital physician charge	incident	380	90	70s
Substance abuse, hospital room and board	incident	5410	90	70s
Insurance and Pensions				
Auto insurance, private passenger	year	547.38	91	63s
Taxes				
Tax, cigarette	pack	18	91	77s
Tax, gasoline	gal	21	91	77s
Taxes, state	capita	1056	91	77s
Transportation				
Driver's license fee		5.00	12/90	43s
Utilities				
Electricity	mil Btu	17.33	90	64s

Hampton Roads, VA

Item	Per	Value	Date	Ref.
Composite ACCRA index		103.90	4Q 92	4c
Alcoholic Beverages				
Beer, Miller Lite or Budweiser, 12-oz containers	6 pack	3.66	4Q 92	4c
Liquor, J & B Scotch	750 ml	16.95	4Q 92	4c
Wine, Gallo Chablis blanc, 1.5 liter	bottle	5.58	4Q 92	4c
Clothing				
Jeans, man's denim		32.79	4Q 92	4c
Shirt, man's dress shirt		24.40	4Q 92	4c
Undervest, boy's size 10-14, cotton	3	4.41	4Q 92	4c
Communications				
Newspaper subscription, daily and Sunday home delivery, large-city	month	9.16	4Q 92	4c
Telephone bill, family of four	month	22.17	4Q 92	4c
Energy and Fuels				
Energy, combined forms, 1,800 sq ft heating area	month	132.62	4Q 92	4c
Gasoline, motor	gal	1.08	4Q 92	4c
Entertainment				
Bowling, evening rate	game	2.17	4Q 92	4c
Monopoly game, Parker Brothers', No. 9		11.51	4Q 92	4c
Movie	admission	5.45	4Q 92	4c
Tennis balls, yellow, Wilson or Penn, 3	can	2.97	4Q 92	4c
Goods and Services				
ACCRA Index, Miscellaneous Goods and Services		102.90	4Q 92	4c

Values are in dollars or fractions of dollars. In the column headed *Ref*, references are shown to sources. Each reference is followed by a letter. These refer to the geographical level for which data were reported: s=State, r=Region, and c=City or metro. The abbreviation *ex* is used to mean *except* or *excluding*; *exp* stands for expenditures. For other abbreviations and further explanations, please see the Introduction.

Hampton Roads, VA - continued

Item	Per	Value	Date	Ref.
Groceries				
ACCRA Index, Groceries		100.80	4Q 92	4c
Babyfood, strained vegetables, lowest price	4-4.5 oz jar	0.32	4Q 92	4c
Bananas	lb	0.46	4Q 92	4c
Bread, white	24 oz	0.84	4Q 92	4c
Cheese, Kraft grated Parmesan	8-oz canister	3.27	4Q 92	4c
Chicken, fryer, whole	lb	0.76	4Q 92	4c
Cigarettes, Winston	carton	16.10	4Q 92	4c
Coffee, vacuum-packed	13-oz can	2.15	4Q 92	4c
Corn, frozen	10 oz	0.54	4Q 92	4c
Corn Flakes, Kellogg's or Post Toasties	18 oz	1.78	4Q 92	4c
Eggs, Grade A large	doz	0.80	4Q 92	4c
Ground beef or hamburger	lb	1.42	4Q 92	4c
Lettuce, iceberg	head	0.93	4Q 92	4c
Margarine, Blue Bonnet or Parkay cubes	lb	0.58	4Q 92	4c
Milk, whole	1/2 gal	1.56	4Q 92	4c
Orange juice, Minute Maid frozen	12-oz can	1.37	4Q 92	4c
Peaches	29-oz can	1.38	4Q 92	4c
Peas Sweet, Del Monte or Green Giant	15-17 oz can	0.62	4Q 92	4c
Potatoes, white or red	10-lb sack	2.13	4Q 92	4c
Sausage, Jimmy Dean, 100% pork	lb	2.23	4Q 92	4c
Shortening, vegetable, Crisco	3-lb can	2.20	4Q 92	4c
Soft drink, Coca Cola	2 liter	0.99	4Q 92	4c
Steak, T-bone	lb	5.71	4Q 92	4c
Sugar, cane or beet	4 lb	1.78	4Q 92	4c
Tomatoes, Hunt's or Del Monte	14.5-oz can	0.59	4Q 92	4c
Tuna, chunk, light	6.125-6.5 oz can	0.66	4Q 92	4c
Health Care				
ACCRA Index, Health Care		90.70	4Q 92	4c
Analgesic, Aspirin, Bayer, 325 mg tablets	100	5.70	4Q 92	4c
Dentist's fee, adult teeth cleaning and periodic oral exam	visit	43.60	4Q 92	4c
Doctor's fee, routine exam, established patient	visit	32.60	4Q 92	4c
Hospital care, semiprivate room	day	242.25	4Q 92	4c
Household Goods				
Appliance repair, home, service call, washing machine	min labor charge	30.87	4Q 92	4c
Laundry detergent, Tide Ultra, Bold, or Cheer	42 oz	3.64	4Q 92	4c
Tissues, facial, Kleenex brand	175-count box	1.17	4Q 92	4c
Housing				
ACCRA Index, Housing		101.20	4Q 92	4c
House, 1,800 sq ft, 8,000 sq ft lot, new, urban	total	108400	4Q 92	4c
House payment, principal and interest, 25% down payment	month	589	4Q 92	4c
Mortgage rate, incl. points & origination fee, 30-year fixed or adjustable rate	percent	7.87	4Q 92	4c
Rent, apartment, 2 bedrooms - 1-1/2 to 2 baths, unfurnished, 950 sq ft, water	month	574	4Q 92	4c
Personal Goods				
Shampoo, Alberto VO5	15 oz	1.61	4Q 92	4c
Toothpaste, Crest or Colgate	6-7 oz	2.17	4Q 92	4c

Hampton Roads, VA - continued

Item	Per	Value	Date	Ref.
Personal Services				
Dry cleaning, man's 2-piece suit		7.01	4Q 92	4c
Haircare, woman's shampoo, trim and blow-dry		16.80	4Q 92	4c
Haircut, man's barbershop, no styling		7.00	4Q 92	4c
Restaurant Food				
Chicken, fried, thigh and drumstick		1.99	4Q 92	4c
Hamburger with cheese	1/4 lb	1.90	4Q 92	4c
Pizza, Pizza Hut or Pizza Inn, cheese, thin crust	12-13 in	7.59	4Q 92	4c
Transportation				
ACCRA Index, Transportation		110.90	4Q 92	4c
Bus fare, up to 10 miles	one-way	1.10	4Q 92	4c
Tire balance, computer or spin balance, front	wheel	7.97	4Q 92	4c
Utilities				
ACCRA Index, Utilities		120.70	4Q 92	4c
Electricity, all electric, 1,800 sq ft living area new home	month	132.62	4Q 92	4c

Hanover, PA

Item	Per	Value	Date	Ref.
Composite ACCRA index		103.70	4Q 92	4c
Alcoholic Beverages				
Beer, Miller Lite or Budweiser, 12-oz containers	6 pack	5.03	4Q 92	4c
Liquor, J & B Scotch	750 ml	16.39	4Q 92	4c
Wine, Gallo Chablis blanc, 1.5 liter	bottle	5.79	4Q 92	4c
Clothing				
Jeans, man's denim		30.66	4Q 92	4c
Shirt, man's dress shirt		19.33	4Q 92	4c
Undervest, boy's size 10-14, cotton	3	4.99	4Q 92	4c
Communications				
Newspaper subscription, daily and Sunday home delivery, large-city	month	8.70	4Q 92	4c
Telephone bill, family of four	month	14.11	4Q 92	4c
Energy and Fuels				
Energy, combined forms, 1,800 sq ft heating area	month	99.58	4Q 92	4c
Energy, exc electricity, 1,800 sq ft heating area	month	44.83	4Q 92	4c
Gasoline, motor	gal	1.09	4Q 92	4c
Entertainment				
Bowling, evening rate	game	2.00	4Q 92	4c
Monopoly game, Parker Brothers', No. 9		11.99	4Q 92	4c
Movie	admission	5.75	4Q 92	4c
Tennis balls, yellow, Wilson or Penn, 3	can	3.49	4Q 92	4c
Goods and Services				
ACCRA Index, Miscellaneous Goods and Services		103.90	4Q 92	4c
Groceries				
ACCRA Index, Groceries		106.80	4Q 92	4c
Babyfood, strained vegetables, lowest price	4-4.5 oz jar	0.37	4Q 92	4c
Bananas	lb	0.47	4Q 92	4c
Bread, white	24 oz	0.95	4Q 92	4c
Cheese, Kraft grated Parmesan	8-oz canister	3.24	4Q 92	4c
Chicken, fryer, whole	lb	0.75	4Q 92	4c
Cigarettes, Winston	carton	18.17	4Q 92	4c
Coffee, vacuum-packed	13-oz can	2.14	4Q 92	4c
Corn, frozen	10 oz	0.73	4Q 92	4c
Corn Flakes, Kellogg's or Post Toasties	18 oz	2.21	4Q 92	4c

Values are in dollars or fractions of dollars. In the column headed *Ref*, references are shown to sources. Each reference is followed by a letter. These refer to the geographical level for which data were reported: s = State, r = Region, and c = City or metro. The abbreviation *ex* is used to mean *except* or *excluding*; *exp* stands for expenditures. For other abbreviations and further explanations, please see the Introduction.

Hanover, PA - continued

Item	Per	Value	Date	Ref.
Groceries				
Eggs, Grade A large	doz	0.83	4Q 92	4c
Ground beef or hamburger	lb	1.68	4Q 92	4c
Lettuce, iceberg	head	0.85	4Q 92	4c
Margarine, Blue Bonnet or Parkay cubes	lb	0.75	4Q 92	4c
Milk, whole	1/2 gal	1.26	4Q 92	4c
Orange juice, Minute Maid frozen	12-oz can	1.62	4Q 92	4c
Peaches	29-oz can	1.35	4Q 92	4c
Peas Sweet, Del Monte or Green Giant	15-17 oz can	0.66	4Q 92	4c
Potatoes, white or red	10-lb sack	1.82	4Q 92	4c
Sausage, Jimmy Dean, 100% pork	lb	2.79	4Q 92	4c
Shortening, vegetable, Crisco	3-lb can	2.72	4Q 92	4c
Soft drink, Coca Cola	2 liter	1.16	4Q 92	4c
Steak, T-bone	lb	5.22	4Q 92	4c
Sugar, cane or beet	4 lb	1.67	4Q 92	4c
Tomatoes, Hunt's or Del Monte	14.5-oz can	0.80	4Q 92	4c
Tuna, chunk, light	6.125-6.5 oz can	0.74	4Q 92	4c
Health Care				
ACCRA Index, Health Care		95.10	4Q 92	4c
Analgesic, Aspirin, Bayer, 325 mg tablets	100	6.52	4Q 92	4c
Dentist's fee, adult teeth cleaning and periodic oral exam	visit	40.75	4Q 92	4c
Doctor's fee, routine exam, established patient	visit	34.25	4Q 92	4c
Hospital care, semiprivate room	day	299.00	4Q 92	4c
Household Goods				
Appliance repair, home, service call, washing machine	min labor charge	33.17	4Q 92	4c
Laundry detergent, Tide Ultra, Bold, or Cheer	42 oz	3.26	4Q 92	4c
Tissues, facial, Kleenex brand	175-count box	1.10	4Q 92	4c
Housing				
ACCRA Index, Housing		110.40	4Q 92	4c
House, 1,800 sq ft, 8,000 sq ft lot, new, urban	total	130600	4Q 92	4c
House payment, principal and interest, 25% down payment	month	742	4Q 92	4c
Mortgage rate, incl. points & origination fee, 30-year fixed or adjustable rate	percent	8.35	4Q 92	4c
Rent, apartment, 2 bedrooms - 1-1/2 to 2 baths, unfurnished, 950 sq ft, water	month	397	4Q 92	4c
Personal Goods				
Shampoo, Alberto VO5	15 oz	1.55	4Q 92	4c
Toothpaste, Crest or Colgate	6-7 oz	2.52	4Q 92	4c
Personal Services				
Dry cleaning, man's 2-piece suit		6.50	4Q 92	4c
Haircare, woman's shampoo, trim and blow-dry		14.60	4Q 92	4c
Haircut, man's barbershop, no styling		6.00	4Q 92	4c
Restaurant Food				
Chicken, fried, thigh and drumstick		2.22	4Q 92	4c
Hamburger with cheese	1/4 lb	1.85	4Q 92	4c
Pizza, Pizza Hut or Pizza Inn, cheese, thin crust	12-13 in	7.99	4Q 92	4c
Transportation				
ACCRA Index, Transportation		97.60	4Q 92	4c
Tire balance, computer or spin balance, front	wheel	6.42	4Q 92	4c

Hanover, PA - continued

Item	Per	Value	Date	Ref.
Utilities				
ACCRA Index, Utilities		89.30	4Q 92	4c
Electricity, partial electric and other energy, 1,800 sq ft living area new home	month	54.75	4Q 92	4c

Harlingen, TX

Item	Per	Value	Date	Ref.
Composite ACCRA index		92.70	4Q 92	4c
Alcoholic Beverages				
Beer, Miller Lite or Budweiser, 12-oz containers	6 pack	3.93	4Q 92	4c
Liquor, J & B Scotch	750 ml	17.49	4Q 92	4c
Wine, Gallo Chablis blanc, 1.5 liter	bottle	4.70	4Q 92	4c
Clothing				
Jeans, man's denim		29.29	4Q 92	4c
Shirt, man's dress shirt		23.50	4Q 92	4c
Undervest, boy's size 10-14, cotton	3	3.79	4Q 92	4c
Communications				
Newspaper subscription, daily and Sunday home delivery, large-city	month	7.00	4Q 92	4c
Telephone, flat rate	month	8.80	91	11c
Telephone bill, family of four	month	15.34	4Q 92	4c
Energy and Fuels				
Energy, combined forms, 1,800 sq ft heating area	month	136.51	4Q 92	4c
Gasoline, motor	gal	1.16	4Q 92	4c
Entertainment				
Bowling, evening rate	game	2.06	4Q 92	4c
Monopoly game, Parker Brothers', No. 9		9.86	4Q 92	4c
Movie	admission	5.00	4Q 92	4c
Tennis balls, yellow, Wilson or Penn, 3	can	1.97	4Q 92	4c
Goods and Services				
ACCRA Index, Miscellaneous Goods and Services		94.10	4Q 92	4c
Groceries				
ACCRA Index, Groceries		97.30	4Q 92	4c
Babyfood, strained vegetables, lowest price	4-4.5 oz jar	0.35	4Q 92	4c
Bananas	lb	0.17	4Q 92	4c
Bread, white	24 oz	0.59	4Q 92	4c
Cheese, Kraft grated Parmesan	8-oz canister	3.77	4Q 92	4c
Chicken, fryer, whole	lb	0.72	4Q 92	4c
Cigarettes, Winston	carton	19.09	4Q 92	4c
Coffee, vacuum-packed	13-oz can	1.91	4Q 92	4c
Corn, frozen	10 oz	0.66	4Q 92	4c
Corn Flakes, Kellogg's or Post Toasties	18 oz	2.00	4Q 92	4c
Eggs, Grade A large	doz	0.92	4Q 92	4c
Ground beef or hamburger	lb	1.55	4Q 92	4c
Lettuce, iceberg	head	0.72	4Q 92	4c
Margarine, Blue Bonnet or Parkay cubes	lb	0.58	4Q 92	4c
Milk, whole	1/2 gal	1.23	4Q 92	4c
Orange juice, Minute Maid frozen	12-oz can	1.67	4Q 92	4c
Peaches	29-oz can	1.38	4Q 92	4c
Peas Sweet, Del Monte or Green Giant	15-17 oz can	0.62	4Q 92	4c
Potatoes, white or red	10-lb sack	1.45	4Q 92	4c
Sausage, Jimmy Dean, 100% pork	lb	2.68	4Q 92	4c
Shortening, vegetable, Crisco	3-lb can	2.51	4Q 92	4c
Soft drink, Coca Cola	2 liter	1.56	4Q 92	4c
Steak, T-bone	lb	4.49	4Q 92	4c
Sugar, cane or beet	4 lb	1.60	4Q 92	4c

Values are in dollars or fractions of dollars. In the column headed *Ref*, references are shown to sources. Each reference is followed by a letter. These refer to the geographical level for which data were reported: s = State, r = Region, and c = City or metro. The abbreviation *ex* is used to mean *except* or *excluding*; *exp* stands for *expenditures*. For other abbreviations and further explanations, please see the Introduction.

Harlingen, TX - continued

Item	Per	Value	Date	Ref.
Groceries				
Tomatoes, Hunt's or Del Monte	14.5-oz can	0.66	4Q 92	4c
Tuna, chunk, light	6.125-6.5 oz can	0.61	4Q 92	4c
Health Care				
ACCRA Index, Health Care		93.60	4Q 92	4c
Analgesic, Aspirin, Bayer, 325 mg tablets	100	5.72	4Q 92	4c
Dentist's fee, adult teeth cleaning and periodic oral exam	visit	40.00	4Q 92	4c
Doctor's fee, routine exam, established patient	visit	35.67	4Q 92	4c
Hospital care, semiprivate room	day	290.00	4Q 92	4c
Household Goods				
Appliance repair, home, service call, washing machine	min labor charge	26.50	4Q 92	4c
Laundry detergent, Tide Ultra, Bold, or Cheer	42 oz	3.24	4Q 92	4c
Tissues, facial, Kleenex brand	175-count box	1.22	4Q 92	4c
Housing				
ACCRA Index, Housing		75.70	4Q 92	4c
House, 1,800 sq ft, 8,000 sq ft lot, new, urban	total	81000	4Q 92	4c
House payment, principal and interest, 25% down payment	month	440	4Q 92	4c
Mortgage rate, incl. points & origination fee, 30-year fixed or adjustable rate	per-cent	7.86	4Q 92	4c
Rent, apartment, 2 bedrooms - 1-1/2 to 2 baths, unfurnished, 950 sq ft, water	month	433	4Q 92	4c
Personal Goods				
Shampoo, Alberto VO5	15 oz	0.99	4Q 92	4c
Toothpaste, Crest or Colgate	6-7 oz	2.46	4Q 92	4c
Personal Services				
Dry cleaning, man's 2-piece suit		6.00	4Q 92	4c
Haircare, woman's shampoo, trim and blow-dry		21.83	4Q 92	4c
Haircut, man's barbershop, no styling		5.67	4Q 92	4c
Restaurant Food				
Chicken, fried, thigh and drumstick		1.84	4Q 92	4c
Hamburger with cheese	1/4 lb	2.09	4Q 92	4c
Pizza, Pizza Hut or Pizza Inn, cheese, thin crust	12-13 in	8.32	4Q 92	4c
Transportation				
ACCRA Index, Transportation		103.90	4Q 92	4c
Tire balance, computer or spin balance, front	wheel	6.83	4Q 92	4c
Utilities				
ACCRA Index, Utilities		120.40	4Q 92	4c
Electricity, all electric, 1,800 sq ft living area new home	month	136.51	4Q 92	4c

Harrisburg, PA

Item	Per	Value	Date	Ref.
Composite ACCRA index		103.90	4Q 92	4c
Alcoholic Beverages				
Beer, Miller Lite or Budweiser, 12-oz containers	6 pack	5.39	4Q 92	4c
Liquor, J & B Scotch	750 ml	16.39	4Q 92	4c
Wine, Gallo Chablis blanc, 1.5 liter	bottle	5.79	4Q 92	4c
Child Care				
Child care fee, average, center	hour	2.18	90	65r
Child care fee, average, nonregulated family day care	hour	1.83	90	65r

Harrisburg, PA - continued

Item	Per	Value	Date	Ref.
Child Care - continued				
Child care fee, average, regulated family day care	hour	2.02	90	65r
Clothing				
Jeans, man's denim		31.32	4Q 92	4c
Shirt, man's dress shirt		20.37	4Q 92	4c
Undervest, boy's size 10-14, cotton	3	4.62	4Q 92	4c
Communications				
Long-distance telephone service, day, initial minute, 0-100 miles	min	0.15-0.29	91	12s
Long-distance telephone service, day, additional minute, 0-100 miles	min	0.06-0.22	91	12s
Long-distance telephone service, evenings/ weekends, 0-100 mi, initial minute	min	0.06-0.14	91	12s
Long-distance telephone service, evenings/ weekends, 0-100 mi, additional minute	min	0.03-0.11	91	12s
Newspaper subscription, daily and Sunday home delivery, large-city	month	13.26	4Q 92	4c
Telephone bill, family of four	month	17.81	4Q 92	4c
Education				
Board, 4-yr private college/university	year	2019	91	22s
Board, 4-yr public college/university	year	1656	91	22s
Expenditures, local gov't, public elementary/secondary	pupil	6980	92	20s
Room, 4-year private college/university	year	2179	91	22s
Room, 4-year public college/university	year	1719	91	22s
Tuition, 2-year private college/university	year	6314	91	22s
Tuition, 2-year public college/university	year	1505	91	22s
Tuition, 4-year private college/university	year	9848	91	22s
Tuition, 4-year public college/university, in-state	year	3401	91	22s
Energy and Fuels				
Coal	mil Btu	1.57	90	64s
Energy	mil Btu	8.63	90	64s
Energy, combined forms, 1,800 sq ft heating area	month	134.59	4Q 92	4c
Energy exp/householder, 1-family unit	year	588	90	28r
Energy exp/householder, <1,000 sq ft heating area	year	477	90	28r
Energy exp/householder, 1,000-1,999 sq ft heating area	year	517	90	28r
Energy exp/householder, 2,000+ sq ft heating area	year	630	90	28r
Energy exp/householder, mobile home	year	412	90	28r
Energy exp/householder, multifamily	year	498	90	28r
Gas, natural	mil Btu	5.24	90	64s
Gas, natural	000 cu ft	6.76	91	46s
Gas, natural, exp	year	703	91	46s
Gasoline, motor	gal	1.10	4Q 92	4c
Gasoline, unleaded regular	mil Btu	9.35	90	64s
Entertainment				
Bowling, evening rate	game	2.11	4Q 92	4c
Monopoly game, Parker Brothers', No. 9		10.78	4Q 92	4c
Movie	admission	4.92	4Q 92	4c
Tennis balls, yellow, Wilson or Penn, 3	can	2.72	4Q 92	4c
Funerals				
Casket, 18-gauge steel, velvet interior		1811.58	91	24r
Cosmetology, hair care, etc.		111.08	91	24r
Embalming		329.42	91	24r
Facility use for ceremony		201.29	91	24r
Hearse, local		135.27	91	24r
Limousine, local		127.24	91	24r
Remains to funeral home, transfer		103.98	91	24r
Service charge, professional		724.98	91	24r
Vault, concrete, non-metallic liner		766.71	91	24r
Viewing facilities, use		260.60	91	24r

Values are in dollars or fractions of dollars. In the column headed *Ref*, references are shown to sources. Each reference is followed by a letter. These refer to the geographical level for which data were reported: s=State, r=Region, and c=City or metro. The abbreviation *ex* is used to mean *except* or *excluding*; *exp* stands for expenditures. For other abbreviations and further explanations, please see the Introduction.

Harrisburg, PA - continued

Item	Per	Value	Date	Ref.
Goods and Services				
ACCRA Index, Miscellaneous Goods and Services		102.40	4Q 92	4c
Groceries				
ACCRA Index, Groceries		96.60	4Q 92	4c
Apples, Red Delicious	lb	0.85	4/93	16r
Babyfood, strained vegetables, lowest price	4-4.5 oz jar	0.35	4Q 92	4c
Bacon	lb	2.12	4/93	16r
Bananas	lb	0.40	4Q 92	4c
Bananas	lb	0.54	4/93	16r
Bread, white	24 oz	0.83	4Q 92	4c
Bread, white, pan	lb	0.81	4/93	16r
Butter	lb	2.02	4/93	16r
Carrots, short trimmed and topped	lb	0.51	4/93	16r
Cheese, Kraft grated Parmesan	8-oz canister	2.91	4Q 92	4c
Chicken, fresh, whole	lb	1.04	4/93	16r
Chicken, fryer, whole	lb	0.60	4Q 92	4c
Chicken breast, bone-in	lb	2.21	4/93	16r
Chicken legs, bone-in	lb	1.16	4/93	16r
Chuck roast, USDA choice, boneless	lb	2.82	4/93	16r
Cigarettes, Winston	carton	17.74	4Q 92	4c
Coffee, 100% ground roast, all sizes	lb	2.66	4/93	16r
Coffee, vacuum-packed	13-oz can	1.84	4Q 92	4c
Corn, frozen	10 oz	0.57	4Q 92	4c
Corn Flakes, Kellogg's or Post Toasties	18 oz	2.01	4Q 92	4c
Cucumbers	lb	0.85	4/93	16r
Eggs, Grade A large	doz	0.74	4Q 92	4c
Eggs, Grade A large	doz	1.15	4/93	16r
Grapefruit	lb	0.45	4/93	16r
Grapes, Thompson Seedless	lb	1.52	4/93	16r
Ground beef, lean and extra lean	lb	2.36	4/93	16r
Ground beef or hamburger	lb	1.33	4Q 92	4c
Ground chuck, 100% beef	lb	2.02	4/93	16r
Honey, jar	8 oz	0.96-1.75	92	5r
Honey, jar	lb	1.50-3.00	92	5r
Honey, squeeze bear	12-oz	1.50-1.99	92	5r
Ice cream, prepackaged, bulk, regular	1/2 gal	2.80	4/93	16r
Lemons	lb	0.96	4/93	16r
Lettuce, iceberg	head	0.97	4Q 92	4c
Lettuce, iceberg	lb	0.95	4/93	16r
Margarine, Blue Bonnet or Parkay cubes	lb	0.66	4Q 92	4c
Margarine, stick	lb	0.81	4/93	16r
Milk, fresh, whole, fortified	1/2 gal	1.30	4/93	16r
Milk, whole	1/2 gal	1.22	4Q 92	4c
Orange juice, Minute Maid frozen	12-oz can	1.30	4Q 92	4c
Oranges, navel	lb	0.56	4/93	16r
Peaches	29-oz can	1.28	4Q 92	4c
Peanut butter, creamy, all sizes	lb	1.88	4/93	16r
Peas Sweet, Del Monte or Green Giant	15-17 oz can	0.54	4Q 92	4c
Pork chops, center cut, bone-in	lb	3.34	4/93	16r
Potato chips	16 oz	2.88	4/93	16r
Potatoes, white	lb	0.37	4/93	16r
Potatoes, white or red	10-lb sack	2.33	4Q 92	4c
Rib roast, USDA choice, bone-in	lb	4.94	4/93	16r
Round roast, USDA choice, boneless	lb	3.17	4/93	16r
Sausage, Jimmy Dean, 100% pork	lb	2.95	4Q 92	4c
Shortening, vegetable oil blends	lb	0.98	4/93	16r
Shortening, vegetable, Crisco	3-lb can	2.26	4Q 92	4c
Soft drink, Coca Cola	2 liter	0.97	4Q 92	4c
Spaghetti and macaroni	lb	0.82	4/93	16r
Steak, round, graded & ungraded, ex USDA prime & choice	lb	4.04	4/93	16r
Steak, round, USDA choice, boneless	lb	3.90	4/93	16r
Steak, sirloin, USDA choice, boneless	lb	4.97	4/93	16r

Harrisburg, PA - continued

Item	Per	Value	Date	Ref.
Groceries - continued				
Steak, T-bone	lb	4.67	4Q 92	4c
Strawberries, dry pint	12 oz	0.90	4/93	16r
Sugar, cane or beet	4 lb	1.52	4Q 92	4c
Sugar, white	lb	0.50	4/93	16r
Sugar, white, 33-80 oz pk	lb	0.41	4/93	16r
Tomatoes, field grown	lb	1.23	4/93	16r
Tomatoes, Hunt's or Del Monte	14.5-oz can	0.75	4Q 92	4c
Tuna, chunk, light	6.125-6.5 oz can	0.62	4Q 92	4c
Tuna, chunk, light	lb	2.22	4/93	16r
Turkey, frozen, whole	lb	1.04	4/93	16r
Health Care				
ACCRA Index, Health Care		99.30	4Q 92	4c
Analgesic, Aspirin, Bayer, 325 mg tablets	100	5.27	4Q 92	4c
Childbirth, cesarean, hospital		5826	91	62r
Childbirth, cesarean, physician's fee		2053	91	62r
Childbirth, normal, hospital		2964	91	62r
Childbirth, normal, physician's fee		1492	91	62r
Dentist's fee, adult teeth cleaning and periodic oral exam	visit	44.60	4Q 92	4c
Doctor's fee, routine exam, established patient	visit	29.00	4Q 92	4c
Hospital care, semiprivate room	day	352.81	90	27c
Hospital care, semiprivate room	day	456.25	4Q 92	4c
Medical insurance premium, per employee, small group comprehensive	month	222.20	10/91	25c
Medical plan per employee	year	3942	91	45r
Mental health care, exp	capita	53.68-118.35	90	38s
Mental health care, exp, state mental health agency	capita	56.85	90	38s
Mental health care, hospital psychiatric services, non-Federal, exp	capita	22.11	88	38s
Mental health care, mental health organization, multiservice, exp	capita	21.01	88	38s
Mental health care, psychiatric hospitals, private, exp	capita	26.48	88	38s
Mental health care, psychiatric out-patient clinics, freestanding, exp	capita	4.17	88	38s
Mental health care, psychiatric partial-care organizations, freestanding, exp	capita	0.94	88	38s
Mental health care, state and county mental hospitals, exp	capita	37.11	88	38s
Mental health care, VA medical centers, exp	capita	9.77	88	38s
Prescription drug co-pay, Medicaid	month	6.00	91	21s
Substance abuse, hospital ancillary charge	incident	720	90	70s
Substance abuse, hospital physician charge	incident	210	90	70s
Substance abuse, hospital room and board	incident	5400	90	70s
Household Goods				
Appliance repair, home, service call, washing machine	min labor charge	31.75	4Q 92	4c
Laundry detergent, Tide Ultra, Bold, or Cheer	42 oz	2.77	4Q 92	4c
Tissues, facial, Kleenex brand	175-count box	1.12	4Q 92	4c
Housing				
ACCRA Index, Housing		100.60	4Q 92	4c
House, 1,800 sq ft, 8,000 sq ft lot, new, urban	total	111100	4Q 92	4c
House payment, principal and interest, 25% down payment	month	602	4Q 92	4c
Mortgage rate, incl. points & origination fee, 30-year fixed or adjustable rate	percent	7.84	4Q 92	4c

Values are in dollars or fractions of dollars. In the column headed *Ref*, references are shown to sources. Each reference is followed by a letter. These refer to the geographical level for which data were reported: s = State, r = Region, and c = City or metro. The abbreviation *ex* is used to mean *except* or *excluding*; *exp* stands for expenditures. For other abbreviations and further explanations, please see the Introduction.

Harrisburg, PA - continued

Item	Per	Value	Date	Ref.
Housing				
Rent, apartment, 2 bedrooms - 1-1/2 to 2 baths, unfurnished, 950 sq ft, water	month	534	4Q 92	4c
Rental unit, 1 bedroom	month	484	93	23c
Rental unit, 2 bedroom	month	572	93	23c
Rental unit, 3 bedroom	month	714	93	23c
Rental unit, 4 bedroom	month	799	93	23c
Rental unit, efficiency	month	403	93	23c
Insurance and Pensions				
Auto insurance, private passenger	year	683.57	91	63s
Personal Goods				
Shampoo, Alberto VO5	15 oz	1.40	4Q 92	4c
Toothpaste, Crest or Colgate	6-7 oz	2.36	4Q 92	4c
Personal Services				
Dry cleaning, man's 2-piece suit		6.32	4Q 92	4c
Haircare, woman's shampoo, trim and blow-dry		18.30	4Q 92	4c
Haircut, man's barbershop, no styling		6.90	4Q 92	4c
Restaurant Food				
Chicken, fried, thigh and drumstick		2.19	4Q 92	4c
Hamburger with cheese	1/4 lb	1.91	4Q 92	4c
Pizza, Pizza Hut or Pizza Inn, cheese, thin crust	12-13 in	7.99	4Q 92	4c
Taxes				
Tax, cigarette	pack	31	91	77s
Tax, gasoline	gal	12	91	77s
Taxes, state	capita	1089	91	77s
Transportation				
ACCRA Index, Transportation		116.00	4Q 92	4c
Bus fare	one-way	0.90	3/93	2c
Bus fare, up to 10 miles	one-way	1.15	4Q 92	4c
Driver's license fee		22.00	12/90	43s
Tire balance, computer or spin balance, front	wheel	8.49	4Q 92	4c
Travel				
Business travel	day	165.00	4/93	89r
Utilities				
ACCRA Index, Utilities		120.10	4Q 92	4c
Electricity	mil Btu	22.46	90	64s
Electricity, all electric, 1,800 sq ft living area new home	month	134.59	4Q 92	4c

Hartford, CT

Item	Per	Value	Date	Ref.
Child Care				
Child care fee, average, center	hour	2.18	90	65r
Child care fee, average, nonregulated family day care	hour	1.83	90	65r
Child care fee, average, regulated family day care	hour	2.02	90	65r
Communications				
Long-distance telephone service, day, initial minute, 0-100 miles	min	0.18-0.45	91	12s
Long-distance telephone service, day, additional minute, 0-100 miles	min	0.10-0.26	91	12s
Long-distance telephone service, evenings/weekends, 0-100 mi, initial minute	min	0.07-0.18	91	12s
Long-distance telephone service, evenings/weekends, 0-100 mi, additional minute	min	0.04-0.10	91	12s
Telephone, flat rate	month	12.79	91	11c
Education				
Board, 4-yr private college/university	year	2182	91	22s
Board, 4-yr public college/university	year	1750	91	22s
Expenditures, local gov't, public elementary/secondary	pupil	8308	92	20s

Hartford, CT - continued

Item	Per	Value	Date	Ref.
Education - continued				
Room, 4-year private college/university	year	2703	91	22s
Room, 4-year public college/university	year	1913	91	22s
Tuition, 2-year private college/university	year	8586	91	22s
Tuition, 2-year public college/university	year	972	91	22s
Tuition, 4-year private college/university	year	12315	91	22s
Tuition, 4-year public college/university, in-state	year	2313	91	22s
Energy and Fuels				
Coal	mil Btu	2.15	90	64s
Energy	mil Btu	11.62	90	64s
Energy exp/householder, 1-family unit	year	588	90	28r
Energy exp/householder, <1,000 sq ft heating area	year	477	90	28r
Energy exp/householder, 1,000-1,999 sq ft heating area	year	517	90	28r
Energy exp/householder, 2,000+ sq ft heating area	year	630	90	28r
Energy exp/householder, mobile home	year	412	90	28r
Energy exp/householder, multifamily	year	498	90	28r
Gas, cooking, 10 therms	month	15.03	92	56c
Gas, cooking, 30 therms	month	32.09	92	56c
Gas, cooking, 50 therms	month	49.15	92	56c
Gas, heating, winter, 100 therms	month	85.21	92	56c
Gas, heating, winter, average use	month	152.36	92	56c
Gas, natural	mil Btu	6.40	90	64s
Gas, natural	000 cu ft	8.74	91	46s
Gas, natural, exp	year	756	91	46s
Gasoline, unleaded regular	mil Btu	10.06	90	64s
Entertainment				
Miniature golf admission	adult	6.18	92	1r
Miniature golf admission	child	5.14	92	1r
Waterpark admission	adult	11.00	92	1r
Waterpark admission	child	8.55	92	1r
Funerals				
Casket, 18-gauge steel, velvet interior		1853.42	91	24r
Cosmetology, hair care, etc.		98.33	91	24r
Embalming		273.94	91	24r
Facility use for ceremony		196.06	91	24r
Hearse, local		145.67	91	24r
Limousine, local		131.07	91	24r
Remains to funeral home, transfer		135.24	91	24r
Service charge, professional		843.16	91	24r
Vault, concrete, non-metallic liner		709.14	91	24r
Viewing facilities, use		229.85	91	24r
Groceries				
Apples, Red Delicious	lb	0.85	4/93	16r
Bacon	lb	2.12	4/93	16r
Bananas	lb	0.54	4/93	16r
Bread, white, pan	lb	0.81	4/93	16r
Butter	lb	2.02	4/93	16r
Carrots, short trimmed and topped	lb	0.51	4/93	16r
Chicken, fresh, whole	lb	1.04	4/93	16r
Chicken breast, bone-in	lb	2.21	4/93	16r
Chicken legs, bone-in	lb	1.16	4/93	16r
Chuck roast, USDA choice, boneless	lb	2.82	4/93	16r
Coffee, 100% ground roast, all sizes	lb	2.66	4/93	16r
Cucumbers	lb	0.85	4/93	16r
Eggs, Grade A large	doz	1.15	4/93	16r
Grapefruit	lb	0.45	4/93	16r
Grapes, Thompson Seedless	lb	1.52	4/93	16r
Ground beef, lean and extra lean	lb	2.36	4/93	16r
Ground chuck, 100% beef	lb	2.02	4/93	16r
Honey, jar	8 oz	0.96-1.75	92	5r
Honey, jar	lb	1.50-3.00	92	5r
Honey, squeeze bear	12-oz	1.50-1.99	92	5r
Ice cream, prepackaged, bulk, regular	1/2 gal	2.80	4/93	16r
Lemons	lb	0.96	4/93	16r
Lettuce, iceberg	lb	0.95	4/93	16r
Margarine, stick	lb	0.81	4/93	16r

Values are in dollars or fractions of dollars. In the column headed *Ref*, references are shown to sources. Each reference is followed by a letter. These refer to the geographical level for which data were reported: s=State, r=Region, and c=City or metro. The abbreviation *ex* is used to mean *except* or *excluding*; *exp* stands for expenditures. For other abbreviations and further explanations, please see the Introduction.

Hartford, CT - continued

Item	Per	Value	Date	Ref.
Groceries				
Milk, fresh, whole, fortified	1/2 gal	1.30	4/93	16r
Oranges, navel	lb	0.56	4/93	16r
Peanut butter, creamy, all sizes	lb	1.88	4/93	16r
Pork chops, center cut, bone-in	lb	3.34	4/93	16r
Potato chips	16 oz	2.88	4/93	16r
Potatoes, white	lb	0.37	4/93	16r
Rib roast, USDA choice, bone-in	lb	4.94	4/93	16r
Round roast, USDA choice, boneless	lb	3.17	4/93	16r
Shortening, vegetable oil blends	lb	0.98	4/93	16r
Spaghetti and macaroni	lb	0.82	4/93	16r
Steak, round, graded & ungraded, ex USDA prime & choice	lb	4.04	4/93	16r
Steak, round, USDA choice, boneless	lb	3.90	4/93	16r
Steak, sirloin, USDA choice, boneless	lb	4.97	4/93	16r
Strawberries, dry pint	12 oz	0.90	4/93	16r
Sugar, white	lb	0.50	4/93	16r
Sugar, white, 33-80 oz pk	lb	0.41	4/93	16r
Tomatoes, field grown	lb	1.23	4/93	16r
Tuna, chunk, light	lb	2.22	4/93	16r
Turkey, frozen, whole	lb	1.04	4/93	16r
Health Care				
Childbirth, cesarean, hospital		5826	91	62r
Childbirth, cesarean, physician's fee		2053	91	62r
Childbirth, normal, hospital		2964	91	62r
Childbirth, normal, physician's fee		1492	91	62r
Hospital care, semiprivate room	day	379.58	90	27c
Medical insurance premium, per employee, small group comprehensive	month	349.45	10/91	25c
Medical plan per employee	year	3958	91	45r
Mental health care, exp	capita	53.68-118.35	90	38s
Mental health care, exp, state mental health agency	capita	72.81	90	38s
Mental health care, hospital psychiatric services, non-Federal, exp	capita	19.30	88	38s
Mental health care, mental health organization, multiservice, exp	capita	19.14	88	38s
Mental health care, psychiatric hospitals, private, exp	capita	35.86	88	38s
Mental health care, psychiatric out-patient clinics, freestanding, exp	capita	5.83	88	38s
Mental health care, psychiatric partial-care organizations, freestanding, exp	capita	0.15	88	38s
Mental health care, state and county mental hospitals, exp	capita	51.85	88	38s
Mental health care, VA medical centers, exp	capita	1.74	88	38s
Prescription drug co-pay, Medicaid	month	10.00	91	21s
Substance abuse, hospital ancillary charge	incident	1200	90	70s
Substance abuse, hospital physician charge	incident	270	90	70s
Substance abuse, hospital room and board	incident	4420	90	70s
Housing				
Home, median price	unit	141.10		26c
Rental unit, 1 bedroom	month	609	93	23c
Rental unit, 2 bedroom	month	713	93	23c
Rental unit, 3 bedroom	month	898	93	23c
Rental unit, 4 bedroom	month	1002	93	23c
Rental unit, efficiency	month	500	93	23c
Insurance and Pensions				
Auto insurance, private passenger	year	928.10	91	63s
Taxes				
Tax, cigarette	pack	45	91	77s
Tax, gasoline	gal	26	91	77s
Taxes, state	capita	1514	91	77s
Transportation				
Auto rental, average	day	46.00	6/91	60c

Hartford, CT - continued

Item	Per	Value	Date	Ref.
Transportation - continued				
Bus fare	one-way	1.00	3/93	2c
Driver's license fee		31.00	12/90	43s
Limo fare, airport-city, average	day	8.00	6/91	60c
Taxi fare, airport-city, average	day	21.00	6/91	60c
Travel				
Breakfast	day	6.28	6/91	60c
Business travel	day	165.00	4/93	89r
Dinner	day	24.65	6/91	60c
Lodging	day	109.00	91	60c
Lunch	day	9.23	6/91	60c
Utilities				
Electricity	mil Btu	26.83	90	64s
Electricity, winter, 250 KWh	month	33.60	92	55c
Electricity, winter, 500 KWh	month	58.85	92	55c
Electricity, winter, 750 KWh	month	84.12	92	55c
Electricity, winter, 1000 KWh	month	109.37	92	55c

Hastings, NE

Item	Per	Value	Date	Ref.
Composite ACCRA index		88.00	4Q 92	4c
Alcoholic Beverages				
Beer, Miller Lite or Budweiser, 12-oz containers	6 pack	3.99	4Q 92	4c
Liquor, J & B Scotch	750 ml	17.73	4Q 92	4c
Wine, Gallo Chablis blanc, 1.5 liter	bottle	5.84	4Q 92	4c
Clothing				
Jeans, man's denim		26.29	4Q 92	4c
Shirt, man's dress shirt		18.23	4Q 92	4c
Undervest, boy's size 10-14, cotton	3	3.68	4Q 92	4c
Communications				
Newspaper subscription, daily and Sunday home delivery, large-city	month	8.70	4Q 92	4c
Telephone bill, family of four	month	17.48	4Q 92	4c
Energy and Fuels				
Energy, combined forms, 1,800 sq ft heating area	month	84.45	4Q 92	4c
Energy, exc electricity, 1,800 sq ft heating area	month	36.07	4Q 92	4c
Gasoline, motor	gal	1.18	4Q 92	4c
Entertainment				
Bowling, evening rate	game	1.75	4Q 92	4c
Monopoly game, Parker Brothers', No. 9		9.14	4Q 92	4c
Movie	admission	4.95	4Q 92	4c
Tennis balls, yellow, Wilson or Penn, 3	can	2.21	4Q 92	4c
Goods and Services				
ACCRA Index, Miscellaneous Goods and Services		90.10	4Q 92	4c
Groceries				
ACCRA Index, Groceries		104.60	4Q 92	4c
Babyfood, strained vegetables, lowest price	4-4.5 oz jar	0.37	4Q 92	4c
Bananas	lb	0.48	4Q 92	4c
Bread, white	24 oz	1.04	4Q 92	4c
Cheese, Kraft grated Parmesan	8-oz canister	3.35	4Q 92	4c
Chicken, fryer, whole	lb	0.76	4Q 92	4c
Cigarettes, Winston	carton	17.72	4Q 92	4c
Coffee, vacuum-packed	13-oz can	1.98	4Q 92	4c
Corn, frozen	10 oz	0.63	4Q 92	4c
Corn Flakes, Kellogg's or Post Toasties	18 oz	1.98	4Q 92	4c
Eggs, Grade A large	doz	0.70	4Q 92	4c
Ground beef or hamburger	lb	1.46	4Q 92	4c
Lettuce, iceberg	head	0.98	4Q 92	4c

Values are in dollars or fractions of dollars. In the column headed *Ref*, references are shown to sources. Each reference is followed by a letter. These refer to the geographical level for which data were reported: s=State, r=Region, and c=City or metro. The abbreviation *ex* is used to mean *except* or *excluding*; *exp* stands for expenditures. For other abbreviations and further explanations, please see the Introduction.

Item	Per	Value	Date	Ref.
Groceries				
Margarine, Blue Bonnet or Parkay cubes	lb	0.58	4Q 92	4c
Milk, whole	1/2 gal	1.37	4Q 92	4c
Orange juice, Minute Maid frozen	12-oz can	1.50	4Q 92	4c
Peaches	29-oz can	1.39	4Q 92	4c
Peas Sweet, Del Monte or Green Giant	15-17 oz can	0.50	4Q 92	4c
Potatoes, white or red	10-lb sack	1.82	4Q 92	4c
Sausage, Jimmy Dean, 100% pork	lb	3.12	4Q 92	4c
Shortening, vegetable, Crisco	3-lb can	2.61	4Q 92	4c
Soft drink, Coca Cola	2 liter	1.37	4Q 92	4c
Steak, T-bone	lb	4.62	4Q 92	4c
Sugar, cane or beet	4 lb	1.38	4Q 92	4c
Tomatoes, Hunt's or Del Monte	14.5-oz can	0.75	4Q 92	4c
Tuna, chunk, light	6.125-6.5 oz can	0.58	4Q 92	4c
Health Care				
ACCRA Index, Health Care		82.30	4Q 92	4c
Analgesic, Aspirin, Bayer, 325 mg tablets	100	4.09	4Q 92	4c
Dentist's fee, adult teeth cleaning and periodic oral exam	visit	41.33	4Q 92	4c
Doctor's fee, routine exam, established patient	visit	29.60	4Q 92	4c
Hospital care, semiprivate room	day	191.24	90	27c
Hospital care, semiprivate room	day	239.00	4Q 92	4c
Household Goods				
Appliance repair, home, service call, washing machine	min labor charge	29.00	4Q 92	4c
Laundry detergent, Tide Ultra, Bold, or Cheer	42 oz	4.06	4Q 92	4c
Tissues, facial, Kleenex brand	175-count box	1.00	4Q 92	4c
Housing				
ACCRA Index, Housing		80.70	4Q 92	4c
House, 1,800 sq ft, 8,000 sq ft lot, new, urban	total	90421	4Q 92	4c
House payment, principal and interest, 25% down payment	month	503	4Q 92	4c
Mortgage rate, incl. points & origination fee, 30-year fixed or adjustable rate	percent	8.12	4Q 92	4c
Rent, apartment, 2 bedrooms - 1-1/2 to 2 baths, unfurnished, 950 sq ft, water	month	382	4Q 92	4c
Personal Goods				
Shampoo, Alberto VO5	15 oz	1.08	4Q 92	4c
Toothpaste, Crest or Colgate	6-7 oz	1.64	4Q 92	4c
Personal Services				
Dry cleaning, man's 2-piece suit		7.28	4Q 92	4c
Haircare, woman's shampoo, trim and blow-dry		17.25	4Q 92	4c
Haircut, man's barbershop, no styling		7.33	4Q 92	4c
Restaurant Food				
Chicken, fried, thigh and drumstick		1.80	4Q 92	4c
Hamburger with cheese	1/4 lb	1.80	4Q 92	4c
Pizza, Pizza Hut or Pizza Inn, cheese, thin crust	12-13 in	7.49	4Q 92	4c
Transportation				
ACCRA Index, Transportation		90.70	4Q 92	4c
Tire balance, computer or spin balance, front	wheel	5.00	4Q 92	4c

Item	Per	Value	Date	Ref.
Utilities				
ACCRA Index, Utilities		78.60	4Q 92	4c
Electricity, partial electric and other energy, 1,800 sq ft living area new home	month	48.38	4Q 92	4c

Hattiesburg, MS

Item	Per	Value	Date	Ref.
Composite ACCRA index		94.80	4Q 92	4c
Alcoholic Beverages				
Beer, Miller Lite or Budweiser, 12-oz containers	6 pack	4.02	4Q 92	4c
Liquor, J & B Scotch	750 ml	15.77	4Q 92	4c
Wine, Gallo Chablis blanc, 1.5 liter	bottle	5.11	4Q 92	4c
Clothing				
Jeans, man's denim		38.75	4Q 92	4c
Shirt, man's dress shirt		27.50	4Q 92	4c
Undervest, boy's size 10-14, cotton	3	4.23	4Q 92	4c
Communications				
Newspaper subscription, daily and Sunday home delivery, large-city	month	9.00	4Q 92	4c
Telephone, flat rate	month	17.25	91	11c
Telephone bill, family of four	month	28.50	4Q 92	4c
Energy and Fuels				
Energy, combined forms, 1,800 sq ft heating area	month	110.10	4Q 92	4c
Gasoline, motor	gal	1.04	4Q 92	4c
Entertainment				
Bowling, evening rate	game	2.00	4Q 92	4c
Monopoly game, Parker Brothers', No. 9		11.68	4Q 92	4c
Movie	admission	5.38	4Q 92	4c
Tennis balls, yellow, Wilson or Penn, 3	can	2.47	4Q 92	4c
Goods and Services				
ACCRA Index, Miscellaneous Goods and Services		102.50	4Q 92	4c
Groceries				
ACCRA Index, Groceries		102.20	4Q 92	4c
Babyfood, strained vegetables, lowest price	4-4.5 oz jar	0.34	4Q 92	4c
Bananas	lb	0.47	4Q 92	4c
Bread, white	24 oz	0.87	4Q 92	4c
Cheese, Kraft grated Parmesan	8-oz canister	3.28	4Q 92	4c
Chicken, fryer, whole	lb	0.75	4Q 92	4c
Cigarettes, Winston	carton	17.00	4Q 92	4c
Coffee, vacuum-packed	13-oz can	2.02	4Q 92	4c
Corn, frozen	10 oz	0.70	4Q 92	4c
Corn Flakes, Kellogg's or Post Toasties	18 oz	1.76	4Q 92	4c
Eggs, Grade A large	doz	0.76	4Q 92	4c
Ground beef or hamburger	lb	1.50	4Q 92	4c
Lettuce, iceberg	head	1.08	4Q 92	4c
Margarine, Blue Bonnet or Parkay cubes	lb	0.64	4Q 92	4c
Milk, whole	1/2 gal	1.47	4Q 92	4c
Orange juice, Minute Maid frozen	12-oz can	1.54	4Q 92	4c
Peaches	29-oz can	1.35	4Q 92	4c
Peas Sweet, Del Monte or Green Giant	15-17 oz can	0.60	4Q 92	4c
Potatoes, white or red	10-lb sack	2.24	4Q 92	4c
Sausage, Jimmy Dean, 100% pork	lb	2.41	4Q 92	4c
Shortening, vegetable, Crisco	3-lb can	2.20	4Q 92	4c
Soft drink, Coca Cola	2 liter	1.26	4Q 92	4c
Steak, T-bone	lb	4.90	4Q 92	4c
Sugar, cane or beet	4 lb	1.54	4Q 92	4c

Values are in dollars or fractions of dollars. In the column headed *Ref*, references are shown to sources. Each reference is followed by a letter. These refer to the geographical level for which data were reported: s=State, r=Region, and c=City or metro. The abbreviation *ex* is used to mean *except* or *excluding*; *exp* stands for *expenditures*. For other abbreviations and further explanations, please see the Introduction.

Hattiesburg, MS - continued

Item	Per	Value	Date	Ref.
Groceries				
Tomatoes, Hunt's or Del Monte	14.5-oz can	0.75	4Q 92	4c
Tuna, chunk, light	6.125-6.5 oz can	0.58	4Q 92	4c
Health Care				
ACCRA Index, Health Care		89.20	4Q 92	4c
Analgesic, Aspirin, Bayer, 325 mg tablets	100	5.48	4Q 92	4c
Dentist's fee, adult teeth cleaning and periodic oral exam	visit	39.80	4Q 92	4c
Doctor's fee, routine exam, established patient	visit	36.70	4Q 92	4c
Hospital care, semiprivate room	day	208.00	4Q 92	4c
Household Goods				
Appliance repair, home, service call, washing machine	min labor charge	29.99	4Q 92	4c
Laundry detergent, Tide Ultra, Bold, or Cheer	42 oz	3.71	4Q 92	4c
Tissues, facial, Kleenex brand	175-count box	1.26	4Q 92	4c
Housing				
ACCRA Index, Housing		79.90	4Q 92	4c
House, 1,800 sq ft, 8,000 sq ft lot, new, urban	total	85360	4Q 92	4c
House payment, principal and interest, 25% down payment	month	479	4Q 92	4c
Mortgage rate, incl. points & origination fee, 30-year fixed or adjustable rate	per-cent	8.21	4Q 92	4c
Rent, apartment, 2 bedrooms - 1-1/2 to 2 baths, unfurnished, 950 sq ft, water	month	422	4Q 92	4c
Personal Goods				
Shampoo, Alberto VO5	15 oz	1.53	4Q 92	4c
Toothpaste, Crest or Colgate	6-7 oz	2.17	4Q 92	4c
Personal Services				
Dry cleaning, man's 2-piece suit		4.70	4Q 92	4c
Haircare, woman's shampoo, trim and blow-dry		19.00	4Q 92	4c
Haircut, man's barbershop, no styling		7.00	4Q 92	4c
Restaurant Food				
Chicken, fried, thigh and drumstick		1.67	4Q 92	4c
Hamburger with cheese	1/4 lb	1.85	4Q 92	4c
Pizza, Pizza Hut or Pizza Inn, cheese, thin crust	12-13 in	8.79	4Q 92	4c
Transportation				
ACCRA Index, Transportation		93.70	4Q 92	4c
Tire balance, computer or spin balance, front	wheel	6.21	4Q 92	4c
Utilities				
ACCRA Index, Utilities		105.40	4Q 92	4c
Electricity, all electric, 1,800 sq ft living area new home	month	110.10	4Q 92	4c

Hays, KS

Item	Per	Value	Date	Ref.
Composite ACCRA index		89.90	4Q 92	4c
Alcoholic Beverages				
Beer, Miller Lite or Budweiser, 12-oz containers	6 pack	3.90	4Q 92	4c
Liquor, J & B Scotch	750 ml	17.39	4Q 92	4c
Wine, Gallo Chablis blanc, 1.5 liter	bottle	5.09	4Q 92	4c
Clothing				
Jeans, man's denim		21.99	4Q 92	4c
Shirt, man's dress shirt		20.67	4Q 92	4c
Undervest, boy's size 10-14, cotton	3	4.99	4Q 92	4c

Hays, KS - continued

Item	Per	Value	Date	Ref.
Communications				
Newspaper subscription, daily and Sunday home delivery, large-city	month	12.83	4Q 92	4c
Telephone, flat rate	month	10.05	91	11c
Telephone bill, family of four	month	15.92	4Q 92	4c
Energy and Fuels				
Energy, combined forms, 1,800 sq ft heating area	month	107.45	4Q 92	4c
Energy, exc electricity, 1,800 sq ft heating area	month	30.70	4Q 92	4c
Gasoline, motor	gal	1.06	4Q 92	4c
Entertainment				
Bowling, evening rate	game	1.90	4Q 92	4c
Monopoly game, Parker Brothers', No. 9		10.72	4Q 92	4c
Movie	admis-sion	4.50	4Q 92	4c
Tennis balls, yellow, Wilson or Penn, 3	can	2.22	4Q 92	4c
Goods and Services				
ACCRA Index, Miscellaneous Goods and Services		95.10	4Q 92	4c
Groceries				
ACCRA Index, Groceries		92.10	4Q 92	4c
Babyfood, strained vegetables, lowest price	4-4.5 oz jar	0.29	4Q 92	4c
Bananas	lb	0.34	4Q 92	4c
Bread, white	24 oz	0.55	4Q 92	4c
Cheese, Kraft grated Parmesan	8-oz canis-ter	3.60	4Q 92	4c
Chicken, fryer, whole	lb	0.64	4Q 92	4c
Cigarettes, Winston	carton	17.36	4Q 92	4c
Coffee, vacuum-packed	13-oz can	1.81	4Q 92	4c
Corn, frozen	10 oz	0.66	4Q 92	4c
Corn Flakes, Kellogg's or Post Toasties	18 oz	2.15	4Q 92	4c
Eggs, Grade A large	doz	0.84	4Q 92	4c
Ground beef or hamburger	lb	1.31	4Q 92	4c
Lettuce, iceberg	head	0.94	4Q 92	4c
Margarine, Blue Bonnet or Parkay cubes	lb	0.40	4Q 92	4c
Milk, whole	1/2 gal	1.33	4Q 92	4c
Orange juice, Minute Maid frozen	12-oz can	1.42	4Q 92	4c
Peaches	29-oz can	1.00	4Q 92	4c
Peas Sweet, Del Monte or Green Giant	15-17 oz can	0.63	4Q 92	4c
Potatoes, white or red	10-lb sack	1.58	4Q 92	4c
Sausage, Jimmy Dean, 100% pork	lb	2.46	4Q 92	4c
Shortening, vegetable, Crisco	3-lb can	2.28	4Q 92	4c
Soft drink, Coca Cola	2 liter	0.91	4Q 92	4c
Steak, T-bone	lb	4.32	4Q 92	4c
Sugar, cane or beet	4 lb	1.69	4Q 92	4c
Tomatoes, Hunt's or Del Monte	14.5-oz can	0.70	4Q 92	4c
Tuna, chunk, light	6.125-6.5 oz can	0.69	4Q 92	4c
Health Care				
ACCRA Index, Health Care		82.30	4Q 92	4c
Analgesic, Aspirin, Bayer, 325 mg tablets	100	3.69	4Q 92	4c
Dentist's fee, adult teeth cleaning and periodic oral exam	visit	39.00	4Q 92	4c
Doctor's fee, routine exam, established patient	visit	28.67	4Q 92	4c
Hospital care, semiprivate room	day	185.00	90	27c
Hospital care, semiprivate room	day	300.00	4Q 92	4c

Values are in dollars or fractions of dollars. In the column headed *Ref*, references are shown to sources. Each reference is followed by a letter. These refer to the geographical level for which data were reported: s = State, r = Region, and c = City or metro. The abbreviation *ex* is used to mean *except* or *excluding*; *exp* stands for expenditures. For other abbreviations and further explanations, please see the Introduction.

Hays, KS - continued

Item	Per	Value	Date	Ref.
Household Goods				
Appliance repair, home, service call, washing machine	min labor charge	32.00	4Q 92	4c
Laundry detergent, Tide Ultra, Bold, or Cheer	42 oz	3.85	4Q 92	4c
Tissues, facial, Kleenex brand	175-count box	1.22	4Q 92	4c
Housing				
ACCRA Index, Housing		78.90	4Q 92	4c
House, 1,800 sq ft, 8,000 sq ft lot, new, urban	total	92750	4Q 92	4c
House payment, principal and interest, 25% down payment	month	513	4Q 92	4c
Mortgage rate, incl. points & origination fee, 30-year fixed or adjustable rate	per-cent	8.04	4Q 92	4c
Rent, apartment, 2 bedrooms - 1-1/2 to 2 baths, unfurnished, 950 sq ft, water	month	325	4Q 92	
Personal Goods				
Shampoo, Alberto VO5	15 oz	1.25	4Q 92	4c
Toothpaste, Crest or Colgate	6-7 oz	1.64	4Q 92	4c
Personal Services				
Dry cleaning, man's 2-piece suit		5.82	4Q 92	4c
Haircare, woman's shampoo, trim and blow-dry		10.00	4Q 92	4c
Haircut, man's barbershop, no styling		7.67	4Q 92	4c
Restaurant Food				
Chicken, fried, thigh and drumstick		2.49	4Q 92	4c
Hamburger with cheese	1/4 lb	1.84	4Q 92	4c
Pizza, Pizza Hut or Pizza Inn, cheese, thin crust	12-13 in	7.49	4Q 92	4c
Transportation				
ACCRA Index, Transportation		97.00	4Q 92	4c
Tire balance, computer or spin balance, front	wheel	6.50	4Q 92	4c
Utilities				
ACCRA Index, Utilities		96.80	4Q 92	4c
Electricity, partial electric and other energy, 1,800 sq ft living area new home	month	76.75	4Q 92	4c

Helena, MT

Item	Per	Value	Date	Ref.
Composite ACCRA index		100.00	4Q 92	4c
Alcoholic Beverages				
Beer, Miller Lite or Budweiser, 12-oz containers	6 pack	4.28	4Q 92	4c
Liquor, J & B Scotch	750 ml	18.10	4Q 92	4c
Wine, Gallo Chablis blanc, 1.5 liter	bottle	5.29	4Q 92	4c
Clothing				
Jeans, man's denim		26.31	4Q 92	4c
Shirt, man's dress shirt		19.93	4Q 92	4c
Undervest, boy's size 10-14, cotton	3	4.03	4Q 92	4c
Communications				
Newspaper subscription, daily and Sunday home delivery, large-city	month	11.25	4Q 92	4c
Telephone, flat rate	month	13.84	91	11c
Telephone bill, family of four	month	19.25	4Q 92	4c
Energy and Fuels				
Energy, combined forms, 1,800 sq ft heating area	month	102.15	4Q 92	4c
Energy, exc electricity, 1,800 sq ft heating area	month	56.15	4Q 92	4c
Gasoline, motor	gal	1.28	4Q 92	4c
Entertainment				
Bowling, evening rate	game	1.44	4Q 92	4c
Monopoly game, Parker Brothers', No. 9		11.15	4Q 92	4c

Helena, MT - continued

Item	Per	Value	Date	Ref.
Entertainment - continued				
Movie	admis-sion	5.00	4Q 92	4c
Tennis balls, yellow, Wilson or Penn, 3	can	2.45	4Q 92	4c
Goods and Services				
ACCRA Index, Miscellaneous Goods and Services		95.50	4Q 92	4c
Groceries				
ACCRA Index, Groceries		106.00	4Q 92	4c
Babyfood, strained vegetables, lowest price	4-4.5 oz jar	0.32	4Q 92	4c
Bananas	lb	0.45	4Q 92	4c
Bread, white	24 oz	0.92	4Q 92	4c
Cheese, Kraft grated Parmesan	8-oz canis-ter	3.37	4Q 92	4c
Chicken, fryer, whole	lb	0.55	4Q 92	4c
Cigarettes, Winston	carton	17.81	4Q 92	4c
Coffee, vacuum-packed	13-oz can	2.49	4Q 92	4c
Corn, frozen	10 oz	0.62	4Q 92	4c
Corn Flakes, Kellogg's or Post Toasties	18 oz	2.17	4Q 92	4c
Eggs, Grade A large	doz	0.91	4Q 92	4c
Ground beef or hamburger	lb	1.23	4Q 92	4c
Lettuce, iceberg	head	0.99	4Q 92	4c
Margarine, Blue Bonnet or Parkay cubes	lb	0.71	4Q 92	4c
Milk, whole	1/2 gal	1.47	4Q 92	4c
Orange juice, Minute Maid frozen	12-oz can	1.50	4Q 92	4c
Peaches	29-oz can	1.43	4Q 92	4c
Peas Sweet, Del Monte or Green Giant	15-17 oz can	0.66	4Q 92	4c
Potatoes, white or red	10-lb sack	2.09	4Q 92	4c
Sausage, Jimmy Dean, 100% pork	lb	3.40	4Q 92	4c
Shortening, vegetable, Crisco	3-lb can	2.35	4Q 92	4c
Soft drink, Coca Cola	2 liter	1.43	4Q 92	4c
Steak, T-bone	lb	4.87	4Q 92	4c
Sugar, cane or beet	4 lb	1.50	4Q 92	4c
Tomatoes, Hunt's or Del Monte	14.5-oz can	0.69	4Q 92	4c
Tuna, chunk, light	6.125-6.5 oz can	0.74	4Q 92	4c
Health Care				
ACCRA Index, Health Care		113.70	4Q 92	4c
Analgesic, Aspirin, Bayer, 325 mg tablets	100	6.04	4Q 92	4c
Dentist's fee, adult teeth cleaning and periodic oral exam	visit	54.33	4Q 92	4c
Doctor's fee, routine exam, established patient	visit	39.58	4Q 92	4c
Hospital care, semiprivate room	day	315.00	90	27c
Hospital care, semiprivate room	day	373.00	4Q 92	4c
Household Goods				
Appliance repair, home, service call, washing machine	min labor charge	27.67	4Q 92	4c
Laundry detergent, Tide Ultra, Bold, or Cheer	42 oz	4.19	4Q 92	4c
Tissues, facial, Kleenex brand	175-count box	1.24	4Q 92	4c
Housing				
ACCRA Index, Housing		101.70	4Q 92	4c
House, 1,800 sq ft, 8,000 sq ft lot, new, urban	total	118000	4Q 92	4c
House payment, principal and interest, 25% down payment	month	674	4Q 92	4c

Values are in dollars or fractions of dollars. In the column headed *Ref*, references are shown to sources. Each reference is followed by a letter. These refer to the geographical level for which data were reported: s = State, r = Region, and c = City or metro. The abbreviation *ex* is used to mean *except* or *excluding*; *exp* stands for *expenditures*. For other abbreviations and further explanations, please see the Introduction.

Helena, MT - continued

Item	Per	Value	Date	Ref.
Housing				
Mortgage rate, incl. points & origination fee, 30-year fixed or adjustable rate	per-cent	8.40	4Q 92	4c
Rent, apartment, 2 bedrooms - 1-1/2 to 2 baths, unfurnished, 950 sq ft, water	month	387	4Q 92	4c
Personal Goods				
Shampoo, Alberto VO5	15 oz	1.63	4Q 92	4c
Toothpaste, Crest or Colgate	6-7 oz	2.44	4Q 92	4c
Personal Services				
Dry cleaning, man's 2-piece suit		6.58	4Q 92	4c
Haircare, woman's shampoo, trim and blow-dry		15.17	4Q 92	4c
Haircut, man's barbershop, no styling		8.32	4Q 92	4c
Restaurant Food				
Chicken, fried, thigh and drumstick		2.10	4Q 92	4c
Hamburger with cheese	1/4 lb	1.92	4Q 92	4c
Pizza, Pizza Hut or Pizza Inn, cheese, thin crust	12-13 in	8.70	4Q 92	4c
Transportation				
ACCRA Index, Transportation		101.50	4Q 92	4c
Tire balance, computer or spin balance, front	wheel	5.83	4Q 92	4c
Utilities				
ACCRA Index, Utilities		94.10	4Q 92	4c
Electricity, partial electric and other energy, 1,800 sq ft living area new home	month	46.00	4Q 92	4c

Hickory, NC

Item	Per	Value	Date	Ref.
Composite ACCRA index		99.40	4Q 92	4c
Alcoholic Beverages				
Beer, Miller Lite or Budweiser, 12-oz containers	6 pack	3.70	4Q 92	4c
Liquor, J & B Scotch	750 ml	17.65	4Q 92	4c
Wine, Gallo Chablis blanc, 1.5 liter	bottle	4.76	4Q 92	4c
Child Care				
Child care fee, average, center	hour	1.29	90	65r
Child care fee, average, nonregulated family day care	hour	0.89	90	65r
Child care fee, average, regulated family day care	hour	1.32	90	65r
Clothing				
Jeans, man's denim		25.99	4Q 92	4c
Shirt, man's dress shirt		26.12	4Q 92	4c
Undervest, boy's size 10-14, cotton	3	3.91	4Q 92	4c
Communications				
Long-distance telephone service, day, initial minute, 0-100 miles	min	0.10-0.33	91	12s
Long-distance telephone service, day, additional minute, 0-100 miles	min	0.10-0.33	91	12s
Long-distance telephone service, evenings/ weekends, 0-100 mi, initial minute	min	0.08-0.24	91	12s
Long-distance telephone service, evenings/ weekends, 0-100 mi, additional minute	min	0.05-0.17	91	12s
Newspaper subscription, daily and Sunday home delivery, large-city	month	10.83	4Q 92	4c
Telephone bill, family of four	month	17.20	4Q 92	4c
Education				
Board, 4-yr private college/university	year	1768	91	22s
Board, 4-yr public college/university	year	1568	91	22s
Expenditures, local gov't, public elementary/secondary	pupil	5078	92	20s
Room, 4-year private college/university	year	1467	91	22s
Room, 4-year public college/university	year	1386	91	22s
Tuition, 2-year private college/university	year	4964	91	22s
Tuition, 2-year public college/university	year	334	91	22s
Tuition, 4-year private college/university	year	7826	91	22s

Hickory, NC - continued

Item	Per	Value	Date	Ref.
Education - continued				
Tuition, 4-year public college/university, in-state	year	1112	91	22s
Energy and Fuels				
Coal	mil Btu	1.79	90	64s
Energy	mil Btu	10.06	90	64s
Energy, combined forms, 1,800 sq ft heating area	month	119.35	4Q 92	4c
Energy exp/householder, 1-family unit	year	487	90	28r
Energy exp/householder, <1,000 sq ft heating area	year	393	90	28r
Energy exp/householder, 1,000-1,999 sq ft heating area	year	442	90	28r
Energy exp/householder, 2,000+ sq ft heating area	year	577	90	28r
Energy exp/householder, mobile home	year	366	90	28r
Energy exp/householder, multifamily	year	382	90	28r
Gas, natural	mil Btu	4.19	90	64s
Gas, natural	000 cu ft	6.24	91	46s
Gas, natural, exp	year	439	91	46s
Gasoline, motor	gal	1.09	4Q 92	4c
Gasoline, unleaded regular	mil Btu	9.44	90	64s
Entertainment				
Bowling, evening rate	game	2.60	4Q 92	4c
Miniature golf admission	adult	6.18	92	1r
Miniature golf admission	child	5.14	92	1r
Monopoly game, Parker Brothers', No. 9		10.73	4Q 92	4c
Movie	admission	5.50	4Q 92	4c
Tennis balls, yellow, Wilson or Penn, 3	can	2.08	4Q 92	4c
Waterpark admission	adult	11.00	92	1r
Waterpark admission	child	8.55	92	1r
Funerals				
Casket, 18-gauge steel, velvet interior		2029.08	91	24r
Cosmetology, hair care, etc.		75.10	91	24r
Embalming		249.24	91	24r
Facility use for ceremony		162.27	91	24r
Hearse, local		114.04	91	24r
Limousine, local		88.57	91	24r
Remains to funeral home, transfer		92.61	91	24r
Service charge, professional		682.42	91	24r
Vault, concrete, non-metallic liner		798.70	91	24r
Viewing facilities, use		163.86	91	24r
Goods and Services				
ACCRA Index, Miscellaneous Goods and Services		99.70	4Q 92	4c
Groceries				
ACCRA Index, Groceries		92.80	4Q 92	4c
Apples, Red Delicious	lb	0.79	4/93	16r
Babyfood, strained vegetables, lowest price	4-4.5 oz jar	0.31	4Q 92	4c
Bacon	lb	1.75	4/93	16r
Bananas	lb	0.46	4Q 92	4c
Bananas	lb	0.42	4/93	16r
Beef, stew, boneless	lb	2.61	4/93	16r
Bologna, all beef or mixed	lb	2.24	4/93	16r
Bread, white	24 oz	0.61	4Q 92	4c
Bread, white, pan	lb	0.64	4/93	16r
Bread, whole wheat, pan	lb	0.96	4/93	16r
Cabbage	lb	0.37	4/93	16r
Carrots, short trimmed and topped	lb	0.47	4/93	16r
Celery	lb	0.64	4/93	16r
Cheese, American	lb	2.98	4/93	16r
Cheese, Cheddar	lb	3.28	4/93	16r
Cheese, Kraft grated Parmesan	8-oz canister	3.25	4Q 92	4c
Chicken, fresh, whole	lb	0.77	4/93	16r
Chicken, fryer, whole	lb	0.81	4Q 92	4c

Values are in dollars or fractions of dollars. In the column headed *Ref*, references are shown to sources. Each reference is followed by a letter. These refer to the geographical level for which data were reported: s=State, r=Region, and c=City or metro. The abbreviation *ex* is used to mean *except* or *excluding*; *exp* stands for *expenditures*. For other abbreviations and further explanations, please see the Introduction.

Hickory, NC - continued

Item	Per	Value	Date	Ref.
Groceries				
Chicken breast, bone-in	lb	1.92	4/93	16r
Chicken legs, bone-in	lb	1.06	4/93	16r
Chuck roast, graded and ungraded, ex USDA prime and choice	lb	2.40	4/93	16r
Chuck roast, USDA choice, bone-in	lb	2.19	4/93	16r
Chuck roast, USDA choice, boneless	lb	2.38	4/93	16r
Cigarettes, Winston	carton	15.25	4Q 92	4c
Coffee, 100% ground roast, all sizes	lb	2.48	4/93	16r
Coffee, vacuum-packed	13-oz can	1.92	4Q 92	4c
Corn, frozen	10 oz	0.52	4Q 92	4c
Corn Flakes, Kellogg's or Post Toasties	18 oz	1.68	4Q 92	4c
Crackers, soda, salted	lb	1.15	4/93	16r
Eggs, Grade A large	doz	0.90	4Q 92	4c
Eggs, Grade A large	doz	0.96	4/93	16r
Flour, white, all purpose	lb	0.24	4/93	16r
Frankfurters, all meat or all beef	lb	2.01	4/93	16r
Grapefruit	lb	0.44	4/93	16r
Grapes, Thompson Seedless	lb	1.40	4/93	16r
Ground beef, 100% beef	lb	1.58	4/93	16r
Ground beef, lean and extra lean	lb	2.09	4/93	16r
Ground beef or hamburger	lb	1.55	4Q 92	4c
Ground chuck, 100% beef	lb	1.98	4/93	16r
Ham, boneless, excluding canned	lb	2.89	4/93	16r
Ham, picnic, shoulder, bone-in, smoked	lb	1.02	4/93	16r
Ham, rump or steak half, bone-in, smoked	lb	1.48	4/93	16r
Ice cream, prepackaged, bulk, regular	1/2 gal	2.41	4/93	16r
Lemons	lb	1.05	4/93	16r
Lettuce, iceberg	head	0.83	4Q 92	4c
Lettuce, iceberg	lb	0.81	4/93	16r
Margarine, Blue Bonnet or Parkay cubes	lb	0.47	4Q 92	4c
Margarine, stick	lb	0.88	4/93	16r
Milk, whole	1/2 gal	1.40	4Q 92	4c
Orange juice, Minute Maid frozen	12-oz can	1.16	4Q 92	4c
Oranges, navel	lb	0.55	4/93	16r
Peaches	29-oz can	1.30	4Q 92	4c
Pears, Anjou	lb	0.92	4/93	16r
Peas Sweet, Del Monte or Green Giant	15-17 oz can	0.46	4Q 92	4c
Pork chops, center cut, bone-in	lb	3.13	4/93	16r
Potato chips	16 oz	2.94	4/93	16r
Potatoes, white	lb	0.43	4/93	16r
Potatoes, white or red	10-lb sack	1.89	4Q 92	4c
Rib roast, USDA choice, bone-in	lb	4.63	4/93	16r
Rice, white, long grain, uncooked	lb	0.45	4/93	16r
Round roast, graded & ungraded, ex USDA prime & choice	lb	3.03	4/93	16r
Round roast, USDA choice, boneless	lb	3.09	4/93	16r
Sausage, fresh, loose	lb	2.08	4/93	16r
Sausage, Jimmy Dean, 100% pork	lb	1.96	4Q 92	4c
Short ribs, bone-in	lb	2.66	4/93	16r
Shortening, vegetable oil blends	lb	0.69	4/93	16r
Shortening, vegetable, Crisco	3-lb can	1.99	4Q 92	4c
Soft drink, Coca Cola	2 liter	1.22	4Q 92	4c
Spaghetti and macaroni	lb	0.81	4/93	16r
Steak, rib eye, USDA choice, boneless	lb	6.24	4/93	16r
Steak, round, graded & ungraded, ex USDA prime & choice	lb	3.31	4/93	16r
Steak, round, USDA choice, boneless	lb	3.34	4/93	16r
Steak, sirloin, graded & ungraded, ex USDA prime & choice	lb	4.19	4/93	16r
Steak, sirloin, USDA choice, boneless	lb	4.46	4/93	16r
Steak, T-bone	lb	5.67	4Q 92	4c
Steak, T-bone, USDA choice, bone-in	lb	5.25	4/93	16r
Strawberries, dry pint	12 oz	0.92	4/93	16r
Sugar, cane or beet	4 lb	1.57	4Q 92	4c
Sugar, white	lb	0.39	4/93	16r
Sugar, white, 33-80 oz pk	lb	0.38	4/93	16r

Hickory, NC - continued

Item	Per	Value	Date	Ref.
Groceries - continued				
Tomatoes, field grown	lb	0.88	4/93	16r
Tomatoes, Hunt's or Del Monte	14.5-oz can	0.48	4Q 92	4c
Tuna, chunk, light	6.125-6.5 oz can	0.52	4Q 92	4c
Tuna, chunk, light	lb	1.79	4/93	16r
Turkey, frozen, whole	lb	1.04	4/93	16r
Yogurt, natural, fruit flavored	1/2 pint	0.57	4/93	16r
Health Care				
ACCRA Index, Health Care		86.90	4Q 92	4c
Analgesic, Aspirin, Bayer, 325 mg tablets	100	4.33	4Q 92	4c
Childbirth, cesarean, hospital		5034	91	62r
Childbirth, cesarean, physician's fee		2053	91	62r
Childbirth, normal, hospital		2712	91	62r
Childbirth, normal, physician's fee		1492	91	62r
Dentist's fee, adult teeth cleaning and periodic oral exam	visit	40.00	4Q 92	4c
Doctor's fee, routine exam, established patient	visit	33.00	4Q 92	4c
Hospital care, semiprivate room	day	182.74	90	27c
Hospital care, semiprivate room	day	270.00	4Q 92	4c
Medical insurance premium, per employee, small group comprehensive	month	273.75	10/91	25c
Medical plan per employee	year	3495	91	45r
Mental health care, exp	capita	37.60-53.67	90	38s
Mental health care, exp, state mental health agency	capita	45.66	90	38s
Mental health care, hospital psychiatric services, non-Federal, exp	capita	12.05	88	38s
Mental health care, mental health organization, multiservice, exp	capita	29.54	88	38s
Mental health care, psychiatric hospitals, private, exp	capita	15.07	88	38s
Mental health care, psychiatric out-patient clinics, freestanding, exp	capita	0.11	88	38s
Mental health care, state and county mental hospitals, exp	capita	26.36	88	38s
Mental health care, VA medical centers, exp	capita	2.23	88	38s
Physician fee, family practice, first-visit		75.00	91	62r
Physician fee, family practice, revisit		34.00	91	62r
Physician fee, general practice, first-visit		61.00	91	62r
Physician fee, general practice, revisit		32.00	91	62r
Physician fee, general surgeon, first-visit		64.00	91	62r
Physician fee, general surgeon, revisit		40.00	91	62r
Physician fee, internal medicine, first-visit		98.00	91	62r
Physician fee, internal medicine, revisit		40.00	91	62r
Physician fee, median, neurosurgeon, first-visit		130.00	91	62r
Physician fee, median, nonsurgical specialist, first-visit		95.00	91	62r
Physician fee, median, orthopedic surgeon, first-visit		91.00	91	62r
Physician fee, median, plastic surgeon, first-visit		66.00	91	62r
Physician fee, median, surgical specialist, first-visit		62.00	91	62r
Physician fee, neurosurgeon, revisit		50.00	91	62r
Physician fee, nonsurgical specialist, revisit		40.00	91	62r
Physician fee, obstetrics/gynecology, first-visit		64.00	91	62r
Physician fee, obstetrics/gynecology, revisit		41.00	91	62r
Physician fee, orthopedic surgeon, revisit		40.00	91	62r
Physician fee, pediatrician, first-visit		49.00	91	62r
Physician fee, pediatrician, revisit		33.00	91	62r
Physician fee, plastic surgeon, revisit		43.00	91	62r
Physician fee, surgical specialist, revisit		37.00	91	62r
Substance abuse, hospital ancillary charge	incident	1090	90	70s

Values are in dollars or fractions of dollars. In the column headed *Ref*, references are shown to sources. Each reference is followed by a letter. These refer to the geographical level for which data were reported: s = State, r = Region, and c = City or metro. The abbreviation *ex* is used to mean *except* or *excluding*; *exp* stands for expenditures. For other abbreviations and further explanations, please see the Introduction.

Hickory, NC - continued

Item	Per	Value	Date	Ref.
Health Care				
Substance abuse, hospital physician charge	incident	460	90	70s
Substance abuse, hospital room and board	incident	4880	90	70s
Household Goods				
Appliance repair, home, service call, washing machine	min labor charge	36.50	4Q 92	4c
Laundry detergent, Tide Ultra, Bold, or Cheer	42 oz	2.60	4Q 92	4c
Tissues, facial, Kleenex brand	175-count box	1.00	4Q 92	4c
Housing				
ACCRA Index, Housing		107.20	4Q 92	4c
House, 1,800 sq ft, 8,000 sq ft lot, new, urban	total	124000	4Q 92	4c
House payment, principal and interest, 25% down payment	month	691	4Q 92	4c
Mortgage rate, incl. points & origination fee, 30-year fixed or adjustable rate	percent	8.13	4Q 92	4c
Rent, apartment, 2 bedrooms - 1-1/2 to 2 baths, unfurnished, 950 sq ft, water	month	455	4Q 92	4c
Rental unit, 1 bedroom	month	369	93	23c
Rental unit, 2 bedroom	month	437	93	23c
Rental unit, 3 bedroom	month	547	93	23c
Rental unit, 4 bedroom	month	615	93	23c
Rental unit, efficiency	month	305	93	23c
Insurance and Pensions				
Auto insurance, private passenger	year	522.39	91	63s
Personal Goods				
Shampoo, Alberto VO5	15 oz	1.05	4Q 92	4c
Toothpaste, Crest or Colgate	6-7 oz	1.85	4Q 92	4c
Personal Services				
Dry cleaning, man's 2-piece suit		5.49	4Q 92	4c
Haircare, woman's shampoo, trim and blow-dry		17.25	4Q 92	4c
Haircut, man's barbershop, no styling		8.06	4Q 92	4c
Restaurant Food				
Chicken, fried, thigh and drumstick		2.30	4Q 92	4c
Hamburger with cheese	1/4 lb	1.79	4Q 92	4c
Pizza, Pizza Hut or Pizza Inn, cheese, thin crust	12-13 in	7.59	4Q 92	4c
Taxes				
Tax, cigarette	pack	5	91	77s
Tax, gasoline	gal	21.90	91	77s
Taxes, state	capita	1165	91	77s
Transportation				
ACCRA Index, Transportation		84.70	4Q 92	4c
Driver's license fee		15.00	12/90	43s
Tire balance, computer or spin balance, front	wheel	4.74	4Q 92	4c
Vehicle registration and license plate	year	35.00	93	50s
Travel				
Business travel	day	193.00	4/93	89r
Utilities				
ACCRA Index, Utilities		107.20	4Q 92	4c
Electricity	mil Btu	18.74	90	64s
Electricity, all electric, 1,800 sq ft living area new home	month	119.35	4Q 92	4c

Hobbs, NM

Item	Per	Value	Date	Ref.
Composite ACCRA index		89.00	4Q 92	4c
Alcoholic Beverages				
Beer, Miller Lite or Budweiser, 12-oz containers	6 pack	3.49	4Q 92	4c
Liquor, J & B Scotch	750 ml	16.85	4Q 92	4c
Wine, Gallo Chablis blanc, 1.5 liter	bottle	4.78	4Q 92	4c
Clothing				
Jeans, man's denim		27.83	4Q 92	4c
Shirt, man's dress shirt		20.98	4Q 92	4c
Undervest, boy's size 10-14, cotton	3	4.37	4Q 92	4c
Communications				
Newspaper subscription, daily and Sunday home delivery, large-city	month	8.67	4Q 92	4c
Telephone bill, family of four	month	20.76	4Q 92	4c
Energy and Fuels				
Energy, combined forms, 1,800 sq ft heating area	month	86.15	4Q 92	4c
Energy, exc electricity, 1,800 sq ft heating area	month	26.21	4Q 92	4c
Gasoline, motor	gal	1.19	4Q 92	4c
Entertainment				
Bowling, evening rate	game	1.55	4Q 92	4c
Monopoly game, Parker Brothers', No. 9		10.47	4Q 92	4c
Movie	admission	5.00	4Q 92	4c
Tennis balls, yellow, Wilson or Penn, 3	can	2.61	4Q 92	4c
Goods and Services				
ACCRA Index, Miscellaneous Goods and Services		95.90	4Q 92	4c
Groceries				
ACCRA Index, Groceries		98.30	4Q 92	4c
Babyfood, strained vegetables, lowest price	4-4.5 oz jar	0.35	4Q 92	4c
Bananas	lb	0.37	4Q 92	4c
Bread, white	24 oz	0.72	4Q 92	4c
Cheese, Kraft grated Parmesan	8-oz canister	3.82	4Q 92	4c
Chicken, fryer, whole	lb	0.62	4Q 92	4c
Cigarettes, Winston	carton	17.12	4Q 92	4c
Coffee, vacuum-packed	13-oz can	2.05	4Q 92	4c
Corn, frozen	10 oz	0.76	4Q 92	4c
Corn Flakes, Kellogg's or Post Toasties	18 oz	2.11	4Q 92	4c
Eggs, Grade A large	doz	0.89	4Q 92	4c
Ground beef or hamburger	lb	0.99	4Q 92	4c
Lettuce, iceberg	head	0.99	4Q 92	4c
Margarine, Blue Bonnet or Parkay cubes	lb	0.70	4Q 92	4c
Milk, whole	1/2 gal	1.47	4Q 92	4c
Orange juice, Minute Maid frozen	12-oz can	1.62	4Q 92	4c
Peaches	29-oz can	1.41	4Q 92	4c
Peas Sweet, Del Monte or Green Giant	15-17 oz can	0.57	4Q 92	4c
Potatoes, white or red	10-lb sack	2.36	4Q 92	4c
Sausage, Jimmy Dean, 100% pork	lb	2.35	4Q 92	4c
Shortening, vegetable, Crisco	3-lb can	2.32	4Q 92	4c
Soft drink, Coca Cola	2 liter	1.36	4Q 92	4c
Steak, T-bone	lb	4.09	4Q 92	4c
Sugar, cane or beet	4 lb	1.72	4Q 92	4c
Tomatoes, Hunt's or Del Monte	14.5-oz can	0.72	4Q 92	4c
Tuna, chunk, light	6.125-6.5 oz can	0.73	4Q 92	4c

Values are in dollars or fractions of dollars. In the column headed *Ref*, references are shown to sources. Each reference is followed by a letter. These refer to the geographical level for which data were reported: s=State, r=Region, and c=City or metro. The abbreviation *ex* is used to mean *except* or *excluding*; *exp* stands for expenditures. For other abbreviations and further explanations, please see the Introduction.

Hobbs, NM - continued

Item	Per	Value	Date	Ref.
Health Care				
ACCRA Index, Health Care		94.70	4Q 92	4c
Analgesic, Aspirin, Bayer, 325 mg tablets	100	5.56	4Q 92	4c
Dentist's fee, adult teeth cleaning and periodic oral exam	visit	45.00	4Q 92	4c
Doctor's fee, routine exam, established patient	visit	34.25	4Q 92	4c
Hospital care, semiprivate room	day	272.00	4Q 92	4c
Household Goods				
Appliance repair, home, service call, washing machine	min labor charge	34.33	4Q 92	4c
Laundry detergent, Tide Ultra, Bold, or Cheer	42 oz	3.92	4Q 92	4c
Tissues, facial, Kleenex brand	175-count box	1.19	4Q 92	4c
Housing				
ACCRA Index, Housing		76.70	4Q 92	4c
House, 1,800 sq ft, 8,000 sq ft lot, new, urban	total	84600	4Q 92	4c
House payment, principal and interest, 25% down payment	month	476	4Q 92	4c
Mortgage rate, incl. points & origination fee, 30-year fixed or adjustable rate	per-cent	8.23	4Q 92	4c
Rent, apartment, 2 bedrooms - 1-1/2 to 2 baths, unfurnished, 950 sq ft, water	month	368	4Q 92	4c
Personal Goods				
Shampoo, Alberto VO5	15 oz	1.26	4Q 92	4c
Toothpaste, Crest or Colgate	6-7 oz	2.19	4Q 92	4c
Personal Services				
Dry cleaning, man's 2-piece suit		5.25	4Q 92	4c
Haircare, woman's shampoo, trim and blow-dry		21.50	4Q 92	4c
Haircut, man's barbershop, no styling		7.17	4Q 92	4c
Restaurant Food				
Chicken, fried, thigh and drumstick		1.89	4Q 92	4c
Hamburger with cheese	1/4 lb	1.88	4Q 92	4c
Pizza, Pizza Hut or Pizza Inn, cheese, thin crust	12-13 in	8.10	4Q 92	4c
Transportation				
ACCRA Index, Transportation		91.00	4Q 92	4c
Tire balance, computer or spin balance, front	wheel	5.00	4Q 92	4c
Utilities				
ACCRA Index, Utilities		81.70	4Q 92	4c
Electricity, partial electric and other energy, 1,800 sq ft living area new home	month	59.94	4Q 92	4c

Holland, MI

Item	Per	Value	Date	Ref.
Composite ACCRA index		103.80	4Q 92	4c
Alcoholic Beverages				
Beer, Miller Lite or Budweiser, 12-oz containers	6 pack	4.22	4Q 92	4c
Liquor, J & B Scotch	750 ml	17.51	4Q 92	4c
Wine, Gallo Chablis blanc, 1.5 liter	bottle	5.99	4Q 92	4c
Clothing				
Jeans, man's denim		35.99	4Q 92	4c
Shirt, man's dress shirt		24.32	4Q 92	4c
Undervest, boy's size 10-14, cotton	3	5.24	4Q 92	4c
Communications				
Newspaper subscription, daily and Sunday home delivery, large-city	month	10.00	4Q 92	4c
Telephone bill, family of four	month	15.67	4Q 92	4c

Holland, MI - continued

Item	Per	Value	Date	Ref.
Energy and Fuels				
Energy, combined forms, 1,800 sq ft heating area	month	88.07	4Q 92	4c
Energy, exc electricity, 1,800 sq ft heating area	month	41.92	4Q 92	4c
Gas, cooking, 10 therms	month	11.28	92	56c
Gas, cooking, 30 therms	month	19.85	92	56c
Gas, cooking, 50 therms	month	28.41	92	56c
Gas, heating, winter, 100 therms	month	49.82	92	56c
Gas, heating, winter, average use	month	89.89	92	56c
Gasoline, motor	gal	1.12	4Q 92	4c
Entertainment				
Bowling, evening rate	game	2.00	4Q 92	4c
Monopoly game, Parker Brothers', No. 9		9.99	4Q 92	4c
Movie	admis-sion	5.50	4Q 92	4c
Tennis balls, yellow, Wilson or Penn, 3	can	2.72	4Q 92	4c
Goods and Services				
ACCRA Index, Miscellaneous Goods and Services		106.70	4Q 92	4c
Groceries				
ACCRA Index, Groceries		102.20	4Q 92	4c
Babyfood, strained vegetables, lowest price	4-4.5 oz jar	0.39	4Q 92	4c
Bananas	lb	0.39	4Q 92	4c
Bread, white	24 oz	0.71	4Q 92	4c
Cheese, Kraft grated Parmesan	8-oz canis-ter	3.29	4Q 92	4c
Chicken, fryer, whole	lb	0.77	4Q 92	4c
Cigarettes, Winston	carton	17.25	4Q 92	4c
Coffee, vacuum-packed	13-oz can	2.15	4Q 92	4c
Corn, frozen	10 oz	0.69	4Q 92	4c
Corn Flakes, Kellogg's or Post Toasties	18 oz	1.81	4Q 92	4c
Eggs, Grade A large	doz	0.81	4Q 92	4c
Ground beef or hamburger	lb	1.49	4Q 92	4c
Lettuce, iceberg	head	0.99	4Q 92	4c
Margarine, Blue Bonnet or Parkay cubes	lb	0.75	4Q 92	4c
Milk, whole	1/2 gal	1.51	4Q 92	4c
Orange juice, Minute Maid frozen	12-oz can	1.35	4Q 92	4c
Peaches	29-oz can	1.39	4Q 92	4c
Peas Sweet, Del Monte or Green Giant	15-17 oz can	0.55	4Q 92	4c
Potatoes, white or red	10-lb sack	1.37	4Q 92	4c
Sausage, Jimmy Dean, 100% pork	lb	2.69	4Q 92	4c
Shortening, vegetable, Crisco	3-lb can	2.39	4Q 92	4c
Soft drink, Coca Cola	2 liter	1.45	4Q 92	4c
Steak, T-bone	lb	5.77	4Q 92	4c
Sugar, cane or beet	4 lb	1.54	4Q 92	4c
Tomatoes, Hunt's or Del Monte	14.5-oz can	0.69	4Q 92	4c
Tuna, chunk, light	6.125-6.5 oz can	0.69	4Q 92	4c
Health Care				
ACCRA Index, Health Care		92.80	4Q 92	4c
Analgesic, Aspirin, Bayer, 325 mg tablets	100	4.90	4Q 92	4c
Dentist's fee, adult teeth cleaning and periodic oral exam	visit	47.00	4Q 92	4c
Doctor's fee, routine exam, established patient	visit	34.35	4Q 92	4c
Hospital care, semiprivate room	day	238.00	4Q 92	4c

Values are in dollars or fractions of dollars. In the column headed *Ref*, references are shown to sources. Each reference is followed by a letter. These refer to the geographical level for which data were reported: s = State, r = Region, and c = City or metro. The abbreviation *ex* is used to mean *except* or *excluding*; *exp* stands for *expenditures*. For other abbreviations and further explanations, please see the Introduction.

Holland, MI - continued

Item	Per	Value	Date	Ref.
Household Goods				
Appliance repair, home, service call, washing machine	min labor charge	34.11	4Q 92	4c
Laundry detergent, Tide Ultra, Bold, or Cheer	42 oz	3.29	4Q 92	4c
Tissues, facial, Kleenex brand	175-count box	0.96	4Q 92	4c
Housing				
ACCRA Index, Housing		111.80	4Q 92	4c
House, 1,800 sq ft, 8,000 sq ft lot, new, urban	total	127340	4Q 92	4c
House payment, principal and interest, 25% down payment	month	722	4Q 92	4c
Mortgage rate, incl. points & origination fee, 30-year fixed or adjustable rate	per-cent	8.31	4Q 92	4c
Rent, apartment, 2 bedrooms - 1-1/2 to 2 baths, unfurnished, 950 sq ft, water	month	472	4Q 92	4c
Personal Goods				
Shampoo, Alberto VO5	15 oz	0.99	4Q 92	4c
Toothpaste, Crest or Colgate	6-7 oz	1.79	4Q 92	4c
Personal Services				
Dry cleaning, man's 2-piece suit		6.69	4Q 92	4c
Haircare, woman's shampoo, trim and blow-dry		19.90	4Q 92	4c
Haircut, man's barbershop, no styling		8.88	4Q 92	4c
Restaurant Food				
Chicken, fried, thigh and drumstick		2.20	4Q 92	4c
Hamburger with cheese	1/4 lb	1.81	4Q 92	4c
Pizza, Pizza Hut or Pizza Inn, cheese, thin crust	12-13 in	7.99	4Q 92	4c
Transportation				
ACCRA Index, Transportation		99.90	4Q 92	4c
Tire balance, computer or spin balance, front	wheel	6.55	4Q 92	4c
Utilities				
ACCRA Index, Utilities		80.60	4Q 92	4c
Electricity, partial electric and other energy, 1,800 sq ft living area new home	month	46.15	4Q 92	4c

Honolulu, HI

Item	Per	Value	Date	Ref.
Child Care				
Child care fee, average, center	hour	1.71	90	65r
Child care fee, average, nonregulated family day care	hour	1.32	90	65r
Child care fee, average, regulated family day care	hour	1.86	90	65r
Communications				
Telephone, residential, private line, rotary, unlimited calling	month	17.59	10/91	78c
Education				
Board, 4-yr private college/university	year	1720	91	22s
Board, 4-yr public college/university	year	2276	91	22s
Expenditures, local gov't, public elementary/secondary	pupil	5453	92	20s
Room, 4-year private college/university	year	1943	91	22s
Room, 4-year public college/university	year	1400	91	22s
Tuition, 2-year public college/university	year	413	91	22s
Tuition, 4-year private college/university	year	4448	91	22s
Tuition, 4-year public college/university, in-state	year	1290	91	22s
Energy and Fuels				
Coal	mil Btu	1.82	90	64s
Energy	mil Btu	9.76	90	64s
Energy exp/householder, 1-family unit	year	362	90	28r

Honolulu, HI - continued

Item	Per	Value	Date	Ref.
Energy and Fuels - continued				
Energy exp/householder, <1,000 sq ft heating area	year	254	90	28r
Energy exp/householder, 1,000-1,999 sq ft heating area	year	358	90	28r
Energy exp/householder, 2,000+ sq ft heating area	year	467	90	28r
Energy exp/householder, mobile home	year	390	90	28r
Energy exp/householder, multifamily	year	252	90	28r
Gas, cooking, 10 therms	month	19.88	92	56c
Gas, cooking, 30 therms	month	47.64	92	56c
Gas, cooking, 50 therms	month	75.40	92	56c
Gas, heating, winter, 100 therms	month	144.80	92	56c
Gas, heating, winter, average use	month	29.46	92	56c
Gas, natural	mil Btu	12.24	90	64s
Gas, natural	000 cu ft	22.93	91	46s
Gas, natural, exp	year	421	91	46s
Gasoline, unleaded regular	mil Btu	11.71	90	64s
Entertainment				
Dinner entree, restaurant		31.50-44.50	92	83c
Miniature golf admission	adult	6.18	92	1r
Miniature golf admission	child	5.14	92	1r
Waterpark admission	adult	11.00	92	1r
Waterpark admission	child	8.55	92	1r
Funerals				
Casket, 18-gauge steel, velvet interior		1781.09	91	24r
Cosmetology, hair care, etc.		84.64	91	24r
Embalming		207.41	91	24r
Facility use for ceremony		205.76	91	24r
Hearse, local		105.14	91	24r
Limousine, local		83.21	91	24r
Remains to funeral home, transfer		113.82	91	24r
Service charge, professional		626.33	91	24r
Vault, concrete, non-metallic liner		599.54	91	24r
Viewing facilities, use		85.81	91	24r
Goods and Services				
Goods and services	year	19227	92	36c
Groceries				
Apples, Red Delicious	lb	0.80	4/93	16r
Bacon	lb	1.79	4/93	16r
Bananas	lb	0.53	4/93	16r
Bologna, all beef or mixed	lb	2.67	4/93	16r
Bread, white, pan	lb	0.81	4/93	16r
Carrots, short trimmed and topped	lb	0.39	4/93	16r
Chicken, fresh, whole	lb	0.94	4/93	16r
Chicken breast, bone-in	lb	2.19	4/93	16r
Chuck roast, graded and ungraded, ex USDA prime and choice	lb	2.26	4/93	16r
Coffee, 100% ground roast, all sizes	lb	2.33	4/93	16r
Eggs, Grade AA large	doz	1.18	4/93	16r
Flour, white, all purpose	lb	0.22	4/93	16r
Grapefruit	lb	0.52	4/93	16r
Grapes, Thompson Seedless	lb	1.50	4/93	16r
Ground beef, 100% beef	lb	1.44	4/93	16r
Ground beef, lean and extra lean	lb	2.34	4/93	16r
Ham, boneless, excluding canned	lb	2.56	4/93	16r
Honey, jar	8 oz	0.89-1.00	92	5r
Honey, jar	lb	1.35-1.97	92	5r
Honey, squeeze bear	12-oz	1.19-1.50	92	5r
Ice cream, prepackaged, bulk, regular	1/2 gal	2.40	4/93	16r
Lemons	lb	0.81	4/93	16r
Lettuce, iceberg	lb	0.84	4/93	16r
Margarine, stick	lb	0.81	4/93	16r
Oranges, navel	lb	0.48	4/93	16r
Pork chops, center cut, bone-in	lb	3.25	4/93	16r
Potato chips	16 oz	2.89	4/93	16r
Potatoes, white	lb	0.38	4/93	16r
Round roast, graded & ungraded, ex USDA prime & choice	lb	3.00	4/93	16r

Values are in dollars or fractions of dollars. In the column headed *Ref*, references are shown to sources. Each reference is followed by a letter. These refer to the geographical level for which data were reported: s=State, r=Region, and c=City or metro. The abbreviation *ex* is used to mean *except* or *excluding*; *exp* stands for expenditures. For other abbreviations and further explanations, please see the Introduction.

Honolulu, HI - continued

Item	Per	Value	Date	Ref.
Groceries				
Round roast, USDA choice, boneless	lb	3.16	4/93	16r
Shortening, vegetable oil blends	lb	0.86	4/93	16r
Spaghetti and macaroni	lb	0.84	4/93	16r
Steak, round, graded & ungraded, ex USDA prime & choice	lb	3.34	4/93	16r
Steak, round, USDA choice, boneless	lb	3.24	4/93	16r
Steak, sirloin, graded & ungraded, ex USDA prime & choice	lb	3.75	4/93	16r
Steak, sirloin, USDA choice, boneless	lb	4.49	4/93	16r
Sugar, white	lb	0.41	4/93	16r
Sugar, white, 33-80 oz pk	lb	0.38	4/93	16r
Tomatoes, field grown	lb	1.01	4/93	16r
Turkey, frozen, whole	lb	1.04	4/93	16r
Health Care				
Childbirth, cesarean, hospital		5533	91	62r
Childbirth, cesarean, physician's fee		2053	91	62r
Childbirth, normal, hospital		2745	91	62r
Childbirth, normal, physician's fee		1492	91	62r
Hospital care, semiprivate room	day	347.49	90	27c
Medical insurance premium, per employee, small group comprehensive	month	372.30	10/91	25c
Medical plan per employee	year	3421	91	45r
Mental health care, exp	capita	28.84-37.59	90	38s
Mental health care, exp, state mental health agency	capita	37.58	90	38s
Mental health care, hospital psychiatric services, non-Federal, exp	capita	14.47	88	38s
Mental health care, mental health organization, multiservice, exp	capita	13.45	88	38s
Mental health care, psychiatric hospitals, private, exp	capita	11.08	88	38s
Mental health care, psychiatric out-patient clinics, freestanding, exp	capita	1.16	88	38s
Mental health care, state and county mental hospitals, exp	capita	12.45	88	38s
Physician fee, family practice, first-visit		111.00	91	62r
Physician fee, family practice, revisit		45.00	91	62r
Physician fee, general practice, first-visit		100.00	91	62r
Physician fee, general practice, revisit		40.00	91	62r
Physician fee, internal medicine, first-visit		137.00	91	62r
Physician fee, internal medicine, revisit		48.00	91	62r
Physician fee, median, neurosurgeon, first-visit		157.00	91	62r
Physician fee, median, nonsurgical specialist, first-visit		131.00	91	62r
Physician fee, median, orthopedic surgeon, first-visit		124.00	91	62r
Physician fee, median, plastic surgeon, first-visit		88.00	91	62r
Physician fee, median, surgical specialist, first-visit		100.00	91	62r
Physician fee, neurosurgeon, revisit		51.00	91	62r
Physician fee, nonsurgical specialist, revisit		47.00	91	62r
Physician fee, obstetrics/gynecology, first-visit		95.00	91	62r
Physician fee, obstetrics/gynecology, revisit		50.00	91	62r
Physician fee, orthopedic surgeon, revisit		51.00	91	62r
Physician fee, pediatrician, first-visit		81.00	91	62r
Physician fee, pediatrician, revisit		42.00	91	62r
Physician fee, plastic surgeon, revisit		48.00	91	62r
Physician fee, surgical specialist, revisit		49.00	91	62r
Housing				
Home, median price	unit	349.00		26c
Rental unit, 1 bedroom	month	782	93	23c
Rental unit, 2 bedroom	month	920	93	23c
Rental unit, 3 bedroom	month	1158	93	23c
Rental unit, 4 bedroom	month	1297	93	23c
Rental unit, efficiency	month	643	93	23c

Honolulu, HI - continued

Item	Per	Value	Date	Ref.
Insurance and Pensions				
Auto insurance, private passenger	year	999.01	91	63s
Taxes				
Tax, cigarette	pack	46	91	77s
Tax, gasoline	gal	24.80-32.50	91	77s
Taxes, hotel room	day	8.64	92	33c
Taxes, state	capita	2324	91	77s
Transportation				
Bus fare	one-way	0.60	3/93	2c
Driver's license fee		3.00-12.00	12/90	43s
Travel				
Business travel	day	178.00	4/93	89r
Utilities				
Electricity	mil Btu	26.53	90	64s
Electricity, winter, 250 KWh	month	27.10	92	55c
Electricity, winter, 500 KWh	month	47.19	92	55c
Electricity, winter, 750 KWh	month	67.29	92	55c
Electricity, winter, 1000 KWh	month	87.38	92	55c

Hot Springs, AR

Item	Per	Value	Date	Ref.
Composite ACCRA index		96.00	4Q 92	4c
Alcoholic Beverages				
Beer, Miller Lite or Budweiser, 12-oz containers	6 pack	3.64	4Q 92	4c
Liquor, J & B Scotch	750 ml	18.15	4Q 92	4c
Wine, Gallo Chablis blanc, 1.5 liter	bottle	5.27	4Q 92	4c
Clothing				
Jeans, man's denim		29.99	4Q 92	4c
Shirt, man's dress shirt		28.75	4Q 92	4c
Undervest, boy's size 10-14, cotton	3	6.15	4Q 92	4c
Communications				
Newspaper subscription, daily and Sunday home delivery, large-city	month	8.00	4Q 92	4c
Telephone, flat rate	month	13.91	91	11c
Telephone bill, family of four	month	19.61	4Q 92	4c
Energy and Fuels				
Energy, combined forms, 1,800 sq ft heating area	month	123.46	4Q 92	4c
Gasoline, motor	gal	1.04	4Q 92	4c
Entertainment				
Bowling, evening rate	game	1.92	4Q 92	4c
Monopoly game, Parker Brothers', No. 9		10.98	4Q 92	4c
Movie	admission	5.00	4Q 92	4c
Tennis balls, yellow, Wilson or Penn, 3	can	2.87	4Q 92	4c
Goods and Services				
ACCRA Index, Miscellaneous Goods and Services		107.20	4Q 92	4c
Groceries				
ACCRA Index, Groceries		102.30	4Q 92	4c
Babyfood, strained vegetables, lowest price	4-4.5 oz jar	0.30	4Q 92	4c
Bananas	lb	0.52	4Q 92	4c
Bread, white	24 oz	0.71	4Q 92	4c
Cheese, Kraft grated Parmesan	8-oz canister	3.44	4Q 92	4c
Chicken, fryer, whole	lb	0.68	4Q 92	4c
Cigarettes, Winston	carton	18.70	4Q 92	4c
Coffee, vacuum-packed	13-oz can	2.19	4Q 92	4c
Corn, frozen	10 oz	0.76	4Q 92	4c
Corn Flakes, Kellogg's or Post Toasties	18 oz	2.24	4Q 92	4c

Values are in dollars or fractions of dollars. In the column headed *Ref*, references are shown to sources. Each reference is followed by a letter. These refer to the geographical level for which data were reported: s = State, r = Region, and c = City or metro. The abbreviation *ex* is used to mean *except* or *excluding*; *exp* stands for expenditures. For other abbreviations and further explanations, please see the Introduction.

Hot Springs, AR - continued

Item	Per	Value	Date	Ref.
Groceries				
Eggs, Grade A large	doz	0.78	4Q 92	4c
Ground beef or hamburger	lb	1.54	4Q 92	4c
Lettuce, iceberg	head	0.96	4Q 92	4c
Margarine, Blue Bonnet or Parkay cubes	lb	0.59	4Q 92	4c
Milk, whole	1/2 gal	1.51	4Q 92	4c
Orange juice, Minute Maid frozen	12-oz can	1.18	4Q 92	4c
Peaches	29-oz can	1.28	4Q 92	4c
Peas Sweet, Del Monte or Green Giant	15-17 oz can	0.63	4Q 92	4c
Potatoes, white or red	10-lb sack	2.28	4Q 92	4c
Sausage, Jimmy Dean, 100% pork	lb	2.56	4Q 92	4c
Shortening, vegetable, Crisco	3-lb can	2.25	4Q 92	4c
Soft drink, Coca Cola	2 liter	1.27	4Q 92	4c
Steak, T-bone	lb	5.54	4Q 92	4c
Sugar, cane or beet	4 lb	1.69	4Q 92	4c
Tomatoes, Hunt's or Del Monte	14.5-oz can	0.78	4Q 92	4c
Tuna, chunk, light	6.125-6.5 oz can	0.61	4Q 92	4c
Health Care				
ACCRA Index, Health Care		84.60	4Q 92	4c
Analgesic, Aspirin, Bayer, 325 mg tablets	100	3.82	4Q 92	4c
Dentist's fee, adult teeth cleaning and periodic oral exam	visit	39.25	4Q 92	4c
Doctor's fee, routine exam, established patient	visit	36.00	4Q 92	4c
Hospital care, semiprivate room	day	210.00	4Q 92	4c
Household Goods				
Appliance repair, home, service call, washing machine	min labor charge	30.00	4Q 92	4c
Laundry detergent, Tide Ultra, Bold, or Cheer	42 oz	3.34	4Q 92	4c
Tissues, facial, Kleenex brand	175-count box	1.19	4Q 92	4c
Housing				
ACCRA Index, Housing		74.90	4Q 92	4c
House, 1,800 sq ft, 8,000 sq ft lot, new, urban	total	84667	4Q 92	4c
House payment, principal and interest, 25% down payment	month	469	4Q 92	4c
Mortgage rate, incl. points & origination fee, 30-yr fixed or adjustable rate	per-cent	8.07	4Q 92	4c
Rent, apartment, 2 bedrooms - 1-1/2 to 2 baths, unfurnished, 950 sq ft, water	month	350	4Q 92	4c
Personal Goods				
Shampoo, Alberto VO5	15 oz	1.51	4Q 92	4c
Toothpaste, Crest or Colgate	6-7 oz	1.82	4Q 92	4c
Personal Services				
Dry cleaning, man's 2-piece suit		3.99	4Q 92	4c
Haircare, woman's shampoo, trim and blow-dry		20.75	4Q 92	4c
Haircut, man's barbershop, no styling		9.00	4Q 92	4c
Restaurant Food				
Chicken, fried, thigh and drumstick		2.39	4Q 92	4c
Hamburger with cheese	1/4 lb	1.90	4Q 92	4c
Pizza, Pizza Hut or Pizza Inn, cheese, thin crust	12-13 in	8.99	4Q 92	4c
Transportation				
ACCRA Index, Transportation		98.90	4Q 92	4c
Tire balance, computer or spin balance, front	wheel	6.88	4Q 92	4c

Hot Springs, AR - continued

Item	Per	Value	Date	Ref.
Utilities				
ACCRA Index, Utilities		111.80	4Q 92	4c
Electricity, all electric, 1,800 sq ft living area new home	month	123.46	4Q 92	4c

Houma-Thibodaux, LA

Item	Per	Value	Date	Ref.
Child Care				
Child care fee, average, center	hour	1.29	90	65r
Child care fee, average, nonregulated family day care	hour	0.89	90	65r
Child care fee, average, regulated family day care	hour	1.32	90	65r
Communications				
Long-distance telephone service, day, initial minute, 0-100 miles	min	0.14-0.41	91	12s
Long-distance telephone service, day, additional minute, 0-100 miles	min	0.09-0.29	91	12s
Long-distance telephone service, evenings/weekends, 0-100 mi, initial minute	min	0.06-0.16	91	12s
Long-distance telephone service, evenings/weekends, 0-100 mi, additional minute	min	0.04-0.12	91	12s
Education				
Board, 4-yr private college/university	year	2125	91	22s
Board, 4-yr public college/university	year	1453	91	22s
Expenditures, local gov't, public elementary/secondary	pupil	4299	92	20s
Room, 4-year private college/university	year	2216	91	22s
Room, 4-year public college/university	year	1323	91	22s
Tuition, 2-year private college/university	year	5671	91	22s
Tuition, 2-year public college/university	year	852	91	22s
Tuition, 4-year private college/university	year	9783	91	22s
Tuition, 4-year public college/university, in-state	year	1791	91	22s
Energy and Fuels				
Coal	mil Btu	1.68	90	64s
Energy	mil Btu	6.05	90	64s
Energy exp/householder, 1-family unit	year	471	90	28r
Energy exp/householder, <1,000 sq ft heating area	year	384	90	28r
Energy exp/householder, 1,000-1,999 sq ft heating area	year	421	90	28r
Energy exp/householder, 2,000+ sq ft heating area	year	625	90	28r
Energy exp/householder, mobile home	year	271	90	28r
Energy exp/householder, multifamily	year	355	90	28r
Gas, natural	mil Btu	2.11	90	64s
Gas, natural	000 cu ft	5.77	91	46s
Gas, natural, exp	year	336	91	46s
Gasoline, unleaded regular	mil Btu	9.47	90	64s
Entertainment				
Miniature golf admission	adult	6.18	92	1r
Miniature golf admission	child	5.14	92	1r
Waterpark admission	adult	11.00	92	1r
Waterpark admission	child	8.55	92	1r
Funerals				
Casket, 18-gauge steel, velvet interior		2274.41	91	24r
Cosmetology, hair care, etc.		74.62	91	24r
Embalming		229.94	91	24r
Facility use for ceremony		176.61	91	24r
Hearse, local		116.34	91	24r
Limousine, local		72.68	91	24r
Remains to funeral home, transfer		87.72	91	24r
Service charge, professional		712.53	91	24r
Vault, concrete, non-metallic liner		750.55	91	24r
Viewing facilities, use		155.31	91	24r

Values are in dollars or fractions of dollars. In the column headed *Ref*, references are shown to sources. Each reference is followed by a letter. These refer to the geographical level for which data were reported: s=State, r=Region, and c=City or metro. The abbreviation *ex* is used to mean *except* or *excluding*; *exp* stands for expenditures. For other abbreviations and further explanations, please see the Introduction.

Houma-Thibodaux, LA - continued

Item	Per	Value	Date	Ref.
Groceries				
Apples, Red Delicious	lb	0.79	4/93	16r
Bacon	lb	1.75	4/93	16r
Bananas	lb	0.42	4/93	16r
Beef, stew, boneless	lb	2.61	4/93	16r
Bologna, all beef or mixed	lb	2.24	4/93	16r
Bread, white, pan	lb	0.64	4/93	16r
Bread, whole wheat, pan	lb	0.96	4/93	16r
Cabbage	lb	0.37	4/93	16r
Carrots, short trimmed and topped	lb	0.47	4/93	16r
Celery	lb	0.64	4/93	16r
Cheese, American	lb	2.98	4/93	16r
Cheese, Cheddar	lb	3.28	4/93	16r
Chicken, fresh, whole	lb	0.77	4/93	16r
Chicken breast, bone-in	lb	1.92	4/93	16r
Chicken legs, bone-in	lb	1.06	4/93	16r
Chuck roast, graded and ungraded, ex USDA prime and choice	lb	2.40	4/93	16r
Chuck roast, USDA choice, bone-in	lb	2.19	4/93	16r
Chuck roast, USDA choice, boneless	lb	2.38	4/93	16r
Coffee, 100% ground roast, all sizes	lb	2.48	4/93	16r
Crackers, soda, salted	lb	1.15	4/93	16r
Eggs, Grade A large	doz	0.96	4/93	16r
Flour, white, all purpose	lb	0.24	4/93	16r
Frankfurters, all meat or all beef	lb	2.01	4/93	16r
Grapefruit	lb	0.44	4/93	16r
Grapes, Thompson Seedless	lb	1.40	4/93	16r
Ground beef, 100% beef	lb	1.58	4/93	16r
Ground beef, lean and extra lean	lb	2.09	4/93	16r
Ground chuck, 100% beef	lb	1.98	4/93	16r
Ham, boneless, excluding canned	lb	2.89	4/93	16r
Ham, picnic, shoulder, bone-in, smoked	lb	1.02	4/93	16r
Ham, rump or steak half, bone-in, smoked	lb	1.48	4/93	16r
Honey, jar	8 oz	0.73-1.19	92	5r
Honey, jar	lb	1.10-1.79	92	5r
Honey, squeeze bear	12-oz	1.19-1.50	92	5r
Ice cream, prepackaged, bulk, regular	1/2 gal	2.41	4/93	16r
Lemons	lb	1.05	4/93	16r
Lettuce, iceberg	lb	0.81	4/93	16r
Margarine, stick	lb	0.88	4/93	16r
Oranges, navel	lb	0.55	4/93	16r
Pears, Anjou	lb	0.92	4/93	16r
Pork chops, center cut, bone-in	lb	3.13	4/93	16r
Potato chips	16 oz	2.94	4/93	16r
Potatoes, white	lb	0.43	4/93	16r
Rib roast, USDA choice, bone-in	lb	4.63	4/93	16r
Rice, white, long grain, uncooked	lb	0.45	4/93	16r
Round roast, graded & ungraded, ex USDA prime & choice	lb	3.03	4/93	16r
Round roast, USDA choice, boneless	lb	3.09	4/93	16r
Sausage, fresh, loose	lb	2.08	4/93	16r
Short ribs, bone-in	lb	2.66	4/93	16r
Shortening, vegetable oil blends	lb	0.69	4/93	16r
Spaghetti and macaroni	lb	0.81	4/93	16r
Steak, rib eye, USDA choice, boneless	lb	6.24	4/93	16r
Steak, round, graded & ungraded, ex USDA prime & choice	lb	3.31	4/93	16r
Steak, round, USDA choice, boneless	lb	3.34	4/93	16r
Steak, sirloin, graded & ungraded, ex USDA prime & choice	lb	4.19	4/93	16r
Steak, sirloin, USDA choice, boneless	lb	4.46	4/93	16r
Steak, T-bone, USDA choice, bone-in	lb	5.25	4/93	16r
Strawberries, dry pint	12 oz	0.92	4/93	16r
Sugar, white	lb	0.39	4/93	16r
Sugar, white, 33-80 oz pk	lb	0.38	4/93	16r
Tomatoes, field grown	lb	0.88	4/93	16r
Tuna, chunk, light	lb	1.79	4/93	16r
Turkey, frozen, whole	lb	1.04	4/93	16r
Yogurt, natural, fruit flavored	1/2 pint	0.57	4/93	16r
Health Care				
Childbirth, cesarean, hospital		5034	91	62r
Childbirth, cesarean, physician's fee		2053	91	62r

Houma-Thibodaux, LA - continued

Item	Per	Value	Date	Ref.
Health Care - continued				
Childbirth, normal, hospital		2712	91	62r
Childbirth, normal, physician's fee		1492	91	62r
Mental health care, exp	capita	20.37-28.83	90	38s
Mental health care, exp, state mental health agency	capita	28.44	90	38s
Mental health care, hospital psychiatric services, non-Federal, exp	capita	8.19	88	38s
Mental health care, mental health organization, multiservice, exp	capita	0.49	88	38s
Mental health care, psychiatric hospitals, private, exp	capita	43.54	88	38s
Mental health care, psychiatric out-patient clinics, freestanding, exp	capita	4.11	88	38s
Mental health care, state and county mental hospitals, exp	capita	18.74	88	38s
Mental health care, VA medical centers, exp	capita	2.60	88	38s
Physician fee, family practice, first-visit		75.00	91	62r
Physician fee, family practice, revisit		34.00	91	62r
Physician fee, general practice, first-visit		61.00	91	62r
Physician fee, general practice, revisit		32.00	91	62r
Physician fee, general surgeon, first-visit		64.00	91	62r
Physician fee, general surgeon, revisit		40.00	91	62r
Physician fee, internal medicine, first-visit		98.00	91	62r
Physician fee, internal medicine, revisit		40.00	91	62r
Physician fee, median, neurosurgeon, first-visit		130.00	91	62r
Physician fee, median, nonsurgical specialist, first-visit		95.00	91	62r
Physician fee, median, orthopedic surgeon, first-visit		91.00	91	62r
Physician fee, median, plastic surgeon, first-visit		66.00	91	62r
Physician fee, median, surgical specialist, first-visit		62.00	91	62r
Physician fee, neurosurgeon, revisit		50.00	91	62r
Physician fee, nonsurgical specialist, revisit		40.00	91	62r
Physician fee, obstetrics/gynecology, first-visit		64.00	91	62r
Physician fee, obstetrics/gynecology, revisit		41.00	91	62r
Physician fee, orthopedic surgeon, revisit		40.00	91	62r
Physician fee, pediatrician, first-visit		49.00	91	62r
Physician fee, pediatrician, revisit		33.00	91	62r
Physician fee, plastic surgeon, revisit		43.00	91	62r
Physician fee, surgical specialist, revisit		37.00	91	62r
Substance abuse, hospital ancillary charge	incident	2600	90	70s
Substance abuse, hospital physician charge	incident	840	90	70s
Substance abuse, hospital room and board	incident	6410	90	70s
Insurance and Pensions				
Auto insurance, private passenger	year	778.70	91	63s
Taxes				
Tax, cigarette	pack	20	91	77s
Tax, gasoline	gal	20	91	77s
Taxes, state	capita	1013	91	77s
Transportation				
Driver's license fee		18.00	12/90	43s
Travel				
Business travel	day	193.00	4/93	89r
Utilities				
Electricity	mil Btu	17.77	90	64s

Values are in dollars or fractions of dollars. In the column headed *Ref*, references are shown to sources. Each reference is followed by a letter. These refer to the geographical level for which data were reported: s=State, r=Region, and c=City or metro. The abbreviation *ex* is used to mean *except* or *excluding*; *exp* stands for expenditures. For other abbreviations and further explanations, please see the Introduction.

Houston, TX

Item	Per	Value	Date	Ref.
Composite ACCRA index		98.40	4Q 92	4c
Alcoholic Beverages				
Beer, Miller Lite or Budweiser, 12-oz containers	6 pack	3.80	4Q 92	4c
Liquor, J & B Scotch	750 ml	15.41	4Q 92	4c
Wine, Gallo Chablis blanc, 1.5 liter	bottle	4.46	4Q 92	4c
Child Care				
Child care fee, average, center	hour	1.29	90	65r
Child care fee, average, nonregulated family day care	hour	0.89	90	65r
Child care fee, average, regulated family day care	hour	1.32	90	65r
Clothing				
Jeans, man's denim		29.30	4Q 92	4c
Shirt, man's dress shirt		18.00	4Q 92	4c
Undervest, boy's size 10-14, cotton	3	4.33	4Q 92	4c
Communications				
Long-distance telephone service, day, initial minute, 0-100 miles	min	0.10-0.46	91	12s
Long-distance telephone service, day, additional minute, 0-100 miles	min	0.06-0.45	91	12s
Newspaper subscription, daily and Sunday home delivery, large-city	month	10.50	4Q 92	4c
Telephone, flat rate	month	11.05	91	11c
Telephone, residential, private line, rotary, unlimited calling	month	18.09	10/91	78c
Telephone bill, family of four	month	18.35	4Q 92	4c
Education				
Board, 4-yr private college/university	year	1883	91	22s
Board, 4-yr public college/university	year	1605	91	22s
Expenditures, local gov't, public elementary/secondary	pupil	4593	92	20s
Room, 4-year private college/university	year	1620	91	22s
Room, 4-year public college/university	year	1532	91	22s
Tuition, 2-year private college/university	year	4394	91	22s
Tuition, 2-year public college/university	year	495	91	22s
Tuition, 4-year private college/university	year	6497	91	22s
Tuition, 4-year public college/university, in-state	year	986	91	22s
Energy and Fuels				
Coal	mil Btu	1.44	90	64s
Energy	mil Btu	6.48	90	64s
Energy, combined forms, 1,800 sq ft heating area	month	112.09	4Q 92	4c
Energy, exc electricity, 1,800 sq ft heating area	month	22.52	4Q 92	4c
Energy exp/householder, 1-family unit	year	471	90	28r
Energy exp/householder, <1,000 sq ft heating area	year	384	90	28r
Energy exp/householder, 1,000-1,999 sq ft heating area	year	421	90	28r
Energy exp/householder, 2,000+ sq ft heating area	year	625	90	28r
Energy exp/householder, mobile home	year	271	90	28r
Energy exp/householder, multifamily	year	355	90	28r
Gas, cooking, winter, 10 therms	month	13.39	92	56c
Gas, cooking, winter, 30 therms	month	21.17	92	56c
Gas, cooking, winter, 50 therms	month	28.95	92	56c
Gas, heating, winter, 100 therms	month	48.40	92	56c
Gas, heating, winter, average use	month	19.42	92	56c
Gas, natural	mil Btu	2.47	90	64s
Gas, natural	000 cu ft	5.71	91	46s
Gas, natural, exp	year	388	91	46s
Gas, piped	100 therms	46.84	4/93	16c
Gas, piped	40 therms	24.76	4/93	16c
Gas, piped	therm	0.49	4/93	16c
Gasoline, all types	gal	1.12	4/93	16c

Houston, TX - continued

Item	Per	Value	Date	Ref.
Energy and Fuels - continued				
Gasoline, motor	gal	1.06	4Q 92	4c
Gasoline, regular unleaded, taxes included, cash, self-service	gal	1.26	4/93	16c
Gasoline, unleaded premium 93 octane	gal	1.06	4/93	16c
Gasoline, unleaded regular	mil Btu	9.16	90	64s
Entertainment				
Bowling, evening rate	game	1.66	4Q 92	4c
Miniature golf admission	adult	6.18	92	1r
Miniature golf admission	child	5.14	92	1r
Monopoly game, Parker Brothers', No. 9		12.64	4Q 92	4c
Movie	admission	5.79	4Q 92	4c
Tennis balls, yellow, Wilson or Penn, 3	can	2.08	4Q 92	4c
Waterpark admission	adult	11.00	92	1r
Waterpark admission	child	8.55	92	1r
Funerals				
Casket, 18-gauge steel, velvet interior		2274.41	91	24r
Cosmetology, hair care, etc.		74.62	91	24r
Embalming		229.94	91	24r
Facility use for ceremony		176.61	91	24r
Hearse, local		116.34	91	24r
Limousine, local		72.68	91	24r
Remains to funeral home, transfer		87.72	91	24r
Service charge, professional		712.53	91	24r
Vault, concrete, non-metallic liner		750.55	91	24r
Viewing facilities, use		155.31	91	24r
Goods and Services				
ACCRA Index, Miscellaneous Goods and Services		95.40	4Q 92	4c
Groceries				
ACCRA Index, Groceries		98.90	4Q 92	4c
Apples, Red Delicious	lb	0.79	4/93	16r
Babyfood, strained vegetables, lowest price	4-4.5 oz jar	0.23	4Q 92	4c
Bacon	lb	1.75	4/93	16r
Bakery products, exp	year	191	89	15c
Bananas	lb	0.42	4Q 92	4c
Bananas	lb	0.42	4/93	16r
Beef, exp	year	194	89	15c
Beef, stew, boneless	lb	2.61	4/93	16r
Bologna, all beef or mixed	lb	2.24	4/93	16r
Bread, white	24 oz	0.66	4Q 92	4c
Bread, white, pan	lb	0.64	4/93	16r
Bread, whole wheat, pan	lb	0.96	4/93	16r
Cabbage	lb	0.37	4/93	16r
Carrots, short trimmed and topped	lb	0.47	4/93	16r
Celery	lb	0.64	4/93	16r
Cereals and bakery products, exp	year	325	89	15c
Cereals and cereal products, exp	year	134	89	15c
Cheese, American	lb	2.98	4/93	16r
Cheese, Cheddar	lb	3.28	4/93	16r
Cheese, Kraft grated Parmesan	8-oz canister	3.33	4Q 92	4c
Chicken, fresh, whole	lb	0.77	4/93	16r
Chicken, fryer, whole	lb	0.76	4Q 92	4c
Chicken breast, bone-in	lb	1.92	4/93	16r
Chicken legs, bone-in	lb	1.06	4/93	16r
Chuck roast, graded and ungraded, ex USDA prime and choice	lb	2.40	4/93	16r
Chuck roast, USDA choice, bone-in	lb	2.19	4/93	16r
Chuck roast, USDA choice, boneless	lb	2.38	4/93	16r
Cigarettes, Winston	carton	19.82	4Q 92	4c
Coffee, 100% ground roast, all sizes	lb	2.48	4/93	16r
Coffee, vacuum-packed	13-oz can	1.90	4Q 92	4c
Corn, frozen	10 oz	0.62	4Q 92	4c
Corn Flakes, Kellogg's or Post Toasties	18 oz	1.87	4Q 92	4c
Crackers, soda, salted	lb	1.15	4/93	16r
Dairy products, exp	year	278	89	15c

Values are in dollars or fractions of dollars. In the column headed *Ref*, references are shown to sources. Each reference is followed by a letter. These refer to the geographical level for which data were reported: s=State, r=Region, and c=City or metro. The abbreviation *ex* is used to mean *except* or *excluding*; *exp* stands for *expenditures*. For other abbreviations and further explanations, please see the Introduction.

Houston, TX - continued

Item	Per	Value	Date	Ref.
Groceries				
Dairy products, miscellaneous, exp	year	137	89	15c
Eggs, exp	year	32	89	15c
Eggs, Grade A large	doz	0.81	4Q 92	4c
Eggs, Grade A large	doz	0.96	4/93	16r
Fish and seafood, exp	year	48	89	15c
Flour, white, all purpose	lb	0.24	4/93	16r
Food, exp	year	4109	89	15c
Food eaten at home, exp	year	2255	89	15c
Frankfurters, all meat or all beef	lb	2.01	4/93	16r
Fruits, fresh, exp	year	110	89	15c
Fruits, processed, exp	year	76	89	15c
Fruits and vegetables, exp	year	371	89	15c
Grapefruit	lb	0.44	4/93	16r
Grapes, Thompson Seedless	lb	1.40	4/93	16r
Ground beef, 100% beef	lb	1.58	4/93	16r
Ground beef, lean and extra lean	lb	2.09	4/93	16r
Ground beef or hamburger	lb	1.72	4Q 92	4c
Ground chuck, 100% beef	lb	1.98	4/93	16r
Ham, boneless, excluding canned	lb	2.89	4/93	16r
Ham, picnic, shoulder, bone-in, smoked	lb	1.02	4/93	16r
Ham, rump or steak half, bone-in, smoked	lb	1.48	4/93	16r
Honey, jar	8 oz	0.73-1.19	92	5r
Honey, jar	lb	1.10-1.79	92	5r
Honey, squeeze bear	12-oz	1.19-1.50	92	5r
Ice cream, prepackaged, bulk, regular	1/2 gal	2.41	4/93	16r
Lemons	lb	1.05	4/93	16r
Lettuce, iceberg	head	0.98	4Q 92	4c
Lettuce, iceberg	lb	0.81	4/93	16r
Margarine, Blue Bonnet or Parkay cubes	lb	0.53	4Q 92	4c
Margarine, stick	lb	0.88	4/93	16r
Meats, poultry, fish and eggs, exp	year	566	89	15c
Milk, whole	1/2 gal	1.33	4Q 92	4c
Milk and cream, fresh, exp	year	141	89	15c
Orange juice, Minute Maid frozen	12-oz can	1.35	4Q 92	4c
Oranges, navel	lb	0.55	4/93	16r
Peaches	29-oz can	1.33	4Q 92	4c
Pears, Anjou	lb	0.92	4/93	16r
Peas Sweet, Del Monte or Green Giant	15-17 oz can	0.54	4Q 92	4c
Pork, exp	year	127	89	15c
Pork chops, center cut, bone-in	lb	3.13	4/93	16r
Potato chips	16 oz	2.94	4/93	16r
Potatoes, white	lb	0.43	4/93	16r
Potatoes, white or red	10-lb sack	2.37	4Q 92	4c
Poultry, exp	year	69	89	15c
Rib roast, USDA choice, bone-in	lb	4.63	4/93	16r
Rice, white, long grain, uncooked	lb	0.45	4/93	16r
Round roast, graded & ungraded, ex USDA prime & choice	lb	3.03	4/93	16r
Round roast, USDA choice, boneless	lb	3.09	4/93	16r
Sausage, fresh, loose	lb	2.08	4/93	16r
Sausage, Jimmy Dean, 100% pork	lb	2.55	4Q 92	4c
Short ribs, bone-in	lb	2.66	4/93	16r
Shortening, vegetable oil blends	lb	0.69	4/93	16r
Shortening, vegetable, Crisco	3-lb can	2.11	4Q 92	4c
Soft drink, Coca Cola	2 liter	1.07	4Q 92	4c
Spaghetti and macaroni	lb	0.81	4/93	16r
Steak, rib eye, USDA choice, boneless	lb	6.24	4/93	16r
Steak, round, graded & ungraded, ex USDA prime & choice	lb	3.31	4/93	16r
Steak, round, USDA choice, boneless	lb	3.34	4/93	16r
Steak, sirloin, graded & ungraded, ex USDA prime & choice	lb	4.19	4/93	16r
Steak, sirloin, USDA choice, boneless	lb	4.46	4/93	16r
Steak, T-bone	lb	5.86	4Q 92	4c
Steak, T-bone, USDA choice, bone-in	lb	5.25	4/93	16r
Strawberries, dry pint	12 oz	0.92	4/93	16r
Sugar, cane or beet	4 lb	1.31	4Q 92	4c

Houston, TX - continued

Item	Per	Value	Date	Ref.
Groceries - continued				
Sugar, white	lb	0.39	4/93	16r
Sugar, white, 33-80 oz pk	lb	0.38	4/93	16r
Tomatoes, field grown	lb	0.88	4/93	16r
Tomatoes, Hunt's or Del Monte	14.5-oz can	0.64	4Q 92	4c
Tuna, chunk, light	6.125-6.5 oz can	0.60	4Q 92	4c
Tuna, chunk, light	lb	1.79	4/93	16r
Turkey, frozen, whole	lb	1.04	4/93	16r
Vegetables, fresh, exp	year	122	89	15c
Vegetables, processed, exp	year	63	89	15c
Yogurt, natural, fruit flavored	1/2 pint	0.57	4/93	16r
Health Care				
ACCRA Index, Health Care		112.30	4Q 92	4c
Analgesic, Aspirin, Bayer, 325 mg tablets	100	5.54	4Q 92	4c
Childbirth, cesarean, hospital		5034	91	62r
Childbirth, cesarean, physician's fee		2053	91	62r
Childbirth, normal, hospital		2712	91	62r
Childbirth, normal, physician's fee		1492	91	62r
Dentist's fee, adult teeth cleaning and periodic oral exam	visit	53.08	4Q 92	4c
Doctor's fee, routine exam, established patient	visit	44.17	4Q 92	4c
Health care spending, state	capita	2192	3/93	84s
Health maintenance organization coverage, employee	year	3575	93	39c
Hospital care, semiprivate room	day	228.09	90	27c
Hospital care, semiprivate room	day	308.00	4Q 92	4c
Insurance coverage, traditional, employee	year	3627	93	39c
Medical insurance premium, per employee, small group comprehensive	month	467.20	10/91	25c
Mental health care, exp	capita	20.37-28.83	90	38s
Mental health care, exp, state mental health agency	capita	22.72	90	38s
Mental health care, hospital psychiatric services, non-Federal, exp	capita	7.95	88	38s
Mental health care, mental health organization, multiservice, exp	capita	12.05	88	38s
Mental health care, psychiatric hospitals, private, exp	capita	37.78	88	38s
Mental health care, psychiatric out-patient clinics, freestanding, exp	capita	0.43	88	38s
Mental health care, state and county mental hospitals, exp	capita	12.54	88	38s
Mental health care, VA medical centers, exp	capita	5.35	88	38s
Physician fee, family practice, first-visit		75.00	91	62r
Physician fee, family practice, revisit		34.00	91	62r
Physician fee, general practice, first-visit		61.00	91	62r
Physician fee, general practice, revisit		32.00	91	62r
Physician fee, general surgeon, first-visit		64.00	91	62r
Physician fee, general surgeon, revisit		40.00	91	62r
Physician fee, internal medicine, first-visit		98.00	91	62r
Physician fee, internal medicine, revisit		40.00	91	62r
Physician fee, median, neurosurgeon, first-visit		130.00	91	62r
Physician fee, median, nonsurgical specialist, first-visit		95.00	91	62r
Physician fee, median, orthopedic surgeon, first-visit		91.00	91	62r
Physician fee, median, plastic surgeon, first-visit		66.00	91	62r
Physician fee, median, surgical specialist, first-visit		62.00	91	62r
Physician fee, neurosurgeon, revisit		50.00	91	62r
Physician fee, nonsurgical specialist, revisit		40.00	91	62r
Physician fee, obstetrics/gynecology, first-visit		64.00	91	62r
Physician fee, obstetrics/gynecology, revisit		41.00	91	62r
Physician fee, orthopedic surgeon, revisit		40.00	91	62r

Values are in dollars or fractions of dollars. In the column headed *Ref*, references are shown to sources. Each reference is followed by a letter. These refer to the geographical level for which data were reported: s=State, r=Region, and c=City or metro. The abbreviation *ex* is used to mean *except* or *excluding*; *exp* stands for *expenditures*. For other abbreviations and further explanations, please see the Introduction.

Houston, TX - continued

Item	Per	Value	Date	Ref.
Health Care				
Physician fee, pediatrician, first-visit		49.00	91	62r
Physician fee, pediatrician, revisit		33.00	91	62r
Physician fee, plastic surgeon, revisit		43.00	91	62r
Physician fee, surgical specialist, revisit		37.00	91	62r
Substance abuse, hospital ancillary charge	incident	3750	90	70s
Substance abuse, hospital physician charge	incident	1080	90	70s
Substance abuse, hospital room and board	incident	5320	90	70s
Household Goods				
Appliance repair, home, service call, washing machine	min labor charge	32.24	4Q 92	4c
Laundry detergent, Tide Ultra, Bold, or Cheer	42 oz	2.78	4Q 92	4c
Tissues, facial, Kleenex brand	175-count box	1.13	4Q 92	4c
Housing				
ACCRA Index, Housing		91.20	4Q 92	4c
Home, median price	unit	80.20		26c
House, 1,800 sq ft, 8,000 sq ft lot, new, urban	total	93047	4Q 92	4c
House payment, principal and interest, 25% down payment	month	508	4Q 92	4c
Mortgage rate, incl. points & origination fee, 30-year fixed or adjustable rate	percent	7.92	4Q 92	4c
Rent, apartment, 2 bedrooms - 1-1/2 to 2 baths, unfurnished, 950 sq ft, water	month	572	4Q 92	4c
Rental unit, 1 bedroom	month	414	93	23c
Rental unit, 2 bedroom	month	488	93	23c
Rental unit, 3 bedroom	month	612	93	23c
Rental unit, 4 bedroom	month	685	93	23c
Rental unit, efficiency	month	341	93	23c
Insurance and Pensions				
Auto insurance, private passenger	year	709.79	91	63s
Personal Goods				
Shampoo, Alberto VO5	15 oz	1.10	4Q 92	4c
Toothpaste, Crest or Colgate	6-7 oz	2.05	4Q 92	4c
Personal Services				
Dry cleaning, man's 2-piece suit		5.71	4Q 92	4c
Haircare, woman's shampoo, trim and blow-dry		22.22	4Q 92	4c
Haircut, man's barbershop, no styling		8.40	4Q 92	4c
Restaurant Food				
Chicken, fried, thigh and drumstick		1.89	4Q 92	4c
Hamburger with cheese	1/4 lb	1.81	4Q 92	4c
Pizza, Pizza Hut or Pizza Inn, cheese, thin crust	12-13 in	7.70	4Q 92	4c
Taxes				
Tax, cigarette	pack	41	91	77s
Tax, gasoline	gal	20	91	77s
Taxes, hotel room	day	8.80	92	33c
Taxes, state	capita	923	91	77s
Transportation				
ACCRA Index, Transportation		118.30	4Q 92	4c
Auto rental, average	day	47.50	6/91	60c
Bus fare	one-way	0.85	3/93	2c
Bus fare, up to 10 miles	one-way	1.85	4Q 92	4c
Driver's license fee		16.00	12/90	43s
Limo fare, airport-city, average	day	8.50	6/91	60c
Taxi fare, airport-city, average	day	26.00	6/91	60c
Tire balance, computer or spin balance, front	wheel	7.88	4Q 92	4c

Houston, TX - continued

Item	Per	Value	Date	Ref.
Travel				
Breakfast	day	8.17	6/91	60c
Business travel	day	193.00	4/93	89r
Dinner	day	19.20	6/91	60c
Dinner	day	22.50	92	85c
Lodging	day	113.16	91	60c
Lodging	day	111.00	92	85c
Lunch	day	11.37	6/91	60c
Travel, business	day	207.29	93	88c
Utilities				
ACCRA Index, Utilities		101.80	4Q 92	4c
Electricity	500 KWh	43.49	4/93	16c
Electricity	KWh	0.08	4/93	16c
Electricity	mil Btu	17.09	90	64s
Electricity, partial electric and other energy, 1,800 sq ft living area new home	month	89.57	4Q 92	4c
Electricity, residential	KWh	5.92	2/93	94s
Electricity, winter, 250 KWh	month	17.77	92	55c
Electricity, winter, 500 KWh	month	43.50	92	55c
Electricity, winter, 750 KWh	month	69.22	92	55c
Electricity, winter, 1000 KWh	month	87.87	92	55c

Huntington, WV

Item	Per	Value	Date	Ref.
Composite ACCRA index		96.00	4Q 92	4c
Alcoholic Beverages				
Beer, Miller Lite or Budweiser, 12-oz containers	6 pack	4.52	4Q 92	4c
Liquor, J & B Scotch	750 ml	17.19	4Q 92	4c
Wine, Gallo Chablis blanc, 1.5 liter	bottle	5.65	4Q 92	4c
Child Care				
Child care fee, average, center	hour	1.29	90	65r
Child care fee, average, nonregulated family day care	hour	0.89	90	65r
Child care fee, average, regulated family day care	hour	1.32	90	65r
Clothing				
Jeans, man's denim		34.99	4Q 92	4c
Shirt, man's dress shirt		26.08	4Q 92	4c
Undervest, boy's size 10-14, cotton	3	5.99	4Q 92	4c
Communications				
Long-distance telephone service, day, initial minute, 0-100 miles	min	0.26-0.70	91	12s
Long-distance telephone service, day, additional minute, 0-100 miles	min	0.13-0.45	91	12s
Long-distance telephone service, evenings/weekends, 0-100 mi, initial minute	min	0.10-0.28	91	12s
Long-distance telephone service, evenings/weekends, 0-100 mi, additional minute	min	0.05-0.18	91	12s
Newspaper subscription, daily and Sunday home delivery, large-city	month	14.13	4Q 92	4c
Telephone, flat rate	month	60.00	91	11c
Telephone, residential, private line, rotary, unlimited calling	month	27.05	10/91	78c
Telephone bill, family of four	month	27.35	4Q 92	4c
Education				
Board, 4-yr private college/university	year	1664	91	22s
Board, 4-yr public college/university	year	1723	91	22s
Expenditures, local gov't, public elementary/secondary	pupil	5401	92	20s
Room, 4-year private college/university	year	1401	91	22s
Room, 4-year public college/university	year	1556	91	22s
Tuition, 2-year private college/university	year	2767	91	22s
Tuition, 2-year public college/university	year	930	91	22s
Tuition, 4-year private college/university	year	8751	91	22s
Tuition, 4-year public college/university, in-state	year	1543	91	22s

Values are in dollars or fractions of dollars. In the column headed *Ref*, references are shown to sources. Each reference is followed by a letter. These refer to the geographical level for which data were reported: s=State, r=Region, and c=City or metro. The abbreviation *ex* is used to mean *except* or *excluding*; *exp* stands for *expenditures*. For other abbreviations and further explanations, please see the Introduction.

Huntington, WV - continued

Item	Per	Value	Date	Ref.
Energy and Fuels				
Coal	mil Btu	1.47	90	64s
Energy	mil Btu	6.77	90	64s
Energy, combined forms, 1,800 sq ft heating area	month	87.83	4Q 92	4c
Energy exp/householder, 1-family unit	year	487	90	28r
Energy exp/householder, <1,000 sq ft heating area	year	393	90	28r
Energy exp/householder, 1,000-1,999 sq ft heating area	year	442	90	28r
Energy exp/householder, 2,000+ sq ft heating area	year	577	90	28r
Energy exp/householder, mobile home	year	366	90	28r
Energy exp/householder, multifamily	year	382	90	28r
Gas, natural	mil Btu	4.40	90	64s
Gas, natural	000 cu ft	6.50	91	46s
Gas, natural, exp	year	605	91	46s
Gasoline, motor	gal	1.15	4Q 92	4c
Gasoline, unleaded regular	mil Btu	9.96	90	64s
Entertainment				
Bowling, evening rate	game	2.25	4Q 92	4c
Miniature golf admission	adult	6.18	92	1r
Miniature golf admission	child	5.14	92	1r
Monopoly game, Parker Brothers', No. 9		10.54	4Q 92	4c
Movie	admission	5.10	4Q 92	4c
Tennis balls, yellow, Wilson or Penn, 3	can	3.04	4Q 92	4c
Waterpark admission	adult	11.00	92	1r
Waterpark admission	child	8.55	92	1r
Funerals				
Casket, 18-gauge steel, velvet interior		2029.08	91	24r
Cosmetology, hair care, etc.		75.10	91	24r
Embalming		249.24	91	24r
Facility use for ceremony		162.27	91	24r
Hearse, local		114.04	91	24r
Limousine, local		88.57	91	24r
Remains to funeral home, transfer		92.61	91	24r
Service charge, professional		682.42	91	24r
Vault, concrete, non-metallic liner		798.70	91	24r
Viewing facilities, use		163.86	91	24r
Goods and Services				
ACCRA Index, Miscellaneous Goods and Services		107.60	4Q 92	4c
Groceries				
ACCRA Index, Groceries		93.40	4Q 92	4c
Apples, Red Delicious	lb	0.79	4/93	16r
Babyfood, strained vegetables, lowest price	4-4.5 oz jar	0.19	4Q 92	4c
Bacon	lb	1.75	4/93	16r
Bananas	lb	0.41	4Q 92	4c
Bananas	lb	0.42	4/93	16r
Beef, stew, boneless	lb	2.61	4/93	16r
Bologna, all beef or mixed	lb	2.24	4/93	16r
Bread, white	24 oz	0.50	4Q 92	4c
Bread, white, pan	lb	0.64	4/93	16r
Bread, whole wheat, pan	lb	0.96	4/93	16r
Cabbage	lb	0.37	4/93	16r
Carrots, short trimmed and topped	lb	0.47	4/93	16r
Celery	lb	0.64	4/93	16r
Cheese, American	lb	2.98	4/93	16r
Cheese, Cheddar	lb	3.28	4/93	16r
Cheese, Kraft grated Parmesan	8-oz canister	2.91	4Q 92	4c
Chicken, fresh, whole	lb	0.77	4/93	16r
Chicken, fryer, whole	lb	0.91	4Q 92	4c
Chicken breast, bone-in	lb	1.92	4/93	16r
Chicken legs, bone-in	lb	1.06	4/93	16r
Chuck roast, graded and ungraded, ex USDA prime and choice	lb	2.40	4/93	16r

Huntington, WV - continued

Item	Per	Value	Date	Ref.
Groceries - continued				
Chuck roast, USDA choice, bone-in	lb	2.19	4/93	16r
Chuck roast, USDA choice, boneless	lb	2.38	4/93	16r
Cigarettes, Winston	carton	17.31	4Q 92	4c
Coffee, 100% ground roast, all sizes	lb	2.48	4/93	16r
Coffee, vacuum-packed	13-oz can	2.23	4Q 92	4c
Corn, frozen	10 oz	0.62	4Q 92	4c
Corn Flakes, Kellogg's or Post Toasties	18 oz	1.98	4Q 92	4c
Crackers, soda, salted	lb	1.15	4/93	16r
Eggs, Grade A large	doz	0.75	4Q 92	4c
Eggs, Grade A large	doz	0.96	4/93	16r
Flour, white, all purpose	lb	0.24	4/93	16r
Frankfurters, all meat or all beef	lb	2.01	4/93	16r
Grapefruit	lb	0.44	4/93	16r
Grapes, Thompson Seedless	lb	1.40	4/93	16r
Ground beef, 100% beef	lb	1.58	4/93	16r
Ground beef, lean and extra lean	lb	2.09	4/93	16r
Ground beef or hamburger	lb	1.18	4Q 92	4c
Ground chuck, 100% beef	lb	1.98	4/93	16r
Ham, boneless, excluding canned	lb	2.89	4/93	16r
Ham, picnic, shoulder, bone-in, smoked	lb	1.02	4/93	16r
Ham, rump or steak half, bone-in, smoked	lb	1.48	4/93	16r
Ice cream, prepackaged, bulk, regular	1/2 gal	2.41	4/93	16r
Lemons	lb	1.05	4/93	16r
Lettuce, iceberg	head	0.90	4Q 92	4c
Lettuce, iceberg	lb	0.81	4/93	16r
Margarine, Blue Bonnet or Parkay cubes	lb	0.49	4Q 92	4c
Margarine, stick	lb	0.88	4/93	16r
Milk, whole	1/2 gal	1.44	4Q 92	4c
Orange juice, Minute Maid frozen	12-oz can	1.29	4Q 92	4c
Oranges, navel	lb	0.55	4/93	16r
Peaches	29-oz can	1.37	4Q 92	4c
Pears, Anjou	lb	0.92	4/93	16r
Peas Sweet, Del Monte or Green Giant	15-17 oz can	0.58	4Q 92	4c
Pork chops, center cut, bone-in	lb	3.13	4/93	16r
Potato chips	16 oz	2.94	4/93	16r
Potatoes, white	lb	0.43	4/93	16r
Potatoes, white or red	10-lb sack	2.16	4Q 92	4c
Rib roast, USDA choice, bone-in	lb	4.63	4/93	16r
Rice, white, long grain, uncooked	lb	0.45	4/93	16r
Round roast, graded & ungraded, ex USDA prime & choice	lb	3.03	4/93	16r
Round roast, USDA choice, boneless	lb	3.09	4/93	16r
Sausage, fresh, loose	lb	2.08	4/93	16r
Sausage, Jimmy Dean, 100% pork	lb	2.48	4Q 92	4c
Short ribs, bone-in	lb	2.66	4/93	16r
Shortening, vegetable oil blends	lb	0.69	4/93	16r
Shortening, vegetable, Crisco	3-lb can	1.86	4Q 92	4c
Soft drink, Coca Cola	2 liter	1.05	4Q 92	4c
Spaghetti and macaroni	lb	0.81	4/93	16r
Steak, rib eye, USDA choice, boneless	lb	6.24	4/93	16r
Steak, round, graded & ungraded, ex USDA prime & choice	lb	3.31	4/93	16r
Steak, round, USDA choice, boneless	lb	3.34	4/93	16r
Steak, sirloin, graded & ungraded, ex USDA prime & choice	lb	4.19	4/93	16r
Steak, sirloin, USDA choice, boneless	lb	4.46	4/93	16r
Steak, T-bone	lb	6.05	4Q 92	4c
Steak, T-bone, USDA choice, bone-in	lb	5.25	4/93	16r
Strawberries, dry pint	12 oz	0.92	4/93	16r
Sugar, cane or beet	4 lb	0.94	4Q 92	4c
Sugar, white	lb	0.39	4/93	16r
Sugar, white, 33-80 oz pk	lb	0.38	4/93	16r
Tomatoes, field grown	lb	0.88	4/93	16r
Tomatoes, Hunt's or Del Monte	14.5-oz can	0.69	4Q 92	4c

Values are in dollars or fractions of dollars. In the column headed *Ref*, references are shown to sources. Each reference is followed by a letter. These refer to the geographical level for which data were reported: s = State, r = Region, and c = City or metro. The abbreviation *ex* is used to mean *except* or *excluding*; *exp* stands for expenditures. For other abbreviations and further explanations, please see the Introduction.

Huntington, WV - continued

Item	Per	Value	Date	Ref.
Groceries				
Tuna, chunk, light	6.125-6.5 oz can	0.57	4Q 92	4c
Tuna, chunk, light	lb	1.79	4/93	16r
Turkey, frozen, whole	lb	1.04	4/93	16r
Yogurt, natural, fruit flavored	1/2 pint	0.57	4/93	16r
Health Care				
ACCRA Index, Health Care		97.70	4Q 92	4c
Analgesic, Aspirin, Bayer, 325 mg tablets	100	5.35	4Q 92	4c
Childbirth, cesarean, hospital		5034	91	62r
Childbirth, cesarean, physician's fee		2053	91	62r
Childbirth, normal, hospital		2712	91	62r
Childbirth, normal, physician's fee		1492	91	62r
Dentist's fee, adult teeth cleaning and periodic oral exam	visit	43.80	4Q 92	4c
Doctor's fee, routine exam, established patient	visit	37.20	4Q 92	4c
Hospital care, semiprivate room	day	278.00	90	27c
Hospital care, semiprivate room	day	299.50	4Q 92	4c
Medical insurance premium, per employee, small group comprehensive	month	306.60	10/91	25c
Medical plan per employee	year	3495	91	45r
Mental health care, exp	capita	20.37-28.83	90	38s
Mental health care, exp, state mental health agency	capita	23.72	90	38s
Mental health care, hospital psychiatric services, non-Federal, exp	capita	9.26	88	38s
Mental health care, mental health organization, multiservice, exp	capita	26.55	88	38s
Mental health care, psychiatric hospitals, private, exp	capita	5.67	88	38s
Mental health care, psychiatric out-patient clinics, freestanding, exp	capita	1.30	88	38s
Mental health care, state and county mental hospitals, exp	capita	11.86	88	38s
Mental health care, VA medical centers, exp	capita	0.70	88	38s
Physician fee, family practice, first-visit		75.00	91	62r
Physician fee, family practice, revisit		34.00	91	62r
Physician fee, general practice, first-visit		61.00	91	62r
Physician fee, general practice, revisit		32.00	91	62r
Physician fee, general surgeon, first-visit		64.00	91	62r
Physician fee, general surgeon, revisit		40.00	91	62r
Physician fee, internal medicine, first-visit		98.00	91	62r
Physician fee, internal medicine, revisit		40.00	91	62r
Physician fee, median, neurosurgeon, first-visit		130.00	91	62r
Physician fee, median, nonsurgical specialist, first-visit		95.00	91	62r
Physician fee, median, orthopedic surgeon, first-visit		91.00	91	62r
Physician fee, median, plastic surgeon, first-visit		66.00	91	62r
Physician fee, median, surgical specialist, first-visit		62.00	91	62r
Physician fee, neurosurgeon, revisit		50.00	91	62r
Physician fee, nonsurgical specialist, revisit		40.00	91	62r
Physician fee, obstetrics/gynecology, first-visit		64.00	91	62r
Physician fee, obstetrics/gynecology, revisit		41.00	91	62r
Physician fee, orthopedic surgeon, revisit		40.00	91	62r
Physician fee, pediatrician, first-visit		49.00	91	62r
Physician fee, pediatrician, revisit		33.00	91	62r
Physician fee, plastic surgeon, revisit		43.00	91	62r
Physician fee, surgical specialist, revisit		37.00	91	62r
Substance abuse, hospital ancillary charge	incident	1900	90	70s
Substance abuse, hospital physician charge	incident	1270	90	70s
Substance abuse, hospital room and board	incident	4590	90	70s

Huntington, WV - continued

Item	Per	Value	Date	Ref.
Household Goods				
Appliance repair, home, service call, washing machine	min labor charge	28.60	4Q 92	4c
Laundry detergent, Tide Ultra, Bold, or Cheer	42 oz	3.49	4Q 92	4c
Tissues, facial, Kleenex brand	175-count box	1.05	4Q 92	4c
Housing				
ACCRA Index, Housing		83.30	4Q 92	4c
House, 1,800 sq ft, 8,000 sq ft lot, new, urban	total	90250	4Q 92	4c
House payment, principal and interest, 25% down payment	month	506	4Q 92	4c
Mortgage rate, incl. points & origination fee, 30-year fixed or adjustable rate	percent	8.20	4Q 92	4c
Rent, apartment, 2 bedrooms - 1-1/2 to 2 baths, unfurnished, 950 sq ft, water	month	425	4Q 92	4c
Rental unit, 1 bedroom	month	389	93	23c
Rental unit, 2 bedroom	month	460	93	23c
Rental unit, 3 bedroom	month	575	93	23c
Rental unit, 4 bedroom	month	647	93	23c
Rental unit, efficiency	month	320	93	23c
Insurance and Pensions				
Auto insurance, private passenger	year	621.65	91	63s
Personal Goods				
Shampoo, Alberto VO5	15 oz	1.58	4Q 92	4c
Toothpaste, Crest or Colgate	6-7 oz	2.01	4Q 92	4c
Personal Services				
Dry cleaning, man's 2-piece suit		6.17	4Q 92	4c
Haircare, woman's shampoo, trim and blow-dry		13.00	4Q 92	4c
Haircut, man's barbershop, no styling		6.30	4Q 92	4c
Restaurant Food				
Chicken, fried, thigh and drumstick		2.00	4Q 92	4c
Hamburger with cheese	1/4 lb	1.90	4Q 92	4c
Pizza, Pizza Hut or Pizza Inn, cheese, thin crust	12-13 in	7.49	4Q 92	4c
Taxes				
Tax, cigarette	pack	17	91	77s
Tax, gasoline	gal	15.50	91	77s
Taxes, state	capita	1293	91	77s
Transportation				
ACCRA Index, Transportation		102.20	4Q 92	4c
Bus fare, up to 10 miles	one-way	0.75	4Q 92	4c
Driver's license fee		10.00	12/90	43s
Tire balance, computer or spin balance, front	wheel	6.90	4Q 92	4c
Vehicle registration and license plate	year	26.50-37.50	93	69s
Travel				
Business travel	day	193.00	4/93	89r
Utilities				
ACCRA Index, Utilities		86.50	4Q 92	4c
Electricity	mil Btu	13.90	90	64s
Electricity, all electric, 1,800 sq ft living area new home	month	87.83	4Q 92	4c
Electricity, winter, 250 KWh	month	21.89	92	55s
Electricity, winter, 500 KWh	month	38.44	92	55s
Electricity, winter, 750 KWh	month	53.70	92	55s
Electricity, winter, 1000 KWh	month	68.96	92	55s

Values are in dollars or fractions of dollars. In the column headed *Ref*, references are shown to sources. Each reference is followed by a letter. These refer to the geographical level for which data were reported: s=State, r=Region, and c=City or metro. The abbreviation *ex* is used to mean *except* or *excluding*; *exp* stands for expenditures. For other abbreviations and further explanations, please see the Introduction.

Huntsville, AL

Item	Per	Value	Date	Ref.
Composite ACCRA index		100.60	4Q 92	4c
Alcoholic Beverages				
Beer, Miller Lite or Budweiser, 12-oz containers	6 pack	4.09	4Q 92	4c
Liquor, J & B Scotch	750 ml	19.99	4Q 92	4c
Wine, Gallo Chablis blanc, 1.5 liter	bottle	5.55	4Q 92	4c
Child Care				
Child care fee, average, center	hour	1.29	90	65r
Child care fee, average, nonregulated family day care	hour	0.89	90	65r
Child care fee, average, regulated family day care	hour	1.32	90	65r
Clothing				
Jeans, man's denim		29.80	4Q 92	4c
Shirt, man's dress shirt		24.09	4Q 92	4c
Undervest, boy's size 10-14, cotton	3	6.07	4Q 92	4c
Communications				
Long-distance telephone service, day, initial minute, 0-100 miles	min	0.11-0.36	91	12s
Long-distance telephone service, day, additional minute, 0-100 miles	min	0.09-0.26	91	12s
Long-distance telephone service, evenings/weekends, 0-100 mi, initial minute	min	0.04-0.14	91	12s
Long-distance telephone service, evenings/weekends, 0-100 mi, additional minute	min	0.04-0.10	91	12s
Newspaper subscription, daily and Sunday home delivery, large-city	month	9.85	4Q 92	4c
Telephone, flat rate	month	17.26	91	11c
Telephone, residential, private line, rotary, unlimited calling	month	23.67	10/91	78c
Telephone bill, family of four	month	23.69	4Q 92	4c
Education				
Board, 4-yr private college/university	year	1795	91	22s
Board, 4-yr public college/university	year	1469	91	22s
Expenditures, local gov't, public elementary/secondary	pupil	3675	92	20s
Room, 4-year private college/university	year	1340	91	22s
Room, 4-year public college/university	year	1295	91	22s
Tuition, 2-year private college/university	year	4148	91	22s
Tuition, 2-year public college/university	year	689	91	22s
Tuition, 4-year private college/university	year	5942	91	22s
Tuition, 4-year public college/university, in-state	year	1593	91	22s
Energy and Fuels				
Coal	mil Btu	1.83	90	64s
Energy	mil Btu	7.92	90	64s
Energy, combined forms, 1,800 sq ft heating area	month	99.89	4Q 92	4c
Energy exp/householder, 1-family unit	year	403	90	28r
Energy exp/householder, <1,000 sq ft heating area	year	342	90	28r
Energy exp/householder, 1,000-1,999 sq ft heating area	year	388	90	28r
Energy exp/householder, 2,000+ sq ft heating area	year	434	90	28r
Energy exp/householder, mobile home	year	320	90	28r
Energy exp/householder, multifamily	year	338	90	28r
Gas, natural	mil Btu	4.07	90	64s
Gas, natural	000 cu ft	7.05	91	46s
Gas, natural, exp	year	461	91	46s
Gasoline, motor	gal	1.13	4Q 92	4c
Gasoline, unleaded regular	mil Btu	8.96	90	64s
Entertainment				
Bowling, evening rate	game	2.08	4Q 92	4c
Miniature golf admission	adult	6.18	92	1r
Miniature golf admission	child	5.14	92	1r
Monopoly game, Parker Brothers', No. 9		11.24	4Q 92	4c

Huntsville, AL - continued

Item	Per	Value	Date	Ref.
Entertainment - continued				
Movie	admission	6.50	4Q 92	4c
Tennis balls, yellow, Wilson or Penn, 3	can	2.48	4Q 92	4c
Waterpark admission	adult	11.00	92	1r
Waterpark admission	child	8.55	92	1r
Funerals				
Casket, 18-gauge steel, velvet interior		2329.05	91	24r
Cosmetology, hair care, etc.		72.78	91	24r
Embalming		240.71	91	24r
Facility use for ceremony		181.67	91	24r
Hearse, local		106.25	91	24r
Limousine, local		70.92	91	24r
Remains to funeral home, transfer		96.30	91	24r
Service charge, professional		687.09	91	24r
Vault, concrete, non-metallic liner		732.09	91	24r
Viewing facilities, use		190.30	91	24r
Goods and Services				
ACCRA Index, Miscellaneous Goods and Services		108.30	4Q 92	4c
Groceries				
ACCRA Index, Groceries		94.30	4Q 92	4c
Apples, Red Delicious	lb	0.79	4/93	16r
Babyfood, strained vegetables, lowest price	4-4.5 oz jar	0.27	4Q 92	4c
Bacon	lb	1.75	4/93	16r
Bananas	lb	0.41	4Q 92	4c
Bananas	lb	0.42	4/93	16r
Beef, stew, boneless	lb	2.61	4/93	16r
Bologna, all beef or mixed	lb	2.24	4/93	16r
Bread, white	24 oz	0.72	4Q 92	4c
Bread, white, pan	lb	0.64	4/93	16r
Bread, whole wheat, pan	lb	0.96	4/93	16r
Cabbage	lb	0.37	4/93	16r
Carrots, short trimmed and topped	lb	0.47	4/93	16r
Celery	lb	0.64	4/93	16r
Cheese, American	lb	2.98	4/93	16r
Cheese, Cheddar	lb	3.28	4/93	16r
Cheese, Kraft grated Parmesan	8-oz canister	3.03	4Q 92	4c
Chicken, fresh, whole	lb	0.77	4/93	16r
Chicken, fryer, whole	lb	0.68	4Q 92	4c
Chicken breast, bone-in	lb	1.92	4/93	16r
Chicken legs, bone-in	lb	1.06	4/93	16r
Chuck roast, graded and ungraded, ex USDA prime and choice	lb	2.40	4/93	16r
Chuck roast, USDA choice, bone-in	lb	2.19	4/93	16r
Chuck roast, USDA choice, boneless	lb	2.38	4/93	16r
Cigarettes, Winston	carton	16.33	4Q 92	4c
Coffee, 100% ground roast, all sizes	lb	2.48	4/93	16r
Coffee, vacuum-packed	13-oz can	1.92	4Q 92	4c
Corn, frozen	10 oz	0.53	4Q 92	4c
Corn Flakes, Kellogg's or Post Toasties	18 oz	1.52	4Q 92	4c
Crackers, soda, salted	lb	1.15	4/93	16r
Eggs, Grade A large	doz	0.78	4Q 92	4c
Eggs, Grade A large	doz	0.96	4/93	16r
Flour, white, all purpose	lb	0.24	4/93	16r
Frankfurters, all meat or all beef	lb	2.01	4/93	16r
Grapefruit	lb	0.44	4/93	16r
Grapes, Thompson Seedless	lb	1.40	4/93	16r
Ground beef, 100% beef	lb	1.58	4/93	16r
Ground beef, lean and extra lean	lb	2.09	4/93	16r
Ground beef or hamburger	lb	1.71	4Q 92	4c
Ground chuck, 100% beef	lb	1.98	4/93	16r
Ham, boneless, excluding canned	lb	2.89	4/93	16r
Ham, picnic, shoulder, bone-in, smoked	lb	1.02	4/93	16r
Ham, rump or steak half, bone-in, smoked	lb	1.48	4/93	16r
Honey, jar	8 oz	0.89-1.09	92	5r
Honey, jar	lb	1.39-2.25	92	5r
Honey, squeeze bear	12-oz	1.00-1.50	92	5r

Values are in dollars or fractions of dollars. In the column headed *Ref*, references are shown to sources. Each reference is followed by a letter. These refer to the geographical level for which data were reported: s=State, r=Region, and c=City or metro. The abbreviation *ex* is used to mean *except* or *excluding*; *exp* stands for expenditures. For other abbreviations and further explanations, please see the Introduction.

Huntsville, AL - continued

Item	Per	Value	Date	Ref.
Groceries				
Ice cream, prepackaged, bulk, regular	1/2 gal	2.41	4/93	16r
Lemons	lb	1.05	4/93	16r
Lettuce, iceberg	head	1.09	4Q 92	4c
Lettuce, iceberg	lb	0.81	4/93	16r
Margarine, Blue Bonnet or Parkay cubes	lb	0.51	4Q 92	4c
Margarine, stick	lb	0.88	4/93	16r
Milk, whole	1/2 gal	1.27	4Q 92	4c
Orange juice, Minute Maid frozen	12-oz can	1.21	4Q 92	4c
Oranges, navel	lb	0.55	4/93	16r
Peaches	29-oz can	1.25	4Q 92	4c
Pears, Anjou	lb	0.92	4/93	16r
Peas Sweet, Del Monte or Green Giant	15-17 oz can	0.56	4Q 92	4c
Pork chops, center cut, bone-in	lb	3.13	4/93	16r
Potato chips	16 oz	2.94	4/93	16r
Potatoes, white	lb	0.43	4/93	16r
Potatoes, white or red	10-lb sack	2.45	4Q 92	4c
Rib roast, USDA choice, bone-in	lb	4.63	4/93	16r
Rice, white, long grain, uncooked	lb	0.45	4/93	16r
Round roast, graded & ungraded, ex USDA prime & choice	lb	3.03	4/93	16r
Round roast, USDA choice, boneless	lb	3.09	4/93	16r
Sausage, fresh, loose	lb	2.08	4/93	16r
Sausage, Jimmy Dean, 100% pork	lb	2.19	4Q 92	4c
Short ribs, bone-in	lb	2.66	4/93	16r
Shortening, vegetable oil blends	lb	0.69	4/93	16r
Shortening, vegetable, Crisco	3-lb can	1.97	4Q 92	4c
Soft drink, Coca Cola	2 liter	1.10	4Q 92	4c
Spaghetti and macaroni	lb	0.81	4/93	16r
Steak, rib eye, USDA choice, boneless	lb	6.24	4/93	16r
Steak, round, graded & ungraded, ex USDA prime & choice	lb	3.31	4/93	16r
Steak, round, USDA choice, boneless	lb	3.34	4/93	16r
Steak, sirloin, graded & ungraded, ex USDA prime & choice	lb	4.19	4/93	16r
Steak, sirloin, USDA choice, boneless	lb	4.46	4/93	16r
Steak, T-bone	lb	5.59	4Q 92	4c
Steak, T-bone, USDA choice, bone-in	lb	5.25	4/93	16r
Strawberries, dry pint	12 oz	0.92	4/93	16r
Sugar, cane or beet	4 lb	1.40	4Q 92	4c
Sugar, white	lb	0.39	4/93	16r
Sugar, white, 33-80 oz pk	lb	0.38	4/93	16r
Tomatoes, field grown	lb	0.88	4/93	16r
Tomatoes, Hunt's or Del Monte	14.5-oz can	0.50	4Q 92	4c
Tuna, chunk, light	6.125-6.5 oz can	0.56	4Q 92	4c
Tuna, chunk, light	lb	1.79	4/93	16r
Turkey, frozen, whole	lb	1.04	4/93	16r
Yogurt, natural, fruit flavored	1/2 pint	0.57	4/93	16r
Health Care				
ACCRA Index, Health Care		95.40	4Q 92	4c
Analgesic, Aspirin, Bayer, 325 mg tablets	100	4.34	4Q 92	4c
Childbirth, cesarean, hospital		5034	91	62r
Childbirth, cesarean, physician's fee		2053	91	62r
Childbirth, normal, hospital		2712	91	62r
Childbirth, normal, physician's fee		1492	91	62r
Dentist's fee, adult teeth cleaning and periodic oral exam	visit	39.83	4Q 92	4c
Doctor's fee, routine exam, established patient	visit	41.67	4Q 92	4c
Hospital care, semiprivate room	day	276.67	4Q 92	4c
Medical insurance premium, per employee, small group comprehensive	month	324.85	10/91	25c
Mental health care, exp	capita	37.60-53.67	90	38s

Huntsville, AL - continued

Item	Per	Value	Date	Ref.
Health Care - continued				
Mental health care, exp, state mental health agency	capita	38.35	90	38s
Mental health care, hospital psychiatric services, non-Federal, exp	capita	13.58	88	38s
Mental health care, mental health organization, multiservice, exp	capita	12.40	88	38s
Mental health care, psychiatric hospitals, private, exp	capita	9.49	88	38s
Mental health care, state and county mental hospitals, exp	capita	22.15	88	38s
Mental health care, VA medical centers, exp	capita	10.94	88	38s
Physician fee, family practice, first-visit		75.00	91	62r
Physician fee, family practice, revisit		34.00	91	62r
Physician fee, general practice, first-visit		61.00	91	62r
Physician fee, general practice, revisit		32.00	91	62r
Physician fee, general surgeon, first-visit		64.00	91	62r
Physician fee, general surgeon, revisit		40.00	91	62r
Physician fee, internal medicine, first-visit		98.00	91	62r
Physician fee, internal medicine, revisit		40.00	91	62r
Physician fee, median, neurosurgeon, first-visit		130.00	91	62r
Physician fee, median, nonsurgical specialist, first-visit		95.00	91	62r
Physician fee, median, orthopedic surgeon, first-visit		91.00	91	62r
Physician fee, median, plastic surgeon, first-visit		66.00	91	62r
Physician fee, median, surgical specialist, first-visit		62.00	91	62r
Physician fee, neurosurgeon, revisit		50.00	91	62r
Physician fee, nonsurgical specialist, revisit		40.00	91	62r
Physician fee, obstetrics/gynecology, first-visit		64.00	91	62r
Physician fee, obstetrics/gynecology, revisit		41.00	91	62r
Physician fee, orthopedic surgeon, revisit		40.00	91	62r
Physician fee, pediatrician, first-visit		49.00	91	62r
Physician fee, pediatrician, revisit		33.00	91	62r
Physician fee, plastic surgeon, revisit		43.00	91	62r
Physician fee, surgical specialist, revisit		37.00	91	62r
Substance abuse, hospital ancillary charge	incident	1390	90	70s
Substance abuse, hospital physician charge	incident	520	90	70s
Substance abuse, hospital room and board	incident	5830	90	70s
Household Goods				
Appliance repair, home, service call, washing machine	min labor charge	35.90	4Q 92	4c
Laundry detergent, Tide Ultra, Bold, or Cheer	42 oz	2.90	4Q 92	4c
Tissues, facial, Kleenex brand	175-count box	1.02	4Q 92	4c
Housing				
ACCRA Index, Housing		94.00	4Q 92	4c
House, 1,800 sq ft, 8,000 sq ft lot, new, urban	total	107068	4Q 92	4c
House payment, principal and interest, 25% down payment	month	590	4Q 92	4c
Mortgage rate, incl. points & origination fee, 30-year fixed or adjustable rate	percent	8.01	4Q 92	4c
Rent, apartment, 2 bedrooms - 1-1/2 to 2 baths, unfurnished, 950 sq ft, water	month	435	4Q 92	4c
Rental unit, 1 bedroom	month	368	93	23c
Rental unit, 2 bedroom	month	432	93	23c
Rental unit, 3 bedroom	month	542	93	23c
Rental unit, 4 bedroom	month	608	93	23c
Rental unit, efficiency	month	304	93	23c

Values are in dollars or fractions of dollars. In the column headed *Ref*, references are shown to sources. Each reference is followed by a letter. These refer to the geographical level for which data were reported: s=State, r=Region, and c=City or metro. The abbreviation *ex* is used to mean *except* or *excluding*; *exp* stands for expenditures. For other abbreviations and further explanations, please see the Introduction.

Huntsville, AL - continued

Item	Per	Value	Date	Ref.
Insurance and Pensions				
Auto insurance, private passenger	year	562.59	91	63s
Personal Goods				
Shampoo, Alberto VO5	15 oz	1.19	4Q 92	4c
Toothpaste, Crest or Colgate	6-7 oz	1.94	4Q 92	4c
Personal Services				
Dry cleaning, man's 2-piece suit		5.29	4Q 92	4c
Haircare, woman's shampoo, trim and blow-dry		13.20	4Q 92	4c
Haircut, man's barbershop, no styling		8.80	4Q 92	4c
Restaurant Food				
Chicken, fried, thigh and drumstick		2.18	4Q 92	4c
Hamburger with cheese	1/4 lb	1.91	4Q 92	4c
Pizza, Pizza Hut or Pizza Inn, cheese, thin crust	12-13 in	9.99	4Q 92	4c
Taxes				
Tax, cigarette	pack	16.50	91	77s
Tax, gasoline	gal	16	91	77s
Taxes, state	capita	964	91	77s
Transportation				
ACCRA Index, Transportation		108.50	4Q 92	4c
Driver's license fee		15.00	12/90	43s
Tire balance, computer or spin balance, front	wheel	7.58	4Q 92	4c
Travel				
Business travel	day	193.00	4/93	89r
Utilities				
ACCRA Index, Utilities		94.50	4Q 92	4c
Electricity	mil Btu	16.46	90	64s
Electricity, all electric, 1,800 sq ft living area new home	month	99.89	4Q 92	4c

Indianapolis, IN

Item	Per	Value	Date	Ref.
Composite ACCRA index		97.90	4Q 92	4c
Alcoholic Beverages				
Beer, Miller Lite or Budweiser, 12-oz containers	6 pack	3.59	4Q 92	4c
Liquor, J & B Scotch	750 ml	14.85	4Q 92	4c
Wine, Gallo Chablis blanc, 1.5 liter	bottle	4.74	4Q 92	4c
Child Care				
Child care fee, average, center	hour	1.63	90	65r
Child care fee, average, nonregulated family day care	hour	1.83	90	65r
Child care fee, average, regulated family day care	hour	1.42	90	65r
Clothing				
Jeans, man's denim		29.59	4Q 92	4c
Shirt, man's dress shirt		23.99	4Q 92	4c
Undervest, boy's size 10-14, cotton	3	4.13	4Q 92	4c
Communications				
Long-distance telephone service, day, initial minute, 0-100 miles	min	0.18-0.45	91	12s
Long-distance telephone service, day, additional minute, 0-100 miles	min	0.10-0.30	91	12s
Long-distance telephone service, evenings/weekends, 0-100 mi, initial minute	min	0.08-0.19	91	12s
Long-distance telephone service, evenings/weekends, 0-100 mi, additional minute	min	0.04-0.13	91	12s
Newspaper subscription, daily and Sunday home delivery, large-city	month	11.96	4Q 92	4c
Telephone, flat rate	month	13.17	91	11c
Telephone, residential, private line, rotary, unlimited calling	month	20.78	10/91	78c
Telephone bill, family of four	month	21.98	4Q 92	4c

Indianapolis, IN - continued

Item	Per	Value	Date	Ref.
Education				
Board, 4-yr private college/university	year	1714	91	22s
Board, 4-yr public college/university	year	1829	91	22s
Expenditures, local gov't, public elementary/secondary	pupil	5545	92	20s
Room, 4-year private college/university	year	1512	91	22s
Room, 4-year public college/university	year	1435	91	22s
Tuition, 2-year private college/university	year	6756	91	22s
Tuition, 2-year public college/university	year	1423	91	22s
Tuition, 4-year private college/university	year	8451	91	22s
Tuition, 4-year public college/university, in-state	year	2067	91	22s
Energy and Fuels				
Coal	mil Btu	1.46	90	64s
Energy	mil Btu	6.77	90	64s
Energy, combined forms, 1,800 sq ft heating area	month	104.06	4Q 92	4c
Energy, exc electricity, 1,800 sq ft heating area	month	55.20	4Q 92	4c
Energy exp/householder, 1-family unit	year	471	90	28r
Energy exp/householder, <1,000 sq ft heating area	year	430	90	28r
Energy exp/householder, 1,000-1,999 sq ft heating area	year	481	90	28r
Energy exp/householder, 2,000+ sq ft heating area	year	473	90	28r
Energy exp/householder, mobile home	year	430	90	28r
Energy exp/householder, multifamily	year	461	90	28r
Gas, cooking, 10 therms	month	9.86	92	56c
Gas, cooking, 30 therms	month	17.57	92	56c
Gas, cooking, 50 therms	month	25.29	92	56c
Gas, heating, winter, 100 therms	month	53.92	92	56c
Gas, heating, winter, average use	month	89.95	92	56c
Gas, natural	mil Btu	4.27	90	64s
Gas, natural	000 cu ft	5.46	91	46s
Gas, natural, exp	year	588	91	46s
Gasoline, motor	gal	1.10	4Q 92	4c
Gasoline, unleaded regular	mil Btu	8.74	90	64s
Entertainment				
Bowling, evening rate	game	2.04	4Q 92	4c
Miniature golf admission	adult	6.18	92	1r
Miniature golf admission	child	5.14	92	1r
Monopoly game, Parker Brothers', No. 9		12.16	4Q 92	4c
Movie	admission	6.25	4Q 92	4c
Tennis balls, yellow, Wilson or Penn, 3	can	2.21	4Q 92	4c
Waterpark admission	adult	11.00	92	1r
Waterpark admission	child	8.55	92	1r
Funerals				
Casket, 18-gauge steel, velvet interior		1926.72	91	24r
Cosmetology, hair care, etc.		97.64	91	24r
Embalming		249.14	91	24r
Facility use for ceremony		208.59	91	24r
Hearse, local		130.12	91	24r
Limousine, local		104.66	91	24r
Remains to funeral home, transfer		93.61	91	24r
Service charge, professional		724.62	91	24r
Vault, concrete, non-metallic liner		734.53	91	24r
Viewing facilities, use		236.06	91	24r
Goods and Services				
ACCRA Index, Miscellaneous Goods and Services		97.90	4Q 92	4c
Groceries				
ACCRA Index, Groceries		98.20	4Q 92	4c
Apples, Red Delicious	lb	0.77	4/93	16r
Babyfood, strained vegetables, lowest price	4-4.5 oz jar	0.30	4Q 92	4c
Bacon	lb	1.85	4/93	16r
Bananas	lb	0.44	4Q 92	4c

Values are in dollars or fractions of dollars. In the column headed *Ref*, references are shown to sources. Each reference is followed by a letter. These refer to the geographical level for which data were reported: s = State, r = Region, and c = City or metro. The abbreviation *ex* is used to mean *except* or *excluding*; *exp* stands for expenditures. For other abbreviations and further explanations, please see the Introduction.

Indianapolis, IN - continued

Item	Per	Value	Date	Ref.
Groceries				
Bananas	lb	0.46	4/93	16r
Beef, stew, boneless	lb	2.53	4/93	16r
Bologna, all beef or mixed	lb	2.19	4/93	16r
Bread, white	24 oz	0.59	4Q 92	4c
Bread, white, pan	lb	0.78	4/93	16r
Butter	lb	1.50	4/93	16r
Cabbage	lb	0.40	4/93	16r
Carrots, short trimmed and topped	lb	0.45	4/93	16r
Cheese, Cheddar	lb	3.47	4/93	16r
Cheese, Kraft grated Parmesan	8-oz canister	3.16	4Q 92	4c
Chicken, fresh, whole	lb	0.84	4/93	16r
Chicken, fryer, whole	lb	0.82	4Q 92	4c
Chicken breast, bone-in	lb	1.94	4/93	16r
Chicken legs, bone-in	lb	1.02	4/93	16r
Chuck roast, graded and ungraded, ex USDA prime and choice	lb	2.43	4/93	16r
Chuck roast, USDA choice, bone-in	lb	2.11	4/93	16r
Chuck roast, USDA choice, boneless	lb	2.44	4/93	16r
Cigarettes, Winston	carton	16.74	4Q 92	4c
Coffee, 100% ground roast, all sizes	lb	2.47	4/93	16r
Coffee, vacuum-packed	13-oz can	2.04	4Q 92	4c
Cookies, chocolate chip	lb	2.73	4/93	16r
Corn, frozen	10 oz	0.67	4Q 92	4c
Corn Flakes, Kellogg's or Post Toasties	18 oz	1.73	4Q 92	4c
Eggs, Grade A large	doz	0.79	4Q 92	4c
Eggs, Grade A large	doz	0.93	4/93	16r
Flour, white, all purpose	lb	0.21	4/93	16r
Grapefruit	lb	0.45	4/93	16r
Grapes, Thompson Seedless	lb	1.46	4/93	16r
Ground beef, 100% beef	lb	1.63	4/93	16r
Ground beef, lean and extra lean	lb	2.08	4/93	16r
Ground beef or hamburger	lb	1.45	4Q 92	4c
Ground chuck, 100% beef	lb	1.94	4/93	16r
Ham, boneless, excluding canned	lb	2.21	4/93	16r
Honey, jar	8 oz	0.97-1.25	92	5r
Honey, jar	lb	1.25-2.25	92	5r
Honey, squeeze bear	12-oz	1.25-1.99	92	5r
Ice cream, prepackaged, bulk, regular	1/2 gal	2.41	4/93	16r
Lemons	lb	0.82	4/93	16r
Lettuce, iceberg	head	0.95	4Q 92	4c
Lettuce, iceberg	lb	0.83	4/93	16r
Margarine, Blue Bonnet or Parkay cubes	lb	0.65	4Q 92	4c
Margarine, stick	lb	0.77	4/93	16r
Milk, whole	1/2 gal	1.54	4Q 92	4c
Orange juice, Minute Maid frozen	12-oz can	1.53	4Q 92	4c
Oranges, navel	lb	0.50	4/93	16r
Peaches	29-oz can	1.26	4Q 92	4c
Peanut butter, creamy, all sizes	lb	1.82	4/93	16r
Pears, Anjou	lb	0.85	4/93	16r
Peas Sweet, Del Monte or Green Giant	15-17 oz can	0.60	4Q 92	4c
Pork chops, center cut, bone-in	lb	3.17	4/93	16r
Potato chips	16 oz	2.68	4/93	16r
Potatoes, white	lb	0.26	4/93	16r
Potatoes, white or red	10-lb sack	1.70	4Q 92	4c
Round roast, graded & ungraded, ex USDA prime & choice	lb	2.88	4/93	16r
Round roast, USDA choice, boneless	lb	2.96	4/93	16r
Sausage, Jimmy Dean, 100% pork	lb	3.03	4Q 92	4c
Shortening, vegetable oil blends	lb	0.79	4/93	16r
Shortening, vegetable, Crisco	3-lb can	1.99	4Q 92	4c
Soft drink, Coca Cola	2 liter	1.05	4Q 92	4c
Spaghetti and macaroni	lb	0.76	4/93	16r
Steak, rib eye, USDA choice, boneless	lb	6.29	4/93	16r
Steak, round, USDA choice, boneless	lb	3.24	4/93	16r

Indianapolis, IN - continued

Item	Per	Value	Date	Ref.
Groceries - continued				
Steak, sirloin, graded & ungraded, ex USDA prime & choice	lb	4.00	4/93	16r
Steak, sirloin, USDA choice, bone-in	lb	3.57	4/93	16r
Steak, sirloin, USDA choice, boneless	lb	4.17	4/93	16r
Steak, T-bone	lb	4.48	4Q 92	4c
Steak, T-bone, USDA choice, bone-in	lb	5.60	4/93	16r
Strawberries, dry pint	12 oz	0.90	4/93	16r
Sugar, cane or beet	4 lb	1.29	4Q 92	4c
Sugar, white	lb	0.36	4/93	16r
Sugar, white, 33-80 oz pk	lb	0.35	4/93	16r
Tomatoes, field grown	lb	0.99	4/93	16r
Tomatoes, Hunt's or Del Monte	14.5-oz can	0.75	4Q 92	4c
Tuna, chunk, light	6.125-6.5 oz can	0.64	4Q 92	4c
Tuna, chunk, light	lb	1.76	4/93	16r
Turkey, frozen, whole	lb	0.91	4/93	16r
Health Care				
ACCRA Index, Health Care		97.00	4Q 92	4c
Analgesic, Aspirin, Bayer, 325 mg tablets	100	5.29	4Q 92	4c
Childbirth, cesarean, hospital		4688	91	62r
Childbirth, cesarean, physician's fee		2053	91	62r
Childbirth, normal, hospital		2657	91	62r
Childbirth, normal, physician's fee		1492	91	62r
Dentist's fee, adult teeth cleaning and periodic oral exam	visit	43.90	4Q 92	4c
Doctor's fee, routine exam, established patient	visit	34.90	4Q 92	4c
Hospital care, semiprivate room	day	243.27	90	27c
Hospital care, semiprivate room	day	327.56	4Q 92	4c
Medical insurance premium, per employee, small group comprehensive	month	317.55	10/91	25c
Medical plan per employee	year	3443	91	45r
Mental health care, exp	capita	37.60-53.67	90	38s
Mental health care, exp, state mental health agency	capita	47.05	90	38s
Mental health care, hospital psychiatric services, non-Federal, exp	capita	22.14	88	38s
Mental health care, mental health organization, multiservice, exp	capita	10.33	88	38s
Mental health care, psychiatric hospitals, private, exp	capita	20.10	88	38s
Mental health care, state and county mental hospitals, exp	capita	24.00	88	38s
Mental health care, VA medical centers, exp	capita	3.20	88	38s
Physician fee, family practice, first-visit		76.00	91	62r
Physician fee, family practice, revisit		33.00	91	62r
Physician fee, general practice, first-visit		61.00	91	62r
Physician fee, general practice, revisit		31.00	91	62r
Physician fee, general surgeon, first-visit		65.00	91	62r
Physician fee, general surgeon, revisit		35.00	91	62r
Physician fee, internal medicine, first-visit		91.00	91	62r
Physician fee, internal medicine, revisit		40.00	91	62r
Physician fee, median, neurosurgeon, first-visit		106.00	91	62r
Physician fee, median, nonsurgical specialist, first-visit		90.00	91	62r
Physician fee, median, orthopedic surgeon, first-visit		83.00	91	62r
Physician fee, median, surgical specialist, first-visit		61.00	91	62r
Physician fee, neurosurgeon, revisit		41.00	91	62r
Physician fee, nonsurgical specialist, revisit		40.00	91	62r
Physician fee, obstetrics/gynecology, first-visit		61.00	91	62r
Physician fee, obstetrics/gynecology, revisit		40.00	91	62r
Physician fee, orthopedic surgeon, revisit		41.00	91	62r
Physician fee, pediatrician, first-visit		46.00	91	62r
Physician fee, pediatrician, revisit		33.00	91	62r
Physician fee, surgical specialist, revisit		36.00	91	62r

Values are in dollars or fractions of dollars. In the column headed *Ref*, references are shown to sources. Each reference is followed by a letter. These refer to the geographical level for which data were reported: s = State, r = Region, and c = City or metro. The abbreviation *ex* is used to mean *except* or *excluding*; *exp* stands for expenditures. For other abbreviations and further explanations, please see the Introduction.

Indianapolis, IN - continued

Item	Per	Value	Date	Ref.
Health Care				
Substance abuse, hospital ancillary charge	incident	1230	90	70s
Substance abuse, hospital physician charge	incident	410	90	70s
Substance abuse, hospital room and board	incident	5510	90	70s
Household Goods				
Appliance repair, home, service call, washing machine	min labor charge	26.08	4Q 92	4c
Laundry detergent, Tide Ultra, Bold, or Cheer	42 oz	3.90	4Q 92	4c
Tissues, facial, Kleenex brand	175-count box	1.16	4Q 92	4c
Housing				
ACCRA Index, Housing		97.80	4Q 92	4c
Home, median price	unit	83.70		26c
House, 1,800 sq ft, 8,000 sq ft lot, new, urban	total	104800	4Q 92	4c
House payment, principal and interest, 25% down payment	month	587	4Q 92	4c
Mortgage rate, incl. points & origination fee, 30-year fixed or adjustable rate	percent	8.19	4Q 92	4c
Rent, apartment, 2 bedrooms - 1-1/2 to 2 baths, unfurnished, 950 sq ft, water	month	515	4Q 92	4c
Rental unit, 1 bedroom	month	432	93	23c
Rental unit, 2 bedroom	month	508	93	23c
Rental unit, 3 bedroom	month	635	93	23c
Rental unit, 4 bedroom	month	711	93	23c
Rental unit, efficiency	month	355	93	23c
Insurance and Pensions				
Auto insurance, private passenger	year	548.99	91	63s
Personal Goods				
Shampoo, Alberto VO5	15 oz	1.37	4Q 92	4c
Toothpaste, Crest or Colgate	6-7 oz	2.16	4Q 92	4c
Personal Services				
Dry cleaning, man's 2-piece suit		6.30	4Q 92	4c
Haircare, woman's shampoo, trim and blow-dry		15.05	4Q 92	4c
Haircut, man's barbershop, no styling		7.85	4Q 92	4c
Restaurant Food				
Chicken, fried, thigh and drumstick		1.99	4Q 92	4c
Hamburger with cheese	1/4 lb	1.77	4Q 92	4c
Pizza, Pizza Hut or Pizza Inn, cheese, thin crust	12-13 in	7.99	4Q 92	4c
Taxes				
Tax, cigarette	pack	15.50	91	77s
Tax, gasoline	gal	15	91	77s
Taxes, state	capita	1102	91	77s
Transportation				
ACCRA Index, Transportation		98.80	4Q 92	4c
Auto rental, average	day	49.00	6/91	60c
Bus fare	one-way	0.75	3/93	2c
Bus fare, up to 10 miles	one-way	1.25	4Q 92	4c
Driver's license fee		6.00	12/90	43s
Limo fare, airport-city, average	day	5.00	6/91	60c
Taxi fare, airport-city, average	day	11.00	6/91	60c
Tire balance, computer or spin balance, front	wheel	5.88	4Q 92	4c
Travel				
Breakfast	day	6.22	6/91	60c
Dinner	day	13.24	6/91	60c
Lodging	day	107.94	91	60c
Lunch	day	7.42	6/91	60c

Indianapolis, IN - continued

Item	Per	Value	Date	Ref.
Utilities				
ACCRA Index, Utilities		97.10	4Q 92	4c
Electricity	mil Btu	15.75	90	64s
Electricity, partial electric and other energy, 1,800 sq ft living area new home	month	48.86	4Q 92	4c
Electricity, winter, 250 KWh	month	20.50	92	55c
Electricity, winter, 500 KWh	month	40.35	92	55c
Electricity, winter, 750 KWh	month	49.75	92	55c
Electricity, winter, 1000 KWh	month	59.15	92	55c

Indio, CA

Item	Per	Value	Date	Ref.
Composite ACCRA index		108.00	4Q 92	4c
Alcoholic Beverages				
Beer, Miller Lite or Budweiser, 12-oz containers	6 pack	4.24	4Q 92	4c
Liquor, J & B Scotch	750 ml	15.65	4Q 92	4c
Wine, Gallo Chablis blanc, 1.5 liter	bottle	3.73	4Q 92	4c
Clothing				
Jeans, man's denim		28.99	4Q 92	4c
Shirt, man's dress shirt		27.25	4Q 92	4c
Undervest, boy's size 10-14, cotton	3	6.09	4Q 92	4c
Communications				
Newspaper subscription, daily and Sunday home delivery, large-city	month	7.50	4Q 92	4c
Telephone bill, family of four	month	17.51	4Q 92	4c
Energy and Fuels				
Energy, combined forms, 1,800 sq ft heating area	month	85.23	4Q 92	4c
Energy, exc electricity, 1,800 sq ft heating area	month	23.52	4Q 92	4c
Gasoline, motor	gal	1.29	4Q 92	4c
Entertainment				
Bowling, evening rate	game	1.00	4Q 92	4c
Monopoly game, Parker Brothers', No. 9		11.59	4Q 92	4c
Movie	admission	7.00	4Q 92	4c
Tennis balls, yellow, Wilson or Penn, 3	can	3.08	4Q 92	4c
Goods and Services				
ACCRA Index, Miscellaneous Goods and Services		108.60	4Q 92	4c
Groceries				
ACCRA Index, Groceries		107.70	4Q 92	4c
Babyfood, strained vegetables, lowest price	4-4.5 oz jar	0.38	4Q 92	4c
Bananas	lb	0.54	4Q 92	4c
Bread, white	24 oz	0.93	4Q 92	4c
Cheese, Kraft grated Parmesan	8-oz canister	2.96	4Q 92	4c
Chicken, fryer, whole	lb	0.96	4Q 92	4c
Cigarettes, Winston	carton	20.59	4Q 92	4c
Coffee, vacuum-packed	13-oz can	2.09	4Q 92	4c
Corn, frozen	10 oz	0.65	4Q 92	4c
Corn Flakes, Kellogg's or Post Toasties	18 oz	1.91	4Q 92	4c
Eggs, Grade A large	doz	1.69	4Q 92	4c
Ground beef or hamburger	lb	1.61	4Q 92	4c
Lettuce, iceberg	head	0.89	4Q 92	4c
Margarine, Blue Bonnet or Parkay cubes	lb	0.64	4Q 92	4c
Milk, whole	1/2 gal	1.32	4Q 92	4c
Orange juice, Minute Maid frozen	12-oz can	1.53	4Q 92	4c
Peaches	29-oz can	1.16	4Q 92	4c
Peas Sweet, Del Monte or Green Giant	15-17 oz can	0.61	4Q 92	4c
Potatoes, white or red	10-lb sack	1.44	4Q 92	4c

Values are in dollars or fractions of dollars. In the column headed *Ref*, references are shown to sources. Each reference is followed by a letter. These refer to the geographical level for which data were reported: s=State, r=Region, and c=City or metro. The abbreviation *ex* is used to mean *except* or *excluding*; *exp* stands for expenditures. For other abbreviations and further explanations, please see the Introduction.

Indio, CA - continued

Item	Per	Value	Date	Ref.
Groceries				
Sausage, Jimmy Dean, 100% pork	lb	2.65	4Q 92	4c
Shortening, vegetable, Crisco	3-lb can	2.30	4Q 92	4c
Soft drink, Coca Cola	2 liter	1.08	4Q 92	4c
Steak, T-bone	lb	5.16	4Q 92	4c
Sugar, cane or beet	4 lb	1.47	4Q 92	4c
Tomatoes, Hunt's or Del Monte	14.5-oz can	0.86	4Q 92	4c
Tuna, chunk, light	6.125-6.5 oz can	0.58	4Q 92	4c
Health Care				
ACCRA Index, Health Care		118.40	4Q 92	4c
Analgesic, Aspirin, Bayer, 325 mg tablets	100	5.84	4Q 92	4c
Dentist's fee, adult teeth cleaning and periodic oral exam	visit	40.00	4Q 92	4c
Doctor's fee, routine exam, established patient	visit	47.00	4Q 92	4c
Hospital care, semiprivate room	day	530.00	4Q 92	4c
Household Goods				
Appliance repair, home, service call, washing machine	min labor charge	38.48	4Q 92	4c
Laundry detergent, Tide Ultra, Bold, or Cheer	42 oz	3.90	4Q 92	4c
Tissues, facial, Kleenex brand	175-count box	1.10	4Q 92	4c
Housing				
ACCRA Index, Housing		109.80	4Q 92	4c
House, 1,800 sq ft, 8,000 sq ft lot, new, urban	total	119258	4Q 92	4c
House payment, principal and interest, 25% down payment	month	672	4Q 92	4c
Mortgage rate, incl. points & origination fee, 30-year fixed or adjustable rate	percent	8.25	4Q 92	4c
Rent, apartment, 2 bedrooms - 1-1/2 to 2 baths, unfurnished, 950 sq ft, water	month	549	4Q 92	4c
Personal Goods				
Shampoo, Alberto VO5	15 oz	1.15	4Q 92	4c
Toothpaste, Crest or Colgate	6-7 oz	2.22	4Q 92	4c
Personal Services				
Dry cleaning, man's 2-piece suit		8.62	4Q 92	4c
Haircare, woman's shampoo, trim and blow-dry		24.80	4Q 92	4c
Haircut, man's barbershop, no styling		9.60	4Q 92	4c
Restaurant Food				
Chicken, fried, thigh and drumstick		1.99	4Q 92	4c
Hamburger with cheese	1/4 lb	1.89	4Q 92	4c
Pizza, Pizza Hut or Pizza Inn, cheese, thin crust	12-13 in	6.30	4Q 92	4c
Transportation				
ACCRA Index, Transportation		121.40	4Q 92	4c
Bus fare, up to 10 miles	one-way	0.50	4Q 92	4c
Tire balance, computer or spin balance, front	wheel	9.29	4Q 92	4c
Utilities				
ACCRA Index, Utilities		79.30	4Q 92	4c
Electricity, partial electric and other energy, 1,800 sq ft living area new home	month	61.71	4Q 92	4c

Iowa City-Coralville, IA

Item	Per	Value	Date	Ref.
Composite ACCRA index		105.60	4Q 92	4c
Alcoholic Beverages				
Beer, Miller Lite or Budweiser, 12-oz containers	6 pack	3.53	4Q 92	4c
Liquor, J & B Scotch	750 ml	18.41	4Q 92	4c
Wine, Gallo Chablis blanc, 1.5 liter	bottle	4.93	4Q 92	4c
Child Care				
Child care fee, average, center	hour	1.63	90	65r
Child care fee, average, nonregulated family day care	hour	1.83	90	65r
Child care fee, average, regulated family day care	hour	1.42	90	65r
Clothing				
Jeans, man's denim		30.59	4Q 92	4c
Shirt, man's dress shirt		24.80	4Q 92	4c
Undervest, boy's size 10-14, cotton	3	3.40	4Q 92	4c
Communications				
Long-distance telephone service, day, initial minute, 0-100 miles	min	0.21-0.41	91	12s
Long-distance telephone service, day, additional minute, 0-100 miles	min	0.11-0.30	91	12s
Long-distance telephone service, evenings/weekends, 0-100 mi, initial minute	min	0.11-0.20	91	12s
Long-distance telephone service, evenings/weekends, 0-100 mi, additional minute	min	0.06-0.15	91	12s
Newspaper subscription, daily and Sunday home delivery, large-city	month	9.78	4Q 92	4c
Telephone, flat rate	month	14.45	91	11c
Telephone bill, family of four	month	18.27	4Q 92	4c
Education				
Board, 4-yr private college/university	year	1703	91	22s
Board, 4-yr public college/university	year	1183	91	22s
Expenditures, local gov't, public elementary/secondary	pupil	5026	92	20s
Room, 4-year private college/university	year	1392	91	22s
Room, 4-year public college/university	year	1188	91	22s
Tuition, 2-year private college/university	year	5119	91	22s
Tuition, 2-year public college/university	year	1298	91	22s
Tuition, 4-year private college/university	year	8703	91	22s
Tuition, 4-year public college/university, in-state	year	1880	91	22s
Energy and Fuels				
Coal	mil Btu	1.16	90	64s
Energy	mil Btu	7.71	90	64s
Energy, combined forms, 1,800 sq ft heating area	month	108.87	4Q 92	4c
Energy, exc electricity, 1,800 sq ft heating area	month	32.39	4Q 92	4c
Energy exp/householder, 1-family unit	year	473	90	28r
Energy exp/householder, <1,000 sq ft heating area	year	429	90	28r
Energy exp/householder, 1,000-1,999 sq ft heating area	year	442	90	28r
Energy exp/householder, 2,000+ sq ft heating area	year	498	90	28r
Energy exp/householder, mobile home	year	442	90	28r
Energy exp/householder, multifamily	year	407	90	28r
Gas, natural	mil Btu	3.81	90	64s
Gas, natural	000 cu ft	4.81	91	46s
Gas, natural, exp	year	530	91	46s
Gasoline, motor	gal	1.12	4Q 92	4c
Gasoline, unleaded regular	mil Btu	9.38	90	64s
Entertainment				
Bowling, evening rate	game	1.72	4Q 92	4c
Miniature golf admission	adult	6.18	92	1r
Miniature golf admission	child	5.14	92	1r
Monopoly game, Parker Brothers', No. 9		8.38	4Q 92	4c

Values are in dollars or fractions of dollars. In the column headed *Ref*, references are shown to sources. Each reference is followed by a letter. These refer to the geographical level for which data were reported: s=State, r=Region, and c=City or metro. The abbreviation *ex* is used to mean *except* or *excluding*; *exp* stands for expenditures. For other abbreviations and further explanations, please see the Introduction.

Iowa City-Coralville, IA - continued

Item	Per	Value	Date	Ref.
Entertainment				
Movie	admission	5.00	4Q 92	4c
Tennis balls, yellow, Wilson or Penn, 3	can	1.98	4Q 92	4c
Waterpark admission	adult	11.00	92	1r
Waterpark admission	child	8.55	92	1r
Funerals				
Casket, 18-gauge steel, velvet interior		1952.97	91	24r
Cosmetology, hair care, etc.		90.03	91	24r
Embalming		251.75	91	24r
Facility use for ceremony		180.75	91	24r
Hearse, local		117.51	91	24r
Limousine, local		71.86	91	24r
Remains to funeral home, transfer		81.14	91	24r
Service charge, professional		740.03	91	24r
Vault, concrete, non-metallic liner		801.47	91	24r
Viewing facilities, use		169.33	91	24r
Goods and Services				
ACCRA Index, Miscellaneous Goods and Services		96.50	4Q 92	4c
Groceries				
ACCRA Index, Groceries		100.40	4Q 92	4c
Apples, Red Delicious	lb	0.77	4/93	16r
Babyfood, strained vegetables, lowest price	4-4.5 oz jar	0.37	4Q 92	4c
Bacon	lb	1.85	4/93	16r
Bananas	lb	0.51	4Q 92	4c
Bananas	lb	0.46	4/93	16r
Beef, stew, boneless	lb	2.53	4/93	16r
Bologna, all beef or mixed	lb	2.19	4/93	16r
Bread, white	24 oz	0.67	4Q 92	4c
Bread, white, pan	lb	0.78	4/93	16r
Butter	lb	1.50	4/93	16r
Cabbage	lb	0.40	4/93	16r
Carrots, short trimmed and topped	lb	0.45	4/93	16r
Cheese, Cheddar	lb	3.47	4/93	16r
Cheese, Kraft grated Parmesan	8-oz canister	3.20	4Q 92	4c
Chicken, fresh, whole	lb	0.84	4/93	16r
Chicken, fryer, whole	lb	0.82	4Q 92	4c
Chicken breast, bone-in	lb	1.94	4/93	16r
Chicken legs, bone-in	lb	1.02	4/93	16r
Chuck roast, graded and ungraded, ex USDA prime and choice	lb	2.43	4/93	16r
Chuck roast, USDA choice, bone-in	lb	2.11	4/93	16r
Chuck roast, USDA choice, boneless	lb	2.44	4/93	16r
Cigarettes, Winston	carton	18.17	4Q 92	4c
Coffee, 100% ground roast, all sizes	lb	2.47	4/93	16r
Coffee, vacuum-packed	13-oz can	1.88	4Q 92	4c
Cookies, chocolate chip	lb	2.73	4/93	16r
Corn, frozen	10 oz	0.73	4Q 92	4c
Corn Flakes, Kellogg's or Post Toasties	18 oz	1.92	4Q 92	4c
Eggs, Grade A large	doz	0.76	4Q 92	4c
Eggs, Grade A large	doz	0.93	4/93	16r
Flour, white, all purpose	lb	0.21	4/93	16r
Grapefruit	lb	0.45	4/93	16r
Grapes, Thompson Seedless	lb	1.46	4/93	16r
Ground beef, 100% beef	lb	1.63	4/93	16r
Ground beef, lean and extra lean	lb	2.08	4/93	16r
Ground beef or hamburger	lb	1.35	4Q 92	4c
Ground chuck, 100% beef	lb	1.94	4/93	16r
Ham, boneless, excluding canned	lb	2.21	4/93	16r
Ice cream, prepackaged, bulk, regular	1/2 gal	2.41	4/93	16r
Lemons	lb	0.82	4/93	16r
Lettuce, iceberg	head	1.06	4Q 92	4c
Lettuce, iceberg	lb	0.83	4/93	16r
Margarine, Blue Bonnet or Parkay cubes	lb	0.68	4Q 92	4c
Margarine, stick	lb	0.77	4/93	16r
Milk, whole	1/2 gal	1.40	4Q 92	4c

Iowa City-Coralville, IA - continued

Item	Per	Value	Date	Ref.
Groceries - continued				
Orange juice, Minute Maid frozen	12-oz can	1.43	4Q 92	4c
Oranges, navel	lb	0.50	4/93	16r
Peaches	29-oz can	1.41	4Q 92	4c
Peanut butter, creamy, all sizes	lb	1.82	4/93	16r
Pears, Anjou	lb	0.85	4/93	16r
Peas Sweet, Del Monte or Green Giant	15-17 oz can	0.56	4Q 92	4c
Pork chops, center cut, bone-in	lb	3.17	4/93	16r
Potato chips	16 oz	2.68	4/93	16r
Potatoes, white	lb	0.26	4/93	16r
Potatoes, white or red	10-lb sack	1.88	4Q 92	4c
Round roast, graded & ungraded, ex USDA prime & choice	lb	2.88	4/93	16r
Round roast, USDA choice, boneless	lb	2.96	4/93	16r
Sausage, Jimmy Dean, 100% pork	lb	2.53	4Q 92	4c
Shortening, vegetable oil blends	lb	0.79	4/93	16r
Shortening, vegetable, Crisco	3-lb can	2.27	4Q 92	4c
Soft drink, Coca Cola	2 liter	1.32	4Q 92	4c
Spaghetti and macaroni	lb	0.76	4/93	16r
Steak, rib eye, USDA choice, boneless	lb	6.29	4/93	16r
Steak, round, USDA choice, boneless	lb	3.24	4/93	16r
Steak, sirloin, graded & ungraded, ex USDA prime & choice	lb	4.00	4/93	16r
Steak, sirloin, USDA choice, bone-in	lb	3.57	4/93	16r
Steak, sirloin, USDA choice, boneless	lb	4.17	4/93	16r
Steak, T-bone	lb	4.87	4Q 92	4c
Steak, T-bone, USDA choice, bone-in	lb	5.60	4/93	16r
Strawberries, dry pint	12 oz	0.90	4/93	16r
Sugar, cane or beet	4 lb	1.68	4Q 92	4c
Sugar, white	lb	0.36	4/93	16r
Sugar, white, 33-80 oz pk	lb	0.35	4/93	16r
Tomatoes, field grown	lb	0.99	4/93	16r
Tomatoes, Hunt's or Del Monte	14.5-oz can	0.73	4Q 92	4c
Tuna, chunk, light	6.125-6.5 oz can	0.57	4Q 92	4c
Tuna, chunk, light	lb	1.76	4/93	16r
Turkey, frozen, whole	lb	0.91	4/93	16r
Health Care				
ACCRA Index, Health Care		91.60	4Q 92	4c
Analgesic, Aspirin, Bayer, 325 mg tablets	100	3.86	4Q 92	4c
Childbirth, cesarean, hospital		4688	91	62r
Childbirth, cesarean, physician's fee		2053	91	62r
Childbirth, normal, hospital		2657	91	62r
Childbirth, normal, physician's fee		1492	91	62r
Dentist's fee, adult teeth cleaning and periodic oral exam	visit	47.80	4Q 92	4c
Doctor's fee, routine exam, established patient	visit	32.00	4Q 92	4c
Health care spending, state	capita	2351	3/93	84s
Hospital care, semiprivate room	day	285.00	4Q 92	4c
Medical insurance premium, per employee, small group comprehensive	month	267.40	10/91	25c
Medical plan per employee	year	3443	91	45r
Mental health care, exp	capita	20.37-28.83	90	38s
Mental health care, exp, state mental health agency	capita	17.07	90	38s
Mental health care, hospital psychiatric services, non-Federal, exp	capita	23.51	88	38s
Mental health care, mental health organization, multiservice, exp	capita	7.66	88	38s
Mental health care, psychiatric hospitals, private, exp	capita	2.86	88	38s
Mental health care, psychiatric out-patient clinics, freestanding, exp	capita	3.02	88	38s

Values are in dollars or fractions of dollars. In the column headed *Ref*, references are shown to sources. Each reference is followed by a letter. These refer to the geographical level for which data were reported: s=State, r=Region, and c=City or metro. The abbreviation *ex* is used to mean *except* or *excluding*; *exp* stands for expenditures. For other abbreviations and further explanations, please see the Introduction.

Iowa City-Coralville, IA - continued

Item	Per	Value	Date	Ref.
Health Care				
Mental health care, state and county mental hospitals, exp	capita	14.54	88	38s
Mental health care, VA medical centers, exp	capita	13.98	88	38s
Physician fee, family practice, first-visit		76.00	91	62r
Physician fee, family practice, revisit		33.00	91	62r
Physician fee, general practice, first-visit		61.00	91	62r
Physician fee, general practice, revisit		31.00	91	62r
Physician fee, general surgeon, first-visit		65.00	91	62r
Physician fee, general surgeon, revisit		35.00	91	62r
Physician fee, internal medicine, first-visit		91.00	91	62r
Physician fee, internal medicine, revisit		40.00	91	62r
Physician fee, median, neurosurgeon, first-visit		106.00	91	62r
Physician fee, median, nonsurgical specialist, first-visit		90.00	91	62r
Physician fee, median, orthopedic surgeon, first-visit		83.00	91	62r
Physician fee, median, surgical specialist, first-visit		61.00	91	62r
Physician fee, neurosurgeon, revisit		41.00	91	62r
Physician fee, nonsurgical specialist, revisit		40.00	91	62r
Physician fee, obstetrics/gynecology, first-visit		61.00	91	62r
Physician fee, obstetrics/gynecology, revisit		40.00	91	62r
Physician fee, orthopedic surgeon, revisit		41.00	91	62r
Physician fee, pediatrician, first-visit		46.00	91	62r
Physician fee, pediatrician, revisit		33.00	91	62r
Physician fee, surgical specialist, revisit		36.00	91	62r
Substance abuse, hospital ancillary charge	incident	950	90	70s
Substance abuse, hospital physician charge	incident	250	90	70s
Substance abuse, hospital room and board	incident	3110	90	70s
Household Goods				
Appliance repair, home, service call, washing machine	min labor charge	36.74	4Q 92	4c
Laundry detergent, Tide Ultra, Bold, or Cheer	42 oz	3.71	4Q 92	4c
Tissues, facial, Kleenex brand	175-count box	1.12	4Q 92	4c
Housing				
ACCRA Index, Housing		124.80	4Q 92	4c
House, 1,800 sq ft, 8,000 sq ft lot, new, urban	total	150500	4Q 92	4c
House payment, principal and interest, 25% down payment	month	830	4Q 92	4c
Mortgage rate, incl. points & origination fee, 30-year fixed or adjustable rate	percent	8.02	4Q 92	4c
Rent, apartment, 2 bedrooms - 1-1/2 to 2 baths, unfurnished, 950 sq ft, water	month	471	4Q 92	4c
Rental unit, 1 bedroom	month	457	93	23c
Rental unit, 2 bedroom	month	537	93	23c
Rental unit, 3 bedroom	month	672	93	23c
Rental unit, 4 bedroom	month	753	93	23c
Rental unit, efficiency	month	374	93	23c
Insurance and Pensions				
Auto insurance, private passenger	year	422.46	91	63s
Personal Goods				
Shampoo, Alberto VO5	15 oz	0.98	4Q 92	4c
Toothpaste, Crest or Colgate	6-7 oz	1.04	4Q 92	4c
Personal Services				
Dry cleaning, man's 2-piece suit		7.41	4Q 92	4c
Haircare, woman's shampoo, trim and blow-dry		18.24	4Q 92	4c
Haircut, man's barbershop, no styling		9.58	4Q 92	4c

Iowa City-Coralville, IA - continued

Item	Per	Value	Date	Ref.
Restaurant Food				
Chicken, fried, thigh and drumstick		1.98	4Q 92	4c
Hamburger with cheese	1/4 lb	1.95	4Q 92	4c
Pizza, Pizza Hut or Pizza Inn, cheese, thin crust	12-13 in	7.79	4Q 92	4c
Taxes				
Tax, cigarette	pack	36	91	77s
Tax, gasoline	gal	20	91	77s
Taxes, state	capita	1233	91	77s
Transportation				
ACCRA Index, Transportation		103.60	4Q 92	4c
Bus fare	one-way	0.50	3/93	2c
Bus fare, up to 10 miles	one-way	0.50	4Q 92	4c
Driver's license fee		16.00	12/90	43s
Tire balance, computer or spin balance, front	wheel	7.70	4Q 92	4c
Utilities				
ACCRA Index, Utilities		99.10	4Q 92	4c
Electricity	mil Btu	17.37	90	64s
Electricity, partial electric and other energy, 1,800 sq ft living area new home	month	76.48	4Q 92	4c

Jackson, MI

Item	Per	Value	Date	Ref.
Child Care				
Child care fee, average, center	hour	1.63	90	65r
Child care fee, average, nonregulated family day care	hour	1.83	90	65r
Child care fee, average, regulated family day care	hour	1.42	90	65r
Communications				
Long-distance telephone service, day, initial minute, 0-100 miles	min	0.14-0.36	91	12s
Long-distance telephone service, day, additional minute, 0-100 miles	min	0.14-0.36	91	12s
Long-distance telephone service, evenings/weekends, 0-100 mi, initial minute	min	0.07-0.19	91	12s
Long-distance telephone service, evenings/weekends, 0-100 mi, additional minute	min	0.04-0.14	91	12s
Education				
Board, 4-yr private college/university	year	1698	91	22s
Board, 4-yr public college/university	year	1962	91	22s
Expenditures, local gov't, public elementary/secondary	pupil	5671	92	20s
Room, 4-year private college/university	year	1440	91	22s
Room, 4-year public college/university	year	1687	91	22s
Tuition, 2-year private college/university	year	4749	91	22s
Tuition, 2-year public college/university	year	1124	91	22s
Tuition, 4-year private college/university	year	6885	91	22s
Tuition, 4-year public college/university, in-state	year	2635	91	22s
Energy and Fuels				
Coal	mil Btu	1.63	90	64s
Energy	mil Btu	8.17	90	64s
Energy exp/householder, 1-family unit	year	471	90	28r
Energy exp/householder, <1,000 sq ft heating area	year	430	90	28r
Energy exp/householder, 1,000-1,999 sq ft heating area	year	481	90	28r
Energy exp/householder, 2,000+ sq ft heating area	year	473	90	28r
Energy exp/householder, mobile home	year	430	90	28r
Energy exp/householder, multifamily	year	461	90	28r
Gas, natural	mil Btu	4.36	90	64s
Gas, natural	000 cu ft	5.07	91	46s
Gas, natural, exp	year	655	91	46s

Values are in dollars or fractions of dollars. In the column headed *Ref*, references are shown to sources. Each reference is followed by a letter. These refer to the geographical level for which data were reported: s=State, r=Region, and c=City or metro. The abbreviation *ex* is used to mean *except* or *excluding*; *exp* stands for expenditures. For other abbreviations and further explanations, please see the Introduction.

Jackson, MI - continued

Item	Per	Value	Date	Ref.
Energy and Fuels				
Gasoline, unleaded regular	mil Btu	8.78	90	64s
Entertainment				
Miniature golf admission	adult	6.18	92	1r
Miniature golf admission	child	5.14	92	1r
Waterpark admission	adult	11.00	92	1r
Waterpark admission	child	8.55	92	1r
Funerals				
Casket, 18-gauge steel, velvet interior		1926.72	91	24r
Cosmetology, hair care, etc.		97.64	91	24r
Embalming		249.14	91	24r
Facility use for ceremony		208.59	91	24r
Hearse, local		130.12	91	24r
Limousine, local		104.66	91	24r
Remains to funeral home, transfer		93.61	91	24r
Service charge, professional		724.62	91	24r
Vault, concrete, non-metallic liner		734.53	91	24r
Viewing facilities, use		236.06	91	24r
Groceries				
Apples, Red Delicious	lb	0.77	4/93	16r
Bacon	lb	1.85	4/93	16r
Bananas	lb	0.46	4/93	16r
Beef, stew, boneless	lb	2.53	4/93	16r
Bologna, all beef or mixed	lb	2.19	4/93	16r
Bread, white, pan	lb	0.78	4/93	16r
Butter	lb	1.50	4/93	16r
Cabbage	lb	0.40	4/93	16r
Carrots, short trimmed and topped	lb	0.45	4/93	16r
Cheese, Cheddar	lb	3.47	4/93	16r
Chicken, fresh, whole	lb	0.84	4/93	16r
Chicken breast, bone-in	lb	1.94	4/93	16r
Chicken legs, bone-in	lb	1.02	4/93	16r
Chuck roast, graded and ungraded, ex USDA prime and choice	lb	2.43	4/93	16r
Chuck roast, USDA choice, bone-in	lb	2.11	4/93	16r
Chuck roast, USDA choice, boneless	lb	2.44	4/93	16r
Coffee, 100% ground roast, all sizes	lb	2.47	4/93	16r
Cookies, chocolate chip	lb	2.73	4/93	16r
Eggs, Grade A large	doz	0.93	4/93	16r
Flour, white, all purpose	lb	0.21	4/93	16r
Grapefruit	lb	0.45	4/93	16r
Grapes, Thompson Seedless	lb	1.46	4/93	16r
Ground beef, 100% beef	lb	1.63	4/93	16r
Ground beef, lean and extra lean	lb	2.08	4/93	16r
Ground chuck, 100% beef	lb	1.94	4/93	16r
Ham, boneless, excluding canned	lb	2.21	4/93	16r
Honey, jar	8 oz	0.97-1.25	92	5r
Honey, jar	lb	1.25-2.25	92	5r
Honey, squeeze bear	12-oz	1.25-1.99	92	5r
Ice cream, prepackaged, bulk, regular	1/2 gal	2.41	4/93	16r
Lemons	lb	0.82	4/93	16r
Lettuce, iceberg	lb	0.83	4/93	16r
Margarine, stick	lb	0.77	4/93	16r
Oranges, navel	lb	0.50	4/93	16r
Peanut butter, creamy, all sizes	lb	1.82	4/93	16r
Pears, Anjou	lb	0.85	4/93	16r
Pork chops, center cut, bone-in	lb	3.17	4/93	16r
Potato chips	16 oz	2.68	4/93	16r
Potatoes, white	lb	0.26	4/93	16r
Round roast, graded & ungraded, ex USDA prime & choice	lb	2.88	4/93	16r
Round roast, USDA choice, boneless	lb	2.96	4/93	16r
Shortening, vegetable oil blends	lb	0.79	4/93	16r
Spaghetti and macaroni	lb	0.76	4/93	16r
Steak, rib eye, USDA choice, boneless	lb	6.29	4/93	16r
Steak, round, USDA choice, boneless	lb	3.24	4/93	16r
Steak, sirloin, graded & ungraded, ex USDA prime & choice	lb	4.00	4/93	16r
Steak, sirloin, USDA choice, bone-in	lb	3.57	4/93	16r
Steak, sirloin, USDA choice, boneless	lb	4.17	4/93	16r
Steak, T-bone, USDA choice, bone-in	lb	5.60	4/93	16r
Strawberries, dry pint	12 oz	0.90	4/93	16r

Jackson, MI - continued

Item	Per	Value	Date	Ref.
Groceries - continued				
Sugar, white	lb	0.36	4/93	16r
Sugar, white, 33-80 oz pk	lb	0.35	4/93	16r
Tomatoes, field grown	lb	0.99	4/93	16r
Tuna, chunk, light	lb	1.76	4/93	16r
Turkey, frozen, whole	lb	0.91	4/93	16r
Health Care				
Childbirth, cesarean, hospital		4688	91	62r
Childbirth, cesarean, physician's fee		2053	91	62r
Childbirth, normal, hospital		2657	91	62r
Childbirth, normal, physician's fee		1492	91	62r
Medical plan per employee	year	3443	91	45r
Mental health care, exp	capita	53.68-118.35	90	38s
Mental health care, exp, state mental health agency	capita	73.73	90	38s
Mental health care, hospital psychiatric services, non-Federal, exp	capita	22.52	88	38s
Mental health care, mental health organization, multiservice, exp	capita	42.68	88	38s
Mental health care, psychiatric hospitals, private, exp	capita	10.80	88	38s
Mental health care, psychiatric out-patient clinics, freestanding, exp	capita	3.47	88	38s
Mental health care, psychiatric partial-care organizations, freestanding, exp	capita	0.73	88	38s
Mental health care, state and county mental hospitals, exp	capita	36.77	88	38s
Mental health care, VA medical centers, exp	capita	4.03	88	38s
Physician fee, family practice, first-visit		76.00	91	62r
Physician fee, family practice, revisit		33.00	91	62r
Physician fee, general practice, first-visit		61.00	91	62r
Physician fee, general practice, revisit		31.00	91	62r
Physician fee, general surgeon, first-visit		65.00	91	62r
Physician fee, general surgeon, revisit		35.00	91	62r
Physician fee, internal medicine, first-visit		91.00	91	62r
Physician fee, internal medicine, revisit		40.00	91	62r
Physician fee, median, neurosurgeon, first-visit		106.00	91	62r
Physician fee, median, nonsurgical specialist, first-visit		90.00	91	62r
Physician fee, median, orthopedic surgeon, first-visit		83.00	91	62r
Physician fee, median, surgical specialist, first-visit		61.00	91	62r
Physician fee, neurosurgeon, revisit		41.00	91	62r
Physician fee, nonsurgical specialist, revisit		40.00	91	62r
Physician fee, obstetrics/gynecology, first-visit		61.00	91	62r
Physician fee, obstetrics/gynecology, revisit		40.00	91	62r
Physician fee, orthopedic surgeon, revisit		41.00	91	62r
Physician fee, pediatrician, first-visit		46.00	91	62r
Physician fee, pediatrician, revisit		33.00	91	62r
Physician fee, surgical specialist, revisit		36.00	91	62r
Substance abuse, hospital ancillary charge	incident	1480	90	70s
Substance abuse, hospital physician charge	incident	250	90	70s
Substance abuse, hospital room and board	incident	4070	90	70s
Insurance and Pensions				
Auto insurance, private passenger	year	716.78	91	63s
Taxes				
Tax, cigarette	pack	25	91	77s
Tax, gasoline	gal	15	91	77s
Taxes, state	capita	1185	91	77s
Transportation				
Driver's license fee		12.00	12/90	43s
Vehicle registration and license plate	year	14.00-200.00	93	40s

Values are in dollars or fractions of dollars. In the column headed *Ref*, references are shown to sources. Each reference is followed by a letter. These refer to the geographical level for which data were reported: s=State, r=Region, and c=City or metro. The abbreviation *ex* is used to mean *except* or *excluding*; *exp* stands for expenditures. For other abbreviations and further explanations, please see the Introduction.

Jackson, MI - continued

Item	Per	Value	Date	Ref.
Utilities				
Electricity	mil Btu	20.85	90	64s

Jackson, MS

Item	Per	Value	Date	Ref.
Child Care				
Child care fee, average, center	hour	1.29	90	65r
Child care fee, average, nonregulated family day care	hour	0.89	90	65r
Child care fee, average, regulated family day care	hour	1.32	90	65r
Communications				
Long-distance telephone service, day, initial minute, 0-100 miles	min	0.19-0.47	91	12s
Long-distance telephone service, day, additional minute, 0-100 miles	min	0.11-0.34	91	12s
Long-distance telephone service, evenings/weekends, 0-100 mi, initial minute	min	0.06-0.19	91	12s
Long-distance telephone service, evenings/weekends, 0-100 mi, additional minute	min	0.04-0.14	91	12s
Telephone, flat rate	month	19.01	91	11c
Education				
Board, 4-yr private college/university	year	1312	91	22s
Board, 4-yr public college/university	year	1924	91	22s
Expenditures, local gov't, public elementary/secondary	pupil	3344	92	20s
Room, 4-year private college/university	year	1002	91	22s
Room, 4-year public college/university	year	1154	91	22s
Tuition, 2-year private college/university	year	3721	91	22s
Tuition, 2-year public college/university	year	722	91	22s
Tuition, 4-year private college/university	year	5238	91	22s
Tuition, 4-year public college/university, in-state	year	1927	91	22s
Energy and Fuels				
Coal	mil Btu	1.65	90	64s
Energy	mil Btu	8.31	90	64s
Energy exp/householder, 1-family unit	year	403	90	28r
Energy exp/householder, <1,000 sq ft heating area	year	342	90	28r
Energy exp/householder, 1,000-1,999 sq ft heating area	year	388	90	28r
Energy exp/householder, 2,000+ sq ft heating area	year	434	90	28r
Energy exp/householder, mobile home	year	320	90	28r
Energy exp/householder, multifamily	year	338	90	28r
Gas, cooking, 10 therms	month	7.23	92	56c
Gas, cooking, 30 therms	month	15.42	92	56c
Gas, cooking, 50 therms	month	23.73	92	56c
Gas, heating, winter, 100 therms	month	44.37	92	56c
Gas, heating, winter, average use	month	55.20	92	56c
Gas, natural	mil Btu	2.75	90	64s
Gas, natural	000 cu ft	5.21	91	46s
Gas, natural, exp	year	348	91	46s
Gasoline, unleaded regular	mil Btu	9.21	90	64s
Entertainment				
Miniature golf admission	adult	6.18	92	1r
Miniature golf admission	child	5.14	92	1r
Waterpark admission	adult	11.00	92	1r
Waterpark admission	child	8.55	92	1r
Funerals				
Casket, 18-gauge steel, velvet interior		2329.05	91	24r
Cosmetology, hair care, etc.		72.78	91	24r
Embalming		240.71	91	24r
Facility use for ceremony		181.67	91	24r
Hearse, local		106.25	91	24r
Limousine, local		70.92	91	24r
Remains to funeral home, transfer		96.30	91	24r
Service charge, professional		687.09	91	24r

Jackson, MS - continued

Item	Per	Value	Date	Ref.
Funerals - continued				
Vault, concrete, non-metallic liner		732.09	91	24r
Viewing facilities, use		190.30	91	24r
Groceries				
Apples, Red Delicious	lb	0.79	4/93	16r
Bacon	lb	1.75	4/93	16r
Bananas	lb	0.42	4/93	16r
Beef, stew, boneless	lb	2.61	4/93	16r
Bologna, all beef or mixed	lb	2.24	4/93	16r
Bread, white, pan	lb	0.64	4/93	16r
Bread, whole wheat, pan	lb	0.96	4/93	16r
Cabbage	lb	0.37	4/93	16r
Carrots, short trimmed and topped	lb	0.47	4/93	16r
Celery	lb	0.64	4/93	16r
Cheese, American	lb	2.98	4/93	16r
Cheese, Cheddar	lb	3.28	4/93	16r
Chicken, fresh, whole	lb	0.77	4/93	16r
Chicken breast, bone-in	lb	1.92	4/93	16r
Chicken legs, bone-in	lb	1.06	4/93	16r
Chuck roast, graded and ungraded, ex USDA prime and choice	lb	2.40	4/93	16r
Chuck roast, USDA choice, bone-in	lb	2.19	4/93	16r
Chuck roast, USDA choice, boneless	lb	2.38	4/93	16r
Coffee, 100% ground roast, all sizes	lb	2.48	4/93	16r
Crackers, soda, salted	lb	1.15	4/93	16r
Eggs, Grade A large	doz	0.96	4/93	16r
Flour, white, all purpose	lb	0.24	4/93	16r
Frankfurters, all meat or all beef	lb	2.01	4/93	16r
Grapefruit	lb	0.44	4/93	16r
Grapes, Thompson Seedless	lb	1.40	4/93	16r
Ground beef, 100% beef	lb	1.58	4/93	16r
Ground beef, lean and extra lean	lb	2.09	4/93	16r
Ground chuck, 100% beef	lb	1.98	4/93	16r
Ham, boneless, excluding canned	lb	2.89	4/93	16r
Ham, picnic, shoulder, bone-in, smoked	lb	1.02	4/93	16r
Ham, rump or steak half, bone-in, smoked	lb	1.48	4/93	16r
Honey, jar	8 oz	0.89-1.09	92	5r
Honey, jar	lb	1.39-2.25	92	5r
Honey, squeeze bear	12-oz	1.00-1.50	92	5r
Ice cream, prepackaged, bulk, regular	1/2 gal	2.41	4/93	16r
Lemons	lb	1.05	4/93	16r
Lettuce, iceberg	lb	0.81	4/93	16r
Margarine, stick	lb	0.88	4/93	16r
Oranges, navel	lb	0.55	4/93	16r
Pears, Anjou	lb	0.92	4/93	16r
Pork chops, center cut, bone-in	lb	3.13	4/93	16r
Potato chips	16 oz	2.94	4/93	16r
Potatoes, white	lb	0.43	4/93	16r
Rib roast, USDA choice, bone-in	lb	4.63	4/93	16r
Rice, white, long grain, uncooked	lb	0.45	4/93	16r
Round roast, graded & ungraded, ex USDA prime & choice	lb	3.03	4/93	16r
Round roast, USDA choice, boneless	lb	3.09	4/93	16r
Sausage, fresh, loose	lb	2.08	4/93	16r
Short ribs, bone-in	lb	2.66	4/93	16r
Shortening, vegetable oil blends	lb	0.69	4/93	16r
Spaghetti and macaroni	lb	0.81	4/93	16r
Steak, rib eye, USDA choice, boneless	lb	6.24	4/93	16r
Steak, round, graded & ungraded, ex USDA prime & choice	lb	3.31	4/93	16r
Steak, round, USDA choice, boneless	lb	3.34	4/93	16r
Steak, sirloin, graded & ungraded, ex USDA prime & choice	lb	4.19	4/93	16r
Steak, sirloin, USDA choice, boneless	lb	4.46	4/93	16r
Steak, T-bone, USDA choice, bone-in	lb	5.25	4/93	16r
Strawberries, dry pint	12 oz	0.92	4/93	16r
Sugar, white	lb	0.39	4/93	16r
Sugar, white, 33-80 oz pk	lb	0.38	4/93	16r
Tomatoes, field grown	lb	0.88	4/93	16r
Tuna, chunk, light	lb	1.79	4/93	16r
Turkey, frozen, whole	lb	1.04	4/93	16r
Yogurt, natural, fruit flavored	1/2 pint	0.57	4/93	16r

Values are in dollars or fractions of dollars. In the column headed *Ref*, references are shown to sources. Each reference is followed by a letter. These refer to the geographical level for which data were reported: s=State, r=Region, and c=City or metro. The abbreviation *ex* is used to mean *except* or *excluding*; *exp* stands for expenditures. For other abbreviations and further explanations, please see the Introduction.

Jackson, MS - continued

Item	Per	Value	Date	Ref.
Health Care				
Childbirth, cesarean, hospital		5034	91	62r
Childbirth, cesarean, physician's fee		2053	91	62r
Childbirth, normal, hospital		2712	91	62r
Childbirth, normal, physician's fee		1492	91	62r
Hospital care, semiprivate room	day	170.00	90	27c
Medical insurance premium, per employee, small group comprehensive	month	222.20	10/91	25c
Mental health care, exp	capita	28.84-37.59	90	38s
Mental health care, exp, state mental health agency	capita	33.71	90	38s
Mental health care, hospital psychiatric services, non-Federal, exp	capita	5.17	88	38s
Mental health care, mental health organization, multiservice, exp	capita	8.65	88	38s
Mental health care, psychiatric hospitals, private, exp	capita	6.85	88	38s
Mental health care, state and county mental hospitals, exp	capita	20.41	88	38s
Mental health care, VA medical centers, exp	capita	7.21	88	38s
Physician fee, family practice, first-visit		75.00	91	62r
Physician fee, family practice, revisit		34.00	91	62r
Physician fee, general practice, first-visit		61.00	91	62r
Physician fee, general practice, revisit		32.00	91	62r
Physician fee, general surgeon, first-visit		64.00	91	62r
Physician fee, general surgeon, revisit		40.00	91	62r
Physician fee, internal medicine, first-visit		98.00	91	62r
Physician fee, internal medicine, revisit		40.00	91	62r
Physician fee, median, neurosurgeon, first-visit		130.00	91	62r
Physician fee, median, nonsurgical specialist, first-visit		95.00	91	62r
Physician fee, median, orthopedic surgeon, first-visit		91.00	91	62r
Physician fee, median, plastic surgeon, first-visit		66.00	91	62r
Physician fee, median, surgical specialist, first-visit		62.00	91	62r
Physician fee, neurosurgeon, revisit		50.00	91	62r
Physician fee, nonsurgical specialist, revisit		40.00	91	62r
Physician fee, obstetrics/gynecology, first-visit		64.00	91	62r
Physician fee, obstetrics/gynecology, revisit		41.00	91	62r
Physician fee, orthopedic surgeon, revisit		40.00	91	62r
Physician fee, pediatrician, first-visit		49.00	91	62r
Physician fee, pediatrician, revisit		33.00	91	62r
Physician fee, plastic surgeon, revisit		43.00	91	62r
Physician fee, surgical specialist, revisit		37.00	91	62r
Substance abuse, hospital ancillary charge	incident	1760	90	70s
Substance abuse, hospital physician charge	incident	540	90	70s
Substance abuse, hospital room and board	incident	4060	90	70s
Housing				
Rental unit, 1 bedroom	month	428	93	23c
Rental unit, 2 bedroom	month	505	93	23c
Rental unit, 3 bedroom	month	633	93	23c
Rental unit, 4 bedroom	month	710	93	23c
Rental unit, efficiency	month	352	93	23c
Insurance and Pensions				
Auto insurance, private passenger	year	576.42	91	63s
Taxes				
Tax, cigarette	pack	18	91	77s
Tax, gasoline	gal	18	91	77s
Taxes, state	capita	949	91	77s
Transportation				
Bus fare	one-way	0.75	3/93	2c
Driver's license fee		13.00	12/90	43s

Jackson, MS - continued

Item	Per	Value	Date	Ref.
Travel				
Business travel	day	193.00	4/93	89r
Utilities				
Electricity	mil Btu	18.05	90	64s
Electricity, winter, 250 KWh	month	29.82	92	55c
Electricity, winter, 500 KWh	month	53.59	92	55c
Electricity, winter, 750 KWh	month	67.31	92	55c
Electricity, winter, 1000 KWh	month	81.02	92	55c

Jackson, TN

Item	Per	Value	Date	Ref.
Composite ACCRA index		96.10	4Q 92	4c
Alcoholic Beverages				
Beer, Miller Lite or Budweiser, 12-oz containers	6 pack	4.32	4Q 92	4c
Liquor, J & B Scotch	750 ml	19.12	4Q 92	4c
Wine, Gallo Chablis blanc, 1.5 liter	bottle	5.88	4Q 92	4c
Child Care				
Child care fee, average, center	hour	1.29	90	65r
Child care fee, average, nonregulated family day care	hour	0.89	90	65r
Child care fee, average, regulated family day care	hour	1.32	90	65r
Clothing				
Jeans, man's denim		32.24	4Q 92	4c
Shirt, man's dress shirt		24.50	4Q 92	4c
Undervest, boy's size 10-14, cotton	3	5.49	4Q 92	4c
Communications				
Long-distance telephone service, day, initial minute, 0-100 miles	min	0.10-0.22	91	12s
Long-distance telephone service, day, additional minute, 0-100 miles	min	0.10-0.22	91	12s
Long-distance telephone service, evenings/weekends, 0-100 mi, initial minute	min	0.05-0.10	91	12s
Long-distance telephone service, evenings/weekends, 0-100 mi, additional minute	min	0.05-0.10	91	12s
Newspaper subscription, daily and Sunday home delivery, large-city	month	10.50	4Q 92	4c
Telephone, flat rate	month	9.05	91	11c
Telephone bill, family of four	month	16.14	4Q 92	4c
Education				
Board, 4-yr private college/university	year	1845	91	22s
Board, 4-yr public college/university	year	1499	91	22s
Expenditures, local gov't, public elementary/secondary	pupil	3736	92	20s
Room, 4-year private college/university	year	1679	91	22s
Room, 4-year public college/university	year	1339	91	22s
Tuition, 2-year private college/university	year	4203	91	22s
Tuition, 2-year public college/university	year	848	91	22s
Tuition, 4-year private college/university	year	6889	91	22s
Tuition, 4-year public college/university, in-state	year	1518	91	22s
Energy and Fuels				
Coal	mil Btu	1.35	90	64s
Energy	mil Btu	8.61	90	64s
Energy, combined forms, 1,800 sq ft heating area	month	19.90	4Q 92	4c
Energy exp/householder, 1-family unit	year	403	90	28r
Energy exp/householder, <1,000 sq ft heating area	year	342	90	28r
Energy exp/householder, 1,000-1,999 sq ft heating area	year	388	90	28r
Energy exp/householder, 2,000+ sq ft heating area	year	434	90	28r
Energy exp/householder, mobile home	year	320	90	28r
Energy exp/householder, multifamily	year	338	90	28r
Gas, natural	mil Btu	3.98	90	64s
Gas, natural	000 cu ft	5.19	91	46s

Values are in dollars or fractions of dollars. In the column headed *Ref*, references are shown to sources. Each reference is followed by a letter. These refer to the geographical level for which data were reported: s=State, r=Region, and c=City or metro. The abbreviation *ex* is used to mean *except* or *excluding*; *exp* stands for expenditures. For other abbreviations and further explanations, please see the Introduction.

Jackson, TN - continued

Item	Per	Value	Date	Ref.
Energy and Fuels				
Gas, natural, exp	year	388	91	46s
Gasoline, motor	gal	1.10	4Q 92	4c
Gasoline, unleaded regular	mil Btu	9.40	90	64s
Entertainment				
Bowling, evening rate	game	2.00	4Q 92	4c
Miniature golf admission	adult	6.18	92	1r
Miniature golf admission	child	5.14	92	1r
Monopoly game, Parker Brothers', No. 9		9.97	4Q 92	4c
Movie	admission	5.00	4Q 92	4c
Tennis balls, yellow, Wilson or Penn, 3	can	2.14	4Q 92	4c
Waterpark admission	adult	11.00	92	1r
Waterpark admission	child	8.55	92	1r
Funerals				
Casket, 18-gauge steel, velvet interior		2329.05	91	24r
Cosmetology, hair care, etc.		72.78	91	24r
Embalming		240.71	91	24r
Facility use for ceremony		181.67	91	24r
Hearse, local		106.25	91	24r
Limousine, local		70.92	91	24r
Remains to funeral home, transfer		96.30	91	24r
Service charge, professional		687.09	91	24r
Vault, concrete, non-metallic liner		732.09	91	24r
Viewing facilities, use		190.30	91	24r
Goods and Services				
ACCRA Index, Miscellaneous Goods and Services		104.00	4Q 92	4c
Groceries				
ACCRA Index, Groceries		102.30	4Q 92	4c
Apples, Red Delicious	lb	0.79	4/93	16r
Babyfood, strained vegetables, lowest price	4-4.5 oz jar	0.36	4Q 92	4c
Bacon	lb	1.75	4/93	16r
Bananas	lb	0.42	4Q 92	4c
Bananas	lb	0.42	4/93	16r
Beef, stew, boneless	lb	2.61	4/93	16r
Bologna, all beef or mixed	lb	2.24	4/93	16r
Bread, white	24 oz	0.64	4Q 92	4c
Bread, white, pan	lb	0.64	4/93	16r
Bread, whole wheat, pan	lb	0.96	4/93	16r
Cabbage	lb	0.37	4/93	16r
Carrots, short trimmed and topped	lb	0.47	4/93	16r
Celery	lb	0.64	4/93	16r
Cheese, American	lb	2.98	4/93	16r
Cheese, Cheddar	lb	3.28	4/93	16r
Cheese, Kraft grated Parmesan	8-oz canister	3.54	4Q 92	4c
Chicken, fresh, whole	lb	0.77	4/93	16r
Chicken, fryer, whole	lb	0.68	4Q 92	4c
Chicken breast, bone-in	lb	1.92	4/93	16r
Chicken legs, bone-in	lb	1.06	4/93	16r
Chuck roast, graded and ungraded, ex USDA prime and choice	lb	2.40	4/93	16r
Chuck roast, USDA choice, bone-in	lb	2.19	4/93	16r
Chuck roast, USDA choice, boneless	lb	2.38	4/93	16r
Cigarettes, Winston	carton	17.02	4Q 92	4c
Coffee, 100% ground roast, all sizes	lb	2.48	4/93	16r
Coffee, vacuum-packed	13-oz can	2.11	4Q 92	4c
Corn, frozen	10 oz	0.80	4Q 92	4c
Corn Flakes, Kellogg's or Post Toasties	18 oz	2.22	4Q 92	4c
Crackers, soda, salted	lb	1.15	4/93	16r
Eggs, Grade A large	doz	0.67	4Q 92	4c
Eggs, Grade A large	doz	0.96	4/93	16r
Flour, white, all purpose	lb	0.24	4/93	16r
Frankfurters, all meat or all beef	lb	2.01	4/93	16r
Grapefruit	lb	0.44	4/93	16r
Grapes, Thompson Seedless	lb	1.40	4/93	16r
Ground beef, 100% beef	lb	1.58	4/93	16r

Jackson, TN - continued

Item	Per	Value	Date	Ref.
Groceries - continued				
Ground beef, lean and extra lean	lb	2.09	4/93	16r
Ground beef or hamburger	lb	1.46	4Q 92	4c
Ground chuck, 100% beef	lb	1.98	4/93	16r
Ham, boneless, excluding canned	lb	2.89	4/93	16r
Ham, picnic, shoulder, bone-in, smoked	lb	1.02	4/93	16r
Ham, rump or steak half, bone-in, smoked	lb	1.48	4/93	16r
Honey, jar	8 oz	0.89-1.09	92	5r
Honey, jar	lb	1.39-2.25	92	5r
Honey, squeeze bear	12-oz	1.00-1.50	92	5r
Ice cream, prepackaged, bulk, regular	1/2 gal	2.41	4/93	16r
Lemons	lb	1.05	4/93	16r
Lettuce, iceberg	head	0.87	4Q 92	4c
Lettuce, iceberg	lb	0.81	4/93	16r
Margarine, Blue Bonnet or Parkay cubes	lb	0.70	4Q 92	4c
Margarine, stick	lb	0.88	4/93	16r
Milk, whole	1/2 gal	1.53	4Q 92	4c
Orange juice, Minute Maid frozen	12-oz can	1.60	4Q 92	4c
Oranges, navel	lb	0.55	4/93	16r
Peaches	29-oz can	1.32	4Q 92	4c
Pears, Anjou	lb	0.92	4/93	16r
Peas Sweet, Del Monte or Green Giant	15-17 oz can	0.70	4Q 92	4c
Pork chops, center cut, bone-in	lb	3.13	4/93	16r
Potato chips	16 oz	2.94	4/93	16r
Potatoes, white	lb	0.43	4/93	16r
Potatoes, white or red	10-lb sack	2.39	4Q 92	4c
Rib roast, USDA choice, bone-in	lb	4.63	4/93	16r
Rice, white, long grain, uncooked	lb	0.45	4/93	16r
Round roast, graded & ungraded, ex USDA prime & choice	lb	3.03	4/93	16r
Round roast, USDA choice, boneless	lb	3.09	4/93	16r
Sausage, fresh, loose	lb	2.08	4/93	16r
Sausage, Jimmy Dean, 100% pork	lb	2.64	4Q 92	4c
Short ribs, bone-in	lb	2.66	4/93	16r
Shortening, vegetable oil blends	lb	0.69	4/93	16r
Shortening, vegetable, Crisco	3-lb can	2.56	4Q 92	4c
Soft drink, Coca Cola	2 liter	0.86	4Q 92	4c
Spaghetti and macaroni	lb	0.81	4/93	16r
Steak, rib eye, USDA choice, boneless	lb	6.24	4/93	16r
Steak, round, graded & ungraded, ex USDA prime & choice	lb	3.31	4/93	16r
Steak, round, USDA choice, boneless	lb	3.34	4/93	16r
Steak, sirloin, graded & ungraded, ex USDA prime & choice	lb	4.19	4/93	16r
Steak, sirloin, USDA choice, boneless	lb	4.46	4/93	16r
Steak, T-bone	lb	5.42	4Q 92	4c
Steak, T-bone, USDA choice, bone-in	lb	5.25	4/93	16r
Strawberries, dry pint	12 oz	0.92	4/93	16r
Sugar, cane or beet	4 lb	1.69	4Q 92	4c
Sugar, white	lb	0.39	4/93	16r
Sugar, white, 33-80 oz pk	lb	0.38	4/93	16r
Tomatoes, field grown	lb	0.88	4/93	16r
Tomatoes, Hunt's or Del Monte	14.5-oz can	0.78	4Q 92	4c
Tuna, chunk, light	6.125-6.5 oz can	0.72	4Q 92	4c
Tuna, chunk, light	lb	1.79	4/93	16r
Turkey, frozen, whole	lb	1.04	4/93	16r
Yogurt, natural, fruit flavored	1/2 pint	0.57	4/93	16r
Health Care				
ACCRA Index, Health Care		86.00	4Q 92	4c
Analgesic, Aspirin, Bayer, 325 mg tablets	100	5.48	4Q 92	4c
Childbirth, cesarean, hospital		5034	91	62r
Childbirth, cesarean, physician's fee		2053	91	62r
Childbirth, normal, hospital		2712	91	62r
Childbirth, normal, physician's fee		1492	91	62r

Values are in dollars or fractions of dollars. In the column headed *Ref*, references are shown to sources. Each reference is followed by a letter. These refer to the geographical level for which data were reported: s=State, r=Region, and c=City or metro. The abbreviation *ex* is used to mean *except* or *excluding*; *exp* stands for expenditures. For other abbreviations and further explanations, please see the Introduction.

Jackson, TN - continued

Item	Per	Value	Date	Ref.
Health Care				
Dentist's fee, adult teeth cleaning and periodic oral exam	visit	45.40	4Q 92	4c
Doctor's fee, routine exam, established patient	visit	27.70	4Q 92	4c
Hospital care, semiprivate room	day	185.69	90	27c
Hospital care, semiprivate room	day	227.50	4Q 92	4c
Medical insurance premium, per employee, small group comprehensive	month	310.25	10/91	25c
Mental health care, exp	capita	20.37-28.83	90	38s
Mental health care, exp, state mental health agency	capita	28.84	90	38s
Mental health care, hospital psychiatric services, non-Federal, exp	capita	13.48	88	38s
Mental health care, mental health organization, multiservice, exp	capita	11.35	88	38s
Mental health care, psychiatric hospitals, private, exp	capita	22.28	88	38s
Mental health care, psychiatric out-patient clinics, freestanding, exp	capita	2.58	88	38s
Mental health care, psychiatric partial-care organizations, freestanding, exp	capita	0.25	88	38s
Mental health care, state and county mental hospitals, exp	capita	20.05	88	38s
Mental health care, VA medical centers, exp	capita	4.98	88	38s
Physician fee, family practice, first-visit		75.00	91	62r
Physician fee, family practice, revisit		34.00	91	62r
Physician fee, general practice, first-visit		61.00	91	62r
Physician fee, general practice, revisit		32.00	91	62r
Physician fee, general surgeon, first-visit		64.00	91	62r
Physician fee, general surgeon, revisit		40.00	91	62r
Physician fee, internal medicine, first-visit		98.00	91	62r
Physician fee, internal medicine, revisit		40.00	91	62r
Physician fee, median, neurosurgeon, first-visit		130.00	91	62r
Physician fee, median, nonsurgical specialist, first-visit		95.00	91	62r
Physician fee, median, orthopedic surgeon, first-visit		91.00	91	62r
Physician fee, median, plastic surgeon, first-visit		66.00	91	62r
Physician fee, median, surgical specialist, first-visit		62.00	91	62r
Physician fee, neurosurgeon, revisit		50.00	91	62r
Physician fee, nonsurgical specialist, revisit		40.00	91	62r
Physician fee, obstetrics/gynecology, first-visit		64.00	91	62r
Physician fee, obstetrics/gynecology, revisit		41.00	91	62r
Physician fee, orthopedic surgeon, revisit		40.00	91	62r
Physician fee, pediatrician, first-visit		49.00	91	62r
Physician fee, pediatrician, revisit		33.00	91	62r
Physician fee, plastic surgeon, revisit		43.00	91	62r
Physician fee, surgical specialist, revisit		37.00	91	62r
Substance abuse, hospital ancillary charge	incident	1330	90	70s
Substance abuse, hospital physician charge	incident	580	90	70s
Substance abuse, hospital room and board	incident	5180	90	70s
Household Goods				
Appliance repair, home, service call, washing machine	min labor charge	32.70	4Q 92	4c
Laundry detergent, Tide Ultra, Bold, or Cheer	42 oz	4.24	4Q 92	4c
Tissues, facial, Kleenex brand	175-count box	1.16	4Q 92	4c
Housing				
ACCRA Index, Housing		91.70	4Q 92	4c

Jackson, TN - continued

Item	Per	Value	Date	Ref.
Housing - continued				
House, 1,800 sq ft, 8,000 sq ft lot, new, urban	total	95900	4Q 92	4c
House payment, principal and interest, 25% down payment	month	533	4Q 92	4c
Mortgage rate, incl. points & origination fee, 30-year fixed or adjustable rate	percent	8.11	4Q 92	4c
Rent, apartment, 2 bedrooms - 1-1/2 to 2 baths, unfurnished, 950 sq ft, water	month	523	4Q 92	4c
Rental unit, 1 bedroom	month	350	93	23c
Rental unit, 2 bedroom	month	416	93	23c
Rental unit, 3 bedroom	month	519	93	23c
Rental unit, 4 bedroom	month	585	93	23c
Rental unit, efficiency	month	292	93	23c
Insurance and Pensions				
Auto insurance, private passenger	year	554.60	91	63s
Personal Goods				
Shampoo, Alberto VO5	15 oz	1.35	4Q 92	4c
Toothpaste, Crest or Colgate	6-7 oz	2.17	4Q 92	4c
Personal Services				
Dry cleaning, man's 2-piece suit		5.67	4Q 92	4c
Haircare, woman's shampoo, trim and blow-dry		19.90	4Q 92	4c
Haircut, man's barbershop, no styling		8.60	4Q 92	4c
Restaurant Food				
Chicken, fried, thigh and drumstick		2.11	4Q 92	4c
Hamburger with cheese	1/4 lb	1.85	4Q 92	4c
Pizza, Pizza Hut or Pizza Inn, cheese, thin crust	12-13 in	8.14	4Q 92	4c
Taxes				
Tax, cigarette	pack	13	91	77s
Tax, gasoline	gal	22.40	91	77s
Taxes, state	capita	870	91	77s
Transportation				
ACCRA Index, Transportation		88.50	4Q 92	4c
Bus fare	one-way	0.75	3/93	2c
Driver's license fee		14.00-16.00	12/90	43s
Tire balance, computer or spin balance, front	wheel	5.20	4Q 92	4c
Travel				
Business travel	day	193.00	4/93	89r
Utilities				
ACCRA Index, Utilities		84.00	4Q 92	4c
Electricity	mil Btu	15.59	90	64s
Electricity, all electric, 1,800 sq ft living area new home	month	91.20	4Q 92	4c

Jacksonville, FL

Item	Per	Value	Date	Ref.
Composite ACCRA index		96.00	4Q 92	4c
Alcoholic Beverages				
Beer, Miller Lite or Budweiser, 12-oz containers	6 pack	3.61	4Q 92	4c
Liquor, J & B Scotch	750 ml	15.97	4Q 92	4c
Wine, Gallo Chablis blanc, 1.5 liter	bottle	4.79	4Q 92	4c
Child Care				
Child care fee, average, center	hour	1.29	90	65r
Child care fee, average, nonregulated family day care	hour	0.89	90	65r
Child care fee, average, regulated family day care	hour	1.32	90	65r
Clothing				
Jeans, man's denim		28.89	4Q 92	4c
Shirt, man's dress shirt		29.50	4Q 92	4c
Undervest, boy's size 10-14, cotton	3	3.64	4Q 92	4c

Values are in dollars or fractions of dollars. In the column headed *Ref*, references are shown to sources. Each reference is followed by a letter. These refer to the geographical level for which data were reported: s=State, r=Region, and c=City or metro. The abbreviation *ex* is used to mean *except* or *excluding*; *exp* stands for expenditures. For other abbreviations and further explanations, please see the Introduction.

Jacksonville, FL - continued

Item	Per	Value	Date	Ref.
Communications				
Long-distance telephone service, day, initial minute, 0-100 miles	min	0.15-0.20	91	12s
Long-distance telephone service, day, additional minute, 0-100 miles	min	0.08-0.20	91	12s
Long-distance telephone service, evenings/weekends, 0-100 mi, initial minute	min	0.09-0.12	91	12s
Long-distance telephone service, evenings/weekends, 0-100 mi, additional minute	min	0.05-0.12	91	12s
Newspaper subscription, daily and Sunday home delivery, large-city	month	9.75	4Q 92	4c
Telephone, flat rate	month	10.05	91	11c
Telephone bill, family of four	month	20.02	4Q 92	4c
Education				
Board, 4-yr private college/university	year	1924	91	22s
Board, 4-yr public college/university	year	1955	91	22s
Expenditures, local gov't, public elementary/secondary	pupil	5235	92	20s
Room, 4-year private college/university	year	1904	91	22s
Room, 4-year public college/university	year	1510	91	22s
Tuition, 2-year private college/university	year	4751	91	22s
Tuition, 2-year public college/university	year	788	91	22s
Tuition, 4-year private college/university	year	7992	91	22s
Tuition, 4-year public college/university, in-state	year	1337	91	22s
Energy and Fuels				
Coal	mil Btu	1.85	90	64s
Energy	mil Btu	10.58	90	64s
Energy, combined forms, 1,800 sq ft heating area	month	117.56	4Q 92	4c
Energy exp/householder, 1-family unit	year	487	90	28r
Energy exp/householder, <1,000 sq ft heating area	year	393	90	28r
Energy exp/householder, 1,000-1,999 sq ft heating area	year	442	90	28r
Energy exp/householder, 2,000+ sq ft heating area	year	577	90	28r
Energy exp/householder, mobile home	year	366	90	28r
Energy exp/householder, multifamily	year	382	90	28r
Gas, natural	mil Btu	3.21	90	64s
Gas, natural	000 cu ft	8.98	91	46s
Gas, natural, exp	year	248	91	46s
Gasoline, motor	gal	1.13	4Q 92	4c
Gasoline, unleaded regular	mil Btu	8.85	90	64s
Entertainment				
Bowling, evening rate	game	2.30	4Q 92	4c
Miniature golf admission	adult	6.18	92	1r
Miniature golf admission	child	5.14	92	1r
Monopoly game, Parker Brothers', No. 9		10.94	4Q 92	4c
Movie	admission	5.45	4Q 92	4c
Tennis balls, yellow, Wilson or Penn, 3	can	2.32	4Q 92	4c
Waterpark admission	adult	11.00	92	1r
Waterpark admission	child	8.55	92	1r
Funerals				
Casket, 18-gauge steel, velvet interior		2029.08	91	24r
Cosmetology, hair care, etc.		75.10	91	24r
Embalming		249.24	91	24r
Facility use for ceremony		162.27	91	24r
Hearse, local		114.04	91	24r
Limousine, local		88.57	91	24r
Remains to funeral home, transfer		92.61	91	24r
Service charge, professional		682.42	91	24r
Vault, concrete, non-metallic liner		798.70	91	24r
Viewing facilities, use		163.86	91	24r
Goods and Services				
ACCRA Index, Miscellaneous Goods and Services		99.70	4Q 92	4c

Jacksonville, FL - continued

Item	Per	Value	Date	Ref.
Groceries				
ACCRA Index, Groceries		95.40	4Q 92	4c
Apples, Red Delicious	lb	0.79	4/93	16r
Babyfood, strained vegetables, lowest price	4-4.5 oz jar	0.32	4Q 92	4c
Bacon	lb	1.75	4/93	16r
Bananas	lb	0.32	4Q 92	4c
Bananas	lb	0.42	4/93	16r
Beef, stew, boneless	lb	2.61	4/93	16r
Bologna, all beef or mixed	lb	2.24	4/93	16r
Bread, white	24 oz	0.74	4Q 92	4c
Bread, white, pan	lb	0.64	4/93	16r
Bread, whole wheat, pan	lb	0.96	4/93	16r
Cabbage	lb	0.37	4/93	16r
Carrots, short trimmed and topped	lb	0.47	4/93	16r
Celery	lb	0.64	4/93	16r
Cheese, American	lb	2.98	4/93	16r
Cheese, Cheddar	lb	3.28	4/93	16r
Cheese, Kraft grated Parmesan	8-oz canister	3.23	4Q 92	4c
Chicken, fresh, whole	lb	0.77	4/93	16r
Chicken, fryer, whole	lb	0.79	4Q 92	4c
Chicken breast, bone-in	lb	1.92	4/93	16r
Chicken legs, bone-in	lb	1.06	4/93	16r
Chuck roast, graded and ungraded, ex USDA prime and choice	lb	2.40	4/93	16r
Chuck roast, USDA choice, bone-in	lb	2.19	4/93	16r
Chuck roast, USDA choice, boneless	lb	2.38	4/93	16r
Cigarettes, Winston	carton	18.31	4Q 92	4c
Coffee, 100% ground roast, all sizes	lb	2.48	4/93	16r
Coffee, vacuum-packed	13-oz can	1.31	4Q 92	4c
Corn, frozen	10 oz	0.55	4Q 92	4c
Corn Flakes, Kellogg's or Post Toasties	18 oz	1.70	4Q 92	4c
Crackers, soda, salted	lb	1.15	4/93	16r
Eggs, Grade A large	doz	0.83	4Q 92	4c
Eggs, Grade A large	doz	0.96	4/93	16r
Flour, white, all purpose	lb	0.24	4/93	16r
Frankfurters, all meat or all beef	lb	2.01	4/93	16r
Grapefruit	lb	0.44	4/93	16r
Grapes, Thompson Seedless	lb	1.40	4/93	16r
Ground beef, 100% beef	lb	1.58	4/93	16r
Ground beef, lean and extra lean	lb	2.09	4/93	16r
Ground beef or hamburger	lb	1.59	4Q 92	4c
Ground chuck, 100% beef	lb	1.98	4/93	16r
Ham, boneless, excluding canned	lb	2.89	4/93	16r
Ham, picnic, shoulder, bone-in, smoked	lb	1.02	4/93	16r
Ham, rump or steak half, bone-in, smoked	lb	1.48	4/93	16r
Ice cream, prepackaged, bulk, regular	1/2 gal	2.41	4/93	16r
Lemons	lb	1.05	4/93	16r
Lettuce, iceberg	head	0.99	4Q 92	4c
Lettuce, iceberg	lb	0.81	4/93	16r
Margarine, Blue Bonnet or Parkay cubes	lb	0.49	4Q 92	4c
Margarine, stick	lb	0.88	4/93	16r
Milk, whole	1/2 gal	1.44	4Q 92	4c
Orange juice, Minute Maid frozen	12-oz can	1.14	4Q 92	4c
Oranges, navel	lb	0.55	4/93	16r
Peaches	29-oz can	1.30	4Q 92	4c
Pears, Anjou	lb	0.92	4/93	16r
Peas Sweet, Del Monte or Green Giant	15-17 oz can	0.47	4Q 92	4c
Pork chops, center cut, bone-in	lb	3.13	4/93	16r
Potato chips	16 oz	2.94	4/93	16r
Potatoes, white	lb	0.43	4/93	16r
Potatoes, white or red	10-lb sack	1.71	4Q 92	4c
Rib roast, USDA choice, bone-in	lb	4.63	4/93	16r
Rice, white, long grain, uncooked	lb	0.45	4/93	16r
Round roast, graded & ungraded, ex USDA prime & choice	lb	3.03	4/93	16r

Values are in dollars or fractions of dollars. In the column headed *Ref*, references are shown to sources. Each reference is followed by a letter. These refer to the geographical level for which data were reported: s=State, r=Region, and c=City or metro. The abbreviation *ex* is used to mean *except* or *excluding*; *exp* stands for expenditures. For other abbreviations and further explanations, please see the Introduction.

Jacksonville, FL - continued

Item	Per	Value	Date	Ref.
Groceries				
Round roast, USDA choice, boneless	lb	3.09	4/93	16r
Sausage, fresh, loose	lb	2.08	4/93	16r
Sausage, Jimmy Dean, 100% pork	lb	2.21	4Q 92	4c
Short ribs, bone-in	lb	2.66	4/93	16r
Shortening, vegetable oil blends	lb	0.69	4/93	16r
Shortening, vegetable, Crisco	3-lb can	2.14	4Q 92	4c
Soft drink, Coca Cola	2 liter	1.17	4Q 92	4c
Spaghetti and macaroni	lb	0.81	4/93	16r
Steak, rib eye, USDA choice, boneless	lb	6.24	4/93	16r
Steak, round, graded & ungraded, ex USDA prime & choice	lb	3.31	4/93	16r
Steak, round, USDA choice, boneless	lb	3.34	4/93	16r
Steak, sirloin, graded & ungraded, ex USDA prime & choice	lb	4.19	4/93	16r
Steak, sirloin, USDA choice, boneless	lb	4.46	4/93	16r
Steak, T-bone	lb	5.51	4Q 92	4c
Steak, T-bone, USDA choice, bone-in	lb	5.25	4/93	16r
Strawberries, dry pint	12 oz	0.92	4/93	16r
Sugar, cane or beet	4 lb	1.89	4Q 92	4c
Sugar, white	lb	0.39	4/93	16r
Sugar, white, 33-80 oz pk	lb	0.38	4/93	16r
Tomatoes, field grown	lb	0.88	4/93	16r
Tomatoes, Hunt's or Del Monte	14.5-oz can	0.60	4Q 92	4c
Tuna, chunk, light	6.125-6.5 oz can	0.53	4Q 92	4c
Tuna, chunk, light	lb	1.79	4/93	16r
Turkey, frozen, whole	lb	1.04	4/93	16r
Yogurt, natural, fruit flavored	1/2 pint	0.57	4/93	16r
Health Care				
ACCRA Index, Health Care		105.70	4Q 92	4c
Analgesic, Aspirin, Bayer, 325 mg tablets	100	3.37	4Q 92	4c
Childbirth, cesarean, hospital		5034	91	62r
Childbirth, cesarean, physician's fee		2053	91	62r
Childbirth, normal, hospital		2712	91	62r
Childbirth, normal, physician's fee		1492	91	62r
Dentist's fee, adult teeth cleaning and periodic oral exam	visit	47.40	4Q 92	4c
Doctor's fee, routine exam, established patient	visit	49.60	4Q 92	4c
Hospital care, semiprivate room	day	222.83	90	27c
Hospital care, semiprivate room	day	261.25	4Q 92	4c
Medical insurance premium, per employee, small group comprehensive	month	375.95	10/91	25c
Medical plan per employee	year	3495	91	45r
Mental health care, exp	capita	28.84-37.59	90	38s
Mental health care, exp, state mental health agency	capita	37.49	90	38s
Mental health care, hospital psychiatric services, non-Federal, exp	capita	9.11	88	38s
Mental health care, mental health organization, multiservice, exp	capita	16.21	88	38s
Mental health care, psychiatric hospitals, private, exp	capita	22.26	88	38s
Mental health care, psychiatric out-patient clinics, freestanding, exp	capita	0.89	88	38s
Mental health care, psychiatric partial-care organizations, freestanding, exp	capita	0.41	88	38s
Mental health care, state and county mental hospitals, exp	capita	16.25	88	38s
Mental health care, VA medical centers, exp	capita	1.69	88	38s
Physician fee, family practice, first-visit		75.00	91	62r
Physician fee, family practice, revisit		34.00	91	62r
Physician fee, general practice, first-visit		61.00	91	62r
Physician fee, general practice, revisit		32.00	91	62r
Physician fee, general surgeon, first-visit		64.00	91	62r
Physician fee, general surgeon, revisit		40.00	91	62r
Physician fee, internal medicine, first-visit		98.00	91	62r

Jacksonville, FL - continued

Item	Per	Value	Date	Ref.
Health Care - continued				
Physician fee, internal medicine, revisit		40.00	91	62r
Physician fee, median, neurosurgeon, first-visit		130.00	91	62r
Physician fee, median, nonsurgical specialist, first-visit		95.00	91	62r
Physician fee, median, orthopedic surgeon, first-visit		91.00	91	62r
Physician fee, median, plastic surgeon, first-visit		66.00	91	62r
Physician fee, median, surgical specialist, first-visit		62.00	91	62r
Physician fee, neurosurgeon, revisit		50.00	91	62r
Physician fee, nonsurgical specialist, revisit		40.00	91	62r
Physician fee, obstetrics/gynecology, first-visit		64.00	91	62r
Physician fee, obstetrics/gynecology, revisit		41.00	91	62r
Physician fee, orthopedic surgeon, revisit		40.00	91	62r
Physician fee, pediatrician, first-visit		49.00	91	62r
Physician fee, pediatrician, revisit		33.00	91	62r
Physician fee, plastic surgeon, revisit		43.00	91	62r
Physician fee, surgical specialist, revisit		37.00	91	62r
Substance abuse, hospital ancillary charge	incident	1390	90	70s
Substance abuse, hospital physician charge	incident	770	90	70s
Substance abuse, hospital room and board	incident	5600	90	70s
Household Goods				
Appliance repair, home, service call, washing machine	min labor charge	32.96	4Q 92	4c
Laundry detergent, Tide Ultra, Bold, or Cheer	42 oz	2.58	4Q 92	4c
Tissues, facial, Kleenex brand	175-count box	1.04	4Q 92	4c
Housing				
ACCRA Index, Housing		82.80	4Q 92	4c
Home, median price	unit	76.80		26c
House, 1,800 sq ft, 8,000 sq ft lot, new, urban	total	89900	4Q 92	4c
House payment, principal and interest, 25% down payment	month	495	4Q 92	4c
Mortgage rate, incl. points & origination fee, 30-year fixed or adjustable rate	percent	8.00	4Q 92	4c
Rent, apartment, 2 bedrooms - 1-1/2 to 2 baths, unfurnished, 950 sq ft, water	month	441	4Q 92	4c
Rental unit, 1 bedroom	month	420	93	23c
Rental unit, 2 bedroom	month	497	93	23c
Rental unit, 3 bedroom	month	620	93	23c
Rental unit, 4 bedroom	month	696	93	23c
Rental unit, efficiency	month	346	93	23c
Insurance and Pensions				
Auto insurance, private passenger	year	727.60	91	63s
Personal Goods				
Shampoo, Alberto VO5	15 oz	0.92	4Q 92	4c
Toothpaste, Crest or Colgate	6-7 oz	1.58	4Q 92	4c
Personal Services				
Dry cleaning, man's 2-piece suit		5.94	4Q 92	4c
Haircare, woman's shampoo, trim and blow-dry		20.50	4Q 92	4c
Haircut, man's barbershop, no styling		7.20	4Q 92	4c
Restaurant Food				
Chicken, fried, thigh and drumstick		2.01	4Q 92	4c
Hamburger with cheese	1/4 lb	1.84	4Q 92	4c
Pizza, Pizza Hut or Pizza Inn, cheese, thin crust	12-13 in	7.99	4Q 92	4c

Values are in dollars or fractions of dollars. In the column headed *Ref*, references are shown to sources. Each reference is followed by a letter. These refer to the geographical level for which data were reported: s=State, r=Region, and c=City or metro. The abbreviation *ex* is used to mean *except* or *excluding*; *exp* stands for *expenditures*. For other abbreviations and further explanations, please see the Introduction.

Jacksonville, FL - continued

Item	Per	Value	Date	Ref.
Taxes				
Tax, cigarette	pack	33.90	91	77s
Tax, gasoline	gal	11.60	91	77s
Taxes, state	capita	1037	91	77s
Transportation				
ACCRA Index, Transportation		105.80	4Q 92	4c
Auto rental, average	day	39.00	6/91	60c
Bus fare	one-way	0.60	3/93	2c
Commuter train fare (automated guideway)	one-way	0.25	3/03	2c
Driver's license fee		15.00	12/90	43s
Taxi fare, airport-city, average	day	19.00	6/91	60c
Tire balance, computer or spin balance, front	wheel	7.28	4Q 92	4c
Travel				
Breakfast	day	5.25	6/91	60c
Business travel	day	193.00	4/93	89r
Dinner	day	18.43	6/91	60c
Lodging	day	108.90	91	60c
Lunch	day	9.19	6/91	60c
Utilities				
ACCRA Index, Utilities		107.20	4Q 92	4c
Electricity	mil Btu	20.62	90	64s
Electricity, all electric, 1,800 sq ft living area new home	month	117.56	4Q 92	4c

Jacksonville, NC

Item	Per	Value	Date	Ref.
Child Care				
Child care fee, average, center	hour	1.29	90	65r
Child care fee, average, nonregulated family day care	hour	0.89	90	65r
Child care fee, average, regulated family day care	hour	1.32	90	65r
Communications				
Long-distance telephone service, day, initial minute, 0-100 miles	min	0.10-0.33	91	12s
Long-distance telephone service, day, additional minute, 0-100 miles	min	0.10-0.33	91	12s
Long-distance telephone service, evenings/weekends, 0-100 mi, initial minute	min	0.08-0.24	91	12s
Long-distance telephone service, evenings/weekends, 0-100 mi, additional minute	min	0.05-0.17	91	12s
Education				
Board, 4-yr private college/university	year	1768	91	22s
Board, 4-yr public college/university	year	1568	91	22s
Expenditures, local gov't, public elementary/secondary	pupil	5078	92	20s
Room, 4-year private college/university	year	1467	91	22s
Room, 4-year public college/university	year	1386	91	22s
Tuition, 2-year private college/university	year	4964	91	22s
Tuition, 2-year public college/university	year	334	91	22s
Tuition, 4-year private college/university	year	7826	91	22s
Tuition, 4-year public college/university, in-state	year	1112	91	22s
Energy and Fuels				
Coal	mil Btu	1.79	90	64s
Energy	mil Btu	10.06	90	64s
Energy exp/householder, 1-family unit	year	487	90	28r
Energy exp/householder, <1,000 sq ft heating area	year	393	90	28r
Energy exp/householder, 1,000-1,999 sq ft heating area	year	442	90	28r
Energy exp/householder, 2,000+ sq ft heating area	year	577	90	28r
Energy exp/householder, mobile home	year	366	90	28r
Energy exp/householder, multifamily	year	382	90	28r
Gas, natural	mil Btu	4.19	90	64s

Jacksonville, NC - continued

Item	Per	Value	Date	Ref.
Energy and Fuels - continued				
Gas, natural	000 cu ft	6.24	91	46s
Gas, natural, exp	year	439	91	46s
Gasoline, unleaded regular	mil Btu	9.44	90	64s
Entertainment				
Miniature golf admission	adult	6.18	92	1r
Miniature golf admission	child	5.14	92	1r
Waterpark admission	adult	11.00	92	1r
Waterpark admission	child	8.55	92	1r
Funerals				
Casket, 18-gauge steel, velvet interior		2029.08	91	24r
Cosmetology, hair care, etc.		75.10	91	24r
Embalming		249.24	91	24r
Facility use for ceremony		162.27	91	24r
Hearse, local		114.04	91	24r
Limousine, local		88.57	91	24r
Remains to funeral home, transfer		92.61	91	24r
Service charge, professional		682.42	91	24r
Vault, concrete, non-metallic liner		798.70	91	24r
Viewing facilities, use		163.86	91	24r
Groceries				
Apples, Red Delicious	lb	0.79	4/93	16r
Bacon	lb	1.75	4/93	16r
Bananas	lb	0.42	4/93	16r
Beef, stew, boneless	lb	2.61	4/93	16r
Bologna, all beef or mixed	lb	2.24	4/93	16r
Bread, white, pan	lb	0.64	4/93	16r
Bread, whole wheat, pan	lb	0.96	4/93	16r
Cabbage	lb	0.37	4/93	16r
Carrots, short trimmed and topped	lb	0.47	4/93	16r
Celery	lb	0.64	4/93	16r
Cheese, American	lb	2.98	4/93	16r
Cheese, Cheddar	lb	3.28	4/93	16r
Chicken, fresh, whole	lb	0.77	4/93	16r
Chicken breast, bone-in	lb	1.92	4/93	16r
Chicken legs, bone-in	lb	1.06	4/93	16r
Chuck roast, graded and ungraded, ex USDA prime and choice	lb	2.40	4/93	16r
Chuck roast, USDA choice, bone-in	lb	2.19	4/93	16r
Chuck roast, USDA choice, boneless	lb	2.38	4/93	16r
Coffee, 100% ground roast, all sizes	lb	2.48	4/93	16r
Crackers, soda, salted	lb	1.15	4/93	16r
Eggs, Grade A large	doz	0.96	4/93	16r
Flour, white, all purpose	lb	0.24	4/93	16r
Frankfurters, all meat or all beef	lb	2.01	4/93	16r
Grapefruit	lb	0.44	4/93	16r
Grapes, Thompson Seedless	lb	1.40	4/93	16r
Ground beef, 100% beef	lb	1.58	4/93	16r
Ground beef, lean and extra lean	lb	2.09	4/93	16r
Ground chuck, 100% beef	lb	1.98	4/93	16r
Ham, boneless, excluding canned	lb	2.89	4/93	16r
Ham, picnic, shoulder, bone-in, smoked	lb	1.02	4/93	16r
Ham, rump or steak half, bone-in, smoked	lb	1.48	4/93	16r
Ice cream, prepackaged, bulk, regular	1/2 gal	2.41	4/93	16r
Lemons	lb	1.05	4/93	16r
Lettuce, iceberg	lb	0.81	4/93	16r
Margarine, stick	lb	0.88	4/93	16r
Oranges, navel	lb	0.55	4/93	16r
Pears, Anjou	lb	0.92	4/93	16r
Pork chops, center cut, bone-in	lb	3.13	4/93	16r
Potato chips	16 oz	2.94	4/93	16r
Potatoes, white	lb	0.43	4/93	16r
Rib roast, USDA choice, bone-in	lb	4.63	4/93	16r
Rice, white, long grain, uncooked	lb	0.45	4/93	16r
Round roast, graded & ungraded, ex USDA prime & choice	lb	3.03	4/93	16r
Round roast, USDA choice, boneless	lb	3.09	4/93	16r
Sausage, fresh, loose	lb	2.08	4/93	16r
Short ribs, bone-in	lb	2.66	4/93	16r
Shortening, vegetable oil blends	lb	0.69	4/93	16r
Spaghetti and macaroni	lb	0.81	4/93	16r

Values are in dollars or fractions of dollars. In the column headed *Ref*, references are shown to sources. Each reference is followed by a letter. These refer to the geographical level for which data were reported: s=State, r=Region, and c=City or metro. The abbreviation *ex* is used to mean *except* or *excluding*; *exp* stands for expenditures. For other abbreviations and further explanations, please see the Introduction.

Jacksonville, NC - continued

Item	Per	Value	Date	Ref.
Groceries				
Steak, rib eye, USDA choice, boneless	lb	6.24	4/93	16r
Steak, round, graded & ungraded, ex USDA prime & choice	lb	3.31	4/93	16r
Steak, round, USDA choice, boneless	lb	3.34	4/93	16r
Steak, sirloin, graded & ungraded, ex USDA prime & choice	lb	4.19	4/93	16r
Steak, sirloin, USDA choice, boneless	lb	4.46	4/93	16r
Steak, T-bone, USDA choice, bone-in	lb	5.25	4/93	16r
Strawberries, dry pint	12 oz	0.92	4/93	16r
Sugar, white	lb	0.39	4/93	16r
Sugar, white, 33-80 oz pk	lb	0.38	4/93	16r
Tomatoes, field grown	lb	0.88	4/93	16r
Tuna, chunk, light	lb	1.79	4/93	16r
Turkey, frozen, whole	lb	1.04	4/93	16r
Yogurt, natural, fruit flavored	1/2 pint	0.57	4/93	16r
Health Care				
Childbirth, cesarean, hospital		5034	91	62r
Childbirth, cesarean, physician's fee		2053	91	62r
Childbirth, normal, hospital		2712	91	62r
Childbirth, normal, physician's fee		1492	91	62r
Medical plan per employee	year	3495	91	45r
Mental health care, exp	capita	37.60-53.67	90	38s
Mental health care, exp, state mental health agency	capita	45.66	90	38s
Mental health care, hospital psychiatric services, non-Federal, exp	capita	12.05	88	38s
Mental health care, mental health organization, multiservice, exp	capita	29.54	88	38s
Mental health care, psychiatric hospitals, private, exp	capita	15.07	88	38s
Mental health care, psychiatric out-patient clinics, freestanding, exp	capita	0.11	88	38s
Mental health care, state and county mental hospitals, exp	capita	26.36	88	38s
Mental health care, VA medical centers, exp	capita	2.23	88	38s
Physician fee, family practice, first-visit		75.00	91	62r
Physician fee, family practice, revisit		34.00	91	62r
Physician fee, general practice, first-visit		61.00	91	62r
Physician fee, general practice, revisit		32.00	91	62r
Physician fee, general surgeon, first-visit		64.00	91	62r
Physician fee, general surgeon, revisit		40.00	91	62r
Physician fee, internal medicine, first-visit		98.00	91	62r
Physician fee, internal medicine, revisit		40.00	91	62r
Physician fee, median, neurosurgeon, first-visit		130.00	91	62r
Physician fee, median, nonsurgical specialist, first-visit		95.00	91	62r
Physician fee, median, orthopedic surgeon, first-visit		91.00	91	62r
Physician fee, median, plastic surgeon, first-visit		66.00	91	62r
Physician fee, median, surgical specialist, first-visit		62.00	91	62r
Physician fee, neurosurgeon, revisit		50.00	91	62r
Physician fee, nonsurgical specialist, revisit		40.00	91	62r
Physician fee, obstetrics/gynecology, first-visit		64.00	91	62r
Physician fee, obstetrics/gynecology, revisit		41.00	91	62r
Physician fee, orthopedic surgeon, revisit		40.00	91	62r
Physician fee, pediatrician, first-visit		49.00	91	62r
Physician fee, pediatrician, revisit		33.00	91	62r
Physician fee, plastic surgeon, revisit		43.00	91	62r
Physician fee, surgical specialist, revisit		37.00	91	62r
Substance abuse, hospital ancillary charge	incident	1090	90	70s
Substance abuse, hospital physician charge	incident	460	90	70s
Substance abuse, hospital room and board	incident	4880	90	70s

Jacksonville, NC - continued

Item	Per	Value	Date	Ref.
Insurance and Pensions				
Auto insurance, private passenger	year	522.39	91	63s
Taxes				
Tax, cigarette	pack	5	91	77s
Tax, gasoline	gal	21.90	91	77s
Taxes, state	capita	1165	91	77s
Transportation				
Driver's license fee		15.00	12/90	43s
Vehicle registration and license plate	year	35.00	93	50s
Travel				
Business travel	day	193.00	4/93	89r
Utilities				
Electricity	mil Btu	18.74	90	64s

Jamestown-Dunkirk, NY

Item	Per	Value	Date	Ref.
Child Care				
Child care fee, average, center	hour	2.18	90	65r
Child care fee, average, nonregulated family day care	hour	1.83	90	65r
Child care fee, average, regulated family day care	hour	2.02	90	65r
Education				
Board, 4-yr private college/university	year	2451	91	22s
Board, 4-yr public college/university	year	1725	91	22s
Expenditures, local gov't, public elementary/secondary	pupil	8603	92	20s
Room, 4-year private college/university	year	2652	91	22s
Room, 4-year public college/university	year	2183	91	22s
Tuition, 2-year private college/university	year	5926	91	22s
Tuition, 2-year public college/university	year	1419	91	22s
Tuition, 4-year private college/university	year	10340	91	22s
Tuition, 4-year public college/university, in-state	year	1587	91	22s
Energy and Fuels				
Coal	mil Btu	1.66	90	64s
Energy	mil Btu	10.68	90	64s
Energy exp/householder, 1-family unit	year	588	90	28r
Energy exp/householder, <1,000 sq ft heating area	year	477	90	28r
Energy exp/householder, 1,000-1,999 sq ft heating area	year	517	90	28r
Energy exp/householder, 2,000+ sq ft heating area	year	630	90	28r
Energy exp/householder, mobile home	year	412	90	28r
Energy exp/householder, multifamily	year	498	90	28r
Gas, natural	mil Btu	5.25	90	64s
Gas, natural	000 cu ft	7.35	91	46s
Gas, natural, exp	year	557	91	46s
Gasoline, unleaded regular	mil Btu	8.83	90	64s
Funerals				
Casket, 18-gauge steel, velvet interior		1811.58	91	24r
Cosmetology, hair care, etc.		111.08	91	24r
Embalming		329.42	91	24r
Facility use for ceremony		201.29	91	24r
Hearse, local		135.27	91	24r
Limousine, local		127.24	91	24r
Remains to funeral home, transfer		103.98	91	24r
Service charge, professional		724.98	91	24r
Vault, concrete, non-metallic liner		766.71	91	24r
Viewing facilities, use		260.60	91	24r
Groceries				
Apples, Red Delicious	lb	0.85	4/93	16r
Bacon	lb	2.12	4/93	16r
Bananas	lb	0.54	4/93	16r
Bread, white, pan	lb	0.81	4/93	16r
Butter	lb	2.02	4/93	16r

Values are in dollars or fractions of dollars. In the column headed *Ref*, references are shown to sources. Each reference is followed by a letter. These refer to the geographical level for which data were reported: s=State, r=Region, and c=City or metro. The abbreviation *ex* is used to mean *except* or *excluding*; *exp* stands for expenditures. For other abbreviations and further explanations, please see the Introduction.

Jamestown-Dunkirk, NY - continued

Item	Per	Value	Date	Ref.
Groceries				
Carrots, short trimmed and topped	lb	0.51	4/93	16r
Chicken, fresh, whole	lb	1.04	4/93	16r
Chicken breast, bone-in	lb	2.21	4/93	16r
Chicken legs, bone-in	lb	1.16	4/93	16r
Chuck roast, USDA choice, boneless	lb	2.82	4/93	16r
Coffee, 100% ground roast, all sizes	lb	2.66	4/93	16r
Cucumbers	lb	0.85	4/93	16r
Eggs, Grade A large	doz	1.15	4/93	16r
Grapefruit	lb	0.45	4/93	16r
Grapes, Thompson Seedless	lb	1.52	4/93	16r
Ground beef, lean and extra lean	lb	2.36	4/93	16r
Ground chuck, 100% beef	lb	2.02	4/93	16r
Honey, jar	8 oz	0.96-1.75	92	5r
Honey, jar	lb	1.50-3.00	92	5r
Honey, squeeze bear	12-oz	1.50-1.99	92	5r
Ice cream, prepackaged, bulk, regular	1/2 gal	2.80	4/93	16r
Lemons	lb	0.96	4/93	16r
Lettuce, iceberg	lb	0.95	4/93	16r
Margarine, stick	lb	0.81	4/93	16r
Milk, fresh, whole, fortified	1/2 gal	1.30	4/93	16r
Oranges, navel	lb	0.56	4/93	16r
Peanut butter, creamy, all sizes	lb	1.88	4/93	16r
Pork chops, center cut, bone-in	lb	3.34	4/93	16r
Potato chips	16 oz	2.88	4/93	16r
Potatoes, white	lb	0.37	4/93	16r
Rib roast, USDA choice, bone-in	lb	4.94	4/93	16r
Round roast, USDA choice, boneless	lb	3.17	4/93	16r
Shortening, vegetable oil blends	lb	0.98	4/93	16r
Spaghetti and macaroni	lb	0.82	4/93	16r
Steak, round, graded & ungraded, ex USDA prime & choice	lb	4.04	4/93	16r
Steak, round, USDA choice, boneless	lb	3.90	4/93	16r
Steak, sirloin, USDA choice, boneless	lb	4.97	4/93	16r
Strawberries, dry pint	12 oz	0.90	4/93	16r
Sugar, white	lb	0.50	4/93	16r
Sugar, white, 33-80 oz pk	lb	0.41	4/93	16r
Tomatoes, field grown	lb	1.23	4/93	16r
Tuna, chunk, light	lb	2.22	4/93	16r
Turkey, frozen, whole	lb	1.04	4/93	16r
Health Care				
Childbirth, cesarean, hospital		5826	91	62r
Childbirth, cesarean, physician's fee		2053	91	62r
Childbirth, normal, hospital		2964	91	62r
Childbirth, normal, physician's fee		1492	91	62r
Medical plan per employee	year	3942	91	45r
Mental health care, exp	capita	53.68-118.35	90	38s
Mental health care, exp, state mental health agency	capita	118.34	90	38s
Mental health care, hospital psychiatric services, non-Federal, exp	capita	29.77	88	38s
Mental health care, mental health organization, multiservice, exp	capita	20.03	88	38s
Mental health care, psychiatric hospitals, private, exp	capita	8.37	88	38s
Mental health care, psychiatric out-patient clinics, freestanding, exp	capita	7.96	88	38s
Mental health care, psychiatric partial-care organizations, freestanding, exp	capita	1.24	88	38s
Mental health care, state and county mental hospitals, exp	capita	89.52	88	38s
Mental health care, VA medical centers, exp	capita	7.12	88	38s
Prescription drug co-pay, Medicaid	month	23.00	91	21s
Substance abuse, hospital ancillary charge	incident	1040	90	70s
Substance abuse, hospital physician charge	incident	360	90	70s
Substance abuse, hospital room and board	incident	6330	90	70s

Jamestown-Dunkirk, NY - continued

Item	Per	Value	Date	Ref.
Insurance and Pensions				
Auto insurance, private passenger	year	840.89	91	63s
Taxes				
Tax, cigarette	pack	39	91	77s
Tax, gasoline	gal	8	91	77s
Taxes, state	capita	1567	91	77s
Transportation				
Driver's license fee		17.50	12/90	43s
Vehicle registration and license plate	2 years	27.50-149.50	93	67s
Travel				
Business travel	day	165.00	4/93	89r
Utilities				
Electricity	mil Btu	27.51	90	64s

Janesville, WI

Item	Per	Value	Date	Ref.
Composite ACCRA index		100.40	4Q 92	4c
Alcoholic Beverages				
Beer, Miller Lite or Budweiser, 12-oz containers	6 pack	3.62	4Q 92	4c
Liquor, J & B Scotch	750 ml	16.66	4Q 92	4c
Wine, Gallo Chablis blanc, 1.5 liter	bottle	4.39	4Q 92	4c
Child Care				
Child care fee, average, center	hour	1.63	90	65r
Child care fee, average, nonregulated family day care	hour	1.83	90	65r
Child care fee, average, regulated family day care	hour	1.42	90	65r
Clothing				
Jeans, man's denim		35.32	4Q 92	4c
Shirt, man's dress shirt		29.25	4Q 92	4c
Undervest, boy's size 10-14, cotton	3	3.79	4Q 92	4c
Communications				
Long-distance telephone service, day, initial minute, 0-100 miles	min	0.15-0.29	91	12s
Long-distance telephone service, day, additional minute, 0-100 miles	min	0.10-0.27	91	12s
Newspaper subscription, daily and Sunday home delivery, large-city	month	11.96	4Q 92	4c
Telephone, flat rate	month	6.00	91	11c
Telephone bill, family of four	month	16.31	4Q 92	4c
Education				
Board, 4-yr private college/university	year	1533	91	22s
Board, 4-yr public college/university	year	1404	91	22s
Expenditures, local gov't, public elementary/secondary	pupil	5972	92	20s
Room, 4-year private college/university	year	1256	91	22s
Room, 4-year public college/university	year	1416	91	22s
Tuition, 2-year private college/university	year	4768	91	22s
Tuition, 2-year public college/university	year	1234	91	22s
Tuition, 4-year private college/university	year	8237	91	22s
Tuition, 4-year public college/university, in-state	year	1951	91	22s
Energy and Fuels				
Coal	mil Btu	1.41	90	64s
Energy	mil Btu	8.27	90	64s
Energy, combined forms, 1,800 sq ft heating area	month	97.71	4Q 92	4c
Energy, exc electricity, 1,800 sq ft heating area	month	56.94	4Q 92	4c
Energy exp/householder, 1-family unit	year	471	90	28r
Energy exp/householder, <1,000 sq ft heating area	year	430	90	28r
Energy exp/householder, 1,000-1,999 sq ft heating area	year	481	90	28r

Values are in dollars or fractions of dollars. In the column headed *Ref*, references are shown to sources. Each reference is followed by a letter. These refer to the geographical level for which data were reported: s=State, r=Region, and c=City or metro. The abbreviation *ex* is used to mean *except* or *excluding*; *exp* stands for expenditures. For other abbreviations and further explanations, please see the Introduction.

Janesville, WI - continued

Item	Per	Value	Date	Ref.
Energy and Fuels				
Energy exp/householder, 2,000+ sq ft heating area	year	473	90	28r
Energy exp/householder, mobile home	year	430	90	28r
Energy exp/householder, multifamily	year	461	90	28r
Gas, cooking, winter, 10 therms	month	9.12	92	56c
Gas, cooking, winter, 30 therms	month	20.35	92	56c
Gas, cooking, winter, 50 therms	month	31.59	92	56c
Gas, heating, winter, 100 therms	month	56.67	92	56c
Gas, heating, winter, average use	month	95.62	92	56c
Gas, natural	mil Btu	4.56	90	64s
Gas, natural	000 cu ft	5.61	91	46s
Gas, natural, exp	year	605	91	46s
Gasoline, motor	gal	1.16	4Q 92	4c
Gasoline, unleaded regular	mil Btu	9.38	90	64s
Entertainment				
Bowling, evening rate	game	1.83	4Q 92	4c
Miniature golf admission	adult	6.18	92	1r
Miniature golf admission	child	5.14	92	1r
Monopoly game, Parker Brothers', No. 9		10.95	4Q 92	4c
Movie	admission	4.88	4Q 92	4c
Tennis balls, yellow, Wilson or Penn, 3	can	1.98	4Q 92	4c
Waterpark admission	adult	11.00	92	1r
Waterpark admission	child	8.55	92	1r
Funerals				
Casket, 18-gauge steel, velvet interior		1926.72	91	24r
Cosmetology, hair care, etc.		97.64	91	24r
Embalming		249.14	91	24r
Facility use for ceremony		208.59	91	24r
Hearse, local		130.12	91	24r
Limousine, local		104.66	91	24r
Remains to funeral home, transfer		93.61	91	24r
Service charge, professional		724.62	91	24r
Vault, concrete, non-metallic liner		734.53	91	24r
Viewing facilities, use		236.06	91	24r
Goods and Services				
ACCRA Index, Miscellaneous Goods and Services		97.90	4Q 92	4c
Groceries				
ACCRA Index, Groceries		102.80	4Q 92	4c
Apples, Red Delicious	lb	0.77	4/93	16r
Babyfood, strained vegetables, lowest price	4-4.5 oz jar	0.39	4Q 92	4c
Bacon	lb	1.85	4/93	16r
Bananas	lb	0.45	4Q 92	4c
Bananas	lb	0.46	4/93	16r
Beef, stew, boneless	lb	2.53	4/93	16r
Bologna, all beef or mixed	lb	2.19	4/93	16r
Bread, white	24 oz	0.88	4Q 92	4c
Bread, white, pan	lb	0.78	4/93	16r
Butter	lb	1.50	4/93	16r
Cabbage	lb	0.40	4/93	16r
Carrots, short trimmed and topped	lb	0.45	4/93	16r
Cheese, Cheddar	lb	3.47	4/93	16r
Cheese, Kraft grated Parmesan	8-oz canister	3.23	4Q 92	4c
Chicken, fresh, whole	lb	0.84	4/93	16r
Chicken, fryer, whole	lb	0.99	4Q 92	4c
Chicken breast, bone-in	lb	1.94	4/93	16r
Chicken legs, bone-in	lb	1.02	4/93	16r
Chuck roast, graded and ungraded, ex USDA prime and choice	lb	2.43	4/93	16r
Chuck roast, USDA choice, bone-in	lb	2.11	4/93	16r
Chuck roast, USDA choice, boneless	lb	2.44	4/93	16r
Cigarettes, Winston	carton	18.55	4Q 92	4c
Coffee, 100% ground roast, all sizes	lb	2.47	4/93	16r
Coffee, vacuum-packed	13-oz can	1.93	4Q 92	4c

Janesville, WI - continued

Item	Per	Value	Date	Ref.
Groceries - continued				
Cookies, chocolate chip	lb	2.73	4/93	16r
Corn, frozen	10 oz	0.68	4Q 92	4c
Corn Flakes, Kellogg's or Post Toasties	18 oz	1.98	4Q 92	4c
Eggs, Grade A large	doz	0.69	4Q 92	4c
Eggs, Grade A large	doz	0.93	4/93	16r
Flour, white, all purpose	lb	0.21	4/93	16r
Grapefruit	lb	0.45	4/93	16r
Grapes, Thompson Seedless	lb	1.46	4/93	16r
Ground beef, 100% beef	lb	1.63	4/93	16r
Ground beef, lean and extra lean	lb	2.08	4/93	16r
Ground beef or hamburger	lb	1.79	4Q 92	4c
Ground chuck, 100% beef	lb	1.94	4/93	16r
Ham, boneless, excluding canned	lb	2.21	4/93	16r
Honey, jar	8 oz	0.97-1.25	92	5r
Honey, jar	lb	1.25-2.25	92	5r
Honey, squeeze bear	12-oz	1.25-1.99	92	5r
Ice cream, prepackaged, bulk, regular	1/2 gal	2.41	4/93	16r
Lemons	lb	0.82	4/93	16r
Lettuce, iceberg	head	1.03	4Q 92	4c
Lettuce, iceberg	lb	0.83	4/93	16r
Margarine, Blue Bonnet or Parkay cubes	lb	0.58	4Q 92	4c
Margarine, stick	lb	0.77	4/93	16r
Milk, whole	1/2 gal	1.21	4Q 92	4c
Orange juice, Minute Maid frozen	12-oz can	1.21	4Q 92	4c
Oranges, navel	lb	0.50	4/93	16r
Peaches	29-oz can	1.10	4Q 92	4c
Peanut butter, creamy, all sizes	lb	1.82	4/93	16r
Pears, Anjou	lb	0.85	4/93	16r
Peas Sweet, Del Monte or Green Giant	15-17 oz can	0.55	4Q 92	4c
Pork chops, center cut, bone-in	lb	3.17	4/93	16r
Potato chips	16 oz	2.68	4/93	16r
Potatoes, white	lb	0.26	4/93	16r
Potatoes, white or red	10-lb sack	1.91	4Q 92	4c
Round roast, graded & ungraded, ex USDA prime & choice	lb	2.88	4/93	16r
Round roast, USDA choice, boneless	lb	2.96	4/93	16r
Sausage, Jimmy Dean, 100% pork	lb	2.59	4Q 92	4c
Shortening, vegetable oil blends	lb	0.79	4/93	16r
Shortening, vegetable, Crisco	3-lb can	2.43	4Q 92	4c
Soft drink, Coca Cola	2 liter	1.09	4Q 92	4c
Spaghetti and macaroni	lb	0.76	4/93	16r
Steak, rib eye, USDA choice, boneless	lb	6.29	4/93	16r
Steak, round, USDA choice, boneless	lb	3.24	4/93	16r
Steak, sirloin, graded & ungraded, ex USDA prime & choice	lb	4.00	4/93	16r
Steak, sirloin, USDA choice, bone-in	lb	3.57	4/93	16r
Steak, sirloin, USDA choice, boneless	lb	4.17	4/93	16r
Steak, T-bone	lb	4.49	4Q 92	4c
Steak, T-bone, USDA choice, bone-in	lb	5.60	4/93	16r
Strawberries, dry pint	12 oz	0.90	4/93	16r
Sugar, cane or beet	4 lb	1.70	4Q 92	4c
Sugar, white	lb	0.36	4/93	16r
Sugar, white, 33-80 oz pk	lb	0.35	4/93	16r
Tomatoes, field grown	lb	0.99	4/93	16r
Tomatoes, Hunt's or Del Monte	14.5-oz can	0.73	4Q 92	4c
Tuna, chunk, light	6.125-6.5 oz can	0.57	4Q 92	4c
Tuna, chunk, light	lb	1.76	4/93	16r
Turkey, frozen, whole	lb	0.91	4/93	16r
Health Care				
ACCRA Index, Health Care		98.50	4Q 92	4c
Analgesic, Aspirin, Bayer, 325 mg tablets	100	4.93	4Q 92	4c
Childbirth, cesarean, hospital		4688	91	62r
Childbirth, cesarean, physician's fee		2053	91	62r
Childbirth, normal, hospital		2657	91	62r

Values are in dollars or fractions of dollars. In the column headed *Ref*, references are shown to sources. Each reference is followed by a letter. These refer to the geographical level for which data were reported: s = State, r = Region, and c = City or metro. The abbreviation *ex* is used to mean *except* or *excluding*; *exp* stands for expenditures. For other abbreviations and further explanations, please see the Introduction.

Janesville, WI - continued

Item	Per	Value	Date	Ref.
Health Care				
Childbirth, normal, physician's fee		1492	91	62r
Dentist's fee, adult teeth cleaning and periodic oral exam	visit	40.44	4Q 92	4c
Doctor's fee, routine exam, established patient	visit	47.75	4Q 92	4c
Hospital care, semiprivate room	day	198.00	4Q 92	4c
Medical insurance premium, per employee, small group comprehensive	month	284.70	10/91	25c
Medical plan per employee	year	3443	91	45r
Mental health care, exp	capita	28.84-37.59	90	38s
Mental health care, exp, state mental health agency	capita	36.62	90	38s
Mental health care, hospital psychiatric services, non-Federal, exp	capita	13.05	88	38s
Mental health care, mental health organization, multiservice, exp	capita	10.93	88	38s
Mental health care, psychiatric hospitals, private, exp	capita	8.71	88	38s
Mental health care, psychiatric out-patient clinics, freestanding, exp	capita	5.33	88	38s
Mental health care, psychiatric partial-care organizations, freestanding, exp	capita	0.20	88	38s
Mental health care, state and county mental hospitals, exp	capita	28.29	88	38s
Mental health care, VA medical centers, exp	capita	7.57	88	38s
Physician fee, family practice, first-visit		76.00	91	62r
Physician fee, family practice, revisit		33.00	91	62r
Physician fee, general practice, first-visit		61.00	91	62r
Physician fee, general practice, revisit		31.00	91	62r
Physician fee, general surgeon, first-visit		65.00	91	62r
Physician fee, general surgeon, revisit		35.00	91	62r
Physician fee, internal medicine, first-visit		91.00	91	62r
Physician fee, internal medicine, revisit		40.00	91	62r
Physician fee, median, neurosurgeon, first-visit		106.00	91	62r
Physician fee, median, nonsurgical specialist, first-visit		90.00	91	62r
Physician fee, median, orthopedic surgeon, first-visit		83.00	91	62r
Physician fee, median, surgical specialist, first-visit		61.00	91	62r
Physician fee, neurosurgeon, revisit		41.00	91	62r
Physician fee, nonsurgical specialist, revisit		40.00	91	62r
Physician fee, obstetrics/gynecology, first-visit		61.00	91	62r
Physician fee, obstetrics/gynecology, revisit		40.00	91	62r
Physician fee, orthopedic surgeon, revisit		41.00	91	62r
Physician fee, pediatrician, first-visit		46.00	91	62r
Physician fee, pediatrician, revisit		33.00	91	62r
Physician fee, surgical specialist, revisit		36.00	91	62r
Substance abuse, hospital ancillary charge	incident	960	90	70s
Substance abuse, hospital physician charge	incident	470	90	70s
Substance abuse, hospital room and board	incident	3980	90	70s
Household Goods				
Appliance repair, home, service call, washing machine	min labor charge	26.18	4Q 92	4c
Laundry detergent, Tide Ultra, Bold, or Cheer	42 oz	3.63	4Q 92	4c
Tissues, facial, Kleenex brand	175-count box	1.14	4Q 92	4c
Housing				
ACCRA Index, Housing		110.30	4Q 92	4c
House, 1,800 sq ft, 8,000 sq ft lot, new, urban	total	127038	4Q 92	4c

Janesville, WI - continued

Item	Per	Value	Date	Ref.
Housing - continued				
House payment, principal and interest, 25% down payment	month	709	4Q 92	4c
Mortgage rate, incl. points & origination fee, 30-year fixed or adjustable rate	percent	8.15	4Q 92	4c
Rent, apartment, 2 bedrooms - 1-1/2 to 2 baths, unfurnished, 950 sq ft, water	month	473	4Q 92	4c
Rental unit, 1 bedroom	month	404	93	23c
Rental unit, 2 bedroom	month	476	93	23c
Rental unit, 3 bedroom	month	596	93	23c
Rental unit, 4 bedroom	month	668	93	23c
Rental unit, efficiency	month	331	93	23c
Insurance and Pensions				
Auto insurance, private passenger	year	510.11	91	63s
Personal Goods				
Shampoo, Alberto VO5	15 oz	1.33	4Q 92	4c
Toothpaste, Crest or Colgate	6-7 oz	2.13	4Q 92	4c
Personal Services				
Dry cleaning, man's 2-piece suit		5.59	4Q 92	4c
Haircare, woman's shampoo, trim and blow-dry		16.78	4Q 92	4c
Haircut, man's barbershop, no styling		7.56	4Q 92	4c
Restaurant Food				
Chicken, fried, thigh and drumstick		2.18	4Q 92	4c
Hamburger with cheese	1/4 lb	1.76	4Q 92	4c
Pizza, Pizza Hut or Pizza Inn, cheese, thin crust	12-13 in	7.00	4Q 92	4c
Taxes				
Tax, cigarette	pack	38	91	77s
Tax, gasoline	gal	22.20	91	77s
Taxes, state	capita	1416	91	77s
Transportation				
ACCRA Index, Transportation		89.60	4Q 92	4c
Bus fare, up to 10 miles	one-way	0.60	4Q 92	4c
Driver's license fee		9.00	12/90	43s
Tire balance, computer or spin balance, front	wheel	5.28	4Q 92	4c
Utilities				
ACCRA Index, Utilities		88.90	4Q 92	4c
Electricity	mil Btu	15.77	90	64s
Electricity, partial electric and other energy, 1,800 sq ft living area new home	month	40.77	4Q 92	4c
Electricity, winter, 250 KWh	month	18.92	92	55c
Electricity, winter, 500 KWh	month	34.34	92	55c
Electricity, winter, 750 KWh	month	49.76	92	55c
Electricity, winter, 1000 KWh	month	65.18	92	55c

Jefferson City, MO

Item	Per	Value	Date	Ref.
Composite ACCRA index		86.00	4Q 92	4c
Alcoholic Beverages				
Beer, Miller Lite or Budweiser, 12-oz containers	6 pack	3.43	4Q 92	4c
Liquor, J & B Scotch	750 ml	14.58	4Q 92	4c
Wine, Gallo Chablis blanc, 1.5 liter	bottle	4.35	4Q 92	4c
Clothing				
Jeans, man's denim		20.66	4Q 92	4c
Shirt, man's dress shirt		22.00	4Q 92	4c
Undervest, boy's size 10-14, cotton	3	3.07	4Q 92	4c
Communications				
Newspaper subscription, daily and Sunday home delivery, large-city	month	6.50	4Q 92	4c
Telephone bill, family of four	month	14.05	4Q 92	4c
Energy and Fuels				
Energy, combined forms, 1,800 sq ft heating area	month	115.58	4Q 92	4c

Values are in dollars or fractions of dollars. In the column headed *Ref*, references are shown to sources. Each reference is followed by a letter. These refer to the geographical level for which data were reported: s = State, r = Region, and c = City or metro. The abbreviation *ex* is used to mean *except* or *excluding*; *exp* stands for expenditures. For other abbreviations and further explanations, please see the Introduction.

Jefferson City, MO - continued

Item	Per	Value	Date	Ref.
Energy and Fuels				
Energy, exc electricity, 1,800 sq ft heating area	month	53.76	4Q 92	4c
Gas, cooking, 10 therms	month	11.67	92	56c
Gas, cooking, 30 therms	month	22.79	92	56c
Gas, cooking, 50 therms	month	33.92	92	56c
Gas, heating, winter, 100 therms	month	61.73	92	56c
Gas, heating, winter, average use	month	80.08	92	56c
Gasoline, motor	gal	1.01	4Q 92	4c
Entertainment				
Bowling, evening rate	game	1.74	4Q 92	4c
Monopoly game, Parker Brothers', No. 9		9.97	4Q 92	4c
Movie	admission	4.50	4Q 92	4c
Tennis balls, yellow, Wilson or Penn, 3	can	1.94	4Q 92	4c
Goods and Services				
ACCRA Index, Miscellaneous Goods and Services		84.90	4Q 92	4c
Groceries				
ACCRA Index, Groceries		82.70	4Q 92	4c
Babyfood, strained vegetables, lowest price	4-4.5 oz jar	0.21	4Q 92	4c
Bananas	lb	0.44	4Q 92	4c
Bread, white	24 oz	0.38	4Q 92	4c
Cheese, Kraft grated Parmesan	8-oz canister	2.92	4Q 92	4c
Chicken, fryer, whole	lb	0.56	4Q 92	4c
Cigarettes, Winston	carton	15.32	4Q 92	4c
Coffee, vacuum-packed	13-oz can	1.57	4Q 92	4c
Corn, frozen	10 oz	0.57	4Q 92	4c
Corn Flakes, Kellogg's or Post Toasties	18 oz	1.64	4Q 92	4c
Eggs, Grade A large	doz	0.74	4Q 92	4c
Ground beef or hamburger	lb	0.97	4Q 92	4c
Lettuce, iceberg	head	0.79	4Q 92	4c
Margarine, Blue Bonnet or Parkay cubes	lb	0.48	4Q 92	4c
Milk, whole	1/2 gal	1.24	4Q 92	4c
Orange juice, Minute Maid frozen	12-oz can	1.43	4Q 92	4c
Peaches	29-oz can	1.31	4Q 92	4c
Peas Sweet, Del Monte or Green Giant	15-17 oz can	0.47	4Q 92	4c
Potatoes, white or red	10-lb sack	1.29	4Q 92	4c
Sausage, Jimmy Dean, 100% pork	lb	2.67	4Q 92	4c
Shortening, vegetable, Crisco	3-lb can	1.83	4Q 92	4c
Soft drink, Coca Cola	2 liter	0.97	4Q 92	4c
Steak, T-bone	lb	4.45	4Q 92	4c
Sugar, cane or beet	4 lb	1.50	4Q 92	4c
Tomatoes, Hunt's or Del Monte	14.5-oz can	0.83	4Q 92	4c
Tuna, chunk, light	6.125-6.5 oz can	0.52	4Q 92	4c
Health Care				
ACCRA Index, Health Care		79.30	4Q 92	4c
Analgesic, Aspirin, Bayer, 325 mg tablets	100	3.88	4Q 92	4c
Dentist's fee, adult teeth cleaning and periodic oral exam	visit	34.33	4Q 92	4c
Doctor's fee, routine exam, established patient	visit	27.67	4Q 92	4c
Hospital care, semiprivate room	day	277.56	90	27c
Hospital care, semiprivate room	day	319.00	4Q 92	4c
Household Goods				
Appliance repair, home, service call, washing machine	min labor charge	30.67	4Q 92	4c

Jefferson City, MO - continued

Item	Per	Value	Date	Ref.
Household Goods - continued				
Laundry detergent, Tide Ultra, Bold, or Cheer	42 oz	3.08	4Q 92	4c
Tissues, facial, Kleenex brand	175-count box	1.01	4Q 92	4c
Housing				
ACCRA Index, Housing		80.50	4Q 92	4c
House, 1,800 sq ft, 8,000 sq ft lot, new, urban	total	90000	4Q 92	4c
House payment, principal and interest, 25% down payment	month	500	4Q 92	4c
Mortgage rate, incl. points & origination fee, 30-year fixed or adjustable rate	percent	8.11	4Q 92	4c
Personal Goods				
Shampoo, Alberto VO5	15 oz	1.07	4Q 92	4c
Toothpaste, Crest or Colgate	6-7 oz	1.60	4Q 92	4c
Personal Services				
Dry cleaning, man's 2-piece suit		4.92	4Q 92	4c
Haircare, woman's shampoo, trim and blow-dry		15.82	4Q 92	4c
Haircut, man's barbershop, no styling		7.33	4Q 92	4c
Restaurant Food				
Chicken, fried, thigh and drumstick		1.98	4Q 92	4c
Hamburger with cheese	1/4 lb	1.96	4Q 92	4c
Pizza, Pizza Hut or Pizza Inn, cheese, thin crust	12-13 in	7.09	4Q 92	4c
Transportation				
ACCRA Index, Transportation		98.50	4Q 92	4c
Tire balance, computer or spin balance, front	wheel	6.98	4Q 92	4c
Utilities				
ACCRA Index, Utilities		102.50	4Q 92	4c
Electricity, partial electric and other energy, 1,800 sq ft living area new home	month	61.82	4Q 92	4c

Jersey City, NJ

Item	Per	Value	Date	Ref.
Child Care				
Child care fee, average, center	hour	2.18	90	65r
Child care fee, average, nonregulated family day care	hour	1.83	90	65r
Child care fee, average, regulated family day care	hour	2.02	90	65r
Communications				
Long-distance telephone service, day, initial minute, 0-100 miles	min	0.09-0.42	91	12s
Long-distance telephone service, day, additional minute, 0-100 miles	min	0.03-0.12	91	12s
Education				
Board, 4-yr private college/university	year	2883	91	22s
Board, 4-yr public college/university	year	1647	91	22s
Expenditures, local gov't, public elementary/secondary	pupil	9940	92	20s
Room, 4-year private college/university	year	2440	91	22s
Room, 4-year public college/university	year	2415	91	22s
Tuition, 2-year private college/university	year	5874	91	22s
Tuition, 2-year public college/university	year	1235	91	22s
Tuition, 4-year private college/university	year	10281	91	22s
Tuition, 4-year public college/university, in-state	year	2860	91	22s
Energy and Fuels				
Coal	mil Btu	1.79	90	64s
Energy	mil Btu	9.32	90	64s
Energy exp/householder, 1-family unit	year	588	90	28r
Energy exp/householder, <1,000 sq ft heating area	year	477	90	28r

Values are in dollars or fractions of dollars. In the column headed *Ref*, references are shown to sources. Each reference is followed by a letter. These refer to the geographical level for which data were reported: s = State, r = Region, and c = City or metro. The abbreviation *ex* is used to mean *except* or *excluding*; *exp* stands for expenditures. For other abbreviations and further explanations, please see the Introduction.

Jersey City, NJ - continued

Item	Per	Value	Date	Ref.
Energy and Fuels				
Energy exp/householder, 1,000-1,999 sq ft heating area	year	517	90	28r
Energy exp/householder, 2,000+ sq ft heating area	year	630	90	28r
Energy exp/householder, mobile home	year	412	90	28r
Energy exp/householder, multifamily	year	498	90	28r
Gas, natural	mil Btu	5.05	90	64s
Gas, natural	000 cu ft	6.73	91	46s
Gas, natural, exp	year	593	91	46s
Gasoline, unleaded regular	mil Btu	9.03	90	64s
Funerals				
Casket, 18-gauge steel, velvet interior		1811.58	91	24r
Cosmetology, hair care, etc.		111.08	91	24r
Embalming		329.42	91	24r
Facility use for ceremony		201.29	91	24r
Hearse, local		135.27	91	24r
Limousine, local		127.24	91	24r
Remains to funeral home, transfer		103.98	91	24r
Service charge, professional		724.98	91	24r
Vault, concrete, non-metallic liner		766.71	91	24r
Viewing facilities, use		260.60	91	24r
Groceries				
Apples, Red Delicious	lb	0.85	4/93	16r
Bacon	lb	2.12	4/93	16r
Bananas	lb	0.54	4/93	16r
Bread, white, pan	lb	0.81	4/93	16r
Butter	lb	2.02	4/93	16r
Carrots, short trimmed and topped	lb	0.51	4/93	16r
Chicken, fresh, whole	lb	1.04	4/93	16r
Chicken breast, bone-in	lb	2.21	4/93	16r
Chicken legs, bone-in	lb	1.16	4/93	16r
Chuck roast, USDA choice, boneless	lb	2.82	4/93	16r
Coffee, 100% ground roast, all sizes	lb	2.66	4/93	16r
Cucumbers	lb	0.85	4/93	16r
Eggs, Grade A large	doz	1.15	4/93	16r
Grapefruit	lb	0.45	4/93	16r
Grapes, Thompson Seedless	lb	1.52	4/93	16r
Ground beef, lean and extra lean	lb	2.36	4/93	16r
Ground chuck, 100% beef	lb	2.02	4/93	16r
Honey, jar	8 oz	0.96-1.75	92	5r
Honey, jar	lb	1.50-3.00	92	5r
Honey, squeeze bear	12-oz	1.50-1.99	92	5r
Ice cream, prepackaged, bulk, regular	1/2 gal	2.80	4/93	16r
Lemons	lb	0.96	4/93	16r
Lettuce, iceberg	lb	0.95	4/93	16r
Margarine, stick	lb	0.81	4/93	16r
Milk, fresh, whole, fortified	1/2 gal	1.30	4/93	16r
Oranges, navel	lb	0.56	4/93	16r
Peanut butter, creamy, all sizes	lb	1.88	4/93	16r
Pork chops, center cut, bone-in	lb	3.34	4/93	16r
Potato chips	16 oz	2.88	4/93	16r
Potatoes, white	lb	0.37	4/93	16r
Rib roast, USDA choice, bone-in	lb	4.94	4/93	16r
Round roast, USDA choice, boneless	lb	3.17	4/93	16r
Shortening, vegetable oil blends	lb	0.98	4/93	16r
Spaghetti and macaroni	lb	0.82	4/93	16r
Steak, round, graded & ungraded, ex USDA prime & choice	lb	4.04	4/93	16r
Steak, round, USDA choice, boneless	lb	3.90	4/93	16r
Steak, sirloin, USDA choice, boneless	lb	4.97	4/93	16r
Strawberries, dry pint	12 oz	0.90	4/93	16r
Sugar, white	lb	0.50	4/93	16r
Sugar, white, 33-80 oz pk	lb	0.41	4/93	16r
Tomatoes, field grown	lb	1.23	4/93	16r
Tuna, chunk, light	lb	2.22	4/93	16r
Turkey, frozen, whole	lb	1.04	4/93	16r
Health Care				
Childbirth, cesarean, hospital		5826	91	62r
Childbirth, cesarean, physician's fee		2053	91	62r
Childbirth, normal, hospital		2964	91	62r

Jersey City, NJ - continued

Item	Per	Value	Date	Ref.
Health Care - continued				
Childbirth, normal, physician's fee		1492	91	62r
Medical plan per employee	year	3942	91	45r
Mental health care, exp	capita	28.84-37.59	90	38s
Mental health care, exp, state mental health agency	capita	57.16	90	38s
Mental health care, hospital psychiatric services, non-Federal, exp	capita	16.04	88	38s
Mental health care, mental health organization, multiservice, exp	capita	11.14	88	38s
Mental health care, psychiatric hospitals, private, exp	capita	17.85	88	38s
Mental health care, psychiatric out-patient clinics, freestanding, exp	capita	1.56	88	38s
Mental health care, psychiatric partial-care organizations, freestanding, exp	capita	0.66	88	38s
Mental health care, state and county mental hospitals, exp	capita	36.80	88	38s
Mental health care, VA medical centers, exp	capita	5.61	88	38s
Prescription drug co-pay, Medicaid	month	5.00	91	21s
Substance abuse, hospital ancillary charge	incident	780	90	70s
Substance abuse, hospital physician charge	incident	550	90	70s
Substance abuse, hospital room and board	incident	6300	90	70s
Insurance and Pensions				
Auto insurance, private passenger	year	1081.45	91	63s
Taxes				
Tax, cigarette	pack	40	91	77s
Tax, gasoline	gal	10.50	91	77s
Taxes, state	capita	1501	91	77s
Transportation				
Driver's license fee		16.00-17.50	12/90	43s
Vehicle registration and license plate	year	32.90-93.90	93	44s
Travel				
Business travel	day	165.00	4/93	89r
Utilities				
Electricity	mil Btu	26.63	90	64s

Johnson City, TN

Item	Per	Value	Date	Ref.
Composite ACCRA index		98.10	4Q 92	4c
Alcoholic Beverages				
Beer, Miller Lite or Budweiser, 12-oz containers	6 pack	3.86	4Q 92	4c
Liquor, J & B Scotch	750 ml	20.01	4Q 92	4c
Wine, Gallo Chablis blanc, 1.5 liter	bottle	6.36	4Q 92	4c
Child Care				
Child care fee, average, center	hour	1.29	90	65r
Child care fee, average, nonregulated family day care	hour	0.89	90	65r
Child care fee, average, regulated family day care	hour	1.32	90	65r
Clothing				
Jeans, man's denim		28.66	4Q 92	4c
Shirt, man's dress shirt		25.00	4Q 92	4c
Undervest, boy's size 10-14, cotton	3	5.39	4Q 92	4c
Communications				
Long-distance telephone service, day, initial minute, 0-100 miles	min	0.10-0.22	91	12s
Long-distance telephone service, day, additional minute, 0-100 miles	min	0.10-0.22	91	12s
Long-distance telephone service, evenings/weekends, 0-100 mi, initial minute	min	0.05-0.10	91	12s

Values are in dollars or fractions of dollars. In the column headed *Ref*, references are shown to sources. Each reference is followed by a letter. These refer to the geographical level for which data were reported: s=State, r=Region, and c=City or metro. The abbreviation *ex* is used to mean *except* or *excluding*; *exp* stands for expenditures. For other abbreviations and further explanations, please see the Introduction.

Johnson City, TN - continued

Item	Per	Value	Date	Ref.
Communications				
Long-distance telephone service, evenings/ weekends, 0-100 mi, additional minute	min	0.05-0.10	91	12s
Newspaper subscription, daily and Sunday home delivery, large-city	month	8.25	4Q 92	4c
Telephone bill, family of four	month	21.60	4Q 92	4c
Education				
Board, 4-yr private college/university	year	1845	91	22s
Board, 4-yr public college/university	year	1499	91	22s
Expenditures, local gov't, public elementary/secondary	pupil	3736	92	20s
Room, 4-year private college/university	year	1679	91	22s
Room, 4-year public college/university	year	1339	91	22s
Tuition, 2-year private college/university	year	4203	91	22s
Tuition, 2-year public college/university	year	848	91	22s
Tuition, 4-year private college/university	year	6889	91	22s
Tuition, 4-year public college/university, in-state	year	1518	91	22s
Energy and Fuels				
Coal	mil Btu	1.35	90	64s
Energy	mil Btu	8.61	90	64s
Energy, combined forms, 1,800 sq ft heating area	month	87.04	4Q 92	4c
Energy, exc electricity, 1,800 sq ft heating area	month	39.75	4Q 92	4c
Energy exp/householder, 1-family unit	year	403	90	28r
Energy exp/householder, <1,000 sq ft heating area	year	342	90	28r
Energy exp/householder, 1,000-1,999 sq ft heating area	year	388	90	28r
Energy exp/householder, 2,000+ sq ft heating area	year	434	90	28r
Energy exp/householder, mobile home	year	320	90	28r
Energy exp/householder, multifamily	year	338	90	28r
Gas, cooking, winter, 10 therms	month	11.11	92	56c
Gas, cooking, winter, 30 therms	month	23.32	92	56c
Gas, cooking, winter, 50 therms	month	35.53	92	56c
Gas, heating, winter, 100 therms	month	66.06	92	56c
Gas, natural	mil Btu	3.98	90	64s
Gas, natural	000 cu ft	5.19	91	46s
Gas, natural, exp	year	388	91	46s
Gasoline, motor	gal	1.12	4Q 92	4c
Gasoline, unleaded regular	mil Btu	9.40	90	64s
Entertainment				
Bowling, evening rate	game	2.08	4Q 92	4c
Miniature golf admission	adult	6.18	92	1r
Miniature golf admission	child	5.14	92	1r
Monopoly game, Parker Brothers', No. 9		9.28	4Q 92	4c
Movie	admission	5.00	4Q 92	4c
Tennis balls, yellow, Wilson or Penn, 3	can	2.10	4Q 92	4c
Waterpark admission	adult	11.00	92	1r
Waterpark admission	child	8.55	92	1r
Funerals				
Casket, 18-gauge steel, velvet interior		2329.05	91	24r
Cosmetology, hair care, etc.		72.78	91	24r
Embalming		240.71	91	24r
Facility use for ceremony		181.67	91	24r
Hearse, local		106.25	91	24r
Limousine, local		70.92	91	24r
Remains to funeral home, transfer		96.30	91	24r
Service charge, professional		687.09	91	24r
Vault, concrete, non-metallic liner		732.09	91	24r
Viewing facilities, use		190.30	91	24r
Goods and Services				
ACCRA Index, Miscellaneous Goods and Services		102.70	4Q 92	4c

Johnson City, TN - continued

Item	Per	Value	Date	Ref.
Groceries				
ACCRA Index, Groceries		92.60	4Q 92	4c
Apples, Red Delicious	lb	0.79	4/93	16r
Babyfood, strained vegetables, lowest price	4-4.5 oz jar	0.32	4Q 92	4c
Bacon	lb	1.75	4/93	16r
Bananas	lb	0.46	4Q 92	4c
Bananas	lb	0.42	4/93	16r
Beef, stew, boneless	lb	2.61	4/93	16r
Bologna, all beef or mixed	lb	2.24	4/93	16r
Bread, white	24 oz	0.68	4Q 92	4c
Bread, white, pan	lb	0.64	4/93	16r
Bread, whole wheat, pan	lb	0.96	4/93	16r
Cabbage	lb	0.37	4/93	16r
Carrots, short trimmed and topped	lb	0.47	4/93	16r
Celery	lb	0.64	4/93	16r
Cheese, American	lb	2.98	4/93	16r
Cheese, Cheddar	lb	3.28	4/93	16r
Cheese, Kraft grated Parmesan	8-oz canister	3.25	4Q 92	4c
Chicken, fresh, whole	lb	0.77	4/93	16r
Chicken, fryer, whole	lb	0.67	4Q 92	4c
Chicken breast, bone-in	lb	1.92	4/93	16r
Chicken legs, bone-in	lb	1.06	4/93	16r
Chuck roast, graded and ungraded, ex USDA prime and choice	lb	2.40	4/93	16r
Chuck roast, USDA choice, bone-in	lb	2.19	4/93	16r
Chuck roast, USDA choice, boneless	lb	2.38	4/93	16r
Cigarettes, Winston	carton	16.62	4Q 92	4c
Coffee, 100% ground roast, all sizes	lb	2.48	4/93	16r
Coffee, vacuum-packed	13-oz can	1.99	4Q 92	4c
Corn, frozen	10 oz	0.55	4Q 92	4c
Corn Flakes, Kellogg's or Post Toasties	18 oz	1.77	4Q 92	4c
Crackers, soda, salted	lb	1.15	4/93	16r
Eggs, Grade A large	doz	0.82	4Q 92	4c
Eggs, Grade A large	doz	0.96	4/93	16r
Flour, white, all purpose	lb	0.24	4/93	16r
Frankfurters, all meat or all beef	lb	2.01	4/93	16r
Grapefruit	lb	0.44	4/93	16r
Grapes, Thompson Seedless	lb	1.40	4/93	16r
Ground beef, 100% beef	lb	1.58	4/93	16r
Ground beef, lean and extra lean	lb	2.09	4/93	16r
Ground beef or hamburger	lb	1.47	4Q 92	4c
Ground chuck, 100% beef	lb	1.98	4/93	16r
Ham, boneless, excluding canned	lb	2.89	4/93	16r
Ham, picnic, shoulder, bone-in, smoked	lb	1.02	4/93	16r
Ham, rump or steak half, bone-in, smoked	lb	1.48	4/93	16r
Honey, jar	8 oz	0.89-1.09	92	5r
Honey, jar	lb	1.39-2.25	92	5r
Honey, squeeze bear	12-oz	1.00-1.50	92	5r
Ice cream, prepackaged, bulk, regular	1/2 gal	2.41	4/93	16r
Lemons	lb	1.05	4/93	16r
Lettuce, iceberg	head	0.99	4Q 92	4c
Lettuce, iceberg	lb	0.81	4/93	16r
Margarine, Blue Bonnet or Parkay cubes	lb	0.49	4Q 92	4c
Margarine, stick	lb	0.88	4/93	16r
Milk, whole	1/2 gal	1.33	4Q 92	4c
Orange juice, Minute Maid frozen	12-oz can	1.31	4Q 92	4c
Oranges, navel	lb	0.55	4/93	16r
Peaches	29-oz can	1.28	4Q 92	4c
Pears, Anjou	lb	0.92	4/93	16r
Peas Sweet, Del Monte or Green Giant	15-17 oz can	0.47	4Q 92	4c
Pork chops, center cut, bone-in	lb	3.13	4/93	16r
Potato chips	16 oz	2.94	4/93	16r
Potatoes, white	lb	0.43	4/93	16r
Potatoes, white or red	10-lb sack	2.03	4Q 92	4c
Rib roast, USDA choice, bone-in	lb	4.63	4/93	16r

Values are in dollars or fractions of dollars. In the column headed *Ref*, references are shown to sources. Each reference is followed by a letter. These refer to the geographical level for which data were reported: s=State, r=Region, and c=City or metro. The abbreviation *ex* is used to mean *except* or *excluding*; *exp* stands for expenditures. For other abbreviations and further explanations, please see the Introduction.

Johnson City, TN - continued

Item	Per	Value	Date	Ref.
Groceries				
Rice, white, long grain, uncooked	lb	0.45	4/93	16r
Round roast, graded & ungraded, ex USDA prime & choice	lb	3.03	4/93	16r
Round roast, USDA choice, boneless	lb	3.09	4/93	16r
Sausage, fresh, loose	lb	2.08	4/93	16r
Sausage, Jimmy Dean, 100% pork	lb	2.02	4Q 92	4c
Short ribs, bone-in	lb	2.66	4/93	16r
Shortening, vegetable oil blends	lb	0.69	4/93	16r
Shortening, vegetable, Crisco	3-lb can	1.99	4Q 92	4c
Soft drink, Coca Cola	2 liter	0.91	4Q 92	4c
Spaghetti and macaroni	lb	0.81	4/93	16r
Steak, rib eye, USDA choice, boneless	lb	6.24	4/93	16r
Steak, round, graded & ungraded, ex USDA prime & choice	lb	3.31	4/93	16r
Steak, round, USDA choice, boneless	lb	3.34	4/93	16r
Steak, sirloin, graded & ungraded, ex USDA prime & choice	lb	4.19	4/93	16r
Steak, sirloin, USDA choice, boneless	lb	4.46	4/93	16r
Steak, T-bone	lb	5.53	4Q 92	4c
Steak, T-bone, USDA choice, bone-in	lb	5.25	4/93	16r
Strawberries, dry pint	12 oz	0.92	4/93	16r
Sugar, cane or beet	4 lb	1.43	4Q 92	4c
Sugar, white	lb	0.39	4/93	16r
Sugar, white, 33-80 oz pk	lb	0.38	4/93	16r
Tomatoes, field grown	lb	0.88	4/93	16r
Tomatoes, Hunt's or Del Monte	14.5-oz can	0.52	4Q 92	4c
Tuna, chunk, light	6.125-6.5 oz can	0.54	4Q 92	4c
Tuna, chunk, light	lb	1.79	4/93	16r
Turkey, frozen, whole	lb	1.04	4/93	16r
Yogurt, natural, fruit flavored	1/2 pint	0.57	4/93	16r
Health Care				
ACCRA Index, Health Care		82.80	4Q 92	4c
Analgesic, Aspirin, Bayer, 325 mg tablets	100	5.55	4Q 92	4c
Childbirth, cesarean, hospital		5034	91	62r
Childbirth, cesarean, physician's fee		2053	91	62r
Childbirth, normal, hospital		2712	91	62r
Childbirth, normal, physician's fee		1492	91	62r
Dentist's fee, adult teeth cleaning and periodic oral exam	visit	33.60	4Q 92	4c
Doctor's fee, routine exam, established patient	visit	33.25	4Q 92	4c
Hospital care, semiprivate room	day	195.00	90	27c
Hospital care, semiprivate room	day	231.67	4Q 92	4c
Medical insurance premium, per employee, small group comprehensive	month	306.60	10/91	25c
Mental health care, exp	capita	20.37-28.83	90	38s
Mental health care, exp, state mental health agency	capita	28.84	90	38s
Mental health care, hospital psychiatric services, non-Federal, exp	capita	13.48	88	38s
Mental health care, mental health organization, multiservice, exp	capita	11.35	88	38s
Mental health care, psychiatric hospitals, private, exp	capita	22.28	88	38s
Mental health care, psychiatric out-patient clinics, freestanding, exp	capita	2.58	88	38s
Mental health care, psychiatric partial-care organizations, freestanding, exp	capita	0.25	88	38s
Mental health care, state and county mental hospitals, exp	capita	20.05	88	38s
Mental health care, VA medical centers, exp	capita	4.98	88	38s
Physician fee, family practice, first-visit		75.00	91	62r
Physician fee, family practice, revisit		34.00	91	62r
Physician fee, general practice, first-visit		61.00	91	62r
Physician fee, general practice, revisit		32.00	91	62r
Physician fee, general surgeon, first-visit		64.00	91	62r

Johnson City, TN - continued

Item	Per	Value	Date	Ref.
Health Care - continued				
Physician fee, general surgeon, revisit		40.00	91	62r
Physician fee, internal medicine, first-visit		98.00	91	62r
Physician fee, internal medicine, revisit		40.00	91	62r
Physician fee, median, neurosurgeon, first-visit		130.00	91	62r
Physician fee, median, nonsurgical specialist, first-visit		95.00	91	62r
Physician fee, median, orthopedic surgeon, first-visit		91.00	91	62r
Physician fee, median, plastic surgeon, first-visit		66.00	91	62r
Physician fee, median, surgical specialist, first-visit		62.00	91	62r
Physician fee, neurosurgeon, revisit		50.00	91	62r
Physician fee, nonsurgical specialist, revisit		40.00	91	62r
Physician fee, obstetrics/gynecology, first-visit		64.00	91	62r
Physician fee, obstetrics/gynecology, revisit		41.00	91	62r
Physician fee, orthopedic surgeon, revisit		40.00	91	62r
Physician fee, pediatrician, first-visit		49.00	91	62r
Physician fee, pediatrician, revisit		33.00	91	62r
Physician fee, plastic surgeon, revisit		43.00	91	62r
Physician fee, surgical specialist, revisit		37.00	91	62r
Substance abuse, hospital ancillary charge	incident	1330	90	70s
Substance abuse, hospital physician charge	incident	580	90	70s
Substance abuse, hospital room and board	incident	5180	90	70s
Household Goods				
Appliance repair, home, service call, washing machine	min labor charge	42.00	4Q 92	4c
Laundry detergent, Tide Ultra, Bold, or Cheer	42 oz	2.69	4Q 92	4c
Tissues, facial, Kleenex brand	175-count box	0.99	4Q 92	4c
Housing				
ACCRA Index, Housing		103.90	4Q 92	4c
House, 1,800 sq ft, 8,000 sq ft lot, new, urban	total	116620	4Q 92	4c
House payment, principal and interest, 25% down payment	month	648	4Q 92	4c
Mortgage rate, incl. points & origination fee, 30-year fixed or adjustable rate	percent	8.11	4Q 92	4c
Rent, apartment, 2 bedrooms - 1-1/2 to 2 baths, unfurnished, 950 sq ft, water	month	490	4Q 92	4c
Rental unit, 1 bedroom	month	327	93	23c
Rental unit, 2 bedroom	month	384	93	23c
Rental unit, 3 bedroom	month	481	93	23c
Rental unit, 4 bedroom	month	540	93	23c
Rental unit, efficiency	month	268	93	23c
Insurance and Pensions				
Auto insurance, private passenger	year	554.60	91	63s
Personal Goods				
Shampoo, Alberto VO5	15 oz	1.16	4Q 92	4c
Toothpaste, Crest or Colgate	6-7 oz	1.85	4Q 92	4c
Personal Services				
Dry cleaning, man's 2-piece suit		5.72	4Q 92	4c
Haircare, woman's shampoo, trim and blow-dry		18.00	4Q 92	4c
Haircut, man's barbershop, no styling		8.40	4Q 92	4c
Restaurant Food				
Chicken, fried, thigh and drumstick		2.00	4Q 92	4c
Hamburger with cheese	1/4 lb	1.78	4Q 92	4c
Pizza, Pizza Hut or Pizza Inn, cheese, thin crust	12-13 in	7.49	4Q 92	4c

Values are in dollars or fractions of dollars. In the column headed *Ref*, references are shown to sources. Each reference is followed by a letter. These refer to the geographical level for which data were reported: s=State, r=Region, and c=City or metro. The abbreviation *ex* is used to mean *except* or *excluding*; *exp* stands for expenditures. For other abbreviations and further explanations, please see the Introduction.

Johnson City, TN - continued

Item	Per	Value	Date	Ref.
Taxes				
Tax, cigarette	pack	13	91	77s
Tax, gasoline	gal	22.40	91	77s
Taxes, state	capita	870	91	77s
Transportation				
ACCRA Index, Transportation		94.80	4Q 92	4c
Driver's license fee		14.00-16.00	12/90	43s
Tire balance, computer or spin balance, front	wheel	5.90	4Q 92	4c
Travel				
Business travel	day	193.00	4/93	89r
Utilities				
ACCRA Index, Utilities		82.80	4Q 92	4c
Electricity	mil Btu	15.59	90	64s
Electricity, partial electric and other energy, 1,800 sq ft living area new home	month	47.29	4Q 92	4c

Johnstown, PA

Item	Per	Value	Date	Ref.
Child Care				
Child care fee, average, center	hour	2.18	90	65s
Child care fee, average, nonregulated family day care	hour	1.83	90	65r
Child care fee, average, regulated family day care	hour	2.02	90	65r
Communications				
Long-distance telephone service, day, initial minute, 0-100 miles	min	0.15-0.29	91	12s
Long-distance telephone service, day, additional minute, 0-100 miles	min	0.06-0.22	91	12s
Long-distance telephone service, evenings/weekends, 0-100 mi, initial minute	min	0.06-0.14	91	12s
Long-distance telephone service, evenings/weekends, 0-100 mi, additional minute	min	0.03-0.11	91	12s
Education				
Board, 4-yr private college/university	year	2019	91	22s
Board, 4-yr public college/university	year	1656	91	22s
Expenditures, local gov't, public elementary/secondary	pupil	6980	92	20s
Room, 4-year private college/university	year	2179	91	22s
Room, 4-year public college/university	year	1719	91	22s
Tuition, 2-year private college/university	year	6314	91	22s
Tuition, 2-year public college/university	year	1505	91	22s
Tuition, 4-year private college/university	year	9848	91	22s
Tuition, 4-year public college/university, in-state	year	3401	91	22s
Energy and Fuels				
Coal	mil Btu	1.57	90	64s
Energy	mil Btu	8.63	90	64s
Energy exp/householder, 1-family unit	year	588	90	28r
Energy exp/householder, <1,000 sq ft heating area	year	477	90	28r
Energy exp/householder, 1,000-1,999 sq ft heating area	year	517	90	28r
Energy exp/householder, 2,000+ sq ft heating area	year	630	90	28r
Energy exp/householder, mobile home	year	412	90	28r
Energy exp/householder, multifamily	year	498	90	28r
Gas, natural	mil Btu	5.24	90	64s
Gas, natural	000 cu ft	6.76	91	46s
Gas, natural, exp	year	703	91	46s
Gasoline, unleaded regular	mil Btu	9.35	90	64s
Funerals				
Casket, 18-gauge steel, velvet interior		1811.58	91	24r
Cosmetology, hair care, etc.		111.08	91	24r
Embalming		329.42	91	24r

Johnstown, PA - continued

Item	Per	Value	Date	Ref.
Funerals - continued				
Facility use for ceremony		201.29	91	24r
Hearse, local		135.27	91	24r
Limousine, local		127.24	91	24r
Remains to funeral home, transfer		103.98	91	24r
Service charge, professional		724.98	91	24r
Vault, concrete, non-metallic liner		766.71	91	24r
Viewing facilities, use		260.60	91	24r
Groceries				
Apples, Red Delicious	lb	0.85	4/93	16r
Bacon	lb	2.12	4/93	16r
Bananas	lb	0.54	4/93	16r
Bread, white, pan	lb	0.81	4/93	16r
Butter	lb	2.02	4/93	16r
Carrots, short trimmed and topped	lb	0.51	4/93	16r
Chicken, fresh, whole	lb	1.04	4/93	16r
Chicken breast, bone-in	lb	2.21	4/93	16r
Chicken legs, bone-in	lb	1.16	4/93	16r
Chuck roast, USDA choice, boneless	lb	2.82	4/93	16r
Coffee, 100% ground roast, all sizes	lb	2.66	4/93	16r
Cucumbers	lb	0.85	4/93	16r
Eggs, Grade A large	doz	1.15	4/93	16r
Grapefruit	lb	0.45	4/93	16r
Grapes, Thompson Seedless	lb	1.52	4/93	16r
Ground beef, lean and extra lean	lb	2.36	4/93	16r
Ground chuck, 100% beef	lb	2.02	4/93	16r
Honey, jar	8 oz	0.96-1.75	92	5r
Honey, jar	lb	1.50-3.00	92	5r
Honey, squeeze bear	12-oz	1.50-1.99	92	5r
Ice cream, prepackaged, bulk, regular	1/2 gal	2.80	4/93	16r
Lemons	lb	0.96	4/93	16r
Lettuce, iceberg	lb	0.95	4/93	16r
Margarine, stick	lb	0.81	4/93	16r
Milk, fresh, whole, fortified	1/2 gal	1.30	4/93	16r
Oranges, navel	lb	0.56	4/93	16r
Peanut butter, creamy, all sizes	lb	1.88	4/93	16r
Pork chops, center cut, bone-in	lb	3.34	4/93	16r
Potato chips	16 oz	2.88	4/93	16r
Potatoes, white	lb	0.37	4/93	16r
Rib roast, USDA choice, bone-in	lb	4.94	4/93	16r
Round roast, USDA choice, boneless	lb	3.17	4/93	16r
Shortening, vegetable oil blends	lb	0.98	4/93	16r
Spaghetti and macaroni	lb	0.82	4/93	16r
Steak, round, graded & ungraded, ex USDA prime & choice	lb	4.04	4/93	16r
Steak, round, USDA choice, boneless	lb	3.90	4/93	16r
Steak, sirloin, USDA choice, boneless	lb	4.97	4/93	16r
Strawberries, dry pint	12 oz	0.90	4/93	16r
Sugar, white	lb	0.50	4/93	16r
Sugar, white, 33-80 oz pk	lb	0.41	4/93	16r
Tomatoes, field grown	lb	1.23	4/93	16r
Tuna, chunk, light	lb	2.22	4/93	16r
Turkey, frozen, whole	lb	1.04	4/93	16r
Health Care				
Childbirth, cesarean, hospital		5826	91	62r
Childbirth, cesarean, physician's fee		2053	91	62r
Childbirth, normal, hospital		2964	91	62r
Childbirth, normal, physician's fee		1492	91	62r
Medical plan per employee	year	3942	91	45r
Mental health care, exp	capita	53.68-118.35	90	38s
Mental health care, exp, state mental health agency	capita	56.85	90	38s
Mental health care, hospital psychiatric services, non-Federal, exp	capita	22.11	88	38s
Mental health care, mental health organization, multiservice, exp	capita	21.01	88	38s
Mental health care, psychiatric hospitals, private, exp	capita	26.48	88	38s
Mental health care, psychiatric out-patient clinics, freestanding, exp	capita	4.17	88	38s

Values are in dollars or fractions of dollars. In the column headed *Ref*, references are shown to sources. Each reference is followed by a letter. These refer to the geographical level for which data were reported: s=State, r=Region, and c=City or metro. The abbreviation *ex* is used to mean *except* or *excluding*; *exp* stands for expenditures. For other abbreviations and further explanations, please see the Introduction.

Johnstown, PA - continued

Item	Per	Value	Date	Ref.
Health Care				
Mental health care, psychiatric partial-care organizations, freestanding, exp	capita	0.94	88	38s
Mental health care, state and county mental hospitals, exp	capita	37.11	88	38s
Mental health care, VA medical centers, exp	capita	9.77	88	38s
Prescription drug co-pay, Medicaid	month	6.00	91	21s
Substance abuse, hospital ancillary charge	incident	720	90	70s
Substance abuse, hospital physician charge	incident	210	90	70s
Substance abuse, hospital room and board	incident	5400	90	70s
Insurance and Pensions				
Auto insurance, private passenger	year	683.57	91	63s
Taxes				
Tax, cigarette	pack	31	91	77s
Tax, gasoline	gal	12	91	77s
Taxes, state	capita	1089	91	77s
Transportation				
Driver's license fee		22.00	12/90	43s
Travel				
Business travel	day	165.00	4/93	89r
Utilities				
Electricity	mil Btu	22.46	90	64s

Joliet, IL

Item	Per	Value	Date	Ref.
Composite ACCRA index		115.10	4Q 92	4c
Alcoholic Beverages				
Beer, Miller Lite or Budweiser, 12-oz containers	6 pack	3.79	4Q 92	4c
Liquor, J & B Scotch	750 ml	14.59	4Q 92	4c
Wine, Gallo Chablis blanc, 1.5 liter	bottle	4.69	4Q 92	4c
Child Care				
Child care fee, average, center	hour	1.63	90	65r
Child care fee, average, nonregulated family day care	hour	1.83	90	65r
Child care fee, average, regulated family day care	hour	1.42	90	65r
Clothing				
Jeans, man's denim		30.19	4Q 92	4c
Shirt, man's dress shirt		25.70	4Q 92	4c
Undervest, boy's size 10-14, cotton	3	5.48	4Q 92	4c
Communications				
Long-distance telephone service, day, initial minute, 0-100 miles	min	0.10-0.34	91	12s
Long-distance telephone service, day, additional minute, 0-100 miles	min	0.04-0.16	91	12s
Long-distance telephone service, evenings/weekends, 0-100 mi, initial minute	min	0.06-0.20	91	12s
Long-distance telephone service, evenings/weekends, 0-100 mi, additional minute	min	0.02-0.10	91	12s
Newspaper subscription, daily and Sunday home delivery, large-city	month	16.52	4Q 92	4c
Telephone bill, family of four	month	19.31	4Q 92	4c
Education				
Board, 4-yr private college/university	year	1797	91	22s
Board, 4-yr public college/university	year	1857	91	22s
Expenditures, local gov't, public elementary/secondary	pupil	5248	92	20s
Room, 4-year private college/university	year	2095	91	22s
Room, 4-year public college/university	year	1454	91	22s
Tuition, 2-year private college/university	year	5279	91	22s
Tuition, 2-year public college/university	year	906	91	22s
Tuition, 4-year private college/university	year	8853	91	22s

Joliet, IL - continued

Item	Per	Value	Date	Ref.
Education - continued				
Tuition, 4-year public college/university, in-state	year	2465	91	22s
Energy and Fuels				
Coal	mil Btu	1.72	90	64s
Energy	mil Btu	8.74	90	64s
Energy, combined forms, 1,800 sq ft heating area	month	135.16	4Q 92	4c
Energy, exc electricity, 1,800 sq ft heating area	month	47.55	4Q 92	4c
Energy exp/householder, 1-family unit	year	471	90	28r
Energy exp/householder, <1,000 sq ft heating area	year	430	90	28r
Energy exp/householder, 1,000-1,999 sq ft heating area	year	481	90	28r
Energy exp/householder, 2,000+ sq ft heating area	year	473	90	28r
Energy exp/householder, mobile home	year	430	90	28r
Energy exp/householder, multifamily	year	461	90	28r
Gas, natural	mil Btu	4.57	90	64s
Gas, natural	000 cu ft	4.95	91	46s
Gas, natural, exp	year	696	91	46s
Gasoline, motor	gal	1.16	4Q 92	4c
Gasoline, unleaded regular	mil Btu	9.35	90	64s
Entertainment				
Bowling, evening rate	game	1.98	4Q 92	4c
Miniature golf admission	adult	6.18	92	1r
Miniature golf admission	child	5.14	92	1r
Monopoly game, Parker Brothers', No. 9		13.47	4Q 92	4c
Movie	admission	5.17	4Q 92	4c
Tennis balls, yellow, Wilson or Penn, 3	can	2.81	4Q 92	4c
Waterpark admission	adult	11.00	92	1r
Waterpark admission	child	8.55	92	1r
Funerals				
Casket, 18-gauge steel, velvet interior		1926.72	91	24r
Cosmetology, hair care, etc.		97.64	91	24r
Embalming		249.14	91	24r
Facility use for ceremony		208.59	91	24r
Hearse, local		130.12	91	24r
Limousine, local		104.66	91	24r
Remains to funeral home, transfer		93.61	91	24r
Service charge, professional		724.62	91	24r
Vault, concrete, non-metallic liner		734.53	91	24r
Viewing facilities, use		236.06	91	24r
Goods and Services				
ACCRA Index, Miscellaneous Goods and Services		104.60	4Q 92	4c
Groceries				
ACCRA Index, Groceries		100.70	4Q 92	4c
Apples, Red Delicious	lb	0.77	4/93	16r
Babyfood, strained vegetables, lowest price	4-4.5 oz jar	0.37	4Q 92	4c
Bacon	lb	1.85	4/93	16r
Bananas	lb	0.52	4Q 92	4c
Bananas	lb	0.46	4/93	16r
Beef, stew, boneless	lb	2.53	4/93	16r
Bologna, all beef or mixed	lb	2.19	4/93	16r
Bread, white	24 oz	0.50	4Q 92	4c
Bread, white, pan	lb	0.78	4/93	16r
Butter	lb	1.50	4/93	16r
Cabbage	lb	0.40	4/93	16r
Carrots, short trimmed and topped	lb	0.45	4/93	16r
Cheese, Cheddar	lb	3.47	4/93	16r
Cheese, Kraft grated Parmesan	8-oz canister	3.21	4Q 92	4c
Chicken, fresh, whole	lb	0.84	4/93	16r
Chicken, fryer, whole	lb	0.80	4Q 92	4c

Values are in dollars or fractions of dollars. In the column headed *Ref*, references are shown to sources. Each reference is followed by a letter. These refer to the geographical level for which data were reported: s=State, r=Region, and c=City or metro. The abbreviation *ex* is used to mean *except* or *excluding*; *exp* stands for *expenditures*. For other abbreviations and further explanations, please see the Introduction.

Joliet, IL - continued

Item	Per	Value	Date	Ref.
Groceries				
Chicken breast, bone-in	lb	1.94	4/93	16r
Chicken legs, bone-in	lb	1.02	4/93	16r
Chuck roast, graded and ungraded, ex USDA prime and choice	lb	2.43	4/93	16r
Chuck roast, USDA choice, bone-in	lb	2.11	4/93	16r
Chuck roast, USDA choice, boneless	lb	2.44	4/93	16r
Cigarettes, Winston	carton	18.74	4Q 92	4c
Coffee, 100% ground roast, all sizes	lb	2.47	4/93	16r
Coffee, vacuum-packed	13-oz can	1.91	4Q 92	4c
Cookies, chocolate chip	lb	2.73	4/93	16r
Corn, frozen	10 oz	0.60	4Q 92	4c
Corn Flakes, Kellogg's or Post Toasties	18 oz	2.00	4Q 92	4c
Eggs, Grade A large	doz	0.74	4Q 92	4c
Eggs, Grade A large	doz	0.93	4/93	16r
Flour, white, all purpose	lb	0.21	4/93	16r
Grapefruit	lb	0.45	4/93	16r
Grapes, Thompson Seedless	lb	1.46	4/93	16r
Ground beef, 100% beef	lb	1.63	4/93	16r
Ground beef, lean and extra lean	lb	2.08	4/93	16r
Ground beef or hamburger	lb	1.67	4Q 92	4c
Ground chuck, 100% beef	lb	1.94	4/93	16r
Ham, boneless, excluding canned	lb	2.21	4/93	16r
Honey, jar	8 oz	0.97-1.25	92	5r
Honey, jar	lb	1.25-2.25	92	5r
Honey, squeeze bear	12-oz	1.25-1.99	92	5r
Ice cream, prepackaged, bulk, regular	1/2 gal	2.41	4/93	16r
Lemons	lb	0.82	4/93	16r
Lettuce, iceberg	head	0.86	4Q 92	4c
Lettuce, iceberg	lb	0.83	4/93	16r
Margarine, Blue Bonnet or Parkay cubes	lb	0.57	4Q 92	4c
Margarine, stick	lb	0.77	4/93	16r
Milk, whole	1/2 gal	1.53	4Q 92	4c
Orange juice, Minute Maid frozen	12-oz can	1.19	4Q 92	4c
Oranges, navel	lb	0.50	4/93	16r
Peaches	29-oz can	1.46	4Q 92	4c
Peanut butter, creamy, all sizes	lb	1.82	4/93	16r
Pears, Anjou	lb	0.85	4/93	16r
Peas Sweet, Del Monte or Green Giant	15-17 oz can	0.58	4Q 92	4c
Pork chops, center cut, bone-in	lb	3.17	4/93	16r
Potato chips	16 oz	2.68	4/93	16r
Potatoes, white	lb	0.26	4/93	16r
Potatoes, white or red	10-lb sack	2.88	4Q 92	4c
Round roast, graded & ungraded, ex USDA prime & choice	lb	2.88	4/93	16r
Round roast, USDA choice, boneless	lb	2.96	4/93	16r
Sausage, Jimmy Dean, 100% pork	lb	2.84	4Q 92	4c
Shortening, vegetable oil blends	lb	0.79	4/93	16r
Shortening, vegetable, Crisco	3-lb can	2.29	4Q 92	4c
Soft drink, Coca Cola	2 liter	1.14	4Q 92	4c
Spaghetti and macaroni	lb	0.76	4/93	16r
Steak, rib eye, USDA choice, boneless	lb	6.29	4/93	16r
Steak, round, USDA choice, boneless	lb	3.24	4/93	16r
Steak, sirloin, graded & ungraded, ex USDA prime & choice	lb	4.00	4/93	16r
Steak, sirloin, USDA choice, bone-in	lb	3.57	4/93	16r
Steak, sirloin, USDA choice, boneless	lb	4.17	4/93	16r
Steak, T-bone	lb	5.26	4Q 92	4c
Steak, T-bone, USDA choice, bone-in	lb	5.60	4/93	16r
Strawberries, dry pint	12 oz	0.90	4/93	16r
Sugar, cane or beet	4 lb	1.34	4Q 92	4c
Sugar, white	lb	0.36	4/93	16r
Sugar, white, 33-80 oz pk	lb	0.35	4/93	16r
Tomatoes, field grown	lb	0.99	4/93	16r
Tomatoes, Hunt's or Del Monte	14.5-oz can	0.68	4Q 92	4c

Joliet, IL - continued

Item	Per	Value	Date	Ref.
Groceries - continued				
Tuna, chunk, light	6.125-6.5 oz can	0.63	4Q 92	4c
Tuna, chunk, light	lb	1.76	4/93	16r
Turkey, frozen, whole	lb	0.91	4/93	16r
Health Care				
ACCRA Index, Health Care		109.40	4Q 92	4c
Analgesic, Aspirin, Bayer, 325 mg tablets	100	4.86	4Q 92	4c
Childbirth, cesarean, hospital		4688	91	62r
Childbirth, cesarean, physician's fee		2053	91	62r
Childbirth, normal, hospital		2657	91	62r
Childbirth, normal, physician's fee		1492	91	62r
Dentist's fee, adult teeth cleaning and periodic oral exam	visit	52.25	4Q 92	4c
Doctor's fee, routine exam, established patient	visit	34.40	4Q 92	4c
Hospital care, semiprivate room	day	457.50	4Q 92	4c
Medical insurance premium, per employee, small group comprehensive	month	375.95	10/91	25c
Medical plan per employee	year	3443	91	45r
Mental health care, exp	capita	28.84-37.59	90	38s
Mental health care, exp, state mental health agency	capita	34.43	90	38s
Mental health care, hospital psychiatric services, non-Federal, exp	capita	18.46	88	38s
Mental health care, mental health organization, multiservice, exp	capita	11.97	88	38s
Mental health care, psychiatric hospitals, private, exp	capita	7.84	88	38s
Mental health care, psychiatric out-patient clinics, freestanding, exp	capita	3.21	88	38s
Mental health care, psychiatric partial-care organizations, freestanding, exp	capita	0.51	88	38s
Mental health care, state and county mental hospitals, exp	capita	18.11	88	38s
Mental health care, VA medical centers, exp	capita	3.69	88	38s
Physician fee, family practice, first-visit		76.00	91	62r
Physician fee, family practice, revisit		33.00	91	62r
Physician fee, general practice, first-visit		61.00	91	62r
Physician fee, general practice, revisit		31.00	91	62r
Physician fee, general surgeon, first-visit		65.00	91	62r
Physician fee, general surgeon, revisit		35.00	91	62r
Physician fee, internal medicine, first-visit		91.00	91	62r
Physician fee, internal medicine, revisit		40.00	91	62r
Physician fee, median, neurosurgeon, first-visit		106.00	91	62r
Physician fee, median, nonsurgical specialist, first-visit		90.00	91	62r
Physician fee, median, orthopedic surgeon, first-visit		83.00	91	62r
Physician fee, median, surgical specialist, first-visit		61.00	91	62r
Physician fee, neurosurgeon, revisit		41.00	91	62r
Physician fee, nonsurgical specialist, revisit		40.00	91	62r
Physician fee, obstetrics/gynecology, first-visit		61.00	91	62r
Physician fee, obstetrics/gynecology, revisit		40.00	91	62r
Physician fee, orthopedic surgeon, revisit		41.00	91	62r
Physician fee, pediatrician, first-visit		46.00	91	62r
Physician fee, pediatrician, revisit		33.00	91	62r
Physician fee, surgical specialist, revisit		36.00	91	62r
Prescription drug co-pay, Medicaid	month	25.00	91	21s
Substance abuse, hospital ancillary charge	incident	1310	90	70s
Substance abuse, hospital physician charge	incident	540	90	70s
Substance abuse, hospital room and board	incident	6150	90	70s

Joliet, IL - continued

Item	Per	Value	Date	Ref.
Household Goods				
Appliance repair, home, service call, washing machine	min labor charge	35.97	4Q 92	4c
Laundry detergent, Tide Ultra, Bold, or Cheer	42 oz	3.06	4Q 92	4c
Tissues, facial, Kleenex brand	175-count box	1.12	4Q 92	4c
Housing				
ACCRA Index, Housing		133.70	4Q 92	4c
House, 1,800 sq ft, 8,000 sq ft lot, new, urban	total	158680	4Q 92	4c
House payment, principal and interest, 25% down payment	month	874	4Q 92	4c
Mortgage rate, incl. points & origination fee, 30-year fixed or adjustable rate	per-cent	8.01	4Q 92	4c
Rent, apartment, 2 bedrooms - 1-1/2 to 2 baths, unfurnished, 950 sq ft, water	month	539	4Q 92	4c
Rental unit, 1 bedroom	month	603	93	23c
Rental unit, 2 bedroom	month	713	93	23c
Rental unit, 3 bedroom	month	891	93	23c
Rental unit, 4 bedroom	month	1001	93	23c
Rental unit, efficiency	month	495	93	23c
Insurance and Pensions				
Auto insurance, private passenger	year	621.37	91	63s
Personal Goods				
Shampoo, Alberto VO5	15 oz	1.19	4Q 92	4c
Toothpaste, Crest or Colgate	6-7 oz	2.02	4Q 92	4c
Personal Services				
Dry cleaning, man's 2-piece suit		5.39	4Q 92	4c
Haircare, woman's shampoo, trim and blow-dry		13.69	4Q 92	4c
Haircut, man's barbershop, no styling		9.10	4Q 92	4c
Restaurant Food				
Chicken, fried, thigh and drumstick		1.46	4Q 92	4c
Hamburger with cheese	1/4 lb	1.93	4Q 92	4c
Pizza, Pizza Hut or Pizza Inn, cheese, thin crust	12-13 in	7.67	4Q 92	4c
Taxes				
Tax, cigarette	pack	30	91	77s
Tax, gasoline	gal	19	91	77s
Taxes, state	capita	1151	91	77s
Transportation				
ACCRA Index, Transportation		116.10	4Q 92	4c
Driver's license fee		10.00	12/90	43s
Tire balance, computer or spin balance, front	wheel	8.40	4Q 92	4c
Vehicle registration and license plate	multi-year	48.00	93	52s
Utilities				
ACCRA Index, Utilities		121.30	4Q 92	4c
Electricity	mil Btu	22.02	90	64s
Electricity, partial electric and other energy, 1,800 sq ft living area new home	month	87.61	4Q 92	4c

Jonesboro, AR

Item	Per	Value	Date	Ref.
Composite ACCRA index		88.20	4Q 92	4c
Alcoholic Beverages				
Beer, Miller Lite or Budweiser, 12-oz containers	6 pack	4.40	4Q 92	4c
Liquor, J & B Scotch	750 ml	17.15	4Q 92	4c
Wine, Gallo Chablis blanc, 1.5 liter	bottle	5.50	4Q 92	4c
Clothing				
Jeans, man's denim		34.99	4Q 92	4c
Shirt, man's dress shirt		23.66	4Q 92	4c

Jonesboro, AR - continued

Item	Per	Value	Date	Ref.
Clothing - continued				
Undervest, boy's size 10-14, cotton	3	3.24	4Q 92	4c
Communications				
Newspaper subscription, daily and Sunday home delivery, large-city	month	7.50	4Q 92	4c
Telephone, flat rate	month	13.91	91	11c
Telephone bill, family of four	month	21.85	4Q 92	4c
Energy and Fuels				
Energy, combined forms, 1,800 sq ft heating area	month	86.93	4Q 92	4c
Energy, exc electricity, 1,800 sq ft heating area	month	38.02	4Q 92	4c
Gasoline, motor	gal	1.04	4Q 92	4c
Entertainment				
Bowling, evening rate	game	1.80	4Q 92	4c
Monopoly game, Parker Brothers', No. 9		11.31	4Q 92	4c
Movie	admis-sion	5.00	4Q 92	4c
Tennis balls, yellow, Wilson or Penn, 3	can	1.97	4Q 92	4c
Goods and Services				
ACCRA Index, Miscellaneous Goods and Services		94.30	4Q 92	4c
Groceries				
ACCRA Index, Groceries		92.80	4Q 92	4c
Babyfood, strained vegetables, lowest price	4-4.5 oz jar	0.29	4Q 92	4c
Bananas	lb	0.41	4Q 92	4c
Bread, white	24 oz	0.58	4Q 92	4c
Cheese, Kraft grated Parmesan	8-oz canis-ter	3.55	4Q 92	4c
Chicken, fryer, whole	lb	0.69	4Q 92	4c
Cigarettes, Winston	carton	17.41	4Q 92	4c
Coffee, vacuum-packed	13-oz can	1.89	4Q 92	4c
Corn, frozen	10 oz	0.81	4Q 92	4c
Corn Flakes, Kellogg's or Post Toasties	18 oz	1.92	4Q 92	4c
Eggs, Grade A large	doz	0.61	4Q 92	4c
Ground beef or hamburger	lb	1.03	4Q 92	4c
Lettuce, iceberg	head	0.91	4Q 92	4c
Margarine, Blue Bonnet or Parkay cubes	lb	0.53	4Q 92	4c
Milk, whole	1/2 gal	1.29	4Q 92	4c
Orange juice, Minute Maid frozen	12-oz can	1.55	4Q 92	4c
Peaches	29-oz can	1.32	4Q 92	4c
Peas Sweet, Del Monte or Green Giant	15-17 oz can	0.66	4Q 92	4c
Potatoes, white or red	10-lb sack	1.79	4Q 92	4c
Sausage, Jimmy Dean, 100% pork	lb	2.32	4Q 92	4c
Shortening, vegetable, Crisco	3-lb can	2.30	4Q 92	4c
Soft drink, Coca Cola	2 liter	1.18	4Q 92	4c
Steak, T-bone	lb	5.41	4Q 92	4c
Sugar, cane or beet	4 lb	1.35	4Q 92	4c
Tomatoes, Hunt's or Del Monte	14.5-oz can	0.75	4Q 92	4c
Tuna, chunk, light	6.125-6.5 oz can	0.65	4Q 92	4c
Health Care				
ACCRA Index, Health Care		81.70	4Q 92	4c
Analgesic, Aspirin, Bayer, 325 mg tablets	100	4.39	4Q 92	4c
Dentist's fee, adult teeth cleaning and periodic oral exam	visit	39.67	4Q 92	4c
Doctor's fee, routine exam, established patient	visit	33.00	4Q 92	4c
Hospital care, semiprivate room	day	157.94	90	27c
Hospital care, semiprivate room	day	182.50	4Q 92	4c

Values are in dollars or fractions of dollars. In the column headed *Ref*, references are shown to sources. Each reference is followed by a letter. These refer to the geographical level for which data were reported: s=State, r=Region, and c=City or metro. The abbreviation *ex* is used to mean *except* or *excluding*; *exp* stands for expenditures. For other abbreviations and further explanations, please see the Introduction.

Jonesboro, AR - continued

Item	Per	Value	Date	Ref.
Household Goods				
Appliance repair, home, service call, washing machine	min labor charge	28.30	4Q 92	4c
Laundry detergent, Tide Ultra, Bold, or Cheer	42 oz	3.07	4Q 92	4c
Tissues, facial, Kleenex brand	175-count box	1.08	4Q 92	4c
Housing				
ACCRA Index, Housing		83.40	4Q 92	4c
House, 1,800 sq ft, 8,000 sq ft lot, new, urban	total	93000	4Q 92	4c
House payment, principal and interest, 25% down payment	month	514	4Q 92	4c
Mortgage rate, incl. points & origination fee, 30-year fixed or adjustable rate	percent	8.04	4Q 92	4c
Rent, apartment, 2 bedrooms - 1-1/2 to 2 baths, unfurnished, 950 sq ft, water	month	408	4Q 92	4c
Personal Goods				
Shampoo, Alberto VO5	15 oz	1.14	4Q 92	4c
Toothpaste, Crest or Colgate	6-7 oz	1.95	4Q 92	4c
Personal Services				
Dry cleaning, man's 2-piece suit		6.07	4Q 92	4c
Haircare, woman's shampoo, trim and blow-dry		13.33	4Q 92	4c
Haircut, man's barbershop, no styling		6.00	4Q 92	4c
Restaurant Food				
Chicken, fried, thigh and drumstick		2.28	4Q 92	4c
Hamburger with cheese	1/4 lb	1.85	4Q 92	4c
Pizza, Pizza Hut or Pizza Inn, cheese, thin crust	12-13 in	7.49	4Q 92	4c
Transportation				
ACCRA Index, Transportation		82.00	4Q 92	4c
Tire balance, computer or spin balance, front	wheel	4.67	4Q 92	4c
Utilities				
ACCRA Index, Utilities		82.90	4Q 92	4c
Electricity, partial electric and other energy, 1,800 sq ft living area new home	month	48.91	4Q 92	4c

Joplin, MO

Item	Per	Value	Date	Ref.
Composite ACCRA index		87.00	4Q 92	4c
Alcoholic Beverages				
Beer, Miller Lite or Budweiser, 12-oz containers	6 pack	3.71	4Q 92	4c
Liquor, J & B Scotch	750 ml	15.85	4Q 92	4c
Wine, Gallo Chablis blanc, 1.5 liter	bottle	4.71	4Q 92	4c
Child Care				
Child care fee, average, center	hour	1.63	90	65r
Child care fee, average, nonregulated family day care	hour	1.83	90	65r
Child care fee, average, regulated family day care	hour	1.42	90	65r
Clothing				
Jeans, man's denim		26.79	4Q 92	4c
Shirt, man's dress shirt		22.66	4Q 92	4c
Undervest, boy's size 10-14, cotton	3	3.34	4Q 92	4c
Communications				
Long-distance telephone service, day, initial minute, 0-100 miles	min	0.10-0.46	91	12s
Long-distance telephone service, day, additional minute, 0-100 miles	min	0.06-0.29	91	12s
Newspaper subscription, daily and Sunday home delivery, large-city	month	10.25	4Q 92	4c
Telephone, flat rate	month	9.10	91	11c

Joplin, MO - continued

Item	Per	Value	Date	Ref.
Communications - continued				
Telephone bill, family of four	month	16.53	4Q 92	4c
Education				
Board, 4-yr private college/university	year	1789	91	22s
Board, 4-yr public college/university	year	1162	91	22s
Expenditures, local gov't, public elementary/secondary	pupil	4537	92	20s
Room, 4-year private college/university	year	1817	91	22s
Room, 4-year public college/university	year	1450	91	22s
Tuition, 2-year private college/university	year	5208	91	22s
Tuition, 2-year public college/university	year	891	91	22s
Tuition, 4-year private college/university	year	7487	91	22s
Tuition, 4-year public college/university, in-state	year	1733	91	22s
Energy and Fuels				
Coal	mil Btu	1.35	90	64s
Energy	mil Btu	8.91	90	64s
Energy, combined forms, 1,800 sq ft heating area	month	78.97	4Q 92	4c
Energy exp/householder, 1-family unit	year	473	90	28r
Energy exp/householder, <1,000 sq ft heating area	year	429	90	28r
Energy exp/householder, 1,000-1,999 sq ft heating area	year	442	90	28r
Energy exp/householder, 2,000+ sq ft heating area	year	498	90	28r
Energy exp/householder, mobile home	year	442	90	28r
Energy exp/householder, multifamily	year	407	90	28r
Gas, natural	mil Btu	4.69	90	64s
Gas, natural	000 cu ft	5.14	91	46s
Gas, natural, exp	year	512	91	46s
Gasoline, motor	gal	0.97	4Q 92	4c
Gasoline, unleaded regular	mil Btu	8.61	90	64s
Entertainment				
Bowling, evening rate	game	1.73	4Q 92	4c
Miniature golf admission	adult	6.18	92	1r
Miniature golf admission	child	5.14	92	1r
Monopoly game, Parker Brothers', No. 9		10.28	4Q 92	4c
Movie	admission	4.67	4Q 92	4c
Tennis balls, yellow, Wilson or Penn, 3	can	2.26	4Q 92	4c
Waterpark admission	adult	11.00	92	1r
Waterpark admission	child	8.55	92	1r
Funerals				
Casket, 18-gauge steel, velvet interior		1952.97	91	24r
Cosmetology, hair care, etc.		90.03	91	24r
Embalming		251.75	91	24r
Facility use for ceremony		180.75	91	24r
Hearse, local		117.51	91	24r
Limousine, local		71.86	91	24r
Remains to funeral home, transfer		81.14	91	24r
Service charge, professional		740.03	91	24r
Vault, concrete, non-metallic liner		801.47	91	24r
Viewing facilities, use		169.33	91	24r
Goods and Services				
ACCRA Index, Miscellaneous Goods and Services		90.10	4Q 92	4c
Groceries				
ACCRA Index, Groceries		95.60	4Q 92	4c
Apples, Red Delicious	lb	0.77	4/93	16r
Babyfood, strained vegetables, lowest price	4-4.5 oz jar	0.36	4Q 92	4c
Bacon	lb	1.85	4/93	16r
Bananas	lb	0.37	4Q 92	4c
Bananas	lb	0.46	4/93	16r
Beef, stew, boneless	lb	2.53	4/93	16r
Bologna, all beef or mixed	lb	2.19	4/93	16r
Bread, white	24 oz	0.58	4Q 92	4c
Bread, white, pan	lb	0.78	4/93	16r

Values are in dollars or fractions of dollars. In the column headed *Ref*, references are shown to sources. Each reference is followed by a letter. These refer to the geographical level for which data were reported: s = State, r = Region, and c = City or metro. The abbreviation *ex* is used to mean *except* or *excluding*; *exp* stands for *expenditures*. For other abbreviations and further explanations, please see the Introduction.

Joplin, MO - continued

Item	Per	Value	Date	Ref.
Groceries				
Butter	lb	1.50	4/93	16r
Cabbage	lb	0.40	4/93	16r
Carrots, short trimmed and topped	lb	0.45	4/93	16r
Cheese, Cheddar	lb	3.47	4/93	16r
Cheese, Kraft grated Parmesan	8-oz canister	3.35	4Q 92	4c
Chicken, fresh, whole	lb	0.84	4/93	16r
Chicken, fryer, whole	lb	0.79	4Q 92	4c
Chicken breast, bone-in	lb	1.94	4/93	16r
Chicken legs, bone-in	lb	1.02	4/93	16r
Chuck roast, graded and ungraded, ex USDA prime and choice	lb	2.43	4/93	16r
Chuck roast, USDA choice, bone-in	lb	2.11	4/93	16r
Chuck roast, USDA choice, boneless	lb	2.44	4/93	16r
Cigarettes, Winston	carton	16.20	4Q 92	4c
Coffee, 100% ground roast, all sizes	lb	2.47	4/93	16r
Coffee, vacuum-packed	13-oz can	2.05	4Q 92	4c
Cookies, chocolate chip	lb	2.73	4/93	16r
Corn, frozen	10 oz	0.67	4Q 92	4c
Corn Flakes, Kellogg's or Post Toasties	18 oz	1.95	4Q 92	4c
Eggs, Grade A large	doz	0.76	4Q 92	4c
Eggs, Grade A large	doz	0.93	4/93	16r
Flour, white, all purpose	lb	0.21	4/93	16r
Grapefruit	lb	0.45	4/93	16r
Grapes, Thompson Seedless	lb	1.46	4/93	16r
Ground beef, 100% beef	lb	1.63	4/93	16r
Ground beef, lean and extra lean	lb	2.08	4/93	16r
Ground beef or hamburger	lb	1.28	4Q 92	4c
Ground chuck, 100% beef	lb	1.94	4/93	16r
Ham, boneless, excluding canned	lb	2.21	4/90	10r
Ice cream, prepackaged, bulk, regular	1/2 gal	2.41	4/93	16r
Lemons	lb	0.82	4/93	16r
Lettuce, iceberg	head	0.97	4Q 92	4c
Lettuce, iceberg	lb	0.83	4/93	16r
Margarine, Blue Bonnet or Parkay cubes	lb	0.56	4Q 92	4c
Margarine, stick	lb	0.77	4/93	16r
Milk, whole	1/2 gal	1.33	4Q 92	4c
Orange juice, Minute Maid frozen	12-oz can	1.63	4Q 92	4c
Oranges, navel	lb	0.50	4/93	16r
Peaches	29-oz can	1.33	4Q 92	4c
Peanut butter, creamy, all sizes	lb	1.82	4/93	16r
Pears, Anjou	lb	0.85	4/93	16r
Peas Sweet, Del Monte or Green Giant	15-17 oz can	0.69	4Q 92	4c
Pork chops, center cut, bone-in	lb	3.17	4/93	16r
Potato chips	16 oz	2.68	4/93	16r
Potatoes, white	lb	0.26	4/93	16r
Potatoes, white or red	10-lb sack	1.55	4Q 92	4c
Round roast, graded & ungraded, ex USDA prime & choice	lb	2.88	4/93	16r
Round roast, USDA choice, boneless	lb	2.96	4/93	16r
Sausage, Jimmy Dean, 100% pork	lb	2.60	4Q 92	4c
Shortening, vegetable oil blends	lb	0.79	4/93	16r
Shortening, vegetable, Crisco	3-lb can	2.40	4Q 92	4c
Soft drink, Coca Cola	2 liter	1.19	4Q 92	4c
Spaghetti and macaroni	lb	0.76	4/93	16r
Steak, rib eye, USDA choice, boneless	lb	6.29	4/93	16r
Steak, round, USDA choice, boneless	lb	3.24	4/93	16r
Steak, sirloin, graded & ungraded, ex USDA prime & choice	lb	4.00	4/93	16r
Steak, sirloin, USDA choice, bone-in	lb	3.57	4/93	16r
Steak, sirloin, USDA choice, boneless	lb	4.17	4/93	16r
Steak, T-bone	lb	4.51	4Q 92	4c
Steak, T-bone, USDA choice, bone-in	lb	5.60	4/93	16r
Strawberries, dry pint	12 oz	0.90	4/93	16r
Sugar, cane or beet	4 lb	1.39	4Q 92	4c

Joplin, MO - continued

Item	Per	Value	Date	Ref.
Groceries - continued				
Sugar, white	lb	0.36	4/93	16r
Sugar, white, 33-80 oz pk	lb	0.35	4/93	16r
Tomatoes, field grown	lb	0.99	4/93	16r
Tomatoes, Hunt's or Del Monte	14.5-oz can	0.76	4Q 92	4c
Tuna, chunk, light	6.125-6.5 oz can	0.69	4Q 92	4c
Tuna, chunk, light	lb	1.76	4/93	16r
Turkey, frozen, whole	lb	0.91	4/93	16r
Health Care				
ACCRA Index, Health Care		87.70	4Q 92	4c
Analgesic, Aspirin, Bayer, 325 mg tablets	100	3.96	4Q 92	4c
Childbirth, cesarean, hospital		4688	91	62r
Childbirth, cesarean, physician's fee		2053	91	62r
Childbirth, normal, hospital		2657	91	62r
Childbirth, normal, physician's fee		1492	91	62r
Dentist's fee, adult teeth cleaning and periodic oral exam	visit	40.89	4Q 92	4c
Doctor's fee, routine exam, established patient	visit	31.43	4Q 92	4c
Hospital care, semiprivate room	day	313.33	4Q 92	4c
Medical insurance premium, per employee, small group comprehensive	month	306.60	10/91	25c
Medical plan per employee	year	3443	91	45r
Mental health care, exp	capita	37.60-53.67	90	38s
Mental health care, exp, state mental health agency	capita	35.47	90	38s
Mental health care, hospital psychiatric services, non-Federal, exp	capita	22.53	88	38s
Mental health care, mental health organization, multiservice, exp	capita	6.98	88	38s
Mental health care, psychiatric hospitals, private, exp	capita	5.96	88	38s
Mental health care, psychiatric out-patient clinics, freestanding, exp	capita	0.79	88	38s
Mental health care, state and county mental hospitals, exp	capita	33.35	88	38s
Mental health care, VA medical centers, exp	capita	3.33	88	38s
Physician fee, family practice, first-visit		76.00	91	62r
Physician fee, family practice, revisit		33.00	91	62r
Physician fee, general practice, first-visit		61.00	91	62r
Physician fee, general practice, revisit		31.00	91	62r
Physician fee, general surgeon, first-visit		65.00	91	62r
Physician fee, general surgeon, revisit		35.00	91	62r
Physician fee, internal medicine, first-visit		91.00	91	62r
Physician fee, internal medicine, revisit		40.00	91	62r
Physician fee, median, neurosurgeon, first-visit		106.00	91	62r
Physician fee, median, nonsurgical specialist, first-visit		90.00	91	62r
Physician fee, median, orthopedic surgeon, first-visit		83.00	91	62r
Physician fee, median, surgical specialist, first-visit		61.00	91	62r
Physician fee, neurosurgeon, revisit		41.00	91	62r
Physician fee, nonsurgical specialist, revisit		40.00	91	62r
Physician fee, obstetrics/gynecology, first-visit		61.00	91	62r
Physician fee, obstetrics/gynecology, revisit		40.00	91	62r
Physician fee, orthopedic surgeon, revisit		41.00	91	62r
Physician fee, pediatrician, first-visit		46.00	91	62r
Physician fee, pediatrician, revisit		33.00	91	62r
Physician fee, surgical specialist, revisit		36.00	91	62r
Substance abuse, hospital ancillary charge	incident	1380	90	70s
Substance abuse, hospital physician charge	incident	560	90	70s
Substance abuse, hospital room and board	incident	5670	90	70s

Values are in dollars or fractions of dollars. In the column headed *Ref*, references are shown to sources. Each reference is followed by a letter. These refer to the geographical level for which data were reported: s=State, r=Region, and c=City or metro. The abbreviation *ex* is used to mean *except* or *excluding*; *exp* stands for expenditures. For other abbreviations and further explanations, please see the Introduction.

Joplin, MO - continued

Item	Per	Value	Date	Ref.
Household Goods				
Appliance repair, home, service call, washing machine	min labor charge	22.80	4Q 92	4c
Laundry detergent, Tide Ultra, Bold, or Cheer	42 oz	3.88	4Q 92	4c
Tissues, facial, Kleenex brand	175-count box	0.95	4Q 92	4c
Housing				
ACCRA Index, Housing		83.90	4Q 92	4c
House, 1,800 sq ft, 8,000 sq ft lot, new, urban	total	95153	4Q 92	4c
House payment, principal and interest, 25% down payment	month	531	4Q 92	4c
Mortgage rate, incl. points & origination fee, 30-year fixed or adjustable rate	per-cent	8.14	4Q 92	4c
Rent, apartment, 2 bedrooms - 1-1/2 to 2 baths, unfurnished, 950 sq ft, water	month	378	4Q 92	4c
Rental unit, 1 bedroom	month	306	93	23c
Rental unit, 2 bedroom	month	360	93	23c
Rental unit, 3 bedroom	month	452	93	23c
Rental unit, 4 bedroom	month	507	93	23c
Rental unit, efficiency	month	251	93	23c
Insurance and Pensions				
Auto insurance, private passenger	year	551.85	91	63s
Personal Goods				
Shampoo, Alberto VO5	15 oz	1.23	4Q 92	4c
Toothpaste, Crest or Colgate	6-7 oz	1.77	4Q 92	4c
Personal Services				
Dry cleaning, man's 2-piece suit		5.63	4Q 92	4c
Haircare, woman's shampoo, trim and blow-dry		14.40	4Q 92	4c
Haircut, man's barbershop, no styling		5.55	4Q 92	4c
Restaurant Food				
Chicken, fried, thigh and drumstick		2.59	4Q 92	4c
Hamburger with cheese	1/4 lb	1.69	4Q 92	4c
Pizza, Pizza Hut or Pizza Inn, cheese, thin crust	12-13 in	8.14	4Q 92	4c
Taxes				
Tax, cigarette	pack	13	91	77s
Tax, gasoline	gal	13	91	77s
Taxes, state	capita	969	91	77s
Transportation				
ACCRA Index, Transportation		85.80	4Q 92	4c
Driver's license fee		7.50	12/90	43s
Tire balance, computer or spin balance, front	wheel	5.57	4Q 92	4c
Vehicle registration and license plate	year	1.65-51.15	93	41s
Utilities				
ACCRA Index, Utilities		73.60	4Q 92	4c
Electricity	mil Btu	18.94	90	64s
Electricity, all electric, 1,800 sq ft living area new home	month	78.97	4Q 92	4c
Electricity, winter, 250 KWh	month	18.96	92	55c
Electricity, winter, 500 KWh	month	35.20	92	55c
Electricity, winter, 750 KWh	month	47.79	92	55c
Electricity, winter, 1000 KWh	month	57.91	92	55c

Juneau, AK

Item	Per	Value	Date	Ref.
Composite ACCRA index		136.50	4Q 92	4c
Alcoholic Beverages				
Beer, Miller Lite or Budweiser, 12-oz containers	6 pack	4.98	4Q 92	4c
Liquor, J & B Scotch	750 ml	21.04	4Q 92	4c
Wine, Gallo Chablis blanc, 1.5 liter	bottle	6.71	4Q 92	4c

Juneau, AK - continued

Item	Per	Value	Date	Ref.
Clothing				
Jeans, man's denim		28.68	4Q 92	4c
Shirt, man's dress shirt		19.67	4Q 92	4c
Undervest, boy's size 10-14, cotton	3	5.57	4Q 92	4c
Communications				
Newspaper subscription, daily and Sunday home delivery, large-city	month	11.91	4Q 92	4c
Telephone bill, family of four	month	14.27	4Q 92	4c
Energy and Fuels				
Energy, combined forms, 1,800 sq ft heating area	month	178.17	4Q 92	4c
Gasoline, motor	gal	1.62	4Q 92	4c
Entertainment				
Bowling, evening rate	game	2.25	4Q 92	4c
Monopoly game, Parker Brothers', No. 9		16.86	4Q 92	4c
Movie	admission	7.50	4Q 92	4c
Tennis balls, yellow, Wilson or Penn, 3	can	3.54	4Q 92	4c
Goods and Services				
ACCRA Index, Miscellaneous Goods and Services		124.20	4Q 92	4c
Groceries				
ACCRA Index, Groceries		135.40	4Q 92	4c
Babyfood, strained vegetables, lowest price	4-4.5 oz jar	0.44	4Q 92	4c
Bananas	lb	0.76	4Q 92	4c
Bread, white	24 oz	0.96	4Q 92	4c
Cheese, Kraft grated Parmesan	8-oz canister	3.81	4Q 92	4c
Chicken, fryer, whole	lb	1.16	4Q 92	4c
Cigarettes, Winston	carton	20.61	4Q 92	4c
Coffee, vacuum-packed	13-oz can	3.01	4Q 92	4c
Corn, frozen	10 oz	0.73	4Q 92	4c
Corn Flakes, Kellogg's or Post Toasties	18 oz	2.73	4Q 92	4c
Eggs, Grade A large	doz	0.99	4Q 92	4c
Ground beef or hamburger	lb	1.85	4Q 92	4c
Lettuce, iceberg	head	1.15	4Q 92	4c
Margarine, Blue Bonnet or Parkay cubes	lb	0.95	4Q 92	4c
Milk, whole	1/2 gal	1.92	4Q 92	4c
Orange juice, Minute Maid frozen	12-oz can	1.48	4Q 92	4c
Peaches	29-oz can	1.94	4Q 92	4c
Peas Sweet, Del Monte or Green Giant	15-17 oz can	0.88	4Q 92	4c
Potatoes, white or red	10-lb sack	3.58	4Q 92	4c
Sausage, Jimmy Dean, 100% pork	lb	3.52	4Q 92	4c
Shortening, vegetable, Crisco	3-lb can	3.13	4Q 92	4c
Soft drink, Coca Cola	2 liter	2.08	4Q 92	4c
Steak, T-bone	lb	6.22	4Q 92	4c
Sugar, cane or beet	4 lb	2.04	4Q 92	4c
Tomatoes, Hunt's or Del Monte	14.5-oz can	0.76	4Q 92	4c
Tuna, chunk, light	6.125-6.5 oz can	0.96	4Q 92	4c
Health Care				
ACCRA Index, Health Care		177.30	4Q 92	4c
Analgesic, Aspirin, Bayer, 325 mg tablets	100	7.38	4Q 92	4c
Dentist's fee, adult teeth cleaning and periodic oral exam	visit	117.33	4Q 92	4c
Doctor's fee, routine exam, established patient	visit	52.60	4Q 92	4c
Hospital care, semiprivate room	day	380.00	4Q 92	4c

Values are in dollars or fractions of dollars. In the column headed *Ref*, references are shown to sources. Each reference is followed by a letter. These refer to the geographical level for which data were reported: s = State, r = Region, and c = City or metro. The abbreviation *ex* is used to mean *except* or *excluding*; *exp* stands for expenditures. For other abbreviations and further explanations, please see the Introduction.

Juneau, AK - continued

Item	Per	Value	Date	Ref.
Household Goods				
Appliance repair, home, service call, washing machine	min labor charge	55.15	4Q 92	4c
Laundry detergent, Tide Ultra, Bold, or Cheer	42 oz	4.66	4Q 92	4c
Tissues, facial, Kleenex brand	175-count box	1.54	4Q 92	4c
Housing				
ACCRA Index, Housing		144.60	4Q 92	4c
House, 1,800 sq ft, 8,000 sq ft lot, new, urban	total	138750	4Q 92	4c
House payment, principal and interest, 25% down payment	month	782	4Q 92	4c
Mortgage rate, incl. points & origination fee, 30-year fixed or adjustable rate	per-cent	8.25	4Q 92	4c
Rent, apartment, 2 bedrooms - 1-1/2 to 2 baths, unfurnished, 950 sq ft, water	month	960	4Q 92	4c
Personal Goods				
Shampoo, Alberto VO5	15 oz	1.87	4Q 92	4c
Toothpaste, Crest or Colgate	6-7 oz	3.06	4Q 92	4c
Personal Services				
Dry cleaning, man's 2-piece suit		8.82	4Q 92	4c
Haircare, woman's shampoo, trim and blow-dry		23.08	4Q 92	4c
Haircut, man's barbershop, no styling		12.88	4Q 92	4c
Restaurant Food				
Chicken, fried, thigh and drumstick		1.78	4Q 92	4c
Hamburger with cheese	1/4 lb	2.55	4Q 92	4c
Pizza, Pizza Hut or Pizza Inn, cheese, thin crust	12-13 in	8.98	4Q 92	4c
Transportation				
ACCRA Index, Transportation		122.30	4Q 92	4c
Bus fare	one-way	1.25	3/93	2c
Bus fare, up to 10 miles	one-way	1.00	4Q 92	4c
Tire balance, computer or spin balance, front	wheel	6.70	4Q 92	4c
Utilities				
ACCRA Index, Utilities		154.20	4Q 92	4c
Electricity, all electric, 1,800 sq ft living area new home	month	178.17	4Q 92	4c
Electricity, winter, 250 KWh	month	28.78	92	55c
Electricity, winter, 500 KWh	month	49.05	92	55c
Electricity, winter, 750 KWh	month	69.33	92	55c
Electricity, winter, 1000 KWh	month	89.60	92	55c

Kalamazoo, MI

Item	Per	Value	Date	Ref.
Child Care				
Child care fee, average, center	hour	1.63	90	65r
Child care fee, average, nonregulated family day care	hour	1.83	90	65r
Child care fee, average, regulated family day care	hour	1.42	90	65r
Communications				
Long-distance telephone service, day, initial minute, 0-100 miles	min	0.14-0.36	91	12s
Long-distance telephone service, day, additional minute, 0-100 miles	min	0.14-0.36	91	12s
Long-distance telephone service, evenings/weekends, 0-100 mi, initial minute	min	0.07-0.19	91	12s
Long-distance telephone service, evenings/weekends, 0-100 mi, additional minute	min	0.04-0.14	91	12s

Kalamazoo, MI - continued

Item	Per	Value	Date	Ref.
Education				
Board, 4-yr private college/university	year	1698	91	22s
Board, 4-yr public college/university	year	1962	91	22s
Expenditures, local gov't, public elementary/secondary	pupil	5671	92	20s
Room, 4-year private college/university	year	1440	91	22s
Room, 4-year public college/university	year	1687	91	22s
Tuition, 2-year private college/university	year	4749	91	22s
Tuition, 2-year public college/university	year	1124	91	22s
Tuition, 4-year private college/university	year	6885	91	22s
Tuition, 4-year public college/university, in-state	year	2635	91	22s
Energy and Fuels				
Coal	mil Btu	1.63	90	64s
Energy	mil Btu	8.17	90	64s
Energy exp/householder, 1-family unit	year	471	90	28r
Energy exp/householder, <1,000 sq ft heating area	year	430	90	28r
Energy exp/householder, 1,000-1,999 sq ft heating area	year	481	90	28r
Energy exp/householder, 2,000+ sq ft heating area	year	473	90	28r
Energy exp/householder, mobile home	year	430	90	28r
Energy exp/householder, multifamily	year	461	90	28r
Gas, natural	mil Btu	4.36	90	64s
Gas, natural	000 cu ft	5.07	91	46s
Gas, natural, exp	year	655	91	46s
Gasoline, unleaded regular	mil Btu	8.78	90	64s
Entertainment				
Miniature golf admission	adult	6.18	92	1r
Miniature golf admission	child	5.14	92	1r
Waterpark admission	adult	11.00	92	1r
Waterpark admission	child	8.55	92	1r
Funerals				
Casket, 18-gauge steel, velvet interior		1926.72	91	24r
Cosmetology, hair care, etc.		97.64	91	24r
Embalming		249.14	91	24r
Facility use for ceremony		208.59	91	24r
Hearse, local		130.12	91	24r
Limousine, local		104.66	91	24r
Remains to funeral home, transfer		93.61	91	24r
Service charge, professional		724.62	91	24r
Vault, concrete, non-metallic liner		734.53	91	24r
Viewing facilities, use		236.06	91	24r
Groceries				
Apples, Red Delicious	lb	0.77	4/93	16r
Bacon	lb	1.85	4/93	16r
Bananas	lb	0.46	4/93	16r
Beef, stew, boneless	lb	2.53	4/93	16r
Bologna, all beef or mixed	lb	2.19	4/93	16r
Bread, white, pan	lb	0.78	4/93	16r
Butter	lb	1.50	4/93	16r
Cabbage	lb	0.40	4/93	16r
Carrots, short trimmed and topped	lb	0.45	4/93	16r
Cheese, Cheddar	lb	3.47	4/93	16r
Chicken, fresh, whole	lb	0.84	4/93	16r
Chicken breast, bone-in	lb	1.94	4/93	16r
Chicken legs, bone-in	lb	1.02	4/93	16r
Chuck roast, graded and ungraded, ex USDA prime and choice	lb	2.43	4/93	16r
Chuck roast, USDA choice, bone-in	lb	2.11	4/93	16r
Chuck roast, USDA choice, boneless	lb	2.44	4/93	16r
Coffee, 100% ground roast, all sizes	lb	2.47	4/93	16r
Cookies, chocolate chip	lb	2.73	4/93	16r
Eggs, Grade A large	doz	0.93	4/93	16r
Flour, white, all purpose	lb	0.21	4/93	16r
Grapefruit	lb	0.45	4/93	16r
Grapes, Thompson Seedless	lb	1.46	4/93	16r
Ground beef, 100% beef	lb	1.63	4/93	16r
Ground beef, lean and extra lean	lb	2.08	4/93	16r

Values are in dollars or fractions of dollars. In the column headed *Ref*, references are shown to sources. Each reference is followed by a letter. These refer to the geographical level for which data were reported: s=State, r=Region, and c=City or metro. The abbreviation *ex* is used to mean *except* or *excluding*; *exp* stands for expenditures. For other abbreviations and further explanations, please see the Introduction.

Kalamazoo, MI - continued

Item	Per	Value	Date	Ref.
Groceries				
Ground chuck, 100% beef	lb	1.94	4/93	16r
Ham, boneless, excluding canned	lb	2.21	4/93	16r
Honey, jar	8 oz	0.97-1.25	92	5r
Honey, jar	lb	1.25-2.25	92	5r
Honey, squeeze bear	12-oz	1.25-1.99	92	5r
Ice cream, prepackaged, bulk, regular	1/2 gal	2.41	4/93	16r
Lemons	lb	0.82	4/93	16r
Lettuce, iceberg	lb	0.83	4/93	16r
Margarine, stick	lb	0.77	4/93	16r
Oranges, navel	lb	0.50	4/93	16r
Peanut butter, creamy, all sizes	lb	1.82	4/93	16r
Pears, Anjou	lb	0.85	4/93	16r
Pork chops, center cut, bone-in	lb	3.17	4/93	16r
Potato chips	16 oz	2.68	4/93	16r
Potatoes, white	lb	0.26	4/93	16r
Round roast, graded & ungraded, ex USDA prime & choice	lb	2.88	4/93	16r
Round roast, USDA choice, boneless	lb	2.96	4/93	16r
Shortening, vegetable oil blends	lb	0.79	4/93	16r
Spaghetti and macaroni	lb	0.76	4/93	16r
Steak, rib eye, USDA choice, boneless	lb	6.29	4/93	16r
Steak, round, USDA choice, boneless	lb	3.24	4/93	16r
Steak, sirloin, graded & ungraded, ex USDA prime & choice	lb	4.00	4/93	16r
Steak, sirloin, USDA choice, bone-in	lb	3.57	4/93	16r
Steak, sirloin, USDA choice, boneless	lb	4.17	4/93	16r
Steak, T-bone, USDA choice, bone-in	lb	5.60	4/93	16r
Strawberries, dry pint	12 oz	0.90	4/93	16r
Sugar, white	lb	0.36	4/93	16r
Sugar, white, 33-80 oz pk	lb	0.35	4/93	16r
Tomatoes, field grown	lb	0.99	4/93	16r
Tuna, chunk, light	lb	1.76	4/93	16r
Turkey, frozen, whole	lb	0.91	4/93	16r
Health Care				
Childbirth, cesarean, hospital		4688	91	62r
Childbirth, cesarean, physician's fee		2053	91	62r
Childbirth, normal, hospital		2657	91	62r
Childbirth, normal, physician's fee		1492	91	62r
Medical plan per employee	year	3443	91	45r
Mental health care, exp	capita	53.68-118.35	90	38s
Mental health care, exp, state mental health agency	capita	73.73	90	38s
Mental health care, hospital psychiatric services, non-Federal, exp	capita	22.52	88	38s
Mental health care, mental health organization, multiservice, exp	capita	42.68	88	38s
Mental health care, psychiatric hospitals, private, exp	capita	10.80	88	38s
Mental health care, psychiatric out-patient clinics, freestanding, exp	capita	3.47	88	38s
Mental health care, psychiatric partial-care organizations, freestanding, exp	capita	0.73	88	38s
Mental health care, state and county mental hospitals, exp	capita	36.77	88	38s
Mental health care, VA medical centers, exp	capita	4.03	88	38s
Physician fee, family practice, first-visit		76.00	91	62r
Physician fee, family practice, revisit		33.00	91	62r
Physician fee, general practice, first-visit		61.00	91	62r
Physician fee, general practice, revisit		31.00	91	62r
Physician fee, general surgeon, first-visit		65.00	91	62r
Physician fee, general surgeon, revisit		35.00	91	62r
Physician fee, internal medicine, first-visit		91.00	91	62r
Physician fee, internal medicine, revisit		40.00	91	62r
Physician fee, median, neurosurgeon, first-visit		106.00	91	62r
Physician fee, median, nonsurgical specialist, first-visit		90.00	91	62r
Physician fee, median, orthopedic surgeon, first-visit		83.00	91	62r
Physician fee, median, surgical specialist, first-visit		61.00	91	62r

Kalamazoo, MI - continued

Item	Per	Value	Date	Ref.
Health Care - continued				
Physician fee, neurosurgeon, revisit		41.00	91	62r
Physician fee, nonsurgical specialist, revisit		40.00	91	62r
Physician fee, obstetrics/gynecology, first-visit		61.00	91	62r
Physician fee, obstetrics/gynecology, revisit		40.00	91	62r
Physician fee, orthopedic surgeon, revisit		41.00	91	62r
Physician fee, pediatrician, first-visit		46.00	91	62r
Physician fee, pediatrician, revisit		33.00	91	62r
Physician fee, surgical specialist, revisit		36.00	91	62r
Substance abuse, hospital ancillary charge	incident	1480	90	70s
Substance abuse, hospital physician charge	incident	250	90	70s
Substance abuse, hospital room and board	incident	4070	90	70s
Insurance and Pensions				
Auto insurance, private passenger	year	716.78	91	63s
Taxes				
Tax, cigarette	pack	25	91	77s
Tax, gasoline	gal	15	91	77s
Taxes, state	capita	1185	91	77s
Transportation				
Driver's license fee		12.00	12/90	43s
Vehicle registration and license plate	year	14.00-200.00	93	40s
Utilities				
Electricity	mil Btu	20.85	90	64s

Kankakee, IL

Item	Per	Value	Date	Ref.
Child Care				
Child care fee, average, center	hour	1.63	90	65r
Child care fee, average, nonregulated family day care	hour	1.83	90	65r
Child care fee, average, regulated family day care	hour	1.42	90	65r
Communications				
Long-distance telephone service, day, initial minute, 0-100 miles	min	0.10-0.34	91	12s
Long-distance telephone service, day, additional minute, 0-100 miles	min	0.04-0.16	91	12s
Long-distance telephone service, evenings/weekends, 0-100 mi, initial minute	min	0.06-0.20	91	12s
Long-distance telephone service, evenings/weekends, 0-100 mi, additional minute	min	0.02-0.10	91	12s
Education				
Board, 4-yr private college/university	year	1797	91	22s
Board, 4-yr public college/university	year	1857	91	22s
Expenditures, local gov't, public elementary/secondary	pupil	5248	92	20s
Room, 4-year private college/university	year	2095	91	22s
Room, 4-year public college/university	year	1454	91	22s
Tuition, 2-year private college/university	year	5279	91	22s
Tuition, 2-year public college/university	year	906	91	22s
Tuition, 4-year private college/university	year	8853	91	22s
Tuition, 4-year public college/university, in-state	year	2465	91	22s
Energy and Fuels				
Coal	mil Btu	1.72	90	64s
Energy	mil Btu	8.74	90	64s
Energy exp/householder, 1-family unit	year	471	90	28r
Energy exp/householder, <1,000 sq ft heating area	year	430	90	28r
Energy exp/householder, 1,000-1,999 sq ft heating area	year	481	90	28r
Energy exp/householder, 2,000+ sq ft heating area	year	473	90	28r

Values are in dollars or fractions of dollars. In the column headed *Ref*, references are shown to sources. Each reference is followed by a letter. These refer to the geographical level for which data were reported: s=State, r=Region, and c=City or metro. The abbreviation *ex* is used to mean *except* or *excluding*; *exp* stands for expenditures. For other abbreviations and further explanations, please see the Introduction.

Kankakee, IL - continued

Item	Per	Value	Date	Ref.
Energy and Fuels				
Energy exp/householder, mobile home	year	430	90	28r
Energy exp/householder, multifamily	year	461	90	28r
Gas, natural	mil Btu	4.57	90	64s
Gas, natural	000 cu ft	4.95	91	46s
Gas, natural, exp	year	696	91	46s
Gasoline, unleaded regular	mil Btu	9.35	90	64s
Entertainment				
Miniature golf admission	adult	6.18	92	1r
Miniature golf admission	child	5.14	92	1r
Waterpark admission	adult	11.00	92	1r
Waterpark admission	child	8.55	92	1r
Funerals				
Casket, 18-gauge steel, velvet interior		1926.72	91	24r
Cosmetology, hair care, etc.		97.64	91	24r
Embalming		249.14	91	24r
Facility use for ceremony		208.59	91	24r
Hearse, local		130.12	91	24r
Limousine, local		104.66	91	24r
Remains to funeral home, transfer		93.61	91	24r
Service charge, professional		724.62	91	24r
Vault, concrete, non-metallic liner		734.53	91	24r
Viewing facilities, use		236.06	91	24r
Groceries				
Apples, Red Delicious	lb	0.77	4/93	16r
Bacon	lb	1.85	4/93	16r
Bananas	lb	0.46	4/93	16r
Beef, stew, boneless	lb	2.53	4/93	16r
Bologna, all beef or mixed	lb	2.19	4/93	16r
Bread, white, pan	lb	0.78	4/93	16r
Butter	lb	1.50	4/93	16r
Cabbage	lb	0.40	4/93	16r
Carrots, short trimmed and topped	lb	0.45	4/93	16r
Cheese, Cheddar	lb	3.47	4/93	16r
Chicken, fresh, whole	lb	0.84	4/93	16r
Chicken breast, bone-in	lb	1.94	4/93	16r
Chicken legs, bone-in	lb	1.02	4/93	16r
Chuck roast, graded and ungraded, ex USDA prime and choice	lb	2.43	4/93	16r
Chuck roast, USDA choice, bone-in	lb	2.11	4/93	16r
Chuck roast, USDA choice, boneless	lb	2.44	4/93	16r
Coffee, 100% ground roast, all sizes	lb	2.47	4/93	16r
Cookies, chocolate chip	lb	2.73	4/93	16r
Eggs, Grade A large	doz	0.93	4/93	16r
Flour, white, all purpose	lb	0.21	4/93	16r
Grapefruit	lb	0.45	4/93	16r
Grapes, Thompson Seedless	lb	1.46	4/93	16r
Ground beef, 100% beef	lb	1.63	4/93	16r
Ground beef, lean and extra lean	lb	2.08	4/93	16r
Ground chuck, 100% beef	lb	1.94	4/93	16r
Ham, boneless, excluding canned	lb	2.21	4/93	16r
Honey, jar	8 oz	0.97-1.25	92	5r
Honey, jar	lb	1.25-2.25	92	5r
Honey, squeeze bear	12-oz	1.25-1.99	92	5r
Ice cream, prepackaged, bulk, regular	1/2 gal	2.41	4/93	16r
Lemons	lb	0.82	4/93	16r
Lettuce, iceberg	lb	0.83	4/93	16r
Margarine, stick	lb	0.77	4/93	16r
Oranges, navel	lb	0.50	4/93	16r
Peanut butter, creamy, all sizes	lb	1.82	4/93	16r
Pears, Anjou	lb	0.85	4/93	16r
Pork chops, center cut, bone-in	lb	3.17	4/93	16r
Potato chips	16 oz	2.68	4/93	16r
Potatoes, white	lb	0.26	4/93	16r
Round roast, graded & ungraded, ex USDA prime & choice	lb	2.88	4/93	16r
Round roast, USDA choice, boneless	lb	2.96	4/93	16r
Shortening, vegetable oil blends	lb	0.79	4/93	16r
Spaghetti and macaroni	lb	0.76	4/93	16r
Steak, rib eye, USDA choice, boneless	lb	6.29	4/93	16r
Steak, round, USDA choice, boneless	lb	3.24	4/93	16r

Kankakee, IL - continued

Item	Per	Value	Date	Ref.
Groceries - continued				
Steak, sirloin, graded & ungraded, ex USDA prime & choice	lb	4.00	4/93	16r
Steak, sirloin, USDA choice, bone-in	lb	3.57	4/93	16r
Steak, sirloin, USDA choice, boneless	lb	4.17	4/93	16r
Steak, T-bone, USDA choice, bone-in	lb	5.60	4/93	16r
Strawberries, dry pint	12 oz	0.90	4/93	16r
Sugar, white	lb	0.36	4/93	16r
Sugar, white, 33-80 oz pk	lb	0.35	4/93	16r
Tomatoes, field grown	lb	0.99	4/93	16r
Tuna, chunk, light	lb	1.76	4/93	16r
Turkey, frozen, whole	lb	0.91	4/93	16r
Health Care				
Childbirth, cesarean, hospital		4688	91	62r
Childbirth, cesarean, physician's fee		2053	91	62r
Childbirth, normal, hospital		2657	91	62r
Childbirth, normal, physician's fee		1492	91	62r
Medical plan per employee	year	3443	91	45r
Mental health care, exp	capita	28.84-37.59	90	38s
Mental health care, exp, state mental health agency	capita	34.43	90	38s
Mental health care, hospital psychiatric services, non-Federal, exp	capita	18.46	88	38s
Mental health care, mental health organization, multiservice, exp	capita	11.97	88	38s
Mental health care, psychiatric hospitals, private, exp	capita	7.84	88	38s
Mental health care, psychiatric out-patient clinics, freestanding, exp	capita	3.21	88	38s
Mental health care, psychiatric partial-care organizations, freestanding, exp	capita	0.51	88	38s
Mental health care, state and county mental hospitals, exp	capita	18.11	88	38s
Mental health care, VA medical centers, exp	capita	3.69	88	38s
Physician fee, family practice, first-visit		76.00	91	62r
Physician fee, family practice, revisit		33.00	91	62r
Physician fee, general practice, first-visit		61.00	91	62r
Physician fee, general practice, revisit		31.00	91	62r
Physician fee, general surgeon, first-visit		65.00	91	62r
Physician fee, general surgeon, revisit		35.00	91	62r
Physician fee, internal medicine, first-visit		91.00	91	62r
Physician fee, internal medicine, revisit		40.00	91	62r
Physician fee, median, neurosurgeon, first-visit		106.00	91	62r
Physician fee, median, nonsurgical specialist, first-visit		90.00	91	62r
Physician fee, median, orthopedic surgeon, first-visit		83.00	91	62r
Physician fee, median, surgical specialist, first-visit		61.00	91	62r
Physician fee, neurosurgeon, revisit		41.00	91	62r
Physician fee, nonsurgical specialist, revisit		40.00	91	62r
Physician fee, obstetrics/gynecology, first-visit		61.00	91	62r
Physician fee, obstetrics/gynecology, revisit		40.00	91	62r
Physician fee, orthopedic surgeon, revisit		41.00	91	62r
Physician fee, pediatrician, first-visit		46.00	91	62r
Physician fee, pediatrician, revisit		33.00	91	62r
Physician fee, surgical specialist, revisit		36.00	91	62r
Prescription drug co-pay, Medicaid	month	25.00	91	21s
Substance abuse, hospital ancillary charge	incident	1310	90	70s
Substance abuse, hospital physician charge	incident	540	90	70s
Substance abuse, hospital room and board	incident	6150	90	70s
Insurance and Pensions				
Auto insurance, private passenger	year	621.37	91	63s
Taxes				
Tax, cigarette	pack	30	91	77s
Tax, gasoline	gal	19	91	77s

Values are in dollars or fractions of dollars. In the column headed *Ref*, references are shown to sources. Each reference is followed by a letter. These refer to the geographical level for which data were reported: s=State, r=Region, and c=City or metro. The abbreviation *ex* is used to mean *except* or *excluding*; *exp* stands for *expenditures*. For other abbreviations and further explanations, please see the Introduction.

Kankakee, IL - continued

Item	Per	Value	Date	Ref.
Taxes				
Taxes, state	capita	1151	91	77s
Transportation				
Driver's license fee		10.00	12/90	43s
Vehicle registration and license plate	multi-year	48.00	93	52s
Utilities				
Electricity	mil Btu	22.02	90	64s

Kansas City, MO, KS

Item	Per	Value	Date	Ref.
Composite ACCRA index		97.50	4Q 92	4c
Alcoholic Beverages				
Alcoholic beverages, exp	year	237	89	15c
Beer, Miller Lite or Budweiser, 12-oz containers	6 pack	4.02	4Q 92	4c
Liquor, J & B Scotch	750 ml	16.28	4Q 92	4c
Wine, Gallo Chablis blanc, 1.5 liter	bottle	5.04	4Q 92	4c
Charity				
Cash contributions	year	845	89	15c
Child Care				
Child care fee, average, center	hour	1.63	90	65r
Child care fee, average, nonregulated family day care	hour	1.83	90	65r
Child care fee, average, regulated family day care	hour	1.42	90	65r
Clothing				
Jeans, man's denim		24.89	4Q 92	4c
Shirt, man's dress shirt		23.10	4Q 92	4c
Undervest, boy's size 10-14, cotton	3	5.23	4Q 92	4c
Communications				
Long-distance telephone service, day, initial minute, 0-100 miles	min	0.10-0.46	91	12s
Long-distance telephone service, day, additional minute, 0-100 miles	min	0.06-0.29	91	12s
Newspaper subscription, daily and Sunday home delivery, large-city	month	11.23	4Q 92	4c
Postage and stationery, exp	year	144	89	15c
Telephone, exp	year	530	89	15c
Telephone, flat rate	month	12.05	91	11c
Telephone, residential, private line, rotary, unlimited calling	month	18.05	10/91	78c
Telephone bill, family of four	month	21.01	4Q 92	4c
Education				
Board, 4-yr private college/university	year	1789	91	22s
Board, 4-yr public college/university	year	1162	91	22s
Education, exp	year	370	89	15c
Expenditures, local gov't, public elementary/secondary	pupil	4537	92	20s
Room, 4-year private college/university	year	1817	91	22s
Room, 4-year public college/university	year	1450	91	22s
Tuition, 2-year private college/university	year	5208	91	22s
Tuition, 2-year public college/university	year	891	91	22s
Tuition, 4-year private college/university	year	7487	91	22s
Tuition, 4-year public college/university, in-state	year	1733	91	22s
Energy and Fuels				
Coal	mil Btu	1.35	90	64s
Energy	mil Btu	8.91	90	64s
Energy, combined forms, 1,800 sq ft heating area	month	98.92	4Q 92	4c
Energy, exc electricity, 1,800 sq ft heating area	month	43.00	4Q 92	4c
Energy exp/householder, 1-family unit	year	473	90	28r
Energy exp/householder, <1,000 sq ft heating area	year	429	90	28r
Energy exp/householder, 1,000-1,999 sq ft heating area	year	442	90	28r

Kansas City, MO, KS - continued

Item	Per	Value	Date	Ref.
Energy and Fuels - continued				
Energy exp/householder, 2,000 + sq ft heating area	year	498	90	28r
Energy exp/householder, mobile home	year	442	90	28r
Energy exp/householder, multifamily	year	407	90	28r
Fuel oil, other fuel, exp	year	13	89	15c
Gas, cooking, 10 therms	month	11.68	92	56c
Gas, cooking, 30 therms	month	19.02	92	56c
Gas, cooking, 50 therms	month	26.38	92	56c
Gas, heating, winter, 100 therms	month	44.76	92	56c
Gas, heating, winter, average use	month	64.25	92	56c
Gas, natural	mil Btu	4.69	90	64s
Gas, natural	000 cu ft	5.14	91	46s
Gas, natural, exp	year	398	89	15c
Gas, natural, exp	year	512	91	46s
Gasoline, motor	gal	1.07	4Q 92	4c
Gasoline, unleaded regular	mil Btu	8.61	90	64s
Entertainment				
Bowling, evening rate	game	1.79	4Q 92	4c
Entertainment exp	year	1426	89	15c
Fees and admissions	year	347	89	15c
Football game expenditures, pro		127.83	91	80c
Miniature golf admission	adult	6.18	92	1r
Miniature golf admission	child	5.14	92	1r
Monopoly game, Parker Brothers', No. 9		10.18	4Q 92	4c
Movie	admission	5.55	4Q 92	4c
Pets, toys, playground equipment, exp	year	233	89	15c
Reading, exp	year	161	89	15c
Supplies, equipment, services, exp	year	447	89	15c
Tennis balls, yellow, Wilson or Penn, 3	can	1.98	4Q 92	4c
Waterpark admission	adult	11.00	92	1r
Waterpark admission	child	8.55	92	1r
Funerals				
Casket, 18-gauge steel, velvet interior		1952.97	91	24r
Cosmetology, hair care, etc.		90.03	91	24r
Embalming		251.75	91	24r
Facility use for ceremony		180.75	91	24r
Hearse, local		117.51	91	24r
Limousine, local		71.86	91	24r
Remains to funeral home, transfer		81.14	91	24r
Service charge, professional		740.03	91	24r
Vault, concrete, non-metallic liner		801.47	91	24r
Viewing facilities, use		169.33	91	24r
Goods and Services				
ACCRA Index, Miscellaneous Goods and Services		98.70	4Q 92	4c
Groceries				
ACCRA Index, Groceries		98.00	4Q 92	4c
Apples, Red Delicious	lb	0.77	4/93	16r
Babyfood, strained vegetables, lowest price	4-4.5 oz jar	0.27	4Q 92	4c
Bacon	lb	1.85	4/93	16r
Bakery products, exp	year	218	89	15c
Bananas	lb	0.51	4Q 92	4c
Bananas	lb	0.46	4/93	16r
Beef, exp	year	179	89	15c
Beef, stew, boneless	lb	2.53	4/93	16r
Beverages, nonalcoholic, exp	year	210	89	15c
Bologna, all beef or mixed	lb	2.19	4/93	16r
Bread, white	24 oz	0.60	4Q 92	4c
Bread, white, pan	lb	0.78	4/93	16r
Butter	lb	1.50	4/93	16r
Cabbage	lb	0.40	4/93	16r
Carrots, short trimmed and topped	lb	0.45	4/93	16r
Cereals and bakery products, exp	year	351	89	15c
Cereals and cereal products, exp	year	133	89	15c
Cheese, Cheddar	lb	3.47	4/93	16r

Values are in dollars or fractions of dollars. In the column headed *Ref*, references are shown to sources. Each reference is followed by a letter. These refer to the geographical level for which data were reported: s = State, r = Region, and c = City or metro. The abbreviation *ex* is used to mean *except* or *excluding*; *exp* stands for expenditures. For other abbreviations and further explanations, please see the Introduction.

Kansas City, MO, KS - continued

Item	Per	Value	Date	Ref.
Groceries				
Cheese, Kraft grated Parmesan	8-oz canis-ter	3.50	4Q 92	4c
Chicken, fresh, whole	lb	0.84	4/93	16r
Chicken, fryer, whole	lb	0.76	4Q 92	4c
Chicken breast, bone-in	lb	1.94	4/93	16r
Chicken legs, bone-in	lb	1.02	4/93	16r
Chuck roast, graded and ungraded, ex USDA prime and choice	lb	2.43	4/93	16r
Chuck roast, USDA choice, bone-in	lb	2.11	4/93	16r
Chuck roast, USDA choice, boneless	lb	2.44	4/93	16r
Cigarettes, Winston	carton	17.29	4Q 92	4c
Coffee, 100% ground roast, all sizes	lb	2.47	4/93	16r
Coffee, vacuum-packed	13-oz can	1.89	4Q 92	4c
Cookies, chocolate chip	lb	2.73	4/93	16r
Corn, frozen	10 oz	0.65	4Q 92	4c
Corn Flakes, Kellogg's or Post Toasties	18 oz	2.09	4Q 92	4c
Dairy products, exp	year	323	89	15c
Dairy products, miscellaneous, exp	year	170	89	15c
Eggs, exp	year	32	89	15c
Eggs, Grade A large	doz	0.81	4Q 92	4c
Eggs, Grade A large	doz	0.93	4/93	16r
Fish and seafood, exp	year	53	89	15c
Flour, white, all purpose	lb	0.21	4/93	16r
Food, exp	year	4049	89	15c
Food eaten at home, exp	year	2374	89	15c
Food eaten away from home, exp	year	1675	89	15c
Food prepared on out-of-town trips, exp	year	37	89	15c
Fruits, fresh, exp	year	175	89	15c
Fruits, processed, exp	year	91	89	15c
Fruits and vegetables, exp	year	455	89	15c
Grapefruit	lb	0.45	4/93	16r
Grapes, Thompson Seedless	lb	1.46	4/93	16r
Ground beef, 100% beef	lb	1.63	4/93	16r
Ground beef, lean and extra lean	lb	2.08	4/93	16r
Ground beef or hamburger	lb	1.44	4Q 92	4c
Ground chuck, 100% beef	lb	1.94	4/93	16r
Ham, boneless, excluding canned	lb	2.21	4/93	16r
Ice cream, prepackaged, bulk, regular	1/2 gal	2.41	4/93	16r
Lemons	lb	0.82	4/93	16r
Lettuce, iceberg	head	0.95	4Q 92	4c
Lettuce, iceberg	lb	0.83	4/93	16r
Margarine, Blue Bonnet or Parkay cubes	lb	0.74	4Q 92	4c
Margarine, stick	lb	0.77	4/93	16r
Meats, miscellaneous, exp	year	71	89	15c
Meats, poultry, fish and eggs, exp	year	529	89	15c
Milk, whole	1/2 gal	1.24	4Q 92	4c
Milk and cream, fresh, exp	year	153	89	15c
Orange juice, Minute Maid frozen	12-oz can	1.54	4Q 92	4c
Oranges, navel	lb	0.50	4/93	16r
Peaches	29-oz can	1.36	4Q 92	4c
Peanut butter, creamy, all sizes	lb	1.82	4/93	16r
Pears, Anjou	lb	0.85	4/93	16r
Peas Sweet, Del Monte or Green Giant	15-17 oz can	0.60	4Q 92	4c
Pork, exp	year	111	89	15c
Pork chops, center cut, bone-in	lb	3.17	4/93	16r
Potato chips	16 oz	2.68	4/93	16r
Potatoes, white	lb	0.26	4/93	16r
Potatoes, white or red	10-lb sack	2.76	4Q 92	4c
Poultry, exp	year	84	89	15c
Round roast, graded & ungraded, ex USDA prime & choice	lb	2.88	4/93	16r
Round roast, USDA choice, boneless	lb	2.96	4/93	16r
Sausage, Jimmy Dean, 100% pork	lb	2.42	4Q 92	4c
Shortening, vegetable oil blends	lb	0.79	4/93	16r
Shortening, vegetable, Crisco	3-lb can	2.10	4Q 92	4c

Kansas City, MO, KS - continued

Item	Per	Value	Date	Ref.
Groceries - continued				
Soft drink, Coca Cola	2 liter	1.22	4Q 92	4c
Spaghetti and macaroni	lb	0.76	4/93	16r
Steak, rib eye, USDA choice, boneless	lb	6.29	4/93	16r
Steak, round, USDA choice, boneless	lb	3.24	4/93	16r
Steak, sirloin, graded & ungraded, ex USDA prime & choice	lb	4.00	4/93	16r
Steak, sirloin, USDA choice, bone-in	lb	3.57	4/93	16r
Steak, sirloin, USDA choice, boneless	lb	4.17	4/93	16r
Steak, T-bone	lb	5.09	4Q 92	4c
Steak, T-bone, USDA choice, bone-in	lb	5.60	4/93	16r
Strawberries, dry pint	12 oz	0.90	4/93	16r
Sugar, cane or beet	4 lb	1.48	4Q 92	4c
Sugar, white	lb	0.36	4/93	16r
Sugar, white, 33-80 oz pk	lb	0.35	4/93	16r
Tobacco products, exp	year	262	89	15c
Tomatoes, field grown	lb	0.99	4/93	16r
Tomatoes, Hunt's or Del Monte	14.5-oz can	0.70	4Q 92	4c
Tuna, chunk, light	6.125-6.5 oz can	0.59	4Q 92	4c
Tuna, chunk, light	lb	1.76	4/93	16r
Turkey, frozen, whole	lb	0.91	4/93	16r
Vegetables, fresh, exp	year	120	89	15c
Vegetables, processed, exp	year	70	89	15c
Health Care				
ACCRA Index, Health Care		99.10	4Q 92	4c
Analgesic, Aspirin, Bayer, 325 mg tablets	100	5.56	4Q 92	4c
Childbirth, cesarean, hospital		4688	91	62r
Childbirth, cesarean, physician's fee		2053	91	62r
Childbirth, normal, hospital		2657	91	62r
Childbirth, normal, physician's fee		1492	91	62r
Dentist's fee, adult teeth cleaning and periodic oral exam	visit	41.60	4Q 92	4c
Doctor's fee, routine exam, established patient	visit	35.70	4Q 92	4c
Drugs, exp	year	269	89	15c
Health care, exp	year	1796	89	15c
Health insurance, exp	year	753	89	15c
Hospital care, semiprivate room	day	290.82	90	27c
Hospital care, semiprivate room	day	369.40	4Q 92	4c
Medical insurance premium, per employee, small group comprehensive	month	365.00	10/91	25c
Medical plan per employee	year	3443	91	45r
Medical services, exp	year	703	89	15c
Medical supplies, exp	year	70	89	15c
Mental health care, exp	capita	37.60-53.67	90	38s
Mental health care, exp, state mental health agency	capita	35.47	90	38s
Mental health care, hospital psychiatric services, non-Federal, exp	capita	22.53	88	38s
Mental health care, mental health organization, multiservice, exp	capita	6.98	88	38s
Mental health care, psychiatric hospitals, private, exp	capita	5.96	88	38s
Mental health care, psychiatric out-patient clinics, freestanding, exp	capita	0.79	88	38s
Mental health care, state and county mental hospitals, exp	capita	33.35	88	38s
Mental health care, VA medical centers, exp	capita	3.33	88	38s
Physician fee, family practice, first-visit		76.00	91	62r
Physician fee, family practice, revisit		33.00	91	62r
Physician fee, general practice, first-visit		61.00	91	62r
Physician fee, general practice, revisit		31.00	91	62r
Physician fee, general surgeon, first-visit		65.00	91	62r
Physician fee, general surgeon, revisit		35.00	91	62r
Physician fee, internal medicine, first-visit		91.00	91	62r
Physician fee, internal medicine, revisit		40.00	91	62r
Physician fee, median, neurosurgeon, first-visit		106.00	91	62r

Values are in dollars or fractions of dollars. In the column headed *Ref*, references are shown to sources. Each reference is followed by a letter. These refer to the geographical level for which data were reported: s = State, r = Region, and c = City or metro. The abbreviation *ex* is used to mean *except* or *excluding*; *exp* stands for expenditures. For other abbreviations and further explanations, please see the Introduction.

Kansas City, MO, KS - continued

Item	Per	Value	Date	Ref.
Health Care				
Physician fee, median, nonsurgical specialist, first-visit		90.00	91	62r
Physician fee, median, orthopedic surgeon, first-visit		83.00	91	62r
Physician fee, median, surgical specialist, first-visit		61.00	91	62r
Physician fee, neurosurgeon, revisit		41.00	91	62r
Physician fee, nonsurgical specialist, revisit		40.00	91	62r
Physician fee, obstetrics/gynecology, first-visit		61.00	91	62r
Physician fee, obstetrics/gynecology, revisit		40.00	91	62r
Physician fee, orthopedic surgeon, revisit		41.00	91	62r
Physician fee, pediatrician, first-visit		46.00	91	62r
Physician fee, pediatrician, revisit		33.00	91	62r
Physician fee, surgical specialist, revisit		36.00	91	62r
Substance abuse, hospital ancillary charge	incident	1380	90	70s
Substance abuse, hospital physician charge	incident	560	90	70s
Substance abuse, hospital room and board	incident	5670	90	70s
Household Goods				
Appliance repair, home, service call, washing machine	min labor charge	34.64	4Q 92	4c
Appliances, major, exp	year	161	89	15c
Appliances, small, exp	year	54	89	15c
Equipment, misc., exp	year	346	89	15c
Floor coverings, exp	year	14	89	15c
Furnishings and equipment, exp	year	1045	89	15c
Furniture, exp	year	378	89	15c
Household products, misc., exp	year	146	89	15c
Household textiles, exp	year	91	89	15c
Housekeeping supplies, exp	year	363	89	15c
Laundry and cleaning supplies, exp	year	73	89	15c
Laundry detergent, Tide Ultra, Bold, or Cheer	42 oz	3.16	4Q 92	4c
Tissues, facial, Kleenex brand	175-count box	1.20	4Q 92	4c
TVs, radios, sound equipment, exp	year	397	89	15c
Housing				
ACCRA Index, Housing		96.20	4Q 92	4c
Dwellings, exp	year	3151	89	15c
Home, median price	unit	79.50		26c
House, 1,800 sq ft, 8,000 sq ft lot, new, urban	total	99000	4Q 92	4c
House payment, principal and interest, 25% down payment	month	551	4Q 92	4c
Household expenses, misc.	year	144	89	15c
Household operations, exp	year	357	89	15c
Housing, exp	year	8510	89	15c
Lodging, exp	year	454	89	15c
Maintenance, repairs, insurance, and other, exp	year	637	89	15c
Mortgage interest, exp	year	2229	89	15c
Mortgage rate, incl. points & origination fee, 30-year fixed or adjustable rate	percent	8.12	4Q 92	4c
Rent, apartment, 2 bedrooms - 1-1/2 to 2 baths, unfurnished, 950 sq ft, water	month	567	4Q 92	4c
Rental unit, 1 bedroom	month	416	93	23c
Rental unit, 2 bedroom	month	489	93	23c
Rental unit, 3 bedroom	month	611	93	23c
Rental unit, 4 bedroom	month	685	93	23c
Rental unit, efficiency	month	342	93	23c
Rented dwellings, exp	year	1177	89	15c
Shelter, exp	year	4781	89	15c
Insurance and Pensions				
Auto insurance, private passenger	year	551.85	91	63s
Insurance, life and other personal, exp	year	386	89	15c
Insurance and pensions, personal, exp	year	2616	89	15c

Kansas City, MO, KS - continued

Item	Per	Value	Date	Ref.
Insurance and Pensions - continued				
Pensions and social security, exp	year	2230	89	15c
Vehicle insurance	year	565	89	15c
Personal Goods				
Products and services, exp	year	293	89	15c
Shampoo, Alberto VO5	15 oz	1.40	4Q 92	4c
Toothpaste, Crest or Colgate	6-7 oz	2.14	4Q 92	4c
Personal Services				
Dry cleaning, man's 2-piece suit		5.93	4Q 92	4c
Haircare, woman's shampoo, trim and blow-dry		15.00	4Q 92	4c
Haircut, man's barbershop, no styling		9.00	4Q 92	4c
Services, exp	year	212	89	15c
Restaurant Food				
Chicken, fried, thigh and drumstick		1.99	4Q 92	4c
Hamburger with cheese	1/4 lb	1.88	4Q 92	4c
Pizza, Pizza Hut or Pizza Inn, cheese, thin crust	12-13 in	7.59	4Q 92	4c
Taxes				
Property tax, exp	year	285	89	15c
Tax, cigarette	pack	13	91	77s
Tax, gasoline	gal	13	91	77s
Taxes, state	capita	969	91	77s
Transportation				
ACCRA Index, Transportation		100.20	4Q 92	4c
Auto rental, average	day	45.50	6/91	60c
Bus fare	one-way	0.90	3/93	2c
Bus fare, up to 10 miles	one-way	0.90	4Q 92	4c
Driver's license fee		7.50	12/90	43s
Limo fare, airport-city, average	day	9.00	6/91	60c
Public transit, exp	year	207	89	15c
Taxi fare, airport-city, average	day	24.00	6/91	60c
Tire balance, computer or spin balance, front	wheel	6.80	4Q 92	4c
Vehicle expenses, misc.	year	1806	89	15c
Vehicle finance charges	year	339	89	15c
Vehicle maintenance	year	545	89	15c
Vehicle registration and license plate	year	1.65-51.15	93	41s
Vehicle rental and license	year	357	89	15c
Travel				
Breakfast	day	5.25	6/91	60c
Dinner	day	19.06	6/91	60c
Lodging	day	113.38	91	60c
Lunch	day	9.76	6/91	60c
Utilities				
ACCRA Index, Utilities		92.30	4Q 92	4c
Electricity	mil Btu	18.94	90	64s
Electricity, exp	year	765	89	15c
Electricity, partial electric and other energy, 1,800 sq ft living area new home	month	55.92	4Q 92	4c
Electricity, winter, 250 KWh	month	25.59	92	55c
Electricity, winter, 500 KWh	month	45.16	92	55c
Electricity, winter, 750 KWh	month	64.73	92	55c
Electricity, winter, 1000 KWh	month	84.28	92	55c
Utilities, fuels, public services, exp	year	1964	89	15c
Water, public services, exp	year	258	89	15c

Kearney, NE

Item	Per	Value	Date	Ref.
Composite ACCRA index		87.60	4Q 92	4c
Alcoholic Beverages				
Beer, Miller Lite or Budweiser, 12-oz containers	6 pack	4.41	4Q 92	4c
Liquor, J & B Scotch	750 ml	18.45	4Q 92	4c
Wine, Gallo Chablis blanc, 1.5 liter	bottle	5.53	4Q 92	4c

Values are in dollars or fractions of dollars. In the column headed *Ref*, references are shown to sources. Each reference is followed by a letter. These refer to the geographical level for which data were reported: s=State, r=Region, and c=City or metro. The abbreviation *ex* is used to mean *except* or *excluding*; *exp* stands for expenditures. For other abbreviations and further explanations, please see the Introduction.

Kearney, NE - continued

Item	Per	Value	Date	Ref.
Clothing				
Jeans, man's denim		25.00	4Q 92	4c
Shirt, man's dress shirt		22.24	4Q 92	4c
Undervest, boy's size 10-14, cotton	3	3.34	4Q 92	4c
Communications				
Newspaper subscription, daily and Sunday home delivery, large-city	month	8.70	4Q 92	4c
Telephone bill, family of four	month	15.44	4Q 92	4c
Energy and Fuels				
Energy, combined forms, 1,800 sq ft heating area	month	102.48	4Q 92	4c
Energy, exc electricity, 1,800 sq ft heating area	month	40.40	4Q 92	4c
Gasoline, motor	gal	1.22	4Q 92	4c
Entertainment				
Bowling, evening rate	game	2.00	4Q 92	4c
Monopoly game, Parker Brothers', No. 9		11.98	4Q 92	4c
Movie	admission	4.75	4Q 92	4c
Tennis balls, yellow, Wilson or Penn, 3	can	2.06	4Q 92	4c
Goods and Services				
ACCRA Index, Miscellaneous Goods and Services		91.50	4Q 92	4c
Groceries				
ACCRA Index, Groceries		103.80	4Q 92	4c
Babyfood, strained vegetables, lowest price	4-4.5 oz jar	0.38	4Q 92	4c
Bananas	lb	0.47	4Q 92	4c
Bread, white	24 oz	0.94	4Q 92	4c
Cheese, Kraft grated Parmesan	8-oz canister	3.77	4Q 92	4c
Chicken, fryer, whole	lb	0.75	4Q 92	4c
Cigarettes, Winston	carton	18.31	4Q 92	4c
Coffee, vacuum-packed	13-oz can	1.98	4Q 92	4c
Corn, frozen	10 oz	0.67	4Q 92	4c
Corn Flakes, Kellogg's or Post Toasties	18 oz	2.09	4Q 92	4c
Eggs, Grade A large	doz	0.85	4Q 92	4c
Ground beef or hamburger	lb	1.24	4Q 92	4c
Lettuce, iceberg	head	0.84	4Q 92	4c
Margarine, Blue Bonnet or Parkay cubes	lb	0.67	4Q 92	4c
Milk, whole	1/2 gal	1.35	4Q 92	4c
Orange juice, Minute Maid frozen	12-oz can	1.53	4Q 92	4c
Peaches	29-oz can	1.50	4Q 92	4c
Peas Sweet, Del Monte or Green Giant	15-17 oz can	0.60	4Q 92	4c
Potatoes, white or red	10-lb sack	2.09	4Q 92	4c
Sausage, Jimmy Dean, 100% pork	lb	2.82	4Q 92	4c
Shortening, vegetable, Crisco	3-lb can	2.57	4Q 92	4c
Soft drink, Coca Cola	2 liter	1.62	4Q 92	4c
Steak, T-bone	lb	4.36	4Q 92	4c
Sugar, cane or beet	4 lb	1.45	4Q 92	4c
Tomatoes, Hunt's or Del Monte	14.5-oz can	0.81	4Q 92	4c
Tuna, chunk, light	6.125-6.5 oz can	0.61	4Q 92	4c
Health Care				
ACCRA Index, Health Care		78.40	4Q 92	4c
Analgesic, Aspirin, Bayer, 325 mg tablets	100	4.26	4Q 92	4c
Dentist's fee, adult teeth cleaning and periodic oral exam	visit	36.00	4Q 92	4c
Doctor's fee, routine exam, established patient	visit	29.00	4Q 92	4c
Hospital care, semiprivate room	day	245.00	4Q 92	4c

Kearney, NE - continued

Item	Per	Value	Date	Ref.
Household Goods				
Appliance repair, home, service call, washing machine	min labor charge	26.32	4Q 92	4c
Laundry detergent, Tide Ultra, Bold, or Cheer	42 oz	3.64	4Q 92	4c
Tissues, facial, Kleenex brand	175-count box	1.10	4Q 92	4c
Housing				
ACCRA Index, Housing		72.20	4Q 92	4c
House, 1,800 sq ft, 8,000 sq ft lot, new, urban	total	78800	4Q 92	4c
House payment, principal and interest, 25% down payment	month	438	4Q 92	4c
Mortgage rate, incl. points & origination fee, 30-year fixed or adjustable rate	percent	8.10	4Q 92	4c
Rent, apartment, 2 bedrooms - 1-1/2 to 2 baths, unfurnished, 950 sq ft, water	month	369	4Q 92	4c
Personal Goods				
Shampoo, Alberto VO5	15 oz	1.26	4Q 92	4c
Toothpaste, Crest or Colgate	6-7 oz	1.84	4Q 92	4c
Personal Services				
Dry cleaning, man's 2-piece suit		7.38	4Q 92	4c
Haircare, woman's shampoo, trim and blow-dry		14.40	4Q 92	4c
Haircut, man's barbershop, no styling		7.10	4Q 92	4c
Restaurant Food				
Chicken, fried, thigh and drumstick		1.99	4Q 92	4c
Hamburger with cheese	1/4 lb	1.80	4Q 92	4c
Pizza, Pizza Hut or Pizza Inn, cheese, thin crust	12-13 in	7.49	4Q 92	4c
Transportation				
ACCRA Index, Transportation		96.70	4Q 92	4c
Tire balance, computer or spin balance, front	wheel	5.56	4Q 92	4c
Utilities				
ACCRA Index, Utilities		92.40	4Q 92	4c
Electricity, partial electric and other energy, 1,800 sq ft living area new home	month	62.08	4Q 92	4c

Kennett, MO

Item	Per	Value	Date	Ref.
Composite ACCRA index		83.30	4Q 92	4c
Alcoholic Beverages				
Beer, Miller Lite or Budweiser, 12-oz containers	6 pack	3.84	4Q 92	4c
Liquor, J & B Scotch	750 ml	15.77	4Q 92	4c
Wine, Gallo Chablis blanc, 1.5 liter	bottle	4.60	4Q 92	4c
Clothing				
Jeans, man's denim		26.50	4Q 92	4c
Shirt, man's dress shirt		24.00	4Q 92	4c
Undervest, boy's size 10-14, cotton	3	3.18	4Q 92	4c
Communications				
Newspaper subscription, daily and Sunday home delivery, large-city	month	12.86	4Q 92	4c
Telephone, flat rate	month	9.10	91	11c
Telephone bill, family of four	month	16.45	4Q 92	4c
Energy and Fuels				
Energy, combined forms, 1,800 sq ft heating area	month	68.51	4Q 92	4c
Energy, exc electricity, 1,800 sq ft heating area	month	37.04	4Q 92	4c
Gasoline, motor	gal	1.06	4Q 92	4c
Entertainment				
Bowling, evening rate	game	1.60	4Q 92	4c
Monopoly game, Parker Brothers', No. 9		9.47	4Q 92	4c

Values are in dollars or fractions of dollars. In the column headed *Ref*, references are shown to sources. Each reference is followed by a letter. These refer to the geographical level for which data were reported: s = State, r = Region, and c = City or metro. The abbreviation *ex* is used to mean *except* or *excluding*; *exp* stands for expenditures. For other abbreviations and further explanations, please see the Introduction.

Kennett, MO - continued

Item	Per	Value	Date	Ref.
Entertainment				
Movie	admis-sion	4.00	4Q 92	4c
Tennis balls, yellow, Wilson or Penn, 3	can	1.92	4Q 92	4c
Goods and Services				
ACCRA Index, Miscellaneous Goods and Services		90.40	4Q 92	4c
Groceries				
ACCRA Index, Groceries		100.40	4Q 92	4c
Babyfood, strained vegetables, lowest price	4-4.5 oz jar	0.38	4Q 92	4c
Bananas	lb	0.46	4Q 92	4c
Bread, white	24 oz	0.59	4Q 92	4c
Cheese, Kraft grated Parmesan	8-oz canis-ter	3.57	4Q 92	4c
Chicken, fryer, whole	lb	0.68	4Q 92	4c
Cigarettes, Winston	carton	15.76	4Q 92	4c
Coffee, vacuum-packed	13-oz can	2.12	4Q 92	4c
Corn, frozen	10 oz	0.81	4Q 92	4c
Corn Flakes, Kellogg's or Post Toasties	18 oz	2.26	4Q 92	4c
Eggs, Grade A large	doz	0.71	4Q 92	4c
Ground beef or hamburger	lb	1.45	4Q 92	4c
Lettuce, iceberg	head	0.95	4Q 92	4c
Margarine, Blue Bonnet or Parkay cubes	lb	0.74	4Q 92	4c
Milk, whole	1/2 gal	1.44	4Q 92	4c
Orange juice, Minute Maid frozen	12-oz can	1.62	4Q 92	4c
Peaches	29-oz can	1.47	4Q 92	4c
Peas Sweet, Del Monte or Green Giant	15-17 oz can	0.72	4Q 92	4c
Potatoes, white or red	10-lb sack	1.95	4Q 92	4c
Sausage, Jimmy Dean, 100% pork	lb	2.65	4Q 92	4c
Shortening, vegetable, Crisco	3-lb can	2.52	4Q 92	4c
Soft drink, Coca Cola	2 liter	1.09	4Q 92	4c
Steak, T-bone	lb	4.29	4Q 92	4c
Sugar, cane or beet	4 lb	1.57	4Q 92	4c
Tomatoes, Hunt's or Del Monte	14.5-oz can	0.78	4Q 92	4c
Tuna, chunk, light	6.125-6.5 oz can	0.73	4Q 92	4c
Health Care				
ACCRA Index, Health Care		85.80	4Q 92	4c
Analgesic, Aspirin, Bayer, 325 mg tablets	100	3.84	4Q 92	4c
Dentist's fee, adult teeth cleaning and periodic oral exam	visit	46.50	4Q 92	4c
Doctor's fee, routine exam, established patient	visit	29.33	4Q 92	4c
Hospital care, semiprivate room	day	245.00	4Q 92	4c
Household Goods				
Appliance repair, home, service call, washing machine	min labor charge	23.33	4Q 92	4c
Laundry detergent, Tide Ultra, Bold, or Cheer	42 oz	3.89	4Q 92	4c
Tissues, facial, Kleenex brand	175-count box	1.29	4Q 92	4c
Housing				
ACCRA Index, Housing		73.60	4Q 92	4c
House, 1,800 sq ft, 8,000 sq ft lot, new, urban	total	82500	4Q 92	4c
House payment, principal and interest, 25% down payment	month	457	4Q 92	4c

Kennett, MO - continued

Item	Per	Value	Date	Ref.
Housing - continued				
Mortgage rate, incl. points & origination fee, 30-year fixed or adjustable rate	per-cent	8.06	4Q 92	4c
Personal Goods				
Shampoo, Alberto VO5	15 oz	0.98	4Q 92	4c
Toothpaste, Crest or Colgate	6-7 oz	1.67	4Q 92	4c
Personal Services				
Dry cleaning, man's 2-piece suit		6.00	4Q 92	4c
Haircare, woman's shampoo, trim and blow-dry		14.00	4Q 92	4c
Haircut, man's barbershop, no styling		7.00	4Q 92	4c
Restaurant Food				
Chicken, fried, thigh and drumstick		2.59	4Q 92	4c
Hamburger with cheese	1/4 lb	1.79	4Q 92	4c
Pizza, Pizza Hut or Pizza Inn, cheese, thin crust	12-13 in	9.39	4Q 92	4c
Transportation				
ACCRA Index, Transportation		78.70	4Q 92	4c
Tire balance, computer or spin balance, front	wheel	4.16	4Q 92	4c
Utilities				
ACCRA Index, Utilities		64.90	4Q 92	4c
Electricity, partial electric and other energy, 1,800 sq ft living area new home	month	31.47	4Q 92	4c

Kenosha, WI

Item	Per	Value	Date	Ref.
Child Care				
Child care fee, average, center	hour	1.63	90	65r
Child care fee, average, nonregulated family day care	hour	1.83	90	65r
Child care fee, average, regulated family day care	hour	1.42	90	65r
Communications				
Long-distance telephone service, day, initial minute, 0-100 miles	min	0.15-0.29	91	12s
Long-distance telephone service, day, additional minute, 0-100 miles	min	0.10-0.27	91	12s
Education				
Board, 4-yr private college/university	year	1533	91	22s
Board, 4-yr public college/university	year	1404	91	22s
Expenditures, local gov't, public elementary/secondary	pupil	5972	92	20s
Room, 4-year private college/university	year	1256	91	22s
Room, 4-year public college/university	year	1416	91	22s
Tuition, 2-year private college/university	year	4768	91	22s
Tuition, 2-year public college/university	year	1234	91	22s
Tuition, 4-year private college/university	year	8237	91	22s
Tuition, 4-year public college/university, in-state	year	1951	91	22s
Energy and Fuels				
Coal	mil Btu	1.41	90	64s
Energy	mil Btu	8.27	90	64s
Energy exp/householder, 1-family unit	year	471	90	28r
Energy exp/householder, <1,000 sq ft heating area	year	430	90	28r
Energy exp/householder, 1,000-1,999 sq ft heating area	year	481	90	28r
Energy exp/householder, 2,000+ sq ft heating area	year	473	90	28r
Energy exp/householder, mobile home	year	430	90	28r
Energy exp/householder, multifamily	year	461	90	28r
Gas, natural	mil Btu	4.56	90	64s
Gas, natural	000 cu ft	5.61	91	46s
Gas, natural, exp	year	605	91	46s
Gasoline, unleaded regular	mil Btu	9.38	90	64s

Values are in dollars or fractions of dollars. In the column headed *Ref*, references are shown to sources. Each reference is followed by a letter. These refer to the geographical level for which data were reported: s = State, r = Region, and c = City or metro. The abbreviation *ex* is used to mean *except* or *excluding*; *exp* stands for expenditures. For other abbreviations and further explanations, please see the Introduction.

Kenosha, WI - continued

Item	Per	Value	Date	Ref.
Entertainment				
Miniature golf admission	adult	6.18	92	1r
Miniature golf admission	child	5.14	92	1r
Waterpark admission	adult	11.00	92	1r
Waterpark admission	child	8.55	92	1r
Funerals				
Casket, 18-gauge steel, velvet interior		1926.72	91	24r
Cosmetology, hair care, etc.		97.64	91	24r
Embalming		249.14	91	24r
Facility use for ceremony		208.59	91	24r
Hearse, local		130.12	91	24r
Limousine, local		104.66	91	24r
Remains to funeral home, transfer		93.61	91	24r
Service charge, professional		724.62	91	24r
Vault, concrete, non-metallic liner		734.53	91	24r
Viewing facilities, use		236.06	91	24r
Groceries				
Apples, Red Delicious	lb	0.77	4/93	16r
Bacon	lb	1.85	4/93	16r
Bananas	lb	0.46	4/93	16r
Beef, stew, boneless	lb	2.53	4/93	16r
Bologna, all beef or mixed	lb	2.19	4/93	16r
Bread, white, pan	lb	0.78	4/93	16r
Butter	lb	1.50	4/93	16r
Cabbage	lb	0.40	4/93	16r
Carrots, short trimmed and topped	lb	0.45	4/93	16r
Cheese, Cheddar	lb	3.47	4/93	16r
Chicken, fresh, whole	lb	0.84	4/93	16r
Chicken breast, bone-in	lb	1.94	4/93	16r
Chicken legs, bone-in	lb	1.02	4/93	16r
Chuck roast, graded and ungraded, ex USDA prime and choice	lb	2.43	4/93	16r
Chuck roast, USDA choice, bone-in	lb	2.11	4/93	16r
Chuck roast, USDA choice, boneless	lb	2.44	4/93	16r
Coffee, 100% ground roast, all sizes	lb	2.47	4/93	16r
Cookies, chocolate chip	lb	2.73	4/93	16r
Eggs, Grade A large	doz	0.93	4/93	16r
Flour, white, all purpose	lb	0.21	4/93	16r
Grapefruit	lb	0.45	4/93	16r
Grapes, Thompson Seedless	lb	1.46	4/93	16r
Ground beef, 100% beef	lb	1.63	4/93	16r
Ground beef, lean and extra lean	lb	2.08	4/93	16r
Ground chuck, 100% beef	lb	1.94	4/93	16r
Ham, boneless, excluding canned	lb	2.21	4/93	16r
Honey, jar	8 oz	0.97-1.25	92	5r
Honey, jar	lb	1.25-2.25	92	5r
Honey, squeeze bear	12-oz	1.25-1.99	92	5r
Ice cream, prepackaged, bulk, regular	1/2 gal	2.41	4/93	16r
Lemons	lb	0.82	4/93	16r
Lettuce, iceberg	lb	0.83	4/93	16r
Margarine, stick	lb	0.77	4/93	16r
Oranges, navel	lb	0.50	4/93	16r
Peanut butter, creamy, all sizes	lb	1.82	4/93	16r
Pears, Anjou	lb	0.85	4/93	16r
Pork chops, center cut, bone-in	lb	3.17	4/93	16r
Potato chips	16 oz	2.68	4/93	16r
Potatoes, white	lb	0.26	4/93	16r
Round roast, graded & ungraded, ex USDA prime & choice	lb	2.88	4/93	16r
Round roast, USDA choice, boneless	lb	2.96	4/93	16r
Shortening, vegetable oil blends	lb	0.79	4/93	16r
Spaghetti and macaroni	lb	0.76	4/93	16r
Steak, rib eye, USDA choice, boneless	lb	6.29	4/93	16r
Steak, round, USDA choice, boneless	lb	3.24	4/93	16r
Steak, sirloin, graded & ungraded, ex USDA prime & choice	lb	4.00	4/93	16r
Steak, sirloin, USDA choice, bone-in	lb	3.57	4/93	16r
Steak, sirloin, USDA choice, boneless	lb	4.17	4/93	16r
Steak, T-bone, USDA choice, bone-in	lb	5.60	4/93	16r
Strawberries, dry pint	12 oz	0.90	4/93	16r
Sugar, white	lb	0.36	4/93	16r
Sugar, white, 33-80 oz pk	lb	0.35	4/93	16r

Kenosha, WI - continued

Item	Per	Value	Date	Ref.
Groceries - continued				
Tomatoes, field grown	lb	0.99	4/93	16r
Tuna, chunk, light	lb	1.76	4/93	16r
Turkey, frozen, whole	lb	0.91	4/93	16r
Health Care				
Childbirth, cesarean, hospital		4688	91	62r
Childbirth, cesarean, physician's fee		2053	91	62r
Childbirth, normal, hospital		2657	91	62r
Childbirth, normal, physician's fee		1492	91	62r
Medical plan per employee	year	3443	91	45r
Mental health care, exp	capita	28.84-	90	38s
		37.59		
Mental health care, exp, state mental health agency	capita	36.62	90	38s
Mental health care, hospital psychiatric services, non-Federal, exp	capita	13.05	88	38s
Mental health care, mental health organization, multiservice, exp	capita	10.93	88	38s
Mental health care, psychiatric hospitals, private, exp	capita	8.71	88	38s
Mental health care, psychiatric out-patient clinics, freestanding, exp	capita	5.33	88	38s
Mental health care, psychiatric partial-care organizations, freestanding, exp	capita	0.20	88	38s
Mental health care, state and county mental hospitals, exp	capita	28.29	88	38s
Mental health care, VA medical centers, exp	capita	7.57	88	38s
Physician fee, family practice, first-visit		76.00	91	62r
Physician fee, family practice, revisit		33.00	91	62r
Physician fee, general practice, first-visit		61.00	91	62r
Physician fee, general practice, revisit		31.00	91	62r
Physician fee, general surgeon, first-visit		65.00	91	62r
Physician fee, general surgeon, revisit		35.00	91	62r
Physician fee, internal medicine, first-visit		91.00	91	62r
Physician fee, internal medicine, revisit		40.00	91	62r
Physician fee, median, neurosurgeon, first-visit		106.00	91	62r
Physician fee, median, nonsurgical specialist, first-visit		90.00	91	62r
Physician fee, median, orthopedic surgeon, first-visit		83.00	91	62r
Physician fee, median, surgical specialist, first-visit		61.00	91	62r
Physician fee, neurosurgeon, revisit		41.00	91	62r
Physician fee, nonsurgical specialist, revisit		40.00	91	62r
Physician fee, obstetrics/gynecology, first-visit		61.00	91	62r
Physician fee, obstetrics/gynecology, revisit		40.00	91	62r
Physician fee, orthopedic surgeon, revisit		41.00	91	62r
Physician fee, pediatrician, first-visit		46.00	91	62r
Physician fee, pediatrician, revisit		33.00	91	62r
Physician fee, surgical specialist, revisit		36.00	91	62r
Substance abuse, hospital ancillary charge	incident	960	90	70s
Substance abuse, hospital physician charge	incident	470	90	70s
Substance abuse, hospital room and board	incident	3980	90	70s
Insurance and Pensions				
Auto insurance, private passenger	year	510.11	91	63s
Taxes				
Tax, cigarette	pack	38	91	77s
Tax, gasoline	gal	22.20	91	77s
Taxes, state	capita	1416	91	77s
Transportation				
Driver's license fee		9.00	12/90	43s
Utilities				
Electricity	mil Btu	15.77	90	64s

Values are in dollars or fractions of dollars. In the column headed *Ref*, references are shown to sources. Each reference is followed by a letter. These refer to the geographical level for which data were reported: s=State, r=Region, and c=City or metro. The abbreviation *ex* is used to mean *except* or *excluding*; *exp* stands for expenditures. For other abbreviations and further explanations, please see the Introduction.

Kerrville, TX

Item	Per	Value	Date	Ref.
Composite ACCRA index		94.30	4Q 92	4c
Alcoholic Beverages				
Beer, Miller Lite or Budweiser, 12-oz containers	6 pack	3.79	4Q 92	4c
Liquor, J & B Scotch	750 ml	16.03	4Q 92	4c
Wine, Gallo Chablis blanc, 1.5 liter	bottle	4.70	4Q 92	4c
Clothing				
Jeans, man's denim		24.66	4Q 92	4c
Shirt, man's dress shirt		23.67	4Q 92	4c
Undervest, boy's size 10-14, cotton	3	4.89	4Q 92	4c
Communications				
Newspaper subscription, daily and Sunday home delivery, large-city	month	7.60	4Q 92	4c
Telephone bill, family of four	month	11.66	4Q 92	4c
Energy and Fuels				
Energy, combined forms, 1,800 sq ft heating area	month	126.39	4Q 92	4c
Energy, exc electricity, 1,800 sq ft heating area	month	9.02	4Q 92	4c
Gasoline, motor	gal	1.16	4Q 92	4c
Entertainment				
Bowling, evening rate	game	1.85	4Q 92	4c
Monopoly game, Parker Brothers', No. 9		10.96	4Q 92	4c
Movie	admission	4.50	4Q 92	4c
Tennis balls, yellow, Wilson or Penn, 3	can	1.97	4Q 92	4c
Goods and Services				
ACCRA Index, Miscellaneous Goods and Services		97.20	4Q 92	4c
Groceries				
ACCRA Index, Groceries		97.70	4Q 92	4c
Babyfood, strained vegetables, lowest price	4-4.5 oz jar	0.25	4Q 92	4c
Bananas	lb	0.38	4Q 92	4c
Bread, white	24 oz	0.72	4Q 92	4c
Cheese, Kraft grated Parmesan	8-oz canister	3.22	4Q 92	4c
Chicken, fryer, whole	lb	0.66	4Q 92	4c
Cigarettes, Winston	carton	19.42	4Q 92	4c
Coffee, vacuum-packed	13-oz can	1.84	4Q 92	4c
Corn, frozen	10 oz	0.69	4Q 92	4c
Corn Flakes, Kellogg's or Post Toasties	18 oz	1.95	4Q 92	4c
Eggs, Grade A large	doz	0.94	4Q 92	4c
Ground beef or hamburger	lb	1.42	4Q 92	4c
Lettuce, iceberg	head	0.83	4Q 92	4c
Margarine, Blue Bonnet or Parkay cubes	lb	0.59	4Q 92	4c
Milk, whole	1/2 gal	1.50	4Q 92	4c
Orange juice, Minute Maid frozen	12-oz can	1.41	4Q 92	4c
Peaches	29-oz can	1.41	4Q 92	4c
Peas Sweet, Del Monte or Green Giant	15-17 oz can	0.43	4Q 92	4c
Potatoes, white or red	10-lb sack	2.36	4Q 92	4c
Sausage, Jimmy Dean, 100% pork	lb	2.61	4Q 92	4c
Shortening, vegetable, Crisco	3-lb can	1.98	4Q 92	4c
Soft drink, Coca Cola	2 liter	1.15	4Q 92	4c
Steak, T-bone	lb	5.42	4Q 92	4c
Sugar, cane or beet	4 lb	1.45	4Q 92	4c
Tomatoes, Hunt's or Del Monte	14.5-oz can	0.65	4Q 92	4c
Tuna, chunk, light	6.125-6.5 oz can	0.59	4Q 92	4c

Kerrville, TX - continued

Item	Per	Value	Date	Ref.
Health Care				
ACCRA Index, Health Care		79.70	4Q 92	4c
Analgesic, Aspirin, Bayer, 325 mg tablets	100	5.34	4Q 92	4c
Dentist's fee, adult teeth cleaning and periodic oral exam	visit	35.33	4Q 92	4c
Doctor's fee, routine exam, established patient	visit	32.00	4Q 92	4c
Hospital care, semiprivate room	day	185.00	4Q 92	4c
Household Goods				
Appliance repair, home, service call, washing machine	min labor charge	35.00	4Q 92	4c
Laundry detergent, Tide Ultra, Bold, or Cheer	42 oz	2.99	4Q 92	4c
Tissues, facial, Kleenex brand	175-count box	1.02	4Q 92	4c
Housing				
ACCRA Index, Housing		85.00	4Q 92	4c
House, 1,800 sq ft, 8,000 sq ft lot, new, urban	total	91800	4Q 92	4c
House payment, principal and interest, 25% down payment	month	510	4Q 92	4c
Mortgage rate, incl. points & origination fee, 30-year fixed or adjustable rate	percent	8.11	4Q 92	4c
Rent, apartment, 2 bedrooms - 1-1/2 to 2 baths, unfurnished, 950 sq ft, water	month	448	4Q 92	4c
Personal Goods				
Shampoo, Alberto VO5	15 oz	1.22	4Q 92	4c
Toothpaste, Crest or Colgate	6-7 oz	2.12	4Q 92	4c
Personal Services				
Dry cleaning, man's 2-piece suit		5.85	4Q 92	4c
Haircare, woman's shampoo, trim and blow-dry		18.17	4Q 92	4c
Haircut, man's barbershop, no styling		7.00	4Q 92	4c
Restaurant Food				
Chicken, fried, thigh and drumstick		1.99	4Q 92	4c
Hamburger with cheese	1/4 lb	1.89	4Q 92	4c
Pizza, Pizza Hut or Pizza Inn, cheese, thin crust	12-13 in	9.69	4Q 92	4c
Transportation				
ACCRA Index, Transportation		98.70	4Q 92	4c
Tire balance, computer or spin balance, front	wheel	6.17	4Q 92	4c
Utilities				
ACCRA Index, Utilities		110.20	4Q 92	4c
Electricity, partial electric and other energy, 1,800 sq ft living area new home	month	117.37	4Q 92	4c

Ketchikan, AK

Item	Per	Value	Date	Ref.
Composite ACCRA index		145.00	4Q 92	4c
Alcoholic Beverages				
Beer, Miller Lite or Budweiser, 12-oz containers	6 pack	4.80	4Q 92	4c
Liquor, J & B Scotch	750 ml	21.25	4Q 92	4c
Wine, Gallo Chablis blanc, 1.5 liter	bottle	6.98	4Q 92	4c
Clothing				
Jeans, man's denim		32.58	4Q 92	4c
Shirt, man's dress shirt		25.31	4Q 92	4c
Undervest, boy's size 10-14, cotton	3	5.24	4Q 92	4c
Communications				
Newspaper subscription, daily and Sunday home delivery, large-city	month	23.30	4Q 92	4c
Telephone bill, family of four	month	12.48	4Q 92	4c

Values are in dollars or fractions of dollars. In the column headed *Ref*, references are shown to sources. Each reference is followed by a letter. These refer to the geographical level for which data were reported: s = State, r = Region, and c = City or metro. The abbreviation *ex* is used to mean *except* or *excluding*; *exp* stands for expenditures. For other abbreviations and further explanations, please see the Introduction.

341

Ketchikan, AK - continued

Item	Per	Value	Date	Ref.
Energy and Fuels				
Energy, combined forms, 1,800 sq ft heating area	month	192.99	4Q 92	4c
Energy, exc electricity, 1,800 sq ft heating area	month	99.50	4Q 92	4c
Gasoline, motor	gal	1.57	4Q 92	4c
Entertainment				
Bowling, evening rate	game	3.00	4Q 92	4c
Monopoly game, Parker Brothers', No. 9		20.49	4Q 92	4c
Movie	admission	7.50	4Q 92	4c
Tennis balls, yellow, Wilson or Penn, 3	can	4.80	4Q 92	4c
Goods and Services				
ACCRA Index, Miscellaneous Goods and Services		135.70	4Q 92	4c
Groceries				
ACCRA Index, Groceries		136.40	4Q 92	4c
Babyfood, strained vegetables, lowest price	4-4.5 oz jar	0.52	4Q 92	4c
Bananas	lb	0.81	4Q 92	4c
Bread, white	24 oz	1.01	4Q 92	4c
Cheese, Kraft grated Parmesan	8-oz canister	4.05	4Q 92	4c
Chicken, fryer, whole	lb	1.10	4Q 92	4c
Cigarettes, Winston	carton	20.68	4Q 92	4c
Coffee, vacuum-packed	13-oz can	2.79	4Q 92	4c
Corn, frozen	10 oz	1.05	4Q 92	4c
Corn Flakes, Kellogg's or Post Toasties	18 oz	2.55	4Q 92	4c
Eggs, Grade A large	doz	1.27	4Q 92	4c
Ground beef or hamburger	lb	1.74	4Q 92	4c
Lettuce, iceberg	head	1.23	4Q 92	4c
Margarine, Blue Bonnet or Parkay cubes	lb	0.72	4Q 92	4c
Milk, whole	1/2 gal	2.08	4Q 92	4c
Orange juice, Minute Maid frozen	12-oz can	1.81	4Q 92	4c
Peaches	29-oz can	1.94	4Q 92	4c
Peas Sweet, Del Monte or Green Giant	15-17 oz can	0.82	4Q 92	4c
Potatoes, white or red	10-lb sack	2.74	4Q 92	4c
Sausage, Jimmy Dean, 100% pork	lb	3.51	4Q 92	4c
Shortening, vegetable, Crisco	3-lb can	3.18	4Q 92	4c
Soft drink, Coca Cola	2 liter	1.98	4Q 92	4c
Steak, T-bone	lb	6.26	4Q 92	4c
Sugar, cane or beet	4 lb	2.54	4Q 92	4c
Tomatoes, Hunt's or Del Monte	14.5-oz can	0.80	4Q 92	4c
Tuna, chunk, light	6.125-6.5 oz can	0.93	4Q 92	4c
Health Care				
ACCRA Index, Health Care		206.20	4Q 92	4c
Analgesic, Aspirin, Bayer, 325 mg tablets	100	8.16	4Q 92	4c
Dentist's fee, adult teeth cleaning and periodic oral exam	visit	103.00	4Q 92	4c
Doctor's fee, routine exam, established patient	visit	88.00	4Q 92	4c
Hospital care, semiprivate room	day	455.00	4Q 92	4c
Household Goods				
Appliance repair, home, service call, washing machine	min labor charge	48.00	4Q 92	4c
Laundry detergent, Tide Ultra, Bold, or Cheer	42 oz	3.74	4Q 92	4c

Ketchikan, AK - continued

Item	Per	Value	Date	Ref.
Household Goods - continued				
Tissues, facial, Kleenex brand	175-count box	1.60	4Q 92	4c
Housing				
ACCRA Index, Housing		146.70	4Q 92	4c
House, 1,800 sq ft, 8,000 sq ft lot, new, urban	total	163333	4Q 92	4c
House payment, principal and interest, 25% down payment	month	911	4Q 92	4c
Mortgage rate, incl. points & origination fee, 30-year fixed or adjustable rate	percent	8.14	4Q 92	4c
Personal Goods				
Shampoo, Alberto VO5	15 oz	1.75	4Q 92	4c
Toothpaste, Crest or Colgate	6-7 oz	3.35	4Q 92	4c
Personal Services				
Dry cleaning, man's 2-piece suit		8.00	4Q 92	4c
Haircare, woman's shampoo, trim and blow-dry		19.80	4Q 92	4c
Haircut, man's barbershop, no styling		11.00	4Q 92	4c
Restaurant Food				
Chicken, fried, thigh and drumstick		2.79	4Q 92	4c
Hamburger with cheese	1/4 lb	2.30	4Q 92	4c
Pizza, Pizza Hut or Pizza Inn, cheese, thin crust	12-13 in	9.63	4Q 92	4c
Transportation				
ACCRA Index, Transportation		134.60	4Q 92	4c
Tire balance, computer or spin balance, front	wheel	8.50	4Q 92	4c
Utilities				
ACCRA Index, Utilities		165.50	4Q 92	4c
Electricity, partial electric and other energy, 1,800 sq ft living area new home	month	93.49	4Q 92	4c

Killeen-Harker Heights, TX

Item	Per	Value	Date	Ref.
Composite ACCRA index		91.80	4Q 92	4c
Alcoholic Beverages				
Beer, Miller Lite or Budweiser, 12-oz containers	6 pack	3.87	4Q 92	4c
Liquor, J & B Scotch	750 ml	18.61	4Q 92	4c
Wine, Gallo Chablis blanc, 1.5 liter	bottle	5.07	4Q 92	4c
Child Care				
Child care fee, average, center	hour	1.29	90	65r
Child care fee, average, nonregulated family day care	hour	0.89	90	65r
Child care fee, average, regulated family day care	hour	1.32	90	65r
Clothing				
Jeans, man's denim		23.00	4Q 92	4c
Shirt, man's dress shirt		20.00	4Q 92	4c
Undervest, boy's size 10-14, cotton	3	4.44	4Q 92	4c
Communications				
Long-distance telephone service, day, initial minute, 0-100 miles	min	0.10-0.46	91	12s
Long-distance telephone service, day, additional minute, 0-100 miles	min	0.06-0.45	91	12s
Newspaper subscription, daily and Sunday home delivery, large-city	month	8.00	4Q 92	4c
Telephone bill, family of four	month	16.55	4Q 92	4c
Education				
Board, 4-yr private college/university	year	1883	91	22s
Board, 4-yr public college/university	year	1605	91	22s
Expenditures, local gov't, public elementary/secondary	pupil	4593	92	20s
Room, 4-year private college/university	year	1620	91	22s
Room, 4-year public college/university	year	1532	91	22s

Values are in dollars or fractions of dollars. In the column headed *Ref*, references are shown to sources. Each reference is followed by a letter. These refer to the geographical level for which data were reported: s=State, r=Region, and c=City or metro. The abbreviation *ex* is used to mean *except* or *excluding*; *exp* stands for expenditures. For other abbreviations and further explanations, please see the Introduction.

Killeen-Harker Heights, TX - continued

Item	Per	Value	Date	Ref.
Education				
Tuition, 2-year private college/university	year	4394	91	22s
Tuition, 2-year public college/university	year	495	91	22s
Tuition, 4-year private college/university	year	6497	91	22s
Tuition, 4-year public college/university, in-state	year	986	91	22s
Energy and Fuels				
Coal	mil Btu	1.44	90	64s
Energy	mil Btu	6.48	90	64s
Energy, combined forms, 1,800 sq ft heating area	month	121.23	4Q 92	4c
Energy, exc electricity, 1,800 sq ft heating area	month	25.43	4Q 92	4c
Energy exp/householder, 1-family unit	year	471	90	28r
Energy exp/householder, <1,000 sq ft heating area	year	384	90	28r
Energy exp/householder, 1,000-1,999 sq ft heating area	year	421	90	28r
Energy exp/householder, 2,000+ sq ft heating area	year	625	90	28r
Energy exp/householder, mobile home	year	271	90	28r
Energy exp/householder, multifamily	year	355	90	28r
Gas, natural	mil Btu	2.47	90	64s
Gas, natural	000 cu ft	5.71	91	46s
Gas, natural, exp	year	388	91	46s
Gasoline, motor	gal	1.05	4Q 92	4c
Gasoline, unleaded regular	mil Btu	9.16	90	64s
Entertainment				
Bowling, evening rate	game	2.21	4Q 92	4c
Miniature golf admission	adult	6.18	92	1r
Miniature golf admission	child	5.14	92	1r
Monopoly game, Parker Brothers', No. 9		11.64	4Q 92	4c
Movie	admission	5.00	4Q 92	4c
Tennis balls, yellow, Wilson or Penn, 3	can	2.24	4Q 92	4c
Waterpark admission	adult	11.00	92	1r
Waterpark admission	child	8.55	92	1r
Funerals				
Casket, 18-gauge steel, velvet interior		2274.41	91	24r
Cosmetology, hair care, etc.		74.62	91	24r
Embalming		229.94	91	24r
Facility use for ceremony		176.61	91	24r
Hearse, local		116.34	91	24r
Limousine, local		72.68	91	24r
Remains to funeral home, transfer		87.72	91	24r
Service charge, professional		712.53	91	24r
Vault, concrete, non-metallic liner		750.55	91	24r
Viewing facilities, use		155.31	91	24r
Goods and Services				
ACCRA Index, Miscellaneous Goods and Services		93.60	4Q 92	4c
Groceries				
ACCRA Index, Groceries		94.50	4Q 92	4c
Apples, Red Delicious	lb	0.79	4/93	16r
Babyfood, strained vegetables, lowest price	4-4.5 oz jar	0.26	4Q 92	4c
Bacon	lb	1.75	4/93	16r
Bananas	lb	0.37	4Q 92	4c
Bananas	lb	0.42	4/93	16r
Beef, stew, boneless	lb	2.61	4/93	16r
Bologna, all beef or mixed	lb	2.24	4/93	16r
Bread, white	24 oz	0.63	4Q 92	4c
Bread, white, pan	lb	0.64	4/93	16r
Bread, whole wheat, pan	lb	0.96	4/93	16r
Cabbage	lb	0.37	4/93	16r
Carrots, short trimmed and topped	lb	0.47	4/93	16r
Celery	lb	0.64	4/93	16r
Cheese, American	lb	2.98	4/93	16r
Cheese, Cheddar	lb	3.28	4/93	16r

Killeen-Harker Heights, TX - continued

Item	Per	Value	Date	Ref.
Groceries - continued				
Cheese, Kraft grated Parmesan	8-oz canister	3.28	4Q 92	4c
Chicken, fresh, whole	lb	0.77	4/93	16r
Chicken, fryer, whole	lb	0.55	4Q 92	4c
Chicken breast, bone-in	lb	1.92	4/93	16r
Chicken legs, bone-in	lb	1.06	4/93	16r
Chuck roast, graded and ungraded, ex USDA prime and choice	lb	2.40	4/93	16r
Chuck roast, USDA choice, bone-in	lb	2.19	4/93	16r
Chuck roast, USDA choice, boneless	lb	2.38	4/93	16r
Cigarettes, Winston	carton	19.18	4Q 92	4c
Coffee, 100% ground roast, all sizes	lb	2.48	4/93	16r
Coffee, vacuum-packed	13-oz can	1.93	4Q 92	4c
Corn, frozen	10 oz	0.58	4Q 92	4c
Corn Flakes, Kellogg's or Post Toasties	18 oz	1.85	4Q 92	4c
Crackers, soda, salted	lb	1.15	4/93	16r
Eggs, Grade A large	doz	0.93	4Q 92	4c
Eggs, Grade A large	doz	0.96	4/93	16r
Flour, white, all purpose	lb	0.24	4/93	16r
Frankfurters, all meat or all beef	lb	2.01	4/93	16r
Grapefruit	lb	0.44	4/93	16r
Grapes, Thompson Seedless	lb	1.40	4/93	16r
Ground beef, 100% beef	lb	1.58	4/93	16r
Ground beef, lean and extra lean	lb	2.09	4/93	16r
Ground beef or hamburger	lb	1.57	4Q 92	4c
Ground chuck, 100% beef	lb	1.98	4/93	16r
Ham, boneless, excluding canned	lb	2.89	4/93	16r
Ham, picnic, shoulder, bone-in, smoked	lb	1.02	4/93	16r
Ham, rump or steak half, bone-in, smoked	lb	1.48	4/93	16r
Honey, jar	8 oz	0.73-1.19	92	5r
Honey, jar	lb	1.10-1.79	92	5r
Honey, squeeze bear	12-oz	1.19-1.50	92	5r
Ice cream, prepackaged, bulk, regular	1/2 gal	2.41	4/93	16r
Lemons	lb	1.05	4/93	16r
Lettuce, iceberg	head	0.88	4Q 92	4c
Lettuce, iceberg	lb	0.81	4/93	16r
Margarine, Blue Bonnet or Parkay cubes	lb	0.56	4Q 92	4c
Margarine, stick	lb	0.88	4/93	16r
Milk, whole	1/2 gal	1.24	4Q 92	4c
Orange juice, Minute Maid frozen	12-oz can	1.36	4Q 92	4c
Oranges, navel	lb	0.55	4/93	16r
Peaches	29-oz can	1.37	4Q 92	4c
Pears, Anjou	lb	0.92	4/93	16r
Peas Sweet, Del Monte or Green Giant	15-17 oz can	0.51	4Q 92	4c
Pork chops, center cut, bone-in	lb	3.13	4/93	16r
Potato chips	16 oz	2.94	4/93	16r
Potatoes, white	lb	0.43	4/93	16r
Potatoes, white or red	10-lb sack	2.27	4Q 92	4c
Rib roast, USDA choice, bone-in	lb	4.63	4/93	16r
Rice, white, long grain, uncooked	lb	0.45	4/93	16r
Round roast, graded & ungraded, ex USDA prime & choice	lb	3.03	4/93	16r
Round roast, USDA choice, boneless	lb	3.09	4/93	16r
Sausage, fresh, loose	lb	2.08	4/93	16r
Sausage, Jimmy Dean, 100% pork	lb	2.56	4Q 92	4c
Short ribs, bone-in	lb	2.66	4/93	16r
Shortening, vegetable oil blends	lb	0.69	4/93	16r
Shortening, vegetable, Crisco	3-lb can	2.04	4Q 92	4c
Soft drink, Coca Cola	2 liter	1.12	4Q 92	4c
Spaghetti and macaroni	lb	0.81	4/93	16r
Steak, rib eye, USDA choice, boneless	lb	6.24	4/93	16r
Steak, round, graded & ungraded, ex USDA prime & choice	lb	3.31	4/93	16r
Steak, round, USDA choice, boneless	lb	3.34	4/93	16r

Values are in dollars or fractions of dollars. In the column headed *Ref*, references are shown to sources. Each reference is followed by a letter. These refer to the geographical level for which data were reported: s=State, r=Region, and c=City or metro. The abbreviation *ex* is used to mean *except* or *excluding*; *exp* stands for expenditures. For other abbreviations and further explanations, please see the Introduction.

Killeen-Harker Heights, TX - continued

Item	Per	Value	Date	Ref.
Groceries				
Steak, sirloin, graded & ungraded, ex USDA prime & choice	lb	4.19	4/93	16r
Steak, sirloin, USDA choice, boneless	lb	4.46	4/93	16r
Steak, T-bone	lb	5.07	4Q 92	4c
Steak, T-bone, USDA choice, bone-in	lb	5.25	4/93	16r
Strawberries, dry pint	12 oz	0.92	4/93	16r
Sugar, cane or beet	4 lb	1.50	4Q 92	4c
Sugar, white	lb	0.39	4/93	16r
Sugar, white, 33-80 oz pk	lb	0.38	4/93	16r
Tomatoes, field grown	lb	0.88	4/93	16r
Tomatoes, Hunt's or Del Monte	14.5-oz can	0.56	4Q 92	4c
Tuna, chunk, light	6.125-6.5 oz can	0.61	4Q 92	4c
Tuna, chunk, light	lb	1.79	4/93	16r
Turkey, frozen, whole	lb	1.04	4/93	16r
Yogurt, natural, fruit flavored	1/2 pint	0.57	4/93	16r
Health Care				
ACCRA Index, Health Care		91.00	4Q 92	4c
Analgesic, Aspirin, Bayer, 325 mg tablets	100	4.31	4Q 92	4c
Childbirth, cesarean, hospital		5034	91	62r
Childbirth, cesarean, physician's fee		2053	91	62r
Childbirth, normal, hospital		2712	91	62r
Childbirth, normal, physician's fee		1492	91	62r
Dentist's fee, adult teeth cleaning and periodic oral exam	visit	37.00	4Q 92	4c
Doctor's fee, routine exam, established patient	visit	38.00	4Q 92	4c
Health care spending, state	capita	2192	3/93	84s
Hospital care, semiprivate room	day	299.00	4Q 92	4c
Mental health care, exp	capita	20.37-28.83	90	38s
Mental health care, exp, state mental health agency	capita	22.72	90	38s
Mental health care, hospital psychiatric services, non-Federal, exp	capita	7.95	88	38s
Mental health care, mental health organization, multiservice, exp	capita	12.05	88	38s
Mental health care, psychiatric hospitals, private, exp	capita	37.78	88	38s
Mental health care, psychiatric out-patient clinics, freestanding, exp	capita	0.43	88	38s
Mental health care, state and county mental hospitals, exp	capita	12.54	88	38s
Mental health care, VA medical centers, exp	capita	5.35	88	38s
Physician fee, family practice, first-visit		75.00	91	62r
Physician fee, family practice, revisit		34.00	91	62r
Physician fee, general practice, first-visit		61.00	91	62r
Physician fee, general practice, revisit		32.00	91	62r
Physician fee, general surgeon, first-visit		64.00	91	62r
Physician fee, general surgeon, revisit		40.00	91	62r
Physician fee, internal medicine, first-visit		98.00	91	62r
Physician fee, internal medicine, revisit		40.00	91	62r
Physician fee, median, neurosurgeon, first-visit		130.00	91	62r
Physician fee, median, nonsurgical specialist, first-visit		95.00	91	62r
Physician fee, median, orthopedic surgeon, first-visit		91.00	91	62r
Physician fee, median, plastic surgeon, first-visit		66.00	91	62r
Physician fee, median, surgical specialist, first-visit		62.00	91	62r
Physician fee, neurosurgeon, revisit		50.00	91	62r
Physician fee, nonsurgical specialist, revisit		40.00	91	62r
Physician fee, obstetrics/gynecology, first-visit		64.00	91	62r
Physician fee, obstetrics/gynecology, revisit		41.00	91	62r
Physician fee, orthopedic surgeon, revisit		40.00	91	62r
Physician fee, pediatrician, first-visit		49.00	91	62r

Killeen-Harker Heights, TX - continued

Item	Per	Value	Date	Ref.
Health Care - continued				
Physician fee, pediatrician, revisit		33.00	91	62r
Physician fee, plastic surgeon, revisit		43.00	91	62r
Physician fee, surgical specialist, revisit		37.00	91	62r
Substance abuse, hospital ancillary charge	incident	3750	90	70s
Substance abuse, hospital physician charge	incident	1080	90	70s
Substance abuse, hospital room and board	incident	5320	90	70s
Household Goods				
Appliance repair, home, service call, washing machine	min labor charge	30.00	4Q 92	4c
Laundry detergent, Tide Ultra, Bold, or Cheer	42 oz	2.87	4Q 92	4c
Tissues, facial, Kleenex brand	175-count box	1.03	4Q 92	4c
Housing				
ACCRA Index, Housing		84.10	4Q 92	4c
House, 1,800 sq ft, 8,000 sq ft lot, new, urban	total	87000	4Q 92	4c
House payment, principal and interest, 25% down payment	month	474	4Q 92	4c
Mortgage rate, incl. points & origination fee, 30-year fixed or adjustable rate	percent	7.89	4Q 92	4c
Rent, apartment, 2 bedrooms - 1-1/2 to 2 baths, unfurnished, 950 sq ft, water	month	515	4Q 92	4c
Insurance and Pensions				
Auto insurance, private passenger	year	709.79	91	63s
Personal Goods				
Shampoo, Alberto VO5	15 oz	0.93	4Q 92	4c
Toothpaste, Crest or Colgate	6-7 oz	1.72	4Q 92	4c
Personal Services				
Dry cleaning, man's 2-piece suit		5.00	4Q 92	4c
Haircare, woman's shampoo, trim and blow-dry		15.30	4Q 92	4c
Haircut, man's barbershop, no styling		8.10	4Q 92	4c
Restaurant Food				
Chicken, fried, thigh and drumstick		2.16	4Q 92	4c
Hamburger with cheese	1/4 lb	1.89	4Q 92	4c
Pizza, Pizza Hut or Pizza Inn, cheese, thin crust	12-13 in	7.99	4Q 92	4c
Taxes				
Tax, cigarette	pack	41	91	77s
Tax, gasoline	gal	20	91	77s
Taxes, state	capita	923	91	77s
Transportation				
ACCRA Index, Transportation		89.50	4Q 92	4c
Driver's license fee		16.00	12/90	43s
Tire balance, computer or spin balance, front	wheel	5.59	4Q 92	4c
Travel				
Business travel	day	193.00	4/93	89r
Utilities				
ACCRA Index, Utilities		108.40	4Q 92	4c
Electricity	mil Btu	17.09	90	64s
Electricity, partial electric and other energy, 1,800 sq ft living area new home	month	95.80	4Q 92	4c
Electricity, residential	KWh	5.92	2/93	94s

Values are in dollars or fractions of dollars. In the column headed *Ref*, references are shown to sources. Each reference is followed by a letter. These refer to the geographical level for which data were reported: s=State, r=Region, and c=City or metro. The abbreviation *ex* is used to mean *except* or *excluding*; *exp* stands for expenditures. For other abbreviations and further explanations, please see the Introduction.

Kirksville, MO

Item	Per	Value	Date	Ref.
Composite ACCRA index		92.50	4Q 92	4c
Alcoholic Beverages				
Beer, Miller Lite or Budweiser, 12-oz containers	6 pack	3.74	4Q 92	4c
Liquor, J & B Scotch	750 ml	15.98	4Q 92	4c
Wine, Gallo Chablis blanc, 1.5 liter	bottle	5.27	4Q 92	4c
Clothing				
Jeans, man's denim		23.43	4Q 92	4c
Shirt, man's dress shirt		24.00	4Q 92	4c
Undervest, boy's size 10-14, cotton	3	2.95	4Q 92	4c
Communications				
Newspaper subscription, daily and Sunday home delivery, large-city	month	17.83	4Q 92	4c
Telephone, flat rate	month	9.10	91	11c
Telephone bill, family of four	month	18.62	4Q 92	4c
Energy and Fuels				
Energy, combined forms, 1,800 sq ft heating area	month	95.35	4Q 92	4c
Energy, exc electricity, 1,800 sq ft heating area	month	33.60	4Q 92	4c
Gas, cooking, 10 therms	month	11.29	92	56c
Gas, cooking, 30 therms	month	19.87	92	56c
Gas, cooking, 50 therms	month	28.46	92	56c
Gas, heating, winter, 100 therms	month	49.91	92	56c
Gas, heating, winter, average use	month	63.65	92	56c
Gasoline, motor	gal	1.05	4Q 92	4c
Entertainment				
Bowling, evening rate	game	1.90	4Q 92	4c
Monopoly game, Parker Brothers', No. 9		9.98	4Q 92	4c
Movie	admission	4.25	4Q 92	4c
Tennis balls, yellow, Wilson or Penn, 3	can	2.02	4Q 92	4c
Goods and Services				
ACCRA Index, Miscellaneous Goods and Services		90.40	4Q 92	4c
Groceries				
ACCRA Index, Groceries		94.10	4Q 92	4c
Babyfood, strained vegetables, lowest price	4-4.5 oz jar	0.37	4Q 92	4c
Bananas	lb	0.49	4Q 92	4c
Bread, white	24 oz	0.48	4Q 92	4c
Cheese, Kraft grated Parmesan	8-oz canister	3.48	4Q 92	4c
Chicken, fryer, whole	lb	0.78	4Q 92	4c
Cigarettes, Winston	carton	15.89	4Q 92	4c
Coffee, vacuum-packed	13-oz can	1.92	4Q 92	4c
Corn, frozen	10 oz	0.65	4Q 92	4c
Corn Flakes, Kellogg's or Post Toasties	18 oz	2.08	4Q 92	4c
Eggs, Grade A large	doz	0.79	4Q 92	4c
Ground beef or hamburger	lb	1.34	4Q 92	4c
Lettuce, iceberg	head	0.72	4Q 92	4c
Margarine, Blue Bonnet or Parkay cubes	lb	0.60	4Q 92	4c
Milk, whole	1/2 gal	1.30	4Q 92	4c
Orange juice, Minute Maid frozen	12-oz can	1.60	4Q 92	4c
Peaches	29-oz can	1.40	4Q 92	4c
Peas Sweet, Del Monte or Green Giant	15-17 oz can	0.64	4Q 92	4c
Potatoes, white or red	10-lb sack	1.72	4Q 92	4c
Sausage, Jimmy Dean, 100% pork	lb	2.42	4Q 92	4c
Shortening, vegetable, Crisco	3-lb can	2.18	4Q 92	4c
Soft drink, Coca Cola	2 liter	0.99	4Q 92	4c
Steak, T-bone	lb	5.48	4Q 92	4c
Sugar, cane or beet	4 lb	1.40	4Q 92	4c

Kirksville, MO - continued

Item	Per	Value	Date	Ref.
Groceries - continued				
Tomatoes, Hunt's or Del Monte	14.5-oz can	0.70	4Q 92	4c
Tuna, chunk, light	6.125-6.5 oz can	0.53	4Q 92	4c
Health Care				
ACCRA Index, Health Care		83.70	4Q 92	4c
Analgesic, Aspirin, Bayer, 325 mg tablets	100	3.43	4Q 92	4c
Dentist's fee, adult teeth cleaning and periodic oral exam	visit	41.80	4Q 92	4c
Doctor's fee, routine exam, established patient	visit	28.49	4Q 92	4c
Hospital care, semiprivate room	day	250.11	90	27c
Hospital care, semiprivate room	day	302.00	4Q 92	4c
Household Goods				
Appliance repair, home, service call, washing machine	min labor charge	31.17	4Q 92	4c
Laundry detergent, Tide Ultra, Bold, or Cheer	42 oz	2.81	4Q 92	4c
Tissues, facial, Kleenex brand	175-count box	1.10	4Q 92	4c
Housing				
ACCRA Index, Housing		99.70	4Q 92	4c
House, 1,800 sq ft, 8,000 sq ft lot, new, urban	total	113500	4Q 92	4c
House payment, principal and interest, 25% down payment	month	644	4Q 92	4c
Mortgage rate, incl. points & origination fee, 30-year fixed or adjustable rate	percent	8.32	4Q 92	4c
Rent, apartment, 2 bedrooms - 1-1/2 to 2 baths, unfurnished, 950 sq ft, water	month	420	4Q 92	4c
Personal Goods				
Shampoo, Alberto VO5	15 oz	0.98	4Q 92	4c
Toothpaste, Crest or Colgate	6-7 oz	1.57	4Q 92	4c
Personal Services				
Dry cleaning, man's 2-piece suit		5.15	4Q 92	4c
Haircare, woman's shampoo, trim and blow-dry		14.67	4Q 92	4c
Haircut, man's barbershop, no styling		5.67	4Q 92	4c
Restaurant Food				
Chicken, fried, thigh and drumstick		2.18	4Q 92	4c
Hamburger with cheese	1/4 lb	1.85	4Q 92	4c
Pizza, Pizza Hut or Pizza Inn, cheese, thin crust	12-13 in	7.39	4Q 92	4c
Transportation				
ACCRA Index, Transportation		85.60	4Q 92	4c
Tire balance, computer or spin balance, front	wheel	5.10	4Q 92	4c
Utilities				
ACCRA Index, Utilities		88.20	4Q 92	4c
Electricity, partial electric and other energy, 1,800 sq ft living area new home	month	61.75	4Q 92	4c

Klamath Falls, OR

Item	Per	Value	Date	Ref.
Composite ACCRA index		99.40	4Q 92	4c
Alcoholic Beverages				
Beer, Miller Lite or Budweiser, 12-oz containers	6 pack	3.48	4Q 92	4c
Liquor, J & B Scotch	750 ml	20.05	4Q 92	4c
Wine, Gallo Chablis blanc, 1.5 liter	bottle	4.89	4Q 92	4c
Clothing				
Jeans, man's denim		40.75	4Q 92	4c
Shirt, man's dress shirt		22.00	4Q 92	4c

Values are in dollars or fractions of dollars. In the column headed *Ref*, references are shown to sources. Each reference is followed by a letter. These refer to the geographical level for which data were reported: s=State, r=Region, and c=City or metro. The abbreviation *ex* is used to mean *except* or *excluding*; *exp* stands for expenditures. For other abbreviations and further explanations, please see the Introduction.

Klamath Falls, OR - continued

Item	Per	Value	Date	Ref.
Clothing				
Undervest, boy's size 10-14, cotton	3	4.05	4Q 92	4c
Communications				
Newspaper subscription, daily and Sunday home delivery, large-city	month	11.95	4Q 92	4c
Telephone, flat rate	month	13.68	91	11c
Telephone bill, family of four	month	16.28	4Q 92	4c
Energy and Fuels				
Energy, combined forms, 1,800 sq ft heating area	month	82.70	4Q 92	4c
Gasoline, motor	gal	1.32	4Q 92	4c
Entertainment				
Bowling, evening rate	game	1.75	4Q 92	4c
Monopoly game, Parker Brothers', No. 9		9.46	4Q 92	4c
Movie	admission	5.00	4Q 92	4c
Tennis balls, yellow, Wilson or Penn, 3	can	2.01	4Q 92	4c
Goods and Services				
ACCRA Index, Miscellaneous Goods and Services		100.10	4Q 92	4c
Groceries				
ACCRA Index, Groceries		101.40	4Q 92	4c
Babyfood, strained vegetables, lowest price	4-4.5 oz jar	0.34	4Q 92	4c
Bananas	lb	0.44	4Q 92	4c
Bread, white	24 oz	0.58	4Q 92	4c
Cheese, Kraft grated Parmesan	8-oz canister	3.38	4Q 92	4c
Chicken, fryer, whole	lb	0.90	4Q 92	4c
Cigarettes, Winston	carton	16.68	4Q 92	4c
Coffee, vacuum-packed	13-oz can	2.87	4Q 92	4c
Corn, frozen	10 oz	0.63	4Q 92	4c
Corn Flakes, Kellogg's or Post Toasties	18 oz	1.96	4Q 92	4c
Eggs, Grade A large	doz	0.91	4Q 92	4c
Ground beef or hamburger	lb	1.58	4Q 92	4c
Lettuce, iceberg	head	0.72	4Q 92	4c
Margarine, Blue Bonnet or Parkay cubes	lb	0.52	4Q 92	4c
Milk, whole	1/2 gal	1.38	4Q 92	4c
Orange juice, Minute Maid frozen	12-oz can	1.17	4Q 92	4c
Peaches	29-oz can	1.74	4Q 92	4c
Peas Sweet, Del Monte or Green Giant	15-17 oz can	0.69	4Q 92	4c
Potatoes, white or red	10-lb sack	1.84	4Q 92	4c
Sausage, Jimmy Dean, 100% pork	lb	3.29	4Q 92	4c
Shortening, vegetable, Crisco	3-lb can	2.11	4Q 92	4c
Soft drink, Coca Cola	2 liter	1.13	4Q 92	4c
Steak, T-bone	lb	4.74	4Q 92	4c
Sugar, cane or beet	4 lb	1.57	4Q 92	4c
Tomatoes, Hunt's or Del Monte	14.5-oz can	0.72	4Q 92	4c
Tuna, chunk, light	6.125-6.5 oz can	0.57	4Q 92	4c
Health Care				
ACCRA Index, Health Care		111.40	4Q 92	4c
Analgesic, Aspirin, Bayer, 325 mg tablets	100	4.81	4Q 92	4c
Dentist's fee, adult teeth cleaning and periodic oral exam	visit	54.00	4Q 92	4c
Doctor's fee, routine exam, established patient	visit	40.50	4Q 92	4c
Hospital care, semiprivate room	day	320.00	90	27c
Hospital care, semiprivate room	day	370.00	4Q 92	4c

Klamath Falls, OR - continued

Item	Per	Value	Date	Ref.
Household Goods				
Appliance repair, home, service call, washing machine	min labor charge	29.70	4Q 92	4c
Laundry detergent, Tide Ultra, Bold, or Cheer	42 oz	3.56	4Q 92	4c
Tissues, facial, Kleenex brand	175-count box	1.17	4Q 92	4c
Housing				
ACCRA Index, Housing		101.70	4Q 92	4c
House, 1,800 sq ft, 8,000 sq ft lot, new, urban	total	114000	4Q 92	4c
House payment, principal and interest, 25% down payment	month	635	4Q 92	4c
Mortgage rate, incl. points & origination fee, 30-year fixed or adjustable rate	percent	8.13	4Q 92	4c
Rent, apartment, 2 bedrooms - 1-1/2 to 2 baths, unfurnished, 950 sq ft, water	month	479	4Q 92	4c
Personal Goods				
Shampoo, Alberto VO5	15 oz	1.33	4Q 92	4c
Toothpaste, Crest or Colgate	6-7 oz	1.85	4Q 92	4c
Personal Services				
Dry cleaning, man's 2-piece suit		6.38	4Q 92	4c
Haircare, woman's shampoo, trim and blow-dry		18.12	4Q 92	4c
Haircut, man's barbershop, no styling		6.50	4Q 92	4c
Restaurant Food				
Chicken, fried, thigh and drumstick		2.40	4Q 92	4c
Hamburger with cheese	1/4 lb	1.85	4Q 92	4c
Pizza, Pizza Hut or Pizza Inn, cheese, thin crust	12-13 in	7.99	4Q 92	4c
Transportation				
ACCRA Index, Transportation		102.80	4Q 92	4c
Bus fare	one-way	0.70	3/93	2c
Tire balance, computer or spin balance, front	wheel	5.81	4Q 92	4c
Utilities				
ACCRA Index, Utilities		76.50	4Q 92	4c
Electricity, all electric, 1,800 sq ft living area new home	month	82.70	4Q 92	4c

Knoxville, TN

Item	Per	Value	Date	Ref.
Composite ACCRA index		94.60	4Q 92	4c
Alcoholic Beverages				
Beer, Miller Lite or Budweiser, 12-oz containers	6 pack	3.87	4Q 92	4c
Liquor, J & B Scotch	750 ml	18.81	4Q 92	4c
Wine, Gallo Chablis blanc, 1.5 liter	bottle	6.09	4Q 92	4c
Child Care				
Child care fee, average, center	hour	1.29	90	65r
Child care fee, average, nonregulated family day care	hour	0.89	90	65r
Child care fee, average, regulated family day care	hour	1.32	90	65r
Clothing				
Jeans, man's denim		28.55	4Q 92	4c
Shirt, man's dress shirt		24.38	4Q 92	4c
Undervest, boy's size 10-14, cotton	3	3.40	4Q 92	4c
Communications				
Long-distance telephone service, day, initial minute, 0-100 miles	min	0.10-0.22	91	12s
Long-distance telephone service, day, additional minute, 0-100 miles	min	0.10-0.22	91	12s

Values are in dollars or fractions of dollars. In the column headed *Ref*, references are shown to sources. Each reference is followed by a letter. These refer to the geographical level for which data were reported: s = State, r = Region, and c = City or metro. The abbreviation *ex* is used to mean *except* or *excluding*; *exp* stands for *expenditures*. For other abbreviations and further explanations, please see the Introduction.

Knoxville, TN - continued

Item	Per	Value	Date	Ref.
Communications				
Long-distance telephone service, evenings/weekends, 0-100 mi, initial minute	min	0.05-0.10	91	12s
Long-distance telephone service, evenings/weekends, 0-100 mi, additional minute	min	0.05-0.10	91	12s
Newspaper subscription, daily and Sunday home delivery, large-city	month	13.55	4Q 92	4c
Telephone, flat rate	month	11.85	91	11c
Telephone bill, family of four	month	19.16	4Q 92	4c
Education				
Board, 4-yr private college/university	year	1845	91	22s
Board, 4-yr public college/university	year	1499	91	22s
Expenditures, local gov't, public elementary/secondary	pupil	3736	92	20s
Room, 4-year private college/university	year	1679	91	22s
Room, 4-year public college/university	year	1339	91	22s
Tuition, 2-year private college/university	year	4203	91	22s
Tuition, 2-year public college/university	year	848	91	22s
Tuition, 4-year private college/university	year	6889	91	22s
Tuition, 4-year public college/university, in-state	year	1518	91	22s
Energy and Fuels				
Coal	mil Btu	1.35	90	64s
Energy	mil Btu	8.61	90	64s
Energy, combined forms, 1,800 sq ft heating area	month	107.39	4Q 92	4c
Energy, exc electricity, 1,800 sq ft heating area	month	41.00	4Q 92	4c
Energy exp/householder, 1-family unit	year	403	90	28r
Energy exp/householder, <1,000 sq ft heating area	year	342	90	28r
Energy exp/householder, 1,000-1,999 sq ft heating area	year	388	90	28r
Energy exp/householder, 2,000+ sq ft heating area	year	434	90	28r
Energy exp/householder, mobile home	year	320	90	28r
Energy exp/householder, multifamily	year	338	90	28r
Gas, natural	mil Btu	3.98	90	64s
Gas, natural	000 cu ft	5.19	91	46s
Gas, natural, exp	year	388	91	46s
Gasoline, motor	gal	1.07	4Q 92	4c
Gasoline, unleaded regular	mil Btu	9.40	90	64s
Entertainment				
Bowling, evening rate	game	1.83	4Q 92	4c
Miniature golf admission	adult	6.18	92	1r
Miniature golf admission	child	5.14	92	1r
Monopoly game, Parker Brothers', No. 9		10.39	4Q 92	4c
Movie	admission	5.50	4Q 92	4c
Tennis balls, yellow, Wilson or Penn, 3	can	2.06	4Q 92	4c
Waterpark admission	adult	11.00	92	1r
Waterpark admission	child	8.55	92	1r
Funerals				
Casket, 18-gauge steel, velvet interior		2329.05	91	24r
Cosmetology, hair care, etc.		72.78	91	24r
Embalming		240.71	91	24r
Facility use for ceremony		181.67	91	24r
Hearse, local		106.25	91	24r
Limousine, local		70.92	91	24r
Remains to funeral home, transfer		96.30	91	24r
Service charge, professional		687.09	91	24r
Vault, concrete, non-metallic liner		732.09	91	24r
Viewing facilities, use		190.30	91	24r
Goods and Services				
ACCRA Index, Miscellaneous Goods and Services		97.40	4Q 92	4c
Groceries				
ACCRA Index, Groceries		93.00	4Q 92	4c
Apples, Red Delicious	lb	0.79	4/93	16r

Knoxville, TN - continued

Item	Per	Value	Date	Ref.
Groceries - continued				
Babyfood, strained vegetables, lowest price	4-4.5 oz jar	0.29	4Q 92	4c
Bacon	lb	1.75	4/93	16r
Bananas	lb	0.43	4Q 92	4c
Bananas	lb	0.42	4/93	16r
Beef, stew, boneless	lb	2.61	4/93	16r
Bologna, all beef or mixed	lb	2.24	4/93	16r
Bread, white	24 oz	0.72	4Q 92	4c
Bread, white, pan	lb	0.64	4/93	16r
Bread, whole wheat, pan	lb	0.96	4/93	16r
Cabbage	lb	0.37	4/93	16r
Carrots, short trimmed and topped	lb	0.47	4/93	16r
Celery	lb	0.64	4/93	16r
Cheese, American	lb	2.98	4/93	16r
Cheese, Cheddar	lb	3.28	4/93	16r
Cheese, Kraft grated Parmesan	8-oz canister	3.29	4Q 92	4c
Chicken, fresh, whole	lb	0.77	4/93	16r
Chicken, fryer, whole	lb	0.59	4Q 92	4c
Chicken breast, bone-in	lb	1.92	4/93	16r
Chicken legs, bone-in	lb	1.06	4/93	16r
Chuck roast, graded and ungraded, ex USDA prime and choice	lb	2.40	4/93	16r
Chuck roast, USDA choice, bone-in	lb	2.19	4/93	16r
Chuck roast, USDA choice, boneless	lb	2.38	4/93	16r
Cigarettes, Winston	carton	16.45	4Q 92	4c
Coffee, 100% ground roast, all sizes	lb	2.48	4/93	16r
Coffee, vacuum-packed	13-oz can	2.03	4Q 92	4c
Corn, frozen	10 oz	0.48	4Q 92	4c
Corn Flakes, Kellogg's or Post Toasties	18 oz	1.73	4Q 92	4c
Crackers, soda, salted	lb	1.15	4/93	16r
Eggs, Grade A large	doz	0.77	4Q 92	4c
Eggs, Grade A large	doz	0.96	4/93	16r
Flour, white, all purpose	lb	0.24	4/93	16r
Frankfurters, all meat or all beef	lb	2.01	4/93	16r
Grapefruit	lb	0.44	4/93	16r
Grapes, Thompson Seedless	lb	1.40	4/93	16r
Ground beef, 100% beef	lb	1.58	4/93	16r
Ground beef, lean and extra lean	lb	2.09	4/93	16r
Ground beef or hamburger	lb	1.45	4Q 92	4c
Ground chuck, 100% beef	lb	1.98	4/93	16r
Ham, boneless, excluding canned	lb	2.89	4/93	16r
Ham, picnic, shoulder, bone-in, smoked	lb	1.02	4/93	16r
Ham, rump or steak half, bone-in, smoked	lb	1.48	4/93	16r
Honey, jar	8 oz	0.89-1.09	92	5r
Honey, jar	lb	1.39-2.25	92	5r
Honey, squeeze bear	12-oz	1.00-1.50	92	5r
Ice cream, prepackaged, bulk, regular	1/2 gal	2.41	4/93	16r
Lemons	lb	1.05	4/93	16r
Lettuce, iceberg	head	0.99	4Q 92	4c
Lettuce, iceberg	lb	0.81	4/93	16r
Margarine, Blue Bonnet or Parkay cubes	lb	0.51	4Q 92	4c
Margarine, stick	lb	0.88	4/93	16r
Milk, whole	1/2 gal	1.31	4Q 92	4c
Orange juice, Minute Maid frozen	12-oz can	1.25	4Q 92	4c
Oranges, navel	lb	0.55	4/93	16r
Peaches	29-oz can	1.26	4Q 92	4c
Pears, Anjou	lb	0.92	4/93	16r
Peas Sweet, Del Monte or Green Giant	15-17 oz can	0.50	4Q 92	4c
Pork chops, center cut, bone-in	lb	3.13	4/93	16r
Potato chips	16 oz	2.94	4/93	16r
Potatoes, white	lb	0.43	4/93	16r
Potatoes, white or red	10-lb sack	2.61	4Q 92	4c
Rib roast, USDA choice, bone-in	lb	4.63	4/93	16r
Rice, white, long grain, uncooked	lb	0.45	4/93	16r

Values are in dollars or fractions of dollars. In the column headed *Ref*, references are shown to sources. Each reference is followed by a letter. These refer to the geographical level for which data were reported: s=State, r=Region, and c=City or metro. The abbreviation *ex* is used to mean *except* or *excluding*; *exp* stands for expenditures. For other abbreviations and further explanations, please see the Introduction.

Knoxville, TN - continued

Item	Per	Value	Date	Ref.
Groceries				
Round roast, graded & ungraded, ex USDA prime & choice	lb	3.03	4/93	16r
Round roast, USDA choice, boneless	lb	3.09	4/93	16r
Sausage, fresh, loose	lb	2.08	4/93	16r
Sausage, Jimmy Dean, 100% pork	lb	2.35	4Q 92	4c
Short ribs, bone-in	lb	2.66	4/93	16r
Shortening, vegetable oil blends	lb	0.69	4/93	16r
Shortening, vegetable, Crisco	3-lb can	1.99	4Q 92	4c
Soft drink, Coca Cola	2 liter	0.94	4Q 92	4c
Spaghetti and macaroni	lb	0.81	4/93	16r
Steak, rib eye, USDA choice, boneless	lb	6.24	4/93	16r
Steak, round, graded & ungraded, ex USDA prime & choice	lb	3.31	4/93	16r
Steak, round, USDA choice, boneless	lb	3.34	4/93	16r
Steak, sirloin, graded & ungraded, ex USDA prime & choice	lb	4.19	4/93	16r
Steak, sirloin, USDA choice, boneless	lb	4.46	4/93	16r
Steak, T-bone	lb	5.41	4Q 92	4c
Steak, T-bone, USDA choice, bone-in	lb	5.25	4/93	16r
Strawberries, dry pint	12 oz	0.92	4/93	16r
Sugar, cane or beet	4 lb	1.47	4Q 92	4c
Sugar, white	lb	0.39	4/93	16r
Sugar, white, 33-80 oz pk	lb	0.38	4/93	16r
Tomatoes, field grown	lb	0.88	4/93	16r
Tomatoes, Hunt's or Del Monte	14.5-oz can	0.56	4Q 92	4c
Tuna, chunk, light	6.125-6.5 oz can	0.55	4Q 92	4c
Tuna, chunk, light	lb	1.79	4/93	16r
Turkey, frozen, whole	lb	1.04	4/93	16r
Yogurt, natural, fruit flavored	1/2 pint	0.57	4/93	16r
Health Care				
ACCRA Index, Health Care		92.20	4Q 92	4c
Analgesic, Aspirin, Bayer, 325 mg tablets	100	4.57	4Q 92	4c
Childbirth, cesarean, hospital		5034	91	62r
Childbirth, cesarean, physician's fee		2053	91	62r
Childbirth, normal, hospital		2712	91	62r
Childbirth, normal, physician's fee		1492	91	62r
Dentist's fee, adult teeth cleaning and periodic oral exam	visit	39.20	4Q 92	4c
Doctor's fee, routine exam, established patient	visit	39.00	4Q 92	4c
Hospital care, semiprivate room	day	197.27	90	27c
Hospital care, semiprivate room	day	264.40	4Q 92	4c
Medical insurance premium, per employee, small group comprehensive	month	328.50	10/91	25c
Mental health care, exp	capita	20.37-28.83	90	38s
Mental health care, exp, state mental health agency	capita	28.84	90	38s
Mental health care, hospital psychiatric services, non-Federal, exp	capita	13.48	88	38s
Mental health care, mental health organization, multiservice, exp	capita	11.35	88	38s
Mental health care, psychiatric hospitals, private, exp	capita	22.28	88	38s
Mental health care, psychiatric out-patient clinics, freestanding, exp	capita	2.58	88	38s
Mental health care, psychiatric partial-care organizations, freestanding, exp	capita	0.25	88	38s
Mental health care, state and county mental hospitals, exp	capita	20.05	88	38s
Mental health care, VA medical centers, exp	capita	4.98	88	38s
Physician fee, family practice, first-visit		75.00	91	62r
Physician fee, family practice, revisit		34.00	91	62r
Physician fee, general practice, first-visit		61.00	91	62r
Physician fee, general practice, revisit		32.00	91	62r
Physician fee, general surgeon, first-visit		64.00	91	62r
Physician fee, general surgeon, revisit		40.00	91	62r

Knoxville, TN - continued

Item	Per	Value	Date	Ref.
Health Care - continued				
Physician fee, internal medicine, first-visit		98.00	91	62r
Physician fee, internal medicine, revisit		40.00	91	62r
Physician fee, median, neurosurgeon, first-visit		130.00	91	62r
Physician fee, median, nonsurgical specialist, first-visit		95.00	91	62r
Physician fee, median, orthopedic surgeon, first-visit		91.00	91	62r
Physician fee, median, plastic surgeon, first-visit		66.00	91	62r
Physician fee, median, surgical specialist, first-visit		62.00	91	62r
Physician fee, neurosurgeon, revisit		50.00	91	62r
Physician fee, nonsurgical specialist, revisit		40.00	91	62r
Physician fee, obstetrics/gynecology, first-visit		64.00	91	62r
Physician fee, obstetrics/gynecology, revisit		41.00	91	62r
Physician fee, orthopedic surgeon, revisit		40.00	91	62r
Physician fee, pediatrician, first-visit		49.00	91	62r
Physician fee, pediatrician, revisit		33.00	91	62r
Physician fee, plastic surgeon, revisit		43.00	91	62r
Physician fee, surgical specialist, revisit		37.00	91	62r
Substance abuse, hospital ancillary charge	incident	1330	90	70s
Substance abuse, hospital physician charge	incident	580	90	70s
Substance abuse, hospital room and board	incident	5180	90	70s
Household Goods				
Appliance repair, home, service call, washing machine	min labor charge	34.78	4Q 92	4c
Laundry detergent, Tide Ultra, Bold, or Cheer	42 oz	2.59	4Q 92	4c
Tissues, facial, Kleenex brand	175-count box	1.03	4Q 92	4c
Housing				
ACCRA Index, Housing		91.50	4Q 92	4c
Home, median price	unit	80.10		26c
House, 1,800 sq ft, 8,000 sq ft lot, new, urban	total	98720	4Q 92	4c
House payment, principal and interest, 25% down payment	month	550	4Q 92	4c
Mortgage rate, incl. points & origination fee, 30-year fixed or adjustable rate	percent	8.12	4Q 92	4c
Rent, apartment, 2 bedrooms - 1-1/2 to 2 baths, unfurnished, 950 sq ft, water	month	481	4Q 92	4c
Rental unit, 1 bedroom	month	360	93	23c
Rental unit, 2 bedroom	month	423	93	23c
Rental unit, 3 bedroom	month	531	93	23c
Rental unit, 4 bedroom	month	595	93	23c
Rental unit, efficiency	month	296	93	23c
Insurance and Pensions				
Auto insurance, private passenger	year	554.60	91	63s
Personal Goods				
Shampoo, Alberto VO5	15 oz	1.17	4Q 92	4c
Toothpaste, Crest or Colgate	6-7 oz	1.93	4Q 92	4c
Personal Services				
Dry cleaning, man's 2-piece suit		5.87	4Q 92	4c
Haircare, woman's shampoo, trim and blow-dry		20.00	4Q 92	4c
Haircut, man's barbershop, no styling		7.10	4Q 92	4c
Restaurant Food				
Chicken, fried, thigh and drumstick		1.99	4Q 92	4c
Hamburger with cheese	1/4 lb	1.79	4Q 92	4c
Pizza, Pizza Hut or Pizza Inn, cheese, thin crust	12-13 in	7.99	4Q 92	4c

Values are in dollars or fractions of dollars. In the column headed *Ref*, references are shown to sources. Each reference is followed by a letter. These refer to the geographical level for which data were reported: s=State, r=Region, and c=City or metro. The abbreviation *ex* is used to mean *except* or *excluding*; *exp* stands for expenditures. For other abbreviations and further explanations, please see the Introduction.

Knoxville, TN - continued

Item	Per	Value	Date	Ref.
Taxes				
Tax, cigarette	pack	13	91	77s
Tax, gasoline	gal	22.40	91	77s
Taxes, state	capita	870	91	77s
Transportation				
ACCRA Index, Transportation		93.50	4Q 92	4c
Auto rental, average	day	46.00	6/91	60c
Bus fare	one-way	1.00	3/93	2c
Driver's license fee		14.00-16.00	12/90	43s
Limo fare, airport-city, average	day	12.50	6/91	60c
Taxi fare, airport-city, average	day	14.00	6/91	60c
Tire balance, computer or spin balance, front	wheel	5.99	4Q 92	4c
Travel				
Breakfast	day	7.42	6/91	60c
Business travel	day	193.00	4/93	89r
Dinner	day	24.84	6/91	60c
Lodging	day	76.72	91	60c
Lunch	day	10.98	6/91	60c
Utilities				
ACCRA Index, Utilities		98.40	4Q 92	4c
Electricity	mil Btu	15.59	90	64s
Electricity, partial electric and other energy, 1,800 sq ft living area new home	month	66.39	4Q 92	4c

Kodiak, AK

Item	Per	Value	Date	Ref.
Composite ACCRA index		149.20	4Q 92	4c
Alcoholic Beverages				
Beer, Miller Lite or Budweiser, 12-oz containers	6 pack	5.37	4Q 92	4c
Liquor, J & B Scotch	750 ml	20.88	4Q 92	4c
Wine, Gallo Chablis blanc, 1.5 liter	bottle	6.66	4Q 92	4c
Clothing				
Jeans, man's denim		33.33	4Q 92	4c
Shirt, man's dress shirt		27.00	4Q 92	4c
Undervest, boy's size 10-14, cotton	3	7.74	4Q 92	4c
Communications				
Newspaper subscription, daily and Sunday home delivery, large-city	month	19.00	4Q 92	4c
Telephone bill, family of four	month	21.51	4Q 92	4c
Energy and Fuels				
Energy, combined forms, 1,800 sq ft heating area	month	211.89	4Q 92	4c
Energy, exc electricity, 1,800 sq ft heating area	month	113.00	4Q 92	4c
Gasoline, motor	gal	1.47	4Q 92	4c
Entertainment				
Bowling, evening rate	game	2.25	4Q 92	4c
Monopoly game, Parker Brothers', No. 9		19.99	4Q 92	4c
Movie	admission	4.00	4Q 92	4c
Tennis balls, yellow, Wilson or Penn, 3	can	5.82	4Q 92	4c
Goods and Services				
ACCRA Index, Miscellaneous Goods and Services		133.50	4Q 92	4c
Groceries				
ACCRA Index, Groceries		158.40	4Q 92	4c
Babyfood, strained vegetables, lowest price	4-4.5 oz jar	0.45	4Q 92	4c
Bananas	lb	0.96	4Q 92	4c
Bread, white	24 oz	1.10	4Q 92	4c
Cheese, Kraft grated Parmesan	8-oz canister	4.51	4Q 92	4c

Kodiak, AK - continued

Item	Per	Value	Date	Ref.
Groceries - continued				
Chicken, fryer, whole	lb	1.66	4Q 92	4c
Cigarettes, Winston	carton	20.59	4Q 92	4c
Coffee, vacuum-packed	13-oz can	2.74	4Q 92	4c
Corn, frozen	10 oz	1.03	4Q 92	4c
Corn Flakes, Kellogg's or Post Toasties	18 oz	2.73	4Q 92	4c
Eggs, Grade A large	doz	1.76	4Q 92	4c
Ground beef or hamburger	lb	2.12	4Q 92	4c
Lettuce, iceberg	head	1.24	4Q 92	4c
Margarine, Blue Bonnet or Parkay cubes	lb	1.38	4Q 92	4c
Milk, whole	1/2 gal	2.34	4Q 92	4c
Orange juice, Minute Maid frozen	12-oz can	2.06	4Q 92	4c
Peaches	29-oz can	2.08	4Q 92	4c
Peas Sweet, Del Monte or Green Giant	15-17 oz can	1.12	4Q 92	4c
Potatoes, white or red	10-lb sack	4.74	4Q 92	4c
Sausage, Jimmy Dean, 100% pork	lb	3.65	4Q 92	4c
Shortening, vegetable, Crisco	3-lb can	3.53	4Q 92	4c
Soft drink, Coca Cola	2 liter	2.46	4Q 92	4c
Steak, T-bone	lb	6.36	4Q 92	4c
Sugar, cane or beet	4 lb	1.90	4Q 92	4c
Tomatoes, Hunt's or Del Monte	14.5-oz can	0.96	4Q 92	4c
Tuna, chunk, light	6.125-6.5 oz can	1.24	4Q 92	4c
Health Care				
ACCRA Index, Health Care		166.60	4Q 92	4c
Analgesic, Aspirin, Bayer, 325 mg tablets	100	8.10	4Q 92	4c
Dentist's fee, adult teeth cleaning and periodic oral exam	visit	103.33	4Q 92	4c
Doctor's fee, routine exam, established patient	visit	49.33	4Q 92	4c
Hospital care, semiprivate room	day	406.00	4Q 92	4c
Household Goods				
Appliance repair, home, service call, washing machine	min labor charge	25.98	4Q 92	4c
Laundry detergent, Tide Ultra, Bold, or Cheer	42 oz	5.97	4Q 92	4c
Tissues, facial, Kleenex brand	175-count box	1.95	4Q 92	4c
Housing				
ACCRA Index, Housing		166.00	4Q 92	4c
House, 1,800 sq ft, 8,000 sq ft lot, new, urban	total	185049	4Q 92	4c
House payment, principal and interest, 25% down payment	month	1045	4Q 92	4c
Mortgage rate, incl. points & origination fee, 30-year fixed or adjustable rate	percent	8.27	4Q 92	4c
Rent, apartment, 2 bedrooms - 1-1/2 to 2 baths, unfurnished, 950 sq ft, water	month	763	4Q 92	4c
Personal Goods				
Shampoo, Alberto VO5	15 oz	2.16	4Q 92	4c
Toothpaste, Crest or Colgate	6-7 oz	3.20	4Q 92	4c
Personal Services				
Dry cleaning, man's 2-piece suit		9.00	4Q 92	4c
Haircare, woman's shampoo, trim and blow-dry		23.62	4Q 92	4c
Haircut, man's barbershop, no styling		9.00	4Q 92	4c
Restaurant Food				
Chicken, fried, thigh and drumstick		2.19	4Q 92	4c
Hamburger with cheese	1/4 lb	2.59	4Q 92	4c

Values are in dollars or fractions of dollars. In the column headed *Ref*, references are shown to sources. Each reference is followed by a letter. These refer to the geographical level for which data were reported: s=State, r=Region, and c=City or metro. The abbreviation *ex* is used to mean *except* or *excluding*; *exp* stands for *expenditures*. For other abbreviations and further explanations, please see the Introduction.

Kodiak, AK - continued

Item	Per	Value	Date	Ref.
Restaurant Food				
Pizza, Pizza Hut or Pizza Inn, cheese, thin crust	12-13 in	10.99	4Q 92	4c
Transportation				
ACCRA Index, Transportation		103.40	4Q 92	4c
Tire balance, computer or spin balance, front	wheel	5.00	4Q 92	4c
Utilities				
ACCRA Index, Utilities		185.70	4Q 92	4c
Electricity, partial electric and other energy, 1,800 sq ft living area new home	month	98.89	4Q 92	4c

Kokomo, IN

Item	Per	Value	Date	Ref.
Child Care				
Child care fee, average, center	hour	1.63	90	65r
Child care fee, average, nonregulated family day care	hour	1.83	90	65r
Child care fee, average, regulated family day care	hour	1.42	90	65r
Communications				
Long-distance telephone service, day, initial minute, 0-100 miles	min	0.18-0.45	91	12s
Long-distance telephone service, day, additional minute, 0-100 miles	min	0.10-0.30	91	12s
Long-distance telephone service, evenings/weekends, 0-100 mi, initial minute	min	0.08-0.19	91	12s
Long-distance telephone service, evenings/weekends, 0-100 mi, additional minute	min	0.04-0.13	91	12s
Education				
Board, 4-yr private college/university	year	1714	91	22s
Board, 4-yr public college/university	year	1829	91	22s
Expenditures, local gov't, public elementary/secondary	pupil	5545	92	20s
Room, 4-year private college/university	year	1512	91	22s
Room, 4-year public college/university	year	1435	91	22s
Tuition, 2-year private college/university	year	6756	91	22s
Tuition, 2-year public college/university	year	1423	91	22s
Tuition, 4-year private college/university	year	8451	91	22s
Tuition, 4-year public college/university, in-state	year	2067	91	22s
Energy and Fuels				
Coal	mil Btu	1.46	90	64s
Energy	mil Btu	6.77	90	64s
Energy exp/householder, 1-family unit	year	471	90	28r
Energy exp/householder, <1,000 sq ft heating area	year	430	90	28r
Energy exp/householder, 1,000-1,999 sq ft heating area	year	481	90	28r
Energy exp/householder, 2,000+ sq ft heating area	year	473	90	28r
Energy exp/householder, mobile home	year	430	90	28r
Energy exp/householder, multifamily	year	461	90	28r
Gas, natural	mil Btu	4.27	90	64s
Gas, natural	000 cu ft	5.46	91	46s
Gas, natural, exp	year	588	91	46s
Gasoline, unleaded regular	mil Btu	8.74	90	64s
Entertainment				
Miniature golf admission	adult	6.18	92	1r
Miniature golf admission	child	5.14	92	1r
Waterpark admission	adult	11.00	92	1r
Waterpark admission	child	8.55	92	1r
Funerals				
Casket, 18-gauge steel, velvet interior		1926.72	91	24r
Cosmetology, hair care, etc.		97.64	91	24r
Embalming		249.14	91	24r
Facility use for ceremony		208.59	91	24r

Kokomo, IN - continued

Item	Per	Value	Date	Ref.
Funerals - continued				
Hearse, local		130.12	91	24r
Limousine, local		104.66	91	24r
Remains to funeral home, transfer		93.61	91	24r
Service charge, professional		724.62	91	24r
Vault, concrete, non-metallic liner		734.53	91	24r
Viewing facilities, use		236.06	91	24r
Groceries				
Apples, Red Delicious	lb	0.77	4/93	16r
Bacon	lb	1.85	4/93	16r
Bananas	lb	0.46	4/93	16r
Beef, stew, boneless	lb	2.53	4/93	16r
Bologna, all beef or mixed	lb	2.19	4/93	16r
Bread, white, pan	lb	0.78	4/93	16r
Butter	lb	1.50	4/93	16r
Cabbage	lb	0.40	4/93	16r
Carrots, short trimmed and topped	lb	0.45	4/93	16r
Cheese, Cheddar	lb	3.47	4/93	16r
Chicken, fresh, whole	lb	0.84	4/93	16r
Chicken breast, bone-in	lb	1.94	4/93	16r
Chicken legs, bone-in	lb	1.02	4/93	16r
Chuck roast, graded and ungraded, ex USDA prime and choice	lb	2.43	4/93	16r
Chuck roast, USDA choice, bone-in	lb	2.11	4/93	16r
Chuck roast, USDA choice, boneless	lb	2.44	4/93	16r
Coffee, 100% ground roast, all sizes	lb	2.47	4/93	16r
Cookies, chocolate chip	lb	2.73	4/93	16r
Eggs, Grade A large	doz	0.93	4/93	16r
Flour, white, all purpose	lb	0.21	4/93	16r
Grapefruit	lb	0.45	4/93	16r
Grapes, Thompson Seedless	lb	1.46	4/93	16r
Ground beef, 100% beef	lb	1.63	4/93	16r
Ground beef, lean and extra lean	lb	2.08	4/93	10r
Ground chuck, 100% beef	lb	1.94	4/93	16r
Ham, boneless, excluding canned	lb	2.21	4/93	16r
Honey, jar	8 oz	0.97-1.25	92	5r
Honey, jar	lb	1.25-2.25	92	5r
Honey, squeeze bear	12-oz	1.25-1.99	92	5r
Ice cream, prepackaged, bulk, regular	1/2 gal	2.41	4/93	16r
Lemons	lb	0.82	4/93	16r
Lettuce, iceberg	lb	0.83	4/93	16r
Margarine, stick	lb	0.77	4/93	16r
Oranges, navel	lb	0.50	4/93	16r
Peanut butter, creamy, all sizes	lb	1.82	4/93	16r
Pears, Anjou	lb	0.85	4/93	16r
Pork chops, center cut, bone-in	lb	3.17	4/93	16r
Potato chips	16 oz	2.68	4/93	16r
Potatoes, white	lb	0.26	4/93	16r
Round roast, graded & ungraded, ex USDA prime & choice	lb	2.88	4/93	16r
Round roast, USDA choice, boneless	lb	2.96	4/93	16r
Shortening, vegetable oil blends	lb	0.79	4/93	16r
Spaghetti and macaroni	lb	0.76	4/93	16r
Steak, rib eye, USDA choice, boneless	lb	6.29	4/93	16r
Steak, round, USDA choice, boneless	lb	3.24	4/93	16r
Steak, sirloin, graded & ungraded, ex USDA prime & choice	lb	4.00	4/93	16r
Steak, sirloin, USDA choice, bone-in	lb	3.57	4/93	16r
Steak, sirloin, USDA choice, boneless	lb	4.17	4/93	16r
Steak, T-bone, USDA choice, bone-in	lb	5.60	4/93	16r
Strawberries, dry pint	12 oz	0.90	4/93	16r
Sugar, white	lb	0.36	4/93	16r
Sugar, white, 33-80 oz pk	lb	0.35	4/93	16r
Tomatoes, field grown	lb	0.99	4/93	16r
Tuna, chunk, light	lb	1.76	4/93	16r
Turkey, frozen, whole	lb	0.91	4/93	16r
Health Care				
Childbirth, cesarean, hospital		4688	91	62r
Childbirth, cesarean, physician's fee		2053	91	62r
Childbirth, normal, hospital		2657	91	62r
Childbirth, normal, physician's fee		1492	91	62r
Medical plan per employee	year	3443	91	45r

Values are in dollars or fractions of dollars. In the column headed *Ref*, references are shown to sources. Each reference is followed by a letter. These refer to the geographical level for which data were reported: s = State, r = Region, and c = City or metro. The abbreviation *ex* is used to mean *except* or *excluding*; *exp* stands for expenditures. For other abbreviations and further explanations, please see the Introduction.

Kokomo, IN - continued

Item	Per	Value	Date	Ref.
Health Care				
Mental health care, exp	capita	37.60-53.67	90	38s
Mental health care, exp, state mental health agency	capita	47.05	90	38s
Mental health care, hospital psychiatric services, non-Federal, exp	capita	22.14	88	38s
Mental health care, mental health organization, multiservice, exp	capita	10.33	88	38s
Mental health care, psychiatric hospitals, private, exp	capita	20.10	88	38s
Mental health care, state and county mental hospitals, exp	capita	24.00	88	38s
Mental health care, VA medical centers, exp	capita	3.20	88	38s
Physician fee, family practice, first-visit		76.00	91	62r
Physician fee, family practice, revisit		33.00	91	62r
Physician fee, general practice, first-visit		61.00	91	62r
Physician fee, general practice, revisit		31.00	91	62r
Physician fee, general surgeon, first-visit		65.00	91	62r
Physician fee, general surgeon, revisit		35.00	91	62r
Physician fee, internal medicine, first-visit		91.00	91	62r
Physician fee, internal medicine, revisit		40.00	91	62r
Physician fee, median, neurosurgeon, first-visit		106.00	91	62r
Physician fee, median, nonsurgical specialist, first-visit		90.00	91	62r
Physician fee, median, orthopedic surgeon, first-visit		83.00	91	62r
Physician fee, median, surgical specialist, first-visit		61.00	91	62r
Physician fee, neurosurgeon, revisit		41.00	91	62r
Physician fee, nonsurgical specialist, revisit		40.00	91	62r
Physician fee, obstetrics/gynecology, first-visit		61.00	91	62r
Physician fee, obstetrics/gynecology, revisit		40.00	91	62r
Physician fee, orthopedic surgeon, revisit		41.00	91	62r
Physician fee, pediatrician, first-visit		46.00	91	62r
Physician fee, pediatrician, revisit		33.00	91	62r
Physician fee, surgical specialist, revisit		36.00	91	62r
Substance abuse, hospital ancillary charge	incident	1230	90	70s
Substance abuse, hospital physician charge	incident	410	90	70s
Substance abuse, hospital room and board	incident	5510	90	70s
Insurance and Pensions				
Auto insurance, private passenger	year	548.99	91	63s
Taxes				
Tax, cigarette	pack	15.50	91	77s
Tax, gasoline	gal	15	91	77s
Taxes, state	capita	1102	91	77s
Transportation				
Driver's license fee		6.00	12/90	43s
Utilities				
Electricity	mil Btu	15.75	90	64s

La Crosse, WI

Item	Per	Value	Date	Ref.
Composite ACCRA index		102.10	4Q 92	4c
Alcoholic Beverages				
Beer, Miller Lite or Budweiser, 12-oz containers	6 pack	3.33	4Q 92	4c
Liquor, J & B Scotch	750 ml	15.92	4Q 92	4c
Wine, Gallo Chablis blanc, 1.5 liter	bottle	4.45	4Q 92	4c
Child Care				
Child care fee, average, center	hour	1.63	90	65r
Child care fee, average, nonregulated family day care	hour	1.83	90	65r

La Crosse, WI - continued

Item	Per	Value	Date	Ref.
Child Care - continued				
Child care fee, average, regulated family day care	hour	1.42	90	65r
Clothing				
Jeans, man's denim		33.30	4Q 92	4c
Shirt, man's dress shirt		26.00	4Q 92	4c
Undervest, boy's size 10-14, cotton	3	3.41	4Q 92	4c
Communications				
Long-distance telephone service, day, initial minute, 0-100 miles	min	0.15-0.29	91	12s
Long-distance telephone service, day, additional minute, 0-100 miles	min	0.10-0.27	91	12s
Newspaper subscription, daily and Sunday home delivery, large-city	month	14.95	4Q 92	4c
Telephone bill, family of four	month	16.06	4Q 92	4c
Education				
Board, 4-yr private college/university	year	1533	91	22s
Board, 4-yr public college/university	year	1404	91	22s
Expenditures, local gov't, public elementary/secondary	pupil	5972	92	20s
Room, 4-year private college/university	year	1256	91	22s
Room, 4-year public college/university	year	1416	91	22s
Tuition, 2-year private college/university	year	4768	91	22s
Tuition, 2-year public college/university	year	1234	91	22s
Tuition, 4-year private college/university	year	8237	91	22s
Tuition, 4-year public college/university, in-state	year	1951	91	22s
Energy and Fuels				
Coal	mil Btu	1.41	90	64s
Energy	mil Btu	8.27	90	64s
Energy, combined forms, 1,800 sq ft heating area	month	106.11	4Q 92	4c
Energy, exc electricity, 1,800 sq ft heating area	month	60.91	4Q 92	4c
Energy exp/householder, 1-family unit	year	471	90	28r
Energy exp/householder, <1,000 sq ft heating area	year	430	90	28r
Energy exp/householder, 1,000-1,999 sq ft heating area	year	481	90	28r
Energy exp/householder, 2,000+ sq ft heating area	year	473	90	28r
Energy exp/householder, mobile home	year	430	90	28r
Energy exp/householder, multifamily	year	461	90	28r
Gas, natural	mil Btu	4.56	90	64s
Gas, natural	000 cu ft	5.61	91	46s
Gas, natural, exp	year	605	91	46s
Gasoline, motor	gal	1.18	4Q 92	4c
Gasoline, unleaded regular	mil Btu	9.38	90	64s
Entertainment				
Bowling, evening rate	game	1.46	4Q 92	4c
Miniature golf admission	adult	6.18	92	1r
Miniature golf admission	child	5.14	92	1r
Monopoly game, Parker Brothers', No. 9		10.95	4Q 92	4c
Movie	admission	5.58	4Q 92	4c
Tennis balls, yellow, Wilson or Penn, 3	can	2.18	4Q 92	4c
Waterpark admission	adult	11.00	92	1r
Waterpark admission	child	8.55	92	1r
Funerals				
Casket, 18-gauge steel, velvet interior		1926.72	91	24r
Cosmetology, hair care, etc.		97.64	91	24r
Embalming		249.14	91	24r
Facility use for ceremony		208.59	91	24r
Hearse, local		130.12	91	24r
Limousine, local		104.66	91	24r
Remains to funeral home, transfer		93.61	91	24r
Service charge, professional		724.62	91	24r
Vault, concrete, non-metallic liner		734.53	91	24r
Viewing facilities, use		236.06	91	24r

Values are in dollars or fractions of dollars. In the column headed *Ref*, references are shown to sources. Each reference is followed by a letter. These refer to the geographical level for which data were reported: s = State, r = Region, and c = City or metro. The abbreviation *ex* is used to mean *except* or *excluding*; *exp* stands for expenditures. For other abbreviations and further explanations, please see the Introduction.

La Crosse, WI - continued

Item	Per	Value	Date	Ref.
Goods and Services				
ACCRA Index, Miscellaneous Goods and Services		97.00	4Q 92	4c
Groceries				
ACCRA Index, Groceries		95.80	4Q 92	4c
Apples, Red Delicious	lb	0.77	4/93	16r
Babyfood, strained vegetables, lowest price	4-4.5 oz jar	0.40	4Q 92	4c
Bacon	lb	1.85	4/93	16r
Bananas	lb	0.29	4Q 92	4c
Bananas	lb	0.46	4/93	16r
Beef, stew, boneless	lb	2.53	4/93	16r
Bologna, all beef or mixed	lb	2.19	4/93	16r
Bread, white	24 oz	0.65	4Q 92	4c
Bread, white, pan	lb	0.78	4/93	16r
Butter	lb	1.50	4/93	16r
Cabbage	lb	0.40	4/93	16r
Carrots, short trimmed and topped	lb	0.45	4/93	16r
Cheese, Cheddar	lb	3.47	4/93	16r
Cheese, Kraft grated Parmesan	8-oz canister	3.29	4Q 92	4c
Chicken, fresh, whole	lb	0.84	4/93	16r
Chicken, fryer, whole	lb	0.85	4Q 92	4c
Chicken breast, bone-in	lb	1.94	4/93	16r
Chicken legs, bone-in	lb	1.02	4/93	16r
Chuck roast, graded and ungraded, ex USDA prime and choice	lb	2.43	4/93	16r
Chuck roast, USDA choice, bone-in	lb	2.11	4/93	16r
Chuck roast, USDA choice, boneless	lb	2.44	4/93	16r
Cigarettes, Winston	carton	18.75	4Q 92	4c
Coffee, 100% ground roast, all sizes	lb	2.47	4/93	16r
Coffee, vacuum-packed	13-oz can	1.89	4Q 92	4c
Cookies, chocolate chip	lb	2.73	4/93	16r
Corn, frozen	10 oz	0.61	4Q 92	4c
Corn Flakes, Kellogg's or Post Toasties	18 oz	1.86	4Q 92	4c
Eggs, Grade A large	doz	0.71	4Q 92	4c
Eggs, Grade A large	doz	0.93	4/93	16r
Flour, white, all purpose	lb	0.21	4/93	16r
Grapefruit	lb	0.45	4/93	16r
Grapes, Thompson Seedless	lb	1.46	4/93	16r
Ground beef, 100% beef	lb	1.63	4/93	16r
Ground beef, lean and extra lean	lb	2.08	4/93	16r
Ground beef or hamburger	lb	1.41	4Q 92	4c
Ground chuck, 100% beef	lb	1.94	4/93	16r
Ham, boneless, excluding canned	lb	2.21	4/93	16r
Honey, jar	8 oz	0.97-1.25	92	5r
Honey, jar	lb	1.25-2.25	92	5r
Honey, squeeze bear	12-oz	1.25-1.99	92	5r
Ice cream, prepackaged, bulk, regular	1/2 gal	2.41	4/93	16r
Lemons	lb	0.82	4/93	16r
Lettuce, iceberg	head	0.81	4Q 92	4c
Lettuce, iceberg	lb	0.83	4/93	16r
Margarine, Blue Bonnet or Parkay cubes	lb	0.59	4Q 92	4c
Margarine, stick	lb	0.77	4/93	16r
Milk, whole	1/2 gal	1.45	4Q 92	4c
Orange juice, Minute Maid frozen	12-oz can	1.29	4Q 92	4c
Oranges, navel	lb	0.50	4/93	16r
Peaches	29-oz can	1.33	4Q 92	4c
Peanut butter, creamy, all sizes	lb	1.82	4/93	16r
Pears, Anjou	lb	0.85	4/93	16r
Peas Sweet, Del Monte or Green Giant	15-17 oz can	0.51	4Q 92	4c
Pork chops, center cut, bone-in	lb	3.17	4/93	16r
Potato chips	16 oz	2.68	4/93	16r
Potatoes, white	lb	0.26	4/93	16r
Potatoes, white or red	10-lb sack	1.97	4Q 92	4c
Round roast, graded & ungraded, ex USDA prime & choice	lb	2.88	4/93	16r

La Crosse, WI - continued

Item	Per	Value	Date	Ref.
Groceries - continued				
Round roast, USDA choice, boneless	lb	2.96	4/93	16r
Sausage, Jimmy Dean, 100% pork	lb	2.55	4Q 92	4c
Shortening, vegetable oil blends	lb	0.79	4/93	16r
Shortening, vegetable, Crisco	3-lb can	2.29	4Q 92	4c
Soft drink, Coca Cola	2 liter	1.03	4Q 92	4c
Spaghetti and macaroni	lb	0.76	4/93	16r
Steak, rib eye, USDA choice, boneless	lb	6.29	4/93	16r
Steak, round, USDA choice, boneless	lb	3.24	4/93	16r
Steak, sirloin, graded & ungraded, ex USDA prime & choice	lb	4.00	4/93	16r
Steak, sirloin, USDA choice, bone-in	lb	3.57	4/93	16r
Steak, sirloin, USDA choice, boneless	lb	4.17	4/93	16r
Steak, T-bone	lb	4.40	4Q 92	4c
Steak, T-bone, USDA choice, bone-in	lb	5.60	4/93	16r
Strawberries, dry pint	12 oz	0.90	4/93	16r
Sugar, cane or beet	4 lb	1.52	4Q 92	4c
Sugar, white	lb	0.36	4/93	16r
Sugar, white, 33-80 oz pk	lb	0.35	4/93	16r
Tomatoes, field grown	lb	0.99	4/93	16r
Tomatoes, Hunt's or Del Monte	14.5-oz can	0.68	4Q 92	4c
Tuna, chunk, light	6.125-6.5 oz can	0.60	4Q 92	4c
Tuna, chunk, light	lb	1.76	4/93	16r
Turkey, frozen, whole	lb	0.91	4/93	16r
Health Care				
ACCRA Index, Health Care		128.60	4Q 92	4c
Analgesic, Aspirin, Bayer, 325 mg tablets	100	5.42	4Q 92	4c
Childbirth, cesarean, hospital		4688	91	62r
Childbirth, cesarean, physician's fee		2053	91	62r
Childbirth, normal, hospital		2657	91	62r
Childbirth, normal, physician's fee		1492	91	62r
Dentist's fee, adult teeth cleaning and periodic oral exam	visit	46.40	4Q 92	4c
Doctor's fee, routine exam, established patient	visit	62.60	4Q 92	4c
Hospital care, semiprivate room	day	208.99	90	27c
Hospital care, semiprivate room	day	380.00	4Q 92	4c
Medical insurance premium, per employee, small group comprehensive	month	273.75	10/91	25c
Medical plan per employee	year	3443	91	45r
Mental health care, exp	capita	28.84-37.59	90	38s
Mental health care, exp, state mental health agency	capita	36.62	90	38s
Mental health care, hospital psychiatric services, non-Federal, exp	capita	13.05	88	38s
Mental health care, mental health organization, multiservice, exp	capita	10.93	88	38s
Mental health care, psychiatric hospitals, private, exp	capita	8.71	88	38s
Mental health care, psychiatric out-patient clinics, freestanding, exp	capita	5.33	88	38s
Mental health care, psychiatric partial-care organizations, freestanding, exp	capita	0.20	88	38s
Mental health care, state and county mental hospitals, exp	capita	28.29	88	38s
Mental health care, VA medical centers, exp	capita	7.57	88	38s
Physician fee, family practice, first-visit		76.00	91	62r
Physician fee, family practice, revisit		33.00	91	62r
Physician fee, general practice, first-visit		61.00	91	62r
Physician fee, general practice, revisit		31.00	91	62r
Physician fee, general surgeon, first-visit		65.00	91	62r
Physician fee, general surgeon, revisit		35.00	91	62r
Physician fee, internal medicine, first-visit		91.00	91	62r
Physician fee, internal medicine, revisit		40.00	91	62r
Physician fee, median, neurosurgeon, first-visit		106.00	91	62r
Physician fee, median, nonsurgical specialist, first-visit		90.00	91	62r

Values are in dollars or fractions of dollars. In the column headed *Ref*, references are shown to sources. Each reference is followed by a letter. These refer to the geographical level for which data were reported: s=State, r=Region, and c=City or metro. The abbreviation *ex* is used to mean *except* or *excluding*; *exp* stands for expenditures. For other abbreviations and further explanations, please see the Introduction.

La Crosse, WI - continued

Item	Per	Value	Date	Ref.
Health Care				
Physician fee, median, orthopedic surgeon, first-visit		83.00	91	62r
Physician fee, median, surgical specialist, first-visit		61.00	91	62r
Physician fee, neurosurgeon, revisit		41.00	91	62r
Physician fee, nonsurgical specialist, revisit		40.00	91	62r
Physician fee, obstetrics/gynecology, first-visit		61.00	91	62r
Physician fee, obstetrics/gynecology, revisit		40.00	91	62r
Physician fee, orthopedic surgeon, revisit		41.00	91	62r
Physician fee, pediatrician, first-visit		46.00	91	62r
Physician fee, pediatrician, revisit		33.00	91	62r
Physician fee, surgical specialist, revisit		36.00	91	62r
Substance abuse, hospital ancillary charge	incident	960	90	70s
Substance abuse, hospital physician charge	incident	470	90	70s
Substance abuse, hospital room and board	incident	3980	90	70s
Household Goods				
Appliance repair, home, service call, washing machine	min labor charge	31.08	4Q 92	4c
Laundry detergent, Tide Ultra, Bold, or Cheer	42 oz	2.87	4Q 92	4c
Tissues, facial, Kleenex brand	175-count box	1.05	4Q 92	4c
Housing				
ACCRA Index, Housing		111.60	4Q 92	4c
House, 1,800 sq ft, 8,000 sq ft lot, new, urban	total	131467	4Q 92	4c
House payment, principal and interest, 25% down payment	month	743	4Q 92	4c
Mortgage rate, incl. points & origination fee, 30-year fixed or adjustable rate	percent	8.29	4Q 92	4c
Rent, apartment, 2 bedrooms - 1-1/2 to 2 baths, unfurnished, 950 sq ft, water	month	418	4Q 92	4c
Rental unit, 1 bedroom	month	432	93	23c
Rental unit, 2 bedroom	month	508	93	23c
Rental unit, 3 bedroom	month	635	93	23c
Rental unit, 4 bedroom	month	712	93	23c
Rental unit, efficiency	month	356	93	23c
Insurance and Pensions				
Auto insurance, private passenger	year	510.11	91	63s
Personal Goods				
Shampoo, Alberto VO5	15 oz	1.39	4Q 92	4c
Toothpaste, Crest or Colgate	6-7 oz	2.15	4Q 92	4c
Personal Services				
Dry cleaning, man's 2-piece suit		6.12	4Q 92	4c
Haircare, woman's shampoo, trim and blow-dry		12.20	4Q 92	4c
Haircut, man's barbershop, no styling		7.65	4Q 92	4c
Restaurant Food				
Chicken, fried, thigh and drumstick		2.12	4Q 92	4c
Hamburger with cheese	1/4 lb	1.75	4Q 92	4c
Pizza, Pizza Hut or Pizza Inn, cheese, thin crust	12-13 in	7.49	4Q 92	4c
Taxes				
Tax, cigarette	pack	38	91	77s
Tax, gasoline	gal	22.20	91	77s
Taxes, state	capita	1416	91	77s
Transportation				
ACCRA Index, Transportation		93.90	4Q 92	4c
Bus fare	one-way	0.65	3/93	2c
Bus fare, up to 10 miles	one-way	0.60	4Q 92	4c

La Crosse, WI - continued

Item	Per	Value	Date	Ref.
Transportation - continued				
Driver's license fee		9.00	12/90	43s
Tire balance, computer or spin balance, front	wheel	5.80	4Q 92	4c
Utilities				
ACCRA Index, Utilities		95.70	4Q 92	4c
Electricity	mil Btu	15.77	90	64s
Electricity, partial electric and other energy, 1,800 sq ft living area new home	month	45.20	4Q 92	4c

LaGrange, GA

Item	Per	Value	Date	Ref.
Composite ACCRA index		97.30	4Q 92	4c
Alcoholic Beverages				
Beer, Miller Lite or Budweiser, 12-oz containers	6 pack	4.42	4Q 92	4c
Liquor, J & B Scotch	750 ml	17.51	4Q 92	4c
Wine, Gallo Chablis blanc, 1.5 liter	bottle	6.65	4Q 92	4c
Clothing				
Jeans, man's denim		30.49	4Q 92	4c
Shirt, man's dress shirt		21.95	4Q 92	4c
Undervest, boy's size 10-14, cotton	3	5.48	4Q 92	4c
Communications				
Newspaper subscription, daily and Sunday home delivery, large-city	month	12.61	4Q 92	4c
Telephone bill, family of four	month	18.13	4Q 92	4c
Energy and Fuels				
Energy, combined forms, 1,800 sq ft heating area	month	111.96	4Q 92	4c
Gasoline, motor	gal	0.97	4Q 92	4c
Entertainment				
Bowling, evening rate	game	2.25	4Q 92	4c
Monopoly game, Parker Brothers', No. 9		10.96	4Q 92	4c
Movie	admission	5.00	4Q 92	4c
Tennis balls, yellow, Wilson or Penn, 3	can	2.26	4Q 92	4c
Groceries				
ACCRA Index, Groceries		97.60	4Q 92	4c
Babyfood, strained vegetables, lowest price	4-4.5 oz jar	0.28	4Q 92	4c
Bananas	lb	0.48	4Q 92	4c
Bread, white	24 oz	0.83	4Q 92	4c
Cheese, Kraft grated Parmesan	8-oz canister	2.98	4Q 92	4c
Cigarettes, Winston	carton	16.44	4Q 92	4c
Coffee, vacuum-packed	13-oz can	2.09	4Q 92	4c
Corn, frozen	10 oz	0.56	4Q 92	4c
Corn Flakes, Kellogg's or Post Toasties	18 oz	1.66	4Q 92	4c
Eggs, Grade A large	doz	0.84	4Q 92	4c
Lettuce, iceberg	head	0.99	4Q 92	4c
Margarine, Blue Bonnet or Parkay cubes	lb	0.49	4Q 92	4c
Orange juice, Minute Maid frozen	12-oz can	1.24	4Q 92	4c
Peaches	29-oz can	1.32	4Q 92	4c
Peas Sweet, Del Monte or Green Giant	15-17 oz can	0.58	4Q 92	4c
Potatoes, white or red	10-lb sack	2.44	4Q 92	4c
Shortening, vegetable, Crisco	3-lb can	2.05	4Q 92	4c
Soft drink, Coca Cola	2 liter	1.07	4Q 92	4c
Sugar, cane or beet	4 lb	1.33	4Q 92	4c
Tomatoes, Hunt's or Del Monte	14.5-oz can	0.54	4Q 92	4c

Values are in dollars or fractions of dollars. In the column headed Ref, references are shown to sources. Each reference is followed by a letter. These refer to the geographical level for which data were reported: s=State, r=Region, and c=City or metro. The abbreviation ex is used to mean except or excluding; exp stands for expenditures. For other abbreviations and further explanations, please see the Introduction.

LaGrange, GA - continued

Item	Per	Value	Date	Ref.
Health Care				
ACCRA Index, Health Care		95.40	4Q 92	4c
Analgesic, Aspirin, Bayer, 325 mg tablets	100	4.29	4Q 92	4c
Dentist's fee, adult teeth cleaning and periodic oral exam	visit	43.33	4Q 92	4c
Doctor's fee, routine exam, established patient	visit	42.20	4Q 92	4c
Hospital care, semiprivate room	day	223.00	4Q 92	4c
Household Goods				
Appliance repair, home, service call, washing machine	min labor charge	32.08	4Q 92	4c
Laundry detergent, Tide Ultra, Bold, or Cheer	42 oz	2.89	4Q 92	4c
Tissues, facial, Kleenex brand	175-count box	0.96	4Q 92	4c
Housing				
ACCRA Index, Housing		88.40	4Q 92	4c
House, 1,800 sq ft, 8,000 sq ft lot, new, urban	total	95700	4Q 92	4c
House payment, principal and interest, 25% down payment	month	531	4Q 92	4c
Mortgage rate, incl. points & origination fee, 30-year fixed or adjustable rate	percent	8.09	4Q 92	4c
Rent, apartment, 2 bedrooms - 1-1/2 to 2 baths, unfurnished, 950 sq ft, water	month	466	4Q 92	4c
Personal Goods				
Shampoo, Alberto VO5	15 oz	1.12	4Q 92	4c
Toothpaste, Crest or Colgate	6-7 oz	1.73	4Q 92	4c
Personal Services				
Dry cleaning, man's 2-piece suit		6.07	4Q 92	4c
Haircare, woman's shampoo, trim and blow-dry		17.60	4Q 92	4c
Haircut, man's barbershop, no styling		8.60	4Q 92	4c
Restaurant Food				
Chicken, fried, thigh and drumstick		2.03	4Q 92	4c
Hamburger with cheese	1/4 lb	1.95	4Q 92	4c
Pizza, Pizza Hut or Pizza Inn, cheese, thin crust	12-13 in	8.24	4Q 92	4c
Transportation				
ACCRA Index, Transportation		97.00	4Q 92	4c
Tire balance, computer or spin balance, front	wheel	7.00	4Q 92	4c
Utilities				
ACCRA Index, Utilities		101.60	4Q 92	4c
Electricity, all electric, 1,800 sq ft living area new home	month	111.96	4Q 92	4c

LaPorte, IN

Item	Per	Value	Date	Ref.
Composite ACCRA index		98.90	4Q 92	4c
Alcoholic Beverages				
Beer, Miller Lite or Budweiser, 12-oz containers	6 pack	3.94	4Q 92	4c
Liquor, J & B Scotch	750 ml	18.79	4Q 92	4c
Wine, Gallo Chablis blanc, 1.5 liter	bottle	5.52	4Q 92	4c
Clothing				
Jeans, man's denim		36.49	4Q 92	4c
Shirt, man's dress shirt		25.67	4Q 92	4c
Undervest, boy's size 10-14, cotton	3	4.18	4Q 92	4c
Communications				
Newspaper subscription, daily and Sunday home delivery, large-city	month	10.00	4Q 92	4c
Telephone bill, family of four	month	25.28	4Q 92	4c

LaPorte, IN - continued

Item	Per	Value	Date	Ref.
Energy and Fuels				
Energy, combined forms, 1,800 sq ft heating area	month	123.43	4Q 92	4c
Energy, exc electricity, 1,800 sq ft heating area	month	52.64	4Q 92	4c
Gasoline, motor	gal	1.10	4Q 92	4c
Entertainment				
Bowling, evening rate	game	1.80	4Q 92	4c
Monopoly game, Parker Brothers', No. 9		13.71	4Q 92	4c
Movie	admission	4.00	4Q 92	4c
Tennis balls, yellow, Wilson or Penn, 3	can	3.34	4Q 92	4c
Goods and Services				
ACCRA Index, Miscellaneous Goods and Services		100.10	4Q 92	4c
Groceries				
ACCRA Index, Groceries		102.60	4Q 92	4c
Babyfood, strained vegetables, lowest price	4-4.5 oz jar	0.40	4Q 92	4c
Bananas	lb	0.40	4Q 92	4c
Bread, white	24 oz	0.62	4Q 92	4c
Cheese, Kraft grated Parmesan	8-oz canister	3.43	4Q 92	4c
Chicken, fryer, whole	lb	0.56	4Q 92	4c
Cigarettes, Winston	carton	16.98	4Q 92	4c
Coffee, vacuum-packed	13-oz can	2.36	4Q 92	4c
Corn, frozen	10 oz	0.66	4Q 92	4c
Corn Flakes, Kellogg's or Post Toasties	18 oz	2.06	4Q 92	4c
Eggs, Grade A large	doz	0.78	4Q 92	4c
Ground beef or hamburger	lb	1.69	4Q 92	4c
Lettuce, iceberg	head	0.96	4Q 92	4c
Margarine, Blue Bonnet or Parkay cubes	lb	0.78	4Q 92	4c
Milk, whole	1/2 gal	1.54	4Q 92	4c
Orange juice, Minute Maid frozen	12-oz can	1.49	4Q 92	4c
Peaches	29-oz can	1.29	4Q 92	4c
Peas Sweet, Del Monte or Green Giant	15-17 oz can	0.66	4Q 92	4c
Potatoes, white or red	10-lb sack	1.16	4Q 92	4c
Sausage, Jimmy Dean, 100% pork	lb	2.94	4Q 92	4c
Shortening, vegetable, Crisco	3-lb can	2.71	4Q 92	4c
Soft drink, Coca Cola	2 liter	0.99	4Q 92	4c
Steak, T-bone	lb	4.92	4Q 92	4c
Sugar, cane or beet	4 lb	1.60	4Q 92	4c
Tomatoes, Hunt's or Del Monte	14.5-oz can	0.78	4Q 92	4c
Tuna, chunk, light	6.125-6.5 oz can	0.85	4Q 92	4c
Health Care				
ACCRA Index, Health Care		99.80	4Q 92	4c
Analgesic, Aspirin, Bayer, 325 mg tablets	100	4.81	4Q 92	4c
Dentist's fee, adult teeth cleaning and periodic oral exam	visit	45.40	4Q 92	4c
Doctor's fee, routine exam, established patient	visit	37.20	4Q 92	4c
Hospital care, semiprivate room	day	336.67	4Q 92	4c
Household Goods				
Appliance repair, home, service call, washing machine	min labor charge	25.97	4Q 92	4c
Laundry detergent, Tide Ultra, Bold, or Cheer	42 oz	3.89	4Q 92	4c

Values are in dollars or fractions of dollars. In the column headed *Ref*, references are shown to sources. Each reference is followed by a letter. These refer to the geographical level for which data were reported: s=State, r=Region, and c=City or metro. The abbreviation *ex* is used to mean *except* or *excluding*; *exp* stands for *expenditures*. For other abbreviations and further explanations, please see the Introduction.

LaPorte, IN - continued

Item	Per	Value	Date	Ref.
Household Goods				
Tissues, facial, Kleenex brand	175-count box	1.12	4Q 92	4c
Housing				
ACCRA Index, Housing		92.00	4Q 92	4c
House, 1,800 sq ft, 8,000 sq ft lot, new, urban	total	103633	4Q 92	4c
House payment, principal and interest, 25% down payment	month	583	4Q 92	4c
Mortgage rate, incl. points & origination fee, 30-year fixed or adjustable rate	per-cent	8.24	4Q 92	4c
Rent, apartment, 2 bedrooms - 1-1/2 to 2 baths, unfurnished, 950 sq ft, water	month	413	4Q 92	4c
Personal Goods				
Shampoo, Alberto VO5	15 oz	1.22	4Q 92	4c
Toothpaste, Crest or Colgate	6-7 oz	1.97	4Q 92	4c
Personal Services				
Dry cleaning, man's 2-piece suit		5.73	4Q 92	4c
Haircare, woman's shampoo, trim and blow-dry		14.67	4Q 92	4c
Haircut, man's barbershop, no styling		6.33	4Q 92	4c
Restaurant Food				
Chicken, fried, thigh and drumstick		1.98	4Q 92	4c
Hamburger with cheese	1/4 lb	1.75	4Q 92	4c
Pizza, Pizza Hut or Pizza Inn, cheese, thin crust	12-13 in	7.59	4Q 92	4c
Transportation				
ACCRA Index, Transportation		94.60	4Q 92	4c
Tire balance, computer or spin balance, front	wheel	6.00	4Q 92	4c
Utilities				
ACCRA Index, Utilities		114.70	4Q 92	4c
Electricity, partial electric and other energy, 1,800 sq ft living area new home	month	70.79	4Q 92	4c

Lafayette, IN

Item	Per	Value	Date	Ref.
Composite ACCRA index		99.30	4Q 92	4c
Alcoholic Beverages				
Beer, Miller Lite or Budweiser, 12-oz containers	6 pack	3.56	4Q 92	4c
Liquor, J & B Scotch	750 ml	14.77	4Q 92	4c
Wine, Gallo Chablis blanc, 1.5 liter	bottle	4.59	4Q 92	4c
Clothing				
Jeans, man's denim		27.19	4Q 92	4c
Shirt, man's dress shirt		19.99	4Q 92	4c
Undervest, boy's size 10-14, cotton	3	4.69	4Q 92	4c
Communications				
Newspaper subscription, daily and Sunday home delivery, large-city	month	13.04	4Q 92	4c
Telephone bill, family of four	month	23.59	4Q 92	4c
Energy and Fuels				
Energy, combined forms, 1,800 sq ft heating area	month	102.49	4Q 92	4c
Energy, exc electricity, 1,800 sq ft heating area	month	48.01	4Q 92	4c
Gasoline, motor	gal	1.06	4Q 92	4c
Entertainment				
Bowling, evening rate	game	1.80	4Q 92	4c
Monopoly game, Parker Brothers', No. 9		10.39	4Q 92	4c
Movie	admis-sion	5.00	4Q 92	4c
Tennis balls, yellow, Wilson or Penn, 3	can	3.10	4Q 92	4c

Lafayette, IN - continued

Item	Per	Value	Date	Ref.
Goods and Services				
ACCRA Index, Miscellaneous Goods and Services		100.40	4Q 92	4c
Groceries				
ACCRA Index, Groceries		100.00	4Q 92	4c
Babyfood, strained vegetables, lowest price	4-4.5 oz jar	0.32	4Q 92	4c
Bananas	lb	0.32	4Q 92	4c
Bread, white	24 oz	0.82	4Q 92	4c
Cheese, Kraft grated Parmesan	8-oz canister	3.36	4Q 92	4c
Chicken, fryer, whole	lb	0.68	4Q 92	4c
Cigarettes, Winston	carton	16.27	4Q 92	4c
Coffee, vacuum-packed	13-oz can	1.93	4Q 92	4c
Corn, frozen	10 oz	0.64	4Q 92	4c
Corn Flakes, Kellogg's or Post Toasties	18 oz	1.94	4Q 92	4c
Eggs, Grade A large	doz	0.72	4Q 92	4c
Ground beef or hamburger	lb	1.54	4Q 92	4c
Lettuce, iceberg	head	0.99	4Q 92	4c
Margarine, Blue Bonnet or Parkay cubes	lb	0.56	4Q 92	4c
Milk, whole	1/2 gal	1.47	4Q 92	4c
Orange juice, Minute Maid frozen	12-oz can	1.16	4Q 92	4c
Peaches	29-oz can	1.28	4Q 92	4c
Peas Sweet, Del Monte or Green Giant	15-17 oz can	0.60	4Q 92	4c
Potatoes, white or red	10-lb sack	2.44	4Q 92	4c
Sausage, Jimmy Dean, 100% pork	lb	3.36	4Q 92	4c
Shortening, vegetable, Crisco	3-lb can	2.34	4Q 92	4c
Soft drink, Coca Cola	2 liter	1.39	4Q 92	4c
Steak, T-bone	lb	4.68	4Q 92	4c
Sugar, cane or beet	4 lb	1.37	4Q 92	4c
Tomatoes, Hunt's or Del Monte	14.5-oz can	0.74	4Q 92	4c
Tuna, chunk, light	6.125-6.5 oz can	0.60	4Q 92	4c
Health Care				
ACCRA Index, Health Care		90.40	4Q 92	4c
Analgesic, Aspirin, Bayer, 325 mg tablets	100	5.38	4Q 92	4c
Dentist's fee, adult teeth cleaning and periodic oral exam	visit	38.00	4Q 92	4c
Doctor's fee, routine exam, established patient	visit	34.00	4Q 92	4c
Hospital care, semiprivate room	day	261.75	90	27c
Hospital care, semiprivate room	day	301.00	4Q 92	4c
Medical insurance premium, per employee, small group comprehensive	month	288.35	10/91	25c
Household Goods				
Appliance repair, home, service call, washing machine	min labor charge	37.77	4Q 92	4c
Laundry detergent, Tide Ultra, Bold, or Cheer	42 oz	3.08	4Q 92	4c
Tissues, facial, Kleenex brand	175-count box	1.16	4Q 92	4c
Housing				
ACCRA Index, Housing		102.90	4Q 92	4c
House, 1,800 sq ft, 8,000 sq ft lot, new, urban	total	112530	4Q 92	4c
House payment, principal and interest, 25% down payment	month	633	4Q 92	4c
Mortgage rate, incl. points & origination fee, 30-year fixed or adjustable rate	per-cent	8.23	4Q 92	4c

Values are in dollars or fractions of dollars. In the column headed *Ref*, references are shown to sources. Each reference is followed by a letter. These refer to the geographical level for which data were reported: s=State, r=Region, and c=City or metro. The abbreviation *ex* is used to mean *except* or *excluding*; *exp* stands for expenditures. For other abbreviations and further explanations, please see the Introduction.

Lafayette, IN - continued

Item	Per	Value	Date	Ref.
Housing				
Rent, apartment, 2 bedrooms - 1-1/2 to 2 baths, unfurnished, 950 sq ft, water	month	506	4Q 92	4c
Rental unit, 1 bedroom	month	403	93	23c
Rental unit, 2 bedroom	month	474	93	23c
Rental unit, 3 bedroom	month	592	93	23c
Rental unit, 4 bedroom	month	665	93	23c
Rental unit, efficiency	month	331	93	23c
Personal Goods				
Shampoo, Alberto VO5	15 oz	1.29	4Q 92	4c
Toothpaste, Crest or Colgate	6-7 oz	2.34	4Q 92	4c
Personal Services				
Dry cleaning, man's 2-piece suit		6.69	4Q 92	4c
Haircare, woman's shampoo, trim and blow-dry		16.40	4Q 92	4c
Haircut, man's barbershop, no styling		6.40	4Q 92	4c
Restaurant Food				
Chicken, fried, thigh and drumstick		2.28	4Q 92	4c
Hamburger with cheese	1/4 lb	1.75	4Q 92	4c
Pizza, Pizza Hut or Pizza Inn, cheese, thin crust	12-13 in	8.21	4Q 92	4c
Transportation				
ACCRA Index, Transportation		91.60	4Q 92	4c
Bus fare	one-way	0.50	3/93	2c
Bus fare, up to 10 miles	one-way	0.50	4Q 92	4c
Tire balance, computer or spin balance, front	wheel	6.30	4Q 92	4c
Utilities				
ACCRA Index, Utilities		96.60	4Q 92	4c
Electricity, partial electric and other energy, 1,800 sq ft living area new home	month	54.48	4Q 92	4c

Lafayette, LA

Item	Per	Value	Date	Ref.
Child Care				
Child care fee, average, center	hour	1.29	90	65r
Child care fee, average, nonregulated family day care	hour	0.89	90	65r
Child care fee, average, regulated family day care	hour	1.32	90	65r
Communications				
Long-distance telephone service, day, initial minute, 0-100 miles	min	0.14-0.41	91	12s
Long-distance telephone service, day, additional minute, 0-100 miles	min	0.09-0.29	91	12s
Long-distance telephone service, evenings/weekends, 0-100 mi, initial minute	min	0.06-0.16	91	12s
Long-distance telephone service, evenings/weekends, 0-100 mi, additional minute	min	0.04-0.12	91	12s
Education				
Board, 4-yr private college/university	year	2125	91	22s
Board, 4-yr public college/university	year	1453	91	22s
Expenditures, local gov't, public elementary/secondary	pupil	4299	92	20s
Room, 4-year private college/university	year	2216	91	22s
Room, 4-year public college/university	year	1323	91	22s
Tuition, 2-year private college/university	year	5671	91	22s
Tuition, 2-year public college/university	year	852	91	22s
Tuition, 4-year private college/university	year	9783	91	22s
Tuition, 4-year public college/university, in-state	year	1791	91	22s
Energy and Fuels				
Coal	mil Btu	1.68	90	64s
Energy	mil Btu	6.05	90	64s
Energy exp/householder, 1-family unit	year	471	90	28r

Lafayette, LA - continued

Item	Per	Value	Date	Ref.
Energy and Fuels - continued				
Energy exp/householder, <1,000 sq ft heating area	year	384	90	28r
Energy exp/householder, 1,000-1,999 sq ft heating area	year	421	90	28r
Energy exp/householder, 2,000+ sq ft heating area	year	625	90	28r
Energy exp/householder, mobile home	year	271	90	28r
Energy exp/householder, multifamily	year	355	90	28r
Gas, cooking, 10 therms	month	11.61	92	56c
Gas, cooking, 30 therms	month	28.24	92	56c
Gas, cooking, 50 therms	month	34.03	92	56c
Gas, heating, winter, 100 therms	month	62.07	92	56c
Gas, heating, winter, average use	month	59.27	92	56c
Gas, natural	mil Btu	2.11	90	64s
Gas, natural	000 cu ft	5.77	91	46s
Gas, natural, exp	year	336	91	46s
Gasoline, unleaded regular	mil Btu	9.47	90	64s
Entertainment				
Miniature golf admission	adult	6.18	92	1r
Miniature golf admission	child	5.14	92	1r
Waterpark admission	adult	11.00	92	1r
Waterpark admission	child	8.55	92	1r
Funerals				
Casket, 18-gauge steel, velvet interior		2274.41	91	24r
Cosmetology, hair care, etc.		74.62	91	24r
Embalming		229.94	91	24r
Facility use for ceremony		176.61	91	24r
Hearse, local		116.34	91	24r
Limousine, local		72.68	91	24r
Remains to funeral home, transfer		87.72	01	24r
Service charge, professional		712.53	91	24r
Vault, concrete, non-metallic liner		750.55	91	24r
Viewing facilities, use		155.31	91	24r
Groceries				
Apples, Red Delicious	lb	0.79	4/93	16r
Bacon	lb	1.75	4/93	16r
Bacon, Oscar Mayer	lb	3.26	3/91	71c
Bananas	lb	0.42	4/93	16r
Bananas, brand name	lb	0.55	3/91	71c
Beef, ground chuck steak, USDA choice	lb	1.92	3/91	71c
Beef, stew, boneless	lb	2.61	4/93	16r
Bologna, all beef or mixed	lb	2.24	4/93	16r
Bologna, Oscar Mayer	8 oz	1.52	3/91	71c
Bread, Pepperidge Farm white	lb	1.48	3/91	71c
Bread, Sunbeam white	20 oz	1.24	3/91	71c
Bread, white, pan	lb	0.64	4/93	16r
Bread, whole wheat, pan	lb	0.96	4/93	16r
Butter, Land O'Lakes, light salt	lb	1.60	3/91	71c
Butter, private label	lb	1.74	3/91	71c
Cabbage	lb	0.37	4/93	16r
Carrots, short trimmed and topped	lb	0.47	4/93	16r
Celery	lb	0.64	4/93	16r
Cereal, Kellogg's Corn Flakes	18 oz	1.92	3/91	71c
Cereal, Nabisco Shredded Wheat	15 oz	2.41	3/91	71c
Cereal, Rice Krispies	13 oz	2.76	3/91	71c
Cheese, American	lb	2.98	4/93	16r
Cheese, Cheddar	lb	3.28	4/93	16r
Cheese, Kraft American singles	16 oz	3.23	3/91	71c
Chicken, fresh, whole	lb	0.77	4/93	16r
Chicken breast, bone-in	lb	1.92	4/93	16r
Chicken fryer breasts	lb	2.07	3/91	71c
Chicken legs, bone-in	lb	1.06	4/93	16r
Chuck roast, graded and ungraded, ex USDA prime and choice	lb	2.40	4/93	16r
Chuck roast, USDA choice, bone-in	lb	2.19	4/93	16r
Chuck roast, USDA choice, boneless	lb	2.38	4/93	16r
Coffee, 100% ground roast, all sizes	lb	2.48	4/93	16r
Coffee, Maxwell House regular grind	11.5 oz	2.26	3/91	71c
Cookies, Nabisco Oreos	20 oz	2.52	3/91	71c
Crackers, soda, salted	lb	1.15	4/93	16r

Values are in dollars or fractions of dollars. In the column headed *Ref*, references are shown to sources. Each reference is followed by a letter. These refer to the geographical level for which data were reported: s=State, r=Region, and c=City or metro. The abbreviation *ex* is used to mean *except* or *excluding*; *exp* stands for expenditures. For other abbreviations and further explanations, please see the Introduction.

Lafayette, LA - continued

Item	Per	Value	Date	Ref.
Groceries				
Eggs, Grade A large	doz	0.96	4/93	16r
Eggs, private label, large, white	doz	1.03	3/91	71c
Flour, white, all purpose	lb	0.24	4/93	16r
Frankfurters, all meat or all beef	lb	2.01	4/93	16r
Frankfurters, Deckerumbo	lb	2.02	3/91	71c
Frozen dinner, Stouffer's Lean Cuisine glazed chicken		2.74	3/91	71c
Grapefruit	lb	0.44	4/93	16r
Grapes, Thompson Seedless	lb	1.40	4/93	16r
Ground beef, 100% beef	lb	1.58	4/93	16r
Ground beef, lean and extra lean	lb	2.09	4/93	16r
Ground chuck, 100% beef	lb	1.98	4/93	16r
Ham, boneless, excluding canned	lb	2.89	4/93	16r
Ham, picnic, shoulder, bone-in, smoked	lb	1.02	4/93	16r
Ham, rump or steak half, bone-in, smoked	lb	1.48	4/93	16r
Honey, jar	8 oz	0.73-1.19	92	5r
Honey, jar	lb	1.10-1.79	92	5r
Honey, squeeze bear	12-oz	1.19-1.50	92	5r
Ice cream, prepackaged, bulk, regular	1/2 gal	2.41	4/93	16r
Jelly, Welch's grape	32 oz	2.00	3/91	71c
Ketchup, Heinz	14 oz	1.57	3/91	71c
Lemons	lb	1.05	4/93	16r
Lettuce, iceberg	head	0.85	3/91	71c
Lettuce, iceberg	lb	0.81	4/93	16r
Margarine, Parkay sticks	lb	0.58	3/91	71c
Margarine, stick	lb	0.88	4/93	16r
Mayonnaise, Hellmann's	quart	1.89	3/91	71c
Milk, private label, whole	gal	2.24	3/91	71c
Muffins, Bay's English	6	1.50	3/91	71c
Orange juice, Minute Maid frozen	12 oz	1.47	3/91	71c
Oranges	10	2.72	3/91	71c
Oranges, navel	lb	0.55	4/93	16r
Peanut butter, Skippy, creamy	18 oz	2.83	3/91	71c
Pears, Anjou	lb	0.92	4/93	16r
Pizza, Jeno's frozen cheese	7.4 oz	1.18	3/91	71c
Pork chops, center cut, bone-in	lb	3.13	4/93	16r
Potato chips	16 oz	2.94	4/93	16r
Potatoes, white	lb	0.43	4/93	16r
Rib roast, USDA choice, bone-in	lb	4.63	4/93	16r
Rice, white, long grain, uncooked	lb	0.45	4/93	16r
Round roast, graded & ungraded, ex USDA prime & choice	lb	3.03	4/93	16r
Round roast, USDA choice, boneless	lb	3.09	4/93	16r
Sausage, fresh, loose	lb	2.08	4/93	16r
Sausage, Jimmy Dean, bulk or link	12	2.56	3/91	71c
Short ribs, bone-in	lb	2.66	4/93	16r
Shortening, vegetable oil blends	lb	0.69	4/93	16r
Soft drink, Coca Cola	2 liter	1.41	3/91	71c
Soft drink, Diet Coca Cola	2 liter	1.41	3/91	71c
Soft drink, Diet Pepsi	2 liter	1.44	3/91	71c
Soft drink, Pepsi	2 liter	1.44	3/91	71c
Spaghetti, Luxury	16 oz	1.03	3/91	71c
Spaghetti and macaroni	lb	0.81	4/93	16r
Spaghetti sauce w/mushrooms, Prego	15 oz	1.27	3/91	71c
Spaghetti sauce w/mushrooms, Ragu	15 oz	1.24	3/91	71c
Steak, rib eye, USDA choice, boneless	lb	6.24	4/93	16r
Steak, round, graded & ungraded, ex USDA prime & choice	lb	3.31	4/93	16r
Steak, round, USDA choice, boneless	lb	3.34	4/93	16r
Steak, sirloin, graded & ungraded, ex USDA prime & choice	lb	4.19	4/93	16r
Steak, sirloin, USDA choice, boneless	lb	4.46	4/93	16r
Steak, T-bone, USDA choice, bone-in	lb	5.25	4/93	16r
Strawberries, dry pint	12 oz	0.92	4/93	16r
Sugar, regular granulated	5 lb	1.89	3/91	71c
Sugar, white	lb	0.39	4/93	16r
Sugar, white, 33-80 oz pk	lb	0.38	4/93	16r
Tea, Lipton tea bags	100	2.97	3/91	71c
Tomato soup, Campbell's	10 3/4 oz	0.49	3/91	71c
Tomatoes, field grown	lb	0.88	4/93	16r
Tuna, Chicken of the Sea chunk light	6.5 oz	0.74	3/91	71c

Lafayette, LA - continued

Item	Per	Value	Date	Ref.
Groceries - continued				
Tuna, chunk, light	lb	1.79	4/93	16r
Turkey, frozen, whole	lb	1.04	4/93	16r
Yogurt, natural, fruit flavored	1/2 pint	0.57	4/93	16r
Health Care				
Childbirth, cesarean, hospital		5034	91	62r
Childbirth, cesarean, physician's fee		2053	91	62r
Childbirth, normal, hospital		2712	91	62r
Childbirth, normal, physician's fee		1492	91	62r
Hospital care, semiprivate room	day	135.00	90	27c
Medical insurance premium, per employee, small group comprehensive	month	350.40	10/91	25c
Mental health care, exp	capita	20.37-28.83	90	38s
Mental health care, exp, state mental health agency	capita	28.44	90	38s
Mental health care, hospital psychiatric services, non-Federal, exp	capita	8.19	88	38s
Mental health care, mental health organization, multiservice, exp	capita	0.49	88	38s
Mental health care, psychiatric hospitals, private, exp	capita	43.54	88	38s
Mental health care, psychiatric out-patient clinics, freestanding, exp	capita	4.11	88	38s
Mental health care, state and county mental hospitals, exp	capita	18.74	88	38s
Mental health care, VA medical centers, exp	capita	2.60	88	38s
Physician fee, family practice, first-visit		75.00	91	62r
Physician fee, family practice, revisit		34.00	91	62r
Physician fee, general practice, first-visit		61.00	91	62r
Physician fee, general practice, revisit		32.00	91	62r
Physician fee, general surgeon, first-visit		64.00	91	62r
Physician fee, general surgeon, revisit		40.00	91	62r
Physician fee, internal medicine, first-visit		98.00	91	62r
Physician fee, internal medicine, revisit		40.00	91	62r
Physician fee, median, neurosurgeon, first-visit		130.00	91	62r
Physician fee, median, nonsurgical specialist, first-visit		95.00	91	62r
Physician fee, median, orthopedic surgeon, first-visit		91.00	91	62r
Physician fee, median, plastic surgeon, first-visit		66.00	91	62r
Physician fee, median, surgical specialist, first-visit		62.00	91	62r
Physician fee, neurosurgeon, revisit		50.00	91	62r
Physician fee, nonsurgical specialist, revisit		40.00	91	62r
Physician fee, obstetrics/gynecology, first-visit		64.00	91	62r
Physician fee, obstetrics/gynecology, revisit		41.00	91	62r
Physician fee, orthopedic surgeon, revisit		40.00	91	62r
Physician fee, pediatrician, first-visit		49.00	91	62r
Physician fee, pediatrician, revisit		33.00	91	62r
Physician fee, plastic surgeon, revisit		43.00	91	62r
Physician fee, surgical specialist, revisit		37.00	91	62r
Substance abuse, hospital ancillary charge	incident	2600	90	70s
Substance abuse, hospital physician charge	incident	840	90	70s
Substance abuse, hospital room and board	incident	6410	90	70s
Household Goods				
Laundry detergent, Tide powder	42 oz	4.06	3/91	71c
Paper towels, Bounty	67 ft	0.92	3/91	71c
Plastic wrap, Saran	50 ft	1.57	3/91	71c
Housing				
Rental unit, 1 bedroom	month	428	93	23c
Rental unit, 2 bedroom	month	504	93	23c
Rental unit, 3 bedroom	month	630	93	23c
Rental unit, 4 bedroom	month	707	93	23c
Rental unit, efficiency	month	353	93	23c

Values are in dollars or fractions of dollars. In the column headed *Ref*, references are shown to sources. Each reference is followed by a letter. These refer to the geographical level for which data were reported: s=State, r=Region, and c=City or metro. The abbreviation *ex* is used to mean *except* or *excluding*; *exp* stands for expenditures. For other abbreviations and further explanations, please see the Introduction.

Lafayette, LA - continued

Item	Per	Value	Date	Ref.
Insurance and Pensions				
Auto insurance, private passenger	year	778.70	91	63s
Personal Goods				
Toothpaste, Crest gel	6.4 oz	2.30	3/91	71c
Taxes				
Tax, cigarette	pack	20	91	77s
Tax, gasoline	gal	20	91	77s
Taxes, state	capita	1013	91	77s
Transportation				
Driver's license fee		18.00	12/90	43s
Travel				
Business travel	day	193.00	4/93	89r
Utilities				
Electricity	mil Btu	17.77	90	64s

Lake Charles, LA

Item	Per	Value	Date	Ref.
Composite ACCRA index		96.00	4Q 92	4c
Alcoholic Beverages				
Beer, Miller Lite or Budweiser, 12-oz containers	6 pack	4.08	4Q 92	4c
Liquor, J & B Scotch	750 ml	15.73	4Q 92	4c
Wine, Gallo Chablis blanc, 1.5 liter	bottle	4.59	4Q 92	4c
Child Care				
Child care fee, average, center	hour	1.29	90	65r
Child care fee, average, nonregulated family day care	hour	0.89	90	65r
Child care fee, average, regulated family day care	hour	1.32	90	65r
Clothing				
Jeans, man's denim		27.72	4Q 92	4c
Shirt, man's dress shirt		27.88	4Q 92	4c
Undervest, boy's size 10-14, cotton	3	5.05	4Q 92	4c
Communications				
Long-distance telephone service, day, initial minute, 0-100 miles	min	0.14-0.41	91	12s
Long-distance telephone service, day, additional minute, 0-100 miles	min	0.09-0.29	91	12s
Long-distance telephone service, evenings/weekends, 0-100 mi, initial minute	min	0.06-0.16	91	12s
Long-distance telephone service, evenings/weekends, 0-100 mi, additional minute	min	0.04-0.12	91	12s
Newspaper subscription, daily and Sunday home delivery, large-city	month	8.00	4Q 92	4c
Telephone, flat rate	month	12.85	91	11c
Telephone bill, family of four	month	22.03	4Q 92	4c
Education				
Board, 4-yr private college/university	year	2125	91	22s
Board, 4-yr public college/university	year	1453	91	22s
Expenditures, local gov't, public elementary/secondary	pupil	4299	92	20s
Room, 4-year private college/university	year	2216	91	22s
Room, 4-year public college/university	year	1323	91	22s
Tuition, 2-year private college/university	year	5671	91	22s
Tuition, 2-year public college/university	year	852	91	22s
Tuition, 4-year private college/university	year	9783	91	22s
Tuition, 4-year public college/university, in-state	year	1791	91	22s
Energy and Fuels				
Coal	mil Btu	1.68	90	64s
Energy	mil Btu	6.05	90	64s
Energy, combined forms, 1,800 sq ft heating area	month	110.56	4Q 92	4c
Energy exp/householder, 1-family unit	year	471	90	28r
Energy exp/householder, <1,000 sq ft heating area	year	384	90	28r

Lake Charles, LA - continued

Item	Per	Value	Date	Ref.
Energy and Fuels - continued				
Energy exp/householder, 1,000-1,999 sq ft heating area	year	421	90	28r
Energy exp/householder, 2,000+ sq ft heating area	year	625	90	28r
Energy exp/householder, mobile home	year	271	90	28r
Energy exp/householder, multifamily	year	355	90	28r
Gas, cooking, 10 therms	month	13.09	92	56c
Gas, cooking, 30 therms	month	20.28	92	56c
Gas, cooking, 50 therms	month	27.47	92	56c
Gas, heating, winter, 100 therms	month	45.44	92	56c
Gas, heating, winter, average use	month	43.64	92	56c
Gas, natural	mil Btu	2.11	90	64s
Gas, natural	000 cu ft	5.77	91	46s
Gas, natural, exp	year	336	91	46s
Gasoline, motor	gal	1.15	4Q 92	4c
Gasoline, unleaded regular	mil Btu	9.47	90	64s
Entertainment				
Bowling, evening rate	game	2.20	4Q 92	4c
Miniature golf admission	adult	6.18	92	1r
Miniature golf admission	child	5.14	92	1r
Monopoly game, Parker Brothers', No. 9		12.67	4Q 92	4c
Movie	admission	5.13	4Q 92	4c
Tennis balls, yellow, Wilson or Penn, 3	can	3.00	4Q 92	4c
Waterpark admission	adult	11.00	92	1r
Waterpark admission	child	8.55	92	1r
Funerals				
Casket, 18-gauge steel, velvet interior		2274.41	91	24r
Cosmetology, hair care, etc.		74.62	91	24r
Embalming		229.94	91	24r
Facility use for ceremony		176.61	91	24r
Hearse, local		116.34	91	24r
Limousine, local		72.68	91	24r
Remains to funeral home, transfer		87.72	91	24r
Service charge, professional		712.53	91	24r
Vault, concrete, non-metallic liner		750.55	91	24r
Viewing facilities, use		155.31	91	24r
Goods and Services				
ACCRA Index, Miscellaneous Goods and Services		103.10	4Q 92	4c
Groceries				
ACCRA Index, Groceries		99.40	4Q 92	4c
Apples, Red Delicious	lb	0.79	4/93	16r
Babyfood, strained vegetables, lowest price	4-4.5 oz jar	0.26	4Q 92	4c
Bacon	lb	1.75	4/93	16r
Bananas	lb	0.45	4Q 92	4c
Bananas	lb	0.42	4/93	16r
Beef, stew, boneless	lb	2.61	4/93	16r
Bologna, all beef or mixed	lb	2.24	4/93	16r
Bread, white	24 oz	0.66	4Q 92	4c
Bread, white, pan	lb	0.64	4/93	16r
Bread, whole wheat, pan	lb	0.96	4/93	16r
Cabbage	lb	0.37	4/93	16r
Carrots, short trimmed and topped	lb	0.47	4/93	16r
Celery	lb	0.64	4/93	16r
Cheese, American	lb	2.98	4/93	16r
Cheese, Cheddar	lb	3.28	4/93	16r
Cheese, Kraft grated Parmesan	8-oz canister	3.08	4Q 92	4c
Chicken, fresh, whole	lb	0.77	4/93	16r
Chicken, fryer, whole	lb	0.67	4Q 92	4c
Chicken breast, bone-in	lb	1.92	4/93	16r
Chicken legs, bone-in	lb	1.06	4/93	16r
Chuck roast, graded and ungraded, ex USDA prime and choice	lb	2.40	4/93	16r
Chuck roast, USDA choice, bone-in	lb	2.19	4/93	16r
Chuck roast, USDA choice, boneless	lb	2.38	4/93	16r

Values are in dollars or fractions of dollars. In the column headed *Ref*, references are shown to sources. Each reference is followed by a letter. These refer to the geographical level for which data were reported: s=State, r=Region, and c=City or metro. The abbreviation *ex* is used to mean *except* or *excluding*; *exp* stands for *expenditures*. For other abbreviations and further explanations, please see the Introduction.

Lake Charles, LA - continued

Item	Per	Value	Date	Ref.
Groceries				
Cigarettes, Winston	carton	16.97	4Q 92	4c
Coffee, 100% ground roast, all sizes	lb	2.48	4/93	16r
Coffee, vacuum-packed	13-oz can	2.08	4Q 92	4c
Corn, frozen	10 oz	0.75	4Q 92	4c
Corn Flakes, Kellogg's or Post Toasties	18 oz	2.10	4Q 92	4c
Crackers, soda, salted	lb	1.15	4/93	16r
Eggs, Grade A large	doz	0.88	4Q 92	4c
Eggs, Grade A large	doz	0.96	4/93	16r
Flour, white, all purpose	lb	0.24	4/93	16r
Frankfurters, all meat or all beef	lb	2.01	4/93	16r
Grapefruit	lb	0.44	4/93	16r
Grapes, Thompson Seedless	lb	1.40	4/93	16r
Ground beef, 100% beef	lb	1.58	4/93	16r
Ground beef, lean and extra lean	lb	2.09	4/93	16r
Ground beef or hamburger	lb	1.32	4Q 92	4c
Ground chuck, 100% beef	lb	1.98	4/93	16r
Ham, boneless, excluding canned	lb	2.89	4/93	16r
Ham, picnic, shoulder, bone-in, smoked	lb	1.02	4/93	16r
Ham, rump or steak half, bone-in, smoked	lb	1.48	4/93	16r
Honey, jar	8 oz	0.73-1.19	92	5r
Honey, jar	lb	1.10-1.79	92	5r
Honey, squeeze bear	12-oz	1.19-1.50	92	5r
Ice cream, prepackaged, bulk, regular	1/2 gal	2.41	4/93	16r
Lemons	lb	1.05	4/93	16r
Lettuce, iceberg	head	1.10	4Q 92	4c
Lettuce, iceberg	lb	0.81	4/93	16r
Margarine, Blue Bonnet or Parkay cubes	lb	0.53	4Q 92	4c
Margarine, stick	lb	0.88	4/93	16r
Milk, whole	1/2 gal	1.65	4Q 92	4c
Orange juice, Minute Maid frozen	12-oz can	1.37	4Q 92	4c
Oranges, navel	lb	0.55	4/93	16r
Peaches	29-oz can	1.50	4Q 92	4c
Pears, Anjou	lb	0.92	4/93	16r
Peas Sweet, Del Monte or Green Giant	15-17 oz can	0.58	4Q 92	4c
Pork chops, center cut, bone-in	lb	3.13	4/93	16r
Potato chips	16 oz	2.94	4/93	16r
Potatoes, white	lb	0.43	4/93	16r
Potatoes, white or red	10-lb sack	2.64	4Q 92	4c
Rib roast, USDA choice, bone-in	lb	4.63	4/93	16r
Rice, white, long grain, uncooked	lb	0.45	4/93	16r
Round roast, graded & ungraded, ex USDA prime & choice	lb	3.03	4/93	16r
Round roast, USDA choice, boneless	lb	3.09	4/93	16r
Sausage, fresh, loose	lb	2.08	4/93	16r
Sausage, Jimmy Dean, 100% pork	lb	2.49	4Q 92	4c
Short ribs, bone-in	lb	2.66	4/93	16r
Shortening, vegetable oil blends	lb	0.69	4/93	16r
Shortening, vegetable, Crisco	3-lb can	2.03	4Q 92	4c
Soft drink, Coca Cola	2 liter	1.21	4Q 92	4c
Spaghetti and macaroni	lb	0.81	4/93	16r
Steak, rib eye, USDA choice, boneless	lb	6.24	4/93	16r
Steak, round, graded & ungraded, ex USDA prime & choice	lb	3.31	4/93	16r
Steak, round, USDA choice, boneless	lb	3.34	4/93	16r
Steak, sirloin, graded & ungraded, ex USDA prime & choice	lb	4.19	4/93	16r
Steak, sirloin, USDA choice, boneless	lb	4.46	4/93	16r
Steak, T-bone	lb	5.49	4Q 92	4c
Steak, T-bone, USDA choice, bone-in	lb	5.25	4/93	16r
Strawberries, dry pint	12 oz	0.92	4/93	16r
Sugar, cane or beet	4 lb	1.55	4Q 92	4c
Sugar, white	lb	0.39	4/93	16r
Sugar, white, 33-80 oz pk	lb	0.38	4/93	16r
Tomatoes, field grown	lb	0.88	4/93	16r
Tomatoes, Hunt's or Del Monte	14.5-oz can	0.66	4Q 92	4c

Lake Charles, LA - continued

Item	Per	Value	Date	Ref.
Groceries - continued				
Tuna, chunk, light	6.125-6.5 oz can	0.68	4Q 92	4c
Tuna, chunk, light	lb	1.79	4/93	16r
Turkey, frozen, whole	lb	1.04	4/93	16r
Yogurt, natural, fruit flavored	1/2 pint	0.57	4/93	16r
Health Care				
ACCRA Index, Health Care		88.70	4Q 92	4c
Analgesic, Aspirin, Bayer, 325 mg tablets	100	5.50	4Q 92	4c
Childbirth, cesarean, hospital		5034	91	62r
Childbirth, cesarean, physician's fee		2053	91	62r
Childbirth, normal, hospital		2712	91	62r
Childbirth, normal, physician's fee		1492	91	62r
Dentist's fee, adult teeth cleaning and periodic oral exam	visit	41.30	4Q 92	4c
Doctor's fee, routine exam, established patient	visit	31.10	4Q 92	4c
Hospital care, semiprivate room	day	185.00	90	27c
Hospital care, semiprivate room	day	270.50	4Q 92	4c
Medical insurance premium, per employee, small group comprehensive	month	350.40	10/91	25c
Mental health care, exp	capita	20.37-28.83	90	38s
Mental health care, exp, state mental health agency	capita	28.44	90	38s
Mental health care, hospital psychiatric services, non-Federal, exp	capita	8.19	88	38s
Mental health care, mental health organization, multiservice, exp	capita	0.49	88	38s
Mental health care, psychiatric hospitals, private, exp	capita	43.54	88	38s
Mental health care, psychiatric out-patient clinics, freestanding, exp	capita	4.11	88	38s
Mental health care, state and county mental hospitals, exp	capita	18.74	88	38s
Mental health care, VA medical centers, exp	capita	2.60	88	38s
Physician fee, family practice, first-visit		75.00	91	62r
Physician fee, family practice, revisit		34.00	91	62r
Physician fee, general practice, first-visit		61.00	91	62r
Physician fee, general practice, revisit		32.00	91	62r
Physician fee, general surgeon, first-visit		64.00	91	62r
Physician fee, general surgeon, revisit		40.00	91	62r
Physician fee, internal medicine, first-visit		98.00	91	62r
Physician fee, internal medicine, revisit		40.00	91	62r
Physician fee, median, neurosurgeon, first-visit		130.00	91	62r
Physician fee, median, nonsurgical specialist, first-visit		95.00	91	62r
Physician fee, median, orthopedic surgeon, first-visit		91.00	91	62r
Physician fee, median, plastic surgeon, first-visit		66.00	91	62r
Physician fee, median, surgical specialist, first-visit		62.00	91	62r
Physician fee, neurosurgeon, revisit		50.00	91	62r
Physician fee, nonsurgical specialist, revisit		40.00	91	62r
Physician fee, obstetrics/gynecology, first-visit		64.00	91	62r
Physician fee, obstetrics/gynecology, revisit		41.00	91	62r
Physician fee, orthopedic surgeon, revisit		40.00	91	62r
Physician fee, pediatrician, first-visit		49.00	91	62r
Physician fee, pediatrician, revisit		33.00	91	62r
Physician fee, plastic surgeon, revisit		43.00	91	62r
Physician fee, surgical specialist, revisit		37.00	91	62r
Substance abuse, hospital ancillary charge	incident	2600	90	70s
Substance abuse, hospital physician charge	incident	840	90	70s
Substance abuse, hospital room and board	incident	6410	90	70s

Values are in dollars or fractions of dollars. In the column headed *Ref*, references are shown to sources. Each reference is followed by a letter. These refer to the geographical level for which data were reported: s=State, r=Region, and c=City or metro. The abbreviation *ex* is used to mean *except* or *excluding*; *exp* stands for expenditures. For other abbreviations and further explanations, please see the Introduction.

Lake Charles, LA - continued

Item	Per	Value	Date	Ref.
Household Goods				
Appliance repair, home, service call, washing machine	min labor charge	33.48	4Q 92	4c
Laundry detergent, Tide Ultra, Bold, or Cheer	42 oz	3.20	4Q 92	4c
Tissues, facial, Kleenex brand	175-count box	1.21	4Q 92	4c
Housing				
ACCRA Index, Housing		82.50	4Q 92	4c
House, 1,800 sq ft, 8,000 sq ft lot, new, urban	total	87963	4Q 92	4c
House payment, principal and interest, 25% down payment	month	497	4Q 92	4c
Mortgage rate, incl. points & origination fee, 30-year fixed or adjustable rate	per-cent	8.29	4Q 92	4c
Rent, apartment, 2 bedrooms - 1-1/2 to 2 baths, unfurnished, 950 sq ft, water	month	430	4Q 92	4c
Rental unit, 1 bedroom	month	350	93	23c
Rental unit, 2 bedroom	month	412	93	23c
Rental unit, 3 bedroom	month	515	93	23c
Rental unit, 4 bedroom	month	576	93	23c
Rental unit, efficiency	month	288	93	23c
Insurance and Pensions				
Auto insurance, private passenger	year	778.70	91	63s
Personal Goods				
Shampoo, Alberto VO5	15 oz	1.27	4Q 92	4c
Toothpaste, Crest or Colgate	6-7 oz	2.71	4Q 92	4c
Personal Services				
Dry cleaning, man's 2-piece suit		6.71	4Q 92	4c
Haircare, woman's shampoo, trim and blow-dry		18.70	4Q 92	4c
Haircut, man's barbershop, no styling		7.45	4Q 92	4c
Restaurant Food				
Chicken, fried, thigh and drumstick		2.09	4Q 92	4c
Hamburger with cheese	1/4 lb	0.99	4Q 92	4c
Pizza, Pizza Hut or Pizza Inn, cheese, thin crust	12-13 in	8.95	4Q 92	4c
Taxes				
Tax, cigarette	pack	20	91	77s
Tax, gasoline	gal	20	91	77s
Taxes, state	capita	1013	91	77s
Transportation				
ACCRA Index, Transportation		102.20	4Q 92	4c
Driver's license fee		18.00	12/90	43s
Tire balance, computer or spin balance, front	wheel	6.68	4Q 92	4c
Travel				
Business travel	day	193.00	4/93	89r
Utilities				
ACCRA Index, Utilities		102.50	4Q 92	4c
Electricity	mil Btu	17.77	90	64s
Electricity, all electric, 1,800 sq ft living area new home	month	110.56	4Q 92	4c

Lake Havasu, AZ

Item	Per	Value	Date	Ref.
Composite ACCRA index		98.40	4Q 92	4c
Alcoholic Beverages				
Beer, Miller Lite or Budweiser, 12-oz containers	6 pack	3.99	4Q 92	4c
Liquor, J & B Scotch	750 ml	15.19	4Q 92	4c
Wine, Gallo Chablis blanc, 1.5 liter	bottle	4.19	4Q 92	4c
Clothing				
Jeans, man's denim		32.47	4Q 92	4c
Shirt, man's dress shirt		17.82	4Q 92	4c

Lake Havasu, AZ - continued

Item	Per	Value	Date	Ref.
Clothing - continued				
Undervest, boy's size 10-14, cotton	3	3.70	4Q 92	4c
Communications				
Newspaper subscription, daily and Sunday home delivery, large-city	month	13.26	4Q 92	4c
Telephone bill, family of four	month	21.80	4Q 92	4c
Energy and Fuels				
Energy, combined forms, 1,800 sq ft heating area	month	91.25	4Q 92	4c
Gasoline, motor	gal	1.28	4Q 92	4c
Entertainment				
Bowling, evening rate	game	1.75	4Q 92	4c
Monopoly game, Parker Brothers', No. 9		10.64	4Q 92	4c
Movie	admis-sion	5.00	4Q 92	4c
Tennis balls, yellow, Wilson or Penn, 3	can	2.48	4Q 92	4c
Goods and Services				
ACCRA Index, Miscellaneous Goods and Services		96.30	4Q 92	4c
Groceries				
ACCRA Index, Groceries		101.60	4Q 92	4c
Babyfood, strained vegetables, lowest price	4-4.5 oz jar	0.35	4Q 92	4c
Bananas	lb	0.36	4Q 92	4c
Bread, white	24 oz	0.71	4Q 92	4c
Cheese, Kraft grated Parmesan	8-oz canis-ter	3.26	4Q 92	4c
Chicken, fryer, whole	lb	0.88	4Q 92	4c
Cigarettes, Winston	carton	17.23	4Q 92	4c
Coffee, vacuum-packed	13-oz can	1.86	4Q 92	4c
Corn, frozen	10 oz	0.74	4Q 92	4c
Corn Flakes, Kellogg's or Post Toasties	18 oz	2.28	4Q 92	4c
Eggs, Grade A large	doz	0.90	4Q 92	4c
Ground beef or hamburger	lb	1.38	4Q 92	4c
Lettuce, iceberg	head	0.99	4Q 92	4c
Margarine, Blue Bonnet or Parkay cubes	lb	0.72	4Q 92	4c
Milk, whole	1/2 gal	1.32	4Q 92	4c
Orange juice, Minute Maid frozen	12-oz can	1.38	4Q 92	4c
Peaches	29-oz can	1.55	4Q 92	4c
Peas Sweet, Del Monte or Green Giant	15-17 oz can	0.66	4Q 92	4c
Potatoes, white or red	10-lb sack	1.75	4Q 92	4c
Sausage, Jimmy Dean, 100% pork	lb	3.09	4Q 92	4c
Shortening, vegetable, Crisco	3-lb can	2.74	4Q 92	4c
Soft drink, Coca Cola	2 liter	1.22	4Q 92	4c
Steak, T-bone	lb	4.82	4Q 92	4c
Sugar, cane or beet	4 lb	1.46	4Q 92	4c
Tomatoes, Hunt's or Del Monte	14.5-oz can	0.75	4Q 92	4c
Tuna, chunk, light	6.125-6.5 oz can	0.53	4Q 92	4c
Health Care				
ACCRA Index, Health Care		110.90	4Q 92	4c
Analgesic, Aspirin, Bayer, 325 mg tablets	100	5.05	4Q 92	4c
Dentist's fee, adult teeth cleaning and periodic oral exam	visit	51.20	4Q 92	4c
Doctor's fee, routine exam, established patient	visit	44.60	4Q 92	4c
Hospital care, semiprivate room	day	320.00	4Q 92	4c

Values are in dollars or fractions of dollars. In the column headed *Ref*, references are shown to sources. Each reference is followed by a letter. These refer to the geographical level for which data were reported: s=State, r=Region, and c=City or metro. The abbreviation *ex* is used to mean *except* or *excluding*; *exp* stands for *expenditures*. For other abbreviations and further explanations, please see the Introduction.

Lake Havasu, AZ - continued

Item	Per	Value	Date	Ref.
Household Goods				
Appliance repair, home, service call, washing machine	min labor charge	30.50	4Q 92	4c
Laundry detergent, Tide Ultra, Bold, or Cheer	42 oz	3.88	4Q 92	4c
Tissues, facial, Kleenex brand	175-count box	1.15	4Q 92	4c
Housing				
ACCRA Index, Housing		101.40	4Q 92	4c
House, 1,800 sq ft, 8,000 sq ft lot, new, urban	total	108333	4Q 92	4c
House payment, principal and interest, 25% down payment	month	604	4Q 92	4c
Mortgage rate, incl. points & origination fee, 30-year fixed or adjustable rate	percent	8.14	4Q 92	4c
Rent, apartment, 2 bedrooms - 1-1/2 to 2 baths, unfurnished, 950 sq ft, water	month	545	4Q 92	4c
Personal Goods				
Shampoo, Alberto VO5	15 oz	1.24	4Q 92	4c
Toothpaste, Crest or Colgate	6-7 oz	2.08	4Q 92	4c
Personal Services				
Dry cleaning, man's 2-piece suit		6.50	4Q 92	4c
Haircare, woman's shampoo, trim and blow-dry		16.50	4Q 92	4c
Haircut, man's barbershop, no styling		6.90	4Q 92	4c
Restaurant Food				
Chicken, fried, thigh and drumstick		2.49	4Q 92	4c
Hamburger with cheese	1/4 lb	1.99	4Q 92	4c
Pizza, Pizza Hut or Pizza Inn, cheese, thin crust	12-13 in	7.50	4Q 92	4c
Transportation				
ACCRA Index, Transportation		97.60	4Q 92	4c
Tire balance, computer or spin balance, front	wheel	5.33	4Q 92	4c
Utilities				
ACCRA Index, Utilities		86.40	4Q 92	4c
Electricity, all electric, 1,800 sq ft living area new home	month	91.25	4Q 92	4c
Electricity, winter, 250 KWh	month	24.23	92	55c
Electricity, winter, 500 KWh	month	42.05	92	55c
Electricity, winter, 750 KWh	month	59.87	92	55c
Electricity, winter, 1000 KWh	month	77.69	92	55c

Lakeland-Winter Haven, FL

Item	Per	Value	Date	Ref.
Child Care				
Child care fee, average, center	hour	1.29	90	65r
Child care fee, average, nonregulated family day care	hour	0.89	90	65r
Child care fee, average, regulated family day care	hour	1.32	90	65r
Communications				
Long-distance telephone service, day, initial minute, 0-100 miles	min	0.15-0.20	91	12s
Long-distance telephone service, day, additional minute, 0-100 miles	min	0.08-0.20	91	12s
Long-distance telephone service, evenings/weekends, 0-100 mi, initial minute	min	0.09-0.12	91	12s
Long-distance telephone service, evenings/weekends, 0-100 mi, additional minute	min	0.05-0.12	91	12s
Education				
Board, 4-yr private college/university	year	1924	91	22s
Board, 4-yr public college/university	year	1955	91	22s
Expenditures, local gov't, public elementary/secondary	pupil	5235	92	20s
Room, 4-year private college/university	year	1904	91	22s

Lakeland-Winter Haven, FL - continued

Item	Per	Value	Date	Ref.
Education - continued				
Room, 4-year public college/university	year	1510	91	22s
Tuition, 2-year private college/university	year	4751	91	22s
Tuition, 2-year public college/university	year	788	91	22s
Tuition, 4-year private college/university	year	7992	91	22s
Tuition, 4-year public college/university, in-state	year	1337	91	22s
Energy and Fuels				
Coal	mil Btu	1.85	90	64s
Energy	mil Btu	10.58	90	64s
Energy exp/householder, 1-family unit	year	487	90	28r
Energy exp/householder, <1,000 sq ft heating area	year	393	90	28r
Energy exp/householder, 1,000-1,999 sq ft heating area	year	442	90	28r
Energy exp/householder, 2,000+ sq ft heating area	year	577	90	28r
Energy exp/householder, mobile home	year	366	90	28r
Energy exp/householder, multifamily	year	382	90	28r
Gas, natural	mil Btu	3.21	90	64s
Gas, natural	000 cu ft	8.98	91	46s
Gas, natural, exp	year	248	91	46s
Gasoline, unleaded regular	mil Btu	8.85	90	64s
Entertainment				
Miniature golf admission	adult	6.18	92	1r
Miniature golf admission	child	5.14	92	1r
Waterpark admission	adult	11.00	92	1r
Waterpark admission	child	8.55	92	1r
Funerals				
Casket, 18-gauge steel, velvet interior		2029.08	91	24r
Cosmetology, hair care, etc.		75.10	91	24r
Embalming		249.24	91	24r
Facility use for ceremony		162.27	91	24r
Hearse, local		114.04	91	24r
Limousine, local		88.57	91	24r
Remains to funeral home, transfer		92.61	91	24r
Service charge, professional		682.42	91	24r
Vault, concrete, non-metallic liner		798.70	91	24r
Viewing facilities, use		163.86	91	24r
Groceries				
Apples, Red Delicious	lb	0.79	4/93	16r
Bacon	lb	1.75	4/93	16r
Bananas	lb	0.42	4/93	16r
Beef, stew, boneless	lb	2.61	4/93	16r
Bologna, all beef or mixed	lb	2.24	4/93	16r
Bread, white, pan	lb	0.64	4/93	16r
Bread, whole wheat, pan	lb	0.96	4/93	16r
Cabbage	lb	0.37	4/93	16r
Carrots, short trimmed and topped	lb	0.47	4/93	16r
Celery	lb	0.64	4/93	16r
Cheese, American	lb	2.98	4/93	16r
Cheese, Cheddar	lb	3.28	4/93	16r
Chicken, fresh, whole	lb	0.77	4/93	16r
Chicken breast, bone-in	lb	1.92	4/93	16r
Chicken legs, bone-in	lb	1.06	4/93	16r
Chuck roast, graded and ungraded, ex USDA prime and choice	lb	2.40	4/93	16r
Chuck roast, USDA choice, bone-in	lb	2.19	4/93	16r
Chuck roast, USDA choice, boneless	lb	2.38	4/93	16r
Coffee, 100% ground roast, all sizes	lb	2.48	4/93	16r
Crackers, soda, salted	lb	1.15	4/93	16r
Eggs, Grade A large	doz	0.96	4/93	16r
Flour, white, all purpose	lb	0.24	4/93	16r
Frankfurters, all meat or all beef	lb	2.01	4/93	16r
Grapefruit	lb	0.44	4/93	16r
Grapes, Thompson Seedless	lb	1.40	4/93	16r
Ground beef, 100% beef	lb	1.58	4/93	16r
Ground beef, lean and extra lean	lb	2.09	4/93	16r
Ground chuck, 100% beef	lb	1.98	4/93	16r
Ham, boneless, excluding canned	lb	2.89	4/93	16r

Values are in dollars or fractions of dollars. In the column headed *Ref*, references are shown to sources. Each reference is followed by a letter. These refer to the geographical level for which data were reported: s = State, r = Region, and c = City or metro. The abbreviation *ex* is used to mean *except* or *excluding*; *exp* stands for expenditures. For other abbreviations and further explanations, please see the Introduction.

Lakeland-Winter Haven, FL - continued

Item	Per	Value	Date	Ref.
Groceries				
Ham, picnic, shoulder, bone-in, smoked	lb	1.02	4/93	16r
Ham, rump or steak half, bone-in, smoked	lb	1.48	4/93	16r
Ice cream, prepackaged, bulk, regular	1/2 gal	2.41	4/93	16r
Lemons	lb	1.05	4/93	16r
Lettuce, iceberg	lb	0.81	4/93	16r
Margarine, stick	lb	0.88	4/93	16r
Oranges, navel	lb	0.55	4/93	16r
Pears, Anjou	lb	0.92	4/93	16r
Pork chops, center cut, bone-in	lb	3.13	4/93	16r
Potato chips	16 oz	2.94	4/93	16r
Potatoes, white	lb	0.43	4/93	16r
Rib roast, USDA choice, bone-in	lb	4.63	4/93	16r
Rice, white, long grain, uncooked	lb	0.45	4/93	16r
Round roast, graded & ungraded, ex USDA prime & choice	lb	3.03	4/93	16r
Round roast, USDA choice, boneless	lb	3.09	4/93	16r
Sausage, fresh, loose	lb	2.08	4/93	16r
Short ribs, bone-in	lb	2.66	4/93	16r
Shortening, vegetable oil blends	lb	0.69	4/93	16r
Spaghetti and macaroni	lb	0.81	4/93	16r
Steak, rib eye, USDA choice, boneless	lb	6.24	4/93	16r
Steak, round, graded & ungraded, ex USDA prime & choice	lb	3.31	4/93	16r
Steak, round, USDA choice, boneless	lb	3.34	4/93	16r
Steak, sirloin, graded & ungraded, ex USDA prime & choice	lb	4.19	4/93	16r
Steak, sirloin, USDA choice, boneless	lb	4.46	4/93	16r
Steak, T-bone, USDA choice, bone-in	lb	5.25	4/93	16r
Strawberries, dry pint	12 oz	0.92	4/93	16r
Sugar, white	lb	0.39	4/93	16r
Sugar, white, 33-80 oz pk	lb	0.38	4/93	16r
Tomatoes, field grown	lb	0.88	4/93	16r
Tuna, chunk, light	lb	1.79	4/93	16r
Turkey, frozen, whole	lb	1.04	4/93	16r
Yogurt, natural, fruit flavored	1/2 pint	0.57	4/93	16r
Health Care				
Childbirth, cesarean, hospital		5034	91	62r
Childbirth, cesarean, physician's fee		2053	91	62r
Childbirth, normal, hospital		2712	91	62r
Childbirth, normal, physician's fee		1492	91	62r
Medical plan per employee	year	3495	91	45r
Mental health care, exp	capita	28.84-37.59	90	38s
Mental health care, exp, state mental health agency	capita	37.49	90	38s
Mental health care, hospital psychiatric services, non-Federal, exp	capita	9.11	88	38s
Mental health care, mental health organization, multiservice, exp	capita	16.21	88	38s
Mental health care, psychiatric hospitals, private, exp	capita	22.26	88	38s
Mental health care, psychiatric out-patient clinics, freestanding, exp	capita	0.89	88	38s
Mental health care, psychiatric partial-care organizations, freestanding, exp	capita	0.41	88	38s
Mental health care, state and county mental hospitals, exp	capita	16.25	88	38s
Mental health care, VA medical centers, exp	capita	1.69	88	38s
Physician fee, family practice, first-visit		75.00	91	62r
Physician fee, family practice, revisit		34.00	91	62r
Physician fee, general practice, first-visit		61.00	91	62r
Physician fee, general practice, revisit		32.00	91	62r
Physician fee, general surgeon, first-visit		64.00	91	62r
Physician fee, general surgeon, revisit		40.00	91	62r
Physician fee, internal medicine, first-visit		98.00	91	62r
Physician fee, internal medicine, revisit		40.00	91	62r
Physician fee, median, neurosurgeon, first-visit		130.00	91	62r
Physician fee, median, nonsurgical specialist, first-visit		95.00	91	62r

Lakeland-Winter Haven, FL - continued

Item	Per	Value	Date	Ref.
Health Care - continued				
Physician fee, median, orthopedic surgeon, first-visit		91.00	91	62r
Physician fee, median, plastic surgeon, first-visit		66.00	91	62r
Physician fee, median, surgical specialist, first-visit		62.00	91	62r
Physician fee, neurosurgeon, revisit		50.00	91	62r
Physician fee, nonsurgical specialist, revisit		40.00	91	62r
Physician fee, obstetrics/gynecology, first-visit		64.00	91	62r
Physician fee, obstetrics/gynecology, revisit		41.00	91	62r
Physician fee, orthopedic surgeon, revisit		40.00	91	62r
Physician fee, pediatrician, first-visit		49.00	91	62r
Physician fee, pediatrician, revisit		33.00	91	62r
Physician fee, plastic surgeon, revisit		43.00	91	62r
Physician fee, surgical specialist, revisit		37.00	91	62r
Substance abuse, hospital ancillary charge	incident	1390	90	70s
Substance abuse, hospital physician charge	incident	770	90	70s
Substance abuse, hospital room and board	incident	5600	90	70s
Insurance and Pensions				
Auto insurance, private passenger	year	727.60	91	63s
Taxes				
Tax, cigarette	pack	33.90	91	77s
Tax, gasoline	gal	11.60	91	77s
Taxes, state	capita	1037	91	77s
Transportation				
Driver's license fee		15.00	12/90	43s
Travel				
Business travel	day	193.00	4/93	89r
Utilities				
Electricity	mil Btu	20.62	90	64s

Lancaster, PA

Item	Per	Value	Date	Ref.
Composite ACCRA index		111.10	4Q 92	4c
Alcoholic Beverages				
Beer, Miller Lite or Budweiser, 12-oz containers	6 pack	5.34	4Q 92	4c
Liquor, J & B Scotch	750 ml	16.39	4Q 92	4c
Wine, Gallo Chablis blanc, 1.5 liter	bottle	5.79	4Q 92	4c
Child Care				
Child care fee, average, center	hour	2.18	90	65r
Child care fee, average, nonregulated family day care	hour	1.83	90	65r
Child care fee, average, regulated family day care	hour	2.02	90	65r
Clothing				
Jeans, man's denim		33.79	4Q 92	4c
Shirt, man's dress shirt		26.00	4Q 92	4c
Undervest, boy's size 10-14, cotton	3	4.27	4Q 92	4c
Communications				
Long-distance telephone service, day, initial minute, 0-100 miles	min	0.15-0.29	91	12s
Long-distance telephone service, day, additional minute, 0-100 miles	min	0.06-0.22	91	12s
Long-distance telephone service, evenings/weekends, 0-100 mi, initial minute	min	0.06-0.14	91	12s
Long-distance telephone service, evenings/weekends, 0-100 mi, additional minute	min	0.03-0.11	91	12s
Newspaper subscription, daily and Sunday home delivery, large-city	month	14.57	4Q 92	4c
Telephone bill, family of four	month	16.32	4Q 92	4c

Values are in dollars or fractions of dollars. In the column headed *Ref*, references are shown to sources. Each reference is followed by a letter. These refer to the geographical level for which data were reported: s=State, r=Region, and c=City or metro. The abbreviation *ex* is used to mean *except* or *excluding*; *exp* stands for expenditures. For other abbreviations and further explanations, please see the Introduction.

Lancaster, PA - continued

Item	Per	Value	Date	Ref.
Education				
Board, 4-yr private college/university	year	2019	91	22s
Board, 4-yr public college/university	year	1656	91	22s
Expenditures, local gov't, public elementary/secondary	pupil	6980	92	20s
Room, 4-year private college/university	year	2179	91	22s
Room, 4-year public college/university	year	1719	91	22s
Tuition, 2-year private college/university	year	6314	91	22s
Tuition, 2-year public college/university	year	1505	91	22s
Tuition, 4-year private college/university	year	9848	91	22s
Tuition, 4-year public college/university, in-state	year	3401	91	22s
Energy and Fuels				
Coal	mil Btu	1.57	90	64s
Energy	mil Btu	8.63	90	64s
Energy, combined forms, 1,800 sq ft heating area	month	149.53	4Q 92	4c
Energy exp/householder, 1-family unit	year	588	90	28r
Energy exp/householder, <1,000 sq ft heating area	year	477	90	28r
Energy exp/householder, 1,000-1,999 sq ft heating area	year	517	90	28r
Energy exp/householder, 2,000+ sq ft heating area	year	630	90	28r
Energy exp/householder, mobile home	year	412	90	28r
Energy exp/householder, multifamily	year	498	90	28r
Gas, natural	mil Btu	5.24	90	64s
Gas, natural	000 cu ft	6.76	91	46s
Gas, natural, exp	year	703	91	46s
Gasoline, motor	gal	1.13	4Q 92	4c
Gasoline, unleaded regular	mil Btu	9.35	90	64s
Entertainment				
Bowling, evening rate	game	2.25	4Q 92	4c
Monopoly game, Parker Brothers', No. 9		11.95	4Q 92	4c
Movie	admission	5.50	4Q 92	4c
Tennis balls, yellow, Wilson or Penn, 3	can	2.96	4Q 92	4c
Funerals				
Casket, 18-gauge steel, velvet interior		1811.58	91	24r
Cosmetology, hair care, etc.		111.08	91	24r
Embalming		329.42	91	24r
Facility use for ceremony		201.29	91	24r
Hearse, local		135.27	91	24r
Limousine, local		127.24	91	24r
Remains to funeral home, transfer		103.98	91	24r
Service charge, professional		724.98	91	24r
Vault, concrete, non-metallic liner		766.71	91	24r
Viewing facilities, use		260.60	91	24r
Goods and Services				
ACCRA Index, Miscellaneous Goods and Services		106.50	4Q 92	4c
Groceries				
ACCRA Index, Groceries		102.80	4Q 92	4c
Apples, Red Delicious	lb	0.85	4/93	16r
Babyfood, strained vegetables, lowest price	4-4.5 oz jar	0.39	4Q 92	4c
Bacon	lb	2.12	4/93	16r
Bananas	lb	0.40	4Q 92	4c
Bananas	lb	0.54	4/93	16r
Bread, white	24 oz	0.84	4Q 92	4c
Bread, white, pan	lb	0.81	4/93	16r
Butter	lb	2.02	4/93	16r
Carrots, short trimmed and topped	lb	0.51	4/93	16r
Cheese, Kraft grated Parmesan	8-oz canister	3.21	4Q 92	4c
Chicken, fresh, whole	lb	1.04	4/93	16r
Chicken, fryer, whole	lb	0.85	4Q 92	4c
Chicken breast, bone-in	lb	2.21	4/93	16r

Lancaster, PA - continued

Item	Per	Value	Date	Ref.
Groceries - continued				
Chicken legs, bone-in	lb	1.16	4/93	16r
Chuck roast, USDA choice, boneless	lb	2.82	4/93	16r
Cigarettes, Winston	carton	17.74	4Q 92	4c
Coffee, 100% ground roast, all sizes	lb	2.66	4/93	16r
Coffee, vacuum-packed	13-oz can	1.97	4Q 92	4c
Corn, frozen	10 oz	0.63	4Q 92	4c
Corn Flakes, Kellogg's or Post Toasties	18 oz	2.13	4Q 92	4c
Cucumbers	lb	0.85	4/93	16r
Eggs, Grade A large	doz	0.85	4Q 92	4c
Eggs, Grade A large	doz	1.15	4/93	16r
Grapefruit	lb	0.45	4/93	16r
Grapes, Thompson Seedless	lb	1.52	4/93	16r
Ground beef, lean and extra lean	lb	2.36	4/93	16r
Ground beef or hamburger	lb	1.58	4Q 92	4c
Ground chuck, 100% beef	lb	2.02	4/93	16r
Honey, jar	8 oz	0.96-1.75	92	5r
Honey, jar	lb	1.50-3.00	92	5r
Honey, squeeze bear	12-oz	1.50-1.99	92	5r
Ice cream, prepackaged, bulk, regular	1/2 gal	2.80	4/93	16r
Lemons	lb	0.96	4/93	16r
Lettuce, iceberg	head	0.93	4Q 92	4c
Lettuce, iceberg	lb	0.95	4/93	16r
Margarine, Blue Bonnet or Parkay cubes	lb	0.73	4Q 92	4c
Margarine, stick	lb	0.81	4/93	16r
Milk, fresh, whole, fortified	1/2 gal	1.30	4/93	16r
Milk, whole	1/2 gal	1.21	4Q 92	4c
Orange juice, Minute Maid frozen	12-oz can	1.51	4Q 92	4c
Oranges, navel	lb	0.56	4/93	16r
Peaches	29-oz can	1.31	4Q 92	4c
Peanut butter, creamy, all sizes	lb	1.88	4/93	16r
Peas Sweet, Del Monte or Green Giant	15-17 oz can	0.55	4Q 92	4c
Pork chops, center cut, bone-in	lb	3.34	4/93	16r
Potato chips	16 oz	2.88	4/93	16r
Potatoes, white	lb	0.37	4/93	16r
Potatoes, white or red	10-lb sack	1.83	4Q 92	4c
Rib roast, USDA choice, bone-in	lb	4.94	4/93	16r
Round roast, USDA choice, boneless	lb	3.17	4/93	16r
Sausage, Jimmy Dean, 100% pork	lb	2.54	4Q 92	4c
Shortening, vegetable oil blends	lb	0.98	4/93	16r
Shortening, vegetable, Crisco	3-lb can	2.40	4Q 92	4c
Soft drink, Coca Cola	2 liter	1.11	4Q 92	4c
Spaghetti and macaroni	lb	0.82	4/93	16r
Steak, round, graded & ungraded, ex USDA prime & choice	lb	4.04	4/93	16r
Steak, round, USDA choice, boneless	lb	3.90	4/93	16r
Steak, sirloin, USDA choice, boneless	lb	4.97	4/93	16r
Steak, T-bone	lb	4.97	4Q 92	4c
Strawberries, dry pint	12 oz	0.90	4/93	16r
Sugar, cane or beet	4 lb	1.47	4Q 92	4c
Sugar, white	lb	0.50	4/93	16r
Sugar, white, 33-80 oz pk	lb	0.41	4/93	16r
Tomatoes, field grown	lb	1.23	4/93	16r
Tomatoes, Hunt's or Del Monte	14.5-oz can	0.71	4Q 92	4c
Tuna, chunk, light	6.125-6.5 oz can	0.69	4Q 92	4c
Tuna, chunk, light	lb	2.22	4/93	16r
Turkey, frozen, whole	lb	1.04	4/93	16r
Health Care				
ACCRA Index, Health Care		92.00	4Q 92	4c
Analgesic, Aspirin, Bayer, 325 mg tablets	100	5.81	4Q 92	4c
Childbirth, cesarean, hospital		5826	91	62r
Childbirth, cesarean, physician's fee		2053	91	62r
Childbirth, normal, hospital		2964	91	62r
Childbirth, normal, physician's fee		1492	91	62r

Values are in dollars or fractions of dollars. In the column headed *Ref*, references are shown to sources. Each reference is followed by a letter. These refer to the geographical level for which data were reported: s = State, r = Region, and c = City or metro. The abbreviation *ex* is used to mean *except* or *excluding*; *exp* stands for expenditures. For other abbreviations and further explanations, please see the Introduction.

Lancaster, PA - continued

Health Care

Item	Per	Value	Date	Ref.
Dentist's fee, adult teeth cleaning and periodic oral exam	visit	48.60	4Q 92	4c
Doctor's fee, routine exam, established patient	visit	29.00	4Q 92	4c
Hospital care, semiprivate room	day	255.25	4Q 92	4c
Medical insurance premium, per employee, small group comprehensive	month	310.25	10/91	25c
Medical plan per employee	year	3942	91	45r
Mental health care, exp	capita	53.68-118.35	90	38s
Mental health care, exp, state mental health agency	capita	56.85	90	38s
Mental health care, hospital psychiatric services, non-Federal, exp	capita	22.11	88	38s
Mental health care, mental health organization, multiservice, exp	capita	21.01	88	38s
Mental health care, psychiatric hospitals, private, exp	capita	26.48	88	38s
Mental health care, psychiatric out-patient clinics, freestanding, exp	capita	4.17	88	38s
Mental health care, psychiatric partial-care organizations, freestanding, exp	capita	0.94	88	38s
Mental health care, state and county mental hospitals, exp	capita	37.11	88	38s
Mental health care, VA medical centers, exp	capita	9.77	88	38s
Prescription drug co-pay, Medicaid	month	6.00	91	21s
Substance abuse, hospital ancillary charge	incident	720	90	70s
Substance abuse, hospital physician charge	incident	210	90	70s
Substance abuse, hospital room and board	incident	5400	90	70s

Household Goods

Item	Per	Value	Date	Ref.
Appliance repair, home, service call, washing machine	min labor charge	26.28	4Q 92	4c
Laundry detergent, Tide Ultra, Bold, or Cheer	42 oz	3.87	4Q 92	4c
Tissues, facial, Kleenex brand	175-count box	1.18	4Q 92	4c

Housing

Item	Per	Value	Date	Ref.
ACCRA Index, Housing		120.10	4Q 92	4c
House, 1,800 sq ft, 8,000 sq ft lot, new, urban	total	137810	4Q 92	4c
House payment, principal and interest, 25% down payment	month	761	4Q 92	4c
Mortgage rate, incl. points & origination fee, 30-year fixed or adjustable rate	percent	8.04	4Q 92	4c
Rent, apartment, 2 bedrooms - 1-1/2 to 2 baths, unfurnished, 950 sq ft, water	month	539	4Q 92	4c

Insurance and Pensions

Item	Per	Value	Date	Ref.
Auto insurance, private passenger	year	683.57	91	63s

Personal Goods

Item	Per	Value	Date	Ref.
Shampoo, Alberto VO5	15 oz	1.41	4Q 92	4c
Toothpaste, Crest or Colgate	6-7 oz	2.59	4Q 92	4c

Personal Services

Item	Per	Value	Date	Ref.
Dry cleaning, man's 2-piece suit		6.78	4Q 92	4c
Haircare, woman's shampoo, trim and blow-dry		20.10	4Q 92	4c
Haircut, man's barbershop, no styling		7.79	4Q 92	4c

Restaurant Food

Item	Per	Value	Date	Ref.
Chicken, fried, thigh and drumstick		2.22	4Q 92	4c
Hamburger with cheese	1/4 lb	1.85	4Q 92	4c
Pizza, Pizza Hut or Pizza Inn, cheese, thin crust	12-13 in	7.69	4Q 92	4c

Lancaster, PA - continued

Taxes

Item	Per	Value	Date	Ref.
Tax, cigarette	pack	31	91	77s
Tax, gasoline	gal	12	91	77s
Taxes, state	capita	1089	91	77s

Transportation

Item	Per	Value	Date	Ref.
ACCRA Index, Transportation		103.70	4Q 92	4c
Bus fare	one-way	0.85	3/93	2c
Driver's license fee		22.00	12/90	43s
Tire balance, computer or spin balance, front	wheel	6.97	4Q 92	4c

Travel

Item	Per	Value	Date	Ref.
Business travel	day	165.00	4/93	89r

Utilities

Item	Per	Value	Date	Ref.
ACCRA Index, Utilities		131.60	4Q 92	4c
Electricity	mil Btu	22.46	90	64s
Electricity, all electric, 1,800 sq ft living area new home	month	149.53	4Q 92	4c

Lansing, MI

Item	Per	Value	Date	Ref.
Composite ACCRA index		104.40	4Q 92	4c

Alcoholic Beverages

Item	Per	Value	Date	Ref.
Beer, Miller Lite or Budweiser, 12-oz containers	6 pack	3.99	4Q 92	4c
Liquor, J & B Scotch	750 ml	17.51	4Q 92	4c
Wine, Gallo Chablis blanc, 1.5 liter	bottle	5.45	4Q 92	4c

Child Care

Item	Per	Value	Date	Ref.
Child care fee, average, center	hour	1.63	90	65r
Child care fee, average, nonregulated family day care	hour	1.83	90	65r
Child care fee, average, regulated family day care	hour	1.42	90	65r

Clothing

Item	Per	Value	Date	Ref.
Jeans, man's denim		23.32	4Q 92	4c
Shirt, man's dress shirt		26.20	4Q 92	4c
Undervest, boy's size 10-14, cotton	3	3.63	4Q 92	4c

Communications

Item	Per	Value	Date	Ref.
Long-distance telephone service, day, initial minute, 0-100 miles	min	0.14-0.36	91	12s
Long-distance telephone service, day, additional minute, 0-100 miles	min	0.14-0.36	91	12s
Long-distance telephone service, evenings/weekends, 0-100 mi, initial minute	min	0.07-0.19	91	12s
Long-distance telephone service, evenings/weekends, 0-100 mi, additional minute	min	0.04-0.14	91	12s
Newspaper subscription, daily and Sunday home delivery, large-city	month	13.04	4Q 92	4c
Telephone, flat rate	month	10.42	91	11c
Telephone bill, family of four	month	17.55	4Q 92	4c

Education

Item	Per	Value	Date	Ref.
Board, 4-yr private college/university	year	1698	91	22s
Board, 4-yr public college/university	year	1962	91	22s
Expenditures, local gov't, public elementary/secondary	pupil	5671	92	20s
Room, 4-year private college/university	year	1440	91	22s
Room, 4-year public college/university	year	1687	91	22s
Tuition, 2-year private college/university	year	4749	91	22s
Tuition, 2-year public college/university	year	1124	91	22s
Tuition, 4-year private college/university	year	6885	91	22s
Tuition, 4-year public college/university, in-state	year	2635	91	22s

Energy and Fuels

Item	Per	Value	Date	Ref.
Coal	mil Btu	1.63	90	64s
Energy	mil Btu	8.17	90	64s
Energy, combined forms, 1,800 sq ft heating area	month	97.58	4Q 92	4c

Values are in dollars or fractions of dollars. In the column headed *Ref*, references are shown to sources. Each reference is followed by a letter. These refer to the geographical level for which data were reported: s=State, r=Region, and c=City or metro. The abbreviation *ex* is used to mean *except* or *excluding*; *exp* stands for *expenditures*. For other abbreviations and further explanations, please see the Introduction.

Lansing, MI - continued

Item	Per	Value	Date	Ref.
Energy and Fuels				
Energy, exc electricity, 1,800 sq ft heating area	month	57.10	4Q 92	4c
Energy exp/householder, 1-family unit	year	471	90	28r
Energy exp/householder, <1,000 sq ft heating area	year	430	90	28r
Energy exp/householder, 1,000-1,999 sq ft heating area	year	481	90	28r
Energy exp/householder, 2,000+ sq ft heating area	year	473	90	28r
Energy exp/householder, mobile home	year	430	90	28r
Energy exp/householder, multifamily	year	461	90	28r
Gas, natural	mil Btu	4.36	90	64s
Gas, natural	000 cu ft	5.07	91	46s
Gas, natural, exp	year	655	91	46s
Gasoline, motor	gal	1.12	4Q 92	4c
Gasoline, unleaded regular	mil Btu	8.78	90	64s
Entertainment				
Bowling, evening rate	game	2.04	4Q 92	4c
Miniature golf admission	adult	6.18	92	1r
Miniature golf admission	child	5.14	92	1r
Monopoly game, Parker Brothers', No. 9		9.99	4Q 92	4c
Movie	admis- sion	5.75	4Q 92	4c
Tennis balls, yellow, Wilson or Penn, 3	can	2.32	4Q 92	4c
Waterpark admission	adult	11.00	92	1r
Waterpark admission	child	8.55	92	1r
Funerals				
Casket, 18-gauge steel, velvet interior		1926.72	91	24r
Cosmetology, hair care, etc.		97.64	91	24r
Embalming		249.14	91	24r
Facility use for ceremony		208.59	91	24r
Hearse, local		130.12	91	24r
Limousine, local		104.66	91	24r
Remains to funeral home, transfer		93.61	91	24r
Service charge, professional		724.62	91	24r
Vault, concrete, non-metallic liner		734.53	91	24r
Viewing facilities, use		236.06	91	24r
Goods and Services				
ACCRA Index, Miscellaneous Goods and Services		96.70	4Q 92	4c
Groceries				
ACCRA Index, Groceries		106.30	4Q 92	4c
Apples, Red Delicious	lb	0.77	4/93	16r
Babyfood, strained vegetables, lowest price	4-4.5 oz jar	0.34	4Q 92	4c
Bacon	lb	1.85	4/93	16r
Bananas	lb	0.42	4Q 92	4c
Bananas	lb	0.46	4/93	16r
Beef, stew, boneless	lb	2.53	4/93	16r
Bologna, all beef or mixed	lb	2.19	4/93	16r
Bread, white	24 oz	0.85	4Q 92	4c
Bread, white, pan	lb	0.78	4/93	16r
Butter	lb	1.50	4/93	16r
Cabbage	lb	0.40	4/93	16r
Carrots, short trimmed and topped	lb	0.45	4/93	16r
Cheese, Cheddar	lb	3.47	4/93	16r
Cheese, Kraft grated Parmesan	8-oz canis- ter	3.03	4Q 92	4c
Chicken, fresh, whole	lb	0.84	4/93	16r
Chicken, fryer, whole	lb	0.89	4Q 92	4c
Chicken breast, bone-in	lb	1.94	4/93	16r
Chicken legs, bone-in	lb	1.02	4/93	16r
Chuck roast, graded and ungraded, ex USDA prime and choice	lb	2.43	4/93	16r
Chuck roast, USDA choice, bone-in	lb	2.11	4/93	16r
Chuck roast, USDA choice, boneless	lb	2.44	4/93	16r
Cigarettes, Winston	carton	17.47	4Q 92	4c
Coffee, 100% ground roast, all sizes	lb	2.47	4/93	16r

Lansing, MI - continued

Item	Per	Value	Date	Ref.
Groceries - continued				
Coffee, vacuum-packed	13-oz can	2.55	4Q 92	4c
Cookies, chocolate chip	lb	2.73	4/93	16r
Corn, frozen	10 oz	0.71	4Q 92	4c
Corn Flakes, Kellogg's or Post Toasties	18 oz	2.01	4Q 92	4c
Eggs, Grade A large	doz	0.85	4Q 92	4c
Eggs, Grade A large	doz	0.93	4/93	16r
Flour, white, all purpose	lb	0.21	4/93	16r
Grapefruit	lb	0.45	4/93	16r
Grapes, Thompson Seedless	lb	1.46	4/93	16r
Ground beef, 100% beef	lb	1.63	4/93	16r
Ground beef, lean and extra lean	lb	2.08	4/93	16r
Ground beef or hamburger	lb	1.53	4Q 92	4c
Ground chuck, 100% beef	lb	1.94	4/93	16r
Ham, boneless, excluding canned	lb	2.21	4/93	16r
Honey, jar	8 oz	0.97-1.25	92	5r
Honey, jar	lb	1.25-2.25	92	5r
Honey, squeeze bear	12-oz	1.25-1.99	92	5r
Ice cream, prepackaged, bulk, regular	1/2 gal	2.41	4/93	16r
Lemons	lb	0.82	4/93	16r
Lettuce, iceberg	head	0.89	4Q 92	4c
Lettuce, iceberg	lb	0.83	4/93	16r
Margarine, Blue Bonnet or Parkay cubes	lb	0.77	4Q 92	4c
Margarine, stick	lb	0.77	4/93	16r
Milk, whole	1/2 gal	1.43	4Q 92	4c
Orange juice, Minute Maid frozen	12-oz can	1.25	4Q 92	4c
Oranges, navel	lb	0.50	4/93	16r
Peaches	29-oz can	1.29	4Q 92	4c
Peanut butter, creamy, all sizes	lb	1.82	4/93	16r
Pears, Anjou	lb	0.85	4/93	16r
Peas Sweet, Del Monte or Green Giant	15-17 oz can	0.70	4Q 92	4c
Pork chops, center cut, bone-in	lb	3.17	4/93	16r
Potato chips	16 oz	2.68	4/93	16r
Potatoes, white	lb	0.26	4/93	16r
Potatoes, white or red	10-lb sack	1.51	4Q 92	4c
Round roast, graded & ungraded, ex USDA prime & choice	lb	2.88	4/93	16r
Round roast, USDA choice, boneless	lb	2.96	4/93	16r
Sausage, Jimmy Dean, 100% pork	lb	2.43	4Q 92	4c
Shortening, vegetable oil blends	lb	0.79	4/93	16r
Shortening, vegetable, Crisco	3-lb can	2.59	4Q 92	4c
Soft drink, Coca Cola	2 liter	1.37	4Q 92	4c
Spaghetti and macaroni	lb	0.76	4/93	16r
Steak, rib eye, USDA choice, boneless	lb	6.29	4/93	16r
Steak, round, USDA choice, boneless	lb	3.24	4/93	16r
Steak, sirloin, graded & ungraded, ex USDA prime & choice	lb	4.00	4/93	16r
Steak, sirloin, USDA choice, bone-in	lb	3.57	4/93	16r
Steak, sirloin, USDA choice, boneless	lb	4.17	4/93	16r
Steak, T-bone	lb	5.85	4Q 92	4c
Steak, T-bone, USDA choice, bone-in	lb	5.60	4/93	16r
Strawberries, dry pint	12 oz	0.90	4/93	16r
Sugar, cane or beet	4 lb	1.41	4Q 92	4c
Sugar, white	lb	0.36	4/93	16r
Sugar, white, 33-80 oz pk	lb	0.35	4/93	16r
Tomatoes, field grown	lb	0.99	4/93	16r
Tomatoes, Hunt's or Del Monte	14.5-oz can	0.84	4Q 92	4c
Tuna, chunk, light	6.125- 6.5 oz can	0.86	4Q 92	4c
Tuna, chunk, light	lb	1.76	4/93	16r
Turkey, frozen, whole	lb	0.91	4/93	16r
Health Care				
ACCRA Index, Health Care		111.70	4Q 92	4c
Analgesic, Aspirin, Bayer, 325 mg tablets	100	4.55	4Q 92	4c
Childbirth, cesarean, hospital		4688	91	62r

Values are in dollars or fractions of dollars. In the column headed *Ref*, references are shown to sources. Each reference is followed by a letter. These refer to the geographical level for which data were reported: s=State, r=Region, and c=City or metro. The abbreviation *ex* is used to mean *except* or *excluding*; *exp* stands for expenditures. For other abbreviations and further explanations, please see the Introduction.

Lansing, MI - continued

Item	Per	Value	Date	Ref.
Health Care				
Childbirth, cesarean, physician's fee		2053	91	62r
Childbirth, normal, hospital		2657	91	62r
Childbirth, normal, physician's fee		1492	91	62r
Dentist's fee, adult teeth cleaning and periodic oral exam	visit	58.00	4Q 92	4c
Doctor's fee, routine exam, established patient	visit	36.00	4Q 92	4c
Hospital care, semiprivate room	day	337.96	90	27c
Hospital care, semiprivate room	day	407.25	4Q 92	4c
Medical insurance premium, per employee, small group comprehensive	month	328.50	10/91	25c
Medical plan per employee	year	3443	91	45r
Mental health care, exp	capita	53.68- 118.35	90	38s
Mental health care, exp, state mental health agency	capita	73.73	90	38s
Mental health care, hospital psychiatric services, non-Federal, exp	capita	22.52	88	38s
Mental health care, mental health organization, multiservice, exp	capita	42.68	88	38s
Mental health care, psychiatric hospitals, private, exp	capita	10.80	88	38s
Mental health care, psychiatric out-patient clinics, freestanding, exp	capita	3.47	88	38s
Mental health care, psychiatric partial-care organizations, freestanding, exp	capita	0.73	88	38s
Mental health care, state and county mental hospitals, exp	capita	36.77	88	38s
Mental health care, VA medical centers, exp	capita	4.03	88	38s
Physician fee, family practice, first-visit		76.00	91	62r
Physician fee, family practice, revisit		33.00	91	62r
Physician fee, general practice, first-visit		61.00	91	62r
Physician fee, general practice, revisit		31.00	91	62r
Physician fee, general surgeon, first-visit		65.00	91	62r
Physician fee, general surgeon, revisit		35.00	91	62r
Physician fee, internal medicine, first-visit		91.00	91	62r
Physician fee, internal medicine, revisit		40.00	91	62r
Physician fee, median, neurosurgeon, first-visit		106.00	91	62r
Physician fee, median, nonsurgical specialist, first-visit		90.00	91	62r
Physician fee, median, orthopedic surgeon, first-visit		83.00	91	62r
Physician fee, median, surgical specialist, first-visit		61.00	91	62r
Physician fee, neurosurgeon, revisit		41.00	91	62r
Physician fee, nonsurgical specialist, revisit		40.00	91	62r
Physician fee, obstetrics/gynecology, first-visit		61.00	91	62r
Physician fee, obstetrics/gynecology, revisit		40.00	91	62r
Physician fee, orthopedic surgeon, revisit		41.00	91	62r
Physician fee, pediatrician, first-visit		46.00	91	62r
Physician fee, pediatrician, revisit		33.00	91	62r
Physician fee, surgical specialist, revisit		36.00	91	62r
Substance abuse, hospital ancillary charge	incident	1480	90	70s
Substance abuse, hospital physician charge	incident	250	90	70s
Substance abuse, hospital room and board	incident	4070	90	70s
Household Goods				
Appliance repair, home, service call, washing machine	min labor charge	30.00	4Q 92	4c
Laundry detergent, Tide Ultra, Bold, or Cheer	42 oz	4.07	4Q 92	4c
Tissues, facial, Kleenex brand	175-count box	1.05	4Q 92	4c

Lansing, MI - continued

Item	Per	Value	Date	Ref.
Housing				
ACCRA Index, Housing		117.50	4Q 92	4c
Home, median price	unit	69.90		26c
House, 1,800 sq ft, 8,000 sq ft lot, new, urban	total	133733	4Q 92	4c
House payment, principal and interest, 25% down payment	month	752	4Q 92	4c
Mortgage rate, incl. points & origination fee, 30-year fixed or adjustable rate	percent	8.23	4Q 92	4c
Rent, apartment, 2 bedrooms - 1-1/2 to 2 baths, unfurnished, 950 sq ft, water	month	511	4Q 92	4c
Rental unit, 1 bedroom	month	429	93	23c
Rental unit, 2 bedroom	month	502	93	23c
Rental unit, 3 bedroom	month	625	93	23c
Rental unit, 4 bedroom	month	698	93	23c
Rental unit, efficiency	month	358	93	23c
Insurance and Pensions				
Auto insurance, private passenger	year	716.78	91	63s
Personal Goods				
Shampoo, Alberto VO5	15 oz	1.00	4Q 92	4c
Toothpaste, Crest or Colgate	6-7 oz	1.47	4Q 92	4c
Personal Services				
Dry cleaning, man's 2-piece suit		6.18	4Q 92	4c
Haircare, woman's shampoo, trim and blow-dry		16.50	4Q 92	4c
Haircut, man's barbershop, no styling		8.25	4Q 92	4c
Restaurant Food				
Chicken, fried, thigh and drumstick		2.07	4Q 92	4c
Hamburger with cheese	1/4 lb	1.69	4Q 92	4c
Pizza, Pizza Hut or Pizza Inn, cheese, thin crust	12-13 in	9.00	4Q 92	4c
Taxes				
Tax, cigarette	pack	25	91	77s
Tax, gasoline	gal	15	91	77s
Taxes, state	capita	1185	91	77s
Transportation				
ACCRA Index, Transportation		101.80	4Q 92	4c
Bus fare	one-way	0.85	3/93	2c
Bus fare, up to 10 miles	one-way	0.85	4Q 92	4c
Driver's license fee		12.00	12/90	43s
Tire balance, computer or spin balance, front	wheel	6.83	4Q 92	4c
Vehicle registration and license plate	year	14.00-200.00	93	40s
Utilities				
ACCRA Index, Utilities		89.50	4Q 92	4c
Electricity	mil Btu	20.85	90	64s
Electricity, partial electric and other energy, 1,800 sq ft living area new home	month	40.48	4Q 92	4c

Laramie, WY

Item	Per	Value	Date	Ref.
Composite ACCRA index		96.90	4Q 92	4c
Alcoholic Beverages				
Beer, Miller Lite or Budweiser, 12-oz containers	6 pack	4.27	4Q 92	4c
Liquor, J & B Scotch	750 ml	17.87	4Q 92	4c
Wine, Gallo Chablis blanc, 1.5 liter	bottle	5.60	4Q 92	4c
Child Care				
Child care fee, average, center	hour	1.71	90	65r
Child care fee, average, nonregulated family day care	hour	1.32	90	65r
Child care fee, average, regulated family day care	hour	1.86	90	65r

Values are in dollars or fractions of dollars. In the column headed *Ref*, references are shown to sources. Each reference is followed by a letter. These refer to the geographical level for which data were reported: s=State, r=Region, and c=City or metro. The abbreviation *ex* is used to mean *except* or *excluding*; *exp* stands for *expenditures*. For other abbreviations and further explanations, please see the Introduction.

Laramie, WY - continued

Item	Per	Value	Date	Ref.
Clothing				
Jeans, man's denim		28.62	4Q 92	4c
Shirt, man's dress shirt		22.95	4Q 92	4c
Undervest, boy's size 10-14, cotton	3	4.24	4Q 92	4c
Communications				
Long-distance telephone service, day, initial minute, 0-100 miles	min	0.19-0.43	91	12s
Long-distance telephone service, day, additional minute, 0-100 miles	min	0.09-0.29	91	12s
Long-distance telephone service, evenings/ weekends, 0-100 mi, initial minute	min	0.10-0.24	91	12s
Long-distance telephone service, evenings/ weekends, 0-100 mi, additional minute	min	0.05-0.16	91	12s
Newspaper subscription, daily and Sunday home delivery, large-city	month	8.48	4Q 92	4c
Telephone, flat rate	month	11.22	91	11c
Telephone bill, family of four	month	17.24	4Q 92	4c
Education				
Board, 4-yr public college/university	year	1767	91	22s
Expenditures, local gov't, public elementary/secondary	pupil	5355	92	20s
Room, 4-year public college/university	year	1312	91	22s
Tuition, 2-year private college/university	year	7500	91	22s
Tuition, 2-year public college/university	year	662	91	22s
Tuition, 4-year public college/university, in-state	year	1148	91	22s
Energy and Fuels				
Coal	mil Btu	0.86	90	64s
Energy	mil Btu	6.46	90	64s
Energy, combined forms, 1,800 sq ft heating area	month	76.74	4Q 92	4c
Energy, exc electricity, 1,800 sq ft heating area	month	40.97	4Q 92	4c
Energy exp/householder, 1-family unit	year	372	90	28r
Energy exp/householder, <1,000 sq ft heating area	year	335	90	28r
Energy exp/householder, 1,000-1,999 sq ft heating area	year	365	90	28r
Energy exp/householder, 2,000+ sq ft heating area	year	411	90	28r
Energy exp/householder, mobile home	year	305	90	28r
Energy exp/householder, multifamily	year	372	90	28r
Gas, natural	mil Btu	3.57	90	64s
Gas, natural	000 cu ft	4.74	91	46s
Gas, natural, exp	year	501	91	46s
Gasoline, motor	gal	1.13	4Q 92	4c
Gasoline, unleaded regular	mil Btu	8.66	90	64s
Entertainment				
Bowling, evening rate	game	1.80	4Q 92	4c
Miniature golf admission	adult	6.18	92	1r
Miniature golf admission	child	5.14	92	1r
Monopoly game, Parker Brothers', No. 9		9.30	4Q 92	4c
Movie	admission	4.75	4Q 92	4c
Tennis balls, yellow, Wilson or Penn, 3	can	2.36	4Q 92	4c
Waterpark admission	adult	11.00	92	1r
Waterpark admission	child	8.55	92	1r
Funerals				
Casket, 18-gauge steel, velvet interior		1929.04	91	24r
Cosmetology, hair care, etc.		88.52	91	24r
Embalming		249.33	91	24r
Facility use for ceremony		182.75	91	24r
Hearse, local		110.04	91	24r
Limousine, local		66.67	91	24r
Remains to funeral home, transfer		84.58	91	24r
Service charge, professional		593.00	91	24r
Vault, concrete, non-metallic liner		647.38	91	24r
Viewing facilities, use		99.87	91	24r

Laramie, WY - continued

Item	Per	Value	Date	Ref.
Goods and Services				
ACCRA Index, Miscellaneous Goods and Services		95.90	4Q 92	4c
Groceries				
ACCRA Index, Groceries		109.50	4Q 92	4c
Apples, Red Delicious	lb	0.80	4/93	16r
Babyfood, strained vegetables, lowest price	4-4.5 oz jar	0.33	4Q 92	4c
Bacon	lb	1.79	4/93	16r
Bananas	lb	0.55	4Q 92	4c
Bananas	lb	0.53	4/93	16r
Bologna, all beef or mixed	lb	2.67	4/93	16r
Bread, white	24 oz	0.77	4Q 92	4c
Bread, white, pan	lb	0.81	4/93	16r
Carrots, short trimmed and topped	lb	0.39	4/93	16r
Cheese, Kraft grated Parmesan	8-oz canister	3.29	4Q 92	4c
Chicken, fresh, whole	lb	0.94	4/93	16r
Chicken, fryer, whole	lb	0.70	4Q 92	4c
Chicken breast, bone-in	lb	2.19	4/93	16r
Chuck roast, graded and ungraded, ex USDA prime and choice	lb	2.26	4/93	16r
Cigarettes, Winston	carton	16.94	4Q 92	4c
Coffee, 100% ground roast, all sizes	lb	2.33	4/93	16r
Coffee, vacuum-packed	13-oz can	2.34	4Q 92	4c
Corn, frozen	10 oz	0.81	4Q 92	4c
Corn Flakes, Kellogg's or Post Toasties	18 oz	2.14	4Q 92	4c
Eggs, Grade A large	doz	0.82	4Q 92	4c
Eggs, Grade AA large	doz	1.18	4/93	16r
Flour, white, all purpose	lb	0.22	4/93	16r
Grapefruit	lb	0.52	4/93	16r
Grapes, Thompson Seedless	lb	1.50	4/93	16r
Ground beef, 100% beef	lb	1.44	4/93	16r
Ground beef, lean and extra lean	lb	2.34	4/93	16r
Ground beef or hamburger	lb	1.56	4Q 92	4c
Ham, boneless, excluding canned	lb	2.56	4/93	16r
Honey, jar	8 oz	0.89-1.00	92	5r
Honey, jar	lb	1.35-1.97	92	5r
Honey, squeeze bear	12-oz	1.00-1.89	92	5r
Ice cream, prepackaged, bulk, regular	1/2 gal	2.40	4/93	16r
Lemons	lb	0.81	4/93	16r
Lettuce, iceberg	head	0.95	4Q 92	4c
Lettuce, iceberg	lb	0.84	4/93	16r
Margarine, Blue Bonnet or Parkay cubes	lb	0.88	4Q 92	4c
Margarine, stick	lb	0.81	4/93	16r
Milk, whole	1/2 gal	1.49	4Q 92	4c
Orange juice, Minute Maid frozen	12-oz can	1.51	4Q 92	4c
Oranges, navel	lb	0.48	4/93	16r
Peaches	29-oz can	1.63	4Q 92	4c
Peas Sweet, Del Monte or Green Giant	15-17 oz can	0.74	4Q 92	4c
Pork chops, center cut, bone-in	lb	3.25	4/93	16r
Potato chips	16 oz	2.89	4/93	16r
Potatoes, white	lb	0.38	4/93	16r
Potatoes, white or red	10-lb sack	2.64	4Q 92	4c
Round roast, graded & ungraded, ex USDA prime & choice	lb	3.00	4/93	16r
Round roast, USDA choice, boneless	lb	3.16	4/93	16r
Sausage, Jimmy Dean, 100% pork	lb	3.39	4Q 92	4c
Shortening, vegetable oil blends	lb	0.86	4/93	16r
Shortening, vegetable, Crisco	3-lb can	2.32	4Q 92	4c
Soft drink, Coca Cola	2 liter	1.59	4Q 92	4c
Spaghetti and macaroni	lb	0.84	4/93	16r
Steak, round, graded & ungraded, ex USDA prime & choice	lb	3.34	4/93	16r
Steak, round, USDA choice, boneless	lb	3.24	4/93	16r

Values are in dollars or fractions of dollars. In the column headed *Ref*, references are shown to sources. Each reference is followed by a letter. These refer to the geographical level for which data were reported: s=State, r=Region, and c=City or metro. The abbreviation *ex* is used to mean *except* or *excluding*; *exp* stands for expenditures. For other abbreviations and further explanations, please see the Introduction.

Laramie, WY - continued

Item	Per	Value	Date	Ref.
Groceries				
Steak, sirloin, graded & ungraded, ex USDA prime & choice	lb	3.75	4/93	16r
Steak, sirloin, USDA choice, boneless	lb	4.49	4/93	16r
Steak, T-bone	lb	4.61	4Q 92	4c
Sugar, cane or beet	4 lb	1.74	4Q 92	4c
Sugar, white	lb	0.41	4/93	16r
Sugar, white, 33-80 oz pk	lb	0.38	4/93	16r
Tomatoes, field grown	lb	1.01	4/93	16r
Tomatoes, Hunt's or Del Monte	14.5-oz can	0.67	4Q 92	4c
Tuna, chunk, light	6.125-6.5 oz can	0.78	4Q 92	4c
Turkey, frozen, whole	lb	1.04	4/93	16r
Health Care				
ACCRA Index, Health Care		105.70	4Q 92	4c
Analgesic, Aspirin, Bayer, 325 mg tablets	100	4.74	4Q 92	4c
Childbirth, cesarean, hospital		5533	91	62r
Childbirth, cesarean, physician's fee		2053	91	62r
Childbirth, normal, hospital		2745	91	62r
Childbirth, normal, physician's fee		1492	91	62r
Dentist's fee, adult teeth cleaning and periodic oral exam	visit	47.80	4Q 92	4c
Doctor's fee, routine exam, established patient	visit	39.33	4Q 92	4c
Hospital care, semiprivate room	day	375.00	4Q 92	4c
Medical plan per employee	year	3218	91	45r
Mental health care, exp	capita	28.84-37.59	90	38s
Mental health care, exp, state mental health agency	capita	34.62	90	38s
Mental health care, hospital psychiatric services, non-Federal, exp	capita	3.06	88	38s
Mental health care, mental health organization, multiservice, exp	capita	9.72	88	38s
Mental health care, psychiatric hospitals, private, exp	capita	24.34	88	38s
Mental health care, psychiatric out-patient clinics, freestanding, exp	capita	9.27	88	38s
Mental health care, state and county mental hospitals, exp	capita	25.55	88	38s
Mental health care, VA medical centers, exp	capita	39.92	88	38s
Physician fee, family practice, first-visit		111.00	91	62r
Physician fee, family practice, revisit		45.00	91	62r
Physician fee, general practice, first-visit		100.00	91	62r
Physician fee, general practice, revisit		40.00	91	62r
Physician fee, internal medicine, first-visit		137.00	91	62r
Physician fee, internal medicine, revisit		48.00	91	62r
Physician fee, median, neurosurgeon, first-visit		157.00	91	62r
Physician fee, median, nonsurgical specialist, first-visit		131.00	91	62r
Physician fee, median, orthopedic surgeon, first-visit		124.00	91	62r
Physician fee, median, plastic surgeon, first-visit		88.00	91	62r
Physician fee, median, surgical specialist, first-visit		100.00	91	62r
Physician fee, neurosurgeon, revisit		51.00	91	62r
Physician fee, nonsurgical specialist, revisit		47.00	91	62r
Physician fee, obstetrics/gynecology, first-visit		95.00	91	62r
Physician fee, obstetrics/gynecology, revisit		50.00	91	62r
Physician fee, orthopedic surgeon, revisit		51.00	91	62r
Physician fee, pediatrician, first-visit		81.00	91	62r
Physician fee, pediatrician, revisit		42.00	91	62r
Physician fee, plastic surgeon, revisit		48.00	91	62r
Physician fee, surgical specialist, revisit		49.00	91	62r

Laramie, WY - continued

Item	Per	Value	Date	Ref.
Household Goods				
Appliance repair, home, service call, washing machine	min labor charge	25.33	4Q 92	4c
Laundry detergent, Tide Ultra, Bold, or Cheer	42 oz	4.11	4Q 92	4c
Tissues, facial, Kleenex brand	175-count box	1.18	4Q 92	4c
Housing				
ACCRA Index, Housing		99.20	4Q 92	4c
House, 1,800 sq ft, 8,000 sq ft lot, new, urban	total	110000	4Q 92	4c
House payment, principal and interest, 25% down payment	month	616	4Q 92	4c
Mortgage rate, incl. points & origination fee, 30-year fixed or adjustable rate	per-cent	8.18	4Q 92	4c
Insurance and Pensions				
Auto insurance, private passenger	year	450.33	91	63s
Personal Goods				
Shampoo, Alberto VO5	15 oz	1.49	4Q 92	4c
Toothpaste, Crest or Colgate	6-7 oz	2.07	4Q 92	4c
Personal Services				
Dry cleaning, man's 2-piece suit		6.35	4Q 92	4c
Haircare, woman's shampoo, trim and blow-dry		13.11	4Q 92	4c
Haircut, man's barbershop, no styling		8.00	4Q 92	4c
Restaurant Food				
Chicken, fried, thigh and drumstick		2.10	4Q 92	4c
Hamburger with cheese	1/4 lb	1.89	4Q 92	4c
Pizza, Pizza Hut or Pizza Inn, cheese, thin crust	12-13 in	9.05	4Q 92	4c
Taxes				
Tax, cigarette	pack	12	91	77s
Tax, gasoline	gal	9	91	77s
Taxes, state	capita	1385	91	77s
Transportation				
ACCRA Index, Transportation		95.20	4Q 92	4c
Driver's license fee		5.00	12/90	43s
Tire balance, computer or spin balance, front	wheel	5.92	4Q 92	4c
Travel				
Business travel	day	178.00	4/93	89r
Utilities				
ACCRA Index, Utilities		72.10	4Q 92	4c
Electricity	mil Btu	12.37	90	64s
Electricity, partial electric and other energy, 1,800 sq ft living area new home	month	35.77	4Q 92	4c

Laredo, TX

Item	Per	Value	Date	Ref.
Child Care				
Child care fee, average, center	hour	1.29	90	65r
Child care fee, average, nonregulated family day care	hour	0.89	90	65r
Child care fee, average, regulated family day care	hour	1.32	90	65r
Communications				
Long-distance telephone service, day, initial minute, 0-100 miles	min	0.10-0.46	91	12s
Long-distance telephone service, day, additional minute, 0-100 miles	min	0.06-0.45	91	12s
Education				
Board, 4-yr private college/university	year	1883	91	22s
Board, 4-yr public college/university	year	1605	91	22s

Values are in dollars or fractions of dollars. In the column headed *Ref*, references are shown to sources. Each reference is followed by a letter. These refer to the geographical level for which data were reported: s=State, r=Region, and c=City or metro. The abbreviation *ex* is used to mean *except* or *excluding*; *exp* stands for expenditures. For other abbreviations and further explanations, please see the Introduction.

Laredo, TX - continued

Item	Per	Value	Date	Ref.
Education				
Expenditures, local gov't, public elementary/secondary	pupil	4593	92	20s
Room, 4-year private college/university	year	1620	91	22s
Room, 4-year public college/university	year	1532	91	22s
Tuition, 2-year private college/university	year	4394	91	22s
Tuition, 2-year public college/university	year	495	91	22s
Tuition, 4-year private college/university	year	6497	91	22s
Tuition, 4-year public college/university, in-state	year	986	91	22s
Energy and Fuels				
Coal	mil Btu	1.44	90	64s
Energy	mil Btu	6.48	90	64s
Energy exp/householder, 1-family unit	year	471	90	28r
Energy exp/householder, <1,000 sq ft heating area	year	384	90	28r
Energy exp/householder, 1,000-1,999 sq ft heating area	year	421	90	28r
Energy exp/householder, 2,000+ sq ft heating area	year	625	90	28r
Energy exp/householder, mobile home	year	271	90	28r
Energy exp/householder, multifamily	year	355	90	28r
Gas, natural	mil Btu	2.47	90	64s
Gas, natural	000 cu ft	5.71	91	46s
Gas, natural, exp	year	388	91	46s
Gasoline, unleaded regular	mil Btu	9.16	90	64s
Entertainment				
Miniature golf admission	adult	6.18	92	1r
Miniature golf admission	child	5.14	92	1r
Waterpark admission	adult	11.00	92	1r
Waterpark admission	child	8.55	92	1r
Funerals				
Casket, 18-gauge steel, velvet interior		2274.41	91	24r
Cosmetology, hair care, etc.		74.62	91	24r
Embalming		229.94	91	24r
Facility use for ceremony		176.61	91	24r
Hearse, local		116.34	91	24r
Limousine, local		72.68	91	24r
Remains to funeral home, transfer		87.72	91	24r
Service charge, professional		712.53	91	24r
Vault, concrete, non-metallic liner		750.55	91	24r
Viewing facilities, use		155.31	91	24r
Groceries				
Apples, Red Delicious	lb	0.79	4/93	16r
Bacon	lb	1.75	4/93	16r
Bananas	lb	0.42	4/93	16r
Beef, stew, boneless	lb	2.61	4/93	16r
Bologna, all beef or mixed	lb	2.24	4/93	16r
Bread, white, pan	lb	0.64	4/93	16r
Bread, whole wheat, pan	lb	0.96	4/93	16r
Cabbage	lb	0.37	4/93	16r
Carrots, short trimmed and topped	lb	0.47	4/93	16r
Celery	lb	0.64	4/93	16r
Cheese, American	lb	2.98	4/93	16r
Cheese, Cheddar	lb	3.28	4/93	16r
Chicken, fresh, whole	lb	0.77	4/93	16r
Chicken breast, bone-in	lb	1.92	4/93	16r
Chicken legs, bone-in	lb	1.06	4/93	16r
Chuck roast, graded and ungraded, ex USDA prime and choice	lb	2.40	4/93	16r
Chuck roast, USDA choice, bone-in	lb	2.19	4/93	16r
Chuck roast, USDA choice, boneless	lb	2.38	4/93	16r
Coffee, 100% ground roast, all sizes	lb	2.48	4/93	16r
Crackers, soda, salted	lb	1.15	4/93	16r
Eggs, Grade A large	doz	0.96	4/93	16r
Flour, white, all purpose	lb	0.24	4/93	16r
Frankfurters, all meat or all beef	lb	2.01	4/93	16r
Grapefruit	lb	0.44	4/93	16r
Grapes, Thompson Seedless	lb	1.40	4/93	16r
Ground beef, 100% beef	lb	1.58	4/93	16r

Laredo, TX - continued

Item	Per	Value	Date	Ref.
Groceries - continued				
Ground beef, lean and extra lean	lb	2.09	4/93	16r
Ground chuck, 100% beef	lb	1.98	4/93	16r
Ham, boneless, excluding canned	lb	2.89	4/93	16r
Ham, picnic, shoulder, bone-in, smoked	lb	1.02	4/93	16r
Ham, rump or steak half, bone-in, smoked	lb	1.48	4/93	16r
Honey, jar	8 oz	0.73-1.19	92	5r
Honey, jar	lb	1.10-1.79	92	5r
Honey, squeeze bear	12-oz	1.19-1.50	92	5r
Ice cream, prepackaged, bulk, regular	1/2 gal	2.41	4/93	16r
Lemons	lb	1.05	4/93	16r
Lettuce, iceberg	lb	0.81	4/93	16r
Margarine, stick	lb	0.88	4/93	16r
Oranges, navel	lb	0.55	4/93	16r
Pears, Anjou	lb	0.92	4/93	16r
Pork chops, center cut, bone-in	lb	3.13	4/93	16r
Potato chips	16 oz	2.94	4/93	16r
Potatoes, white	lb	0.43	4/93	16r
Rib roast, USDA choice, bone-in	lb	4.63	4/93	16r
Rice, white, long grain, uncooked	lb	0.45	4/93	16r
Round roast, graded & ungraded, ex USDA prime & choice	lb	3.03	4/93	16r
Round roast, USDA choice, boneless	lb	3.09	4/93	16r
Sausage, fresh, loose	lb	2.08	4/93	16r
Short ribs, bone-in	lb	2.66	4/93	16r
Shortening, vegetable oil blends	lb	0.69	4/93	16r
Spaghetti and macaroni	lb	0.81	4/93	16r
Steak, rib eye, USDA choice, boneless	lb	6.24	4/93	16r
Steak, round, graded & ungraded, ex USDA prime & choice	lb	3.31	4/93	16r
Steak, round, USDA choice, boneless	lb	3.34	4/93	16r
Steak, sirloin, graded & ungraded, ex USDA prime & choice	lb	4.19	4/93	16r
Steak, sirloin, USDA choice, boneless	lb	4.46	4/93	16r
Steak, T-bone, USDA choice, bone-in	lb	5.25	4/93	16r
Strawberries, dry pint	12 oz	0.92	4/93	16r
Sugar, white	lb	0.39	4/93	16r
Sugar, white, 33-80 oz pk	lb	0.38	4/93	16r
Tomatoes, field grown	lb	0.88	4/93	16r
Tuna, chunk, light	lb	1.79	4/93	16r
Turkey, frozen, whole	lb	1.04	4/93	16r
Yogurt, natural, fruit flavored	1/2 pint	0.57	4/93	16r
Health Care				
Childbirth, cesarean, hospital		5034	91	62r
Childbirth, cesarean, physician's fee		2053	91	62r
Childbirth, normal, hospital		2712	91	62r
Childbirth, normal, physician's fee		1492	91	62r
Health care spending, state	capita	2192	3/93	84s
Mental health care, exp	capita	20.37-28.83	90	38s
Mental health care, exp, state mental health agency	capita	22.72	90	38s
Mental health care, hospital psychiatric services, non-Federal, exp	capita	7.95	88	38s
Mental health care, mental health organization, multiservice, exp	capita	12.05	88	38s
Mental health care, psychiatric hospitals, private, exp	capita	37.78	88	38s
Mental health care, psychiatric out-patient clinics, freestanding, exp	capita	0.43	88	38s
Mental health care, state and county mental hospitals, exp	capita	12.54	88	38s
Mental health care, VA medical centers, exp	capita	5.35	88	38s
Physician fee, family practice, first-visit		75.00	91	62r
Physician fee, family practice, revisit		34.00	91	62r
Physician fee, general practice, first-visit		61.00	91	62r
Physician fee, general practice, revisit		32.00	91	62r
Physician fee, general surgeon, first-visit		64.00	91	62r
Physician fee, general surgeon, revisit		40.00	91	62r
Physician fee, internal medicine, first-visit		98.00	91	62r
Physician fee, internal medicine, revisit		40.00	91	62r

Values are in dollars or fractions of dollars. In the column headed *Ref*, references are shown to sources. Each reference is followed by a letter. These refer to the geographical level for which data were reported: s=State, r=Region, and c=City or metro. The abbreviation *ex* is used to mean *except* or *excluding*; *exp* stands for expenditures. For other abbreviations and further explanations, please see the Introduction.

Laredo, TX - continued

Item	Per	Value	Date	Ref.
Health Care				
Physician fee, median, neurosurgeon, first-visit		130.00	91	62r
Physician fee, median, nonsurgical specialist, first-visit		95.00	91	62r
Physician fee, median, orthopedic surgeon, first-visit		91.00	91	62r
Physician fee, median, plastic surgeon, first-visit		66.00	91	62r
Physician fee, median, surgical specialist, first-visit		62.00	91	62r
Physician fee, neurosurgeon, revisit		50.00	91	62r
Physician fee, nonsurgical specialist, revisit		40.00	91	62r
Physician fee, obstetrics/gynecology, first-visit		64.00	91	62r
Physician fee, obstetrics/gynecology, revisit		41.00	91	62r
Physician fee, orthopedic surgeon, revisit		40.00	91	62r
Physician fee, pediatrician, first-visit		49.00	91	62r
Physician fee, pediatrician, revisit		33.00	91	62r
Physician fee, plastic surgeon, revisit		43.00	91	62r
Physician fee, surgical specialist, revisit		37.00	91	62r
Substance abuse, hospital ancillary charge	incident	3750	90	70s
Substance abuse, hospital physician charge	incident	1080	90	70s
Substance abuse, hospital room and board	incident	5320	90	70s
Insurance and Pensions				
Auto insurance, private passenger	year	709.79	91	63s
Taxes				
Tax, cigarette	pack	41	91	77s
Tax, gasoline	gal	20	91	77s
Taxes, state	capita	923	91	77s
Transportation				
Driver's license fee		16.00	12/90	43s
Travel				
Business travel	day	193.00	4/93	89r
Utilities				
Electricity	mil Btu	17.09	90	64s
Electricity, residential	KWh	5.92	2/93	94s

Las Cruces, NM

Item	Per	Value	Date	Ref.
Composite ACCRA index		100.40	4Q 92	4c
Alcoholic Beverages				
Beer, Miller Lite or Budweiser, 12-oz containers	6 pack	3.56	4Q 92	4c
Liquor, J & B Scotch	750 ml	14.61	4Q 92	4c
Wine, Gallo Chablis blanc, 1.5 liter	bottle	5.11	4Q 92	4c
Child Care				
Child care fee, average, center	hour	1.71	90	65r
Child care fee, average, nonregulated family day care	hour	1.32	90	65r
Child care fee, average, regulated family day care	hour	1.86	90	65r
Clothing				
Jeans, man's denim		24.78	4Q 92	4c
Shirt, man's dress shirt		24.60	4Q 92	4c
Undervest, boy's size 10-14, cotton	3	5.12	4Q 92	4c
Communications				
Long-distance telephone service, day, initial minute, 0-100 miles	min	0.19-0.32	91	12s
Long-distance telephone service, day, additional minute, 0-100 miles	min	0.11-0.24	91	12s
Long-distance telephone service, evenings/weekends, 0-100 mi, initial minute	min	0.11-0.20	91	12s
Long-distance telephone service, evenings/weekends, 0-100 mi, additional minute	min	0.07-0.14	91	12s

Las Cruces, NM - continued

Item	Per	Value	Date	Ref.
Communications - continued				
Newspaper subscription, daily and Sunday home delivery, large-city	month	9.70	4Q 92	4c
Telephone bill, family of four	month	19.15	4Q 92	4c
Education				
Board, 4-yr private college/university	year	1890	91	22s
Board, 4-yr public college/university	year	1527	91	22s
Expenditures, local gov't, public elementary/secondary	pupil	4524	92	20s
Room, 4-year private college/university	year	1468	91	22s
Room, 4-year public college/university	year	1321	91	22s
Tuition, 2-year private college/university	year	3594	91	22s
Tuition, 2-year public college/university	year	536	91	22s
Tuition, 4-year private college/university	year	8187	91	22s
Tuition, 4-year public college/university, in-state	year	1409	91	22s
Energy and Fuels				
Coal	mil Btu	1.32	90	64s
Energy	mil Btu	9.22	90	64s
Energy, combined forms, 1,800 sq ft heating area	month	99.59	4Q 92	4c
Energy, exc electricity, 1,800 sq ft heating area	month	25.06	4Q 92	4c
Energy exp/householder, 1-family unit	year	372	90	28r
Energy exp/householder, <1,000 sq ft heating area	year	335	90	28r
Energy exp/householder, 1,000-1,999 sq ft heating area	year	365	90	28r
Energy exp/householder, 2,000+ sq ft heating area	year	411	90	28r
Energy exp/householder, mobile home	year	305	90	28r
Energy exp/householder, multifamily	year	372	90	28r
Gas, natural	mil Btu	3.84	90	64s
Gas, natural	000 cu ft	5.40	91	46s
Gas, natural, exp	year	424	91	46s
Gasoline, motor	gal	1.18	4Q 92	4c
Gasoline, unleaded regular	mil Btu	9.23	90	64s
Entertainment				
Bowling, evening rate	game	2.35	4Q 92	4c
Miniature golf admission	adult	6.18	92	1r
Miniature golf admission	child	5.14	92	1r
Monopoly game, Parker Brothers', No. 9		12.28	4Q 92	4c
Movie	admission	5.00	4Q 92	4c
Tennis balls, yellow, Wilson or Penn, 3	can	2.42	4Q 92	4c
Waterpark admission	adult	11.00	92	1r
Waterpark admission	child	8.55	92	1r
Funerals				
Casket, 18-gauge steel, velvet interior		1929.04	91	24r
Cosmetology, hair care, etc.		88.52	91	24r
Embalming		249.33	91	24r
Facility use for ceremony		182.75	91	24r
Hearse, local		110.04	91	24r
Limousine, local		66.67	91	24r
Remains to funeral home, transfer		84.58	91	24r
Service charge, professional		593.00	91	24r
Vault, concrete, non-metallic liner		647.38	91	24r
Viewing facilities, use		99.87	91	24r
Goods and Services				
ACCRA Index, Miscellaneous Goods and Services		99.30	4Q 92	4c
Groceries				
ACCRA Index, Groceries		94.00	4Q 92	4c
Apples, Red Delicious	lb	0.80	4/93	16r
Babyfood, strained vegetables, lowest price	4-4.5 oz jar	0.28	4Q 92	4c
Bacon	lb	1.79	4/93	16r
Bananas	lb	0.30	4Q 92	4c
Bananas	lb	0.53	4/93	16r

Values are in dollars or fractions of dollars. In the column headed *Ref*, references are shown to sources. Each reference is followed by a letter. These refer to the geographical level for which data were reported: s=State, r=Region, and c=City or metro. The abbreviation *ex* is used to mean *except* or *excluding*; *exp* stands for expenditures. For other abbreviations and further explanations, please see the Introduction.

Las Cruces, NM - continued

Item	Per	Value	Date	Ref.
Groceries				
Bologna, all beef or mixed	lb	2.67	4/93	16r
Bread, white	24 oz	0.57	4Q 92	4c
Bread, white, pan	lb	0.81	4/93	16r
Carrots, short trimmed and topped	lb	0.39	4/93	16r
Cheese, Kraft grated Parmesan	8-oz canister	3.45	4Q 92	4c
Chicken, fresh, whole	lb	0.94	4/93	16r
Chicken, fryer, whole	lb	0.65	4Q 92	4c
Chicken breast, bone-in	lb	2.19	4/93	16r
Chuck roast, graded and ungraded, ex USDA prime and choice	lb	2.26	4/93	16r
Cigarettes, Winston	carton	16.47	4Q 92	4c
Coffee, 100% ground roast, all sizes	lb	2.33	4/93	16r
Coffee, vacuum-packed	13-oz can	1.95	4Q 92	4c
Corn, frozen	10 oz	0.71	4Q 92	4c
Corn Flakes, Kellogg's or Post Toasties	18 oz	2.06	4Q 92	4c
Eggs, Grade A large	doz	0.85	4Q 92	4c
Eggs, Grade AA large	doz	1.18	4/93	16r
Flour, white, all purpose	lb	0.22	4/93	16r
Grapefruit	lb	0.52	4/93	16r
Grapes, Thompson Seedless	lb	1.50	4/93	16r
Ground beef, 100% beef	lb	1.44	4/93	16r
Ground beef, lean and extra lean	lb	2.34	4/93	16r
Ground beef or hamburger	lb	1.09	4Q 92	4c
Ham, boneless, excluding canned	lb	2.56	4/93	16r
Honey, jar	8 oz	0.99-1.19	92	5r
Honey, jar	lb	1.35-1.97	92	5r
Honey, squeeze bear	12-oz	1.00-1.89	92	5r
Ice cream, prepackaged, bulk, regular	1/2 gal	2.40	4/93	16r
Lemons	lb	0.81	4/93	16r
Lettuce, iceberg	head	0.92	4Q 92	4c
Lettuce, iceberg	lb	0.84	4/93	16r
Margarine, Blue Bonnet or Parkay cubes	lb	0.83	4Q 92	4c
Margarine, stick	lb	0.81	4/93	16r
Milk, whole	1/2 gal	1.38	4Q 92	4c
Orange juice, Minute Maid frozen	12-oz can	1.36	4Q 92	4c
Oranges, navel	lb	0.48	4/93	16r
Peaches	29-oz can	1.43	4Q 92	4c
Peas Sweet, Del Monte or Green Giant	15-17 oz can	0.60	4Q 92	4c
Pork chops, center cut, bone-in	lb	3.25	4/93	16r
Potato chips	16 oz	2.89	4/93	16r
Potatoes, white	lb	0.38	4/93	16r
Potatoes, white or red	10-lb sack	2.15	4Q 92	4c
Round roast, graded & ungraded, ex USDA prime & choice	lb	3.00	4/93	16r
Round roast, USDA choice, boneless	lb	3.16	4/93	16r
Sausage, Jimmy Dean, 100% pork	lb	2.23	4Q 92	4c
Shortening, vegetable oil blends	lb	0.86	4/93	16r
Shortening, vegetable, Crisco	3-lb can	2.12	4Q 92	4c
Soft drink, Coca Cola	2 liter	1.23	4Q 92	4c
Spaghetti and macaroni	lb	0.84	4/93	16r
Steak, round, graded & ungraded, ex USDA prime & choice	lb	3.34	4/93	16r
Steak, round, USDA choice, boneless	lb	3.24	4/93	16r
Steak, sirloin, graded & ungraded, ex USDA prime & choice	lb	3.75	4/93	16r
Steak, sirloin, USDA choice, boneless	lb	4.49	4/93	16r
Steak, T-bone	lb	4.77	4Q 92	4c
Sugar, cane or beet	4 lb	1.63	4Q 92	4c
Sugar, white	lb	0.41	4/93	16r
Sugar, white, 33-80 oz pk	lb	0.38	4/93	16r
Tomatoes, field grown	lb	1.01	4/93	16r
Tomatoes, Hunt's or Del Monte	14.5-oz can	0.74	4Q 92	4c

Las Cruces, NM - continued

Item	Per	Value	Date	Ref.
Groceries - continued				
Tuna, chunk, light	6.125-6.5 oz can	0.71	4Q 92	4c
Turkey, frozen, whole	lb	1.04	4/93	16r
Health Care				
ACCRA Index, Health Care		93.90	4Q 92	4c
Analgesic, Aspirin, Bayer, 325 mg tablets	100	4.99	4Q 92	4c
Childbirth, cesarean, hospital		5533	91	62r
Childbirth, cesarean, physician's fee		2053	91	62r
Childbirth, normal, hospital		2745	91	62r
Childbirth, normal, physician's fee		1492	91	62r
Dentist's fee, adult teeth cleaning and periodic oral exam	visit	47.84	4Q 92	4c
Doctor's fee, routine exam, established patient	visit	32.43	4Q 92	4c
Hospital care, semiprivate room	day	273.00	4Q 92	4c
Medical insurance premium, per employee, small group comprehensive	month	292.00	10/91	25c
Medical plan per employee	year	3218	91	45r
Mental health care, exp	capita	20.37-28.83	90	38s
Mental health care, exp, state mental health agency	capita	22.88	90	38s
Mental health care, hospital psychiatric services, non-Federal, exp	capita	7.77	88	38s
Mental health care, mental health organization, multiservice, exp	capita	16.77	88	38s
Mental health care, psychiatric hospitals, private, exp	capita	32.81	88	38s
Mental health care, psychiatric out-patient clinics, freestanding, exp	capita	2.18	88	38s
Mental health care, psychiatric partial-care organizations, freestanding, exp	capita	1.80	88	38s
Mental health care, state and county mental hospitals, exp	capita	20.94	88	38s
Mental health care, VA medical centers, exp	capita	2.32	88	38s
Physician fee, family practice, first-visit		111.00	91	62r
Physician fee, family practice, revisit		45.00	91	62r
Physician fee, general practice, first-visit		100.00	91	62r
Physician fee, general practice, revisit		40.00	91	62r
Physician fee, internal medicine, first-visit		137.00	91	62r
Physician fee, internal medicine, revisit		48.00	91	62r
Physician fee, median, neurosurgeon, first-visit		157.00	91	62r
Physician fee, median, nonsurgical specialist, first-visit		131.00	91	62r
Physician fee, median, orthopedic surgeon, first-visit		124.00	91	62r
Physician fee, median, plastic surgeon, first-visit		88.00	91	62r
Physician fee, median, surgical specialist, first-visit		100.00	91	62r
Physician fee, neurosurgeon, revisit		51.00	91	62r
Physician fee, nonsurgical specialist, revisit		47.00	91	62r
Physician fee, obstetrics/gynecology, first-visit		95.00	91	62r
Physician fee, obstetrics/gynecology, revisit		50.00	91	62r
Physician fee, orthopedic surgeon, revisit		51.00	91	62r
Physician fee, pediatrician, first-visit		81.00	91	62r
Physician fee, pediatrician, revisit		42.00	91	62r
Physician fee, plastic surgeon, revisit		48.00	91	62r
Physician fee, surgical specialist, revisit		49.00	91	62r
Substance abuse, hospital ancillary charge	incident	2630	90	70s
Substance abuse, hospital physician charge	incident	840	90	70s
Substance abuse, hospital room and board	incident	6500	90	70s

Values are in dollars or fractions of dollars. In the column headed *Ref*, references are shown to sources. Each reference is followed by a letter. These refer to the geographical level for which data were reported: s=State, r=Region, and c=City or metro. The abbreviation *ex* is used to mean *except* or *excluding*; *exp* stands for expenditures. For other abbreviations and further explanations, please see the Introduction.

Las Cruces, NM - continued

Item	Per	Value	Date	Ref.
Household Goods				
Appliance repair, home, service call, washing machine	min labor charge	33.32	4Q 92	4c
Laundry detergent, Tide Ultra, Bold, or Cheer	42 oz	3.24	4Q 92	4c
Tissues, facial, Kleenex brand	175-count box	1.25	4Q 92	4c
Housing				
ACCRA Index, Housing		105.20	4Q 92	4c
House, 1,800 sq ft, 8,000 sq ft lot, new, urban	total	115250	4Q 92	4c
House payment, principal and interest, 25% down payment	month	645	4Q 92	4c
Mortgage rate, incl. points & origination fee, 30-year fixed or adjustable rate	percent	8.18	4Q 92	4c
Rent, apartment, 2 bedrooms - 1-1/2 to 2 baths, unfurnished, 950 sq ft, water	month	524	4Q 92	4c
Rental unit, 1 bedroom	month	379	93	23c
Rental unit, 2 bedroom	month	446	93	23c
Rental unit, 3 bedroom	month	559	93	23c
Rental unit, 4 bedroom	month	627	93	23c
Rental unit, efficiency	month	313	93	23c
Insurance and Pensions				
Auto insurance, private passenger	year	628.37	91	63s
Personal Goods				
Shampoo, Alberto VO5	15 oz	1.13	4Q 92	4c
Toothpaste, Crest or Colgate	6-7 oz	1.91	4Q 92	4c
Personal Services				
Dry cleaning, man's 2-piece suit		5.97	4Q 92	4c
Haircare, woman's shampoo, trim and blow-dry		19.27	4Q 92	4c
Haircut, man's barbershop, no styling		6.11	4Q 92	4c
Restaurant Food				
Chicken, fried, thigh and drumstick		1.82	4Q 92	4c
Hamburger with cheese	1/4 lb	1.86	4Q 92	4c
Pizza, Pizza Hut or Pizza Inn, cheese, thin crust	12-13 in	7.89	4Q 92	4c
Taxes				
Tax, cigarette	pack	15	91	77s
Tax, gasoline	gal	16	91	77s
Taxes, state	capita	1347	91	77s
Transportation				
ACCRA Index, Transportation		110.20	4Q 92	4c
Driver's license fee		10.00	12/90	43s
Tire balance, computer or spin balance, front	wheel	7.56	4Q 92	4c
Travel				
Business travel	day	178.00	4/93	89r
Utilities				
ACCRA Index, Utilities		91.90	4Q 92	4c
Electricity	mil Btu	20.99	90	64s
Electricity, partial electric and other energy, 1,800 sq ft living area new home	month	74.53	4Q 92	4c
Electricity, residential	KWh	9.58	2/93	94s
Electricity, winter, 250 KWh	month	30.91	92	55c
Electricity, winter, 500 KWh	month	55.83	92	55c
Electricity, winter, 750 KWh	month	80.73	92	55c
Electricity, winter, 1000 KWh	month	105.64	92	55c

Las Vegas, NV

Item	Per	Value	Date	Ref.
Composite ACCRA index		106.70	4Q 92	4c

Las Vegas, NV - continued

Item	Per	Value	Date	Ref.
Alcoholic Beverages				
Beer, Miller Lite or Budweiser, 12-oz containers	6 pack	4.20	4Q 92	4c
Liquor, J & B Scotch	750 ml	15.98	4Q 92	4c
Wine, Gallo Chablis blanc, 1.5 liter	bottle	4.74	4Q 92	4c
Child Care				
Child care fee, average, center	hour	1.71	90	65r
Child care fee, average, nonregulated family day care	hour	1.32	90	65r
Child care fee, average, regulated family day care	hour	1.86	90	65r
Clothing				
Jeans, man's denim		29.59	4Q 92	4c
Shirt, man's dress shirt		27.40	4Q 92	4c
Undervest, boy's size 10-14, cotton	3	5.19	4Q 92	4c
Communications				
Long-distance telephone service, day, initial minute, 0-100 miles	min	0.16-0.39	91	12s
Long-distance telephone service, day, additional minute, 0-100 miles	min	0.06-0.25	91	12s
Long-distance telephone service, evenings/weekends, 0-100 mi, initial minute	min	0.08-0.20	91	12s
Long-distance telephone service, evenings/weekends, 0-100 mi, additional minute	min	0.03-0.13	91	12s
Newspaper subscription, daily and Sunday home delivery, large-city	month	9.78	4Q 92	4c
Telephone bill, family of four	month	11.43	4Q 92	4c
Education				
Board, 4-yr public college/university	year	1709	91	22s
Expenditures, local gov't, public elementary/secondary	pupil	4891	92	20s
Room, 4-year private college/university	year	2100	91	22s
Room, 4-year public college/university	year	2489	91	22s
Tuition, 2-year public college/university	year	651	91	22s
Tuition, 4-year private college/university	year	6200	91	22s
Tuition, 4-year public college/university, in-state	year	1275	91	22s
Energy and Fuels				
Coal	mil Btu	1.49	90	64s
Energy	mil Btu	9.01	90	64s
Energy, combined forms, 1,800 sq ft heating area	month	100.21	4Q 92	4c
Energy, exc electricity, 1,800 sq ft heating area	month	30.76	4Q 92	4c
Energy exp/householder, 1-family unit	year	372	90	28r
Energy exp/householder, <1,000 sq ft heating area	year	335	90	28r
Energy exp/householder, 1,000-1,999 sq ft heating area	year	365	90	28r
Energy exp/householder, 2,000+ sq ft heating area	year	411	90	28r
Energy exp/householder, mobile home	year	305	90	28r
Energy exp/householder, multifamily	year	372	90	28r
Gas, cooking, winter, 10 therms	month	10.26	92	56c
Gas, cooking, winter, 30 therms	month	19.57	92	56c
Gas, cooking, winter, 50 therms	month	22.60	92	56c
Gas, heating, winter, 100 therms	month	49.76	92	56c
Gas, heating, winter, average use	month	45.32	92	56c
Gas, natural	mil Btu	3.68	90	64s
Gas, natural	000 cu ft	5.61	91	46s
Gas, natural, exp	year	379	91	46s
Gasoline, motor	gal	1.20	4Q 92	4c
Gasoline, unleaded regular	mil Btu	9.10	90	64s
Entertainment				
Bowling, evening rate	game	1.33	4Q 92	4c
Miniature golf admission	adult	6.18	92	1r
Miniature golf admission	child	5.14	92	1r
Monopoly game, Parker Brothers', No. 9		13.79	4Q 92	4c

Values are in dollars or fractions of dollars. In the column headed *Ref*, references are shown to sources. Each reference is followed by a letter. These refer to the geographical level for which data were reported: s=State, r=Region, and c=City or metro. The abbreviation *ex* is used to mean *except* or *excluding*; *exp* stands for expenditures. For other abbreviations and further explanations, please see the Introduction.

Las Vegas, NV - continued

Item	Per	Value	Date	Ref.
Entertainment				
Movie	admission	6.60	4Q 92	4c
Tennis balls, yellow, Wilson or Penn, 3	can	2.43	4Q 92	4c
Waterpark admission	adult	11.00	92	1r
Waterpark admission	child	8.55	92	1r
Funerals				
Casket, 18-gauge steel, velvet interior		1929.04	91	24r
Cosmetology, hair care, etc.		88.52	91	24r
Embalming		249.33	91	24r
Facility use for ceremony		182.75	91	24r
Hearse, local		110.04	91	24r
Limousine, local		66.67	91	24r
Remains to funeral home, transfer		84.58	91	24r
Service charge, professional		593.00	91	24r
Vault, concrete, non-metallic liner		647.38	91	24r
Viewing facilities, use		99.87	91	24r
Goods and Services				
ACCRA Index, Miscellaneous Goods and Services		104.40	4Q 92	4c
Groceries				
ACCRA Index, Groceries		97.40	4Q 92	4c
Apples, Red Delicious	lb	0.80	4/93	16r
Babyfood, strained vegetables, lowest price	4-4.5 oz jar	0.36	4Q 92	4c
Bacon	lb	1.79	4/93	16r
Bananas	lb	0.43	4Q 92	4c
Bananas	lb	0.53	4/93	16r
Bologna, all beef or mixed	lb	2.67	4/93	16r
Bread, white	24 oz	0.61	4Q 92	4c
Bread, white, pan	lb	0.81	4/93	16r
Carrots, short trimmed and topped	lb	0.39	4/93	16r
Cheese, Kraft grated Parmesan	8-oz canister	2.90	4Q 92	4c
Chicken, fresh, whole	lb	0.94	4/93	16r
Chicken, fryer, whole	lb	0.85	4Q 92	4c
Chicken breast, bone-in	lb	2.19	4/93	16r
Chuck roast, graded and ungraded, ex USDA prime and choice	lb	2.26	4/93	16r
Cigarettes, Winston	carton	19.81	4Q 92	4c
Coffee, 100% ground roast, all sizes	lb	2.33	4/93	16r
Coffee, vacuum-packed	13-oz can	1.88	4Q 92	4c
Corn, frozen	10 oz	0.76	4Q 92	4c
Corn Flakes, Kellogg's or Post Toasties	18 oz	1.73	4Q 92	4c
Eggs, Grade A large	doz	1.36	4Q 92	4c
Eggs, Grade AA large	doz	1.18	4/93	16r
Flour, white, all purpose	lb	0.22	4/93	16r
Grapefruit	lb	0.52	4/93	16r
Grapes, Thompson Seedless	lb	1.50	4/93	16r
Ground beef, 100% beef	lb	1.44	4/93	16r
Ground beef, lean and extra lean	lb	2.34	4/93	16r
Ground beef or hamburger	lb	1.25	4Q 92	4c
Ham, boneless, excluding canned	lb	2.56	4/93	16r
Honey, jar	8 oz	0.89-1.00	92	5r
Honey, jar	lb	1.35-1.97	92	5r
Honey, squeeze bear	12-oz	1.00-1.89	92	5r
Ice cream, prepackaged, bulk, regular	1/2 gal	2.40	4/93	16r
Lemons	lb	0.81	4/93	16r
Lettuce, iceberg	head	0.73	4Q 92	4c
Lettuce, iceberg	lb	0.84	4/93	16r
Margarine, Blue Bonnet or Parkay cubes	lb	0.50	4Q 92	4c
Margarine, stick	lb	0.81	4/93	16r
Milk, whole	1/2 gal	1.35	4Q 92	4c
Orange juice, Minute Maid frozen	12-oz can	1.18	4Q 92	4c
Oranges, navel	lb	0.48	4/93	16r
Peaches	29-oz can	1.13	4Q 92	4c
Peas Sweet, Del Monte or Green Giant	15-17 oz can	0.61	4Q 92	4c

Las Vegas, NV - continued

Item	Per	Value	Date	Ref.
Groceries - continued				
Pork chops, center cut, bone-in	lb	3.25	4/93	16r
Potato chips	16 oz	2.89	4/93	16r
Potatoes, white	lb	0.38	4/93	16r
Potatoes, white or red	10-lb sack	1.87	4Q 92	4c
Round roast, graded & ungraded, ex USDA prime & choice	lb	3.00	4/93	16r
Round roast, USDA choice, boneless	lb	3.16	4/93	16r
Sausage, Jimmy Dean, 100% pork	lb	2.75	4Q 92	4c
Shortening, vegetable oil blends	lb	0.86	4/93	16r
Shortening, vegetable, Crisco	3-lb can	2.28	4Q 92	4c
Soft drink, Coca Cola	2 liter	1.12	4Q 92	4c
Spaghetti and macaroni	lb	0.84	4/93	16r
Steak, round, graded & ungraded, ex USDA prime & choice	lb	3.34	4/93	16r
Steak, round, USDA choice, boneless	lb	3.24	4/93	16r
Steak, sirloin, graded & ungraded, ex USDA prime & choice	lb	3.75	4/93	16r
Steak, sirloin, USDA choice, boneless	lb	4.49	4/93	16r
Steak, T-bone	lb	4.48	4Q 92	4c
Sugar, cane or beet	4 lb	1.69	4Q 92	4c
Sugar, white	lb	0.41	4/93	16r
Sugar, white, 33-80 oz pk	lb	0.38	4/93	16r
Tomatoes, field grown	lb	1.01	4/93	16r
Tomatoes, Hunt's or Del Monte	14.5-oz can	0.65	4Q 92	4c
Tuna, chunk, light	6.125-6.5 oz can	0.62	4Q 92	4c
Turkey, frozen, whole	lb	1.04	4/93	16r
Health Care				
ACCRA Index, Health Care		107.00	4Q 92	4c
Analgesic, Aspirin, Bayer, 325 mg tablets	100	5.07	4Q 92	4c
Childbirth, cesarean, hospital		5533	91	62r
Childbirth, cesarean, physician's fee		2053	91	62r
Childbirth, normal, hospital		2745	91	62r
Childbirth, normal, physician's fee		1492	91	62r
Dentist's fee, adult teeth cleaning and periodic oral exam	visit	46.80	4Q 92	4c
Doctor's fee, routine exam, established patient	visit	47.60	4Q 92	4c
Hospital care, semiprivate room	day	270.46	90	27c
Hospital care, semiprivate room	day	259.40	4Q 92	4c
Medical insurance premium, per employee, small group comprehensive	month	456.25	10/91	25c
Medical plan per employee	year	3218	91	45r
Mental health care, exp	capita	28.84-37.59	90	38s
Mental health care, exp, state mental health agency	capita	33.47	90	38s
Mental health care, hospital psychiatric services, non-Federal, exp	capita	6.90	88	38s
Mental health care, mental health organization, multiservice, exp	capita	3.34	88	38s
Mental health care, psychiatric hospitals, private, exp	capita	42.05	88	38s
Mental health care, state and county mental hospitals, exp	capita	20.24	88	38s
Mental health care, VA medical centers, exp	capita	4.74	88	38s
Physician fee, family practice, first-visit		111.00	91	62r
Physician fee, family practice, revisit		45.00	91	62r
Physician fee, general practice, first-visit		100.00	91	62r
Physician fee, general practice, revisit		40.00	91	62r
Physician fee, internal medicine, first-visit		137.00	91	62r
Physician fee, internal medicine, revisit		48.00	91	62r
Physician fee, median, neurosurgeon, first-visit		157.00	91	62r
Physician fee, median, nonsurgical specialist, first-visit		131.00	91	62r
Physician fee, median, orthopedic surgeon, first-visit		124.00	91	62r

Values are in dollars or fractions of dollars. In the column headed *Ref*, references are shown to sources. Each reference is followed by a letter. These refer to the geographical level for which data were reported: s = State, r = Region, and c = City or metro. The abbreviation *ex* is used to mean *except* or *excluding*; *exp* stands for expenditures. For other abbreviations and further explanations, please see the Introduction.

Las Vegas, NV - continued

Item	Per	Value	Date	Ref.
Health Care				
Physician fee, median, plastic surgeon, first-visit		88.00	91	62r
Physician fee, median, surgical specialist, first-visit		100.00	91	62r
Physician fee, neurosurgeon, revisit		51.00	91	62r
Physician fee, nonsurgical specialist, revisit		47.00	91	62r
Physician fee, obstetrics/gynecology, first-visit		95.00	91	62r
Physician fee, obstetrics/gynecology, revisit		50.00	91	62r
Physician fee, orthopedic surgeon, revisit		51.00	91	62r
Physician fee, pediatrician, first-visit		81.00	91	62r
Physician fee, pediatrician, revisit		42.00	91	62r
Physician fee, plastic surgeon, revisit		48.00	91	62r
Physician fee, surgical specialist, revisit		49.00	91	62r
Substance abuse, hospital ancillary charge	incident	1420	90	70s
Substance abuse, hospital physician charge	incident	660	90	70s
Substance abuse, hospital room and board	incident	5240	90	70s
Household Goods				
Appliance repair, home, service call, washing machine	min labor charge	29.00	4Q 92	4c
Laundry detergent, Tide Ultra, Bold, or Cheer	42 oz	3.90	4Q 92	4c
Tissues, facial, Kleenex brand	175-count box	1.05	4Q 92	4c
Housing				
ACCRA Index, Housing		119.80	4Q 92	4c
Home, median price	unit	104.30		26c
House, 1,800 sq ft, 8,000 sq ft lot, new, urban	total	132250	4Q 92	4c
House payment, principal and interest, 25% down payment	month	725	4Q 92	4c
Mortgage rate, incl. points & origination fee, 30-year fixed or adjustable rate	percent	7.96	4Q 92	4c
Rent, apartment, 2 bedrooms - 1-1/2 to 2 baths, unfurnished, 950 sq ft, water	month	618	4Q 92	4c
Rental unit, 1 bedroom	month	583	93	23c
Rental unit, 2 bedroom	month	687	93	23c
Rental unit, 3 bedroom	month	862	93	23c
Rental unit, 4 bedroom	month	965	93	23c
Rental unit, efficiency	month	481	93	23c
Insurance and Pensions				
Auto insurance, private passenger	year	752.76	91	63s
Personal Goods				
Shampoo, Alberto VO5	15 oz	1.21	4Q 92	4c
Toothpaste, Crest or Colgate	6-7 oz	2.05	4Q 92	4c
Personal Services				
Dry cleaning, man's 2-piece suit		8.00	4Q 92	4c
Haircare, woman's shampoo, trim and blow-dry		19.00	4Q 92	4c
Haircut, man's barbershop, no styling		9.40	4Q 92	4c
Restaurant Food				
Chicken, fried, thigh and drumstick		1.99	4Q 92	4c
Hamburger with cheese	1/4 lb	1.93	4Q 92	4c
Pizza, Pizza Hut or Pizza Inn, cheese, thin crust	12-13 in	7.49	4Q 92	4c
Taxes				
Tax, cigarette	pack	35	91	77s
Tax, gasoline	gal	23	91	77s
Taxes, state	capita	1310	91	77s
Transportation				
ACCRA Index, Transportation		106.50	4Q 92	4c
Auto rental, average	day	42.00	6/91	60c

Las Vegas, NV - continued

Item	Per	Value	Date	Ref.
Transportation - continued				
Bus fare	one-way	1.00	3/93	2c
Bus fare, up to 10 miles	one-way	1.00	4Q 92	4c
Driver's license fee		9.00	12/90	43s
Limo fare, airport-city, average	day	4.25	6/91	60c
Taxi fare, airport-city, average	day	17.00	6/91	60c
Tire balance, computer or spin balance, front	wheel	6.80	4Q 92	4c
Travel				
Breakfast	day	4.94	6/91	60c
Business travel	day	178.00	4/93	89r
Dinner	day	17.85	6/91	60c
Lodging	day	90.71	91	60c
Lunch	day	10.06	6/91	60c
Utilities				
ACCRA Index, Utilities		88.50	4Q 92	4c
Electricity	mil Btu	15.77	90	64s
Electricity, partial electric and other energy, 1,800 sq ft living area new home	month	69.45	4Q 92	4c
Electricity, winter, 250 KWh	month	16.84	92	55c
Electricity, winter, 500 KWh	month	30.18	92	55c
Electricity, winter, 750 KWh	month	43.52	92	55c
Electricity, winter, 1000 KWh	month	56.85	92	55c

Lawrence, KS

Item	Per	Value	Date	Ref.
Composite ACCRA index		94.50	4Q 92	4c
Alcoholic Beverages				
Beer, Miller Lite or Budweiser, 12-oz containers	6 pack	3.99	4Q 92	4c
Liquor, J & B Scotch	750 ml	17.67	4Q 92	4c
Wine, Gallo Chablis blanc, 1.5 liter	bottle	5.22	4Q 92	4c
Child Care				
Child care fee, average, center	hour	1.63	90	65r
Child care fee, average, nonregulated family day care	hour	1.83	90	65r
Child care fee, average, regulated family day care	hour	1.42	90	65r
Clothing				
Jeans, man's denim		27.29	4Q 92	4c
Shirt, man's dress shirt		27.16	4Q 92	4c
Undervest, boy's size 10-14, cotton	3	4.82	4Q 92	4c
Communications				
Long-distance telephone service, day, initial minute, 0-100 miles	min	0.18-0.40	91	12s
Long-distance telephone service, day, additional minute, 0-100 miles	min	0.09-0.30	91	12s
Newspaper subscription, daily and Sunday home delivery, large-city	month	13.58	4Q 92	4c
Telephone bill, family of four	month	19.21	4Q 92	4c
Education				
Board, 4-yr private college/university	year	1719	91	22s
Board, 4-yr public college/university	year	1294	91	22s
Expenditures, local gov't, public elementary/secondary	pupil	5105	92	20s
Room, 4-year private college/university	year	1269	91	22s
Room, 4-year public college/university	year	1301	91	22s
Tuition, 2-year private college/university	year	4135	91	22s
Tuition, 2-year public college/university	year	748	91	22s
Tuition, 4-year private college/university	year	5997	91	22s
Tuition, 4-year public college/university, in-state	year	1569	91	22s
Energy and Fuels				
Coal	mil Btu	1.24	90	64s
Energy	mil Btu	7.59	90	64s

Values are in dollars or fractions of dollars. In the column headed *Ref*, references are shown to sources. Each reference is followed by a letter. These refer to the geographical level for which data were reported: s = State, r = Region, and c = City or metro. The abbreviation *ex* is used to mean *except* or *excluding*; *exp* stands for expenditures. For other abbreviations and further explanations, please see the Introduction.

Lawrence, KS - continued

Item	Per	Value	Date	Ref.
Energy and Fuels				
Energy, combined forms, 1,800 sq ft heating area	month	87.94	4Q 92	4c
Energy, exc electricity, 1,800 sq ft heating area	month	33.02	4Q 92	4c
Energy exp/householder, 1-family unit	year	473	90	28r
Energy exp/householder, <1,000 sq ft heating area	year	429	90	28r
Energy exp/householder, 1,000-1,999 sq ft heating area	year	442	90	28r
Energy exp/householder, 2,000+ sq ft heating area	year	498	90	28r
Energy exp/householder, mobile home	year	442	90	28r
Energy exp/householder, multifamily	year	407	90	28r
Gas, cooking, 10 therms	month	8.04	92	56c
Gas, cooking, 30 therms	month	16.22	92	56c
Gas, cooking, 50 therms	month	24.40	92	56c
Gas, heating, winter, 100 therms	month	44.87	92	56c
Gas, heating, winter, average use	month	76.34	92	56c
Gas, natural	mil Btu	3.30	90	64s
Gas, natural	000 cu ft	4.38	91	46s
Gas, natural, exp	year	435	91	46s
Gasoline, motor	gal	1.09	4Q 92	4c
Gasoline, unleaded regular	mil Btu	8.90	90	64s
Entertainment				
Bowling, evening rate	game	1.75	4Q 92	4c
Miniature golf admission	adult	6.18	92	1r
Miniature golf admission	child	5.14	92	1r
Monopoly game, Parker Brothers', No. 9		10.57	4Q 92	4c
Movie	admission	4.83	4Q 92	4c
Tennis balls, yellow, Wilson or Penn, 3	can	2.86	4Q 92	4c
Waterpark admission	adult	11.00	92	1r
Waterpark admission	child	8.55	92	1r
Funerals				
Casket, 18-gauge steel, velvet interior		1952.97	91	24r
Cosmetology, hair care, etc.		90.03	91	24r
Embalming		251.75	91	24r
Facility use for ceremony		180.75	91	24r
Hearse, local		117.51	91	24r
Limousine, local		71.86	91	24r
Remains to funeral home, transfer		81.14	91	24r
Service charge, professional		740.03	91	24r
Vault, concrete, non-metallic liner		801.47	91	24r
Viewing facilities, use		169.33	91	24r
Goods and Services				
ACCRA Index, Miscellaneous Goods and Services		101.10	4Q 92	4c
Groceries				
ACCRA Index, Groceries		88.40	4Q 92	4c
Apples, Red Delicious	lb	0.77	4/93	16r
Babyfood, strained vegetables, lowest price	4-4.5 oz jar	0.30	4Q 92	4c
Bacon	lb	1.85	4/93	16r
Bananas	lb	0.44	4Q 92	4c
Bananas	lb	0.46	4/93	16r
Beef, stew, boneless	lb	2.53	4/93	16r
Bologna, all beef or mixed	lb	2.19	4/93	16r
Bread, white	24 oz	0.54	4Q 92	4c
Bread, white, pan	lb	0.78	4/93	16r
Butter	lb	1.50	4/93	16r
Cabbage	lb	0.40	4/93	16r
Carrots, short trimmed and topped	lb	0.45	4/93	16r
Cheese, Cheddar	lb	3.47	4/93	16r
Cheese, Kraft grated Parmesan	8-oz canister	3.34	4Q 92	4c
Chicken, fresh, whole	lb	0.84	4/93	16r
Chicken, fryer, whole	lb	0.64	4Q 92	4c
Chicken breast, bone-in	lb	1.94	4/93	16r

Lawrence, KS - continued

Item	Per	Value	Date	Ref.
Groceries - continued				
Chicken legs, bone-in	lb	1.02	4/93	16r
Chuck roast, graded and ungraded, ex USDA prime and choice	lb	2.43	4/93	16r
Chuck roast, USDA choice, bone-in	lb	2.11	4/93	16r
Chuck roast, USDA choice, boneless	lb	2.44	4/93	16r
Cigarettes, Winston	carton	17.00	4Q 92	4c
Coffee, 100% ground roast, all sizes	lb	2.47	4/93	16r
Coffee, vacuum-packed	13-oz can	1.76	4Q 92	4c
Cookies, chocolate chip	lb	2.73	4/93	16r
Corn, frozen	10 oz	0.60	4Q 92	4c
Corn Flakes, Kellogg's or Post Toasties	18 oz	1.97	4Q 92	4c
Eggs, Grade A large	doz	0.78	4Q 92	4c
Eggs, Grade A large	doz	0.93	4/93	16r
Flour, white, all purpose	lb	0.21	4/93	16r
Grapefruit	lb	0.45	4/93	16r
Grapes, Thompson Seedless	lb	1.46	4/93	16r
Ground beef, 100% beef	lb	1.63	4/93	16r
Ground beef, lean and extra lean	lb	2.08	4/93	16r
Ground beef or hamburger	lb	1.31	4Q 92	4c
Ground chuck, 100% beef	lb	1.94	4/93	16r
Ham, boneless, excluding canned	lb	2.21	4/93	16r
Ice cream, prepackaged, bulk, regular	1/2 gal	2.41	4/93	16r
Lemons	lb	0.82	4/93	16r
Lettuce, iceberg	head	0.73	4Q 92	4c
Lettuce, iceberg	lb	0.83	4/93	16r
Margarine, Blue Bonnet or Parkay cubes	lb	0.39	4Q 92	4c
Margarine, stick	lb	0.77	4/93	16r
Milk, whole	1/2 gal	1.36	4Q 92	4c
Orange juice, Minute Maid frozen	12-oz can	1.38	4Q 92	4c
Oranges, navel	lb	0.50	4/93	16r
Peaches	29-oz can	1.38	4Q 92	4c
Peanut butter, creamy, all sizes	lb	1.82	4/93	16r
Pears, Anjou	lb	0.85	4/93	16r
Peas Sweet, Del Monte or Green Giant	15-17 oz can	0.54	4Q 92	4c
Pork chops, center cut, bone-in	lb	3.17	4/93	16r
Potato chips	16 oz	2.68	4/93	16r
Potatoes, white	lb	0.26	4/93	16r
Potatoes, white or red	10-lb sack	1.68	4Q 92	4c
Round roast, graded & ungraded, ex USDA prime & choice	lb	2.88	4/93	16r
Round roast, USDA choice, boneless	lb	2.96	4/93	16r
Sausage, Jimmy Dean, 100% pork	lb	2.34	4Q 92	4c
Shortening, vegetable oil blends	lb	0.79	4/93	16r
Shortening, vegetable, Crisco	3-lb can	1.94	4Q 92	4c
Soft drink, Coca Cola	2 liter	1.06	4Q 92	4c
Spaghetti and macaroni	lb	0.76	4/93	16r
Steak, rib eye, USDA choice, boneless	lb	6.29	4/93	16r
Steak, round, USDA choice, boneless	lb	3.24	4/93	16r
Steak, sirloin, graded & ungraded, ex USDA prime & choice	lb	4.00	4/93	16r
Steak, sirloin, USDA choice, bone-in	lb	3.57	4/93	16r
Steak, sirloin, USDA choice, boneless	lb	4.17	4/93	16r
Steak, T-bone	lb	4.38	4Q 92	4c
Steak, T-bone, USDA choice, bone-in	lb	5.60	4/93	16r
Strawberries, dry pint	12 oz	0.90	4/93	16r
Sugar, cane or beet	4 lb	0.87	4Q 92	4c
Sugar, white	lb	0.36	4/93	16r
Sugar, white, 33-80 oz pk	lb	0.35	4/93	16r
Tomatoes, field grown	lb	0.99	4/93	16r
Tomatoes, Hunt's or Del Monte	14.5-oz can	0.69	4Q 92	4c
Tuna, chunk, light	6.125-6.5 oz can	0.48	4Q 92	4c
Tuna, chunk, light	lb	1.76	4/93	16r
Turkey, frozen, whole	lb	0.91	4/93	16r

Values are in dollars or fractions of dollars. In the column headed *Ref*, references are shown to sources. Each reference is followed by a letter. These refer to the geographical level for which data were reported: s=State, r=Region, and c=City or metro. The abbreviation *ex* is used to mean *except* or *excluding*; *exp* stands for *expenditures*. For other abbreviations and further explanations, please see the Introduction.

Lawrence, KS - continued

Item	Per	Value	Date	Ref.
Health Care				
ACCRA Index, Health Care		86.80	4Q 92	4c
Analgesic, Aspirin, Bayer, 325 mg tablets	100	4.09	4Q 92	4c
Childbirth, cesarean, hospital		4688	91	62r
Childbirth, cesarean, physician's fee		2053	91	62r
Childbirth, normal, hospital		2657	91	62r
Childbirth, normal, physician's fee		1492	91	62r
Dentist's fee, adult teeth cleaning and periodic oral exam	visit	39.75	4Q 92	4c
Doctor's fee, routine exam, established patient	visit	34.50	4Q 92	4c
Hospital care, semiprivate room	day	257.00	4Q 92	4c
Medical insurance premium, per employee, small group comprehensive	month	332.15	10/91	25c
Medical plan per employee	year	3443	91	45r
Mental health care, exp	capita	28.84-37.59	90	38s
Mental health care, exp, state mental health agency	capita	35.41	90	38s
Mental health care, hospital psychiatric services, non-Federal, exp	capita	11.07	88	38s
Mental health care, mental health organization, multiservice, exp	capita	12.68	88	38s
Mental health care, psychiatric hospitals, private, exp	capita	21.42	88	38s
Mental health care, psychiatric out-patient clinics, freestanding, exp	capita	3.45	88	38s
Mental health care, state and county mental hospitals, exp	capita	26.34	88	38s
Mental health care, VA medical centers, exp	capita	22.97	88	38s
Physician fee, family practice, first-visit		76.00	91	62r
Physician fee, family practice, revisit		33.00	91	62r
Physician fee, general practice, first-visit		61.00	91	62r
Physician fee, general practice, revisit		31.00	91	62r
Physician fee, general surgeon, first-visit		65.00	91	62r
Physician fee, general surgeon, revisit		35.00	91	62r
Physician fee, internal medicine, first-visit		91.00	91	62r
Physician fee, internal medicine, revisit		40.00	91	62r
Physician fee, median, neurosurgeon, first-visit		106.00	91	62r
Physician fee, median, nonsurgical specialist, first-visit		90.00	91	62r
Physician fee, median, orthopedic surgeon, first-visit		83.00	91	62r
Physician fee, median, surgical specialist, first-visit		61.00	91	62r
Physician fee, neurosurgeon, revisit		41.00	91	62r
Physician fee, nonsurgical specialist, revisit		40.00	91	62r
Physician fee, obstetrics/gynecology, first-visit		61.00	91	62r
Physician fee, obstetrics/gynecology, revisit		40.00	91	62r
Physician fee, orthopedic surgeon, revisit		41.00	91	62r
Physician fee, pediatrician, first-visit		46.00	91	62r
Physician fee, pediatrician, revisit		33.00	91	62r
Physician fee, surgical specialist, revisit		36.00	91	62r
Substance abuse, hospital ancillary charge	incident	1170	90	70s
Substance abuse, hospital physician charge	incident	560	90	70s
Substance abuse, hospital room and board	incident	5920	90	70s
Household Goods				
Appliance repair, home, service call, washing machine	min labor charge	33.30	4Q 92	4c
Laundry detergent, Tide Ultra, Bold, or Cheer	42 oz	2.93	4Q 92	4c
Tissues, facial, Kleenex brand	175-count box	1.16	4Q 92	4c

Lawrence, KS - continued

Item	Per	Value	Date	Ref.
Housing				
ACCRA Index, Housing		93.80	4Q 92	4c
House, 1,800 sq ft, 8,000 sq ft lot, new, urban	total	103831	4Q 92	4c
House payment, principal and interest, 25% down payment	month	578	4Q 92	4c
Mortgage rate, incl. points & origination fee, 30-year fixed or adjustable rate	percent	8.13	4Q 92	4c
Rent, apartment, 2 bedrooms - 1-1/2 to 2 baths, unfurnished, 950 sq ft, water	month	459	4Q 92	4c
Rental unit, 1 bedroom	month	438	93	23c
Rental unit, 2 bedroom	month	516	93	23c
Rental unit, 3 bedroom	month	644	93	23c
Rental unit, 4 bedroom	month	724	93	23c
Rental unit, efficiency	month	361	93	23c
Insurance and Pensions				
Auto insurance, private passenger	year	459.62	91	63s
Personal Goods				
Shampoo, Alberto VO5	15 oz	1.18	4Q 92	4c
Toothpaste, Crest or Colgate	6-7 oz	1.52	4Q 92	4c
Personal Services				
Dry cleaning, man's 2-piece suit		6.27	4Q 92	4c
Haircare, woman's shampoo, trim and blow-dry		15.00	4Q 92	4c
Haircut, man's barbershop, no styling		7.00	4Q 92	4c
Restaurant Food				
Chicken, fried, thigh and drumstick		1.99	4Q 92	4c
Hamburger with cheese	1/4 lb	1.89	4Q 92	4c
Pizza, Pizza Hut or Pizza Inn, cheese, thin crust	12-13 in	7.59	4Q 92	4c
Taxes				
Tax, cigarette	pack	24	91	77s
Tax, gasoline	gal	18	91	77s
Taxes, state	capita	1121	91	77s
Transportation				
ACCRA Index, Transportation		95.90	4Q 92	4c
Driver's license fee		8.00-12.00	12/90	43s
Tire balance, computer or spin balance, front	wheel	6.19	4Q 92	4c
Vehicle registration and license plate	year	27.25-37.25	93	32s
Utilities				
ACCRA Index, Utilities		82.40	4Q 92	4c
Electricity	mil Btu	19.31	90	64s
Electricity, partial electric and other energy, 1,800 sq ft living area new home	month	54.92	4Q 92	4c

Lawrence-Haverhill, MA

Item	Per	Value	Date	Ref.
Child Care				
Child care fee, average, center	hour	2.18	90	65r
Child care fee, average, nonregulated family day care	hour	1.83	90	65r
Child care fee, average, regulated family day care	hour	2.02	90	65r
Communications				
Long-distance telephone service, day, initial minute, 0-100 miles	min	0.18-0.31	91	12s
Long-distance telephone service, day, additional minute, 0-100 miles	min	0.08-0.13	91	12s
Long-distance telephone service, evenings/weekends, 0-100 mi, initial minute	min	0.67-0.12	91	12s
Long-distance telephone service, evenings/weekends, 0-100 mi, additional minute	min	0.04-0.05	91	12s

Values are in dollars or fractions of dollars. In the column headed *Ref*, references are shown to sources. Each reference is followed by a letter. These refer to the geographical level for which data were reported: s=State, r=Region, and c=City or metro. The abbreviation *ex* is used to mean *except* or *excluding*; *exp* stands for *expenditures*. For other abbreviations and further explanations, please see the Introduction.

Lawrence-Haverhill, MA - continued

Item	Per	Value	Date	Ref.
Education				
Board, 4-yr private college/university	year	2698	91	22s
Board, 4-yr public college/university	year	1741	91	22s
Expenditures, local gov't, public elementary/secondary	pupil	6687	92	20s
Room, 4-year private college/university	year	2945	91	22s
Room, 4-year public college/university	year	2144	91	22s
Tuition, 2-year private college/university	year	7750	91	22s
Tuition, 2-year public college/university	year	1528	91	22s
Tuition, 4-year private college/university	year	12446	91	22s
Tuition, 4-year public college/university, in-state	year	2580	91	22s
Energy and Fuels				
Coal	mil Btu	1.77	90	64s
Energy	mil Btu	10.57	90	64s
Energy exp/householder, 1-family unit	year	588	90	28r
Energy exp/householder, <1,000 sq ft heating area	year	477	90	28r
Energy exp/householder, 1,000-1,999 sq ft heating area	year	517	90	28r
Energy exp/householder, 2,000+ sq ft heating area	year	630	90	28r
Energy exp/householder, mobile home	year	412	90	28r
Energy exp/householder, multifamily	year	498	90	28r
Gas, natural	mil Btu	5.55	90	64s
Gas, natural	000 cu ft	8.11	91	46s
Gas, natural, exp	year	741	91	46s
Gasoline, unleaded regular	mil Btu	9.53	90	64s
Entertainment				
Miniature golf admission	adult	6.18	92	1r
Miniature golf admission	child	5.14	92	1r
Waterpark admission	adult	11.00	92	1r
Waterpark admission	child	8.55	92	1r
Funerals				
Casket, 18-gauge steel, velvet interior		1853.42	91	24r
Cosmetology, hair care, etc.		98.33	91	24r
Embalming		273.94	91	24r
Facility use for ceremony		196.06	91	24r
Hearse, local		145.67	91	24r
Limousine, local		131.07	91	24r
Remains to funeral home, transfer		135.24	91	24r
Service charge, professional		843.16	91	24r
Vault, concrete, non-metallic liner		709.14	91	24r
Viewing facilities, use		229.85	91	24r
Groceries				
Apples, Red Delicious	lb	0.85	4/93	16r
Bacon	lb	2.12	4/93	16r
Bananas	lb	0.54	4/93	16r
Bread, white, pan	lb	0.81	4/93	16r
Butter	lb	2.02	4/93	16r
Carrots, short trimmed and topped	lb	0.51	4/93	16r
Chicken, fresh, whole	lb	1.04	4/93	16r
Chicken breast, bone-in	lb	2.21	4/93	16r
Chicken legs, bone-in	lb	1.16	4/93	16r
Chuck roast, USDA choice, boneless	lb	2.82	4/93	16r
Coffee, 100% ground roast, all sizes	lb	2.66	4/93	16r
Cucumbers	lb	0.85	4/93	16r
Eggs, Grade A large	doz	1.15	4/93	16r
Grapefruit	lb	0.45	4/93	16r
Grapes, Thompson Seedless	lb	1.52	4/93	16r
Ground beef, lean and extra lean	lb	2.36	4/93	16r
Ground chuck, 100% beef	lb	2.02	4/93	16r
Honey, jar	8 oz	0.96-1.75	92	5r
Honey, jar	lb	1.50-3.00	92	5r
Honey, squeeze bear	12-oz	1.50-1.99	92	5r
Ice cream, prepackaged, bulk, regular	1/2 gal	2.80	4/93	16r
Lemons	lb	0.96	4/93	16r
Lettuce, iceberg	lb	0.95	4/93	16r
Margarine, stick	lb	0.81	4/93	16r
Milk, fresh, whole, fortified	1/2 gal	1.30	4/93	16r

Lawrence-Haverhill, MA - continued

Item	Per	Value	Date	Ref.
Groceries - continued				
Oranges, navel	lb	0.56	4/93	16r
Peanut butter, creamy, all sizes	lb	1.88	4/93	16r
Pork chops, center cut, bone-in	lb	3.34	4/93	16r
Potato chips	16 oz	2.88	4/93	16r
Potatoes, white	lb	0.37	4/93	16r
Rib roast, USDA choice, bone-in	lb	4.94	4/93	16r
Round roast, USDA choice, boneless	lb	3.17	4/93	16r
Shortening, vegetable oil blends	lb	0.98	4/93	16r
Spaghetti and macaroni	lb	0.82	4/93	16r
Steak, round, graded & ungraded, ex USDA prime & choice	lb	4.04	4/93	16r
Steak, round, USDA choice, boneless	lb	3.90	4/93	16r
Steak, sirloin, USDA choice, boneless	lb	4.97	4/93	16r
Strawberries, dry pint	12 oz	0.90	4/93	16r
Sugar, white	lb	0.50	4/93	16r
Sugar, white, 33-80 oz pk	lb	0.41	4/93	16r
Tomatoes, field grown	lb	1.23	4/93	16r
Tuna, chunk, light	lb	2.22	4/93	16r
Turkey, frozen, whole	lb	1.04	4/93	16r
Health Care				
Childbirth, cesarean, hospital		5826	91	62r
Childbirth, cesarean, physician's fee		2053	91	62r
Childbirth, normal, hospital		2964	91	62r
Childbirth, normal, physician's fee		1492	91	62r
Health care spending, state	capita	3031	3/93	84s
Medical plan per employee	year	3958	91	45r
Mental health care, exp	capita	53.68-118.35	90	38s
Mental health care, exp, state mental health agency	capita	83.91	90	38s
Mental health care, hospital psychiatric services, non-Federal, exp	capita	22.67	88	38s
Mental health care, mental health organization, multiservice, exp	capita	36.07	88	38s
Mental health care, psychiatric hospitals, private, exp	capita	38.65	88	38s
Mental health care, psychiatric out-patient clinics, freestanding, exp	capita	4.41	88	38s
Mental health care, psychiatric partial-care organizations, freestanding, exp	capita	0.92	88	38s
Mental health care, state and county mental hospitals, exp	capita	30.59	88	38s
Mental health care, VA medical centers, exp	capita	21.14	88	38s
Substance abuse, hospital ancillary charge	incident	1310	90	70s
Substance abuse, hospital physician charge	incident	460	90	70s
Substance abuse, hospital room and board	incident	3450	90	70s
Insurance and Pensions				
Auto insurance, private passenger	year	912.83	91	63s
Taxes				
Tax, cigarette	pack	26	91	77s
Tax, gasoline	gal	21	91	77s
Taxes, state	capita	1615	91	77s
Transportation				
Driver's license fee		35.00	12/90	43s
Travel				
Business travel	day	165.00	4/93	89r
Utilities				
Electricity	mil Btu	25.93	90	64s

Lawton, OK

Item	Per	Value	Date	Ref.
Composite ACCRA index		94.40	4Q 92	4c

Values are in dollars or fractions of dollars. In the column headed *Ref*, references are shown to sources. Each reference is followed by a letter. These refer to the geographical level for which data were reported: s=State, r=Region, and c=City or metro. The abbreviation *ex* is used to mean *except* or *excluding*; *exp* stands for expenditures. For other abbreviations and further explanations, please see the Introduction.

Lawton, OK - continued

Item	Per	Value	Date	Ref.
Alcoholic Beverages				
Beer, Miller Lite or Budweiser, 12-oz containers	6 pack	3.28	4Q 92	4c
Liquor, J & B Scotch	750 ml	15.49	4Q 92	4c
Wine, Gallo Chablis blanc, 1.5 liter	bottle	5.91	4Q 92	4c
Child Care				
Child care fee, average, center	hour	1.29	90	65r
Child care fee, average, nonregulated family day care	hour	0.89	90	65r
Child care fee, average, regulated family day care	hour	1.32	90	65r
Clothing				
Jeans, man's denim		23.98	4Q 92	4c
Shirt, man's dress shirt		22.70	4Q 92	4c
Undervest, boy's size 10-14, cotton	3	4.23	4Q 92	4c
Communications				
Long-distance telephone service, day, initial minute, 0-100 miles	min	0.12-0.45	91	12s
Long-distance telephone service, day, additional minute, 0-100 miles	min	0.07-0.39	91	12s
Newspaper subscription, daily and Sunday home delivery, large-city	month	12.85	4Q 92	4c
Telephone, flat rate	month	11.32	91	11c
Telephone bill, family of four	month	17.99	4Q 92	4c
Education				
Board, 4-yr private college/university	year	1664	91	22s
Board, 4-yr public college/university	year	1368	91	22s
Expenditures, local gov't, public elementary/secondary	pupil	3901	92	20s
Room, 4-year private college/university	year	1384	91	22s
Room, 4-year public college/university	year	1119	91	22s
Tuition, 2-year private college/university	year	5732	91	22s
Tuition, 2-year public college/university	year	864	91	22s
Tuition, 4-year private college/university	year	5852	91	22s
Tuition, 4-year public college/university, in-state	year	1340	91	22s
Energy and Fuels				
Coal	mil Btu	1.40	90	64s
Energy	mil Btu	7.46	90	64s
Energy, combined forms, 1,800 sq ft heating area	month	116.18	4Q 92	4c
Energy, exc electricity, 1,800 sq ft heating area	month	37.94	4Q 92	4c
Energy exp/householder, 1-family unit	year	471	90	28r
Energy exp/householder, <1,000 sq ft heating area	year	384	90	28r
Energy exp/householder, 1,000-1,999 sq ft heating area	year	421	90	28r
Energy exp/householder, 2,000+ sq ft heating area	year	625	90	28r
Energy exp/householder, mobile home	year	271	90	28r
Energy exp/householder, multifamily	year	355	90	28r
Gas, cooking, winter, 10 therms	month	19.28	92	56c
Gas, cooking, winter, 30 therms	month	18.03	92	56c
Gas, cooking, winter, 50 therms	month	26.52	92	56c
Gas, heating, winter, 100 therms	month	47.75	92	56c
Gas, heating, winter, average use	month	55.44	92	56c
Gas, natural	mil Btu	2.80	90	64s
Gas, natural	000 cu ft	4.72	91	46s
Gas, natural, exp	year	396	91	46s
Gasoline, motor	gal	1.10	4Q 92	4c
Gasoline, unleaded regular	mil Btu	9.00	90	64s
Entertainment				
Bowling, evening rate	game	1.95	4Q 92	4c
Miniature golf admission	adult	6.18	92	1r
Miniature golf admission	child	5.14	92	1r
Monopoly game, Parker Brothers', No. 9		12.74	4Q 92	4c
Movie	admission	5.50	4Q 92	4c

Lawton, OK - continued

Item	Per	Value	Date	Ref.
Entertainment - continued				
Tennis balls, yellow, Wilson or Penn, 3	can	2.51	4Q 92	4c
Waterpark admission	adult	11.00	92	1r
Waterpark admission	child	8.55	92	1r
Funerals				
Casket, 18-gauge steel, velvet interior		2274.41	91	24r
Cosmetology, hair care, etc.		74.62	91	24r
Embalming		229.94	91	24r
Facility use for ceremony		176.61	91	24r
Hearse, local		116.34	91	24r
Limousine, local		72.68	91	24r
Remains to funeral home, transfer		87.72	91	24r
Service charge, professional		712.53	91	24r
Vault, concrete, non-metallic liner		750.55	91	24r
Viewing facilities, use		155.31	91	24r
Goods and Services				
ACCRA Index, Miscellaneous Goods and Services		97.80	4Q 92	4c
Groceries				
ACCRA Index, Groceries		97.80	4Q 92	4c
Apples, Red Delicious	lb	0.79	4/93	16r
Babyfood, strained vegetables, lowest price	4-4.5 oz jar	0.30	4Q 92	4c
Bacon	lb	1.75	4/93	16r
Bananas	lb	0.47	4Q 92	4c
Bananas	lb	0.42	4/93	16r
Beef, stew, boneless	lb	2.61	4/93	16r
Bologna, all beef or mixed	lb	2.24	4/93	16r
Bread, white	24 oz	0.62	4Q 92	4c
Bread, white, pan	lb	0.64	4/93	16r
Bread, whole wheat, pan	lb	0.96	4/93	16r
Cabbage	lb	0.37	4/93	16r
Carrots, short trimmed and topped	lb	0.47	4/93	16r
Celery	lb	0.64	4/93	16r
Cheese, American	lb	2.98	4/93	16r
Cheese, Cheddar	lb	3.28	4/93	16r
Cheese, Kraft grated Parmesan	8-oz canister	3.35	4Q 92	4c
Chicken, fresh, whole	lb	0.77	4/93	16r
Chicken, fryer, whole	lb	0.77	4Q 92	4c
Chicken breast, bone-in	lb	1.92	4/93	16r
Chicken legs, bone-in	lb	1.06	4/93	16r
Chuck roast, graded and ungraded, ex USDA prime and choice	lb	2.40	4/93	16r
Chuck roast, USDA choice, bone-in	lb	2.19	4/93	16r
Chuck roast, USDA choice, boneless	lb	2.38	4/93	16r
Cigarettes, Winston	carton	17.21	4Q 92	4c
Coffee, 100% ground roast, all sizes	lb	2.48	4/93	16r
Coffee, vacuum-packed	13-oz can	1.85	4Q 92	4c
Corn, frozen	10 oz	0.60	4Q 92	4c
Corn Flakes, Kellogg's or Post Toasties	18 oz	1.88	4Q 92	4c
Crackers, soda, salted	lb	1.15	4/93	16r
Eggs, Grade A large	doz	0.89	4Q 92	4c
Eggs, Grade A large	doz	0.96	4/93	16r
Flour, white, all purpose	lb	0.24	4/93	16r
Frankfurters, all meat or all beef	lb	2.01	4/93	16r
Grapefruit	lb	0.44	4/93	16r
Grapes, Thompson Seedless	lb	1.40	4/93	16r
Ground beef, 100% beef	lb	1.58	4/93	16r
Ground beef, lean and extra lean	lb	2.09	4/93	16r
Ground beef or hamburger	lb	1.65	4Q 92	4c
Ground chuck, 100% beef	lb	1.98	4/93	16r
Ham, boneless, excluding canned	lb	2.89	4/93	16r
Ham, picnic, shoulder, bone-in, smoked	lb	1.02	4/93	16r
Ham, rump or steak half, bone-in, smoked	lb	1.48	4/93	16r
Honey, jar	8 oz	0.73-1.19	92	5r
Honey, jar	lb	1.10-1.79	92	5r
Honey, squeeze bear	12-oz	1.19-1.50	92	5r
Ice cream, prepackaged, bulk, regular	1/2 gal	2.41	4/93	16r
Lemons	lb	1.05	4/93	16r

Values are in dollars or fractions of dollars. In the column headed *Ref*, references are shown to sources. Each reference is followed by a letter. These refer to the geographical level for which data were reported: s=State, r=Region, and c=City or metro. The abbreviation *ex* is used to mean *except* or *excluding*; *exp* stands for *expenditures*. For other abbreviations and further explanations, please see the Introduction.

Lawton, OK - continued

Item	Per	Value	Date	Ref.
Groceries				
Lettuce, iceberg	head	1.08	4Q 92	4c
Lettuce, iceberg	lb	0.81	4/93	16r
Margarine, Blue Bonnet or Parkay cubes	lb	0.51	4Q 92	4c
Margarine, stick	lb	0.88	4/93	16r
Milk, whole	1/2 gal	1.14	4Q 92	4c
Orange juice, Minute Maid frozen	12-oz can	1.35	4Q 92	4c
Oranges, navel	lb	0.55	4/93	16r
Peaches	29-oz can	1.34	4Q 92	4c
Pears, Anjou	lb	0.92	4/93	16r
Peas Sweet, Del Monte or Green Giant	15-17 oz can	0.54	4Q 92	4c
Pork chops, center cut, bone-in	lb	3.13	4/93	16r
Potato chips	16 oz	2.94	4/93	16r
Potatoes, white	lb	0.43	4/93	16r
Potatoes, white or red	10-lb sack	2.65	4Q 92	4c
Rib roast, USDA choice, bone-in	lb	4.63	4/93	16r
Rice, white, long grain, uncooked	lb	0.45	4/93	16r
Round roast, graded & ungraded, ex USDA prime & choice	lb	3.03	4/93	16r
Round roast, USDA choice, boneless	lb	3.09	4/93	16r
Sausage, fresh, loose	lb	2.08	4/93	16r
Sausage, Jimmy Dean, 100% pork	lb	2.72	4Q 92	4c
Short ribs, bone-in	lb	2.66	4/93	16r
Shortening, vegetable oil blends	lb	0.69	4/93	16r
Shortening, vegetable, Crisco	3-lb can	2.21	4Q 92	4c
Soft drink, Coca Cola	2 liter	1.26	4Q 92	4c
Spaghetti and macaroni	lb	0.81	4/93	16r
Steak, rib eye, USDA choice, boneless	lb	6.24	4/93	16r
Steak, round, graded & ungraded, ex USDA prime & choice	lb	3.31	4/93	16r
Steak, round, USDA choice, boneless	lb	3.34	4/93	16r
Steak, sirloin, graded & ungraded, ex USDA prime & choice	lb	4.19	4/93	16r
Steak, sirloin, USDA choice, boneless	lb	4.46	4/93	16r
Steak, T-bone	lb	4.29	4Q 92	4c
Steak, T-bone, USDA choice, bone-in	lb	5.25	4/93	16r
Strawberries, dry pint	12 oz	0.92	4/93	16r
Sugar, cane or beet	4 lb	1.77	4Q 92	4c
Sugar, white	lb	0.39	4/93	16r
Sugar, white, 33-80 oz pk	lb	0.38	4/93	16r
Tomatoes, field grown	lb	0.88	4/93	16r
Tomatoes, Hunt's or Del Monte	14.5-oz can	0.64	4Q 92	4c
Tuna, chunk, light	6.125-6.5 oz can	0.71	4Q 92	4c
Tuna, chunk, light	lb	1.79	4/93	16r
Turkey, frozen, whole	lb	1.04	4/93	16r
Yogurt, natural, fruit flavored	1/2 pint	0.57	4/93	16r
Health Care				
ACCRA Index, Health Care		94.30	4Q 92	4c
Analgesic, Aspirin, Bayer, 325 mg tablets	100	5.15	4Q 92	4c
Childbirth, cesarean, hospital		5034	91	62r
Childbirth, cesarean, physician's fee		2053	91	62r
Childbirth, normal, hospital		2712	91	62r
Childbirth, normal, physician's fee		1492	91	62r
Dentist's fee, adult teeth cleaning and periodic oral exam	visit	50.17	4Q 92	4c
Doctor's fee, routine exam, established patient	visit	34.25	4Q 92	4c
Hospital care, semiprivate room	day	186.22	90	27c
Hospital care, semiprivate room	day	211.90	4Q 92	4c
Medical insurance premium, per employee, small group comprehensive	month	306.60	10/91	25c
Mental health care, exp	capita	28.84-37.59	90	38s

Lawton, OK - continued

Item	Per	Value	Date	Ref.
Health Care - continued				
Mental health care, exp, state mental health agency	capita	35.92	90	38s
Mental health care, hospital psychiatric services, non-Federal, exp	capita	11.62	88	38s
Mental health care, mental health organization, multiservice, exp	capita	13.80	88	38s
Mental health care, psychiatric hospitals, private, exp	capita	21.32	88	38s
Mental health care, psychiatric out-patient clinics, freestanding, exp	capita	3.63	88	38s
Mental health care, psychiatric partial-care organizations, freestanding, exp	capita	0.04	88	38s
Mental health care, state and county mental hospitals, exp	capita	20.87	88	38s
Mental health care, VA medical centers, exp	capita	0.46	88	38s
Physician fee, family practice, first-visit		75.00	91	62r
Physician fee, family practice, revisit		34.00	91	62r
Physician fee, general practice, first-visit		61.00	91	62r
Physician fee, general practice, revisit		32.00	91	62r
Physician fee, general surgeon, first-visit		64.00	91	62r
Physician fee, general surgeon, revisit		40.00	91	62r
Physician fee, internal medicine, first-visit		98.00	91	62r
Physician fee, internal medicine, revisit		40.00	91	62r
Physician fee, median, neurosurgeon, first-visit		130.00	91	62r
Physician fee, median, nonsurgical specialist, first-visit		95.00	91	62r
Physician fee, median, orthopedic surgeon, first-visit		91.00	91	62r
Physician fee, median, plastic surgeon, first-visit		66.00	91	62r
Physician fee, median, surgical specialist, first-visit		62.00	91	62r
Physician fee, neurosurgeon, revisit		50.00	91	62r
Physician fee, nonsurgical specialist, revisit		40.00	91	62r
Physician fee, obstetrics/gynecology, first-visit		64.00	91	62r
Physician fee, obstetrics/gynecology, revisit		41.00	91	62r
Physician fee, orthopedic surgeon, revisit		40.00	91	62r
Physician fee, pediatrician, first-visit		49.00	91	62r
Physician fee, pediatrician, revisit		33.00	91	62r
Physician fee, plastic surgeon, revisit		43.00	91	62r
Physician fee, surgical specialist, revisit		37.00	91	62r
Substance abuse, hospital ancillary charge	incident	1220	90	70s
Substance abuse, hospital physician charge	incident	160	90	70s
Substance abuse, hospital room and board	incident	5490	90	70s
Household Goods				
Appliance repair, home, service call, washing machine	min labor charge	33.49	4Q 92	4c
Laundry detergent, Tide Ultra, Bold, or Cheer	42 oz	3.17	4Q 92	4c
Tissues, facial, Kleenex brand	175-count box	1.08	4Q 92	4c
Housing				
ACCRA Index, Housing		81.90	4Q 92	4c
House, 1,800 sq ft, 8,000 sq ft lot, new, urban	total	89000	4Q 92	4c
House payment, principal and interest, 25% down payment	month	498	4Q 92	4c
Mortgage rate, incl. points & origination fee, 30-year fixed or adjustable rate	per-cent	8.18	4Q 92	4c
Rent, apartment, 2 bedrooms - 1-1/2 to 2 baths, unfurnished, 950 sq ft, water	month	416	4Q 92	4c
Rental unit, 1 bedroom	month	346	93	23c
Rental unit, 2 bedroom	month	409	93	23c
Rental unit, 3 bedroom	month	509	93	23c

Values are in dollars or fractions of dollars. In the column headed *Ref*, references are shown to sources. Each reference is followed by a letter. These refer to the geographical level for which data were reported: s = State, r = Region, and c = City or metro. The abbreviation *ex* is used to mean *except* or *excluding*; *exp* stands for expenditures. For other abbreviations and further explanations, please see the Introduction.

Lawton, OK - continued

Item	Per	Value	Date	Ref.
Housing				
Rental unit, 4 bedroom	month	571	93	23c
Rental unit, efficiency	month	284	93	23c
Insurance and Pensions				
Auto insurance, private passenger	year	554.09	91	63s
Personal Goods				
Shampoo, Alberto VO5	15 oz	1.23	4Q 92	4c
Toothpaste, Crest or Colgate	6-7 oz	1.97	4Q 92	4c
Personal Services				
Dry cleaning, man's 2-piece suit		5.82	4Q 92	4c
Haircare, woman's shampoo, trim and blow-dry		17.33	4Q 92	4c
Haircut, man's barbershop, no styling		6.17	4Q 92	4c
Restaurant Food				
Chicken, fried, thigh and drumstick		2.07	4Q 92	4c
Hamburger with cheese	1/4 lb	1.76	4Q 92	4c
Pizza, Pizza Hut or Pizza Inn, cheese, thin crust	12-13 in	8.60	4Q 92	4c
Taxes				
Tax, cigarette	pack	23	91	77s
Tax, gasoline	gal	17	91	77s
Taxes, state	capita	1216	91	77s
Transportation				
ACCRA Index, Transportation		103.10	4Q 92	4c
Driver's license fee		7.00-14.00	12/90	43s
Tire balance, computer or spin balance, front	wheel	7.08	4Q 92	4c
Travel				
Business travel	day	193.00	4/93	89r
Utilities				
ACCRA Index, Utilities		105.00	4Q 92	4c
Electricity	mil Btu	16.08	90	64s
Electricity, partial electric and other energy, 1,800 sq ft living area new home	month	78.24	4Q 92	4c
Electricity, residential	KWh	6.24	2/93	94s

Lewiston-Auburn, ME

Item	Per	Value	Date	Ref.
Child Care				
Child care fee, average, center	hour	2.18	90	65r
Child care fee, average, nonregulated family day care	hour	1.83	90	65r
Child care fee, average, regulated family day care	hour	2.02	90	65r
Communications				
Long-distance telephone service, day, initial minute, 0-100 miles	min	0.19-0.64	91	12s
Long-distance telephone service, day, additional minute, 0-100 miles	min	0.15-0.40	91	12s
Long-distance telephone service, evenings/weekends, 0-100 mi, initial minute	min	0.08-0.26	91	12s
Long-distance telephone service, evenings/weekends, 0-100 mi, additional minute	min	0.80-0.16	91	12s
Education				
Board, 4-yr private college/university	year	2441	91	22s
Board, 4-yr public college/university	year	1855	91	22s
Expenditures, local gov't, public elementary/secondary	pupil	5969	92	20s
Room, 4-year private college/university	year	2344	91	22s
Room, 4-year public college/university	year	1886	91	22s
Tuition, 2-year private college/university	year	3899	91	22s
Tuition, 2-year public college/university	year	1497	91	22s
Tuition, 4-year private college/university	year	10928	91	22s
Tuition, 4-year public college/university, in-state	year	2263	91	22s

Lewiston-Auburn, ME - continued

Item	Per	Value	Date	Ref.
Energy and Fuels				
Coal	mil Btu	2.72	90	64s
Energy	mil Btu	9.54	90	64s
Energy exp/householder, 1-family unit	year	588	90	28r
Energy exp/householder, <1,000 sq ft heating area	year	477	90	28r
Energy exp/householder, 1,000-1,999 sq ft heating area	year	517	90	28r
Energy exp/householder, 2,000+ sq ft heating area	year	630	90	28r
Energy exp/householder, mobile home	year	412	90	28r
Energy exp/householder, multifamily	year	498	90	28r
Gas, natural	mil Btu	6.05	90	64s
Gas, natural	000 cu ft	6.86	91	46s
Gas, natural, exp	year	399	91	46s
Gasoline, unleaded regular	mil Btu	9.74	90	64s
Entertainment				
Miniature golf admission	adult	6.18	92	1r
Miniature golf admission	child	5.14	92	1r
Waterpark admission	adult	11.00	92	1r
Waterpark admission	child	8.55	92	1r
Funerals				
Casket, 18-gauge steel, velvet interior		1853.42	91	24r
Cosmetology, hair care, etc.		98.33	91	24r
Embalming		273.94	91	24r
Facility use for ceremony		196.06	91	24r
Hearse, local		145.67	91	24r
Limousine, local		131.07	91	24r
Remains to funeral home, transfer		135.24	91	24r
Service charge, professional		843.16	91	24r
Vault, concrete, non-metallic liner		709.14	91	24r
Viewing facilities, use		229.85	91	24r
Groceries				
Apples, Red Delicious	lb	0.85	4/93	16r
Bacon	lb	2.12	4/93	16r
Bananas	lb	0.54	4/93	16r
Bread, white, pan	lb	0.81	4/93	16r
Butter	lb	2.02	4/93	16r
Carrots, short trimmed and topped	lb	0.51	4/93	16r
Chicken, fresh, whole	lb	1.04	4/93	16r
Chicken breast, bone-in	lb	2.21	4/93	16r
Chicken legs, bone-in	lb	1.16	4/93	16r
Chuck roast, USDA choice, boneless	lb	2.82	4/93	16r
Coffee, 100% ground roast, all sizes	lb	2.66	4/93	16r
Cucumbers	lb	0.85	4/93	16r
Eggs, Grade A large	doz	1.15	4/93	16r
Grapefruit	lb	0.45	4/93	16r
Grapes, Thompson Seedless	lb	1.52	4/93	16r
Ground beef, lean and extra lean	lb	2.36	4/93	16r
Ground chuck, 100% beef	lb	2.02	4/93	16r
Honey, jar	8 oz	0.96-1.75	92	5r
Honey, jar	lb	1.50-3.00	92	5r
Honey, squeeze bear	12-oz	1.50-1.99	92	5r
Ice cream, prepackaged, bulk, regular	1/2 gal	2.80	4/93	16r
Lemons	lb	0.96	4/93	16r
Lettuce, iceberg	lb	0.95	4/93	16r
Margarine, stick	lb	0.81	4/93	16r
Milk, fresh, whole, fortified	1/2 gal	1.30	4/93	16r
Oranges, navel	lb	0.56	4/93	16r
Peanut butter, creamy, all sizes	lb	1.88	4/93	16r
Pork chops, center cut, bone-in	lb	3.34	4/93	16r
Potato chips	16 oz	2.88	4/93	16r
Potatoes, white	lb	0.37	4/93	16r
Rib roast, USDA choice, bone-in	lb	4.94	4/93	16r
Round roast, USDA choice, boneless	lb	3.17	4/93	16r
Shortening, vegetable oil blends	lb	0.98	4/93	16r
Spaghetti and macaroni	lb	0.82	4/93	16r
Steak, round, graded & ungraded, ex USDA prime & choice	lb	4.04	4/93	16r
Steak, round, USDA choice, boneless	lb	3.90	4/93	16r
Steak, sirloin, USDA choice, boneless	lb	4.97	4/93	16r

Values are in dollars or fractions of dollars. In the column headed *Ref*, references are shown to sources. Each reference is followed by a letter. These refer to the geographical level for which data were reported: s = State, r = Region, and c = City or metro. The abbreviation *ex* is used to mean *except* or *excluding*; *exp* stands for expenditures. For other abbreviations and further explanations, please see the Introduction.

Lewiston-Auburn, ME - continued

Item	Per	Value	Date	Ref.
Groceries				
Strawberries, dry pint	12 oz	0.90	4/93	16r
Sugar, white	lb	0.50	4/93	16r
Sugar, white, 33-80 oz pk	lb	0.41	4/93	16r
Tomatoes, field grown	lb	1.23	4/93	16r
Tuna, chunk, light	lb	2.22	4/93	16r
Turkey, frozen, whole	lb	1.04	4/93	16r
Health Care				
Childbirth, cesarean, hospital		5826	91	62r
Childbirth, cesarean, physician's fee		2053	91	62r
Childbirth, normal, hospital		2964	91	62r
Childbirth, normal, physician's fee		1492	91	62r
Medical plan per employee	year	3958	91	45r
Mental health care, exp	capita	53.68-118.35	90	38s
Mental health care, exp, state mental health agency	capita	67.29	90	38s
Mental health care, hospital psychiatric services, non-Federal, exp	capita	16.12	88	38s
Mental health care, mental health organization, multiservice, exp	capita	17.98	88	38s
Mental health care, psychiatric hospitals, private, exp	capita	7.97	88	38s
Mental health care, psychiatric out-patient clinics, freestanding, exp	capita	1.60	88	38s
Mental health care, psychiatric partial-care organizations, freestanding, exp	capita	0.38	88	38s
Mental health care, state and county mental hospitals, exp	capita	29.80	88	38s
Mental health care, VA medical centers, exp	capita	8.16	88	38s
Prescription drug co-pay, Medicaid	month	3.00-5.00	91	21s
Substance abuse, hospital ancillary charge	incident	840	90	70s
Substance abuse, hospital physician charge	incident	170	90	70s
Substance abuse, hospital room and board	incident	4720	90	70s
Insurance and Pensions				
Auto insurance, private passenger	year	558.21	91	63s
Taxes				
Tax, cigarette	pack	37	91	77s
Tax, gasoline	gal	19	91	77s
Taxes, state	capita	1262	91	77s
Transportation				
Driver's license fee		18.00	12/90	43s
Vehicle registration and license plate	year	22.00	93	61s
Travel				
Business travel	day	165.00	4/93	89r
Utilities				
Electricity	mil Btu	22.42	90	64s

Lexington, KY

Item	Per	Value	Date	Ref.
Composite ACCRA index		101.60	4Q 92	4c
Alcoholic Beverages				
Beer, Miller Lite or Budweiser, 12-oz containers	6 pack	3.55	4Q 92	4c
Liquor, J & B Scotch	750 ml	17.18	4Q 92	4c
Wine, Gallo Chablis blanc, 1.5 liter	bottle	5.79	4Q 92	4c
Clothing				
Jeans, man's denim		32.14	4Q 92	4c
Shirt, man's dress shirt		26.35	4Q 92	4c
Undervest, boy's size 10-14, cotton	3	5.26	4Q 92	4c
Communications				
Newspaper subscription, daily and Sunday home delivery, large-city	month	15.95	4Q 92	4c
Telephone bill, family of four	month	26.22	4Q 92	4c

Lexington, KY - continued

Item	Per	Value	Date	Ref.
Energy and Fuels				
Energy, combined forms, 1,800 sq ft heating area	month	84.22	4Q 92	4c
Energy, exc electricity, 1,800 sq ft heating area	month	48.94	4Q 92	4c
Gas, cooking, 10 therms	month	5.02	92	56c
Gas, cooking, 30 therms	month	15.05	92	56c
Gas, cooking, 50 therms	month	25.09	92	56c
Gas, heating, winter, 100 therms	month	50.18	92	56c
Gas, heating, winter, average use	month	50.18	92	56c
Gasoline, motor	gal	1.08	4Q 92	4c
Entertainment				
Bowling, evening rate	game	2.04	4Q 92	4c
Monopoly game, Parker Brothers', No. 9		12.62	4Q 92	4c
Movie	admission	5.21	4Q 92	4c
Tennis balls, yellow, Wilson or Penn, 3	can	2.66	4Q 92	4c
Goods and Services				
ACCRA Index, Miscellaneous Goods and Services		106.30	4Q 92	4c
Groceries				
ACCRA Index, Groceries		97.50	4Q 92	4c
Babyfood, strained vegetables, lowest price	4-4.5 oz jar	0.29	4Q 92	4c
Bananas	lb	0.54	4Q 92	4c
Bread, white	24 oz	0.75	4Q 92	4c
Cheese, Kraft grated Parmesan	8-oz canister	3.02	4Q 92	4c
Chicken, fryer, whole	lb	0.84	4Q 92	4c
Cigarettes, Winston	carton	15.38	4Q 92	4c
Coffee, vacuum-packed	13-oz can	1.96	4Q 92	4c
Corn, frozen	10 oz	0.64	4Q 92	4c
Corn Flakes, Kellogg's or Post Toasties	18 oz	2.03	4Q 92	4c
Eggs, Grade A large	doz	0.70	4Q 92	4c
Ground beef or hamburger	lb	1.41	4Q 92	4c
Lettuce, iceberg	head	1.08	4Q 92	4c
Margarine, Blue Bonnet or Parkay cubes	lb	0.45	4Q 92	4c
Milk, whole	1/2 gal	1.50	4Q 92	4c
Orange juice, Minute Maid frozen	12-oz can	1.37	4Q 92	4c
Peaches	29-oz can	1.45	4Q 92	4c
Peas Sweet, Del Monte or Green Giant	15-17 oz can	0.58	4Q 92	4c
Potatoes, white or red	10-lb sack	2.47	4Q 92	4c
Sausage, Jimmy Dean, 100% pork	lb	2.21	4Q 92	4c
Shortening, vegetable, Crisco	3-lb can	1.99	4Q 92	4c
Soft drink, Coca Cola	2 liter	1.09	4Q 92	4c
Steak, T-bone	lb	5.49	4Q 92	4c
Sugar, cane or beet	4 lb	1.38	4Q 92	4c
Tomatoes, Hunt's or Del Monte	14.5-oz can	0.72	4Q 92	4c
Tuna, chunk, light	6.125-6.5 oz can	0.51	4Q 92	4c
Health Care				
ACCRA Index, Health Care		110.40	4Q 92	4c
Analgesic, Aspirin, Bayer, 325 mg tablets	100	5.42	4Q 92	4c
Dentist's fee, adult teeth cleaning and periodic oral exam	visit	48.50	4Q 92	4c
Doctor's fee, routine exam, established patient	visit	45.50	4Q 92	4c
Hospital care, semiprivate room	day	248.97	90	27c
Hospital care, semiprivate room	day	318.13	4Q 92	4c
Medical insurance premium, per employee, small group comprehensive	month	299.30	10/91	25c

Values are in dollars or fractions of dollars. In the column headed *Ref*, references are shown to sources. Each reference is followed by a letter. These refer to the geographical level for which data were reported: s=State, r=Region, and c=City or metro. The abbreviation *ex* is used to mean *except* or *excluding*; *exp* stands for expenditures. For other abbreviations and further explanations, please see the Introduction.

Lexington, KY - continued

Item	Per	Value	Date	Ref.
Household Goods				
Appliance repair, home, service call, washing machine	min labor charge	32.39	4Q 92	4c
Laundry detergent, Tide Ultra, Bold, or Cheer	42 oz	3.43	4Q 92	4c
Tissues, facial, Kleenex brand	175-count box	1.06	4Q 92	4c
Housing				
ACCRA Index, Housing		104.70	4Q 92	4c
House, 1,800 sq ft, 8,000 sq ft lot, new, urban	total	114472	4Q 92	4c
House payment, principal and interest, 25% down payment	month	632	4Q 92	4c
Mortgage rate, incl. points & origination fee, 30-year fixed or adjustable rate	percent	8.03	4Q 92	4c
Rent, apartment, 2 bedrooms - 1-1/2 to 2 baths, unfurnished, 950 sq ft, water	month	543	4Q 92	4c
Personal Goods				
Shampoo, Alberto VO5	15 oz	1.24	4Q 92	4c
Toothpaste, Crest or Colgate	6-7 oz	2.08	4Q 92	4c
Personal Services				
Dry cleaning, man's 2-piece suit		5.47	4Q 92	4c
Haircare, woman's shampoo, trim and blow-dry		22.44	4Q 92	4c
Haircut, man's barbershop, no styling		8.06	4Q 92	4c
Restaurant Food				
Chicken, fried, thigh and drumstick		2.05	4Q 92	4c
Hamburger with cheese	1/4 lb	1.75	4Q 92	4c
Pizza, Pizza Hut or Pizza Inn, cheese, thin crust	12-13 in	7.49	4Q 92	4c
Transportation				
ACCRA Index, Transportation		94.00	4Q 92	4c
Bus fare, up to 10 miles	one-way	0.80	4Q 92	4c
Tire balance, computer or spin balance, front	wheel	6.06	4Q 92	4c
Utilities				
ACCRA Index, Utilities		82.90	4Q 92	4c
Electricity, partial electric and other energy, 1,800 sq ft living area new home	month	35.28	4Q 92	4c
Electricity, winter, 250 KWh	month	14.44	92	55c
Electricity, winter, 500 KWh	month	25.26	92	55c
Electricity, winter, 750 KWh	month	35.47	92	55c
Electricity, winter, 1000 KWh	month	45.67	92	55c

Lexington-Fayette, KY

Item	Per	Value	Date	Ref.
Child Care				
Child care fee, average, center	hour	1.29	90	65r
Child care fee, average, nonregulated family day care	hour	0.89	90	65r
Child care fee, average, regulated family day care	hour	1.32	90	65r
Communications				
Long-distance telephone service, day, initial minute, 0-100 miles	min	0.20-0.55	91	12s
Long-distance telephone service, day, additional minute, 0-100 miles	min	0.14-0.44	91	12s
Long-distance telephone service, evenings/weekends, 0-100 mi, initial minute	min	0.08-0.22	91	12s
Long-distance telephone service, evenings/weekends, 0-100 mi, additional minute	min	0.06-0.16	91	12s
Education				
Board, 4-yr private college/university	year	1522	91	22s
Board, 4-yr public college/university	year	1862	91	22s

Lexington-Fayette, KY - continued

Item	Per	Value	Date	Ref.
Education - continued				
Expenditures, local gov't, public elementary/secondary	pupil	4616	92	20s
Room, 4-year private college/university	year	1193	91	22s
Room, 4-year public college/university	year	1153	91	22s
Tuition, 2-year private college/university	year	4662	91	22s
Tuition, 2-year public college/university	year	771	91	22s
Tuition, 4-year private college/university	year	5200	91	22s
Tuition, 4-year public college/university, in-state	year	1444	91	22s
Energy and Fuels				
Coal	mil Btu	1.27	90	64s
Energy	mil Btu	7.91	90	64s
Energy exp/householder, 1-family unit	year	403	90	28r
Energy exp/householder, <1,000 sq ft heating area	year	342	90	28r
Energy exp/householder, 1,000-1,999 sq ft heating area	year	388	90	28r
Energy exp/householder, 2,000+ sq ft heating area	year	434	90	28r
Energy exp/householder, mobile home	year	320	90	28r
Energy exp/householder, multifamily	year	338	90	28r
Gas, natural	mil Btu	4.10	90	64s
Gas, natural	000 cu ft	4.87	91	46s
Gas, natural, exp	year	457	91	46s
Gasoline, unleaded regular	mil Btu	9.25	90	64s
Entertainment				
Miniature golf admission	adult	6.18	92	1r
Miniature golf admission	child	5.14	92	1r
Waterpark admission	adult	11.00	92	1r
Waterpark admission	child	8.55	92	1r
Funerals				
Casket, 18-gauge steel, velvet interior		2329.05	91	24r
Cosmetology, hair care, etc.		72.78	91	24r
Embalming		240.71	91	24r
Facility use for ceremony		181.67	91	24r
Hearse, local		106.25	91	24r
Limousine, local		70.92	91	24r
Remains to funeral home, transfer		96.30	91	24r
Service charge, professional		687.09	91	24r
Vault, concrete, non-metallic liner		732.09	91	24r
Viewing facilities, use		190.30	91	24r
Groceries				
Apples, Red Delicious	lb	0.79	4/93	16r
Bacon	lb	1.75	4/93	16r
Bananas	lb	0.42	4/93	16r
Beef, stew, boneless	lb	2.61	4/93	16r
Bologna, all beef or mixed	lb	2.24	4/93	16r
Bread, white, pan	lb	0.64	4/93	16r
Bread, whole wheat, pan	lb	0.96	4/93	16r
Cabbage	lb	0.37	4/93	16r
Carrots, short trimmed and topped	lb	0.47	4/93	16r
Celery	lb	0.64	4/93	16r
Cheese, American	lb	2.98	4/93	16r
Cheese, Cheddar	lb	3.28	4/93	16r
Chicken, fresh, whole	lb	0.77	4/93	16r
Chicken breast, bone-in	lb	1.92	4/93	16r
Chicken legs, bone-in	lb	1.06	4/93	16r
Chuck roast, graded and ungraded, ex USDA prime and choice	lb	2.40	4/93	16r
Chuck roast, USDA choice, bone-in	lb	2.19	4/93	16r
Chuck roast, USDA choice, boneless	lb	2.38	4/93	16r
Coffee, 100% ground roast, all sizes	lb	2.48	4/93	16r
Crackers, soda, salted	lb	1.15	4/93	16r
Eggs, Grade A large	doz	0.96	4/93	16r
Flour, white, all purpose	lb	0.24	4/93	16r
Frankfurters, all meat or all beef	lb	2.01	4/93	16r
Grapefruit	lb	0.44	4/93	16r
Grapes, Thompson Seedless	lb	1.40	4/93	16r
Ground beef, 100% beef	lb	1.58	4/93	16r

Values are in dollars or fractions of dollars. In the column headed *Ref*, references are shown to sources. Each reference is followed by a letter. These refer to the geographical level for which data were reported: s=State, r=Region, and c=City or metro. The abbreviation *ex* is used to mean *except* or *excluding*; *exp* stands for expenditures. For other abbreviations and further explanations, please see the Introduction.

Lexington-Fayette, KY - continued

Item	Per	Value	Date	Ref.
Groceries				
Ground beef, lean and extra lean	lb	2.09	4/93	16r
Ground chuck, 100% beef	lb	1.98	4/93	16r
Ham, boneless, excluding canned	lb	2.89	4/93	16r
Ham, picnic, shoulder, bone-in, smoked	lb	1.02	4/93	16r
Ham, rump or steak half, bone-in, smoked	lb	1.48	4/93	16r
Honey, jar	8 oz	0.89-1.09	92	5r
Honey, jar	lb	1.39-2.25	92	5r
Honey, squeeze bear	12-oz	1.00-1.50	92	5r
Ice cream, prepackaged, bulk, regular	1/2 gal	2.41	4/93	16r
Lemons	lb	1.05	4/93	16r
Lettuce, iceberg	lb	0.81	4/93	16r
Margarine, stick	lb	0.88	4/93	16r
Oranges, navel	lb	0.55	4/93	16r
Pears, Anjou	lb	0.92	4/93	16r
Pork chops, center cut, bone-in	lb	3.13	4/93	16r
Potato chips	16 oz	2.94	4/93	16r
Potatoes, white	lb	0.43	4/93	16r
Rib roast, USDA choice, bone-in	lb	4.63	4/93	16r
Rice, white, long grain, uncooked	lb	0.45	4/93	16r
Round roast, graded & ungraded, ex USDA prime & choice	lb	3.03	4/93	16r
Round roast, USDA choice, boneless	lb	3.09	4/93	16r
Sausage, fresh, loose	lb	2.08	4/93	16r
Short ribs, bone-in	lb	2.66	4/93	16r
Shortening, vegetable oil blends	lb	0.69	4/93	16r
Spaghetti and macaroni	lb	0.81	4/93	16r
Steak, rib eye, USDA choice, boneless	lb	6.24	4/93	16r
Steak, round, graded & ungraded, ex USDA prime & choice	lb	3.31	4/93	16r
Steak, round, USDA choice, boneless	lb	3.34	4/93	16r
Steak, sirloin, graded & ungraded, ex USDA prime & choice	lb	4.19	4/93	16r
Steak, sirloin, USDA choice, boneless	lb	4.46	4/93	16r
Steak, T-bone, USDA choice, bone-in	lb	5.25	4/93	16r
Strawberries, dry pint	12 oz	0.92	4/93	16r
Sugar, white	lb	0.39	4/93	16r
Sugar, white, 33-80 oz pk	lb	0.38	4/93	16r
Tomatoes, field grown	lb	0.88	4/93	16r
Tuna, chunk, light	lb	1.79	4/93	16r
Turkey, frozen, whole	lb	1.04	4/93	16r
Yogurt, natural, fruit flavored	1/2 pint	0.57	4/93	16r
Health Care				
Childbirth, cesarean, hospital		5034	91	62r
Childbirth, cesarean, physician's fee		2053	91	62r
Childbirth, normal, hospital		2712	91	62r
Childbirth, normal, physician's fee		1492	91	62r
Mental health care, exp	capita	20.37-28.83	90	38s
Mental health care, exp, state mental health agency	capita	23.24	90	38s
Mental health care, hospital psychiatric services, non-Federal, exp	capita	7.35	88	38s
Mental health care, mental health organization, multiservice, exp	capita	29.19	88	38s
Mental health care, psychiatric hospitals, private, exp	capita	21.55	88	38s
Mental health care, psychiatric partial-care organizations, freestanding, exp	capita	0.24	88	38s
Mental health care, state and county mental hospitals, exp	capita	14.97	88	38s
Mental health care, VA medical centers, exp	capita	1.60	88	38s
Physician fee, family practice, first-visit		75.00	91	62r
Physician fee, family practice, revisit		34.00	91	62r
Physician fee, general practice, first-visit		61.00	91	62r
Physician fee, general practice, revisit		32.00	91	62r
Physician fee, general surgeon, first-visit		64.00	91	62r
Physician fee, general surgeon, revisit		40.00	91	62r
Physician fee, internal medicine, first-visit		98.00	91	62r
Physician fee, internal medicine, revisit		40.00	91	62r
Physician fee, median, neurosurgeon, first-visit		130.00	91	62r

Lexington-Fayette, KY - continued

Item	Per	Value	Date	Ref.
Health Care - continued				
Physician fee, median, nonsurgical specialist, first-visit		95.00	91	62r
Physician fee, median, orthopedic surgeon, first-visit		91.00	91	62r
Physician fee, median, plastic surgeon, first-visit		66.00	91	62r
Physician fee, median, surgical specialist, first-visit		62.00	91	62r
Physician fee, neurosurgeon, revisit		50.00	91	62r
Physician fee, nonsurgical specialist, revisit		40.00	91	62r
Physician fee, obstetrics/gynecology, first-visit		64.00	91	62r
Physician fee, obstetrics/gynecology, revisit		41.00	91	62r
Physician fee, orthopedic surgeon, revisit		40.00	91	62r
Physician fee, pediatrician, first-visit		49.00	91	62r
Physician fee, pediatrician, revisit		33.00	91	62r
Physician fee, plastic surgeon, revisit		43.00	91	62r
Physician fee, surgical specialist, revisit		37.00	91	62r
Substance abuse, hospital ancillary charge	incident	1090	90	70s
Substance abuse, hospital physician charge	incident	640	90	70s
Substance abuse, hospital room and board	incident	5780	90	70s
Housing				
Home, median price	unit	78.70		26c
Rental unit, 1 bedroom	month	405	93	23c
Rental unit, 2 bedroom	month	474	93	23c
Rental unit, 3 bedroom	month	596	93	23c
Rental unit, 4 bedroom	month	667	93	23c
Rental unit, efficiency	month	332	93	23c
Insurance and Pensions				
Auto insurance, private passenger	year	543.37	91	63s
Taxes				
Tax, cigarette	pack	3	91	77s
Tax, gasoline	gal	15	91	77s
Taxes, state	capita	1358	91	77s
Transportation				
Driver's license fee		8.00	12/90	43s
Travel				
Business travel	day	193.00	4/93	89r
Utilities				
Electricity	mil Btu	13.17	90	64s

Lima, OH

Item	Per	Value	Date	Ref.
Child Care				
Child care fee, average, center	hour	1.63	90	65r
Child care fee, average, nonregulated family day care	hour	1.83	90	65r
Child care fee, average, regulated family day care	hour	1.42	90	65r
Communications				
Long-distance telephone service, day, initial minute, 0-100 miles	min	0.26-0.43	91	12s
Long-distance telephone service, day, additional minute, 0-100 miles	min	0.14-0.24	91	12s
Long-distance telephone service, evenings/weekends, 0-100 mi, initial minute	min	0.11-0.17	91	12s
Long-distance telephone service, evenings/weekends, 0-100 mi, additional minute	min	0.06-0.10	91	12s
Education				
Board, 4-yr private college/university	year	1872	91	22s
Board, 4-yr public college/university	year	1742	91	22s
Expenditures, local gov't, public elementary/secondary	pupil	5451	92	20s
Room, 4-year private college/university	year	1695	91	22s

Values are in dollars or fractions of dollars. In the column headed *Ref*, references are shown to sources. Each reference is followed by a letter. These refer to the geographical level for which data were reported: s=State, r=Region, and c=City or metro. The abbreviation *ex* is used to mean *except* or *excluding*; *exp* stands for expenditures. For other abbreviations and further explanations, please see the Introduction.

Lima, OH - continued

Item	Per	Value	Date	Ref.
Education				
Room, 4-year public college/university	year	2259	91	22s
Tuition, 2-year private college/university	year	6093	91	22s
Tuition, 2-year public college/university	year	1768	91	22s
Tuition, 4-year private college/university	year	8729	91	22s
Tuition, 4-year public college/university, in-state	year	2622	91	22s
Energy and Fuels				
Coal	mil Btu	1.54	90	64s
Energy	mil Btu	8.32	90	64s
Energy exp/householder, 1-family unit	year	471	90	28r
Energy exp/householder, <1,000 sq ft heating area	year	430	90	28r
Energy exp/householder, 1,000-1,999 sq ft heating area	year	481	90	28r
Energy exp/householder, 2,000+ sq ft heating area	year	473	90	28r
Energy exp/householder, mobile home	year	430	90	28r
Energy exp/householder, multifamily	year	461	90	28r
Gas, natural	mil Btu	4.54	90	64s
Gas, natural	000 cu ft	5.28	91	46s
Gas, natural, exp	year	606	91	46s
Gasoline, unleaded regular	mil Btu	9.35	90	64s
Entertainment				
Miniature golf admission	adult	6.18	92	1r
Miniature golf admission	child	5.14	92	1r
Waterpark admission	adult	11.00	92	1r
Waterpark admission	child	8.55	92	1r
Funerals				
Casket, 18-gauge steel, velvet interior		1926.72	91	24r
Cosmetology, hair care, etc.		97.64	91	24r
Embalming		249.14	91	24r
Facility use for ceremony		208.59	91	24r
Hearse, local		130.12	91	24r
Limousine, local		104.66	91	24r
Remains to funeral home, transfer		93.61	91	24r
Service charge, professional		724.62	91	24r
Vault, concrete, non-metallic liner		734.53	91	24r
Viewing facilities, use		236.06	91	24r
Groceries				
Apples, Red Delicious	lb	0.77	4/93	16r
Bacon	lb	1.85	4/93	16r
Bananas	lb	0.46	4/93	16r
Beef, stew, boneless	lb	2.53	4/93	16r
Bologna, all beef or mixed	lb	2.19	4/93	16r
Bread, white, pan	lb	0.78	4/93	16r
Butter	lb	1.50	4/93	16r
Cabbage	lb	0.40	4/93	16r
Carrots, short trimmed and topped	lb	0.45	4/93	16r
Cheese, Cheddar	lb	3.47	4/93	16r
Chicken, fresh, whole	lb	0.84	4/93	16r
Chicken breast, bone-in	lb	1.94	4/93	16r
Chicken legs, bone-in	lb	1.02	4/93	16r
Chuck roast, graded and ungraded, ex USDA prime and choice	lb	2.43	4/93	16r
Chuck roast, USDA choice, bone-in	lb	2.11	4/93	16r
Chuck roast, USDA choice, boneless	lb	2.44	4/93	16r
Coffee, 100% ground roast, all sizes	lb	2.47	4/93	16r
Cookies, chocolate chip	lb	2.73	4/93	16r
Eggs, Grade A large	doz	0.93	4/93	16r
Flour, white, all purpose	lb	0.21	4/93	16r
Grapefruit	lb	0.45	4/93	16r
Grapes, Thompson Seedless	lb	1.46	4/93	16r
Ground beef, 100% beef	lb	1.63	4/93	16r
Ground beef, lean and extra lean	lb	2.08	4/93	16r
Ground chuck, 100% beef	lb	1.94	4/93	16r
Ham, boneless, excluding canned	lb	2.21	4/93	16r
Honey, jar	8 oz	0.97-1.25	92	5r
Honey, jar	lb	1.25-2.25	92	5r
Honey, squeeze bear	12-oz	1.25-1.99	92	5r

Lima, OH - continued

Item	Per	Value	Date	Ref.
Groceries - continued				
Ice cream, prepackaged, bulk, regular	1/2 gal	2.41	4/93	16r
Lemons	lb	0.82	4/93	16r
Lettuce, iceberg	lb	0.83	4/93	16r
Margarine, stick	lb	0.77	4/93	16r
Oranges, navel	lb	0.50	4/93	16r
Peanut butter, creamy, all sizes	lb	1.82	4/93	16r
Pears, Anjou	lb	0.85	4/93	16r
Pork chops, center cut, bone-in	lb	3.17	4/93	16r
Potato chips	16 oz	2.68	4/93	16r
Potatoes, white	lb	0.26	4/93	16r
Round roast, graded & ungraded, ex USDA prime & choice	lb	2.88	4/93	16r
Round roast, USDA choice, boneless	lb	2.96	4/93	16r
Shortening, vegetable oil blends	lb	0.79	4/93	16r
Spaghetti and macaroni	lb	0.76	4/93	16r
Steak, rib eye, USDA choice, boneless	lb	6.29	4/93	16r
Steak, round, USDA choice, boneless	lb	3.24	4/93	16r
Steak, sirloin, graded & ungraded, ex USDA prime & choice	lb	4.00	4/93	16r
Steak, sirloin, USDA choice, bone-in	lb	3.57	4/93	16r
Steak, sirloin, USDA choice, boneless	lb	4.17	4/93	16r
Steak, T-bone, USDA choice, bone-in	lb	5.60	4/93	16r
Strawberries, dry pint	12 oz	0.90	4/93	16r
Sugar, white	lb	0.36	4/93	16r
Sugar, white, 33-80 oz pk	lb	0.35	4/93	16r
Tomatoes, field grown	lb	0.99	4/93	16r
Tuna, chunk, light	lb	1.76	4/93	16r
Turkey, frozen, whole	lb	0.91	4/93	16r
Health Care				
Childbirth, cesarean, hospital		4688	91	62r
Childbirth, cesarean, physician's fee		2053	91	62r
Childbirth, normal, hospital		2657	91	62r
Childbirth, normal, physician's fee		1492	91	62r
Medical plan per employee	year	3443	91	45r
Mental health care, exp	capita	37.60-53.67	90	38s
Mental health care, exp, state mental health agency	capita	40.93	90	38s
Mental health care, hospital psychiatric services, non-Federal, exp	capita	15.03	88	38s
Mental health care, mental health organization, multiservice, exp	capita	14.46	88	38s
Mental health care, psychiatric hospitals, private, exp	capita	7.93	88	38s
Mental health care, psychiatric out-patient clinics, freestanding, exp	capita	2.93	88	38s
Mental health care, psychiatric partial-care organizations, freestanding, exp	capita	0.32	88	38s
Mental health care, state and county mental hospitals, exp	capita	23.79	88	38s
Mental health care, VA medical centers, exp	capita	7.76	88	38s
Physician fee, family practice, first-visit		76.00	91	62r
Physician fee, family practice, revisit		33.00	91	62r
Physician fee, general practice, first-visit		61.00	91	62r
Physician fee, general practice, revisit		31.00	91	62r
Physician fee, general surgeon, first-visit		65.00	91	62r
Physician fee, general surgeon, revisit		35.00	91	62r
Physician fee, internal medicine, first-visit		91.00	91	62r
Physician fee, internal medicine, revisit		40.00	91	62r
Physician fee, median, neurosurgeon, first-visit		106.00	91	62r
Physician fee, median, nonsurgical specialist, first-visit		90.00	91	62r
Physician fee, median, orthopedic surgeon, first-visit		83.00	91	62r
Physician fee, median, surgical specialist, first-visit		61.00	91	62r
Physician fee, neurosurgeon, revisit		41.00	91	62r
Physician fee, nonsurgical specialist, revisit		40.00	91	62r
Physician fee, obstetrics/gynecology, first-visit		61.00	91	62r
Physician fee, obstetrics/gynecology, revisit		40.00	91	62r

Values are in dollars or fractions of dollars. In the column headed *Ref*, references are shown to sources. Each reference is followed by a letter. These refer to the geographical level for which data were reported: s=State, r=Region, and c=City or metro. The abbreviation *ex* is used to mean *except* or *excluding*; *exp* stands for expenditures. For other abbreviations and further explanations, please see the Introduction.

Lima, OH - continued

Item	Per	Value	Date	Ref.
Health Care				
Physician fee, orthopedic surgeon, revisit		41.00	91	62r
Physician fee, pediatrician, first-visit		46.00	91	62r
Physician fee, pediatrician, revisit		33.00	91	62r
Physician fee, surgical specialist, revisit		36.00	91	62r
Substance abuse, hospital ancillary charge	inci-dent	940	90	70s
Substance abuse, hospital physician charge	inci-dent	380	90	70s
Substance abuse, hospital room and board	inci-dent	5410	90	70s
Insurance and Pensions				
Auto insurance, private passenger	year	547.38	91	63s
Taxes				
Tax, cigarette	pack	18	91	77s
Tax, gasoline	gal	21	91	77s
Taxes, state	capita	1056	91	77s
Transportation				
Driver's license fee		5.00	12/90	43s
Utilities				
Electricity	mil Btu	17.33	90	64s

Lincoln, NE

Item	Per	Value	Date	Ref.
Composite ACCRA index		89.60	4Q 92	4c
Alcoholic Beverages				
Beer, Miller Lite or Budweiser, 12-oz containers	6 pack	3.98	4Q 92	4c
Liquor, J & B Scotch	750 ml	15.36	4Q 92	4c
Wine, Gallo Chablis blanc, 1.5 liter	bottle	5.14	4Q 92	4c
Child Care				
Child care fee, average, center	hour	1.63	90	65r
Child care fee, average, nonregulated family day care	hour	1.83	90	65r
Child care fee, average, regulated family day care	hour	1.42	90	65r
Clothing				
Jeans, man's denim		19.35	4Q 92	4c
Shirt, man's dress shirt		17.64	4Q 92	4c
Undervest, boy's size 10-14, cotton	3	3.57	4Q 92	4c
Communications				
Long-distance telephone service, day, initial minute, 0-100 miles	min	0.30-0.44	91	12s
Long-distance telephone service, day, additional minute, 0-100 miles	min	0.16-0.29	91	12s
Long-distance telephone service, evenings/weekends, 0-100 mi, initial minute	min	0.15-0.25	91	12s
Long-distance telephone service, evenings/weekends, 0-100 mi, additional minute	min	0.06-0.15	91	12s
Newspaper subscription, daily and Sunday home delivery, large-city	month	9.35	4Q 92	4c
Telephone bill, family of four	month	16.46	4Q 92	4c
Education				
Board, 4-yr private college/university	year	1666	91	22s
Board, 4-yr public college/university	year	963	91	22s
Expenditures, local gov't, public elementary/secondary	pupil	4567	92	20s
Room, 4-year private college/university	year	1436	91	22s
Room, 4-year public college/university	year	749	91	22s
Tuition, 2-year public college/university	year	990	91	22s
Tuition, 4-year private college/university	year	6893	91	22s
Tuition, 4-year public college/university, in-state	year	1592	91	22s
Energy and Fuels				
Coal	mil Btu	0.78	90	64s
Energy	mil Btu	8.43	90	64s

Lincoln, NE - continued

Item	Per	Value	Date	Ref.
Energy and Fuels - continued				
Energy, combined forms, 1,800 sq ft heating area	month	92.29	4Q 92	4c
Energy, exc electricity, 1,800 sq ft heating area	month	25.12	4Q 92	4c
Energy exp/householder, 1-family unit	year	473	90	28r
Energy exp/householder, <1,000 sq ft heating area	year	429	90	28r
Energy exp/householder, 1,000-1,999 sq ft heating area	year	442	90	28r
Energy exp/householder, 2,000+ sq ft heating area	year	498	90	28r
Energy exp/householder, mobile home	year	442	90	28r
Energy exp/householder, multifamily	year	407	90	28r
Gas, natural	mil Btu	3.93	90	64s
Gas, natural	000 cu ft	4.64	91	46s
Gas, natural, exp	year	502	91	46s
Gasoline, motor	gal	1.17	4Q 92	4c
Gasoline, unleaded regular	mil Btu	9.49	90	64s
Entertainment				
Bowling, evening rate	game	1.81	4Q 92	4c
Miniature golf admission	adult	6.18	92	1r
Miniature golf admission	child	5.14	92	1r
Monopoly game, Parker Brothers', No. 9		9.49	4Q 92	4c
Movie	admission	4.50	4Q 92	4c
Tennis balls, yellow, Wilson or Penn, 3	can	3.06	4Q 92	4c
Waterpark admission	adult	11.00	92	1r
Waterpark admission	child	8.55	92	1r
Funerals				
Casket, 18-gauge steel, velvet interior		1952.97	91	24r
Cosmetology, hair care, etc.		90.03	91	24r
Embalming		251.75	91	24r
Facility use for ceremony		180.75	91	24r
Hearse, local		117.51	91	24r
Limousine, local		71.86	91	24r
Remains to funeral home, transfer		81.14	91	24r
Service charge, professional		740.03	91	24r
Vault, concrete, non-metallic liner		801.47	91	24r
Viewing facilities, use		169.33	91	24r
Goods and Services				
ACCRA Index, Miscellaneous Goods and Services		90.10	4Q 92	4c
Goods and services	year	14898	92	36c
Groceries				
ACCRA Index, Groceries		96.60	4Q 92	4c
Apples, Red Delicious	lb	0.77	4/93	16r
Babyfood, strained vegetables, lowest price	4-4.5 oz jar	0.34	4Q 92	4c
Bacon	lb	1.85	4/93	16r
Bananas	lb	0.28	4Q 92	4c
Bananas	lb	0.46	4/93	16r
Beef, stew, boneless	lb	2.53	4/93	16r
Bologna, all beef or mixed	lb	2.19	4/93	16r
Bread, white	24 oz	0.94	4Q 92	4c
Bread, white, pan	lb	0.78	4/93	16r
Butter	lb	1.50	4/93	16r
Cabbage	lb	0.40	4/93	16r
Carrots, short trimmed and topped	lb	0.45	4/93	16r
Cheese, Cheddar	lb	3.47	4/93	16r
Cheese, Kraft grated Parmesan	8-oz canister	2.95	4Q 92	4c
Chicken, fresh, whole	lb	0.84	4/93	16r
Chicken, fryer, whole	lb	0.77	4Q 92	4c
Chicken breast, bone-in	lb	1.94	4/93	16r
Chicken legs, bone-in	lb	1.02	4/93	16r
Chuck roast, graded and ungraded, ex USDA prime and choice	lb	2.43	4/93	16r
Chuck roast, USDA choice, bone-in	lb	2.11	4/93	16r

Values are in dollars or fractions of dollars. In the column headed *Ref*, references are shown to sources. Each reference is followed by a letter. These refer to the geographical level for which data were reported: s=State, r=Region, and c=City or metro. The abbreviation *ex* is used to mean *except* or *excluding*; *exp* stands for expenditures. For other abbreviations and further explanations, please see the Introduction.

Lincoln, NE - continued

Item	Per	Value	Date	Ref.
Groceries				
Chuck roast, USDA choice, boneless	lb	2.44	4/93	16r
Cigarettes, Winston	carton	17.75	4Q 92	4c
Coffee, 100% ground roast, all sizes	lb	2.47	4/93	16r
Coffee, vacuum-packed	13-oz can	2.10	4Q 92	4c
Cookies, chocolate chip	lb	2.73	4/93	16r
Corn, frozen	10 oz	0.63	4Q 92	4c
Corn Flakes, Kellogg's or Post Toasties	18 oz	1.72	4Q 92	4c
Eggs, Grade A large	doz	0.70	4Q 92	4c
Eggs, Grade A large	doz	0.93	4/93	16r
Flour, white, all purpose	lb	0.21	4/93	16r
Grapefruit	lb	0.45	4/93	16r
Grapes, Thompson Seedless	lb	1.46	4/93	16r
Ground beef, 100% beef	lb	1.63	4/93	16r
Ground beef, lean and extra lean	lb	2.08	4/93	16r
Ground beef or hamburger	lb	1.44	4Q 92	4c
Ground chuck, 100% beef	lb	1.94	4/93	16r
Ham, boneless, excluding canned	lb	2.21	4/93	16r
Ice cream, prepackaged, bulk, regular	1/2 gal	2.41	4/93	16r
Lemons	lb	0.82	4/93	16r
Lettuce, iceberg	head	0.46	4Q 92	4c
Lettuce, iceberg	lb	0.83	4/93	16r
Margarine, Blue Bonnet or Parkay cubes	lb	0.60	4Q 92	4c
Margarine, stick	lb	0.77	4/93	16r
Milk, whole	1/2 gal	1.31	4Q 92	4c
Orange juice, Minute Maid frozen	12-oz can	1.34	4Q 92	4c
Oranges, navel	lb	0.50	4/93	16r
Peaches	29-oz can	1.23	4Q 92	4c
Peanut butter, creamy, all sizes	lb	1.82	4/93	16r
Pears, Anjou	lb	0.85	4/93	16r
Peas Sweet, Del Monte or Green Giant	15-17 oz can	0.54	4Q 92	4c
Pork chops, center cut, bone-in	lb	3.17	4/93	16r
Potato chips	16 oz	2.68	4/93	16r
Potatoes, white	lb	0.26	4/93	16r
Potatoes, white or red	10-lb sack	1.47	4Q 92	4c
Round roast, graded & ungraded, ex USDA prime & choice	lb	2.88	4/93	16r
Round roast, USDA choice, boneless	lb	2.96	4/93	16r
Sausage, Jimmy Dean, 100% pork	lb	2.59	4Q 92	4c
Shortening, vegetable oil blends	lb	0.79	4/93	16r
Shortening, vegetable, Crisco	3-lb can	2.14	4Q 92	4c
Soft drink, Coca Cola	2 liter	1.17	4Q 92	4c
Spaghetti and macaroni	lb	0.76	4/93	16r
Steak, rib eye, USDA choice, boneless	lb	6.29	4/93	16r
Steak, round, USDA choice, boneless	lb	3.24	4/93	16r
Steak, sirloin, graded & ungraded, ex USDA prime & choice	lb	4.00	4/93	16r
Steak, sirloin, USDA choice, bone-in	lb	3.57	4/93	16r
Steak, sirloin, USDA choice, boneless	lb	4.17	4/93	16r
Steak, T-bone	lb	4.43	4Q 92	4c
Steak, T-bone, USDA choice, bone-in	lb	5.60	4/93	16r
Strawberries, dry pint	12 oz	0.90	4/93	16r
Sugar, cane or beet	4 lb	1.62	4Q 92	4c
Sugar, white	lb	0.36	4/93	16r
Sugar, white, 33-80 oz pk	lb	0.35	4/93	16r
Tomatoes, field grown	lb	0.99	4/93	16r
Tomatoes, Hunt's or Del Monte	14.5-oz can	0.70	4Q 92	4c
Tuna, chunk, light	6.125-6.5 oz can	0.53	4Q 92	4c
Tuna, chunk, light	lb	1.76	4/93	16r
Turkey, frozen, whole	lb	0.91	4/93	16r
Health Care				
ACCRA Index, Health Care		82.30	4Q 92	4c
Analgesic, Aspirin, Bayer, 325 mg tablets	100	4.89	4Q 92	4c
Childbirth, cesarean, hospital		4688	91	62r

Lincoln, NE - continued

Item	Per	Value	Date	Ref.
Health Care - continued				
Childbirth, cesarean, physician's fee		2053	91	62r
Childbirth, normal, hospital		2657	91	62r
Childbirth, normal, physician's fee		1492	91	62r
Dentist's fee, adult teeth cleaning and periodic oral exam	visit	32.80	4Q 92	4c
Doctor's fee, routine exam, established patient	visit	32.40	4Q 92	4c
Hospital care, semiprivate room	day	222.79	90	27c
Hospital care, semiprivate room	day	275.00	4Q 92	4c
Medical insurance premium, per employee, small group comprehensive	month	299.30	10/91	25c
Medical plan per employee	year	3443	91	45r
Mental health care, exp, state mental health agency	capita	29.07	90	38s
Mental health care, hospital psychiatric services, non-Federal, exp	capita	12.29	88	38s
Mental health care, mental health organization, multiservice, exp	capita	10.57	88	38s
Mental health care, psychiatric hospitals, private, exp	capita	7.24	88	38s
Mental health care, psychiatric out-patient clinics, freestanding, exp	capita	1.81	88	38s
Mental health care, psychiatric partial-care organizations, freestanding, exp	capita	0.05	88	38s
Mental health care, state and county mental hospitals, exp	capita	19.63	88	38s
Mental health care, VA medical centers, exp	capita	0.85	88	38s
Physician fee, family practice, first-visit		76.00	91	62r
Physician fee, family practice, revisit		33.00	91	62r
Physician fee, general practice, first-visit		61.00	91	62r
Physician fee, general practice, revisit		31.00	91	62r
Physician fee, general surgeon, first-visit		65.00	91	62r
Physician fee, general surgeon, revisit		35.00	91	62r
Physician fee, internal medicine, first-visit		91.00	91	62r
Physician fee, internal medicine, revisit		40.00	91	62r
Physician fee, median, neurosurgeon, first-visit		106.00	91	62r
Physician fee, median, nonsurgical specialist, first-visit		90.00	91	62r
Physician fee, median, orthopedic surgeon, first-visit		83.00	91	62r
Physician fee, median, surgical specialist, first-visit		61.00	91	62r
Physician fee, neurosurgeon, revisit		41.00	91	62r
Physician fee, nonsurgical specialist, revisit		40.00	91	62r
Physician fee, obstetrics/gynecology, first-visit		61.00	91	62r
Physician fee, obstetrics/gynecology, revisit		40.00	91	62r
Physician fee, orthopedic surgeon, revisit		41.00	91	62r
Physician fee, pediatrician, first-visit		46.00	91	62r
Physician fee, pediatrician, revisit		33.00	91	62r
Physician fee, surgical specialist, revisit		36.00	91	62r
Household Goods				
Appliance repair, home, service call, washing machine	min labor charge	29.60	4Q 92	4c
Laundry detergent, Tide Ultra, Bold, or Cheer	42 oz	3.69	4Q 92	4c
Tissues, facial, Kleenex brand	175-count box	1.09	4Q 92	4c
Housing				
ACCRA Index, Housing		84.20	4Q 92	4c
Home, median price	unit	67.70		26c
House, 1,800 sq ft, 8,000 sq ft lot, new, urban	total	92875	4Q 92	4c
House payment, principal and interest, 25% down payment	month	511	4Q 92	4c
Mortgage rate, incl. points & origination fee, 30-year fixed or adjustable rate	percent	8.00	4Q 92	4c

Values are in dollars or fractions of dollars. In the column headed *Ref*, references are shown to sources. Each reference is followed by a letter. These refer to the geographical level for which data were reported: s=State, r=Region, and c=City or metro. The abbreviation *ex* is used to mean *except* or *excluding*; *exp* stands for expenditures. For other abbreviations and further explanations, please see the Introduction.

Lincoln, NE - continued

Item	Per	Value	Date	Ref.
Housing				
Rent, apartment, 2 bedrooms - 1-1/2 to 2 baths, unfurnished, 950 sq ft, water	month	430	4Q 92	4c
Rental unit, 1 bedroom	month	402	93	23c
Rental unit, 2 bedroom	month	474	93	23c
Rental unit, 3 bedroom	month	594	93	23c
Rental unit, 4 bedroom	month	665	93	23c
Rental unit, efficiency	month	331	93	23c
Insurance and Pensions				
Auto insurance, private passenger	year	424.72	91	63s
Personal Goods				
Shampoo, Alberto VO5	15 oz	1.35	4Q 92	4c
Toothpaste, Crest or Colgate	6-7 oz	1.87	4Q 92	4c
Personal Services				
Dry cleaning, man's 2-piece suit		6.17	4Q 92	4c
Haircare, woman's shampoo, trim and blow-dry		20.80	4Q 92	4c
Haircut, man's barbershop, no styling		7.90	4Q 92	4c
Restaurant Food				
Chicken, fried, thigh and drumstick		1.99	4Q 92	4c
Hamburger with cheese	1/4 lb	1.79	4Q 92	4c
Pizza, Pizza Hut or Pizza Inn, cheese, thin crust	12-13 in	7.99	4Q 92	4c
Taxes				
Tax, cigarette	pack	27	91	77s
Tax, gasoline	gal	24	91	77s
Taxes, state	capita	1109	91	77s
Transportation				
ACCRA Index, Transportation		102.40	4Q 92	4c
Bus fare	one-way	0.75	3/93	2c
Bus fare, up to 10 miles	one-way	0.79	4Q 92	4c
Driver's license fee		10.00	12/90	43s
Tire balance, computer or spin balance, front	wheel	6.76	4Q 92	4c
Vehicle registration and license plate	year	17.50	93	47s
Utilities				
ACCRA Index, Utilities		84.50	4Q 92	4c
Electricity	mil Btu	16.34	90	64s
Electricity, partial electric and other energy, 1,800 sq ft living area new home	month	67.17	4Q 92	4c

Little Rock, AR

Item	Per	Value	Date	Ref.
Composite ACCRA index		92.70	4Q 92	4c
Alcoholic Beverages				
Beer, Miller Lite or Budweiser, 12-oz containers	6 pack	3.31	4Q 92	4c
Liquor, J & B Scotch	750 ml	15.87	4Q 92	4c
Wine, Gallo Chablis blanc, 1.5 liter	bottle	4.99	4Q 92	4c
Child Care				
Child care fee, average, center	hour	1.29	90	65r
Child care fee, average, nonregulated family day care	hour	0.89	90	65r
Child care fee, average, regulated family day care	hour	1.32	90	65r
Clothing				
Jeans, man's denim		24.39	4Q 92	4c
Shirt, man's dress shirt		21.79	4Q 92	4c
Undervest, boy's size 10-14, cotton	3	2.99	4Q 92	4c
Communications				
Long-distance telephone service, day, initial minute, 0-100 miles	min	0.10-0.42	91	12s
Long-distance telephone service, day, additional minute, 0-100 miles	min	0.08-0.34	91	12s

Little Rock, AR - continued

Item	Per	Value	Date	Ref.
Communications - continued				
Long-distance telephone service, evenings/weekends, 0-100 mi, initial minute	min	0.06-0.23	91	12s
Long-distance telephone service, evenings/weekends, 0-100 mi, additional minute	min	0.04-0.19	91	12s
Newspaper subscription, daily and Sunday home delivery, large-city	month	8.25	4Q 92	4c
Telephone, flat rate	month	15.31	91	11c
Telephone bill, family of four	month	23.63	4Q 92	4c
Education				
Board, 4-yr private college/university	year	1651	91	22s
Board, 4-yr public college/university	year	1253	91	22s
Expenditures, local gov't, public elementary/secondary	pupil	3770	92	20s
Room, 4-year private college/university	year	1111	91	22s
Room, 4-year public college/university	year	1173	91	22s
Tuition, 2-year private college/university	year	2482	91	22s
Tuition, 2-year public college/university	year	648	91	22s
Tuition, 4-year private college/university	year	4464	91	22s
Tuition, 4-year public college/university, in-state	year	1418	91	22s
Energy and Fuels				
Coal	mil Btu	1.62	90	64s
Energy	mil Btu	8.81	90	64s
Energy, combined forms, 1,800 sq ft heating area	month	126.75	4Q 92	4c
Energy, exc electricity, 1,800 sq ft heating area	month	42.57	4Q 92	4c
Energy exp/householder, 1-family unit	year	471	90	28r
Energy exp/householder, <1,000 sq ft heating area	year	384	90	28r
Energy exp/householder, 1,000-1,999 sq ft heating area	year	421	90	28r
Energy exp/householder, 2,000+ sq ft heating area	year	625	90	28r
Energy exp/householder, mobile home	year	271	90	28r
Energy exp/householder, multifamily	year	355	90	28r
Gas, cooking, 10 therms	month	9.54	92	56c
Gas, cooking, 30 therms	month	19.31	92	56c
Gas, cooking, 50 therms	month	27.34	92	56c
Gas, heating, winter, 100 therms	month	47.42	92	56c
Gas, heating, winter, average use	month	61.87	92	56c
Gas, natural	mil Btu	3.27	90	64s
Gas, natural	000 cu ft	4.98	91	46s
Gas, natural, exp	year	408	91	46s
Gasoline, motor	gal	1.08	4Q 92	4c
Gasoline, unleaded regular	mil Btu	8.86	90	64s
Entertainment				
Bowling, evening rate	game	2.25	4Q 92	4c
Miniature golf admission	adult	6.18	92	1r
Miniature golf admission	child	5.14	92	1r
Monopoly game, Parker Brothers', No. 9		8.13	4Q 92	4c
Movie	admission	5.15	4Q 92	4c
Tennis balls, yellow, Wilson or Penn, 3	can	1.98	4Q 92	4c
Waterpark admission	adult	11.00	92	1r
Waterpark admission	child	8.55	92	1r
Funerals				
Casket, 18-gauge steel, velvet interior		2274.41	91	24r
Cosmetology, hair care, etc.		74.62	91	24r
Embalming		229.94	91	24r
Facility use for ceremony		176.61	91	24r
Hearse, local		116.34	91	24r
Limousine, local		72.68	91	24r
Remains to funeral home, transfer		87.72	91	24r
Service charge, professional		712.53	91	24r
Vault, concrete, non-metallic liner		750.55	91	24r
Viewing facilities, use		155.31	91	24r

Values are in dollars or fractions of dollars. In the column headed *Ref*, references are shown to sources. Each reference is followed by a letter. These refer to the geographical level for which data were reported: s = State, r = Region, and c = City or metro. The abbreviation *ex* is used to mean *except* or *excluding*; *exp* stands for expenditures. For other abbreviations and further explanations, please see the Introduction.

Little Rock, AR - continued

Item	Per	Value	Date	Ref.
Goods and Services				
ACCRA Index, Miscellaneous Goods and Services		92.30	4Q 92	4c
Groceries				
ACCRA Index, Groceries		95.70	4Q 92	4c
Apples, Red Delicious	lb	0.79	4/93	16r
Babyfood, strained vegetables, lowest price	4-4.5 oz jar	0.28	4Q 92	4c
Bacon	lb	1.75	4/93	16r
Bananas	lb	0.59	4Q 92	4c
Bananas	lb	0.42	4/93	16r
Beef, stew, boneless	lb	2.61	4/93	16r
Bologna, all beef or mixed	lb	2.24	4/93	16r
Bread, white	24 oz	0.46	4Q 92	4c
Bread, white, pan	lb	0.64	4/93	16r
Bread, whole wheat, pan	lb	0.96	4/93	16r
Cabbage	lb	0.37	4/93	16r
Carrots, short trimmed and topped	lb	0.47	4/93	16r
Celery	lb	0.64	4/93	16r
Cheese, American	lb	2.98	4/93	16r
Cheese, Cheddar	lb	3.28	4/93	16r
Cheese, Kraft grated Parmesan	8-oz canister	3.49	4Q 92	4c
Chicken, fresh, whole	lb	0.77	4/93	16r
Chicken, fryer, whole	lb	0.60	4Q 92	4c
Chicken breast, bone-in	lb	1.92	4/93	16r
Chicken legs, bone-in	lb	1.06	4/93	16r
Chuck roast, graded and ungraded, ex USDA prime and choice	lb	2.40	4/93	16r
Chuck roast, USDA choice, bone-in	lb	2.19	4/93	16r
Chuck roast, USDA choice, boneless	lb	2.38	4/93	16r
Cigarettes, Winston	carton	16.84	4Q 92	4c
Coffee, 100% ground roast, all sizes	lb	2.48	4/93	16r
Coffee, vacuum-packed	13-oz can	2.08	4Q 92	4c
Corn, frozen	10 oz	0.93	4Q 92	4c
Corn Flakes, Kellogg's or Post Toasties	18 oz	2.18	4Q 92	4c
Crackers, soda, salted	lb	1.15	4/93	16r
Eggs, Grade A large	doz	0.66	4Q 92	4c
Eggs, Grade A large	doz	0.96	4/93	16r
Flour, white, all purpose	lb	0.24	4/93	16r
Frankfurters, all meat or all beef	lb	2.01	4/93	16r
Grapefruit	lb	0.44	4/93	16r
Grapes, Thompson Seedless	lb	1.40	4/93	16r
Ground beef, 100% beef	lb	1.58	4/93	16r
Ground beef, lean and extra lean	lb	2.09	4/93	16r
Ground beef or hamburger	lb	1.41	4Q 92	4c
Ground chuck, 100% beef	lb	1.98	4/93	16r
Ham, boneless, excluding canned	lb	2.89	4/93	16r
Ham, picnic, shoulder, bone-in, smoked	lb	1.02	4/93	16r
Ham, rump or steak half, bone-in, smoked	lb	1.48	4/93	16r
Honey, jar	8 oz	0.73-1.19	92	5r
Honey, jar	lb	1.10-1.79	92	5r
Honey, squeeze bear	12-oz	1.19-1.50	92	5r
Ice cream, prepackaged, bulk, regular	1/2 gal	2.41	4/93	16r
Lemons	lb	1.05	4/93	16r
Lettuce, iceberg	head	0.81	4Q 92	4c
Lettuce, iceberg	lb	0.81	4/93	16r
Margarine, Blue Bonnet or Parkay cubes	lb	0.49	4Q 92	4c
Margarine, stick	lb	0.88	4/93	16r
Milk, whole	1/2 gal	1.48	4Q 92	4c
Orange juice, Minute Maid frozen	12-oz can	1.29	4Q 92	4c
Oranges, navel	lb	0.55	4/93	16r
Peaches	29-oz can	1.37	4Q 92	4c
Pears, Anjou	lb	0.92	4/93	16r
Peas Sweet, Del Monte or Green Giant	15-17 oz can	0.59	4Q 92	4c
Pork chops, center cut, bone-in	lb	3.13	4/93	16r
Potato chips	16 oz	2.94	4/93	16r
Potatoes, white	lb	0.43	4/93	16r

Little Rock, AR - continued

Item	Per	Value	Date	Ref.
Groceries - continued				
Potatoes, white or red	10-lb sack	2.63	4Q 92	4c
Rib roast, USDA choice, bone-in	lb	4.63	4/93	16r
Rice, white, long grain, uncooked	lb	0.45	4/93	16r
Round roast, graded & ungraded, ex USDA prime & choice	lb	3.03	4/93	16r
Round roast, USDA choice, boneless	lb	3.09	4/93	16r
Sausage, fresh, loose	lb	2.08	4/93	16r
Sausage, Jimmy Dean, 100% pork	lb	2.53	4Q 92	4c
Short ribs, bone-in	lb	2.66	4/93	16r
Shortening, vegetable oil blends	lb	0.69	4/93	16r
Shortening, vegetable, Crisco	3-lb can	2.22	4Q 92	4c
Soft drink, Coca Cola	2 liter	1.11	4Q 92	4c
Spaghetti and macaroni	lb	0.81	4/93	16r
Steak, rib eye, USDA choice, boneless	lb	6.24	4/93	16r
Steak, round, graded & ungraded, ex USDA prime & choice	lb	3.31	4/93	16r
Steak, round, USDA choice, boneless	lb	3.34	4/93	16r
Steak, sirloin, graded & ungraded, ex USDA prime & choice	lb	4.19	4/93	16r
Steak, sirloin, USDA choice, boneless	lb	4.46	4/93	16r
Steak, T-bone	lb	4.94	4Q 92	4c
Steak, T-bone, USDA choice, bone-in	lb	5.25	4/93	16r
Strawberries, dry pint	12 oz	0.92	4/93	16r
Sugar, cane or beet	4 lb	1.63	4Q 92	4c
Sugar, white	lb	0.39	4/93	16r
Sugar, white, 33-80 oz pk	lb	0.38	4/93	16r
Tomatoes, field grown	lb	0.88	4/93	16r
Tomatoes, Hunt's or Del Monte	14.5-oz can	0.83	4Q 92	4c
Tuna, chunk, light	6.125-6.5 oz can	0.54	4Q 92	4c
Tuna, chunk, light	lb	1.79	4/93	16r
Turkey, frozen, whole	lb	1.04	4/93	16r
Yogurt, natural, fruit flavored	1/2 pint	0.57	4/93	16r
Health Care				
ACCRA Index, Health Care		88.10	4Q 92	4c
Analgesic, Aspirin, Bayer, 325 mg tablets	100	5.23	4Q 92	4c
Childbirth, cesarean, hospital		5034	91	62r
Childbirth, cesarean, physician's fee		2053	91	62r
Childbirth, normal, hospital		2712	91	62r
Childbirth, normal, physician's fee		1492	91	62r
Dentist's fee, adult teeth cleaning and periodic oral exam	visit	42.60	4Q 92	4c
Doctor's fee, routine exam, established patient	visit	33.00	4Q 92	4c
Health care spending, state	capita	1944	3/93	84s
Hospital care, semiprivate room	day	169.80	90	27c
Hospital care, semiprivate room	day	221.80	4Q 92	4c
Medical insurance premium, per employee, small group comprehensive	month	335.80	10/91	25c
Mental health care, exp	capita	20.37-28.83	90	38s
Mental health care, exp, state mental health agency	capita	25.92	90	38s
Mental health care, hospital psychiatric services, non-Federal, exp	capita	5.26	88	38s
Mental health care, mental health organization, multiservice, exp	capita	15.69	88	38s
Mental health care, psychiatric hospitals, private, exp	capita	15.15	88	38s
Mental health care, psychiatric out-patient clinics, freestanding, exp	capita	0.46	88	38s
Mental health care, state and county mental hospitals, exp	capita	6.78	88	38s
Mental health care, VA medical centers, exp	capita	7.18	88	38s
Physician fee, family practice, first-visit		75.00	91	62r
Physician fee, family practice, revisit		34.00	91	62r
Physician fee, general practice, first-visit		61.00	91	62r

Values are in dollars or fractions of dollars. In the column headed *Ref*, references are shown to sources. Each reference is followed by a letter. These refer to the geographical level for which data were reported: s=State, r=Region, and c=City or metro. The abbreviation *ex* is used to mean *except* or *excluding*; *exp* stands for expenditures. For other abbreviations and further explanations, please see the Introduction.

Little Rock, AR - continued

Item	Per	Value	Date	Ref.
Health Care				
Physician fee, general practice, revisit		32.00	91	62r
Physician fee, general surgeon, first-visit		64.00	91	62r
Physician fee, general surgeon, revisit		40.00	91	62r
Physician fee, internal medicine, first-visit		98.00	91	62r
Physician fee, internal medicine, revisit		40.00	91	62r
Physician fee, median, neurosurgeon, first-visit		130.00	91	62r
Physician fee, median, nonsurgical specialist, first-visit		95.00	91	62r
Physician fee, median, orthopedic surgeon, first-visit		91.00	91	62r
Physician fee, median, plastic surgeon, first-visit		66.00	91	62r
Physician fee, median, surgical specialist, first-visit		62.00	91	62r
Physician fee, neurosurgeon, revisit		50.00	91	62r
Physician fee, nonsurgical specialist, revisit		40.00	91	62r
Physician fee, obstetrics/gynecology, first-visit		64.00	91	62r
Physician fee, obstetrics/gynecology, revisit		41.00	91	62r
Physician fee, orthopedic surgeon, revisit		40.00	91	62r
Physician fee, pediatrician, first-visit		49.00	91	62r
Physician fee, pediatrician, revisit		33.00	91	62r
Physician fee, plastic surgeon, revisit		43.00	91	62r
Physician fee, surgical specialist, revisit		37.00	91	62r
Substance abuse, hospital ancillary charge	incident	1680	90	70s
Substance abuse, hospital physician charge	incident	450	90	70s
Substance abuse, hospital room and board	incident	4490	90	70s
Household Goods				
Appliance repair, home, service call, washing machine	min labor charge	28.50	4Q 92	4c
Laundry detergent, Tide Ultra, Bold, or Cheer	42 oz	3.65	4Q 92	4c
Tissues, facial, Kleenex brand	175-count box	1.15	4Q 92	4c
Housing				
ACCRA Index, Housing		83.00	4Q 92	4c
House, 1,800 sq ft, 8,000 sq ft lot, new, urban	total	92000	4Q 92	4c
House payment, principal and interest, 25% down payment	month	512	4Q 92	4c
Mortgage rate, incl. points & origination fee, 30-year fixed or adjustable rate	percent	8.12	4Q 92	4c
Rent, apartment, 2 bedrooms - 1-1/2 to 2 baths, unfurnished, 950 sq ft, water	month	405	4Q 92	4c
Rental unit, 1 bedroom	month	397	93	23c
Rental unit, 2 bedroom	month	467	93	23c
Rental unit, 3 bedroom	month	587	93	23c
Rental unit, 4 bedroom	month	657	93	23c
Rental unit, efficiency	month	327	93	23c
Insurance and Pensions				
Auto insurance, private passenger	year	501.00	91	63s
Personal Goods				
Shampoo, Alberto VO5	15 oz	1.53	4Q 92	4c
Toothpaste, Crest or Colgate	6-7 oz	2.13	4Q 92	4c
Personal Services				
Dry cleaning, man's 2-piece suit		5.44	4Q 92	4c
Haircare, woman's shampoo, trim and blow-dry		24.40	4Q 92	4c
Haircut, man's barbershop, no styling		8.40	4Q 92	4c
Restaurant Food				
Chicken, fried, thigh and drumstick		2.56	4Q 92	4c
Hamburger with cheese	1/4 lb	1.81	4Q 92	4c

Little Rock, AR - continued

Item	Per	Value	Date	Ref.
Restaurant Food - continued				
Pizza, Pizza Hut or Pizza Inn, cheese, thin crust	12-13 in	7.69	4Q 92	4c
Taxes				
Tax, cigarette	pack	22	91	77s
Tax, gasoline	gal	18.50	91	77s
Taxes, state	capita	997	91	77s
Transportation				
ACCRA Index, Transportation		98.00	4Q 92	4c
Auto rental, average	day	42.67	6/91	60c
Bus fare	one-way	0.80	3/93	2c
Bus fare, up to 10 miles	one-way	0.80	4Q 92	4c
Driver's license fee		14.25	12/90	43s
Limo fare, airport-city, average	day	15.00	6/91	60c
Taxi fare, airport-city, average	day	7.50	6/91	60c
Tire balance, computer or spin balance, front	wheel	6.60	4Q 92	4c
Vehicle registration and license plate	year	17.00-30.00	93	10s
Travel				
Breakfast	day	5.14	6/91	60c
Business travel	day	193.00	4/93	89r
Dinner	day	16.37	6/91	60c
Lodging	day	78.36	91	60c
Lunch	day	6.97	6/91	60c
Utilities				
ACCRA Index, Utilities		116.60	4Q 92	4c
Electricity	mil Btu	19.78	90	64s
Electricity, partial electric and other energy, 1,800 sq ft living area new home	month	84.18	4Q 92	4c
Electricity, winter, 250 KWh	month	31.83	92	55c
Electricity, winter, 500 KWh	month	56.38	92	55c
Electricity, winter, 750 KWh	month	80.91	92	55c
Electricity, winter, 1000 KWh	month	105.43	92	55c

Longview, TX

Item	Per	Value	Date	Ref.
Composite ACCRA index		92.60	4Q 92	4c
Alcoholic Beverages				
Beer, Miller Lite or Budweiser, 12-oz containers	6 pack	4.07	4Q 92	4c
Liquor, J & B Scotch	750 ml	16.60	4Q 92	4c
Wine, Gallo Chablis blanc, 1.5 liter	bottle	4.64	4Q 92	4c
Child Care				
Child care fee, average, center	hour	1.29	90	65r
Child care fee, average, nonregulated family day care	hour	0.89	90	65r
Child care fee, average, regulated family day care	hour	1.32	90	65r
Clothing				
Jeans, man's denim		31.97	4Q 92	4c
Shirt, man's dress shirt		23.50	4Q 92	4c
Undervest, boy's size 10-14, cotton	3	5.19	4Q 92	4c
Communications				
Long-distance telephone service, day, initial minute, 0-100 miles	min	0.10-0.46	91	12s
Long-distance telephone service, day, additional minute, 0-100 miles	min	0.06-0.45	91	12s
Newspaper subscription, daily and Sunday home delivery, large-city	month	7.75	4Q 92	4c
Telephone, flat rate	month	8.80	91	11c
Telephone bill, family of four	month	13.80	4Q 92	4c
Education				
Board, 4-yr private college/university	year	1883	91	22s
Board, 4-yr public college/university	year	1605	91	22s

Values are in dollars or fractions of dollars. In the column headed *Ref*, references are shown to sources. Each reference is followed by a letter. These refer to the geographical level for which data were reported: s=State, r=Region, and c=City or metro. The abbreviation *ex* is used to mean *except* or *excluding*; *exp* stands for expenditures. For other abbreviations and further explanations, please see the Introduction.

Longview, TX - continued

Item	Per	Value	Date	Ref.
Education				
Expenditures, local gov't, public elementary/secondary	pupil	4593	92	20s
Room, 4-year private college/university	year	1620	91	22s
Room, 4-year public college/university	year	1532	91	22s
Tuition, 2-year private college/university	year	4394	91	22s
Tuition, 2-year public college/university	year	495	91	22s
Tuition, 4-year private college/university	year	6497	91	22s
Tuition, 4-year public college/university, in-state	year	986	91	22s
Energy and Fuels				
Coal	mil Btu	1.44	90	64s
Energy	mil Btu	6.48	90	64s
Energy, combined forms, 1,800 sq ft heating area	month	95.21	4Q 92	4c
Energy, exc electricity, 1,800 sq ft heating area	month	27.21	4Q 92	4c
Energy exp/householder, 1-family unit	year	471	90	28r
Energy exp/householder, <1,000 sq ft heating area	year	384	90	28r
Energy exp/householder, 1,000-1,999 sq ft heating area	year	421	90	28r
Energy exp/householder, 2,000+ sq ft heating area	year	625	90	28r
Energy exp/householder, mobile home	year	271	90	28r
Energy exp/householder, multifamily	year	355	90	28r
Gas, natural	mil Btu	2.47	90	64s
Gas, natural	000 cu ft	5.71	91	46s
Gas, natural, exp	year	388	91	46s
Gasoline, motor	gal	1.11	4Q 92	4c
Gasoline, unleaded regular	mil Btu	9.16	90	64s
Entertainment				
Bowling, evening rate	game	2.08	4Q 92	4c
Miniature golf admission	adult	6.18	92	1r
Miniature golf admission	child	5.14	92	1r
Monopoly game, Parker Brothers', No. 9		11.41	4Q 92	4c
Movie	admission	5.00	4Q 92	4c
Tennis balls, yellow, Wilson or Penn, 3	can	2.38	4Q 92	4c
Waterpark admission	adult	11.00	92	1r
Waterpark admission	child	8.55	92	1r
Funerals				
Casket, 18-gauge steel, velvet interior		2274.41	91	24r
Cosmetology, hair care, etc.		74.62	91	24r
Embalming		229.94	91	24r
Facility use for ceremony		176.61	91	24r
Hearse, local		116.34	91	24r
Limousine, local		72.68	91	24r
Remains to funeral home, transfer		87.72	91	24r
Service charge, professional		712.53	91	24r
Vault, concrete, non-metallic liner		750.55	91	24r
Viewing facilities, use		155.31	91	24r
Goods and Services				
ACCRA Index, Miscellaneous Goods and Services		102.30	4Q 92	4c
Groceries				
ACCRA Index, Groceries		95.80	4Q 92	4c
Apples, Red Delicious	lb	0.79	4/93	16r
Babyfood, strained vegetables, lowest price	4-4.5 oz jar	0.23	4Q 92	4c
Bacon	lb	1.75	4/93	16r
Bananas	lb	0.43	4Q 92	4c
Bananas	lb	0.42	4/93	16r
Beef, stew, boneless	lb	2.61	4/93	16r
Bologna, all beef or mixed	lb	2.24	4/93	16r
Bread, white	24 oz	0.59	4Q 92	4c
Bread, white, pan	lb	0.64	4/93	16r
Bread, whole wheat, pan	lb	0.96	4/93	16r
Cabbage	lb	0.37	4/93	16r

Longview, TX - continued

Item	Per	Value	Date	Ref.
Groceries - continued				
Carrots, short trimmed and topped	lb	0.47	4/93	16r
Celery	lb	0.64	4/93	16r
Cheese, American	lb	2.98	4/93	16r
Cheese, Cheddar	lb	3.28	4/93	16r
Cheese, Kraft grated Parmesan	8-oz canister	3.39	4Q 92	4c
Chicken, fresh, whole	lb	0.77	4/93	16r
Chicken, fryer, whole	lb	0.63	4Q 92	4c
Chicken breast, bone-in	lb	1.92	4/93	16r
Chicken legs, bone-in	lb	1.06	4/93	16r
Chuck roast, graded and ungraded, ex USDA prime and choice	lb	2.40	4/93	16r
Chuck roast, USDA choice, bone-in	lb	2.19	4/93	16r
Chuck roast, USDA choice, boneless	lb	2.38	4/93	16r
Cigarettes, Winston	carton	18.35	4Q 92	4c
Coffee, 100% ground roast, all sizes	lb	2.48	4/93	16r
Coffee, vacuum-packed	13-oz can	1.74	4Q 92	4c
Corn, frozen	10 oz	0.53	4Q 92	4c
Corn Flakes, Kellogg's or Post Toasties	18 oz	1.85	4Q 92	4c
Crackers, soda, salted	lb	1.15	4/93	16r
Eggs, Grade A large	doz	0.87	4Q 92	4c
Eggs, Grade A large	doz	0.96	4/93	16r
Flour, white, all purpose	lb	0.24	4/93	16r
Frankfurters, all meat or all beef	lb	2.01	4/93	16r
Grapefruit	lb	0.44	4/93	16r
Grapes, Thompson Seedless	lb	1.40	4/93	16r
Ground beef, 100% beef	lb	1.58	4/93	16r
Ground beef, lean and extra lean	lb	2.09	4/93	16r
Ground beef or hamburger	lb	1.45	4Q 92	4c
Ground chuck, 100% beef	lb	1.98	4/93	16r
Ham, boneless, excluding canned	lb	2.89	4/93	16r
Ham, picnic, shoulder, bone-in, smoked	lb	1.02	4/93	16r
Ham, rump or steak half, bone-in, smoked	lb	1.48	4/93	16r
Honey, jar	8 oz	0.73-1.19	92	5r
Honey, jar	lb	1.10-1.79	92	5r
Honey, squeeze bear	12-oz	1.19-1.50	92	5r
Ice cream, prepackaged, bulk, regular	1/2 gal	2.41	4/93	16r
Lemons	lb	1.05	4/93	16r
Lettuce, iceberg	head	0.92	4Q 92	4c
Lettuce, iceberg	lb	0.81	4/93	16r
Margarine, Blue Bonnet or Parkay cubes	lb	0.52	4Q 92	4c
Margarine, stick	lb	0.88	4/93	16r
Milk, whole	1/2 gal	1.48	4Q 92	4c
Orange juice, Minute Maid frozen	12-oz can	1.27	4Q 92	4c
Oranges, navel	lb	0.55	4/93	16r
Peaches	29-oz can	1.44	4Q 92	4c
Pears, Anjou	lb	0.92	4/93	16r
Peas Sweet, Del Monte or Green Giant	15-17 oz can	0.44	4Q 92	4c
Pork chops, center cut, bone-in	lb	3.13	4/93	16r
Potato chips	16 oz	2.94	4/93	16r
Potatoes, white	lb	0.43	4/93	16r
Potatoes, white or red	10-lb sack	2.67	4Q 92	4c
Rib roast, USDA choice, bone-in	lb	4.63	4/93	16r
Rice, white, long grain, uncooked	lb	0.45	4/93	16r
Round roast, graded & ungraded, ex USDA prime & choice	lb	3.03	4/93	16r
Round roast, USDA choice, boneless	lb	3.09	4/93	16r
Sausage, fresh, loose	lb	2.08	4/93	16r
Sausage, Jimmy Dean, 100% pork	lb	2.85	4Q 92	4c
Short ribs, bone-in	lb	2.66	4/93	16r
Shortening, vegetable oil blends	lb	0.69	4/93	16r
Shortening, vegetable, Crisco	3-lb can	1.81	4Q 92	4c
Soft drink, Coca Cola	2 liter	1.04	4Q 92	4c
Spaghetti and macaroni	lb	0.81	4/93	16r
Steak, rib eye, USDA choice, boneless	lb	6.24	4/93	16r

Values are in dollars or fractions of dollars. In the column headed *Ref*, references are shown to sources. Each reference is followed by a letter. These refer to the geographical level for which data were reported: s=State, r=Region, and c=City or metro. The abbreviation *ex* is used to mean *except* or *excluding*; *exp* stands for expenditures. For other abbreviations and further explanations, please see the Introduction.

Longview, TX - continued

Item	Per	Value	Date	Ref.
Groceries				
Steak, round, graded & ungraded, ex USDA prime & choice	lb	3.31	4/93	16r
Steak, round, USDA choice, boneless	lb	3.34	4/93	16r
Steak, sirloin, graded & ungraded, ex USDA prime & choice	lb	4.19	4/93	16r
Steak, sirloin, USDA choice, boneless	lb	4.46	4/93	16r
Steak, T-bone	lb	5.13	4Q 92	4c
Steak, T-bone, USDA choice, bone-in	lb	5.25	4/93	16r
Strawberries, dry pint	12 oz	0.92	4/93	16r
Sugar, cane or beet	4 lb	1.46	4Q 92	4c
Sugar, white	lb	0.39	4/93	16r
Sugar, white, 33-80 oz pk	lb	0.38	4/93	16r
Tomatoes, field grown	lb	0.88	4/93	16r
Tomatoes, Hunt's or Del Monte	14.5-oz can	0.56	4Q 92	4c
Tuna, chunk, light	6.125-6.5 oz can	0.57	4Q 92	4c
Tuna, chunk, light	lb	1.79	4/93	16r
Turkey, frozen, whole	lb	1.04	4/93	16r
Yogurt, natural, fruit flavored	1/2 pint	0.57	4/93	16r
Health Care				
ACCRA Index, Health Care		83.10	4Q 92	4c
Analgesic, Aspirin, Bayer, 325 mg tablets	100	4.86	4Q 92	4c
Childbirth, cesarean, hospital		5034	91	62r
Childbirth, cesarean, physician's fee		2053	91	62r
Childbirth, normal, hospital		2712	91	62r
Childbirth, normal, physician's fee		1492	91	62r
Dentist's fee, adult teeth cleaning and periodic oral exam	visit	37.00	4Q 92	4c
Doctor's fee, routine exam, established patient	visit	29.80	4Q 92	4c
Health care spending, state	capita	2192	3/93	84s
Hospital care, semiprivate room	day	214.88	90	27c
Hospital care, semiprivate room	day	277.00	4Q 92	4c
Medical insurance premium, per employee, small group comprehensive	month	349.45	10/91	25c
Mental health care, exp	capita	20.37-28.83	90	38s
Mental health care, exp, state mental health agency	capita	22.72	90	38s
Mental health care, hospital psychiatric services, non-Federal, exp	capita	7.95	88	38s
Mental health care, mental health organization, multiservice, exp	capita	12.05	88	38s
Mental health care, psychiatric hospitals, private, exp	capita	37.78	88	38s
Mental health care, psychiatric out-patient clinics, freestanding, exp	capita	0.43	88	38s
Mental health care, state and county mental hospitals, exp	capita	12.54	88	38s
Mental health care, VA medical centers, exp	capita	5.35	88	38s
Physician fee, family practice, first-visit		75.00	91	62r
Physician fee, family practice, revisit		34.00	91	62r
Physician fee, general practice, first-visit		61.00	91	62r
Physician fee, general practice, revisit		32.00	91	62r
Physician fee, general surgeon, first-visit		64.00	91	62r
Physician fee, general surgeon, revisit		40.00	91	62r
Physician fee, internal medicine, first-visit		98.00	91	62r
Physician fee, internal medicine, revisit		40.00	91	62r
Physician fee, median, neurosurgeon, first-visit		130.00	91	62r
Physician fee, median, nonsurgical specialist, first-visit		95.00	91	62r
Physician fee, median, orthopedic surgeon, first-visit		91.00	91	62r
Physician fee, median, plastic surgeon, first-visit		66.00	91	62r
Physician fee, median, surgical specialist, first-visit		62.00	91	62r
Physician fee, neurosurgeon, revisit		50.00	91	62r

Longview, TX - continued

Item	Per	Value	Date	Ref.
Health Care - continued				
Physician fee, nonsurgical specialist, revisit		40.00	91	62r
Physician fee, obstetrics/gynecology, first-visit		64.00	91	62r
Physician fee, obstetrics/gynecology, revisit		41.00	91	62r
Physician fee, orthopedic surgeon, revisit		40.00	91	62r
Physician fee, pediatrician, first-visit		49.00	91	62r
Physician fee, pediatrician, revisit		33.00	91	62r
Physician fee, plastic surgeon, revisit		43.00	91	62r
Physician fee, surgical specialist, revisit		37.00	91	62r
Substance abuse, hospital ancillary charge	incident	3750	90	70s
Substance abuse, hospital physician charge	incident	1080	90	70s
Substance abuse, hospital room and board	incident	5320	90	70s
Household Goods				
Appliance repair, home, service call, washing machine	min labor charge	37.30	4Q 92	4c
Laundry detergent, Tide Ultra, Bold, or Cheer	42 oz	3.70	4Q 92	4c
Tissues, facial, Kleenex brand	175-count box	1.13	4Q 92	4c
Housing				
ACCRA Index, Housing		80.90	4Q 92	4c
House, 1,800 sq ft, 8,000 sq ft lot, new, urban	total	88325	4Q 92	4c
House payment, principal and interest, 25% down payment	month	493	4Q 92	4c
Mortgage rate, incl. points & origination fee, 30-year fixed or adjustable rate	percent	8.16	4Q 92	4c
Rent, apartment, 2 bedrooms - 1-1/2 to 2 baths, unfurnished, 950 sq ft, water	month	409	4Q 92	4c
Rental unit, 1 bedroom	month	409	93	23c
Rental unit, 2 bedroom	month	480	93	23c
Rental unit, 3 bedroom	month	599	93	23c
Rental unit, 4 bedroom	month	673	93	23c
Rental unit, efficiency	month	337	93	23c
Insurance and Pensions				
Auto insurance, private passenger	year	709.79	91	63s
Personal Goods				
Shampoo, Alberto VO5	15 oz	1.03	4Q 92	4c
Toothpaste, Crest or Colgate	6-7 oz	1.75	4Q 92	4c
Personal Services				
Dry cleaning, man's 2-piece suit		5.35	4Q 92	4c
Haircare, woman's shampoo, trim and blow-dry		20.60	4Q 92	4c
Haircut, man's barbershop, no styling		7.85	4Q 92	4c
Restaurant Food				
Chicken, fried, thigh and drumstick		1.84	4Q 92	4c
Hamburger with cheese	1/4 lb	1.90	4Q 92	4c
Pizza, Pizza Hut or Pizza Inn, cheese, thin crust	12-13 in	8.70	4Q 92	4c
Taxes				
Tax, cigarette	pack	41	91	77s
Tax, gasoline	gal	20	91	77s
Taxes, state	capita	923	91	77s
Transportation				
ACCRA Index, Transportation		98.50	4Q 92	4c
Driver's license fee		16.00	12/90	43s
Tire balance, computer or spin balance, front	wheel	6.40	4Q 92	4c
Travel				
Business travel	day	193.00	4/93	89r

Values are in dollars or fractions of dollars. In the column headed *Ref*, references are shown to sources. Each reference is followed by a letter. These refer to the geographical level for which data were reported: s=State, r=Region, and c=City or metro. The abbreviation *ex* is used to mean *except* or *excluding*; *exp* stands for expenditures. For other abbreviations and further explanations, please see the Introduction.

Longview, TX - continued

Item	Per	Value	Date	Ref.
Utilities				
ACCRA Index, Utilities		85.60	4Q 92	4c
Electricity	mil Btu	17.09	90	64s
Electricity, partial electric and other energy, 1,800 sq ft living area new home	month	68.00	4Q 92	4c
Electricity, residential	KWh	5.92	2/93	94s
Electricity, winter, 250 KWh	month	21.46	92	55c
Electricity, winter, 500 KWh	month	35.94	92	55c
Electricity, winter, 750 KWh	month	48.16	92	55c
Electricity, winter, 1000 KWh	month	58.91	92	55c

Lorain-Elyria, OH

Item	Per	Value	Date	Ref.
Child Care				
Child care fee, average, center	hour	1.63	90	65r
Child care fee, average, nonregulated family day care	hour	1.83	90	65r
Child care fee, average, regulated family day care	hour	1.42	90	65r
Communications				
Long-distance telephone service, day, initial minute, 0-100 miles	min	0.26-0.43	91	12s
Long-distance telephone service, day, additional minute, 0-100 miles	min	0.14-0.24	91	12s
Long-distance telephone service, evenings/weekends, 0-100 mi, initial minute	min	0.11-0.17	91	12s
Long-distance telephone service, evenings/weekends, 0-100 mi, additional minute	min	0.06-0.10	91	12s
Education				
Board, 4-yr private college/university	year	1872	91	22s
Board, 4-yr public college/university	year	1742	91	22s
Expenditures, local gov't, public elementary/secondary	pupil	5451	92	20s
Room, 4-year private college/university	year	1695	91	22s
Room, 4-year public college/university	year	2259	91	22s
Tuition, 2-year private college/university	year	6093	91	22s
Tuition, 2-year public college/university	year	1768	91	22s
Tuition, 4-year private college/university	year	8729	91	22s
Tuition, 4-year public college/university, in-state	year	2622	91	22s
Energy and Fuels				
Coal	mil Btu	1.54	90	64s
Energy	mil Btu	8.32	90	64s
Energy exp/householder, 1-family unit	year	471	90	28r
Energy exp/householder, <1,000 sq ft heating area	year	430	90	28r
Energy exp/householder, 1,000-1,999 sq ft heating area	year	481	90	28r
Energy exp/householder, 2,000+ sq ft heating area	year	473	90	28r
Energy exp/householder, mobile home	year	430	90	28r
Energy exp/householder, multifamily	year	461	90	28r
Gas, natural	mil Btu	4.54	90	64s
Gas, natural	000 cu ft	5.28	91	46s
Gas, natural, exp	year	606	91	46s
Gasoline, unleaded regular	mil Btu	9.35	90	64s
Entertainment				
Miniature golf admission	adult	6.18	92	1r
Miniature golf admission	child	5.14	92	1r
Waterpark admission	adult	11.00	92	1r
Waterpark admission	child	8.55	92	1r
Funerals				
Casket, 18-gauge steel, velvet interior		1926.72	91	24r
Cosmetology, hair care, etc.		97.64	91	24r
Embalming		249.14	91	24r
Facility use for ceremony		208.59	91	24r
Hearse, local		130.12	91	24r
Limousine, local		104.66	91	24r

Lorain-Elyria, OH - continued

Item	Per	Value	Date	Ref.
Funerals - continued				
Remains to funeral home, transfer		93.61	91	24r
Service charge, professional		724.62	91	24r
Vault, concrete, non-metallic liner		734.53	91	24r
Viewing facilities, use		236.06	91	24r
Groceries				
Apples, Red Delicious	lb	0.77	4/93	16r
Bacon	lb	1.85	4/93	16r
Bananas	lb	0.46	4/93	16r
Beef, stew, boneless	lb	2.53	4/93	16r
Bologna, all beef or mixed	lb	2.19	4/93	16r
Bread, white, pan	lb	0.78	4/93	16r
Butter	lb	1.50	4/93	16r
Cabbage	lb	0.40	4/93	16r
Carrots, short trimmed and topped	lb	0.45	4/93	16r
Cheese, Cheddar	lb	3.47	4/93	16r
Chicken, fresh, whole	lb	0.84	4/93	16r
Chicken breast, bone-in	lb	1.94	4/93	16r
Chicken legs, bone-in	lb	1.02	4/93	16r
Chuck roast, graded and ungraded, ex USDA prime and choice	lb	2.43	4/93	16r
Chuck roast, USDA choice, bone-in	lb	2.11	4/93	16r
Chuck roast, USDA choice, boneless	lb	2.44	4/93	16r
Coffee, 100% ground roast, all sizes	lb	2.47	4/93	16r
Cookies, chocolate chip	lb	2.73	4/93	16r
Eggs, Grade A large	doz	0.93	4/93	16r
Flour, white, all purpose	lb	0.21	4/93	16r
Grapefruit	lb	0.45	4/93	16r
Grapes, Thompson Seedless	lb	1.46	4/93	16r
Ground beef, 100% beef	lb	1.63	4/93	16r
Ground beef, lean and extra lean	lb	2.08	4/93	16r
Ground chuck, 100% beef	lb	1.94	4/93	16r
Ham, boneless, excluding canned	lb	2.21	4/93	16r
Honey, jar	8 oz	0.97-1.25	92	5r
Honey, jar	lb	1.25-2.25	92	5r
Honey, squeeze bear	12-oz	1.25-1.99	92	5r
Ice cream, prepackaged, bulk, regular	1/2 gal	2.41	4/93	16r
Lemons	lb	0.82	4/93	16r
Lettuce, iceberg	lb	0.83	4/93	16r
Margarine, stick	lb	0.77	4/93	16r
Oranges, navel	lb	0.50	4/93	16r
Peanut butter, creamy, all sizes	lb	1.82	4/93	16r
Pears, Anjou	lb	0.85	4/93	16r
Pork chops, center cut, bone-in	lb	3.17	4/93	16r
Potato chips	16 oz	2.68	4/93	16r
Potatoes, white	lb	0.26	4/93	16r
Round roast, graded & ungraded, ex USDA prime & choice	lb	2.88	4/93	16r
Round roast, USDA choice, boneless	lb	2.96	4/93	16r
Shortening, vegetable oil blends	lb	0.79	4/93	16r
Spaghetti and macaroni	lb	0.76	4/93	16r
Steak, rib eye, USDA choice, boneless	lb	6.29	4/93	16r
Steak, round, USDA choice, boneless	lb	3.24	4/93	16r
Steak, sirloin, graded & ungraded, ex USDA prime & choice	lb	4.00	4/93	16r
Steak, sirloin, USDA choice, bone-in	lb	3.57	4/93	16r
Steak, sirloin, USDA choice, boneless	lb	4.17	4/93	16r
Steak, T-bone, USDA choice, bone-in	lb	5.60	4/93	16r
Strawberries, dry pint	12 oz	0.90	4/93	16r
Sugar, white	lb	0.36	4/93	16r
Sugar, white, 33-80 oz pk	lb	0.35	4/93	16r
Tomatoes, field grown	lb	0.99	4/93	16r
Tuna, chunk, light	lb	1.76	4/93	16r
Turkey, frozen, whole	lb	0.91	4/93	16r
Health Care				
Childbirth, cesarean, hospital		4688	91	62r
Childbirth, cesarean, physician's fee		2053	91	62r
Childbirth, normal, hospital		2657	91	62r
Childbirth, normal, physician's fee		1492	91	62r
Medical plan per employee	year	3443	91	45r
Mental health care, exp	capita	37.60-53.67	90	38s

Values are in dollars or fractions of dollars. In the column headed *Ref*, references are shown to sources. Each reference is followed by a letter. These refer to the geographical level for which data were reported: s=State, r=Region, and c=City or metro. The abbreviation *ex* is used to mean *except* or *excluding*; *exp* stands for *expenditures*. For other abbreviations and further explanations, please see the Introduction.

Lorain-Elyria, OH - continued

Item	Per	Value	Date	Ref.
Health Care				
Mental health care, exp, state mental health agency	capita	40.93	90	38s
Mental health care, hospital psychiatric services, non-Federal, exp	capita	15.03	88	38s
Mental health care, mental health organization, multiservice, exp	capita	14.46	88	38s
Mental health care, psychiatric hospitals, private, exp	capita	7.93	88	38s
Mental health care, psychiatric out-patient clinics, freestanding, exp	capita	2.93	88	38s
Mental health care, psychiatric partial-care organizations, freestanding, exp	capita	0.32	88	38s
Mental health care, state and county mental hospitals, exp	capita	23.79	88	38s
Mental health care, VA medical centers, exp	capita	7.76	88	38s
Physician fee, family practice, first-visit		76.00	91	62r
Physician fee, family practice, revisit		33.00	91	62r
Physician fee, general practice, first-visit		61.00	91	62r
Physician fee, general practice, revisit		31.00	91	62r
Physician fee, general surgeon, first-visit		65.00	91	62r
Physician fee, general surgeon, revisit		35.00	91	62r
Physician fee, internal medicine, first-visit		91.00	91	62r
Physician fee, internal medicine, revisit		40.00	91	62r
Physician fee, median, neurosurgeon, first-visit		106.00	91	62r
Physician fee, median, nonsurgical specialist, first-visit		90.00	91	62r
Physician fee, median, orthopedic surgeon, first-visit		83.00	91	62r
Physician fee, median, surgical specialist, first-visit		61.00	91	62r
Physician fee, neurosurgeon, revisit		41.00	91	62r
Physician fee, nonsurgical specialist, revisit		40.00	91	62r
Physician fee, obstetrics/gynecology, first-visit		61.00	91	62r
Physician fee, obstetrics/gynecology, revisit		40.00	91	62r
Physician fee, orthopedic surgeon, revisit		41.00	91	62r
Physician fee, pediatrician, first-visit		46.00	91	62r
Physician fee, pediatrician, revisit		33.00	91	62r
Physician fee, surgical specialist, revisit		36.00	91	62r
Substance abuse, hospital ancillary charge	incident	940	90	70s
Substance abuse, hospital physician charge	incident	380	90	70s
Substance abuse, hospital room and board	incident	5410	90	70s
Insurance and Pensions				
Auto insurance, private passenger	year	547.38	91	63s
Taxes				
Tax, cigarette	pack	18	91	77s
Tax, gasoline	gal	21	91	77s
Taxes, state	capita	1056	91	77s
Transportation				
Driver's license fee		5.00	12/90	43s
Utilities				
Electricity	mil Btu	17.33	90	64s

Los Angeles, CA

Item	Per	Value	Date	Ref.
Composite ACCRA index		134.70	4Q 92	4c
Alcoholic Beverages				
Beer, Miller Lite or Budweiser, 12-oz containers	6 pack	4.03	4Q 92	4c
Liquor, J & B Scotch	750 ml	14.69	4Q 92	4c
Wine, Gallo Chablis blanc, 1.5 liter	bottle	3.88	4Q 92	4c
Child Care				
Child care, on-site	year	4108	93	17c
Child care fee, average, center	hour	1.71	90	65r

Los Angeles, CA - continued

Item	Per	Value	Date	Ref.
Child Care - continued				
Child care fee, average, nonregulated family day care	hour	1.32	90	65r
Child care fee, average, regulated family day care	hour	1.86	90	65r
Clothing				
Jeans, man's denim		29.56	4Q 92	4c
Shirt, man's dress shirt		20.50	4Q 92	4c
Undervest, boy's size 10-14, cotton	3	7.70	4Q 92	4c
Communications				
Long-distance telephone service, day, initial minute, 0-100 miles	min	0.17-0.40	91	12s
Long-distance telephone service, day, additional minute, 0-100 miles	min	0.07-0.31	91	12s
Long-distance telephone service, evenings/weekends, 0-100 mi, initial minute	min	0.07-0.16	91	12s
Long-distance telephone service, evenings/weekends, 0-100 mi, additional minute	min	0.03-0.12	91	12s
Newspaper subscription, daily and Sunday home delivery, large-city	month	16.35	4Q 92	4c
Telephone, flat rate	month	8.35	91	11c
Telephone, residential, private line, rotary, unlimited calling	month	13.50	10/91	78c
Telephone bill, family of four	month	14.14	4Q 92	4c
Education				
Board, 4-yr private college/university	year	2515	91	22s
Board, 4-yr public college/university	year	2268	91	22s
Expenditures, local gov't, public elementary/secondary	pupil	4866	92	20s
Room, 4-year private college/university	year	2622	91	22s
Room, 4-year public college/university	year	2406	91	22s
Tuition, 2-year private college/university	year	7942	91	22s
Tuition, 2-year public college/university	year	114	91	22s
Tuition, 4-year private college/university	year	10863	91	22s
Tuition, 4-year public college/university, in-state	year	1220	91	22s
Energy and Fuels				
Coal	mil Btu	2.01	90	64s
Energy	mil Btu	9.08	90	64s
Energy, combined forms, 1,800 sq ft heating area	month	90.95	4Q 92	4c
Energy, exc electricity, 1,800 sq ft heating area	month	28.94	4Q 92	4c
Energy exp/householder, 1-family unit	year	362	90	28r
Energy exp/householder, <1,000 sq ft heating area	year	254	90	28r
Energy exp/householder, 1,000-1,999 sq ft heating area	year	358	90	28r
Energy exp/householder, 2,000+ sq ft heating area	year	467	90	28r
Energy exp/householder, mobile home	year	390	90	28r
Energy exp/householder, multifamily	year	252	90	28r
Gas, cooking, 10 therms	month	7.76	92	56c
Gas, cooking, 30 therms	month	17.14	92	56c
Gas, cooking, 50 therms	month	26.53	92	56c
Gas, heating, winter, 100 therms	month	67.87	92	56c
Gas, heating, winter, average use	month	45.68	92	56c
Gas, natural	mil Btu	4.31	90	64s
Gas, natural	000 cu ft	6.27	91	46s
Gas, natural, exp	year	369	91	46s
Gas, piped	100 therms	64.99	4/93	16c
Gas, piped	40 therms	24.28	4/93	16c
Gas, piped	therm	0.67	4/93	16c
Gasoline, all types	gal	1.35	4/93	16c
Gasoline, motor	gal	1.26	4Q 92	4c
Gasoline, regular unleaded, taxes included, cash, self-service	gal	1.46	4/93	16c
Gasoline, unleaded premium 93 octane	gal	1.25	4/93	16c

Values are in dollars or fractions of dollars. In the column headed *Ref*, references are shown to sources. Each reference is followed by a letter. These refer to the geographical level for which data were reported: s=State, r=Region, and c=City or metro. The abbreviation *ex* is used to mean *except* or *excluding*; *exp* stands for expenditures. For other abbreviations and further explanations, please see the Introduction.

Los Angeles, CA - continued

Item	Per	Value	Date	Ref.
Energy and Fuels				
Gasoline, unleaded regular	mil Btu	8.57	90	64s
Entertainment				
Bowling, evening rate	game	2.32	4Q 92	4c
Miniature golf admission	adult	6.18	92	1r
Miniature golf admission	child	5.14	92	1r
Monopoly game, Parker Brothers', No. 9		15.18	4Q 92	4c
Movie	admission	7.17	4Q 92	4c
Tennis balls, yellow, Wilson or Penn, 3	can	2.69	4Q 92	4c
Waterpark admission	adult	11.00	92	1r
Waterpark admission	child	8.55	92	1r
Funerals				
Casket, 18-gauge steel, velvet interior		1781.09	91	24r
Cosmetology, hair care, etc.		84.64	91	24r
Embalming		207.41	91	24r
Facility use for ceremony		205.76	91	24r
Hearse, local		105.14	91	24r
Limousine, local		83.21	91	24r
Remains to funeral home, transfer		113.82	91	24r
Service charge, professional		626.33	91	24r
Vault, concrete, non-metallic liner		599.54	91	24r
Viewing facilities, use		85.81	91	24r
Goods and Services				
ACCRA Index, Miscellaneous Goods and Services		118.80	4Q 92	4c
Goods and services	year	16638	92	36c
Groceries				
ACCRA Index, Groceries		111.70	4Q 92	4c
Apples, Red Delicious	lb	0.80	4/93	16r
Babyfood, strained vegetables, lowest price	4-4.5 oz jar	0.38	4Q 92	4c
Bacon	lb	1.79	4/93	16r
Bananas	lb	0.48	4Q 92	4c
Bananas	lb	0.53	4/93	16r
Bologna, all beef or mixed	lb	2.67	4/93	16r
Bread, white	24 oz	1.15	4Q 92	4c
Bread, white, pan	lb	0.81	4/93	16r
Carrots, short trimmed and topped	lb	0.39	4/93	16r
Cheese, Kraft grated Parmesan	8-oz canister	3.51	4Q 92	4c
Chicken, fresh, whole	lb	0.94	4/93	16r
Chicken, fryer, whole	lb	0.92	4Q 92	4c
Chicken breast, bone-in	lb	2.19	4/93	16r
Chuck roast, graded and ungraded, ex USDA prime and choice	lb	2.26	4/93	16r
Cigarettes, Winston	carton	20.64	4Q 92	4c
Coffee, 100% ground roast, all sizes	lb	2.33	4/93	16r
Coffee, vacuum-packed	13-oz can	2.23	4Q 92	4c
Corn, frozen	10 oz	0.89	4Q 92	4c
Corn Flakes, Kellogg's or Post Toasties	18 oz	1.95	4Q 92	4c
Eggs, Grade A large	doz	1.58	4Q 92	4c
Eggs, Grade AA large	doz	1.18	4/93	16r
Flour, white, all purpose	lb	0.22	4/93	16r
Grapefruit	lb	0.52	4/93	16r
Grapes, Thompson Seedless	lb	1.50	4/93	16r
Ground beef, 100% beef	lb	1.44	4/93	16r
Ground beef, lean and extra lean	lb	2.34	4/93	16r
Ground beef or hamburger	lb	1.75	4Q 92	4c
Ham, boneless, excluding canned	lb	2.56	4/93	16r
Honey, jar	8 oz	0.89-1.00	92	5r
Honey, jar	lb	1.35-1.97	92	5r
Honey, squeeze bear	12-oz	1.19-1.50	92	5r
Ice cream, prepackaged, bulk, regular	1/2 gal	2.40	4/93	16r
Lemons	lb	0.81	4/93	16r
Lettuce, iceberg	head	0.87	4Q 92	4c
Lettuce, iceberg	lb	0.84	4/93	16r
Margarine, Blue Bonnet or Parkay cubes	lb	0.77	4Q 92	4c
Margarine, stick	lb	0.81	4/93	16r

Los Angeles, CA - continued

Item	Per	Value	Date	Ref.
Groceries - continued				
Milk, whole	1/2 gal	1.40	4Q 92	4c
Orange juice, Minute Maid frozen	12-oz can	1.52	4Q 92	4c
Oranges, navel	lb	0.48	4/93	16r
Peaches	29-oz can	1.14	4Q 92	4c
Peas Sweet, Del Monte or Green Giant	15-17 oz can	0.70	4Q 92	4c
Pork chops, center cut, bone-in	lb	3.25	4/93	16r
Potato chips	16 oz	2.89	4/93	16r
Potatoes, white	lb	0.38	4/93	16r
Potatoes, white or red	10-lb sack	2.35	4Q 92	4c
Round roast, graded & ungraded, ex USDA prime & choice	lb	3.00	4/93	16r
Round roast, USDA choice, boneless	lb	3.16	4/93	16r
Sausage, Jimmy Dean, 100% pork	lb	2.56	4Q 92	4c
Shortening, vegetable oil blends	lb	0.86	4/93	16r
Shortening, vegetable, Crisco	3-lb can	2.51	4Q 92	4c
Soft drink, Coca Cola	2 liter	1.11	4Q 92	4c
Spaghetti and macaroni	lb	0.84	4/93	16r
Steak, round, graded & ungraded, ex USDA prime & choice	lb	3.34	4/93	16r
Steak, round, USDA choice, boneless	lb	3.24	4/93	16r
Steak, sirloin, graded & ungraded, ex USDA prime & choice	lb	3.75	4/93	16r
Steak, sirloin, USDA choice, boneless	lb	4.49	4/93	16r
Steak, T-bone	lb	4.09	4Q 92	4c
Sugar, cane or beet	4 lb	1.74	4Q 92	4c
Sugar, white	lb	0.41	4/93	16r
Sugar, white, 33-80 oz pk	lb	0.38	4/93	16r
Tomatoes, field grown	lb	1.01	4/93	16r
Tomatoes, Hunt's or Del Monte	14.5-oz can	0.88	4Q 92	4c
Tuna, chunk, light	6.125-6.5 oz can	0.64	4Q 92	4c
Turkey, frozen, whole	lb	1.04	4/93	16r
Health Care				
ACCRA Index, Health Care		143.30	4Q 92	4c
Analgesic, Aspirin, Bayer, 325 mg tablets	100	6.32	4Q 92	4c
Appendectomy		1268	91	62c
Cardizem 60 mg tablets	30	24.04	92	49s
Cector 250 mg tablets	15	35.87	92	49s
Childbirth, cesarean		2554	91	62c
Childbirth, cesarean, hospital		5533	91	62r
Childbirth, cesarean, physician's fee		2053	91	62r
Childbirth, normal, hospital		2745	91	62r
Childbirth, normal, physician's fee		1492	91	62r
Cholecystectomy		1944	91	62c
Coronary bypass surgery, triple		6375	91	62c
Dentist's fee, adult teeth cleaning and periodic oral exam	visit	58.75	4Q 92	4c
Doctor's fee, routine exam, established patient	visit	57.80	4Q 92	4c
Health care spending, state	capita	2894	3/93	84s
Health maintenance organization coverage, employee	year	3189	93	39c
Health maintenance organization medical coverage, employee	year	3189	92	34c
Health maintenance organization medical coverage, employee	year	3189	92	42c
Hospital care, semiprivate room	day	385.89	90	27c
Hospital care, semiprivate room	day	517.40	4Q 92	4c
Hysterectomy		2622	91	62c
Indemnity plan medical coverage, employee	year	4350	92	42c
Indemnity plan medical coverage, employee	year	4350	92	34c
Insurance coverage, traditional, employee	year	4350	93	39c
Lumpectomy		737	91	62c
Medical insurance premium, per employee, small group comprehensive	month	631.45	10/91	25c

Values are in dollars or fractions of dollars. In the column headed *Ref*, references are shown to sources. Each reference is followed by a letter. These refer to the geographical level for which data were reported: s=State, r=Region, and c=City or metro. The abbreviation *ex* is used to mean *except* or *excluding*; *exp* stands for expenditures. For other abbreviations and further explanations, please see the Introduction.

Los Angeles, CA - continued

Item	Per	Value	Date	Ref.
Health Care				
Medical plan per employee	year	3421	91	45r
Mental health care, exp	capita	37.60-	90	38s
		53.67		
Mental health care, exp, state mental health agency	capita	42.32	90	38s
Mental health care, hospital psychiatric services, non-Federal, exp	capita	10.64	88	38s
Mental health care, mental health organization, multiservice, exp	capita	28.56	88	38s
Mental health care, psychiatric hospitals, private, exp	capita	18.60	88	38s
Mental health care, psychiatric out-patient clinics, freestanding, exp	capita	2.28	88	38s
Mental health care, psychiatric partial-care organizations, freestanding, exp	capita	0.24	88	38s
Mental health care, state and county mental hospitals, exp	capita	13.60	88	38s
Mental health care, VA medical centers, exp	capita	2.33	88	38s
Mevacor 20 mg tablets	30	67.62	92	49s
Oophorectomy		1629	91	62c
Physician fee, family practice, first-visit		111.00	91	62r
Physician fee, family practice, revisit		45.00	91	62r
Physician fee, general practice, first-visit		100.00	91	62r
Physician fee, general practice, revisit		40.00	91	62r
Physician fee, internal medicine, first-visit		137.00	91	62r
Physician fee, internal medicine, revisit		48.00	91	62r
Physician fee, median, neurosurgeon, first-visit		157.00	91	62r
Physician fee, median, nonsurgical specialist, first-visit		131.00	91	62r
Physician fee, median, orthopedic surgeon, first-visit		124.00	91	62r
Physician fee, median, plastic surgeon, first-visit		88.00	91	62r
Physician fee, median, surgical specialist, first-visit		100.00	91	62r
Physician fee, neurosurgeon, revisit		51.00	91	62r
Physician fee, nonsurgical specialist, revisit		47.00	91	62r
Physician fee, obstetrics/gynecology, first-visit		95.00	91	62r
Physician fee, obstetrics/gynecology, revisit		50.00	91	62r
Physician fee, orthopedic surgeon, revisit		51.00	91	62r
Physician fee, pediatrician, first-visit		81.00	91	62r
Physician fee, pediatrician, revisit		42.00	91	62r
Physician fee, plastic surgeon, revisit		48.00	91	62r
Physician fee, surgical specialist, revisit		49.00	91	62r
Preferred provider organization medical coverage, employee	year	4457	92	42c
Preferred provider organization medical coverage, employee	year	4457	92	34c
Prostatectomy, retro-pubic		2444	91	62c
Prozac 20 mg tablets	14	33.22	92	49s
Salpingo-oophorectomy		1328	91	62c
Substance abuse, hospital ancillary charge	inci-dent	1760	90	70s
Substance abuse, hospital physician charge	inci-dent	750	90	70s
Substance abuse, hospital room and board	inci-dent	6390	90	70s
Tagamet 300 mg tablets	100	77.08	92	49s
Vasectomy		486	91	62c
Xanax 0.25 mg tablets	90	64.08	92	49s
Zantac 160 mg tablets	60	92.31	92	49s
Household Goods				
Appliance repair, home, service call, washing machine	min labor charge	44.95	4Q 92	4c
Laundry detergent, Tide Ultra, Bold, or Cheer	42 oz	3.22	4Q 92	4c
Tissues, facial, Kleenex brand	175-count box	1.13	4Q 92	4c

Los Angeles, CA - continued

Item	Per	Value	Date	Ref.
Housing				
ACCRA Index, Housing		185.30	4Q 92	4c
Home, median price	unit	213.80		26c
Home, median price	unit	131,200	92	58s
House, 1,800 sq ft, 8,000 sq ft lot, new, urban	total	211420	4Q 92	4c
House payment, principal and interest, 25% down payment	month	1206	4Q 92	4c
Mortgage rate, incl. points & origination fee, 30-year fixed or adjustable rate	per-cent	8.38	4Q 92	4c
Rent, apartment, 2 bedrooms - 1-1/2 to 2 baths, unfurnished, 950 sq ft, water	month	759	4Q 92	4c
Rental unit, 1 bedroom	month	704	93	23c
Rental unit, 2 bedroom	month	829	93	23c
Rental unit, 3 bedroom	month	1036	93	23c
Rental unit, 4 bedroom	month	1161	93	23c
Rental unit, efficiency	month	579	93	23c
Insurance and Pensions				
Auto insurance	year	1513.00	4/93	35c
Auto insurance, private passenger	year	904.37	91	63s
Personal Goods				
Shampoo, Alberto VO5	15 oz	1.31	4Q 92	4c
Toothpaste, Crest or Colgate	6-7 oz	2.20	4Q 92	4c
Personal Services				
Dry cleaning, man's 2-piece suit		6.92	4Q 92	4c
Haircare, woman's shampoo, trim and blow-dry		15.25	4Q 92	4c
Haircut, man's barbershop, no styling		10.20	4Q 92	4c
Restaurant Food				
Chicken, fried, thigh and drumstick		2.12	4Q 92	4c
Hamburger with cheese	1/4 lb	1.99	4Q 92	4c
Pizza, Pizza Hut or Pizza Inn, cheese, thin crust	12-13 in	10.21	4Q 92	4c
Taxes				
Tax, cigarette	pack	35	91	77s
Tax, gasoline	gal	16	91	77s
Taxes, hotel room	day	8.78	92	33c
Taxes, state	capita	1477	91	77s
Transportation				
ACCRA Index, Transportation		121.60	4Q 92	4c
Auto fixed costs, midsize		5787	91	60c
Auto operating cost, midsize		1478	91	60c
Auto rental, average	day	47.25	6/91	60c
Bus fare	one-way	0.25	3/93	2c
Bus fare, up to 10 miles	one-way	1.35	4Q 92	4c
Driver's license fee		10.00	12/90	43s
Limo fare, airport-city, average	day	11.00	6/91	60c
Railway fare, commuter	one-way	6.00	3/93	2c
Railway fare, heavy rail	one-way	1.10	3/93	2c
Railway fare, light rail	one-way	1.10	93	2c
Taxi fare, airport-city, average	day	26.50	6/91	60c
Tire balance, computer or spin balance, front	wheel	8.05	4Q 92	4c
Travel				
Breakfast	day	8.55	6/91	60c
Business travel	day	178.00	4/93	89r
Dinner	day	27.00	6/91	60c
Dinner	day	25.80	92	85c
Lodging	day	145.74	91	60c
Lodging	day	142.00	92	85c
Lunch	day	13.12	6/91	60c
Travel, business	day	209.97	93	88c

Values are in dollars or fractions of dollars. In the column headed *Ref*, references are shown to sources. Each reference is followed by a letter. These refer to the geographical level for which data were reported: s = State, r = Region, and c = City or metro. The abbreviation *ex* is used to mean *except* or *excluding*; *exp* stands for expenditures. For other abbreviations and further explanations, please see the Introduction.

Los Angeles, CA - continued

Item	Per	Value	Date	Ref.
Utilities				
ACCRA Index, Utilities		82.20	4Q 92	4c
Electricity	500 KWh	61.27	4/93	16c
Electricity	KWh	0.12	4/93	16c
Electricity	mil Btu	25.98	90	64s
Electricity, partial electric and other energy, 1,800 sq ft living area new home	month	62.01	4Q 92	4c

Louisville, KY

Item	Per	Value	Date	Ref.
Composite ACCRA index		91.10	4Q 92	4c
Alcoholic Beverages				
Beer, Miller Lite or Budweiser, 12-oz containers	6 pack	3.29	4Q 92	4c
Liquor, J & B Scotch	750 ml	17.76	4Q 92	4c
Wine, Gallo Chablis blanc, 1.5 liter	bottle	4.77	4Q 92	4c
Child Care				
Child care fee, average, center	hour	1.29	90	65r
Child care fee, average, nonregulated family day care	hour	0.89	90	65r
Child care fee, average, regulated family day care	hour	1.32	90	65r
Clothing				
Jeans, man's denim		28.19	4Q 92	4c
Shirt, man's dress shirt		22.20	4Q 92	4c
Undervest, boy's size 10-14, cotton	3	3.04	4Q 92	4c
Communications				
Long-distance telephone service, day, initial minute, 0-100 miles	min	0.20-0.55	91	12s
Long-distance telephone service, day, additional minute, 0-100 miles	min	0.14-0.44	91	12s
Long-distance telephone service, evenings/weekends, 0-100 mi, initial minute	min	0.08-0.22	91	12s
Long-distance telephone service, evenings/weekends, 0-100 mi, additional minute	min	0.06-0.16	91	12s
Newspaper subscription, daily and Sunday home delivery, large-city	month	13.00	4Q 92	4c
Telephone, flat rate	month	16.55	91	11c
Telephone, residential, private line, rotary, unlimited calling	month	22.02	10/91	78c
Telephone bill, family of four	month	25.31	4Q 92	4c
Education				
Board, 4-yr private college/university	year	1522	91	22s
Board, 4-yr public college/university	year	1862	91	22s
Expenditures, local gov't, public elementary/secondary	pupil	4616	92	20s
Room, 4-year private college/university	year	1193	91	22s
Room, 4-year public college/university	year	1153	91	22s
Tuition, 2-year private college/university	year	4662	91	22s
Tuition, 2-year public college/university	year	771	91	22s
Tuition, 4-year private college/university	year	5200	91	22s
Tuition, 4-year public college/university, in-state	year	1444	91	22s
Energy and Fuels				
Coal	mil Btu	1.27	90	64s
Energy	mil Btu	7.91	90	64s
Energy, combined forms, 1,800 sq ft heating area	month	80.43	4Q 92	4c
Energy, exc electricity, 1,800 sq ft heating area	month	38.09	4Q 92	4c
Energy exp/householder, 1-family unit	year	403	90	28r
Energy exp/householder, <1,000 sq ft heating area	year	342	90	28r
Energy exp/householder, 1,000-1,999 sq ft heating area	year	388	90	28r
Energy exp/householder, 2,000+ sq ft heating area	year	434	90	28r
Energy exp/householder, mobile home	year	320	90	28r

Louisville, KY - continued

Item	Per	Value	Date	Ref.
Energy and Fuels - continued				
Energy exp/householder, multifamily	year	338	90	28r
Gas, cooking, 10 therms	month	3.36	92	56c
Gas, cooking, 30 therms	month	10.07	92	56c
Gas, cooking, 50 therms	month	16.79	92	56c
Gas, heating, winter, 100 therms	month	33.58	92	56c
Gas, heating, winter, average use	month	33.58	92	56c
Gas, natural	mil Btu	4.10	90	64s
Gas, natural	000 cu ft	4.87	91	46s
Gas, natural, exp	year	457	91	46s
Gasoline, motor	gal	1.03	4Q 92	4c
Gasoline, unleaded regular	mil Btu	9.25	90	64s
Entertainment				
Bowling, evening rate	game	1.98	4Q 92	4c
Miniature golf admission	adult	6.18	92	1r
Miniature golf admission	child	5.14	92	1r
Monopoly game, Parker Brothers', No. 9		9.88	4Q 92	4c
Movie	admission	6.50	4Q 92	4c
Tennis balls, yellow, Wilson or Penn, 3	can	2.43	4Q 92	4c
Waterpark admission	adult	11.00	92	1r
Waterpark admission	child	8.55	92	1r
Funerals				
Casket, 18-gauge steel, velvet interior		2329.05	91	24r
Cosmetology, hair care, etc.		72.78	91	24r
Embalming		240.71	91	24r
Facility use for ceremony		181.67	91	24r
Hearse, local		106.25	91	24r
Limousine, local		70.92	91	24r
Remains to funeral home, transfer		96.30	91	24r
Service charge, professional		687.09	91	24r
Vault, concrete, non-metallic liner		732.09	91	24r
Viewing facilities, use		190.30	91	24r
Goods and Services				
ACCRA Index, Miscellaneous Goods and Services		95.40	4Q 92	4c
Groceries				
ACCRA Index, Groceries		93.80	4Q 92	4c
Apples, Red Delicious	lb	0.79	4/93	16r
Babyfood, strained vegetables, lowest price	4-4.5 oz jar	0.25	4Q 92	4c
Bacon	lb	1.75	4/93	16r
Bananas	lb	0.46	4Q 92	4c
Bananas	lb	0.42	4/93	16r
Beef, stew, boneless	lb	2.61	4/93	16r
Bologna, all beef or mixed	lb	2.24	4/93	16r
Bread, white	24 oz	0.64	4Q 92	4c
Bread, white, pan	lb	0.64	4/93	16r
Bread, whole wheat, pan	lb	0.96	4/93	16r
Cabbage	lb	0.37	4/93	16r
Carrots, short trimmed and topped	lb	0.47	4/93	16r
Celery	lb	0.64	4/93	16r
Cheese, American	lb	2.98	4/93	16r
Cheese, Cheddar	lb	3.28	4/93	16r
Cheese, Kraft grated Parmesan	8-oz canister	3.29	4Q 92	4c
Chicken, fresh, whole	lb	0.77	4/93	16r
Chicken, fryer, whole	lb	0.71	4Q 92	4c
Chicken breast, bone-in	lb	1.92	4/93	16r
Chicken legs, bone-in	lb	1.06	4/93	16r
Chuck roast, graded and ungraded, ex USDA prime and choice	lb	2.40	4/93	16r
Chuck roast, USDA choice, bone-in	lb	2.19	4/93	16r
Chuck roast, USDA choice, boneless	lb	2.38	4/93	16r
Cigarettes, Winston	carton	15.37	4Q 92	4c
Coffee, 100% ground roast, all sizes	lb	2.48	4/93	16r
Coffee, vacuum-packed	13-oz can	1.90	4Q 92	4c
Corn, frozen	10 oz	0.61	4Q 92	4c

Values are in dollars or fractions of dollars. In the column headed *Ref*, references are shown to sources. Each reference is followed by a letter. These refer to the geographical level for which data were reported: s=State, r=Region, and c=City or metro. The abbreviation *ex* is used to mean *except* or *excluding*; *exp* stands for expenditures. For other abbreviations and further explanations, please see the Introduction.

Louisville, KY - continued

Item	Per	Value	Date	Ref.
Groceries				
Corn Flakes, Kellogg's or Post Toasties	18 oz	1.99	4Q 92	4c
Crackers, soda, salted	lb	1.15	4/93	16r
Eggs, Grade A large	doz	0.78	4Q 92	4c
Eggs, Grade A large	doz	0.96	4/93	16r
Flour, white, all purpose	lb	0.24	4/93	16r
Frankfurters, all meat or all beef	lb	2.01	4/93	16r
Grapefruit	lb	0.44	4/93	16r
Grapes, Thompson Seedless	lb	1.40	4/93	16r
Ground beef, 100% beef	lb	1.58	4/93	16r
Ground beef, lean and extra lean	lb	2.09	4/93	16r
Ground beef or hamburger	lb	1.71	4Q 92	4c
Ground chuck, 100% beef	lb	1.98	4/93	16r
Ham, boneless, excluding canned	lb	2.89	4/93	16r
Ham, picnic, shoulder, bone-in, smoked	lb	1.02	4/93	16r
Ham, rump or steak half, bone-in, smoked	lb	1.48	4/93	16r
Honey, jar	8 oz	0.89-1.09	92	5r
Honey, jar	lb	1.39-2.25	92	5r
Honey, squeeze bear	12-oz	1.00-1.50	92	5r
Ice cream, prepackaged, bulk, regular	1/2 gal	2.41	4/93	16r
Lemons	lb	1.05	4/93	16r
Lettuce, iceberg	head	0.95	4Q 92	4c
Lettuce, iceberg	lb	0.81	4/93	16r
Margarine, Blue Bonnet or Parkay cubes	lb	0.53	4Q 92	4c
Margarine, stick	lb	0.88	4/93	16r
Milk, whole	1/2 gal	1.50	4Q 92	4c
Orange juice, Minute Maid frozen	12-oz can	1.16	4Q 92	4c
Oranges, navel	lb	0.55	4/93	16r
Peaches	29-oz can	1.32	4Q 92	4c
Pears, Anjou	lb	0.92	4/93	16r
Peas Sweet, Del Monte or Green Giant	15-17 oz can	0.54	4Q 92	4c
Pork chops, center cut, bone-in	lb	3.13	4/93	16r
Potato chips	16 oz	2.94	4/93	16r
Potatoes, white	lb	0.43	4/93	16r
Potatoes, white or red	10-lb sack	1.75	4Q 92	4c
Rib roast, USDA choice, bone-in	lb	4.63	4/93	16r
Rice, white, long grain, uncooked	lb	0.45	4/93	16r
Round roast, graded & ungraded, ex USDA prime & choice	lb	3.03	4/93	16r
Round roast, USDA choice, boneless	lb	3.09	4/93	16r
Sausage, fresh, loose	lb	2.08	4/93	16r
Sausage, Jimmy Dean, 100% pork	lb	2.09	4Q 92	4c
Short ribs, bone-in	lb	2.66	4/93	16r
Shortening, vegetable oil blends	lb	0.69	4/93	16r
Shortening, vegetable, Crisco	3-lb can	2.11	4Q 92	4c
Soft drink, Coca Cola	2 liter	0.89	4Q 92	4c
Spaghetti and macaroni	lb	0.81	4/93	16r
Steak, rib eye, USDA choice, boneless	lb	6.24	4/93	16r
Steak, round, graded & ungraded, ex USDA prime & choice	lb	3.31	4/93	16r
Steak, round, USDA choice, boneless	lb	3.34	4/93	16r
Steak, sirloin, graded & ungraded, ex USDA prime & choice	lb	4.19	4/93	16r
Steak, sirloin, USDA choice, boneless	lb	4.46	4/93	16r
Steak, T-bone	lb	5.26	4Q 92	4c
Steak, T-bone, USDA choice, bone-in	lb	5.25	4/93	16r
Strawberries, dry pint	12 oz	0.92	4/93	16r
Sugar, cane or beet	4 lb	1.46	4Q 92	4c
Sugar, white	lb	0.39	4/93	16r
Sugar, white, 33-80 oz pk	lb	0.38	4/93	16r
Tomatoes, field grown	lb	0.88	4/93	16r
Tomatoes, Hunt's or Del Monte	14.5-oz can	0.76	4Q 92	4c
Tuna, chunk, light	6.125-6.5 oz can	0.53	4Q 92	4c
Tuna, chunk, light	lb	1.79	4/93	16r
Turkey, frozen, whole	lb	1.04	4/93	16r

Louisville, KY - continued

Item	Per	Value	Date	Ref.
Groceries - continued				
Yogurt, natural, fruit flavored	1/2 pint	0.57	4/93	16r
Health Care				
ACCRA Index, Health Care		85.40	4Q 92	4c
Analgesic, Aspirin, Bayer, 325 mg tablets	100	3.84	4Q 92	4c
Childbirth, cesarean, hospital		5034	91	62r
Childbirth, cesarean, physician's fee		2053	91	62r
Childbirth, normal, hospital		2712	91	62r
Childbirth, normal, physician's fee		1492	91	62r
Dentist's fee, adult teeth cleaning and periodic oral exam	visit	32.40	4Q 92	4c
Doctor's fee, routine exam, established patient	visit	34.80	4Q 92	4c
Hospital care, semiprivate room	day	265.66	90	27c
Hospital care, semiprivate room	day	334.57	4Q 92	4c
Medical insurance premium, per employee, small group comprehensive	month	328.50	10/91	25c
Mental health care, exp	capita	20.37-28.83	90	38s
Mental health care, exp, state mental health agency	capita	23.24	90	38s
Mental health care, hospital psychiatric services, non-Federal, exp	capita	7.35	88	38s
Mental health care, mental health organization, multiservice, exp	capita	29.19	88	38s
Mental health care, psychiatric hospitals, private, exp	capita	21.55	88	38s
Mental health care, psychiatric partial-care organizations, freestanding, exp	capita	0.24	88	38s
Mental health care, state and county mental hospitals, exp	capita	14.97	88	38s
Mental health care, VA medical centers, exp	capita	1.60	88	38s
Physician fee, family practice, first-visit		75.00	91	62r
Physician fee, family practice, revisit		34.00	91	62r
Physician fee, general practice, first-visit		61.00	91	62r
Physician fee, general practice, revisit		32.00	91	62r
Physician fee, general surgeon, first-visit		64.00	91	62r
Physician fee, general surgeon, revisit		40.00	91	62r
Physician fee, internal medicine, first-visit		98.00	91	62r
Physician fee, internal medicine, revisit		40.00	91	62r
Physician fee, median, neurosurgeon, first-visit		130.00	91	62r
Physician fee, median, nonsurgical specialist, first-visit		95.00	91	62r
Physician fee, median, orthopedic surgeon, first-visit		91.00	91	62r
Physician fee, median, plastic surgeon, first-visit		66.00	91	62r
Physician fee, median, surgical specialist, first-visit		62.00	91	62r
Physician fee, neurosurgeon, revisit		50.00	91	62r
Physician fee, nonsurgical specialist, revisit		40.00	91	62r
Physician fee, obstetrics/gynecology, first-visit		64.00	91	62r
Physician fee, obstetrics/gynecology, revisit		41.00	91	62r
Physician fee, orthopedic surgeon, revisit		40.00	91	62r
Physician fee, pediatrician, first-visit		49.00	91	62r
Physician fee, pediatrician, revisit		33.00	91	62r
Physician fee, plastic surgeon, revisit		43.00	91	62r
Physician fee, surgical specialist, revisit		37.00	91	62r
Substance abuse, hospital ancillary charge	incident	1090	90	70s
Substance abuse, hospital physician charge	incident	640	90	70s
Substance abuse, hospital room and board	incident	5780	90	70s
Household Goods				
Appliance repair, home, service call, washing machine	min labor charge	32.29	4Q 92	4c

Values are in dollars or fractions of dollars. In the column headed *Ref*, references are shown to sources. Each reference is followed by a letter. These refer to the geographical level for which data were reported: s = State, r = Region, and c = City or metro. The abbreviation *ex* is used to mean *except* or *excluding*; *exp* stands for expenditures. For other abbreviations and further explanations, please see the Introduction.

Louisville, KY - continued

Item	Per	Value	Date	Ref.
Household Goods				
Laundry detergent, Tide Ultra, Bold, or Cheer	42 oz	3.03	4Q 92	4c
Tissues, facial, Kleenex brand	175-count box	1.07	4Q 92	4c
Housing				
ACCRA Index, Housing		88.80	4Q 92	4c
Home, median price	unit	69.50		26c
House, 1,800 sq ft, 8,000 sq ft lot, new, urban	total	96800	4Q 92	4c
House payment, principal and interest, 25% down payment	month	540	4Q 92	4c
Mortgage rate, incl. points & origination fee, 30-year fixed or adjustable rate	per-cent	8.15	4Q 92	4c
Rent, apartment, 2 bedrooms - 1-1/2 to 2 baths, unfurnished, 950 sq ft, water	month	451	4Q 92	4c
Rental unit, 1 bedroom	month	347	93	23c
Rental unit, 2 bedroom	month	408	93	23c
Rental unit, 3 bedroom	month	508	93	23c
Rental unit, 4 bedroom	month	570	93	23c
Rental unit, efficiency	month	287	93	23c
Insurance and Pensions				
Auto insurance, private passenger	year	543.37	91	63s
Personal Goods				
Shampoo, Alberto VO5	15 oz	0.97	4Q 92	4c
Toothpaste, Crest or Colgate	6-7 oz	1.64	4Q 92	4c
Personal Services				
Dry cleaning, man's 2-piece suit		6.54	4Q 92	4c
Haircare, woman's shampoo, trim and blow-dry		14.90	4Q 92	4c
Haircut, man's barbershop, no styling		6.70	4Q 92	4c
Restaurant Food				
Chicken, fried, thigh and drumstick		2.22	4Q 92	4c
Hamburger with cheese	1/4 lb	1.76	4Q 92	4c
Pizza, Pizza Hut or Pizza Inn, cheese, thin crust	12-13 in	7.69	4Q 92	4c
Taxes				
Tax, cigarette	pack	3	91	77s
Tax, gasoline	gal	15	91	77s
Taxes, state	capita	1358	91	77s
Transportation				
ACCRA Index, Transportation		92.20	4Q 92	4c
Auto rental, average	day	48.00	6/91	60c
Bus fare	one-way	0.35	3/93	2c
Bus fare, up to 10 miles	one-way	0.60	4Q 92	4c
Driver's license fee		8.00	12/90	43s
Limo fare, airport-city, average	day	4.50	6/91	60c
Taxi fare, airport-city, average	day	10.00	6/91	60c
Tire balance, computer or spin balance, front	wheel	6.40	4Q 92	4c
Travel				
Breakfast	day	5.01	6/91	60c
Business travel	day	193.00	4/93	89r
Dinner	day	15.46	6/91	60c
Lodging	day	81.12	91	60c
Lunch	day	9.14	6/91	60c
Utilities				
ACCRA Index, Utilities		79.30	4Q 92	4c
Electricity	mil Btu	13.17	90	64s
Electricity, partial electric and other energy, 1,800 sq ft living area new home	month	42.34	4Q 92	4c
Electricity, winter, 250 KWh	month	17.49	92	55c
Electricity, winter, 500 KWh	month	31.69	92	55c
Electricity, winter, 750 KWh	month	43.90	92	55c
Electricity, winter, 1000 KWh	month	54.79	92	55c

Loveland, CO

Item	Per	Value	Date	Ref.
Composite ACCRA index		89.50	4Q 92	4c
Alcoholic Beverages				
Beer, Miller Lite or Budweiser, 12-oz containers	6 pack	4.20	4Q 92	4c
Liquor, J & B Scotch	750 ml	16.75	4Q 92	4c
Wine, Gallo Chablis blanc, 1.5 liter	bottle	4.37	4Q 92	4c
Clothing				
Jeans, man's denim		26.79	4Q 92	4c
Shirt, man's dress shirt		20.24	4Q 92	4c
Undervest, boy's size 10-14, cotton	3	3.08	4Q 92	4c
Communications				
Newspaper subscription, daily and Sunday home delivery, large-city	month	10.88	4Q 92	4c
Telephone, flat rate	month	14.22	91	11c
Telephone bill, family of four	month	20.22	4Q 92	4c
Energy and Fuels				
Energy, combined forms, 1,800 sq ft heating area	month	79.62	4Q 92	4c
Energy, exc electricity, 1,800 sq ft heating area	month	40.06	4Q 92	4c
Gasoline, motor	gal	1.21	4Q 92	4c
Entertainment				
Bowling, evening rate	game	2.02	4Q 92	4c
Monopoly game, Parker Brothers', No. 9		7.70	4Q 92	4c
Movie	admission	5.75	4Q 92	4c
Tennis balls, yellow, Wilson or Penn, 3	can	2.14	4Q 92	4c
Goods and Services				
ACCRA Index, Miscellaneous Goods and Services		88.60	4Q 92	4c
Groceries				
ACCRA Index, Groceries		102.00	4Q 92	4c
Babyfood, strained vegetables, lowest price	4-4.5 oz jar	0.32	4Q 92	4c
Bananas	lb	0.59	4Q 92	4c
Bread, white	24 oz	0.50	4Q 92	4c
Cheese, Kraft grated Parmesan	8-oz canister	2.76	4Q 92	4c
Chicken, fryer, whole	lb	0.67	4Q 92	4c
Cigarettes, Winston	carton	16.78	4Q 92	4c
Coffee, vacuum-packed	13-oz can	2.15	4Q 92	4c
Corn, frozen	10 oz	0.66	4Q 92	4c
Corn Flakes, Kellogg's or Post Toasties	18 oz	1.80	4Q 92	4c
Eggs, Grade A large	doz	0.74	4Q 92	4c
Ground beef or hamburger	lb	1.72	4Q 92	4c
Lettuce, iceberg	head	0.91	4Q 92	4c
Margarine, Blue Bonnet or Parkay cubes	lb	0.72	4Q 92	4c
Milk, whole	1/2 gal	1.45	4Q 92	4c
Orange juice, Minute Maid frozen	12-oz can	1.50	4Q 92	4c
Peaches	29-oz can	1.51	4Q 92	4c
Peas Sweet, Del Monte or Green Giant	15-17 oz can	0.72	4Q 92	4c
Potatoes, white or red	10-lb sack	2.58	4Q 92	4c
Sausage, Jimmy Dean, 100% pork	lb	3.53	4Q 92	4c
Shortening, vegetable, Crisco	3-lb can	2.32	4Q 92	4c
Soft drink, Coca Cola	2 liter	1.24	4Q 92	4c
Steak, T-bone	lb	4.81	4Q 92	4c
Sugar, cane or beet	4 lb	1.51	4Q 92	4c
Tomatoes, Hunt's or Del Monte	14.5-oz can	0.81	4Q 92	4c
Tuna, chunk, light	6.125-6.5 oz can	0.67	4Q 92	4c

Values are in dollars or fractions of dollars. In the column headed *Ref*, references are shown to sources. Each reference is followed by a letter. These refer to the geographical level for which data were reported: s=State, r=Region, and c=City or metro. The abbreviation *ex* is used to mean *except* or *excluding*; *exp* stands for expenditures. For other abbreviations and further explanations, please see the Introduction.

Loveland, CO - continued

Item	Per	Value	Date	Ref.
Health Care				
ACCRA Index, Health Care		101.90	4Q 92	4c
Analgesic, Aspirin, Bayer, 325 mg tablets	100	5.10	4Q 92	4c
Dentist's fee, adult teeth cleaning and periodic oral exam	visit	44.40	4Q 92	4c
Doctor's fee, routine exam, established patient	visit	38.10	4Q 92	4c
Hospital care, semiprivate room	day	360.20	4Q 92	4c
Household Goods				
Appliance repair, home, service call, washing machine	min labor charge	22.10	4Q 92	4c
Laundry detergent, Tide Ultra, Bold, or Cheer	42 oz	3.07	4Q 92	4c
Tissues, facial, Kleenex brand	175-count box	1.03	4Q 92	4c
Housing				
ACCRA Index, Housing		84.00	4Q 92	4c
House, 1,800 sq ft, 8,000 sq ft lot, new, urban	total	86575	4Q 92	4c
House payment, principal and interest, 25% down payment	month	482	4Q 92	4c
Mortgage rate, incl. points & origination fee, 30-year fixed or adjustable rate	per-cent	8.12	4Q 92	4c
Rent, apartment, 2 bedrooms - 1-1/2 to 2 baths, unfurnished, 950 sq ft, water	month	493	4Q 92	4c
Personal Goods				
Shampoo, Alberto VO5	15 oz	1.22	4Q 92	4c
Toothpaste, Crest or Colgate	6-7 oz	2.17	4Q 92	4c
Personal Services				
Dry cleaning, man's 2-piece suit		6.10	4Q 92	4c
Haircare, woman's shampoo, trim and blow-dry		9.79	4Q 92	4c
Haircut, man's barbershop, no styling		6.39	4Q 92	4c
Restaurant Food				
Chicken, fried, thigh and drumstick		2.06	4Q 92	4c
Hamburger with cheese	1/4 lb	1.95	4Q 92	4c
Pizza, Pizza Hut or Pizza Inn, cheese, thin crust	12-13 in	7.69	4Q 92	4c
Transportation				
ACCRA Index, Transportation		98.10	4Q 92	4c
Tire balance, computer or spin balance, front	wheel	5.80	4Q 92	4c
Utilities				
ACCRA Index, Utilities		76.00	4Q 92	4c
Electricity, partial electric and other energy, 1,800 sq ft living area new home	month	39.56	4Q 92	4c

Lowell, MA

Item	Per	Value	Date	Ref.
Child Care				
Child care fee, average, center	hour	2.18	90	65r
Child care fee, average, nonregulated family day care	hour	1.83	90	65r
Child care fee, average, regulated family day care	hour	2.02	90	65r
Communications				
Long-distance telephone service, day, initial minute, 0-100 miles	min	0.18-0.31	91	12s
Long-distance telephone service, day, additional minute, 0-100 miles	min	0.08-0.13	91	12s
Long-distance telephone service, evenings/weekends, 0-100 mi, initial minute	min	0.67-0.12	91	12s
Long-distance telephone service, evenings/weekends, 0-100 mi, additional minute	min	0.04-0.05	91	12s

Lowell, MA - continued

Item	Per	Value	Date	Ref.
Education				
Board, 4-yr private college/university	year	2698	91	22s
Board, 4-yr public college/university	year	1741	91	22s
Expenditures, local gov't, public elementary/secondary	pupil	6687	92	20s
Room, 4-year private college/university	year	2945	91	22s
Room, 4-year public college/university	year	2144	91	22s
Tuition, 2-year private college/university	year	7750	91	22s
Tuition, 2-year public college/university	year	1528	91	22s
Tuition, 4-year private college/university	year	12446	91	22s
Tuition, 4-year public college/university, in-state	year	2580	91	22s
Energy and Fuels				
Coal	mil Btu	1.77	90	64s
Energy	mil Btu	10.57	90	64s
Energy exp/householder, 1-family unit	year	588	90	28r
Energy exp/householder, <1,000 sq ft heating area	year	477	90	28r
Energy exp/householder, 1,000-1,999 sq ft heating area	year	517	90	28r
Energy exp/householder, 2,000+ sq ft heating area	year	630	90	28r
Energy exp/householder, mobile home	year	412	90	28r
Energy exp/householder, multifamily	year	498	90	28r
Gas, natural	mil Btu	5.55	90	64s
Gas, natural	000 cu ft	8.11	91	46s
Gas, natural, exp	year	741	91	46s
Gasoline, unleaded regular	mil Btu	9.53	90	64s
Entertainment				
Miniature golf admission	adult	6.18	92	1r
Miniature golf admission	child	5.14	92	1r
Waterpark admission	adult	11.00	92	1r
Waterpark admission	child	8.55	92	1r
Funerals				
Casket, 18-gauge steel, velvet interior		1853.42	91	24r
Cosmetology, hair care, etc.		98.33	91	24r
Embalming		273.94	91	24r
Facility use for ceremony		196.06	91	24r
Hearse, local		145.67	91	24r
Limousine, local		131.07	91	24r
Remains to funeral home, transfer		135.24	91	24r
Service charge, professional		843.16	91	24r
Vault, concrete, non-metallic liner		709.14	91	24r
Viewing facilities, use		229.85	91	24r
Groceries				
Apples, Red Delicious	lb	0.85	4/93	16r
Bacon	lb	2.12	4/93	16r
Bananas	lb	0.54	4/93	16r
Bread, white, pan	lb	0.81	4/93	16r
Butter	lb	2.02	4/93	16r
Carrots, short trimmed and topped	lb	0.51	4/93	16r
Chicken, fresh, whole	lb	1.04	4/93	16r
Chicken breast, bone-in	lb	2.21	4/93	16r
Chicken legs, bone-in	lb	1.16	4/93	16r
Chuck roast, USDA choice, boneless	lb	2.82	4/93	16r
Coffee, 100% ground roast, all sizes	lb	2.66	4/93	16r
Cucumbers	lb	0.85	4/93	16r
Eggs, Grade A large	doz	1.15	4/93	16r
Grapefruit	lb	0.45	4/93	16r
Grapes, Thompson Seedless	lb	1.52	4/93	16r
Ground beef, lean and extra lean	lb	2.36	4/93	16r
Ground chuck, 100% beef	lb	2.02	4/93	16r
Honey, jar	8 oz	0.96-1.75	92	5r
Honey, jar	lb	1.50-3.00	92	5r
Honey, squeeze bear	12-oz	1.50-1.99	92	5r
Ice cream, prepackaged, bulk, regular	1/2 gal	2.80	4/93	16r
Lemons	lb	0.96	4/93	16r
Lettuce, iceberg	lb	0.95	4/93	16r
Margarine, stick	lb	0.81	4/93	16r
Milk, fresh, whole, fortified	1/2 gal	1.30	4/93	16r

Values are in dollars or fractions of dollars. In the column headed *Ref*, references are shown to sources. Each reference is followed by a letter. These refer to the geographical level for which data were reported: s=State, r=Region, and c=City or metro. The abbreviation *ex* is used to mean *except* or *excluding*; *exp* stands for expenditures. For other abbreviations and further explanations, please see the Introduction.

Lowell, MA - continued

Item	Per	Value	Date	Ref.
Groceries				
Oranges, navel	lb	0.56	4/93	16r
Peanut butter, creamy, all sizes	lb	1.88	4/93	16r
Pork chops, center cut, bone-in	lb	3.34	4/93	16r
Potato chips	16 oz	2.88	4/93	16r
Potatoes, white	lb	0.37	4/93	16r
Rib roast, USDA choice, bone-in	lb	4.94	4/93	16r
Round roast, USDA choice, boneless	lb	3.17	4/93	16r
Shortening, vegetable oil blends	lb	0.98	4/93	16r
Spaghetti and macaroni	lb	0.82	4/93	16r
Steak, round, graded & ungraded, ex USDA prime & choice	lb	4.04	4/93	16r
Steak, round, USDA choice, boneless	lb	3.90	4/93	16r
Steak, sirloin, USDA choice, boneless	lb	4.97	4/93	16r
Strawberries, dry pint	12 oz	0.90	4/93	16r
Sugar, white	lb	0.50	4/93	16r
Sugar, white, 33-80 oz pk	lb	0.41	4/93	16r
Tomatoes, field grown	lb	1.23	4/93	16r
Tuna, chunk, light	lb	2.22	4/93	16r
Turkey, frozen, whole	lb	1.04	4/93	16r
Health Care				
Childbirth, cesarean, hospital		5826	91	62r
Childbirth, cesarean, physician's fee		2053	91	62r
Childbirth, normal, hospital		2964	91	62r
Childbirth, normal, physician's fee		1492	91	62r
Health care spending, state	capita	3031	3/93	84s
Medical plan per employee	year	3958	91	45r
Mental health care, exp	capita	53.68-118.35	90	38s
Mental health care, exp, state mental health agency	capita	83.91	90	38s
Mental health care, hospital psychiatric services, non-Federal, exp	capita	22.67	88	38s
Mental health care, mental health organization, multiservice, exp	capita	36.07	88	38s
Mental health care, psychiatric hospitals, private, exp	capita	38.65	88	38s
Mental health care, psychiatric out-patient clinics, freestanding, exp	capita	4.41	88	38s
Mental health care, psychiatric partial-care organizations, freestanding, exp	capita	0.92	88	38s
Mental health care, state and county mental hospitals, exp	capita	30.59	88	38s
Mental health care, VA medical centers, exp	capita	21.14	88	38s
Substance abuse, hospital ancillary charge	incident	1310	90	70s
Substance abuse, hospital physician charge	incident	460	90	70s
Substance abuse, hospital room and board	incident	3450	90	70s
Insurance and Pensions				
Auto insurance, private passenger	year	912.83	91	63s
Taxes				
Tax, cigarette	pack	26	91	77s
Tax, gasoline	gal	21	91	77s
Taxes, state	capita	1615	91	77s
Transportation				
Driver's license fee		35.00	12/90	43s
Travel				
Business travel	day	165.00	4/93	89r
Utilities				
Electricity	mil Btu	25.93	90	64s

Lubbock, TX

Item	Per	Value	Date	Ref.
Composite ACCRA index		95.20	4Q 92	4c

Lubbock, TX - continued

Item	Per	Value	Date	Ref.
Alcoholic Beverages				
Beer, Miller Lite or Budweiser, 12-oz containers	6 pack	5.27	4Q 92	4c
Liquor, J & B Scotch	750 ml	18.89	4Q 92	4c
Wine, Gallo Chablis blanc, 1.5 liter	bottle	5.59	4Q 92	4c
Child Care				
Child care fee, average, center	hour	1.29	90	65r
Child care fee, average, nonregulated family day care	hour	0.89	90	65r
Child care fee, average, regulated family day care	hour	1.32	90	65r
Clothing				
Jeans, man's denim		30.19	4Q 92	4c
Shirt, man's dress shirt		23.80	4Q 92	4c
Undervest, boy's size 10-14, cotton	3	4.69	4Q 92	4c
Communications				
Long-distance telephone service, day, initial minute, 0-100 miles	min	0.10-0.46	91	12s
Long-distance telephone service, day, additional minute, 0-100 miles	min	0.06-0.45	91	12s
Newspaper subscription, daily and Sunday home delivery, large-city	month	8.75	4Q 92	4c
Telephone, flat rate	month	9.10	91	11c
Telephone bill, family of four	month	16.57	4Q 92	4c
Education				
Board, 4-yr private college/university	year	1883	91	22s
Board, 4-yr public college/university	year	1605	91	22s
Expenditures, local gov't, public elementary/secondary	pupil	4593	92	20s
Room, 4-year private college/university	year	1620	91	22s
Room, 4-year public college/university	year	1532	91	22s
Tuition, 2-year private college/university	year	4394	91	22s
Tuition, 2-year public college/university	year	495	91	22s
Tuition, 4-year private college/university	year	6497	91	22s
Tuition, 4-year public college/university, in-state	year	986	91	22s
Energy and Fuels				
Coal	mil Btu	1.44	90	64s
Energy	mil Btu	6.48	90	64s
Energy, combined forms, 1,800 sq ft heating area	month	92.56	4Q 92	4c
Energy, exc electricity, 1,800 sq ft heating area	month	34.89	4Q 92	4c
Energy exp/householder, 1-family unit	year	471	90	28r
Energy exp/householder, <1,000 sq ft heating area	year	384	90	28r
Energy exp/householder, 1,000-1,999 sq ft heating area	year	421	90	28r
Energy exp/householder, 2,000+ sq ft heating area	year	625	90	28r
Energy exp/householder, mobile home	year	271	90	28r
Energy exp/householder, multifamily	year	355	90	28r
Gas, natural	mil Btu	2.47	90	64s
Gas, natural	000 cu ft	5.71	91	46s
Gas, natural, exp	year	388	91	46s
Gasoline, motor	gal	1.16	4Q 92	4c
Gasoline, unleaded regular	mil Btu	9.16	90	64s
Entertainment				
Bowling, evening rate	game	2.19	4Q 92	4c
Miniature golf admission	adult	6.18	92	1r
Miniature golf admission	child	5.14	92	1r
Monopoly game, Parker Brothers', No. 9		10.24	4Q 92	4c
Movie	admission	5.37	4Q 92	4c
Tennis balls, yellow, Wilson or Penn, 3	can	2.37	4Q 92	4c
Waterpark admission	adult	11.00	92	1r
Waterpark admission	child	8.55	92	1r

Values are in dollars or fractions of dollars. In the column headed *Ref*, references are shown to sources. Each reference is followed by a letter. These refer to the geographical level for which data were reported: s=State, r=Region, and c=City or metro. The abbreviation *ex* is used to mean *except* or *excluding*; *exp* stands for expenditures. For other abbreviations and further explanations, please see the Introduction.

Lubbock, TX - continued

Item	Per	Value	Date	Ref.
Funerals				
Casket, 18-gauge steel, velvet interior		2274.41	91	24r
Cosmetology, hair care, etc.		74.62	91	24r
Embalming		229.94	91	24r
Facility use for ceremony		176.61	91	24r
Hearse, local		116.34	91	24r
Limousine, local		72.68	91	24r
Remains to funeral home, transfer		87.72	91	24r
Service charge, professional		712.53	91	24r
Vault, concrete, non-metallic liner		750.55	91	24r
Viewing facilities, use		155.31	91	24r
Goods and Services				
ACCRA Index, Miscellaneous Goods and Services		101.50	4Q 92	4c
Groceries				
ACCRA Index, Groceries		96.80	4Q 92	4c
Apples, Red Delicious	lb	0.79	4/93	16r
Babyfood, strained vegetables, lowest price	4-4.5 oz jar	0.24	4Q 92	4c
Bacon	lb	1.75	4/93	16r
Bananas	lb	0.45	4Q 92	4c
Bananas	lb	0.42	4/93	16r
Beef, stew, boneless	lb	2.61	4/93	16r
Bologna, all beef or mixed	lb	2.24	4/93	16r
Bread, white	24 oz	0.77	4Q 92	4c
Bread, white, pan	lb	0.64	4/93	16r
Bread, whole wheat, pan	lb	0.96	4/93	16r
Cabbage	lb	0.37	4/93	16r
Carrots, short trimmed and topped	lb	0.47	4/93	16r
Celery	lb	0.64	4/93	16r
Cheese, American	lb	2.98	4/93	16r
Cheese, Cheddar	lb	3.28	4/93	16r
Cheese, Kraft grated Parmesan	8-oz canister	3.73	4Q 92	4c
Chicken, fresh, whole	lb	0.77	4/93	16r
Chicken, fryer, whole	lb	0.57	4Q 92	4c
Chicken breast, bone-in	lb	1.92	4/93	16r
Chicken legs, bone-in	lb	1.06	4/93	16r
Chuck roast, graded and ungraded, ex USDA prime and choice	lb	2.40	4/93	16r
Chuck roast, USDA choice, bone-in	lb	2.19	4/93	16r
Chuck roast, USDA choice, boneless	lb	2.38	4/93	16r
Cigarettes, Winston	carton	18.51	4Q 92	4c
Coffee, 100% ground roast, all sizes	lb	2.48	4/93	16r
Coffee, vacuum-packed	13-oz can	1.85	4Q 92	4c
Corn, frozen	10 oz	0.61	4Q 92	4c
Corn Flakes, Kellogg's or Post Toasties	18 oz	2.13	4Q 92	4c
Crackers, soda, salted	lb	1.15	4/93	16r
Eggs, Grade A large	doz	0.85	4Q 92	4c
Eggs, Grade A large	doz	0.96	4/93	16r
Flour, white, all purpose	lb	0.24	4/93	16r
Frankfurters, all meat or all beef	lb	2.01	4/93	16r
Grapefruit	lb	0.44	4/93	16r
Grapes, Thompson Seedless	lb	1.40	4/93	16r
Ground beef, 100% beef	lb	1.58	4/93	16r
Ground beef, lean and extra lean	lb	2.09	4/93	16r
Ground beef or hamburger	lb	1.54	4Q 92	4c
Ground chuck, 100% beef	lb	1.98	4/93	16r
Ham, boneless, excluding canned	lb	2.89	4/93	16r
Ham, picnic, shoulder, bone-in, smoked	lb	1.02	4/93	16r
Ham, rump or steak half, bone-in, smoked	lb	1.48	4/93	16r
Honey, jar	8 oz	0.73-1.19	92	5r
Honey, jar	lb	1.10-1.79	92	5r
Honey, squeeze bear	12-oz	1.19-1.50	92	5r
Ice cream, prepackaged, bulk, regular	1/2 gal	2.41	4/93	16r
Lemons	lb	1.05	4/93	16r
Lettuce, iceberg	head	1.07	4Q 92	4c
Lettuce, iceberg	lb	0.81	4/93	16r
Margarine, Blue Bonnet or Parkay cubes	lb	0.57	4Q 92	4c
Margarine, stick	lb	0.88	4/93	16r

Lubbock, TX - continued

Item	Per	Value	Date	Ref.
Groceries - continued				
Milk, whole	1/2 gal	1.29	4Q 92	4c
Orange juice, Minute Maid frozen	12-oz can	1.23	4Q 92	4c
Oranges, navel	lb	0.55	4/93	16r
Peaches	29-oz can	1.44	4Q 92	4c
Pears, Anjou	lb	0.92	4/93	16r
Peas Sweet, Del Monte or Green Giant	15-17 oz can	0.52	4Q 92	4c
Pork chops, center cut, bone-in	lb	3.13	4/93	16r
Potato chips	16 oz	2.94	4/93	16r
Potatoes, white	lb	0.43	4/93	16r
Potatoes, white or red	10-lb sack	2.18	4Q 92	4c
Rib roast, USDA choice, bone-in	lb	4.63	4/93	16r
Rice, white, long grain, uncooked	lb	0.45	4/93	16r
Round roast, graded & ungraded, ex USDA prime & choice	lb	3.03	4/93	16r
Round roast, USDA choice, boneless	lb	3.09	4/93	16r
Sausage, fresh, loose	lb	2.08	4/93	16r
Sausage, Jimmy Dean, 100% pork	lb	2.29	4Q 92	4c
Short ribs, bone-in	lb	2.66	4/93	16r
Shortening, vegetable oil blends	lb	0.69	4/93	16r
Shortening, vegetable, Crisco	3-lb can	1.98	4Q 92	4c
Soft drink, Coca Cola	2 liter	1.31	4Q 92	4c
Spaghetti and macaroni	lb	0.81	4/93	16r
Steak, rib eye, USDA choice, boneless	lb	6.24	4/93	16r
Steak, round, graded & ungraded, ex USDA prime & choice	lb	3.31	4/93	16r
Steak, round, USDA choice, boneless	lb	3.34	4/93	16r
Steak, sirloin, graded & ungraded, ex USDA prime & choice	lb	4.19	4/93	16r
Steak, sirloin, USDA choice, boneless	lb	4.46	4/93	16r
Steak, T-bone	lb	5.11	4Q 92	4c
Steak, T-bone, USDA choice, bone-in	lb	5.25	4/93	16r
Strawberries, dry pint	12 oz	0.92	4/93	16r
Sugar, cane or beet	4 lb	1.50	4Q 92	4c
Sugar, white	lb	0.39	4/93	16r
Sugar, white, 33-80 oz pk	lb	0.38	4/93	16r
Tomatoes, field grown	lb	0.88	4/93	16r
Tomatoes, Hunt's or Del Monte	14.5-oz can	0.72	4Q 92	4c
Tuna, chunk, light	6.125-6.5 oz can	0.59	4Q 92	4c
Tuna, chunk, light	lb	1.79	4/93	16r
Turkey, frozen, whole	lb	1.04	4/93	16r
Yogurt, natural, fruit flavored	1/2 pint	0.57	4/93	16r
Health Care				
ACCRA Index, Health Care		90.70	4Q 92	4c
Analgesic, Aspirin, Bayer, 325 mg tablets	100	5.91	4Q 92	4c
Childbirth, cesarean, hospital		5034	91	62r
Childbirth, cesarean, physician's fee		2053	91	62r
Childbirth, normal, hospital		2712	91	62r
Childbirth, normal, physician's fee		1492	91	62r
Dentist's fee, adult teeth cleaning and periodic oral exam	visit	43.11	4Q 92	4c
Doctor's fee, routine exam, established patient	visit	31.11	4Q 92	4c
Health care spending, state	capita	2192	3/93	84s
Hospital care, semiprivate room	day	197.26	90	27c
Hospital care, semiprivate room	day	266.80	4Q 92	4c
Medical insurance premium, per employee, small group comprehensive	month	349.45	10/91	25c
Mental health care, exp	capita	20.37-28.83	90	38s
Mental health care, exp, state mental health agency	capita	22.72	90	38s
Mental health care, hospital psychiatric services, non-Federal, exp	capita	7.95	88	38s

Values are in dollars or fractions of dollars. In the column headed *Ref*, references are shown to sources. Each reference is followed by a letter. These refer to the geographical level for which data were reported: s=State, r=Region, and c=City or metro. The abbreviation *ex* is used to mean *except* or *excluding*; *exp* stands for expenditures. For other abbreviations and further explanations, please see the Introduction.

Lubbock, TX - continued

Item	Per	Value	Date	Ref.
Health Care				
Mental health care, mental health organization, multiservice, exp	capita	12.05	88	38s
Mental health care, psychiatric hospitals, private, exp	capita	37.78	88	38s
Mental health care, psychiatric out-patient clinics, freestanding, exp	capita	0.43	88	38s
Mental health care, state and county mental hospitals, exp	capita	12.54	88	38s
Mental health care, VA medical centers, exp	capita	5.35	88	38s
Physician fee, family practice, first-visit		75.00	91	62r
Physician fee, family practice, revisit		34.00	91	62r
Physician fee, general practice, first-visit		61.00	91	62r
Physician fee, general practice, revisit		32.00	91	62r
Physician fee, general surgeon, first-visit		64.00	91	62r
Physician fee, general surgeon, revisit		40.00	91	62r
Physician fee, internal medicine, first-visit		98.00	91	62r
Physician fee, internal medicine, revisit		40.00	91	62r
Physician fee, median, neurosurgeon, first-visit		130.00	91	62r
Physician fee, median, nonsurgical specialist, first-visit		95.00	91	62r
Physician fee, median, orthopedic surgeon, first-visit		91.00	91	62r
Physician fee, median, plastic surgeon, first-visit		66.00	91	62r
Physician fee, median, surgical specialist, first-visit		62.00	91	62r
Physician fee, neurosurgeon, revisit		50.00	91	62r
Physician fee, nonsurgical specialist, revisit		40.00	91	62r
Physician fee, obstetrics/gynecology, first-visit		64.00	91	62r
Physician fee, obstetrics/gynecology, revisit		41.00	91	62r
Physician fee, orthopedic surgeon, revisit		40.00	91	62r
Physician fee, pediatrician, first-visit		49.00	91	62r
Physician fee, pediatrician, revisit		33.00	91	62r
Physician fee, plastic surgeon, revisit		43.00	91	62r
Physician fee, surgical specialist, revisit		37.00	91	62r
Substance abuse, hospital ancillary charge	incident	3750	90	70s
Substance abuse, hospital physician charge	incident	1080	90	70s
Substance abuse, hospital room and board	incident	5320	90	70s
Household Goods				
Appliance repair, home, service call, washing machine	min labor charge	32.50	4Q 92	4c
Laundry detergent, Tide Ultra, Bold, or Cheer	42 oz	3.03	4Q 92	4c
Tissues, facial, Kleenex brand	175-count box	1.03	4Q 92	4c
Housing				
ACCRA Index, Housing		90.20	4Q 92	4c
House, 1,800 sq ft, 8,000 sq ft lot, new, urban	total	94960	4Q 92	4c
House payment, principal and interest, 25% down payment	month	531	4Q 92	4c
Mortgage rate, incl. points & origination fee, 30-year fixed or adjustable rate	percent	8.18	4Q 92	4c
Rent, apartment, 2 bedrooms - 1-1/2 to 2 baths, unfurnished, 950 sq ft, water	month	500	4Q 92	4c
Rental unit, 1 bedroom	month	313	93	23c
Rental unit, 2 bedroom	month	411	93	23c
Rental unit, 3 bedroom	month	521	93	23c
Rental unit, 4 bedroom	month	574	93	23c
Rental unit, efficiency	month	250	93	23c
Insurance and Pensions				
Auto insurance, private passenger	year	709.79	91	63s

Lubbock, TX - continued

Item	Per	Value	Date	Ref.
Personal Goods				
Shampoo, Alberto VO5	15 oz	1.06	4Q 92	4c
Toothpaste, Crest or Colgate	6-7 oz	1.99	4Q 92	4c
Personal Services				
Dry cleaning, man's 2-piece suit		5.47	4Q 92	4c
Haircare, woman's shampoo, trim and blow-dry		18.60	4Q 92	4c
Haircut, man's barbershop, no styling		6.80	4Q 92	4c
Restaurant Food				
Chicken, fried, thigh and drumstick		1.99	4Q 92	4c
Hamburger with cheese	1/4 lb	1.75	4Q 92	4c
Pizza, Pizza Hut or Pizza Inn, cheese, thin crust	12-13 in	9.75	4Q 92	4c
Taxes				
Tax, cigarette	pack	41	91	77s
Tax, gasoline	gal	20	91	77s
Taxes, state	capita	923	91	77s
Transportation				
ACCRA Index, Transportation		97.00	4Q 92	4c
Bus fare	one-way	0.75	3/93	2c
Driver's license fee		16.00	12/90	43s
Tire balance, computer or spin balance, front	wheel	5.98	4Q 92	4c
Travel				
Business travel	day	193.00	4/93	89r
Utilities				
ACCRA Index, Utilities		84.80	4Q 92	4c
Electricity	mil Btu	17.09	90	64s
Electricity, partial electric and other energy, 1,800 sq ft living area new home	month	57.67	4Q 92	4c
Electricity, residential	KWh	5.92	2/93	94s

Lynchburg, VA

Item	Per	Value	Date	Ref.
Composite ACCRA index		93.70	4Q 92	4c
Alcoholic Beverages				
Beer, Miller Lite or Budweiser, 12-oz containers	6 pack	3.51	4Q 92	4c
Liquor, J & B Scotch	750 ml	16.95	4Q 92	4c
Wine, Gallo Chablis blanc, 1.5 liter	bottle	5.10	4Q 92	4c
Child Care				
Child care fee, average, center	hour	1.29	90	65r
Child care fee, average, nonregulated family day care	hour	0.89	90	65r
Child care fee, average, regulated family day care	hour	1.32	90	65r
Clothing				
Jeans, man's denim		35.83	4Q 92	4c
Shirt, man's dress shirt		22.75	4Q 92	4c
Undervest, boy's size 10-14, cotton	3	3.95	4Q 92	4c
Communications				
Long-distance telephone service, day, initial minute, 0-100 miles	min	0.21-0.35	91	12s
Long-distance telephone service, day, additional minute, 0-100 miles	min	0.12-0.21	91	12s
Long-distance telephone service, evenings/weekends, 0-100 mi, initial minute	min	0.08-0.14	91	12s
Long-distance telephone service, evenings/weekends, 0-100 mi, additional minute	min	0.05-0.08	91	12s
Newspaper subscription, daily and Sunday home delivery, large-city	month	9.78	4Q 92	4c
Telephone, flat rate	month	11.91	91	11c
Telephone bill, family of four	month	17.31	4Q 92	4c
Education				
Board, 4-yr private college/university	year	1804	91	22s
Board, 4-yr public college/university	year	1688	91	22s

Values are in dollars or fractions of dollars. In the column headed *Ref*, references are shown to sources. Each reference is followed by a letter. These refer to the geographical level for which data were reported: s=State, r=Region, and c=City or metro. The abbreviation *ex* is used to mean *except* or *excluding*; *exp* stands for expenditures. For other abbreviations and further explanations, please see the Introduction.

Lynchburg, VA - continued

Item	Per	Value	Date	Ref.
Education				
Expenditures, local gov't, public elementary/secondary	pupil	5487	92	20s
Room, 4-year private college/university	year	1659	91	22s
Room, 4-year public college/university	year	1916	91	22s
Tuition, 2-year private college/university	year	4852	91	22s
Tuition, 2-year public college/university	year	867	91	22s
Tuition, 4-year private college/university	year	7621	91	22s
Tuition, 4-year public college/university, in-state	year	2691	91	22s
Energy and Fuels				
Coal	mil Btu	1.60	90	64s
Energy	mil Btu	8.89	90	64s
Energy, combined forms, 1,800 sq ft heating area	month	93.33	4Q 92	4c
Energy exp/householder, 1-family unit	year	487	90	28r
Energy exp/householder, <1,000 sq ft heating area	year	393	90	28r
Energy exp/householder, 1,000-1,999 sq ft heating area	year	442	90	28r
Energy exp/householder, 2,000+ sq ft heating area	year	577	90	28r
Energy exp/householder, mobile home	year	366	90	28r
Energy exp/householder, multifamily	year	382	90	28r
Gas, natural	mil Btu	4.67	90	64s
Gas, natural	000 cu ft	6.80	91	46s
Gas, natural, exp	year	566	91	46s
Gasoline, motor	gal	1.06	4Q 92	4c
Gasoline, unleaded regular	mil Btu	9.46	90	64s
Entertainment				
Bowling, evening rate	game	2.25	4Q 92	4c
Miniature golf admission	adult	6.18	92	1r
Miniature golf admission	child	5.14	92	1r
Monopoly game, Parker Brothers', No. 9		10.20	4Q 92	4c
Movie	admission	3.19	4Q 92	4c
Tennis balls, yellow, Wilson or Penn, 3	can	2.15	4Q 92	4c
Waterpark admission	adult	11.00	92	1r
Waterpark admission	child	8.55	92	1r
Funerals				
Casket, 18-gauge steel, velvet interior		2029.08	91	24r
Cosmetology, hair care, etc.		75.10	91	24r
Embalming		249.24	91	24r
Facility use for ceremony		162.27	91	24r
Hearse, local		114.04	91	24r
Limousine, local		88.57	91	24r
Remains to funeral home, transfer		92.61	91	24r
Service charge, professional		682.42	91	24r
Vault, concrete, non-metallic liner		798.70	91	24r
Viewing facilities, use		163.86	91	24r
Goods and Services				
ACCRA Index, Miscellaneous Goods and Services		96.60	4Q 92	4c
Groceries				
ACCRA Index, Groceries		94.50	4Q 92	4c
Apples, Red Delicious	lb	0.79	4/93	16r
Babyfood, strained vegetables, lowest price	4-4.5 oz jar	0.32	4Q 92	4c
Bacon	lb	1.75	4/93	16r
Bananas	lb	0.51	4Q 92	4c
Bananas	lb	0.42	4/93	16r
Beef, stew, boneless	lb	2.61	4/93	16r
Bologna, all beef or mixed	lb	2.24	4/93	16r
Bread, white	24 oz	0.68	4Q 92	4c
Bread, white, pan	lb	0.64	4/93	16r
Bread, whole wheat, pan	lb	0.96	4/93	16r
Cabbage	lb	0.37	4/93	16r
Carrots, short trimmed and topped	lb	0.47	4/93	16r
Celery	lb	0.64	4/93	16r

Lynchburg, VA - continued

Item	Per	Value	Date	Ref.
Groceries - continued				
Cheese, American	lb	2.98	4/93	16r
Cheese, Cheddar	lb	3.28	4/93	16r
Cheese, Kraft grated Parmesan	8-oz canister	3.24	4Q 92	4c
Chicken, fresh, whole	lb	0.77	4/93	16r
Chicken, fryer, whole	lb	0.80	4Q 92	4c
Chicken breast, bone-in	lb	1.92	4/93	16r
Chicken legs, bone-in	lb	1.06	4/93	16r
Chuck roast, graded and ungraded, ex USDA prime and choice	lb	2.40	4/93	16r
Chuck roast, USDA choice, bone-in	lb	2.19	4/93	16r
Chuck roast, USDA choice, boneless	lb	2.38	4/93	16r
Cigarettes, Winston	carton	15.14	4Q 92	4c
Coffee, 100% ground roast, all sizes	lb	2.48	4/93	16r
Coffee, vacuum-packed	13-oz can	1.90	4Q 92	4c
Corn, frozen	10 oz	0.52	4Q 92	4c
Corn Flakes, Kellogg's or Post Toasties	18 oz	1.73	4Q 92	4c
Crackers, soda, salted	lb	1.15	4/93	16r
Eggs, Grade A large	doz	0.86	4Q 92	4c
Eggs, Grade A large	doz	0.96	4/93	16r
Flour, white, all purpose	lb	0.24	4/93	16r
Frankfurters, all meat or all beef	lb	2.01	4/93	16r
Grapefruit	lb	0.44	4/93	16r
Grapes, Thompson Seedless	lb	1.40	4/93	16r
Ground beef, 100% beef	lb	1.58	4/93	16r
Ground beef, lean and extra lean	lb	2.09	4/93	16r
Ground beef or hamburger	lb	1.64	4Q 92	4c
Ground chuck, 100% beef	lb	1.98	4/93	16r
Ham, boneless, excluding canned	lb	2.89	4/93	16r
Ham, picnic, shoulder, bone-in, smoked	lb	1.02	4/93	16r
Ham, rump or steak half, bone-in, smoked	lb	1.48	4/93	16r
Ice cream, prepackaged, bulk, regular	1/2 gal	2.41	4/93	16r
Lemons	lb	1.05	4/93	16r
Lettuce, iceberg	head	0.89	4Q 92	4c
Lettuce, iceberg	lb	0.81	4/93	16r
Margarine, Blue Bonnet or Parkay cubes	lb	0.46	4Q 92	4c
Margarine, stick	lb	0.88	4/93	16r
Milk, whole	1/2 gal	1.38	4Q 92	4c
Orange juice, Minute Maid frozen	12-oz can	1.27	4Q 92	4c
Oranges, navel	lb	0.55	4/93	16r
Peaches	29-oz can	1.30	4Q 92	4c
Pears, Anjou	lb	0.92	4/93	16r
Peas Sweet, Del Monte or Green Giant	15-17 oz can	0.48	4Q 92	4c
Pork chops, center cut, bone-in	lb	3.13	4/93	16r
Potato chips	16 oz	2.94	4/93	16r
Potatoes, white	lb	0.43	4/93	16r
Potatoes, white or red	10-lb sack	2.00	4Q 92	4c
Rib roast, USDA choice, bone-in	lb	4.63	4/93	16r
Rice, white, long grain, uncooked	lb	0.45	4/93	16r
Round roast, graded & ungraded, ex USDA prime & choice	lb	3.03	4/93	16r
Round roast, USDA choice, boneless	lb	3.09	4/93	16r
Sausage, fresh, loose	lb	2.08	4/93	16r
Sausage, Jimmy Dean, 100% pork	lb	2.19	4Q 92	4c
Short ribs, bone-in	lb	2.66	4/93	16r
Shortening, vegetable oil blends	lb	0.69	4/93	16r
Shortening, vegetable, Crisco	3-lb can	1.97	4Q 92	4c
Soft drink, Coca Cola	2 liter	0.92	4Q 92	4c
Spaghetti and macaroni	lb	0.81	4/93	16r
Steak, rib eye, USDA choice, boneless	lb	6.24	4/93	16r
Steak, round, graded & ungraded, ex USDA prime & choice	lb	3.31	4/93	16r
Steak, round, USDA choice, boneless	lb	3.34	4/93	16r
Steak, sirloin, graded & ungraded, ex USDA prime & choice	lb	4.19	4/93	16r

Values are in dollars or fractions of dollars. In the column headed *Ref*, references are shown to sources. Each reference is followed by a letter. These refer to the geographical level for which data were reported: s = State, r = Region, and c = City or metro. The abbreviation *ex* is used to mean *except* or *excluding*; *exp* stands for expenditures. For other abbreviations and further explanations, please see the Introduction.

Lynchburg, VA - continued

Item	Per	Value	Date	Ref.
Groceries				
Steak, sirloin, USDA choice, boneless	lb	4.46	4/93	16r
Steak, T-bone	lb	5.75	4Q 92	4c
Steak, T-bone, USDA choice, bone-in	lb	5.25	4/93	16r
Strawberries, dry pint	12 oz	0.92	4/93	16r
Sugar, cane or beet	4 lb	1.43	4Q 92	4c
Sugar, white	lb	0.39	4/93	16r
Sugar, white, 33-80 oz pk	lb	0.38	4/93	16r
Tomatoes, field grown	lb	0.88	4/93	16r
Tomatoes, Hunt's or Del Monte	14.5-oz can	0.53	4Q 92	4c
Tuna, chunk, light	6.125-6.5 oz can	0.52	4Q 92	4c
Tuna, chunk, light	lb	1.79	4/93	16r
Turkey, frozen, whole	lb	1.04	4/93	16r
Yogurt, natural, fruit flavored	1/2 pint	0.57	4/93	16r
Health Care				
ACCRA Index, Health Care		88.60	4Q 92	4c
Analgesic, Aspirin, Bayer, 325 mg tablets	100	5.24	4Q 92	4c
Childbirth, cesarean, hospital		5034	91	62r
Childbirth, cesarean, physician's fee		2053	91	62r
Childbirth, normal, hospital		2712	91	62r
Childbirth, normal, physician's fee		1492	91	62r
Dentist's fee, adult teeth cleaning and periodic oral exam	visit	42.20	4Q 92	4c
Doctor's fee, routine exam, established patient	visit	31.40	4Q 92	4c
Hospital care, semiprivate room	day	263.00	4Q 92	4c
Medical insurance premium, per employee, small group comprehensive	month	284.70	10/91	25c
Medical plan per employee	year	3495	91	45r
Mental health care, exp	capita	37.60-53.67	90	38s
Mental health care, exp, state mental health agency	capita	44.54	90	38s
Mental health care, hospital psychiatric services, non-Federal, exp	capita	9.90	88	38s
Mental health care, mental health organization, multiservice, exp	capita	17.29	88	38s
Mental health care, psychiatric hospitals, private, exp	capita	32.58	88	38s
Mental health care, psychiatric out-patient clinics, freestanding, exp	capita	0.93	88	38s
Mental health care, psychiatric partial-care organizations, freestanding, exp	capita	0.25	88	38s
Mental health care, state and county mental hospitals, exp	capita	28.61	88	38s
Mental health care, VA medical centers, exp	capita	3.95	88	38s
Physician fee, family practice, first-visit		75.00	91	62r
Physician fee, family practice, revisit		34.00	91	62r
Physician fee, general practice, first-visit		61.00	91	62r
Physician fee, general practice, revisit		32.00	91	62r
Physician fee, general surgeon, first-visit		64.00	91	62r
Physician fee, general surgeon, revisit		40.00	91	62r
Physician fee, internal medicine, first-visit		98.00	91	62r
Physician fee, internal medicine, revisit		40.00	91	62r
Physician fee, median, neurosurgeon, first-visit		130.00	91	62r
Physician fee, median, nonsurgical specialist, first-visit		95.00	91	62r
Physician fee, median, orthopedic surgeon, first-visit		91.00	91	62r
Physician fee, median, plastic surgeon, first-visit		66.00	91	62r
Physician fee, median, surgical specialist, first-visit		62.00	91	62r
Physician fee, neurosurgeon, revisit		50.00	91	62r
Physician fee, nonsurgical specialist, revisit		40.00	91	62r
Physician fee, obstetrics/gynecology, first-visit		64.00	91	62r
Physician fee, obstetrics/gynecology, revisit		41.00	91	62r

Lynchburg, VA - continued

Item	Per	Value	Date	Ref.
Health Care - continued				
Physician fee, orthopedic surgeon, revisit		40.00	91	62r
Physician fee, pediatrician, first-visit		49.00	91	62r
Physician fee, pediatrician, revisit		33.00	91	62r
Physician fee, plastic surgeon, revisit		43.00	91	62r
Physician fee, surgical specialist, revisit		37.00	91	62r
Substance abuse, hospital ancillary charge	incident	1220	90	70s
Substance abuse, hospital physician charge	incident	590	90	70s
Substance abuse, hospital room and board	incident	6280	90	70s
Household Goods				
Appliance repair, home, service call, washing machine	min labor charge	31.23	4Q 92	4c
Laundry detergent, Tide Ultra, Bold, or Cheer	42 oz	2.63	4Q 92	4c
Tissues, facial, Kleenex brand	175-count box	0.99	4Q 92	4c
Housing				
ACCRA Index, Housing		95.10	4Q 92	4c
House, 1,800 sq ft, 8,000 sq ft lot, new, urban	total	109414	4Q 92	4c
House payment, principal and interest, 25% down payment	month	609	4Q 92	4c
Mortgage rate, incl. points & origination fee, 30-year fixed or adjustable rate	percent	8.13	4Q 92	4c
Rent, apartment, 2 bedrooms - 1-1/2 to 2 baths, unfurnished, 950 sq ft, water	month	412	4Q 92	4c
Rental unit, 1 bedroom	month	385	93	23c
Rental unit, 2 bedroom	month	444	93	23c
Rental unit, 3 bedroom	month	542	93	23c
Rental unit, 4 bedroom	month	622	93	23c
Rental unit, efficiency	month	310	93	23c
Insurance and Pensions				
Auto insurance, private passenger	year	559.45	91	63s
Personal Goods				
Shampoo, Alberto VO5	15 oz	1.04	4Q 92	4c
Toothpaste, Crest or Colgate	6-7 oz	1.93	4Q 92	4c
Personal Services				
Dry cleaning, man's 2-piece suit		6.51	4Q 92	4c
Haircare, woman's shampoo, trim and blow-dry		20.34	4Q 92	4c
Haircut, man's barbershop, no styling		7.69	4Q 92	4c
Restaurant Food				
Chicken, fried, thigh and drumstick		1.99	4Q 92	4c
Hamburger with cheese	1/4 lb	1.79	4Q 92	4c
Pizza, Pizza Hut or Pizza Inn, cheese, thin crust	12-13 in	7.47	4Q 92	4c
Taxes				
Tax, cigarette	pack	2.50	91	77s
Tax, gasoline	gal	17.50	91	77s
Taxes, state	capita	1090	91	77s
Transportation				
ACCRA Index, Transportation		87.80	4Q 92	4c
Bus fare	one-way	0.75	3/93	2c
Driver's license fee		12.00	12/90	43s
Tire balance, computer or spin balance, front	wheel	5.30	4Q 92	4c
Vehicle registration and license plate	year	26.50-37.50	93	90s
Travel				
Business travel	day	193.00	4/93	89r

Values are in dollars or fractions of dollars. In the column headed *Ref*, references are shown to sources. Each reference is followed by a letter. These refer to the geographical level for which data were reported: s=State, r=Region, and c=City or metro. The abbreviation *ex* is used to mean *except* or *excluding*; *exp* stands for expenditures. For other abbreviations and further explanations, please see the Introduction.

Lynchburg, VA - continued

Item	Per	Value	Date	Ref.
Utilities				
ACCRA Index, Utilities		85.80	4Q 92	4c
Electricity	mil Btu	17.70	90	64s
Electricity, all electric, 1,800 sq ft living area new home	month	93.33	4Q 92	4c

Macon, GA

Item	Per	Value	Date	Ref.
Composite ACCRA index		99.60	4Q 92	4c
Alcoholic Beverages				
Beer, Miller Lite or Budweiser, 12-oz containers	6 pack	4.64	4Q 92	4c
Liquor, J & B Scotch	750 ml	16.91	4Q 92	4c
Wine, Gallo Chablis blanc, 1.5 liter	bottle	6.12	4Q 92	4c
Child Care				
Child care fee, average, center	hour	1.29	90	65r
Child care fee, average, nonregulated family day care	hour	0.89	90	65r
Child care fee, average, regulated family day care	hour	1.32	90	65r
Clothing				
Jeans, man's denim		28.39	4Q 92	4c
Shirt, man's dress shirt		28.28	4Q 92	4c
Undervest, boy's size 10-14, cotton	3	4.49	4Q 92	4c
Communications				
Long-distance telephone service, day, initial minute, 0-100 miles	min	0.16-0.26	91	12s
Long-distance telephone service, day, additional minute, 0-100 miles	min	0.08-0.23	91	12s
Long-distance telephone service, evenings/ weekends, 0-100 mi, initial minute	min	0.06-0.13	91	12s
Long-distance telephone service, evenings/ weekends, 0-100 mi, additional minute	min	0.04-0.12	91	12s
Newspaper subscription, daily and Sunday home delivery, large-city	month	11.57	4Q 92	4c
Telephone, flat rate	month	13.55	91	11c
Telephone bill, family of four	month	19.34	4Q 92	4c
Education				
Board, 4-yr private college/university	year	1801	91	22s
Board, 4-yr public college/university	year	1501	91	22s
Expenditures, local gov't, public elementary/secondary	pupil	4747	92	20s
Room, 4-year private college/university	year	2139	91	22s
Room, 4-year public college/university	year	1192	91	22s
Tuition, 2-year private college/university	year	4457	91	22s
Tuition, 2-year public college/university	year	946	91	22s
Tuition, 4-year private college/university	year	7542	91	22s
Tuition, 4-year public college/university, in-state	year	1680	91	22s
Energy and Fuels				
Coal	mil Btu	1.79	90	64s
Energy	mil Btu	8.88	90	64s
Energy, combined forms, 1,800 sq ft heating area	month	117.82	4Q 92	4c
Energy, exc electricity, 1,800 sq ft heating area	month	40.62	4Q 92	4c
Energy exp/householder, 1-family unit	year	487	90	28r
Energy exp/householder, <1,000 sq ft heating area	year	393	90	28r
Energy exp/householder, 1,000-1,999 sq ft heating area	year	442	90	28r
Energy exp/householder, 2,000+ sq ft heating area	year	577	90	28r
Energy exp/householder, mobile home	year	366	90	28r
Energy exp/householder, multifamily	year	382	90	28r
Gas, natural	mil Btu	4.80	90	64s
Gas, natural	000 cu ft	6.70	91	46s
Gas, natural, exp	year	475	91	46s

Macon, GA - continued

Item	Per	Value	Date	Ref.
Energy and Fuels - continued				
Gasoline, motor	gal	0.99	4Q 92	4c
Gasoline, unleaded regular	mil Btu	8.24	90	64s
Entertainment				
Bowling, evening rate	game	2.28	4Q 92	4c
Miniature golf admission	adult	6.18	92	1r
Miniature golf admission	child	5.14	92	1r
Monopoly game, Parker Brothers', No. 9		10.10	4Q 92	4c
Movie	admission	5.50	4Q 92	4c
Tennis balls, yellow, Wilson or Penn, 3	can	2.60	4Q 92	4c
Waterpark admission	adult	11.00	92	1r
Waterpark admission	child	8.55	92	1r
Funerals				
Casket, 18-gauge steel, velvet interior		2029.08	91	24r
Cosmetology, hair care, etc.		75.10	91	24r
Embalming		249.24	91	24r
Facility use for ceremony		162.27	91	24r
Hearse, local		114.04	91	24r
Limousine, local		88.57	91	24r
Remains to funeral home, transfer		92.61	91	24r
Service charge, professional		682.42	91	24r
Vault, concrete, non-metallic liner		798.70	91	24r
Viewing facilities, use		163.86	91	24r
Goods and Services				
ACCRA Index, Miscellaneous Goods and Services		103.00	4Q 92	4c
Groceries				
ACCRA Index, Groceries		93.90	4Q 92	4c
Apples, Red Delicious	lb	0.79	4/93	16r
Babyfood, strained vegetables, lowest price	4-4.5 oz jar	0.26	4Q 92	4c
Bacon	lb	1.75	4/93	16r
Bananas	lb	0.43	4Q 92	4c
Bananas	lb	0.42	4/93	16r
Beef, stew, boneless	lb	2.61	4/93	16r
Bologna, all beef or mixed	lb	2.24	4/93	16r
Bread, white	24 oz	0.72	4Q 92	4c
Bread, white, pan	lb	0.64	4/93	16r
Bread, whole wheat, pan	lb	0.96	4/93	16r
Cabbage	lb	0.37	4/93	16r
Carrots, short trimmed and topped	lb	0.47	4/93	16r
Celery	lb	0.64	4/93	16r
Cheese, American	lb	2.98	4/93	16r
Cheese, Cheddar	lb	3.28	4/93	16r
Cheese, Kraft grated Parmesan	8-oz canister	3.17	4Q 92	4c
Chicken, fresh, whole	lb	0.77	4/93	16r
Chicken, fryer, whole	lb	0.65	4Q 92	4c
Chicken breast, bone-in	lb	1.92	4/93	16r
Chicken legs, bone-in	lb	1.06	4/93	16r
Chuck roast, graded and ungraded, ex USDA prime and choice	lb	2.40	4/93	16r
Chuck roast, USDA choice, bone-in	lb	2.19	4/93	16r
Chuck roast, USDA choice, boneless	lb	2.38	4/93	16r
Cigarettes, Winston	carton	15.66	4Q 92	4c
Coffee, 100% ground roast, all sizes	lb	2.48	4/93	16r
Coffee, vacuum-packed	13-oz can	2.09	4Q 92	4c
Corn, frozen	10 oz	0.63	4Q 92	4c
Corn Flakes, Kellogg's or Post Toasties	18 oz	1.71	4Q 92	4c
Crackers, soda, salted	lb	1.15	4/93	16r
Eggs, Grade A large	doz	0.73	4Q 92	4c
Eggs, Grade A large	doz	0.96	4/93	16r
Flour, white, all purpose	lb	0.24	4/93	16r
Frankfurters, all meat or all beef	lb	2.01	4/93	16r
Grapefruit	lb	0.44	4/93	16r
Grapes, Thompson Seedless	lb	1.40	4/93	16r
Ground beef, 100% beef	lb	1.58	4/93	16r
Ground beef, lean and extra lean	lb	2.09	4/93	16r

Values are in dollars or fractions of dollars. In the column headed *Ref*, references are shown to sources. Each reference is followed by a letter. These refer to the geographical level for which data were reported: s = State, r = Region, and c = City or metro. The abbreviation *ex* is used to mean *except* or *excluding*; *exp* stands for expenditures. For other abbreviations and further explanations, please see the Introduction.

Macon, GA - continued

Item	Per	Value	Date	Ref.
Groceries				
Ground beef or hamburger	lb	1.66	4Q 92	4c
Ground chuck, 100% beef	lb	1.98	4/93	16r
Ham, boneless, excluding canned	lb	2.89	4/93	16r
Ham, picnic, shoulder, bone-in, smoked	lb	1.02	4/93	16r
Ham, rump or steak half, bone-in, smoked	lb	1.48	4/93	16r
Ice cream, prepackaged, bulk, regular	1/2 gal	2.41	4/93	16r
Lemons	lb	1.05	4/93	16r
Lettuce, iceberg	head	0.98	4Q 92	4c
Lettuce, iceberg	lb	0.81	4/93	16r
Margarine, Blue Bonnet or Parkay cubes	lb	0.49	4Q 92	4c
Margarine, stick	lb	0.88	4/93	16r
Milk, whole	1/2 gal	1.44	4Q 92	4c
Orange juice, Minute Maid frozen	12-oz can	1.09	4Q 92	4c
Oranges, navel	lb	0.55	4/93	16r
Peaches	29-oz can	1.18	4Q 92	4c
Pears, Anjou	lb	0.92	4/93	16r
Peas Sweet, Del Monte or Green Giant	15-17 oz can	0.60	4Q 92	4c
Pork chops, center cut, bone-in	lb	3.13	4/93	16r
Potato chips	16 oz	2.94	4/93	16r
Potatoes, white	lb	0.43	4/93	16r
Potatoes, white or red	10-lb sack	2.23	4Q 92	4c
Rib roast, USDA choice, bone-in	lb	4.63	4/93	16r
Rice, white, long grain, uncooked	lb	0.45	4/93	16r
Round roast, graded & ungraded, ex USDA prime & choice	lb	3.03	4/93	16r
Round roast, USDA choice, boneless	lb	3.09	4/93	16r
Sausage, fresh, loose	lb	2.08	4/93	16r
Sausage, Jimmy Dean, 100% pork	lb	2.03	4Q 92	4c
Short ribs, bone-in	lb	2.66	4/93	16r
Shortening, vegetable oil blends	lb	0.69	4/93	16r
Shortening, vegetable, Crisco	3-lb can	1.86	4Q 92	4c
Soft drink, Coca Cola	2 liter	1.07	4Q 92	4c
Spaghetti and macaroni	lb	0.81	4/93	16r
Steak, rib eye, USDA choice, boneless	lb	6.24	4/93	16r
Steak, round, graded & ungraded, ex USDA prime & choice	lb	3.31	4/93	16r
Steak, round, USDA choice, boneless	lb	3.34	4/93	16r
Steak, sirloin, graded & ungraded, ex USDA prime & choice	lb	4.19	4/93	16r
Steak, sirloin, USDA choice, boneless	lb	4.46	4/93	16r
Steak, T-bone	lb	5.78	4Q 92	4c
Steak, T-bone, USDA choice, bone-in	lb	5.25	4/93	16r
Strawberries, dry pint	12 oz	0.92	4/93	16r
Sugar, cane or beet	4 lb	1.47	4Q 92	4c
Sugar, white	lb	0.39	4/93	16r
Sugar, white, 33-80 oz pk	lb	0.38	4/93	16r
Tomatoes, field grown	lb	0.88	4/93	16r
Tomatoes, Hunt's or Del Monte	14.5-oz can	0.56	4Q 92	4c
Tuna, chunk, light	6.125-6.5 oz can	0.58	4Q 92	4c
Tuna, chunk, light	lb	1.79	4/93	16r
Turkey, frozen, whole	lb	1.04	4/93	16r
Yogurt, natural, fruit flavored	1/2 pint	0.57	4/93	16r
Health Care				
ACCRA Index, Health Care		88.30	4Q 92	4c
Analgesic, Aspirin, Bayer, 325 mg tablets	100	4.58	4Q 92	4c
Childbirth, cesarean, hospital		5034	91	62r
Childbirth, cesarean, physician's fee		2053	91	62r
Childbirth, normal, hospital		2712	91	62r
Childbirth, normal, physician's fee		1492	91	62r
Dentist's fee, adult teeth cleaning and periodic oral exam	visit	43.25	4Q 92	4c
Doctor's fee, routine exam, established patient	visit	34.00	4Q 92	4c

Macon, GA - continued

Item	Per	Value	Date	Ref.
Health Care - continued				
Hospital care, semiprivate room	day	166.68	90	27c
Hospital care, semiprivate room	day	226.00	4Q 92	4c
Medical insurance premium, per employee, small group comprehensive	month	335.80	10/91	25c
Medical plan per employee	year	3495	91	45r
Mental health care, exp	capita	37.60-53.67	90	38s
Mental health care, exp, state mental health agency	capita	50.98	90	38s
Mental health care, hospital psychiatric services, non-Federal, exp	capita	9.66	88	38s
Mental health care, mental health organization, multiservice, exp	capita	16.40	88	38s
Mental health care, psychiatric hospitals, private, exp	capita	26.36	88	38s
Mental health care, psychiatric out-patient clinics, freestanding, exp	capita	0.13	88	38s
Mental health care, state and county mental hospitals, exp	capita	38.94	88	38s
Mental health care, VA medical centers, exp	capita	3.91	88	38s
Physician fee, family practice, first-visit		75.00	91	62r
Physician fee, family practice, revisit		34.00	91	62r
Physician fee, general practice, first-visit		61.00	91	62r
Physician fee, general practice, revisit		32.00	91	62r
Physician fee, general surgeon, first-visit		64.00	91	62r
Physician fee, general surgeon, revisit		40.00	91	62r
Physician fee, internal medicine, first-visit		98.00	91	62r
Physician fee, internal medicine, revisit		40.00	91	62r
Physician fee, median, neurosurgeon, first-visit		130.00	91	62r
Physician fee, median, nonsurgical specialist, first-visit		95.00	91	62r
Physician fee, median, orthopedic surgeon, first-visit		91.00	91	62r
Physician fee, median, plastic surgeon, first-visit		66.00	91	62r
Physician fee, median, surgical specialist, first-visit		62.00	91	62r
Physician fee, neurosurgeon, revisit		50.00	91	62r
Physician fee, nonsurgical specialist, revisit		40.00	91	62r
Physician fee, obstetrics/gynecology, first-visit		64.00	91	62r
Physician fee, obstetrics/gynecology, revisit		41.00	91	62r
Physician fee, orthopedic surgeon, revisit		40.00	91	62r
Physician fee, pediatrician, first-visit		49.00	91	62r
Physician fee, pediatrician, revisit		33.00	91	62r
Physician fee, plastic surgeon, revisit		43.00	91	62r
Physician fee, surgical specialist, revisit		37.00	91	62r
Substance abuse, hospital ancillary charge	incident	1800	90	70s
Substance abuse, hospital physician charge	incident	890	90	70s
Substance abuse, hospital room and board	incident	5560	90	70s
Household Goods				
Appliance repair, home, service call, washing machine	min labor charge	33.98	4Q 92	4c
Laundry detergent, Tide Ultra, Bold, or Cheer	42 oz	2.99	4Q 92	4c
Tissues, facial, Kleenex brand	175-count box	0.91	4Q 92	4c
Housing				
ACCRA Index, Housing		98.60	4Q 92	4c
House, 1,800 sq ft, 8,000 sq ft lot, new, urban	total	107700	4Q 92	4c
House payment, principal and interest, 25% down payment	month	600	4Q 92	4c
Mortgage rate, incl. points & origination fee, 30-year fixed or adjustable rate	percent	8.13	4Q 92	4c

Values are in dollars or fractions of dollars. In the column headed *Ref*, references are shown to sources. Each reference is followed by a letter. These refer to the geographical level for which data were reported: s=State, r=Region, and c=City or metro. The abbreviation *ex* is used to mean *except* or *excluding*; *exp* stands for expenditures. For other abbreviations and further explanations, please see the Introduction.

Macon, GA - continued

Item	Per	Value	Date	Ref.
Housing				
Rent, apartment, 2 bedrooms - 1-1/2 to 2 baths, unfurnished, 950 sq ft, water	month	500	4Q 92	4c
Rental unit, 1 bedroom	month	365	93	23c
Rental unit, 2 bedroom	month	429	93	23c
Rental unit, 3 bedroom	month	536	93	23c
Rental unit, 4 bedroom	month	597	93	23c
Rental unit, efficiency	month	297	93	23c
Insurance and Pensions				
Auto insurance, private passenger	year	651.31	91	63s
Personal Goods				
Shampoo, Alberto VO5	15 oz	1.19	4Q 92	4c
Toothpaste, Crest or Colgate	6-7 oz	2.02	4Q 92	4c
Personal Services				
Dry cleaning, man's 2-piece suit		5.52	4Q 92	4c
Haircare, woman's shampoo, trim and blow-dry		15.54	4Q 92	4c
Haircut, man's barbershop, no styling		6.78	4Q 92	4c
Restaurant Food				
Chicken, fried, thigh and drumstick		1.99	4Q 92	4c
Hamburger with cheese	1/4 lb	1.89	4Q 92	4c
Pizza, Pizza Hut or Pizza Inn, cheese, thin crust	12-13 in	8.05	4Q 92	4c
Taxes				
Tax, cigarette	pack	12	91	77s
Tax, gasoline	gal	7.50	91	77s
Taxes, state	capita	1080	91	77s
Transportation				
ACCRA Index, Transportation		96.90	4Q 92	4c
Driver's license fee		4.50	12/90	43s
Tire balance, computer or spin balance, front	wheel	6.92	4Q 92	4c
Travel				
Business travel	day	193.00	4/93	89r
Utilities				
ACCRA Index, Utilities		107.10	4Q 92	4c
Electricity	mil Btu	19.25	90	64s
Electricity, partial electric and other energy, 1,800 sq ft living area new home	month	77.20	4Q 92	4c

Madison, WI

Item	Per	Value	Date	Ref.
Child Care				
Child care fee, average, center	hour	1.63	90	65r
Child care fee, average, nonregulated family day care	hour	1.83	90	65r
Child care fee, average, regulated family day care	hour	1.42	90	65r
Communications				
Long-distance telephone service, day, initial minute, 0-100 miles	min	0.15-0.29	91	12s
Long-distance telephone service, day, additional minute, 0-100 miles	min	0.10-0.27	91	12s
Telephone, flat rate	month	6.00	91	11c
Education				
Board, 4-yr private college/university	year	1533	91	22s
Board, 4-yr public college/university	year	1404	91	22s
Expenditures, local gov't, public elementary/secondary	pupil	5972	92	20s
Room, 4-year private college/university	year	1256	91	22s
Room, 4-year public college/university	year	1416	91	22s
Tuition, 2-year private college/university	year	4768	91	22s
Tuition, 2-year public college/university	year	1234	91	22s
Tuition, 4-year private college/university	year	8237	91	22s
Tuition, 4-year public college/university, in-state	year	1951	91	22s

Madison, WI - continued

Item	Per	Value	Date	Ref.
Energy and Fuels				
Coal	mil Btu	1.41	90	64s
Energy	mil Btu	8.27	90	64s
Energy exp/householder, 1-family unit	year	471	90	28r
Energy exp/householder, <1,000 sq ft heating area	year	430	90	28r
Energy exp/householder, 1,000-1,999 sq ft heating area	year	481	90	28r
Energy exp/householder, 2,000+ sq ft heating area	year	473	90	28r
Energy exp/householder, mobile home	year	430	90	28r
Energy exp/householder, multifamily	year	461	90	28r
Gas, cooking, winter, 10 therms	month	8.97	92	56c
Gas, cooking, winter, 30 therms	month	19.92	92	56c
Gas, cooking, winter, 50 therms	month	30.87	92	56c
Gas, heating, winter, 100 therms	month	58.23	92	56c
Gas, heating, winter, average use	month	92.71	92	56c
Gas, natural	mil Btu	4.56	90	64s
Gas, natural	000 cu ft	5.61	91	46s
Gas, natural, exp	year	605	91	46s
Gasoline, unleaded regular	mil Btu	9.38	90	64s
Entertainment				
Miniature golf admission	adult	6.18	92	1r
Miniature golf admission	child	5.14	92	1r
Waterpark admission	adult	11.00	92	1r
Waterpark admission	child	8.55	92	1r
Funerals				
Casket, 18-gauge steel, velvet interior		1926.72	91	24r
Cosmetology, hair care, etc.		97.64	91	24r
Embalming		249.14	91	24r
Facility use for ceremony		208.59	91	24r
Hearse, local		130.12	91	24r
Limousine, local		104.66	91	24r
Remains to funeral home, transfer		93.61	91	24r
Service charge, professional		724.62	91	24r
Vault, concrete, non-metallic liner		734.53	91	24r
Viewing facilities, use		236.06	91	24r
Groceries				
Apples, Red Delicious	lb	0.77	4/93	16r
Bacon	lb	1.85	4/93	16r
Bananas	lb	0.46	4/93	16r
Beef, stew, boneless	lb	2.53	4/93	16r
Bologna, all beef or mixed	lb	2.19	4/93	16r
Bread, white, pan	lb	0.78	4/93	16r
Butter	lb	1.50	4/93	16r
Cabbage	lb	0.40	4/93	16r
Carrots, short trimmed and topped	lb	0.45	4/93	16r
Cheese, Cheddar	lb	3.47	4/93	16r
Chicken, fresh, whole	lb	0.84	4/93	16r
Chicken breast, bone-in	lb	1.94	4/93	16r
Chicken legs, bone-in	lb	1.02	4/93	16r
Chuck roast, graded and ungraded, ex USDA prime and choice	lb	2.43	4/93	16r
Chuck roast, USDA choice, bone-in	lb	2.11	4/93	16r
Chuck roast, USDA choice, boneless	lb	2.44	4/93	16r
Coffee, 100% ground roast, all sizes	lb	2.47	4/93	16r
Cookies, chocolate chip	lb	2.73	4/93	16r
Eggs, Grade A large	doz	0.93	4/93	16r
Flour, white, all purpose	lb	0.21	4/93	16r
Grapefruit	lb	0.45	4/93	16r
Grapes, Thompson Seedless	lb	1.46	4/93	16r
Ground beef, 100% beef	lb	1.63	4/93	16r
Ground beef, lean and extra lean	lb	2.08	4/93	16r
Ground chuck, 100% beef	lb	1.94	4/93	16r
Ham, boneless, excluding canned	lb	2.21	4/93	16r
Honey, jar	8 oz	0.97-1.25	92	5r
Honey, jar	lb	1.25-2.25	92	5r
Honey, squeeze bear	12-oz	1.25-1.99	92	5r
Ice cream, prepackaged, bulk, regular	1/2 gal	2.41	4/93	16r
Lemons	lb	0.82	4/93	16r
Lettuce, iceberg	lb	0.83	4/93	16r

Values are in dollars or fractions of dollars. In the column headed *Ref*, references are shown to sources. Each reference is followed by a letter. These refer to the geographical level for which data were reported: s=State, r=Region, and c=City or metro. The abbreviation *ex* is used to mean *except* or *excluding*; *exp* stands for expenditures. For other abbreviations and further explanations, please see the Introduction.

Madison, WI - continued

Item	Per	Value	Date	Ref.
Groceries				
Margarine, stick	lb	0.77	4/93	16r
Oranges, navel	lb	0.50	4/93	16r
Peanut butter, creamy, all sizes	lb	1.82	4/93	16r
Pears, Anjou	lb	0.85	4/93	16r
Pork chops, center cut, bone-in	lb	3.17	4/93	16r
Potato chips	16 oz	2.68	4/93	16r
Potatoes, white	lb	0.26	4/93	16r
Round roast, graded & ungraded, ex USDA prime & choice	lb	2.88	4/93	16r
Round roast, USDA choice, boneless	lb	2.96	4/93	16r
Shortening, vegetable oil blends	lb	0.79	4/93	16r
Spaghetti and macaroni	lb	0.76	4/93	16r
Steak, rib eye, USDA choice, boneless	lb	6.29	4/93	16r
Steak, round, USDA choice, boneless	lb	3.24	4/93	16r
Steak, sirloin, graded & ungraded, ex USDA prime & choice	lb	4.00	4/93	16r
Steak, sirloin, USDA choice, bone-in	lb	3.57	4/93	16r
Steak, sirloin, USDA choice, boneless	lb	4.17	4/93	16r
Steak, T-bone, USDA choice, bone-in	lb	5.60	4/93	16r
Strawberries, dry pint	12 oz	0.90	4/93	16r
Sugar, white	lb	0.36	4/93	16r
Sugar, white, 33-80 oz pk	lb	0.35	4/93	16r
Tomatoes, field grown	lb	0.99	4/93	16r
Tuna, chunk, light	lb	1.76	4/93	16r
Turkey, frozen, whole	lb	0.91	4/93	16r
Health Care				
Childbirth, cesarean, hospital		4688	91	62r
Childbirth, cesarean, physician's fee		2053	91	62r
Childbirth, normal, hospital		2657	91	62r
Childbirth, normal, physician's fee		1492	91	62r
Hospital care, semiprivate room	day	199.29	90	27c
Medical insurance premium, per employee, small group comprehensive	month	299.30	10/91	25c
Medical plan per employee	year	3443	91	45r
Mental health care, exp	capita	28.84-37.59	90	38s
Mental health care, exp, state mental health agency	capita	36.62	90	38s
Mental health care, hospital psychiatric services, non-Federal, exp	capita	13.05	88	38s
Mental health care, mental health organization, multiservice, exp	capita	10.93	88	38s
Mental health care, psychiatric hospitals, private, exp	capita	8.71	88	38s
Mental health care, psychiatric out-patient clinics, freestanding, exp	capita	5.33	88	38s
Mental health care, psychiatric partial-care organizations, freestanding, exp	capita	0.20	88	38s
Mental health care, state and county mental hospitals, exp	capita	28.29	88	38s
Mental health care, VA medical centers, exp	capita	7.57	88	38s
Physician fee, family practice, first-visit		76.00	91	62r
Physician fee, family practice, revisit		33.00	91	62r
Physician fee, general practice, first-visit		61.00	91	62r
Physician fee, general practice, revisit		31.00	91	62r
Physician fee, general surgeon, first-visit		65.00	91	62r
Physician fee, general surgeon, revisit		35.00	91	62r
Physician fee, internal medicine, first-visit		91.00	91	62r
Physician fee, internal medicine, revisit		40.00	91	62r
Physician fee, median, neurosurgeon, first-visit		106.00	91	62r
Physician fee, median, nonsurgical specialist, first-visit		90.00	91	62r
Physician fee, median, orthopedic surgeon, first-visit		83.00	91	62r
Physician fee, median, surgical specialist, first-visit		61.00	91	62r
Physician fee, neurosurgeon, revisit		41.00	91	62r
Physician fee, nonsurgical specialist, revisit		40.00	91	62r
Physician fee, obstetrics/gynecology, first-visit		61.00	91	62r
Physician fee, obstetrics/gynecology, revisit		40.00	91	62r

Madison, WI - continued

Item	Per	Value	Date	Ref.
Health Care - continued				
Physician fee, orthopedic surgeon, revisit		41.00	91	62r
Physician fee, pediatrician, first-visit		46.00	91	62r
Physician fee, pediatrician, revisit		33.00	91	62r
Physician fee, surgical specialist, revisit		36.00	91	62r
Substance abuse, hospital ancillary charge	incident	960	90	70s
Substance abuse, hospital physician charge	incident	470	90	70s
Substance abuse, hospital room and board	incident	3980	90	70s
Housing				
Home, median price	unit	94.90		26c
Rental unit, 1 bedroom	month	467	93	23c
Rental unit, 2 bedroom	month	571	93	23c
Rental unit, 3 bedroom	month	714	93	23c
Rental unit, 4 bedroom	month	799	93	23c
Rental unit, efficiency	month	400	93	23c
Insurance and Pensions				
Auto insurance, private passenger	year	510.11	91	63s
Taxes				
Tax, cigarette	pack	38	91	77s
Tax, gasoline	gal	22.20	91	77s
Taxes, state	capita	1416	91	77s
Transportation				
Bus fare	one-way	1.00	3/93	2c
Driver's license fee		9.00	12/90	43s
Utilities				
Electricity	mil Btu	15.77	90	64s
Electricity, winter, 250 KWh	month	20.75	92	55c
Electricity, winter, 500 KWh	month	38.00	92	55c
Electricity, winter, 750 KWh	month	55.25	92	55c
Electricity, winter, 1000 KWh	month	72.50	92	55c

Manchester, NH

Item	Per	Value	Date	Ref.
Composite ACCRA index		115.90	4Q 92	4c
Alcoholic Beverages				
Beer, Miller Lite or Budweiser, 12-oz containers	6 pack	3.94	4Q 92	4c
Liquor, J & B Scotch	750 ml	14.50	4Q 92	4c
Wine, Gallo Chablis blanc, 1.5 liter	bottle	4.47	4Q 92	4c
Clothing				
Jeans, man's denim		28.66	4Q 92	4c
Shirt, man's dress shirt		29.00	4Q 92	4c
Undervest, boy's size 10-14, cotton	3	3.45	4Q 92	4c
Communications				
Newspaper subscription, daily and Sunday home delivery, large-city	month	18.26	4Q 92	4c
Telephone bill, family of four	month	21.04	4Q 92	4c
Energy and Fuels				
Energy, combined forms, 1,800 sq ft heating area	month	172.43	4Q 92	4c
Energy, exc electricity, 1,800 sq ft heating area	month	82.63	4Q 92	4c
Gas, cooking, winter, 10 therms	month	10.88	92	56c
Gas, cooking, winter, 30 therms	month	25.09	92	56c
Gas, cooking, winter, 50 therms	month	39.29	92	56c
Gas, heating, winter, 100 therms	month	73.59	92	56c
Gas, heating, winter, average use	month	122.86	92	56c
Gasoline, motor	gal	1.14	4Q 92	4c
Entertainment				
Bowling, evening rate	game	1.65	4Q 92	4c
Monopoly game, Parker Brothers', No. 9		10.58	4Q 92	4c
Movie	admission	6.25	4Q 92	4c

Values are in dollars or fractions of dollars. In the column headed *Ref*, references are shown as sources. Each reference is followed by a letter. These refer to the geographical level for which data were reported: s=State, r=Region, and c=City or metro. The abbreviation *ex* is used to mean *except* or *excluding*; *exp* stands for expenditures. For other abbreviations and further explanations, please see the Introduction.

Manchester, NH - continued

Item	Per	Value	Date	Ref.
Entertainment				
Tennis balls, yellow, Wilson or Penn, 3	can	2.43	4Q 92	4c
Goods and Services				
ACCRA Index, Miscellaneous Goods and Services		107.10	4Q 92	4c
Groceries				
ACCRA Index, Groceries		103.20	4Q 92	4c
Babyfood, strained vegetables, lowest price	4-4.5 oz jar	0.33	4Q 92	4c
Bananas	lb	0.59	4Q 92	4c
Bread, white	24 oz	0.93	4Q 92	4c
Cheese, Kraft grated Parmesan	8-oz canister	2.96	4Q 92	4c
Chicken, fryer, whole	lb	0.89	4Q 92	4c
Cigarettes, Winston	carton	17.31	4Q 92	4c
Coffee, vacuum-packed	13-oz can	1.75	4Q 92	4c
Corn, frozen	10 oz	0.58	4Q 92	4c
Corn Flakes, Kellogg's or Post Toasties	18 oz	2.06	4Q 92	4c
Eggs, Grade A large	doz	0.96	4Q 92	4c
Ground beef or hamburger	lb	1.45	4Q 92	4c
Lettuce, iceberg	head	0.99	4Q 92	4c
Margarine, Blue Bonnet or Parkay cubes	lb	0.54	4Q 92	4c
Milk, whole	1/2 gal	1.11	4Q 92	4c
Orange juice, Minute Maid frozen	12-oz can	1.32	4Q 92	4c
Peaches	29-oz can	1.46	4Q 92	4c
Peas Sweet, Del Monte or Green Giant	15-17 oz can	0.42	4Q 92	4c
Potatoes, white or red	10-lb sack	1.62	4Q 92	4c
Sausage, Jimmy Dean, 100% pork	lb	2.54	4Q 92	4c
Shortening, vegetable, Crisco	3-lb can	2.79	4Q 92	4c
Soft drink, Coca Cola	2 liter	1.12	4Q 92	4c
Steak, T-bone	lb	5.52	4Q 92	4c
Sugar, cane or beet	4 lb	1.46	4Q 92	4c
Tomatoes, Hunt's or Del Monte	14.5-oz can	0.66	4Q 92	4c
Tuna, chunk, light	6.125-6.5 oz can	0.90	4Q 92	4c
Health Care				
ACCRA Index, Health Care		116.20	4Q 92	4c
Analgesic, Aspirin, Bayer, 325 mg tablets	100	5.15	4Q 92	4c
Dentist's fee, adult teeth cleaning and periodic oral exam	visit	53.00	4Q 92	4c
Doctor's fee, routine exam, established patient	visit	44.20	4Q 92	4c
Hospital care, semiprivate room	day	298.44	90	27c
Hospital care, semiprivate room	day	392.50	4Q 92	4c
Medical insurance premium, per employee, small group comprehensive	month	295.65	10/91	25c
Household Goods				
Appliance repair, home, service call, washing machine	min labor charge	47.19	4Q 92	4c
Laundry detergent, Tide Ultra, Bold, or Cheer	42 oz	3.05	4Q 92	4c
Tissues, facial, Kleenex brand	175-count box	1.14	4Q 92	4c
Housing				
ACCRA Index, Housing		123.90	4Q 92	4c
House, 1,800 sq ft, 8,000 sq ft lot, new, urban	total	136750	4Q 92	4c
House payment, principal and interest, 25% down payment	month	767	4Q 92	4c

Manchester, NH - continued

Item	Per	Value	Date	Ref.
Housing - continued				
Mortgage rate, incl. points & origination fee, 30-year fixed or adjustable rate	percent	8.20	4Q 92	4c
Rent, apartment, 2 bedrooms - 1-1/2 to 2 baths, unfurnished, 950 sq ft, water	month	600	4Q 92	4c
Rental unit, 1 bedroom	month	572	93	23c
Rental unit, 2 bedroom	month	673	93	23c
Rental unit, 3 bedroom	month	841	93	23c
Rental unit, 4 bedroom	month	946	93	23c
Rental unit, efficiency	month	470	93	23c
Personal Goods				
Shampoo, Alberto VO5	15 oz	1.15	4Q 92	4c
Toothpaste, Crest or Colgate	6-7 oz	2.02	4Q 92	4c
Personal Services				
Dry cleaning, man's 2-piece suit		7.08	4Q 92	4c
Haircare, woman's shampoo, trim and blow-dry		15.90	4Q 92	4c
Haircut, man's barbershop, no styling		8.59	4Q 92	4c
Restaurant Food				
Chicken, fried, thigh and drumstick		2.58	4Q 92	4c
Hamburger with cheese	1/4 lb	1.99	4Q 92	4c
Pizza, Pizza Hut or Pizza Inn, cheese, thin crust	12-13 in	7.69	4Q 92	4c
Transportation				
ACCRA Index, Transportation		107.60	4Q 92	4c
Auto rental, average	day	41.67	6/91	60c
Bus fare, up to 10 miles	one-way	0.90	4Q 92	4c
Limo fare, airport-city, average	day	45.00	6/91	60c
Taxi fare, airport-city, average	day	9.00	6/91	60c
Tire balance, computer or spin balance, front	wheel	7.50	4Q 92	4c
Travel				
Lodging	day	98.70	91	60c
Utilities				
ACCRA Index, Utilities		152.90	4Q 92	4c
Electricity, partial electric and other energy, 1,800 sq ft living area new home	month	89.80	4Q 92	4c
Electricity, winter, 250 KWh	month	28.78	92	55c
Electricity, winter, 500 KWh	month	60.92	92	55c
Electricity, winter, 750 KWh	month	93.05	92	55c
Electricity, winter, 1000 KWh	month	121.56	92	55c

Manhattan, KS

Item	Per	Value	Date	Ref.
Composite ACCRA index		93.20	4Q 92	4c
Alcoholic Beverages				
Beer, Miller Lite or Budweiser, 12-oz containers	6 pack	3.83	4Q 92	4c
Liquor, J & B Scotch	750 ml	17.59	4Q 92	4c
Wine, Gallo Chablis blanc, 1.5 liter	bottle	4.66	4Q 92	4c
Clothing				
Jeans, man's denim		26.33	4Q 92	4c
Shirt, man's dress shirt		19.33	4Q 92	4c
Undervest, boy's size 10-14, cotton	3	3.04	4Q 92	4c
Communications				
Newspaper subscription, daily and Sunday home delivery, large-city	month	10.02	4Q 92	4c
Telephone, flat rate	month	10.70	91	11c
Telephone bill, family of four	month	17.34	4Q 92	4c
Energy and Fuels				
Energy, combined forms, 1,800 sq ft heating area	month	95.70	4Q 92	4c
Energy, exc electricity, 1,800 sq ft heating area	month	47.16	4Q 92	4c
Gasoline, motor	gal	1.14	4Q 92	4c

Values are in dollars or fractions of dollars. In the column headed *Ref*, references are shown to sources. Each reference is followed by a letter. These refer to the geographical level for which data were reported: s=State, r=Region, and c=City or metro. The abbreviation *ex* is used to mean *except* or *excluding*; *exp* stands for *expenditures*. For other abbreviations and further explanations, please see the Introduction.

Manhattan, KS - continued

Item	Per	Value	Date	Ref.
Entertainment				
Bowling, evening rate	game	1.48	4Q 92	4c
Monopoly game, Parker Brothers', No. 9		10.98	4Q 92	4c
Movie	admis-sion	5.50	4Q 92	4c
Tennis balls, yellow, Wilson or Penn, 3	can	1.92	4Q 92	4c
Goods and Services				
ACCRA Index, Miscellaneous Goods and Services		89.20	4Q 92	4c
Groceries				
ACCRA Index, Groceries		97.30	4Q 92	4c
Babyfood, strained vegetables, lowest price	4-4.5 oz jar	0.37	4Q 92	4c
Bananas	lb	0.40	4Q 92	4c
Bread, white	24 oz	0.53	4Q 92	4c
Cheese, Kraft grated Parmesan	8-oz canis-ter	3.78	4Q 92	4c
Chicken, fryer, whole	lb	0.66	4Q 92	4c
Cigarettes, Winston	carton	16.79	4Q 92	4c
Coffee, vacuum-packed	13-oz can	1.99	4Q 92	4c
Corn, frozen	10 oz	0.66	4Q 92	4c
Corn Flakes, Kellogg's or Post Toasties	18 oz	1.99	4Q 92	4c
Eggs, Grade A large	doz	0.83	4Q 92	4c
Ground beef or hamburger	lb	1.46	4Q 92	4c
Lettuce, iceberg	head	0.95	4Q 92	4c
Margarine, Blue Bonnet or Parkay cubes	lb	0.62	4Q 92	4c
Milk, whole	1/2 gal	1.36	4Q 92	4c
Orange juice, Minute Maid frozen	12-oz can	1.50	4Q 92	4c
Peaches	29-oz can	1.39	4Q 92	4c
Peas Sweet, Del Monte or Green Giant	15-17 oz can	0.64	4Q 92	4c
Potatoes, white or red	10-lb sack	2.12	4Q 92	4c
Sausage, Jimmy Dean, 100% pork	lb	2.36	4Q 92	4c
Shortening, vegetable, Crisco	3-lb can	2.89	4Q 92	4c
Soft drink, Coca Cola	2 liter	1.37	4Q 92	4c
Steak, T-bone	lb	4.82	4Q 92	4c
Sugar, cane or beet	4 lb	1.51	4Q 92	4c
Tomatoes, Hunt's or Del Monte	14.5-oz can	0.69	4Q 92	4c
Tuna, chunk, light	6.125-6.5 oz can	0.61	4Q 92	4c
Health Care				
ACCRA Index, Health Care		93.80	4Q 92	4c
Analgesic, Aspirin, Bayer, 325 mg tablets	100	3.79	4Q 92	4c
Dentist's fee, adult teeth cleaning and periodic oral exam	visit	43.67	4Q 92	4c
Doctor's fee, routine exam, established patient	visit	33.50	4Q 92	4c
Hospital care, semiprivate room	day	355.00	4Q 92	4c
Household Goods				
Appliance repair, home, service call, washing machine	min labor charge	28.33	4Q 92	4c
Laundry detergent, Tide Ultra, Bold, or Cheer	42 oz	3.35	4Q 92	4c
Tissues, facial, Kleenex brand	175-count box	1.19	4Q 92	4c
Housing				
ACCRA Index, Housing		97.70	4Q 92	4c
House, 1,800 sq ft, 8,000 sq ft lot, new, urban	total	110700	4Q 92	4c

Manhattan, KS - continued

Item	Per	Value	Date	Ref.
Housing - continued				
House payment, principal and interest, 25% down payment	month	616	4Q 92	4c
Mortgage rate, incl. points & origination fee, 30-year fixed or adjustable rate	per-cent	8.12	4Q 92	4c
Rent, apartment, 2 bedrooms - 1-1/2 to 2 baths, unfurnished, 950 sq ft, water	month	446	4Q 92	4c
Personal Goods				
Shampoo, Alberto VO5	15 oz	1.39	4Q 92	4c
Toothpaste, Crest or Colgate	6-7 oz	2.06	4Q 92	4c
Personal Services				
Dry cleaning, man's 2-piece suit		6.18	4Q 92	4c
Haircare, woman's shampoo, trim and blow-dry		14.32	4Q 92	4c
Haircut, man's barbershop, no styling		5.83	4Q 92	4c
Restaurant Food				
Chicken, fried, thigh and drumstick		2.18	4Q 92	4c
Hamburger with cheese	1/4 lb	1.95	4Q 92	4c
Pizza, Pizza Hut or Pizza Inn, cheese, thin crust	12-13 in	7.75	4Q 92	4c
Transportation				
ACCRA Index, Transportation		93.90	4Q 92	4c
Tire balance, computer or spin balance, front	wheel	5.67	4Q 92	4c
Utilities				
ACCRA Index, Utilities		87.80	4Q 92	4c
Electricity, partial electric and other energy, 1,800 sq ft living area new home	month	48.54	4Q 92	4c

Manitowoc-Two Rivers, WI

Item	Per	Value	Date	Ref.
Composite ACCRA index		99.60	4Q 92	4c
Alcoholic Beverages				
Beer, Miller Lite or Budweiser, 12-oz containers	6 pack	3.69	4Q 92	4c
Liquor, J & B Scotch	750 ml	16.79	4Q 92	4c
Wine, Gallo Chablis blanc, 1.5 liter	bottle	4.99	4Q 92	4c
Clothing				
Jeans, man's denim		28.74	4Q 92	4c
Shirt, man's dress shirt		26.75	4Q 92	4c
Undervest, boy's size 10-14, cotton	3	3.74	4Q 92	4c
Communications				
Newspaper subscription, daily and Sunday home delivery, large-city	month	10.65	4Q 92	4c
Telephone bill, family of four	month	16.31	4Q 92	4c
Energy and Fuels				
Energy, combined forms, 1,800 sq ft heating area	month	96.85	4Q 92	4c
Energy, exc electricity, 1,800 sq ft heating area	month	52.33	4Q 92	4c
Gasoline, motor	gal	1.18	4Q 92	4c
Entertainment				
Bowling, evening rate	game	1.44	4Q 92	4c
Monopoly game, Parker Brothers', No. 9		8.22	4Q 92	4c
Movie	admis-sion	5.75	4Q 92	4c
Tennis balls, yellow, Wilson or Penn, 3	can	2.25	4Q 92	4c
Goods and Services				
ACCRA Index, Miscellaneous Goods and Services		95.90	4Q 92	4c
Groceries				
ACCRA Index, Groceries		96.60	4Q 92	4c
Babyfood, strained vegetables, lowest price	4-4.5 oz jar	0.37	4Q 92	4c
Bananas	lb	0.43	4Q 92	4c
Bread, white	24 oz	0.58	4Q 92	4c

Values are in dollars or fractions of dollars. In the column headed *Ref*, references are shown to sources. Each reference is followed by a letter. These refer to the geographical level for which data were reported: s=State, r=Region, and c=City or metro. The abbreviation *ex* is used to mean *except* or *excluding*; *exp* stands for expenditures. For other abbreviations and further explanations, please see the Introduction.

Manitowoc-Two Rivers, WI - continued

Item	Per	Value	Date	Ref.
Groceries				
Cheese, Kraft grated Parmesan	8-oz canis-ter	3.07	4Q 92	4c
Chicken, fryer, whole	lb	0.77	4Q 92	4c
Cigarettes, Winston	carton	18.70	4Q 92	4c
Coffee, vacuum-packed	13-oz can	1.90	4Q 92	4c
Corn, frozen	10 oz	0.61	4Q 92	4c
Corn Flakes, Kellogg's or Post Toasties	18 oz	1.87	4Q 92	4c
Eggs, Grade A large	doz	0.76	4Q 92	4c
Ground beef or hamburger	lb	1.56	4Q 92	4c
Lettuce, iceberg	head	0.94	4Q 92	4c
Margarine, Blue Bonnet or Parkay cubes	lb	0.56	4Q 92	4c
Milk, whole	1/2 gal	1.36	4Q 92	4c
Orange juice, Minute Maid frozen	12-oz can	1.29	4Q 92	4c
Peaches	29-oz can	1.46	4Q 92	4c
Peas Sweet, Del Monte or Green Giant	15-17 oz can	0.47	4Q 92	4c
Potatoes, white or red	10-lb sack	2.79	4Q 92	4c
Sausage, Jimmy Dean, 100% pork	lb	2.54	4Q 92	4c
Shortening, vegetable, Crisco	3-lb can	2.39	4Q 92	4c
Soft drink, Coca Cola	2 liter	1.00	4Q 92	4c
Steak, T-bone	lb	4.78	4Q 92	4c
Sugar, cane or beet	4 lb	1.67	4Q 92	4c
Tomatoes, Hunt's or Del Monte	14.5-oz can	0.72	4Q 92	4c
Tuna, chunk, light	6.125-6.5 oz can	0.54	4Q 92	4c
Health Care				
ACCRA Index, Health Care		97.30	4Q 92	4c
Analgesic, Aspirin, Bayer, 325 mg tablets	100	5.38	4Q 92	4c
Dentist's fee, adult teeth cleaning and periodic oral exam	visit	49.67	4Q 92	4c
Doctor's fee, routine exam, established patient	visit	35.55	4Q 92	4c
Hospital care, semiprivate room	day	240.50	4Q 92	4c
Household Goods				
Appliance repair, home, service call, washing machine	min labor charge	28.45	4Q 92	4c
Laundry detergent, Tide Ultra, Bold, or Cheer	42 oz	2.86	4Q 92	4c
Tissues, facial, Kleenex brand	175-count box	0.94	4Q 92	4c
Housing				
ACCRA Index, Housing		111.70	4Q 92	4c
House, 1,800 sq ft, 8,000 sq ft lot, new, urban	total	123625	4Q 92	4c
House payment, principal and interest, 25% down payment	month	694	4Q 92	4c
Mortgage rate, incl. points & origination fee, 30-year fixed or adjustable rate	per-cent	8.21	4Q 92	4c
Personal Goods				
Shampoo, Alberto VO5	15 oz	1.17	4Q 92	4c
Toothpaste, Crest or Colgate	6-7 oz	1.81	4Q 92	4c
Personal Services				
Dry cleaning, man's 2-piece suit		6.05	4Q 92	4c
Haircare, woman's shampoo, trim and blow-dry		14.30	4Q 92	4c
Haircut, man's barbershop, no styling		7.38	4Q 92	4c
Restaurant Food				
Chicken, fried, thigh and drumstick		2.19	4Q 92	4c
Hamburger with cheese	1/4 lb	1.74	4Q 92	4c

Manitowoc-Two Rivers, WI - continued

Item	Per	Value	Date	Ref.
Restaurant Food - continued				
Pizza, Pizza Hut or Pizza Inn, cheese, thin crust	12-13 in	9.35	4Q 92	4c
Transportation				
ACCRA Index, Transportation		93.60	4Q 92	4c
Tire balance, computer or spin balance, front	wheel	5.40	4Q 92	4c
Utilities				
ACCRA Index, Utilities		88.20	4Q 92	4c
Electricity, partial electric and other energy, 1,800 sq ft living area new home	month	44.52	4Q 92	4c

Mansfield, OH

Item	Per	Value	Date	Ref.
Composite ACCRA index		97.70	4Q 92	4c
Alcoholic Beverages				
Beer, Miller Lite or Budweiser, 12-oz containers	6 pack	3.90	4Q 92	4c
Liquor, J & B Scotch	750 ml	18.35	4Q 92	4c
Wine, Gallo Chablis blanc, 1.5 liter	bottle	5.71	4Q 92	4c
Child Care				
Child care fee, average, center	hour	1.63	90	65r
Child care fee, average, nonregulated family day care	hour	1.83	90	65r
Child care fee, average, regulated family day care	hour	1.42	90	65r
Clothing				
Jeans, man's denim		29.99	4Q 92	4c
Shirt, man's dress shirt		27.25	4Q 92	4c
Undervest, boy's size 10-14, cotton	3	3.72	4Q 92	4c
Communications				
Long-distance telephone service, day, initial minute, 0-100 miles	min	0.26-0.43	91	12s
Long-distance telephone service, day, additional minute, 0-100 miles	min	0.14-0.24	91	12s
Long-distance telephone service, evenings/weekends, 0-100 mi, initial minute	min	0.11-0.17	91	12s
Long-distance telephone service, evenings/weekends, 0-100 mi, additional minute	min	0.06-0.10	91	12s
Newspaper subscription, daily and Sunday home delivery, large-city	month	11.96	4Q 92	4c
Telephone bill, family of four	month	22.71	4Q 92	4c
Education				
Board, 4-yr private college/university	year	1872	91	22s
Board, 4-yr public college/university	year	1742	91	22s
Expenditures, local gov't, public elementary/secondary	pupil	5451	92	20s
Room, 4-year private college/university	year	1695	91	22s
Room, 4-year public college/university	year	2259	91	22s
Tuition, 2-year private college/university	year	6093	91	22s
Tuition, 2-year public college/university	year	1768	91	22s
Tuition, 4-year private college/university	year	8729	91	22s
Tuition, 4-year public college/university, in-state	year	2622	91	22s
Energy and Fuels				
Coal	mil Btu	1.54	90	64s
Energy	mil Btu	8.32	90	64s
Energy, combined forms, 1,800 sq ft heating area	month	136.86	4Q 92	4c
Energy, exc electricity, 1,800 sq ft heating area	month	52.63	4Q 92	4c
Energy exp/householder, 1-family unit	year	471	90	28r
Energy exp/householder, <1,000 sq ft heating area	year	430	90	28r
Energy exp/householder, 1,000-1,999 sq ft heating area	year	481	90	28r
Energy exp/householder, 2,000+ sq ft heating area	year	473	90	28r

Values are in dollars or fractions of dollars. In the column headed *Ref*, references are shown to sources. Each reference is followed by a letter. These refer to the geographical level for which data were reported: s = State, r = Region, and c = City or metro. The abbreviation *ex* is used to mean *except* or *excluding*; *exp* stands for expenditures. For other abbreviations and further explanations, please see the Introduction.

Mansfield, OH - continued

Item	Per	Value	Date	Ref.
Energy and Fuels				
Energy exp/householder, mobile home	year	430	90	28r
Energy exp/householder, multifamily	year	461	90	28r
Gas, natural	mil Btu	4.54	90	64s
Gas, natural	000 cu ft	5.28	91	46s
Gas, natural, exp	year	606	91	46s
Gasoline, motor	gal	1.05	4Q 92	4c
Gasoline, unleaded regular	mil Btu	9.35	90	64s
Entertainment				
Bowling, evening rate	game	2.15	4Q 92	4c
Miniature golf admission	adult	6.18	92	1r
Miniature golf admission	child	5.14	92	1r
Monopoly game, Parker Brothers', No. 9		11.48	4Q 92	4c
Movie	admission	4.88	4Q 92	4c
Tennis balls, yellow, Wilson or Penn, 3	can	2.30	4Q 92	4c
Waterpark admission	adult	11.00	92	1r
Waterpark admission	child	8.55	92	1r
Funerals				
Casket, 18-gauge steel, velvet interior		1926.72	91	24r
Cosmetology, hair care, etc.		97.64	91	24r
Embalming		249.14	91	24r
Facility use for ceremony		208.59	91	24r
Hearse, local		130.12	91	24r
Limousine, local		104.66	91	24r
Remains to funeral home, transfer		93.61	91	24r
Service charge, professional		724.62	91	24r
Vault, concrete, non-metallic liner		734.53	91	24r
Viewing facilities, use		236.06	91	24r
Goods and Services				
ACCRA Index, Miscellaneous Goods and Services		99.00	4Q 92	4c
Groceries				
ACCRA Index, Groceries		100.20	4Q 92	4c
Apples, Red Delicious	lb	0.77	4/93	16r
Babyfood, strained vegetables, lowest price	4-4.5 oz jar	0.26	4Q 92	4c
Bacon	lb	1.85	4/93	16r
Bananas	lb	0.49	4Q 92	4c
Bananas	lb	0.46	4/93	16r
Beef, stew, boneless	lb	2.53	4/93	16r
Bologna, all beef or mixed	lb	2.19	4/93	16r
Bread, white	24 oz	0.60	4Q 92	4c
Bread, white, pan	lb	0.78	4/93	16r
Butter	lb	1.50	4/93	16r
Cabbage	lb	0.40	4/93	16r
Carrots, short trimmed and topped	lb	0.45	4/93	16r
Cheese, Cheddar	lb	3.47	4/93	16r
Cheese, Kraft grated Parmesan	8-oz canister	3.11	4Q 92	4c
Chicken, fresh, whole	lb	0.84	4/93	16r
Chicken, fryer, whole	lb	0.88	4Q 92	4c
Chicken breast, bone-in	lb	1.94	4/93	16r
Chicken legs, bone-in	lb	1.02	4/93	16r
Chuck roast, graded and ungraded, ex USDA prime and choice	lb	2.43	4/93	16r
Chuck roast, USDA choice, bone-in	lb	2.11	4/93	16r
Chuck roast, USDA choice, boneless	lb	2.44	4/93	16r
Cigarettes, Winston	carton	17.09	4Q 92	4c
Coffee, 100% ground roast, all sizes	lb	2.47	4/93	16r
Coffee, vacuum-packed	13-oz can	2.10	4Q 92	4c
Cookies, chocolate chip	lb	2.73	4/93	16r
Corn, frozen	10 oz	0.64	4Q 92	4c
Corn Flakes, Kellogg's or Post Toasties	18 oz	1.97	4Q 92	4c
Eggs, Grade A large	doz	0.80	4Q 92	4c
Eggs, Grade A large	doz	0.93	4/93	16r
Flour, white, all purpose	lb	0.21	4/93	16r
Grapefruit	lb	0.45	4/93	16r

Mansfield, OH - continued

Item	Per	Value	Date	Ref.
Groceries - continued				
Grapes, Thompson Seedless	lb	1.46	4/93	16r
Ground beef, 100% beef	lb	1.63	4/93	16r
Ground beef, lean and extra lean	lb	2.08	4/93	16r
Ground beef or hamburger	lb	1.63	4Q 92	4c
Ground chuck, 100% beef	lb	1.94	4/93	16r
Ham, boneless, excluding canned	lb	2.21	4/93	16r
Honey, jar	8 oz	0.97-1.25	92	5r
Honey, jar	lb	1.25-2.25	92	5r
Honey, squeeze bear	12-oz	1.25-1.99	92	5r
Ice cream, prepackaged, bulk, regular	1/2 gal	2.41	4/93	16r
Lemons	lb	0.82	4/93	16r
Lettuce, iceberg	head	0.97	4Q 92	4c
Lettuce, iceberg	lb	0.83	4/93	16r
Margarine, Blue Bonnet or Parkay cubes	lb	0.63	4Q 92	4c
Margarine, stick	lb	0.77	4/93	16r
Milk, whole	1/2 gal	1.30	4Q 92	4c
Orange juice, Minute Maid frozen	12-oz can	1.53	4Q 92	4c
Oranges, navel	lb	0.50	4/93	16r
Peaches	29-oz can	1.49	4Q 92	4c
Peanut butter, creamy, all sizes	lb	1.82	4/93	16r
Pears, Anjou	lb	0.85	4/93	16r
Peas Sweet, Del Monte or Green Giant	15-17 oz can	0.63	4Q 92	4c
Pork chops, center cut, bone-in	lb	3.17	4/93	16r
Potato chips	16 oz	2.68	4/93	16r
Potatoes, white	lb	0.26	4/93	16r
Potatoes, white or red	10-lb sack	1.37	4Q 92	4c
Round roast, graded & ungraded, ex USDA prime & choice	lb	2.88	4/93	16r
Round roast, USDA choice, boneless	lb	2.96	4/93	16r
Sausage, Jimmy Dean, 100% pork	lb	2.61	4Q 92	4c
Shortening, vegetable oil blends	lb	0.79	4/93	16r
Shortening, vegetable, Crisco	3-lb can	2.27	4Q 92	4c
Soft drink, Coca Cola	2 liter	1.11	4Q 92	4c
Spaghetti and macaroni	lb	0.76	4/93	16r
Steak, rib eye, USDA choice, boneless	lb	6.29	4/93	16r
Steak, round, USDA choice, boneless	lb	3.24	4/93	16r
Steak, sirloin, graded & ungraded, ex USDA prime & choice	lb	4.00	4/93	16r
Steak, sirloin, USDA choice, bone-in	lb	3.57	4/93	16r
Steak, sirloin, USDA choice, boneless	lb	4.17	4/93	16r
Steak, T-bone	lb	5.59	4Q 92	4c
Steak, T-bone, USDA choice, bone-in	lb	5.60	4/93	16r
Strawberries, dry pint	12 oz	0.90	4/93	16r
Sugar, cane or beet	4 lb	1.36	4Q 92	4c
Sugar, white	lb	0.36	4/93	16r
Sugar, white, 33-80 oz pk	lb	0.35	4/93	16r
Tomatoes, field grown	lb	0.99	4/93	16r
Tomatoes, Hunt's or Del Monte	14.5-oz can	0.77	4Q 92	4c
Tuna, chunk, light	6.125-6.5 oz can	0.68	4Q 92	4c
Tuna, chunk, light	lb	1.76	4/93	16r
Turkey, frozen, whole	lb	0.91	4/93	16r
Health Care				
ACCRA Index, Health Care		89.40	4Q 92	4c
Analgesic, Aspirin, Bayer, 325 mg tablets	100	4.57	4Q 92	4c
Childbirth, cesarean, hospital		4688	91	62r
Childbirth, cesarean, physician's fee		2053	91	62r
Childbirth, normal, hospital		2657	91	62r
Childbirth, normal, physician's fee		1492	91	62r
Dentist's fee, adult teeth cleaning and periodic oral exam	visit	39.33	4Q 92	4c
Doctor's fee, routine exam, established patient	visit	31.50	4Q 92	4c
Hospital care, semiprivate room	day	265.10	90	27c
Hospital care, semiprivate room	day	339.00	4Q 92	4c

Values are in dollars or fractions of dollars. In the column headed *Ref*, references are shown to sources. Each reference is followed by a letter. These refer to the geographical level for which data were reported: s=State, r=Region, and c=City or metro. The abbreviation *ex* is used to mean *except* or *excluding*; *exp* stands for expenditures. For other abbreviations and further explanations, please see the Introduction.

Mansfield, OH - continued

Item	Per	Value	Date	Ref.
Health Care				
Medical insurance premium, per employee, small group comprehensive	month	299.30	10/91	25c
Medical plan per employee	year	3443	91	45r
Mental health care, exp	capita	37.60-53.67	90	38s
Mental health care, exp, state mental health agency	capita	40.93	90	38s
Mental health care, hospital psychiatric services, non-Federal, exp	capita	15.03	88	38s
Mental health care, mental health organization, multiservice, exp	capita	14.46	88	38s
Mental health care, psychiatric hospitals, private, exp	capita	7.93	88	38s
Mental health care, psychiatric out-patient clinics, freestanding, exp	capita	2.93	88	38s
Mental health care, psychiatric partial-care organizations, freestanding, exp	capita	0.32	88	38s
Mental health care, state and county mental hospitals, exp	capita	23.79	88	38s
Mental health care, VA medical centers, exp	capita	7.76	88	38s
Physician fee, family practice, first-visit		76.00	91	62r
Physician fee, family practice, revisit		33.00	91	62r
Physician fee, general practice, first-visit		61.00	91	62r
Physician fee, general practice, revisit		31.00	91	62r
Physician fee, general surgeon, first-visit		65.00	91	62r
Physician fee, general surgeon, revisit		35.00	91	62r
Physician fee, internal medicine, first-visit		91.00	91	62r
Physician fee, internal medicine, revisit		40.00	91	62r
Physician fee, median, neurosurgeon, first-visit		106.00	91	62r
Physician fee, median, nonsurgical specialist, first-visit		90.00	91	62r
Physician fee, median, orthopedic surgeon, first-visit		83.00	91	62r
Physician fee, median, surgical specialist, first-visit		61.00	91	62r
Physician fee, neurosurgeon, revisit		41.00	91	62r
Physician fee, nonsurgical specialist, revisit		40.00	91	62r
Physician fee, obstetrics/gynecology, first-visit		61.00	91	62r
Physician fee, obstetrics/gynecology, revisit		40.00	91	62r
Physician fee, orthopedic surgeon, revisit		41.00	91	62r
Physician fee, pediatrician, first-visit		46.00	91	62r
Physician fee, pediatrician, revisit		33.00	91	62r
Physician fee, surgical specialist, revisit		36.00	91	62r
Substance abuse, hospital ancillary charge	incident	940	90	70s
Substance abuse, hospital physician charge	incident	380	90	70s
Substance abuse, hospital room and board	incident	5410	90	70s
Household Goods				
Appliance repair, home, service call, washing machine	min labor charge	31.09	4Q 92	4c
Laundry detergent, Tide Ultra, Bold, or Cheer	42 oz	3.53	4Q 92	4c
Tissues, facial, Kleenex brand	175-count box	1.19	4Q 92	4c
Housing				
ACCRA Index, Housing		91.00	4Q 92	4c
House, 1,800 sq ft, 8,000 sq ft lot, new, urban	total	108828	4Q 92	4c
House payment, principal and interest, 25% down payment	month	607	4Q 92	4c
Mortgage rate, incl. points & origination fee, 30-year fixed or adjustable rate	percent	8.14	4Q 92	4c
Rent, apartment, 2 bedrooms - 1-1/2 to 2 baths, unfurnished, 950 sq ft, water	month	339	4Q 92	4c
Rental unit, 1 bedroom	month	337	93	23c

Mansfield, OH - continued

Item	Per	Value	Date	Ref.
Housing - continued				
Rental unit, 2 bedroom	month	393	93	23c
Rental unit, 3 bedroom	month	495	93	23c
Rental unit, 4 bedroom	month	552	93	23c
Rental unit, efficiency	month	274	93	23c
Insurance and Pensions				
Auto insurance, private passenger	year	547.38	91	63s
Personal Goods				
Shampoo, Alberto VO5	15 oz	1.18	4Q 92	4c
Toothpaste, Crest or Colgate	6-7 oz	1.85	4Q 92	4c
Personal Services				
Dry cleaning, man's 2-piece suit		6.09	4Q 92	4c
Haircare, woman's shampoo, trim and blow-dry		18.30	4Q 92	4c
Haircut, man's barbershop, no styling		7.15	4Q 92	4c
Restaurant Food				
Chicken, fried, thigh and drumstick		1.89	4Q 92	4c
Hamburger with cheese	1/4 lb	1.80	4Q 92	4c
Pizza, Pizza Hut or Pizza Inn, cheese, thin crust	12-13 in	7.95	4Q 92	4c
Taxes				
Tax, cigarette	pack	18	91	77s
Tax, gasoline	gal	21	91	77s
Taxes, state	capita	1056	91	77s
Transportation				
ACCRA Index, Transportation		88.70	4Q 92	4c
Driver's license fee		5.00	12/90	43s
Tire balance, computer or spin balance, front	wheel	5.50	4Q 92	4c
Utilities				
ACCRA Index, Utilities		124.50	4Q 92	4c
Electricity	mil Btu	17.33	90	64s
Electricity, partial electric and other energy, 1,800 sq ft living area new home	month	84.23	4Q 92	4c

Marietta, OH

Item	Per	Value	Date	Ref.
Composite ACCRA index		93.10	4Q 92	4c
Alcoholic Beverages				
Beer, Miller Lite or Budweiser, 12-oz containers	6 pack	3.85	4Q 92	4c
Liquor, J & B Scotch	750 ml	18.35	4Q 92	4c
Wine, Gallo Chablis blanc, 1.5 liter	bottle	5.73	4Q 92	4c
Clothing				
Jeans, man's denim		31.00	4Q 92	4c
Shirt, man's dress shirt		21.00	4Q 92	4c
Undervest, boy's size 10-14, cotton	3	3.98	4Q 92	4c
Communications				
Newspaper subscription, daily and Sunday home delivery, large-city	month	10.65	4Q 92	4c
Telephone bill, family of four	month	25.77	4Q 92	4c
Energy and Fuels				
Energy, combined forms, 1,800 sq ft heating area	month	94.78	4Q 92	4c
Energy, exc electricity, 1,800 sq ft heating area	month	49.30	4Q 92	4c
Gas, cooking, winter, 10 therms	month	11.66	92	56c
Gas, cooking, winter, 30 therms	month	23.17	92	56c
Gas, cooking, winter, 50 therms	month	34.68	92	56c
Gas, heating, winter, 100 therms	month	63.46	92	56c
Gas, heating, winter, average use	month	141.17	92	56c
Gasoline, motor	gal	1.14	4Q 92	4c
Entertainment				
Bowling, evening rate	game	1.92	4Q 92	4c
Monopoly game, Parker Brothers', No. 9		9.64	4Q 92	4c

Values are in dollars or fractions of dollars. In the column headed *Ref*, references are shown to sources. Each reference is followed by a letter. These refer to the geographical level for which data were reported: s=State, r=Region, and c=City or metro. The abbreviation *ex* is used to mean *except* or *excluding*; *exp* stands for expenditures. For other abbreviations and further explanations, please see the Introduction.

Marietta, OH - continued

Item	Per	Value	Date	Ref.
Entertainment				
Movie	admission	5.00	4Q 92	4c
Tennis balls, yellow, Wilson or Penn, 3	can	2.87	4Q 92	4c
Goods and Services				
ACCRA Index, Miscellaneous Goods and Services		97.80	4Q 92	4c
Groceries				
ACCRA Index, Groceries		95.10	4Q 92	4c
Babyfood, strained vegetables, lowest price	4-4.5 oz jar	0.25	4Q 92	4c
Bananas	lb	0.40	4Q 92	4c
Bread, white	24 oz	0.65	4Q 92	4c
Cheese, Kraft grated Parmesan	8-oz canister	2.88	4Q 92	4c
Chicken, fryer, whole	lb	0.87	4Q 92	4c
Cigarettes, Winston	carton	16.84	4Q 92	4c
Coffee, vacuum-packed	13-oz can	2.21	4Q 92	4c
Corn, frozen	10 oz	0.68	4Q 92	4c
Corn Flakes, Kellogg's or Post Toasties	18 oz	1.87	4Q 92	4c
Eggs, Grade A large	doz	0.85	4Q 92	4c
Ground beef or hamburger	lb	1.44	4Q 92	4c
Lettuce, iceberg	head	0.87	4Q 92	4c
Margarine, Blue Bonnet or Parkay cubes	lb	0.50	4Q 92	4c
Milk, whole	1/2 gal	1.42	4Q 92	4c
Orange juice, Minute Maid frozen	12-oz can	1.33	4Q 92	4c
Peaches	29-oz can	1.40	4Q 92	4c
Peas Sweet, Del Monte or Green Giant	15-17 oz can	0.69	4Q 92	4c
Potatoes, white or red	10-lb sack	1.35	4Q 92	4c
Sausage, Jimmy Dean, 100% pork	lb	2.07	4Q 92	4c
Shortening, vegetable, Crisco	3-lb can	2.13	4Q 92	4c
Soft drink, Coca Cola	2 liter	1.07	4Q 92	4c
Steak, T-bone	lb	5.59	4Q 92	4c
Sugar, cane or beet	4 lb	1.43	4Q 92	4c
Tomatoes, Hunt's or Del Monte	14.5-oz can	0.70	4Q 92	4c
Tuna, chunk, light	6.125-6.5 oz can	0.58	4Q 92	4c
Health Care				
ACCRA Index, Health Care		87.30	4Q 92	4c
Analgesic, Aspirin, Bayer, 325 mg tablets	100	4.46	4Q 92	4c
Dentist's fee, adult teeth cleaning and periodic oral exam	visit	38.38	4Q 92	4c
Doctor's fee, routine exam, established patient	visit	31.62	4Q 92	4c
Hospital care, semiprivate room	day	317.00	4Q 92	4c
Household Goods				
Appliance repair, home, service call, washing machine	min labor charge	35.48	4Q 92	4c
Laundry detergent, Tide Ultra, Bold, or Cheer	42 oz	2.99	4Q 92	4c
Tissues, facial, Kleenex brand	175-count box	1.19	4Q 92	4c
Housing				
ACCRA Index, Housing		88.80	4Q 92	4c
House, 1,800 sq ft, 8,000 sq ft lot, new, urban	total	101750	4Q 92	4c
House payment, principal and interest, 25% down payment	month	572	4Q 92	4c

Marietta, OH - continued

Item	Per	Value	Date	Ref.
Housing - continued				
Mortgage rate, incl. points & origination fee, 30-year fixed or adjustable rate	percent	8.22	4Q 92	4c
Rent, apartment, 2 bedrooms - 1-1/2 to 2 baths, unfurnished, 950 sq ft, water	month	378	4Q 92	4c
Personal Goods				
Shampoo, Alberto VO5	15 oz	1.26	4Q 92	4c
Toothpaste, Crest or Colgate	6-7 oz	1.91	4Q 92	4c
Personal Services				
Dry cleaning, man's 2-piece suit		5.67	4Q 92	4c
Haircare, woman's shampoo, trim and blow-dry		18.00	4Q 92	4c
Haircut, man's barbershop, no styling		6.70	4Q 92	4c
Restaurant Food				
Chicken, fried, thigh and drumstick		1.99	4Q 92	4c
Hamburger with cheese	1/4 lb	1.75	4Q 92	4c
Pizza, Pizza Hut or Pizza Inn, cheese, thin crust	12-13 in	7.49	4Q 92	4c
Transportation				
ACCRA Index, Transportation		90.70	4Q 92	4c
Tire balance, computer or spin balance, front	wheel	5.52	4Q 92	4c
Utilities				
ACCRA Index, Utilities		91.40	4Q 92	4c
Electricity, partial electric and other energy, 1,800 sq ft living area new home	month	45.48	4Q 92	4c
Electricity, winter, 250 KWh	month	15.76	92	55c
Electricity, winter, 500 KWh	month	28.54	92	55c
Electricity, winter, 750 KWh	month	41.31	92	55c
Electricity, winter, 1000 KWh	month	54.09	92	55c

Marinette, WI

Item	Per	Value	Date	Ref.
Composite ACCRA index		93.60	4Q 92	4c
Alcoholic Beverages				
Beer, Miller Lite or Budweiser, 12-oz containers	6 pack	3.26	4Q 92	4c
Liquor, J & B Scotch	750 ml	15.42	4Q 92	4c
Wine, Gallo Chablis blanc, 1.5 liter	bottle	4.49	4Q 92	4c
Clothing				
Jeans, man's denim		29.99	4Q 92	4c
Shirt, man's dress shirt		23.00	4Q 92	4c
Undervest, boy's size 10-14, cotton	3	3.45	4Q 92	4c
Communications				
Newspaper subscription, daily and Sunday home delivery, large-city	month	11.96	4Q 92	4c
Telephone bill, family of four	month	16.31	4Q 92	4c
Energy and Fuels				
Energy, combined forms, 1,800 sq ft heating area	month	95.27	4Q 92	4c
Energy, exc electricity, 1,800 sq ft heating area	month	55.18	4Q 92	4c
Gasoline, motor	gal	1.17	4Q 92	4c
Entertainment				
Bowling, evening rate	game	1.75	4Q 92	4c
Monopoly game, Parker Brothers', No. 9		9.97	4Q 92	4c
Movie	admission	5.00	4Q 92	4c
Tennis balls, yellow, Wilson or Penn, 3	can	2.66	4Q 92	4c
Goods and Services				
ACCRA Index, Miscellaneous Goods and Services		98.00	4Q 92	4c
Groceries				
ACCRA Index, Groceries		102.20	4Q 92	4c
Babyfood, strained vegetables, lowest price	4-4.5 oz jar	0.39	4Q 92	4c

Values are in dollars or fractions of dollars. In the column headed *Ref*, references are shown to sources. Each reference is followed by a letter. These refer to the geographical level for which data were reported: s=State, r=Region, and c=City or metro. The abbreviation *ex* is used to mean *except* or *excluding*; *exp* stands for *expenditures*. For other abbreviations and further explanations, please see the Introduction.

Marinette, WI - continued

Item	Per	Value	Date	Ref.
Groceries				
Bananas	lb	0.30	4Q 92	4c
Bread, white	24 oz	0.58	4Q 92	4c
Cheese, Kraft grated Parmesan	8-oz canister	2.96	4Q 92	4c
Chicken, fryer, whole	lb	0.92	4Q 92	4c
Cigarettes, Winston	carton	19.38	4Q 92	4c
Coffee, vacuum-packed	13-oz can	1.96	4Q 92	4c
Corn, frozen	10 oz	0.63	4Q 92	4c
Corn Flakes, Kellogg's or Post Toasties	18 oz	2.21	4Q 92	4c
Eggs, Grade A large	doz	0.76	4Q 92	4c
Ground beef or hamburger	lb	1.64	4Q 92	4c
Lettuce, iceberg	head	1.09	4Q 92	4c
Margarine, Blue Bonnet or Parkay cubes	lb	0.59	4Q 92	4c
Milk, whole	1/2 gal	1.53	4Q 92	4c
Orange juice, Minute Maid frozen	12-oz can	1.58	4Q 92	4c
Peaches	29-oz can	1.52	4Q 92	4c
Peas Sweet, Del Monte or Green Giant	15-17 oz can	0.65	4Q 92	4c
Potatoes, white or red	10-lb sack	2.49	4Q 92	4c
Sausage, Jimmy Dean, 100% pork	lb	2.75	4Q 92	4c
Shortening, vegetable, Crisco	3-lb can	2.16	4Q 92	4c
Soft drink, Coca Cola	2 liter	1.14	4Q 92	4c
Steak, T-bone	lb	4.64	4Q 92	4c
Sugar, cane or beet	4 lb	1.44	4Q 92	4c
Tomatoes, Hunt's or Del Monte	14.5-oz can	0.72	4Q 92	4c
Tuna, chunk, light	6.125-6.5 oz can	0.50	4Q 92	4c
Health Care				
ACCRA Index, Health Care		96.60	4Q 92	4c
Analgesic, Aspirin, Bayer, 325 mg tablets	100	5.27	4Q 92	4c
Dentist's fee, adult teeth cleaning and periodic oral exam	visit	40.67	4Q 92	4c
Doctor's fee, routine exam, established patient	visit	45.00	4Q 92	4c
Hospital care, semiprivate room	day	195.00	4Q 92	4c
Household Goods				
Appliance repair, home, service call, washing machine	min labor charge	36.32	4Q 92	4c
Laundry detergent, Tide Ultra, Bold, or Cheer	42 oz	4.16	4Q 92	4c
Tissues, facial, Kleenex brand	175-count box	1.19	4Q 92	4c
Housing				
ACCRA Index, Housing		83.20	4Q 92	4c
House, 1,800 sq ft, 8,000 sq ft lot, new, urban	total	95167	4Q 92	4c
House payment, principal and interest, 25% down payment	month	541	4Q 92	4c
Mortgage rate, incl. points & origination fee, 30-year fixed or adjustable rate	percent	8.34	4Q 92	4c
Rent, apartment, 2 bedrooms - 1-1/2 to 2 baths, unfurnished, 950 sq ft, water	month	343	4Q 92	4c
Personal Goods				
Shampoo, Alberto VO5	15 oz	1.49	4Q 92	4c
Toothpaste, Crest or Colgate	6-7 oz	2.43	4Q 92	4c
Personal Services				
Dry cleaning, man's 2-piece suit		6.33	4Q 92	4c
Haircare, woman's shampoo, trim and blow-dry		13.75	4Q 92	4c

Marinette, WI - continued

Item	Per	Value	Date	Ref.
Personal Services - continued				
Haircut, man's barbershop, no styling		8.17	4Q 92	4c
Restaurant Food				
Chicken, fried, thigh and drumstick		2.12	4Q 92	4c
Hamburger with cheese	1/4 lb	1.89	4Q 92	4c
Pizza, Pizza Hut or Pizza Inn, cheese, thin crust	12-13 in	8.39	4Q 92	4c
Transportation				
ACCRA Index, Transportation		100.30	4Q 92	4c
Tire balance, computer or spin balance, front	wheel	6.33	4Q 92	4c
Utilities				
ACCRA Index, Utilities		86.90	4Q 92	4c
Electricity, partial electric and other energy, 1,800 sq ft living area new home	month	40.09	4Q 92	4c

Marshfield, WI

Item	Per	Value	Date	Ref.
Composite ACCRA index		99.20	4Q 92	4c
Alcoholic Beverages				
Beer, Miller Lite or Budweiser, 12-oz containers	6 pack	3.40	4Q 92	4c
Liquor, J & B Scotch	750 ml	15.62	4Q 92	4c
Wine, Gallo Chablis blanc, 1.5 liter	bottle	4.92	4Q 92	4c
Clothing				
Jeans, man's denim		39.99	4Q 92	4c
Shirt, man's dress shirt		23.67	4Q 92	4c
Undervest, boy's size 10-14, cotton	3	3.41	4Q 92	4c
Communications				
Newspaper subscription, daily and Sunday home delivery, large-city	month	13.52	4Q 92	4c
Telephone bill, family of four	month	22.75	4Q 92	4c
Energy and Fuels				
Energy, combined forms, 1,800 sq ft heating area	month	101.97	4Q 92	4c
Energy, exc electricity, 1,800 sq ft heating area	month	69.91	4Q 92	4c
Gasoline, motor	gal	1.17	4Q 92	4c
Entertainment				
Bowling, evening rate	game	1.70	4Q 92	4c
Monopoly game, Parker Brothers', No. 9		9.99	4Q 92	4c
Movie	admission	5.25	4Q 92	4c
Tennis balls, yellow, Wilson or Penn, 3	can	2.12	4Q 92	4c
Goods and Services				
ACCRA Index, Miscellaneous Goods and Services		98.50	4Q 92	4c
Groceries				
ACCRA Index, Groceries		99.90	4Q 92	4c
Babyfood, strained vegetables, lowest price	4-4.5 oz jar	0.41	4Q 92	4c
Bananas	lb	0.37	4Q 92	4c
Bread, white	24 oz	0.70	4Q 92	4c
Cheese, Kraft grated Parmesan	8-oz canister	3.04	4Q 92	4c
Chicken, fryer, whole	lb	0.89	4Q 92	4c
Cigarettes, Winston	carton	18.71	4Q 92	4c
Coffee, vacuum-packed	13-oz can	2.10	4Q 92	4c
Corn, frozen	10 oz	0.62	4Q 92	4c
Corn Flakes, Kellogg's or Post Toasties	18 oz	2.03	4Q 92	4c
Eggs, Grade A large	doz	0.77	4Q 92	4c
Ground beef or hamburger	lb	1.53	4Q 92	4c
Lettuce, iceberg	head	0.79	4Q 92	4c
Margarine, Blue Bonnet or Parkay cubes	lb	0.54	4Q 92	4c
Milk, whole	1/2 gal	1.45	4Q 92	4c

Values are in dollars or fractions of dollars. In the column headed *Ref*, references are shown to sources. Each reference is followed by a letter. These refer to the geographical level for which data were reported: s = State, r = Region, and c = City or metro. The abbreviation *ex* is used to mean *except* or *excluding*; *exp* stands for *expenditures*. For other abbreviations and further explanations, please see the Introduction.

Marshfield, WI - continued

Item	Per	Value	Date	Ref.
Groceries				
Orange juice, Minute Maid frozen	12-oz can	1.33	4Q 92	4c
Peaches	29-oz can	1.40	4Q 92	4c
Peas Sweet, Del Monte or Green Giant	15-17 oz can	0.51	4Q 92	4c
Potatoes, white or red	10-lb sack	1.69	4Q 92	4c
Sausage, Jimmy Dean, 100% pork	lb	2.67	4Q 92	4c
Shortening, vegetable, Crisco	3-lb can	2.30	4Q 92	4c
Soft drink, Coca Cola	2 liter	1.02	4Q 92	4c
Steak, T-bone	lb	4.49	4Q 92	4c
Sugar, cane or beet	4 lb	1.63	4Q 92	4c
Tomatoes, Hunt's or Del Monte	14.5-oz can	0.74	4Q 92	4c
Tuna, chunk, light	6.125-6.5 oz can	0.62	4Q 92	4c
Health Care				
ACCRA Index, Health Care		105.90	4Q 92	4c
Analgesic, Aspirin, Bayer, 325 mg tablets	100	4.40	4Q 92	4c
Dentist's fee, adult teeth cleaning and periodic oral exam	visit	41.75	4Q 92	4c
Doctor's fee, routine exam, established patient	visit	54.00	4Q 92	4c
Hospital care, semiprivate room	day	228.00	4Q 92	4c
Household Goods				
Appliance repair, home, service call, washing machine	min labor charge	31.00	4Q 92	4c
Laundry detergent, Tide Ultra, Bold, or Cheer	42 oz	3.47	4Q 92	4c
Tissues, facial, Kleenex brand	175-count box	1.16	4Q 92	4c
Housing				
ACCRA Index, Housing		100.10	4Q 92	4c
House, 1,800 sq ft, 8,000 sq ft lot, new, urban	total	107967	4Q 92	4c
House payment, principal and interest, 25% down payment	month	610	4Q 92	4c
Mortgage rate, incl. points & origination fee, 30-year fixed or adjustable rate	per-cent	8.29	4Q 92	4c
Rent, apartment, 2 bedrooms - 1-1/2 to 2 baths, unfurnished, 950 sq ft, water	month	506	4Q 92	4c
Personal Goods				
Shampoo, Alberto VO5	15 oz	1.07	4Q 92	4c
Toothpaste, Crest or Colgate	6-7 oz	1.87	4Q 92	4c
Personal Services				
Dry cleaning, man's 2-piece suit		5.74	4Q 92	4c
Haircare, woman's shampoo, trim and blow-dry		14.90	4Q 92	4c
Haircut, man's barbershop, no styling		8.40	4Q 92	4c
Restaurant Food				
Chicken, fried, thigh and drumstick		2.12	4Q 92	4c
Hamburger with cheese	1/4 lb	1.77	4Q 92	4c
Pizza, Pizza Hut or Pizza Inn, cheese, thin crust	12-13 in	8.39	4Q 92	4c
Transportation				
ACCRA Index, Transportation		97.80	4Q 92	4c
Tire balance, computer or spin balance, front	wheel	6.00	4Q 92	4c
Utilities				
ACCRA Index, Utilities		95.70	4Q 92	4c
Electricity, partial electric and other energy, 1,800 sq ft living area new home	month	32.06	4Q 92	4c

Martinsburg, WV

Item	Per	Value	Date	Ref.
Composite ACCRA index		90.60	4Q 92	4c
Alcoholic Beverages				
Beer, Miller Lite or Budweiser, 12-oz containers	6 pack	3.95	4Q 92	4c
Liquor, J & B Scotch	750 ml	16.81	4Q 92	4c
Wine, Gallo Chablis blanc, 1.5 liter	bottle	5.76	4Q 92	4c
Clothing				
Jeans, man's denim		25.79	4Q 92	4c
Shirt, man's dress shirt		16.79	4Q 92	4c
Undervest, boy's size 10-14, cotton	3	3.99	4Q 92	4c
Communications				
Newspaper subscription, daily and Sunday home delivery, large-city	month	8.00	4Q 92	4c
Telephone, flat rate	month	60.00	91	11c
Telephone bill, family of four	month	22.17	4Q 92	4c
Energy and Fuels				
Energy, combined forms, 1,800 sq ft heating area	month	93.89	4Q 92	4c
Gasoline, motor	gal	1.05	4Q 92	4c
Entertainment				
Bowling, evening rate	game	2.00	4Q 92	4c
Monopoly game, Parker Brothers', No. 9		12.81	4Q 92	4c
Movie	admis-sion	4.50	4Q 92	4c
Tennis balls, yellow, Wilson or Penn, 3	can	2.08	4Q 92	4c
Goods and Services				
ACCRA Index, Miscellaneous Goods and Services		90.20	4Q 92	4c
Groceries				
ACCRA Index, Groceries		91.40	4Q 92	4c
Babyfood, strained vegetables, lowest price	4-4.5 oz jar	0.34	4Q 92	4c
Bananas	lb	0.49	4Q 92	4c
Bread, white	24 oz	0.62	4Q 92	4c
Cheese, Kraft grated Parmesan	8-oz canis-ter	3.20	4Q 92	4c
Chicken, fryer, whole	lb	0.58	4Q 92	4c
Cigarettes, Winston	carton	16.57	4Q 92	4c
Coffee, vacuum-packed	13-oz can	1.92	4Q 92	4c
Corn, frozen	10 oz	0.64	4Q 92	4c
Corn Flakes, Kellogg's or Post Toasties	18 oz	1.94	4Q 92	4c
Eggs, Grade A large	doz	0.83	4Q 92	4c
Ground beef or hamburger	lb	1.43	4Q 92	4c
Lettuce, iceberg	head	0.91	4Q 92	4c
Margarine, Blue Bonnet or Parkay cubes	lb	0.58	4Q 92	4c
Milk, whole	1/2 gal	1.06	4Q 92	4c
Orange juice, Minute Maid frozen	12-oz can	1.37	4Q 92	4c
Peaches	29-oz can	1.34	4Q 92	4c
Peas Sweet, Del Monte or Green Giant	15-17 oz can	0.52	4Q 92	4c
Potatoes, white or red	10-lb sack	1.53	4Q 92	4c
Sausage, Jimmy Dean, 100% pork	lb	2.24	4Q 92	4c
Shortening, vegetable, Crisco	3-lb can	2.31	4Q 92	4c
Soft drink, Coca Cola	2 liter	1.03	4Q 92	4c
Steak, T-bone	lb	4.70	4Q 92	4c
Sugar, cane or beet	4 lb	1.34	4Q 92	4c
Tomatoes, Hunt's or Del Monte	14.5-oz can	0.65	4Q 92	4c
Tuna, chunk, light	6.125-6.5 oz can	0.63	4Q 92	4c

Values are in dollars or fractions of dollars. In the column headed *Ref*, references are shown to sources. Each reference is followed by a letter. These refer to the geographical level for which data were reported: s = State, r = Region, and c = City or metro. The abbreviation *ex* is used to mean *except* or *excluding*; *exp* stands for *expenditures*. For other abbreviations and further explanations, please see the Introduction.

Martinsburg, WV - continued

Item	Per	Value	Date	Ref.
Health Care				
ACCRA Index, Health Care		82.20	4Q 92	4c
Analgesic, Aspirin, Bayer, 325 mg tablets	100	4.99	4Q 92	4c
Dentist's fee, adult teeth cleaning and periodic oral exam	visit	36.67	4Q 92	4c
Doctor's fee, routine exam, established patient	visit	31.60	4Q 92	4c
Hospital care, semiprivate room	day	185.00	90	27c
Hospital care, semiprivate room	day	231.00	4Q 92	4c
Household Goods				
Appliance repair, home, service call, washing machine	min labor charge	29.67	4Q 92	4c
Laundry detergent, Tide Ultra, Bold, or Cheer	42 oz	3.04	4Q 92	4c
Tissues, facial, Kleenex brand	175-count box	0.99	4Q 92	4c
Housing				
ACCRA Index, Housing		95.50	4Q 92	4c
House, 1,800 sq ft, 8,000 sq ft lot, new, urban	total	110020	4Q 92	4c
House payment, principal and interest, 25% down payment	month	605	4Q 92	4c
Mortgage rate, incl. points & origination fee, 30-year fixed or adjustable rate	percent	8.00	4Q 92	4c
Rent, apartment, 2 bedrooms - 1-1/2 to 2 baths, unfurnished, 950 sq ft, water	month	430	4Q 92	4c
Personal Goods				
Shampoo, Alberto VO5	15 oz	1.31	4Q 92	4c
Toothpaste, Crest or Colgate	6-7 oz	1.95	4Q 92	4c
Personal Services				
Dry cleaning, man's 2-piece suit		5.80	4Q 92	4c
Haircare, woman's shampoo, trim and blow-dry		10.68	4Q 92	4c
Haircut, man's barbershop, no styling		5.05	4Q 92	4c
Restaurant Food				
Chicken, fried, thigh and drumstick		2.36	4Q 92	4c
Hamburger with cheese	1/4 lb	1.80	4Q 92	4c
Pizza, Pizza Hut or Pizza Inn, cheese, thin crust	12-13 in	7.49	4Q 92	4c
Transportation				
ACCRA Index, Transportation		83.20	4Q 92	4c
Tire balance, computer or spin balance, front	wheel	4.80	4Q 92	4c
Utilities				
ACCRA Index, Utilities		88.80	4Q 92	4c
Electricity, all electric, 1,800 sq ft living area new home	month	93.89	4Q 92	4c

Mason City, IA

Item	Per	Value	Date	Ref.
Composite ACCRA index		94.70	4Q 92	4c
Alcoholic Beverages				
Beer, Miller Lite or Budweiser, 12-oz containers	6 pack	3.66	4Q 92	4c
Liquor, J & B Scotch	750 ml	16.99	4Q 92	4c
Wine, Gallo Chablis blanc, 1.5 liter	bottle	5.65	4Q 92	4c
Clothing				
Jeans, man's denim		28.99	4Q 92	4c
Shirt, man's dress shirt		25.00	4Q 92	4c
Undervest, boy's size 10-14, cotton	3	3.35	4Q 92	4c
Communications				
Newspaper subscription, daily and Sunday home delivery, large-city	month	16.30	4Q 92	4c
Telephone, flat rate	month	14.45	91	11c
Telephone bill, family of four	month	20.38	4Q 92	4c

Mason City, IA - continued

Item	Per	Value	Date	Ref.
Energy and Fuels				
Energy, combined forms, 1,800 sq ft heating area	month	105.85	4Q 92	4c
Energy, exc electricity, 1,800 sq ft heating area	month	52.74	4Q 92	4c
Gas, cooking, 10 therms	month	9.45	92	56c
Gas, cooking, 30 therms	month	18.35	92	56c
Gas, cooking, 50 therms	month	27.26	92	56c
Gas, heating, winter, 100 therms	month	49.51	92	56c
Gas, heating, winter, average use	month	90.92	92	56c
Gasoline, motor	gal	1.09	4Q 92	4c
Entertainment				
Bowling, evening rate	game	1.58	4Q 92	4c
Monopoly game, Parker Brothers', No. 9		9.98	4Q 92	4c
Movie	admission	4.50	4Q 92	4c
Tennis balls, yellow, Wilson or Penn, 3	can	2.96	4Q 92	4c
Goods and Services				
ACCRA Index, Miscellaneous Goods and Services		94.70	4Q 92	4c
Groceries				
ACCRA Index, Groceries		97.40	4Q 92	4c
Babyfood, strained vegetables, lowest price	4-4.5 oz jar	0.32	4Q 92	4c
Bananas	lb	0.46	4Q 92	4c
Bread, white	24 oz	0.65	4Q 92	4c
Cheese, Kraft grated Parmesan	8-oz canister	3.31	4Q 92	4c
Chicken, fryer, whole	lb	0.78	4Q 92	4c
Cigarettes, Winston	carton	19.14	4Q 92	4c
Coffee, vacuum-packed	13-oz can	1.91	4Q 92	4c
Corn, frozen	10 oz	0.73	4Q 92	4c
Corn Flakes, Kellogg's or Post Toasties	18 oz	1.95	4Q 92	4c
Eggs, Grade A large	doz	0.72	4Q 92	4c
Ground beef or hamburger	lb	1.35	4Q 92	4c
Lettuce, iceberg	head	0.81	4Q 92	4c
Margarine, Blue Bonnet or Parkay cubes	lb	0.54	4Q 92	4c
Milk, whole	1/2 gal	1.18	4Q 92	4c
Orange juice, Minute Maid frozen	12-oz can	1.55	4Q 92	4c
Peaches	29-oz can	1.37	4Q 92	4c
Peas Sweet, Del Monte or Green Giant	15-17 oz can	0.64	4Q 92	4c
Potatoes, white or red	10-lb sack	1.77	4Q 92	4c
Sausage, Jimmy Dean, 100% pork	lb	2.50	4Q 92	4c
Shortening, vegetable, Crisco	3-lb can	2.34	4Q 92	4c
Soft drink, Coca Cola	2 liter	1.29	4Q 92	4c
Steak, T-bone	lb	5.27	4Q 92	4c
Sugar, cane or beet	4 lb	1.61	4Q 92	4c
Tomatoes, Hunt's or Del Monte	14.5-oz can	0.67	4Q 92	4c
Tuna, chunk, light	6.125-6.5 oz can	0.49	4Q 92	4c
Health Care				
ACCRA Index, Health Care		90.60	4Q 92	4c
Analgesic, Aspirin, Bayer, 325 mg tablets	100	4.43	4Q 92	4c
Dentist's fee, adult teeth cleaning and periodic oral exam	visit	43.20	4Q 92	4c
Doctor's fee, routine exam, established patient	visit	32.25	4Q 92	4c
Hospital care, semiprivate room	day	302.50	4Q 92	4c

Values are in dollars or fractions of dollars. In the column headed *Ref*, references are shown to sources. Each reference is followed by a letter. These refer to the geographical level for which data were reported: s=State, r=Region, and c=City or metro. The abbreviation *ex* is used to mean *except* or *excluding*; *exp* stands for expenditures. For other abbreviations and further explanations, please see the Introduction.

Mason City, IA - continued

Item	Per	Value	Date	Ref.
Household Goods				
Appliance repair, home, service call, washing machine	min labor charge	21.82	4Q 92	4c
Laundry detergent, Tide Ultra, Bold, or Cheer	42 oz	3.62	4Q 92	4c
Tissues, facial, Kleenex brand	175-count box	1.10	4Q 92	4c
Housing				
ACCRA Index, Housing		90.00	4Q 92	4c
House, 1,800 sq ft, 8,000 sq ft lot, new, urban	total	104363	4Q 92	4c
House payment, principal and interest, 25% down payment	month	583	4Q 92	4c
Mortgage rate, incl. points & origination fee, 30-year fixed or adjustable rate	per-cent	8.16	4Q 92	4c
Rent, apartment, 2 bedrooms - 1-1/2 to 2 baths, unfurnished, 950 sq ft, water	month	376	4Q 92	4c
Personal Goods				
Shampoo, Alberto VO5	15 oz	1.53	4Q 92	4c
Toothpaste, Crest or Colgate	6-7 oz	1.80	4Q 92	4c
Personal Services				
Dry cleaning, man's 2-piece suit		6.00	4Q 92	4c
Haircare, woman's shampoo, trim and blow-dry		16.65	4Q 92	4c
Haircut, man's barbershop, no styling		7.85	4Q 92	4c
Restaurant Food				
Chicken, fried, thigh and drumstick		1.90	4Q 92	4c
Hamburger with cheese	1/4 lb	1.89	4Q 92	4c
Pizza, Pizza Hut or Pizza Inn, cheese, thin crust	12-13 in	7.49	4Q 92	4c
Transportation				
ACCRA Index, Transportation		103.40	4Q 92	4c
Tire balance, computer or spin balance, front	wheel	7.18	4Q 92	4c
Utilities				
ACCRA Index, Utilities		97.70	4Q 92	4c
Electricity, partial electric and other energy, 1,800 sq ft living area new home	month	53.11	4Q 92	4c

McAlester, OK

Item	Per	Value	Date	Ref.
Composite ACCRA index		89.70	4Q 92	4c
Alcoholic Beverages				
Beer, Miller Lite or Budweiser, 12-oz containers	6 pack	3.84	4Q 92	4c
Liquor, J & B Scotch	750 ml	15.08	4Q 92	4c
Wine, Gallo Chablis blanc, 1.5 liter	bottle	5.32	4Q 92	4c
Clothing				
Jeans, man's denim		27.99	4Q 92	4c
Shirt, man's dress shirt		14.50	4Q 92	4c
Undervest, boy's size 10-14, cotton	3	4.15	4Q 92	4c
Communications				
Newspaper subscription, daily and Sunday home delivery, large-city	month	12.85	4Q 92	4c
Telephone, flat rate	month	10.87	91	11c
Telephone bill, family of four	month	18.03	4Q 92	4c
Energy and Fuels				
Energy, combined forms, 1,800 sq ft heating area	month	114.46	4Q 92	4c
Energy, exc electricity, 1,800 sq ft heating area	month	37.86	4Q 92	4c
Gasoline, motor	gal	1.07	4Q 92	4c
Entertainment				
Bowling, evening rate	game	1.85	4Q 92	4c
Monopoly game, Parker Brothers', No. 9		11.98	4Q 92	4c

McAlester, OK - continued

Item	Per	Value	Date	Ref.
Entertainment - continued				
Movie	admis-sion	2.50	4Q 92	4c
Tennis balls, yellow, Wilson or Penn, 3	can	2.48	4Q 92	4c
Goods and Services				
ACCRA Index, Miscellaneous Goods and Services		89.60	4Q 92	4c
Groceries				
ACCRA Index, Groceries		97.30	4Q 92	4c
Babyfood, strained vegetables, lowest price	4-4.5 oz jar	0.31	4Q 92	4c
Bananas	lb	0.39	4Q 92	4c
Bread, white	24 oz	0.63	4Q 92	4c
Cheese, Kraft grated Parmesan	8-oz canis-ter	3.45	4Q 92	4c
Chicken, fryer, whole	lb	0.74	4Q 92	4c
Cigarettes, Winston	carton	17.31	4Q 92	4c
Coffee, vacuum-packed	13-oz can	1.86	4Q 92	4c
Corn, frozen	10 oz	0.56	4Q 92	4c
Corn Flakes, Kellogg's or Post Toasties	18 oz	1.98	4Q 92	4c
Eggs, Grade A large	doz	0.86	4Q 92	4c
Ground beef or hamburger	lb	1.63	4Q 92	4c
Lettuce, iceberg	head	1.02	4Q 92	4c
Margarine, Blue Bonnet or Parkay cubes	lb	0.54	4Q 92	4c
Milk, whole	1/2 gal	1.31	4Q 92	4c
Orange juice, Minute Maid frozen	12-oz can	1.48	4Q 92	4c
Peaches	29-oz can	1.25	4Q 92	4c
Peas Sweet, Del Monte or Green Giant	15-17 oz can	0.56	4Q 92	4c
Potatoes, white or red	10-lb sack	2.26	4Q 92	4c
Sausage, Jimmy Dean, 100% pork	lb	2.58	4Q 92	4c
Shortening, vegetable, Crisco	3-lb can	2.06	4Q 92	4c
Soft drink, Coca Cola	2 liter	1.22	4Q 92	4c
Steak, T-bone	lb	4.58	4Q 92	4c
Sugar, cane or beet	4 lb	1.58	4Q 92	4c
Tomatoes, Hunt's or Del Monte	14.5-oz can	0.67	4Q 92	4c
Tuna, chunk, light	6.125-6.5 oz can	0.68	4Q 92	4c
Health Care				
ACCRA Index, Health Care		106.20	4Q 92	4c
Analgesic, Aspirin, Bayer, 325 mg tablets	100	4.93	4Q 92	4c
Dentist's fee, adult teeth cleaning and periodic oral exam	visit	52.50	4Q 92	4c
Doctor's fee, routine exam, established patient	visit	44.60	4Q 92	4c
Hospital care, semiprivate room	day	150.00	90	27c
Hospital care, semiprivate room	day	225.00	4Q 92	4c
Household Goods				
Appliance repair, home, service call, washing machine	min labor charge	30.90	4Q 92	4c
Laundry detergent, Tide Ultra, Bold, or Cheer	42 oz	3.01	4Q 92	4c
Tissues, facial, Kleenex brand	175-count box	1.15	4Q 92	4c
Housing				
ACCRA Index, Housing		79.80	4Q 92	4c
House, 1,800 sq ft, 8,000 sq ft lot, new, urban	total	90000	4Q 92	4c
House payment, principal and interest, 25% down payment	month	504	4Q 92	4c

Values are in dollars or fractions of dollars. In the column headed *Ref*, references are shown as sources. Each reference is followed by a letter. These refer to the geographical level for which data were reported: s = State, r = Region, and c = City or metro. The abbreviation *ex* is used to mean *except* or *excluding*; *exp* stands for expenditures. For other abbreviations and further explanations, please see the Introduction.

McAlester, OK - continued

Item	Per	Value	Date	Ref.
Housing				
Mortgage rate, incl. points & origination fee, 30-year fixed or adjustable rate	per-cent	8.18	4Q 92	4c
Rent, apartment, 2 bedrooms - 1-1/2 to 2 baths, unfurnished, 950 sq ft, water	month	362	4Q 92	4c
Personal Goods				
Shampoo, Alberto VO5	15 oz	1.30	4Q 92	4c
Toothpaste, Crest or Colgate	6-7 oz	2.03	4Q 92	4c
Personal Services				
Dry cleaning, man's 2-piece suit		5.00	4Q 92	4c
Haircare, woman's shampoo, trim and blow-dry		17.17	4Q 92	4c
Haircut, man's barbershop, no styling		5.00	4Q 92	4c
Restaurant Food				
Chicken, fried, thigh and drumstick		2.13	4Q 92	4c
Hamburger with cheese	1/4 lb	1.70	4Q 92	4c
Pizza, Pizza Hut or Pizza Inn, cheese, thin crust	12-13 in	8.14	4Q 92	4c
Transportation				
ACCRA Index, Transportation		87.00	4Q 92	4c
Tire balance, computer or spin balance, front	wheel	5.17	4Q 92	4c
Utilities				
ACCRA Index, Utilities		103.60	4Q 92	4c
Electricity, partial electric and other energy, 1,800 sq ft living area new home	month	76.60	4Q 92	4c

Mcallen-Edinburg-Mission, TX

Item	Per	Value	Date	Ref.
Child Care				
Child care fee, average, center	hour	1.29	90	65r
Child care fee, average, nonregulated family day care	hour	0.89	90	65r
Child care fee, average, regulated family day care	hour	1.32	90	65r
Communications				
Long-distance telephone service, day, initial minute, 0-100 miles	min	0.10-0.46	91	12s
Long-distance telephone service, day, additional minute, 0-100 miles	min	0.06-0.45	91	12s
Education				
Board, 4-yr private college/university	year	1883	91	22s
Board, 4-yr public college/university	year	1605	91	22s
Expenditures, local gov't, public elementary/secondary	pupil	4593	92	20s
Room, 4-year private college/university	year	1620	91	22s
Room, 4-year public college/university	year	1532	91	22s
Tuition, 2-year private college/university	year	4394	91	22s
Tuition, 2-year public college/university	year	495	91	22s
Tuition, 4-year private college/university	year	6497	91	22s
Tuition, 4-year public college/university, in-state	year	986	91	22s
Energy and Fuels				
Coal	mil Btu	1.44	90	64s
Energy	mil Btu	6.48	90	64s
Energy exp/householder, 1-family unit	year	471	90	28r
Energy exp/householder, <1,000 sq ft heating area	year	384	90	28r
Energy exp/householder, 1,000-1,999 sq ft heating area	year	421	90	28r
Energy exp/householder, 2,000+ sq ft heating area	year	625	90	28r
Energy exp/householder, mobile home	year	271	90	28r
Energy exp/householder, multifamily	year	355	90	28r
Gas, natural	mil Btu	2.47	90	64s
Gas, natural	000 cu ft	5.71	91	46s
Gas, natural, exp	year	388	91	46s

Mcallen-Edinburg-Mission, TX - continued

Item	Per	Value	Date	Ref.
Energy and Fuels - continued				
Gasoline, unleaded regular	mil Btu	9.16	90	64s
Entertainment				
Miniature golf admission	adult	6.18	92	1r
Miniature golf admission	child	5.14	92	1r
Waterpark admission	adult	11.00	92	1r
Waterpark admission	child	8.55	92	1r
Funerals				
Casket, 18-gauge steel, velvet interior		2274.41	91	24r
Cosmetology, hair care, etc.		74.62	91	24r
Embalming		229.94	91	24r
Facility use for ceremony		176.61	91	24r
Hearse, local		116.34	91	24r
Limousine, local		72.68	91	24r
Remains to funeral home, transfer		87.72	91	24r
Service charge, professional		712.53	91	24r
Vault, concrete, non-metallic liner		750.55	91	24r
Viewing facilities, use		155.31	91	24r
Groceries				
Apples, Red Delicious	lb	0.79	4/93	16r
Bacon	lb	1.75	4/93	16r
Bananas	lb	0.42	4/93	16r
Beef, stew, boneless	lb	2.61	4/93	16r
Bologna, all beef or mixed	lb	2.24	4/93	16r
Bread, white, pan	lb	0.64	4/93	16r
Bread, whole wheat, pan	lb	0.96	4/93	16r
Cabbage	lb	0.37	4/93	16r
Carrots, short trimmed and topped	lb	0.47	4/93	16r
Celery	lb	0.64	4/93	16r
Cheese, American	lb	2.98	4/93	16r
Cheese, Cheddar	lb	3.28	4/93	16r
Chicken, fresh, whole	lb	0.77	4/93	16r
Chicken breast, bone-in	lb	1.92	4/93	16r
Chicken legs, bone-in	lb	1.06	4/93	16r
Chuck roast, graded and ungraded, ex USDA prime and choice	lb	2.40	4/93	16r
Chuck roast, USDA choice, bone-in	lb	2.19	4/93	16r
Chuck roast, USDA choice, boneless	lb	2.38	4/93	16r
Coffee, 100% ground roast, all sizes	lb	2.48	4/93	16r
Crackers, soda, salted	lb	1.15	4/93	16r
Eggs, Grade A large	doz	0.96	4/93	16r
Flour, white, all purpose	lb	0.24	4/93	16r
Frankfurters, all meat or all beef	lb	2.01	4/93	16r
Grapefruit	lb	0.44	4/93	16r
Grapes, Thompson Seedless	lb	1.40	4/93	16r
Ground beef, 100% beef	lb	1.58	4/93	16r
Ground beef, lean and extra lean	lb	2.09	4/93	16r
Ground chuck, 100% beef	lb	1.98	4/93	16r
Ham, boneless, excluding canned	lb	2.89	4/93	16r
Ham, picnic, shoulder, bone-in, smoked	lb	1.02	4/93	16r
Ham, rump or steak half, bone-in, smoked	lb	1.48	4/93	16r
Honey, jar	8 oz	0.73-1.19	92	5r
Honey, jar	lb	1.10-1.79	92	5r
Honey, squeeze bear	12-oz	1.19-1.50	92	5r
Ice cream, prepackaged, bulk, regular	1/2 gal	2.41	4/93	16r
Lemons	lb	1.05	4/93	16r
Lettuce, iceberg	lb	0.81	4/93	16r
Margarine, stick	lb	0.88	4/93	16r
Oranges, navel	lb	0.55	4/93	16r
Pears, Anjou	lb	0.92	4/93	16r
Pork chops, center cut, bone-in	lb	3.13	4/93	16r
Potato chips	16 oz	2.94	4/93	16r
Potatoes, white	lb	0.43	4/93	16r
Rib roast, USDA choice, bone-in	lb	4.63	4/93	16r
Rice, white, long grain, uncooked	lb	0.45	4/93	16r
Round roast, graded & ungraded, ex USDA prime & choice	lb	3.03	4/93	16r
Round roast, USDA choice, boneless	lb	3.09	4/93	16r
Sausage, fresh, loose	lb	2.08	4/93	16r
Short ribs, bone-in	lb	2.66	4/93	16r
Shortening, vegetable oil blends	lb	0.69	4/93	16r
Spaghetti and macaroni	lb	0.81	4/93	16r

Values are in dollars or fractions of dollars. In the column headed *Ref*, references are shown to sources. Each reference is followed by a letter. These refer to the geographical level for which data were reported: s = State, r = Region, and c = City or metro. The abbreviation *ex* is used to mean *except* or *excluding*; *exp* stands for expenditures. For other abbreviations and further explanations, please see the Introduction.

McAllen-Edinburg-Mission, TX - continued

Item	Per	Value	Date	Ref.
Groceries				
Steak, rib eye, USDA choice, boneless	lb	6.24	4/93	16r
Steak, round, graded & ungraded, ex USDA prime & choice	lb	3.31	4/93	16r
Steak, round, USDA choice, boneless	lb	3.34	4/93	16r
Steak, sirloin, graded & ungraded, ex USDA prime & choice	lb	4.19	4/93	16r
Steak, sirloin, USDA choice, boneless	lb	4.46	4/93	16r
Steak, T-bone, USDA choice, bone-in	lb	5.25	4/93	16r
Strawberries, dry pint	12 oz	0.92	4/93	16r
Sugar, white	lb	0.39	4/93	16r
Sugar, white, 33-80 oz pk	lb	0.38	4/93	16r
Tomatoes, field grown	lb	0.88	4/93	16r
Tuna, chunk, light	lb	1.79	4/93	16r
Turkey, frozen, whole	lb	1.04	4/93	16r
Yogurt, natural, fruit flavored	1/2 pint	0.57	4/93	16r
Health Care				
Childbirth, cesarean, hospital		5034	91	62r
Childbirth, cesarean, physician's fee		2053	91	62r
Childbirth, normal, hospital		2712	91	62r
Childbirth, normal, physician's fee		1492	91	62r
Health care spending, state	capita	2192	3/93	84s
Mental health care, exp	capita	20.37-28.83	90	38s
Mental health care, exp, state mental health agency	capita	22.72	90	38s
Mental health care, hospital psychiatric services, non-Federal, exp	capita	7.95	88	38s
Mental health care, mental health organization, multiservice, exp	capita	12.05	88	38s
Mental health care, psychiatric hospitals, private, exp	capita	37.78	88	38s
Mental health care, psychiatric out-patient clinics, freestanding, exp	capita	0.43	88	38s
Mental health care, state and county mental hospitals, exp	capita	12.54	88	38s
Mental health care, VA medical centers, exp	capita	5.35	88	38s
Physician fee, family practice, first-visit		75.00	91	62r
Physician fee, family practice, revisit		34.00	91	62r
Physician fee, general practice, first-visit		61.00	91	62r
Physician fee, general practice, revisit		32.00	91	62r
Physician fee, general surgeon, first-visit		64.00	91	62r
Physician fee, general surgeon, revisit		40.00	91	62r
Physician fee, internal medicine, first-visit		98.00	91	62r
Physician fee, internal medicine, revisit		40.00	91	62r
Physician fee, median, neurosurgeon, first-visit		130.00	91	62r
Physician fee, median, nonsurgical specialist, first-visit		95.00	91	62r
Physician fee, median, orthopedic surgeon, first-visit		91.00	91	62r
Physician fee, median, plastic surgeon, first-visit		66.00	91	62r
Physician fee, median, surgical specialist, first-visit		62.00	91	62r
Physician fee, neurosurgeon, revisit		50.00	91	62r
Physician fee, nonsurgical specialist, revisit		40.00	91	62r
Physician fee, obstetrics/gynecology, first-visit		64.00	91	62r
Physician fee, obstetrics/gynecology, revisit		41.00	91	62r
Physician fee, orthopedic surgeon, revisit		40.00	91	62r
Physician fee, pediatrician, first-visit		49.00	91	62r
Physician fee, pediatrician, revisit		33.00	91	62r
Physician fee, plastic surgeon, revisit		43.00	91	62r
Physician fee, surgical specialist, revisit		37.00	91	62r
Substance abuse, hospital ancillary charge	incident	3750	90	70s
Substance abuse, hospital physician charge	incident	1080	90	70s
Substance abuse, hospital room and board	incident	5320	90	70s

McAllen-Edinburg-Mission, TX - continued

Item	Per	Value	Date	Ref.
Insurance and Pensions				
Auto insurance, private passenger	year	709.79	91	63s
Taxes				
Tax, cigarette	pack	41	91	77s
Tax, gasoline	gal	20	91	77s
Taxes, state	capita	923	91	77s
Transportation				
Driver's license fee		16.00	12/90	43s
Travel				
Business travel	day	193.00	4/93	89r
Utilities				
Electricity	mil Btu	17.09	90	64s
Electricity, residential	KWh	5.92	2/93	94s

Medford, OR

Item	Per	Value	Date	Ref.
Child Care				
Child care fee, average, center	hour	1.71	90	65r
Child care fee, average, nonregulated family day care	hour	1.32	90	65r
Child care fee, average, regulated family day care	hour	1.86	90	65r
Communications				
Long-distance telephone service, day, initial minute, 0-100 miles	min	0.13-0.26	91	12s
Long-distance telephone service, day, additional minute, 0-100 miles	min	0.10-0.21	91	12s
Long-distance telephone service, evenings/weekends, 0-100 mi, initial minute	min	0.07-0.13	91	12s
Long-distance telephone service, evenings/weekends, 0-100 mi, additional minute	min	0.04-0.07	91	12s
Education				
Board, 4-yr private college/university	year	2004	91	22s
Board, 4-yr public college/university	year	1954	91	22s
Expenditures, local gov't, public elementary/secondary	pupil	5463	92	20s
Room, 4-year private college/university	year	1621	91	22s
Room, 4-year public college/university	year	1329	91	22s
Tuition, 2-year private college/university	year	7570	91	22s
Tuition, 2-year public college/university	year	794	91	22s
Tuition, 4-year private college/university	year	9606	91	22s
Tuition, 4-year public college/university, in-state	year	1906	91	22s
Energy and Fuels				
Coal	mil Btu	1.22	90	64s
Energy	mil Btu	8.39	90	64s
Energy exp/householder, 1-family unit	year	362	90	28r
Energy exp/householder, <1,000 sq ft heating area	year	254	90	28r
Energy exp/householder, 1,000-1,999 sq ft heating area	year	358	90	28r
Energy exp/householder, 2,000+ sq ft heating area	year	467	90	28r
Energy exp/householder, mobile home	year	390	90	28r
Energy exp/householder, multifamily	year	252	90	28r
Gas, natural	mil Btu	4.28	90	64s
Gas, natural	000 cu ft	6.13	91	46s
Gas, natural, exp	year	429	91	46s
Gasoline, unleaded regular	mil Btu	9.45	90	64s
Entertainment				
Miniature golf admission	adult	6.18	92	1r
Miniature golf admission	child	5.14	92	1r
Waterpark admission	adult	11.00	92	1r
Waterpark admission	child	8.55	92	1r

Values are in dollars or fractions of dollars. In the column headed *Ref*, references are shown to sources. Each reference is followed by a letter. These refer to the geographical level for which data were reported: s=State, r=Region, and c=City or metro. The abbreviation *ex* is used to mean *except* or *excluding*; *exp* stands for expenditures. For other abbreviations and further explanations, please see the Introduction.

Medford, OR - continued

Item	Per	Value	Date	Ref.
Funerals				
Casket, 18-gauge steel, velvet interior		1781.09	91	24r
Cosmetology, hair care, etc.		84.64	91	24r
Embalming		207.41	91	24r
Facility use for ceremony		205.76	91	24r
Hearse, local		105.14	91	24r
Limousine, local		83.21	91	24r
Remains to funeral home, transfer		113.82	91	24r
Service charge, professional		626.33	91	24r
Vault, concrete, non-metallic liner		599.54	91	24r
Viewing facilities, use		85.81	91	24r
Groceries				
Apples, Red Delicious	lb	0.80	4/93	16r
Bacon	lb	1.79	4/93	16r
Bananas	lb	0.53	4/93	16r
Bologna, all beef or mixed	lb	2.67	4/93	16r
Bread, white, pan	lb	0.81	4/93	16r
Carrots, short trimmed and topped	lb	0.39	4/93	16r
Chicken, fresh, whole	lb	0.94	4/93	16r
Chicken breast, bone-in	lb	2.19	4/93	16r
Chuck roast, graded and ungraded, ex USDA prime and choice	lb	2.26	4/93	16r
Coffee, 100% ground roast, all sizes	lb	2.33	4/93	16r
Eggs, Grade AA large	doz	1.18	4/93	16r
Flour, white, all purpose	lb	0.22	4/93	16r
Grapefruit	lb	0.52	4/93	16r
Grapes, Thompson Seedless	lb	1.50	4/93	16r
Ground beef, 100% beef	lb	1.44	4/93	16r
Ground beef, lean and extra lean	lb	2.34	4/93	16r
Ham, boneless, excluding canned	lb	2.56	4/93	16r
Honey, jar	8 oz	0.89-1.00	92	5r
Honey, jar	lb	1.35-1.97	92	5r
Honey, squeeze bear	12-oz	1.19-1.50	92	5r
Ice cream, prepackaged, bulk, regular	1/2 gal	2.40	4/93	16r
Lemons	lb	0.81	4/93	16r
Lettuce, iceberg	lb	0.84	4/93	16r
Margarine, stick	lb	0.81	4/93	16r
Oranges, navel	lb	0.48	4/93	16r
Pork chops, center cut, bone-in	lb	3.25	4/93	16r
Potato chips	16 oz	2.89	4/93	16r
Potatoes, white	lb	0.38	4/93	16r
Round roast, graded & ungraded, ex USDA prime & choice	lb	3.00	4/93	16r
Round roast, USDA choice, boneless	lb	3.16	4/93	16r
Shortening, vegetable oil blends	lb	0.86	4/93	16r
Spaghetti and macaroni	lb	0.84	4/93	16r
Steak, round, graded & ungraded, ex USDA prime & choice	lb	3.34	4/93	16r
Steak, round, USDA choice, boneless	lb	3.24	4/93	16r
Steak, sirloin, graded & ungraded, ex USDA prime & choice	lb	3.75	4/93	16r
Steak, sirloin, USDA choice, boneless	lb	4.49	4/93	16r
Sugar, white	lb	0.41	4/93	16r
Sugar, white, 33-80 oz pk	lb	0.38	4/93	16r
Tomatoes, field grown	lb	1.01	4/93	16r
Turkey, frozen, whole	lb	1.04	4/93	16r
Health Care				
Childbirth, cesarean, hospital		5533	91	62r
Childbirth, cesarean, physician's fee		2053	91	62r
Childbirth, normal, hospital		2745	91	62r
Childbirth, normal, physician's fee		1492	91	62r
Medical plan per employee	year	3421	91	45r
Mental health care, exp, state mental health agency	capita	40.68	90	38s
Mental health care, hospital psychiatric services, non-Federal, exp	capita	9.91	88	38s
Mental health care, mental health organization, multiservice, exp	capita	25.94	88	38s
Mental health care, psychiatric hospitals, private, exp	capita	1.48	88	38s
Mental health care, psychiatric out-patient clinics, freestanding, exp	capita	3.50	88	38s

Medford, OR - continued

Item	Per	Value	Date	Ref.
Health Care - continued				
Mental health care, psychiatric partial-care organizations, freestanding, exp	capita	0.58	88	38s
Mental health care, state and county mental hospitals, exp	capita	18.67	88	38s
Mental health care, VA medical centers, exp	capita	2.53	88	38s
Physician fee, family practice, first-visit		111.00	91	62r
Physician fee, family practice, revisit		45.00	91	62r
Physician fee, general practice, first-visit		100.00	91	62r
Physician fee, general practice, revisit		40.00	91	62r
Physician fee, internal medicine, first-visit		137.00	91	62r
Physician fee, internal medicine, revisit		48.00	91	62r
Physician fee, median, neurosurgeon, first-visit		157.00	91	62r
Physician fee, median, nonsurgical specialist, first-visit		131.00	91	62r
Physician fee, median, orthopedic surgeon, first-visit		124.00	91	62r
Physician fee, median, plastic surgeon, first-visit		88.00	91	62r
Physician fee, median, surgical specialist, first-visit		100.00	91	62r
Physician fee, neurosurgeon, revisit		51.00	91	62r
Physician fee, nonsurgical specialist, revisit		47.00	91	62r
Physician fee, obstetrics/gynecology, first-visit		95.00	91	62r
Physician fee, obstetrics/gynecology, revisit		50.00	91	62r
Physician fee, orthopedic surgeon, revisit		51.00	91	62r
Physician fee, pediatrician, first-visit		81.00	91	62r
Physician fee, pediatrician, revisit		42.00	91	62r
Physician fee, plastic surgeon, revisit		48.00	91	62r
Physician fee, surgical specialist, revisit		49.00	91	62r
Substance abuse, hospital ancillary charge	incident	710	90	70s
Substance abuse, hospital physician charge	incident	70	90	70s
Substance abuse, hospital room and board	incident	3330	90	70s
Insurance and Pensions				
Auto insurance, private passenger	year	598.04	91	63s
Taxes				
Tax, cigarette	pack	28	91	77s
Tax, gasoline	gal	22	91	77s
Taxes, state	capita	1037	91	77s
Transportation				
Driver's license fee		15.00	12/90	43s
Vehicle registration and license plate	year	32.50	93	53s
Travel				
Business travel	day	178.00	4/93	89r
Utilities				
Electricity	mil Btu	12.25	90	64s

Melbourne-Titusville-Palm Bay, FL

Item	Per	Value	Date	Ref.
Child Care				
Child care fee, average, center	hour	1.29	90	65r
Child care fee, average, nonregulated family day care	hour	0.89	90	65r
Child care fee, average, regulated family day care	hour	1.32	90	65r
Communications				
Long-distance telephone service, day, initial minute, 0-100 miles	min	0.15-0.20	91	12s
Long-distance telephone service, day, additional minute, 0-100 miles	min	0.08-0.20	91	12s
Long-distance telephone service, evenings/weekends, 0-100 mi, initial minute	min	0.09-0.12	91	12s
Long-distance telephone service, evenings/weekends, 0-100 mi, additional minute	min	0.05-0.12	91	12s

Values are in dollars or fractions of dollars. In the column headed *Ref*, references are shown to sources. Each reference is followed by a letter. These refer to the geographical level for which data were reported: s=State, r=Region, and c=City or metro. The abbreviation *ex* is used to mean *except* or *excluding*; *exp* stands for expenditures. For other abbreviations and further explanations, please see the Introduction.

Melbourne-Titusville-Palm Bay, FL - continued

Item	Per	Value	Date	Ref.
Education				
Board, 4-yr private college/university	year	1924	91	22s
Board, 4-yr public college/university	year	1955	91	22s
Expenditures, local gov't, public elementary/secondary	pupil	5235	92	20s
Room, 4-year private college/university	year	1904	91	22s
Room, 4-year public college/university	year	1510	91	22s
Tuition, 2-year private college/university	year	4751	91	22s
Tuition, 2-year public college/university	year	788	91	22s
Tuition, 4-year private college/university	year	7992	91	22s
Tuition, 4-year public college/university, in-state	year	1337	91	22s
Energy and Fuels				
Coal	mil Btu	1.85	90	64s
Energy	mil Btu	10.58	90	64s
Energy exp/householder, 1-family unit	year	487	90	28r
Energy exp/householder, <1,000 sq ft heating area	year	393	90	28r
Energy exp/householder, 1,000-1,999 sq ft heating area	year	442	90	28r
Energy exp/householder, 2,000+ sq ft heating area	year	577	90	28r
Energy exp/householder, mobile home	year	366	90	28r
Energy exp/householder, multifamily	year	382	90	28r
Gas, natural	mil Btu	3.21	90	64s
Gas, natural	000 cu ft	8.98	91	46s
Gas, natural, exp	year	248	91	46s
Gasoline, unleaded regular	mil Btu	8.85	90	64s
Entertainment				
Miniature golf admission	adult	6.18	92	1r
Miniature golf admission	child	5.14	92	1r
Waterpark admission	adult	11.00	92	1r
Waterpark admission	child	8.55	92	1r
Funerals				
Casket, 18-gauge steel, velvet interior		2029.08	91	24r
Cosmetology, hair care, etc.		75.10	91	24r
Embalming		249.24	91	24r
Facility use for ceremony		162.27	91	24r
Hearse, local		114.04	91	24r
Limousine, local		88.57	91	24r
Remains to funeral home, transfer		92.61	91	24r
Service charge, professional		682.42	91	24r
Vault, concrete, non-metallic liner		798.70	91	24r
Viewing facilities, use		163.86	91	24r
Groceries				
Apples, Red Delicious	lb	0.79	4/93	16r
Bacon	lb	1.75	4/93	16r
Bananas	lb	0.42	4/93	16r
Beef, stew, boneless	lb	2.61	4/93	16r
Bologna, all beef or mixed	lb	2.24	4/93	16r
Bread, white, pan	lb	0.64	4/93	16r
Bread, whole wheat, pan	lb	0.96	4/93	16r
Cabbage	lb	0.37	4/93	16r
Carrots, short trimmed and topped	lb	0.47	4/93	16r
Celery	lb	0.64	4/93	16r
Cheese, American	lb	2.98	4/93	16r
Cheese, Cheddar	lb	3.28	4/93	16r
Chicken, fresh, whole	lb	0.77	4/93	16r
Chicken breast, bone-in	lb	1.92	4/93	16r
Chicken legs, bone-in	lb	1.06	4/93	16r
Chuck roast, graded and ungraded, ex USDA prime and choice	lb	2.40	4/93	16r
Chuck roast, USDA choice, bone-in	lb	2.19	4/93	16r
Chuck roast, USDA choice, boneless	lb	2.38	4/93	16r
Coffee, 100% ground roast, all sizes	lb	2.48	4/93	16r
Crackers, soda, salted	lb	1.15	4/93	16r
Eggs, Grade A large	doz	0.96	4/93	16r
Flour, white, all purpose	lb	0.24	4/93	16r
Frankfurters, all meat or all beef	lb	2.01	4/93	16r
Grapefruit	lb	0.44	4/93	16r

Melbourne-Titusville-Palm Bay, FL - continued

Item	Per	Value	Date	Ref.
Groceries - continued				
Grapes, Thompson Seedless	lb	1.40	4/93	16r
Ground beef, 100% beef	lb	1.58	4/93	16r
Ground beef, lean and extra lean	lb	2.09	4/93	16r
Ground chuck, 100% beef	lb	1.98	4/93	16r
Ham, boneless, excluding canned	lb	2.89	4/93	16r
Ham, picnic, shoulder, bone-in, smoked	lb	1.02	4/93	16r
Ham, rump or steak half, bone-in, smoked	lb	1.48	4/93	16r
Ice cream, prepackaged, bulk, regular	1/2 gal	2.41	4/93	16r
Lemons	lb	1.05	4/93	16r
Lettuce, iceberg	lb	0.81	4/93	16r
Margarine, stick	lb	0.88	4/93	16r
Oranges, navel	lb	0.55	4/93	16r
Pears, Anjou	lb	0.92	4/93	16r
Pork chops, center cut, bone-in	lb	3.13	4/93	16r
Potato chips	16 oz	2.94	4/93	16r
Potatoes, white	lb	0.43	4/93	16r
Rib roast, USDA choice, bone-in	lb	4.63	4/93	16r
Rice, white, long grain, uncooked	lb	0.45	4/93	16r
Round roast, graded & ungraded, ex USDA prime & choice	lb	3.03	4/93	16r
Round roast, USDA choice, boneless	lb	3.09	4/93	16r
Sausage, fresh, loose	lb	2.08	4/93	16r
Short ribs, bone-in	lb	2.66	4/93	16r
Shortening, vegetable oil blends	lb	0.69	4/93	16r
Spaghetti and macaroni	lb	0.81	4/93	16r
Steak, rib eye, USDA choice, boneless	lb	6.24	4/93	16r
Steak, round, graded & ungraded, ex USDA prime & choice	lb	3.31	4/93	16r
Steak, round, USDA choice, boneless	lb	3.34	4/93	16r
Steak, sirloin, graded & ungraded, ex USDA prime & choice	lb	4.19	4/93	16r
Steak, sirloin, USDA choice, boneless	lb	4.46	4/93	16r
Steak, T-bone, USDA choice, bone-in	lb	5.25	4/93	16r
Strawberries, dry pint	12 oz	0.92	4/93	16r
Sugar, white	lb	0.39	4/93	16r
Sugar, white, 33-80 oz pk	lb	0.38	4/93	16r
Tomatoes, field grown	lb	0.88	4/93	16r
Tuna, chunk, light	lb	1.79	4/93	16r
Turkey, frozen, whole	lb	1.04	4/93	16r
Yogurt, natural, fruit flavored	1/2 pint	0.57	4/93	16r
Health Care				
Childbirth, cesarean, hospital		5034	91	62r
Childbirth, cesarean, physician's fee		2053	91	62r
Childbirth, normal, hospital		2712	91	62r
Childbirth, normal, physician's fee		1492	91	62r
Medical plan per employee	year	3495	91	45r
Mental health care, exp	capita	28.84-37.59	90	38s
Mental health care, exp, state mental health agency	capita	37.49	90	38s
Mental health care, hospital psychiatric services, non-Federal, exp	capita	9.11	88	38s
Mental health care, mental health organization, multiservice, exp	capita	16.21	88	38s
Mental health care, psychiatric hospitals, private, exp	capita	22.26	88	38s
Mental health care, psychiatric out-patient clinics, freestanding, exp	capita	0.89	88	38s
Mental health care, psychiatric partial-care organizations, freestanding, exp	capita	0.41	88	38s
Mental health care, state and county mental hospitals, exp	capita	16.25	88	38s
Mental health care, VA medical centers, exp	capita	1.69	88	38s
Physician fee, family practice, first-visit		75.00	91	62r
Physician fee, family practice, revisit		34.00	91	62r
Physician fee, general practice, first-visit		61.00	91	62r
Physician fee, general practice, revisit		32.00	91	62r
Physician fee, general surgeon, first-visit		64.00	91	62r
Physician fee, general surgeon, revisit		40.00	91	62r
Physician fee, internal medicine, first-visit		98.00	91	62r
Physician fee, internal medicine, revisit		40.00	91	62r

Values are in dollars or fractions of dollars. In the column headed *Ref*, references are shown to sources. Each reference is followed by a letter. These refer to the geographical level for which data were reported: s=State, r=Region, and c=City or metro. The abbreviation *ex* is used to mean *except* or *excluding*; *exp* stands for expenditures. For other abbreviations and further explanations, please see the Introduction.

Melbourne-Titusville-Palm Bay, FL - continued

Item	Per	Value	Date	Ref.
Health Care				
Physician fee, median, neurosurgeon, first-visit		130.00	91	62r
Physician fee, median, nonsurgical specialist, first-visit		95.00	91	62r
Physician fee, median, orthopedic surgeon, first-visit		91.00	91	62r
Physician fee, median, plastic surgeon, first-visit		66.00	91	62r
Physician fee, median, surgical specialist, first-visit		62.00	91	62r
Physician fee, neurosurgeon, revisit		50.00	91	62r
Physician fee, nonsurgical specialist, revisit		40.00	91	62r
Physician fee, obstetrics/gynecology, first-visit		64.00	91	62r
Physician fee, obstetrics/gynecology, revisit		41.00	91	62r
Physician fee, orthopedic surgeon, revisit		40.00	91	62r
Physician fee, pediatrician, first-visit		49.00	91	62r
Physician fee, pediatrician, revisit		33.00	91	62r
Physician fee, plastic surgeon, revisit		43.00	91	62r
Physician fee, surgical specialist, revisit		37.00	91	62r
Substance abuse, hospital ancillary charge	incident	1390	90	70s
Substance abuse, hospital physician charge	incident	770	90	70s
Substance abuse, hospital room and board	incident	5600	90	70s
Insurance and Pensions				
Auto insurance, private passenger	year	727.60	91	63s
Taxes				
Tax, cigarette	pack	33.90	91	77s
Tax, gasoline	gal	11.60	91	77s
Taxes, state	capita	1037	91	77s
Transportation				
Driver's license fee		15.00	12/90	43s
Travel				
Business travel	day	193.00	4/93	89r
Utilities				
Electricity	mil Btu	20.62	90	64s

Memphis, TN

Item	Per	Value	Date	Ref.
Composite ACCRA index		94.50	4Q 92	4c
Alcoholic Beverages				
Beer, Miller Lite or Budweiser, 12-oz containers	6 pack	3.85	4Q 92	4c
Liquor, J & B Scotch	750 ml	17.22	4Q 92	4c
Wine, Gallo Chablis blanc, 1.5 liter	bottle	5.91	4Q 92	4c
Child Care				
Child care fee, average, center	hour	1.29	90	65r
Child care fee, average, nonregulated family day care	hour	0.89	90	65r
Child care fee, average, regulated family day care	hour	1.32	90	65r
Clothing				
Jeans, man's denim		26.20	4Q 92	4c
Shirt, man's dress shirt		28.80	4Q 92	4c
Undervest, boy's size 10-14, cotton	3	3.56	4Q 92	4c
Communications				
Long-distance telephone service, day, initial minute, 0-100 miles	min	0.10-0.22	91	12s
Long-distance telephone service, day, additional minute, 0-100 miles	min	0.10-0.22	91	12s
Long-distance telephone service, evenings/weekends, 0-100 mi, initial minute	min	0.05-0.10	91	12s
Long-distance telephone service, evenings/weekends, 0-100 mi, additional minute	min	0.05-0.10	91	12s

Memphis, TN - continued

Item	Per	Value	Date	Ref.
Communications - continued				
Newspaper subscription, daily and Sunday home delivery, large-city	month	13.95	4Q 92	4c
Telephone, flat rate	month	12.15	91	11c
Telephone, residential, private line, rotary, unlimited calling	month	18.51	10/91	78c
Telephone bill, family of four	month	20.04	4Q 92	4c
Education				
Board, 4-yr private college/university	year	1845	91	22s
Board, 4-yr public college/university	year	1499	91	22s
Expenditures, local gov't, public elementary/secondary	pupil	3736	92	20s
Room, 4-year private college/university	year	1679	91	22s
Room, 4-year public college/university	year	1339	91	22s
Tuition, 2-year private college/university	year	4203	91	22s
Tuition, 2-year public college/university	year	848	91	22s
Tuition, 4-year private college/university	year	6889	91	22s
Tuition, 4-year public college/university, in-state	year	1518	91	22s
Energy and Fuels				
Coal	mil Btu	1.35	90	64s
Energy	mil Btu	8.61	90	64s
Energy, combined forms, 1,800 sq ft heating area	month	94.75	4Q 92	4c
Energy, exc electricity, 1,800 sq ft heating area	month	24.49	4Q 92	4c
Energy exp/householder, 1-family unit	year	403	90	28r
Energy exp/householder, <1,000 sq ft heating area	year	342	90	28r
Energy exp/householder, 1,000-1,999 sq ft heating area	year	388	90	28r
Energy exp/householder, 2,000+ sq ft heating area	year	434	90	28r
Energy exp/householder, mobile home	year	320	90	28r
Energy exp/householder, multifamily	year	338	90	28r
Gas, natural	mil Btu	3.98	90	64s
Gas, natural	000 cu ft	5.19	91	46s
Gas, natural, exp	year	388	91	46s
Gasoline, motor	gal	1.12	4Q 92	4c
Gasoline, unleaded regular	mil Btu	9.40	90	64s
Entertainment				
Bowling, evening rate	game	2.03	4Q 92	4c
Miniature golf admission	adult	6.18	92	1r
Miniature golf admission	child	5.14	92	1r
Monopoly game, Parker Brothers', No. 9		9.75	4Q 92	4c
Movie	admission	6.00	4Q 92	4c
Tennis balls, yellow, Wilson or Penn, 3	can	2.14	4Q 92	4c
Waterpark admission	adult	11.00	92	1r
Waterpark admission	child	8.55	92	1r
Funerals				
Casket, 18-gauge steel, velvet interior		2329.05	91	24r
Cosmetology, hair care, etc.		72.78	91	24r
Embalming		240.71	91	24r
Facility use for ceremony		181.67	91	24r
Hearse, local		106.25	91	24r
Limousine, local		70.92	91	24r
Remains to funeral home, transfer		96.30	91	24r
Service charge, professional		687.09	91	24r
Vault, concrete, non-metallic liner		732.09	91	24r
Viewing facilities, use		190.30	91	24r
Goods and Services				
ACCRA Index, Miscellaneous Goods and Services		98.10	4Q 92	4c
Goods and services	year	16387	92	36c
Goods and services, misc.	year	16387	92	37c
Groceries				
ACCRA Index, Groceries		99.90	4Q 92	4c
Apples, Red Delicious	lb	0.79	4/93	16r

Values are in dollars or fractions of dollars. In the column headed *Ref*, references are shown to sources. Each reference is followed by a letter. These refer to the geographical level for which data were reported: s=State, r=Region, and c=City or metro. The abbreviation *ex* is used to mean *except* or *excluding*; *exp* stands for expenditures. For other abbreviations and further explanations, please see the Introduction.

Memphis, TN - continued

Groceries

Item	Per	Value	Date	Ref.
Babyfood, strained vegetables, lowest price	4-4.5 oz jar	0.25	4Q 92	4c
Bacon	lb	1.75	4/93	16r
Bananas	lb	0.55	4Q 92	4c
Bananas	lb	0.42	4/93	16r
Beef, stew, boneless	lb	2.61	4/93	16r
Bologna, all beef or mixed	lb	2.24	4/93	16r
Bread, white	24 oz	0.64	4Q 92	4c
Bread, white, pan	lb	0.64	4/93	16r
Bread, whole wheat, pan	lb	0.96	4/93	16r
Cabbage	lb	0.37	4/93	16r
Carrots, short trimmed and topped	lb	0.47	4/93	16r
Celery	lb	0.64	4/93	16r
Cheese, American	lb	2.98	4/93	16r
Cheese, Cheddar	lb	3.28	4/93	16r
Cheese, Kraft grated Parmesan	8-oz canis-ter	3.50	4Q 92	4c
Chicken, fresh, whole	lb	0.77	4/93	16r
Chicken, fryer, whole	lb	0.65	4Q 92	4c
Chicken breast, bone-in	lb	1.92	4/93	16r
Chicken legs, bone-in	lb	1.06	4/93	16r
Chuck roast, graded and ungraded, ex USDA prime and choice	lb	2.40	4/93	16r
Chuck roast, USDA choice, bone-in	lb	2.19	4/93	16r
Chuck roast, USDA choice, boneless	lb	2.38	4/93	16r
Cigarettes, Winston	carton	17.25	4Q 92	4c
Coffee, 100% ground roast, all sizes	lb	2.48	4/93	16r
Coffee, vacuum-packed	13-oz can	2.14	4Q 92	4c
Corn, frozen	10 oz	0.77	4Q 92	4c
Corn Flakes, Kellogg's or Post Toasties	18 oz	2.14	4Q 92	4c
Crackers, soda, salted	lb	1.15	4/93	16r
Eggs, Grade A large	doz	0.76	4Q 92	4c
Eggs, Grade A large	doz	0.96	4/93	16r
Flour, white, all purpose	lb	0.24	4/93	16r
Frankfurters, all meat or all beef	lb	2.01	4/93	16r
Grapefruit	lb	0.44	4/93	16r
Grapes, Thompson Seedless	lb	1.40	4/93	16r
Ground beef, 100% beef	lb	1.58	4/93	16r
Ground beef, lean and extra lean	lb	2.09	4/93	16r
Ground beef or hamburger	lb	1.49	4Q 92	4c
Ground chuck, 100% beef	lb	1.98	4/93	16r
Ham, boneless, excluding canned	lb	2.89	4/93	16r
Ham, picnic, shoulder, bone-in, smoked	lb	1.02	4/93	16r
Ham, rump or steak half, bone-in, smoked	lb	1.48	4/93	16r
Honey, jar	8 oz	0.89-1.09	92	5r
Honey, jar	lb	1.39-2.25	92	5r
Honey, squeeze bear	12-oz	1.00-1.50	92	5r
Ice cream, prepackaged, bulk, regular	1/2 gal	2.41	4/93	16r
Lemons	lb	1.05	4/93	16r
Lettuce, iceberg	head	0.99	4Q 92	4c
Lettuce, iceberg	lb	0.81	4/93	16r
Margarine, Blue Bonnet or Parkay cubes	lb	0.61	4Q 92	4c
Margarine, stick	lb	0.88	4/93	16r
Milk, whole	1/2 gal	1.45	4Q 92	4c
Orange juice, Minute Maid frozen	12-oz can	1.62	4Q 92	4c
Oranges, navel	lb	0.55	4/93	16r
Peaches	29-oz can	1.48	4Q 92	4c
Pears, Anjou	lb	0.92	4/93	16r
Peas Sweet, Del Monte or Green Giant	15-17 oz can	0.69	4Q 92	4c
Pork chops, center cut, bone-in	lb	3.13	4/93	16r
Potato chips	16 oz	2.94	4/93	16r
Potatoes, white	lb	0.43	4/93	16r
Potatoes, white or red	10-lb sack	2.75	4Q 92	4c
Rib roast, USDA choice, bone-in	lb	4.63	4/93	16r
Rice, white, long grain, uncooked	lb	0.45	4/93	16r

Memphis, TN - continued

Groceries - continued

Item	Per	Value	Date	Ref.
Round roast, graded & ungraded, ex USDA prime & choice	lb	3.03	4/93	16r
Round roast, USDA choice, boneless	lb	3.09	4/93	16r
Sausage, fresh, loose	lb	2.08	4/93	16r
Sausage, Jimmy Dean, 100% pork	lb	2.54	4Q 92	4c
Short ribs, bone-in	lb	2.66	4/93	16r
Shortening, vegetable oil blends	lb	0.69	4/93	16r
Shortening, vegetable, Crisco	3-lb can	2.25	4Q 92	4c
Soft drink, Coca Cola	2 liter	0.99	4Q 92	4c
Spaghetti and macaroni	lb	0.81	4/93	16r
Steak, rib eye, USDA choice, boneless	lb	6.24	4/93	16r
Steak, round, graded & ungraded, ex USDA prime & choice	lb	3.31	4/93	16r
Steak, round, USDA choice, boneless	lb	3.34	4/93	16r
Steak, sirloin, graded & ungraded, ex USDA prime & choice	lb	4.19	4/93	16r
Steak, sirloin, USDA choice, boneless	lb	4.46	4/93	16r
Steak, T-bone	lb	5.10	4Q 92	4c
Steak, T-bone, USDA choice, bone-in	lb	5.25	4/93	16r
Strawberries, dry pint	12 oz	0.92	4/93	16r
Sugar, cane or beet	4 lb	1.49	4Q 92	4c
Sugar, white	lb	0.39	4/93	16r
Sugar, white, 33-80 oz pk	lb	0.38	4/93	16r
Tomatoes, field grown	lb	0.88	4/93	16r
Tomatoes, Hunt's or Del Monte	14.5-oz can	0.81	4Q 92	4c
Tuna, chunk, light	6.125-6.5 oz can	0.67	4Q 92	4c
Tuna, chunk, light	lb	1.79	4/93	16r
Turkey, frozen, whole	lb	1.04	4/93	16r
Yogurt, natural, fruit flavored	1/2 pint	0.57	4/93	16r

Health Care

Item	Per	Value	Date	Ref.
ACCRA Index, Health Care		98.00	4Q 92	4c
Analgesic, Aspirin, Bayer, 325 mg tablets	100	5.89	4Q 92	4c
Childbirth, cesarean, hospital		5034	91	62r
Childbirth, cesarean, physician's fee		2053	91	62r
Childbirth, normal, hospital		2712	91	62r
Childbirth, normal, physician's fee		1492	91	62r
Dentist's fee, adult teeth cleaning and periodic oral exam	visit	43.20	4Q 92	4c
Doctor's fee, routine exam, established patient	visit	40.00	4Q 92	4c
Hospital care, semiprivate room	day	200.22	90	27c
Hospital care, semiprivate room	day	244.60	4Q 92	4c
Medical insurance premium, per employee, small group comprehensive	month	368.65	10/91	25c
Mental health care, exp	capita	20.37-28.83	90	38s
Mental health care, exp, state mental health agency	capita	28.84	90	38s
Mental health care, hospital psychiatric services, non-Federal, exp	capita	13.48	88	38s
Mental health care, mental health organization, multiservice, exp	capita	11.35	88	38s
Mental health care, psychiatric hospitals, private, exp	capita	22.28	88	38s
Mental health care, psychiatric out-patient clinics, freestanding, exp	capita	2.58	88	38s
Mental health care, psychiatric partial-care organizations, freestanding, exp	capita	0.25	88	38s
Mental health care, state and county mental hospitals, exp	capita	20.05	88	38s
Mental health care, VA medical centers, exp	capita	4.98	88	38s
Physician fee, family practice, first-visit		75.00	91	62r
Physician fee, family practice, revisit		34.00	91	62r
Physician fee, general practice, first-visit		61.00	91	62r
Physician fee, general practice, revisit		32.00	91	62r
Physician fee, general surgeon, first-visit		64.00	91	62r
Physician fee, general surgeon, revisit		40.00	91	62r

Values are in dollars or fractions of dollars. In the column headed *Ref*, references are shown to sources. Each reference is followed by a letter. These refer to the geographical level for which data were reported: s = State, r = Region, and c = City or metro. The abbreviation *ex* is used to mean *except* or *excluding*; *exp* stands for expenditures. For other abbreviations and further explanations, please see the Introduction.

Memphis, TN - continued

Item	Per	Value	Date	Ref.
Health Care				
Physician fee, internal medicine, first-visit		98.00	91	62r
Physician fee, internal medicine, revisit		40.00	91	62r
Physician fee, median, neurosurgeon, first-visit		130.00	91	62r
Physician fee, median, nonsurgical specialist, first-visit		95.00	91	62r
Physician fee, median, orthopedic surgeon, first-visit		91.00	91	62r
Physician fee, median, plastic surgeon, first-visit		66.00	91	62r
Physician fee, median, surgical specialist, first-visit		62.00	91	62r
Physician fee, neurosurgeon, revisit		50.00	91	62r
Physician fee, nonsurgical specialist, revisit		40.00	91	62r
Physician fee, obstetrics/gynecology, first-visit		64.00	91	62r
Physician fee, obstetrics/gynecology, revisit		41.00	91	62r
Physician fee, orthopedic surgeon, revisit		40.00	91	62r
Physician fee, pediatrician, first-visit		49.00	91	62r
Physician fee, pediatrician, revisit		33.00	91	62r
Physician fee, plastic surgeon, revisit		43.00	91	62r
Physician fee, surgical specialist, revisit		37.00	91	62r
Substance abuse, hospital ancillary charge	incident	1330	90	70s
Substance abuse, hospital physician charge	incident	580	90	70s
Substance abuse, hospital room and board	incident	5180	90	70s
Household Goods				
Appliance repair, home, service call, washing machine	min labor charge	30.30	4Q 92	4c
Laundry detergent, Tide Ultra, Bold, or Cheer	42 oz	3.02	4Q 92	4c
Tissues, facial, Kleenex brand	175-count box	1.09	4Q 92	4c
Housing				
ACCRA Index, Housing		84.20	4Q 92	4c
Home, median price	unit	85.30		26c
House, 1,800 sq ft, 8,000 sq ft lot, new, urban	total	91612	4Q 92	4c
House payment, principal and interest, 25% down payment	month	513	4Q 92	4c
Mortgage rate, incl. points & origination fee, 30-year fixed or adjustable rate	percent	8.18	4Q 92	4c
Rent, apartment, 2 bedrooms - 1-1/2 to 2 baths, unfurnished, 950 sq ft, water	month	426	4Q 92	4c
Rental unit, 1 bedroom	month	383	93	23c
Rental unit, 2 bedroom	month	451	93	23c
Rental unit, 3 bedroom	month	562	93	23c
Rental unit, 4 bedroom	month	629	93	23c
Rental unit, efficiency	month	316	93	23c
Insurance and Pensions				
Auto insurance, private passenger	year	554.60	91	63s
Personal Goods				
Shampoo, Alberto VO5	15 oz	1.58	4Q 92	4c
Toothpaste, Crest or Colgate	6-7 oz	2.31	4Q 92	4c
Personal Services				
Dry cleaning, man's 2-piece suit		6.03	4Q 92	4c
Haircare, woman's shampoo, trim and blow-dry		14.39	4Q 92	4c
Haircut, man's barbershop, no styling		7.80	4Q 92	4c
Restaurant Food				
Chicken, fried, thigh and drumstick		1.46	4Q 92	4c
Hamburger with cheese	1/4 lb	1.85	4Q 92	4c
Pizza, Pizza Hut or Pizza Inn, cheese, thin crust	12-13 in	8.79	4Q 92	4c

Memphis, TN - continued

Item	Per	Value	Date	Ref.
Taxes				
Tax, cigarette	pack	13	91	77s
Tax, gasoline	gal	22.40	91	77s
Taxes, sales	year	1278	92	37c
Taxes, state	capita	870	91	77s
Transportation				
ACCRA Index, Transportation		107.40	4Q 92	4c
Auto rental, average	day	43.75	6/91	60c
Bus fare	one-way	1.00	3/93	2c
Bus fare, up to 10 miles	one-way	1.00	4Q 92	4c
Driver's license fee		14.00-16.00	12/90	43s
Limo fare, airport-city, average	day	6.00	6/91	60c
Railway fare, light rail	one-way	1.10	93	2c
Taxi fare, airport-city, average	day	14.50	6/91	60c
Tire balance, computer or spin balance, front	wheel	7.39	4Q 92	4c
Travel				
Breakfast	day	5.94	6/91	60c
Business travel	day	111.00	92	86c
Business travel	day	193.00	4/93	89r
Dinner	day	18.83	6/91	60c
Dinner	day	18.75	92	85c
Lodging	day	90.75	91	60c
Lodging	day	77.00	92	85c
Lunch	day	7.53	6/91	60c
Utilities				
ACCRA Index, Utilities		88.40	4Q 92	4c
Electricity	mil Btu	15.59	90	64s
Electricity, partial electric and other energy, 1,800 sq ft living area new home	month	70.26	4Q 92	4c

Merced, CA

Item	Per	Value	Date	Ref.
Child Care				
Child care fee, average, center	hour	1.71	90	65r
Child care fee, average, nonregulated family day care	hour	1.32	90	65r
Child care fee, average, regulated family day care	hour	1.86	90	65r
Communications				
Long-distance telephone service, day, initial minute, 0-100 miles	min	0.17-0.40	91	12s
Long-distance telephone service, day, additional minute, 0-100 miles	min	0.07-0.31	91	12s
Long-distance telephone service, evenings/weekends, 0-100 mi, initial minute	min	0.07-0.16	91	12s
Long-distance telephone service, evenings/weekends, 0-100 mi, additional minute	min	0.03-0.12	91	12s
Education				
Board, 4-yr private college/university	year	2515	91	22s
Board, 4-yr public college/university	year	2268	91	22s
Expenditures, local gov't, public elementary/secondary	pupil	4866	92	20s
Room, 4-year private college/university	year	2622	91	22s
Room, 4-year public college/university	year	2406	91	22s
Tuition, 2-year private college/university	year	7942	91	22s
Tuition, 2-year public college/university	year	114	91	22s
Tuition, 4-year private college/university	year	10863	91	22s
Tuition, 4-year public college/university, in-state	year	1220	91	22s
Energy and Fuels				
Coal	mil Btu	2.01	90	64s
Energy	mil Btu	9.08	90	64s
Energy exp/householder, 1-family unit	year	362	90	28r

Values are in dollars or fractions of dollars. In the column headed *Ref*, references are shown to sources. Each reference is followed by a letter. These refer to the geographical level for which data were reported: s = State, r = Region, and c = City or metro. The abbreviation *ex* is used to mean *except* or *excluding*; *exp* stands for *expenditures*. For other abbreviations and further explanations, please see the Introduction.

Merced, CA - continued

Item	Per	Value	Date	Ref.
Energy and Fuels				
Energy exp/householder, <1,000 sq ft heating area	year	254	90	28r
Energy exp/householder, 1,000-1,999 sq ft heating area	year	358	90	28r
Energy exp/householder, 2,000+ sq ft heating area	year	467	90	28r
Energy exp/householder, mobile home	year	390	90	28r
Energy exp/householder, multifamily	year	252	90	28r
Gas, natural	mil Btu	4.31	90	64s
Gas, natural	000 cu ft	6.27	91	46s
Gas, natural, exp	year	369	91	46s
Gasoline, unleaded regular	mil Btu	8.57	90	64s
Entertainment				
Miniature golf admission	adult	6.18	92	1r
Miniature golf admission	child	5.14	92	1r
Waterpark admission	adult	11.00	92	1r
Waterpark admission	child	8.55	92	1r
Funerals				
Casket, 18-gauge steel, velvet interior		1781.09	91	24r
Cosmetology, hair care, etc.		84.64	91	24r
Embalming		207.41	91	24r
Facility use for ceremony		205.76	91	24r
Hearse, local		105.14	91	24r
Limousine, local		83.21	91	24r
Remains to funeral home, transfer		113.82	91	24r
Service charge, professional		626.33	91	24r
Vault, concrete, non-metallic liner		599.54	91	24r
Viewing facilities, use		85.81	91	24r
Groceries				
Apples, Red Delicious	lb	0.80	4/93	16r
Bacon	lb	1.79	4/93	16r
Bananas	lb	0.53	4/93	16r
Bologna, all beef or mixed	lb	2.67	4/93	16r
Bread, white, pan	lb	0.81	4/93	16r
Carrots, short trimmed and topped	lb	0.39	4/93	16r
Chicken, fresh, whole	lb	0.94	4/93	16r
Chicken breast, bone-in	lb	2.19	4/93	16r
Chuck roast, graded and ungraded, ex USDA prime and choice	lb	2.26	4/93	16r
Coffee, 100% ground roast, all sizes	lb	2.33	4/93	16r
Eggs, Grade AA large	doz	1.18	4/93	16r
Flour, white, all purpose	lb	0.22	4/93	16r
Grapefruit	lb	0.52	4/93	16r
Grapes, Thompson Seedless	lb	1.50	4/93	16r
Ground beef, 100% beef	lb	1.44	4/93	16r
Ground beef, lean and extra lean	lb	2.34	4/93	16r
Ham, boneless, excluding canned	lb	2.56	4/93	16r
Honey, jar	8 oz	0.89-1.00	92	5r
Honey, jar	lb	1.35-1.97	92	5r
Honey, squeeze bear	12-oz	1.19-1.50	92	5r
Ice cream, prepackaged, bulk, regular	1/2 gal	2.40	4/93	16r
Lemons	lb	0.81	4/93	16r
Lettuce, iceberg	lb	0.84	4/93	16r
Margarine, stick	lb	0.81	4/93	16r
Oranges, navel	lb	0.48	4/93	16r
Pork chops, center cut, bone-in	lb	3.25	4/93	16r
Potato chips	16 oz	2.89	4/93	16r
Potatoes, white	lb	0.38	4/93	16r
Round roast, graded & ungraded, ex USDA prime & choice	lb	3.00	4/93	16r
Round roast, USDA choice, boneless	lb	3.16	4/93	16r
Shortening, vegetable oil blends	lb	0.86	4/93	16r
Spaghetti and macaroni	lb	0.84	4/93	16r
Steak, round, graded & ungraded, ex USDA prime & choice	lb	3.34	4/93	16r
Steak, round, USDA choice, boneless	lb	3.24	4/93	16r
Steak, sirloin, graded & ungraded, ex USDA prime & choice	lb	3.75	4/93	16r
Steak, sirloin, USDA choice, boneless	lb	4.49	4/93	16r
Sugar, white	lb	0.41	4/93	16r

Merced, CA - continued

Item	Per	Value	Date	Ref.
Groceries - continued				
Sugar, white, 33-80 oz pk	lb	0.38	4/93	16r
Tomatoes, field grown	lb	1.01	4/93	16r
Turkey, frozen, whole	lb	1.04	4/93	16r
Health Care				
Cardizem 60 mg tablets	30	24.04	92	49s
Cector 250 mg tablets	15	35.87	92	49s
Childbirth, cesarean, hospital		5533	91	62r
Childbirth, cesarean, physician's fee		2053	91	62r
Childbirth, normal, hospital		2745	91	62r
Childbirth, normal, physician's fee		1492	91	62r
Health care spending, state	capita	2894	3/93	84s
Medical plan per employee	year	3421	91	45r
Mental health care, exp	capita	37.60-53.67	90	38s
Mental health care, exp, state mental health agency	capita	42.32	90	38s
Mental health care, hospital psychiatric services, non-Federal, exp	capita	10.64	88	38s
Mental health care, mental health organization, multiservice, exp	capita	28.56	88	38s
Mental health care, psychiatric hospitals, private, exp	capita	18.60	88	38s
Mental health care, psychiatric out-patient clinics, freestanding, exp	capita	2.28	88	38s
Mental health care, psychiatric partial-care organizations, freestanding, exp	capita	0.24	88	38s
Mental health care, state and county mental hospitals, exp	capita	13.60	88	38s
Mental health care, VA medical centers, exp	capita	2.33	88	38s
Mevacor 20 mg tablets	30	67.62	92	49s
Physician fee, family practice, first-visit		111.00	91	02r
Physician fee, family practice, revisit		45.00	91	62r
Physician fee, general practice, first-visit		100.00	91	62r
Physician fee, general practice, revisit		40.00	91	62r
Physician fee, internal medicine, first-visit		137.00	91	62r
Physician fee, internal medicine, revisit		48.00	91	62r
Physician fee, median, neurosurgeon, first-visit		157.00	91	62r
Physician fee, median, nonsurgical specialist, first-visit		131.00	91	62r
Physician fee, median, orthopedic surgeon, first-visit		124.00	91	62r
Physician fee, median, plastic surgeon, first-visit		88.00	91	62r
Physician fee, median, surgical specialist, first-visit		100.00	91	62r
Physician fee, neurosurgeon, revisit		51.00	91	62r
Physician fee, nonsurgical specialist, revisit		47.00	91	62r
Physician fee, obstetrics/gynecology, first-visit		95.00	91	62r
Physician fee, obstetrics/gynecology, revisit		50.00	91	62r
Physician fee, orthopedic surgeon, revisit		51.00	91	62r
Physician fee, pediatrician, first-visit		81.00	91	62r
Physician fee, pediatrician, revisit		42.00	91	62r
Physician fee, plastic surgeon, revisit		48.00	91	62r
Physician fee, surgical specialist, revisit		49.00	91	62r
Prozac 20 mg tablets	14	33.22	92	49s
Substance abuse, hospital ancillary charge	incident	1760	90	70s
Substance abuse, hospital physician charge	incident	750	90	70s
Substance abuse, hospital room and board	incident	6390	90	70s
Tagamet 300 mg tablets	100	77.08	92	49s
Xanax 0.25 mg tablets	90	64.08	92	49s
Zantac 160 mg tablets	60	92.31	92	49s
Housing				
Home, median price	unit	131,200	92	58s
Insurance and Pensions				
Auto insurance, private passenger	year	904.37	91	63s

Values are in dollars or fractions of dollars. In the column headed *Ref*, references are shown to sources. Each reference is followed by a letter. These refer to the geographical level for which data were reported: s=State, r=Region, and c=City or metro. The abbreviation *ex* is used to mean *except* or *excluding*; *exp* stands for expenditures. For other abbreviations and further explanations, please see the Introduction.

Merced, CA - continued

Item	Per	Value	Date	Ref.
Taxes				
Tax, cigarette	pack	35	91	77s
Tax, gasoline	gal	16	91	77s
Taxes, state	capita	1477	91	77s
Transportation				
Driver's license fee		10.00	12/90	43s
Travel				
Business travel	day	178.00	4/93	89r
Utilities				
Electricity	mil Btu	25.98	90	64s

Miami, FL

Item	Per	Value	Date	Ref.
Child Care				
Child care fee, average, center	hour	1.29	90	65r
Child care fee, average, nonregulated family day care	hour	0.89	90	65r
Child care fee, average, regulated family day care	hour	1.32	90	65r
Communications				
Long-distance telephone service, day, initial minute, 0-100 miles	min	0.15-0.20	91	12s
Long-distance telephone service, day, additional minute, 0-100 miles	min	0.08-0.20	91	12s
Long-distance telephone service, evenings/weekends, 0-100 mi, initial minute	min	0.09-0.12	91	12s
Long-distance telephone service, evenings/weekends, 0-100 mi, additional minute	min	0.05-0.12	91	12s
Telephone, flat rate	month	10.65	91	11c
Telephone, residential, private line, rotary, unlimited calling	month	17.28	10/91	78c
Construction				
Plywood, post-Hurricane Andrew	4x8 sheet	11.99	92	13c
Plywood, pre-Hurricane Andrew	4x8 sheet	7.84	92	13c
Education				
Board, 4-yr private college/university	year	1924	91	22s
Board, 4-yr public college/university	year	1955	91	22s
Expenditures, local gov't, public elementary/secondary	pupil	5235	92	20s
Room, 4-year private college/university	year	1904	91	22s
Room, 4-year public college/university	year	1510	91	22s
Tuition, 2-year private college/university	year	4751	91	22s
Tuition, 2-year public college/university	year	788	91	22s
Tuition, 4-year private college/university	year	7992	91	22s
Tuition, 4-year public college/university, in-state	year	1337	91	22s
Energy and Fuels				
Coal	mil Btu	1.85	90	64s
Energy	mil Btu	10.58	90	64s
Energy exp/householder, 1-family unit	year	487	90	28r
Energy exp/householder, <1,000 sq ft heating area	year	393	90	28r
Energy exp/householder, 1,000-1,999 sq ft heating area	year	442	90	28r
Energy exp/householder, 2,000+ sq ft heating area	year	577	90	28r
Energy exp/householder, mobile home	year	366	90	28r
Energy exp/householder, multifamily	year	382	90	28r
Gas, cooking, 10 therms	month	11.51	92	56c
Gas, cooking, 30 therms	month	22.52	92	56c
Gas, cooking, 50 therms	month	33.53	92	56c
Gas, heating, winter, 100 therms	month	61.06	92	56c
Gas, heating, winter, average use	month	23.62	92	56c
Gas, natural	mil Btu	3.21	90	64s
Gas, natural	000 cu ft	8.98	91	46s

Miami, FL - continued

Item	Per	Value	Date	Ref.
Energy and Fuels - continued				
Gas, natural, exp	year	248	91	46s
Gas, piped	100 therms	90.90	4/93	16c
Gas, piped	40 therms	40.17	4/93	16c
Gas, piped	therm	1.19	4/93	16c
Gasoline, all types	gal	1.23	4/93	16c
Gasoline, regular unleaded, taxes included, cash, self-service	gal	1.33	4/93	16c
Gasoline, unleaded premium 93 octane	gal	1.15	4/93	16c
Gasoline, unleaded regular	mil Btu	8.85	90	64s
Entertainment				
Miniature golf admission	adult	6.18	92	1r
Miniature golf admission	child	5.14	92	1r
Waterpark admission	adult	11.00	92	1r
Waterpark admission	child	8.55	92	1r
Funerals				
Casket, 18-gauge steel, velvet interior		2029.08	91	24r
Cosmetology, hair care, etc.		75.10	91	24r
Embalming		249.24	91	24r
Facility use for ceremony		162.27	91	24r
Hearse, local		114.04	91	24r
Limousine, local		88.57	91	24r
Remains to funeral home, transfer		92.61	91	24r
Service charge, professional		682.42	91	24r
Vault, concrete, non-metallic liner		798.70	91	24r
Viewing facilities, use		163.86	91	24r
Groceries				
Apples, Red Delicious	lb	0.79	4/93	16r
Bacon	lb	1.75	4/93	16r
Bakery products, exp	year	193	89	15c
Bananas	lb	0.42	4/93	16r
Beef, exp	year	198	89	15c
Beef, stew, boneless	lb	2.61	4/93	16r
Bologna, all beef or mixed	lb	2.24	4/93	16r
Bread, white, pan	lb	0.64	4/93	16r
Bread, whole wheat, pan	lb	0.96	4/93	16r
Cabbage	lb	0.37	4/93	16r
Carrots, short trimmed and topped	lb	0.47	4/93	16r
Celery	lb	0.64	4/93	16r
Cereals and bakery products, exp	year	296	89	15c
Cereals and cereal products, exp	year	103	89	15c
Cheese, American	lb	2.98	4/93	16r
Cheese, Cheddar	lb	3.28	4/93	16r
Chicken, fresh, whole	lb	0.77	4/93	16r
Chicken breast, bone-in	lb	1.92	4/93	16r
Chicken legs, bone-in	lb	1.06	4/93	16r
Chuck roast, graded and ungraded, ex USDA prime and choice	lb	2.40	4/93	16r
Chuck roast, USDA choice, bone-in	lb	2.19	4/93	16r
Chuck roast, USDA choice, boneless	lb	2.38	4/93	16r
Coffee, 100% ground roast, all sizes	lb	2.48	4/93	16r
Crackers, soda, salted	lb	1.15	4/93	16r
Dairy products, exp	year	273	89	15c
Dairy products, miscellaneous, exp	year	136	89	15c
Eggs, exp	year	30	89	15c
Eggs, Grade A large	doz	0.96	4/93	16r
Fish and seafood, exp	year	121	89	15c
Flour, white, all purpose	lb	0.24	4/93	16r
Food, exp	year	4489	89	15c
Food eaten at home, exp	year	2165	89	15c
Frankfurters, all meat or all beef	lb	2.01	4/93	16r
Fruits, fresh, exp	year	118	89	15c
Fruits, processed, exp	year	113	89	15c
Fruits and vegetables, exp	year	416	89	15c
Grapefruit	lb	0.44	4/93	16r
Grapes, Thompson Seedless	lb	1.40	4/93	16r
Ground beef, 100% beef	lb	1.58	4/93	16r
Ground beef, lean and extra lean	lb	2.09	4/93	16r
Ground chuck, 100% beef	lb	1.98	4/93	16r
Ham, boneless, excluding canned	lb	2.89	4/93	16r

Values are in dollars or fractions of dollars. In the column headed *Ref*, references are shown to sources. Each reference is followed by a letter. These refer to the geographical level for which data were reported: s=State, r=Region, and c=City or metro. The abbreviation *ex* is used to mean *except* or *excluding*; *exp* stands for expenditures. For other abbreviations and further explanations, please see the Introduction.

Miami, FL - continued

Item	Per	Value	Date	Ref.
Groceries				
Ham, picnic, shoulder, bone-in, smoked	lb	1.02	4/93	16r
Ham, rump or steak half, bone-in, smoked	lb	1.48	4/93	16r
Ice cream, prepackaged, bulk, regular	1/2 gal	2.41	4/93	16r
Lemons	lb	1.05	4/93	16r
Lettuce, iceberg	lb	0.81	4/93	16r
Margarine, stick	lb	0.88	4/93	16r
Meats, poultry, fish and eggs, exp	year	615	89	15c
Milk and cream, fresh, exp	year	137	89	15c
Oranges, navel	lb	0.55	4/93	16r
Pears, Anjou	lb	0.92	4/93	16r
Pork, exp	year	88	89	15c
Pork chops, center cut, bone-in	lb	3.13	4/93	16r
Potato chips	16 oz	2.94	4/93	16r
Potatoes, white	lb	0.43	4/93	16r
Poultry, exp	year	106	89	15c
Rib roast, USDA choice, bone-in	lb	4.63	4/93	16r
Rice, white, long grain, uncooked	lb	0.45	4/93	16r
Round roast, graded & ungraded, ex USDA prime & choice	lb	3.03	4/93	16r
Round roast, USDA choice, boneless	lb	3.09	4/93	16r
Sausage, fresh, loose	lb	2.08	4/93	16r
Short ribs, bone-in	lb	2.66	4/93	16r
Shortening, vegetable oil blends	lb	0.69	4/93	16r
Spaghetti and macaroni	lb	0.81	4/93	16r
Steak, rib eye, USDA choice, boneless	lb	6.24	4/93	16r
Steak, round, graded & ungraded, ex USDA prime & choice	lb	3.31	4/93	16r
Steak, round, USDA choice, boneless	lb	3.34	4/93	16r
Steak, sirloin, graded & ungraded, ex USDA prime & choice	lb	4.19	4/93	16r
Steak, sirloin, USDA choice, boneless	lb	4.46	4/93	16r
Steak, T-bone, USDA choice, bone-in	lb	5.25	4/93	16r
Strawberries, dry pint	12 oz	0.92	4/93	16r
Sugar, white	lb	0.39	4/93	16r
Sugar, white, 33-80 oz pk	lb	0.38	4/93	16r
Tomatoes, field grown	lb	0.88	4/93	16r
Tuna, chunk, light	lb	1.79	4/93	16r
Turkey, frozen, whole	lb	1.04	4/93	16r
Vegetables, fresh, exp	year	120	89	15c
Vegetables, processed, exp	year	65	89	15c
Yogurt, natural, fruit flavored	1/2 pint	0.57	4/93	16r
Health Care				
Childbirth, cesarean, hospital		5034	91	62r
Childbirth, cesarean, physician's fee		2053	91	62r
Childbirth, normal, hospital		2712	91	62r
Childbirth, normal, physician's fee		1492	91	62r
Hospital care, semiprivate room	day	301.57	90	27c
Medical insurance premium, per employee, small group comprehensive	month	620.50	10/91	25c
Medical plan per employee	year	3495	91	45r
Mental health care, exp	capita	28.84-37.59	90	38s
Mental health care, exp, state mental health agency	capita	37.49	90	38s
Mental health care, hospital psychiatric services, non-Federal, exp	capita	9.11	88	38s
Mental health care, mental health organization, multiservice, exp	capita	16.21	88	38s
Mental health care, psychiatric hospitals, private, exp	capita	22.26	88	38s
Mental health care, psychiatric out-patient clinics, freestanding, exp	capita	0.89	88	38s
Mental health care, psychiatric partial-care organizations, freestanding, exp	capita	0.41	88	38s
Mental health care, state and county mental hospitals, exp	capita	16.25	88	38s
Mental health care, VA medical centers, exp	capita	1.69	88	38s
Physician fee, family practice, first-visit		75.00	91	62r
Physician fee, family practice, revisit		34.00	91	62r
Physician fee, general practice, first-visit		61.00	91	62r
Physician fee, general practice, revisit		32.00	91	62r

Miami, FL - continued

Item	Per	Value	Date	Ref.
Health Care - continued				
Physician fee, general surgeon, first-visit		64.00	91	62r
Physician fee, general surgeon, revisit		40.00	91	62r
Physician fee, internal medicine, first-visit		98.00	91	62r
Physician fee, internal medicine, revisit		40.00	91	62r
Physician fee, median, neurosurgeon, first-visit		130.00	91	62r
Physician fee, median, nonsurgical specialist, first-visit		95.00	91	62r
Physician fee, median, orthopedic surgeon, first-visit		91.00	91	62r
Physician fee, median, plastic surgeon, first-visit		66.00	91	62r
Physician fee, median, surgical specialist, first-visit		62.00	91	62r
Physician fee, neurosurgeon, revisit		50.00	91	62r
Physician fee, nonsurgical specialist, revisit		40.00	91	62r
Physician fee, obstetrics/gynecology, first-visit		64.00	91	62r
Physician fee, obstetrics/gynecology, revisit		41.00	91	62r
Physician fee, orthopedic surgeon, revisit		40.00	91	62r
Physician fee, pediatrician, first-visit		49.00	91	62r
Physician fee, pediatrician, revisit		33.00	91	62r
Physician fee, plastic surgeon, revisit		43.00	91	62r
Physician fee, surgical specialist, revisit		37.00	91	62r
Substance abuse, hospital ancillary charge	incident	1390	90	70s
Substance abuse, hospital physician charge	incident	770	90	70s
Substance abuse, hospital room and board	incident	5600	90	70s
Housing				
Home, median price	unit	97.10		26c
Rental unit, 1 bedroom	month	611	93	23c
Rental unit, 2 bedroom	month	719	93	23c
Rental unit, 3 bedroom	month	899	93	23c
Rental unit, 4 bedroom	month	1007	93	23c
Rental unit, efficiency	month	504	93	23c
Insurance and Pensions				
Auto insurance, private passenger	year	727.60	91	63s
Taxes				
Tax, cigarette	pack	33.90	91	77s
Tax, gasoline	gal	11.60	91	77s
Taxes, hotel room	day	8.23	92	33c
Taxes, state	capita	1037	91	77s
Transportation				
Auto rental, average	day	30.00	6/91	60c
Bus fare	one-way	1.25	3/93	2c
Commuter train fare (automated guideway)	one-way	0.25	3/03	2c
Driver's license fee		15.00	12/90	43s
Railway fare, commuter	one-way	3.00	3/93	2c
Railway fare, heavy rail	one-way	1.25	3/93	2c
Taxi fare, airport-city, average	day	13.00	6/91	60c
Travel				
Breakfast	day	6.90	6/91	60c
Business travel	day	193.00	4/93	89r
Dinner	day	21.91	6/91	60c
Dinner	day	21.75	92	85c
Lodging	day	142.46	91	60c
Lodging	day	90.00	92	85c
Lunch	day	10.62	6/91	60c
Travel, business	day	181.29	93	88c
Utilities				
Electricity	500 KWh	45.15	4/93	16c
Electricity	KWh	0.09	4/93	16c

Values are in dollars or fractions of dollars. In the column headed *Ref*, references are shown to sources. Each reference is followed by a letter. These refer to the geographical level for which data were reported: s=State, r=Region, and c=City or metro. The abbreviation *ex* is used to mean *except* or *excluding*; *exp* stands for *expenditures*. For other abbreviations and further explanations, please see the Introduction.

Miami, FL - continued

Item	Per	Value	Date	Ref.
Utilities				
Electricity	mil Btu	20.62	90	64s
Electricity, winter, 250 KWh	month	22.38	92	55c
Electricity, winter, 500 KWh	month	30.09	92	55c
Electricity, winter, 750 KWh	month	55.85	92	55c
Electricity, winter, 1000 KWh	month	75.06	92	55c

Michigan City, IN

Item	Per	Value	Date	Ref.
Composite ACCRA index		98.30	4Q 92	4c
Alcoholic Beverages				
Beer, Miller Lite or Budweiser, 12-oz containers	6 pack	3.71	4Q 92	4c
Liquor, J & B Scotch	750 ml	15.35	4Q 92	4c
Wine, Gallo Chablis blanc, 1.5 liter	bottle	4.63	4Q 92	4c
Clothing				
Jeans, man's denim		29.69	4Q 92	4c
Shirt, man's dress shirt		15.59	4Q 92	4c
Undervest, boy's size 10-14, cotton	3	3.89	4Q 92	4c
Communications				
Newspaper subscription, daily and Sunday home delivery, large-city	month	14.89	4Q 92	4c
Telephone, flat rate	month	9.85	91	11c
Telephone bill, family of four	month	20.42	4Q 92	4c
Energy and Fuels				
Energy, combined forms, 1,800 sq ft heating area	month	123.43	4Q 92	4c
Energy, exc electricity, 1,800 sq ft heating area	month	52.64	4Q 92	4c
Gasoline, motor	gal	1.06	4Q 92	4c
Entertainment				
Bowling, evening rate	game	1.30	4Q 92	4c
Monopoly game, Parker Brothers', No. 9		12.77	4Q 92	4c
Movie	admission	4.00	4Q 92	4c
Tennis balls, yellow, Wilson or Penn, 3	can	3.28	4Q 92	4c
Goods and Services				
ACCRA Index, Miscellaneous Goods and Services		95.20	4Q 92	4c
Groceries				
ACCRA Index, Groceries		100.90	4Q 92	4c
Babyfood, strained vegetables, lowest price	4-4.5 oz jar	0.40	4Q 92	4c
Bananas	lb	0.46	4Q 92	4c
Bread, white	24 oz	0.47	4Q 92	4c
Cheese, Kraft grated Parmesan	8-oz canister	3.36	4Q 92	4c
Chicken, fryer, whole	lb	0.77	4Q 92	4c
Cigarettes, Winston	carton	16.62	4Q 92	4c
Coffee, vacuum-packed	13-oz can	1.99	4Q 92	4c
Corn, frozen	10 oz	0.66	4Q 92	4c
Corn Flakes, Kellogg's or Post Toasties	18 oz	2.01	4Q 92	4c
Eggs, Grade A large	doz	0.87	4Q 92	4c
Ground beef or hamburger	lb	1.46	4Q 92	4c
Lettuce, iceberg	head	1.03	4Q 92	4c
Margarine, Blue Bonnet or Parkay cubes	lb	0.74	4Q 92	4c
Milk, whole	1/2 gal	1.59	4Q 92	4c
Orange juice, Minute Maid frozen	12-oz can	1.32	4Q 92	4c
Peaches	29-oz can	1.48	4Q 92	4c
Peas Sweet, Del Monte or Green Giant	15-17 oz can	0.64	4Q 92	4c
Potatoes, white or red	10-lb sack	2.03	4Q 92	4c
Sausage, Jimmy Dean, 100% pork	lb	2.70	4Q 92	4c

Michigan City, IN - continued

Item	Per	Value	Date	Ref.
Groceries - continued				
Shortening, vegetable, Crisco	3-lb can	2.47	4Q 92	4c
Soft drink, Coca Cola	2 liter	1.25	4Q 92	4c
Steak, T-bone	lb	5.22	4Q 92	4c
Sugar, cane or beet	4 lb	1.39	4Q 92	4c
Tomatoes, Hunt's or Del Monte	14.5-oz can	0.72	4Q 92	4c
Tuna, chunk, light	6.125-6.5 oz can	0.68	4Q 92	4c
Health Care				
ACCRA Index, Health Care		102.00	4Q 92	4c
Analgesic, Aspirin, Bayer, 325 mg tablets	100	5.06	4Q 92	4c
Dentist's fee, adult teeth cleaning and periodic oral exam	visit	48.88	4Q 92	4c
Doctor's fee, routine exam, established patient	visit	37.88	4Q 92	4c
Hospital care, semiprivate room	day	307.50	4Q 92	4c
Household Goods				
Appliance repair, home, service call, washing machine	min labor charge	36.50	4Q 92	4c
Laundry detergent, Tide Ultra, Bold, or Cheer	42 oz	3.94	4Q 92	4c
Tissues, facial, Kleenex brand	175-count box	1.17	4Q 92	4c
Housing				
ACCRA Index, Housing		96.70	4Q 92	4c
House, 1,800 sq ft, 8,000 sq ft lot, new, urban	total	104341	4Q 92	4c
House payment, principal and interest, 25% down payment	month	595	4Q 92	4c
Mortgage rate, incl. points & origination fee, 30-year fixed or adjustable rate	percent	8.38	4Q 92	4c
Rent, apartment, 2 bedrooms - 1-1/2 to 2 baths, unfurnished, 950 sq ft, water	month	475	4Q 92	4c
Personal Goods				
Shampoo, Alberto VO5	15 oz	1.15	4Q 92	4c
Toothpaste, Crest or Colgate	6-7 oz	1.85	4Q 92	4c
Personal Services				
Dry cleaning, man's 2-piece suit		5.59	4Q 92	4c
Haircare, woman's shampoo, trim and blow-dry		17.60	4Q 92	4c
Haircut, man's barbershop, no styling		7.20	4Q 92	4c
Restaurant Food				
Chicken, fried, thigh and drumstick		2.25	4Q 92	4c
Hamburger with cheese	1/4 lb	1.75	4Q 92	4c
Pizza, Pizza Hut or Pizza Inn, cheese, thin crust	12-13 in	7.59	4Q 92	4c
Transportation				
ACCRA Index, Transportation		95.50	4Q 92	4c
Tire balance, computer or spin balance, front	wheel	6.30	4Q 92	4c
Utilities				
ACCRA Index, Utilities		112.20	4Q 92	4c
Electricity, partial electric and other energy, 1,800 sq ft living area new home	month	70.79	4Q 92	4c

Middlesex-Somerset-Hunterdon, NJ

Item	Per	Value	Date	Ref.
Child Care				
Child care fee, average, center	hour	2.18	90	65r
Child care fee, average, nonregulated family day care	hour	1.83	90	65r
Child care fee, average, regulated family day care	hour	2.02	90	65r

Values are in dollars or fractions of dollars. In the column headed *Ref*, references are shown to sources. Each reference is followed by a letter. These refer to the geographical level for which data were reported: s=State, r=Region, and c=City or metro. The abbreviation *ex* is used to mean *except* or *excluding*; *exp* stands for expenditures. For other abbreviations and further explanations, please see the Introduction.

Middlesex-Somerset-Hunterdon, NJ - continued

Item	Per	Value	Date	Ref.
Communications				
Long-distance telephone service, day, initial minute, 0-100 miles	min	0.09-0.42	91	12s
Long-distance telephone service, day, additional minute, 0-100 miles	min	0.03-0.12	91	12s
Education				
Board, 4-yr private college/university	year	2883	91	22s
Board, 4-yr public college/university	year	1647	91	22s
Expenditures, local gov't, public elementary/secondary	pupil	9940	92	20s
Room, 4-year private college/university	year	2440	91	22s
Room, 4-year public college/university	year	2415	91	22s
Tuition, 2-year private college/university	year	5874	91	22s
Tuition, 2-year public college/university	year	1235	91	22s
Tuition, 4-year private college/university	year	10281	91	22s
Tuition, 4-year public college/university, in-state	year	2860	91	22s
Energy and Fuels				
Coal	mil Btu	1.79	90	64s
Energy	mil Btu	9.32	90	64s
Energy exp/householder, 1-family unit	year	588	90	28r
Energy exp/householder, <1,000 sq ft heating area	year	477	90	28r
Energy exp/householder, 1,000-1,999 sq ft heating area	year	517	90	28r
Energy exp/householder, 2,000+ sq ft heating area	year	630	90	28r
Energy exp/householder, mobile home	year	412	90	28r
Energy exp/householder, multifamily	year	498	90	28r
Gas, natural	mil Btu	5.05	90	64s
Gas, natural	000 cu ft	6.73	91	46s
Gas, natural, exp	year	593	91	46s
Gasoline, unleaded regular	mil Btu	9.03	90	64s
Funerals				
Casket, 18-gauge steel, velvet interior		1811.58	91	24r
Cosmetology, hair care, etc.		111.08	91	24r
Embalming		329.42	91	24r
Facility use for ceremony		201.29	91	24r
Hearse, local		135.27	91	24r
Limousine, local		127.24	91	24r
Remains to funeral home, transfer		103.98	91	24r
Service charge, professional		724.98	91	24r
Vault, concrete, non-metallic liner		766.71	91	24r
Viewing facilities, use		260.60	91	24r
Groceries				
Apples, Red Delicious	lb	0.85	4/93	16r
Bacon	lb	2.12	4/93	16r
Bananas	lb	0.54	4/93	16r
Bread, white, pan	lb	0.81	4/93	16r
Butter	lb	2.02	4/93	16r
Carrots, short trimmed and topped	lb	0.51	4/93	16r
Chicken, fresh, whole	lb	1.04	4/93	16r
Chicken breast, bone-in	lb	2.21	4/93	16r
Chicken legs, bone-in	lb	1.16	4/93	16r
Chuck roast, USDA choice, boneless	lb	2.82	4/93	16r
Coffee, 100% ground roast, all sizes	lb	2.66	4/93	16r
Cucumbers	lb	0.85	4/93	16r
Eggs, Grade A large	doz	1.15	4/93	16r
Grapefruit	lb	0.45	4/93	16r
Grapes, Thompson Seedless	lb	1.52	4/93	16r
Ground beef, lean and extra lean	lb	2.36	4/93	16r
Ground chuck, 100% beef	lb	2.02	4/93	16r
Honey, jar	8 oz	0.96-1.75	92	5r
Honey, jar	lb	1.50-3.00	92	5r
Honey, squeeze bear	12-oz	1.50-1.99	92	5r
Ice cream, prepackaged, bulk, regular	1/2 gal	2.80	4/93	16r
Lemons	lb	0.96	4/93	16r
Lettuce, iceberg	lb	0.95	4/93	16r
Margarine, stick	lb	0.81	4/93	16r
Milk, fresh, whole, fortified	1/2 gal	1.30	4/93	16r

Middlesex-Somerset-Hunterdon, NJ - continued

Item	Per	Value	Date	Ref.
Groceries - continued				
Oranges, navel	lb	0.56	4/93	16r
Peanut butter, creamy, all sizes	lb	1.88	4/93	16r
Pork chops, center cut, bone-in	lb	3.34	4/93	16r
Potato chips	16 oz	2.88	4/93	16r
Potatoes, white	lb	0.37	4/93	16r
Rib roast, USDA choice, bone-in	lb	4.94	4/93	16r
Round roast, USDA choice, boneless	lb	3.17	4/93	16r
Shortening, vegetable oil blends	lb	0.98	4/93	16r
Spaghetti and macaroni	lb	0.82	4/93	16r
Steak, round, graded & ungraded, ex USDA prime & choice	lb	4.04	4/93	16r
Steak, round, USDA choice, boneless	lb	3.90	4/93	16r
Steak, sirloin, USDA choice, boneless	lb	4.97	4/93	16r
Strawberries, dry pint	12 oz	0.90	4/93	16r
Sugar, white	lb	0.50	4/93	16r
Sugar, white, 33-80 oz pk	lb	0.41	4/93	16r
Tomatoes, field grown	lb	1.23	4/93	16r
Tuna, chunk, light	lb	2.22	4/93	16r
Turkey, frozen, whole	lb	1.04	4/93	16r
Health Care				
Childbirth, cesarean, hospital		5826	91	62r
Childbirth, cesarean, physician's fee		2053	91	62r
Childbirth, normal, hospital		2964	91	62r
Childbirth, normal, physician's fee		1492	91	62r
Medical plan per employee	year	3942	91	45r
Mental health care, exp	capita	28.84-37.59	90	38s
Mental health care, exp, state mental health agency	capita	57.16	90	38s
Mental health care, hospital psychiatric services, non-Federal, exp	capita	16.04	88	38s
Mental health care, mental health organization, multiservice, exp	capita	11.14	88	38s
Mental health care, psychiatric hospitals, private, exp	capita	17.85	88	38s
Mental health care, psychiatric out-patient clinics, freestanding, exp	capita	1.56	88	38s
Mental health care, psychiatric partial-care organizations, freestanding, exp	capita	0.66	88	38s
Mental health care, state and county mental hospitals, exp	capita	36.80	88	38s
Mental health care, VA medical centers, exp	capita	5.61	88	38s
Prescription drug co-pay, Medicaid	month	5.00	91	21s
Substance abuse, hospital ancillary charge	incident	780	90	70s
Substance abuse, hospital physician charge	incident	550	90	70s
Substance abuse, hospital room and board	incident	6300	90	70s
Insurance and Pensions				
Auto insurance, private passenger	year	1081.45	91	63s
Taxes				
Tax, cigarette	pack	40	91	77s
Tax, gasoline	gal	10.50	91	77s
Taxes, state	capita	1501	91	77s
Transportation				
Driver's license fee		16.00-17.50	12/90	43s
Vehicle registration and license plate	year	32.90-93.90	93	44s
Travel				
Business travel	day	165.00	4/93	89r
Utilities				
Electricity	mil Btu	26.63	90	64s

Values are in dollars or fractions of dollars. In the column headed *Ref*, references are shown to sources. Each reference is followed by a letter. These refer to the geographical level for which data were reported: s=State, r=Region, and c=City or metro. The abbreviation *ex* is used to mean *except* or *excluding*; *exp* stands for expenditures. For other abbreviations and further explanations, please see the Introduction.

Middletown, CT

Item	Per	Value	Date	Ref.
Child Care				
Child care fee, average, center	hour	2.18	90	65r
Child care fee, average, nonregulated family day care	hour	1.83	90	65r
Child care fee, average, regulated family day care	hour	2.02	90	65r
Communications				
Long-distance telephone service, day, initial minute, 0-100 miles	min	0.18-0.45	91	12s
Long-distance telephone service, day, additional minute, 0-100 miles	min	0.10-0.26	91	12s
Long-distance telephone service, evenings/weekends, 0-100 mi, initial minute	min	0.07-0.18	91	12s
Long-distance telephone service, evenings/weekends, 0-100 mi, additional minute	min	0.04-0.10	91	12s
Education				
Board, 4-yr private college/university	year	2182	91	22s
Board, 4-yr public college/university	year	1750	91	22s
Expenditures, local gov't, public elementary/secondary	pupil	8308	92	20s
Room, 4-year private college/university	year	2703	91	22s
Room, 4-year public college/university	year	1913	91	22s
Tuition, 2-year private college/university	year	8586	91	22s
Tuition, 2-year public college/university	year	972	91	22s
Tuition, 4-year private college/university	year	12315	91	22s
Tuition, 4-year public college/university, in-state	year	2313	91	22s
Energy and Fuels				
Coal	mil Btu	2.15	90	64s
Energy	mil Btu	11.62	90	64s
Energy exp/householder, 1-family unit	year	588	90	28r
Energy exp/householder, <1,000 sq ft heating area	year	477	90	28r
Energy exp/householder, 1,000-1,999 sq ft heating area	year	517	90	28r
Energy exp/householder, 2,000+ sq ft heating area	year	630	90	28r
Energy exp/householder, mobile home	year	412	90	28r
Energy exp/householder, multifamily	year	498	90	28r
Gas, natural	mil Btu	6.40	90	64s
Gas, natural	000 cu ft	8.74	91	46s
Gas, natural, exp	year	756	91	46s
Gasoline, unleaded regular	mil Btu	10.06	90	64s
Entertainment				
Miniature golf admission	adult	6.18	92	1r
Miniature golf admission	child	5.14	92	1r
Waterpark admission	adult	11.00	92	1r
Waterpark admission	child	8.55	92	1r
Funerals				
Casket, 18-gauge steel, velvet interior		1853.42	91	24r
Cosmetology, hair care, etc.		98.33	91	24r
Embalming		273.94	91	24r
Facility use for ceremony		196.06	91	24r
Hearse, local		145.67	91	24r
Limousine, local		131.07	91	24r
Remains to funeral home, transfer		135.24	91	24r
Service charge, professional		843.16	91	24r
Vault, concrete, non-metallic liner		709.14	91	24r
Viewing facilities, use		229.85	91	24r
Groceries				
Apples, Red Delicious	lb	0.85	4/93	16r
Bacon	lb	2.12	4/93	16r
Bananas	lb	0.54	4/93	16r
Bread, white, pan	lb	0.81	4/93	16r
Butter	lb	2.02	4/93	16r
Carrots, short trimmed and topped	lb	0.51	4/93	16r
Chicken, fresh, whole	lb	1.04	4/93	16r
Chicken breast, bone-in	lb	2.21	4/93	16r

Middletown, CT - continued

Item	Per	Value	Date	Ref.
Groceries - continued				
Chicken legs, bone-in	lb	1.16	4/93	16r
Chuck roast, USDA choice, boneless	lb	2.82	4/93	16r
Coffee, 100% ground roast, all sizes	lb	2.66	4/93	16r
Cucumbers	lb	0.85	4/93	16r
Eggs, Grade A large	doz	1.15	4/93	16r
Grapefruit	lb	0.45	4/93	16r
Grapes, Thompson Seedless	lb	1.52	4/93	16r
Ground beef, lean and extra lean	lb	2.36	4/93	16r
Ground chuck, 100% beef	lb	2.02	4/93	16r
Honey, jar	8 oz	0.96-1.75	92	5r
Honey, jar	lb	1.50-3.00	92	5r
Honey, squeeze bear	12-oz	1.50-1.99	92	5r
Ice cream, prepackaged, bulk, regular	1/2 gal	2.80	4/93	16r
Lemons	lb	0.96	4/93	16r
Lettuce, iceberg	lb	0.95	4/93	16r
Margarine, stick	lb	0.81	4/93	16r
Milk, fresh, whole, fortified	1/2 gal	1.30	4/93	16r
Oranges, navel	lb	0.56	4/93	16r
Peanut butter, creamy, all sizes	lb	1.88	4/93	16r
Pork chops, center cut, bone-in	lb	3.34	4/93	16r
Potato chips	16 oz	2.88	4/93	16r
Potatoes, white	lb	0.37	4/93	16r
Rib roast, USDA choice, bone-in	lb	4.94	4/93	16r
Round roast, USDA choice, boneless	lb	3.17	4/93	16r
Shortening, vegetable oil blends	lb	0.98	4/93	16r
Spaghetti and macaroni	lb	0.82	4/93	16r
Steak, round, graded & ungraded, ex USDA prime & choice	lb	4.04	4/93	16r
Steak, round, USDA choice, boneless	lb	3.90	4/93	16r
Steak, sirloin, USDA choice, boneless	lb	4.97	4/93	16r
Strawberries, dry pint	12 oz	0.90	4/93	16r
Sugar, white	lb	0.50	4/93	16r
Sugar, white, 33-80 oz pk	lb	0.41	4/93	16r
Tomatoes, field grown	lb	1.23	4/93	16r
Tuna, chunk, light	lb	2.22	4/93	16r
Turkey, frozen, whole	lb	1.04	4/93	16r
Health Care				
Childbirth, cesarean, hospital		5826	91	62r
Childbirth, cesarean, physician's fee		2053	91	62r
Childbirth, normal, hospital		2964	91	62r
Childbirth, normal, physician's fee		1492	91	62r
Medical plan per employee	year	3958	91	45r
Mental health care, exp	capita	53.68-118.35	90	38s
Mental health care, exp, state mental health agency	capita	72.81	90	38s
Mental health care, hospital psychiatric services, non-Federal, exp	capita	19.30	88	38s
Mental health care, mental health organization, multiservice, exp	capita	19.14	88	38s
Mental health care, psychiatric hospitals, private, exp	capita	35.86	88	38s
Mental health care, psychiatric out-patient clinics, freestanding, exp	capita	5.83	88	38s
Mental health care, psychiatric partial-care organizations, freestanding, exp	capita	0.15	88	38s
Mental health care, state and county mental hospitals, exp	capita	51.85	88	38s
Mental health care, VA medical centers, exp	capita	1.74	88	38s
Prescription drug co-pay, Medicaid	month	10.00	91	21s
Substance abuse, hospital ancillary charge	incident	1200	90	70s
Substance abuse, hospital physician charge	incident	270	90	70s
Substance abuse, hospital room and board	incident	4420	90	70s
Insurance and Pensions				
Auto insurance, private passenger	year	928.10	91	63s
Taxes				
Tax, cigarette	pack	45	91	77s
Tax, gasoline	gal	26	91	77s

Values are in dollars or fractions of dollars. In the column headed *Ref*, references are shown to sources. Each reference is followed by a letter. These refer to the geographical level for which data were reported: s=State, r=Region, and c=City or metro. The abbreviation *ex* is used to mean *except* or *excluding*; *exp* stands for expenditures. For other abbreviations and further explanations, please see the Introduction.

Middletown, CT - continued

Item	Per	Value	Date	Ref.
Taxes				
Taxes, state	capita	1514	91	77s
Transportation				
Driver's license fee		31.00	12/90	43s
Travel				
Business travel	day	165.00	4/93	89r
Utilities				
Electricity	mil Btu	26.83	90	64s

Midland, TX

Item	Per	Value	Date	Ref.
Composite ACCRA index		94.80	4Q 92	4c
Alcoholic Beverages				
Beer, Miller Lite or Budweiser, 12-oz containers	6 pack	3.89	4Q 92	4c
Liquor, J & B Scotch	750 ml	17.98	4Q 92	4c
Wine, Gallo Chablis blanc, 1.5 liter	bottle	4.36	4Q 92	4c
Child Care				
Child care fee, average, center	hour	1.29	90	65r
Child care fee, average, nonregulated family day care	hour	0.89	90	65r
Child care fee, average, regulated family day care	hour	1.32	90	65r
Clothing				
Jeans, man's denim		24.80	4Q 92	4c
Shirt, man's dress shirt		22.00	4Q 92	4c
Undervest, boy's size 10-14, cotton	3	4.50	4Q 92	4c
Communications				
Long-distance telephone service, day, initial minute, 0-100 miles	min	0.10-0.46	91	12s
Long-distance telephone service, day, additional minute, 0-100 miles	min	0.06-0.45	91	12s
Newspaper subscription, daily and Sunday home delivery, large-city	month	10.00	4Q 92	4c
Telephone, flat rate	month	9.10	91	11c
Telephone bill, family of four	month	15.51	4Q 92	4c
Education				
Board, 4-yr private college/university	year	1883	91	22s
Board, 4-yr public college/university	year	1605	91	22s
Expenditures, local gov't, public elementary/secondary	pupil	4593	92	20s
Room, 4-year private college/university	year	1620	91	22s
Room, 4-year public college/university	year	1532	91	22s
Tuition, 2-year private college/university	year	4394	91	22s
Tuition, 2-year public college/university	year	495	91	22s
Tuition, 4-year private college/university	year	6497	91	22s
Tuition, 4-year public college/university, in-state	year	986	91	22s
Energy and Fuels				
Coal	mil Btu	1.44	90	64s
Energy	mil Btu	6.48	90	64s
Energy, combined forms, 1,800 sq ft heating area	month	120.19	4Q 92	4c
Energy, exc electricity, 1,800 sq ft heating area	month	35.07	4Q 92	4c
Energy exp/householder, 1-family unit	year	471	90	28r
Energy exp/householder, <1,000 sq ft heating area	year	384	90	28r
Energy exp/householder, 1,000-1,999 sq ft heating area	year	421	90	28r
Energy exp/householder, 2,000+ sq ft heating area	year	625	90	28r
Energy exp/householder, mobile home	year	271	90	28r
Energy exp/householder, multifamily	year	355	90	28r
Gas, natural	mil Btu	2.47	90	64s
Gas, natural	000 cu ft	5.71	91	46s
Gas, natural, exp	year	388	91	46s

Midland, TX - continued

Item	Per	Value	Date	Ref.
Energy and Fuels - continued				
Gasoline, motor	gal	1.14	4Q 92	4c
Gasoline, unleaded regular	mil Btu	9.16	90	64s
Entertainment				
Bowling, evening rate	game	1.88	4Q 92	4c
Miniature golf admission	adult	6.18	92	1r
Miniature golf admission	child	5.14	92	1r
Monopoly game, Parker Brothers', No. 9		11.24	4Q 92	4c
Movie	admission	5.50	4Q 92	4c
Tennis balls, yellow, Wilson or Penn, 3	can	2.84	4Q 92	4c
Waterpark admission	adult	11.00	92	1r
Waterpark admission	child	8.55	92	1r
Funerals				
Casket, 18-gauge steel, velvet interior		2274.41	91	24r
Cosmetology, hair care, etc.		74.62	91	24r
Embalming		229.94	91	24r
Facility use for ceremony		176.61	91	24r
Hearse, local		116.34	91	24r
Limousine, local		72.68	91	24r
Remains to funeral home, transfer		87.72	91	24r
Service charge, professional		712.53	91	24r
Vault, concrete, non-metallic liner		750.55	91	24r
Viewing facilities, use		155.31	91	24r
Goods and Services				
ACCRA Index, Miscellaneous Goods and Services		99.70	4Q 92	4c
Groceries				
ACCRA Index, Groceries		91.80	4Q 92	4c
Apples, Red Delicious	lb	0.79	4/93	16r
Babyfood, strained vegetables, lowest price	4-4.5 oz jar	0.23	4Q 92	4c
Bacon	lb	1.75	4/93	16r
Bananas	lb	0.49	4Q 92	4c
Bananas	lb	0.42	4/93	16r
Beef, stew, boneless	lb	2.61	4/93	16r
Bologna, all beef or mixed	lb	2.24	4/93	16r
Bread, white	24 oz	0.61	4Q 92	4c
Bread, white, pan	lb	0.64	4/93	16r
Bread, whole wheat, pan	lb	0.96	4/93	16r
Cabbage	lb	0.37	4/93	16r
Carrots, short trimmed and topped	lb	0.47	4/93	16r
Celery	lb	0.64	4/93	16r
Cheese, American	lb	2.98	4/93	16r
Cheese, Cheddar	lb	3.28	4/93	16r
Cheese, Kraft grated Parmesan	8-oz canister	3.57	4Q 92	4c
Chicken, fresh, whole	lb	0.77	4/93	16r
Chicken, fryer, whole	lb	0.61	4Q 92	4c
Chicken breast, bone-in	lb	1.92	4/93	16r
Chicken legs, bone-in	lb	1.06	4/93	16r
Chuck roast, graded and ungraded, ex USDA prime and choice	lb	2.40	4/93	16r
Chuck roast, USDA choice, bone-in	lb	2.19	4/93	16r
Chuck roast, USDA choice, boneless	lb	2.38	4/93	16r
Cigarettes, Winston	carton	18.99	4Q 92	4c
Coffee, 100% ground roast, all sizes	lb	2.48	4/93	16r
Coffee, vacuum-packed	13-oz can	1.73	4Q 92	4c
Corn, frozen	10 oz	0.62	4Q 92	4c
Corn Flakes, Kellogg's or Post Toasties	18 oz	2.15	4Q 92	4c
Crackers, soda, salted	lb	1.15	4/93	16r
Eggs, Grade A large	doz	0.87	4Q 92	4c
Eggs, Grade A large	doz	0.96	4/93	16r
Flour, white, all purpose	lb	0.24	4/93	16r
Frankfurters, all meat or all beef	lb	2.01	4/93	16r
Grapefruit	lb	0.44	4/93	16r
Grapes, Thompson Seedless	lb	1.40	4/93	16r
Ground beef, 100% beef	lb	1.58	4/93	16r
Ground beef, lean and extra lean	lb	2.09	4/93	16r

Values are in dollars or fractions of dollars. In the column headed *Ref*, references are shown to sources. Each reference is followed by a letter. These refer to the geographical level for which data were reported: s=State, r=Region, and c=City or metro. The abbreviation *ex* is used to mean *except* or *excluding*; *exp* stands for expenditures. For other abbreviations and further explanations, please see the Introduction.

Midland, TX - continued

Item	Per	Value	Date	Ref.
Groceries				
Ground beef or hamburger	lb	0.98	4Q 92	4c
Ground chuck, 100% beef	lb	1.98	4/93	16r
Ham, boneless, excluding canned	lb	2.89	4/93	16r
Ham, picnic, shoulder, bone-in, smoked	lb	1.02	4/93	16r
Ham, rump or steak half, bone-in, smoked	lb	1.48	4/93	16r
Honey, jar	8 oz	0.73-1.19	92	5r
Honey, jar	lb	1.10-1.79	92	5r
Honey, squeeze bear	12-oz	1.19-1.50	92	5r
Ice cream, prepackaged, bulk, regular	1/2 gal	2.41	4/93	16r
Lemons	lb	1.05	4/93	16r
Lettuce, iceberg	head	1.05	4Q 92	4c
Lettuce, iceberg	lb	0.81	4/93	16r
Margarine, Blue Bonnet or Parkay cubes	lb	0.54	4Q 92	4c
Margarine, stick	lb	0.88	4/93	16r
Milk, whole	1/2 gal	1.29	4Q 92	4c
Orange juice, Minute Maid frozen	12-oz can	0.99	4Q 92	4c
Oranges, navel	lb	0.55	4/93	16r
Peaches	29-oz can	1.43	4Q 92	4c
Pears, Anjou	lb	0.92	4/93	16r
Peas Sweet, Del Monte or Green Giant	15-17 oz can	0.51	4Q 92	4c
Pork chops, center cut, bone-in	lb	3.13	4/93	16r
Potato chips	16 oz	2.94	4/93	16r
Potatoes, white	lb	0.43	4/93	16r
Potatoes, white or red	10-lb sack	2.66	4Q 92	4c
Rib roast, USDA choice, bone-in	lb	4.63	4/93	16r
Rice, white, long grain, uncooked	lb	0.45	4/93	16r
Round roast, graded & ungraded, ex USDA prime & choice	lb	3.03	4/93	16r
Round roast, USDA choice, boneless	lb	3.09	4/93	16r
Sausage, fresh, loose	lb	2.08	4/93	16r
Sausage, Jimmy Dean, 100% pork	lb	2.71	4Q 92	4c
Short ribs, bone-in	lb	2.66	4/93	16r
Shortening, vegetable oil blends	lb	0.69	4/93	16r
Shortening, vegetable, Crisco	3-lb can	1.98	4Q 92	4c
Soft drink, Coca Cola	2 liter	1.43	4Q 92	4c
Spaghetti and macaroni	lb	0.81	4/93	16r
Steak, rib eye, USDA choice, boneless	lb	6.24	4/93	16r
Steak, round, graded & ungraded, ex USDA prime & choice	lb	3.31	4/93	16r
Steak, round, USDA choice, boneless	lb	3.34	4/93	16r
Steak, sirloin, graded & ungraded, ex USDA prime & choice	lb	4.19	4/93	16r
Steak, sirloin, USDA choice, boneless	lb	4.46	4/93	16r
Steak, T-bone	lb	4.21	4Q 92	4c
Steak, T-bone, USDA choice, bone-in	lb	5.25	4/93	16r
Strawberries, dry pint	12 oz	0.92	4/93	16r
Sugar, cane or beet	4 lb	1.41	4Q 92	4c
Sugar, white	lb	0.39	4/93	16r
Sugar, white, 33-80 oz pk	lb	0.38	4/93	16r
Tomatoes, field grown	lb	0.88	4/93	16r
Tomatoes, Hunt's or Del Monte	14.5-oz can	0.60	4Q 92	4c
Tuna, chunk, light	6.125-6.5 oz can	0.54	4Q 92	4c
Tuna, chunk, light	lb	1.79	4/93	16r
Turkey, frozen, whole	lb	1.04	4/93	16r
Yogurt, natural, fruit flavored	1/2 pint	0.57	4/93	16r
Health Care				
ACCRA Index, Health Care		109.10	4Q 92	4c
Analgesic, Aspirin, Bayer, 325 mg tablets	100	4.79	4Q 92	4c
Childbirth, cesarean, hospital		5034	91	62r
Childbirth, cesarean, physician's fee		2053	91	62r
Childbirth, normal, hospital		2712	91	62r
Childbirth, normal, physician's fee		1492	91	62r

Midland, TX - continued

Item	Per	Value	Date	Ref.
Health Care - continued				
Dentist's fee, adult teeth cleaning and periodic oral exam	visit	51.02	4Q 92	4c
Doctor's fee, routine exam, established patient	visit	46.40	4Q 92	4c
Health care spending, state	capita	2192	3/93	84s
Hospital care, semiprivate room	day	271.50	4Q 92	4c
Medical insurance premium, per employee, small group comprehensive	month	343.10	10/91	25c
Mental health care, exp	capita	20.37-28.83	90	38s
Mental health care, exp, state mental health agency	capita	22.72	90	38s
Mental health care, hospital psychiatric services, non-Federal, exp	capita	7.95	88	38s
Mental health care, mental health organization, multiservice, exp	capita	12.05	88	38s
Mental health care, psychiatric hospitals, private, exp	capita	37.78	88	38s
Mental health care, psychiatric out-patient clinics, freestanding, exp	capita	0.43	88	38s
Mental health care, state and county mental hospitals, exp	capita	12.54	88	38s
Mental health care, VA medical centers, exp	capita	5.35	88	38s
Physician fee, family practice, first-visit		75.00	91	62r
Physician fee, family practice, revisit		34.00	91	62r
Physician fee, general practice, first-visit		61.00	91	62r
Physician fee, general practice, revisit		32.00	91	62r
Physician fee, general surgeon, first-visit		64.00	91	62r
Physician fee, general surgeon, revisit		40.00	91	62r
Physician fee, internal medicine, first-visit		98.00	91	62r
Physician fee, internal medicine, revisit		40.00	91	62r
Physician fee, median, neurosurgeon, first-visit		130.00	91	62r
Physician fee, median, nonsurgical specialist, first-visit		95.00	91	62r
Physician fee, median, orthopedic surgeon, first-visit		91.00	91	62r
Physician fee, median, plastic surgeon, first-visit		66.00	91	62r
Physician fee, median, surgical specialist, first-visit		62.00	91	62r
Physician fee, neurosurgeon, revisit		50.00	91	62r
Physician fee, nonsurgical specialist, revisit		40.00	91	62r
Physician fee, obstetrics/gynecology, first-visit		64.00	91	62r
Physician fee, obstetrics/gynecology, revisit		41.00	91	62r
Physician fee, orthopedic surgeon, revisit		40.00	91	62r
Physician fee, pediatrician, first-visit		49.00	91	62r
Physician fee, pediatrician, revisit		33.00	91	62r
Physician fee, plastic surgeon, revisit		43.00	91	62r
Physician fee, surgical specialist, revisit		37.00	91	62r
Substance abuse, hospital ancillary charge	incident	3750	90	70s
Substance abuse, hospital physician charge	incident	1080	90	70s
Substance abuse, hospital room and board	incident	5320	90	70s
Household Goods				
Appliance repair, home, service call, washing machine	min labor charge	34.00	4Q 92	4c
Laundry detergent, Tide Ultra, Bold, or Cheer	42 oz	2.89	4Q 92	4c
Tissues, facial, Kleenex brand	175-count box	1.08	4Q 92	4c
Housing				
ACCRA Index, Housing		81.40	4Q 92	4c
House, 1,800 sq ft, 8,000 sq ft lot, new, urban	total	87333	4Q 92	4c

Values are in dollars or fractions of dollars. In the column headed *Ref*, references are shown to sources. Each reference is followed by a letter. These refer to the geographical level for which data were reported: s=State, r=Region, and c=City or metro. The abbreviation *ex* is used to mean *except* or *excluding*; *exp* stands for *expenditures*. For other abbreviations and further explanations, please see the Introduction.

Midland, TX - continued

Item	Per	Value	Date	Ref.
Housing				
House payment, principal and interest, 25% down payment	month	486	4Q 92	4c
Mortgage rate, incl. points & origination fee, 30-year fixed or adjustable rate	per-cent	8.11	4Q 92	4c
Rent, apartment, 2 bedrooms - 1-1/2 to 2 baths, unfurnished, 950 sq ft, water	month	434	4Q 92	4c
Rental unit, 1 bedroom	month	469	93	23c
Rental unit, 2 bedroom	month	553	93	23c
Rental unit, 3 bedroom	month	693	93	23c
Rental unit, 4 bedroom	month	775	93	23c
Rental unit, efficiency	month	385	93	23c
Insurance and Pensions				
Auto insurance, private passenger	year	709.79	91	63s
Personal Goods				
Shampoo, Alberto VO5	15 oz	1.27	4Q 92	4c
Toothpaste, Crest or Colgate	6-7 oz	1.99	4Q 92	4c
Personal Services				
Dry cleaning, man's 2-piece suit		6.12	4Q 92	4c
Haircare, woman's shampoo, trim and blow-dry		23.80	4Q 92	4c
Haircut, man's barbershop, no styling		6.90	4Q 92	4c
Restaurant Food				
Chicken, fried, thigh and drumstick		1.99	4Q 92	4c
Hamburger with cheese	1/4 lb	1.87	4Q 92	4c
Pizza, Pizza Hut or Pizza Inn, cheese, thin crust	12-13 in	8.79	4Q 92	4c
Taxes				
Tax, cigarette	pack	41	91	77s
Tax, gasoline	gal	20	91	77s
Taxes, state	capita	923	91	77s
Transportation				
ACCRA Index, Transportation		101.00	4Q 92	4c
Driver's license fee		16.00	12/90	43s
Tire balance, computer or spin balance, front	wheel	6.59	4Q 92	4c
Travel				
Business travel	day	193.00	4/93	89r
Utilities				
ACCRA Index, Utilities		107.00	4Q 92	4c
Electricity	mil Btu	17.09	90	64s
Electricity, partial electric and other energy, 1,800 sq ft living area new home	month	85.12	4Q 92	4c
Electricity, residential	KWh	5.92	2/93	94s

Milwaukee, WI

Item	Per	Value	Date	Ref.
Alcoholic Beverages				
Alcoholic beverages, exp	year	299	89	15c
Charity				
Cash contributions	year	584	89	15c
Child Care				
Child care fee, average, center	hour	1.63	90	65r
Child care fee, average, nonregulated family day care	hour	1.83	90	65r
Child care fee, average, regulated family day care	hour	1.42	90	65r
Communications				
Long-distance telephone service, day, initial minute, 0-100 miles	min	0.15-0.29	91	12s
Long-distance telephone service, day, additional minute, 0-100 miles	min	0.10-0.27	91	12s
Postage and stationery, exp	year	118	89	15c
Telephone, exp	year	473	89	15c
Telephone, flat rate	month	6.00	91	11c

Milwaukee, WI - continued

Item	Per	Value	Date	Ref.
Communications - continued				
Telephone, residential, private line, rotary, unlimited calling	month	17.55	10/91	78c
Education				
Board, 4-yr private college/university	year	1533	91	22s
Board, 4-yr public college/university	year	1404	91	22s
Education, exp	year	259	89	15c
Expenditures, local gov't, public elementary/secondary	pupil	5972	92	20s
Room, 4-year private college/university	year	1256	91	22s
Room, 4-year public college/university	year	1416	91	22s
Tuition, 2-year private college/university	year	4768	91	22s
Tuition, 2-year public college/university	year	1234	91	22s
Tuition, 4-year private college/university	year	8237	91	22s
Tuition, 4-year public college/university, in-state	year	1951	91	22s
Energy and Fuels				
Coal	mil Btu	1.41	90	64s
Energy	mil Btu	8.27	90	64s
Energy exp/householder, 1-family unit	year	471	90	28r
Energy exp/householder, <1,000 sq ft heating area	year	430	90	28r
Energy exp/householder, 1,000-1,999 sq ft heating area	year	481	90	28r
Energy exp/householder, 2,000+ sq ft heating area	year	473	90	28r
Energy exp/householder, mobile home	year	430	90	28r
Energy exp/householder, multifamily	year	461	90	28r
Fuel oil, other fuel, exp	year	65	89	15c
Gas, cooking, winter, 10 therms	month	8.99	92	56c
Gas, cooking, winter, 30 therms	month	19.96	92	56c
Gas, cooking, winter, 50 therms	month	30.93	92	56c
Gas, heating, winter, 100 therms	month	58.35	92	56c
Gas, heating, winter, average use	month	86.65	92	56c
Gas, natural	mil Btu	4.56	90	64s
Gas, natural	000 cu ft	5.61	91	46s
Gas, natural, exp	year	450	89	15c
Gas, natural, exp	year	605	91	46s
Gasoline, unleaded premium	gal	61.56	12/92	31c
Gasoline, unleaded regular	mil Btu	9.38	90	64s
Entertainment				
Entertainment exp	year	1220	89	15c
Fees and admissions	year	334	89	15c
Miniature golf admission	adult	6.18	92	1r
Miniature golf admission	child	5.14	92	1r
Pets, toys, playground equipment, exp	year	239	89	15c
Reading, exp	year	142	89	15c
Supplies, equipment, services, exp	year	248	89	15c
Waterpark admission	adult	11.00	92	1r
Waterpark admission	child	8.55	92	1r
Funerals				
Casket, 18-gauge steel, velvet interior		1926.72	91	24r
Cosmetology, hair care, etc.		97.64	91	24r
Embalming		249.14	91	24r
Facility use for ceremony		208.59	91	24r
Hearse, local		130.12	91	24r
Limousine, local		104.66	91	24r
Remains to funeral home, transfer		93.61	91	24r
Service charge, professional		724.62	91	24r
Vault, concrete, non-metallic liner		734.53	91	24r
Viewing facilities, use		236.06	91	24r
Goods and Services				
Police protection expense	resident	175.00	92	18c
Groceries				
Apples, Red Delicious	lb	0.77	4/93	16r
Bacon	lb	1.85	4/93	16r
Bakery products, exp	year	245	89	15c
Bananas	lb	0.46	4/93	16r

Values are in dollars or fractions of dollars. In the column headed *Ref*, references are shown to sources. Each reference is followed by a letter. These refer to the geographical level for which data were reported: s=State, r=Region, and c=City or metro. The abbreviation *ex* is used to mean *except* or *excluding*; *exp* stands for expenditures. For other abbreviations and further explanations, please see the Introduction.

Milwaukee, WI - continued

Item	Per	Value	Date	Ref.
Groceries				
Beef, exp	year	167	89	15c
Beef, stew, boneless	lb	2.53	4/93	16r
Beverages, nonalcoholic, exp	year	218	89	15c
Bologna, all beef or mixed	lb	2.19	4/93	16r
Bread, white, pan	lb	0.78	4/93	16r
Butter	lb	1.50	4/93	16r
Cabbage	lb	0.40	4/93	16r
Carrots, short trimmed and topped	lb	0.45	4/93	16r
Cereals and bakery products, exp	year	364	89	15c
Cereals and cereal products, exp	year	119	89	15c
Cheese, Cheddar	lb	3.47	4/93	16r
Chicken, fresh, whole	lb	0.84	4/93	16r
Chicken breast, bone-in	lb	1.94	4/93	16r
Chicken legs, bone-in	lb	1.02	4/93	16r
Chuck roast, graded and ungraded, ex USDA prime and choice	lb	2.43	4/93	16r
Chuck roast, USDA choice, bone-in	lb	2.11	4/93	16r
Chuck roast, USDA choice, boneless	lb	2.44	4/93	16r
Coffee, 100% ground roast, all sizes	lb	2.47	4/93	16r
Cookies, chocolate chip	lb	2.73	4/93	16r
Dairy products, exp	year	352	89	15c
Dairy products, miscellaneous, exp	year	182	89	15c
Eggs, exp	year	27	89	15c
Eggs, Grade A large	doz	0.93	4/93	16r
Fats and oils, exp	year	62	89	15c
Fish and seafood, exp	year	58	89	15c
Flour, white, all purpose	lb	0.21	4/93	16r
Food, exp	year	3729	89	15c
Food eaten at home, exp	year	2468	89	15c
Food eaten away from home, exp	year	1260	89	15c
Food prepared on out-of-town trips, exp	year	20	89	15c
Foods, miscellaneous, exp	year	313	89	15c
Fruits, fresh, exp	year	146	89	15c
Fruits, processed, exp	year	96	89	15c
Fruits and vegetables, exp	year	437	89	15c
Grapefruit	lb	0.45	4/93	16r
Grapes, Thompson Seedless	lb	1.46	4/93	16r
Ground beef, 100% beef	lb	1.63	4/93	16r
Ground beef, lean and extra lean	lb	2.08	4/93	16r
Ground chuck, 100% beef	lb	1.94	4/93	16r
Ham, boneless, excluding canned	lb	2.21	4/93	16r
Honey, jar	8 oz	0.97-1.25	92	5r
Honey, jar	lb	1.25-2.25	92	5r
Honey, squeeze bear	12-oz	1.25-1.99	92	5r
Ice cream, prepackaged, bulk, regular	1/2 gal	2.41	4/93	16r
Lemons	lb	0.82	4/93	16r
Lettuce, iceberg	lb	0.83	4/93	16r
Margarine, stick	lb	0.77	4/93	16r
Meats, miscellaneous, exp	year	115	89	15c
Meats, poultry, fish and eggs, exp	year	599	89	15c
Milk and cream, fresh, exp	year	170	89	15c
Oranges, navel	lb	0.50	4/93	16r
Peanut butter, creamy, all sizes	lb	1.82	4/93	16r
Pears, Anjou	lb	0.85	4/93	16r
Pork, exp	year	125	89	15c
Pork chops, center cut, bone-in	lb	3.17	4/93	16r
Potato chips	16 oz	2.68	4/93	16r
Potatoes, white	lb	0.26	4/93	16r
Poultry, exp	year	106	89	15c
Round roast, graded & ungraded, ex USDA prime & choice	lb	2.88	4/93	16r
Round roast, USDA choice, boneless	lb	2.96	4/93	16r
Shortening, vegetable oil blends	lb	0.79	4/93	16r
Spaghetti and macaroni	lb	0.76	4/93	16r
Steak, rib eye, USDA choice, boneless	lb	6.29	4/93	16r
Steak, round, USDA choice, boneless	lb	3.24	4/93	16r
Steak, sirloin, graded & ungraded, ex USDA prime & choice	lb	4.00	4/93	16r
Steak, sirloin, USDA choice, bone-in	lb	3.57	4/93	16r
Steak, sirloin, USDA choice, boneless	lb	4.17	4/93	16r
Steak, T-bone, USDA choice, bone-in	lb	5.60	4/93	16r
Strawberries, dry pint	12 oz	0.90	4/93	16r

Milwaukee, WI - continued

Item	Per	Value	Date	Ref.
Groceries - continued				
Sugar, white	lb	0.36	4/93	16r
Sugar, white, 33-80 oz pk	lb	0.35	4/93	16r
Sugar and other sweets, exp	year	103	89	15c
Tobacco products, exp	year	245	89	15c
Tomatoes, field grown	lb	0.99	4/93	16r
Tuna, chunk, light	lb	1.76	4/93	16r
Turkey, frozen, whole	lb	0.91	4/93	16r
Vegetables, fresh, exp	year	128	89	15c
Vegetables, processed, exp	year	66	89	15c
Health Care				
Childbirth, cesarean, hospital		4688	91	62r
Childbirth, cesarean, physician's fee		2053	91	62r
Childbirth, normal, hospital		2657	91	62r
Childbirth, normal, physician's fee		1492	91	62r
Drugs, exp	year	177	89	15c
Health care, exp	year	1192	89	15c
Health insurance, exp	year	459	89	15c
Hospital care, semiprivate room	day	222.09	90	27c
Medical insurance premium, per employee, small group comprehensive	month	324.85	10/91	25c
Medical plan per employee	year	3443	91	45r
Medical services, exp	year	492	89	15c
Medical supplies, exp	year	64	89	15c
Mental health care, exp	capita	28.84-37.59	90	38s
Mental health care, exp, state mental health agency	capita	36.62	90	38s
Mental health care, hospital psychiatric services, non-Federal, exp	capita	13.05	88	38s
Mental health care, mental health organization, multiservice, exp	capita	10.93	88	38s
Mental health care, psychiatric hospitals, private, exp	capita	8.71	88	38s
Mental health care, psychiatric out-patient clinics, freestanding, exp	capita	5.33	88	38s
Mental health care, psychiatric partial-care organizations, freestanding, exp	capita	0.20	88	38s
Mental health care, state and county mental hospitals, exp	capita	28.29	88	38s
Mental health care, VA medical centers, exp	capita	7.57	88	38s
Physician fee, family practice, first-visit		76.00	91	62r
Physician fee, family practice, revisit		33.00	91	62r
Physician fee, general practice, first-visit		61.00	91	62r
Physician fee, general practice, revisit		31.00	91	62r
Physician fee, general surgeon, first-visit		65.00	91	62r
Physician fee, general surgeon, revisit		35.00	91	62r
Physician fee, internal medicine, first-visit		91.00	91	62r
Physician fee, internal medicine, revisit		40.00	91	62r
Physician fee, median, neurosurgeon, first-visit		106.00	91	62r
Physician fee, median, nonsurgical specialist, first-visit		90.00	91	62r
Physician fee, median, orthopedic surgeon, first-visit		83.00	91	62r
Physician fee, median, surgical specialist, first-visit		61.00	91	62r
Physician fee, neurosurgeon, revisit		41.00	91	62r
Physician fee, nonsurgical specialist, revisit		40.00	91	62r
Physician fee, obstetrics/gynecology, first-visit		61.00	91	62r
Physician fee, obstetrics/gynecology, revisit		40.00	91	62r
Physician fee, orthopedic surgeon, revisit		41.00	91	62r
Physician fee, pediatrician, first-visit		46.00	91	62r
Physician fee, pediatrician, revisit		33.00	91	62r
Physician fee, surgical specialist, revisit		36.00	91	62r
Substance abuse, hospital ancillary charge	incident	960	90	70s
Substance abuse, hospital physician charge	incident	470	90	70s
Substance abuse, hospital room and board	incident	3980	90	70s

Values are in dollars or fractions of dollars. In the column headed *Ref*, references are shown to sources. Each reference is followed by a letter. These refer to the geographical level for which data were reported: s=State, r=Region, and c=City or metro. The abbreviation *ex* is used to mean *except* or *excluding*; *exp* stands for expenditures. For other abbreviations and further explanations, please see the Introduction.

Milwaukee, WI - continued

Item	Per	Value	Date	Ref.
Household Goods				
Appliances, major, exp	year	154	89	15c
Appliances, small, exp	year	46	89	15c
Equipment, misc., exp	year	306	89	15c
Floor coverings, exp	year	97	89	15c
Furnishings and equipment, exp	year	920	89	15c
Furniture, exp	year	225	89	15c
Household products, misc., exp	year	166	89	15c
Household textiles, exp	year	91	89	15c
Housekeeping supplies, exp	year	388	89	15c
Laundry and cleaning supplies, exp	year	104	89	15c
TVs, radios, sound equipment, exp	year	399	89	15c
Housing				
Dwellings, exp	year	3236	89	15c
Home, median price	unit	97.00		26c
Household expenses, misc.	year	111	89	15c
Household operations, exp	year	276	89	15c
Housing, exp	year	8171	89	15c
Lodging, exp	year	316	89	15c
Maintenance, repairs, insurance, and other, exp	year	424	89	15c
Mortgage interest, exp	year	1464	89	15c
Rental unit, 1 bedroom	month	433	93	23c
Rental unit, 2 bedroom	month	513	93	23c
Rental unit, 3 bedroom	month	642	93	23c
Rental unit, 4 bedroom	month	716	93	23c
Rental unit, efficiency	month	359	93	23c
Rented dwellings, exp	year	1482	89	15c
Shelter, exp	year	5033	89	15c
Insurance and Pensions				
Auto insurance, private passenger	year	510.11	91	63s
Insurance, life and other personal, exp	year	254	89	15c
Insurance and pensions, personal, exp	year	1955	89	15c
Pensions and social security, exp	year	1701	89	15c
Vehicle insurance	year	404	89	15c
Legal Assistance				
Living trust, 77-year-old, $80,000 estate		540	9/92	3c
Living trust, married couple with $150,000 home and $50,000 in stocks		795	9/92	3c
Will		149	9/92	3c
Will and probate, $80,000 estate		1654	9/92	3c
Will and probate, $80,000 estate, 77-year-old		1654	9/92	3c
Personal Goods				
Products and services, exp	year	316	89	15c
Personal Services				
Services, exp	year	165	89	15c
Taxes				
Property tax, exp	year	1347	89	15c
Tax, cigarette	pack	38	91	77s
Tax, gasoline	gal	22.20	91	77s
Taxes, state	capita	1416	91	77s
Transportation				
Auto fixed costs, midsize		3475	91	60c
Auto operating cost, midsize		1433	91	60c
Auto rental, average	day	41.25	6/91	60c
Bus fare	one-way	1.10	3/93	2c
Driver's license fee		9.00	12/90	43s
Limo fare, airport-city, average	day	6.50	6/91	60c
Public transit, exp	year	210	89	15c
Taxi fare, airport-city, average	day	15.00	6/91	60c
Vehicle expenses, misc.	year	1186	89	15c
Vehicle finance charges	year	199	89	15c
Vehicle maintenance	year	448	89	15c
Vehicle rental and license	year	136	89	15c
Travel				
Breakfast	day	5.94	6/91	60c
Dinner	day	19.86	6/91	60c
Lodging	day	113.21	91	60c

Milwaukee, WI - continued

Item	Per	Value	Date	Ref.
Travel - continued				
Lunch	day	9.70	6/91	60c
Travel, business	day	189.29	93	88c
Utilities				
Electricity	mil Btu	15.77	90	64s
Electricity, exp	year	479	89	15c
Electricity, winter, 250 KWh	month	20.43	92	55c
Electricity, winter, 500 KWh	month	37.35	92	55c
Electricity, winter, 750 KWh	month	54.28	92	55c
Electricity, winter, 1000 KWh	month	60.26	92	55c
Utilities, fuels, public services, exp	year	1554	89	15c
Water, public services, exp	year	87	89	15c

Minneapolis, MN

Item	Per	Value	Date	Ref.
Composite ACCRA index		103.70	4Q 92	4c
Alcoholic Beverages				
Beer, Miller Lite or Budweiser, 12-oz containers	6 pack	3.99	4Q 92	4c
Liquor, J & B Scotch	750 ml	13.99	4Q 92	4c
Wine, Gallo Chablis blanc, 1.5 liter	bottle	4.79	4Q 92	4c
Clothing				
Jeans, man's denim		21.79	4Q 92	4c
Shirt, man's dress shirt		24.19	4Q 92	4c
Undervest, boy's size 10-14, cotton	3	4.79	4Q 92	4c
Communications				
Newspaper subscription, daily and Sunday home delivery, large-city	month	13.00	4Q 92	4c
Telephone, residential, private line, rotary, unlimited calling	month	19.85	10/91	78c
Telephone bill, family of four	month	20.74	4Q 92	4c
Energy and Fuels				
Energy, combined forms, 1,800 sq ft heating area	month	99.30	4Q 92	4c
Energy, exc electricity, 1,800 sq ft heating area	month	48.14	4Q 92	4c
Gas, cooking, 10 therms	month	5.28	92	56c
Gas, cooking, 30 therms	month	12.66	92	56c
Gas, cooking, 50 therms	month	20.07	92	56c
Gas, heating, winter, 100 therms	month	38.58	92	56c
Gas, heating, winter, average use	month	62.29	92	56c
Gasoline, motor	gal	1.13	4Q 92	4c
Entertainment				
Bowling, evening rate	game	2.00	4Q 92	4c
Monopoly game, Parker Brothers', No. 9		10.49	4Q 92	4c
Movie	admission	6.00	4Q 92	4c
Tennis balls, yellow, Wilson or Penn, 3	can	3.59	4Q 92	4c
Goods and Services				
ACCRA Index, Miscellaneous Goods and Services		102.30	4Q 92	4c
Groceries				
ACCRA Index, Groceries		95.40	4Q 92	4c
Babyfood, strained vegetables, lowest price	4-4.5 oz jar	0.34	4Q 92	4c
Bananas	lb	0.40	4Q 92	4c
Bread, white	24 oz	0.66	4Q 92	4c
Cheese, Kraft grated Parmesan	8-oz canister	3.03	4Q 92	4c
Chicken, fryer, whole	lb	0.94	4Q 92	4c
Cigarettes, Winston	carton	19.52	4Q 92	4c
Coffee, vacuum-packed	13-oz can	1.96	4Q 92	4c
Corn, frozen	10 oz	0.64	4Q 92	4c
Corn Flakes, Kellogg's or Post Toasties	18 oz	1.79	4Q 92	4c
Eggs, Grade A large	doz	0.64	4Q 92	4c
Ground beef or hamburger	lb	1.26	4Q 92	4c

Values are in dollars or fractions of dollars. In the column headed *Ref*, references are shown to sources. Each reference is followed by a letter. These refer to the geographical level for which data were reported: s=State, r=Region, and c=City or metro. The abbreviation *ex* is used to mean *except* or *excluding*; *exp* stands for expenditures. For other abbreviations and further explanations, please see the Introduction.

Minneapolis, MN - continued

Item	Per	Value	Date	Ref.
Groceries				
Lettuce, iceberg	head	0.79	4Q 92	4c
Margarine, Blue Bonnet or Parkay cubes	lb	0.65	4Q 92	4c
Milk, whole	1/2 gal	1.42	4Q 92	4c
Orange juice, Minute Maid frozen	12-oz can	1.30	4Q 92	4c
Peaches	29-oz can	1.15	4Q 92	4c
Peas Sweet, Del Monte or Green Giant	15-17 oz can	0.56	4Q 92	4c
Potatoes, white or red	10-lb sack	1.65	4Q 92	4c
Sausage, Jimmy Dean, 100% pork	lb	2.22	4Q 92	4c
Shortening, vegetable, Crisco	3-lb can	2.01	4Q 92	4c
Soft drink, Coca Cola	2 liter	1.15	4Q 92	4c
Steak, T-bone	lb	4.46	4Q 92	4c
Sugar, cane or beet	4 lb	1.78	4Q 92	4c
Tomatoes, Hunt's or Del Monte	14.5-oz can	0.65	4Q 92	4c
Tuna, chunk, light	6.125-6.5 oz can	0.57	4Q 92	4c
Health Care				
ACCRA Index, Health Care		105.50	4Q 92	4c
Analgesic, Aspirin, Bayer, 325 mg tablets	100	4.46	4Q 92	4c
Dentist's fee, adult teeth cleaning and periodic oral exam	visit	49.60	4Q 92	4c
Doctor's fee, routine exam, established patient	visit	35.00	4Q 92	4c
Hospital care, semiprivate room	day	321.82	90	27c
Hospital care, semiprivate room	day	430.60	4Q 92	4c
Medical insurance premium, per employee, small group comprehensive	month	222.20	10/91	25c
Household Goods				
Appliance repair, home, service call, washing machine	min labor charge	30.98	4Q 92	4c
Laundry detergent, Tide Ultra, Bold, or Cheer	42 oz	3.57	4Q 92	4c
Tissues, facial, Kleenex brand	175-count box	0.96	4Q 92	4c
Housing				
ACCRA Index, Housing		112.50	4Q 92	4c
House, 1,800 sq ft, 8,000 sq ft lot, new, urban	total	124650	4Q 92	4c
House payment, principal and interest, 25% down payment	month	693	4Q 92	4c
Mortgage rate, incl. points & origination fee, 30-year fixed or adjustable rate	per-cent	8.11	4Q 92	4c
Rent, apartment, 2 bedrooms - 1-1/2 to 2 baths, unfurnished, 950 sq ft, water	month	552	4Q 92	4c
Personal Goods				
Shampoo, Alberto VO5	15 oz	1.29	4Q 92	4c
Toothpaste, Crest or Colgate	6-7 oz	1.79	4Q 92	4c
Personal Services				
Dry cleaning, man's 2-piece suit		6.17	4Q 92	4c
Haircare, woman's shampoo, trim and blow-dry		18.40	4Q 92	4c
Haircut, man's barbershop, no styling		9.70	4Q 92	4c
Restaurant Food				
Chicken, fried, thigh and drumstick		2.15	4Q 92	4c
Hamburger with cheese	1/4 lb	1.89	4Q 92	4c
Pizza, Pizza Hut or Pizza Inn, cheese, thin crust	12-13 in	7.59	4Q 92	4c
Transportation				
ACCRA Index, Transportation		104.20	4Q 92	4c

Minneapolis, MN - continued

Item	Per	Value	Date	Ref.
Transportation - continued				
Bus fare	one-way	0.85	3/93	2c
Bus fare, up to 10 miles	one-way	1.10	4Q 92	4c
Tire balance, computer or spin balance, front	wheel	6.70	4Q 92	4c
Travel				
Business travel	day	125.00	92	86c
Dinner	day	21.10	92	85c
Lodging	day	88.00	92	85c
Utilities				
ACCRA Index, Utilities		92.50	4Q 92	4c
Electricity, partial electric and other energy, 1,800 sq ft living area new home	month	51.16	4Q 92	4c
Electricity, winter, 250 KWh	month	17.14	92	55c
Electricity, winter, 500 KWh	month	35.94	92	55c
Electricity, winter, 750 KWh	month	51.42	92	55c
Electricity, winter, 1000 KWh	month	67.03	92	55c

Minneapolis-Saint Paul, MN

Item	Per	Value	Date	Ref.
Alcoholic Beverages				
Alcoholic beverages, exp	year	423	89	15c
Charity				
Cash contributions	year	803	89	15c
Child Care				
Child care fee, average, center	hour	1.63	90	65r
Child care fee, average, nonregulated family day care	hour	1.83	90	65r
Child care fee, average, regulated family day care	hour	1.42	90	65r
Communications				
Long-distance telephone service, day, initial minute, 0-100 miles	min	0.14-0.52	91	12s
Long-distance telephone service, day, additional minute, 0-100 miles	min	0.05-0.35	91	12s
Long-distance telephone service, evenings/weekends, 0-100 mi, initial minute	min	0.08-0.31	91	12s
Long-distance telephone service, evenings/weekends, 0-100 mi, additional minute	min	0.03-0.21	91	12s
Postage and stationery, exp	year	140	89	15c
Telephone, exp	year	492	89	15c
Education				
Board, 4-yr private college/university	year	1718	91	22s
Board, 4-yr public college/university	year	1321	91	22s
Education, exp	year	530	89	15c
Expenditures, local gov't, public elementary/secondary	pupil	5500	92	20s
Room, 4-year private college/university	year	1587	91	22s
Room, 4-year public college/university	year	1344	91	22s
Tuition, 2-year private college/university	year	7664	91	22s
Tuition, 2-year public college/university	year	1578	91	22s
Tuition, 4-year private college/university	year	9507	91	22s
Tuition, 4-year public college/university, in-state	year	2216	91	22s
Energy and Fuels				
Coal	mil Btu	1.32	90	64s
Energy	mil Btu	8.17	90	64s
Energy exp/householder, 1-family unit	year	473	90	28r
Energy exp/householder, <1,000 sq ft heating area	year	429	90	28r
Energy exp/householder, 1,000-1,999 sq ft heating area	year	442	90	28r
Energy exp/householder, 2,000+ sq ft heating area	year	498	90	28r
Energy exp/householder, mobile home	year	442	90	28r
Energy exp/householder, multifamily	year	407	90	28r

Values are in dollars or fractions of dollars. In the column headed *Ref*, references are shown to sources. Each reference is followed by a letter. These refer to the geographical level for which data were reported: s = State, r = Region, and c = City or metro. The abbreviation *ex* is used to mean *except* or *excluding*; *exp* stands for expenditures. For other abbreviations and further explanations, please see the Introduction.

Minneapolis-Saint Paul, MN - continued

Item	Per	Value	Date	Ref.
Energy and Fuels				
Fuel oil, other fuel, exp	year	58	89	15c
Gas, natural	mil Btu	3.87	90	64s
Gas, natural	000 cu ft	4.52	91	46s
Gas, natural, exp	year	406	89	15c
Gas, natural, exp	year	545	91	46s
Gasoline, unleaded regular	mil Btu	9.56	90	64s
Entertainment				
Entertainment exp	year	1470	89	15c
Fees and admissions	year	517	89	15c
Miniature golf admission	adult	6.18	92	1r
Miniature golf admission	child	5.14	92	1r
Pets, toys, playground equipment, exp	year	234	89	15c
Reading, exp	year	223	89	15c
Supplies, equipment, services, exp	year	284	89	15c
Waterpark admission	adult	11.00	92	1r
Waterpark admission	child	8.55	92	1r
Funerals				
Casket, 18-gauge steel, velvet interior		1952.97	91	24r
Cosmetology, hair care, etc.		90.03	91	24r
Embalming		251.75	91	24r
Facility use for ceremony		180.75	91	24r
Hearse, local		117.51	91	24r
Limousine, local		71.86	91	24r
Remains to funeral home, transfer		81.14	91	24r
Service charge, professional		740.03	91	24r
Vault, concrete, non-metallic liner		801.47	91	24r
Viewing facilities, use		169.33	91	24r
Groceries				
Apples, Red Delicious	lb	0.77	4/93	16r
Bacon	lb	1.85	4/93	16r
Bakery products, exp	year	240	89	15c
Bananas	lb	0.46	4/93	16r
Beef, exp	year	142	89	15c
Beef, stew, boneless	lb	2.53	4/93	16r
Beverages, nonalcoholic, exp	year	216	89	15c
Bologna, all beef or mixed	lb	2.19	4/93	16r
Bread, white, pan	lb	0.78	4/93	16r
Butter	lb	1.50	4/93	16r
Cabbage	lb	0.40	4/93	16r
Carrots, short trimmed and topped	lb	0.45	4/93	16r
Cereals and bakery products, exp	year	336	89	15c
Cereals and cereal products, exp	year	96	89	15c
Cheese, Cheddar	lb	3.47	4/93	16r
Chicken, fresh, whole	lb	0.84	4/93	16r
Chicken breast, bone-in	lb	1.94	4/93	16r
Chicken legs, bone-in	lb	1.02	4/93	16r
Chuck roast, graded and ungraded, ex USDA prime and choice	lb	2.43	4/93	16r
Chuck roast, USDA choice, bone-in	lb	2.11	4/93	16r
Chuck roast, USDA choice, boneless	lb	2.44	4/93	16r
Coffee, 100% ground roast, all sizes	lb	2.47	4/93	16r
Cookies, chocolate chip	lb	2.73	4/93	16r
Dairy products, exp	year	288	89	15c
Dairy products, miscellaneous, exp	year	163	89	15c
Eggs, exp	year	17	89	15c
Eggs, Grade A large	doz	0.93	4/93	16r
Fats and oils, exp	year	59	89	15c
Fish and seafood, exp	year	49	89	15c
Flour, white, all purpose	lb	0.21	4/93	16r
Food, exp	year	4197	89	15c
Food eaten at home, exp	year	2167	89	15c
Food eaten away from home, exp	year	2030	89	15c
Food prepared on out-of-town trips, exp	year	74	89	15c
Foods, miscellaneous, exp	year	301	89	15c
Fruits, fresh, exp	year	147	89	15c
Fruits, processed, exp	year	79	89	15c
Fruits and vegetables, exp	year	372	89	15c
Grapefruit	lb	0.45	4/93	16r
Grapes, Thompson Seedless	lb	1.46	4/93	16r
Ground beef, 100% beef	lb	1.63	4/93	16r

Minneapolis-Saint Paul, MN - continued

Item	Per	Value	Date	Ref.
Groceries - continued				
Ground beef, lean and extra lean	lb	2.08	4/93	16r
Ground chuck, 100% beef	lb	1.94	4/93	16r
Ham, boneless, excluding canned	lb	2.21	4/93	16r
Ice cream, prepackaged, bulk, regular	1/2 gal	2.41	4/93	16r
Lemons	lb	0.82	4/93	16r
Lettuce, iceberg	lb	0.83	4/93	16r
Margarine, stick	lb	0.77	4/93	16r
Meats, miscellaneous, exp	year	72	89	15c
Meats, poultry, fish and eggs, exp	year	449	89	15c
Milk and cream, fresh, exp	year	125	89	15c
Oranges, navel	lb	0.50	4/93	16r
Peanut butter, creamy, all sizes	lb	1.82	4/93	16r
Pears, Anjou	lb	0.85	4/93	16r
Pork, exp	year	88	89	15c
Pork chops, center cut, bone-in	lb	3.17	4/93	16r
Potato chips	16 oz	2.68	4/93	16r
Potatoes, white	lb	0.26	4/93	16r
Poultry, exp	year	81	89	15c
Round roast, graded & ungraded, ex USDA prime & choice	lb	2.88	4/93	16r
Round roast, USDA choice, boneless	lb	2.96	4/93	16r
Shortening, vegetable oil blends	lb	0.79	4/93	16r
Spaghetti and macaroni	lb	0.76	4/93	16r
Steak, rib eye, USDA choice, boneless	lb	6.29	4/93	16r
Steak, round, USDA choice, boneless	lb	3.24	4/93	16r
Steak, sirloin, graded & ungraded, ex USDA prime & choice	lb	4.00	4/93	16r
Steak, sirloin, USDA choice, bone-in	lb	3.57	4/93	16r
Steak, sirloin, USDA choice, boneless	lb	4.17	4/93	16r
Steak, T-bone, USDA choice, bone-in	lb	5.60	4/93	16r
Strawberries, dry pint	12 oz	0.90	4/93	16r
Sugar, white	lb	0.36	4/03	16r
Sugar, white, 33-80 oz pk	lb	0.35	4/93	16r
Sugar and other sweets, exp	year	73	89	15c
Tobacco products, exp	year	225	89	15c
Tomatoes, field grown	lb	0.99	4/93	16r
Tuna, chunk, light	lb	1.76	4/93	16r
Turkey, frozen, whole	lb	0.91	4/93	16r
Vegetables, fresh, exp	year	92	89	15c
Vegetables, processed, exp	year	54	89	15c
Health Care				
Childbirth, cesarean, hospital		4688	91	62r
Childbirth, cesarean, physician's fee		2053	91	62r
Childbirth, normal, hospital		2657	91	62r
Childbirth, normal, physician's fee		1492	91	62r
Drugs, exp	year	177	89	15c
Health care, exp	year	1284	89	15c
Health insurance, exp	year	459	89	15c
Health maintenance organization coverage, employee	year	2969	93	39c
Health maintenance organization medical coverage, employee	year	2969	92	42c
Health maintenance organization medical coverage, employee	year	2969	92	34c
Indemnity plan medical coverage, employee	year	3347	92	42c
Indemnity plan medical coverage, employee	year	3347	92	34c
Insurance coverage, traditional, employee	year	3347	93	39c
Medical plan per employee	year	3443	91	45r
Medical services, exp	year	492	89	15c
Medical supplies, exp	year	64	89	15c
Mental health care, exp	capita	20.37-28.83	90	38s
Mental health care, exp, state mental health agency	capita	53.67	90	38s
Mental health care, hospital psychiatric services, non-Federal, exp	capita	18.62	88	38s
Mental health care, mental health organization, multiservice, exp	capita	9.59	88	38s
Mental health care, psychiatric hospitals, private, exp	capita	2.70	88	38s
Mental health care, psychiatric out-patient clinics, freestanding, exp	capita	8.41	88	38s

Values are in dollars or fractions of dollars. In the column headed *Ref*, references are shown to sources. Each reference is followed by a letter. These refer to the geographical level for which data were reported: s=State, r=Region, and c=City or metro. The abbreviation *ex* is used to mean *except* or *excluding*; *exp* stands for expenditures. For other abbreviations and further explanations, please see the Introduction.

Minneapolis-Saint Paul, MN - continued

Item	Per	Value	Date	Ref.
Health Care				
Mental health care, state and county mental hospitals, exp	capita	27.18	88	38s
Mental health care, VA medical centers, exp	capita	7.88	88	38s
Physician fee, family practice, first-visit		76.00	91	62r
Physician fee, family practice, revisit		33.00	91	62r
Physician fee, general practice, first-visit		61.00	91	62r
Physician fee, general practice, revisit		31.00	91	62r
Physician fee, general surgeon, first-visit		65.00	91	62r
Physician fee, general surgeon, revisit		35.00	91	62r
Physician fee, internal medicine, first-visit		91.00	91	62r
Physician fee, internal medicine, revisit		40.00	91	62r
Physician fee, median, neurosurgeon, first-visit		106.00	91	62r
Physician fee, median, nonsurgical specialist, first-visit		90.00	91	62r
Physician fee, median, orthopedic surgeon, first-visit		83.00	91	62r
Physician fee, median, surgical specialist, first-visit		61.00	91	62r
Physician fee, neurosurgeon, revisit		41.00	91	62r
Physician fee, nonsurgical specialist, revisit		40.00	91	62r
Physician fee, obstetrics/gynecology, first-visit		61.00	91	62r
Physician fee, obstetrics/gynecology, revisit		40.00	91	62r
Physician fee, orthopedic surgeon, revisit		41.00	91	62r
Physician fee, pediatrician, first-visit		46.00	91	62r
Physician fee, pediatrician, revisit		33.00	91	62r
Physician fee, surgical specialist, revisit		36.00	91	62r
Preferred provider organization medical coverage, employee	year	3121	92	34c
Preferred provider organization medical coverage, employee	year	3121	92	42c
Substance abuse, hospital ancillary charge	incident	670	90	70s
Substance abuse, hospital physician charge	incident	310	90	70s
Substance abuse, hospital room and board	incident	3800	90	70s
Household Goods				
Appliances, major, exp	year	136	89	15c
Appliances, small, exp	year	85	89	15c
Equipment, misc., exp	year	424	89	15c
Floor coverings, exp	year	31	89	15c
Furnishings and equipment, exp	year	1078	89	15c
Furniture, exp	year	319	89	15c
Household products, misc., exp	year	237	89	15c
Household textiles, exp	year	82	89	15c
Housekeeping supplies, exp	year	490	89	15c
Laundry and cleaning supplies, exp	year	113	89	15c
TVs, radios, sound equipment, exp	year	436	89	15c
Housing				
Dwellings, exp	year	4412	89	15c
Home, median price	unit	94.20		26c
Household expenses, misc.	year	352	89	15c
Household operations, exp	year	629	89	15c
Housing, exp	year	10353	89	15c
Lodging, exp	year	564	89	15c
Maintenance, repairs, insurance, and other, exp	year	799	89	15c
Mortgage interest, exp	year	2591	89	15c
Rental unit, 1 bedroom	month	535	93	23c
Rental unit, 2 bedroom	month	630	93	23c
Rental unit, 3 bedroom	month	788	93	23c
Rental unit, 4 bedroom	month	882	93	23c
Rental unit, efficiency	month	440	93	23c
Rented dwellings, exp	year	1492	89	15c
Shelter, exp	year	6469	89	15c
Insurance and Pensions				
Auto insurance, private passenger	year	584.92	91	63s
Insurance, life and other personal, exp	year	322	89	15c
Insurance and pensions, personal, exp	year	3130	89	15c

Minneapolis-Saint Paul, MN - continued

Item	Per	Value	Date	Ref.
Insurance and Pensions - continued				
Pensions and social security, exp	year	2808	89	15c
Vehicle insurance	year	606	89	15c
Personal Goods				
Products and services, exp	year	422	89	15c
Personal Services				
Services, exp	year	277	89	15c
Taxes				
Property tax, exp	year	1023	89	15c
Tax, cigarette	pack	48	91	77s
Tax, gasoline	gal	20	91	77s
Taxes, state	capita	1591	91	77s
Transportation				
Auto rental, average	day	42.00	6/91	60c
Driver's license fee		15.00	12/90	43s
Limo fare, airport-city, average	day	7.50	6/91	60c
Public transit, exp	year	415	89	15c
Taxi fare, airport-city, average	day	18.00	6/91	60c
Vehicle expenses, misc.	year	1890	89	15c
Vehicle finance charges	year	337	89	15c
Vehicle maintenance	year	713	89	15c
Vehicle registration and license plate	year	10.00	93	66s
Vehicle rental and license	year	235	89	15c
Travel				
Breakfast	day	8.27	6/91	60c
Dinner	day	20.89	6/91	60c
Lodging	day	97.61	91	60c
Lunch	day	9.76	6/91	60c
Utilities				
Electricity	mil Btu	15.68	90	64s
Electricity, exp	year	548	89	15c
Utilities, fuels, public services, exp	year	1687	89	15c
Water, public services, exp	year	185	89	15c

Minot, ND

Item	Per	Value	Date	Ref.
Composite ACCRA index		97.40	4Q 92	4c
Alcoholic Beverages				
Beer, Miller Lite or Budweiser, 12-oz containers	6 pack	3.96	4Q 92	4c
Liquor, J & B Scotch	750 ml	17.47	4Q 92	4c
Wine, Gallo Chablis blanc, 1.5 liter	bottle	5.28	4Q 92	4c
Clothing				
Jeans, man's denim		33.33	4Q 92	4c
Shirt, man's dress shirt		20.67	4Q 92	4c
Undervest, boy's size 10-14, cotton	3	4.20	4Q 92	4c
Communications				
Newspaper subscription, daily and Sunday home delivery, large-city	month	9.25	4Q 92	4c
Telephone, flat rate	month	10.82	91	11c
Telephone bill, family of four	month	9.32	4Q 92	4c
Energy and Fuels				
Energy, combined forms, 1,800 sq ft heating area	month	89.91	4Q 92	4c
Energy, exc electricity, 1,800 sq ft heating area	month	47.53	4Q 92	4c
Gasoline, motor	gal	1.20	4Q 92	4c
Entertainment				
Bowling, evening rate	game	2.25	4Q 92	4c
Monopoly game, Parker Brothers', No. 9		9.98	4Q 92	4c
Movie	admission	5.00	4Q 92	4c
Tennis balls, yellow, Wilson or Penn, 3	can	2.43	4Q 92	4c
Goods and Services				
ACCRA Index, Miscellaneous Goods and Services		99.80	4Q 92	4c

Values are in dollars or fractions of dollars. In the column headed *Ref*, references are shown in sources. Each reference is followed by a letter. These refer to the geographical level for which data were reported: s = State, r = Region, and c = City or metro. The abbreviation *ex* is used to mean *except* or *excluding*; *exp* stands for expenditures. For other abbreviations and further explanations, please see the Introduction.

Minot, ND - continued

Groceries

Item	Per	Value	Date	Ref.
ACCRA Index, Groceries		102.70	4Q 92	4c
Babyfood, strained vegetables, lowest price	4-4.5 oz jar	0.29	4Q 92	4c
Bananas	lb	0.44	4Q 92	4c
Bread, white	24 oz	0.69	4Q 92	4c
Cheese, Kraft grated Parmesan	8-oz canister	3.53	4Q 92	4c
Chicken, fryer, whole	lb	0.88	4Q 92	4c
Cigarettes, Winston	carton	17.42	4Q 92	4c
Coffee, vacuum-packed	13-oz can	1.92	4Q 92	4c
Corn, frozen	10 oz	0.76	4Q 92	4c
Corn Flakes, Kellogg's or Post Toasties	18 oz	1.59	4Q 92	4c
Eggs, Grade A large	doz	0.80	4Q 92	4c
Ground beef or hamburger	lb	1.69	4Q 92	4c
Lettuce, iceberg	head	0.96	4Q 92	4c
Margarine, Blue Bonnet or Parkay cubes	lb	0.49	4Q 92	4c
Milk, whole	1/2 gal	1.48	4Q 92	4c
Orange juice, Minute Maid frozen	12-oz can	1.61	4Q 92	4c
Peaches	29-oz can	1.41	4Q 92	4c
Peas Sweet, Del Monte or Green Giant	15-17 oz can	0.72	4Q 92	4c
Potatoes, white or red	10-lb sack	2.19	4Q 92	4c
Sausage, Jimmy Dean, 100% pork	lb	2.53	4Q 92	4c
Shortening, vegetable, Crisco	3-lb can	2.57	4Q 92	4c
Soft drink, Coca Cola	2 liter	1.46	4Q 92	4c
Steak, T-bone	lb	4.79	4Q 92	4c
Sugar, cane or beet	4 lb	1.50	4Q 92	4c
Tomatoes, Hunt's or Del Monte	14.5-oz can	0.77	4Q 92	4c
Tuna, chunk, light	6.125-6.5 oz can	0.64	4Q 92	4c

Health Care

Item	Per	Value	Date	Ref.
ACCRA Index, Health Care		97.80	4Q 92	4c
Analgesic, Aspirin, Bayer, 325 mg tablets	100	5.53	4Q 92	4c
Dentist's fee, adult teeth cleaning and periodic oral exam	visit	39.00	4Q 92	4c
Doctor's fee, routine exam, established patient	visit	40.00	4Q 92	4c
Hospital care, semiprivate room	day	228.32	90	27c
Hospital care, semiprivate room	day	311.14	4Q 92	4c

Household Goods

Item	Per	Value	Date	Ref.
Appliance repair, home, service call, washing machine	min labor charge	35.33	4Q 92	4c
Laundry detergent, Tide Ultra, Bold, or Cheer	42 oz	3.94	4Q 92	4c
Tissues, facial, Kleenex brand	175-count box	1.21	4Q 92	4c

Housing

Item	Per	Value	Date	Ref.
ACCRA Index, Housing		99.80	4Q 92	4c
House, 1,800 sq ft, 8,000 sq ft lot, new, urban	total	118750	4Q 92	4c
House payment, principal and interest, 25% down payment	month	668	4Q 92	4c
Mortgage rate, incl. points & origination fee, 30-year fixed or adjustable rate	percent	8.23	4Q 92	4c
Rent, apartment, 2 bedrooms - 1-1/2 to 2 baths, unfurnished, 950 sq ft, water	month	368	4Q 92	4c

Personal Goods

Item	Per	Value	Date	Ref.
Shampoo, Alberto VO5	15 oz	1.57	4Q 92	4c
Toothpaste, Crest or Colgate	6-7 oz	2.39	4Q 92	4c

Minot, ND - continued

Personal Services

Item	Per	Value	Date	Ref.
Dry cleaning, man's 2-piece suit		5.45	4Q 92	4c
Haircare, woman's shampoo, trim and blow-dry		15.00	4Q 92	4c
Haircut, man's barbershop, no styling		7.50	4Q 92	4c

Restaurant Food

Item	Per	Value	Date	Ref.
Chicken, fried, thigh and drumstick		1.96	4Q 92	4c
Hamburger with cheese	1/4 lb	1.89	4Q 92	4c
Pizza, Pizza Hut or Pizza Inn, cheese, thin crust	12-13 in	8.59	4Q 92	4c

Transportation

Item	Per	Value	Date	Ref.
ACCRA Index, Transportation		91.40	4Q 92	4c
Tire balance, computer or spin balance, front	wheel	5.00	4Q 92	4c

Utilities

Item	Per	Value	Date	Ref.
ACCRA Index, Utilities		78.90	4Q 92	4c
Electricity, partial electric and other energy, 1,800 sq ft living area new home	month	42.38	4Q 92	4c

Missoula, MT

Item	Per	Value	Date	Ref.
Composite ACCRA index		103.80	4Q 92	4c

Alcoholic Beverages

Item	Per	Value	Date	Ref.
Beer, Miller Lite or Budweiser, 12-oz containers	6 pack	4.01	4Q 92	4c
Liquor, J & B Scotch	750 ml	18.10	4Q 92	4c
Wine, Gallo Chablis blanc, 1.5 liter	bottle	5.99	4Q 92	4c

Clothing

Item	Per	Value	Date	Ref.
Jeans, man's denim		29.79	4Q 92	4c
Shirt, man's dress shirt		25.20	4Q 92	4c
Undervest, boy's size 10-14, cotton	3	5.19	4Q 92	4c

Communications

Item	Per	Value	Date	Ref.
Newspaper subscription, daily and Sunday home delivery, large-city	month	12.77	4Q 92	4c
Telephone, flat rate	month	13.84	91	11c
Telephone bill, family of four	month	19.24	4Q 92	4c

Energy and Fuels

Item	Per	Value	Date	Ref.
Energy, combined forms, 1,800 sq ft heating area	month	96.34	4Q 92	4c
Energy, exc electricity, 1,800 sq ft heating area	month	50.34	4Q 92	4c
Gas, cooking, 10 therms	month	8.21	92	56c
Gas, cooking, 30 therms	month	15.64	92	56c
Gas, cooking, 50 therms	month	23.06	92	56c
Gas, heating, winter, 100 therms	month	41.62	92	56c
Gas, heating, winter, average use	month	58.32	92	56c
Gasoline, motor	gal	1.28	4Q 92	4c

Entertainment

Item	Per	Value	Date	Ref.
Bowling, evening rate	game	1.58	4Q 92	4c
Monopoly game, Parker Brothers', No. 9		13.97	4Q 92	4c
Movie	admission	5.00	4Q 92	4c
Tennis balls, yellow, Wilson or Penn, 3	can	2.63	4Q 92	4c

Goods and Services

Item	Per	Value	Date	Ref.
ACCRA Index, Miscellaneous Goods and Services		106.90	4Q 92	4c

Groceries

Item	Per	Value	Date	Ref.
ACCRA Index, Groceries		111.70	4Q 92	4c
Babyfood, strained vegetables, lowest price	4-4.5 oz jar	0.30	4Q 92	4c
Bananas	lb	0.54	4Q 92	4c
Bread, white	24 oz	0.83	4Q 92	4c
Cheese, Kraft grated Parmesan	8-oz canister	3.81	4Q 92	4c
Chicken, fryer, whole	lb	0.93	4Q 92	4c
Cigarettes, Winston	carton	17.71	4Q 92	4c

Values are in dollars or fractions of dollars. In the column headed *Ref*, references are shown to sources. Each reference is followed by a letter. These refer to the geographical level for which data were reported: s = State, r = Region, and c = City or metro. The abbreviation *ex* is used to mean *except* or *excluding*; *exp* stands for expenditures. For other abbreviations and further explanations, please see the Introduction.

Missoula, MT - continued

Item	Per	Value	Date	Ref.
Groceries				
Coffee, vacuum-packed	13-oz can	2.19	4Q 92	4c
Corn, frozen	10 oz	0.62	4Q 92	4c
Corn Flakes, Kellogg's or Post Toasties	18 oz	1.95	4Q 92	4c
Eggs, Grade A large	doz	0.95	4Q 92	4c
Ground beef or hamburger	lb	1.69	4Q 92	4c
Lettuce, iceberg	head	1.11	4Q 92	4c
Margarine, Blue Bonnet or Parkay cubes	lb	0.83	4Q 92	4c
Milk, whole	1/2 gal	1.47	4Q 92	4c
Orange juice, Minute Maid frozen	12-oz can	1.59	4Q 92	4c
Peaches	29-oz can	1.44	4Q 92	4c
Peas Sweet, Del Monte or Green Giant	15-17 oz can	0.67	4Q 92	4c
Potatoes, white or red	10-lb sack	1.85	4Q 92	4c
Sausage, Jimmy Dean, 100% pork	lb	3.36	4Q 92	4c
Shortening, vegetable, Crisco	3-lb can	2.13	4Q 92	4c
Soft drink, Coca Cola	2 liter	1.72	4Q 92	4c
Steak, T-bone	lb	4.93	4Q 92	4c
Sugar, cane or beet	4 lb	1.49	4Q 92	4c
Tomatoes, Hunt's or Del Monte	14.5-oz can	0.68	4Q 92	4c
Tuna, chunk, light	6.125-6.5 oz can	0.93	4Q 92	4c
Health Care				
ACCRA Index, Health Care		111.80	4Q 92	4c
Analgesic, Aspirin, Bayer, 325 mg tablets	100	5.87	4Q 92	4c
Dentist's fee, adult teeth cleaning and periodic oral exam	visit	61.20	4Q 92	4c
Doctor's fee, routine exam, established patient	visit	35.00	4Q 92	4c
Hospital care, semiprivate room	day	270.09	90	27c
Hospital care, semiprivate room	day	331.00	4Q 92	4c
Household Goods				
Appliance repair, home, service call, washing machine	min labor charge	35.74	4Q 92	4c
Laundry detergent, Tide Ultra, Bold, or Cheer	42 oz	3.20	4Q 92	4c
Tissues, facial, Kleenex brand	175-count box	1.26	4Q 92	4c
Housing				
ACCRA Index, Housing		98.50	4Q 92	4c
House, 1,800 sq ft, 8,000 sq ft lot, new, urban	total	102230	4Q 92	4c
House payment, principal and interest, 25% down payment	month	580	4Q 92	4c
Mortgage rate, incl. points & origination fee, 30-year fixed or adjustable rate	percent	8.33	4Q 92	4c
Rent, apartment, 2 bedrooms - 1-1/2 to 2 baths, unfurnished, 950 sq ft, water	month	545	4Q 92	4c
Personal Goods				
Shampoo, Alberto VO5	15 oz	1.54	4Q 92	4c
Toothpaste, Crest or Colgate	6-7 oz	2.42	4Q 92	4c
Personal Services				
Dry cleaning, man's 2-piece suit		7.15	4Q 92	4c
Haircare, woman's shampoo, trim and blow-dry		19.30	4Q 92	4c
Haircut, man's barbershop, no styling		8.20	4Q 92	4c
Restaurant Food				
Chicken, fried, thigh and drumstick		2.10	4Q 92	4c
Hamburger with cheese	1/4 lb	1.87	4Q 92	4c
Pizza, Pizza Hut or Pizza Inn, cheese, thin crust	12-13 in	8.80	4Q 92	4c

Missoula, MT - continued

Item	Per	Value	Date	Ref.
Transportation				
ACCRA Index, Transportation		106.70	4Q 92	4c
Bus fare, up to 10 miles	one-way	0.65	4Q 92	4c
Tire balance, computer or spin balance, front	wheel	6.99	4Q 92	4c
Utilities				
ACCRA Index, Utilities		89.30	4Q 92	4c
Electricity, partial electric and other energy, 1,800 sq ft living area new home	month	46.00	4Q 92	4c

Mobile, AL

Item	Per	Value	Date	Ref.
Composite ACCRA index		95.20	4Q 92	4c
Alcoholic Beverages				
Beer, Miller Lite or Budweiser, 12-oz containers	6 pack	3.93	4Q 92	4c
Liquor, J & B Scotch	750 ml	19.99	4Q 92	4c
Wine, Gallo Chablis blanc, 1.5 liter	bottle	6.21	4Q 92	4c
Child Care				
Child care fee, average, center	hour	1.29	90	65r
Child care fee, average, nonregulated family day care	hour	0.89	90	65r
Child care fee, average, regulated family day care	hour	1.32	90	65r
Clothing				
Jeans, man's denim		23.82	4Q 92	4c
Shirt, man's dress shirt		24.40	4Q 92	4c
Undervest, boy's size 10-14, cotton	3	3.92	4Q 92	4c
Communications				
Long-distance telephone service, day, initial minute, 0-100 miles	min	0.11-0.36	91	12s
Long-distance telephone service, day, additional minute, 0-100 miles	min	0.09-0.26	91	12s
Long-distance telephone service, evenings/weekends, 0-100 mi, initial minute	min	0.04-0.14	91	12s
Long-distance telephone service, evenings/weekends, 0-100 mi, additional minute	min	0.04-0.10	91	12s
Newspaper subscription, daily and Sunday home delivery, large-city	month	9.00	4Q 92	4c
Telephone, flat rate	month	17.61	91	11c
Telephone bill, family of four	month	23.89	4Q 92	4c
Education				
Board, 4-yr private college/university	year	1795	91	22s
Board, 4-yr public college/university	year	1469	91	22s
Expenditures, local gov't, public elementary/secondary	pupil	3675	92	20s
Room, 4-year private college/university	year	1340	91	22s
Room, 4-year public college/university	year	1295	91	22s
Tuition, 2-year private college/university	year	4148	91	22s
Tuition, 2-year public college/university	year	689	91	22s
Tuition, 4-year private college/university	year	5942	91	22s
Tuition, 4-year public college/university, in-state	year	1593	91	22s
Energy and Fuels				
Coal	mil Btu	1.83	90	64s
Energy	mil Btu	7.92	90	64s
Energy, combined forms, 1,800 sq ft heating area	month	126.99	4Q 92	4c
Energy, exc electricity, 1,800 sq ft heating area	month	33.47	4Q 92	4c
Energy exp/householder, 1-family unit	year	403	90	28r
Energy exp/householder, <1,000 sq ft heating area	year	342	90	28r
Energy exp/householder, 1,000-1,999 sq ft heating area	year	388	90	28r
Energy exp/householder, 2,000+ sq ft heating area	year	434	90	28r
Energy exp/householder, mobile home	year	320	90	28r

Values are in dollars or fractions of dollars. In the column headed *Ref*, references are shown to sources. Each reference is followed by a letter. These refer to the geographical level for which data were reported: s=State, r=Region, and c=City or metro. The abbreviation *ex* is used to mean *except* or *excluding*; *exp* stands for expenditures. For other abbreviations and further explanations, please see the Introduction.

Mobile, AL - continued

Item	Per	Value	Date	Ref.
Energy and Fuels				
Energy exp/householder, multifamily	year	338	90	28r
Gas, cooking, 10 therms	month	13.37	92	56c
Gas, cooking, 30 therms	month	25.71	92	56c
Gas, cooking, 50 therms	month	36.31	92	56c
Gas, heating, winter, 100 therms	month	62.81	92	56c
Gas, heating, winter, average use	month	66.83	92	56c
Gas, natural	mil Btu	4.07	90	64s
Gas, natural	000 cu ft	7.05	91	46s
Gas, natural, exp	year	461	91	46s
Gasoline, motor	gal	1.11	4Q 92	4c
Gasoline, unleaded regular	mil Btu	8.96	90	64s
Entertainment				
Bowling, evening rate	game	2.43	4Q 92	4c
Miniature golf admission	adult	6.18	92	1r
Miniature golf admission	child	5.14	92	1r
Monopoly game, Parker Brothers', No. 9		11.15	4Q 92	4c
Movie	admission	5.00	4Q 92	4c
Tennis balls, yellow, Wilson or Penn, 3	can	2.24	4Q 92	4c
Waterpark admission	adult	11.00	92	1r
Waterpark admission	child	8.55	92	1r
Funerals				
Casket, 18-gauge steel, velvet interior		2329.05	91	24r
Cosmetology, hair care, etc.		72.78	91	24r
Embalming		240.71	91	24r
Facility use for ceremony		181.67	91	24r
Hearse, local		106.25	91	24r
Limousine, local		70.92	91	24r
Remains to funeral home, transfer		96.30	91	24r
Service charge, professional		687.09	91	24r
Vault, concrete, non-metallic liner		732.09	91	24r
Viewing facilities, use		190.30	91	24r
Goods and Services				
ACCRA Index, Miscellaneous Goods and Services		97.00	4Q 92	4c
Groceries				
ACCRA Index, Groceries		99.40	4Q 92	4c
Apples, Red Delicious	lb	0.79	4/93	16r
Babyfood, strained vegetables, lowest price	4-4.5 oz jar	0.28	4Q 92	4c
Bacon	lb	1.75	4/93	16r
Bananas	lb	0.41	4Q 92	4c
Bananas	lb	0.42	4/93	16r
Beef, stew, boneless	lb	2.61	4/93	16r
Bologna, all beef or mixed	lb	2.24	4/93	16r
Bread, white	24 oz	0.84	4Q 92	4c
Bread, white, pan	lb	0.64	4/93	16r
Bread, whole wheat, pan	lb	0.96	4/93	16r
Cabbage	lb	0.37	4/93	16r
Carrots, short trimmed and topped	lb	0.47	4/93	16r
Celery	lb	0.64	4/93	16r
Cheese, American	lb	2.98	4/93	16r
Cheese, Cheddar	lb	3.28	4/93	16r
Cheese, Kraft grated Parmesan	8-oz canister	3.25	4Q 92	4c
Chicken, fresh, whole	lb	0.77	4/93	16r
Chicken, fryer, whole	lb	0.70	4Q 92	4c
Chicken breast, bone-in	lb	1.92	4/93	16r
Chicken legs, bone-in	lb	1.06	4/93	16r
Chuck roast, graded and ungraded, ex USDA prime and choice	lb	2.40	4/93	16r
Chuck roast, USDA choice, bone-in	lb	2.19	4/93	16r
Chuck roast, USDA choice, boneless	lb	2.38	4/93	16r
Cigarettes, Winston	carton	17.48	4Q 92	4c
Coffee, 100% ground roast, all sizes	lb	2.48	4/93	16r
Coffee, vacuum-packed	13-oz can	1.79	4Q 92	4c
Corn, frozen	10 oz	0.58	4Q 92	4c

Mobile, AL - continued

Item	Per	Value	Date	Ref.
Groceries - continued				
Corn Flakes, Kellogg's or Post Toasties	18 oz	1.49	4Q 92	4c
Crackers, soda, salted	lb	1.15	4/93	16r
Eggs, Grade A large	doz	0.78	4Q 92	4c
Eggs, Grade A large	doz	0.96	4/93	16r
Flour, white, all purpose	lb	0.24	4/93	16r
Frankfurters, all meat or all beef	lb	2.01	4/93	16r
Grapefruit	lb	0.44	4/93	16r
Grapes, Thompson Seedless	lb	1.40	4/93	16r
Ground beef, 100% beef	lb	1.58	4/93	16r
Ground beef, lean and extra lean	lb	2.09	4/93	16r
Ground beef or hamburger	lb	1.73	4Q 92	4c
Ground chuck, 100% beef	lb	1.98	4/93	16r
Ham, boneless, excluding canned	lb	2.89	4/93	16r
Ham, picnic, shoulder, bone-in, smoked	lb	1.02	4/93	16r
Ham, rump or steak half, bone-in, smoked	lb	1.48	4/93	16r
Honey, jar	8 oz	0.89-1.09	92	5r
Honey, jar	lb	1.39-2.25	92	5r
Honey, squeeze bear	12-oz	1.00-1.50	92	5r
Ice cream, prepackaged, bulk, regular	1/2 gal	2.41	4/93	16r
Lemons	lb	1.05	4/93	16r
Lettuce, iceberg	head	1.07	4Q 92	4c
Lettuce, iceberg	lb	0.81	4/93	16r
Margarine, Blue Bonnet or Parkay cubes	lb	0.52	4Q 92	4c
Margarine, stick	lb	0.88	4/93	16r
Milk, whole	1/2 gal	1.45	4Q 92	4c
Orange juice, Minute Maid frozen	12-oz can	1.31	4Q 92	4c
Oranges, navel	lb	0.55	4/93	16r
Peaches	29-oz can	1.35	4Q 92	4c
Pears, Anjou	lb	0.92	4/93	16r
Peas Sweet, Del Monte or Green Giant	15-17 oz can	0.59	4Q 92	4c
Pork chops, center cut, bone-in	lb	3.13	4/93	16r
Potato chips	16 oz	2.94	4/93	16r
Potatoes, white	lb	0.43	4/93	16r
Potatoes, white or red	10-lb sack	3.25	4Q 92	4c
Rib roast, USDA choice, bone-in	lb	4.63	4/93	16r
Rice, white, long grain, uncooked	lb	0.45	4/93	16r
Round roast, graded & ungraded, ex USDA prime & choice	lb	3.03	4/93	16r
Round roast, USDA choice, boneless	lb	3.09	4/93	16r
Sausage, fresh, loose	lb	2.08	4/93	16r
Sausage, Jimmy Dean, 100% pork	lb	2.27	4Q 92	4c
Short ribs, bone-in	lb	2.66	4/93	16r
Shortening, vegetable oil blends	lb	0.69	4/93	16r
Shortening, vegetable, Crisco	3-lb can	2.19	4Q 92	4c
Soft drink, Coca Cola	2 liter	0.99	4Q 92	4c
Spaghetti and macaroni	lb	0.81	4/93	16r
Steak, rib eye, USDA choice, boneless	lb	6.24	4/93	16r
Steak, round, graded & ungraded, ex USDA prime & choice	lb	3.31	4/93	16r
Steak, round, USDA choice, boneless	lb	3.34	4/93	16r
Steak, sirloin, graded & ungraded, ex USDA prime & choice	lb	4.19	4/93	16r
Steak, sirloin, USDA choice, boneless	lb	4.46	4/93	16r
Steak, T-bone	lb	5.91	4Q 92	4c
Steak, T-bone, USDA choice, bone-in	lb	5.25	4/93	16r
Strawberries, dry pint	12 oz	0.92	4/93	16r
Sugar, cane or beet	4 lb	1.43	4Q 92	4c
Sugar, white	lb	0.39	4/93	16r
Sugar, white, 33-80 oz pk	lb	0.38	4/93	16r
Tomatoes, field grown	lb	0.88	4/93	16r
Tomatoes, Hunt's or Del Monte	14.5-oz can	0.72	4Q 92	4c
Tuna, chunk, light	6.125-6.5 oz can	0.55	4Q 92	4c
Tuna, chunk, light	lb	1.79	4/93	16r
Turkey, frozen, whole	lb	1.04	4/93	16r

Values are in dollars or fractions of dollars. In the column headed *Ref*, references are shown to sources. Each reference is followed by a letter. These refer to the geographical level for which data were reported: s=State, r=Region, and c=City or metro. The abbreviation *ex* is used to mean *except* or *excluding; exp* stands for expenditures. For other abbreviations and further explanations, please see the Introduction.

Mobile, AL - continued

Item	Per	Value	Date	Ref.
Groceries				
Yogurt, natural, fruit flavored	1/2 pint	0.57	4/93	16r
Health Care				
ACCRA Index, Health Care		92.10	4Q 92	4c
Analgesic, Aspirin, Bayer, 325 mg tablets	100	4.62	4Q 92	4c
Childbirth, cesarean, hospital		5034	91	62r
Childbirth, cesarean, physician's fee		2053	91	62r
Childbirth, normal, hospital		2712	91	62r
Childbirth, normal, physician's fee		1492	91	62r
Dentist's fee, adult teeth cleaning and periodic oral exam	visit	39.00	4Q 92	4c
Doctor's fee, routine exam, established patient	visit	44.00	4Q 92	4c
Hospital care, semiprivate room	day	181.00	4Q 92	4c
Medical insurance premium, per employee, small group comprehensive	month	349.45	10/91	25c
Mental health care, exp	capita	37.60-53.67	90	38s
Mental health care, exp, state mental health agency	capita	38.35	90	38s
Mental health care, hospital psychiatric services, non-Federal, exp	capita	13.58	88	38s
Mental health care, mental health organization, multiservice, exp	capita	12.40	88	38s
Mental health care, psychiatric hospitals, private, exp	capita	9.49	88	38s
Mental health care, state and county mental hospitals, exp	capita	22.15	88	38s
Mental health care, VA medical centers, exp	capita	10.94	88	38s
Physician fee, family practice, first-visit		75.00	91	62r
Physician fee, family practice, revisit		34.00	91	62r
Physician fee, general practice, first-visit		61.00	91	62r
Physician fee, general practice, revisit		32.00	91	62r
Physician fee, general surgeon, first-visit		64.00	91	62r
Physician fee, general surgeon, revisit		40.00	91	62r
Physician fee, internal medicine, first-visit		98.00	91	62r
Physician fee, internal medicine, revisit		40.00	91	62r
Physician fee, median, neurosurgeon, first-visit		130.00	91	62r
Physician fee, median, nonsurgical specialist, first-visit		95.00	91	62r
Physician fee, median, orthopedic surgeon, first-visit		91.00	91	62r
Physician fee, median, plastic surgeon, first-visit		66.00	91	62r
Physician fee, median, surgical specialist, first-visit		62.00	91	62r
Physician fee, neurosurgeon, revisit		50.00	91	62r
Physician fee, nonsurgical specialist, revisit		40.00	91	62r
Physician fee, obstetrics/gynecology, first-visit		64.00	91	62r
Physician fee, obstetrics/gynecology, revisit		41.00	91	62r
Physician fee, orthopedic surgeon, revisit		40.00	91	62r
Physician fee, pediatrician, first-visit		49.00	91	62r
Physician fee, pediatrician, revisit		33.00	91	62r
Physician fee, plastic surgeon, revisit		43.00	91	62r
Physician fee, surgical specialist, revisit		37.00	91	62r
Substance abuse, hospital ancillary charge	incident	1390	90	70s
Substance abuse, hospital physician charge	incident	520	90	70s
Substance abuse, hospital room and board	incident	5830	90	70s
Household Goods				
Appliance repair, home, service call, washing machine	min labor charge	34.48	4Q 92	4c
Laundry detergent, Tide Ultra, Bold, or Cheer	42 oz	3.15	4Q 92	4c

Mobile, AL - continued

Item	Per	Value	Date	Ref.
Household Goods - continued				
Tissues, facial, Kleenex brand	175-count box	1.07	4Q 92	4c
Housing				
ACCRA Index, Housing		79.70	4Q 92	4c
Home, median price	unit	64.80		26c
House, 1,800 sq ft, 8,000 sq ft lot, new, urban	total	91980	4Q 92	4c
House payment, principal and interest, 25% down payment	month	509	4Q 92	4c
Mortgage rate, incl. points & origination fee, 30-year fixed or adjustable rate	percent	8.06	4Q 92	4c
Rent, apartment, 2 bedrooms - 1-1/2 to 2 baths, unfurnished, 950 sq ft, water	month	349	4Q 92	4c
Rental unit, 1 bedroom	month	380	93	23c
Rental unit, 2 bedroom	month	447	93	23c
Rental unit, 3 bedroom	month	560	93	23c
Rental unit, 4 bedroom	month	629	93	23c
Rental unit, efficiency	month	313	93	23c
Insurance and Pensions				
Auto insurance, private passenger	year	562.59	91	63s
Personal Goods				
Shampoo, Alberto VO5	15 oz	1.29	4Q 92	4c
Toothpaste, Crest or Colgate	6-7 oz	2.09	4Q 92	4c
Personal Services				
Dry cleaning, man's 2-piece suit		5.09	4Q 92	4c
Haircare, woman's shampoo, trim and blow-dry		18.90	4Q 92	4c
Haircut, man's barbershop, no styling		7.80	4Q 92	4c
Restaurant Food				
Chicken, fried, thigh and drumstick		1.93	4Q 92	4c
Hamburger with cheese	1/4 lb	1.83	4Q 92	4c
Pizza, Pizza Hut or Pizza Inn, cheese, thin crust	12-13 in	7.49	4Q 92	4c
Taxes				
Tax, cigarette	pack	16.50	91	77s
Tax, gasoline	gal	16	91	77s
Taxes, state	capita	964	91	77s
Transportation				
ACCRA Index, Transportation		109.00	4Q 92	4c
Bus fare	one-way	0.75	3/93	2c
Bus fare, up to 10 miles	one-way	0.75	4Q 92	4c
Driver's license fee		15.00	12/90	43s
Tire balance, computer or spin balance, front	wheel	8.10	4Q 92	4c
Travel				
Business travel	day	193.00	4/93	89r
Utilities				
ACCRA Index, Utilities		117.00	4Q 92	4c
Electricity	mil Btu	16.46	90	64s
Electricity, partial electric and other energy, 1,800 sq ft living area new home	month	93.52	4Q 92	4c

Modesto, CA

Item	Per	Value	Date	Ref.
Child Care				
Child care fee, average, center	hour	1.71	90	65r
Child care fee, average, nonregulated family day care	hour	1.32	90	65r
Child care fee, average, regulated family day care	hour	1.86	90	65r
Communications				
Long-distance telephone service, day, initial minute, 0-100 miles	min	0.17-0.40	91	12s

Values are in dollars or fractions of dollars. In the column headed *Ref*, references are shown to sources. Each reference is followed by a letter. These refer to the geographical level for which data were reported: s = State, r = Region, and c = City or metro. The abbreviation *ex* is used to mean *except* or *excluding*; *exp* stands for expenditures. For other abbreviations and further explanations, please see the Introduction.

Modesto, CA - continued

Item	Per	Value	Date	Ref.
Communications				
Long-distance telephone service, day, additional minute, 0-100 miles	min	0.07-0.31	91	12s
Long-distance telephone service, evenings/weekends, 0-100 mi, initial minute	min	0.07-0.16	91	12s
Long-distance telephone service, evenings/weekends, 0-100 mi, additional minute	min	0.03-0.12	91	12s
Education				
Board, 4-yr private college/university	year	2515	91	22s
Board, 4-yr public college/university	year	2268	91	22s
Expenditures, local gov't, public elementary/secondary	pupil	4866	92	20s
Room, 4-year private college/university	year	2622	91	22s
Room, 4-year public college/university	year	2406	91	22s
Tuition, 2-year private college/university	year	7942	91	22s
Tuition, 2-year public college/university	year	114	91	22s
Tuition, 4-year private college/university	year	10863	91	22s
Tuition, 4-year public college/university, in-state	year	1220	91	22s
Energy and Fuels				
Coal	mil Btu	2.01	90	64s
Energy	mil Btu	9.08	90	64s
Energy exp/householder, 1-family unit	year	362	90	28r
Energy exp/householder, <1,000 sq ft heating area	year	254	90	28r
Energy exp/householder, 1,000-1,999 sq ft heating area	year	358	90	28r
Energy exp/householder, 2,000+ sq ft heating area	year	467	90	28r
Energy exp/householder, mobile home	year	390	90	28r
Energy exp/householder, multifamily	year	252	90	28r
Gas, natural	mil Btu	4.31	90	64s
Gas, natural	000 cu ft	6.27	91	46s
Gas, natural, exp	year	369	91	46s
Gasoline, unleaded regular	mil Btu	8.57	90	64s
Entertainment				
Miniature golf admission	adult	6.18	92	1r
Miniature golf admission	child	5.14	92	1r
Waterpark admission	adult	11.00	92	1r
Waterpark admission	child	8.55	92	1r
Funerals				
Casket, 18-gauge steel, velvet interior		1781.09	91	24r
Cosmetology, hair care, etc.		84.64	91	24r
Embalming		207.41	91	24r
Facility use for ceremony		205.76	91	24r
Hearse, local		105.14	91	24r
Limousine, local		83.21	91	24r
Remains to funeral home, transfer		113.82	91	24r
Service charge, professional		626.33	91	24r
Vault, concrete, non-metallic liner		599.54	91	24r
Viewing facilities, use		85.81	91	24r
Groceries				
Apples, Red Delicious	lb	0.80	4/93	16r
Bacon	lb	1.79	4/93	16r
Bananas	lb	0.53	4/93	16r
Bologna, all beef or mixed	lb	2.67	4/93	16r
Bread, white, pan	lb	0.81	4/93	16r
Carrots, short trimmed and topped	lb	0.39	4/93	16r
Chicken, fresh, whole	lb	0.94	4/93	16r
Chicken breast, bone-in	lb	2.19	4/93	16r
Chuck roast, graded and ungraded, ex USDA prime and choice	lb	2.26	4/93	16r
Coffee, 100% ground roast, all sizes	lb	2.33	4/93	16r
Eggs, Grade AA large	doz	1.18	4/93	16r
Flour, white, all purpose	lb	0.22	4/93	16r
Grapefruit	lb	0.52	4/93	16r
Grapes, Thompson Seedless	lb	1.50	4/93	16r
Ground beef, 100% beef	lb	1.44	4/93	16r
Ground beef, lean and extra lean	lb	2.34	4/93	16r

Modesto, CA - continued

Item	Per	Value	Date	Ref.
Groceries - continued				
Ham, boneless, excluding canned	lb	2.56	4/93	16r
Honey, jar	8 oz	0.89-1.00	92	5r
Honey, jar	lb	1.35-1.97	92	5r
Honey, squeeze bear	12-oz	1.19-1.50	92	5r
Ice cream, prepackaged, bulk, regular	1/2 gal	2.40	4/93	16r
Lemons	lb	0.81	4/93	16r
Lettuce, iceberg	lb	0.84	4/93	16r
Margarine, stick	lb	0.81	4/93	16r
Oranges, navel	lb	0.48	4/93	16r
Pork chops, center cut, bone-in	lb	3.25	4/93	16r
Potato chips	16 oz	2.89	4/93	16r
Potatoes, white	lb	0.38	4/93	16r
Round roast, graded & ungraded, ex USDA prime & choice	lb	3.00	4/93	16r
Round roast, USDA choice, boneless	lb	3.16	4/93	16r
Shortening, vegetable oil blends	lb	0.86	4/93	16r
Spaghetti and macaroni	lb	0.84	4/93	16r
Steak, round, graded & ungraded, ex USDA prime & choice	lb	3.34	4/93	16r
Steak, round, USDA choice, boneless	lb	3.24	4/93	16r
Steak, sirloin, graded & ungraded, ex USDA prime & choice	lb	3.75	4/93	16r
Steak, sirloin, USDA choice, boneless	lb	4.49	4/93	16r
Sugar, white	lb	0.41	4/93	16r
Sugar, white, 33-80 oz pk	lb	0.38	4/93	16r
Tomatoes, field grown	lb	1.01	4/93	16r
Turkey, frozen, whole	lb	1.04	4/93	16r
Health Care				
Cardizem 60 mg tablets	30	24.04	92	49s
Cector 250 mg tablets	15	35.87	92	49s
Childbirth, cesarean, hospital		5533	91	62r
Childbirth, cesarean, physician's fee		2053	91	62r
Childbirth, normal, hospital		2745	91	62r
Childbirth, normal, physician's fee		1492	91	62r
Health care spending, state	capita	2894	3/93	84s
Medical plan per employee	year	3421	91	45r
Mental health care, exp	capita	37.60-53.67	90	38s
Mental health care, exp, state mental health agency	capita	42.32	90	38s
Mental health care, hospital psychiatric services, non-Federal, exp	capita	10.64	88	38s
Mental health care, mental health organization, multiservice, exp	capita	28.56	88	38s
Mental health care, psychiatric hospitals, private, exp	capita	18.60	88	38s
Mental health care, psychiatric out-patient clinics, freestanding, exp	capita	2.28	88	38s
Mental health care, psychiatric partial-care organizations, freestanding, exp	capita	0.24	88	38s
Mental health care, state and county mental hospitals, exp	capita	13.60	88	38s
Mental health care, VA medical centers, exp	capita	2.33	88	38s
Mevacor 20 mg tablets	30	67.62	92	49s
Physician fee, family practice, first-visit		111.00	91	62r
Physician fee, family practice, revisit		45.00	91	62r
Physician fee, general practice, first-visit		100.00	91	62r
Physician fee, general practice, revisit		40.00	91	62r
Physician fee, internal medicine, first-visit		137.00	91	62r
Physician fee, internal medicine, revisit		48.00	91	62r
Physician fee, median, neurosurgeon, first-visit		157.00	91	62r
Physician fee, median, nonsurgical specialist, first-visit		131.00	91	62r
Physician fee, median, orthopedic surgeon, first-visit		124.00	91	62r
Physician fee, median, plastic surgeon, first-visit		88.00	91	62r
Physician fee, median, surgical specialist, first-visit		100.00	91	62r
Physician fee, neurosurgeon, revisit		51.00	91	62r
Physician fee, nonsurgical specialist, revisit		47.00	91	62r

Values are in dollars or fractions of dollars. In the column headed *Ref*, references are shown to sources. Each reference is followed by a letter. These refer to the geographical level for which data were reported: s=State, r=Region, and c=City or metro. The abbreviation *ex* is used to mean *except* or *excluding*; *exp* stands for expenditures. For other abbreviations and further explanations, please see the Introduction.

Modesto, CA - continued

Item	Per	Value	Date	Ref.
Health Care				
Physician fee, obstetrics/gynecology, first-visit		95.00	91	62r
Physician fee, obstetrics/gynecology, revisit		50.00	91	62r
Physician fee, orthopedic surgeon, revisit		51.00	91	62r
Physician fee, pediatrician, first-visit		81.00	91	62r
Physician fee, pediatrician, revisit		42.00	91	62r
Physician fee, plastic surgeon, revisit		48.00	91	62r
Physician fee, surgical specialist, revisit		49.00	91	62r
Prozac 20 mg tablets	14	33.22	92	49s
Substance abuse, hospital ancillary charge	incident	1760	90	70s
Substance abuse, hospital physician charge	incident	750	90	70s
Substance abuse, hospital room and board	incident	6390	90	70s
Tagamet 300 mg tablets	100	77.08	92	49s
Xanax 0.25 mg tablets	90	64.08	92	49s
Zantac 160 mg tablets	60	92.31	92	49s
Housing				
Home, median price	unit	131,200	92	58s
Insurance and Pensions				
Auto insurance, private passenger	year	904.37	91	63s
Taxes				
Tax, cigarette	pack	35	91	77s
Tax, gasoline	gal	16	91	77s
Taxes, state	capita	1477	91	77s
Transportation				
Driver's license fee		10.00	12/90	43s
Travel				
Business travel	day	178.00	4/93	89r
Utilities				
Electricity	mil Btu	25.98	90	64s

Monmouth-Ocean, NJ

Item	Per	Value	Date	Ref.
Child Care				
Child care fee, average, center	hour	2.18	90	65r
Child care fee, average, nonregulated family day care	hour	1.83	90	65r
Child care fee, average, regulated family day care	hour	2.02	90	65r
Communications				
Long-distance telephone service, day, initial minute, 0-100 miles	min	0.09-0.42	91	12s
Long-distance telephone service, day, additional minute, 0-100 miles	min	0.03-0.12	91	12s
Education				
Board, 4-yr private college/university	year	2883	91	22s
Board, 4-yr public college/university	year	1647	91	22s
Expenditures, local gov't, public elementary/secondary	pupil	9940	92	20s
Room, 4-year private college/university	year	2440	91	22s
Room, 4-year public college/university	year	2415	91	22s
Tuition, 2-year private college/university	year	5874	91	22s
Tuition, 2-year public college/university	year	1235	91	22s
Tuition, 4-year private college/university	year	10281	91	22s
Tuition, 4-year public college/university, in-state	year	2860	91	22s
Energy and Fuels				
Coal	mil Btu	1.79	90	64s
Energy	mil Btu	9.32	90	64s
Energy exp/householder, 1-family unit	year	588	90	28r
Energy exp/householder, <1,000 sq ft heating area	year	477	90	28r
Energy exp/householder, 1,000-1,999 sq ft heating area	year	517	90	28r

Monmouth-Ocean, NJ - continued

Item	Per	Value	Date	Ref.
Energy and Fuels - continued				
Energy exp/householder, 2,000+ sq ft heating area	year	630	90	28r
Energy exp/householder, mobile home	year	412	90	28r
Energy exp/householder, multifamily	year	498	90	28r
Gas, natural	mil Btu	5.05	90	64s
Gas, natural	000 cu ft	6.73	91	46s
Gas, natural, exp	year	593	91	46s
Gasoline, unleaded regular	mil Btu	9.03	90	64s
Funerals				
Casket, 18-gauge steel, velvet interior		1811.58	91	24r
Cosmetology, hair care, etc.		111.08	91	24r
Embalming		329.42	91	24r
Facility use for ceremony		201.29	91	24r
Hearse, local		135.27	91	24r
Limousine, local		127.24	91	24r
Remains to funeral home, transfer		103.98	91	24r
Service charge, professional		724.98	91	24r
Vault, concrete, non-metallic liner		766.71	91	24r
Viewing facilities, use		260.60	91	24r
Groceries				
Apples, Red Delicious	lb	0.85	4/93	16r
Bacon	lb	2.12	4/93	16r
Bananas	lb	0.54	4/93	16r
Bread, white, pan	lb	0.81	4/93	16r
Butter	lb	2.02	4/93	16r
Carrots, short trimmed and topped	lb	0.51	4/93	16r
Chicken, fresh, whole	lb	1.04	4/93	16r
Chicken breast, bone-in	lb	2.21	4/93	16r
Chicken legs, bone-in	lb	1.16	4/93	16r
Chuck roast, USDA choice, boneless	lb	2.82	4/93	16r
Coffee, 100% ground roast, all sizes	lb	2.66	4/93	16r
Cucumbers	lb	0.85	4/93	16r
Eggs, Grade A large	doz	1.15	4/93	16r
Grapefruit	lb	0.45	4/93	16r
Grapes, Thompson Seedless	lb	1.52	4/93	16r
Ground beef, lean and extra lean	lb	2.36	4/93	16r
Ground chuck, 100% beef	lb	2.02	4/93	16r
Honey, jar	8 oz	0.96-1.75	92	5r
Honey, jar	lb	1.50-3.00	92	5r
Honey, squeeze bear	12-oz	1.50-1.99	92	5r
Ice cream, prepackaged, bulk, regular	1/2 gal	2.80	4/93	16r
Lemons	lb	0.96	4/93	16r
Lettuce, iceberg	lb	0.95	4/93	16r
Margarine, stick	lb	0.81	4/93	16r
Milk, fresh, whole, fortified	1/2 gal	1.30	4/93	16r
Oranges, navel	lb	0.56	4/93	16r
Peanut butter, creamy, all sizes	lb	1.88	4/93	16r
Pork chops, center cut, bone-in	lb	3.34	4/93	16r
Potato chips	16 oz	2.88	4/93	16r
Potatoes, white	lb	0.37	4/93	16r
Rib roast, USDA choice, bone-in	lb	4.94	4/93	16r
Round roast, USDA choice, boneless	lb	3.17	4/93	16r
Shortening, vegetable oil blends	lb	0.98	4/93	16r
Spaghetti and macaroni	lb	0.82	4/93	16r
Steak, round, graded & ungraded, ex USDA prime & choice	lb	4.04	4/93	16r
Steak, round, USDA choice, boneless	lb	3.90	4/93	16r
Steak, sirloin, USDA choice, boneless	lb	4.97	4/93	16r
Strawberries, dry pint	12 oz	0.90	4/93	16r
Sugar, white	lb	0.50	4/93	16r
Sugar, white, 33-80 oz pk	lb	0.41	4/93	16r
Tomatoes, field grown	lb	1.23	4/93	16r
Tuna, chunk, light	lb	2.22	4/93	16r
Turkey, frozen, whole	lb	1.04	4/93	16r
Health Care				
Childbirth, cesarean, hospital		5826	91	62r
Childbirth, cesarean, physician's fee		2053	91	62r
Childbirth, normal, hospital		2964	91	62r
Childbirth, normal, physician's fee		1492	91	62r
Medical plan per employee	year	3942	91	45r

Values are in dollars or fractions of dollars. In the column headed *Ref*, references are shown to sources. Each reference is followed by a letter. These refer to the geographical level for which data were reported: s = State, r = Region, and c = City or metro. The abbreviation *ex* is used to mean *except* or *excluding*; *exp* stands for expenditures. For other abbreviations and further explanations, please see the Introduction.

Monmouth-Ocean, NJ - continued

Item	Per	Value	Date	Ref.
Health Care				
Mental health care, exp	capita	28.84-37.59	90	38s
Mental health care, exp, state mental health agency	capita	57.16	90	38s
Mental health care, hospital psychiatric services, non-Federal, exp	capita	16.04	88	38s
Mental health care, mental health organization, multiservice, exp	capita	11.14	88	38s
Mental health care, psychiatric hospitals, private, exp	capita	17.85	88	38s
Mental health care, psychiatric out-patient clinics, freestanding, exp	capita	1.56	88	38s
Mental health care, psychiatric partial-care organizations, freestanding, exp	capita	0.66	88	38s
Mental health care, state and county mental hospitals, exp	capita	36.80	88	38s
Mental health care, VA medical centers, exp	capita	5.61	88	38s
Prescription drug co-pay, Medicaid	month	5.00	91	21s
Substance abuse, hospital ancillary charge	incident	780	90	70s
Substance abuse, hospital physician charge	incident	550	90	70s
Substance abuse, hospital room and board	incident	6300	90	70s
Insurance and Pensions				
Auto insurance, private passenger	year	1081.45	91	63s
Taxes				
Tax, cigarette	pack	40	91	77s
Tax, gasoline	gal	10.50	91	77s
Taxes, state	capita	1501	91	77s
Transportation				
Driver's license fee		16.00-17.50	12/90	43s
Vehicle registration and license plate	year	32.90-93.90	93	44s
Travel				
Business travel	day	165.00	4/93	89r
Utilities				
Electricity	mil Btu	26.63	90	64s

Monroe, LA

Item	Per	Value	Date	Ref.
Composite ACCRA index		99.90	4Q 92	4c
Alcoholic Beverages				
Beer, Miller Lite or Budweiser, 12-oz containers	6 pack	3.98	4Q 92	4c
Liquor, J & B Scotch	750 ml	16.06	4Q 92	4c
Wine, Gallo Chablis blanc, 1.5 liter	bottle	4.62	4Q 92	4c
Child Care				
Child care fee, average, center	hour	1.29	90	65r
Child care fee, average, nonregulated family day care	hour	0.89	90	65r
Child care fee, average, regulated family day care	hour	1.32	90	65r
Clothing				
Jeans, man's denim		30.99	4Q 92	4c
Shirt, man's dress shirt		23.60	4Q 92	4c
Undervest, boy's size 10-14, cotton	3	6.18	4Q 92	4c
Communications				
Long-distance telephone service, day, initial minute, 0-100 miles	min	0.14-0.41	91	12s
Long-distance telephone service, day, additional minute, 0-100 miles	min	0.09-0.29	91	12s
Long-distance telephone service, evenings/weekends, 0-100 mi, initial minute	min	0.06-0.16	91	12s
Long-distance telephone service, evenings/weekends, 0-100 mi, additional minute	min	0.04-0.12	91	12s

Monroe, LA - continued

Item	Per	Value	Date	Ref.
Communications - continued				
Newspaper subscription, daily and Sunday home delivery, large-city	month	11.00	4Q 92	4c
Telephone, flat rate	month	12.64	91	11c
Telephone bill, family of four	month	19.33	4Q 92	4c
Education				
Board, 4-yr private college/university	year	2125	91	22s
Board, 4-yr public college/university	year	1453	91	22s
Expenditures, local gov't, public elementary/secondary	pupil	4299	92	20s
Room, 4-year private college/university	year	2216	91	22s
Room, 4-year public college/university	year	1323	91	22s
Tuition, 2-year private college/university	year	5671	91	22s
Tuition, 2-year public college/university	year	852	91	22s
Tuition, 4-year private college/university	year	9783	91	22s
Tuition, 4-year public college/university, in-state	year	1791	91	22s
Energy and Fuels				
Coal	mil Btu	1.68	90	64s
Energy	mil Btu	6.05	90	64s
Energy, combined forms, 1,800 sq ft heating area	month	150.11	4Q 92	4c
Energy exp/householder, 1-family unit	year	471	90	28r
Energy exp/householder, <1,000 sq ft heating area	year	384	90	28r
Energy exp/householder, 1,000-1,999 sq ft heating area	year	421	90	28r
Energy exp/householder, 2,000+ sq ft heating area	year	625	90	28r
Energy exp/householder, mobile home	year	271	90	28r
Energy exp/householder, multifamily	year	355	90	28r
Gas, natural	mil Btu	2.11	90	64s
Gas, natural	000 cu ft	5.77	91	46s
Gas, natural, exp	year	336	91	46s
Gasoline, motor	gal	1.16	4Q 92	4c
Gasoline, unleaded regular	mil Btu	9.47	90	64s
Entertainment				
Bowling, evening rate	game	2.25	4Q 92	4c
Miniature golf admission	adult	6.18	92	1r
Miniature golf admission	child	5.14	92	1r
Monopoly game, Parker Brothers', No. 9		11.48	4Q 92	4c
Movie	admission	5.00	4Q 92	4c
Tennis balls, yellow, Wilson or Penn, 3	can	2.65	4Q 92	4c
Waterpark admission	adult	11.00	92	1r
Waterpark admission	child	8.55	92	1r
Funerals				
Casket, 18-gauge steel, velvet interior		2274.41	91	24r
Cosmetology, hair care, etc.		74.62	91	24r
Embalming		229.94	91	24r
Facility use for ceremony		176.61	91	24r
Hearse, local		116.34	91	24r
Limousine, local		72.68	91	24r
Remains to funeral home, transfer		87.72	91	24r
Service charge, professional		712.53	91	24r
Vault, concrete, non-metallic liner		750.55	91	24r
Viewing facilities, use		155.31	91	24r
Goods and Services				
ACCRA Index, Miscellaneous Goods and Services		106.00	4Q 92	4c
Groceries				
ACCRA Index, Groceries		99.10	4Q 92	4c
Apples, Red Delicious	lb	0.79	4/93	16r
Babyfood, strained vegetables, lowest price	4-4.5 oz jar	0.27	4Q 92	4c
Bacon	lb	1.75	4/93	16r
Bananas	lb	0.42	4Q 92	4c
Bananas	lb	0.42	4/93	16r
Beef, stew, boneless	lb	2.61	4/93	16r

Values are in dollars or fractions of dollars. In the column headed *Ref*, references are shown to sources. Each reference is followed by a letter. These refer to the geographical level for which data were reported: s=State, r=Region, and c=City or metro. The abbreviation *ex* is used to mean *except* or *excluding*; *exp* stands for *expenditures*. For other abbreviations and further explanations, please see the Introduction.

Monroe, LA - continued

Item	Per	Value	Date	Ref.
Groceries				
Bologna, all beef or mixed	lb	2.24	4/93	16r
Bread, white	24 oz	0.82	4Q 92	4c
Bread, white, pan	lb	0.64	4/93	16r
Bread, whole wheat, pan	lb	0.96	4/93	16r
Cabbage	lb	0.37	4/93	16r
Carrots, short trimmed and topped	lb	0.47	4/93	16r
Celery	lb	0.64	4/93	16r
Cheese, American	lb	2.98	4/93	16r
Cheese, Cheddar	lb	3.28	4/93	16r
Cheese, Kraft grated Parmesan	8-oz canister	3.18	4Q 92	4c
Chicken, fresh, whole	lb	0.77	4/93	16r
Chicken, fryer, whole	lb	0.69	4Q 92	4c
Chicken breast, bone-in	lb	1.92	4/93	16r
Chicken legs, bone-in	lb	1.06	4/93	16r
Chuck roast, graded and ungraded, ex USDA prime and choice	lb	2.40	4/93	16r
Chuck roast, USDA choice, bone-in	lb	2.19	4/93	16r
Chuck roast, USDA choice, boneless	lb	2.38	4/93	16r
Cigarettes, Winston	carton	17.01	4Q 92	4c
Coffee, 100% ground roast, all sizes	lb	2.48	4/93	16r
Coffee, vacuum-packed	13-oz can	2.01	4Q 92	4c
Corn, frozen	10 oz	0.82	4Q 92	4c
Corn Flakes, Kellogg's or Post Toasties	18 oz	1.67	4Q 92	4c
Crackers, soda, salted	lb	1.15	4/93	16r
Eggs, Grade A large	doz	0.84	4Q 92	4c
Eggs, Grade A large	doz	0.96	4/93	16r
Flour, white, all purpose	lb	0.24	4/93	16r
Frankfurters, all meat or all beef	lb	2.01	4/93	16r
Grapefruit	lb	0.44	4/93	16r
Grapes, Thompson Seedless	lb	1.40	4/93	16r
Ground beef, 100% beef	lb	1.58	4/93	16r
Ground beef, lean and extra lean	lb	2.09	4/93	16r
Ground beef or hamburger	lb	1.54	4Q 92	4c
Ground chuck, 100% beef	lb	1.98	4/93	16r
Ham, boneless, excluding canned	lb	2.89	4/93	16r
Ham, picnic, shoulder, bone-in, smoked	lb	1.02	4/93	16r
Ham, rump or steak half, bone-in, smoked	lb	1.48	4/93	16r
Honey, jar	8 oz	0.73-1.19	92	5r
Honey, jar	lb	1.10-1.79	92	5r
Honey, squeeze bear	12-oz	1.19-1.50	92	5r
Ice cream, prepackaged, bulk, regular	1/2 gal	2.41	4/93	16r
Lemons	lb	1.05	4/93	16r
Lettuce, iceberg	head	1.01	4Q 92	4c
Lettuce, iceberg	lb	0.81	4/93	16r
Margarine, Blue Bonnet or Parkay cubes	lb	0.58	4Q 92	4c
Margarine, stick	lb	0.88	4/93	16r
Milk, whole	1/2 gal	1.32	4Q 92	4c
Orange juice, Minute Maid frozen	12-oz can	1.35	4Q 92	4c
Oranges, navel	lb	0.55	4/93	16r
Peaches	29-oz can	1.36	4Q 92	4c
Pears, Anjou	lb	0.92	4/93	16r
Peas Sweet, Del Monte or Green Giant	15-17 oz can	0.61	4Q 92	4c
Pork chops, center cut, bone-in	lb	3.13	4/93	16r
Potato chips	16 oz	2.94	4/93	16r
Potatoes, white	lb	0.43	4/93	16r
Potatoes, white or red	10-lb sack	2.48	4Q 92	4c
Rib roast, USDA choice, bone-in	lb	4.63	4/93	16r
Rice, white, long grain, uncooked	lb	0.45	4/93	16r
Round roast, graded & ungraded, ex USDA prime & choice	lb	3.03	4/93	16r
Round roast, USDA choice, boneless	lb	3.09	4/93	16r
Sausage, fresh, loose	lb	2.08	4/93	16r
Sausage, Jimmy Dean, 100% pork	lb	2.37	4Q 92	4c
Short ribs, bone-in	lb	2.66	4/93	16r
Shortening, vegetable oil blends	lb	0.69	4/93	16r

Monroe, LA - continued

Item	Per	Value	Date	Ref.
Groceries - continued				
Shortening, vegetable, Crisco	3-lb can	2.18	4Q 92	4c
Soft drink, Coca Cola	2 liter	1.08	4Q 92	4c
Spaghetti and macaroni	lb	0.81	4/93	16r
Steak, rib eye, USDA choice, boneless	lb	6.24	4/93	16r
Steak, round, graded & ungraded, ex USDA prime & choice	lb	3.31	4/93	16r
Steak, round, USDA choice, boneless	lb	3.34	4/93	16r
Steak, sirloin, graded & ungraded, ex USDA prime & choice	lb	4.19	4/93	16r
Steak, sirloin, USDA choice, boneless	lb	4.46	4/93	16r
Steak, T-bone	lb	5.23	4Q 92	4c
Steak, T-bone, USDA choice, bone-in	lb	5.25	4/93	16r
Strawberries, dry pint	12 oz	0.92	4/93	16r
Sugar, cane or beet	4 lb	1.50	4Q 92	4c
Sugar, white	lb	0.39	4/93	16r
Sugar, white, 33-80 oz pk	lb	0.38	4/93	16r
Tomatoes, field grown	lb	0.88	4/93	16r
Tomatoes, Hunt's or Del Monte	14.5-oz can	0.71	4Q 92	4c
Tuna, chunk, light	6.125-6.5 oz can	0.71	4Q 92	4c
Tuna, chunk, light	lb	1.79	4/93	16r
Turkey, frozen, whole	lb	1.04	4/93	16r
Yogurt, natural, fruit flavored	1/2 pint	0.57	4/93	16r
Health Care				
ACCRA Index, Health Care		94.50	4Q 92	4c
Analgesic, Aspirin, Bayer, 325 mg tablets	100	4.03	4Q 92	4c
Childbirth, cesarean, hospital		5034	91	62r
Childbirth, cesarean, physician's fee		2053	91	62r
Childbirth, normal, hospital		2712	91	62r
Childbirth, normal, physician's fee		1492	91	62r
Dentist's fee, adult teeth cleaning and periodic oral exam	visit	48.33	4Q 92	4c
Doctor's fee, routine exam, established patient	visit	39.00	4Q 92	4c
Hospital care, semiprivate room	day	123.67	90	27c
Hospital care, semiprivate room	day	204.50	4Q 92	4c
Medical insurance premium, per employee, small group comprehensive	month	332.15	10/91	25c
Mental health care, exp	capita	20.37-28.83	90	38s
Mental health care, exp, state mental health agency	capita	28.44	90	38s
Mental health care, hospital psychiatric services, non-Federal, exp	capita	8.19	88	38s
Mental health care, mental health organization, multiservice, exp	capita	0.49	88	38s
Mental health care, psychiatric hospitals, private, exp	capita	43.54	88	38s
Mental health care, psychiatric out-patient clinics, freestanding, exp	capita	4.11	88	38s
Mental health care, state and county mental hospitals, exp	capita	18.74	88	38s
Mental health care, VA medical centers, exp	capita	2.60	88	38s
Physician fee, family practice, first-visit		75.00	91	62r
Physician fee, family practice, revisit		34.00	91	62r
Physician fee, general practice, first-visit		61.00	91	62r
Physician fee, general practice, revisit		32.00	91	62r
Physician fee, general surgeon, first-visit		64.00	91	62r
Physician fee, general surgeon, revisit		40.00	91	62r
Physician fee, internal medicine, first-visit		98.00	91	62r
Physician fee, internal medicine, revisit		40.00	91	62r
Physician fee, median, neurosurgeon, first-visit		130.00	91	62r
Physician fee, median, nonsurgical specialist, first-visit		95.00	91	62r
Physician fee, median, orthopedic surgeon, first-visit		91.00	91	62r

Values are in dollars or fractions of dollars. In the column headed *Ref*, references are shown to sources. Each reference is followed by a letter. These refer to the geographical level for which data were reported: s = State, r = Region, and c = City or metro. The abbreviation *ex* is used to mean *except* or *excluding*; *exp* stands for expenditures. For other abbreviations and further explanations, please see the Introduction.

Monroe, LA - continued

Item	Per	Value	Date	Ref.
Health Care				
Physician fee, median, plastic surgeon, first-visit		66.00	91	62r
Physician fee, median, surgical specialist, first-visit		62.00	91	62r
Physician fee, neurosurgeon, revisit		50.00	91	62r
Physician fee, nonsurgical specialist, revisit		40.00	91	62r
Physician fee, obstetrics/gynecology, first-visit		64.00	91	62r
Physician fee, obstetrics/gynecology, revisit		41.00	91	62r
Physician fee, orthopedic surgeon, revisit		40.00	91	62r
Physician fee, pediatrician, first-visit		49.00	91	62r
Physician fee, pediatrician, revisit		33.00	91	62r
Physician fee, plastic surgeon, revisit		43.00	91	62r
Physician fee, surgical specialist, revisit		37.00	91	62r
Substance abuse, hospital ancillary charge	incident	2600	90	70s
Substance abuse, hospital physician charge	incident	840	90	70s
Substance abuse, hospital room and board	incident	6410	90	70s
Household Goods				
Appliance repair, home, service call, washing machine	min labor charge	36.58	4Q 92	4c
Laundry detergent, Tide Ultra, Bold, or Cheer	42 oz	3.51	4Q 92	4c
Tissues, facial, Kleenex brand	175-count box	1.10	4Q 92	4c
Housing				
ACCRA Index, Housing		81.30	4Q 92	4c
House, 1,800 sq ft, 8,000 sq ft lot, new, urban	total	87017	4Q 92	4c
House payment, principal and interest, 25% down payment	month	485	4Q 92	4c
Mortgage rate, incl. points & origination fee, 30-year fixed or adjustable rate	percent	8.13	4Q 92	4c
Rent, apartment, 2 bedrooms - 1-1/2 to 2 baths, unfurnished, 950 sq ft, water	month	436	4Q 92	4c
Rental unit, 1 bedroom	month	341	93	23c
Rental unit, 2 bedroom	month	400	93	23c
Rental unit, 3 bedroom	month	501	93	23c
Rental unit, 4 bedroom	month	560	93	23c
Rental unit, efficiency	month	279	93	23c
Insurance and Pensions				
Auto insurance, private passenger	year	778.70	91	63s
Personal Goods				
Shampoo, Alberto VO5	15 oz	1.16	4Q 92	4c
Toothpaste, Crest or Colgate	6-7 oz	1.95	4Q 92	4c
Personal Services				
Dry cleaning, man's 2-piece suit		6.74	4Q 92	4c
Haircare, woman's shampoo, trim and blow-dry		13.71	4Q 92	4c
Haircut, man's barbershop, no styling		10.14	4Q 92	4c
Restaurant Food				
Chicken, fried, thigh and drumstick		1.65	4Q 92	4c
Hamburger with cheese	1/4 lb	1.76	4Q 92	4c
Pizza, Pizza Hut or Pizza Inn, cheese, thin crust	12-13 in	8.79	4Q 92	4c
Taxes				
Tax, cigarette	pack	20	91	77s
Tax, gasoline	gal	20	91	77s
Taxes, state	capita	1013	91	77s
Transportation				
ACCRA Index, Transportation		103.70	4Q 92	4c
Bus fare	one-way	0.60	3/93	2c
Driver's license fee		18.00	12/90	43s

Monroe, LA - continued

Item	Per	Value	Date	Ref.
Transportation - continued				
Tire balance, computer or spin balance, front	wheel	6.79	4Q 92	4c
Travel				
Business travel	day	193.00	4/93	89r
Utilities				
ACCRA Index, Utilities		133.70	4Q 92	4c
Electricity	mil Btu	17.77	90	64s
Electricity, all electric, 1,800 sq ft living area new home	month	150.11	4Q 92	4c

Montgomery, AL

Item	Per	Value	Date	Ref.
Composite ACCRA index		99.00	4Q 92	4c
Alcoholic Beverages				
Beer, Miller Lite or Budweiser, 12-oz containers	6 pack	3.87	4Q 92	4c
Liquor, J & B Scotch	750 ml	19.99	4Q 92	4c
Wine, Gallo Chablis blanc, 1.5 liter	bottle	6.29	4Q 92	4c
Child Care				
Child care fee, average, center	hour	1.29	90	65r
Child care fee, average, nonregulated family day care	hour	0.89	90	65r
Child care fee, average, regulated family day care	hour	1.32	90	65r
Clothing				
Jeans, man's denim		36.99	4Q 92	4c
Shirt, man's dress shirt		26.40	4Q 92	4c
Undervest, boy's size 10-14, cotton	3	3.97	4Q 92	4c
Communications				
Long-distance telephone service, day, initial minute, 0-100 miles	min	0.11-0.36	91	12s
Long-distance telephone service, day, additional minute, 0-100 miles	min	0.09-0.26	91	12s
Long-distance telephone service, evenings/weekends, 0-100 mi, initial minute	min	0.04-0.14	91	12s
Long-distance telephone service, evenings/weekends, 0-100 mi, additional minute	min	0.04-0.10	91	12s
Newspaper subscription, daily and Sunday home delivery, large-city	month	10.44	4Q 92	4c
Telephone, flat rate	month	17.26	91	11c
Telephone bill, family of four	month	22.26	4Q 92	4c
Education				
Board, 4-yr private college/university	year	1795	91	22s
Board, 4-yr public college/university	year	1469	91	22s
Expenditures, local gov't, public elementary/secondary	pupil	3675	92	20s
Room, 4-year private college/university	year	1340	91	22s
Room, 4-year public college/university	year	1295	91	22s
Tuition, 2-year private college/university	year	4148	91	22s
Tuition, 2-year public college/university	year	689	91	22s
Tuition, 4-year private college/university	year	5942	91	22s
Tuition, 4-year public college/university, in-state	year	1593	91	22s
Energy and Fuels				
Coal	mil Btu	1.83	90	64s
Energy	mil Btu	7.92	90	64s
Energy, combined forms, 1,800 sq ft heating area	month	136.10	4Q 92	4c
Energy, exc electricity, 1,800 sq ft heating area	month	42.92	4Q 92	4c
Energy exp/householder, 1-family unit	year	403	90	28r
Energy exp/householder, <1,000 sq ft heating area	year	342	90	28r
Energy exp/householder, 1,000-1,999 sq ft heating area	year	388	90	28r
Energy exp/householder, 2,000+ sq ft heating area	year	434	90	28r

Values are in dollars or fractions of dollars. In the column headed *Ref*, references are shown to sources. Each reference is followed by a letter. These refer to the geographical level for which data were reported: s=State, r=Region, and c=City or metro. The abbreviation *ex* is used to mean *except* or *excluding*; *exp* stands for *expenditures*. For other abbreviations and further explanations, please see the Introduction.

Montgomery, AL - continued

Item	Per	Value	Date	Ref.
Energy and Fuels				
Energy exp/householder, mobile home	year	320	90	28r
Energy exp/householder, multifamily	year	338	90	28r
Gas, natural	mil Btu	4.07	90	64s
Gas, natural	000 cu ft	7.05	91	46s
Gas, natural, exp	year	461	91	46s
Gasoline, motor	gal	1.08	4Q 92	4c
Gasoline, unleaded regular	mil Btu	8.96	90	64s
Entertainment				
Bowling, evening rate	game	2.60	4Q 92	4c
Miniature golf admission	adult	6.18	92	1r
Miniature golf admission	child	5.14	92	1r
Monopoly game, Parker Brothers', No. 9		10.97	4Q 92	4c
Movie	admission	5.25	4Q 92	4c
Tennis balls, yellow, Wilson or Penn, 3	can	2.96	4Q 92	4c
Waterpark admission	adult	11.00	92	1r
Waterpark admission	child	8.55	92	1r
Funerals				
Casket, 18-gauge steel, velvet interior		2329.05	91	24r
Cosmetology, hair care, etc.		72.78	91	24r
Embalming		240.71	91	24r
Facility use for ceremony		181.67	91	24r
Hearse, local		106.25	91	24r
Limousine, local		70.92	91	24r
Remains to funeral home, transfer		96.30	91	24r
Service charge, professional		687.09	91	24r
Vault, concrete, non-metallic liner		732.09	91	24r
Viewing facilities, use		190.30	91	24r
Goods and Services				
ACCRA Index, Miscellaneous Goods and Services		105.70	4Q 92	4c
Groceries				
ACCRA Index, Groceries		96.80	4Q 92	4c
Apples, Red Delicious	lb	0.79	4/93	16r
Babyfood, strained vegetables, lowest price	4-4.5 oz jar	0.27	4Q 92	4c
Bacon	lb	1.75	4/93	16r
Bananas	lb	0.37	4Q 92	4c
Bananas	lb	0.42	4/93	16r
Beef, stew, boneless	lb	2.61	4/93	16r
Bologna, all beef or mixed	lb	2.24	4/93	16r
Bread, white	24 oz	0.65	4Q 92	4c
Bread, white, pan	lb	0.64	4/93	16r
Bread, whole wheat, pan	lb	0.96	4/93	16r
Cabbage	lb	0.37	4/93	16r
Carrots, short trimmed and topped	lb	0.47	4/93	16r
Celery	lb	0.64	4/93	16r
Cheese, American	lb	2.98	4/93	16r
Cheese, Cheddar	lb	3.28	4/93	16r
Cheese, Kraft grated Parmesan	8-oz canister	3.19	4Q 92	4c
Chicken, fresh, whole	lb	0.77	4/93	16r
Chicken, fryer, whole	lb	0.64	4Q 92	4c
Chicken breast, bone-in	lb	1.92	4/93	16r
Chicken legs, bone-in	lb	1.06	4/93	16r
Chuck roast, graded and ungraded, ex USDA prime and choice	lb	2.40	4/93	16r
Chuck roast, USDA choice, bone-in	lb	2.19	4/93	16r
Chuck roast, USDA choice, boneless	lb	2.38	4/93	16r
Cigarettes, Winston	carton	15.63	4Q 92	4c
Coffee, 100% ground roast, all sizes	lb	2.48	4/93	16r
Coffee, vacuum-packed	13-oz can	2.10	4Q 92	4c
Corn, frozen	10 oz	0.58	4Q 92	4c
Corn Flakes, Kellogg's or Post Toasties	18 oz	1.77	4Q 92	4c
Crackers, soda, salted	lb	1.15	4/93	16r
Eggs, Grade A large	doz	0.66	4Q 92	4c
Eggs, Grade A large	doz	0.96	4/93	16r

Montgomery, AL - continued

Item	Per	Value	Date	Ref.
Groceries - continued				
Flour, white, all purpose	lb	0.24	4/93	16r
Frankfurters, all meat or all beef	lb	2.01	4/93	16r
Grapefruit	lb	0.44	4/93	16r
Grapes, Thompson Seedless	lb	1.40	4/93	16r
Ground beef, 100% beef	lb	1.58	4/93	16r
Ground beef, lean and extra lean	lb	2.09	4/93	16r
Ground beef or hamburger	lb	1.84	4Q 92	4c
Ground chuck, 100% beef	lb	1.98	4/93	16r
Ham, boneless, excluding canned	lb	2.89	4/93	16r
Ham, picnic, shoulder, bone-in, smoked	lb	1.02	4/93	16r
Ham, rump or steak half, bone-in, smoked	lb	1.48	4/93	16r
Honey, jar	8 oz	0.89-1.09	92	5r
Honey, jar	lb	1.39-2.25	92	5r
Honey, squeeze bear	12-oz	1.00-1.50	92	5r
Ice cream, prepackaged, bulk, regular	1/2 gal	2.41	4/93	16r
Lemons	lb	1.05	4/93	16r
Lettuce, iceberg	head	0.95	4Q 92	4c
Lettuce, iceberg	lb	0.81	4/93	16r
Margarine, Blue Bonnet or Parkay cubes	lb	0.54	4Q 92	4c
Margarine, stick	lb	0.88	4/93	16r
Milk, whole	1/2 gal	1.40	4Q 92	4c
Orange juice, Minute Maid frozen	12-oz can	1.29	4Q 92	4c
Oranges, navel	lb	0.55	4/93	16r
Peaches	29-oz can	1.32	4Q 92	4c
Pears, Anjou	lb	0.92	4/93	16r
Peas Sweet, Del Monte or Green Giant	15-17 oz can	0.52	4Q 92	4c
Pork chops, center cut, bone-in	lb	3.13	4/93	16r
Potato chips	16 oz	2.94	4/93	16r
Potatoes, white	lb	0.43	4/93	16r
Potatoes, white or red	10-lb sack	2.93	4Q 92	4c
Rib roast, USDA choice, bone-in	lb	4.63	4/93	16r
Rice, white, long grain, uncooked	lb	0.45	4/93	16r
Round roast, graded & ungraded, ex USDA prime & choice	lb	3.03	4/93	16r
Round roast, USDA choice, boneless	lb	3.09	4/93	16r
Sausage, fresh, loose	lb	2.08	4/93	16r
Sausage, Jimmy Dean, 100% pork	lb	2.27	4Q 92	4c
Short ribs, bone-in	lb	2.66	4/93	16r
Shortening, vegetable oil blends	lb	0.69	4/93	16r
Shortening, vegetable, Crisco	3-lb can	2.15	4Q 92	4c
Soft drink, Coca Cola	2 liter	1.01	4Q 92	4c
Spaghetti and macaroni	lb	0.81	4/93	16r
Steak, rib eye, USDA choice, boneless	lb	6.24	4/93	16r
Steak, round, graded & ungraded, ex USDA prime & choice	lb	3.31	4/93	16r
Steak, round, USDA choice, boneless	lb	3.34	4/93	16r
Steak, sirloin, graded & ungraded, ex USDA prime & choice	lb	4.19	4/93	16r
Steak, sirloin, USDA choice, boneless	lb	4.46	4/93	16r
Steak, T-bone	lb	6.07	4Q 92	4c
Steak, T-bone, USDA choice, bone-in	lb	5.25	4/93	16r
Strawberries, dry pint	12 oz	0.92	4/93	16r
Sugar, cane or beet	4 lb	1.71	4Q 92	4c
Sugar, white	lb	0.39	4/93	16r
Sugar, white, 33-80 oz pk	lb	0.38	4/93	16r
Tomatoes, field grown	lb	0.88	4/93	16r
Tomatoes, Hunt's or Del Monte	14.5-oz can	0.52	4Q 92	4c
Tuna, chunk, light	6.125-6.5 oz can	0.57	4Q 92	4c
Tuna, chunk, light	lb	1.79	4/93	16r
Turkey, frozen, whole	lb	1.04	4/93	16r
Yogurt, natural, fruit flavored	1/2 pint	0.57	4/93	16r

Values are in dollars or fractions of dollars. In the column headed *Ref*, references are shown to sources. Each reference is followed by a letter. These refer to the geographical level for which data were reported: s=State, r=Region, and c=City or metro. The abbreviation *ex* is used to mean *except* or *excluding*; *exp* stands for expenditures. For other abbreviations and further explanations, please see the Introduction.

Montgomery, AL - continued

Item	Per	Value	Date	Ref.
Health Care				
ACCRA Index, Health Care		94.30	4Q 92	4c
Analgesic, Aspirin, Bayer, 325 mg tablets	100	3.86	4Q 92	4c
Childbirth, cesarean, hospital		5034	91	62r
Childbirth, cesarean, physician's fee		2053	91	62r
Childbirth, normal, hospital		2712	91	62r
Childbirth, normal, physician's fee		1492	91	62r
Dentist's fee, adult teeth cleaning and periodic oral exam	visit	40.60	4Q 92	4c
Doctor's fee, routine exam, established patient	visit	40.00	4Q 92	4c
Hospital care, semiprivate room	day	190.18	90	27c
Hospital care, semiprivate room	day	294.60	4Q 92	4c
Medical insurance premium, per employee, small group comprehensive	month	335.80	10/91	25c
Mental health care, exp	capita	37.60-53.67	90	38s
Mental health care, exp, state mental health agency	capita	38.35	90	38s
Mental health care, hospital psychiatric services, non-Federal, exp	capita	13.58	88	38s
Mental health care, mental health organization, multiservice, exp	capita	12.40	88	38s
Mental health care, psychiatric hospitals, private, exp	capita	9.49	88	38s
Mental health care, state and county mental hospitals, exp	capita	22.15	88	38s
Mental health care, VA medical centers, exp	capita	10.94	88	38s
Physician fee, family practice, first-visit		75.00	91	62r
Physician fee, family practice, revisit		34.00	91	62r
Physician fee, general practice, first-visit		61.00	91	62r
Physician fee, general practice, revisit		32.00	91	62r
Physician fee, general surgeon, first-visit		64.00	91	62r
Physician fee, general surgeon, revisit		40.00	91	62r
Physician fee, internal medicine, first-visit		98.00	91	62r
Physician fee, internal medicine, revisit		40.00	91	62r
Physician fee, median, neurosurgeon, first-visit		130.00	91	62r
Physician fee, median, nonsurgical specialist, first-visit		95.00	91	62r
Physician fee, median, orthopedic surgeon, first-visit		91.00	91	62r
Physician fee, median, plastic surgeon, first-visit		66.00	91	62r
Physician fee, median, surgical specialist, first-visit		62.00	91	62r
Physician fee, neurosurgeon, revisit		50.00	91	62r
Physician fee, nonsurgical specialist, revisit		40.00	91	62r
Physician fee, obstetrics/gynecology, first-visit		64.00	91	62r
Physician fee, obstetrics/gynecology, revisit		41.00	91	62r
Physician fee, orthopedic surgeon, revisit		40.00	91	62r
Physician fee, pediatrician, first-visit		49.00	91	62r
Physician fee, pediatrician, revisit		33.00	91	62r
Physician fee, plastic surgeon, revisit		43.00	91	62r
Physician fee, surgical specialist, revisit		37.00	91	62r
Substance abuse, hospital ancillary charge	incident	1390	90	70s
Substance abuse, hospital physician charge	incident	520	90	70s
Substance abuse, hospital room and board	incident	5830	90	70s
Household Goods				
Appliance repair, home, service call, washing machine	min labor charge	32.68	4Q 92	4c
Laundry detergent, Tide Ultra, Bold, or Cheer	42 oz	3.15	4Q 92	4c
Tissues, facial, Kleenex brand	175-count box	1.07	4Q 92	4c

Montgomery, AL - continued

Item	Per	Value	Date	Ref.
Housing				
ACCRA Index, Housing		83.70	4Q 92	4c
Home, median price	unit	79.70		26c
House, 1,800 sq ft, 8,000 sq ft lot, new, urban	total	91800	4Q 92	4c
House payment, principal and interest, 25% down payment	month	507	4Q 92	4c
Mortgage rate, incl. points & origination fee, 30-year fixed or adjustable rate	percent	8.03	4Q 92	4c
Rent, apartment, 2 bedrooms - 1-1/2 to 2 baths, unfurnished, 950 sq ft, water	month	431	4Q 92	4c
Rental unit, 1 bedroom	month	338	93	23c
Rental unit, 2 bedroom	month	397	93	23c
Rental unit, 3 bedroom	month	498	93	23c
Rental unit, 4 bedroom	month	558	93	23c
Rental unit, efficiency	month	276	93	23c
Insurance and Pensions				
Auto insurance, private passenger	year	562.59	91	63s
Personal Goods				
Shampoo, Alberto VO5	15 oz	0.92	4Q 92	4c
Toothpaste, Crest or Colgate	6-7 oz	1.84	4Q 92	4c
Personal Services				
Dry cleaning, man's 2-piece suit		5.75	4Q 92	4c
Haircare, woman's shampoo, trim and blow-dry		22.50	4Q 92	4c
Haircut, man's barbershop, no styling		7.40	4Q 92	4c
Restaurant Food				
Chicken, fried, thigh and drumstick		1.89	4Q 92	4c
Hamburger with cheese	1/4 lb	1.85	4Q 92	4c
Pizza, Pizza Hut or Pizza Inn, cheese, thin crust	12-13 in	8.27	4Q 92	4c
Taxes				
Tax, cigarette	pack	16.50	91	77s
Tax, gasoline	gal	16	91	77s
Taxes, state	capita	964	91	77s
Transportation				
ACCRA Index, Transportation		101.40	4Q 92	4c
Bus fare, up to 10 miles	one-way	1.00	4Q 92	4c
Driver's license fee		15.00	12/90	43s
Tire balance, computer or spin balance, front	wheel	6.78	4Q 92	4c
Travel				
Business travel	day	193.00	4/93	89r
Utilities				
ACCRA Index, Utilities		123.60	4Q 92	4c
Cable-television service, more than one provider	month	17.95	92	81c
Cable-television service, with no competition	month	17.95	92	81c
Electricity	mil Btu	16.46	90	64s
Electricity, partial electric and other energy, 1,800 sq ft living area new home	month	93.18	4Q 92	4c

Montpelier-Barre, VT

Item	Per	Value	Date	Ref.
Composite ACCRA index		110.20	4Q 92	4c
Alcoholic Beverages				
Beer, Miller Lite or Budweiser, 12-oz containers	6 pack	3.89	4Q 92	4c
Liquor, J & B Scotch	750 ml	14.70	4Q 92	4c
Wine, Gallo Chablis blanc, 1.5 liter	bottle	6.49	4Q 92	4c
Clothing				
Jeans, man's denim		25.99	4Q 92	4c
Shirt, man's dress shirt		23.00	4Q 92	4c
Undervest, boy's size 10-14, cotton	3	4.14	4Q 92	4c

Values are in dollars or fractions of dollars. In the column headed *Ref*, references are shown to sources. Each reference is followed by a letter. These refer to the geographical level for which data were reported: s=State, r=Region, and c=City or metro. The abbreviation *ex* is used to mean *except* or *excluding*; *exp* stands for expenditures. For other abbreviations and further explanations, please see the Introduction.

Montpelier-Barre, VT - continued

Item	Per	Value	Date	Ref.
Communications				
Newspaper subscription, daily and Sunday home delivery, large-city	month	10.65	4Q 92	4c
Telephone bill, family of four	month	27.48	4Q 92	4c
Energy and Fuels				
Energy, combined forms, 1,800 sq ft heating area	month	119.65	4Q 92	4c
Energy, exc electricity, 1,800 sq ft heating area	month	55.28	4Q 92	4c
Gasoline, motor	gal	1.21	4Q 92	4c
Entertainment				
Bowling, evening rate	game	1.82	4Q 92	4c
Monopoly game, Parker Brothers', No. 9		10.96	4Q 92	4c
Movie	admission	5.00	4Q 92	4c
Tennis balls, yellow, Wilson or Penn, 3	can	3.77	4Q 92	4c
Goods and Services				
ACCRA Index, Miscellaneous Goods and Services		102.40	4Q 92	4c
Groceries				
ACCRA Index, Groceries		118.30	4Q 92	4c
Babyfood, strained vegetables, lowest price	4-4.5 oz jar	0.35	4Q 92	4c
Bananas	lb	0.44	4Q 92	4c
Bread, white	24 oz	0.98	4Q 92	4c
Cheese, Kraft grated Parmesan	8-oz canister	2.99	4Q 92	4c
Chicken, fryer, whole	lb	1.29	4Q 92	4c
Cigarettes, Winston	carton	17.85	4Q 92	4c
Coffee, vacuum-packed	13-oz can	2.64	4Q 92	4c
Corn, frozen	10 oz	0.69	4Q 92	4c
Corn Flakes, Kellogg's or Post Toasties	18 oz	2.29	4Q 92	4c
Eggs, Grade A large	doz	1.24	4Q 92	4c
Ground beef or hamburger	lb	1.68	4Q 92	4c
Lettuce, iceberg	head	0.99	4Q 92	4c
Margarine, Blue Bonnet or Parkay cubes	lb	0.74	4Q 92	4c
Milk, whole	1/2 gal	1.49	4Q 92	4c
Orange juice, Minute Maid frozen	12-oz can	1.59	4Q 92	4c
Peaches	29-oz can	1.59	4Q 92	4c
Peas Sweet, Del Monte or Green Giant	15-17 oz can	0.66	4Q 92	4c
Potatoes, white or red	10-lb sack	1.99	4Q 92	4c
Sausage, Jimmy Dean, 100% pork	lb	3.45	4Q 92	4c
Shortening, vegetable, Crisco	3-lb can	3.19	4Q 92	4c
Soft drink, Coca Cola	2 liter	1.42	4Q 92	4c
Steak, T-bone	lb	6.03	4Q 92	4c
Sugar, cane or beet	4 lb	1.43	4Q 92	4c
Tomatoes, Hunt's or Del Monte	14.5-oz can	1.04	4Q 92	4c
Tuna, chunk, light	6.125-6.5 oz can	0.59	4Q 92	4c
Health Care				
ACCRA Index, Health Care		113.20	4Q 92	4c
Analgesic, Aspirin, Bayer, 325 mg tablets	100	5.19	4Q 92	4c
Dentist's fee, adult teeth cleaning and periodic oral exam	visit	53.50	4Q 92	4c
Doctor's fee, routine exam, established patient	visit	35.00	4Q 92	4c
Hospital care, semiprivate room	day	486.00	4Q 92	4c
Household Goods				
Appliance repair, home, service call, washing machine	min labor charge	39.00	4Q 92	4c

Montpelier-Barre, VT - continued

Item	Per	Value	Date	Ref.
Household Goods - continued				
Laundry detergent, Tide Ultra, Bold, or Cheer	42 oz	4.39	4Q 92	4c
Tissues, facial, Kleenex brand	175-count box	1.24	4Q 92	4c
Housing				
ACCRA Index, Housing		121.50	4Q 92	4c
House, 1,800 sq ft, 8,000 sq ft lot, new, urban	total	141000	4Q 92	4c
House payment, principal and interest, 25% down payment	month	798	4Q 92	4c
Mortgage rate, incl. points & origination fee, 30-year fixed or adjustable rate	percent	8.30	4Q 92	4c
Rent, apartment, 2 bedrooms - 1-1/2 to 2 baths, unfurnished, 950 sq ft, water	month	482	4Q 92	4c
Personal Goods				
Shampoo, Alberto VO5	15 oz	1.64	4Q 92	4c
Toothpaste, Crest or Colgate	6-7 oz	2.19	4Q 92	4c
Personal Services				
Dry cleaning, man's 2-piece suit		6.12	4Q 92	4c
Haircare, woman's shampoo, trim and blow-dry		15.83	4Q 92	4c
Haircut, man's barbershop, no styling		7.75	4Q 92	4c
Restaurant Food				
Chicken, fried, thigh and drumstick		2.00	4Q 92	4c
Hamburger with cheese	1/4 lb	1.99	4Q 92	4c
Pizza, Pizza Hut or Pizza Inn, cheese, thin crust	12-13 in	7.75	4Q 92	4c
Transportation				
ACCRA Index, Transportation		91.90	4Q 92	4c
Tire balance, computer or spin balance, front	wheel	5.00	4Q 92	4c
Utilities				
ACCRA Index, Utilities		112.70	4Q 92	4c
Electricity, partial electric and other energy, 1,800 sq ft living area new home	month	64.37	4Q 92	4c

Morristown, TN

Item	Per	Value	Date	Ref.
Composite ACCRA index		87.70	4Q 92	4c
Alcoholic Beverages				
Beer, Miller Lite or Budweiser, 12-oz containers	6 pack	3.86	4Q 92	4c
Liquor, J & B Scotch	750 ml	18.83	4Q 92	4c
Wine, Gallo Chablis blanc, 1.5 liter	bottle	6.99	4Q 92	4c
Clothing				
Jeans, man's denim		33.99	4Q 92	4c
Shirt, man's dress shirt		22.00	4Q 92	4c
Undervest, boy's size 10-14, cotton	3	3.12	4Q 92	4c
Communications				
Newspaper subscription, daily and Sunday home delivery, large-city	month	8.26	4Q 92	4c
Telephone bill, family of four	month	16.36	4Q 92	4c
Energy and Fuels				
Energy, combined forms, 1,800 sq ft heating area	month	94.27	4Q 92	4c
Gas, cooking, winter, 10 therms	month	11.40	92	56c
Gas, cooking, winter, 30 therms	month	24.20	92	56c
Gas, cooking, winter, 50 therms	month	37.01	92	56c
Gas, heating, winter, 100 therms	month	69.01	92	56c
Gasoline, motor	gal	1.07	4Q 92	4c
Entertainment				
Bowling, evening rate	game	1.85	4Q 92	4c
Monopoly game, Parker Brothers', No. 9		10.06	4Q 92	4c
Movie	admission	5.00	4Q 92	4c

Values are in dollars or fractions of dollars. In the column headed *Ref*, references are shown to sources. Each reference is followed by a letter. These refer to the geographical level for which data were reported: s=State, r=Region, and c=City or metro. The abbreviation *ex* is used to mean *except* or *excluding*; *exp* stands for expenditures. For other abbreviations and further explanations, please see the Introduction.

451

Morristown, TN - continued

Item	Per	Value	Date	Ref.
Entertainment				
Tennis balls, yellow, Wilson or Penn, 3	can	2.05	4Q 92	4c
Goods and Services				
ACCRA Index, Miscellaneous Goods and Services		93.50	4Q 92	4c
Groceries				
ACCRA Index, Groceries		96.00	4Q 92	4c
Babyfood, strained vegetables, lowest price	4-4.5 oz jar	0.31	4Q 92	4c
Bananas	lb	0.49	4Q 92	4c
Bread, white	24 oz	0.72	4Q 92	4c
Cheese, Kraft grated Parmesan	8-oz canister	3.23	4Q 92	4c
Chicken, fryer, whole	lb	0.63	4Q 92	4c
Cigarettes, Winston	carton	16.09	4Q 92	4c
Coffee, vacuum-packed	13-oz can	1.64	4Q 92	4c
Corn, frozen	10 oz	0.55	4Q 92	4c
Corn Flakes, Kellogg's or Post Toasties	18 oz	1.67	4Q 92	4c
Eggs, Grade A large	doz	0.87	4Q 92	4c
Ground beef or hamburger	lb	1.76	4Q 92	4c
Lettuce, iceberg	head	0.99	4Q 92	4c
Margarine, Blue Bonnet or Parkay cubes	lb	0.53	4Q 92	4c
Milk, whole	1/2 gal	1.32	4Q 92	4c
Orange juice, Minute Maid frozen	12-oz can	1.33	4Q 92	4c
Peaches	29-oz can	1.24	4Q 92	4c
Peas Sweet, Del Monte or Green Giant	15-17 oz can	0.48	4Q 92	4c
Potatoes, white or red	10-lb sack	1.95	4Q 92	4c
Sausage, Jimmy Dean, 100% pork	lb	2.33	4Q 92	4c
Shortening, vegetable, Crisco	3-lb can	1.99	4Q 92	4c
Soft drink, Coca Cola	2 liter	0.90	4Q 92	4c
Steak, T-bone	lb	5.79	4Q 92	4c
Sugar, cane or beet	4 lb	1.50	4Q 92	4c
Tomatoes, Hunt's or Del Monte	14.5-oz can	0.51	4Q 92	4c
Tuna, chunk, light	6.125-6.5 oz can	0.54	4Q 92	4c
Health Care				
ACCRA Index, Health Care		76.90	4Q 92	4c
Analgesic, Aspirin, Bayer, 325 mg tablets	100	5.20	4Q 92	4c
Dentist's fee, adult teeth cleaning and periodic oral exam	visit	37.80	4Q 92	4c
Doctor's fee, routine exam, established patient	visit	26.50	4Q 92	4c
Hospital care, semiprivate room	day	200.00	4Q 92	4c
Household Goods				
Appliance repair, home, service call, washing machine	min labor charge	30.00	4Q 92	4c
Laundry detergent, Tide Ultra, Bold, or Cheer	42 oz	3.47	4Q 92	4c
Tissues, facial, Kleenex brand	175-count box	1.09	4Q 92	4c
Housing				
ACCRA Index, Housing		77.80	4Q 92	4c
House, 1,800 sq ft, 8,000 sq ft lot, new, urban	total	84500	4Q 92	4c
House payment, principal and interest, 25% down payment	month	471	4Q 92	4c
Mortgage rate, incl. points & origination fee, 30-year fixed or adjustable rate	percent	8.13	4Q 92	4c

Morristown, TN - continued

Item	Per	Value	Date	Ref.
Housing - continued				
Rent, apartment, 2 bedrooms - 1-1/2 to 2 baths, unfurnished, 950 sq ft, water	month	400	4Q 92	4c
Personal Goods				
Shampoo, Alberto VO5	15 oz	1.20	4Q 92	4c
Toothpaste, Crest or Colgate	6-7 oz	2.00	4Q 92	4c
Personal Services				
Dry cleaning, man's 2-piece suit		5.35	4Q 92	4c
Haircare, woman's shampoo, trim and blow-dry		15.33	4Q 92	4c
Haircut, man's barbershop, no styling		5.67	4Q 92	4c
Restaurant Food				
Chicken, fried, thigh and drumstick		2.15	4Q 92	4c
Hamburger with cheese	1/4 lb	1.79	4Q 92	4c
Pizza, Pizza Hut or Pizza Inn, cheese, thin crust	12-13 in	7.74	4Q 92	4c
Transportation				
ACCRA Index, Transportation		91.10	4Q 92	4c
Tire balance, computer or spin balance, front	wheel	5.67	4Q 92	4c
Utilities				
ACCRA Index, Utilities		86.10	4Q 92	4c
Electricity, all electric, 1,800 sq ft living area new home	month	94.27	4Q 92	4c

Moultrie, GA

Item	Per	Value	Date	Ref.
Composite ACCRA index		86.90	4Q 92	4c
Alcoholic Beverages				
Beer, Miller Lite or Budweiser, 12-oz containers	6 pack	4.19	4Q 92	4c
Liquor, J & B Scotch	750 ml	15.68	4Q 92	4c
Wine, Gallo Chablis blanc, 1.5 liter	bottle	6.21	4Q 92	4c
Clothing				
Jeans, man's denim		37.49	4Q 92	4c
Shirt, man's dress shirt		28.00	4Q 92	4c
Undervest, boy's size 10-14, cotton	3	2.98	4Q 92	4c
Communications				
Newspaper subscription, daily and Sunday home delivery, large-city	month	6.50	4Q 92	4c
Telephone bill, family of four	month	21.11	4Q 92	4c
Energy and Fuels				
Energy, combined forms, 1,800 sq ft heating area	month	116.28	4Q 92	4c
Gasoline, motor	gal	1.04	4Q 92	4c
Entertainment				
Bowling, evening rate	game	1.70	4Q 92	4c
Monopoly game, Parker Brothers', No. 9		10.48	4Q 92	4c
Movie	admission	3.00	4Q 92	4c
Tennis balls, yellow, Wilson or Penn, 3	can	1.94	4Q 92	4c
Goods and Services				
ACCRA Index, Miscellaneous Goods and Services		91.80	4Q 92	4c
Groceries				
ACCRA Index, Groceries		98.70	4Q 92	4c
Babyfood, strained vegetables, lowest price	4-4.5 oz jar	0.33	4Q 92	4c
Bananas	lb	0.41	4Q 92	4c
Bread, white	24 oz	0.77	4Q 92	4c
Cheese, Kraft grated Parmesan	8-oz canister	3.36	4Q 92	4c
Chicken, fryer, whole	lb	0.65	4Q 92	4c
Cigarettes, Winston	carton	15.83	4Q 92	4c

Values are in dollars or fractions of dollars. In the column headed *Ref*, references are shown to sources. Each reference is followed by a letter. These refer to the geographical level for which data were reported: s=State, r=Region, and c=City or metro. The abbreviation *ex* is used to mean *except* or *excluding*; *exp* stands for *expenditures*. For other abbreviations and further explanations, please see the Introduction.

Moultrie, GA - continued

Item	Per	Value	Date	Ref.
Groceries				
Coffee, vacuum-packed	13-oz can	2.16	4Q 92	4c
Corn, frozen	10 oz	0.55	4Q 92	4c
Corn Flakes, Kellogg's or Post Toasties	18 oz	1.69	4Q 92	4c
Eggs, Grade A large	doz	0.84	4Q 92	4c
Ground beef or hamburger	lb	1.68	4Q 92	4c
Lettuce, iceberg	head	0.99	4Q 92	4c
Margarine, Blue Bonnet or Parkay cubes	lb	0.64	4Q 92	4c
Milk, whole	1/2 gal	1.45	4Q 92	4c
Orange juice, Minute Maid frozen	12-oz can	1.46	4Q 92	4c
Peaches	29-oz can	1.32	4Q 92	4c
Peas Sweet, Del Monte or Green Giant	15-17 oz can	0.61	4Q 92	4c
Potatoes, white or red	10-lb sack	2.52	4Q 92	4c
Sausage, Jimmy Dean, 100% pork	lb	2.29	4Q 92	4c
Shortening, vegetable, Crisco	3-lb can	2.19	4Q 92	4c
Soft drink, Coca Cola	2 liter	1.09	4Q 92	4c
Steak, T-bone	lb	5.41	4Q 92	4c
Sugar, cane or beet	4 lb	1.45	4Q 92	4c
Tomatoes, Hunt's or Del Monte	14.5-oz can	0.60	4Q 92	4c
Tuna, chunk, light	6.125-6.5 oz can	0.62	4Q 92	4c
Health Care				
ACCRA Index, Health Care		67.80	4Q 92	4c
Analgesic, Aspirin, Bayer, 325 mg tablets	100	3.66	4Q 92	4c
Dentist's fee, adult teeth cleaning and periodic oral exam	visit	32.33	4Q 92	4c
Doctor's fee, routine exam, established patient	visit	26.33	4Q 92	4c
Hospital care, semiprivate room	day	176.00	4Q 92	4c
Household Goods				
Appliance repair, home, service call, washing machine	min labor charge	26.65	4Q 92	4c
Laundry detergent, Tide Ultra, Bold, or Cheer	42 oz	2.79	4Q 92	4c
Tissues, facial, Kleenex brand	175-count box	1.11	4Q 92	4c
Housing				
ACCRA Index, Housing		73.40	4Q 92	4c
House, 1,800 sq ft, 8,000 sq ft lot, new, urban	total	82000	4Q 92	4c
House payment, principal and interest, 25% down payment	month	456	4Q 92	4c
Mortgage rate, incl. points & origination fee, 30-year fixed or adjustable rate	percent	8.11	4Q 92	4c
Rent, apartment, 2 bedrooms - 1-1/2 to 2 baths, unfurnished, 950 sq ft, water	month	352	4Q 92	4c
Personal Goods				
Shampoo, Alberto VO5	15 oz	0.98	4Q 92	4c
Toothpaste, Crest or Colgate	6-7 oz	1.46	4Q 92	4c
Personal Services				
Dry cleaning, man's 2-piece suit		4.42	4Q 92	4c
Haircare, woman's shampoo, trim and blow-dry		15.67	4Q 92	4c
Haircut, man's barbershop, no styling		5.00	4Q 92	4c
Restaurant Food				
Chicken, fried, thigh and drumstick		2.27	4Q 92	4c
Hamburger with cheese	1/4 lb	1.80	4Q 92	4c
Pizza, Pizza Hut or Pizza Inn, cheese, thin crust	12-13 in	8.39	4Q 92	4c

Moultrie, GA - continued

Item	Per	Value	Date	Ref.
Transportation				
ACCRA Index, Transportation		84.30	4Q 92	4c
Tire balance, computer or spin balance, front	wheel	5.00	4Q 92	4c
Utilities				
ACCRA Index, Utilities		106.70	4Q 92	4c
Electricity, all electric, 1,800 sq ft living area new home	month	116.28	4Q 92	4c

Mount Vernon, OH

Item	Per	Value	Date	Ref.
Composite ACCRA index		97.10	4Q 92	4c
Alcoholic Beverages				
Beer, Miller Lite or Budweiser, 12-oz containers	6 pack	3.90	4Q 92	4c
Liquor, J & B Scotch	750 ml	18.20	4Q 92	4c
Wine, Gallo Chablis blanc, 1.5 liter	bottle	4.19	4Q 92	4c
Clothing				
Jeans, man's denim		39.97	4Q 92	4c
Shirt, man's dress shirt		24.33	4Q 92	4c
Undervest, boy's size 10-14, cotton	3	3.66	4Q 92	4c
Communications				
Newspaper subscription, daily and Sunday home delivery, large-city	month	11.30	4Q 92	4c
Telephone bill, family of four	month	21.59	4Q 92	4c
Energy and Fuels				
Energy, combined forms, 1,800 sq ft heating area	month	125.29	4Q 92	4c
Energy, exc electricity, 1,800 sq ft heating area	month	49.08	4Q 92	4c
Gasoline, motor	gal	1.09	4Q 92	4c
Entertainment				
Bowling, evening rate	game	1.78	4Q 92	4c
Monopoly game, Parker Brothers', No. 9		10.90	4Q 92	4c
Movie	admission	4.75	4Q 92	4c
Tennis balls, yellow, Wilson or Penn, 3	can	2.65	4Q 92	4c
Goods and Services				
ACCRA Index, Miscellaneous Goods and Services		97.40	4Q 92	4c
Groceries				
ACCRA Index, Groceries		99.90	4Q 92	4c
Babyfood, strained vegetables, lowest price	4-4.5 oz jar	0.26	4Q 92	4c
Bananas	lb	0.47	4Q 92	4c
Bread, white	24 oz	0.54	4Q 92	4c
Cheese, Kraft grated Parmesan	8-oz canister	3.50	4Q 92	4c
Chicken, fryer, whole	lb	0.92	4Q 92	4c
Cigarettes, Winston	carton	17.14	4Q 92	4c
Coffee, vacuum-packed	13-oz can	2.04	4Q 92	4c
Corn, frozen	10 oz	0.69	4Q 92	4c
Corn Flakes, Kellogg's or Post Toasties	18 oz	2.07	4Q 92	4c
Eggs, Grade A large	doz	0.81	4Q 92	4c
Ground beef or hamburger	lb	1.52	4Q 92	4c
Lettuce, iceberg	head	0.99	4Q 92	4c
Margarine, Blue Bonnet or Parkay cubes	lb	0.82	4Q 92	4c
Milk, whole	1/2 gal	1.39	4Q 92	4c
Orange juice, Minute Maid frozen	12-oz can	1.36	4Q 92	4c
Peaches	29-oz can	1.55	4Q 92	4c
Peas Sweet, Del Monte or Green Giant	15-17 oz can	0.61	4Q 92	4c
Potatoes, white or red	10-lb sack	1.19	4Q 92	4c

Values are in dollars or fractions of dollars. In the column headed *Ref*, references are shown to sources. Each reference is followed by a letter. These refer to the geographical level for which data were reported: s=State, r=Region, and c=City or metro. The abbreviation *ex* is used to mean *except* or *excluding*; *exp* stands for *expenditures*. For other abbreviations and further explanations, please see the Introduction.

Mount Vernon, OH - continued

Item	Per	Value	Date	Ref.
Groceries				
Sausage, Jimmy Dean, 100% pork	lb	2.22	4Q 92	4c
Shortening, vegetable, Crisco	3-lb can	2.22	4Q 92	4c
Soft drink, Coca Cola	2 liter	1.12	4Q 92	4c
Steak, T-bone	lb	5.79	4Q 92	4c
Sugar, cane or beet	4 lb	1.11	4Q 92	4c
Tomatoes, Hunt's or Del Monte	14.5-oz can	0.84	4Q 92	4c
Tuna, chunk, light	6.125-6.5 oz can	0.71	4Q 92	4c
Health Care				
ACCRA Index, Health Care		92.70	4Q 92	4c
Analgesic, Aspirin, Bayer, 325 mg tablets	100	4.54	4Q 92	4c
Dentist's fee, adult teeth cleaning and periodic oral exam	visit	41.33	4Q 92	4c
Doctor's fee, routine exam, established patient	visit	35.33	4Q 92	4c
Hospital care, semiprivate room	day	307.00	4Q 92	4c
Household Goods				
Appliance repair, home, service call, washing machine	min labor charge	26.97	4Q 92	4c
Laundry detergent, Tide Ultra, Bold, or Cheer	42 oz	4.02	4Q 92	4c
Tissues, facial, Kleenex brand	175-count box	1.19	4Q 92	4c
Housing				
ACCRA Index, Housing		90.20	4Q 92	4c
House, 1,800 sq ft, 8,000 sq ft lot, new, urban	total	100500	4Q 92	4c
House payment, principal and interest, 25% down payment	month	567	4Q 92	4c
Mortgage rate, incl. points & origination fee, 30-year fixed or adjustable rate	per-cent	8.26	4Q 92	4c
Rent, apartment, 2 bedrooms - 1-1/2 to 2 baths, unfurnished, 950 sq ft, water	month	417	4Q 92	4c
Personal Goods				
Shampoo, Alberto VO5	15 oz	1.40	4Q 92	4c
Toothpaste, Crest or Colgate	6-7 oz	1.81	4Q 92	4c
Personal Services				
Dry cleaning, man's 2-piece suit		6.08	4Q 92	4c
Haircare, woman's shampoo, trim and blow-dry		14.00	4Q 92	4c
Haircut, man's barbershop, no styling		6.25	4Q 92	4c
Restaurant Food				
Chicken, fried, thigh and drumstick		1.98	4Q 92	4c
Hamburger with cheese	1/4 lb	1.69	4Q 92	4c
Pizza, Pizza Hut or Pizza Inn, cheese, thin crust	12-13 in	7.20	4Q 92	4c
Transportation				
ACCRA Index, Transportation		98.30	4Q 92	4c
Tire balance, computer or spin balance, front	wheel	6.50	4Q 92	4c
Utilities				
ACCRA Index, Utilities		114.40	4Q 92	4c
Electricity, partial electric and other energy, 1,800 sq ft living area new home	month	76.21	4Q 92	4c

Muncie, IN

Item	Per	Value	Date	Ref.
Composite ACCRA index		102.40	4Q 92	4c
Alcoholic Beverages				
Beer, Miller Lite or Budweiser, 12-oz containers	6 pack	3.92	4Q 92	4c

Muncie, IN - continued

Item	Per	Value	Date	Ref.
Alcoholic Beverages - continued				
Liquor, J & B Scotch	750 ml	17.36	4Q 92	4c
Wine, Gallo Chablis blanc, 1.5 liter	bottle	4.82	4Q 92	4c
Child Care				
Child care fee, average, center	hour	1.63	90	65r
Child care fee, average, nonregulated family day care	hour	1.83	90	65r
Child care fee, average, regulated family day care	hour	1.42	90	65r
Clothing				
Jeans, man's denim		27.74	4Q 92	4c
Shirt, man's dress shirt		23.37	4Q 92	4c
Undervest, boy's size 10-14, cotton	3	5.90	4Q 92	4c
Communications				
Long-distance telephone service, day, initial minute, 0-100 miles	min	0.18-0.45	91	12s
Long-distance telephone service, day, additional minute, 0-100 miles	min	0.10-0.30	91	12s
Long-distance telephone service, evenings/ weekends, 0-100 mi, initial minute	min	0.08-0.19	91	12s
Long-distance telephone service, evenings/ weekends, 0-100 mi, additional minute	min	0.04-0.13	91	12s
Newspaper subscription, daily and Sunday home delivery, large-city	month	10.87	4Q 92	4c
Telephone, flat rate	month	11.11	91	11c
Telephone bill, family of four	month	20.61	4Q 92	4c
Education				
Board, 4-yr private college/university	year	1714	91	22s
Board, 4-yr public college/university	year	1829	91	22s
Expenditures, local gov't, public elementary/secondary	pupil	5545	92	20s
Room, 4-year private college/university	year	1512	91	22s
Room, 4-year public college/university	year	1435	91	22s
Tuition, 2-year private college/university	year	6756	91	22s
Tuition, 2-year public college/university	year	1423	91	22s
Tuition, 4-year private college/university	year	8451	91	22s
Tuition, 4-year public college/university, in-state	year	2067	91	22s
Energy and Fuels				
Coal	mil Btu	1.46	90	64s
Energy	mil Btu	6.77	90	64s
Energy, combined forms, 1,800 sq ft heating area	month	101.71	4Q 92	4c
Energy, exc electricity, 1,800 sq ft heating area	month	43.71	4Q 92	4c
Energy exp/householder, 1-family unit	year	471	90	28r
Energy exp/householder, <1,000 sq ft heating area	year	430	90	28r
Energy exp/householder, 1,000-1,999 sq ft heating area	year	481	90	28r
Energy exp/householder, 2,000+ sq ft heating area	year	473	90	28r
Energy exp/householder, mobile home	year	430	90	28r
Energy exp/householder, multifamily	year	461	90	28r
Gas, cooking, 10 therms	month	13.97	92	56c
Gas, cooking, 30 therms	month	23.89	92	56c
Gas, cooking, 50 therms	month	33.82	92	56c
Gas, heating, winter, 100 therms	month	58.63	92	56c
Gas, heating, winter, average use	month	100.32	92	56c
Gas, natural	mil Btu	4.27	90	64s
Gas, natural	000 cu ft	5.46	91	46s
Gas, natural, exp	year	588	91	46s
Gasoline, motor	gal	1.09	4Q 92	4c
Gasoline, unleaded regular	mil Btu	8.74	90	64s
Entertainment				
Bowling, evening rate	game	1.75	4Q 92	4c
Miniature golf admission	adult	6.18	92	1r
Miniature golf admission	child	5.14	92	1r
Monopoly game, Parker Brothers', No. 9		12.96	4Q 92	4c

Values are in dollars or fractions of dollars. In the column headed *Ref*, references are shown to sources. Each reference is followed by a letter. These refer to the geographical level for which data were reported: s=State, r=Region, and c=City or metro. The abbreviation *ex* is used to mean *except* or *excluding*; *exp* stands for expenditures. For other abbreviations and further explanations, please see the Introduction.

Muncie, IN - continued

Item	Per	Value	Date	Ref.
Entertainment				
Movie	admission	5.00	4Q 92	4c
Tennis balls, yellow, Wilson or Penn, 3	can	2.72	4Q 92	4c
Waterpark admission	adult	11.00	92	1r
Waterpark admission	child	8.55	92	1r
Funerals				
Casket, 18-gauge steel, velvet interior		1926.72	91	24r
Cosmetology, hair care, etc.		97.64	91	24r
Embalming		249.14	91	24r
Facility use for ceremony		208.59	91	24r
Hearse, local		130.12	91	24r
Limousine, local		104.66	91	24r
Remains to funeral home, transfer		93.61	91	24r
Service charge, professional		724.62	91	24r
Vault, concrete, non-metallic liner		734.53	91	24r
Viewing facilities, use		236.06	91	24r
Goods and Services				
ACCRA Index, Miscellaneous Goods and Services		101.00	4Q 92	4c
Groceries				
ACCRA Index, Groceries		101.50	4Q 92	4c
Apples, Red Delicious	lb	0.77	4/93	16r
Babyfood, strained vegetables, lowest price	4-4.5 oz jar	0.31	4Q 92	4c
Bacon	lb	1.85	4/93	16r
Bananas	lb	0.27	4Q 92	4c
Bananas	lb	0.46	4/93	16r
Beef, stew, boneless	lb	2.53	4/93	16r
Bologna, all beef or mixed	lb	2.19	4/93	16r
Bread, white	24 oz	0.82	4Q 92	4c
Bread, white, pan	lb	0.78	4/93	16r
Butter	lb	1.50	4/93	16r
Cabbage	lb	0.40	4/93	16r
Carrots, short trimmed and topped	lb	0.45	4/93	16r
Cheese, Cheddar	lb	3.47	4/93	16r
Cheese, Kraft grated Parmesan	8-oz canister	3.23	4Q 92	4c
Chicken, fresh, whole	lb	0.84	4/93	16r
Chicken, fryer, whole	lb	0.91	4Q 92	4c
Chicken breast, bone-in	lb	1.94	4/93	16r
Chicken legs, bone-in	lb	1.02	4/93	16r
Chuck roast, graded and ungraded, ex USDA prime and choice	lb	2.43	4/93	16r
Chuck roast, USDA choice, bone-in	lb	2.11	4/93	16r
Chuck roast, USDA choice, boneless	lb	2.44	4/93	16r
Cigarettes, Winston	carton	16.47	4Q 92	4c
Coffee, 100% ground roast, all sizes	lb	2.47	4/93	16r
Coffee, vacuum-packed	13-oz can	2.05	4Q 92	4c
Cookies, chocolate chip	lb	2.73	4/93	16r
Corn, frozen	10 oz	0.70	4Q 92	4c
Corn Flakes, Kellogg's or Post Toasties	18 oz	2.04	4Q 92	4c
Eggs, Grade A large	doz	0.67	4Q 92	4c
Eggs, Grade A large	doz	0.93	4/93	16r
Flour, white, all purpose	lb	0.21	4/93	16r
Grapefruit	lb	0.45	4/93	16r
Grapes, Thompson Seedless	lb	1.46	4/93	16r
Ground beef, 100% beef	lb	1.63	4/93	16r
Ground beef, lean and extra lean	lb	2.08	4/93	16r
Ground beef or hamburger	lb	1.57	4Q 92	4c
Ground chuck, 100% beef	lb	1.94	4/93	16r
Ham, boneless, excluding canned	lb	2.21	4/93	16r
Honey, jar	8 oz	0.97-1.25	92	5r
Honey, jar	lb	1.25-2.25	92	5r
Honey, squeeze bear	12-oz	1.25-1.99	92	5r
Ice cream, prepackaged, bulk, regular	1/2 gal	2.41	4/93	16r
Lemons	lb	0.82	4/93	16r
Lettuce, iceberg	head	0.95	4Q 92	4c
Lettuce, iceberg	lb	0.83	4/93	16r
Margarine, Blue Bonnet or Parkay cubes	lb	0.67	4Q 92	4c

Muncie, IN - continued

Item	Per	Value	Date	Ref.
Groceries - continued				
Margarine, stick	lb	0.77	4/93	16r
Milk, whole	1/2 gal	1.41	4Q 92	4c
Orange juice, Minute Maid frozen	12-oz can	1.61	4Q 92	4c
Oranges, navel	lb	0.50	4/93	16r
Peaches	29-oz can	1.19	4Q 92	4c
Peanut butter, creamy, all sizes	lb	1.82	4/93	16r
Pears, Anjou	lb	0.85	4/93	16r
Peas Sweet, Del Monte or Green Giant	15-17 oz can	0.61	4Q 92	4c
Pork chops, center cut, bone-in	lb	3.17	4/93	16r
Potato chips	16 oz	2.68	4/93	16r
Potatoes, white	lb	0.26	4/93	16r
Potatoes, white or red	10-lb sack	1.78	4Q 92	4c
Round roast, graded & ungraded, ex USDA prime & choice	lb	2.88	4/93	16r
Round roast, USDA choice, boneless	lb	2.96	4/93	16r
Sausage, Jimmy Dean, 100% pork	lb	3.05	4Q 92	4c
Shortening, vegetable oil blends	lb	0.79	4/93	16r
Shortening, vegetable, Crisco	3-lb can	2.17	4Q 92	4c
Soft drink, Coca Cola	2 liter	1.29	4Q 92	4c
Spaghetti and macaroni	lb	0.76	4/93	16r
Steak, rib eye, USDA choice, boneless	lb	6.29	4/93	16r
Steak, round, USDA choice, boneless	lb	3.24	4/93	16r
Steak, sirloin, graded & ungraded, ex USDA prime & choice	lb	4.00	4/93	16r
Steak, sirloin, USDA choice, bone-in	lb	3.57	4/93	16r
Steak, sirloin, USDA choice, boneless	lb	4.17	4/93	16r
Steak, T-bone	lb	4.51	4Q 92	4c
Steak, T-bone, USDA choice, bone-in	lb	5.60	4/93	16r
Strawberries, dry pint	12 oz	0.90	4/93	16r
Sugar, cane or beet	4 lb	1.51	4Q 92	4c
Sugar, white	lb	0.36	4/93	16r
Sugar, white, 33-80 oz pk	lb	0.35	4/93	16r
Tomatoes, field grown	lb	0.99	4/93	16r
Tomatoes, Hunt's or Del Monte	14.5-oz can	0.89	4Q 92	4c
Tuna, chunk, light	6.125-6.5 oz can	0.59	4Q 92	4c
Tuna, chunk, light	lb	1.76	4/93	16r
Turkey, frozen, whole	lb	0.91	4/93	16r
Health Care				
ACCRA Index, Health Care		86.80	4Q 92	4c
Analgesic, Aspirin, Bayer, 325 mg tablets	100	5.48	4Q 92	4c
Childbirth, cesarean, hospital		4688	91	62r
Childbirth, cesarean, physician's fee		2053	91	62r
Childbirth, normal, hospital		2657	91	62r
Childbirth, normal, physician's fee		1492	91	62r
Dentist's fee, adult teeth cleaning and periodic oral exam	visit	38.22	4Q 92	4c
Doctor's fee, routine exam, established patient	visit	32.03	4Q 92	4c
Hospital care, semiprivate room	day	188.14	90	27c
Hospital care, semiprivate room	day	265.00	4Q 92	4c
Medical insurance premium, per employee, small group comprehensive	month	267.40	10/91	25c
Medical plan per employee	year	3443	91	45r
Mental health care, exp	capita	37.60-53.67	90	38s
Mental health care, exp, state mental health agency	capita	47.05	90	38s
Mental health care, hospital psychiatric services, non-Federal, exp	capita	22.14	88	38s
Mental health care, mental health organization, multiservice, exp	capita	10.33	88	38s
Mental health care, psychiatric hospitals, private, exp	capita	20.10	88	38s

Values are in dollars or fractions of dollars. In the column headed *Ref*, references are shown to sources. Each reference is followed by a letter. These refer to the geographical level for which data were reported: s=State, r=Region, and c=City or metro. The abbreviation *ex* is used to mean *except* or *excluding*; *exp* stands for *expenditures*. For other abbreviations and further explanations, please see the Introduction.

Muncie, IN - continued

Item	Per	Value	Date	Ref.
Health Care				
Mental health care, state and county mental hospitals, exp	capita	24.00	88	38s
Mental health care, VA medical centers, exp	capita	3.20	88	38s
Physician fee, family practice, first-visit		76.00	91	62r
Physician fee, family practice, revisit		33.00	91	62r
Physician fee, general practice, first-visit		61.00	91	62r
Physician fee, general practice, revisit		31.00	91	62r
Physician fee, general surgeon, first-visit		65.00	91	62r
Physician fee, general surgeon, revisit		35.00	91	62r
Physician fee, internal medicine, first-visit		91.00	91	62r
Physician fee, internal medicine, revisit		40.00	91	62r
Physician fee, median, neurosurgeon, first-visit		106.00	91	62r
Physician fee, median, nonsurgical specialist, first-visit		90.00	91	62r
Physician fee, median, orthopedic surgeon, first-visit		83.00	91	62r
Physician fee, median, surgical specialist, first-visit		61.00	91	62r
Physician fee, neurosurgeon, revisit		41.00	91	62r
Physician fee, nonsurgical specialist, revisit		40.00	91	62r
Physician fee, obstetrics/gynecology, first-visit		61.00	91	62r
Physician fee, obstetrics/gynecology, revisit		40.00	91	62r
Physician fee, orthopedic surgeon, revisit		41.00	91	62r
Physician fee, pediatrician, first-visit		46.00	91	62r
Physician fee, pediatrician, revisit		33.00	91	62r
Physician fee, surgical specialist, revisit		36.00	91	62r
Substance abuse, hospital ancillary charge	incident	1230	90	70s
Substance abuse, hospital physician charge	incident	410	90	70s
Substance abuse, hospital room and board	incident	5510	90	70s
Household Goods				
Appliance repair, home, service call, washing machine	min labor charge	30.98	4Q 92	4c
Laundry detergent, Tide Ultra, Bold, or Cheer	42 oz	3.71	4Q 92	4c
Tissues, facial, Kleenex brand	175-count box	1.17	4Q 92	4c
Housing				
ACCRA Index, Housing		108.70	4Q 92	4c
House, 1,800 sq ft, 8,000 sq ft lot, new, urban	total	117075	4Q 92	4c
House payment, principal and interest, 25% down payment	month	667	4Q 92	4c
Mortgage rate, incl. points & origination fee, 30-year fixed or adjustable rate	percent	8.37	4Q 92	4c
Rent, apartment, 2 bedrooms - 1-1/2 to 2 baths, unfurnished, 950 sq ft, water	month	540	4Q 92	4c
Rental unit, 1 bedroom	month	328	93	23c
Rental unit, 2 bedroom	month	387	93	23c
Rental unit, 3 bedroom	month	480	93	23c
Rental unit, 4 bedroom	month	538	93	23c
Rental unit, efficiency	month	272	93	23c
Insurance and Pensions				
Auto insurance, private passenger	year	548.99	91	63s
Personal Goods				
Shampoo, Alberto VO5	15 oz	1.34	4Q 92	4c
Toothpaste, Crest or Colgate	6-7 oz	2.26	4Q 92	4c
Personal Services				
Dry cleaning, man's 2-piece suit		5.90	4Q 92	4c
Haircare, woman's shampoo, trim and blow-dry		19.00	4Q 92	4c
Haircut, man's barbershop, no styling		7.12	4Q 92	4c

Muncie, IN - continued

Item	Per	Value	Date	Ref.
Restaurant Food				
Chicken, fried, thigh and drumstick		1.78	4Q 92	4c
Hamburger with cheese	1/4 lb	1.69	4Q 92	4c
Pizza, Pizza Hut or Pizza Inn, cheese, thin crust	12-13 in	7.50	4Q 92	4c
Taxes				
Tax, cigarette	pack	15.50	91	77s
Tax, gasoline	gal	15	91	77s
Taxes, state	capita	1102	91	77s
Transportation				
ACCRA Index, Transportation		105.60	4Q 92	4c
Bus fare	one-way	0.40	3/93	2c
Driver's license fee		6.00	12/90	43s
Tire balance, computer or spin balance, front	wheel	7.44	4Q 92	4c
Utilities				
ACCRA Index, Utilities		94.40	4Q 92	4c
Electricity	mil Btu	15.75	90	64s
Electricity, partial electric and other energy, 1,800 sq ft living area new home	month	58.00	4Q 92	4c

Murfreesboro-Smyrna, TN

Item	Per	Value	Date	Ref.
Composite ACCRA index		94.40	4Q 92	4c
Alcoholic Beverages				
Beer, Miller Lite or Budweiser, 12-oz containers	6 pack	3.83	4Q 92	4c
Liquor, J & B Scotch	750 ml	18.48	4Q 92	4c
Wine, Gallo Chablis blanc, 1.5 liter	bottle	5.85	4Q 92	4c
Clothing				
Jeans, man's denim		32.18	4Q 92	4c
Shirt, man's dress shirt		25.60	4Q 92	4c
Undervest, boy's size 10-14, cotton	3	3.34	4Q 92	4c
Communications				
Newspaper subscription, daily and Sunday home delivery, large-city	month	14.13	4Q 92	4c
Telephone bill, family of four	month	19.65	4Q 92	4c
Energy and Fuels				
Energy, combined forms, 1,800 sq ft heating area	month	101.12	4Q 92	4c
Energy, exc electricity, 1,800 sq ft heating area	month	40.61	4Q 92	4c
Gas, cooking, winter, 10 therms	month	10.70	92	56c
Gas, cooking, winter, 30 therms	month	22.09	92	56c
Gas, cooking, winter, 50 therms	month	33.48	92	56c
Gas, heating, winter, 100 therms	month	61.95	92	56c
Gasoline, motor	gal	1.07	4Q 92	4c
Entertainment				
Bowling, evening rate	game	2.25	4Q 92	4c
Monopoly game, Parker Brothers', No. 9		10.23	4Q 92	4c
Movie	admission	5.00	4Q 92	4c
Tennis balls, yellow, Wilson or Penn, 3	can	2.59	4Q 92	4c
Goods and Services				
ACCRA Index, Miscellaneous Goods and Services		99.30	4Q 92	4c
Groceries				
ACCRA Index, Groceries		97.60	4Q 92	4c
Babyfood, strained vegetables, lowest price	4-4.5 oz jar	0.29	4Q 92	4c
Bananas	lb	0.37	4Q 92	4c
Bread, white	24 oz	0.86	4Q 92	4c
Cheese, Kraft grated Parmesan	8-oz canister	3.27	4Q 92	4c
Chicken, fryer, whole	lb	0.67	4Q 92	4c

Values are in dollars or fractions of dollars. In the column headed *Ref*, references are shown to sources. Each reference is followed by a letter. These refer to the geographical level for which data were reported: s=State, r=Region, and c=City or metro. The abbreviation *ex* is used to mean *except* or *excluding*; *exp* stands for expenditures. For other abbreviations and further explanations, please see the Introduction.

Murfreesboro-Smyrna, TN - continued

Item	Per	Value	Date	Ref.
Groceries				
Cigarettes, Winston	carton	15.84	4Q 92	4c
Coffee, vacuum-packed	13-oz can	2.16	4Q 92	4c
Corn, frozen	10 oz	0.68	4Q 92	4c
Corn Flakes, Kellogg's or Post Toasties	18 oz	1.81	4Q 92	4c
Eggs, Grade A large	doz	0.77	4Q 92	4c
Ground beef or hamburger	lb	1.61	4Q 92	4c
Lettuce, iceberg	head	0.99	4Q 92	4c
Margarine, Blue Bonnet or Parkay cubes	lb	0.51	4Q 92	4c
Milk, whole	1/2 gal	1.25	4Q 92	4c
Orange juice, Minute Maid frozen	12-oz can	1.39	4Q 92	4c
Peaches	29-oz can	1.31	4Q 92	4c
Peas Sweet, Del Monte or Green Giant	15-17 oz can	0.50	4Q 92	4c
Potatoes, white or red	10-lb sack	2.89	4Q 92	4c
Sausage, Jimmy Dean, 100% pork	lb	2.33	4Q 92	4c
Shortening, vegetable, Crisco	3-lb can	2.03	4Q 92	4c
Soft drink, Coca Cola	2 liter	1.25	4Q 92	4c
Steak, T-bone	lb	5.11	4Q 92	4c
Sugar, cane or beet	4 lb	1.48	4Q 92	4c
Tomatoes, Hunt's or Del Monte	14.5-oz can	0.58	4Q 92	4c
Tuna, chunk, light	6.125-6.5 oz can	0.57	4Q 92	4c
Health Care				
ACCRA Index, Health Care		85.60	4Q 92	4c
Analgesic, Aspirin, Bayer, 325 mg tablets	100	4.48	4Q 92	4c
Dentist's fee, adult teeth cleaning and periodic oral exam	visit	40.50	4Q 92	4c
Doctor's fee, routine exam, established patient	visit	33.17	4Q 92	4c
Hospital care, semiprivate room	day	232.00	4Q 92	4c
Household Goods				
Appliance repair, home, service call, washing machine	min labor charge	32.48	4Q 92	4c
Laundry detergent, Tide Ultra, Bold, or Cheer	42 oz	3.35	4Q 92	4c
Tissues, facial, Kleenex brand	175-count box	1.11	4Q 92	4c
Housing				
ACCRA Index, Housing		87.70	4Q 92	4c
House, 1,800 sq ft, 8,000 sq ft lot, new, urban	total	95491	4Q 92	4c
House payment, principal and interest, 25% down payment	month	530	4Q 92	4c
Mortgage rate, incl. points & origination fee, 30-year fixed or adjustable rate	percent	8.09	4Q 92	4c
Rent, apartment, 2 bedrooms - 1-1/2 to 2 baths, unfurnished, 950 sq ft, water	month	453	4Q 92	4c
Personal Goods				
Shampoo, Alberto VO5	15 oz	1.22	4Q 92	4c
Toothpaste, Crest or Colgate	6-7 oz	1.67	4Q 92	4c
Personal Services				
Dry cleaning, man's 2-piece suit		5.64	4Q 92	4c
Haircare, woman's shampoo, trim and blow-dry		16.33	4Q 92	4c
Haircut, man's barbershop, no styling		7.00	4Q 92	4c
Restaurant Food				
Chicken, fried, thigh and drumstick		1.91	4Q 92	4c
Hamburger with cheese	1/4 lb	1.83	4Q 92	4c
Pizza, Pizza Hut or Pizza Inn, cheese, thin crust	12-13 in	7.99	4Q 92	4c

Murfreesboro-Smyrna, TN - continued

Item	Per	Value	Date	Ref.
Transportation				
ACCRA Index, Transportation		97.30	4Q 92	4c
Tire balance, computer or spin balance, front	wheel	6.49	4Q 92	4c
Utilities				
ACCRA Index, Utilities		93.40	4Q 92	4c
Electricity, partial electric and other energy, 1,800 sq ft living area new home	month	60.51	4Q 92	4c

Murray, KY

Item	Per	Value	Date	Ref.
Composite ACCRA index		86.80	4Q 92	4c
Alcoholic Beverages				
Beer, Miller Lite or Budweiser, 12-oz containers	6 pack	3.78	4Q 92	4c
Liquor, J & B Scotch	750 ml	16.21	4Q 92	4c
Wine, Gallo Chablis blanc, 1.5 liter	bottle	6.72	4Q 92	4c
Clothing				
Jeans, man's denim		31.99	4Q 92	4c
Shirt, man's dress shirt		22.00	4Q 92	4c
Undervest, boy's size 10-14, cotton	3	5.49	4Q 92	4c
Communications				
Newspaper subscription, daily and Sunday home delivery, large-city	month	9.90	4Q 92	4c
Telephone, flat rate	month	12.02	91	11c
Telephone bill, family of four	month	22.59	4Q 92	4c
Energy and Fuels				
Energy, combined forms, 1,800 sq ft heating area	month	86.32	4Q 92	4c
Energy, exc electricity, 1,800 sq ft heating area	month	29.83	4Q 92	4c
Gasoline, motor	gal	1.06	4Q 92	4c
Entertainment				
Bowling, evening rate	game	1.75	4Q 92	4c
Monopoly game, Parker Brothers', No. 9		10.98	4Q 92	4c
Movie	admission	4.50	4Q 92	4c
Tennis balls, yellow, Wilson or Penn, 3	can	1.98	4Q 92	4c
Goods and Services				
ACCRA Index, Miscellaneous Goods and Services		98.60	4Q 92	4c
Groceries				
ACCRA Index, Groceries		97.40	4Q 92	4c
Babyfood, strained vegetables, lowest price	4-4.5 oz jar	0.34	4Q 92	4c
Bananas	lb	0.52	4Q 92	4c
Bread, white	24 oz	0.70	4Q 92	4c
Cheese, Kraft grated Parmesan	8-oz canister	3.46	4Q 92	4c
Chicken, fryer, whole	lb	0.76	4Q 92	4c
Cigarettes, Winston	carton	15.17	4Q 92	4c
Coffee, vacuum-packed	13-oz can	1.92	4Q 92	4c
Corn, frozen	10 oz	0.76	4Q 92	4c
Corn Flakes, Kellogg's or Post Toasties	18 oz	2.06	4Q 92	4c
Eggs, Grade A large	doz	0.77	4Q 92	4c
Ground beef or hamburger	lb	1.22	4Q 92	4c
Lettuce, iceberg	head	0.99	4Q 92	4c
Margarine, Blue Bonnet or Parkay cubes	lb	0.58	4Q 92	4c
Milk, whole	1/2 gal	1.43	4Q 92	4c
Orange juice, Minute Maid frozen	12-oz can	1.52	4Q 92	4c
Peaches	29-oz can	1.28	4Q 92	4c
Peas Sweet, Del Monte or Green Giant	15-17 oz can	0.60	4Q 92	4c

Values are in dollars or fractions of dollars. In the column headed *Ref*, references are shown to sources. Each reference is followed by a letter. These refer to the geographical level for which data were reported: s=State, r=Region, and c=City or metro. The abbreviation *ex* is used to mean *except* or *excluding*; *exp* stands for expenditures. For other abbreviations and further explanations, please see the Introduction.

457

Murray, KY - continued

Item	Per	Value	Date	Ref.
Groceries				
Potatoes, white or red	10-lb sack	1.92	4Q 92	4c
Sausage, Jimmy Dean, 100% pork	lb	2.19	4Q 92	4c
Shortening, vegetable, Crisco	3-lb can	2.26	4Q 92	4c
Soft drink, Coca Cola	2 liter	1.14	4Q 92	4c
Steak, T-bone	lb	5.82	4Q 92	4c
Sugar, cane or beet	4 lb	1.47	4Q 92	4c
Tomatoes, Hunt's or Del Monte	14.5-oz can	0.76	4Q 92	4c
Tuna, chunk, light	6.125-6.5 oz can	0.53	4Q 92	4c
Health Care				
ACCRA Index, Health Care		86.50	4Q 92	4c
Analgesic, Aspirin, Bayer, 325 mg tablets	100	5.82	4Q 92	4c
Dentist's fee, adult teeth cleaning and periodic oral exam	visit	39.00	4Q 92	4c
Doctor's fee, routine exam, established patient	visit	32.40	4Q 92	4c
Hospital care, semiprivate room	day	230.00	4Q 92	4c
Household Goods				
Appliance repair, home, service call, washing machine	min labor charge	28.75	4Q 92	4c
Laundry detergent, Tide Ultra, Bold, or Cheer	42 oz	3.28	4Q 92	4c
Tissues, facial, Kleenex brand	175-count box	1.20	4Q 92	4c
Housing				
ACCRA Index, Housing		70.40	4Q 92	4c
House, 1,800 sq ft, 8,000 sq ft lot, new, urban	total	78700	4Q 92	4c
House payment, principal and interest, 25% down payment	month	437	4Q 92	4c
Mortgage rate, incl. points & origination fee, 30-year fixed or adjustable rate	percent	8.09	4Q 92	4c
Personal Goods				
Shampoo, Alberto VO5	15 oz	1.61	4Q 92	4c
Toothpaste, Crest or Colgate	6-7 oz	1.59	4Q 92	4c
Personal Services				
Dry cleaning, man's 2-piece suit		5.28	4Q 92	4c
Haircare, woman's shampoo, trim and blow-dry		14.25	4Q 92	4c
Haircut, man's barbershop, no styling		6.75	4Q 92	4c
Restaurant Food				
Chicken, fried, thigh and drumstick		2.14	4Q 92	4c
Hamburger with cheese	1/4 lb	1.89	4Q 92	4c
Pizza, Pizza Hut or Pizza Inn, cheese, thin crust	12-13 in	8.49	4Q 92	4c
Transportation				
ACCRA Index, Transportation		81.30	4Q 92	4c
Tire balance, computer or spin balance, front	wheel	4.50	4Q 92	4c
Utilities				
ACCRA Index, Utilities		82.80	4Q 92	4c
Electricity, partial electric and other energy, 1,800 sq ft living area new home	month	56.49	4Q 92	4c

Muskegon, MI

Item	Per	Value	Date	Ref.
Child Care				
Child care fee, average, center	hour	1.63	90	65r
Child care fee, average, nonregulated family day care	hour	1.83	90	65r

Muskegon, MI - continued

Item	Per	Value	Date	Ref.
Child Care - continued				
Child care fee, average, regulated family day care	hour	1.42	90	65r
Communications				
Long-distance telephone service, day, initial minute, 0-100 miles	min	0.14-0.36	91	12s
Long-distance telephone service, day, additional minute, 0-100 miles	min	0.14-0.36	91	12s
Long-distance telephone service, evenings/weekends, 0-100 mi, initial minute	min	0.07-0.19	91	12s
Long-distance telephone service, evenings/weekends, 0-100 mi, additional minute	min	0.04-0.14	91	12s
Education				
Board, 4-yr private college/university	year	1698	91	22s
Board, 4-yr public college/university	year	1962	91	22s
Expenditures, local gov't, public elementary/secondary	pupil	5671	92	20s
Room, 4-year private college/university	year	1440	91	22s
Room, 4-year public college/university	year	1687	91	22s
Tuition, 2-year private college/university	year	4749	91	22s
Tuition, 2-year public college/university	year	1124	91	22s
Tuition, 4-year private college/university	year	6885	91	22s
Tuition, 4-year public college/university, in-state	year	2635	91	22s
Energy and Fuels				
Coal	mil Btu	1.63	90	64s
Energy	mil Btu	8.17	90	64s
Energy exp/householder, 1-family unit	year	471	90	28r
Energy exp/householder, <1,000 sq ft heating area	year	430	90	28r
Energy exp/householder, 1,000-1,999 sq ft heating area	year	481	90	28r
Energy exp/householder, 2,000+ sq ft heating area	year	473	90	28r
Energy exp/householder, mobile home	year	430	90	28r
Energy exp/householder, multifamily	year	461	90	28r
Gas, natural	mil Btu	4.36	90	64s
Gas, natural	000 cu ft	5.07	91	46s
Gas, natural, exp	year	655	91	46s
Gasoline, unleaded regular	mil Btu	8.78	90	64s
Entertainment				
Miniature golf admission	adult	6.18	92	1r
Miniature golf admission	child	5.14	92	1r
Waterpark admission	adult	11.00	92	1r
Waterpark admission	child	8.55	92	1r
Funerals				
Casket, 18-gauge steel, velvet interior		1926.72	91	24r
Cosmetology, hair care, etc.		97.64	91	24r
Embalming		249.14	91	24r
Facility use for ceremony		208.59	91	24r
Hearse, local		130.12	91	24r
Limousine, local		104.66	91	24r
Remains to funeral home, transfer		93.61	91	24r
Service charge, professional		724.62	91	24r
Vault, concrete, non-metallic liner		734.53	91	24r
Viewing facilities, use		236.06	91	24r
Groceries				
Apples, Red Delicious	lb	0.77	4/93	16r
Bacon	lb	1.85	4/93	16r
Bananas	lb	0.46	4/93	16r
Beef, stew, boneless	lb	2.53	4/93	16r
Bologna, all beef or mixed	lb	2.19	4/93	16r
Bread, white, pan	lb	0.78	4/93	16r
Butter	lb	1.50	4/93	16r
Cabbage	lb	0.40	4/93	16r
Carrots, short trimmed and topped	lb	0.45	4/93	16r
Cheese, Cheddar	lb	3.47	4/93	16r
Chicken, fresh, whole	lb	0.84	4/93	16r
Chicken breast, bone-in	lb	1.94	4/93	16r

Values are in dollars or fractions of dollars. In the column headed *Ref*, references are shown to sources. Each reference is followed by a letter. These refer to the geographical level for which data were reported: s=State, r=Region, and c=City or metro. The abbreviation *ex* is used to mean *except* or *excluding*; *exp* stands for expenditures. For other abbreviations and further explanations, please see the Introduction.

Muskegon, MI - continued

Item	Per	Value	Date	Ref.
Groceries				
Chicken legs, bone-in	lb	1.02	4/93	16r
Chuck roast, graded and ungraded, ex USDA prime and choice	lb	2.43	4/93	16r
Chuck roast, USDA choice, bone-in	lb	2.11	4/93	16r
Chuck roast, USDA choice, boneless	lb	2.44	4/93	16r
Coffee, 100% ground roast, all sizes	lb	2.47	4/93	16r
Cookies, chocolate chip	lb	2.73	4/93	16r
Eggs, Grade A large	doz	0.93	4/93	16r
Flour, white, all purpose	lb	0.21	4/93	16r
Grapefruit	lb	0.45	4/93	16r
Grapes, Thompson Seedless	lb	1.46	4/93	16r
Ground beef, 100% beef	lb	1.63	4/93	16r
Ground beef, lean and extra lean	lb	2.08	4/93	16r
Ground chuck, 100% beef	lb	1.94	4/93	16r
Ham, boneless, excluding canned	lb	2.21	4/93	16r
Honey, jar	8 oz	0.97-1.25	92	5r
Honey, jar	lb	1.25-2.25	92	5r
Honey, squeeze bear	12-oz	1.25-1.99	92	5r
Ice cream, prepackaged, bulk, regular	1/2 gal	2.41	4/93	16r
Lemons	lb	0.82	4/93	16r
Lettuce, iceberg	lb	0.83	4/93	16r
Margarine, stick	lb	0.77	4/93	16r
Oranges, navel	lb	0.50	4/93	16r
Peanut butter, creamy, all sizes	lb	1.82	4/93	16r
Pears, Anjou	lb	0.85	4/93	16r
Pork chops, center cut, bone-in	lb	3.17	4/93	16r
Potato chips	16 oz	2.68	4/93	16r
Potatoes, white	lb	0.26	4/93	16r
Round roast, graded & ungraded, ex USDA prime & choice	lb	2.88	4/93	16r
Round roast, USDA choice, boneless	lb	2.96	4/93	16r
Shortening, vegetable oil blends	lb	0.79	4/93	16r
Spaghetti and macaroni	lb	0.76	4/93	16r
Steak, rib eye, USDA choice, boneless	lb	6.29	4/93	16r
Steak, round, USDA choice, boneless	lb	3.24	4/93	16r
Steak, sirloin, graded & ungraded, ex USDA prime & choice	lb	4.00	4/93	16r
Steak, sirloin, USDA choice, bone-in	lb	3.57	4/93	16r
Steak, sirloin, USDA choice, boneless	lb	4.17	4/93	16r
Steak, T-bone, USDA choice, bone-in	lb	5.60	4/93	16r
Strawberries, dry pint	12 oz	0.90	4/93	16r
Sugar, white	lb	0.36	4/93	16r
Sugar, white, 33-80 oz pk	lb	0.35	4/93	16r
Tomatoes, field grown	lb	0.99	4/93	16r
Tuna, chunk, light	lb	1.76	4/93	16r
Turkey, frozen, whole	lb	0.91	4/93	16r
Health Care				
Childbirth, cesarean, hospital		4688	91	62r
Childbirth, cesarean, physician's fee		2053	91	62r
Childbirth, normal, hospital		2657	91	62r
Childbirth, normal, physician's fee		1492	91	62r
Medical plan per employee	year	3443	91	45r
Mental health care, exp	capita	53.68-118.35	90	38s
Mental health care, exp, state mental health agency	capita	73.73	90	38s
Mental health care, hospital psychiatric services, non-Federal, exp	capita	22.52	88	38s
Mental health care, mental health organization, multiservice, exp	capita	42.68	88	38s
Mental health care, psychiatric hospitals, private, exp	capita	10.80	88	38s
Mental health care, psychiatric out-patient clinics, freestanding, exp	capita	3.47	88	38s
Mental health care, psychiatric partial-care organizations, freestanding, exp	capita	0.73	88	38s
Mental health care, state and county mental hospitals, exp	capita	36.77	88	38s
Mental health care, VA medical centers, exp	capita	4.03	88	38s
Physician fee, family practice, first-visit		76.00	91	62r
Physician fee, family practice, revisit		33.00	91	62r
Physician fee, general practice, first-visit		61.00	91	62r

Muskegon, MI - continued

Item	Per	Value	Date	Ref.
Health Care - continued				
Physician fee, general practice, revisit		31.00	91	62r
Physician fee, general surgeon, first-visit		65.00	91	62r
Physician fee, general surgeon, revisit		35.00	91	62r
Physician fee, internal medicine, first-visit		91.00	91	62r
Physician fee, internal medicine, revisit		40.00	91	62r
Physician fee, median, neurosurgeon, first-visit		106.00	91	62r
Physician fee, median, nonsurgical specialist, first-visit		90.00	91	62r
Physician fee, median, orthopedic surgeon, first-visit		83.00	91	62r
Physician fee, median, surgical specialist, first-visit		61.00	91	62r
Physician fee, neurosurgeon, revisit		41.00	91	62r
Physician fee, nonsurgical specialist, revisit		40.00	91	62r
Physician fee, obstetrics/gynecology, first-visit		61.00	91	62r
Physician fee, obstetrics/gynecology, revisit		40.00	91	62r
Physician fee, orthopedic surgeon, revisit		41.00	91	62r
Physician fee, pediatrician, first-visit		46.00	91	62r
Physician fee, pediatrician, revisit		33.00	91	62r
Physician fee, surgical specialist, revisit		36.00	91	62r
Substance abuse, hospital ancillary charge	incident	1480	90	70s
Substance abuse, hospital physician charge	incident	250	90	70s
Substance abuse, hospital room and board	incident	4070	90	70s
Insurance and Pensions				
Auto insurance, private passenger	year	716.78	91	63s
Taxes				
Tax, cigarette	pack	25	91	77s
Tax, gasoline	gal	15	91	77s
Taxes, state	capita	1185	91	77s
Transportation				
Driver's license fee		12.00	12/90	43s
Vehicle registration and license plate	year	14.00-200.00	93	40s
Utilities				
Electricity	mil Btu	20.85	90	64s

Myrtle Beach, SC

Item	Per	Value	Date	Ref.
Composite ACCRA index		94.30	4Q 92	4c
Alcoholic Beverages				
Beer, Miller Lite or Budweiser, 12-oz containers	6 pack	3.82	4Q 92	4c
Liquor, J & B Scotch	750 ml	17.49	4Q 92	4c
Wine, Gallo Chablis blanc, 1.5 liter	bottle	5.49	4Q 92	4c
Clothing				
Jeans, man's denim		24.79	4Q 92	4c
Shirt, man's dress shirt		24.60	4Q 92	4c
Undervest, boy's size 10-14, cotton	3	3.37	4Q 92	4c
Communications				
Newspaper subscription, daily and Sunday home delivery, large-city	month	8.17	4Q 92	4c
Telephone bill, family of four	month	17.97	4Q 92	4c
Energy and Fuels				
Energy, combined forms, 1,800 sq ft heating area	month	94.78	4Q 92	4c
Gasoline, motor	gal	1.16	4Q 92	4c
Entertainment				
Bowling, evening rate	game	2.25	4Q 92	4c
Monopoly game, Parker Brothers', No. 9		9.86	4Q 92	4c
Movie	admission	5.50	4Q 92	4c
Tennis balls, yellow, Wilson or Penn, 3	can	2.00	4Q 92	4c

Values are in dollars or fractions of dollars. In the column headed *Ref*, references are shown to sources. Each reference is followed by a letter. These refer to the geographical level for which data were reported: s = State, r = Region, and c = City or metro. The abbreviation *ex* is used to mean *except* or *excluding*; *exp* stands for expenditures. For other abbreviations and further explanations, please see the Introduction.

Myrtle Beach, SC - continued

Item	Per	Value	Date	Ref.
Goods and Services				
ACCRA Index, Miscellaneous Goods and Services		94.10	4Q 92	4c
Groceries				
ACCRA Index, Groceries		94.40	4Q 92	4c
Babyfood, strained vegetables, lowest price	4-4.5 oz jar	0.30	4Q 92	4c
Bananas	lb	0.46	4Q 92	4c
Bread, white	24 oz	0.67	4Q 92	4c
Cheese, Kraft grated Parmesan	8-oz canister	3.12	4Q 92	4c
Chicken, fryer, whole	lb	0.64	4Q 92	4c
Cigarettes, Winston	carton	15.44	4Q 92	4c
Coffee, vacuum-packed	13-oz can	1.96	4Q 92	4c
Corn, frozen	10 oz	0.54	4Q 92	4c
Corn Flakes, Kellogg's or Post Toasties	18 oz	1.76	4Q 92	4c
Eggs, Grade A large	doz	0.87	4Q 92	4c
Ground beef or hamburger	lb	1.66	4Q 92	4c
Lettuce, iceberg	head	0.99	4Q 92	4c
Margarine, Blue Bonnet or Parkay cubes	lb	0.48	4Q 92	4c
Milk, whole	1/2 gal	1.40	4Q 92	4c
Orange juice, Minute Maid frozen	12-oz can	1.18	4Q 92	4c
Peaches	29-oz can	1.32	4Q 92	4c
Peas Sweet, Del Monte or Green Giant	15-17 oz can	0.52	4Q 92	4c
Potatoes, white or red	10-lb sack	2.19	4Q 92	4c
Sausage, Jimmy Dean, 100% pork	lb	2.14	4Q 92	4c
Shortening, vegetable, Crisco	3-lb can	2.02	4Q 92	4c
Soft drink, Coca Cola	2 liter	1.23	4Q 92	4c
Steak, T-bone	lb	5.88	4Q 92	4c
Sugar, cane or beet	4 lb	1.42	4Q 92	4c
Tomatoes, Hunt's or Del Monte	14.5-oz can	0.52	4Q 92	4c
Tuna, chunk, light	6.125-6.5 oz can	0.54	4Q 92	4c
Health Care				
ACCRA Index, Health Care		89.80	4Q 92	4c
Analgesic, Aspirin, Bayer, 325 mg tablets	100	4.28	4Q 92	4c
Dentist's fee, adult teeth cleaning and periodic oral exam	visit	41.88	4Q 92	4c
Doctor's fee, routine exam, established patient	visit	30.60	4Q 92	4c
Hospital care, semiprivate room	day	338.00	4Q 92	4c
Household Goods				
Appliance repair, home, service call, washing machine	min labor charge	30.00	4Q 92	4c
Laundry detergent, Tide Ultra, Bold, or Cheer	42 oz	2.90	4Q 92	4c
Tissues, facial, Kleenex brand	175-count box	0.93	4Q 92	4c
Housing				
ACCRA Index, Housing		96.50	4Q 92	4c
House, 1,800 sq ft, 8,000 sq ft lot, new, urban	total	109920	4Q 92	4c
House payment, principal and interest, 25% down payment	month	617	4Q 92	4c
Mortgage rate, incl. points & origination fee, 30-year fixed or adjustable rate	percent	8.21	4Q 92	4c
Rent, apartment, 2 bedrooms - 1-1/2 to 2 baths, unfurnished, 950 sq ft, water	month	422	4Q 92	4c

Myrtle Beach, SC - continued

Item	Per	Value	Date	Ref.
Personal Goods				
Shampoo, Alberto VO5	15 oz	0.96	4Q 92	4c
Toothpaste, Crest or Colgate	6-7 oz	1.81	4Q 92	4c
Personal Services				
Dry cleaning, man's 2-piece suit		5.68	4Q 92	4c
Haircare, woman's shampoo, trim and blow-dry		19.29	4Q 92	4c
Haircut, man's barbershop, no styling		6.75	4Q 92	4c
Restaurant Food				
Chicken, fried, thigh and drumstick		2.19	4Q 92	4c
Hamburger with cheese	1/4 lb	1.94	4Q 92	4c
Pizza, Pizza Hut or Pizza Inn, cheese, thin crust	12-13 in	7.99	4Q 92	4c
Transportation				
ACCRA Index, Transportation		97.40	4Q 92	4c
Tire balance, computer or spin balance, front	wheel	6.00	4Q 92	4c
Utilities				
ACCRA Index, Utilities		87.40	4Q 92	4c
Electricity, all electric, 1,800 sq ft living area new home	month	94.78	4Q 92	4c

Naples, FL

Item	Per	Value	Date	Ref.
Child Care				
Child care fee, average, center	hour	1.29	90	65r
Child care fee, average, nonregulated family day care	hour	0.89	90	65r
Child care fee, average, regulated family day care	hour	1.32	90	65r
Communications				
Long-distance telephone service, day, initial minute, 0-100 miles	min	0.15-0.20	91	12s
Long-distance telephone service, day, additional minute, 0-100 miles	min	0.08-0.20	91	12s
Long-distance telephone service, evenings/weekends, 0-100 mi, initial minute	min	0.09-0.12	91	12s
Long-distance telephone service, evenings/weekends, 0-100 mi, additional minute	min	0.05-0.12	91	12s
Education				
Board, 4-yr private college/university	year	1924	91	22s
Board, 4-yr public college/university	year	1955	91	22s
Expenditures, local gov't, public elementary/secondary	pupil	5235	92	20s
Room, 4-year private college/university	year	1904	91	22s
Room, 4-year public college/university	year	1510	91	22s
Tuition, 2-year private college/university	year	4751	91	22s
Tuition, 2-year public college/university	year	788	91	22s
Tuition, 4-year private college/university	year	7992	91	22s
Tuition, 4-year public college/university, in-state	year	1337	91	22s
Energy and Fuels				
Coal	mil Btu	1.85	90	64s
Energy	mil Btu	10.58	90	64s
Energy exp/householder, 1-family unit	year	487	90	28r
Energy exp/householder, <1,000 sq ft heating area	year	393	90	28r
Energy exp/householder, 1,000-1,999 sq ft heating area	year	442	90	28r
Energy exp/householder, 2,000+ sq ft heating area	year	577	90	28r
Energy exp/householder, mobile home	year	366	90	28r
Energy exp/householder, multifamily	year	382	90	28r
Gas, natural	mil Btu	3.21	90	64s
Gas, natural	000 cu ft	8.98	91	46s
Gas, natural, exp	year	248	91	46s
Gasoline, unleaded regular	mil Btu	8.85	90	64s

Values are in dollars or fractions of dollars. In the column headed *Ref*, references are shown to sources. Each reference is followed by a letter. These refer to the geographical level for which data were reported: s=State, r=Region, and c=City or metro. The abbreviation *ex* is used to mean *except* or *excluding*; *exp* stands for expenditures. For other abbreviations and further explanations, please see the Introduction.

Naples, FL - continued

Item	Per	Value	Date	Ref.
Entertainment				
Miniature golf admission	adult	6.18	92	1r
Miniature golf admission	child	5.14	92	1r
Waterpark admission	adult	11.00	92	1r
Waterpark admission	child	8.55	92	1r
Funerals				
Casket, 18-gauge steel, velvet interior		2029.08	91	24r
Cosmetology, hair care, etc.		75.10	91	24r
Embalming		249.24	91	24r
Facility use for ceremony		162.27	91	24r
Hearse, local		114.04	91	24r
Limousine, local		88.57	91	24r
Remains to funeral home, transfer		92.61	91	24r
Service charge, professional		682.42	91	24r
Vault, concrete, non-metallic liner		798.70	91	24r
Viewing facilities, use		163.86	91	24r
Groceries				
Apples, Red Delicious	lb	0.79	4/93	16r
Bacon	lb	1.75	4/93	16r
Bananas	lb	0.42	4/93	16r
Beef, stew, boneless	lb	2.61	4/93	16r
Bologna, all beef or mixed	lb	2.24	4/93	16r
Bread, white, pan	lb	0.64	4/93	16r
Bread, whole wheat, pan	lb	0.96	4/93	16r
Cabbage	lb	0.37	4/93	16r
Carrots, short trimmed and topped	lb	0.47	4/93	16r
Celery	lb	0.64	4/93	16r
Cheese, American	lb	2.98	4/93	16r
Cheese, Cheddar	lb	3.28	4/93	16r
Chicken, fresh, whole	lb	0.77	4/93	16r
Chicken breast, bone-in	lb	1.92	4/93	16r
Chicken legs, bone-in	lb	1.06	4/93	16r
Chuck roast, graded and ungraded, ex USDA prime and choice	lb	2.40	4/93	16r
Chuck roast, USDA choice, bone-in	lb	2.19	4/93	16r
Chuck roast, USDA choice, boneless	lb	2.38	4/93	16r
Coffee, 100% ground roast, all sizes	lb	2.48	4/93	16r
Crackers, soda, salted	lb	1.15	4/93	16r
Eggs, Grade A large	doz	0.96	4/93	16r
Flour, white, all purpose	lb	0.24	4/93	16r
Frankfurters, all meat or all beef	lb	2.01	4/93	16r
Grapefruit	lb	0.44	4/93	16r
Grapes, Thompson Seedless	lb	1.40	4/93	16r
Ground beef, 100% beef	lb	1.58	4/93	16r
Ground beef, lean and extra lean	lb	2.09	4/93	16r
Ground chuck, 100% beef	lb	1.98	4/93	16r
Ham, boneless, excluding canned	lb	2.89	4/93	16r
Ham, picnic, shoulder, bone-in, smoked	lb	1.02	4/93	16r
Ham, rump or steak half, bone-in, smoked	lb	1.48	4/93	16r
Ice cream, prepackaged, bulk, regular	1/2 gal	2.41	4/93	16r
Lemons	lb	1.05	4/93	16r
Lettuce, iceberg	lb	0.81	4/93	16r
Margarine, stick	lb	0.88	4/93	16r
Oranges, navel	lb	0.55	4/93	16r
Pears, Anjou	lb	0.92	4/93	16r
Pork chops, center cut, bone-in	lb	3.13	4/93	16r
Potato chips	16 oz	2.94	4/93	16r
Potatoes, white	lb	0.43	4/93	16r
Rib roast, USDA choice, bone-in	lb	4.63	4/93	16r
Rice, white, long grain, uncooked	lb	0.45	4/93	16r
Round roast, graded & ungraded, ex USDA prime & choice	lb	3.03	4/93	16r
Round roast, USDA choice, boneless	lb	3.09	4/93	16r
Sausage, fresh, loose	lb	2.08	4/93	16r
Short ribs, bone-in	lb	2.66	4/93	16r
Shortening, vegetable oil blends	lb	0.69	4/93	16r
Spaghetti and macaroni	lb	0.81	4/93	16r
Steak, rib eye, USDA choice, boneless	lb	6.24	4/93	16r
Steak, round, graded & ungraded, ex USDA prime & choice	lb	3.31	4/93	16r
Steak, round, USDA choice, boneless	lb	3.34	4/93	16r

Naples, FL - continued

Item	Per	Value	Date	Ref.
Groceries - continued				
Steak, sirloin, graded & ungraded, ex USDA prime & choice	lb	4.19	4/93	16r
Steak, sirloin, USDA choice, boneless	lb	4.46	4/93	16r
Steak, T-bone, USDA choice, bone-in	lb	5.25	4/93	16r
Strawberries, dry pint	12 oz	0.92	4/93	16r
Sugar, white	lb	0.39	4/93	16r
Sugar, white, 33-80 oz pk	lb	0.38	4/93	16r
Tomatoes, field grown	lb	0.88	4/93	16r
Tuna, chunk, light	lb	1.79	4/93	16r
Turkey, frozen, whole	lb	1.04	4/93	16r
Yogurt, natural, fruit flavored	1/2 pint	0.57	4/93	16r
Health Care				
Childbirth, cesarean, hospital		5034	91	62r
Childbirth, cesarean, physician's fee		2053	91	62r
Childbirth, normal, hospital		2712	91	62r
Childbirth, normal, physician's fee		1492	91	62r
Medical plan per employee	year	3495	91	45r
Mental health care, exp	capita	28.84-37.59	90	38s
Mental health care, exp, state mental health agency	capita	37.49	90	38s
Mental health care, hospital psychiatric services, non-Federal, exp	capita	9.11	88	38s
Mental health care, mental health organization, multiservice, exp	capita	16.21	88	38s
Mental health care, psychiatric hospitals, private, exp	capita	22.26	88	38s
Mental health care, psychiatric out-patient clinics, freestanding, exp	capita	0.89	88	38s
Mental health care, psychiatric partial-care organizations, freestanding, exp	capita	0.41	88	38s
Mental health care, state and county mental hospitals, exp	capita	16.25	88	38s
Mental health care, VA medical centers, exp	capita	1.69	88	38s
Physician fee, family practice, first-visit		75.00	91	62r
Physician fee, family practice, revisit		34.00	91	62r
Physician fee, general practice, first-visit		61.00	91	62r
Physician fee, general practice, revisit		32.00	91	62r
Physician fee, general surgeon, first-visit		64.00	91	62r
Physician fee, general surgeon, revisit		40.00	91	62r
Physician fee, internal medicine, first-visit		98.00	91	62r
Physician fee, internal medicine, revisit		40.00	91	62r
Physician fee, median, neurosurgeon, first-visit		130.00	91	62r
Physician fee, median, nonsurgical specialist, first-visit		95.00	91	62r
Physician fee, median, orthopedic surgeon, first-visit		91.00	91	62r
Physician fee, median, plastic surgeon, first-visit		66.00	91	62r
Physician fee, median, surgical specialist, first-visit		62.00	91	62r
Physician fee, neurosurgeon, revisit		50.00	91	62r
Physician fee, nonsurgical specialist, revisit		40.00	91	62r
Physician fee, obstetrics/gynecology, first-visit		64.00	91	62r
Physician fee, obstetrics/gynecology, revisit		41.00	91	62r
Physician fee, orthopedic surgeon, revisit		40.00	91	62r
Physician fee, pediatrician, first-visit		49.00	91	62r
Physician fee, pediatrician, revisit		33.00	91	62r
Physician fee, plastic surgeon, revisit		43.00	91	62r
Physician fee, surgical specialist, revisit		37.00	91	62r
Substance abuse, hospital ancillary charge	incident	1390	90	70s
Substance abuse, hospital physician charge	incident	770	90	70s
Substance abuse, hospital room and board	incident	5600	90	70s

Values are in dollars or fractions of dollars. In the column headed *Ref*, references are shown to sources. Each reference is followed by a letter. These refer to the geographical level for which data were reported: s = State, r = Region, and c = City or metro. The abbreviation *ex* is used to mean *except* or *excluding*; *exp* stands for expenditures. For other abbreviations and further explanations, please see the Introduction.

Naples, FL - continued

Item	Per	Value	Date	Ref.
Insurance and Pensions				
Auto insurance, private passenger	year	727.60	91	63s
Taxes				
Tax, cigarette	pack	33.90	91	77s
Tax, gasoline	gal	11.60	91	77s
Taxes, state	capita	1037	91	77s
Transportation				
Driver's license fee		15.00	12/90	43s
Travel				
Business travel	day	193.00	4/93	89r
Utilities				
Electricity	mil Btu	20.62	90	64s

Nashville-Franklin, TN

Item	Per	Value	Date	Ref.
Composite ACCRA index		93.20	4Q 92	4c
Alcoholic Beverages				
Beer, Miller Lite or Budweiser, 12-oz containers	6 pack	3.99	4Q 92	4c
Liquor, J & B Scotch	750 ml	16.65	4Q 92	4c
Wine, Gallo Chablis blanc, 1.5 liter	bottle	5.73	4Q 92	4c
Child Care				
Child care fee, average, center	hour	1.29	90	65r
Child care fee, average, nonregulated family day care	hour	0.89	90	65r
Child care fee, average, regulated family day care	hour	1.32	90	65r
Clothing				
Jeans, man's denim		33.98	4Q 92	4c
Shirt, man's dress shirt		23.20	4Q 92	4c
Undervest, boy's size 10-14, cotton	3	3.84	4Q 92	4c
Communications				
Long-distance telephone service, day, initial minute, 0-100 miles	min	0.10-0.22	91	12s
Long-distance telephone service, day, additional minute, 0-100 miles	min	0.10-0.22	91	12s
Long-distance telephone service, evenings/weekends, 0-100 mi, initial minute	min	0.05-0.10	91	12s
Long-distance telephone service, evenings/weekends, 0-100 mi, additional minute	min	0.05-0.10	91	12s
Newspaper subscription, daily and Sunday home delivery, large-city	month	13.04	4Q 92	4c
Telephone, flat rate	month	12.15	91	11c
Telephone, residential, private line, rotary, unlimited calling	month	17.36	10/91	78c
Telephone bill, family of four	month	18.99	4Q 92	4c
Education				
Board, 4-yr private college/university	year	1845	91	22s
Board, 4-yr public college/university	year	1499	91	22s
Expenditures, local gov't, public elementary/secondary	pupil	3736	92	20s
Room, 4-year private college/university	year	1679	91	22s
Room, 4-year public college/university	year	1339	91	22s
Tuition, 2-year private college/university	year	4203	91	22s
Tuition, 2-year public college/university	year	848	91	22s
Tuition, 4-year private college/university	year	6889	91	22s
Tuition, 4-year public college/university, in-state	year	1518	91	22s
Energy and Fuels				
Coal	mil Btu	1.35	90	64s
Energy	mil Btu	8.61	90	64s
Energy, combined forms, 1,800 sq ft heating area	month	98.67	4Q 92	4c
Energy exp/householder, 1-family unit	year	403	90	28r
Energy exp/householder, <1,000 sq ft heating area	year	342	90	28r

Nashville-Franklin, TN - continued

Item	Per	Value	Date	Ref.
Energy and Fuels - continued				
Energy exp/householder, 1,000-1,999 sq ft heating area	year	388	90	28r
Energy exp/householder, 2,000+ sq ft heating area	year	434	90	28r
Energy exp/householder, mobile home	year	320	90	28r
Energy exp/householder, multifamily	year	338	90	28r
Gas, cooking, winter, 10 therms	month	9.95	92	56c
Gas, cooking, winter, 30 therms	month	19.85	92	56c
Gas, cooking, winter, 50 therms	month	29.74	92	56c
Gas, heating, winter, 100 therms	month	54.49	92	56c
Gas, natural	mil Btu	3.98	90	64s
Gas, natural	000 cu ft	5.19	91	46s
Gas, natural, exp	year	388	91	46s
Gasoline, motor	gal	1.08	4Q 92	4c
Gasoline, unleaded regular	mil Btu	9.40	90	64s
Entertainment				
Bowling, evening rate	game	2.07	4Q 92	4c
Miniature golf admission	adult	6.18	92	1r
Miniature golf admission	child	5.14	92	1r
Monopoly game, Parker Brothers', No. 9		10.58	4Q 92	4c
Movie	admission	5.50	4Q 92	4c
Tennis balls, yellow, Wilson or Penn, 3	can	1.96	4Q 92	4c
Waterpark admission	adult	11.00	92	1r
Waterpark admission	child	8.55	92	1r
Funerals				
Casket, 18-gauge steel, velvet interior		2329.05	91	24r
Cosmetology, hair care, etc.		72.78	91	24r
Embalming		240.71	91	24r
Facility use for ceremony		181.67	91	24r
Hearse, local		106.25	91	24r
Limousine, local		70.92	91	24r
Remains to funeral home, transfer		96.30	91	24r
Service charge, professional		687.09	91	24r
Vault, concrete, non-metallic liner		732.09	91	24r
Viewing facilities, use		190.30	91	24r
Goods and Services				
ACCRA Index, Miscellaneous Goods and Services		97.10	4Q 92	4c
Groceries				
ACCRA Index, Groceries		98.00	4Q 92	4c
Apples, Red Delicious	lb	0.79	4/93	16r
Babyfood, strained vegetables, lowest price	4-4.5 oz jar	0.32	4Q 92	4c
Bacon	lb	1.75	4/93	16r
Bananas	lb	0.41	4Q 92	4c
Bananas	lb	0.42	4/93	16r
Beef, stew, boneless	lb	2.61	4/93	16r
Bologna, all beef or mixed	lb	2.24	4/93	16r
Bread, white	24 oz	0.93	4Q 92	4c
Bread, white, pan	lb	0.64	4/93	16r
Bread, whole wheat, pan	lb	0.96	4/93	16r
Cabbage	lb	0.37	4/93	16r
Carrots, short trimmed and topped	lb	0.47	4/93	16r
Celery	lb	0.64	4/93	16r
Cheese, American	lb	2.98	4/93	16r
Cheese, Cheddar	lb	3.28	4/93	16r
Cheese, Kraft grated Parmesan	8-oz canister	3.33	4Q 92	4c
Chicken, fresh, whole	lb	0.77	4/93	16r
Chicken, fryer, whole	lb	0.62	4Q 92	4c
Chicken breast, bone-in	lb	1.92	4/93	16r
Chicken legs, bone-in	lb	1.06	4/93	16r
Chuck roast, graded and ungraded, ex USDA prime and choice	lb	2.40	4/93	16r
Chuck roast, USDA choice, bone-in	lb	2.19	4/93	16r
Chuck roast, USDA choice, boneless	lb	2.38	4/93	16r
Cigarettes, Winston	carton	16.19	4Q 92	4c

Values are in dollars or fractions of dollars. In the column headed *Ref*, references are shown to sources. Each reference is followed by a letter. These refer to the geographical level for which data were reported: s=State, r=Region, and c=City or metro. The abbreviation *ex* is used to mean *except* or *excluding*; *exp* stands for expenditures. For other abbreviations and further explanations, please see the Introduction.

Nashville-Franklin, TN - continued

Item	Per	Value	Date	Ref.
Groceries				
Coffee, 100% ground roast, all sizes	lb	2.48	4/93	16r
Coffee, vacuum-packed	13-oz can	2.06	4Q 92	4c
Corn, frozen	10 oz	0.65	4Q 92	4c
Corn Flakes, Kellogg's or Post Toasties	18 oz	1.83	4Q 92	4c
Crackers, soda, salted	lb	1.15	4/93	16r
Eggs, Grade A large	doz	0.77	4Q 92	4c
Eggs, Grade A large	doz	0.96	4/93	16r
Flour, white, all purpose	lb	0.24	4/93	16r
Frankfurters, all meat or all beef	lb	2.01	4/93	16r
Grapefruit	lb	0.44	4/93	16r
Grapes, Thompson Seedless	lb	1.40	4/93	16r
Ground beef, 100% beef	lb	1.58	4/93	16r
Ground beef, lean and extra lean	lb	2.09	4/93	16r
Ground beef or hamburger	lb	1.46	4Q 92	4c
Ground chuck, 100% beef	lb	1.98	4/93	16r
Ham, boneless, excluding canned	lb	2.89	4/93	16r
Ham, picnic, shoulder, bone-in, smoked	lb	1.02	4/93	16r
Ham, rump or steak half, bone-in, smoked	lb	1.48	4/93	16r
Honey, jar	8 oz	0.89-1.09	92	5r
Honey, jar	lb	1.39-2.25	92	5r
Honey, squeeze bear	12-oz	1.00-1.50	92	5r
Ice cream, prepackaged, bulk, regular	1/2 gal	2.41	4/93	16r
Lemons	lb	1.05	4/93	16r
Lettuce, iceberg	head	0.88	4Q 92	4c
Lettuce, iceberg	lb	0.81	4/93	16r
Margarine, Blue Bonnet or Parkay cubes	lb	0.57	4Q 92	4c
Margarine, stick	lb	0.88	4/93	16r
Milk, whole	1/2 gal	1.39	4Q 92	4c
Orange juice, Minute Maid frozen	12-oz can	1.24	4Q 92	4c
Oranges, navel	lb	0.55	4/93	16r
Peaches	29-oz can	1.33	4Q 92	4c
Pears, Anjou	lb	0.92	4/93	16r
Peas Sweet, Del Monte or Green Giant	15-17 oz can	0.59	4Q 92	4c
Pork chops, center cut, bone-in	lb	3.13	4/93	16r
Potato chips	16 oz	2.94	4/93	16r
Potatoes, white	lb	0.43	4/93	16r
Potatoes, white or red	10-lb sack	2.85	4Q 92	4c
Rib roast, USDA choice, bone-in	lb	4.63	4/93	16r
Rice, white, long grain, uncooked	lb	0.45	4/93	16r
Round roast, graded & ungraded, ex USDA prime & choice	lb	3.03	4/93	16r
Round roast, USDA choice, boneless	lb	3.09	4/93	16r
Sausage, fresh, loose	lb	2.08	4/93	16r
Sausage, Jimmy Dean, 100% pork	lb	2.12	4Q 92	4c
Short ribs, bone-in	lb	2.66	4/93	16r
Shortening, vegetable oil blends	lb	0.69	4/93	16r
Shortening, vegetable, Crisco	3-lb can	2.13	4Q 92	4c
Soft drink, Coca Cola	2 liter	1.31	4Q 92	4c
Spaghetti and macaroni	lb	0.81	4/93	16r
Steak, rib eye, USDA choice, boneless	lb	6.24	4/93	16r
Steak, round, graded & ungraded, ex USDA prime & choice	lb	3.31	4/93	16r
Steak, round, USDA choice, boneless	lb	3.34	4/93	16r
Steak, sirloin, graded & ungraded, ex USDA prime & choice	lb	4.19	4/93	16r
Steak, sirloin, USDA choice, boneless	lb	4.46	4/93	16r
Steak, T-bone	lb	5.50	4Q 92	4c
Steak, T-bone, USDA choice, bone-in	lb	5.25	4/93	16r
Strawberries, dry pint	12 oz	0.92	4/93	16r
Sugar, cane or beet	4 lb	1.53	4Q 92	4c
Sugar, white	lb	0.39	4/93	16r
Sugar, white, 33-80 oz pk	lb	0.38	4/93	16r
Tomatoes, field grown	lb	0.88	4/93	16r
Tomatoes, Hunt's or Del Monte	14.5-oz can	0.51	4Q 92	4c

Nashville-Franklin, TN - continued

Item	Per	Value	Date	Ref.
Groceries - continued				
Tuna, chunk, light	6.125-6.5 oz can	0.58	4Q 92	4c
Tuna, chunk, light	lb	1.79	4/93	16r
Turkey, frozen, whole	lb	1.04	4/93	16r
Yogurt, natural, fruit flavored	1/2 pint	0.57	4/93	16r
Health Care				
ACCRA Index, Health Care		82.30	4Q 92	4c
Analgesic, Aspirin, Bayer, 325 mg tablets	100	4.56	4Q 92	4c
Childbirth, cesarean, hospital		5034	91	62r
Childbirth, cesarean, physician's fee		2053	91	62r
Childbirth, normal, hospital		2712	91	62r
Childbirth, normal, physician's fee		1492	91	62r
Dentist's fee, adult teeth cleaning and periodic oral exam	visit	36.80	4Q 92	4c
Doctor's fee, routine exam, established patient	visit	33.40	4Q 92	4c
Hospital care, semiprivate room	day	176.16	90	27c
Hospital care, semiprivate room	day	218.00	4Q 92	4c
Medical insurance premium, per employee, small group comprehensive	month	346.75	10/91	25c
Mental health care, exp	capita	20.37-28.83	90	38s
Mental health care, exp, state mental health agency	capita	28.84	90	38s
Mental health care, hospital psychiatric services, non-Federal, exp	capita	13.48	88	38s
Mental health care, mental health organization, multiservice, exp	capita	11.35	88	38s
Mental health care, psychiatric hospitals, private, exp	capita	22.28	88	38s
Mental health care, psychiatric out-patient clinics, freestanding, exp	capita	2.58	88	38s
Mental health care, psychiatric partial-care organizations, freestanding, exp	capita	0.25	88	38s
Mental health care, state and county mental hospitals, exp	capita	20.05	88	38s
Mental health care, VA medical centers, exp	capita	4.98	88	38s
Physician fee, family practice, first-visit		75.00	91	62r
Physician fee, family practice, revisit		34.00	91	62r
Physician fee, general practice, first-visit		61.00	91	62r
Physician fee, general practice, revisit		32.00	91	62r
Physician fee, general surgeon, first-visit		64.00	91	62r
Physician fee, general surgeon, revisit		40.00	91	62r
Physician fee, internal medicine, first-visit		98.00	91	62r
Physician fee, internal medicine, revisit		40.00	91	62r
Physician fee, median, neurosurgeon, first-visit		130.00	91	62r
Physician fee, median, nonsurgical specialist, first-visit		95.00	91	62r
Physician fee, median, orthopedic surgeon, first-visit		91.00	91	62r
Physician fee, median, plastic surgeon, first-visit		66.00	91	62r
Physician fee, median, surgical specialist, first-visit		62.00	91	62r
Physician fee, neurosurgeon, revisit		50.00	91	62r
Physician fee, nonsurgical specialist, revisit		40.00	91	62r
Physician fee, obstetrics/gynecology, first-visit		64.00	91	62r
Physician fee, obstetrics/gynecology, revisit		41.00	91	62r
Physician fee, orthopedic surgeon, revisit		40.00	91	62r
Physician fee, pediatrician, first-visit		49.00	91	62r
Physician fee, pediatrician, revisit		33.00	91	62r
Physician fee, plastic surgeon, revisit		43.00	91	62r
Physician fee, surgical specialist, revisit		37.00	91	62r
Substance abuse, hospital ancillary charge	incident	1330	90	70s
Substance abuse, hospital physician charge	incident	580	90	70s

Values are in dollars or fractions of dollars. In the column headed *Ref*, references are shown to sources. Each reference is followed by a letter. These refer to the geographical level for which data were reported: s = State, r = Region, and c = City or metro. The abbreviation *ex* is used to mean *except* or *excluding*; *exp* stands for expenditures. For other abbreviations and further explanations, please see the Introduction.

Nashville-Franklin, TN - continued

Item	Per	Value	Date	Ref.
Health Care				
Substance abuse, hospital room and board	incident	5180	90	70s
Household Goods				
Appliance repair, home, service call, washing machine	min labor charge	29.99	4Q 92	4c
Laundry detergent, Tide Ultra, Bold, or Cheer	42 oz	3.01	4Q 92	4c
Tissues, facial, Kleenex brand	175-count box	1.03	4Q 92	4c
Housing				
ACCRA Index, Housing		88.80	4Q 92	4c
Home, median price	unit	88.80		26c
House, 1,800 sq ft, 8,000 sq ft lot, new, urban	total	97864	4Q 92	4c
House payment, principal and interest, 25% down payment	month	540	4Q 92	4c
Mortgage rate, incl. points & origination fee, 30-year fixed or adjustable rate	percent	8.03	4Q 92	4c
Rent, apartment, 2 bedrooms - 1-1/2 to 2 baths, unfurnished, 950 sq ft, water	month	452	4Q 92	4c
Rental unit, 1 bedroom	month	429	93	23c
Rental unit, 2 bedroom	month	505	93	23c
Rental unit, 3 bedroom	month	631	93	23c
Rental unit, 4 bedroom	month	709	93	23c
Rental unit, efficiency	month	351	93	23c
Insurance and Pensions				
Auto insurance, private passenger	year	554.60	91	63s
Personal Goods				
Shampoo, Alberto VO5	15 oz	1.11	4Q 92	4c
Toothpaste, Crest or Colgate	6-7 oz	1.22	4Q 92	4c
Personal Services				
Dry cleaning, man's 2-piece suit		5.14	4Q 92	4c
Haircare, woman's shampoo, trim and blow-dry		18.00	4Q 92	4c
Haircut, man's barbershop, no styling		6.75	4Q 92	4c
Restaurant Food				
Chicken, fried, thigh and drumstick		2.05	4Q 92	4c
Hamburger with cheese	1/4 lb	1.79	4Q 92	4c
Pizza, Pizza Hut or Pizza Inn, cheese, thin crust	12-13 in	7.84	4Q 92	4c
Taxes				
Tax, cigarette	pack	13	91	77s
Tax, gasoline	gal	22.40	91	77s
Taxes, state	capita	870	91	77s
Transportation				
ACCRA Index, Transportation		92.60	4Q 92	4c
Auto rental, average	day	44.00	6/91	60c
Bus fare	one-way	1.05	3/93	2c
Bus fare, up to 10 miles	one-way	1.05	4Q 92	4c
Driver's license fee		14.00-16.00	12/90	43s
Limo fare, airport-city, average	day	8.00	6/91	60c
Taxi fare, airport-city, average	day	13.00	6/91	60c
Tire balance, computer or spin balance, front	wheel	5.40	4Q 92	4c
Travel				
Breakfast	day	6.62	6/91	60c
Business travel	day	193.00	4/93	89r
Dinner	day	21.22	6/91	60c
Lodging	day	95.19	91	60c
Lunch	day	12.67	6/91	60c

Nashville-Franklin, TN - continued

Item	Per	Value	Date	Ref.
Utilities				
ACCRA Index, Utilities		91.10	4Q 92	4c
Cable-television, expanded service	month	23.30	92	92c
Electricity	mil Btu	15.59	90	64s
Electricity, all electric, 1,800 sq ft living area new home	month	98.67	4Q 92	4c

Nassau-Suffolk, NY

Item	Per	Value	Date	Ref.
Child Care				
Child care fee, average, center	hour	2.18	90	65r
Child care fee, average, nonregulated family day care	hour	1.83	90	65r
Child care fee, average, regulated family day care	hour	2.02	90	65r
Education				
Board, 4-yr private college/university	year	2451	91	22s
Board, 4-yr public college/university	year	1725	91	22s
Expenditures, local gov't, public elementary/secondary	pupil	8603	92	20s
Room, 4-year private college/university	year	2652	91	22s
Room, 4-year public college/university	year	2183	91	22s
Tuition, 2-year private college/university	year	5926	91	22s
Tuition, 2-year public college/university	year	1419	91	22s
Tuition, 4-year private college/university	year	10340	91	22s
Tuition, 4-year public college/university, in-state	year	1587	91	22s
Energy and Fuels				
Coal	mil Btu	1.66	90	64s
Energy	mil Btu	10.68	90	64s
Energy exp/householder, 1-family unit	year	588	90	28r
Energy exp/householder, <1,000 sq ft heating area	year	477	90	28r
Energy exp/householder, 1,000-1,999 sq ft heating area	year	517	90	28r
Energy exp/householder, 2,000+ sq ft heating area	year	630	90	28r
Energy exp/householder, mobile home	year	412	90	28r
Energy exp/householder, multifamily	year	498	90	28r
Gas, natural	mil Btu	5.25	90	64s
Gas, natural	000 cu ft	7.35	91	46s
Gas, natural, exp	year	557	91	46s
Gasoline, unleaded regular	mil Btu	8.83	90	64s
Funerals				
Casket, 18-gauge steel, velvet interior		1811.58	91	24r
Cosmetology, hair care, etc.		111.08	91	24r
Embalming		329.42	91	24r
Facility use for ceremony		201.29	91	24r
Hearse, local		135.27	91	24r
Limousine, local		127.24	91	24r
Remains to funeral home, transfer		103.98	91	24r
Service charge, professional		724.98	91	24r
Vault, concrete, non-metallic liner		766.71	91	24r
Viewing facilities, use		260.60	91	24r
Groceries				
Apples, Red Delicious	lb	0.85	4/93	16r
Bacon	lb	2.12	4/93	16r
Bananas	lb	0.54	4/93	16r
Bread, white, pan	lb	0.81	4/93	16r
Butter	lb	2.02	4/93	16r
Carrots, short trimmed and topped	lb	0.51	4/93	16r
Chicken, fresh, whole	lb	1.04	4/93	16r
Chicken breast, bone-in	lb	2.21	4/93	16r
Chicken legs, bone-in	lb	1.16	4/93	16r
Chuck roast, USDA choice, boneless	lb	2.82	4/93	16r
Coffee, 100% ground roast, all sizes	lb	2.66	4/93	16r
Cucumbers	lb	0.85	4/93	16r
Eggs, Grade A large	doz	1.15	4/93	16r
Grapefruit	lb	0.45	4/93	16r

Values are in dollars or fractions of dollars. In the column headed *Ref*, references are shown to sources. Each reference is followed by a letter. These refer to the geographical level for which data were reported: s=State, r=Region, and c=City or metro. The abbreviation *ex* is used to mean *except* or *excluding*; *exp* stands for expenditures. For other abbreviations and further explanations, please see the Introduction.

Nassau-Suffolk, NY - continued

Item	Per	Value	Date	Ref.
Groceries				
Grapes, Thompson Seedless	lb	1.52	4/93	16r
Ground beef, lean and extra lean	lb	2.36	4/93	16r
Ground chuck, 100% beef	lb	2.02	4/93	16r
Honey, jar	8 oz	0.96-1.75	92	5r
Honey, jar	lb	1.50-3.00	92	5r
Honey, squeeze bear	12-oz	1.50-1.99	92	5r
Ice cream, prepackaged, bulk, regular	1/2 gal	2.80	4/93	16r
Lemons	lb	0.96	4/93	16r
Lettuce, iceberg	lb	0.95	4/93	16r
Margarine, stick	lb	0.81	4/93	16r
Milk, fresh, whole, fortified	1/2 gal	1.30	4/93	16r
Oranges, navel	lb	0.56	4/93	16r
Peanut butter, creamy, all sizes	lb	1.88	4/93	16r
Pork chops, center cut, bone-in	lb	3.34	4/93	16r
Potato chips	16 oz	2.88	4/93	16r
Potatoes, white	lb	0.37	4/93	16r
Rib roast, USDA choice, bone-in	lb	4.94	4/93	16r
Round roast, USDA choice, boneless	lb	3.17	4/93	16r
Shortening, vegetable oil blends	lb	0.98	4/93	16r
Spaghetti and macaroni	lb	0.82	4/93	16r
Steak, round, graded & ungraded, ex USDA prime & choice	lb	4.04	4/93	16r
Steak, round, USDA choice, boneless	lb	3.90	4/93	16r
Steak, sirloin, USDA choice, boneless	lb	4.97	4/93	16r
Strawberries, dry pint	12 oz	0.90	4/93	16r
Sugar, white	lb	0.50	4/93	16r
Sugar, white, 33-80 oz pk	lb	0.41	4/93	16r
Tomatoes, field grown	lb	1.23	4/93	16r
Tuna, chunk, light	lb	2.22	4/93	16r
Turkey, frozen, whole	lb	1.04	4/93	16r
Health Care				
Childbirth, cesarean, hospital		5826	91	62r
Childbirth, cesarean, physician's fee		2053	91	62r
Childbirth, normal, hospital		2964	91	62r
Childbirth, normal, physician's fee		1492	91	62r
Medical plan per employee	year	3942	91	45r
Mental health care, exp	capita	53.68-118.35	90	38s
Mental health care, exp, state mental health agency	capita	118.34	90	38s
Mental health care, hospital psychiatric services, non-Federal, exp	capita	29.77	88	38s
Mental health care, mental health organization, multiservice, exp	capita	20.03	88	38s
Mental health care, psychiatric hospitals, private, exp	capita	8.37	88	38s
Mental health care, psychiatric out-patient clinics, freestanding, exp	capita	7.96	88	38s
Mental health care, psychiatric partial-care organizations, freestanding, exp	capita	1.24	88	38s
Mental health care, state and county mental hospitals, exp	capita	89.52	88	38s
Mental health care, VA medical centers, exp	capita	7.12	88	38s
Prescription drug co-pay, Medicaid	month	23.00	91	21s
Substance abuse, hospital ancillary charge	incident	1040	90	70s
Substance abuse, hospital physician charge	incident	360	90	70s
Substance abuse, hospital room and board	incident	6330	90	70s
Insurance and Pensions				
Auto insurance, private passenger	year	840.89	91	63s
Taxes				
Tax, cigarette	pack	39	91	77s
Tax, gasoline	gal	8	91	77s
Taxes, state	capita	1567	91	77s
Transportation				
Driver's license fee		17.50	12/90	43s
Vehicle registration and license plate	2 years	27.50-149.50	93	67s

Nassau-Suffolk, NY - continued

Item	Per	Value	Date	Ref.
Travel				
Business travel	day	165.00	4/93	89r
Utilities				
Electricity	mil Btu	27.51	90	64s

Nevada, MO

Item	Per	Value	Date	Ref.
Composite ACCRA index		86.00	4Q 92	4c
Alcoholic Beverages				
Beer, Miller Lite or Budweiser, 12-oz containers	6 pack	4.06	4Q 92	4c
Liquor, J & B Scotch	750 ml	18.35	4Q 92	4c
Wine, Gallo Chablis blanc, 1.5 liter	bottle	5.57	4Q 92	4c
Clothing				
Jeans, man's denim		28.87	4Q 92	4c
Shirt, man's dress shirt		26.00	4Q 92	4c
Undervest, boy's size 10-14, cotton	3	3.95	4Q 92	4c
Communications				
Newspaper subscription, daily and Sunday home delivery, large-city	month	10.39	4Q 92	4c
Telephone, flat rate	month	9.10	91	11c
Telephone bill, family of four	month	17.06	4Q 92	4c
Energy and Fuels				
Energy, combined forms, 1,800 sq ft heating area	month	89.99	4Q 92	4c
Gasoline, motor	gal	1.01	4Q 92	4c
Entertainment				
Bowling, evening rate	game	1.50	4Q 92	4c
Monopoly game, Parker Brothers', No. 9		9.97	4Q 92	4c
Movie	admission	4.00	4Q 92	4c
Tennis balls, yellow, Wilson or Penn, 3	can	2.81	4Q 92	4c
Goods and Services				
ACCRA Index, Miscellaneous Goods and Services		94.10	4Q 92	4c
Groceries				
ACCRA Index, Groceries		93.50	4Q 92	4c
Babyfood, strained vegetables, lowest price	4-4.5 oz jar	0.39	4Q 92	4c
Bananas	lb	0.40	4Q 92	4c
Bread, white	24 oz	0.41	4Q 92	4c
Cheese, Kraft grated Parmesan	8-oz canister	3.88	4Q 92	4c
Chicken, fryer, whole	lb	0.68	4Q 92	4c
Cigarettes, Winston	carton	15.82	4Q 92	4c
Coffee, vacuum-packed	13-oz can	1.91	4Q 92	4c
Corn, frozen	10 oz	0.65	4Q 92	4c
Corn Flakes, Kellogg's or Post Toasties	18 oz	2.22	4Q 92	4c
Eggs, Grade A large	doz	0.68	4Q 92	4c
Ground beef or hamburger	lb	1.29	4Q 92	4c
Lettuce, iceberg	head	0.89	4Q 92	4c
Margarine, Blue Bonnet or Parkay cubes	lb	0.63	4Q 92	4c
Milk, whole	1/2 gal	1.32	4Q 92	4c
Orange juice, Minute Maid frozen	12-oz can	1.63	4Q 92	4c
Peaches	29-oz can	1.47	4Q 92	4c
Peas Sweet, Del Monte or Green Giant	15-17 oz can	0.67	4Q 92	4c
Potatoes, white or red	10-lb sack	1.69	4Q 92	4c
Sausage, Jimmy Dean, 100% pork	lb	2.47	4Q 92	4c
Shortening, vegetable, Crisco	3-lb can	2.70	4Q 92	4c
Soft drink, Coca Cola	2 liter	1.03	4Q 92	4c
Steak, T-bone	lb	4.83	4Q 92	4c

Values are in dollars or fractions of dollars. In the column headed *Ref*, references are shown to sources. Each reference is followed by a letter. These refer to the geographical level for which data were reported: s = State, r = Region, and c = City or metro. The abbreviation *ex* is used to mean *except* or *excluding*; *exp* stands for expenditures. For other abbreviations and further explanations, please see the Introduction.

Nevada, MO - continued

Item	Per	Value	Date	Ref.
Groceries				
Sugar, cane or beet	4 lb	1.33	4Q 92	4c
Tomatoes, Hunt's or Del Monte	14.5-oz can	0.78	4Q 92	4c
Tuna, chunk, light	6.125-6.5 oz can	0.68	4Q 92	4c
Health Care				
ACCRA Index, Health Care		77.40	4Q 92	4c
Analgesic, Aspirin, Bayer, 325 mg tablets	100	4.69	4Q 92	4c
Dentist's fee, adult teeth cleaning and periodic oral exam	visit	34.67	4Q 92	4c
Doctor's fee, routine exam, established patient	visit	24.00	4Q 92	4c
Hospital care, semiprivate room	day	311.50	4Q 92	4c
Household Goods				
Appliance repair, home, service call, washing machine	min labor charge	19.73	4Q 92	4c
Laundry detergent, Tide Ultra, Bold, or Cheer	42 oz	3.23	4Q 92	4c
Tissues, facial, Kleenex brand	175-count box	1.00	4Q 92	4c
Housing				
ACCRA Index, Housing		78.60	4Q 92	4c
House, 1,800 sq ft, 8,000 sq ft lot, new, urban	total	87000	4Q 92	4c
House payment, principal and interest, 25% down payment	month	488	4Q 92	4c
Mortgage rate, incl. points & origination fee, 30-year fixed or adjustable rate	percent	8.21	4Q 92	4c
Personal Goods				
Shampoo, Alberto VO5	15 oz	1.15	4Q 92	4c
Toothpaste, Crest or Colgate	6-7 oz	1.96	4Q 92	4c
Personal Services				
Dry cleaning, man's 2-piece suit		5.45	4Q 92	4c
Haircare, woman's shampoo, trim and blow-dry		14.33	4Q 92	4c
Haircut, man's barbershop, no styling		2.63	4Q 92	4c
Restaurant Food				
Chicken, fried, thigh and drumstick		2.58	4Q 92	4c
Hamburger with cheese	1/4 lb	1.89	4Q 92	4c
Pizza, Pizza Hut or Pizza Inn, cheese, thin crust	12-13 in	9.25	4Q 92	4c
Transportation				
ACCRA Index, Transportation		75.50	4Q 92	4c
Tire balance, computer or spin balance, front	wheel	4.00	4Q 92	4c
Utilities				
ACCRA Index, Utilities		82.90	4Q 92	4c
Electricity, all electric, 1,800 sq ft living area new home	month	89.99	4Q 92	4c

New Bedford, MA

Item	Per	Value	Date	Ref.
Child Care				
Child care fee, average, center	hour	2.18	90	65r
Child care fee, average, nonregulated family day care	hour	1.83	90	65r
Child care fee, average, regulated family day care	hour	2.02	90	65r
Communications				
Long-distance telephone service, day, initial minute, 0-100 miles	min	0.18-0.31	91	12s
Long-distance telephone service, day, additional minute, 0-100 miles	min	0.08-0.13	91	12s

New Bedford, MA - continued

Item	Per	Value	Date	Ref.
Communications - continued				
Long-distance telephone service, evenings/ weekends, 0-100 mi, initial minute	min	0.67-0.12	91	12s
Long-distance telephone service, evenings/ weekends, 0-100 mi, additional minute	min	0.04-0.05	91	12s
Education				
Board, 4-yr private college/university	year	2698	91	22s
Board, 4-yr public college/university	year	1741	91	22s
Expenditures, local gov't, public elementary/secondary	pupil	6687	92	20s
Room, 4-year private college/university	year	2945	91	22s
Room, 4-year public college/university	year	2144	91	22s
Tuition, 2-year private college/university	year	7750	91	22s
Tuition, 2-year public college/university	year	1528	91	22s
Tuition, 4-year private college/university	year	12446	91	22s
Tuition, 4-year public college/university, in-state	year	2580	91	22s
Energy and Fuels				
Coal	mil Btu	1.77	90	64s
Energy	mil Btu	10.57	90	64s
Energy exp/householder, 1-family unit	year	588	90	28r
Energy exp/householder, <1,000 sq ft heating area	year	477	90	28r
Energy exp/householder, 1,000-1,999 sq ft heating area	year	517	90	28r
Energy exp/householder, 2,000+ sq ft heating area	year	630	90	28r
Energy exp/householder, mobile home	year	412	90	28r
Energy exp/householder, multifamily	year	498	90	28r
Gas, natural	mil Btu	5.55	90	64s
Gas, natural	000 cu ft	8.11	91	46s
Gas, natural, exp	year	741	91	46s
Gasoline, unleaded regular	mil Btu	9.53	90	64s
Entertainment				
Miniature golf admission	adult	6.18	92	1r
Miniature golf admission	child	5.14	92	1r
Waterpark admission	adult	11.00	92	1r
Waterpark admission	child	8.55	92	1r
Funerals				
Casket, 18-gauge steel, velvet interior		1853.42	91	24r
Cosmetology, hair care, etc.		98.33	91	24r
Embalming		273.94	91	24r
Facility use for ceremony		196.06	91	24r
Hearse, local		145.67	91	24r
Limousine, local		131.07	91	24r
Remains to funeral home, transfer		135.24	91	24r
Service charge, professional		843.16	91	24r
Vault, concrete, non-metallic liner		709.14	91	24r
Viewing facilities, use		229.85	91	24r
Groceries				
Apples, Red Delicious	lb	0.85	4/93	16r
Bacon	lb	2.12	4/93	16r
Bananas	lb	0.54	4/93	16r
Bread, white, pan	lb	0.81	4/93	16r
Butter	lb	2.02	4/93	16r
Carrots, short trimmed and topped	lb	0.51	4/93	16r
Chicken, fresh, whole	lb	1.04	4/93	16r
Chicken breast, bone-in	lb	2.21	4/93	16r
Chicken legs, bone-in	lb	1.16	4/93	16r
Chuck roast, USDA choice, boneless	lb	2.82	4/93	16r
Coffee, 100% ground roast, all sizes	lb	2.66	4/93	16r
Cucumbers	lb	0.85	4/93	16r
Eggs, Grade A large	doz	1.15	4/93	16r
Grapefruit	lb	0.45	4/93	16r
Grapes, Thompson Seedless	lb	1.52	4/93	16r
Ground beef, lean and extra lean	lb	2.36	4/93	16r
Ground chuck, 100% beef	lb	2.02	4/93	16r
Honey, jar	8 oz	0.96-1.75	92	5r
Honey, jar	lb	1.50-3.00	92	5r

Values are in dollars or fractions of dollars. In the column headed *Ref*, references are shown to sources. Each reference is followed by a letter. These refer to the geographical level for which data were reported: s = State, r = Region, and c = City or metro. The abbreviation *ex* is used to mean *except* or *excluding*; *exp* stands for expenditures. For other abbreviations and further explanations, please see the Introduction.

New Bedford, MA - continued

Item	Per	Value	Date	Ref.
Groceries				
Honey, squeeze bear	12-oz	1.50-1.99	92	5r
Ice cream, prepackaged, bulk, regular	1/2 gal	2.80	4/93	16r
Lemons	lb	0.96	4/93	16r
Lettuce, iceberg	lb	0.95	4/93	16r
Margarine, stick	lb	0.81	4/93	16r
Milk, fresh, whole, fortified	1/2 gal	1.30	4/93	16r
Oranges, navel	lb	0.56	4/93	16r
Peanut butter, creamy, all sizes	lb	1.88	4/93	16r
Pork chops, center cut, bone-in	lb	3.34	4/93	16r
Potato chips	16 oz	2.88	4/93	16r
Potatoes, white	lb	0.37	4/93	16r
Rib roast, USDA choice, bone-in	lb	4.94	4/93	16r
Round roast, USDA choice, boneless	lb	3.17	4/93	16r
Shortening, vegetable oil blends	lb	0.98	4/93	16r
Spaghetti and macaroni	lb	0.82	4/93	16r
Steak, round, graded & ungraded, ex USDA prime & choice	lb	4.04	4/93	16r
Steak, round, USDA choice, boneless	lb	3.90	4/93	16r
Steak, sirloin, USDA choice, boneless	lb	4.97	4/93	16r
Strawberries, dry pint	12 oz	0.90	4/93	16r
Sugar, white	lb	0.50	4/93	16r
Sugar, white, 33-80 oz pk	lb	0.41	4/93	16r
Tomatoes, field grown	lb	1.23	4/93	16r
Tuna, chunk, light	lb	2.22	4/93	16r
Turkey, frozen, whole	lb	1.04	4/93	16r
Health Care				
Childbirth, cesarean, hospital		5826	91	62r
Childbirth, cesarean, physician's fee		2053	91	62r
Childbirth, normal, hospital		2964	91	62r
Childbirth, normal, physician's fee		1492	91	62r
Health care spending, state	capita	3031	3/93	84s
Medical plan per employee	year	3958	91	45r
Mental health care, exp	capita	53.68-118.35	90	38s
Mental health care, exp, state mental health agency	capita	83.91	90	38s
Mental health care, hospital psychiatric services, non-Federal, exp	capita	22.67	88	38s
Mental health care, mental health organization, multiservice, exp	capita	36.07	88	38s
Mental health care, psychiatric hospitals, private, exp	capita	38.65	88	38s
Mental health care, psychiatric out-patient clinics, freestanding, exp	capita	4.41	88	38s
Mental health care, psychiatric partial-care organizations, freestanding, exp	capita	0.92	88	38s
Mental health care, state and county mental hospitals, exp	capita	30.59	88	38s
Mental health care, VA medical centers, exp	capita	21.14	88	38s
Substance abuse, hospital ancillary charge	incident	1310	90	70s
Substance abuse, hospital physician charge	incident	460	90	70s
Substance abuse, hospital room and board	incident	3450	90	70s
Insurance and Pensions				
Auto insurance, private passenger	year	912.83	91	63s
Taxes				
Tax, cigarette	pack	26	91	77s
Tax, gasoline	gal	21	91	77s
Taxes, state	capita	1615	91	77s
Transportation				
Driver's license fee		35.00	12/90	43s
Travel				
Business travel	day	165.00	4/93	89r
Utilities				
Electricity	mil Btu	25.93	90	64s

New Britain, CT

Item	Per	Value	Date	Ref.
Child Care				
Child care fee, average, center	hour	2.18	90	65r
Child care fee, average, nonregulated family day care	hour	1.83	90	65r
Child care fee, average, regulated family day care	hour	2.02	90	65r
Communications				
Long-distance telephone service, day, initial minute, 0-100 miles	min	0.18-0.45	91	12s
Long-distance telephone service, day, additional minute, 0-100 miles	min	0.10-0.26	91	12s
Long-distance telephone service, evenings/weekends, 0-100 mi, initial minute	min	0.07-0.18	91	12s
Long-distance telephone service, evenings/weekends, 0-100 mi, additional minute	min	0.04-0.10	91	12s
Education				
Board, 4-yr private college/university	year	2182	91	22s
Board, 4-yr public college/university	year	1750	91	22s
Expenditures, local gov't, public elementary/secondary	pupil	8308	92	20s
Room, 4-year private college/university	year	2703	91	22s
Room, 4-year public college/university	year	1913	91	22s
Tuition, 2-year private college/university	year	8586	91	22s
Tuition, 2-year public college/university	year	972	91	22s
Tuition, 4-year private college/university	year	12315	91	22s
Tuition, 4-year public college/university, in-state	year	2313	91	22s
Energy and Fuels				
Coal	mil Btu	2.15	90	64s
Energy	mil Btu	11.62	90	64s
Energy exp/householder, 1-family unit	year	588	90	28r
Energy exp/householder, <1,000 sq ft heating area	year	477	90	28r
Energy exp/householder, 1,000-1,999 sq ft heating area	year	517	90	28r
Energy exp/householder, 2,000+ sq ft heating area	year	630	90	28r
Energy exp/householder, mobile home	year	412	90	28r
Energy exp/householder, multifamily	year	498	90	28r
Gas, natural	mil Btu	6.40	90	64s
Gas, natural	000 cu ft	8.74	91	46s
Gas, natural, exp	year	756	91	46s
Gasoline, unleaded regular	mil Btu	10.06	90	64s
Entertainment				
Miniature golf admission	adult	6.18	92	1r
Miniature golf admission	child	5.14	92	1r
Waterpark admission	adult	11.00	92	1r
Waterpark admission	child	8.55	92	1r
Funerals				
Casket, 18-gauge steel, velvet interior		1853.42	91	24r
Cosmetology, hair care, etc.		98.33	91	24r
Embalming		273.94	91	24r
Facility use for ceremony		196.06	91	24r
Hearse, local		145.67	91	24r
Limousine, local		131.07	91	24r
Remains to funeral home, transfer		135.24	91	24r
Service charge, professional		843.16	91	24r
Vault, concrete, non-metallic liner		709.14	91	24r
Viewing facilities, use		229.85	91	24r
Groceries				
Apples, Red Delicious	lb	0.85	4/93	16r
Bacon	lb	2.12	4/93	16r
Bananas	lb	0.54	4/93	16r
Bread, white, pan	lb	0.81	4/93	16r
Butter	lb	2.02	4/93	16r
Carrots, short trimmed and topped	lb	0.51	4/93	16r
Chicken, fresh, whole	lb	1.04	4/93	16r
Chicken breast, bone-in	lb	2.21	4/93	16r

Values are in dollars or fractions of dollars. In the column headed *Ref*, references are shown to sources. Each reference is followed by a letter. These refer to the geographical level for which data were reported: s = State, r = Region, and c = City or metro. The abbreviation *ex* is used to mean *except* or *excluding*; *exp* stands for expenditures. For other abbreviations and further explanations, please see the Introduction.

New Britain, CT - continued

Item	Per	Value	Date	Ref.
Groceries				
Chicken legs, bone-in	lb	1.16	4/93	16r
Chuck roast, USDA choice, boneless	lb	2.82	4/93	16r
Coffee, 100% ground roast, all sizes	lb	2.66	4/93	16r
Cucumbers	lb	0.85	4/93	16r
Eggs, Grade A large	doz	1.15	4/93	16r
Grapefruit	lb	0.45	4/93	16r
Grapes, Thompson Seedless	lb	1.52	4/93	16r
Ground beef, lean and extra lean	lb	2.36	4/93	16r
Ground chuck, 100% beef	lb	2.02	4/93	16r
Honey, jar	8 oz	0.96-1.75	92	5r
Honey, jar	lb	1.50-3.00	92	5r
Honey, squeeze bear	12-oz	1.50-1.99	92	5r
Ice cream, prepackaged, bulk, regular	1/2 gal	2.80	4/93	16r
Lemons	lb	0.96	4/93	16r
Lettuce, iceberg	lb	0.95	4/93	16r
Margarine, stick	lb	0.81	4/93	16r
Milk, fresh, whole, fortified	1/2 gal	1.30	4/93	16r
Oranges, navel	lb	0.56	4/93	16r
Peanut butter, creamy, all sizes	lb	1.88	4/93	16r
Pork chops, center cut, bone-in	lb	3.34	4/93	16r
Potato chips	16 oz	2.88	4/93	16r
Potatoes, white	lb	0.37	4/93	16r
Rib roast, USDA choice, bone-in	lb	4.94	4/93	16r
Round roast, USDA choice, boneless	lb	3.17	4/93	16r
Shortening, vegetable oil blends	lb	0.98	4/93	16r
Spaghetti and macaroni	lb	0.82	4/93	16r
Steak, round, graded & ungraded, ex USDA prime & choice	lb	4.04	4/93	16r
Steak, round, USDA choice, boneless	lb	3.90	4/93	16r
Steak, sirloin, USDA choice, boneless	lb	4.97	4/93	16r
Strawberries, dry pint	12 oz	0.90	4/93	16r
Sugar, white	lb	0.50	4/93	16r
Sugar, white, 33-80 oz pk	lb	0.41	4/93	16r
Tomatoes, field grown	lb	1.23	4/93	16r
Tuna, chunk, light	lb	2.22	4/93	16r
Turkey, frozen, whole	lb	1.04	4/93	16r
Health Care				
Childbirth, cesarean, hospital		5826	91	62r
Childbirth, cesarean, physician's fee		2053	91	62r
Childbirth, normal, hospital		2964	91	62r
Childbirth, normal, physician's fee		1492	91	62r
Medical plan per employee	year	3958	91	45r
Mental health care, exp	capita	53.68-118.35	90	38s
Mental health care, exp, state mental health agency	capita	72.81	90	38s
Mental health care, hospital psychiatric services, non-Federal, exp	capita	19.30	88	38s
Mental health care, mental health organization, multiservice, exp	capita	19.14	88	38s
Mental health care, psychiatric hospitals, private, exp	capita	35.86	88	38s
Mental health care, psychiatric out-patient clinics, freestanding, exp	capita	5.83	88	38s
Mental health care, psychiatric partial-care organizations, freestanding, exp	capita	0.15	88	38s
Mental health care, state and county mental hospitals, exp	capita	51.85	88	38s
Mental health care, VA medical centers, exp	capita	1.74	88	38s
Prescription drug co-pay, Medicaid	month	10.00	91	21s
Substance abuse, hospital ancillary charge	incident	1200	90	70s
Substance abuse, hospital physician charge	incident	270	90	70s
Substance abuse, hospital room and board	incident	4420	90	70s
Insurance and Pensions				
Auto insurance, private passenger	year	928.10	91	63s
Taxes				
Tax, cigarette	pack	45	91	77s
Tax, gasoline	gal	26	91	77s

New Britain, CT - continued

Item	Per	Value	Date	Ref.
Taxes - continued				
Taxes, state	capita	1514	91	77s
Transportation				
Driver's license fee		31.00	12/90	43s
Travel				
Business travel	day	165.00	4/93	89r
Utilities				
Electricity	mil Btu	26.83	90	64s

New Haven, CT

Item	Per	Value	Date	Ref.
Child Care				
Child care fee, average, center	hour	2.18	90	65r
Child care fee, average, nonregulated family day care	hour	1.83	90	65r
Child care fee, average, regulated family day care	hour	2.02	90	65r
Communications				
Long-distance telephone service, day, initial minute, 0-100 miles	min	0.18-0.45	91	12s
Long-distance telephone service, day, additional minute, 0-100 miles	min	0.10-0.26	91	12s
Long-distance telephone service, evenings/weekends, 0-100 mi, initial minute	min	0.07-0.18	91	12s
Long-distance telephone service, evenings/weekends, 0-100 mi, additional minute	min	0.04-0.10	91	12s
Telephone, flat rate	month	12.79	91	11c
Education				
Board, 4-yr private college/university	year	2182	91	22s
Board, 4-yr public college/university	year	1750	91	22s
Expenditures, local gov't, public elementary/secondary	pupil	8308	92	20s
Room, 4-year private college/university	year	2703	91	22s
Room, 4-year public college/university	year	1913	91	22s
Tuition, 2-year private college/university	year	8586	91	22s
Tuition, 2-year public college/university	year	972	91	22s
Tuition, 4-year private college/university	year	12315	91	22s
Tuition, 4-year public college/university, in-state	year	2313	91	22s
Energy and Fuels				
Coal	mil Btu	2.15	90	64s
Energy	mil Btu	11.62	90	64s
Energy exp/householder, 1-family unit	year	588	90	28r
Energy exp/householder, <1,000 sq ft heating area	year	477	90	28r
Energy exp/householder, 1,000-1,999 sq ft heating area	year	517	90	28r
Energy exp/householder, 2,000+ sq ft heating area	year	630	90	28r
Energy exp/householder, mobile home	year	412	90	28r
Energy exp/householder, multifamily	year	498	90	28r
Gas, natural	mil Btu	6.40	90	64s
Gas, natural	000 cu ft	8.74	91	46s
Gas, natural, exp	year	756	91	46s
Gasoline, unleaded premium	gal	61.25-73.46	12/92	31c
Gasoline, unleaded regular	mil Btu	10.06	90	64s
Entertainment				
Miniature golf admission	adult	6.18	92	1r
Miniature golf admission	child	5.14	92	1r
Waterpark admission	adult	11.00	92	1r
Waterpark admission	child	8.55	92	1r
Funerals				
Casket, 18-gauge steel, velvet interior		1853.42	91	24r
Cosmetology, hair care, etc.		98.33	91	24r
Embalming		273.94	91	24r
Facility use for ceremony		196.06	91	24r

Values are in dollars or fractions of dollars. In the column headed *Ref*, references are shown to sources. Each reference is followed by a letter. These refer to the geographical level for which data were reported: s = State, r = Region, and c = City or metro. The abbreviation *ex* is used to mean *except* or *excluding*; *exp* stands for expenditures. For other abbreviations and further explanations, please see the Introduction.

New Haven, CT - continued

Item	Per	Value	Date	Ref.
Funerals				
Hearse, local		145.67	91	24r
Limousine, local		131.07	91	24r
Remains to funeral home, transfer		135.24	91	24r
Service charge, professional		843.16	91	24r
Vault, concrete, non-metallic liner		709.14	91	24r
Viewing facilities, use		229.85	91	24r
Goods and Services				
Goods and services	year	17464	92	36c
Groceries				
Apples, Red Delicious	lb	0.85	4/93	16r
Bacon	lb	2.12	4/93	16r
Bananas	lb	0.54	4/93	16r
Bread, white, pan	lb	0.81	4/93	16r
Butter	lb	2.02	4/93	16r
Carrots, short trimmed and topped	lb	0.51	4/93	16r
Chicken, fresh, whole	lb	1.04	4/93	16r
Chicken breast, bone-in	lb	2.21	4/93	16r
Chicken legs, bone-in	lb	1.16	4/93	16r
Chuck roast, USDA choice, boneless	lb	2.82	4/93	16r
Coffee, 100% ground roast, all sizes	lb	2.66	4/93	16r
Cucumbers	lb	0.85	4/93	16r
Eggs, Grade A large	doz	1.15	4/93	16r
Grapefruit	lb	0.45	4/93	16r
Grapes, Thompson Seedless	lb	1.52	4/93	16r
Ground beef, lean and extra lean	lb	2.36	4/93	16r
Ground chuck, 100% beef	lb	2.02	4/93	16r
Honey, jar	8 oz	0.96-1.75	92	5r
Honey, jar	lb	1.50-3.00	92	5r
Honey, squeeze bear	12-oz	1.50-1.99	92	5r
Ice cream, prepackaged, bulk, regular	1/2 gal	2.80	4/93	16r
Lemons	lb	0.96	4/93	16r
Lettuce, iceberg	lb	0.95	4/93	16r
Margarine, stick	lb	0.81	4/93	16r
Milk, fresh, whole, fortified	1/2 gal	1.30	4/93	16r
Oranges, navel	lb	0.56	4/93	16r
Peanut butter, creamy, all sizes	lb	1.88	4/93	16r
Pork chops, center cut, bone-in	lb	3.34	4/93	16r
Potato chips	16 oz	2.88	4/93	16r
Potatoes, white	lb	0.37	4/93	16r
Rib roast, USDA choice, bone-in	lb	4.94	4/93	16r
Round roast, USDA choice, boneless	lb	3.17	4/93	16r
Shortening, vegetable oil blends	lb	0.98	4/93	16r
Spaghetti and macaroni	lb	0.82	4/93	16r
Steak, round, graded & ungraded, ex USDA prime & choice	lb	4.04	4/93	16r
Steak, round, USDA choice, boneless	lb	3.90	4/93	16r
Steak, sirloin, USDA choice, boneless	lb	4.97	4/93	16r
Strawberries, dry pint	12 oz	0.90	4/93	16r
Sugar, white	lb	0.50	4/93	16r
Sugar, white, 33-80 oz pk	lb	0.41	4/93	16r
Tomatoes, field grown	lb	1.23	4/93	16r
Tuna, chunk, light	lb	2.22	4/93	16r
Turkey, frozen, whole	lb	1.04	4/93	16r
Health Care				
Childbirth, cesarean, hospital		5826	91	62r
Childbirth, cesarean, physician's fee		2053	91	62r
Childbirth, normal, hospital		2964	91	62r
Childbirth, normal, physician's fee		1492	91	62r
Hospital care, semiprivate room	day	383.83	90	27c
Medical insurance premium, per employee, small group comprehensive	month	375.95	10/91	25c
Medical plan per employee	year	3958	91	45r
Mental health care, exp	capita	53.68-118.35	90	38s
Mental health care, exp, state mental health agency	capita	72.81	90	38s
Mental health care, hospital psychiatric services, non-Federal, exp	capita	19.30	88	38s
Mental health care, mental health organization, multiservice, exp	capita	19.14	88	38s

New Haven, CT - continued

Item	Per	Value	Date	Ref.
Health Care - continued				
Mental health care, psychiatric hospitals, private, exp	capita	35.86	88	38s
Mental health care, psychiatric out-patient clinics, freestanding, exp	capita	5.83	88	38s
Mental health care, psychiatric partial-care organizations, freestanding, exp	capita	0.15	88	38s
Mental health care, state and county mental hospitals, exp	capita	51.85	88	38s
Mental health care, VA medical centers, exp	capita	1.74	88	38s
Prescription drug co-pay, Medicaid	month	10.00	91	21s
Substance abuse, hospital ancillary charge	incident	1200	90	70s
Substance abuse, hospital physician charge	incident	270	90	70s
Substance abuse, hospital room and board	incident	4420	90	70s
Housing				
Home, median price	unit	145.80		26c
Rental unit, 1 bedroom	month	655	93	23c
Rental unit, 2 bedroom	month	773	93	23c
Rental unit, 3 bedroom	month	968	93	23c
Rental unit, 4 bedroom	month	1082	93	23c
Rental unit, efficiency	month	539	93	23c
Insurance and Pensions				
Auto insurance, private passenger	year	928.10	91	63s
Taxes				
Tax, cigarette	pack	45	91	77s
Tax, gasoline	gal	26	91	77s
Taxes, state	capita	1514	91	77s
Transportation				
Auto rental, average	day	46.00	6/91	60c
Bus fare	one-way	0.85	3/93	2c
Driver's license fee		31.00	12/90	43s
Railway fare, commuter	one-way	2.00	3/93	2c
Taxi fare, airport-city, average	day	3.00	6/91	60c
Travel				
Breakfast	day	6.23	6/91	60c
Business travel	day	165.00	4/93	89r
Dinner	day	19.44	6/91	60c
Lodging	day	87.50	91	60c
Lunch	day	9.29	6/91	60c
Utilities				
Electricity	mil Btu	26.83	90	64s

New London, CT

Item	Per	Value	Date	Ref.
Child Care				
Child care fee, average, center	hour	2.18	90	65r
Child care fee, average, nonregulated family day care	hour	1.83	90	65r
Child care fee, average, regulated family day care	hour	2.02	90	65r
Communications				
Long-distance telephone service, day, initial minute, 0-100 miles	min	0.18-0.45	91	12s
Long-distance telephone service, day, additional minute, 0-100 miles	min	0.10-0.26	91	12s
Long-distance telephone service, evenings/weekends, 0-100 mi, initial minute	min	0.07-0.18	91	12s
Long-distance telephone service, evenings/weekends, 0-100 mi, additional minute	min	0.04-0.10	91	12s
Education				
Board, 4-yr private college/university	year	2182	91	22s
Board, 4-yr public college/university	year	1750	91	22s

Values are in dollars or fractions of dollars. In the column headed *Ref*, references are shown to sources. Each reference is followed by a letter. These refer to the geographical level for which data were reported: s=State, r=Region, and c=City or metro. The abbreviation *ex* is used to mean *except* or *excluding*; *exp* stands for expenditures. For other abbreviations and further explanations, please see the Introduction.

New London, CT - continued

Item	Per	Value	Date	Ref.
Education				
Expenditures, local gov't, public elementary/secondary	pupil	8308	92	20s
Room, 4-year private college/university	year	2703	91	22s
Room, 4-year public college/university	year	1913	91	22s
Tuition, 2-year private college/university	year	8586	91	22s
Tuition, 2-year public college/university	year	972	91	22s
Tuition, 4-year private college/university	year	12315	91	22s
Tuition, 4-year public college/university, in-state	year	2313	91	22s
Energy and Fuels				
Coal	mil Btu	2.15	90	64s
Energy	mil Btu	11.62	90	64s
Energy exp/householder, 1-family unit	year	588	90	28r
Energy exp/householder, <1,000 sq ft heating area	year	477	90	28r
Energy exp/householder, 1,000-1,999 sq ft heating area	year	517	90	28r
Energy exp/householder, 2,000+ sq ft heating area	year	630	90	28r
Energy exp/householder, mobile home	year	412	90	28r
Energy exp/householder, multifamily	year	498	90	28r
Gas, natural	mil Btu	6.40	90	64s
Gas, natural	000 cu ft	8.74	91	46s
Gas, natural, exp	year	756	91	46s
Gasoline, unleaded regular	mil Btu	10.06	90	64s
Entertainment				
Miniature golf admission	adult	6.18	92	1r
Miniature golf admission	child	5.14	92	1r
Waterpark admission	adult	11.00	92	1r
Waterpark admission	child	8.55	92	1r
Funerals				
Casket, 18-gauge steel, velvet interior		1853.42	91	24r
Cosmetology, hair care, etc.		98.33	91	24r
Embalming		273.94	91	24r
Facility use for ceremony		196.06	91	24r
Hearse, local		145.67	91	24r
Limousine, local		131.07	91	24r
Remains to funeral home, transfer		135.24	91	24r
Service charge, professional		843.16	91	24r
Vault, concrete, non-metallic liner		709.14	91	24r
Viewing facilities, use		229.85	91	24r
Groceries				
Apples, Red Delicious	lb	0.85	4/93	16r
Bacon	lb	2.12	4/93	16r
Bananas	lb	0.54	4/93	16r
Bread, white, pan	lb	0.81	4/93	16r
Butter	lb	2.02	4/93	16r
Carrots, short trimmed and topped	lb	0.51	4/93	16r
Chicken, fresh, whole	lb	1.04	4/93	16r
Chicken breast, bone-in	lb	2.21	4/93	16r
Chicken legs, bone-in	lb	1.16	4/93	16r
Chuck roast, USDA choice, boneless	lb	2.82	4/93	16r
Coffee, 100% ground roast, all sizes	lb	2.66	4/93	16r
Cucumbers	lb	0.85	4/93	16r
Eggs, Grade A large	doz	1.15	4/93	16r
Grapefruit	lb	0.45	4/93	16r
Grapes, Thompson Seedless	lb	1.52	4/93	16r
Ground beef, lean and extra lean	lb	2.36	4/93	16r
Ground chuck, 100% beef	lb	2.02	4/93	16r
Honey, jar	8 oz	0.96-1.75	92	5r
Honey, jar	lb	1.50-3.00	92	5r
Honey, squeeze bear	12-oz	1.50-1.99	92	5r
Ice cream, prepackaged, bulk, regular	1/2 gal	2.80	4/93	16r
Lemons	lb	0.96	4/93	16r
Lettuce, iceberg	lb	0.95	4/93	16r
Margarine, stick	lb	0.81	4/93	16r
Milk, fresh, whole, fortified	1/2 gal	1.30	4/93	16r
Oranges, navel	lb	0.56	4/93	16r
Peanut butter, creamy, all sizes	lb	1.88	4/93	16r

New London, CT - continued

Item	Per	Value	Date	Ref.
Groceries - continued				
Pork chops, center cut, bone-in	lb	3.34	4/93	16r
Potato chips	16 oz	2.88	4/93	16r
Potatoes, white	lb	0.37	4/93	16r
Rib roast, USDA choice, bone-in	lb	4.94	4/93	16r
Round roast, USDA choice, boneless	lb	3.17	4/93	16r
Shortening, vegetable oil blends	lb	0.98	4/93	16r
Spaghetti and macaroni	lb	0.82	4/93	16r
Steak, round, graded & ungraded, ex USDA prime & choice	lb	4.04	4/93	16r
Steak, round, USDA choice, boneless	lb	3.90	4/93	16r
Steak, sirloin, USDA choice, boneless	lb	4.97	4/93	16r
Strawberries, dry pint	12 oz	0.90	4/93	16r
Sugar, white	lb	0.50	4/93	16r
Sugar, white, 33-80 oz pk	lb	0.41	4/93	16r
Tomatoes, field grown	lb	1.23	4/93	16r
Tuna, chunk, light	lb	2.22	4/93	16r
Turkey, frozen, whole	lb	1.04	4/93	16r
Health Care				
Childbirth, cesarean, hospital		5826	91	62r
Childbirth, cesarean, physician's fee		2053	91	62r
Childbirth, normal, hospital		2964	91	62r
Childbirth, normal, physician's fee		1492	91	62r
Medical plan per employee	year	3958	91	45r
Mental health care, exp	capita	53.68-118.35	90	38s
Mental health care, exp, state mental health agency	capita	72.81	90	38s
Mental health care, hospital psychiatric services, non-Federal, exp	capita	19.30	88	38s
Mental health care, mental health organization, multiservice, exp	capita	19.14	88	38s
Mental health care, psychiatric hospitals, private, exp	capita	35.86	88	38s
Mental health care, psychiatric out-patient clinics, freestanding, exp	capita	5.83	88	38s
Mental health care, psychiatric partial-care organizations, freestanding, exp	capita	0.15	88	38s
Mental health care, state and county mental hospitals, exp	capita	51.85	88	38s
Mental health care, VA medical centers, exp	capita	1.74	88	38s
Prescription drug co-pay, Medicaid	month	10.00	91	21s
Substance abuse, hospital ancillary charge	incident	1200	90	70s
Substance abuse, hospital physician charge	incident	270	90	70s
Substance abuse, hospital room and board	incident	4420	90	70s
Insurance and Pensions				
Auto insurance, private passenger	year	928.10	91	63s
Taxes				
Tax, cigarette	pack	45	91	77s
Tax, gasoline	gal	26	91	77s
Taxes, state	capita	1514	91	77s
Transportation				
Driver's license fee		31.00	12/90	43s
Travel				
Business travel	day	165.00	4/93	89r
Utilities				
Electricity	mil Btu	26.83	90	64s

New Orleans, LA

Item	Per	Value	Date	Ref.
Composite ACCRA index		95.70	4Q 92	4c
Alcoholic Beverages				
Beer, Miller Lite or Budweiser, 12-oz containers	6 pack	3.90	4Q 92	4c
Liquor, J & B Scotch	750 ml	18.64	4Q 92	4c
Wine, Gallo Chablis blanc, 1.5 liter	bottle	4.62	4Q 92	4c

Values are in dollars or fractions of dollars. In the column headed *Ref*, references are shown to sources. Each reference is followed by a letter. These refer to the geographical level for which data were reported: s=State, r=Region, and c=City or metro. The abbreviation *ex* is used to mean *except* or *excluding*; *exp* stands for expenditures. For other abbreviations and further explanations, please see the Introduction.

New Orleans, LA - continued

Item	Per	Value	Date	Ref.
Child Care				
Child care fee, average, center	hour	1.29	90	65r
Child care fee, average, nonregulated family day care	hour	0.89	90	65r
Child care fee, average, regulated family day care	hour	1.32	90	65r
Clothing				
Jeans, man's denim		24.40	4Q 92	4c
Shirt, man's dress shirt		18.80	4Q 92	4c
Undervest, boy's size 10-14, cotton	3	3.78	4Q 92	4c
Communications				
Long-distance telephone service, day, initial minute, 0-100 miles	min	0.14-0.41	91	12s
Long-distance telephone service, day, additional minute, 0-100 miles	min	0.09-0.29	91	12s
Long-distance telephone service, evenings/ weekends, 0-100 mi, initial minute	min	0.06-0.16	91	12s
Long-distance telephone service, evenings/ weekends, 0-100 mi, additional minute	min	0.04-0.12	91	12s
Newspaper subscription, daily and Sunday home delivery, large-city	month	9.50	4Q 92	4c
Telephone, flat rate	month	14.42	91	11c
Telephone, residential, private line, rotary, unlimited calling	month	22.27	10/91	78c
Telephone bill, family of four	month	22.90	4Q 92	4c
Education				
Board, 4-yr private college/university	year	2125	91	22s
Board, 4-yr public college/university	year	1453	91	22s
Expenditures, local gov't, public elementary/secondary	pupil	4299	92	20s
Room, 4-year private college/university	year	2216	91	22s
Room, 4-year public college/university	year	1323	91	22s
Tuition, 2-year private college/university	year	5671	91	22s
Tuition, 2-year public college/university	year	852	91	22s
Tuition, 4-year private college/university	year	9783	91	22s
Tuition, 4-year public college/university, in-state	year	1791	91	22s
Energy and Fuels				
Coal	mil Btu	1.68	90	64s
Energy	mil Btu	6.05	90	64s
Energy, combined forms, 1,800 sq ft heating area	month	132.26	4Q 92	4c
Energy, exc electricity, 1,800 sq ft heating area	month	28.58	4Q 92	4c
Energy exp/householder, 1-family unit	year	471	90	28r
Energy exp/householder, <1,000 sq ft heating area	year	384	90	28r
Energy exp/householder, 1,000-1,999 sq ft heating area	year	421	90	28r
Energy exp/householder, 2,000+ sq ft heating area	year	625	90	28r
Energy exp/householder, mobile home	year	271	90	28r
Energy exp/householder, multifamily	year	355	90	28r
Gas, cooking, 10 therms	month	5.54	92	56c
Gas, cooking, 30 therms	month	11.59	92	56c
Gas, cooking, 50 therms	month	17.66	92	56c
Gas, heating, winter, 100 therms	month	32.83	92	56c
Gas, heating, winter, average use	month	37.90	92	56c
Gas, natural	mil Btu	2.11	90	64s
Gas, natural	000 cu ft	5.77	91	46s
Gas, natural, exp	year	336	91	46s
Gasoline, motor	gal	1.16	4Q 92	4c
Gasoline, unleaded regular	mil Btu	9.47	90	64s
Entertainment				
Bowling, evening rate	game	1.74	4Q 92	4c
Dinner entree, restaurant		25.00-30.00	92	83c
Miniature golf admission	adult	6.18	92	1r
Miniature golf admission	child	5.14	92	1r

New Orleans, LA - continued

Item	Per	Value	Date	Ref.
Entertainment - continued				
Monopoly game, Parker Brothers', No. 9		10.95	4Q 92	4c
Movie	admission	5.80	4Q 92	4c
Tennis balls, yellow, Wilson or Penn, 3	can	2.19	4Q 92	4c
Waterpark admission	adult	11.00	92	1r
Waterpark admission	child	8.55	92	1r
Funerals				
Casket, 18-gauge steel, velvet interior		2274.41	91	24r
Cosmetology, hair care, etc.		74.62	91	24r
Embalming		229.94	91	24r
Facility use for ceremony		176.61	91	24r
Hearse, local		116.34	91	24r
Limousine, local		72.68	91	24r
Remains to funeral home, transfer		87.72	91	24r
Service charge, professional		712.53	91	24r
Vault, concrete, non-metallic liner		750.55	91	24r
Viewing facilities, use		155.31	91	24r
Goods and Services				
ACCRA Index, Miscellaneous Goods and Services		92.30	4Q 92	4c
Groceries				
ACCRA Index, Groceries		102.80	4Q 92	4c
Apples, Red Delicious	lb	0.79	4/93	16r
Babyfood, strained vegetables, lowest price	4-4.5 oz jar	0.30	4Q 92	4c
Bacon	lb	1.75	4/93	16r
Bananas	lb	0.48	4Q 92	4c
Bananas	lb	0.42	4/93	16r
Beef, stew, boneless	lb	2.61	4/93	16r
Bologna, all beef or mixed	lb	2.24	4/93	16r
Bread, white	24 oz	0.80	4Q 92	4c
Bread, white, pan	lb	0.64	4/93	16r
Bread, whole wheat, pan	lb	0.96	4/93	16r
Cabbage	lb	0.37	4/93	16r
Carrots, short trimmed and topped	lb	0.47	4/93	16r
Celery	lb	0.64	4/93	16r
Cheese, American	lb	2.98	4/93	16r
Cheese, Cheddar	lb	3.28	4/93	16r
Cheese, Kraft grated Parmesan	8-oz canister	3.33	4Q 92	4c
Chicken, fresh, whole	lb	0.77	4/93	16r
Chicken, fryer, whole	lb	0.66	4Q 92	4c
Chicken breast, bone-in	lb	1.92	4/93	16r
Chicken legs, bone-in	lb	1.06	4/93	16r
Chuck roast, graded and ungraded, ex USDA prime and choice	lb	2.40	4/93	16r
Chuck roast, USDA choice, bone-in	lb	2.19	4/93	16r
Chuck roast, USDA choice, boneless	lb	2.38	4/93	16r
Cigarettes, Winston	carton	19.12	4Q 92	4c
Coffee, 100% ground roast, all sizes	lb	2.48	4/93	16r
Coffee, vacuum-packed	13-oz can	2.29	4Q 92	4c
Corn, frozen	10 oz	0.75	4Q 92	4c
Corn Flakes, Kellogg's or Post Toasties	18 oz	2.21	4Q 92	4c
Crackers, soda, salted	lb	1.15	4/93	16r
Eggs, Grade A large	doz	0.95	4Q 92	4c
Eggs, Grade A large	doz	0.96	4/93	16r
Flour, white, all purpose	lb	0.24	4/93	16r
Frankfurters, all meat or all beef	lb	2.01	4/93	16r
Grapefruit	lb	0.44	4/93	16r
Grapes, Thompson Seedless	lb	1.40	4/93	16r
Ground beef, 100% beef	lb	1.58	4/93	16r
Ground beef, lean and extra lean	lb	2.09	4/93	16r
Ground beef or hamburger	lb	1.49	4Q 92	4c
Ground chuck, 100% beef	lb	1.98	4/93	16r
Ham, boneless, excluding canned	lb	2.89	4/93	16r
Ham, picnic, shoulder, bone-in, smoked	lb	1.02	4/93	16r
Ham, rump or steak half, bone-in, smoked	lb	1.48	4/93	16r
Honey, jar	8 oz	0.73-1.19	92	5r
Honey, jar	lb	1.10-1.79	92	5r

Values are in dollars or fractions of dollars. In the column headed Ref, references are shown to sources. Each reference is followed by a letter. These refer to the geographical level for which data were reported: s=State, r=Region, and c=City or metro. The abbreviation ex is used to mean except or excluding; exp stands for expenditures. For other abbreviations and further explanations, please see the Introduction.

New Orleans, LA - continued

Item	Per	Value	Date	Ref.
Groceries				
Honey, squeeze bear	12-oz	1.19-1.50	92	5r
Ice cream, prepackaged, bulk, regular	1/2 gal	2.41	4/93	16r
Lemons	lb	1.05	4/93	16r
Lettuce, iceberg	head	0.89	4Q 92	4c
Lettuce, iceberg	lb	0.81	4/93	16r
Margarine, Blue Bonnet or Parkay cubes	lb	0.63	4Q 92	4c
Margarine, stick	lb	0.88	4/93	16r
Milk, whole	1/2 gal	1.37	4Q 92	4c
Orange juice, Minute Maid frozen	12-oz can	1.60	4Q 92	4c
Oranges, navel	lb	0.55	4/93	16r
Peaches	29-oz can	1.51	4Q 92	4c
Pears, Anjou	lb	0.92	4/93	16r
Peas Sweet, Del Monte or Green Giant	15-17 oz can	0.65	4Q 92	4c
Pork chops, center cut, bone-in	lb	3.13	4/93	16r
Potato chips	16 oz	2.94	4/93	16r
Potatoes, white	lb	0.43	4/93	16r
Potatoes, white or red	10-lb sack	2.17	4Q 92	4c
Rib roast, USDA choice, bone-in	lb	4.63	4/93	16r
Rice, white, long grain, uncooked	lb	0.45	4/93	16r
Round roast, graded & ungraded, ex USDA prime & choice	lb	3.03	4/93	16r
Round roast, USDA choice, boneless	lb	3.09	4/93	16r
Sausage, fresh, loose	lb	2.08	4/93	16r
Sausage, Jimmy Dean, 100% pork	lb	2.03	4Q 92	4c
Short ribs, bone-in	lb	2.66	4/93	16r
Shortening, vegetable oil blends	lb	0.69	4/93	16r
Shortening, vegetable, Crisco	3-lb can	2.55	4Q 92	4c
Soft drink, Coca Cola	2 liter	1.14	4Q 92	4c
Spaghetti and macaroni	lb	0.81	4/93	16r
Steak, rib eye, USDA choice, boneless	lb	6.24	4/93	16r
Steak, round, graded & ungraded, ex USDA prime & choice	lb	3.31	4/93	16r
Steak, round, USDA choice, boneless	lb	3.34	4/93	16r
Steak, sirloin, graded & ungraded, ex USDA prime & choice	lb	4.19	4/93	16r
Steak, sirloin, USDA choice, boneless	lb	4.46	4/93	16r
Steak, T-bone	lb	6.35	4Q 92	4c
Steak, T-bone, USDA choice, bone-in	lb	5.25	4/93	16r
Strawberries, dry pint	12 oz	0.92	4/93	16r
Sugar, cane or beet	4 lb	1.65	4Q 92	4c
Sugar, white	lb	0.39	4/93	16r
Sugar, white, 33-80 oz pk	lb	0.38	4/93	16r
Tomatoes, field grown	lb	0.88	4/93	16r
Tomatoes, Hunt's or Del Monte	14.5-oz can	0.81	4Q 92	4c
Tuna, chunk, light	6.125-6.5 oz can	0.54	4Q 92	4c
Tuna, chunk, light	lb	1.79	4/93	16r
Turkey, frozen, whole	lb	1.04	4/93	16r
Yogurt, natural, fruit flavored	1/2 pint	0.57	4/93	16r
Health Care				
ACCRA Index, Health Care		84.20	4Q 92	4c
Analgesic, Aspirin, Bayer, 325 mg tablets	100	3.79	4Q 92	4c
Childbirth, cesarean, hospital		5034	91	62r
Childbirth, cesarean, physician's fee		2053	91	62r
Childbirth, normal, hospital		2712	91	62r
Childbirth, normal, physician's fee		1492	91	62r
Dentist's fee, adult teeth cleaning and periodic oral exam	visit	37.40	4Q 92	4c
Doctor's fee, routine exam, established patient	visit	31.40	4Q 92	4c
Hospital care, semiprivate room	day	262.72	90	27c
Hospital care, semiprivate room	day	306.00	4Q 92	4c
Medical insurance premium, per employee, small group comprehensive	month	448.95	10/91	25c

New Orleans, LA - continued

Item	Per	Value	Date	Ref.
Health Care - continued				
Mental health care, exp	capita	20.37-28.83	90	38s
Mental health care, exp, state mental health agency	capita	28.44	90	38s
Mental health care, hospital psychiatric services, non-Federal, exp	capita	8.19	88	38s
Mental health care, mental health organization, multiservice, exp	capita	0.49	88	38s
Mental health care, psychiatric hospitals, private, exp	capita	43.54	88	38s
Mental health care, psychiatric out-patient clinics, freestanding, exp	capita	4.11	88	38s
Mental health care, state and county mental hospitals, exp	capita	18.74	88	38s
Mental health care, VA medical centers, exp	capita	2.60	88	38s
Physician fee, family practice, first-visit		75.00	91	62r
Physician fee, family practice, revisit		34.00	91	62r
Physician fee, general practice, first-visit		61.00	91	62r
Physician fee, general practice, revisit		32.00	91	62r
Physician fee, general surgeon, first-visit		64.00	91	62r
Physician fee, general surgeon, revisit		40.00	91	62r
Physician fee, internal medicine, first-visit		98.00	91	62r
Physician fee, internal medicine, revisit		40.00	91	62r
Physician fee, median, neurosurgeon, first-visit		130.00	91	62r
Physician fee, median, nonsurgical specialist, first-visit		95.00	91	62r
Physician fee, median, orthopedic surgeon, first-visit		91.00	91	62r
Physician fee, median, plastic surgeon, first-visit		66.00	91	62r
Physician fee, median, surgical specialist, first-visit		62.00	91	62r
Physician fee, neurosurgeon, revisit		50.00	91	62r
Physician fee, nonsurgical specialist, revisit		40.00	91	62r
Physician fee, obstetrics/gynecology, first-visit		64.00	91	62r
Physician fee, obstetrics/gynecology, revisit		41.00	91	62r
Physician fee, orthopedic surgeon, revisit		40.00	91	62r
Physician fee, pediatrician, first-visit		49.00	91	62r
Physician fee, pediatrician, revisit		33.00	91	62r
Physician fee, plastic surgeon, revisit		43.00	91	62r
Physician fee, surgical specialist, revisit		37.00	91	62r
Substance abuse, hospital ancillary charge	incident	2600	90	70s
Substance abuse, hospital physician charge	incident	840	90	70s
Substance abuse, hospital room and board	incident	6410	90	70s
Household Goods				
Appliance repair, home, service call, washing machine	min labor charge	26.00	4Q 92	4c
Laundry detergent, Tide Ultra, Bold, or Cheer	42 oz	3.09	4Q 92	4c
Tissues, facial, Kleenex brand	175-count box	1.17	4Q 92	4c
Housing				
ACCRA Index, Housing		87.70	4Q 92	4c
Home, median price	unit	73.80		26c
House, 1,800 sq ft, 8,000 sq ft lot, new, urban	total	90500	4Q 92	4c
House payment, principal and interest, 25% down payment	month	502	4Q 92	4c
Mortgage rate, incl. points & origination fee, 30-year fixed or adjustable rate	percent	8.08	4Q 92	4c
Rent, apartment, 2 bedrooms - 1-1/2 to 2 baths, unfurnished, 950 sq ft, water	month	519	4Q 92	4c
Rental unit, 1 bedroom	month	383	93	23c
Rental unit, 2 bedroom	month	451	93	23c

Values are in dollars or fractions of dollars. In the column headed *Ref*, references are shown to sources. Each reference is followed by a letter. These refer to the geographical level for which data were reported: s=State, r=Region, and c=City or metro. The abbreviation *ex* is used to mean *except* or *excluding*; *exp* stands for expenditures. For other abbreviations and further explanations, please see the Introduction.

New Orleans, LA - continued

Item	Per	Value	Date	Ref.
Housing				
Rental unit, 3 bedroom	month	564	93	23c
Rental unit, 4 bedroom	month	631	93	23c
Rental unit, efficiency	month	316	93	23c
Insurance and Pensions				
Auto insurance, private passenger	year	778.70	91	63s
Personal Goods				
Shampoo, Alberto VO5	15 oz	0.98	4Q 92	4c
Toothpaste, Crest or Colgate	6-7 oz	1.70	4Q 92	4c
Personal Services				
Dry cleaning, man's 2-piece suit		5.46	4Q 92	4c
Haircare, woman's shampoo, trim and blow-dry		23.80	4Q 92	4c
Haircut, man's barbershop, no styling		8.30	4Q 92	4c
Restaurant Food				
Chicken, fried, thigh and drumstick		2.13	4Q 92	4c
Hamburger with cheese	1/4 lb	1.96	4Q 92	4c
Pizza, Pizza Hut or Pizza Inn, cheese, thin crust	12-13 in	7.85	4Q 92	4c
Taxes				
Tax, cigarette	pack	20	91	77s
Tax, gasoline	gal	20	91	77s
Taxes, hotel room	day	9.04	92	33c
Taxes, state	capita	1013	91	77s
Transportation				
ACCRA Index, Transportation		104.40	4Q 92	4c
Auto rental, average	day	43.50	6/91	60c
Bus fare	one-way	1.00	3/93	2c
Bus fare, up to 10 miles	one-way	1.25	4Q 92	4c
Driver's license fee		18.00	12/90	43s
Limo fare, airport-city, average	day	7.00	6/91	60c
Railway fare, light rail	one-way	1.00	93	2c
Taxi fare, airport-city, average	day	18.00	6/91	60c
Tire balance, computer or spin balance, front	wheel	6.35	4Q 92	4c
Travel				
Breakfast	day	7.36	6/91	60c
Business travel	day	132.00	92	86c
Business travel	day	193.00	4/93	89r
Dinner	day	24.09	6/91	60c
Dinner	day	21.05	92	85c
Lodging	day	130.69	91	60c
Lodging	day	94.00	92	85c
Lunch	day	11.59	6/91	60c
Utilities				
ACCRA Index, Utilities		120.80	4Q 92	4c
Electricity	mil Btu	17.77	90	64s
Electricity, partial electric and other energy, 1,800 sq ft living area new home	month	103.68	4Q 92	4c

New York, NY

Item	Per	Value	Date	Ref.
Composite ACCRA index		206.30	4Q 92	4c
Alcoholic Beverages				
Beer, Miller Lite or Budweiser, 12-oz containers	6 pack	4.65	4Q 92	4c
Liquor, J & B Scotch	750 ml	18.49	4Q 92	4c
Wine, Gallo Chablis blanc, 1.5 liter	bottle	6.99	4Q 92	4c
Child Care				
Child care, on-site	year	6136	93	17c
Child care fee, average, center	hour	2.18	90	65r
Child care fee, average, nonregulated family day care	hour	1.83	90	65r

New York, NY - continued

Item	Per	Value	Date	Ref.
Child Care - continued				
Child care fee, average, regulated family day care	hour	2.02	90	65r
Clothing				
Jeans, man's denim		35.19	4Q 92	4c
Shirt, man's dress shirt		25.00	4Q 92	4c
Undervest, boy's size 10-14, cotton	3	10.39	4Q 92	4c
Communications				
Newspaper subscription, daily and Sunday home delivery, large-city	month	21.74	4Q 92	4c
Telephone, exp	year	718	89	15c
Telephone, residential, private line, rotary, unlimited calling	month	25.29	10/91	78c
Telephone bill, family of four	month	47.20	4Q 92	4c
Education				
Board, 4-yr private college/university	year	2451	91	22s
Board, 4-yr public college/university	year	1725	91	22s
Cooking lessons		370.00	93	48c
Expenditures, local gov't, public elementary/secondary	pupil	8603	92	20s
Room, 4-year private college/university	year	2652	91	22s
Room, 4-year public college/university	year	2183	91	22s
Tuition, 2-year private college/university	year	5926	91	22s
Tuition, 2-year public college/university	year	1419	91	22s
Tuition, 4-year private college/university	year	10340	91	22s
Tuition, 4-year public college/university, in-state	year	1587	91	22s
Energy and Fuels				
Coal	mil Btu	1.66	90	64s
Energy	mil Btu	10.68	90	64s
Energy, combined forms, 1,800 sq ft heating area	month	149.50	4Q 92	4c
Energy, exc electricity, 1,800 sq ft heating area	month	39.69	4Q 92	4c
Energy exp/householder, 1-family unit	year	588	90	28r
Energy exp/householder, <1,000 sq ft heating area	year	477	90	28r
Energy exp/householder, 1,000-1,999 sq ft heating area	year	517	90	28r
Energy exp/householder, 2,000+ sq ft heating area	year	630	90	28r
Energy exp/householder, mobile home	year	412	90	28r
Energy exp/householder, multifamily	year	498	90	28r
Fuel oil #2	gal	1.09	4/93	16c
Fuel oil, other fuel, exp	year	261	89	15c
Gas, cooking, winter, 10 therms	month	15.21	92	56c
Gas, cooking, winter, 30 therms	month	28.74	92	56c
Gas, cooking, winter, 50 therms	month	42.28	92	56c
Gas, heating, winter, 100 therms	month	75.67	92	56c
Gas, heating, winter, average use	month	139.04	92	56c
Gas, natural	mil Btu	5.25	90	64s
Gas, natural	000 cu ft	7.35	91	46s
Gas, natural, exp	year	349	89	15c
Gas, natural, exp	year	557	91	46s
Gas, piped	100 therms	84.59	4/93	16c
Gas, piped	40 therms	40.45	4/93	16c
Gas, piped	therm	0.90	4/93	16c
Gasoline, all types	gal	1.24	4/93	16c
Gasoline, motor	gal	1.33	4Q 92	4c
Gasoline, regular unleaded, taxes included, cash, self-service	gal	1.37	4/93	16c
Gasoline, unleaded premium 93 octane	gal	1.12	4/93	16c
Gasoline, unleaded regular	mil Btu	8.83	90	64s
Entertainment				
Bowling, evening rate	game	3.37	4Q 92	4c
Dinner entree, restaurant		54.50	92	83c
Monopoly game, Parker Brothers', No. 9		18.38	4Q 92	4c

Values are in dollars or fractions of dollars. In the column headed *Ref*, references are shown to sources. Each reference is followed by a letter. These refer to the geographical level for which data were reported: s = State, r = Region, and c = City or metro. The abbreviation *ex* is used to mean *except* or *excluding*; *exp* stands for expenditures. For other abbreviations and further explanations, please see the Introduction.

New York, NY - continued

Item	Per	Value	Date	Ref.
Entertainment				
Movie	admission	7.90	4Q 92	4c
Tennis balls, yellow, Wilson or Penn, 3	can	3.06	4Q 92	4c
Funerals				
Casket, 18-gauge steel, velvet interior		1811.58	91	24r
Cosmetology, hair care, etc.		111.08	91	24r
Embalming		329.42	91	24r
Facility use for ceremony		201.29	91	24r
Hearse, local		135.27	91	24r
Limousine, local		127.24	91	24r
Remains to funeral home, transfer		103.98	91	24r
Service charge, professional		724.98	91	24r
Vault, concrete, non-metallic liner		766.71	91	24r
Viewing facilities, use		260.60	91	24r
Goods and Services				
ACCRA Index, Miscellaneous Goods and Services		150.50	4Q 92	4c
Police protection expense	resident	221.00	92	18c
Groceries				
ACCRA Index, Groceries		142.20	4Q 92	4c
Apples, Red Delicious	lb	0.85	4/93	16r
Babyfood, strained vegetables, lowest price	4-4.5 oz jar	0.46	4Q 92	4c
Bacon	lb	2.12	4/93	16r
Bakery products, exp	year	267	89	15c
Bananas	lb	0.55	4Q 92	4c
Bananas	lb	0.54	4/93	16r
Beef, exp	year	220	89	15c
Beverages, nonalcoholic, exp	year	211	89	15c
Bread, white	24 oz	1.14	4Q 92	4c
Bread, white, pan	lb	0.81	4/93	16r
Butter	lb	2.02	4/93	16r
Carrots, short trimmed and topped	lb	0.51	4/93	16r
Cereals and baking products, exp	year	387	89	15c
Cereals and cereal products, exp	year	120	89	15c
Cheese, Kraft grated Parmesan	8-oz canister	4.38	4Q 92	4c
Chicken, fresh, whole	lb	1.04	4/93	16r
Chicken, fryer, whole	lb	1.47	4Q 92	4c
Chicken breast, bone-in	lb	2.21	4/93	16r
Chicken legs, bone-in	lb	1.16	4/93	16r
Chuck roast, USDA choice, boneless	lb	2.82	4/93	16r
Cigarettes, Winston	carton	21.55	4Q 92	4c
Coffee, 100% ground roast, all sizes	lb	2.66	4/93	16r
Coffee, vacuum-packed	13-oz can	3.25	4Q 92	4c
Corn, frozen	10 oz	1.04	4Q 92	4c
Corn Flakes, Kellogg's or Post Toasties	18 oz	2.72	4Q 92	4c
Cucumbers	lb	0.85	4/93	16r
Dairy product purchases	year	296	89	15c
Dairy products, miscellaneous, exp	year	160	89	15c
Eggs, exp	year	35	89	15c
Eggs, Grade A large	doz	1.27	4Q 92	4c
Eggs, Grade A large	doz	1.15	4/93	16r
Fats and oils, exp	year	51	89	15c
Fish and seafood, exp	year	116	89	15c
Food, exp	year	4779	89	15c
Food eaten at home, exp	year	600	89	15c
Food eaten at home, exp	year	2477	89	15c
Food purchased away from home, exp	year	2303	89	15c
Foods, miscellaneous, exp	year	229	89	15c
Fruits, fresh, exp	year	145	89	15c
Fruits, processed, exp	year	118	89	15c
Fruits and vegetables, exp	year	472	89	15c
Grapefruit	lb	0.45	4/93	16r
Grapes, Thompson Seedless	lb	1.52	4/93	16r
Ground beef, lean and extra lean	lb	2.36	4/93	16r
Ground beef or hamburger	lb	1.99	4Q 92	4c
Ground chuck, 100% beef	lb	2.02	4/93	16r

New York, NY - continued

Item	Per	Value	Date	Ref.
Groceries - continued				
Honey, jar	8 oz	0.96-1.75	92	5r
Honey, jar	lb	1.50-3.00	92	5r
Honey, squeeze bear	12-oz	1.50-1.99	92	5r
Ice cream, prepackaged, bulk, regular	1/2 gal	2.80	4/93	16r
Lemons	lb	0.96	4/93	16r
Lettuce, iceberg	head	1.03	4Q 92	4c
Lettuce, iceberg	lb	0.95	4/93	16r
Margarine, Blue Bonnet or Parkay cubes	lb	1.18	4Q 92	4c
Margarine, stick	lb	0.81	4/93	16r
Meats, miscellaneous, exp	year	103	89	15c
Meats, poultry, fish and eggs, exp	year	721	89	15c
Milk, fresh, whole, fortified	1/2 gal	1.30	4/93	16r
Milk, whole	1/2 gal	1.63	4Q 92	4c
Milk and cream, fresh, exp	year	136	89	15c
Orange juice, Minute Maid frozen	12-oz can	2.39	4Q 92	4c
Oranges, navel	lb	0.56	4/93	16r
Peaches	29-oz can	1.63	4Q 92	4c
Peanut butter, creamy, all sizes	lb	1.88	4/93	16r
Peas Sweet, Del Monte or Green Giant	15-17 oz can	0.95	4Q 92	4c
Pork, exp	year	109	89	15c
Pork chops, center cut, bone-in	lb	3.34	4/93	16r
Potato chips	16 oz	2.88	4/93	16r
Potatoes, white	lb	0.37	4/93	16r
Potatoes, white or red	10-lb sack	1.83	4Q 92	4c
Poultry, exp	year	138	89	15c
Rib roast, USDA choice, bone-in	lb	4.94	4/93	16r
Round roast, USDA choice, boneless	lb	3.17	4/93	16r
Sausage, Jimmy Dean, 100% pork	lb	2.95	4Q 92	4c
Shortening, vegetable oil blends	lb	0.98	4/93	16r
Shortening, vegetable, Crisco	3-lb can	3.93	4Q 92	4c
Soft drink, Coca Cola	2 liter	1.29	4Q 92	4c
Spaghetti and macaroni	lb	0.82	4/93	16r
Steak, round, graded & ungraded, ex USDA prime & choice	lb	4.04	4/93	16r
Steak, round, USDA choice, boneless	lb	3.90	4/93	16r
Steak, sirloin, USDA choice, boneless	lb	4.97	4/93	16r
Steak, T-bone	lb	7.07	4Q 92	4c
Strawberries, dry pint	12 oz	0.90	4/93	16r
Sugar, cane or beet	4 lb	2.82	4Q 92	4c
Sugar, white	lb	0.50	4/93	16r
Sugar, white, 33-80 oz pk	lb	0.41	4/93	16r
Sugar and other sweets, exp	year	79	89	15c
Tomatoes, field grown	lb	1.23	4/93	16r
Tomatoes, Hunt's or Del Monte	14.5-oz can	1.09	4Q 92	4c
Tuna, chunk, light	6.125-6.5 oz can	1.33	4Q 92	4c
Tuna, chunk, light	lb	2.22	4/93	16r
Turkey, frozen, whole	lb	1.04	4/93	16r
Vegetables, fresh, exp	year	147	89	15c
Vegetables, processed, exp	year	62	89	15c
Health Care				
ACCRA Index, Health Care		204.20	4Q 92	4c
Analgesic, Aspirin, Bayer, 325 mg tablets	100	7.31	4Q 92	4c
Appendectomy		1901	91	62c
Childbirth, cesarean		4789	91	62c
Childbirth, cesarean, hospital		5826	91	62r
Childbirth, cesarean, physician's fee		2053	91	62r
Childbirth, normal, hospital		2964	91	62r
Childbirth, normal, physician's fee		1492	91	62r
Cholecystectomy		3048	91	62c
Coronary bypass surgery, triple		8189	91	62c
Dentist's fee, adult teeth cleaning and periodic oral exam	visit	86.00	4Q 92	4c
Doctor's fee, routine exam, established patient	visit	76.00	4Q 92	4c

Values are in dollars or fractions of dollars. In the column headed *Ref*, references are shown to sources. Each reference is followed by a letter. These refer to the geographical level for which data were reported: s=State, r=Region, and c=City or metro. The abbreviation *ex* is used to mean *except* or *excluding*; *exp* stands for expenditures. For other abbreviations and further explanations, please see the Introduction.

New York, NY - continued

Item	Per	Value	Date	Ref.
Health Care				
Health maintenance organization coverage, employee	year	3448	93	39c
Health maintenance organization medical coverage, employee	year	3448	92	34c
Health maintenance organization medical coverage, employee	year	3448	92	42c
Hospital care, semiprivate room	day	634.53	90	27c
Hospital care, semiprivate room	day	880.40	4Q 92	4c
Hysterectomy		4997	91	62c
Indemnity plan medical coverage, employee	year	4852	92	42c
Indemnity plan medical coverage, employee	year	4852	92	34c
Insurance coverage, traditional, employee	year	4852	93	39c
Lumpectomy		1252	91	62c
Medical insurance premium, per employee, small group comprehensive	month	507.35	10/91	25c
Medical plan per employee	year	3942	91	45r
Mental health care, exp	capita	53.68-118.35	90	38s
Mental health care, exp, state mental health agency	capita	118.34	90	38s
Mental health care, hospital psychiatric services, non-Federal, exp	capita	29.77	88	38s
Mental health care, mental health organization, multiservice, exp	capita	20.03	88	38s
Mental health care, psychiatric hospitals, private, exp	capita	8.37	88	38s
Mental health care, psychiatric out-patient clinics, freestanding, exp	capita	7.96	88	38s
Mental health care, psychiatric partial-care organizations, freestanding, exp	capita	1.24	88	38s
Mental health care, state and county mental hospitals, exp	capita	89.52	88	38s
Mental health care, VA medical centers, exp	capita	7.12	88	38s
Oophorectomy		2734	91	62c
Preferred provider organization medical coverage, employee	year	3871	92	42c
Preferred provider organization medical coverage, employee	year	3871	92	34c
Prescription drug co-pay, Medicaid	month	23.00	91	21s
Prostatectomy, retro-pubic		3268	91	62c
Salpingo-oophorectomy		3318	91	62c
Substance abuse, hospital ancillary charge	incident	1040	90	70s
Substance abuse, hospital physician charge	incident	360	90	70s
Substance abuse, hospital room and board	incident	6330	90	70s
Vasectomy		670	91	62c
Household Goods				
Appliance repair, home, service call, washing machine	min labor charge	51.97	4Q 92	4c
Appliances, major, exp	year	153	89	15c
Appliances, small, misc. housewares, exp	year	89	89	15c
Floor coverings, exp	year	74	89	15c
Household equipment, misc., exp	year	331	89	15c
Laundry detergent, Tide Ultra, Bold, or Cheer	42 oz	5.08	4Q 92	4c
Tissues, facial, Kleenex brand	175-count box	1.19	4Q 92	4c
Housing				
ACCRA Index, Housing		352.70	4Q 92	4c
Home, median price	unit	172.60		26c
House, 1,800 sq ft, 8,000 sq ft lot, new, urban	total	372500	4Q 92	4c
House payment, principal and interest, 25% down payment	month	2142	4Q 92	4c
Mortgage rate, incl. points & origination fee, 30-year fixed or adjustable rate	percent	8.47	4Q 92	4c

New York, NY - continued

Item	Per	Value	Date	Ref.
Housing - continued				
Rent, apartment, 2 bedrooms - 1-1/2 to 2 baths, unfurnished, 950 sq ft, water	month	1799	4Q 92	4c
Rental unit, 1 bedroom	month	579	93	23c
Rental unit, 2 bedroom	month	681	93	23c
Rental unit, 3 bedroom	month	854	93	23c
Rental unit, 4 bedroom	month	957	93	23c
Rental unit, efficiency	month	477	93	23c
Insurance and Pensions				
Auto insurance, private passenger	year	840.89	91	63s
Personal Goods				
Shampoo, Alberto VO5	15 oz	2.05	4Q 92	4c
Toothpaste, Crest or Colgate	6-7 oz	2.79	4Q 92	4c
Personal Services				
Dry cleaning, man's 2-piece suit		8.70	4Q 92	4c
Haircare, woman's shampoo, trim and blow-dry		42.88	4Q 92	4c
Haircut, man's barbershop, no styling		14.15	4Q 92	4c
Restaurant Food				
Chicken, fried, thigh and drumstick		2.55	4Q 92	4c
Hamburger with cheese	1/4 lb	2.87	4Q 92	4c
Pizza, Pizza Hut or Pizza Inn, cheese, thin crust	12-13 in	8.14	4Q 92	4c
Taxes				
Tax, cigarette	pack	39	91	77s
Tax, gasoline	gal	8	91	77s
Taxes, hotel room	day	23.76	92	33c
Taxes, state	capita	1567	91	77s
Transportation				
ACCRA Index, Transportation		129.20	4Q 92	4c
Auto fixed costs, midsize		4434	91	60c
Auto operating cost, midsize		1598	91	60c
Auto rental, average	day	63.50	6/91	60c
Bus fare	one-way	0.50	3/93	2c
Bus fare, up to 10 miles	one-way	1.25	4Q 92	4c
Driver's license fee		17.50	12/90	43s
Ferry boat fare	one-way	2.00	3/93	2c
Limo fare, airport-city, average	day	11.00	6/91	60c
Railway fare, commuter	one-way	1.20	3/93	2c
Railway fare, heavy rail	one-way	1.25	3/93	2c
Railway fare, light rail	one-way	1.00	93	2c
Taxi fare, airport-city, average	day	27.00	6/91	60c
Tire balance, computer or spin balance, front	wheel	8.90	4Q 92	4c
Vehicle registration and license plate	2 years	27.50-149.50	93	67s
Travel				
Breakfast	day	11.62	6/91	60c
Business travel	day	297.00	92	86c
Business travel	day	165.00	4/93	89r
Dinner	day	35.70	6/91	60c
Dinner	day	36.75	92	85c
Lodging	day	218.98	91	60c
Lodging	day	227.00	92	85c
Lunch	day	18.59	6/91	60c
Travel, business	day	320.56	92	82c
Travel, business	day	329.93	93	88c
Utilities				
ACCRA Index, Utilities		147.50	4Q 92	4c
Electricity	500 KWh	69.06	4/93	16c
Electricity	KWh	0.14	4/93	16c
Electricity	mil Btu	27.51	90	64s

Values are in dollars or fractions of dollars. In the column headed *Ref*, references are shown to sources. Each reference is followed by a letter. These refer to the geographical level for which data were reported: s=State, r=Region, and c=City or metro. The abbreviation *ex* is used to mean *except* or *excluding*; *exp* stands for expenditures. For other abbreviations and further explanations, please see the Introduction.

New York, NY - continued

Item	Per	Value	Date	Ref.
Utilities				
Electricity, exp	year	674	89	15c
Electricity, partial electric and other energy, 1,800 sq ft living area new home	month	109.81	4Q 92	4c
Electricity, winter, 250 KWh	month	37.32	92	55c
Electricity, winter, 500 KWh	month	68.54	92	55c
Electricity, winter, 750 KWh	month	99.76	92	55c
Electricity, winter, 1000 KWh	month	130.98	92	55c
Utilities, fuels, public services, exp	year	2137	89	15c
Water, other public service, exp	year	135	89	15c

Newark, NJ

Item	Per	Value	Date	Ref.
Child Care				
Child care fee, average, center	hour	2.18	90	65r
Child care fee, average, nonregulated family day care	hour	1.83	90	65r
Child care fee, average, regulated family day care	hour	2.02	90	65r
Communications				
Long-distance telephone service, day, initial minute, 0-100 miles	min	0.09-0.42	91	12s
Long-distance telephone service, day, additional minute, 0-100 miles	min	0.03-0.12	91	12s
Telephone, flat rate	month	8.19	91	11c
Education				
Board, 4-yr private college/university	year	2883	91	22s
Board, 4-yr public college/university	year	1647	91	22s
Expenditures, local gov't, public elementary/secondary	pupil	9940	92	20s
Room, 4-year private college/university	year	2440	91	22s
Room, 4-year public college/university	year	2415	91	22s
Tuition, 2-year private college/university	year	5874	91	22s
Tuition, 2-year public college/university	year	1235	91	22s
Tuition, 4-year private college/university	year	10281	91	22s
Tuition, 4-year public college/university, in-state	year	2860	91	22s
Energy and Fuels				
Coal	mil Btu	1.79	90	64s
Energy	mil Btu	9.32	90	64s
Energy exp/householder, 1-family unit	year	588	90	28r
Energy exp/householder, <1,000 sq ft heating area	year	477	90	28r
Energy exp/householder, 1,000-1,999 sq ft heating area	year	517	90	28r
Energy exp/householder, 2,000+ sq ft heating area	year	630	90	28r
Energy exp/householder, mobile home	year	412	90	28r
Energy exp/householder, multifamily	year	498	90	28r
Gas, cooking, winter, 10 therms	month	10.21	92	56c
Gas, cooking, winter, 30 therms	month	20.29	92	56c
Gas, cooking, winter, 50 therms	month	30.37	92	56c
Gas, heating, winter, 100 therms	month	55.56	92	56c
Gas, heating, winter, average use	month	116.03	92	56c
Gas, natural	mil Btu	5.05	90	64s
Gas, natural	000 cu ft	6.73	91	46s
Gas, natural, exp	year	593	91	46s
Gasoline, unleaded regular	mil Btu	9.03	90	64s
Funerals				
Casket, 18-gauge steel, velvet interior		1811.58	91	24r
Cosmetology, hair care, etc.		111.08	91	24r
Embalming		329.42	91	24r
Facility use for ceremony		201.29	91	24r
Hearse, local		135.27	91	24r
Limousine, local		127.24	91	24r
Remains to funeral home, transfer		103.98	91	24r
Service charge, professional		724.98	91	24r
Vault, concrete, non-metallic liner		766.71	91	24r
Viewing facilities, use		260.60	91	24r

Newark, NJ - continued

Item	Per	Value	Date	Ref.
Groceries				
Apples, Red Delicious	lb	0.85	4/93	16r
Bacon	lb	2.12	4/93	16r
Bananas	lb	0.54	4/93	16r
Bread, white, pan	lb	0.81	4/93	16r
Butter	lb	2.02	4/93	16r
Carrots, short trimmed and topped	lb	0.51	4/93	16r
Chicken, fresh, whole	lb	1.04	4/93	16r
Chicken breast, bone-in	lb	2.21	4/93	16r
Chicken legs, bone-in	lb	1.16	4/93	16r
Chuck roast, USDA choice, boneless	lb	2.82	4/93	16r
Coffee, 100% ground roast, all sizes	lb	2.66	4/93	16r
Cucumbers	lb	0.85	4/93	16r
Eggs, Grade A large	doz	1.15	4/93	16r
Grapefruit	lb	0.45	4/93	16r
Grapes, Thompson Seedless	lb	1.52	4/93	16r
Ground beef, lean and extra lean	lb	2.36	4/93	16r
Ground chuck, 100% beef	lb	2.02	4/93	16r
Honey, jar	8 oz	0.96-1.75	92	5r
Honey, jar	lb	1.50-3.00	92	5r
Honey, squeeze bear	12-oz	1.50-1.99	92	5r
Ice cream, prepackaged, bulk, regular	1/2 gal	2.80	4/93	16r
Lemons	lb	0.96	4/93	16r
Lettuce, iceberg	lb	0.95	4/93	16r
Margarine, stick	lb	0.81	4/93	16r
Milk, fresh, whole, fortified	1/2 gal	1.30	4/93	16r
Oranges, navel	lb	0.56	4/93	16r
Peanut butter, creamy, all sizes	lb	1.88	4/93	16r
Pork chops, center cut, bone-in	lb	3.34	4/93	16r
Potato chips	16 oz	2.88	4/93	16r
Potatoes, white	lb	0.37	4/93	16r
Rib roast, USDA choice, bone-in	lb	4.94	4/93	16r
Round roast, USDA choice, boneless	lb	3.17	4/93	16r
Shortening, vegetable oil blends	lb	0.98	4/93	16r
Spaghetti and macaroni	lb	0.82	4/93	16r
Steak, round, graded & ungraded, ex USDA prime & choice	lb	4.04	4/93	16r
Steak, round, USDA choice, boneless	lb	3.90	4/93	16r
Steak, sirloin, USDA choice, boneless	lb	4.97	4/93	16r
Strawberries, dry pint	12 oz	0.90	4/93	16r
Sugar, white	lb	0.50	4/93	16r
Sugar, white, 33-80 oz pk	lb	0.41	4/93	16r
Tomatoes, field grown	lb	1.23	4/93	16r
Tuna, chunk, light	lb	2.22	4/93	16r
Turkey, frozen, whole	lb	1.04	4/93	16r
Health Care				
Childbirth, cesarean, hospital		5826	91	62r
Childbirth, cesarean, physician's fee		2053	91	62r
Childbirth, normal, hospital		2964	91	62r
Childbirth, normal, physician's fee		1492	91	62r
Hospital care, semiprivate room	day	313.24	90	27c
Medical insurance premium, per employee, small group comprehensive	month	390.55	10/91	25c
Medical plan per employee	year	3942	91	45r
Mental health care, exp	capita	28.84-37.59	90	38s
Mental health care, exp, state mental health agency	capita	57.16	90	38s
Mental health care, hospital psychiatric services, non-Federal, exp	capita	16.04	88	38s
Mental health care, mental health organization, multiservice, exp	capita	11.14	88	38s
Mental health care, psychiatric hospitals, private, exp	capita	17.85	88	38s
Mental health care, psychiatric out-patient clinics, freestanding, exp	capita	1.56	88	38s
Mental health care, psychiatric partial-care organizations, freestanding, exp	capita	0.66	88	38s
Mental health care, state and county mental hospitals, exp	capita	36.80	88	38s
Mental health care, VA medical centers, exp	capita	5.61	88	38s
Prescription drug co-pay, Medicaid	month	5.00	91	21s

Values are in dollars or fractions of dollars. In the column headed *Ref*, references are shown to sources. Each reference is followed by a letter. These refer to the geographical level for which data were reported: s=State, r=Region, and c=City or metro. The abbreviation *ex* is used to mean *except* or *excluding*; *exp* stands for expenditures. For other abbreviations and further explanations, please see the Introduction.

Newark, NJ - continued

Item	Per	Value	Date	Ref.
Health Care				
Substance abuse, hospital ancillary charge	incident	780	90	70s
Substance abuse, hospital physician charge	incident	550	90	70s
Substance abuse, hospital room and board	incident	6300	90	70s
Housing				
Home, median price	unit	184.40		26c
Rental unit, 1 bedroom	month	650	93	23c
Rental unit, 2 bedroom	month	765	93	23c
Rental unit, 3 bedroom	month	956	93	23c
Rental unit, 4 bedroom	month	1071	93	23c
Rental unit, efficiency	month	535	93	23c
Insurance and Pensions				
Auto insurance, private passenger	year	1081.45	91	63s
Taxes				
Tax, cigarette	pack	40	91	77s
Tax, gasoline	gal	10.50	91	77s
Taxes, state	capita	1501	91	77s
Transportation				
Auto rental, average	day	52.50	6/91	60c
Driver's license fee		16.00-17.50	12/90	43s
Taxi fare, airport-city, average	day	12.00	6/91	60c
Vehicle registration and license plate	year	32.90-93.90	93	44s
Travel				
Breakfast	day	6.86	6/91	60c
Business travel	day	165.00	4/93	89r
Dinner	day	25.39	6/91	60c
Lodging	day	135.09	91	60c
Lunch	day	9.52	6/91	60c
Travel, business	day	220.07	92	82c
Travel, business	day	225.40	93	88c
Utilities				
Electricity	mil Btu	26.63	90	64s

Newark, OH

Item	Per	Value	Date	Ref.
Composite ACCRA index		95.10	4Q 92	4c
Alcoholic Beverages				
Beer, Miller Lite or Budweiser, 12-oz containers	6 pack	3.59	4Q 92	4c
Liquor, J & B Scotch	750 ml	18.30	4Q 92	4c
Wine, Gallo Chablis blanc, 1.5 liter	bottle	5.92	4Q 92	4c
Clothing				
Jeans, man's denim		28.66	4Q 92	4c
Shirt, man's dress shirt		30.67	4Q 92	4c
Undervest, boy's size 10-14, cotton	3	3.68	4Q 92	4c
Communications				
Newspaper subscription, daily and Sunday home delivery, large-city	month	9.30	4Q 92	4c
Telephone bill, family of four	month	17.17	4Q 92	4c
Energy and Fuels				
Energy, combined forms, 1,800 sq ft heating area	month	123.96	4Q 92	4c
Energy, exc electricity, 1,800 sq ft heating area	month	56.50	4Q 92	4c
Gasoline, motor	gal	1.13	4Q 92	4c
Entertainment				
Bowling, evening rate	game	1.87	4Q 92	4c
Monopoly game, Parker Brothers', No. 9		10.69	4Q 92	4c
Movie	admission	5.00	4Q 92	4c
Tennis balls, yellow, Wilson or Penn, 3	can	2.22	4Q 92	4c

Newark, OH - continued

Item	Per	Value	Date	Ref.
Goods and Services				
ACCRA Index, Miscellaneous Goods and Services		96.40	4Q 92	4c
Groceries				
ACCRA Index, Groceries		98.60	4Q 92	4c
Babyfood, strained vegetables, lowest price	4-4.5 oz jar	0.42	4Q 92	4c
Bananas	lb	0.41	4Q 92	4c
Bread, white	24 oz	0.56	4Q 92	4c
Cheese, Kraft grated Parmesan	8-oz canister	3.32	4Q 92	4c
Chicken, fryer, whole	lb	1.02	4Q 92	4c
Cigarettes, Winston	carton	16.98	4Q 92	4c
Coffee, vacuum-packed	13-oz can	2.08	4Q 92	4c
Corn, frozen	10 oz	0.67	4Q 92	4c
Corn Flakes, Kellogg's or Post Toasties	18 oz	2.00	4Q 92	4c
Eggs, Grade A large	doz	0.76	4Q 92	4c
Ground beef or hamburger	lb	1.16	4Q 92	4c
Lettuce, iceberg	head	0.72	4Q 92	4c
Margarine, Blue Bonnet or Parkay cubes	lb	0.66	4Q 92	4c
Milk, whole	1/2 gal	1.40	4Q 92	4c
Orange juice, Minute Maid frozen	12-oz can	1.27	4Q 92	4c
Peaches	29-oz can	1.54	4Q 92	4c
Peas Sweet, Del Monte or Green Giant	15-17 oz can	0.50	4Q 92	4c
Potatoes, white or red	10-lb sack	1.32	4Q 92	4c
Sausage, Jimmy Dean, 100% pork	lb	2.22	4Q 92	4c
Shortening, vegetable, Crisco	3-lb can	2.34	4Q 92	4c
Soft drink, Coca Cola	2 liter	1.01	4Q 92	4c
Steak, T-bone	lb	5.39	4Q 92	4c
Sugar, cane or beet	4 lb	1.60	4Q 92	4c
Tomatoes, Hunt's or Del Monte	14.5-oz can	0.82	4Q 92	4c
Tuna, chunk, light	6.125-6.5 oz can	0.66	4Q 92	4c
Health Care				
ACCRA Index, Health Care		90.80	4Q 92	4c
Analgesic, Aspirin, Bayer, 325 mg tablets	100	4.54	4Q 92	4c
Dentist's fee, adult teeth cleaning and periodic oral exam	visit	45.00	4Q 92	4c
Doctor's fee, routine exam, established patient	visit	33.57	4Q 92	4c
Hospital care, semiprivate room	day	255.00	4Q 92	4c
Household Goods				
Appliance repair, home, service call, washing machine	min labor charge	28.74	4Q 92	4c
Laundry detergent, Tide Ultra, Bold, or Cheer	42 oz	3.97	4Q 92	4c
Tissues, facial, Kleenex brand	175-count box	1.19	4Q 92	4c
Housing				
ACCRA Index, Housing		85.10	4Q 92	4c
House, 1,800 sq ft, 8,000 sq ft lot, new, urban	total	94000	4Q 92	4c
House payment, principal and interest, 25% down payment	month	523	4Q 92	4c
Mortgage rate, incl. points & origination fee, 30-year fixed or adjustable rate	percent	8.12	4Q 92	4c
Rent, apartment, 2 bedrooms - 1-1/2 to 2 baths, unfurnished, 950 sq ft, water	month	420	4Q 92	4c

Values are in dollars or fractions of dollars. In the column headed *Ref*, references are shown to sources. Each reference is followed by a letter. These refer to the geographical level for which data were reported: s=State, r=Region, and c=City or metro. The abbreviation *ex* is used to mean *except* or *excluding*; *exp* stands for expenditures. For other abbreviations and further explanations, please see the Introduction.

Newark, OH - continued

Item	Per	Value	Date	Ref.
Personal Goods				
Shampoo, Alberto VO5	15 oz	1.12	4Q 92	4c
Toothpaste, Crest or Colgate	6-7 oz	1.82	4Q 92	4c
Personal Services				
Dry cleaning, man's 2-piece suit		6.65	4Q 92	4c
Haircare, woman's shampoo, trim and blow-dry		14.00	4Q 92	4c
Haircut, man's barbershop, no styling		6.50	4Q 92	4c
Restaurant Food				
Chicken, fried, thigh and drumstick		1.94	4Q 92	4c
Hamburger with cheese	1/4 lb	1.69	4Q 92	4c
Pizza, Pizza Hut or Pizza Inn, cheese, thin crust	12-13 in	7.59	4Q 92	4c
Transportation				
ACCRA Index, Transportation		101.70	4Q 92	4c
Tire balance, computer or spin balance, front	wheel	6.75	4Q 92	4c
Utilities				
ACCRA Index, Utilities		111.00	4Q 92	4c
Electricity, partial electric and other energy, 1,800 sq ft living area new home	month	67.46	4Q 92	4c

Niagara Falls, NY

Item	Per	Value	Date	Ref.
Child Care				
Child care fee, average, center	hour	2.18	90	65r
Child care fee, average, nonregulated family day care	hour	1.83	90	65r
Child care fee, average, regulated family day care	hour	2.02	90	65r
Education				
Board, 4-yr private college/university	year	2451	91	22s
Board, 4-yr public college/university	year	1725	91	22s
Expenditures, local gov't, public elementary/secondary	pupil	8603	92	20s
Room, 4-year private college/university	year	2652	91	22s
Room, 4-year public college/university	year	2183	91	22s
Tuition, 2-year private college/university	year	5926	91	22s
Tuition, 2-year public college/university	year	1419	91	22s
Tuition, 4-year private college/university	year	10340	91	22s
Tuition, 4-year public college/university, in-state	year	1587	91	22s
Energy and Fuels				
Coal	mil Btu	1.66	90	64s
Energy	mil Btu	10.68	90	64s
Energy exp/householder, 1-family unit	year	588	90	28r
Energy exp/householder, <1,000 sq ft heating area	year	477	90	28r
Energy exp/householder, 1,000-1,999 sq ft heating area	year	517	90	28r
Energy exp/householder, 2,000+ sq ft heating area	year	630	90	28r
Energy exp/householder, mobile home	year	412	90	28r
Energy exp/householder, multifamily	year	498	90	28r
Gas, natural	mil Btu	5.25	90	64s
Gas, natural	000 cu ft	7.35	91	46s
Gas, natural, exp	year	557	91	46s
Gasoline, unleaded regular	mil Btu	8.83	90	64s
Funerals				
Casket, 18-gauge steel, velvet interior		1811.58	91	24r
Cosmetology, hair care, etc.		111.08	91	24r
Embalming		329.42	91	24r
Facility use for ceremony		201.29	91	24r
Hearse, local		135.27	91	24r
Limousine, local		127.24	91	24r
Remains to funeral home, transfer		103.98	91	24r
Service charge, professional		724.98	91	24r

Niagara Falls, NY - continued

Item	Per	Value	Date	Ref.
Funerals - continued				
Vault, concrete, non-metallic liner		766.71	91	24r
Viewing facilities, use		260.60	91	24r
Groceries				
Apples, Red Delicious	lb	0.85	4/93	16r
Bacon	lb	2.12	4/93	16r
Bananas	lb	0.54	4/93	16r
Bread, white, pan	lb	0.81	4/93	16r
Butter	lb	2.02	4/93	16r
Carrots, short trimmed and topped	lb	0.51	4/93	16r
Chicken, fresh, whole	lb	1.04	4/93	16r
Chicken breast, bone-in	lb	2.21	4/93	16r
Chicken legs, bone-in	lb	1.16	4/93	16r
Chuck roast, USDA choice, boneless	lb	2.82	4/93	16r
Coffee, 100% ground roast, all sizes	lb	2.66	4/93	16r
Cucumbers	lb	0.85	4/93	16r
Eggs, Grade A large	doz	1.15	4/93	16r
Grapefruit	lb	0.45	4/93	16r
Grapes, Thompson Seedless	lb	1.52	4/93	16r
Ground beef, lean and extra lean	lb	2.36	4/93	16r
Ground chuck, 100% beef	lb	2.02	4/93	16r
Honey, jar	8 oz	0.96-1.75	92	5r
Honey, jar	lb	1.50-3.00	92	5r
Honey, squeeze bear	12-oz	1.50-1.99	92	5r
Ice cream, prepackaged, bulk, regular	1/2 gal	2.80	4/93	16r
Lemons	lb	0.96	4/93	16r
Lettuce, iceberg	lb	0.95	4/93	16r
Margarine, stick	lb	0.81	4/93	16r
Milk, fresh, whole, fortified	1/2 gal	1.30	4/93	16r
Oranges, navel	lb	0.56	4/93	16r
Peanut butter, creamy, all sizes	lb	1.88	4/93	16r
Pork chops, center cut, bone-in	lb	3.34	4/93	16r
Potato chips	16 oz	2.88	4/93	16r
Potatoes, white	lb	0.37	4/93	16r
Rib roast, USDA choice, bone-in	lb	4.94	4/93	16r
Round roast, USDA choice, boneless	lb	3.17	4/93	16r
Shortening, vegetable oil blends	lb	0.98	4/93	16r
Spaghetti and macaroni	lb	0.82	4/93	16r
Steak, round, graded & ungraded, ex USDA prime & choice	lb	4.04	4/93	16r
Steak, round, USDA choice, boneless	lb	3.90	4/93	16r
Steak, sirloin, USDA choice, boneless	lb	4.97	4/93	16r
Strawberries, dry pint	12 oz	0.90	4/93	16r
Sugar, white	lb	0.50	4/93	16r
Sugar, white, 33-80 oz pk	lb	0.41	4/93	16r
Tomatoes, field grown	lb	1.23	4/93	16r
Tuna, chunk, light	lb	2.22	4/93	16r
Turkey, frozen, whole	lb	1.04	4/93	16r
Health Care				
Childbirth, cesarean, hospital		5826	91	62r
Childbirth, cesarean, physician's fee		2053	91	62r
Childbirth, normal, hospital		2964	91	62r
Childbirth, normal, physician's fee		1492	91	62r
Medical plan per employee	year	3942	91	45r
Mental health care, exp	capita	53.68-118.35	90	38s
Mental health care, exp, state mental health agency	capita	118.34	90	38s
Mental health care, hospital psychiatric services, non-Federal, exp	capita	29.77	88	38s
Mental health care, mental health organization, multiservice, exp	capita	20.03	88	38s
Mental health care, psychiatric hospitals, private, exp	capita	8.37	88	38s
Mental health care, psychiatric out-patient clinics, freestanding, exp	capita	7.96	88	38s
Mental health care, psychiatric partial-care organizations, freestanding, exp	capita	1.24	88	38s
Mental health care, state and county mental hospitals, exp	capita	89.52	88	38s
Mental health care, VA medical centers, exp	capita	7.12	88	38s
Prescription drug co-pay, Medicaid	month	23.00	91	21s

Values are in dollars or fractions of dollars. In the column headed *Ref*, references are shown to sources. Each reference is followed by a letter. These refer to the geographical level for which data were reported: s=State, r=Region, and c=City or metro. The abbreviation *ex* is used to mean *except* or *excluding; exp* stands for expenditures. For other abbreviations and further explanations, please see the Introduction.

Niagara Falls, NY - continued

Item	Per	Value	Date	Ref.
Health Care				
Substance abuse, hospital ancillary charge	incident	1040	90	70s
Substance abuse, hospital physician charge	incident	360	90	70s
Substance abuse, hospital room and board	incident	6330	90	70s
Insurance and Pensions				
Auto insurance, private passenger	year	840.89	91	63s
Taxes				
Tax, cigarette	pack	39	91	77s
Tax, gasoline	gal	8	91	77s
Taxes, state	capita	1567	91	77s
Transportation				
Driver's license fee		17.50	12/90	43s
Vehicle registration and license plate	2 years	27.50-149.50	93	67s
Travel				
Business travel	day	165.00	4/93	89r
Utilities				
Electricity	mil Btu	27.51	90	64s

Norfolk, VA

Item	Per	Value	Date	Ref.
Child Care				
Child care fee, average, center	hour	1.29	90	65r
Child care fee, average, nonregulated family day care	hour	0.89	90	65r
Child care fee, average, regulated family day care	hour	1.32	90	65r
Communications				
Long-distance telephone service, day, initial minute, 0-100 miles	min	0.21-0.35	91	12s
Long-distance telephone service, day, additional minute, 0-100 miles	min	0.12-0.21	91	12s
Long-distance telephone service, evenings/weekends, 0-100 mi, initial minute	min	0.08-0.14	91	12s
Long-distance telephone service, evenings/weekends, 0-100 mi, additional minute	min	0.05-0.08	91	12s
Construction				
Plywood, post-Hurricane Andrew	4x8 sheet	10.99	92	13c
Plywood, pre-Hurricane Andrew	4x8 sheet	7.84	92	13c
Education				
Board, 4-yr private college/university	year	1804	91	22s
Board, 4-yr public college/university	year	1688	91	22s
Expenditures, local gov't, public elementary/secondary	pupil	5487	92	20s
Room, 4-year private college/university	year	1659	91	22s
Room, 4-year public college/university	year	1916	91	22s
Tuition, 2-year private college/university	year	4852	91	22s
Tuition, 2-year public college/university	year	867	91	22s
Tuition, 4-year private college/university	year	7621	91	22s
Tuition, 4-year public college/university, in-state	year	2691	91	22s
Energy and Fuels				
Coal	mil Btu	1.60	90	64s
Energy	mil Btu	8.89	90	64s
Energy exp/householder, 1-family unit	year	487	90	28r
Energy exp/householder, <1,000 sq ft heating area	year	393	90	28r
Energy exp/householder, 1,000-1,999 sq ft heating area	year	442	90	28r
Energy exp/householder, 2,000+ sq ft heating area	year	577	90	28r
Energy exp/householder, mobile home	year	366	90	28r

Norfolk, VA - continued

Item	Per	Value	Date	Ref.
Energy and Fuels - continued				
Energy exp/householder, multifamily	year	382	90	28r
Gas, cooking, winter, 10 therms	month	13.38	92	56c
Gas, cooking, winter, 30 therms	month	26.15	92	56c
Gas, cooking, winter, 50 therms	month	38.56	92	56c
Gas, heating, winter, 100 therms	month	69.31	92	56c
Gas, heating, winter, average use	month	76.69	92	56c
Gas, natural	mil Btu	4.67	90	64s
Gas, natural	000 cu ft	6.80	91	46s
Gas, natural, exp	year	566	91	46s
Gasoline, unleaded premium	gal	65.05	12/92	31c
Gasoline, unleaded regular	mil Btu	9.46	90	64s
Entertainment				
Miniature golf admission	adult	6.18	92	1r
Miniature golf admission	child	5.14	92	1r
Waterpark admission	adult	11.00	92	1r
Waterpark admission	child	8.55	92	1r
Funerals				
Casket, 18-gauge steel, velvet interior		2029.08	91	24r
Cosmetology, hair care, etc.		75.10	91	24r
Embalming		249.24	91	24r
Facility use for ceremony		162.27	91	24r
Hearse, local		114.04	91	24r
Limousine, local		88.57	91	24r
Remains to funeral home, transfer		92.61	91	24r
Service charge, professional		682.42	91	24r
Vault, concrete, non-metallic liner		798.70	91	24r
Viewing facilities, use		163.86	91	24r
Groceries				
Apples, Red Delicious	lb	0.79	4/93	16r
Bacon	lb	1.75	4/93	16r
Bananas	lb	0.42	4/93	16r
Beef, stew, boneless	lb	2.61	4/93	16r
Bologna, all beef or mixed	lb	2.24	4/93	16r
Bread, white, pan	lb	0.64	4/93	16r
Bread, whole wheat, pan	lb	0.96	4/93	16r
Cabbage	lb	0.37	4/93	16r
Carrots, short trimmed and topped	lb	0.47	4/93	16r
Celery	lb	0.64	4/93	16r
Cheese, American	lb	2.98	4/93	16r
Cheese, Cheddar	lb	3.28	4/93	16r
Chicken, fresh, whole	lb	0.77	4/93	16r
Chicken breast, bone-in	lb	1.92	4/93	16r
Chicken legs, bone-in	lb	1.06	4/93	16r
Chuck roast, graded and ungraded, ex USDA prime and choice	lb	2.40	4/93	16r
Chuck roast, USDA choice, bone-in	lb	2.19	4/93	16r
Chuck roast, USDA choice, boneless	lb	2.38	4/93	16r
Coffee, 100% ground roast, all sizes	lb	2.48	4/93	16r
Crackers, soda, salted	lb	1.15	4/93	16r
Eggs, Grade A large	doz	0.96	4/93	16r
Flour, white, all purpose	lb	0.24	4/93	16r
Frankfurters, all meat or all beef	lb	2.01	4/93	16r
Grapefruit	lb	0.44	4/93	16r
Grapes, Thompson Seedless	lb	1.40	4/93	16r
Ground beef, 100% beef	lb	1.58	4/93	16r
Ground beef, lean and extra lean	lb	2.09	4/93	16r
Ground chuck, 100% beef	lb	1.98	4/93	16r
Ham, boneless, excluding canned	lb	2.89	4/93	16r
Ham, picnic, shoulder, bone-in, smoked	lb	1.02	4/93	16r
Ham, rump or steak half, bone-in, smoked	lb	1.48	4/93	16r
Ice cream, prepackaged, bulk, regular	1/2 gal	2.41	4/93	16r
Lemons	lb	1.05	4/93	16r
Lettuce, iceberg	lb	0.81	4/93	16r
Margarine, stick	lb	0.88	4/93	16r
Oranges, navel	lb	0.55	4/93	16r
Pears, Anjou	lb	0.92	4/93	16r
Pork chops, center cut, bone-in	lb	3.13	4/93	16r
Potato chips	16 oz	2.94	4/93	16r
Potatoes, white	lb	0.43	4/93	16r
Rib roast, USDA choice, bone-in	lb	4.63	4/93	16r

Values are in dollars or fractions of dollars. In the column headed *Ref*, references are shown to sources. Each reference is followed by a letter. These refer to the geographical level for which data were reported: s=State, r=Region, and c=City or metro. The abbreviation *ex* is used to mean *except* or *excluding*; *exp* stands for expenditures. For other abbreviations and further explanations, please see the Introduction.

Norfolk, VA - continued

Item	Per	Value	Date	Ref.
Groceries				
Rice, white, long grain, uncooked	lb	0.45	4/93	16r
Round roast, graded & ungraded, ex USDA prime & choice	lb	3.03	4/93	16r
Round roast, USDA choice, boneless	lb	3.09	4/93	16r
Sausage, fresh, loose	lb	2.08	4/93	16r
Short ribs, bone-in	lb	2.66	4/93	16r
Shortening, vegetable oil blends	lb	0.69	4/93	16r
Spaghetti and macaroni	lb	0.81	4/93	16r
Steak, rib eye, USDA choice, boneless	lb	6.24	4/93	16r
Steak, round, graded & ungraded, ex USDA prime & choice	lb	3.31	4/93	16r
Steak, round, USDA choice, boneless	lb	3.34	4/93	16r
Steak, sirloin, graded & ungraded, ex USDA prime & choice	lb	4.19	4/93	16r
Steak, sirloin, USDA choice, boneless	lb	4.46	4/93	16r
Steak, T-bone, USDA choice, bone-in	lb	5.25	4/93	16r
Strawberries, dry pint	12 oz	0.92	4/93	16r
Sugar, white	lb	0.39	4/93	16r
Sugar, white, 33-80 oz pk	lb	0.38	4/93	16r
Tomatoes, field grown	lb	0.88	4/93	16r
Tuna, chunk, light	lb	1.79	4/93	16r
Turkey, frozen, whole	lb	1.04	4/93	16r
Yogurt, natural, fruit flavored	1/2 pint	0.57	4/93	16r
Health Care				
Childbirth, cesarean, hospital		5034	91	62r
Childbirth, cesarean, physician's fee		2053	91	62r
Childbirth, normal, hospital		2712	91	62r
Childbirth, normal, physician's fee		1492	91	62r
Hospital care, semiprivate room	day	280.26	90	27c
Medical insurance premium, per employee, small group comprehensive	month	349.45	10/91	25c
Medical plan per employee	year	3495	91	45r
Mental health care, exp	capita	37.60-53.67	90	38s
Mental health care, exp, state mental health agency	capita	44.54	90	38s
Mental health care, hospital psychiatric services, non-Federal, exp	capita	9.90	88	38s
Mental health care, mental health organization, multiservice, exp	capita	17.29	88	38s
Mental health care, psychiatric hospitals, private, exp	capita	32.58	88	38s
Mental health care, psychiatric out-patient clinics, freestanding, exp	capita	0.93	88	38s
Mental health care, psychiatric partial-care organizations, freestanding, exp	capita	0.25	88	38s
Mental health care, state and county mental hospitals, exp	capita	28.61	88	38s
Mental health care, VA medical centers, exp	capita	3.95	88	38s
Physician fee, family practice, first-visit		75.00	91	62r
Physician fee, family practice, revisit		34.00	91	62r
Physician fee, general practice, first-visit		61.00	91	62r
Physician fee, general practice, revisit		32.00	91	62r
Physician fee, general surgeon, first-visit		64.00	91	62r
Physician fee, general surgeon, revisit		40.00	91	62r
Physician fee, internal medicine, first-visit		98.00	91	62r
Physician fee, internal medicine, revisit		40.00	91	62r
Physician fee, median, neurosurgeon, first-visit		130.00	91	62r
Physician fee, median, nonsurgical specialist, first-visit		95.00	91	62r
Physician fee, median, orthopedic surgeon, first-visit		91.00	91	62r
Physician fee, median, plastic surgeon, first-visit		66.00	91	62r
Physician fee, median, surgical specialist, first-visit		62.00	91	62r
Physician fee, neurosurgeon, revisit		50.00	91	62r
Physician fee, nonsurgical specialist, revisit		40.00	91	62r
Physician fee, obstetrics/gynecology, first-visit		64.00	91	62r

Norfolk, VA - continued

Item	Per	Value	Date	Ref.
Health Care - continued				
Physician fee, obstetrics/gynecology, revisit		41.00	91	62r
Physician fee, orthopedic surgeon, revisit		40.00	91	62r
Physician fee, pediatrician, first-visit		49.00	91	62r
Physician fee, pediatrician, revisit		33.00	91	62r
Physician fee, plastic surgeon, revisit		43.00	91	62r
Physician fee, surgical specialist, revisit		37.00	91	62r
Substance abuse, hospital ancillary charge	incident	1220	90	70s
Substance abuse, hospital physician charge	incident	590	90	70s
Substance abuse, hospital room and board	incident	6280	90	70s
Housing				
Home, median price	unit	94.80		26c
Rental unit, 1 bedroom	month	468	93	23c
Rental unit, 2 bedroom	month	550	93	23c
Rental unit, 3 bedroom	month	688	93	23c
Rental unit, 4 bedroom	month	771	93	23c
Rental unit, efficiency	month	385	93	23c
Insurance and Pensions				
Auto insurance, private passenger	year	559.45	91	63s
Taxes				
Tax, cigarette	pack	2.50	91	77s
Tax, gasoline	gal	17.50	91	77s
Taxes, state	capita	1090	91	77s
Transportation				
Auto rental, average	day	43.25	6/91	60c
Bus fare	one-way	0.75	3/93	2c
Driver's license fee		12.00	12/90	40s
Ferry boat fare	one-way	0.80	3/93	2c
Limo fare, airport-city, average	day	7.50	6/91	60c
Taxi fare, airport-city, average	day	15.00	6/91	60c
Vehicle registration and license plate	year	26.50-37.50	93	90s
Travel				
Breakfast	day	5.42	6/91	60c
Business travel	day	193.00	4/93	89r
Dinner	day	20.03	6/91	60c
Lodging	day	97.00	91	60c
Lunch	day	7.53	6/91	60c
Utilities				
Electricity	mil Btu	17.70	90	64s

North Haven, CT

Item	Per	Value	Date	Ref.
Groceries				
Bacon	lb	1.68	12/91	72c
Barbecue sauce	oz	0.09	12/91	72c
Bread, Wonder	oz	0.07	12/91	72c
Butter	6 oz	2.01	12/91	72c
Candy, M&Ms	lb	2.60	12/91	72c
Cat food, Purina Cat Chow	lb	0.90	12/91	72c
Cereal, Cheerios	oz	0.19	12/91	72c
Cheese, American	oz	0.19	12/91	72c
Cheese, Cheddar	oz	0.17	12/91	72c
Coffee, Maxwell House	oz	0.14	12/91	72c
Cookies, Nabisco Oreos	oz	0.14	12/91	72c
Dog food, Purina Dog Chow	lb	0.40	12/91	72c
Eggs	1	0.05	12/91	72c
Frankfurters, Hebrew National	1	0.40	12/91	72c
Ham, canned	lb	3.62	12/91	72c
Jelly, Welch's grape	oz	0.12	12/91	72c
Ketchup, Heinz	oz	0.08	12/91	72c
Lasagna, Stouffer's	oz	1.17	12/91	72c
Margarine	lb	0.53	12/91	72c
Mayonnaise, Hellmann's	48 oz	4.04	12/91	72c

Values are in dollars or fractions of dollars. In the column headed *Ref*, references are shown to sources. Each reference is followed by a letter. These refer to the geographical level for which data were reported: s=State, r=Region, and c=City or metro. The abbreviation *ex* is used to mean *except* or *excluding*; *exp* stands for expenditures. For other abbreviations and further explanations, please see the Introduction.

North Haven, CT - continued

Item	Per	Value	Date	Ref.
Groceries				
Milk	1/2 gal	0.20	12/91	72c
Muffins, Thomas English	oz	0.10	12/91	72c
Orange juice, frozen	oz	0.05	12/91	72c
Orange juice, Tropicana	96 oz	3.45	12/91	72c
Oranges	1	0.22	12/91	72c
Peanut butter, Skippy	12 oz	0.89	12/91	72c
Sausage, bulk or link	oz	0.18	12/91	72c
Snacks, Doritos corn chips	oz	0.15	12/91	72c
Spaghetti	lb	0.53	12/91	72c
Spaghetti sauce	oz	0.05	12/91	72c
Sugar	5 lb	1.98	12/91	72c
Tomato soup, Campbell's	10 3/4 oz	1.39	12/91	72c
Health Care				
Analgesic, Advil	1	0.11	12/91	72c
Household Goods				
Aluminum foil, Reynolds	ft	0.02	12/91	72c
Dishwashing detergent, Cascade	oz	0.05	12/91	72c
Laundry detergent, Tide liquid	1/2 gal	3.45	12/91	72c
Laundry detergent, Tide powder	oz	0.13	12/91	72c
Laundry supplies, Bounce fabric softener	sheet	0.16	12/91	72c
Paper towels	ft	0.02	12/91	72c
Pet products, cat litter	lb	0.32	12/91	72c
Plastic wrap	ft	0.01	12/91	72c
Personal Goods				
Deodorant, Secret Solid	2.7 oz	3.48	12/91	72c
Diapers, disposable	1	0.31	12/91	72c
Feminine hygiene product, Stayfree	24	2.72	12/91	72c
Mouthwash, Listerine	oz	0.13	12/91	72c
Mouthwash, Scope	oz	0.19	12/91	72c
Shampoo, Pert Plus	oz	0.24	12/91	72c
Toothpaste	oz	0.33	12/91	72c

Norwalk, CT

Item	Per	Value	Date	Ref.
Child Care				
Child care fee, average, center	hour	2.18	90	65r
Child care fee, average, nonregulated family day care	hour	1.83	90	65r
Child care fee, average, regulated family day care	hour	2.02	90	65r
Communications				
Long-distance telephone service, day, initial minute, 0-100 miles	min	0.18-0.45	91	12s
Long-distance telephone service, day, additional minute, 0-100 miles	min	0.10-0.26	91	12s
Long-distance telephone service, evenings/weekends, 0-100 mi, initial minute	min	0.07-0.18	91	12s
Long-distance telephone service, evenings/weekends, 0-100 mi, additional minute	min	0.04-0.10	91	12s
Education				
Board, 4-yr private college/university	year	2182	91	22s
Board, 4-yr public college/university	year	1750	91	22s
Expenditures, local gov't, public elementary/secondary	pupil	8308	92	20s
Room, 4-year private college/university	year	2703	91	22s
Room, 4-year public college/university	year	1913	91	22s
Tuition, 2-year private college/university	year	8586	91	22s
Tuition, 2-year public college/university	year	972	91	22s
Tuition, 4-year private college/university	year	12315	91	22s
Tuition, 4-year public college/university, in-state	year	2313	91	22s
Energy and Fuels				
Coal	mil Btu	2.15	90	64s
Energy	mil Btu	11.62	90	64s
Energy exp/householder, 1-family unit	year	588	90	28r
Energy exp/householder, <1,000 sq ft heating area	year	477	90	28r

Norwalk, CT - continued

Item	Per	Value	Date	Ref.
Energy and Fuels - continued				
Energy exp/householder, 1,000-1,999 sq ft heating area	year	517	90	28r
Energy exp/householder, 2,000+ sq ft heating area	year	630	90	28r
Energy exp/householder, mobile home	year	412	90	28r
Energy exp/householder, multifamily	year	498	90	28r
Gas, natural	mil Btu	6.40	90	64s
Gas, natural	000 cu ft	8.74	91	46s
Gas, natural, exp	year	756	91	46s
Gasoline, unleaded regular	mil Btu	10.06	90	64s
Entertainment				
Miniature golf admission	adult	6.18	92	1r
Miniature golf admission	child	5.14	92	1r
Waterpark admission	adult	11.00	92	1r
Waterpark admission	child	8.55	92	1r
Funerals				
Casket, 18-gauge steel, velvet interior		1853.42	91	24r
Cosmetology, hair care, etc.		98.33	91	24r
Embalming		273.94	91	24r
Facility use for ceremony		196.06	91	24r
Hearse, local		145.67	91	24r
Limousine, local		131.07	91	24r
Remains to funeral home, transfer		135.24	91	24r
Service charge, professional		843.16	91	24r
Vault, concrete, non-metallic liner		709.14	91	24r
Viewing facilities, use		229.85	91	24r
Groceries				
Apples, Red Delicious	lb	0.85	4/93	16r
Bacon	lb	2.12	4/93	16r
Bananas	lb	0.54	4/93	16r
Bread, white, pan	lb	0.81	4/93	16r
Butter	lb	2.02	4/93	16r
Carrots, short trimmed and topped	lb	0.51	4/93	16r
Chicken, fresh, whole	lb	1.04	4/93	16r
Chicken breast, bone-in	lb	2.21	4/93	16r
Chicken legs, bone-in	lb	1.16	4/93	16r
Chuck roast, USDA choice, boneless	lb	2.82	4/93	16r
Coffee, 100% ground roast, all sizes	lb	2.66	4/93	16r
Cucumbers	lb	0.85	4/93	16r
Eggs, Grade A large	doz	1.15	4/93	16r
Grapefruit	lb	0.45	4/93	16r
Grapes, Thompson Seedless	lb	1.52	4/93	16r
Ground beef, lean and extra lean	lb	2.36	4/93	16r
Ground chuck, 100% beef	lb	2.02	4/93	16r
Honey, jar	8 oz	0.96-1.75	92	5r
Honey, jar	lb	1.50-3.00	92	5r
Honey, squeeze bear	12-oz	1.50-1.99	92	5r
Ice cream, prepackaged, bulk, regular	1/2 gal	2.80	4/93	16r
Lemons	lb	0.96	4/93	16r
Lettuce, iceberg	lb	0.95	4/93	16r
Margarine, stick	lb	0.81	4/93	16r
Milk, fresh, whole, fortified	1/2 gal	1.30	4/93	16r
Oranges, navel	lb	0.56	4/93	16r
Peanut butter, creamy, all sizes	lb	1.88	4/93	16r
Pork chops, center cut, bone-in	lb	3.34	4/93	16r
Potato chips	16 oz	2.88	4/93	16r
Potatoes, white	lb	0.37	4/93	16r
Rib roast, USDA choice, bone-in	lb	4.94	4/93	16r
Round roast, USDA choice, boneless	lb	3.17	4/93	16r
Shortening, vegetable oil blends	lb	0.98	4/93	16r
Spaghetti and macaroni	lb	0.82	4/93	16r
Steak, round, graded & ungraded, ex USDA prime & choice	lb	4.04	4/93	16r
Steak, round, USDA choice, boneless	lb	3.90	4/93	16r
Steak, sirloin, USDA choice, boneless	lb	4.97	4/93	16r
Strawberries, dry pint	12 oz	0.90	4/93	16r
Sugar, white	lb	0.50	4/93	16r
Sugar, white, 33-80 oz pk	lb	0.41	4/93	16r
Tomatoes, field grown	lb	1.23	4/93	16r
Tuna, chunk, light	lb	2.22	4/93	16r

Values are in dollars or fractions of dollars. In the column headed *Ref*, references are shown to sources. Each reference is followed by a letter. These refer to the geographical level for which data were reported: s=State, r=Region, and c=City or metro. The abbreviation *ex* is used to mean *except* or *excluding*; *exp* stands for expenditures. For other abbreviations and further explanations, please see the Introduction.

Norwalk, CT - continued

Item	Per	Value	Date	Ref.
Groceries				
Turkey, frozen, whole	lb	1.04	4/93	16r
Health Care				
Childbirth, cesarean, hospital		5826	91	62r
Childbirth, cesarean, physician's fee		2053	91	62r
Childbirth, normal, hospital		2964	91	62r
Childbirth, normal, physician's fee		1492	91	62r
Medical plan per employee	year	3958	91	45r
Mental health care, exp	capita	53.68-118.35	90	38s
Mental health care, exp, state mental health agency	capita	72.81	90	38s
Mental health care, hospital psychiatric services, non-Federal, exp	capita	19.30	88	38s
Mental health care, mental health organization, multiservice, exp	capita	19.14	88	38s
Mental health care, psychiatric hospitals, private, exp	capita	35.86	88	38s
Mental health care, psychiatric out-patient clinics, freestanding, exp	capita	5.83	88	38s
Mental health care, psychiatric partial-care organizations, freestanding, exp	capita	0.15	88	38s
Mental health care, state and county mental hospitals, exp	capita	51.85	88	38s
Mental health care, VA medical centers, exp	capita	1.74	88	38s
Prescription drug co-pay, Medicaid	month	10.00	91	21s
Substance abuse, hospital ancillary charge	incident	1200	90	70s
Substance abuse, hospital physician charge	incident	270	90	70s
Substance abuse, hospital room and board	incident	4420	90	70s
Insurance and Pensions				
Auto insurance, private passenger	year	928.10	91	63s
Taxes				
Tax, cigarette	pack	45	91	77s
Tax, gasoline	gal	26	91	77s
Taxes, state	capita	1514	91	77s
Transportation				
Driver's license fee		31.00	12/90	43s
Travel				
Business travel	day	165.00	4/93	89r
Utilities				
Electricity	mil Btu	26.83	90	64s

Oakland, CA

Item	Per	Value	Date	Ref.
Child Care				
Child care fee, average, center	hour	1.71	90	65r
Child care fee, average, nonregulated family day care	hour	1.32	90	65r
Child care fee, average, regulated family day care	hour	1.86	90	65r
Communications				
Long-distance telephone service, day, initial minute, 0-100 miles	min	0.17-0.40	91	12s
Long-distance telephone service, day, additional minute, 0-100 miles	min	0.07-0.31	91	12s
Long-distance telephone service, evenings/weekends, 0-100 mi, initial minute	min	0.07-0.16	91	12s
Long-distance telephone service, evenings/weekends, 0-100 mi, additional minute	min	0.03-0.12	91	12s
Telephone, flat rate	month	8.35	91	11c
Telephone, residential, private line, rotary, unlimited calling	month	13.07	10/91	78c
Education				
Board, 4-yr private college/university	year	2515	91	22s
Board, 4-yr public college/university	year	2268	91	22s

Oakland, CA - continued

Item	Per	Value	Date	Ref.
Education - continued				
Expenditures, local gov't, public elementary/secondary	pupil	4866	92	20s
Room, 4-year private college/university	year	2622	91	22s
Room, 4-year public college/university	year	2406	91	22s
Tuition, 2-year private college/university	year	7942	91	22s
Tuition, 2-year public college/university	year	114	91	22s
Tuition, 4-year private college/university	year	10863	91	22s
Tuition, 4-year public college/university, in-state	year	1220	91	22s
Energy and Fuels				
Coal	mil Btu	2.01	90	64s
Energy	mil Btu	9.08	90	64s
Energy exp/householder, 1-family unit	year	362	90	28r
Energy exp/householder, <1,000 sq ft heating area	year	254	90	28r
Energy exp/householder, 1,000-1,999 sq ft heating area	year	358	90	28r
Energy exp/householder, 2,000+ sq ft heating area	year	467	90	28r
Energy exp/householder, mobile home	year	390	90	28r
Energy exp/householder, multifamily	year	252	90	28r
Gas, natural	mil Btu	4.31	90	64s
Gas, natural	000 cu ft	6.27	91	46s
Gas, natural, exp	year	369	91	46s
Gasoline, unleaded regular	mil Btu	8.57	90	64s
Entertainment				
Miniature golf admission	adult	6.18	92	1r
Miniature golf admission	child	5.14	92	1r
Waterpark admission	adult	11.00	92	1r
Watorpark admission	child	8.55	92	1r
Funerals				
Casket, 18-gauge steel, velvet interior		1781.09	91	24r
Cosmetology, hair care, etc.		84.64	91	24r
Embalming		207.41	91	24r
Facility use for ceremony		205.76	91	24r
Hearse, local		105.14	91	24r
Limousine, local		83.21	91	24r
Remains to funeral home, transfer		113.82	91	24r
Service charge, professional		626.33	91	24r
Vault, concrete, non-metallic liner		599.54	91	24r
Viewing facilities, use		85.81	91	24r
Groceries				
Apples, Red Delicious	lb	0.80	4/93	16r
Bacon	lb	1.79	4/93	16r
Bananas	lb	0.53	4/93	16r
Bologna, all beef or mixed	lb	2.67	4/93	16r
Bread, white, pan	lb	0.81	4/93	16r
Carrots, short trimmed and topped	lb	0.39	4/93	16r
Chicken, fresh, whole	lb	0.94	4/93	16r
Chicken breast, bone-in	lb	2.19	4/93	16r
Chuck roast, graded and ungraded, ex USDA prime and choice	lb	2.26	4/93	16r
Coffee, 100% ground roast, all sizes	lb	2.33	4/93	16r
Eggs, Grade AA large	doz	1.18	4/93	16r
Flour, white, all purpose	lb	0.22	4/93	16r
Grapefruit	lb	0.52	4/93	16r
Grapes, Thompson Seedless	lb	1.50	4/93	16r
Ground beef, 100% beef	lb	1.44	4/93	16r
Ground beef, lean and extra lean	lb	2.34	4/93	16r
Ham, boneless, excluding canned	lb	2.56	4/93	16r
Honey, jar	8 oz	0.89-1.00	92	5r
Honey, jar	lb	1.35-1.97	92	5r
Honey, squeeze bear	12-oz	1.19-1.50	92	5r
Ice cream, prepackaged, bulk, regular	1/2 gal	2.40	4/93	16r
Lemons	lb	0.81	4/93	16r
Lettuce, iceberg	lb	0.84	4/93	16r
Margarine, stick	lb	0.81	4/93	16r
Oranges, navel	lb	0.48	4/93	16r
Pork chops, center cut, bone-in	lb	3.25	4/93	16r

Values are in dollars or fractions of dollars. In the column headed *Ref*, references are shown to sources. Each reference is followed by a letter. These refer to the geographical level for which data were reported: s = State, r = Region, and c = City or metro. The abbreviation *ex* is used to mean *except* or *excluding*; *exp* stands for expenditures. For other abbreviations and further explanations, please see the Introduction.

Oakland, CA - continued

Item	Per	Value	Date	Ref.
Groceries				
Potato chips	16 oz	2.89	4/93	16r
Potatoes, white	lb	0.38	4/93	16r
Round roast, graded & ungraded, ex USDA prime & choice	lb	3.00	4/93	16r
Round roast, USDA choice, boneless	lb	3.16	4/93	16r
Shortening, vegetable oil blends	lb	0.86	4/93	16r
Spaghetti and macaroni	lb	0.84	4/93	16r
Steak, round, graded & ungraded, ex USDA prime & choice	lb	3.34	4/93	16r
Steak, round, USDA choice, boneless	lb	3.24	4/93	16r
Steak, sirloin, graded & ungraded, ex USDA prime & choice	lb	3.75	4/93	16r
Steak, sirloin, USDA choice, boneless	lb	4.49	4/93	16r
Sugar, white	lb	0.41	4/93	16r
Sugar, white, 33-80 oz pk	lb	0.38	4/93	16r
Tomatoes, field grown	lb	1.01	4/93	16r
Turkey, frozen, whole	lb	1.04	4/93	16r
Health Care				
Cardizem 60 mg tablets	30	24.04	92	49s
Cector 250 mg tablets	15	35.87	92	49s
Childbirth, cesarean, hospital		5533	91	62r
Childbirth, cesarean, physician's fee		2053	91	62r
Childbirth, normal, hospital		2745	91	62r
Childbirth, normal, physician's fee		1492	91	62r
Health care spending, state	capita	2894	3/93	84s
Hospital care, semiprivate room	day	566.30	90	27c
Medical insurance premium, per employee, small group comprehensive	month	459.90	10/91	25c
Medical plan per employee	year	3421	91	45r
Mental health care, exp	capita	37.60-53.67	90	38s
Mental health care, exp, state mental health agency	capita	42.32	90	38s
Mental health care, hospital psychiatric services, non-Federal, exp	capita	10.64	88	38s
Mental health care, mental health organization, multiservice, exp	capita	28.56	88	38s
Mental health care, psychiatric hospitals, private, exp	capita	18.60	88	38s
Mental health care, psychiatric out-patient clinics, freestanding, exp	capita	2.28	88	38s
Mental health care, psychiatric partial-care organizations, freestanding, exp	capita	0.24	88	38s
Mental health care, state and county mental hospitals, exp	capita	13.60	88	38s
Mental health care, VA medical centers, exp	capita	2.33	88	38s
Mevacor 20 mg tablets	30	67.62	92	49s
Physician fee, family practice, first-visit		111.00	91	62r
Physician fee, family practice, revisit		45.00	91	62r
Physician fee, general practice, first-visit		100.00	91	62r
Physician fee, general practice, revisit		40.00	91	62r
Physician fee, internal medicine, first-visit		137.00	91	62r
Physician fee, internal medicine, revisit		48.00	91	62r
Physician fee, median, neurosurgeon, first-visit		157.00	91	62r
Physician fee, median, nonsurgical specialist, first-visit		131.00	91	62r
Physician fee, median, orthopedic surgeon, first-visit		124.00	91	62r
Physician fee, median, plastic surgeon, first-visit		88.00	91	62r
Physician fee, median, surgical specialist, first-visit		100.00	91	62r
Physician fee, neurosurgeon, revisit		51.00	91	62r
Physician fee, nonsurgical specialist, revisit		47.00	91	62r
Physician fee, obstetrics/gynecology, first-visit		95.00	91	62r
Physician fee, obstetrics/gynecology, revisit		50.00	91	62r
Physician fee, orthopedic surgeon, revisit		51.00	91	62r
Physician fee, pediatrician, first-visit		81.00	91	62r
Physician fee, pediatrician, revisit		42.00	91	62r
Physician fee, plastic surgeon, revisit		48.00	91	62r

Oakland, CA - continued

Item	Per	Value	Date	Ref.
Health Care - continued				
Physician fee, surgical specialist, revisit		49.00	91	62r
Prozac 20 mg tablets	14	33.22	92	49s
Substance abuse, hospital ancillary charge	incident	1760	90	70s
Substance abuse, hospital physician charge	incident	750	90	70s
Substance abuse, hospital room and board	incident	6390	90	70s
Tagamet 300 mg tablets	100	77.08	92	49s
Xanax 0.25 mg tablets	90	64.08	92	49s
Zantac 160 mg tablets	60	92.31	92	49s
Housing				
Home, median price	unit	131,200	92	58s
Rental unit, 1 bedroom	month	706	93	23c
Rental unit, 2 bedroom	month	832	93	23c
Rental unit, 3 bedroom	month	1040	93	23c
Rental unit, 4 bedroom	month	1165	93	23c
Rental unit, efficiency	month	581	93	23c
Insurance and Pensions				
Auto insurance, private passenger	year	904.37	91	63s
Taxes				
Tax, cigarette	pack	35	91	77s
Tax, gasoline	gal	16	91	77s
Taxes, state	capita	1477	91	77s
Transportation				
Auto rental, average	day	40.75	6/91	60c
Driver's license fee		10.00	12/90	43s
Taxi fare, airport-city, average	day	16.50	6/91	60c
Travel				
Breakfast	day	7.60	6/91	60c
Business travel	day	178.00	4/93	89r
Dinner	day	20.52	6/91	60c
Lodging	day	115.00	91	60c
Lunch	day	12.81	6/91	60c
Utilities				
Electricity	mil Btu	25.98	90	64s

Ocala, FL

Item	Per	Value	Date	Ref.
Composite ACCRA index		94.50	4Q 92	4c
Alcoholic Beverages				
Beer, Miller Lite or Budweiser, 12-oz containers	6 pack	3.59	4Q 92	4c
Liquor, J & B Scotch	750 ml	16.29	4Q 92	4c
Wine, Gallo Chablis blanc, 1.5 liter	bottle	4.99	4Q 92	4c
Child Care				
Child care fee, average, center	hour	1.29	90	65r
Child care fee, average, nonregulated family day care	hour	0.89	90	65r
Child care fee, average, regulated family day care	hour	1.32	90	65r
Clothing				
Jeans, man's denim		36.39	4Q 92	4c
Shirt, man's dress shirt		22.67	4Q 92	4c
Undervest, boy's size 10-14, cotton	3	4.68	4Q 92	4c
Communications				
Long-distance telephone service, day, initial minute, 0-100 miles	min	0.15-0.20	91	12s
Long-distance telephone service, day, additional minute, 0-100 miles	min	0.08-0.20	91	12s
Long-distance telephone service, evenings/weekends, 0-100 mi, initial minute	min	0.09-0.12	91	12s
Long-distance telephone service, evenings/weekends, 0-100 mi, additional minute	min	0.05-0.12	91	12s
Newspaper subscription, daily and Sunday home delivery, large-city	month	9.50	4Q 92	4c

Values are in dollars or fractions of dollars. In the column headed *Ref*, references are shown to sources. Each reference is followed by a letter. These refer to the geographical level for which data were reported: s=State, r=Region, and c=City or metro. The abbreviation *ex* is used to mean *except* or *excluding*; *exp* stands for expenditures. For other abbreviations and further explanations, please see the Introduction.

Ocala, FL - continued

Item	Per	Value	Date	Ref.
Communications				
Telephone bill, family of four	month	14.08	4Q 92	4c
Education				
Board, 4-yr private college/university	year	1924	91	22s
Board, 4-yr public college/university	year	1955	91	22s
Expenditures, local gov't, public elementary/secondary	pupil	5235	92	20s
Room, 4-year private college/university	year	1904	91	22s
Room, 4-year public college/university	year	1510	91	22s
Tuition, 2-year private college/university	year	4751	91	22s
Tuition, 2-year public college/university	year	788	91	22s
Tuition, 4-year private college/university	year	7992	91	22s
Tuition, 4-year public college/university, in-state	year	1337	91	22s
Energy and Fuels				
Coal	mil Btu	1.85	90	64s
Energy	mil Btu	10.58	90	64s
Energy, combined forms, 1,800 sq ft heating area	month	116.13	4Q 92	4c
Energy exp/householder, 1-family unit	year	487	90	28r
Energy exp/householder, <1,000 sq ft heating area	year	393	90	28r
Energy exp/householder, 1,000-1,999 sq ft heating area	year	442	90	28r
Energy exp/householder, 2,000+ sq ft heating area	year	577	90	28r
Energy exp/householder, mobile home	year	366	90	28r
Energy exp/householder, multifamily	year	382	90	28r
Gas, natural	mil Btu	3.21	90	64s
Gas, natural	000 cu ft	8.98	91	46s
Gas, natural, exp	year	248	91	46s
Gasoline, motor	gal	1.13	4Q 92	4c
Gasoline, unleaded regular	mil Btu	8.85	90	64s
Entertainment				
Bowling, evening rate	game	2.25	4Q 92	4c
Miniature golf admission	adult	6.18	92	1r
Miniature golf admission	child	5.14	92	1r
Monopoly game, Parker Brothers', No. 9		11.32	4Q 92	4c
Movie	admission	5.33	4Q 92	4c
Tennis balls, yellow, Wilson or Penn, 3	can	2.15	4Q 92	4c
Waterpark admission	adult	11.00	92	1r
Waterpark admission	child	8.55	92	1r
Funerals				
Casket, 18-gauge steel, velvet interior		2029.08	91	24r
Cosmetology, hair care, etc.		75.10	91	24r
Embalming		249.24	91	24r
Facility use for ceremony		162.27	91	24r
Hearse, local		114.04	91	24r
Limousine, local		88.57	91	24r
Remains to funeral home, transfer		92.61	91	24r
Service charge, professional		682.42	91	24r
Vault, concrete, non-metallic liner		798.70	91	24r
Viewing facilities, use		163.86	91	24r
Goods and Services				
ACCRA Index, Miscellaneous Goods and Services		101.50	4Q 92	4c
Groceries				
ACCRA Index, Groceries		101.80	4Q 92	4c
Apples, Red Delicious	lb	0.79	4/93	16r
Babyfood, strained vegetables, lowest price	4-4.5 oz jar	0.31	4Q 92	4c
Bacon	lb	1.75	4/93	16r
Bananas	lb	0.33	4Q 92	4c
Bananas	lb	0.42	4/93	16r
Beef, stew, boneless	lb	2.61	4/93	16r
Bologna, all beef or mixed	lb	2.24	4/93	16r
Bread, white	24 oz	0.86	4Q 92	4c
Bread, white, pan	lb	0.64	4/93	16r

Ocala, FL - continued

Item	Per	Value	Date	Ref.
Groceries - continued				
Bread, whole wheat, pan	lb	0.96	4/93	16r
Cabbage	lb	0.37	4/93	16r
Carrots, short trimmed and topped	lb	0.47	4/93	16r
Celery	lb	0.64	4/93	16r
Cheese, American	lb	2.98	4/93	16r
Cheese, Cheddar	lb	3.28	4/93	16r
Cheese, Kraft grated Parmesan	8-oz canister	2.93	4Q 92	4c
Chicken, fresh, whole	lb	0.77	4/93	16r
Chicken, fryer, whole	lb	0.82	4Q 92	4c
Chicken breast, bone-in	lb	1.92	4/93	16r
Chicken legs, bone-in	lb	1.06	4/93	16r
Chuck roast, graded and ungraded, ex USDA prime and choice	lb	2.40	4/93	16r
Chuck roast, USDA choice, bone-in	lb	2.19	4/93	16r
Chuck roast, USDA choice, boneless	lb	2.38	4/93	16r
Cigarettes, Winston	carton	18.31	4Q 92	4c
Coffee, 100% ground roast, all sizes	lb	2.48	4/93	16r
Coffee, vacuum-packed	13-oz can	2.20	4Q 92	4c
Corn, frozen	10 oz	0.54	4Q 92	4c
Corn Flakes, Kellogg's or Post Toasties	18 oz	1.71	4Q 92	4c
Crackers, soda, salted	lb	1.15	4/93	16r
Eggs, Grade A large	doz	0.82	4Q 92	4c
Eggs, Grade A large	doz	0.96	4/93	16r
Flour, white, all purpose	lb	0.24	4/93	16r
Frankfurters, all meat or all beef	lb	2.01	4/93	16r
Grapefruit	lb	0.44	4/93	16r
Grapes, Thompson Seedless	lb	1.40	4/93	16r
Ground beef, 100% beef	lb	1.58	4/93	16r
Ground beef, lean and extra lean	lb	2.09	4/93	16r
Ground beef or hamburger	lb	1.73	4Q 92	4c
Ground chuck, 100% beef	lb	1.98	4/93	16r
Ham, boneless, excluding canned	lb	2.89	4/93	16r
Ham, picnic, shoulder, bone-in, smoked	lb	1.02	4/93	16r
Ham, rump or steak half, bone-in, smoked	lb	1.48	4/93	16r
Ice cream, prepackaged, bulk, regular	1/2 gal	2.41	4/93	16r
Lemons	lb	1.05	4/93	16r
Lettuce, iceberg	head	1.01	4Q 92	4c
Lettuce, iceberg	lb	0.81	4/93	16r
Margarine, Blue Bonnet or Parkay cubes	lb	0.54	4Q 92	4c
Margarine, stick	lb	0.88	4/93	16r
Milk, whole	1/2 gal	1.57	4Q 92	4c
Orange juice, Minute Maid frozen	12-oz can	1.24	4Q 92	4c
Oranges, navel	lb	0.55	4/93	16r
Peaches	29-oz can	1.48	4Q 92	4c
Pears, Anjou	lb	0.92	4/93	16r
Peas Sweet, Del Monte or Green Giant	15-17 oz can	0.52	4Q 92	4c
Pork chops, center cut, bone-in	lb	3.13	4/93	16r
Potato chips	16 oz	2.94	4/93	16r
Potatoes, white	lb	0.43	4/93	16r
Potatoes, white or red	10-lb sack	2.35	4Q 92	4c
Rib roast, USDA choice, bone-in	lb	4.63	4/93	16r
Rice, white, long grain, uncooked	lb	0.45	4/93	16r
Round roast, graded & ungraded, ex USDA prime & choice	lb	3.03	4/93	16r
Round roast, USDA choice, boneless	lb	3.09	4/93	16r
Sausage, fresh, loose	lb	2.08	4/93	16r
Sausage, Jimmy Dean, 100% pork	lb	2.31	4Q 92	4c
Short ribs, bone-in	lb	2.66	4/93	16r
Shortening, vegetable oil blends	lb	0.69	4/93	16r
Shortening, vegetable, Crisco	3-lb can	2.07	4Q 92	4c
Soft drink, Coca Cola	2 liter	1.13	4Q 92	4c
Spaghetti and macaroni	lb	0.81	4/93	16r
Steak, rib eye, USDA choice, boneless	lb	6.24	4/93	16r

Values are in dollars or fractions of dollars. In the column headed *Ref*, references are shown to sources. Each reference is followed by a letter. These refer to the geographical level for which data were reported: s=State, r=Region, and c=City or metro. The abbreviation *ex* is used to mean *except* or *excluding*; *exp* stands for expenditures. For other abbreviations and further explanations, please see the Introduction.

Ocala, FL - continued

Item	Per	Value	Date	Ref.
Groceries				
Steak, round, graded & ungraded, ex USDA prime & choice	lb	3.31	4/93	16r
Steak, round, USDA choice, boneless	lb	3.34	4/93	16r
Steak, sirloin, graded & ungraded, ex USDA prime & choice	lb	4.19	4/93	16r
Steak, sirloin, USDA choice, boneless	lb	4.46	4/93	16r
Steak, T-bone	lb	4.97	4Q 92	4c
Steak, T-bone, USDA choice, bone-in	lb	5.25	4/93	16r
Strawberries, dry pint	12 oz	0.92	4/93	16r
Sugar, cane or beet	4 lb	1.93	4Q 92	4c
Sugar, white	lb	0.39	4/93	16r
Sugar, white, 33-80 oz pk	lb	0.38	4/93	16r
Tomatoes, field grown	lb	0.88	4/93	16r
Tomatoes, Hunt's or Del Monte	14.5-oz can	0.73	4Q 92	4c
Tuna, chunk, light	6.125-6.5 oz can	0.56	4Q 92	4c
Tuna, chunk, light	lb	1.79	4/93	16r
Turkey, frozen, whole	lb	1.04	4/93	16r
Yogurt, natural, fruit flavored	1/2 pint	0.57	4/93	16r
Health Care				
ACCRA Index, Health Care		91.60	4Q 92	4c
Analgesic, Aspirin, Bayer, 325 mg tablets	100	4.34	4Q 92	4c
Childbirth, cesarean, hospital		5034	91	62r
Childbirth, cesarean, physician's fee		2053	91	62r
Childbirth, normal, hospital		2712	91	62r
Childbirth, normal, physician's fee		1492	91	62r
Dentist's fee, adult teeth cleaning and periodic oral exam	visit	38.60	4Q 92	4c
Doctor's fee, routine exam, established patient	visit	38.00	4Q 92	4c
Hospital care, semiprivate room	day	287.50	4Q 92	4c
Medical insurance premium, per employee, small group comprehensive	month	354.05	10/91	25c
Medical plan per employee	year	3495	91	45r
Mental health care, exp	capita	28.84-37.59	90	38s
Mental health care, exp, state mental health agency	capita	37.49	90	38s
Mental health care, hospital psychiatric services, non-Federal, exp	capita	9.11	88	38s
Mental health care, mental health organization, multiservice, exp	capita	16.21	88	38s
Mental health care, psychiatric hospitals, private, exp	capita	22.26	88	38s
Mental health care, psychiatric out-patient clinics, freestanding, exp	capita	0.89	88	38s
Mental health care, psychiatric partial-care organizations, freestanding, exp	capita	0.41	88	38s
Mental health care, state and county mental hospitals, exp	capita	16.25	88	38s
Mental health care, VA medical centers, exp	capita	1.69	88	38s
Physician fee, family practice, first-visit		75.00	91	62r
Physician fee, family practice, revisit		34.00	91	62r
Physician fee, general practice, first-visit		61.00	91	62r
Physician fee, general practice, revisit		32.00	91	62r
Physician fee, general surgeon, first-visit		64.00	91	62r
Physician fee, general surgeon, revisit		40.00	91	62r
Physician fee, internal medicine, first-visit		98.00	91	62r
Physician fee, internal medicine, revisit		40.00	91	62r
Physician fee, median, neurosurgeon, first-visit		130.00	91	62r
Physician fee, median, nonsurgical specialist, first-visit		95.00	91	62r
Physician fee, median, orthopedic surgeon, first-visit		91.00	91	62r
Physician fee, median, plastic surgeon, first-visit		66.00	91	62r
Physician fee, median, surgical specialist, first-visit		62.00	91	62r

Ocala, FL - continued

Item	Per	Value	Date	Ref.
Health Care - continued				
Physician fee, neurosurgeon, revisit		50.00	91	62r
Physician fee, nonsurgical specialist, revisit		40.00	91	62r
Physician fee, obstetrics/gynecology, first-visit		64.00	91	62r
Physician fee, obstetrics/gynecology, revisit		41.00	91	62r
Physician fee, orthopedic surgeon, revisit		40.00	91	62r
Physician fee, pediatrician, first-visit		49.00	91	62r
Physician fee, pediatrician, revisit		33.00	91	62r
Physician fee, plastic surgeon, revisit		43.00	91	62r
Physician fee, surgical specialist, revisit		37.00	91	62r
Substance abuse, hospital ancillary charge	incident	1390	90	70s
Substance abuse, hospital physician charge	incident	770	90	70s
Substance abuse, hospital room and board	incident	5600	90	70s
Household Goods				
Appliance repair, home, service call, washing machine	min labor charge	33.70	4Q 92	4c
Laundry detergent, Tide Ultra, Bold, or Cheer	42 oz	3.55	4Q 92	4c
Tissues, facial, Kleenex brand	175-count box	1.13	4Q 92	4c
Housing				
ACCRA Index, Housing		79.20	4Q 92	4c
House, 1,800 sq ft, 8,000 sq ft lot, new, urban	total	89160	4Q 92	4c
House payment, principal and interest, 25% down payment	month	498	4Q 92	4c
Mortgage rate, incl. points & origination fee, 30-year fixed or adjustable rate	percent	8.15	4Q 92	4c
Rent, apartment, 2 bedrooms - 1-1/2 to 2 baths, unfurnished, 950 sq ft, water	month	366	4Q 92	4c
Rental unit, 1 bedroom	month	402	93	23c
Rental unit, 2 bedroom	month	445	93	23c
Rental unit, 3 bedroom	month	556	93	23c
Rental unit, 4 bedroom	month	622	93	23c
Rental unit, efficiency	month	311	93	23c
Insurance and Pensions				
Auto insurance, private passenger	year	727.60	91	63s
Personal Goods				
Shampoo, Alberto VO5	15 oz	1.16	4Q 92	4c
Toothpaste, Crest or Colgate	6-7 oz	1.89	4Q 92	4c
Personal Services				
Dry cleaning, man's 2-piece suit		5.72	4Q 92	4c
Haircare, woman's shampoo, trim and blow-dry		18.00	4Q 92	4c
Haircut, man's barbershop, no styling		5.38	4Q 92	4c
Restaurant Food				
Chicken, fried, thigh and drumstick		2.11	4Q 92	4c
Hamburger with cheese	1/4 lb	1.96	4Q 92	4c
Pizza, Pizza Hut or Pizza Inn, cheese, thin crust	12-13 in	7.99	4Q 92	4c
Taxes				
Tax, cigarette	pack	33.90	91	77s
Tax, gasoline	gal	11.60	91	77s
Taxes, state	capita	1037	91	77s
Transportation				
ACCRA Index, Transportation		97.60	4Q 92	4c
Driver's license fee		15.00	12/90	43s
Tire balance, computer or spin balance, front	wheel	6.20	4Q 92	4c
Travel				
Business travel	day	193.00	4/93	89r

Values are in dollars or fractions of dollars. In the column headed *Ref*, references are shown to sources. Each reference is followed by a letter. These refer to the geographical level for which data were reported: s=State, r=Region, and c=City or metro. The abbreviation *ex* is used to mean *except* or *excluding*; *exp* stands for expenditures. For other abbreviations and further explanations, please see the Introduction.

Ocala, FL - continued

Item	Per	Value	Date	Ref.
Utilities				
ACCRA Index, Utilities		103.00	4Q 92	4c
Electricity	mil Btu	20.62	90	64s
Electricity, all electric, 1,800 sq ft living area new home	month	116.13	4Q 92	4c

Odessa, TX

Item	Per	Value	Date	Ref.
Composite ACCRA index		93.90	4Q 92	4c
Alcoholic Beverages				
Beer, Miller Lite or Budweiser, 12-oz containers	6 pack	3.89	4Q 92	4c
Liquor, J & B Scotch	750 ml	18.64	4Q 92	4c
Wine, Gallo Chablis blanc, 1.5 liter	bottle	4.30	4Q 92	4c
Child Care				
Child care fee, average, center	hour	1.29	90	65r
Child care fee, average, nonregulated family day care	hour	0.89	90	65r
Child care fee, average, regulated family day care	hour	1.32	90	65r
Clothing				
Jeans, man's denim		23.00	4Q 92	4c
Shirt, man's dress shirt		21.00	4Q 92	4c
Undervest, boy's size 10-14, cotton	3	4.30	4Q 92	4c
Communications				
Long-distance telephone service, day, initial minute, 0-100 miles	min	0.10-0.46	91	12s
Long-distance telephone service, day, additional minute, 0-100 miles	min	0.06-0.45	91	12s
Newspaper subscription, daily and Sunday home delivery, large-city	month	8.75	4Q 92	4c
Telephone, flat rate	month	8.80	91	11c
Telephone bill, family of four	month	15.51	4Q 92	4c
Education				
Board, 4-yr private college/university	year	1883	91	22s
Board, 4-yr public college/university	year	1605	91	22s
Expenditures, local gov't, public elementary/secondary	pupil	4593	92	20s
Room, 4-year private college/university	year	1620	91	22s
Room, 4-year public college/university	year	1532	91	22s
Tuition, 2-year private college/university	year	4394	91	22s
Tuition, 2-year public college/university	year	495	91	22s
Tuition, 4-year private college/university	year	6497	91	22s
Tuition, 4-year public college/university, in-state	year	986	91	22s
Energy and Fuels				
Coal	mil Btu	1.44	90	64s
Energy	mil Btu	6.48	90	64s
Energy, combined forms, 1,800 sq ft heating area	month	120.19	4Q 92	4c
Energy, exc electricity, 1,800 sq ft heating area	month	35.07	4Q 92	4c
Energy exp/householder, 1-family unit	year	471	90	28r
Energy exp/householder, <1,000 sq ft heating area	year	384	90	28r
Energy exp/householder, 1,000-1,999 sq ft heating area	year	421	90	28r
Energy exp/householder, 2,000+ sq ft heating area	year	625	90	28r
Energy exp/householder, mobile home	year	271	90	28r
Energy exp/householder, multifamily	year	355	90	28r
Gas, natural	mil Btu	2.47	90	64s
Gas, natural	000 cu ft	5.71	91	46s
Gas, natural, exp	year	388	91	46s
Gasoline, motor	gal	1.17	4Q 92	4c
Gasoline, unleaded regular	mil Btu	9.16	90	64s

Item	Per	Value	Date	Ref.
Entertainment				
Bowling, evening rate	game	1.62	4Q 92	4c
Miniature golf admission	adult	6.18	92	1r
Miniature golf admission	child	5.14	92	1r
Monopoly game, Parker Brothers', No. 9		12.58	4Q 92	4c
Movie	admission	5.50	4Q 92	4c
Tennis balls, yellow, Wilson or Penn, 3	can	2.70	4Q 92	4c
Waterpark admission	adult	11.00	92	1r
Waterpark admission	child	8.55	92	1r
Funerals				
Casket, 18-gauge steel, velvet interior		2274.41	91	24r
Cosmetology, hair care, etc.		74.62	91	24r
Embalming		229.94	91	24r
Facility use for ceremony		176.61	91	24r
Hearse, local		116.34	91	24r
Limousine, local		72.68	91	24r
Remains to funeral home, transfer		87.72	91	24r
Service charge, professional		712.53	91	24r
Vault, concrete, non-metallic liner		750.55	91	24r
Viewing facilities, use		155.31	91	24r
Goods and Services				
ACCRA Index, Miscellaneous Goods and Services		95.90	4Q 92	4c
Groceries				
ACCRA Index, Groceries		99.20	4Q 92	4c
Apples, Red Delicious	lb	0.79	4/93	16r
Babyfood, strained vegetables, lowest price	4-4.5 oz jar	0.25	4Q 92	4c
Bacon	lb	1.75	4/93	16r
Bananas	lb	0.49	4Q 92	4c
Bananas	lb	0.42	4/93	16r
Beef, stew, boneless	lb	2.61	4/93	16r
Bologna, all beef or mixed	lb	2.24	4/93	16r
Bread, white	24 oz	0.67	4Q 92	4c
Bread, white, pan	lb	0.64	4/93	16r
Bread, whole wheat, pan	lb	0.96	4/93	16r
Cabbage	lb	0.37	4/93	16r
Carrots, short trimmed and topped	lb	0.47	4/93	16r
Celery	lb	0.64	4/93	16r
Cheese, American	lb	2.98	4/93	16r
Cheese, Cheddar	lb	3.28	4/93	16r
Cheese, Kraft grated Parmesan	8-oz canister	3.51	4Q 92	4c
Chicken, fresh, whole	lb	0.77	4/93	16r
Chicken, fryer, whole	lb	0.70	4Q 92	4c
Chicken breast, bone-in	lb	1.92	4/93	16r
Chicken legs, bone-in	lb	1.06	4/93	16r
Chuck roast, graded and ungraded, ex USDA prime and choice	lb	2.40	4/93	16r
Chuck roast, USDA choice, bone-in	lb	2.19	4/93	16r
Chuck roast, USDA choice, boneless	lb	2.38	4/93	16r
Cigarettes, Winston	carton	18.95	4Q 92	4c
Coffee, 100% ground roast, all sizes	lb	2.48	4/93	16r
Coffee, vacuum-packed	13-oz can	1.97	4Q 92	4c
Corn, frozen	10 oz	0.67	4Q 92	4c
Corn Flakes, Kellogg's or Post Toasties	18 oz	2.22	4Q 92	4c
Crackers, soda, salted	lb	1.15	4/93	16r
Eggs, Grade A large	doz	0.84	4Q 92	4c
Eggs, Grade A large	doz	0.96	4/93	16r
Flour, white, all purpose	lb	0.24	4/93	16r
Frankfurters, all meat or all beef	lb	2.01	4/93	16r
Grapefruit	lb	0.44	4/93	16r
Grapes, Thompson Seedless	lb	1.40	4/93	16r
Ground beef, 100% beef	lb	1.58	4/93	16r
Ground beef, lean and extra lean	lb	2.09	4/93	16r
Ground beef or hamburger	lb	1.26	4Q 92	4c
Ground chuck, 100% beef	lb	1.98	4/93	16r
Ham, boneless, excluding canned	lb	2.89	4/93	16r
Ham, picnic, shoulder, bone-in, smoked	lb	1.02	4/93	16r

Values are in dollars or fractions of dollars. In the column headed *Ref*, references are shown to sources. Each reference is followed by a letter. These refer to the geographical level for which data were reported: s=State, r=Region, and c=City or metro. The abbreviation *ex* is used to mean *except* or *excluding*; *exp* stands for expenditures. For other abbreviations and further explanations, please see the Introduction.

Odessa, TX - continued

Item	Per	Value	Date	Ref.
Groceries				
Ham, rump or steak half, bone-in, smoked	lb	1.48	4/93	16r
Honey, jar	8 oz	0.73-1.19	92	5r
Honey, jar	lb	1.10-1.79	92	5r
Honey, squeeze bear	12-oz	1.19-1.50	92	5r
Ice cream, prepackaged, bulk, regular	1/2 gal	2.41	4/93	16r
Lemons	lb	1.05	4/93	16r
Lettuce, iceberg	head	1.16	4Q 92	4c
Lettuce, iceberg	lb	0.81	4/93	16r
Margarine, Blue Bonnet or Parkay cubes	lb	0.66	4Q 92	4c
Margarine, stick	lb	0.88	4/93	16r
Milk, whole	1/2 gal	1.33	4Q 92	4c
Orange juice, Minute Maid frozen	12-oz can	1.39	4Q 92	4c
Oranges, navel	lb	0.55	4/93	16r
Peaches	29-oz can	1.44	4Q 92	4c
Pears, Anjou	lb	0.92	4/93	16r
Peas Sweet, Del Monte or Green Giant	15-17 oz can	0.59	4Q 92	4c
Pork chops, center cut, bone-in	lb	3.13	4/93	16r
Potato chips	16 oz	2.94	4/93	16r
Potatoes, white	lb	0.43	4/93	16r
Potatoes, white or red	10-lb sack	2.07	4Q 92	4c
Rib roast, USDA choice, bone-in	lb	4.63	4/93	16r
Rice, white, long grain, uncooked	lb	0.45	4/93	16r
Round roast, graded & ungraded, ex USDA prime & choice	lb	3.03	4/93	16r
Round roast, USDA choice, boneless	lb	3.09	4/93	16r
Sausage, fresh, loose	lb	2.08	4/93	16r
Sausage, Jimmy Dean, 100% pork	lb	2.36	4Q 92	4c
Short ribs, bone-in	lb	2.66	4/93	16r
Shortening, vegetable oil blends	lb	0.69	4/93	16r
Shortening, vegetable, Crisco	3-lb can	1.97	4Q 92	4c
Soft drink, Coca Cola	2 liter	1.41	4Q 92	4c
Spaghetti and macaroni	lb	0.81	4/93	16r
Steak, rib eye, USDA choice, boneless	lb	6.24	4/93	16r
Steak, round, graded & ungraded, ex USDA prime & choice	lb	3.31	4/93	16r
Steak, round, USDA choice, boneless	lb	3.34	4/93	16r
Steak, sirloin, graded & ungraded, ex USDA prime & choice	lb	4.19	4/93	16r
Steak, sirloin, USDA choice, boneless	lb	4.46	4/93	16r
Steak, T-bone	lb	4.60	4Q 92	4c
Steak, T-bone, USDA choice, bone-in	lb	5.25	4/93	16r
Strawberries, dry pint	12 oz	0.92	4/93	16r
Sugar, cane or beet	4 lb	1.55	4Q 92	4c
Sugar, white	lb	0.39	4/93	16r
Sugar, white, 33-80 oz pk	lb	0.38	4/93	16r
Tomatoes, field grown	lb	0.88	4/93	16r
Tomatoes, Hunt's or Del Monte	14.5-oz can	0.75	4Q 92	4c
Tuna, chunk, light	6.125-6.5 oz can	0.77	4Q 92	4c
Tuna, chunk, light	lb	1.79	4/93	16r
Turkey, frozen, whole	lb	1.04	4/93	16r
Yogurt, natural, fruit flavored	1/2 pint	0.57	4/93	16r
Health Care				
ACCRA Index, Health Care		98.10	4Q 92	4c
Analgesic, Aspirin, Bayer, 325 mg tablets	100	5.05	4Q 92	4c
Childbirth, cesarean, hospital		5034	91	62r
Childbirth, cesarean, physician's fee		2053	91	62r
Childbirth, normal, hospital		2712	91	62r
Childbirth, normal, physician's fee		1492	91	62r
Dentist's fee, adult teeth cleaning and periodic oral exam	visit	44.40	4Q 92	4c
Doctor's fee, routine exam, established patient	visit	40.20	4Q 92	4c
Health care spending, state	capita	2192	3/93	84s

Odessa, TX - continued

Item	Per	Value	Date	Ref.
Health Care - continued				
Hospital care, semiprivate room	day	260.00	4Q 92	4c
Medical insurance premium, per employee, small group comprehensive	month	339.45	10/91	25c
Mental health care, exp	capita	20.37-28.83	90	38s
Mental health care, exp, state mental health agency	capita	22.72	90	38s
Mental health care, hospital psychiatric services, non-Federal, exp	capita	7.95	88	38s
Mental health care, mental health organization, multiservice, exp	capita	12.05	88	38s
Mental health care, psychiatric hospitals, private, exp	capita	37.78	88	38s
Mental health care, psychiatric out-patient clinics, freestanding, exp	capita	0.43	88	38s
Mental health care, state and county mental hospitals, exp	capita	12.54	88	38s
Mental health care, VA medical centers, exp	capita	5.35	88	38s
Physician fee, family practice, first-visit		75.00	91	62r
Physician fee, family practice, revisit		34.00	91	62r
Physician fee, general practice, first-visit		61.00	91	62r
Physician fee, general practice, revisit		32.00	91	62r
Physician fee, general surgeon, first-visit		64.00	91	62r
Physician fee, general surgeon, revisit		40.00	91	62r
Physician fee, internal medicine, first-visit		98.00	91	62r
Physician fee, internal medicine, revisit		40.00	91	62r
Physician fee, median, neurosurgeon, first-visit		130.00	91	62r
Physician fee, median, nonsurgical specialist, first-visit		95.00	91	62r
Physician fee, median, orthopedic surgeon, first-visit		91.00	91	62r
Physician fee, median, plastic surgeon, first-visit		66.00	91	62r
Physician fee, median, surgical specialist, first-visit		62.00	91	62r
Physician fee, neurosurgeon, revisit		50.00	91	62r
Physician fee, nonsurgical specialist, revisit		40.00	91	62r
Physician fee, obstetrics/gynecology, first-visit		64.00	91	62r
Physician fee, obstetrics/gynecology, revisit		41.00	91	62r
Physician fee, orthopedic surgeon, revisit		40.00	91	62r
Physician fee, pediatrician, first-visit		49.00	91	62r
Physician fee, pediatrician, revisit		33.00	91	62r
Physician fee, plastic surgeon, revisit		43.00	91	62r
Physician fee, surgical specialist, revisit		37.00	91	62r
Substance abuse, hospital ancillary charge	incident	3750	90	70s
Substance abuse, hospital physician charge	incident	1080	90	70s
Substance abuse, hospital room and board	incident	5320	90	70s
Household Goods				
Appliance repair, home, service call, washing machine	min labor charge	36.10	4Q 92	4c
Laundry detergent, Tide Ultra, Bold, or Cheer	42 oz	4.01	4Q 92	4c
Tissues, facial, Kleenex brand	175-count box	1.10	4Q 92	4c
Housing				
ACCRA Index, Housing		80.90	4Q 92	4c
House, 1,800 sq ft, 8,000 sq ft lot, new, urban	total	90158	4Q 92	4c
House payment, principal and interest, 25% down payment	month	501	4Q 92	4c
Mortgage rate, incl. points & origination fee, 30-year fixed or adjustable rate	percent	8.10	4Q 92	4c
Rent, apartment, 2 bedrooms - 1-1/2 to 2 baths, unfurnished, 950 sq ft, water	month	391	4Q 92	4c

Values are in dollars or fractions of dollars. In the column headed *Ref*, references are shown to sources. Each reference is followed by a letter. These refer to the geographical level for which data were reported: s = State, r = Region, and c = City or metro. The abbreviation *ex* is used to mean *except* or *excluding*; *exp* stands for expenditures. For other abbreviations and further explanations, please see the Introduction.

Odessa, TX - continued

Item	Per	Value	Date	Ref.
Housing				
Rental unit, 1 bedroom	month	467	93	23c
Rental unit, 2 bedroom	month	550	93	23c
Rental unit, 3 bedroom	month	686	93	23c
Rental unit, 4 bedroom	month	770	93	23c
Rental unit, efficiency	month	383	93	23c
Insurance and Pensions				
Auto insurance, private passenger	year	709.79	91	63s
Personal Goods				
Shampoo, Alberto VO5	15 oz	1.23	4Q 92	4c
Toothpaste, Crest or Colgate	6-7 oz	2.11	4Q 92	4c
Personal Services				
Dry cleaning, man's 2-piece suit		5.24	4Q 92	4c
Haircare, woman's shampoo, trim and blow-dry		14.40	4Q 92	4c
Haircut, man's barbershop, no styling		6.80	4Q 92	4c
Restaurant Food				
Chicken, fried, thigh and drumstick		1.95	4Q 92	4c
Hamburger with cheese	1/4 lb	1.89	4Q 92	4c
Pizza, Pizza Hut or Pizza Inn, cheese, thin crust	12-13 in	8.79	4Q 92	4c
Taxes				
Tax, cigarette	pack	41	91	77s
Tax, gasoline	gal	20	91	77s
Taxes, state	capita	923	91	77s
Transportation				
ACCRA Index, Transportation		102.50	4Q 92	4c
Driver's license fee		16.00	12/90	43s
Tire balance, computer or spin balance, front	wheel	6.60	4Q 92	4c
Travel				
Business travel	day	193.00	4/93	89r
Utilities				
ACCRA Index, Utilities		107.00	4Q 92	4c
Electricity	mil Btu	17.09	90	64s
Electricity, partial electric and other energy, 1,800 sq ft living area new home	month	85.12	4Q 92	4c
Electricity, residential	KWh	5.92	2/93	94s

Oklahoma City, OK

Item	Per	Value	Date	Ref.
Composite ACCRA index		91.00	4Q 92	4c
Alcoholic Beverages				
Beer, Miller Lite or Budweiser, 12-oz containers	6 pack	3.56	4Q 92	4c
Liquor, J & B Scotch	750 ml	14.41	4Q 92	4c
Wine, Gallo Chablis blanc, 1.5 liter	bottle	4.92	4Q 92	4c
Child Care				
Child care fee, average, center	hour	1.29	90	65r
Child care fee, average, nonregulated family day care	hour	0.89	90	65r
Child care fee, average, regulated family day care	hour	1.32	90	65r
Clothing				
Jeans, man's denim		22.39	4Q 92	4c
Shirt, man's dress shirt		18.60	4Q 92	4c
Undervest, boy's size 10-14, cotton	3	4.50	4Q 92	4c
Communications				
Long-distance telephone service, day, initial minute, 0-100 miles	min	0.12-0.45	91	12s
Long-distance telephone service, day, additional minute, 0-100 miles	min	0.07-0.39	91	12s
Newspaper subscription, daily and Sunday home delivery, large-city	month	11.75	4Q 92	4c
Telephone, flat rate	month	12.97	91	11c
Telephone bill, family of four	month	20.27	4Q 92	4c

Oklahoma City, OK - continued

Item	Per	Value	Date	Ref.
Education				
Board, 4-yr private college/university	year	1664	91	22s
Board, 4-yr public college/university	year	1368	91	22s
Expenditures, local gov't, public elementary/secondary	pupil	3901	92	20s
Room, 4-year private college/university	year	1384	91	22s
Room, 4-year public college/university	year	1119	91	22s
Tuition, 2-year private college/university	year	5732	91	22s
Tuition, 2-year public college/university	year	864	91	22s
Tuition, 4-year private college/university	year	5852	91	22s
Tuition, 4-year public college/university, in-state	year	1340	91	22s
Energy and Fuels				
Coal	mil Btu	1.40	90	64s
Energy	mil Btu	7.46	90	64s
Energy, combined forms, 1,800 sq ft heating area	month	117.70	4Q 92	4c
Energy, exc electricity, 1,800 sq ft heating area	month	36.02	4Q 92	4c
Energy exp/householder, 1-family unit	year	471	90	28r
Energy exp/householder, <1,000 sq ft heating area	year	384	90	28r
Energy exp/householder, 1,000-1,999 sq ft heating area	year	421	90	28r
Energy exp/householder, 2,000+ sq ft heating area	year	625	90	28r
Energy exp/householder, mobile home	year	271	90	28r
Energy exp/householder, multifamily	year	355	90	28r
Gas, cooking, winter, 10 therms	month	8.72	92	56c
Gas, cooking, winter, 30 therms	month	20.03	92	56c
Gas, cooking, winter, 50 therms	month	27.63	92	56c
Gas, heating, winter, 100 therms	month	46.63	92	56c
Gas, heating, winter, average use	month	58.23	92	56c
Gas, natural	mil Btu	2.80	90	64s
Gas, natural	000 cu ft	4.72	91	46s
Gas, natural, exp	year	396	91	46s
Gasoline, motor	gal	1.06	4Q 92	4c
Gasoline, unleaded regular	mil Btu	9.00	90	64s
Entertainment				
Bowling, evening rate	game	2.01	4Q 92	4c
Miniature golf admission	adult	6.18	92	1r
Miniature golf admission	child	5.14	92	1r
Monopoly game, Parker Brothers', No. 9		12.09	4Q 92	4c
Movie	admission	5.65	4Q 92	4c
Tennis balls, yellow, Wilson or Penn, 3	can	2.32	4Q 92	4c
Waterpark admission	adult	11.00	92	1r
Waterpark admission	child	8.55	92	1r
Funerals				
Casket, 18-gauge steel, velvet interior		2274.41	91	24r
Cosmetology, hair care, etc.		74.62	91	24r
Embalming		229.94	91	24r
Facility use for ceremony		176.61	91	24r
Hearse, local		116.34	91	24r
Limousine, local		72.68	91	24r
Remains to funeral home, transfer		87.72	91	24r
Service charge, professional		712.53	91	24r
Vault, concrete, non-metallic liner		750.55	91	24r
Viewing facilities, use		155.31	91	24r
Goods and Services				
ACCRA Index, Miscellaneous Goods and Services		92.90	4Q 92	4c
Groceries				
ACCRA Index, Groceries		92.00	4Q 92	4c
Apples, Red Delicious	lb	0.79	4/93	16r
Babyfood, strained vegetables, lowest price	4-4.5 oz jar	0.27	4Q 92	4c
Bacon	lb	1.75	4/93	16r
Bananas	lb	0.39	4Q 92	4c

Values are in dollars or fractions of dollars. In the column headed *Ref*, references are shown to sources. Each reference is followed by a letter. These refer to the geographical level for which data were reported: s=State, r=Region, and c=City or metro. The abbreviation *ex* is used to mean *except* or *excluding*; *exp* stands for *expenditures*. For other abbreviations and further explanations, please see the Introduction.

Oklahoma City, OK - continued

Item	Per	Value	Date	Ref.
Groceries				
Bananas	lb	0.42	4/93	16r
Beef, stew, boneless	lb	2.61	4/93	16r
Bologna, all beef or mixed	lb	2.24	4/93	16r
Bread, white	24 oz	0.56	4Q 92	4c
Bread, white, pan	lb	0.64	4/93	16r
Bread, whole wheat, pan	lb	0.96	4/93	16r
Cabbage	lb	0.37	4/93	16r
Carrots, short trimmed and topped	lb	0.47	4/93	16r
Celery	lb	0.64	4/93	16r
Cheese, American	lb	2.98	4/93	16r
Cheese, Cheddar	lb	3.28	4/93	16r
Cheese, Kraft grated Parmesan	8-oz canis-ter	3.38	4Q 92	4c
Chicken, fresh, whole	lb	0.77	4/93	16r
Chicken, fryer, whole	lb	0.73	4Q 92	4c
Chicken breast, bone-in	lb	1.92	4/93	16r
Chicken legs, bone-in	lb	1.06	4/93	16r
Chuck roast, graded and ungraded, ex USDA prime and choice	lb	2.40	4/93	16r
Chuck roast, USDA choice, bone-in	lb	2.19	4/93	16r
Chuck roast, USDA choice, boneless	lb	2.38	4/93	16r
Cigarettes, Winston	carton	17.45	4Q 92	4c
Coffee, 100% ground roast, all sizes	lb	2.48	4/93	16r
Coffee, vacuum-packed	13-oz can	1.91	4Q 92	4c
Corn, frozen	10 oz	0.66	4Q 92	4c
Corn Flakes, Kellogg's or Post Toasties	18 oz	1.92	4Q 92	4c
Crackers, soda, salted	lb	1.15	4/93	16r
Eggs, Grade A large	doz	0.84	4Q 92	4c
Eggs, Grade A large	doz	0.96	4/93	16r
Flour, white, all purpose	lb	0.24	4/93	16r
Frankfurters, all meat or all beef	lb	2.01	4/93	16r
Grapefruit	lb	0.44	4/93	16r
Grapes, Thompson Seedless	lb	1.40	4/93	16r
Ground beef, 100% beef	lb	1.58	4/93	16r
Ground beef, lean and extra lean	lb	2.09	4/93	16r
Ground beef or hamburger	lb	1.29	4Q 92	4c
Ground chuck, 100% beef	lb	1.98	4/93	16r
Ham, boneless, excluding canned	lb	2.89	4/93	16r
Ham, picnic, shoulder, bone-in, smoked	lb	1.02	4/93	16r
Ham, rump or steak half, bone-in, smoked	lb	1.48	4/93	16r
Honey, jar	8 oz	0.73-1.19	92	5r
Honey, jar	lb	1.10-1.79	92	5r
Honey, squeeze bear	12-oz	1.19-1.50	92	5r
Ice cream, prepackaged, bulk, regular	1/2 gal	2.41	4/93	16r
Lemons	lb	1.05	4/93	16r
Lettuce, iceberg	head	0.89	4Q 92	4c
Lettuce, iceberg	lb	0.81	4/93	16r
Margarine, Blue Bonnet or Parkay cubes	lb	0.53	4Q 92	4c
Margarine, stick	lb	0.88	4/93	16r
Milk, whole	1/2 gal	1.28	4Q 92	4c
Orange juice, Minute Maid frozen	12-oz can	1.36	4Q 92	4c
Oranges, navel	lb	0.55	4/93	16r
Peaches	29-oz can	1.25	4Q 92	4c
Pears, Anjou	lb	0.92	4/93	16r
Peas Sweet, Del Monte or Green Giant	15-17 oz can	0.52	4Q 92	4c
Pork chops, center cut, bone-in	lb	3.13	4/93	16r
Potato chips	16 oz	2.94	4/93	16r
Potatoes, white	lb	0.43	4/93	16r
Potatoes, white or red	10-lb sack	1.95	4Q 92	4c
Rib roast, USDA choice, bone-in	lb	4.63	4/93	16r
Rice, white, long grain, uncooked	lb	0.45	4/93	16r
Round roast, graded & ungraded, ex USDA prime & choice	lb	3.03	4/93	16r
Round roast, USDA choice, boneless	lb	3.09	4/93	16r
Sausage, fresh, loose	lb	2.08	4/93	16r
Sausage, Jimmy Dean, 100% pork	lb	2.25	4Q 92	4c

Oklahoma City, OK - continued

Item	Per	Value	Date	Ref.
Groceries - continued				
Short ribs, bone-in	lb	2.66	4/93	16r
Shortening, vegetable oil blends	lb	0.69	4/93	16r
Shortening, vegetable, Crisco	3-lb can	2.05	4Q 92	4c
Soft drink, Coca Cola	2 liter	1.28	4Q 92	4c
Spaghetti and macaroni	lb	0.81	4/93	16r
Steak, rib eye, USDA choice, boneless	lb	6.24	4/93	16r
Steak, round, graded & ungraded, ex USDA prime & choice	lb	3.31	4/93	16r
Steak, round, USDA choice, boneless	lb	3.34	4/93	16r
Steak, sirloin, graded & ungraded, ex USDA prime & choice	lb	4.19	4/93	16r
Steak, sirloin, USDA choice, boneless	lb	4.46	4/93	16r
Steak, T-bone	lb	4.69	4Q 92	4c
Steak, T-bone, USDA choice, bone-in	lb	5.25	4/93	16r
Strawberries, dry pint	12 oz	0.92	4/93	16r
Sugar, cane or beet	4 lb	1.57	4Q 92	4c
Sugar, white	lb	0.39	4/93	16r
Sugar, white, 33-80 oz pk	lb	0.38	4/93	16r
Tomatoes, field grown	lb	0.88	4/93	16r
Tomatoes, Hunt's or Del Monte	14.5-oz can	0.64	4Q 92	4c
Tuna, chunk, light	6.125-6.5 oz can	0.58	4Q 92	4c
Tuna, chunk, light	lb	1.79	4/93	16r
Turkey, frozen, whole	lb	1.04	4/93	16r
Yogurt, natural, fruit flavored	1/2 pint	0.57	4/93	16r
Health Care				
ACCRA Index, Health Care		98.60	4Q 92	4c
Analgesic, Aspirin, Bayer, 325 mg tablets	100	5.56	4Q 92	4c
Childbirth, cesarean, hospital		5034	91	62r
Childbirth, cesarean, physician's fee		2053	91	62r
Childbirth, normal, hospital		2712	91	62r
Childbirth, normal, physician's fee		1492	91	62r
Dentist's fee, adult teeth cleaning and periodic oral exam	visit	51.00	4Q 92	4c
Doctor's fee, routine exam, established patient	visit	35.20	4Q 92	4c
Hospital care, semiprivate room	day	224.62	90	27c
Hospital care, semiprivate room	day	245.30	4Q 92	4c
Medical insurance premium, per employee, small group comprehensive	month	343.75	10/91	25c
Mental health care, exp	capita	28.84-37.59	90	38s
Mental health care, exp, state mental health agency	capita	35.92	90	38s
Mental health care, hospital psychiatric services, non-Federal, exp	capita	11.62	88	38s
Mental health care, mental health organization, multiservice, exp	capita	13.80	88	38s
Mental health care, psychiatric hospitals, private, exp	capita	21.32	88	38s
Mental health care, psychiatric out-patient clinics, freestanding, exp	capita	3.63	88	38s
Mental health care, psychiatric partial-care organizations, freestanding, exp	capita	0.04	88	38s
Mental health care, state and county mental hospitals, exp	capita	20.87	88	38s
Mental health care, VA medical centers, exp	capita	0.46	88	38s
Physician fee, family practice, first-visit		75.00	91	62r
Physician fee, family practice, revisit		34.00	91	62r
Physician fee, general practice, first-visit		61.00	91	62r
Physician fee, general practice, revisit		32.00	91	62r
Physician fee, general surgeon, first-visit		64.00	91	62r
Physician fee, general surgeon, revisit		40.00	91	62r
Physician fee, internal medicine, first-visit		98.00	91	62r
Physician fee, internal medicine, revisit		40.00	91	62r
Physician fee, median, neurosurgeon, first-visit		130.00	91	62r

Values are in dollars or fractions of dollars. In the column headed *Ref*, references are shown to sources. Each reference is followed by a letter. These refer to the geographical level for which data were reported: s = State, r = Region, and c = City or metro. The abbreviation *ex* is used to mean *except* or *excluding*; *exp* stands for expenditures. For other abbreviations and further explanations, please see the Introduction.

Oklahoma City, OK - continued

Item	Per	Value	Date	Ref.
Health Care				
Physician fee, median, nonsurgical specialist, first-visit		95.00	91	62r
Physician fee, median, orthopedic surgeon, first-visit		91.00	91	62r
Physician fee, median, plastic surgeon, first-visit		66.00	91	62r
Physician fee, median, surgical specialist, first-visit		62.00	91	62r
Physician fee, neurosurgeon, revisit		50.00	91	62r
Physician fee, nonsurgical specialist, revisit		40.00	91	62r
Physician fee, obstetrics/gynecology, first-visit		64.00	91	62r
Physician fee, obstetrics/gynecology, revisit		41.00	91	62r
Physician fee, orthopedic surgeon, revisit		40.00	91	62r
Physician fee, pediatrician, first-visit		49.00	91	62r
Physician fee, pediatrician, revisit		33.00	91	62r
Physician fee, plastic surgeon, revisit		43.00	91	62r
Physician fee, surgical specialist, revisit		37.00	91	62r
Substance abuse, hospital ancillary charge	incident	1220	90	70s
Substance abuse, hospital physician charge	incident	160	90	70s
Substance abuse, hospital room and board	incident	5490	90	70s
Household Goods				
Appliance repair, home, service call, washing machine	min labor charge	25.13	4Q 92	4c
Laundry detergent, Tide Ultra, Bold, or Cheer	42 oz	2.99	4Q 92	4c
Tissues, facial, Kleenex brand	175-count box	1.12	4Q 92	4c
Housing				
ACCRA Index, Housing		79.30	4Q 92	4c
Home, median price	unit	61.60		26c
House, 1,800 sq ft, 8,000 sq ft lot, new, urban	total	85050	4Q 92	4c
House payment, principal and interest, 25% down payment	month	473	4Q 92	4c
Mortgage rate, incl. points & origination fee, 30-year fixed or adjustable rate	percent	8.11	4Q 92	4c
Rent, apartment, 2 bedrooms - 1-1/2 to 2 baths, unfurnished, 950 sq ft, water	month	425	4Q 92	4c
Rental unit, 1 bedroom	month	375	93	23c
Rental unit, 2 bedroom	month	440	93	23c
Rental unit, 3 bedroom	month	552	93	23c
Rental unit, 4 bedroom	month	618	93	23c
Rental unit, efficiency	month	308	93	23c
Insurance and Pensions				
Auto insurance, private passenger	year	554.09	91	63s
Personal Goods				
Shampoo, Alberto VO5	15 oz	1.27	4Q 92	4c
Toothpaste, Crest or Colgate	6-7 oz	2.10	4Q 92	4c
Personal Services				
Dry cleaning, man's 2-piece suit		5.98	4Q 92	4c
Haircare, woman's shampoo, trim and blow-dry		18.95	4Q 92	4c
Haircut, man's barbershop, no styling		6.61	4Q 92	4c
Restaurant Food				
Chicken, fried, thigh and drumstick		1.79	4Q 92	4c
Hamburger with cheese	1/4 lb	1.78	4Q 92	4c
Pizza, Pizza Hut or Pizza Inn, cheese, thin crust	12-13 in	8.69	4Q 92	4c
Taxes				
Tax, cigarette	pack	23	91	77s
Tax, gasoline	gal	17	91	77s
Taxes, state	capita	1216	91	77s

Oklahoma City, OK - continued

Item	Per	Value	Date	Ref.
Transportation				
ACCRA Index, Transportation		97.10	4Q 92	4c
Auto rental, average	day	39.25	6/91	60c
Bus fare	one-way	0.75	3/93	2c
Bus fare, up to 10 miles	one-way	0.75	4Q 92	4c
Driver's license fee		7.00-14.00	12/90	43s
Limo fare, airport-city, average	day	6.00	6/91	60c
Taxi fare, airport-city, average	day	12.00	6/91	60c
Tire balance, computer or spin balance, front	wheel	6.70	4Q 92	4c
Travel				
Breakfast	day	5.59	6/91	60c
Business travel	day	193.00	4/93	89r
Dinner	day	20.03	6/91	60c
Lodging	day	81.75	91	60c
Lunch	day	9.52	6/91	60c
Utilities				
ACCRA Index, Utilities		107.40	4Q 92	4c
Electricity	mil Btu	16.08	90	64s
Electricity, partial electric and other energy, 1,800 sq ft living area new home	month	81.68	4Q 92	4c
Electricity, residential	KWh	6.24	2/93	94s
Electricity, winter, 250 KWh	month	26.23	92	55c
Electricity, winter, 500 KWh	month	45.82	92	55c
Electricity, winter, 750 KWh	month	59.22	92	55c
Electricity, winter, 1000 KWh	month	68.49	92	55c

Olympia, WA

Item	Per	Value	Date	Ref.
Composite ACCRA index		106.40	4Q 92	4c
Alcoholic Beverages				
Beer, Miller Lite or Budweiser, 12-oz containers	6 pack	2.80	4Q 92	4c
Liquor, J & B Scotch	750 ml	17.95	4Q 92	4c
Wine, Gallo Chablis blanc, 1.5 liter	bottle	4.49	4Q 92	4c
Child Care				
Child care fee, average, center	hour	1.71	90	65r
Child care fee, average, nonregulated family day care	hour	1.32	90	65r
Child care fee, average, regulated family day care	hour	1.86	90	65r
Clothing				
Jeans, man's denim		35.79	4Q 92	4c
Shirt, man's dress shirt		23.75	4Q 92	4c
Undervest, boy's size 10-14, cotton	3	5.96	4Q 92	4c
Communications				
Long-distance telephone service, day, initial minute, 0-100 miles	min	0.15-0.37	91	12s
Long-distance telephone service, day, additional minute, 0-100 miles	min	0.01-0.03	91	12s
Long-distance telephone service, evenings/weekends, 0-100 mi, initial minute	min	0.05-0.19	91	12s
Long-distance telephone service, evenings/weekends, 0-100 mi, additional minute	min	0.00-0.01	91	12s
Newspaper subscription, daily and Sunday home delivery, large-city	month	11.25	4Q 92	4c
Telephone, flat rate	month	9.75	91	11c
Telephone bill, family of four	month	14.58	4Q 92	4c
Education				
Board, 4-yr private college/university	year	1811	91	22s
Board, 4-yr public college/university	year	1539	91	22s
Expenditures, local gov't, public elementary/secondary	pupil	5317	92	20s
Room, 4-year private college/university	year	1885	91	22s
Room, 4-year public college/university	year	1698	91	22s
Tuition, 2-year private college/university	year	6743	91	22s

Values are in dollars or fractions of dollars. In the column headed *Ref*, references are shown to sources. Each reference is followed by a letter. These refer to the geographical level for which data were reported: s = State, r = Region, and c = City or metro. The abbreviation *ex* is used to mean *except* or *excluding*; *exp* stands for *expenditures*. For other abbreviations and further explanations, please see the Introduction.

Olympia, WA - continued

Item	Per	Value	Date	Ref.
Education				
Tuition, 2-year public college/university	year	844	91	22s
Tuition, 4-year private college/university	year	9463	91	22s
Tuition, 4-year public college/university, in-state	year	1823	91	22s
Energy and Fuels				
Energy	mil Btu	7.39	90	64s
Energy, combined forms, 1,800 sq ft heating area	month	74.30	4Q 92	4c
Energy, exc electricity, 1,800 sq ft heating area	month	40.83	4Q 92	4c
Energy exp/householder, 1-family unit	year	362	90	28r
Energy exp/householder, <1,000 sq ft heating area	year	254	90	28r
Energy exp/householder, 1,000-1,999 sq ft heating area	year	358	90	28r
Energy exp/householder, 2,000+ sq ft heating area	year	467	90	28r
Energy exp/householder, mobile home	year	390	90	28r
Energy exp/householder, multifamily	year	252	90	28r
Gas, natural	mil Btu	3.60	90	64s
Gas, natural	000 cu ft	4.68	91	46s
Gas, natural, exp	year	440	91	46s
Gasoline, motor	gal	1.24	4Q 92	4c
Gasoline, unleaded regular	mil Btu	9.45	90	64s
Entertainment				
Bowling, evening rate	game	1.72	4Q 92	4c
Miniature golf admission	adult	6.18	92	1r
Miniature golf admission	child	5.14	92	1r
Monopoly game, Parker Brothers', No. 9		9.99	4Q 92	4c
Movie	admission	6.00	4Q 92	4c
Tennis balls, yellow, Wilson or Penn, 3	can	2.26	4Q 92	4c
Waterpark admission	adult	11.00	92	1r
Waterpark admission	child	8.55	92	1r
Funerals				
Casket, 18-gauge steel, velvet interior		1781.09	91	24r
Cosmetology, hair care, etc.		84.64	91	24r
Embalming		207.41	91	24r
Facility use for ceremony		205.76	91	24r
Hearse, local		105.14	91	24r
Limousine, local		83.21	91	24r
Remains to funeral home, transfer		113.82	91	24r
Service charge, professional		626.33	91	24r
Vault, concrete, non-metallic liner		599.54	91	24r
Viewing facilities, use		85.81	91	24r
Goods and Services				
ACCRA Index, Miscellaneous Goods and Services		107.00	4Q 92	4c
Groceries				
ACCRA Index, Groceries		105.30	4Q 92	4c
Apples, Red Delicious	lb	0.80	4/93	16r
Babyfood, strained vegetables, lowest price	4-4.5 oz jar	0.31	4Q 92	4c
Bacon	lb	1.79	4/93	16r
Bananas	lb	0.50	4Q 92	4c
Bananas	lb	0.53	4/93	16r
Bologna, all beef or mixed	lb	2.67	4/93	16r
Bread, white	24 oz	0.52	4Q 92	4c
Bread, white, pan	lb	0.81	4/93	16r
Carrots, short trimmed and topped	lb	0.39	4/93	16r
Cheese, Kraft grated Parmesan	8-oz canister	3.69	4Q 92	4c
Chicken, fresh, whole	lb	0.94	4/93	16r
Chicken, fryer, whole	lb	1.23	4Q 92	4c
Chicken breast, bone-in	lb	2.19	4/93	16r
Chuck roast, graded and ungraded, ex USDA prime and choice	lb	2.26	4/93	16r

Olympia, WA - continued

Item	Per	Value	Date	Ref.
Groceries - continued				
Cigarettes, Winston	carton	20.65	4Q 92	4c
Coffee, 100% ground roast, all sizes	lb	2.33	4/93	16r
Coffee, vacuum-packed	13-oz can	2.44	4Q 92	4c
Corn, frozen	10 oz	0.69	4Q 92	4c
Corn Flakes, Kellogg's or Post Toasties	18 oz	2.14	4Q 92	4c
Eggs, Grade A large	doz	0.87	4Q 92	4c
Eggs, Grade AA large	doz	1.18	4/93	16r
Flour, white, all purpose	lb	0.22	4/93	16r
Grapefruit	lb	0.52	4/93	16r
Grapes, Thompson Seedless	lb	1.50	4/93	16r
Ground beef, 100% beef	lb	1.44	4/93	16r
Ground beef, lean and extra lean	lb	2.34	4/93	16r
Ground beef or hamburger	lb	1.38	4Q 92	4c
Ham, boneless, excluding canned	lb	2.56	4/93	16r
Honey, jar	8 oz	0.89-1.00	92	5r
Honey, jar	lb	1.35-1.97	92	5r
Honey, squeeze bear	12-oz	1.19-1.50	92	5r
Ice cream, prepackaged, bulk, regular	1/2 gal	2.40	4/93	16r
Lemons	lb	0.81	4/93	16r
Lettuce, iceberg	head	0.87	4Q 92	4c
Lettuce, iceberg	lb	0.84	4/93	16r
Margarine, Blue Bonnet or Parkay cubes	lb	0.56	4Q 92	4c
Margarine, stick	lb	0.81	4/93	16r
Milk, whole	1/2 gal	1.47	4Q 92	4c
Orange juice, Minute Maid frozen	12-oz can	1.39	4Q 92	4c
Oranges, navel	lb	0.48	4/93	16r
Peaches	29-oz can	1.55	4Q 92	4c
Peas Sweet, Del Monte or Green Giant	15-17 oz can	0.68	4Q 92	4c
Pork chops, center cut, bone-in	lb	3.25	4/93	16r
Potato chips	16 oz	2.89	4/93	16r
Potatoes, white	lb	0.38	4/93	16r
Potatoes, white or red	10-lb sack	1.60	4Q 92	4c
Round roast, graded & ungraded, ex USDA prime & choice	lb	3.00	4/93	16r
Round roast, USDA choice, boneless	lb	3.16	4/93	16r
Sausage, Jimmy Dean, 100% pork	lb	3.23	4Q 92	4c
Shortening, vegetable oil blends	lb	0.86	4/93	16r
Shortening, vegetable, Crisco	3-lb can	2.06	4Q 92	4c
Soft drink, Coca Cola	2 liter	1.13	4Q 92	4c
Spaghetti and macaroni	lb	0.84	4/93	16r
Steak, round, graded & ungraded, ex USDA prime & choice	lb	3.34	4/93	16r
Steak, round, USDA choice, boneless	lb	3.24	4/93	16r
Steak, sirloin, graded & ungraded, ex USDA prime & choice	lb	3.75	4/93	16r
Steak, sirloin, USDA choice, boneless	lb	4.49	4/93	16r
Steak, T-bone	lb	4.57	4Q 92	4c
Sugar, cane or beet	4 lb	1.30	4Q 92	4c
Sugar, white	lb	0.41	4/93	16r
Sugar, white, 33-80 oz pk	lb	0.38	4/93	16r
Tomatoes, field grown	lb	1.01	4/93	16r
Tomatoes, Hunt's or Del Monte	14.5-oz can	0.62	4Q 92	4c
Tuna, chunk, light	6.125-6.5 oz can	0.63	4Q 92	4c
Turkey, frozen, whole	lb	1.04	4/93	16r
Health Care				
ACCRA Index, Health Care		137.10	4Q 92	4c
Analgesic, Aspirin, Bayer, 325 mg tablets	100	5.02	4Q 92	4c
Childbirth, cesarean, hospital		5533	91	62r
Childbirth, cesarean, physician's fee		2053	91	62r
Childbirth, normal, hospital		2745	91	62r
Childbirth, normal, physician's fee		1492	91	62r
Dentist's fee, adult teeth cleaning and periodic oral exam	visit	70.40	4Q 92	4c

Values are in dollars or fractions of dollars. In the column headed *Ref*, references are shown to sources. Each reference is followed by a letter. These refer to the geographical level for which data were reported: s = State, r = Region, and c = City or metro. The abbreviation *ex* is used to mean *except* or *excluding*; *exp* stands for expenditures. For other abbreviations and further explanations, please see the Introduction.

Olympia, WA - continued

Item	Per	Value	Date	Ref.
Health Care				
Doctor's fee, routine exam, established patient	visit	45.93	4Q 92	4c
Hospital care, semiprivate room	day	353.40	90	27c
Hospital care, semiprivate room	day	502.88	4Q 92	4c
Medical insurance premium, per employee, small group comprehensive	month	281.05	10/91	25c
Medical plan per employee	year	3421	91	45r
Mental health care, exp	capita	37.60-53.67	90	38s
Physician fee, family practice, first-visit		111.00	91	62r
Physician fee, family practice, revisit		45.00	91	62r
Physician fee, general practice, first-visit		100.00	91	62r
Physician fee, general practice, revisit		40.00	91	62r
Physician fee, internal medicine, first-visit		137.00	91	62r
Physician fee, internal medicine, revisit		48.00	91	62r
Physician fee, median, neurosurgeon, first-visit		157.00	91	62r
Physician fee, median, nonsurgical specialist, first-visit		131.00	91	62r
Physician fee, median, orthopedic surgeon, first-visit		124.00	91	62r
Physician fee, median, plastic surgeon, first-visit		88.00	91	62r
Physician fee, median, surgical specialist, first-visit		100.00	91	62r
Physician fee, neurosurgeon, revisit		51.00	91	62r
Physician fee, nonsurgical specialist, revisit		47.00	91	62r
Physician fee, obstetrics/gynecology, first-visit		95.00	91	62r
Physician fee, obstetrics/gynecology, revisit		50.00	91	62r
Physician fee, orthopedic surgeon, revisit		51.00	91	62r
Physician fee, pediatrician, first-visit		81.00	91	02r
Physician fee, pediatrician, revisit		42.00	91	62r
Physician fee, plastic surgeon, revisit		48.00	91	62r
Physician fee, surgical specialist, revisit		49.00	91	62r
Substance abuse, hospital ancillary charge	incident	1360	90	70s
Substance abuse, hospital physician charge	incident	150	90	70s
Substance abuse, hospital room and board	incident	4200	90	70s
Household Goods				
Appliance repair, home, service call, washing machine	min labor charge	27.50	4Q 92	4c
Laundry detergent, Tide Ultra, Bold, or Cheer	42 oz	4.11	4Q 92	4c
Tissues, facial, Kleenex brand	175-count box	1.40	4Q 92	4c
Housing				
ACCRA Index, Housing		114.70	4Q 92	4c
House, 1,800 sq ft, 8,000 sq ft lot, new, urban	total	136190	4Q 92	4c
House payment, principal and interest, 25% down payment	month	767	4Q 92	4c
Mortgage rate, incl. points & origination fee, 30-year fixed or adjustable rate	percent	8.25	4Q 92	4c
Rent, apartment, 2 bedrooms - 1-1/2 to 2 baths, unfurnished, 950 sq ft, water	month	423	4Q 92	4c
Rental unit, 1 bedroom	month	505	93	23c
Rental unit, 2 bedroom	month	595	93	23c
Rental unit, 3 bedroom	month	745	93	23c
Rental unit, 4 bedroom	month	836	93	23c
Rental unit, efficiency	month	416	93	23c
Insurance and Pensions				
Auto insurance, private passenger	year	627.71	91	63s
Personal Goods				
Shampoo, Alberto VO5	15 oz	1.35	4Q 92	4c
Toothpaste, Crest or Colgate	6-7 oz	2.11	4Q 92	4c

Olympia, WA - continued

Item	Per	Value	Date	Ref.
Personal Services				
Dry cleaning, man's 2-piece suit		7.18	4Q 92	4c
Haircare, woman's shampoo, trim and blow-dry		19.60	4Q 92	4c
Haircut, man's barbershop, no styling		7.40	4Q 92	4c
Restaurant Food				
Chicken, fried, thigh and drumstick		2.56	4Q 92	4c
Hamburger with cheese	1/4 lb	1.84	4Q 92	4c
Pizza, Pizza Hut or Pizza Inn, cheese, thin crust	12-13 in	9.76	4Q 92	4c
Taxes				
Tax, cigarette	pack	34	91	77s
Tax, gasoline	gal	23	91	77s
Taxes, state	capita	1592	91	77s
Transportation				
ACCRA Index, Transportation		101.30	4Q 92	4c
Bus fare	one-way	0.35	3/93	2c
Driver's license fee		14.00	12/90	43s
Tire balance, computer or spin balance, front	wheel	6.04	4Q 92	4c
Travel				
Business travel	day	178.00	4/93	89r
Utilities				
ACCRA Index, Utilities		68.70	4Q 92	4c
Electricity	mil Btu	10.03	90	64s
Electricity, partial electric and other energy, 1,800 sq ft living area new home	month	33.47	4Q 92	4c

Omaha, NE

Item	Per	Value	Date	Ref.
Composite ACCRA index		91.50	4Q 92	4c
Alcoholic Beverages				
Beer, Miller Lite or Budweiser, 12-oz containers	6 pack	3.81	4Q 92	4c
Liquor, J & B Scotch	750 ml	15.99	4Q 92	4c
Wine, Gallo Chablis blanc, 1.5 liter	bottle	4.47	4Q 92	4c
Child Care				
Child care fee, average, center	hour	1.63	90	65r
Child care fee, average, nonregulated family day care	hour	1.83	90	65r
Child care fee, average, regulated family day care	hour	1.42	90	65r
Clothing				
Jeans, man's denim		28.24	4Q 92	4c
Shirt, man's dress shirt		25.00	4Q 92	4c
Undervest, boy's size 10-14, cotton	3	2.94	4Q 92	4c
Communications				
Long-distance telephone service, day, initial minute, 0-100 miles	min	0.30-0.44	91	12s
Long-distance telephone service, day, additional minute, 0-100 miles	min	0.16-0.29	91	12s
Long-distance telephone service, evenings/weekends, 0-100 mi, initial minute	min	0.15-0.25	91	12s
Long-distance telephone service, evenings/weekends, 0-100 mi, additional minute	min	0.06-0.15	91	12s
Newspaper subscription, daily and Sunday home delivery, large-city	month	8.70	4Q 92	4c
Telephone, flat rate	month	14.90	91	11c
Telephone bill, family of four	month	24.15	4Q 92	4c
Education				
Board, 4-yr private college/university	year	1666	91	22s
Board, 4-yr public college/university	year	963	91	22s
Expenditures, local gov't, public elementary/secondary	pupil	4567	92	20s
Room, 4-year private college/university	year	1436	91	22s
Room, 4-year public college/university	year	749	91	22s

Values are in dollars or fractions of dollars. In the column headed *Ref*, references are shown to sources. Each reference is followed by a letter. These refer to the geographical level for which data were reported: s=State, r=Region, and c=City or metro. The abbreviation *ex* is used to mean *except* or *excluding*; *exp* stands for expenditures. For other abbreviations and further explanations, please see the Introduction.

Omaha, NE - continued

Item	Per	Value	Date	Ref.
Education				
Tuition, 2-year public college/university	year	990	91	22s
Tuition, 4-year private college/university	year	6893	91	22s
Tuition, 4-year public college/university, in-state	year	1592	91	22s
Energy and Fuels				
Coal	mil Btu	0.78	90	64s
Energy	mil Btu	8.43	90	64s
Energy, combined forms, 1,800 sq ft heating area	month	105.75	4Q 92	4c
Energy, exc electricity, 1,800 sq ft heating area	month	46.35	4Q 92	4c
Energy exp/householder, 1-family unit	year	473	90	28r
Energy exp/householder, <1,000 sq ft heating area	year	429	90	28r
Energy exp/householder, 1,000-1,999 sq ft heating area	year	442	90	28r
Energy exp/householder, 2,000+ sq ft heating area	year	498	90	28r
Energy exp/householder, mobile home	year	442	90	28r
Energy exp/householder, multifamily	year	407	90	28r
Gas, natural	mil Btu	3.93	90	64s
Gas, natural	000 cu ft	4.64	91	46s
Gas, natural, exp	year	502	91	46s
Gasoline, motor	gal	1.11	4Q 92	4c
Gasoline, unleaded regular	mil Btu	9.49	90	64s
Entertainment				
Bowling, evening rate	game	1.36	4Q 92	4c
Miniature golf admission	adult	6.18	92	1r
Miniature golf admission	child	5.14	92	1r
Monopoly game, Parker Brothers', No. 9		9.93	4Q 92	4c
Movie	admission	4.90	4Q 92	4c
Tennis balls, yellow, Wilson or Penn, 3	can	2.17	4Q 92	4c
Waterpark admission	adult	11.00	92	1r
Waterpark admission	child	8.55	92	1r
Funerals				
Casket, 18-gauge steel, velvet interior		1952.97	91	24r
Cosmetology, hair care, etc.		90.03	91	24r
Embalming		251.75	91	24r
Facility use for ceremony		180.75	91	24r
Hearse, local		117.51	91	24r
Limousine, local		71.86	91	24r
Remains to funeral home, transfer		81.14	91	24r
Service charge, professional		740.03	91	24r
Vault, concrete, non-metallic liner		801.47	91	24r
Viewing facilities, use		169.33	91	24r
Goods and Services				
ACCRA Index, Miscellaneous Goods and Services		88.30	4Q 92	4c
Groceries				
ACCRA Index, Groceries		96.10	4Q 92	4c
Apples, Red Delicious	lb	0.77	4/93	16r
Babyfood, strained vegetables, lowest price	4-4.5 oz jar	0.23	4Q 92	4c
Bacon	lb	1.85	4/93	16r
Bananas	lb	0.51	4Q 92	4c
Bananas	lb	0.46	4/93	16r
Beef, stew, boneless	lb	2.53	4/93	16r
Bologna, all beef or mixed	lb	2.19	4/93	16r
Bread, white	24 oz	0.71	4Q 92	4c
Bread, white, pan	lb	0.78	4/93	16r
Butter	lb	1.50	4/93	16r
Cabbage	lb	0.40	4/93	16r
Carrots, short trimmed and topped	lb	0.45	4/93	16r
Cheese, Cheddar	lb	3.47	4/93	16r
Cheese, Kraft grated Parmesan	8-oz canister	3.20	4Q 92	4c

Omaha, NE - continued

Item	Per	Value	Date	Ref.
Groceries - continued				
Chicken, fresh, whole	lb	0.84	4/93	16r
Chicken, fryer, whole	lb	0.76	4Q 92	4c
Chicken breast, bone-in	lb	1.94	4/93	16r
Chicken legs, bone-in	lb	1.02	4/93	16r
Chuck roast, graded and ungraded, ex USDA prime and choice	lb	2.43	4/93	16r
Chuck roast, USDA choice, bone-in	lb	2.11	4/93	16r
Chuck roast, USDA choice, boneless	lb	2.44	4/93	16r
Cigarettes, Winston	carton	17.75	4Q 92	4c
Coffee, 100% ground roast, all sizes	lb	2.47	4/93	16r
Coffee, vacuum-packed	13-oz can	1.89	4Q 92	4c
Cookies, chocolate chip	lb	2.73	4/93	16r
Corn, frozen	10 oz	0.60	4Q 92	4c
Corn Flakes, Kellogg's or Post Toasties	18 oz	1.83	4Q 92	4c
Eggs, Grade A large	doz	0.75	4Q 92	4c
Eggs, Grade A large	doz	0.93	4/93	16r
Flour, white, all purpose	lb	0.21	4/93	16r
Grapefruit	lb	0.45	4/93	16r
Grapes, Thompson Seedless	lb	1.46	4/93	16r
Ground beef, 100% beef	lb	1.63	4/93	16r
Ground beef, lean and extra lean	lb	2.08	4/93	16r
Ground beef or hamburger	lb	1.43	4Q 92	4c
Ground chuck, 100% beef	lb	1.94	4/93	16r
Ham, boneless, excluding canned	lb	2.21	4/93	16r
Ice cream, prepackaged, bulk, regular	1/2 gal	2.41	4/93	16r
Lemons	lb	0.82	4/93	16r
Lettuce, iceberg	head	0.84	4Q 92	4c
Lettuce, iceberg	lb	0.83	4/93	16r
Margarine, Blue Bonnet or Parkay cubes	lb	0.56	4Q 92	4c
Margarine, stick	lb	0.77	4/93	16r
Milk, whole	1/2 gal	1.39	4Q 92	4c
Orange juice, Minute Maid frozen	12-oz can	1.40	4Q 92	4c
Oranges, navel	lb	0.50	4/93	16r
Peaches	29-oz can	1.34	4Q 92	4c
Peanut butter, creamy, all sizes	lb	1.82	4/93	16r
Pears, Anjou	lb	0.85	4/93	16r
Peas Sweet, Del Monte or Green Giant	15-17 oz can	0.50	4Q 92	4c
Pork chops, center cut, bone-in	lb	3.17	4/93	16r
Potato chips	16 oz	2.68	4/93	16r
Potatoes, white	lb	0.26	4/93	16r
Potatoes, white or red	10-lb sack	2.05	4Q 92	4c
Round roast, graded & ungraded, ex USDA prime & choice	lb	2.88	4/93	16r
Round roast, USDA choice, boneless	lb	2.96	4/93	16r
Sausage, Jimmy Dean, 100% pork	lb	2.91	4Q 92	4c
Shortening, vegetable oil blends	lb	0.79	4/93	16r
Shortening, vegetable, Crisco	3-lb can	2.02	4Q 92	4c
Soft drink, Coca Cola	2 liter	1.06	4Q 92	4c
Spaghetti and macaroni	lb	0.76	4/93	16r
Steak, rib eye, USDA choice, boneless	lb	6.29	4/93	16r
Steak, round, USDA choice, boneless	lb	3.24	4/93	16r
Steak, sirloin, graded & ungraded, ex USDA prime & choice	lb	4.00	4/93	16r
Steak, sirloin, USDA choice, bone-in	lb	3.57	4/93	16r
Steak, sirloin, USDA choice, boneless	lb	4.17	4/93	16r
Steak, T-bone	lb	4.99	4Q 92	4c
Steak, T-bone, USDA choice, bone-in	lb	5.60	4/93	16r
Strawberries, dry pint	12 oz	0.90	4/93	16r
Sugar, cane or beet	4 lb	1.31	4Q 92	4c
Sugar, white	lb	0.36	4/93	16r
Sugar, white, 33-80 oz pk	lb	0.35	4/93	16r
Tomatoes, field grown	lb	0.99	4/93	16r
Tomatoes, Hunt's or Del Monte	14.5-oz can	0.71	4Q 92	4c

Values are in dollars or fractions of dollars. In the column headed *Ref*, references are shown to sources. Each reference is followed by a letter. These refer to the geographical level for which data were reported: s=State, r=Region, and c=City or metro. The abbreviation *ex* is used to mean *except* or *excluding*; *exp* stands for expenditures. For other abbreviations and further explanations, please see the Introduction.

Omaha, NE - continued

Item	Per	Value	Date	Ref.
Groceries				
Tuna, chunk, light	6.125-6.5 oz can	0.50	4Q 92	4c
Tuna, chunk, light	lb	1.76	4/93	16r
Turkey, frozen, whole	lb	0.91	4/93	16r
Health Care				
ACCRA Index, Health Care		97.60	4Q 92	4c
Analgesic, Aspirin, Bayer, 325 mg tablets	100	3.04	4Q 92	4c
Childbirth, cesarean, hospital		4688	91	62r
Childbirth, cesarean, physician's fee		2053	91	62r
Childbirth, normal, hospital		2657	91	62r
Childbirth, normal, physician's fee		1492	91	62r
Dentist's fee, adult teeth cleaning and periodic oral exam	visit	49.20	4Q 92	4c
Doctor's fee, routine exam, established patient	visit	39.00	4Q 92	4c
Hospital care, semiprivate room	day	216.22	90	27c
Hospital care, semiprivate room	day	285.20	4Q 92	4c
Medical insurance premium, per employee, small group comprehensive	month	222.20	10/91	25c
Medical plan per employee	year	3443	91	45r
Mental health care, exp, state mental health agency	capita	29.07	90	38s
Mental health care, hospital psychiatric services, non-Federal, exp	capita	12.29	88	38s
Mental health care, mental health organization, multiservice, exp	capita	10.57	88	38s
Mental health care, psychiatric hospitals, private, exp	capita	7.24	88	38s
Mental health care, psychiatric out-patient clinics, freestanding, exp	capita	1.81	88	38s
Mental health care, psychiatric partial-care organizations, freestanding, exp	capita	0.05	88	38s
Mental health care, state and county mental hospitals, exp	capita	19.63	88	38s
Mental health care, VA medical centers, exp	capita	0.85	88	38s
Physician fee, family practice, first-visit		76.00	91	62r
Physician fee, family practice, revisit		33.00	91	62r
Physician fee, general practice, first-visit		61.00	91	62r
Physician fee, general practice, revisit		31.00	91	62r
Physician fee, general surgeon, first-visit		65.00	91	62r
Physician fee, general surgeon, revisit		35.00	91	62r
Physician fee, internal medicine, first-visit		91.00	91	62r
Physician fee, internal medicine, revisit		40.00	91	62r
Physician fee, median, neurosurgeon, first-visit		106.00	91	62r
Physician fee, median, nonsurgical specialist, first-visit		90.00	91	62r
Physician fee, median, orthopedic surgeon, first-visit		83.00	91	62r
Physician fee, median, surgical specialist, first-visit		61.00	91	62r
Physician fee, neurosurgeon, revisit		41.00	91	62r
Physician fee, nonsurgical specialist, revisit		40.00	91	62r
Physician fee, obstetrics/gynecology, first-visit		61.00	91	62r
Physician fee, obstetrics/gynecology, revisit		40.00	91	62r
Physician fee, orthopedic surgeon, revisit		41.00	91	62r
Physician fee, pediatrician, first-visit		46.00	91	62r
Physician fee, pediatrician, revisit		33.00	91	62r
Physician fee, surgical specialist, revisit		36.00	91	62r
Household Goods				
Appliance repair, home, service call, washing machine	min labor charge	26.77	4Q 92	4c
Laundry detergent, Tide Ultra, Bold, or Cheer	42 oz	2.77	4Q 92	4c
Tissues, facial, Kleenex brand	175-count box	1.13	4Q 92	4c

Omaha, NE - continued

Item	Per	Value	Date	Ref.
Housing				
ACCRA Index, Housing		85.10	4Q 92	4c
Home, median price	unit	69.40		26c
House, 1,800 sq ft, 8,000 sq ft lot, new, urban	total	93704	4Q 92	4c
House payment, principal and interest, 25% down payment	month	516	4Q 92	4c
Mortgage rate, incl. points & origination fee, 30-year fixed or adjustable rate	percent	8.00	4Q 92	4c
Rent, apartment, 2 bedrooms - 1-1/2 to 2 baths, unfurnished, 950 sq ft, water	month	438	4Q 92	4c
Rental unit, 1 bedroom	month	395	93	23c
Rental unit, 2 bedroom	month	464	93	23c
Rental unit, 3 bedroom	month	581	93	23c
Rental unit, 4 bedroom	month	655	93	23c
Rental unit, efficiency	month	326	93	23c
Insurance and Pensions				
Auto insurance, private passenger	year	424.72	91	63s
Personal Goods				
Shampoo, Alberto VO5	15 oz	0.93	4Q 92	4c
Toothpaste, Crest or Colgate	6-7 oz	1.49	4Q 92	4c
Personal Services				
Dry cleaning, man's 2-piece suit		5.20	4Q 92	4c
Haircare, woman's shampoo, trim and blow-dry		14.79	4Q 92	4c
Haircut, man's barbershop, no styling		7.80	4Q 92	4c
Restaurant Food				
Chicken, fried, thigh and drumstick		1.98	4Q 92	4c
Hamburger with cheese	1/4 lb	1.79	4Q 92	4c
Pizza, Pizza Hut or Pizza Inn, cheese, thin crust	12-13 in	7.49	4Q 92	4c
Taxes				
Tax, cigarette	pack	27	91	77s
Tax, gasoline	gal	24	91	77s
Taxes, state	capita	1109	91	77s
Transportation				
ACCRA Index, Transportation		104.60	4Q 92	4c
Auto rental, average	day	41.75	6/91	60c
Bus fare	one-way	0.90	3/93	2c
Bus fare, up to 10 miles	one-way	0.90	4Q 92	4c
Driver's license fee		10.00	12/90	43s
Limo fare, airport-city, average	day	5.50	6/91	60c
Taxi fare, airport-city, average	day	5.50	6/91	60c
Tire balance, computer or spin balance, front	wheel	7.20	4Q 92	4c
Vehicle registration and license plate	year	17.50	93	47s
Travel				
Breakfast	day	5.08	6/91	60c
Dinner	day	13.92	6/91	60c
Lodging	day	90.18	91	60c
Lunch	day	9.14	6/91	60c
Utilities				
ACCRA Index, Utilities		99.60	4Q 92	4c
Electricity	mil Btu	16.34	90	64s
Electricity, partial electric and other energy, 1,800 sq ft living area new home	month	59.40	4Q 92	4c

Orlando, FL

Item	Per	Value	Date	Ref.
Composite ACCRA index		99.10	4Q 92	4c
Alcoholic Beverages				
Beer, Miller Lite or Budweiser, 12-oz containers	6 pack	3.65	4Q 92	4c
Liquor, J & B Scotch	750 ml	16.44	4Q 92	4c
Wine, Gallo Chablis blanc, 1.5 liter	bottle	5.08	4Q 92	4c

Values are in dollars or fractions of dollars. In the column headed *Ref*, references are shown to sources. Each reference is followed by a letter. These refer to the geographical level for which data were reported: s=State, r=Region, and c=City or metro. The abbreviation *ex* is used to mean *except* or *excluding*; *exp* stands for expenditures. For other abbreviations and further explanations, please see the Introduction.

Orlando, FL - continued

Item	Per	Value	Date	Ref.
Child Care				
Child care fee, average, center	hour	1.29	90	65r
Child care fee, average, nonregulated family day care	hour	0.89	90	65r
Child care fee, average, regulated family day care	hour	1.32	90	65r
Clothing				
Jeans, man's denim		30.39	4Q 92	4c
Shirt, man's dress shirt		20.60	4Q 92	4c
Undervest, boy's size 10-14, cotton	3	4.08	4Q 92	4c
Communications				
Long-distance telephone service, day, initial minute, 0-100 miles	min	0.15-0.20	91	12s
Long-distance telephone service, day, additional minute, 0-100 miles	min	0.08-0.20	91	12s
Long-distance telephone service, evenings/weekends, 0-100 mi, initial minute	min	0.09-0.12	91	12s
Long-distance telephone service, evenings/weekends, 0-100 mi, additional minute	min	0.05-0.12	91	12s
Newspaper subscription, daily and Sunday home delivery, large-city	month	13.00	4Q 92	4c
Telephone, flat rate	month	10.30	91	11c
Telephone bill, family of four	month	18.91	4Q 92	4c
Construction				
Plywood, post-Hurricane Andrew	4x8 sheet	11.99	92	13c
Plywood, pre-Hurricane Andrew	4x8 sheet	7.84	92	13c
Education				
Board, 4-yr private college/university	year	1924	91	22s
Board, 4-yr public college/university	year	1955	91	22s
Expenditures, local gov't, public elementary/secondary	pupil	5235	92	20s
Room, 4-year private college/university	year	1904	91	22s
Room, 4-year public college/university	year	1510	91	22s
Tuition, 2-year private college/university	year	4751	91	22s
Tuition, 2-year public college/university	year	788	91	22s
Tuition, 4-year private college/university	year	7992	91	22s
Tuition, 4-year public college/university, in-state	year	1337	91	22s
Energy and Fuels				
Coal	mil Btu	1.85	90	64s
Energy	mil Btu	10.58	90	64s
Energy, combined forms, 1,800 sq ft heating area	month	107.31	4Q 92	4c
Energy exp/householder, 1-family unit	year	487	90	28r
Energy exp/householder, <1,000 sq ft heating area	year	393	90	28r
Energy exp/householder, 1,000-1,999 sq ft heating area	year	442	90	28r
Energy exp/householder, 2,000+ sq ft heating area	year	577	90	28r
Energy exp/householder, mobile home	year	366	90	28r
Energy exp/householder, multifamily	year	382	90	28r
Gas, natural	mil Btu	3.21	90	64s
Gas, natural	000 cu ft	8.98	91	46s
Gas, natural, exp	year	248	91	46s
Gasoline, motor	gal	1.12	4Q 92	4c
Gasoline, unleaded regular	mil Btu	8.85	90	64s
Entertainment				
Bowling, evening rate	game	2.19	4Q 92	4c
Miniature golf admission	adult	6.18	92	1r
Miniature golf admission	child	5.14	92	1r
Monopoly game, Parker Brothers', No. 9		12.07	4Q 92	4c
Movie	admission	6.03	4Q 92	4c
Tennis balls, yellow, Wilson or Penn, 3	can	2.26	4Q 92	4c
Waterpark admission	adult	11.00	92	1r
Waterpark admission	child	8.55	92	1r

Orlando, FL - continued

Item	Per	Value	Date	Ref.
Funerals				
Casket, 18-gauge steel, velvet interior		2029.08	91	24r
Cosmetology, hair care, etc.		75.10	91	24r
Embalming		249.24	91	24r
Facility use for ceremony		162.27	91	24r
Hearse, local		114.04	91	24r
Limousine, local		88.57	91	24r
Remains to funeral home, transfer		92.61	91	24r
Service charge, professional		682.42	91	24r
Vault, concrete, non-metallic liner		798.70	91	24r
Viewing facilities, use		163.86	91	24r
Goods and Services				
ACCRA Index, Miscellaneous Goods and Services		99.30	4Q 92	4c
Groceries				
ACCRA Index, Groceries		95.10	4Q 92	4c
Apples, Red Delicious	lb	0.79	4/93	16r
Babyfood, strained vegetables, lowest price	4-4.5 oz jar	0.32	4Q 92	4c
Bacon	lb	1.75	4/93	16r
Bananas	lb	0.36	4Q 92	4c
Bananas	lb	0.42	4/93	16r
Beef, stew, boneless	lb	2.61	4/93	16r
Bologna, all beef or mixed	lb	2.24	4/93	16r
Bread, white	24 oz	0.72	4Q 92	4c
Bread, white, pan	lb	0.64	4/93	16r
Bread, whole wheat, pan	lb	0.96	4/93	16r
Cabbage	lb	0.37	4/93	16r
Carrots, short trimmed and topped	lb	0.47	4/93	16r
Celery	lb	0.64	4/93	16r
Cheese, American	lb	2.98	4/93	16r
Cheese, Cheddar	lb	3.28	4/93	16r
Cheese, Kraft grated Parmesan	8-oz canister	3.28	4Q 92	4c
Chicken, fresh, whole	lb	0.77	4/93	16r
Chicken, fryer, whole	lb	0.71	4Q 92	4c
Chicken breast, bone-in	lb	1.92	4/93	16r
Chicken legs, bone-in	lb	1.06	4/93	16r
Chuck roast, graded and ungraded, ex USDA prime and choice	lb	2.40	4/93	16r
Chuck roast, USDA choice, bone-in	lb	2.19	4/93	16r
Chuck roast, USDA choice, boneless	lb	2.38	4/93	16r
Cigarettes, Winston	carton	18.28	4Q 92	4c
Coffee, 100% ground roast, all sizes	lb	2.48	4/93	16r
Coffee, vacuum-packed	13-oz can	1.59	4Q 92	4c
Corn, frozen	10 oz	0.60	4Q 92	4c
Corn Flakes, Kellogg's or Post Toasties	18 oz	1.73	4Q 92	4c
Crackers, soda, salted	lb	1.15	4/93	16r
Eggs, Grade A large	doz	0.82	4Q 92	4c
Eggs, Grade A large	doz	0.96	4/93	16r
Flour, white, all purpose	lb	0.24	4/93	16r
Frankfurters, all meat or all beef	lb	2.01	4/93	16r
Grapefruit	lb	0.44	4/93	16r
Grapes, Thompson Seedless	lb	1.40	4/93	16r
Ground beef, 100% beef	lb	1.58	4/93	16r
Ground beef, lean and extra lean	lb	2.09	4/93	16r
Ground beef or hamburger	lb	1.39	4Q 92	4c
Ground chuck, 100% beef	lb	1.98	4/93	16r
Ham, boneless, excluding canned	lb	2.89	4/93	16r
Ham, picnic, shoulder, bone-in, smoked	lb	1.02	4/93	16r
Ham, rump or steak half, bone-in, smoked	lb	1.48	4/93	16r
Ice cream, prepackaged, bulk, regular	1/2 gal	2.41	4/93	16r
Lemons	lb	1.05	4/93	16r
Lettuce, iceberg	head	0.90	4Q 92	4c
Lettuce, iceberg	lb	0.81	4/93	16r
Margarine, Blue Bonnet or Parkay cubes	lb	0.49	4Q 92	4c
Margarine, stick	lb	0.88	4/93	16r
Milk, whole	1/2 gal	1.66	4Q 92	4c
Orange juice, Minute Maid frozen	12-oz can	1.20	4Q 92	4c

Values are in dollars or fractions of dollars. In the column headed *Ref*, references are shown to sources. Each reference is followed by a letter. These refer to the geographical level for which data were reported: s=State, r=Region, and c=City or metro. The abbreviation *ex* is used to mean *except* or *excluding*; *exp* stands for expenditures. For other abbreviations and further explanations, please see the Introduction.

Orlando, FL - continued

Item	Per	Value	Date	Ref.
Groceries				
Oranges, navel	lb	0.55	4/93	16r
Peaches	29-oz can	1.36	4Q 92	4c
Pears, Anjou	lb	0.92	4/93	16r
Peas Sweet, Del Monte or Green Giant	15-17 oz can	0.52	4Q 92	4c
Pork chops, center cut, bone-in	lb	3.13	4/93	16r
Potato chips	16 oz	2.94	4/93	16r
Potatoes, white	lb	0.43	4/93	16r
Potatoes, white or red	10-lb sack	2.11	4Q 92	4c
Rib roast, USDA choice, bone-in	lb	4.63	4/93	16r
Rice, white, long grain, uncooked	lb	0.45	4/93	16r
Round roast, graded & ungraded, ex USDA prime & choice	lb	3.03	4/93	16r
Round roast, USDA choice, boneless	lb	3.09	4/93	16r
Sausage, fresh, loose	lb	2.08	4/93	16r
Sausage, Jimmy Dean, 100% pork	lb	2.26	4Q 92	4c
Short ribs, bone-in	lb	2.66	4/93	16r
Shortening, vegetable oil blends	lb	0.69	4/93	16r
Shortening, vegetable, Crisco	3-lb can	2.05	4Q 92	4c
Soft drink, Coca Cola	2 liter	1.11	4Q 92	4c
Spaghetti and macaroni	lb	0.81	4/93	16r
Steak, rib eye, USDA choice, boneless	lb	6.24	4/93	16r
Steak, round, graded & ungraded, ex USDA prime & choice	lb	3.31	4/93	16r
Steak, round, USDA choice, boneless	lb	3.34	4/93	16r
Steak, sirloin, graded & ungraded, ex USDA prime & choice	lb	4.19	4/93	16r
Steak, sirloin, USDA choice, boneless	lb	4.46	4/93	16r
Steak, T-bone	lb	4.86	4Q 92	4c
Steak, T-bone, USDA choice, bone-in	lb	5.25	4/93	16r
Strawberries, dry pint	12 oz	0.92	4/93	16r
Sugar, cane or beet	4 lb	1.48	4Q 92	4c
Sugar, white	lb	0.39	4/93	16r
Sugar, white, 33-80 oz pk	lb	0.38	4/93	16r
Tomatoes, field grown	lb	0.88	4/93	16r
Tomatoes, Hunt's or Del Monte	14.5-oz can	0.56	4Q 92	4c
Tuna, chunk, light	6.125-6.5 oz can	0.56	4Q 92	4c
Tuna, chunk, light	lb	1.79	4/93	16r
Turkey, frozen, whole	lb	1.04	4/93	16r
Yogurt, natural, fruit flavored	1/2 pint	0.57	4/93	16r
Health Care				
ACCRA Index, Health Care		115.90	4Q 92	4c
Analgesic, Aspirin, Bayer, 325 mg tablets	100	4.25	4Q 92	4c
Childbirth, cesarean, hospital		5034	91	62r
Childbirth, cesarean, physician's fee		2053	91	62r
Childbirth, normal, hospital		2712	91	62r
Childbirth, normal, physician's fee		1492	91	62r
Dentist's fee, adult teeth cleaning and periodic oral exam	visit	66.20	4Q 92	4c
Doctor's fee, routine exam, established patient	visit	39.00	4Q 92	4c
Hospital care, semiprivate room	day	252.68	90	27c
Hospital care, semiprivate room	day	333.56	4Q 92	4c
Medical insurance premium, per employee, small group comprehensive	month	365.00	10/91	25c
Medical plan per employee	year	3495	91	45r
Mental health care, exp	capita	28.84-37.59	90	38s
Mental health care, exp, state mental health agency	capita	37.49	90	38s
Mental health care, hospital psychiatric services, non-Federal, exp	capita	9.11	88	38s
Mental health care, mental health organization, multiservice, exp	capita	16.21	88	38s

Orlando, FL - continued

Item	Per	Value	Date	Ref.
Health Care - continued				
Mental health care, psychiatric hospitals, private, exp	capita	22.26	88	38s
Mental health care, psychiatric out-patient clinics, freestanding, exp	capita	0.89	88	38s
Mental health care, psychiatric partial-care organizations, freestanding, exp	capita	0.41	88	38s
Mental health care, state and county mental hospitals, exp	capita	16.25	88	38s
Mental health care, VA medical centers, exp	capita	1.69	88	38s
Physician fee, family practice, first-visit		75.00	91	62r
Physician fee, family practice, revisit		34.00	91	62r
Physician fee, general practice, first-visit		61.00	91	62r
Physician fee, general practice, revisit		32.00	91	62r
Physician fee, general surgeon, first-visit		64.00	91	62r
Physician fee, general surgeon, revisit		40.00	91	62r
Physician fee, internal medicine, first-visit		98.00	91	62r
Physician fee, internal medicine, revisit		40.00	91	62r
Physician fee, median, neurosurgeon, first-visit		130.00	91	62r
Physician fee, median, nonsurgical specialist, first-visit		95.00	91	62r
Physician fee, median, orthopedic surgeon, first-visit		91.00	91	62r
Physician fee, median, plastic surgeon, first-visit		66.00	91	62r
Physician fee, median, surgical specialist, first-visit		62.00	91	62r
Physician fee, neurosurgeon, revisit		50.00	91	62r
Physician fee, nonsurgical specialist, revisit		40.00	91	62r
Physician fee, obstetrics/gynecology, first-visit		64.00	91	62r
Physician fee, obstetrics/gynecology, revisit		41.00	91	62r
Physician fee, orthopedic surgeon, revisit		40.00	91	62r
Physician fee, pediatrician, first-visit		49.00	91	62r
Physician fee, pediatrician, revisit		33.00	91	62r
Physician fee, plastic surgeon, revisit		43.00	91	62r
Physician fee, surgical specialist, revisit		37.00	91	62r
Substance abuse, hospital ancillary charge	incident	1390	90	70s
Substance abuse, hospital physician charge	incident	770	90	70s
Substance abuse, hospital room and board	incident	5600	90	70s
Household Goods				
Appliance repair, home, service call, washing machine	min labor charge	30.85	4Q 92	4c
Laundry detergent, Tide Ultra, Bold, or Cheer	42 oz	3.31	4Q 92	4c
Tissues, facial, Kleenex brand	175-count box	1.06	4Q 92	4c
Housing				
ACCRA Index, Housing		97.30	4Q 92	4c
Home, median price	unit	87.60		26c
House, 1,800 sq ft, 8,000 sq ft lot, new, urban	total	101898	4Q 92	4c
House payment, principal and interest, 25% down payment	month	565	4Q 92	4c
Mortgage rate, incl. points & origination fee, 30-year fixed or adjustable rate	percent	8.09	4Q 92	4c
Rent, apartment, 2 bedrooms - 1-1/2 to 2 baths, unfurnished, 950 sq ft, water	month	556	4Q 92	4c
Rental unit, 1 bedroom	month	466	93	23c
Rental unit, 2 bedroom	month	548	93	23c
Rental unit, 3 bedroom	month	667	93	23c
Rental unit, 4 bedroom	month	746	93	23c
Rental unit, efficiency	month	382	93	23c
Insurance and Pensions				
Auto insurance, private passenger	year	727.60	91	63s

Values are in dollars or fractions of dollars. In the column headed *Ref*, references are shown to sources. Each reference is followed by a letter. These refer to the geographical level for which data were reported: s=State, r=Region, and c=City or metro. The abbreviation *ex* is used to mean *except* or *excluding*; *exp* stands for expenditures. For other abbreviations and further explanations, please see the Introduction.

Orlando, FL - continued

Item	Per	Value	Date	Ref.
Personal Goods				
Shampoo, Alberto VO5	15 oz	0.94	4Q 92	4c
Toothpaste, Crest or Colgate	6-7 oz	1.64	4Q 92	4c
Personal Services				
Dry cleaning, man's 2-piece suit		6.28	4Q 92	4c
Haircare, woman's shampoo, trim and blow-dry		21.80	4Q 92	4c
Haircut, man's barbershop, no styling		8.30	4Q 92	4c
Restaurant Food				
Chicken, fried, thigh and drumstick		1.99	4Q 92	4c
Hamburger with cheese	1/4 lb	1.82	4Q 92	4c
Pizza, Pizza Hut or Pizza Inn, cheese, thin crust	12-13 in	8.18	4Q 92	4c
Taxes				
Tax, cigarette	pack	33.90	91	77s
Tax, gasoline	gal	11.60	91	77s
Taxes, state	capita	1037	91	77s
Transportation				
ACCRA Index, Transportation		100.70	4Q 92	4c
Auto fixed costs, midsize		3475	91	60c
Auto operating cost, midsize		1418	91	60c
Auto rental, average	day	26.50	6/91	60c
Bus fare	one-way	0.75	3/93	2c
Bus fare, up to 10 miles	one-way	0.75	4Q 92	4c
Driver's license fee		15.00	12/90	43s
Limo fare, airport-city, average	day	10.00	6/91	60c
Taxi fare, airport-city, average	day	18.50	6/91	60c
Tire balance, computer or spin balance, front	wheel	6.85	4Q 92	4c
Travel				
Breakfast	day	7.42	6/91	60c
Business travel	day	108.00	92	86c
Business travel	day	193.00	4/93	89r
Dinner	day	21.68	6/91	60c
Dinner	day	16.70	92	85c
Lodging	day	127.75	91	60c
Lodging	day	77.00	92	85c
Lunch	day	11.80	6/91	60c
Utilities				
ACCRA Index, Utilities		98.20	4Q 92	4c
Electricity	mil Btu	20.62	90	64s
Electricity, all electric, 1,800 sq ft living area new home	month	107.31	4Q 92	4c

Oshkosh, WI

Item	Per	Value	Date	Ref.
Composite ACCRA index		97.80	4Q 92	4c
Alcoholic Beverages				
Beer, Miller Lite or Budweiser, 12-oz containers	6 pack	3.52	4Q 92	4c
Liquor, J & B Scotch	750 ml	15.41	4Q 92	4c
Wine, Gallo Chablis blanc, 1.5 liter	bottle	4.75	4Q 92	4c
Clothing				
Jeans, man's denim		30.99	4Q 92	4c
Shirt, man's dress shirt		21.39	4Q 92	4c
Undervest, boy's size 10-14, cotton	3	4.15	4Q 92	4c
Communications				
Newspaper subscription, daily and Sunday home delivery, large-city	month	12.39	4Q 92	4c
Telephone, flat rate	month	6.00	91	11c
Telephone bill, family of four	month	19.28	4Q 92	4c
Energy and Fuels				
Energy, combined forms, 1,800 sq ft heating area	month	91.66	4Q 92	4c

Oshkosh, WI - continued

Item	Per	Value	Date	Ref.
Energy and Fuels - continued				
Energy, exc electricity, 1,800 sq ft heating area	month	50.91	4Q 92	4c
Gasoline, motor	gal	1.14	4Q 92	4c
Entertainment				
Bowling, evening rate	game	1.60	4Q 92	4c
Monopoly game, Parker Brothers', No. 9		9.99	4Q 92	4c
Movie	admission	5.75	4Q 92	4c
Tennis balls, yellow, Wilson or Penn, 3	can	2.17	4Q 92	4c
Goods and Services				
ACCRA Index, Miscellaneous Goods and Services		97.10	4Q 92	4c
Groceries				
ACCRA Index, Groceries		99.20	4Q 92	4c
Babyfood, strained vegetables, lowest price	4-4.5 oz jar	0.39	4Q 92	4c
Bananas	lb	0.41	4Q 92	4c
Bread, white	24 oz	0.62	4Q 92	4c
Cheese, Kraft grated Parmesan	8-oz canister	3.16	4Q 92	4c
Chicken, fryer, whole	lb	0.93	4Q 92	4c
Cigarettes, Winston	carton	18.77	4Q 92	4c
Coffee, vacuum-packed	13-oz can	1.88	4Q 92	4c
Corn, frozen	10 oz	0.66	4Q 92	4c
Corn Flakes, Kellogg's or Post Toasties	18 oz	1.84	4Q 92	4c
Eggs, Grade A large	doz	0.71	4Q 92	4c
Ground beef or hamburger	lb	1.58	4Q 92	4c
Lettuce, iceberg	head	0.95	4Q 92	4c
Margarine, Blue Bonnet or Parkay cubes	lb	0.51	4Q 92	4c
Milk, whole	1/2 gal	1.45	4Q 92	4c
Orange juice, Minute Maid frozen	12-oz can	1.17	4Q 92	4c
Peaches	29-oz can	1.41	4Q 92	4c
Peas Sweet, Del Monte or Green Giant	15-17 oz can	0.57	4Q 92	4c
Potatoes, white or red	10-lb sack	1.58	4Q 92	4c
Sausage, Jimmy Dean, 100% pork	lb	2.56	4Q 92	4c
Shortening, vegetable, Crisco	3-lb can	2.38	4Q 92	4c
Soft drink, Coca Cola	2 liter	1.03	4Q 92	4c
Steak, T-bone	lb	5.37	4Q 92	4c
Sugar, cane or beet	4 lb	1.46	4Q 92	4c
Tomatoes, Hunt's or Del Monte	14.5-oz can	0.71	4Q 92	4c
Tuna, chunk, light	6.125-6.5 oz can	0.55	4Q 92	4c
Health Care				
ACCRA Index, Health Care		95.50	4Q 92	4c
Analgesic, Aspirin, Bayer, 325 mg tablets	100	5.77	4Q 92	4c
Dentist's fee, adult teeth cleaning and periodic oral exam	visit	41.80	4Q 92	4c
Doctor's fee, routine exam, established patient	visit	37.50	4Q 92	4c
Hospital care, semiprivate room	day	193.95	90	27c
Hospital care, semiprivate room	day	271.00	4Q 92	4c
Household Goods				
Appliance repair, home, service call, washing machine	min labor charge	25.18	4Q 92	4c
Laundry detergent, Tide Ultra, Bold, or Cheer	42 oz	3.73	4Q 92	4c
Tissues, facial, Kleenex brand	175-count box	1.04	4Q 92	4c

Values are in dollars or fractions of dollars. In the column headed *Ref*, references are shown as sources. Each reference is followed by a letter. These refer to the geographical level for which data were reported: s=State, r=Region, and c=City or metro. The abbreviation *ex* is used to mean *except* or *excluding*; *exp* stands for expenditures. For other abbreviations and further explanations, please see the Introduction.

Oshkosh, WI - continued

Item	Per	Value	Date	Ref.
Housing				
ACCRA Index, Housing		103.20	4Q 92	4c
House, 1,800 sq ft, 8,000 sq ft lot, new, urban	total	119100	4Q 92	4c
House payment, principal and interest, 25% down payment	month	676	4Q 92	4c
Mortgage rate, incl. points & origination fee, 30-year fixed or adjustable rate	per-cent	8.32	4Q 92	4c
Rent, apartment, 2 bedrooms - 1-1/2 to 2 baths, unfurnished, 950 sq ft, water	month	413	4Q 92	4c
Personal Goods				
Shampoo, Alberto VO5	15 oz	1.29	4Q 92	4c
Toothpaste, Crest or Colgate	6-7 oz	2.22	4Q 92	4c
Personal Services				
Dry cleaning, man's 2-piece suit		6.15	4Q 92	4c
Haircare, woman's shampoo, trim and blow-dry		17.80	4Q 92	4c
Haircut, man's barbershop, no styling		8.00	4Q 92	4c
Restaurant Food				
Chicken, fried, thigh and drumstick		2.38	4Q 92	4c
Hamburger with cheese	1/4 lb	1.86	4Q 92	4c
Pizza, Pizza Hut or Pizza Inn, cheese, thin crust	12-13 in	8.74	4Q 92	4c
Transportation				
ACCRA Index, Transportation		95.30	4Q 92	4c
Bus fare	one-way	0.50	3/93	2c
Bus fare, up to 10 miles	one-way	0.50	4Q 92	4c
Tire balance, computer or spin balance, front	wheel	6.38	4Q 92	4c
Utilities				
ACCRA Index, Utilities		85.50	4Q 92	4c
Electricity, partial electric and other energy, 1,800 sq ft living area new home	month	40.75	4Q 92	4c

Owensboro, KY

Item	Per	Value	Date	Ref.
Composite ACCRA index		94.40	4Q 92	4c
Alcoholic Beverages				
Beer, Miller Lite or Budweiser, 12-oz containers	6 pack	3.95	4Q 92	4c
Liquor, J & B Scotch	750 ml	17.66	4Q 92	4c
Wine, Gallo Chablis blanc, 1.5 liter	bottle	5.30	4Q 92	4c
Child Care				
Child care fee, average, center	hour	1.29	90	65r
Child care fee, average, nonregulated family day care	hour	0.89	90	65r
Child care fee, average, regulated family day care	hour	1.32	90	65r
Clothing				
Jeans, man's denim		32.59	4Q 92	4c
Shirt, man's dress shirt		26.24	4Q 92	4c
Undervest, boy's size 10-14, cotton	3	6.09	4Q 92	4c
Communications				
Long-distance telephone service, day, initial minute, 0-100 miles	min	0.20-0.55	91	12s
Long-distance telephone service, day, additional minute, 0-100 miles	min	0.14-0.44	91	12s
Long-distance telephone service, evenings/weekends, 0-100 mi, initial minute	min	0.08-0.22	91	12s
Long-distance telephone service, evenings/weekends, 0-100 mi, additional minute	min	0.06-0.16	91	12s
Newspaper subscription, daily and Sunday home delivery, large-city	month	9.95	4Q 92	4c
Telephone, flat rate	month	12.69	91	11c
Telephone bill, family of four	month	20.26	4Q 92	4c

Owensboro, KY - continued

Item	Per	Value	Date	Ref.
Education				
Board, 4-yr private college/university	year	1522	91	22s
Board, 4-yr public college/university	year	1862	91	22s
Expenditures, local gov't, public elementary/secondary	pupil	4616	92	20s
Room, 4-year private college/university	year	1193	91	22s
Room, 4-year public college/university	year	1153	91	22s
Tuition, 2-year private college/university	year	4662	91	22s
Tuition, 2-year public college/university	year	771	91	22s
Tuition, 4-year private college/university	year	5200	91	22s
Tuition, 4-year public college/university, in-state	year	1444	91	22s
Energy and Fuels				
Coal	mil Btu	1.27	90	64s
Energy	mil Btu	7.91	90	64s
Energy, combined forms, 1,800 sq ft heating area	month	87.81	4Q 92	4c
Energy, exc electricity, 1,800 sq ft heating area	month	28.32	4Q 92	4c
Energy exp/householder, 1-family unit	year	403	90	28r
Energy exp/householder, <1,000 sq ft heating area	year	342	90	28r
Energy exp/householder, 1,000-1,999 sq ft heating area	year	388	90	28r
Energy exp/householder, 2,000+ sq ft heating area	year	434	90	28r
Energy exp/householder, mobile home	year	320	90	28r
Energy exp/householder, multifamily	year	338	90	28r
Gas, cooking, 10 therms	month	4.38	92	56c
Gas, cooking, 30 therms	month	13.13	92	56c
Gas, cooking, 50 therms	month	21.88	92	56c
Gas, heating, winter, 100 therms	month	43.76	92	56c
Gas, heating, winter, average use	month	43.76	92	56c
Gas, natural	mil Btu	4.10	90	64s
Gas, natural	000 cu ft	4.87	91	46s
Gas, natural, exp	year	457	91	46s
Gasoline, motor	gal	1.06	4Q 92	4c
Gasoline, unleaded regular	mil Btu	9.25	90	64s
Entertainment				
Bowling, evening rate	game	1.88	4Q 92	4c
Miniature golf admission	adult	6.18	92	1r
Miniature golf admission	child	5.14	92	1r
Monopoly game, Parker Brothers', No. 9		9.95	4Q 92	4c
Movie	admission	5.00	4Q 92	4c
Tennis balls, yellow, Wilson or Penn, 3	can	2.44	4Q 92	4c
Waterpark admission	adult	11.00	92	1r
Waterpark admission	child	8.55	92	1r
Funerals				
Casket, 18-gauge steel, velvet interior		2329.05	91	24r
Cosmetology, hair care, etc.		72.78	91	24r
Embalming		240.71	91	24r
Facility use for ceremony		181.67	91	24r
Hearse, local		106.25	91	24r
Limousine, local		70.92	91	24r
Remains to funeral home, transfer		96.30	91	24r
Service charge, professional		687.09	91	24r
Vault, concrete, non-metallic liner		732.09	91	24r
Viewing facilities, use		190.30	91	24r
Goods and Services				
ACCRA Index, Miscellaneous Goods and Services		103.00	4Q 92	4c
Groceries				
ACCRA Index, Groceries		103.70	4Q 92	4c
Apples, Red Delicious	lb	0.79	4/93	16r
Babyfood, strained vegetables, lowest price	4-4.5 oz jar	0.33	4Q 92	4c
Bacon	lb	1.75	4/93	16r
Bananas	lb	0.48	4Q 92	4c

Values are in dollars or fractions of dollars. In the column headed *Ref*, references are shown to sources. Each reference is followed by a letter. These refer to the geographical level for which data were reported: s = State, r = Region, and c = City or metro. The abbreviation *ex* is used to mean *except* or *excluding*; *exp* stands for expenditures. For other abbreviations and further explanations, please see the Introduction.

Owensboro, KY - continued

Item	Per	Value	Date	Ref.
Groceries				
Bananas	lb	0.42	4/93	16r
Beef, stew, boneless	lb	2.61	4/93	16r
Bologna, all beef or mixed	lb	2.24	4/93	16r
Bread, white	24 oz	1.24	4Q 92	4c
Bread, white, pan	lb	0.64	4/93	16r
Bread, whole wheat, pan	lb	0.96	4/93	16r
Cabbage	lb	0.37	4/93	16r
Carrots, short trimmed and topped	lb	0.47	4/93	16r
Celery	lb	0.64	4/93	16r
Cheese, American	lb	2.98	4/93	16r
Cheese, Cheddar	lb	3.28	4/93	16r
Cheese, Kraft grated Parmesan	8-oz canister	3.17	4Q 92	4c
Chicken, fresh, whole	lb	0.77	4/93	16r
Chicken, fryer, whole	lb	0.77	4Q 92	4c
Chicken breast, bone-in	lb	1.92	4/93	16r
Chicken legs, bone-in	lb	1.06	4/93	16r
Chuck roast, graded and ungraded, ex USDA prime and choice	lb	2.40	4/93	16r
Chuck roast, USDA choice, bone-in	lb	2.19	4/93	16r
Chuck roast, USDA choice, boneless	lb	2.38	4/93	16r
Cigarettes, Winston	carton	14.96	4Q 92	4c
Coffee, 100% ground roast, all sizes	lb	2.48	4/93	16r
Coffee, vacuum-packed	13-oz can	2.03	4Q 92	4c
Corn, frozen	10 oz	0.75	4Q 92	4c
Corn Flakes, Kellogg's or Post Toasties	18 oz	1.95	4Q 92	4c
Crackers, soda, salted	lb	1.15	4/93	16r
Eggs, Grade A large	doz	0.59	4Q 92	4c
Eggs, Grade A large	doz	0.96	4/93	16r
Flour, white, all purpose	lb	0.24	4/93	16r
Frankfurters, all meat or all beef	lb	2.01	4/93	16r
Grapefruit	lb	0.44	4/93	16r
Grapes, Thompson Seedless	lb	1.40	4/93	16r
Ground beef, 100% beef	lb	1.58	4/93	16r
Ground beef, lean and extra lean	lb	2.09	4/93	16r
Ground beef or hamburger	lb	1.57	4Q 92	4c
Ground chuck, 100% beef	lb	1.98	4/93	16r
Ham, boneless, excluding canned	lb	2.89	4/93	16r
Ham, picnic, shoulder, bone-in, smoked	lb	1.02	4/93	16r
Ham, rump or steak half, bone-in, smoked	lb	1.48	4/93	16r
Honey, jar	8 oz	0.89-1.09	92	5r
Honey, jar	lb	1.39-2.25	92	5r
Honey, squeeze bear	12-oz	1.00-1.50	92	5r
Ice cream, prepackaged, bulk, regular	1/2 gal	2.41	4/93	16r
Lemons	lb	1.05	4/93	16r
Lettuce, iceberg	head	0.85	4Q 92	4c
Lettuce, iceberg	lb	0.81	4/93	16r
Margarine, Blue Bonnet or Parkay cubes	lb	0.39	4Q 92	4c
Margarine, stick	lb	0.88	4/93	16r
Milk, whole	1/2 gal	1.49	4Q 92	4c
Orange juice, Minute Maid frozen	12-oz can	1.57	4Q 92	4c
Oranges, navel	lb	0.55	4/93	16r
Peaches	29-oz can	1.41	4Q 92	4c
Pears, Anjou	lb	0.92	4/93	16r
Peas Sweet, Del Monte or Green Giant	15-17 oz can	0.69	4Q 92	4c
Pork chops, center cut, bone-in	lb	3.13	4/93	16r
Potato chips	16 oz	2.94	4/93	16r
Potatoes, white	lb	0.43	4/93	16r
Potatoes, white or red	10-lb sack	2.19	4Q 92	4c
Rib roast, USDA choice, bone-in	lb	4.63	4/93	16r
Rice, white, long grain, uncooked	lb	0.45	4/93	16r
Round roast, graded & ungraded, ex USDA prime & choice	lb	3.03	4/93	16r
Round roast, USDA choice, boneless	lb	3.09	4/93	16r
Sausage, fresh, loose	lb	2.08	4/93	16r
Sausage, Jimmy Dean, 100% pork	lb	2.59	4Q 92	4c

Owensboro, KY - continued

Item	Per	Value	Date	Ref.
Groceries - continued				
Short ribs, bone-in	lb	2.66	4/93	16r
Shortening, vegetable oil blends	lb	0.69	4/93	16r
Shortening, vegetable, Crisco	3-lb can	1.81	4Q 92	4c
Soft drink, Coca Cola	2 liter	1.13	4Q 92	4c
Spaghetti and macaroni	lb	0.81	4/93	16r
Steak, rib eye, USDA choice, boneless	lb	6.24	4/93	16r
Steak, round, graded & ungraded, ex USDA prime & choice	lb	3.31	4/93	16r
Steak, round, USDA choice, boneless	lb	3.34	4/93	16r
Steak, sirloin, graded & ungraded, ex USDA prime & choice	lb	4.19	4/93	16r
Steak, sirloin, USDA choice, boneless	lb	4.46	4/93	16r
Steak, T-bone	lb	5.61	4Q 92	4c
Steak, T-bone, USDA choice, bone-in	lb	5.25	4/93	16r
Strawberries, dry pint	12 oz	0.92	4/93	16r
Sugar, cane or beet	4 lb	1.48	4Q 92	4c
Sugar, white	lb	0.39	4/93	16r
Sugar, white, 33-80 oz pk	lb	0.38	4/93	16r
Tomatoes, field grown	lb	0.88	4/93	16r
Tomatoes, Hunt's or Del Monte	14.5-oz can	0.77	4Q 92	4c
Tuna, chunk, light	6.125-6.5 oz can	0.49	4Q 92	4c
Tuna, chunk, light	lb	1.79	4/93	16r
Turkey, frozen, whole	lb	1.04	4/93	16r
Yogurt, natural, fruit flavored	1/2 pint	0.57	4/93	16r
Health Care				
ACCRA Index, Health Care		89.70	4Q 92	4c
Analgesic, Aspirin, Bayer, 325 mg tablets	100	4.48	4Q 92	4c
Childbirth, cesarean, hospital		5034	91	62r
Childbirth, cesarean, physician's fee		2053	91	62r
Childbirth, normal, hospital		2712	91	62r
Childbirth, normal, physician's fee		1492	91	62r
Dentist's fee, adult teeth cleaning and periodic oral exam	visit	41.60	4Q 92	4c
Doctor's fee, routine exam, established patient	visit	32.20	4Q 92	4c
Hospital care, semiprivate room	day	214.09	90	27c
Hospital care, semiprivate room	day	306.00	4Q 92	4c
Medical insurance premium, per employee, small group comprehensive	month	299.30	10/91	25c
Mental health care, exp	capita	20.37-28.83	90	38s
Mental health care, exp, state mental health agency	capita	23.24	90	38s
Mental health care, hospital psychiatric services, non-Federal, exp	capita	7.35	88	38s
Mental health care, mental health organization, multiservice, exp	capita	29.19	88	38s
Mental health care, psychiatric hospitals, private, exp	capita	21.55	88	38s
Mental health care, psychiatric partial-care organizations, freestanding, exp	capita	0.24	88	38s
Mental health care, state and county mental hospitals, exp	capita	14.97	88	38s
Mental health care, VA medical centers, exp	capita	1.60	88	38s
Physician fee, family practice, first-visit		75.00	91	62r
Physician fee, family practice, revisit		34.00	91	62r
Physician fee, general practice, first-visit		61.00	91	62r
Physician fee, general practice, revisit		32.00	91	62r
Physician fee, general surgeon, first-visit		64.00	91	62r
Physician fee, general surgeon, revisit		40.00	91	62r
Physician fee, internal medicine, first-visit		98.00	91	62r
Physician fee, internal medicine, revisit		40.00	91	62r
Physician fee, median, neurosurgeon, first-visit		130.00	91	62r
Physician fee, median, nonsurgical specialist, first-visit		95.00	91	62r

Values are in dollars or fractions of dollars. In the column headed *Ref*, references are shown to sources. Each reference is followed by a letter. These refer to the geographical level for which data were reported: s = State, r = Region, and c = City or metro. The abbreviation *ex* is used to mean *except* or *excluding*; *exp* stands for *expenditures*. For other abbreviations and further explanations, please see the Introduction.

Owensboro, KY - continued

Item	Per	Value	Date	Ref.
Health Care				
Physician fee, median, orthopedic surgeon, first-visit		91.00	91	62r
Physician fee, median, plastic surgeon, first-visit		66.00	91	62r
Physician fee, median, surgical specialist, first-visit		62.00	91	62r
Physician fee, neurosurgeon, revisit		50.00	91	62r
Physician fee, nonsurgical specialist, revisit		40.00	91	62r
Physician fee, obstetrics/gynecology, first-visit		64.00	91	62r
Physician fee, obstetrics/gynecology, revisit		41.00	91	62r
Physician fee, orthopedic surgeon, revisit		40.00	91	62r
Physician fee, pediatrician, first-visit		49.00	91	62r
Physician fee, pediatrician, revisit		33.00	91	62r
Physician fee, plastic surgeon, revisit		43.00	91	62r
Physician fee, surgical specialist, revisit		37.00	91	62r
Substance abuse, hospital ancillary charge	incident	1090	90	70s
Substance abuse, hospital physician charge	incident	640	90	70s
Substance abuse, hospital room and board	incident	5780	90	70s
Household Goods				
Appliance repair, home, service call, washing machine	min labor charge	26.50	4Q 92	4c
Laundry detergent, Tide Ultra, Bold, or Cheer	42 oz	3.18	4Q 92	4c
Tissues, facial, Kleenex brand	175-count box	1.11	4Q 92	4c
Housing				
ACCRA Index, Housing		85.80	4Q 92	4c
House, 1,800 sq ft, 8,000 sq ft lot, new, urban	total	96000	4Q 92	4c
House payment, principal and interest, 25% down payment	month	540	4Q 92	4c
Mortgage rate, incl. points & origination fee, 30-year fixed or adjustable rate	percent	8.24	4Q 92	4c
Rent, apartment, 2 bedrooms - 1-1/2 to 2 baths, unfurnished, 950 sq ft, water	month	395	4Q 92	4c
Rental unit, 1 bedroom	month	315	93	23c
Rental unit, 2 bedroom	month	373	93	23c
Rental unit, 3 bedroom	month	465	93	23c
Rental unit, 4 bedroom	month	522	93	23c
Rental unit, efficiency	month	260	93	23c
Insurance and Pensions				
Auto insurance, private passenger	year	543.37	91	63s
Personal Goods				
Shampoo, Alberto VO5	15 oz	1.45	4Q 92	4c
Toothpaste, Crest or Colgate	6-7 oz	1.75	4Q 92	4c
Personal Services				
Dry cleaning, man's 2-piece suit		5.22	4Q 92	4c
Haircare, woman's shampoo, trim and blow-dry		15.19	4Q 92	4c
Haircut, man's barbershop, no styling		8.80	4Q 92	4c
Restaurant Food				
Chicken, fried, thigh and drumstick		2.19	4Q 92	4c
Hamburger with cheese	1/4 lb	1.79	4Q 92	4c
Pizza, Pizza Hut or Pizza Inn, cheese, thin crust	12-13 in	7.69	4Q 92	4c
Taxes				
Tax, cigarette	pack	3	91	77s
Tax, gasoline	gal	15	91	77s
Taxes, state	capita	1358	91	77s
Transportation				
ACCRA Index, Transportation		89.30	4Q 92	4c

Owensboro, KY - continued

Item	Per	Value	Date	Ref.
Transportation - continued				
Bus fare	one-way	1.00	3/93	2c
Driver's license fee		8.00	12/90	43s
Tire balance, computer or spin balance, front	wheel	5.50	4Q 92	4c
Travel				
Business travel	day	193.00	4/93	89r
Utilities				
ACCRA Index, Utilities		82.80	4Q 92	4c
Electricity	mil Btu	13.17	90	64s
Electricity, partial electric and other energy, 1,800 sq ft living area new home	month	59.49	4Q 92	4c

Oxnard-Ventura, CA

Item	Per	Value	Date	Ref.
Child Care				
Child care fee, average, center	hour	1.71	90	65r
Child care fee, average, nonregulated family day care	hour	1.32	90	65r
Child care fee, average, regulated family day care	hour	1.86	90	65r
Communications				
Long-distance telephone service, day, initial minute, 0-100 miles	min	0.17-0.40	91	12s
Long-distance telephone service, day, additional minute, 0-100 miles	min	0.07-0.31	91	12s
Long-distance telephone service, evenings/weekends, 0-100 mi, initial minute	min	0.07-0.16	91	12s
Long-distance telephone service, evenings/weekends, 0-100 mi, additional minute	min	0.03-0.12	91	12s
Education				
Board, 4-yr private college/university	year	2515	91	22s
Board, 4-yr public college/university	year	2268	91	22s
Expenditures, local gov't, public elementary/secondary	pupil	4866	92	20s
Room, 4-year private college/university	year	2622	91	22s
Room, 4-year public college/university	year	2406	91	22s
Tuition, 2-year private college/university	year	7942	91	22s
Tuition, 2-year public college/university	year	114	91	22s
Tuition, 4-year private college/university	year	10863	91	22s
Tuition, 4-year public college/university, in-state	year	1220	91	22s
Energy and Fuels				
Coal	mil Btu	2.01	90	64s
Energy	mil Btu	9.08	90	64s
Energy exp/householder, 1-family unit	year	362	90	28r
Energy exp/householder, <1,000 sq ft heating area	year	254	90	28r
Energy exp/householder, 1,000-1,999 sq ft heating area	year	358	90	28r
Energy exp/householder, 2,000+ sq ft heating area	year	467	90	28r
Energy exp/householder, mobile home	year	390	90	28r
Energy exp/householder, multifamily	year	252	90	28r
Gas, natural	mil Btu	4.31	90	64s
Gas, natural	000 cu ft	6.27	91	46s
Gas, natural, exp	year	369	91	46s
Gasoline, unleaded regular	mil Btu	8.57	90	64s
Entertainment				
Miniature golf admission	adult	6.18	92	1r
Miniature golf admission	child	5.14	92	1r
Waterpark admission	adult	11.00	92	1r
Waterpark admission	child	8.55	92	1r
Funerals				
Casket, 18-gauge steel, velvet interior		1781.09	91	24r
Cosmetology, hair care, etc.		84.64	91	24r

Values are in dollars or fractions of dollars. In the column headed *Ref*, references are shown to sources. Each reference is followed by a letter. These refer to the geographical level for which data were reported: s=State, r=Region, and c=City or metro. The abbreviation *ex* is used to mean *except* or *excluding*; *exp* stands for expenditures. For other abbreviations and further explanations, please see the Introduction.

Oxnard-Ventura, CA - continued

Item	Per	Value	Date	Ref.
Funerals				
Embalming		207.41	91	24r
Facility use for ceremony		205.76	91	24r
Hearse, local		105.14	91	24r
Limousine, local		83.21	91	24r
Remains to funeral home, transfer		113.82	91	24r
Service charge, professional		626.33	91	24r
Vault, concrete, non-metallic liner		599.54	91	24r
Viewing facilities, use		85.81	91	24r
Groceries				
Apples, Red Delicious	lb	0.80	4/93	16r
Bacon	lb	1.79	4/93	16r
Bananas	lb	0.53	4/93	16r
Bologna, all beef or mixed	lb	2.67	4/93	16r
Bread, white, pan	lb	0.81	4/93	16r
Carrots, short trimmed and topped	lb	0.39	4/93	16r
Chicken, fresh, whole	lb	0.94	4/93	16r
Chicken breast, bone-in	lb	2.19	4/93	16r
Chuck roast, graded and ungraded, ex USDA prime and choice	lb	2.26	4/93	16r
Coffee, 100% ground roast, all sizes	lb	2.33	4/93	16r
Eggs, Grade AA large	doz	1.18	4/93	16r
Flour, white, all purpose	lb	0.22	4/93	16r
Grapefruit	lb	0.52	4/93	16r
Grapes, Thompson Seedless	lb	1.50	4/93	16r
Ground beef, 100% beef	lb	1.44	4/93	16r
Ground beef, lean and extra lean	lb	2.34	4/93	16r
Ham, boneless, excluding canned	lb	2.56	4/93	16r
Honey, jar	8 oz	0.89-1.00	92	5r
Honey, jar	lb	1.35-1.97	92	5r
Honey, squeeze bear	12-oz	1.19-1.50	92	5r
Ice cream, prepackaged, bulk, regular	1/2 gal	2.40	4/93	16r
Lemons	lb	0.81	4/93	16r
Lettuce, iceberg	lb	0.84	4/93	16r
Margarine, stick	lb	0.81	4/93	16r
Oranges, navel	lb	0.48	4/93	16r
Pork chops, center cut, bone-in	lb	3.25	4/93	16r
Potato chips	16 oz	2.89	4/93	16r
Potatoes, white	lb	0.38	4/93	16r
Round roast, graded & ungraded, ex USDA prime & choice	lb	3.00	4/93	16r
Round roast, USDA choice, boneless	lb	3.16	4/93	16r
Shortening, vegetable oil blends	lb	0.86	4/93	16r
Spaghetti and macaroni	lb	0.84	4/93	16r
Steak, round, graded & ungraded, ex USDA prime & choice	lb	3.34	4/93	16r
Steak, round, USDA choice, boneless	lb	3.24	4/93	16r
Steak, sirloin, graded & ungraded, ex USDA prime & choice	lb	3.75	4/93	16r
Steak, sirloin, USDA choice, boneless	lb	4.49	4/93	16r
Sugar, white	lb	0.41	4/93	16r
Sugar, white, 33-80 oz pk	lb	0.38	4/93	16r
Tomatoes, field grown	lb	1.01	4/93	16r
Turkey, frozen, whole	lb	1.04	4/93	16r
Health Care				
Cardizem 60 mg tablets	30	24.04	92	49s
Cector 250 mg tablets	15	35.87	92	49s
Childbirth, cesarean, hospital		5533	91	62r
Childbirth, cesarean, physician's fee		2053	91	62r
Childbirth, normal, hospital		2745	91	62r
Childbirth, normal, physician's fee		1492	91	62r
Health care spending, state	capita	2894	3/93	84s
Medical plan per employee	year	3421	91	45r
Mental health care, exp	capita	37.60-53.67	90	38s
Mental health care, exp, state mental health agency	capita	42.32	90	38s
Mental health care, hospital psychiatric services, non-Federal, exp	capita	10.64	88	38s
Mental health care, mental health organization, multiservice, exp	capita	28.56	88	38s

Oxnard-Ventura, CA - continued

Item	Per	Value	Date	Ref.
Health Care - continued				
Mental health care, psychiatric hospitals, private, exp	capita	18.60	88	38s
Mental health care, psychiatric out-patient clinics, freestanding, exp	capita	2.28	88	38s
Mental health care, psychiatric partial-care organizations, freestanding, exp	capita	0.24	88	38s
Mental health care, state and county mental hospitals, exp	capita	13.60	88	38s
Mental health care, VA medical centers, exp	capita	2.33	88	38s
Mevacor 20 mg tablets	30	67.62	92	49s
Physician fee, family practice, first-visit		111.00	91	62r
Physician fee, family practice, revisit		45.00	91	62r
Physician fee, general practice, first-visit		100.00	91	62r
Physician fee, general practice, revisit		40.00	91	62r
Physician fee, internal medicine, first-visit		137.00	91	62r
Physician fee, internal medicine, revisit		48.00	91	62r
Physician fee, median, neurosurgeon, first-visit		157.00	91	62r
Physician fee, median, nonsurgical specialist, first-visit		131.00	91	62r
Physician fee, median, orthopedic surgeon, first-visit		124.00	91	62r
Physician fee, median, plastic surgeon, first-visit		88.00	91	62r
Physician fee, median, surgical specialist, first-visit		100.00	91	62r
Physician fee, neurosurgeon, revisit		51.00	91	62r
Physician fee, nonsurgical specialist, revisit		47.00	91	62r
Physician fee, obstetrics/gynecology, first-visit		95.00	91	62r
Physician fee, obstetrics/gynecology, revisit		50.00	91	62r
Physician fee, orthopedic surgeon, revisit		51.00	91	62r
Physician fee, pediatrician, first-visit		81.00	91	62r
Physician fee, pediatrician, revisit		42.00	91	62r
Physician fee, plastic surgeon, revisit		48.00	91	62r
Physician fee, surgical specialist, revisit		49.00	91	62r
Prozac 20 mg tablets	14	33.22	92	49s
Substance abuse, hospital ancillary charge	incident	1760	90	70s
Substance abuse, hospital physician charge	incident	750	90	70s
Substance abuse, hospital room and board	incident	6390	90	70s
Tagamet 300 mg tablets	100	77.08	92	49s
Xanax 0.25 mg tablets	90	64.08	92	49s
Zantac 160 mg tablets	60	92.31	92	49s
Housing				
Home, median price	unit	131,200	92	58s
Insurance and Pensions				
Auto insurance, private passenger	year	904.37	91	63s
Taxes				
Tax, cigarette	pack	35	91	77s
Tax, gasoline	gal	16	91	77s
Taxes, state	capita	1477	91	77s
Transportation				
Driver's license fee		10.00	12/90	43s
Travel				
Business travel	day	178.00	4/93	89r
Utilities				
Electricity	mil Btu	25.98	90	64s

Paducah, KY

Item	Per	Value	Date	Ref.
Composite ACCRA index		91.20	4Q 92	4c
Alcoholic Beverages				
Beer, Miller Lite or Budweiser, 12-oz containers	6 pack	3.78	4Q 92	4c

Values are in dollars or fractions of dollars. In the column headed *Ref*, references are shown to sources. Each reference is followed by a letter. These refer to the geographical level for which data were reported: s=State, r=Region, and c=City or metro. The abbreviation *ex* is used to mean *except* or *excluding*; *exp* stands for *expenditures*. For other abbreviations and further explanations, please see the Introduction.

Paducah, KY - continued

Item	Per	Value	Date	Ref.
Alcoholic Beverages				
Liquor, J & B Scotch	750 ml	16.21	4Q 92	4c
Wine, Gallo Chablis blanc, 1.5 liter	bottle	6.72	4Q 92	4c
Clothing				
Jeans, man's denim		27.90	4Q 92	4c
Shirt, man's dress shirt		24.65	4Q 92	4c
Undervest, boy's size 10-14, cotton	3	4.62	4Q 92	4c
Communications				
Newspaper subscription, daily and Sunday home delivery, large-city	month	9.30	4Q 92	4c
Telephone, flat rate	month	12.69	91	11c
Telephone bill, family of four	month	20.43	4Q 92	4c
Energy and Fuels				
Energy, combined forms, 1,800 sq ft heating area	month	94.86	4Q 92	4c
Energy, exc electricity, 1,800 sq ft heating area	month	37.90	4Q 92	4c
Gasoline, motor	gal	1.01	4Q 92	4c
Entertainment				
Bowling, evening rate	game	2.00	4Q 92	4c
Monopoly game, Parker Brothers', No. 9		12.98	4Q 92	4c
Movie	admission	5.00	4Q 92	4c
Tennis balls, yellow, Wilson or Penn, 3	can	1.95	4Q 92	4c
Goods and Services				
ACCRA Index, Miscellaneous Goods and Services		98.30	4Q 92	4c
Groceries				
ACCRA Index, Groceries		104.50	4Q 92	4c
Babyfood, strained vegetables, lowest price	4-4.5 oz jar	0.34	4Q 92	4c
Bananas	lb	0.46	4Q 92	4c
Bread, white	24 oz	1.10	4Q 92	4c
Cheese, Kraft grated Parmesan	8-oz canister	3.23	4Q 92	4c
Chicken, fryer, whole	lb	0.78	4Q 92	4c
Cigarettes, Winston	carton	15.12	4Q 92	4c
Coffee, vacuum-packed	13-oz can	2.12	4Q 92	4c
Corn, frozen	10 oz	0.77	4Q 92	4c
Corn Flakes, Kellogg's or Post Toasties	18 oz	2.09	4Q 92	4c
Eggs, Grade A large	doz	0.77	4Q 92	4c
Ground beef or hamburger	lb	1.36	4Q 92	4c
Lettuce, iceberg	head	0.94	4Q 92	4c
Margarine, Blue Bonnet or Parkay cubes	lb	0.60	4Q 92	4c
Milk, whole	1/2 gal	1.59	4Q 92	4c
Orange juice, Minute Maid frozen	12-oz can	1.59	4Q 92	4c
Peaches	29-oz can	1.36	4Q 92	4c
Peas Sweet, Del Monte or Green Giant	15-17 oz can	0.60	4Q 92	4c
Potatoes, white or red	10-lb sack	2.32	4Q 92	4c
Sausage, Jimmy Dean, 100% pork	lb	2.56	4Q 92	4c
Shortening, vegetable, Crisco	3-lb can	2.36	4Q 92	4c
Soft drink, Coca Cola	2 liter	1.11	4Q 92	4c
Steak, T-bone	lb	5.09	4Q 92	4c
Sugar, cane or beet	4 lb	1.56	4Q 92	4c
Tomatoes, Hunt's or Del Monte	14.5-oz can	0.80	4Q 92	4c
Tuna, chunk, light	6.125-6.5 oz can	0.67	4Q 92	4c
Health Care				
ACCRA Index, Health Care		82.30	4Q 92	4c
Analgesic, Aspirin, Bayer, 325 mg tablets	100	5.78	4Q 92	4c

Paducah, KY - continued

Item	Per	Value	Date	Ref.
Health Care - continued				
Dentist's fee, adult teeth cleaning and periodic oral exam	visit	36.00	4Q 92	4c
Doctor's fee, routine exam, established patient	visit	30.80	4Q 92	4c
Hospital care, semiprivate room	day	211.99	90	27c
Hospital care, semiprivate room	day	223.50	4Q 92	4c
Household Goods				
Appliance repair, home, service call, washing machine	min labor charge	30.00	4Q 92	4c
Laundry detergent, Tide Ultra, Bold, or Cheer	42 oz	3.39	4Q 92	4c
Tissues, facial, Kleenex brand	175-count box	1.15	4Q 92	4c
Housing				
ACCRA Index, Housing		79.70	4Q 92	4c
House, 1,800 sq ft, 8,000 sq ft lot, new, urban	total	89951	4Q 92	4c
House payment, principal and interest, 25% down payment	month	498	4Q 92	4c
Mortgage rate, incl. points & origination fee, 30-year fixed or adjustable rate	percent	8.06	4Q 92	4c
Rent, apartment, 2 bedrooms - 1-1/2 to 2 baths, unfurnished, 950 sq ft, water	month	375	4Q 92	4c
Personal Goods				
Shampoo, Alberto VO5	15 oz	1.56	4Q 92	4c
Toothpaste, Crest or Colgate	6-7 oz	2.29	4Q 92	4c
Personal Services				
Dry cleaning, man's 2-piece suit		5.50	4Q 92	4c
Haircare, woman's shampoo, trim and blow-dry		16.00	4Q 92	4c
Haircut, man's barbershop, no styling		6.33	4Q 92	4c
Restaurant Food				
Chicken, fried, thigh and drumstick		2.29	4Q 92	4c
Hamburger with cheese	1/4 lb	1.84	4Q 92	4c
Pizza, Pizza Hut or Pizza Inn, cheese, thin crust	12-13 in	7.24	4Q 92	4c
Transportation				
ACCRA Index, Transportation		87.80	4Q 92	4c
Bus fare	one-way	0.75	3/93	2c
Tire balance, computer or spin balance, front	wheel	5.60	4Q 92	4c
Utilities				
ACCRA Index, Utilities		88.70	4Q 92	4c
Electricity, partial electric and other energy, 1,800 sq ft living area new home	month	56.96	4Q 92	4c

Palm Springs, CA

Item	Per	Value	Date	Ref.
Composite ACCRA index		123.70	4Q 92	4c
Alcoholic Beverages				
Beer, Miller Lite or Budweiser, 12-oz containers	6 pack	4.02	4Q 92	4c
Liquor, J & B Scotch	750 ml	15.29	4Q 92	4c
Wine, Gallo Chablis blanc, 1.5 liter	bottle	3.92	4Q 92	4c
Clothing				
Jeans, man's denim		30.00	4Q 92	4c
Shirt, man's dress shirt		27.83	4Q 92	4c
Undervest, boy's size 10-14, cotton	3	5.99	4Q 92	4c
Communications				
Newspaper subscription, daily and Sunday home delivery, large-city	month	7.50	4Q 92	4c
Telephone bill, family of four	month	16.38	4Q 92	4c

Values are in dollars or fractions of dollars. In the column headed *Ref*, references are shown to sources. Each reference is followed by a letter. These refer to the geographical level for which data were reported: s = State, r = Region, and c = City or metro. The abbreviation *ex* is used to mean *except* or *excluding*; *exp* stands for *expenditures*. For other abbreviations and further explanations, please see the Introduction.

Palm Springs, CA - continued

Item	Per	Value	Date	Ref.
Energy and Fuels				
Energy, combined forms, 1,800 sq ft heating area	month	115.23	4Q 92	4c
Energy, exc electricity, 1,800 sq ft heating area	month	18.14	4Q 92	4c
Gasoline, motor	gal	1.32	4Q 92	4c
Entertainment				
Bowling, evening rate	game	2.75	4Q 92	4c
Monopoly game, Parker Brothers', No. 9		13.65	4Q 92	4c
Movie	admission	7.00	4Q 92	4c
Tennis balls, yellow, Wilson or Penn, 3	can	2.96	4Q 92	4c
Goods and Services				
ACCRA Index, Miscellaneous Goods and Services		118.20	4Q 92	4c
Groceries				
ACCRA Index, Groceries		107.30	4Q 92	4c
Babyfood, strained vegetables, lowest price	4-4.5 oz jar	0.37	4Q 92	4c
Bananas	lb	0.56	4Q 92	4c
Bread, white	24 oz	0.96	4Q 92	4c
Cheese, Kraft grated Parmesan	8-oz canister	3.33	4Q 92	4c
Chicken, fryer, whole	lb	0.96	4Q 92	4c
Cigarettes, Winston	carton	20.75	4Q 92	4c
Coffee, vacuum-packed	13-oz can	1.66	4Q 92	4c
Corn, frozen	10 oz	0.70	4Q 92	4c
Corn Flakes, Kellogg's or Post Toasties	18 oz	2.04	4Q 92	4c
Eggs, Grade A large	doz	1.68	4Q 92	4c
Ground beef or hamburger	lb	1.54	4Q 92	4c
Lettuce, iceberg	head	0.80	4Q 92	4c
Margarine, Blue Bonnet or Parkay cubes	lb	0.61	4Q 92	4c
Milk, whole	1/2 gal	1.37	4Q 92	4c
Orange juice, Minute Maid frozen	12-oz can	1.35	4Q 92	4c
Peaches	29-oz can	1.22	4Q 92	4c
Peas Sweet, Del Monte or Green Giant	15-17 oz can	0.63	4Q 92	4c
Potatoes, white or red	10-lb sack	1.82	4Q 92	4c
Sausage, Jimmy Dean, 100% pork	lb	2.68	4Q 92	4c
Shortening, vegetable, Crisco	3-lb can	2.50	4Q 92	4c
Soft drink, Coca Cola	2 liter	1.16	4Q 92	4c
Steak, T-bone	lb	4.78	4Q 92	4c
Sugar, cane or beet	4 lb	1.89	4Q 92	4c
Tomatoes, Hunt's or Del Monte	14.5-oz can	0.79	4Q 92	4c
Tuna, chunk, light	6.125-6.5 oz can	0.55	4Q 92	4c
Health Care				
ACCRA Index, Health Care		128.40	4Q 92	4c
Analgesic, Aspirin, Bayer, 325 mg tablets	100	6.11	4Q 92	4c
Dentist's fee, adult teeth cleaning and periodic oral exam	visit	48.00	4Q 92	4c
Doctor's fee, routine exam, established patient	visit	47.80	4Q 92	4c
Hospital care, semiprivate room	day	375.47	90	27c
Hospital care, semiprivate room	day	575.00	4Q 92	4c
Household Goods				
Appliance repair, home, service call, washing machine	min labor charge	41.78	4Q 92	4c
Laundry detergent, Tide Ultra, Bold, or Cheer	42 oz	3.22	4Q 92	4c

Palm Springs, CA - continued

Item	Per	Value	Date	Ref.
Household Goods - continued				
Tissues, facial, Kleenex brand	175-count box	1.12	4Q 92	4c
Housing				
ACCRA Index, Housing		144.30	4Q 92	4c
House, 1,800 sq ft, 8,000 sq ft lot, new, urban	total	159821	4Q 92	4c
House payment, principal and interest, 25% down payment	month	912	4Q 92	4c
Mortgage rate, incl. points & origination fee, 30-year fixed or adjustable rate	percent	8.39	4Q 92	4c
Rent, apartment, 2 bedrooms - 1-1/2 to 2 baths, unfurnished, 950 sq ft, water	month	655	4Q 92	4c
Personal Goods				
Shampoo, Alberto VO5	15 oz	1.29	4Q 92	4c
Toothpaste, Crest or Colgate	6-7 oz	2.21	4Q 92	4c
Personal Services				
Dry cleaning, man's 2-piece suit		7.94	4Q 92	4c
Haircare, woman's shampoo, trim and blow-dry		34.80	4Q 92	4c
Haircut, man's barbershop, no styling		12.00	4Q 92	4c
Restaurant Food				
Chicken, fried, thigh and drumstick		1.99	4Q 92	4c
Hamburger with cheese	1/4 lb	1.99	4Q 92	4c
Pizza, Pizza Hut or Pizza Inn, cheese, thin crust	12-13 in	7.99	4Q 92	4c
Transportation				
ACCRA Index, Transportation		122.20	4Q 92	4c
Bus fare	one-way	0.75	3/93	2c
Bus fare, up to 10 miles	one-way	0.50	4Q 92	4c
Tire balance, computer or spin balance, front	wheel	9.19	4Q 92	4c
Utilities				
ACCRA Index, Utilities		103.40	4Q 92	4c
Electricity, partial electric and other energy, 1,800 sq ft living area new home	month	97.09	4Q 92	4c

Panama City, FL

Item	Per	Value	Date	Ref.
Child Care				
Child care fee, average, center	hour	1.29	90	65r
Child care fee, average, nonregulated family day care	hour	0.89	90	65r
Child care fee, average, regulated family day care	hour	1.32	90	65r
Communications				
Long-distance telephone service, day, initial minute, 0-100 miles	min	0.15-0.20	91	12s
Long-distance telephone service, day, additional minute, 0-100 miles	min	0.08-0.20	91	12s
Long-distance telephone service, evenings/weekends, 0-100 mi, initial minute	min	0.09-0.12	91	12s
Long-distance telephone service, evenings/weekends, 0-100 mi, additional minute	min	0.05-0.12	91	12s
Education				
Board, 4-yr private college/university	year	1924	91	22s
Board, 4-yr public college/university	year	1955	91	22s
Expenditures, local gov't, public elementary/secondary	pupil	5235	92	20s
Room, 4-year private college/university	year	1904	91	22s
Room, 4-year public college/university	year	1510	91	22s
Tuition, 2-year private college/university	year	4751	91	22s
Tuition, 2-year public college/university	year	788	91	22s
Tuition, 4-year private college/university	year	7992	91	22s

Values are in dollars or fractions of dollars. In the column headed *Ref*, references are shown to sources. Each reference is followed by a letter. These refer to the geographical level for which data were reported: s = State, r = Region, and c = City or metro. The abbreviation *ex* is used to mean *except* or *excluding*; *exp* stands for expenditures. For other abbreviations and further explanations, please see the Introduction.

Panama City, FL - continued

Item	Per	Value	Date	Ref.
Education				
Tuition, 4-year public college/university, in-state	year	1337	91	22s
Energy and Fuels				
Coal	mil Btu	1.85	90	64s
Energy	mil Btu	10.58	90	64s
Energy exp/householder, 1-family unit	year	487	90	28r
Energy exp/householder, <1,000 sq ft heating area	year	393	90	28r
Energy exp/householder, 1,000-1,999 sq ft heating area	year	442	90	28r
Energy exp/householder, 2,000+ sq ft heating area	year	577	90	28r
Energy exp/householder, mobile home	year	366	90	28r
Energy exp/householder, multifamily	year	382	90	28r
Gas, natural	mil Btu	3.21	90	64s
Gas, natural	000 cu ft	8.98	91	46s
Gas, natural, exp	year	248	91	46s
Gasoline, unleaded regular	mil Btu	8.85	90	64s
Entertainment				
Miniature golf admission	adult	6.18	92	1r
Miniature golf admission	child	5.14	92	1r
Waterpark admission	adult	11.00	92	1r
Waterpark admission	child	8.55	92	1r
Funerals				
Casket, 18-gauge steel, velvet interior		2029.08	91	24r
Cosmetology, hair care, etc.		75.10	91	24r
Embalming		249.24	91	24r
Facility use for ceremony		162.27	91	24r
Hearse, local		114.04	91	24r
Limousine, local		88.57	91	24r
Remains to funeral home, transfer		92.61	91	24r
Service charge, professional		682.42	91	24r
Vault, concrete, non-metallic liner		798.70	91	24r
Viewing facilities, use		163.86	91	24r
Groceries				
Apples, Red Delicious	lb	0.79	4/93	16r
Bacon	lb	1.75	4/93	16r
Bananas	lb	0.42	4/93	16r
Beef, stew, boneless	lb	2.61	4/93	16r
Bologna, all beef or mixed	lb	2.24	4/93	16r
Bread, white, pan	lb	0.64	4/93	16r
Bread, whole wheat, pan	lb	0.96	4/93	16r
Cabbage	lb	0.37	4/93	16r
Carrots, short trimmed and topped	lb	0.47	4/93	16r
Celery	lb	0.64	4/93	16r
Cheese, American	lb	2.98	4/93	16r
Cheese, Cheddar	lb	3.28	4/93	16r
Chicken, fresh, whole	lb	0.77	4/93	16r
Chicken breast, bone-in	lb	1.92	4/93	16r
Chicken legs, bone-in	lb	1.06	4/93	16r
Chuck roast, graded and ungraded, ex USDA prime and choice	lb	2.40	4/93	16r
Chuck roast, USDA choice, bone-in	lb	2.19	4/93	16r
Chuck roast, USDA choice, boneless	lb	2.38	4/93	16r
Coffee, 100% ground roast, all sizes	lb	2.48	4/93	16r
Crackers, soda, salted	lb	1.15	4/93	16r
Eggs, Grade A large	doz	0.96	4/93	16r
Flour, white, all purpose	lb	0.24	4/93	16r
Frankfurters, all meat or all beef	lb	2.01	4/93	16r
Grapefruit	lb	0.44	4/93	16r
Grapes, Thompson Seedless	lb	1.40	4/93	16r
Ground beef, 100% beef	lb	1.58	4/93	16r
Ground beef, lean and extra lean	lb	2.09	4/93	16r
Ground chuck, 100% beef	lb	1.98	4/93	16r
Ham, boneless, excluding canned	lb	2.89	4/93	16r
Ham, picnic, shoulder, bone-in, smoked	lb	1.02	4/93	16r
Ham, rump or steak half, bone-in, smoked	lb	1.48	4/93	16r
Ice cream, prepackaged, bulk, regular	1/2 gal	2.41	4/93	16r
Lemons	lb	1.05	4/93	16r

Panama City, FL - continued

Item	Per	Value	Date	Ref.
Groceries - continued				
Lettuce, iceberg	lb	0.81	4/93	16r
Margarine, stick	lb	0.88	4/93	16r
Oranges, navel	lb	0.55	4/93	16r
Pears, Anjou	lb	0.92	4/93	16r
Pork chops, center cut, bone-in	lb	3.13	4/93	16r
Potato chips	16 oz	2.94	4/93	16r
Potatoes, white	lb	0.43	4/93	16r
Rib roast, USDA choice, bone-in	lb	4.63	4/93	16r
Rice, white, long grain, uncooked	lb	0.45	4/93	16r
Round roast, graded & ungraded, ex USDA prime & choice	lb	3.03	4/93	16r
Round roast, USDA choice, boneless	lb	3.09	4/93	16r
Sausage, fresh, loose	lb	2.08	4/93	16r
Short ribs, bone-in	lb	2.66	4/93	16r
Shortening, vegetable oil blends	lb	0.69	4/93	16r
Spaghetti and macaroni	lb	0.81	4/93	16r
Steak, rib eye, USDA choice, boneless	lb	6.24	4/93	16r
Steak, round, graded & ungraded, ex USDA prime & choice	lb	3.31	4/93	16r
Steak, round, USDA choice, boneless	lb	3.34	4/93	16r
Steak, sirloin, graded & ungraded, ex USDA prime & choice	lb	4.19	4/93	16r
Steak, sirloin, USDA choice, boneless	lb	4.46	4/93	16r
Steak, T-bone, USDA choice, bone-in	lb	5.25	4/93	16r
Strawberries, dry pint	12 oz	0.92	4/93	16r
Sugar, white	lb	0.39	4/93	16r
Sugar, white, 33-80 oz pk	lb	0.38	4/93	16r
Tomatoes, field grown	lb	0.88	4/93	16r
Tuna, chunk, light	lb	1.79	4/93	16r
Turkey, frozen, whole	lb	1.04	4/93	16r
Yogurt, natural, fruit flavored	1/2 pint	0.57	4/93	16r
Health Care				
Childbirth, cesarean, hospital		5034	91	62r
Childbirth, cesarean, physician's fee		2053	91	62r
Childbirth, normal, hospital		2712	91	62r
Childbirth, normal, physician's fee		1492	91	62r
Medical plan per employee	year	3495	91	45r
Mental health care, exp	capita	28.84-37.59	90	38s
Mental health care, exp, state mental health agency	capita	37.49	90	38s
Mental health care, hospital psychiatric services, non-Federal, exp	capita	9.11	88	38s
Mental health care, mental health organization, multiservice, exp	capita	16.21	88	38s
Mental health care, psychiatric hospitals, private, exp	capita	22.26	88	38s
Mental health care, psychiatric out-patient clinics, freestanding, exp	capita	0.89	88	38s
Mental health care, psychiatric partial-care organizations, freestanding, exp	capita	0.41	88	38s
Mental health care, state and county mental hospitals, exp	capita	16.25	88	38s
Mental health care, VA medical centers, exp	capita	1.69	88	38s
Physician fee, family practice, first-visit		75.00	91	62r
Physician fee, family practice, revisit		34.00	91	62r
Physician fee, general practice, first-visit		61.00	91	62r
Physician fee, general practice, revisit		32.00	91	62r
Physician fee, general surgeon, first-visit		64.00	91	62r
Physician fee, general surgeon, revisit		40.00	91	62r
Physician fee, internal medicine, first-visit		98.00	91	62r
Physician fee, internal medicine, revisit		40.00	91	62r
Physician fee, median, neurosurgeon, first-visit		130.00	91	62r
Physician fee, median, nonsurgical specialist, first-visit		95.00	91	62r
Physician fee, median, orthopedic surgeon, first-visit		91.00	91	62r
Physician fee, median, plastic surgeon, first-visit		66.00	91	62r

Values are in dollars or fractions of dollars. In the column headed *Ref*, references are shown to sources. Each reference is followed by a letter. These refer to the geographical level for which data were reported: s=State, r=Region, and c=City or metro. The abbreviation *ex* is used to mean *except* or *excluding*; *exp* stands for expenditures. For other abbreviations and further explanations, please see the Introduction.

Panama City, FL - continued

Item	Per	Value	Date	Ref.
Health Care				
Physician fee, median, surgical specialist, first-visit		62.00	91	62r
Physician fee, neurosurgeon, revisit		50.00	91	62r
Physician fee, nonsurgical specialist, revisit		40.00	91	62r
Physician fee, obstetrics/gynecology, first-visit		64.00	91	62r
Physician fee, obstetrics/gynecology, revisit		41.00	91	62r
Physician fee, orthopedic surgeon, revisit		40.00	91	62r
Physician fee, pediatrician, first-visit		49.00	91	62r
Physician fee, pediatrician, revisit		33.00	91	62r
Physician fee, plastic surgeon, revisit		43.00	91	62r
Physician fee, surgical specialist, revisit		37.00	91	62r
Substance abuse, hospital ancillary charge	incident	1390	90	70s
Substance abuse, hospital physician charge	incident	770	90	70s
Substance abuse, hospital room and board	incident	5600	90	70s
Insurance and Pensions				
Auto insurance, private passenger	year	727.60	91	63s
Taxes				
Tax, cigarette	pack	33.90	91	77s
Tax, gasoline	gal	11.60	91	77s
Taxes, state	capita	1037	91	77s
Transportation				
Driver's license fee		15.00	12/90	43s
Travel				
Business travel	day	193.00	4/93	89r
Utilities				
Electricity	mil Btu	20.62	90	64s

Parkersburg-Marietta, WV, OH

Item	Per	Value	Date	Ref.
Child Care				
Child care fee, average, center	hour	1.29	90	65r
Child care fee, average, nonregulated family day care	hour	0.89	90	65r
Child care fee, average, regulated family day care	hour	1.32	90	65r
Communications				
Long-distance telephone service, day, initial minute, 0-100 miles	min	0.26-0.70	91	12s
Long-distance telephone service, day, additional minute, 0-100 miles	min	0.13-0.45	91	12s
Long-distance telephone service, evenings/weekends, 0-100 mi, initial minute	min	0.10-0.28	91	12s
Long-distance telephone service, evenings/weekends, 0-100 mi, additional minute	min	0.05-0.18	91	12s
Education				
Board, 4-yr private college/university	year	1664	91	22s
Board, 4-yr public college/university	year	1723	91	22s
Expenditures, local gov't, public elementary/secondary	pupil	5401	92	20s
Room, 4-year private college/university	year	1401	91	22s
Room, 4-year public college/university	year	1556	91	22s
Tuition, 2-year private college/university	year	2767	91	22s
Tuition, 2-year public college/university	year	930	91	22s
Tuition, 4-year private college/university	year	8751	91	22s
Tuition, 4-year public college/university, in-state	year	1543	91	22s
Energy and Fuels				
Coal	mil Btu	1.47	90	64s
Energy	mil Btu	6.77	90	64s
Energy exp/householder, 1-family unit	year	487	90	28r
Energy exp/householder, <1,000 sq ft heating area	year	393	90	28r

Parkersburg-Marietta, WV, OH - continued

Item	Per	Value	Date	Ref.
Energy and Fuels - continued				
Energy exp/householder, 1,000-1,999 sq ft heating area	year	442	90	28r
Energy exp/householder, 2,000+ sq ft heating area	year	577	90	28r
Energy exp/householder, mobile home	year	366	90	28r
Energy exp/householder, multifamily	year	382	90	28r
Gas, natural	mil Btu	4.40	90	64s
Gas, natural	000 cu ft	6.50	91	46s
Gas, natural, exp	year	605	91	46s
Gasoline, unleaded regular	mil Btu	9.96	90	64s
Entertainment				
Miniature golf admission	adult	6.18	92	1r
Miniature golf admission	child	5.14	92	1r
Waterpark admission	adult	11.00	92	1r
Waterpark admission	child	8.55	92	1r
Funerals				
Casket, 18-gauge steel, velvet interior		2029.08	91	24r
Cosmetology, hair care, etc.		75.10	91	24r
Embalming		249.24	91	24r
Facility use for ceremony		162.27	91	24r
Hearse, local		114.04	91	24r
Limousine, local		88.57	91	24r
Remains to funeral home, transfer		92.61	91	24r
Service charge, professional		682.42	91	24r
Vault, concrete, non-metallic liner		798.70	91	24r
Viewing facilities, use		163.86	91	24r
Groceries				
Apples, Red Delicious	lb	0.79	4/93	16r
Bacon	lb	1.75	4/93	16r
Bananas	lb	0.42	4/93	16r
Beef, stew, boneless	lb	2.61	4/93	16r
Bologna, all beef or mixed	lb	2.24	4/93	16r
Bread, white, pan	lb	0.64	4/93	16r
Bread, whole wheat, pan	lb	0.96	4/93	16r
Cabbage	lb	0.37	4/93	16r
Carrots, short trimmed and topped	lb	0.47	4/93	16r
Celery	lb	0.64	4/93	16r
Cheese, American	lb	2.98	4/93	16r
Cheese, Cheddar	lb	3.28	4/93	16r
Chicken, fresh, whole	lb	0.77	4/93	16r
Chicken breast, bone-in	lb	1.92	4/93	16r
Chicken legs, bone-in	lb	1.06	4/93	16r
Chuck roast, graded and ungraded, ex USDA prime and choice	lb	2.40	4/93	16r
Chuck roast, USDA choice, bone-in	lb	2.19	4/93	16r
Chuck roast, USDA choice, boneless	lb	2.38	4/93	16r
Coffee, 100% ground roast, all sizes	lb	2.48	4/93	16r
Crackers, soda, salted	lb	1.15	4/93	16r
Eggs, Grade A large	doz	0.96	4/93	16r
Flour, white, all purpose	lb	0.24	4/93	16r
Frankfurters, all meat or all beef	lb	2.01	4/93	16r
Grapefruit	lb	0.44	4/93	16r
Grapes, Thompson Seedless	lb	1.40	4/93	16r
Ground beef, 100% beef	lb	1.58	4/93	16r
Ground beef, lean and extra lean	lb	2.09	4/93	16r
Ground chuck, 100% beef	lb	1.98	4/93	16r
Ham, boneless, excluding canned	lb	2.89	4/93	16r
Ham, picnic, shoulder, bone-in, smoked	lb	1.02	4/93	16r
Ham, rump or steak half, bone-in, smoked	lb	1.48	4/93	16r
Ice cream, prepackaged, bulk, regular	1/2 gal	2.41	4/93	16r
Lemons	lb	1.05	4/93	16r
Lettuce, iceberg	lb	0.81	4/93	16r
Margarine, stick	lb	0.88	4/93	16r
Oranges, navel	lb	0.55	4/93	16r
Pears, Anjou	lb	0.92	4/93	16r
Pork chops, center cut, bone-in	lb	3.13	4/93	16r
Potato chips	16 oz	2.94	4/93	16r
Potatoes, white	lb	0.43	4/93	16r
Rib roast, USDA choice, bone-in	lb	4.63	4/93	16r
Rice, white, long grain, uncooked	lb	0.45	4/93	16r

Values are in dollars or fractions of dollars. In the column headed *Ref*, references are shown to sources. Each reference is followed by a letter. These refer to the geographical level for which data were reported: s = State, r = Region, and c = City or metro. The abbreviation *ex* is used to mean *except* or *excluding*; *exp* stands for expenditures. For other abbreviations and further explanations, please see the Introduction.

Parkersburg-Marietta, WV, OH - continued

Item	Per	Value	Date	Ref.
Groceries				
Round roast, graded & ungraded, ex USDA prime & choice	lb	3.03	4/93	16r
Round roast, USDA choice, boneless	lb	3.09	4/93	16r
Sausage, fresh, loose	lb	2.08	4/93	16r
Short ribs, bone-in	lb	2.66	4/93	16r
Shortening, vegetable oil blends	lb	0.69	4/93	16r
Spaghetti and macaroni	lb	0.81	4/93	16r
Steak, rib eye, USDA choice, boneless	lb	6.24	4/93	16r
Steak, round, graded & ungraded, ex USDA prime & choice	lb	3.31	4/93	16r
Steak, round, USDA choice, boneless	lb	3.34	4/93	16r
Steak, sirloin, graded & ungraded, ex USDA prime & choice	lb	4.19	4/93	16r
Steak, sirloin, USDA choice, boneless	lb	4.46	4/93	16r
Steak, T-bone, USDA choice, bone-in	lb	5.25	4/93	16r
Strawberries, dry pint	12 oz	0.92	4/93	16r
Sugar, white	lb	0.39	4/93	16r
Sugar, white, 33-80 oz pk	lb	0.38	4/93	16r
Tomatoes, field grown	lb	0.88	4/93	16r
Tuna, chunk, light	lb	1.79	4/93	16r
Turkey, frozen, whole	lb	1.04	4/93	16r
Yogurt, natural, fruit flavored	1/2 pint	0.57	4/93	16r
Health Care				
Childbirth, cesarean, hospital		5034	91	62r
Childbirth, cesarean, physician's fee		2053	91	62r
Childbirth, normal, hospital		2712	91	62r
Childbirth, normal, physician's fee		1492	91	62r
Medical plan per employee	year	3495	91	45r
Mental health care, exp	capita	20.37-28.83	90	38s
Mental health care, exp, state mental health agency	capita	23.72	90	38s
Mental health care, hospital psychiatric services, non-Federal, exp	capita	9.26	88	38s
Mental health care, mental health organization, multiservice, exp	capita	26.55	88	38s
Mental health care, psychiatric hospitals, private, exp	capita	5.67	88	38s
Mental health care, psychiatric out-patient clinics, freestanding, exp	capita	1.30	88	38s
Mental health care, state and county mental hospitals, exp	capita	11.86	88	38s
Mental health care, VA medical centers, exp	capita	0.70	88	38s
Physician fee, family practice, first-visit		75.00	91	62r
Physician fee, family practice, revisit		34.00	91	62r
Physician fee, general practice, first-visit		61.00	91	62r
Physician fee, general practice, revisit		32.00	91	62r
Physician fee, general surgeon, first-visit		64.00	91	62r
Physician fee, general surgeon, revisit		40.00	91	62r
Physician fee, internal medicine, first-visit		98.00	91	62r
Physician fee, internal medicine, revisit		40.00	91	62r
Physician fee, median, neurosurgeon, first-visit		130.00	91	62r
Physician fee, median, nonsurgical specialist, first-visit		95.00	91	62r
Physician fee, median, orthopedic surgeon, first-visit		91.00	91	62r
Physician fee, median, plastic surgeon, first-visit		66.00	91	62r
Physician fee, median, surgical specialist, first-visit		62.00	91	62r
Physician fee, neurosurgeon, revisit		50.00	91	62r
Physician fee, nonsurgical specialist, revisit		40.00	91	62r
Physician fee, obstetrics/gynecology, first-visit		64.00	91	62r
Physician fee, obstetrics/gynecology, revisit		41.00	91	62r
Physician fee, orthopedic surgeon, revisit		40.00	91	62r
Physician fee, pediatrician, first-visit		49.00	91	62r
Physician fee, pediatrician, revisit		33.00	91	62r
Physician fee, plastic surgeon, revisit		43.00	91	62r
Physician fee, surgical specialist, revisit		37.00	91	62r

Parkersburg-Marietta, WV, OH - continued

Item	Per	Value	Date	Ref.
Health Care - continued				
Substance abuse, hospital ancillary charge	incident	1900	90	70s
Substance abuse, hospital physician charge	incident	1270	90	70s
Substance abuse, hospital room and board	incident	4590	90	70s
Insurance and Pensions				
Auto insurance, private passenger	year	621.65	91	63s
Taxes				
Tax, cigarette	pack	17	91	77s
Tax, gasoline	gal	15.50	91	77s
Taxes, state	capita	1293	91	77s
Transportation				
Driver's license fee		10.00	12/90	43s
Vehicle registration and license plate	year	26.50-37.50	93	69s
Travel				
Business travel	day	193.00	4/93	89r
Utilities				
Electricity	mil Btu	13.90	90	64s
Electricity, winter, 250 KWh	month	21.89	92	55s
Electricity, winter, 500 KWh	month	38.44	92	55s
Electricity, winter, 750 KWh	month	53.70	92	55s
Electricity, winter, 1000 KWh	month	68.96	92	55s

Pascagoula, MS

Item	Per	Value	Date	Ref.
Child Care				
Child care fee, average, center	hour	1.29	90	65r
Child care fee, average, nonregulated family day care	hour	0.89	90	65r
Child care fee, average, regulated family day care	hour	1.32	90	65r
Communications				
Long-distance telephone service, day, initial minute, 0-100 miles	min	0.19-0.47	91	12s
Long-distance telephone service, day, additional minute, 0-100 miles	min	0.11-0.34	91	12s
Long-distance telephone service, evenings/weekends, 0-100 mi, initial minute	min	0.06-0.19	91	12s
Long-distance telephone service, evenings/weekends, 0-100 mi, additional minute	min	0.04-0.14	91	12s
Education				
Board, 4-yr private college/university	year	1312	91	22s
Board, 4-yr public college/university	year	1924	91	22s
Expenditures, local gov't, public elementary/secondary	pupil	3344	92	20s
Room, 4-year private college/university	year	1002	91	22s
Room, 4-year public college/university	year	1154	91	22s
Tuition, 2-year private college/university	year	3721	91	22s
Tuition, 2-year public college/university	year	722	91	22s
Tuition, 4-year private college/university	year	5238	91	22s
Tuition, 4-year public college/university, in-state	year	1927	91	22s
Energy and Fuels				
Coal	mil Btu	1.65	90	64s
Energy	mil Btu	8.31	90	64s
Energy exp/householder, 1-family unit	year	403	90	28r
Energy exp/householder, <1,000 sq ft heating area	year	342	90	28r
Energy exp/householder, 1,000-1,999 sq ft heating area	year	388	90	28r
Energy exp/householder, 2,000+ sq ft heating area	year	434	90	28r
Energy exp/householder, mobile home	year	320	90	28r
Energy exp/householder, multifamily	year	338	90	28r
Gas, natural	mil Btu	2.75	90	64s

Values are in dollars or fractions of dollars. In the column headed *Ref*, references are shown to sources. Each reference is followed by a letter. These refer to the geographical level for which data were reported: s=State, r=Region, and c=City or metro. The abbreviation *ex* is used to mean *except* or *excluding*; *exp* stands for expenditures. For other abbreviations and further explanations, please see the Introduction.

Pascagoula, MS - continued

Item	Per	Value	Date	Ref.
Energy and Fuels				
Gas, natural	000 cu ft	5.21	91	46s
Gas, natural, exp	year	348	91	46s
Gasoline, unleaded regular	mil Btu	9.21	90	64s
Entertainment				
Miniature golf admission	adult	6.18	92	1r
Miniature golf admission	child	5.14	92	1r
Waterpark admission	adult	11.00	92	1r
Waterpark admission	child	8.55	92	1r
Funerals				
Casket, 18-gauge steel, velvet interior		2329.05	91	24r
Cosmetology, hair care, etc.		72.78	91	24r
Embalming		240.71	91	24r
Facility use for ceremony		181.67	91	24r
Hearse, local		106.25	91	24r
Limousine, local		70.92	91	24r
Remains to funeral home, transfer		96.30	91	24r
Service charge, professional		687.09	91	24r
Vault, concrete, non-metallic liner		732.09	91	24r
Viewing facilities, use		190.30	91	24r
Groceries				
Apples, Red Delicious	lb	0.79	4/93	16r
Bacon	lb	1.75	4/93	16r
Bananas	lb	0.42	4/93	16r
Beef, stew, boneless	lb	2.61	4/93	16r
Bologna, all beef or mixed	lb	2.24	4/93	16r
Bread, white, pan	lb	0.64	4/93	16r
Bread, whole wheat, pan	lb	0.96	4/93	16r
Cabbage	lb	0.37	4/93	16r
Carrots, short trimmed and topped	lb	0.47	4/93	16r
Celery	lb	0.64	4/93	16r
Cheese, American	lb	2.98	4/93	16r
Cheese, Cheddar	lb	3.28	4/93	16r
Chicken, fresh, whole	lb	0.77	4/93	16r
Chicken breast, bone-in	lb	1.92	4/93	16r
Chicken legs, bone-in	lb	1.06	4/93	16r
Chuck roast, graded and ungraded, ex USDA prime and choice	lb	2.40	4/93	16r
Chuck roast, USDA choice, bone-in	lb	2.19	4/93	16r
Chuck roast, USDA choice, boneless	lb	2.38	4/93	16r
Coffee, 100% ground roast, all sizes	lb	2.48	4/93	16r
Crackers, soda, salted	lb	1.15	4/93	16r
Eggs, Grade A large	doz	0.96	4/93	16r
Flour, white, all purpose	lb	0.24	4/93	16r
Frankfurters, all meat or all beef	lb	2.01	4/93	16r
Grapefruit	lb	0.44	4/93	16r
Grapes, Thompson Seedless	lb	1.40	4/93	16r
Ground beef, 100% beef	lb	1.58	4/93	16r
Ground beef, lean and extra lean	lb	2.09	4/93	16r
Ground chuck, 100% beef	lb	1.98	4/93	16r
Ham, boneless, excluding canned	lb	2.89	4/93	16r
Ham, picnic, shoulder, bone-in, smoked	lb	1.02	4/93	16r
Ham, rump or steak half, bone-in, smoked	lb	1.48	4/93	16r
Honey, jar	8 oz	0.89-1.09	92	5r
Honey, jar	lb	1.39-2.25	92	5r
Honey, squeeze bear	12-oz	1.00-1.50	92	5r
Ice cream, prepackaged, bulk, regular	1/2 gal	2.41	4/93	16r
Lemons	lb	1.05	4/93	16r
Lettuce, iceberg	lb	0.81	4/93	16r
Margarine, stick	lb	0.88	4/93	16r
Oranges, navel	lb	0.55	4/93	16r
Pears, Anjou	lb	0.92	4/93	16r
Pork chops, center cut, bone-in	lb	3.13	4/93	16r
Potato chips	16 oz	2.94	4/93	16r
Potatoes, white	lb	0.43	4/93	16r
Rib roast, USDA choice, bone-in	lb	4.63	4/93	16r
Rice, white, long grain, uncooked	lb	0.45	4/93	16r
Round roast, graded & ungraded, ex USDA prime & choice	lb	3.03	4/93	16r
Round roast, USDA choice, boneless	lb	3.09	4/93	16r
Sausage, fresh, loose	lb	2.08	4/93	16r

Pascagoula, MS - continued

Item	Per	Value	Date	Ref.
Groceries - continued				
Short ribs, bone-in	lb	2.66	4/93	16r
Shortening, vegetable oil blends	lb	0.69	4/93	16r
Spaghetti and macaroni	lb	0.81	4/93	16r
Steak, rib eye, USDA choice, boneless	lb	6.24	4/93	16r
Steak, round, graded & ungraded, ex USDA prime & choice	lb	3.31	4/93	16r
Steak, round, USDA choice, boneless	lb	3.34	4/93	16r
Steak, sirloin, graded & ungraded, ex USDA prime & choice	lb	4.19	4/93	16r
Steak, sirloin, USDA choice, boneless	lb	4.46	4/93	16r
Steak, T-bone, USDA choice, bone-in	lb	5.25	4/93	16r
Strawberries, dry pint	12 oz	0.92	4/93	16r
Sugar, white	lb	0.39	4/93	16r
Sugar, white, 33-80 oz pk	lb	0.38	4/93	16r
Tomatoes, field grown	lb	0.88	4/93	16r
Tuna, chunk, light	lb	1.79	4/93	16r
Turkey, frozen, whole	lb	1.04	4/93	16r
Yogurt, natural, fruit flavored	1/2 pint	0.57	4/93	16r
Health Care				
Childbirth, cesarean, hospital		5034	91	62r
Childbirth, cesarean, physician's fee		2053	91	62r
Childbirth, normal, hospital		2712	91	62r
Childbirth, normal, physician's fee		1492	91	62r
Mental health care, exp	capita	28.84-37.59	90	38s
Mental health care, exp, state mental health agency	capita	33.71	90	38s
Mental health care, hospital psychiatric services, non-Federal, exp	capita	5.17	88	38s
Mental health care, mental health organization, multiservice, exp	capita	8.65	88	38s
Mental health care, psychiatric hospitals, private, exp	capita	6.85	88	38s
Mental health care, state and county mental hospitals, exp	capita	20.41	88	38s
Mental health care, VA medical centers, exp	capita	7.21	88	38s
Physician fee, family practice, first-visit		75.00	91	62r
Physician fee, family practice, revisit		34.00	91	62r
Physician fee, general practice, first-visit		61.00	91	62r
Physician fee, general practice, revisit		32.00	91	62r
Physician fee, general surgeon, first-visit		64.00	91	62r
Physician fee, general surgeon, revisit		40.00	91	62r
Physician fee, internal medicine, first-visit		98.00	91	62r
Physician fee, internal medicine, revisit		40.00	91	62r
Physician fee, median, neurosurgeon, first-visit		130.00	91	62r
Physician fee, median, nonsurgical specialist, first-visit		95.00	91	62r
Physician fee, median, orthopedic surgeon, first-visit		91.00	91	62r
Physician fee, median, plastic surgeon, first-visit		66.00	91	62r
Physician fee, median, surgical specialist, first-visit		62.00	91	62r
Physician fee, neurosurgeon, revisit		50.00	91	62r
Physician fee, nonsurgical specialist, revisit		40.00	91	62r
Physician fee, obstetrics/gynecology, first-visit		64.00	91	62r
Physician fee, obstetrics/gynecology, revisit		41.00	91	62r
Physician fee, orthopedic surgeon, revisit		40.00	91	62r
Physician fee, pediatrician, first-visit		49.00	91	62r
Physician fee, pediatrician, revisit		33.00	91	62r
Physician fee, plastic surgeon, revisit		43.00	91	62r
Physician fee, surgical specialist, revisit		37.00	91	62r
Substance abuse, hospital ancillary charge	incident	1760	90	70s
Substance abuse, hospital physician charge	incident	540	90	70s
Substance abuse, hospital room and board	incident	4060	90	70s

Values are in dollars or fractions of dollars. In the column headed *Ref*, references are shown to sources. Each reference is followed by a letter. These refer to the geographical level for which data were reported: s=State, r=Region, and c=City or metro. The abbreviation *ex* is used to mean *except* or *excluding*; *exp* stands for expenditures. For other abbreviations and further explanations, please see the Introduction.

Pascagoula, MS - continued

Item	Per	Value	Date	Ref.
Insurance and Pensions				
Auto insurance, private passenger	year	576.42	91	63s
Taxes				
Tax, cigarette	pack	18	91	77s
Tax, gasoline	gal	18	91	77s
Taxes, state	capita	949	91	77s
Transportation				
Driver's license fee		13.00	12/90	43s
Travel				
Business travel	day	193.00	4/93	89r
Utilities				
Electricity	mil Btu	18.05	90	64s

Pawtucket-Woonsocket-Attleboro, RI, MA

Item	Per	Value	Date	Ref.
Child Care				
Child care fee, average, center	hour	2.18	90	65r
Child care fee, average, nonregulated family day care	hour	1.83	90	65r
Child care fee, average, regulated family day care	hour	2.02	90	65r
Communications				
Long-distance telephone service, day, initial minute, 0-100 miles	min	0.31-0.37	91	12s
Long-distance telephone service, day, additional minute, 0-100 miles	min	0.14-0.18	91	12s
Long-distance telephone service, evenings/weekends, 0-100 mi, initial minute	min	0.12-0.15	91	12s
Long-distance telephone service, evenings/weekends, 0-100 mi, additional minute	min	0.06-0.07	91	12s
Education				
Board, 4-yr private college/university	year	2476	91	22s
Board, 4-yr public college/university	year	2064	91	22s
Expenditures, local gov't, public elementary/secondary	pupil	6834	92	20s
Room, 4-year private college/university	year	2252	91	22s
Room, 4-year public college/university	year	2256	91	22s
Tuition, 2-year public college/university	year	1100	91	22s
Tuition, 4-year private college/university	year	10885	91	22s
Tuition, 4-year public college/university, in-state	year	2311	91	22s
Energy and Fuels				
Coal	mil Btu	3.58	90	64s
Energy	mil Btu	10.80	90	64s
Energy exp/householder, 1-family unit	year	588	90	28r
Energy exp/householder, <1,000 sq ft heating area	year	477	90	28r
Energy exp/householder, 1,000-1,999 sq ft heating area	year	517	90	28r
Energy exp/householder, 2,000+ sq ft heating area	year	630	90	28r
Energy exp/householder, mobile home	year	412	90	28r
Energy exp/householder, multifamily	year	498	90	28r
Gas, natural	mil Btu	5.80	90	64s
Gas, natural	000 cu ft	7.63	91	46s
Gas, natural, exp	year	675	91	46s
Gasoline, unleaded regular	mil Btu	10.03	90	64s
Entertainment				
Miniature golf admission	adult	6.18	92	1r
Miniature golf admission	child	5.14	92	1r
Waterpark admission	adult	11.00	92	1r
Waterpark admission	child	8.55	92	1r
Funerals				
Casket, 18-gauge steel, velvet interior		1853.42	91	24r
Cosmetology, hair care, etc.		98.33	91	24r
Embalming		273.94	91	24r

Pawtucket-Woonsocket-Attleboro, RI, MA - continued

Item	Per	Value	Date	Ref.
Funerals - continued				
Facility use for ceremony		196.06	91	24r
Hearse, local		145.67	91	24r
Limousine, local		131.07	91	24r
Remains to funeral home, transfer		135.24	91	24r
Service charge, professional		843.16	91	24r
Vault, concrete, non-metallic liner		709.14	91	24r
Viewing facilities, use		229.85	91	24r
Groceries				
Apples, Red Delicious	lb	0.85	4/93	16r
Bacon	lb	2.12	4/93	16r
Bananas	lb	0.54	4/93	16r
Bread, white, pan	lb	0.81	4/93	16r
Butter	lb	2.02	4/93	16r
Carrots, short trimmed and topped	lb	0.51	4/93	16r
Chicken, fresh, whole	lb	1.04	4/93	16r
Chicken breast, bone-in	lb	2.21	4/93	16r
Chicken legs, bone-in	lb	1.16	4/93	16r
Chuck roast, USDA choice, boneless	lb	2.82	4/93	16r
Coffee, 100% ground roast, all sizes	lb	2.66	4/93	16r
Cucumbers	lb	0.85	4/93	16r
Eggs, Grade A large	doz	1.15	4/93	16r
Grapefruit	lb	0.45	4/93	16r
Grapes, Thompson Seedless	lb	1.52	4/93	16r
Ground beef, lean and extra lean	lb	2.36	4/93	16r
Ground chuck, 100% beef	lb	2.02	4/93	16r
Honey, jar	8 oz	0.96-1.75	92	5r
Honey, jar	lb	1.50-3.00	92	5r
Honey, squeeze bear	12-oz	1.50-1.99	92	5r
Ice cream, prepackaged, bulk, regular	1/2 gal	2.80	4/93	16r
Lemons	lb	0.96	4/93	16r
Lettuce, iceberg	lb	0.95	4/93	16r
Margarine, stick	lb	0.81	4/93	16r
Milk, fresh, whole, fortified	1/2 gal	1.30	4/93	16r
Oranges, navel	lb	0.56	4/93	16r
Peanut butter, creamy, all sizes	lb	1.88	4/93	16r
Pork chops, center cut, bone-in	lb	3.34	4/93	16r
Potato chips	16 oz	2.88	4/93	16r
Potatoes, white	lb	0.37	4/93	16r
Rib roast, USDA choice, bone-in	lb	4.94	4/93	16r
Round roast, USDA choice, boneless	lb	3.17	4/93	16r
Shortening, vegetable oil blends	lb	0.98	4/93	16r
Spaghetti and macaroni	lb	0.82	4/93	16r
Steak, round, graded & ungraded, ex USDA prime & choice	lb	4.04	4/93	16r
Steak, round, USDA choice, boneless	lb	3.90	4/93	16r
Steak, sirloin, USDA choice, boneless	lb	4.97	4/93	16r
Strawberries, dry pint	12 oz	0.90	4/93	16r
Sugar, white	lb	0.50	4/93	16r
Sugar, white, 33-80 oz pk	lb	0.41	4/93	16r
Tomatoes, field grown	lb	1.23	4/93	16r
Tuna, chunk, light	lb	2.22	4/93	16r
Turkey, frozen, whole	lb	1.04	4/93	16r
Health Care				
Childbirth, cesarean, hospital		5826	91	62r
Childbirth, cesarean, physician's fee		2053	91	62r
Childbirth, normal, hospital		2964	91	62r
Childbirth, normal, physician's fee		1492	91	62r
Medical plan per employee	year	3958	91	45r
Mental health care, exp	capita	53.68-118.35	90	38s
Mental health care, exp, state mental health agency	capita	50.37	90	38s
Mental health care, hospital psychiatric services, non-Federal	capita	6.39	88	38s
Mental health care, mental health organization, multiservice, exp	capita	32.12	88	38s
Mental health care, psychiatric hospitals, private, exp	capita	30.73	88	38s
Mental health care, psychiatric out-patient clinics, freestanding, exp	capita	3.69	88	38s

Values are in dollars or fractions of dollars. In the column headed *Ref*, references are shown to sources. Each reference is followed by a letter. These refer to the geographical level for which data were reported: s = State, r = Region, and c = City or metro. The abbreviation *ex* is used to mean *except* or *excluding*; *exp* stands for expenditures. For other abbreviations and further explanations, please see the Introduction.

Pawtucket-Woonsocket-Attleboro, RI, MA - continued

Item	Per	Value	Date	Ref.
Health Care				
Mental health care, state and county mental hospitals, exp	capita	23.91	88	38s
Mental health care, VA medical centers, exp	capita	1.68	88	38s
Substance abuse, hospital ancillary charge	incident	400	90	70s
Substance abuse, hospital physician charge	incident	70	90	70s
Substance abuse, hospital room and board	incident	5400	90	70s
Insurance and Pensions				
Auto insurance, private passenger	year	939.06	91	63s
Taxes				
Tax, cigarette	pack	37	91	77s
Tax, gasoline	gal	26	91	77s
Taxes, state	capita	1251	91	77s
Transportation				
Driver's license fee		30.00	12/90	43s
Vehicle registration	2 years	30.00	93	57s
Travel				
Business travel	day	165.00	4/93	89r
Utilities				
Electricity	mil Btu	26.85	90	64s

Pensacola, FL

Item	Per	Value	Date	Ref.
Child Care				
Child care fee, average, center	hour	1.29	90	65r
Child care fee, average, nonregulated family day care	hour	0.89	90	65r
Child care fee, average, regulated family day care	hour	1.32	90	65r
Communications				
Long-distance telephone service, day, initial minute, 0-100 miles	min	0.15-0.20	91	12s
Long-distance telephone service, day, additional minute, 0-100 miles	min	0.08-0.20	91	12s
Long-distance telephone service, evenings/weekends, 0-100 mi, initial minute	min	0.09-0.12	91	12s
Long-distance telephone service, evenings/weekends, 0-100 mi, additional minute	min	0.05-0.12	91	12s
Education				
Board, 4-yr private college/university	year	1924	91	22s
Board, 4-yr public college/university	year	1955	91	22s
Expenditures, local gov't, public elementary/secondary	pupil	5235	92	20s
Room, 4-year private college/university	year	1904	91	22s
Room, 4-year public college/university	year	1510	91	22s
Tuition, 2-year private college/university	year	4751	91	22s
Tuition, 2-year public college/university	year	788	91	22s
Tuition, 4-year private college/university	year	7992	91	22s
Tuition, 4-year public college/university, in-state	year	1337	91	22s
Energy and Fuels				
Coal	mil Btu	1.85	90	64s
Energy	mil Btu	10.58	90	64s
Energy exp/householder, 1-family unit	year	487	90	28r
Energy exp/householder, <1,000 sq ft heating area	year	393	90	28r
Energy exp/householder, 1,000-1,999 sq ft heating area	year	442	90	28r
Energy exp/householder, 2,000+ sq ft heating area	year	577	90	28r
Energy exp/householder, mobile home	year	366	90	28r
Energy exp/householder, multifamily	year	382	90	28r
Gas, natural	mil Btu	3.21	90	64s
Gas, natural	000 cu ft	8.98	91	46s

Pensacola, FL - continued

Item	Per	Value	Date	Ref.
Energy and Fuels - continued				
Gas, natural, exp	year	248	91	46s
Gasoline, unleaded regular	mil Btu	8.85	90	64s
Entertainment				
Miniature golf admission	adult	6.18	92	1r
Miniature golf admission	child	5.14	92	1r
Waterpark admission	adult	11.00	92	1r
Waterpark admission	child	8.55	92	1r
Funerals				
Casket, 18-gauge steel, velvet interior		2029.08	91	24r
Cosmetology, hair care, etc.		75.10	91	24r
Embalming		249.24	91	24r
Facility use for ceremony		162.27	91	24r
Hearse, local		114.04	91	24r
Limousine, local		88.57	91	24r
Remains to funeral home, transfer		92.61	91	24r
Service charge, professional		682.42	91	24r
Vault, concrete, non-metallic liner		798.70	91	24r
Viewing facilities, use		163.86	91	24r
Groceries				
Apples, Red Delicious	lb	0.79	4/93	16r
Bacon	lb	1.75	4/93	16r
Bananas	lb	0.42	4/93	16r
Beef, stew, boneless	lb	2.61	4/93	16r
Bologna, all beef or mixed	lb	2.24	4/93	16r
Bread, white, pan	lb	0.64	4/93	16r
Bread, whole wheat, pan	lb	0.96	4/93	16r
Cabbage	lb	0.37	4/93	16r
Carrots, short trimmed and topped	lb	0.47	4/93	16r
Celery	lb	0.64	4/93	16r
Cheese, American	lb	2.98	4/93	16r
Cheese, Cheddar	lb	3.28	4/93	16r
Chicken, fresh, whole	lb	0.77	4/93	16r
Chicken breast, bone-in	lb	1.92	4/93	16r
Chicken legs, bone-in	lb	1.06	4/93	16r
Chuck roast, graded and ungraded, ex USDA prime and choice	lb	2.40	4/93	16r
Chuck roast, USDA choice, bone-in	lb	2.19	4/93	16r
Chuck roast, USDA choice, boneless	lb	2.38	4/93	16r
Coffee, 100% ground roast, all sizes	lb	2.48	4/93	16r
Crackers, soda, salted	lb	1.15	4/93	16r
Eggs, Grade A large	doz	0.96	4/93	16r
Flour, white, all purpose	lb	0.24	4/93	16r
Frankfurters, all meat or all beef	lb	2.01	4/93	16r
Grapefruit	lb	0.44	4/93	16r
Grapes, Thompson Seedless	lb	1.40	4/93	16r
Ground beef, 100% beef	lb	1.58	4/93	16r
Ground beef, lean and extra lean	lb	2.09	4/93	16r
Ground chuck, 100% beef	lb	1.98	4/93	16r
Ham, boneless, excluding canned	lb	2.89	4/93	16r
Ham, picnic, shoulder, bone-in, smoked	lb	1.02	4/93	16r
Ham, rump or steak half, bone-in, smoked	lb	1.48	4/93	16r
Ice cream, prepackaged, bulk, regular	1/2 gal	2.41	4/93	16r
Lemons	lb	1.05	4/93	16r
Lettuce, iceberg	lb	0.81	4/93	16r
Margarine, stick	lb	0.88	4/93	16r
Oranges, navel	lb	0.55	4/93	16r
Pears, Anjou	lb	0.92	4/93	16r
Pork chops, center cut, bone-in	lb	3.13	4/93	16r
Potato chips	16 oz	2.94	4/93	16r
Potatoes, white	lb	0.43	4/93	16r
Rib roast, USDA choice, bone-in	lb	4.63	4/93	16r
Rice, white, long grain, uncooked	lb	0.45	4/93	16r
Round roast, graded & ungraded, ex USDA prime & choice	lb	3.03	4/93	16r
Round roast, USDA choice, boneless	lb	3.09	4/93	16r
Sausage, fresh, loose	lb	2.08	4/93	16r
Short ribs, bone-in	lb	2.66	4/93	16r
Shortening, vegetable oil blends	lb	0.69	4/93	16r
Spaghetti and macaroni	lb	0.81	4/93	16r
Steak, rib eye, USDA choice, boneless	lb	6.24	4/93	16r

Values are in dollars or fractions of dollars. In the column headed *Ref*, references are shown to sources. Each reference is followed by a letter. These refer to the geographical level for which data were reported: s = State, r = Region, and c = City or metro. The abbreviation *ex* is used to mean *except* or *excluding*; *exp* stands for expenditures. For other abbreviations and further explanations, please see the Introduction.

Pensacola, FL - continued

Item	Per	Value	Date	Ref.
Groceries				
Steak, round, graded & ungraded, ex USDA prime & choice	lb	3.31	4/93	16r
Steak, round, USDA choice, boneless	lb	3.34	4/93	16r
Steak, sirloin, graded & ungraded, ex USDA prime & choice	lb	4.19	4/93	16r
Steak, sirloin, USDA choice, boneless	lb	4.46	4/93	16r
Steak, T-bone, USDA choice, bone-in	lb	5.25	4/93	16r
Strawberries, dry pint	12 oz	0.92	4/93	16r
Sugar, white	lb	0.39	4/93	16r
Sugar, white, 33-80 oz pk	lb	0.38	4/93	16r
Tomatoes, field grown	lb	0.88	4/93	16r
Tuna, chunk, light	lb	1.79	4/93	16r
Turkey, frozen, whole	lb	1.04	4/93	16r
Yogurt, natural, fruit flavored	1/2 pint	0.57	4/93	16r
Health Care				
Childbirth, cesarean, hospital		5034	91	62r
Childbirth, cesarean, physician's fee		2053	91	62r
Childbirth, normal, hospital		2712	91	62r
Childbirth, normal, physician's fee		1492	91	62r
Medical plan per employee	year	3495	91	45r
Mental health care, exp	capita	28.84-37.59	90	38s
Mental health care, exp, state mental health agency	capita	37.49	90	38s
Mental health care, hospital psychiatric services, non-Federal, exp	capita	9.11	88	38s
Mental health care, mental health organization, multiservice, exp	capita	16.21	88	38s
Mental health care, psychiatric hospitals, private, exp	capita	22.26	88	38s
Mental health care, psychiatric out-patient clinics, freestanding, exp	capita	0.89	88	38s
Mental health care, psychiatric partial-care organizations, freestanding, exp	capita	0.41	88	38s
Mental health care, state and county mental hospitals, exp	capita	16.25	88	38s
Mental health care, VA medical centers, exp	capita	1.69	88	38s
Physician fee, family practice, first-visit		75.00	91	62r
Physician fee, family practice, revisit		34.00	91	62r
Physician fee, general practice, first-visit		61.00	91	62r
Physician fee, general practice, revisit		32.00	91	62r
Physician fee, general surgeon, first-visit		64.00	91	62r
Physician fee, general surgeon, revisit		40.00	91	62r
Physician fee, internal medicine, first-visit		98.00	91	62r
Physician fee, internal medicine, revisit		40.00	91	62r
Physician fee, median, neurosurgeon, first-visit		130.00	91	62r
Physician fee, median, nonsurgical specialist, first-visit		95.00	91	62r
Physician fee, median, orthopedic surgeon, first-visit		91.00	91	62r
Physician fee, median, plastic surgeon, first-visit		66.00	91	62r
Physician fee, median, surgical specialist, first-visit		62.00	91	62r
Physician fee, neurosurgeon, revisit		50.00	91	62r
Physician fee, nonsurgical specialist, revisit		40.00	91	62r
Physician fee, obstetrics/gynecology, first-visit		64.00	91	62r
Physician fee, obstetrics/gynecology, revisit		41.00	91	62r
Physician fee, orthopedic surgeon, revisit		40.00	91	62r
Physician fee, pediatrician, first-visit		49.00	91	62r
Physician fee, pediatrician, revisit		33.00	91	62r
Physician fee, plastic surgeon, revisit		43.00	91	62r
Physician fee, surgical specialist, revisit		37.00	91	62r
Substance abuse, hospital ancillary charge	incident	1390	90	70s
Substance abuse, hospital physician charge	incident	770	90	70s
Substance abuse, hospital room and board	incident	5600	90	70s

Pensacola, FL - continued

Item	Per	Value	Date	Ref.
Insurance and Pensions				
Auto insurance, private passenger	year	727.60	91	63s
Taxes				
Tax, cigarette	pack	33.90	91	77s
Tax, gasoline	gal	11.60	91	77s
Taxes, state	capita	1037	91	77s
Transportation				
Driver's license fee		15.00	12/90	43s
Travel				
Business travel	day	193.00	4/93	89r
Utilities				
Electricity	mil Btu	20.62	90	64s

Peoria, IL

Item	Per	Value	Date	Ref.
Composite ACCRA index		104.90	4Q 92	4c
Alcoholic Beverages				
Beer, Miller Lite or Budweiser, 12-oz containers	6 pack	3.77	4Q 92	4c
Liquor, J & B Scotch	750 ml	15.97	4Q 92	4c
Wine, Gallo Chablis blanc, 1.5 liter	bottle	4.81	4Q 92	4c
Child Care				
Child care fee, average, center	hour	1.63	90	65r
Child care fee, average, nonregulated family day care	hour	1.83	90	65r
Child care fee, average, regulated family day care	hour	1.42	90	65r
Clothing				
Jeans, man's denim		27.39	4Q 92	4c
Shirt, man's dress shirt		24.80	4Q 92	4c
Undervest, boy's size 10-14, cotton	3	4.42	4Q 92	4c
Communications				
Long-distance telephone service, day, initial minute, 0-100 miles	min	0.10-0.34	91	12s
Long-distance telephone service, day, additional minute, 0-100 miles	min	0.04-0.16	91	12s
Long-distance telephone service, evenings/weekends, 0-100 mi, initial minute	min	0.06-0.20	91	12s
Long-distance telephone service, evenings/weekends, 0-100 mi, additional minute	min	0.02-0.10	91	12s
Newspaper subscription, daily and Sunday home delivery, large-city	month	14.13	4Q 92	4c
Telephone bill, family of four	month	19.98	4Q 92	4c
Education				
Board, 4-yr private college/university	year	1797	91	22s
Board, 4-yr public college/university	year	1857	91	22s
Expenditures, local gov't, public elementary/secondary	pupil	5248	92	20s
Room, 4-year private college/university	year	2095	91	22s
Room, 4-year public college/university	year	1454	91	22s
Tuition, 2-year private college/university	year	5279	91	22s
Tuition, 2-year public college/university	year	906	91	22s
Tuition, 4-year private college/university	year	8853	91	22s
Tuition, 4-year public college/university, in-state	year	2465	91	22s
Energy and Fuels				
Coal	mil Btu	1.72	90	64s
Energy	mil Btu	8.74	90	64s
Energy, combined forms, 1,800 sq ft heating area	month	105.46	4Q 92	4c
Energy, exc electricity, 1,800 sq ft heating area	month	43.17	4Q 92	4c
Energy exp/householder, 1-family unit	year	471	90	28r
Energy exp/householder, <1,000 sq ft heating area	year	430	90	28r
Energy exp/householder, 1,000-1,999 sq ft heating area	year	481	90	28r

Values are in dollars or fractions of dollars. In the column headed *Ref*, references are shown to sources. Each reference is followed by a letter. These refer to the geographical level for which data were reported: s=State, r=Region, and c=City or metro. The abbreviation *ex* is used to mean *except* or *excluding*; *exp* stands for expenditures. For other abbreviations and further explanations, please see the Introduction.

Peoria, IL - continued

Item	Per	Value	Date	Ref.
Energy and Fuels				
Energy exp/householder, 2,000+ sq ft heating area	year	473	90	28r
Energy exp/householder, mobile home	year	430	90	28r
Energy exp/householder, multifamily	year	461	90	28r
Gas, cooking, 10 therms	month	11.38	92	56c
Gas, cooking, 30 therms	month	20.63	92	56c
Gas, cooking, 50 therms	month	29.89	92	56c
Gas, heating, winter, 100 therms	month	51.22	92	56c
Gas, heating, winter, average use	month	115.19	92	56c
Gas, natural	mil Btu	4.57	90	64s
Gas, natural	000 cu ft	4.95	91	46s
Gas, natural, exp	year	696	91	46s
Gasoline, motor	gal	1.15	4Q 92	4c
Gasoline, unleaded regular	mil Btu	9.35	90	64s
Entertainment				
Bowling, evening rate	game	1.89	4Q 92	4c
Miniature golf admission	adult	6.18	92	1r
Miniature golf admission	child	5.14	92	1r
Monopoly game, Parker Brothers', No. 9		11.99	4Q 92	4c
Movie	admission	5.20	4Q 92	4c
Tennis balls, yellow, Wilson or Penn, 3	can	3.06	4Q 92	4c
Waterpark admission	adult	11.00	92	1r
Waterpark admission	child	8.55	92	1r
Funerals				
Casket, 18-gauge steel, velvet interior		1926.72	91	24r
Cosmetology, hair care, etc.		97.64	91	24r
Embalming		249.14	91	24r
Facility use for ceremony		208.59	91	24r
Hearse, local		130.12	91	24r
Limousine, local		104.66	91	24r
Remains to funeral home, transfer		93.61	91	24r
Service charge, professional		724.62	91	24r
Vault, concrete, non-metallic liner		734.53	91	24r
Viewing facilities, use		236.06	91	24r
Goods and Services				
ACCRA Index, Miscellaneous Goods and Services		103.30	4Q 92	4c
Groceries				
ACCRA Index, Groceries		105.60	4Q 92	4c
Apples, Red Delicious	lb	0.77	4/93	16r
Babyfood, strained vegetables, lowest price	4-4.5 oz jar	0.36	4Q 92	4c
Bacon	lb	1.85	4/93	16r
Bananas	lb	0.46	4Q 92	4c
Bananas	lb	0.46	4/93	16r
Beef, stew, boneless	lb	2.53	4/93	16r
Bologna, all beef or mixed	lb	2.19	4/93	16r
Bread, white	24 oz	0.58	4Q 92	4c
Bread, white, pan	lb	0.78	4/93	16r
Butter	lb	1.50	4/93	16r
Cabbage	lb	0.40	4/93	16r
Carrots, short trimmed and topped	lb	0.45	4/93	16r
Cheese, Cheddar	lb	3.47	4/93	16r
Cheese, Kraft grated Parmesan	8-oz canister	3.33	4Q 92	4c
Chicken, fresh, whole	lb	0.84	4/93	16r
Chicken, fryer, whole	lb	0.85	4Q 92	4c
Chicken breast, bone-in	lb	1.94	4/93	16r
Chicken legs, bone-in	lb	1.02	4/93	16r
Chuck roast, graded and ungraded, ex USDA prime and choice	lb	2.43	4/93	16r
Chuck roast, USDA choice, bone-in	lb	2.11	4/93	16r
Chuck roast, USDA choice, boneless	lb	2.44	4/93	16r
Cigarettes, Winston	carton	17.86	4Q 92	4c
Coffee, 100% ground roast, all sizes	lb	2.47	4/93	16r
Coffee, vacuum-packed	13-oz can	2.28	4Q 92	4c

Peoria, IL - continued

Item	Per	Value	Date	Ref.
Groceries - continued				
Cookies, chocolate chip	lb	2.73	4/93	16r
Corn, frozen	10 oz	0.72	4Q 92	4c
Corn Flakes, Kellogg's or Post Toasties	18 oz	1.89	4Q 92	4c
Eggs, Grade A large	doz	0.82	4Q 92	4c
Eggs, Grade A large	doz	0.93	4/93	16r
Flour, white, all purpose	lb	0.21	4/93	16r
Grapefruit	lb	0.45	4/93	16r
Grapes, Thompson Seedless	lb	1.46	4/93	16r
Ground beef, 100% beef	lb	1.63	4/93	16r
Ground beef, lean and extra lean	lb	2.08	4/93	16r
Ground beef or hamburger	lb	1.41	4Q 92	4c
Ground chuck, 100% beef	lb	1.94	4/93	16r
Ham, boneless, excluding canned	lb	2.21	4/93	16r
Honey, jar	8 oz	0.97-1.25	92	5r
Honey, jar	lb	1.25-2.25	92	5r
Honey, squeeze bear	12-oz	1.25-1.99	92	5r
Ice cream, prepackaged, bulk, regular	1/2 gal	2.41	4/93	16r
Lemons	lb	0.82	4/93	16r
Lettuce, iceberg	head	1.05	4Q 92	4c
Lettuce, iceberg	lb	0.83	4/93	16r
Margarine, Blue Bonnet or Parkay cubes	lb	0.74	4Q 92	4c
Margarine, stick	lb	0.77	4/93	16r
Milk, whole	1/2 gal	1.70	4Q 92	4c
Orange juice, Minute Maid frozen	12-oz can	1.58	4Q 92	4c
Oranges, navel	lb	0.50	4/93	16r
Peaches	29-oz can	1.39	4Q 92	4c
Peanut butter, creamy, all sizes	lb	1.82	4/93	16r
Pears, Anjou	lb	0.85	4/93	16r
Peas Sweet, Del Monte or Green Giant	15-17 oz can	0.61	4Q 92	4c
Pork chops, center cut, bone-in	lb	3.17	4/93	16r
Potato chips	16 oz	2.68	4/93	16r
Potatoes, white	lb	0.26	4/93	16r
Potatoes, white or red	10-lb sack	2.81	4Q 92	4c
Round roast, graded & ungraded, ex USDA prime & choice	lb	2.88	4/93	16r
Round roast, USDA choice, boneless	lb	2.96	4/93	16r
Sausage, Jimmy Dean, 100% pork	lb	2.77	4Q 92	4c
Shortening, vegetable oil blends	lb	0.79	4/93	16r
Shortening, vegetable, Crisco	3-lb can	2.41	4Q 92	4c
Soft drink, Coca Cola	2 liter	1.19	4Q 92	4c
Spaghetti and macaroni	lb	0.76	4/93	16r
Steak, rib eye, USDA choice, boneless	lb	6.29	4/93	16r
Steak, round, USDA choice, boneless	lb	3.24	4/93	16r
Steak, sirloin, graded & ungraded, ex USDA prime & choice	lb	4.00	4/93	16r
Steak, sirloin, USDA choice, bone-in	lb	3.57	4/93	16r
Steak, sirloin, USDA choice, boneless	lb	4.17	4/93	16r
Steak, T-bone	lb	6.05	4Q 92	4c
Steak, T-bone, USDA choice, bone-in	lb	5.60	4/93	16r
Strawberries, dry pint	12 oz	0.90	4/93	16r
Sugar, cane or beet	4 lb	1.32	4Q 92	4c
Sugar, white	lb	0.36	4/93	16r
Sugar, white, 33-80 oz pk	lb	0.35	4/93	16r
Tomatoes, field grown	lb	0.99	4/93	16r
Tomatoes, Hunt's or Del Monte	14.5-oz can	0.78	4Q 92	4c
Tuna, chunk, light	6.125-6.5 oz can	0.68	4Q 92	4c
Tuna, chunk, light	lb	1.76	4/93	16r
Turkey, frozen, whole	lb	0.91	4/93	16r
Health Care				
ACCRA Index, Health Care		90.10	4Q 92	4c
Analgesic, Aspirin, Bayer, 325 mg tablets	100	5.03	4Q 92	4c
Childbirth, cesarean, hospital		4688	91	62r
Childbirth, cesarean, physician's fee		2053	91	62r
Childbirth, normal, hospital		2657	91	62r

Values are in dollars or fractions of dollars. In the column headed *Ref*, references are shown to sources. Each reference is followed by a letter. These refer to the geographical level for which data were reported: s=State, r=Region, and c=City or metro. The abbreviation *ex* is used to mean *except* or *excluding*; *exp* stands for expenditures. For other abbreviations and further explanations, please see the Introduction.

Peoria, IL - continued

Item	Per	Value	Date	Ref.
Health Care				
Childbirth, normal, physician's fee		1492	91	62r
Dentist's fee, adult teeth cleaning and periodic oral exam	visit	44.40	4Q 92	4c
Doctor's fee, routine exam, established patient	visit	31.60	4Q 92	4c
Hospital care, semiprivate room	day	265.25	90	27c
Hospital care, semiprivate room	day	265.00	4Q 92	4c
Medical insurance premium, per employee, small group comprehensive	month	313.90	10/91	25c
Medical plan per employee	year	3443	91	45r
Mental health care, exp	capita	28.84-37.59	90	38s
Mental health care, exp, state mental health agency	capita	34.43	90	38s
Mental health care, hospital psychiatric services, non-Federal, exp	capita	18.46	88	38s
Mental health care, mental health organization, multiservice, exp	capita	11.97	88	38s
Mental health care, psychiatric hospitals, private, exp	capita	7.84	88	38s
Mental health care, psychiatric out-patient clinics, freestanding, exp	capita	3.21	88	38s
Mental health care, psychiatric partial-care organizations, freestanding, exp	capita	0.51	88	38s
Mental health care, state and county mental hospitals, exp	capita	18.11	88	38s
Mental health care, VA medical centers, exp	capita	3.69	88	38s
Physician fee, family practice, first-visit		76.00	91	62r
Physician fee, family practice, revisit		33.00	91	62r
Physician fee, general practice, first-visit		61.00	91	62r
Physician fee, general practice, revisit		31.00	91	62r
Physician fee, general surgeon, first-visit		65.00	91	62r
Physician fee, general surgeon, revisit		35.00	91	62r
Physician fee, internal medicine, first-visit		91.00	91	62r
Physician fee, internal medicine, revisit		40.00	91	62r
Physician fee, median, neurosurgeon, first-visit		106.00	91	62r
Physician fee, median, nonsurgical specialist, first-visit		90.00	91	62r
Physician fee, median, orthopedic surgeon, first-visit		83.00	91	62r
Physician fee, median, surgical specialist, first-visit		61.00	91	62r
Physician fee, neurosurgeon, revisit		41.00	91	62r
Physician fee, nonsurgical specialist, revisit		40.00	91	62r
Physician fee, obstetrics/gynecology, first-visit		61.00	91	62r
Physician fee, obstetrics/gynecology, revisit		40.00	91	62r
Physician fee, orthopedic surgeon, revisit		41.00	91	62r
Physician fee, pediatrician, first-visit		46.00	91	62r
Physician fee, pediatrician, revisit		33.00	91	62r
Physician fee, surgical specialist, revisit		36.00	91	62r
Prescription drug co-pay, Medicaid	month	25.00	91	21s
Substance abuse, hospital ancillary charge	incident	1310	90	70s
Substance abuse, hospital physician charge	incident	540	90	70s
Substance abuse, hospital room and board	incident	6150	90	70s
Household Goods				
Appliance repair, home, service call, washing machine	min labor charge	31.89	4Q 92	4c
Laundry detergent, Tide Ultra, Bold, or Cheer	42 oz	3.92	4Q 92	4c
Tissues, facial, Kleenex brand	175-count box	1.15	4Q 92	4c
Housing				
ACCRA Index, Housing		112.00	4Q 92	4c
Home, median price	unit	59.00		26c

Peoria, IL - continued

Item	Per	Value	Date	Ref.
Housing - continued				
House, 1,800 sq ft, 8,000 sq ft lot, new, urban	total	131075	4Q 92	4c
House payment, principal and interest, 25% down payment	month	725	4Q 92	4c
Mortgage rate, incl. points & origination fee, 30-year fixed or adjustable rate	percent	8.05	4Q 92	4c
Rent, apartment, 2 bedrooms - 1-1/2 to 2 baths, unfurnished, 950 sq ft, water	month	469	4Q 92	4c
Rental unit, 1 bedroom	month	469	93	23c
Rental unit, 2 bedroom	month	552	93	23c
Rental unit, 3 bedroom	month	692	93	23c
Rental unit, 4 bedroom	month	774	93	23c
Rental unit, efficiency	month	387	93	23c
Insurance and Pensions				
Auto insurance, private passenger	year	621.37	91	63s
Personal Goods				
Shampoo, Alberto VO5	15 oz	1.43	4Q 92	4c
Toothpaste, Crest or Colgate	6-7 oz	2.26	4Q 92	4c
Personal Services				
Dry cleaning, man's 2-piece suit		6.39	4Q 92	4c
Haircare, woman's shampoo, trim and blow-dry		24.40	4Q 92	4c
Haircut, man's barbershop, no styling		8.10	4Q 92	4c
Restaurant Food				
Chicken, fried, thigh and drumstick		2.14	4Q 92	4c
Hamburger with cheese	1/4 lb	1.85	4Q 92	4c
Pizza, Pizza Hut or Pizza Inn, cheese, thin crust	12-13 in	7.87	4Q 92	4c
Taxes				
Tax, cigarette	pack	30	91	77s
Tax, gasoline	gal	19	91	77s
Taxes, state	capita	1151	91	77s
Transportation				
ACCRA Index, Transportation		104.00	4Q 92	4c
Bus fare	one-way	0.75	3/93	2c
Bus fare, up to 10 miles	one-way	0.60	4Q 92	4c
Driver's license fee		10.00	12/90	43s
Tire balance, computer or spin balance, front	wheel	7.40	4Q 92	4c
Vehicle registration and license plate	multi-year	48.00	93	52s
Utilities				
ACCRA Index, Utilities		97.20	4Q 92	4c
Electricity	mil Btu	22.02	90	64s
Electricity, partial electric and other energy, 1,800 sq ft living area new home	month	62.29	4Q 92	4c
Electricity, winter, 250 KWh	month	20.08	92	55c
Electricity, winter, 500 KWh	month	36.47	92	55c
Electricity, winter, 750 KWh	month	52.85	92	55c
Electricity, winter, 1000 KWh	month	66.94	92	55c

Philadelphia, PA

Item	Per	Value	Date	Ref.
Composite ACCRA index		133.40	4Q 92	4c
Alcoholic Beverages				
Beer, Miller Lite or Budweiser, 12-oz containers	6 pack	4.66	4Q 92	4c
Liquor, J & B Scotch	750 ml	16.39	4Q 92	4c
Wine, Gallo Chablis blanc, 1.5 liter	bottle	5.79	4Q 92	4c
Child Care				
Child care fee, average, center	hour	2.18	90	65r
Child care fee, average, nonregulated family day care	hour	1.83	90	65r
Child care fee, average, regulated family day care	hour	2.02	90	65r

Values are in dollars or fractions of dollars. In the column headed *Ref*, references are shown to sources. Each reference is followed by a letter. These refer to the geographical level for which data were reported: s=State, r=Region, and c=City or metro. The abbreviation *ex* is used to mean *except* or *excluding*; *exp* stands for expenditures. For other abbreviations and further explanations, please see the Introduction.

Philadelphia, PA - continued

Item	Per	Value	Date	Ref.
Clothing				
Jeans, man's denim		27.75	4Q 92	4c
Shirt, man's dress shirt		25.00	4Q 92	4c
Undervest, boy's size 10-14, cotton	3	6.91	4Q 92	4c
Communications				
Long-distance telephone service, day, initial minute, 0-100 miles	min	0.15-0.29	91	12s
Long-distance telephone service, day, additional minute, 0-100 miles	min	0.06-0.22	91	12s
Long-distance telephone service, evenings/weekends, 0-100 mi, initial minute	min	0.06-0.14	91	12s
Long-distance telephone service, evenings/weekends, 0-100 mi, additional minute	min	0.03-0.11	91	12s
Newspaper subscription, daily and Sunday home delivery, large-city	month	13.10	4Q 92	4c
Telephone, exp	year	499	89	15c
Telephone, residential, private line, rotary, unlimited calling	month	16.41	10/91	78c
Telephone bill, family of four	month	14.92	4Q 92	4c
Construction				
Plywood, post-Hurricane Andrew	4x8 sheet	10.69	92	13c
Plywood, pre-Hurricane Andrew	4x8 sheet	7.95	92	13c
Education				
Board, 4-yr private college/university	year	2019	91	22s
Board, 4-yr public college/university	year	1656	91	22s
Expenditures, local gov't, public elementary/secondary	pupil	6980	92	20s
Room, 4-year private college/university	year	2179	91	22s
Room, 4-year public college/university	year	1719	91	22s
Tuition, 2-year private college/university	year	6314	91	22s
Tuition, 2-year public college/university	year	1505	91	22s
Tuition, 4-year private college/university	year	9848	91	22s
Tuition, 4-year public college/university, in-state	year	3401	91	22s
Energy and Fuels				
Coal	mil Btu	1.57	90	64s
Energy	mil Btu	8.63	90	64s
Energy, combined forms, 1,800 sq ft heating area	month	220.18	4Q 92	4c
Energy exp/householder, 1-family unit	year	588	90	28r
Energy exp/householder, <1,000 sq ft heating area	year	477	90	28r
Energy exp/householder, 1,000-1,999 sq ft heating area	year	517	90	28r
Energy exp/householder, 2,000+ sq ft heating area	year	630	90	28r
Energy exp/householder, mobile home	year	412	90	28r
Energy exp/householder, multifamily	year	498	90	28r
Fuel oil #2	gal	0.96	4/93	16c
Fuel oil, other fuel, exp	year	171	89	15c
Gas, cooking, winter, 10 therms	month	13.45	92	56c
Gas, cooking, winter, 30 therms	month	25.02	92	56c
Gas, cooking, winter, 50 therms	month	36.60	92	56c
Gas, heating, winter, 100 therms	month	65.52	92	56c
Gas, heating, winter, average use	month	131.87	92	56c
Gas, natural	mil Btu	5.24	90	64s
Gas, natural	000 cu ft	6.76	91	46s
Gas, natural, exp	year	262	89	15c
Gas, natural, exp	year	703	91	46s
Gas, piped	100 therms	71.82	4/93	16c
Gas, piped	40 therms	31.95	4/93	16c
Gas, piped	therm	0.72	4/93	16c
Gasoline, all types	gal	1.17	4/93	16c
Gasoline, motor	gal	1.17	4Q 92	4c
Gasoline, regular unleaded, taxes included, cash, self-service	gal	1.30	4/93	16c

Philadelphia, PA - continued

Item	Per	Value	Date	Ref.
Energy and Fuels - continued				
Gasoline, unleaded premium 93 octane	gal	1.05	4/93	16c
Gasoline, unleaded regular	mil Btu	9.35	90	64s
Entertainment				
Bowling, evening rate	game	2.29	4Q 92	4c
Dinner entree, restaurant		92.00	92	83c
Monopoly game, Parker Brothers', No. 9		13.79	4Q 92	4c
Movie	admission	6.00	4Q 92	4c
Tennis balls, yellow, Wilson or Penn, 3	can	3.09	4Q 92	4c
Funerals				
Casket, 18-gauge steel, velvet interior		1811.58	91	24r
Cosmetology, hair care, etc.		111.08	91	24r
Embalming		329.42	91	24r
Facility use for ceremony		201.29	91	24r
Hearse, local		135.27	91	24r
Limousine, local		127.24	91	24r
Remains to funeral home, transfer		103.98	91	24r
Service charge, professional		724.98	91	24r
Vault, concrete, non-metallic liner		766.71	91	24r
Viewing facilities, use		260.60	91	24r
Goods and Services				
ACCRA Index, Miscellaneous Goods and Services		116.80	4Q 92	4c
Police protection expense	resident	181.00	92	18c
Groceries				
ACCRA Index, Groceries		122.90	4Q 92	4c
Apples, Red Delicious	lb	0.85	4/93	16r
Babyfood, strained vegetables, lowest price	4-4.5 oz jar	0.38	4Q 92	4c
Bacon	lb	2.12	4/93	16r
Bakery products, exp	year	261	89	15c
Bananas	lb	0.66	4Q 92	4c
Bananas	lb	0.54	4/93	16r
Beef, exp	year	191	89	15c
Beverages, nonalcoholic, exp	year	219	89	15c
Bread, white	24 oz	1.01	4Q 92	4c
Bread, white, pan	lb	0.81	4/93	16r
Butter	lb	2.02	4/93	16r
Carrots, short trimmed and topped	lb	0.51	4/93	16r
Cereals and baking products, exp	year	388	89	15c
Cereals and cereal products, exp	year	127	89	15c
Cheese, Kraft grated Parmesan	8-oz canister	3.59	4Q 92	4c
Chicken, fresh, whole	lb	1.04	4/93	16r
Chicken, fryer, whole	lb	1.06	4Q 92	4c
Chicken breast, bone-in	lb	2.21	4/93	16r
Chicken legs, bone-in	lb	1.16	4/93	16r
Chuck roast, USDA choice, boneless	lb	2.82	4/93	16r
Cigarettes, Winston	carton	17.40	4Q 92	4c
Coffee, 100% ground roast, all sizes	lb	2.66	4/93	16r
Coffee, vacuum-packed	13-oz can	2.84	4Q 92	4c
Corn, frozen	10 oz	0.78	4Q 92	4c
Corn Flakes, Kellogg's or Post Toasties	18 oz	1.84	4Q 92	4c
Cucumbers	lb	0.85	4/93	16r
Dairy product purchases	year	291	89	15c
Dairy products, miscellaneous, exp	year	167	89	15c
Eggs, exp	year	30	89	15c
Eggs, Grade A large	doz	1.04	4Q 92	4c
Eggs, Grade A large	doz	1.15	4/93	16r
Fats and oils, exp	year	47	89	15c
Fish and seafood, exp	year	91	89	15c
Food, exp	year	4417	89	15c
Food eaten at home, exp	year	647	89	15c
Food eaten at home, exp	year	2384	89	15c
Food purchased away from home, exp	year	2033	89	15c
Foods, miscellaneous, exp	year	274	89	15c
Fruits, fresh, exp	year	117	89	15c

Values are in dollars or fractions of dollars. In the column headed *Ref*, references are shown to sources. Each reference is followed by a letter. These refer to the geographical level for which data were reported: s=State, r=Region, and c=City or metro. The abbreviation *ex* is used to mean *except* or *excluding*; *exp* stands for expenditures. For other abbreviations and further explanations, please see the Introduction.

Philadelphia, PA - continued

Item	Per	Value	Date	Ref.
Groceries				
Fruits, processed, exp	year	104	89	15c
Fruits and vegetables, exp	year	391	89	15c
Grapefruit	lb	0.45	4/93	16r
Grapes, Thompson Seedless	lb	1.52	4/93	16r
Ground beef, lean and extra lean	lb	2.36	4/93	16r
Ground beef or hamburger	lb	1.99	4Q 92	4c
Ground chuck, 100% beef	lb	2.02	4/93	16r
Honey, jar	8 oz	0.96-1.75	92	5r
Honey, jar	lb	1.50-3.00	92	5r
Honey, squeeze bear	12-oz	1.50-1.99	92	5r
Ice cream, prepackaged, bulk, regular	1/2 gal	2.80	4/93	16r
Lemons	lb	0.96	4/93	16r
Lettuce, iceberg	head	0.91	4Q 92	4c
Lettuce, iceberg	lb	0.95	4/93	16r
Margarine, Blue Bonnet or Parkay cubes	lb	1.04	4Q 92	4c
Margarine, stick	lb	0.81	4/93	16r
Meats, miscellaneous, exp	year	107	89	15c
Meats, poultry, fish and eggs, exp	year	667	89	15c
Milk, fresh, whole, fortified	1/2 gal	1.30	4/93	16r
Milk, whole	1/2 gal	1.30	4Q 92	4c
Milk and cream, fresh, exp	year	125	89	15c
Orange juice, Minute Maid frozen	12-oz can	1.73	4Q 92	4c
Oranges, navel	lb	0.56	4/93	16r
Peaches	29-oz can	1.47	4Q 92	4c
Peanut butter, creamy, all sizes	lb	1.88	4/93	16r
Peas Sweet, Del Monte or Green Giant	15-17 oz can	0.63	4Q 92	4c
Pork, exp	year	131	89	15c
Pork chops, center cut, bone-in	lb	3.34	4/93	16r
Potato chips	16 oz	2.88	4/93	16r
Potatoes, white	lb	0.37	4/93	16r
Potatoes, white or red	10-lb sack	2.41	4Q 92	4c
Poultry, exp	year	116	89	15c
Rib roast, USDA choice, bone-in	lb	4.94	4/93	16r
Round roast, USDA choice, boneless	lb	3.17	4/93	16r
Sausage, Jimmy Dean, 100% pork	lb	3.46	4Q 92	4c
Shortening, vegetable oil blends	lb	0.98	4/93	16r
Shortening, vegetable, Crisco	3-lb can	2.86	4Q 92	4c
Soft drink, Coca Cola	2 liter	1.34	4Q 92	4c
Spaghetti and macaroni	lb	0.82	4/93	16r
Steak, round, graded & ungraded, ex USDA prime & choice	lb	4.04	4/93	16r
Steak, round, USDA choice, boneless	lb	3.90	4/93	16r
Steak, sirloin, USDA choice, boneless	lb	4.97	4/93	16r
Steak, T-bone	lb	5.56	4Q 92	4c
Strawberries, dry pint	12 oz	0.90	4/93	16r
Sugar, cane or beet	4 lb	2.07	4Q 92	4c
Sugar, white	lb	0.50	4/93	16r
Sugar, white, 33-80 oz pk	lb	0.41	4/93	16r
Sugar and other sweets, exp	year	84	89	15c
Tomatoes, field grown	lb	1.23	4/93	16r
Tomatoes, Hunt's or Del Monte	14.5-oz can	0.98	4Q 92	4c
Tuna, chunk, light	6.125-6.5 oz can	1.13	4Q 92	4c
Tuna, chunk, light	lb	2.22	4/93	16r
Turkey, frozen, whole	lb	1.04	4/93	16r
Vegetables, fresh, exp	year	116	89	15c
Vegetables, processed, exp	year	54	89	15c
Health Care				
ACCRA Index, Health Care		125.00	4Q 92	4c
Analgesic, Aspirin, Bayer, 325 mg tablets	100	4.87	4Q 92	4c
Appendectomy		1039	91	62c
Childbirth, cesarean		2285	91	62c
Childbirth, cesarean, hospital		5826	91	62r
Childbirth, cesarean, physician's fee		2053	91	62r
Childbirth, normal, hospital		2964	91	62r

Philadelphia, PA - continued

Item	Per	Value	Date	Ref.
Health Care - continued				
Childbirth, normal, physician's fee		1492	91	62r
Cholecystectomy		1535	91	62c
Coronary bypass surgery, triple		6118	91	62c
Dentist's fee, adult teeth cleaning and periodic oral exam	visit	62.50	4Q 92	4c
Doctor's fee, routine exam, established patient	visit	43.75	4Q 92	4c
Health maintenance organization coverage, employee	year	3319	93	39c
Health maintenance organization medical coverage, employee	year	3319	92	42c
Hospital care, semiprivate room	day	594.94	90	27c
Hospital care, semiprivate room	day	438.75	4Q 92	4c
Hysterectomy		2443	91	62c
Indemnity plan medical coverage, employee	year	4696	92	42c
Insurance coverage, traditional, employee	year	4696	93	39c
Lumpectomy		595	91	62c
Medical insurance premium, per employee, small group comprehensive	month	423.40	10/91	25c
Medical plan per employee	year	3942	91	45r
Mental health care, exp	capita	53.68-118.35	90	38s
Mental health care, exp, state mental health agency	capita	56.85	90	38s
Mental health care, hospital psychiatric services, non-Federal, exp	capita	22.11	88	38s
Mental health care, mental health organization, multiservice, exp	capita	21.01	88	38s
Mental health care, psychiatric hospitals, private, exp	capita	26.48	88	38s
Mental health care, psychiatric out-patient clinics, freestanding, exp	capita	4.17	88	38s
Mental health care, psychiatric partial-care organizations, freestanding, exp	capita	0.94	88	38s
Mental health care, state and county mental hospitals, exp	capita	37.11	88	38s
Mental health care, VA medical centers, exp	capita	9.77	88	38s
Oophorectomy		1705	91	62c
Preferred provider organization medical coverage, employee	year	3708	92	42c
Prescription drug co-pay, Medicaid	month	6.00	91	21s
Prostatectomy, retro-pubic		1938	91	62c
Salpingo-oophorectomy		1798	91	62c
Substance abuse, hospital ancillary charge	incident	720	90	70s
Substance abuse, hospital physician charge	incident	210	90	70s
Substance abuse, hospital room and board	incident	5400	90	70s
Vasectomy		464	91	62c
Household Goods				
Appliance repair, home, service call, washing machine	min labor charge	37.36	4Q 92	4c
Appliances, major, exp	year	178	89	15c
Appliances, small, misc. housewares, exp	year	61	89	15c
Floor coverings, exp	year	67	89	15c
Household equipment, misc., exp	year	418	89	15c
Laundry detergent, Tide Ultra, Bold, or Cheer	42 oz	3.66	4Q 92	4c
Tissues, facial, Kleenex brand	175-count box	1.10	4Q 92	4c
Housing				
ACCRA Index, Housing		149.80	4Q 92	4c
Home, median price	unit	117.60		26c
House, 1,800 sq ft, 8,000 sq ft lot, new, urban	total	165600	4Q 92	4c
House payment, principal and interest, 25% down payment	month	929	4Q 92	4c

Values are in dollars or fractions of dollars. In the column headed *Ref*, references are shown to sources. Each reference is followed by a letter. These refer to the geographical level for which data were reported: s = State, r = Region, and c = City or metro. The abbreviation *ex* is used to mean *except* or *excluding*; *exp* stands for *expenditures*. For other abbreviations and further explanations, please see the Introduction.

Philadelphia, PA - continued

Item	Per	Value	Date	Ref.
Housing				
Mortgage rate, incl. points & origination fee, 30-year fixed or adjustable rate	percent	8.20	4Q 92	4c
Rent, apartment, 2 bedrooms - 1-1/2 to 2 baths, unfurnished, 950 sq ft, water	month	721	4Q 92	4c
Rental unit, 1 bedroom	month	538	93	23c
Rental unit, 2 bedroom	month	634	93	23c
Rental unit, 3 bedroom	month	793	93	23c
Rental unit, 4 bedroom	month	889	93	23c
Rental unit, efficiency	month	444	93	23c
Insurance and Pensions				
Auto insurance, private passenger	year	683.57	91	63s
Personal Goods				
Shampoo, Alberto VO5	15 oz	1.84	4Q 92	4c
Toothpaste, Crest or Colgate	6-7 oz	2.30	4Q 92	4c
Personal Services				
Dry cleaning, man's 2-piece suit		6.50	4Q 92	4c
Haircare, woman's shampoo, trim and blow-dry		25.20	4Q 92	4c
Haircut, man's barbershop, no styling		11.25	4Q 92	4c
Restaurant Food				
Chicken, fried, thigh and drumstick		2.35	4Q 92	4c
Hamburger with cheese	1/4 lb	1.90	4Q 92	4c
Pizza, Pizza Hut or Pizza Inn, cheese, thin crust	12-13 in	7.93	4Q 92	4c
Taxes				
Tax, cigarette	pack	31	91	77s
Tax, gasoline	gal	12	91	77s
Taxes, hotel room	day	8.16	92	33c
Taxes, state	capita	1089	91	77s
Transportation				
ACCRA Index, Transportation		113.50	4Q 92	4c
Auto rental, average	day	46.00	6/91	60c
Bus fare	one-way	1.10	3/93	2c
Bus fare, up to 10 miles	one-way	1.45	4Q 92	4c
Driver's license fee		22.00	12/90	43s
Limo fare, airport-city, average	day	8.00	6/91	60c
Railway fare, commuter	one-way	2.00	3/93	2c
Railway fare, heavy rail	one-way	1.50	3/93	2c
Railway fare, light rail	one-way	1.50	93	2c
Taxi fare, airport-city, average	day	19.00	6/91	60c
Tire balance, computer or spin balance, front	wheel	7.26	4Q 92	4c
Trolley fare	one-way	1.50	3/93	2c
Travel				
Breakfast	day	8.27	6/91	60c
Business travel	day	165.00	4/93	89r
Dinner	day	24.81	6/91	60c
Dinner	day	20.55	92	85c
Lodging	day	127.52	91	60c
Lodging	day	122.00	92	85c
Lunch	day	11.30	6/91	60c
Travel, business	day	224.89	93	88c
Utilities				
ACCRA Index, Utilities		189.20	4Q 92	4c
Electricity	500 KWh	59.10	4/93	16c
Electricity	KWh	0.11	4/93	16c
Electricity	mil Btu	22.46	90	64s
Electricity, all electric, 1,800 sq ft living area new home	month	220.18	4Q 92	4c
Electricity, exp	year	764	89	15c
Electricity, winter, 250 KWh	month	40.67	92	55c

Philadelphia, PA - continued

Item	Per	Value	Date	Ref.
Utilities - continued				
Electricity, winter, 500 KWh	month	76.07	92	55c
Electricity, winter, 750 KWh	month	111.46	92	55c
Electricity, winter, 1000 KWh	month	146.85	92	55c
Utilities, fuels, public services, exp	year	1869	89	15c
Water, other public service, exp	year	173	89	15c

Phoenix, AZ

Item	Per	Value	Date	Ref.
Composite ACCRA index		101.20	4Q 92	4c
Alcoholic Beverages				
Beer, Miller Lite or Budweiser, 12-oz containers	6 pack	3.63	4Q 92	4c
Liquor, J & B Scotch	750 ml	15.79	4Q 92	4c
Wine, Gallo Chablis blanc, 1.5 liter	bottle	5.81	4Q 92	4c
Child Care				
Child care fee, average, center	hour	1.71	90	65r
Child care fee, average, nonregulated family day care	hour	1.32	90	65r
Child care fee, average, regulated family day care	hour	1.86	90	65r
Clothing				
Jeans, man's denim		26.15	4Q 92	4c
Shirt, man's dress shirt		25.16	4Q 92	4c
Undervest, boy's size 10-14, cotton	3	4.62	4Q 92	4c
Communications				
Long-distance telephone service, day, initial minute, 0-100 miles	min	0.24-0.42	91	12s
Long-distance telephone service, day, additional minute, 0-100 miles	min	0.10-0.26	91	12s
Long-distance telephone service, evenings/weekends, 0-100 mi initial minute	min	0.14-0.25	91	12s
Long-distance telephone service, evenings/weekends, 0-100 mi, additional minute	min	0.06-0.17	91	12s
Newspaper subscription, daily and Sunday home delivery, large-city	month	13.26	4Q 92	4c
Telephone, flat rate	month	12.40	91	11c
Telephone bill, family of four	month	18.90	4Q 92	4c
Education				
Board, 4-yr private college/university	year	1460	91	22s
Board, 4-yr public college/university	year	1697	91	22s
Expenditures, local gov't, public elementary/secondary	pupil	4489	92	20s
Room, 4-year private college/university	year	1350	91	22s
Room, 4-year public college/university	year	1556	91	22s
Tuition, 2-year private college/university	year	8977	91	22s
Tuition, 2-year public college/university	year	579	91	22s
Tuition, 4-year private college/university	year	4660	91	22s
Tuition, 4-year public college/university, in-state	year	1478	91	22s
Energy and Fuels				
Coal	mil Btu	1.45	90	64s
Energy	mil Btu	11.37	90	64s
Energy, combined forms, 1,800 sq ft heating area	month	97.94	4Q 92	4c
Energy exp/householder, 1-family unit	year	372	90	28r
Energy exp/householder, <1,000 sq ft heating area	year	335	90	28r
Energy exp/householder, 1,000-1,999 sq ft heating area	year	365	90	28r
Energy exp/householder, 2,000+ sq ft heating area	year	411	90	28r
Energy exp/householder, mobile home	year	305	90	28r
Energy exp/householder, multifamily	year	372	90	28r
Gas, cooking, 10 therms	month	11.68	92	56c
Gas, cooking, 30 therms	month	24.02	92	56c
Gas, cooking, 50 therms	month	36.36	92	56c
Gas, heating, winter, 100 therms	month	67.21	92	56c
Gas, natural	mil Btu	4.48	90	64s

Values are in dollars or fractions of dollars. In the column headed *Ref*, references are shown to sources. Each reference is followed by a letter. These refer to the geographical level for which data were reported: s=State, r=Region, and c=City or metro. The abbreviation *ex* is used to mean *except* or *excluding*; *exp* stands for expenditures. For other abbreviations and further explanations, please see the Introduction.

Phoenix, AZ - continued

Item	Per	Value	Date	Ref.
Energy and Fuels				
Gas, natural	000 cu ft	6.99	91	46s
Gas, natural, exp	year	341	91	46s
Gasoline, motor	gal	1.19	4Q 92	4c
Gasoline, unleaded regular	mil Btu	9.22	90	64s
Entertainment				
Bowling, evening rate	game	1.51	4Q 92	4c
Miniature golf admission	adult	6.18	92	1r
Miniature golf admission	child	5.14	92	1r
Monopoly game, Parker Brothers', No. 9		10.32	4Q 92	4c
Movie	admission	5.67	4Q 92	4c
Tennis balls, yellow, Wilson or Penn, 3	can	2.47	4Q 92	4c
Waterpark admission	adult	11.00	92	1r
Waterpark admission	child	8.55	92	1r
Funerals				
Casket, 18-gauge steel, velvet interior		1929.04	91	24r
Cosmetology, hair care, etc.		88.52	91	24r
Embalming		249.33	91	24r
Facility use for ceremony		182.75	91	24r
Hearse, local		110.04	91	24r
Limousine, local		66.67	91	24r
Remains to funeral home, transfer		84.58	91	24r
Service charge, professional		593.00	91	24r
Vault, concrete, non-metallic liner		647.38	91	24r
Viewing facilities, use		99.87	91	24r
Goods and Services				
ACCRA Index, Miscellaneous Goods and Services		102.50	4Q 92	4c
Groceries				
ACCRA Index, Groceries		100.10	4Q 92	4c
Apples, Red Delicious	lb	0.80	4/93	16r
Babyfood, strained vegetables, lowest price	4-4.5 oz jar	0.28	4Q 92	4c
Bacon	lb	1.79	4/93	16r
Bananas	lb	0.37	4Q 92	4c
Bananas	lb	0.53	4/93	16r
Bologna, all beef or mixed	lb	2.67	4/93	16r
Bread, white	24 oz	0.73	4Q 92	4c
Bread, white, pan	lb	0.81	4/93	16r
Carrots, short trimmed and topped	lb	0.39	4/93	16r
Cheese, Kraft grated Parmesan	8-oz canister	3.41	4Q 92	4c
Chicken, fresh, whole	lb	0.94	4/93	16r
Chicken, fryer, whole	lb	0.81	4Q 92	4c
Chicken breast, bone-in	lb	2.19	4/93	16r
Chuck roast, graded and ungraded, ex USDA prime and choice	lb	2.26	4/93	16r
Cigarettes, Winston	carton	16.71	4Q 92	4c
Coffee, 100% ground roast, all sizes	lb	2.33	4/93	16r
Coffee, vacuum-packed	13-oz can	2.03	4Q 92	4c
Corn, frozen	10 oz	0.64	4Q 92	4c
Corn Flakes, Kellogg's or Post Toasties	18 oz	2.23	4Q 92	4c
Eggs, Grade A large	doz	0.73	4Q 92	4c
Eggs, Grade AA large	doz	1.18	4/93	16r
Flour, white, all purpose	lb	0.22	4/93	16r
Grapefruit	lb	0.52	4/93	16r
Grapes, Thompson Seedless	lb	1.50	4/93	16r
Ground beef, 100% beef	lb	1.44	4/93	16r
Ground beef, lean and extra lean	lb	2.34	4/93	16r
Ground beef or hamburger	lb	1.25	4Q 92	4c
Ham, boneless, excluding canned	lb	2.56	4/93	16r
Honey, jar	8 oz	0.89-1.00	92	5r
Honey, jar	lb	1.35-1.97	92	5r
Honey, squeeze bear	12-oz	1.00-1.89	92	5r
Ice cream, prepackaged, bulk, regular	1/2 gal	2.40	4/93	16r
Lemons	lb	0.81	4/93	16r
Lettuce, iceberg	head	0.77	4Q 92	4c

Phoenix, AZ - continued

Item	Per	Value	Date	Ref.
Groceries - continued				
Lettuce, iceberg	lb	0.84	4/93	16r
Margarine, Blue Bonnet or Parkay cubes	lb	0.70	4Q 92	4c
Margarine, stick	lb	0.81	4/93	16r
Milk, whole	1/2 gal	1.32	4Q 92	4c
Orange juice, Minute Maid frozen	12-oz can	1.50	4Q 92	4c
Oranges, navel	lb	0.48	4/93	16r
Peaches	29-oz can	1.42	4Q 92	4c
Peas Sweet, Del Monte or Green Giant	15-17 oz can	0.59	4Q 92	4c
Pork chops, center cut, bone-in	lb	3.25	4/93	16r
Potato chips	16 oz	2.89	4/93	16r
Potatoes, white	lb	0.38	4/93	16r
Potatoes, white or red	10-lb sack	2.18	4Q 92	4c
Round roast, graded & ungraded, ex USDA prime & choice	lb	3.00	4/93	16r
Round roast, USDA choice, boneless	lb	3.16	4/93	16r
Sausage, Jimmy Dean, 100% pork	lb	2.81	4Q 92	4c
Shortening, vegetable oil blends	lb	0.86	4/93	16r
Shortening, vegetable, Crisco	3-lb can	2.61	4Q 92	4c
Soft drink, Coca Cola	2 liter	1.07	4Q 92	4c
Spaghetti and macaroni	lb	0.84	4/93	16r
Steak, round, graded & ungraded, ex USDA prime & choice	lb	3.34	4/93	16r
Steak, round, USDA choice, boneless	lb	3.24	4/93	16r
Steak, sirloin, graded & ungraded, ex USDA prime & choice	lb	3.75	4/93	16r
Steak, sirloin, USDA choice, boneless	lb	4.49	4/93	16r
Steak, T-bone	lb	4.98	4Q 92	4c
Sugar, cane or beet	4 lb	1.66	4Q 92	4c
Sugar, white	lb	0.41	4/93	16r
Sugar, white, 33-80 oz pk	lb	0.38	4/93	16r
Tomatoes, field grown	lb	1.01	4/93	16r
Tomatoes, Hunt's or Del Monte	14.5-oz can	0.75	4Q 92	4c
Tuna, chunk, light	6.125-6.5 oz can	0.76	4Q 92	4c
Turkey, frozen, whole	lb	1.04	4/93	16r
Health Care				
ACCRA Index, Health Care		111.30	4Q 92	4c
Analgesic, Aspirin, Bayer, 325 mg tablets	100	5.50	4Q 92	4c
Childbirth, cesarean, hospital		5533	91	62r
Childbirth, cesarean, physician's fee		2053	91	62r
Childbirth, normal, hospital		2745	91	62r
Childbirth, normal, physician's fee		1492	91	62r
Dentist's fee, adult teeth cleaning and periodic oral exam	visit	52.12	4Q 92	4c
Doctor's fee, routine exam, established patient	visit	41.00	4Q 92	4c
Hospital care, semiprivate room	day	278.97	90	27c
Hospital care, semiprivate room	day	356.95	4Q 92	4c
Medical insurance premium, per employee, small group comprehensive	month	401.50	10/91	25c
Medical plan per employee	year	3218	91	45r
Mental health care, exp	capita	20.37-28.83	90	38s
Mental health care, exp, state mental health agency	capita	27.27	90	38s
Mental health care, hospital psychiatric services, non-Federal, exp	capita	8.91	88	38s
Mental health care, mental health organization, multiservice, exp	capita	11.35	88	38s
Mental health care, psychiatric hospitals, private, exp	capita	36.59	88	38s
Mental health care, psychiatric out-patient clinics, freestanding, exp	capita	1.11	88	38s
Mental health care, state and county mental hospitals, exp	capita	8.18	88	38s

Values are in dollars or fractions of dollars. In the column headed *Ref*, references are shown to sources. Each reference is followed by a letter. These refer to the geographical level for which data were reported: s=State, r=Region, and c=City or metro. The abbreviation *ex* is used to mean *except* or *excluding*; *exp* stands for expenditures. For other abbreviations and further explanations, please see the Introduction.

Phoenix, AZ - continued

Item	Per	Value	Date	Ref.
Health Care				
Mental health care, VA medical centers, exp	capita	2.60	88	38s
Physician fee, family practice, first-visit		111.00	91	62r
Physician fee, family practice, revisit		45.00	91	62r
Physician fee, general practice, first-visit		100.00	91	62r
Physician fee, general practice, revisit		40.00	91	62r
Physician fee, internal medicine, first-visit		137.00	91	62r
Physician fee, internal medicine, revisit		48.00	91	62r
Physician fee, median, neurosurgeon, first-visit		157.00	91	62r
Physician fee, median, nonsurgical specialist, first-visit		131.00	91	62r
Physician fee, median, orthopedic surgeon, first-visit		124.00	91	62r
Physician fee, median, plastic surgeon, first-visit		88.00	91	62r
Physician fee, median, surgical specialist, first-visit		100.00	91	62r
Physician fee, neurosurgeon, revisit		51.00	91	62r
Physician fee, nonsurgical specialist, revisit		47.00	91	62r
Physician fee, obstetrics/gynecology, first-visit		95.00	91	62r
Physician fee, obstetrics/gynecology, revisit		50.00	91	62r
Physician fee, orthopedic surgeon, revisit		51.00	91	62r
Physician fee, pediatrician, first-visit		81.00	91	62r
Physician fee, pediatrician, revisit		42.00	91	62r
Physician fee, plastic surgeon, revisit		48.00	91	62r
Physician fee, surgical specialist, revisit		49.00	91	62r
Substance abuse, hospital ancillary charge	incident	1800	90	70s
Substance abuse, hospital physician charge	incident	800	90	70s
Substance abuse, hospital room and board	incident	6480	90	70s
Household Goods				
Appliance repair, home, service call, washing machine	min labor charge	34.47	4Q 92	4c
Laundry detergent, Tide Ultra, Bold, or Cheer	42 oz	3.86	4Q 92	4c
Tissues, facial, Kleenex brand	175-count box	1.18	4Q 92	4c
Housing				
ACCRA Index, Housing		96.40	4Q 92	4c
Home, median price	unit	86.80		26c
House, 1,800 sq ft, 8,000 sq ft lot, new, urban	total	102796	4Q 92	4c
House payment, principal and interest, 25% down payment	month	574	4Q 92	4c
Mortgage rate, incl. points & origination fee, 30-year fixed or adjustable rate	percent	8.15	4Q 92	4c
Rent, apartment, 2 bedrooms - 1-1/2 to 2 baths, unfurnished, 950 sq ft, water	month	520	4Q 92	4c
Rental unit, 1 bedroom	month	429	93	23c
Rental unit, 2 bedroom	month	505	93	23c
Rental unit, 3 bedroom	month	631	93	23c
Rental unit, 4 bedroom	month	707	93	23c
Rental unit, efficiency	month	354	93	23c
Insurance and Pensions				
Auto insurance, private passenger	year	704.41	91	63s
Personal Goods				
Shampoo, Alberto VO5	15 oz	1.20	4Q 92	4c
Toothpaste, Crest or Colgate	6-7 oz	2.24	4Q 92	4c
Personal Services				
Dry cleaning, man's 2-piece suit		7.33	4Q 92	4c
Haircare, woman's shampoo, trim and blow-dry		20.69	4Q 92	4c
Haircut, man's barbershop, no styling		7.87	4Q 92	4c

Phoenix, AZ - continued

Item	Per	Value	Date	Ref.
Restaurant Food				
Chicken, fried, thigh and drumstick		2.18	4Q 92	4c
Hamburger with cheese	1/4 lb	1.99	4Q 92	4c
Pizza, Pizza Hut or Pizza Inn, cheese, thin crust	12-13 in	8.32	4Q 92	4c
Taxes				
Tax, cigarette	pack	18	91	77s
Tax, gasoline	gal	18	91	77s
Taxes, hotel room	day	7.87	92	33c
Taxes, state	capita	1256	91	77s
Transportation				
ACCRA Index, Transportation		116.00	4Q 92	4c
Auto rental, average	day	36.50	6/91	60c
Bus fare	one-way	1.00	3/93	2c
Bus fare, up to 10 miles	one-way	1.00	4Q 92	4c
Driver's license fee		7.00	12/90	43s
Limo fare, airport-city, average	day	5.00	6/91	60c
Taxi fare, airport-city, average	day	8.00	6/91	60c
Tire balance, computer or spin balance, front	wheel	8.25	4Q 92	4c
Travel				
Breakfast	day	6.53	6/91	60c
Business travel	day	178.00	4/93	89r
Dinner	day	16.66	6/91	60c
Lodging	day	137.33	91	60c
Lunch	day	8.30	6/91	60c
Travel, business	day	197.62	93	88c
Utilities				
ACCRA Index, Utilities		90.40	4Q 92	4c
Electricity	mil Btu	22.82	90	64s
Electricity, all electric, 1,800 sq ft living area new home	month	97.94	4Q 92	4c
Electricity, residential	KWh	10.69	2/93	94s
Electricity, winter, 250 KWh	month	30.15	92	55c
Electricity, winter, 500 KWh	month	52.79	92	55c
Electricity, winter, 750 KWh	month	75.43	92	55c
Electricity, winter, 1000 KWh	month	98.05	92	55c

Pikeville, KY

Item	Per	Value	Date	Ref.
Composite ACCRA index		103.10	4Q 92	4c
Alcoholic Beverages				
Beer, Miller Lite or Budweiser, 12-oz containers	6 pack	3.76	4Q 92	4c
Liquor, J & B Scotch	750 ml	17.83	4Q 92	4c
Wine, Gallo Chablis blanc, 1.5 liter	bottle	6.29	4Q 92	4c
Clothing				
Jeans, man's denim		33.33	4Q 92	4c
Shirt, man's dress shirt		29.50	4Q 92	4c
Undervest, boy's size 10-14, cotton	3	4.56	4Q 92	4c
Communications				
Newspaper subscription, daily and Sunday home delivery, large-city	month	15.95	4Q 92	4c
Telephone, flat rate	month	12.02	91	11c
Telephone bill, family of four	month	19.32	4Q 92	4c
Energy and Fuels				
Energy, combined forms, 1,800 sq ft heating area	month	98.74	4Q 92	4c
Gasoline, motor	gal	1.20	4Q 92	4c
Entertainment				
Bowling, evening rate	game	1.75	4Q 92	4c
Monopoly game, Parker Brothers', No. 9		10.92	4Q 92	4c
Movie	admission	5.00	4Q 92	4c
Tennis balls, yellow, Wilson or Penn, 3	can	2.31	4Q 92	4c

Values are in dollars or fractions of dollars. In the column headed *Ref*, references are shown to sources. Each reference is followed by a letter. These refer to the geographical level for which data were reported: s = State, r = Region, and c = City or metro. The abbreviation *ex* is used to mean *except* or *excluding*; *exp* stands for expenditures. For other abbreviations and further explanations, please see the Introduction.

Pikeville, KY - continued

Item	Per	Value	Date	Ref.
Goods and Services				
ACCRA Index, Miscellaneous Goods and Services		104.70	4Q 92	4c
Groceries				
ACCRA Index, Groceries		94.30	4Q 92	4c
Babyfood, strained vegetables, lowest price	4-4.5 oz jar	0.32	4Q 92	4c
Bananas	lb	0.44	4Q 92	4c
Bread, white	24 oz	0.57	4Q 92	4c
Cheese, Kraft grated Parmesan	8-oz canister	3.28	4Q 92	4c
Chicken, fryer, whole	lb	0.72	4Q 92	4c
Cigarettes, Winston	carton	15.36	4Q 92	4c
Coffee, vacuum-packed	13-oz can	1.95	4Q 92	4c
Corn, frozen	10 oz	0.67	4Q 92	4c
Corn Flakes, Kellogg's or Post Toasties	18 oz	1.82	4Q 92	4c
Eggs, Grade A large	doz	0.74	4Q 92	4c
Ground beef or hamburger	lb	1.52	4Q 92	4c
Lettuce, iceberg	head	0.86	4Q 92	4c
Margarine, Blue Bonnet or Parkay cubes	lb	0.58	4Q 92	4c
Milk, whole	1/2 gal	1.51	4Q 92	4c
Orange juice, Minute Maid frozen	12-oz can	1.49	4Q 92	4c
Peaches	29-oz can	1.43	4Q 92	4c
Peas Sweet, Del Monte or Green Giant	15-17 oz can	0.56	4Q 92	4c
Potatoes, white or red	10-lb sack	2.22	4Q 92	4c
Sausage, Jimmy Dean, 100% pork	lb	1.99	4Q 92	4c
Shortening, vegetable, Crisco	3-lb can	2.16	4Q 92	4c
Soft drink, Coca Cola	2 liter	1.04	4Q 92	4c
Steak, T-bone	lb	5.26	4Q 92	4c
Sugar, cane or beet	4 lb	1.44	4Q 92	4c
Tomatoes, Hunt's or Del Monte	14.5-oz can	0.63	4Q 92	4c
Tuna, chunk, light	6.125-6.5 oz can	0.54	4Q 92	4c
Health Care				
ACCRA Index, Health Care		103.00	4Q 92	4c
Analgesic, Aspirin, Bayer, 325 mg tablets	100	5.35	4Q 92	4c
Dentist's fee, adult teeth cleaning and periodic oral exam	visit	46.14	4Q 92	4c
Doctor's fee, routine exam, established patient	visit	40.00	4Q 92	4c
Hospital care, semiprivate room	day	314.00	4Q 92	4c
Household Goods				
Appliance repair, home, service call, washing machine	min labor charge	36.65	4Q 92	4c
Laundry detergent, Tide Ultra, Bold, or Cheer	42 oz	3.07	4Q 92	4c
Tissues, facial, Kleenex brand	175-count box	1.14	4Q 92	4c
Housing				
ACCRA Index, Housing		111.70	4Q 92	4c
House, 1,800 sq ft, 8,000 sq ft lot, new, urban	total	126200	4Q 92	4c
House payment, principal and interest, 25% down payment	month	709	4Q 92	4c
Mortgage rate, incl. points & origination fee, 30-year fixed or adjustable rate	percent	8.21	4Q 92	4c
Rent, apartment, 2 bedrooms - 1-1/2 to 2 baths, unfurnished, 950 sq ft, water	month	500	4Q 92	4c

Pikeville, KY - continued

Item	Per	Value	Date	Ref.
Personal Goods				
Shampoo, Alberto VO5	15 oz	1.13	4Q 92	4c
Toothpaste, Crest or Colgate	6-7 oz	2.15	4Q 92	4c
Personal Services				
Dry cleaning, man's 2-piece suit		5.50	4Q 92	4c
Haircare, woman's shampoo, trim and blow-dry		13.62	4Q 92	4c
Haircut, man's barbershop, no styling		8.19	4Q 92	4c
Restaurant Food				
Chicken, fried, thigh and drumstick		2.00	4Q 92	4c
Hamburger with cheese	1/4 lb	1.75	4Q 92	4c
Pizza, Pizza Hut or Pizza Inn, cheese, thin crust	12-13 in	8.79	4Q 92	4c
Transportation				
ACCRA Index, Transportation		95.70	4Q 92	4c
Tire balance, computer or spin balance, front	wheel	5.56	4Q 92	4c
Utilities				
ACCRA Index, Utilities		91.30	4Q 92	4c
Electricity, all electric, 1,800 sq ft living area new home	month	98.74	4Q 92	4c

Pine Bluff, AR

Item	Per	Value	Date	Ref.
Child Care				
Child care fee, average, center	hour	1.29	90	65r
Child care fee, average, nonregulated family day care	hour	0.89	90	65r
Child care fee, average, regulated family day care	hour	1.32	90	65r
Communications				
Long-distance telephone service, day, initial minute, 0-100 miles	min	0.10-0.42	91	12s
Long-distance telephone service, day, additional minute, 0-100 miles	min	0.08-0.34	91	12s
Long-distance telephone service, evenings/weekends, 0-100 mi, initial minute	min	0.06-0.23	91	12s
Long-distance telephone service, evenings/weekends, 0-100 mi, additional minute	min	0.04-0.19	91	12s
Education				
Board, 4-yr private college/university	year	1651	91	22s
Board, 4-yr public college/university	year	1253	91	22s
Expenditures, local gov't, public elementary/secondary	pupil	3770	92	20s
Room, 4-year private college/university	year	1111	91	22s
Room, 4-year public college/university	year	1173	91	22s
Tuition, 2-year private college/university	year	2482	91	22s
Tuition, 2-year public college/university	year	648	91	22s
Tuition, 4-year private college/university	year	4464	91	22s
Tuition, 4-year public college/university, in-state	year	1418	91	22s
Energy and Fuels				
Coal	mil Btu	1.62	90	64s
Energy	mil Btu	8.81	90	64s
Energy exp/householder, 1-family unit	year	471	90	28r
Energy exp/householder, <1,000 sq ft heating area	year	384	90	28r
Energy exp/householder, 1,000-1,999 sq ft heating area	year	421	90	28r
Energy exp/householder, 2,000+ sq ft heating area	year	625	90	28r
Energy exp/householder, mobile home	year	271	90	28r
Energy exp/householder, multifamily	year	355	90	28r
Gas, natural	mil Btu	3.27	90	64s
Gas, natural	000 cu ft	4.98	91	46s
Gas, natural, exp	year	408	91	46s
Gasoline, unleaded regular	mil Btu	8.86	90	64s

Values are in dollars or fractions of dollars. In the column headed *Ref*, references are shown to sources. Each reference is followed by a letter. These refer to the geographical level for which data were reported: s=State, r=Region, and c=City or metro. The abbreviation *ex* is used to mean *except* or *excluding*; *exp* stands for expenditures. For other abbreviations and further explanations, please see the Introduction.

Pine Bluff, AR - continued

Item	Per	Value	Date	Ref.
Entertainment				
Miniature golf admission	adult	6.18	92	1r
Miniature golf admission	child	5.14	92	1r
Waterpark admission	adult	11.00	92	1r
Waterpark admission	child	8.55	92	1r
Funerals				
Casket, 18-gauge steel, velvet interior		2274.41	91	24r
Cosmetology, hair care, etc.		74.62	91	24r
Embalming		229.94	91	24r
Facility use for ceremony		176.61	91	24r
Hearse, local		116.34	91	24r
Limousine, local		72.68	91	24r
Remains to funeral home, transfer		87.72	91	24r
Service charge, professional		712.53	91	24r
Vault, concrete, non-metallic liner		750.55	91	24r
Viewing facilities, use		155.31	91	24r
Groceries				
Apples, Red Delicious	lb	0.79	4/93	16r
Bacon	lb	1.75	4/93	16r
Bananas	lb	0.42	4/93	16r
Beef, stew, boneless	lb	2.61	4/93	16r
Bologna, all beef or mixed	lb	2.24	4/93	16r
Bread, white, pan	lb	0.64	4/93	16r
Bread, whole wheat, pan	lb	0.96	4/93	16r
Cabbage	lb	0.37	4/93	16r
Carrots, short trimmed and topped	lb	0.47	4/93	16r
Celery	lb	0.64	4/93	16r
Cheese, American	lb	2.98	4/93	16r
Cheese, Cheddar	lb	3.28	4/93	16r
Chicken, fresh, whole	lb	0.77	4/93	16r
Chicken breast, bone-in	lb	1.92	4/93	16r
Chicken legs, bone-in	lb	1.06	4/93	16r
Chuck roast, graded and ungraded, ex USDA prime and choice	lb	2.40	4/93	16r
Chuck roast, USDA choice, bone-in	lb	2.19	4/93	16r
Chuck roast, USDA choice, boneless	lb	2.38	4/93	16r
Coffee, 100% ground roast, all sizes	lb	2.48	4/93	16r
Crackers, soda, salted	lb	1.15	4/93	16r
Eggs, Grade A large	doz	0.96	4/93	16r
Flour, white, all purpose	lb	0.24	4/93	16r
Frankfurters, all meat or all beef	lb	2.01	4/93	16r
Grapefruit	lb	0.44	4/93	16r
Grapes, Thompson Seedless	lb	1.40	4/93	16r
Ground beef, 100% beef	lb	1.58	4/93	16r
Ground beef, lean and extra lean	lb	2.09	4/93	16r
Ground chuck, 100% beef	lb	1.98	4/93	16r
Ham, boneless, excluding canned	lb	2.89	4/93	16r
Ham, picnic, shoulder, bone-in, smoked	lb	1.02	4/93	16r
Ham, rump or steak half, bone-in, smoked	lb	1.48	4/93	16r
Honey, jar	8 oz	0.73-1.19	92	5r
Honey, jar	lb	1.10-1.79	92	5r
Honey, squeeze bear	12-oz	1.19-1.50	92	5r
Ice cream, prepackaged, bulk, regular	1/2 gal	2.41	4/93	16r
Lemons	lb	1.05	4/93	16r
Lettuce, iceberg	lb	0.81	4/93	16r
Margarine, stick	lb	0.88	4/93	16r
Oranges, navel	lb	0.55	4/93	16r
Pears, Anjou	lb	0.92	4/93	16r
Pork chops, center cut, bone-in	lb	3.13	4/93	16r
Potato chips	16 oz	2.94	4/93	16r
Potatoes, white	lb	0.43	4/93	16r
Rib roast, USDA choice, bone-in	lb	4.63	4/93	16r
Rice, white, long grain, uncooked	lb	0.45	4/93	16r
Round roast, graded & ungraded, ex USDA prime & choice	lb	3.03	4/93	16r
Round roast, USDA choice, boneless	lb	3.09	4/93	16r
Sausage, fresh, loose	lb	2.08	4/93	16r
Short ribs, bone-in	lb	2.66	4/93	16r
Shortening, vegetable oil blends	lb	0.69	4/93	16r
Spaghetti and macaroni	lb	0.81	4/93	16r
Steak, rib eye, USDA choice, boneless	lb	6.24	4/93	16r

Pine Bluff, AR - continued

Item	Per	Value	Date	Ref.
Groceries - continued				
Steak, round, graded & ungraded, ex USDA prime & choice	lb	3.31	4/93	16r
Steak, round, USDA choice, boneless	lb	3.34	4/93	16r
Steak, sirloin, graded & ungraded, ex USDA prime & choice	lb	4.19	4/93	16r
Steak, sirloin, USDA choice, boneless	lb	4.46	4/93	16r
Steak, T-bone, USDA choice, bone-in	lb	5.25	4/93	16r
Strawberries, dry pint	12 oz	0.92	4/93	16r
Sugar, white	lb	0.39	4/93	16r
Sugar, white, 33-80 oz pk	lb	0.38	4/93	16r
Tomatoes, field grown	lb	0.88	4/93	16r
Tuna, chunk, light	lb	1.79	4/93	16r
Turkey, frozen, whole	lb	1.04	4/93	16r
Yogurt, natural, fruit flavored	1/2 pint	0.57	4/93	16r
Health Care				
Childbirth, cesarean, hospital		5034	91	62r
Childbirth, cesarean, physician's fee		2053	91	62r
Childbirth, normal, hospital		2712	91	62r
Childbirth, normal, physician's fee		1492	91	62r
Health care spending, state	capita	1944	3/93	84s
Mental health care, exp	capita	20.37-28.83	90	38s
Mental health care, exp, state mental health agency	capita	25.92	90	38s
Mental health care, hospital psychiatric services, non-Federal, exp	capita	5.26	88	38s
Mental health care, mental health organization, multiservice, exp	capita	15.69	88	38s
Mental health care, psychiatric hospitals, private, exp	capita	15.15	88	38s
Mental health care, psychiatric out-patient clinics, freestanding, exp	capita	0.46	88	38s
Mental health care, state and county mental hospitals, exp	capita	6.78	88	38s
Mental health care, VA medical centers, exp	capita	7.18	88	38s
Physician fee, family practice, first-visit		75.00	91	62r
Physician fee, family practice, revisit		34.00	91	62r
Physician fee, general practice, first-visit		61.00	91	62r
Physician fee, general practice, revisit		32.00	91	62r
Physician fee, general surgeon, first-visit		64.00	91	62r
Physician fee, general surgeon, revisit		40.00	91	62r
Physician fee, internal medicine, first-visit		98.00	91	62r
Physician fee, internal medicine, revisit		40.00	91	62r
Physician fee, median, neurosurgeon, first-visit		130.00	91	62r
Physician fee, median, nonsurgical specialist, first-visit		95.00	91	62r
Physician fee, median, orthopedic surgeon, first-visit		91.00	91	62r
Physician fee, median, plastic surgeon, first-visit		66.00	91	62r
Physician fee, median, surgical specialist, first-visit		62.00	91	62r
Physician fee, neurosurgeon, revisit		50.00	91	62r
Physician fee, nonsurgical specialist, revisit		40.00	91	62r
Physician fee, obstetrics/gynecology, first-visit		64.00	91	62r
Physician fee, obstetrics/gynecology, revisit		41.00	91	62r
Physician fee, orthopedic surgeon, revisit		40.00	91	62r
Physician fee, pediatrician, first-visit		49.00	91	62r
Physician fee, pediatrician, revisit		33.00	91	62r
Physician fee, plastic surgeon, revisit		43.00	91	62r
Physician fee, surgical specialist, revisit		37.00	91	62r
Substance abuse, hospital ancillary charge	incident	1680	90	70s
Substance abuse, hospital physician charge	incident	450	90	70s
Substance abuse, hospital room and board	incident	4490	90	70s

Values are in dollars or fractions of dollars. In the column headed *Ref*, references are shown to sources. Each reference is followed by a letter. These refer to the geographical level for which data were reported: s=State, r=Region, and c=City or metro. The abbreviation *ex* is used to mean *except* or *excluding*; *exp* stands for expenditures. For other abbreviations and further explanations, please see the Introduction.

Pine Bluff, AR - continued

Item	Per	Value	Date	Ref.
Insurance and Pensions				
Auto insurance, private passenger	year	501.00	91	63s
Taxes				
Tax, cigarette	pack	22	91	77s
Tax, gasoline	gal	18.50	91	77s
Taxes, state	capita	997	91	77s
Transportation				
Driver's license fee		14.25	12/90	43s
Vehicle registration and license plate	year	17.00-30.00	93	10s
Travel				
Business travel	day	193.00	4/93	89r
Utilities				
Electricity	mil Btu	19.78	90	64s

Pittsburgh, PA

Item	Per	Value	Date	Ref.
Child Care				
Child care fee, average, center	hour	2.18	90	65r
Child care fee, average, nonregulated family day care	hour	1.83	90	65r
Child care fee, average, regulated family day care	hour	2.02	90	65r
Communications				
Long-distance telephone service, day, initial minute, 0-100 miles	min	0.15-0.29	91	12s
Long-distance telephone service, day, additional minute, 0-100 miles	min	0.06-0.22	91	12s
Long-distance telephone service, evenings/weekends, 0-100 mi, initial minute	min	0.06-0.14	91	12s
Long-distance telephone service, evenings/weekends, 0-100 mi, additional minute	min	0.03-0.11	91	12s
Telephone, exp	year	430	89	15c
Telephone, residential, private line, rotary, unlimited calling	month	16.41	10/91	78c
Education				
Board, 4-yr private college/university	year	2019	91	22s
Board, 4-yr public college/university	year	1656	91	22s
Expenditures, local gov't, public elementary/secondary	pupil	6980	92	20s
Room, 4-year private college/university	year	2179	91	22s
Room, 4-year public college/university	year	1719	91	22s
Tuition, 2-year private college/university	year	6314	91	22s
Tuition, 2-year public college/university	year	1505	91	22s
Tuition, 4-year private college/university	year	9848	91	22s
Tuition, 4-year public college/university, in-state	year	3401	91	22s
Energy and Fuels				
Coal	mil Btu	1.57	90	64s
Energy	mil Btu	8.63	90	64s
Energy exp/householder, 1-family unit	year	588	90	28r
Energy exp/householder, <1,000 sq ft heating area	year	477	90	28r
Energy exp/householder, 1,000-1,999 sq ft heating area	year	517	90	28r
Energy exp/householder, 2,000+ sq ft heating area	year	630	90	28r
Energy exp/householder, mobile home	year	412	90	28r
Energy exp/householder, multifamily	year	498	90	28r
Fuel oil #2	gal	0.89	4/93	16c
Fuel oil, other fuel, exp	year	51	89	15c
Gas, cooking, winter, 10 therms	month	5.49	92	56c
Gas, cooking, winter, 30 therms	month	16.48	92	56c
Gas, cooking, winter, 50 therms	month	27.47	92	56c
Gas, heating, winter, 100 therms	month	78.78	92	56c
Gas, natural	mil Btu	5.24	90	64s
Gas, natural	000 cu ft	6.76	91	46s

Pittsburgh, PA - continued

Item	Per	Value	Date	Ref.
Energy and Fuels - continued				
Gas, natural, exp	year	503	89	15c
Gas, natural, exp	year	703	91	46s
Gas, piped	100 therms	63.49	4/93	16c
Gas, piped	40 therms	34.40	4/93	16c
Gas, piped	therm	0.62	4/93	16c
Gasoline, all types	gal	1.13	4/93	16c
Gasoline, regular unleaded, taxes included, cash, self-service	gal	1.28	4/93	16c
Gasoline, unleaded premium 93 octane	gal	1.07	4/93	16c
Gasoline, unleaded regular	mil Btu	9.35	90	64s
Funerals				
Casket, 18-gauge steel, velvet interior		1811.58	91	24r
Cosmetology, hair care, etc.		111.08	91	24r
Embalming		329.42	91	24r
Facility use for ceremony		201.29	91	24r
Hearse, local		135.27	91	24r
Limousine, local		127.24	91	24r
Remains to funeral home, transfer		103.98	91	24r
Service charge, professional		724.98	91	24r
Vault, concrete, non-metallic liner		766.71	91	24r
Viewing facilities, use		260.60	91	24r
Groceries				
Apples, Red Delicious	lb	0.85	4/93	16r
Bacon	lb	2.12	4/93	16r
Bakery products, exp	year	225	89	15c
Bananas	lb	0.54	4/93	16r
Beef, exp	year	157	89	15c
Beverages, nonalcoholic, exp	year	206	89	15c
Bread, white, pan	lb	0.81	4/93	16r
Butter	lb	2.02	4/93	16r
Carrots, short trimmed and topped	lb	0.51	4/93	16r
Cereals and baking products, exp	year	334	89	15c
Cereals and cereal products, exp	year	109	89	15c
Chicken, fresh, whole	lb	1.04	4/93	16r
Chicken breast, bone-in	lb	2.21	4/93	16r
Chicken legs, bone-in	lb	1.16	4/93	16r
Chuck roast, USDA choice, boneless	lb	2.82	4/93	16r
Coffee, 100% ground roast, all sizes	lb	2.66	4/93	16r
Cucumbers	lb	0.85	4/93	16r
Dairy product purchases	year	288	89	15c
Dairy products, miscellaneous, exp	year	154	89	15c
Eggs, exp	year	25	89	15c
Eggs, Grade A large	doz	1.15	4/93	16r
Fats and oils, exp	year	52	89	15c
Fish and seafood, exp	year	50	89	15c
Food, exp	year	3560	89	15c
Food eaten at home, exp	year	610	89	15c
Food eaten at home, exp	year	2099	89	15c
Food purchased away from home, exp	year	1461	89	15c
Foods, miscellaneous, exp	year	250	91	15c
Fruits, fresh, exp	year	113	89	15c
Fruits, processed, exp	year	78	89	15c
Fruits and vegetables, exp	year	371	89	15c
Grapefruit	lb	0.45	4/93	16r
Grapes, Thompson Seedless	lb	1.52	4/93	16r
Ground beef, lean and extra lean	lb	2.36	4/93	16r
Ground chuck, 100% beef	lb	2.02	4/93	16r
Honey, jar	8 oz	0.96-1.75	92	5r
Honey, jar	lb	1.50-3.00	92	5r
Honey, squeeze bear	12-oz	1.50-1.99	92	5r
Ice cream, prepackaged, bulk, regular	1/2 gal	2.80	4/93	16r
Lemons	lb	0.96	4/93	16r
Lettuce, iceberg	lb	0.95	4/93	16r
Margarine, stick	lb	0.81	4/93	16r
Meats, miscellaneous, exp	year	82	89	15c
Meats, poultry, fish and eggs, exp	year	496	89	15c
Milk, fresh, whole, fortified	1/2 gal	1.30	4/93	16r
Milk and cream, fresh, exp	year	134	89	15c
Oranges, navel	lb	0.56	4/93	16r

Values are in dollars or fractions of dollars. In the column headed *Ref*, references are shown to sources. Each reference is followed by a letter. These refer to the geographical level for which data were reported: s=State, r=Region, and c=City or metro. The abbreviation *ex* is used to mean *except* or *excluding*; *exp* stands for expenditures. For other abbreviations and further explanations, please see the Introduction.

Pittsburgh, PA - continued

Item	Per	Value	Date	Ref.
Groceries				
Peanut butter, creamy, all sizes	lb	1.88	4/93	16r
Pork, exp	year	93	89	15c
Pork chops, center cut, bone-in	lb	3.34	4/93	16r
Potato chips	16 oz	2.88	4/93	16r
Potatoes, white	lb	0.37	4/93	16r
Poultry, exp	year	87	89	15c
Rib roast, USDA choice, bone-in	lb	4.94	4/93	16r
Round roast, USDA choice, boneless	lb	3.17	4/93	16r
Shortening, vegetable oil blends	lb	0.98	4/93	16r
Spaghetti and macaroni	lb	0.82	4/93	16r
Steak, round, graded & ungraded, ex USDA prime & choice	lb	4.04	4/93	16r
Steak, round, USDA choice, boneless	lb	3.90	4/93	16r
Steak, sirloin, USDA choice, boneless	lb	4.97	4/93	16r
Strawberries, dry pint	12 oz	0.90	4/93	16r
Sugar, white	lb	0.50	4/93	16r
Sugar, white, 33-80 oz pk	lb	0.41	4/93	16r
Sugar and other sweets, exp	year	72	89	15c
Tomatoes, field grown	lb	1.23	4/93	16r
Tuna, chunk, light	lb	2.22	4/93	16r
Turkey, frozen, whole	lb	1.04	4/93	16r
Vegetables, fresh, exp	year	123	89	15c
Vegetables, processed, exp	year	57	89	15c
Health Care				
Childbirth, cesarean, hospital		5826	91	62r
Childbirth, cesarean, physician's fee		2053	91	62r
Childbirth, normal, hospital		2964	91	62r
Childbirth, normal, physician's fee		1492	91	62r
Hospital care, semiprivate room	day	337.42	90	27c
Medical insurance premium, per employee, small group comprehensive	month	372.30	10/91	25c
Medical plan per employee	year	3942	91	45r
Mental health care, exp	capita	53.68-118.35	90	38s
Mental health care, exp, state mental health agency	capita	56.85	90	38s
Mental health care, hospital psychiatric services, non-Federal, exp	capita	22.11	88	38s
Mental health care, mental health organization, multiservice, exp	capita	21.01	88	38s
Mental health care, psychiatric hospitals, private, exp	capita	26.48	88	38s
Mental health care, psychiatric out-patient clinics, freestanding, exp	capita	4.17	88	38s
Mental health care, psychiatric partial-care organizations, freestanding, exp	capita	0.94	88	38s
Mental health care, state and county mental hospitals, exp	capita	37.11	88	38s
Mental health care, VA medical centers, exp	capita	9.77	88	38s
Prescription drug co-pay, Medicaid	month	6.00	91	21s
Substance abuse, hospital ancillary charge	incident	720	90	70s
Substance abuse, hospital physician charge	incident	210	90	70s
Substance abuse, hospital room and board	incident	5400	90	70s
Household Goods				
Appliances, major, exp	year	187	89	15c
Appliances, small, misc. housewares, exp	year	43	89	15c
Floor coverings, exp	year	73	89	15c
Household equipment, misc., exp	year	247	89	15c
Housing				
Home, median price	unit	78.70		26c
Insurance and Pensions				
Auto insurance, private passenger	year	683.57	91	63s
Taxes				
Tax, cigarette	pack	31	91	77s
Tax, gasoline	gal	12	91	77s
Taxes, state	capita	1089	91	77s

Pittsburgh, PA - continued

Item	Per	Value	Date	Ref.
Transportation				
Auto rental, average	day	52.25	6/91	60c
Bus fare	one-way	1.00	3/93	2c
Commuter train fare (inclined plane)	one-way	1.00	3/93	2c
Driver's license fee		22.00	12/90	43s
Limo fare, airport-city, average	day	8.00	6/91	60c
Railway fare, light rail	one-way	1.25	93	2c
Taxi fare, airport-city, average	day	25.00	6/91	60c
Travel				
Breakfast	day	7.01	6/91	60c
Business travel	day	165.00	4/93	89r
Dinner	day	21.83	6/91	60c
Lodging	day	114.43	91	60c
Lunch	day	8.50	6/91	60c
Travel, business	day	184.51	93	88c
Utilities				
Electricity	500 KWh	53.94	4/93	16c
Electricity	KWh	0.10	4/93	16c
Electricity	mil Btu	22.46	90	64s
Electricity, exp	year	599	89	15c
Electricity, winter, 250 KWh	month	39.79	92	55c
Electricity, winter, 500 KWh	month	72.55	92	55c
Electricity, winter, 750 KWh	month	105.30	92	55c
Electricity, winter, 1000 KWh	month	138.05	92	55c
Utilities, fuels, public services, exp	year	1762	89	15c
Water, other public service, exp	year	179	89	15c

Pittsfield, MA

Item	Per	Value	Date	Ref.
Child Care				
Child care fee, average, center	hour	2.18	90	65r
Child care fee, average, nonregulated family day care	hour	1.83	90	65r
Child care fee, average, regulated family day care	hour	2.02	90	65r
Communications				
Long-distance telephone service, day, initial minute, 0-100 miles	min	0.18-0.31	91	12s
Long-distance telephone service, day, additional minute, 0-100 miles	min	0.08-0.13	91	12s
Long-distance telephone service, evenings/weekends, 0-100 mi, initial minute	min	0.67-0.12	91	12s
Long-distance telephone service, evenings/weekends, 0-100 mi, additional minute	min	0.04-0.05	91	12s
Education				
Board, 4-yr private college/university	year	2698	91	22s
Board, 4-yr public college/university	year	1741	91	22s
Expenditures, local gov't, public elementary/secondary	pupil	6687	92	20s
Room, 4-year private college/university	year	2945	91	22s
Room, 4-year public college/university	year	2144	91	22s
Tuition, 2-year private college/university	year	7750	91	22s
Tuition, 2-year public college/university	year	1528	91	22s
Tuition, 4-year private college/university	year	12446	91	22s
Tuition, 4-year public college/university, in-state	year	2580	91	22s
Energy and Fuels				
Coal	mil Btu	1.77	90	64s
Energy	mil Btu	10.57	90	64s
Energy exp/householder, 1-family unit	year	588	90	28r
Energy exp/householder, <1,000 sq ft heating area	year	477	90	28r
Energy exp/householder, 1,000-1,999 sq ft heating area	year	517	90	28r

Values are in dollars or fractions of dollars. In the column headed *Ref*, references are shown to sources. Each reference is followed by a letter. These refer to the geographical level for which data were reported: s = State, r = Region, and c = City or metro. The abbreviation *ex* is used to mean *except* or *excluding*; *exp* stands for expenditures. For other abbreviations and further explanations, please see the Introduction.

Pittsfield, MA - continued

Item	Per	Value	Date	Ref.
Energy and Fuels				
Energy exp/householder, 2,000+ sq ft heating area	year	630	90	28r
Energy exp/householder, mobile home	year	412	90	28r
Energy exp/householder, multifamily	year	498	90	28r
Gas, natural	mil Btu	5.55	90	64s
Gas, natural	000 cu ft	8.11	91	46s
Gas, natural, exp	year	741	91	46s
Gasoline, unleaded regular	mil Btu	9.53	90	64s
Entertainment				
Miniature golf admission	adult	6.18	92	1r
Miniature golf admission	child	5.14	92	1r
Waterpark admission	adult	11.00	92	1r
Waterpark admission	child	8.55	92	1r
Funerals				
Casket, 18-gauge steel, velvet interior		1853.42	91	24r
Cosmetology, hair care, etc.		98.33	91	24r
Embalming		273.94	91	24r
Facility use for ceremony		196.06	91	24r
Hearse, local		145.67	91	24r
Limousine, local		131.07	91	24r
Remains to funeral home, transfer		135.24	91	24r
Service charge, professional		843.16	91	24r
Vault, concrete, non-metallic liner		709.14	91	24r
Viewing facilities, use		229.85	91	24r
Groceries				
Apples, Red Delicious	lb	0.85	4/93	16r
Bacon	lb	2.12	4/93	16r
Bananas	lb	0.54	4/93	16r
Bread, white, pan	lb	0.81	4/93	16r
Butter	lb	2.02	4/93	16r
Carrots, short trimmed and topped	lb	0.51	4/93	16r
Chicken, fresh, whole	lb	1.04	4/93	16r
Chicken breast, bone-in	lb	2.21	4/93	16r
Chicken legs, bone-in	lb	1.16	4/93	16r
Chuck roast, USDA choice, boneless	lb	2.82	4/93	16r
Coffee, 100% ground roast, all sizes	lb	2.66	4/93	16r
Cucumbers	lb	0.85	4/93	16r
Eggs, Grade A large	doz	1.15	4/93	16r
Grapefruit	lb	0.45	4/93	16r
Grapes, Thompson Seedless	lb	1.52	4/93	16r
Ground beef, lean and extra lean	lb	2.36	4/93	16r
Ground chuck, 100% beef	lb	2.02	4/93	16r
Honey, jar	8 oz	0.96-1.75	92	5r
Honey, jar	lb	1.50-3.00	92	5r
Honey, squeeze bear	12-oz	1.50-1.99	92	5r
Ice cream, prepackaged, bulk, regular	1/2 gal	2.80	4/93	16r
Lemons	lb	0.96	4/93	16r
Lettuce, iceberg	lb	0.95	4/93	16r
Margarine, stick	lb	0.81	4/93	16r
Milk, fresh, whole, fortified	1/2 gal	1.30	4/93	16r
Oranges, navel	lb	0.56	4/93	16r
Peanut butter, creamy, all sizes	lb	1.88	4/93	16r
Pork chops, center cut, bone-in	lb	3.34	4/93	16r
Potato chips	16 oz	2.88	4/93	16r
Potatoes, white	lb	0.37	4/93	16r
Rib roast, USDA choice, bone-in	lb	4.94	4/93	16r
Round roast, USDA choice, boneless	lb	3.17	4/93	16r
Shortening, vegetable oil blends	lb	0.98	4/93	16r
Spaghetti and macaroni	lb	0.82	4/93	16r
Steak, round, graded & ungraded, ex USDA prime & choice	lb	4.04	4/93	16r
Steak, round, USDA choice, boneless	lb	3.90	4/93	16r
Steak, sirloin, USDA choice, boneless	lb	4.97	4/93	16r
Strawberries, dry pint	12 oz	0.90	4/93	16r
Sugar, white	lb	0.50	4/93	16r
Sugar, white, 33-80 oz pk	lb	0.41	4/93	16r
Tomatoes, field grown	lb	1.23	4/93	16r
Tuna, chunk, light	lb	2.22	4/93	16r
Turkey, frozen, whole	lb	1.04	4/93	16r

Pittsfield, MA - continued

Item	Per	Value	Date	Ref.
Health Care				
Childbirth, cesarean, hospital		5826	91	62r
Childbirth, cesarean, physician's fee		2053	91	62r
Childbirth, normal, hospital		2964	91	62r
Childbirth, normal, physician's fee		1492	91	62r
Health care spending, state	capita	3031	3/93	84s
Medical plan per employee	year	3958	91	45r
Mental health care, exp	capita	53.68-118.35	90	38s
Mental health care, exp, state mental health agency	capita	83.91	90	38s
Mental health care, hospital psychiatric services, non-Federal, exp	capita	22.67	88	38s
Mental health care, mental health organization, multiservice, exp	capita	36.07	88	38s
Mental health care, psychiatric hospitals, private, exp	capita	38.65	88	38s
Mental health care, psychiatric out-patient clinics, freestanding, exp	capita	4.41	88	38s
Mental health care, psychiatric partial-care organizations, freestanding, exp	capita	0.92	88	38s
Mental health care, state and county mental hospitals, exp	capita	30.59	88	38s
Mental health care, VA medical centers, exp	capita	21.14	88	38s
Substance abuse, hospital ancillary charge	incident	1310	90	70s
Substance abuse, hospital physician charge	incident	460	90	70s
Substance abuse, hospital room and board	incident	3450	90	70s
Insurance and Pensions				
Auto insurance, private passenger	year	912.83	91	63s
Taxes				
Tax, cigarette	pack	26	91	77s
Tax, gasoline	gal	21	91	77s
Taxes, state	capita	1615	91	77s
Transportation				
Driver's license fee		35.00	12/90	43s
Travel				
Business travel	day	165.00	4/93	89r
Utilities				
Electricity	mil Btu	25.93	90	64s

Plymouth, IN

Item	Per	Value	Date	Ref.
Composite ACCRA index		94.90	4Q 92	4c
Alcoholic Beverages				
Beer, Miller Lite or Budweiser, 12-oz containers	6 pack	4.08	4Q 92	4c
Liquor, J & B Scotch	750 ml	19.89	4Q 92	4c
Wine, Gallo Chablis blanc, 1.5 liter	bottle	5.70	4Q 92	4c
Clothing				
Jeans, man's denim		32.50	4Q 92	4c
Shirt, man's dress shirt		23.00	4Q 92	4c
Undervest, boy's size 10-14, cotton	3	3.48	4Q 92	4c
Communications				
Newspaper subscription, daily and Sunday home delivery, large-city	month	10.00	4Q 92	4c
Telephone bill, family of four	month	21.50	4Q 92	4c
Energy and Fuels				
Energy, combined forms, 1,800 sq ft heating area	month	104.90	4Q 92	4c
Energy, exc electricity, 1,800 sq ft heating area	month	34.50	4Q 92	4c
Gasoline, motor	gal	1.03	4Q 92	4c

Values are in dollars or fractions of dollars. In the column headed *Ref*, references are shown to sources. Each reference is followed by a letter. These refer to the geographical level for which data were reported: s=State, r=Region, and c=City or metro. The abbreviation *ex* is used to mean *except* or *excluding*; *exp* stands for expenditures. For other abbreviations and further explanations, please see the Introduction.

Plymouth, IN - continued

Item	Per	Value	Date	Ref.
Entertainment				
Bowling, evening rate	game	1.65	4Q 92	4c
Monopoly game, Parker Brothers', No. 9		12.99	4Q 92	4c
Movie	admission	6.50	4Q 92	4c
Tennis balls, yellow, Wilson or Penn, 3	can	3.01	4Q 92	4c
Goods and Services				
ACCRA Index, Miscellaneous Goods and Services		98.10	4Q 92	4c
Groceries				
ACCRA Index, Groceries		94.40	4Q 92	4c
Babyfood, strained vegetables, lowest price	4-4.5 oz jar	0.31	4Q 92	4c
Bananas	lb	0.39	4Q 92	4c
Bread, white	24 oz	0.54	4Q 92	4c
Cheese, Kraft grated Parmesan	8-oz canister	3.36	4Q 92	4c
Chicken, fryer, whole	lb	0.64	4Q 92	4c
Cigarettes, Winston	carton	15.09	4Q 92	4c
Coffee, vacuum-packed	13-oz can	2.04	4Q 92	4c
Corn, frozen	10 oz	0.65	4Q 92	4c
Corn Flakes, Kellogg's or Post Toasties	18 oz	1.69	4Q 92	4c
Eggs, Grade A large	doz	0.83	4Q 92	4c
Ground beef or hamburger	lb	1.59	4Q 92	4c
Lettuce, iceberg	head	0.86	4Q 92	4c
Margarine, Blue Bonnet or Parkay cubes	lb	0.55	4Q 92	4c
Milk, whole	1/2 gal	1.42	4Q 92	4c
Orange juice, Minute Maid frozen	12-oz can	1.57	4Q 92	4c
Peaches	29-oz can	1.21	4Q 92	4c
Peas Sweet, Del Monte or Green Giant	15-17 oz can	0.56	4Q 92	4c
Potatoes, white or red	10-lb sack	1.39	4Q 92	4c
Sausage, Jimmy Dean, 100% pork	lb	2.80	4Q 92	4c
Shortening, vegetable, Crisco	3-lb can	1.91	4Q 92	4c
Soft drink, Coca Cola	2 liter	1.51	4Q 92	4c
Steak, T-bone	lb	4.82	4Q 92	4c
Sugar, cane or beet	4 lb	1.16	4Q 92	4c
Tomatoes, Hunt's or Del Monte	14.5-oz can	0.81	4Q 92	4c
Tuna, chunk, light	6.125-6.5 oz can	0.63	4Q 92	4c
Health Care				
ACCRA Index, Health Care		92.00	4Q 92	4c
Analgesic, Aspirin, Bayer, 325 mg tablets	100	4.88	4Q 92	4c
Dentist's fee, adult teeth cleaning and periodic oral exam	visit	39.29	4Q 92	4c
Doctor's fee, routine exam, established patient	visit	29.20	4Q 92	4c
Hospital care, semiprivate room	day	411.00	4Q 92	4c
Household Goods				
Appliance repair, home, service call, washing machine	min labor charge	30.50	4Q 92	4c
Laundry detergent, Tide Ultra, Bold, or Cheer	42 oz	3.11	4Q 92	4c
Tissues, facial, Kleenex brand	175-count box	1.05	4Q 92	4c
Housing				
ACCRA Index, Housing		93.70	4Q 92	4c
House, 1,800 sq ft, 8,000 sq ft lot, new, urban	total	105875	4Q 92	4c

Plymouth, IN - continued

Item	Per	Value	Date	Ref.
Housing - continued				
House payment, principal and interest, 25% down payment	month	593	4Q 92	4c
Mortgage rate, incl. points & origination fee, 30-year fixed or adjustable rate	percent	8.20	4Q 92	4c
Rent, apartment, 2 bedrooms - 1-1/2 to 2 baths, unfurnished, 950 sq ft, water	month	423	4Q 92	4c
Personal Goods				
Shampoo, Alberto VO5	15 oz	1.31	4Q 92	4c
Toothpaste, Crest or Colgate	6-7 oz	1.94	4Q 92	4c
Personal Services				
Dry cleaning, man's 2-piece suit		6.50	4Q 92	4c
Haircare, woman's shampoo, trim and blow-dry		13.88	4Q 92	4c
Haircut, man's barbershop, no styling		7.20	4Q 92	4c
Restaurant Food				
Chicken, fried, thigh and drumstick		1.90	4Q 92	4c
Hamburger with cheese	1/4 lb	1.69	4Q 92	4c
Pizza, Pizza Hut or Pizza Inn, cheese, thin crust	12-13 in	6.35	4Q 92	4c
Transportation				
ACCRA Index, Transportation		86.70	4Q 92	4c
Tire balance, computer or spin balance, front	wheel	5.33	4Q 92	4c
Utilities				
ACCRA Index, Utilities		97.50	4Q 92	4c
Electricity, partial electric and other energy, 1,800 sq ft living area new home	month	70.40	4Q 92	4c

Pocatello, ID

Item	Per	Value	Date	Ref.
Composite ACCRA index		95.40	4Q 92	4c
Alcoholic Beverages				
Beer, Miller Lite or Budweiser, 12-oz containers	6 pack	3.78	4Q 92	4c
Liquor, J & B Scotch	750 ml	18.15	4Q 92	4c
Wine, Gallo Chablis blanc, 1.5 liter	bottle	5.24	4Q 92	4c
Clothing				
Jeans, man's denim		28.86	4Q 92	4c
Shirt, man's dress shirt		21.16	4Q 92	4c
Undervest, boy's size 10-14, cotton	3	4.67	4Q 92	4c
Communications				
Newspaper subscription, daily and Sunday home delivery, large-city	month	10.17	4Q 92	4c
Telephone, flat rate	month	11.04	91	11c
Telephone bill, family of four	month	16.32	4Q 92	4c
Energy and Fuels				
Energy, combined forms, 1,800 sq ft heating area	month	83.69	4Q 92	4c
Gasoline, motor	gal	1.21	4Q 92	4c
Entertainment				
Bowling, evening rate	game	1.68	4Q 92	4c
Monopoly game, Parker Brothers', No. 9		14.99	4Q 92	4c
Movie	admission	5.00	4Q 92	4c
Tennis balls, yellow, Wilson or Penn, 3	can	2.52	4Q 92	4c
Goods and Services				
ACCRA Index, Miscellaneous Goods and Services		98.90	4Q 92	4c
Groceries				
ACCRA Index, Groceries		94.40	4Q 92	4c
Babyfood, strained vegetables, lowest price	4-4.5 oz jar	0.31	4Q 92	4c
Bananas	lb	0.34	4Q 92	4c
Bread, white	24 oz	0.64	4Q 92	4c

Pocatello, ID - continued

Item	Per	Value	Date	Ref.
Groceries				
Cheese, Kraft grated Parmesan	8-oz canister	3.92	4Q 92	4c
Chicken, fryer, whole	lb	0.79	4Q 92	4c
Cigarettes, Winston	carton	17.48	4Q 92	4c
Coffee, vacuum-packed	13-oz can	2.22	4Q 92	4c
Corn, frozen	10 oz	0.48	4Q 92	4c
Corn Flakes, Kellogg's or Post Toasties	18 oz	1.87	4Q 92	4c
Eggs, Grade A large	doz	0.56	4Q 92	4c
Ground beef or hamburger	lb	1.32	4Q 92	4c
Lettuce, iceberg	head	0.53	4Q 92	4c
Margarine, Blue Bonnet or Parkay cubes	lb	0.52	4Q 92	4c
Milk, whole	1/2 gal	1.53	4Q 92	4c
Orange juice, Minute Maid frozen	12-oz can	1.58	4Q 92	4c
Peaches	29-oz can	1.19	4Q 92	4c
Peas Sweet, Del Monte or Green Giant	15-17 oz can	0.49	4Q 92	4c
Potatoes, white or red	10-lb sack	0.83	4Q 92	4c
Sausage, Jimmy Dean, 100% pork	lb	3.20	4Q 92	4c
Shortening, vegetable, Crisco	3-lb can	2.38	4Q 92	4c
Soft drink, Coca Cola	2 liter	1.19	4Q 92	4c
Steak, T-bone	lb	3.29	4Q 92	4c
Sugar, cane or beet	4 lb	1.57	4Q 92	4c
Tomatoes, Hunt's or Del Monte	14.5-oz can	0.66	4Q 92	4c
Tuna, chunk, light	6.125-6.5 oz can	0.57	4Q 92	4c
Health Care				
ACCRA Index, Health Care		99.10	4Q 92	4c
Analgesic, Aspirin, Bayer, 325 mg tablets	100	5.26	4Q 92	4c
Dentist's fee, adult teeth cleaning and periodic oral exam	visit	43.75	4Q 92	4c
Doctor's fee, routine exam, established patient	visit	35.33	4Q 92	4c
Hospital care, semiprivate room	day	245.00	90	27c
Hospital care, semiprivate room	day	360.00	4Q 92	4c
Household Goods				
Appliance repair, home, service call, washing machine	min labor charge	30.50	4Q 92	4c
Laundry detergent, Tide Ultra, Bold, or Cheer	42 oz	4.29	4Q 92	4c
Tissues, facial, Kleenex brand	175-count box	0.91	4Q 92	4c
Housing				
ACCRA Index, Housing		95.20	4Q 92	4c
House, 1,800 sq ft, 8,000 sq ft lot, new, urban	total	106770	4Q 92	4c
House payment, principal and interest, 25% down payment	month	591	4Q 92	4c
Mortgage rate, incl. points & origination fee, 30-year fixed or adjustable rate	percent	8.06	4Q 92	4c
Personal Goods				
Shampoo, Alberto VO5	15 oz	1.60	4Q 92	4c
Toothpaste, Crest or Colgate	6-7 oz	1.86	4Q 92	4c
Personal Services				
Dry cleaning, man's 2-piece suit		6.30	4Q 92	4c
Haircare, woman's shampoo, trim and blow-dry		16.50	4Q 92	4c
Haircut, man's barbershop, no styling		6.67	4Q 92	4c

Pocatello, ID - continued

Item	Per	Value	Date	Ref.
Restaurant Food				
Chicken, fried, thigh and drumstick		1.80	4Q 92	4c
Hamburger with cheese	1/4 lb	1.89	4Q 92	4c
Pizza, Pizza Hut or Pizza Inn, cheese, thin crust	12-13 in	8.95	4Q 92	4c
Transportation				
ACCRA Index, Transportation		99.70	4Q 92	4c
Tire balance, computer or spin balance, front	wheel	6.00	4Q 92	4c
Utilities				
ACCRA Index, Utilities		77.40	4Q 92	4c
Electricity, all electric, 1,800 sq ft living area new home	month	83.69	4Q 92	4c

Poplar Bluff, MO

Item	Per	Value	Date	Ref.
Composite ACCRA index		84.60	4Q 92	4c
Alcoholic Beverages				
Beer, Miller Lite or Budweiser, 12-oz containers	6 pack	3.69	4Q 92	4c
Liquor, J & B Scotch	750 ml	14.61	4Q 92	4c
Wine, Gallo Chablis blanc, 1.5 liter	bottle	4.74	4Q 92	4c
Clothing				
Jeans, man's denim		27.63	4Q 92	4c
Shirt, man's dress shirt		22.50	4Q 92	4c
Undervest, boy's size 10-14, cotton	3	3.74	4Q 92	4c
Communications				
Newspaper subscription, daily and Sunday home delivery, large-city	month	12.55	4Q 92	4c
Telephone, flat rate	month	9.10	91	11c
Telephone bill, family of four	month	16.78	4Q 92	4c
Energy and Fuels				
Energy, combined forms, 1,800 sq ft heating area	month	79.06	4Q 92	4c
Gasoline, motor	gal	1.04	4Q 92	4c
Entertainment				
Bowling, evening rate	game	1.83	4Q 92	4c
Monopoly game, Parker Brothers', No. 9		9.97	4Q 92	4c
Movie	admission	1.50	4Q 92	4c
Tennis balls, yellow, Wilson or Penn, 3	can	2.07	4Q 92	4c
Goods and Services				
ACCRA Index, Miscellaneous Goods and Services		86.30	4Q 92	4c
Groceries				
ACCRA Index, Groceries		98.30	4Q 92	4c
Babyfood, strained vegetables, lowest price	4-4.5 oz jar	0.37	4Q 92	4c
Bananas	lb	0.56	4Q 92	4c
Bread, white	24 oz	0.46	4Q 92	4c
Cheese, Kraft grated Parmesan	8-oz canister	3.54	4Q 92	4c
Chicken, fryer, whole	lb	0.59	4Q 92	4c
Cigarettes, Winston	carton	16.48	4Q 92	4c
Coffee, vacuum-packed	13-oz can	2.04	4Q 92	4c
Corn, frozen	10 oz	0.80	4Q 92	4c
Corn Flakes, Kellogg's or Post Toasties	18 oz	2.32	4Q 92	4c
Eggs, Grade A large	doz	0.82	4Q 92	4c
Ground beef or hamburger	lb	1.14	4Q 92	4c
Lettuce, iceberg	head	1.02	4Q 92	4c
Margarine, Blue Bonnet or Parkay cubes	lb	0.67	4Q 92	4c
Milk, whole	1/2 gal	1.48	4Q 92	4c
Orange juice, Minute Maid frozen	12-oz can	1.34	4Q 92	4c
Peaches	29-oz can	1.47	4Q 92	4c

Values are in dollars or fractions of dollars. In the column headed *Ref*, references are shown to sources. Each reference is followed by a letter. These refer to the geographical level for which data were reported: s=State, r=Region, and c=City or metro. The abbreviation *ex* is used to mean *except* or *excluding*; *exp* stands for *expenditures*. For other abbreviations and further explanations, please see the Introduction.

Poplar Bluff, MO - continued

Item	Per	Value	Date	Ref.
Groceries				
Peas Sweet, Del Monte or Green Giant	15-17 oz can	0.61	4Q 92	4c
Potatoes, white or red	10-lb sack	2.39	4Q 92	4c
Sausage, Jimmy Dean, 100% pork	lb	2.71	4Q 92	4c
Shortening, vegetable, Crisco	3-lb can	2.35	4Q 92	4c
Soft drink, Coca Cola	2 liter	1.32	4Q 92	4c
Steak, T-bone	lb	5.42	4Q 92	4c
Sugar, cane or beet	4 lb	1.44	4Q 92	4c
Tomatoes, Hunt's or Del Monte	14.5-oz can	0.83	4Q 92	4c
Tuna, chunk, light	6.125-6.5 oz can	0.62	4Q 92	4c
Health Care				
ACCRA Index, Health Care		83.30	4Q 92	4c
Analgesic, Aspirin, Bayer, 325 mg tablets	100	4.42	4Q 92	4c
Dentist's fee, adult teeth cleaning and periodic oral exam	visit	41.67	4Q 92	4c
Doctor's fee, routine exam, established patient	visit	30.00	4Q 92	4c
Hospital care, semiprivate room	day	232.50	4Q 92	4c
Household Goods				
Appliance repair, home, service call, washing machine	min labor charge	21.67	4Q 92	4c
Laundry detergent, Tide Ultra, Bold, or Cheer	42 oz	3.32	4Q 92	4c
Tissues, facial, Kleenex brand	175-count box	1.26	4Q 92	4c
Housing				
ACCRA Index, Housing		76.70	4Q 92	4c
House, 1,800 sq ft, 8,000 sq ft lot, new, urban	total	84950	4Q 92	4c
House payment, principal and interest, 25% down payment	month	476	4Q 92	4c
Mortgage rate, incl. points & origination fee, 30-year fixed or adjustable rate	per-cent	8.21	4Q 92	4c
Personal Goods				
Shampoo, Alberto VO5	15 oz	1.05	4Q 92	4c
Toothpaste, Crest or Colgate	6-7 oz	1.52	4Q 92	4c
Personal Services				
Dry cleaning, man's 2-piece suit		5.08	4Q 92	4c
Haircare, woman's shampoo, trim and blow-dry		15.48	4Q 92	4c
Haircut, man's barbershop, no styling		7.98	4Q 92	4c
Restaurant Food				
Chicken, fried, thigh and drumstick		1.99	4Q 92	4c
Hamburger with cheese	1/4 lb	1.86	4Q 92	4c
Pizza, Pizza Hut or Pizza Inn, cheese, thin crust	12-13 in	7.77	4Q 92	4c
Transportation				
ACCRA Index, Transportation		93.50	4Q 92	4c
Tire balance, computer or spin balance, front	wheel	6.17	4Q 92	4c
Utilities				
ACCRA Index, Utilities		73.80	4Q 92	4c
Electricity, all electric, 1,800 sq ft living area new home	month	79.06	4Q 92	4c

Portland, ME

Item	Per	Value	Date	Ref.
Child Care				
Child care fee, average, center	hour	2.18	90	65r
Child care fee, average, nonregulated family day care	hour	1.83	90	65r
Child care fee, average, regulated family day care	hour	2.02	90	65r
Communications				
Long-distance telephone service, day, initial minute, 0-100 miles	min	0.19-0.64	91	12s
Long-distance telephone service, day, additional minute, 0-100 miles	min	0.15-0.40	91	12s
Long-distance telephone service, evenings/weekends, 0-100 mi, initial minute	min	0.08-0.26	91	12s
Long-distance telephone service, evenings/weekends, 0-100 mi, additional minute	min	0.80-0.16	91	12s
Telephone, flat rate	month	12.46	91	11c
Telephone, residential, private line, rotary, unlimited calling	month	17.43	10/91	78c
Education				
Board, 4-yr private college/university	year	2441	91	22s
Board, 4-yr public college/university	year	1855	91	22s
Expenditures, local gov't, public elementary/secondary	pupil	5969	92	20s
Room, 4-year private college/university	year	2344	91	22s
Room, 4-year public college/university	year	1886	91	22s
Tuition, 2-year private college/university	year	3899	91	22s
Tuition, 2-year public college/university	year	1497	91	22s
Tuition, 4-year private college/university	year	10928	91	22s
Tuition, 4-year public college/university, in-state	year	2263	91	22s
Energy and Fuels				
Coal	mil Btu	2.72	90	64s
Energy	mil Btu	9.54	90	64s
Energy exp/householder, 1-family unit	year	588	90	28r
Energy exp/householder, <1,000 sq ft heating area	year	477	90	28r
Energy exp/householder, 1,000-1,999 sq ft heating area	year	517	90	28r
Energy exp/householder, 2,000+ sq ft heating area	year	630	90	28r
Energy exp/householder, mobile home	year	412	90	28r
Energy exp/householder, multifamily	year	498	90	28r
Gas, cooking, 10 therms	month	9.60	92	56c
Gas, cooking, 30 therms	month	24.70	92	56c
Gas, cooking, 50 therms	month	39.80	92	56c
Gas, heating, winter, 100 therms	month	70.72	92	56c
Gas, heating, winter, average use	month	99.78	92	56c
Gas, natural	mil Btu	6.05	90	64s
Gas, natural	000 cu ft	6.86	91	46s
Gas, natural, exp	year	399	91	46s
Gasoline, unleaded premium	gal	61.65-73.30	12/92	31c
Gasoline, unleaded regular	mil Btu	9.74	90	64s
Entertainment				
Miniature golf admission	adult	6.18	92	1r
Miniature golf admission	child	5.14	92	1r
Waterpark admission	adult	11.00	92	1r
Waterpark admission	child	8.55	92	1r
Funerals				
Casket, 18-gauge steel, velvet interior		1853.42	91	24r
Cosmetology, hair care, etc.		98.33	91	24r
Embalming		273.94	91	24r
Facility use for ceremony		196.06	91	24r
Hearse, local		145.67	91	24r
Limousine, local		131.07	91	24r
Remains to funeral home, transfer		135.24	91	24r
Service charge, professional		843.16	91	24r
Vault, concrete, non-metallic liner		709.14	91	24r
Viewing facilities, use		229.85	91	24r

Values are in dollars or fractions of dollars. In the column headed *Ref*, references are shown to sources. Each reference is followed by a letter. These refer to the geographical level for which data were reported: s = State, r = Region, and c = City or metro. The abbreviation *ex* is used to mean *except* or *excluding*; *exp* stands for expenditures. For other abbreviations and further explanations, please see the Introduction.

Portland, ME - continued

Item	Per	Value	Date	Ref.
Groceries				
Apples, Red Delicious	lb	0.85	4/93	16r
Bacon	lb	2.12	4/93	16r
Bananas	lb	0.54	4/93	16r
Bread, white, pan	lb	0.81	4/93	16r
Butter	lb	2.02	4/93	16r
Carrots, short trimmed and topped	lb	0.51	4/93	16r
Chicken, fresh, whole	lb	1.04	4/93	16r
Chicken breast, bone-in	lb	2.21	4/93	16r
Chicken legs, bone-in	lb	1.16	4/93	16r
Chuck roast, USDA choice, boneless	lb	2.82	4/93	16r
Coffee, 100% ground roast, all sizes	lb	2.66	4/93	16r
Cucumbers	lb	0.85	4/93	16r
Eggs, Grade A large	doz	1.15	4/93	16r
Grapefruit	lb	0.45	4/93	16r
Grapes, Thompson Seedless	lb	1.52	4/93	16r
Ground beef, lean and extra lean	lb	2.36	4/93	16r
Ground chuck, 100% beef	lb	2.02	4/93	16r
Honey, jar	8 oz	0.96-1.75	92	5r
Honey, jar	lb	1.50-3.00	92	5r
Honey, squeeze bear	12-oz	1.50-1.99	92	5r
Ice cream, prepackaged, bulk, regular	1/2 gal	2.80	4/93	16r
Lemons	lb	0.96	4/93	16r
Lettuce, iceberg	lb	0.95	4/93	16r
Margarine, stick	lb	0.81	4/93	16r
Milk, fresh, whole, fortified	1/2 gal	1.30	4/93	16r
Oranges, navel	lb	0.56	4/93	16r
Peanut butter, creamy, all sizes	lb	1.88	4/93	16r
Pork chops, center cut, bone-in	lb	3.34	4/93	16r
Potato chips	16 oz	2.88	4/93	16r
Potatoes, white	lb	0.37	4/93	16r
Rib roast, USDA choice, bone-in	lb	4.94	4/93	16r
Round roast, USDA choice, boneless	lb	3.17	4/93	16r
Shortening, vegetable oil blends	lb	0.98	4/93	16r
Spaghetti and macaroni	lb	0.82	4/93	16r
Steak, round, graded & ungraded, ex USDA prime & choice	lb	4.04	4/93	16r
Steak, round, USDA choice, boneless	lb	3.90	4/93	16r
Steak, sirloin, USDA choice, boneless	lb	4.97	4/93	16r
Strawberries, dry pint	12 oz	0.90	4/93	16r
Sugar, white	lb	0.50	4/93	16r
Sugar, white, 33-80 oz pk	lb	0.41	4/93	16r
Tomatoes, field grown	lb	1.23	4/93	16r
Tuna, chunk, light	lb	2.22	4/93	16r
Turkey, frozen, whole	lb	1.04	4/93	16r
Health Care				
Childbirth, cesarean, hospital		5826	91	62r
Childbirth, cesarean, physician's fee		2053	91	62r
Childbirth, normal, hospital		2964	91	62r
Childbirth, normal, physician's fee		1492	91	62r
Hospital care, semiprivate room	day	349.99	90	27c
Medical insurance premium, per employee, small group comprehensive	month	299.30	10/91	25c
Medical plan per employee	year	3958	91	45r
Mental health care, exp	capita	53.68-118.35	90	38s
Mental health care, exp, state mental health agency	capita	67.29	90	38s
Mental health care, hospital psychiatric services, non-Federal, exp	capita	16.12	88	38s
Mental health care, mental health organization, multiservice, exp	capita	17.98	88	38s
Mental health care, psychiatric hospitals, private, exp	capita	7.97	88	38s
Mental health care, psychiatric out-patient clinics, freestanding, exp	capita	1.60	88	38s
Mental health care, psychiatric partial-care organizations, freestanding, exp	capita	0.38	88	38s
Mental health care, state and county mental hospitals, exp	capita	29.80	88	38s
Mental health care, VA medical centers, exp	capita	8.16	88	38s
Prescription drug co-pay, Medicaid	month	3.00-5.00	91	21s

Portland, ME - continued

Item	Per	Value	Date	Ref.
Health Care - continued				
Substance abuse, hospital ancillary charge	incident	840	90	70s
Substance abuse, hospital physician charge	incident	170	90	70s
Substance abuse, hospital room and board	incident	4720	90	70s
Housing				
Rental unit, 1 bedroom	month	577	93	23c
Rental unit, 2 bedroom	month	731	93	23c
Rental unit, 3 bedroom	month	819	93	23c
Rental unit, 4 bedroom	month	984	93	23c
Rental unit, efficiency	month	454	93	23c
Insurance and Pensions				
Auto insurance, private passenger	year	558.21	91	63s
Taxes				
Tax, cigarette	pack	37	91	77s
Tax, gasoline	gal	19	91	77s
Taxes, state	capita	1262	91	77s
Transportation				
Auto rental, average	day	44.00	6/91	60c
Driver's license fee		18.00	12/90	43s
Taxi fare, airport-city, average	day	8.00	6/91	60c
Vehicle registration and license plate	year	22.00	93	61s
Travel				
Business travel	day	165.00	4/93	89r
Lodging	day	142.69	91	60c
Utilities				
Electricity	mil Btu	22.42	90	64s
Electricity, winter, 250 KWh	month	24.86	92	55c
Electricity, winter, 500 KWh	month	52.22	92	55c
Electricity, winter, 750 KWh	month	83.32	92	55c
Electricity, winter, 1000 KWh	month	114.43	92	55c

Portland, OR

Item	Per	Value	Date	Ref.
Composite ACCRA index		110.60	4Q 92	4c
Alcoholic Beverages				
Beer, Miller Lite or Budweiser, 12-oz containers	6 pack	3.93	4Q 92	4c
Liquor, J & B Scotch	750 ml	20.05	4Q 92	4c
Wine, Gallo Chablis blanc, 1.5 liter	bottle	4.78	4Q 92	4c
Child Care				
Child care fee, average, center	hour	1.71	90	65r
Child care fee, average, nonregulated family day care	hour	1.32	90	65r
Child care fee, average, regulated family day care	hour	1.86	90	65r
Clothing				
Jeans, man's denim		27.17	4Q 92	4c
Shirt, man's dress shirt		23.80	4Q 92	4c
Undervest, boy's size 10-14, cotton	3	4.29	4Q 92	4c
Communications				
Long-distance telephone service, day, initial minute, 0-100 miles	min	0.13-0.26	91	12s
Long-distance telephone service, day, additional minute, 0-100 miles	min	0.10-0.21	91	12s
Long-distance telephone service, evenings/weekends, 0-100 mi, initial minute	min	0.07-0.13	91	12s
Long-distance telephone service, evenings/weekends, 0-100 mi, additional minute	min	0.04-0.07	91	12s
Newspaper subscription, daily and Sunday home delivery, large-city	month	11.96	4Q 92	4c
Telephone, flat rate	month	13.68	91	11c
Telephone, residential, private line, rotary, unlimited calling	month	21.76	10/91	78c
Telephone bill, family of four	month	22.42	4Q 92	4c

Values are in dollars or fractions of dollars. In the column headed *Ref*, references are shown to sources. Each reference is followed by a letter. These refer to the geographical level for which data were reported: s=State, r=Region, and c=City or metro. The abbreviation *ex* is used to mean *except* or *excluding*; *exp* stands for expenditures. For other abbreviations and further explanations, please see the Introduction.

Portland, OR - continued

Item	Per	Value	Date	Ref.
Education				
Board, 4-yr private college/university	year	2004	91	22s
Board, 4-yr public college/university	year	1954	91	22s
Expenditures, local gov't, public elementary/secondary	pupil	5463	92	20s
Room, 4-year private college/university	year	1621	91	22s
Room, 4-year public college/university	year	1329	91	22s
Tuition, 2-year private college/university	year	7570	91	22s
Tuition, 2-year public college/university	year	794	91	22s
Tuition, 4-year private college/university	year	9606	91	22s
Tuition, 4-year public college/university, in-state	year	1906	91	22s
Energy and Fuels				
Coal	mil Btu	1.22	90	64s
Energy	mil Btu	8.39	90	64s
Energy, combined forms, 1,800 sq ft heating area	month	74.04	4Q 92	4c
Energy, exc electricity, 1,800 sq ft heating area	month	39.03	4Q 92	4c
Energy exp/householder, 1-family unit	year	362	90	28r
Energy exp/householder, <1,000 sq ft heating area	year	254	90	28r
Energy exp/householder, 1,000-1,999 sq ft heating area	year	358	90	28r
Energy exp/householder, 2,000+ sq ft heating area	year	467	90	28r
Energy exp/householder, mobile home	year	390	90	28r
Energy exp/householder, multifamily	year	252	90	28r
Gas, cooking, winter, 10 therms	month	8.58	92	56c
Gas, cooking, winter, 30 therms	month	19.73	92	56c
Gas, cooking, winter, 50 therms	month	30.88	92	56c
Gas, heating, winter, 100 therms	month	58.76	92	56c
Gas, heating, winter, average use	month	55.97	92	56c
Gas, natural	mil Btu	4.28	90	64s
Gas, natural	000 cu ft	6.13	91	46s
Gas, natural, exp	year	429	91	46s
Gasoline, motor	gal	1.28	4Q 92	4c
Gasoline, unleaded regular	mil Btu	9.45	90	64s
Entertainment				
Bowling, evening rate	game	2.08	4Q 92	4c
Miniature golf admission	adult	6.18	92	1r
Miniature golf admission	child	5.14	92	1r
Monopoly game, Parker Brothers', No. 9		11.19	4Q 92	4c
Movie	admission	5.88	4Q 92	4c
Tennis balls, yellow, Wilson or Penn, 3	can	2.53	4Q 92	4c
Waterpark admission	adult	11.00	92	1r
Waterpark admission	child	8.55	92	1r
Funerals				
Casket, 18-gauge steel, velvet interior		1781.09	91	24r
Cosmetology, hair care, etc.		84.64	91	24r
Embalming		207.41	91	24r
Facility use for ceremony		205.76	91	24r
Hearse, local		105.14	91	24r
Limousine, local		83.21	91	24r
Remains to funeral home, transfer		113.82	91	24r
Service charge, professional		626.33	91	24r
Vault, concrete, non-metallic liner		599.54	91	24r
Viewing facilities, use		85.81	91	24r
Goods and Services				
ACCRA Index, Miscellaneous Goods and Services		105.10	4Q 92	4c
Groceries				
ACCRA Index, Groceries		104.20	4Q 92	4c
Apples, Red Delicious	lb	0.80	4/93	16r
Babyfood, strained vegetables, lowest price	4-4.5 oz jar	0.31	4Q 92	4c
Bacon	lb	1.79	4/93	16r
Bananas	lb	0.40	4Q 92	4c

Portland, OR - continued

Item	Per	Value	Date	Ref.
Groceries - continued				
Bananas	lb	0.53	4/93	16r
Bologna, all beef or mixed	lb	2.67	4/93	16r
Bread, white	24 oz	0.66	4Q 92	4c
Bread, white, pan	lb	0.81	4/93	16r
Carrots, short trimmed and topped	lb	0.39	4/93	16r
Cheese, Kraft grated Parmesan	8-oz canister	3.44	4Q 92	4c
Chicken, fresh, whole	lb	0.94	4/93	16r
Chicken, fryer, whole	lb	0.90	4Q 92	4c
Chicken breast, bone-in	lb	2.19	4/93	16r
Chuck roast, graded and ungraded, ex USDA prime and choice	lb	2.26	4/93	16r
Cigarettes, Winston	carton	17.77	4Q 92	4c
Coffee, 100% ground roast, all sizes	lb	2.33	4/93	16r
Coffee, vacuum-packed	13-oz can	2.54	4Q 92	4c
Corn, frozen	10 oz	0.69	4Q 92	4c
Corn Flakes, Kellogg's or Post Toasties	18 oz	2.09	4Q 92	4c
Eggs, Grade A large	doz	0.93	4Q 92	4c
Eggs, Grade AA large	doz	1.18	4/93	16r
Flour, white, all purpose	lb	0.22	4/93	16r
Grapefruit	lb	0.52	4/93	16r
Grapes, Thompson Seedless	lb	1.50	4/93	16r
Ground beef, 100% beef	lb	1.44	4/93	16r
Ground beef, lean and extra lean	lb	2.34	4/93	16r
Ground beef or hamburger	lb	1.67	4Q 92	4c
Ham, boneless, excluding canned	lb	2.56	4/93	16r
Honey, jar	8 oz	0.89-1.00	92	5r
Honey, jar	lb	1.35-1.97	92	5r
Honey, squeeze bear	12-oz	1.19-1.50	92	5r
Ice cream, prepackaged, bulk, regular	1/2 gal	2.40	4/93	16r
Lemons	lb	0.81	4/93	16r
Lettuce, iceberg	head	0.95	4Q 92	4c
Lettuce, iceberg	lb	0.84	4/93	16r
Margarine, Blue Bonnet or Parkay cubes	lb	0.58	4Q 92	4c
Margarine, stick	lb	0.81	4/93	16r
Milk, whole	1/2 gal	1.35	4Q 92	4c
Orange juice, Minute Maid frozen	12-oz can	1.23	4Q 92	4c
Oranges, navel	lb	0.48	4/93	16r
Peaches	29-oz can	1.58	4Q 92	4c
Peas Sweet, Del Monte or Green Giant	15-17 oz can	0.72	4Q 92	4c
Pork chops, center cut, bone-in	lb	3.25	4/93	16r
Potato chips	16 oz	2.89	4/93	16r
Potatoes, white	lb	0.38	4/93	16r
Potatoes, white or red	10-lb sack	1.69	4Q 92	4c
Round roast, graded & ungraded, ex USDA prime & choice	lb	3.00	4/93	16r
Round roast, USDA choice, boneless	lb	3.16	4/93	16r
Sausage, Jimmy Dean, 100% pork	lb	3.43	4Q 92	4c
Shortening, vegetable oil blends	lb	0.86	4/93	16r
Shortening, vegetable, Crisco	3-lb can	2.07	4Q 92	4c
Soft drink, Coca Cola	2 liter	1.31	4Q 92	4c
Spaghetti and macaroni	lb	0.84	4/93	16r
Steak, round, graded & ungraded, ex USDA prime & choice	lb	3.34	4/93	16r
Steak, round, USDA choice, boneless	lb	3.24	4/93	16r
Steak, sirloin, graded & ungraded, ex USDA prime & choice	lb	3.75	4/93	16r
Steak, sirloin, USDA choice, boneless	lb	4.49	4/93	16r
Steak, T-bone	lb	4.93	4Q 92	4c
Sugar, cane or beet	4 lb	1.32	4Q 92	4c
Sugar, white	lb	0.41	4/93	16r
Sugar, white, 33-80 oz pk	lb	0.38	4/93	16r
Tomatoes, field grown	lb	1.01	4/93	16r
Tomatoes, Hunt's or Del Monte	14.5-oz can	0.66	4Q 92	4c

Values are in dollars or fractions of dollars. In the column headed *Ref*, references are shown to sources. Each reference is followed by a letter. These refer to the geographical level for which data were reported: s = State, r = Region, and c = City or metro. The abbreviation *ex* is used to mean *except* or *excluding*; *exp* stands for expenditures. For other abbreviations and further explanations, please see the Introduction.

Portland, OR - continued

Item	Per	Value	Date	Ref.
Groceries				
Tuna, chunk, light	6.125-6.5 oz can	0.54	4Q 92	4c
Turkey, frozen, whole	lb	1.04	4/93	16r
Health Care				
ACCRA Index, Health Care		131.10	4Q 92	4c
Analgesic, Aspirin, Bayer, 325 mg tablets	100	5.37	4Q 92	4c
Childbirth, cesarean, hospital		5533	91	62r
Childbirth, cesarean, physician's fee		2053	91	62r
Childbirth, normal, hospital		2745	91	62r
Childbirth, normal, physician's fee		1492	91	62r
Dentist's fee, adult teeth cleaning and periodic oral exam	visit	68.20	4Q 92	4c
Doctor's fee, routine exam, established patient	visit	44.25	4Q 92	4c
Hospital care, semiprivate room	day	384.53	90	27c
Hospital care, semiprivate room	day	441.07	4Q 92	4c
Medical insurance premium, per employee, small group comprehensive	month	313.90	10/91	25c
Medical plan per employee	year	3421	91	45r
Mental health care, exp, state mental health agency	capita	40.68	90	38s
Mental health care, hospital psychiatric services, non-Federal, exp	capita	9.91	88	38s
Mental health care, mental health organization, multiservice, exp	capita	25.94	88	38s
Mental health care, psychiatric hospitals, private, exp	capita	1.48	88	38s
Mental health care, psychiatric out-patient clinics, freestanding, exp	capita	3.50	88	38s
Mental health care, psychiatric partial-care organizations, freestanding, exp	capita	0.58	88	38s
Mental health care, state and county mental hospitals, exp	capita	18.67	88	38s
Mental health care, VA medical centers, exp	capita	2.53	88	38s
Physician fee, family practice, first-visit		111.00	91	62r
Physician fee, family practice, revisit		45.00	91	62r
Physician fee, general practice, first-visit		100.00	91	62r
Physician fee, general practice, revisit		40.00	91	62r
Physician fee, internal medicine, first-visit		137.00	91	62r
Physician fee, internal medicine, revisit		48.00	91	62r
Physician fee, median, neurosurgeon, first-visit		157.00	91	62r
Physician fee, median, nonsurgical specialist, first-visit		131.00	91	62r
Physician fee, median, orthopedic surgeon, first-visit		124.00	91	62r
Physician fee, median, plastic surgeon, first-visit		88.00	91	62r
Physician fee, median, surgical specialist, first-visit		100.00	91	62r
Physician fee, neurosurgeon, revisit		51.00	91	62r
Physician fee, nonsurgical specialist, revisit		47.00	91	62r
Physician fee, obstetrics/gynecology, first-visit		95.00	91	62r
Physician fee, obstetrics/gynecology, revisit		50.00	91	62r
Physician fee, orthopedic surgeon, revisit		51.00	91	62r
Physician fee, pediatrician, first-visit		81.00	91	62r
Physician fee, pediatrician, revisit		42.00	91	62r
Physician fee, plastic surgeon, revisit		48.00	91	62r
Physician fee, surgical specialist, revisit		49.00	91	62r
Substance abuse, hospital ancillary charge	incident	710	90	70s
Substance abuse, hospital physician charge	incident	70	90	70s
Substance abuse, hospital room and board	incident	3330	90	70s
Household Goods				
Appliance repair, home, service call, washing machine	min labor charge	36.18	4Q 92	4c

Portland, OR - continued

Item	Per	Value	Date	Ref.
Household Goods - continued				
Laundry detergent, Tide Ultra, Bold, or Cheer	42 oz	3.75	4Q 92	4c
Tissues, facial, Kleenex brand	175-count box	1.41	4Q 92	4c
Housing				
ACCRA Index, Housing		129.10	4Q 92	4c
Home, median price	unit	97.70		26c
House, 1,800 sq ft, 8,000 sq ft lot, new, urban	total	141950	4Q 92	4c
House payment, principal and interest, 25% down payment	month	788	4Q 92	4c
Mortgage rate, incl. points & origination fee, 30-year fixed or adjustable rate	percent	8.09	4Q 92	4c
Rent, apartment, 2 bedrooms - 1-1/2 to 2 baths, unfurnished, 950 sq ft, water	month	650	4Q 92	4c
Rental unit, 1 bedroom	month	435	93	23c
Rental unit, 2 bedroom	month	512	93	23c
Rental unit, 3 bedroom	month	676	93	23c
Rental unit, 4 bedroom	month	748	93	23c
Rental unit, efficiency	month	358	93	23c
Insurance and Pensions				
Auto insurance, private passenger	year	598.04	91	63s
Personal Goods				
Shampoo, Alberto VO5	15 oz	1.40	4Q 92	4c
Toothpaste, Crest or Colgate	6-7 oz	2.27	4Q 92	4c
Personal Services				
Dry cleaning, man's 2-piece suit		7.86	4Q 92	4c
Haircare, woman's shampoo, trim and blow-dry		19.39	4Q 92	4c
Haircut, man's barbershop, no styling		8.10	4Q 92	4c
Restaurant Food				
Chicken, fried, thigh and drumstick		2.30	4Q 92	4c
Hamburger with cheese	1/4 lb	1.95	4Q 92	4c
Pizza, Pizza Hut or Pizza Inn, cheese, thin crust	12-13 in	8.99	4Q 92	4c
Taxes				
Tax, cigarette	pack	28	91	77s
Tax, gasoline	gal	22	91	77s
Taxes, state	capita	1037	91	77s
Transportation				
ACCRA Index, Transportation		110.80	4Q 92	4c
Auto rental, average	day	44.50	6/91	60c
Bus fare	one-way	0.60	3/93	2c
Bus fare, up to 10 miles	one-way	1.25	4Q 92	4c
Driver's license fee		15.00	12/90	43s
Limo fare, airport-city, average	day	6.00	6/91	60c
Railway fare, light rail	one-way	0.95	93	2c
Taxi fare, airport-city, average	day	20.50	6/91	60c
Tire balance, computer or spin balance, front	wheel	6.55	4Q 92	4c
Vehicle registration and license plate	year	32.50	93	53s
Travel				
Breakfast	day	4.66	6/91	60c
Business travel	day	178.00	4/93	89r
Dinner	day	16.66	6/91	60c
Lodging	day	105.71	91	60c
Lunch	day	7.27	6/91	60c
Utilities				
ACCRA Index, Utilities		72.60	4Q 92	4c
Electricity	mil Btu	12.25	90	64s
Electricity, partial electric and other energy, 1,800 sq ft living area new home	month	35.01	4Q 92	4c
Electricity, winter, 250 KWh	month	14.67	92	55c

Values are in dollars or fractions of dollars. In the column headed *Ref*, references are shown to sources. Each reference is followed by a letter. These refer to the geographical level for which data were reported: s=State, r=Region, and c=City or metro. The abbreviation *ex* is used to mean *except* or *excluding*; *exp* stands for expenditures. For other abbreviations and further explanations, please see the Introduction.

Portland, OR - continued

Utilities

Item	Per	Value	Date	Ref.
Electricity, winter, 500 KWh	month	25.94	92	55c
Electricity, winter, 750 KWh	month	37.60	92	55c
Electricity, winter, 1000 KWh	month	49.27	92	55c

Poughkeepsie, NY

Item	Per	Value	Date	Ref.

Child Care

Item	Per	Value	Date	Ref.
Child care fee, average, center	hour	2.18	90	65r
Child care fee, average, nonregulated family day care	hour	1.83	90	65r
Child care fee, average, regulated family day care	hour	2.02	90	65r

Education

Item	Per	Value	Date	Ref.
Board, 4-yr private college/university	year	2451	91	22s
Board, 4-yr public college/university	year	1725	91	22s
Expenditures, local gov't, public elementary/secondary	pupil	8603	92	20s
Room, 4-year private college/university	year	2652	91	22s
Room, 4-year public college/university	year	2183	91	22s
Tuition, 2-year private college/university	year	5926	91	22s
Tuition, 2-year public college/university	year	1419	91	22s
Tuition, 4-year private college/university	year	10340	91	22s
Tuition, 4-year public college/university, in-state	year	1587	91	22s

Energy and Fuels

Item	Per	Value	Date	Ref.
Coal	mil Btu	1.66	90	64s
Energy	mil Btu	10.68	90	64s
Energy exp/householder, 1-family unit	year	588	90	28r
Energy exp/householder, <1,000 sq ft heating area	year	477	90	28r
Energy exp/householder, 1,000-1,999 sq ft heating area	year	517	90	28r
Energy exp/householder, 2,000+ sq ft heating area	year	630	90	28r
Energy exp/householder, mobile home	year	412	90	28r
Energy exp/householder, multifamily	year	498	90	28r
Gas, natural	mil Btu	5.25	90	64s
Gas, natural	000 cu ft	7.35	91	46s
Gas, natural, exp	year	557	91	46s
Gasoline, unleaded regular	mil Btu	8.83	90	64s

Funerals

Item	Per	Value	Date	Ref.
Casket, 18-gauge steel, velvet interior		1811.58	91	24r
Cosmetology, hair care, etc.		111.08	91	24r
Embalming		329.42	91	24r
Facility use for ceremony		201.29	91	24r
Hearse, local		135.27	91	24r
Limousine, local		127.24	91	24r
Remains to funeral home, transfer		103.98	91	24r
Service charge, professional		724.98	91	24r
Vault, concrete, non-metallic liner		766.71	91	24r
Viewing facilities, use		260.60	91	24r

Groceries

Item	Per	Value	Date	Ref.
Apples, Red Delicious	lb	0.85	4/93	16r
Bacon	lb	2.12	4/93	16r
Bananas	lb	0.54	4/93	16r
Bread, white, pan	lb	0.81	4/93	16r
Butter	lb	2.02	4/93	16r
Carrots, short trimmed and topped	lb	0.51	4/93	16r
Chicken, fresh, whole	lb	1.04	4/93	16r
Chicken breast, bone-in	lb	2.21	4/93	16r
Chicken legs, bone-in	lb	1.16	4/93	16r
Chuck roast, USDA choice, boneless	lb	2.82	4/93	16r
Coffee, 100% ground roast, all sizes	lb	2.66	4/93	16r
Cucumbers	lb	0.85	4/93	16r
Eggs, Grade A large	doz	1.15	4/93	16r
Grapefruit	lb	0.45	4/93	16r
Grapes, Thompson Seedless	lb	1.52	4/93	16r
Ground beef, lean and extra lean	lb	2.36	4/93	16r

Poughkeepsie, NY - continued

Groceries - continued

Item	Per	Value	Date	Ref.
Ground chuck, 100% beef	lb	2.02	4/93	16r
Honey, jar	8 oz	0.96-1.75	92	5r
Honey, jar	lb	1.50-3.00	92	5r
Honey, squeeze bear	12-oz	1.50-1.99	92	5r
Ice cream, prepackaged, bulk, regular	1/2 gal	2.80	4/93	16r
Lemons	lb	0.96	4/93	16r
Lettuce, iceberg	lb	0.95	4/93	16r
Margarine, stick	lb	0.81	4/93	16r
Milk, fresh, whole, fortified	1/2 gal	1.30	4/93	16r
Oranges, navel	lb	0.56	4/93	16r
Peanut butter, creamy, all sizes	lb	1.88	4/93	16r
Pork chops, center cut, bone-in	lb	3.34	4/93	16r
Potato chips	16 oz	2.88	4/93	16r
Potatoes, white	lb	0.37	4/93	16r
Rib roast, USDA choice, bone-in	lb	4.94	4/93	16r
Round roast, USDA choice, boneless	lb	3.17	4/93	16r
Shortening, vegetable oil blends	lb	0.98	4/93	16r
Spaghetti and macaroni	lb	0.82	4/93	16r
Steak, round, graded & ungraded, ex USDA prime & choice	lb	4.04	4/93	16r
Steak, round, USDA choice, boneless	lb	3.90	4/93	16r
Steak, sirloin, USDA choice, boneless	lb	4.97	4/93	16r
Strawberries, dry pint	12 oz	0.90	4/93	16r
Sugar, white	lb	0.50	4/93	16r
Sugar, white, 33-80 oz pk	lb	0.41	4/93	16r
Tomatoes, field grown	lb	1.23	4/93	16r
Tuna, chunk, light	lb	2.22	4/93	16r
Turkey, frozen, whole	lb	1.04	4/93	16r

Health Care

Item	Per	Value	Date	Ref.
Childbirth, cesarean, hospital		5826	91	62r
Childbirth, cesarean, physician's fee		2053	91	62r
Childbirth, normal, hospital		2964	91	62r
Childbirth, normal, physician's fee		1492	91	62r
Medical plan per employee	year	3942	91	45r
Mental health care, exp	capita	53.68-118.35	90	38s
Mental health care, exp, state mental health agency	capita	118.34	90	38s
Mental health care, hospital psychiatric services, non-Federal, exp	capita	29.77	88	38s
Mental health care, mental health organization, multiservice, exp	capita	20.03	88	38s
Mental health care, psychiatric hospitals, private, exp	capita	8.37	88	38s
Mental health care, psychiatric out-patient clinics, freestanding, exp	capita	7.96	88	38s
Mental health care, psychiatric partial-care organizations, freestanding, exp	capita	1.24	88	38s
Mental health care, state and county mental hospitals, exp	capita	89.52	88	38s
Mental health care, VA medical centers, exp	capita	7.12	88	38s
Prescription drug co-pay, Medicaid	month	23.00	91	21s
Substance abuse, hospital ancillary charge	incident	1040	90	70s
Substance abuse, hospital physician charge	incident	360	90	70s
Substance abuse, hospital room and board	incident	6330	90	70s

Insurance and Pensions

Item	Per	Value	Date	Ref.
Auto insurance, private passenger	year	840.89	91	63s

Taxes

Item	Per	Value	Date	Ref.
Tax, cigarette	pack	39	91	77s
Tax, gasoline	gal	8	91	77s
Taxes, state	capita	1567	91	77s

Transportation

Item	Per	Value	Date	Ref.
Driver's license fee		17.50	12/90	43s
Vehicle registration and license plate	2 years	27.50-149.50	93	67s

Values are in dollars or fractions of dollars. In the column headed *Ref*, references are shown to sources. Each reference is followed by a letter. These refer to the geographical level for which data were reported: s=State, r=Region, and c=City or metro. The abbreviation *ex* is used to mean *except* or *excluding*; *exp* stands for expenditures. For other abbreviations and further explanations, please see the Introduction.

Poughkeepsie, NY - continued

Item	Per	Value	Date	Ref.
Travel				
Business travel	day	165.00	4/93	89r
Utilities				
Electricity	mil Btu	27.51	90	64s

Prescott, AZ

Item	Per	Value	Date	Ref.
Composite ACCRA index		106.20	4Q 92	4c
Alcoholic Beverages				
Beer, Miller Lite or Budweiser, 12-oz containers	6 pack	3.91	4Q 92	4c
Liquor, J & B Scotch	750 ml	15.85	4Q 92	4c
Wine, Gallo Chablis blanc, 1.5 liter	bottle	4.35	4Q 92	4c
Clothing				
Jeans, man's denim		27.39	4Q 92	4c
Shirt, man's dress shirt		22.39	4Q 92	4c
Undervest, boy's size 10-14, cotton	3	5.34	4Q 92	4c
Communications				
Newspaper subscription, daily and Sunday home delivery, large-city	month	13.26	4Q 92	4c
Telephone, flat rate	month	12.40	91	11c
Telephone bill, family of four	month	19.64	4Q 92	4c
Energy and Fuels				
Energy, combined forms, 1,800 sq ft heating area	month	90.87	4Q 92	4c
Energy, exc electricity, 1,800 sq ft heating area	month	35.16	4Q 92	4c
Gasoline, motor	gal	1.26	4Q 92	4c
Entertainment				
Bowling, evening rate	game	2.25	4Q 92	4c
Monopoly game, Parker Brothers', No. 9		11.65	4Q 92	4c
Movie	admission	4.50	4Q 92	4c
Tennis balls, yellow, Wilson or Penn, 3	can	2.58	4Q 92	4c
Goods and Services				
ACCRA Index, Miscellaneous Goods and Services		102.70	4Q 92	4c
Groceries				
ACCRA Index, Groceries		99.10	4Q 92	4c
Babyfood, strained vegetables, lowest price	4-4.5 oz jar	0.28	4Q 92	4c
Bananas	lb	0.38	4Q 92	4c
Bread, white	24 oz	0.69	4Q 92	4c
Cheese, Kraft grated Parmesan	8-oz canister	3.36	4Q 92	4c
Chicken, fryer, whole	lb	0.85	4Q 92	4c
Cigarettes, Winston	carton	16.90	4Q 92	4c
Coffee, vacuum-packed	13-oz can	2.23	4Q 92	4c
Corn, frozen	10 oz	0.61	4Q 92	4c
Corn Flakes, Kellogg's or Post Toasties	18 oz	2.17	4Q 92	4c
Eggs, Grade A large	doz	0.85	4Q 92	4c
Ground beef or hamburger	lb	1.30	4Q 92	4c
Lettuce, iceberg	head	0.85	4Q 92	4c
Margarine, Blue Bonnet or Parkay cubes	lb	0.63	4Q 92	4c
Milk, whole	1/2 gal	1.35	4Q 92	4c
Orange juice, Minute Maid frozen	12-oz can	1.55	4Q 92	4c
Peaches	29-oz can	1.38	4Q 92	4c
Peas Sweet, Del Monte or Green Giant	15-17 oz can	0.66	4Q 92	4c
Potatoes, white or red	10-lb sack	1.51	4Q 92	4c
Sausage, Jimmy Dean, 100% pork	lb	3.03	4Q 92	4c
Shortening, vegetable, Crisco	3-lb can	2.37	4Q 92	4c

Prescott, AZ - continued

Item	Per	Value	Date	Ref.
Groceries - continued				
Soft drink, Coca Cola	2 liter	1.10	4Q 92	4c
Steak, T-bone	lb	4.15	4Q 92	4c
Sugar, cane or beet	4 lb	1.65	4Q 92	4c
Tomatoes, Hunt's or Del Monte	14.5-oz can	0.71	4Q 92	4c
Tuna, chunk, light	6.125-6.5 oz can	0.65	4Q 92	4c
Health Care				
ACCRA Index, Health Care		106.10	4Q 92	4c
Analgesic, Aspirin, Bayer, 325 mg tablets	100	4.43	4Q 92	4c
Dentist's fee, adult teeth cleaning and periodic oral exam	visit	51.75	4Q 92	4c
Doctor's fee, routine exam, established patient	visit	37.60	4Q 92	4c
Hospital care, semiprivate room	day	275.04	90	27c
Hospital care, semiprivate room	day	370.00	4Q 92	4c
Household Goods				
Appliance repair, home, service call, washing machine	min labor charge	32.30	4Q 92	4c
Laundry detergent, Tide Ultra, Bold, or Cheer	42 oz	4.05	4Q 92	4c
Tissues, facial, Kleenex brand	175-count box	1.23	4Q 92	4c
Housing				
ACCRA Index, Housing		120.00	4Q 92	4c
House, 1,800 sq ft, 8,000 sq ft lot, new, urban	total	139747	4Q 92	4c
House payment, principal and interest, 25% down payment	month	776	4Q 92	4c
Mortgage rate, incl. points & origination fee, 30-year fixed or adjustable rate	percent	8.10	4Q 92	4c
Rent, apartment, 2 bedrooms - 1-1/2 to 2 baths, unfurnished, 950 sq ft, water	month	502	4Q 92	4c
Personal Goods				
Shampoo, Alberto VO5	15 oz	1.17	4Q 92	4c
Toothpaste, Crest or Colgate	6-7 oz	1.94	4Q 92	4c
Personal Services				
Dry cleaning, man's 2-piece suit		6.12	4Q 92	4c
Haircare, woman's shampoo, trim and blow-dry		23.60	4Q 92	4c
Haircut, man's barbershop, no styling		7.80	4Q 92	4c
Restaurant Food				
Chicken, fried, thigh and drumstick		2.00	4Q 92	4c
Hamburger with cheese	1/4 lb	1.95	4Q 92	4c
Pizza, Pizza Hut or Pizza Inn, cheese, thin crust	12-13 in	8.69	4Q 92	4c
Transportation				
ACCRA Index, Transportation		107.80	4Q 92	4c
Tire balance, computer or spin balance, front	wheel	6.78	4Q 92	4c
Utilities				
ACCRA Index, Utilities		85.00	4Q 92	4c
Electricity, partial electric and other energy, 1,800 sq ft living area new home	month	55.71	4Q 92	4c

Providence, RI

Item	Per	Value	Date	Ref.
Child Care				
Child care fee, average, center	hour	2.18	90	65r
Child care fee, average, nonregulated family day care	hour	1.83	90	65r
Child care fee, average, regulated family day care	hour	2.02	90	65r

Values are in dollars or fractions of dollars. In the column headed *Ref*, references are shown to sources. Each reference is followed by a letter. These refer to the geographical level for which data were reported: s=State, r=Region, and c=City or metro. The abbreviation *ex* is used to mean *except* or *excluding*; *exp* stands for expenditures. For other abbreviations and further explanations, please see the Introduction.

Providence, RI - continued

Item	Per	Value	Date	Ref.
Communications				
Long-distance telephone service, day, initial minute, 0-100 miles	min	0.31-0.37	91	12s
Long-distance telephone service, day, additional minute, 0-100 miles	min	0.14-0.18	91	12s
Long-distance telephone service, evenings/weekends, 0-100 mi, initial minute	min	0.12-0.15	91	12s
Long-distance telephone service, evenings/weekends, 0-100 mi, additional minute	min	0.06-0.07	91	12s
Telephone, flat rate	month	16.64	91	11c
Telephone, residential, private line, rotary, unlimited calling	month	21.94	10/91	78c
Education				
Board, 4-yr private college/university	year	2476	91	22s
Board, 4-yr public college/university	year	2064	91	22s
Expenditures, local gov't, public elementary/secondary	pupil	6834	92	20s
Room, 4-year private college/university	year	2252	91	22s
Room, 4-year public college/university	year	2256	91	22s
Tuition, 2-year college/university	year	1100	91	22s
Tuition, 4-year private college/university	year	10885	91	22s
Tuition, 4-year public college/university, in-state	year	2311	91	22s
Energy and Fuels				
Coal	mil Btu	3.58	90	64s
Energy	mil Btu	10.80	90	64s
Energy exp/householder, 1-family unit	year	588	90	28r
Energy exp/householder, <1,000 sq ft heating area	year	477	90	28r
Energy exp/householder, 1,000-1,999 sq ft heating area	year	517	90	28r
Energy exp/householder, 2,000+ sq ft heating area	year	630	90	28r
Energy exp/householder, mobile home	year	412	90	28r
Energy exp/householder, multifamily	year	498	90	28r
Gas, cooking, winter, 10 therms	month	12.83	92	56c
Gas, cooking, winter, 30 therms	month	26.58	92	56c
Gas, cooking, winter, 50 therms	month	40.33	92	56c
Gas, heating, winter, 100 therms	month	74.71	92	56c
Gas, heating, winter, average use	month	129.96	92	56c
Gas, natural	mil Btu	5.80	90	64s
Gas, natural	000 cu ft	7.63	91	46s
Gas, natural, exp	year	675	91	46s
Gasoline, unleaded premium	gal	61.25-74.30	12/92	31c
Gasoline, unleaded regular	mil Btu	10.03	90	64s
Entertainment				
Miniature golf admission	adult	6.18	92	1r
Miniature golf admission	child	5.14	92	1r
Waterpark admission	adult	11.00	92	1r
Waterpark admission	child	8.55	92	1r
Funerals				
Casket, 18-gauge steel, velvet interior		1853.42	91	24r
Cosmetology, hair care, etc.		98.33	91	24r
Embalming		273.94	91	24r
Facility use for ceremony		196.06	91	24r
Hearse, local		145.67	91	24r
Limousine, local		131.07	91	24r
Remains to funeral home, transfer		135.24	91	24r
Service charge, professional		843.16	91	24r
Vault, concrete, non-metallic liner		709.14	91	24r
Viewing facilities, use		229.85	91	24r
Groceries				
Apples, Red Delicious	lb	0.85	4/93	16r
Bacon	lb	2.12	4/93	16r
Bananas	lb	0.54	4/93	16r
Bread, white, pan	lb	0.81	4/93	16r
Butter	lb	2.02	4/93	16r
Carrots, short trimmed and topped	lb	0.51	4/93	16r

Providence, RI - continued

Item	Per	Value	Date	Ref.
Groceries - continued				
Chicken, fresh, whole	lb	1.04	4/93	16r
Chicken breast, bone-in	lb	2.21	4/93	16r
Chicken legs, bone-in	lb	1.16	4/93	16r
Chuck roast, USDA choice, boneless	lb	2.82	4/93	16r
Coffee, 100% ground roast, all sizes	lb	2.66	4/93	16r
Cucumbers	lb	0.85	4/93	16r
Eggs, Grade A large	doz	1.15	4/93	16r
Grapefruit	lb	0.45	4/93	16r
Grapes, Thompson Seedless	lb	1.52	4/93	16r
Ground beef, lean and extra lean	lb	2.36	4/93	16r
Ground chuck, 100% beef	lb	2.02	4/93	16r
Honey, jar	8 oz	0.96-1.75	92	5r
Honey, jar	lb	1.50-3.00	92	5r
Honey, squeeze bear	12-oz	1.50-1.99	92	5r
Ice cream, prepackaged, bulk, regular	1/2 gal	2.80	4/93	16r
Lemons	lb	0.96	4/93	16r
Lettuce, iceberg	lb	0.95	4/93	16r
Margarine, stick	lb	0.81	4/93	16r
Milk, fresh, whole, fortified	1/2 gal	1.30	4/93	16r
Oranges, navel	lb	0.56	4/93	16r
Peanut butter, creamy, all sizes	lb	1.88	4/93	16r
Pork chops, center cut, bone-in	lb	3.34	4/93	16r
Potato chips	16 oz	2.88	4/93	16r
Potatoes, white	lb	0.37	4/93	16r
Rib roast, USDA choice, bone-in	lb	4.94	4/93	16r
Round roast, USDA choice, boneless	lb	3.17	4/93	16r
Shortening, vegetable oil blends	lb	0.98	4/93	16r
Spaghetti and macaroni	lb	0.82	4/93	16r
Steak, round, graded & ungraded, ex USDA prime & choice	lb	4.04	4/93	16r
Steak, round, USDA choice, boneless	lb	3.90	4/93	16r
Steak, sirloin, USDA choice, boneless	lb	4.97	4/93	16r
Strawberries, dry pint	12 oz	0.90	4/93	16r
Sugar, white	lb	0.50	4/93	16r
Sugar, white, 33-80 oz pk	lb	0.41	4/93	16r
Tomatoes, field grown	lb	1.23	4/93	16r
Tuna, chunk, light	lb	2.22	4/93	16r
Turkey, frozen, whole	lb	1.04	4/93	16r
Health Care				
Childbirth, cesarean, hospital		5826	91	62r
Childbirth, cesarean, physician's fee		2053	91	62r
Childbirth, normal, hospital		2964	91	62r
Childbirth, normal, physician's fee		1492	91	62r
Hospital care, semiprivate room	day	355.00	90	27c
Medical insurance premium, per employee, small group comprehensive	month	349.45	10/91	25c
Medical plan per employee	year	3958	91	45r
Mental health care, exp	capita	53.68-118.35	90	38s
Mental health care, exp, state mental health agency	capita	50.37	90	38s
Mental health care, hospital psychiatric services, non-Federal, exp	capita	6.39	88	38s
Mental health care, mental health organization, multiservice, exp	capita	32.12	88	38s
Mental health care, psychiatric hospitals, private, exp	capita	30.73	88	38s
Mental health care, psychiatric out-patient clinics, freestanding, exp	capita	3.69	88	38s
Mental health care, state and county mental hospitals, exp	capita	23.91	88	38s
Mental health care, VA medical centers, exp	capita	1.68	88	38s
Substance abuse, hospital ancillary charge	incident	400	90	70s
Substance abuse, hospital physician charge	incident	70	90	70s
Substance abuse, hospital room and board	incident	5400	90	70s
Housing				
Home, median price	unit	118.50		26c
Rental unit, 1 bedroom	month	555	93	23c

Values are in dollars or fractions of dollars. In the column headed *Ref*, references are shown to sources. Each reference is followed by a letter. These refer to the geographical level for which data were reported: s = State, r = Region, and c = City or metro. The abbreviation *ex* is used to mean *except* or *excluding*; *exp* stands for *expenditures*. For other abbreviations and further explanations, please see the Introduction.

Providence, RI - continued

Item	Per	Value	Date	Ref.
Housing				
Rental unit, 2 bedroom	month	653	93	23c
Rental unit, 3 bedroom	month	818	93	23c
Rental unit, 4 bedroom	month	916	93	23c
Rental unit, efficiency	month	457	93	23c
Insurance and Pensions				
Auto insurance, private passenger	year	939.06	91	63s
Taxes				
Tax, cigarette	pack	37	91	77s
Tax, gasoline	gal	26	91	77s
Taxes, state	capita	1251	91	77s
Transportation				
Auto rental, average	day	41.50	6/91	60c
Bus fare	one-way	0.85	3/93	2c
Driver's license fee		30.00	12/90	43s
Limo fare, airport-city, average	day	5.75	6/91	60c
Taxi fare, airport-city, average	day	15.00	6/91	60c
Vehicle registration	2 years	30.00	93	57s
Travel				
Breakfast	day	5.75	6/91	60c
Business travel	day	165.00	4/93	89r
Dinner	day	15.07	6/91	60c
Lodging	day	100.67	91	60c
Lunch	day	8.86	6/91	60c
Utilities				
Electricity	mil Btu	26.85	90	64s
Electricity, winter, 250 KWh	month	28.75	92	55c
Electricity, winter, 500 KWh	month	55.89	92	55c
Electricity, winter, 750 KWh	month	83.02	92	55c
Electricity, winter, 1000 KWh	month	110.16	92	55c

Provo-Orem, UT

Item	Per	Value	Date	Ref.
Composite ACCRA index		93.00	4Q 92	4c
Alcoholic Beverages				
Beer, Miller Lite or Budweiser, 12-oz containers	6 pack	3.70	4Q 92	4c
Liquor, J & B Scotch	750 ml	19.25	4Q 92	4c
Wine, Gallo Chablis blanc, 1.5 liter	bottle	4.95	4Q 92	4c
Child Care				
Child care fee, average, center	hour	1.71	90	65r
Child care fee, average, nonregulated family day care	hour	1.32	90	65r
Child care fee, average, regulated family day care	hour	1.86	90	65r
Clothing				
Jeans, man's denim		30.99	4Q 92	4c
Shirt, man's dress shirt		23.25	4Q 92	4c
Undervest, boy's size 10-14, cotton	3	3.96	4Q 92	4c
Communications				
Long-distance telephone service, day, initial minute, 0-100 miles	min	0.11-0.25	91	12s
Long-distance telephone service, day, additional minute, 0-100 miles	min	0.06-0.21	91	12s
Long-distance telephone service, evenings/weekends, 0-100 mi, initial minute	min	0.07-0.15	91	12s
Long-distance telephone service, evenings/weekends, 0-100 mi, additional minute	min	0.05-0.13	91	12s
Newspaper subscription, daily and Sunday home delivery, large-city	month	8.25	4Q 92	4c
Telephone, flat rate	month	7.98	91	11c
Telephone bill, family of four	month	16.33	4Q 92	4c
Education				
Board, 4-yr private college/university	year	1791	91	22s
Board, 4-yr public college/university	year	1571	91	22s

Provo-Orem, UT - continued

Item	Per	Value	Date	Ref.
Education - continued				
Expenditures, local gov't, public elementary/secondary	pupil	3092	92	20s
Room, 4-year private college/university	year	1195	91	22s
Room, 4-year public college/university	year	1170	91	22s
Tuition, 2-year private college/university	year	4319	91	22s
Tuition, 2-year public college/university	year	1173	91	22s
Tuition, 4-year private college/university	year	2182	91	22s
Tuition, 4-year public college/university, in-state	year	1524	91	22s
Energy and Fuels				
Coal	mil Btu	1.24	90	64s
Energy	mil Btu	7.16	90	64s
Energy, combined forms, 1,800 sq ft heating area	month	95.97	4Q 92	4c
Energy, exc electricity, 1,800 sq ft heating area	month	49.46	4Q 92	4c
Energy exp/householder, 1-family unit	year	372	90	28r
Energy exp/householder, <1,000 sq ft heating area	year	335	90	28r
Energy exp/householder, 1,000-1,999 sq ft heating area	year	365	90	28r
Energy exp/householder, 2,000+ sq ft heating area	year	411	90	28r
Energy exp/householder, mobile home	year	305	90	28r
Energy exp/householder, multifamily	year	372	90	28r
Gas, natural	mil Btu	4.17	90	64s
Gas, natural	000 cu ft	5.44	91	46s
Gas, natural, exp	year	603	91	46s
Gasoline, motor	gal	1.18	4Q 92	4c
Gasoline, unleaded regular	mil Btu	9.09	90	64s
Entertainment				
Bowling, evening rate	game	1.88	4Q 92	4c
Miniature golf admission	adult	6.18	92	1r
Miniature golf admission	child	5.14	92	1r
Monopoly game, Parker Brothers', No. 9		9.65	4Q 92	4c
Movie	admission	5.33	4Q 92	4c
Tennis balls, yellow, Wilson or Penn, 3	can	2.28	4Q 92	4c
Waterpark admission	adult	11.00	92	1r
Waterpark admission	child	8.55	92	1r
Funerals				
Casket, 18-gauge steel, velvet interior		1929.04	91	24r
Cosmetology, hair care, etc.		88.52	91	24r
Embalming		249.33	91	24r
Facility use for ceremony		182.75	91	24r
Hearse, local		110.04	91	24r
Limousine, local		66.67	91	24r
Remains to funeral home, transfer		84.58	91	24r
Service charge, professional		593.00	91	24r
Vault, concrete, non-metallic liner		647.38	91	24r
Viewing facilities, use		99.87	91	24r
Goods and Services				
ACCRA Index, Miscellaneous Goods and Services		96.60	4Q 92	4c
Groceries				
ACCRA Index, Groceries		96.80	4Q 92	4c
Apples, Red Delicious	lb	0.80	4/93	16r
Babyfood, strained vegetables, lowest price	4-4.5 oz jar	0.37	4Q 92	4c
Bacon	lb	1.79	4/93	16r
Bananas	lb	0.29	4Q 92	4c
Bananas	lb	0.53	4/93	16r
Bologna, all beef or mixed	lb	2.67	4/93	16r
Bread, white	24 oz	0.76	4Q 92	4c
Bread, white, pan	lb	0.81	4/93	16r
Carrots, short trimmed and topped	lb	0.39	4/93	16r

Values are in dollars or fractions of dollars. In the column headed *Ref*, references are shown to sources. Each reference is followed by a letter. These refer to the geographical level for which data were reported: s=State, r=Region, and c=City or metro. The abbreviation *ex* is used to mean *except* or *excluding*; *exp* stands for expenditures. For other abbreviations and further explanations, please see the Introduction.

Provo-Orem, UT - continued

Item	Per	Value	Date	Ref.
Groceries				
Cheese, Kraft grated Parmesan	8-oz canister	3.89	4Q 92	4c
Chicken, fresh, whole	lb	0.94	4/93	16r
Chicken, fryer, whole	lb	0.85	4Q 92	4c
Chicken breast, bone-in	lb	2.19	4/93	16r
Chuck roast, graded and ungraded, ex USDA prime and choice	lb	2.26	4/93	16r
Cigarettes, Winston	carton	18.49	4Q 92	4c
Coffee, 100% ground roast, all sizes	lb	2.33	4/93	16r
Coffee, vacuum-packed	13-oz can	2.01	4Q 92	4c
Corn, frozen	10 oz	0.57	4Q 92	4c
Corn Flakes, Kellogg's or Post Toasties	18 oz	1.98	4Q 92	4c
Eggs, Grade A large	doz	0.73	4Q 92	4c
Eggs, Grade AA large	doz	1.18	4/93	16r
Flour, white, all purpose	lb	0.22	4/93	16r
Grapefruit	lb	0.52	4/93	16r
Grapes, Thompson Seedless	lb	1.50	4/93	16r
Ground beef, 100% beef	lb	1.44	4/93	16r
Ground beef, lean and extra lean	lb	2.34	4/93	16r
Ground beef or hamburger	lb	1.48	4Q 92	4c
Ham, boneless, excluding canned	lb	2.56	4/93	16r
Honey, jar	8 oz	0.89-1.00	92	5r
Honey, jar	lb	1.35-1.97	92	5r
Honey, squeeze bear	12-oz	1.19-1.50	92	5r
Ice cream, prepackaged, bulk, regular	1/2 gal	2.40	4/93	16r
Lemons	lb	0.81	4/93	16r
Lettuce, iceberg	head	0.67	4Q 92	4c
Lettuce, iceberg	lb	0.84	4/93	16r
Margarine, Blue Bonnet or Parkay cubes	lb	0.49	4Q 92	4c
Margarine, stick	lb	0.81	4/93	16r
Milk, whole	1/2 gal	1.28	4Q 92	4c
Orange juice, Minute Maid frozen	12-oz can	1.40	4Q 92	4c
Oranges, navel	lb	0.48	4/93	16r
Peaches	29-oz can	1.22	4Q 92	4c
Peas Sweet, Del Monte or Green Giant	15-17 oz can	0.60	4Q 92	4c
Pork chops, center cut, bone-in	lb	3.25	4/93	16r
Potato chips	16 oz	2.89	4/93	16r
Potatoes, white	lb	0.38	4/93	16r
Potatoes, white or red	10-lb sack	0.98	4Q 92	4c
Round roast, graded & ungraded, ex USDA prime & choice	lb	3.00	4/93	16r
Round roast, USDA choice, boneless	lb	3.16	4/93	16r
Sausage, Jimmy Dean, 100% pork	lb	2.81	4Q 92	4c
Shortening, vegetable oil blends	lb	0.86	4/93	16r
Shortening, vegetable, Crisco	3-lb can	2.38	4Q 92	4c
Soft drink, Coca Cola	2 liter	1.09	4Q 92	4c
Spaghetti and macaroni	lb	0.84	4/93	16r
Steak, round, graded & ungraded, ex USDA prime & choice	lb	3.34	4/93	16r
Steak, round, USDA choice, boneless	lb	3.24	4/93	16r
Steak, sirloin, graded & ungraded, ex USDA prime & choice	lb	3.75	4/93	16r
Steak, sirloin, USDA choice, boneless	lb	4.49	4/93	16r
Steak, T-bone	lb	4.06	4Q 92	4c
Sugar, cane or beet	4 lb	1.59	4Q 92	4c
Sugar, white	lb	0.41	4/93	16r
Sugar, white, 33-80 oz pk	lb	0.38	4/93	16r
Tomatoes, field grown	lb	1.01	4/93	16r
Tomatoes, Hunt's or Del Monte	14.5-oz can	0.66	4Q 92	4c
Tuna, chunk, light	6.125-6.5 oz can	0.63	4Q 92	4c
Turkey, frozen, whole	lb	1.04	4/93	16r

Provo-Orem, UT - continued

Item	Per	Value	Date	Ref.
Health Care				
ACCRA Index, Health Care		106.60	4Q 92	4c
Analgesic, Aspirin, Bayer, 325 mg tablets	100	5.16	4Q 92	4c
Childbirth, cesarean, hospital		5533	91	62r
Childbirth, cesarean, physician's fee		2053	91	62r
Childbirth, normal, hospital		2745	91	62r
Childbirth, normal, physician's fee		1492	91	62r
Dentist's fee, adult teeth cleaning and periodic oral exam	visit	47.33	4Q 92	4c
Doctor's fee, routine exam, established patient	visit	40.00	4Q 92	4c
Hospital care, semiprivate room	day	279.65	90	27c
Hospital care, semiprivate room	day	368.40	4Q 92	4c
Medical insurance premium, per employee, small group comprehensive	month	313.90	10/91	25c
Medical plan per employee	year	3218	91	45r
Mental health care, exp	capita	20.37-28.83	90	38s
Mental health care, exp, state mental health agency	capita	20.57	90	38s
Mental health care, hospital psychiatric services, non-Federal, exp	capita	15.78	88	38s
Mental health care, mental health organization, multiservice, exp	capita	25.60	88	38s
Mental health care, psychiatric hospitals, private, exp	capita	27.77	88	38s
Mental health care, psychiatric out-patient clinics, freestanding, exp	capita	0.25	88	38s
Mental health care, state and county mental hospitals, exp	capita	9.29	88	38s
Mental health care, VA medical centers, exp	capita	7.36	88	38s
Physician fee, family practice, first-visit		111.00	91	62r
Physician fee, family practice, revisit		45.00	91	62r
Physician fee, general practice, first-visit		100.00	91	62r
Physician fee, general practice, revisit		40.00	91	62r
Physician fee, internal medicine, first-visit		137.00	91	62r
Physician fee, internal medicine, revisit		48.00	91	62r
Physician fee, median, neurosurgeon, first-visit		157.00	91	62r
Physician fee, median, nonsurgical specialist, first-visit		131.00	91	62r
Physician fee, median, orthopedic surgeon, first-visit		124.00	91	62r
Physician fee, median, plastic surgeon, first-visit		88.00	91	62r
Physician fee, median, surgical specialist, first-visit		100.00	91	62r
Physician fee, neurosurgeon, revisit		51.00	91	62r
Physician fee, nonsurgical specialist, revisit		47.00	91	62r
Physician fee, obstetrics/gynecology, first-visit		95.00	91	62r
Physician fee, obstetrics/gynecology, revisit		50.00	91	62r
Physician fee, orthopedic surgeon, revisit		51.00	91	62r
Physician fee, pediatrician, first-visit		81.00	91	62r
Physician fee, pediatrician, revisit		42.00	91	62r
Physician fee, plastic surgeon, revisit		48.00	91	62r
Physician fee, surgical specialist, revisit		49.00	91	62r
Substance abuse, hospital ancillary charge	incident	1890	90	70s
Substance abuse, hospital physician charge	incident	470	90	70s
Substance abuse, hospital room and board	incident	5560	90	70s
Household Goods				
Appliance repair, home, service call, washing machine	min labor charge	27.75	4Q 92	4c
Laundry detergent, Tide Ultra, Bold, or Cheer	42 oz	3.13	4Q 92	4c
Tissues, facial, Kleenex brand	175-count box	1.14	4Q 92	4c

Values are in dollars or fractions of dollars. In the column headed *Ref*, references are shown to sources. Each reference is followed by a letter. These refer to the geographical level for which data were reported: s = State, r = Region, and c = City or metro. The abbreviation *ex* is used to mean *except* or *excluding*; *exp* stands for expenditures. For other abbreviations and further explanations, please see the Introduction.

Provo-Orem, UT - continued

Item	Per	Value	Date	Ref.
Housing				
ACCRA Index, Housing		85.30	4Q 92	4c
House, 1,800 sq ft, 8,000 sq ft lot, new, urban	total	90000	4Q 92	4c
House payment, principal and interest, 25% down payment	month	498	4Q 92	4c
Mortgage rate, incl. points & origination fee, 30-year fixed or adjustable rate	per-cent	8.07	4Q 92	4c
Rent, apartment, 2 bedrooms - 1-1/2 to 2 baths, unfurnished, 950 sq ft, water	month	480	4Q 92	4c
Rental unit, 1 bedroom	month	394	93	23c
Rental unit, 2 bedroom	month	462	93	23c
Rental unit, 3 bedroom	month	579	93	23c
Rental unit, 4 bedroom	month	650	93	23c
Rental unit, efficiency	month	323	93	23c
Insurance and Pensions				
Auto insurance, private passenger	year	525.15	91	63s
Personal Goods				
Shampoo, Alberto VO5	15 oz	1.19	4Q 92	4c
Toothpaste, Crest or Colgate	6-7 oz	2.03	4Q 92	4c
Personal Services				
Dry cleaning, man's 2-piece suit		7.17	4Q 92	4c
Haircare, woman's shampoo, trim and blow-dry		14.33	4Q 92	4c
Haircut, man's barbershop, no styling		9.67	4Q 92	4c
Restaurant Food				
Chicken, fried, thigh and drumstick		1.95	4Q 92	4c
Hamburger with cheese	1/4 lb	1.99	4Q 92	4c
Pizza, Pizza Hut or Pizza Inn, cheese, thin crust	12-13 in	7.29	4Q 92	4c
Taxes				
Tax, cigarette	pack	26.50	91	77s
Tax, gasoline	gal	19.50	91	77s
Taxes, state	capita	1051	91	77s
Transportation				
ACCRA Index, Transportation		95.40	4Q 92	4c
Bus fare	one-way	0.65	3/93	2c
Driver's license fee		10.00	12/90	43s
Tire balance, computer or spin balance, front	wheel	5.65	4Q 92	4c
Travel				
Business travel	day	178.00	4/93	89r
Utilities				
ACCRA Index, Utilities		87.50	4Q 92	4c
Electricity	mil Btu	16.09	90	64s
Electricity, partial electric and other energy, 1,800 sq ft living area new home	month	46.51	4Q 92	4c

Pryor, OK

Item	Per	Value	Date	Ref.
Composite ACCRA index		86.10	4Q 92	4c
Alcoholic Beverages				
Beer, Miller Lite or Budweiser, 12-oz containers	6 pack	3.69	4Q 92	4c
Liquor, J & B Scotch	750 ml	15.38	4Q 92	4c
Wine, Gallo Chablis blanc, 1.5 liter	bottle	5.06	4Q 92	4c
Clothing				
Jeans, man's denim		20.99	4Q 92	4c
Shirt, man's dress shirt		19.50	4Q 92	4c
Undervest, boy's size 10-14, cotton	3	3.83	4Q 92	4c
Communications				
Newspaper subscription, daily and Sunday home delivery, large-city	month	8.25	4Q 92	4c
Telephone, flat rate	month	10.87	91	11c
Telephone bill, family of four	month	19.30	4Q 92	4c

Pryor, OK - continued

Item	Per	Value	Date	Ref.
Energy and Fuels				
Energy, combined forms, 1,800 sq ft heating area	month	72.43	4Q 92	4c
Energy, exc electricity, 1,800 sq ft heating area	month	20.66	4Q 92	4c
Gasoline, motor	gal	1.09	4Q 92	4c
Entertainment				
Bowling, evening rate	game	1.95	4Q 92	4c
Monopoly game, Parker Brothers', No. 9		9.97	4Q 92	4c
Movie	admission	5.64	4Q 92	4c
Tennis balls, yellow, Wilson or Penn, 3	can	2.78	4Q 92	4c
Goods and Services				
ACCRA Index, Miscellaneous Goods and Services		92.90	4Q 92	4c
Groceries				
ACCRA Index, Groceries		93.80	4Q 92	4c
Babyfood, strained vegetables, lowest price	4-4.5 oz jar	0.36	4Q 92	4c
Bananas	lb	0.42	4Q 92	4c
Bread, white	24 oz	0.51	4Q 92	4c
Cheese, Kraft grated Parmesan	8-oz canister	3.52	4Q 92	4c
Chicken, fryer, whole	lb	0.68	4Q 92	4c
Cigarettes, Winston	carton	17.63	4Q 92	4c
Coffee, vacuum-packed	13-oz can	1.92	4Q 92	4c
Corn, frozen	10 oz	0.58	4Q 92	4c
Corn Flakes, Kellogg's or Post Toasties	18 oz	2.00	4Q 92	4c
Eggs, Grade A large	doz	0.80	4Q 92	4c
Ground beef or hamburger	lb	1.35	4Q 92	4c
Lettuce, iceberg	head	1.10	4Q 92	4c
Margarine, Blue Bonnet or Parkay cubes	lb	0.50	4Q 92	4c
Milk, whole	1/2 gal	1.13	4Q 92	4c
Orange juice, Minute Maid frozen	12-oz can	1.42	4Q 92	4c
Peaches	29-oz can	1.12	4Q 92	4c
Peas Sweet, Del Monte or Green Giant	15-17 oz can	0.47	4Q 92	4c
Potatoes, white or red	10-lb sack	2.32	4Q 92	4c
Sausage, Jimmy Dean, 100% pork	lb	2.69	4Q 92	4c
Shortening, vegetable, Crisco	3-lb can	1.99	4Q 92	4c
Soft drink, Coca Cola	2 liter	1.10	4Q 92	4c
Steak, T-bone	lb	5.01	4Q 92	4c
Sugar, cane or beet	4 lb	1.43	4Q 92	4c
Tomatoes, Hunt's or Del Monte	14.5-oz can	0.73	4Q 92	4c
Tuna, chunk, light	6.125-6.5 oz can	0.59	4Q 92	4c
Health Care				
ACCRA Index, Health Care		94.10	4Q 92	4c
Analgesic, Aspirin, Bayer, 325 mg tablets	100	4.97	4Q 92	4c
Dentist's fee, adult teeth cleaning and periodic oral exam	visit	51.00	4Q 92	4c
Doctor's fee, routine exam, established patient	visit	32.40	4Q 92	4c
Hospital care, semiprivate room	day	235.00	4Q 92	4c
Household Goods				
Appliance repair, home, service call, washing machine	min labor charge	29.49	4Q 92	4c
Laundry detergent, Tide Ultra, Bold, or Cheer	42 oz	3.01	4Q 92	4c

Values are in dollars or fractions of dollars. In the column headed *Ref*, references are shown to sources. Each reference is followed by a letter. These refer to the geographical level for which data were reported: s = State, r = Region, and c = City or metro. The abbreviation *ex* is used to mean *except* or *excluding*; *exp* stands for expenditures. For other abbreviations and further explanations, please see the Introduction.

Pryor, OK - continued

Item	Per	Value	Date	Ref.
Household Goods				
Tissues, facial, Kleenex brand	175-count box	1.18	4Q 92	4c
Housing				
ACCRA Index, Housing		77.10	4Q 92	4c
House, 1,800 sq ft, 8,000 sq ft lot, new, urban	total	88250	4Q 92	4c
House payment, principal and interest, 25% down payment	month	496	4Q 92	4c
Mortgage rate, incl. points & origination fee, 30-year fixed or adjustable rate	percent	8.23	4Q 92	4c
Rent, apartment, 2 bedrooms - 1-1/2 to 2 baths, unfurnished, 950 sq ft, water	month	330	4Q 92	4c
Personal Goods				
Shampoo, Alberto VO5	15 oz	1.45	4Q 92	4c
Toothpaste, Crest or Colgate	6-7 oz	1.70	4Q 92	4c
Personal Services				
Dry cleaning, man's 2-piece suit		5.41	4Q 92	4c
Haircare, woman's shampoo, trim and blow-dry		17.58	4Q 92	4c
Haircut, man's barbershop, no styling		6.32	4Q 92	4c
Restaurant Food				
Chicken, fried, thigh and drumstick		2.59	4Q 92	4c
Hamburger with cheese	1/4 lb	1.90	4Q 92	4c
Pizza, Pizza Hut or Pizza Inn, cheese, thin crust	12-13 in	7.48	4Q 92	4c
Transportation				
ACCRA Index, Transportation		88.60	4Q 92	4c
Tire balance, computer or spin balance, front	wheel	5.25	4Q 92	4c
Utilities				
ACCRA Index, Utilities		69.60	4Q 92	4c
Electricity, partial electric and other energy, 1,800 sq ft living area new home	month	51.77	4Q 92	4c

Pueblo, CO

Item	Per	Value	Date	Ref.
Composite ACCRA index		86.80	4Q 92	4c
Alcoholic Beverages				
Beer, Miller Lite or Budweiser, 12-oz containers	6 pack	4.14	4Q 92	4c
Liquor, J & B Scotch	750 ml	15.72	4Q 92	4c
Wine, Gallo Chablis blanc, 1.5 liter	bottle	4.52	4Q 92	4c
Child Care				
Child care fee, average, center	hour	1.71	90	65r
Child care fee, average, nonregulated family day care	hour	1.32	90	65r
Child care fee, average, regulated family day care	hour	1.86	90	65r
Clothing				
Jeans, man's denim		23.99	4Q 92	4c
Shirt, man's dress shirt		24.00	4Q 92	4c
Undervest, boy's size 10-14, cotton	3	3.91	4Q 92	4c
Communications				
Long-distance telephone service, day, initial minute, 0-100 miles	min	0.11-0.35	91	12s
Long-distance telephone service, day, additional minute, 0-100 miles	min	0.13-0.27	91	12s
Long-distance telephone service, evenings/weekends, 0-100 mi, initial minute	min	0.08-0.17	91	12s
Long-distance telephone service, evenings/weekends, 0-100 mi, additional minute	min	0.06-0.14	91	12s
Newspaper subscription, daily and Sunday home delivery, large-city	month	8.00	4Q 92	4c
Telephone, flat rate	month	14.22	91	11c
Telephone bill, family of four	month	17.35	4Q 92	4c

Pueblo, CO - continued

Item	Per	Value	Date	Ref.
Education				
Board, 4-yr private college/university	year	2162	91	22s
Board, 4-yr public college/university	year	1747	91	22s
Expenditures, local gov't, public elementary/secondary	pupil	5259	92	20s
Room, 4-year private college/university	year	1984	91	22s
Room, 4-year public college/university	year	1546	91	22s
Tuition, 2-year private college/university	year	6731	91	22s
Tuition, 2-year public college/university	year	943	91	22s
Tuition, 4-year private college/university	year	9516	91	22s
Tuition, 4-year public college/university, in-state	year	1919	91	22s
Energy and Fuels				
Coal	mil Btu	1.07	90	64s
Energy	mil Btu	8.14	90	64s
Energy, combined forms, 1,800 sq ft heating area	month	85.58	4Q 92	4c
Energy, exc electricity, 1,800 sq ft heating area	month	36.45	4Q 92	4c
Energy exp/householder, 1-family unit	year	372	90	28r
Energy exp/householder, <1,000 sq ft heating area	year	335	90	28r
Energy exp/householder, 1,000-1,999 sq ft heating area	year	365	90	28r
Energy exp/householder, 2,000+ sq ft heating area	year	411	90	28r
Energy exp/householder, mobile home	year	305	90	28r
Energy exp/householder, multifamily	year	372	90	28r
Gas, natural	mil Btu	3.92	90	64s
Gas, natural	000 cu ft	4.59	91	46s
Gas, natural, exp	year	446	91	46s
Gasoline, motor	gal	1.16	4Q 92	4c
Gasoline, unleaded regular	mil Btu	9.29	90	64s
Entertainment				
Bowling, evening rate	game	1.50	4Q 92	4c
Miniature golf admission	adult	6.18	92	1r
Miniature golf admission	child	5.14	92	1r
Monopoly game, Parker Brothers', No. 9		12.61	4Q 92	4c
Movie	admission	5.25	4Q 92	4c
Tennis balls, yellow, Wilson or Penn, 3	can	2.46	4Q 92	4c
Waterpark admission	adult	11.00	92	1r
Waterpark admission	child	8.55	92	1r
Funerals				
Casket, 18-gauge steel, velvet interior		1929.04	91	24r
Cosmetology, hair care, etc.		88.52	91	24r
Embalming		249.33	91	24r
Facility use for ceremony		182.75	91	24r
Hearse, local		110.04	91	24r
Limousine, local		66.67	91	24r
Remains to funeral home, transfer		84.58	91	24r
Service charge, professional		593.00	91	24r
Vault, concrete, non-metallic liner		647.38	91	24r
Viewing facilities, use		99.87	91	24r
Goods and Services				
ACCRA Index, Miscellaneous Goods and Services		91.60	4Q 92	4c
Groceries				
ACCRA Index, Groceries		98.10	4Q 92	4c
Apples, Red Delicious	lb	0.80	4/93	16r
Babyfood, strained vegetables, lowest price	4-4.5 oz jar	0.33	4Q 92	4c
Bacon	lb	1.79	4/93	16r
Bananas	lb	0.41	4Q 92	4c
Bananas	lb	0.53	4/93	16r
Bologna, all beef or mixed	lb	2.67	4/93	16r
Bread, white	24 oz	0.64	4Q 92	4c
Bread, white, pan	lb	0.81	4/93	16r
Carrots, short trimmed and topped	lb	0.39	4/93	16r

Values are in dollars or fractions of dollars. In the column headed *Ref*, references are shown to sources. Each reference is followed by a letter. These refer to the geographical level for which data were reported: s = State, r = Region, and c = City or metro. The abbreviation *ex* is used to mean *except* or *excluding*; *exp* stands for expenditures. For other abbreviations and further explanations, please see the Introduction.

Pueblo, CO - continued

Item	Per	Value	Date	Ref.
Groceries				
Cheese, Kraft grated Parmesan	8-oz canis-ter	3.23	4Q 92	4c
Chicken, fresh, whole	lb	0.94	4/93	16r
Chicken, fryer, whole	lb	0.68	4Q 92	4c
Chicken breast, bone-in	lb	2.19	4/93	16r
Chuck roast, graded and ungraded, ex USDA prime and choice	lb	2.26	4/93	16r
Cigarettes, Winston	carton	16.55	4Q 92	4c
Coffee, 100% ground roast, all sizes	lb	2.33	4/93	16r
Coffee, vacuum-packed	13-oz can	2.27	4Q 92	4c
Corn, frozen	10 oz	0.68	4Q 92	4c
Corn Flakes, Kellogg's or Post Toasties	18 oz	2.06	4Q 92	4c
Eggs, Grade A large	doz	0.72	4Q 92	4c
Eggs, Grade AA large	doz	1.18	4/93	16r
Flour, white, all purpose	lb	0.22	4/93	16r
Grapefruit	lb	0.52	4/93	16r
Grapes, Thompson Seedless	lb	1.50	4/93	16r
Ground beef, 100% beef	lb	1.44	4/93	16r
Ground beef, lean and extra lean	lb	2.34	4/93	16r
Ground beef or hamburger	lb	1.25	4Q 92	4c
Ham, boneless, excluding canned	lb	2.56	4/93	16r
Honey, jar	8 oz	0.89-1.00	92	5r
Honey, jar	lb	1.35-1.97	92	5r
Honey, squeeze bear	12-oz	1.19-1.50	92	5r
Ice cream, prepackaged, bulk, regular	1/2 gal	2.40	4/93	16r
Lemons	lb	0.81	4/93	16r
Lettuce, iceberg	head	0.91	4Q 92	4c
Lettuce, iceberg	lb	0.84	4/93	16r
Margarine, Blue Bonnet or Parkay cubes	lb	0.49	4Q 92	4c
Margarine, stick	lb	0.81	4/93	16r
Milk, whole	1/2 gal	1.50	4Q 92	4c
Orange juice, Minute Maid frozen	12-oz can	1.57	4Q 92	4c
Oranges, navel	lb	0.48	4/93	16r
Peaches	29-oz can	1.61	4Q 92	4c
Peas Sweet, Del Monte or Green Giant	15-17 oz can	0.64	4Q 92	4c
Pork chops, center cut, bone-in	lb	3.25	4/93	16r
Potato chips	16 oz	2.89	4/93	16r
Potatoes, white	lb	0.38	4/93	16r
Potatoes, white or red	10-lb sack	1.99	4Q 92	4c
Round roast, graded & ungraded, ex USDA prime & choice	lb	3.00	4/93	16r
Round roast, USDA choice, boneless	lb	3.16	4/93	16r
Sausage, Jimmy Dean, 100% pork	lb	3.44	4Q 92	4c
Shortening, vegetable oil blends	lb	0.86	4/93	16r
Shortening, vegetable, Crisco	3-lb can	2.38	4Q 92	4c
Soft drink, Coca Cola	2 liter	1.07	4Q 92	4c
Spaghetti and macaroni	lb	0.84	4/93	16r
Steak, round, graded & ungraded, ex USDA prime & choice	lb	3.34	4/93	16r
Steak, round, USDA choice, boneless	lb	3.24	4/93	16r
Steak, sirloin, graded & ungraded, ex USDA prime & choice	lb	3.75	4/93	16r
Steak, sirloin, USDA choice, boneless	lb	4.49	4/93	16r
Steak, T-bone	lb	3.97	4Q 92	4c
Sugar, cane or beet	4 lb	1.40	4Q 92	4c
Sugar, white	lb	0.41	4/93	16r
Sugar, white, 33-80 oz pk	lb	0.38	4/93	16r
Tomatoes, field grown	lb	1.01	4/93	16r
Tomatoes, Hunt's or Del Monte	14.5-oz can	0.75	4Q 92	4c
Tuna, chunk, light	6.125-6.5 oz can	0.67	4Q 92	4c
Turkey, frozen, whole	lb	1.04	4/93	16r

Pueblo, CO - continued

Item	Per	Value	Date	Ref.
Health Care				
ACCRA Index, Health Care		97.60	4Q 92	4c
Analgesic, Aspirin, Bayer, 325 mg tablets	100	4.99	4Q 92	4c
Childbirth, cesarean, hospital		5533	91	62r
Childbirth, cesarean, physician's fee		2053	91	62r
Childbirth, normal, hospital		2745	91	62r
Childbirth, normal, physician's fee		1492	91	62r
Dentist's fee, adult teeth cleaning and periodic oral exam	visit	46.60	4Q 92	4c
Doctor's fee, routine exam, established patient	visit	36.00	4Q 92	4c
Hospital care, semiprivate room	day	280.11	90	27c
Hospital care, semiprivate room	day	295.00	4Q 92	4c
Medical insurance premium, per employee, small group comprehensive	month	306.60	10/91	25c
Medical plan per employee	year	3218	91	45r
Mental health care, exp	capita	28.84-37.59	90	38s
Mental health care, exp, state mental health agency	capita	33.55	90	38s
Mental health care, hospital psychiatric services, non-Federal, exp	capita	11.38	88	38s
Mental health care, mental health organization, multiservice, exp	capita	21.76	88	38s
Mental health care, psychiatric hospitals, private, exp	capita	14.39	88	38s
Mental health care, psychiatric out-patient clinics, freestanding, exp	capita	0.11	88	38s
Mental health care, state and county mental hospitals, exp	capita	19.03	88	38s
Mental health care, VA medical centers, exp	capita	3.80	88	38s
Physician fee, family practice, first-visit		111.00	91	62r
Physician fee, family practice, revisit		45.00	91	62r
Physician fee, general practice, first-visit		100.00	91	62r
Physician fee, general practice, revisit		40.00	91	62r
Physician fee, internal medicine, first-visit		137.00	91	62r
Physician fee, internal medicine, revisit		48.00	91	62r
Physician fee, median, neurosurgeon, first-visit		157.00	91	62r
Physician fee, median, nonsurgical specialist, first-visit		131.00	91	62r
Physician fee, median, orthopedic surgeon, first-visit		124.00	91	62r
Physician fee, median, plastic surgeon, first-visit		88.00	91	62r
Physician fee, median, surgical specialist, first-visit		100.00	91	62r
Physician fee, neurosurgeon, revisit		51.00	91	62r
Physician fee, nonsurgical specialist, revisit		47.00	91	62r
Physician fee, obstetrics/gynecology, first-visit		95.00	91	62r
Physician fee, obstetrics/gynecology, revisit		50.00	91	62r
Physician fee, orthopedic surgeon, revisit		51.00	91	62r
Physician fee, pediatrician, first-visit		81.00	91	62r
Physician fee, pediatrician, revisit		42.00	91	62r
Physician fee, plastic surgeon, revisit		48.00	91	62r
Physician fee, surgical specialist, revisit		49.00	91	62r
Substance abuse, hospital ancillary charge	incident	1040	90	70s
Substance abuse, hospital physician charge	incident	380	90	70s
Substance abuse, hospital room and board	incident	4880	90	70s
Household Goods				
Appliance repair, home, service call, washing machine	min labor charge	23.37	4Q 92	4c
Laundry detergent, Tide Ultra, Bold, or Cheer	42 oz	3.67	4Q 92	4c
Tissues, facial, Kleenex brand	175-count box	1.11	4Q 92	4c

Values are in dollars or fractions of dollars. In the column headed *Ref*, references are shown to sources. Each reference is followed by a letter. These refer to the geographical level for which data were reported: s=State, r=Region, and c=City or metro. The abbreviation *ex* is used to mean *except* or *excluding*; *exp* stands for expenditures. For other abbreviations and further explanations, please see the Introduction.

Pueblo, CO - continued

Item	Per	Value	Date	Ref.
Housing				
ACCRA Index, Housing		74.10	4Q 92	4c
House, 1,800 sq ft, 8,000 sq ft lot, new, urban	total	82150	4Q 92	4c
House payment, principal and interest, 25% down payment	month	462	4Q 92	4c
Mortgage rate, incl. points & origination fee, 30-year fixed or adjustable rate	per-cent	8.24	4Q 92	4c
Rent, apartment, 2 bedrooms - 1-1/2 to 2 baths, unfurnished, 950 sq ft, water	month	350	4Q 92	4c
Rental unit, 1 bedroom	month	424	93	23c
Rental unit, 2 bedroom	month	499	93	23c
Rental unit, 3 bedroom	month	626	93	23c
Rental unit, 4 bedroom	month	702	93	23c
Rental unit, efficiency	month	350	93	23c
Insurance and Pensions				
Auto insurance, private passenger	year	684.81	91	63s
Personal Goods				
Shampoo, Alberto VO5	15 oz	1.15	4Q 92	4c
Toothpaste, Crest or Colgate	6-7 oz	2.29	4Q 92	4c
Personal Services				
Dry cleaning, man's 2-piece suit		5.67	4Q 92	4c
Haircare, woman's shampoo, trim and blow-dry		14.60	4Q 92	4c
Haircut, man's barbershop, no styling		6.60	4Q 92	4c
Restaurant Food				
Chicken, fried, thigh and drumstick		1.95	4Q 92	4c
Hamburger with cheese	1/4 lb	1.99	4Q 92	4c
Pizza, Pizza Hut or Pizza Inn, cheese, thin crust	12-13 in	7.74	4Q 92	4c
Taxes				
Tax, cigarette	pack	20	91	77s
Tax, gasoline	gal	22	91	77s
Taxes, state	capita	951	91	77s
Transportation				
ACCRA Index, Transportation		91.90	4Q 92	4c
Bus fare, up to 10 miles	one-way	0.50	4Q 92	4c
Driver's license fee		15.00	12/90	43s
Tire balance, computer or spin balance, front	wheel	5.80	4Q 92	4c
Travel				
Business travel	day	178.00	4/93	89r
Utilities				
ACCRA Index, Utilities		79.50	4Q 92	4c
Electricity	mil Btu	17.31	90	64s
Electricity, partial electric and other energy, 1,800 sq ft living area new home	month	49.13	4Q 92	4c
Electricity, residential	KWh	7.70	2/93	94s
Electricity, winter, 250 KWh	month	22.16	92	55c
Electricity, winter, 500 KWh	month	38.72	92	55c
Electricity, winter, 750 KWh	month	55.28	92	55c
Electricity, winter, 1000 KWh	month	71.84	92	55c

Quincy, IL

Item	Per	Value	Date	Ref.
Composite ACCRA index		93.50	4Q 92	4c
Alcoholic Beverages				
Beer, Miller Lite or Budweiser, 12-oz containers	6 pack	3.67	4Q 92	4c
Liquor, J & B Scotch	750 ml	15.83	4Q 92	4c
Wine, Gallo Chablis blanc, 1.5 liter	bottle	4.25	4Q 92	4c
Clothing				
Jeans, man's denim		29.99	4Q 92	4c
Shirt, man's dress shirt		21.71	4Q 92	4c
Undervest, boy's size 10-14, cotton	3	3.94	4Q 92	4c

Quincy, IL - continued

Item	Per	Value	Date	Ref.
Communications				
Newspaper subscription, daily and Sunday home delivery, large-city	month	8.38	4Q 92	4c
Telephone, flat rate	month	12.66	91	11c
Telephone bill, family of four	month	19.12	4Q 92	4c
Energy and Fuels				
Energy, combined forms, 1,800 sq ft heating area	month	127.37	4Q 92	4c
Gas, cooking, 10 therms	month	11.38	92	56c
Gas, cooking, 30 therms	month	21.02	92	56c
Gas, cooking, 50 therms	month	30.66	92	56c
Gas, heating, winter, 100 therms	month	54.76	92	56c
Gas, heating, winter, average use	month	117.42	92	56c
Gasoline, motor	gal	1.11	4Q 92	4c
Entertainment				
Bowling, evening rate	game	1.33	4Q 92	4c
Monopoly game, Parker Brothers', No. 9		11.98	4Q 92	4c
Movie	admission	4.50	4Q 92	4c
Tennis balls, yellow, Wilson or Penn, 3	can	2.17	4Q 92	4c
Goods and Services				
ACCRA Index, Miscellaneous Goods and Services		90.60	4Q 92	4c
Groceries				
ACCRA Index, Groceries		88.80	4Q 92	4c
Babyfood, strained vegetables, lowest price	4-4.5 oz jar	0.28	4Q 92	4c
Bananas	lb	0.45	4Q 92	4c
Bread, white	24 oz	0.41	4Q 92	4c
Cheese, Kraft grated Parmesan	8-oz canister	3.23	4Q 92	4c
Chicken, fryer, whole	lb	0.65	4Q 92	4c
Cigarettes, Winston	carton	18.00	4Q 92	4c
Coffee, vacuum-packed	13-oz can	1.96	4Q 92	4c
Corn, frozen	10 oz	0.67	4Q 92	4c
Corn Flakes, Kellogg's or Post Toasties	18 oz	1.63	4Q 92	4c
Eggs, Grade A large	doz	0.65	4Q 92	4c
Ground beef or hamburger	lb	1.15	4Q 92	4c
Lettuce, iceberg	head	0.93	4Q 92	4c
Margarine, Blue Bonnet or Parkay cubes	lb	0.57	4Q 92	4c
Milk, whole	1/2 gal	1.37	4Q 92	4c
Orange juice, Minute Maid frozen	12-oz can	1.25	4Q 92	4c
Peaches	29-oz can	1.19	4Q 92	4c
Peas Sweet, Del Monte or Green Giant	15-17 oz can	0.52	4Q 92	4c
Potatoes, white or red	10-lb sack	1.55	4Q 92	4c
Sausage, Jimmy Dean, 100% pork	lb	2.47	4Q 92	4c
Shortening, vegetable, Crisco	3-lb can	1.86	4Q 92	4c
Soft drink, Coca Cola	2 liter	1.27	4Q 92	4c
Steak, T-bone	lb	5.13	4Q 92	4c
Sugar, cane or beet	4 lb	1.06	4Q 92	4c
Tomatoes, Hunt's or Del Monte	14.5-oz can	0.67	4Q 92	4c
Tuna, chunk, light	6.125-6.5 oz can	0.51	4Q 92	4c
Health Care				
ACCRA Index, Health Care		88.90	4Q 92	4c
Analgesic, Aspirin, Bayer, 325 mg tablets	100	5.26	4Q 92	4c
Dentist's fee, adult teeth cleaning and periodic oral exam	visit	41.80	4Q 92	4c
Doctor's fee, routine exam, established patient	visit	30.67	4Q 92	4c
Hospital care, semiprivate room	day	214.09	90	27c

Values are in dollars or fractions of dollars. In the column headed *Ref*, references are shown to sources. Each reference is followed by a letter. These refer to the geographical level for which data were reported: s=State, r=Region, and c=City or metro. The abbreviation *ex* is used to mean *except* or *excluding*; *exp* stands for expenditures. For other abbreviations and further explanations, please see the Introduction.

Quincy, IL - continued

Item	Per	Value	Date	Ref.
Health Care				
Hospital care, semiprivate room	day	285.00	4Q 92	4c
Household Goods				
Appliance repair, home, service call, washing machine	min labor charge	23.99	4Q 92	4c
Laundry detergent, Tide Ultra, Bold, or Cheer	42 oz	2.89	4Q 92	4c
Tissues, facial, Kleenex brand	175-count box	1.09	4Q 92	4c
Housing				
ACCRA Index, Housing		93.10	4Q 92	4c
House, 1,800 sq ft, 8,000 sq ft lot, new, urban	total	108450	4Q 92	4c
House payment, principal and interest, 25% down payment	month	607	4Q 92	4c
Mortgage rate, incl. points & origination fee, 30-year fixed or adjustable rate	per-cent	8.18	4Q 92	4c
Rent, apartment, 2 bedrooms - 1-1/2 to 2 baths, unfurnished, 950 sq ft, water	month	379	4Q 92	4c
Personal Goods				
Shampoo, Alberto VO5	15 oz	1.32	4Q 92	4c
Toothpaste, Crest or Colgate	6-7 oz	1.99	4Q 92	4c
Personal Services				
Dry cleaning, man's 2-piece suit		5.51	4Q 92	4c
Haircare, woman's shampoo, trim and blow-dry		17.70	4Q 92	4c
Haircut, man's barbershop, no styling		7.90	4Q 92	4c
Restaurant Food				
Chicken, fried, thigh and drumstick		2.00	4Q 92	4c
Hamburger with cheese	1/4 lb	1.89	4Q 92	4c
Pizza, Pizza Hut or Pizza Inn, cheese, thin crust	12-13 in	7.10	4Q 92	4c
Transportation				
ACCRA Index, Transportation		93.60	4Q 92	4c
Tire balance, computer or spin balance, front	wheel	5.80	4Q 92	4c
Utilities				
ACCRA Index, Utilities		114.80	4Q 92	4c
Electricity, all electric, 1,800 sq ft living area new home	month	127.37	4Q 92	4c
Electricity, winter, 250 KWh	month	23.06	92	55c
Electricity, winter, 500 KWh	month	42.24	92	55c
Electricity, winter, 750 KWh	month	61.42	92	55c
Electricity, winter, 1000 KWh	month	80.60	92	55c

Racine, WI

Item	Per	Value	Date	Ref.
Child Care				
Child care fee, average, center	hour	1.63	90	65r
Child care fee, average, nonregulated family day care	hour	1.83	90	65r
Child care fee, average, regulated family day care	hour	1.42	90	65r
Communications				
Long-distance telephone service, day, initial minute, 0-100 miles	min	0.15-0.29	91	12s
Long-distance telephone service, day, additional minute, 0-100 miles	min	0.10-0.27	91	12s
Education				
Board, 4-yr private college/university	year	1533	91	22s
Board, 4-yr public college/university	year	1404	91	22s
Expenditures, local gov't, public elementary/secondary	pupil	5972	92	20s
Room, 4-year private college/university	year	1256	91	22s
Room, 4-year public college/university	year	1416	91	22s

Racine, WI - continued

Item	Per	Value	Date	Ref.
Education - continued				
Tuition, 2-year private college/university	year	4768	91	22s
Tuition, 2-year public college/university	year	1234	91	22s
Tuition, 4-year private college/university	year	8237	91	22s
Tuition, 4-year public college/university, in-state	year	1951	91	22s
Energy and Fuels				
Coal	mil Btu	1.41	90	64s
Energy	mil Btu	8.27	90	64s
Energy exp/householder, 1-family unit	year	471	90	28r
Energy exp/householder, <1,000 sq ft heating area	year	430	90	28r
Energy exp/householder, 1,000-1,999 sq ft heating area	year	481	90	28r
Energy exp/householder, 2,000+ sq ft heating area	year	473	90	28r
Energy exp/householder, mobile home	year	430	90	28r
Energy exp/householder, multifamily	year	461	90	28r
Gas, natural	mil Btu	4.56	90	64s
Gas, natural	000 cu ft	5.61	91	46s
Gas, natural, exp	year	605	91	46s
Gasoline, unleaded regular	mil Btu	9.38	90	64s
Entertainment				
Miniature golf admission	adult	6.18	92	1r
Miniature golf admission	child	5.14	92	1r
Waterpark admission	adult	11.00	92	1r
Waterpark admission	child	8.55	92	1r
Funerals				
Casket, 18-gauge steel, velvet interior		1926.72	91	24r
Cosmetology, hair care, etc.		97.64	91	24r
Embalming		249.14	91	24r
Facility use for ceremony		208.59	91	24r
Hearse, local		130.12	91	24r
Limousine, local		104.66	91	24r
Remains to funeral home, transfer		93.61	91	24r
Service charge, professional		724.62	91	24r
Vault, concrete, non-metallic liner		734.53	91	24r
Viewing facilities, use		236.06	91	24r
Groceries				
Apples, Red Delicious	lb	0.77	4/93	16r
Bacon	lb	1.85	4/93	16r
Bananas	lb	0.46	4/93	16r
Beef, stew, boneless	lb	2.53	4/93	16r
Bologna, all beef or mixed	lb	2.19	4/93	16r
Bread, white, pan	lb	0.78	4/93	16r
Butter	lb	1.50	4/93	16r
Cabbage	lb	0.40	4/93	16r
Carrots, short trimmed and topped	lb	0.45	4/93	16r
Cheese, Cheddar	lb	3.47	4/93	16r
Chicken, fresh, whole	lb	0.84	4/93	16r
Chicken breast, bone-in	lb	1.94	4/93	16r
Chicken legs, bone-in	lb	1.02	4/93	16r
Chuck roast, graded and ungraded, ex USDA prime and choice	lb	2.43	4/93	16r
Chuck roast, USDA choice, bone-in	lb	2.11	4/93	16r
Chuck roast, USDA choice, boneless	lb	2.44	4/93	16r
Coffee, 100% ground roast, all sizes	lb	2.47	4/93	16r
Cookies, chocolate chip	lb	2.73	4/93	16r
Eggs, Grade A large	doz	0.93	4/93	16r
Flour, white, all purpose	lb	0.21	4/93	16r
Grapefruit	lb	0.45	4/93	16r
Grapes, Thompson Seedless	lb	1.46	4/93	16r
Ground beef, 100% beef	lb	1.63	4/93	16r
Ground beef, lean and extra lean	lb	2.08	4/93	16r
Ground chuck, 100% beef	lb	1.94	4/93	16r
Ham, boneless, excluding canned	lb	2.21	4/93	16r
Honey, jar	8 oz	0.97-1.25	92	5r
Honey, jar	lb	1.25-2.25	92	5r
Honey, squeeze bear	12-oz	1.25-1.99	92	5r
Ice cream, prepackaged, bulk, regular	1/2 gal	2.41	4/93	16r

Values are in dollars or fractions of dollars. In the column headed *Ref*, references are shown to sources. Each reference is followed by a letter. These refer to the geographical level for which data were reported: s = State, r = Region, and c = City or metro. The abbreviation *ex* is used to mean *except* or *excluding*; *exp* stands for expenditures. For other abbreviations and further explanations, please see the Introduction.

Racine, WI - continued

Item	Per	Value	Date	Ref.
Groceries				
Lemons	lb	0.82	4/93	16r
Lettuce, iceberg	lb	0.83	4/93	16r
Margarine, stick	lb	0.77	4/93	16r
Oranges, navel	lb	0.50	4/93	16r
Peanut butter, creamy, all sizes	lb	1.82	4/93	16r
Pears, Anjou	lb	0.85	4/93	16r
Pork chops, center cut, bone-in	lb	3.17	4/93	16r
Potato chips	16 oz	2.68	4/93	16r
Potatoes, white	lb	0.26	4/93	16r
Round roast, graded & ungraded, ex USDA prime & choice	lb	2.88	4/93	16r
Round roast, USDA choice, boneless	lb	2.96	4/93	16r
Shortening, vegetable oil blends	lb	0.79	4/93	16r
Spaghetti and macaroni	lb	0.76	4/93	16r
Steak, rib eye, USDA choice, boneless	lb	6.29	4/93	16r
Steak, round, USDA choice, boneless	lb	3.24	4/93	16r
Steak, sirloin, graded & ungraded, ex USDA prime & choice	lb	4.00	4/93	16r
Steak, sirloin, USDA choice, bone-in	lb	3.57	4/93	16r
Steak, sirloin, USDA choice, boneless	lb	4.17	4/93	16r
Steak, T-bone, USDA choice, bone-in	lb	5.60	4/93	16r
Strawberries, dry pint	12 oz	0.90	4/93	16r
Sugar, white	lb	0.36	4/93	16r
Sugar, white, 33-80 oz pk	lb	0.35	4/93	16r
Tomatoes, field grown	lb	0.99	4/93	16r
Tuna, chunk, light	lb	1.76	4/93	16r
Turkey, frozen, whole	lb	0.91	4/93	16r
Health Care				
Childbirth, cesarean, hospital		4688	91	62r
Childbirth, cesarean, physician's fee		2053	91	62r
Childbirth, normal, hospital		2657	91	62r
Childbirth, normal, physician's fee		1492	91	62r
Medical plan per employee	year	3443	91	45r
Mental health care, exp	capita	28.84-37.59	90	38s
Mental health care, exp, state mental health agency	capita	36.62	90	38s
Mental health care, hospital psychiatric services, non-Federal, exp	capita	13.05	88	38s
Mental health care, mental health organization, multiservice, exp	capita	10.93	88	38s
Mental health care, psychiatric hospitals, private, exp	capita	8.71	88	38s
Mental health care, psychiatric out-patient clinics, freestanding, exp	capita	5.33	88	38s
Mental health care, psychiatric partial-care organizations, freestanding, exp	capita	0.20	88	38s
Mental health care, state and county mental hospitals, exp	capita	28.29	88	38s
Mental health care, VA medical centers, exp	capita	7.57	88	38s
Physician fee, family practice, first-visit		76.00	91	62r
Physician fee, family practice, revisit		33.00	91	62r
Physician fee, general practice, first-visit		61.00	91	62r
Physician fee, general practice, revisit		31.00	91	62r
Physician fee, general surgeon, first-visit		65.00	91	62r
Physician fee, general surgeon, revisit		35.00	91	62r
Physician fee, internal medicine, first-visit		91.00	91	62r
Physician fee, internal medicine, revisit		40.00	91	62r
Physician fee, median, neurosurgeon, first-visit		106.00	91	62r
Physician fee, median, nonsurgical specialist, first-visit		90.00	91	62r
Physician fee, median, orthopedic surgeon, first-visit		83.00	91	62r
Physician fee, median, surgical specialist, first-visit		61.00	91	62r
Physician fee, neurosurgeon, revisit		41.00	91	62r
Physician fee, nonsurgical specialist, revisit		40.00	91	62r
Physician fee, obstetrics/gynecology, first-visit		61.00	91	62r
Physician fee, obstetrics/gynecology, revisit		40.00	91	62r
Physician fee, orthopedic surgeon, revisit		41.00	91	62r

Racine, WI - continued

Item	Per	Value	Date	Ref.
Health Care - continued				
Physician fee, pediatrician, first-visit		46.00	91	62r
Physician fee, pediatrician, revisit		33.00	91	62r
Physician fee, surgical specialist, revisit		36.00	91	62r
Substance abuse, hospital ancillary charge	incident	960	90	70s
Substance abuse, hospital physician charge	incident	470	90	70s
Substance abuse, hospital room and board	incident	3980	90	70s
Insurance and Pensions				
Auto insurance, private passenger	year	510.11	91	63s
Taxes				
Tax, cigarette	pack	38	91	77s
Tax, gasoline	gal	22.20	91	77s
Taxes, state	capita	1416	91	77s
Transportation				
Driver's license fee		9.00	12/90	43s
Utilities				
Electricity	mil Btu	15.77	90	64s

Raleigh-Durham, NC

Item	Per	Value	Date	Ref.
Composite ACCRA index		98.70	4Q 92	4c
Alcoholic Beverages				
Beer, Miller Lite or Budweiser, 12-oz containers	6 pack	3.67	4Q 92	4c
Liquor, J & B Scotch	750 ml	17.65	4Q 92	4c
Wine, Gallo Chablis blanc, 1.5 liter	bottle	4.76	4Q 92	4c
Child Care				
Child care fee, average, center	hour	1.29	90	65r
Child care fee, average, nonregulated family day care	hour	0.89	90	65r
Child care fee, average, regulated family day care	hour	1.32	90	65r
Clothing				
Jeans, man's denim		27.86	4Q 92	4c
Shirt, man's dress shirt		24.50	4Q 92	4c
Undervest, boy's size 10-14, cotton	3	3.80	4Q 92	4c
Communications				
Long-distance telephone service, day, initial minute, 0-100 miles	min	0.10-0.33	91	12s
Long-distance telephone service, day, additional minute, 0-100 miles	min	0.10-0.33	91	12s
Long-distance telephone service, evenings/weekends, 0-100 mi, initial minute	min	0.08-0.24	91	12s
Long-distance telephone service, evenings/weekends, 0-100 mi, additional minute	min	0.05-0.17	91	12s
Newspaper subscription, daily and Sunday home delivery, large-city	month	11.96	4Q 92	4c
Telephone bill, family of four	month	18.51	4Q 92	4c
Education				
Board, 4-yr private college/university	year	1768	91	22s
Board, 4-yr public college/university	year	1568	91	22s
Expenditures, local gov't, public elementary/secondary	pupil	5078	92	20s
Room, 4-year private college/university	year	1467	91	22s
Room, 4-year public college/university	year	1386	91	22s
Tuition, 2-year private college/university	year	4964	91	22s
Tuition, 2-year public college/university	year	334	91	22s
Tuition, 4-year private college/university	year	7826	91	22s
Tuition, 4-year public college/university, in-state	year	1112	91	22s
Energy and Fuels				
Coal	mil Btu	1.79	90	64s
Energy	mil Btu	10.06	90	64s

Values are in dollars or fractions of dollars. In the column headed *Ref*, references are shown to sources. Each reference is followed by a letter. These refer to the geographical level for which data were reported: s=State, r=Region, and c=City or metro. The abbreviation *ex* is used to mean *except* or *excluding*; *exp* stands for expenditures. For other abbreviations and further explanations, please see the Introduction.

Raleigh-Durham, NC - continued

Item	Per	Value	Date	Ref.
Energy and Fuels				
Energy, combined forms, 1,800 sq ft heating area	month	122.90	4Q 92	4c
Energy exp/householder, 1-family unit	year	487	90	28r
Energy exp/householder, <1,000 sq ft heating area	year	393	90	28r
Energy exp/householder, 1,000-1,999 sq ft heating area	year	442	90	28r
Energy exp/householder, 2,000+ sq ft heating area	year	577	90	28r
Energy exp/householder, mobile home	year	366	90	28r
Energy exp/householder, multifamily	year	382	90	28r
Gas, cooking, winter, 10 therms	month	12.08	92	56c
Gas, cooking, winter, 30 therms	month	22.23	92	56c
Gas, cooking, winter, 50 therms	month	32.38	92	56c
Gas, heating, winter, 100 therms	month	64.32	92	56c
Gas, heating, winter, average use	month	70.84	92	56c
Gas, natural	mil Btu	4.19	90	64s
Gas, natural	000 cu ft	6.24	91	46s
Gas, natural, exp	year	439	91	46s
Gasoline, motor	gal	1.09	4Q 92	4c
Gasoline, unleaded regular	mil Btu	9.44	90	64s
Entertainment				
Bowling, evening rate	game	1.93	4Q 92	4c
Miniature golf admission	adult	6.18	92	1r
Miniature golf admission	child	5.14	92	1r
Monopoly game, Parker Brothers', No. 9		10.23	4Q 92	4c
Movie	admission	5.50	4Q 92	4c
Tennis balls, yellow, Wilson or Penn, 3	can	2.18	4Q 92	4c
Waterpark admission	adult	11.00	92	1r
Waterpark admission	child	8.55	92	1r
Funerals				
Casket, 18-gauge steel, velvet interior		2029.08	91	24r
Cosmetology, hair care, etc.		75.10	91	24r
Embalming		249.24	91	24r
Facility use for ceremony		162.27	91	24r
Hearse, local		114.04	91	24r
Limousine, local		88.57	91	24r
Remains to funeral home, transfer		92.61	91	24r
Service charge, professional		682.42	91	24r
Vault, concrete, non-metallic liner		798.70	91	24r
Viewing facilities, use		163.86	91	24r
Goods and Services				
ACCRA Index, Miscellaneous Goods and Services		96.00	4Q 92	4c
Groceries				
ACCRA Index, Groceries		92.80	4Q 92	4c
Apples, Red Delicious	lb	0.79	4/93	16r
Babyfood, strained vegetables, lowest price	4-4.5 oz jar	0.31	4Q 92	4c
Bacon	lb	1.75	4/93	16r
Bananas	lb	0.48	4Q 92	4c
Bananas	lb	0.42	4/93	16r
Beef, stew, boneless	lb	2.61	4/93	16r
Bologna, all beef or mixed	lb	2.24	4/93	16r
Bread, white	24 oz	0.64	4Q 92	4c
Bread, white, pan	lb	0.64	4/93	16r
Bread, whole wheat, pan	lb	0.96	4/93	16r
Cabbage	lb	0.37	4/93	16r
Carrots, short trimmed and topped	lb	0.47	4/93	16r
Celery	lb	0.64	4/93	16r
Cheese, American	lb	2.98	4/93	16r
Cheese, Cheddar	lb	3.28	4/93	16r
Cheese, Kraft grated Parmesan	8-oz canister	3.26	4Q 92	4c
Chicken, fresh, whole	lb	0.77	4/93	16r
Chicken, fryer, whole	lb	0.76	4Q 92	4c
Chicken breast, bone-in	lb	1.92	4/93	16r

Raleigh-Durham, NC - continued

Item	Per	Value	Date	Ref.
Groceries - continued				
Chicken legs, bone-in	lb	1.06	4/93	16r
Chuck roast, graded and ungraded, ex USDA prime and choice	lb	2.40	4/93	16r
Chuck roast, USDA choice, bone-in	lb	2.19	4/93	16r
Chuck roast, USDA choice, boneless	lb	2.38	4/93	16r
Cigarettes, Winston	carton	15.28	4Q 92	4c
Coffee, 100% ground roast, all sizes	lb	2.48	4/93	16r
Coffee, vacuum-packed	13-oz can	1.76	4Q 92	4c
Corn, frozen	10 oz	0.52	4Q 92	4c
Corn Flakes, Kellogg's or Post Toasties	18 oz	1.69	4Q 92	4c
Crackers, soda, salted	lb	1.15	4/93	16r
Eggs, Grade A large	doz	0.90	4Q 92	4c
Eggs, Grade A large	doz	0.96	4/93	16r
Flour, white, all purpose	lb	0.24	4/93	16r
Frankfurters, all meat or all beef	lb	2.01	4/93	16r
Grapefruit	lb	0.44	4/93	16r
Grapes, Thompson Seedless	lb	1.40	4/93	16r
Ground beef, 100% beef	lb	1.58	4/93	16r
Ground beef, lean and extra lean	lb	2.09	4/93	16r
Ground beef or hamburger	lb	1.41	4Q 92	4c
Ground chuck, 100% beef	lb	1.98	4/93	16r
Ham, boneless, excluding canned	lb	2.89	4/93	16r
Ham, picnic, shoulder, bone-in, smoked	lb	1.02	4/93	16r
Ham, rump or steak half, bone-in, smoked	lb	1.48	4/93	16r
Ice cream, prepackaged, bulk, regular	1/2 gal	2.41	4/93	16r
Lemons	lb	1.05	4/93	16r
Lettuce, iceberg	head	0.89	4Q 92	4c
Lettuce, iceberg	lb	0.81	4/93	16r
Margarine, Blue Bonnet or Parkay cubes	lb	0.48	4Q 92	4c
Margarine, stick	lb	0.88	4/93	16r
Milk, whole	1/2 gal	1.38	4Q 92	4c
Orange juice, Minute Maid frozen	12-oz can	1.28	4Q 92	4c
Oranges, navel	lb	0.55	4/93	16r
Peaches	29-oz can	1.29	4Q 92	4c
Pears, Anjou	lb	0.92	4/93	16r
Peas Sweet, Del Monte or Green Giant	15-17 oz can	0.47	4Q 92	4c
Pork chops, center cut, bone-in	lb	3.13	4/93	16r
Potato chips	16 oz	2.94	4/93	16r
Potatoes, white	lb	0.43	4/93	16r
Potatoes, white or red	10-lb sack	2.06	4Q 92	4c
Rib roast, USDA choice, bone-in	lb	4.63	4/93	16r
Rice, white, long grain, uncooked	lb	0.45	4/93	16r
Round roast, graded & ungraded, ex USDA prime & choice	lb	3.03	4/93	16r
Round roast, USDA choice, boneless	lb	3.09	4/93	16r
Sausage, fresh, loose	lb	2.08	4/93	16r
Sausage, Jimmy Dean, 100% pork	lb	2.00	4Q 92	4c
Short ribs, bone-in	lb	2.66	4/93	16r
Shortening, vegetable oil blends	lb	0.69	4/93	16r
Shortening, vegetable, Crisco	3-lb can	1.98	4Q 92	4c
Soft drink, Coca Cola	2 liter	1.24	4Q 92	4c
Spaghetti and macaroni	lb	0.81	4/93	16r
Steak, rib eye, USDA choice, boneless	lb	6.24	4/93	16r
Steak, round, graded & ungraded, ex USDA prime & choice	lb	3.31	4/93	16r
Steak, round, USDA choice, boneless	lb	3.34	4/93	16r
Steak, sirloin, graded & ungraded, ex USDA prime & choice	lb	4.19	4/93	16r
Steak, sirloin, USDA choice, boneless	lb	4.46	4/93	16r
Steak, T-bone	lb	5.86	4Q 92	4c
Steak, T-bone, USDA choice, bone-in	lb	5.25	4/93	16r
Strawberries, dry pint	12 oz	0.92	4/93	16r
Sugar, cane or beet	4 lb	1.41	4Q 92	4c
Sugar, white	lb	0.39	4/93	16r
Sugar, white, 33-80 oz pk	lb	0.38	4/93	16r
Tomatoes, field grown	lb	0.88	4/93	16r

Values are in dollars or fractions of dollars. In the column headed *Ref*, references are shown to sources. Each reference is followed by a letter. These refer to the geographical level for which data were reported: s=State, r=Region, and c=City or metro. The abbreviation *ex* is used to mean *except* or *excluding*; *exp* stands for expenditures. For other abbreviations and further explanations, please see the Introduction.

Raleigh-Durham, NC - continued

Item	Per	Value	Date	Ref.
Groceries				
Tomatoes, Hunt's or Del Monte	14.5-oz can	0.49	4Q 92	4c
Tuna, chunk, light	6.125-6.5 oz can	0.53	4Q 92	4c
Tuna, chunk, light	lb	1.79	4/93	16r
Turkey, frozen, whole	lb	1.04	4/93	16r
Yogurt, natural, fruit flavored	1/2 pint	0.57	4/93	16r
Health Care				
ACCRA Index, Health Care		103.50	4Q 92	4c
Analgesic, Aspirin, Bayer, 325 mg tablets	100	4.56	4Q 92	4c
Childbirth, cesarean, hospital		5034	91	62r
Childbirth, cesarean, physician's fee		2053	91	62r
Childbirth, normal, hospital		2712	91	62r
Childbirth, normal, physician's fee		1492	91	62r
Dentist's fee, adult teeth cleaning and periodic oral exam	visit	48.17	4Q 92	4c
Doctor's fee, routine exam, established patient	visit	44.00	4Q 92	4c
Hospital care, semiprivate room	day	259.75	4Q 92	4c
Medical plan per employee	year	3495	91	45r
Mental health care, exp	capita	37.60-53.67	90	38s
Mental health care, exp, state mental health agency	capita	45.66	90	38s
Mental health care, hospital psychiatric services, non-Federal, exp	capita	12.05	88	38s
Mental health care, mental health organization, multiservice, exp	capita	29.54	88	38s
Mental health care, psychiatric hospitals, private, exp	capita	15.07	88	38s
Mental health care, psychiatric out-patient clinics, freestanding, exp	capita	0.11	88	38s
Mental health care, state and county mental hospitals, exp	capita	26.36	88	38s
Mental health care, VA medical centers, exp	capita	2.23	88	38s
Physician fee, family practice, first-visit		75.00	91	62r
Physician fee, family practice, revisit		34.00	91	62r
Physician fee, general practice, first-visit		61.00	91	62r
Physician fee, general practice, revisit		32.00	91	62r
Physician fee, general surgeon, first-visit		64.00	91	62r
Physician fee, general surgeon, revisit		40.00	91	62r
Physician fee, internal medicine, first-visit		98.00	91	62r
Physician fee, internal medicine, revisit		40.00	91	62r
Physician fee, median, neurosurgeon, first-visit		130.00	91	62r
Physician fee, median, nonsurgical specialist, first-visit		95.00	91	62r
Physician fee, median, orthopedic surgeon, first-visit		91.00	91	62r
Physician fee, median, plastic surgeon, first-visit		66.00	91	62r
Physician fee, median, surgical specialist, first-visit		62.00	91	62r
Physician fee, neurosurgeon, revisit		50.00	91	62r
Physician fee, nonsurgical specialist, revisit		40.00	91	62r
Physician fee, obstetrics/gynecology, first-visit		64.00	91	62r
Physician fee, obstetrics/gynecology, revisit		41.00	91	62r
Physician fee, orthopedic surgeon, revisit		40.00	91	62r
Physician fee, pediatrician, first-visit		49.00	91	62r
Physician fee, pediatrician, revisit		33.00	91	62r
Physician fee, plastic surgeon, revisit		43.00	91	62r
Physician fee, surgical specialist, revisit		37.00	91	62r
Substance abuse, hospital ancillary charge	incident	1090	90	70s
Substance abuse, hospital physician charge	incident	460	90	70s
Substance abuse, hospital room and board	incident	4880	90	70s

Raleigh-Durham, NC - continued

Item	Per	Value	Date	Ref.
Household Goods				
Appliance repair, home, service call, washing machine	min labor charge	31.40	4Q 92	4c
Laundry detergent, Tide Ultra, Bold, or Cheer	42 oz	2.72	4Q 92	4c
Tissues, facial, Kleenex brand	175-count box	1.00	4Q 92	4c
Housing				
ACCRA Index, Housing		101.70	4Q 92	4c
Home, median price	unit	105.90		26c
House, 1,800 sq ft, 8,000 sq ft lot, new, urban	total	116488	4Q 92	4c
House payment, principal and interest, 25% down payment	month	640	4Q 92	4c
Mortgage rate, incl. points & origination fee, 30-year fixed or adjustable rate	percent	7.98	4Q 92	4c
Rent, apartment, 2 bedrooms - 1-1/2 to 2 baths, unfurnished, 950 sq ft, water	month	469	4Q 92	4c
Rental unit, 1 bedroom	month	418	93	23c
Rental unit, 2 bedroom	month	494	93	23c
Rental unit, 3 bedroom	month	617	93	23c
Rental unit, 4 bedroom	month	691	93	23c
Rental unit, efficiency	month	344	93	23c
Insurance and Pensions				
Auto insurance, private passenger	year	522.39	91	63s
Personal Goods				
Shampoo, Alberto VO5	15 oz	1.03	4Q 92	4c
Toothpaste, Crest or Colgate	6-7 oz	1.74	4Q 92	4c
Personal Services				
Dry cleaning, man's 2-piece suit		5.36	4Q 92	4c
Haircare, woman's shampoo, trim and blow-dry		18.86	4Q 92	4c
Haircut, man's barbershop, no styling		8.00	4Q 92	4c
Restaurant Food				
Chicken, fried, thigh and drumstick		1.99	4Q 92	4c
Hamburger with cheese	1/4 lb	1.82	4Q 92	4c
Pizza, Pizza Hut or Pizza Inn, cheese, thin crust	12-13 in	7.69	4Q 92	4c
Taxes				
Tax, cigarette	pack	5	91	77s
Tax, gasoline	gal	21.90	91	77s
Taxes, state	capita	1165	91	77s
Transportation				
ACCRA Index, Transportation		94.60	4Q 92	4c
Auto rental, average	day	54.25	6/91	60c
Bus fare, up to 10 miles	one-way	0.50	4Q 92	4c
Driver's license fee		15.00	12/90	43s
Limo fare, airport-city, average	day	14.00	6/91	60c
Taxi fare, airport-city, average	day	20.50	6/91	60c
Tire balance, computer or spin balance, front	wheel	6.56	4Q 92	4c
Vehicle registration and license plate	year	35.00	93	50s
Travel				
Breakfast	day	6.24	6/91	60c
Business travel	day	193.00	4/93	89r
Dinner	day	22.89	6/91	60c
Lodging	day	90.66	91	60c
Lunch	day	10.58	6/91	60c
Utilities				
ACCRA Index, Utilities		110.80	4Q 92	4c
Electricity	mil Btu	18.74	90	64s
Electricity, all electric, 1,800 sq ft living area new home	month	122.90	4Q 92	4c

Values are in dollars or fractions of dollars. In the column headed *Ref*, references are shown to sources. Each reference is followed by a letter. These refer to the geographical level for which data were reported: s=State, r=Region, and c=City or metro. The abbreviation *ex* is used to mean *except* or *excluding*; *exp* stands for expenditures. For other abbreviations and further explanations, please see the Introduction.

Rapid City, SD

Item	Per	Value	Date	Ref.
Composite ACCRA index		100.70	4Q 92	4c
Alcoholic Beverages				
Beer, Miller Lite or Budweiser, 12-oz containers	6 pack	3.62	4Q 92	4c
Liquor, J & B Scotch	750 ml	18.08	4Q 92	4c
Wine, Gallo Chablis blanc, 1.5 liter	bottle	5.28	4Q 92	4c
Child Care				
Child care fee, average, center	hour	1.63	90	65r
Child care fee, average, nonregulated family day care	hour	1.83	90	65r
Child care fee, average, regulated family day care	hour	1.42	90	65r
Clothing				
Jeans, man's denim		28.97	4Q 92	4c
Shirt, man's dress shirt		24.60	4Q 92	4c
Undervest, boy's size 10-14, cotton	3	4.10	4Q 92	4c
Communications				
Long-distance telephone service, day, initial minute, 0-100 miles	min	0.21-0.41	91	12s
Long-distance telephone service, day, additional minute, 0-100 miles	min	0.15-0.27	91	12s
Long-distance telephone service, evenings/ weekends, 0-100 mi, initial minute	min	0.08-0.16	91	12s
Long-distance telephone service, evenings/ weekends, 0-100 mi, additional minute	min	0.06-0.11	91	12s
Newspaper subscription, daily and Sunday home delivery, large-city	month	10.50	4Q 92	4c
Telephone, flat rate	month	32.95	91	11c
Telephone bill, family of four	month	22.46	4Q 92	4c
Education				
Board, 4-yr private college/university	year	1452	91	22s
Board, 4-yr public college/university	year	1234	91	22s
Expenditures, local gov't, public elementary/secondary	pupil	4255	92	20s
Room, 4-year private college/university	year	1282	91	22s
Room, 4-year public college/university	year	739	91	22s
Tuition, 2-year private college/university	year	4515	91	22s
Tuition, 2-year public college/university	year	1920	91	22s
Tuition, 4-year private college/university	year	6346	91	22s
Tuition, 4-year public college/university, in-state	year	1854	91	22s
Energy and Fuels				
Coal	mil Btu	1.22	90	64s
Energy	mil Btu	8.65	90	64s
Energy, combined forms, 1,800 sq ft heating area	month	115.10	4Q 92	4c
Energy, exc electricity, 1,800 sq ft heating area	month	56.89	4Q 92	4c
Energy exp/householder, 1-family unit	year	473	90	28r
Energy exp/householder, <1,000 sq ft heating area	year	429	90	28r
Energy exp/householder, 1,000-1,999 sq ft heating area	year	442	90	28r
Energy exp/householder, 2,000+ sq ft heating area	year	498	90	28r
Energy exp/householder, mobile home	year	442	90	28r
Energy exp/householder, multifamily	year	407	90	28r
Gas, cooking, winter, 10 therms	month	10.30	92	56c
Gas, cooking, winter, 30 therms	month	19.22	92	56c
Gas, cooking, winter, 50 therms	month	28.14	92	56c
Gas, heating, winter, 100 therms	month	50.44	92	56c
Gas, natural	mil Btu	4.41	90	64s
Gas, natural	000 cu ft	4.94	91	46s
Gas, natural, exp	year	514	91	46s
Gasoline, motor	gal	1.26	4Q 92	4c
Gasoline, unleaded regular	mil Btu	9.40	90	64s
Entertainment				
Bowling, evening rate	game	1.90	4Q 92	4c

Rapid City, SD - continued

Item	Per	Value	Date	Ref.
Entertainment - continued				
Miniature golf admission	adult	6.18	92	1r
Miniature golf admission	child	5.14	92	1r
Monopoly game, Parker Brothers', No. 9		10.98	4Q 92	4c
Movie	admission	5.00	4Q 92	4c
Tennis balls, yellow, Wilson or Penn, 3	can	1.98	4Q 92	4c
Waterpark admission	adult	11.00	92	1r
Waterpark admission	child	8.55	92	1r
Funerals				
Casket, 18-gauge steel, velvet interior		1952.97	91	24r
Cosmetology, hair care, etc.		90.03	91	24r
Embalming		251.75	91	24r
Facility use for ceremony		180.75	91	24r
Hearse, local		117.51	91	24r
Limousine, local		71.86	91	24r
Remains to funeral home, transfer		81.14	91	24r
Service charge, professional		740.03	91	24r
Vault, concrete, non-metallic liner		801.47	91	24r
Viewing facilities, use		169.33	91	24r
Goods and Services				
ACCRA Index, Miscellaneous Goods and Services		97.10	4Q 92	4c
Groceries				
ACCRA Index, Groceries		104.80	4Q 92	4c
Apples, Red Delicious	lb	0.77	4/93	16r
Babyfood, strained vegetables, lowest price	4-4.5 oz jar	0.33	4Q 92	4c
Bacon	lb	1.85	4/93	16r
Bananas	lb	0.56	4Q 92	4c
Bananas	lb	0.46	4/93	16r
Beef, stew, boneless	lb	2.53	4/93	16r
Bologna, all beef or mixed	lb	2.19	4/93	16r
Bread, white	24 oz	0.53	4Q 92	4c
Bread, white, pan	lb	0.78	4/93	16r
Butter	lb	1.50	4/93	16r
Cabbage	lb	0.40	4/93	16r
Carrots, short trimmed and topped	lb	0.45	4/93	16r
Cheese, Cheddar	lb	3.47	4/93	16r
Cheese, Kraft grated Parmesan	8-oz canister	3.36	4Q 92	4c
Chicken, fresh, whole	lb	0.84	4/93	16r
Chicken, fryer, whole	lb	0.68	4Q 92	4c
Chicken breast, bone-in	lb	1.94	4/93	16r
Chicken legs, bone-in	lb	1.02	4/93	16r
Chuck roast, graded and ungraded, ex USDA prime and choice	lb	2.43	4/93	16r
Chuck roast, USDA choice, bone-in	lb	2.11	4/93	16r
Chuck roast, USDA choice, boneless	lb	2.44	4/93	16r
Cigarettes, Winston	carton	17.89	4Q 92	4c
Coffee, 100% ground roast, all sizes	lb	2.47	4/93	16r
Coffee, vacuum-packed	13-oz can	2.80	4Q 92	4c
Cookies, chocolate chip	lb	2.73	4/93	16r
Corn, frozen	10 oz	0.71	4Q 92	4c
Corn Flakes, Kellogg's or Post Toasties	18 oz	1.96	4Q 92	4c
Eggs, Grade A large	doz	0.80	4Q 92	4c
Eggs, Grade A large	doz	0.93	4/93	16r
Flour, white, all purpose	lb	0.21	4/93	16r
Grapefruit	lb	0.45	4/93	16r
Grapes, Thompson Seedless	lb	1.46	4/93	16r
Ground beef, 100% beef	lb	1.63	4/93	16r
Ground beef, lean and extra lean	lb	2.08	4/93	16r
Ground beef or hamburger	lb	1.48	4Q 92	4c
Ground chuck, 100% beef	lb	1.94	4/93	16r
Ham, boneless, excluding canned	lb	2.21	4/93	16r
Ice cream, prepackaged, bulk, regular	1/2 gal	2.41	4/93	16r
Lemons	lb	0.82	4/93	16r
Lettuce, iceberg	head	1.00	4Q 92	4c
Lettuce, iceberg	lb	0.83	4/93	16r
Margarine, Blue Bonnet or Parkay cubes	lb	0.56	4Q 92	4c

Values are in dollars or fractions of dollars. In the column headed *Ref*, references are shown to sources. Each reference is followed by a letter. These refer to the geographical level for which data were reported: s=State, r=Region, and c=City or metro. The abbreviation *ex* is used to mean *except* or *excluding*; *exp* stands for expenditures. For other abbreviations and further explanations, please see the Introduction.

Rapid City, SD - continued

Item	Per	Value	Date	Ref.
Groceries				
Margarine, stick	lb	0.77	4/93	16r
Milk, whole	1/2 gal	1.61	4Q 92	4c
Orange juice, Minute Maid frozen	12-oz can	1.53	4Q 92	4c
Oranges, navel	lb	0.50	4/93	16r
Peaches	29-oz can	1.53	4Q 92	4c
Peanut butter, creamy, all sizes	lb	1.82	4/93	16r
Pears, Anjou	lb	0.85	4/93	16r
Peas Sweet, Del Monte or Green Giant	15-17 oz can	0.57	4Q 92	4c
Pork chops, center cut, bone-in	lb	3.17	4/93	16r
Potato chips	16 oz	2.68	4/93	16r
Potatoes, white	lb	0.26	4/93	16r
Potatoes, white or red	10-lb sack	1.62	4Q 92	4c
Round roast, graded & ungraded, ex USDA prime & choice	lb	2.88	4/93	16r
Round roast, USDA choice, boneless	lb	2.96	4/93	16r
Sausage, Jimmy Dean, 100% pork	lb	3.20	4Q 92	4c
Shortening, vegetable oil blends	lb	0.79	4/93	16r
Shortening, vegetable, Crisco	3-lb can	2.69	4Q 92	4c
Soft drink, Coca Cola	2 liter	1.86	4Q 92	4c
Spaghetti and macaroni	lb	0.76	4/93	16r
Steak, rib eye, USDA choice, boneless	lb	6.29	4/93	16r
Steak, round, USDA choice, boneless	lb	3.24	4/93	16r
Steak, sirloin, graded & ungraded, ex USDA prime & choice	lb	4.00	4/93	16r
Steak, sirloin, USDA choice, bone-in	lb	3.57	4/93	16r
Steak, sirloin, USDA choice, boneless	lb	4.17	4/93	16r
Steak, T-bone	lb	4.52	4Q 92	4c
Steak, T-bone, USDA choice, bone-in	lb	5.60	4/93	16r
Strawberries, dry pint	12 oz	0.90	4/93	16r
Sugar, cane or beet	4 lb	1.47	4Q 92	4c
Sugar, white	lb	0.36	4/93	16r
Sugar, white, 33-80 oz pk	lb	0.35	4/93	16r
Tomatoes, field grown	lb	0.99	4/93	16r
Tomatoes, Hunt's or Del Monte	14.5-oz can	0.71	4Q 92	4c
Tuna, chunk, light	6.125-6.5 oz can	0.83	4Q 92	4c
Tuna, chunk, light	lb	1.76	4/93	16r
Turkey, frozen, whole	lb	0.91	4/93	16r
Health Care				
ACCRA Index, Health Care		93.30	4Q 92	4c
Analgesic, Aspirin, Bayer, 325 mg tablets	100	4.50	4Q 92	4c
Childbirth, cesarean, hospital		4688	91	62r
Childbirth, cesarean, physician's fee		2053	91	62r
Childbirth, normal, hospital		2657	91	62r
Childbirth, normal, physician's fee		1492	91	62r
Dentist's fee, adult teeth cleaning and periodic oral exam	visit	51.20	4Q 92	4c
Doctor's fee, routine exam, established patient	visit	31.00	4Q 92	4c
Hospital care, semiprivate room	day	224.91	90	27c
Hospital care, semiprivate room	day	260.00	4Q 92	4c
Medical insurance premium, per employee, small group comprehensive	month	267.40	10/91	25c
Medical plan per employee	year	3443	91	45r
Mental health care, exp	capita	20.37-28.83	90	38s
Mental health care, exp, state mental health agency	capita	25.34	90	38s
Mental health care, hospital psychiatric services, non-Federal, exp	capita	4.36	88	38s
Mental health care, mental health organization, multiservice, exp	capita	16.71	88	38s
Mental health care, psychiatric out-patient clinics, freestanding, exp	capita	0.33	88	38s

Rapid City, SD - continued

Item	Per	Value	Date	Ref.
Health Care - continued				
Mental health care, state and county mental hospitals, exp	capita	20.13	88	38s
Mental health care, VA medical centers, exp	capita	20.15	88	38s
Physician fee, family practice, first-visit		76.00	91	62r
Physician fee, family practice, revisit		33.00	91	62r
Physician fee, general practice, first-visit		61.00	91	62r
Physician fee, general practice, revisit		31.00	91	62r
Physician fee, general surgeon, first-visit		65.00	91	62r
Physician fee, general surgeon, revisit		35.00	91	62r
Physician fee, internal medicine, first-visit		91.00	91	62r
Physician fee, internal medicine, revisit		40.00	91	62r
Physician fee, median, neurosurgeon, first-visit		106.00	91	62r
Physician fee, median, nonsurgical specialist, first-visit		90.00	91	62r
Physician fee, median, orthopedic surgeon, first-visit		83.00	91	62r
Physician fee, median, surgical specialist, first-visit		61.00	91	62r
Physician fee, neurosurgeon, revisit		41.00	91	62r
Physician fee, nonsurgical specialist, revisit		40.00	91	62r
Physician fee, obstetrics/gynecology, first-visit		61.00	91	62r
Physician fee, obstetrics/gynecology, revisit		40.00	91	62r
Physician fee, orthopedic surgeon, revisit		41.00	91	62r
Physician fee, pediatrician, first-visit		46.00	91	62r
Physician fee, pediatrician, revisit		33.00	91	62r
Physician fee, surgical specialist, revisit		36.00	91	62r
Household Goods				
Appliance repair, home, service call, washing machine	min labor charge	27.30	4Q 92	4c
Laundry detergent, Tide Ultra, Bold, or Cheer	42 oz	3.48	4Q 92	4c
Tissues, facial, Kleenex brand	175-count box	1.15	4Q 92	4c
Housing				
ACCRA Index, Housing		103.30	4Q 92	4c
House, 1,800 sq ft, 8,000 sq ft lot, new, urban	total	108000	4Q 92	4c
House payment, principal and interest, 25% down payment	month	619	4Q 92	4c
Mortgage rate, incl. points & origination fee, 30-year fixed or adjustable rate	percent	8.43	4Q 92	4c
Rent, apartment, 2 bedrooms - 1-1/2 to 2 baths, unfurnished, 950 sq ft, water	month	547	4Q 92	4c
Rental unit, 1 bedroom	month	368	93	23c
Rental unit, 2 bedroom	month	428	93	23c
Rental unit, 3 bedroom	month	530	93	23c
Rental unit, 4 bedroom	month	594	93	23c
Rental unit, efficiency	month	305	93	23c
Insurance and Pensions				
Auto insurance, private passenger	year	409.16	91	63s
Personal Goods				
Shampoo, Alberto VO5	15 oz	1.46	4Q 92	4c
Toothpaste, Crest or Colgate	6-7 oz	1.97	4Q 92	4c
Personal Services				
Dry cleaning, man's 2-piece suit		6.34	4Q 92	4c
Haircare, woman's shampoo, trim and blow-dry		16.50	4Q 92	4c
Haircut, man's barbershop, no styling		8.71	4Q 92	4c
Restaurant Food				
Chicken, fried, thigh and drumstick		2.10	4Q 92	4c
Hamburger with cheese	1/4 lb	1.80	4Q 92	4c
Pizza, Pizza Hut or Pizza Inn, cheese, thin crust	12-13 in	8.59	4Q 92	4c

Values are in dollars or fractions of dollars. In the column headed *Ref*, references are shown to sources. Each reference is followed by a letter. These refer to the geographical level for which data were reported: s = State, r = Region, and c = City or metro. The abbreviation *ex* is used to mean *except* or *excluding*; *exp* stands for expenditures. For other abbreviations and further explanations, please see the Introduction.

Rapid City, SD - continued

Item	Per	Value	Date	Ref.
Taxes				
Tax, cigarette	pack	23	91	77s
Tax, gasoline	gal	18	91	77s
Taxes, state	capita	751	91	77s
Transportation				
ACCRA Index, Transportation		99.40	4Q 92	4c
Driver's license fee		6.00	12/90	43s
Tire balance, computer or spin balance, front	wheel	5.70	4Q 92	4c
Utilities				
ACCRA Index, Utilities		106.40	4Q 92	4c
Electricity	mil Btu	17.95	90	64s
Electricity, partial electric and other energy, 1,800 sq ft living area new home	month	58.21	4Q 92	4c
Electricity, winter, 250 KWh	month	24.62	92	55c
Electricity, winter, 500 KWh	month	42.25	92	55c
Electricity, winter, 750 KWh	month	59.87	92	55c
Electricity, winter, 1000 KWh	month	77.49	92	55c

Reading, PA

Item	Per	Value	Date	Ref.
Child Care				
Child care fee, average, center	hour	2.18	90	65r
Child care fee, average, nonregulated family day care	hour	1.83	90	65r
Child care fee, average, regulated family day care	hour	2.02	90	65r
Communications				
Long-distance telephone service, day, initial minute, 0-100 miles	min	0.15-0.29	91	12s
Long-distance telephone service, day, additional minute, 0-100 miles	min	0.06-0.22	91	12s
Long-distance telephone service, evenings/weekends, 0-100 mi, initial minute	min	0.06-0.14	91	12s
Long-distance telephone service, evenings/weekends, 0-100 mi, additional minute	min	0.03-0.11	91	12s
Education				
Board, 4-yr private college/university	year	2019	91	22s
Board, 4-yr public college/university	year	1656	91	22s
Expenditures, local gov't, public elementary/secondary	pupil	6980	92	20s
Room, 4-year private college/university	year	2179	91	22s
Room, 4-year public college/university	year	1719	91	22s
Tuition, 2-year private college/university	year	6314	91	22s
Tuition, 2-year public college/university	year	1505	91	22s
Tuition, 4-year private college/university	year	9848	91	22s
Tuition, 4-year public college/university, in-state	year	3401	91	22s
Energy and Fuels				
Coal	mil Btu	1.57	90	64s
Energy	mil Btu	8.63	90	64s
Energy exp/householder, 1-family unit	year	588	90	28r
Energy exp/householder, <1,000 sq ft heating area	year	477	90	28r
Energy exp/householder, 1,000-1,999 sq ft heating area	year	517	90	28r
Energy exp/householder, 2,000+ sq ft heating area	year	630	90	28r
Energy exp/householder, mobile home	year	412	90	28r
Energy exp/householder, multifamily	year	498	90	28r
Gas, natural	mil Btu	5.24	90	64s
Gas, natural	000 cu ft	6.76	91	46s
Gas, natural, exp	year	703	91	46s
Gasoline, unleaded regular	mil Btu	9.35	90	64s
Funerals				
Casket, 18-gauge steel, velvet interior		1811.58	91	24r
Cosmetology, hair care, etc.		111.08	91	24r
Embalming		329.42	91	24r

Reading, PA - continued

Item	Per	Value	Date	Ref.
Funerals - continued				
Facility use for ceremony		201.29	91	24r
Hearse, local		135.27	91	24r
Limousine, local		127.24	91	24r
Remains to funeral home, transfer		103.98	91	24r
Service charge, professional		724.98	91	24r
Vault, concrete, non-metallic liner		766.71	91	24r
Viewing facilities, use		260.60	91	24r
Groceries				
Apples, Red Delicious	lb	0.85	4/93	16r
Bacon	lb	2.12	4/93	16r
Bananas	lb	0.54	4/93	16r
Bread, white, pan	lb	0.81	4/93	16r
Butter	lb	2.02	4/93	16r
Carrots, short trimmed and topped	lb	0.51	4/93	16r
Chicken, fresh, whole	lb	1.04	4/93	16r
Chicken breast, bone-in	lb	2.21	4/93	16r
Chicken legs, bone-in	lb	1.16	4/93	16r
Chuck roast, USDA choice, boneless	lb	2.82	4/93	16r
Coffee, 100% ground roast, all sizes	lb	2.66	4/93	16r
Cucumbers	lb	0.85	4/93	16r
Eggs, Grade A large	doz	1.15	4/93	16r
Grapefruit	lb	0.45	4/93	16r
Grapes, Thompson Seedless	lb	1.52	4/93	16r
Ground beef, lean and extra lean	lb	2.36	4/93	16r
Ground chuck, 100% beef	lb	2.02	4/93	16r
Honey, jar	8 oz	0.96-1.75	92	5r
Honey, jar	lb	1.50-3.00	92	5r
Honey, squeeze bear	12-oz	1.50-1.99	92	5r
Ice cream, prepackaged, bulk, regular	1/2 gal	2.80	4/93	16r
Lemons	lb	0.96	4/93	16r
Lettuce, iceberg	lb	0.95	4/93	16r
Margarine, stick	lb	0.81	4/93	16r
Milk, fresh, whole, fortified	1/2 gal	1.30	4/93	16r
Oranges, navel	lb	0.56	4/93	16r
Peanut butter, creamy, all sizes	lb	1.88	4/93	16r
Pork chops, center cut, bone-in	lb	3.34	4/93	16r
Potato chips	16 oz	2.88	4/93	16r
Potatoes, white	lb	0.37	4/93	16r
Rib roast, USDA choice, bone-in	lb	4.94	4/93	16r
Round roast, USDA choice, boneless	lb	3.17	4/93	16r
Shortening, vegetable oil blends	lb	0.98	4/93	16r
Spaghetti and macaroni	lb	0.82	4/93	16r
Steak, round, graded & ungraded, ex USDA prime & choice	lb	4.04	4/93	16r
Steak, round, USDA choice, boneless	lb	3.90	4/93	16r
Steak, sirloin, USDA choice, boneless	lb	4.97	4/93	16r
Strawberries, dry pint	12 oz	0.90	4/93	16r
Sugar, white	lb	0.50	4/93	16r
Sugar, white, 33-80 oz pk	lb	0.41	4/93	16r
Tomatoes, field grown	lb	1.23	4/93	16r
Tuna, chunk, light	lb	2.22	4/93	16r
Turkey, frozen, whole	lb	1.04	4/93	16r
Health Care				
Childbirth, cesarean, hospital		5826	91	62r
Childbirth, cesarean, physician's fee		2053	91	62r
Childbirth, normal, hospital		2964	91	62r
Childbirth, normal, physician's fee		1492	91	62r
Medical plan per employee	year	3942	91	45r
Mental health care, exp	capita	53.68-118.35	90	38s
Mental health care, exp, state mental health agency	capita	56.85	90	38s
Mental health care, hospital psychiatric services, non-Federal, exp	capita	22.11	88	38s
Mental health care, mental health organization, multiservice, exp	capita	21.01	88	38s
Mental health care, psychiatric hospitals, private, exp	capita	26.48	88	38s
Mental health care, psychiatric out-patient clinics, freestanding, exp	capita	4.17	88	38s

Values are in dollars or fractions of dollars. In the column headed *Ref*, references are shown to sources. Each reference is followed by a letter. These refer to the geographical level for which data were reported: s = State, r = Region, and c = City or metro. The abbreviation *ex* is used to mean *except* or *excluding*; *exp* stands for expenditures. For other abbreviations and further explanations, please see the Introduction.

Reading, PA - continued

Item	Per	Value	Date	Ref.
Health Care				
Mental health care, psychiatric partial-care organizations, freestanding, exp	capita	0.94	88	38s
Mental health care, state and county mental hospitals, exp	capita	37.11	88	38s
Mental health care, VA medical centers, exp	capita	9.77	88	38s
Prescription drug co-pay, Medicaid	month	6.00	91	21s
Substance abuse, hospital ancillary charge	incident	720	90	70s
Substance abuse, hospital physician charge	incident	210	90	70s
Substance abuse, hospital room and board	incident	5400	90	70s
Insurance and Pensions				
Auto insurance, private passenger	year	683.57	91	63s
Taxes				
Tax, cigarette	pack	31	91	77s
Tax, gasoline	gal	12	91	77s
Taxes, state	capita	1089	91	77s
Transportation				
Driver's license fee		22.00	12/90	43s
Travel				
Business travel	day	165.00	4/93	89r
Utilities				
Electricity	mil Btu	22.46	90	64s

Redding, CA

Item	Per	Value	Date	Ref.
Child Care				
Child care fee, average, center	hour	1.71	90	65r
Child care fee, average, nonregulated family day care	hour	1.32	90	65r
Child care fee, average, regulated family day care	hour	1.86	90	65r
Communications				
Long-distance telephone service, day, initial minute, 0-100 miles	min	0.17-0.40	91	12s
Long-distance telephone service, day, additional minute, 0-100 miles	min	0.07-0.31	91	12s
Long-distance telephone service, evenings/weekends, 0-100 mi, initial minute	min	0.07-0.16	91	12s
Long-distance telephone service, evenings/weekends, 0-100 mi, additional minute	min	0.03-0.12	91	12s
Education				
Board, 4-yr private college/university	year	2515	91	22s
Board, 4-yr public college/university	year	2268	91	22s
Expenditures, local gov't, public elementary/secondary	pupil	4866	92	20s
Room, 4-year private college/university	year	2622	91	22s
Room, 4-year public college/university	year	2406	91	22s
Tuition, 2-year private college/university	year	7942	91	22s
Tuition, 2-year public college/university	year	114	91	22s
Tuition, 4-year private college/university	year	10863	91	22s
Tuition, 4-year public college/university, in-state	year	1220	91	22s
Energy and Fuels				
Coal	mil Btu	2.01	90	64s
Energy	mil Btu	9.08	90	64s
Energy exp/householder, 1-family unit	year	362	90	28r
Energy exp/householder, <1,000 sq ft heating area	year	254	90	28r
Energy exp/householder, 1,000-1,999 sq ft heating area	year	358	90	28r
Energy exp/householder, 2,000+ sq ft heating area	year	467	90	28r
Energy exp/householder, mobile home	year	390	90	28r
Energy exp/householder, multifamily	year	252	90	28r
Gas, natural	mil Btu	4.31	90	64s

Redding, CA - continued

Item	Per	Value	Date	Ref.
Energy and Fuels - continued				
Gas, natural	000 cu ft	6.27	91	46s
Gas, natural, exp	year	369	91	46s
Gasoline, unleaded regular	mil Btu	8.57	90	64s
Entertainment				
Miniature golf admission	adult	6.18	92	1r
Miniature golf admission	child	5.14	92	1r
Waterpark admission	adult	11.00	92	1r
Waterpark admission	child	8.55	92	1r
Funerals				
Casket, 18-gauge steel, velvet interior		1781.09	91	24r
Cosmetology, hair care, etc.		84.64	91	24r
Embalming		207.41	91	24r
Facility use for ceremony		205.76	91	24r
Hearse, local		105.14	91	24r
Limousine, local		83.21	91	24r
Remains to funeral home, transfer		113.82	91	24r
Service charge, professional		626.33	91	24r
Vault, concrete, non-metallic liner		599.54	91	24r
Viewing facilities, use		85.81	91	24r
Groceries				
Apples, Red Delicious	lb	0.80	4/93	16r
Bacon	lb	1.79	4/93	16r
Bananas	lb	0.53	4/93	16r
Bologna, all beef or mixed	lb	2.67	4/93	16r
Bread, white, pan	lb	0.81	4/93	16r
Carrots, short trimmed and topped	lb	0.39	4/93	16r
Chicken, fresh, whole	lb	0.94	4/93	16r
Chicken breast, bone-in	lb	2.19	4/93	16r
Chuck roast, graded and ungraded, ex USDA prime and choice	lb	2.26	4/93	16r
Coffee, 100% ground roast, all sizes	lb	2.33	4/93	16r
Eggs, Grade AA large	doz	1.18	4/93	16r
Flour, white, all purpose	lb	0.22	4/93	16r
Grapefruit	lb	0.52	4/93	16r
Grapes, Thompson Seedless	lb	1.50	4/93	16r
Ground beef, 100% beef	lb	1.44	4/93	16r
Ground beef, lean and extra lean	lb	2.34	4/93	16r
Ham, boneless, excluding canned	lb	2.56	4/93	16r
Honey, jar	8 oz	0.89-1.00	92	5r
Honey, jar	lb	1.35-1.97	92	5r
Honey, squeeze bear	12-oz	1.19-1.50	92	5r
Ice cream, prepackaged, bulk, regular	1/2 gal	2.40	4/93	16r
Lemons	lb	0.81	4/93	16r
Lettuce, iceberg	lb	0.84	4/93	16r
Margarine, stick	lb	0.81	4/93	16r
Oranges, navel	lb	0.48	4/93	16r
Pork chops, center cut, bone-in	lb	3.25	4/93	16r
Potato chips	16 oz	2.89	4/93	16r
Potatoes, white	lb	0.38	4/93	16r
Round roast, graded & ungraded, ex USDA prime & choice	lb	3.00	4/93	16r
Round roast, USDA choice, boneless	lb	3.16	4/93	16r
Shortening, vegetable oil blends	lb	0.86	4/93	16r
Spaghetti and macaroni	lb	0.84	4/93	16r
Steak, round, graded & ungraded, ex USDA prime & choice	lb	3.34	4/93	16r
Steak, round, USDA choice, boneless	lb	3.24	4/93	16r
Steak, sirloin, graded & ungraded, ex USDA prime & choice	lb	3.75	4/93	16r
Steak, sirloin, USDA choice, boneless	lb	4.49	4/93	16r
Sugar, white	lb	0.41	4/93	16r
Sugar, white, 33-80 oz pk	lb	0.38	4/93	16r
Tomatoes, field grown	lb	1.01	4/93	16r
Turkey, frozen, whole	lb	1.04	4/93	16r
Health Care				
Cardizem 60 mg tablets	30	24.04	92	49s
Cector 250 mg tablets	15	35.87	92	49s
Childbirth, cesarean, hospital		5533	91	62r
Childbirth, cesarean, physician's fee		2053	91	62r

Values are in dollars or fractions of dollars. In the column headed *Ref*, references are shown to sources. Each reference is followed by a letter. These refer to the geographical level for which data were reported: s=State, r=Region, and c=City or metro. The abbreviation *ex* is used to mean *except* or *excluding; exp* stands for *expenditures*. For other abbreviations and further explanations, please see the Introduction.

Redding, CA - continued

Item	Per	Value	Date	Ref.
Health Care				
Childbirth, normal, hospital		2745	91	62r
Childbirth, normal, physician's fee		1492	91	62r
Health care spending, state	capita	2894	3/93	84s
Medical plan per employee	year	3421	91	45r
Mental health care, exp	capita	37.60- 53.67	90	38s
Mental health care, exp, state mental health agency	capita	42.32	90	38s
Mental health care, hospital psychiatric services, non-Federal, exp	capita	10.64	88	38s
Mental health care, mental health organization, multiservice, exp	capita	28.56	88	38s
Mental health care, psychiatric hospitals, private, exp	capita	18.60	88	38s
Mental health care, psychiatric out-patient clinics, freestanding, exp	capita	2.28	88	38s
Mental health care, psychiatric partial-care organizations, freestanding, exp	capita	0.24	88	38s
Mental health care, state and county mental hospitals, exp	capita	13.60	88	38s
Mental health care, VA medical centers, exp	capita	2.33	88	38s
Mevacor 20 mg tablets	30	67.62	92	49s
Physician fee, family practice, first-visit		111.00	91	62r
Physician fee, family practice, revisit		45.00	91	62r
Physician fee, general practice, first-visit		100.00	91	62r
Physician fee, general practice, revisit		40.00	91	62r
Physician fee, internal medicine, first-visit		137.00	91	62r
Physician fee, internal medicine, revisit		48.00	91	62r
Physician fee, median, neurosurgeon, first-visit		157.00	91	62r
Physician fee, median, nonsurgical specialist, first-visit		131.00	91	62r
Physician fee, median, orthopedic surgeon, first-visit		124.00	91	62r
Physician fee, median, plastic surgeon, first-visit		88.00	91	62r
Physician fee, median, surgical specialist, first-visit		100.00	91	62r
Physician fee, neurosurgeon, revisit		51.00	91	62r
Physician fee, nonsurgical specialist, revisit		47.00	91	62r
Physician fee, obstetrics/gynecology, first-visit		95.00	91	62r
Physician fee, obstetrics/gynecology, revisit		50.00	91	62r
Physician fee, orthopedic surgeon, revisit		51.00	91	62r
Physician fee, pediatrician, first-visit		81.00	91	62r
Physician fee, pediatrician, revisit		42.00	91	62r
Physician fee, plastic surgeon, revisit		48.00	91	62r
Physician fee, surgical specialist, revisit		49.00	91	62r
Prozac 20 mg tablets	14	33.22	92	49s
Substance abuse, hospital ancillary charge	incident	1760	90	70s
Substance abuse, hospital physician charge	incident	750	90	70s
Substance abuse, hospital room and board	incident	6390	90	70s
Tagamet 300 mg tablets	100	77.08	92	49s
Xanax 0.25 mg tablets	90	64.08	92	49s
Zantac 160 mg tablets	60	92.31	92	49s
Housing				
Home, median price	unit	131,200	92	58s
Insurance and Pensions				
Auto insurance, private passenger	year	904.37	91	63s
Taxes				
Tax, cigarette	pack	35	91	77s
Tax, gasoline	gal	16	91	77s
Taxes, state	capita	1477	91	77s
Transportation				
Driver's license fee		10.00	12/90	43s

Redding, CA - continued

Item	Per	Value	Date	Ref.
Travel				
Business travel	day	178.00	4/93	89r
Utilities				
Electricity	mil Btu	25.98	90	64s

Reno, NV

Item	Per	Value	Date	Ref.
Alcoholic Beverages				
Beer, Miller Lite or Budweiser, 12-oz containers	6 pack	4.01	4Q 92	4c
Liquor, J & B Scotch	750 ml	15.89	4Q 92	4c
Wine, Gallo Chablis blanc, 1.5 liter	bottle	3.95	4Q 92	4c
Child Care				
Child care fee, average, center	hour	1.71	90	65r
Child care fee, average, nonregulated family day care	hour	1.32	90	65r
Child care fee, average, regulated family day care	hour	1.86	90	65r
Clothing				
Jeans, man's denim		34.40	4Q 92	4c
Shirt, man's dress shirt		22.80	4Q 92	4c
Undervest, boy's size 10-14, cotton	3	3.84	4Q 92	4c
Communications				
Long-distance telephone service, day, initial minute, 0-100 miles	min	0.16-0.39	91	12s
Long-distance telephone service, day, additional minute, 0-100 miles	min	0.06-0.25	91	12s
Long-distance telephone service, evenings/weekends, 0-100 mi, initial minute	min	0.08-0.20	91	12s
Long-distance telephone service, evenings/weekends, 0-100 mi, additional minute	min	0.03-0.13	91	12s
Newspaper subscription, daily and Sunday home delivery, large-city	month	14.13	4Q 92	4c
Telephone bill, family of four	month	13.50	4Q 92	4c
Education				
Board, 4-yr public college/university	year	1709	91	22s
Expenditures, local gov't, public elementary/secondary	pupil	4891	92	20s
Room, 4-year private college/university	year	2100	91	22s
Room, 4-year public college/university	year	2489	91	22s
Tuition, 2-year public college/university	year	651	91	22s
Tuition, 4-year private college/university	year	6200	91	22s
Tuition, 4-year public college/university, in-state	year	1275	91	22s
Energy and Fuels				
Coal	mil Btu	1.49	90	64s
Energy	mil Btu	9.01	90	64s
Energy, combined forms, 1,800 sq ft heating area	month	83.30	4Q 92	4c
Energy, exc electricity, 1,800 sq ft heating area	month	34.95	4Q 92	4c
Energy exp/householder, 1-family unit	year	372	90	28r
Energy exp/householder, <1,000 sq ft heating area	year	335	90	28r
Energy exp/householder, 1,000-1,999 sq ft heating area	year	365	90	28r
Energy exp/householder, 2,000+ sq ft heating area	year	411	90	28r
Energy exp/householder, mobile home	year	305	90	28r
Energy exp/householder, multifamily	year	372	90	28r
Gas, cooking, winter, 10 therms	month	7.74	92	56c
Gas, cooking, winter, 30 therms	month	16.72	92	56c
Gas, cooking, winter, 50 therms	month	25.70	92	56c
Gas, heating, winter, 100 therms	month	48.16	92	56c
Gas, heating, winter, average use	month	47.71	92	56c
Gas, natural	mil Btu	3.68	90	64s
Gas, natural	000 cu ft	5.61	91	46s
Gas, natural, exp	year	379	91	46s

Values are in dollars or fractions of dollars. In the column headed *Ref*, references are shown to sources. Each reference is followed by a letter. These refer to the geographical level for which data were reported: s=State, r=Region, and c=City or metro. The abbreviation *ex* is used to mean *except* or *excluding*; *exp* stands for expenditures. For other abbreviations and further explanations, please see the Introduction.

Reno, NV - continued

Item	Per	Value	Date	Ref.
Energy and Fuels				
Gasoline, motor	gal	1.28	4Q 92	4c
Gasoline, unleaded regular	mil Btu	9.10	90	64s
Entertainment				
Bowling, evening rate	game	1.76	4Q 92	4c
Miniature golf admission	adult	6.18	92	1r
Miniature golf admission	child	5.14	92	1r
Monopoly game, Parker Brothers', No. 9		10.89	4Q 92	4c
Movie	admission	4.25	4Q 92	4c
Tennis balls, yellow, Wilson or Penn, 3	can	2.38	4Q 92	4c
Waterpark admission	adult	11.00	92	1r
Waterpark admission	child	8.55	92	1r
Funerals				
Casket, 18-gauge steel, velvet interior		1929.04	91	24r
Cosmetology, hair care, etc.		88.52	91	24r
Embalming		249.33	91	24r
Facility use for ceremony		182.75	91	24r
Hearse, local		110.04	91	24r
Limousine, local		66.67	91	24r
Remains to funeral home, transfer		84.58	91	24r
Service charge, professional		593.00	91	24r
Vault, concrete, non-metallic liner		647.38	91	24r
Viewing facilities, use		99.87	91	24r
Groceries				
Apples, Red Delicious	lb	0.80	4/93	16r
Babyfood, strained vegetables, lowest price	4-4.5 oz jar	0.35	4Q 92	4c
Bacon	lb	1.79	4/93	16r
Bananas	lb	0.42	4Q 92	4c
Bananas	lb	0.53	4/93	16r
Bologna, all beef or mixed	lb	2.67	4/93	16r
Bread, white	24 oz	0.83	4Q 92	4c
Bread, white, pan	lb	0.81	4/93	16r
Carrots, short trimmed and topped	lb	0.39	4/93	16r
Cheese, Kraft grated Parmesan	8-oz canister	3.55	4Q 92	4c
Chicken, fresh, whole	lb	0.94	4/93	16r
Chicken, fryer, whole	lb	0.89	4Q 92	4c
Chicken breast, bone-in	lb	2.19	4/93	16r
Chuck roast, graded and ungraded, ex USDA prime and choice	lb	2.26	4/93	16r
Cigarettes, Winston	carton	19.14	4Q 92	4c
Coffee, 100% ground roast, all sizes	lb	2.33	4/93	16r
Coffee, vacuum-packed	13-oz can	2.00	4Q 92	4c
Corn, frozen	10 oz	0.58	4Q 92	4c
Corn Flakes, Kellogg's or Post Toasties	18 oz	1.91	4Q 92	4c
Eggs, Grade A large	doz	0.90	4Q 92	4c
Eggs, Grade AA large	doz	1.18	4/93	16r
Flour, white, all purpose	lb	0.22	4/93	16r
Grapefruit	lb	0.52	4/93	16r
Grapes, Thompson Seedless	lb	1.50	4/93	16r
Ground beef, 100% beef	lb	1.44	4/93	16r
Ground beef, lean and extra lean	lb	2.34	4/93	16r
Ground beef or hamburger	lb	1.53	4Q 92	4c
Ham, boneless, excluding canned	lb	2.56	4/93	16r
Honey, jar	8 oz	0.89-1.00	92	5r
Honey, jar	lb	1.35-1.97	92	5r
Honey, squeeze bear	12-oz	1.00-1.89	92	5r
Ice cream, prepackaged, bulk, regular	1/2 gal	2.40	4/93	16r
Lemons	lb	0.81	4/93	16r
Lettuce, iceberg	head	0.75	4Q 92	4c
Lettuce, iceberg	lb	0.84	4/93	16r
Margarine, Blue Bonnet or Parkay cubes	lb	0.67	4Q 92	4c
Margarine, stick	lb	0.81	4/93	16r
Milk, whole	1/2 gal	1.30	4Q 92	4c
Orange juice, Minute Maid frozen	12-oz can	1.59	4Q 92	4c
Oranges, navel	lb	0.48	4/93	16r

Reno, NV - continued

Item	Per	Value	Date	Ref.
Groceries - continued				
Peaches	29-oz can	1.23	4Q 92	4c
Peas Sweet, Del Monte or Green Giant	15-17 oz can	0.62	4Q 92	4c
Pork chops, center cut, bone-in	lb	3.25	4/93	16r
Potato chips	16 oz	2.89	4/93	16r
Potatoes, white	lb	0.38	4/93	16r
Potatoes, white or red	10-lb sack	1.79	4Q 92	4c
Round roast, graded & ungraded, ex USDA prime & choice	lb	3.00	4/93	16r
Round roast, USDA choice, boneless	lb	3.16	4/93	16r
Sausage, Jimmy Dean, 100% pork	lb	3.16	4Q 92	4c
Shortening, vegetable oil blends	lb	0.86	4/93	16r
Shortening, vegetable, Crisco	3-lb can	2.51	4Q 92	4c
Soft drink, Coca Cola	2 liter	1.30	4Q 92	4c
Spaghetti and macaroni	lb	0.84	4/93	16r
Steak, round, graded & ungraded, ex USDA prime & choice	lb	3.34	4/93	16r
Steak, round, USDA choice, boneless	lb	3.24	4/93	16r
Steak, sirloin, graded & ungraded, ex USDA prime & choice	lb	3.75	4/93	16r
Steak, sirloin, USDA choice, boneless	lb	4.49	4/93	16r
Steak, T-bone	lb	4.42	4Q 92	4c
Sugar, cane or beet	4 lb	1.48	4Q 92	4c
Sugar, white	lb	0.41	4/93	16r
Sugar, white, 33-80 oz pk	lb	0.38	4/93	16r
Tomatoes, field grown	lb	1.01	4/93	16r
Tomatoes, Hunt's or Del Monte	14.5-oz can	0.70	4Q 92	4c
Tuna, chunk, light	6.125-6.5 oz can	0.68	4Q 92	4c
Turkey, frozen, whole	lb	1.04	4/93	16r
Health Care				
Analgesic, Aspirin, Bayer, 325 mg tablets	100	5.16	4Q 92	4c
Childbirth, cesarean, hospital		5533	91	62r
Childbirth, cesarean, physician's fee		2053	91	62r
Childbirth, normal, hospital		2745	91	62r
Childbirth, normal, physician's fee		1492	91	62r
Dentist's fee, adult teeth cleaning and periodic oral exam	visit	66.20	4Q 92	4c
Doctor's fee, routine exam, established patient	visit	37.00	4Q 92	4c
Hospital care, semiprivate room	day	316.00	90	27c
Hospital care, semiprivate room	day	438.53	4Q 92	4c
Medical insurance premium, per employee, small group comprehensive	month	430.70	10/91	25c
Medical plan per employee	year	3218	91	45r
Mental health care, exp	capita	28.84-37.59	90	38s
Mental health care, exp, state mental health agency	capita	33.47	90	38s
Mental health care, hospital psychiatric services, non-Federal, exp	capita	6.90	88	38s
Mental health care, mental health organization, multiservice, exp	capita	3.34	88	38s
Mental health care, psychiatric hospitals, private, exp	capita	42.05	88	38s
Mental health care, state and county mental hospitals, exp	capita	20.24	88	38s
Mental health care, VA medical centers, exp	capita	4.74	88	38s
Physician fee, family practice, first-visit		111.00	91	62r
Physician fee, family practice, revisit		45.00	91	62r
Physician fee, general practice, first-visit		100.00	91	62r
Physician fee, general practice, revisit		40.00	91	62r
Physician fee, internal medicine, first-visit		137.00	91	62r
Physician fee, internal medicine, revisit		48.00	91	62r
Physician fee, median, neurosurgeon, first-visit		157.00	91	62r

Values are in dollars or fractions of dollars. In the column headed *Ref*, references are shown to sources. Each reference is followed by a letter. These refer to the geographical level for which data were reported: s = State, r = Region, and c = City or metro. The abbreviation *ex* is used to mean *except* or *excluding*; *exp* stands for expenditures. For other abbreviations and further explanations, please see the Introduction.

Reno, NV - continued

Item	Per	Value	Date	Ref.
Health Care				
Physician fee, median, nonsurgical specialist, first-visit		131.00	91	62r
Physician fee, median, orthopedic surgeon, first-visit		124.00	91	62r
Physician fee, median, plastic surgeon, first-visit		88.00	91	62r
Physician fee, median, surgical specialist, first-visit		100.00	91	62r
Physician fee, neurosurgeon, revisit		51.00	91	62r
Physician fee, nonsurgical specialist, revisit		47.00	91	62r
Physician fee, obstetrics/gynecology, first-visit		95.00	91	62r
Physician fee, obstetrics/gynecology, revisit		50.00	91	62r
Physician fee, orthopedic surgeon, revisit		51.00	91	62r
Physician fee, pediatrician, first-visit		81.00	91	62r
Physician fee, pediatrician, revisit		42.00	91	62r
Physician fee, plastic surgeon, revisit		48.00	91	62r
Physician fee, surgical specialist, revisit		49.00	91	62r
Substance abuse, hospital ancillary charge	incident	1420	90	70s
Substance abuse, hospital physician charge	incident	660	90	70s
Substance abuse, hospital room and board	incident	5240	90	70s
Household Goods				
Appliance repair, home, service call, washing machine	min labor charge	38.68	4Q 92	4c
Laundry detergent, Tide Ultra, Bold, or Cheer	42 oz	3.95	4Q 92	4c
Tissues, facial, Kleenex brand	175-count box	1.20	4Q 92	4c
Housing				
Home, median price	unit	117.90		26c
House, 1,800 sq ft, 8,000 sq ft lot, new, urban	total	142710	4Q 92	4c
House payment, principal and interest, 25% down payment	month	791	4Q 92	4c
Mortgage rate, incl. points & origination fee, 30-year fixed or adjustable rate	percent	8.08	4Q 92	4c
Rent, apartment, 2 bedrooms - 1-1/2 to 2 baths, unfurnished, 950 sq ft, water	month	604	4Q 92	4c
Rental unit, 1 bedroom	month	489	93	23c
Rental unit, 2 bedroom	month	575	93	23c
Rental unit, 3 bedroom	month	719	93	23c
Rental unit, 4 bedroom	month	805	93	23c
Rental unit, efficiency	month	403	93	23c
Insurance and Pensions				
Auto insurance, private passenger	year	752.76	91	63s
Personal Goods				
Shampoo, Alberto VO5	15 oz	1.49	4Q 92	4c
Toothpaste, Crest or Colgate	6-7 oz	2.18	4Q 92	4c
Personal Services				
Dry cleaning, man's 2-piece suit		6.63	4Q 92	4c
Haircare, woman's shampoo, trim and blow-dry		14.79	4Q 92	4c
Haircut, man's barbershop, no styling		9.19	4Q 92	4c
Restaurant Food				
Chicken, fried, thigh and drumstick		2.15	4Q 92	4c
Hamburger with cheese	1/4 lb	1.84	4Q 92	4c
Pizza, Pizza Hut or Pizza Inn, cheese, thin crust	12-13 in	8.75	4Q 92	4c
Taxes				
Tax, cigarette	pack	35	91	77s
Tax, gasoline	gal	23	91	77s
Taxes, state	capita	1310	91	77s

Reno, NV - continued

Item	Per	Value	Date	Ref.
Transportation				
Bus fare	one-way	0.75	3/93	2c
Bus fare, up to 10 miles	one-way	0.75	4Q 92	4c
Driver's license fee		9.00	12/90	43s
Tire balance, computer or spin balance, front	wheel	6.28	4Q 92	4c
Travel				
Business travel	day	178.00	4/93	89r
Utilities				
Electricity	mil Btu	15.77	90	64s
Electricity, partial electric and other energy, 1,800 sq ft living area new home	month	48.35	4Q 92	4c
Electricity, winter, 250 KWh	month	22.96	92	55c
Electricity, winter, 500 KWh	month	42.86	92	55c
Electricity, winter, 750 KWh	month	62.76	92	55c
Electricity, winter, 1000 KWh	month	82.67	92	55c

Richland-Kennewick-Pasco, WA

Item	Per	Value	Date	Ref.
Composite ACCRA index		107.40	4Q 92	4c
Alcoholic Beverages				
Beer, Miller Lite or Budweiser, 12-oz containers	6 pack	3.94	4Q 92	4c
Liquor, J & B Scotch	750 ml	17.95	4Q 92	4c
Wine, Gallo Chablis blanc, 1.5 liter	bottle	4.41	4Q 92	4c
Child Care				
Child care fee, average, center	hour	1.71	90	65r
Child care fee, average, nonregulated family day care	hour	1.32	90	65r
Child care fee, average, regulated family day care	hour	1.86	90	65r
Clothing				
Jeans, man's denim		32.99	4Q 92	4c
Shirt, man's dress shirt		22.90	4Q 92	4c
Undervest, boy's size 10-14, cotton	3	4.85	4Q 92	4c
Communications				
Long-distance telephone service, day, initial minute, 0-100 miles	min	0.15-0.37	91	12s
Long-distance telephone service, day, additional minute, 0-100 miles	min	0.01-0.03	91	12s
Long-distance telephone service, evenings/weekends, 0-100 mi, initial minute	min	0.05-0.19	91	12s
Long-distance telephone service, evenings/weekends, 0-100 mi, additional minute	min	0.00-0.01	91	12s
Newspaper subscription, daily and Sunday home delivery, large-city	month	9.00	4Q 92	4c
Telephone bill, family of four	month	16.94	4Q 92	4c
Education				
Board, 4-yr private college/university	year	1811	91	22s
Board, 4-yr public college/university	year	1539	91	22s
Expenditures, local gov't, public elementary/secondary	pupil	5317	92	20s
Room, 4-year private college/university	year	1885	91	22s
Room, 4-year public college/university	year	1698	91	22s
Tuition, 2-year private college/university	year	6743	91	22s
Tuition, 2-year public college/university	year	844	91	22s
Tuition, 4-year private college/university	year	9463	91	22s
Tuition, 4-year public college/university, in-state	year	1823	91	22s
Energy and Fuels				
Energy	mil Btu	7.39	90	64s
Energy, combined forms, 1,800 sq ft heating area	month	82.22	4Q 92	4c
Energy exp/householder, 1-family unit	year	362	90	28r
Energy exp/householder, <1,000 sq ft heating area	year	254	90	28r

Values are in dollars or fractions of dollars. In the column headed *Ref*, references are shown to sources. Each reference is followed by a letter. These refer to the geographical level for which data were reported: s=State, r=Region, and c=City or metro. The abbreviation *ex* is used to mean *except* or *excluding*; *exp* stands for expenditures. For other abbreviations and further explanations, please see the Introduction.

Richland-Kennewick-Pasco, WA - continued

Item	Per	Value	Date	Ref.
Energy and Fuels				
Energy exp/householder, 1,000-1,999 sq ft heating area	year	358	90	28r
Energy exp/householder, 2,000+ sq ft heating area	year	467	90	28r
Energy exp/householder, mobile home	year	390	90	28r
Energy exp/householder, multifamily	year	252	90	28r
Gas, natural	mil Btu	3.60	90	64s
Gas, natural	000 cu ft	4.68	91	46s
Gas, natural, exp	year	440	91	46s
Gasoline, motor	gal	1.30	4Q 92	4c
Gasoline, unleaded regular	mil Btu	9.45	90	64s
Entertainment				
Bowling, evening rate	game	2.05	4Q 92	4c
Miniature golf admission	adult	6.18	92	1r
Miniature golf admission	child	5.14	92	1r
Monopoly game, Parker Brothers', No. 9		13.27	4Q 92	4c
Movie	admission	5.50	4Q 92	4c
Tennis balls, yellow, Wilson or Penn, 3	can	2.84	4Q 92	4c
Waterpark admission	adult	11.00	92	1r
Waterpark admission	child	8.55	92	1r
Funerals				
Casket, 18-gauge steel, velvet interior		1781.09	91	24r
Cosmetology, hair care, etc.		84.64	91	24r
Embalming		207.41	91	24r
Facility use for ceremony		205.76	91	24r
Hearse, local		105.14	91	24r
Limousine, local		83.21	91	24r
Remains to funeral home, transfer		113.82	91	24r
Service charge, professional		626.33	91	24r
Vault, concrete, non-metallic liner		599.54	91	24r
Viewing facilities, use		85.81	91	24r
Goods and Services				
ACCRA Index, Miscellaneous Goods and Services		107.60	4Q 92	4c
Groceries				
ACCRA Index, Groceries		102.20	4Q 92	4c
Apples, Red Delicious	lb	0.80	4/93	16r
Babyfood, strained vegetables, lowest price	4-4.5 oz jar	0.30	4Q 92	4c
Bacon	lb	1.79	4/93	16r
Bananas	lb	0.43	4Q 92	4c
Bananas	lb	0.53	4/93	16r
Bologna, all beef or mixed	lb	2.67	4/93	16r
Bread, white	24 oz	0.55	4Q 92	4c
Bread, white, pan	lb	0.81	4/93	16r
Carrots, short trimmed and topped	lb	0.39	4/93	16r
Cheese, Kraft grated Parmesan	8-oz canister	3.85	4Q 92	4c
Chicken, fresh, whole	lb	0.94	4/93	16r
Chicken, fryer, whole	lb	0.88	4Q 92	4c
Chicken breast, bone-in	lb	2.19	4/93	16r
Chuck roast, graded and ungraded, ex USDA prime and choice	lb	2.26	4/93	16r
Cigarettes, Winston	carton	18.63	4Q 92	4c
Coffee, 100% ground roast, all sizes	lb	2.33	4/93	16r
Coffee, vacuum-packed	13-oz can	2.23	4Q 92	4c
Corn, frozen	10 oz	0.62	4Q 92	4c
Corn Flakes, Kellogg's or Post Toasties	18 oz	2.16	4Q 92	4c
Eggs, Grade A large	doz	0.89	4Q 92	4c
Eggs, Grade AA large	doz	1.18	4/93	16r
Flour, white, all purpose	lb	0.22	4/93	16r
Grapefruit	lb	0.52	4/93	16r
Grapes, Thompson Seedless	lb	1.50	4/93	16r
Ground beef, 100% beef	lb	1.44	4/93	16r
Ground beef, lean and extra lean	lb	2.34	4/93	16r
Ground beef or hamburger	lb	1.32	4Q 92	4c

Richland-Kennewick-Pasco, WA - continued

Item	Per	Value	Date	Ref.
Groceries - continued				
Ham, boneless, excluding canned	lb	2.56	4/93	16r
Honey, jar	8 oz	0.89-1.00	92	5r
Honey, jar	lb	1.35-1.97	92	5r
Honey, squeeze bear	12-oz	1.19-1.50	92	5r
Ice cream, prepackaged, bulk, regular	1/2 gal	2.40	4/93	16r
Lemons	lb	0.81	4/93	16r
Lettuce, iceberg	head	0.92	4Q 92	4c
Lettuce, iceberg	lb	0.84	4/93	16r
Margarine, Blue Bonnet or Parkay cubes	lb	0.71	4Q 92	4c
Margarine, stick	lb	0.81	4/93	16r
Milk, whole	1/2 gal	1.27	4Q 92	4c
Orange juice, Minute Maid frozen	12-oz can	1.37	4Q 92	4c
Oranges, navel	lb	0.48	4/93	16r
Peaches	29-oz can	1.46	4Q 92	4c
Peas Sweet, Del Monte or Green Giant	15-17 oz can	0.69	4Q 92	4c
Pork chops, center cut, bone-in	lb	3.25	4/93	16r
Potato chips	16 oz	2.89	4/93	16r
Potatoes, white	lb	0.38	4/93	16r
Potatoes, white or red	10-lb sack	1.87	4Q 92	4c
Round roast, graded & ungraded, ex USDA prime & choice	lb	3.00	4/93	16r
Round roast, USDA choice, boneless	lb	3.16	4/93	16r
Sausage, Jimmy Dean, 100% pork	lb	3.19	4Q 92	4c
Shortening, vegetable oil blends	lb	0.86	4/93	16r
Shortening, vegetable, Crisco	3-lb can	2.57	4Q 92	4c
Soft drink, Coca Cola	2 liter	1.09	4Q 92	4c
Spaghetti and macaroni	lb	0.84	4/93	16r
Steak, round, graded & ungraded, ex USDA prime & choice	lb	3.34	4/93	16r
Steak, round, USDA choice, boneless	lb	3.24	4/93	16r
Steak, sirloin, graded & ungraded, ex USDA prime & choice	lb	3.75	4/93	16r
Steak, sirloin, USDA choice, boneless	lb	4.49	4/93	16r
Steak, T-bone	lb	5.04	4Q 92	4c
Sugar, cane or beet	4 lb	1.22	4Q 92	4c
Sugar, white	lb	0.41	4/93	16r
Sugar, white, 33-80 oz pk	lb	0.38	4/93	16r
Tomatoes, field grown	lb	1.01	4/93	16r
Tomatoes, Hunt's or Del Monte	14.5-oz can	0.59	4Q 92	4c
Tuna, chunk, light	6.125-6.5 oz can	0.71	4Q 92	4c
Turkey, frozen, whole	lb	1.04	4/93	16r
Health Care				
ACCRA Index, Health Care		134.60	4Q 92	4c
Analgesic, Aspirin, Bayer, 325 mg tablets	100	5.54	4Q 92	4c
Childbirth, cesarean, hospital		5533	91	62r
Childbirth, cesarean, physician's fee		2053	91	62r
Childbirth, normal, hospital		2745	91	62r
Childbirth, normal, physician's fee		1492	91	62r
Dentist's fee, adult teeth cleaning and periodic oral exam	visit	72.25	4Q 92	4c
Doctor's fee, routine exam, established patient	visit	45.92	4Q 92	4c
Hospital care, semiprivate room	day	415.00	4Q 92	4c
Medical insurance premium, per employee, small group comprehensive	month	281.05	10/91	25c
Medical plan per employee	year	3421	91	45r
Mental health care, exp	capita	37.60-53.67	90	38s
Physician fee, family practice, first-visit		111.00	91	62r
Physician fee, family practice, revisit		45.00	91	62r
Physician fee, general practice, first-visit		100.00	91	62r
Physician fee, general practice, revisit		40.00	91	62r
Physician fee, internal medicine, first-visit		137.00	91	62r
Physician fee, internal medicine, revisit		48.00	91	62r

Values are in dollars or fractions of dollars. In the column headed *Ref*, references are shown to sources. Each reference is followed by a letter. These refer to the geographical level for which data were reported: s=State, r=Region, and c=City or metro. The abbreviation *ex* is used to mean *except* or *excluding*; *exp* stands for expenditures. For other abbreviations and further explanations, please see the Introduction.

Richland-Kennewick-Pasco, WA - continued

Item	Per	Value	Date	Ref.
Health Care				
Physician fee, median, neurosurgeon, first-visit		157.00	91	62r
Physician fee, median, nonsurgical specialist, first-visit		131.00	91	62r
Physician fee, median, orthopedic surgeon, first-visit		124.00	91	62r
Physician fee, median, plastic surgeon, first-visit		88.00	91	62r
Physician fee, median, surgical specialist, first-visit		100.00	91	62r
Physician fee, neurosurgeon, revisit		51.00	91	62r
Physician fee, nonsurgical specialist, revisit		47.00	91	62r
Physician fee, obstetrics/gynecology, first-visit		95.00	91	62r
Physician fee, obstetrics/gynecology, revisit		50.00	91	62r
Physician fee, orthopedic surgeon, revisit		51.00	91	62r
Physician fee, pediatrician, first-visit		81.00	91	62r
Physician fee, pediatrician, revisit		42.00	91	62r
Physician fee, plastic surgeon, revisit		48.00	91	62r
Physician fee, surgical specialist, revisit		49.00	91	62r
Substance abuse, hospital ancillary charge	incident	1360	90	70s
Substance abuse, hospital physician charge	incident	150	90	70s
Substance abuse, hospital room and board	incident	4200	90	70s
Household Goods				
Appliance repair, home, service call, washing machine	min labor charge	36.97	4Q 92	4c
Laundry detergent, Tide Ultra, Bold, or Cheer	42 oz	4.35	4Q 92	4c
Tissues, facial, Kleenex brand	175-count box	1.36	4Q 92	4c
Housing				
ACCRA Index, Housing		116.30	4Q 92	4c
Home, median price	unit	84.10		26c
House, 1,800 sq ft, 8,000 sq ft lot, new, urban	total	124700	4Q 92	4c
House payment, principal and interest, 25% down payment	month	698	4Q 92	4c
Mortgage rate, incl. points & origination fee, 30-year fixed or adjustable rate	percent	8.18	4Q 92	4c
Rent, apartment, 2 bedrooms - 1-1/2 to 2 baths, unfurnished, 950 sq ft, water	month	612	4Q 92	4c
Rental unit, 1 bedroom	month	424	93	23c
Rental unit, 2 bedroom	month	499	93	23c
Rental unit, 3 bedroom	month	624	93	23c
Rental unit, 4 bedroom	month	699	93	23c
Rental unit, efficiency	month	349	93	23c
Insurance and Pensions				
Auto insurance, private passenger	year	627.71	91	63s
Personal Goods				
Shampoo, Alberto VO5	15 oz	1.52	4Q 92	4c
Toothpaste, Crest or Colgate	6-7 oz	2.31	4Q 92	4c
Personal Services				
Dry cleaning, man's 2-piece suit		7.11	4Q 92	4c
Haircare, woman's shampoo, trim and blow-dry		24.00	4Q 92	4c
Haircut, man's barbershop, no styling		7.75	4Q 92	4c
Restaurant Food				
Chicken, fried, thigh and drumstick		1.95	4Q 92	4c
Hamburger with cheese	1/4 lb	1.89	4Q 92	4c
Pizza, Pizza Hut or Pizza Inn, cheese, thin crust	12-13 in	9.69	4Q 92	4c

Richland-Kennewick-Pasco, WA - continued

Item	Per	Value	Date	Ref.
Taxes				
Tax, cigarette	pack	34	91	77s
Tax, gasoline	gal	23	91	77s
Taxes, state	capita	1592	91	77s
Transportation				
ACCRA Index, Transportation		102.30	4Q 92	4c
Bus fare	one-way	0.40	3/93	2c
Driver's license fee		14.00	12/90	43s
Tire balance, computer or spin balance, front	wheel	5.87	4Q 92	4c
Travel				
Business travel	day	178.00	4/93	89r
Utilities				
ACCRA Index, Utilities		76.50	4Q 92	4c
Electricity	mil Btu	10.03	90	64s
Electricity, all electric, 1,800 sq ft living area new home	month	82.22	4Q 92	4c

Richmond, VA

Item	Per	Value	Date	Ref.
Composite ACCRA index		108.50	4Q 92	4c
Alcoholic Beverages				
Beer, Miller Lite or Budweiser, 12-oz containers	6 pack	3.76	4Q 92	4c
Liquor, J & B Scotch	750 ml	16.95	4Q 92	4c
Wine, Gallo Chablis blanc, 1.5 liter	bottle	5.80	4Q 92	4c
Child Care				
Child care fee, average, center	hour	1.29	90	65r
Child care fee, average, nonregulated family day care	hour	0.89	90	65r
Child care fee, average, regulated family day care	hour	1.32	90	65r
Clothing				
Jeans, man's denim		39.80	4Q 92	4c
Shirt, man's dress shirt		27.80	4Q 92	4c
Undervest, boy's size 10-14, cotton	3	6.53	4Q 92	4c
Communications				
Long-distance telephone service, day, initial minute, 0-100 miles	min	0.21-0.35	91	12s
Long-distance telephone service, day, additional minute, 0-100 miles	min	0.12-0.21	91	12s
Long-distance telephone service, evenings/weekends, 0-100 mi, initial minute	min	0.08-0.14	91	12s
Long-distance telephone service, evenings/weekends, 0-100 mi, additional minute	min	0.05-0.08	91	12s
Newspaper subscription, daily and Sunday home delivery, large-city	month	11.80	4Q 92	4c
Telephone, flat rate	month	13.59	91	11c
Telephone, residential, private line, rotary, unlimited calling	month	22.85	10/91	78c
Telephone bill, family of four	month	21.15	4Q 92	4c
Education				
Board, 4-yr private college/university	year	1804	91	22s
Board, 4-yr public college/university	year	1688	91	22s
Expenditures, local gov't, public elementary/secondary	pupil	5487	92	20s
Room, 4-year private college/university	year	1659	91	22s
Room, 4-year public college/university	year	1916	91	22s
Tuition, 2-year private college/university	year	4852	91	22s
Tuition, 2-year public college/university	year	867	91	22s
Tuition, 4-year private college/university	year	7621	91	22s
Tuition, 4-year public college/university, in-state	year	2691	91	22s
Energy and Fuels				
Coal	mil Btu	1.60	90	64s
Energy	mil Btu	8.89	90	64s

Values are in dollars or fractions of dollars. In the column headed *Ref*, references are shown to sources. Each reference is followed by a letter. These refer to the geographical level for which data were reported: s=State, r=Region, and c=City or metro. The abbreviation *ex* is used to mean *except* or *excluding*; *exp* stands for expenditures. For other abbreviations and further explanations, please see the Introduction.

Richmond, VA - continued

Item	Per	Value	Date	Ref.
Energy and Fuels				
Energy, combined forms, 1,800 sq ft heating area	month	132.63	4Q 92	4c
Energy exp/householder, 1-family unit	year	487	90	28r
Energy exp/householder, <1,000 sq ft heating area	year	393	90	28r
Energy exp/householder, 1,000-1,999 sq ft heating area	year	442	90	28r
Energy exp/householder, 2,000+ sq ft heating area	year	577	90	28r
Energy exp/householder, mobile home	year	366	90	28r
Energy exp/householder, multifamily	year	382	90	28r
Gas, natural	mil Btu	4.67	90	64s
Gas, natural	000 cu ft	6.80	91	46s
Gas, natural, exp	year	566	91	46s
Gasoline, motor	gal	1.08	4Q 92	4c
Gasoline, unleaded regular	mil Btu	9.46	90	64s
Entertainment				
Bowling, evening rate	game	2.68	4Q 92	4c
Miniature golf admission	adult	6.18	92	1r
Miniature golf admission	child	5.14	92	1r
Monopoly game, Parker Brothers', No. 9		10.28	4Q 92	4c
Movie	admission	5.50	4Q 92	4c
Tennis balls, yellow, Wilson or Penn, 3	can	2.28	4Q 92	4c
Waterpark admission	adult	11.00	92	1r
Waterpark admission	child	8.55	92	1r
Funerals				
Casket, 18-gauge steel, velvet interior		2029.08	91	24r
Cosmetology, hair care, etc.		75.10	91	24r
Embalming		249.24	91	24r
Facility use for ceremony		162.27	91	24r
Hearse, local		114.04	91	24r
Limousine, local		88.57	91	24r
Remains to funeral home, transfer		92.61	91	24r
Service charge, professional		682.42	91	24r
Vault, concrete, non-metallic liner		798.70	91	24r
Viewing facilities, use		163.86	91	24r
Goods and Services				
ACCRA Index, Miscellaneous Goods and Services		114.90	4Q 92	4c
Groceries				
ACCRA Index, Groceries		100.80	4Q 92	4c
Apples, Red Delicious	lb	0.79	4/93	16r
Babyfood, strained vegetables, lowest price	4-4.5 oz jar	0.32	4Q 92	4c
Bacon	lb	1.75	4/93	16r
Bananas	lb	0.48	4Q 92	4c
Bananas	lb	0.42	4/93	16r
Beef, stew, boneless	lb	2.61	4/93	16r
Bologna, all beef or mixed	lb	2.24	4/93	16r
Bread, white	24 oz	0.67	4Q 92	4c
Bread, white, pan	lb	0.64	4/93	16r
Bread, whole wheat, pan	lb	0.96	4/93	16r
Cabbage	lb	0.37	4/93	16r
Carrots, short trimmed and topped	lb	0.47	4/93	16r
Celery	lb	0.64	4/93	16r
Cheese, American	lb	2.98	4/93	16r
Cheese, Cheddar	lb	3.28	4/93	16r
Cheese, Kraft grated Parmesan	8-oz canister	3.41	4Q 92	4c
Chicken, fresh, whole	lb	0.77	4/93	16r
Chicken, fryer, whole	lb	0.81	4Q 92	4c
Chicken breast, bone-in	lb	1.92	4/93	16r
Chicken legs, bone-in	lb	1.06	4/93	16r
Chuck roast, graded and ungraded, ex USDA prime and choice	lb	2.40	4/93	16r
Chuck roast, USDA choice, bone-in	lb	2.19	4/93	16r
Chuck roast, USDA choice, boneless	lb	2.38	4/93	16r

Richmond, VA - continued

Item	Per	Value	Date	Ref.
Groceries - continued				
Cigarettes, Winston	carton	14.81	4Q 92	4c
Coffee, 100% ground roast, all sizes	lb	2.48	4/93	16r
Coffee, vacuum-packed	13-oz can	2.48	4Q 92	4c
Corn, frozen	10 oz	0.56	4Q 92	4c
Corn Flakes, Kellogg's or Post Toasties	18 oz	1.73	4Q 92	4c
Crackers, soda, salted	lb	1.15	4/93	16r
Eggs, Grade A large	doz	0.85	4Q 92	4c
Eggs, Grade A large	doz	0.96	4/93	16r
Flour, white, all purpose	lb	0.24	4/93	16r
Frankfurters, all meat or all beef	lb	2.01	4/93	16r
Grapefruit	lb	0.44	4/93	16r
Grapes, Thompson Seedless	lb	1.40	4/93	16r
Ground beef, 100% beef	lb	1.58	4/93	16r
Ground beef, lean and extra lean	lb	2.09	4/93	16r
Ground beef or hamburger	lb	1.77	4Q 92	4c
Ground chuck, 100% beef	lb	1.98	4/93	16r
Ham, boneless, excluding canned	lb	2.89	4/93	16r
Ham, picnic, shoulder, bone-in, smoked	lb	1.02	4/93	16r
Ham, rump or steak half, bone-in, smoked	lb	1.48	4/93	16r
Ice cream, prepackaged, bulk, regular	1/2 gal	2.41	4/93	16r
Lemons	lb	1.05	4/93	16r
Lettuce, iceberg	head	1.07	4Q 92	4c
Lettuce, iceberg	lb	0.81	4/93	16r
Margarine, Blue Bonnet or Parkay cubes	lb	0.54	4Q 92	4c
Margarine, stick	lb	0.88	4/93	16r
Milk, whole	1/2 gal	1.43	4Q 92	4c
Orange juice, Minute Maid frozen	12-oz can	1.40	4Q 92	4c
Oranges, navel	lb	0.55	4/93	16r
Peaches	29-oz can	1.43	4Q 92	4c
Pears, Anjou	lb	0.92	4/93	16r
Peas Sweet, Del Monte or Green Giant	15-17 oz can	0.54	4Q 92	4c
Pork chops, center cut, bone-in	lb	3.13	4/93	16r
Potato chips	16 oz	2.94	4/93	16r
Potatoes, white	lb	0.43	4/93	16r
Potatoes, white or red	10-lb sack	2.17	4Q 92	4c
Rib roast, USDA choice, bone-in	lb	4.63	4/93	16r
Rice, white, long grain, uncooked	lb	0.45	4/93	16r
Round roast, graded & ungraded, ex USDA prime & choice	lb	3.03	4/93	16r
Round roast, USDA choice, boneless	lb	3.09	4/93	16r
Sausage, fresh, loose	lb	2.08	4/93	16r
Sausage, Jimmy Dean, 100% pork	lb	2.21	4Q 92	4c
Short ribs, bone-in	lb	2.66	4/93	16r
Shortening, vegetable oil blends	lb	0.69	4/93	16r
Shortening, vegetable, Crisco	3-lb can	2.17	4Q 92	4c
Soft drink, Coca Cola	2 liter	0.99	4Q 92	4c
Spaghetti and macaroni	lb	0.81	4/93	16r
Steak, rib eye, USDA choice, boneless	lb	6.24	4/93	16r
Steak, round, graded & ungraded, ex USDA prime & choice	lb	3.31	4/93	16r
Steak, round, USDA choice, boneless	lb	3.34	4/93	16r
Steak, sirloin, graded & ungraded, ex USDA prime & choice	lb	4.19	4/93	16r
Steak, sirloin, USDA choice, boneless	lb	4.46	4/93	16r
Steak, T-bone	lb	6.07	4Q 92	4c
Steak, T-bone, USDA choice, bone-in	lb	5.25	4/93	16r
Strawberries, dry pint	12 oz	0.92	4/93	16r
Sugar, cane or beet	4 lb	1.48	4Q 92	4c
Sugar, white	lb	0.39	4/93	16r
Sugar, white, 33-80 oz pk	lb	0.38	4/93	16r
Tomatoes, field grown	lb	0.88	4/93	16r
Tomatoes, Hunt's or Del Monte	14.5-oz can	0.57	4Q 92	4c
Tuna, chunk, light	6.125-6.5 oz can	0.67	4Q 92	4c

Values are in dollars or fractions of dollars. In the column headed *Ref*, references are shown to sources. Each reference is followed by a letter. These refer to the geographical level for which data were reported: s = State, r = Region, and c = City or metro. The abbreviation *ex* is used to mean *except* or *excluding*; *exp* stands for expenditures. For other abbreviations and further explanations, please see the Introduction.

Richmond, VA - continued

Item	Per	Value	Date	Ref.
Groceries				
Tuna, chunk, light	lb	1.79	4/93	16r
Turkey, frozen, whole	lb	1.04	4/93	16r
Yogurt, natural, fruit flavored	1/2 pint	0.57	4/93	16r
Health Care				
ACCRA Index, Health Care		106.00	4Q 92	4c
Analgesic, Aspirin, Bayer, 325 mg tablets	100	5.12	4Q 92	4c
Childbirth, cesarean, hospital		5034	91	62r
Childbirth, cesarean, physician's fee		2053	91	62r
Childbirth, normal, hospital		2712	91	62r
Childbirth, normal, physician's fee		1492	91	62r
Dentist's fee, adult teeth cleaning and periodic oral exam	visit	49.20	4Q 92	4c
Doctor's fee, routine exam, established patient	visit	42.20	4Q 92	4c
Hospital care, semiprivate room	day	228.89	90	27c
Hospital care, semiprivate room	day	298.76	4Q 92	4c
Medical insurance premium, per employee, small group comprehensive	month	328.50	10/91	25c
Medical plan per employee	year	3495	91	45r
Mental health care, exp	capita	37.60-53.67	90	38s
Mental health care, exp, state mental health agency	capita	44.54	90	38s
Mental health care, hospital psychiatric services, non-Federal, exp	capita	9.90	88	38s
Mental health care, mental health organization, multiservice, exp	capita	17.29	88	38s
Mental health care, psychiatric hospitals, private, exp	capita	32.58	88	38s
Mental health care, psychiatric out-patient clinics, freestanding, exp	capita	0.93	88	38s
Mental health care, psychiatric partial-care organizations, freestanding, exp	capita	0.25	88	38s
Mental health care, state and county mental hospitals, exp	capita	28.61	88	38s
Mental health care, VA medical centers, exp	capita	3.95	88	38s
Physician fee, family practice, first-visit		75.00	91	62r
Physician fee, family practice, revisit		34.00	91	62r
Physician fee, general practice, first-visit		61.00	91	62r
Physician fee, general practice, revisit		32.00	91	62r
Physician fee, general surgeon, first-visit		64.00	91	62r
Physician fee, general surgeon, revisit		40.00	91	62r
Physician fee, internal medicine, first-visit		98.00	91	62r
Physician fee, internal medicine, revisit		40.00	91	62r
Physician fee, median, neurosurgeon, first-visit		130.00	91	62r
Physician fee, median, nonsurgical specialist, first-visit		95.00	91	62r
Physician fee, median, orthopedic surgeon, first-visit		91.00	91	62r
Physician fee, median, plastic surgeon, first-visit		66.00	91	62r
Physician fee, median, surgical specialist, first-visit		62.00	91	62r
Physician fee, neurosurgeon, revisit		50.00	91	62r
Physician fee, nonsurgical specialist, revisit		40.00	91	62r
Physician fee, obstetrics/gynecology, first-visit		64.00	91	62r
Physician fee, obstetrics/gynecology, revisit		41.00	91	62r
Physician fee, orthopedic surgeon, revisit		40.00	91	62r
Physician fee, pediatrician, first-visit		49.00	91	62r
Physician fee, pediatrician, revisit		33.00	91	62r
Physician fee, plastic surgeon, revisit		43.00	91	62r
Physician fee, surgical specialist, revisit		37.00	91	62r
Substance abuse, hospital ancillary charge	incident	1220	90	70s
Substance abuse, hospital physician charge	incident	590	90	70s
Substance abuse, hospital room and board	incident	6280	90	70s

Richmond, VA - continued

Item	Per	Value	Date	Ref.
Household Goods				
Appliance repair, home, service call, washing machine	min labor charge	37.00	4Q 92	4c
Laundry detergent, Tide Ultra, Bold, or Cheer	42 oz	3.75	4Q 92	4c
Tissues, facial, Kleenex brand	175-count box	1.11	4Q 92	4c
Housing				
ACCRA Index, Housing		100.10	4Q 92	4c
Home, median price	unit	93.90		26c
House, 1,800 sq ft, 8,000 sq ft lot, new, urban	total	105270	4Q 92	4c
House payment, principal and interest, 25% down payment	month	581	4Q 92	4c
Mortgage rate, incl. points & origination fee, 30-year fixed or adjustable rate	percent	8.03	4Q 92	4c
Rent, apartment, 2 bedrooms - 1-1/2 to 2 baths, unfurnished, 950 sq ft, water	month	574	4Q 92	4c
Rental unit, 1 bedroom	month	414	93	23c
Rental unit, 2 bedroom	month	482	93	23c
Rental unit, 3 bedroom	month	605	93	23c
Rental unit, 4 bedroom	month	679	93	23c
Rental unit, efficiency	month	344	93	23c
Insurance and Pensions				
Auto insurance, private passenger	year	559.45	91	63s
Personal Goods				
Shampoo, Alberto VO5	15 oz	1.27	4Q 92	4c
Toothpaste, Crest or Colgate	6-7 oz	2.22	4Q 92	4c
Personal Services				
Dry cleaning, man's 2-piece suit		6.78	4Q 92	4c
Haircare, woman's shampoo, trim and blow-dry		24.45	4Q 92	4c
Haircut, man's barbershop, no styling		8.30	4Q 92	4c
Restaurant Food				
Chicken, fried, thigh and drumstick		1.99	4Q 92	4c
Hamburger with cheese	1/4 lb	1.83	4Q 92	4c
Pizza, Pizza Hut or Pizza Inn, cheese, thin crust	12-13 in	7.99	4Q 92	4c
Taxes				
Tax, cigarette	pack	2.50	91	77s
Tax, gasoline	gal	17.50	91	77s
Taxes, state	capita	1090	91	77s
Transportation				
ACCRA Index, Transportation		110.00	4Q 92	4c
Auto rental, average	day	42.00	6/91	60c
Bus fare	one-way	1.00	3/93	2c
Bus fare, up to 10 miles	one-way	1.25	4Q 92	4c
Driver's license fee		12.00	12/90	43s
Limo fare, airport-city, average	day	10.75	6/91	60c
Taxi fare, airport-city, average	day	17.00	6/91	60c
Tire balance, computer or spin balance, front	wheel	7.60	4Q 92	4c
Vehicle registration and license plate	year	26.50-37.50	93	90s
Travel				
Breakfast	day	7.64	6/91	60c
Business travel	day	193.00	4/93	89r
Dinner	day	24.27	6/91	60c
Lodging	day	109.57	91	60c
Lunch	day	11.62	6/91	60c
Utilities				
ACCRA Index, Utilities		120.20	4Q 92	4c
Electricity	mil Btu	17.70	90	64s

Values are in dollars or fractions of dollars. In the column headed *Ref*, references are shown to sources. Each reference is followed by a letter. These refer to the geographical level for which data were reported: s=State, r=Region, and c=City or metro. The abbreviation *ex* is used to mean *except* or *excluding*; *exp* stands for expenditures. For other abbreviations and further explanations, please see the Introduction.

Richmond, VA - continued

Item	Per	Value	Date	Ref.
Utilities				
Electricity, all electric, 1,800 sq ft living area new home	month	132.63	4Q 92	4c

Riverside, CA

Item	Per	Value	Date	Ref.
Composite ACCRA index		117.90	4Q 92	4c
Alcoholic Beverages				
Beer, Miller Lite or Budweiser, 12-oz containers	6 pack	3.74	4Q 92	4c
Liquor, J & B Scotch	750 ml	14.59	4Q 92	4c
Wine, Gallo Chablis blanc, 1.5 liter	bottle	3.72	4Q 92	4c
Child Care				
Child care fee, average, center	hour	1.71	90	65r
Child care fee, average, nonregulated family day care	hour	1.32	90	65r
Child care fee, average, regulated family day care	hour	1.86	90	65r
Clothing				
Jeans, man's denim		32.66	4Q 92	4c
Shirt, man's dress shirt		21.15	4Q 92	4c
Undervest, boy's size 10-14, cotton	3	9.81	4Q 92	4c
Communications				
Long-distance telephone service, day, initial minute, 0-100 miles	min	0.17-0.40	91	12s
Long-distance telephone service, day, additional minute, 0-100 miles	min	0.07-0.31	91	12s
Long-distance telephone service, evenings/weekends, 0-100 mi, initial minute	min	0.07-0.16	91	12s
Long-distance telephone service, evenings/weekends, 0-100 mi, additional minute	min	0.03-0.12	91	12s
Newspaper subscription, daily and Sunday home delivery, large-city	month	7.27	4Q 92	4c
Telephone bill, family of four	month	9.35	4Q 92	4c
Education				
Board, 4-yr private college/university	year	2515	91	22s
Board, 4-yr public college/university	year	2268	91	22s
Expenditures, local gov't, public elementary/secondary	pupil	4866	92	20s
Room, 4-year private college/university	year	2622	91	22s
Room, 4-year public college/university	year	2406	91	22s
Tuition, 2-year private college/university	year	7942	91	22s
Tuition, 2-year public college/university	year	114	91	22s
Tuition, 4-year private college/university	year	10863	91	22s
Tuition, 4-year public college/university, in-state	year	1220	91	22s
Energy and Fuels				
Coal	mil Btu	2.01	90	64s
Energy	mil Btu	9.08	90	64s
Energy, combined forms, 1,800 sq ft heating area	month	78.90	4Q 92	4c
Energy, exc electricity, 1,800 sq ft heating area	month	24.60	4Q 92	4c
Energy exp/householder, 1-family unit	year	362	90	28r
Energy exp/householder, <1,000 sq ft heating area	year	254	90	28r
Energy exp/householder, 1,000-1,999 sq ft heating area	year	358	90	28r
Energy exp/householder, 2,000+ sq ft heating area	year	467	90	28r
Energy exp/householder, mobile home	year	390	90	28r
Energy exp/householder, multifamily	year	252	90	28r
Gas, natural	mil Btu	4.31	90	64s
Gas, natural	000 cu ft	6.27	91	46s
Gas, natural, exp	year	369	91	46s
Gasoline, motor	gal	1.28	4Q 92	4c
Gasoline, unleaded regular	mil Btu	8.57	90	64s

Riverside, CA - continued

Item	Per	Value	Date	Ref.
Entertainment				
Bowling, evening rate	game	2.50	4Q 92	4c
Miniature golf admission	adult	6.18	92	1r
Miniature golf admission	child	5.14	92	1r
Monopoly game, Parker Brothers', No. 9		13.59	4Q 92	4c
Movie	admission	6.00	4Q 92	4c
Tennis balls, yellow, Wilson or Penn, 3	can	2.66	4Q 92	4c
Waterpark admission	adult	11.00	92	1r
Waterpark admission	child	8.55	92	1r
Funerals				
Casket, 18-gauge steel, velvet interior		1781.09	91	24r
Cosmetology, hair care, etc.		84.64	91	24r
Embalming		207.41	91	24r
Facility use for ceremony		205.76	91	24r
Hearse, local		105.14	91	24r
Limousine, local		83.21	91	24r
Remains to funeral home, transfer		113.82	91	24r
Service charge, professional		626.33	91	24r
Vault, concrete, non-metallic liner		599.54	91	24r
Viewing facilities, use		85.81	91	24r
Goods and Services				
ACCRA Index, Miscellaneous Goods and Services		117.80	4Q 92	4c
Groceries				
ACCRA Index, Groceries		104.80	4Q 92	4c
Apples, Red Delicious	lb	0.80	4/93	16r
Babyfood, strained vegetables, lowest price	4-4.5 oz jar	0.38	4Q 92	4c
Bacon	lb	1.79	4/93	16r
Bananas	lb	0.49	4Q 92	4c
Bananas	lb	0.53	4/93	16r
Bologna, all beef or mixed	lb	2.67	4/93	16r
Bread, white	24 oz	0.93	4Q 92	4c
Bread, white, pan	lb	0.81	4/93	16r
Carrots, short trimmed and topped	lb	0.39	4/93	16r
Cheese, Kraft grated Parmesan	8-oz canister	3.08	4Q 92	4c
Chicken, fresh, whole	lb	0.94	4/93	16r
Chicken, fryer, whole	lb	0.79	4Q 92	4c
Chicken breast, bone-in	lb	2.19	4/93	16r
Chuck roast, graded and ungraded, ex USDA prime and choice	lb	2.26	4/93	16r
Cigarettes, Winston	carton	20.35	4Q 92	4c
Coffee, 100% ground roast, all sizes	lb	2.33	4/93	16r
Coffee, vacuum-packed	13-oz can	2.05	4Q 92	4c
Corn, frozen	10 oz	0.61	4Q 92	4c
Corn Flakes, Kellogg's or Post Toasties	18 oz	1.94	4Q 92	4c
Eggs, Grade A large	doz	1.40	4Q 92	4c
Eggs, Grade AA large	doz	1.18	4/93	16r
Flour, white, all purpose	lb	0.22	4/93	16r
Grapefruit	lb	0.52	4/93	16r
Grapes, Thompson Seedless	lb	1.50	4/93	16r
Ground beef, 100% beef	lb	1.44	4/93	16r
Ground beef, lean and extra lean	lb	2.34	4/93	16r
Ground beef or hamburger	lb	1.38	4Q 92	4c
Ham, boneless, excluding canned	lb	2.56	4/93	16r
Honey, jar	8 oz	0.89-1.00	92	5r
Honey, jar	lb	1.35-1.97	92	5r
Honey, squeeze bear	12-oz	1.19-1.50	92	5r
Ice cream, prepackaged, bulk, regular	1/2 gal	2.40	4/93	16r
Lemons	lb	0.81	4/93	16r
Lettuce, iceberg	head	0.74	4Q 92	4c
Lettuce, iceberg	lb	0.84	4/93	16r
Margarine, Blue Bonnet or Parkay cubes	lb	0.69	4Q 92	4c
Margarine, stick	lb	0.81	4/93	16r
Milk, whole	1/2 gal	1.32	4Q 92	4c
Orange juice, Minute Maid frozen	12-oz can	1.33	4Q 92	4c
Oranges, navel	lb	0.48	4/93	16r

Values are in dollars or fractions of dollars. In the column headed *Ref*, references are shown to sources. Each reference is followed by a letter. These refer to the geographical level for which data were reported: s = State, r = Region, and c = City or metro. The abbreviation *ex* is used to mean *except* or *excluding*; *exp* stands for expenditures. For other abbreviations and further explanations, please see the Introduction.

Riverside, CA - continued

Item	Per	Value	Date	Ref.
Groceries				
Peaches	29-oz can	1.16	4Q 92	4c
Peas Sweet, Del Monte or Green Giant	15-17 oz can	0.65	4Q 92	4c
Pork chops, center cut, bone-in	lb	3.25	4/93	16r
Potato chips	16 oz	2.89	4/93	16r
Potatoes, white	lb	0.38	4/93	16r
Potatoes, white or red	10-lb sack	1.75	4Q 92	4c
Round roast, graded & ungraded, ex USDA prime & choice	lb	3.00	4/93	16r
Round roast, USDA choice, boneless	lb	3.16	4/93	16r
Sausage, Jimmy Dean, 100% pork	lb	2.56	4Q 92	4c
Shortening, vegetable oil blends	lb	0.86	4/93	16r
Shortening, vegetable, Crisco	3-lb can	2.36	4Q 92	4c
Soft drink, Coca Cola	2 liter	1.11	4Q 92	4c
Spaghetti and macaroni	lb	0.84	4/93	16r
Steak, round, graded & ungraded, ex USDA prime & choice	lb	3.34	4/93	16r
Steak, round, USDA choice, boneless	lb	3.24	4/93	16r
Steak, sirloin, graded & ungraded, ex USDA prime & choice	lb	3.75	4/93	16r
Steak, sirloin, USDA choice, boneless	lb	4.49	4/93	16r
Steak, T-bone	lb	4.98	4Q 92	4c
Sugar, cane or beet	4 lb	1.92	4Q 92	4c
Sugar, white	lb	0.41	4/93	16r
Sugar, white, 33-80 oz pk	lb	0.38	4/93	16r
Tomatoes, field grown	lb	1.01	4/93	16r
Tomatoes, Hunt's or Del Monte	14.5-oz can	0.72	4Q 92	4c
Tuna, chunk, light	6.125-6.5 oz can	0.60	4Q 92	4c
Turkey, frozen, whole	lb	1.04	4/93	16r
Health Care				
ACCRA Index, Health Care		116.80	4Q 92	4c
Analgesic, Aspirin, Bayer, 325 mg tablets	100	6.03	4Q 92	4c
Cardizem 60 mg tablets	30	24.04	92	49s
Cector 250 mg tablets	15	35.87	92	49s
Childbirth, cesarean, hospital		5533	91	62r
Childbirth, cesarean, physician's fee		2053	91	62r
Childbirth, normal, hospital		2745	91	62r
Childbirth, normal, physician's fee		1492	91	62r
Dentist's fee, adult teeth cleaning and periodic oral exam	visit	48.12	4Q 92	4c
Doctor's fee, routine exam, established patient	visit	38.50	4Q 92	4c
Health care spending, state	capita	2894	3/93	84s
Hospital care, semiprivate room	day	529.00	4Q 92	4c
Medical insurance premium, per employee, small group comprehensive	month	467.20	10/91	25c
Medical plan per employee	year	3421	91	45r
Mental health care, exp	capita	37.60-53.67	90	38s
Mental health care, exp, state mental health agency	capita	42.32	90	38s
Mental health care, hospital psychiatric services, non-Federal, exp	capita	10.64	88	38s
Mental health care, mental health organization, multiservice, exp	capita	28.56	88	38s
Mental health care, psychiatric hospitals, private, exp	capita	18.60	88	38s
Mental health care, psychiatric out-patient clinics, freestanding, exp	capita	2.28	88	38s
Mental health care, psychiatric partial-care organizations, freestanding, exp	capita	0.24	88	38s
Mental health care, state and county mental hospitals, exp	capita	13.60	88	38s
Mental health care, VA medical centers, exp	capita	2.33	88	38s
Mevacor 20 mg tablets	30	67.62	92	49s
Physician fee, family practice, first-visit		111.00	91	62r

Riverside, CA - continued

Item	Per	Value	Date	Ref.
Health Care - continued				
Physician fee, family practice, revisit		45.00	91	62r
Physician fee, general practice, first-visit		100.00	91	62r
Physician fee, general practice, revisit		40.00	91	62r
Physician fee, internal medicine, first-visit		137.00	91	62r
Physician fee, internal medicine, revisit		48.00	91	62r
Physician fee, median, neurosurgeon, first-visit		157.00	91	62r
Physician fee, median, nonsurgical specialist, first-visit		131.00	91	62r
Physician fee, median, orthopedic surgeon, first-visit		124.00	91	62r
Physician fee, median, plastic surgeon, first-visit		88.00	91	62r
Physician fee, median, surgical specialist, first-visit		100.00	91	62r
Physician fee, neurosurgeon, revisit		51.00	91	62r
Physician fee, nonsurgical specialist, revisit		47.00	91	62r
Physician fee, obstetrics/gynecology, first-visit		95.00	91	62r
Physician fee, obstetrics/gynecology, revisit		50.00	91	62r
Physician fee, orthopedic surgeon, revisit		51.00	91	62r
Physician fee, pediatrician, first-visit		81.00	91	62r
Physician fee, pediatrician, revisit		42.00	91	62r
Physician fee, plastic surgeon, revisit		48.00	91	62r
Physician fee, surgical specialist, revisit		49.00	91	62r
Prozac 20 mg tablets	14	33.22	92	49s
Substance abuse, hospital ancillary charge	incident	1760	90	70s
Substance abuse, hospital physician charge	incident	750	90	70s
Substance abuse, hospital room and board	incident	6390	90	70s
Tagamet 300 mg tablets	100	77.08	92	49s
Xanax 0.25 mg tablets	90	64.08	92	49s
Zantac 160 mg tablets	60	92.31	92	49s
Household Goods				
Appliance repair, home, service call, washing machine	min labor charge	31.98	4Q 92	4c
Laundry detergent, Tide Ultra, Bold, or Cheer	42 oz	4.51	4Q 92	4c
Tissues, facial, Kleenex brand	175-count box	1.04	4Q 92	4c
Housing				
ACCRA Index, Housing		140.10	4Q 92	4c
Home, median price	unit	136.20		26c
Home, median price	unit	131,200	92	58s
House, 1,800 sq ft, 8,000 sq ft lot, new, urban	total	162575	4Q 92	4c
House payment, principal and interest, 25% down payment	month	892	4Q 92	4c
Mortgage rate, incl. points & origination fee, 30-year fixed or adjustable rate	percent	7.98	4Q 92	4c
Rent, apartment, 2 bedrooms - 1-1/2 to 2 baths, unfurnished, 950 sq ft, water	month	619	4Q 92	4c
Rental unit, 1 bedroom	month	555	93	23c
Rental unit, 2 bedroom	month	647	93	23c
Rental unit, 3 bedroom	month	838	93	23c
Rental unit, 4 bedroom	month	943	93	23c
Rental unit, efficiency	month	470	93	23c
Insurance and Pensions				
Auto insurance, private passenger	year	904.37	91	63s
Personal Goods				
Shampoo, Alberto VO5	15 oz	1.21	4Q 92	4c
Toothpaste, Crest or Colgate	6-7 oz	2.13	4Q 92	4c
Personal Services				
Dry cleaning, man's 2-piece suit		6.74	4Q 92	4c

Values are in dollars or fractions of dollars. In the column headed *Ref*, references are shown to sources. Each reference is followed by a letter. These refer to the geographical level for which data were reported: s=State, r=Region, and c=City or metro. The abbreviation *ex* is used to mean *except* or *excluding*; *exp* stands for expenditures. For other abbreviations and further explanations, please see the Introduction.

Riverside, CA - continued

Item	Per	Value	Date	Ref.
Personal Services				
Haircare, woman's shampoo, trim and blow-dry		22.75	4Q 92	4c
Haircut, man's barbershop, no styling		9.25	4Q 92	4c
Restaurant Food				
Chicken, fried, thigh and drumstick		2.18	4Q 92	4c
Hamburger with cheese	1/4 lb	1.86	4Q 92	4c
Pizza, Pizza Hut or Pizza Inn, cheese, thin crust	12-13 in	9.81	4Q 92	4c
Taxes				
Tax, cigarette	pack	35	91	77s
Tax, gasoline	gal	16	91	77s
Taxes, state	capita	1477	91	77s
Transportation				
ACCRA Index, Transportation		117.30	4Q 92	4c
Auto rental, average	day	51.00	6/91	60c
Bus fare	one-way	0.75	3/93	2c
Bus fare, up to 10 miles	one-way	0.60	4Q 92	4c
Driver's license fee		10.00	12/90	43s
Limo fare, airport-city, average	day	17.50	6/91	60c
Taxi fare, airport-city, average	day	24.00	6/91	60c
Tire balance, computer or spin balance, front	wheel	8.60	4Q 92	4c
Travel				
Breakfast	day	5.94	6/91	60c
Business travel	day	178.00	4/93	89r
Dinner	day	12.11	6/91	60c
Lodging	day	138.40	91	60c
Lunch	day	7.24	6/91	60c
Utilities				
ACCRA Index, Utilities		69.80	4Q 92	4c
Electricity	mil Btu	25.98	90	64s
Electricity, partial electric and other energy, 1,800 sq ft living area new home	month	54.30	4Q 92	4c

Roanoke, VA

Item	Per	Value	Date	Ref.
Composite ACCRA index		94.70	4Q 92	4c
Alcoholic Beverages				
Beer, Miller Lite or Budweiser, 12-oz containers	6 pack	3.57	4Q 92	4c
Liquor, J & B Scotch	750 ml	16.95	4Q 92	4c
Wine, Gallo Chablis blanc, 1.5 liter	bottle	5.11	4Q 92	4c
Child Care				
Child care fee, average, center	hour	1.29	90	65r
Child care fee, average, nonregulated family day care	hour	0.89	90	65r
Child care fee, average, regulated family day care	hour	1.32	90	65r
Clothing				
Jeans, man's denim		32.79	4Q 92	4c
Shirt, man's dress shirt		24.80	4Q 92	4c
Undervest, boy's size 10-14, cotton	3	3.68	4Q 92	4c
Communications				
Long-distance telephone service, day, initial minute, 0-100 miles	min	0.21-0.35	91	12s
Long-distance telephone service, day, additional minute, 0-100 miles	min	0.12-0.21	91	12s
Long-distance telephone service, evenings/weekends, 0-100 mi, initial minute	min	0.08-0.14	91	12s
Long-distance telephone service, evenings/weekends, 0-100 mi, additional minute	min	0.05-0.08	91	12s
Newspaper subscription, daily and Sunday home delivery, large-city	month	9.75	4Q 92	4c
Telephone, flat rate	month	12.64	91	11c
Telephone bill, family of four	month	19.37	4Q 92	4c

Roanoke, VA - continued

Item	Per	Value	Date	Ref.
Education				
Board, 4-yr private college/university	year	1804	91	22s
Board, 4-yr public college/university	year	1688	91	22s
Expenditures, local gov't, public elementary/secondary	pupil	5487	92	20s
Room, 4-year private college/university	year	1659	91	22s
Room, 4-year public college/university	year	1916	91	22s
Tuition, 2-year private college/university	year	4852	91	22s
Tuition, 2-year public college/university	year	867	91	22s
Tuition, 4-year private college/university	year	7621	91	22s
Tuition, 4-year public college/university, in-state	year	2691	91	22s
Energy and Fuels				
Coal	mil Btu	1.60	90	64s
Energy	mil Btu	8.89	90	64s
Energy, combined forms, 1,800 sq ft heating area	month	93.25	4Q 92	4c
Energy exp/householder, 1-family unit	year	487	90	28r
Energy exp/householder, <1,000 sq ft heating area	year	393	90	28r
Energy exp/householder, 1,000-1,999 sq ft heating area	year	442	90	28r
Energy exp/householder, 2,000+ sq ft heating area	year	577	90	28r
Energy exp/householder, mobile home	year	366	90	28r
Energy exp/householder, multifamily	year	382	90	28r
Gas, cooking, winter, 10 therms	month	21.59	92	56c
Gas, cooking, winter, 30 therms	month	17.92	92	56c
Gas, cooking, winter, 50 therms	month	26.42	92	56c
Gas, heating, winter, 100 therms	month	45.71	92	56c
Gas, heating, winter, average use	month	66.39	92	56c
Gas, natural	mil Btu	4.67	90	64s
Gas, natural	000 cu ft	6.80	91	46s
Gas, natural, exp	year	566	91	46s
Gasoline, motor	gal	1.08	4Q 92	4c
Gasoline, unleaded regular	mil Btu	9.46	90	64s
Entertainment				
Bowling, evening rate	game	2.00	4Q 92	4c
Miniature golf admission	adult	6.18	92	1r
Miniature golf admission	child	5.14	92	1r
Monopoly game, Parker Brothers', No. 9		9.35	4Q 92	4c
Movie	admission	5.33	4Q 92	4c
Tennis balls, yellow, Wilson or Penn, 3	can	2.14	4Q 92	4c
Waterpark admission	adult	11.00	92	1r
Waterpark admission	child	8.55	92	1r
Funerals				
Casket, 18-gauge steel, velvet interior		2029.08	91	24r
Cosmetology, hair care, etc.		75.10	91	24r
Embalming		249.24	91	24r
Facility use for ceremony		162.27	91	24r
Hearse, local		114.04	91	24r
Limousine, local		88.57	91	24r
Remains to funeral home, transfer		92.61	91	24r
Service charge, professional		682.42	91	24r
Vault, concrete, non-metallic liner		798.70	91	24r
Viewing facilities, use		163.86	91	24r
Goods and Services				
ACCRA Index, Miscellaneous Goods and Services		98.30	4Q 92	4c
Groceries				
ACCRA Index, Groceries		93.00	4Q 92	4c
Apples, Red Delicious	lb	0.79	4/93	16r
Babyfood, strained vegetables, lowest price	4-4.5 oz jar	0.30	4Q 92	4c
Bacon	lb	1.75	4/93	16r
Bananas	lb	0.42	4Q 92	4c
Bananas	lb	0.42	4/93	16r
Beef, stew, boneless	lb	2.61	4/93	16r

Values are in dollars or fractions of dollars. In the column headed *Ref*, references are shown to sources. Each reference is followed by a letter. These refer to the geographical level for which data were reported: s=State, r=Region, and c=City or metro. The abbreviation *ex* is used to mean *except* or *excluding*; *exp* stands for expenditures. For other abbreviations and further explanations, please see the Introduction.

Roanoke, VA - continued

Item	Per	Value	Date	Ref.
Groceries				
Bologna, all beef or mixed	lb	2.24	4/93	16r
Bread, white	24 oz	0.84	4Q 92	4c
Bread, white, pan	lb	0.64	4/93	16r
Bread, whole wheat, pan	lb	0.96	4/93	16r
Cabbage	lb	0.37	4/93	16r
Carrots, short trimmed and topped	lb	0.47	4/93	16r
Celery	lb	0.64	4/93	16r
Cheese, American	lb	2.98	4/93	16r
Cheese, Cheddar	lb	3.28	4/93	16r
Cheese, Kraft grated Parmesan	8-oz canister	3.19	4Q 92	4c
Chicken, fresh, whole	lb	0.77	4/93	16r
Chicken, fryer, whole	lb	0.79	4Q 92	4c
Chicken breast, bone-in	lb	1.92	4/93	16r
Chicken legs, bone-in	lb	1.06	4/93	16r
Chuck roast, graded and ungraded, ex USDA prime and choice	lb	2.40	4/93	16r
Chuck roast, USDA choice, bone-in	lb	2.19	4/93	16r
Chuck roast, USDA choice, boneless	lb	2.38	4/93	16r
Cigarettes, Winston	carton	15.17	4Q 92	4c
Coffee, 100% ground roast, all sizes	lb	2.48	4/93	16r
Coffee, vacuum-packed	13-oz can	1.89	4Q 92	4c
Corn, frozen	10 oz	0.51	4Q 92	4c
Corn Flakes, Kellogg's or Post Toasties	18 oz	1.77	4Q 92	4c
Crackers, soda, salted	lb	1.15	4/93	16r
Eggs, Grade A large	doz	0.88	4Q 92	4c
Eggs, Grade A large	doz	0.96	4/93	16r
Flour, white, all purpose	lb	0.24	4/93	16r
Frankfurters, all meat or all beef	lb	2.01	4/93	16r
Grapefruit	lb	0.44	4/93	16r
Grapes, Thompson Seedless	lb	1.40	4/93	16r
Ground beef, 100% beef	lb	1.58	4/93	16r
Ground beef, lean and extra lean	lb	2.09	4/93	16r
Ground beef or hamburger	lb	1.49	4Q 92	4c
Ground chuck, 100% beef	lb	1.98	4/93	16r
Ham, boneless, excluding canned	lb	2.89	4/93	16r
Ham, picnic, shoulder, bone-in, smoked	lb	1.02	4/93	16r
Ham, rump or steak half, bone-in, smoked	lb	1.48	4/93	16r
Ice cream, prepackaged, bulk, regular	1/2 gal	2.41	4/93	16r
Lemons	lb	1.05	4/93	16r
Lettuce, iceberg	head	0.75	4Q 92	4c
Lettuce, iceberg	lb	0.81	4/93	16r
Margarine, Blue Bonnet or Parkay cubes	lb	0.49	4Q 92	4c
Margarine, stick	lb	0.88	4/93	16r
Milk, whole	1/2 gal	1.41	4Q 92	4c
Orange juice, Minute Maid frozen	12-oz can	1.22	4Q 92	4c
Oranges, navel	lb	0.55	4/93	16r
Peaches	29-oz can	1.27	4Q 92	4c
Pears, Anjou	lb	0.92	4/93	16r
Peas Sweet, Del Monte or Green Giant	15-17 oz can	0.53	4Q 92	4c
Pork chops, center cut, bone-in	lb	3.13	4/93	16r
Potato chips	16 oz	2.94	4/93	16r
Potatoes, white	lb	0.43	4/93	16r
Potatoes, white or red	10-lb sack	1.77	4Q 92	4c
Rib roast, USDA choice, bone-in	lb	4.63	4/93	16r
Rice, white, long grain, uncooked	lb	0.45	4/93	16r
Round roast, graded & ungraded, ex USDA prime & choice	lb	3.03	4/93	16r
Round roast, USDA choice, boneless	lb	3.09	4/93	16r
Sausage, fresh, loose	lb	2.08	4/93	16r
Sausage, Jimmy Dean, 100% pork	lb	1.91	4Q 92	4c
Short ribs, bone-in	lb	2.66	4/93	16r
Shortening, vegetable oil blends	lb	0.69	4/93	16r
Shortening, vegetable, Crisco	3-lb can	1.99	4Q 92	4c
Soft drink, Coca Cola	2 liter	0.95	4Q 92	4c

Roanoke, VA - continued

Item	Per	Value	Date	Ref.
Groceries - continued				
Spaghetti and macaroni	lb	0.81	4/93	16r
Steak, rib eye, USDA choice, boneless	lb	6.24	4/93	16r
Steak, round, graded & ungraded, ex USDA prime & choice	lb	3.31	4/93	16r
Steak, round, USDA choice, boneless	lb	3.34	4/93	16r
Steak, sirloin, graded & ungraded, ex USDA prime & choice	lb	4.19	4/93	16r
Steak, sirloin, USDA choice, boneless	lb	4.46	4/93	16r
Steak, T-bone	lb	5.47	4Q 92	4c
Steak, T-bone, USDA choice, bone-in	lb	5.25	4/93	16r
Strawberries, dry pint	12 oz	0.92	4/93	16r
Sugar, cane or beet	4 lb	1.19	4Q 92	4c
Sugar, white	lb	0.39	4/93	16r
Sugar, white, 33-80 oz pk	lb	0.38	4/93	16r
Tomatoes, field grown	lb	0.88	4/93	16r
Tomatoes, Hunt's or Del Monte	14.5-oz can	0.52	4Q 92	4c
Tuna, chunk, light	6.125-6.5 oz can	0.52	4Q 92	4c
Tuna, chunk, light	lb	1.79	4/93	16r
Turkey, frozen, whole	lb	1.04	4/93	16r
Yogurt, natural, fruit flavored	1/2 pint	0.57	4/93	16r
Health Care				
ACCRA Index, Health Care		91.40	4Q 92	4c
Analgesic, Aspirin, Bayer, 325 mg tablets	100	4.53	4Q 92	4c
Childbirth, cesarean, hospital		5034	91	62r
Childbirth, cesarean, physician's fee		2053	91	62r
Childbirth, normal, hospital		2712	91	62r
Childbirth, normal, physician's fee		1492	91	62r
Dentist's fee, adult teeth cleaning and periodic oral exam	visit	42.60	4Q 92	4c
Doctor's fee, routine exam, established patient	visit	35.20	4Q 92	4c
Hospital care, semiprivate room	day	226.24	90	27c
Hospital care, semiprivate room	day	271.33	4Q 92	4c
Medical insurance premium, per employee, small group comprehensive	month	292.00	10/91	25c
Medical plan per employee	year	3495	91	45r
Mental health care, exp	capita	37.60-53.67	90	38s
Mental health care, exp, state mental health agency	capita	44.54	90	38s
Mental health care, hospital psychiatric services, non-Federal, exp	capita	9.90	88	38s
Mental health care, mental health organization, multiservice, exp	capita	17.29	88	38s
Mental health care, psychiatric hospitals, private, exp	capita	32.58	88	38s
Mental health care, psychiatric out-patient clinics, freestanding, exp	capita	0.93	88	38s
Mental health care, psychiatric partial-care organizations, freestanding, exp	capita	0.25	88	38s
Mental health care, state and county mental hospitals, exp	capita	28.61	88	38s
Mental health care, VA medical centers, exp	capita	3.95	88	38s
Physician fee, family practice, first-visit		75.00	91	62r
Physician fee, family practice, revisit		34.00	91	62r
Physician fee, general practice, first-visit		61.00	91	62r
Physician fee, general practice, revisit		32.00	91	62r
Physician fee, general surgeon, first-visit		64.00	91	62r
Physician fee, general surgeon, revisit		40.00	91	62r
Physician fee, internal medicine, first-visit		98.00	91	62r
Physician fee, internal medicine, revisit		40.00	91	62r
Physician fee, median, neurosurgeon, first-visit		130.00	91	62r
Physician fee, median, nonsurgical specialist, first-visit		95.00	91	62r
Physician fee, median, orthopedic surgeon, first-visit		91.00	91	62r

Values are in dollars or fractions of dollars. In the column headed *Ref*, references are shown to sources. Each reference is followed by a letter. These refer to the geographical level for which data were reported: s=State, r=Region, and c=City or metro. The abbreviation *ex* is used to mean *except* or *excluding*; *exp* stands for expenditures. For other abbreviations and further explanations, please see the Introduction.

Roanoke, VA - continued

Item	Per	Value	Date	Ref.
Health Care				
Physician fee, median, plastic surgeon, first-visit		66.00	91	62r
Physician fee, median, surgical specialist, first-visit		62.00	91	62r
Physician fee, neurosurgeon, revisit		50.00	91	62r
Physician fee, nonsurgical specialist, revisit		40.00	91	62r
Physician fee, obstetrics/gynecology, first-visit		64.00	91	62r
Physician fee, obstetrics/gynecology, revisit		41.00	91	62r
Physician fee, orthopedic surgeon, revisit		40.00	91	62r
Physician fee, pediatrician, first-visit		49.00	91	62r
Physician fee, pediatrician, revisit		33.00	91	62r
Physician fee, plastic surgeon, revisit		43.00	91	62r
Physician fee, surgical specialist, revisit		37.00	91	62r
Substance abuse, hospital ancillary charge	incident	1220	90	70s
Substance abuse, hospital physician charge	incident	590	90	70s
Substance abuse, hospital room and board	incident	6280	90	70s
Household Goods				
Appliance repair, home, service call, washing machine	min labor charge	35.49	4Q 92	4c
Laundry detergent, Tide Ultra, Bold, or Cheer	42 oz	3.04	4Q 92	4c
Tissues, facial, Kleenex brand	175-count box	0.97	4Q 92	4c
Housing				
ACCRA Index, Housing		92.60	4Q 92	4c
House, 1,800 sq ft, 8,000 sq ft lot, new, urban	total	105950	4Q 92	4c
House payment, principal and interest, 25% down payment	month	588	4Q 92	4c
Mortgage rate, incl. points & origination fee, 30-year fixed or adjustable rate	percent	8.09	4Q 92	4c
Rent, apartment, 2 bedrooms - 1-1/2 to 2 baths, unfurnished, 950 sq ft, water	month	414	4Q 92	4c
Rental unit, 1 bedroom	month	368	93	23c
Rental unit, 2 bedroom	month	431	93	23c
Rental unit, 3 bedroom	month	541	93	23c
Rental unit, 4 bedroom	month	605	93	23c
Rental unit, efficiency	month	302	93	23c
Insurance and Pensions				
Auto insurance, private passenger	year	559.45	91	63s
Personal Goods				
Shampoo, Alberto VO5	15 oz	1.06	4Q 92	4c
Toothpaste, Crest or Colgate	6-7 oz	1.95	4Q 92	4c
Personal Services				
Dry cleaning, man's 2-piece suit		6.18	4Q 92	4c
Haircare, woman's shampoo, trim and blow-dry		14.80	4Q 92	4c
Haircut, man's barbershop, no styling		7.60	4Q 92	4c
Restaurant Food				
Chicken, fried, thigh and drumstick		2.20	4Q 92	4c
Hamburger with cheese	1/4 lb	1.89	4Q 92	4c
Pizza, Pizza Hut or Pizza Inn, cheese, thin crust	12-13 in	7.49	4Q 92	4c
Taxes				
Tax, cigarette	pack	2.50	91	77s
Tax, gasoline	gal	17.50	91	77s
Taxes, state	capita	1090	91	77s
Transportation				
ACCRA Index, Transportation		99.40	4Q 92	4c
Bus fare, up to 10 miles	one-way	1.00	4Q 92	4c
Driver's license fee		12.00	12/90	43s

Roanoke, VA - continued

Item	Per	Value	Date	Ref.
Transportation - continued				
Tire balance, computer or spin balance, front	wheel	6.49	4Q 92	4c
Vehicle registration and license plate	year	26.50-37.50	93	90s
Travel				
Business travel	day	193.00	4/93	89r
Utilities				
ACCRA Index, Utilities		86.80	4Q 92	4c
Electricity	mil Btu	17.70	90	64s
Electricity, all electric, 1,800 sq ft living area new home	month	93.25	4Q 92	4c
Electricity, winter, 250 KWh	month	19.26	92	55c
Electricity, winter, 500 KWh	month	32.84	92	55c
Electricity, winter, 750 KWh	month	46.41	92	55c
Electricity, winter, 1000 KWh	month	58.99	92	55c

Rochester, MN

Item	Per	Value	Date	Ref.
Composite ACCRA index		101.90	4Q 92	4c
Alcoholic Beverages				
Beer, Miller Lite or Budweiser, 12-oz containers	6 pack	3.75	4Q 92	4c
Liquor, J & B Scotch	750 ml	16.74	4Q 92	4c
Wine, Gallo Chablis blanc, 1.5 liter	bottle	5.06	4Q 92	4c
Child Care				
Child care fee, average, center	hour	1.63	90	65r
Child care fee, average, nonregulated family day care	hour	1.83	90	65r
Child care fee, average, regulated family day care	hour	1.42	90	65r
Clothing				
Jeans, man's denim		28.95	4Q 92	4c
Shirt, man's dress shirt		23.98	4Q 92	4c
Undervest, boy's size 10-14, cotton	3	3.76	4Q 92	4c
Communications				
Long-distance telephone service, day, initial minute, 0-100 miles	min	0.14-0.52	91	12s
Long-distance telephone service, day, additional minute, 0-100 miles	min	0.05-0.35	91	12s
Long-distance telephone service, evenings/weekends, 0-100 mi, initial minute	min	0.08-0.31	91	12s
Long-distance telephone service, evenings/weekends, 0-100 mi, additional minute	min	0.03-0.21	91	12s
Newspaper subscription, daily and Sunday home delivery, large-city	month	11.52	4Q 92	4c
Telephone, flat rate	month	17.89	91	11c
Telephone bill, family of four	month	23.10	4Q 92	4c
Education				
Board, 4-yr private college/university	year	1718	91	22s
Board, 4-yr public college/university	year	1321	91	22s
Expenditures, local gov't, public elementary/secondary	pupil	5500	92	20s
Room, 4-year private college/university	year	1587	91	22s
Room, 4-year public college/university	year	1344	91	22s
Tuition, 2-year private college/university	year	7664	91	22s
Tuition, 2-year public college/university	year	1578	91	22s
Tuition, 4-year private college/university	year	9507	91	22s
Tuition, 4-year public college/university, in-state	year	2216	91	22s
Energy and Fuels				
Coal	mil Btu	1.32	90	64s
Energy	mil Btu	8.17	90	64s
Energy, combined forms, 1,800 sq ft heating area	month	102.50	4Q 92	4c
Energy, exc electricity, 1,800 sq ft heating area	month	46.99	4Q 92	4c
Energy exp/householder, 1-family unit	year	473	90	28r

Values are in dollars or fractions of dollars. In the column headed *Ref*, references are shown to sources. Each reference is followed by a letter. These refer to the geographical level for which data were reported: s=State, r=Region, and c=City or metro. The abbreviation *ex* is used to mean *except* or *excluding*; *exp* stands for expenditures. For other abbreviations and further explanations, please see the Introduction.

Rochester, MN - continued

Item	Per	Value	Date	Ref.
Energy and Fuels				
Energy exp/householder, <1,000 sq ft heating area	year	429	90	28r
Energy exp/householder, 1,000-1,999 sq ft heating area	year	442	90	28r
Energy exp/householder, 2,000+ sq ft heating area	year	498	90	28r
Energy exp/householder, mobile home	year	442	90	28r
Energy exp/householder, multifamily	year	407	90	28r
Gas, cooking, 10 therms	month	8.25	92	56c
Gas, cooking, 30 therms	month	16.75	92	56c
Gas, cooking, 50 therms	month	25.25	92	56c
Gas, heating, winter, 100 therms	month	46.51	92	56c
Gas, heating, winter, average use	month	77.53	92	56c
Gas, natural	mil Btu	3.87	90	64s
Gas, natural	000 cu ft	4.52	91	46s
Gas, natural, exp	year	545	91	46s
Gasoline, motor	gal	1.15	4Q 92	4c
Gasoline, unleaded regular	mil Btu	9.56	90	64s
Entertainment				
Bowling, evening rate	game	1.69	4Q 92	4c
Miniature golf admission	adult	6.18	92	1r
Miniature golf admission	child	5.14	92	1r
Monopoly game, Parker Brothers', No. 9		9.93	4Q 92	4c
Movie	admission	5.50	4Q 92	4c
Tennis balls, yellow, Wilson or Penn, 3	can	2.78	4Q 92	4c
Waterpark admission	adult	11.00	92	1r
Waterpark admission	child	8.55	92	1r
Funerals				
Casket, 18-gauge steel, velvet interior		1952.97	91	24r
Cosmetology, hair care, etc.		90.03	91	24r
Embalming		251.75	91	24r
Facility use for ceremony		180.75	91	24r
Hearse, local		117.51	91	24r
Limousine, local		71.86	91	24r
Remains to funeral home, transfer		81.14	91	24r
Service charge, professional		740.03	91	24r
Vault, concrete, non-metallic liner		801.47	91	24r
Viewing facilities, use		169.33	91	24r
Goods and Services				
ACCRA Index, Miscellaneous Goods and Services		99.40	4Q 92	4c
Groceries				
ACCRA Index, Groceries		99.10	4Q 92	4c
Apples, Red Delicious	lb	0.77	4/93	16r
Babyfood, strained vegetables, lowest price	4-4.5 oz jar	0.32	4Q 92	4c
Bacon	lb	1.85	4/93	16r
Bananas	lb	0.37	4Q 92	4c
Bananas	lb	0.46	4/93	16r
Beef, stew, boneless	lb	2.53	4/93	16r
Bologna, all beef or mixed	lb	2.19	4/93	16r
Bread, white	24 oz	0.62	4Q 92	4c
Bread, white, pan	lb	0.78	4/93	16r
Butter	lb	1.50	4/93	16r
Cabbage	lb	0.40	4/93	16r
Carrots, short trimmed and topped	lb	0.45	4/93	16r
Cheese, Cheddar	lb	3.47	4/93	16r
Cheese, Kraft grated Parmesan	8-oz canister	3.17	4Q 92	4c
Chicken, fresh, whole	lb	0.84	4/93	16r
Chicken, fryer, whole	lb	0.74	4Q 92	4c
Chicken breast, bone-in	lb	1.94	4/93	16r
Chicken legs, bone-in	lb	1.02	4/93	16r
Chuck roast, graded and ungraded, ex USDA prime and choice	lb	2.43	4/93	16r
Chuck roast, USDA choice, bone-in	lb	2.11	4/93	16r
Chuck roast, USDA choice, boneless	lb	2.44	4/93	16r

Rochester, MN - continued

Item	Per	Value	Date	Ref.
Groceries - continued				
Cigarettes, Winston	carton	18.80	4Q 92	4c
Coffee, 100% ground roast, all sizes	lb	2.47	4/93	16r
Coffee, vacuum-packed	13-oz can	2.34	4Q 92	4c
Cookies, chocolate chip	lb	2.73	4/93	16r
Corn, frozen	10 oz	0.66	4Q 92	4c
Corn Flakes, Kellogg's or Post Toasties	18 oz	2.02	4Q 92	4c
Eggs, Grade A large	doz	0.67	4Q 92	4c
Eggs, Grade A large	doz	0.93	4/93	16r
Flour, white, all purpose	lb	0.21	4/93	16r
Grapefruit	lb	0.45	4/93	16r
Grapes, Thompson Seedless	lb	1.46	4/93	16r
Ground beef, 100% beef	lb	1.63	4/93	16r
Ground beef, lean and extra lean	lb	2.08	4/93	16r
Ground beef or hamburger	lb	1.50	4Q 92	4c
Ground chuck, 100% beef	lb	1.94	4/93	16r
Ham, boneless, excluding canned	lb	2.21	4/93	16r
Ice cream, prepackaged, bulk, regular	1/2 gal	2.41	4/93	16r
Lemons	lb	0.82	4/93	16r
Lettuce, iceberg	head	0.76	4Q 92	4c
Lettuce, iceberg	lb	0.83	4/93	16r
Margarine, Blue Bonnet or Parkay cubes	lb	0.70	4Q 92	4c
Margarine, stick	lb	0.77	4/93	16r
Milk, whole	1/2 gal	1.36	4Q 92	4c
Orange juice, Minute Maid frozen	12-oz can	1.42	4Q 92	4c
Oranges, navel	lb	0.50	4/93	16r
Peaches	29-oz can	1.37	4Q 92	4c
Peanut butter, creamy, all sizes	lb	1.82	4/93	16r
Pears, Anjou	lb	0.85	4/93	16r
Peas Sweet, Del Monte or Green Giant	15-17 oz can	0.59	4Q 92	4c
Pork chops, center cut, bone-in	lb	3.17	4/93	16r
Potato chips	16 oz	2.68	4/93	16r
Potatoes, white	lb	0.26	4/93	16r
Potatoes, white or red	10-lb sack	2.03	4Q 92	4c
Round roast, graded & ungraded, ex USDA prime & choice	lb	2.88	4/93	16r
Round roast, USDA choice, boneless	lb	2.96	4/93	16r
Sausage, Jimmy Dean, 100% pork	lb	2.61	4Q 92	4c
Shortening, vegetable oil blends	lb	0.79	4/93	16r
Shortening, vegetable, Crisco	3-lb can	2.24	4Q 92	4c
Soft drink, Coca Cola	2 liter	1.29	4Q 92	4c
Spaghetti and macaroni	lb	0.76	4/93	16r
Steak, rib eye, USDA choice, boneless	lb	6.29	4/93	16r
Steak, round, USDA choice, boneless	lb	3.24	4/93	16r
Steak, sirloin, graded & ungraded, ex USDA prime & choice	lb	4.00	4/93	16r
Steak, sirloin, USDA choice, bone-in	lb	3.57	4/93	16r
Steak, sirloin, USDA choice, boneless	lb	4.17	4/93	16r
Steak, T-bone	lb	4.72	4Q 92	4c
Steak, T-bone, USDA choice, bone-in	lb	5.60	4/93	16r
Strawberries, dry pint	12 oz	0.90	4/93	16r
Sugar, cane or beet	4 lb	1.67	4Q 92	4c
Sugar, white	lb	0.36	4/93	16r
Sugar, white, 33-80 oz pk	lb	0.35	4/93	16r
Tomatoes, field grown	lb	0.99	4/93	16r
Tomatoes, Hunt's or Del Monte	14.5-oz can	0.74	4Q 92	4c
Tuna, chunk, light	6.125-6.5 oz can	0.62	4Q 92	4c
Tuna, chunk, light	lb	1.76	4/93	16r
Turkey, frozen, whole	lb	0.91	4/93	16r
Health Care				
ACCRA Index, Health Care		105.80	4Q 92	4c
Analgesic, Aspirin, Bayer, 325 mg tablets	100	4.81	4Q 92	4c
Childbirth, cesarean, hospital		4688	91	62r
Childbirth, cesarean, physician's fee		2053	91	62r

Values are in dollars or fractions of dollars. In the column headed *Ref*, references are shown to sources. Each reference is followed by a letter. These refer to the geographical level for which data were reported: s=State, r=Region, and c=City or metro. The abbreviation *ex* is used to mean *except* or *excluding*; *exp* stands for expenditures. For other abbreviations and further explanations, please see the Introduction.

Rochester, MN - continued

Item	Per	Value	Date	Ref.
Health Care				
Childbirth, normal, hospital		2657	91	62r
Childbirth, normal, physician's fee		1492	91	62r
Dentist's fee, adult teeth cleaning and periodic oral exam	visit	43.96	4Q 92	4c
Doctor's fee, routine exam, established patient	visit	41.67	4Q 92	4c
Hospital care, semiprivate room	day	258.19	90	27c
Hospital care, semiprivate room	day	385.00	4Q 92	4c
Medical insurance premium, per employee, small group comprehensive	month	284.70	10/91	25c
Medical plan per employee	year	3443	91	45r
Mental health care, exp	capita	20.37-28.83	90	38s
Mental health care, exp, state mental health agency	capita	53.67	90	38s
Mental health care, hospital psychiatric services, non-Federal, exp	capita	18.62	88	38s
Mental health care, mental health organization, multiservice, exp	capita	9.59	88	38s
Mental health care, psychiatric hospitals, private, exp	capita	2.70	88	38s
Mental health care, psychiatric out-patient clinics, freestanding, exp	capita	8.41	88	38s
Mental health care, state and county mental hospitals, exp	capita	27.18	88	38s
Mental health care, VA medical centers, exp	capita	7.88	88	38s
Physician fee, family practice, first-visit		76.00	91	62r
Physician fee, family practice, revisit		33.00	91	62r
Physician fee, general practice, first-visit		61.00	91	62r
Physician fee, general practice, revisit		31.00	91	62r
Physician fee, general surgeon, first-visit		65.00	91	62r
Physician fee, general surgeon, revisit		35.00	91	62r
Physician fee, internal medicine, first-visit		91.00	91	62r
Physician fee, internal medicine, revisit		40.00	91	62r
Physician fee, median, neurosurgeon, first-visit		106.00	91	62r
Physician fee, median, nonsurgical specialist, first-visit		90.00	91	62r
Physician fee, median, orthopedic surgeon, first-visit		83.00	91	62r
Physician fee, median, surgical specialist, first-visit		61.00	91	62r
Physician fee, neurosurgeon, revisit		41.00	91	62r
Physician fee, nonsurgical specialist, revisit		40.00	91	62r
Physician fee, obstetrics/gynecology, first-visit		61.00	91	62r
Physician fee, obstetrics/gynecology, revisit		40.00	91	62r
Physician fee, orthopedic surgeon, revisit		41.00	91	62r
Physician fee, pediatrician, first-visit		46.00	91	62r
Physician fee, pediatrician, revisit		33.00	91	62r
Physician fee, surgical specialist, revisit		36.00	91	62r
Substance abuse, hospital ancillary charge	incident	670	90	70s
Substance abuse, hospital physician charge	incident	310	90	70s
Substance abuse, hospital room and board	incident	3800	90	70s
Household Goods				
Appliance repair, home, service call, washing machine	min labor charge	33.67	4Q 92	4c
Laundry detergent, Tide Ultra, Bold, or Cheer	42 oz	3.87	4Q 92	4c
Tissues, facial, Kleenex brand	175-count box	1.10	4Q 92	4c
Housing				
ACCRA Index, Housing		104.90	4Q 92	4c
House, 1,800 sq ft, 8,000 sq ft lot, new, urban	total	107789	4Q 92	4c

Rochester, MN - continued

Item	Per	Value	Date	Ref.
Housing - continued				
House payment, principal and interest, 25% down payment	month	610	4Q 92	4c
Mortgage rate, incl. points & origination fee, 30-year fixed or adjustable rate	percent	8.29	4Q 92	4c
Rent, apartment, 2 bedrooms - 1-1/2 to 2 baths, unfurnished, 950 sq ft, water	month	599	4Q 92	4c
Rental unit, 1 bedroom	month	427	93	23c
Rental unit, 2 bedroom	month	504	93	23c
Rental unit, 3 bedroom	month	630	93	23c
Rental unit, 4 bedroom	month	705	93	23c
Rental unit, efficiency	month	352	93	23c
Insurance and Pensions				
Auto insurance, private passenger	year	584.92	91	63s
Personal Goods				
Shampoo, Alberto VO5	15 oz	1.27	4Q 92	4c
Toothpaste, Crest or Colgate	6-7 oz	1.68	4Q 92	4c
Personal Services				
Dry cleaning, man's 2-piece suit		6.99	4Q 92	4c
Haircare, woman's shampoo, trim and blow-dry		16.02	4Q 92	4c
Haircut, man's barbershop, no styling		9.93	4Q 92	4c
Restaurant Food				
Chicken, fried, thigh and drumstick		2.11	4Q 92	4c
Hamburger with cheese	1/4 lb	1.83	4Q 92	4c
Pizza, Pizza Hut or Pizza Inn, cheese, thin crust	12-13 in	7.95	4Q 92	4c
Taxes				
Tax, cigarette	pack	48	91	77s
Tax, gasoline	gal	20	91	77s
Taxes, state	capita	1591	91	77s
Transportation				
ACCRA Index, Transportation		109.00	4Q 92	4c
Driver's license fee		15.00	12/90	43s
Tire balance, computer or spin balance, front	wheel	7.54	4Q 92	4c
Vehicle registration and license plate	year	10.00	93	66s
Utilities				
ACCRA Index, Utilities		96.40	4Q 92	4c
Electricity	mil Btu	15.68	90	64s
Electricity, partial electric and other energy, 1,800 sq ft living area new home	month	55.51	4Q 92	4c

Rochester, NY

Item	Per	Value	Date	Ref.
Composite ACCRA index		113.40	4Q 92	4c
Alcoholic Beverages				
Beer, Miller Lite or Budweiser, 12-oz containers	6 pack	4.49	4Q 92	4c
Liquor, J & B Scotch	750 ml	18.32	4Q 92	4c
Wine, Gallo Chablis blanc, 1.5 liter	bottle	5.95	4Q 92	4c
Child Care				
Child care fee, average, center	hour	2.18	90	65r
Child care fee, average, nonregulated family day care	hour	1.83	90	65r
Child care fee, average, regulated family day care	hour	2.02	90	65r
Clothing				
Jeans, man's denim		29.25	4Q 92	4c
Shirt, man's dress shirt		23.50	4Q 92	4c
Undervest, boy's size 10-14, cotton	3	4.49	4Q 92	4c
Communications				
Newspaper subscription, daily and Sunday home delivery, large-city	month	13.26	4Q 92	4c
Telephone, residential, private line, rotary, unlimited calling	month	19.47	10/91	78c
Telephone bill, family of four	month	20.68	4Q 92	4c

Values are in dollars or fractions of dollars. In the column headed *Ref*, references are shown to sources. Each reference is followed by a letter. These refer to the geographical level for which data were reported: s=State, r=Region, and c=City or metro. The abbreviation *ex* is used to mean *except* or *excluding*; *exp* stands for expenditures. For other abbreviations and further explanations, please see the Introduction.

Rochester, NY - continued

Item	Per	Value	Date	Ref.
Education				
Board, 4-yr private college/university	year	2451	91	22s
Board, 4-yr public college/university	year	1725	91	22s
Expenditures, local gov't, public elementary/secondary	pupil	8603	92	20s
Room, 4-year private college/university	year	2652	91	22s
Room, 4-year public college/university	year	2183	91	22s
Tuition, 2-year private college/university	year	5926	91	22s
Tuition, 2-year public college/university	year	1419	91	22s
Tuition, 4-year private college/university	year	10340	91	22s
Tuition, 4-year public college/university, in-state	year	1587	91	22s
Energy and Fuels				
Coal	mil Btu	1.66	90	64s
Energy	mil Btu	10.68	90	64s
Energy, combined forms, 1,800 sq ft heating area	month	123.31	4Q 92	4c
Energy, exc electricity, 1,800 sq ft heating area	month	56.52	4Q 92	4c
Energy exp/householder, 1-family unit	year	588	90	28r
Energy exp/householder, <1,000 sq ft heating area	year	477	90	28r
Energy exp/householder, 1,000-1,999 sq ft heating area	year	517	90	28r
Energy exp/householder, 2,000+ sq ft heating area	year	630	90	28r
Energy exp/householder, mobile home	year	412	90	28r
Energy exp/householder, multifamily	year	498	90	28r
Gas, cooking, winter, 10 therms	month	10.85	92	56c
Gas, cooking, winter, 30 therms	month	22.88	92	56c
Gas, cooking, winter, 50 therms	month	34.92	92	56c
Gas, heating, winter, 100 therms	month	65.01	92	56c
Gas, heating, winter, average use	month	185.36	92	56c
Gas, natural	mil Btu	5.25	90	64s
Gas, natural	000 cu ft	7.35	91	46s
Gas, natural, exp	year	557	91	46s
Gasoline, motor	gal	1.24	4Q 92	4c
Gasoline, unleaded regular	mil Btu	8.83	90	64s
Entertainment				
Bowling, evening rate	game	2.00	4Q 92	4c
Monopoly game, Parker Brothers', No. 9		12.24	4Q 92	4c
Movie	admission	6.45	4Q 92	4c
Tennis balls, yellow, Wilson or Penn, 3	can	2.41	4Q 92	4c
Funerals				
Casket, 18-gauge steel, velvet interior		1811.58	91	24r
Cosmetology, hair care, etc.		111.08	91	24r
Embalming		329.42	91	24r
Facility use for ceremony		201.29	91	24r
Hearse, local		135.27	91	24r
Limousine, local		127.24	91	24r
Remains to funeral home, transfer		103.98	91	24r
Service charge, professional		724.98	91	24r
Vault, concrete, non-metallic liner		766.71	91	24r
Viewing facilities, use		260.60	91	24r
Goods and Services				
ACCRA Index, Miscellaneous Goods and Services		104.20	4Q 92	4c
Groceries				
ACCRA Index, Groceries		115.10	4Q 92	4c
Apples, Red Delicious	lb	0.85	4/93	16r
Babyfood, strained vegetables, lowest price	4-4.5 oz jar	0.42	4Q 92	4c
Bacon	lb	2.12	4/93	16r
Bananas	lb	0.48	4Q 92	4c
Bananas	lb	0.54	4/93	16r
Bread, white	24 oz	0.87	4Q 92	4c
Bread, white, pan	lb	0.81	4/93	16r
Butter	lb	2.02	4/93	16r

Rochester, NY - continued

Item	Per	Value	Date	Ref.
Groceries - continued				
Carrots, short trimmed and topped	lb	0.51	4/93	16r
Cheese, Kraft grated Parmesan	8-oz canister	3.37	4Q 92	4c
Chicken, fresh, whole	lb	1.04	4/93	16r
Chicken, fryer, whole	lb	0.87	4Q 92	4c
Chicken breast, bone-in	lb	2.21	4/93	16r
Chicken legs, bone-in	lb	1.16	4/93	16r
Chuck roast, USDA choice, boneless	lb	2.82	4/93	16r
Cigarettes, Winston	carton	19.64	4Q 92	4c
Coffee, 100% ground roast, all sizes	lb	2.66	4/93	16r
Coffee, vacuum-packed	13-oz can	2.49	4Q 92	4c
Corn, frozen	10 oz	0.74	4Q 92	4c
Corn Flakes, Kellogg's or Post Toasties	18 oz	2.00	4Q 92	4c
Cucumbers	lb	0.85	4/93	16r
Eggs, Grade A large	doz	0.88	4Q 92	4c
Eggs, Grade A large	doz	1.15	4/93	16r
Grapefruit	lb	0.45	4/93	16r
Grapes, Thompson Seedless	lb	1.52	4/93	16r
Ground beef, lean and extra lean	lb	2.36	4/93	16r
Ground beef or hamburger	lb	1.76	4Q 92	4c
Ground chuck, 100% beef	lb	2.02	4/93	16r
Honey, jar	8 oz	0.96-1.75	92	5r
Honey, jar	lb	1.50-3.00	92	5r
Honey, squeeze bear	12-oz	1.50-1.99	92	5r
Ice cream, prepackaged, bulk, regular	1/2 gal	2.80	4/93	16r
Lemons	lb	0.96	4/93	16r
Lettuce, iceberg	head	0.99	4Q 92	4c
Lettuce, iceberg	lb	0.95	4/93	16r
Margarine, Blue Bonnet or Parkay cubes	lb	0.66	4Q 92	4c
Margarine, stick	lb	0.81	4/93	16r
Milk, fresh, whole, fortified	1/2 gal	1.30	4/93	16r
Milk, whole	1/2 gal	1.29	4Q 92	4c
Orange juice, Minute Maid frozen	12-oz can	1.65	4Q 92	4c
Oranges, navel	lb	0.56	4/93	16r
Peaches	29-oz can	1.51	4Q 92	4c
Peanut butter, creamy, all sizes	lb	1.88	4/93	16r
Peas Sweet, Del Monte or Green Giant	15-17 oz can	0.64	4Q 92	4c
Pork chops, center cut, bone-in	lb	3.34	4/93	16r
Potato chips	16 oz	2.88	4/93	16r
Potatoes, white	lb	0.37	4/93	16r
Potatoes, white or red	10-lb sack	1.93	4Q 92	4c
Rib roast, USDA choice, bone-in	lb	4.94	4/93	16r
Round roast, USDA choice, boneless	lb	3.17	4/93	16r
Sausage, Jimmy Dean, 100% pork	lb	3.32	4Q 92	4c
Shortening, vegetable oil blends	lb	0.98	4/93	16r
Shortening, vegetable, Crisco	3-lb can	2.95	4Q 92	4c
Soft drink, Coca Cola	2 liter	1.69	4Q 92	4c
Spaghetti and macaroni	lb	0.82	4/93	16r
Steak, round, graded & ungraded, ex USDA prime & choice	lb	4.04	4/93	16r
Steak, round, USDA choice, boneless	lb	3.90	4/93	16r
Steak, sirloin, USDA choice, boneless	lb	4.97	4/93	16r
Steak, T-bone	lb	5.81	4Q 92	4c
Strawberries, dry pint	12 oz	0.90	4/93	16r
Sugar, cane or beet	4 lb	1.88	4Q 92	4c
Sugar, white	lb	0.50	4/93	16r
Sugar, white, 33-80 oz pk	lb	0.41	4/93	16r
Tomatoes, field grown	lb	1.23	4/93	16r
Tomatoes, Hunt's or Del Monte	14.5-oz can	0.75	4Q 92	4c
Tuna, chunk, light	6.125-6.5 oz can	0.78	4Q 92	4c
Tuna, chunk, light	lb	2.22	4/93	16r
Turkey, frozen, whole	lb	1.04	4/93	16r

Values are in dollars or fractions of dollars. In the column headed *Ref*, references are shown to sources. Each reference is followed by a letter. These refer to the geographical level for which data were reported: s=State, r=Region, and c=City or metro. The abbreviation *ex* is used to mean *except* or *excluding*; *exp* stands for expenditures. For other abbreviations and further explanations, please see the Introduction.

Rochester, NY - continued

Item	Per	Value	Date	Ref.
Health Care				
ACCRA Index, Health Care		113.50	4Q 92	4c
Analgesic, Aspirin, Bayer, 325 mg tablets	100	4.69	4Q 92	4c
Childbirth, cesarean, hospital		5826	91	62r
Childbirth, cesarean, physician's fee		2053	91	62r
Childbirth, normal, hospital		2964	91	62r
Childbirth, normal, physician's fee		1492	91	62r
Dentist's fee, adult teeth cleaning and periodic oral exam	visit	42.60	4Q 92	4c
Doctor's fee, routine exam, established patient	visit	46.40	4Q 92	4c
Hospital care, semiprivate room	day	251.97	90	27c
Hospital care, semiprivate room	day	464.80	4Q 92	4c
Medical insurance premium, per employee, small group comprehensive	month	306.60	10/91	25c
Medical plan per employee	year	3942	91	45r
Mental health care, exp	capita	53.68-118.35	90	38s
Mental health care, exp, state mental health agency	capita	118.34	90	38s
Mental health care, hospital psychiatric services, non-Federal, exp	capita	29.77	88	38s
Mental health care, mental health organization, multiservice, exp	capita	20.03	88	38s
Mental health care, psychiatric hospitals, private, exp	capita	8.37	88	38s
Mental health care, psychiatric out-patient clinics, freestanding, exp	capita	7.96	88	38s
Mental health care, psychiatric partial-care organizations, freestanding, exp	capita	1.24	88	38s
Mental health care, state and county mental hospitals, exp	capita	89.52	88	38s
Mental health care, VA medical centers, exp	capita	7.12	88	38s
Prescription drug co-pay, Medicaid	month	23.00	91	21s
Substance abuse, hospital ancillary charge	incident	1040	90	70s
Substance abuse, hospital physician charge	incident	360	90	70s
Substance abuse, hospital room and board	incident	6330	90	70s
Household Goods				
Appliance repair, home, service call, washing machine	min labor charge	26.40	4Q 92	4c
Laundry detergent, Tide Ultra, Bold, or Cheer	42 oz	4.07	4Q 92	4c
Tissues, facial, Kleenex brand	175-count box	1.25	4Q 92	4c
Housing				
ACCRA Index, Housing		121.50	4Q 92	4c
Home, median price	unit	84.70		26c
House, 1,800 sq ft, 8,000 sq ft lot, new, urban	total	135000	4Q 92	4c
House payment, principal and interest, 25% down payment	month	774	4Q 92	4c
Mortgage rate, incl. points & origination fee, 30-year fixed or adjustable rate	percent	8.44	4Q 92	4c
Rent, apartment, 2 bedrooms - 1-1/2 to 2 baths, unfurnished, 950 sq ft, water	month	537	4Q 92	4c
Rental unit, 1 bedroom	month	506	93	23c
Rental unit, 2 bedroom	month	596	93	23c
Rental unit, 3 bedroom	month	745	93	23c
Rental unit, 4 bedroom	month	830	93	23c
Rental unit, efficiency	month	413	93	23c
Insurance and Pensions				
Auto insurance, private passenger	year	840.89	91	63s
Personal Goods				
Shampoo, Alberto VO5	15 oz	1.21	4Q 92	4c
Toothpaste, Crest or Colgate	6-7 oz	2.08	4Q 92	4c

Rochester, NY - continued

Item	Per	Value	Date	Ref.
Personal Services				
Dry cleaning, man's 2-piece suit		7.46	4Q 92	4c
Haircare, woman's shampoo, trim and blow-dry		17.81	4Q 92	4c
Haircut, man's barbershop, no styling		7.60	4Q 92	4c
Restaurant Food				
Chicken, fried, thigh and drumstick		2.41	4Q 92	4c
Hamburger with cheese	1/4 lb	2.15	4Q 92	4c
Pizza, Pizza Hut or Pizza Inn, cheese, thin crust	12-13 in	7.99	4Q 92	4c
Taxes				
Tax, cigarette	pack	39	91	77s
Tax, gasoline	gal	8	91	77s
Taxes, state	capita	1567	91	77s
Transportation				
ACCRA Index, Transportation		121.90	4Q 92	4c
Auto rental, average	day	48.50	6/91	60c
Bus fare	one-way	1.00	3/93	2c
Bus fare, up to 10 miles	one-way	1.25	4Q 92	4c
Driver's license fee		17.50	12/90	43s
Taxi fare, airport-city, average	day	9.00	6/91	60c
Tire balance, computer or spin balance, front	wheel	8.38	4Q 92	4c
Vehicle registration and license plate	2 years	27.50-149.50	93	67s
Travel				
Breakfast	day	6.33	6/91	60c
Business travel	day	165.00	4/93	89r
Dinner	day	20.26	6/91	60c
Lodging	day	104.17	91	60c
Lunch	day	9.37	6/91	60c
Utilities				
ACCRA Index, Utilities		112.30	4Q 92	4c
Electricity	mil Btu	27.51	90	64s
Electricity, partial electric and other energy, 1,800 sq ft living area new home	month	66.79	4Q 92	4c
Electricity, winter, 250 KWh	month	30.46	92	55c
Electricity, winter, 500 KWh	month	53.85	92	55c
Electricity, winter, 750 KWh	month	77.23	92	55c
Electricity, winter, 1000 KWh	month	100.62	92	55c

Rockford, IL

Item	Per	Value	Date	Ref.
Composite ACCRA index		108.50	4Q 92	4c
Alcoholic Beverages				
Beer, Miller Lite or Budweiser, 12-oz containers	6 pack	3.59	4Q 92	4c
Liquor, J & B Scotch	750 ml	13.60	4Q 92	4c
Wine, Gallo Chablis blanc, 1.5 liter	bottle	3.81	4Q 92	4c
Child Care				
Child care fee, average, center	hour	1.63	90	65r
Child care fee, average, nonregulated family day care	hour	1.83	90	65r
Child care fee, average, regulated family day care	hour	1.42	90	65r
Clothing				
Jeans, man's denim		30.99	4Q 92	4c
Shirt, man's dress shirt		27.20	4Q 92	4c
Undervest, boy's size 10-14, cotton	3	5.52	4Q 92	4c
Communications				
Long-distance telephone service, day, initial minute, 0-100 miles	min	0.10-0.34	91	12s
Long-distance telephone service, day, additional minute, 0-100 miles	min	0.04-0.16	91	12s
Long-distance telephone service, evenings/weekends, 0-100 mi, initial minute	min	0.06-0.20	91	12s

Rockford, IL - continued

Item	Per	Value	Date	Ref.
Communications				
Long-distance telephone service, evenings/ weekends, 0-100 mi, additional minute	min	0.02-0.10	91	12s
Newspaper subscription, daily and Sunday home delivery, large-city	month	13.04	4Q 92	4c
Telephone bill, family of four	month	21.60	4Q 92	4c
Education				
Board, 4-yr private college/university	year	1797	91	22s
Board, 4-yr public college/university	year	1857	91	22s
Expenditures, local gov't, public elemen- tary/secondary	pupil	5248	92	20s
Room, 4-year private college/university	year	2095	91	22s
Room, 4-year public college/university	year	1454	91	22s
Tuition, 2-year private college/university	year	5279	91	22s
Tuition, 2-year public college/university	year	906	91	22s
Tuition, 4-year private college/university	year	8853	91	22s
Tuition, 4-year public college/university, in- state	year	2465	91	22s
Energy and Fuels				
Coal	mil Btu	1.72	90	64s
Energy	mil Btu	8.74	90	64s
Energy, combined forms, 1,800 sq ft heating area	month	147.59	4Q 92	4c
Energy, exc electricity, 1,800 sq ft heating area	month	53.98	4Q 92	4c
Energy exp/householder, 1-family unit	year	471	90	28r
Energy exp/householder, <1,000 sq ft heating area	year	430	90	28r
Energy exp/householder, 1,000-1,999 sq ft heating area	year	481	90	28r
Energy exp/householder, 2,000+ sq ft heating area	year	473	90	28r
Energy exp/householder, mobile home	year	430	90	28r
Energy exp/householder, multifamily	year	461	90	28r
Gas, cooking, 10 therms	month	8.31	92	56c
Gas, cooking, 30 therms	month	16.94	92	56c
Gas, cooking, 50 therms	month	25.57	92	56c
Gas, heating, winter, 100 therms	month	42.86	92	56c
Gas, heating, winter, average use	month	105.10	92	56c
Gas, natural	mil Btu	4.57	90	64s
Gas, natural	000 cu ft	4.95	91	46s
Gas, natural, exp	year	696	91	46s
Gasoline, motor	gal	1.12	4Q 92	4c
Gasoline, unleaded regular	mil Btu	9.35	90	64s
Entertainment				
Bowling, evening rate	game	1.90	4Q 92	4c
Miniature golf admission	adult	6.18	92	1r
Miniature golf admission	child	5.14	92	1r
Monopoly game, Parker Brothers', No. 9		9.78	4Q 92	4c
Movie	admis- sion	5.50	4Q 92	4c
Tennis balls, yellow, Wilson or Penn, 3	can	2.16	4Q 92	4c
Waterpark admission	adult	11.00	92	1r
Waterpark admission	child	8.55	92	1r
Funerals				
Casket, 18-gauge steel, velvet interior		1926.72	91	24r
Cosmetology, hair care, etc.		97.64	91	24r
Embalming		249.14	91	24r
Facility use for ceremony		208.59	91	24r
Hearse, local		130.12	91	24r
Limousine, local		104.66	91	24r
Remains to funeral home, transfer		93.61	91	24r
Service charge, professional		724.62	91	24r
Vault, concrete, non-metallic liner		734.53	91	24r
Viewing facilities, use		236.06	91	24r
Goods and Services				
ACCRA Index, Miscellaneous Goods and Services		104.60	4Q 92	4c

Rockford, IL - continued

Item	Per	Value	Date	Ref.
Groceries				
ACCRA Index, Groceries		97.90	4Q 92	4c
Apples, Red Delicious	lb	0.77	4/93	16r
Babyfood, strained vegetables, lowest price	4-4.5 oz jar	0.37	4Q 92	4c
Bacon	lb	1.85	4/93	16r
Bananas	lb	0.40	4Q 92	4c
Bananas	lb	0.46	4/93	16r
Beef, stew, boneless	lb	2.53	4/93	16r
Bologna, all beef or mixed	lb	2.19	4/93	16r
Bread, white	24 oz	0.63	4Q 92	4c
Bread, white, pan	lb	0.78	4/93	16r
Butter	lb	1.50	4/93	16r
Cabbage	lb	0.40	4/93	16r
Carrots, short trimmed and topped	lb	0.45	4/93	16r
Cheese, Cheddar	lb	3.47	4/93	16r
Cheese, Kraft grated Parmesan	8-oz canis- ter	2.89	4Q 92	4c
Chicken, fresh, whole	lb	0.84	4/93	16r
Chicken, fryer, whole	lb	0.75	4Q 92	4c
Chicken breast, bone-in	lb	1.94	4/93	16r
Chicken legs, bone-in	lb	1.02	4/93	16r
Chuck roast, graded and ungraded, ex USDA prime and choice	lb	2.43	4/93	16r
Chuck roast, USDA choice, bone-in	lb	2.11	4/93	16r
Chuck roast, USDA choice, boneless	lb	2.44	4/93	16r
Cigarettes, Winston	carton	17.78	4Q 92	4c
Coffee, 100% ground roast, all sizes	lb	2.47	4/93	16r
Coffee, vacuum-packed	13-oz can	1.97	4Q 92	4c
Cookies, chocolate chip	lb	2.73	4/93	16r
Corn, frozen	10 oz	0.65	4Q 92	4c
Corn Flakes, Kellogg's or Post Toasties	18 oz	2.04	4Q 92	4c
Eggs, Grade A large	doz	0.70	4Q 92	4c
Eggs, Grade A large	doz	0.93	4/93	16r
Flour, white, all purpose	lb	0.21	4/93	16r
Grapefruit	lb	0.45	4/93	16r
Grapes, Thompson Seedless	lb	1.46	4/93	16r
Ground beef, 100% beef	lb	1.63	4/93	16r
Ground beef, lean and extra lean	lb	2.08	4/93	16r
Ground beef or hamburger	lb	1.53	4Q 92	4c
Ground chuck, 100% beef	lb	1.94	4/93	16r
Ham, boneless, excluding canned	lb	2.21	4/93	16r
Honey, jar	8 oz	0.97-1.25	92	5r
Honey, jar	lb	1.25-2.25	92	5r
Honey, squeeze bear	12-oz	1.25-1.99	92	5r
Ice cream, prepackaged, bulk, regular	1/2 gal	2.41	4/93	16r
Lemons	lb	0.82	4/93	16r
Lettuce, iceberg	head	0.89	4Q 92	4c
Lettuce, iceberg	lb	0.83	4/93	16r
Margarine, Blue Bonnet or Parkay cubes	lb	0.65	4Q 92	4c
Margarine, stick	lb	0.77	4/93	16r
Milk, whole	1/2 gal	1.35	4Q 92	4c
Orange juice, Minute Maid frozen	12-oz can	1.26	4Q 92	4c
Oranges, navel	lb	0.50	4/93	16r
Peaches	29-oz can	1.49	4Q 92	4c
Peanut butter, creamy, all sizes	lb	1.82	4/93	16r
Pears, Anjou	lb	0.85	4/93	16r
Peas Sweet, Del Monte or Green Giant	15-17 oz can	0.59	4Q 92	4c
Pork chops, center cut, bone-in	lb	3.17	4/93	16r
Potato chips	16 oz	2.68	4/93	16r
Potatoes, white	lb	0.26	4/93	16r
Potatoes, white or red	10-lb sack	1.80	4Q 92	4c
Round roast, graded & ungraded, ex USDA prime & choice	lb	2.88	4/93	16r
Round roast, USDA choice, boneless	lb	2.96	4/93	16r
Sausage, Jimmy Dean, 100% pork	lb	2.47	4Q 92	4c
Shortening, vegetable oil blends	lb	0.79	4/93	16r

Values are in dollars or fractions of dollars. In the column headed *Ref*, references are shown to sources. Each reference is followed by a letter. These refer to the geographical level for which data were reported: s=State, r=Region, and c=City or metro. The abbreviation *ex* is used to mean *except* or *excluding*; *exp* stands for expenditures. For other abbreviations and further explanations, please see the Introduction.

Rockford, IL - continued

Item	Per	Value	Date	Ref.
Groceries				
Shortening, vegetable, Crisco	3-lb can	2.35	4Q 92	4c
Soft drink, Coca Cola	2 liter	1.23	4Q 92	4c
Spaghetti and macaroni	lb	0.76	4/93	16r
Steak, rib eye, USDA choice, boneless	lb	6.29	4/93	16r
Steak, round, USDA choice, boneless	lb	3.24	4/93	16r
Steak, sirloin, graded & ungraded, ex USDA prime & choice	lb	4.00	4/93	16r
Steak, sirloin, USDA choice, bone-in	lb	3.57	4/93	16r
Steak, sirloin, USDA choice, boneless	lb	4.17	4/93	16r
Steak, T-bone	lb	4.83	4Q 92	4c
Steak, T-bone, USDA choice, bone-in	lb	5.60	4/93	16r
Strawberries, dry pint	12 oz	0.90	4/93	16r
Sugar, cane or beet	4 lb	1.71	4Q 92	4c
Sugar, white	lb	0.36	4/93	16r
Sugar, white, 33-80 oz pk	lb	0.35	4/93	16r
Tomatoes, field grown	lb	0.99	4/93	16r
Tomatoes, Hunt's or Del Monte	14.5-oz can	0.70	4Q 92	4c
Tuna, chunk, light	6.125-6.5 oz can	0.59	4Q 92	4c
Tuna, chunk, light	lb	1.76	4/93	16r
Turkey, frozen, whole	lb	0.91	4/93	16r
Health Care				
ACCRA Index, Health Care		109.60	4Q 92	4c
Analgesic, Aspirin, Bayer, 325 mg tablets	100	5.98	4Q 92	4c
Childbirth, cesarean, hospital		4688	91	62r
Childbirth, cesarean, physician's fee		2053	91	62r
Childbirth, normal, hospital		2657	91	62r
Childbirth, normal, physician's fee		1492	91	62r
Dentist's fee, adult teeth cleaning and periodic oral exam	visit	49.40	4Q 92	4c
Doctor's fee, routine exam, established patient	visit	41.00	4Q 92	4c
Hospital care, semiprivate room	day	235.77	90	27c
Hospital care, semiprivate room	day	345.00	4Q 92	4c
Medical insurance premium, per employee, small group comprehensive	month	306.60	10/91	25c
Medical plan per employee	year	3443	91	45r
Mental health care, exp	capita	28.84-37.59	90	38s
Mental health care, exp, state mental health agency	capita	34.43	90	38s
Mental health care, hospital psychiatric services, non-Federal, exp	capita	18.46	88	38s
Mental health care, mental health organization, multiservice, exp	capita	11.97	88	38s
Mental health care, psychiatric hospitals, private, exp	capita	7.84	88	38s
Mental health care, psychiatric out-patient clinics, freestanding, exp	capita	3.21	88	38s
Mental health care, psychiatric partial-care organizations, freestanding, exp	capita	0.51	88	38s
Mental health care, state and county mental hospitals, exp	capita	18.11	88	38s
Mental health care, VA medical centers, exp	capita	3.69	88	38s
Physician fee, family practice, first-visit		76.00	91	62r
Physician fee, family practice, revisit		33.00	91	62r
Physician fee, general practice, first-visit		61.00	91	62r
Physician fee, general practice, revisit		31.00	91	62r
Physician fee, general surgeon, first-visit		65.00	91	62r
Physician fee, general surgeon, revisit		35.00	91	62r
Physician fee, internal medicine, first-visit		91.00	91	62r
Physician fee, internal medicine, revisit		40.00	91	62r
Physician fee, median, neurosurgeon, first-visit		106.00	91	62r
Physician fee, median, nonsurgical specialist, first-visit		90.00	91	62r
Physician fee, median, orthopedic surgeon, first-visit		83.00	91	62r

Rockford, IL - continued

Item	Per	Value	Date	Ref.
Health Care - continued				
Physician fee, median, surgical specialist, first-visit		61.00	91	62r
Physician fee, neurosurgeon, revisit		41.00	91	62r
Physician fee, nonsurgical specialist, revisit		40.00	91	62r
Physician fee, obstetrics/gynecology, first-visit		61.00	91	62r
Physician fee, obstetrics/gynecology, revisit		40.00	91	62r
Physician fee, orthopedic surgeon, revisit		41.00	91	62r
Physician fee, pediatrician, first-visit		46.00	91	62r
Physician fee, pediatrician, revisit		33.00	91	62r
Physician fee, surgical specialist, revisit		36.00	91	62r
Prescription drug co-pay, Medicaid	month	25.00	91	21s
Substance abuse, hospital ancillary charge	incident	1310	90	70s
Substance abuse, hospital physician charge	incident	540	90	70s
Substance abuse, hospital room and board	incident	6150	90	70s
Household Goods				
Appliance repair, home, service call, washing machine	min labor charge	35.60	4Q 92	4c
Laundry detergent, Tide Ultra, Bold, or Cheer	42 oz	3.39	4Q 92	4c
Tissues, facial, Kleenex brand	175-count box	1.17	4Q 92	4c
Housing				
ACCRA Index, Housing		110.80	4Q 92	4c
Home, median price	unit	75.70		26c
House, 1,800 sq ft, 8,000 sq ft lot, new, urban	total	122662	4Q 92	4c
House payment, principal and interest, 25% down payment	month	683	4Q 92	4c
Mortgage rate, incl. points & origination fee, 30-year fixed or adjustable rate	percent	8.12	4Q 92	4c
Rent, apartment, 2 bedrooms - 1-1/2 to 2 baths, unfurnished, 950 sq ft, water	month	542	4Q 92	4c
Rental unit, 1 bedroom	month	427	93	23c
Rental unit, 2 bedroom	month	502	93	23c
Rental unit, 3 bedroom	month	627	93	23c
Rental unit, 4 bedroom	month	702	93	23c
Rental unit, efficiency	month	350	93	23c
Insurance and Pensions				
Auto insurance, private passenger	year	621.37	91	63s
Personal Goods				
Shampoo, Alberto VO5	15 oz	1.32	4Q 92	4c
Toothpaste, Crest or Colgate	6-7 oz	2.00	4Q 92	4c
Personal Services				
Dry cleaning, man's 2-piece suit		6.56	4Q 92	4c
Haircare, woman's shampoo, trim and blow-dry		20.80	4Q 92	4c
Haircut, man's barbershop, no styling		6.05	4Q 92	4c
Restaurant Food				
Chicken, fried, thigh and drumstick		2.18	4Q 92	4c
Hamburger with cheese	1/4 lb	1.69	4Q 92	4c
Pizza, Pizza Hut or Pizza Inn, cheese, thin crust	12-13 in	9.03	4Q 92	4c
Taxes				
Tax, cigarette	pack	30	91	77s
Tax, gasoline	gal	19	91	77s
Taxes, state	capita	1151	91	77s
Transportation				
ACCRA Index, Transportation		107.30	4Q 92	4c
Bus fare	one-way	0.80	3/93	2c
Bus fare, up to 10 miles	one-way	0.80	4Q 92	4c

Values are in dollars or fractions of dollars. In the column headed *Ref*, references are shown to sources. Each reference is followed by a letter. These refer to the geographical level for which data were reported: s = State, r = Region, and c = City or metro. The abbreviation *ex* is used to mean *except* or *excluding*; *exp* stands for *expenditures*. For other abbreviations and further explanations, please see the Introduction.

Rockford, IL - continued

Item	Per	Value	Date	Ref.
Transportation				
Driver's license fee		10.00	12/90	43s
Tire balance, computer or spin balance, front	wheel	7.74	4Q 92	4c
Vehicle registration and license plate	multi-year	48.00	93	52s
Utilities				
ACCRA Index, Utilities		132.80	4Q 92	4c
Electricity	mil Btu	22.02	90	64s
Electricity, partial electric and other energy, 1,800 sq ft living area new home	month	93.61	4Q 92	4c

Rocky Mount, NC

Item	Per	Value	Date	Ref.
Composite ACCRA index		101.40	4Q 92	4c
Alcoholic Beverages				
Beer, Miller Lite or Budweiser, 12-oz containers	6 pack	3.59	4Q 92	4c
Liquor, J & B Scotch	750 ml	17.65	4Q 92	4c
Wine, Gallo Chablis blanc, 1.5 liter	bottle	4.46	4Q 92	4c
Clothing				
Jeans, man's denim		32.49	4Q 92	4c
Shirt, man's dress shirt		23.50	4Q 92	4c
Undervest, boy's size 10-14, cotton	3	4.40	4Q 92	4c
Communications				
Newspaper subscription, daily and Sunday home delivery, large-city	month	11.00	4Q 92	4c
Telephone bill, family of four	month	23.31	4Q 92	4c
Energy and Fuels				
Energy, combined forms, 1,800 sq ft heating area	month	138.21	4Q 92	4c
Gasoline, motor	gal	1.09	4Q 92	4c
Entertainment				
Bowling, evening rate	game	2.45	4Q 92	4c
Monopoly game, Parker Brothers', No. 9		11.98	4Q 92	4c
Movie	admission	5.00	4Q 92	4c
Tennis balls, yellow, Wilson or Penn, 3	can	2.08	4Q 92	4c
Goods and Services				
ACCRA Index, Miscellaneous Goods and Services		102.30	4Q 92	4c
Groceries				
ACCRA Index, Groceries		99.70	4Q 92	4c
Babyfood, strained vegetables, lowest price	4-4.5 oz jar	0.36	4Q 92	4c
Bananas	lb	0.39	4Q 92	4c
Bread, white	24 oz	0.81	4Q 92	4c
Cheese, Kraft grated Parmesan	8-oz canister	3.44	4Q 92	4c
Chicken, fryer, whole	lb	0.78	4Q 92	4c
Cigarettes, Winston	carton	15.57	4Q 92	4c
Coffee, vacuum-packed	13-oz can	1.87	4Q 92	4c
Corn, frozen	10 oz	1.01	4Q 92	4c
Corn Flakes, Kellogg's or Post Toasties	18 oz	1.84	4Q 92	4c
Eggs, Grade A large	doz	0.92	4Q 92	4c
Ground beef or hamburger	lb	1.85	4Q 92	4c
Lettuce, iceberg	head	0.92	4Q 92	4c
Margarine, Blue Bonnet or Parkay cubes	lb	0.47	4Q 92	4c
Milk, whole	1/2 gal	1.40	4Q 92	4c
Orange juice, Minute Maid frozen	12-oz can	1.30	4Q 92	4c
Peaches	29-oz can	1.42	4Q 92	4c
Peas Sweet, Del Monte or Green Giant	15-17 oz can	0.53	4Q 92	4c

Rocky Mount, NC - continued

Item	Per	Value	Date	Ref.
Groceries - continued				
Potatoes, white or red	10-lb sack	1.92	4Q 92	4c
Sausage, Jimmy Dean, 100% pork	lb	2.09	4Q 92	4c
Shortening, vegetable, Crisco	3-lb can	2.27	4Q 92	4c
Soft drink, Coca Cola	2 liter	1.14	4Q 92	4c
Steak, T-bone	lb	5.84	4Q 92	4c
Sugar, cane or beet	4 lb	1.86	4Q 92	4c
Tomatoes, Hunt's or Del Monte	14.5-oz can	0.49	4Q 92	4c
Tuna, chunk, light	6.125-6.5 oz can	0.57	4Q 92	4c
Health Care				
ACCRA Index, Health Care		95.00	4Q 92	4c
Analgesic, Aspirin, Bayer, 325 mg tablets	100	5.01	4Q 92	4c
Dentist's fee, adult teeth cleaning and periodic oral exam	visit	50.60	4Q 92	4c
Doctor's fee, routine exam, established patient	visit	30.75	4Q 92	4c
Hospital care, semiprivate room	day	190.00	90	27c
Hospital care, semiprivate room	day	283.50	4Q 92	4c
Household Goods				
Appliance repair, home, service call, washing machine	min labor charge	34.99	4Q 92	4c
Laundry detergent, Tide Ultra, Bold, or Cheer	42 oz	2.60	4Q 92	4c
Tissues, facial, Kleenex brand	175-count box	1.02	4Q 92	4c
Housing				
ACCRA Index, Housing		95.80	4Q 92	4c
House, 1,800 sq ft, 8,000 sq ft lot, new, urban	total	102300	4Q 92	4c
House payment, principal and interest, 25% down payment	month	599	4Q 92	4c
Mortgage rate, incl. points & origination fee, 30-year fixed or adjustable rate	percent	8.67	4Q 92	4c
Rent, apartment, 2 bedrooms - 1-1/2 to 2 baths, unfurnished, 950 sq ft, water	month	449	4Q 92	4c
Personal Goods				
Shampoo, Alberto VO5	15 oz	1.29	4Q 92	4c
Toothpaste, Crest or Colgate	6-7 oz	2.07	4Q 92	4c
Personal Services				
Dry cleaning, man's 2-piece suit		6.45	4Q 92	4c
Haircare, woman's shampoo, trim and blow-dry		19.00	4Q 92	4c
Haircut, man's barbershop, no styling		8.00	4Q 92	4c
Restaurant Food				
Chicken, fried, thigh and drumstick		2.04	4Q 92	4c
Hamburger with cheese	1/4 lb	2.00	4Q 92	4c
Pizza, Pizza Hut or Pizza Inn, cheese, thin crust	12-13 in	7.79	4Q 92	4c
Transportation				
ACCRA Index, Transportation		97.70	4Q 92	4c
Tire balance, computer or spin balance, front	wheel	6.44	4Q 92	4c
Utilities				
ACCRA Index, Utilities		125.90	4Q 92	4c
Electricity, all electric, 1,800 sq ft living area new home	month	138.21	4Q 92	4c

Values are in dollars or fractions of dollars. In the column headed *Ref*, references are shown to sources. Each reference is followed by a letter. These refer to the geographical level for which data were reported: s = State, r = Region, and c = City or metro. The abbreviation *ex* is used to mean *except* or *excluding*; *exp* stands for expenditures. For other abbreviations and further explanations, please see the Introduction.

Roswell, NM

Item	Per	Value	Date	Ref.
Composite ACCRA index		91.10	4Q 92	4c
Alcoholic Beverages				
Beer, Miller Lite or Budweiser, 12-oz containers	6 pack	3.79	4Q 92	4c
Liquor, J & B Scotch	750 ml	15.26	4Q 92	4c
Wine, Gallo Chablis blanc, 1.5 liter	bottle	4.66	4Q 92	4c
Clothing				
Jeans, man's denim		28.99	4Q 92	4c
Shirt, man's dress shirt		24.50	4Q 92	4c
Undervest, boy's size 10-14, cotton	3	4.05	4Q 92	4c
Communications				
Newspaper subscription, daily and Sunday home delivery, large-city	month	13.00	4Q 92	4c
Telephone, flat rate	month	12.93	91	11c
Telephone bill, family of four	month	23.56	4Q 92	4c
Energy and Fuels				
Energy, combined forms, 1,800 sq ft heating area	month	80.55	4Q 92	4c
Energy, exc electricity, 1,800 sq ft heating area	month	37.23	4Q 92	4c
Gasoline, motor	gal	1.14	4Q 92	4c
Entertainment				
Bowling, evening rate	game	1.75	4Q 92	4c
Monopoly game, Parker Brothers', No. 9		11.73	4Q 92	4c
Movie	admission	4.50	4Q 92	4c
Tennis balls, yellow, Wilson or Penn, 3	can	2.51	4Q 92	4c
Goods and Services				
ACCRA Index, Miscellaneous Goods and Services		98.10	4Q 92	4c
Groceries				
ACCRA Index, Groceries		93.40	4Q 92	4c
Babyfood, strained vegetables, lowest price	4-4.5 oz jar	0.25	4Q 92	4c
Bananas	lb	0.24	4Q 92	4c
Bread, white	24 oz	0.66	4Q 92	4c
Cheese, Kraft grated Parmesan	8-oz canister	3.59	4Q 92	4c
Chicken, fryer, whole	lb	0.58	4Q 92	4c
Cigarettes, Winston	carton	16.01	4Q 92	4c
Coffee, vacuum-packed	13-oz can	2.15	4Q 92	4c
Corn, frozen	10 oz	0.74	4Q 92	4c
Corn Flakes, Kellogg's or Post Toasties	18 oz	2.06	4Q 92	4c
Eggs, Grade A large	doz	0.88	4Q 92	4c
Ground beef or hamburger	lb	1.06	4Q 92	4c
Lettuce, iceberg	head	0.99	4Q 92	4c
Margarine, Blue Bonnet or Parkay cubes	lb	0.82	4Q 92	4c
Milk, whole	1/2 gal	1.50	4Q 92	4c
Orange juice, Minute Maid frozen	12-oz can	1.38	4Q 92	4c
Peaches	29-oz can	1.54	4Q 92	4c
Peas Sweet, Del Monte or Green Giant	15-17 oz can	0.66	4Q 92	4c
Potatoes, white or red	10-lb sack	2.12	4Q 92	4c
Sausage, Jimmy Dean, 100% pork	lb	2.01	4Q 92	4c
Shortening, vegetable, Crisco	3-lb can	2.06	4Q 92	4c
Soft drink, Coca Cola	2 liter	1.51	4Q 92	4c
Steak, T-bone	lb	4.62	4Q 92	4c
Sugar, cane or beet	4 lb	1.48	4Q 92	4c
Tomatoes, Hunt's or Del Monte	14.5-oz can	0.69	4Q 92	4c
Tuna, chunk, light	6.125-6.5 oz can	0.68	4Q 92	4c

Roswell, NM - continued

Item	Per	Value	Date	Ref.
Health Care				
ACCRA Index, Health Care		80.00	4Q 92	4c
Analgesic, Aspirin, Bayer, 325 mg tablets	100	5.09	4Q 92	4c
Dentist's fee, adult teeth cleaning and periodic oral exam	visit	37.20	4Q 92	4c
Doctor's fee, routine exam, established patient	visit	26.60	4Q 92	4c
Hospital care, semiprivate room	day	265.00	4Q 92	4c
Household Goods				
Appliance repair, home, service call, washing machine	min labor charge	37.58	4Q 92	4c
Laundry detergent, Tide Ultra, Bold, or Cheer	42 oz	3.25	4Q 92	4c
Tissues, facial, Kleenex brand	175-count box	1.06	4Q 92	4c
Housing				
ACCRA Index, Housing		86.90	4Q 92	4c
House, 1,800 sq ft, 8,000 sq ft lot, new, urban	total	99960	4Q 92	4c
House payment, principal and interest, 25% down payment	month	551	4Q 92	4c
Mortgage rate, incl. points & origination fee, 30-year fixed or adjustable rate	percent	8.02	4Q 92	4c
Rent, apartment, 2 bedrooms - 1-1/2 to 2 baths, unfurnished, 950 sq ft, water	month	390	4Q 92	4c
Personal Goods				
Shampoo, Alberto VO5	15 oz	1.30	4Q 92	4c
Toothpaste, Crest or Colgate	6-7 oz	2.07	4Q 92	4c
Personal Services				
Dry cleaning, man's 2-piece suit		5.37	4Q 92	4c
Haircare, woman's shampoo, trim and blow-dry		15.90	4Q 92	4c
Haircut, man's barbershop, no styling		7.60	4Q 92	4c
Restaurant Food				
Chicken, fried, thigh and drumstick		1.84	4Q 92	4c
Hamburger with cheese	1/4 lb	1.89	4Q 92	4c
Pizza, Pizza Hut or Pizza Inn, cheese, thin crust	12-13 in	7.79	4Q 92	4c
Transportation				
ACCRA Index, Transportation		92.60	4Q 92	4c
Tire balance, computer or spin balance, front	wheel	5.50	4Q 92	4c
Utilities				
ACCRA Index, Utilities		78.50	4Q 92	4c
Electricity, partial electric and other energy, 1,800 sq ft living area new home	month	42.32	4Q 92	4c
Electricity, winter, 250 KWh	month	19.37	92	55c
Electricity, winter, 500 KWh	month	33.75	92	55c
Electricity, winter, 750 KWh	month	48.12	92	55c
Electricity, winter, 1000 KWh	month	62.49	92	55c

Sacramento, CA

Item	Per	Value	Date	Ref.
Child Care				
Child care fee, average, center	hour	1.71	90	65r
Child care fee, average, nonregulated family day care	hour	1.32	90	65r
Child care fee, average, regulated family day care	hour	1.86	90	65r
Communications				
Long-distance telephone service, day, initial minute, 0-100 miles	min	0.17-0.40	91	12s
Long-distance telephone service, day, additional minute, 0-100 miles	min	0.07-0.31	91	12s
Long-distance telephone service, evenings/weekends, 0-100 mi, initial minute	min	0.07-0.16	91	12s

Values are in dollars or fractions of dollars. In the column headed *Ref*, references are shown to sources. Each reference is followed by a letter. These refer to the geographical level for which data were reported: s = State, r = Region, and c = City or metro. The abbreviation *ex* is used to mean *except* or *excluding*; *exp* stands for expenditures. For other abbreviations and further explanations, please see the Introduction.

Sacramento, CA - continued

Item	Per	Value	Date	Ref.
Communications				
Long-distance telephone service, evenings/ weekends, 0-100 mi, additional minute	min	0.03-0.12	91	12s
Telephone, flat rate	month	8.35	91	11c
Education				
Board, 4-yr private college/university	year	2515	91	22s
Board, 4-yr public college/university	year	2268	91	22s
Expenditures, local gov't, public elementary/secondary	pupil	4866	92	20s
Room, 4-year private college/university	year	2622	91	22s
Room, 4-year public college/university	year	2406	91	22s
Tuition, 2-year private college/university	year	7942	91	22s
Tuition, 2-year public college/university	year	114	91	22s
Tuition, 4-year private college/university	year	10863	91	22s
Tuition, 4-year public college/university, in-state	year	1220	91	22s
Energy and Fuels				
Coal	mil Btu	2.01	90	64s
Energy	mil Btu	9.08	90	64s
Energy exp/householder, 1-family unit	year	362	90	28r
Energy exp/householder, <1,000 sq ft heating area	year	254	90	28r
Energy exp/householder, 1,000-1,999 sq ft heating area	year	358	90	28r
Energy exp/householder, 2,000+ sq ft heating area	year	467	90	28r
Energy exp/householder, mobile home	year	390	90	28r
Energy exp/householder, multifamily	year	252	90	28r
Gas, natural	mil Btu	4.31	90	64s
Gas, natural	000 cu ft	6.27	91	46s
Gas, natural, exp	year	369	91	46s
Gasoline, unleaded regular	mil Btu	8.57	90	64s
Entertainment				
Miniature golf admission	adult	6.18	92	1r
Miniature golf admission	child	5.14	92	1r
Waterpark admission	adult	11.00	92	1r
Waterpark admission	child	8.55	92	1r
Funerals				
Casket, 18-gauge steel, velvet interior		1781.09	91	24r
Cosmetology, hair care, etc.		84.64	91	24r
Embalming		207.41	91	24r
Facility use for ceremony		205.76	91	24r
Hearse, local		105.14	91	24r
Limousine, local		83.21	91	24r
Remains to funeral home, transfer		113.82	91	24r
Service charge, professional		626.33	91	24r
Vault, concrete, non-metallic liner		599.54	91	24r
Viewing facilities, use		85.81	91	24r
Groceries				
Apples, Red Delicious	lb	0.80	4/93	16r
Bacon	lb	1.79	4/93	16r
Bananas	lb	0.53	4/93	16r
Bologna, all beef or mixed	lb	2.67	4/93	16r
Bread, white, pan	lb	0.81	4/93	16r
Carrots, short trimmed and topped	lb	0.39	4/93	16r
Chicken, fresh, whole	lb	0.94	4/93	16r
Chicken breast, bone-in	lb	2.19	4/93	16r
Chuck roast, graded and ungraded, ex USDA prime and choice	lb	2.26	4/93	16r
Coffee, 100% ground roast, all sizes	lb	2.33	4/93	16r
Eggs, Grade AA large	doz	1.18	4/93	16r
Flour, white, all purpose	lb	0.22	4/93	16r
Grapefruit	lb	0.52	4/93	16r
Grapes, Thompson Seedless	lb	1.50	4/93	16r
Ground beef, 100% beef	lb	1.44	4/93	16r
Ground beef, lean and extra lean	lb	2.34	4/93	16r
Ham, boneless, excluding canned	lb	2.56	4/93	16r
Honey, jar	8 oz	0.89-1.00	92	5r
Honey, jar	lb	1.35-1.97	92	5r

Sacramento, CA - continued

Item	Per	Value	Date	Ref.
Groceries - continued				
Honey, squeeze bear	12-oz	1.19-1.50	92	5r
Ice cream, prepackaged, bulk, regular	1/2 gal	2.40	4/93	16r
Lemons	lb	0.81	4/93	16r
Lettuce, iceberg	lb	0.84	4/93	16r
Margarine, stick	lb	0.81	4/93	16r
Oranges, navel	lb	0.48	4/93	16r
Pork chops, center cut, bone-in	lb	3.25	4/93	16r
Potato chips	16 oz	2.89	4/93	16r
Potatoes, white	lb	0.38	4/93	16r
Round roast, graded & ungraded, ex USDA prime & choice	lb	3.00	4/93	16r
Round roast, USDA choice, boneless	lb	3.16	4/93	16r
Shortening, vegetable oil blends	lb	0.86	4/93	16r
Spaghetti and macaroni	lb	0.84	4/93	16r
Steak, round, graded & ungraded, ex USDA prime & choice	lb	3.34	4/93	16r
Steak, round, USDA choice, boneless	lb	3.24	4/93	16r
Steak, sirloin, graded & ungraded, ex USDA prime & choice	lb	3.75	4/93	16r
Steak, sirloin, USDA choice, boneless	lb	4.49	4/93	16r
Sugar, white	lb	0.41	4/93	16r
Sugar, white, 33-80 oz pk	lb	0.38	4/93	16r
Tomatoes, field grown	lb	1.01	4/93	16r
Turkey, frozen, whole	lb	1.04	4/93	16r
Health Care				
Cardizem 60 mg tablets	30	24.04	92	49s
Cector 250 mg tablets	15	35.87	92	49s
Childbirth, cesarean, hospital		5533	91	62r
Childbirth, cesarean, physician's fee		2053	91	62r
Childbirth, normal, hospital		2745	91	62r
Childbirth, normal, physician's fee		1492	91	62r
Health care spending, state	capita	2894	3/93	84s
Hospital care, semiprivate room	day	585.85	90	27c
Medical insurance premium, per employee, small group comprehensive	month	390.55	10/91	25c
Medical plan per employee	year	3421	91	45r
Mental health care, exp	capita	37.60-53.67	90	38s
Mental health care, exp, state mental health agency	capita	42.32	90	38s
Mental health care, hospital psychiatric services, non-Federal, exp	capita	10.64	88	38s
Mental health care, mental health organization, multiservice, exp	capita	28.56	88	38s
Mental health care, psychiatric hospitals, private, exp	capita	18.60	88	38s
Mental health care, psychiatric out-patient clinics, freestanding, exp	capita	2.28	88	38s
Mental health care, psychiatric partial-care organizations, freestanding, exp	capita	0.24	88	38s
Mental health care, state and county mental hospitals, exp	capita	13.60	88	38s
Mental health care, VA medical centers, exp	capita	2.33	88	38s
Mevacor 20 mg tablets	30	67.62	92	49s
Physician fee, family practice, first-visit		111.00	91	62r
Physician fee, family practice, revisit		45.00	91	62r
Physician fee, general practice, first-visit		100.00	91	62r
Physician fee, general practice, revisit		40.00	91	62r
Physician fee, internal medicine, first-visit		137.00	91	62r
Physician fee, internal medicine, revisit		48.00	91	62r
Physician fee, median, neurosurgeon, first-visit		157.00	91	62r
Physician fee, median, nonsurgical specialist, first-visit		131.00	91	62r
Physician fee, median, orthopedic surgeon, first-visit		124.00	91	62r
Physician fee, median, plastic surgeon, first-visit		88.00	91	62r
Physician fee, median, surgical specialist, first-visit		100.00	91	62r
Physician fee, neurosurgeon, revisit		51.00	91	62r
Physician fee, nonsurgical specialist, revisit		47.00	91	62r

Values are in dollars or fractions of dollars. In the column headed *Ref*, references are shown to sources. Each reference is followed by a letter. These refer to the geographical level for which data were reported: s = State, r = Region, and c = City or metro. The abbreviation *ex* is used to mean *except* or *excluding*; *exp* stands for expenditures. For other abbreviations and further explanations, please see the Introduction.

Sacramento, CA - continued

Item	Per	Value	Date	Ref.
Health Care				
Physician fee, obstetrics/gynecology, first-visit		95.00	91	62r
Physician fee, obstetrics/gynecology, revisit		50.00	91	62r
Physician fee, orthopedic surgeon, revisit		51.00	91	62r
Physician fee, pediatrician, first-visit		81.00	91	62r
Physician fee, pediatrician, revisit		42.00	91	62r
Physician fee, plastic surgeon, revisit		48.00	91	62r
Physician fee, surgical specialist, revisit		49.00	91	62r
Prozac 20 mg tablets	14	33.22	92	49s
Substance abuse, hospital ancillary charge	incident	1760	90	70s
Substance abuse, hospital physician charge	incident	750	90	70s
Substance abuse, hospital room and board	incident	6390	90	70s
Tagamet 300 mg tablets	100	77.08	92	49s
Xanax 0.25 mg tablets	90	64.08	92	49s
Zantac 160 mg tablets	60	92.31	92	49s
Housing				
Home, median price	unit	134.50		26c
Home, median price	unit	131,200	92	58s
Rent, apartment, 1 bedroom - 1 bath	month	350-450	92	58c
Rent, apartment, 2 bedrooms - 1 bath	month	400-550	92	58c
Rent, apartment, 2 bedrooms - 2 baths	month	500-650	92	58c
Rent, apartment, 3 bedrooms - 2 baths	month	700-1000	92	58c
Rent, townhouse	month	650-1000	92	58c
Rental unit, 1 bedroom	month	497	93	23c
Rental unit, 2 bedroom	month	595	93	23c
Rental unit, 3 bedroom	month	864	93	23c
Rental unit, 4 bedroom	month	918	93	23c
Rental unit, efficiency	month	417	93	23c
Insurance and Pensions				
Auto insurance, private passenger	year	904.37	91	63s
Taxes				
Tax, cigarette	pack	35	91	77s
Tax, gasoline	gal	16	91	77s
Taxes, state	capita	1477	91	77s
Transportation				
Auto rental, average	day	48.75	6/91	60c
Bus fare	one-way	1.25	3/93	2c
Driver's license fee		10.00	12/90	43s
Limo fare, airport-city, average	day	7.50	6/91	60c
Railway fare, light rail	one-way	1.25	93	2c
Taxi fare, airport-city, average	day	26.00	6/91	60c
Travel				
Breakfast	day	6.08	6/91	60c
Business travel	day	178.00	4/93	89r
Dinner	day	16.71	6/91	60c
Lodging	day	100.77	91	60c
Lunch	day	9.21	6/91	60c
Utilities				
Electricity	mil Btu	25.98	90	64s

Saginaw-Bay City-Midland, MI

Item	Per	Value	Date	Ref.
Child Care				
Child care fee, average, center	hour	1.63	90	65r
Child care fee, average, nonregulated family day care	hour	1.83	90	65r
Child care fee, average, regulated family day care	hour	1.42	90	65r
Communications				
Long-distance telephone service, day, initial minute, 0-100 miles	min	0.14-0.36	91	12s

Saginaw-Bay City-Midland, MI - continued

Item	Per	Value	Date	Ref.
Communications - continued				
Long-distance telephone service, day, additional minute, 0-100 miles	min	0.14-0.36	91	12s
Long-distance telephone service, evenings/weekends, 0-100 mi, initial minute	min	0.07-0.19	91	12s
Long-distance telephone service, evenings/weekends, 0-100 mi, additional minute	min	0.04-0.14	91	12s
Education				
Board, 4-yr private college/university	year	1698	91	22s
Board, 4-yr public college/university	year	1962	91	22s
Expenditures, local gov't, public elementary/secondary	pupil	5671	92	20s
Room, 4-year private college/university	year	1440	91	22s
Room, 4-year public college/university	year	1687	91	22s
Tuition, 2-year private college/university	year	4749	91	22s
Tuition, 2-year public college/university	year	1124	91	22s
Tuition, 4-year private college/university	year	6885	91	22s
Tuition, 4-year public college/university, in-state	year	2635	91	22s
Energy and Fuels				
Coal	mil Btu	1.63	90	64s
Energy	mil Btu	8.17	90	64s
Energy exp/householder, 1-family unit	year	471	90	28r
Energy exp/householder, <1,000 sq ft heating area	year	430	90	28r
Energy exp/householder, 1,000-1,999 sq ft heating area	year	481	90	28r
Energy exp/householder, 2,000+ sq ft heating area	year	473	90	28r
Energy exp/householder, mobile home	year	430	90	28r
Energy exp/householder, multifamily	year	461	90	28r
Gas, natural	mil Btu	4.36	90	64s
Gas, natural	000 cu ft	5.07	91	46s
Gas, natural, exp	year	655	91	46s
Gasoline, unleaded regular	mil Btu	8.78	90	64s
Entertainment				
Miniature golf admission	adult	6.18	92	1r
Miniature golf admission	child	5.14	92	1r
Waterpark admission	adult	11.00	92	1r
Waterpark admission	child	8.55	92	1r
Funerals				
Casket, 18-gauge steel, velvet interior		1926.72	91	24r
Cosmetology, hair care, etc.		97.64	91	24r
Embalming		249.14	91	24r
Facility use for ceremony		208.59	91	24r
Hearse, local		130.12	91	24r
Limousine, local		104.66	91	24r
Remains to funeral home, transfer		93.61	91	24r
Service charge, professional		724.62	91	24r
Vault, concrete, non-metallic liner		734.53	91	24r
Viewing facilities, use		236.06	91	24r
Groceries				
Apples, Red Delicious	lb	0.77	4/93	16r
Bacon	lb	1.85	4/93	16r
Bananas	lb	0.46	4/93	16r
Beef, stew, boneless	lb	2.53	4/93	16r
Bologna, all beef or mixed	lb	2.19	4/93	16r
Bread, white, pan	lb	0.78	4/93	16r
Butter	lb	1.50	4/93	16r
Cabbage	lb	0.40	4/93	16r
Carrots, short trimmed and topped	lb	0.45	4/93	16r
Cheese, Cheddar	lb	3.47	4/93	16r
Chicken, fresh, whole	lb	0.84	4/93	16r
Chicken breast, bone-in	lb	1.94	4/93	16r
Chicken legs, bone-in	lb	1.02	4/93	16r
Chuck roast, graded and ungraded, ex USDA prime and choice	lb	2.43	4/93	16r
Chuck roast, USDA choice, bone-in	lb	2.11	4/93	16r
Chuck roast, USDA choice, boneless	lb	2.44	4/93	16r

Values are in dollars or fractions of dollars. In the column headed *Ref*, references are shown to sources. Each reference is followed by a letter. These refer to the geographical level for which data were reported: s = State, r = Region, and c = City or metro. The abbreviation *ex* is used to mean *except* or *excluding*; *exp* stands for expenditures. For other abbreviations and further explanations, please see the Introduction.

Saginaw-Bay City-Midland, MI - continued

Item	Per	Value	Date	Ref.
Groceries				
Coffee, 100% ground roast, all sizes	lb	2.47	4/93	16r
Cookies, chocolate chip	lb	2.73	4/93	16r
Eggs, Grade A large	doz	0.93	4/93	16r
Flour, white, all purpose	lb	0.21	4/93	16r
Grapefruit	lb	0.45	4/93	16r
Grapes, Thompson Seedless	lb	1.46	4/93	16r
Ground beef, 100% beef	lb	1.63	4/93	16r
Ground beef, lean and extra lean	lb	2.08	4/93	16r
Ground chuck, 100% beef	lb	1.94	4/93	16r
Ham, boneless, excluding canned	lb	2.21	4/93	16r
Honey, jar	8 oz	0.97-1.25	92	5r
Honey, jar	lb	1.25-2.25	92	5r
Honey, squeeze bear	12-oz	1.25-1.99	92	5r
Ice cream, prepackaged, bulk, regular	1/2 gal	2.41	4/93	16r
Lemons	lb	0.82	4/93	16r
Lettuce, iceberg	lb	0.83	4/93	16r
Margarine, stick	lb	0.77	4/93	16r
Oranges, navel	lb	0.50	4/93	16r
Peanut butter, creamy, all sizes	lb	1.82	4/93	16r
Pears, Anjou	lb	0.85	4/93	16r
Pork chops, center cut, bone-in	lb	3.17	4/93	16r
Potato chips	16 oz	2.68	4/93	16r
Potatoes, white	lb	0.26	4/93	16r
Round roast, graded & ungraded, ex USDA prime & choice	lb	2.88	4/93	16r
Round roast, USDA choice, boneless	lb	2.96	4/93	16r
Shortening, vegetable oil blends	lb	0.79	4/93	16r
Spaghetti and macaroni	lb	0.76	4/93	16r
Steak, rib eye, USDA choice, boneless	lb	6.29	4/93	16r
Steak, round, USDA choice, boneless	lb	3.24	4/93	16r
Steak, sirloin, graded & ungraded, ex USDA prime & choice	lb	4.00	4/93	16r
Steak, sirloin, USDA choice, bone-in	lb	3.57	4/93	16r
Steak, sirloin, USDA choice, boneless	lb	4.17	4/93	16r
Steak, T-bone, USDA choice, bone-in	lb	5.60	4/93	16r
Strawberries, dry pint	12 oz	0.90	4/93	16r
Sugar, white	lb	0.36	4/93	16r
Sugar, white, 33-80 oz pk	lb	0.35	4/93	16r
Tomatoes, field grown	lb	0.99	4/93	16r
Tuna, chunk, light	lb	1.76	4/93	16r
Turkey, frozen, whole	lb	0.91	4/93	16r
Health Care				
Childbirth, cesarean, hospital		4688	91	62r
Childbirth, cesarean, physician's fee		2053	91	62r
Childbirth, normal, hospital		2657	91	62r
Childbirth, normal, physician's fee		1492	91	62r
Medical plan per employee	year	3443	91	45r
Mental health care, exp	capita	53.68-118.35	90	38s
Mental health care, exp, state mental health agency	capita	73.73	90	38s
Mental health care, hospital psychiatric services, non-Federal, exp	capita	22.52	88	38s
Mental health care, mental health organization, multiservice, exp	capita	42.68	88	38s
Mental health care, psychiatric hospitals, private, exp	capita	10.80	88	38s
Mental health care, psychiatric out-patient clinics, freestanding, exp	capita	3.47	88	38s
Mental health care, psychiatric partial-care organizations, freestanding, exp	capita	0.73	88	38s
Mental health care, state and county mental hospitals, exp	capita	36.77	88	38s
Mental health care, VA medical centers, exp	capita	4.03	88	38s
Physician fee, family practice, first-visit		76.00	91	62r
Physician fee, family practice, revisit		33.00	91	62r
Physician fee, general practice, first-visit		61.00	91	62r
Physician fee, general practice, revisit		31.00	91	62r
Physician fee, general surgeon, first-visit		65.00	91	62r
Physician fee, general surgeon, revisit		35.00	91	62r
Physician fee, internal medicine, first-visit		91.00	91	62r
Physician fee, internal medicine, revisit		40.00	91	62r

Saginaw-Bay City-Midland, MI - continued

Item	Per	Value	Date	Ref.
Health Care - continued				
Physician fee, median, neurosurgeon, first-visit		106.00	91	62r
Physician fee, median, nonsurgical specialist, first-visit		90.00	91	62r
Physician fee, median, orthopedic surgeon, first-visit		83.00	91	62r
Physician fee, median, surgical specialist, first-visit		61.00	91	62r
Physician fee, neurosurgeon, revisit		41.00	91	62r
Physician fee, nonsurgical specialist, revisit		40.00	91	62r
Physician fee, obstetrics/gynecology, first-visit		61.00	91	62r
Physician fee, obstetrics/gynecology, revisit		40.00	91	62r
Physician fee, orthopedic surgeon, revisit		41.00	91	62r
Physician fee, pediatrician, first-visit		46.00	91	62r
Physician fee, pediatrician, revisit		33.00	91	62r
Physician fee, surgical specialist, revisit		36.00	91	62r
Substance abuse, hospital ancillary charge	incident	1480	90	70s
Substance abuse, hospital physician charge	incident	250	90	70s
Substance abuse, hospital room and board	incident	4070	90	70s
Insurance and Pensions				
Auto insurance, private passenger	year	716.78	91	63s
Taxes				
Tax, cigarette	pack	25	91	77s
Tax, gasoline	gal	15	91	77s
Taxes, state	capita	1185	91	77s
Transportation				
Driver's license fee		12.00	12/90	43s
Vehicle registration and license plate	year	14.00-200.00	93	40s
Utilities				
Electricity	mil Btu	20.85	90	64s

Saint Charles, MO

Item	Per	Value	Date	Ref.
Composite ACCRA index		95.20	4Q 92	4c
Alcoholic Beverages				
Beer, Miller Lite or Budweiser, 12-oz containers	6 pack	3.74	4Q 92	4c
Liquor, J & B Scotch	750 ml	16.49	4Q 92	4c
Wine, Gallo Chablis blanc, 1.5 liter	bottle	4.86	4Q 92	4c
Clothing				
Jeans, man's denim		24.49	4Q 92	4c
Shirt, man's dress shirt		17.00	4Q 92	4c
Undervest, boy's size 10-14, cotton	3	3.28	4Q 92	4c
Communications				
Newspaper subscription, daily and Sunday home delivery, large-city	month	14.50	4Q 92	4c
Telephone bill, family of four	month	17.72	4Q 92	4c
Energy and Fuels				
Energy, combined forms, 1,800 sq ft heating area	month	115.62	4Q 92	4c
Energy, exc electricity, 1,800 sq ft heating area	month	53.72	4Q 92	4c
Gasoline, motor	gal	1.00	4Q 92	4c
Entertainment				
Bowling, evening rate	game	1.62	4Q 92	4c
Monopoly game, Parker Brothers', No. 9		9.96	4Q 92	4c
Movie	admission	5.75	4Q 92	4c
Tennis balls, yellow, Wilson or Penn, 3	can	1.93	4Q 92	4c

Values are in dollars or fractions of dollars. In the column headed *Ref*, references are shown to sources. Each reference is followed by a letter. These refer to the geographical level for which data were reported: s = State, r = Region, and c = City or metro. The abbreviation *ex* is used to mean *except* or *excluding*; *exp* stands for expenditures. For other abbreviations and further explanations, please see the Introduction.

Saint Charles, MO - continued

Item	Per	Value	Date	Ref.
Goods and Services				
ACCRA Index, Miscellaneous Goods and Services		87.70	4Q 92	4c
Groceries				
ACCRA Index, Groceries		108.50	4Q 92	4c
Babyfood, strained vegetables, lowest price	4-4.5 oz jar	0.31	4Q 92	4c
Bananas	lb	0.52	4Q 92	4c
Bread, white	24 oz	0.95	4Q 92	4c
Cheese, Kraft grated Parmesan	8-oz canister	3.31	4Q 92	4c
Chicken, fryer, whole	lb	0.83	4Q 92	4c
Cigarettes, Winston	carton	16.68	4Q 92	4c
Coffee, vacuum-packed	13-oz can	2.17	4Q 92	4c
Corn, frozen	10 oz	0.80	4Q 92	4c
Corn Flakes, Kellogg's or Post Toasties	18 oz	2.07	4Q 92	4c
Eggs, Grade A large	doz	0.91	4Q 92	4c
Ground beef or hamburger	lb	1.54	4Q 92	4c
Lettuce, iceberg	head	0.83	4Q 92	4c
Margarine, Blue Bonnet or Parkay cubes	lb	0.79	4Q 92	4c
Milk, whole	1/2 gal	1.76	4Q 92	4c
Orange juice, Minute Maid frozen	12-oz can	1.59	4Q 92	4c
Peaches	29-oz can	1.35	4Q 92	4c
Peas Sweet, Del Monte or Green Giant	15-17 oz can	0.61	4Q 92	4c
Potatoes, white or red	10-lb sack	2.48	4Q 92	4c
Sausage, Jimmy Dean, 100% pork	lb	2.67	4Q 92	4c
Shortening, vegetable, Crisco	3-lb can	2.64	4Q 92	4c
Soft drink, Coca Cola	2 liter	1.05	4Q 92	4c
Steak, T-bone	lb	5.03	4Q 92	4c
Sugar, cane or beet	4 lb	1.71	4Q 92	4c
Tomatoes, Hunt's or Del Monte	14.5-oz can	0.74	4Q 92	4c
Tuna, chunk, light	6.125-6.5 oz can	0.78	4Q 92	4c
Health Care				
ACCRA Index, Health Care		97.30	4Q 92	4c
Analgesic, Aspirin, Bayer, 325 mg tablets	100	3.68	4Q 92	4c
Dentist's fee, adult teeth cleaning and periodic oral exam	visit	45.33	4Q 92	4c
Doctor's fee, routine exam, established patient	visit	37.90	4Q 92	4c
Hospital care, semiprivate room	day	292.00	90	27c
Hospital care, semiprivate room	day	326.25	4Q 92	4c
Household Goods				
Appliance repair, home, service call, washing machine	min labor charge	27.83	4Q 92	4c
Laundry detergent, Tide Ultra, Bold, or Cheer	42 oz	3.63	4Q 92	4c
Tissues, facial, Kleenex brand	175-count box	1.17	4Q 92	4c
Housing				
ACCRA Index, Housing		97.20	4Q 92	4c
House, 1,800 sq ft, 8,000 sq ft lot, new, urban	total	109333	4Q 92	4c
House payment, principal and interest, 25% down payment	month	606	4Q 92	4c
Mortgage rate, incl. points & origination fee, 30-year fixed or adjustable rate	percent	8.08	4Q 92	4c
Rent, apartment, 2 bedrooms - 1-1/2 to 2 baths, unfurnished, 950 sq ft, water	month	460	4Q 92	4c

Saint Charles, MO - continued

Item	Per	Value	Date	Ref.
Personal Goods				
Shampoo, Alberto VO5	15 oz	0.84	4Q 92	4c
Toothpaste, Crest or Colgate	6-7 oz	1.76	4Q 92	4c
Personal Services				
Dry cleaning, man's 2-piece suit		5.56	4Q 92	4c
Haircare, woman's shampoo, trim and blow-dry		16.00	4Q 92	4c
Haircut, man's barbershop, no styling		7.63	4Q 92	4c
Restaurant Food				
Chicken, fried, thigh and drumstick		1.90	4Q 92	4c
Hamburger with cheese	1/4 lb	1.82	4Q 92	4c
Pizza, Pizza Hut or Pizza Inn, cheese, thin crust	12-13 in	7.59	4Q 92	4c
Transportation				
ACCRA Index, Transportation		89.40	4Q 92	4c
Tire balance, computer or spin balance, front	wheel	5.88	4Q 92	4c
Utilities				
ACCRA Index, Utilities		104.40	4Q 92	4c
Electricity, partial electric and other energy, 1,800 sq ft living area new home	month	61.90	4Q 92	4c

Saint Cloud, MN

Item	Per	Value	Date	Ref.
Composite ACCRA index		95.30	4Q 92	4c
Alcoholic Beverages				
Beer, Miller Lite or Budweiser, 12-oz containers	6 pack	3.99	4Q 92	4c
Liquor, J & B Scotch	750 ml	13.99	4Q 92	4c
Wine, Gallo Chablis blanc, 1.5 liter	bottle	4.19	4Q 92	4c
Child Care				
Child care fee, average, center	hour	1.63	90	65r
Child care fee, average, nonregulated family day care	hour	1.83	90	65r
Child care fee, average, regulated family day care	hour	1.42	90	65r
Clothing				
Jeans, man's denim		26.99	4Q 92	4c
Shirt, man's dress shirt		25.30	4Q 92	4c
Undervest, boy's size 10-14, cotton	3	3.61	4Q 92	4c
Communications				
Long-distance telephone service, day, initial minute, 0-100 miles	min	0.14-0.52	91	12s
Long-distance telephone service, day, additional minute, 0-100 miles	min	0.05-0.35	91	12s
Long-distance telephone service, evenings/weekends, 0-100 mi, initial minute	min	0.08-0.31	91	12s
Long-distance telephone service, evenings/weekends, 0-100 mi, additional minute	min	0.03-0.21	91	12s
Newspaper subscription, daily and Sunday home delivery, large-city	month	11.96	4Q 92	4c
Telephone, flat rate	month	17.89	91	11c
Telephone bill, family of four	month	22.35	4Q 92	4c
Education				
Board, 4-yr private college/university	year	1718	91	22s
Board, 4-yr public college/university	year	1321	91	22s
Expenditures, local gov't, public elementary/secondary	pupil	5500	92	20s
Room, 4-year private college/university	year	1587	91	22s
Room, 4-year public college/university	year	1344	91	22s
Tuition, 2-year private college/university	year	7664	91	22s
Tuition, 2-year public college/university	year	1578	91	22s
Tuition, 4-year private college/university	year	9507	91	22s
Tuition, 4-year public college/university, in-state	year	2216	91	22s

Values are in dollars or fractions of dollars. In the column headed *Ref*, references are shown to sources. Each reference is followed by a letter. These refer to the geographical level for which data were reported: s = State, r = Region, and c = City or metro. The abbreviation *ex* is used to mean *except* or *excluding*; *exp* stands for expenditures. For other abbreviations and further explanations, please see the Introduction.

Saint Cloud, MN - continued

Item	Per	Value	Date	Ref.
Energy and Fuels				
Coal	mil Btu	1.32	90	64s
Energy	mil Btu	8.17	90	64s
Energy, combined forms, 1,800 sq ft heating area	month	109.58	4Q 92	4c
Energy, exc electricity, 1,800 sq ft heating area	month	46.28	4Q 92	4c
Energy exp/householder, 1-family unit	year	473	90	28r
Energy exp/householder, <1,000 sq ft heating area	year	429	90	28r
Energy exp/householder, 1,000-1,999 sq ft heating area	year	442	90	28r
Energy exp/householder, 2,000+ sq ft heating area	year	498	90	28r
Energy exp/householder, mobile home	year	442	90	28r
Energy exp/householder, multifamily	year	407	90	28r
Gas, natural	mil Btu	3.87	90	64s
Gas, natural	000 cu ft	4.52	91	46s
Gas, natural, exp	year	545	91	46s
Gasoline, motor	gal	1.17	4Q 92	4c
Gasoline, unleaded regular	mil Btu	9.56	90	64s
Entertainment				
Bowling, evening rate	game	1.73	4Q 92	4c
Miniature golf admission	adult	6.18	92	1r
Miniature golf admission	child	5.14	92	1r
Monopoly game, Parker Brothers', No. 9		9.32	4Q 92	4c
Movie	admission	5.00	4Q 92	4c
Tennis balls, yellow, Wilson or Penn, 3	can	2.76	4Q 92	4c
Waterpark admission	adult	11.00	92	1r
Waterpark admission	child	8.55	92	1r
Funerals				
Casket, 18-gauge steel, velvet interior		1952.97	91	24r
Cosmetology, hair care, etc.		90.03	91	24r
Embalming		251.75	91	24r
Facility use for ceremony		180.75	91	24r
Hearse, local		117.51	91	24r
Limousine, local		71.86	91	24r
Remains to funeral home, transfer		81.14	91	24r
Service charge, professional		740.03	91	24r
Vault, concrete, non-metallic liner		801.47	91	24r
Viewing facilities, use		169.33	91	24r
Goods and Services				
ACCRA Index, Miscellaneous Goods and Services		96.80	4Q 92	4c
Groceries				
ACCRA Index, Groceries		104.20	4Q 92	4c
Apples, Red Delicious	lb	0.77	4/93	16r
Babyfood, strained vegetables, lowest price	4-4.5 oz jar	0.36	4Q 92	4c
Bacon	lb	1.85	4/93	16r
Bananas	lb	0.45	4Q 92	4c
Bananas	lb	0.46	4/93	16r
Beef, stew, boneless	lb	2.53	4/93	16r
Bologna, all beef or mixed	lb	2.19	4/93	16r
Bread, white	24 oz	0.63	4Q 92	4c
Bread, white, pan	lb	0.78	4/93	16r
Butter	lb	1.50	4/93	16r
Cabbage	lb	0.40	4/93	16r
Carrots, short trimmed and topped	lb	0.45	4/93	16r
Cheese, Cheddar	lb	3.47	4/93	16r
Cheese, Kraft grated Parmesan	8-oz canister	3.03	4Q 92	4c
Chicken, fresh, whole	lb	0.84	4/93	16r
Chicken, fryer, whole	lb	0.87	4Q 92	4c
Chicken breast, bone-in	lb	1.94	4/93	16r
Chicken legs, bone-in	lb	1.02	4/93	16r
Chuck roast, graded and ungraded, ex USDA prime and choice	lb	2.43	4/93	16r

Saint Cloud, MN - continued

Item	Per	Value	Date	Ref.
Groceries - continued				
Chuck roast, USDA choice, bone-in	lb	2.11	4/93	16r
Chuck roast, USDA choice, boneless	lb	2.44	4/93	16r
Cigarettes, Winston	carton	20.79	4Q 92	4c
Coffee, 100% ground roast, all sizes	lb	2.47	4/93	16r
Coffee, vacuum-packed	13-oz can	2.07	4Q 92	4c
Cookies, chocolate chip	lb	2.73	4/93	16r
Corn, frozen	10 oz	0.67	4Q 92	4c
Corn Flakes, Kellogg's or Post Toasties	18 oz	2.05	4Q 92	4c
Eggs, Grade A large	doz	0.79	4Q 92	4c
Eggs, Grade A large	doz	0.93	4/93	16r
Flour, white, all purpose	lb	0.21	4/93	16r
Grapefruit	lb	0.45	4/93	16r
Grapes, Thompson Seedless	lb	1.46	4/93	16r
Ground beef, 100% beef	lb	1.63	4/93	16r
Ground beef, lean and extra lean	lb	2.08	4/93	16r
Ground beef or hamburger	lb	1.90	4Q 92	4c
Ground chuck, 100% beef	lb	1.94	4/93	16r
Ham, boneless, excluding canned	lb	2.21	4/93	16r
Ice cream, prepackaged, bulk, regular	1/2 gal	2.41	4/93	16r
Lemons	lb	0.82	4/93	16r
Lettuce, iceberg	head	0.95	4Q 92	4c
Lettuce, iceberg	lb	0.83	4/93	16r
Margarine, Blue Bonnet or Parkay cubes	lb	0.68	4Q 92	4c
Margarine, stick	lb	0.77	4/93	16r
Milk, whole	1/2 gal	1.43	4Q 92	4c
Orange juice, Minute Maid frozen	12-oz can	1.24	4Q 92	4c
Oranges, navel	lb	0.50	4/93	16r
Peaches	29-oz can	1.23	4Q 92	4c
Peanut butter, creamy, all sizes	lb	1.82	4/93	16r
Pears, Anjou	lb	0.85	4/93	16r
Peas Sweet, Del Monte or Green Giant	15-17 oz can	0.59	4Q 92	4c
Pork chops, center cut, bone-in	lb	3.17	4/93	16r
Potato chips	16 oz	2.68	4/93	16r
Potatoes, white	lb	0.26	4/93	16r
Potatoes, white or red	10-lb sack	1.70	4Q 92	4c
Round roast, graded & ungraded, ex USDA prime & choice	lb	2.88	4/93	16r
Round roast, USDA choice, boneless	lb	2.96	4/93	16r
Sausage, Jimmy Dean, 100% pork	lb	2.52	4Q 92	4c
Shortening, vegetable oil blends	lb	0.79	4/93	16r
Shortening, vegetable, Crisco	3-lb can	2.31	4Q 92	4c
Soft drink, Coca Cola	2 liter	1.22	4Q 92	4c
Spaghetti and macaroni	lb	0.76	4/93	16r
Steak, rib eye, USDA choice, boneless	lb	6.29	4/93	16r
Steak, round, USDA choice, boneless	lb	3.24	4/93	16r
Steak, sirloin, graded & ungraded, ex USDA prime & choice	lb	4.00	4/93	16r
Steak, sirloin, USDA choice, bone-in	lb	3.57	4/93	16r
Steak, sirloin, USDA choice, boneless	lb	4.17	4/93	16r
Steak, T-bone	lb	4.91	4Q 92	4c
Steak, T-bone, USDA choice, bone-in	lb	5.60	4/93	16r
Strawberries, dry pint	12 oz	0.90	4/93	16r
Sugar, cane or beet	4 lb	1.89	4Q 92	4c
Sugar, white	lb	0.36	4/93	16r
Sugar, white, 33-80 oz pk	lb	0.35	4/93	16r
Tomatoes, field grown	lb	0.99	4/93	16r
Tomatoes, Hunt's or Del Monte	14.5-oz can	0.68	4Q 92	4c
Tuna, chunk, light	6.125-6.5 oz can	0.64	4Q 92	4c
Tuna, chunk, light	lb	1.76	4/93	16r
Turkey, frozen, whole	lb	0.91	4/93	16r
Health Care				
ACCRA Index, Health Care		96.30	4Q 92	4c
Analgesic, Aspirin, Bayer, 325 mg tablets	100	4.97	4Q 92	4c

Values are in dollars or fractions of dollars. In the column headed *Ref*, references are shown to sources. Each reference is followed by a letter. These refer to the geographical level for which data were reported: s=State, r=Region, and c=City or metro. The abbreviation *ex* is used to mean *except* or *excluding*; *exp* stands for expenditures. For other abbreviations and further explanations, please see the Introduction.

Saint Cloud, MN - continued

Item	Per	Value	Date	Ref.
Health Care				
Childbirth, cesarean, hospital		4688	91	62r
Childbirth, cesarean, physician's fee		2053	91	62r
Childbirth, normal, hospital		2657	91	62r
Childbirth, normal, physician's fee		1492	91	62r
Dentist's fee, adult teeth cleaning and periodic oral exam	visit	45.60	4Q 92	4c
Doctor's fee, routine exam, established patient	visit	32.25	4Q 92	4c
Hospital care, semiprivate room	day	349.00	4Q 92	4c
Medical insurance premium, per employee, small group comprehensive	month	281.05	10/91	25c
Medical plan per employee	year	3443	91	45r
Mental health care, exp	capita	20.37-28.83	90	38s
Mental health care, exp, state mental health agency	capita	53.67	90	38s
Mental health care, hospital psychiatric services, non-Federal, exp	capita	18.62	88	38s
Mental health care, mental health organization, multiservice, exp	capita	9.59	88	38s
Mental health care, psychiatric hospitals, private, exp	capita	2.70	88	38s
Mental health care, psychiatric out-patient clinics, freestanding, exp	capita	8.41	88	38s
Mental health care, state and county mental hospitals, exp	capita	27.18	88	38s
Mental health care, VA medical centers, exp	capita	7.88	88	38s
Physician fee, family practice, first-visit		76.00	91	62r
Physician fee, family practice, revisit		33.00	91	62r
Physician fee, general practice, first-visit		61.00	91	62r
Physician fee, general practice, revisit		31.00	91	62r
Physician fee, general surgeon, first-visit		65.00	91	62r
Physician fee, general surgeon, revisit		35.00	91	62r
Physician fee, internal medicine, first-visit		91.00	91	62r
Physician fee, internal medicine, revisit		40.00	91	62r
Physician fee, median, neurosurgeon, first-visit		106.00	91	62r
Physician fee, median, nonsurgical specialist, first-visit		90.00	91	62r
Physician fee, median, orthopedic surgeon, first-visit		83.00	91	62r
Physician fee, median, surgical specialist, first-visit		61.00	91	62r
Physician fee, neurosurgeon, revisit		41.00	91	62r
Physician fee, nonsurgical specialist, revisit		40.00	91	62r
Physician fee, obstetrics/gynecology, first-visit		61.00	91	62r
Physician fee, obstetrics/gynecology, revisit		40.00	91	62r
Physician fee, orthopedic surgeon, revisit		41.00	91	62r
Physician fee, pediatrician, first-visit		46.00	91	62r
Physician fee, pediatrician, revisit		33.00	91	62r
Physician fee, surgical specialist, revisit		36.00	91	62r
Substance abuse, hospital ancillary charge	incident	670	90	70s
Substance abuse, hospital physician charge	incident	310	90	70s
Substance abuse, hospital room and board	incident	3800	90	70s
Household Goods				
Appliance repair, home, service call, washing machine	min labor charge	31.61	4Q 92	4c
Laundry detergent, Tide Ultra, Bold, or Cheer	42 oz	4.01	4Q 92	4c
Tissues, facial, Kleenex brand	175-count box	1.14	4Q 92	4c
Housing				
ACCRA Index, Housing		82.90	4Q 92	4c
House, 1,800 sq ft, 8,000 sq ft lot, new, urban	total	88633	4Q 92	4c

Saint Cloud, MN - continued

Item	Per	Value	Date	Ref.
Housing - continued				
House payment, principal and interest, 25% down payment	month	493	4Q 92	4c
Mortgage rate, incl. points & origination fee, 30-year fixed or adjustable rate	percent	8.11	4Q 92	4c
Rent, apartment, 2 bedrooms - 1-1/2 to 2 baths, unfurnished, 950 sq ft, water	month	447	4Q 92	4c
Rental unit, 1 bedroom	month	407	93	23c
Rental unit, 2 bedroom	month	480	93	23c
Rental unit, 3 bedroom	month	602	93	23c
Rental unit, 4 bedroom	month	672	93	23c
Rental unit, efficiency	month	334	93	23c
Insurance and Pensions				
Auto insurance, private passenger	year	584.92	91	63s
Personal Goods				
Shampoo, Alberto VO5	15 oz	1.38	4Q 92	4c
Toothpaste, Crest or Colgate	6-7 oz	1.79	4Q 92	4c
Personal Services				
Dry cleaning, man's 2-piece suit		6.53	4Q 92	4c
Haircare, woman's shampoo, trim and blow-dry		16.10	4Q 92	4c
Haircut, man's barbershop, no styling		9.35	4Q 92	4c
Restaurant Food				
Chicken, fried, thigh and drumstick		1.90	4Q 92	4c
Hamburger with cheese	1/4 lb	1.80	4Q 92	4c
Pizza, Pizza Hut or Pizza Inn, cheese, thin crust	12-13 in	8.59	4Q 92	4c
Taxes				
Tax, cigarette	pack	48	91	77s
Tax, gasoline	gal	20	91	77s
Taxes, state	capita	1591	91	77s
Transportation				
ACCRA Index, Transportation		107.30	4Q 92	4c
Driver's license fee		15.00	12/90	43s
Tire balance, computer or spin balance, front	wheel	7.20	4Q 92	4c
Vehicle registration and license plate	year	10.00	93	66s
Utilities				
ACCRA Index, Utilities		101.80	4Q 92	4c
Electricity	mil Btu	15.68	90	64s
Electricity, partial electric and other energy, 1,800 sq ft living area new home	month	63.30	4Q 92	4c

Saint George, UT

Item	Per	Value	Date	Ref.
Composite ACCRA index		101.30	4Q 92	4c
Alcoholic Beverages				
Beer, Miller Lite or Budweiser, 12-oz containers	6 pack	4.01	4Q 92	4c
Liquor, J & B Scotch	750 ml	19.25	4Q 92	4c
Wine, Gallo Chablis blanc, 1.5 liter	bottle	4.95	4Q 92	4c
Clothing				
Jeans, man's denim		31.32	4Q 92	4c
Shirt, man's dress shirt		25.17	4Q 92	4c
Undervest, boy's size 10-14, cotton	3	4.33	4Q 92	4c
Communications				
Newspaper subscription, daily and Sunday home delivery, large-city	month	11.00	4Q 92	4c
Telephone, flat rate	month	7.98	91	11c
Telephone bill, family of four	month	13.67	4Q 92	4c
Energy and Fuels				
Energy, combined forms, 1,800 sq ft heating area	month	90.85	4Q 92	4c
Gasoline, motor	gal	1.23	4Q 92	4c

Values are in dollars or fractions of dollars. In the column headed *Ref*, references are shown as sources. Each reference is followed by a letter. These refer to the geographical level for which data were reported: s = State, r = Region, and c = City or metro. The abbreviation *ex* is used to mean *except* or *excluding*; *exp* stands for expenditures. For other abbreviations and further explanations, please see the Introduction.

Saint George, UT - continued

Item	Per	Value	Date	Ref.
Entertainment				
Bowling, evening rate	game	1.70	4Q 92	4c
Monopoly game, Parker Brothers', No. 9		12.58	4Q 92	4c
Movie	admission	5.00	4Q 92	4c
Tennis balls, yellow, Wilson or Penn, 3	can	2.68	4Q 92	4c
Goods and Services				
ACCRA Index, Miscellaneous Goods and Services		100.10	4Q 92	4c
Groceries				
ACCRA Index, Groceries		103.30	4Q 92	4c
Babyfood, strained vegetables, lowest price	4-4.5 oz jar	0.37	4Q 92	4c
Bananas	lb	0.41	4Q 92	4c
Bread, white	24 oz	0.67	4Q 92	4c
Cheese, Kraft grated Parmesan	8-oz canister	3.96	4Q 92	4c
Chicken, fryer, whole	lb	0.82	4Q 92	4c
Cigarettes, Winston	carton	18.89	4Q 92	4c
Coffee, vacuum-packed	13-oz can	2.24	4Q 92	4c
Corn, frozen	10 oz	0.59	4Q 92	4c
Corn Flakes, Kellogg's or Post Toasties	18 oz	2.04	4Q 92	4c
Eggs, Grade A large	doz	0.84	4Q 92	4c
Ground beef or hamburger	lb	1.47	4Q 92	4c
Lettuce, iceberg	head	0.80	4Q 92	4c
Margarine, Blue Bonnet or Parkay cubes	lb	0.66	4Q 92	4c
Milk, whole	1/2 gal	1.50	4Q 92	4c
Orange juice, Minute Maid frozen	12-oz can	1.52	4Q 92	4c
Peaches	29-oz can	1.38	4Q 92	4c
Peas Sweet, Del Monte or Green Giant	15-17 oz can	0.61	4Q 92	4c
Potatoes, white or red	10-lb sack	2.35	4Q 92	4c
Sausage, Jimmy Dean, 100% pork	lb	2.96	4Q 92	4c
Shortening, vegetable, Crisco	3-lb can	2.48	4Q 92	4c
Soft drink, Coca Cola	2 liter	1.19	4Q 92	4c
Steak, T-bone	lb	4.82	4Q 92	4c
Sugar, cane or beet	4 lb	1.50	4Q 92	4c
Tomatoes, Hunt's or Del Monte	14.5-oz can	0.73	4Q 92	4c
Tuna, chunk, light	6.125-6.5 oz can	0.68	4Q 92	4c
Health Care				
ACCRA Index, Health Care		106.20	4Q 92	4c
Analgesic, Aspirin, Bayer, 325 mg tablets	100	5.29	4Q 92	4c
Dentist's fee, adult teeth cleaning and periodic oral exam	visit	53.60	4Q 92	4c
Doctor's fee, routine exam, established patient	visit	35.00	4Q 92	4c
Hospital care, semiprivate room	day	357.00	4Q 92	4c
Household Goods				
Appliance repair, home, service call, washing machine	min labor charge	26.70	4Q 92	4c
Laundry detergent, Tide Ultra, Bold, or Cheer	42 oz	2.99	4Q 92	4c
Tissues, facial, Kleenex brand	175-count box	1.23	4Q 92	4c
Housing				
ACCRA Index, Housing		104.70	4Q 92	4c
House, 1,800 sq ft, 8,000 sq ft lot, new, urban	total	120000	4Q 92	4c

Saint George, UT - continued

Item	Per	Value	Date	Ref.
Housing - continued				
House payment, principal and interest, 25% down payment	month	664	4Q 92	4c
Mortgage rate, incl. points & origination fee, 30-year fixed or adjustable rate	percent	8.07	4Q 92	4c
Rent, apartment, 2 bedrooms - 1-1/2 to 2 baths, unfurnished, 950 sq ft, water	month	468	4Q 92	4c
Personal Goods				
Shampoo, Alberto VO5	15 oz	1.31	4Q 92	4c
Toothpaste, Crest or Colgate	6-7 oz	1.96	4Q 92	4c
Personal Services				
Dry cleaning, man's 2-piece suit		7.47	4Q 92	4c
Haircare, woman's shampoo, trim and blow-dry		17.00	4Q 92	4c
Haircut, man's barbershop, no styling		5.33	4Q 92	4c
Restaurant Food				
Chicken, fried, thigh and drumstick		2.09	4Q 92	4c
Hamburger with cheese	1/4 lb	1.94	4Q 92	4c
Pizza, Pizza Hut or Pizza Inn, cheese, thin crust	12-13 in	7.99	4Q 92	4c
Transportation				
ACCRA Index, Transportation		108.20	4Q 92	4c
Tire balance, computer or spin balance, front	wheel	6.99	4Q 92	4c
Utilities				
ACCRA Index, Utilities		81.90	4Q 92	4c
Electricity, all electric, 1,800 sq ft living area new home	month	90.85	4Q 92	4c

Saint Joseph, MO

Item	Per	Value	Date	Ref.
Composite ACCRA index		89.90	4Q 92	4c
Alcoholic Beverages				
Beer, Miller Lite or Budweiser, 12-oz containers	6 pack	3.70	4Q 92	4c
Liquor, J & B Scotch	750 ml	15.84	4Q 92	4c
Wine, Gallo Chablis blanc, 1.5 liter	bottle	4.56	4Q 92	4c
Clothing				
Jeans, man's denim		24.22	4Q 92	4c
Shirt, man's dress shirt		24.00	4Q 92	4c
Undervest, boy's size 10-14, cotton	3	3.02	4Q 92	4c
Communications				
Newspaper subscription, daily and Sunday home delivery, large-city	month	8.55	4Q 92	4c
Telephone bill, family of four	month	16.12	4Q 92	4c
Energy and Fuels				
Energy, combined forms, 1,800 sq ft heating area	month	97.71	4Q 92	4c
Energy, exc electricity, 1,800 sq ft heating area	month	39.62	4Q 92	4c
Gasoline, motor	gal	0.99	4Q 92	4c
Entertainment				
Bowling, evening rate	game	1.90	4Q 92	4c
Monopoly game, Parker Brothers', No. 9		10.31	4Q 92	4c
Movie	admission	4.50	4Q 92	4c
Tennis balls, yellow, Wilson or Penn, 3	can	1.91	4Q 92	4c
Goods and Services				
ACCRA Index, Miscellaneous Goods and Services		85.20	4Q 92	4c
Groceries				
ACCRA Index, Groceries		95.10	4Q 92	4c
Babyfood, strained vegetables, lowest price	4-4.5 oz jar	0.36	4Q 92	4c
Bananas	lb	0.50	4Q 92	4c
Bread, white	24 oz	0.55	4Q 92	4c

Values are in dollars or fractions of dollars. In the column headed *Ref*, references are shown to sources. Each reference is followed by a letter. These refer to the geographical level for which data were reported: s=State, r=Region, and c=City or metro. The abbreviation *ex* is used to mean *except* or *excluding*; *exp* stands for expenditures. For other abbreviations and further explanations, please see the Introduction.

Saint Joseph, MO - continued

Item	Per	Value	Date	Ref.
Groceries				
Cheese, Kraft grated Parmesan	8-oz canister	2.95	4Q 92	4c
Chicken, fryer, whole	lb	0.72	4Q 92	4c
Cigarettes, Winston	carton	16.01	4Q 92	4c
Coffee, vacuum-packed	13-oz can	1.88	4Q 92	4c
Corn, frozen	10 oz	0.60	4Q 92	4c
Corn Flakes, Kellogg's or Post Toasties	18 oz	2.03	4Q 92	4c
Eggs, Grade A large	doz	0.79	4Q 92	4c
Ground beef or hamburger	lb	1.22	4Q 92	4c
Lettuce, iceberg	head	0.75	4Q 92	4c
Margarine, Blue Bonnet or Parkay cubes	lb	0.63	4Q 92	4c
Milk, whole	1/2 gal	1.35	4Q 92	4c
Orange juice, Minute Maid frozen	12-oz can	1.40	4Q 92	4c
Peaches	29-oz can	1.34	4Q 92	4c
Peas Sweet, Del Monte or Green Giant	15-17 oz can	0.59	4Q 92	4c
Potatoes, white or red	10-lb sack	2.07	4Q 92	4c
Sausage, Jimmy Dean, 100% pork	lb	2.77	4Q 92	4c
Shortening, vegetable, Crisco	3-lb can	2.15	4Q 92	4c
Soft drink, Coca Cola	2 liter	1.22	4Q 92	4c
Steak, T-bone	lb	5.06	4Q 92	4c
Sugar, cane or beet	4 lb	1.55	4Q 92	4c
Tomatoes, Hunt's or Del Monte	14.5-oz can	0.67	4Q 92	4c
Tuna, chunk, light	6.125-6.5 oz can	0.61	4Q 92	4c
Health Care				
ACCRA Index, Health Care		85.80	4Q 92	4c
Analgesic, Aspirin, Bayer, 325 mg tablets	100	3.22	4Q 92	4c
Dentist's fee, adult teeth cleaning and periodic oral exam	visit	41.50	4Q 92	4c
Doctor's fee, routine exam, established patient	visit	26.40	4Q 92	4c
Hospital care, semiprivate room	day	260.50	90	27c
Hospital care, semiprivate room	day	385.00	4Q 92	4c
Medical insurance premium, per employee, small group comprehensive	month	324.85	10/91	25c
Household Goods				
Appliance repair, home, service call, washing machine	min labor charge	23.80	4Q 92	4c
Laundry detergent, Tide Ultra, Bold, or Cheer	42 oz	2.91	4Q 92	4c
Tissues, facial, Kleenex brand	175-count box	1.16	4Q 92	4c
Housing				
ACCRA Index, Housing		95.10	4Q 92	4c
House, 1,800 sq ft, 8,000 sq ft lot, new, urban	total	113700	4Q 92	4c
House payment, principal and interest, 25% down payment	month	639	4Q 92	4c
Mortgage rate, incl. points & origination fee, 30-year fixed or adjustable rate	percent	8.22	4Q 92	4c
Rent, apartment, 2 bedrooms - 1-1/2 to 2 baths, unfurnished, 950 sq ft, water	month	344	4Q 92	4c
Rental unit, 1 bedroom	month	325	93	23c
Rental unit, 2 bedroom	month	383	93	23c
Rental unit, 3 bedroom	month	478	93	23c
Rental unit, 4 bedroom	month	539	93	23c
Rental unit, efficiency	month	268	93	23c

Saint Joseph, MO - continued

Item	Per	Value	Date	Ref.
Personal Goods				
Shampoo, Alberto VO5	15 oz	0.98	4Q 92	4c
Toothpaste, Crest or Colgate	6-7 oz	1.64	4Q 92	4c
Personal Services				
Dry cleaning, man's 2-piece suit		4.71	4Q 92	4c
Haircare, woman's shampoo, trim and blow-dry		12.19	4Q 92	4c
Haircut, man's barbershop, no styling		5.00	4Q 92	4c
Restaurant Food				
Chicken, fried, thigh and drumstick		2.00	4Q 92	4c
Hamburger with cheese	1/4 lb	1.89	4Q 92	4c
Pizza, Pizza Hut or Pizza Inn, cheese, thin crust	12-13 in	7.59	4Q 92	4c
Transportation				
ACCRA Index, Transportation		88.10	4Q 92	4c
Tire balance, computer or spin balance, front	wheel	5.75	4Q 92	4c
Utilities				
ACCRA Index, Utilities		88.80	4Q 92	4c
Electricity, partial electric and other energy, 1,800 sq ft living area new home	month	58.09	4Q 92	4c
Electricity, winter, 250 KWh	month	18.29	92	55c
Electricity, winter, 500 KWh	month	33.95	92	55c
Electricity, winter, 750 KWh	month	47.59	92	55c
Electricity, winter, 1000 KWh	month	58.20	92	55c

Saint Louis, MO

Item	Per	Value	Date	Ref.
Composite ACCRA index		96.60	4Q 92	4c
Alcoholic Beverages				
Alcoholic beverages, exp	year	299	89	15c
Beer, Miller Lite or Budweiser, 12-oz containers	6 pack	3.38	4Q 92	4c
Liquor, J & B Scotch	750 ml	16.12	4Q 92	4c
Wine, Gallo Chablis blanc, 1.5 liter	bottle	4.61	4Q 92	4c
Charity				
Cash contributions	year	982	89	15c
Child Care				
Child care fee, average, center	hour	1.63	90	65r
Child care fee, average, nonregulated family day care	hour	1.83	90	65r
Child care fee, average, regulated family day care	hour	1.42	90	65r
Clothing				
Jeans, man's denim		24.10	4Q 92	4c
Shirt, man's dress shirt		20.40	4Q 92	4c
Undervest, boy's size 10-14, cotton	3	3.46	4Q 92	4c
Communications				
Long-distance telephone service, day, initial minute, 0-100 miles	min	0.10-0.46	91	12s
Long-distance telephone service, day, additional minute, 0-100 miles	min	0.06-0.29	91	12s
Newspaper subscription, daily and Sunday home delivery, large-city	month	13.26	4Q 92	4c
Postage and stationery, exp	year	117	89	15c
Telephone, exp	year	561	89	15c
Telephone, residential, private line, rotary, unlimited calling	month	17.93	10/91	78c
Telephone bill, family of four	month	17.97	4Q 92	4c
Education				
Board, 4-yr private college/university	year	1789	91	22s
Board, 4-yr public college/university	year	1162	91	22s
Education, exp	year	487	89	15c
Expenditures, local gov't, public elementary/secondary	pupil	4537	92	20s
Room, 4-year private college/university	year	1817	91	22s
Room, 4-year public college/university	year	1450	91	22s

Values are in dollars or fractions of dollars. In the column headed *Ref*, references are shown to sources. Each reference is followed by a letter. These refer to the geographical level for which data were reported: s=State, r=Region, and c=City or metro. The abbreviation *ex* is used to mean *except* or *excluding*; *exp* stands for expenditures. For other abbreviations and further explanations, please see the Introduction.

Saint Louis, MO - continued

Item	Per	Value	Date	Ref.
Education				
Tuition, 2-year private college/university	year	5208	91	22s
Tuition, 2-year public college/university	year	891	91	22s
Tuition, 4-year private college/university	year	7487	91	22s
Tuition, 4-year public college/university, in-state	year	1733	91	22s
Energy and Fuels				
Coal	mil Btu	1.35	90	64s
Energy	mil Btu	8.91	90	64s
Energy, combined forms, 1,800 sq ft heating area	month	116.65	4Q 92	4c
Energy, exc electricity, 1,800 sq ft heating area	month	54.75	4Q 92	4c
Energy exp/householder, 1-family unit	year	473	90	28r
Energy exp/householder, <1,000 sq ft heating area	year	429	90	28r
Energy exp/householder, 1,000-1,999 sq ft heating area	year	442	90	28r
Energy exp/householder, 2,000+ sq ft heating area	year	498	90	28r
Energy exp/householder, mobile home	year	442	90	28r
Energy exp/householder, multifamily	year	407	90	28r
Fuel oil, other fuel, exp	year	47	89	15c
Gas, cooking, 10 therms	month	11.79	92	56c
Gas, cooking, 30 therms	month	19.36	92	56c
Gas, cooking, 50 therms	month	26.93	92	56c
Gas, heating, winter, 100 therms	month	45.86	92	56c
Gas, heating, winter, average use	month	59.87	92	56c
Gas, natural	mil Btu	4.69	90	64s
Gas, natural	000 cu ft	5.14	91	46s
Gas, natural, exp	year	418	89	15c
Gas, natural, exp	year	512	91	46s
Gas, piped	100 therms	53.60	4/93	16c
Gas, piped	40 therms	28.51	4/93	16c
Gas, piped	therm	0.52	4/93	16c
Gasoline, all types	gal	1.06	4/93	16c
Gasoline, motor	gal	1.01	4Q 92	4c
Gasoline, regular unleaded, taxes included, cash, self-service	gal	1.21	4/93	16c
Gasoline, unleaded premium 93 octane	gal	0.99	4/93	16c
Gasoline, unleaded regular	mil Btu	8.61	90	64s
Entertainment				
Bowling, evening rate	game	1.90	4Q 92	4c
Dinner entree, restaurant		18.75-28.50	92	83c
Entertainment exp	year	1332	89	15c
Fees and admissions	year	395	89	15c
Miniature golf admission	adult	6.18	92	1r
Miniature golf admission	child	5.14	92	1r
Monopoly game, Parker Brothers', No. 9		9.67	4Q 92	4c
Movie	admission	5.40	4Q 92	4c
Pets, toys, playground equipment, exp	year	239	89	15c
Reading, exp	year	163	89	15c
Supplies, equipment, services, exp	year	276	89	15c
Tennis balls, yellow, Wilson or Penn, 3	can	2.01	4Q 92	4c
Waterpark admission	adult	11.00	92	1r
Waterpark admission	child	8.55	92	1r
Funerals				
Casket, 18-gauge steel, velvet interior		1952.97	91	24r
Cosmetology, hair care, etc.		90.03	91	24r
Embalming		251.75	91	24r
Facility use for ceremony		180.75	91	24r
Hearse, local		117.51	91	24r
Limousine, local		71.86	91	24r
Remains to funeral home, transfer		81.14	91	24r
Service charge, professional		740.03	91	24r
Vault, concrete, non-metallic liner		801.47	91	24r
Viewing facilities, use		169.33	91	24r

Saint Louis, MO - continued

Item	Per	Value	Date	Ref.
Goods and Services				
ACCRA Index, Miscellaneous Goods and Services		91.60	4Q 92	4c
Groceries				
ACCRA Index, Groceries		100.10	4Q 92	4c
Apples, Red Delicious	lb	0.77	4/93	16r
Babyfood, strained vegetables, lowest price	4-4.5 oz jar	0.29	4Q 92	4c
Bacon	lb	1.85	4/93	16r
Bakery products, exp	year	205	89	15c
Bananas	lb	0.43	4Q 92	4c
Bananas	lb	0.46	4/93	16r
Beef, exp	year	191	89	15c
Beef, stew, boneless	lb	2.53	4/93	16r
Beverages, nonalcoholic, exp	year	196	89	15c
Bologna, all beef or mixed	lb	2.19	4/93	16r
Bread, white	24 oz	0.91	4Q 92	4c
Bread, white, pan	lb	0.78	4/93	16r
Butter	lb	1.50	4/93	16r
Cabbage	lb	0.40	4/93	16r
Carrots, short trimmed and topped	lb	0.45	4/93	16r
Cereals and bakery products, exp	year	304	89	15c
Cereals and cereal products, exp	year	99	89	15c
Cheese, Cheddar	lb	3.47	4/93	16r
Cheese, Kraft grated Parmesan	8-oz canister	3.31	4Q 92	4c
Chicken, fresh, whole	lb	0.84	4/93	16r
Chicken, fryer, whole	lb	0.71	4Q 92	4c
Chicken breast, bone-in	lb	1.94	4/93	16r
Chicken legs, bone-in	lb	1.02	4/93	16r
Chuck roast, graded and ungraded, ex USDA prime and choice	lb	2.43	4/93	16r
Chuck roast, USDA choice, bone-in	lb	2.11	4/93	16r
Chuck roast, USDA choice, boneless	lb	2.44	4/93	16r
Cigarettes, Winston	carton	16.29	4Q 92	4c
Coffee, 100% ground roast, all sizes	lb	2.47	4/93	16r
Coffee, vacuum-packed	13-oz can	1.63	4Q 92	4c
Cookies, chocolate chip	lb	2.73	4/93	16r
Corn, frozen	10 oz	0.74	4Q 92	4c
Corn Flakes, Kellogg's or Post Toasties	18 oz	1.85	4Q 92	4c
Dairy products, exp	year	241	89	15c
Dairy products, miscellaneous, exp	year	116	89	15c
Eggs, exp	year	22	89	15c
Eggs, Grade A large	doz	0.77	4Q 92	4c
Eggs, Grade A large	doz	0.93	4/93	16r
Fats and oils, exp	year	44	89	15c
Fish and seafood, exp	year	58	89	15c
Flour, white, all purpose	lb	0.21	4/93	16r
Food, exp	year	3756	89	15c
Food eaten at home, exp	year	2106	89	15c
Food eaten away from home, exp	year	1650	89	15c
Food prepared on out-of-town trips, exp	year	39	89	15c
Foods, miscellaneous, exp	year	307	89	15c
Fruits, fresh, exp	year	98	89	15c
Fruits, processed, exp	year	81	89	15c
Fruits and vegetables, exp	year	331	89	15c
Grapefruit	lb	0.45	4/93	16r
Grapes, Thompson Seedless	lb	1.46	4/93	16r
Ground beef, 100% beef	lb	1.63	4/93	16r
Ground beef, lean and extra lean	lb	2.08	4/93	16r
Ground beef or hamburger	lb	1.49	4Q 92	4c
Ground chuck, 100% beef	lb	1.94	4/93	16r
Ham, boneless, excluding canned	lb	2.21	4/93	16r
Ice cream, prepackaged, bulk, regular	1/2 gal	2.41	4/93	16r
Lemons	lb	0.82	4/93	16r
Lettuce, iceberg	head	0.82	4Q 92	4c
Lettuce, iceberg	lb	0.83	4/93	16r
Margarine, Blue Bonnet or Parkay cubes	lb	0.74	4Q 92	4c
Margarine, stick	lb	0.77	4/93	16r
Meats, miscellaneous, exp	year	96	89	15c
Meats, poultry, fish and eggs, exp	year	570	89	15c

Values are in dollars or fractions of dollars. In the column headed *Ref*, references are shown to sources. Each reference is followed by a letter. These refer to the geographical level for which data were reported: s=State, r=Region, and c=City or metro. The abbreviation *ex* is used to mean *except* or *excluding*; *exp* stands for expenditures. For other abbreviations and further explanations, please see the Introduction.

Saint Louis, MO - continued

Item	Per	Value	Date	Ref.
Groceries				
Milk, whole	1/2 gal	1.37	4Q 92	4c
Milk and cream, fresh, exp	year	126	89	15c
Orange juice, Minute Maid frozen	12-oz can	1.54	4Q 92	4c
Oranges, navel	lb	0.50	4/93	16r
Peaches	29-oz can	1.33	4Q 92	4c
Peanut butter, creamy, all sizes	lb	1.82	4/93	16r
Pears, Anjou	lb	0.85	4/93	16r
Peas Sweet, Del Monte or Green Giant	15-17 oz can	0.64	4Q 92	4c
Pork, exp	year	130	89	15c
Pork chops, center cut, bone-in	lb	3.17	4/93	16r
Potato chips	16 oz	2.68	4/93	16r
Potatoes, white	lb	0.26	4/93	16r
Potatoes, white or red	10-lb sack	2.63	4Q 92	4c
Poultry, exp	year	73	89	15c
Round roast, graded & ungraded, ex USDA prime & choice	lb	2.88	4/93	16r
Round roast, USDA choice, boneless	lb	2.96	4/93	16r
Sausage, Jimmy Dean, 100% pork	lb	2.67	4Q 92	4c
Shortening, vegetable oil blends	lb	0.79	4/93	16r
Shortening, vegetable, Crisco	3-lb can	2.47	4Q 92	4c
Soft drink, Coca Cola	2 liter	1.01	4Q 92	4c
Spaghetti and macaroni	lb	0.76	4/93	16r
Steak, rib eye, USDA choice, boneless	lb	6.29	4/93	16r
Steak, round, USDA choice, boneless	lb	3.24	4/93	16r
Steak, sirloin, graded & ungraded, ex USDA prime & choice	lb	4.00	4/93	16r
Steak, sirloin, USDA choice, bone-in	lb	3.57	4/93	16r
Steak, sirloin, USDA choice, boneless	lb	4.17	4/93	16r
Steak, T-bone	lb	5.01	4Q 92	4c
Steak, T-bone, USDA choice, bone-in	lb	5.60	4/93	16r
Strawberries, dry pint	12 oz	0.90	4/93	16r
Sugar, cane or beet	4 lb	1.33	4Q 92	4c
Sugar, white	lb	0.36	4/93	16r
Sugar, white, 33-80 oz pk	lb	0.35	4/93	16r
Sugar and other sweets, exp	year	74	89	15c
Tobacco products, exp	year	289	89	15c
Tomatoes, field grown	lb	0.99	4/93	16r
Tomatoes, Hunt's or Del Monte	14.5-oz can	0.83	4Q 92	4c
Tuna, chunk, light	6.125-6.5 oz can	0.64	4Q 92	4c
Tuna, chunk, light	lb	1.76	4/93	16r
Turkey, frozen, whole	lb	0.91	4/93	16r
Vegetables, fresh, exp	year	86	89	15c
Vegetables, processed, exp	year	66	89	15c
Health Care				
ACCRA Index, Health Care		100.20	4Q 92	4c
Analgesic, Aspirin, Bayer, 325 mg tablets	100	4.34	4Q 92	4c
Childbirth, cesarean, hospital		4688	91	62r
Childbirth, cesarean, physician's fee		2053	91	62r
Childbirth, normal, hospital		2657	91	62r
Childbirth, normal, physician's fee		1492	91	62r
Dentist's fee, adult teeth cleaning and periodic oral exam	visit	45.30	4Q 92	4c
Doctor's fee, routine exam, established patient	visit	38.70	4Q 92	4c
Drugs, exp	year	319	89	15c
Health care, exp	year	1377	89	15c
Health insurance, exp	year	527	89	15c
Hospital care, semiprivate room	day	273.83	90	27c
Hospital care, semiprivate room	day	338.60	4Q 92	4c
Medical insurance premium, per employee, small group comprehensive	month	360.35	10/91	25c
Medical plan per employee	year	3443	91	45r
Medical services, exp	year	463	89	15c
Medical supplies, exp	year	68	89	15c

Saint Louis, MO - continued

Item	Per	Value	Date	Ref.
Health Care - continued				
Mental health care, exp	capita	37.60-53.67	90	38s
Mental health care, exp, state mental health agency	capita	35.47	90	38s
Mental health care, hospital psychiatric services, non-Federal, exp	capita	22.53	88	38s
Mental health care, mental health organization, multiservice, exp	capita	6.98	88	38s
Mental health care, psychiatric hospitals, private, exp	capita	5.96	88	38s
Mental health care, psychiatric out-patient clinics, freestanding, exp	capita	0.79	88	38s
Mental health care, state and county mental hospitals, exp	capita	33.35	88	38s
Mental health care, VA medical centers, exp	capita	3.33	88	38s
Nursing home, semi-private room, average	month	2498	92	59c
Physician fee, family practice, first-visit		76.00	91	62r
Physician fee, family practice, revisit		33.00	91	62r
Physician fee, general practice, first-visit		61.00	91	62r
Physician fee, general practice, revisit		31.00	91	62r
Physician fee, general surgeon, first-visit		65.00	91	62r
Physician fee, general surgeon, revisit		35.00	91	62r
Physician fee, internal medicine, first-visit		91.00	91	62r
Physician fee, internal medicine, revisit		40.00	91	62r
Physician fee, median, neurosurgeon, first-visit		106.00	91	62r
Physician fee, median, nonsurgical specialist, first-visit		90.00	91	62r
Physician fee, median, orthopedic surgeon, first-visit		83.00	91	62r
Physician fee, median, surgical specialist, first-visit		61.00	91	62r
Physician fee, neurosurgeon, revisit		41.00	91	62r
Physician fee, nonsurgical specialist, revisit		40.00	91	62r
Physician fee, obstetrics/gynecology, first-visit		61.00	91	62r
Physician fee, obstetrics/gynecology, revisit		40.00	91	62r
Physician fee, orthopedic surgeon, revisit		41.00	91	62r
Physician fee, pediatrician, first-visit		46.00	91	62r
Physician fee, pediatrician, revisit		33.00	91	62r
Physician fee, surgical specialist, revisit		36.00	91	62r
Substance abuse, hospital ancillary charge	incident	1380	90	70s
Substance abuse, hospital physician charge	incident	560	90	70s
Substance abuse, hospital room and board	incident	5670	90	70s
Household Goods				
Appliance repair, home, service call, washing machine	min labor charge	26.98	4Q 92	4c
Appliances, major, exp	year	144	89	15c
Appliances, small, exp	year	56	89	15c
Equipment, misc., exp	year	435	89	15c
Floor coverings, exp	year	48	89	15c
Furnishings and equipment, exp	year	1078	89	15c
Furniture, exp	year	309	89	15c
Household products, misc., exp	year	140	89	15c
Household textiles, exp	year	87	89	15c
Housekeeping supplies, exp	year	350	89	15c
Laundry and cleaning supplies, exp	year	94	89	15c
Laundry detergent, Tide Ultra, Bold, or Cheer	42 oz	3.39	4Q 92	4c
Tissues, facial, Kleenex brand	175-count box	1.06	4Q 92	4c
TVs, radios, sound equipment, exp	year	422	89	15c
Housing				
ACCRA Index, Housing		96.40	4Q 92	4c
Dwellings, exp	year	2995	89	15c
Home, median price	unit	83.20		26c

Values are in dollars or fractions of dollars. In the column headed *Ref*, references are shown to sources. Each reference is followed by a letter. These refer to the geographical level for which data were reported: s=State, r=Region, and c=City or metro. The abbreviation *ex* is used to mean *except* or *excluding*; *exp* stands for expenditures. For other abbreviations and further explanations, please see the Introduction.

Saint Louis, MO - continued

Item	Per	Value	Date	Ref.
Housing				
House, 1,800 sq ft, 8,000 sq ft lot, new, urban	total	102204	4Q 92	4c
House payment, principal and interest, 25% down payment	month	564	4Q 92	4c
Household expenses, misc.	year	238	89	15c
Household operations, exp	year	470	89	15c
Housing, exp	year	8351	89	15c
Lodging, exp	year	380	89	15c
Maintenance, repairs, insurance, and other, exp	year	724	89	15c
Mortgage interest, exp	year	1832	89	15c
Mortgage rate, incl. points & origination fee, 30-year fixed or adjustable rate	per-cent	8.04	4Q 92	4c
Rent, apartment, 2 bedrooms - 1-1/2 to 2 baths, unfurnished, 950 sq ft, water	month	542	4Q 92	4c
Rental unit, 1 bedroom	month	426	93	23c
Rental unit, 2 bedroom	month	503	93	23c
Rental unit, 3 bedroom	month	628	93	23c
Rental unit, 4 bedroom	month	704	93	23c
Rental unit, efficiency	month	351	93	23c
Rented dwellings, exp	year	862	89	15c
Shelter, exp	year	4237	89	15c
Insurance and Pensions				
Auto insurance, private passenger	year	551.85	91	63s
Insurance, life and other personal, exp	year	434	89	15c
Insurance and pensions, personal, exp	year	2304	89	15c
Pensions and social security, exp	year	1870	89	15c
Vehicle insurance	year	591	89	15c
Personal Goods				
Products and services, exp	year	320	89	15c
Shampoo, Alberto VO5	15 oz	1.28	4Q 92	4c
Toothpaste, Crest or Colgate	6-7 oz	1.86	4Q 92	4c
Personal Services				
Dry cleaning, man's 2-piece suit		6.00	4Q 92	4c
Haircare, woman's shampoo, trim and blow-dry		21.20	4Q 92	4c
Haircut, man's barbershop, no styling		8.80	4Q 92	4c
Services, exp	year	231	89	15c
Restaurant Food				
Chicken, fried, thigh and drumstick		2.06	4Q 92	4c
Hamburger with cheese	1/4 lb	1.82	4Q 92	4c
Pizza, Pizza Hut or Pizza Inn, cheese, thin crust	12-13 in	7.63	4Q 92	4c
Taxes				
Property tax, exp	year	440	89	15c
Tax, cigarette	pack	13	91	77s
Tax, gasoline	gal	13	91	77s
Taxes, state	capita	969	91	77s
Transportation				
ACCRA Index, Transportation		100.50	4Q 92	4c
Auto rental, average	day	46.25	6/91	60c
Bus fare	one-way	1.00	3/93	2c
Bus fare, up to 10 miles	one-way	1.30	4Q 92	4c
Driver's license fee		7.50	12/90	43s
Limo fare, airport-city, average	day	6.00	6/91	60c
Public transit, exp	year	214	89	15c
Taxi fare, airport-city, average	day	16.50	6/91	60c
Tire balance, computer or spin balance, front	wheel	6.52	4Q 92	4c
Vehicle expenses, misc.	year	1575	89	15c
Vehicle finance charges	year	346	89	15c
Vehicle maintenance	year	504	89	15c
Vehicle registration and license plate	year	1.65-51.15	93	41s
Vehicle rental and license	year	134	89	15c

Saint Louis, MO - continued

Item	Per	Value	Date	Ref.
Travel				
Breakfast	day	6.68	6/91	60c
Business travel	day	152.00	92	86c
Dinner	day	20.19	6/91	60c
Dinner	day	22.15	92	85c
Lodging	day	108.87	91	60c
Lodging	day	113.00	92	85c
Lunch	day	11.01	6/91	60c
Travel, business	day	197.53	93	88c
Utilities				
ACCRA Index, Utilities		105.40	4Q 92	4c
Electricity	500 KWh	41.03	4/93	16c
Electricity	KWh	0.07	4/93	16c
Electricity	mil Btu	18.94	90	64s
Electricity, exp	year	943	89	15c
Electricity, partial electric and other energy, 1,800 sq ft living area new home	month	61.90	4Q 92	4c
Electricity, winter, 250 KWh	month	22.62	92	55c
Electricity, winter, 500 KWh	month	39.17	92	55c
Electricity, winter, 750 KWh	month	55.72	92	55c
Electricity, winter, 1000 KWh	month	66.69	92	55c
Utilities, fuels, public services, exp	year	2216	89	15c
Water, public services, exp	year	246	89	15c

Saint Paul, MN

Item	Per	Value	Date	Ref.
Composite ACCRA index		107.30	4Q 92	4c
Alcoholic Beverages				
Beer, Miller Lite or Budweiser, 12-oz containers	6 pack	3.93	4Q 92	4c
Liquor, J & B Scotch	750 ml	14.56	4Q 92	4c
Wine, Gallo Chablis blanc, 1.5 liter	bottle	6.59	4Q 92	4c
Clothing				
Jeans, man's denim		31.99	4Q 92	4c
Shirt, man's dress shirt		28.79	4Q 92	4c
Undervest, boy's size 10-14, cotton	3	4.99	4Q 92	4c
Communications				
Newspaper subscription, daily and Sunday home delivery, large-city	month	11.00	4Q 92	4c
Telephone bill, family of four	month	23.34	4Q 92	4c
Energy and Fuels				
Energy, combined forms, 1,800 sq ft heating area	month	96.32	4Q 92	4c
Energy, exc electricity, 1,800 sq ft heating area	month	48.14	4Q 92	4c
Gas, cooking, 10 therms	month	8.01	92	56c
Gas, cooking, 30 therms	month	16.02	92	56c
Gas, cooking, 50 therms	month	24.03	92	56c
Gas, heating, winter, 100 therms	month	44.06	92	56c
Gas, heating, winter, average use	month	92.13	92	56c
Gasoline, motor	gal	1.16	4Q 92	4c
Entertainment				
Bowling, evening rate	game	1.92	4Q 92	4c
Monopoly game, Parker Brothers', No. 9		12.79	4Q 92	4c
Movie	admis-sion	5.90	4Q 92	4c
Tennis balls, yellow, Wilson or Penn, 3	can	2.09	4Q 92	4c
Goods and Services				
ACCRA Index, Miscellaneous Goods and Services		106.20	4Q 92	4c
Groceries				
ACCRA Index, Groceries		100.00	4Q 92	4c
Babyfood, strained vegetables, lowest price	4-4.5 oz jar	0.38	4Q 92	4c
Bananas	lb	0.45	4Q 92	4c
Bread, white	24 oz	0.56	4Q 92	4c

Values are in dollars or fractions of dollars. In the column headed *Ref*, references are shown to sources. Each reference is followed by a letter. These refer to the geographical level for which data were reported: s=State, r=Region, and c=City or metro. The abbreviation *ex* is used to mean *except* or *excluding*; *exp* stands for expenditures. For other abbreviations and further explanations, please see the Introduction.

Saint Paul, MN - continued

Item	Per	Value	Date	Ref.
Groceries				
Cheese, Kraft grated Parmesan	8-oz canis-ter	3.13	4Q 92	4c
Chicken, fryer, whole	lb	0.91	4Q 92	4c
Cigarettes, Winston	carton	18.10	4Q 92	4c
Coffee, vacuum-packed	13-oz can	2.03	4Q 92	4c
Corn, frozen	10 oz	0.65	4Q 92	4c
Corn Flakes, Kellogg's or Post Toasties	18 oz	1.99	4Q 92	4c
Eggs, Grade A large	doz	0.67	4Q 92	4c
Ground beef or hamburger	lb	1.37	4Q 92	4c
Lettuce, iceberg	head	0.81	4Q 92	4c
Margarine, Blue Bonnet or Parkay cubes	lb	0.74	4Q 92	4c
Milk, whole	1/2 gal	1.36	4Q 92	4c
Orange juice, Minute Maid frozen	12-oz can	1.28	4Q 92	4c
Peaches	29-oz can	1.22	4Q 92	4c
Peas Sweet, Del Monte or Green Giant	15-17 oz can	0.60	4Q 92	4c
Potatoes, white or red	10-lb sack	1.67	4Q 92	4c
Sausage, Jimmy Dean, 100% pork	lb	2.77	4Q 92	4c
Shortening, vegetable, Crisco	3-lb can	2.11	4Q 92	4c
Soft drink, Coca Cola	2 liter	1.13	4Q 92	4c
Steak, T-bone	lb	4.87	4Q 92	4c
Sugar, cane or beet	4 lb	1.87	4Q 92	4c
Tomatoes, Hunt's or Del Monte	14.5-oz can	0.70	4Q 92	4c
Tuna, chunk, light	6.125-6.5 oz can	0.68	4Q 92	4c
Health Care				
ACCRA Index, Health Care		104.40	4Q 92	4c
Analgesic, Aspirin, Bayer, 325 mg tablets	100	5.49	4Q 92	4c
Dentist's fee, adult teeth cleaning and periodic oral exam	visit	45.80	4Q 92	4c
Doctor's fee, routine exam, established patient	visit	33.00	4Q 92	4c
Hospital care, semiprivate room	day	282.97	90	27c
Hospital care, semiprivate room	day	455.60	4Q 92	4c
Medical insurance premium, per employee, small group comprehensive	month	324.85	10/91	25c
Household Goods				
Appliance repair, home, service call, washing machine	min labor charge	31.79	4Q 92	4c
Laundry detergent, Tide Ultra, Bold, or Cheer	42 oz	4.07	4Q 92	4c
Tissues, facial, Kleenex brand	175-count box	1.22	4Q 92	4c
Housing				
ACCRA Index, Housing		117.10	4Q 92	4c
House, 1,800 sq ft, 8,000 sq ft lot, new, urban	total	125000	4Q 92	4c
House payment, principal and interest, 25% down payment	month	700	4Q 92	4c
Mortgage rate, incl. points & origination fee, 30-year fixed or adjustable rate	per-cent	8.18	4Q 92	4c
Rent, apartment, 2 bedrooms - 1-1/2 to 2 baths, unfurnished, 950 sq ft, water	month	624	4Q 92	4c
Personal Goods				
Shampoo, Alberto VO5	15 oz	1.75	4Q 92	4c
Toothpaste, Crest or Colgate	6-7 oz	2.31	4Q 92	4c
Personal Services				
Dry cleaning, man's 2-piece suit		6.77	4Q 92	4c

Saint Paul, MN - continued

Item	Per	Value	Date	Ref.
Personal Services - continued				
Haircare, woman's shampoo, trim and blow-dry		19.60	4Q 92	4c
Haircut, man's barbershop, no styling		9.25	4Q 92	4c
Restaurant Food				
Chicken, fried, thigh and drumstick		1.97	4Q 92	4c
Hamburger with cheese	1/4 lb	1.85	4Q 92	4c
Pizza, Pizza Hut or Pizza Inn, cheese, thin crust	12-13 in	7.59	4Q 92	4c
Transportation				
ACCRA Index, Transportation		109.30	4Q 92	4c
Bus fare, up to 10 miles	one-way	1.10	4Q 92	4c
Tire balance, computer or spin balance, front	wheel	7.30	4Q 92	4c
Utilities				
ACCRA Index, Utilities		91.40	4Q 92	4c
Electricity, partial electric and other energy, 1,800 sq ft living area new home	month	48.18	4Q 92	4c

Salem, OR

Item	Per	Value	Date	Ref.
Composite ACCRA index		104.50	4Q 92	4c
Alcoholic Beverages				
Beer, Miller Lite or Budweiser, 12-oz containers	6 pack	3.67	4Q 92	4c
Liquor, J & B Scotch	750 ml	20.05	4Q 92	4c
Wine, Gallo Chablis blanc, 1.5 liter	bottle	4.60	4Q 92	4c
Child Care				
Child care fee, average, center	hour	1.71	90	65r
Child care fee, average, nonregulated family day care	hour	1.32	90	65r
Child care fee, average, regulated family day care	hour	1.86	90	65r
Clothing				
Jeans, man's denim		35.18	4Q 92	4c
Shirt, man's dress shirt		24.10	4Q 92	4c
Undervest, boy's size 10-14, cotton	3	5.93	4Q 92	4c
Communications				
Long-distance telephone service, day, initial minute, 0-100 miles	min	0.13-0.26	91	12s
Long-distance telephone service, day, additional minute, 0-100 miles	min	0.10-0.21	91	12s
Long-distance telephone service, evenings/weekends, 0-100 mi, initial minute	min	0.07-0.13	91	12s
Long-distance telephone service, evenings/weekends, 0-100 mi, additional minute	min	0.04-0.07	91	12s
Newspaper subscription, daily and Sunday home delivery, large-city	month	10.50	4Q 92	4c
Telephone, flat rate	month	13.68	91	11c
Telephone bill, family of four	month	17.78	4Q 92	4c
Education				
Board, 4-yr private college/university	year	2004	91	22s
Board, 4-yr public college/university	year	1954	91	22s
Expenditures, local gov't, public elementary/secondary	pupil	5463	92	20s
Room, 4-year private college/university	year	1621	91	22s
Room, 4-year public college/university	year	1329	91	22s
Tuition, 2-year private college/university	year	7570	91	22s
Tuition, 2-year public college/university	year	794	91	22s
Tuition, 4-year private college/university	year	9606	91	22s
Tuition, 4-year public college/university, in-state	year	1906	91	22s
Energy and Fuels				
Coal	mil Btu	1.22	90	64s
Energy	mil Btu	8.39	90	64s
Energy, combined forms, 1,800 sq ft heating area	month	86.99	4Q 92	4c

Values are in dollars or fractions of dollars. In the column headed *Ref*, references are shown as sources. Each reference is followed by a letter. These refer to the geographical level for which data were reported: s=State, r=Region, and c=City or metro. The abbreviation *ex* is used to mean *except* or *excluding*; *exp* stands for expenditures. For other abbreviations and further explanations, please see the Introduction.

Salem, OR - continued

Item	Per	Value	Date	Ref.
Energy and Fuels				
Energy exp/householder, 1-family unit	year	362	90	28r
Energy exp/householder, <1,000 sq ft heating area	year	254	90	28r
Energy exp/householder, 1,000-1,999 sq ft heating area	year	358	90	28r
Energy exp/householder, 2,000+ sq ft heating area	year	467	90	28r
Energy exp/householder, mobile home	year	390	90	28r
Energy exp/householder, multifamily	year	252	90	28r
Gas, natural	mil Btu	4.28	90	64s
Gas, natural	000 cu ft	6.13	91	46s
Gas, natural, exp	year	429	91	46s
Gasoline, motor	gal	1.25	4Q 92	4c
Gasoline, unleaded regular	mil Btu	9.45	90	64s
Entertainment				
Bowling, evening rate	game	1.81	4Q 92	4c
Miniature golf admission	adult	6.18	92	1r
Miniature golf admission	child	5.14	92	1r
Monopoly game, Parker Brothers', No. 9		12.79	4Q 92	4c
Movie	admission	5.50	4Q 92	4c
Tennis balls, yellow, Wilson or Penn, 3	can	2.26	4Q 92	4c
Waterpark admission	adult	11.00	92	1r
Waterpark admission	child	8.55	92	1r
Funerals				
Casket, 18-gauge steel, velvet interior		1781.09	91	24r
Cosmetology, hair care, etc.		84.64	91	24r
Embalming		207.41	91	24r
Facility use for ceremony		205.76	91	24r
Hearse, local		105.14	91	24r
Limousine, local		83.21	91	24r
Remains to funeral home, transfer		113.82	91	24r
Service charge, professional		626.33	91	24r
Vault, concrete, non-metallic liner		599.54	91	24r
Viewing facilities, use		85.81	91	24r
Goods and Services				
ACCRA Index, Miscellaneous Goods and Services		108.00	4Q 92	4c
Groceries				
ACCRA Index, Groceries		94.40	4Q 92	4c
Apples, Red Delicious	lb	0.80	4/93	16r
Babyfood, strained vegetables, lowest price	4-4.5 oz jar	0.33	4Q 92	4c
Bacon	lb	1.79	4/93	16r
Bananas	lb	0.29	4Q 92	4c
Bananas	lb	0.53	4/93	16r
Bologna, all beef or mixed	lb	2.67	4/93	16r
Bread, white	24 oz	0.54	4Q 92	4c
Bread, white, pan	lb	0.81	4/93	16r
Carrots, short trimmed and topped	lb	0.39	4/93	16r
Cheese, Kraft grated Parmesan	8-oz canister	2.98	4Q 92	4c
Chicken, fresh, whole	lb	0.94	4/93	16r
Chicken, fryer, whole	lb	0.82	4Q 92	4c
Chicken breast, bone-in	lb	2.19	4/93	16r
Chuck roast, graded and ungraded, ex USDA prime and choice	lb	2.26	4/93	16r
Cigarettes, Winston	carton	16.70	4Q 92	4c
Coffee, 100% ground roast, all sizes	lb	2.33	4/93	16r
Coffee, vacuum-packed	13-oz can	2.44	4Q 92	4c
Corn, frozen	10 oz	0.62	4Q 92	4c
Corn Flakes, Kellogg's or Post Toasties	18 oz	1.55	4Q 92	4c
Eggs, Grade A large	doz	0.84	4Q 92	4c
Eggs, Grade AA large	doz	1.18	4/93	16r
Flour, white, all purpose	lb	0.22	4/93	16r
Grapefruit	lb	0.52	4/93	16r
Grapes, Thompson Seedless	lb	1.50	4/93	16r

Salem, OR - continued

Item	Per	Value	Date	Ref.
Groceries - continued				
Ground beef, 100% beef	lb	1.44	4/93	16r
Ground beef, lean and extra lean	lb	2.34	4/93	16r
Ground beef or hamburger	lb	1.47	4Q 92	4c
Ham, boneless, excluding canned	lb	2.56	4/93	16r
Honey, jar	8 oz	0.89-1.00	92	5r
Honey, jar	lb	1.35-1.97	92	5r
Honey, squeeze bear	12-oz	1.19-1.50	92	5r
Ice cream, prepackaged, bulk, regular	1/2 gal	2.40	4/93	16r
Lemons	lb	0.81	4/93	16r
Lettuce, iceberg	head	0.72	4Q 92	4c
Lettuce, iceberg	lb	0.84	4/93	16r
Margarine, Blue Bonnet or Parkay cubes	lb	0.40	4Q 92	4c
Margarine, stick	lb	0.81	4/93	16r
Milk, whole	1/2 gal	1.26	4Q 92	4c
Orange juice, Minute Maid frozen	12-oz can	1.05	4Q 92	4c
Oranges, navel	lb	0.48	4/93	16r
Peaches	29-oz can	1.35	4Q 92	4c
Peas Sweet, Del Monte or Green Giant	15-17 oz can	0.70	4Q 92	4c
Pork chops, center cut, bone-in	lb	3.25	4/93	16r
Potato chips	16 oz	2.89	4/93	16r
Potatoes, white	lb	0.38	4/93	16r
Potatoes, white or red	10-lb sack	1.83	4Q 92	4c
Round roast, graded & ungraded, ex USDA prime & choice	lb	3.00	4/93	16r
Round roast, USDA choice, boneless	lb	3.16	4/93	16r
Sausage, Jimmy Dean, 100% pork	lb	3.37	4Q 92	4c
Shortening, vegetable oil blends	lb	0.86	4/93	16r
Shortening, vegetable, Crisco	3-lb can	1.89	4Q 92	4c
Soft drink, Coca Cola	2 liter	1.28	4Q 92	4c
Spaghetti and macaroni	lb	0.84	4/93	16r
Steak, round, graded & ungraded, ex USDA prime & choice	lb	3.34	4/93	16r
Steak, round, USDA choice, boneless	lb	3.24	4/93	16r
Steak, sirloin, graded & ungraded, ex USDA prime & choice	lb	3.75	4/93	16r
Steak, sirloin, USDA choice, boneless	lb	4.49	4/93	16r
Steak, T-bone	lb	4.35	4Q 92	4c
Sugar, cane or beet	4 lb	1.11	4Q 92	4c
Sugar, white	lb	0.41	4/93	16r
Sugar, white, 33-80 oz pk	lb	0.38	4/93	16r
Tomatoes, field grown	lb	1.01	4/93	16r
Tomatoes, Hunt's or Del Monte	14.5-oz can	0.85	4Q 92	4c
Tuna, chunk, light	6.125-6.5 oz can	0.54	4Q 92	4c
Turkey, frozen, whole	lb	1.04	4/93	16r
Health Care				
ACCRA Index, Health Care		119.10	4Q 92	4c
Analgesic, Aspirin, Bayer, 325 mg tablets	100	4.15	4Q 92	4c
Childbirth, cesarean, hospital		5533	91	62r
Childbirth, cesarean, physician's fee		2053	91	62r
Childbirth, normal, hospital		2745	91	62r
Childbirth, normal, physician's fee		1492	91	62r
Dentist's fee, adult teeth cleaning and periodic oral exam	visit	71.40	4Q 92	4c
Doctor's fee, routine exam, established patient	visit	39.00	4Q 92	4c
Hospital care, semiprivate room	day	277.87	90	27c
Hospital care, semiprivate room	day	325.00	4Q 92	4c
Medical insurance premium, per employee, small group comprehensive	month	284.70	10/91	25c
Medical plan per employee	year	3421	91	45r
Mental health care, exp, state mental health agency	capita	40.68	90	38s
Mental health care, hospital psychiatric services, non-Federal, exp	capita	9.91	88	38s

Values are in dollars or fractions of dollars. In the column headed *Ref*, references are shown to sources. Each reference is followed by a letter. These refer to the geographical level for which data were reported: s=State, r=Region, and c=City or metro. The abbreviation *ex* is used to mean *except* or *excluding*; *exp* stands for expenditures. For other abbreviations and further explanations, please see the Introduction.

Salem, OR - continued

Health Care

Item	Per	Value	Date	Ref.
Mental health care, mental health organization, multiservice, exp	capita	25.94	88	38s
Mental health care, psychiatric hospitals, private, exp	capita	1.48	88	38s
Mental health care, psychiatric out-patient clinics, freestanding, exp	capita	3.50	88	38s
Mental health care, psychiatric partial-care organizations, freestanding, exp	capita	0.58	88	38s
Mental health care, state and county mental hospitals, exp	capita	18.67	88	38s
Mental health care, VA medical centers, exp	capita	2.53	88	38s
Physician fee, family practice, first-visit		111.00	91	62r
Physician fee, family practice, revisit		45.00	91	62r
Physician fee, general practice, first-visit		100.00	91	62r
Physician fee, general practice, revisit		40.00	91	62r
Physician fee, internal medicine, first-visit		137.00	91	62r
Physician fee, internal medicine, revisit		48.00	91	62r
Physician fee, median, neurosurgeon, first-visit		157.00	91	62r
Physician fee, median, nonsurgical specialist, first-visit		131.00	91	62r
Physician fee, median, orthopedic surgeon, first-visit		124.00	91	62r
Physician fee, median, plastic surgeon, first-visit		88.00	91	62r
Physician fee, median, surgical specialist, first-visit		100.00	91	62r
Physician fee, neurosurgeon, revisit		51.00	91	62r
Physician fee, nonsurgical specialist, revisit		47.00	91	62r
Physician fee, obstetrics/gynecology, first-visit		95.00	91	62r
Physician fee, obstetrics/gynecology, revisit		50.00	91	62r
Physician fee, orthopedic surgeon, revisit		51.00	91	62r
Physician fee, pediatrician, first-visit		81.00	91	62r
Physician fee, pediatrician, revisit		42.00	91	62r
Physician fee, plastic surgeon, revisit		48.00	91	62r
Physician fee, surgical specialist, revisit		49.00	91	62r
Substance abuse, hospital ancillary charge	incident	710	90	70s
Substance abuse, hospital physician charge	incident	70	90	70s
Substance abuse, hospital room and board	incident	3330	90	70s

Household Goods

Item	Per	Value	Date	Ref.
Appliance repair, home, service call, washing machine	min labor charge	30.69	4Q 92	4c
Laundry detergent, Tide Ultra, Bold, or Cheer	42 oz	3.69	4Q 92	4c
Tissues, facial, Kleenex brand	175-count box	1.24	4Q 92	4c

Housing

Item	Per	Value	Date	Ref.
ACCRA Index, Housing		106.90	4Q 92	4c
House, 1,800 sq ft, 8,000 sq ft lot, new, urban	total	121500	4Q 92	4c
House payment, principal and interest, 25% down payment	month	674	4Q 92	4c
Mortgage rate, incl. points & origination fee, 30-year fixed or adjustable rate	percent	8.08	4Q 92	4c
Rent, apartment, 2 bedrooms - 1-1/2 to 2 baths, unfurnished, 950 sq ft, water	month	488	4Q 92	4c
Rental unit, 1 bedroom	month	483	93	23c
Rental unit, 2 bedroom	month	568	93	23c
Rental unit, 3 bedroom	month	710	93	23c
Rental unit, 4 bedroom	month	795	93	23c
Rental unit, efficiency	month	394	93	23c

Insurance and Pensions

Item	Per	Value	Date	Ref.
Auto insurance, private passenger	year	598.04	91	63s

Salem, OR - continued

Personal Goods

Item	Per	Value	Date	Ref.
Shampoo, Alberto VO5	15 oz	1.25	4Q 92	4c
Toothpaste, Crest or Colgate	6-7 oz	1.90	4Q 92	4c

Personal Services

Item	Per	Value	Date	Ref.
Dry cleaning, man's 2-piece suit		7.24	4Q 92	4c
Haircare, woman's shampoo, trim and blow-dry		17.99	4Q 92	4c
Haircut, man's barbershop, no styling		7.60	4Q 92	4c

Restaurant Food

Item	Per	Value	Date	Ref.
Chicken, fried, thigh and drumstick		2.54	4Q 92	4c
Hamburger with cheese	1/4 lb	1.82	4Q 92	4c
Pizza, Pizza Hut or Pizza Inn, cheese, thin crust	12-13 in	9.30	4Q 92	4c

Taxes

Item	Per	Value	Date	Ref.
Tax, cigarette	pack	28	91	77s
Tax, gasoline	gal	22	91	77s
Taxes, state	capita	1037	91	77s

Transportation

Item	Per	Value	Date	Ref.
ACCRA Index, Transportation		112.40	4Q 92	4c
Bus fare	one-way	0.50	3/93	2c
Driver's license fee		15.00	12/90	43s
Tire balance, computer or spin balance, front	wheel	7.45	4Q 92	4c
Vehicle registration and license plate	year	32.50	93	53s

Travel

Item	Per	Value	Date	Ref.
Business travel	day	178.00	4/93	89r

Utilities

Item	Per	Value	Date	Ref.
ACCRA Index, Utilities		80.80	4Q 92	4c
Electricity	mil Btu	12.25	90	64s
Electricity, all electric, 1,800 sq ft living area new home	month	86.99	4Q 92	4c

Salem-Gloucester, MA

Child Care

Item	Per	Value	Date	Ref.
Child care fee, average, center	hour	2.18	90	65r
Child care fee, average, nonregulated family day care	hour	1.83	90	65r
Child care fee, average, regulated family day care	hour	2.02	90	65r

Communications

Item	Per	Value	Date	Ref.
Long-distance telephone service, day, initial minute, 0-100 miles	min	0.18-0.31	91	12s
Long-distance telephone service, day, additional minute, 0-100 miles	min	0.08-0.13	91	12s
Long-distance telephone service, evenings/weekends, 0-100 mi, initial minute	min	0.67-0.12	91	12s
Long-distance telephone service, evenings/weekends, 0-100 mi, additional minute	min	0.04-0.05	91	12s

Education

Item	Per	Value	Date	Ref.
Board, 4-yr private college/university	year	2698	91	22s
Board, 4-yr public college/university	year	1741	91	22s
Expenditures, local gov't, public elementary/secondary	pupil	6687	92	20s
Room, 4-year private college/university	year	2945	91	22s
Room, 4-year public college/university	year	2144	91	22s
Tuition, 2-year private college/university	year	7750	91	22s
Tuition, 2-year public college/university	year	1528	91	22s
Tuition, 4-year private college/university	year	12446	91	22s
Tuition, 4-year public college/university, in-state	year	2580	91	22s

Energy and Fuels

Item	Per	Value	Date	Ref.
Coal	mil Btu	1.77	90	64s
Energy	mil Btu	10.57	90	64s
Energy exp/householder, 1-family unit	year	588	90	28r

Values are in dollars or fractions of dollars. In the column headed *Ref*, references are shown to sources. Each reference is followed by a letter. These refer to the geographical level for which data were reported: s = State, r = Region, and c = City or metro. The abbreviation *ex* is used to mean *except* or *excluding*; *exp* stands for expenditures. For other abbreviations and further explanations, please see the Introduction.

Salem-Gloucester, MA - continued

Item	Per	Value	Date	Ref.
Energy and Fuels				
Energy exp/householder, <1,000 sq ft heating area	year	477	90	28r
Energy exp/householder, 1,000-1,999 sq ft heating area	year	517	90	28r
Energy exp/householder, 2,000+ sq ft heating area	year	630	90	28r
Energy exp/householder, mobile home	year	412	90	28r
Energy exp/householder, multifamily	year	498	90	28r
Gas, natural	mil Btu	5.55	90	64s
Gas, natural	000 cu ft	8.11	91	46s
Gas, natural, exp	year	741	91	46s
Gasoline, unleaded regular	mil Btu	9.53	90	64s
Entertainment				
Miniature golf admission	adult	6.18	92	1r
Miniature golf admission	child	5.14	92	1r
Waterpark admission	adult	11.00	92	1r
Waterpark admission	child	8.55	92	1r
Funerals				
Casket, 18-gauge steel, velvet interior		1853.42	91	24r
Cosmetology, hair care, etc.		98.33	91	24r
Embalming		273.94	91	24r
Facility use for ceremony		196.06	91	24r
Hearse, local		145.67	91	24r
Limousine, local		131.07	91	24r
Remains to funeral home, transfer		135.24	91	24r
Service charge, professional		843.16	91	24r
Vault, concrete, non-metallic liner		709.14	91	24r
Viewing facilities, use		229.85	91	24r
Groceries				
Apples, Red Delicious	lb	0.85	4/93	16r
Bacon	lb	2.12	4/93	16r
Bananas	lb	0.54	4/93	16r
Bread, white, pan	lb	0.81	4/93	16r
Butter	lb	2.02	4/93	16r
Carrots, short trimmed and topped	lb	0.51	4/93	16r
Chicken, fresh, whole	lb	1.04	4/93	16r
Chicken breast, bone-in	lb	2.21	4/93	16r
Chicken legs, bone-in	lb	1.16	4/93	16r
Chuck roast, USDA choice, boneless	lb	2.82	4/93	16r
Coffee, 100% ground roast, all sizes	lb	2.66	4/93	16r
Cucumbers	lb	0.85	4/93	16r
Eggs, Grade A large	doz	1.15	4/93	16r
Grapefruit	lb	0.45	4/93	16r
Grapes, Thompson Seedless	lb	1.52	4/93	16r
Ground beef, lean and extra lean	lb	2.36	4/93	16r
Ground chuck, 100% beef	lb	2.02	4/93	16r
Honey, jar	8 oz	0.96-1.75	92	5r
Honey, jar	lb	1.50-3.00	92	5r
Honey, squeeze bear	12-oz	1.50-1.99	92	5r
Ice cream, prepackaged, bulk, regular	1/2 gal	2.80	4/93	16r
Lemons	lb	0.96	4/93	16r
Lettuce, iceberg	lb	0.95	4/93	16r
Margarine, stick	lb	0.81	4/93	16r
Milk, fresh, whole, fortified	1/2 gal	1.30	4/93	16r
Oranges, navel	lb	0.56	4/93	16r
Peanut butter, creamy, all sizes	lb	1.88	4/93	16r
Pork chops, center cut, bone-in	lb	3.34	4/93	16r
Potato chips	16 oz	2.88	4/93	16r
Potatoes, white	lb	0.37	4/93	16r
Rib roast, USDA choice, bone-in	lb	4.94	4/93	16r
Round roast, USDA choice, boneless	lb	3.17	4/93	16r
Shortening, vegetable oil blends	lb	0.98	4/93	16r
Spaghetti and macaroni	lb	0.82	4/93	16r
Steak, round, graded & ungraded, ex USDA prime & choice	lb	4.04	4/93	16r
Steak, round, USDA choice, boneless	lb	3.90	4/93	16r
Steak, sirloin, USDA choice, boneless	lb	4.97	4/93	16r
Strawberries, dry pint	12 oz	0.90	4/93	16r
Sugar, white	lb	0.50	4/93	16r
Sugar, white, 33-80 oz pk	lb	0.41	4/93	16r

Salem-Gloucester, MA - continued

Item	Per	Value	Date	Ref.
Groceries - continued				
Tomatoes, field grown	lb	1.23	4/93	16r
Tuna, chunk, light	lb	2.22	4/93	16r
Turkey, frozen, whole	lb	1.04	4/93	16r
Health Care				
Childbirth, cesarean, hospital		5826	91	62r
Childbirth, cesarean, physician's fee		2053	91	62r
Childbirth, normal, hospital		2964	91	62r
Childbirth, normal, physician's fee		1492	91	62r
Health care spending, state	capita	3031	3/93	84s
Medical plan per employee	year	3958	91	45r
Mental health care, exp	capita	53.68-118.35	90	38s
Mental health care, exp, state mental health agency	capita	83.91	90	38s
Mental health care, hospital psychiatric services, non-Federal, exp	capita	22.67	88	38s
Mental health care, mental health organization, multiservice, exp	capita	36.07	88	38s
Mental health care, psychiatric hospitals, private, exp	capita	38.65	88	38s
Mental health care, psychiatric out-patient clinics, freestanding, exp	capita	4.41	88	38s
Mental health care, psychiatric partial-care organizations, freestanding, exp	capita	0.92	88	38s
Mental health care, state and county mental hospitals, exp	capita	30.59	88	38s
Mental health care, VA medical centers, exp	capita	21.14	88	38s
Substance abuse, hospital ancillary charge	incident	1310	90	70s
Substance abuse, hospital physician charge	incident	460	90	70s
Substance abuse, hospital room and board	incident	3450	90	70s
Insurance and Pensions				
Auto insurance, private passenger	year	912.83	91	63s
Taxes				
Tax, cigarette	pack	26	91	77s
Tax, gasoline	gal	21	91	77s
Taxes, state	capita	1615	91	77s
Transportation				
Driver's license fee		35.00	12/90	43s
Travel				
Business travel	day	165.00	4/93	89r
Utilities				
Electricity	mil Btu	25.93	90	64s

Salina, KS

Item	Per	Value	Date	Ref.
Composite ACCRA index		96.10	4Q 92	4c
Alcoholic Beverages				
Beer, Miller Lite or Budweiser, 12-oz containers	6 pack	3.66	4Q 92	4c
Liquor, J & B Scotch	750 ml	17.32	4Q 92	4c
Wine, Gallo Chablis blanc, 1.5 liter	bottle	5.16	4Q 92	4c
Clothing				
Jeans, man's denim		29.00	4Q 92	4c
Shirt, man's dress shirt		21.33	4Q 92	4c
Undervest, boy's size 10-14, cotton	3	4.37	4Q 92	4c
Communications				
Newspaper subscription, daily and Sunday home delivery, large-city	month	11.50	4Q 92	4c
Telephone, flat rate	month	10.70	91	11c
Telephone bill, family of four	month	17.40	4Q 92	4c
Energy and Fuels				
Energy, combined forms, 1,800 sq ft heating area	month	84.24	4Q 92	4c

Values are in dollars or fractions of dollars. In the column headed *Ref*, references are shown to sources. Each reference is followed by a letter. These refer to the geographical level for which data were reported: s=State, r=Region, and c=City or metro. The abbreviation *ex* is used to mean *except* or *excluding*; *exp* stands for expenditures. For other abbreviations and further explanations, please see the Introduction.

Salina, KS - continued

Item	Per	Value	Date	Ref.
Energy and Fuels				
Energy, exc electricity, 1,800 sq ft heating area	month	31.07	4Q 92	4c
Gas, cooking, 10 therms	month	9.19	92	56c
Gas, cooking, 30 therms	month	17.57	92	56c
Gas, cooking, 50 therms	month	25.95	92	56c
Gas, heating, winter, 100 therms	month	46.95	92	56c
Gas, heating, winter, average use	month	92.99	92	56c
Gasoline, motor	gal	1.10	4Q 92	4c
Entertainment				
Bowling, evening rate	game	1.48	4Q 92	4c
Monopoly game, Parker Brothers', No. 9		9.96	4Q 92	4c
Movie	admission	4.50	4Q 92	4c
Tennis balls, yellow, Wilson or Penn, 3	can	2.70	4Q 92	4c
Goods and Services				
ACCRA Index, Miscellaneous Goods and Services		95.40	4Q 92	4c
Groceries				
ACCRA Index, Groceries		97.80	4Q 92	4c
Babyfood, strained vegetables, lowest price	4-4.5 oz jar	0.38	4Q 92	4c
Bananas	lb	0.42	4Q 92	4c
Bread, white	24 oz	0.56	4Q 92	4c
Cheese, Kraft grated Parmesan	8-oz canister	3.51	4Q 92	4c
Chicken, fryer, whole	lb	0.62	4Q 92	4c
Cigarettes, Winston	carton	18.04	4Q 92	4c
Coffee, vacuum-packed	13-oz can	1.94	4Q 92	4c
Corn, frozen	10 oz	0.76	4Q 92	4c
Corn Flakes, Kellogg's or Post Toasties	18 oz	2.10	4Q 92	4c
Eggs, Grade A large	doz	0.74	4Q 92	4c
Ground beef or hamburger	lb	1.39	4Q 92	4c
Lettuce, iceberg	head	0.72	4Q 92	4c
Margarine, Blue Bonnet or Parkay cubes	lb	0.72	4Q 92	4c
Milk, whole	1/2 gal	1.37	4Q 92	4c
Orange juice, Minute Maid frozen	12-oz can	1.47	4Q 92	4c
Peaches	29-oz can	1.61	4Q 92	4c
Peas Sweet, Del Monte or Green Giant	15-17 oz can	0.63	4Q 92	4c
Potatoes, white or red	10-lb sack	2.08	4Q 92	4c
Sausage, Jimmy Dean, 100% pork	lb	2.07	4Q 92	4c
Shortening, vegetable, Crisco	3-lb can	2.89	4Q 92	4c
Soft drink, Coca Cola	2 liter	1.02	4Q 92	4c
Steak, T-bone	lb	5.09	4Q 92	4c
Sugar, cane or beet	4 lb	1.42	4Q 92	4c
Tomatoes, Hunt's or Del Monte	14.5-oz can	0.89	4Q 92	4c
Tuna, chunk, light	6.125-6.5 oz can	0.68	4Q 92	4c
Health Care				
ACCRA Index, Health Care		94.00	4Q 92	4c
Analgesic, Aspirin, Bayer, 325 mg tablets	100	4.83	4Q 92	4c
Dentist's fee, adult teeth cleaning and periodic oral exam	visit	41.00	4Q 92	4c
Doctor's fee, routine exam, established patient	visit	35.67	4Q 92	4c
Hospital care, semiprivate room	day	245.00	90	27c
Hospital care, semiprivate room	day	318.50	4Q 92	4c
Household Goods				
Appliance repair, home, service call, washing machine	min labor charge	32.00	4Q 92	4c

Salina, KS - continued

Item	Per	Value	Date	Ref.
Household Goods - continued				
Laundry detergent, Tide Ultra, Bold, or Cheer	42 oz	4.15	4Q 92	4c
Tissues, facial, Kleenex brand	175-count box	1.12	4Q 92	4c
Housing				
ACCRA Index, Housing		98.70	4Q 92	4c
House, 1,800 sq ft, 8,000 sq ft lot, new, urban	total	117800	4Q 92	4c
House payment, principal and interest, 25% down payment	month	670	4Q 92	4c
Mortgage rate, incl. points & origination fee, 30-year fixed or adjustable rate	percent	8.36	4Q 92	4c
Rent, apartment, 2 bedrooms - 1-1/2 to 2 baths, unfurnished, 950 sq ft, water	month	340	4Q 92	4c
Personal Goods				
Shampoo, Alberto VO5	15 oz	1.15	4Q 92	4c
Toothpaste, Crest or Colgate	6-7 oz	1.97	4Q 92	4c
Personal Services				
Dry cleaning, man's 2-piece suit		5.33	4Q 92	4c
Haircare, woman's shampoo, trim and blow-dry		17.67	4Q 92	4c
Haircut, man's barbershop, no styling		8.25	4Q 92	4c
Restaurant Food				
Chicken, fried, thigh and drumstick		2.04	4Q 92	4c
Hamburger with cheese	1/4 lb	1.86	4Q 92	4c
Pizza, Pizza Hut or Pizza Inn, cheese, thin crust	12-13 in	7.00	4Q 92	4c
Transportation				
ACCRA Index, Transportation		106.30	4Q 92	4c
Tire balance, computer or spin balance, front	wheel	7.50	4Q 92	4c
Utilities				
ACCRA Index, Utilities		78.40	4Q 92	4c
Electricity, partial electric and other energy, 1,800 sq ft living area new home	month	53.17	4Q 92	4c

Salinas-Seaside-Monterey, CA

Item	Per	Value	Date	Ref.
Child Care				
Child care fee, average, center	hour	1.71	90	65r
Child care fee, average, nonregulated family day care	hour	1.32	90	65r
Child care fee, average, regulated family day care	hour	1.86	90	65r
Communications				
Long-distance telephone service, day, initial minute, 0-100 miles	min	0.17-0.40	91	12s
Long-distance telephone service, day, additional minute, 0-100 miles	min	0.07-0.31	91	12s
Long-distance telephone service, evenings/ weekends, 0-100 mi, initial minute	min	0.07-0.16	91	12s
Long-distance telephone service, evenings/ weekends, 0-100 mi, additional minute	min	0.03-0.12	91	12s
Education				
Board, 4-yr private college/university	year	2515	91	22s
Board, 4-yr public college/university	year	2268	91	22s
Expenditures, local gov't, public elementary/secondary	pupil	4866	92	20s
Room, 4-year private college/university	year	2622	91	22s
Room, 4-year public college/university	year	2406	91	22s
Tuition, 2-year private college/university	year	7942	91	22s
Tuition, 2-year public college/university	year	114	91	22s
Tuition, 4-year private college/university	year	10863	91	22s
Tuition, 4-year public college/university, in-state	year	1220	91	22s

Values are in dollars or fractions of dollars. In the column headed *Ref*, references are shown to sources. Each reference is followed by a letter. These refer to the geographical level for which data were reported: s = State, r = Region, and c = City or metro. The abbreviation *ex* is used to mean *except* or *excluding*; *exp* stands for expenditures. For other abbreviations and further explanations, please see the Introduction.

Salinas-Seaside-Monterey, CA - continued

Item	Per	Value	Date	Ref.
Energy and Fuels				
Coal	mil Btu	2.01	90	64s
Energy	mil Btu	9.08	90	64s
Energy exp/householder, 1-family unit	year	362	90	28r
Energy exp/householder, <1,000 sq ft heating area	year	254	90	28r
Energy exp/householder, 1,000-1,999 sq ft heating area	year	358	90	28r
Energy exp/householder, 2,000+ sq ft heating area	year	467	90	28r
Energy exp/householder, mobile home	year	390	90	28r
Energy exp/householder, multifamily	year	252	90	28r
Gas, natural	mil Btu	4.31	90	64s
Gas, natural	000 cu ft	6.27	91	46s
Gas, natural, exp	year	369	91	46s
Gasoline, unleaded regular	mil Btu	8.57	90	64s
Entertainment				
Miniature golf admission	adult	6.18	92	1r
Miniature golf admission	child	5.14	92	1r
Waterpark admission	adult	11.00	92	1r
Waterpark admission	child	8.55	92	1r
Funerals				
Casket, 18-gauge steel, velvet interior		1781.09	91	24r
Cosmetology, hair care, etc.		84.64	91	24r
Embalming		207.41	91	24r
Facility use for ceremony		205.76	91	24r
Hearse, local		105.14	91	24r
Limousine, local		83.21	91	24r
Remains to funeral home, transfer		113.82	91	24r
Service charge, professional		626.33	91	24r
Vault, concrete, non-metallic liner		599.54	91	24r
Viewing facilities, use		85.81	91	24r
Groceries				
Apples, Red Delicious	lb	0.80	4/93	16r
Bacon	lb	1.79	4/93	16r
Bananas	lb	0.53	4/93	16r
Bologna, all beef or mixed	lb	2.67	4/93	16r
Bread, white, pan	lb	0.81	4/93	16r
Carrots, short trimmed and topped	lb	0.39	4/93	16r
Chicken, fresh, whole	lb	0.94	4/93	16r
Chicken breast, bone-in	lb	2.19	4/93	16r
Chuck roast, graded and ungraded, ex USDA prime and choice	lb	2.26	4/93	16r
Coffee, 100% ground roast, all sizes	lb	2.33	4/93	16r
Eggs, Grade AA large	doz	1.18	4/93	16r
Flour, white, all purpose	lb	0.22	4/93	16r
Grapefruit	lb	0.52	4/93	16r
Grapes, Thompson Seedless	lb	1.50	4/93	16r
Ground beef, 100% beef	lb	1.44	4/93	16r
Ground beef, lean and extra lean	lb	2.34	4/93	16r
Ham, boneless, excluding canned	lb	2.56	4/93	16r
Honey, jar	8 oz	0.89-1.00	92	5r
Honey, jar	lb	1.35-1.97	92	5r
Honey, squeeze bear	12-oz	1.19-1.50	92	5r
Ice cream, prepackaged, bulk, regular	1/2 gal	2.40	4/93	16r
Lemons	lb	0.81	4/93	16r
Lettuce, iceberg	lb	0.84	4/93	16r
Margarine, stick	lb	0.81	4/93	16r
Oranges, navel	lb	0.48	4/93	16r
Pork chops, center cut, bone-in	lb	3.25	4/93	16r
Potato chips	16 oz	2.89	4/93	16r
Potatoes, white	lb	0.38	4/93	16r
Round roast, graded & ungraded, ex USDA prime & choice	lb	3.00	4/93	16r
Round roast, USDA choice, boneless	lb	3.16	4/93	16r
Shortening, vegetable oil blends	lb	0.86	4/93	16r
Spaghetti and macaroni	lb	0.84	4/93	16r
Steak, round, graded & ungraded, ex USDA prime & choice	lb	3.34	4/93	16r
Steak, round, USDA choice, boneless	lb	3.24	4/93	16r

Salinas-Seaside-Monterey, CA - continued

Item	Per	Value	Date	Ref.
Groceries - continued				
Steak, sirloin, graded & ungraded, ex USDA prime & choice	lb	3.75	4/93	16r
Steak, sirloin, USDA choice, boneless	lb	4.49	4/93	16r
Sugar, white	lb	0.41	4/93	16r
Sugar, white, 33-80 oz pk	lb	0.38	4/93	16r
Tomatoes, field grown	lb	1.01	4/93	16r
Turkey, frozen, whole	lb	1.04	4/93	16r
Health Care				
Cardizem 60 mg tablets	30	24.04	92	49s
Cector 250 mg tablets	15	35.87	92	49s
Childbirth, cesarean, hospital		5533	91	62r
Childbirth, cesarean, physician's fee		2053	91	62r
Childbirth, normal, hospital		2745	91	62r
Childbirth, normal, physician's fee		1492	91	62r
Health care spending, state	capita	2894	3/93	84s
Medical plan per employee	year	3421	91	45r
Mental health care, exp	capita	37.60-53.67	90	38s
Mental health care, exp, state mental health agency	capita	42.32	90	38s
Mental health care, hospital psychiatric services, non-Federal, exp	capita	10.64	88	38s
Mental health care, mental health organization, multiservice, exp	capita	28.56	88	38s
Mental health care, psychiatric hospitals, private, exp	capita	18.60	88	38s
Mental health care, psychiatric out-patient clinics, freestanding, exp	capita	2.28	88	38s
Mental health care, psychiatric partial-care organizations, freestanding, exp	capita	0.24	88	38s
Mental health care, state and county mental hospitals, exp	capita	13.60	88	38s
Mental health care, VA medical centers, exp	capita	2.33	88	38s
Mevacor 20 mg tablets	30	67.62	92	49s
Physician fee, family practice, first-visit		111.00	91	62r
Physician fee, family practice, revisit		45.00	91	62r
Physician fee, general practice, first-visit		100.00	91	62r
Physician fee, general practice, revisit		40.00	91	62r
Physician fee, internal medicine, first-visit		137.00	91	62r
Physician fee, internal medicine, revisit		48.00	91	62r
Physician fee, median, neurosurgeon, first-visit		157.00	91	62r
Physician fee, median, nonsurgical specialist, first-visit		131.00	91	62r
Physician fee, median, orthopedic surgeon, first-visit		124.00	91	62r
Physician fee, median, plastic surgeon, first-visit		88.00	91	62r
Physician fee, median, surgical specialist, first-visit		100.00	91	62r
Physician fee, neurosurgeon, revisit		51.00	91	62r
Physician fee, nonsurgical specialist, revisit		47.00	91	62r
Physician fee, obstetrics/gynecology, first-visit		95.00	91	62r
Physician fee, obstetrics/gynecology, revisit		50.00	91	62r
Physician fee, orthopedic surgeon, revisit		51.00	91	62r
Physician fee, pediatrician, first-visit		81.00	91	62r
Physician fee, pediatrician, revisit		42.00	91	62r
Physician fee, plastic surgeon, revisit		48.00	91	62r
Physician fee, surgical specialist, revisit		49.00	91	62r
Prozac 20 mg tablets	14	33.22	92	49s
Substance abuse, hospital ancillary charge	incident	1760	90	70s
Substance abuse, hospital physician charge	incident	750	90	70s
Substance abuse, hospital room and board	incident	6390	90	70s
Tagamet 300 mg tablets	100	77.08	92	49s
Xanax 0.25 mg tablets	90	64.08	92	49s
Zantac 160 mg tablets	60	92.31	92	49s

Values are in dollars or fractions of dollars. In the column headed *Ref*, references are shown to sources. Each reference is followed by a letter. These refer to the geographical level for which data were reported: s=State, r=Region, and c=City or metro. The abbreviation *ex* is used to mean *except* or *excluding*; *exp* stands for expenditures. For other abbreviations and further explanations, please see the Introduction.

Salinas-Seaside-Monterey, CA - continued

Item	Per	Value	Date	Ref.
Housing				
Home, median price	unit	131,200	92	58s
Insurance and Pensions				
Auto insurance, private passenger	year	904.37	91	63s
Taxes				
Tax, cigarette	pack	35	91	77s
Tax, gasoline	gal	16	91	77s
Taxes, state	capita	1477	91	77s
Transportation				
Driver's license fee		10.00	12/90	43s
Travel				
Business travel	day	178.00	4/93	89r
Utilities				
Electricity	mil Btu	25.98	90	64s

Salt Lake City, UT

Item	Per	Value	Date	Ref.
Composite ACCRA index		97.00	4Q 92	4c
Alcoholic Beverages				
Beer, Miller Lite or Budweiser, 12-oz containers	6 pack	3.89	4Q 92	4c
Liquor, J & B Scotch	750 ml	19.25	4Q 92	4c
Wine, Gallo Chablis blanc, 1.5 liter	bottle	4.95	4Q 92	4c
Child Care				
Child care fee, average, center	hour	1.71	90	65r
Child care fee, average, nonregulated family day care	hour	1.32	90	65r
Child care fee, average, regulated family day care	hour	1.86	90	65r
Clothing				
Jeans, man's denim		23.59	4Q 92	4c
Shirt, man's dress shirt		22.40	4Q 92	4c
Undervest, boy's size 10-14, cotton	3	5.18	4Q 92	4c
Communications				
Long-distance telephone service, day, initial minute, 0-100 miles	min	0.11-0.25	91	12s
Long-distance telephone service, day, additional minute, 0-100 miles	min	0.06-0.21	91	12s
Long-distance telephone service, evenings/ weekends, 0-100 mi, initial minute	min	0.07-0.15	91	12s
Long-distance telephone service, evenings/ weekends, 0-100 mi, additional minute	min	0.05-0.13	91	12s
Newspaper subscription, daily and Sunday home delivery, large-city	month	12.00	4Q 92	4c
Telephone, flat rate	month	7.98	91	11c
Telephone bill, family of four	month	17.95	4Q 92	4c
Education				
Board, 4-yr private college/university	year	1791	91	22s
Board, 4-yr public college/university	year	1571	91	22s
Expenditures, local gov't, public elementary/secondary	pupil	3092	92	20s
Room, 4-year private college/university	year	1195	91	22s
Room, 4-year public college/university	year	1170	91	22s
Tuition, 2-year private college/university	year	4319	91	22s
Tuition, 2-year public college/university	year	1173	91	22s
Tuition, 4-year private college/university	year	2182	91	22s
Tuition, 4-year public college/university, in-state	year	1524	91	22s
Energy and Fuels				
Coal	mil Btu	1.24	90	64s
Energy	mil Btu	7.16	90	64s
Energy, combined forms, 1,800 sq ft heating area	month	98.19	4Q 92	4c
Energy, exc electricity, 1,800 sq ft heating area	month	48.83	4Q 92	4c
Energy exp/householder, 1-family unit	year	372	90	28r

Salt Lake City, UT - continued

Item	Per	Value	Date	Ref.
Energy and Fuels - continued				
Energy exp/householder, <1,000 sq ft heating area	year	335	90	28r
Energy exp/householder, 1,000-1,999 sq ft heating area	year	365	90	28r
Energy exp/householder, 2,000+ sq ft heating area	year	411	90	28r
Energy exp/householder, mobile home	year	305	90	28r
Energy exp/householder, multifamily	year	372	90	28r
Gas, cooking, winter, 10 therms	month	9.82	92	56c
Gas, cooking, winter, 30 therms	month	19.46	92	56c
Gas, cooking, winter, 50 therms	month	29.11	92	56c
Gas, heating, winter, 100 therms	month	53.21	92	56c
Gas, heating, winter, average use	month	84.55	92	56c
Gas, natural	mil Btu	4.17	90	64s
Gas, natural	000 cu ft	5.44	91	46s
Gas, natural, exp	year	603	91	46s
Gasoline, motor	gal	1.13	4Q 92	4c
Gasoline, unleaded regular	mil Btu	9.09	90	64s
Entertainment				
Bowling, evening rate	game	1.83	4Q 92	4c
Miniature golf admission	adult	6.18	92	1r
Miniature golf admission	child	5.14	92	1r
Monopoly game, Parker Brothers', No. 9		11.93	4Q 92	4c
Movie	admission	5.50	4Q 92	4c
Tennis balls, yellow, Wilson or Penn, 3	can	2.31	4Q 92	4c
Waterpark admission	adult	11.00	92	1r
Waterpark admission	child	8.55	92	1r
Funerals				
Casket, 18-gauge steel, velvet interior		1929.04	91	24r
Cosmetology, hair care, etc.		88.52	91	24r
Embalming		249.33	91	24r
Facility use for ceremony		182.75	91	24r
Hearse, local		110.04	91	24r
Limousine, local		66.67	91	24r
Remains to funeral home, transfer		84.58	91	24r
Service charge, professional		593.00	91	24r
Vault, concrete, non-metallic liner		647.38	91	24r
Viewing facilities, use		99.87	91	24r
Goods and Services				
ACCRA Index, Miscellaneous Goods and Services		101.80	4Q 92	4c
Groceries				
ACCRA Index, Groceries		99.60	4Q 92	4c
Apples, Red Delicious	lb	0.80	4/93	16r
Babyfood, strained vegetables, lowest price	4-4.5 oz jar	0.39	4Q 92	4c
Bacon	lb	1.79	4/93	16r
Bananas	lb	0.40	4Q 92	4c
Bananas	lb	0.53	4/93	16r
Bologna, all beef or mixed	lb	2.67	4/93	16r
Bread, white	24 oz	0.80	4Q 92	4c
Bread, white, pan	lb	0.81	4/93	16r
Carrots, short trimmed and topped	lb	0.39	4/93	16r
Cheese, Kraft grated Parmesan	8-oz canister	3.99	4Q 92	4c
Chicken, fresh, whole	lb	0.94	4/93	16r
Chicken, fryer, whole	lb	0.91	4Q 92	4c
Chicken breast, bone-in	lb	2.19	4/93	16r
Chuck roast, graded and ungraded, ex USDA prime and choice	lb	2.26	4/93	16r
Cigarettes, Winston	carton	18.29	4Q 92	4c
Coffee, 100% ground roast, all sizes	lb	2.33	4/93	16r
Coffee, vacuum-packed	13-oz can	2.27	4Q 92	4c
Corn, frozen	10 oz	0.59	4Q 92	4c
Corn Flakes, Kellogg's or Post Toasties	18 oz	2.07	4Q 92	4c
Eggs, Grade A large	doz	0.77	4Q 92	4c

Values are in dollars or fractions of dollars. In the column headed *Ref*, references are shown to sources. Each reference is followed by a letter. These refer to the geographical level for which data were reported: s=State, r=Region, and c=City or metro. The abbreviation *ex* is used to mean *except* or *excluding*; *exp* stands for expenditures. For other abbreviations and further explanations, please see the Introduction.

Salt Lake City, UT - continued

Item	Per	Value	Date	Ref.
Groceries				
Eggs, Grade AA large	doz	1.18	4/93	16r
Flour, white, all purpose	lb	0.22	4/93	16r
Grapefruit	lb	0.52	4/93	16r
Grapes, Thompson Seedless	lb	1.50	4/93	16r
Ground beef, 100% beef	lb	1.44	4/93	16r
Ground beef, lean and extra lean	lb	2.34	4/93	16r
Ground beef or hamburger	lb	1.00	4Q 92	4c
Ham, boneless, excluding canned	lb	2.56	4/93	16r
Honey, jar	8 oz	0.89-1.00	92	5r
Honey, jar	lb	1.49-2.25	92	5r
Honey, squeeze bear	12-oz	1.00-1.89	92	5r
Ice cream, prepackaged, bulk, regular	1/2 gal	2.40	4/93	16r
Lemons	lb	0.81	4/93	16r
Lettuce, iceberg	head	0.52	4Q 92	4c
Lettuce, iceberg	lb	0.84	4/93	16r
Margarine, Blue Bonnet or Parkay cubes	lb	0.50	4Q 92	4c
Margarine, stick	lb	0.81	4/93	16r
Milk, whole	1/2 gal	1.59	4Q 92	4c
Orange juice, Minute Maid frozen	12-oz can	1.38	4Q 92	4c
Oranges, navel	lb	0.48	4/93	16r
Peaches	29-oz can	1.35	4Q 92	4c
Peas Sweet, Del Monte or Green Giant	15-17 oz can	0.75	4Q 92	4c
Pork chops, center cut, bone-in	lb	3.25	4/93	16r
Potato chips	16 oz	2.89	4/93	16r
Potatoes, white	lb	0.38	4/93	16r
Potatoes, white or red	10-lb sack	2.01	4Q 92	4c
Round roast, graded & ungraded, ex USDA prime & choice	lb	3.00	4/93	16r
Round roast, USDA choice, boneless	lb	3.16	4/93	16r
Sausage, Jimmy Dean, 100% pork	lb	2.97	4Q 92	4c
Shortening, vegetable oil blends	lb	0.86	4/93	16r
Shortening, vegetable, Crisco	3-lb can	2.49	4Q 92	4c
Soft drink, Coca Cola	2 liter	1.04	4Q 92	4c
Spaghetti and macaroni	lb	0.84	4/93	16r
Steak, round, graded & ungraded, ex USDA prime & choice	lb	3.34	4/93	16r
Steak, round, USDA choice, boneless	lb	3.24	4/93	16r
Steak, sirloin, graded & ungraded, ex USDA prime & choice	lb	3.75	4/93	16r
Steak, sirloin, USDA choice, boneless	lb	4.49	4/93	16r
Steak, T-bone	lb	4.02	4Q 92	4c
Sugar, cane or beet	4 lb	1.51	4Q 92	4c
Sugar, white	lb	0.41	4/93	16r
Sugar, white, 33-80 oz pk	lb	0.38	4/93	16r
Tomatoes, field grown	lb	1.01	4/93	16r
Tomatoes, Hunt's or Del Monte	14.5-oz can	0.73	4Q 92	4c
Tuna, chunk, light	6.125-6.5 oz can	0.60	4Q 92	4c
Turkey, frozen, whole	lb	1.04	4/93	16r
Health Care				
ACCRA Index, Health Care		102.40	4Q 92	4c
Analgesic, Aspirin, Bayer, 325 mg tablets	100	4.59	4Q 92	4c
Childbirth, cesarean, hospital		5533	91	62r
Childbirth, cesarean, physician's fee		2053	91	62r
Childbirth, normal, hospital		2745	91	62r
Childbirth, normal, physician's fee		1492	91	62r
Dentist's fee, adult teeth cleaning and periodic oral exam	visit	44.00	4Q 92	4c
Doctor's fee, routine exam, established patient	visit	40.00	4Q 92	4c
Hospital care, semiprivate room	day	351.12	90	27c
Hospital care, semiprivate room	day	362.00	4Q 92	4c
Medical insurance premium, per employee, small group comprehensive	month	332.15	10/91	25c
Medical plan per employee	year	3218	91	45r

Salt Lake City, UT - continued

Item	Per	Value	Date	Ref.
Health Care - continued				
Mental health care, exp	capita	20.37-28.83	90	38s
Mental health care, exp, state mental health agency	capita	20.57	90	38s
Mental health care, hospital psychiatric services, non-Federal, exp	capita	15.78	88	38s
Mental health care, mental health organization, multiservice, exp	capita	25.60	88	38s
Mental health care, psychiatric hospitals, private, exp	capita	27.77	88	38s
Mental health care, psychiatric out-patient clinics, freestanding, exp	capita	0.25	88	38s
Mental health care, state and county mental hospitals, exp	capita	9.29	88	38s
Mental health care, VA medical centers, exp	capita	7.36	88	38s
Physician fee, family practice, first-visit		111.00	91	62r
Physician fee, family practice, revisit		45.00	91	62r
Physician fee, general practice, first-visit		100.00	91	62r
Physician fee, general practice, revisit		40.00	91	62r
Physician fee, internal medicine, first-visit		137.00	91	62r
Physician fee, internal medicine, revisit		48.00	91	62r
Physician fee, median, neurosurgeon, first-visit		157.00	91	62r
Physician fee, median, nonsurgical specialist, first-visit		131.00	91	62r
Physician fee, median, orthopedic surgeon, first-visit		124.00	91	62r
Physician fee, median, plastic surgeon, first-visit		88.00	91	62r
Physician fee, median, surgical specialist, first-visit		100.00	91	62r
Physician fee, neurosurgeon, revisit		51.00	91	62r
Physician fee, nonsurgical specialist, revisit		47.00	91	62r
Physician fee, obstetrics/gynecology, first-visit		95.00	91	62r
Physician fee, obstetrics/gynecology, revisit		50.00	91	62r
Physician fee, orthopedic surgeon, revisit		51.00	91	62r
Physician fee, pediatrician, first-visit		81.00	91	62r
Physician fee, pediatrician, revisit		42.00	91	62r
Physician fee, plastic surgeon, revisit		48.00	91	62r
Physician fee, surgical specialist, revisit		49.00	91	62r
Substance abuse, hospital ancillary charge	incident	1890	90	70s
Substance abuse, hospital physician charge	incident	470	90	70s
Substance abuse, hospital room and board	incident	5560	90	70s
Household Goods				
Appliance repair, home, service call, washing machine	min labor charge	40.00	4Q 92	4c
Laundry detergent, Tide Ultra, Bold, or Cheer	42 oz	3.46	4Q 92	4c
Tissues, facial, Kleenex brand	175-count box	1.14	4Q 92	4c
Housing				
ACCRA Index, Housing		88.00	4Q 92	4c
Home, median price	unit	76.50		26c
House, 1,800 sq ft, 8,000 sq ft lot, new, urban	total	91131	4Q 92	4c
House payment, principal and interest, 25% down payment	month	513	4Q 92	4c
Mortgage rate, incl. points & origination fee, 30-year fixed or adjustable rate	percent	8.23	4Q 92	4c
Rent, apartment, 2 bedrooms - 1-1/2 to 2 baths, unfurnished, 950 sq ft, water	month	499	4Q 92	4c
Rental unit, 1 bedroom	month	343	93	23c
Rental unit, 2 bedroom	month	429	93	23c
Rental unit, 3 bedroom	month	536	93	23c
Rental unit, 4 bedroom	month	601	93	23c

Values are in dollars or fractions of dollars. In the column headed *Ref*, references are shown to sources. Each reference is followed by a letter. These refer to the geographical level for which data were reported: s=State, r=Region, and c=City or metro. The abbreviation *ex* is used to mean *except* or *excluding*; *exp* stands for expenditures. For other abbreviations and further explanations, please see the Introduction.

Salt Lake City, UT - continued

Item	Per	Value	Date	Ref.
Housing				
Rental unit, efficiency	month	300	93	23c
Insurance and Pensions				
Auto insurance, private passenger	year	525.15	91	63s
Personal Goods				
Shampoo, Alberto VO5	15 oz	1.19	4Q 92	4c
Toothpaste, Crest or Colgate	6-7 oz	1.79	4Q 92	4c
Personal Services				
Dry cleaning, man's 2-piece suit		7.48	4Q 92	4c
Haircare, woman's shampoo, trim and blow-dry		16.38	4Q 92	4c
Haircut, man's barbershop, no styling		8.00	4Q 92	4c
Restaurant Food				
Chicken, fried, thigh and drumstick		2.05	4Q 92	4c
Hamburger with cheese	1/4 lb	1.97	4Q 92	4c
Pizza, Pizza Hut or Pizza Inn, cheese, thin crust	12-13 in	7.50	4Q 92	4c
Taxes				
Tax, cigarette	pack	26.50	91	77s
Tax, gasoline	gal	19.50	91	77s
Taxes, state	capita	1051	91	77s
Transportation				
ACCRA Index, Transportation		105.10	4Q 92	4c
Auto rental, average	day	43.25	6/91	60c
Bus fare	one-way	0.65	3/93	2c
Bus fare, up to 10 miles	one-way	0.65	4Q 92	4c
Driver's license fee		10.00	12/90	43s
Taxi fare, airport-city, average	day	10.00	6/91	60c
Tire balance, computer or spin balance, front	wheel	7.61	4Q 92	4c
Travel				
Breakfast	day	6.74	6/91	60c
Business travel	day	178.00	4/93	89r
Dinner	day	15.77	6/91	60c
Lodging	day	95.93	91	60c
Lunch	day	8.81	6/91	60c
Utilities				
ACCRA Index, Utilities		90.20	4Q 92	4c
Electricity	mil Btu	16.09	90	64s
Electricity, partial electric and other energy, 1,800 sq ft living area new home	month	49.38	4Q 92	4c
Electricity, winter, 250 KWh	month	18.91	92	55c
Electricity, winter, 500 KWh	month	36.96	92	55c
Electricity, winter, 750 KWh	month	54.94	92	55c
Electricity, winter, 1000 KWh	month	72.92	92	55c

San Angelo, TX

Item	Per	Value	Date	Ref.
Child Care				
Child care fee, average, center	hour	1.29	90	65r
Child care fee, average, nonregulated family day care	hour	0.89	90	65r
Child care fee, average, regulated family day care	hour	1.32	90	65r
Communications				
Long-distance telephone service, day, initial minute, 0-100 miles	min	0.10-0.46	91	12s
Long-distance telephone service, day, additional minute, 0-100 miles	min	0.06-0.45	91	12s
Education				
Board, 4-yr private college/university	year	1883	91	22s
Board, 4-yr public college/university	year	1605	91	22s
Expenditures, local gov't, public elementary/secondary	pupil	4593	92	20s
Room, 4-year private college/university	year	1620	91	22s

San Angelo, TX - continued

Item	Per	Value	Date	Ref.
Education - continued				
Room, 4-year public college/university	year	1532	91	22s
Tuition, 2-year private college/university	year	4394	91	22s
Tuition, 2-year public college/university	year	495	91	22s
Tuition, 4-year private college/university	year	6497	91	22s
Tuition, 4-year public college/university, in-state	year	986	91	22s
Energy and Fuels				
Coal	mil Btu	1.44	90	64s
Energy	mil Btu	6.48	90	64s
Energy exp/householder, 1-family unit	year	471	90	28r
Energy exp/householder, <1,000 sq ft heating area	year	384	90	28r
Energy exp/householder, 1,000-1,999 sq ft heating area	year	421	90	28r
Energy exp/householder, 2,000+ sq ft heating area	year	625	90	28r
Energy exp/householder, mobile home	year	271	90	28r
Energy exp/householder, multifamily	year	355	90	28r
Gas, natural	mil Btu	2.47	90	64s
Gas, natural	000 cu ft	5.71	91	46s
Gas, natural, exp	year	388	91	46s
Gasoline, unleaded regular	mil Btu	9.16	90	64s
Entertainment				
Miniature golf admission	adult	6.18	92	1r
Miniature golf admission	child	5.14	92	1r
Waterpark admission	adult	11.00	92	1r
Waterpark admission	child	8.55	92	1r
Funerals				
Casket, 18-gauge steel, velvet interior		2274.41	91	24r
Cosmetology, hair care, etc.		74.62	91	24r
Embalming		229.94	91	24r
Facility use for ceremony		176.61	91	24r
Hearse, local		116.34	91	24r
Limousine, local		72.68	91	24r
Remains to funeral home, transfer		87.72	91	24r
Service charge, professional		712.53	91	24r
Vault, concrete, non-metallic liner		750.55	91	24r
Viewing facilities, use		155.31	91	24r
Groceries				
Apples, Red Delicious	lb	0.79	4/93	16r
Bacon	lb	1.75	4/93	16r
Bananas	lb	0.42	4/93	16r
Beef, stew, boneless	lb	2.61	4/93	16r
Bologna, all beef or mixed	lb	2.24	4/93	16r
Bread, white, pan	lb	0.64	4/93	16r
Bread, whole wheat, pan	lb	0.96	4/93	16r
Cabbage	lb	0.37	4/93	16r
Carrots, short trimmed and topped	lb	0.47	4/93	16r
Celery	lb	0.64	4/93	16r
Cheese, American	lb	2.98	4/93	16r
Cheese, Cheddar	lb	3.28	4/93	16r
Chicken, fresh, whole	lb	0.77	4/93	16r
Chicken breast, bone-in	lb	1.92	4/93	16r
Chicken legs, bone-in	lb	1.06	4/93	16r
Chuck roast, graded and ungraded, ex USDA prime and choice	lb	2.40	4/93	16r
Chuck roast, USDA choice, bone-in	lb	2.19	4/93	16r
Chuck roast, USDA choice, boneless	lb	2.38	4/93	16r
Coffee, 100% ground roast, all sizes	lb	2.48	4/93	16r
Crackers, soda, salted	lb	1.15	4/93	16r
Eggs, Grade A large	doz	0.96	4/93	16r
Flour, white, all purpose	lb	0.24	4/93	16r
Frankfurters, all meat or all beef	lb	2.01	4/93	16r
Grapefruit	lb	0.44	4/93	16r
Grapes, Thompson Seedless	lb	1.40	4/93	16r
Ground beef, 100% beef	lb	1.58	4/93	16r
Ground beef, lean and extra lean	lb	2.09	4/93	16r
Ground chuck, 100% beef	lb	1.98	4/93	16r
Ham, boneless, excluding canned	lb	2.89	4/93	16r

Values are in dollars or fractions of dollars. In the column headed *Ref*, references are shown to sources. Each reference is followed by a letter. These refer to the geographical level for which data were reported: s = State, r = Region, and c = City or metro. The abbreviation *ex* is used to mean *except* or *excluding*; *exp* stands for *expenditures*. For other abbreviations and further explanations, please see the Introduction.

San Angelo, TX - continued

Item	Per	Value	Date	Ref.
Groceries				
Ham, picnic, shoulder, bone-in, smoked	lb	1.02	4/93	16r
Ham, rump or steak half, bone-in, smoked	lb	1.48	4/93	16r
Honey, jar	8 oz	0.73-1.19	92	5r
Honey, jar	lb	1.10-1.79	92	5r
Honey, squeeze bear	12-oz	1.19-1.50	92	5r
Ice cream, prepackaged, bulk, regular	1/2 gal	2.41	4/93	16r
Lemons	lb	1.05	4/93	16r
Lettuce, iceberg	lb	0.81	4/93	16r
Margarine, stick	lb	0.88	4/93	16r
Oranges, navel	lb	0.55	4/93	16r
Pears, Anjou	lb	0.92	4/93	16r
Pork chops, center cut, bone-in	lb	3.13	4/93	16r
Potato chips	16 oz	2.94	4/93	16r
Potatoes, white	lb	0.43	4/93	16r
Rib roast, USDA choice, bone-in	lb	4.63	4/93	16r
Rice, white, long grain, uncooked	lb	0.45	4/93	16r
Round roast, graded & ungraded, ex USDA prime & choice	lb	3.03	4/93	16r
Round roast, USDA choice, boneless	lb	3.09	4/93	16r
Sausage, fresh, loose	lb	2.08	4/93	16r
Short ribs, bone-in	lb	2.66	4/93	16r
Shortening, vegetable oil blends	lb	0.69	4/93	16r
Spaghetti and macaroni	lb	0.81	4/93	16r
Steak, rib eye, USDA choice, boneless	lb	6.24	4/93	16r
Steak, round, graded & ungraded, ex USDA prime & choice	lb	3.31	4/93	16r
Steak, round, USDA choice, boneless	lb	3.34	4/93	16r
Steak, sirloin, graded & ungraded, ex USDA prime & choice	lb	4.19	4/93	16r
Steak, sirloin, USDA choice, boneless	lb	4.46	4/93	16r
Steak, T-bone, USDA choice, bone-in	lb	5.25	4/93	16r
Strawberries, dry pint	12 oz	0.92	4/93	16r
Sugar, white	lb	0.39	4/93	16r
Sugar, white, 33-80 oz pk	lb	0.38	4/93	16r
Tomatoes, field grown	lb	0.88	4/93	16r
Tuna, chunk, light	lb	1.79	4/93	16r
Turkey, frozen, whole	lb	1.04	4/93	16r
Yogurt, natural, fruit flavored	1/2 pint	0.57	4/93	16r
Health Care				
Childbirth, cesarean, hospital		5034	91	62r
Childbirth, cesarean, physician's fee		2053	91	62r
Childbirth, normal, hospital		2712	91	62r
Childbirth, normal, physician's fee		1492	91	62r
Health care spending, state	capita	2192	3/93	84s
Mental health care, exp	capita	20.37-28.83	90	38s
Mental health care, exp, state mental health agency	capita	22.72	90	38s
Mental health care, hospital psychiatric services, non-Federal, exp	capita	7.95	88	38s
Mental health care, mental health organization, multiservice, exp	capita	12.05	88	38s
Mental health care, psychiatric hospitals, private, exp	capita	37.78	88	38s
Mental health care, psychiatric out-patient clinics, freestanding, exp	capita	0.43	88	38s
Mental health care, state and county mental hospitals, exp	capita	12.54	88	38s
Mental health care, VA medical centers, exp	capita	5.35	88	38s
Physician fee, family practice, first-visit		75.00	91	62r
Physician fee, family practice, revisit		34.00	91	62r
Physician fee, general practice, first-visit		61.00	91	62r
Physician fee, general practice, revisit		32.00	91	62r
Physician fee, general surgeon, first-visit		64.00	91	62r
Physician fee, general surgeon, revisit		40.00	91	62r
Physician fee, internal medicine, first-visit		98.00	91	62r
Physician fee, internal medicine, revisit		40.00	91	62r
Physician fee, median, neurosurgeon, first-visit		130.00	91	62r
Physician fee, median, nonsurgical specialist, first-visit		95.00	91	62r

San Angelo, TX - continued

Item	Per	Value	Date	Ref.
Health Care - continued				
Physician fee, median, orthopedic surgeon, first-visit		91.00	91	62r
Physician fee, median, plastic surgeon, first-visit		66.00	91	62r
Physician fee, median, surgical specialist, first-visit		62.00	91	62r
Physician fee, neurosurgeon, revisit		50.00	91	62r
Physician fee, nonsurgical specialist, revisit		40.00	91	62r
Physician fee, obstetrics/gynecology, first-visit		64.00	91	62r
Physician fee, obstetrics/gynecology, revisit		41.00	91	62r
Physician fee, orthopedic surgeon, revisit		40.00	91	62r
Physician fee, pediatrician, first-visit		49.00	91	62r
Physician fee, pediatrician, revisit		33.00	91	62r
Physician fee, plastic surgeon, revisit		43.00	91	62r
Physician fee, surgical specialist, revisit		37.00	91	62r
Substance abuse, hospital ancillary charge	incident	3750	90	70s
Substance abuse, hospital physician charge	incident	1080	90	70s
Substance abuse, hospital room and board	incident	5320	90	70s
Insurance and Pensions				
Auto insurance, private passenger	year	709.79	91	63s
Taxes				
Tax, cigarette	pack	41	91	77s
Tax, gasoline	gal	20	91	77s
Taxes, state	capita	923	91	77s
Transportation				
Driver's license fee		16.00	12/90	43s
Travel				
Business travel	day	193.00	4/93	89r
Utilities				
Electricity	mil Btu	17.09	90	64s
Electricity, residential	KWh	5.92	2/93	94s

San Antonio, TX

Item	Per	Value	Date	Ref.
Composite ACCRA index		96.80	4Q 92	4c
Alcoholic Beverages				
Beer, Miller Lite or Budweiser, 12-oz containers	6 pack	3.87	4Q 92	4c
Liquor, J & B Scotch	750 ml	18.58	4Q 92	4c
Wine, Gallo Chablis blanc, 1.5 liter	bottle	4.45	4Q 92	4c
Child Care				
Child care fee, average, center	hour	1.29	90	65r
Child care fee, average, nonregulated family day care	hour	0.89	90	65r
Child care fee, average, regulated family day care	hour	1.32	90	65r
Clothing				
Jeans, man's denim		25.59	4Q 92	4c
Shirt, man's dress shirt		28.39	4Q 92	4c
Undervest, boy's size 10-14, cotton	3	4.91	4Q 92	4c
Communications				
Long-distance telephone service, day, initial minute, 0-100 miles	min	0.10-0.46	91	12s
Long-distance telephone service, day, additional minute, 0-100 miles	min	0.06-0.45	91	12s
Newspaper subscription, daily and Sunday home delivery, large-city	month	7.50	4Q 92	4c
Telephone, flat rate	month	9.85	91	11c
Telephone, residential, private line, rotary, unlimited calling	month	15.48	10/91	78c
Telephone bill, family of four	month	17.33	4Q 92	4c

Values are in dollars or fractions of dollars. In the column headed *Ref*, references are shown to sources. Each reference is followed by a letter. These refer to the geographical level for which data were reported: s = State, r = Region, and c = City or metro. The abbreviation *ex* is used to mean *except* or *excluding*; *exp* stands for expenditures. For other abbreviations and further explanations, please see the Introduction.

San Antonio, TX - continued

Item	Per	Value	Date	Ref.
Education				
Board, 4-yr private college/university	year	1883	91	22s
Board, 4-yr public college/university	year	1605	91	22s
Expenditures, local gov't, public elementary/secondary	pupil	4593	92	20s
Room, 4-year private college/university	year	1620	91	22s
Room, 4-year public college/university	year	1532	91	22s
Tuition, 2-year private college/university	year	4394	91	22s
Tuition, 2-year public college/university	year	495	91	22s
Tuition, 4-year private college/university	year	6497	91	22s
Tuition, 4-year public college/university, in-state	year	986	91	22s
Energy and Fuels				
Coal	mil Btu	1.44	90	64s
Energy	mil Btu	6.48	90	64s
Energy, combined forms, 1,800 sq ft heating area	month	89.85	4Q 92	4c
Energy, exc electricity, 1,800 sq ft heating area	month	26.43	4Q 92	4c
Energy exp/householder, 1-family unit	year	471	90	28r
Energy exp/householder, <1,000 sq ft heating area	year	384	90	28r
Energy exp/householder, 1,000-1,999 sq ft heating area	year	421	90	28r
Energy exp/householder, 2,000+ sq ft heating area	year	625	90	28r
Energy exp/householder, mobile home	year	271	90	28r
Energy exp/householder, multifamily	year	355	90	28r
Gas, natural	mil Btu	2.47	90	64s
Gas, natural	000 cu ft	5.71	91	46s
Gas, natural, exp	year	388	91	46s
Gasoline, motor	gal	1.15	4Q 92	4c
Gasoline, unleaded regular	mil Btu	9.16	90	64s
Entertainment				
Bowling, evening rate	game	2.33	4Q 92	4c
Miniature golf admission	adult	6.18	92	1r
Miniature golf admission	child	5.14	92	1r
Monopoly game, Parker Brothers', No. 9		10.98	4Q 92	4c
Movie	admission	5.50	4Q 92	4c
Tennis balls, yellow, Wilson or Penn, 3	can	2.38	4Q 92	4c
Waterpark admission	adult	11.00	92	1r
Waterpark admission	child	8.55	92	1r
Funerals				
Casket, 18-gauge steel, velvet interior		2274.41	91	24r
Cosmetology, hair care, etc.		74.62	91	24r
Embalming		229.94	91	24r
Facility use for ceremony		176.61	91	24r
Hearse, local		116.34	91	24r
Limousine, local		72.68	91	24r
Remains to funeral home, transfer		87.72	91	24r
Service charge, professional		712.53	91	24r
Vault, concrete, non-metallic liner		750.55	91	24r
Viewing facilities, use		155.31	91	24r
Goods and Services				
ACCRA Index, Miscellaneous Goods and Services		100.50	4Q 92	4c
Goods and services	year	14669	92	36c
Goods and services, misc.	year	14669	92	37c
Groceries				
ACCRA Index, Groceries		94.30	4Q 92	4c
Apples, Red Delicious	lb	0.79	4/93	16r
Babyfood, strained vegetables, lowest price	4-4.5 oz jar	0.23	4Q 92	4c
Bacon	lb	1.75	4/93	16r
Bananas	lb	0.47	4Q 92	4c
Bananas	lb	0.42	4/93	16r
Beef, stew, boneless	lb	2.61	4/93	16r
Bologna, all beef or mixed	lb	2.24	4/93	16r

San Antonio, TX - continued

Item	Per	Value	Date	Ref.
Groceries - continued				
Bread, white	24 oz	0.53	4Q 92	4c
Bread, white, pan	lb	0.64	4/93	16r
Bread, whole wheat, pan	lb	0.96	4/93	16r
Cabbage	lb	0.37	4/93	16r
Carrots, short trimmed and topped	lb	0.47	4/93	16r
Celery	lb	0.64	4/93	16r
Cheese, American	lb	2.98	4/93	16r
Cheese, Cheddar	lb	3.28	4/93	16r
Cheese, Kraft grated Parmesan	8-oz canister	3.10	4Q 92	4c
Chicken, fresh, whole	lb	0.77	4/93	16r
Chicken, fryer, whole	lb	0.63	4Q 92	4c
Chicken breast, bone-in	lb	1.92	4/93	16r
Chicken legs, bone-in	lb	1.06	4/93	16r
Chuck roast, graded and ungraded, ex USDA prime and choice	lb	2.40	4/93	16r
Chuck roast, USDA choice, bone-in	lb	2.19	4/93	16r
Chuck roast, USDA choice, boneless	lb	2.38	4/93	16r
Cigarettes, Winston	carton	19.09	4Q 92	4c
Coffee, 100% ground roast, all sizes	lb	2.48	4/93	16r
Coffee, vacuum-packed	13-oz can	1.75	4Q 92	4c
Corn, frozen	10 oz	0.61	4Q 92	4c
Corn Flakes, Kellogg's or Post Toasties	18 oz	1.84	4Q 92	4c
Crackers, soda, salted	lb	1.15	4/93	16r
Eggs, Grade A large	doz	0.75	4Q 92	4c
Eggs, Grade A large	doz	0.96	4/93	16r
Flour, white, all purpose	lb	0.24	4/93	16r
Frankfurters, all meat or all beef	lb	2.01	4/93	16r
Grapefruit	lb	0.44	4/93	16r
Grapes, Thompson Seedless	lb	1.40	4/93	16r
Ground beef, 100% beef	lb	1.58	4/93	16r
Ground beef, lean and extra lean	lb	2.09	4/93	16r
Ground beef or hamburger	lb	1.27	4Q 92	4c
Ground chuck, 100% beef	lb	1.98	4/93	16r
Ham, boneless, excluding canned	lb	2.89	4/93	16r
Ham, picnic, shoulder, bone-in, smoked	lb	1.02	4/93	16r
Ham, rump or steak half, bone-in, smoked	lb	1.48	4/93	16r
Honey, jar	8 oz	0.73-1.19	92	5r
Honey, jar	lb	1.10-1.79	92	5r
Honey, squeeze bear	12-oz	1.19-1.50	92	5r
Ice cream, prepackaged, bulk, regular	1/2 gal	2.41	4/93	16r
Lemons	lb	1.05	4/93	16r
Lettuce, iceberg	head	0.89	4Q 92	4c
Lettuce, iceberg	lb	0.81	4/93	16r
Margarine, Blue Bonnet or Parkay cubes	lb	0.53	4Q 92	4c
Margarine, stick	lb	0.88	4/93	16r
Milk, whole	1/2 gal	1.21	4Q 92	4c
Orange juice, Minute Maid frozen	12-oz can	1.27	4Q 92	4c
Oranges, navel	lb	0.55	4/93	16r
Peaches	29-oz can	1.41	4Q 92	4c
Pears, Anjou	lb	0.92	4/93	16r
Peas Sweet, Del Monte or Green Giant	15-17 oz can	0.58	4Q 92	4c
Pork chops, center cut, bone-in	lb	3.13	4/93	16r
Potato chips	16 oz	2.94	4/93	16r
Potatoes, white	lb	0.43	4/93	16r
Potatoes, white or red	10-lb sack	2.09	4Q 92	4c
Rib roast, USDA choice, bone-in	lb	4.63	4/93	16r
Rice, white, long grain, uncooked	lb	0.45	4/93	16r
Round roast, graded & ungraded, ex USDA prime & choice	lb	3.03	4/93	16r
Round roast, USDA choice, boneless	lb	3.09	4/93	16r
Sausage, fresh, loose	lb	2.08	4/93	16r
Sausage, Jimmy Dean, 100% pork	lb	2.43	4Q 92	4c
Short ribs, bone-in	lb	2.66	4/93	16r
Shortening, vegetable oil blends	lb	0.69	4/93	16r

Values are in dollars or fractions of dollars. In the column headed *Ref*, references are shown to sources. Each reference is followed by a letter. These refer to the geographical level for which data were reported: s=State, r=Region, and c=City or metro. The abbreviation *ex* is used to mean *except* or *excluding*; *exp* stands for expenditures. For other abbreviations and further explanations, please see the Introduction.

San Antonio, TX - continued

Item	Per	Value	Date	Ref.
Groceries				
Shortening, vegetable, Crisco	3-lb can	1.97	4Q 92	4c
Soft drink, Coca Cola	2 liter	1.77	4Q 92	4c
Spaghetti and macaroni	lb	0.81	4/93	16r
Steak, rib eye, USDA choice, boneless	lb	6.24	4/93	16r
Steak, round, graded & ungraded, ex USDA prime & choice	lb	3.31	4/93	16r
Steak, round, USDA choice, boneless	lb	3.34	4/93	16r
Steak, sirloin, graded & ungraded, ex USDA prime & choice	lb	4.19	4/93	16r
Steak, sirloin, USDA choice, boneless	lb	4.46	4/93	16r
Steak, T-bone	lb	5.45	4Q 92	4c
Steak, T-bone, USDA choice, bone-in	lb	5.25	4/93	16r
Strawberries, dry pint	12 oz	0.92	4/93	16r
Sugar, cane or beet	4 lb	1.45	4Q 92	4c
Sugar, white	lb	0.39	4/93	16r
Sugar, white, 33-80 oz pk	lb	0.38	4/93	16r
Tomatoes, field grown	lb	0.88	4/93	16r
Tomatoes, Hunt's or Del Monte	14.5-oz can	0.62	4Q 92	4c
Tuna, chunk, light	6.125-6.5 oz can	0.65	4Q 92	4c
Tuna, chunk, light	lb	1.79	4/93	16r
Turkey, frozen, whole	lb	1.04	4/93	16r
Yogurt, natural, fruit flavored	1/2 pint	0.57	4/93	16r
Health Care				
ACCRA Index, Health Care		104.10	4Q 92	4c
Analgesic, Aspirin, Bayer, 325 mg tablets	100	4.87	4Q 92	4c
Childbirth, cesarean, hospital		5034	91	62r
Childbirth, cesarean, physician's fee		2053	91	62r
Childbirth, normal, hospital		2712	91	62r
Childbirth, normal, physician's fee		1492	91	62r
Dentist's fee, adult teeth cleaning and periodic oral exam	visit	41.00	4Q 92	4c
Doctor's fee, routine exam, established patient	visit	47.00	4Q 92	4c
Health care spending, state	capita	2192	3/93	84s
Hospital care, semiprivate room	day	212.30	90	27c
Hospital care, semiprivate room	day	303.40	4Q 92	4c
Medical insurance premium, per employee, small group comprehensive	month	343.10	10/91	25c
Mental health care, exp	capita	20.37-28.83	90	38s
Mental health care, exp, state mental health agency	capita	22.72	90	38s
Mental health care, hospital psychiatric services, non-Federal, exp	capita	7.95	88	38s
Mental health care, mental health organization, multiservice, exp	capita	12.05	88	38s
Mental health care, psychiatric hospitals, private, exp	capita	37.78	88	38s
Mental health care, psychiatric out-patient clinics, freestanding, exp	capita	0.43	88	38s
Mental health care, state and county mental hospitals, exp	capita	12.54	88	38s
Mental health care, VA medical centers, exp	capita	5.35	88	38s
Physician fee, family practice, first-visit		75.00	91	62r
Physician fee, family practice, revisit		34.00	91	62r
Physician fee, general practice, first-visit		61.00	91	62r
Physician fee, general practice, revisit		32.00	91	62r
Physician fee, general surgeon, first-visit		64.00	91	62r
Physician fee, general surgeon, revisit		40.00	91	62r
Physician fee, internal medicine, first-visit		98.00	91	62r
Physician fee, internal medicine, revisit		40.00	91	62r
Physician fee, median, neurosurgeon, first-visit		130.00	91	62r
Physician fee, median, nonsurgical specialist, first-visit		95.00	91	62r
Physician fee, median, orthopedic surgeon, first-visit		91.00	91	62r

San Antonio, TX - continued

Item	Per	Value	Date	Ref.
Health Care - continued				
Physician fee, median, plastic surgeon, first-visit		66.00	91	62r
Physician fee, median, surgical specialist, first-visit		62.00	91	62r
Physician fee, neurosurgeon, revisit		50.00	91	62r
Physician fee, nonsurgical specialist, revisit		40.00	91	62r
Physician fee, obstetrics/gynecology, first-visit		64.00	91	62r
Physician fee, obstetrics/gynecology, revisit		41.00	91	62r
Physician fee, orthopedic surgeon, revisit		40.00	91	62r
Physician fee, pediatrician, first-visit		49.00	91	62r
Physician fee, pediatrician, revisit		33.00	91	62r
Physician fee, plastic surgeon, revisit		43.00	91	62r
Physician fee, surgical specialist, revisit		37.00	91	62r
Substance abuse, hospital ancillary charge	incident	3750	90	70s
Substance abuse, hospital physician charge	incident	1080	90	70s
Substance abuse, hospital room and board	incident	5320	90	70s
Household Goods				
Appliance repair, home, service call, washing machine	min labor charge	26.99	4Q 92	4c
Laundry detergent, Tide Ultra, Bold, or Cheer	42 oz	3.48	4Q 92	4c
Tissues, facial, Kleenex brand	175-count box	1.04	4Q 92	4c
Housing				
ACCRA Index, Housing		88.90	4Q 92	4c
Home, median price	unit	70.40		26c
House, 1,800 sq ft, 8,000 sq ft lot, new, urban	total	94300	4Q 92	4c
House payment, principal and interest, 25% down payment	month	519	4Q 92	4c
Mortgage rate, incl. points & origination fee, 30-year fixed or adjustable rate	percent	7.99	4Q 92	4c
Rent, apartment, 2 bedrooms - 1-1/2 to 2 baths, unfurnished, 950 sq ft, water	month	502	4Q 92	4c
Rental unit, 1 bedroom	month	402	93	23c
Rental unit, 2 bedroom	month	473	93	23c
Rental unit, 3 bedroom	month	591	93	23c
Rental unit, 4 bedroom	month	662	93	23c
Rental unit, efficiency	month	331	93	23c
Insurance and Pensions				
Auto insurance, private passenger	year	709.79	91	63s
Personal Goods				
Shampoo, Alberto VO5	15 oz	0.99	4Q 92	4c
Toothpaste, Crest or Colgate	6-7 oz	1.69	4Q 92	4c
Personal Services				
Dry cleaning, man's 2-piece suit		5.79	4Q 92	4c
Haircare, woman's shampoo, trim and blow-dry		19.70	4Q 92	4c
Haircut, man's barbershop, no styling		7.00	4Q 92	4c
Restaurant Food				
Chicken, fried, thigh and drumstick		1.94	4Q 92	4c
Hamburger with cheese	1/4 lb	1.89	4Q 92	4c
Pizza, Pizza Hut or Pizza Inn, cheese, thin crust	12-13 in	9.47	4Q 92	4c
Taxes				
Tax, cigarette	pack	41	91	77s
Tax, gasoline	gal	20	91	77s
Taxes, sales	year	791	92	37c
Taxes, state	capita	923	91	77s
Transportation				
ACCRA Index, Transportation		117.50	4Q 92	4c
Auto fixed costs, midsize		3878	91	60c

Values are in dollars or fractions of dollars. In the column headed *Ref*, references are shown to sources. Each reference is followed by a letter. These refer to the geographical level for which data were reported: s=State, r=Region, and c=City or metro. The abbreviation *ex* is used to mean *except* or *excluding*; *exp* stands for expenditures. For other abbreviations and further explanations, please see the Introduction.

San Antonio, TX - continued

Item	Per	Value	Date	Ref.
Transportation				
Auto operating cost, midsize		1388	91	60c
Auto rental, average	day	41.50	6/91	60c
Bus fare	one-way	0.40	3/93	2c
Bus fare, up to 10 miles	one-way	1.55	4Q 92	4c
Driver's license fee		16.00	12/90	43s
Limo fare, airport-city, average	day	7.00	6/91	60c
Taxi fare, airport-city, average	day	12.00	6/91	60c
Tire balance, computer or spin balance, front	wheel	7.80	4Q 92	4c
Travel				
Breakfast	day	5.59	6/91	60c
Business travel	day	114.00	92	86c
Business travel	day	193.00	4/93	89r
Dinner	day	24.93	6/91	60c
Dinner	day	19.10	92	85c
Lodging	day	115.08	91	60c
Lodging	day	79.00	92	85c
Lunch	day	9.14	6/91	60c
Utilities				
ACCRA Index, Utilities		83.00	4Q 92	4c
Electricity	mil Btu	17.09	90	64s
Electricity, partial electric and other energy, 1,800 sq ft living area new home	month	63.42	4Q 92	4c
Electricity, residential	KWh	5.92	2/93	94s

San Diego, CA

Item	Per	Value	Date	Ref.
Child Care				
Child care fee, average, center	hour	1.71	90	65r
Child care fee, average, nonregulated family day care	hour	1.32	90	65r
Child care fee, average, regulated family day care	hour	1.86	90	65r
Communications				
Long-distance telephone service, day, initial minute, 0-100 miles	min	0.17-0.40	91	12s
Long-distance telephone service, day, additional minute, 0-100 miles	min	0.07-0.31	91	12s
Long-distance telephone service, evenings/weekends, 0-100 mi, initial minute	min	0.07-0.16	91	12s
Long-distance telephone service, evenings/weekends, 0-100 mi, additional minute	min	0.03-0.12	91	12s
Telephone, flat rate	month	8.35	91	11c
Telephone, residential, private line, rotary, unlimited calling	month	12.72	10/91	78c
Education				
Board, 4-yr private college/university	year	2515	91	22s
Board, 4-yr public college/university	year	2268	91	22s
Expenditures, local gov't, public elementary/secondary	pupil	4866	92	20s
Room, 4-year private college/university	year	2622	91	22s
Room, 4-year public college/university	year	2406	91	22s
Tuition, 2-year private college/university	year	7942	91	22s
Tuition, 2-year public college/university	year	114	91	22s
Tuition, 4-year private college/university	year	10863	91	22s
Tuition, 4-year public college/university, in-state	year	1220	91	22s
Energy and Fuels				
Coal	mil Btu	2.01	90	64s
Energy	mil Btu	9.08	90	64s
Energy exp/householder, 1-family unit	year	362	90	28r
Energy exp/householder, <1,000 sq ft heating area	year	254	90	28r
Energy exp/householder, 1,000-1,999 sq ft heating area	year	358	90	28r

San Diego, CA - continued

Item	Per	Value	Date	Ref.
Energy and Fuels - continued				
Energy exp/householder, 2,000+ sq ft heating area	year	467	90	28r
Energy exp/householder, mobile home	year	390	90	28r
Energy exp/householder, multifamily	year	252	90	28r
Gas, cooking, 10 therms	month	5.41	92	56c
Gas, cooking, 30 therms	month	16.22	92	56c
Gas, cooking, 50 therms	month	28.39	92	56c
Gas, heating, winter, 100 therms	month	65.09	92	56c
Gas, heating, winter, average use	month	29.86	92	56c
Gas, natural	mil Btu	4.31	90	64s
Gas, natural	000 cu ft	6.27	91	46s
Gas, natural, exp	year	369	91	46s
Gasoline, unleaded regular	mil Btu	8.57	90	64s
Entertainment				
Football game expenditures, pro		124.67	91	80c
Miniature golf admission	adult	6.18	92	1r
Miniature golf admission	child	5.14	92	1r
Waterpark admission	adult	11.00	92	1r
Waterpark admission	child	8.55	92	1r
Funerals				
Casket, 18-gauge steel, velvet interior		1781.09	91	24r
Cosmetology, hair care, etc.		84.64	91	24r
Embalming		207.41	91	24r
Facility use for ceremony		205.76	91	24r
Hearse, local		105.14	91	24r
Limousine, local		83.21	91	24r
Remains to funeral home, transfer		113.82	91	24r
Service charge, professional		626.33	91	24r
Vault, concrete, non-metallic liner		599.54	91	24r
Viewing facilities, use		85.81	91	24r
Groceries				
Apples, Red Delicious	lb	0.80	4/93	16r
Bacon	lb	1.79	4/93	16r
Bananas	lb	0.53	4/93	16r
Bologna, all beef or mixed	lb	2.67	4/93	16r
Bread, white, pan	lb	0.81	4/93	16r
Carrots, short trimmed and topped	lb	0.39	4/93	16r
Chicken, fresh, whole	lb	0.94	4/93	16r
Chicken breast, bone-in	lb	2.19	4/93	16r
Chuck roast, graded and ungraded, ex USDA prime and choice	lb	2.26	4/93	16r
Coffee, 100% ground roast, all sizes	lb	2.33	4/93	16r
Eggs, Grade AA large	doz	1.18	4/93	16r
Flour, white, all purpose	lb	0.22	4/93	16r
Grapefruit	lb	0.52	4/93	16r
Grapes, Thompson Seedless	lb	1.50	4/93	16r
Ground beef, 100% beef	lb	1.44	4/93	16r
Ground beef, lean and extra lean	lb	2.34	4/93	16r
Ham, boneless, excluding canned	lb	2.56	4/93	16r
Honey, jar	8 oz	0.89-1.00	92	5r
Honey, jar	lb	1.35-1.97	92	5r
Honey, squeeze bear	12-oz	1.19-1.50	92	5r
Ice cream, prepackaged, bulk, regular	1/2 gal	2.40	4/93	16r
Lemons	lb	0.81	4/93	16r
Lettuce, iceberg	lb	0.84	4/93	16r
Margarine, stick	lb	0.81	4/93	16r
Oranges, navel	lb	0.48	4/93	16r
Pork chops, center cut, bone-in	lb	3.25	4/93	16r
Potato chips	16 oz	2.89	4/93	16r
Potatoes, white	lb	0.38	4/93	16r
Round roast, graded & ungraded, ex USDA prime & choice	lb	3.00	4/93	16r
Round roast, USDA choice, boneless	lb	3.16	4/93	16r
Shortening, vegetable oil blends	lb	0.86	4/93	16r
Spaghetti and macaroni	lb	0.84	4/93	16r
Steak, round, graded & ungraded, ex USDA prime & choice	lb	3.34	4/93	16r
Steak, round, USDA choice, boneless	lb	3.24	4/93	16r
Steak, sirloin, graded & ungraded, ex USDA prime & choice	lb	3.75	4/93	16r

Values are in dollars or fractions of dollars. In the column headed *Ref*, references are shown to sources. Each reference is followed by a letter. These refer to the geographical level for which data were reported: s=State, r=Region, and c=City or metro. The abbreviation *ex* is used to mean *except* or *excluding*; *exp* stands for expenditures. For other abbreviations and further explanations, please see the Introduction.

San Diego, CA - continued

Item	Per	Value	Date	Ref.
Groceries				
Steak, sirloin, USDA choice, boneless	lb	4.49	4/93	16r
Sugar, white	lb	0.41	4/93	16r
Sugar, white, 33-80 oz pk	lb	0.38	4/93	16r
Tomatoes, field grown	lb	1.01	4/93	16r
Turkey, frozen, whole	lb	1.04	4/93	16r
Health Care				
Cardizem 60 mg tablets	30	24.04	92	49s
Cector 250 mg tablets	15	35.87	92	49s
Childbirth, cesarean, hospital		5533	91	62r
Childbirth, cesarean, physician's fee		2053	91	62r
Childbirth, normal, hospital		2745	91	62r
Childbirth, normal, physician's fee		1492	91	62r
Health care spending, state	capita	2894	3/93	84s
Hospital care, semiprivate room	day	389.65	90	27c
Medical insurance premium, per employee, small group comprehensive	month	445.30	10/91	25c
Medical plan per employee	year	3421	91	45r
Mental health care, exp	capita	37.60-53.67	90	38s
Mental health care, exp, state mental health agency	capita	42.32	90	38s
Mental health care, hospital psychiatric services, non-Federal, exp	capita	10.64	88	38s
Mental health care, mental health organization, multiservice, exp	capita	28.56	88	38s
Mental health care, psychiatric hospitals, private, exp	capita	18.60	88	38s
Mental health care, psychiatric out-patient clinics, freestanding, exp	capita	2.28	88	38s
Mental health care, psychiatric partial-care organizations, freestanding, exp	capita	0.24	88	38s
Mental health care, state and county mental hospitals, exp	capita	13.60	88	38s
Mental health care, VA medical centers, exp	capita	2.33	88	38s
Mevacor 20 mg tablets	30	67.62	92	49s
Physician fee, family practice, first-visit		111.00	91	62r
Physician fee, family practice, revisit		45.00	91	62r
Physician fee, general practice, first-visit		100.00	91	62r
Physician fee, general practice, revisit		40.00	91	62r
Physician fee, internal medicine, first-visit		137.00	91	62r
Physician fee, internal medicine, revisit		48.00	91	62r
Physician fee, median, neurosurgeon, first-visit		157.00	91	62r
Physician fee, median, nonsurgical specialist, first-visit		131.00	91	62r
Physician fee, median, orthopedic surgeon, first-visit		124.00	91	62r
Physician fee, median, plastic surgeon, first-visit		88.00	91	62r
Physician fee, median, surgical specialist, first-visit		100.00	91	62r
Physician fee, neurosurgeon, revisit		51.00	91	62r
Physician fee, nonsurgical specialist, revisit		47.00	91	62r
Physician fee, obstetrics/gynecology, first-visit		95.00	91	62r
Physician fee, obstetrics/gynecology, revisit		50.00	91	62r
Physician fee, orthopedic surgeon, revisit		51.00	91	62r
Physician fee, pediatrician, first-visit		81.00	91	62r
Physician fee, pediatrician, revisit		42.00	91	62r
Physician fee, plastic surgeon, revisit		48.00	91	62r
Physician fee, surgical specialist, revisit		49.00	91	62r
Prozac 20 mg tablets	14	33.22	92	49s
Substance abuse, hospital ancillary charge	incident	1760	90	70s
Substance abuse, hospital physician charge	incident	750	90	70s
Substance abuse, hospital room and board	incident	6390	90	70s
Tagamet 300 mg tablets	100	77.08	92	49s
Xanax 0.25 mg tablets	90	64.08	92	49s
Zantac 160 mg tablets	60	92.31	92	49s

San Diego, CA - continued

Item	Per	Value	Date	Ref.
Housing				
Home, median price	unit	183.80		26c
Home, median price	unit	131,200	92	58s
Rental unit, 1 bedroom	month	618	93	23c
Rental unit, 2 bedroom	month	725	93	23c
Rental unit, 3 bedroom	month	908	93	23c
Rental unit, 4 bedroom	month	1016	93	23c
Rental unit, efficiency	month	503	93	23c
Insurance and Pensions				
Auto insurance, private passenger	year	904.37	91	63s
Legal Assistance				
Living trust, 77-year-old, $80,000 estate		598	9/92	3c
Living trust, married couple with $150,000 home and $50,000 in stocks		956	9/92	3c
Will		173	9/92	3c
Will and probate, $80,000 estate		1971	9/92	3c
Will and probate, $80,000 estate, 77-year-old		1971	9/92	3c
Taxes				
Tax, cigarette	pack	35	91	77s
Tax, gasoline	gal	16	91	77s
Taxes, state	capita	1477	91	77s
Transportation				
Auto rental, average	day	50.50	6/91	60c
Bus fare	one-way	1.00	3/93	2c
Driver's license fee		10.00	12/90	43s
Limo fare, airport-city, average	day	12.00	6/91	60c
Taxi fare, airport-city, average	day	6.00	6/91	60c
Travel				
Breakfast	day	6.71	6/91	60c
Business travel	day	145.00	92	86c
Business travel	day	178.00	4/93	89r
Dinner	day	18.18	6/91	60c
Dinner	day	22.55	92	85c
Lodging	day	127.18	91	60c
Lodging	day	102.00	92	85c
Lunch	day	11.99	6/91	60c
Utilities				
Electricity	mil Btu	25.98	90	64s
Electricity, winter, 250 KWh	month	25.22	92	55c
Electricity, winter, 500 KWh	month	58.08	92	55c
Electricity, winter, 750 KWh	month	90.94	92	55c
Electricity, winter, 1000 KWh	month	123.80	92	55c

San Francisco, CA

Item	Per	Value	Date	Ref.
Child Care				
Child care fee, average, center	hour	1.71	90	65r
Child care fee, average, nonregulated family day care	hour	1.32	90	65r
Child care fee, average, regulated family day care	hour	1.86	90	65r
Communications				
Long-distance telephone service, day, initial minute, 0-100 miles	min	0.17-0.40	91	12s
Long-distance telephone service, day, additional minute, 0-100 miles	min	0.07-0.31	91	12s
Long-distance telephone service, evenings/weekends, 0-100 mi, initial minute	min	0.07-0.16	91	12s
Long-distance telephone service, evenings/weekends, 0-100 mi, additional minute	min	0.03-0.12	91	12s
Telephone, flat rate	month	8.35	91	11c
Telephone, residential, private line, rotary, unlimited calling	month	12.95	10/91	78c
Education				
Board, 4-yr private college/university	year	2515	91	22s
Board, 4-yr public college/university	year	2268	91	22s

Values are in dollars or fractions of dollars. In the column headed *Ref*, references are shown to sources. Each reference is followed by a letter. These refer to the geographical level for which data were reported: s=State, r=Region, and c=City or metro. The abbreviation *ex* is used to mean *except* or *excluding*; *exp* stands for expenditures. For other abbreviations and further explanations, please see the Introduction.

San Francisco, CA - continued

Item	Per	Value	Date	Ref.
Education				
Expenditures, local gov't, public elementary/secondary	pupil	4866	92	20s
Room, 4-year private college/university	year	2622	91	22s
Room, 4-year public college/university	year	2406	91	22s
Tuition, 2-year private college/university	year	7942	91	22s
Tuition, 2-year public college/university	year	114	91	22s
Tuition, 4-year private college/university	year	10863	91	22s
Tuition, 4-year public college/university, in-state	year	1220	91	22s
Energy and Fuels				
Coal	mil Btu	2.01	90	64s
Energy	mil Btu	9.08	90	64s
Energy exp/householder, 1-family unit	year	362	90	28r
Energy exp/householder, <1,000 sq ft heating area	year	254	90	28r
Energy exp/householder, 1,000-1,999 sq ft heating area	year	358	90	28r
Energy exp/householder, 2,000+ sq ft heating area	year	467	90	28r
Energy exp/householder, mobile home	year	390	90	28r
Energy exp/householder, multifamily	year	252	90	28r
Gas, natural	mil Btu	4.31	90	64s
Gas, natural	000 cu ft	6.27	91	46s
Gas, natural, exp	year	369	91	46s
Gas, piped	100 therms	59.48	4/93	16c
Gas, piped	40 therms	20.47	4/93	16c
Gas, piped	therm	0.58	4/93	16c
Gasoline, all types	gal	1.32	4/93	16c
Gasoline, regular unleaded, taxes included, cash, self-service	gal	1.46	4/93	16c
Gasoline, unleaded premium 93 octane	gal	1.26	4/93	16c
Gasoline, unleaded regular	mil Btu	8.57	90	64s
Entertainment				
Dinner entree, restaurant		20.00-30.00	92	83c
Football game expenditures, pro		197.50	91	80c
Miniature golf admission	adult	6.18	92	1r
Miniature golf admission	child	5.14	92	1r
Waterpark admission	adult	11.00	92	1r
Waterpark admission	child	8.55	92	1r
Funerals				
Casket, 18-gauge steel, velvet interior		1781.09	91	24r
Cosmetology, hair care, etc.		84.64	91	24r
Embalming		207.41	91	24r
Facility use for ceremony		205.76	91	24r
Hearse, local		105.14	91	24r
Limousine, local		83.21	91	24r
Remains to funeral home, transfer		113.82	91	24r
Service charge, professional		626.33	91	24r
Vault, concrete, non-metallic liner		599.54	91	24r
Viewing facilities, use		85.81	91	24r
Goods and Services				
Goods and services	year	16675	92	36c
Goods and services, misc.	year	16675	92	37c
Police protection expense	resident	247.00	92	18c
Groceries				
Apples, Red Delicious	lb	0.80	4/93	16r
Bacon	lb	1.79	4/93	16r
Bananas	lb	0.53	4/93	16r
Bologna, all beef or mixed	lb	2.67	4/93	16r
Bread, white, pan	lb	0.81	4/93	16r
Carrots, short trimmed and topped	lb	0.39	4/93	16r
Chicken, fresh, whole	lb	0.94	4/93	16r
Chicken breast, bone-in	lb	2.19	4/93	16r

San Francisco, CA - continued

Item	Per	Value	Date	Ref.
Groceries - continued				
Chuck roast, graded and ungraded, ex USDA prime and choice	lb	2.26	4/93	16r
Coffee, 100% ground roast, all sizes	lb	2.33	4/93	16r
Eggs, Grade AA large	doz	1.18	4/93	16r
Flour, white, all purpose	lb	0.22	4/93	16r
Grapefruit	lb	0.52	4/93	16r
Grapes, Thompson Seedless	lb	1.50	4/93	16r
Ground beef, 100% beef	lb	1.44	4/93	16r
Ground beef, lean and extra lean	lb	2.34	4/93	16r
Ham, boneless, excluding canned	lb	2.56	4/93	16r
Honey, jar	8 oz	0.89-1.00	92	5r
Honey, jar	lb	1.35-1.97	92	5r
Honey, squeeze bear	12-oz	1.19-1.50	92	5r
Ice cream, prepackaged, bulk, regular	1/2 gal	2.40	4/93	16r
Lemons	lb	0.81	4/93	16r
Lettuce, iceberg	lb	0.84	4/93	16r
Margarine, stick	lb	0.81	4/93	16r
Oranges, navel	lb	0.48	4/93	16r
Pork chops, center cut, bone-in	lb	3.25	4/93	16r
Potato chips	16 oz	2.89	4/93	16r
Potatoes, white	lb	0.38	4/93	16r
Round roast, graded & ungraded, ex USDA prime & choice	lb	3.00	4/93	16r
Round roast, USDA choice, boneless	lb	3.16	4/93	16r
Shortening, vegetable oil blends	lb	0.86	4/93	16r
Spaghetti and macaroni	lb	0.84	4/93	16r
Steak, round, graded & ungraded, ex USDA prime & choice	lb	3.34	4/93	16r
Steak, round, USDA choice, boneless	lb	3.24	4/93	16r
Steak, sirloin, graded & ungraded, ex USDA prime & choice	lb	3.75	4/93	16r
Steak, sirloin, USDA choice, boneless	lb	4.49	4/93	16r
Sugar, white	lb	0.41	4/93	16r
Sugar, white, 33-80 oz pk	lb	0.38	4/93	16r
Tomatoes, field grown	lb	1.01	4/93	16r
Turkey, frozen, whole	lb	1.04	4/93	16r
Health Care				
Cardizem 60 mg tablets	30	24.04	92	49s
Cector 250 mg tablets	15	35.87	92	49s
Childbirth, cesarean, hospital		5533	91	62r
Childbirth, cesarean, physician's fee		2053	91	62r
Childbirth, normal, hospital		2745	91	62r
Childbirth, normal, physician's fee		1492	91	62r
Health care spending, state	capita	2894	3/93	84s
Health maintenance organization coverage, employee	year	3092	93	39c
Health maintenance organization medical coverage, employee	year	3092	92	42c
Health maintenance organization medical coverage, employee	year	3092	92	34c
Hospital care, semiprivate room	day	711.74	90	27c
Indemnity plan medical coverage, employee	year	4531	92	42c
Indemnity plan medical coverage, employee	year	4531	92	34c
Insurance coverage, traditional, employee	year	4531	93	39c
Medical insurance premium, per employee, small group comprehensive	month	489.10	10/91	25c
Medical plan per employee	year	3421	91	45r
Mental health care, exp	capita	37.60-53.67	90	38s
Mental health care, exp, state mental health agency	capita	42.32	90	38s
Mental health care, hospital psychiatric services, non-Federal, exp	capita	10.64	88	38s
Mental health care, mental health organization, multiservice, exp	capita	28.56	88	38s
Mental health care, psychiatric hospitals, private, exp	capita	18.60	88	38s
Mental health care, psychiatric out-patient clinics, freestanding, exp	capita	2.28	88	38s
Mental health care, psychiatric partial-care organizations, freestanding, exp	capita	0.24	88	38s

Values are in dollars or fractions of dollars. In the column headed *Ref*, references are shown to sources. Each reference is followed by a letter. These refer to the geographical level for which data were reported: s = State, r = Region, and c = City or metro. The abbreviation *ex* is used to mean *except* or *excluding*; *exp* stands for expenditures. For other abbreviations and further explanations, please see the Introduction.

San Francisco, CA - continued

Item	Per	Value	Date	Ref.
Health Care				
Mental health care, state and county mental hospitals, exp	capita	13.60	88	38s
Mental health care, VA medical centers, exp	capita	2.33	88	38s
Mevacor 20 mg tablets	30	67.62	92	49s
Physician fee, family practice, first-visit		111.00	91	62r
Physician fee, family practice, revisit		45.00	91	62r
Physician fee, general practice, first-visit		100.00	91	62r
Physician fee, general practice, revisit		40.00	91	62r
Physician fee, internal medicine, first-visit		137.00	91	62r
Physician fee, internal medicine, revisit		48.00	91	62r
Physician fee, median, neurosurgeon, first-visit		157.00	91	62r
Physician fee, median, nonsurgical specialist, first-visit		131.00	91	62r
Physician fee, median, orthopedic surgeon, first-visit		124.00	91	62r
Physician fee, median, plastic surgeon, first-visit		88.00	91	62r
Physician fee, median, surgical specialist, first-visit		100.00	91	62r
Physician fee, neurosurgeon, revisit		51.00	91	62r
Physician fee, nonsurgical specialist, revisit		47.00	91	62r
Physician fee, obstetrics/gynecology, first-visit		95.00	91	62r
Physician fee, obstetrics/gynecology, revisit		50.00	91	62r
Physician fee, orthopedic surgeon, revisit		51.00	91	62r
Physician fee, pediatrician, first-visit		81.00	91	62r
Physician fee, pediatrician, revisit		42.00	91	62r
Physician fee, plastic surgeon, revisit		48.00	91	62r
Physician fee, surgical specialist, revisit		49.00	91	62r
Preferred provider organization medical coverage, employee	year	4459	92	42c
Preferred provider organization medical coverage, employee	year	4459	92	34c
Prozac 20 mg tablets	14	33.22	92	49s
Substance abuse, hospital ancillary charge	incident	1760	90	70s
Substance abuse, hospital physician charge	incident	750	90	70s
Substance abuse, hospital room and board	incident	6390	90	70s
Tagamet 300 mg tablets	100	77.08	92	49s
Xanax 0.25 mg tablets	90	64.08	92	49s
Zantac 160 mg tablets	60	92.31	92	49s
Housing				
Home, median price	unit	254.80		26c
Home, median price	unit	131,200	92	58s
Rental unit, 1 bedroom	month	845	93	23c
Rental unit, 2 bedroom	month	1002	93	23c
Rental unit, 3 bedroom	month	1247	93	23c
Rental unit, 4 bedroom	month	1397	93	23c
Rental unit, efficiency	month	697	93	23c
Insurance and Pensions				
Auto insurance, private passenger	year	904.37	91	63s
Taxes				
Tax, cigarette	pack	35	91	77s
Tax, gasoline	gal	16	91	77s
Taxes, hotel room	day	8.94	92	33c
Taxes, sales	year	1015	92	37c
Taxes, state	capita	1477	91	77s
Transportation				
Auto rental, average	day	49.25	6/91	60c
Auto rental, midsize car	day	39.06	92	91c
Bus fare	one-way	0.75	3/93	2c
Cable car fare	one-way	3.00	3/93	2c
Driver's license fee		10.00	12/90	43s
Ferry boat fare	one-way	3.75	3/93	2c

San Francisco, CA - continued

Item	Per	Value	Date	Ref.
Transportation - continued				
Limo fare, airport-city, average	day	6.00	6/91	60c
Railway fare, commuter	one-way	1.00	3/93	2c
Railway fare, heavy rail	one-way	0.80	3/93	2c
Taxi fare, airport-city, average	day	24.00	6/91	60c
Trolley fare	one-way	1.00	3/93	2c
Travel				
Breakfast	day	12.75	6/91	60c
Business travel	day	194.00	92	86c
Business travel	day	178.00	4/93	89r
Dinner	day	43.75	6/91	60c
Dinner	day	24.90	92	85c
Lodging	day	157.34	91	60c
Lodging	day	135.00	92	85c
Lunch	day	17.90	6/91	60c
Travel, business	day	220.97	93	88c
Utilities				
Electricity	500 KWh	63.08	4/93	16c
Electricity	KWh	0.13	4/93	16c
Electricity	mil Btu	25.98	90	64s

San Jose, CA

Item	Per	Value	Date	Ref.
Child Care				
Child care fee, average, center	hour	1.71	90	65r
Child care fee, average, nonregulated family day care	hour	1.32	90	65r
Child care fee, average, regulated family day care	hour	1.86	90	65r
Communications				
Long-distance telephone service, day, initial minute, 0-100 miles	min	0.17-0.40	91	12s
Long-distance telephone service, day, additional minute, 0-100 miles	min	0.07-0.31	91	12s
Long-distance telephone service, evenings/weekends, 0-100 mi, initial minute	min	0.07-0.16	91	12s
Long-distance telephone service, evenings/weekends, 0-100 mi, additional minute	min	0.03-0.12	91	12s
Telephone, residential, private line, rotary, unlimited calling	month	12.89	10/91	78c
Education				
Board, 4-yr private college/university	year	2515	91	22s
Board, 4-yr public college/university	year	2268	91	22s
Expenditures, local gov't, public elementary/secondary	pupil	4866	92	20s
Room, 4-year private college/university	year	2622	91	22s
Room, 4-year public college/university	year	2406	91	22s
Tuition, 2-year private college/university	year	7942	91	22s
Tuition, 2-year public college/university	year	114	91	22s
Tuition, 4-year private college/university	year	10863	91	22s
Tuition, 4-year public college/university, in-state	year	1220	91	22s
Energy and Fuels				
Coal	mil Btu	2.01	90	64s
Energy	mil Btu	9.08	90	64s
Energy exp/householder, 1-family unit	year	362	90	28r
Energy exp/householder, <1,000 sq ft heating area	year	254	90	28r
Energy exp/householder, 1,000-1,999 sq ft heating area	year	358	90	28r
Energy exp/householder, 2,000+ sq ft heating area	year	467	90	28r
Energy exp/householder, mobile home	year	390	90	28r
Energy exp/householder, multifamily	year	252	90	28r
Gas, cooking, 10 therms	month	5.25	92	56c

Values are in dollars or fractions of dollars. In the column headed *Ref*, references are shown to sources. Each reference is followed by a letter. These refer to the geographical level for which data were reported: s=State, r=Region, and c=City or metro. The abbreviation *ex* is used to mean *except* or *excluding*; *exp* stands for expenditures. For other abbreviations and further explanations, please see the Introduction.

San Jose, CA - continued

Item	Per	Value	Date	Ref.
Energy and Fuels				
Gas, cooking, 30 therms	month	15.76	92	56c
Gas, cooking, 50 therms	month	26.27	92	56c
Gas, heating, winter, 100 therms	month	61.50	92	56c
Gas, heating, winter, average use	month	46.28	92	56c
Gas, natural	mil Btu	4.31	90	64s
Gas, natural	000 cu ft	6.27	91	46s
Gas, natural, exp	year	369	91	46s
Gasoline, unleaded regular	mil Btu	8.57	90	64s
Entertainment				
Miniature golf admission	adult	6.18	92	1r
Miniature golf admission	child	5.14	92	1r
Waterpark admission	adult	11.00	92	1r
Waterpark admission	child	8.55	92	1r
Funerals				
Casket, 18-gauge steel, velvet interior		1781.09	91	24r
Cosmetology, hair care, etc.		84.64	91	24r
Embalming		207.41	91	24r
Facility use for ceremony		205.76	91	24r
Hearse, local		105.14	91	24r
Limousine, local		83.21	91	24r
Remains to funeral home, transfer		113.82	91	24r
Service charge, professional		626.33	91	24r
Vault, concrete, non-metallic liner		599.54	91	24r
Viewing facilities, use		85.81	91	24r
Groceries				
Apples, Red Delicious	lb	0.80	4/93	16r
Bacon	lb	1.79	4/93	16r
Bananas	lb	0.53	4/93	16r
Bologna, all beef or mixed	lb	2.67	4/93	16r
Bread, white, pan	lb	0.81	4/93	16r
Carrots, short trimmed and topped	lb	0.39	4/93	16r
Chicken, fresh, whole	lb	0.94	4/93	16r
Chicken breast, bone-in	lb	2.19	4/93	16r
Chuck roast, graded and ungraded, ex USDA prime and choice	lb	2.26	4/93	16r
Coffee, 100% ground roast, all sizes	lb	2.33	4/93	16r
Eggs, Grade AA large	doz	1.18	4/93	16r
Flour, white, all purpose	lb	0.22	4/93	16r
Grapefruit	lb	0.52	4/93	16r
Grapes, Thompson Seedless	lb	1.50	4/93	16r
Ground beef, 100% beef	lb	1.44	4/93	16r
Ground beef, lean and extra lean	lb	2.34	4/93	16r
Ham, boneless, excluding canned	lb	2.56	4/93	16r
Honey, jar	8 oz	0.89-1.00	92	5r
Honey, jar	lb	1.35-1.97	92	5r
Honey, squeeze bear	12-oz	1.19-1.50	92	5r
Ice cream, prepackaged, bulk, regular	1/2 gal	2.40	4/93	16r
Lemons	lb	0.81	4/93	16r
Lettuce, iceberg	lb	0.84	4/93	16r
Margarine, stick	lb	0.81	4/93	16r
Oranges, navel	lb	0.48	4/93	16r
Pork chops, center cut, bone-in	lb	3.25	4/93	16r
Potato chips	16 oz	2.89	4/93	16r
Potatoes, white	lb	0.38	4/93	16r
Round roast, graded & ungraded, ex USDA prime & choice	lb	3.00	4/93	16r
Round roast, USDA choice, boneless	lb	3.16	4/93	16r
Shortening, vegetable oil blends	lb	0.86	4/93	16r
Spaghetti and macaroni	lb	0.84	4/93	16r
Steak, round, graded & ungraded, ex USDA prime & choice	lb	3.34	4/93	16r
Steak, round, USDA choice, boneless	lb	3.24	4/93	16r
Steak, sirloin, graded & ungraded, ex USDA prime & choice	lb	3.75	4/93	16r
Steak, sirloin, USDA choice, boneless	lb	4.49	4/93	16r
Sugar, white	lb	0.41	4/93	16r
Sugar, white, 33-80 oz pk	lb	0.38	4/93	16r
Tomatoes, field grown	lb	1.01	4/93	16r
Turkey, frozen, whole	lb	1.04	4/93	16r

San Jose, CA - continued

Item	Per	Value	Date	Ref.
Health Care				
Cardizem 60 mg tablets	30	24.04	92	49s
Cector 250 mg tablets	15	35.87	92	49s
Childbirth, cesarean, hospital		5533	91	62r
Childbirth, cesarean, physician's fee		2053	91	62r
Childbirth, normal, hospital		2745	91	62r
Childbirth, normal, physician's fee		1492	91	62r
Health care spending, state	capita	2894	3/93	84s
Hospital care, semiprivate room	day	490.00	90	27c
Medical insurance premium, per employee, small group comprehensive	month	430.70	10/91	25c
Medical plan per employee	year	3421	91	45r
Mental health care, exp	capita	37.60-53.67	90	38s
Mental health care, exp, state mental health agency	capita	42.32	90	38s
Mental health care, hospital psychiatric services, non-Federal, exp	capita	10.64	88	38s
Mental health care, mental health organization, multiservice, exp	capita	28.56	88	38s
Mental health care, psychiatric hospitals, private, exp	capita	18.60	88	38s
Mental health care, psychiatric out-patient clinics, freestanding, exp	capita	2.28	88	38s
Mental health care, psychiatric partial-care organizations, freestanding, exp	capita	0.24	88	38s
Mental health care, state and county mental hospitals, exp	capita	13.60	88	38s
Mental health care, VA medical centers, exp	capita	2.33	88	38s
Mevacor 20 mg tablets	30	67.62	92	49s
Physician fee, family practice, first-visit		111.00	91	62r
Physician fee, family practice, revisit		45.00	91	62r
Physician fee, general practice, first-visit		100.00	91	62r
Physician fee, general practice, revisit		40.00	91	62r
Physician fee, internal medicine, first-visit		137.00	91	62r
Physician fee, internal medicine, revisit		48.00	91	62r
Physician fee, median, neurosurgeon, first-visit		157.00	91	62r
Physician fee, median, nonsurgical specialist, first-visit		131.00	91	62r
Physician fee, median, orthopedic surgeon, first-visit		124.00	91	62r
Physician fee, median, plastic surgeon, first-visit		88.00	91	62r
Physician fee, median, surgical specialist, first-visit		100.00	91	62r
Physician fee, neurosurgeon, revisit		51.00	91	62r
Physician fee, nonsurgical specialist, revisit		47.00	91	62r
Physician fee, obstetrics/gynecology, first-visit		95.00	91	62r
Physician fee, obstetrics/gynecology, revisit		50.00	91	62r
Physician fee, orthopedic surgeon, revisit		51.00	91	62r
Physician fee, pediatrician, first-visit		81.00	91	62r
Physician fee, pediatrician, revisit		42.00	91	62r
Physician fee, plastic surgeon, revisit		48.00	91	62r
Physician fee, surgical specialist, revisit		49.00	91	62r
Prozac 20 mg tablets	14	33.22	92	49s
Substance abuse, hospital ancillary charge	incident	1760	90	70s
Substance abuse, hospital physician charge	incident	750	90	70s
Substance abuse, hospital room and board	incident	6390	90	70s
Tagamet 300 mg tablets	100	77.08	92	49s
Xanax 0.25 mg tablets	90	64.08	92	49s
Zantac 160 mg tablets	60	92.31	92	49s
Housing				
Home, median price	unit	131,200	92	58s
Rental unit, 1 bedroom	month	780	93	23c
Rental unit, 2 bedroom	month	920	93	23c
Rental unit, 3 bedroom	month	1149	93	23c
Rental unit, 4 bedroom	month	1288	93	23c
Rental unit, efficiency	month	643	93	23c

Values are in dollars or fractions of dollars. In the column headed *Ref*, references are shown to sources. Each reference is followed by a letter. These refer to the geographical level for which data were reported: s = State, r = Region, and c = City or metro. The abbreviation *ex* is used to mean *except* or *excluding*; *exp* stands for expenditures. For other abbreviations and further explanations, please see the Introduction.

San Jose, CA - continued

Item	Per	Value	Date	Ref.
Insurance and Pensions				
Auto insurance, private passenger	year	904.37	91	63s
Taxes				
Tax, cigarette	pack	35	91	77s
Tax, gasoline	gal	16	91	77s
Taxes, state	capita	1477	91	77s
Transportation				
Auto rental, average	day	47.25	6/91	60c
Bus fare	one-way	1.00	3/93	2c
Driver's license fee		10.00	12/90	43s
Taxi fare, airport-city, average	day	9.75	6/91	60c
Travel				
Breakfast	day	7.31	6/91	60c
Business travel	day	178.00	4/93	89r
Dinner	day	18.93	6/91	60c
Lodging	day	119.31	91	60c
Lunch	day	11.44	6/91	60c
Utilities				
Electricity	mil Btu	25.98	90	64s
Electricity, winter, 250 KWh	month	27.82	92	55c
Electricity, winter, 500 KWh	month	59.69	92	55c
Electricity, winter, 750 KWh	month	94.40	92	55c
Electricity, winter, 1000 KWh	month	129.11	92	55c

Santa Barbara-Santa Maria-Lompoc, CA

Item	Per	Value	Date	Ref.
Child Care				
Child care fee, average, center	hour	1.71	90	65r
Child care fee, average, nonregulated family day care	hour	1.32	90	65r
Child care fee, average, regulated family day care	hour	1.86	90	65r
Communications				
Long-distance telephone service, day, initial minute, 0-100 miles	min	0.17-0.40	91	12s
Long-distance telephone service, day, additional minute, 0-100 miles	min	0.07-0.31	91	12s
Long-distance telephone service, evenings/ weekends, 0-100 mi, initial minute	min	0.07-0.16	91	12s
Long-distance telephone service, evenings/ weekends, 0-100 mi, additional minute	min	0.03-0.12	91	12s
Education				
Board, 4-yr private college/university	year	2515	91	22s
Board, 4-yr public college/university	year	2268	91	22s
Expenditures, local gov't, public elementary/secondary	pupil	4866	92	20s
Room, 4-year private college/university	year	2622	91	22s
Room, 4-year public college/university	year	2406	91	22s
Tuition, 2-year private college/university	year	7942	91	22s
Tuition, 2-year public college/university	year	114	91	22s
Tuition, 4-year private college/university	year	10863	91	22s
Tuition, 4-year public college/university, in-state	year	1220	91	22s
Energy and Fuels				
Coal	mil Btu	2.01	90	64s
Energy	mil Btu	9.08	90	64s
Energy exp/householder, 1-family unit	year	362	90	28r
Energy exp/householder, <1,000 sq ft heating area	year	254	90	28r
Energy exp/householder, 1,000-1,999 sq ft heating area	year	358	90	28r
Energy exp/householder, 2,000+ sq ft heating area	year	467	90	28r
Energy exp/householder, mobile home	year	390	90	28r
Energy exp/householder, multifamily	year	252	90	28r
Gas, natural	mil Btu	4.31	90	64s

Santa Barbara-Santa Maria-Lompoc, CA - continued

Item	Per	Value	Date	Ref.
Energy and Fuels - continued				
Gas, natural	000 cu ft	6.27	91	46s
Gas, natural, exp	year	369	91	46s
Gasoline, unleaded regular	mil Btu	8.57	90	64s
Entertainment				
Miniature golf admission	adult	6.18	92	1r
Miniature golf admission	child	5.14	92	1r
Waterpark admission	adult	11.00	92	1r
Waterpark admission	child	8.55	92	1r
Funerals				
Casket, 18-gauge steel, velvet interior		1781.09	91	24r
Cosmetology, hair care, etc.		84.64	91	24r
Embalming		207.41	91	24r
Facility use for ceremony		205.76	91	24r
Hearse, local		105.14	91	24r
Limousine, local		83.21	91	24r
Remains to funeral home, transfer		113.82	91	24r
Service charge, professional		626.33	91	24r
Vault, concrete, non-metallic liner		599.54	91	24r
Viewing facilities, use		85.81	91	24r
Groceries				
Apples, Red Delicious	lb	0.80	4/93	16r
Bacon	lb	1.79	4/93	16r
Bananas	lb	0.53	4/93	16r
Bologna, all beef or mixed	lb	2.67	4/93	16r
Bread, white, pan	lb	0.81	4/93	16r
Carrots, short trimmed and topped	lb	0.39	4/93	16r
Chicken, fresh, whole	lb	0.94	4/93	16r
Chicken breast, bone-in	lb	2.19	4/93	16r
Chuck roast, graded and ungraded, ex USDA prime and choice	lb	2.26	4/93	16r
Coffee, 100% ground roast, all sizes	lb	2.33	4/93	16r
Eggs, Grade AA large	doz	1.18	4/93	16r
Flour, white, all purpose	lb	0.22	4/93	16r
Grapefruit	lb	0.52	4/93	16r
Grapes, Thompson Seedless	lb	1.50	4/93	16r
Ground beef, 100% beef	lb	1.44	4/93	16r
Ground beef, lean and extra lean	lb	2.34	4/93	16r
Ham, boneless, excluding canned	lb	2.56	4/93	16r
Honey, jar	8 oz	0.89-1.00	92	5r
Honey, jar	lb	1.35-1.97	92	5r
Honey, squeeze bear	12-oz	1.19-1.50	92	5r
Ice cream, prepackaged, bulk, regular	1/2 gal	2.40	4/93	16r
Lemons	lb	0.81	4/93	16r
Lettuce, iceberg	lb	0.84	4/93	16r
Margarine, stick	lb	0.81	4/93	16r
Oranges, navel	lb	0.48	4/93	16r
Pork chops, center cut, bone-in	lb	3.25	4/93	16r
Potato chips	16 oz	2.89	4/93	16r
Potatoes, white	lb	0.38	4/93	16r
Round roast, graded & ungraded, ex USDA prime & choice	lb	3.00	4/93	16r
Round roast, USDA choice, boneless	lb	3.16	4/93	16r
Shortening, vegetable oil blends	lb	0.86	4/93	16r
Spaghetti and macaroni	lb	0.84	4/93	16r
Steak, round, graded & ungraded, ex USDA prime & choice	lb	3.34	4/93	16r
Steak, round, USDA choice, boneless	lb	3.24	4/93	16r
Steak, sirloin, graded & ungraded, ex USDA prime & choice	lb	3.75	4/93	16r
Steak, sirloin, USDA choice, boneless	lb	4.49	4/93	16r
Sugar, white	lb	0.41	4/93	16r
Sugar, white, 33-80 oz pk	lb	0.38	4/93	16r
Tomatoes, field grown	lb	1.01	4/93	16r
Turkey, frozen, whole	lb	1.04	4/93	16r
Health Care				
Cardizem 60 mg tablets	30	24.04	92	49s
Cector 250 mg tablets	15	35.87	92	49s
Childbirth, cesarean, hospital		5533	91	62r
Childbirth, cesarean, physician's fee		2053	91	62r

Values are in dollars or fractions of dollars. In the column headed *Ref*, references are shown to sources. Each reference is followed by a letter. These refer to the geographical level for which data were reported: s = State, r = Region, and c = City or metro. The abbreviation *ex* is used to mean *except* or *excluding*; *exp* stands for expenditures. For other abbreviations and further explanations, please see the Introduction.

Santa Barbara-Santa Maria-Lompoc, CA - continued

Item	Per	Value	Date	Ref.
Health Care				
Childbirth, normal, hospital		2745	91	62r
Childbirth, normal, physician's fee		1492	91	62r
Health care spending, state	capita	2894	3/93	84s
Medical plan per employee	year	3421	91	45r
Mental health care, exp	capita	37.60-53.67	90	38s
Mental health care, exp, state mental health agency	capita	42.32	90	38s
Mental health care, hospital psychiatric services, non-Federal, exp	capita	10.64	88	38s
Mental health care, mental health organization, multiservice, exp	capita	28.56	88	38s
Mental health care, psychiatric hospitals, private, exp	capita	18.60	88	38s
Mental health care, psychiatric out-patient clinics, freestanding, exp	capita	2.28	88	38s
Mental health care, psychiatric partial-care organizations, freestanding, exp	capita	0.24	88	38s
Mental health care, state and county mental hospitals, exp	capita	13.60	88	38s
Mental health care, VA medical centers, exp	capita	2.33	88	38s
Mevacor 20 mg tablets	30	67.62	92	49s
Physician fee, family practice, first-visit		111.00	91	62r
Physician fee, family practice, revisit		45.00	91	62r
Physician fee, general practice, first-visit		100.00	91	62r
Physician fee, general practice, revisit		40.00	91	62r
Physician fee, internal medicine, first-visit		137.00	91	62r
Physician fee, internal medicine, revisit		48.00	91	62r
Physician fee, median, neurosurgeon, first-visit		157.00	91	62r
Physician fee, median, nonsurgical specialist, first-visit		131.00	91	62r
Physician fee, median, orthopedic surgeon, first-visit		124.00	91	62r
Physician fee, median, plastic surgeon, first-visit		88.00	91	62r
Physician fee, median, surgical specialist, first-visit		100.00	91	62r
Physician fee, neurosurgeon, revisit		51.00	91	62r
Physician fee, nonsurgical specialist, revisit		47.00	91	62r
Physician fee, obstetrics/gynecology, first-visit		95.00	91	62r
Physician fee, obstetrics/gynecology, revisit		50.00	91	62r
Physician fee, orthopedic surgeon, revisit		51.00	91	62r
Physician fee, pediatrician, first-visit		81.00	91	62r
Physician fee, pediatrician, revisit		42.00	91	62r
Physician fee, plastic surgeon, revisit		48.00	91	62r
Physician fee, surgical specialist, revisit		49.00	91	62r
Prozac 20 mg tablets	14	33.22	92	49s
Substance abuse, hospital ancillary charge	incident	1760	90	70s
Substance abuse, hospital physician charge	incident	750	90	70s
Substance abuse, hospital room and board	incident	6390	90	70s
Tagamet 300 mg tablets	100	77.08	92	49s
Xanax 0.25 mg tablets	90	64.08	92	49s
Zantac 160 mg tablets	60	92.31	92	49s
Housing				
Home, median price	unit	131,200	92	58s
Insurance and Pensions				
Auto insurance, private passenger	year	904.37	91	63s
Taxes				
Tax, cigarette	pack	35	91	77s
Tax, gasoline	gal	16	91	77s
Taxes, state	capita	1477	91	77s
Transportation				
Driver's license fee		10.00	12/90	43s

Santa Barbara-Santa Maria-Lompoc, CA - continued

Item	Per	Value	Date	Ref.
Travel				
Business travel	day	178.00	4/93	89r
Utilities				
Electricity	mil Btu	25.98	90	64s

Santa Cruz, CA

Item	Per	Value	Date	Ref.
Child Care				
Child care fee, average, center	hour	1.71	90	65r
Child care fee, average, nonregulated family day care	hour	1.32	90	65r
Child care fee, average, regulated family day care	hour	1.86	90	65r
Communications				
Long-distance telephone service, day, initial minute, 0-100 miles	min	0.17-0.40	91	12s
Long-distance telephone service, day, additional minute, 0-100 miles	min	0.07-0.31	91	12s
Long-distance telephone service, evenings/weekends, 0-100 mi, initial minute	min	0.07-0.16	91	12s
Long-distance telephone service, evenings/weekends, 0-100 mi, additional minute	min	0.03-0.12	91	12s
Education				
Board, 4-yr private college/university	year	2515	91	22s
Board, 4-yr public college/university	year	2268	91	22s
Expenditures, local gov't, public elementary/secondary	pupil	4866	92	20s
Room, 4-year private college/university	year	2622	91	22s
Room, 4-year public college/university	year	2406	91	22s
Tuition, 2-year private college/university	year	7942	91	22s
Tuition, 2-year public college/university	year	114	91	22s
Tuition, 4-year private college/university	year	10863	91	22s
Tuition, 4-year public college/university, in-state	year	1220	91	22s
Energy and Fuels				
Coal	mil Btu	2.01	90	64s
Energy	mil Btu	9.08	90	64s
Energy exp/householder, 1-family unit	year	362	90	28r
Energy exp/householder, <1,000 sq ft heating area	year	254	90	28r
Energy exp/householder, 1,000-1,999 sq ft heating area	year	358	90	28r
Energy exp/householder, 2,000+ sq ft heating area	year	467	90	28r
Energy exp/householder, mobile home	year	390	90	28r
Energy exp/householder, multifamily	year	252	90	28r
Gas, natural	mil Btu	4.31	90	64s
Gas, natural	000 cu ft	6.27	91	46s
Gas, natural, exp	year	369	91	46s
Gasoline, unleaded regular	mil Btu	8.57	90	64s
Entertainment				
Miniature golf admission	adult	6.18	92	1r
Miniature golf admission	child	5.14	92	1r
Waterpark admission	adult	11.00	92	1r
Waterpark admission	child	8.55	92	1r
Funerals				
Casket, 18-gauge steel, velvet interior		1781.09	91	24r
Cosmetology, hair care, etc.		84.64	91	24r
Embalming		207.41	91	24r
Facility use for ceremony		205.76	91	24r
Hearse, local		105.14	91	24r
Limousine, local		83.21	91	24r
Remains to funeral home, transfer		113.82	91	24r
Service charge, professional		626.33	91	24r
Vault, concrete, non-metallic liner		599.54	91	24r
Viewing facilities, use		85.81	91	24r

Values are in dollars or fractions of dollars. In the column headed *Ref*, references are shown to sources. Each reference is followed by a letter. These refer to the geographical level for which data were reported: s=State, r=Region, and c=City or metro. The abbreviation *ex* is used to mean *except* or *excluding*; *exp* stands for expenditures. For other abbreviations and further explanations, please see the Introduction.

Santa Cruz, CA - continued

Groceries

Item	Per	Value	Date	Ref.
Apples, Red Delicious	lb	0.80	4/93	16r
Bacon	lb	1.79	4/93	16r
Bananas	lb	0.53	4/93	16r
Bologna, all beef or mixed	lb	2.67	4/93	16r
Bread, white, pan	lb	0.81	4/93	16r
Carrots, short trimmed and topped	lb	0.39	4/93	16r
Chicken, fresh, whole	lb	0.94	4/93	16r
Chicken breast, bone-in	lb	2.19	4/93	16r
Chuck roast, graded and ungraded, ex USDA prime and choice	lb	2.26	4/93	16r
Coffee, 100% ground roast, all sizes	lb	2.33	4/93	16r
Eggs, Grade AA large	doz	1.18	4/93	16r
Flour, white, all purpose	lb	0.22	4/93	16r
Grapefruit	lb	0.52	4/93	16r
Grapes, Thompson Seedless	lb	1.50	4/93	16r
Ground beef, 100% beef	lb	1.44	4/93	16r
Ground beef, lean and extra lean	lb	2.34	4/93	16r
Ham, boneless, excluding canned	lb	2.56	4/93	16r
Honey, jar	8 oz	0.89-1.00	92	5r
Honey, jar	lb	1.35-1.97	92	5r
Honey, squeeze bear	12-oz	1.19-1.50	92	5r
Ice cream, prepackaged, bulk, regular	1/2 gal	2.40	4/93	16r
Lemons	lb	0.81	4/93	16r
Lettuce, iceberg	lb	0.84	4/93	16r
Margarine, stick	lb	0.81	4/93	16r
Oranges, navel	lb	0.48	4/93	16r
Pork chops, center cut, bone-in	lb	3.25	4/93	16r
Potato chips	16 oz	2.89	4/93	16r
Potatoes, white	lb	0.38	4/93	16r
Round roast, graded & ungraded, ex USDA prime & choice	lb	3.00	4/93	16r
Round roast, USDA choice, boneless	lb	3.16	4/93	16r
Shortening, vegetable oil blends	lb	0.86	4/93	16r
Spaghetti and macaroni	lb	0.84	4/93	16r
Steak, round, graded & ungraded, ex USDA prime & choice	lb	3.34	4/93	16r
Steak, round, USDA choice, boneless	lb	3.24	4/93	16r
Steak, sirloin, graded & ungraded, ex USDA prime & choice	lb	3.75	4/93	16r
Steak, sirloin, USDA choice, boneless	lb	4.49	4/93	16r
Sugar, white	lb	0.41	4/93	16r
Sugar, white, 33-80 oz pk	lb	0.38	4/93	16r
Tomatoes, field grown	lb	1.01	4/93	16r
Turkey, frozen, whole	lb	1.04	4/93	16r

Health Care

Item	Per	Value	Date	Ref.
Cardizem 60 mg tablets	30	24.04	92	49s
Cector 250 mg tablets	15	35.87	92	49s
Childbirth, cesarean, hospital		5533	91	62r
Childbirth, cesarean, physician's fee		2053	91	62r
Childbirth, normal, hospital		2745	91	62r
Childbirth, normal, physician's fee		1492	91	62r
Health care spending, state	capita	2894	3/93	84s
Medical plan per employee	year	3421	91	45r
Mental health care, exp	capita	37.60-53.67	90	38s
Mental health care, exp, state mental health agency	capita	42.32	90	38s
Mental health care, hospital psychiatric services, non-Federal, exp	capita	10.64	88	38s
Mental health care, mental health organization, multiservice, exp	capita	28.56	88	38s
Mental health care, psychiatric hospitals, private, exp	capita	18.60	88	38s
Mental health care, psychiatric out-patient clinics, freestanding, exp	capita	2.28	88	38s
Mental health care, psychiatric partial-care organizations, freestanding, exp	capita	0.24	88	38s
Mental health care, state and county mental hospitals, exp	capita	13.60	88	38s
Mental health care, VA medical centers, exp	capita	2.33	88	38s
Mevacor 20 mg tablets	30	67.62	92	49s
Physician fee, family practice, first-visit		111.00	91	62r

Santa Cruz, CA - continued

Health Care - continued

Item	Per	Value	Date	Ref.
Physician fee, family practice, revisit		45.00	91	62r
Physician fee, general practice, first-visit		100.00	91	62r
Physician fee, general practice, revisit		40.00	91	62r
Physician fee, internal medicine, first-visit		137.00	91	62r
Physician fee, internal medicine, revisit		48.00	91	62r
Physician fee, median, neurosurgeon, first-visit		157.00	91	62r
Physician fee, median, nonsurgical specialist, first-visit		131.00	91	62r
Physician fee, median, orthopedic surgeon, first-visit		124.00	91	62r
Physician fee, median, plastic surgeon, first-visit		88.00	91	62r
Physician fee, median, surgical specialist, first-visit		100.00	91	62r
Physician fee, neurosurgeon, revisit		51.00	91	62r
Physician fee, nonsurgical specialist, revisit		47.00	91	62r
Physician fee, obstetrics/gynecology, first-visit		95.00	91	62r
Physician fee, obstetrics/gynecology, revisit		50.00	91	62r
Physician fee, orthopedic surgeon, revisit		51.00	91	62r
Physician fee, pediatrician, first-visit		81.00	91	62r
Physician fee, pediatrician, revisit		42.00	91	62r
Physician fee, plastic surgeon, revisit		48.00	91	62r
Physician fee, surgical specialist, revisit		49.00	91	62r
Prozac 20 mg tablets	14	33.22	92	49s
Substance abuse, hospital ancillary charge	incident	1760	90	70s
Substance abuse, hospital physician charge	incident	750	90	70s
Substance abuse, hospital room and board	incident	6390	90	70s
Tagamet 300 mg tablets	100	77.08	92	49s
Xanax 0.25 mg tablets	90	64.08	92	49s
Zantac 160 mg tablets	60	92.31	92	49s

Housing

Item	Per	Value	Date	Ref.
Home, median price	unit	131,200	92	58s

Insurance and Pensions

Item	Per	Value	Date	Ref.
Auto insurance, private passenger	year	904.37	91	63s

Taxes

Item	Per	Value	Date	Ref.
Tax, cigarette	pack	35	91	77s
Tax, gasoline	gal	16	91	77s
Taxes, state	capita	1477	91	77s

Transportation

Item	Per	Value	Date	Ref.
Driver's license fee		10.00	12/90	43s

Travel

Item	Per	Value	Date	Ref.
Business travel	day	178.00	4/93	89r

Utilities

Item	Per	Value	Date	Ref.
Electricity	mil Btu	25.98	90	64s

Santa Fe, NM

Alcoholic Beverages

Item	Per	Value	Date	Ref.
Beer, Miller Lite or Budweiser, 12-oz containers	6 pack	3.41	4Q 92	4c
Liquor, J & B Scotch	750 ml	17.29	4Q 92	4c
Wine, Gallo Chablis blanc, 1.5 liter	bottle	4.55	4Q 92	4c

Child Care

Item	Per	Value	Date	Ref.
Child care fee, average, center	hour	1.71	90	65r
Child care fee, average, nonregulated family day care	hour	1.32	90	65r
Child care fee, average, regulated family day care	hour	1.86	90	65r

Clothing

Item	Per	Value	Date	Ref.
Jeans, man's denim		28.60	4Q 92	4c
Shirt, man's dress shirt		22.87	4Q 92	4c
Undervest, boy's size 10-14, cotton	3	3.92	4Q 92	4c

Values are in dollars or fractions of dollars. In the column headed *Ref*, references are shown to sources. Each reference is followed by a letter. These refer to the geographical level for which data were reported: s=State, r=Region, and c=City or metro. The abbreviation *ex* is used to mean *except* or *excluding*; *exp* stands for expenditures. For other abbreviations and further explanations, please see the Introduction.

Santa Fe, NM - continued

Item	Per	Value	Date	Ref.
Communications				
Long-distance telephone service, day, initial minute, 0-100 miles	min	0.19-0.32	91	12s
Long-distance telephone service, day, additional minute, 0-100 miles	min	0.11-0.24	91	12s
Long-distance telephone service, evenings/weekends, 0-100 mi, initial minute	min	0.11-0.20	91	12s
Long-distance telephone service, evenings/weekends, 0-100 mi, additional minute	min	0.07-0.14	91	12s
Newspaper subscription, daily and Sunday home delivery, large-city	month	11.96	4Q 92	4c
Telephone, flat rate	month	12.93	91	11c
Telephone bill, family of four	month	18.71	4Q 92	4c
Education				
Board, 4-yr private college/university	year	1890	91	22s
Board, 4-yr public college/university	year	1527	91	22s
Expenditures, local gov't, public elementary/secondary	pupil	4524	92	20s
Room, 4-year private college/university	year	1468	91	22s
Room, 4-year public college/university	year	1321	91	22s
Tuition, 2-year private college/university	year	3594	91	22s
Tuition, 2-year public college/university	year	536	91	22s
Tuition, 4-year private college/university	year	8187	91	22s
Tuition, 4-year public college/university, in-state	year	1409	91	22s
Energy and Fuels				
Coal	mil Btu	1.32	90	64s
Energy	mil Btu	9.22	90	64s
Energy, combined forms, 1,800 sq ft heating area	month	93.68	4Q 92	4c
Energy, exc electricity, 1,800 sq ft heating area	month	35.00	4Q 92	4c
Energy exp/householder, 1-family unit	year	372	90	28r
Energy exp/householder, <1,000 sq ft heating area	year	335	90	28r
Energy exp/householder, 1,000-1,999 sq ft heating area	year	365	90	28r
Energy exp/householder, 2,000+ sq ft heating area	year	411	90	28r
Energy exp/householder, mobile home	year	305	90	28r
Energy exp/householder, multifamily	year	372	90	28r
Gas, natural	mil Btu	3.84	90	64s
Gas, natural	000 cu ft	5.40	91	46s
Gas, natural, exp	year	424	91	46s
Gasoline, motor	gal	1.24	4Q 92	4c
Gasoline, unleaded regular	mil Btu	9.23	90	64s
Entertainment				
Bowling, evening rate	game	2.30	4Q 92	4c
Miniature golf admission	adult	6.18	92	1r
Miniature golf admission	child	5.14	92	1r
Monopoly game, Parker Brothers', No. 9		10.49	4Q 92	4c
Movie	admission	6.00	4Q 92	4c
Tennis balls, yellow, Wilson or Penn, 3	can	2.75	4Q 92	4c
Waterpark admission	adult	11.00	92	1r
Waterpark admission	child	8.55	92	1r
Funerals				
Casket, 18-gauge steel, velvet interior		1929.04	91	24r
Cosmetology, hair care, etc.		88.52	91	24r
Embalming		249.33	91	24r
Facility use for ceremony		182.75	91	24r
Hearse, local		110.04	91	24r
Limousine, local		66.67	91	24r
Remains to funeral home, transfer		84.58	91	24r
Service charge, professional		593.00	91	24r
Vault, concrete, non-metallic liner		647.38	91	24r
Viewing facilities, use		99.87	91	24r
Groceries				
Apples, Red Delicious	lb	0.80	4/93	16r

Santa Fe, NM - continued

Item	Per	Value	Date	Ref.
Groceries - continued				
Babyfood, strained vegetables, lowest price	4-4.5 oz jar	0.23	4Q 92	4c
Bacon	lb	1.79	4/93	16r
Bananas	lb	0.47	4Q 92	4c
Bananas	lb	0.53	4/93	16r
Bologna, all beef or mixed	lb	2.67	4/93	16r
Bread, white	24 oz	0.66	4Q 92	4c
Bread, white, pan	lb	0.81	4/93	16r
Carrots, short trimmed and topped	lb	0.39	4/93	16r
Cheese, Kraft grated Parmesan	8-oz canister	3.52	4Q 92	4c
Chicken, fresh, whole	lb	0.94	4/93	16r
Chicken, fryer, whole	lb	0.58	4Q 92	4c
Chicken breast, bone-in	lb	2.19	4/93	16r
Chuck roast, graded and ungraded, ex USDA prime and choice	lb	2.26	4/93	16r
Cigarettes, Winston	carton	15.46	4Q 92	4c
Coffee, 100% ground roast, all sizes	lb	2.33	4/93	16r
Coffee, vacuum-packed	13-oz can	2.29	4Q 92	4c
Corn, frozen	10 oz	0.72	4Q 92	4c
Corn Flakes, Kellogg's or Post Toasties	18 oz	1.84	4Q 92	4c
Eggs, Grade A large	doz	0.78	4Q 92	4c
Eggs, Grade AA large	doz	1.18	4/93	16r
Flour, white, all purpose	lb	0.22	4/93	16r
Grapefruit	lb	0.52	4/93	16r
Grapes, Thompson Seedless	lb	1.50	4/93	16r
Ground beef, 100% beef	lb	1.44	4/93	16r
Ground beef, lean and extra lean	lb	2.34	4/93	16r
Ground beef or hamburger	lb	1.39	4Q 92	4c
Ham, boneless, excluding canned	lb	2.56	4/93	16r
Honey, jar	8 oz	0.99-1.19	92	5r
Honey, jar	lb	1.49-2.25	92	5r
Honey, squeeze bear	12-oz	1.00-1.89	92	5r
Ice cream, prepackaged, bulk, regular	1/2 gal	2.40	4/93	16r
Lemons	lb	0.81	4/93	16r
Lettuce, iceberg	head	0.96	4Q 92	4c
Lettuce, iceberg	lb	0.84	4/93	16r
Margarine, Blue Bonnet or Parkay cubes	lb	0.86	4Q 92	4c
Margarine, stick	lb	0.81	4/93	16r
Milk, whole	1/2 gal	1.58	4Q 92	4c
Orange juice, Minute Maid frozen	12-oz can	1.42	4Q 92	4c
Oranges, navel	lb	0.48	4/93	16r
Peaches	29-oz can	1.56	4Q 92	4c
Peas Sweet, Del Monte or Green Giant	15-17 oz can	0.61	4Q 92	4c
Pork chops, center cut, bone-in	lb	3.25	4/93	16r
Potato chips	16 oz	2.89	4/93	16r
Potatoes, white	lb	0.38	4/93	16r
Potatoes, white or red	10-lb sack	1.82	4Q 92	4c
Round roast, graded & ungraded, ex USDA prime & choice	lb	3.00	4/93	16r
Round roast, USDA choice, boneless	lb	3.16	4/93	16r
Sausage, Jimmy Dean, 100% pork	lb	2.15	4Q 92	4c
Shortening, vegetable oil blends	lb	0.86	4/93	16r
Shortening, vegetable, Crisco	3-lb can	1.99	4Q 92	4c
Soft drink, Coca Cola	2 liter	1.49	4Q 92	4c
Spaghetti and macaroni	lb	0.84	4/93	16r
Steak, round, graded & ungraded, ex USDA prime & choice	lb	3.34	4/93	16r
Steak, round, USDA choice, boneless	lb	3.24	4/93	16r
Steak, sirloin, graded & ungraded, ex USDA prime & choice	lb	3.75	4/93	16r
Steak, sirloin, USDA choice, boneless	lb	4.49	4/93	16r
Steak, T-bone	lb	4.76	4Q 92	4c
Sugar, cane or beet	4 lb	1.86	4Q 92	4c
Sugar, white	lb	0.41	4/93	16r

Values are in dollars or fractions of dollars. In the column headed *Ref*, references are shown to sources. Each reference is followed by a letter. These refer to the geographical level for which data were reported: s=State, r=Region, and c=City or metro. The abbreviation *ex* is used to mean *except* or *excluding*; *exp* stands for expenditures. For other abbreviations and further explanations, please see the Introduction.

Santa Fe, NM - continued

Item	Per	Value	Date	Ref.
Groceries				
Sugar, white, 33-80 oz pk	lb	0.38	4/93	16r
Tomatoes, field grown	lb	1.01	4/93	16r
Tomatoes, Hunt's or Del Monte	14.5-oz can	0.66	4Q 92	4c
Tuna, chunk, light	6.125-6.5 oz can	0.66	4Q 92	4c
Turkey, frozen, whole	lb	1.04	4/93	16r
Health Care				
Analgesic, Aspirin, Bayer, 325 mg tablets	100	4.79	4Q 92	4c
Childbirth, cesarean, hospital		5533	91	62r
Childbirth, cesarean, physician's fee		2053	91	62r
Childbirth, normal, hospital		2745	91	62r
Childbirth, normal, physician's fee		1492	91	62r
Dentist's fee, adult teeth cleaning and periodic oral exam	visit	54.75	4Q 92	4c
Doctor's fee, routine exam, established patient	visit	38.26	4Q 92	4c
Hospital care, semiprivate room	day	270.00	4Q 92	4c
Medical insurance premium, per employee, small group comprehensive	month	306.60	10/91	25c
Medical plan per employee	year	3218	91	45r
Mental health care, exp	capita	20.37-28.83	90	38s
Mental health care, exp, state mental health agency	capita	22.88	90	38s
Mental health care, hospital psychiatric services, non-Federal, exp	capita	7.77	88	38s
Mental health care, mental health organization, multiservice, exp	capita	16.77	88	38s
Mental health care, psychiatric hospitals, private, exp	capita	32.81	88	38s
Mental health care, psychiatric out-patient clinics, freestanding, exp	capita	2.18	88	38s
Mental health care, psychiatric partial-care organizations, freestanding, exp	capita	1.80	88	38s
Mental health care, state and county mental hospitals, exp	capita	20.94	88	38s
Mental health care, VA medical centers, exp	capita	2.32	88	38s
Physician fee, family practice, first-visit		111.00	91	62r
Physician fee, family practice, revisit		45.00	91	62r
Physician fee, general practice, first-visit		100.00	91	62r
Physician fee, general practice, revisit		40.00	91	62r
Physician fee, internal medicine, first-visit		137.00	91	62r
Physician fee, internal medicine, revisit		48.00	91	62r
Physician fee, median, neurosurgeon, first-visit		157.00	91	62r
Physician fee, median, nonsurgical specialist, first-visit		131.00	91	62r
Physician fee, median, orthopedic surgeon, first-visit		124.00	91	62r
Physician fee, median, plastic surgeon, first-visit		88.00	91	62r
Physician fee, median, surgical specialist, first-visit		100.00	91	62r
Physician fee, neurosurgeon, revisit		51.00	91	62r
Physician fee, nonsurgical specialist, revisit		47.00	91	62r
Physician fee, obstetrics/gynecology, first-visit		95.00	91	62r
Physician fee, obstetrics/gynecology, revisit		50.00	91	62r
Physician fee, orthopedic surgeon, revisit		51.00	91	62r
Physician fee, pediatrician, first-visit		81.00	91	62r
Physician fee, pediatrician, revisit		42.00	91	62r
Physician fee, plastic surgeon, revisit		48.00	91	62r
Physician fee, surgical specialist, revisit		49.00	91	62r
Substance abuse, hospital ancillary charge	incident	2630	90	70s
Substance abuse, hospital physician charge	incident	840	90	70s
Substance abuse, hospital room and board	incident	6500	90	70s

Santa Fe, NM - continued

Item	Per	Value	Date	Ref.
Household Goods				
Appliance repair, home, service call, washing machine	min labor charge	35.79	4Q 92	4c
Laundry detergent, Tide Ultra, Bold, or Cheer	42 oz	4.26	4Q 92	4c
Tissues, facial, Kleenex brand	175-count box	1.22	4Q 92	4c
Housing				
House, 1,800 sq ft, 8,000 sq ft lot, new, urban	total	157200	4Q 92	4c
House payment, principal and interest, 25% down payment	month	889	4Q 92	4c
Mortgage rate, incl. points & origination fee, 30-year fixed or adjustable rate	percent	8.29	4Q 92	4c
Rent, apartment, 2 bedrooms - 1-1/2 to 2 baths, unfurnished, 950 sq ft, water	month	672	4Q 92	4c
Rental unit, 1 bedroom	month	557	93	23c
Rental unit, 2 bedroom	month	657	93	23c
Rental unit, 3 bedroom	month	819	93	23c
Rental unit, 4 bedroom	month	919	93	23c
Rental unit, efficiency	month	458	93	23c
Insurance and Pensions				
Auto insurance, private passenger	year	628.37	91	63s
Personal Goods				
Shampoo, Alberto VO5	15 oz	1.36	4Q 92	4c
Toothpaste, Crest or Colgate	6-7 oz	1.89	4Q 92	4c
Personal Services				
Dry cleaning, man's 2-piece suit		6.65	4Q 92	4c
Haircare, woman's shampoo, trim and blow-dry		23.67	4Q 92	4c
Haircut, man's barbershop, no styling		7.01	4Q 92	4c
Restaurant Food				
Chicken, fried, thigh and drumstick		2.11	4Q 92	4c
Hamburger with cheese	1/4 lb	1.99	4Q 92	4c
Pizza, Pizza Hut or Pizza Inn, cheese, thin crust	12-13 in	7.59	4Q 92	4c
Taxes				
Tax, cigarette	pack	15	91	77s
Tax, gasoline	gal	16	91	77s
Taxes, state	capita	1347	91	77s
Transportation				
Driver's license fee		10.00	12/90	43s
Tire balance, computer or spin balance, front	wheel	6.79	4Q 92	4c
Travel				
Business travel	day	178.00	4/93	89r
Utilities				
Electricity	mil Btu	20.99	90	64s
Electricity, partial electric and other energy, 1,800 sq ft living area new home	month	58.68	4Q 92	4c
Electricity, residential	KWh	9.58	2/93	94s

Santa Rosa-Petaluma, CA

Item	Per	Value	Date	Ref.
Child Care				
Child care fee, average, center	hour	1.71	90	65r
Child care fee, average, nonregulated family day care	hour	1.32	90	65r
Child care fee, average, regulated family day care	hour	1.86	90	65r
Communications				
Long-distance telephone service, day, initial minute, 0-100 miles	min	0.17-0.40	91	12s
Long-distance telephone service, day, additional minute, 0-100 miles	min	0.07-0.31	91	12s

Values are in dollars or fractions of dollars. In the column headed *Ref*, references are shown to sources. Each reference is followed by a letter. These refer to the geographical level for which data were reported: s = State, r = Region, and c = City or metro. The abbreviation *ex* is used to mean *except* or *excluding*; *exp* stands for expenditures. For other abbreviations and further explanations, please see the Introduction.

Santa Rosa-Petaluma, CA - continued

Item	Per	Value	Date	Ref.
Communications				
Long-distance telephone service, evenings/ weekends, 0-100 mi, initial minute	min	0.07-0.16	91	12s
Long-distance telephone service, evenings/ weekends, 0-100 mi, additional minute	min	0.03-0.12	91	12s
Education				
Board, 4-yr private college/university	year	2515	91	22s
Board, 4-yr public college/university	year	2268	91	22s
Expenditures, local gov't, public elementary/secondary	pupil	4866	92	20s
Room, 4-year private college/university	year	2622	91	22s
Room, 4-year public college/university	year	2406	91	22s
Tuition, 2-year private college/university	year	7942	91	22s
Tuition, 2-year public college/university	year	114	91	22s
Tuition, 4-year private college/university	year	10863	91	22s
Tuition, 4-year public college/university, in-state	year	1220	91	22s
Energy and Fuels				
Coal	mil Btu	2.01	90	64s
Energy	mil Btu	9.08	90	64s
Energy exp/householder, 1-family unit	year	362	90	28r
Energy exp/householder, <1,000 sq ft heating area	year	254	90	28r
Energy exp/householder, 1,000-1,999 sq ft heating area	year	358	90	28r
Energy exp/householder, 2,000+ sq ft heating area	year	467	90	28r
Energy exp/householder, mobile home	year	390	90	28r
Energy exp/householder, multifamily	year	252	90	28r
Gas, natural	mil Btu	4.31	90	64s
Gas, natural	000 cu ft	6.27	91	46s
Gas, natural, exp	year	369	91	46s
Gasoline, unleaded regular	mil Btu	8.57	90	64s
Entertainment				
Miniature golf admission	adult	6.18	92	1r
Miniature golf admission	child	5.14	92	1r
Waterpark admission	adult	11.00	92	1r
Waterpark admission	child	8.55	92	1r
Funerals				
Casket, 18-gauge steel, velvet interior		1781.09	91	24r
Cosmetology, hair care, etc.		84.64	91	24r
Embalming		207.41	91	24r
Facility use for ceremony		205.76	91	24r
Hearse, local		105.14	91	24r
Limousine, local		83.21	91	24r
Remains to funeral home, transfer		113.82	91	24r
Service charge, professional		626.33	91	24r
Vault, concrete, non-metallic liner		599.54	91	24r
Viewing facilities, use		85.81	91	24r
Groceries				
Apples, Red Delicious	lb	0.80	4/93	16r
Bacon	lb	1.79	4/93	16r
Bananas	lb	0.53	4/93	16r
Bologna, all beef or mixed	lb	2.67	4/93	16r
Bread, white, pan	lb	0.81	4/93	16r
Carrots, short trimmed and topped	lb	0.39	4/93	16r
Chicken, fresh, whole	lb	0.94	4/93	16r
Chicken breast, bone-in	lb	2.19	4/93	16r
Chuck roast, graded and ungraded, ex USDA prime and choice	lb	2.26	4/93	16r
Coffee, 100% ground roast, all sizes	lb	2.33	4/93	16r
Eggs, Grade AA large	doz	1.18	4/93	16r
Flour, white, all purpose	lb	0.22	4/93	16r
Grapefruit	lb	0.52	4/93	16r
Grapes, Thompson Seedless	lb	1.50	4/93	16r
Ground beef, 100% beef	lb	1.44	4/93	16r
Ground beef, lean and extra lean	lb	2.34	4/93	16r
Ham, boneless, excluding canned	lb	2.56	4/93	16r
Honey, jar	8 oz	0.89-1.00	92	5r

Santa Rosa-Petaluma, CA - continued

Item	Per	Value	Date	Ref.
Groceries - continued				
Honey, jar	lb	1.35-1.97	92	5r
Honey, squeeze bear	12-oz	1.19-1.50	92	5r
Ice cream, prepackaged, bulk, regular	1/2 gal	2.40	4/93	16r
Lemons	lb	0.81	4/93	16r
Lettuce, iceberg	lb	0.84	4/93	16r
Margarine, stick	lb	0.81	4/93	16r
Oranges, navel	lb	0.48	4/93	16r
Pork chops, center cut, bone-in	lb	3.25	4/93	16r
Potato chips	16 oz	2.89	4/93	16r
Potatoes, white	lb	0.38	4/93	16r
Round roast, graded & ungraded, ex USDA prime & choice	lb	3.00	4/93	16r
Round roast, USDA choice, boneless	lb	3.16	4/93	16r
Shortening, vegetable oil blends	lb	0.86	4/93	16r
Spaghetti and macaroni	lb	0.84	4/93	16r
Steak, round, graded & ungraded, ex USDA prime & choice	lb	3.34	4/93	16r
Steak, round, USDA choice, boneless	lb	3.24	4/93	16r
Steak, sirloin, graded & ungraded, ex USDA prime & choice	lb	3.75	4/93	16r
Steak, sirloin, USDA choice, boneless	lb	4.49	4/93	16r
Sugar, white	lb	0.41	4/93	16r
Sugar, white, 33-80 oz pk	lb	0.38	4/93	16r
Tomatoes, field grown	lb	1.01	4/93	16r
Turkey, frozen, whole	lb	1.04	4/93	16r
Health Care				
Cardizem 60 mg tablets	30	24.04	92	49s
Cector 250 mg tablets	15	35.87	92	49s
Childbirth, cesarean, hospital		5533	91	62r
Childbirth, cesarean, physician's fee		2053	91	62r
Childbirth, normal, hospital		2745	91	62r
Childbirth, normal, physician's fee		1492	91	62r
Health care spending, state	capita	2894	3/93	84s
Medical plan per employee	year	3421	91	45r
Mental health care, exp	capita	37.60-53.67	90	38s
Mental health care, exp, state mental health agency	capita	42.32	90	38s
Mental health care, hospital psychiatric services, non-Federal, exp	capita	10.64	88	38s
Mental health care, mental health organization, multiservice, exp	capita	28.56	88	38s
Mental health care, psychiatric hospitals, private, exp	capita	18.60	88	38s
Mental health care, psychiatric out-patient clinics, freestanding, exp	capita	2.28	88	38s
Mental health care, psychiatric partial-care organizations, freestanding, exp	capita	0.24	88	38s
Mental health care, state and county mental hospitals, exp	capita	13.60	88	38s
Mental health care, VA medical centers, exp	capita	2.33	88	38s
Mevacor 20 mg tablets	30	67.62	92	49s
Physician fee, family practice, first-visit		111.00	91	62r
Physician fee, family practice, revisit		45.00	91	62r
Physician fee, general practice, first-visit		100.00	91	62r
Physician fee, general practice, revisit		40.00	91	62r
Physician fee, internal medicine, first-visit		137.00	91	62r
Physician fee, internal medicine, revisit		48.00	91	62r
Physician fee, median, neurosurgeon, first-visit		157.00	91	62r
Physician fee, median, nonsurgical specialist, first-visit		131.00	91	62r
Physician fee, median, orthopedic surgeon, first-visit		124.00	91	62r
Physician fee, median, plastic surgeon, first-visit		88.00	91	62r
Physician fee, median, surgical specialist, first-visit		100.00	91	62r
Physician fee, neurosurgeon, revisit		51.00	91	62r
Physician fee, nonsurgical specialist, revisit		47.00	91	62r
Physician fee, obstetrics/gynecology, first-visit		95.00	91	62r

Values are in dollars or fractions of dollars. In the column headed *Ref*, references are shown to sources. Each reference is followed by a letter. These refer to the geographical level for which data were reported: s = State, r = Region, and c = City or metro. The abbreviation *ex* is used to mean *except* or *excluding; exp* stands for expenditures. For other abbreviations and further explanations, please see the Introduction.

Santa Rosa-Petaluma, CA - continued

Item	Per	Value	Date	Ref.
Health Care				
Physician fee, obstetrics/gynecology, revisit		50.00	91	62r
Physician fee, orthopedic surgeon, revisit		51.00	91	62r
Physician fee, pediatrician, first-visit		81.00	91	62r
Physician fee, pediatrician, revisit		42.00	91	62r
Physician fee, plastic surgeon, revisit		48.00	91	62r
Physician fee, surgical specialist, revisit		49.00	91	62r
Prozac 20 mg tablets	14	33.22	92	49s
Substance abuse, hospital ancillary charge	incident	1760	90	70s
Substance abuse, hospital physician charge	incident	750	90	70s
Substance abuse, hospital room and board	incident	6390	90	70s
Tagamet 300 mg tablets	100	77.08	92	49s
Xanax 0.25 mg tablets	90	64.08	92	49s
Zantac 160 mg tablets	60	92.31	92	49s
Housing				
Home, median price	unit	131,200	92	58s
Insurance and Pensions				
Auto insurance, private passenger	year	904.37	91	63s
Taxes				
Tax, cigarette	pack	35	91	77s
Tax, gasoline	gal	16	91	77s
Taxes, state	capita	1477	91	77s
Transportation				
Driver's license fee		10.00	12/90	43s
Travel				
Business travel	day	178.00	4/93	89r
Utilities				
Electricity	mil Btu	25.98	90	64s

Sarasota, FL

Item	Per	Value	Date	Ref.
Child Care				
Child care fee, average, center	hour	1.29	90	65r
Child care fee, average, nonregulated family day care	hour	0.89	90	65r
Child care fee, average, regulated family day care	hour	1.32	90	65r
Communications				
Long-distance telephone service, day, initial minute, 0-100 miles	min	0.15-0.20	91	12s
Long-distance telephone service, day, additional minute, 0-100 miles	min	0.08-0.20	91	12s
Long-distance telephone service, evenings/weekends, 0-100 mi, initial minute	min	0.09-0.12	91	12s
Long-distance telephone service, evenings/weekends, 0-100 mi, additional minute	min	0.05-0.12	91	12s
Education				
Board, 4-yr private college/university	year	1924	91	22s
Board, 4-yr public college/university	year	1955	91	22s
Expenditures, local gov't, public elementary/secondary	pupil	5235	92	20s
Room, 4-year private college/university	year	1904	91	22s
Room, 4-year public college/university	year	1510	91	22s
Tuition, 2-year private college/university	year	4751	91	22s
Tuition, 2-year public college/university	year	788	91	22s
Tuition, 4-year private college/university	year	7992	91	22s
Tuition, 4-year public college/university, in-state	year	1337	91	22s
Energy and Fuels				
Coal	mil Btu	1.85	90	64s
Energy	mil Btu	10.58	90	64s
Energy exp/householder, 1-family unit	year	487	90	28r
Energy exp/householder, <1,000 sq ft heating area	year	393	90	28r

Sarasota, FL - continued

Item	Per	Value	Date	Ref.
Energy and Fuels - continued				
Energy exp/householder, 1,000-1,999 sq ft heating area	year	442	90	28r
Energy exp/householder, 2,000+ sq ft heating area	year	577	90	28r
Energy exp/householder, mobile home	year	366	90	28r
Energy exp/householder, multifamily	year	382	90	28r
Gas, natural	mil Btu	3.21	90	64s
Gas, natural	000 cu ft	8.98	91	46s
Gas, natural, exp	year	248	91	46s
Gasoline, unleaded regular	mil Btu	8.85	90	64s
Entertainment				
Miniature golf admission	adult	6.18	92	1r
Miniature golf admission	child	5.14	92	1r
Waterpark admission	adult	11.00	92	1r
Waterpark admission	child	8.55	92	1r
Funerals				
Casket, 18-gauge steel, velvet interior		2029.08	91	24r
Cosmetology, hair care, etc.		75.10	91	24r
Embalming		249.24	91	24r
Facility use for ceremony		162.27	91	24r
Hearse, local		114.04	91	24r
Limousine, local		88.57	91	24r
Remains to funeral home, transfer		92.61	91	24r
Service charge, professional		682.42	91	24r
Vault, concrete, non-metallic liner		798.70	91	24r
Viewing facilities, use		163.86	91	24r
Groceries				
Apples, Red Delicious	lb	0.79	4/93	16r
Bacon	lb	1.75	4/93	16r
Bananas	lb	0.42	4/93	16r
Beef, stew, boneless	lb	2.61	4/93	16r
Bologna, all beef or mixed	lb	2.24	4/93	16r
Bread, white, pan	lb	0.64	4/93	16r
Bread, whole wheat, pan	lb	0.96	4/93	16r
Cabbage	lb	0.37	4/93	16r
Carrots, short trimmed and topped	lb	0.47	4/93	16r
Celery	lb	0.64	4/93	16r
Cheese, American	lb	2.98	4/93	16r
Cheese, Cheddar	lb	3.28	4/93	16r
Chicken, fresh, whole	lb	0.77	4/93	16r
Chicken breast, bone-in	lb	1.92	4/93	16r
Chicken legs, bone-in	lb	1.06	4/93	16r
Chuck roast, graded and ungraded, ex USDA prime and choice	lb	2.40	4/93	16r
Chuck roast, USDA choice, bone-in	lb	2.19	4/93	16r
Chuck roast, USDA choice, boneless	lb	2.38	4/93	16r
Coffee, 100% ground roast, all sizes	lb	2.48	4/93	16r
Crackers, soda, salted	lb	1.15	4/93	16r
Eggs, Grade A large	doz	0.96	4/93	16r
Flour, white, all purpose	lb	0.24	4/93	16r
Frankfurters, all meat or all beef	lb	2.01	4/93	16r
Grapefruit	lb	0.44	4/93	16r
Grapes, Thompson Seedless	lb	1.40	4/93	16r
Ground beef, 100% beef	lb	1.58	4/93	16r
Ground beef, lean and extra lean	lb	2.09	4/93	16r
Ground chuck, 100% beef	lb	1.98	4/93	16r
Ham, boneless, excluding canned	lb	2.89	4/93	16r
Ham, picnic, shoulder, bone-in, smoked	lb	1.02	4/93	16r
Ham, rump or steak half, bone-in, smoked	lb	1.48	4/93	16r
Ice cream, prepackaged, bulk, regular	1/2 gal	2.41	4/93	16r
Lemons	lb	1.05	4/93	16r
Lettuce, iceberg	lb	0.81	4/93	16r
Margarine, stick	lb	0.88	4/93	16r
Oranges, navel	lb	0.55	4/93	16r
Pears, Anjou	lb	0.92	4/93	16r
Pork chops, center cut, bone-in	lb	3.13	4/93	16r
Potato chips	16 oz	2.94	4/93	16r
Potatoes, white	lb	0.43	4/93	16r
Rib roast, USDA choice, bone-in	lb	4.63	4/93	16r
Rice, white, long grain, uncooked	lb	0.45	4/93	16r

Values are in dollars or fractions of dollars. In the column headed *Ref*, references are shown to sources. Each reference is followed by a letter. These refer to the geographical level for which data were reported: s=State, r=Region, and c=City or metro. The abbreviation *ex* is used to mean *except* or *excluding*; *exp* stands for expenditures. For other abbreviations and further explanations, please see the Introduction.

Sarasota, FL - continued

Item	Per	Value	Date	Ref.
Groceries				
Round roast, graded & ungraded, ex USDA prime & choice	lb	3.03	4/93	16r
Round roast, USDA choice, boneless	lb	3.09	4/93	16r
Sausage, fresh, loose	lb	2.08	4/93	16r
Short ribs, bone-in	lb	2.66	4/93	16r
Shortening, vegetable oil blends	lb	0.69	4/93	16r
Spaghetti and macaroni	lb	0.81	4/93	16r
Steak, rib eye, USDA choice, boneless	lb	6.24	4/93	16r
Steak, round, graded & ungraded, ex USDA prime & choice	lb	3.31	4/93	16r
Steak, round, USDA choice, boneless	lb	3.34	4/93	16r
Steak, sirloin, graded & ungraded, ex USDA prime & choice	lb	4.19	4/93	16r
Steak, sirloin, USDA choice, boneless	lb	4.46	4/93	16r
Steak, T-bone, USDA choice, bone-in	lb	5.25	4/93	16r
Strawberries, dry pint	12 oz	0.92	4/93	16r
Sugar, white	lb	0.39	4/93	16r
Sugar, white, 33-80 oz pk	lb	0.38	4/93	16r
Tomatoes, field grown	lb	0.88	4/93	16r
Tuna, chunk, light	lb	1.79	4/93	16r
Turkey, frozen, whole	lb	1.04	4/93	16r
Yogurt, natural, fruit flavored	1/2 pint	0.57	4/93	16r
Health Care				
Childbirth, cesarean, hospital		5034	91	62r
Childbirth, cesarean, physician's fee		2053	91	62r
Childbirth, normal, hospital		2712	91	62r
Childbirth, normal, physician's fee		1492	91	62r
Medical plan per employee	year	3495	91	45r
Mental health care, exp	capita	28.84-37.59	90	38s
Mental health care, exp, state mental health agency	capita	37.49	90	38s
Mental health care, hospital psychiatric services, non-Federal, exp	capita	9.11	88	38s
Mental health care, mental health organization, multiservice, exp	capita	16.21	88	38s
Mental health care, psychiatric hospitals, private, exp	capita	22.26	88	38s
Mental health care, psychiatric out-patient clinics, freestanding, exp	capita	0.89	88	38s
Mental health care, psychiatric partial-care organizations, freestanding, exp	capita	0.41	88	38s
Mental health care, state and county mental hospitals, exp	capita	16.25	88	38s
Mental health care, VA medical centers, exp	capita	1.69	88	38s
Physician fee, family practice, first-visit		75.00	91	62r
Physician fee, family practice, revisit		34.00	91	62r
Physician fee, general practice, first-visit		61.00	91	62r
Physician fee, general practice, revisit		32.00	91	62r
Physician fee, general surgeon, first-visit		64.00	91	62r
Physician fee, general surgeon, revisit		40.00	91	62r
Physician fee, internal medicine, first-visit		98.00	91	62r
Physician fee, internal medicine, revisit		40.00	91	62r
Physician fee, median, neurosurgeon, first-visit		130.00	91	62r
Physician fee, median, nonsurgical specialist, first-visit		95.00	91	62r
Physician fee, median, orthopedic surgeon, first-visit		91.00	91	62r
Physician fee, median, plastic surgeon, first-visit		66.00	91	62r
Physician fee, median, surgical specialist, first-visit		62.00	91	62r
Physician fee, neurosurgeon, revisit		50.00	91	62r
Physician fee, nonsurgical specialist, revisit		40.00	91	62r
Physician fee, obstetrics/gynecology, first-visit		64.00	91	62r
Physician fee, obstetrics/gynecology, revisit		41.00	91	62r
Physician fee, orthopedic surgeon, revisit		40.00	91	62r
Physician fee, pediatrician, first-visit		49.00	91	62r
Physician fee, pediatrician, revisit		33.00	91	62r

Sarasota, FL - continued

Item	Per	Value	Date	Ref.
Health Care - continued				
Physician fee, plastic surgeon, revisit		43.00	91	62r
Physician fee, surgical specialist, revisit		37.00	91	62r
Substance abuse, hospital ancillary charge	incident	1390	90	70s
Substance abuse, hospital physician charge	incident	770	90	70s
Substance abuse, hospital room and board	incident	5600	90	70s
Insurance and Pensions				
Auto insurance, private passenger	year	727.60	91	63s
Taxes				
Tax, cigarette	pack	33.90	91	77s
Tax, gasoline	gal	11.60	91	77s
Taxes, state	capita	1037	91	77s
Transportation				
Driver's license fee		15.00	12/90	43s
Travel				
Business travel	day	193.00	4/93	89r
Utilities				
Electricity	mil Btu	20.62	90	64s

Savannah, GA

Item	Per	Value	Date	Ref.
Child Care				
Child care fee, average, center	hour	1.29	90	65r
Child care fee, average, nonregulated family day care	hour	0.89	90	65r
Child care fee, average, regulated family day care	hour	1.32	90	65r
Communications				
Long-distance telephone service, day, initial minute, 0-100 miles	min	0.16-0.26	91	12s
Long-distance telephone service, day, additional minute, 0-100 miles	min	0.08-0.23	91	12s
Long-distance telephone service, evenings/weekends, 0-100 mi, initial minute	min	0.06-0.13	91	12s
Long-distance telephone service, evenings/weekends, 0-100 mi, additional minute	min	0.04-0.12	91	12s
Education				
Board, 4-yr private college/university	year	1801	91	22s
Board, 4-yr public college/university	year	1501	91	22s
Expenditures, local gov't, public elementary/secondary	pupil	4747	92	20s
Room, 4-year private college/university	year	2139	91	22s
Room, 4-year public college/university	year	1192	91	22s
Tuition, 2-year private college/university	year	4457	91	22s
Tuition, 2-year public college/university	year	946	91	22s
Tuition, 4-year private college/university	year	7542	91	22s
Tuition, 4-year public college/university, in-state	year	1680	91	22s
Energy and Fuels				
Coal	mil Btu	1.79	90	64s
Energy	mil Btu	8.88	90	64s
Energy exp/householder, 1-family unit	year	487	90	28r
Energy exp/householder, <1,000 sq ft heating area	year	393	90	28r
Energy exp/householder, 1,000-1,999 sq ft heating area	year	442	90	28r
Energy exp/householder, 2,000+ sq ft heating area	year	577	90	28r
Energy exp/householder, mobile home	year	366	90	28r
Energy exp/householder, multifamily	year	382	90	28r
Gas, natural	mil Btu	4.80	90	64s
Gas, natural	000 cu ft	6.70	91	46s
Gas, natural, exp	year	475	91	46s
Gasoline, unleaded regular	mil Btu	8.24	90	64s

Values are in dollars or fractions of dollars. In the column headed *Ref*, references are shown to sources. Each reference is followed by a letter. These refer to the geographical level for which data were reported: s=State, r=Region, and c=City or metro. The abbreviation *ex* is used to mean *except* or *excluding*; *exp* stands for expenditures. For other abbreviations and further explanations, please see the Introduction.

Savannah, GA - continued

Item	Per	Value	Date	Ref.
Entertainment				
Miniature golf admission	adult	6.18	92	1r
Miniature golf admission	child	5.14	92	1r
Waterpark admission	adult	11.00	92	1r
Waterpark admission	child	8.55	92	1r
Funerals				
Casket, 18-gauge steel, velvet interior		2029.08	91	24r
Cosmetology, hair care, etc.		75.10	91	24r
Embalming		249.24	91	24r
Facility use for ceremony		162.27	91	24r
Hearse, local		114.04	91	24r
Limousine, local		88.57	91	24r
Remains to funeral home, transfer		92.61	91	24r
Service charge, professional		682.42	91	24r
Vault, concrete, non-metallic liner		798.70	91	24r
Viewing facilities, use		163.86	91	24r
Groceries				
Apples, Red Delicious	lb	0.79	4/93	16r
Bacon	lb	1.75	4/93	16r
Bananas	lb	0.42	4/93	16r
Beef, stew, boneless	lb	2.61	4/93	16r
Bologna, all beef or mixed	lb	2.24	4/93	16r
Bread, white, pan	lb	0.64	4/93	16r
Bread, whole wheat, pan	lb	0.96	4/93	16r
Cabbage	lb	0.37	4/93	16r
Carrots, short trimmed and topped	lb	0.47	4/93	16r
Celery	lb	0.64	4/93	16r
Cheese, American	lb	2.98	4/93	16r
Cheese, Cheddar	lb	3.28	4/93	16r
Chicken, fresh, whole	lb	0.77	4/93	16r
Chicken breast, bone-in	lb	1.92	4/93	16r
Chicken legs, bone-in	lb	1.06	4/93	16r
Chuck roast, graded and ungraded, ex USDA prime and choice	lb	2.40	4/93	16r
Chuck roast, USDA choice, bone-in	lb	2.19	4/93	16r
Chuck roast, USDA choice, boneless	lb	2.38	4/93	16r
Coffee, 100% ground roast, all sizes	lb	2.48	4/93	16r
Crackers, soda, salted	lb	1.15	4/93	16r
Eggs, Grade A large	doz	0.96	4/93	16r
Flour, white, all purpose	lb	0.24	4/93	16r
Frankfurters, all meat or all beef	lb	2.01	4/93	16r
Grapefruit	lb	0.44	4/93	16r
Grapes, Thompson Seedless	lb	1.40	4/93	16r
Ground beef, 100% beef	lb	1.58	4/93	16r
Ground beef, lean and extra lean	lb	2.09	4/93	16r
Ground chuck, 100% beef	lb	1.98	4/93	16r
Ham, boneless, excluding canned	lb	2.89	4/93	16r
Ham, picnic, shoulder, bone-in, smoked	lb	1.02	4/93	16r
Ham, rump or steak half, bone-in, smoked	lb	1.48	4/93	16r
Ice cream, prepackaged, bulk, regular	1/2 gal	2.41	4/93	16r
Lemons	lb	1.05	4/93	16r
Lettuce, iceberg	lb	0.81	4/93	16r
Margarine, stick	lb	0.88	4/93	16r
Oranges, navel	lb	0.55	4/93	16r
Pears, Anjou	lb	0.92	4/93	16r
Pork chops, center cut, bone-in	lb	3.13	4/93	16r
Potato chips	16 oz	2.94	4/93	16r
Potatoes, white	lb	0.43	4/93	16r
Rib roast, USDA choice, bone-in	lb	4.63	4/93	16r
Rice, white, long grain, uncooked	lb	0.45	4/93	16r
Round roast, graded & ungraded, ex USDA prime & choice	lb	3.03	4/93	16r
Round roast, USDA choice, boneless	lb	3.09	4/93	16r
Sausage, fresh, loose	lb	2.08	4/93	16r
Short ribs, bone-in	lb	2.66	4/93	16r
Shortening, vegetable oil blends	lb	0.69	4/93	16r
Spaghetti and macaroni	lb	0.81	4/93	16r
Steak, rib eye, USDA choice, boneless	lb	6.24	4/93	16r
Steak, round, graded & ungraded, ex USDA prime & choice	lb	3.31	4/93	16r
Steak, round, USDA choice, boneless	lb	3.34	4/93	16r

Savannah, GA - continued

Item	Per	Value	Date	Ref.
Groceries - continued				
Steak, sirloin, graded & ungraded, ex USDA prime & choice	lb	4.19	4/93	16r
Steak, sirloin, USDA choice, boneless	lb	4.46	4/93	16r
Steak, T-bone, USDA choice, bone-in	lb	5.25	4/93	16r
Strawberries, dry pint	12 oz	0.92	4/93	16r
Sugar, white	lb	0.39	4/93	16r
Sugar, white, 33-80 oz pk	lb	0.38	4/93	16r
Tomatoes, field grown	lb	0.88	4/93	16r
Tuna, chunk, light	lb	1.79	4/93	16r
Turkey, frozen, whole	lb	1.04	4/93	16r
Yogurt, natural, fruit flavored	1/2 pint	0.57	4/93	16r
Health Care				
Childbirth, cesarean, hospital		5034	91	62r
Childbirth, cesarean, physician's fee		2053	91	62r
Childbirth, normal, hospital		2712	91	62r
Childbirth, normal, physician's fee		1492	91	62r
Medical plan per employee	year	3495	91	45r
Mental health care, exp	capita	37.60-53.67	90	38s
Mental health care, exp, state mental health agency	capita	50.98	90	38s
Mental health care, hospital psychiatric services, non-Federal, exp	capita	9.66	88	38s
Mental health care, mental health organization, multiservice, exp	capita	16.40	88	38s
Mental health care, psychiatric hospitals, private, exp	capita	26.36	88	38s
Mental health care, psychiatric out-patient clinics, freestanding, exp	capita	0.13	88	38s
Mental health care, state and county mental hospitals, exp	capita	38.94	88	38s
Mental health care, VA medical centers, exp	capita	3.91	88	38s
Physician fee, family practice, first-visit		75.00	91	62r
Physician fee, family practice, revisit		34.00	91	62r
Physician fee, general practice, first-visit		61.00	91	62r
Physician fee, general practice, revisit		32.00	91	62r
Physician fee, general surgeon, first-visit		64.00	91	62r
Physician fee, general surgeon, revisit		40.00	91	62r
Physician fee, internal medicine, first-visit		98.00	91	62r
Physician fee, internal medicine, revisit		40.00	91	62r
Physician fee, median, neurosurgeon, first-visit		130.00	91	62r
Physician fee, median, nonsurgical specialist, first-visit		95.00	91	62r
Physician fee, median, orthopedic surgeon, first-visit		91.00	91	62r
Physician fee, median, plastic surgeon, first-visit		66.00	91	62r
Physician fee, median, surgical specialist, first-visit		62.00	91	62r
Physician fee, neurosurgeon, revisit		50.00	91	62r
Physician fee, nonsurgical specialist, revisit		40.00	91	62r
Physician fee, obstetrics/gynecology, first-visit		64.00	91	62r
Physician fee, obstetrics/gynecology, revisit		41.00	91	62r
Physician fee, orthopedic surgeon, revisit		40.00	91	62r
Physician fee, pediatrician, first-visit		49.00	91	62r
Physician fee, pediatrician, revisit		33.00	91	62r
Physician fee, plastic surgeon, revisit		43.00	91	62r
Physician fee, surgical specialist, revisit		37.00	91	62r
Substance abuse, hospital ancillary charge	incident	1800	90	70s
Substance abuse, hospital physician charge	incident	890	90	70s
Substance abuse, hospital room and board	incident	5560	90	70s
Insurance and Pensions				
Auto insurance, private passenger	year	651.31	91	63s

Values are in dollars or fractions of dollars. In the column headed *Ref*, references are shown to sources. Each reference is followed by a letter. These refer to the geographical level for which data were reported: s = State, r = Region, and c = City or metro. The abbreviation *ex* is used to mean *except* or *excluding*; *exp* stands for expenditures. For other abbreviations and further explanations, please see the Introduction.

Savannah, GA - continued

Item	Per	Value	Date	Ref.
Taxes				
Tax, cigarette	pack	12	91	77s
Tax, gasoline	gal	7.50	91	77s
Taxes, state	capita	1080	91	77s
Transportation				
Driver's license fee		4.50	12/90	43s
Travel				
Business travel	day	193.00	4/93	89r
Utilities				
Electricity	mil Btu	19.25	90	64s

Scottsdale, AZ

Item	Per	Value	Date	Ref.
Composite ACCRA index		101.40	4Q 92	4c
Alcoholic Beverages				
Beer, Miller Lite or Budweiser, 12-oz containers	6 pack	3.69	4Q 92	4c
Liquor, J & B Scotch	750 ml	14.49	4Q 92	4c
Wine, Gallo Chablis blanc, 1.5 liter	bottle	4.35	4Q 92	4c
Clothing				
Jeans, man's denim		31.33	4Q 92	4c
Shirt, man's dress shirt		20.00	4Q 92	4c
Undervest, boy's size 10-14, cotton	3	2.99	4Q 92	4c
Communications				
Newspaper subscription, daily and Sunday home delivery, large-city	month	13.26	4Q 92	4c
Telephone bill, family of four	month	16.75	4Q 92	4c
Energy and Fuels				
Energy, combined forms, 1,800 sq ft heating area	month	97.94	4Q 92	4c
Gasoline, motor	gal	1.21	4Q 92	4c
Entertainment				
Bowling, evening rate	game	1.91	4Q 92	4c
Dinner entree, restaurant		18.00-45.00	92	83c
Monopoly game, Parker Brothers', No. 9		9.98	4Q 92	4c
Movie	admission	5.75	4Q 92	4c
Tennis balls, yellow, Wilson or Penn, 3	can	1.88	4Q 92	4c
Goods and Services				
ACCRA Index, Miscellaneous Goods and Services		94.10	4Q 92	4c
Groceries				
ACCRA Index, Groceries		96.90	4Q 92	4c
Babyfood, strained vegetables, lowest price	4-4.5 oz jar	0.28	4Q 92	4c
Bananas	lb	0.32	4Q 92	4c
Bread, white	24 oz	0.55	4Q 92	4c
Cheese, Kraft grated Parmesan	8-oz canister	3.43	4Q 92	4c
Chicken, fryer, whole	lb	0.83	4Q 92	4c
Cigarettes, Winston	carton	16.54	4Q 92	4c
Coffee, vacuum-packed	13-oz can	2.03	4Q 92	4c
Corn, frozen	10 oz	0.62	4Q 92	4c
Corn Flakes, Kellogg's or Post Toasties	18 oz	2.20	4Q 92	4c
Eggs, Grade A large	doz	0.83	4Q 92	4c
Ground beef or hamburger	lb	1.49	4Q 92	4c
Lettuce, iceberg	head	0.87	4Q 92	4c
Margarine, Blue Bonnet or Parkay cubes	lb	0.67	4Q 92	4c
Milk, whole	1/2 gal	1.35	4Q 92	4c
Orange juice, Minute Maid frozen	12-oz can	1.45	4Q 92	4c
Peaches	29-oz can	1.17	4Q 92	4c

Scottsdale, AZ - continued

Item	Per	Value	Date	Ref.
Groceries - continued				
Peas Sweet, Del Monte or Green Giant	15-17 oz can	0.61	4Q 92	4c
Potatoes, white or red	10-lb sack	1.99	4Q 92	4c
Sausage, Jimmy Dean, 100% pork	lb	2.95	4Q 92	4c
Shortening, vegetable, Crisco	3-lb can	2.59	4Q 92	4c
Soft drink, Coca Cola	2 liter	1.11	4Q 92	4c
Steak, T-bone	lb	4.47	4Q 92	4c
Sugar, cane or beet	4 lb	1.38	4Q 92	4c
Tomatoes, Hunt's or Del Monte	14.5-oz can	0.72	4Q 92	4c
Tuna, chunk, light	6.125-6.5 oz can	0.70	4Q 92	4c
Health Care				
ACCRA Index, Health Care		105.70	4Q 92	4c
Analgesic, Aspirin, Bayer, 325 mg tablets	100	5.39	4Q 92	4c
Dentist's fee, adult teeth cleaning and periodic oral exam	visit	43.40	4Q 92	4c
Doctor's fee, routine exam, established patient	visit	41.40	4Q 92	4c
Hospital care, semiprivate room	day	372.75	4Q 92	4c
Medical insurance premium, per employee, small group comprehensive	month	397.85	10/91	25c
Household Goods				
Appliance repair, home, service call, washing machine	min labor charge	24.39	4Q 92	4c
Laundry detergent, Tide Ultra, Bold, or Cheer	42 oz	3.23	4Q 92	4c
Tissues, facial, Kleenex brand	175-count box	1.19	4Q 92	4c
Housing				
ACCRA Index, Housing		111.10	4Q 92	4c
House, 1,800 sq ft, 8,000 sq ft lot, new, urban	total	128130	4Q 92	4c
House payment, principal and interest, 25% down payment	month	702	4Q 92	4c
Mortgage rate, incl. points & origination fee, 30-year fixed or adjustable rate	percent	7.95	4Q 92	4c
Rent, apartment, 2 bedrooms - 1-1/2 to 2 baths, unfurnished, 950 sq ft, water	month	506	4Q 92	4c
Personal Goods				
Shampoo, Alberto VO5	15 oz	1.21	4Q 92	4c
Toothpaste, Crest or Colgate	6-7 oz	2.21	4Q 92	4c
Personal Services				
Dry cleaning, man's 2-piece suit		6.54	4Q 92	4c
Haircare, woman's shampoo, trim and blow-dry		24.99	4Q 92	4c
Haircut, man's barbershop, no styling		8.70	4Q 92	4c
Restaurant Food				
Chicken, fried, thigh and drumstick		1.92	4Q 92	4c
Hamburger with cheese	1/4 lb	1.95	4Q 92	4c
Pizza, Pizza Hut or Pizza Inn, cheese, thin crust	12-13 in	8.61	4Q 92	4c
Transportation				
ACCRA Index, Transportation		114.40	4Q 92	4c
Bus fare, up to 10 miles	one-way	1.00	4Q 92	4c
Tire balance, computer or spin balance, front	wheel	7.90	4Q 92	4c
Utilities				
ACCRA Index, Utilities		89.30	4Q 92	4c
Electricity, all electric, 1,800 sq ft living area new home	month	97.94	4Q 92	4c

Values are in dollars or fractions of dollars. In the column headed *Ref*, references are shown to sources. Each reference is followed by a letter. These refer to the geographical level for which data were reported: s=State, r=Region, and c=City or metro. The abbreviation *ex* is used to mean *except* or *excluding*; *exp* stands for expenditures. For other abbreviations and further explanations, please see the Introduction.

Scranton, PA

Item	Per	Value	Date	Ref.
Child Care				
Child care fee, average, center	hour	2.18	90	65r
Child care fee, average, nonregulated family day care	hour	1.83	90	65r
Child care fee, average, regulated family day care	hour	2.02	90	65r
Communications				
Long-distance telephone service, day, initial minute, 0-100 miles	min	0.15-0.29	91	12s
Long-distance telephone service, day, additional minute, 0-100 miles	min	0.06-0.22	91	12s
Long-distance telephone service, evenings/weekends, 0-100 mi, initial minute	min	0.06-0.14	91	12s
Long-distance telephone service, evenings/weekends, 0-100 mi, additional minute	min	0.03-0.11	91	12s
Telephone, residential, private line, rotary, unlimited calling	month	15.07	10/91	78c
Education				
Board, 4-yr private college/university	year	2019	91	22s
Board, 4-yr public college/university	year	1656	91	22s
Expenditures, local gov't, public elementary/secondary	pupil	6980	92	20s
Room, 4-year private college/university	year	2179	91	22s
Room, 4-year public college/university	year	1719	91	22s
Tuition, 2-year private college/university	year	6314	91	22s
Tuition, 2-year public college/university	year	1505	91	22s
Tuition, 4-year private college/university	year	9848	91	22s
Tuition, 4-year public college/university, in-state	year	3401	91	22s
Energy and Fuels				
Coal	mil Btu	1.57	90	64s
Energy	mil Btu	8.63	90	64s
Energy exp/householder, 1-family unit	year	588	90	28r
Energy exp/householder, <1,000 sq ft heating area	year	477	90	28r
Energy exp/householder, 1,000-1,999 sq ft heating area	year	517	90	28r
Energy exp/householder, 2,000+ sq ft heating area	year	630	90	28r
Energy exp/householder, mobile home	year	412	90	28r
Energy exp/householder, multifamily	year	498	90	28r
Gas, cooking, winter, 10 therms	month	9.40	92	56c
Gas, cooking, winter, 30 therms	month	19.87	92	56c
Gas, cooking, winter, 50 therms	month	30.34	92	56c
Gas, heating, winter, 100 therms	month	56.50	92	56c
Gas, heating, winter, average use	month	107.90	92	56c
Gas, natural	mil Btu	5.24	90	64s
Gas, natural	000 cu ft	6.76	91	46s
Gas, natural, exp	year	703	91	46s
Gasoline, unleaded regular	mil Btu	9.35	90	64s
Funerals				
Casket, 18-gauge steel, velvet interior		1811.58	91	24r
Cosmetology, hair care, etc.		111.08	91	24r
Embalming		329.42	91	24r
Facility use for ceremony		201.29	91	24r
Hearse, local		135.27	91	24r
Limousine, local		127.24	91	24r
Remains to funeral home, transfer		103.98	91	24r
Service charge, professional		724.98	91	24r
Vault, concrete, non-metallic liner		766.71	91	24r
Viewing facilities, use		260.60	91	24r
Groceries				
Apples, Red Delicious	lb	0.85	4/93	16r
Bacon	lb	2.12	4/93	16r
Bananas	lb	0.54	4/93	16r
Bread, white, pan	lb	0.81	4/93	16r
Butter	lb	2.02	4/93	16r
Carrots, short trimmed and topped	lb	0.51	4/93	16r
Chicken, fresh, whole	lb	1.04	4/93	16r

Scranton, PA - continued

Item	Per	Value	Date	Ref.
Groceries - continued				
Chicken breast, bone-in	lb	2.21	4/93	16r
Chicken legs, bone-in	lb	1.16	4/93	16r
Chuck roast, USDA choice, boneless	lb	2.82	4/93	16r
Coffee, 100% ground roast, all sizes	lb	2.66	4/93	16r
Cucumbers	lb	0.85	4/93	16r
Eggs, Grade A large	doz	1.15	4/93	16r
Grapefruit	lb	0.45	4/93	16r
Grapes, Thompson Seedless	lb	1.52	4/93	16r
Ground beef, lean and extra lean	lb	2.36	4/93	16r
Ground chuck, 100% beef	lb	2.02	4/93	16r
Honey, jar	8 oz	0.96-1.75	92	5r
Honey, jar	lb	1.50-3.00	92	5r
Honey, squeeze bear	12-oz	1.50-1.99	92	5r
Ice cream, prepackaged, bulk, regular	1/2 gal	2.80	4/93	16r
Lemons	lb	0.96	4/93	16r
Lettuce, iceberg	lb	0.95	4/93	16r
Margarine, stick	lb	0.81	4/93	16r
Milk, fresh, whole, fortified	1/2 gal	1.30	4/93	16r
Oranges, navel	lb	0.56	4/93	16r
Peanut butter, creamy, all sizes	lb	1.88	4/93	16r
Pork chops, center cut, bone-in	lb	3.34	4/93	16r
Potato chips	16 oz	2.88	4/93	16r
Potatoes, white	lb	0.37	4/93	16r
Rib roast, USDA choice, bone-in	lb	4.94	4/93	16r
Round roast, USDA choice, boneless	lb	3.17	4/93	16r
Shortening, vegetable oil blends	lb	0.98	4/93	16r
Spaghetti and macaroni	lb	0.82	4/93	16r
Steak, round, graded & ungraded, ex USDA prime & choice	lb	4.04	4/93	16r
Steak, round, USDA choice, boneless	lb	3.90	4/93	16r
Steak, sirloin, USDA choice, boneless	lb	4.97	4/93	16r
Strawberries, dry pint	12 oz	0.90	4/93	16r
Sugar, white	lb	0.50	4/93	16r
Sugar, white, 33-80 oz pk	lb	0.41	4/93	16r
Tomatoes, field grown	lb	1.23	4/93	16r
Tuna, chunk, light	lb	2.22	4/93	16r
Turkey, frozen, whole	lb	1.04	4/93	16r
Health Care				
Childbirth, cesarean, hospital		5826	91	62r
Childbirth, cesarean, physician's fee		2053	91	62r
Childbirth, normal, hospital		2964	91	62r
Childbirth, normal, physician's fee		1492	91	62r
Hospital care, semiprivate room	day	284.86	90	27c
Medical insurance premium, per employee, small group comprehensive	month	317.55	10/91	25c
Medical plan per employee	year	3942	91	45r
Mental health care, exp	capita	53.68-118.35	90	38s
Mental health care, exp, state mental health agency	capita	56.85	90	38s
Mental health care, hospital psychiatric services, non-Federal, exp	capita	22.11	88	38s
Mental health care, mental health organization, multiservice, exp	capita	21.01	88	38s
Mental health care, psychiatric hospitals, private, exp	capita	26.48	88	38s
Mental health care, psychiatric out-patient clinics, freestanding, exp	capita	4.17	88	38s
Mental health care, psychiatric partial-care organizations, freestanding, exp	capita	0.94	88	38s
Mental health care, state and county mental hospitals, exp	capita	37.11	88	38s
Mental health care, VA medical centers, exp	capita	9.77	88	38s
Prescription drug co-pay, Medicaid	month	6.00	91	21s
Substance abuse, hospital ancillary charge	incident	720	90	70s
Substance abuse, hospital physician charge	incident	210	90	70s
Substance abuse, hospital room and board	incident	5400	90	70s

Values are in dollars or fractions of dollars. In the column headed *Ref*, references are shown to sources. Each reference is followed by a letter. These refer to the geographical level for which data were reported: s=State, r=Region, and c=City or metro. The abbreviation *ex* is used to mean *except* or *excluding*; *exp* stands for expenditures. For other abbreviations and further explanations, please see the Introduction.

Scranton, PA - continued

Item	Per	Value	Date	Ref.
Insurance and Pensions				
Auto insurance, private passenger	year	683.57	91	63s
Taxes				
Tax, cigarette	pack	31	91	77s
Tax, gasoline	gal	12	91	77s
Taxes, state	capita	1089	91	77s
Transportation				
Auto rental, average	day	47.00	6/91	60c
Bus fare	one-way	0.90	3/93	2c
Driver's license fee		22.00	12/90	43s
Limo fare, airport-city, average	day	10.50	6/91	60c
Taxi fare, airport-city, average	day	12.00	6/91	60c
Travel				
Business travel	day	165.00	4/93	89r
Lodging	day	68.64	91	60c
Utilities				
Electricity	mil Btu	22.46	90	64s

Seattle, WA

Item	Per	Value	Date	Ref.
Composite ACCRA index		119.10	4Q 92	4c
Alcoholic Beverages				
Beer, Miller Lite or Budweiser, 12-oz containers	6 pack	4.40	4Q 92	4c
Liquor, J & B Scotch	750 ml	17.95	4Q 92	4c
Wine, Gallo Chablis blanc, 1.5 liter	bottle	4.96	4Q 92	4c
Child Care				
Child care fee, average, center	hour	1.71	90	65r
Child care fee, average, nonregulated family day care	hour	1.32	90	65r
Child care fee, average, regulated family day care	hour	1.86	90	65r
Clothing				
Jeans, man's denim		25.99	4Q 92	4c
Shirt, man's dress shirt		23.50	4Q 92	4c
Undervest, boy's size 10-14, cotton	3	4.99	4Q 92	4c
Communications				
Long-distance telephone service, day, initial minute, 0-100 miles	min	0.15-0.37	91	12s
Long-distance telephone service, day, additional minute, 0-100 miles	min	0.01-0.03	91	12s
Long-distance telephone service, evenings/weekends, 0-100 mi, initial minute	min	0.05-0.19	91	12s
Long-distance telephone service, evenings/weekends, 0-100 mi, additional minute	min	0.00-0.01	91	12s
Newspaper subscription, daily and Sunday home delivery, large-city	month	8.50	4Q 92	4c
Telephone, flat rate	month	10.75	91	11c
Telephone, residential, private line, rotary, unlimited calling	month	16.35	10/91	78c
Telephone bill, family of four	month	18.50	4Q 92	4c
Education				
Board, 4-yr private college/university	year	1811	91	22s
Board, 4-yr public college/university	year	1539	91	22s
Cooking lessons		295.00	93	48c
Expenditures, local gov't, public elementary/secondary	pupil	5317	92	20s
Room, 4-year private college/university	year	1885	91	22s
Room, 4-year public college/university	year	1698	91	22s
Tuition, 2-year private college/university	year	6743	91	22s
Tuition, 2-year public college/university	year	844	91	22s
Tuition, 4-year private college/university	year	9463	91	22s
Tuition, 4-year public college/university, in-state	year	1823	91	22s

Seattle, WA - continued

Item	Per	Value	Date	Ref.
Energy and Fuels				
Energy	mil Btu	7.39	90	64s
Energy, combined forms, 1,800 sq ft heating area	month	64.12	4Q 92	4c
Energy exp/householder, 1-family unit	year	362	90	28r
Energy exp/householder, <1,000 sq ft heating area	year	254	90	28r
Energy exp/householder, 1,000-1,999 sq ft heating area	year	358	90	28r
Energy exp/householder, 2,000+ sq ft heating area	year	467	90	28r
Energy exp/householder, mobile home	year	390	90	28r
Energy exp/householder, multifamily	year	252	90	28r
Gas, cooking, winter, 10 therms	month	9.66	92	56c
Gas, cooking, winter, 30 therms	month	19.39	92	56c
Gas, cooking, winter, 50 therms	month	27.45	92	56c
Gas, heating, winter, 100 therms	month	47.08	92	56c
Gas, heating, winter, average use	month	59.34	92	56c
Gas, natural	mil Btu	3.60	90	64s
Gas, natural	000 cu ft	4.68	91	46s
Gas, natural, exp	year	440	91	46s
Gasoline, motor	gal	1.23	4Q 92	4c
Gasoline, unleaded regular	mil Btu	9.45	90	64s
Entertainment				
Bowling, evening rate	game	2.30	4Q 92	4c
Miniature golf admission	adult	6.18	92	1r
Miniature golf admission	child	5.14	92	1r
Monopoly game, Parker Brothers', No. 9		9.99	4Q 92	4c
Movie	admission	6.50	4Q 92	4c
Tennis balls, yellow, Wilson or Penn, 3	can	3.37	4Q 92	4c
Waterpark admission	adult	11.00	92	1r
Waterpark admission	child	8.55	92	1r
Funerals				
Casket, 18-gauge steel, velvet interior		1781.09	91	24r
Cosmetology, hair care, etc.		84.64	91	24r
Embalming		207.41	91	24r
Facility use for ceremony		205.76	91	24r
Hearse, local		105.14	91	24r
Limousine, local		83.21	91	24r
Remains to funeral home, transfer		113.82	91	24r
Service charge, professional		626.33	91	24r
Vault, concrete, non-metallic liner		599.54	91	24r
Viewing facilities, use		85.81	91	24r
Goods and Services				
ACCRA Index, Miscellaneous Goods and Services		106.90	4Q 92	4c
Goods and services	year	16314	92	36c
Groceries				
ACCRA Index, Groceries		117.60	4Q 92	4c
Apples, Red Delicious	lb	0.80	4/93	16r
Babyfood, strained vegetables, lowest price	4-4.5 oz jar	0.29	4Q 92	4c
Bacon	lb	1.79	4/93	16r
Bananas	lb	0.49	4Q 92	4c
Bananas	lb	0.53	4/93	16r
Bologna, all beef or mixed	lb	2.67	4/93	16r
Bread, white	24 oz	0.79	4Q 92	4c
Bread, white, pan	lb	0.81	4/93	16r
Carrots, short trimmed and topped	lb	0.39	4/93	16r
Cheese, Kraft grated Parmesan	8-oz canister	3.86	4Q 92	4c
Chicken, fresh, whole	lb	0.94	4/93	16r
Chicken, fryer, whole	lb	1.32	4Q 92	4c
Chicken breast, bone-in	lb	2.19	4/93	16r
Chuck roast, graded and ungraded, ex USDA prime and choice	lb	2.26	4/93	16r
Cigarettes, Winston	carton	20.69	4Q 92	4c
Coffee, 100% ground roast, all sizes	lb	2.33	4/93	16r

Values are in dollars or fractions of dollars. In the column headed *Ref*, references are shown to sources. Each reference is followed by a letter. These refer to the geographical level for which data were reported: s=State, r=Region, and c=City or metro. The abbreviation *ex* is used to mean *except* or *excluding*; *exp* stands for expenditures. For other abbreviations and further explanations, please see the Introduction.

Seattle, WA - continued

Item	Per	Value	Date	Ref.
Groceries				
Coffee, vacuum-packed	13-oz can	2.46	4Q 92	4c
Corn, frozen	10 oz	0.67	4Q 92	4c
Corn Flakes, Kellogg's or Post Toasties	18 oz	2.34	4Q 92	4c
Eggs, Grade A large	doz	1.14	4Q 92	4c
Eggs, Grade AA large	doz	1.18	4/93	16r
Flour, white, all purpose	lb	0.22	4/93	16r
Grapefruit	lb	0.52	4/93	16r
Grapes, Thompson Seedless	lb	1.50	4/93	16r
Ground beef, 100% beef	lb	1.44	4/93	16r
Ground beef, lean and extra lean	lb	2.34	4/93	16r
Ground beef or hamburger	lb	1.46	4Q 92	4c
Ham, boneless, excluding canned	lb	2.56	4/93	16r
Honey, jar	8 oz	0.89-1.00	92	5r
Honey, jar	lb	1.35-1.97	92	5r
Honey, squeeze bear	12-oz	1.19-1.50	92	5r
Ice cream, prepackaged, bulk, regular	1/2 gal	2.40	4/93	16r
Lemons	lb	0.81	4/93	16r
Lettuce, iceberg	head	0.99	4Q 92	4c
Lettuce, iceberg	lb	0.84	4/93	16r
Margarine, Blue Bonnet or Parkay cubes	lb	0.74	4Q 92	4c
Margarine, stick	lb	0.81	4/93	16r
Milk, whole	1/2 gal	1.59	4Q 92	4c
Orange juice, Minute Maid frozen	12-oz can	1.54	4Q 92	4c
Oranges, navel	lb	0.48	4/93	16r
Peaches	29-oz can	1.59	4Q 92	4c
Peas Sweet, Del Monte or Green Giant	15-17 oz can	0.76	4Q 92	4c
Pork chops, center cut, bone-in	lb	3.25	4/93	16r
Potato chips	16 oz	2.89	4/93	16r
Potatoes, white	lb	0.38	4/93	16r
Potatoes, white or red	10-lb sack	1.96	4Q 92	4c
Round roast, graded & ungraded, ex USDA prime & choice	lb	3.00	4/93	16r
Round roast, USDA choice, boneless	lb	3.16	4/93	16r
Sausage, Jimmy Dean, 100% pork	lb	3.22	4Q 92	4c
Shortening, vegetable oil blends	lb	0.86	4/93	16r
Shortening, vegetable, Crisco	3-lb can	2.99	4Q 92	4c
Soft drink, Coca Cola	2 liter	1.02	4Q 92	4c
Spaghetti and macaroni	lb	0.84	4/93	16r
Steak, round, graded & ungraded, ex USDA prime & choice	lb	3.34	4/93	16r
Steak, round, USDA choice, boneless	lb	3.24	4/93	16r
Steak, sirloin, graded & ungraded, ex USDA prime & choice	lb	3.75	4/93	16r
Steak, sirloin, USDA choice, boneless	lb	4.49	4/93	16r
Steak, T-bone	lb	5.42	4Q 92	4c
Sugar, cane or beet	4 lb	1.39	4Q 92	4c
Sugar, white	lb	0.41	4/93	16r
Sugar, white, 33-80 oz pk	lb	0.38	4/93	16r
Tomatoes, field grown	lb	1.01	4/93	16r
Tomatoes, Hunt's or Del Monte	14.5-oz can	0.74	4Q 92	4c
Tuna, chunk, light	6.125-6.5 oz can	0.94	4Q 92	4c
Turkey, frozen, whole	lb	1.04	4/93	16r
Health Care				
ACCRA Index, Health Care		132.50	4Q 92	4c
Analgesic, Aspirin, Bayer, 325 mg tablets	100	5.23	4Q 92	4c
Childbirth, cesarean, hospital		5533	91	62r
Childbirth, cesarean, physician's fee		2053	91	62r
Childbirth, normal, hospital		2745	91	62r
Childbirth, normal, physician's fee		1492	91	62r
Dentist's fee, adult teeth cleaning and periodic oral exam	visit	70.50	4Q 92	4c
Doctor's fee, routine exam, established patient	visit	43.67	4Q 92	4c

Seattle, WA - continued

Item	Per	Value	Date	Ref.
Health Care - continued				
Health maintenance organization coverage, employee	year	3092	93	39c
Health maintenance organization medical coverage, employee	year	3092	92	34c
Hospital care, semiprivate room	day	357.88	90	27c
Hospital care, semiprivate room	day	451.80	4Q 92	4c
Indemnity plan medical coverage, employee	year	3554	92	34c
Insurance coverage, traditional, employee	year	3554	93	39c
Medical insurance premium, per employee, small group comprehensive	month	310.25	10/91	25c
Medical plan per employee	year	3421	91	45r
Mental health care, exp	capita	37.60-53.67	90	38s
Physician fee, family practice, first-visit		111.00	91	62r
Physician fee, family practice, revisit		45.00	91	62r
Physician fee, general practice, first-visit		100.00	91	62r
Physician fee, general practice, revisit		40.00	91	62r
Physician fee, internal medicine, first-visit		137.00	91	62r
Physician fee, internal medicine, revisit		48.00	91	62r
Physician fee, median, neurosurgeon, first-visit		157.00	91	62r
Physician fee, median, nonsurgical specialist, first-visit		131.00	91	62r
Physician fee, median, orthopedic surgeon, first-visit		124.00	91	62r
Physician fee, median, plastic surgeon, first-visit		88.00	91	62r
Physician fee, median, surgical specialist, first-visit		100.00	91	62r
Physician fee, neurosurgeon, revisit		51.00	91	62r
Physician fee, nonsurgical specialist, revisit		47.00	91	62r
Physician fee, obstetrics/gynecology, first-visit		95.00	91	62r
Physician fee, obstetrics/gynecology, revisit		50.00	91	62r
Physician fee, orthopedic surgeon, revisit		51.00	91	62r
Physician fee, pediatrician, first-visit		81.00	91	62r
Physician fee, pediatrician, revisit		42.00	91	62r
Physician fee, plastic surgeon, revisit		48.00	91	62r
Physician fee, surgical specialist, revisit		49.00	91	62r
Preferred provider organization medical coverage, employee	year	3114	92	34c
Substance abuse, hospital ancillary charge	incident	1360	90	70s
Substance abuse, hospital physician charge	incident	150	90	70s
Substance abuse, hospital room and board	incident	4200	90	70s
Household Goods				
Appliance repair, home, service call, washing machine	min labor charge	31.98	4Q 92	4c
Laundry detergent, Tide Ultra, Bold, or Cheer	42 oz	4.73	4Q 92	4c
Tissues, facial, Kleenex brand	175-count box	1.64	4Q 92	4c
Housing				
ACCRA Index, Housing		153.60	4Q 92	4c
Home, median price	unit	145.70		26c
House, 1,800 sq ft, 8,000 sq ft lot, new, urban	total	188116	4Q 92	4c
House payment, principal and interest, 25% down payment	month	1036	4Q 92	4c
Mortgage rate, incl. points & origination fee, 30-year fixed or adjustable rate	percent	8.00	4Q 92	4c
Rent, apartment, 2 bedrooms - 1-1/2 to 2 baths, unfurnished, 950 sq ft, water	month	546	4Q 92	4c
Rental unit, 1 bedroom	month	536	93	23c
Rental unit, 2 bedroom	month	630	93	23c
Rental unit, 3 bedroom	month	813	93	23c
Rental unit, 4 bedroom	month	895	93	23c

Values are in dollars or fractions of dollars. In the column headed *Ref*, references are shown to sources. Each reference is followed by a letter. These refer to the geographical level for which data were reported: s=State, r=Region, and c=City or metro. The abbreviation *ex* is used to mean *except* or *excluding*; *exp* stands for expenditures. For other abbreviations and further explanations, please see the Introduction.

Seattle, WA - continued

Item	Per	Value	Date	Ref.
Housing				
Rental unit, efficiency	month	441	93	23c
Insurance and Pensions				
Auto insurance, private passenger	year	627.71	91	63s
Personal Goods				
Shampoo, Alberto VO5	15 oz	1.44	4Q 92	4c
Toothpaste, Crest or Colgate	6-7 oz	2.14	4Q 92	4c
Personal Services				
Dry cleaning, man's 2-piece suit		6.47	4Q 92	4c
Haircare, woman's shampoo, trim and blow-dry		18.49	4Q 92	4c
Haircut, man's barbershop, no styling		10.00	4Q 92	4c
Restaurant Food				
Chicken, fried, thigh and drumstick		2.15	4Q 92	4c
Hamburger with cheese	1/4 lb	2.00	4Q 92	4c
Pizza, Pizza Hut or Pizza Inn, cheese, thin crust	12-13 in	9.51	4Q 92	4c
Taxes				
Tax, cigarette	pack	34	91	77s
Tax, gasoline	gal	23	91	77s
Taxes, state	capita	1592	91	77s
Transportation				
ACCRA Index, Transportation		111.10	4Q 92	4c
Auto rental, average	day	49.25	6/91	60c
Bus fare	one-way	0.80	3/93	2c
Bus fare, up to 10 miles	one-way	1.50	4Q 92	4c
Driver's license fee		14.00	12/90	43s
Ferry boat fare	one-way	1.65	3/93	2c
Limo fare, airport-city, average	day	6.00	6/91	60c
Taxi fare, airport-city, average	day	25.25	6/91	60c
Tire balance, computer or spin balance, front	wheel	6.49	4Q 92	4c
Trolley fare	one-way	0.85	3/93	2c
Travel				
Breakfast	day	8.53	6/91	60c
Business travel	day	178.00	4/93	89c
Dinner	day	19.67	6/91	60c
Dinner	day	21.70	92	85c
Lodging	day	125.37	91	60c
Lodging	day	105.00	92	85c
Lunch	day	9.72	6/91	60c
Travel, business	day	187.50	93	88c
Utilities				
ACCRA Index, Utilities		62.40	4Q 92	4c
Electricity	mil Btu	10.03	90	64s
Electricity, all electric, 1,800 sq ft living area new home	month	64.12	4Q 92	4c

Sharon, PA

Item	Per	Value	Date	Ref.
Child Care				
Child care fee, average, center	hour	2.18	90	65r
Child care fee, average, nonregulated family day care	hour	1.83	90	65r
Child care fee, average, regulated family day care	hour	2.02	90	65r
Communications				
Long-distance telephone service, day, initial minute, 0-100 miles	min	0.15-0.29	91	12s
Long-distance telephone service, day, additional minute, 0-100 miles	min	0.06-0.22	91	12s
Long-distance telephone service, evenings/weekends, 0-100 mi, initial minute	min	0.06-0.14	91	12s

Sharon, PA - continued

Item	Per	Value	Date	Ref.
Communications - continued				
Long-distance telephone service, evenings/weekends, 0-100 mi, additional minute	min	0.03-0.11	91	12s
Education				
Board, 4-yr private college/university	year	2019	91	22s
Board, 4-yr public college/university	year	1656	91	22s
Expenditures, local gov't, public elementary/secondary	pupil	6980	92	20s
Room, 4-year private college/university	year	2179	91	22s
Room, 4-year public college/university	year	1719	91	22s
Tuition, 2-year private college/university	year	6314	91	22s
Tuition, 2-year public college/university	year	1505	91	22s
Tuition, 4-year private college/university	year	9848	91	22s
Tuition, 4-year public college/university, in-state	year	3401	91	22s
Energy and Fuels				
Coal	mil Btu	1.57	90	64s
Energy	mil Btu	8.63	90	64s
Energy exp/householder, 1-family unit	year	588	90	28r
Energy exp/householder, <1,000 sq ft heating area	year	477	90	28r
Energy exp/householder, 1,000-1,999 sq ft heating area	year	517	90	28r
Energy exp/householder, 2,000+ sq ft heating area	year	630	90	28r
Energy exp/householder, mobile home	year	412	90	28r
Energy exp/householder, multifamily	year	498	90	28r
Gas, natural	mil Btu	5.24	90	64s
Gas, natural	000 cu ft	6.76	91	46s
Gas, natural, exp	year	703	91	46s
Gasoline, unleaded regular	mil Btu	9.35	90	64s
Funerals				
Casket, 18-gauge steel, velvet interior		1811.58	91	24r
Cosmetology, hair care, etc.		111.08	91	24r
Embalming		329.42	91	24r
Facility use for ceremony		201.29	91	24r
Hearse, local		135.27	91	24r
Limousine, local		127.24	91	24r
Remains to funeral home, transfer		103.98	91	24r
Service charge, professional		724.98	91	24r
Vault, concrete, non-metallic liner		766.71	91	24r
Viewing facilities, use		260.60	91	24r
Groceries				
Apples, Red Delicious	lb	0.85	4/93	16r
Bacon	lb	2.12	4/93	16r
Bananas	lb	0.54	4/93	16r
Bread, white, pan	lb	0.81	4/93	16r
Butter	lb	2.02	4/93	16r
Carrots, short trimmed and topped	lb	0.51	4/93	16r
Chicken, fresh, whole	lb	1.04	4/93	16r
Chicken breast, bone-in	lb	2.21	4/93	16r
Chicken legs, bone-in	lb	1.16	4/93	16r
Chuck roast, USDA choice, boneless	lb	2.82	4/93	16r
Coffee, 100% ground roast, all sizes	lb	2.66	4/93	16r
Cucumbers	lb	0.85	4/93	16r
Eggs, Grade A large	doz	1.15	4/93	16r
Grapefruit	lb	0.45	4/93	16r
Grapes, Thompson Seedless	lb	1.52	4/93	16r
Ground beef, lean and extra lean	lb	2.36	4/93	16r
Ground chuck, 100% beef	lb	2.02	4/93	16r
Honey, jar	8 oz	0.96-1.75	92	5r
Honey, jar	lb	1.50-3.00	92	5r
Honey, squeeze bear	12-oz	1.50-1.99	92	5r
Ice cream, prepackaged, bulk, regular	1/2 gal	2.80	4/93	16r
Lemons	lb	0.96	4/93	16r
Lettuce, iceberg	lb	0.95	4/93	16r
Margarine, stick	lb	0.81	4/93	16r
Milk, fresh, whole, fortified	1/2 gal	1.30	4/93	16r
Oranges, navel	lb	0.56	4/93	16r
Peanut butter, creamy, all sizes	lb	1.88	4/93	16r

Values are in dollars or fractions of dollars. In the column headed *Ref*, references are shown to sources. Each reference is followed by a letter. These refer to the geographical level for which data were reported: s = State, r = Region, and c = City or metro. The abbreviation *ex* is used to mean *except* or *excluding*; *exp* stands for expenditures. For other abbreviations and further explanations, please see the Introduction.

Sharon, PA - continued

Item	Per	Value	Date	Ref.
Groceries				
Pork chops, center cut, bone-in	lb	3.34	4/93	16r
Potato chips	16 oz	2.88	4/93	16r
Potatoes, white	lb	0.37	4/93	16r
Rib roast, USDA choice, bone-in	lb	4.94	4/93	16r
Round roast, USDA choice, boneless	lb	3.17	4/93	16r
Shortening, vegetable oil blends	lb	0.98	4/93	16r
Spaghetti and macaroni	lb	0.82	4/93	16r
Steak, round, graded & ungraded, ex USDA prime & choice	lb	4.04	4/93	16r
Steak, round, USDA choice, boneless	lb	3.90	4/93	16r
Steak, sirloin, USDA choice, boneless	lb	4.97	4/93	16r
Strawberries, dry pint	12 oz	0.90	4/93	16r
Sugar, white	lb	0.50	4/93	16r
Sugar, white, 33-80 oz pk	lb	0.41	4/93	16r
Tomatoes, field grown	lb	1.23	4/93	16r
Tuna, chunk, light	lb	2.22	4/93	16r
Turkey, frozen, whole	lb	1.04	4/93	16r
Health Care				
Childbirth, cesarean, hospital		5826	91	62r
Childbirth, cesarean, physician's fee		2053	91	62r
Childbirth, normal, hospital		2964	91	62r
Childbirth, normal, physician's fee		1492	91	62r
Medical plan per employee	year	3942	91	45r
Mental health care, exp	capita	53.68-118.35	90	38s
Mental health care, exp, state mental health agency	capita	56.85	90	38s
Mental health care, hospital psychiatric services, non-Federal, exp	capita	22.11	88	38s
Mental health care, mental health organization, multiservice, exp	capita	21.01	88	38s
Mental health care, psychiatric hospitals, private, exp	capita	26.48	88	38s
Mental health care, psychiatric out-patient clinics, freestanding, exp	capita	4.17	88	38s
Mental health care, psychiatric partial-care organizations, freestanding, exp	capita	0.94	88	38s
Mental health care, state and county mental hospitals, exp	capita	37.11	88	38s
Mental health care, VA medical centers, exp	capita	9.77	88	38s
Prescription drug co-pay, Medicaid	month	6.00	91	21s
Substance abuse, hospital ancillary charge	incident	720	90	70s
Substance abuse, hospital physician charge	incident	210	90	70s
Substance abuse, hospital room and board	incident	5400	90	70s
Insurance and Pensions				
Auto insurance, private passenger	year	683.57	91	63s
Taxes				
Tax, cigarette	pack	31	91	77s
Tax, gasoline	gal	12	91	77s
Taxes, state	capita	1089	91	77s
Transportation				
Driver's license fee		22.00	12/90	43s
Travel				
Business travel	day	165.00	4/93	89r
Utilities				
Electricity	mil Btu	22.46	90	64s

Sheboygan, WI

Item	Per	Value	Date	Ref.
Child Care				
Child care fee, average, center	hour	1.63	90	65r
Child care fee, average, nonregulated family day care	hour	1.83	90	65r
Child care fee, average, regulated family day care	hour	1.42	90	65r

Sheboygan, WI - continued

Item	Per	Value	Date	Ref.
Communications				
Long-distance telephone service, day, initial minute, 0-100 miles	min	0.15-0.29	91	12s
Long-distance telephone service, day, additional minute, 0-100 miles	min	0.10-0.27	91	12s
Education				
Board, 4-yr private college/university	year	1533	91	22s
Board, 4-yr public college/university	year	1404	91	22s
Expenditures, local gov't, public elementary/secondary	pupil	5972	92	20s
Room, 4-year private college/university	year	1256	91	22s
Room, 4-year public college/university	year	1416	91	22s
Tuition, 2-year private college/university	year	4768	91	22s
Tuition, 2-year public college/university	year	1234	91	22s
Tuition, 4-year private college/university	year	8237	91	22s
Tuition, 4-year public college/university, in-state	year	1951	91	22s
Energy and Fuels				
Coal	mil Btu	1.41	90	64s
Energy	mil Btu	8.27	90	64s
Energy exp/householder, 1-family unit	year	471	90	28r
Energy exp/householder, <1,000 sq ft heating area	year	430	90	28r
Energy exp/householder, 1,000-1,999 sq ft heating area	year	481	90	28r
Energy exp/householder, 2,000+ sq ft heating area	year	473	90	28r
Energy exp/householder, mobile home	year	430	90	28r
Energy exp/householder, multifamily	year	461	90	28r
Gas, natural	mil Btu	4.56	90	64s
Gas, natural	000 cu ft	5.61	91	46s
Gas, natural, exp	year	605	91	46s
Gasoline, unleaded regular	mil Btu	9.38	90	64s
Entertainment				
Miniature golf admission	adult	6.18	92	1r
Miniature golf admission	child	5.14	92	1r
Waterpark admission	adult	11.00	92	1r
Waterpark admission	child	8.55	92	1r
Funerals				
Casket, 18-gauge steel, velvet interior		1926.72	91	24r
Cosmetology, hair care, etc.		97.64	91	24r
Embalming		249.14	91	24r
Facility use for ceremony		208.59	91	24r
Hearse, local		130.12	91	24r
Limousine, local		104.66	91	24r
Remains to funeral home, transfer		93.61	91	24r
Service charge, professional		724.62	91	24r
Vault, concrete, non-metallic liner		734.53	91	24r
Viewing facilities, use		236.06	91	24r
Groceries				
Apples, Red Delicious	lb	0.77	4/93	16r
Bacon	lb	1.85	4/93	16r
Bananas	lb	0.46	4/93	16r
Beef, stew, boneless	lb	2.53	4/93	16r
Bologna, all beef or mixed	lb	2.19	4/93	16r
Bread, white, pan	lb	0.78	4/93	16r
Butter	lb	1.50	4/93	16r
Cabbage	lb	0.40	4/93	16r
Carrots, short trimmed and topped	lb	0.45	4/93	16r
Cheese, Cheddar	lb	3.47	4/93	16r
Chicken, fresh, whole	lb	0.84	4/93	16r
Chicken breast, bone-in	lb	1.94	4/93	16r
Chicken legs, bone-in	lb	1.02	4/93	16r
Chuck roast, graded and ungraded, ex USDA prime and choice	lb	2.43	4/93	16r
Chuck roast, USDA choice, bone-in	lb	2.11	4/93	16r
Chuck roast, USDA choice, boneless	lb	2.44	4/93	16r
Coffee, 100% ground roast, all sizes	lb	2.47	4/93	16r
Cookies, chocolate chip	lb	2.73	4/93	16r

Values are in dollars or fractions of dollars. In the column headed *Ref*, references are shown to sources. Each reference is followed by a letter. These refer to the geographical level for which data were reported: s=State, r=Region, and c=City or metro. The abbreviation *ex* is used to mean *except* or *excluding*; *exp* stands for expenditures. For other abbreviations and further explanations, please see the Introduction.

Sheboygan, WI - continued

Item	Per	Value	Date	Ref.
Groceries				
Eggs, Grade A large	doz	0.93	4/93	16r
Flour, white, all purpose	lb	0.21	4/93	16r
Grapefruit	lb	0.45	4/93	16r
Grapes, Thompson Seedless	lb	1.46	4/93	16r
Ground beef, 100% beef	lb	1.63	4/93	16r
Ground beef, lean and extra lean	lb	2.08	4/93	16r
Ground chuck, 100% beef	lb	1.94	4/93	16r
Ham, boneless, excluding canned	lb	2.21	4/93	16r
Honey, jar	8 oz	0.97-1.25	92	5r
Honey, jar	lb	1.25-2.25	92	5r
Honey, squeeze bear	12-oz	1.25-1.99	92	5r
Ice cream, prepackaged, bulk, regular	1/2 gal	2.41	4/93	16r
Lemons	lb	0.82	4/93	16r
Lettuce, iceberg	lb	0.83	4/93	16r
Margarine, stick	lb	0.77	4/93	16r
Oranges, navel	lb	0.50	4/93	16r
Peanut butter, creamy, all sizes	lb	1.82	4/93	16r
Pears, Anjou	lb	0.85	4/93	16r
Pork chops, center cut, bone-in	lb	3.17	4/93	16r
Potato chips	16 oz	2.68	4/93	16r
Potatoes, white	lb	0.26	4/93	16r
Round roast, graded & ungraded, ex USDA prime & choice	lb	2.88	4/93	16r
Round roast, USDA choice, boneless	lb	2.96	4/93	16r
Shortening, vegetable oil blends	lb	0.79	4/93	16r
Spaghetti and macaroni	lb	0.76	4/93	16r
Steak, rib eye, USDA choice, boneless	lb	6.29	4/93	16r
Steak, round, USDA choice, boneless	lb	3.24	4/93	16r
Steak, sirloin, graded & ungraded, ex USDA prime & choice	lb	4.00	4/93	16r
Steak, sirloin, USDA choice, bone-in	lb	3.57	4/93	16r
Steak, sirloin, USDA choice, boneless	lb	4.17	4/93	16r
Steak, T-bone, USDA choice, bone-in	lb	5.60	4/93	16r
Strawberries, dry pint	12 oz	0.90	4/93	16r
Sugar, white	lb	0.36	4/93	16r
Sugar, white, 33-80 oz pk	lb	0.35	4/93	16r
Tomatoes, field grown	lb	0.99	4/93	16r
Tuna, chunk, light	lb	1.76	4/93	16r
Turkey, frozen, whole	lb	0.91	4/93	16r
Health Care				
Childbirth, cesarean, hospital		4688	91	62r
Childbirth, cesarean, physician's fee		2053	91	62r
Childbirth, normal, hospital		2657	91	62r
Childbirth, normal, physician's fee		1492	91	62r
Medical plan per employee	year	3443	91	45r
Mental health care, exp	capita	28.84-37.59	90	38s
Mental health care, exp, state mental health agency	capita	36.62	90	38s
Mental health care, hospital psychiatric services, non-Federal, exp	capita	13.05	88	38s
Mental health care, mental health organization, multiservice, exp	capita	10.93	88	38s
Mental health care, psychiatric hospitals, private, exp	capita	8.71	88	38s
Mental health care, psychiatric out-patient clinics, freestanding, exp	capita	5.33	88	38s
Mental health care, psychiatric partial-care organizations, freestanding, exp	capita	0.20	88	38s
Mental health care, state and county mental hospitals, exp	capita	28.29	88	38s
Mental health care, VA medical centers, exp	capita	7.57	88	38s
Physician fee, family practice, first-visit		76.00	91	62r
Physician fee, family practice, revisit		33.00	91	62r
Physician fee, general practice, first-visit		61.00	91	62r
Physician fee, general practice, revisit		31.00	91	62r
Physician fee, general surgeon, first-visit		65.00	91	62r
Physician fee, general surgeon, revisit		35.00	91	62r
Physician fee, internal medicine, first-visit		91.00	91	62r
Physician fee, internal medicine, revisit		40.00	91	62r
Physician fee, median, neurosurgeon, first-visit		106.00	91	62r

Sheboygan, WI - continued

Item	Per	Value	Date	Ref.
Health Care - continued				
Physician fee, median, nonsurgical specialist, first-visit		90.00	91	62r
Physician fee, median, orthopedic surgeon, first-visit		83.00	91	62r
Physician fee, median, surgical specialist, first-visit		61.00	91	62r
Physician fee, neurosurgeon, revisit		41.00	91	62r
Physician fee, nonsurgical specialist, revisit		40.00	91	62r
Physician fee, obstetrics/gynecology, first-visit		61.00	91	62r
Physician fee, obstetrics/gynecology, revisit		40.00	91	62r
Physician fee, orthopedic surgeon, revisit		41.00	91	62r
Physician fee, pediatrician, first-visit		46.00	91	62r
Physician fee, pediatrician, revisit		33.00	91	62r
Physician fee, surgical specialist, revisit		36.00	91	62r
Substance abuse, hospital ancillary charge	incident	960	90	70s
Substance abuse, hospital physician charge	incident	470	90	70s
Substance abuse, hospital room and board	incident	3980	90	70s
Insurance and Pensions				
Auto insurance, private passenger	year	510.11	91	63s
Taxes				
Tax, cigarette	pack	38	91	77s
Tax, gasoline	gal	22.20	91	77s
Taxes, state	capita	1416	91	77s
Transportation				
Driver's license fee		9.00	12/90	43s
Utilities				
Electricity	mil Btu	15.77	90	64s

Sherman-Denison, TX

Item	Per	Value	Date	Ref.
Child Care				
Child care fee, average, center	hour	1.29	90	65r
Child care fee, average, nonregulated family day care	hour	0.89	90	65r
Child care fee, average, regulated family day care	hour	1.32	90	65r
Communications				
Long-distance telephone service, day, initial minute, 0-100 miles	min	0.10-0.46	91	12s
Long-distance telephone service, day, additional minute, 0-100 miles	min	0.06-0.45	91	12s
Education				
Board, 4-yr private college/university	year	1883	91	22s
Board, 4-yr public college/university	year	1605	91	22s
Expenditures, local gov't, public elementary/secondary	pupil	4593	92	20s
Room, 4-year private college/university	year	1620	91	22s
Room, 4-year public college/university	year	1532	91	22s
Tuition, 2-year private college/university	year	4394	91	22s
Tuition, 2-year public college/university	year	495	91	22s
Tuition, 4-year private college/university	year	6497	91	22s
Tuition, 4-year public college/university, in-state	year	986	91	22s
Energy and Fuels				
Coal	mil Btu	1.44	90	64s
Energy	mil Btu	6.48	90	64s
Energy exp/householder, 1-family unit	year	471	90	28r
Energy exp/householder, <1,000 sq ft heating area	year	384	90	28r
Energy exp/householder, 1,000-1,999 sq ft heating area	year	421	90	28r
Energy exp/householder, 2,000+ sq ft heating area	year	625	90	28r

Values are in dollars or fractions of dollars. In the column headed *Ref*, references are shown to sources. Each reference is followed by a letter. These refer to the geographical level for which data were reported: s=State, r=Region, and c=City or metro. The abbreviation *ex* is used to mean *except* or *excluding*; *exp* stands for *expenditures*. For other abbreviations and further explanations, please see the Introduction.

Sherman-Denison, TX - continued

Item	Per	Value	Date	Ref.
Energy and Fuels				
Energy exp/householder, mobile home	year	271	90	28r
Energy exp/householder, multifamily	year	355	90	28r
Gas, natural	mil Btu	2.47	90	64s
Gas, natural	000 cu ft	5.71	91	46s
Gas, natural, exp	year	388	91	46s
Gasoline, unleaded regular	mil Btu	9.16	90	64s
Entertainment				
Miniature golf admission	adult	6.18	92	1r
Miniature golf admission	child	5.14	92	1r
Waterpark admission	adult	11.00	92	1r
Waterpark admission	child	8.55	92	1r
Funerals				
Casket, 18-gauge steel, velvet interior		2274.41	91	24r
Cosmetology, hair care, etc.		74.62	91	24r
Embalming		229.94	91	24r
Facility use for ceremony		176.61	91	24r
Hearse, local		116.34	91	24r
Limousine, local		72.68	91	24r
Remains to funeral home, transfer		87.72	91	24r
Service charge, professional		712.53	91	24r
Vault, concrete, non-metallic liner		750.55	91	24r
Viewing facilities, use		155.31	91	24r
Groceries				
Apples, Red Delicious	lb	0.79	4/93	16r
Bacon	lb	1.75	4/93	16r
Bananas	lb	0.42	4/93	16r
Beef, stew, boneless	lb	2.61	4/93	16r
Bologna, all beef or mixed	lb	2.24	4/93	16r
Bread, white, pan	lb	0.64	4/93	16r
Bread, whole wheat, pan	lb	0.96	4/93	16r
Cabbage	lb	0.37	4/93	16r
Carrots, short trimmed and topped	lb	0.47	4/93	16r
Celery	lb	0.64	4/93	16r
Cheese, American	lb	2.98	4/93	16r
Cheese, Cheddar	lb	3.28	4/93	16r
Chicken, fresh, whole	lb	0.77	4/93	16r
Chicken breast, bone-in	lb	1.92	4/93	16r
Chicken legs, bone-in	lb	1.06	4/93	16r
Chuck roast, graded and ungraded, ex USDA prime and choice	lb	2.40	4/93	16r
Chuck roast, USDA choice, bone-in	lb	2.19	4/93	16r
Chuck roast, USDA choice, boneless	lb	2.38	4/93	16r
Coffee, 100% ground roast, all sizes	lb	2.48	4/93	16r
Crackers, soda, salted	lb	1.15	4/93	16r
Eggs, Grade A large	doz	0.96	4/93	16r
Flour, white, all purpose	lb	0.24	4/93	16r
Frankfurters, all meat or all beef	lb	2.01	4/93	16r
Grapefruit	lb	0.44	4/93	16r
Grapes, Thompson Seedless	lb	1.40	4/93	16r
Ground beef, 100% beef	lb	1.58	4/93	16r
Ground beef, lean and extra lean	lb	2.09	4/93	16r
Ground chuck, 100% beef	lb	1.98	4/93	16r
Ham, boneless, excluding canned	lb	2.89	4/93	16r
Ham, picnic, shoulder, bone-in, smoked	lb	1.02	4/93	16r
Ham, rump or steak half, bone-in, smoked	lb	1.48	4/93	16r
Honey, jar	8 oz	0.73-1.19	92	5r
Honey, jar	lb	1.10-1.79	92	5r
Honey, squeeze bear	12-oz	1.19-1.50	92	5r
Ice cream, prepackaged, bulk, regular	1/2 gal	2.41	4/93	16r
Lemons	lb	1.05	4/93	16r
Lettuce, iceberg	lb	0.81	4/93	16r
Margarine, stick	lb	0.88	4/93	16r
Oranges, navel	lb	0.55	4/93	16r
Pears, Anjou	lb	0.92	4/93	16r
Pork chops, center cut, bone-in	lb	3.13	4/93	16r
Potato chips	16 oz	2.94	4/93	16r
Potatoes, white	lb	0.43	4/93	16r
Rib roast, USDA choice, bone-in	lb	4.63	4/93	16r
Rice, white, long grain, uncooked	lb	0.45	4/93	16r

Sherman-Denison, TX - continued

Item	Per	Value	Date	Ref.
Groceries - continued				
Round roast, graded & ungraded, ex USDA prime & choice	lb	3.03	4/93	16r
Round roast, USDA choice, boneless	lb	3.09	4/93	16r
Sausage, fresh, loose	lb	2.08	4/93	16r
Short ribs, bone-in	lb	2.66	4/93	16r
Shortening, vegetable oil blends	lb	0.69	4/93	16r
Spaghetti and macaroni	lb	0.81	4/93	16r
Steak, rib eye, USDA choice, boneless	lb	6.24	4/93	16r
Steak, round, graded & ungraded, ex USDA prime & choice	lb	3.31	4/93	16r
Steak, round, USDA choice, boneless	lb	3.34	4/93	16r
Steak, sirloin, graded & ungraded, ex USDA prime & choice	lb	4.19	4/93	16r
Steak, sirloin, USDA choice, boneless	lb	4.46	4/93	16r
Steak, T-bone, USDA choice, bone-in	lb	5.25	4/93	16r
Strawberries, dry pint	12 oz	0.92	4/93	16r
Sugar, white	lb	0.39	4/93	16r
Sugar, white, 33-80 oz pk	lb	0.38	4/93	16r
Tomatoes, field grown	lb	0.88	4/93	16r
Tuna, chunk, light	lb	1.79	4/93	16r
Turkey, frozen, whole	lb	1.04	4/93	16r
Yogurt, natural, fruit flavored	1/2 pint	0.57	4/93	16r
Health Care				
Childbirth, cesarean, hospital		5034	91	62r
Childbirth, cesarean, physician's fee		2053	91	62r
Childbirth, normal, hospital		2712	91	62r
Childbirth, normal, physician's fee		1492	91	62r
Health care spending, state	capita	2192	3/93	84s
Mental health care, exp	capita	20.37-28.83	90	38s
Mental health care, exp, state mental health agency	capita	22.72	90	38s
Mental health care, hospital psychiatric services, non-Federal, exp	capita	7.95	88	38s
Mental health care, mental health organization, multiservice, exp	capita	12.05	88	38s
Mental health care, psychiatric hospitals, private, exp	capita	37.78	88	38s
Mental health care, psychiatric out-patient clinics, freestanding, exp	capita	0.43	88	38s
Mental health care, state and county mental hospitals, exp	capita	12.54	88	38s
Mental health care, VA medical centers, exp	capita	5.35	88	38s
Physician fee, family practice, first-visit		75.00	91	62r
Physician fee, family practice, revisit		34.00	91	62r
Physician fee, general practice, first-visit		61.00	91	62r
Physician fee, general practice, revisit		32.00	91	62r
Physician fee, general surgeon, first-visit		64.00	91	62r
Physician fee, general surgeon, revisit		40.00	91	62r
Physician fee, internal medicine, first-visit		98.00	91	62r
Physician fee, internal medicine, revisit		40.00	91	62r
Physician fee, median, neurosurgeon, first-visit		130.00	91	62r
Physician fee, median, nonsurgical specialist, first-visit		95.00	91	62r
Physician fee, median, orthopedic surgeon, first-visit		91.00	91	62r
Physician fee, median, plastic surgeon, first-visit		66.00	91	62r
Physician fee, median, surgical specialist, first-visit		62.00	91	62r
Physician fee, neurosurgeon, revisit		50.00	91	62r
Physician fee, nonsurgical specialist, revisit		40.00	91	62r
Physician fee, obstetrics/gynecology, first-visit		64.00	91	62r
Physician fee, obstetrics/gynecology, revisit		41.00	91	62r
Physician fee, orthopedic surgeon, revisit		40.00	91	62r
Physician fee, pediatrician, first-visit		49.00	91	62r
Physician fee, pediatrician, revisit		33.00	91	62r
Physician fee, plastic surgeon, revisit		43.00	91	62r
Physician fee, surgical specialist, revisit		37.00	91	62r

Values are in dollars or fractions of dollars. In the column headed *Ref*, references are shown to sources. Each reference is followed by a letter. These refer to the geographical level for which data were reported: s = State, r = Region, and c = City or metro. The abbreviation *ex* is used to mean *except* or *excluding*; *exp* stands for expenditures. For other abbreviations and further explanations, please see the Introduction.

Sherman-Denison, TX - continued

Item	Per	Value	Date	Ref.
Health Care				
Substance abuse, hospital ancillary charge	incident	3750	90	70s
Substance abuse, hospital physician charge	incident	1080	90	70s
Substance abuse, hospital room and board	incident	5320	90	70s
Insurance and Pensions				
Auto insurance, private passenger	year	709.79	91	63s
Taxes				
Tax, cigarette	pack	41	91	77s
Tax, gasoline	gal	20	91	77s
Taxes, state	capita	923	91	77s
Transportation				
Driver's license fee		16.00	12/90	43s
Travel				
Business travel	day	193.00	4/93	89r
Utilities				
Electricity	mil Btu	17.09	90	64s
Electricity, residential	KWh	5.92	2/93	94s

Shreveport, LA

Item	Per	Value	Date	Ref.
Child Care				
Child care fee, average, center	hour	1.29	90	65r
Child care fee, average, nonregulated family day care	hour	0.89	90	65r
Child care fee, average, regulated family day care	hour	1.32	90	65r
Communications				
Long-distance telephone service, day, initial minute, 0-100 miles	min	0.14-0.41	91	12s
Long-distance telephone service, day, additional minute, 0-100 miles	min	0.09-0.29	91	12s
Long-distance telephone service, evenings/ weekends, 0-100 mi, initial minute	min	0.06-0.16	91	12s
Long-distance telephone service, evenings/ weekends, 0-100 mi, additional minute	min	0.04-0.12	91	12s
Education				
Board, 4-yr private college/university	year	2125	91	22s
Board, 4-yr public college/university	year	1453	91	22s
Expenditures, local gov't, public elementary/secondary	pupil	4299	92	20s
Room, 4-year private college/university	year	2216	91	22s
Room, 4-year public college/university	year	1323	91	22s
Tuition, 2-year private college/university	year	5671	91	22s
Tuition, 2-year public college/university	year	852	91	22s
Tuition, 4-year private college/university	year	9783	91	22s
Tuition, 4-year public college/university, in-state	year	1791	91	22s
Energy and Fuels				
Coal	mil Btu	1.68	90	64s
Energy	mil Btu	6.05	90	64s
Energy exp/householder, 1-family unit	year	471	90	28r
Energy exp/householder, <1,000 sq ft heating area	year	384	90	28r
Energy exp/householder, 1,000-1,999 sq ft heating area	year	421	90	28r
Energy exp/householder, 2,000+ sq ft heating area	year	625	90	28r
Energy exp/householder, mobile home	year	271	90	28r
Energy exp/householder, multifamily	year	355	90	28r
Gas, cooking, 10 therms	month	10.72	92	56c
Gas, cooking, 30 therms	month	22.16	92	56c
Gas, cooking, 50 therms	month	33.60	92	56c
Gas, heating, winter, 100 therms	month	62.19	92	56c
Gas, heating, winter, average use	month	71.92	92	56c
Gas, natural	mil Btu	2.11	90	64s

Shreveport, LA - continued

Item	Per	Value	Date	Ref.
Energy and Fuels - continued				
Gas, natural	000 cu ft	5.77	91	46s
Gas, natural, exp	year	336	91	46s
Gasoline, unleaded regular	mil Btu	9.47	90	64s
Entertainment				
Miniature golf admission	adult	6.18	92	1r
Miniature golf admission	child	5.14	92	1r
Waterpark admission	adult	11.00	92	1r
Waterpark admission	child	8.55	92	1r
Funerals				
Casket, 18-gauge steel, velvet interior		2274.41	91	24r
Cosmetology, hair care, etc.		74.62	91	24r
Embalming		229.94	91	24r
Facility use for ceremony		176.61	91	24r
Hearse, local		116.34	91	24r
Limousine, local		72.68	91	24r
Remains to funeral home, transfer		87.72	91	24r
Service charge, professional		712.53	91	24r
Vault, concrete, non-metallic liner		750.55	91	24r
Viewing facilities, use		155.31	91	24r
Groceries				
Apples, Red Delicious	lb	0.79	4/93	16r
Bacon	lb	1.75	4/93	16r
Bananas	lb	0.42	4/93	16r
Beef, stew, boneless	lb	2.61	4/93	16r
Bologna, all beef or mixed	lb	2.24	4/93	16r
Bread, white, pan	lb	0.64	4/93	16r
Bread, whole wheat, pan	lb	0.96	4/93	16r
Cabbage	lb	0.37	4/93	16r
Carrots, short trimmed and topped	lb	0.47	4/93	16r
Celery	lb	0.64	4/93	16r
Cheese, American	lb	2.98	4/93	16r
Cheese, Cheddar	lb	3.28	4/93	16r
Chicken, fresh, whole	lb	0.77	4/93	16r
Chicken breast, bone-in	lb	1.92	4/93	16r
Chicken legs, bone-in	lb	1.06	4/93	16r
Chuck roast, graded and ungraded, ex USDA prime and choice	lb	2.40	4/93	16r
Chuck roast, USDA choice, bone-in	lb	2.19	4/93	16r
Chuck roast, USDA choice, boneless	lb	2.38	4/93	16r
Coffee, 100% ground roast, all sizes	lb	2.48	4/93	16r
Crackers, soda, salted	lb	1.15	4/93	16r
Eggs, Grade A large	doz	0.96	4/93	16r
Flour, white, all purpose	lb	0.24	4/93	16r
Frankfurters, all meat or all beef	lb	2.01	4/93	16r
Grapefruit	lb	0.44	4/93	16r
Grapes, Thompson Seedless	lb	1.40	4/93	16r
Ground beef, 100% beef	lb	1.58	4/93	16r
Ground beef, lean and extra lean	lb	2.09	4/93	16r
Ground chuck, 100% beef	lb	1.98	4/93	16r
Ham, boneless, excluding canned	lb	2.89	4/93	16r
Ham, picnic, shoulder, bone-in, smoked	lb	1.02	4/93	16r
Ham, rump or steak half, bone-in, smoked	lb	1.48	4/93	16r
Honey, jar	8 oz	0.73-1.19	92	5r
Honey, jar	lb	1.10-1.79	92	5r
Honey, squeeze bear	12-oz	1.19-1.50	92	5r
Ice cream, prepackaged, bulk, regular	1/2 gal	2.41	4/93	16r
Lemons	lb	1.05	4/93	16r
Lettuce, iceberg	lb	0.81	4/93	16r
Margarine, stick	lb	0.88	4/93	16r
Oranges, navel	lb	0.55	4/93	16r
Pears, Anjou	lb	0.92	4/93	16r
Pork chops, center cut, bone-in	lb	3.13	4/93	16r
Potato chips	16 oz	2.94	4/93	16r
Potatoes, white	lb	0.43	4/93	16r
Rib roast, USDA choice, bone-in	lb	4.63	4/93	16r
Rice, white, long grain, uncooked	lb	0.45	4/93	16r
Round roast, graded & ungraded, ex USDA prime & choice	lb	3.03	4/93	16r
Round roast, USDA choice, boneless	lb	3.09	4/93	16r
Sausage, fresh, loose	lb	2.08	4/93	16r

Values are in dollars or fractions of dollars. In the column headed *Ref*, references are shown to sources. Each reference is followed by a letter. These refer to the geographical level for which data were reported: s = State, r = Region, and c = City or metro. The abbreviation *ex* is used to mean *except* or *excluding*; *exp* stands for expenditures. For other abbreviations and further explanations, please see the Introduction.

Shreveport, LA - continued

Item	Per	Value	Date	Ref.
Groceries				
Short ribs, bone-in	lb	2.66	4/93	16r
Shortening, vegetable oil blends	lb	0.69	4/93	16r
Spaghetti and macaroni	lb	0.81	4/93	16r
Steak, rib eye, USDA choice, boneless	lb	6.24	4/93	16r
Steak, round, graded & ungraded, ex USDA prime & choice	lb	3.31	4/93	16r
Steak, round, USDA choice, boneless	lb	3.34	4/93	16r
Steak, sirloin, graded & ungraded, ex USDA prime & choice	lb	4.19	4/93	16r
Steak, sirloin, USDA choice, boneless	lb	4.46	4/93	16r
Steak, T-bone, USDA choice, bone-in	lb	5.25	4/93	16r
Strawberries, dry pint	12 oz	0.92	4/93	16r
Sugar, white	lb	0.39	4/93	16r
Sugar, white, 33-80 oz pk	lb	0.38	4/93	16r
Tomatoes, field grown	lb	0.88	4/93	16r
Tuna, chunk, light	lb	1.79	4/93	16r
Turkey, frozen, whole	lb	1.04	4/93	16r
Yogurt, natural, fruit flavored	1/2 pint	0.57	4/93	16r
Health Care				
Childbirth, cesarean, hospital		5034	91	62r
Childbirth, cesarean, physician's fee		2053	91	62r
Childbirth, normal, hospital		2712	91	62r
Childbirth, normal, physician's fee		1492	91	62r
Hospital care, semiprivate room	day	213.95	90	27c
Medical insurance premium, per employee, small group comprehensive	month	357.70	10/91	25c
Mental health care, exp	capita	20.37-28.83	90	38s
Mental health care, exp, state mental health agency	capita	28.44	90	38s
Mental health care, hospital psychiatric services, non-Federal, exp	capita	8.19	88	38s
Mental health care, mental health organization, multiservice, exp	capita	0.49	88	38s
Mental health care, psychiatric hospitals, private, exp	capita	43.54	88	38s
Mental health care, psychiatric out-patient clinics, freestanding, exp	capita	4.11	88	38s
Mental health care, state and county mental hospitals, exp	capita	18.74	88	38s
Mental health care, VA medical centers, exp	capita	2.60	88	38s
Physician fee, family practice, first-visit		75.00	91	62r
Physician fee, family practice, revisit		34.00	91	62r
Physician fee, general practice, first-visit		61.00	91	62r
Physician fee, general practice, revisit		32.00	91	62r
Physician fee, general surgeon, first-visit		64.00	91	62r
Physician fee, general surgeon, revisit		40.00	91	62r
Physician fee, internal medicine, first-visit		98.00	91	62r
Physician fee, internal medicine, revisit		40.00	91	62r
Physician fee, median, neurosurgeon, first-visit		130.00	91	62r
Physician fee, median, nonsurgical specialist, first-visit		95.00	91	62r
Physician fee, median, orthopedic surgeon, first-visit		91.00	91	62r
Physician fee, median, plastic surgeon, first-visit		66.00	91	62r
Physician fee, median, surgical specialist, first-visit		62.00	91	62r
Physician fee, neurosurgeon, revisit		50.00	91	62r
Physician fee, nonsurgical specialist, revisit		40.00	91	62r
Physician fee, obstetrics/gynecology, first-visit		64.00	91	62r
Physician fee, obstetrics/gynecology, revisit		41.00	91	62r
Physician fee, orthopedic surgeon, revisit		40.00	91	62r
Physician fee, pediatrician, first-visit		49.00	91	62r
Physician fee, pediatrician, revisit		33.00	91	62r
Physician fee, plastic surgeon, revisit		43.00	91	62r
Physician fee, surgical specialist, revisit		37.00	91	62r
Substance abuse, hospital ancillary charge	incident	2600	90	70s

Shreveport, LA - continued

Item	Per	Value	Date	Ref.
Health Care - continued				
Substance abuse, hospital physician charge	incident	840	90	70s
Substance abuse, hospital room and board	incident	6410	90	70s
Housing				
Home, median price	unit	66.30		26c
Rental unit, 1 bedroom	month	385	93	23c
Rental unit, 2 bedroom	month	457	93	23c
Rental unit, 3 bedroom	month	570	93	23c
Rental unit, 4 bedroom	month	638	93	23c
Rental unit, efficiency	month	317	93	23c
Insurance and Pensions				
Auto insurance, private passenger	year	778.70	91	63s
Taxes				
Tax, cigarette	pack	20	91	77s
Tax, gasoline	gal	20	91	77s
Taxes, state	capita	1013	91	77s
Transportation				
Bus fare	one-way	0.75	3/93	2c
Driver's license fee		18.00	12/90	43s
Travel				
Business travel	day	193.00	4/93	89r
Utilities				
Electricity	mil Btu	17.77	90	64s
Electricity, winter, 250 KWh	month	19.32	92	55c
Electricity, winter, 500 KWh	month	34.84	92	55c
Electricity, winter, 750 KWh	month	50.26	92	55c
Electricity, winter, 1000 KWh	month	65.67	92	55c

Sioux City, IA

Item	Per	Value	Date	Ref.
Composite ACCRA index		100.80	4Q 92	4c
Alcoholic Beverages				
Beer, Miller Lite or Budweiser, 12-oz containers	6 pack	3.67	4Q 92	4c
Liquor, J & B Scotch	750 ml	18.94	4Q 92	4c
Wine, Gallo Chablis blanc, 1.5 liter	bottle	5.24	4Q 92	4c
Child Care				
Child care fee, average, center	hour	1.63	90	65r
Child care fee, average, nonregulated family day care	hour	1.83	90	65r
Child care fee, average, regulated family day care	hour	1.42	90	65r
Clothing				
Jeans, man's denim		28.24	4Q 92	4c
Shirt, man's dress shirt		25.33	4Q 92	4c
Undervest, boy's size 10-14, cotton	3	3.47	4Q 92	4c
Communications				
Long-distance telephone service, day, initial minute, 0-100 miles	min	0.21-0.41	91	12s
Long-distance telephone service, day, additional minute, 0-100 miles	min	0.11-0.30	91	12s
Long-distance telephone service, evenings/weekends, 0-100 mi, initial minute	min	0.11-0.20	91	12s
Long-distance telephone service, evenings/weekends, 0-100 mi, additional minute	min	0.06-0.15	91	12s
Newspaper subscription, daily and Sunday home delivery, large-city	month	10.50	4Q 92	4c
Telephone, flat rate	month	14.45	91	11c
Telephone bill, family of four	month	20.08	4Q 92	4c
Education				
Board, 4-yr private college/university	year	1703	91	22s
Board, 4-yr public college/university	year	1183	91	22s
Expenditures, local gov't, public elementary/secondary	pupil	5026	92	20s

Values are in dollars or fractions of dollars. In the column headed *Ref*, references are shown to sources. Each reference is followed by a letter. These refer to the geographical level for which data were reported: s=State, r=Region, and c=City or metro. The abbreviation *ex* is used to mean *except* or *excluding*; *exp* stands for expenditures. For other abbreviations and further explanations, please see the Introduction.

Sioux City, IA - continued

Item	Per	Value	Date	Ref.
Education				
Room, 4-year private college/university	year	1392	91	22s
Room, 4-year public college/university	year	1188	91	22s
Tuition, 2-year private college/university	year	5119	91	22s
Tuition, 2-year public college/university	year	1298	91	22s
Tuition, 4-year private college/university	year	8703	91	22s
Tuition, 4-year public college/university, in-state	year	1880	91	22s
Energy and Fuels				
Coal	mil Btu	1.16	90	64s
Energy	mil Btu	7.71	90	64s
Energy, combined forms, 1,800 sq ft heating area	month	99.69	4Q 92	4c
Energy, exc electricity, 1,800 sq ft heating area	month	53.36	4Q 92	4c
Energy exp/householder, 1-family unit	year	473	90	28r
Energy exp/householder, <1,000 sq ft heating area	year	429	90	28r
Energy exp/householder, 1,000-1,999 sq ft heating area	year	442	90	28r
Energy exp/householder, 2,000+ sq ft heating area	year	498	90	28r
Energy exp/householder, mobile home	year	442	90	28r
Energy exp/householder, multifamily	year	407	90	28r
Gas, natural	mil Btu	3.81	90	64s
Gas, natural	000 cu ft	4.81	91	46s
Gas, natural, exp	year	530	91	46s
Gasoline, motor	gal	1.14	4Q 92	4c
Gasoline, unleaded regular	mil Btu	9.38	90	64s
Entertainment				
Bowling, evening rate	game	1.97	4Q 92	4c
Miniature golf admission	adult	6.18	92	1r
Miniature golf admission	child	5.14	92	1r
Monopoly game, Parker Brothers', No. 9		10.14	4Q 92	4c
Movie	admission	5.00	4Q 92	4c
Tennis balls, yellow, Wilson or Penn, 3	can	2.17	4Q 92	4c
Waterpark admission	adult	11.00	92	1r
Waterpark admission	child	8.55	92	1r
Funerals				
Casket, 18-gauge steel, velvet interior		1952.97	91	24r
Cosmetology, hair care, etc.		90.03	91	24r
Embalming		251.75	91	24r
Facility use for ceremony		180.75	91	24r
Hearse, local		117.51	91	24r
Limousine, local		71.86	91	24r
Remains to funeral home, transfer		81.14	91	24r
Service charge, professional		740.03	91	24r
Vault, concrete, non-metallic liner		801.47	91	24r
Viewing facilities, use		169.33	91	24r
Goods and Services				
ACCRA Index, Miscellaneous Goods and Services		95.40	4Q 92	4c
Groceries				
ACCRA Index, Groceries		101.00	4Q 92	4c
Apples, Red Delicious	lb	0.77	4/93	16r
Babyfood, strained vegetables, lowest price	4-4.5 oz jar	0.31	4Q 92	4c
Bacon	lb	1.85	4/93	16r
Bananas	lb	0.33	4Q 92	4c
Bananas	lb	0.46	4/93	16r
Beef, stew, boneless	lb	2.53	4/93	16r
Bologna, all beef or mixed	lb	2.19	4/93	16r
Bread, white	24 oz	0.82	4Q 92	4c
Bread, white, pan	lb	0.78	4/93	16r
Butter	lb	1.50	4/93	16r
Cabbage	lb	0.40	4/93	16r
Carrots, short trimmed and topped	lb	0.45	4/93	16r
Cheese, Cheddar	lb	3.47	4/93	16r

Sioux City, IA - continued

Item	Per	Value	Date	Ref.
Groceries - continued				
Cheese, Kraft grated Parmesan	8-oz canister	3.44	4Q 92	4c
Chicken, fresh, whole	lb	0.84	4/93	16r
Chicken, fryer, whole	lb	0.80	4Q 92	4c
Chicken breast, bone-in	lb	1.94	4/93	16r
Chicken legs, bone-in	lb	1.02	4/93	16r
Chuck roast, graded and ungraded, ex USDA prime and choice	lb	2.43	4/93	16r
Chuck roast, USDA choice, bone-in	lb	2.11	4/93	16r
Chuck roast, USDA choice, boneless	lb	2.44	4/93	16r
Cigarettes, Winston	carton	18.90	4Q 92	4c
Coffee, 100% ground roast, all sizes	lb	2.47	4/93	16r
Coffee, vacuum-packed	13-oz can	1.99	4Q 92	4c
Cookies, chocolate chip	lb	2.73	4/93	16r
Corn, frozen	10 oz	0.76	4Q 92	4c
Corn Flakes, Kellogg's or Post Toasties	18 oz	2.11	4Q 92	4c
Eggs, Grade A large	doz	0.76	4Q 92	4c
Eggs, Grade A large	doz	0.93	4/93	16r
Flour, white, all purpose	lb	0.21	4/93	16r
Grapefruit	lb	0.45	4/93	16r
Grapes, Thompson Seedless	lb	1.46	4/93	16r
Ground beef, 100% beef	lb	1.63	4/93	16r
Ground beef, lean and extra lean	lb	2.08	4/93	16r
Ground beef or hamburger	lb	1.31	4Q 92	4c
Ground chuck, 100% beef	lb	1.94	4/93	16r
Ham, boneless, excluding canned	lb	2.21	4/93	16r
Ice cream, prepackaged, bulk, regular	1/2 gal	2.41	4/93	16r
Lemons	lb	0.82	4/93	16r
Lettuce, iceberg	head	0.87	4Q 92	4c
Lettuce, iceberg	lb	0.83	4/93	16r
Margarine, Blue Bonnet or Parkay cubes	lb	0.66	4Q 92	4c
Margarine, stick	lb	0.77	4/93	16r
Milk, whole	1/2 gal	1.22	4Q 92	4c
Orange juice, Minute Maid frozen	12-oz can	1.51	4Q 92	4c
Oranges, navel	lb	0.50	4/93	16r
Peaches	29-oz can	1.48	4Q 92	4c
Peanut butter, creamy, all sizes	lb	1.82	4/93	16r
Pears, Anjou	lb	0.85	4/93	16r
Peas Sweet, Del Monte or Green Giant	15-17 oz can	0.64	4Q 92	4c
Pork chops, center cut, bone-in	lb	3.17	4/93	16r
Potato chips	16 oz	2.68	4/93	16r
Potatoes, white	lb	0.26	4/93	16r
Potatoes, white or red	10-lb sack	2.11	4Q 92	4c
Round roast, graded & ungraded, ex USDA prime & choice	lb	2.88	4/93	16r
Round roast, USDA choice, boneless	lb	2.96	4/93	16r
Sausage, Jimmy Dean, 100% pork	lb	2.88	4Q 92	4c
Shortening, vegetable oil blends	lb	0.79	4/93	16r
Shortening, vegetable, Crisco	3-lb can	2.36	4Q 92	4c
Soft drink, Coca Cola	2 liter	1.27	4Q 92	4c
Spaghetti and macaroni	lb	0.76	4/93	16r
Steak, rib eye, USDA choice, boneless	lb	6.29	4/93	16r
Steak, round, USDA choice, boneless	lb	3.24	4/93	16r
Steak, sirloin, graded & ungraded, ex USDA prime & choice	lb	4.00	4/93	16r
Steak, sirloin, USDA choice, bone-in	lb	3.57	4/93	16r
Steak, sirloin, USDA choice, boneless	lb	4.17	4/93	16r
Steak, T-bone	lb	5.28	4Q 92	4c
Steak, T-bone, USDA choice, bone-in	lb	5.60	4/93	16r
Strawberries, dry pint	12 oz	0.90	4/93	16r
Sugar, cane or beet	4 lb	1.23	4Q 92	4c
Sugar, white	lb	0.36	4/93	16r
Sugar, white, 33-80 oz pk	lb	0.35	4/93	16r
Tomatoes, field grown	lb	0.99	4/93	16r

Values are in dollars or fractions of dollars. In the column headed *Ref*, references are shown to sources. Each reference is followed by a letter. These refer to the geographical level for which data were reported: s=State, r=Region, and c=City or metro. The abbreviation *ex* is used to mean *except* or *excluding*; *exp* stands for expenditures. For other abbreviations and further explanations, please see the Introduction.

Sioux City, IA - continued

Item	Per	Value	Date	Ref.
Groceries				
Tomatoes, Hunt's or Del Monte	14.5-oz can	0.77	4Q 92	4c
Tuna, chunk, light	6.125-6.5 oz can	0.58	4Q 92	4c
Tuna, chunk, light	lb	1.76	4/93	16r
Turkey, frozen, whole	lb	0.91	4/93	16r
Health Care				
ACCRA Index, Health Care		100.70	4Q 92	4c
Analgesic, Aspirin, Bayer, 325 mg tablets	100	5.06	4Q 92	4c
Childbirth, cesarean, hospital		4688	91	62r
Childbirth, cesarean, physician's fee		2053	91	62r
Childbirth, normal, hospital		2657	91	62r
Childbirth, normal, physician's fee		1492	91	62r
Dentist's fee, adult teeth cleaning and periodic oral exam	visit	44.20	4Q 92	4c
Doctor's fee, routine exam, established patient	visit	36.60	4Q 92	4c
Health care spending, state	capita	2351	3/93	84s
Hospital care, semiprivate room	day	250.00	90	27c
Hospital care, semiprivate room	day	367.50	4Q 92	4c
Medical insurance premium, per employee, small group comprehensive	month	284.70	10/91	25c
Medical plan per employee	year	3443	91	45r
Mental health care, exp	capita	20.37-28.83	90	38s
Mental health care, exp, state mental health agency	capita	17.07	90	38s
Mental health care, hospital psychiatric services, non-Federal, exp	capita	23.51	88	38s
Mental health care, mental health organization, multiservice, exp	capita	7.66	88	38s
Mental health care, psychiatric hospitals, private, exp	capita	2.86	88	38s
Mental health care, psychiatric out-patient clinics, freestanding, exp	capita	3.02	88	38s
Mental health care, state and county mental hospitals, exp	capita	14.54	88	38s
Mental health care, VA medical centers, exp	capita	13.98	88	38s
Physician fee, family practice, first-visit		76.00	91	62r
Physician fee, family practice, revisit		33.00	91	62r
Physician fee, general practice, first-visit		61.00	91	62r
Physician fee, general practice, revisit		31.00	91	62r
Physician fee, general surgeon, first-visit		65.00	91	62r
Physician fee, general surgeon, revisit		35.00	91	62r
Physician fee, internal medicine, first-visit		91.00	91	62r
Physician fee, internal medicine, revisit		40.00	91	62r
Physician fee, median, neurosurgeon, first-visit		106.00	91	62r
Physician fee, median, nonsurgical specialist, first-visit		90.00	91	62r
Physician fee, median, orthopedic surgeon, first-visit		83.00	91	62r
Physician fee, median, surgical specialist, first-visit		61.00	91	62r
Physician fee, neurosurgeon, revisit		41.00	91	62r
Physician fee, nonsurgical specialist, revisit		40.00	91	62r
Physician fee, obstetrics/gynecology, first-visit		61.00	91	62r
Physician fee, obstetrics/gynecology, revisit		40.00	91	62r
Physician fee, orthopedic surgeon, revisit		41.00	91	62r
Physician fee, pediatrician, first-visit		46.00	91	62r
Physician fee, pediatrician, revisit		33.00	91	62r
Physician fee, surgical specialist, revisit		36.00	91	62r
Substance abuse, hospital ancillary charge	incident	950	90	70s
Substance abuse, hospital physician charge	incident	250	90	70s
Substance abuse, hospital room and board	incident	3110	90	70s

Sioux City, IA - continued

Item	Per	Value	Date	Ref.
Household Goods				
Appliance repair, home, service call, washing machine	min labor charge	28.10	4Q 92	4c
Laundry detergent, Tide Ultra, Bold, or Cheer	42 oz	3.86	4Q 92	4c
Tissues, facial, Kleenex brand	175-count box	1.11	4Q 92	4c
Housing				
ACCRA Index, Housing		110.80	4Q 92	4c
House, 1,800 sq ft, 8,000 sq ft lot, new, urban	total	125000	4Q 92	4c
House payment, principal and interest, 25% down payment	month	698	4Q 92	4c
Mortgage rate, incl. points & origination fee, 30-year fixed or adjustable rate	per-cent	8.16	4Q 92	4c
Rent, apartment, 2 bedrooms - 1-1/2 to 2 baths, unfurnished, 950 sq ft, water	month	507	4Q 92	4c
Rental unit, 1 bedroom	month	392	93	23c
Rental unit, 2 bedroom	month	461	93	23c
Rental unit, 3 bedroom	month	576	93	23c
Rental unit, 4 bedroom	month	647	93	23c
Rental unit, efficiency	month	322	93	23c
Insurance and Pensions				
Auto insurance, private passenger	year	422.46	91	63s
Personal Goods				
Shampoo, Alberto VO5	15 oz	1.03	4Q 92	4c
Toothpaste, Crest or Colgate	6-7 oz	1.70	4Q 92	4c
Personal Services				
Dry cleaning, man's 2-piece suit		5.88	4Q 92	4c
Haircare, woman's shampoo, trim and blow-dry		15.62	4Q 92	4c
Haircut, man's barbershop, no styling		9.19	4Q 92	4c
Restaurant Food				
Chicken, fried, thigh and drumstick		2.20	4Q 92	4c
Hamburger with cheese	1/4 lb	1.96	4Q 92	4c
Pizza, Pizza Hut or Pizza Inn, cheese, thin crust	12-13 in	7.49	4Q 92	4c
Taxes				
Tax, cigarette	pack	36	91	77s
Tax, gasoline	gal	20	91	77s
Taxes, state	capita	1233	91	77s
Transportation				
ACCRA Index, Transportation		99.40	4Q 92	4c
Driver's license fee		16.00	12/90	43s
Tire balance, computer or spin balance, front	wheel	6.40	4Q 92	4c
Utilities				
ACCRA Index, Utilities		92.50	4Q 92	4c
Electricity	mil Btu	17.37	90	64s
Electricity, partial electric and other energy, 1,800 sq ft living area new home	month	46.33	4Q 92	4c
Electricity, winter, 250 KWh	month	23.16	92	55c
Electricity, winter, 250 KWh	month	23.44	2/93	30c
Electricity, winter, 500 KWh	month	42.94	92	55c
Electricity, winter, 500 KWh	month	41.00	2/93	30c
Electricity, winter, 750 KWh	month	61.33	92	55c
Electricity, winter, 750 KWh	month	58.88	2/93	30c
Electricity, winter, 1000 KWh	month	79.71	92	55c
Electricity, winter, 1000 KWh	month	74.23	2/93	30c

Sioux Falls, SD

Item	Per	Value	Date	Ref.
Composite ACCRA index		95.10	4Q 92	4c

Values are in dollars or fractions of dollars. In the column headed *Ref*, references are shown to sources. Each reference is followed by a letter. These refer to the geographical level for which data were reported: s=State, r=Region, and c=City or metro. The abbreviation *ex* is used to mean *except* or *excluding*; *exp* stands for expenditures. For other abbreviations and further explanations, please see the Introduction.

Sioux Falls, SD - continued

Item	Per	Value	Date	Ref.
Alcoholic Beverages				
Beer, Miller Lite or Budweiser, 12-oz containers	6 pack	3.69	4Q 92	4c
Liquor, J & B Scotch	750 ml	16.17	4Q 92	4c
Wine, Gallo Chablis blanc, 1.5 liter	bottle	5.67	4Q 92	4c
Child Care				
Child care fee, average, center	hour	1.63	90	65r
Child care fee, average, nonregulated family day care	hour	1.83	90	65r
Child care fee, average, regulated family day care	hour	1.42	90	65r
Clothing				
Jeans, man's denim		24.39	4Q 92	4c
Shirt, man's dress shirt		20.00	4Q 92	4c
Undervest, boy's size 10-14, cotton	3	4.29	4Q 92	4c
Communications				
Long-distance telephone service, day, initial minute, 0-100 miles	min	0.21-0.41	91	12s
Long-distance telephone service, day, additional minute, 0-100 miles	min	0.15-0.27	91	12s
Long-distance telephone service, evenings/weekends, 0-100 mi, initial minute	min	0.08-0.16	91	12s
Long-distance telephone service, evenings/weekends, 0-100 mi, additional minute	min	0.06-0.11	91	12s
Newspaper subscription, daily and Sunday home delivery, large-city	month	13.00	4Q 92	4c
Telephone, flat rate	month	34.75	91	11c
Telephone bill, family of four	month	22.63	4Q 92	4c
Education				
Board, 4-yr private college/university	year	1452	91	22s
Board, 4-yr public college/university	year	1234	91	22s
Expenditures, local gov't, public elementary/secondary	pupil	4255	92	20s
Room, 4-year private college/university	year	1282	91	22s
Room, 4-year public college/university	year	739	91	22s
Tuition, 2-year private college/university	year	4515	91	22s
Tuition, 2-year public college/university	year	1920	91	22s
Tuition, 4-year private college/university	year	6346	91	22s
Tuition, 4-year public college/university, in-state	year	1854	91	22s
Energy and Fuels				
Coal	mil Btu	1.22	90	64s
Energy	mil Btu	8.65	90	64s
Energy, combined forms, 1,800 sq ft heating area	month	93.33	4Q 92	4c
Energy, exc electricity, 1,800 sq ft heating area	month	47.55	4Q 92	4c
Energy exp/householder, 1-family unit	year	473	90	28r
Energy exp/householder, <1,000 sq ft heating area	year	429	90	28r
Energy exp/householder, 1,000-1,999 sq ft heating area	year	442	90	28r
Energy exp/householder, 2,000+ sq ft heating area	year	498	90	28r
Energy exp/householder, mobile home	year	442	90	28r
Energy exp/householder, multifamily	year	407	90	28r
Gas, cooking, winter, 10 therms	month	7.45	92	56c
Gas, cooking, winter, 30 therms	month	15.05	92	56c
Gas, cooking, winter, 50 therms	month	22.65	92	56c
Gas, heating, winter, 100 therms	month	41.65	92	56c
Gas, natural	mil Btu	4.41	90	64s
Gas, natural	000 cu ft	4.94	91	46s
Gas, natural, exp	year	514	91	46s
Gasoline, motor	gal	1.10	4Q 92	4c
Gasoline, unleaded regular	mil Btu	9.40	90	64s
Entertainment				
Bowling, evening rate	game	2.00	4Q 92	4c
Miniature golf admission	adult	6.18	92	1r
Miniature golf admission	child	5.14	92	1r

Sioux Falls, SD - continued

Item	Per	Value	Date	Ref.
Entertainment - continued				
Monopoly game, Parker Brothers', No. 9		10.97	4Q 92	4c
Movie	admission	5.00	4Q 92	4c
Tennis balls, yellow, Wilson or Penn, 3	can	2.17	4Q 92	4c
Waterpark admission	adult	11.00	92	1r
Waterpark admission	child	8.55	92	1r
Funerals				
Casket, 18-gauge steel, velvet interior		1952.97	91	24r
Cosmetology, hair care, etc.		90.03	91	24r
Embalming		251.75	91	24r
Facility use for ceremony		180.75	91	24r
Hearse, local		117.51	91	24r
Limousine, local		71.86	91	24r
Remains to funeral home, transfer		81.14	91	24r
Service charge, professional		740.03	91	24r
Vault, concrete, non-metallic liner		801.47	91	24r
Viewing facilities, use		169.33	91	24r
Goods and Services				
ACCRA Index, Miscellaneous Goods and Services		93.70	4Q 92	4c
Groceries				
ACCRA Index, Groceries		98.20	4Q 92	4c
Apples, Red Delicious	lb	0.77	4/93	16r
Babyfood, strained vegetables, lowest price	4-4.5 oz jar	0.31	4Q 92	4c
Bacon	lb	1.85	4/93	16r
Bananas	lb	0.46	4Q 92	4c
Bananas	lb	0.46	4/93	16r
Beef, stew, boneless	lb	2.53	4/93	16r
Bologna, all beef or mixed	lb	2.19	4/93	16r
Bread, white	24 oz	0.74	4Q 92	4c
Bread, white, pan	lb	0.78	4/93	16r
Butter	lb	1.50	4/93	16r
Cabbage	lb	0.40	4/93	16r
Carrots, short trimmed and topped	lb	0.45	4/93	16r
Cheese, Cheddar	lb	3.47	4/93	16r
Cheese, Kraft grated Parmesan	8-oz canister	3.56	4Q 92	4c
Chicken, fresh, whole	lb	0.84	4/93	16r
Chicken, fryer, whole	lb	0.78	4Q 92	4c
Chicken breast, bone-in	lb	1.94	4/93	16r
Chicken legs, bone-in	lb	1.02	4/93	16r
Chuck roast, graded and ungraded, ex USDA prime and choice	lb	2.43	4/93	16r
Chuck roast, USDA choice, bone-in	lb	2.11	4/93	16r
Chuck roast, USDA choice, boneless	lb	2.44	4/93	16r
Cigarettes, Winston	carton	17.43	4Q 92	4c
Coffee, 100% ground roast, all sizes	lb	2.47	4/93	16r
Coffee, vacuum-packed	13-oz can	2.02	4Q 92	4c
Cookies, chocolate chip	lb	2.73	4/93	16r
Corn, frozen	10 oz	0.72	4Q 92	4c
Corn Flakes, Kellogg's or Post Toasties	18 oz	1.95	4Q 92	4c
Eggs, Grade A large	doz	0.71	4Q 92	4c
Eggs, Grade A large	doz	0.93	4/93	16r
Flour, white, all purpose	lb	0.21	4/93	16r
Grapefruit	lb	0.45	4/93	16r
Grapes, Thompson Seedless	lb	1.46	4/93	16r
Ground beef, 100% beef	lb	1.63	4/93	16r
Ground beef, lean and extra lean	lb	2.08	4/93	16r
Ground beef or hamburger	lb	1.35	4Q 92	4c
Ground chuck, 100% beef	lb	1.94	4/93	16r
Ham, boneless, excluding canned	lb	2.21	4/93	16r
Ice cream, prepackaged, bulk, regular	1/2 gal	2.41	4/93	16r
Lemons	lb	0.82	4/93	16r
Lettuce, iceberg	head	0.87	4Q 92	4c
Lettuce, iceberg	lb	0.83	4/93	16r
Margarine, Blue Bonnet or Parkay cubes	lb	0.63	4Q 92	4c
Margarine, stick	lb	0.77	4/93	16r
Milk, whole	1/2 gal	1.21	4Q 92	4c

Values are in dollars or fractions of dollars. In the column headed *Ref*, references are shown to sources. Each reference is followed by a letter. These refer to the geographical level for which data were reported: s=State, r=Region, and c=City or metro. The abbreviation *ex* is used to mean *except* or *excluding*; *exp* stands for expenditures. For other abbreviations and further explanations, please see the Introduction.

Sioux Falls, SD - continued

Item	Per	Value	Date	Ref.
Groceries				
Orange juice, Minute Maid frozen	12-oz can	1.63	4Q 92	4c
Oranges, navel	lb	0.50	4/93	16r
Peaches	29-oz can	1.40	4Q 92	4c
Peanut butter, creamy, all sizes	lb	1.82	4/93	16r
Pears, Anjou	lb	0.85	4/93	16r
Peas Sweet, Del Monte or Green Giant	15-17 oz can	0.50	4Q 92	4c
Pork chops, center cut, bone-in	lb	3.17	4/93	16r
Potato chips	16 oz	2.68	4/93	16r
Potatoes, white	lb	0.26	4/93	16r
Potatoes, white or red	10-lb sack	2.23	4Q 92	4c
Round roast, graded & ungraded, ex USDA prime & choice	lb	2.88	4/93	16r
Round roast, USDA choice, boneless	lb	2.96	4/93	16r
Sausage, Jimmy Dean, 100% pork	lb	2.41	4Q 92	4c
Shortening, vegetable oil blends	lb	0.79	4/93	16r
Shortening, vegetable, Crisco	3-lb can	2.23	4Q 92	4c
Soft drink, Coca Cola	2 liter	1.15	4Q 92	4c
Spaghetti and macaroni	lb	0.76	4/93	16r
Steak, rib eye, USDA choice, boneless	lb	6.29	4/93	16r
Steak, round, USDA choice, boneless	lb	3.24	4/93	16r
Steak, sirloin, graded & ungraded, ex USDA prime & choice	lb	4.00	4/93	16r
Steak, sirloin, USDA choice, bone-in	lb	3.57	4/93	16r
Steak, sirloin, USDA choice, boneless	lb	4.17	4/93	16r
Steak, T-bone	lb	5.33	4Q 92	4c
Steak, T-bone, USDA choice, bone-in	lb	5.60	4/93	16r
Strawberries, dry pint	12 oz	0.90	4/93	16r
Sugar, cane or beet	4 lb	1.74	4Q 92	4c
Sugar, white	lb	0.36	4/93	16r
Sugar, white, 33-80 oz pk	lb	0.35	4/93	16r
Tomatoes, field grown	lb	0.99	4/93	16r
Tomatoes, Hunt's or Del Monte	14.5-oz can	0.61	4Q 92	4c
Tuna, chunk, light	6.125-6.5 oz can	0.56	4Q 92	4c
Tuna, chunk, light	lb	1.76	4/93	16r
Turkey, frozen, whole	lb	0.91	4/93	16r
Health Care				
ACCRA Index, Health Care		97.30	4Q 92	4c
Analgesic, Aspirin, Bayer, 325 mg tablets	100	5.27	4Q 92	4c
Childbirth, cesarean, hospital		4688	91	62r
Childbirth, cesarean, physician's fee		2053	91	62r
Childbirth, normal, hospital		2657	91	62r
Childbirth, normal, physician's fee		1492	91	62r
Dentist's fee, adult teeth cleaning and periodic oral exam	visit	48.75	4Q 92	4c
Doctor's fee, routine exam, established patient	visit	32.38	4Q 92	4c
Hospital care, semiprivate room	day	185.92	90	27c
Hospital care, semiprivate room	day	310.00	4Q 92	4c
Medical insurance premium, per employee, small group comprehensive	month	281.05	10/91	25c
Medical plan per employee	year	3443	91	45r
Mental health care, exp	capita	20.37-28.83	90	38s
Mental health care, exp, state mental health agency	capita	25.34	90	38s
Mental health care, hospital psychiatric services, non-Federal, exp	capita	4.36	88	38s
Mental health care, mental health organization, multiservice, exp	capita	16.71	88	38s
Mental health care, psychiatric out-patient clinics, freestanding, exp	capita	0.33	88	38s
Mental health care, state and county mental hospitals, exp	capita	20.13	88	38s
Mental health care, VA medical centers, exp	capita	20.15	88	38s

Sioux Falls, SD - continued

Item	Per	Value	Date	Ref.
Health Care - continued				
Physician fee, family practice, first-visit		76.00	91	62r
Physician fee, family practice, revisit		33.00	91	62r
Physician fee, general practice, first-visit		61.00	91	62r
Physician fee, general practice, revisit		31.00	91	62r
Physician fee, general surgeon, first-visit		65.00	91	62r
Physician fee, general surgeon, revisit		35.00	91	62r
Physician fee, internal medicine, first-visit		91.00	91	62r
Physician fee, internal medicine, revisit		40.00	91	62r
Physician fee, median, neurosurgeon, first-visit		106.00	91	62r
Physician fee, median, nonsurgical specialist, first-visit		90.00	91	62r
Physician fee, median, orthopedic surgeon, first-visit		83.00	91	62r
Physician fee, median, surgical specialist, first-visit		61.00	91	62r
Physician fee, neurosurgeon, revisit		41.00	91	62r
Physician fee, nonsurgical specialist, revisit		40.00	91	62r
Physician fee, obstetrics/gynecology, first-visit		61.00	91	62r
Physician fee, obstetrics/gynecology, revisit		40.00	91	62r
Physician fee, orthopedic surgeon, revisit		41.00	91	62r
Physician fee, pediatrician, first-visit		46.00	91	62r
Physician fee, pediatrician, revisit		33.00	91	62r
Physician fee, surgical specialist, revisit		36.00	91	62r
Household Goods				
Appliance repair, home, service call, washing machine	min labor charge	29.18	4Q 92	4c
Laundry detergent, Tide Ultra, Bold, or Cheer	42 oz	3.02	4Q 92	4c
Tissues, facial, Kleenex brand	175-count box	1.11	4Q 92	4c
Housing				
ACCRA Index, Housing		96.40	4Q 92	4c
Home, median price	unit	69.00		26c
House, 1,800 sq ft, 8,000 sq ft lot, new, urban	total	99700	4Q 92	4c
House payment, principal and interest, 25% down payment	month	559	4Q 92	4c
Mortgage rate, incl. points & origination fee, 30-year fixed or adjustable rate	per-cent	8.20	4Q 92	4c
Rent, apartment, 2 bedrooms - 1-1/2 to 2 baths, unfurnished, 950 sq ft, water	month	553	4Q 92	4c
Rental unit, 1 bedroom	month	391	93	23c
Rental unit, 2 bedroom	month	459	93	23c
Rental unit, 3 bedroom	month	577	93	23c
Rental unit, 4 bedroom	month	645	93	23c
Rental unit, efficiency	month	321	93	23c
Insurance and Pensions				
Auto insurance, private passenger	year	409.16	91	63s
Personal Goods				
Shampoo, Alberto VO5	15 oz	1.25	4Q 92	4c
Toothpaste, Crest or Colgate	6-7 oz	1.71	4Q 92	4c
Personal Services				
Dry cleaning, man's 2-piece suit		5.86	4Q 92	4c
Haircare, woman's shampoo, trim and blow-dry		15.80	4Q 92	4c
Haircut, man's barbershop, no styling		8.50	4Q 92	4c
Restaurant Food				
Chicken, fried, thigh and drumstick		2.05	4Q 92	4c
Hamburger with cheese	1/4 lb	1.85	4Q 92	4c
Pizza, Pizza Hut or Pizza Inn, cheese, thin crust	12-13 in	7.07	4Q 92	4c
Taxes				
Tax, cigarette	pack	23	91	77s
Tax, gasoline	gal	18	91	77s

Values are in dollars or fractions of dollars. In the column headed *Ref*, references are shown to sources. Each reference is followed by a letter. These refer to the geographical level for which data were reported: s=State, r=Region, and c=City or metro. The abbreviation *ex* is used to mean *except* or *excluding*; *exp* stands for expenditures. For other abbreviations and further explanations, please see the Introduction.

Sioux Falls, SD - continued

Item	Per	Value	Date	Ref.
Taxes				
Taxes, state	capita	751	91	77s
Transportation				
ACCRA Index, Transportation		97.40	4Q 92	4c
Bus fare	one-way	0.60	3/93	2c
Driver's license fee		6.00	12/90	43s
Tire balance, computer or spin balance, front	wheel	6.35	4Q 92	4c
Utilities				
ACCRA Index, Utilities		88.60	4Q 92	4c
Electricity	mil Btu	17.95	90	64s
Electricity, partial electric and other energy, 1,800 sq ft living area new home	month	45.78	4Q 92	4c
Electricity, winter, 250 KWh	month	20.45	92	55c
Electricity, winter, 500 KWh	month	34.35	92	55c
Electricity, winter, 750 KWh	month	48.25	92	55c
Electricity, winter, 1000 KWh	month	62.15	92	55c

South Bend, IN

Item	Per	Value	Date	Ref.
Composite ACCRA index		93.70	4Q 92	4c
Alcoholic Beverages				
Beer, Miller Lite or Budweiser, 12-oz containers	6 pack	3.50	4Q 92	4c
Liquor, J & B Scotch	750 ml	14.24	4Q 92	4c
Wine, Gallo Chablis blanc, 1.5 liter	bottle	4.09	4Q 92	4c
Child Care				
Child care fee, average, center	hour	1.63	90	65r
Child care fee, average, nonregulated family day care	hour	1.83	90	65r
Child care fee, average, regulated family day care	hour	1.42	90	65r
Clothing				
Jeans, man's denim		28.32	4Q 92	4c
Shirt, man's dress shirt		26.30	4Q 92	4c
Undervest, boy's size 10-14, cotton	3	3.96	4Q 92	4c
Communications				
Long-distance telephone service, day, initial minute, 0-100 miles	min	0.18-0.45	91	12s
Long-distance telephone service, day, additional minute, 0-100 miles	min	0.10-0.30	91	12s
Long-distance telephone service, evenings/weekends, 0-100 mi, initial minute	min	0.08-0.19	91	12s
Long-distance telephone service, evenings/weekends, 0-100 mi, additional minute	min	0.04-0.13	91	12s
Newspaper subscription, daily and Sunday home delivery, large-city	month	10.00	4Q 92	4c
Telephone, flat rate	month	11.11	91	11c
Telephone bill, family of four	month	22.10	4Q 92	4c
Education				
Board, 4-yr private college/university	year	1714	91	22s
Board, 4-yr public college/university	year	1829	91	22s
Expenditures, local gov't, public elementary/secondary	pupil	5545	92	20s
Room, 4-year private college/university	year	1512	91	22s
Room, 4-year public college/university	year	1435	91	22s
Tuition, 2-year private college/university	year	6756	91	22s
Tuition, 2-year public college/university	year	1423	91	22s
Tuition, 4-year private college/university	year	8451	91	22s
Tuition, 4-year public college/university, in-state	year	2067	91	22s
Energy and Fuels				
Coal	mil Btu	1.46	90	64s
Energy	mil Btu	6.77	90	64s
Energy, combined forms, 1,800 sq ft heating area	month	106.30	4Q 92	4c

South Bend, IN - continued

Item	Per	Value	Date	Ref.
Energy and Fuels - continued				
Energy, exc electricity, 1,800 sq ft heating area	month	57.32	4Q 92	4c
Energy exp/householder, 1-family unit	year	471	90	28r
Energy exp/householder, <1,000 sq ft heating area	year	430	90	28r
Energy exp/householder, 1,000-1,999 sq ft heating area	year	481	90	28r
Energy exp/householder, 2,000+ sq ft heating area	year	473	90	28r
Energy exp/householder, mobile home	year	430	90	28r
Energy exp/householder, multifamily	year	461	90	28r
Gas, natural	mil Btu	4.27	90	64s
Gas, natural	000 cu ft	5.46	91	46s
Gas, natural, exp	year	588	91	46s
Gasoline, motor	gal	1.06	4Q 92	4c
Gasoline, unleaded regular	mil Btu	8.74	90	64s
Entertainment				
Bowling, evening rate	game	1.72	4Q 92	4c
Miniature golf admission	adult	6.18	92	1r
Miniature golf admission	child	5.14	92	1r
Monopoly game, Parker Brothers', No. 9		9.99	4Q 92	4c
Movie	admission	5.70	4Q 92	4c
Tennis balls, yellow, Wilson or Penn, 3	can	2.15	4Q 92	4c
Waterpark admission	adult	11.00	92	1r
Waterpark admission	child	8.55	92	1r
Funerals				
Casket, 18-gauge steel, velvet interior		1926.72	91	24r
Cosmetology, hair care, etc.		97.64	91	24r
Embalming		249.14	91	24r
Facility use for ceremony		208.59	91	24r
Hearse, local		130.12	91	24r
Limousine, local		104.66	91	24r
Remains to funeral home, transfer		93.61	91	24r
Service charge, professional		724.62	91	24r
Vault, concrete, non-metallic liner		734.53	91	24r
Viewing facilities, use		236.06	91	24r
Goods and Services				
ACCRA Index, Miscellaneous Goods and Services		96.70	4Q 92	4c
Groceries				
ACCRA Index, Groceries		89.80	4Q 92	4c
Apples, Red Delicious	lb	0.77	4/93	16r
Babyfood, strained vegetables, lowest price	4-4.5 oz jar	0.31	4Q 92	4c
Bacon	lb	1.85	4/93	16r
Bananas	lb	0.39	4Q 92	4c
Bananas	lb	0.46	4/93	16r
Beef, stew, boneless	lb	2.53	4/93	16r
Bologna, all beef or mixed	lb	2.19	4/93	16r
Bread, white	24 oz	0.62	4Q 92	4c
Bread, white, pan	lb	0.78	4/93	16r
Butter	lb	1.50	4/93	16r
Cabbage	lb	0.40	4/93	16r
Carrots, short trimmed and topped	lb	0.45	4/93	16r
Cheese, Cheddar	lb	3.47	4/93	16r
Cheese, Kraft grated Parmesan	8-oz canister	3.14	4Q 92	4c
Chicken, fresh, whole	lb	0.84	4/93	16r
Chicken, fryer, whole	lb	0.49	4Q 92	4c
Chicken breast, bone-in	lb	1.94	4/93	16r
Chicken legs, bone-in	lb	1.02	4/93	16r
Chuck roast, graded and ungraded, ex USDA prime and choice	lb	2.43	4/93	16r
Chuck roast, USDA choice, bone-in	lb	2.11	4/93	16r
Chuck roast, USDA choice, boneless	lb	2.44	4/93	16r
Cigarettes, Winston	carton	16.44	4Q 92	4c
Coffee, 100% ground roast, all sizes	lb	2.47	4/93	16r

Values are in dollars or fractions of dollars. In the column headed *Ref*, references are shown to sources. Each reference is followed by a letter. These refer to the geographical level for which data were reported: s=State, r=Region, and c=City or metro. The abbreviation *ex* is used to mean *except* or *excluding*; *exp* stands for expenditures. For other abbreviations and further explanations, please see the Introduction.

South Bend, IN - continued

Item	Per	Value	Date	Ref.
Groceries				
Coffee, vacuum-packed	13-oz can	1.99	4Q 92	4c
Cookies, chocolate chip	lb	2.73	4/93	16r
Corn, frozen	10 oz	0.61	4Q 92	4c
Corn Flakes, Kellogg's or Post Toasties	18 oz	1.51	4Q 92	4c
Eggs, Grade A large	doz	0.78	4Q 92	4c
Eggs, Grade A large	doz	0.93	4/93	16r
Flour, white, all purpose	lb	0.21	4/93	16r
Grapefruit	lb	0.45	4/93	16r
Grapes, Thompson Seedless	lb	1.46	4/93	16r
Ground beef, 100% beef	lb	1.63	4/93	16r
Ground beef, lean and extra lean	lb	2.08	4/93	16r
Ground beef or hamburger	lb	1.22	4Q 92	4c
Ground chuck, 100% beef	lb	1.94	4/93	16r
Ham, boneless, excluding canned	lb	2.21	4/93	16r
Honey, jar	8 oz	0.97-1.25	92	5r
Honey, jar	lb	1.25-2.25	92	5r
Honey, squeeze bear	12-oz	1.25-1.99	92	5r
Ice cream, prepackaged, bulk, regular	1/2 gal	2.41	4/93	16r
Lemons	lb	0.82	4/93	16r
Lettuce, iceberg	head	0.75	4Q 92	4c
Lettuce, iceberg	lb	0.83	4/93	16r
Margarine, Blue Bonnet or Parkay cubes	lb	0.51	4Q 92	4c
Margarine, stick	lb	0.77	4/93	16r
Milk, whole	1/2 gal	1.32	4Q 92	4c
Orange juice, Minute Maid frozen	12-oz can	1.48	4Q 92	4c
Oranges, navel	lb	0.50	4/93	16r
Peaches	29-oz can	1.29	4Q 92	4c
Peanut butter, creamy, all sizes	lb	1.82	4/93	16r
Pears, Anjou	lb	0.85	4/93	16r
Peas Sweet, Del Monte or Green Giant	15-17 oz can	0.56	4Q 92	4c
Pork chops, center cut, bone-in	lb	3.17	4/93	16r
Potato chips	16 oz	2.68	4/93	16r
Potatoes, white	lb	0.26	4/93	16r
Potatoes, white or red	10-lb sack	1.36	4Q 92	4c
Round roast, graded & ungraded, ex USDA prime & choice	lb	2.88	4/93	16r
Round roast, USDA choice, boneless	lb	2.96	4/93	16r
Sausage, Jimmy Dean, 100% pork	lb	2.83	4Q 92	4c
Shortening, vegetable oil blends	lb	0.79	4/93	16r
Shortening, vegetable, Crisco	3-lb can	1.92	4Q 92	4c
Soft drink, Coca Cola	2 liter	1.32	4Q 92	4c
Spaghetti and macaroni	lb	0.76	4/93	16r
Steak, rib eye, USDA choice, boneless	lb	6.29	4/93	16r
Steak, round, USDA choice, boneless	lb	3.24	4/93	16r
Steak, sirloin, graded & ungraded, ex USDA prime & choice	lb	4.00	4/93	16r
Steak, sirloin, USDA choice, bone-in	lb	3.57	4/93	16r
Steak, sirloin, USDA choice, boneless	lb	4.17	4/93	16r
Steak, T-bone	lb	4.17	4Q 92	4c
Steak, T-bone, USDA choice, bone-in	lb	5.60	4/93	16r
Strawberries, dry pint	12 oz	0.90	4/93	16r
Sugar, cane or beet	4 lb	1.15	4Q 92	4c
Sugar, white	lb	0.36	4/93	16r
Sugar, white, 33-80 oz pk	lb	0.35	4/93	16r
Tomatoes, field grown	lb	0.99	4/93	16r
Tomatoes, Hunt's or Del Monte	14.5-oz can	0.68	4Q 92	4c
Tuna, chunk, light	6.125-6.5 oz can	0.64	4Q 92	4c
Tuna, chunk, light	lb	1.76	4/93	16r
Turkey, frozen, whole	lb	0.91	4/93	16r
Health Care				
ACCRA Index, Health Care		90.70	4Q 92	4c
Analgesic, Aspirin, Bayer, 325 mg tablets	100	3.92	4Q 92	4c
Childbirth, cesarean, hospital		4688	91	62r

South Bend, IN - continued

Item	Per	Value	Date	Ref.
Health Care - continued				
Childbirth, cesarean, physician's fee		2053	91	62r
Childbirth, normal, hospital		2657	91	62r
Childbirth, normal, physician's fee		1492	91	62r
Dentist's fee, adult teeth cleaning and periodic oral exam	visit	38.83	4Q 92	4c
Doctor's fee, routine exam, established patient	visit	29.50	4Q 92	4c
Hospital care, semiprivate room	day	292.03	90	27c
Hospital care, semiprivate room	day	427.25	4Q 92	4c
Medical insurance premium, per employee, small group comprehensive	month	281.05	10/91	25c
Medical plan per employee	year	3443	91	45r
Mental health care, exp	capita	37.60-53.67	90	38s
Mental health care, exp, state mental health agency	capita	47.05	90	38s
Mental health care, hospital psychiatric services, non-Federal, exp	capita	22.14	88	38s
Mental health care, mental health organization, multiservice, exp	capita	10.33	88	38s
Mental health care, psychiatric hospitals, private, exp	capita	20.10	88	38s
Mental health care, state and county mental hospitals, exp	capita	24.00	88	38s
Mental health care, VA medical centers, exp	capita	3.20	88	38s
Physician fee, family practice, first-visit		76.00	91	62r
Physician fee, family practice, revisit		33.00	91	62r
Physician fee, general practice, first-visit		61.00	91	62r
Physician fee, general practice, revisit		31.00	91	62r
Physician fee, general surgeon, first-visit		65.00	91	62r
Physician fee, general surgeon, revisit		35.00	91	62r
Physician fee, internal medicine, first-visit		91.00	91	62r
Physician fee, internal medicine, revisit		40.00	91	62r
Physician fee, median, neurosurgeon, first-visit		106.00	91	62r
Physician fee, median, nonsurgical specialist, first-visit		90.00	91	62r
Physician fee, median, orthopedic surgeon, first-visit		83.00	91	62r
Physician fee, median, surgical specialist, first-visit		61.00	91	62r
Physician fee, neurosurgeon, revisit		41.00	91	62r
Physician fee, nonsurgical specialist, revisit		40.00	91	62r
Physician fee, obstetrics/gynecology, first-visit		61.00	91	62r
Physician fee, obstetrics/gynecology, revisit		40.00	91	62r
Physician fee, orthopedic surgeon, revisit		41.00	91	62r
Physician fee, pediatrician, first-visit		46.00	91	62r
Physician fee, pediatrician, revisit		33.00	91	62r
Physician fee, surgical specialist, revisit		36.00	91	62r
Substance abuse, hospital ancillary charge	incident	1230	90	70s
Substance abuse, hospital physician charge	incident	410	90	70s
Substance abuse, hospital room and board	incident	5510	90	70s
Household Goods				
Appliance repair, home, service call, washing machine	min labor charge	32.39	4Q 92	4c
Laundry detergent, Tide Ultra, Bold, or Cheer	42 oz	2.92	4Q 92	4c
Tissues, facial, Kleenex brand	175-count box	1.08	4Q 92	4c
Housing				
ACCRA Index, Housing		92.10	4Q 92	4c
Home, median price	unit	62.90		26c
House, 1,800 sq ft, 8,000 sq ft lot, new, urban	total	95371	4Q 92	4c

Values are in dollars or fractions of dollars. In the column headed *Ref*, references are shown to sources. Each reference is followed by a letter. These refer to the geographical level for which data were reported: s=State, r=Region, and c=City or metro. The abbreviation *ex* is used to mean *except* or *excluding*; *exp* stands for expenditures. For other abbreviations and further explanations, please see the Introduction.

South Bend, IN - continued

Item	Per	Value	Date	Ref.
Housing				
House payment, principal and interest, 25% down payment	month	536	4Q 92	4c
Mortgage rate, incl. points & origination fee, 30-year fixed or adjustable rate	percent	8.23	4Q 92	4c
Rent, apartment, 2 bedrooms - 1-1/2 to 2 baths, unfurnished, 950 sq ft, water	month	525	4Q 92	4c
Rental unit, 1 bedroom	month	374	93	23c
Rental unit, 2 bedroom	month	437	93	23c
Rental unit, 3 bedroom	month	543	93	23c
Rental unit, 4 bedroom	month	605	93	23c
Rental unit, efficiency	month	309	93	23c
Insurance and Pensions				
Auto insurance, private passenger	year	548.99	91	63s
Personal Goods				
Shampoo, Alberto VO5	15 oz	1.02	4Q 92	4c
Toothpaste, Crest or Colgate	6-7 oz	1.42	4Q 92	4c
Personal Services				
Dry cleaning, man's 2-piece suit		5.64	4Q 92	4c
Haircare, woman's shampoo, trim and blow-dry		22.00	4Q 92	4c
Haircut, man's barbershop, no styling		8.57	4Q 92	4c
Restaurant Food				
Chicken, fried, thigh and drumstick		2.12	4Q 92	4c
Hamburger with cheese	1/4 lb	1.72	4Q 92	4c
Pizza, Pizza Hut or Pizza Inn, cheese, thin crust	12-13 in	7.99	4Q 92	4c
Taxes				
Tax, cigarette	pack	15.50	91	77s
Tax, gasoline	gal	15	91	77s
Taxes, state	capita	1102	91	77s
Transportation				
ACCRA Index, Transportation		89.60	4Q 92	4c
Bus fare	one-way	0.75	3/93	2c
Bus fare, up to 10 miles	one-way	0.60	4Q 92	4c
Driver's license fee		6.00	12/90	43s
Tire balance, computer or spin balance, front	wheel	5.83	4Q 92	4c
Utilities				
ACCRA Index, Utilities		99.00	4Q 92	4c
Electricity	mil Btu	15.75	90	64s
Electricity, partial electric and other energy, 1,800 sq ft living area new home	month	48.98	4Q 92	4c

Spartanburg, SC

Item	Per	Value	Date	Ref.
Composite ACCRA index		94.20	4Q 92	4c
Alcoholic Beverages				
Beer, Miller Lite or Budweiser, 12-oz containers	6 pack	3.84	4Q 92	4c
Liquor, J & B Scotch	750 ml	16.11	4Q 92	4c
Wine, Gallo Chablis blanc, 1.5 liter	bottle	5.01	4Q 92	4c
Child Care				
Child care fee, average, center	hour	1.29	90	65r
Child care fee, average, nonregulated family day care	hour	0.89	90	65r
Child care fee, average, regulated family day care	hour	1.32	90	65r
Clothing				
Jeans, man's denim		31.80	4Q 92	4c
Shirt, man's dress shirt		25.00	4Q 92	4c
Undervest, boy's size 10-14, cotton	3	4.17	4Q 92	4c
Communications				
Long-distance telephone service, day, initial minute, 0-100 miles	min	0.24-0.52	91	12s

Spartanburg, SC - continued

Item	Per	Value	Date	Ref.
Communications - continued				
Long-distance telephone service, day, additional minute, 0-100 miles	min	0.13-0.35	91	12s
Long-distance telephone service, evenings/weekends, 0-100 mi, initial minute	min	0.12-0.26	91	12s
Long-distance telephone service, evenings/weekends, 0-100 mi, additional minute	min	0.07-0.16	91	12s
Newspaper subscription, daily and Sunday home delivery, large-city	month	8.25	4Q 92	4c
Telephone bill, family of four	month	22.35	4Q 92	4c
Education				
Board, 4-yr private college/university	year	1468	91	22s
Board, 4-yr public college/university	year	1632	91	22s
Expenditures, local gov't, public elementary/secondary	pupil	4312	92	20s
Room, 4-year private college/university	year	1393	91	22s
Room, 4-year public college/university	year	1492	91	22s
Tuition, 2-year private college/university	year	5110	91	22s
Tuition, 2-year public college/university	year	813	91	22s
Tuition, 4-year private college/university	year	6434	91	22s
Tuition, 4-year public college/university, in-state	year	2317	91	22s
Energy and Fuels				
Coal	mil Btu	1.73	90	64s
Energy	mil Btu	8.93	90	64s
Energy, combined forms, 1,800 sq ft heating area	month	117.15	4Q 92	4c
Energy exp/householder, 1-family unit	year	487	90	28r
Energy exp/householder, <1,000 sq ft heating area	year	393	90	28r
Energy exp/householder, 1,000-1,999 sq ft heating area	year	442	90	28r
Energy exp/householder, 2,000+ sq ft heating area	year	577	90	28r
Energy exp/householder, mobile home	year	366	90	28r
Energy exp/householder, multifamily	year	382	90	28r
Gas, natural	mil Btu	4.01	90	64s
Gas, natural	000 cu ft	6.98	91	46s
Gas, natural, exp	year	397	91	46s
Gasoline, motor	gal	1.03	4Q 92	4c
Gasoline, unleaded regular	mil Btu	8.80	90	64s
Entertainment				
Bowling, evening rate	game	2.37	4Q 92	4c
Miniature golf admission	adult	6.18	92	1r
Miniature golf admission	child	5.14	92	1r
Monopoly game, Parker Brothers', No. 9		9.86	4Q 92	4c
Movie	admission	5.50	4Q 92	4c
Tennis balls, yellow, Wilson or Penn, 3	can	2.06	4Q 92	4c
Waterpark admission	adult	11.00	92	1r
Waterpark admission	child	8.55	92	1r
Funerals				
Casket, 18-gauge steel, velvet interior		2029.08	91	24r
Cosmetology, hair care, etc.		75.10	91	24r
Embalming		249.24	91	24r
Facility use for ceremony		162.27	91	24r
Hearse, local		114.04	91	24r
Limousine, local		88.57	91	24r
Remains to funeral home, transfer		92.61	91	24r
Service charge, professional		682.42	91	24r
Vault, concrete, non-metallic liner		798.70	91	24r
Viewing facilities, use		163.86	91	24r
Goods and Services				
ACCRA Index, Miscellaneous Goods and Services		98.70	4Q 92	4c
Groceries				
ACCRA Index, Groceries		95.80	4Q 92	4c
Apples, Red Delicious	lb	0.79	4/93	16r

Values are in dollars or fractions of dollars. In the column headed *Ref*, references are shown to sources. Each reference is followed by a letter. These refer to the geographical level for which data were reported: s = State, r = Region, and c = City or metro. The abbreviation *ex* is used to mean *except* or *excluding*; *exp* stands for *expenditures*. For other abbreviations and further explanations, please see the Introduction.

Spartanburg, SC - continued

Item	Per	Value	Date	Ref.
Groceries				
Babyfood, strained vegetables, lowest price	4-4.5 oz jar	0.31	4Q 92	4c
Bacon	lb	1.75	4/93	16r
Bananas	lb	0.51	4Q 92	4c
Bananas	lb	0.42	4/93	16r
Beef, stew, boneless	lb	2.61	4/93	16r
Bologna, all beef or mixed	lb	2.24	4/93	16r
Bread, white	24 oz	0.67	4Q 92	4c
Bread, white, pan	lb	0.64	4/93	16r
Bread, whole wheat, pan	lb	0.96	4/93	16r
Cabbage	lb	0.37	4/93	16r
Carrots, short trimmed and topped	lb	0.47	4/93	16r
Celery	lb	0.64	4/93	16r
Cheese, American	lb	2.98	4/93	16r
Cheese, Cheddar	lb	3.28	4/93	16r
Cheese, Kraft grated Parmesan	8-oz canister	3.27	4Q 92	4c
Chicken, fresh, whole	lb	0.77	4/93	16r
Chicken, fryer, whole	lb	0.82	4Q 92	4c
Chicken breast, bone-in	lb	1.92	4/93	16r
Chicken legs, bone-in	lb	1.06	4/93	16r
Chuck roast, graded and ungraded, ex USDA prime and choice	lb	2.40	4/93	16r
Chuck roast, USDA choice, bone-in	lb	2.19	4/93	16r
Chuck roast, USDA choice, boneless	lb	2.38	4/93	16r
Cigarettes, Winston	carton	15.39	4Q 92	4c
Coffee, 100% ground roast, all sizes	lb	2.48	4/93	16r
Coffee, vacuum-packed	13-oz can	1.95	4Q 92	4c
Corn, frozen	10 oz	0.55	4Q 92	4c
Corn Flakes, Kellogg's or Post Toasties	18 oz	1.67	4Q 92	4c
Crackers, soda, salted	lb	1.15	4/93	16r
Eggs, Grade A large	doz	0.90	4Q 92	4c
Eggs, Grade A large	doz	0.96	4/93	16r
Flour, white, all purpose	lb	0.24	4/93	16r
Frankfurters, all meat or all beef	lb	2.01	4/93	16r
Grapefruit	lb	0.44	4/93	16r
Grapes, Thompson Seedless	lb	1.40	4/93	16r
Ground beef, 100% beef	lb	1.58	4/93	16r
Ground beef, lean and extra lean	lb	2.09	4/93	16r
Ground beef or hamburger	lb	1.50	4Q 92	4c
Ground chuck, 100% beef	lb	1.98	4/93	16r
Ham, boneless, excluding canned	lb	2.89	4/93	16r
Ham, picnic, shoulder, bone-in, smoked	lb	1.02	4/93	16r
Ham, rump or steak half, bone-in, smoked	lb	1.48	4/93	16r
Ice cream, prepackaged, bulk, regular	1/2 gal	2.41	4/93	16r
Lemons	lb	1.05	4/93	16r
Lettuce, iceberg	head	0.91	4Q 92	4c
Lettuce, iceberg	lb	0.81	4/93	16r
Margarine, Blue Bonnet or Parkay cubes	lb	0.50	4Q 92	4c
Margarine, stick	lb	0.88	4/93	16r
Milk, whole	1/2 gal	1.43	4Q 92	4c
Orange juice, Minute Maid frozen	12-oz can	1.35	4Q 92	4c
Oranges, navel	lb	0.55	4/93	16r
Peaches	29-oz can	1.28	4Q 92	4c
Pears, Anjou	lb	0.92	4/93	16r
Peas Sweet, Del Monte or Green Giant	15-17 oz can	0.52	4Q 92	4c
Pork chops, center cut, bone-in	lb	3.13	4/93	16r
Potato chips	16 oz	2.94	4/93	16r
Potatoes, white	lb	0.43	4/93	16r
Potatoes, white or red	10-lb sack	2.25	4Q 92	4c
Rib roast, USDA choice, bone-in	lb	4.63	4/93	16r
Rice, white, long grain, uncooked	lb	0.45	4/93	16r
Round roast, graded & ungraded, ex USDA prime & choice	lb	3.03	4/93	16r
Round roast, USDA choice, boneless	lb	3.09	4/93	16r
Sausage, fresh, loose	lb	2.08	4/93	16r

Spartanburg, SC - continued

Item	Per	Value	Date	Ref.
Groceries - continued				
Sausage, Jimmy Dean, 100% pork	lb	2.33	4Q 92	4c
Short ribs, bone-in	lb	2.66	4/93	16r
Shortening, vegetable oil blends	lb	0.69	4/93	16r
Shortening, vegetable, Crisco	3-lb can	1.99	4Q 92	4c
Soft drink, Coca Cola	2 liter	1.09	4Q 92	4c
Spaghetti and macaroni	lb	0.81	4/93	16r
Steak, rib eye, USDA choice, boneless	lb	6.24	4/93	16r
Steak, round, graded & ungraded, ex USDA prime & choice	lb	3.31	4/93	16r
Steak, round, USDA choice, boneless	lb	3.34	4/93	16r
Steak, sirloin, graded & ungraded, ex USDA prime & choice	lb	4.19	4/93	16r
Steak, sirloin, USDA choice, boneless	lb	4.46	4/93	16r
Steak, T-bone	lb	5.65	4Q 92	4c
Steak, T-bone, USDA choice, bone-in	lb	5.25	4/93	16r
Strawberries, dry pint	12 oz	0.92	4/93	16r
Sugar, cane or beet	4 lb	1.52	4Q 92	4c
Sugar, white	lb	0.39	4/93	16r
Sugar, white, 33-80 oz pk	lb	0.38	4/93	16r
Tomatoes, field grown	lb	0.88	4/93	16r
Tomatoes, Hunt's or Del Monte	14.5-oz can	0.54	4Q 92	4c
Tuna, chunk, light	6.125-6.5 oz can	0.52	4Q 92	4c
Tuna, chunk, light	lb	1.79	4/93	16r
Turkey, frozen, whole	lb	1.04	4/93	16r
Yogurt, natural, fruit flavored	1/2 pint	0.57	4/93	16r
Health Care				
ACCRA Index, Health Care		90.70	4Q 92	4c
Analgesic, Aspirin, Bayer, 325 mg tablets	100	3.93	4Q 92	4c
Childbirth, cesarean, hospital		5034	91	62r
Childbirth, cesarean, physician's fee		2053	91	62r
Childbirth, normal, hospital		2712	91	62r
Childbirth, normal, physician's fee		1492	91	62r
Dentist's fee, adult teeth cleaning and periodic oral exam	visit	39.20	4Q 92	4c
Doctor's fee, routine exam, established patient	visit	41.60	4Q 92	4c
Health care spending, state	capita	1689	3/93	84s
Hospital care, semiprivate room	day	135.00	90	27c
Hospital care, semiprivate room	day	219.67	4Q 92	4c
Medical plan per employee	year	3495	91	45r
Mental health care, exp	capita	37.60-53.67	90	38s
Mental health care, exp, state mental health agency	capita	51.12	90	38s
Mental health care, hospital psychiatric services, non-Federal, exp	capita	10.67	88	38s
Mental health care, mental health organization, multiservice, exp	capita	11.38	88	38s
Mental health care, psychiatric hospitals, private, exp	capita	9.21	88	38s
Mental health care, psychiatric out-patient clinics, freestanding, exp	capita	0.68	88	38s
Mental health care, state and county mental hospitals, exp	capita	25.02	88	38s
Mental health care, VA medical centers, exp	capita	0.62	88	38s
Physician fee, family practice, first-visit		75.00	91	62r
Physician fee, family practice, revisit		34.00	91	62r
Physician fee, general practice, first-visit		61.00	91	62r
Physician fee, general practice, revisit		32.00	91	62r
Physician fee, general surgeon, first-visit		64.00	91	62r
Physician fee, general surgeon, revisit		40.00	91	62r
Physician fee, internal medicine, first-visit		98.00	91	62r
Physician fee, internal medicine, revisit		40.00	91	62r
Physician fee, median, neurosurgeon, first-visit		130.00	91	62r
Physician fee, median, nonsurgical specialist, first-visit		95.00	91	62r

Values are in dollars or fractions of dollars. In the column headed *Ref*, references are shown to sources. Each reference is followed by a letter. These refer to the geographical level for which data were reported: s=State, r=Region, and c=City or metro. The abbreviation *ex* is used to mean *except* or *excluding*; *exp* stands for expenditures. For other abbreviations and further explanations, please see the Introduction.

Spartanburg, SC - continued

Item	Per	Value	Date	Ref.
Health Care				
Physician fee, median, orthopedic surgeon, first-visit		91.00	91	62r
Physician fee, median, plastic surgeon, first-visit		66.00	91	62r
Physician fee, median, surgical specialist, first-visit		62.00	91	62r
Physician fee, neurosurgeon, revisit		50.00	91	62r
Physician fee, nonsurgical specialist, revisit		40.00	91	62r
Physician fee, obstetrics/gynecology, first-visit		64.00	91	62r
Physician fee, obstetrics/gynecology, revisit		41.00	91	62r
Physician fee, orthopedic surgeon, revisit		40.00	91	62r
Physician fee, pediatrician, first-visit		49.00	91	62r
Physician fee, pediatrician, revisit		33.00	91	62r
Physician fee, plastic surgeon, revisit		43.00	91	62r
Physician fee, surgical specialist, revisit		37.00	91	62r
Substance abuse, hospital ancillary charge	incident	1250	90	70s
Substance abuse, hospital physician charge	incident	250	90	70s
Substance abuse, hospital room and board	incident	6100	90	70s
Household Goods				
Appliance repair, home, service call, washing machine	min labor charge	34.00	4Q 92	4c
Laundry detergent, Tide Ultra, Bold, or Cheer	42 oz	2.60	4Q 92	4c
Tissues, facial, Kleenex brand	175-count box	1.06	4Q 92	4c
Housing				
ACCRA Index, Housing		87.30	4Q 92	4c
House, 1,800 sq ft, 8,000 sq ft lot, new, urban	total	93800	4Q 92	4c
House payment, principal and interest, 25% down payment	month	526	4Q 92	4c
Mortgage rate, incl. points & origination fee, 30-year fixed or adjustable rate	percent	8.21	4Q 92	4c
Rent, apartment, 2 bedrooms - 1-1/2 to 2 baths, unfurnished, 950 sq ft, water	month	455	4Q 92	4c
Insurance and Pensions				
Auto insurance, private passenger	year	605.26	91	63s
Personal Goods				
Shampoo, Alberto VO5	15 oz	1.03	4Q 92	4c
Toothpaste, Crest or Colgate	6-7 oz	1.55	4Q 92	4c
Personal Services				
Dry cleaning, man's 2-piece suit		5.62	4Q 92	4c
Haircare, woman's shampoo, trim and blow-dry		15.30	4Q 92	4c
Haircut, man's barbershop, no styling		7.80	4Q 92	4c
Restaurant Food				
Chicken, fried, thigh and drumstick		2.07	4Q 92	4c
Hamburger with cheese	1/4 lb	1.79	4Q 92	4c
Pizza, Pizza Hut or Pizza Inn, cheese, thin crust	12-13 in	8.03	4Q 92	4c
Taxes				
Tax, cigarette	pack	7	91	77s
Tax, gasoline	gal	16	91	77s
Taxes, state	capita	1105	91	77s
Transportation				
ACCRA Index, Transportation		84.60	4Q 92	4c
Driver's license fee		10.00	12/90	43s
Tire balance, computer or spin balance, front	wheel	5.10	4Q 92	4c

Spartanburg, SC - continued

Item	Per	Value	Date	Ref.
Travel				
Business travel	day	193.00	4/93	89r
Utilities				
ACCRA Index, Utilities		108.10	4Q 92	4c
Electricity	mil Btu	16.39	90	64s
Electricity, all electric, 1,800 sq ft living area new home	month	117.15	4Q 92	4c

Spokane, WA

Item	Per	Value	Date	Ref.
Composite ACCRA index		103.30	4Q 92	4c
Alcoholic Beverages				
Beer, Miller Lite or Budweiser, 12-oz containers	6 pack	3.27	4Q 92	4c
Liquor, J & B Scotch	750 ml	17.95	4Q 92	4c
Wine, Gallo Chablis blanc, 1.5 liter	bottle	3.96	4Q 92	4c
Child Care				
Child care fee, average, center	hour	1.71	90	65r
Child care fee, average, nonregulated family day care	hour	1.32	90	65r
Child care fee, average, regulated family day care	hour	1.86	90	65r
Clothing				
Jeans, man's denim		24.49	4Q 92	4c
Shirt, man's dress shirt		23.30	4Q 92	4c
Undervest, boy's size 10-14, cotton	3	3.59	4Q 92	4c
Communications				
Long-distance telephone service, day, initial minute, 0-100 miles	min	0.15-0.37	91	12s
Long-distance telephone service, day, additional minute, 0-100 miles	min	0.01-0.03	91	12s
Long-distance telephone service, evenings/weekends, 0-100 mi, initial minute	min	0.05-0.19	91	12s
Long-distance telephone service, evenings/weekends, 0-100 mi, additional minute	min	0.00-0.01	91	12s
Newspaper subscription, daily and Sunday home delivery, large-city	month	11.00	4Q 92	4c
Telephone, flat rate	month	10.75	91	11c
Telephone bill, family of four	month	15.92	4Q 92	4c
Education				
Board, 4-yr private college/university	year	1811	91	22s
Board, 4-yr public college/university	year	1539	91	22s
Expenditures, local gov't, public elementary/secondary	pupil	5317	92	20s
Room, 4-year private college/university	year	1885	91	22s
Room, 4-year public college/university	year	1698	91	22s
Tuition, 2-year private college/university	year	6743	91	22s
Tuition, 2-year public college/university	year	844	91	22s
Tuition, 4-year private college/university	year	9463	91	22s
Tuition, 4-year public college/university, in-state	year	1823	91	22s
Energy and Fuels				
Energy	mil Btu	7.39	90	64s
Energy, combined forms, 1,800 sq ft heating area	month	67.19	4Q 92	4c
Energy, exc electricity, 1,800 sq ft heating area	month	27.99	4Q 92	4c
Energy exp/householder, 1-family unit	year	362	90	28r
Energy exp/householder, <1,000 sq ft heating area	year	254	90	28r
Energy exp/householder, 1,000-1,999 sq ft heating area	year	358	90	28r
Energy exp/householder, 2,000+ sq ft heating area	year	467	90	28r
Energy exp/householder, mobile home	year	390	90	28r
Energy exp/householder, multifamily	year	252	90	28r
Gas, cooking, winter, 10 therms	month	6.13	92	56c
Gas, cooking, winter, 30 therms	month	11.88	92	56c
Gas, cooking, winter, 50 therms	month	17.63	92	56c

Values are in dollars or fractions of dollars. In the column headed *Ref*, references are shown to sources. Each reference is followed by a letter. These refer to the geographical level for which data were reported: s = State, r = Region, and c = City or metro. The abbreviation *ex* is used to mean *except* or *excluding*; *exp* stands for expenditures. For other abbreviations and further explanations, please see the Introduction.

Spokane, WA - continued

Item	Per	Value	Date	Ref.
Energy and Fuels				
Gas, heating, winter, 100 therms	month	32.02	92	56c
Gas, heating, winter, average use	month	38.64	92	56c
Gas, natural	mil Btu	3.60	90	64s
Gas, natural	000 cu ft	4.68	91	46s
Gas, natural, exp	year	440	91	46s
Gasoline, motor	gal	1.25	4Q 92	4c
Gasoline, unleaded regular	mil Btu	9.45	90	64s
Entertainment				
Bowling, evening rate	game	1.97	4Q 92	4c
Miniature golf admission	adult	6.18	92	1r
Miniature golf admission	child	5.14	92	1r
Monopoly game, Parker Brothers', No. 9		13.34	4Q 92	4c
Movie	admission	5.80	4Q 92	4c
Tennis balls, yellow, Wilson or Penn, 3	can	2.89	4Q 92	4c
Waterpark admission	adult	11.00	92	1r
Waterpark admission	child	8.55	92	1r
Funerals				
Casket, 18-gauge steel, velvet interior		1781.09	91	24r
Cosmetology, hair care, etc.		84.64	91	24r
Embalming		207.41	91	24r
Facility use for ceremony		205.76	91	24r
Hearse, local		105.14	91	24r
Limousine, local		83.21	91	24r
Remains to funeral home, transfer		113.82	91	24r
Service charge, professional		626.33	91	24r
Vault, concrete, non-metallic liner		599.54	91	24r
Viewing facilities, use		85.81	91	24r
Goods and Services				
ACCRA Index, Miscellaneous Goods and Services		98.30	4Q 92	4c
Groceries				
ACCRA Index, Groceries		101.40	4Q 92	4c
Apples, Red Delicious	lb	0.80	4/93	16r
Babyfood, strained vegetables, lowest price	4-4.5 oz jar	0.33	4Q 92	4c
Bacon	lb	1.79	4/93	16r
Bananas	lb	0.40	4Q 92	4c
Bananas	lb	0.53	4/93	16r
Bologna, all beef or mixed	lb	2.67	4/93	16r
Bread, white	24 oz	0.71	4Q 92	4c
Bread, white, pan	lb	0.81	4/93	16r
Carrots, short trimmed and topped	lb	0.39	4/93	16r
Cheese, Kraft grated Parmesan	8-oz canister	3.72	4Q 92	4c
Chicken, fresh, whole	lb	0.94	4/93	16r
Chicken, fryer, whole	lb	0.85	4Q 92	4c
Chicken breast, bone-in	lb	2.19	4/93	16r
Chuck roast, graded and ungraded, ex USDA prime and choice	lb	2.26	4/93	16r
Cigarettes, Winston	carton	20.22	4Q 92	4c
Coffee, 100% ground roast, all sizes	lb	2.33	4/93	16r
Coffee, vacuum-packed	13-oz can	2.38	4Q 92	4c
Corn, frozen	10 oz	0.58	4Q 92	4c
Corn Flakes, Kellogg's or Post Toasties	18 oz	2.02	4Q 92	4c
Eggs, Grade A large	doz	0.87	4Q 92	4c
Eggs, Grade AA large	doz	1.18	4/93	16r
Flour, white, all purpose	lb	0.22	4/93	16r
Grapefruit	lb	0.52	4/93	16r
Grapes, Thompson Seedless	lb	1.50	4/93	16r
Ground beef, 100% beef	lb	1.44	4/93	16r
Ground beef, lean and extra lean	lb	2.34	4/93	16r
Ground beef or hamburger	lb	1.24	4Q 92	4c
Ham, boneless, excluding canned	lb	2.56	4/93	16r
Honey, jar	8 oz	0.89-1.00	92	5r
Honey, jar	lb	1.35-1.97	92	5r
Honey, squeeze bear	12-oz	1.19-1.50	92	5r

Spokane, WA - continued

Item	Per	Value	Date	Ref.
Groceries - continued				
Ice cream, prepackaged, bulk, regular	1/2 gal	2.40	4/93	16r
Lemons	lb	0.81	4/93	16r
Lettuce, iceberg	head	0.78	4Q 92	4c
Lettuce, iceberg	lb	0.84	4/93	16r
Margarine, Blue Bonnet or Parkay cubes	lb	0.61	4Q 92	4c
Margarine, stick	lb	0.81	4/93	16r
Milk, whole	1/2 gal	1.51	4Q 92	4c
Orange juice, Minute Maid frozen	12-oz can	1.52	4Q 92	4c
Oranges, navel	lb	0.48	4/93	16r
Peaches	29-oz can	1.44	4Q 92	4c
Peas Sweet, Del Monte or Green Giant	15-17 oz can	0.61	4Q 92	4c
Pork chops, center cut, bone-in	lb	3.25	4/93	16r
Potato chips	16 oz	2.89	4/93	16r
Potatoes, white	lb	0.38	4/93	16r
Potatoes, white or red	10-lb sack	1.64	4Q 92	4c
Round roast, graded & ungraded, ex USDA prime & choice	lb	3.00	4/93	16r
Round roast, USDA choice, boneless	lb	3.16	4/93	16r
Sausage, Jimmy Dean, 100% pork	lb	2.72	4Q 92	4c
Shortening, vegetable oil blends	lb	0.86	4/93	16r
Shortening, vegetable, Crisco	3-lb can	1.96	4Q 92	4c
Soft drink, Coca Cola	2 liter	1.21	4Q 92	4c
Spaghetti and macaroni	lb	0.84	4/93	16r
Steak, round, graded & ungraded, ex USDA prime & choice	lb	3.34	4/93	16r
Steak, round, USDA choice, boneless	lb	3.24	4/93	16r
Steak, sirloin, graded & ungraded, ex USDA prime & choice	lb	3.75	4/93	16r
Steak, sirloin, USDA choice, boneless	lb	4.49	4/93	16r
Steak, T-bone	lb	4.38	4Q 92	4c
Sugar, cane or beet	4 lb	1.40	4Q 92	4c
Sugar, white	lb	0.41	4/93	16r
Sugar, white, 33-80 oz pk	lb	0.38	4/93	16r
Tomatoes, field grown	lb	1.01	4/93	16r
Tomatoes, Hunt's or Del Monte	14.5-oz can	0.63	4Q 92	4c
Tuna, chunk, light	6.125-6.5 oz can	0.70	4Q 92	4c
Turkey, frozen, whole	lb	1.04	4/93	16r
Health Care				
ACCRA Index, Health Care		123.00	4Q 92	4c
Analgesic, Aspirin, Bayer, 325 mg tablets	100	6.08	4Q 92	4c
Childbirth, cesarean, hospital		5533	91	62r
Childbirth, cesarean, physician's fee		2053	91	62r
Childbirth, normal, hospital		2745	91	62r
Childbirth, normal, physician's fee		1492	91	62r
Dentist's fee, adult teeth cleaning and periodic oral exam	visit	62.12	4Q 92	4c
Doctor's fee, routine exam, established patient	visit	41.22	4Q 92	4c
Hospital care, semiprivate room	day	321.90	90	27c
Hospital care, semiprivate room	day	404.60	4Q 92	4c
Medical insurance premium, per employee, small group comprehensive	month	299.30	10/91	25c
Medical plan per employee	year	3421	91	45r
Mental health care, exp	capita	37.60-53.67	90	38s
Physician fee, family practice, first-visit		111.00	91	62r
Physician fee, family practice, revisit		45.00	91	62r
Physician fee, general practice, first-visit		100.00	91	62r
Physician fee, general practice, revisit		40.00	91	62r
Physician fee, internal medicine, first-visit		137.00	91	62r
Physician fee, internal medicine, revisit		48.00	91	62r
Physician fee, median, neurosurgeon, first-visit		157.00	91	62r

Values are in dollars or fractions of dollars. In the column headed *Ref*, references are shown to sources. Each reference is followed by a letter. These refer to the geographical level for which data were reported: s=State, r=Region, and c=City or metro. The abbreviation *ex* is used to mean *except* or *excluding*; *exp* stands for expenditures. For other abbreviations and further explanations, please see the Introduction.

Spokane, WA - continued

Item	Per	Value	Date	Ref.
Health Care				
Physician fee, median, nonsurgical specialist, first-visit		131.00	91	62r
Physician fee, median, orthopedic surgeon, first-visit		124.00	91	62r
Physician fee, median, plastic surgeon, first-visit		88.00	91	62r
Physician fee, median, surgical specialist, first-visit		100.00	91	62r
Physician fee, neurosurgeon, revisit		51.00	91	62r
Physician fee, nonsurgical specialist, revisit		47.00	91	62r
Physician fee, obstetrics/gynecology, first-visit		95.00	91	62r
Physician fee, obstetrics/gynecology, revisit		50.00	91	62r
Physician fee, orthopedic surgeon, revisit		51.00	91	62r
Physician fee, pediatrician, first-visit		81.00	91	62r
Physician fee, pediatrician, revisit		42.00	91	62r
Physician fee, plastic surgeon, revisit		48.00	91	62r
Physician fee, surgical specialist, revisit		49.00	91	62r
Substance abuse, hospital ancillary charge	incident	1360	90	70s
Substance abuse, hospital physician charge	incident	150	90	70s
Substance abuse, hospital room and board	incident	4200	90	70s
Household Goods				
Appliance repair, home, service call, washing machine	min labor charge	28.18	4Q 92	4c
Laundry detergent, Tide Ultra, Bold, or Cheer	42 oz	3.92	4Q 92	4c
Tissues, facial, Kleenex brand	175-count box	1.25	4Q 92	4c
Housing				
ACCRA Index, Housing		123.10	4Q 92	4c
Home, median price	unit	76.30		26c
House, 1,800 sq ft, 8,000 sq ft lot, new, urban	total	140705	4Q 92	4c
House payment, principal and interest, 25% down payment	month	779	4Q 92	4c
Mortgage rate, incl. points & origination fee, 30-year fixed or adjustable rate	percent	8.06	4Q 92	4c
Rent, apartment, 2 bedrooms - 1-1/2 to 2 baths, unfurnished, 950 sq ft, water	month	556	4Q 92	4c
Rental unit, 1 bedroom	month	425	93	23c
Rental unit, 2 bedroom	month	501	93	23c
Rental unit, 3 bedroom	month	641	93	23c
Rental unit, 4 bedroom	month	708	93	23c
Rental unit, efficiency	month	364	93	23c
Insurance and Pensions				
Auto insurance, private passenger	year	627.71	91	63s
Personal Goods				
Shampoo, Alberto VO5	15 oz	1.40	4Q 92	4c
Toothpaste, Crest or Colgate	6-7 oz	2.10	4Q 92	4c
Personal Services				
Dry cleaning, man's 2-piece suit		7.16	4Q 92	4c
Haircare, woman's shampoo, trim and blow-dry		17.22	4Q 92	4c
Haircut, man's barbershop, no styling		7.31	4Q 92	4c
Restaurant Food				
Chicken, fried, thigh and drumstick		2.18	4Q 92	4c
Hamburger with cheese	1/4 lb	1.86	4Q 92	4c
Pizza, Pizza Hut or Pizza Inn, cheese, thin crust	12-13 in	8.95	4Q 92	4c
Taxes				
Tax, cigarette	pack	34	91	77s
Tax, gasoline	gal	23	91	77s
Taxes, state	capita	1592	91	77s

Spokane, WA - continued

Item	Per	Value	Date	Ref.
Transportation				
ACCRA Index, Transportation		94.10	4Q 92	4c
Auto rental, average	day	46.00	6/91	60c
Bus fare	one-way	0.75	3/93	2c
Bus fare, up to 10 miles	one-way	0.75	4Q 92	4c
Driver's license fee		14.00	12/90	43s
Taxi fare, airport-city, average	day	12.00	6/91	60c
Tire balance, computer or spin balance, front	wheel	5.18	4Q 92	4c
Travel				
Business travel	day	178.00	4/93	89r
Lodging	day	73.28	91	60c
Utilities				
ACCRA Index, Utilities		63.60	4Q 92	4c
Electricity	mil Btu	10.03	90	64s
Electricity, partial electric and other energy, 1,800 sq ft living area new home	month	39.20	4Q 92	4c
Electricity, winter, 250 KWh	month	12.55	92	55c
Electricity, winter, 500 KWh	month	22.10	92	55c
Electricity, winter, 750 KWh	month	32.81	92	55c
Electricity, winter, 1000 KWh	month	44.31	92	55c

Springfield, IL

Item	Per	Value	Date	Ref.
Composite ACCRA index		92.20	4Q 92	4c
Alcoholic Beverages				
Beer, Miller Lite or Budweiser, 12-oz containers	6 pack	3.51	4Q 92	4c
Liquor, J & B Scotch	750 ml	14.83	4Q 92	4c
Wine, Gallo Chablis blanc, 1.5 liter	bottle	3.83	4Q 92	4c
Child Care				
Child care fee, average, center	hour	1.63	90	65r
Child care fee, average, nonregulated family day care	hour	1.83	90	65r
Child care fee, average, regulated family day care	hour	1.42	90	65r
Clothing				
Jeans, man's denim		27.39	4Q 92	4c
Shirt, man's dress shirt		24.80	4Q 92	4c
Undervest, boy's size 10-14, cotton	3	3.81	4Q 92	4c
Communications				
Long-distance telephone service, day, initial minute, 0-100 miles	min	0.10-0.34	91	12s
Long-distance telephone service, day, additional minute, 0-100 miles	min	0.04-0.16	91	12s
Long-distance telephone service, evenings/weekends, 0-100 mi, initial minute	min	0.06-0.20	91	12s
Long-distance telephone service, evenings/weekends, 0-100 mi, additional minute	min	0.02-0.10	91	12s
Newspaper subscription, daily and Sunday home delivery, large-city	month	9.61	4Q 92	4c
Telephone bill, family of four	month	21.83	4Q 92	4c
Education				
Board, 4-yr private college/university	year	1797	91	22s
Board, 4-yr public college/university	year	1857	91	22s
Expenditures, local gov't, public elementary/secondary	pupil	5248	92	20s
Room, 4-year private college/university	year	2095	91	22s
Room, 4-year public college/university	year	1454	91	22s
Tuition, 2-year private college/university	year	5279	91	22s
Tuition, 2-year public college/university	year	906	91	22s
Tuition, 4-year private college/university	year	8853	91	22s
Tuition, 4-year public college/university, in-state	year	2465	91	22s

Values are in dollars or fractions of dollars. In the column headed *Ref*, references are shown to sources. Each reference is followed by a letter. These refer to the geographical level for which data were reported: s=State, r=Region, and c=City or metro. The abbreviation *ex* is used to mean *except* or *excluding*; *exp* stands for expenditures. For other abbreviations and further explanations, please see the Introduction.

Springfield, IL - continued

Item	Per	Value	Date	Ref.
Energy and Fuels				
Coal	mil Btu	1.72	90	64s
Energy	mil Btu	8.74	90	64s
Energy, combined forms, 1,800 sq ft heating area	month	94.72	4Q 92	4c
Energy, exc electricity, 1,800 sq ft heating area	month	36.86	4Q 92	4c
Energy exp/householder, 1-family unit	year	471	90	28r
Energy exp/householder, <1,000 sq ft heating area	year	430	90	28r
Energy exp/householder, 1,000-1,999 sq ft heating area	year	481	90	28r
Energy exp/householder, 2,000+ sq ft heating area	year	473	90	28r
Energy exp/householder, mobile home	year	430	90	28r
Energy exp/householder, multifamily	year	461	90	28r
Gas, natural	mil Btu	4.57	90	64s
Gas, natural	000 cu ft	4.95	91	46s
Gas, natural, exp	year	696	91	46s
Gasoline, motor	gal	1.13	4Q 92	4c
Gasoline, unleaded regular	mil Btu	9.35	90	64s
Entertainment				
Bowling, evening rate	game	1.81	4Q 92	4c
Miniature golf admission	adult	6.18	92	1r
Miniature golf admission	child	5.14	92	1r
Monopoly game, Parker Brothers', No. 9		10.74	4Q 92	4c
Movie	admission	5.00	4Q 92	4c
Tennis balls, yellow, Wilson or Penn, 3	can	2.61	4Q 92	4c
Waterpark admission	adult	11.00	92	1r
Waterpark admission	child	8.55	92	1r
Funerals				
Casket, 18-gauge steel, velvet interior		1926.72	91	24r
Cosmetology, hair care, etc.		97.64	91	24r
Embalming		249.14	91	24r
Facility use for ceremony		208.59	91	24r
Hearse, local		130.12	91	24r
Limousine, local		104.66	91	24r
Remains to funeral home, transfer		93.61	91	24r
Service charge, professional		724.62	91	24r
Vault, concrete, non-metallic liner		734.53	91	24r
Viewing facilities, use		236.06	91	24r
Goods and Services				
ACCRA Index, Miscellaneous Goods and Services		93.30	4Q 92	4c
Groceries				
ACCRA Index, Groceries		99.90	4Q 92	4c
Apples, Red Delicious	lb	0.77	4/93	16r
Babyfood, strained vegetables, lowest price	4-4.5 oz jar	0.34	4Q 92	4c
Bacon	lb	1.85	4/93	16r
Bananas	lb	0.48	4Q 92	4c
Bananas	lb	0.46	4/93	16r
Beef, stew, boneless	lb	2.53	4/93	16r
Bologna, all beef or mixed	lb	2.19	4/93	16r
Bread, white	24 oz	0.79	4Q 92	4c
Bread, white, pan	lb	0.78	4/93	16r
Butter	lb	1.50	4/93	16r
Cabbage	lb	0.40	4/93	16r
Carrots, short trimmed and topped	lb	0.45	4/93	16r
Cheese, Cheddar	lb	3.47	4/93	16r
Cheese, Kraft grated Parmesan	8-oz canister	3.00	4Q 92	4c
Chicken, fresh, whole	lb	0.84	4/93	16r
Chicken, fryer, whole	lb	0.71	4Q 92	4c
Chicken breast, bone-in	lb	1.94	4/93	16r
Chicken legs, bone-in	lb	1.02	4/93	16r
Chuck roast, graded and ungraded, ex USDA prime and choice	lb	2.43	4/93	16r

Springfield, IL - continued

Item	Per	Value	Date	Ref.
Groceries - continued				
Chuck roast, USDA choice, bone-in	lb	2.11	4/93	16r
Chuck roast, USDA choice, boneless	lb	2.44	4/93	16r
Cigarettes, Winston	carton	18.65	4Q 92	4c
Coffee, 100% ground roast, all sizes	lb	2.47	4/93	16r
Coffee, vacuum-packed	13-oz can	1.86	4Q 92	4c
Cookies, chocolate chip	lb	2.73	4/93	16r
Corn, frozen	10 oz	0.63	4Q 92	4c
Corn Flakes, Kellogg's or Post Toasties	18 oz	1.64	4Q 92	4c
Eggs, Grade A large	doz	0.72	4Q 92	4c
Eggs, Grade A large	doz	0.93	4/93	16r
Flour, white, all purpose	lb	0.21	4/93	16r
Grapefruit	lb	0.45	4/93	16r
Grapes, Thompson Seedless	lb	1.46	4/93	16r
Ground beef, 100% beef	lb	1.63	4/93	16r
Ground beef, lean and extra lean	lb	2.08	4/93	16r
Ground beef or hamburger	lb	1.57	4Q 92	4c
Ground chuck, 100% beef	lb	1.94	4/93	16r
Ham, boneless, excluding canned	lb	2.21	4/93	16r
Honey, jar	8 oz	0.97-1.25	92	5r
Honey, jar	lb	1.25-2.25	92	5r
Honey, squeeze bear	12-oz	1.25-1.99	92	5r
Ice cream, prepackaged, bulk, regular	1/2 gal	2.41	4/93	16r
Lemons	lb	0.82	4/93	16r
Lettuce, iceberg	head	0.84	4Q 92	4c
Lettuce, iceberg	lb	0.83	4/93	16r
Margarine, Blue Bonnet or Parkay cubes	lb	0.53	4Q 92	4c
Margarine, stick	lb	0.77	4/93	16r
Milk, whole	1/2 gal	1.51	4Q 92	4c
Orange juice, Minute Maid frozen	12-oz can	1.06	4Q 92	4c
Oranges, navel	lb	0.50	4/93	16r
Peaches	29-oz can	1.45	4Q 92	4c
Peanut butter, creamy, all sizes	lb	1.82	4/93	16r
Pears, Anjou	lb	0.85	4/93	16r
Peas Sweet, Del Monte or Green Giant	15-17 oz can	0.62	4Q 92	4c
Pork chops, center cut, bone-in	lb	3.17	4/93	16r
Potato chips	16 oz	2.68	4/93	16r
Potatoes, white	lb	0.26	4/93	16r
Potatoes, white or red	10-lb sack	2.76	4Q 92	4c
Round roast, graded & ungraded, ex USDA prime & choice	lb	2.88	4/93	16r
Round roast, USDA choice, boneless	lb	2.96	4/93	16r
Sausage, Jimmy Dean, 100% pork	lb	2.65	4Q 92	4c
Shortening, vegetable oil blends	lb	0.79	4/93	16r
Shortening, vegetable, Crisco	3-lb can	2.29	4Q 92	4c
Soft drink, Coca Cola	2 liter	1.04	4Q 92	4c
Spaghetti and macaroni	lb	0.76	4/93	16r
Steak, rib eye, USDA choice, boneless	lb	6.29	4/93	16r
Steak, round, USDA choice, boneless	lb	3.24	4/93	16r
Steak, sirloin, graded & ungraded, ex USDA prime & choice	lb	4.00	4/93	16r
Steak, sirloin, USDA choice, bone-in	lb	3.57	4/93	16r
Steak, sirloin, USDA choice, boneless	lb	4.17	4/93	16r
Steak, T-bone	lb	5.41	4Q 92	4c
Steak, T-bone, USDA choice, bone-in	lb	5.60	4/93	16r
Strawberries, dry pint	12 oz	0.90	4/93	16r
Sugar, cane or beet	4 lb	1.11	4Q 92	4c
Sugar, white	lb	0.36	4/93	16r
Sugar, white, 33-80 oz pk	lb	0.35	4/93	16r
Tomatoes, field grown	lb	0.99	4/93	16r
Tomatoes, Hunt's or Del Monte	14.5-oz can	0.65	4Q 92	4c
Tuna, chunk, light	6.125-6.5 oz can	0.65	4Q 92	4c
Tuna, chunk, light	lb	1.76	4/93	16r
Turkey, frozen, whole	lb	0.91	4/93	16r

Values are in dollars or fractions of dollars. In the column headed *Ref*, references are shown to sources. Each reference is followed by a letter. These refer to the geographical level for which data were reported: s=State, r=Region, and c=City or metro. The abbreviation *ex* is used to mean *except* or *excluding*; *exp* stands for expenditures. For other abbreviations and further explanations, please see the Introduction.

Springfield, IL - continued

Health Care

Item	Per	Value	Date	Ref.
ACCRA Index, Health Care		97.50	4Q 92	4c
Analgesic, Aspirin, Bayer, 325 mg tablets	100	5.13	4Q 92	4c
Childbirth, cesarean, hospital		4688	91	62r
Childbirth, cesarean, physician's fee		2053	91	62r
Childbirth, normal, hospital		2657	91	62r
Childbirth, normal, physician's fee		1492	91	62r
Dentist's fee, adult teeth cleaning and periodic oral exam	visit	46.60	4Q 92	4c
Doctor's fee, routine exam, established patient	visit	35.40	4Q 92	4c
Hospital care, semiprivate room	day	224.80	90	27c
Hospital care, semiprivate room	day	297.00	4Q 92	4c
Medical insurance premium, per employee, small group comprehensive	month	313.90	10/91	25c
Medical plan per employee	year	3443	91	45r
Mental health care, exp	capita	28.84-37.59	90	38s
Mental health care, exp, state mental health agency	capita	34.43	90	38s
Mental health care, hospital psychiatric services, non-Federal, exp	capita	18.46	88	38s
Mental health care, mental health organization, multiservice, exp	capita	11.97	88	38s
Mental health care, psychiatric hospitals, private, exp	capita	7.84	88	38s
Mental health care, psychiatric out-patient clinics, freestanding, exp	capita	3.21	88	38s
Mental health care, psychiatric partial-care organizations, freestanding, exp	capita	0.51	88	38s
Mental health care, state and county mental hospitals, exp	capita	18.11	88	38s
Mental health care, VA medical centers, exp	capita	3.69	88	38s
Physician fee, family practice, first-visit		76.00	91	62r
Physician fee, family practice, revisit		33.00	91	62r
Physician fee, general practice, first-visit		61.00	91	62r
Physician fee, general practice, revisit		31.00	91	62r
Physician fee, general surgeon, first-visit		65.00	91	62r
Physician fee, general surgeon, revisit		35.00	91	62r
Physician fee, internal medicine, first-visit		91.00	91	62r
Physician fee, internal medicine, revisit		40.00	91	62r
Physician fee, median, neurosurgeon, first-visit		106.00	91	62r
Physician fee, median, nonsurgical specialist, first-visit		90.00	91	62r
Physician fee, median, orthopedic surgeon, first-visit		83.00	91	62r
Physician fee, median, surgical specialist, first-visit		61.00	91	62r
Physician fee, neurosurgeon, revisit		41.00	91	62r
Physician fee, nonsurgical specialist, revisit		40.00	91	62r
Physician fee, obstetrics/gynecology, first-visit		61.00	91	62r
Physician fee, obstetrics/gynecology, revisit		40.00	91	62r
Physician fee, orthopedic surgeon, revisit		41.00	91	62r
Physician fee, pediatrician, first-visit		46.00	91	62r
Physician fee, pediatrician, revisit		33.00	91	62r
Physician fee, surgical specialist, revisit		36.00	91	62r
Prescription drug co-pay, Medicaid	month	25.00	91	21s
Substance abuse, hospital ancillary charge	incident	1310	90	70s
Substance abuse, hospital physician charge	incident	540	90	70s
Substance abuse, hospital room and board	incident	6150	90	70s

Household Goods

Item	Per	Value	Date	Ref.
Appliance repair, home, service call, washing machine	min labor charge	23.70	4Q 92	4c
Laundry detergent, Tide Ultra, Bold, or Cheer	42 oz	3.23	4Q 92	4c

Springfield, IL - continued

Household Goods - continued

Item	Per	Value	Date	Ref.
Tissues, facial, Kleenex brand	175-count box	1.07	4Q 92	4c

Housing

Item	Per	Value	Date	Ref.
ACCRA Index, Housing		86.80	4Q 92	4c
Home, median price	unit	67.70		26c
House, 1,800 sq ft, 8,000 sq ft lot, new, urban	total	96050	4Q 92	4c
House payment, principal and interest, 25% down payment	month	540	4Q 92	4c
Mortgage rate, incl. points & origination fee, 30-year fixed or adjustable rate	percent	8.23	4Q 92	4c
Rent, apartment, 2 bedrooms - 1-1/2 to 2 baths, unfurnished, 950 sq ft, water	month	414	4Q 92	4c
Rental unit, 1 bedroom	month	428	93	23c
Rental unit, 2 bedroom	month	503	93	23c
Rental unit, 3 bedroom	month	629	93	23c
Rental unit, 4 bedroom	month	704	93	23c
Rental unit, efficiency	month	351	93	23c

Insurance and Pensions

Item	Per	Value	Date	Ref.
Auto insurance, private passenger	year	621.37	91	63s

Personal Goods

Item	Per	Value	Date	Ref.
Shampoo, Alberto VO5	15 oz	1.23	4Q 92	4c
Toothpaste, Crest or Colgate	6-7 oz	2.05	4Q 92	4c

Personal Services

Item	Per	Value	Date	Ref.
Dry cleaning, man's 2-piece suit		4.78	4Q 92	4c
Haircare, woman's shampoo, trim and blow-dry		18.57	4Q 92	4c
Haircut, man's barbershop, no styling		6.75	4Q 92	4c

Restaurant Food

Item	Per	Value	Date	Ref.
Chicken, fried, thigh and drumstick		2.18	4Q 92	4c
Hamburger with cheese	1/4 lb	1.89	4Q 92	4c
Pizza, Pizza Hut or Pizza Inn, cheese, thin crust	12-13 in	7.79	4Q 92	4c

Taxes

Item	Per	Value	Date	Ref.
Tax, cigarette	pack	30	91	77s
Tax, gasoline	gal	19	91	77s
Taxes, state	capita	1151	91	77s

Transportation

Item	Per	Value	Date	Ref.
ACCRA Index, Transportation		93.00	4Q 92	4c
Bus fare	one-way	0.50	3/93	2c
Bus fare, up to 10 miles	one-way	0.50	4Q 92	4c
Driver's license fee		10.00	12/90	43s
Tire balance, computer or spin balance, front	wheel	6.09	4Q 92	4c
Vehicle registration and license plate	multi-year	48.00	93	52s

Utilities

Item	Per	Value	Date	Ref.
ACCRA Index, Utilities		89.30	4Q 92	4c
Electricity	mil Btu	22.02	90	64s
Electricity, partial electric and other energy, 1,800 sq ft living area new home	month	57.86	4Q 92	4c

Springfield, MA

Child Care

Item	Per	Value	Date	Ref.
Child care fee, average, center	hour	2.18	90	65r
Child care fee, average, nonregulated family day care	hour	1.83	90	65r
Child care fee, average, regulated family day care	hour	2.02	90	65r

Communications

Item	Per	Value	Date	Ref.
Long-distance telephone service, day, initial minute, 0-100 miles	min	0.18-0.31	91	12s

Values are in dollars or fractions of dollars. In the column headed *Ref*, references are shown to sources. Each reference is followed by a letter. These refer to the geographical level for which data were reported: s = State, r = Region, and c = City or metro. The abbreviation *ex* is used to mean *except* or *excluding*; *exp* stands for *expenditures*. For other abbreviations and further explanations, please see the Introduction.

Springfield, MA - continued

Item	Per	Value	Date	Ref.
Communications				
Long-distance telephone service, day, additional minute, 0-100 miles	min	0.08-0.13	91	12s
Long-distance telephone service, evenings/ weekends, 0-100 mi, initial minute	min	0.67-0.12	91	12s
Long-distance telephone service, evenings/ weekends, 0-100 mi, additional minute	min	0.04-0.05	91	12s
Telephone, residential, private line, rotary, unlimited calling	month	17.38	10/91	78c
Education				
Board, 4-yr private college/university	year	2698	91	22s
Board, 4-yr public college/university	year	1741	91	22s
Expenditures, local gov't, public elementary/secondary	pupil	6687	92	20s
Room, 4-year private college/university	year	2945	91	22s
Room, 4-year public college/university	year	2144	91	22s
Tuition, 2-year private college/university	year	7750	91	22s
Tuition, 2-year public college/university	year	1528	91	22s
Tuition, 4-year private college/university	year	12446	91	22s
Tuition, 4-year public college/university, in-state	year	2580	91	22s
Energy and Fuels				
Coal	mil Btu	1.77	90	64s
Energy	mil Btu	10.57	90	64s
Energy exp/householder, 1-family unit	year	588	90	28r
Energy exp/householder, <1,000 sq ft heating area	year	477	90	28r
Energy exp/householder, 1,000-1,999 sq ft heating area	year	517	90	28r
Energy exp/householder, 2,000+ sq ft heating area	year	630	90	28r
Energy exp/householder, mobile home	year	412	90	28r
Energy exp/householder, multifamily	year	498	90	28r
Gas, heating, winter, 100 therms	month	91.08	92	56c
Gas, heating, winter, average use	month	144.19	92	56c
Gas, natural	mil Btu	5.55	90	64s
Gas, natural	000 cu ft	8.11	91	46s
Gas, natural, exp	year	741	91	46s
Gasoline, unleaded regular	mil Btu	9.53	90	64s
Entertainment				
Miniature golf admission	adult	6.18	92	1r
Miniature golf admission	child	5.14	92	1r
Waterpark admission	adult	11.00	92	1r
Waterpark admission	child	8.55	92	1r
Funerals				
Casket, 18-gauge steel, velvet interior		1853.42	91	24r
Cosmetology, hair care, etc.		98.33	91	24r
Embalming		273.94	91	24r
Facility use for ceremony		196.06	91	24r
Hearse, local		145.67	91	24r
Limousine, local		131.07	91	24r
Remains to funeral home, transfer		135.24	91	24r
Service charge, professional		843.16	91	24r
Vault, concrete, non-metallic liner		709.14	91	24r
Viewing facilities, use		229.85	91	24r
Groceries				
Apples, Red Delicious	lb	0.85	4/93	16r
Bacon	lb	2.12	4/93	16r
Bananas	lb	0.54	4/93	16r
Bread, white, pan	lb	0.81	4/93	16r
Butter	lb	2.02	4/93	16r
Carrots, short trimmed and topped	lb	0.51	4/93	16r
Chicken, fresh, whole	lb	1.04	4/93	16r
Chicken breast, bone-in	lb	2.21	4/93	16r
Chicken legs, bone-in	lb	1.16	4/93	16r
Chuck roast, USDA choice, boneless	lb	2.82	4/93	16r
Coffee, 100% ground roast, all sizes	lb	2.66	4/93	16r
Cucumbers	lb	0.85	4/93	16r
Eggs, Grade A large	doz	1.15	4/93	16r

Springfield, MA - continued

Item	Per	Value	Date	Ref.
Groceries - continued				
Grapefruit	lb	0.45	4/93	16r
Grapes, Thompson Seedless	lb	1.52	4/93	16r
Ground beef, lean and extra lean	lb	2.36	4/93	16r
Ground chuck, 100% beef	lb	2.02	4/93	16r
Honey, jar	8 oz	0.96-1.75	92	5r
Honey, jar	lb	1.50-3.00	92	5r
Honey, squeeze bear	12-oz	1.50-1.99	92	5r
Ice cream, prepackaged, bulk, regular	1/2 gal	2.80	4/93	16r
Lemons	lb	0.96	4/93	16r
Lettuce, iceberg	lb	0.95	4/93	16r
Margarine, stick	lb	0.81	4/93	16r
Milk, fresh, whole, fortified	1/2 gal	1.30	4/93	16r
Oranges, navel	lb	0.56	4/93	16r
Peanut butter, creamy, all sizes	lb	1.88	4/93	16r
Pork chops, center cut, bone-in	lb	3.34	4/93	16r
Potato chips	16 oz	2.88	4/93	16r
Potatoes, white	lb	0.37	4/93	16r
Rib roast, USDA choice, bone-in	lb	4.94	4/93	16r
Round roast, USDA choice, boneless	lb	3.17	4/93	16r
Shortening, vegetable oil blends	lb	0.98	4/93	16r
Spaghetti and macaroni	lb	0.82	4/93	16r
Steak, round, graded & ungraded, ex USDA prime & choice	lb	4.04	4/93	16r
Steak, round, USDA choice, boneless	lb	3.90	4/93	16r
Steak, sirloin, USDA choice, boneless	lb	4.97	4/93	16r
Strawberries, dry pint	12 oz	0.90	4/93	16r
Sugar, white	lb	0.50	4/93	16r
Sugar, white, 33-80 oz pk	lb	0.41	4/93	16r
Tomatoes, field grown	lb	1.23	4/93	16r
Tuna, chunk, light	lb	2.22	4/93	16r
Turkey, frozen, whole	lb	1.04	4/93	16r
Health Care				
Childbirth, cesarean, hospital		5826	91	62r
Childbirth, cesarean, physician's fee		2053	91	62r
Childbirth, normal, hospital		2964	91	62r
Childbirth, normal, physician's fee		1492	91	62r
Health care spending, state	capita	3031	3/93	84s
Hospital care, semiprivate room	day	329.54	90	27c
Medical insurance premium, per employee, small group comprehensive	month	350.40	10/91	25c
Medical plan per employee	year	3958	91	45r
Mental health care, exp	capita	53.68-118.35	90	38s
Mental health care, exp, state mental health agency	capita	83.91	90	38s
Mental health care, hospital psychiatric services, non-Federal, exp	capita	22.67	88	38s
Mental health care, mental health organization, multiservice, exp	capita	36.07	88	38s
Mental health care, psychiatric hospitals, private, exp	capita	38.65	88	38s
Mental health care, psychiatric out-patient clinics, freestanding, exp	capita	4.41	88	38s
Mental health care, psychiatric partial-care organizations, freestanding, exp	capita	0.92	88	38s
Mental health care, state and county mental hospitals, exp	capita	30.59	88	38s
Mental health care, VA medical centers, exp	capita	21.14	88	38s
Substance abuse, hospital ancillary charge	incident	1310	90	70s
Substance abuse, hospital physician charge	incident	460	90	70s
Substance abuse, hospital room and board	incident	3450	90	70s
Housing				
Home, median price	unit	115.10		26c
Rental unit, 1 bedroom	month	502	93	23c
Rental unit, 2 bedroom	month	591	93	23c
Rental unit, 3 bedroom	month	739	93	23c
Rental unit, 4 bedroom	month	827	93	23c
Rental unit, efficiency	month	414	93	23c

Values are in dollars or fractions of dollars. In the column headed *Ref*, references are shown to sources. Each reference is followed by a letter. These refer to the geographical level for which data were reported: s=State, r=Region, and c=City or metro. The abbreviation *ex* is used to mean *except* or *excluding*; *exp* stands for expenditures. For other abbreviations and further explanations, please see the Introduction.

Springfield, MA - continued

Item	Per	Value	Date	Ref.
Insurance and Pensions				
Auto insurance, private passenger	year	912.83	91	63s
Taxes				
Tax, cigarette	pack	26	91	77s
Tax, gasoline	gal	21	91	77s
Taxes, state	capita	1615	91	77s
Transportation				
Auto rental, average	day	49.00	6/91	60c
Bus fare	one-way	0.65	3/93	2c
Driver's license fee		35.00	12/90	43s
Taxi fare, airport-city, average	day	28.00	6/91	60c
Travel				
Breakfast	day	7.40	6/91	60c
Business travel	day	165.00	4/93	89r
Dinner	day	17.50	6/91	60c
Lodging	day	101.58	91	60c
Lunch	day	8.24	6/91	60c
Utilities				
Electricity	mil Btu	25.93	90	64s
Electricity, winter, 250 KWh	month	39.17	92	55c
Electricity, winter, 500 KWh	month	68.44	92	55c
Electricity, winter, 750 KWh	month	97.72	92	55c
Electricity, winter, 1000 KWh	month	126.99	92	55c

Springfield, MO

Item	Per	Value	Date	Ref.
Composite ACCRA index		92.40	4Q 92	4c
Alcoholic Beverages				
Beer, Miller Lite or Budweiser, 12-oz containers	6 pack	3.97	4Q 92	4c
Liquor, J & B Scotch	750 ml	15.99	4Q 92	4c
Wine, Gallo Chablis blanc, 1.5 liter	bottle	4.77	4Q 92	4c
Child Care				
Child care fee, average, center	hour	1.63	90	65r
Child care fee, average, nonregulated family day care	hour	1.83	90	65r
Child care fee, average, regulated family day care	hour	1.42	90	65r
Clothing				
Jeans, man's denim		28.23	4Q 92	4c
Shirt, man's dress shirt		26.88	4Q 92	4c
Undervest, boy's size 10-14, cotton	3	3.78	4Q 92	4c
Communications				
Long-distance telephone service, day, initial minute, 0-100 miles	min	0.10-0.46	91	12s
Long-distance telephone service, day, additional minute, 0-100 miles	min	0.06-0.29	91	12s
Newspaper subscription, daily and Sunday home delivery, large-city	month	11.95	4Q 92	4c
Telephone, flat rate	month	9.80	91	11c
Telephone bill, family of four	month	17.92	4Q 92	4c
Education				
Board, 4-yr private college/university	year	1789	91	22s
Board, 4-yr public college/university	year	1162	91	22s
Expenditures, local gov't, public elementary/secondary	pupil	4537	92	20s
Room, 4-year private college/university	year	1817	91	22s
Room, 4-year public college/university	year	1450	91	22s
Tuition, 2-year private college/university	year	5208	91	22s
Tuition, 2-year public college/university	year	891	91	22s
Tuition, 4-year private college/university	year	7487	91	22s
Tuition, 4-year public college/university, in-state	year	1733	91	22s
Energy and Fuels				
Coal	mil Btu	1.35	90	64s
Energy	mil Btu	8.91	90	64s

Springfield, MO - continued

Item	Per	Value	Date	Ref.
Energy and Fuels - continued				
Energy, combined forms, 1,800 sq ft heating area	month	91.56	4Q 92	4c
Energy, exc electricity, 1,800 sq ft heating area	month	45.77	4Q 92	4c
Energy exp/householder, 1-family unit	year	473	90	28r
Energy exp/householder, <1,000 sq ft heating area	year	429	90	28r
Energy exp/householder, 1,000-1,999 sq ft heating area	year	442	90	28r
Energy exp/householder, 2,000+ sq ft heating area	year	498	90	28r
Energy exp/householder, mobile home	year	442	90	28r
Energy exp/householder, multifamily	year	407	90	28r
Gas, natural	mil Btu	4.69	90	64s
Gas, natural	000 cu ft	5.14	91	46s
Gas, natural, exp	year	512	91	46s
Gasoline, motor	gal	0.99	4Q 92	4c
Gasoline, unleaded regular	mil Btu	8.61	90	64s
Entertainment				
Bowling, evening rate	game	1.71	4Q 92	4c
Miniature golf admission	adult	6.18	92	1r
Miniature golf admission	child	5.14	92	1r
Monopoly game, Parker Brothers', No. 9		8.64	4Q 92	4c
Movie	admission	5.31	4Q 92	4c
Tennis balls, yellow, Wilson or Penn, 3	can	2.45	4Q 92	4c
Waterpark admission	adult	11.00	92	1r
Waterpark admission	child	8.55	92	1r
Funerals				
Casket, 18-gauge steel, velvet interior		1952.97	91	24r
Cosmetology, hair care, etc.		90.03	91	24r
Embalming		251.75	91	24r
Facility use for ceremony		180.75	91	24r
Hearse, local		117.51	91	24r
Limousine, local		71.86	91	24r
Remains to funeral home, transfer		81.14	91	24r
Service charge, professional		740.03	91	24r
Vault, concrete, non-metallic liner		801.47	91	24r
Viewing facilities, use		169.33	91	24r
Goods and Services				
ACCRA Index, Miscellaneous Goods and Services		99.00	4Q 92	4c
Groceries				
ACCRA Index, Groceries		96.50	4Q 92	4c
Apples, Red Delicious	lb	0.77	4/93	16r
Babyfood, strained vegetables, lowest price	4-4.5 oz jar	0.36	4Q 92	4c
Bacon	lb	1.85	4/93	16r
Bananas	lb	0.35	4Q 92	4c
Bananas	lb	0.46	4/93	16r
Beef, stew, boneless	lb	2.53	4/93	16r
Bologna, all beef or mixed	lb	2.19	4/93	16r
Bread, white	24 oz	0.90	4Q 92	4c
Bread, white, pan	lb	0.78	4/93	16r
Butter	lb	1.50	4/93	16r
Cabbage	lb	0.40	4/93	16r
Carrots, short trimmed and topped	lb	0.45	4/93	16r
Cheese, Cheddar	lb	3.47	4/93	16r
Cheese, Kraft grated Parmesan	8-oz canister	3.56	4Q 92	4c
Chicken, fresh, whole	lb	0.84	4/93	16r
Chicken, fryer, whole	lb	0.69	4Q 92	4c
Chicken breast, bone-in	lb	1.94	4/93	16r
Chicken legs, bone-in	lb	1.02	4/93	16r
Chuck roast, graded and ungraded, ex USDA prime and choice	lb	2.43	4/93	16r
Chuck roast, USDA choice, bone-in	lb	2.11	4/93	16r
Chuck roast, USDA choice, boneless	lb	2.44	4/93	16r

Values are in dollars or fractions of dollars. In the column headed *Ref*, references are shown to sources. Each reference is followed by a letter. These refer to the geographical level for which data were reported: s = State, r = Region, and c = City or metro. The abbreviation *ex* is used to mean *except* or *excluding*; *exp* stands for expenditures. For other abbreviations and further explanations, please see the Introduction.

Springfield, MO - continued

Item	Per	Value	Date	Ref.
Groceries				
Cigarettes, Winston	carton	15.79	4Q 92	4c
Coffee, 100% ground roast, all sizes	lb	2.47	4/93	16r
Coffee, vacuum-packed	13-oz can	1.98	4Q 92	4c
Cookies, chocolate chip	lb	2.73	4/93	16r
Corn, frozen	10 oz	0.70	4Q 92	4c
Corn Flakes, Kellogg's or Post Toasties	18 oz	2.09	4Q 92	4c
Eggs, Grade A large	doz	0.71	4Q 92	4c
Eggs, Grade A large	doz	0.93	4/93	16r
Flour, white, all purpose	lb	0.21	4/93	16r
Grapefruit	lb	0.45	4/93	16r
Grapes, Thompson Seedless	lb	1.46	4/93	16r
Ground beef, 100% beef	lb	1.63	4/93	16r
Ground beef, lean and extra lean	lb	2.08	4/93	16r
Ground beef or hamburger	lb	0.97	4Q 92	4c
Ground chuck, 100% beef	lb	1.94	4/93	16r
Ham, boneless, excluding canned	lb	2.21	4/93	16r
Ice cream, prepackaged, bulk, regular	1/2 gal	2.41	4/93	16r
Lemons	lb	0.82	4/93	16r
Lettuce, iceberg	head	0.92	4Q 92	4c
Lettuce, iceberg	lb	0.83	4/93	16r
Margarine, Blue Bonnet or Parkay cubes	lb	0.77	4Q 92	4c
Margarine, stick	lb	0.77	4/93	16r
Milk, whole	1/2 gal	1.31	4Q 92	4c
Orange juice, Minute Maid frozen	12-oz can	1.65	4Q 92	4c
Oranges, navel	lb	0.50	4/93	16r
Peaches	29-oz can	1.44	4Q 92	4c
Peanut butter, creamy, all sizes	lb	1.82	4/93	16r
Pears, Anjou	lb	0.85	4/93	16r
Peas Sweet, Del Monte or Green Giant	15-17 oz can	0.67	4Q 92	4c
Pork chops, center cut, bone-in	lb	3.17	4/93	16r
Potato chips	16 oz	2.68	4/93	16r
Potatoes, white	lb	0.26	4/93	16r
Potatoes, white or red	10-lb sack	1.49	4Q 92	4c
Round roast, graded & ungraded, ex USDA prime & choice	lb	2.88	4/93	16r
Round roast, USDA choice, boneless	lb	2.96	4/93	16r
Sausage, Jimmy Dean, 100% pork	lb	2.37	4Q 92	4c
Shortening, vegetable oil blends	lb	0.79	4/93	16r
Shortening, vegetable, Crisco	3-lb can	2.48	4Q 92	4c
Soft drink, Coca Cola	2 liter	1.02	4Q 92	4c
Spaghetti and macaroni	lb	0.76	4/93	16r
Steak, rib eye, USDA choice, boneless	lb	6.29	4/93	16r
Steak, round, USDA choice, boneless	lb	3.24	4/93	16r
Steak, sirloin, graded & ungraded, ex USDA prime & choice	lb	4.00	4/93	16r
Steak, sirloin, USDA choice, bone-in	lb	3.57	4/93	16r
Steak, sirloin, USDA choice, boneless	lb	4.17	4/93	16r
Steak, T-bone	lb	4.07	4Q 92	4c
Steak, T-bone, USDA choice, bone-in	lb	5.60	4/93	16r
Strawberries, dry pint	12 oz	0.90	4/93	16r
Sugar, cane or beet	4 lb	1.49	4Q 92	4c
Sugar, white	lb	0.36	4/93	16r
Sugar, white, 33-80 oz pk	lb	0.35	4/93	16r
Tomatoes, field grown	lb	0.99	4/93	16r
Tomatoes, Hunt's or Del Monte	14.5-oz can	0.76	4Q 92	4c
Tuna, chunk, light	6.125-6.5 oz can	0.69	4Q 92	4c
Tuna, chunk, light	lb	1.76	4/93	16r
Turkey, frozen, whole	lb	0.91	4/93	16r
Health Care				
ACCRA Index, Health Care		99.50	4Q 92	4c
Analgesic, Aspirin, Bayer, 325 mg tablets	100	5.39	4Q 92	4c
Childbirth, cesarean, hospital		4688	91	62r
Childbirth, cesarean, physician's fee		2053	91	62r

Springfield, MO - continued

Item	Per	Value	Date	Ref.
Health Care - continued				
Childbirth, normal, hospital		2657	91	62r
Childbirth, normal, physician's fee		1492	91	62r
Dentist's fee, adult teeth cleaning and periodic oral exam	visit	45.33	4Q 92	4c
Doctor's fee, routine exam, established patient	visit	37.83	4Q 92	4c
Hospital care, semiprivate room	day	181.62	90	27c
Hospital care, semiprivate room	day	298.50	4Q 92	4c
Medical insurance premium, per employee, small group comprehensive	month	306.60	10/91	25c
Medical plan per employee	year	3443	91	45r
Mental health care, exp	capita	37.60-53.67	90	38s
Mental health care, exp, state mental health agency	capita	35.47	90	38s
Mental health care, hospital psychiatric services, non-Federal, exp	capita	22.53	88	38s
Mental health care, mental health organization, multiservice, exp	capita	6.98	88	38s
Mental health care, psychiatric hospitals, private, exp	capita	5.96	88	38s
Mental health care, psychiatric out-patient clinics, freestanding, exp	capita	0.79	88	38s
Mental health care, state and county mental hospitals, exp	capita	33.35	88	38s
Mental health care, VA medical centers, exp	capita	3.33	88	38s
Physician fee, family practice, first-visit		76.00	91	62r
Physician fee, family practice, revisit		33.00	91	62r
Physician fee, general practice, first-visit		61.00	91	62r
Physician fee, general practice, revisit		31.00	91	62r
Physician fee, general surgeon, first-visit		65.00	91	62r
Physician fee, general surgeon, revisit		35.00	91	62r
Physician fee, internal medicine, first-visit		91.00	91	62r
Physician fee, internal medicine, revisit		40.00	91	62r
Physician fee, median, neurosurgeon, first-visit		106.00	91	62r
Physician fee, median, nonsurgical specialist, first-visit		90.00	91	62r
Physician fee, median, orthopedic surgeon, first-visit		83.00	91	62r
Physician fee, median, surgical specialist, first-visit		61.00	91	62r
Physician fee, neurosurgeon, revisit		41.00	91	62r
Physician fee, nonsurgical specialist, revisit		40.00	91	62r
Physician fee, obstetrics/gynecology, first-visit		61.00	91	62r
Physician fee, obstetrics/gynecology, revisit		40.00	91	62r
Physician fee, orthopedic surgeon, revisit		41.00	91	62r
Physician fee, pediatrician, first-visit		46.00	91	62r
Physician fee, pediatrician, revisit		33.00	91	62r
Physician fee, surgical specialist, revisit		36.00	91	62r
Substance abuse, hospital ancillary charge	incident	1380	90	70s
Substance abuse, hospital physician charge	incident	560	90	70s
Substance abuse, hospital room and board	incident	5670	90	70s
Household Goods				
Appliance repair, home, service call, washing machine	min labor charge	31.73	4Q 92	4c
Laundry detergent, Tide Ultra, Bold, or Cheer	42 oz	4.17	4Q 92	4c
Tissues, facial, Kleenex brand	175-count box	1.07	4Q 92	4c
Housing				
ACCRA Index, Housing		80.30	4Q 92	4c
House, 1,800 sq ft, 8,000 sq ft lot, new, urban	total	90433	4Q 92	4c

Values are in dollars or fractions of dollars. In the column headed *Ref*, references are shown to sources. Each reference is followed by a letter. These refer to the geographical level for which data were reported: s=State, r=Region, and c=City or metro. The abbreviation *ex* is used to mean *except* or *excluding*; *exp* stands for *expenditures*. For other abbreviations and further explanations, please see the Introduction.

Springfield, MO - continued

Item	Per	Value	Date	Ref.
Housing				
House payment, principal and interest, 25% down payment	month	502	4Q 92	4c
Mortgage rate, incl. points & origination fee, 30-year fixed or adjustable rate	percent	8.09	4Q 92	4c
Rent, apartment, 2 bedrooms - 1-1/2 to 2 baths, unfurnished, 950 sq ft, water	month	377	4Q 92	4c
Rental unit, 1 bedroom	month	341	93	23c
Rental unit, 2 bedroom	month	401	93	23c
Rental unit, 3 bedroom	month	504	93	23c
Rental unit, 4 bedroom	month	561	93	23c
Rental unit, efficiency	month	278	93	23c
Insurance and Pensions				
Auto insurance, private passenger	year	551.85	91	63s
Personal Goods				
Shampoo, Alberto VO5	15 oz	1.48	4Q 92	4c
Toothpaste, Crest or Colgate	6-7 oz	1.96	4Q 92	4c
Personal Services				
Dry cleaning, man's 2-piece suit		5.00	4Q 92	4c
Haircare, woman's shampoo, trim and blow-dry		18.00	4Q 92	4c
Haircut, man's barbershop, no styling		7.13	4Q 92	4c
Restaurant Food				
Chicken, fried, thigh and drumstick		2.75	4Q 92	4c
Hamburger with cheese	1/4 lb	1.79	4Q 92	4c
Pizza, Pizza Hut or Pizza Inn, cheese, thin crust	12-13 in	8.14	4Q 92	4c
Taxes				
Tax, cigarette	pack	13	91	77s
Tax, gasoline	gal	13	91	77s
Taxes, state	capita	969	91	77s
Transportation				
ACCRA Index, Transportation		100.80	4Q 92	4c
Bus fare	one-way	0.50	3/93	2c
Driver's license fee		7.50	12/90	43s
Tire balance, computer or spin balance, front	wheel	7.37	4Q 92	4c
Vehicle registration and license plate	year	1.65-51.15	93	41s
Utilities				
ACCRA Index, Utilities		84.70	4Q 92	4c
Electricity	mil Btu	18.94	90	64s
Electricity, partial electric and other energy, 1,800 sq ft living area new home	month	45.79	4Q 92	4c

State College, PA

Item	Per	Value	Date	Ref.
Child Care				
Child care fee, average, center	hour	2.18	90	65r
Child care fee, average, nonregulated family day care	hour	1.83	90	65r
Child care fee, average, regulated family day care	hour	2.02	90	65r
Communications				
Long-distance telephone service, day, initial minute, 0-100 miles	min	0.15-0.29	91	12s
Long-distance telephone service, day, additional minute, 0-100 miles	min	0.06-0.22	91	12s
Long-distance telephone service, evenings/weekends, 0-100 mi, initial minute	min	0.06-0.14	91	12s
Long-distance telephone service, evenings/weekends, 0-100 mi, additional minute	min	0.03-0.11	91	12s

State College, PA - continued

Item	Per	Value	Date	Ref.
Education				
Board, 4-yr private college/university	year	2019	91	22s
Board, 4-yr public college/university	year	1656	91	22s
Expenditures, local gov't, public elementary/secondary	pupil	6980	92	20s
Room, 4-year private college/university	year	2179	91	22s
Room, 4-year public college/university	year	1719	91	22s
Tuition, 2-year private college/university	year	6314	91	22s
Tuition, 2-year public college/university	year	1505	91	22s
Tuition, 4-year private college/university	year	9848	91	22s
Tuition, 4-year public college/university, in-state	year	3401	91	22s
Energy and Fuels				
Coal	mil Btu	1.57	90	64s
Energy	mil Btu	8.63	90	64s
Energy exp/householder, 1-family unit	year	588	90	28r
Energy exp/householder, <1,000 sq ft heating area	year	477	90	28r
Energy exp/householder, 1,000-1,999 sq ft heating area	year	517	90	28r
Energy exp/householder, 2,000+ sq ft heating area	year	630	90	28r
Energy exp/householder, mobile home	year	412	90	28r
Energy exp/householder, multifamily	year	498	90	28r
Gas, natural	mil Btu	5.24	90	64s
Gas, natural	000 cu ft	6.76	91	46s
Gas, natural, exp	year	703	91	46s
Gasoline, unleaded regular	mil Btu	9.35	90	64s
Funerals				
Casket, 18-gauge steel, velvet interior		1811.58	91	24r
Cosmetology, hair care, etc.		111.08	91	24r
Embalming		329.42	91	24r
Facility use for ceremony		201.29	91	24r
Hearse, local		135.27	91	24r
Limousine, local		127.24	91	24r
Remains to funeral home, transfer		103.98	91	24r
Service charge, professional		724.98	91	24r
Vault, concrete, non-metallic liner		766.71	91	24r
Viewing facilities, use		260.60	91	24r
Groceries				
Apples, Red Delicious	lb	0.85	4/93	16r
Bacon	lb	2.12	4/93	16r
Bananas	lb	0.54	4/93	16r
Bread, white, pan	lb	0.81	4/93	16r
Butter	lb	2.02	4/93	16r
Carrots, short trimmed and topped	lb	0.51	4/93	16r
Chicken, fresh, whole	lb	1.04	4/93	16r
Chicken breast, bone-in	lb	2.21	4/93	16r
Chicken legs, bone-in	lb	1.16	4/93	16r
Chuck roast, USDA choice, boneless	lb	2.82	4/93	16r
Coffee, 100% ground roast, all sizes	lb	2.66	4/93	16r
Cucumbers	lb	0.85	4/93	16r
Eggs, Grade A large	doz	1.15	4/93	16r
Grapefruit	lb	0.45	4/93	16r
Grapes, Thompson Seedless	lb	1.52	4/93	16r
Ground beef, lean and extra lean	lb	2.36	4/93	16r
Ground chuck, 100% beef	lb	2.02	4/93	16r
Honey, jar	8 oz	0.96-1.75	92	5r
Honey, jar	lb	1.50-3.00	92	5r
Honey, squeeze bear	12-oz	1.50-1.99	92	5r
Ice cream, prepackaged, bulk, regular	1/2 gal	2.80	4/93	16r
Lemons	lb	0.96	4/93	16r
Lettuce, iceberg	lb	0.95	4/93	16r
Margarine, stick	lb	0.81	4/93	16r
Milk, fresh, whole, fortified	1/2 gal	1.30	4/93	16r

Values are in dollars or fractions of dollars. In the column headed *Ref*, references are shown to sources. Each reference is followed by a letter. These refer to the geographical level for which data were reported: s=State, r=Region, and c=City or metro. The abbreviation *ex* is used to mean *except* or *excluding*; *exp* stands for expenditures. For other abbreviations and further explanations, please see the Introduction.

State College, PA - continued

Item	Per	Value	Date	Ref.
Groceries				
Oranges, navel	lb	0.56	4/93	16r
Peanut butter, creamy, all sizes	lb	1.88	4/93	16r
Pork chops, center cut, bone-in	lb	3.34	4/93	16r
Potato chips	16 oz	2.88	4/93	16r
Potatoes, white	lb	0.37	4/93	16r
Rib roast, USDA choice, bone-in	lb	4.94	4/93	16r
Round roast, USDA choice, boneless	lb	3.17	4/93	16r
Shortening, vegetable oil blends	lb	0.98	4/93	16r
Spaghetti and macaroni	lb	0.82	4/93	16r
Steak, round, graded & ungraded, ex USDA prime & choice	lb	4.04	4/93	16r
Steak, round, USDA choice, boneless	lb	3.90	4/93	16r
Steak, sirloin, USDA choice, boneless	lb	4.97	4/93	16r
Strawberries, dry pint	12 oz	0.90	4/93	16r
Sugar, white	lb	0.50	4/93	16r
Sugar, white, 33-80 oz pk	lb	0.41	4/93	16r
Tomatoes, field grown	lb	1.23	4/93	16r
Tuna, chunk, light	lb	2.22	4/93	16r
Turkey, frozen, whole	lb	1.04	4/93	16r
Health Care				
Childbirth, cesarean, hospital		5826	91	62r
Childbirth, cesarean, physician's fee		2053	91	62r
Childbirth, normal, hospital		2964	91	62r
Childbirth, normal, physician's fee		1492	91	62r
Medical plan per employee	year	3942	91	45r
Mental health care, exp	capita	53.68-118.35	90	38s
Mental health care, exp, state mental health agency	capita	56.85	90	38s
Mental health care, hospital psychiatric services, non-Federal, exp	capita	22.11	88	38s
Mental health care, mental health organization, multiservice, exp	capita	21.01	88	38s
Mental health care, psychiatric hospitals, private, exp	capita	26.48	88	38s
Mental health care, psychiatric out-patient clinics, freestanding, exp	capita	4.17	88	38s
Mental health care, psychiatric partial-care organizations, freestanding, exp	capita	0.94	88	38s
Mental health care, state and county mental hospitals, exp	capita	37.11	88	38s
Mental health care, VA medical centers, exp	capita	9.77	88	38s
Prescription drug co-pay, Medicaid	month	6.00	91	21s
Substance abuse, hospital ancillary charge	incident	720	90	70s
Substance abuse, hospital physician charge	incident	210	90	70s
Substance abuse, hospital room and board	incident	5400	90	70s
Insurance and Pensions				
Auto insurance, private passenger	year	683.57	91	63s
Taxes				
Tax, cigarette	pack	31	91	77s
Tax, gasoline	gal	12	91	77s
Taxes, state	capita	1089	91	77s
Transportation				
Driver's license fee		22.00	12/90	43s
Travel				
Business travel	day	165.00	4/93	89r
Utilities				
Electricity	mil Btu	22.46	90	64s

Steubenville-Weirton, OH

Item	Per	Value	Date	Ref.
Child Care				
Child care fee, average, center	hour	1.63	90	65r

Steubenville-Weirton, OH - continued

Item	Per	Value	Date	Ref.
Child Care - continued				
Child care fee, average, nonregulated family day care	hour	1.83	90	65r
Child care fee, average, regulated family day care	hour	1.42	90	65r
Communications				
Long-distance telephone service, day, initial minute, 0-100 miles	min	0.26-0.43	91	12s
Long-distance telephone service, day, additional minute, 0-100 miles	min	0.14-0.24	91	12s
Long-distance telephone service, evenings/weekends, 0-100 mi, initial minute	min	0.11-0.17	91	12s
Long-distance telephone service, evenings/weekends, 0-100 mi, additional minute	min	0.06-0.10	91	12s
Education				
Board, 4-yr private college/university	year	1872	91	22s
Board, 4-yr public college/university	year	1742	91	22s
Expenditures, local gov't, public elementary/secondary	pupil	5451	92	20s
Room, 4-year private college/university	year	1695	91	22s
Room, 4-year public college/university	year	2259	91	22s
Tuition, 2-year private college/university	year	6093	91	22s
Tuition, 2-year public college/university	year	1768	91	22s
Tuition, 4-year private college/university	year	8729	91	22s
Tuition, 4-year public college/university, in-state	year	2622	91	22s
Energy and Fuels				
Coal	mil Btu	1.54	90	64s
Energy	mil Btu	8.32	90	64s
Energy exp/householder, 1-family unit	year	471	90	28r
Energy exp/householder, <1,000 sq ft heating area	year	430	90	28r
Energy exp/householder, 1,000-1,999 sq ft heating area	year	481	90	28r
Energy exp/householder, 2,000+ sq ft heating area	year	473	90	28r
Energy exp/householder, mobile home	year	430	90	28r
Energy exp/householder, multifamily	year	461	90	28r
Gas, natural	mil Btu	4.54	90	64s
Gas, natural	000 cu ft	5.28	91	46s
Gas, natural, exp	year	606	91	46s
Gasoline, unleaded regular	mil Btu	9.35	90	64s
Entertainment				
Miniature golf admission	adult	6.18	92	1r
Miniature golf admission	child	5.14	92	1r
Waterpark admission	adult	11.00	92	1r
Waterpark admission	child	8.55	92	1r
Funerals				
Casket, 18-gauge steel, velvet interior		1926.72	91	24r
Cosmetology, hair care, etc.		97.64	91	24r
Embalming		249.14	91	24r
Facility use for ceremony		208.59	91	24r
Hearse, local		130.12	91	24r
Limousine, local		104.66	91	24r
Remains to funeral home, transfer		93.61	91	24r
Service charge, professional		724.62	91	24r
Vault, concrete, non-metallic liner		734.53	91	24r
Viewing facilities, use		236.06	91	24r
Groceries				
Apples, Red Delicious	lb	0.77	4/93	16r
Bacon	lb	1.85	4/93	16r
Bananas	lb	0.46	4/93	16r
Beef, stew, boneless	lb	2.53	4/93	16r
Bologna, all beef or mixed	lb	2.19	4/93	16r
Bread, white, pan	lb	0.78	4/93	16r
Butter	lb	1.50	4/93	16r
Cabbage	lb	0.40	4/93	16r
Carrots, short trimmed and topped	lb	0.45	4/93	16r
Cheese, Cheddar	lb	3.47	4/93	16r

Values are in dollars or fractions of dollars. In the column headed *Ref*, references are shown to sources. Each reference is followed by a letter. These refer to the geographical level for which data were reported: s=State, r=Region, and c=City or metro. The abbreviation *ex* is used to mean *except* or *excluding*; *exp* stands for expenditures. For other abbreviations and further explanations, please see the Introduction.

Steubenville-Weirton, OH - continued

Item	Per	Value	Date	Ref.
Groceries				
Chicken, fresh, whole	lb	0.84	4/93	16r
Chicken breast, bone-in	lb	1.94	4/93	16r
Chicken legs, bone-in	lb	1.02	4/93	16r
Chuck roast, graded and ungraded, ex USDA prime and choice	lb	2.43	4/93	16r
Chuck roast, USDA choice, bone-in	lb	2.11	4/93	16r
Chuck roast, USDA choice, boneless	lb	2.44	4/93	16r
Coffee, 100% ground roast, all sizes	lb	2.47	4/93	16r
Cookies, chocolate chip	lb	2.73	4/93	16r
Eggs, Grade A large	doz	0.93	4/93	16r
Flour, white, all purpose	lb	0.21	4/93	16r
Grapefruit	lb	0.45	4/93	16r
Grapes, Thompson Seedless	lb	1.46	4/93	16r
Ground beef, 100% beef	lb	1.63	4/93	16r
Ground beef, lean and extra lean	lb	2.08	4/93	16r
Ground chuck, 100% beef	lb	1.94	4/93	16r
Ham, boneless, excluding canned	lb	2.21	4/93	16r
Honey, jar	8 oz	0.97-1.25	92	5r
Honey, jar	lb	1.25-2.25	92	5r
Honey, squeeze bear	12-oz	1.25-1.99	92	5r
Ice cream, prepackaged, bulk, regular	1/2 gal	2.41	4/93	16r
Lemons	lb	0.82	4/93	16r
Lettuce, iceberg	lb	0.83	4/93	16r
Margarine, stick	lb	0.77	4/93	16r
Oranges, navel	lb	0.50	4/93	16r
Peanut butter, creamy, all sizes	lb	1.82	4/93	16r
Pears, Anjou	lb	0.85	4/93	16r
Pork chops, center cut, bone-in	lb	3.17	4/93	16r
Potato chips	16 oz	2.68	4/93	16r
Potatoes, white	lb	0.26	4/93	16r
Round roast, graded & ungraded, ex USDA prime & choice	lb	2.88	4/93	16r
Round roast, USDA choice, boneless	lb	2.96	4/93	16r
Shortening, vegetable oil blends	lb	0.79	4/93	16r
Spaghetti and macaroni	lb	0.76	4/93	16r
Steak, rib eye, USDA choice, boneless	lb	6.29	4/93	16r
Steak, round, USDA choice, boneless	lb	3.24	4/93	16r
Steak, sirloin, graded & ungraded, ex USDA prime & choice	lb	4.00	4/93	16r
Steak, sirloin, USDA choice, bone-in	lb	3.57	4/93	16r
Steak, sirloin, USDA choice, boneless	lb	4.17	4/93	16r
Steak, T-bone, USDA choice, bone-in	lb	5.60	4/93	16r
Strawberries, dry pint	12 oz	0.90	4/93	16r
Sugar, white	lb	0.36	4/93	16r
Sugar, white, 33-80 oz pk	lb	0.35	4/93	16r
Tomatoes, field grown	lb	0.99	4/93	16r
Tuna, chunk, light	lb	1.76	4/93	16r
Turkey, frozen, whole	lb	0.91	4/93	16r
Health Care				
Childbirth, cesarean, hospital		4688	91	62r
Childbirth, cesarean, physician's fee		2053	91	62r
Childbirth, normal, hospital		2657	91	62r
Childbirth, normal, physician's fee		1492	91	62r
Medical plan per employee	year	3443	91	45r
Mental health care, exp	capita	37.60-53.67	90	38s
Mental health care, exp, state mental health agency	capita	40.93	90	38s
Mental health care, hospital psychiatric services, non-Federal, exp	capita	15.03	88	38s
Mental health care, mental health organization, multiservice, exp	capita	14.46	88	38s
Mental health care, psychiatric hospitals, private, exp	capita	7.93	88	38s
Mental health care, psychiatric out-patient clinics, freestanding, exp	capita	2.93	88	38s
Mental health care, psychiatric partial-care organizations, freestanding, exp	capita	0.32	88	38s
Mental health care, state and county mental hospitals, exp	capita	23.79	88	38s
Mental health care, VA medical centers, exp	capita	7.76	88	38s
Physician fee, family practice, first-visit		76.00	91	62r

Steubenville-Weirton, OH - continued

Item	Per	Value	Date	Ref.
Health Care - continued				
Physician fee, family practice, revisit		33.00	91	62r
Physician fee, general practice, first-visit		61.00	91	62r
Physician fee, general practice, revisit		31.00	91	62r
Physician fee, general surgeon, first-visit		65.00	91	62r
Physician fee, general surgeon, revisit		35.00	91	62r
Physician fee, internal medicine, first-visit		91.00	91	62r
Physician fee, internal medicine, revisit		40.00	91	62r
Physician fee, median, neurosurgeon, first-visit		106.00	91	62r
Physician fee, median, nonsurgical specialist, first-visit		90.00	91	62r
Physician fee, median, orthopedic surgeon, first-visit		83.00	91	62r
Physician fee, median, surgical specialist, first-visit		61.00	91	62r
Physician fee, neurosurgeon, revisit		41.00	91	62r
Physician fee, nonsurgical specialist, revisit		40.00	91	62r
Physician fee, obstetrics/gynecology, first-visit		61.00	91	62r
Physician fee, obstetrics/gynecology, revisit		40.00	91	62r
Physician fee, orthopedic surgeon, revisit		41.00	91	62r
Physician fee, pediatrician, first-visit		46.00	91	62r
Physician fee, pediatrician, revisit		33.00	91	62r
Physician fee, surgical specialist, revisit		36.00	91	62r
Substance abuse, hospital ancillary charge	incident	940	90	70s
Substance abuse, hospital physician charge	incident	380	90	70s
Substance abuse, hospital room and board	incident	5410	90	70s
Insurance and Pensions				
Auto insurance, private passenger	year	547.38	91	63s
Taxes				
Tax, cigarette	pack	18	91	77s
Tax, gasoline	gal	21	91	77s
Taxes, state	capita	1056	91	77s
Transportation				
Driver's license fee		5.00	12/90	43s
Utilities				
Electricity	mil Btu	17.33	90	64s

Stillwater, OK

Item	Per	Value	Date	Ref.
Composite ACCRA index		94.60	4Q 92	4c
Alcoholic Beverages				
Beer, Miller Lite or Budweiser, 12-oz containers	6 pack	3.77	4Q 92	4c
Liquor, J & B Scotch	750 ml	14.98	4Q 92	4c
Wine, Gallo Chablis blanc, 1.5 liter	bottle	5.33	4Q 92	4c
Clothing				
Jeans, man's denim		29.70	4Q 92	4c
Shirt, man's dress shirt		23.00	4Q 92	4c
Undervest, boy's size 10-14, cotton	3	4.16	4Q 92	4c
Communications				
Newspaper subscription, daily and Sunday home delivery, large-city	month	12.85	4Q 92	4c
Telephone, flat rate	month	11.32	91	11c
Telephone bill, family of four	month	18.56	4Q 92	4c
Energy and Fuels				
Energy, combined forms, 1,800 sq ft heating area	month	110.35	4Q 92	4c
Energy, exc electricity, 1,800 sq ft heating area	month	37.86	4Q 92	4c
Gasoline, motor	gal	1.07	4Q 92	4c
Entertainment				
Bowling, evening rate	game	1.90	4Q 92	4c
Monopoly game, Parker Brothers', No. 9		9.97	4Q 92	4c

Values are in dollars or fractions of dollars. In the column headed *Ref*, references are shown to sources. Each reference is followed by a letter. These refer to the geographical level for which data were reported: s = State, r = Region, and c = City or metro. The abbreviation *ex* is used to mean *except* or *excluding*; *exp* stands for expenditures. For other abbreviations and further explanations, please see the Introduction.

Stillwater, OK - continued

Item	Per	Value	Date	Ref.
Entertainment				
Movie	admission	5.00	4Q 92	4c
Tennis balls, yellow, Wilson or Penn, 3	can	2.81	4Q 92	4c
Goods and Services				
ACCRA Index, Miscellaneous Goods and Services		97.60	4Q 92	4c
Groceries				
ACCRA Index, Groceries		97.80	4Q 92	4c
Babyfood, strained vegetables, lowest price	4-4.5 oz jar	0.36	4Q 92	4c
Bananas	lb	0.40	4Q 92	4c
Bread, white	24 oz	0.62	4Q 92	4c
Cheese, Kraft grated Parmesan	8-oz canister	3.36	4Q 92	4c
Chicken, fryer, whole	lb	0.85	4Q 92	4c
Cigarettes, Winston	carton	17.33	4Q 92	4c
Coffee, vacuum-packed	13-oz can	1.90	4Q 92	4c
Corn, frozen	10 oz	0.68	4Q 92	4c
Corn Flakes, Kellogg's or Post Toasties	18 oz	2.05	4Q 92	4c
Eggs, Grade A large	doz	0.80	4Q 92	4c
Ground beef or hamburger	lb	1.52	4Q 92	4c
Lettuce, iceberg	head	0.92	4Q 92	4c
Margarine, Blue Bonnet or Parkay cubes	lb	0.64	4Q 92	4c
Milk, whole	1/2 gal	1.16	4Q 92	4c
Orange juice, Minute Maid frozen	12-oz can	1.51	4Q 92	4c
Peaches	29-oz can	1.39	4Q 92	4c
Peas Sweet, Del Monte or Green Giant	15-17 oz can	0.62	4Q 92	4c
Potatoes, white or red	10-lb sack	1.33	4Q 92	4c
Sausage, Jimmy Dean, 100% pork	lb	2.42	4Q 92	4c
Shortening, vegetable, Crisco	3-lb can	2.24	4Q 92	4c
Soft drink, Coca Cola	2 liter	1.19	4Q 92	4c
Steak, T-bone	lb	4.88	4Q 92	4c
Sugar, cane or beet	4 lb	1.60	4Q 92	4c
Tomatoes, Hunt's or Del Monte	14.5-oz can	0.71	4Q 92	4c
Tuna, chunk, light	6.125-6.5 oz can	0.71	4Q 92	4c
Health Care				
ACCRA Index, Health Care		98.50	4Q 92	4c
Analgesic, Aspirin, Bayer, 325 mg tablets	100	5.33	4Q 92	4c
Dentist's fee, adult teeth cleaning and periodic oral exam	visit	45.67	4Q 92	4c
Doctor's fee, routine exam, established patient	visit	40.48	4Q 92	4c
Hospital care, semiprivate room	day	235.00	4Q 92	4c
Household Goods				
Appliance repair, home, service call, washing machine	min labor charge	27.17	4Q 92	4c
Laundry detergent, Tide Ultra, Bold, or Cheer	42 oz	3.07	4Q 92	4c
Tissues, facial, Kleenex brand	175-count box	1.20	4Q 92	4c
Housing				
ACCRA Index, Housing		85.00	4Q 92	4c
House, 1,800 sq ft, 8,000 sq ft lot, new, urban	total	91493	4Q 92	4c
House payment, principal and interest, 25% down payment	month	513	4Q 92	4c

Stillwater, OK - continued

Item	Per	Value	Date	Ref.
Housing - continued				
Mortgage rate, incl. points & origination fee, 30-year fixed or adjustable rate	percent	8.19	4Q 92	4c
Rent, apartment, 2 bedrooms - 1-1/2 to 2 baths, unfurnished, 950 sq ft, water	month	442	4Q 92	4c
Personal Goods				
Shampoo, Alberto VO5	15 oz	1.24	4Q 92	4c
Toothpaste, Crest or Colgate	6-7 oz	1.92	4Q 92	4c
Personal Services				
Dry cleaning, man's 2-piece suit		6.44	4Q 92	4c
Haircare, woman's shampoo, trim and blow-dry		18.17	4Q 92	4c
Haircut, man's barbershop, no styling		6.00	4Q 92	4c
Restaurant Food				
Chicken, fried, thigh and drumstick		2.18	4Q 92	4c
Hamburger with cheese	1/4 lb	1.89	4Q 92	4c
Pizza, Pizza Hut or Pizza Inn, cheese, thin crust	12-13 in	7.48	4Q 92	4c
Transportation				
ACCRA Index, Transportation		99.40	4Q 92	4c
Tire balance, computer or spin balance, front	wheel	6.75	4Q 92	4c
Utilities				
ACCRA Index, Utilities		100.50	4Q 92	4c
Electricity, partial electric and other energy, 1,800 sq ft living area new home	month	72.49	4Q 92	4c

Stockton, CA

Item	Per	Value	Date	Ref.
Child Care				
Child care fee, average, center	hour	1.71	90	65r
Child care fee, average, nonregulated family day care	hour	1.32	90	65r
Child care fee, average, regulated family day care	hour	1.86	90	65r
Communications				
Long-distance telephone service, day, initial minute, 0-100 miles	min	0.17-0.40	91	12s
Long-distance telephone service, day, additional minute, 0-100 miles	min	0.07-0.31	91	12s
Long-distance telephone service, evenings/weekends, 0-100 mi, initial minute	min	0.07-0.16	91	12s
Long-distance telephone service, evenings/weekends, 0-100 mi, additional minute	min	0.03-0.12	91	12s
Education				
Board, 4-yr private college/university	year	2515	91	22s
Board, 4-yr public college/university	year	2268	91	22s
Expenditures, local gov't, public elementary/secondary	pupil	4866	92	20s
Room, 4-year private college/university	year	2622	91	22s
Room, 4-year public college/university	year	2406	91	22s
Tuition, 2-year private college/university	year	7942	91	22s
Tuition, 2-year public college/university	year	114	91	22s
Tuition, 4-year private college/university	year	10863	91	22s
Tuition, 4-year public college/university, in-state	year	1220	91	22s
Energy and Fuels				
Coal	mil Btu	2.01	90	64s
Energy	mil Btu	9.08	90	64s
Energy exp/householder, 1-family unit	year	362	90	28r
Energy exp/householder, <1,000 sq ft heating area	year	254	90	28r
Energy exp/householder, 1,000-1,999 sq ft heating area	year	358	90	28r
Energy exp/householder, 2,000+ sq ft heating area	year	467	90	28r
Energy exp/householder, mobile home	year	390	90	28r
Energy exp/householder, multifamily	year	252	90	28r

Values are in dollars or fractions of dollars. In the column headed *Ref*, references are shown to sources. Each reference is followed by a letter. These refer to the geographical level for which data were reported: s=State, r=Region, and c=City or metro. The abbreviation *ex* is used to mean *except* or *excluding*; *exp* stands for expenditures. For other abbreviations and further explanations, please see the Introduction.

Stockton, CA - continued

Item	Per	Value	Date	Ref.
Energy and Fuels				
Gas, natural	mil Btu	4.31	90	64s
Gas, natural	000 cu ft	6.27	91	46s
Gas, natural, exp	year	369	91	46s
Gasoline, unleaded regular	mil Btu	8.57	90	64s
Entertainment				
Miniature golf admission	adult	6.18	92	1r
Miniature golf admission	child	5.14	92	1r
Waterpark admission	adult	11.00	92	1r
Waterpark admission	child	8.55	92	1r
Funerals				
Casket, 18-gauge steel, velvet interior		1781.09	91	24r
Cosmetology, hair care, etc.		84.64	91	24r
Embalming		207.41	91	24r
Facility use for ceremony		205.76	91	24r
Hearse, local		105.14	91	24r
Limousine, local		83.21	91	24r
Remains to funeral home, transfer		113.82	91	24r
Service charge, professional		626.33	91	24r
Vault, concrete, non-metallic liner		599.54	91	24r
Viewing facilities, use		85.81	91	24r
Groceries				
Apples, Red Delicious	lb	0.80	4/93	16r
Bacon	lb	1.79	4/93	16r
Bananas	lb	0.53	4/93	16r
Bologna, all beef or mixed	lb	2.67	4/93	16r
Bread, white, pan	lb	0.81	4/93	16r
Carrots, short trimmed and topped	lb	0.39	4/93	16r
Chicken, fresh, whole	lb	0.94	4/93	16r
Chicken breast, bone-in	lb	2.19	4/93	16r
Chuck roast, graded and ungraded, ex USDA prime and choice	lb	2.26	4/93	16r
Coffee, 100% ground roast, all sizes	lb	2.33	4/93	16r
Eggs, Grade AA large	doz	1.18	4/93	16r
Flour, white, all purpose	lb	0.22	4/93	16r
Grapefruit	lb	0.52	4/93	16r
Grapes, Thompson Seedless	lb	1.50	4/93	16r
Ground beef, 100% beef	lb	1.44	4/93	16r
Ground beef, lean and extra lean	lb	2.34	4/93	16r
Ham, boneless, excluding canned	lb	2.56	4/93	16r
Honey, jar	8 oz	0.89-1.00	92	5r
Honey, jar	lb	1.35-1.97	92	5r
Honey, squeeze bear	12-oz	1.19-1.50	92	5r
Ice cream, prepackaged, bulk, regular	1/2 gal	2.40	4/93	16r
Lemons	lb	0.81	4/93	16r
Lettuce, iceberg	lb	0.84	4/93	16r
Margarine, stick	lb	0.81	4/93	16r
Oranges, navel	lb	0.48	4/93	16r
Pork chops, center cut, bone-in	lb	3.25	4/93	16r
Potato chips	16 oz	2.89	4/93	16r
Potatoes, white	lb	0.38	4/93	16r
Round roast, graded & ungraded, ex USDA prime & choice	lb	3.00	4/93	16r
Round roast, USDA choice, boneless	lb	3.16	4/93	16r
Shortening, vegetable oil blends	lb	0.86	4/93	16r
Spaghetti and macaroni	lb	0.84	4/93	16r
Steak, round, graded & ungraded, ex USDA prime & choice	lb	3.34	4/93	16r
Steak, round, USDA choice, boneless	lb	3.24	4/93	16r
Steak, sirloin, graded & ungraded, ex USDA prime & choice	lb	3.75	4/93	16r
Steak, sirloin, USDA choice, boneless	lb	4.49	4/93	16r
Sugar, white	lb	0.41	4/93	16r
Sugar, white, 33-80 oz pk	lb	0.38	4/93	16r
Tomatoes, field grown	lb	1.01	4/93	16r
Turkey, frozen, whole	lb	1.04	4/93	16r
Health Care				
Cardizem 60 mg tablets	30	24.04	92	49s
Cector 250 mg tablets	15	35.87	92	49s
Childbirth, cesarean, hospital		5533	91	62r

Stockton, CA - continued

Item	Per	Value	Date	Ref.
Health Care - continued				
Childbirth, cesarean, physician's fee		2053	91	62r
Childbirth, normal, hospital		2745	91	62r
Childbirth, normal, physician's fee		1492	91	62r
Health care spending, state	capita	2894	3/93	84s
Medical plan per employee	year	3421	91	45r
Mental health care, exp	capita	37.60-53.67	90	38s
Mental health care, exp, state mental health agency	capita	42.32	90	38s
Mental health care, hospital psychiatric services, non-Federal, exp	capita	10.64	88	38s
Mental health care, mental health organization, multiservice, exp	capita	28.56	88	38s
Mental health care, psychiatric hospitals, private, exp	capita	18.60	88	38s
Mental health care, psychiatric out-patient clinics, freestanding, exp	capita	2.28	88	38s
Mental health care, psychiatric partial-care organizations, freestanding, exp	capita	0.24	88	38s
Mental health care, state and county mental hospitals, exp	capita	13.60	88	38s
Mental health care, VA medical centers, exp	capita	2.33	88	38s
Mevacor 20 mg tablets	30	67.62	92	49s
Physician fee, family practice, first-visit		111.00	91	62r
Physician fee, family practice, revisit		45.00	91	62r
Physician fee, general practice, first-visit		100.00	91	62r
Physician fee, general practice, revisit		40.00	91	62r
Physician fee, internal medicine, first-visit		137.00	91	62r
Physician fee, internal medicine, revisit		48.00	91	62r
Physician fee, median, neurosurgeon, first-visit		157.00	91	62r
Physician fee, median, nonsurgical specialist, first-visit		131.00	91	62r
Physician fee, median, orthopedic surgeon, first-visit		124.00	91	62r
Physician fee, median, plastic surgeon, first-visit		88.00	91	62r
Physician fee, median, surgical specialist, first-visit		100.00	91	62r
Physician fee, neurosurgeon, revisit		51.00	91	62r
Physician fee, nonsurgical specialist, revisit		47.00	91	62r
Physician fee, obstetrics/gynecology, first-visit		95.00	91	62r
Physician fee, obstetrics/gynecology, revisit		50.00	91	62r
Physician fee, orthopedic surgeon, revisit		51.00	91	62r
Physician fee, pediatrician, first-visit		81.00	91	62r
Physician fee, pediatrician, revisit		42.00	91	62r
Physician fee, plastic surgeon, revisit		48.00	91	62r
Physician fee, surgical specialist, revisit		49.00	91	62r
Prozac 20 mg tablets	14	33.22	92	49s
Substance abuse, hospital ancillary charge	incident	1760	90	70s
Substance abuse, hospital physician charge	incident	750	90	70s
Substance abuse, hospital room and board	incident	6390	90	70s
Tagamet 300 mg tablets	100	77.08	92	49s
Xanax 0.25 mg tablets	90	64.08	92	49s
Zantac 160 mg tablets	60	92.31	92	49s
Housing				
Home, median price	unit	131,200	92	58s
Insurance and Pensions				
Auto insurance, private passenger	year	904.37	91	63s
Taxes				
Tax, cigarette	pack	35	91	77s
Tax, gasoline	gal	16	91	77s
Taxes, state	capita	1477	91	77s
Transportation				
Driver's license fee		10.00	12/90	43s

Values are in dollars or fractions of dollars. In the column headed *Ref*, references are shown to sources. Each reference is followed by a letter. These refer to the geographical level for which data were reported: s=State, r=Region, and c=City or metro. The abbreviation *ex* is used to mean *except* or *excluding*; *exp* stands for expenditures. For other abbreviations and further explanations, please see the Introduction.

Stockton, CA - continued

Item	Per	Value	Date	Ref.
Travel				
Business travel	day	178.00	4/93	89r
Utilities				
Electricity	mil Btu	25.98	90	64s

Sumter, SC

Item	Per	Value	Date	Ref.
Composite ACCRA index		91.80	4Q 92	4c
Alcoholic Beverages				
Beer, Miller Lite or Budweiser, 12-oz containers	6 pack	3.92	4Q 92	4c
Liquor, J & B Scotch	750 ml	17.86	4Q 92	4c
Wine, Gallo Chablis blanc, 1.5 liter	bottle	4.85	4Q 92	4c
Clothing				
Jeans, man's denim		36.81	4Q 92	4c
Shirt, man's dress shirt		24.67	4Q 92	4c
Undervest, boy's size 10-14, cotton	3	4.76	4Q 92	4c
Communications				
Newspaper subscription, daily and Sunday home delivery, large-city	month	10.42	4Q 92	4c
Telephone bill, family of four	month	21.80	4Q 92	4c
Energy and Fuels				
Energy, combined forms, 1,800 sq ft heating area	month	118.70	4Q 92	4c
Gasoline, motor	gal	1.03	4Q 92	4c
Entertainment				
Bowling, evening rate	game	2.25	4Q 92	4c
Monopoly game, Parker Brothers', No. 9		11.11	4Q 92	4c
Movie	admission	5.00	4Q 92	4c
Tennis balls, yellow, Wilson or Penn, 3	can	2.27	4Q 92	4c
Goods and Services				
ACCRA Index, Miscellaneous Goods and Services		100.10	4Q 92	4c
Groceries				
ACCRA Index, Groceries		96.20	4Q 92	4c
Babyfood, strained vegetables, lowest price	4-4.5 oz jar	0.33	4Q 92	4c
Bananas	lb	0.47	4Q 92	4c
Bread, white	24 oz	0.68	4Q 92	4c
Cheese, Kraft grated Parmesan	8-oz canister	3.21	4Q 92	4c
Chicken, fryer, whole	lb	0.75	4Q 92	4c
Cigarettes, Winston	carton	15.43	4Q 92	4c
Coffee, vacuum-packed	13-oz can	1.81	4Q 92	4c
Corn, frozen	10 oz	0.61	4Q 92	4c
Corn Flakes, Kellogg's or Post Toasties	18 oz	1.81	4Q 92	4c
Eggs, Grade A large	doz	0.87	4Q 92	4c
Ground beef or hamburger	lb	1.76	4Q 92	4c
Lettuce, iceberg	head	0.99	4Q 92	4c
Margarine, Blue Bonnet or Parkay cubes	lb	0.57	4Q 92	4c
Milk, whole	1/2 gal	1.38	4Q 92	4c
Orange juice, Minute Maid frozen	12-oz can	1.19	4Q 92	4c
Peaches	29-oz can	1.30	4Q 92	4c
Peas Sweet, Del Monte or Green Giant	15-17 oz can	0.48	4Q 92	4c
Potatoes, white or red	10-lb sack	2.19	4Q 92	4c
Sausage, Jimmy Dean, 100% pork	lb	2.14	4Q 92	4c
Shortening, vegetable, Crisco	3-lb can	2.01	4Q 92	4c
Soft drink, Coca Cola	2 liter	1.08	4Q 92	4c
Steak, T-bone	lb	5.41	4Q 92	4c
Sugar, cane or beet	4 lb	1.39	4Q 92	4c

Sumter, SC - continued

Item	Per	Value	Date	Ref.
Groceries - continued				
Tomatoes, Hunt's or Del Monte	14.5-oz can	0.55	4Q 92	4c
Tuna, chunk, light	6.125-6.5 oz can	0.57	4Q 92	4c
Health Care				
ACCRA Index, Health Care		69.30	4Q 92	4c
Analgesic, Aspirin, Bayer, 325 mg tablets	100	5.08	4Q 92	4c
Dentist's fee, adult teeth cleaning and periodic oral exam	visit	29.37	4Q 92	4c
Doctor's fee, routine exam, established patient	visit	25.80	4Q 92	4c
Hospital care, semiprivate room	day	194.00	4Q 92	4c
Household Goods				
Appliance repair, home, service call, washing machine	min labor charge	31.90	4Q 92	4c
Laundry detergent, Tide Ultra, Bold, or Cheer	42 oz	3.53	4Q 92	4c
Tissues, facial, Kleenex brand	175-count box	0.97	4Q 92	4c
Housing				
ACCRA Index, Housing		76.00	4Q 92	4c
House, 1,800 sq ft, 8,000 sq ft lot, new, urban	total	81900	4Q 92	4c
House payment, principal and interest, 25% down payment	month	455	4Q 92	4c
Mortgage rate, incl. points & origination fee, 30-year fixed or adjustable rate	percent	8.11	4Q 92	4c
Rent, apartment, 2 bedrooms - 1-1/2 to 2 baths, unfurnished, 950 sq ft, water	month	404	4Q 92	4c
Personal Goods				
Shampoo, Alberto VO5	15 oz	0.97	4Q 92	4c
Toothpaste, Crest or Colgate	6-7 oz	1.97	4Q 92	4c
Personal Services				
Dry cleaning, man's 2-piece suit		5.36	4Q 92	4c
Haircare, woman's shampoo, trim and blow-dry		17.50	4Q 92	4c
Haircut, man's barbershop, no styling		10.40	4Q 92	4c
Restaurant Food				
Chicken, fried, thigh and drumstick		1.77	4Q 92	4c
Hamburger with cheese	1/4 lb	1.67	4Q 92	4c
Pizza, Pizza Hut or Pizza Inn, cheese, thin crust	12-13 in	5.46	4Q 92	4c
Transportation				
ACCRA Index, Transportation		97.30	4Q 92	4c
Tire balance, computer or spin balance, front	wheel	6.70	4Q 92	4c
Utilities				
ACCRA Index, Utilities		109.00	4Q 92	4c
Electricity, all electric, 1,800 sq ft living area new home	month	118.70	4Q 92	4c

Syracuse, NY

Item	Per	Value	Date	Ref.
Composite ACCRA index		103.80	4Q 92	4c
Alcoholic Beverages				
Beer, Miller Lite or Budweiser, 12-oz containers	6 pack	4.43	4Q 92	4c
Liquor, J & B Scotch	750 ml	17.39	4Q 92	4c
Wine, Gallo Chablis blanc, 1.5 liter	bottle	5.29	4Q 92	4c
Child Care				
Child care fee, average, center	hour	2.18	90	65r
Child care fee, average, nonregulated family day care	hour	1.83	90	65r

Values are in dollars or fractions of dollars. In the column headed *Ref*, references are shown to sources. Each reference is followed by a letter. These refer to the geographical level for which data were reported: s=State, r=Region, and c=City or metro. The abbreviation *ex* is used to mean *except* or *excluding*; *exp* stands for expenditures. For other abbreviations and further explanations, please see the Introduction.

Syracuse, NY - continued

Item	Per	Value	Date	Ref.
Child Care				
Child care fee, average, regulated family day care	hour	2.02	90	65r
Clothing				
Jeans, man's denim		30.19	4Q 92	4c
Shirt, man's dress shirt		21.59	4Q 92	4c
Undervest, boy's size 10-14, cotton	3	4.52	4Q 92	4c
Communications				
Newspaper subscription, daily and Sunday home delivery, large-city	month	14.35	4Q 92	4c
Telephone bill, family of four	month	32.90	4Q 92	4c
Education				
Board, 4-yr private college/university	year	2451	91	22s
Board, 4-yr public college/university	year	1725	91	22s
Expenditures, local gov't, public elementary/secondary	pupil	8603	92	20s
Room, 4-year private college/university	year	2652	91	22s
Room, 4-year public college/university	year	2183	91	22s
Tuition, 2-year private college/university	year	5926	91	22s
Tuition, 2-year public college/university	year	1419	91	22s
Tuition, 4-year private college/university	year	10340	91	22s
Tuition, 4-year public college/university, in-state	year	1587	91	22s
Energy and Fuels				
Coal	mil Btu	1.66	90	64s
Energy	mil Btu	10.68	90	64s
Energy, combined forms, 1,800 sq ft heating area	month	144.12	4Q 92	4c
Energy, exc electricity, 1,800 sq ft heating area	month	63.67	4Q 92	4c
Energy exp/householder, 1-family unit	year	588	90	28r
Energy exp/householder, <1,000 sq ft heating area	year	477	90	28r
Energy exp/householder, 1,000-1,999 sq ft heating area	year	517	90	28r
Energy exp/householder, 2,000+ sq ft heating area	year	630	90	28r
Energy exp/householder, mobile home	year	412	90	28r
Energy exp/householder, multifamily	year	498	90	28r
Gas, cooking, winter, 10 therms	month	10.84	92	56c
Gas, cooking, winter, 30 therms	month	24.80	92	56c
Gas, cooking, winter, 50 therms	month	36.93	92	56c
Gas, heating, winter, 100 therms	month	62.68	92	56c
Gas, heating, winter, average use	month	165.69	92	56c
Gas, natural	mil Btu	5.25	90	64s
Gas, natural	000 cu ft	7.35	91	46s
Gas, natural, exp	year	557	91	46s
Gasoline, motor	gal	1.19	4Q 92	4c
Gasoline, unleaded premium	gal	65.94-70.80	12/92	31c
Gasoline, unleaded regular	mil Btu	8.83	90	64s
Entertainment				
Bowling, evening rate	game	1.84	4Q 92	4c
Monopoly game, Parker Brothers', No. 9		9.58	4Q 92	4c
Movie	admission	6.20	4Q 92	4c
Tennis balls, yellow, Wilson or Penn, 3	can	2.63	4Q 92	4c
Funerals				
Casket, 18-gauge steel, velvet interior		1811.58	91	24r
Cosmetology, hair care, etc.		111.08	91	24r
Embalming		329.42	91	24r
Facility use for ceremony		201.29	91	24r
Hearse, local		135.27	91	24r
Limousine, local		127.24	91	24r
Remains to funeral home, transfer		103.98	91	24r
Service charge, professional		724.98	91	24r
Vault, concrete, non-metallic liner		766.71	91	24r
Viewing facilities, use		260.60	91	24r

Syracuse, NY - continued

Item	Per	Value	Date	Ref.
Goods and Services				
ACCRA Index, Miscellaneous Goods and Services		100.40	4Q 92	4c
Groceries				
ACCRA Index, Groceries		109.60	4Q 92	4c
Apples, Red Delicious	lb	0.85	4/93	16r
Babyfood, strained vegetables, lowest price	4-4.5 oz jar	0.36	4Q 92	4c
Bacon	lb	2.12	4/93	16r
Bananas	lb	0.53	4Q 92	4c
Bananas	lb	0.54	4/93	16r
Bread, white	24 oz	0.86	4Q 92	4c
Bread, white, pan	lb	0.81	4/93	16r
Butter	lb	2.02	4/93	16r
Carrots, short trimmed and topped	lb	0.51	4/93	16r
Cheese, Kraft grated Parmesan	8-oz canister	2.95	4Q 92	4c
Chicken, fresh, whole	lb	1.04	4/93	16r
Chicken, fryer, whole	lb	0.88	4Q 92	4c
Chicken breast, bone-in	lb	2.21	4/93	16r
Chicken legs, bone-in	lb	1.16	4/93	16r
Chuck roast, USDA choice, boneless	lb	2.82	4/93	16r
Cigarettes, Winston	carton	18.48	4Q 92	4c
Coffee, 100% ground roast, all sizes	lb	2.66	4/93	16r
Coffee, vacuum-packed	13-oz can	2.47	4Q 92	4c
Corn, frozen	10 oz	0.68	4Q 92	4c
Corn Flakes, Kellogg's or Post Toasties	18 oz	1.87	4Q 92	4c
Cucumbers	lb	0.85	4/93	16r
Eggs, Grade A large	doz	0.93	4Q 92	4c
Eggs, Grade A large	doz	1.15	4/93	16r
Grapefruit	lb	0.45	4/93	16r
Grapes, Thompson Seedless	lb	1.52	4/93	16r
Ground beef, lean and extra lean	lb	2.36	4/93	16r
Ground beef or hamburger	lb	1.85	4Q 92	4c
Ground chuck, 100% beef	lb	2.02	4/93	16r
Honey, jar	8 oz	0.96-1.75	92	5r
Honey, jar	lb	1.50-3.00	92	5r
Honey, squeeze bear	12-oz	1.50-1.99	92	5r
Ice cream, prepackaged, bulk, regular	1/2 gal	2.80	4/93	16r
Lemons	lb	0.96	4/93	16r
Lettuce, iceberg	head	0.99	4Q 92	4c
Lettuce, iceberg	lb	0.95	4/93	16r
Margarine, Blue Bonnet or Parkay cubes	lb	0.58	4Q 92	4c
Margarine, stick	lb	0.81	4/93	16r
Milk, fresh, whole, fortified	1/2 gal	1.30	4/93	16r
Milk, whole	1/2 gal	1.33	4Q 92	4c
Orange juice, Minute Maid frozen	12-oz can	1.63	4Q 92	4c
Oranges, navel	lb	0.56	4/93	16r
Peaches	29-oz can	1.55	4Q 92	4c
Peanut butter, creamy, all sizes	lb	1.88	4/93	16r
Peas Sweet, Del Monte or Green Giant	15-17 oz can	0.71	4Q 92	4c
Pork chops, center cut, bone-in	lb	3.34	4/93	16r
Potato chips	16 oz	2.88	4/93	16r
Potatoes, white	lb	0.37	4/93	16r
Potatoes, white or red	10-lb sack	2.07	4Q 92	4c
Rib roast, USDA choice, bone-in	lb	4.94	4/93	16r
Round roast, USDA choice, boneless	lb	3.17	4/93	16r
Sausage, Jimmy Dean, 100% pork	lb	2.84	4Q 92	4c
Shortening, vegetable oil blends	lb	0.98	4/93	16r
Shortening, vegetable, Crisco	3-lb can	2.83	4Q 92	4c
Soft drink, Coca Cola	2 liter	1.47	4Q 92	4c
Spaghetti and macaroni	lb	0.82	4/93	16r
Steak, round, graded & ungraded, ex USDA prime & choice	lb	4.04	4/93	16r
Steak, round, USDA choice, boneless	lb	3.90	4/93	16r
Steak, sirloin, USDA choice, boneless	lb	4.97	4/93	16r

Values are in dollars or fractions of dollars. In the column headed *Ref*, references are shown to sources. Each reference is followed by a letter. These refer to the geographical level for which data were reported: s = State, r = Region, and c = City or metro. The abbreviation *ex* is used to mean *except* or *excluding*; *exp* stands for expenditures. For other abbreviations and further explanations, please see the Introduction.

Syracuse, NY - continued

Item	Per	Value	Date	Ref.
Groceries				
Steak, T-bone	lb	4.85	4Q 92	4c
Strawberries, dry pint	12 oz	0.90	4/93	16r
Sugar, cane or beet	4 lb	1.46	4Q 92	4c
Sugar, white	lb	0.50	4/93	16r
Sugar, white, 33-80 oz pk	lb	0.41	4/93	16r
Tomatoes, field grown	lb	1.23	4/93	16r
Tomatoes, Hunt's or Del Monte	14.5-oz can	0.78	4Q 92	4c
Tuna, chunk, light	6.125-6.5 oz can	0.72	4Q 92	4c
Tuna, chunk, light	lb	2.22	4/93	16r
Turkey, frozen, whole	lb	1.04	4/93	16r
Health Care				
ACCRA Index, Health Care		107.90	4Q 92	4c
Analgesic, Aspirin, Bayer, 325 mg tablets	100	4.85	4Q 92	4c
Childbirth, cesarean, hospital		5826	91	62r
Childbirth, cesarean, physician's fee		2053	91	62r
Childbirth, normal, hospital		2964	91	62r
Childbirth, normal, physician's fee		1492	91	62r
Dentist's fee, adult teeth cleaning and periodic oral exam	visit	45.80	4Q 92	4c
Doctor's fee, routine exam, established patient	visit	44.60	4Q 92	4c
Hospital care, semiprivate room	day	213.77	90	27c
Hospital care, semiprivate room	day	347.50	4Q 92	4c
Medical plan per employee	year	3942	91	45r
Mental health care, exp	capita	53.68-118.35	90	38s
Mental health care, exp, state mental health agency	capita	118.34	90	38s
Mental health care, hospital psychiatric services, non-Federal, exp	capita	29.77	88	38s
Mental health care, mental health organization, multiservice, exp	capita	20.03	88	38s
Mental health care, psychiatric hospitals, private, exp	capita	8.37	88	38s
Mental health care, psychiatric out-patient clinics, freestanding, exp	capita	7.96	88	38s
Mental health care, psychiatric partial-care organizations, freestanding, exp	capita	1.24	88	38s
Mental health care, state and county mental hospitals, exp	capita	89.52	88	38s
Mental health care, VA medical centers, exp	capita	7.12	88	38s
Prescription drug co-pay, Medicaid	month	23.00	91	21s
Substance abuse, hospital ancillary charge	incident	1040	90	70s
Substance abuse, hospital physician charge	incident	360	90	70s
Substance abuse, hospital room and board	incident	6330	90	70s
Household Goods				
Appliance repair, home, service call, washing machine	min labor charge	27.09	4Q 92	4c
Laundry detergent, Tide Ultra, Bold, or Cheer	42 oz	4.21	4Q 92	4c
Tissues, facial, Kleenex brand	175-count box	1.11	4Q 92	4c
Housing				
ACCRA Index, Housing		92.60	4Q 92	4c
Home, median price	unit	80.40		26c
House, 1,800 sq ft, 8,000 sq ft lot, new, urban	total	100500	4Q 92	4c
House payment, principal and interest, 25% down payment	month	561	4Q 92	4c
Mortgage rate, incl. points & origination fee, 30-year fixed or adjustable rate	percent	8.15	4Q 92	4c
Rent, apartment, 2 bedrooms - 1-1/2 to 2 baths, unfurnished, 950 sq ft, water	month	477	4Q 92	4c

Syracuse, NY - continued

Item	Per	Value	Date	Ref.
Housing - continued				
Rental unit, 1 bedroom	month	436	93	23c
Rental unit, 2 bedroom	month	511	93	23c
Rental unit, 3 bedroom	month	639	93	23c
Rental unit, 4 bedroom	month	716	93	23c
Rental unit, efficiency	month	364	93	23c
Insurance and Pensions				
Auto insurance, private passenger	year	840.89	91	63s
Personal Goods				
Shampoo, Alberto VO5	15 oz	1.55	4Q 92	4c
Toothpaste, Crest or Colgate	6-7 oz	2.21	4Q 92	4c
Personal Services				
Dry cleaning, man's 2-piece suit		6.32	4Q 92	4c
Haircare, woman's shampoo, trim and blow-dry		15.00	4Q 92	4c
Haircut, man's barbershop, no styling		6.45	4Q 92	4c
Restaurant Food				
Chicken, fried, thigh and drumstick		2.39	4Q 92	4c
Hamburger with cheese	1/4 lb	1.89	4Q 92	4c
Pizza, Pizza Hut or Pizza Inn, cheese, thin crust	12-13 in	7.49	4Q 92	4c
Taxes				
Tax, cigarette	pack	39	91	77s
Tax, gasoline	gal	8	91	77s
Taxes, state	capita	1567	91	77s
Transportation				
ACCRA Index, Transportation		108.60	4Q 92	4c
Auto rental, average	day	48.25	6/91	60c
Bus fare	one-way	0.75	3/93	2c
Bus fare, up to 10 miles	one-way	0.75	4Q 92	4c
Driver's license fee		17.50	12/90	43s
Taxi fare, airport-city, average	day	10.50	6/91	60c
Tire balance, computer or spin balance, front	wheel	7.59	4Q 92	4c
Vehicle registration and license plate	2 years	27.50-149.50	93	67s
Travel				
Breakfast	day	6.12	6/91	60c
Business travel	day	165.00	4/93	89r
Dinner	day	18.69	6/91	60c
Lodging	day	94.50	91	60c
Lunch	day	9.65	6/91	60c
Utilities				
ACCRA Index, Utilities		135.70	4Q 92	4c
Electricity	mil Btu	27.51	90	64s
Electricity, partial electric and other energy, 1,800 sq ft living area new home	month	80.45	4Q 92	4c

Tacoma, WA

Item	Per	Value	Date	Ref.
Composite ACCRA index		104.80	4Q 92	4c
Alcoholic Beverages				
Beer, Miller Lite or Budweiser, 12-oz containers	6 pack	4.18	4Q 92	4c
Liquor, J & B Scotch	750 ml	17.95	4Q 92	4c
Wine, Gallo Chablis blanc, 1.5 liter	bottle	4.70	4Q 92	4c
Child Care				
Child care fee, average, center	hour	1.71	90	65r
Child care fee, average, nonregulated family day care	hour	1.32	90	65r
Child care fee, average, regulated family day care	hour	1.86	90	65r
Clothing				
Jeans, man's denim		33.79	4Q 92	4c
Shirt, man's dress shirt		25.60	4Q 92	4c

Values are in dollars or fractions of dollars. In the column headed *Ref*, references are shown to sources. Each reference is followed by a letter. These refer to the geographical level for which data were reported: s=State, r=Region, and c=City or metro. The abbreviation *ex* is used to mean *except* or *excluding*; *exp* stands for expenditures. For other abbreviations and further explanations, please see the Introduction.

Tacoma, WA - continued

Item	Per	Value	Date	Ref.
Clothing				
Undervest, boy's size 10-14, cotton	3	4.69	4Q 92	4c
Communications				
Long-distance telephone service, day, initial minute, 0-100 miles	min	0.15-0.37	91	12s
Long-distance telephone service, day, additional minute, 0-100 miles	min	0.01-0.03	91	12s
Long-distance telephone service, evenings/ weekends, 0-100 mi, initial minute	min	0.05-0.19	91	12s
Long-distance telephone service, evenings/ weekends, 0-100 mi, additional minute	min	0.00-0.01	91	12s
Newspaper subscription, daily and Sunday home delivery, large-city	month	10.00	4Q 92	4c
Telephone, flat rate	month	10.75	91	11c
Telephone bill, family of four	month	16.57	4Q 92	4c
Education				
Board, 4-yr private college/university	year	1811	91	22s
Board, 4-yr public college/university	year	1539	91	22s
Expenditures, local gov't, public elementary/secondary	pupil	5317	92	20s
Room, 4-year private college/university	year	1885	91	22s
Room, 4-year public college/university	year	1698	91	22s
Tuition, 2-year private college/university	year	6743	91	22s
Tuition, 2-year public college/university	year	844	91	22s
Tuition, 4-year private college/university	year	9463	91	22s
Tuition, 4-year public college/university, in-state	year	1823	91	22s
Energy and Fuels				
Energy	mil Btu	7.39	90	64s
Energy, combined forms, 1,800 sq ft heating area	month	65.25	4Q 92	4c
Energy exp/householder, 1-family unit	year	362	90	28r
Energy exp/householder, <1,000 sq ft heating area	year	254	90	28r
Energy exp/householder, 1,000-1,999 sq ft heating area	year	358	90	28r
Energy exp/householder, 2,000+ sq ft heating area	year	467	90	28r
Energy exp/householder, mobile home	year	390	90	28r
Energy exp/householder, multifamily	year	252	90	28r
Gas, natural	mil Btu	3.60	90	64s
Gas, natural	000 cu ft	4.68	91	46s
Gas, natural, exp	year	440	91	46s
Gasoline, motor	gal	1.17	4Q 92	4c
Gasoline, unleaded regular	mil Btu	9.45	90	64s
Entertainment				
Bowling, evening rate	game	1.93	4Q 92	4c
Miniature golf admission	adult	6.18	92	1r
Miniature golf admission	child	5.14	92	1r
Monopoly game, Parker Brothers', No. 9		11.41	4Q 92	4c
Movie	admission	6.35	4Q 92	4c
Tennis balls, yellow, Wilson or Penn, 3	can	2.27	4Q 92	4c
Waterpark admission	adult	11.00	92	1r
Waterpark admission	child	8.55	92	1r
Funerals				
Casket, 18-gauge steel, velvet interior		1781.09	91	24r
Cosmetology, hair care, etc.		84.64	91	24r
Embalming		207.41	91	24r
Facility use for ceremony		205.76	91	24r
Hearse, local		105.14	91	24r
Limousine, local		83.21	91	24r
Remains to funeral home, transfer		113.82	91	24r
Service charge, professional		626.33	91	24r
Vault, concrete, non-metallic liner		599.54	91	24r
Viewing facilities, use		85.81	91	24r
Goods and Services				
ACCRA Index, Miscellaneous Goods and Services		106.50	4Q 92	4c

Tacoma, WA - continued

Item	Per	Value	Date	Ref.
Groceries				
ACCRA Index, Groceries		112.90	4Q 92	4c
Apples, Red Delicious	lb	0.80	4/93	16r
Babyfood, strained vegetables, lowest price	4-4.5 oz jar	0.35	4Q 92	4c
Bacon	lb	1.79	4/93	16r
Bananas	lb	0.32	4Q 92	4c
Bananas	lb	0.53	4/93	16r
Bologna, all beef or mixed	lb	2.67	4/93	16r
Bread, white	24 oz	0.60	4Q 92	4c
Bread, white, pan	lb	0.81	4/93	16r
Carrots, short trimmed and topped	lb	0.39	4/93	16r
Cheese, Kraft grated Parmesan	8-oz canister	3.83	4Q 92	4c
Chicken, fresh, whole	lb	0.94	4/93	16r
Chicken, fryer, whole	lb	1.17	4Q 92	4c
Chicken breast, bone-in	lb	2.19	4/93	16r
Chuck roast, graded and ungraded, ex USDA prime and choice	lb	2.26	4/93	16r
Cigarettes, Winston	carton	19.63	4Q 92	4c
Coffee, 100% ground roast, all sizes	lb	2.33	4/93	16r
Coffee, vacuum-packed	13-oz can	2.51	4Q 92	4c
Corn, frozen	10 oz	0.72	4Q 92	4c
Corn Flakes, Kellogg's or Post Toasties	18 oz	2.32	4Q 92	4c
Eggs, Grade A large	doz	0.96	4Q 92	4c
Eggs, Grade AA large	doz	1.18	4/93	16r
Flour, white, all purpose	lb	0.22	4/93	16r
Grapefruit	lb	0.52	4/93	16r
Grapes, Thompson Seedless	lb	1.50	4/93	16r
Ground beef, 100% beef	lb	1.44	4/93	16r
Ground beef, lean and extra lean	lb	2.34	4/93	16r
Ground beef or hamburger	lb	1.53	4Q 92	4c
Ham, boneless, excluding canned	lb	2.56	4/93	16r
Honey, jar	8 oz	0.89-1.00	92	5r
Honey, jar	lb	1.35-1.97	92	5r
Honey, squeeze bear	12-oz	1.19-1.50	92	5r
Ice cream, prepackaged, bulk, regular	1/2 gal	2.40	4/93	16r
Lemons	lb	0.81	4/93	16r
Lettuce, iceberg	head	0.83	4Q 92	4c
Lettuce, iceberg	lb	0.84	4/93	16r
Margarine, Blue Bonnet or Parkay cubes	lb	0.80	4Q 92	4c
Margarine, stick	lb	0.81	4/93	16r
Milk, whole	1/2 gal	1.44	4Q 92	4c
Orange juice, Minute Maid frozen	12-oz can	1.56	4Q 92	4c
Oranges, navel	lb	0.48	4/93	16r
Peaches	29-oz can	1.57	4Q 92	4c
Peas Sweet, Del Monte or Green Giant	15-17 oz can	0.70	4Q 92	4c
Pork chops, center cut, bone-in	lb	3.25	4/93	16r
Potato chips	16 oz	2.89	4/93	16r
Potatoes, white	lb	0.38	4/93	16r
Potatoes, white or red	10-lb sack	1.65	4Q 92	4c
Round roast, graded & ungraded, ex USDA prime & choice	lb	3.00	4/93	16r
Round roast, USDA choice, boneless	lb	3.16	4/93	16r
Sausage, Jimmy Dean, 100% pork	lb	3.59	4Q 92	4c
Shortening, vegetable oil blends	lb	0.86	4/93	16r
Shortening, vegetable, Crisco	3-lb can	2.72	4Q 92	4c
Soft drink, Coca Cola	2 liter	1.27	4Q 92	4c
Spaghetti and macaroni	lb	0.84	4/93	16r
Steak, round, graded & ungraded, ex USDA prime & choice	lb	3.34	4/93	16r
Steak, round, USDA choice, boneless	lb	3.24	4/93	16r
Steak, sirloin, graded & ungraded, ex USDA prime & choice	lb	3.75	4/93	16r
Steak, sirloin, USDA choice, boneless	lb	4.49	4/93	16r
Steak, T-bone	lb	5.15	4Q 92	4c

Values are in dollars or fractions of dollars. In the column headed *Ref*, references are shown to sources. Each reference is followed by a letter. These refer to the geographical level for which data were reported: s=State, r=Region, and c=City or metro. The abbreviation *ex* is used to mean *except* or *excluding*; *exp* stands for expenditures. For other abbreviations and further explanations, please see the Introduction.

Tacoma, WA - continued

Item	Per	Value	Date	Ref.
Groceries				
Sugar, cane or beet	4 lb	1.48	4Q 92	4c
Sugar, white	lb	0.41	4/93	16r
Sugar, white, 33-80 oz pk	lb	0.38	4/93	16r
Tomatoes, field grown	lb	1.01	4/93	16r
Tomatoes, Hunt's or Del Monte	14.5-oz can	0.71	4Q 92	4c
Tuna, chunk, light	6.125-6.5 oz can	0.92	4Q 92	4c
Turkey, frozen, whole	lb	1.04	4/93	16r
Health Care				
ACCRA Index, Health Care		156.60	4Q 92	4c
Analgesic, Aspirin, Bayer, 325 mg tablets	100	5.44	4Q 92	4c
Childbirth, cesarean, hospital		5533	91	62r
Childbirth, cesarean, physician's fee		2053	91	62r
Childbirth, normal, hospital		2745	91	62r
Childbirth, normal, physician's fee		1492	91	62r
Dentist's fee, adult teeth cleaning and periodic oral exam	visit	89.00	4Q 92	4c
Doctor's fee, routine exam, established patient	visit	54.00	4Q 92	4c
Hospital care, semiprivate room	day	337.58	90	27c
Hospital care, semiprivate room	day	446.00	4Q 92	4c
Medical insurance premium, per employee, small group comprehensive	month	302.95	10/91	25c
Medical plan per employee	year	3421	91	45r
Mental health care, exp	capita	37.60-53.67	90	38s
Physician fee, family practice, first-visit		111.00	91	62r
Physician fee, family practice, revisit		45.00	91	62r
Physician fee, general practice, first-visit		100.00	91	62r
Physician fee, general practice, revisit		40.00	91	62r
Physician fee, internal medicine, first-visit		137.00	91	62r
Physician fee, internal medicine, revisit		48.00	91	62r
Physician fee, median, neurosurgeon, first-visit		157.00	91	62r
Physician fee, median, nonsurgical specialist, first-visit		131.00	91	62r
Physician fee, median, orthopedic surgeon, first-visit		124.00	91	62r
Physician fee, median, plastic surgeon, first-visit		88.00	91	62r
Physician fee, median, surgical specialist, first-visit		100.00	91	62r
Physician fee, neurosurgeon, revisit		51.00	91	62r
Physician fee, nonsurgical specialist, revisit		47.00	91	62r
Physician fee, obstetrics/gynecology, first-visit		95.00	91	62r
Physician fee, obstetrics/gynecology, revisit		50.00	91	62r
Physician fee, orthopedic surgeon, revisit		51.00	91	62r
Physician fee, pediatrician, first-visit		81.00	91	62r
Physician fee, pediatrician, revisit		42.00	91	62r
Physician fee, plastic surgeon, revisit		48.00	91	62r
Physician fee, surgical specialist, revisit		49.00	91	62r
Substance abuse, hospital ancillary charge	incident	1360	90	70s
Substance abuse, hospital physician charge	incident	150	90	70s
Substance abuse, hospital room and board	incident	4200	90	70s
Household Goods				
Appliance repair, home, service call, washing machine	min labor charge	32.76	4Q 92	4c
Laundry detergent, Tide Ultra, Bold, or Cheer	42 oz	4.25	4Q 92	4c
Tissues, facial, Kleenex brand	175-count box	1.65	4Q 92	4c

Tacoma, WA - continued

Item	Per	Value	Date	Ref.
Housing				
ACCRA Index, Housing		102.30	4Q 92	4c
Home, median price	unit	107.80		26c
House, 1,800 sq ft, 8,000 sq ft lot, new, urban	total	112500	4Q 92	4c
House payment, principal and interest, 25% down payment	month	624	4Q 92	4c
Mortgage rate, incl. points & origination fee, 30-year fixed or adjustable rate	percent	8.09	4Q 92	4c
Rent, apartment, 2 bedrooms - 1-1/2 to 2 baths, unfurnished, 950 sq ft, water	month	515	4Q 92	4c
Rental unit, 1 bedroom	month	453	93	23c
Rental unit, 2 bedroom	month	525	93	23c
Rental unit, 3 bedroom	month	713	93	23c
Rental unit, 4 bedroom	month	793	93	23c
Rental unit, efficiency	month	373	93	23c
Insurance and Pensions				
Auto insurance, private passenger	year	627.71	91	63s
Personal Goods				
Shampoo, Alberto VO5	15 oz	1.52	4Q 92	4c
Toothpaste, Crest or Colgate	6-7 oz	2.35	4Q 92	4c
Personal Services				
Dry cleaning, man's 2-piece suit		7.20	4Q 92	4c
Haircare, woman's shampoo, trim and blow-dry		18.40	4Q 92	4c
Haircut, man's barbershop, no styling		7.15	4Q 92	4c
Restaurant Food				
Chicken, fried, thigh and drumstick		2.19	4Q 92	4c
Hamburger with cheese	1/4 lb	1.87	4Q 92	4c
Pizza, Pizza Hut or Pizza Inn, cheese, thin crust	12-13 in	9.76	4Q 92	4c
Taxes				
Tax, cigarette	pack	34	91	77s
Tax, gasoline	gal	23	91	77s
Taxes, state	capita	1592	91	77s
Transportation				
ACCRA Index, Transportation		107.40	4Q 92	4c
Auto rental, average	day	43.63	6/91	60c
Bus fare	one-way	0.75	3/93	2c
Driver's license fee		14.00	12/90	43s
Taxi fare, airport-city, average	day	36.00	6/91	60c
Tire balance, computer or spin balance, front	wheel	7.26	4Q 92	4c
Travel				
Business travel	day	178.00	4/93	89r
Lodging	day	59.20	91	60c
Utilities				
ACCRA Index, Utilities		62.30	4Q 92	4c
Electricity	mil Btu	10.03	90	64s
Electricity, all electric, 1,800 sq ft living area new home	month	65.25	4Q 92	4c

Tallahassee, FL

Item	Per	Value	Date	Ref.
Composite ACCRA index		99.00	4Q 92	4c
Alcoholic Beverages				
Beer, Miller Lite or Budweiser, 12-oz containers	6 pack	3.57	4Q 92	4c
Liquor, J & B Scotch	750 ml	15.69	4Q 92	4c
Wine, Gallo Chablis blanc, 1.5 liter	bottle	4.79	4Q 92	4c
Child Care				
Child care fee, average, center	hour	1.29	90	65r
Child care fee, average, nonregulated family day care	hour	0.89	90	65r
Child care fee, average, regulated family day care	hour	1.32	90	65r

Values are in dollars or fractions of dollars. In the column headed *Ref*, references are shown to sources. Each reference is followed by a letter. These refer to the geographical level for which data were reported: s=State, r=Region, and c=City or metro. The abbreviation *ex* is used to mean *except* or *excluding*; *exp* stands for expenditures. For other abbreviations and further explanations, please see the Introduction.

Tallahassee, FL - continued

Item	Per	Value	Date	Ref.
Clothing				
Jeans, man's denim		31.79	4Q 92	4c
Shirt, man's dress shirt		21.99	4Q 92	4c
Undervest, boy's size 10-14, cotton	3	6.29	4Q 92	4c
Communications				
Long-distance telephone service, day, initial minute, 0-100 miles	min	0.15-0.20	91	12s
Long-distance telephone service, day, additional minute, 0-100 miles	min	0.08-0.20	91	12s
Long-distance telephone service, evenings/ weekends, 0-100 mi, initial minute	min	0.09-0.12	91	12s
Long-distance telephone service, evenings/ weekends, 0-100 mi, additional minute	min	0.05-0.12	91	12s
Newspaper subscription, daily and Sunday home delivery, large-city	month	12.86	4Q 92	4c
Telephone bill, family of four	month	16.28	4Q 92	4c
Education				
Board, 4-yr private college/university	year	1924	91	22s
Board, 4-yr public college/university	year	1955	91	22s
Expenditures, local gov't, public elementary/secondary	pupil	5235	92	20s
Room, 4-year private college/university	year	1904	91	22s
Room, 4-year public college/university	year	1510	91	22s
Tuition, 2-year private college/university	year	4751	91	22s
Tuition, 2-year public college/university	year	788	91	22s
Tuition, 4-year private college/university	year	7992	91	22s
Tuition, 4-year public college/university, in-state	year	1337	91	22s
Energy and Fuels				
Coal	mil Btu	1.85	90	64s
Energy	mil Btu	10.58	90	64s
Energy, combined forms, 1,800 sq ft heating area	month	117.33	4Q 92	4c
Energy exp/householder, 1-family unit	year	487	90	28r
Energy exp/householder, <1,000 sq ft heating area	year	393	90	28r
Energy exp/householder, 1,000-1,999 sq ft heating area	year	442	90	28r
Energy exp/householder, 2,000+ sq ft heating area	year	577	90	28r
Energy exp/householder, mobile home	year	366	90	28r
Energy exp/householder, multifamily	year	382	90	28r
Gas, natural	mil Btu	3.21	90	64s
Gas, natural	000 cu ft	8.98	91	46s
Gas, natural, exp	year	248	91	46s
Gasoline, motor	gal	1.16	4Q 92	4c
Gasoline, unleaded regular	mil Btu	8.85	90	64s
Entertainment				
Bowling, evening rate	game	2.04	4Q 92	4c
Miniature golf admission	adult	6.18	92	1r
Miniature golf admission	child	5.14	92	1r
Monopoly game, Parker Brothers', No. 9		10.33	4Q 92	4c
Movie	admission	5.25	4Q 92	4c
Tennis balls, yellow, Wilson or Penn, 3	can	1.98	4Q 92	4c
Waterpark admission	adult	11.00	92	1r
Waterpark admission	child	8.55	92	1r
Funerals				
Casket, 18-gauge steel, velvet interior		2029.08	91	24r
Cosmetology, hair care, etc.		75.10	91	24r
Embalming		249.24	91	24r
Facility use for ceremony		162.27	91	24r
Hearse, local		114.04	91	24r
Limousine, local		88.57	91	24r
Remains to funeral home, transfer		92 61	91	24r
Service charge, professional		682.42	91	24r
Vault, concrete, non-metallic liner		798.70	91	24r
Viewing facilities, use		163.86	91	24r

Tallahassee, FL - continued

Item	Per	Value	Date	Ref.
Goods and Services				
ACCRA Index, Miscellaneous Goods and Services		99.80	4Q 92	4c
Groceries				
ACCRA Index, Groceries		98.30	4Q 92	4c
Apples, Red Delicious	lb	0.79	4/93	16r
Babyfood, strained vegetables, lowest price	4-4.5 oz jar	0.32	4Q 92	4c
Bacon	lb	1.75	4/93	16r
Bananas	lb	0.32	4Q 92	4c
Bananas	lb	0.42	4/93	16r
Beef, stew, boneless	lb	2.61	4/93	16r
Bologna, all beef or mixed	lb	2.24	4/93	16r
Bread, white	24 oz	0.83	4Q 92	4c
Bread, white, pan	lb	0.64	4/93	16r
Bread, whole wheat, pan	lb	0.96	4/93	16r
Cabbage	lb	0.37	4/93	16r
Carrots, short trimmed and topped	lb	0.47	4/93	16r
Celery	lb	0.64	4/93	16r
Cheese, American	lb	2.98	4/93	16r
Cheese, Cheddar	lb	3.28	4/93	16r
Cheese, Kraft grated Parmesan	8-oz canister	3.23	4Q 92	4c
Chicken, fresh, whole	lb	0.77	4/93	16r
Chicken, fryer, whole	lb	0.83	4Q 92	4c
Chicken breast, bone-in	lb	1.92	4/93	16r
Chicken legs, bone-in	lb	1.06	4/93	16r
Chuck roast, graded and ungraded, ex USDA prime and choice	lb	2.40	4/93	16r
Chuck roast, USDA choice, bone-in	lb	2.19	4/93	16r
Chuck roast, USDA choice, boneless	lb	2.38	4/93	16r
Cigarettes, Winston	carton	18.31	4Q 92	4c
Coffee, 100% ground roast, all sizes	lb	2.48	4/93	16r
Coffee, vacuum-packed	13-oz can	1.69	4Q 92	4c
Corn, frozen	10 oz	0.59	4Q 92	4c
Corn Flakes, Kellogg's or Post Toasties	18 oz	1.70	4Q 92	4c
Crackers, soda, salted	lb	1.15	4/93	16r
Eggs, Grade A large	doz	0.83	4Q 92	4c
Eggs, Grade A large	doz	0.96	4/93	16r
Flour, white, all purpose	lb	0.24	4/93	16r
Frankfurters, all meat or all beef	lb	2.01	4/93	16r
Grapefruit	lb	0.44	4/93	16r
Grapes, Thompson Seedless	lb	1.40	4/93	16r
Ground beef, 100% beef	lb	1.58	4/93	16r
Ground beef, lean and extra lean	lb	2.09	4/93	16r
Ground beef or hamburger	lb	1.73	4Q 92	4c
Ground chuck, 100% beef	lb	1.98	4/93	16r
Ham, boneless, excluding canned	lb	2.89	4/93	16r
Ham, picnic, shoulder, bone-in, smoked	lb	1.02	4/93	16r
Ham, rump or steak half, bone-in, smoked	lb	1.48	4/93	16r
Ice cream, prepackaged, bulk, regular	1/2 gal	2.41	4/93	16r
Lemons	lb	1.05	4/93	16r
Lettuce, iceberg	head	1.12	4Q 92	4c
Lettuce, iceberg	lb	0.81	4/93	16r
Margarine, Blue Bonnet or Parkay cubes	lb	0.49	4Q 92	4c
Margarine, stick	lb	0.88	4/93	16r
Milk, whole	1/2 gal	1.41	4Q 92	4c
Orange juice, Minute Maid frozen	12-oz can	1.22	4Q 92	4c
Oranges, navel	lb	0.55	4/93	16r
Peaches	29-oz can	1.25	4Q 92	4c
Pears, Anjou	lb	0.92	4/93	16r
Peas Sweet, Del Monte or Green Giant	15-17 oz can	0.50	4Q 92	4c
Pork chops, center cut, bone-in	lb	3.13	4/93	16r
Potato chips	16 oz	2.94	4/93	16r
Potatoes, white	lb	0.43	4/93	16r
Potatoes, white or red	10-lb sack	1.85	4Q 92	4c
Rib roast, USDA choice, bone-in	lb	4.63	4/93	16r

Values are in dollars or fractions of dollars. In the column headed *Ref*, references are shown to sources. Each reference is followed by a letter. These refer to the geographical level for which data were reported: s=State, r=Region, and c=City or metro. The abbreviation *ex* is used to mean *except* or *excluding*; *exp* stands for expenditures. For other abbreviations and further explanations, please see the Introduction.

Tallahassee, FL - continued

Item	Per	Value	Date	Ref.
Groceries				
Rice, white, long grain, uncooked	lb	0.45	4/93	16r
Round roast, graded & ungraded, ex USDA prime & choice	lb	3.03	4/93	16r
Round roast, USDA choice, boneless	lb	3.09	4/93	16r
Sausage, fresh, loose	lb	2.08	4/93	16r
Sausage, Jimmy Dean, 100% pork	lb	2.21	4Q 92	4c
Short ribs, bone-in	lb	2.66	4/93	16r
Shortening, vegetable oil blends	lb	0.69	4/93	16r
Shortening, vegetable, Crisco	3-lb can	2.11	4Q 92	4c
Soft drink, Coca Cola	2 liter	1.07	4Q 92	4c
Spaghetti and macaroni	lb	0.81	4/93	16r
Steak, rib eye, USDA choice, boneless	lb	6.24	4/93	16r
Steak, round, graded & ungraded, ex USDA prime & choice	lb	3.31	4/93	16r
Steak, round, USDA choice, boneless	lb	3.34	4/93	16r
Steak, sirloin, graded & ungraded, ex USDA prime & choice	lb	4.19	4/93	16r
Steak, sirloin, USDA choice, boneless	lb	4.46	4/93	16r
Steak, T-bone	lb	5.81	4Q 92	4c
Steak, T-bone, USDA choice, bone-in	lb	5.25	4/93	16r
Strawberries, dry pint	12 oz	0.92	4/93	16r
Sugar, cane or beet	4 lb	1.44	4Q 92	4c
Sugar, white	lb	0.39	4/93	16r
Sugar, white, 33-80 oz pk	lb	0.38	4/93	16r
Tomatoes, field grown	lb	0.88	4/93	16r
Tomatoes, Hunt's or Del Monte	14.5-oz can	0.55	4Q 92	4c
Tuna, chunk, light	6.125-6.5 oz can	0.55	4Q 92	4c
Tuna, chunk, light	lb	1.79	4/93	16r
Turkey, frozen, whole	lb	1.04	4/93	16r
Yogurt, natural, fruit flavored	1/2 pint	0.57	4/93	16r
Health Care				
ACCRA Index, Health Care		96.20	4Q 92	4c
Analgesic, Aspirin, Bayer, 325 mg tablets	100	3.92	4Q 92	4c
Childbirth, cesarean, hospital		5034	91	62r
Childbirth, cesarean, physician's fee		2053	91	62r
Childbirth, normal, hospital		2712	91	62r
Childbirth, normal, physician's fee		1492	91	62r
Dentist's fee, adult teeth cleaning and periodic oral exam	visit	39.40	4Q 92	4c
Doctor's fee, routine exam, established patient	visit	40.00	4Q 92	4c
Hospital care, semiprivate room	day	205.82	90	27c
Hospital care, semiprivate room	day	341.00	4Q 92	4c
Medical insurance premium, per employee, small group comprehensive	month	343.10	10/91	25c
Medical plan per employee	year	3495	91	45r
Mental health care, exp	capita	28.84-37.59	90	38s
Mental health care, exp, state mental health agency	capita	37.49	90	38s
Mental health care, hospital psychiatric services, non-Federal, exp	capita	9.11	88	38s
Mental health care, mental health organization, multiservice, exp	capita	16.21	88	38s
Mental health care, psychiatric hospitals, private, exp	capita	22.26	88	38s
Mental health care, psychiatric out-patient clinics, freestanding, exp	capita	0.89	88	38s
Mental health care, psychiatric partial-care organizations, freestanding, exp	capita	0.41	88	38s
Mental health care, state and county mental hospitals, exp	capita	16.25	88	38s
Mental health care, VA medical centers, exp	capita	1.69	88	38s
Physician fee, family practice, first-visit		75.00	91	62r
Physician fee, family practice, revisit		34.00	91	62r
Physician fee, general practice, first-visit		61.00	91	62r
Physician fee, general practice, revisit		32.00	91	62r

Tallahassee, FL - continued

Item	Per	Value	Date	Ref.
Health Care - continued				
Physician fee, general surgeon, first-visit		64.00	91	62r
Physician fee, general surgeon, revisit		40.00	91	62r
Physician fee, internal medicine, first-visit		98.00	91	62r
Physician fee, internal medicine, revisit		40.00	91	62r
Physician fee, median, neurosurgeon, first-visit		130.00	91	62r
Physician fee, median, nonsurgical specialist, first-visit		95.00	91	62r
Physician fee, median, orthopedic surgeon, first-visit		91.00	91	62r
Physician fee, median, plastic surgeon, first-visit		66.00	91	62r
Physician fee, median, surgical specialist, first-visit		62.00	91	62r
Physician fee, neurosurgeon, revisit		50.00	91	62r
Physician fee, nonsurgical specialist, revisit		40.00	91	62r
Physician fee, obstetrics/gynecology, first-visit		64.00	91	62r
Physician fee, obstetrics/gynecology, revisit		41.00	91	62r
Physician fee, orthopedic surgeon, revisit		40.00	91	62r
Physician fee, pediatrician, first-visit		49.00	91	62r
Physician fee, pediatrician, revisit		33.00	91	62r
Physician fee, plastic surgeon, revisit		43.00	91	62r
Physician fee, surgical specialist, revisit		37.00	91	62r
Substance abuse, hospital ancillary charge	incident	1390	90	70s
Substance abuse, hospital physician charge	incident	770	90	70s
Substance abuse, hospital room and board	incident	5600	90	70s
Household Goods				
Appliance repair, home, service call, washing machine	min labor charge	34.49	4Q 92	4c
Laundry detergent, Tide Ultra, Bold, or Cheer	42 oz	2.86	4Q 92	4c
Tissues, facial, Kleenex brand	175-count box	1.07	4Q 92	4c
Housing				
ACCRA Index, Housing		98.10	4Q 92	4c
House, 1,800 sq ft, 8,000 sq ft lot, new, urban	total	112975	4Q 92	4c
House payment, principal and interest, 25% down payment	month	625	4Q 92	4c
Mortgage rate, incl. points & origination fee, 30-year fixed or adjustable rate	percent	8.06	4Q 92	4c
Rent, apartment, 2 bedrooms - 1-1/2 to 2 baths, unfurnished, 950 sq ft, water	month	432	4Q 92	4c
Rental unit, 1 bedroom	month	396	93	23c
Rental unit, 2 bedroom	month	467	93	23c
Rental unit, 3 bedroom	month	585	93	23c
Rental unit, 4 bedroom	month	654	93	23c
Rental unit, efficiency	month	327	93	23c
Insurance and Pensions				
Auto insurance, private passenger	year	727.60	91	63s
Personal Goods				
Shampoo, Alberto VO5	15 oz	0.92	4Q 92	4c
Toothpaste, Crest or Colgate	6-7 oz	1.57	4Q 92	4c
Personal Services				
Dry cleaning, man's 2-piece suit		6.16	4Q 92	4c
Haircare, woman's shampoo, trim and blow-dry		18.18	4Q 92	4c
Haircut, man's barbershop, no styling		7.70	4Q 92	4c
Restaurant Food				
Chicken, fried, thigh and drumstick		0.99	4Q 92	4c
Hamburger with cheese	1/4 lb	1.89	4Q 92	4c
Pizza, Pizza Hut or Pizza Inn, cheese, thin crust	12-13 in	7.49	4Q 92	4c

Values are in dollars or fractions of dollars. In the column headed *Ref*, references are shown to sources. Each reference is followed by a letter. These refer to the geographical level for which data were reported: s=State, r=Region, and c=City or metro. The abbreviation *ex* is used to mean *except* or *excluding*; *exp* stands for expenditures. For other abbreviations and further explanations, please see the Introduction.

Tallahassee, FL - continued

Item	Per	Value	Date	Ref.
Taxes				
Tax, cigarette	pack	33.90	91	77s
Tax, gasoline	gal	11.60	91	77s
Taxes, state	capita	1037	91	77s
Transportation				
ACCRA Index, Transportation		96.00	4Q 92	4c
Bus fare	one-way	0.75	3/93	2c
Bus fare, up to 10 miles	one-way	0.75	4Q 92	4c
Driver's license fee		15.00	12/90	43s
Tire balance, computer or spin balance, front	wheel	5.98	4Q 92	4c
Travel				
Business travel	day	193.00	4/93	89r
Utilities				
ACCRA Index, Utilities		105.10	4Q 92	4c
Electricity	mil Btu	20.62	90	64s
Electricity, all electric, 1,800 sq ft living area new home	month	117.33	4Q 92	4c

Tampa, FL

Item	Per	Value	Date	Ref.
Composite ACCRA index		97.00	4Q 92	4c
Alcoholic Beverages				
Beer, Miller Lite or Budweiser, 12-oz containers	6 pack	3.79	4Q 92	4c
Liquor, J & B Scotch	750 ml	16.93	4Q 92	4c
Wine, Gallo Chablis blanc, 1.5 liter	bottle	4.94	4Q 92	4c
Child Care				
Child care, on-site	year	2964	93	17c
Child care fee, average, center	hour	1.29	90	65r
Child care fee, average, nonregulated family day care	hour	0.89	90	65r
Child care fee, average, regulated family day care	hour	1.32	90	65r
Clothing				
Jeans, man's denim		31.39	4Q 92	4c
Shirt, man's dress shirt		19.13	4Q 92	4c
Undervest, boy's size 10-14, cotton	3	4.47	4Q 92	4c
Communications				
Long-distance telephone service, day, initial minute, 0-100 miles	min	0.15-0.20	91	12s
Long-distance telephone service, day, additional minute, 0-100 miles	min	0.08-0.20	91	12s
Long-distance telephone service, evenings/weekends, 0-100 mi, initial minute	min	0.09-0.12	91	12s
Long-distance telephone service, evenings/weekends, 0-100 mi, additional minute	min	0.05-0.12	91	12s
Newspaper subscription, daily and Sunday home delivery, large-city	month	9.75	4Q 92	4c
Telephone, residential, private line, rotary, unlimited calling	month	17.35	10/91	78c
Telephone bill, family of four	month	20.39	4Q 92	4c
Education				
Board, 4-yr private college/university	year	1924	91	22s
Board, 4-yr public college/university	year	1955	91	22s
Expenditures, local gov't, public elementary/secondary	pupil	5235	92	20s
Room, 4-year private college/university	year	1904	91	22s
Room, 4-year public college/university	year	1510	91	22s
Tuition, 2-year private college/university	year	4751	91	22s
Tuition, 2-year public college/university	year	788	91	22s
Tuition, 4-year private college/university	year	7992	91	22s
Tuition, 4-year public college/university, in-state	year	1337	91	22s

Tampa, FL - continued

Item	Per	Value	Date	Ref.
Energy and Fuels				
Coal	mil Btu	1.85	90	64s
Energy	mil Btu	10.58	90	64s
Energy, combined forms, 1,800 sq ft heating area	month	107.73	4Q 92	4c
Energy exp/householder, 1-family unit	year	487	90	28r
Energy exp/householder, <1,000 sq ft heating area	year	393	90	28r
Energy exp/householder, 1,000-1,999 sq ft heating area	year	442	90	28r
Energy exp/householder, 2,000+ sq ft heating area	year	577	90	28r
Energy exp/householder, mobile home	year	366	90	28r
Energy exp/householder, multifamily	year	382	90	28r
Gas, cooking, 10 therms	month	12.65	92	56c
Gas, cooking, 30 therms	month	23.95	92	56c
Gas, cooking, 50 therms	month	35.25	92	56c
Gas, heating, winter, 100 therms	month	63.49	92	56c
Gas, heating, winter, average use	month	27.90	92	56c
Gas, natural	mil Btu	3.21	90	64s
Gas, natural	000 cu ft	8.98	91	46s
Gas, natural, exp	year	248	91	46s
Gasoline, motor	gal	1.12	4Q 92	4c
Gasoline, unleaded premium	gal	63.85	12/92	31c
Gasoline, unleaded regular	mil Btu	8.85	90	64s
Entertainment				
Bowling, evening rate	game	2.24	4Q 92	4c
Miniature golf admission	adult	6.18	92	1r
Miniature golf admission	child	5.14	92	1r
Monopoly game, Parker Brothers', No. 9		12.11	4Q 92	4c
Movie	admission	5.67	4Q 92	4c
Tennis balls, yellow, Wilson or Penn, 3	can	2.54	4Q 92	4c
Waterpark admission	adult	11.00	92	1r
Waterpark admission	child	8.55	92	1r
Funerals				
Casket, 18-gauge steel, velvet interior		2029.08	91	24r
Cosmetology, hair care, etc.		75.10	91	24r
Embalming		249.24	91	24r
Facility use for ceremony		162.27	91	24r
Hearse, local		114.04	91	24r
Limousine, local		88.57	91	24r
Remains to funeral home, transfer		92.61	91	24r
Service charge, professional		682.42	91	24r
Vault, concrete, non-metallic liner		798.70	91	24r
Viewing facilities, use		163.86	91	24r
Goods and Services				
ACCRA Index, Miscellaneous Goods and Services		95.80	4Q 92	4c
Groceries				
ACCRA Index, Groceries		97.90	4Q 92	4c
Apples, Red Delicious	lb	0.79	4/93	16r
Babyfood, strained vegetables, lowest price	4-4.5 oz jar	0.33	4Q 92	4c
Bacon	lb	1.75	4/93	16r
Bananas	lb	0.34	4Q 92	4c
Bananas	lb	0.42	4/93	16r
Beef, stew, boneless	lb	2.61	4/93	16r
Bologna, all beef or mixed	lb	2.24	4/93	16r
Bread, white	24 oz	0.76	4Q 92	4c
Bread, white, pan	lb	0.64	4/93	16r
Bread, whole wheat, pan	lb	0.96	4/93	16r
Cabbage	lb	0.37	4/93	16r
Carrots, short trimmed and topped	lb	0.47	4/93	16r
Celery	lb	0.64	4/93	16r
Cheese, American	lb	2.98	4/93	16r
Cheese, Cheddar	lb	3.28	4/93	16r
Cheese, Kraft grated Parmesan	8-oz canister	3.12	4Q 92	4c

Values are in dollars or fractions of dollars. In the column headed *Ref*, references are shown to sources. Each reference is followed by a letter. These refer to the geographical level for which data were reported: s = State, r = Region, and c = City or metro. The abbreviation *ex* is used to mean *except* or *excluding*; *exp* stands for expenditures. For other abbreviations and further explanations, please see the Introduction.

Tampa, FL - continued

Item	Per	Value	Date	Ref.
Groceries				
Chicken, fresh, whole	lb	0.77	4/93	16r
Chicken, fryer, whole	lb	0.69	4Q 92	4c
Chicken breast, bone-in	lb	1.92	4/93	16r
Chicken legs, bone-in	lb	1.06	4/93	16r
Chuck roast, graded and ungraded, ex USDA prime and choice	lb	2.40	4/93	16r
Chuck roast, USDA choice, bone-in	lb	2.19	4/93	16r
Chuck roast, USDA choice, boneless	lb	2.38	4/93	16r
Cigarettes, Winston	carton	18.43	4Q 92	4c
Coffee, 100% ground roast, all sizes	lb	2.48	4/93	16r
Coffee, vacuum-packed	13-oz can	1.81	4Q 92	4c
Corn, frozen	10 oz	0.67	4Q 92	4c
Corn Flakes, Kellogg's or Post Toasties	18 oz	1.72	4Q 92	4c
Crackers, soda, salted	lb	1.15	4/93	16r
Eggs, Grade A large	doz	0.87	4Q 92	4c
Eggs, Grade A large	doz	0.96	4/93	16r
Flour, white, all purpose	lb	0.24	4/93	16r
Frankfurters, all meat or all beef	lb	2.01	4/93	16r
Grapefruit	lb	0.44	4/93	16r
Grapes, Thompson Seedless	lb	1.40	4/93	16r
Ground beef, 100% beef	lb	1.58	4/93	16r
Ground beef, lean and extra lean	lb	2.09	4/93	16r
Ground beef or hamburger	lb	1.60	4Q 92	4c
Ground chuck, 100% beef	lb	1.98	4/93	16r
Ham, boneless, excluding canned	lb	2.89	4/93	16r
Ham, picnic, shoulder, bone-in, smoked	lb	1.02	4/93	16r
Ham, rump or steak half, bone-in, smoked	lb	1.48	4/93	16r
Ice cream, prepackaged, bulk, regular	1/2 gal	2.41	4/93	16r
Lemons	lb	1.05	4/93	16r
Lettuce, iceberg	head	0.84	4Q 92	4c
Lettuce, iceberg	lb	0.81	4/93	16r
Margarine, Blue Bonnet or Parkay cubes	lb	0.51	4Q 92	4c
Margarine, stick	lb	0.88	4/93	16r
Milk, whole	1/2 gal	1.79	4Q 92	4c
Orange juice, Minute Maid frozen	12-oz can	1.23	4Q 92	4c
Oranges, navel	lb	0.55	4/93	16r
Peaches	29-oz can	1.32	4Q 92	4c
Pears, Anjou	lb	0.92	4/93	16r
Peas Sweet, Del Monte or Green Giant	15-17 oz can	0.49	4Q 92	4c
Pork chops, center cut, bone-in	lb	3.13	4/93	16r
Potato chips	16 oz	2.94	4/93	16r
Potatoes, white	lb	0.43	4/93	16r
Potatoes, white or red	10-lb sack	2.18	4Q 92	4c
Rib roast, USDA choice, bone-in	lb	4.63	4/93	16r
Rice, white, long grain, uncooked	lb	0.45	4/93	16r
Round roast, graded & ungraded, ex USDA prime & choice	lb	3.03	4/93	16r
Round roast, USDA choice, boneless	lb	3.09	4/93	16r
Sausage, fresh, loose	lb	2.08	4/93	16r
Sausage, Jimmy Dean, 100% pork	lb	2.65	4Q 92	4c
Short ribs, bone-in	lb	2.66	4/93	16r
Shortening, vegetable oil blends	lb	0.69	4/93	16r
Shortening, vegetable, Crisco	3-lb can	2.00	4Q 92	4c
Soft drink, Coca Cola	2 liter	1.15	4Q 92	4c
Spaghetti and macaroni	lb	0.81	4/93	16r
Steak, rib eye, USDA choice, boneless	lb	6.24	4/93	16r
Steak, round, graded & ungraded, ex USDA prime & choice	lb	3.31	4/93	16r
Steak, round, USDA choice, boneless	lb	3.34	4/93	16r
Steak, sirloin, graded & ungraded, ex USDA prime & choice	lb	4.19	4/93	16r
Steak, sirloin, USDA choice, boneless	lb	4.46	4/93	16r
Steak, T-bone	lb	4.10	4Q 92	4c
Steak, T-bone, USDA choice, bone-in	lb	5.25	4/93	16r
Strawberries, dry pint	12 oz	0.92	4/93	16r
Sugar, cane or beet	4 lb	1.63	4Q 92	4c

Tampa, FL - continued

Item	Per	Value	Date	Ref.
Groceries - continued				
Sugar, white	lb	0.39	4/93	16r
Sugar, white, 33-80 oz pk	lb	0.38	4/93	16r
Tomatoes, field grown	lb	0.88	4/93	16r
Tomatoes, Hunt's or Del Monte	14.5-oz can	0.62	4Q 92	4c
Tuna, chunk, light	6.125-6.5 oz can	0.54	4Q 92	4c
Tuna, chunk, light	lb	1.79	4/93	16r
Turkey, frozen, whole	lb	1.04	4/93	16r
Yogurt, natural, fruit flavored	1/2 pint	0.57	4/93	16r
Health Care				
ACCRA Index, Health Care		91.90	4Q 92	4c
Analgesic, Aspirin, Bayer, 325 mg tablets	100	4.44	4Q 92	4c
Childbirth, cesarean, hospital		5034	91	62r
Childbirth, cesarean, physician's fee		2053	91	62r
Childbirth, normal, hospital		2712	91	62r
Childbirth, normal, physician's fee		1492	91	62r
Dentist's fee, adult teeth cleaning and periodic oral exam	visit	41.40	4Q 92	4c
Doctor's fee, routine exam, established patient	visit	35.20	4Q 92	4c
Hospital care, semiprivate room	day	254.46	90	27c
Hospital care, semiprivate room	day	299.20	4Q 92	4c
Medical insurance premium, per employee, small group comprehensive	month	368.65	10/91	25c
Medical plan per employee	year	3495	91	45r
Mental health care, exp	capita	28.84-37.59	90	38s
Mental health care, exp, state mental health agency	capita	37.49	90	38s
Mental health care, hospital psychiatric services, non-Federal, exp	capita	9.11	88	38s
Mental health care, mental health organization, multiservice, exp	capita	16.21	88	38s
Mental health care, psychiatric hospitals, private, exp	capita	22.26	88	38s
Mental health care, psychiatric out-patient clinics, freestanding, exp	capita	0.89	88	38s
Mental health care, psychiatric partial-care organizations, freestanding, exp	capita	0.41	88	38s
Mental health care, state and county mental hospitals, exp	capita	16.25	88	38s
Mental health care, VA medical centers, exp	capita	1.69	88	38s
Physician fee, family practice, first-visit		75.00	91	62r
Physician fee, family practice, revisit		34.00	91	62r
Physician fee, general practice, first-visit		61.00	91	62r
Physician fee, general practice, revisit		32.00	91	62r
Physician fee, general surgeon, first-visit		64.00	91	62r
Physician fee, general surgeon, revisit		40.00	91	62r
Physician fee, internal medicine, first-visit		98.00	91	62r
Physician fee, internal medicine, revisit		40.00	91	62r
Physician fee, median, neurosurgeon, first-visit		130.00	91	62r
Physician fee, median, nonsurgical specialist, first-visit		95.00	91	62r
Physician fee, median, orthopedic surgeon, first-visit		91.00	91	62r
Physician fee, median, plastic surgeon, first-visit		66.00	91	62r
Physician fee, median, surgical specialist, first-visit		62.00	91	62r
Physician fee, neurosurgeon, revisit		50.00	91	62r
Physician fee, nonsurgical specialist, revisit		40.00	91	62r
Physician fee, obstetrics/gynecology, first-visit		64.00	91	62r
Physician fee, obstetrics/gynecology, revisit		41.00	91	62r
Physician fee, orthopedic surgeon, revisit		40.00	91	62r
Physician fee, pediatrician, first-visit		49.00	91	62r
Physician fee, pediatrician, revisit		33.00	91	62r
Physician fee, plastic surgeon, revisit		43.00	91	62r

Values are in dollars or fractions of dollars. In the column headed *Ref*, references are shown to sources. Each reference is followed by a letter. These refer to the geographical level for which data were reported: s=State, r=Region, and c=City or metro. The abbreviation *ex* is used to mean *except* or *excluding*; *exp* stands for expenditures. For other abbreviations and further explanations, please see the Introduction.

Tampa, FL - continued

Item	Per	Value	Date	Ref.
Health Care				
Physician fee, surgical specialist, revisit		37.00	91	62r
Substance abuse, hospital ancillary charge	incident	1390	90	70s
Substance abuse, hospital physician charge	incident	770	90	70s
Substance abuse, hospital room and board	incident	5600	90	70s
Household Goods				
Appliance repair, home, service call, washing machine	min labor charge	27.18	4Q 92	4c
Laundry detergent, Tide Ultra, Bold, or Cheer	42 oz	3.07	4Q 92	4c
Tissues, facial, Kleenex brand	175-count box	1.19	4Q 92	4c
Housing				
ACCRA Index, Housing		97.40	4Q 92	4c
Home, median price	unit	72.60		26c
House, 1,800 sq ft, 8,000 sq ft lot, new, urban	total	102840	4Q 92	4c
House payment, principal and interest, 25% down payment	month	578	4Q 92	4c
Mortgage rate, incl. points & origination fee, 30-year fixed or adjustable rate	percent	8.23	4Q 92	4c
Rent, apartment, 2 bedrooms - 1-1/2 to 2 baths, unfurnished, 950 sq ft, water	month	528	4Q 92	4c
Rental unit, 1 bedroom	month	453	93	23c
Rental unit, 2 bedroom	month	534	93	23c
Rental unit, 3 bedroom	month	665	93	23c
Rental unit, 4 bedroom	month	747	93	23c
Rental unit, efficiency	month	373	93	23c
Insurance and Pensions				
Auto insurance, private passenger	year	727.60	91	63s
Personal Goods				
Shampoo, Alberto VO5	15 oz	1.08	4Q 92	4c
Toothpaste, Crest or Colgate	6-7 oz	1.73	4Q 92	4c
Personal Services				
Dry cleaning, man's 2-piece suit		6.15	4Q 92	4c
Haircare, woman's shampoo, trim and blow-dry		16.60	4Q 92	4c
Haircut, man's barbershop, no styling		7.30	4Q 92	4c
Restaurant Food				
Chicken, fried, thigh and drumstick		1.99	4Q 92	4c
Hamburger with cheese	1/4 lb	1.29	4Q 92	4c
Pizza, Pizza Hut or Pizza Inn, cheese, thin crust	12-13 in	7.99	4Q 92	4c
Taxes				
Tax, cigarette	pack	33.90	91	77s
Tax, gasoline	gal	11.60	91	77s
Taxes, state	capita	1037	91	77s
Transportation				
ACCRA Index, Transportation		99.40	4Q 92	4c
Auto rental, average	day	37.50	6/91	60c
Bus fare	one-way	0.85	3/93	2c
Bus fare, up to 10 miles	one-way	0.85	4Q 92	4c
Driver's license fee		15.00	12/90	43s
Limo fare, airport-city, average	day	10.00	6/91	60c
Taxi fare, airport-city, average	day	14.00	6/91	60c
Tire balance, computer or spin balance, front	wheel	6.49	4Q 92	4c
Travel				
Breakfast	day	7.47	6/91	60c
Business travel	day	117.00	92	86c
Business travel	day	193.00	4/93	89r

Tampa, FL - continued

Item	Per	Value	Date	Ref.
Travel - continued				
Dinner	day	19.74	6/91	60c
Dinner	day	19.20	92	85c
Lodging	day	128.56	91	60c
Lodging	day	83.00	92	85c
Lunch	day	7.88	6/91	60c
Utilities				
ACCRA Index, Utilities		99.30	4Q 92	4c
Electricity	mil Btu	20.62	90	64s
Electricity, all electric, 1,800 sq ft living area new home	month	107.73	4Q 92	4c
Electricity, winter, 250 KWh	month	25.37	92	55c
Electricity, winter, 500 KWh	month	43.73	92	55c
Electricity, winter, 750 KWh	month	62.10	92	55c
Electricity, winter, 1000 KWh	month	80.45	92	55c

Terre Haute, IN

Item	Per	Value	Date	Ref.
Child Care				
Child care fee, average, center	hour	1.63	90	65r
Child care fee, average, nonregulated family day care	hour	1.83	90	65r
Child care fee, average, regulated family day care	hour	1.42	90	65r
Communications				
Long-distance telephone service, day, initial minute, 0-100 miles	min	0.18-0.45	91	12s
Long-distance telephone service, day, additional minute, 0-100 miles	min	0.10-0.30	91	12s
Long-distance telephone service, evenings/weekends, 0-100 mi, initial minute	min	0.08-0.19	91	12s
Long-distance telephone service, evenings/weekends, 0-100 mi, additional minute	min	0.04-0.13	91	12s
Education				
Board, 4-yr private college/university	year	1714	91	22s
Board, 4-yr public college/university	year	1829	91	22s
Expenditures, local gov't, public elementary/secondary	pupil	5545	92	20s
Room, 4-year private college/university	year	1512	91	22s
Room, 4-year public college/university	year	1435	91	22s
Tuition, 2-year private college/university	year	6756	91	22s
Tuition, 2-year public college/university	year	1423	91	22s
Tuition, 4-year private college/university	year	8451	91	22s
Tuition, 4-year public college/university, in-state	year	2067	91	22s
Energy and Fuels				
Coal	mil Btu	1.46	90	64s
Energy	mil Btu	6.77	90	64s
Energy exp/householder, 1-family unit	year	471	90	28r
Energy exp/householder, <1,000 sq ft heating area	year	430	90	28r
Energy exp/householder, 1,000-1,999 sq ft heating area	year	481	90	28r
Energy exp/householder, 2,000+ sq ft heating area	year	473	90	28r
Energy exp/householder, mobile home	year	430	90	28r
Energy exp/householder, multifamily	year	461	90	28r
Gas, natural	mil Btu	4.27	90	64s
Gas, natural	000 cu ft	5.46	91	46s
Gas, natural, exp	year	588	91	46s
Gasoline, unleaded regular	mil Btu	8.74	90	64s
Entertainment				
Miniature golf admission	adult	6.18	92	1r
Miniature golf admission	child	5.14	92	1r
Waterpark admission	adult	11.00	92	1r
Waterpark admission	child	8.55	92	1r

Values are in dollars or fractions of dollars. In the column headed *Ref*, references are shown to sources. Each reference is followed by a letter. These refer to the geographical level for which data were reported: s=State, r=Region, and c=City or metro. The abbreviation *ex* is used to mean *except* or *excluding*; *exp* stands for expenditures. For other abbreviations and further explanations, please see the Introduction.

Terre Haute, IN - continued

Item	Per	Value	Date	Ref.
Funerals				
Casket, 18-gauge steel, velvet interior		1926.72	91	24r
Cosmetology, hair care, etc.		97.64	91	24r
Embalming		249.14	91	24r
Facility use for ceremony		208.59	91	24r
Hearse, local		130.12	91	24r
Limousine, local		104.66	91	24r
Remains to funeral home, transfer		93.61	91	24r
Service charge, professional		724.62	91	24r
Vault, concrete, non-metallic liner		734.53	91	24r
Viewing facilities, use		236.06	91	24r
Groceries				
Apples, Red Delicious	lb	0.77	4/93	16r
Bacon	lb	1.85	4/93	16r
Bananas	lb	0.46	4/93	16r
Beef, stew, boneless	lb	2.53	4/93	16r
Bologna, all beef or mixed	lb	2.19	4/93	16r
Bread, white, pan	lb	0.78	4/93	16r
Butter	lb	1.50	4/93	16r
Cabbage	lb	0.40	4/93	16r
Carrots, short trimmed and topped	lb	0.45	4/93	16r
Cheese, Cheddar	lb	3.47	4/93	16r
Chicken, fresh, whole	lb	0.84	4/93	16r
Chicken breast, bone-in	lb	1.94	4/93	16r
Chicken legs, bone-in	lb	1.02	4/93	16r
Chuck roast, graded and ungraded, ex USDA prime and choice	lb	2.43	4/93	16r
Chuck roast, USDA choice, bone-in	lb	2.11	4/93	16r
Chuck roast, USDA choice, boneless	lb	2.44	4/93	16r
Coffee, 100% ground roast, all sizes	lb	2.47	4/93	16r
Cookies, chocolate chip	lb	2.73	4/93	16r
Eggs, Grade A large	doz	0.93	4/93	16r
Flour, white, all purpose	lb	0.21	4/93	16r
Grapefruit	lb	0.45	4/93	16r
Grapes, Thompson Seedless	lb	1.46	4/93	16r
Ground beef, 100% beef	lb	1.63	4/93	16r
Ground beef, lean and extra lean	lb	2.08	4/93	16r
Ground chuck, 100% beef	lb	1.94	4/93	16r
Ham, boneless, excluding canned	lb	2.21	4/93	16r
Honey, jar	8 oz	0.97-1.25	92	5r
Honey, jar	lb	1.25-2.25	92	5r
Honey, squeeze bear	12-oz	1.25-1.99	92	5r
Ice cream, prepackaged, bulk, regular	1/2 gal	2.41	4/93	16r
Lemons	lb	0.82	4/93	16r
Lettuce, iceberg	lb	0.83	4/93	16r
Margarine, stick	lb	0.77	4/93	16r
Oranges, navel	lb	0.50	4/93	16r
Peanut butter, creamy, all sizes	lb	1.82	4/93	16r
Pears, Anjou	lb	0.85	4/93	16r
Pork chops, center cut, bone-in	lb	3.17	4/93	16r
Potato chips	16 oz	2.68	4/93	16r
Potatoes, white	lb	0.26	4/93	16r
Round roast, graded & ungraded, ex USDA prime & choice	lb	2.88	4/93	16r
Round roast, USDA choice, boneless	lb	2.96	4/93	16r
Shortening, vegetable oil blends	lb	0.79	4/93	16r
Spaghetti and macaroni	lb	0.76	4/93	16r
Steak, rib eye, USDA choice, boneless	lb	6.29	4/93	16r
Steak, round, USDA choice, boneless	lb	3.24	4/93	16r
Steak, sirloin, graded & ungraded, ex USDA prime & choice	lb	4.00	4/93	16r
Steak, sirloin, USDA choice, bone-in	lb	3.57	4/93	16r
Steak, sirloin, USDA choice, boneless	lb	4.17	4/93	16r
Steak, T-bone, USDA choice, bone-in	lb	5.60	4/93	16r
Strawberries, dry pint	12 oz	0.90	4/93	16r
Sugar, white	lb	0.36	4/93	16r
Sugar, white, 33-80 oz pk	lb	0.35	4/93	16r
Tomatoes, field grown	lb	0.99	4/93	16r
Tuna, chunk, light	lb	1.76	4/93	16r
Turkey, frozen, whole	lb	0.91	4/93	16r

Terre Haute, IN - continued

Item	Per	Value	Date	Ref.
Health Care				
Childbirth, cesarean, hospital		4688	91	62r
Childbirth, cesarean, physician's fee		2053	91	62r
Childbirth, normal, hospital		2657	91	62r
Childbirth, normal, physician's fee		1492	91	62r
Medical plan per employee	year	3443	91	45r
Mental health care, exp	capita	37.60-53.67	90	38s
Mental health care, exp, state mental health agency	capita	47.05	90	38s
Mental health care, hospital psychiatric services, non-Federal, exp	capita	22.14	88	38s
Mental health care, mental health organization, multiservice, exp	capita	10.33	88	38s
Mental health care, psychiatric hospitals, private, exp	capita	20.10	88	38s
Mental health care, state and county mental hospitals, exp	capita	24.00	88	38s
Mental health care, VA medical centers, exp	capita	3.20	88	38s
Physician fee, family practice, first-visit		76.00	91	62r
Physician fee, family practice, revisit		33.00	91	62r
Physician fee, general practice, first-visit		61.00	91	62r
Physician fee, general practice, revisit		31.00	91	62r
Physician fee, general surgeon, first-visit		65.00	91	62r
Physician fee, general surgeon, revisit		35.00	91	62r
Physician fee, internal medicine, first-visit		91.00	91	62r
Physician fee, internal medicine, revisit		40.00	91	62r
Physician fee, median, neurosurgeon, first-visit		106.00	91	62r
Physician fee, median, nonsurgical specialist, first-visit		90.00	91	62r
Physician fee, median, orthopedic surgeon, first-visit		83.00	91	62r
Physician fee, median, surgical specialist, first-visit		61.00	91	62r
Physician fee, neurosurgeon, revisit		41.00	91	62r
Physician fee, nonsurgical specialist, revisit		40.00	91	62r
Physician fee, obstetrics/gynecology, first-visit		61.00	91	62r
Physician fee, obstetrics/gynecology, revisit		40.00	91	62r
Physician fee, orthopedic surgeon, revisit		41.00	91	62r
Physician fee, pediatrician, first-visit		46.00	91	62r
Physician fee, pediatrician, revisit		33.00	91	62r
Physician fee, surgical specialist, revisit		36.00	91	62r
Substance abuse, hospital ancillary charge	incident	1230	90	70s
Substance abuse, hospital physician charge	incident	410	90	70s
Substance abuse, hospital room and board	incident	5510	90	70s
Insurance and Pensions				
Auto insurance, private passenger	year	548.99	91	63s
Taxes				
Tax, cigarette	pack	15.50	91	77s
Tax, gasoline	gal	15	91	77s
Taxes, state	capita	1102	91	77s
Transportation				
Driver's license fee		6.00	12/90	43s
Utilities				
Electricity	mil Btu	15.75	90	64s

Texarkana, TX, AR

Item	Per	Value	Date	Ref.
Composite ACCRA index		92.70	4Q 92	4c
Alcoholic Beverages				
Beer, Miller Lite or Budweiser, 12-oz containers	6 pack	4.40	4Q 92	4c
Liquor, J & B Scotch	750 ml	17.29	4Q 92	4c
Wine, Gallo Chablis blanc, 1.5 liter	bottle	5.60	4Q 92	4c

Values are in dollars or fractions of dollars. In the column headed *Ref*, references are shown to sources. Each reference is followed by a letter. These refer to the geographical level for which data were reported: s=State, r=Region, and c=City or metro. The abbreviation *ex* is used to mean *except* or *excluding*; *exp* stands for expenditures. For other abbreviations and further explanations, please see the Introduction.

Texarkana, TX, AR - continued

Item	Per	Value	Date	Ref.
Child Care				
Child care fee, average, center	hour	1.29	90	65r
Child care fee, average, nonregulated family day care	hour	0.89	90	65r
Child care fee, average, regulated family day care	hour	1.32	90	65r
Clothing				
Jeans, man's denim		30.20	4Q 92	4c
Shirt, man's dress shirt		27.60	4Q 92	4c
Undervest, boy's size 10-14, cotton	3	3.72	4Q 92	4c
Communications				
Long-distance telephone service, day, initial minute, 0-100 miles	min	0.10-0.46	91	12s
Long-distance telephone service, day, additional minute, 0-100 miles	min	0.06-0.45	91	12s
Newspaper subscription, daily and Sunday home delivery, large-city	month	8.95	4Q 92	4c
Telephone bill, family of four	month	15.96	4Q 92	4c
Education				
Board, 4-yr private college/university	year	1883	91	22s
Board, 4-yr public college/university	year	1605	91	22s
Expenditures, local gov't, public elementary/secondary	pupil	4593	92	20s
Room, 4-year private college/university	year	1620	91	22s
Room, 4-year public college/university	year	1532	91	22s
Tuition, 2-year private college/university	year	4394	91	22s
Tuition, 2-year public college/university	year	495	91	22s
Tuition, 4-year private college/university	year	6497	91	22s
Tuition, 4-year public college/university, in-state	year	986	91	22s
Energy and Fuels				
Coal	mil Btu	1.44	90	64s
Energy	mil Btu	6.48	90	64s
Energy, combined forms, 1,800 sq ft heating area	month	107.11	4Q 92	4c
Energy, exc electricity, 1,800 sq ft heating area	month	31.29	4Q 92	4c
Energy exp/householder, 1-family unit	year	471	90	28r
Energy exp/householder, <1,000 sq ft heating area	year	384	90	28r
Energy exp/householder, 1,000-1,999 sq ft heating area	year	421	90	28r
Energy exp/householder, 2,000+ sq ft heating area	year	625	90	28r
Energy exp/householder, mobile home	year	271	90	28r
Energy exp/householder, multifamily	year	355	90	28r
Gas, natural	mil Btu	2.47	90	64s
Gas, natural	000 cu ft	5.71	91	46s
Gas, natural, exp	year	388	91	46s
Gasoline, motor	gal	1.12	4Q 92	4c
Gasoline, unleaded regular	mil Btu	9.16	90	64s
Entertainment				
Bowling, evening rate	game	1.92	4Q 92	4c
Miniature golf admission	adult	6.18	92	1r
Miniature golf admission	child	5.14	92	1r
Monopoly game, Parker Brothers', No. 9		10.96	4Q 92	4c
Movie	admission	5.00	4Q 92	4c
Tennis balls, yellow, Wilson or Penn, 3	can	2.33	4Q 92	4c
Waterpark admission	adult	11.00	92	1r
Waterpark admission	child	8.55	92	1r
Funerals				
Casket, 18-gauge steel, velvet interior		2274.41	91	24r
Cosmetology, hair care, etc.		74.62	91	24r
Embalming		229.94	91	24r
Facility use for ceremony		176.61	91	24r
Hearse, local		116.34	91	24r
Limousine, local		72.68	91	24r
Remains to funeral home, transfer		87.72	91	24r

Texarkana, TX, AR - continued

Item	Per	Value	Date	Ref.
Funerals - continued				
Service charge, professional		712.53	91	24r
Vault, concrete, non-metallic liner		750.55	91	24r
Viewing facilities, use		155.31	91	24r
Goods and Services				
ACCRA Index, Miscellaneous Goods and Services		99.20	4Q 92	4c
Groceries				
ACCRA Index, Groceries		94.90	4Q 92	4c
Apples, Red Delicious	lb	0.79	4/93	16r
Babyfood, strained vegetables, lowest price	4-4.5 oz jar	0.30	4Q 92	4c
Bacon	lb	1.75	4/93	16r
Bananas	lb	0.35	4Q 92	4c
Bananas	lb	0.42	4/93	16r
Beef, stew, boneless	lb	2.61	4/93	16r
Bologna, all beef or mixed	lb	2.24	4/93	16r
Bread, white	24 oz	0.55	4Q 92	4c
Bread, white, pan	lb	0.64	4/93	16r
Bread, whole wheat, pan	lb	0.96	4/93	16r
Cabbage	lb	0.37	4/93	16r
Carrots, short trimmed and topped	lb	0.47	4/93	16r
Celery	lb	0.64	4/93	16r
Cheese, American	lb	2.98	4/93	16r
Cheese, Cheddar	lb	3.28	4/93	16r
Cheese, Kraft grated Parmesan	8-oz canister	3.37	4Q 92	4c
Chicken, fresh, whole	lb	0.77	4/93	16r
Chicken, fryer, whole	lb	0.70	4Q 92	4c
Chicken breast, bone-in	lb	1.92	4/93	16r
Chicken legs, bone-in	lb	1.06	4/93	16r
Chuck roast, graded and ungraded, ex USDA prime and choice	lb	2.40	4/93	16r
Chuck roast, USDA choice, bone-in	lb	2.19	4/93	16r
Chuck roast, USDA choice, boneless	lb	2.38	4/93	16r
Cigarettes, Winston	carton	18.42	4Q 92	4c
Coffee, 100% ground roast, all sizes	lb	2.48	4/93	16r
Coffee, vacuum-packed	13-oz can	1.87	4Q 92	4c
Corn, frozen	10 oz	0.69	4Q 92	4c
Corn Flakes, Kellogg's or Post Toasties	18 oz	2.17	4Q 92	4c
Crackers, soda, salted	lb	1.15	4/93	16r
Eggs, Grade A large	doz	0.88	4Q 92	4c
Eggs, Grade A large	doz	0.96	4/93	16r
Flour, white, all purpose	lb	0.24	4/93	16r
Frankfurters, all meat or all beef	lb	2.01	4/93	16r
Grapefruit	lb	0.44	4/93	16r
Grapes, Thompson Seedless	lb	1.40	4/93	16r
Ground beef, 100% beef	lb	1.58	4/93	16r
Ground beef, lean and extra lean	lb	2.09	4/93	16r
Ground beef or hamburger	lb	0.98	4Q 92	4c
Ground chuck, 100% beef	lb	1.98	4/93	16r
Ham, boneless, excluding canned	lb	2.89	4/93	16r
Ham, picnic, shoulder, bone-in, smoked	lb	1.02	4/93	16r
Ham, rump or steak half, bone-in, smoked	lb	1.48	4/93	16r
Honey, jar	8 oz	0.73-1.19	92	5r
Honey, jar	lb	1.10-1.79	92	5r
Honey, squeeze bear	12-oz	1.19-1.50	92	5r
Ice cream, prepackaged, bulk, regular	1/2 gal	2.41	4/93	16r
Lemons	lb	1.05	4/93	16r
Lettuce, iceberg	head	0.99	4Q 92	4c
Lettuce, iceberg	lb	0.81	4/93	16r
Margarine, Blue Bonnet or Parkay cubes	lb	0.62	4Q 92	4c
Margarine, stick	lb	0.88	4/93	16r
Milk, whole	1/2 gal	1.32	4Q 92	4c
Orange juice, Minute Maid frozen	12-oz can	1.40	4Q 92	4c
Oranges, navel	lb	0.55	4/93	16r
Peaches	29-oz can	1.29	4Q 92	4c
Pears, Anjou	lb	0.92	4/93	16r

Values are in dollars or fractions of dollars. In the column headed *Ref*, references are shown to sources. Each reference is followed by a letter. These refer to the geographical level for which data were reported: s=State, r=Region, and c=City or metro. The abbreviation *ex* is used to mean *except* or *excluding*; *exp* stands for expenditures. For other abbreviations and further explanations, please see the Introduction.

Texarkana, TX, AR - continued

Item	Per	Value	Date	Ref.
Groceries				
Peas Sweet, Del Monte or Green Giant	15-17 oz can	0.58	4Q 92	4c
Pork chops, center cut, bone-in	lb	3.13	4/93	16r
Potato chips	16 oz	2.94	4/93	16r
Potatoes, white	lb	0.43	4/93	16r
Potatoes, white or red	10-lb sack	2.97	4Q 92	4c
Rib roast, USDA choice, bone-in	lb	4.63	4/93	16r
Rice, white, long grain, uncooked	lb	0.45	4/93	16r
Round roast, graded & ungraded, ex USDA prime & choice	lb	3.03	4/93	16r
Round roast, USDA choice, boneless	lb	3.09	4/93	16r
Sausage, fresh, loose	lb	2.08	4/93	16r
Sausage, Jimmy Dean, 100% pork	lb	2.71	4Q 92	4c
Short ribs, bone-in	lb	2.66	4/93	16r
Shortening, vegetable oil blends	lb	0.69	4/93	16r
Shortening, vegetable, Crisco	3-lb can	2.24	4Q 92	4c
Soft drink, Coca Cola	2 liter	1.25	4Q 92	4c
Spaghetti and macaroni	lb	0.81	4/93	16r
Steak, rib eye, USDA choice, boneless	lb	6.24	4/93	16r
Steak, round, graded & ungraded, ex USDA prime & choice	lb	3.31	4/93	16r
Steak, round, USDA choice, boneless	lb	3.34	4/93	16r
Steak, sirloin, graded & ungraded, ex USDA prime & choice	lb	4.19	4/93	16r
Steak, sirloin, USDA choice, boneless	lb	4.46	4/93	16r
Steak, T-bone	lb	4.83	4Q 92	4c
Steak, T-bone, USDA choice, bone-in	lb	5.25	4/93	16r
Strawberries, dry pint	12 oz	0.92	4/93	16r
Sugar, cane or beet	4 lb	1.53	4Q 92	4c
Sugar, white	lb	0.39	4/93	16r
Sugar, white, 33-80 oz pk	lb	0.38	4/93	16r
Tomatoes, field grown	lb	0.88	4/93	16r
Tomatoes, Hunt's or Del Monte	14.5-oz can	0.75	4Q 92	4c
Tuna, chunk, light	6.125-6.5 oz can	0.65	4Q 92	4c
Tuna, chunk, light	lb	1.79	4/93	16r
Turkey, frozen, whole	lb	1.04	4/93	16r
Yogurt, natural, fruit flavored	1/2 pint	0.57	4/93	16r
Health Care				
ACCRA Index, Health Care		94.00	4Q 92	4c
Analgesic, Aspirin, Bayer, 325 mg tablets	100	4.50	4Q 92	4c
Childbirth, cesarean, hospital		5034	91	62r
Childbirth, cesarean, physician's fee		2053	91	62r
Childbirth, normal, hospital		2712	91	62r
Childbirth, normal, physician's fee		1492	91	62r
Dentist's fee, adult teeth cleaning and periodic oral exam	visit	33.20	4Q 92	4c
Doctor's fee, routine exam, established patient	visit	43.49	4Q 92	4c
Health care spending, state	capita	2192	3/93	84s
Hospital care, semiprivate room	day	304.00	4Q 92	4c
Mental health care, exp	capita	20.37-28.83	90	38s
Mental health care, exp, state mental health agency	capita	22.72	90	38s
Mental health care, hospital psychiatric services, non-Federal, exp	capita	7.95	88	38s
Mental health care, mental health organization, multiservice, exp	capita	12.05	88	38s
Mental health care, psychiatric hospitals, private, exp	capita	37.78	88	38s
Mental health care, psychiatric out-patient clinics, freestanding, exp	capita	0.43	88	38s
Mental health care, state and county mental hospitals, exp	capita	12.54	88	38s
Mental health care, VA medical centers, exp	capita	5.35	88	38s
Physician fee, family practice, first-visit		75.00	91	62r

Texarkana, TX, AR - continued

Item	Per	Value	Date	Ref.
Health Care - continued				
Physician fee, family practice, revisit		34.00	91	62r
Physician fee, general practice, first-visit		61.00	91	62r
Physician fee, general practice, revisit		32.00	91	62r
Physician fee, general surgeon, first-visit		64.00	91	62r
Physician fee, general surgeon, revisit		40.00	91	62r
Physician fee, internal medicine, first-visit		98.00	91	62r
Physician fee, internal medicine, revisit		40.00	91	62r
Physician fee, median, neurosurgeon, first-visit		130.00	91	62r
Physician fee, median, nonsurgical specialist, first-visit		95.00	91	62r
Physician fee, median, orthopedic surgeon, first-visit		91.00	91	62r
Physician fee, median, plastic surgeon, first-visit		66.00	91	62r
Physician fee, median, surgical specialist, first-visit		62.00	91	62r
Physician fee, neurosurgeon, revisit		50.00	91	62r
Physician fee, nonsurgical specialist, revisit		40.00	91	62r
Physician fee, obstetrics/gynecology, first-visit		64.00	91	62r
Physician fee, obstetrics/gynecology, revisit		41.00	91	62r
Physician fee, orthopedic surgeon, revisit		40.00	91	62r
Physician fee, pediatrician, first-visit		49.00	91	62r
Physician fee, pediatrician, revisit		33.00	91	62r
Physician fee, plastic surgeon, revisit		43.00	91	62r
Physician fee, surgical specialist, revisit		37.00	91	62r
Substance abuse, hospital ancillary charge	incident	3750	90	70s
Substance abuse, hospital physician charge	incident	1080	90	70s
Substance abuse, hospital room and board	incident	5320	90	70s
Household Goods				
Appliance repair, home, service call, washing machine	min labor charge	35.60	4Q 92	4c
Laundry detergent, Tide Ultra, Bold, or Cheer	42 oz	3.48	4Q 92	4c
Tissues, facial, Kleenex brand	175-count box	1.06	4Q 92	4c
Housing				
ACCRA Index, Housing		79.50	4Q 92	4c
House, 1,800 sq ft, 8,000 sq ft lot, new, urban	total	86125	4Q 92	4c
House payment, principal and interest, 25% down payment	month	478	4Q 92	4c
Mortgage rate, incl. points & origination fee, 30-year fixed or adjustable rate	percent	8.10	4Q 92	4c
Rent, apartment, 2 bedrooms - 1-1/2 to 2 baths, unfurnished, 950 sq ft, water	month	417	4Q 92	4c
Rental unit, 1 bedroom	month	329	93	23c
Rental unit, 2 bedroom	month	389	93	23c
Rental unit, 3 bedroom	month	489	93	23c
Rental unit, 4 bedroom	month	545	93	23c
Rental unit, efficiency	month	271	93	23c
Insurance and Pensions				
Auto insurance, private passenger	year	709.79	91	63s
Personal Goods				
Shampoo, Alberto VO5	15 oz	1.05	4Q 92	4c
Toothpaste, Crest or Colgate	6-7 oz	1.84	4Q 92	4c
Personal Services				
Dry cleaning, man's 2-piece suit		6.65	4Q 92	4c
Haircare, woman's shampoo, trim and blow-dry		17.20	4Q 92	4c
Haircut, man's barbershop, no styling		8.20	4Q 92	4c

Values are in dollars or fractions of dollars. In the column headed *Ref*, references are shown to sources. Each reference is followed by a letter. These refer to the geographical level for which data were reported: s=State, r=Region, and c=City or metro. The abbreviation *ex* is used to mean *except* or *excluding*; *exp* stands for *expenditures*. For other abbreviations and further explanations, please see the Introduction.

Texarkana, TX, AR - continued

Item	Per	Value	Date	Ref.
Restaurant Food				
Chicken, fried, thigh and drumstick		1.82	4Q 92	4c
Hamburger with cheese	1/4 lb	1.85	4Q 92	4c
Pizza, Pizza Hut or Pizza Inn, cheese, thin crust	12-13 in	7.49	4Q 92	4c
Taxes				
Tax, cigarette	pack	41	91	77s
Tax, gasoline	gal	20	91	77s
Taxes, state	capita	923	91	77s
Transportation				
ACCRA Index, Transportation		100.20	4Q 92	4c
Driver's license fee		16.00	12/90	43s
Tire balance, computer or spin balance, front	wheel	6.60	4Q 92	4c
Travel				
Business travel	day	193.00	4/93	89r
Utilities				
ACCRA Index, Utilities		96.50	4Q 92	4c
Electricity	mil Btu	17.09	90	64s
Electricity, partial electric and other energy, 1,800 sq ft living area new home	month	75.82	4Q 92	4c
Electricity, residential	KWh	5.92	2/93	94s

Tifton, GA

Item	Per	Value	Date	Ref.
Composite ACCRA index		94.70	4Q 92	4c
Alcoholic Beverages				
Beer, Miller Lite or Budweiser, 12-oz containers	6 pack	4.09	4Q 92	4c
Liquor, J & B Scotch	750 ml	16.61	4Q 92	4c
Wine, Gallo Chablis blanc, 1.5 liter	bottle	5.03	4Q 92	4c
Clothing				
Jeans, man's denim		37.33	4Q 92	4c
Shirt, man's dress shirt		26.50	4Q 92	4c
Undervest, boy's size 10-14, cotton	3	5.03	4Q 92	4c
Communications				
Newspaper subscription, daily and Sunday home delivery, large-city	month	6.77	4Q 92	4c
Telephone, flat rate	month	11.55	91	11c
Telephone bill, family of four	month	20.74	4Q 92	4c
Energy and Fuels				
Energy, combined forms, 1,800 sq ft heating area	month	124.70	4Q 92	4c
Gasoline, motor	gal	0.97	4Q 92	4c
Entertainment				
Bowling, evening rate	game	1.75	4Q 92	4c
Monopoly game, Parker Brothers', No. 9		10.47	4Q 92	4c
Movie	admission	5.00	4Q 92	4c
Tennis balls, yellow, Wilson or Penn, 3	can	2.52	4Q 92	4c
Goods and Services				
ACCRA Index, Miscellaneous Goods and Services		104.10	4Q 92	4c
Groceries				
ACCRA Index, Groceries		95.50	4Q 92	4c
Babyfood, strained vegetables, lowest price	4-4.5 oz jar	0.31	4Q 92	4c
Bananas	lb	0.46	4Q 92	4c
Bread, white	24 oz	0.69	4Q 92	4c
Cheese, Kraft grated Parmesan	8-oz canister	3.21	4Q 92	4c
Chicken, fryer, whole	lb	0.68	4Q 92	4c
Cigarettes, Winston	carton	15.87	4Q 92	4c
Coffee, vacuum-packed	13-oz can	1.86	4Q 92	4c
Corn, frozen	10 oz	0.77	4Q 92	4c

Tifton, GA - continued

Item	Per	Value	Date	Ref.
Groceries - continued				
Corn Flakes, Kellogg's or Post Toasties	18 oz	1.67	4Q 92	4c
Eggs, Grade A large	doz	0.87	4Q 92	4c
Ground beef or hamburger	lb	1.63	4Q 92	4c
Lettuce, iceberg	head	0.98	4Q 92	4c
Margarine, Blue Bonnet or Parkay cubes	lb	0.51	4Q 92	4c
Milk, whole	1/2 gal	1.37	4Q 92	4c
Orange juice, Minute Maid frozen	12-oz can	1.30	4Q 92	4c
Peaches	29-oz can	1.27	4Q 92	4c
Peas Sweet, Del Monte or Green Giant	15-17 oz can	0.55	4Q 92	4c
Potatoes, white or red	10-lb sack	2.58	4Q 92	4c
Sausage, Jimmy Dean, 100% pork	lb	2.11	4Q 92	4c
Shortening, vegetable, Crisco	3-lb can	2.02	4Q 92	4c
Soft drink, Coca Cola	2 liter	1.10	4Q 92	4c
Steak, T-bone	lb	5.58	4Q 92	4c
Sugar, cane or beet	4 lb	1.45	4Q 92	4c
Tomatoes, Hunt's or Del Monte	14.5-oz can	0.66	4Q 92	4c
Tuna, chunk, light	6.125-6.5 oz can	0.53	4Q 92	4c
Health Care				
ACCRA Index, Health Care		77.80	4Q 92	4c
Analgesic, Aspirin, Bayer, 325 mg tablets	100	4.49	4Q 92	4c
Dentist's fee, adult teeth cleaning and periodic oral exam	visit	38.40	4Q 92	4c
Doctor's fee, routine exam, established patient	visit	29.50	4Q 92	4c
Hospital care, semiprivate room	day	185.00	4Q 92	4c
Household Goods				
Appliance repair, home, service call, washing machine	min labor charge	35.75	4Q 92	4c
Laundry detergent, Tide Ultra, Bold, or Cheer	42 oz	3.01	4Q 92	4c
Tissues, facial, Kleenex brand	175-count box	1.04	4Q 92	4c
Housing				
ACCRA Index, Housing		80.70	4Q 92	4c
House, 1,800 sq ft, 8,000 sq ft lot, new, urban	total	87975	4Q 92	4c
House payment, principal and interest, 25% down payment	month	489	4Q 92	4c
Mortgage rate, incl. points & origination fee, 30-year fixed or adjustable rate	percent	8.11	4Q 92	4c
Rent, apartment, 2 bedrooms - 1-1/2 to 2 baths, unfurnished, 950 sq ft, water	month	415	4Q 92	4c
Personal Goods				
Shampoo, Alberto VO5	15 oz	1.08	4Q 92	4c
Toothpaste, Crest or Colgate	6-7 oz	1.76	4Q 92	4c
Personal Services				
Dry cleaning, man's 2-piece suit		5.15	4Q 92	4c
Haircare, woman's shampoo, trim and blow-dry		20.50	4Q 92	4c
Haircut, man's barbershop, no styling		6.00	4Q 92	4c
Restaurant Food				
Chicken, fried, thigh and drumstick		2.26	4Q 92	4c
Hamburger with cheese	1/4 lb	1.99	4Q 92	4c
Pizza, Pizza Hut or Pizza Inn, cheese, thin crust	12-13 in	7.99	4Q 92	4c
Transportation				
ACCRA Index, Transportation		91.10	4Q 92	4c

Values are in dollars or fractions of dollars. In the column headed *Ref*, references are shown to sources. Each reference is followed by a letter. These refer to the geographical level for which data were reported: s = State, r = Region, and c = City or metro. The abbreviation *ex* is used to mean *except* or *excluding*; *exp* stands for expenditures. For other abbreviations and further explanations, please see the Introduction.

Tifton, GA - continued

Item	Per	Value	Date	Ref.
Transportation				
Tire balance, computer or spin balance, front	wheel	6.25	4Q 92	4c
Utilities				
ACCRA Index, Utilities		113.40	4Q 92	4c
Electricity, all electric, 1,800 sq ft living area new home	month	124.70	4Q 92	4c

Toledo, OH

Item	Per	Value	Date	Ref.
Composite ACCRA index		104.20	4Q 92	4c
Alcoholic Beverages				
Beer, Miller Lite or Budweiser, 12-oz containers	6 pack	3.92	4Q 92	4c
Liquor, J & B Scotch	750 ml	18.30	4Q 92	4c
Wine, Gallo Chablis blanc, 1.5 liter	bottle	5.73	4Q 92	4c
Child Care				
Child care fee, average, center	hour	1.63	90	65r
Child care fee, average, nonregulated family day care	hour	1.83	90	65r
Child care fee, average, regulated family day care	hour	1.42	90	65r
Clothing				
Jeans, man's denim		24.99	4Q 92	4c
Shirt, man's dress shirt		22.99	4Q 92	4c
Undervest, boy's size 10-14, cotton	3	4.64	4Q 92	4c
Communications				
Long-distance telephone service, day, initial minute, 0-100 miles	min	0.26-0.43	91	12s
Long-distance telephone service, day, additional minute, 0-100 miles	min	0.14-0.24	91	12s
Long-distance telephone service, evenings/weekends, 0-100 mi, initial minute	min	0.11-0.17	91	12s
Long-distance telephone service, evenings/weekends, 0-100 mi, additional minute	min	0.06-0.10	91	12s
Newspaper subscription, daily and Sunday home delivery, large-city	month	10.00	4Q 92	4c
Telephone, residential, private line, rotary, unlimited calling	month	19.44	10/91	78c
Telephone bill, family of four	month	21.91	4Q 92	4c
Education				
Board, 4-yr private college/university	year	1872	91	22s
Board, 4-yr public college/university	year	1742	91	22s
Expenditures, local gov't, public elementary/secondary	pupil	5451	92	20s
Room, 4-year private college/university	year	1695	91	22s
Room, 4-year public college/university	year	2259	91	22s
Tuition, 2-year private college/university	year	6093	91	22s
Tuition, 2-year public college/university	year	1768	91	22s
Tuition, 4-year private college/university	year	8729	91	22s
Tuition, 4-year public college/university, in-state	year	2622	91	22s
Energy and Fuels				
Coal	mil Btu	1.54	90	64s
Energy	mil Btu	8.32	90	64s
Energy, combined forms, 1,800 sq ft heating area	month	130.97	4Q 92	4c
Energy, exc electricity, 1,800 sq ft heating area	month	58.14	4Q 92	4c
Energy exp/householder, 1-family unit	year	471	90	28r
Energy exp/householder, <1,000 sq ft heating area	year	430	90	28r
Energy exp/householder, 1,000-1,999 sq ft heating area	year	481	90	28r
Energy exp/householder, 2,000+ sq ft heating area	year	473	90	28r
Energy exp/householder, mobile home	year	430	90	28r
Energy exp/householder, multifamily	year	461	90	28r
Gas, natural	mil Btu	4.54	90	64s

Toledo, OH - continued

Item	Per	Value	Date	Ref.
Energy and Fuels - continued				
Gas, natural	000 cu ft	5.28	91	46s
Gas, natural, exp	year	606	91	46s
Gasoline, motor	gal	1.04	4Q 92	4c
Gasoline, unleaded regular	mil Btu	9.35	90	64s
Entertainment				
Bowling, evening rate	game	1.69	4Q 92	4c
Miniature golf admission	adult	6.18	92	1r
Miniature golf admission	child	5.14	92	1r
Monopoly game, Parker Brothers', No. 9		9.58	4Q 92	4c
Movie	admission	5.75	4Q 92	4c
Tennis balls, yellow, Wilson or Penn, 3	can	2.59	4Q 92	4c
Waterpark admission	adult	11.00	92	1r
Waterpark admission	child	8.55	92	1r
Funerals				
Casket, 18-gauge steel, velvet interior		1926.72	91	24r
Cosmetology, hair care, etc.		97.64	91	24r
Embalming		249.14	91	24r
Facility use for ceremony		208.59	91	24r
Hearse, local		130.12	91	24r
Limousine, local		104.66	91	24r
Remains to funeral home, transfer		93.61	91	24r
Service charge, professional		724.62	91	24r
Vault, concrete, non-metallic liner		734.53	91	24r
Viewing facilities, use		236.06	91	24r
Goods and Services				
ACCRA Index, Miscellaneous Goods and Services		99.90	4Q 92	4c
Groceries				
ACCRA Index, Groceries		100.80	4Q 92	4c
Apples, Red Delicious	lb	0.77	4/93	16r
Babyfood, strained vegetables, lowest price	4-4.5 oz jar	0.27	4Q 92	4c
Bacon	lb	1.85	4/93	16r
Bananas	lb	0.42	4Q 92	4c
Bananas	lb	0.46	4/93	16r
Beef, stew, boneless	lb	2.53	4/93	16r
Bologna, all beef or mixed	lb	2.19	4/93	16r
Bread, white	24 oz	0.79	4Q 92	4c
Bread, white, pan	lb	0.78	4/93	16r
Butter	lb	1.50	4/93	16r
Cabbage	lb	0.40	4/93	16r
Carrots, short trimmed and topped	lb	0.45	4/93	16r
Cheese, Cheddar	lb	3.47	4/93	16r
Cheese, Kraft grated Parmesan	8-oz canister	3.38	4Q 92	4c
Chicken, fresh, whole	lb	0.84	4/93	16r
Chicken, fryer, whole	lb	0.79	4Q 92	4c
Chicken breast, bone-in	lb	1.94	4/93	16r
Chicken legs, bone-in	lb	1.02	4/93	16r
Chuck roast, graded and ungraded, ex USDA prime and choice	lb	2.43	4/93	16r
Chuck roast, USDA choice, bone-in	lb	2.11	4/93	16r
Chuck roast, USDA choice, boneless	lb	2.44	4/93	16r
Cigarettes, Winston	carton	17.12	4Q 92	4c
Coffee, 100% ground roast, all sizes	lb	2.47	4/93	16r
Coffee, vacuum-packed	13-oz can	2.39	4Q 92	4c
Cookies, chocolate chip	lb	2.73	4/93	16r
Corn, frozen	10 oz	0.70	4Q 92	4c
Corn Flakes, Kellogg's or Post Toasties	18 oz	2.07	4Q 92	4c
Eggs, Grade A large	doz	0.85	4Q 92	4c
Eggs, Grade A large	doz	0.93	4/93	16r
Flour, white, all purpose	lb	0.21	4/93	16r
Grapefruit	lb	0.45	4/93	16r
Grapes, Thompson Seedless	lb	1.46	4/93	16r
Ground beef, 100% beef	lb	1.63	4/93	16r
Ground beef, lean and extra lean	lb	2.08	4/93	16r

Values are in dollars or fractions of dollars. In the column headed *Ref*, references are shown to sources. Each reference is followed by a letter. These refer to the geographical level for which data were reported: s=State, r=Region, and c=City or metro. The abbreviation *ex* is used to mean *except* or *excluding*; *exp* stands for expenditures. For other abbreviations and further explanations, please see the Introduction.

Toledo, OH - continued

Item	Per	Value	Date	Ref.
Groceries				
Ground beef or hamburger	lb	1.25	4Q 92	4c
Ground chuck, 100% beef	lb	1.94	4/93	16r
Ham, boneless, excluding canned	lb	2.21	4/93	16r
Honey, jar	8 oz	0.97-1.25	92	5r
Honey, jar	lb	1.25-2.25	92	5r
Honey, squeeze bear	12-oz	1.25-1.99	92	5r
Ice cream, prepackaged, bulk, regular	1/2 gal	2.41	4/93	16r
Lemons	lb	0.82	4/93	16r
Lettuce, iceberg	head	0.81	4Q 92	4c
Lettuce, iceberg	lb	0.83	4/93	16r
Margarine, Blue Bonnet or Parkay cubes	lb	0.68	4Q 92	4c
Margarine, stick	lb	0.77	4/93	16r
Milk, whole	1/2 gal	1.39	4Q 92	4c
Orange juice, Minute Maid frozen	12-oz can	1.48	4Q 92	4c
Oranges, navel	lb	0.50	4/93	16r
Peaches	29-oz can	1.60	4Q 92	4c
Peanut butter, creamy, all sizes	lb	1.82	4/93	16r
Pears, Anjou	lb	0.85	4/93	16r
Peas Sweet, Del Monte or Green Giant	15-17 oz can	0.63	4Q 92	4c
Pork chops, center cut, bone-in	lb	3.17	4/93	16r
Potato chips	16 oz	2.68	4/93	16r
Potatoes, white	lb	0.26	4/93	16r
Potatoes, white or red	10-lb sack	1.35	4Q 92	4c
Round roast, graded & ungraded, ex USDA prime & choice	lb	2.88	4/93	16r
Round roast, USDA choice, boneless	lb	2.96	4/93	16r
Sausage, Jimmy Dean, 100% pork	lb	2.52	4Q 92	4c
Shortening, vegetable oil blends	lb	0.79	4/93	16r
Shortening, vegetable, Crisco	3-lb can	2.39	4Q 92	4c
Soft drink, Coca Cola	2 liter	1.11	4Q 92	4c
Spaghetti and macaroni	lb	0.76	4/93	16r
Steak, rib eye, USDA choice, boneless	lb	6.29	4/93	16r
Steak, round, USDA choice, boneless	lb	3.24	4/93	16r
Steak, sirloin, graded & ungraded, ex USDA prime & choice	lb	4.00	4/93	16r
Steak, sirloin, USDA choice, bone-in	lb	3.57	4/93	16r
Steak, sirloin, USDA choice, boneless	lb	4.17	4/93	16r
Steak, T-bone	lb	5.81	4Q 92	4c
Steak, T-bone, USDA choice, bone-in	lb	5.60	4/93	16r
Strawberries, dry pint	12 oz	0.90	4/93	16r
Sugar, cane or beet	4 lb	1.33	4Q 92	4c
Sugar, white	lb	0.36	4/93	16r
Sugar, white, 33-80 oz pk	lb	0.35	4/93	16r
Tomatoes, field grown	lb	0.99	4/93	16r
Tomatoes, Hunt's or Del Monte	14.5-oz can	0.79	4Q 92	4c
Tuna, chunk, light	6.125-6.5 oz can	0.68	4Q 92	4c
Tuna, chunk, light	lb	1.76	4/93	16r
Turkey, frozen, whole	lb	0.91	4/93	16r
Health Care				
ACCRA Index, Health Care		93.70	4Q 92	4c
Analgesic, Aspirin, Bayer, 325 mg tablets	100	4.86	4Q 92	4c
Childbirth, cesarean, hospital		4688	91	62r
Childbirth, cesarean, physician's fee		2053	91	62r
Childbirth, normal, hospital		2657	91	62r
Childbirth, normal, physician's fee		1492	91	62r
Dentist's fee, adult teeth cleaning and periodic oral exam	visit	46.90	4Q 92	4c
Doctor's fee, routine exam, established patient	visit	33.80	4Q 92	4c
Hospital care, semiprivate room	day	240.51	90	27c
Hospital care, semiprivate room	day	264.60	4Q 92	4c
Medical insurance premium, per employee, small group comprehensive	month	357.70	10/91	25c
Medical plan per employee	year	3443	91	45r

Toledo, OH - continued

Item	Per	Value	Date	Ref.
Health Care - continued				
Mental health care, exp	capita	37.60-53.67	90	38s
Mental health care, exp, state mental health agency	capita	40.93	90	38s
Mental health care, hospital psychiatric services, non-Federal, exp	capita	15.03	88	38s
Mental health care, mental health organization, multiservice, exp	capita	14.46	88	38s
Mental health care, psychiatric hospitals, private, exp	capita	7.93	88	38s
Mental health care, psychiatric out-patient clinics, freestanding, exp	capita	2.93	88	38s
Mental health care, psychiatric partial-care organizations, freestanding, exp	capita	0.32	88	38s
Mental health care, state and county mental hospitals, exp	capita	23.79	88	38s
Mental health care, VA medical centers, exp	capita	7.76	88	38s
Physician fee, family practice, first-visit		76.00	91	62r
Physician fee, family practice, revisit		33.00	91	62r
Physician fee, general practice, first-visit		61.00	91	62r
Physician fee, general practice, revisit		31.00	91	62r
Physician fee, general surgeon, first-visit		65.00	91	62r
Physician fee, general surgeon, revisit		35.00	91	62r
Physician fee, internal medicine, first-visit		91.00	91	62r
Physician fee, internal medicine, revisit		40.00	91	62r
Physician fee, median, neurosurgeon, first-visit		106.00	91	62r
Physician fee, median, nonsurgical specialist, first-visit		90.00	91	62r
Physician fee, median, orthopedic surgeon, first-visit		83.00	91	62r
Physician fee, median, surgical specialist, first-visit		61.00	91	62r
Physician fee, neurosurgeon, revisit		41.00	91	62r
Physician fee, nonsurgical specialist, revisit		40.00	91	62r
Physician fee, obstetrics/gynecology, first-visit		61.00	91	62r
Physician fee, obstetrics/gynecology, revisit		40.00	91	62r
Physician fee, orthopedic surgeon, revisit		41.00	91	62r
Physician fee, pediatrician, first-visit		46.00	91	62r
Physician fee, pediatrician, revisit		33.00	91	62r
Physician fee, surgical specialist, revisit		36.00	91	62r
Substance abuse, hospital ancillary charge	incident	940	90	70s
Substance abuse, hospital physician charge	incident	380	90	70s
Substance abuse, hospital room and board	incident	5410	90	70s
Household Goods				
Appliance repair, home, service call, washing machine	min labor charge	36.55	4Q 92	4c
Laundry detergent, Tide Ultra, Bold, or Cheer	42 oz	4.25	4Q 92	4c
Tissues, facial, Kleenex brand	175-count box	1.17	4Q 92	4c
Housing				
ACCRA Index, Housing		109.40	4Q 92	4c
Home, median price	unit	71.50		26c
House, 1,800 sq ft, 8,000 sq ft lot, new, urban	total	119750	4Q 92	4c
House payment, principal and interest, 25% down payment	month	679	4Q 92	4c
Mortgage rate, incl. points & origination fee, 30-year fixed or adjustable rate	percent	8.32	4Q 92	4c
Rent, apartment, 2 bedrooms - 1-1/2 to 2 baths, unfurnished, 950 sq ft, water	month	525	4Q 92	4c
Rental unit, 1 bedroom	month	425	93	23c
Rental unit, 2 bedroom	month	502	93	23c
Rental unit, 3 bedroom	month	626	93	23c

Values are in dollars or fractions of dollars. In the column headed *Ref*, references are shown to sources. Each reference is followed by a letter. These refer to the geographical level for which data were reported: s=State, r=Region, and c=City or metro. The abbreviation *ex* is used to mean *except* or *excluding*; *exp* stands for expenditures. For other abbreviations and further explanations, please see the Introduction.

Toledo, OH - continued

Item	Per	Value	Date	Ref.
Housing				
Rental unit, 4 bedroom	month	702	93	23c
Rental unit, efficiency	month	348	93	23c
Insurance and Pensions				
Auto insurance, private passenger	year	547.38	91	63s
Personal Goods				
Shampoo, Alberto VO5	15 oz	1.27	4Q 92	4c
Toothpaste, Crest or Colgate	6-7 oz	2.06	4Q 92	4c
Personal Services				
Dry cleaning, man's 2-piece suit		6.67	4Q 92	4c
Haircare, woman's shampoo, trim and blow-dry		18.80	4Q 92	4c
Haircut, man's barbershop, no styling		8.05	4Q 92	4c
Restaurant Food				
Chicken, fried, thigh and drumstick		2.20	4Q 92	4c
Hamburger with cheese	1/4 lb	1.75	4Q 92	4c
Pizza, Pizza Hut or Pizza Inn, cheese, thin crust	12-13 in	7.59	4Q 92	4c
Taxes				
Tax, cigarette	pack	18	91	77s
Tax, gasoline	gal	21	91	77s
Taxes, state	capita	1056	91	77s
Transportation				
ACCRA Index, Transportation		101.10	4Q 92	4c
Auto rental, average	day	38.25	6/91	60c
Bus fare	one-way	0.85	3/93	2c
Bus fare, up to 10 miles	one-way	0.75	4Q 92	4c
Driver's license fee		5.00	12/90	43s
Limo fare, airport-city, average	day	15.00	6/91	60c
Taxi fare, airport-city, average	day	28.00	6/91	60c
Tire balance, computer or spin balance, front	wheel	7.38	4Q 92	4c
Travel				
Breakfast	day	5.53	6/91	60c
Dinner	day	18.10	6/91	60c
Lodging	day	86.00	91	60c
Lunch	day	6.90	6/91	60c
Utilities				
ACCRA Index, Utilities		119.20	4Q 92	4c
Electricity	mil Btu	17.33	90	64s
Electricity, partial electric and other energy, 1,800 sq ft living area new home	month	72.83	4Q 92	4c
Electricity, winter, 250 KWh	month	30.76	92	55c
Electricity, winter, 500 KWh	month	57.57	92	55c
Electricity, winter, 750 KWh	month	84.36	92	55c
Electricity, winter, 1000 KWh	month	111.16	92	55c

Topeka, KS

Item	Per	Value	Date	Ref.
Child Care				
Child care fee, average, center	hour	1.63	90	65r
Child care fee, average, nonregulated family day care	hour	1.83	90	65r
Child care fee, average, regulated family day care	hour	1.42	90	65r
Communications				
Long-distance telephone service, day, initial minute, 0-100 miles	min	0.18-0.40	91	12s
Long-distance telephone service, day, additional minute, 0-100 miles	min	0.09-0.30	91	12s
Education				
Board, 4-yr private college/university	year	1719	91	22s
Board, 4-yr public college/university	year	1294	91	22s
Expenditures, local gov't, public elementary/secondary	pupil	5105	92	20s

Topeka, KS - continued

Item	Per	Value	Date	Ref.
Education - continued				
Room, 4-year private college/university	year	1269	91	22s
Room, 4-year public college/university	year	1301	91	22s
Tuition, 2-year private college/university	year	4135	91	22s
Tuition, 2-year public college/university	year	748	91	22s
Tuition, 4-year private college/university	year	5997	91	22s
Tuition, 4-year public college/university, in-state	year	1569	91	22s
Energy and Fuels				
Coal	mil Btu	1.24	90	64s
Energy	mil Btu	7.59	90	64s
Energy exp/householder, 1-family unit	year	473	90	28r
Energy exp/householder, <1,000 sq ft heating area	year	429	90	28r
Energy exp/householder, 1,000-1,999 sq ft heating area	year	442	90	28r
Energy exp/householder, 2,000+ sq ft heating area	year	498	90	28r
Energy exp/householder, mobile home	year	442	90	28r
Energy exp/householder, multifamily	year	407	90	28r
Gas, natural	mil Btu	3.30	90	64s
Gas, natural	000 cu ft	4.38	91	46s
Gas, natural, exp	year	435	91	46s
Gasoline, unleaded regular	mil Btu	8.90	90	64s
Entertainment				
Miniature golf admission	adult	6.18	92	1r
Miniature golf admission	child	5.14	92	1r
Waterpark admission	adult	11.00	92	1r
Waterpark admission	child	8.55	92	1r
Funerals				
Casket, 18-gauge steel, velvet interior		1952.97	91	24r
Cosmetology, hair care, etc.		90.03	91	24r
Embalming		251.75	91	24r
Facility use for ceremony		180.75	91	24r
Hearse, local		117.51	91	24r
Limousine, local		71.86	91	24r
Remains to funeral home, transfer		81.14	91	24r
Service charge, professional		740.03	91	24r
Vault, concrete, non-metallic liner		801.47	91	24r
Viewing facilities, use		169.33	91	24r
Groceries				
Apples, Red Delicious	lb	0.77	4/93	16r
Bacon	lb	1.85	4/93	16r
Bananas	lb	0.46	4/93	16r
Beef, stew, boneless	lb	2.53	4/93	16r
Bologna, all beef or mixed	lb	2.19	4/93	16r
Bread, white, pan	lb	0.78	4/93	16r
Butter	lb	1.50	4/93	16r
Cabbage	lb	0.40	4/93	16r
Carrots, short trimmed and topped	lb	0.45	4/93	16r
Cheese, Cheddar	lb	3.47	4/93	16r
Chicken, fresh, whole	lb	0.84	4/93	16r
Chicken breast, bone-in	lb	1.94	4/93	16r
Chicken legs, bone-in	lb	1.02	4/93	16r
Chuck roast, graded and ungraded, ex USDA prime and choice	lb	2.43	4/93	16r
Chuck roast, USDA choice, bone-in	lb	2.11	4/93	16r
Chuck roast, USDA choice, boneless	lb	2.44	4/93	16r
Coffee, 100% ground roast, all sizes	lb	2.47	4/93	16r
Cookies, chocolate chip	lb	2.73	4/93	16r
Eggs, Grade A large	doz	0.93	4/93	16r
Flour, white, all purpose	lb	0.21	4/93	16r
Grapefruit	lb	0.45	4/93	16r
Grapes, Thompson Seedless	lb	1.46	4/93	16r
Ground beef, 100% beef	lb	1.63	4/93	16r
Ground beef, lean and extra lean	lb	2.08	4/93	16r
Ground chuck, 100% beef	lb	1.94	4/93	16r
Ham, boneless, excluding canned	lb	2.21	4/93	16r
Ice cream, prepackaged, bulk, regular	1/2 gal	2.41	4/93	16r
Lemons	lb	0.82	4/93	16r

Values are in dollars or fractions of dollars. In the column headed *Ref*, references are shown to sources. Each reference is followed by a letter. These refer to the geographical level for which data were reported: s=State, r=Region, and c=City or metro. The abbreviation *ex* is used to mean *except* or *excluding*; *exp* stands for expenditures. For other abbreviations and further explanations, please see the Introduction.

Topeka, KS - continued

Item	Per	Value	Date	Ref.
Groceries				
Lettuce, iceberg	lb	0.83	4/93	16r
Margarine, stick	lb	0.77	4/93	16r
Oranges, navel	lb	0.50	4/93	16r
Peanut butter, creamy, all sizes	lb	1.82	4/93	16r
Pears, Anjou	lb	0.85	4/93	16r
Pork chops, center cut, bone-in	lb	3.17	4/93	16r
Potato chips	16 oz	2.68	4/93	16r
Potatoes, white	lb	0.26	4/93	16r
Round roast, graded & ungraded, ex USDA prime & choice	lb	2.88	4/93	16r
Round roast, USDA choice, boneless	lb	2.96	4/93	16r
Shortening, vegetable oil blends	lb	0.79	4/93	16r
Spaghetti and macaroni	lb	0.76	4/93	16r
Steak, rib eye, USDA choice, boneless	lb	6.29	4/93	16r
Steak, round, USDA choice, boneless	lb	3.24	4/93	16r
Steak, sirloin, graded & ungraded, ex USDA prime & choice	lb	4.00	4/93	16r
Steak, sirloin, USDA choice, bone-in	lb	3.57	4/93	16r
Steak, sirloin, USDA choice, boneless	lb	4.17	4/93	16r
Steak, T-bone, USDA choice, bone-in	lb	5.60	4/93	16r
Strawberries, dry pint	12 oz	0.90	4/93	16r
Sugar, white	lb	0.36	4/93	16r
Sugar, white, 33-80 oz pk	lb	0.35	4/93	16r
Tomatoes, field grown	lb	0.99	4/93	16r
Tuna, chunk, light	lb	1.76	4/93	16r
Turkey, frozen, whole	lb	0.91	4/93	16r
Health Care				
Childbirth, cesarean, hospital		4688	91	62r
Childbirth, cesarean, physician's fee		2053	91	62r
Childbirth, normal, hospital		2657	91	62r
Childbirth, normal, physician's fee		1492	91	62r
Medical plan per employee	year	3443	91	45r
Mental health care, exp	capita	28.84-37.59	90	38s
Mental health care, exp, state mental health agency	capita	35.41	90	38s
Mental health care, hospital psychiatric services, non-Federal, exp	capita	11.07	88	38s
Mental health care, mental health organization, multiservice, exp	capita	12.68	88	38s
Mental health care, psychiatric hospitals, private, exp	capita	21.42	88	38s
Mental health care, psychiatric out-patient clinics, freestanding, exp	capita	3.45	88	38s
Mental health care, state and county mental hospitals, exp	capita	26.34	88	38s
Mental health care, VA medical centers, exp	capita	22.97	88	38s
Physician fee, family practice, first-visit		76.00	91	62r
Physician fee, family practice, revisit		33.00	91	62r
Physician fee, general practice, first-visit		61.00	91	62r
Physician fee, general practice, revisit		31.00	91	62r
Physician fee, general surgeon, first-visit		65.00	91	62r
Physician fee, general surgeon, revisit		35.00	91	62r
Physician fee, internal medicine, first-visit		91.00	91	62r
Physician fee, internal medicine, revisit		40.00	91	62r
Physician fee, median, neurosurgeon, first-visit		106.00	91	62r
Physician fee, median, nonsurgical specialist, first-visit		90.00	91	62r
Physician fee, median, orthopedic surgeon, first-visit		83.00	91	62r
Physician fee, median, surgical specialist, first-visit		61.00	91	62r
Physician fee, neurosurgeon, revisit		41.00	91	62r
Physician fee, nonsurgical specialist, revisit		40.00	91	62r
Physician fee, obstetrics/gynecology, first-visit		61.00	91	62r
Physician fee, obstetrics/gynecology, revisit		40.00	91	62r
Physician fee, orthopedic surgeon, revisit		41.00	91	62r
Physician fee, pediatrician, first-visit		46.00	91	62r
Physician fee, pediatrician, revisit		33.00	91	62r
Physician fee, surgical specialist, revisit		36.00	91	62r

Topeka, KS - continued

Item	Per	Value	Date	Ref.
Health Care - continued				
Substance abuse, hospital ancillary charge	incident	1170	90	70s
Substance abuse, hospital physician charge	incident	560	90	70s
Substance abuse, hospital room and board	incident	5920	90	70s
Insurance and Pensions				
Auto insurance, private passenger	year	459.62	91	63s
Taxes				
Tax, cigarette	pack	24	91	77s
Tax, gasoline	gal	18	91	77s
Taxes, state	capita	1121	91	77s
Transportation				
Driver's license fee		8.00-12.00	12/90	43s
Vehicle registration and license plate	year	27.25-37.25	93	32s
Utilities				
Electricity	mil Btu	19.31	90	64s

Trenton, NJ

Item	Per	Value	Date	Ref.
Child Care				
Child care fee, average, center	hour	2.18	90	65r
Child care fee, average, nonregulated family day care	hour	1.83	90	65r
Child care fee, average, regulated family day care	hour	2.02	90	65r
Communications				
Long-distance telephone service, day, initial minute, 0-100 miles	min	0.09-0.42	91	12s
Long-distance telephone service, day, additional minute, 0-100 miles	min	0.03-0.12	91	12s
Education				
Board, 4-yr private college/university	year	2883	91	22s
Board, 4-yr public college/university	year	1647	91	22s
Expenditures, local gov't, public elementary/secondary	pupil	9940	92	20s
Room, 4-year private college/university	year	2440	91	22s
Room, 4-year public college/university	year	2415	91	22s
Tuition, 2-year private college/university	year	5874	91	22s
Tuition, 2-year public college/university	year	1235	91	22s
Tuition, 4-year private college/university	year	10281	91	22s
Tuition, 4-year public college/university, in-state	year	2860	91	22s
Energy and Fuels				
Coal	mil Btu	1.79	90	64s
Energy	mil Btu	9.32	90	64s
Energy exp/householder, 1-family unit	year	588	90	28r
Energy exp/householder, <1,000 sq ft heating area	year	477	90	28r
Energy exp/householder, 1,000-1,999 sq ft heating area	year	517	90	28r
Energy exp/householder, 2,000+ sq ft heating area	year	630	90	28r
Energy exp/householder, mobile home	year	412	90	28r
Energy exp/householder, multifamily	year	498	90	28r
Gas, natural	mil Btu	5.05	90	64s
Gas, natural	000 cu ft	6.73	91	46s
Gas, natural, exp	year	593	91	46s
Gasoline, unleaded regular	mil Btu	9.03	90	64s
Funerals				
Casket, 18-gauge steel, velvet interior		1811.58	91	24r
Cosmetology, hair care, etc.		111.08	91	24r
Embalming		329.42	91	24r
Facility use for ceremony		201.29	91	24r

Values are in dollars or fractions of dollars. In the column headed *Ref*, references are shown to sources. Each reference is followed by a letter. These refer to the geographical level for which data were reported: s = State, r = Region, and c = City or metro. The abbreviation *ex* is used to mean *except* or *excluding*; *exp* stands for expenditures. For other abbreviations and further explanations, please see the Introduction.

Trenton, NJ - continued

Item	Per	Value	Date	Ref.
Funerals				
Hearse, local		135.27	91	24r
Limousine, local		127.24	91	24r
Remains to funeral home, transfer		103.98	91	24r
Service charge, professional		724.98	91	24r
Vault, concrete, non-metallic liner		766.71	91	24r
Viewing facilities, use		260.60	91	24r
Groceries				
Apples, Red Delicious	lb	0.85	4/93	16r
Bacon	lb	2.12	4/93	16r
Bananas	lb	0.54	4/93	16r
Bread, white, pan	lb	0.81	4/93	16r
Butter	lb	2.02	4/93	16r
Carrots, short trimmed and topped	lb	0.51	4/93	16r
Chicken, fresh, whole	lb	1.04	4/93	16r
Chicken breast, bone-in	lb	2.21	4/93	16r
Chicken legs, bone-in	lb	1.16	4/93	16r
Chuck roast, USDA choice, boneless	lb	2.82	4/93	16r
Coffee, 100% ground roast, all sizes	lb	2.66	4/93	16r
Cucumbers	lb	0.85	4/93	16r
Eggs, Grade A large	doz	1.15	4/93	16r
Grapefruit	lb	0.45	4/93	16r
Grapes, Thompson Seedless	lb	1.52	4/93	16r
Ground beef, lean and extra lean	lb	2.36	4/93	16r
Ground chuck, 100% beef	lb	2.02	4/93	16r
Honey, jar	8 oz	0.96-1.75	92	5r
Honey, jar	lb	1.50-3.00	92	5r
Honey, squeeze bear	12-oz	1.50-1.99	92	5r
Ice cream, prepackaged, bulk, regular	1/2 gal	2.80	4/93	16r
Lemons	lb	0.96	4/93	16r
Lettuce, iceberg	lb	0.95	4/93	16r
Margarine, stick	lb	0.81	4/93	16r
Milk, fresh, whole, fortified	1/2 gal	1.30	4/93	16r
Oranges, navel	lb	0.56	4/93	16r
Peanut butter, creamy, all sizes	lb	1.88	4/93	16r
Pork chops, center cut, bone-in	lb	3.34	4/93	16r
Potato chips	16 oz	2.88	4/93	16r
Potatoes, white	lb	0.37	4/93	16r
Rib roast, USDA choice, bone-in	lb	4.94	4/93	16r
Round roast, USDA choice, boneless	lb	3.17	4/93	16r
Shortening, vegetable oil blends	lb	0.98	4/93	16r
Spaghetti and macaroni	lb	0.82	4/93	16r
Steak, round, graded & ungraded, ex USDA prime & choice	lb	4.04	4/93	16r
Steak, round, USDA choice, boneless	lb	3.90	4/93	16r
Steak, sirloin, USDA choice, boneless	lb	4.97	4/93	16r
Strawberries, dry pint	12 oz	0.90	4/93	16r
Sugar, white	lb	0.50	4/93	16r
Sugar, white, 33-80 oz pk	lb	0.41	4/93	16r
Tomatoes, field grown	lb	1.23	4/93	16r
Tuna, chunk, light	lb	2.22	4/93	16r
Turkey, frozen, whole	lb	1.04	4/93	16r
Health Care				
Childbirth, cesarean, hospital		5826	91	62r
Childbirth, cesarean, physician's fee		2053	91	62r
Childbirth, normal, hospital		2964	91	62r
Childbirth, normal, physician's fee		1492	91	62r
Medical plan per employee	year	3942	91	45r
Mental health care, exp	capita	28.84-37.59	90	38s
Mental health care, exp, state mental health agency	capita	57.16	90	38s
Mental health care, hospital psychiatric services, non-Federal, exp	capita	16.04	88	38s
Mental health care, mental health organization, multiservice, exp	capita	11.14	88	38s
Mental health care, psychiatric hospitals, private, exp	capita	17.85	88	38s
Mental health care, psychiatric out-patient clinics, freestanding, exp	capita	1.56	88	38s
Mental health care, psychiatric partial-care organizations, freestanding, exp	capita	0.66	88	38s

Trenton, NJ - continued

Item	Per	Value	Date	Ref.
Health Care - continued				
Mental health care, state and county mental hospitals, exp	capita	36.80	88	38s
Mental health care, VA medical centers, exp	capita	5.61	88	38s
Prescription drug co-pay, Medicaid	month	5.00	91	21s
Substance abuse, hospital ancillary charge	incident	780	90	70s
Substance abuse, hospital physician charge	incident	550	90	70s
Substance abuse, hospital room and board	incident	6300	90	70s
Insurance and Pensions				
Auto insurance, private passenger	year	1081.45	91	63s
Taxes				
Tax, cigarette	pack	40	91	77s
Tax, gasoline	gal	10.50	91	77s
Taxes, state	capita	1501	91	77s
Transportation				
Driver's license fee		16.00-17.50	12/90	43s
Vehicle registration and license plate	year	32.90-93.90	93	44s
Travel				
Business travel	day	165.00	4/93	89r
Utilities				
Electricity	mil Btu	26.63	90	64s

Tucson, AZ

Item	Per	Value	Date	Ref.
Composite ACCRA index		102.00	4Q 92	4c
Alcoholic Beverages				
Beer, Miller Lite or Budweiser, 12-oz containers	6 pack	3.59	4Q 92	4c
Liquor, J & B Scotch	750 ml	17.00	4Q 92	4c
Wine, Gallo Chablis blanc, 1.5 liter	bottle	4.80	4Q 92	4c
Child Care				
Child care fee, average, center	hour	1.71	90	65r
Child care fee, average, nonregulated family day care	hour	1.32	90	65r
Child care fee, average, regulated family day care	hour	1.86	90	65r
Clothing				
Jeans, man's denim		30.91	4Q 92	4c
Shirt, man's dress shirt		28.20	4Q 92	4c
Undervest, boy's size 10-14, cotton	3	4.50	4Q 92	4c
Communications				
Long-distance telephone service, day, initial minute, 0-100 miles	min	0.24-0.42	91	12s
Long-distance telephone service, day, additional minute, 0-100 miles	min	0.10-0.26	91	12s
Long-distance telephone service, evenings/weekends, 0-100 mi, initial minute	min	0.14-0.25	91	12s
Long-distance telephone service, evenings/weekends, 0-100 mi, additional minute	min	0.06-0.17	91	12s
Newspaper subscription, daily and Sunday home delivery, large-city	month	11.74	4Q 92	4c
Telephone, flat rate	month	12.40	91	11c
Telephone, residential, private line, rotary, unlimited calling	month	18.19	10/91	78c
Telephone bill, family of four	month	17.40	4Q 92	4c
Education				
Board, 4-yr private college/university	year	1460	91	22s
Board, 4-yr public college/university	year	1697	91	22s
Expenditures, local gov't, public elementary/secondary	pupil	4489	92	20s
Room, 4-year private college/university	year	1350	91	22s
Room, 4-year public college/university	year	1556	91	22s

Values are in dollars or fractions of dollars. In the column headed *Ref*, references are shown to sources. Each reference is followed by a letter. These refer to the geographical level for which data were reported: s=State, r=Region, and c=City or metro. The abbreviation *ex* is used to mean *except* or *excluding*; *exp* stands for expenditures. For other abbreviations and further explanations, please see the Introduction.

Tucson, AZ - continued

Item	Per	Value	Date	Ref.
Education				
Tuition, 2-year private college/university	year	8977	91	22s
Tuition, 2-year public college/university	year	579	91	22s
Tuition, 4-year private college/university	year	4660	91	22s
Tuition, 4-year public college/university, in-state	year	1478	91	22s
Energy and Fuels				
Coal	mil Btu	1.45	90	64s
Energy	mil Btu	11.37	90	64s
Energy, combined forms, 1,800 sq ft heating area	month	110.36	4Q 92	4c
Energy, exc electricity, 1,800 sq ft heating area	month	31.74	4Q 92	4c
Energy exp/householder, 1-family unit	year	372	90	28r
Energy exp/householder, <1,000 sq ft heating area	year	335	90	28r
Energy exp/householder, 1,000-1,999 sq ft heating area	year	365	90	28r
Energy exp/householder, 2,000+ sq ft heating area	year	411	90	28r
Energy exp/householder, mobile home	year	305	90	28r
Energy exp/householder, multifamily	year	372	90	28r
Gas, cooking, 10 therms	month	11.04	92	56c
Gas, cooking, 30 therms	month	22.11	92	56c
Gas, cooking, 50 therms	month	33.17	92	56c
Gas, heating, winter, 100 therms	month	60.85	92	56c
Gas, natural	mil Btu	4.48	90	64s
Gas, natural	000 cu ft	6.99	91	46s
Gas, natural, exp	year	341	91	46s
Gasoline, motor	gal	1.13	4Q 92	4c
Gasoline, unleaded regular	mil Btu	9.22	90	64s
Entertainment				
Bowling, evening rate	game	2.19	4Q 92	4c
Dinner entree, restaurant		24.50-32.50	92	83c
Miniature golf admission	adult	6.18	92	1r
Miniature golf admission	child	5.14	92	1r
Monopoly game, Parker Brothers', No. 9		10.53	4Q 92	4c
Movie	admission	6.80	4Q 92	4c
Tennis balls, yellow, Wilson or Penn, 3	can	1.93	4Q 92	4c
Waterpark admission	adult	11.00	92	1r
Waterpark admission	child	8.55	92	1r
Funerals				
Casket, 18-gauge steel, velvet interior		1929.04	91	24r
Cosmetology, hair care, etc.		88.52	91	24r
Embalming		249.33	91	24r
Facility use for ceremony		182.75	91	24r
Hearse, local		110.04	91	24r
Limousine, local		66.67	91	24r
Remains to funeral home, transfer		84.58	91	24r
Service charge, professional		593.00	91	24r
Vault, concrete, non-metallic liner		647.38	91	24r
Viewing facilities, use		99.87	91	24r
Goods and Services				
ACCRA Index, Miscellaneous Goods and Services		103.10	4Q 92	4c
Groceries				
ACCRA Index, Groceries		103.20	4Q 92	4c
Apples, Red Delicious	lb	0.80	4/93	16r
Babyfood, strained vegetables, lowest price	4-4.5 oz jar	0.31	4Q 92	4c
Bacon	lb	1.79	4/93	16r
Bananas	lb	0.37	4Q 92	4c
Bananas	lb	0.53	4/93	16r
Bologna, all beef or mixed	lb	2.67	4/93	16r
Bread, white	24 oz	0.77	4Q 92	4c
Bread, white, pan	lb	0.81	4/93	16r
Carrots, short trimmed and topped	lb	0.39	4/93	16r

Tucson, AZ - continued

Item	Per	Value	Date	Ref.
Groceries - continued				
Cheese, Kraft grated Parmesan	8-oz canister	3.47	4Q 92	4c
Chicken, fresh, whole	lb	0.94	4/93	16r
Chicken, fryer, whole	lb	0.93	4Q 92	4c
Chicken breast, bone-in	lb	2.19	4/93	16r
Chuck roast, graded and ungraded, ex USDA prime and choice	lb	2.26	4/93	16r
Cigarettes, Winston	carton	16.73	4Q 92	4c
Coffee, 100% ground roast, all sizes	lb	2.33	4/93	16r
Coffee, vacuum-packed	13-oz can	2.01	4Q 92	4c
Corn, frozen	10 oz	0.85	4Q 92	4c
Corn Flakes, Kellogg's or Post Toasties	18 oz	2.38	4Q 92	4c
Eggs, Grade A large	doz	0.92	4Q 92	4c
Eggs, Grade AA large	doz	1.18	4/93	16r
Flour, white, all purpose	lb	0.22	4/93	16r
Grapefruit	lb	0.52	4/93	16r
Grapes, Thompson Seedless	lb	1.50	4/93	16r
Ground beef, 100% beef	lb	1.44	4/93	16r
Ground beef, lean and extra lean	lb	2.34	4/93	16r
Ground beef or hamburger	lb	1.39	4Q 92	4c
Ham, boneless, excluding canned	lb	2.56	4/93	16r
Honey, jar	8 oz	0.89-1.00	92	5r
Honey, jar	lb	1.35-1.97	92	5r
Honey, squeeze bear	12-oz	1.00-1.89	92	5r
Ice cream, prepackaged, bulk, regular	1/2 gal	2.40	4/93	16r
Lemons	lb	0.81	4/93	16r
Lettuce, iceberg	head	0.85	4Q 92	4c
Lettuce, iceberg	lb	0.84	4/93	16r
Margarine, Blue Bonnet or Parkay cubes	lb	0.71	4Q 92	4c
Margarine, stick	lb	0.81	4/93	16r
Milk, whole	1/2 gal	1.46	4Q 92	4c
Orange juice, Minute Maid frozen	12-oz can	1.39	4Q 92	4c
Oranges, navel	lb	0.48	4/93	16r
Peaches	29-oz can	1.49	4Q 92	4c
Peas Sweet, Del Monte or Green Giant	15-17 oz can	0.68	4Q 92	4c
Pork chops, center cut, bone-in	lb	3.25	4/93	16r
Potato chips	16 oz	2.89	4/93	16r
Potatoes, white	lb	0.38	4/93	16r
Potatoes, white or red	10-lb sack	1.33	4Q 92	4c
Round roast, graded & ungraded, ex USDA prime & choice	lb	3.00	4/93	16r
Round roast, USDA choice, boneless	lb	3.16	4/93	16r
Sausage, Jimmy Dean, 100% pork	lb	2.76	4Q 92	4c
Shortening, vegetable oil blends	lb	0.86	4/93	16r
Shortening, vegetable, Crisco	3-lb can	2.64	4Q 92	4c
Soft drink, Coca Cola	2 liter	1.35	4Q 92	4c
Spaghetti and macaroni	lb	0.84	4/93	16r
Steak, round, graded & ungraded, ex USDA prime & choice	lb	3.34	4/93	16r
Steak, round, USDA choice, boneless	lb	3.24	4/93	16r
Steak, sirloin, graded & ungraded, ex USDA prime & choice	lb	3.75	4/93	16r
Steak, sirloin, USDA choice, boneless	lb	4.49	4/93	16r
Steak, T-bone	lb	4.79	4Q 92	4c
Sugar, cane or beet	4 lb	1.73	4Q 92	4c
Sugar, white	lb	0.41	4/93	16r
Sugar, white, 33-80 oz pk	lb	0.38	4/93	16r
Tomatoes, field grown	lb	1.01	4/93	16r
Tomatoes, Hunt's or Del Monte	14.5-oz can	0.70	4Q 92	4c
Tuna, chunk, light	6.125-6.5 oz can	0.61	4Q 92	4c
Turkey, frozen, whole	lb	1.04	4/93	16r

Values are in dollars or fractions of dollars. In the column headed *Ref*, references are shown to sources. Each reference is followed by a letter. These refer to the geographical level for which data were reported: s=State, r=Region, and c=City or metro. The abbreviation *ex* is used to mean *except* or *excluding*; *exp* stands for expenditures. For other abbreviations and further explanations, please see the Introduction.

Tucson, AZ - continued

Item	Per	Value	Date	Ref.
Health Care				
ACCRA Index, Health Care		115.40	4Q 92	4c
Analgesic, Aspirin, Bayer, 325 mg tablets	100	5.43	4Q 92	4c
Childbirth, cesarean, hospital		5533	91	62r
Childbirth, cesarean, physician's fee		2053	91	62r
Childbirth, normal, hospital		2745	91	62r
Childbirth, normal, physician's fee		1492	91	62r
Dentist's fee, adult teeth cleaning and periodic oral exam	visit	50.20	4Q 92	4c
Doctor's fee, routine exam, established patient	visit	41.60	4Q 92	4c
Hospital care, semiprivate room	day	302.17	90	27c
Hospital care, semiprivate room	day	448.00	4Q 92	4c
Medical insurance premium, per employee, small group comprehensive	month	368.65	10/91	25c
Medical plan per employee	year	3218	91	45r
Mental health care, exp	capita	20.37-28.83	90	38s
Mental health care, exp, state mental health agency	capita	27.27	90	38s
Mental health care, hospital psychiatric services, non-Federal, exp	capita	8.91	88	38s
Mental health care, mental health organization, multiservice, exp	capita	11.35	88	38s
Mental health care, psychiatric hospitals, private, exp	capita	36.59	88	38s
Mental health care, psychiatric out-patient clinics, freestanding, exp	capita	1.11	88	38s
Mental health care, state and county mental hospitals, exp	capita	8.18	88	38s
Mental health care, VA medical centers, exp	capita	2.60	88	38s
Physician fee, family practice, first-visit		111.00	91	62r
Physician fee, family practice, revisit		45.00	91	62r
Physician fee, general practice, first-visit		100.00	91	62r
Physician fee, general practice, revisit		40.00	91	62r
Physician fee, internal medicine, first-visit		137.00	91	62r
Physician fee, internal medicine, revisit		48.00	91	62r
Physician fee, median, neurosurgeon, first-visit		157.00	91	62r
Physician fee, median, nonsurgical specialist, first-visit		131.00	91	62r
Physician fee, median, orthopedic surgeon, first-visit		124.00	91	62r
Physician fee, median, plastic surgeon, first-visit		88.00	91	62r
Physician fee, median, surgical specialist, first-visit		100.00	91	62r
Physician fee, neurosurgeon, revisit		51.00	91	62r
Physician fee, nonsurgical specialist, revisit		47.00	91	62r
Physician fee, obstetrics/gynecology, first-visit		95.00	91	62r
Physician fee, obstetrics/gynecology, revisit		50.00	91	62r
Physician fee, orthopedic surgeon, revisit		51.00	91	62r
Physician fee, pediatrician, first-visit		81.00	91	62r
Physician fee, pediatrician, revisit		42.00	91	62r
Physician fee, plastic surgeon, revisit		48.00	91	62r
Physician fee, surgical specialist, revisit		49.00	91	62r
Substance abuse, hospital ancillary charge	incident	1800	90	70s
Substance abuse, hospital physician charge	incident	800	90	70s
Substance abuse, hospital room and board	incident	6480	90	70s
Household Goods				
Appliance repair, home, service call, washing machine	min labor charge	22.97	4Q 92	4c
Laundry detergent, Tide Ultra, Bold, or Cheer	42 oz	4.25	4Q 92	4c
Tissues, facial, Kleenex brand	175-count box	1.19	4Q 92	4c

Tucson, AZ - continued

Item	Per	Value	Date	Ref.
Housing				
ACCRA Index, Housing		98.60	4Q 92	4c
House, 1,800 sq ft, 8,000 sq ft lot, new, urban	total	110875	4Q 92	4c
House, median price	unit	80,000	90	79c
House payment, principal and interest, 25% down payment	month	617	4Q 92	4c
Mortgage rate, incl. points & origination fee, 30-year fixed or adjustable rate	percent	8.11	4Q 92	4c
Rent, apartment, 2 bedrooms - 1-1/2 to 2 baths, unfurnished, 950 sq ft, water	month	462	4Q 92	4c
Rental unit, 1 bedroom	month	392	93	23c
Rental unit, 2 bedroom	month	490	93	23c
Rental unit, 3 bedroom	month	612	93	23c
Rental unit, 4 bedroom	month	686	93	23c
Rental unit, efficiency	month	343	93	23c
Insurance and Pensions				
Auto insurance, private passenger	year	704.41	91	63s
Personal Goods				
Shampoo, Alberto VO5	15 oz	1.19	4Q 92	4c
Toothpaste, Crest or Colgate	6-7 oz	2.21	4Q 92	4c
Personal Services				
Dry cleaning, man's 2-piece suit		6.10	4Q 92	4c
Haircare, woman's shampoo, trim and blow-dry		23.90	4Q 92	4c
Haircut, man's barbershop, no styling		7.40	4Q 92	4c
Restaurant Food				
Chicken, fried, thigh and drumstick		2.14	4Q 92	4c
Hamburger with cheese	1/4 lb	2.05	4Q 92	4c
Pizza, Pizza Hut or Pizza Inn, cheese, thin crust	12-13 in	8.65	4Q 92	4c
Taxes				
Tax, cigarette	pack	18	91	77s
Tax, gasoline	gal	18	91	77s
Taxes, state	capita	1256	91	77s
Transportation				
ACCRA Index, Transportation		101.70	4Q 92	4c
Auto rental, average	day	35.00	6/91	60c
Bus fare	one-way	0.75	3/93	2c
Bus fare, up to 10 miles	one-way	0.75	4Q 92	4c
Driver's license fee		7.00	12/90	43s
Limo fare, airport-city, average	day	10.25	6/91	60c
Taxi fare, airport-city, average	day	14.50	6/91	60c
Tire balance, computer or spin balance, front	wheel	6.93	4Q 92	4c
Travel				
Breakfast	day	7.27	6/91	60c
Business travel	day	178.00	4/93	89r
Dinner	day	18.03	6/91	60c
Lodging	day	95.12	91	60c
Lunch	day	9.32	6/91	60c
Utilities				
ACCRA Index, Utilities		99.90	4Q 92	4c
Electricity	mil Btu	22.82	90	64s
Electricity, partial electric and other energy, 1,800 sq ft living area new home	month	78.62	4Q 92	4c
Electricity, residential	KWh	10.69	2/93	94s
Electricity, winter, 250 KWh	month	24.62	92	55c
Electricity, winter, 500 KWh	month	44.23	92	55c
Electricity, winter, 750 KWh	month	63.83	92	55c
Electricity, winter, 1000 KWh	month	83.43	92	55c

Values are in dollars or fractions of dollars. In the column headed *Ref*, references are shown to sources. Each reference is followed by a letter. These refer to the geographical level for which data were reported: s=State, r=Region, and c=City or metro. The abbreviation *ex* is used to mean *except* or *excluding*; *exp* stands for expenditures. For other abbreviations and further explanations, please see the Introduction.

Tulsa, OK

Item	Per	Value	Date	Ref.
Composite ACCRA index		89.60	4Q 92	4c
Alcoholic Beverages				
Beer, Miller Lite or Budweiser, 12-oz containers	6 pack	3.82	4Q 92	4c
Liquor, J & B Scotch	750 ml	13.83	4Q 92	4c
Wine, Gallo Chablis blanc, 1.5 liter	bottle	4.56	4Q 92	4c
Child Care				
Child care fee, average, center	hour	1.29	90	65r
Child care fee, average, nonregulated family day care	hour	0.89	90	65r
Child care fee, average, regulated family day care	hour	1.32	90	65r
Clothing				
Jeans, man's denim		24.19	4Q 92	4c
Shirt, man's dress shirt		22.80	4Q 92	4c
Undervest, boy's size 10-14, cotton	3	4.40	4Q 92	4c
Communications				
Long-distance telephone service, day, initial minute, 0-100 miles	min	0.12-0.45	91	12s
Long-distance telephone service, day, additional minute, 0-100 miles	min	0.07-0.39	91	12s
Newspaper subscription, daily and Sunday home delivery, large-city	month	8.25	4Q 92	4c
Telephone, flat rate	month	12.07	91	11c
Telephone bill, family of four	month	18.86	4Q 92	4c
Education				
Board, 4-yr private college/university	year	1664	91	22s
Board, 4-yr public college/university	year	1368	91	22s
Expenditures, local gov't, public elementary/secondary	pupil	3901	92	20s
Room, 4-year private college/university	year	1384	91	22s
Room, 4-year public college/university	year	1119	91	22s
Tuition, 2-year private college/university	year	5732	91	22s
Tuition, 2-year public college/university	year	864	91	22s
Tuition, 4-year private college/university	year	5852	91	22s
Tuition, 4-year public college/university, in-state	year	1340	91	22s
Energy and Fuels				
Coal	mil Btu	1.40	90	64s
Energy	mil Btu	7.46	90	64s
Energy, combined forms, 1,800 sq ft heating area	month	99.42	4Q 92	4c
Energy, exc electricity, 1,800 sq ft heating area	month	36.91	4Q 92	4c
Energy exp/householder, 1-family unit	year	471	90	28r
Energy exp/householder, <1,000 sq ft heating area	year	384	90	28r
Energy exp/householder, 1,000-1,999 sq ft heating area	year	421	90	28r
Energy exp/householder, 2,000+ sq ft heating area	year	625	90	28r
Energy exp/householder, mobile home	year	271	90	28r
Energy exp/householder, multifamily	year	355	90	28r
Gas, natural	mil Btu	2.80	90	64s
Gas, natural	000 cu ft	4.72	91	46s
Gas, natural, exp	year	396	91	46s
Gasoline, motor	gal	1.12	4Q 92	4c
Gasoline, unleaded regular	mil Btu	9.00	90	64s
Entertainment				
Bowling, evening rate	game	1.78	4Q 92	4c
Miniature golf admission	adult	6.18	92	1r
Miniature golf admission	child	5.14	92	1r
Monopoly game, Parker Brothers', No. 9		10.58	4Q 92	4c
Movie	admission	5.60	4Q 92	4c
Tennis balls, yellow, Wilson or Penn, 3	can	2.53	4Q 92	4c
Waterpark admission	adult	11.00	92	1r
Waterpark admission	child	8.55	92	1r

Tulsa, OK - continued

Item	Per	Value	Date	Ref.
Funerals				
Casket, 18-gauge steel, velvet interior		2274.41	91	24r
Cosmetology, hair care, etc.		74.62	91	24r
Embalming		229.94	91	24r
Facility use for ceremony		176.61	91	24r
Hearse, local		116.34	91	24r
Limousine, local		72.68	91	24r
Remains to funeral home, transfer		87.72	91	24r
Service charge, professional		712.53	91	24r
Vault, concrete, non-metallic liner		750.55	91	24r
Viewing facilities, use		155.31	91	24r
Goods and Services				
ACCRA Index, Miscellaneous Goods and Services		95.70	4Q 92	4c
Groceries				
ACCRA Index, Groceries		92.60	4Q 92	4c
Apples, Red Delicious	lb	0.79	4/93	16r
Babyfood, strained vegetables, lowest price	4-4.5 oz jar	0.27	4Q 92	4c
Bacon	lb	1.75	4/93	16r
Bananas	lb	0.31	4Q 92	4c
Bananas	lb	0.42	4/93	16r
Beef, stew, boneless	lb	2.61	4/93	16r
Bologna, all beef or mixed	lb	2.24	4/93	16r
Bread, white	24 oz	0.63	4Q 92	4c
Bread, white, pan	lb	0.64	4/93	16r
Bread, whole wheat, pan	lb	0.96	4/93	16r
Cabbage	lb	0.37	4/93	16r
Carrots, short trimmed and topped	lb	0.47	4/93	16r
Celery	lb	0.64	4/93	16r
Cheese, American	lb	2.98	4/93	16r
Cheese, Cheddar	lb	3.28	4/93	16r
Cheese, Kraft grated Parmesan	8-oz canister	3.49	4Q 92	4c
Chicken, fresh, whole	lb	0.77	4/93	16r
Chicken, fryer, whole	lb	0.71	4Q 92	4c
Chicken breast, bone-in	lb	1.92	4/93	16r
Chicken legs, bone-in	lb	1.06	4/93	16r
Chuck roast, graded and ungraded, ex USDA prime and choice	lb	2.40	4/93	16r
Chuck roast, USDA choice, bone-in	lb	2.19	4/93	16r
Chuck roast, USDA choice, boneless	lb	2.38	4/93	16r
Cigarettes, Winston	carton	17.67	4Q 92	4c
Coffee, 100% ground roast, all sizes	lb	2.48	4/93	16r
Coffee, vacuum-packed	13-oz can	1.93	4Q 92	4c
Corn, frozen	10 oz	0.66	4Q 92	4c
Corn Flakes, Kellogg's or Post Toasties	18 oz	2.06	4Q 92	4c
Crackers, soda, salted	lb	1.15	4/93	16r
Eggs, Grade A large	doz	0.74	4Q 92	4c
Eggs, Grade A large	doz	0.96	4/93	16r
Flour, white, all purpose	lb	0.24	4/93	16r
Frankfurters, all meat or all beef	lb	2.01	4/93	16r
Grapefruit	lb	0.44	4/93	16r
Grapes, Thompson Seedless	lb	1.40	4/93	16r
Ground beef, 100% beef	lb	1.58	4/93	16r
Ground beef, lean and extra lean	lb	2.09	4/93	16r
Ground beef or hamburger	lb	1.21	4Q 92	4c
Ground chuck, 100% beef	lb	1.98	4/93	16r
Ham, boneless, excluding canned	lb	2.89	4/93	16r
Ham, picnic, shoulder, bone-in, smoked	lb	1.02	4/93	16r
Ham, rump or steak half, bone-in, smoked	lb	1.48	4/93	16r
Honey, jar	8 oz	0.73-1.19	92	5r
Honey, jar	lb	1.10-1.79	92	5r
Honey, squeeze bear	12-oz	1.19-1.50	92	5r
Ice cream, prepackaged, bulk, regular	1/2 gal	2.41	4/93	16r
Lemons	lb	1.05	4/93	16r
Lettuce, iceberg	head	0.89	4Q 92	4c
Lettuce, iceberg	lb	0.81	4/93	16r
Margarine, Blue Bonnet or Parkay cubes	lb	0.55	4Q 92	4c
Margarine, stick	lb	0.88	4/93	16r

Values are in dollars or fractions of dollars. In the column headed *Ref*, references are shown to sources. Each reference is followed by a letter. These refer to the geographical level for which data were reported: s=State, r=Region, and c=City or metro. The abbreviation *ex* is used to mean *except* or *excluding*; *exp* stands for expenditures. For other abbreviations and further explanations, please see the Introduction.

Tulsa, OK - continued

Item	Per	Value	Date	Ref.
Groceries				
Milk, whole	1/2 gal	1.30	4Q 92	4c
Orange juice, Minute Maid frozen	12-oz can	1.31	4Q 92	4c
Oranges, navel	lb	0.55	4/93	16r
Peaches	29-oz can	1.37	4Q 92	4c
Pears, Anjou	lb	0.92	4/93	16r
Peas Sweet, Del Monte or Green Giant	15-17 oz can	0.56	4Q 92	4c
Pork chops, center cut, bone-in	lb	3.13	4/93	16r
Potato chips	16 oz	2.94	4/93	16r
Potatoes, white	lb	0.43	4/93	16r
Potatoes, white or red	10-lb sack	2.19	4Q 92	4c
Rib roast, USDA choice, bone-in	lb	4.63	4/93	16r
Rice, white, long grain, uncooked	lb	0.45	4/93	16r
Round roast, graded & ungraded, ex USDA prime & choice	lb	3.03	4/93	16r
Round roast, USDA choice, boneless	lb	3.09	4/93	16r
Sausage, fresh, loose	lb	2.08	4/93	16r
Sausage, Jimmy Dean, 100% pork	lb	2.26	4Q 92	4c
Short ribs, bone-in	lb	2.66	4/93	16r
Shortening, vegetable oil blends	lb	0.69	4/93	16r
Shortening, vegetable, Crisco	3-lb can	1.85	4Q 92	4c
Soft drink, Coca Cola	2 liter	1.10	4Q 92	4c
Spaghetti and macaroni	lb	0.81	4/93	16r
Steak, rib eye, USDA choice, boneless	lb	6.24	4/93	16r
Steak, round, graded & ungraded, ex USDA prime & choice	lb	3.31	4/93	16r
Steak, round, USDA choice, boneless	lb	3.34	4/93	16r
Steak, sirloin, graded & ungraded, ex USDA prime & choice	lb	4.19	4/93	16r
Steak, sirloin, USDA choice, boneless	lb	4.46	4/93	16r
Steak, T-bone	lb	4.89	4Q 92	4c
Steak, T-bone, USDA choice, bone-in	lb	5.25	4/93	16r
Strawberries, dry pint	12 oz	0.92	4/93	16r
Sugar, cane or beet	4 lb	1.65	4Q 92	4c
Sugar, white	lb	0.39	4/93	16r
Sugar, white, 33-80 oz pk	lb	0.38	4/93	16r
Tomatoes, field grown	lb	0.88	4/93	16r
Tomatoes, Hunt's or Del Monte	14.5-oz can	0.71	4Q 92	4c
Tuna, chunk, light	6.125-6.5 oz can	0.57	4Q 92	4c
Tuna, chunk, light	lb	1.79	4/93	16r
Turkey, frozen, whole	lb	1.04	4/93	16r
Yogurt, natural, fruit flavored	1/2 pint	0.57	4/93	16r
Health Care				
ACCRA Index, Health Care		89.30	4Q 92	4c
Analgesic, Aspirin, Bayer, 325 mg tablets	100	5.50	4Q 92	4c
Childbirth, cesarean, hospital		5034	91	62r
Childbirth, cesarean, physician's fee		2053	91	62r
Childbirth, normal, hospital		2712	91	62r
Childbirth, normal, physician's fee		1492	91	62r
Dentist's fee, adult teeth cleaning and periodic oral exam	visit	37.43	4Q 92	4c
Doctor's fee, routine exam, established patient	visit	35.70	4Q 92	4c
Hospital care, semiprivate room	day	215.73	90	27c
Hospital care, semiprivate room	day	256.80	4Q 92	4c
Medical insurance premium, per employee, small group comprehensive	month	357.70	10/91	25c
Mental health care, exp	capita	28.84-37.59	90	38s
Mental health care, exp, state mental health agency	capita	35.92	90	38s
Mental health care, hospital psychiatric services, non-Federal, exp	capita	11.62	88	38s

Tulsa, OK - continued

Item	Per	Value	Date	Ref.
Health Care - continued				
Mental health care, mental health organization, multiservice, exp	capita	13.80	88	38s
Mental health care, psychiatric hospitals, private, exp	capita	21.32	88	38s
Mental health care, psychiatric out-patient clinics, freestanding, exp	capita	3.63	88	38s
Mental health care, psychiatric partial-care organizations, freestanding, exp	capita	0.04	88	38s
Mental health care, state and county mental hospitals, exp	capita	20.87	88	38s
Mental health care, VA medical centers, exp	capita	0.46	88	38s
Physician fee, family practice, first-visit		75.00	91	62r
Physician fee, family practice, revisit		34.00	91	62r
Physician fee, general practice, first-visit		61.00	91	62r
Physician fee, general practice, revisit		32.00	91	62r
Physician fee, general surgeon, first-visit		64.00	91	62r
Physician fee, general surgeon, revisit		40.00	91	62r
Physician fee, internal medicine, first-visit		98.00	91	62r
Physician fee, internal medicine, revisit		40.00	91	62r
Physician fee, median, neurosurgeon, first-visit		130.00	91	62r
Physician fee, median, nonsurgical specialist, first-visit		95.00	91	62r
Physician fee, median, orthopedic surgeon, first-visit		91.00	91	62r
Physician fee, median, plastic surgeon, first-visit		66.00	91	62r
Physician fee, median, surgical specialist, first-visit		62.00	91	62r
Physician fee, neurosurgeon, revisit		50.00	91	62r
Physician fee, nonsurgical specialist, revisit		40.00	91	62r
Physician fee, obstetrics/gynecology, first-visit		64.00	91	62r
Physician fee, obstetrics/gynecology, revisit		41.00	91	62r
Physician fee, orthopedic surgeon, revisit		40.00	91	62r
Physician fee, pediatrician, first-visit		49.00	91	62r
Physician fee, pediatrician, revisit		33.00	91	62r
Physician fee, plastic surgeon, revisit		43.00	91	62r
Physician fee, surgical specialist, revisit		37.00	91	62r
Substance abuse, hospital ancillary charge	incident	1220	90	70s
Substance abuse, hospital physician charge	incident	160	90	70s
Substance abuse, hospital room and board	incident	5490	90	70s
Household Goods				
Appliance repair, home, service call, washing machine	min labor charge	37.77	4Q 92	4c
Laundry detergent, Tide Ultra, Bold, or Cheer	42 oz	3.31	4Q 92	4c
Tissues, facial, Kleenex brand	175-count box	1.18	4Q 92	4c
Housing				
ACCRA Index, Housing		79.60	4Q 92	4c
Home, median price	unit	68.30		26c
House, 1,800 sq ft, 8,000 sq ft lot, new, urban	total	85450	4Q 92	4c
House payment, principal and interest, 25% down payment	month	475	4Q 92	4c
Mortgage rate, incl. points & origination fee, 30-year fixed or adjustable rate	percent	8.11	4Q 92	4c
Rent, apartment, 2 bedrooms - 1-1/2 to 2 baths, unfurnished, 950 sq ft, water	month	426	4Q 92	4c
Rental unit, 1 bedroom	month	337	93	23c
Rental unit, 2 bedroom	month	396	93	23c
Rental unit, 3 bedroom	month	495	93	23c
Rental unit, 4 bedroom	month	554	93	23c
Rental unit, efficiency	month	277	93	23c

Values are in dollars or fractions of dollars. In the column headed *Ref*, references are shown to sources. Each reference is followed by a letter. These refer to the geographical level for which data were reported: s=State, r=Region, and c=City or metro. The abbreviation *ex* is used to mean *except* or *excluding*; *exp* stands for expenditures. For other abbreviations and further explanations, please see the Introduction.

Tulsa, OK - continued

Item	Per	Value	Date	Ref.
Insurance and Pensions				
Auto insurance, private passenger	year	554.09	91	63s
Personal Goods				
Shampoo, Alberto VO5	15 oz	1.36	4Q 92	4c
Toothpaste, Crest or Colgate	6-7 oz	2.12	4Q 92	4c
Personal Services				
Dry cleaning, man's 2-piece suit		5.36	4Q 92	4c
Haircare, woman's shampoo, trim and blow-dry		15.60	4Q 92	4c
Haircut, man's barbershop, no styling		7.00	4Q 92	4c
Restaurant Food				
Chicken, fried, thigh and drumstick		1.85	4Q 92	4c
Hamburger with cheese	1/4 lb	1.87	4Q 92	4c
Pizza, Pizza Hut or Pizza Inn, cheese, thin crust	12-13 in	7.49	4Q 92	4c
Taxes				
Tax, cigarette	pack	23	91	77s
Tax, gasoline	gal	17	91	77s
Taxes, state	capita	1216	91	77s
Transportation				
ACCRA Index, Transportation		90.90	4Q 92	4c
Auto rental, average	day	45.67	6/91	60c
Bus fare	one-way	0.75	3/93	2c
Driver's license fee		7.00-14.00	12/90	43s
Taxi fare, airport-city, average	day	12.75	6/91	60c
Tire balance, computer or spin balance, front	wheel	5.40	4Q 92	4c
Travel				
Breakfast	day	5.50	6/91	60c
Business travel	day	193.00	4/93	89r
Dinner	day	17.81	6/91	60c
Lodging	day	87.50	91	60c
Lunch	day	8.27	6/91	60c
Utilities				
ACCRA Index, Utilities		91.60	4Q 92	4c
Electricity	mil Btu	16.08	90	64s
Electricity, partial electric and other energy, 1,800 sq ft living area new home	month	62.51	4Q 92	4c
Electricity, residential	KWh	6.24	2/93	94s
Electricity, winter, 250 KWh	month	21.29	92	55c
Electricity, winter, 500 KWh	month	35.70	92	55c
Electricity, winter, 750 KWh	month	46.80	92	55c
Electricity, winter, 1000 KWh	month	55.69	92	55c

Tuscaloosa, AL

Item	Per	Value	Date	Ref.
Composite ACCRA index		97.20	4Q 92	4c
Alcoholic Beverages				
Beer, Miller Lite or Budweiser, 12-oz containers	6 pack	4.19	4Q 92	4c
Liquor, J & B Scotch	750 ml	19.99	4Q 92	4c
Wine, Gallo Chablis blanc, 1.5 liter	bottle	5.43	4Q 92	4c
Child Care				
Child care fee, average, center	hour	1.29	90	65r
Child care fee, average, nonregulated family day care	hour	0.89	90	65r
Child care fee, average, regulated family day care	hour	1.32	90	65r
Clothing				
Jeans, man's denim		35.58	4Q 92	4c
Shirt, man's dress shirt		25.66	4Q 92	4c
Undervest, boy's size 10-14, cotton	3	3.74	4Q 92	4c
Communications				
Long-distance telephone service, day, initial minute, 0-100 miles	min	0.11-0.36	91	12s

Tuscaloosa, AL - continued

Item	Per	Value	Date	Ref.
Communications - continued				
Long-distance telephone service, day, additional minute, 0-100 miles	min	0.09-0.26	91	12s
Long-distance telephone service, evenings/weekends, 0-100 mi, initial minute	min	0.04-0.14	91	12s
Long-distance telephone service, evenings/weekends, 0-100 mi, additional minute	min	0.04-0.10	91	12s
Newspaper subscription, daily and Sunday home delivery, large-city	month	10.25	4Q 92	4c
Telephone, flat rate	month	16.56	91	11c
Telephone bill, family of four	month	22.68	4Q 92	4c
Education				
Board, 4-yr private college/university	year	1795	91	22s
Board, 4-yr public college/university	year	1469	91	22s
Expenditures, local gov't, public elementary/secondary	pupil	3675	92	20s
Room, 4-year private college/university	year	1340	91	22s
Room, 4-year public college/university	year	1295	91	22s
Tuition, 2-year private college/university	year	4148	91	22s
Tuition, 2-year public college/university	year	689	91	22s
Tuition, 4-year private college/university	year	5942	91	22s
Tuition, 4-year public college/university, in-state	year	1593	91	22s
Energy and Fuels				
Coal	mil Btu	1.83	90	64s
Energy	mil Btu	7.92	90	64s
Energy, combined forms, 1,800 sq ft heating area	month	124.05	4Q 92	4c
Energy, exc electricity, 1,800 sq ft heating area	month	42.92	4Q 92	4c
Energy exp/householder, 1-family unit	year	403	90	28r
Energy exp/householder, <1,000 sq ft heating area	year	342	90	28r
Energy exp/householder, 1,000-1,999 sq ft heating area	year	388	90	28r
Energy exp/householder, 2,000+ sq ft heating area	year	434	90	28r
Energy exp/householder, mobile home	year	320	90	28r
Energy exp/householder, multifamily	year	338	90	28r
Gas, natural	mil Btu	4.07	90	64s
Gas, natural	000 cu ft	7.05	91	46s
Gas, natural, exp	year	461	91	46s
Gasoline, motor	gal	1.12	4Q 92	4c
Gasoline, unleaded regular	mil Btu	8.96	90	64s
Entertainment				
Bowling, evening rate	game	2.10	4Q 92	4c
Miniature golf admission	adult	6.18	92	1r
Miniature golf admission	child	5.14	92	1r
Monopoly game, Parker Brothers', No. 9		11.10	4Q 92	4c
Movie	admission	5.25	4Q 92	4c
Tennis balls, yellow, Wilson or Penn, 3	can	2.20	4Q 92	4c
Waterpark admission	adult	11.00	92	1r
Waterpark admission	child	8.55	92	1r
Funerals				
Casket, 18-gauge steel, velvet interior		2329.05	91	24r
Cosmetology, hair care, etc.		72.78	91	24r
Embalming		240.71	91	24r
Facility use for ceremony		181.67	91	24r
Hearse, local		106.25	91	24r
Limousine, local		70.92	91	24r
Remains to funeral home, transfer		96.30	91	24r
Service charge, professional		687.09	91	24r
Vault, concrete, non-metallic liner		732.09	91	24r
Viewing facilities, use		190.30	91	24r
Goods and Services				
ACCRA Index, Miscellaneous Goods and Services		101.80	4Q 92	4c

Values are in dollars or fractions of dollars. In the column headed *Ref*, references are shown to sources. Each reference is followed by a letter. These refer to the geographical level for which data were reported: s=State, r=Region, and c=City or metro. The abbreviation *ex* is used to mean *except* or *excluding*; *exp* stands for expenditures. For other abbreviations and further explanations, please see the Introduction.

Tuscaloosa, AL - continued

Item	Per	Value	Date	Ref.
Groceries				
ACCRA Index, Groceries		94.60	4Q 92	4c
Apples, Red Delicious	lb	0.79	4/93	16r
Babyfood, strained vegetables, lowest price	4-4.5 oz jar	0.26	4Q 92	4c
Bacon	lb	1.75	4/93	16r
Bananas	lb	0.38	4Q 92	4c
Bananas	lb	0.42	4/93	16r
Beef, stew, boneless	lb	2.61	4/93	16r
Bologna, all beef or mixed	lb	2.24	4/93	16r
Bread, white	24 oz	0.71	4Q 92	4c
Bread, white, pan	lb	0.64	4/93	16r
Bread, whole wheat, pan	lb	0.96	4/93	16r
Cabbage	lb	0.37	4/93	16r
Carrots, short trimmed and topped	lb	0.47	4/93	16r
Celery	lb	0.64	4/93	16r
Cheese, American	lb	2.98	4/93	16r
Cheese, Cheddar	lb	3.28	4/93	16r
Cheese, Kraft grated Parmesan	8-oz canister	3.33	4Q 92	4c
Chicken, fresh, whole	lb	0.77	4/93	16r
Chicken, fryer, whole	lb	0.60	4Q 92	4c
Chicken breast, bone-in	lb	1.92	4/93	16r
Chicken legs, bone-in	lb	1.06	4/93	16r
Chuck roast, graded and ungraded, ex USDA prime and choice	lb	2.40	4/93	16r
Chuck roast, USDA choice, bone-in	lb	2.19	4/93	16r
Chuck roast, USDA choice, boneless	lb	2.38	4/93	16r
Cigarettes, Winston	carton	16.80	4Q 92	4c
Coffee, 100% ground roast, all sizes	lb	2.48	4/93	16r
Coffee, vacuum-packed	13-oz can	2.02	4Q 92	4c
Corn, frozen	10 oz	0.66	4Q 92	4c
Corn Flakes, Kellogg's or Post Toasties	18 oz	1.60	4Q 92	4c
Crackers, soda, salted	lb	1.15	4/93	16r
Eggs, Grade A large	doz	0.76	4Q 92	4c
Eggs, Grade A large	doz	0.96	4/93	16r
Flour, white, all purpose	lb	0.24	4/93	16r
Frankfurters, all meat or all beef	lb	2.01	4/93	16r
Grapefruit	lb	0.44	4/93	16r
Grapes, Thompson Seedless	lb	1.40	4/93	16r
Ground beef, 100% beef	lb	1.58	4/93	16r
Ground beef, lean and extra lean	lb	2.09	4/93	16r
Ground beef or hamburger	lb	1.70	4Q 92	4c
Ground chuck, 100% beef	lb	1.98	4/93	16r
Ham, boneless, excluding canned	lb	2.89	4/93	16r
Ham, picnic, shoulder, bone-in, smoked	lb	1.02	4/93	16r
Ham, rump or steak half, bone-in, smoked	lb	1.48	4/93	16r
Honey, jar	8 oz	0.89-1.09	92	5r
Honey, jar	lb	1.39-2.25	92	5r
Honey, squeeze bear	12-oz	1.00-1.50	92	5r
Ice cream, prepackaged, bulk, regular	1/2 gal	2.41	4/93	16r
Lemons	lb	1.05	4/93	16r
Lettuce, iceberg	head	0.92	4Q 92	4c
Lettuce, iceberg	lb	0.81	4/93	16r
Margarine, Blue Bonnet or Parkay cubes	lb	0.48	4Q 92	4c
Margarine, stick	lb	0.88	4/93	16r
Milk, whole	1/2 gal	1.36	4Q 92	4c
Orange juice, Minute Maid frozen	12-oz can	1.21	4Q 92	4c
Oranges, navel	lb	0.55	4/93	16r
Peaches	29-oz can	1.28	4Q 92	4c
Pears, Anjou	lb	0.92	4/93	16r
Peas Sweet, Del Monte or Green Giant	15-17 oz can	0.52	4Q 92	4c
Pork chops, center cut, bone-in	lb	3.13	4/93	16r
Potato chips	16 oz	2.94	4/93	16r
Potatoes, white	lb	0.43	4/93	16r
Potatoes, white or red	10-lb sack	2.76	4Q 92	4c
Rib roast, USDA choice, bone-in	lb	4.63	4/93	16r

Tuscaloosa, AL - continued

Item	Per	Value	Date	Ref.
Groceries - continued				
Rice, white, long grain, uncooked	lb	0.45	4/93	16r
Round roast, graded & ungraded, ex USDA prime & choice	lb	3.03	4/93	16r
Round roast, USDA choice, boneless	lb	3.09	4/93	16r
Sausage, fresh, loose	lb	2.08	4/93	16r
Sausage, Jimmy Dean, 100% pork	lb	2.33	4Q 92	4c
Short ribs, bone-in	lb	2.66	4/93	16r
Shortening, vegetable oil blends	lb	0.69	4/93	16r
Shortening, vegetable, Crisco	3-lb can	2.19	4Q 92	4c
Soft drink, Coca Cola	2 liter	1.05	4Q 92	4c
Spaghetti and macaroni	lb	0.81	4/93	16r
Steak, rib eye, USDA choice, boneless	lb	6.24	4/93	16r
Steak, round, graded & ungraded, ex USDA prime & choice	lb	3.31	4/93	16r
Steak, round, USDA choice, boneless	lb	3.34	4/93	16r
Steak, sirloin, graded & ungraded, ex USDA prime & choice	lb	4.19	4/93	16r
Steak, sirloin, USDA choice, boneless	lb	4.46	4/93	16r
Steak, T-bone	lb	5.49	4Q 92	4c
Steak, T-bone, USDA choice, bone-in	lb	5.25	4/93	16r
Strawberries, dry pint	12 oz	0.92	4/93	16r
Sugar, cane or beet	4 lb	1.40	4Q 92	4c
Sugar, white	lb	0.39	4/93	16r
Sugar, white, 33-80 oz pk	lb	0.38	4/93	16r
Tomatoes, field grown	lb	0.88	4/93	16r
Tomatoes, Hunt's or Del Monte	14.5-oz can	0.56	4Q 92	4c
Tuna, chunk, light	6.125-6.5 oz can	0.52	4Q 92	4c
Tuna, chunk, light	lb	1.79	4/93	16r
Turkey, frozen, whole	lb	1.04	4/93	16r
Yogurt, natural, fruit flavored	1/2 pint	0.57	4/93	16r
Health Care				
ACCRA Index, Health Care		90.60	4Q 92	4c
Analgesic, Aspirin, Bayer, 325 mg tablets	100	4.17	4Q 92	4c
Childbirth, cesarean, hospital		5034	91	62r
Childbirth, cesarean, physician's fee		2053	91	62r
Childbirth, normal, hospital		2712	91	62r
Childbirth, normal, physician's fee		1492	91	62r
Dentist's fee, adult teeth cleaning and periodic oral exam	visit	42.79	4Q 92	4c
Doctor's fee, routine exam, established patient	visit	35.00	4Q 92	4c
Hospital care, semiprivate room	day	272.00	4Q 92	4c
Medical insurance premium, per employee, small group comprehensive	month	222.20	10/91	25c
Mental health care, exp	capita	37.60-53.67	90	38s
Mental health care, exp, state mental health agency	capita	38.35	90	38s
Mental health care, hospital psychiatric services, non-Federal, exp	capita	13.58	88	38s
Mental health care, mental health organization, multiservice, exp	capita	12.40	88	38s
Mental health care, psychiatric hospitals, private, exp	capita	9.49	88	38s
Mental health care, state and county mental hospitals, exp	capita	22.15	88	38s
Mental health care, VA medical centers, exp	capita	10.94	88	38s
Physician fee, family practice, first-visit		75.00	91	62r
Physician fee, family practice, revisit		34.00	91	62r
Physician fee, general practice, first-visit		61.00	91	62r
Physician fee, general practice, revisit		32.00	91	62r
Physician fee, general surgeon, first-visit		64.00	91	62r
Physician fee, general surgeon, revisit		40.00	91	62r
Physician fee, internal medicine, first-visit		98.00	91	62r
Physician fee, internal medicine, revisit		40.00	91	62r
Physician fee, median, neurosurgeon, first-visit		130.00	91	62r

Values are in dollars or fractions of dollars. In the column headed *Ref*, references are shown to sources. Each reference is followed by a letter. These refer to the geographical level for which data were reported: s=State, r=Region, and c=City or metro. The abbreviation *ex* is used to mean *except* or *excluding*; *exp* stands for expenditures. For other abbreviations and further explanations, please see the Introduction.

Tuscaloosa, AL - continued

Item	Per	Value	Date	Ref.
Health Care				
Physician fee, median, nonsurgical specialist, first-visit		95.00	91	62r
Physician fee, median, orthopedic surgeon, first-visit		91.00	91	62r
Physician fee, median, plastic surgeon, first-visit		66.00	91	62r
Physician fee, median, surgical specialist, first-visit		62.00	91	62r
Physician fee, neurosurgeon, revisit		50.00	91	62r
Physician fee, nonsurgical specialist, revisit		40.00	91	62r
Physician fee, obstetrics/gynecology, first-visit		64.00	91	62r
Physician fee, obstetrics/gynecology, revisit		41.00	91	62r
Physician fee, orthopedic surgeon, revisit		40.00	91	62r
Physician fee, pediatrician, first-visit		49.00	91	62r
Physician fee, pediatrician, revisit		33.00	91	62r
Physician fee, plastic surgeon, revisit		43.00	91	62r
Physician fee, surgical specialist, revisit		37.00	91	62r
Substance abuse, hospital ancillary charge	incident	1390	90	70s
Substance abuse, hospital physician charge	incident	520	90	70s
Substance abuse, hospital room and board	incident	5830	90	70s
Household Goods				
Appliance repair, home, service call, washing machine	min labor charge	35.69	4Q 92	4c
Laundry detergent, Tide Ultra, Bold, or Cheer	42 oz	2.84	4Q 92	4c
Tissues, facial, Kleenex brand	175-count box	1.07	4Q 92	4c
Housing				
ACCRA Index, Housing		87.30	4Q 92	4c
House, 1,800 sq ft, 8,000 sq ft lot, new, urban	total	97217	4Q 92	4c
House payment, principal and interest, 25% down payment	month	539	4Q 92	4c
Mortgage rate, incl. points & origination fee, 30-year fixed or adjustable rate	percent	8.08	4Q 92	4c
Rent, apartment, 2 bedrooms - 1-1/2 to 2 baths, unfurnished, 950 sq ft, water	month	425	4Q 92	4c
Rental unit, 1 bedroom	month	353	93	23c
Rental unit, 2 bedroom	month	417	93	23c
Rental unit, 3 bedroom	month	521	93	23c
Rental unit, 4 bedroom	month	585	93	23c
Rental unit, efficiency	month	291	93	23c
Insurance and Pensions				
Auto insurance, private passenger	year	562.59	91	63s
Personal Goods				
Shampoo, Alberto VO5	15 oz	1.10	4Q 92	4c
Toothpaste, Crest or Colgate	6-7 oz	1.88	4Q 92	4c
Personal Services				
Dry cleaning, man's 2-piece suit		6.88	4Q 92	4c
Haircare, woman's shampoo, trim and blow-dry		17.98	4Q 92	4c
Haircut, man's barbershop, no styling		8.40	4Q 92	4c
Restaurant Food				
Chicken, fried, thigh and drumstick		1.84	4Q 92	4c
Hamburger with cheese	1/4 lb	1.71	4Q 92	4c
Pizza, Pizza Hut or Pizza Inn, cheese, thin crust	12-13 in	8.27	4Q 92	4c
Taxes				
Tax, cigarette	pack	16.50	91	77s
Tax, gasoline	gal	16	91	77s
Taxes, state	capita	964	91	77s

Tuscaloosa, AL - continued

Item	Per	Value	Date	Ref.
Transportation				
ACCRA Index, Transportation		100.90	4Q 92	4c
Driver's license fee		15.00	12/90	43s
Tire balance, computer or spin balance, front	wheel	6.70	4Q 92	4c
Travel				
Business travel	day	193.00	4/93	89r
Utilities				
ACCRA Index, Utilities		113.90	4Q 92	4c
Electricity	mil Btu	16.46	90	64s
Electricity, partial electric and other energy, 1,800 sq ft living area new home	month	81.13	4Q 92	4c

Tyler, TX

Item	Per	Value	Date	Ref.
Composite ACCRA index		95.30	4Q 92	4c
Alcoholic Beverages				
Beer, Miller Lite or Budweiser, 12-oz containers	6 pack	3.98	4Q 92	4c
Liquor, J & B Scotch	750 ml	17.99	4Q 92	4c
Wine, Gallo Chablis blanc, 1.5 liter	bottle	5.59	4Q 92	4c
Child Care				
Child care fee, average, center	hour	1.29	90	65r
Child care fee, average, nonregulated family day care	hour	0.89	90	65r
Child care fee, average, regulated family day care	hour	1.32	90	65r
Clothing				
Jeans, man's denim		24.79	4Q 92	4c
Shirt, man's dress shirt		23.50	4Q 92	4c
Undervest, boy's size 10-14, cotton	3	4.35	4Q 92	4c
Communications				
Long-distance telephone service, day, initial minute, 0-100 miles	min	0.10-0.46	91	12s
Long-distance telephone service, day, additional minute, 0-100 miles	min	0.06-0.45	91	12s
Newspaper subscription, daily and Sunday home delivery, large-city	month	11.96	4Q 92	4c
Telephone, flat rate	month	9.10	91	11c
Telephone bill, family of four	month	15.36	4Q 92	4c
Education				
Board, 4-yr private college/university	year	1883	91	22s
Board, 4-yr public college/university	year	1605	91	22s
Expenditures, local gov't, public elementary/secondary	pupil	4593	92	20s
Room, 4-year private college/university	year	1620	91	22s
Room, 4-year public college/university	year	1532	91	22s
Tuition, 2-year private college/university	year	4394	91	22s
Tuition, 2-year public college/university	year	495	91	22s
Tuition, 4-year private college/university	year	6497	91	22s
Tuition, 4-year public college/university, in-state	year	986	91	22s
Energy and Fuels				
Coal	mil Btu	1.44	90	64s
Energy	mil Btu	6.48	90	64s
Energy, combined forms, 1,800 sq ft heating area	month	123.02	4Q 92	4c
Energy, exc electricity, 1,800 sq ft heating area	month	30.06	4Q 92	4c
Energy exp/householder, 1-family unit	year	471	90	28r
Energy exp/householder, <1,000 sq ft heating area	year	384	90	28r
Energy exp/householder, 1,000-1,999 sq ft heating area	year	421	90	28r
Energy exp/householder, 2,000+ sq ft heating area	year	625	90	28r
Energy exp/householder, mobile home	year	271	90	28r
Energy exp/householder, multifamily	year	355	90	28r

Values are in dollars or fractions of dollars. In the column headed *Ref*, references are shown to sources. Each reference is followed by a letter. These refer to the geographical level for which data were reported: s=State, r=Region, and c=City or metro. The abbreviation *ex* is used to mean *except* or *excluding*; *exp* stands for expenditures. For other abbreviations and further explanations, please see the Introduction.

Tyler, TX - continued

Item	Per	Value	Date	Ref.
Energy and Fuels				
Gas, natural	mil Btu	2.47	90	64s
Gas, natural	000 cu ft	5.71	91	46s
Gas, natural, exp	year	388	91	46s
Gasoline, motor	gal	1.07	4Q 92	4c
Gasoline, unleaded regular	mil Btu	9.16	90	64s
Entertainment				
Bowling, evening rate	game	2.40	4Q 92	4c
Miniature golf admission	adult	6.18	92	1r
Miniature golf admission	child	5.14	92	1r
Monopoly game, Parker Brothers', No. 9		11.23	4Q 92	4c
Movie	admission	5.00	4Q 92	4c
Tennis balls, yellow, Wilson or Penn, 3	can	2.10	4Q 92	4c
Waterpark admission	adult	11.00	92	1r
Waterpark admission	child	8.55	92	1r
Funerals				
Casket, 18-gauge steel, velvet interior		2274.41	91	24r
Cosmetology, hair care, etc.		74.62	91	24r
Embalming		229.94	91	24r
Facility use for ceremony		176.61	91	24r
Hearse, local		116.34	91	24r
Limousine, local		72.68	91	24r
Remains to funeral home, transfer		87.72	91	24r
Service charge, professional		712.53	91	24r
Vault, concrete, non-metallic liner		750.55	91	24r
Viewing facilities, use		155.31	91	24r
Goods and Services				
ACCRA Index, Miscellaneous Goods and Services		99.20	4Q 92	4c
Groceries				
ACCRA Index, Groceries		88.00	4Q 92	4c
Apples, Red Delicious	lb	0.79	4/93	16r
Babyfood, strained vegetables, lowest price	4-4.5 oz jar	0.24	4Q 92	4c
Bacon	lb	1.75	4/93	16r
Bananas	lb	0.38	4Q 92	4c
Bananas	lb	0.42	4/93	16r
Beef, stew, boneless	lb	2.61	4/93	16r
Bologna, all beef or mixed	lb	2.24	4/93	16r
Bread, white	24 oz	0.66	4Q 92	4c
Bread, white, pan	lb	0.64	4/93	16r
Bread, whole wheat, pan	lb	0.96	4/93	16r
Cabbage	lb	0.37	4/93	16r
Carrots, short trimmed and topped	lb	0.47	4/93	16r
Celery	lb	0.64	4/93	16r
Cheese, American	lb	2.98	4/93	16r
Cheese, Cheddar	lb	3.28	4/93	16r
Cheese, Kraft grated Parmesan	8-oz canister	3.45	4Q 92	4c
Chicken, fresh, whole	lb	0.77	4/93	16r
Chicken, fryer, whole	lb	0.59	4Q 92	4c
Chicken breast, bone-in	lb	1.92	4/93	16r
Chicken legs, bone-in	lb	1.06	4/93	16r
Chuck roast, graded and ungraded, ex USDA prime and choice	lb	2.40	4/93	16r
Chuck roast, USDA choice, bone-in	lb	2.19	4/93	16r
Chuck roast, USDA choice, boneless	lb	2.38	4/93	16r
Cigarettes, Winston	carton	18.32	4Q 92	4c
Coffee, 100% ground roast, all sizes	lb	2.48	4/93	16r
Coffee, vacuum-packed	13-oz can	1.83	4Q 92	4c
Corn, frozen	10 oz	0.77	4Q 92	4c
Corn Flakes, Kellogg's or Post Toasties	18 oz	1.88	4Q 92	4c
Crackers, soda, salted	lb	1.15	4/93	16r
Eggs, Grade A large	doz	0.63	4Q 92	4c
Eggs, Grade A large	doz	0.96	4/93	16r
Flour, white, all purpose	lb	0.24	4/93	16r
Frankfurters, all meat or all beef	lb	2.01	4/93	16r

Tyler, TX - continued

Item	Per	Value	Date	Ref.
Groceries - continued				
Grapefruit	lb	0.44	4/93	16r
Grapes, Thompson Seedless	lb	1.40	4/93	16r
Ground beef, 100% beef	lb	1.58	4/93	16r
Ground beef, lean and extra lean	lb	2.09	4/93	16r
Ground beef or hamburger	lb	1.11	4Q 92	4c
Ground chuck, 100% beef	lb	1.98	4/93	16r
Ham, boneless, excluding canned	lb	2.89	4/93	16r
Ham, picnic, shoulder, bone-in, smoked	lb	1.02	4/93	16r
Ham, rump or steak half, bone-in, smoked	lb	1.48	4/93	16r
Honey, jar	8 oz	0.73-1.19	92	5r
Honey, jar	lb	1.10-1.79	92	5r
Honey, squeeze bear	12-oz	1.19-1.50	92	5r
Ice cream, prepackaged, bulk, regular	1/2 gal	2.41	4/93	16r
Lemons	lb	1.05	4/93	16r
Lettuce, iceberg	head	0.86	4Q 92	4c
Lettuce, iceberg	lb	0.81	4/93	16r
Margarine, Blue Bonnet or Parkay cubes	lb	0.48	4Q 92	4c
Margarine, stick	lb	0.88	4/93	16r
Milk, whole	1/2 gal	1.21	4Q 92	4c
Orange juice, Minute Maid frozen	12-oz can	1.19	4Q 92	4c
Oranges, navel	lb	0.55	4/93	16r
Peaches	29-oz can	1.42	4Q 92	4c
Pears, Anjou	lb	0.92	4/93	16r
Peas Sweet, Del Monte or Green Giant	15-17 oz can	0.51	4Q 92	4c
Pork chops, center cut, bone-in	lb	3.13	4/93	16r
Potato chips	16 oz	2.94	4/93	16r
Potatoes, white	lb	0.43	4/93	16r
Potatoes, white or red	10-lb sack	2.62	4Q 92	4c
Rib roast, USDA choice, bone-in	lb	4.63	4/93	16r
Rice, white, long grain, uncooked	lb	0.45	4/93	16r
Round roast, graded & ungraded, ex USDA prime & choice	lb	3.03	4/93	16r
Round roast, USDA choice, boneless	lb	3.09	4/93	16r
Sausage, fresh, loose	lb	2.08	4/93	16r
Sausage, Jimmy Dean, 100% pork	lb	1.91	4Q 92	4c
Short ribs, bone-in	lb	2.66	4/93	16r
Shortening, vegetable oil blends	lb	0.69	4/93	16r
Shortening, vegetable, Crisco	3-lb can	1.97	4Q 92	4c
Soft drink, Coca Cola	2 liter	0.92	4Q 92	4c
Spaghetti and macaroni	lb	0.81	4/93	16r
Steak, rib eye, USDA choice, boneless	lb	6.24	4/93	16r
Steak, round, graded & ungraded, ex USDA prime & choice	lb	3.31	4/93	16r
Steak, round, USDA choice, boneless	lb	3.34	4/93	16r
Steak, sirloin, graded & ungraded, ex USDA prime & choice	lb	4.19	4/93	16r
Steak, sirloin, USDA choice, boneless	lb	4.46	4/93	16r
Steak, T-bone	lb	4.29	4Q 92	4c
Steak, T-bone, USDA choice, bone-in	lb	5.25	4/93	16r
Strawberries, dry pint	12 oz	0.92	4/93	16r
Sugar, cane or beet	4 lb	1.35	4Q 92	4c
Sugar, white	lb	0.39	4/93	16r
Sugar, white, 33-80 oz pk	lb	0.38	4/93	16r
Tomatoes, field grown	lb	0.88	4/93	16r
Tomatoes, Hunt's or Del Monte	14.5-oz can	0.64	4Q 92	4c
Tuna, chunk, light	6.125-6.5 oz can	0.53	4Q 92	4c
Tuna, chunk, light	lb	1.79	4/93	16r
Turkey, frozen, whole	lb	1.04	4/93	16r
Yogurt, natural, fruit flavored	1/2 pint	0.57	4/93	16r
Health Care				
ACCRA Index, Health Care		86.80	4Q 92	4c
Analgesic, Aspirin, Bayer, 325 mg tablets	100	5.36	4Q 92	4c
Childbirth, cesarean, hospital		5034	91	62r

Values are in dollars or fractions of dollars. In the column headed *Ref*, references are shown to sources. Each reference is followed by a letter. These refer to the geographical level for which data were reported: s=State, r=Region, and c=City or metro. The abbreviation *ex* is used to mean *except* or *excluding*; *exp* stands for expenditures. For other abbreviations and further explanations, please see the Introduction.

Tyler, TX - continued

Item	Per	Value	Date	Ref.
Health Care				
Childbirth, cesarean, physician's fee		2053	91	62r
Childbirth, normal, hospital		2712	91	62r
Childbirth, normal, physician's fee		1492	91	62r
Dentist's fee, adult teeth cleaning and periodic oral exam	visit	30.60	4Q 92	4c
Doctor's fee, routine exam, established patient	visit	35.00	4Q 92	4c
Health care spending, state	capita	2192	3/93	84s
Hospital care, semiprivate room	day	254.12	90	27c
Hospital care, semiprivate room	day	320.00	4Q 92	4c
Medical insurance premium, per employee, small group comprehensive	month	349.45	10/91	25c
Mental health care, exp	capita	20.37-28.83	90	38s
Mental health care, exp, state mental health agency	capita	22.72	90	38s
Mental health care, hospital psychiatric services, non-Federal, exp	capita	7.95	88	38s
Mental health care, mental health organization, multiservice, exp	capita	12.05	88	38s
Mental health care, psychiatric hospitals, private, exp	capita	37.78	88	38s
Mental health care, psychiatric out-patient clinics, freestanding, exp	capita	0.43	88	38s
Mental health care, state and county mental hospitals, exp	capita	12.54	88	38s
Mental health care, VA medical centers, exp	capita	5.35	88	38s
Physician fee, family practice, first-visit		75.00	91	62r
Physician fee, family practice, revisit		34.00	91	62r
Physician fee, general practice, first-visit		61.00	91	62r
Physician fee, general practice, revisit		32.00	91	62r
Physician fee, general surgeon, first-visit		64.00	91	62r
Physician fee, general surgeon, revisit		40.00	91	62r
Physician fee, internal medicine, first-visit		98.00	91	62r
Physician fee, internal medicine, revisit		40.00	91	62r
Physician fee, median, neurosurgeon, first-visit		130.00	91	62r
Physician fee, median, nonsurgical specialist, first-visit		95.00	91	62r
Physician fee, median, orthopedic surgeon, first-visit		91.00	91	62r
Physician fee, median, plastic surgeon, first-visit		66.00	91	62r
Physician fee, median, surgical specialist, first-visit		62.00	91	62r
Physician fee, neurosurgeon, revisit		50.00	91	62r
Physician fee, nonsurgical specialist, revisit		40.00	91	62r
Physician fee, obstetrics/gynecology, first-visit		64.00	91	62r
Physician fee, obstetrics/gynecology, revisit		41.00	91	62r
Physician fee, orthopedic surgeon, revisit		40.00	91	62r
Physician fee, pediatrician, first-visit		49.00	91	62r
Physician fee, pediatrician, revisit		33.00	91	62r
Physician fee, plastic surgeon, revisit		43.00	91	62r
Physician fee, surgical specialist, revisit		37.00	91	62r
Substance abuse, hospital ancillary charge	incident	3750	90	70s
Substance abuse, hospital physician charge	incident	1080	90	70s
Substance abuse, hospital room and board	incident	5320	90	70s
Household Goods				
Appliance repair, home, service call, washing machine	min labor charge	38.83	4Q 92	4c
Laundry detergent, Tide Ultra, Bold, or Cheer	42 oz	3.60	4Q 92	4c
Tissues, facial, Kleenex brand	175-count box	1.07	4Q 92	4c

Tyler, TX - continued

Item	Per	Value	Date	Ref.
Housing				
ACCRA Index, Housing		92.30	4Q 92	4c
House, 1,800 sq ft, 8,000 sq ft lot, new, urban	total	103333	4Q 92	4c
House payment, principal and interest, 25% down payment	month	572	4Q 92	4c
Mortgage rate, incl. points & origination fee, 30-year fixed or adjustable rate	percent	8.05	4Q 92	4c
Rent, apartment, 2 bedrooms - 1-1/2 to 2 baths, unfurnished, 950 sq ft, water	month	445	4Q 92	4c
Rental unit, 1 bedroom	month	413	93	23c
Rental unit, 2 bedroom	month	488	93	23c
Rental unit, 3 bedroom	month	609	93	23c
Rental unit, 4 bedroom	month	681	93	23c
Rental unit, efficiency	month	341	93	23c
Insurance and Pensions				
Auto insurance, private passenger	year	709.79	91	63s
Personal Goods				
Shampoo, Alberto VO5	15 oz	1.17	4Q 92	4c
Toothpaste, Crest or Colgate	6-7 oz	2.01	4Q 92	4c
Personal Services				
Dry cleaning, man's 2-piece suit		4.69	4Q 92	4c
Haircare, woman's shampoo, trim and blow-dry		21.39	4Q 92	4c
Haircut, man's barbershop, no styling		7.70	4Q 92	4c
Restaurant Food				
Chicken, fried, thigh and drumstick		1.83	4Q 92	4c
Hamburger with cheese	1/4 lb	1.89	4Q 92	4c
Pizza, Pizza Hut or Pizza Inn, cheese, thin crust	12-13 in	7.99	4Q 92	4c
Taxes				
Tax, cigarette	pack	41	91	77s
Tax, gasoline	gal	20	91	77s
Taxes, state	capita	923	91	77s
Transportation				
ACCRA Index, Transportation		91.50	4Q 92	4c
Driver's license fee		16.00	12/90	43s
Tire balance, computer or spin balance, front	wheel	5.75	4Q 92	4c
Travel				
Business travel	day	193.00	4/93	89r
Utilities				
ACCRA Index, Utilities		109.30	4Q 92	4c
Electricity	mil Btu	17.09	90	64s
Electricity, partial electric and other energy, 1,800 sq ft living area new home	month	92.96	4Q 92	4c
Electricity, residential	KWh	5.92	2/93	94s

Utica-Rome, NY

Item	Per	Value	Date	Ref.
Composite ACCRA index		106.30	4Q 92	4c
Alcoholic Beverages				
Beer, Miller Lite or Budweiser, 12-oz containers	6 pack	5.16	4Q 92	4c
Liquor, J & B Scotch	750 ml	18.25	4Q 92	4c
Wine, Gallo Chablis blanc, 1.5 liter	bottle	5.69	4Q 92	4c
Child Care				
Child care fee, average, center	hour	2.18	90	65r
Child care fee, average, nonregulated family day care	hour	1.83	90	65r
Child care fee, average, regulated family day care	hour	2.02	90	65r
Clothing				
Jeans, man's denim		34.19	4Q 92	4c
Shirt, man's dress shirt		25.40	4Q 92	4c
Undervest, boy's size 10-14, cotton	3	4.99	4Q 92	4c

Values are in dollars or fractions of dollars. In the column headed *Ref*, references are shown to sources. Each reference is followed by a letter. These refer to the geographical level for which data were reported: s = State, r = Region, and c = City or metro. The abbreviation *ex* is used to mean *except* or *excluding*; *exp* stands for expenditures. For other abbreviations and further explanations, please see the Introduction.

Utica-Rome, NY - continued

Item	Per	Value	Date	Ref.
Communications				
Newspaper subscription, daily and Sunday home delivery, large-city	month	13.26	4Q 92	4c
Telephone bill, family of four	month	32.98	4Q 92	4c
Education				
Board, 4-yr private college/university	year	2451	91	22s
Board, 4-yr public college/university	year	1725	91	22s
Expenditures, local gov't, public elementary/secondary	pupil	8603	92	20s
Room, 4-year private college/university	year	2652	91	22s
Room, 4-year public college/university	year	2183	91	22s
Tuition, 2-year private college/university	year	5926	91	22s
Tuition, 2-year public college/university	year	1419	91	22s
Tuition, 4-year private college/university	year	10340	91	22s
Tuition, 4-year public college/university, in-state	year	1587	91	22s
Energy and Fuels				
Coal	mil Btu	1.66	90	64s
Energy	mil Btu	10.68	90	64s
Energy, combined forms, 1,800 sq ft heating area	month	132.55	4Q 92	4c
Energy, exc electricity, 1,800 sq ft heating area	month	61.31	4Q 92	4c
Energy exp/householder, 1-family unit	year	588	90	28r
Energy exp/householder, <1,000 sq ft heating area	year	477	90	28r
Energy exp/householder, 1,000-1,999 sq ft heating area	year	517	90	28r
Energy exp/householder, 2,000+ sq ft heating area	year	630	90	28r
Energy exp/householder, mobile home	year	412	90	28r
Energy exp/householder, multifamily	year	498	90	28r
Gas, natural	mil Btu	5.25	90	64s
Gas, natural	000 cu ft	7.35	91	46s
Gas, natural, exp	year	557	91	46s
Gasoline, motor	gal	1.21	4Q 92	4c
Gasoline, unleaded regular	mil Btu	8.83	90	64s
Entertainment				
Bowling, evening rate	game	1.71	4Q 92	4c
Monopoly game, Parker Brothers', No. 9		13.11	4Q 92	4c
Movie	admission	4.75	4Q 92	4c
Tennis balls, yellow, Wilson or Penn, 3	can	2.63	4Q 92	4c
Funerals				
Casket, 18-gauge steel, velvet interior		1811.58	91	24r
Cosmetology, hair care, etc.		111.08	91	24r
Embalming		329.42	91	24r
Facility use for ceremony		201.29	91	24r
Hearse, local		135.27	91	24r
Limousine, local		127.24	91	24r
Remains to funeral home, transfer		103.98	91	24r
Service charge, professional		724.98	91	24r
Vault, concrete, non-metallic liner		766.71	91	24r
Viewing facilities, use		260.60	91	24r
Goods and Services				
ACCRA Index, Miscellaneous Goods and Services		103.80	4Q 92	4c
Groceries				
ACCRA Index, Groceries		106.10	4Q 92	4c
Apples, Red Delicious	lb	0.85	4/93	16r
Babyfood, strained vegetables, lowest price	4-4.5 oz jar	0.33	4Q 92	4c
Bacon	lb	2.12	4/93	16r
Bananas	lb	0.47	4Q 92	4c
Bananas	lb	0.54	4/93	16r
Bread, white	24 oz	0.83	4Q 92	4c
Bread, white, pan	lb	0.81	4/93	16r
Butter	lb	2.02	4/93	16r
Carrots, short trimmed and topped	lb	0.51	4/93	16r

Utica-Rome, NY - continued

Item	Per	Value	Date	Ref.
Groceries - continued				
Cheese, Kraft grated Parmesan	8-oz canister	2.91	4Q 92	4c
Chicken, fresh, whole	lb	1.04	4/93	16r
Chicken, fryer, whole	lb	0.70	4Q 92	4c
Chicken breast, bone-in	lb	2.21	4/93	16r
Chicken legs, bone-in	lb	1.16	4/93	16r
Chuck roast, USDA choice, boneless	lb	2.82	4/93	16r
Cigarettes, Winston	carton	20.77	4Q 92	4c
Coffee, 100% ground roast, all sizes	lb	2.66	4/93	16r
Coffee, vacuum-packed	13-oz can	2.02	4Q 92	4c
Corn, frozen	10 oz	0.67	4Q 92	4c
Corn Flakes, Kellogg's or Post Toasties	18 oz	2.04	4Q 92	4c
Cucumbers	lb	0.85	4/93	16r
Eggs, Grade A large	doz	0.91	4Q 92	4c
Eggs, Grade A large	doz	1.15	4/93	16r
Grapefruit	lb	0.45	4/93	16r
Grapes, Thompson Seedless	lb	1.52	4/93	16r
Ground beef, lean and extra lean	lb	2.36	4/93	16r
Ground beef or hamburger	lb	1.73	4Q 92	4c
Ground chuck, 100% beef	lb	2.02	4/93	16r
Honey, jar	8 oz	0.96-1.75	92	5r
Honey, jar	lb	1.50-3.00	92	5r
Honey, squeeze bear	12-oz	1.50-1.99	92	5r
Ice cream, prepackaged, bulk, regular	1/2 gal	2.80	4/93	16r
Lemons	lb	0.96	4/93	16r
Lettuce, iceberg	head	0.99	4Q 92	4c
Lettuce, iceberg	lb	0.95	4/93	16r
Margarine, Blue Bonnet or Parkay cubes	lb	0.58	4Q 92	4c
Margarine, stick	lb	0.81	4/93	16r
Milk, fresh, whole, fortified	1/2 gal	1.30	4/93	16r
Milk, whole	1/2 gal	1.15	4Q 92	4c
Orange juice, Minute Maid frozen	12-oz can	1.44	4Q 92	4c
Oranges, navel	lb	0.56	4/93	16r
Peaches	29-oz can	1.32	4Q 92	4c
Peanut butter, creamy, all sizes	lb	1.88	4/93	16r
Peas Sweet, Del Monte or Green Giant	15-17 oz can	0.59	4Q 92	4c
Pork chops, center cut, bone-in	lb	3.34	4/93	16r
Potato chips	16 oz	2.88	4/93	16r
Potatoes, white	lb	0.37	4/93	16r
Potatoes, white or red	10-lb sack	1.59	4Q 92	4c
Rib roast, USDA choice, bone-in	lb	4.94	4/93	16r
Round roast, USDA choice, boneless	lb	3.17	4/93	16r
Sausage, Jimmy Dean, 100% pork	lb	3.50	4Q 92	4c
Shortening, vegetable oil blends	lb	0.98	4/93	16r
Shortening, vegetable, Crisco	3-lb can	2.65	4Q 92	4c
Soft drink, Coca Cola	2 liter	1.14	4Q 92	4c
Spaghetti and macaroni	lb	0.82	4/93	16r
Steak, round, graded & ungraded, ex USDA prime & choice	lb	4.04	4/93	16r
Steak, round, USDA choice, boneless	lb	3.90	4/93	16r
Steak, sirloin, USDA choice, boneless	lb	4.97	4/93	16r
Steak, T-bone	lb	5.65	4Q 92	4c
Strawberries, dry pint	12 oz	0.90	4/93	16r
Sugar, cane or beet	4 lb	1.59	4Q 92	4c
Sugar, white	lb	0.50	4/93	16r
Sugar, white, 33-80 oz pk	lb	0.41	4/93	16r
Tomatoes, field grown	lb	1.23	4/93	16r
Tomatoes, Hunt's or Del Monte	14.5-oz can	0.79	4Q 92	4c
Tuna, chunk, light	6.125-6.5 oz can	0.71	4Q 92	4c
Tuna, chunk, light	lb	2.22	4/93	16r
Turkey, frozen, whole	lb	1.04	4/93	16r

Values are in dollars or fractions of dollars. In the column headed *Ref*, references are shown to sources. Each reference is followed by a letter. These refer to the geographical level for which data were reported: s = State, r = Region, and c = City or metro. The abbreviation *ex* is used to mean *except* or *excluding*; *exp* stands for expenditures. For other abbreviations and further explanations, please see the Introduction.

Utica-Rome, NY - continued

Item	Per	Value	Date	Ref.
Health Care				
ACCRA Index, Health Care		113.30	4Q 92	4c
Analgesic, Aspirin, Bayer, 325 mg tablets	100	5.33	4Q 92	4c
Childbirth, cesarean, hospital		5826	91	62r
Childbirth, cesarean, physician's fee		2053	91	62r
Childbirth, normal, hospital		2964	91	62r
Childbirth, normal, physician's fee		1492	91	62r
Dentist's fee, adult teeth cleaning and periodic oral exam	visit	45.40	4Q 92	4c
Doctor's fee, routine exam, established patient	visit	55.00	4Q 92	4c
Hospital care, semiprivate room	day	207.80	90	27c
Hospital care, semiprivate room	day	256.00	4Q 92	4c
Medical insurance premium, per employee, small group comprehensive	month	284.70	10/91	25c
Medical plan per employee	year	3942	91	45r
Mental health care, exp	capita	53.68-118.35	90	38s
Mental health care, exp, state mental health agency	capita	118.34	90	38s
Mental health care, hospital psychiatric services, non-Federal, exp	capita	29.77	88	38s
Mental health care, mental health organization, multiservice, exp	capita	20.03	88	38s
Mental health care, psychiatric hospitals, private, exp	capita	8.37	88	38s
Mental health care, psychiatric out-patient clinics, freestanding, exp	capita	7.96	88	38s
Mental health care, psychiatric partial-care organizations, freestanding, exp	capita	1.24	88	38s
Mental health care, state and county mental hospitals, exp	capita	89.52	88	38s
Mental health care, VA medical centers, exp	capita	7.12	88	38s
Prescription drug co-pay, Medicaid	month	23.00	91	21s
Substance abuse, hospital ancillary charge	incident	1040	90	70s
Substance abuse, hospital physician charge	incident	360	90	70s
Substance abuse, hospital room and board	incident	6330	90	70s
Household Goods				
Appliance repair, home, service call, washing machine	min labor charge	27.20	4Q 92	4c
Laundry detergent, Tide Ultra, Bold, or Cheer	42 oz	3.14	4Q 92	4c
Tissues, facial, Kleenex brand	175-count box	1.11	4Q 92	4c
Housing				
ACCRA Index, Housing		100.70	4Q 92	4c
House, 1,800 sq ft, 8,000 sq ft lot, new, urban	total	108563	4Q 92	4c
House payment, principal and interest, 25% down payment	month	613	4Q 92	4c
Mortgage rate, incl. points & origination fee, 30-year fixed or adjustable rate	percent	8.27	4Q 92	4c
Rent, apartment, 2 bedrooms - 1-1/2 to 2 baths, unfurnished, 950 sq ft, water	month	510	4Q 92	4c
Rental unit, 1 bedroom	month	405	93	23c
Rental unit, 2 bedroom	month	477	93	23c
Rental unit, 3 bedroom	month	596	93	23c
Rental unit, 4 bedroom	month	668	93	23c
Rental unit, efficiency	month	334	93	23c
Insurance and Pensions				
Auto insurance, private passenger	year	840.89	91	63s
Personal Goods				
Shampoo, Alberto VO5	15 oz	1.25	4Q 92	4c
Toothpaste, Crest or Colgate	6-7 oz	2.12	4Q 92	4c

Utica-Rome, NY - continued

Item	Per	Value	Date	Ref.
Personal Services				
Dry cleaning, man's 2-piece suit		7.19	4Q 92	4c
Haircare, woman's shampoo, trim and blow-dry		14.80	4Q 92	4c
Haircut, man's barbershop, no styling		6.90	4Q 92	4c
Restaurant Food				
Chicken, fried, thigh and drumstick		2.00	4Q 92	4c
Hamburger with cheese	1/4 lb	1.91	4Q 92	4c
Pizza, Pizza Hut or Pizza Inn, cheese, thin crust	12-13 in	7.93	4Q 92	4c
Taxes				
Tax, cigarette	pack	39	91	77s
Tax, gasoline	gal	8	91	77s
Taxes, state	capita	1567	91	77s
Transportation				
ACCRA Index, Transportation		109.60	4Q 92	4c
Bus fare	one-way	0.75	3/93	2c
Bus fare, up to 10 miles	one-way	1.30	4Q 92	4c
Driver's license fee		17.50	12/90	43s
Tire balance, computer or spin balance, front	wheel	6.70	4Q 92	4c
Vehicle registration and license plate	2 years	27.50-149.50	93	67s
Travel				
Business travel	day	165.00	4/93	89r
Utilities				
ACCRA Index, Utilities		126.20	4Q 92	4c
Electricity	mil Btu	27.51	90	64s
Electricity, partial electric and other energy, 1,800 sq ft living area new home	month	71.24	4Q 92	4c

Valdosta, GA

Item	Per	Value	Date	Ref.
Composite ACCRA index		98.00	4Q 92	4c
Alcoholic Beverages				
Beer, Miller Lite or Budweiser, 12-oz containers	6 pack	4.16	4Q 92	4c
Liquor, J & B Scotch	750 ml	17.06	4Q 92	4c
Wine, Gallo Chablis blanc, 1.5 liter	bottle	6.59	4Q 92	4c
Clothing				
Jeans, man's denim		36.64	4Q 92	4c
Shirt, man's dress shirt		25.00	4Q 92	4c
Undervest, boy's size 10-14, cotton	3	4.71	4Q 92	4c
Communications				
Newspaper subscription, daily and Sunday home delivery, large-city	month	10.35	4Q 92	4c
Telephone, flat rate	month	12.25	91	11c
Telephone bill, family of four	month	18.69	4Q 92	4c
Energy and Fuels				
Energy, combined forms, 1,800 sq ft heating area	month	124.70	4Q 92	4c
Gasoline, motor	gal	1.00	4Q 92	4c
Entertainment				
Bowling, evening rate	game	1.80	4Q 92	4c
Monopoly game, Parker Brothers', No. 9		11.63	4Q 92	4c
Movie	admission	5.00	4Q 92	4c
Tennis balls, yellow, Wilson or Penn, 3	can	2.43	4Q 92	4c
Goods and Services				
ACCRA Index, Miscellaneous Goods and Services		102.70	4Q 92	4c
Groceries				
ACCRA Index, Groceries		95.00	4Q 92	4c

Values are in dollars or fractions of dollars. In the column headed *Ref*, references are shown to sources. Each reference is followed by a letter. These refer to the geographical level for which data were reported: s = State, r = Region, and c = City or metro. The abbreviation *ex* is used to mean *except* or *excluding*; *exp* stands for expenditures. For other abbreviations and further explanations, please see the Introduction.

Valdosta, GA - continued

Item	Per	Value	Date	Ref.
Groceries				
Babyfood, strained vegetables, lowest price	4-4.5 oz jar	0.31	4Q 92	4c
Bananas	lb	0.42	4Q 92	4c
Bread, white	24 oz	0.69	4Q 92	4c
Cheese, Kraft grated Parmesan	8-oz canis-ter	3.12	4Q 92	4c
Chicken, fryer, whole	lb	0.66	4Q 92	4c
Cigarettes, Winston	carton	16.16	4Q 92	4c
Coffee, vacuum-packed	13-oz can	1.95	4Q 92	4c
Corn, frozen	10 oz	0.52	4Q 92	4c
Corn Flakes, Kellogg's or Post Toasties	18 oz	1.81	4Q 92	4c
Eggs, Grade A large	doz	0.80	4Q 92	4c
Ground beef or hamburger	lb	1.71	4Q 92	4c
Lettuce, iceberg	head	0.98	4Q 92	4c
Margarine, Blue Bonnet or Parkay cubes	lb	0.51	4Q 92	4c
Milk, whole	1/2 gal	1.41	4Q 92	4c
Orange juice, Minute Maid frozen	12-oz can	1.29	4Q 92	4c
Peaches	29-oz can	1.30	4Q 92	4c
Peas Sweet, Del Monte or Green Giant	15-17 oz can	0.51	4Q 92	4c
Potatoes, white or red	10-lb sack	1.79	4Q 92	4c
Sausage, Jimmy Dean, 100% pork	lb	2.06	4Q 92	4c
Shortening, vegetable, Crisco	3-lb can	2.12	4Q 92	4c
Soft drink, Coca Cola	2 liter	1.01	4Q 92	4c
Steak, T-bone	lb	5.62	4Q 92	4c
Sugar, cane or beet	4 lb	1.45	4Q 92	4c
Tomatoes, Hunt's or Del Monte	14.5-oz can	0.61	4Q 92	4c
Tuna, chunk, light	6.125-6.5 oz can	0.54	4Q 92	4c
Health Care				
ACCRA Index, Health Care		92.70	4Q 92	4c
Analgesic, Aspirin, Bayer, 325 mg tablets	100	5.55	4Q 92	4c
Dentist's fee, adult teeth cleaning and periodic oral exam	visit	49.50	4Q 92	4c
Doctor's fee, routine exam, established patient	visit	31.67	4Q 92	4c
Hospital care, semiprivate room	day	156.76	90	27c
Hospital care, semiprivate room	day	220.00	4Q 92	4c
Household Goods				
Appliance repair, home, service call, washing machine	min labor charge	33.99	4Q 92	4c
Laundry detergent, Tide Ultra, Bold, or Cheer	42 oz	3.44	4Q 92	4c
Tissues, facial, Kleenex brand	175-count box	1.02	4Q 92	4c
Housing				
ACCRA Index, Housing		89.40	4Q 92	4c
House, 1,800 sq ft, 8,000 sq ft lot, new, urban	total	97800	4Q 92	4c
House payment, principal and interest, 25% down payment	month	549	4Q 92	4c
Mortgage rate, incl. points & origination fee, 30-year fixed or adjustable rate	per-cent	8.22	4Q 92	4c
Rent, apartment, 2 bedrooms - 1-1/2 to 2 baths, unfurnished, 950 sq ft, water	month	442	4Q 92	4c
Personal Goods				
Shampoo, Alberto VO5	15 oz	1.02	4Q 92	4c
Toothpaste, Crest or Colgate	6-7 oz	2.02	4Q 92	4c

Valdosta, GA - continued

Item	Per	Value	Date	Ref.
Personal Services				
Dry cleaning, man's 2-piece suit		5.88	4Q 92	4c
Haircare, woman's shampoo, trim and blow-dry		19.00	4Q 92	4c
Haircut, man's barbershop, no styling		5.83	4Q 92	4c
Restaurant Food				
Chicken, fried, thigh and drumstick		1.95	4Q 92	4c
Hamburger with cheese	1/4 lb	1.92	4Q 92	4c
Pizza, Pizza Hut or Pizza Inn, cheese, thin crust	12-13 in	7.49	4Q 92	4c
Transportation				
ACCRA Index, Transportation		99.30	4Q 92	4c
Tire balance, computer or spin balance, front	wheel	7.17	4Q 92	4c
Utilities				
ACCRA Index, Utilities		112.40	4Q 92	4c
Electricity, all electric, 1,800 sq ft living area new home	month	124.70	4Q 92	4c

Vallejo-Fairfield-Napa, CA

Item	Per	Value	Date	Ref.
Child Care				
Child care fee, average, center	hour	1.71	90	65r
Child care fee, average, nonregulated family day care	hour	1.32	90	65r
Child care fee, average, regulated family day care	hour	1.86	90	65r
Communications				
Long-distance telephone service, day, initial minute, 0-100 miles	min	0.17-0.40	91	12s
Long-distance telephone service, day, additional minute, 0-100 miles	min	0.07-0.31	91	12s
Long-distance telephone service, evenings/weekends, 0-100 mi, initial minute	min	0.07-0.16	91	12s
Long-distance telephone service, evenings/weekends, 0-100 mi, additional minute	min	0.03-0.12	91	12s
Education				
Board, 4-yr private college/university	year	2515	91	22s
Board, 4-yr public college/university	year	2268	91	22s
Expenditures, local gov't, public elementary/secondary	pupil	4866	92	20s
Room, 4-year private college/university	year	2622	91	22s
Room, 4-year public college/university	year	2406	91	22s
Tuition, 2-year private college/university	year	7942	91	22s
Tuition, 2-year public college/university	year	114	91	22s
Tuition, 4-year private college/university	year	10863	91	22s
Tuition, 4-year public college/university, in-state	year	1220	91	22s
Energy and Fuels				
Coal	mil Btu	2.01	90	64s
Energy	mil Btu	9.08	90	64s
Energy exp/householder, 1-family unit	year	362	90	28r
Energy exp/householder, <1,000 sq ft heating area	year	254	90	28r
Energy exp/householder, 1,000-1,999 sq ft heating area	year	358	90	28r
Energy exp/householder, 2,000+ sq ft heating area	year	467	90	28r
Energy exp/householder, mobile home	year	390	90	28r
Energy exp/householder, multifamily	year	252	90	28r
Gas, natural	mil Btu	4.31	90	64s
Gas, natural	000 cu ft	6.27	91	46s
Gas, natural, exp	year	369	91	46s
Gasoline, unleaded regular	mil Btu	8.57	90	64s
Entertainment				
Miniature golf admission	adult	6.18	92	1r
Miniature golf admission	child	5.14	92	1r

Values are in dollars or fractions of dollars. In the column headed *Ref*, references are shown to sources. Each reference is followed by a letter. These refer to the geographical level for which data were reported: s=State, r=Region, and c=City or metro. The abbreviation *ex* is used to mean *except* or *excluding*; *exp* stands for expenditures. For other abbreviations and further explanations, please see the Introduction.

Vallejo-Fairfield-Napa, CA - continued

Item	Per	Value	Date	Ref.
Entertainment				
Waterpark admission	adult	11.00	92	1r
Waterpark admission	child	8.55	92	1r
Funerals				
Casket, 18-gauge steel, velvet interior		1781.09	91	24r
Cosmetology, hair care, etc.		84.64	91	24r
Embalming		207.41	91	24r
Facility use for ceremony		205.76	91	24r
Hearse, local		105.14	91	24r
Limousine, local		83.21	91	24r
Remains to funeral home, transfer		113.82	91	24r
Service charge, professional		626.33	91	24r
Vault, concrete, non-metallic liner		599.54	91	24r
Viewing facilities, use		85.81	91	24r
Groceries				
Apples, Red Delicious	lb	0.80	4/93	16r
Bacon	lb	1.79	4/93	16r
Bananas	lb	0.53	4/93	16r
Bologna, all beef or mixed	lb	2.67	4/93	16r
Bread, white, pan	lb	0.81	4/93	16r
Carrots, short trimmed and topped	lb	0.39	4/93	16r
Chicken, fresh, whole	lb	0.94	4/93	16r
Chicken breast, bone-in	lb	2.19	4/93	16r
Chuck roast, graded and ungraded, ex USDA prime and choice	lb	2.26	4/93	16r
Coffee, 100% ground roast, all sizes	lb	2.33	4/93	16r
Eggs, Grade AA large	doz	1.18	4/93	16r
Flour, white, all purpose	lb	0.22	4/93	16r
Grapefruit	lb	0.52	4/93	16r
Grapes, Thompson Seedless	lb	1.50	4/93	16r
Ground beef, 100% beef	lb	1.44	4/93	16r
Ground beef, lean and extra lean	lb	2.34	4/93	16r
Ham, boneless, excluding canned	lb	2.56	4/93	16r
Honey, jar	8 oz	0.89-1.00	92	5r
Honey, jar	lb	1.35-1.97	92	5r
Honey, squeeze bear	12-oz	1.19-1.50	92	5r
Ice cream, prepackaged, bulk, regular	1/2 gal	2.40	4/93	16r
Lemons	lb	0.81	4/93	16r
Lettuce, iceberg	lb	0.84	4/93	16r
Margarine, stick	lb	0.81	4/93	16r
Oranges, navel	lb	0.48	4/93	16r
Pork chops, center cut, bone-in	lb	3.25	4/93	16r
Potato chips	16 oz	2.89	4/93	16r
Potatoes, white	lb	0.38	4/93	16r
Round roast, graded & ungraded, ex USDA prime & choice	lb	3.00	4/93	16r
Round roast, USDA choice, boneless	lb	3.16	4/93	16r
Shortening, vegetable oil blends	lb	0.86	4/93	16r
Spaghetti and macaroni	lb	0.84	4/93	16r
Steak, round, graded & ungraded, ex USDA prime & choice	lb	3.34	4/93	16r
Steak, round, USDA choice, boneless	lb	3.24	4/93	16r
Steak, sirloin, graded & ungraded, ex USDA prime & choice	lb	3.75	4/93	16r
Steak, sirloin, USDA choice, boneless	lb	4.49	4/93	16r
Sugar, white	lb	0.41	4/93	16r
Sugar, white, 33-80 oz pk	lb	0.38	4/93	16r
Tomatoes, field grown	lb	1.01	4/93	16r
Turkey, frozen, whole	lb	1.04	4/93	16r
Health Care				
Cardizem 60 mg tablets	30	24.04	92	49s
Cector 250 mg tablets	15	35.87	92	49s
Childbirth, cesarean, hospital		5533	91	62r
Childbirth, cesarean, physician's fee		2053	91	62r
Childbirth, normal, hospital		2745	91	62r
Childbirth, normal, physician's fee		1492	91	62r
Health care spending, state	capita	2894	3/93	84s
Medical plan per employee	year	3421	91	45r
Mental health care, exp	capita	37.60-53.67	90	38s
Mental health care, exp, state mental health agency	capita	42.32	90	38s

Vallejo-Fairfield-Napa, CA - continued

Item	Per	Value	Date	Ref.
Health Care - continued				
Mental health care, hospital psychiatric services, non-Federal, exp	capita	10.64	88	38s
Mental health care, mental health organization, multiservice, exp	capita	28.56	88	38s
Mental health care, psychiatric hospitals, private, exp	capita	18.60	88	38s
Mental health care, psychiatric out-patient clinics, freestanding, exp	capita	2.28	88	38s
Mental health care, psychiatric partial-care organizations, freestanding, exp	capita	0.24	88	38s
Mental health care, state and county mental hospitals, exp	capita	13.60	88	38s
Mental health care, VA medical centers, exp	capita	2.33	88	38s
Mevacor 20 mg tablets	30	67.62	92	49s
Physician fee, family practice, first-visit		111.00	91	62r
Physician fee, family practice, revisit		45.00	91	62r
Physician fee, general practice, first-visit		100.00	91	62r
Physician fee, general practice, revisit		40.00	91	62r
Physician fee, internal medicine, first-visit		137.00	91	62r
Physician fee, internal medicine, revisit		48.00	91	62r
Physician fee, median, neurosurgeon, first-visit		157.00	91	62r
Physician fee, median, nonsurgical specialist, first-visit		131.00	91	62r
Physician fee, median, orthopedic surgeon, first-visit		124.00	91	62r
Physician fee, median, plastic surgeon, first-visit		88.00	91	62r
Physician fee, median, surgical specialist, first-visit		100.00	91	62r
Physician fee, neurosurgeon, revisit		51.00	91	62r
Physician fee, nonsurgical specialist, revisit		47.00	91	62r
Physician fee, obstetrics/gynecology, first-visit		95.00	91	62r
Physician fee, obstetrics/gynecology, revisit		50.00	91	62r
Physician fee, orthopedic surgeon, revisit		51.00	91	62r
Physician fee, pediatrician, first-visit		81.00	91	62r
Physician fee, pediatrician, revisit		42.00	91	62r
Physician fee, plastic surgeon, revisit		48.00	91	62r
Physician fee, surgical specialist, revisit		49.00	91	62r
Prozac 20 mg tablets	14	33.22	92	49s
Substance abuse, hospital ancillary charge	incident	1760	90	70s
Substance abuse, hospital physician charge	incident	750	90	70s
Substance abuse, hospital room and board	incident	6390	90	70s
Tagamet 300 mg tablets	100	77.08	92	49s
Xanax 0.25 mg tablets	90	64.08	92	49s
Zantac 160 mg tablets	60	92.31	92	49s
Housing				
Home, median price	unit	131,200	92	58s
Insurance and Pensions				
Auto insurance, private passenger	year	904.37	91	63s
Taxes				
Tax, cigarette	pack	35	91	77s
Tax, gasoline	gal	16	91	77s
Taxes, state	capita	1477	91	77s
Transportation				
Driver's license fee		10.00	12/90	43s
Travel				
Business travel	day	178.00	4/93	89r
Utilities				
Electricity	mil Btu	25.98	90	64s

Values are in dollars or fractions of dollars. In the column headed *Ref*, references are shown to sources. Each reference is followed by a letter. These refer to the geographical level for which data were reported: s=State, r=Region, and c=City or metro. The abbreviation *ex* is used to mean *except* or *excluding*; *exp* stands for expenditures. For other abbreviations and further explanations, please see the Introduction.

Vancouver, WA

Item	Per	Value	Date	Ref.
Child Care				
Child care fee, average, center	hour	1.71	90	65r
Child care fee, average, nonregulated family day care	hour	1.32	90	65r
Child care fee, average, regulated family day care	hour	1.86	90	65r
Communications				
Long-distance telephone service, day, initial minute, 0-100 miles	min	0.15-0.37	91	12s
Long-distance telephone service, day, additional minute, 0-100 miles	min	0.01-0.03	91	12s
Long-distance telephone service, evenings/weekends, 0-100 mi, initial minute	min	0.05-0.19	91	12s
Long-distance telephone service, evenings/weekends, 0-100 mi, additional minute	min	0.00-0.01	91	12s
Education				
Board, 4-yr private college/university	year	1811	91	22s
Board, 4-yr public college/university	year	1539	91	22s
Expenditures, local gov't, public elementary/secondary	pupil	5317	92	20s
Room, 4-year private college/university	year	1885	91	22s
Room, 4-year public college/university	year	1698	91	22s
Tuition, 2-year private college/university	year	6743	91	22s
Tuition, 2-year public college/university	year	844	91	22s
Tuition, 4-year private college/university	year	9463	91	22s
Tuition, 4-year public college/university, in-state	year	1823	91	22s
Energy and Fuels				
Energy	mil Btu	7.39	90	64s
Energy exp/householder, 1-family unit	year	362	90	28r
Energy exp/householder, <1,000 sq ft heating area	year	254	90	28r
Energy exp/householder, 1,000-1,999 sq ft heating area	year	358	90	28r
Energy exp/householder, 2,000+ sq ft heating area	year	467	90	28r
Energy exp/householder, mobile home	year	390	90	28r
Energy exp/householder, multifamily	year	252	90	28r
Gas, natural	mil Btu	3.60	90	64s
Gas, natural	000 cu ft	4.68	91	46s
Gas, natural, exp	year	440	91	46s
Gasoline, unleaded regular	mil Btu	9.45	90	64s
Entertainment				
Miniature golf admission	adult	6.18	92	1r
Miniature golf admission	child	5.14	92	1r
Waterpark admission	adult	11.00	92	1r
Waterpark admission	child	8.55	92	1r
Funerals				
Casket, 18-gauge steel, velvet interior		1781.09	91	24r
Cosmetology, hair care, etc.		84.64	91	24r
Embalming		207.41	91	24r
Facility use for ceremony		205.76	91	24r
Hearse, local		105.14	91	24r
Limousine, local		83.21	91	24r
Remains to funeral home, transfer		113.82	91	24r
Service charge, professional		626.33	91	24r
Vault, concrete, non-metallic liner		599.54	91	24r
Viewing facilities, use		85.81	91	24r
Groceries				
Apples, Red Delicious	lb	0.80	4/93	16r
Bacon	lb	1.79	4/93	16r
Bananas	lb	0.53	4/93	16r
Bologna, all beef or mixed	lb	2.67	4/93	16r
Bread, white, pan	lb	0.81	4/93	16r
Carrots, short trimmed and topped	lb	0.39	4/93	16r
Chicken, fresh, whole	lb	0.94	4/93	16r
Chicken breast, bone-in	lb	2.19	4/93	16r

Vancouver, WA - continued

Item	Per	Value	Date	Ref.
Groceries - continued				
Chuck roast, graded and ungraded, ex USDA prime and choice	lb	2.26	4/93	16r
Coffee, 100% ground roast, all sizes	lb	2.33	4/93	16r
Eggs, Grade AA large	doz	1.18	4/93	16r
Flour, white, all purpose	lb	0.22	4/93	16r
Grapefruit	lb	0.52	4/93	16r
Grapes, Thompson Seedless	lb	1.50	4/93	16r
Ground beef, 100% beef	lb	1.44	4/93	16r
Ground beef, lean and extra lean	lb	2.34	4/93	16r
Ham, boneless, excluding canned	lb	2.56	4/93	16r
Honey, jar	8 oz	0.89-1.00	92	5r
Honey, jar	lb	1.35-1.97	92	5r
Honey, squeeze bear	12-oz	1.19-1.50	92	5r
Ice cream, prepackaged, bulk, regular	1/2 gal	2.40	4/93	16r
Lemons	lb	0.81	4/93	16r
Lettuce, iceberg	lb	0.84	4/93	16r
Margarine, stick	lb	0.81	4/93	16r
Oranges, navel	lb	0.48	4/93	16r
Pork chops, center cut, bone-in	lb	3.25	4/93	16r
Potato chips	16 oz	2.89	4/93	16r
Potatoes, white	lb	0.38	4/93	16r
Round roast, graded & ungraded, ex USDA prime & choice	lb	3.00	4/93	16r
Round roast, USDA choice, boneless	lb	3.16	4/93	16r
Shortening, vegetable oil blends	lb	0.86	4/93	16r
Spaghetti and macaroni	lb	0.84	4/93	16r
Steak, round, graded & ungraded, ex USDA prime & choice	lb	3.34	4/93	16r
Steak, round, USDA choice, boneless	lb	3.24	4/93	16r
Steak, sirloin, graded & ungraded, ex USDA prime & choice	lb	3.75	4/93	16r
Steak, sirloin, USDA choice, boneless	lb	4.49	4/93	16r
Sugar, white	lb	0.41	4/93	16r
Sugar, white, 33-80 oz pk	lb	0.38	4/93	16r
Tomatoes, field grown	lb	1.01	4/93	16r
Turkey, frozen, whole	lb	1.04	4/93	16r
Health Care				
Childbirth, cesarean, hospital		5533	91	62r
Childbirth, cesarean, physician's fee		2053	91	62r
Childbirth, normal, hospital		2745	91	62r
Childbirth, normal, physician's fee		1492	91	62r
Medical plan per employee	year	3421	91	45r
Mental health care, exp	capita	37.60-53.67	90	38s
Physician fee, family practice, first-visit		111.00	91	62r
Physician fee, family practice, revisit		45.00	91	62r
Physician fee, general practice, first-visit		100.00	91	62r
Physician fee, general practice, revisit		40.00	91	62r
Physician fee, internal medicine, first-visit		137.00	91	62r
Physician fee, internal medicine, revisit		48.00	91	62r
Physician fee, median, neurosurgeon, first-visit		157.00	91	62r
Physician fee, median, nonsurgical specialist, first-visit		131.00	91	62r
Physician fee, median, orthopedic surgeon, first-visit		124.00	91	62r
Physician fee, median, plastic surgeon, first-visit		88.00	91	62r
Physician fee, median, surgical specialist, first-visit		100.00	91	62r
Physician fee, neurosurgeon, revisit		51.00	91	62r
Physician fee, nonsurgical specialist, revisit		47.00	91	62r
Physician fee, obstetrics/gynecology, first-visit		95.00	91	62r
Physician fee, obstetrics/gynecology, revisit		50.00	91	62r
Physician fee, orthopedic surgeon, revisit		51.00	91	62r
Physician fee, pediatrician, first-visit		81.00	91	62r
Physician fee, pediatrician, revisit		42.00	91	62r
Physician fee, plastic surgeon, revisit		48.00	91	62r
Physician fee, surgical specialist, revisit		49.00	91	62r
Substance abuse, hospital ancillary charge	incident	1360	90	70s

Values are in dollars or fractions of dollars. In the column headed *Ref*, references are shown to sources. Each reference is followed by a letter. These refer to the geographical level for which data were reported: s = State, r = Region, and c = City or metro. The abbreviation *ex* is used to mean *except* or *excluding*; *exp* stands for expenditures. For other abbreviations and further explanations, please see the Introduction.

Vancouver, WA - continued

Item	Per	Value	Date	Ref.
Health Care				
Substance abuse, hospital physician charge	incident	150	90	70s
Substance abuse, hospital room and board	incident	4200	90	70s
Insurance and Pensions				
Auto insurance, private passenger	year	627.71	91	63s
Taxes				
Tax, cigarette	pack	34	91	77s
Tax, gasoline	gal	23	91	77s
Taxes, state	capita	1592	91	77s
Transportation				
Driver's license fee		14.00	12/90	43s
Travel				
Business travel	day	178.00	4/93	89r
Utilities				
Electricity	mil Btu	10.03	90	64s

Vermillion, SD

Item	Per	Value	Date	Ref.
Composite ACCRA index		98.80	4Q 92	4c
Alcoholic Beverages				
Beer, Miller Lite or Budweiser, 12-oz containers	6 pack	3.69	4Q 92	4c
Liquor, J & B Scotch	750 ml	17.49	4Q 92	4c
Wine, Gallo Chablis blanc, 1.5 liter	bottle	4.99	4Q 92	4c
Clothing				
Jeans, man's denim		24.30	4Q 92	4c
Shirt, man's dress shirt		22.00	4Q 92	4c
Undervest, boy's size 10-14, cotton	3	4.49	4Q 92	4c
Communications				
Newspaper subscription, daily and Sunday home delivery, large-city	month	13.04	4Q 92	4c
Telephone, flat rate	month	26.00	91	11c
Telephone bill, family of four	month	19.96	4Q 92	4c
Energy and Fuels				
Energy, combined forms, 1,800 sq ft heating area	month	111.79	4Q 92	4c
Energy, exc electricity, 1,800 sq ft heating area	month	46.08	4Q 92	4c
Gasoline, motor	gal	1.13	4Q 92	4c
Entertainment				
Bowling, evening rate	game	1.75	4Q 92	4c
Monopoly game, Parker Brothers', No. 9		11.49	4Q 92	4c
Movie	admission	4.00	4Q 92	4c
Tennis balls, yellow, Wilson or Penn, 3	can	2.84	4Q 92	4c
Goods and Services				
ACCRA Index, Miscellaneous Goods and Services		95.70	4Q 92	4c
Groceries				
ACCRA Index, Groceries		100.90	4Q 92	4c
Babyfood, strained vegetables, lowest price	4-4.5 oz jar	0.36	4Q 92	4c
Bananas	lb	0.52	4Q 92	4c
Bread, white	24 oz	0.67	4Q 92	4c
Cheese, Kraft grated Parmesan	8-oz canister	3.19	4Q 92	4c
Chicken, fryer, whole	lb	0.84	4Q 92	4c
Cigarettes, Winston	carton	17.39	4Q 92	4c
Coffee, vacuum-packed	13-oz can	2.16	4Q 92	4c
Corn, frozen	10 oz	0.71	4Q 92	4c
Corn Flakes, Kellogg's or Post Toasties	18 oz	1.77	4Q 92	4c
Eggs, Grade A large	doz	0.73	4Q 92	4c

Vermillion, SD - continued

Item	Per	Value	Date	Ref.
Groceries - continued				
Ground beef or hamburger	lb	1.39	4Q 92	4c
Lettuce, iceberg	head	0.98	4Q 92	4c
Margarine, Blue Bonnet or Parkay cubes	lb	0.66	4Q 92	4c
Milk, whole	1/2 gal	1.45	4Q 92	4c
Orange juice, Minute Maid frozen	12-oz can	1.68	4Q 92	4c
Peaches	29-oz can	1.49	4Q 92	4c
Peas Sweet, Del Monte or Green Giant	15-17 oz can	0.65	4Q 92	4c
Potatoes, white or red	10-lb sack	1.64	4Q 92	4c
Sausage, Jimmy Dean, 100% pork	lb	2.60	4Q 92	4c
Shortening, vegetable, Crisco	3-lb can	2.38	4Q 92	4c
Soft drink, Coca Cola	2 liter	1.39	4Q 92	4c
Steak, T-bone	lb	4.99	4Q 92	4c
Sugar, cane or beet	4 lb	1.30	4Q 92	4c
Tomatoes, Hunt's or Del Monte	14.5-oz can	0.66	4Q 92	4c
Tuna, chunk, light	6.125-6.5 oz can	0.46	4Q 92	4c
Health Care				
ACCRA Index, Health Care		100.50	4Q 92	4c
Analgesic, Aspirin, Bayer, 325 mg tablets	100	4.98	4Q 92	4c
Dentist's fee, adult teeth cleaning and periodic oral exam	visit	51.00	4Q 92	4c
Doctor's fee, routine exam, established patient	visit	36.00	4Q 92	4c
Hospital care, semiprivate room	day	287.00	4Q 92	4c
Household Goods				
Appliance repair, home, service call, washing machine	min labor charge	30.00	4Q 92	4c
Laundry detergent, Tide Ultra, Bold, or Cheer	42 oz	3.93	4Q 92	4c
Tissues, facial, Kleenex brand	175-count box	1.19	4Q 92	4c
Housing				
ACCRA Index, Housing		102.70	4Q 92	4c
House, 1,800 sq ft, 8,000 sq ft lot, new, urban	total	117000	4Q 92	4c
House payment, principal and interest, 25% down payment	month	662	4Q 92	4c
Mortgage rate, incl. points & origination fee, 30-year fixed or adjustable rate	percent	8.29	4Q 92	4c
Rent, apartment, 2 bedrooms - 1-1/2 to 2 baths, unfurnished, 950 sq ft, water	month	435	4Q 92	4c
Personal Goods				
Shampoo, Alberto VO5	15 oz	1.34	4Q 92	4c
Toothpaste, Crest or Colgate	6-7 oz	2.14	4Q 92	4c
Personal Services				
Dry cleaning, man's 2-piece suit		6.00	4Q 92	4c
Haircare, woman's shampoo, trim and blow-dry		15.67	4Q 92	4c
Haircut, man's barbershop, no styling		6.75	4Q 92	4c
Restaurant Food				
Chicken, fried, thigh and drumstick		2.23	4Q 92	4c
Hamburger with cheese	1/4 lb	1.79	4Q 92	4c
Pizza, Pizza Hut or Pizza Inn, cheese, thin crust	12-13 in	7.49	4Q 92	4c
Transportation				
ACCRA Index, Transportation		92.20	4Q 92	4c
Tire balance, computer or spin balance, front	wheel	5.50	4Q 92	4c

Values are in dollars or fractions of dollars. In the column headed *Ref*, references are shown to sources. Each reference is followed by a letter. These refer to the geographical level for which data were reported: s=State, r=Region, and c=City or metro. The abbreviation *ex* is used to mean *except* or *excluding*; *exp* stands for *expenditures*. For other abbreviations and further explanations, please see the Introduction.

Vermillion, SD - continued

Item	Per	Value	Date	Ref.
Utilities				
ACCRA Index, Utilities		102.40	4Q 92	4c
Electricity, partial electric and other energy, 1,800 sq ft living area new home	month	65.71	4Q 92	4c

Victoria, TX

Item	Per	Value	Date	Ref.
Child Care				
Child care fee, average, center	hour	1.29	90	65r
Child care fee, average, nonregulated family day care	hour	0.89	90	65r
Child care fee, average, regulated family day care	hour	1.32	90	65r
Communications				
Long-distance telephone service, day, initial minute, 0-100 miles	min	0.10-0.46	91	12s
Long-distance telephone service, day, additional minute, 0-100 miles	min	0.06-0.45	91	12s
Education				
Board, 4-yr private college/university	year	1883	91	22s
Board, 4-yr public college/university	year	1605	91	22s
Expenditures, local gov't, public elementary/secondary	pupil	4593	92	20s
Room, 4-year private college/university	year	1620	91	22s
Room, 4-year public college/university	year	1532	91	22s
Tuition, 2-year private college/university	year	4394	91	22s
Tuition, 2-year public college/university	year	495	91	22s
Tuition, 4-year private college/university	year	6497	91	22s
Tuition, 4-year public college/university, in-state	year	986	91	22s
Energy and Fuels				
Coal	mil Btu	1.44	90	64s
Energy	mil Btu	6.48	90	64s
Energy exp/householder, 1-family unit	year	471	90	28r
Energy exp/householder, <1,000 sq ft heating area	year	384	90	28r
Energy exp/householder, 1,000-1,999 sq ft heating area	year	421	90	28r
Energy exp/householder, 2,000+ sq ft heating area	year	625	90	28r
Energy exp/householder, mobile home	year	271	90	28r
Energy exp/householder, multifamily	year	355	90	28r
Gas, natural	mil Btu	2.47	90	64s
Gas, natural	000 cu ft	5.71	91	46s
Gas, natural, exp	year	388	91	46s
Gasoline, unleaded regular	mil Btu	9.16	90	64s
Entertainment				
Miniature golf admission	adult	6.18	92	1r
Miniature golf admission	child	5.14	92	1r
Waterpark admission	adult	11.00	92	1r
Waterpark admission	child	8.55	92	1r
Funerals				
Casket, 18-gauge steel, velvet interior		2274.41	91	24r
Cosmetology, hair care, etc.		74.62	91	24r
Embalming		229.94	91	24r
Facility use for ceremony		176.61	91	24r
Hearse, local		116.34	91	24r
Limousine, local		72.68	91	24r
Remains to funeral home, transfer		87.72	91	24r
Service charge, professional		712.53	91	24r
Vault, concrete, non-metallic liner		750.55	91	24r
Viewing facilities, use		155.31	91	24r
Groceries				
Apples, Red Delicious	lb	0.79	4/93	16r
Bacon	lb	1.75	4/93	16r
Bananas	lb	0.42	4/93	16r
Beef, stew, boneless	lb	2.61	4/93	16r
Bologna, all beef or mixed	lb	2.24	4/93	16r

Victoria, TX - continued

Item	Per	Value	Date	Ref.
Groceries - continued				
Bread, white, pan	lb	0.64	4/93	16r
Bread, whole wheat, pan	lb	0.96	4/93	16r
Cabbage	lb	0.37	4/93	16r
Carrots, short trimmed and topped	lb	0.47	4/93	16r
Celery	lb	0.64	4/93	16r
Cheese, American	lb	2.98	4/93	16r
Cheese, Cheddar	lb	3.28	4/93	16r
Chicken, fresh, whole	lb	0.77	4/93	16r
Chicken breast, bone-in	lb	1.92	4/93	16r
Chicken legs, bone-in	lb	1.06	4/93	16r
Chuck roast, graded and ungraded, ex USDA prime and choice	lb	2.40	4/93	16r
Chuck roast, USDA choice, bone-in	lb	2.19	4/93	16r
Chuck roast, USDA choice, boneless	lb	2.38	4/93	16r
Coffee, 100% ground roast, all sizes	lb	2.48	4/93	16r
Crackers, soda, salted	lb	1.15	4/93	16r
Eggs, Grade A large	doz	0.96	4/93	16r
Flour, white, all purpose	lb	0.24	4/93	16r
Frankfurters, all meat or all beef	lb	2.01	4/93	16r
Grapefruit	lb	0.44	4/93	16r
Grapes, Thompson Seedless	lb	1.40	4/93	16r
Ground beef, 100% beef	lb	1.58	4/93	16r
Ground beef, lean and extra lean	lb	2.09	4/93	16r
Ground chuck, 100% beef	lb	1.98	4/93	16r
Ham, boneless, excluding canned	lb	2.89	4/93	16r
Ham, picnic, shoulder, bone-in, smoked	lb	1.02	4/93	16r
Ham, rump or steak half, bone-in, smoked	lb	1.48	4/93	16r
Honey, jar	8 oz	0.73-1.19	92	5r
Honey, jar	lb	1.10-1.79	92	5r
Honey, squeeze bear	12-oz	1.19-1.50	92	5r
Ice cream, prepackaged, bulk, regular	1/2 gal	2.41	4/93	16r
Lemons	lb	1.05	4/93	16r
Lettuce, iceberg	lb	0.81	4/93	16r
Margarine, stick	lb	0.88	4/93	16r
Oranges, navel	lb	0.55	4/93	16r
Pears, Anjou	lb	0.92	4/93	16r
Pork chops, center cut, bone-in	lb	3.13	4/93	16r
Potato chips	16 oz	2.94	4/93	16r
Potatoes, white	lb	0.43	4/93	16r
Rib roast, USDA choice, bone-in	lb	4.63	4/93	16r
Rice, white, long grain, uncooked	lb	0.45	4/93	16r
Round roast, graded & ungraded, ex USDA prime & choice	lb	3.03	4/93	16r
Round roast, USDA choice, boneless	lb	3.09	4/93	16r
Sausage, fresh, loose	lb	2.08	4/93	16r
Short ribs, bone-in	lb	2.66	4/93	16r
Shortening, vegetable oil blends	lb	0.69	4/93	16r
Spaghetti and macaroni	lb	0.81	4/93	16r
Steak, rib eye, USDA choice, boneless	lb	6.24	4/93	16r
Steak, round, graded & ungraded, ex USDA prime & choice	lb	3.31	4/93	16r
Steak, round, USDA choice, boneless	lb	3.34	4/93	16r
Steak, sirloin, graded & ungraded, ex USDA prime & choice	lb	4.19	4/93	16r
Steak, sirloin, USDA choice, boneless	lb	4.46	4/93	16r
Steak, T-bone, USDA choice, bone-in	lb	5.25	4/93	16r
Strawberries, dry pint	12 oz	0.92	4/93	16r
Sugar, white	lb	0.39	4/93	16r
Sugar, white, 33-80 oz pk	lb	0.38	4/93	16r
Tomatoes, field grown	lb	0.88	4/93	16r
Tuna, chunk, light	lb	1.79	4/93	16r
Turkey, frozen, whole	lb	1.04	4/93	16r
Yogurt, natural, fruit flavored	1/2 pint	0.57	4/93	16r
Health Care				
Childbirth, cesarean, hospital		5034	91	62r
Childbirth, cesarean, physician's fee		2053	91	62r
Childbirth, normal, hospital		2712	91	62r
Childbirth, normal, physician's fee		1492	91	62r
Health care spending, state	capita	2192	3/93	84s
Mental health care, exp	capita	20.37-28.83	90	38s

Values are in dollars or fractions of dollars. In the column headed *Ref*, references are shown to sources. Each reference is followed by a letter. These refer to the geographical level for which data were reported: s=State, r=Region, and c=City or metro. The abbreviation *ex* is used to mean *except* or *excluding*; *exp* stands for *expenditures*. For other abbreviations and further explanations, please see the Introduction.

Victoria, TX - continued

Item	Per	Value	Date	Ref.
Health Care				
Mental health care, exp, state mental health agency	capita	22.72	90	38s
Mental health care, hospital psychiatric services, non-Federal, exp	capita	7.95	88	38s
Mental health care, mental health organization, multiservice, exp	capita	12.05	88	38s
Mental health care, psychiatric hospitals, private, exp	capita	37.78	88	38s
Mental health care, psychiatric out-patient clinics, freestanding, exp	capita	0.43	88	38s
Mental health care, state and county mental hospitals, exp	capita	12.54	88	38s
Mental health care, VA medical centers, exp	capita	5.35	88	38s
Physician fee, family practice, first-visit		75.00	91	62r
Physician fee, family practice, revisit		34.00	91	62r
Physician fee, general practice, first-visit		61.00	91	62r
Physician fee, general practice, revisit		32.00	91	62r
Physician fee, general surgeon, first-visit		64.00	91	62r
Physician fee, general surgeon, revisit		40.00	91	62r
Physician fee, internal medicine, first-visit		98.00	91	62r
Physician fee, internal medicine, revisit		40.00	91	62r
Physician fee, median, neurosurgeon, first-visit		130.00	91	62r
Physician fee, median, nonsurgical specialist, first-visit		95.00	91	62r
Physician fee, median, orthopedic surgeon, first-visit		91.00	91	62r
Physician fee, median, plastic surgeon, first-visit		66.00	91	62r
Physician fee, median, surgical specialist, first-visit		62.00	91	62r
Physician fee, neurosurgeon, revisit		50.00	91	62r
Physician fee, nonsurgical specialist, revisit		40.00	91	62r
Physician fee, obstetrics/gynecology, first-visit		64.00	91	62r
Physician fee, obstetrics/gynecology, revisit		41.00	91	62r
Physician fee, orthopedic surgeon, revisit		40.00	91	62r
Physician fee, pediatrician, first-visit		49.00	91	62r
Physician fee, pediatrician, revisit		33.00	91	62r
Physician fee, plastic surgeon, revisit		43.00	91	62r
Physician fee, surgical specialist, revisit		37.00	91	62r
Substance abuse, hospital ancillary charge	incident	3750	90	70s
Substance abuse, hospital physician charge	incident	1080	90	70s
Substance abuse, hospital room and board	incident	5320	90	70s
Insurance and Pensions				
Auto insurance, private passenger	year	709.79	91	63s
Taxes				
Tax, cigarette	pack	41	91	77s
Tax, gasoline	gal	20	91	77s
Taxes, state	capita	923	91	77s
Transportation				
Driver's license fee		16.00	12/90	43s
Travel				
Business travel	day	193.00	4/93	89r
Utilities				
Electricity	mil Btu	17.09	90	64s
Electricity, residential	KWh	5.92	2/93	94s

Vineland-Millville-Bridgeton, NJ

Item	Per	Value	Date	Ref.
Child Care				
Child care fee, average, center	hour	2.18	90	65r
Child care fee, average, nonregulated family day care	hour	1.83	90	65r

Vineland-Millville-Bridgeton, NJ - continued

Item	Per	Value	Date	Ref.
Child Care - continued				
Child care fee, average, regulated family day care	hour	2.02	90	65r
Communications				
Long-distance telephone service, day, initial minute, 0-100 miles	min	0.09-0.42	91	12s
Long-distance telephone service, day, additional minute, 0-100 miles	min	0.03-0.12	91	12s
Education				
Board, 4-yr private college/university	year	2883	91	22s
Board, 4-yr public college/university	year	1647	91	22s
Expenditures, local gov't, public elementary/secondary	pupil	9940	92	20s
Room, 4-year private college/university	year	2440	91	22s
Room, 4-year public college/university	year	2415	91	22s
Tuition, 2-year private college/university	year	5874	91	22s
Tuition, 2-year public college/university	year	1235	91	22s
Tuition, 4-year private college/university	year	10281	91	22s
Tuition, 4-year public college/university, in-state	year	2860	91	22s
Energy and Fuels				
Coal	mil Btu	1.79	90	64s
Energy	mil Btu	9.32	90	64s
Energy exp/householder, 1-family unit	year	588	90	28r
Energy exp/householder, <1,000 sq ft heating area	year	477	90	28r
Energy exp/householder, 1,000-1,999 sq ft heating area	year	517	90	28r
Energy exp/householder, 2,000+ sq ft heating area	year	630	90	28r
Energy exp/householder, mobile home	year	412	90	28r
Energy exp/householder, multifamily	year	498	90	28r
Gas, natural	mil Btu	5.05	90	64s
Gas, natural	000 cu ft	6.73	91	46s
Gas, natural, exp	year	593	91	46s
Gasoline, unleaded regular	mil Btu	9.03	90	64s
Funerals				
Casket, 18-gauge steel, velvet interior		1811.58	91	24r
Cosmetology, hair care, etc.		111.08	91	24r
Embalming		329.42	91	24r
Facility use for ceremony		201.29	91	24r
Hearse, local		135.27	91	24r
Limousine, local		127.24	91	24r
Remains to funeral home, transfer		103.98	91	24r
Service charge, professional		724.98	91	24r
Vault, concrete, non-metallic liner		766.71	91	24r
Viewing facilities, use		260.60	91	24r
Groceries				
Apples, Red Delicious	lb	0.85	4/93	16r
Bacon	lb	2.12	4/93	16r
Bananas	lb	0.54	4/93	16r
Bread, white, pan	lb	0.81	4/93	16r
Butter	lb	2.02	4/93	16r
Carrots, short trimmed and topped	lb	0.51	4/93	16r
Chicken, fresh, whole	lb	1.04	4/93	16r
Chicken breast, bone-in	lb	2.21	4/93	16r
Chicken legs, bone-in	lb	1.16	4/93	16r
Chuck roast, USDA choice, boneless	lb	2.82	4/93	16r
Coffee, 100% ground roast, all sizes	lb	2.66	4/93	16r
Cucumbers	lb	0.85	4/93	16r
Eggs, Grade A large	doz	1.15	4/93	16r
Grapefruit	lb	0.45	4/93	16r
Grapes, Thompson Seedless	lb	1.52	4/93	16r
Ground beef, lean and extra lean	lb	2.36	4/93	16r
Ground chuck, 100% beef	lb	2.02	4/93	16r
Honey, jar	8 oz	0.96-1.75	92	5r
Honey, jar	lb	1.50-3.00	92	5r
Honey, squeeze bear	12-oz	1.50-1.99	92	5r
Ice cream, prepackaged, bulk, regular	1/2 gal	2.80	4/93	16r

Values are in dollars or fractions of dollars. In the column headed *Ref*, references are shown to sources. Each reference is followed by a letter. These refer to the geographical level for which data were reported: s=State, r=Region, and c=City or metro. The abbreviation *ex* is used to mean *except* or *excluding*; *exp* stands for *expenditures*. For other abbreviations and further explanations, please see the Introduction.

Vineland-Millville-Bridgeton, NJ - continued

Item	Per	Value	Date	Ref.
Groceries				
Lemons	lb	0.96	4/93	16r
Lettuce, iceberg	lb	0.95	4/93	16r
Margarine, stick	lb	0.81	4/93	16r
Milk, fresh, whole, fortified	1/2 gal	1.30	4/93	16r
Oranges, navel	lb	0.56	4/93	16r
Peanut butter, creamy, all sizes	lb	1.88	4/93	16r
Pork chops, center cut, bone-in	lb	3.34	4/93	16r
Potato chips	16 oz	2.88	4/93	16r
Potatoes, white	lb	0.37	4/93	16r
Rib roast, USDA choice, bone-in	lb	4.94	4/93	16r
Round roast, USDA choice, boneless	lb	3.17	4/93	16r
Shortening, vegetable oil blends	lb	0.98	4/93	16r
Spaghetti and macaroni	lb	0.82	4/93	16r
Steak, round, graded & ungraded, ex USDA prime & choice	lb	4.04	4/93	16r
Steak, round, USDA choice, boneless	lb	3.90	4/93	16r
Steak, sirloin, USDA choice, boneless	lb	4.97	4/93	16r
Strawberries, dry pint	12 oz	0.90	4/93	16r
Sugar, white	lb	0.50	4/93	16r
Sugar, white, 33-80 oz pk	lb	0.41	4/93	16r
Tomatoes, field grown	lb	1.23	4/93	16r
Tuna, chunk, light	lb	2.22	4/93	16r
Turkey, frozen, whole	lb	1.04	4/93	16r
Health Care				
Childbirth, cesarean, hospital		5826	91	62r
Childbirth, cesarean, physician's fee		2053	91	62r
Childbirth, normal, hospital		2964	91	62r
Childbirth, normal, physician's fee		1492	91	62r
Medical plan per employee	year	3942	91	45r
Mental health care, exp	capita	28.84-37.59	90	38s
Mental health care, exp, state mental health agency	capita	57.16	90	38s
Mental health care, hospital psychiatric services, non-Federal, exp	capita	16.04	88	38s
Mental health care, mental health organization, multiservice, exp	capita	11.14	88	38s
Mental health care, psychiatric hospitals, private, exp	capita	17.85	88	38s
Mental health care, psychiatric out-patient clinics, freestanding, exp	capita	1.56	88	38s
Mental health care, psychiatric partial-care organizations, freestanding, exp	capita	0.66	88	38s
Mental health care, state and county mental hospitals, exp	capita	36.80	88	38s
Mental health care, VA medical centers, exp	capita	5.61	88	38s
Prescription drug co-pay, Medicaid	month	5.00	91	21s
Substance abuse, hospital ancillary charge	incident	780	90	70s
Substance abuse, hospital physician charge	incident	550	90	70s
Substance abuse, hospital room and board	incident	6300	90	70s
Insurance and Pensions				
Auto insurance, private passenger	year	1081.45	91	63s
Taxes				
Tax, cigarette	pack	40	91	77s
Tax, gasoline	gal	10.50	91	77s
Taxes, state	capita	1501	91	77s
Transportation				
Driver's license fee		16.00-17.50	12/90	43s
Vehicle registration and license plate	year	32.90-93.90	93	44s
Travel				
Business travel	day	165.00	4/93	89r
Utilities				
Electricity	mil Btu	26.63	90	64s

Visalia, CA

Item	Per	Value	Date	Ref.
Composite ACCRA index		114.50	4Q 92	4c
Alcoholic Beverages				
Beer, Miller Lite or Budweiser, 12-oz containers	6 pack	4.25	4Q 92	4c
Liquor, J & B Scotch	750 ml	18.39	4Q 92	4c
Wine, Gallo Chablis blanc, 1.5 liter	bottle	4.60	4Q 92	4c
Child Care				
Child care fee, average, center	hour	1.71	90	65r
Child care fee, average, nonregulated family day care	hour	1.32	90	65r
Child care fee, average, regulated family day care	hour	1.86	90	65r
Clothing				
Jeans, man's denim		30.00	4Q 92	4c
Shirt, man's dress shirt		25.00	4Q 92	4c
Undervest, boy's size 10-14, cotton	3	5.47	4Q 92	4c
Communications				
Long-distance telephone service, day, initial minute, 0-100 miles	min	0.17-0.40	91	12s
Long-distance telephone service, day, additional minute, 0-100 miles	min	0.07-0.31	91	12s
Long-distance telephone service, evenings/weekends, 0-100 mi, initial minute	min	0.07-0.16	91	12s
Long-distance telephone service, evenings/weekends, 0-100 mi, additional minute	min	0.03-0.12	91	12s
Newspaper subscription, daily and Sunday home delivery, large-city	month	15.69	4Q 92	4c
Telephone, flat rate	month	8.35	91	11c
Telephone bill, family of four	month	12.18	4Q 92	4c
Education				
Board, 4-yr private college/university	year	2515	91	22s
Board, 4-yr public college/university	year	2268	91	22s
Expenditures, local gov't, public elementary/secondary	pupil	4866	92	20s
Room, 4-year private college/university	year	2622	91	22s
Room, 4-year public college/university	year	2406	91	22s
Tuition, 2-year private college/university	year	7942	91	22s
Tuition, 2-year public college/university	year	114	91	22s
Tuition, 4-year private college/university	year	10863	91	22s
Tuition, 4-year public college/university, in-state	year	1220	91	22s
Energy and Fuels				
Coal	mil Btu	2.01	90	64s
Energy	mil Btu	9.08	90	64s
Energy, combined forms, 1,800 sq ft heating area	month	142.59	4Q 92	4c
Energy, exc electricity, 1,800 sq ft heating area	month	41.35	4Q 92	4c
Energy exp/householder, 1-family unit	year	362	90	28r
Energy exp/householder, <1,000 sq ft heating area	year	254	90	28r
Energy exp/householder, 1,000-1,999 sq ft heating area	year	358	90	28r
Energy exp/householder, 2,000+ sq ft heating area	year	467	90	28r
Energy exp/householder, mobile home	year	390	90	28r
Energy exp/householder, multifamily	year	252	90	28r
Gas, natural	mil Btu	4.31	90	64s
Gas, natural	000 cu ft	6.27	91	46s
Gas, natural, exp	year	369	91	46s
Gasoline, motor	gal	1.19	4Q 92	4c
Gasoline, unleaded regular	mil Btu	8.57	90	64s
Entertainment				
Bowling, evening rate	game	2.25	4Q 92	4c
Miniature golf admission	adult	6.18	92	1r
Miniature golf admission	child	5.14	92	1r
Monopoly game, Parker Brothers', No. 9		12.39	4Q 92	4c

Values are in dollars or fractions of dollars. In the column headed *Ref*, references are shown to sources. Each reference is followed by a letter. These refer to the geographical level for which data were reported: s=State, r=Region, and c=City or metro. The abbreviation *ex* is used to mean *except* or *excluding*; *exp* stands for expenditures. For other abbreviations and further explanations, please see the Introduction.

Visalia, CA - continued

Item	Per	Value	Date	Ref.
Entertainment				
Movie	admission	5.75	4Q 92	4c
Tennis balls, yellow, Wilson or Penn, 3	can	2.65	4Q 92	4c
Waterpark admission	adult	11.00	92	1r
Waterpark admission	child	8.55	92	1r
Funerals				
Casket, 18-gauge steel, velvet interior		1781.09	91	24r
Cosmetology, hair care, etc.		84.64	91	24r
Embalming		207.41	91	24r
Facility use for ceremony		205.76	91	24r
Hearse, local		105.14	91	24r
Limousine, local		83.21	91	24r
Remains to funeral home, transfer		113.82	91	24r
Service charge, professional		626.33	91	24r
Vault, concrete, non-metallic liner		599.54	91	24r
Viewing facilities, use		85.81	91	24r
Goods and Services				
ACCRA Index, Miscellaneous Goods and Services		111.00	4Q 92	4c
Groceries				
ACCRA Index, Groceries		108.60	4Q 92	4c
Apples, Red Delicious	lb	0.80	4/93	16r
Babyfood, strained vegetables, lowest price	4-4.5 oz jar	0.38	4Q 92	4c
Bacon	lb	1.79	4/93	16r
Bananas	lb	0.28	4Q 92	4c
Bananas	lb	0.53	4/93	16r
Bologna, all beef or mixed	lb	2.67	4/93	16r
Bread, white	24 oz	1.15	4Q 92	4c
Bread, white, pan	lb	0.81	4/93	16r
Carrots, short trimmed and topped	lb	0.39	4/93	16r
Cheese, Kraft grated Parmesan	8-oz canister	3.40	4Q 92	4c
Chicken, fresh, whole	lb	0.94	4/93	16r
Chicken, fryer, whole	lb	0.88	4Q 92	4c
Chicken breast, bone-in	lb	2.19	4/93	16r
Chuck roast, graded and ungraded, ex USDA prime and choice	lb	2.26	4/93	16r
Cigarettes, Winston	carton	19.58	4Q 92	4c
Coffee, 100% ground roast, all sizes	lb	2.33	4/93	16r
Coffee, vacuum-packed	13-oz can	2.13	4Q 92	4c
Corn, frozen	10 oz	0.76	4Q 92	4c
Corn Flakes, Kellogg's or Post Toasties	18 oz	1.96	4Q 92	4c
Eggs, Grade A large	doz	1.29	4Q 92	4c
Eggs, Grade AA large	doz	1.18	4/93	16r
Flour, white, all purpose	lb	0.22	4/93	16r
Grapefruit	lb	0.52	4/93	16r
Grapes, Thompson Seedless	lb	1.50	4/93	16r
Ground beef, 100% beef	lb	1.44	4/93	16r
Ground beef, lean and extra lean	lb	2.34	4/93	16r
Ground beef or hamburger	lb	1.31	4Q 92	4c
Ham, boneless, excluding canned	lb	2.56	4/93	16r
Honey, jar	8 oz	0.89-1.00	92	5r
Honey, jar	lb	1.35-1.97	92	5r
Honey, squeeze bear	12-oz	1.19-1.50	92	5r
Ice cream, prepackaged, bulk, regular	1/2 gal	2.40	4/93	16r
Lemons	lb	0.81	4/93	16r
Lettuce, iceberg	head	0.67	4Q 92	4c
Lettuce, iceberg	lb	0.84	4/93	16r
Margarine, Blue Bonnet or Parkay cubes	lb	0.76	4Q 92	4c
Margarine, stick	lb	0.81	4/93	16r
Milk, whole	1/2 gal	1.34	4Q 92	4c
Orange juice, Minute Maid frozen	12-oz can	1.50	4Q 92	4c
Oranges, navel	lb	0.48	4/93	16r
Peaches	29-oz can	1.11	4Q 92	4c
Peas Sweet, Del Monte or Green Giant	15-17 oz can	0.69	4Q 92	4c

Visalia, CA - continued

Item	Per	Value	Date	Ref.
Groceries - continued				
Pork chops, center cut, bone-in	lb	3.25	4/93	16r
Potato chips	16 oz	2.89	4/93	16r
Potatoes, white	lb	0.38	4/93	16r
Potatoes, white or red	10-lb sack	1.97	4Q 92	4c
Round roast, graded & ungraded, ex USDA prime & choice	lb	3.00	4/93	16r
Round roast, USDA choice, boneless	lb	3.16	4/93	16r
Sausage, Jimmy Dean, 100% pork	lb	3.05	4Q 92	4c
Shortening, vegetable oil blends	lb	0.86	4/93	16r
Shortening, vegetable, Crisco	3-lb can	2.52	4Q 92	4c
Soft drink, Coca Cola	2 liter	1.33	4Q 92	4c
Spaghetti and macaroni	lb	0.84	4/93	16r
Steak, round, graded & ungraded, ex USDA prime & choice	lb	3.34	4/93	16r
Steak, round, USDA choice, boneless	lb	3.24	4/93	16r
Steak, sirloin, graded & ungraded, ex USDA prime & choice	lb	3.75	4/93	16r
Steak, sirloin, USDA choice, boneless	lb	4.49	4/93	16r
Steak, T-bone	lb	4.49	4Q 92	4c
Sugar, cane or beet	4 lb	1.90	4Q 92	4c
Sugar, white	lb	0.41	4/93	16r
Sugar, white, 33-80 oz pk	lb	0.38	4/93	16r
Tomatoes, field grown	lb	1.01	4/93	16r
Tomatoes, Hunt's or Del Monte	14.5-oz can	0.87	4Q 92	4c
Tuna, chunk, light	6.125-6.5 oz can	0.61	4Q 92	4c
Turkey, frozen, whole	lb	1.04	4/93	16r
Health Care				
ACCRA Index, Health Care		105.40	4Q 92	4c
Analgesic, Aspirin, Bayer, 325 mg tablets	100	5.11	4Q 92	4c
Cardizem 60 mg tablets	30	24.04	92	49s
Cector 250 mg tablets	15	35.87	92	49s
Childbirth, cesarean, hospital		5533	91	62r
Childbirth, cesarean, physician's fee		2053	91	62r
Childbirth, normal, hospital		2745	91	62r
Childbirth, normal, physician's fee		1492	91	62r
Dentist's fee, adult teeth cleaning and periodic oral exam	visit	44.80	4Q 92	4c
Doctor's fee, routine exam, established patient	visit	39.00	4Q 92	4c
Health care spending, state	capita	2894	3/93	84s
Hospital care, semiprivate room	day	400.50	4Q 92	4c
Medical insurance premium, per employee, small group comprehensive	month	401.50	10/91	25c
Medical plan per employee	year	3421	91	45r
Mental health care, exp	capita	37.60-53.67	90	38s
Mental health care, exp, state mental health agency	capita	42.32	90	38s
Mental health care, hospital psychiatric services, non-Federal, exp	capita	10.64	88	38s
Mental health care, mental health organization, multiservice, exp	capita	28.56	88	38s
Mental health care, psychiatric hospitals, private, exp	capita	18.60	88	38s
Mental health care, psychiatric out-patient clinics, freestanding, exp	capita	2.28	88	38s
Mental health care, psychiatric partial-care organizations, freestanding, exp	capita	0.24	88	38s
Mental health care, state and county mental hospitals, exp	capita	13.60	88	38s
Mental health care, VA medical centers, exp	capita	2.33	88	38s
Mevacor 20 mg tablets	30	67.62	92	49s
Physician fee, family practice, first-visit		111.00	91	62r
Physician fee, family practice, revisit		45.00	91	62r
Physician fee, general practice, first-visit		100.00	91	62r
Physician fee, general practice, revisit		40.00	91	62r
Physician fee, internal medicine, first-visit		137.00	91	62r

Values are in dollars or fractions of dollars. In the column headed *Ref*, references are shown to sources. Each reference is followed by a letter. These refer to the geographical level for which data were reported: s = State, r = Region, and c = City or metro. The abbreviation *ex* is used to mean *except* or *excluding*; *exp* stands for expenditures. For other abbreviations and further explanations, please see the Introduction.

Visalia, CA - continued

Item	Per	Value	Date	Ref.
Health Care				
Physician fee, internal medicine, revisit		48.00	91	62r
Physician fee, median, neurosurgeon, first-visit		157.00	91	62r
Physician fee, median, nonsurgical specialist, first-visit		131.00	91	62r
Physician fee, median, orthopedic surgeon, first-visit		124.00	91	62r
Physician fee, median, plastic surgeon, first-visit		88.00	91	62r
Physician fee, median, surgical specialist, first-visit		100.00	91	62r
Physician fee, neurosurgeon, revisit		51.00	91	62r
Physician fee, nonsurgical specialist, revisit		47.00	91	62r
Physician fee, obstetrics/gynecology, first-visit		95.00	91	62r
Physician fee, obstetrics/gynecology, revisit		50.00	91	62r
Physician fee, orthopedic surgeon, revisit		51.00	91	62r
Physician fee, pediatrician, first-visit		81.00	91	62r
Physician fee, pediatrician, revisit		42.00	91	62r
Physician fee, plastic surgeon, revisit		48.00	91	62r
Physician fee, surgical specialist, revisit		49.00	91	62r
Prozac 20 mg tablets	14	33.22	92	49s
Substance abuse, hospital ancillary charge	incident	1760	90	70s
Substance abuse, hospital physician charge	incident	750	90	70s
Substance abuse, hospital room and board	incident	6390	90	70s
Tagamet 300 mg tablets	100	77.08	92	49s
Xanax 0.25 mg tablets	90	64.08	92	49s
Zantac 160 mg tablets	60	92.31	92	49s
Household Goods				
Appliance repair, home, service call, washing machine	min labor charge	39.80	4Q 92	4c
Laundry detergent, Tide Ultra, Bold, or Cheer	42 oz	4.36	4Q 92	4c
Tissues, facial, Kleenex brand	175-count box	1.22	4Q 92	4c
Housing				
ACCRA Index, Housing		121.90	4Q 92	4c
Home, median price	unit	131,200	92	58s
House, 1,800 sq ft, 8,000 sq ft lot, new, urban	total	138200	4Q 92	4c
House payment, principal and interest, 25% down payment	month	783	4Q 92	4c
Mortgage rate, incl. points & origination fee, 30-year fixed or adjustable rate	percent	8.31	4Q 92	4c
Rent, apartment, 2 bedrooms - 1-1/2 to 2 baths, unfurnished, 950 sq ft, water	month	524	4Q 92	4c
Insurance and Pensions				
Auto insurance, private passenger	year	904.37	91	63s
Personal Goods				
Shampoo, Alberto VO5	15 oz	1.51	4Q 92	4c
Toothpaste, Crest or Colgate	6-7 oz	2.04	4Q 92	4c
Personal Services				
Dry cleaning, man's 2-piece suit		6.48	4Q 92	4c
Haircare, woman's shampoo, trim and blow-dry		17.60	4Q 92	4c
Haircut, man's barbershop, no styling		7.00	4Q 92	4c
Restaurant Food				
Chicken, fried, thigh and drumstick		2.54	4Q 92	4c
Hamburger with cheese	1/4 lb	1.92	4Q 92	4c
Pizza, Pizza Hut or Pizza Inn, cheese, thin crust	12-13 in	8.60	4Q 92	4c

Visalia, CA - continued

Item	Per	Value	Date	Ref.
Taxes				
Tax, cigarette	pack	35	91	77s
Tax, gasoline	gal	16	91	77s
Taxes, state	capita	1477	91	77s
Transportation				
ACCRA Index, Transportation		110.30	4Q 92	4c
Bus fare	one-way	1.50	3/93	2c
Driver's license fee		10.00	12/90	43s
Tire balance, computer or spin balance, front	wheel	7.50	4Q 92	4c
Travel				
Business travel	day	178.00	4/93	89r
Utilities				
ACCRA Index, Utilities		123.80	4Q 92	4c
Electricity	mil Btu	25.98	90	64s
Electricity, partial electric and other energy, 1,800 sq ft living area new home	month	101.24	4Q 92	4c

Waco, TX

Item	Per	Value	Date	Ref.
Composite ACCRA index		95.80	4Q 92	4c
Alcoholic Beverages				
Beer, Miller Lite or Budweiser, 12-oz containers	6 pack	3.83	4Q 92	4c
Liquor, J & B Scotch	750 ml	17.68	4Q 92	4c
Wine, Gallo Chablis blanc, 1.5 liter	bottle	4.51	4Q 92	4c
Child Care				
Child care fee, average, center	hour	1.29	90	65r
Child care fee, average, nonregulated family day care	hour	0.89	90	65r
Child care fee, average, regulated family day care	hour	1.32	90	65r
Clothing				
Jeans, man's denim		28.66	4Q 92	4c
Shirt, man's dress shirt		21.66	4Q 92	4c
Undervest, boy's size 10-14, cotton	3	5.33	4Q 92	4c
Communications				
Long-distance telephone service, day, initial minute, 0-100 miles	min	0.10-0.46	91	12s
Long-distance telephone service, day, additional minute, 0-100 miles	min	0.06-0.45	91	12s
Newspaper subscription, daily and Sunday home delivery, large-city	month	11.50	4Q 92	4c
Telephone, flat rate	month	9.10	91	11c
Telephone bill, family of four	month	17.56	4Q 92	4c
Education				
Board, 4-yr private college/university	year	1883	91	22s
Board, 4-yr public college/university	year	1605	91	22s
Expenditures, local gov't, public elementary/secondary	pupil	4593	92	20s
Room, 4-year private college/university	year	1620	91	22s
Room, 4-year public college/university	year	1532	91	22s
Tuition, 2-year private college/university	year	4394	91	22s
Tuition, 2-year public college/university	year	495	91	22s
Tuition, 4-year private college/university	year	6497	91	22s
Tuition, 4-year public college/university, in-state	year	986	91	22s
Energy and Fuels				
Coal	mil Btu	1.44	90	64s
Energy	mil Btu	6.48	90	64s
Energy, combined forms, 1,800 sq ft heating area	month	125.47	4Q 92	4c
Energy, exc electricity, 1,800 sq ft heating area	month	31.71	4Q 92	4c
Energy exp/householder, 1-family unit	year	471	90	28r
Energy exp/householder, <1,000 sq ft heating area	year	384	90	28r

Values are in dollars or fractions of dollars. In the column headed *Ref*, references are shown to sources. Each reference is followed by a letter. These refer to the geographical level for which data were reported: s=State, r=Region, and c=City or metro. The abbreviation *ex* is used to mean *except* or *excluding*; *exp* stands for expenditures. For other abbreviations and further explanations, please see the Introduction.

Waco, TX - continued

Item	Per	Value	Date	Ref.
Energy and Fuels				
Energy exp/householder, 1,000-1,999 sq ft heating area	year	421	90	28r
Energy exp/householder, 2,000+ sq ft heating area	year	625	90	28r
Energy exp/householder, mobile home	year	271	90	28r
Energy exp/householder, multifamily	year	355	90	28r
Gas, natural	mil Btu	2.47	90	64s
Gas, natural	000 cu ft	5.71	91	46s
Gas, natural, exp	year	388	91	46s
Gasoline, motor	gal	1.08	4Q 92	4c
Gasoline, unleaded regular	mil Btu	9.16	90	64s
Entertainment				
Bowling, evening rate	game	1.49	4Q 92	4c
Miniature golf admission	adult	6.18	92	1r
Miniature golf admission	child	5.14	92	1r
Monopoly game, Parker Brothers', No. 9		9.95	4Q 92	4c
Movie	admission	5.50	4Q 92	4c
Tennis balls, yellow, Wilson or Penn, 3	can	2.08	4Q 92	4c
Waterpark admission	adult	11.00	92	1r
Waterpark admission	child	8.55	92	1r
Funerals				
Casket, 18-gauge steel, velvet interior		2274.41	91	24r
Cosmetology, hair care, etc.		74.62	91	24r
Embalming		229.94	91	24r
Facility use for ceremony		176.61	91	24r
Hearse, local		116.34	91	24r
Limousine, local		72.68	91	24r
Remains to funeral home, transfer		87.72	91	24r
Service charge, professional		712.53	91	24r
Vault, concrete, non-metallic liner		750.55	91	24r
Viewing facilities, use		155.31	91	24r
Goods and Services				
ACCRA Index, Miscellaneous Goods and Services		99.50	4Q 92	4c
Groceries				
ACCRA Index, Groceries		93.50	4Q 92	4c
Apples, Red Delicious	lb	0.79	4/93	16r
Babyfood, strained vegetables, lowest price	4-4.5 oz jar	0.25	4Q 92	4c
Bacon	lb	1.75	4/93	16r
Bananas	lb	0.38	4Q 92	4c
Bananas	lb	0.42	4/93	16r
Beef, stew, boneless	lb	2.61	4/93	16r
Bologna, all beef or mixed	lb	2.24	4/93	16r
Bread, white	24 oz	0.54	4Q 92	4c
Bread, white, pan	lb	0.64	4/93	16r
Bread, whole wheat, pan	lb	0.96	4/93	16r
Cabbage	lb	0.37	4/93	16r
Carrots, short trimmed and topped	lb	0.47	4/93	16r
Celery	lb	0.64	4/93	16r
Cheese, American	lb	2.98	4/93	16r
Cheese, Cheddar	lb	3.28	4/93	16r
Cheese, Kraft grated Parmesan	8-oz canister	3.33	4Q 92	4c
Chicken, fresh, whole	lb	0.77	4/93	16r
Chicken, fryer, whole	lb	0.56	4Q 92	4c
Chicken breast, bone-in	lb	1.92	4/93	16r
Chicken legs, bone-in	lb	1.06	4/93	16r
Chuck roast, graded and ungraded, ex USDA prime and choice	lb	2.40	4/93	16r
Chuck roast, USDA choice, bone-in	lb	2.19	4/93	16r
Chuck roast, USDA choice, boneless	lb	2.38	4/93	16r
Cigarettes, Winston	carton	19.45	4Q 92	4c
Coffee, 100% ground roast, all sizes	lb	2.48	4/93	16r
Coffee, vacuum-packed	13-oz can	1.88	4Q 92	4c
Corn, frozen	10 oz	0.56	4Q 92	4c

Waco, TX - continued

Item	Per	Value	Date	Ref.
Groceries - continued				
Corn Flakes, Kellogg's or Post Toasties	18 oz	1.89	4Q 92	4c
Crackers, soda, salted	lb	1.15	4/93	16r
Eggs, Grade A large	doz	0.89	4Q 92	4c
Eggs, Grade A large	doz	0.96	4/93	16r
Flour, white, all purpose	lb	0.24	4/93	16r
Frankfurters, all meat or all beef	lb	2.01	4/93	16r
Grapefruit	lb	0.44	4/93	16r
Grapes, Thompson Seedless	lb	1.40	4/93	16r
Ground beef, 100% beef	lb	1.58	4/93	16r
Ground beef, lean and extra lean	lb	2.09	4/93	16r
Ground beef or hamburger	lb	1.61	4Q 92	4c
Ground chuck, 100% beef	lb	1.98	4/93	16r
Ham, boneless, excluding canned	lb	2.89	4/93	16r
Ham, picnic, shoulder, bone-in, smoked	lb	1.02	4/93	16r
Ham, rump or steak half, bone-in, smoked	lb	1.48	4/93	16r
Honey, jar	8 oz	0.73-1.19	92	5r
Honey, jar	lb	1.10-1.79	92	5r
Honey, squeeze bear	12-oz	1.19-1.50	92	5r
Ice cream, prepackaged, bulk, regular	1/2 gal	2.41	4/93	16r
Lemons	lb	1.05	4/93	16r
Lettuce, iceberg	head	0.85	4Q 92	4c
Lettuce, iceberg	lb	0.81	4/93	16r
Margarine, Blue Bonnet or Parkay cubes	lb	0.51	4Q 92	4c
Margarine, stick	lb	0.88	4/93	16r
Milk, whole	1/2 gal	1.28	4Q 92	4c
Orange juice, Minute Maid frozen	12-oz can	1.32	4Q 92	4c
Oranges, navel	lb	0.55	4/93	16r
Peaches	29-oz can	1.33	4Q 92	4c
Pears, Anjou	lb	0.92	4/93	16r
Peas Sweet, Del Monte or Green Giant	15-17 oz can	0.50	4Q 92	4c
Pork chops, center cut, bone-in	lb	3.13	4/93	16r
Potato chips	16 oz	2.94	4/93	16r
Potatoes, white	lb	0.43	4/93	16r
Potatoes, white or red	10-lb sack	2.62	4Q 92	4c
Rib roast, USDA choice, bone-in	lb	4.63	4/93	16r
Rice, white, long grain, uncooked	lb	0.45	4/93	16r
Round roast, graded & ungraded, ex USDA prime & choice	lb	3.03	4/93	16r
Round roast, USDA choice, boneless	lb	3.09	4/93	16r
Sausage, fresh, loose	lb	2.08	4/93	16r
Sausage, Jimmy Dean, 100% pork	lb	2.44	4Q 92	4c
Short ribs, bone-in	lb	2.66	4/93	16r
Shortening, vegetable oil blends	lb	0.69	4/93	16r
Shortening, vegetable, Crisco	3-lb can	1.98	4Q 92	4c
Soft drink, Coca Cola	2 liter	1.10	4Q 92	4c
Spaghetti and macaroni	lb	0.81	4/93	16r
Steak, rib eye, USDA choice, boneless	lb	6.24	4/93	16r
Steak, round, graded & ungraded, ex USDA prime & choice	lb	3.31	4/93	16r
Steak, round, USDA choice, boneless	lb	3.34	4/93	16r
Steak, sirloin, graded & ungraded, ex USDA prime & choice	lb	4.19	4/93	16r
Steak, sirloin, USDA choice, boneless	lb	4.46	4/93	16r
Steak, T-bone	lb	4.81	4Q 92	4c
Steak, T-bone, USDA choice, bone-in	lb	5.25	4/93	16r
Strawberries, dry pint	12 oz	0.92	4/93	16r
Sugar, cane or beet	4 lb	1.14	4Q 92	4c
Sugar, white	lb	0.39	4/93	16r
Sugar, white, 33-80 oz pk	lb	0.38	4/93	16r
Tomatoes, field grown	lb	0.88	4/93	16r
Tomatoes, Hunt's or Del Monte	14.5-oz can	0.61	4Q 92	4c
Tuna, chunk, light	6.125-6.5 oz can	0.59	4Q 92	4c
Tuna, chunk, light	lb	1.79	4/93	16r
Turkey, frozen, whole	lb	1.04	4/93	16r

Values are in dollars or fractions of dollars. In the column headed *Ref*, references are shown to sources. Each reference is followed by a letter. These refer to the geographical level for which data were reported: s = State, r = Region, and c = City or metro. The abbreviation *ex* is used to mean *except* or *excluding*; *exp* stands for expenditures. For other abbreviations and further explanations, please see the Introduction.

Waco, TX - continued

Item	Per	Value	Date	Ref.
Groceries				
Yogurt, natural, fruit flavored	1/2 pint	0.57	4/93	16r
Health Care				
ACCRA Index, Health Care		92.30	4Q 92	4c
Analgesic, Aspirin, Bayer, 325 mg tablets	100	4.98	4Q 92	4c
Childbirth, cesarean, hospital		5034	91	62r
Childbirth, cesarean, physician's fee		2053	91	62r
Childbirth, normal, hospital		2712	91	62r
Childbirth, normal, physician's fee		1492	91	62r
Dentist's fee, adult teeth cleaning and periodic oral exam	visit	44.40	4Q 92	4c
Doctor's fee, routine exam, established patient	visit	32.33	4Q 92	4c
Health care spending, state	capita	2192	3/93	84s
Hospital care, semiprivate room	day	214.00	90	27c
Hospital care, semiprivate room	day	293.50	4Q 92	4c
Medical insurance premium, per employee, small group comprehensive	month	332.15	10/91	25c
Mental health care, exp	capita	20.37-28.83	90	38s
Mental health care, exp, state mental health agency	capita	22.72	90	38s
Mental health care, hospital psychiatric services, non-Federal, exp	capita	7.95	88	38s
Mental health care, mental health organization, multiservice, exp	capita	12.05	88	38s
Mental health care, psychiatric hospitals, private, exp	capita	37.78	88	38s
Mental health care, psychiatric out-patient clinics, freestanding, exp	capita	0.43	88	38s
Mental health care, state and county mental hospitals, exp	capita	12.54	88	38s
Mental health care, VA medical centers, exp	capita	5.35	88	38s
Physician fee, family practice, first-visit		75.00	91	62r
Physician fee, family practice, revisit		34.00	91	62r
Physician fee, general practice, first-visit		61.00	91	62r
Physician fee, general practice, revisit		32.00	91	62r
Physician fee, general surgeon, first-visit		64.00	91	62r
Physician fee, general surgeon, revisit		40.00	91	62r
Physician fee, internal medicine, first-visit		98.00	91	62r
Physician fee, internal medicine, revisit		40.00	91	62r
Physician fee, median, neurosurgeon, first-visit		130.00	91	62r
Physician fee, median, nonsurgical specialist, first-visit		95.00	91	62r
Physician fee, median, orthopedic surgeon, first-visit		91.00	91	62r
Physician fee, median, plastic surgeon, first-visit		66.00	91	62r
Physician fee, median, surgical specialist, first-visit		62.00	91	62r
Physician fee, neurosurgeon, revisit		50.00	91	62r
Physician fee, nonsurgical specialist, revisit		40.00	91	62r
Physician fee, obstetrics/gynecology, first-visit		64.00	91	62r
Physician fee, obstetrics/gynecology, revisit		41.00	91	62r
Physician fee, orthopedic surgeon, revisit		40.00	91	62r
Physician fee, pediatrician, first-visit		49.00	91	62r
Physician fee, pediatrician, revisit		33.00	91	62r
Physician fee, plastic surgeon, revisit		43.00	91	62r
Physician fee, surgical specialist, revisit		37.00	91	62r
Substance abuse, hospital ancillary charge	incident	3750	90	70s
Substance abuse, hospital physician charge	incident	1080	90	70s
Substance abuse, hospital room and board	incident	5320	90	70s
Household Goods				
Appliance repair, home, service call, washing machine	min labor charge	31.98	4Q 92	4c

Waco, TX - continued

Item	Per	Value	Date	Ref.
Household Goods - continued				
Laundry detergent, Tide Ultra, Bold, or Cheer	42 oz	3.73	4Q 92	4c
Tissues, facial, Kleenex brand	175-count box	1.10	4Q 92	4c
Housing				
ACCRA Index, Housing		85.40	4Q 92	4c
House, 1,800 sq ft, 8,000 sq ft lot, new, urban	total	89480	4Q 92	4c
House payment, principal and interest, 25% down payment	month	502	4Q 92	4c
Mortgage rate, incl. points & origination fee, 30-year fixed or adjustable rate	percent	8.21	4Q 92	4c
Rent, apartment, 2 bedrooms - 1-1/2 to 2 baths, unfurnished, 950 sq ft, water	month	474	4Q 92	4c
Rental unit, 1 bedroom	month	337	93	23c
Rental unit, 2 bedroom	month	394	93	23c
Rental unit, 3 bedroom	month	492	93	23c
Rental unit, 4 bedroom	month	547	93	23c
Rental unit, efficiency	month	280	93	23c
Insurance and Pensions				
Auto insurance, private passenger	year	709.79	91	63s
Personal Goods				
Shampoo, Alberto VO5	15 oz	1.02	4Q 92	4c
Toothpaste, Crest or Colgate	6-7 oz	2.05	4Q 92	4c
Personal Services				
Dry cleaning, man's 2-piece suit		5.82	4Q 92	4c
Haircare, woman's shampoo, trim and blow-dry		21.50	4Q 92	4c
Haircut, man's barbershop, no styling		7.00	4Q 92	4c
Restaurant Food				
Chicken, fried, thigh and drumstick		2.38	4Q 92	4c
Hamburger with cheese	1/4 lb	1.89	4Q 92	4c
Pizza, Pizza Hut or Pizza Inn, cheese, thin crust	12-13 in	8.09	4Q 92	4c
Taxes				
Tax, cigarette	pack	41	91	77s
Tax, gasoline	gal	20	91	77s
Taxes, state	capita	923	91	77s
Transportation				
ACCRA Index, Transportation		101.60	4Q 92	4c
Bus fare	one-way	0.75	3/93	2c
Driver's license fee		16.00	12/90	43s
Tire balance, computer or spin balance, front	wheel	7.00	4Q 92	4c
Travel				
Business travel	day	193.00	4/93	89r
Utilities				
ACCRA Index, Utilities		112.40	4Q 92	4c
Electricity	mil Btu	17.09	90	64s
Electricity, partial electric and other energy, 1,800 sq ft living area new home	month	93.76	4Q 92	4c
Electricity, residential	KWh	5.92	2/93	94s

Washington, DC, MD, VA

Item	Per	Value	Date	Ref.
Communications				
Telephone, flat rate	month	14.82	91	11c
Telephone, residential, private line, rotary, unlimited calling	month	20.97	10/91	78c
Construction				
Plywood, post-Hurricane Andrew	4x8 sheet	10.69	92	13c
Plywood, pre-Hurricane Andrew	4x8 sheet	7.79	92	13c

Values are in dollars or fractions of dollars. In the column headed *Ref*, references are shown to sources. Each reference is followed by a letter. These refer to the geographical level for which data were reported: s=State, r=Region, and c=City or metro. The abbreviation *ex* is used to mean *except* or *excluding*; *exp* stands for *expenditures*. For other abbreviations and further explanations, please see the Introduction.

Washington, DC, MD, VA - continued

Item	Per	Value	Date	Ref.
Education				
Board, 4-yr private college/university	year	2664	91	22s
Expenditures, local gov't, public elementary/secondary	pupil	8116	92	20s
Room, 4-year private college/university	year	3387	91	22s
Tuition, 4-year private college/university	year	11939	91	22s
Tuition, 4-year public college/university, in-state	year	664	91	22s
Energy and Fuels				
Coal	mil Btu	1.96	90	64s
Energy	mil Btu	11.31	90	64s
Energy exp/householder, 1-family unit	year	487	90	28r
Energy exp/householder, <1,000 sq ft heating area	year	393	90	28r
Energy exp/householder, 1,000-1,999 sq ft heating area	year	442	90	28r
Energy exp/householder, 2,000+ sq ft heating area	year	577	90	28r
Energy exp/householder, mobile home	year	366	90	28r
Energy exp/householder, multifamily	year	382	90	28r
Fuel oil #2	gal	1.10	4/93	16c
Gas, cooking, 10 therms	month	9.98	92	56c
Gas, cooking, 30 therms	month	22.13	92	56c
Gas, cooking, 50 therms	month	34.29	92	56c
Gas, heating, winter, 100 therms	month	46.20	92	56c
Gas, heating, winter, average use	month	13.56	92	56c
Gas, natural	mil Btu	6.40	90	64s
Gas, piped	100 therms	80.29	4/93	16c
Gas, piped	40 therms	37.17	4/93	16c
Gas, piped	therm	0.84	4/93	16c
Gasoline, all types	gal	1.19	4/93	16c
Gasoline, regular unleaded, taxes included, cash, self-service	gal	1.30	4/93	16c
Gasoline, unleaded premium 93 octane	gal	1.11	4/93	16c
Gasoline, unleaded regular	mil Btu	10.66	90	64s
Entertainment				
Dinner entree, restaurant		78.00-88.00	92	83c
Football game expenditures, pro		181.50	91	80c
Miniature golf admission	adult	6.18	92	1r
Miniature golf admission	child	5.14	92	1r
Waterpark admission	adult	11.00	92	1r
Waterpark admission	child	8.55	92	1r
Funerals				
Casket, 18-gauge steel, velvet interior		2029.08	91	24r
Cosmetology, hair care, etc.		75.10	91	24r
Embalming		249.24	91	24r
Facility use for ceremony		162.27	91	24r
Hearse, local		114.04	91	24r
Limousine, local		88.57	91	24r
Remains to funeral home, transfer		92.61	91	24r
Service charge, professional		682.42	91	24r
Vault, concrete, non-metallic liner		798.70	91	24r
Viewing facilities, use		163.86	91	24r
Goods and Services				
Goods and services	year	17798	92	36c
Police protection expense	resident	343.00	92	18c
Groceries				
Bakery products, exp	year	217	89	15c
Beef, exp	year	180	89	15c
Cereals and bakery products, exp	year	328	89	15c
Cereals and cereal products, exp	year	111	89	15c
Dairy products, exp	year	265	89	15c
Dairy products, miscellaneous, exp	year	159	89	15c
Eggs, exp	year	21	89	15c
Fish and seafood, exp	year	100	89	15c
Food, exp	year	4710	89	15c

Washington, DC, MD, VA - continued

Item	Per	Value	Date	Ref.
Groceries - continued				
Food eaten at home, exp	year	2317	89	15c
Fruits, fresh, exp	year	133	89	15c
Fruits, processed, exp	year	96	89	15c
Fruits and vegetables, exp	year	413	89	15c
Meats, poultry, fish and eggs, exp	year	605	89	15c
Milk and cream, fresh, exp	year	106	89	15c
Pork, exp	year	91	89	15c
Poultry, exp	year	135	89	15c
Vegetables, fresh, exp	year	126	89	15c
Vegetables, processed, exp	year	59	89	15c
Health Care				
Hospital care, semiprivate room	day	325.00	90	27c
Medical insurance premium, per employee, small group comprehensive	month	445.30	10/91	25c
Medical plan per employee	year	3495	91	45r
Mental health care, exp	capita	53.68-118.35	90	38s
Mental health care, exp, state mental health agency	capita	267.86	90	38s
Mental health care, hospital psychiatric services, non-Federal, exp	capita	10.61	88	38s
Mental health care, mental health organization, multiservice, exp	capita	20.41	88	38s
Mental health care, psychiatric hospitals, private, exp	capita	4.40	88	38s
Mental health care, psychiatric out-patient clinics, freestanding, exp	capita	2.81	88	38s
Mental health care, psychiatric partial-care organizations, freestanding, exp	capita	0.14	88	38s
Mental health care, state and county mental hospitals, exp	capita	256.56	88	38s
Mental health care, VA medical centers, exp	capita	1.99	88	38s
Housing				
Home, median price	unit	157.80		26c
Rental unit, 1 bedroom	month	725	93	23c
Rental unit, 2 bedroom	month	854	93	23c
Rental unit, 3 bedroom	month	1067	93	23c
Rental unit, 4 bedroom	month	1195	93	23c
Rental unit, efficiency	month	597	93	23c
Insurance and Pensions				
Auto insurance, private passenger	year	980.88	91	63s
Taxes				
Tax, cigarette	pack	50	91	77s
Tax, gasoline	gal	20	91	77s
Taxes, hotel room	day	10.48	92	33c
Taxes, state	capita	4037	91	77s
Transportation				
Auto fixed costs, midsize		3673	91	60c
Auto operating cost, midsize		1575	91	60c
Auto rental, average	day	54.00	6/91	60c
Bus fare	one-way	0.35	3/93	2c
Driver's license fee		15.00	12/90	43s
Railway fare, commuter	one-way	3.15	3/93	2c
Railway fare, heavy rail	one-way	1.00	3/93	2c
Taxi fare, airport-city, average	day	11.50	6/91	60c
Travel				
Breakfast	day	8.56	6/91	60c
Business travel	day	248.00	92	86c
Dinner	day	24.14	6/91	60c
Dinner	day	27.45	92	85c
Lodging	day	197.50	91	60c
Lodging	day	196.00	92	85c
Lunch	day	15.23	6/91	60c
Travel, business	day	237.82	92	82c
Travel, business	day	260.46	93	68c

Values are in dollars or fractions of dollars. In the column headed *Ref*, references are shown to sources. Each reference is followed by a letter. These refer to the geographical level for which data were reported: s = State, r = Region, and c = City or metro. The abbreviation *ex* is used to mean *except* or *excluding*; *exp* stands for expenditures. For other abbreviations and further explanations, please see the Introduction.

Washington, DC, MD, VA - continued

Item	Per	Value	Date	Ref.
Utilities				
Electricity	500 KWh	41.62	4/93	16c
Electricity	KWh	0.08	4/93	16c
Electricity	mil Btu	17.38	90	64s
Electricity, winter, 250 KWh	month	12.62	92	55c
Electricity, winter, 500 KWh	month	27.09	92	55c
Electricity, winter, 750 KWh	month	45.32	92	55c
Electricity, winter, 1000 KWh	month	63.55	92	55c

Waterloo-Cedar Falls, IA

Item	Per	Value	Date	Ref.
Composite ACCRA index		96.10	4Q 92	4c
Alcoholic Beverages				
Beer, Miller Lite or Budweiser, 12-oz containers	6 pack	3.60	4Q 92	4c
Liquor, J & B Scotch	750 ml	18.22	4Q 92	4c
Wine, Gallo Chablis blanc, 1.5 liter	bottle	4.97	4Q 92	4c
Child Care				
Child care fee, average, center	hour	1.63	90	65r
Child care fee, average, nonregulated family day care	hour	1.83	90	65r
Child care fee, average, regulated family day care	hour	1.42	90	65r
Clothing				
Jeans, man's denim		33.50	4Q 92	4c
Shirt, man's dress shirt		27.39	4Q 92	4c
Undervest, boy's size 10-14, cotton	3	3.72	4Q 92	4c
Communications				
Long-distance telephone service, day, initial minute, 0-100 miles	min	0.21-0.41	91	12s
Long-distance telephone service, day, additional minute, 0-100 miles	min	0.11-0.30	91	12s
Long-distance telephone service, evenings/weekends, 0-100 mi, initial minute	min	0.11-0.20	91	12s
Long-distance telephone service, evenings/weekends, 0-100 mi, additional minute	min	0.06-0.15	91	12s
Newspaper subscription, daily and Sunday home delivery, large-city	month	11.74	4Q 92	4c
Telephone, flat rate	month	15.95	91	11c
Telephone bill, family of four	month	25.45	4Q 92	4c
Education				
Board, 4-yr private college/university	year	1703	91	22s
Board, 4-yr public college/university	year	1183	91	22s
Expenditures, local gov't, public elementary/secondary	pupil	5026	92	20s
Room, 4-year private college/university	year	1392	91	22s
Room, 4-year public college/university	year	1188	91	22s
Tuition, 2-year private college/university	year	5119	91	22s
Tuition, 2-year public college/university	year	1298	91	22s
Tuition, 4-year private college/university	year	8703	91	22s
Tuition, 4-year public college/university, in-state	year	1880	91	22s
Energy and Fuels				
Coal	mil Btu	1.16	90	64s
Energy	mil Btu	7.71	90	64s
Energy, combined forms, 1,800 sq ft heating area	month	88.45	4Q 92	4c
Energy, exc electricity, 1,800 sq ft heating area	month	43.67	4Q 92	4c
Energy exp/householder, 1-family unit	year	473	90	28r
Energy exp/householder, <1,000 sq ft heating area	year	429	90	28r
Energy exp/householder, 1,000-1,999 sq ft heating area	year	442	90	28r
Energy exp/householder, 2,000+ sq ft heating area	year	498	90	28r
Energy exp/householder, mobile home	year	442	90	28r
Energy exp/householder, multifamily	year	407	90	28r

Waterloo-Cedar Falls, IA - continued

Item	Per	Value	Date	Ref.
Energy and Fuels - continued				
Gas, natural	mil Btu	3.81	90	64s
Gas, natural	000 cu ft	4.81	91	46s
Gas, natural, exp	year	530	91	46s
Gasoline, motor	gal	1.15	4Q 92	4c
Gasoline, unleaded regular	mil Btu	9.38	90	64s
Entertainment				
Bowling, evening rate	game	1.68	4Q 92	4c
Miniature golf admission	adult	6.18	92	1r
Miniature golf admission	child	5.14	92	1r
Monopoly game, Parker Brothers', No. 9		10.30	4Q 92	4c
Movie	admission	5.00	4Q 92	4c
Tennis balls, yellow, Wilson or Penn, 3	can	1.98	4Q 92	4c
Waterpark admission	adult	11.00	92	1r
Waterpark admission	child	8.55	92	1r
Funerals				
Casket, 18-gauge steel, velvet interior		1952.97	91	24r
Cosmetology, hair care, etc.		90.03	91	24r
Embalming		251.75	91	24r
Facility use for ceremony		180.75	91	24r
Hearse, local		117.51	91	24r
Limousine, local		71.86	91	24r
Remains to funeral home, transfer		81.14	91	24r
Service charge, professional		740.03	91	24r
Vault, concrete, non-metallic liner		801.47	91	24r
Viewing facilities, use		169.33	91	24r
Goods and Services				
ACCRA Index, Miscellaneous Goods and Services		97.90	4Q 92	4c
Groceries				
ACCRA Index, Groceries		98.40	4Q 92	4c
Apples, Red Delicious	lb	0.77	4/93	16r
Babyfood, strained vegetables, lowest price	4-4.5 oz jar	0.29	4Q 92	4c
Bacon	lb	1.85	4/93	16r
Bananas	lb	0.50	4Q 92	4c
Bananas	lb	0.46	4/93	16r
Beef, stew, boneless	lb	2.53	4/93	16r
Bologna, all beef or mixed	lb	2.19	4/93	16r
Bread, white	24 oz	0.66	4Q 92	4c
Bread, white, pan	lb	0.78	4/93	16r
Butter	lb	1.50	4/93	16r
Cabbage	lb	0.40	4/93	16r
Carrots, short trimmed and topped	lb	0.45	4/93	16r
Cheese, Cheddar	lb	3.47	4/93	16r
Cheese, Kraft grated Parmesan	8-oz canister	3.22	4Q 92	4c
Chicken, fresh, whole	lb	0.84	4/93	16r
Chicken, fryer, whole	lb	0.80	4Q 92	4c
Chicken breast, bone-in	lb	1.94	4/93	16r
Chicken legs, bone-in	lb	1.02	4/93	16r
Chuck roast, graded and ungraded, ex USDA prime and choice	lb	2.43	4/93	16r
Chuck roast, USDA choice, bone-in	lb	2.11	4/93	16r
Chuck roast, USDA choice, boneless	lb	2.44	4/93	16r
Cigarettes, Winston	carton	18.57	4Q 92	4c
Coffee, 100% ground roast, all sizes	lb	2.47	4/93	16r
Coffee, vacuum-packed	13-oz can	1.99	4Q 92	4c
Cookies, chocolate chip	lb	2.73	4/93	16r
Corn, frozen	10 oz	0.66	4Q 92	4c
Corn Flakes, Kellogg's or Post Toasties	18 oz	1.61	4Q 92	4c
Eggs, Grade A large	doz	0.70	4Q 92	4c
Eggs, Grade A large	doz	0.93	4/93	16r
Flour, white, all purpose	lb	0.21	4/93	16r
Grapefruit	lb	0.45	4/93	16r
Grapes, Thompson Seedless	lb	1.46	4/93	16r
Ground beef, 100% beef	lb	1.63	4/93	16r

Values are in dollars or fractions of dollars. In the column headed *Ref*, references are shown to sources. Each reference is followed by a letter. These refer to the geographical level for which data were reported: s=State, r=Region, and c=City or metro. The abbreviation *ex* is used to mean *except* or *excluding*; *exp* stands for expenditures. For other abbreviations and further explanations, please see the Introduction.

Waterloo-Cedar Falls, IA - continued

Item	Per	Value	Date	Ref.
Groceries				
Ground beef, lean and extra lean	lb	2.08	4/93	16r
Ground beef or hamburger	lb	1.42	4Q 92	4c
Ground chuck, 100% beef	lb	1.94	4/93	16r
Ham, boneless, excluding canned	lb	2.21	4/93	16r
Ice cream, prepackaged, bulk, regular	1/2 gal	2.41	4/93	16r
Lemons	lb	0.82	4/93	16r
Lettuce, iceberg	head	0.90	4Q 92	4c
Lettuce, iceberg	lb	0.83	4/93	16r
Margarine, Blue Bonnet or Parkay cubes	lb	0.61	4Q 92	4c
Margarine, stick	lb	0.77	4/93	16r
Milk, whole	1/2 gal	1.18	4Q 92	4c
Orange juice, Minute Maid frozen	12-oz can	1.58	4Q 92	4c
Oranges, navel	lb	0.50	4/93	16r
Peaches	29-oz can	1.41	4Q 92	4c
Peanut butter, creamy, all sizes	lb	1.82	4/93	16r
Pears, Anjou	lb	0.85	4/93	16r
Peas Sweet, Del Monte or Green Giant	15-17 oz can	0.59	4Q 92	4c
Pork chops, center cut, bone-in	lb	3.17	4/93	16r
Potato chips	16 oz	2.68	4/93	16r
Potatoes, white	lb	0.26	4/93	16r
Potatoes, white or red	10-lb sack	2.12	4Q 92	4c
Round roast, graded & ungraded, ex USDA prime & choice	lb	2.88	4/93	16r
Round roast, USDA choice, boneless	lb	2.96	4/93	16r
Sausage, Jimmy Dean, 100% pork	lb	2.98	4Q 92	4c
Shortening, vegetable oil blends	lb	0.79	4/93	16r
Shortening, vegetable, Crisco	3-lb can	2.14	4Q 92	4c
Soft drink, Coca Cola	2 liter	1.03	4Q 92	4c
Spaghetti and macaroni	lb	0.76	4/93	16r
Steak, rib eye, USDA choice, boneless	lb	6.29	4/93	16r
Steak, round, USDA choice, boneless	lb	3.24	4/93	16r
Steak, sirloin, graded & ungraded, ex USDA prime & choice	lb	4.00	4/93	16r
Steak, sirloin, USDA choice, bone-in	lb	3.57	4/93	16r
Steak, sirloin, USDA choice, boneless	lb	4.17	4/93	16r
Steak, T-bone	lb	5.10	4Q 92	4c
Steak, T-bone, USDA choice, bone-in	lb	5.60	4/93	16r
Strawberries, dry pint	12 oz	0.90	4/93	16r
Sugar, cane or beet	4 lb	1.29	4Q 92	4c
Sugar, white	lb	0.36	4/93	16r
Sugar, white, 33-80 oz pk	lb	0.35	4/93	16r
Tomatoes, field grown	lb	0.99	4/93	16r
Tomatoes, Hunt's or Del Monte	14.5-oz can	0.71	4Q 92	4c
Tuna, chunk, light	6.125-6.5 oz can	0.62	4Q 92	4c
Tuna, chunk, light	lb	1.76	4/93	16r
Turkey, frozen, whole	lb	0.91	4/93	16r
Health Care				
ACCRA Index, Health Care		84.10	4Q 92	4c
Analgesic, Aspirin, Bayer, 325 mg tablets	100	4.52	4Q 92	4c
Childbirth, cesarean, hospital		4688	91	62r
Childbirth, cesarean, physician's fee		2053	91	62r
Childbirth, normal, hospital		2657	91	62r
Childbirth, normal, physician's fee		1492	91	62r
Dentist's fee, adult teeth cleaning and periodic oral exam	visit	42.00	4Q 92	4c
Doctor's fee, routine exam, established patient	visit	27.13	4Q 92	4c
Health care spending, state	capita	2351	3/93	84s
Hospital care, semiprivate room	day	220.87	90	27c
Hospital care, semiprivate room	day	285.33	4Q 92	4c
Medical insurance premium, per employee, small group comprehensive	month	284.70	10/91	25c
Medical plan per employee	year	3443	91	45r

Waterloo-Cedar Falls, IA - continued

Item	Per	Value	Date	Ref.
Health Care - continued				
Mental health care, exp	capita	20.37-28.83	90	38s
Mental health care, exp, state mental health agency	capita	17.07	90	38s
Mental health care, hospital psychiatric services, non-Federal, exp	capita	23.51	88	38s
Mental health care, mental health organization, multiservice, exp	capita	7.66	88	38s
Mental health care, psychiatric hospitals, private, exp	capita	2.86	88	38s
Mental health care, psychiatric out-patient clinics, freestanding, exp	capita	3.02	88	38s
Mental health care, state and county mental hospitals, exp	capita	14.54	88	38s
Mental health care, VA medical centers, exp	capita	13.98	88	38s
Physician fee, family practice, first-visit		76.00	91	62r
Physician fee, family practice, revisit		33.00	91	62r
Physician fee, general practice, first-visit		61.00	91	62r
Physician fee, general practice, revisit		31.00	91	62r
Physician fee, general surgeon, first-visit		65.00	91	62r
Physician fee, general surgeon, revisit		35.00	91	62r
Physician fee, internal medicine, first-visit		91.00	91	62r
Physician fee, internal medicine, revisit		40.00	91	62r
Physician fee, median, neurosurgeon, first-visit		106.00	91	62r
Physician fee, median, nonsurgical specialist, first-visit		90.00	91	62r
Physician fee, median, orthopedic surgeon, first-visit		83.00	91	62r
Physician fee, median, surgical specialist, first-visit		61.00	91	62r
Physician fee, neurosurgeon, revisit		41.00	91	62r
Physician fee, nonsurgical specialist, revisit		40.00	91	62r
Physician fee, obstetrics/gynecology, first-visit		61.00	91	62r
Physician fee, obstetrics/gynecology, revisit		40.00	91	62r
Physician fee, orthopedic surgeon, revisit		41.00	91	62r
Physician fee, pediatrician, first-visit		46.00	91	62r
Physician fee, pediatrician, revisit		33.00	91	62r
Physician fee, surgical specialist, revisit		36.00	91	62r
Substance abuse, hospital ancillary charge	incident	950	90	70s
Substance abuse, hospital physician charge	incident	250	90	70s
Substance abuse, hospital room and board	incident	3110	90	70s
Household Goods				
Appliance repair, home, service call, washing machine	min labor charge	28.04	4Q 92	4c
Laundry detergent, Tide Ultra, Bold, or Cheer	42 oz	3.29	4Q 92	4c
Tissues, facial, Kleenex brand	175-count box	1.16	4Q 92	4c
Housing				
ACCRA Index, Housing		93.30	4Q 92	4c
Home, median price	unit	47.20		26c
House, 1,800 sq ft, 8,000 sq ft lot, new, urban	total	107538	4Q 92	4c
House payment, principal and interest, 25% down payment	month	602	4Q 92	4c
Mortgage rate, incl. points & origination fee, 30-year fixed or adjustable rate	percent	8.18	4Q 92	4c
Rent, apartment, 2 bedrooms - 1-1/2 to 2 baths, unfurnished, 950 sq ft, water	month	394	4Q 92	4c
Rental unit, 1 bedroom	month	434	93	23c
Rental unit, 2 bedroom	month	512	93	23c
Rental unit, 3 bedroom	month	642	93	23c
Rental unit, 4 bedroom	month	721	93	23c
Rental unit, efficiency	month	360	93	23c

Values are in dollars or fractions of dollars. In the column headed *Ref*, references are shown to sources. Each reference is followed by a letter. These refer to the geographical level for which data were reported: s = State, r = Region, and c = City or metro. The abbreviation *ex* is used to mean *except* or *excluding*; *exp* stands for expenditures. For other abbreviations and further explanations, please see the Introduction.

Waterloo-Cedar Falls, IA - continued

Item	Per	Value	Date	Ref.
Insurance and Pensions				
Auto insurance, private passenger	year	422.46	91	63s
Personal Goods				
Shampoo, Alberto VO5	15 oz	1.35	4Q 92	4c
Toothpaste, Crest or Colgate	6-7 oz	1.87	4Q 92	4c
Personal Services				
Dry cleaning, man's 2-piece suit		6.10	4Q 92	4c
Haircare, woman's shampoo, trim and blow-dry		15.05	4Q 92	4c
Haircut, man's barbershop, no styling		9.40	4Q 92	4c
Restaurant Food				
Chicken, fried, thigh and drumstick		2.12	4Q 92	4c
Hamburger with cheese	1/4 lb	1.84	4Q 92	4c
Pizza, Pizza Hut or Pizza Inn, cheese, thin crust	12-13 in	7.79	4Q 92	4c
Taxes				
Tax, cigarette	pack	36	91	77s
Tax, gasoline	gal	20	91	77s
Taxes, state	capita	1233	91	77s
Transportation				
ACCRA Index, Transportation		109.50	4Q 92	4c
Bus fare, up to 10 miles	one-way	1.00	4Q 92	4c
Driver's license fee		16.00	12/90	43s
Tire balance, computer or spin balance, front	wheel	7.52	4Q 92	4c
Utilities				
ACCRA Index, Utilities		86.00	4Q 92	4c
Electricity	mil Btu	17.37	90	64s
Electricity, partial electric and other energy, 1,800 sq ft living area new home	month	44.78	4Q 92	4c

Wausau, WI

Item	Per	Value	Date	Ref.
Composite ACCRA index		106.20	4Q 92	4c
Alcoholic Beverages				
Beer, Miller Lite or Budweiser, 12-oz containers	6 pack	3.26	4Q 92	4c
Liquor, J & B Scotch	750 ml	14.59	4Q 92	4c
Wine, Gallo Chablis blanc, 1.5 liter	bottle	4.33	4Q 92	4c
Child Care				
Child care fee, average, center	hour	1.63	90	65r
Child care fee, average, nonregulated family day care	hour	1.83	90	65r
Child care fee, average, regulated family day care	hour	1.42	90	65r
Clothing				
Jeans, man's denim		32.89	4Q 92	4c
Shirt, man's dress shirt		25.73	4Q 92	4c
Undervest, boy's size 10-14, cotton	3	3.57	4Q 92	4c
Communications				
Long-distance telephone service, day, initial minute, 0-100 miles	min	0.15-0.29	91	12s
Long-distance telephone service, day, additional minute, 0-100 miles	min	0.10-0.27	91	12s
Newspaper subscription, daily and Sunday home delivery, large-city	month	11.52	4Q 92	4c
Telephone bill, family of four	month	24.33	4Q 92	4c
Education				
Board, 4-yr private college/university	year	1533	91	22s
Board, 4-yr public college/university	year	1404	91	22s
Expenditures, local gov't, public elementary/secondary	pupil	5972	92	20s
Room, 4-year private college/university	year	1256	91	22s
Room, 4-year public college/university	year	1416	91	22s
Tuition, 2-year private college/university	year	4768	91	22s
Tuition, 2-year public college/university	year	1234	91	22s

Wausau, WI - continued

Item	Per	Value	Date	Ref.
Education - continued				
Tuition, 4-year private college/university	year	8237	91	22s
Tuition, 4-year public college/university, in-state	year	1951	91	22s
Energy and Fuels				
Coal	mil Btu	1.41	90	64s
Energy	mil Btu	8.27	90	64s
Energy, combined forms, 1,800 sq ft heating area	month	104.11	4Q 92	4c
Energy, exc electricity, 1,800 sq ft heating area	month	60.21	4Q 92	4c
Energy exp/householder, 1-family unit	year	471	90	28r
Energy exp/householder, <1,000 sq ft heating area	year	430	90	28r
Energy exp/householder, 1,000-1,999 sq ft heating area	year	481	90	28r
Energy exp/householder, 2,000+ sq ft heating area	year	473	90	28r
Energy exp/householder, mobile home	year	430	90	28r
Energy exp/householder, multifamily	year	461	90	28r
Gas, cooking, winter, 10 therms	month	8.66	92	56c
Gas, cooking, winter, 30 therms	month	18.99	92	56c
Gas, cooking, winter, 50 therms	month	29.31	92	56c
Gas, heating, winter, 100 therms	month	55.12	92	56c
Gas, heating, winter, average use	month	80.41	92	56c
Gas, natural	mil Btu	4.56	90	64s
Gas, natural	000 cu ft	5.61	91	46s
Gas, natural, exp	year	605	91	46s
Gasoline, motor	gal	1.18	4Q 92	4c
Gasoline, unleaded regular	mil Btu	9.38	90	64s
Entertainment				
Bowling, evening rate	game	1.73	4Q 92	4c
Miniature golf admission	adult	6.18	92	1r
Miniature golf admission	child	5.14	92	1r
Monopoly game, Parker Brothers', No. 9		10.75	4Q 92	4c
Movie	admission	5.37	4Q 92	4c
Tennis balls, yellow, Wilson or Penn, 3	can	2.17	4Q 92	4c
Waterpark admission	adult	11.00	92	1r
Waterpark admission	child	8.55	92	1r
Funerals				
Casket, 18-gauge steel, velvet interior		1926.72	91	24r
Cosmetology, hair care, etc.		97.64	91	24r
Embalming		249.14	91	24r
Facility use for ceremony		208.59	91	24r
Hearse, local		130.12	91	24r
Limousine, local		104.66	91	24r
Remains to funeral home, transfer		93.61	91	24r
Service charge, professional		724.62	91	24r
Vault, concrete, non-metallic liner		734.53	91	24r
Viewing facilities, use		236.06	91	24r
Goods and Services				
ACCRA Index, Miscellaneous Goods and Services		96.70	4Q 92	4c
Groceries				
ACCRA Index, Groceries		97.90	4Q 92	4c
Apples, Red Delicious	lb	0.77	4/93	16r
Babyfood, strained vegetables, lowest price	4-4.5 oz jar	0.39	4Q 92	4c
Bacon	lb	1.85	4/93	16r
Bananas	lb	0.38	4Q 92	4c
Bananas	lb	0.46	4/93	16r
Beef, stew, boneless	lb	2.53	4/93	16r
Bologna, all beef or mixed	lb	2.19	4/93	16r
Bread, white	24 oz	0.67	4Q 92	4c
Bread, white, pan	lb	0.78	4/93	16r
Butter	lb	1.50	4/93	16r
Cabbage	lb	0.40	4/93	16r
Carrots, short trimmed and topped	lb	0.45	4/93	16r

Values are in dollars or fractions of dollars. In the column headed *Ref*, references are shown to sources. Each reference is followed by a letter. These refer to the geographical level for which data were reported: s=State, r=Region, and c=City or metro. The abbreviation *ex* is used to mean *except* or *excluding*; *exp* stands for expenditures. For other abbreviations and further explanations, please see the Introduction.

American Cost of Living Survey

Wausau, WI

Wausau, WI - continued

Item	Per	Value	Date	Ref.
Groceries				
Cheese, Cheddar	lb	3.47	4/93	16r
Cheese, Kraft grated Parmesan	8-oz canister	3.13	4Q 92	4c
Chicken, fresh, whole	lb	0.84	4/93	16r
Chicken, fryer, whole	lb	0.95	4Q 92	4c
Chicken breast, bone-in	lb	1.94	4/93	16r
Chicken legs, bone-in	lb	1.02	4/93	16r
Chuck roast, graded and ungraded, ex USDA prime and choice	lb	2.43	4/93	16r
Chuck roast, USDA choice, bone-in	lb	2.11	4/93	16r
Chuck roast, USDA choice, boneless	lb	2.44	4/93	16r
Cigarettes, Winston	carton	18.94	4Q 92	4c
Coffee, 100% ground roast, all sizes	lb	2.47	4/93	16r
Coffee, vacuum-packed	13-oz can	1.86	4Q 92	4c
Cookies, chocolate chip	lb	2.73	4/93	16r
Corn, frozen	10 oz	0.63	4Q 92	4c
Corn Flakes, Kellogg's or Post Toasties	18 oz	2.05	4Q 92	4c
Eggs, Grade A large	doz	0.74	4Q 92	4c
Eggs, Grade A large	doz	0.93	4/93	16r
Flour, white, all purpose	lb	0.21	4/93	16r
Grapefruit	lb	0.45	4/93	16r
Grapes, Thompson Seedless	lb	1.46	4/93	16r
Ground beef, 100% beef	lb	1.63	4/93	16r
Ground beef, lean and extra lean	lb	2.08	4/93	16r
Ground beef or hamburger	lb	1.59	4Q 92	4c
Ground chuck, 100% beef	lb	1.94	4/93	16r
Ham, boneless, excluding canned	lb	2.21	4/93	16r
Honey, jar	8 oz	0.97-1.25	92	5r
Honey, jar	lb	1.25-2.25	92	5r
Honey, squeeze bear	12-oz	1.25-1.99	92	5r
Ice cream, prepackaged, bulk, regular	1/2 gal	2.41	4/93	16r
Lemons	lb	0.82	4/93	16r
Lettuce, iceberg	head	0.87	4Q 92	4c
Lettuce, iceberg	lb	0.83	4/93	16r
Margarine, Blue Bonnet or Parkay cubes	lb	0.55	4Q 92	4c
Margarine, stick	lb	0.77	4/93	16r
Milk, whole	1/2 gal	1.26	4Q 92	4c
Orange juice, Minute Maid frozen	12-oz can	1.27	4Q 92	4c
Oranges, navel	lb	0.50	4/93	16r
Peaches	29-oz can	1.39	4Q 92	4c
Peanut butter, creamy, all sizes	lb	1.82	4/93	16r
Pears, Anjou	lb	0.85	4/93	16r
Peas Sweet, Del Monte or Green Giant	15-17 oz can	0.57	4Q 92	4c
Pork chops, center cut, bone-in	lb	3.17	4/93	16r
Potato chips	16 oz	2.68	4/93	16r
Potatoes, white	lb	0.26	4/93	16r
Potatoes, white or red	10-lb sack	1.35	4Q 92	4c
Round roast, graded & ungraded, ex USDA prime & choice	lb	2.88	4/93	16r
Round roast, USDA choice, boneless	lb	2.96	4/93	16r
Sausage, Jimmy Dean, 100% pork	lb	2.25	4Q 92	4c
Shortening, vegetable oil blends	lb	0.79	4/93	16r
Shortening, vegetable, Crisco	3-lb can	2.44	4Q 92	4c
Soft drink, Coca Cola	2 liter	1.29	4Q 92	4c
Spaghetti and macaroni	lb	0.76	4/93	16r
Steak, rib eye, USDA choice, boneless	lb	6.29	4/93	16r
Steak, round, USDA choice, boneless	lb	3.24	4/93	16r
Steak, sirloin, graded & ungraded, ex USDA prime & choice	lb	4.00	4/93	16r
Steak, sirloin, USDA choice, bone-in	lb	3.57	4/93	16r
Steak, sirloin, USDA choice, boneless	lb	4.17	4/93	16r
Steak, T-bone	lb	4.99	4Q 92	4c
Steak, T-bone, USDA choice, bone-in	lb	5.60	4/93	16r
Strawberries, dry pint	12 oz	0.90	4/93	16r
Sugar, cane or beet	4 lb	1.39	4Q 92	4c

Wausau, WI - continued

Item	Per	Value	Date	Ref.
Groceries - continued				
Sugar, white	lb	0.36	4/93	16r
Sugar, white, 33-80 oz pk	lb	0.35	4/93	16r
Tomatoes, field grown	lb	0.99	4/93	16r
Tomatoes, Hunt's or Del Monte	14.5-oz can	0.69	4Q 92	4c
Tuna, chunk, light	6.125-6.5 oz can	0.63	4Q 92	4c
Tuna, chunk, light	lb	1.76	4/93	16r
Turkey, frozen, whole	lb	0.91	4/93	16r
Health Care				
ACCRA Index, Health Care		106.70	4Q 92	4c
Analgesic, Aspirin, Bayer, 325 mg tablets	100	5.76	4Q 92	4c
Childbirth, cesarean, hospital		4688	91	62r
Childbirth, cesarean, physician's fee		2053	91	62r
Childbirth, normal, hospital		2657	91	62r
Childbirth, normal, physician's fee		1492	91	62r
Dentist's fee, adult teeth cleaning and periodic oral exam	visit	44.40	4Q 92	4c
Doctor's fee, routine exam, established patient	visit	49.25	4Q 92	4c
Hospital care, semiprivate room	day	272.63	90	27c
Hospital care, semiprivate room	day	233.00	4Q 92	4c
Medical insurance premium, per employee, small group comprehensive	month	270.10	10/91	25c
Medical plan per employee	year	3443	91	45r
Mental health care, exp	capita	28.84-37.59	90	38s
Mental health care, exp, state mental health agency	capita	36.62	90	38s
Mental health care, hospital psychiatric services, non-Federal, exp	capita	13.05	88	38s
Mental health care, mental health organization, multiservice, exp	capita	10.93	88	38s
Mental health care, psychiatric hospitals, private, exp	capita	8.71	88	38s
Mental health care, psychiatric out-patient clinics, freestanding, exp	capita	5.33	88	38s
Mental health care, psychiatric partial-care organizations, freestanding, exp	capita	0.20	88	38s
Mental health care, state and county mental hospitals, exp	capita	28.29	88	38s
Mental health care, VA medical centers, exp	capita	7.57	88	38s
Physician fee, family practice, first-visit		76.00	91	62r
Physician fee, family practice, revisit		33.00	91	62r
Physician fee, general practice, first-visit		61.00	91	62r
Physician fee, general practice, revisit		31.00	91	62r
Physician fee, general surgeon, first-visit		65.00	91	62r
Physician fee, general surgeon, revisit		35.00	91	62r
Physician fee, internal medicine, first-visit		91.00	91	62r
Physician fee, internal medicine, revisit		40.00	91	62r
Physician fee, median, neurosurgeon, first-visit		106.00	91	62r
Physician fee, median, nonsurgical specialist, first-visit		90.00	91	62r
Physician fee, median, orthopedic surgeon, first-visit		83.00	91	62r
Physician fee, median, surgical specialist, first-visit		61.00	91	62r
Physician fee, neurosurgeon, revisit		41.00	91	62r
Physician fee, nonsurgical specialist, revisit		40.00	91	62r
Physician fee, obstetrics/gynecology, first-visit		61.00	91	62r
Physician fee, obstetrics/gynecology, revisit		40.00	91	62r
Physician fee, orthopedic surgeon, revisit		41.00	91	62r
Physician fee, pediatrician, first-visit		46.00	91	62r
Physician fee, pediatrician, revisit		33.00	91	62r
Physician fee, surgical specialist, revisit		36.00	91	62r
Substance abuse, hospital ancillary charge	incident	960	90	70s
Substance abuse, hospital physician charge	incident	470	90	70s

Values are in dollars or fractions of dollars. In the column headed *Ref*, references are shown to sources. Each reference is followed by a letter. These refer to the geographical level for which data were reported: s = State, r = Region, and c = City or metro. The abbreviation *ex* is used to mean *except* or *excluding*; *exp* stands for expenditures. For other abbreviations and further explanations, please see the Introduction.

679

Wausau, WI - continued

Item	Per	Value	Date	Ref.
Health Care				
Substance abuse, hospital room and board	incident	3980	90	70s
Household Goods				
Appliance repair, home, service call, washing machine	min labor charge	27.22	4Q 92	4c
Laundry detergent, Tide Ultra, Bold, or Cheer	42 oz	3.37	4Q 92	4c
Tissues, facial, Kleenex brand	175-count box	0.88	4Q 92	4c
Housing				
ACCRA Index, Housing		129.00	4Q 92	4c
House, 1,800 sq ft, 8,000 sq ft lot, new, urban	total	150450	4Q 92	4c
House payment, principal and interest, 25% down payment	month	851	4Q 92	4c
Mortgage rate, incl. points & origination fee, 30-year fixed or adjustable rate	percent	8.29	4Q 92	4c
Rent, apartment, 2 bedrooms - 1-1/2 to 2 baths, unfurnished, 950 sq ft, water	month	502	4Q 92	4c
Rental unit, 1 bedroom	month	365	93	23c
Rental unit, 2 bedroom	month	432	93	23c
Rental unit, 3 bedroom	month	539	93	23c
Rental unit, 4 bedroom	month	603	93	23c
Rental unit, efficiency	month	300	93	23c
Insurance and Pensions				
Auto insurance, private passenger	year	510.11	91	63s
Personal Goods				
Shampoo, Alberto VO5	15 oz	1.27	4Q 92	4c
Toothpaste, Crest or Colgate	6-7 oz	2.42	4Q 92	4c
Personal Services				
Dry cleaning, man's 2-piece suit		6.28	4Q 92	4c
Haircare, woman's shampoo, trim and blow-dry		16.50	4Q 92	4c
Haircut, man's barbershop, no styling		6.75	4Q 92	4c
Restaurant Food				
Chicken, fried, thigh and drumstick		2.12	4Q 92	4c
Hamburger with cheese	1/4 lb	1.80	4Q 92	4c
Pizza, Pizza Hut or Pizza Inn, cheese, thin crust	12-13 in	8.43	4Q 92	4c
Taxes				
Tax, cigarette	pack	38	91	77s
Tax, gasoline	gal	22.20	91	77s
Taxes, state	capita	1416	91	77s
Transportation				
ACCRA Index, Transportation		93.10	4Q 92	4c
Bus fare, up to 10 miles	one-way	0.60	4Q 92	4c
Driver's license fee		9.00	12/90	43s
Tire balance, computer or spin balance, front	wheel	5.69	4Q 92	4c
Utilities				
ACCRA Index, Utilities		98.20	4Q 92	4c
Electricity	mil Btu	15.77	90	64s
Electricity, partial electric and other energy, 1,800 sq ft living area new home	month	43.80	4Q 92	4c

Weatherford, TX

Item	Per	Value	Date	Ref.
Composite ACCRA index		89.60	4Q 92	4c
Alcoholic Beverages				
Beer, Miller Lite or Budweiser, 12-oz containers	6 pack	4.09	4Q 92	4c
Liquor, J & B Scotch	750 ml	17.99	4Q 92	4c
Wine, Gallo Chablis blanc, 1.5 liter	bottle	5.79	4Q 92	4c

Weatherford, TX - continued

Item	Per	Value	Date	Ref.
Clothing				
Jeans, man's denim		23.77	4Q 92	4c
Shirt, man's dress shirt		22.50	4Q 92	4c
Undervest, boy's size 10-14, cotton	3	3.46	4Q 92	4c
Communications				
Newspaper subscription, daily and Sunday home delivery, large-city	month	10.95	4Q 92	4c
Telephone, flat rate	month	8.35	91	11c
Telephone bill, family of four	month	22.25	4Q 92	4c
Energy and Fuels				
Energy, combined forms, 1,800 sq ft heating area	month	110.49	4Q 92	4c
Energy, exc electricity, 1,800 sq ft heating area	month	9.15	4Q 92	4c
Gasoline, motor	gal	1.13	4Q 92	4c
Entertainment				
Bowling, evening rate	game	1.90	4Q 92	4c
Monopoly game, Parker Brothers', No. 9		10.97	4Q 92	4c
Movie	admission	4.00	4Q 92	4c
Tennis balls, yellow, Wilson or Penn, 3	can	1.97	4Q 92	4c
Goods and Services				
ACCRA Index, Miscellaneous Goods and Services		92.60	4Q 92	4c
Groceries				
ACCRA Index, Groceries		87.10	4Q 92	4c
Babyfood, strained vegetables, lowest price	4-4.5 oz jar	0.25	4Q 92	4c
Bananas	lb	0.27	4Q 92	4c
Bread, white	24 oz	0.52	4Q 92	4c
Cheese, Kraft grated Parmesan	8-oz canister	3.54	4Q 92	4c
Chicken, fryer, whole	lb	0.54	4Q 92	4c
Cigarettes, Winston	carton	18.84	4Q 92	4c
Coffee, vacuum-packed	13-oz can	1.76	4Q 92	4c
Corn, frozen	10 oz	0.61	4Q 92	4c
Corn Flakes, Kellogg's or Post Toasties	18 oz	1.89	4Q 92	4c
Eggs, Grade A large	doz	0.80	4Q 92	4c
Ground beef or hamburger	lb	0.88	4Q 92	4c
Lettuce, iceberg	head	0.78	4Q 92	4c
Margarine, Blue Bonnet or Parkay cubes	lb	0.52	4Q 92	4c
Milk, whole	1/2 gal	1.30	4Q 92	4c
Orange juice, Minute Maid frozen	12-oz can	1.28	4Q 92	4c
Peaches	29-oz can	1.42	4Q 92	4c
Peas Sweet, Del Monte or Green Giant	15-17 oz can	0.53	4Q 92	4c
Potatoes, white or red	10-lb sack	1.59	4Q 92	4c
Sausage, Jimmy Dean, 100% pork	lb	2.27	4Q 92	4c
Shortening, vegetable, Crisco	3-lb can	2.06	4Q 92	4c
Soft drink, Coca Cola	2 liter	1.04	4Q 92	4c
Steak, T-bone	lb	5.24	4Q 92	4c
Sugar, cane or beet	4 lb	1.37	4Q 92	4c
Tomatoes, Hunt's or Del Monte	14.5-oz can	0.66	4Q 92	4c
Tuna, chunk, light	6.125-6.5 oz can	0.66	4Q 92	4c
Health Care				
ACCRA Index, Health Care		90.40	4Q 92	4c
Analgesic, Aspirin, Bayer, 325 mg tablets	100	4.92	4Q 92	4c
Dentist's fee, adult teeth cleaning and periodic oral exam	visit	40.20	4Q 92	4c
Doctor's fee, routine exam, established patient	visit	34.60	4Q 92	4c

Values are in dollars or fractions of dollars. In the column headed *Ref*, references are shown to sources. Each reference is followed by a letter. These refer to the geographical level for which data were reported: s=State, r=Region, and c=City or metro. The abbreviation *ex* is used to mean *except* or *excluding*; *exp* stands for expenditures. For other abbreviations and further explanations, please see the Introduction.

Weatherford, TX - continued

Item	Per	Value	Date	Ref.
Health Care				
Hospital care, semiprivate room	day	280.00	4Q 92	4c
Household Goods				
Appliance repair, home, service call, washing machine	min labor charge	32.00	4Q 92	4c
Laundry detergent, Tide Ultra, Bold, or Cheer	42 oz	3.07	4Q 92	4c
Tissues, facial, Kleenex brand	175-count box	0.96	4Q 92	4c
Housing				
ACCRA Index, Housing		79.60	4Q 92	4c
House, 1,800 sq ft, 8,000 sq ft lot, new, urban	total	82600	4Q 92	4c
House payment, principal and interest, 25% down payment	month	461	4Q 92	4c
Mortgage rate, incl. points & origination fee, 30-year fixed or adjustable rate	per-cent	8.14	4Q 92	4c
Rent, apartment, 2 bedrooms - 1-1/2 to 2 baths, unfurnished, 950 sq ft, water	month	460	4Q 92	4c
Personal Goods				
Shampoo, Alberto VO5	15 oz	1.08	4Q 92	4c
Toothpaste, Crest or Colgate	6-7 oz	1.81	4Q 92	4c
Personal Services				
Dry cleaning, man's 2-piece suit		5.21	4Q 92	4c
Haircare, woman's shampoo, trim and blow-dry		18.40	4Q 92	4c
Haircut, man's barbershop, no styling		6.82	4Q 92	4c
Restaurant Food				
Chicken, fried, thigh and drumstick		2.30	4Q 92	4c
Hamburger with cheese	1/4 lb	1.79	4Q 92	4c
Pizza, Pizza Hut or Pizza Inn, cheese, thin crust	12-13 in	8.95	4Q 92	4c
Transportation				
ACCRA Index, Transportation		98.00	4Q 92	4c
Tire balance, computer or spin balance, front	wheel	6.25	4Q 92	4c
Utilities				
ACCRA Index, Utilities		102.50	4Q 92	4c
Electricity, partial electric and other energy, 1,800 sq ft living area new home	month	101.34	4Q 92	4c

West Palm Beach-Boca Raton-Delray Beach, FL

Item	Per	Value	Date	Ref.
Child Care				
Child care fee, average, center	hour	1.29	90	65r
Child care fee, average, nonregulated family day care	hour	0.89	90	65r
Child care fee, average, regulated family day care	hour	1.32	90	65r
Communications				
Long-distance telephone service, day, initial minute, 0-100 miles	min	0.15-0.20	91	12s
Long-distance telephone service, day, additional minute, 0-100 miles	min	0.08-0.20	91	12s
Long-distance telephone service, evenings/weekends, 0-100 mi, initial minute	min	0.09-0.12	91	12s
Long-distance telephone service, evenings/weekends, 0-100 mi, additional minute	min	0.05-0.12	91	12s
Telephone, residential, private line, rotary, unlimited calling	month	16.02	10/91	78c
Education				
Board, 4-yr private college/university	year	1924	91	22s
Board, 4-yr public college/university	year	1955	91	22s
Expenditures, local gov't, public elementary/secondary	pupil	5235	92	20s

West Palm Beach-Boca Raton-Delray Beach, FL - continued

Item	Per	Value	Date	Ref.
Education - continued				
Room, 4-year private college/university	year	1904	91	22s
Room, 4-year public college/university	year	1510	91	22s
Tuition, 2-year private college/university	year	4751	91	22s
Tuition, 2-year public college/university	year	788	91	22s
Tuition, 4-year private college/university	year	7992	91	22s
Tuition, 4-year public college/university, in-state	year	1337	91	22s
Energy and Fuels				
Coal	mil Btu	1.85	90	64s
Energy	mil Btu	10.58	90	64s
Energy exp/householder, 1-family unit	year	487	90	28r
Energy exp/householder, <1,000 sq ft heating area	year	393	90	28r
Energy exp/householder, 1,000-1,999 sq ft heating area	year	442	90	28r
Energy exp/householder, 2,000+ sq ft heating area	year	577	90	28r
Energy exp/householder, mobile home	year	366	90	28r
Energy exp/householder, multifamily	year	382	90	28r
Gas, cooking, 10 therms	month	13.80	92	56c
Gas, cooking, 30 therms	month	25.41	92	56c
Gas, cooking, 50 therms	month	37.02	92	56c
Gas, heating, winter, 100 therms	month	66.04	92	56c
Gas, heating, winter, average use	month	31.80	92	56c
Gas, natural	mil Btu	3.21	90	64s
Gas, natural	000 cu ft	8.98	91	46s
Gas, natural, exp	year	248	91	46s
Gasoline, unleaded regular	mil Btu	8.85	90	64s
Entertainment				
Miniature golf admission	adult	6.18	92	1r
Miniature golf admission	child	5.14	92	1r
Waterpark admission	adult	11.00	92	1r
Waterpark admission	child	8.55	92	1r
Funerals				
Casket, 18-gauge steel, velvet interior		2029.08	91	24r
Cosmetology, hair care, etc.		75.10	91	24r
Embalming		249.24	91	24r
Facility use for ceremony		162.27	91	24r
Hearse, local		114.04	91	24r
Limousine, local		88.57	91	24r
Remains to funeral home, transfer		92.61	91	24r
Service charge, professional		682.42	91	24r
Vault, concrete, non-metallic liner		798.70	91	24r
Viewing facilities, use		163.86	91	24r
Groceries				
Apples, Red Delicious	lb	0.79	4/93	16r
Bacon	lb	1.75	4/93	16r
Bananas	lb	0.42	4/93	16r
Beef, stew, boneless	lb	2.61	4/93	16r
Bologna, all beef or mixed	lb	2.24	4/93	16r
Bread, white, pan	lb	0.64	4/93	16r
Bread, whole wheat, pan	lb	0.96	4/93	16r
Cabbage	lb	0.37	4/93	16r
Carrots, short trimmed and topped	lb	0.47	4/93	16r
Celery	lb	0.64	4/93	16r
Cheese, American	lb	2.98	4/93	16r
Cheese, Cheddar	lb	3.28	4/93	16r
Chicken, fresh, whole	lb	0.77	4/93	16r
Chicken breast, bone-in	lb	1.92	4/93	16r
Chicken legs, bone-in	lb	1.06	4/93	16r
Chuck roast, graded and ungraded, ex USDA prime and choice	lb	2.40	4/93	16r
Chuck roast, USDA choice, bone-in	lb	2.19	4/93	16r
Chuck roast, USDA choice, boneless	lb	2.38	4/93	16r
Coffee, 100% ground roast, all sizes	lb	2.48	4/93	16r
Crackers, soda, salted	lb	1.15	4/93	16r
Eggs, Grade A large	doz	0.96	4/93	16r
Flour, white, all purpose	lb	0.24	4/93	16r
Frankfurters, all meat or all beef	lb	2.01	4/93	16r

Values are in dollars or fractions of dollars. In the column headed *Ref*, references are shown to sources. Each reference is followed by a letter. These refer to the geographical level for which data were reported: s=State, r=Region, and c=City or metro. The abbreviation *ex* is used to mean *except* or *excluding*; *exp* stands for expenditures. For other abbreviations and further explanations, please see the Introduction.

West Palm Beach-Boca Raton-Delray Beach, FL - continued

Item	Per	Value	Date	Ref.
Groceries				
Grapefruit	lb	0.44	4/93	16r
Grapes, Thompson Seedless	lb	1.40	4/93	16r
Ground beef, 100% beef	lb	1.58	4/93	16r
Ground beef, lean and extra lean	lb	2.09	4/93	16r
Ground chuck, 100% beef	lb	1.98	4/93	16r
Ham, boneless, excluding canned	lb	2.89	4/93	16r
Ham, picnic, shoulder, bone-in, smoked	lb	1.02	4/93	16r
Ham, rump or steak half, bone-in, smoked	lb	1.48	4/93	16r
Ice cream, prepackaged, bulk, regular	1/2 gal	2.41	4/93	16r
Lemons	lb	1.05	4/93	16r
Lettuce, iceberg	lb	0.81	4/93	16r
Margarine, stick	lb	0.88	4/93	16r
Oranges, navel	lb	0.55	4/93	16r
Pears, Anjou	lb	0.92	4/93	16r
Pork chops, center cut, bone-in	lb	3.13	4/93	16r
Potato chips	16 oz	2.94	4/93	16r
Potatoes, white	lb	0.43	4/93	16r
Rib roast, USDA choice, bone-in	lb	4.63	4/93	16r
Rice, white, long grain, uncooked	lb	0.45	4/93	16r
Round roast, graded & ungraded, ex USDA prime & choice	lb	3.03	4/93	16r
Round roast, USDA choice, boneless	lb	3.09	4/93	16r
Sausage, fresh, loose	lb	2.08	4/93	16r
Short ribs, bone-in	lb	2.66	4/93	16r
Shortening, vegetable oil blends	lb	0.69	4/93	16r
Spaghetti and macaroni	lb	0.81	4/93	16r
Steak, rib eye, USDA choice, boneless	lb	6.24	4/93	16r
Steak, round, graded & ungraded, ex USDA prime & choice	lb	3.31	4/93	16r
Steak, round, USDA choice, boneless	lb	3.34	4/93	16r
Steak, sirloin, graded & ungraded, ex USDA prime & choice	lb	4.19	4/93	16r
Steak, sirloin, USDA choice, boneless	lb	4.46	4/93	16r
Steak, T-bone, USDA choice, bone-in	lb	5.25	4/93	16r
Strawberries, dry pint	12 oz	0.92	4/93	16r
Sugar, white	lb	0.39	4/93	16r
Sugar, white, 33-80 oz pk	lb	0.38	4/93	16r
Tomatoes, field grown	lb	0.88	4/93	16r
Tuna, chunk, light	lb	1.79	4/93	16r
Turkey, frozen, whole	lb	1.04	4/93	16r
Yogurt, natural, fruit flavored	1/2 pint	0.57	4/93	16r
Health Care				
Childbirth, cesarean, hospital		5034	91	62r
Childbirth, cesarean, physician's fee		2053	91	62r
Childbirth, normal, hospital		2712	91	62r
Childbirth, normal, physician's fee		1492	91	62r
Medical insurance premium, per employee, small group comprehensive	month	427.05	10/91	25c
Medical plan per employee	year	3495	91	45r
Mental health care, exp	capita	28.84-37.59	90	38s
Mental health care, exp, state mental health agency	capita	37.49	90	38s
Mental health care, hospital psychiatric services, non-Federal, exp	capita	9.11	88	38s
Mental health care, mental health organization, multiservice, exp	capita	16.21	88	38s
Mental health care, psychiatric hospitals, private, exp	capita	22.26	88	38s
Mental health care, psychiatric out-patient clinics, freestanding, exp	capita	0.89	88	38s
Mental health care, psychiatric partial-care organizations, freestanding, exp	capita	0.41	88	38s
Mental health care, state and county mental hospitals, exp	capita	16.25	88	38s
Mental health care, VA medical centers, exp	capita	1.69	88	38s
Physician fee, family practice, first-visit		75.00	91	62r
Physician fee, family practice, revisit		34.00	91	62r
Physician fee, general practice, first-visit		61.00	91	62r
Physician fee, general practice, revisit		32.00	91	62r
Physician fee, general surgeon, first-visit		64.00	91	62r

West Palm Beach-Boca Raton-Delray Beach, FL - continued

Item	Per	Value	Date	Ref.
Health Care - continued				
Physician fee, general surgeon, revisit		40.00	91	62r
Physician fee, internal medicine, first-visit		98.00	91	62r
Physician fee, internal medicine, revisit		40.00	91	62r
Physician fee, median, neurosurgeon, first-visit		130.00	91	62r
Physician fee, median, nonsurgical specialist, first-visit		95.00	91	62r
Physician fee, median, orthopedic surgeon, first-visit		91.00	91	62r
Physician fee, median, plastic surgeon, first-visit		66.00	91	62r
Physician fee, median, surgical specialist, first-visit		62.00	91	62r
Physician fee, neurosurgeon, revisit		50.00	91	62r
Physician fee, nonsurgical specialist, revisit		40.00	91	62r
Physician fee, obstetrics/gynecology, first-visit		64.00	91	62r
Physician fee, obstetrics/gynecology, revisit		41.00	91	62r
Physician fee, orthopedic surgeon, revisit		40.00	91	62r
Physician fee, pediatrician, first-visit		49.00	91	62r
Physician fee, pediatrician, revisit		33.00	91	62r
Physician fee, plastic surgeon, revisit		43.00	91	62r
Physician fee, surgical specialist, revisit		37.00	91	62r
Substance abuse, hospital ancillary charge	incident	1390	90	70s
Substance abuse, hospital physician charge	incident	770	90	70s
Substance abuse, hospital room and board	incident	5600	90	70s
Housing				
Home, median price	unit	114.10		26c
Rental unit, 1 bedroom	month	477	93	23c
Rental unit, 2 bedroom	month	556	93	23c
Rental unit, 3 bedroom	month	680	93	23c
Rental unit, 4 bedroom	month	749	93	23c
Rental unit, efficiency	month	400	93	23c
Insurance and Pensions				
Auto insurance, private passenger	year	727.60	91	63s
Taxes				
Tax, cigarette	pack	33.90	91	77s
Tax, gasoline	gal	11.60	91	77s
Taxes, state	capita	1037	91	77s
Transportation				
Auto rental, average	day	31.68	6/91	60c
Bus fare	one-way	0.90	3/93	2c
Driver's license fee		15.00	12/90	43s
Taxi fare, airport-city, average	day	7.50	6/91	60c
Travel				
Breakfast	day	5.42	6/91	60c
Business travel	day	193.00	4/93	89r
Dinner	day	20.42	6/91	60c
Lodging	day	132.29	91	60c
Lunch	day	8.78	6/91	60c
Utilities				
Electricity	mil Btu	20.62	90	64s

Westborough, MA

Item	Per	Value	Date	Ref.
Groceries				
Bananas	lb	0.48	4/92	75c
Barbecue sauce, Hunt's	oz	0.06	4/92	75c
Beef, ground chuck steak, 80% lean	lb	1.82	4/92	75c
Bologna, Oscar Mayer	oz	0.20	4/92	75c
Bread, white	oz	0.07	4/92	75c
Butter	lb	1.41	4/92	75c
Candy, M&Ms	lb	2.54	4/92	75c
Cat food, Meow Mix	lb	0.84	4/92	75c

Values are in dollars or fractions of dollars. In the column headed *Ref*, references are shown to sources. Each reference is followed by a letter. These refer to the geographical level for which data were reported: s = State, r = Region, and c = City or metro. The abbreviation *ex* is used to mean *except* or *excluding*; *exp* stands for expenditures. For other abbreviations and further explanations, please see the introduction.

Westborough, MA - continued

Item	Per	Value	Date	Ref.
Groceries				
Cereal, Cheerios	oz	0.19	4/92	75c
Cereal, Kellogg's Corn Flakes	oz	0.10	4/92	75c
Cereal, Quaker Oats Instant 10-pk	pk	0.25	4/92	75c
Cheese, Kraft American singles	slice	0.13	4/92	75c
Chicken, Perdue	lb	0.93	4/92	75c
Cigarettes, Marlboro	carton	17.06	4/92	75c
Coffee, Maxwell House	13 oz	2.28	4/92	75c
Cookies, Nabisco Oreos	20 oz	1.97	4/92	75c
Crackers, Premium saltines	16 oz	1.79	4/92	75c
Dog food, Purina Dog Chow	lb	0.37	4/92	75c
Eggs	1	0.07	4/92	75c
Frankfurters, Kahn's	lb	2.35	4/92	75c
Frozen dinner, Healthy Choice chicken Parmesan		2.48	4/92	75c
Jelly, Welch's grape	32 oz	1.50	4/92	75c
Ketchup, Heinz	oz	0.05	4/92	75c
Lettuce, iceberg	head	0.79	4/92	75c
Margarine, Blue Bonnet	lb	0.66	4/92	75c
Mayonnaise, Hellmann's	oz	0.07	4/92	75c
Milk, whole	gal	2.20	4/92	75c
Muffins, Thomas English	6	2.19	4/92	75c
Orange juice, Minute Maid frozen	oz	0.14	4/92	75c
Orange juice, Tropicana	oz	0.04	4/92	75c
Oranges	lb	0.58	4/92	75c
Peanut butter, Skippy, creamy	oz	0.11	4/92	75c
Peas, Green Giant, canned	15 oz	0.57	4/92	75c
Pizza, Ellio's frozen cheese	9 slices	2.65	4/92	75c
Potatoes	lb	0.29	4/92	75c
Snacks, Doritos corn chips	oz	0.17	4/92	75c
Snacks, potato chips	oz	0.17	4/92	75c
Soft drink, Diet Coca Cola	2 liter	1.02	4/92	75c
Soft drink, Pepsi	2 liter	1.39	4/92	75c
Spaghetti	lb	0.52	4/92	75c
Spaghetti sauce, Ragu	oz	0.05	4/92	75c
Sugar	5 lb	2.07	4/92	75c
Tea, Lipton tea bags	bag	0.02	4/92	75c
Tomato soup, Campbell's	10 3/4 oz	0.60	4/92	75c
Tuna, Bumble Bee	6 1/8 oz	1.41	4/92	75c
Yogurt, Columbo	32 oz	1.74	4/92	75c
Health Care				
Analgesic, Advil	100	7.48	4/92	75c
Household Goods				
Laundry detergent, Tide Ultra	oz	0.08	4/92	75c
Aluminum foil, Reynolds	50 ft	1.29	4/92	75c
Cat litter, Tidy Cat 3	lb	0.14	4/92	75c
Dishwashing detergent, Cascade	oz	0.06	4/92	75c
Laundry detergent, Tide liquid	1/2 gal	3.90	4/92	75c
Laundry supplies, Bounce fabric softener	sheet	0.06	4/92	75c
Paper towels, Bounty	roll	0.92	4/92	75c
Plastic wrap, Glad Cling	100 ft	0.97	4/92	75c
Toilet tissue, Charmin	4 rolls	1.09	4/92	75c
Personal Goods				
Deodorant, Ban	oz	1.51	4/92	75c
Feminine hygiene product, Kotex	24	1.06	4/92	75c
Mouthwash, Listerine	oz	0.13	4/92	75c
Mouthwash, Scope	oz	0.14	4/92	75c
Razor blades, Gillette Trac II	blade	0.63	4/92	75c
Razors, Gillette Good News Disposables	razor	0.34	4/92	75c
Shampoo, Pert Plus	oz	0.22	4/92	75c
Toothpaste, Crest	oz	0.33	4/92	75c

Wheeling, WV, OH

Item	Per	Value	Date	Ref.
Child Care				
Child care fee, average, center	hour	1.29	90	65r
Child care fee, average, nonregulated family day care	hour	0.89	90	65r

Wheeling, WV, OH - continued

Item	Per	Value	Date	Ref.
Child Care - continued				
Child care fee, average, regulated family day care	hour	1.32	90	65r
Communications				
Long-distance telephone service, day, initial minute, 0-100 miles	min	0.26-0.70	91	12s
Long-distance telephone service, day, additional minute, 0-100 miles	min	0.13-0.45	91	12s
Long-distance telephone service, evenings/weekends, 0-100 mi, initial minute	min	0.10-0.28	91	12s
Long-distance telephone service, evenings/weekends, 0-100 mi, additional minute	min	0.05-0.18	91	12s
Education				
Board, 4-yr private college/university	year	1664	91	22s
Board, 4-yr public college/university	year	1723	91	22s
Expenditures, local gov't, public elementary/secondary	pupil	5401	92	20s
Room, 4-year private college/university	year	1401	91	22s
Room, 4-year public college/university	year	1556	91	22s
Tuition, 2-year private college/university	year	2767	91	22s
Tuition, 2-year public college/university	year	930	91	22s
Tuition, 4-year private college/university	year	8751	91	22s
Tuition, 4-year public college/university, in-state	year	1543	91	22s
Energy and Fuels				
Coal	mil Btu	1.47	90	64s
Energy	mil Btu	6.77	90	64s
Energy exp/householder, 1-family unit	year	487	90	28r
Energy exp/householder, <1,000 sq ft heating area	year	393	90	28r
Energy exp/householder, 1,000-1,999 sq ft heating area	year	442	90	28r
Energy exp/householder, 2,000+ sq ft heating area	year	577	90	28r
Energy exp/householder, mobile home	year	366	90	28r
Energy exp/householder, multifamily	year	382	90	28r
Gas, natural	mil Btu	4.40	90	64s
Gas, natural	000 cu ft	6.50	91	46s
Gas, natural, exp	year	605	91	46s
Gasoline, unleaded regular	mil Btu	9.96	90	64s
Entertainment				
Miniature golf admission	adult	6.18	92	1r
Miniature golf admission	child	5.14	92	1r
Waterpark admission	adult	11.00	92	1r
Waterpark admission	child	8.55	92	1r
Funerals				
Casket, 18-gauge steel, velvet interior		2029.08	91	24r
Cosmetology, hair care, etc.		75.10	91	24r
Embalming		249.24	91	24r
Facility use for ceremony		162.27	91	24r
Hearse, local		114.04	91	24r
Limousine, local		88.57	91	24r
Remains to funeral home, transfer		92.61	91	24r
Service charge, professional		682.42	91	24r
Vault, concrete, non-metallic liner		798.70	91	24r
Viewing facilities, use		163.86	91	24r
Groceries				
Apples, Red Delicious	lb	0.79	4/93	16r
Bacon	lb	1.75	4/93	16r
Bananas	lb	0.42	4/93	16r
Beef, stew, boneless	lb	2.61	4/93	16r
Bologna, all beef or mixed	lb	2.24	4/93	16r
Bread, white, pan	lb	0.64	4/93	16r
Bread, whole wheat, pan	lb	0.96	4/93	16r
Cabbage	lb	0.37	4/93	16r
Carrots, short trimmed and topped	lb	0.47	4/93	16r
Celery	lb	0.64	4/93	16r
Cheese, American	lb	2.98	4/93	16r
Cheese, Cheddar	lb	3.28	4/93	16r

Values are in dollars or fractions of dollars. In the column headed *Ref*, references are shown to sources. Each reference is followed by a letter. These refer to the geographical level for which data were reported: s = State, r = Region, and c = City or metro. The abbreviation *ex* is used to mean *except* or *excluding*; *exp* stands for expenditures. For other abbreviations and further explanations, please see the Introduction.

Wheeling, WV, OH - continued

Item	Per	Value	Date	Ref.
Groceries				
Chicken, fresh, whole	lb	0.77	4/93	16r
Chicken breast, bone-in	lb	1.92	4/93	16r
Chicken legs, bone-in	lb	1.06	4/93	16r
Chuck roast, graded and ungraded, ex USDA prime and choice	lb	2.40	4/93	16r
Chuck roast, USDA choice, bone-in	lb	2.19	4/93	16r
Chuck roast, USDA choice, boneless	lb	2.38	4/93	16r
Coffee, 100% ground roast, all sizes	lb	2.48	4/93	16r
Crackers, soda, salted	lb	1.15	4/93	16r
Eggs, Grade A large	doz	0.96	4/93	16r
Flour, white, all purpose	lb	0.24	4/93	16r
Frankfurters, all meat or all beef	lb	2.01	4/93	16r
Grapefruit	lb	0.44	4/93	16r
Grapes, Thompson Seedless	lb	1.40	4/93	16r
Ground beef, 100% beef	lb	1.58	4/93	16r
Ground beef, lean and extra lean	lb	2.09	4/93	16r
Ground chuck, 100% beef	lb	1.98	4/93	16r
Ham, boneless, excluding canned	lb	2.89	4/93	16r
Ham, picnic, shoulder, bone-in, smoked	lb	1.02	4/93	16r
Ham, rump or steak half, bone-in, smoked	lb	1.48	4/93	16r
Ice cream, prepackaged, bulk, regular	1/2 gal	2.41	4/93	16r
Lemons	lb	1.05	4/93	16r
Lettuce, iceberg	lb	0.81	4/93	16r
Margarine, stick	lb	0.88	4/93	16r
Oranges, navel	lb	0.55	4/93	16r
Pears, Anjou	lb	0.92	4/93	16r
Pork chops, center cut, bone-in	lb	3.13	4/93	16r
Potato chips	16 oz	2.94	4/93	16r
Potatoes, white	lb	0.43	4/93	16r
Rib roast, USDA choice, bone-in	lb	4.63	4/93	16r
Rice, white, long grain, uncooked	lb	0.45	4/93	16r
Round roast, graded & ungraded, ex USDA prime & choice	lb	3.03	4/93	16r
Round roast, USDA choice, boneless	lb	3.09	4/93	16r
Sausage, fresh, loose	lb	2.08	4/93	16r
Short ribs, bone-in	lb	2.66	4/93	16r
Shortening, vegetable oil blends	lb	0.69	4/93	16r
Spaghetti and macaroni	lb	0.81	4/93	16r
Steak, rib eye, USDA choice, boneless	lb	6.24	4/93	16r
Steak, round, graded & ungraded, ex USDA prime & choice	lb	3.31	4/93	16r
Steak, round, USDA choice, boneless	lb	3.34	4/93	16r
Steak, sirloin, graded & ungraded, ex USDA prime & choice	lb	4.19	4/93	16r
Steak, sirloin, USDA choice, boneless	lb	4.46	4/93	16r
Steak, T-bone, USDA choice, bone-in	lb	5.25	4/93	16r
Strawberries, dry pint	12 oz	0.92	4/93	16r
Sugar, white	lb	0.39	4/93	16r
Sugar, white, 33-80 oz pk	lb	0.38	4/93	16r
Tomatoes, field grown	lb	0.88	4/93	16r
Tuna, chunk, light	lb	1.79	4/93	16r
Turkey, frozen, whole	lb	1.04	4/93	16r
Yogurt, natural, fruit flavored	1/2 pint	0.57	4/93	16r
Health Care				
Childbirth, cesarean, hospital		5034	91	62r
Childbirth, cesarean, physician's fee		2053	91	62r
Childbirth, normal, hospital		2712	91	62r
Childbirth, normal, physician's fee		1492	91	62r
Medical plan per employee	year	3495	91	45r
Mental health care, exp	capita	20.37-28.83	90	38s
Mental health care, exp, state mental health agency	capita	23.72	90	38s
Mental health care, hospital psychiatric services, non-Federal, exp	capita	9.26	88	38s
Mental health care, mental health organization, multiservice, exp	capita	26.55	88	38s
Mental health care, psychiatric hospitals, private, exp	capita	5.67	88	38s
Mental health care, psychiatric out-patient clinics, freestanding, exp	capita	1.30	88	38s

Wheeling, WV, OH - continued

Item	Per	Value	Date	Ref.
Health Care - continued				
Mental health care, state and county mental hospitals, exp	capita	11.86	88	38s
Mental health care, VA medical centers, exp	capita	0.70	88	38s
Physician fee, family practice, first-visit		75.00	91	62r
Physician fee, family practice, revisit		34.00	91	62r
Physician fee, general practice, first-visit		61.00	91	62r
Physician fee, general practice, revisit		32.00	91	62r
Physician fee, general surgeon, first-visit		64.00	91	62r
Physician fee, general surgeon, revisit		40.00	91	62r
Physician fee, internal medicine, first-visit		98.00	91	62r
Physician fee, internal medicine, revisit		40.00	91	62r
Physician fee, median, neurosurgeon, first-visit		130.00	91	62r
Physician fee, median, nonsurgical specialist, first-visit		95.00	91	62r
Physician fee, median, orthopedic surgeon, first-visit		91.00	91	62r
Physician fee, median, plastic surgeon, first-visit		66.00	91	62r
Physician fee, median, surgical specialist, first-visit		62.00	91	62r
Physician fee, neurosurgeon, revisit		50.00	91	62r
Physician fee, nonsurgical specialist, revisit		40.00	91	62r
Physician fee, obstetrics/gynecology, first-visit		64.00	91	62r
Physician fee, obstetrics/gynecology, revisit		41.00	91	62r
Physician fee, orthopedic surgeon, revisit		40.00	91	62r
Physician fee, pediatrician, first-visit		49.00	91	62r
Physician fee, pediatrician, revisit		33.00	91	62r
Physician fee, plastic surgeon, revisit		43.00	91	62r
Physician fee, surgical specialist, revisit		37.00	91	62r
Substance abuse, hospital ancillary charge	incident	1900	90	70s
Substance abuse, hospital physician charge	incident	1270	90	70s
Substance abuse, hospital room and board	incident	4590	90	70s
Insurance and Pensions				
Auto insurance, private passenger	year	621.65	91	63s
Taxes				
Tax, cigarette	pack	17	91	77s
Tax, gasoline	gal	15.50	91	77s
Taxes, state	capita	1293	91	77s
Transportation				
Driver's license fee		10.00	12/90	43s
Vehicle registration and license plate	year	26.50-37.50	93	69s
Travel				
Business travel	day	193.00	4/93	89r
Utilities				
Electricity	mil Btu	13.90	90	64s
Electricity, winter, 250 KWh	month	21.89	92	55s
Electricity, winter, 500 KWh	month	38.44	92	55s
Electricity, winter, 750 KWh	month	53.70	92	55s
Electricity, winter, 1000 KWh	month	68.96	92	55s

Wichita, KS

Item	Per	Value	Date	Ref.
Composite ACCRA index		96.40	4Q 92	4c
Alcoholic Beverages				
Beer, Miller Lite or Budweiser, 12-oz containers	6 pack	3.88	4Q 92	4c
Liquor, J & B Scotch	750 ml	16.75	4Q 92	4c
Wine, Gallo Chablis blanc, 1.5 liter	bottle	4.71	4Q 92	4c
Child Care				
Child care fee, average, center	hour	1.63	90	65r
Child care fee, average, nonregulated family day care	hour	1.83	90	65r

Values are in dollars or fractions of dollars. In the column headed *Ref*, references are shown to sources. Each reference is followed by a letter. These refer to the geographical level for which data were reported: s=State, r=Region, and c=City or metro. The abbreviation *ex* is used to mean *except* or *excluding*; *exp* stands for *expenditures*. For other abbreviations and further explanations, please see the Introduction.

Wichita, KS - continued

Item	Per	Value	Date	Ref.
Child Care				
Child care fee, average, regulated family day care	hour	1.42	90	65r
Clothing				
Jeans, man's denim		25.71	4Q 92	4c
Shirt, man's dress shirt		26.07	4Q 92	4c
Undervest, boy's size 10-14, cotton	3	3.31	4Q 92	4c
Communications				
Long-distance telephone service, day, initial minute, 0-100 miles	min	0.18-0.40	91	12s
Long-distance telephone service, day, additional minute, 0-100 miles	min	0.09-0.30	91	12s
Newspaper subscription, daily and Sunday home delivery, large-city	month	13.70	4Q 92	4c
Telephone, flat rate	month	11.35	91	11c
Telephone bill, family of four	month	17.66	4Q 92	4c
Education				
Board, 4-yr private college/university	year	1719	91	22s
Board, 4-yr public college/university	year	1294	91	22s
Expenditures, local gov't, public elementary/secondary	pupil	5105	92	20s
Room, 4-year private college/university	year	1269	91	22s
Room, 4-year public college/university	year	1301	91	22s
Tuition, 2-year private college/university	year	4135	91	22s
Tuition, 2-year public college/university	year	748	91	22s
Tuition, 4-year private college/university	year	5997	91	22s
Tuition, 4-year public college/university, in-state	year	1569	91	22s
Energy and Fuels				
Coal	mil Btu	1.24	90	64s
Energy	mil Btu	7.59	90	64s
Energy, combined forms, 1,800 sq ft heating area	month	101.94	4Q 92	4c
Energy, exc electricity, 1,800 sq ft heating area	month	30.33	4Q 92	4c
Energy exp/householder, 1-family unit	year	473	90	28r
Energy exp/householder, <1,000 sq ft heating area	year	429	90	28r
Energy exp/householder, 1,000-1,999 sq ft heating area	year	442	90	28r
Energy exp/householder, 2,000+ sq ft heating area	year	498	90	28r
Energy exp/householder, mobile home	year	442	90	28r
Energy exp/householder, multifamily	year	407	90	28r
Gas, cooking, 10 therms	month	9.27	92	56c
Gas, cooking, 30 therms	month	17.81	92	56c
Gas, cooking, 50 therms	month	26.35	92	56c
Gas, heating, winter, 100 therms	month	46.80	92	56c
Gas, heating, winter, average use	month	87.60	92	56c
Gas, natural	mil Btu	3.30	90	64s
Gas, natural	000 cu ft	4.38	91	46s
Gas, natural, exp	year	435	91	46s
Gasoline, motor	gal	1.08	4Q 92	4c
Gasoline, unleaded regular	mil Btu	8.90	90	64s
Entertainment				
Bowling, evening rate	game	2.30	4Q 92	4c
Miniature golf admission	adult	6.18	92	1r
Miniature golf admission	child	5.14	92	1r
Monopoly game, Parker Brothers', No. 9		9.98	4Q 92	4c
Movie	admission	5.75	4Q 92	4c
Tennis balls, yellow, Wilson or Penn, 3	can	2.24	4Q 92	4c
Waterpark admission	adult	11.00	92	1r
Waterpark admission	child	8.55	92	1r
Funerals				
Casket, 18-gauge steel, velvet interior		1952.97	91	24r
Cosmetology, hair care, etc.		90.03	91	24r
Embalming		251.75	91	24r
Facility use for ceremony		180.75	91	24r

Wichita, KS - continued

Item	Per	Value	Date	Ref.
Funerals - continued				
Hearse, local		117.51	91	24r
Limousine, local		71.86	91	24r
Remains to funeral home, transfer		81.14	91	24r
Service charge, professional		740.03	91	24r
Vault, concrete, non-metallic liner		801.47	91	24r
Viewing facilities, use		169.33	91	24r
Goods and Services				
ACCRA Index, Miscellaneous Goods and Services		98.10	4Q 92	4c
Groceries				
ACCRA Index, Groceries		89.20	4Q 92	4c
Apples, Red Delicious	lb	0.77	4/93	16r
Babyfood, strained vegetables, lowest price	4-4.5 oz jar	0.24	4Q 92	4c
Bacon	lb	1.85	4/93	16r
Bananas	lb	0.44	4Q 92	4c
Bananas	lb	0.46	4/93	16r
Beef, stew, boneless	lb	2.53	4/93	16r
Bologna, all beef or mixed	lb	2.19	4/93	16r
Bread, white	24 oz	0.47	4Q 92	4c
Bread, white, pan	lb	0.78	4/93	16r
Butter	lb	1.50	4/93	16r
Cabbage	lb	0.40	4/93	16r
Carrots, short trimmed and topped	lb	0.45	4/93	16r
Cheese, Cheddar	lb	3.47	4/93	16r
Cheese, Kraft grated Parmesan	8-oz canister	3.49	4Q 92	4c
Chicken, fresh, whole	lb	0.84	4/93	16r
Chicken, fryer, whole	lb	0.67	4Q 92	4c
Chicken breast, bone-in	lb	1.94	4/93	16r
Chicken legs, bone-in	lb	1.02	4/93	16r
Chuck roast, graded and ungraded, ex USDA prime and choice	lb	2.43	4/93	16r
Chuck roast, USDA choice, bone-in	lb	2.11	4/93	16r
Chuck roast, USDA choice, boneless	lb	2.44	4/93	16r
Cigarettes, Winston	carton	17.37	4Q 92	4c
Coffee, 100% ground roast, all sizes	lb	2.47	4/93	16r
Coffee, vacuum-packed	13-oz can	1.62	4Q 92	4c
Cookies, chocolate chip	lb	2.73	4/93	16r
Corn, frozen	10 oz	0.63	4Q 92	4c
Corn Flakes, Kellogg's or Post Toasties	18 oz	2.02	4Q 92	4c
Eggs, Grade A large	doz	0.75	4Q 92	4c
Eggs, Grade A large	doz	0.93	4/93	16r
Flour, white, all purpose	lb	0.21	4/93	16r
Grapefruit	lb	0.45	4/93	16r
Grapes, Thompson Seedless	lb	1.46	4/93	16r
Ground beef, 100% beef	lb	1.63	4/93	16r
Ground beef, lean and extra lean	lb	2.08	4/93	16r
Ground beef or hamburger	lb	1.27	4Q 92	4c
Ground chuck, 100% beef	lb	1.94	4/93	16r
Ham, boneless, excluding canned	lb	2.21	4/93	16r
Ice cream, prepackaged, bulk, regular	1/2 gal	2.41	4/93	16r
Lemons	lb	0.82	4/93	16r
Lettuce, iceberg	head	0.94	4Q 92	4c
Lettuce, iceberg	lb	0.83	4/93	16r
Margarine, Blue Bonnet or Parkay cubes	lb	0.64	4Q 92	4c
Margarine, stick	lb	0.77	4/93	16r
Milk, whole	1/2 gal	1.16	4Q 92	4c
Orange juice, Minute Maid frozen	12-oz can	1.42	4Q 92	4c
Oranges, navel	lb	0.50	4/93	16r
Peaches	29-oz can	1.27	4Q 92	4c
Peanut butter, creamy, all sizes	lb	1.82	4/93	16r
Pears, Anjou	lb	0.85	4/93	16r
Peas Sweet, Del Monte or Green Giant	15-17 oz can	0.57	4Q 92	4c
Pork chops, center cut, bone-in	lb	3.17	4/93	16r
Potato chips	16 oz	2.68	4/93	16r

Values are in dollars or fractions of dollars. In the column headed *Ref*, references are shown to sources. Each reference is followed by a letter. These refer to the geographical level for which data were reported: s=State, r=Region, and c=City or metro. The abbreviation *ex* is used to mean *except* or *excluding*; *exp* stands for expenditures. For other abbreviations and further explanations, please see the Introduction.

Wichita, KS - continued

Item	Per	Value	Date	Ref.
Groceries				
Potatoes, white	lb	0.26	4/93	16r
Potatoes, white or red	10-lb sack	2.53	4Q 92	4c
Round roast, graded & ungraded, ex USDA prime & choice	lb	2.88	4/93	16r
Round roast, USDA choice, boneless	lb	2.96	4/93	16r
Sausage, Jimmy Dean, 100% pork	lb	2.27	4Q 92	4c
Shortening, vegetable oil blends	lb	0.79	4/93	16r
Shortening, vegetable, Crisco	3-lb can	2.01	4Q 92	4c
Soft drink, Coca Cola	2 liter	1.04	4Q 92	4c
Spaghetti and macaroni	lb	0.76	4/93	16r
Steak, rib eye, USDA choice, boneless	lb	6.29	4/93	16r
Steak, round, USDA choice, boneless	lb	3.24	4/93	16r
Steak, sirloin, graded & ungraded, ex USDA prime & choice	lb	4.00	4/93	16r
Steak, sirloin, USDA choice, bone-in	lb	3.57	4/93	16r
Steak, sirloin, USDA choice, boneless	lb	4.17	4/93	16r
Steak, T-bone	lb	4.81	4Q 92	4c
Steak, T-bone, USDA choice, bone-in	lb	5.60	4/93	16r
Strawberries, dry pint	12 oz	0.90	4/93	16r
Sugar, cane or beet	4 lb	1.29	4Q 92	4c
Sugar, white	lb	0.36	4/93	16r
Sugar, white, 33-80 oz pk	lb	0.35	4/93	16r
Tomatoes, field grown	lb	0.99	4/93	16r
Tomatoes, Hunt's or Del Monte	14.5-oz can	0.64	4Q 92	4c
Tuna, chunk, light	6.125-6.5 oz can	0.50	4Q 92	4c
Tuna, chunk, light	lb	1.76	4/93	16r
Turkey, frozen, whole	lb	0.91	4/93	16r
Health Care				
ACCRA Index, Health Care		103.00	4Q 92	4c
Analgesic, Aspirin, Bayer, 325 mg tablets	100	4.26	4Q 92	4c
Childbirth, cesarean, hospital		4688	91	62r
Childbirth, cesarean, physician's fee		2053	91	62r
Childbirth, normal, hospital		2657	91	62r
Childbirth, normal, physician's fee		1492	91	62r
Dentist's fee, adult teeth cleaning and periodic oral exam	visit	50.10	4Q 92	4c
Doctor's fee, routine exam, established patient	visit	35.70	4Q 92	4c
Hospital care, semiprivate room	day	273.97	90	27c
Hospital care, semiprivate room	day	375.50	4Q 92	4c
Medical insurance premium, per employee, small group comprehensive	month	335.80	10/91	25c
Medical plan per employee	year	3443	91	45r
Mental health care, exp	capita	28.84-37.59	90	38s
Mental health care, exp, state mental health agency	capita	35.41	90	38s
Mental health care, hospital psychiatric services, non-Federal, exp	capita	11.07	88	38s
Mental health care, mental health organization, multiservice, exp	capita	12.68	88	38s
Mental health care, psychiatric hospitals, private, exp	capita	21.42	88	38s
Mental health care, psychiatric out-patient clinics, freestanding, exp	capita	3.45	88	38s
Mental health care, state and county mental hospitals, exp	capita	26.34	88	38s
Mental health care, VA medical centers, exp	capita	22.97	88	38s
Physician fee, family practice, first-visit		76.00	91	62r
Physician fee, family practice, revisit		33.00	91	62r
Physician fee, general practice, first-visit		61.00	91	62r
Physician fee, general practice, revisit		31.00	91	62r
Physician fee, general surgeon, first-visit		65.00	91	62r
Physician fee, general surgeon, revisit		35.00	91	62r
Physician fee, internal medicine, first-visit		91.00	91	62r
Physician fee, internal medicine, revisit		40.00	91	62r

Wichita, KS - continued

Item	Per	Value	Date	Ref.
Health Care - continued				
Physician fee, median, neurosurgeon, first-visit		106.00	91	62r
Physician fee, median, nonsurgical specialist, first-visit		90.00	91	62r
Physician fee, median, orthopedic surgeon, first-visit		83.00	91	62r
Physician fee, median, surgical specialist, first-visit		61.00	91	62r
Physician fee, neurosurgeon, revisit		41.00	91	62r
Physician fee, nonsurgical specialist, revisit		40.00	91	62r
Physician fee, obstetrics/gynecology, first-visit		61.00	91	62r
Physician fee, obstetrics/gynecology, revisit		40.00	91	62r
Physician fee, orthopedic surgeon, revisit		41.00	91	62r
Physician fee, pediatrician, first-visit		46.00	91	62r
Physician fee, pediatrician, revisit		33.00	91	62r
Physician fee, surgical specialist, revisit		36.00	91	62r
Substance abuse, hospital ancillary charge	incident	1170	90	70s
Substance abuse, hospital physician charge	incident	560	90	70s
Substance abuse, hospital room and board	incident	5920	90	70s
Household Goods				
Appliance repair, home, service call, washing machine	min labor charge	33.11	4Q 92	4c
Laundry detergent, Tide Ultra, Bold, or Cheer	42 oz	2.96	4Q 92	4c
Tissues, facial, Kleenex brand	175-count box	1.06	4Q 92	4c
Housing				
ACCRA Index, Housing		96.00	4Q 92	4c
Home, median price	unit	68.80		26c
House, 1,800 sq ft, 8,000 sq ft lot, new, urban	total	109421	4Q 92	4c
House payment, principal and interest, 25% down payment	month	605	4Q 92	4c
Mortgage rate, incl. points & origination fee, 30-year fixed or adjustable rate	percent	8.05	4Q 92	4c
Rent, apartment, 2 bedrooms - 1-1/2 to 2 baths, unfurnished, 950 sq ft, water	month	440	4Q 92	4c
Rental unit, 1 bedroom	month	423	93	23c
Rental unit, 2 bedroom	month	503	93	23c
Rental unit, 3 bedroom	month	627	93	23c
Rental unit, 4 bedroom	month	698	93	23c
Rental unit, efficiency	month	348	93	23c
Insurance and Pensions				
Auto insurance, private passenger	year	459.62	91	63s
Personal Goods				
Shampoo, Alberto VO5	15 oz	1.18	4Q 92	4c
Toothpaste, Crest or Colgate	6-7 oz	1.82	4Q 92	4c
Personal Services				
Dry cleaning, man's 2-piece suit		5.89	4Q 92	4c
Haircare, woman's shampoo, trim and blow-dry		18.19	4Q 92	4c
Haircut, man's barbershop, no styling		9.09	4Q 92	4c
Restaurant Food				
Chicken, fried, thigh and drumstick		2.12	4Q 92	4c
Hamburger with cheese	1/4 lb	1.83	4Q 92	4c
Pizza, Pizza Hut or Pizza Inn, cheese, thin crust	12-13 in	7.59	4Q 92	4c
Taxes				
Tax, cigarette	pack	24	91	77s
Tax, gasoline	gal	18	91	77s
Taxes, state	capita	1121	91	77s

Values are in dollars or fractions of dollars. In the column headed *Ref*, references are shown to sources. Each reference is followed by a letter. These refer to the geographical level for which data were reported: s=State, r=Region, and c=City or metro. The abbreviation *ex* is used to mean *except* or *excluding*; *exp* stands for expenditures. For other abbreviations and further explanations, please see the Introduction.

Wichita, KS - continued

Item	Per	Value	Date	Ref.
Transportation				
ACCRA Index, Transportation		100.60	4Q 92	4c
Auto rental, average	day	39.50	6/91	60c
Bus fare, up to 10 miles	one-way	0.85	4Q 92	4c
Driver's license fee		8.00-12.00	12/90	43s
Taxi fare, airport-city, average	day	7.50	6/91	60c
Tire balance, computer or spin balance, front	wheel	6.90	4Q 92	4c
Vehicle registration and license plate	year	27.25-37.25	93	32s
Travel				
Breakfast	day	6.17	6/91	60c
Dinner	day	11.30	6/91	60c
Lodging	day	83.00	91	60c
Lunch	day	6.50	6/91	60c
Utilities				
ACCRA Index, Utilities		93.10	4Q 92	4c
Electricity	mil Btu	19.31	90	64s
Electricity, partial electric and other energy, 1,800 sq ft living area new home	month	71.61	4Q 92	4c
Electricity, winter, 250 KWh	month	31.79	92	55c
Electricity, winter, 500 KWh	month	54.97	92	55c
Electricity, winter, 750 KWh	month	78.13	92	55c
Electricity, winter, 1000 KWh	month	101.30	92	55c

Wichita Falls, TX

Item	Per	Value	Date	Ref.
Composite ACCRA index		94.40	4Q 92	4c
Alcoholic Beverages				
Beer, Miller Lite or Budweiser, 12-oz containers	6 pack	3.58	4Q 92	4c
Liquor, J & B Scotch	750 ml	17.22	4Q 92	4c
Wine, Gallo Chablis blanc, 1.5 liter	bottle	4.48	4Q 92	4c
Child Care				
Child care fee, average, center	hour	1.29	90	65r
Child care fee, average, nonregulated family day care	hour	0.89	90	65r
Child care fee, average, regulated family day care	hour	1.32	90	65r
Clothing				
Jeans, man's denim		28.49	4Q 92	4c
Shirt, man's dress shirt		25.19	4Q 92	4c
Undervest, boy's size 10-14, cotton	3	3.62	4Q 92	4c
Communications				
Long-distance telephone service, day, initial minute, 0-100 miles	min	0.10-0.46	91	12s
Long-distance telephone service, day, additional minute, 0-100 miles	min	0.06-0.45	91	12s
Newspaper subscription, daily and Sunday home delivery, large-city	month	9.50	4Q 92	4c
Telephone, flat rate	month	9.10	91	11c
Telephone bill, family of four	month	15.08	4Q 92	4c
Education				
Board, 4-yr private college/university	year	1883	91	22s
Board, 4-yr public college/university	year	1605	91	22s
Expenditures, local gov't, public elementary/secondary	pupil	4593	92	20s
Room, 4-year private college/university	year	1620	91	22s
Room, 4-year public college/university	year	1532	91	22s
Tuition, 2-year private college/university	year	4394	91	22s
Tuition, 2-year public college/university	year	495	91	22s
Tuition, 4-year private college/university	year	6497	91	22s
Tuition, 4-year public college/university, in-state	year	986	91	22s

Wichita Falls, TX - continued

Item	Per	Value	Date	Ref.
Energy and Fuels				
Coal	mil Btu	1.44	90	64s
Energy	mil Btu	6.48	90	64s
Energy, combined forms, 1,800 sq ft heating area	month	115.26	4Q 92	4c
Energy, exc electricity, 1,800 sq ft heating area	month	38.02	4Q 92	4c
Energy exp/householder, 1-family unit	year	471	90	28r
Energy exp/householder, <1,000 sq ft heating area	year	384	90	28r
Energy exp/householder, 1,000-1,999 sq ft heating area	year	421	90	28r
Energy exp/householder, 2,000+ sq ft heating area	year	625	90	28r
Energy exp/householder, mobile home	year	271	90	28r
Energy exp/householder, multifamily	year	355	90	28r
Gas, natural	mil Btu	2.47	90	64s
Gas, natural	000 cu ft	5.71	91	46s
Gas, natural, exp	year	388	91	46s
Gasoline, motor	gal	1.12	4Q 92	4c
Gasoline, unleaded regular	mil Btu	9.16	90	64s
Entertainment				
Bowling, evening rate	game	2.12	4Q 92	4c
Miniature golf admission	adult	6.18	92	1r
Miniature golf admission	child	5.14	92	1r
Monopoly game, Parker Brothers', No. 9		12.33	4Q 92	4c
Movie	admission	4.50	4Q 92	4c
Tennis balls, yellow, Wilson or Penn, 3	can	2.73	4Q 92	4c
Waterpark admission	adult	11.00	92	1r
Waterpark admission	child	8.55	92	1r
Funerals				
Casket, 18-gauge steel, velvet interior		2274.41	91	24r
Cosmetology, hair care, etc.		74.62	91	24r
Embalming		229.94	91	24r
Facility use for ceremony		176.61	91	24r
Hearse, local		116.34	91	24r
Limousine, local		72.68	91	24r
Remains to funeral home, transfer		87.72	91	24r
Service charge, professional		712.53	91	24r
Vault, concrete, non-metallic liner		750.55	91	24r
Viewing facilities, use		155.31	91	24r
Goods and Services				
ACCRA Index, Miscellaneous Goods and Services		96.20	4Q 92	4c
Groceries				
ACCRA Index, Groceries		95.90	4Q 92	4c
Apples, Red Delicious	lb	0.79	4/93	16r
Babyfood, strained vegetables, lowest price	4-4.5 oz jar	0.31	4Q 92	4c
Bacon	lb	1.75	4/93	16r
Bananas	lb	0.32	4Q 92	4c
Bananas	lb	0.42	4/93	16r
Beef, stew, boneless	lb	2.61	4/93	16r
Bologna, all beef or mixed	lb	2.24	4/93	16r
Bread, white	24 oz	0.67	4Q 92	4c
Bread, white, pan	lb	0.64	4/93	16r
Bread, whole wheat, pan	lb	0.96	4/93	16r
Cabbage	lb	0.37	4/93	16r
Carrots, short trimmed and topped	lb	0.47	4/93	16r
Celery	lb	0.64	4/93	16r
Cheese, American	lb	2.98	4/93	16r
Cheese, Cheddar	lb	3.28	4/93	16r
Cheese, Kraft grated Parmesan	8-oz canister	3.51	4Q 92	4c
Chicken, fresh, whole	lb	0.77	4/93	16r
Chicken, fryer, whole	lb	0.43	4Q 92	4c
Chicken breast, bone-in	lb	1.92	4/93	16r
Chicken legs, bone-in	lb	1.06	4/93	16r

Values are in dollars or fractions of dollars. In the column headed *Ref*, references are shown to sources. Each reference is followed by a letter. These refer to the geographical level for which data were reported: s=State, r=Region, and c=City or metro. The abbreviation *ex* is used to mean *except* or *excluding*; *exp* stands for *expenditures*. For other abbreviations and further explanations, please see the Introduction.

Wichita Falls, TX - continued

Item	Per	Value	Date	Ref.
Groceries				
Chuck roast, graded and ungraded, ex USDA prime and choice	lb	2.40	4/93	16r
Chuck roast, USDA choice, bone-in	lb	2.19	4/93	16r
Chuck roast, USDA choice, boneless	lb	2.38	4/93	16r
Cigarettes, Winston	carton	19.63	4Q 92	4c
Coffee, 100% ground roast, all sizes	lb	2.48	4/93	16r
Coffee, vacuum-packed	13-oz can	1.83	4Q 92	4c
Corn, frozen	10 oz	0.62	4Q 92	4c
Corn Flakes, Kellogg's or Post Toasties	18 oz	1.99	4Q 92	4c
Crackers, soda, salted	lb	1.15	4/93	16r
Eggs, Grade A large	doz	0.90	4Q 92	4c
Eggs, Grade A large	doz	0.96	4/93	16r
Flour, white, all purpose	lb	0.24	4/93	16r
Frankfurters, all meat or all beef	lb	2.01	4/93	16r
Grapefruit	lb	0.44	4/93	16r
Grapes, Thompson Seedless	lb	1.40	4/93	16r
Ground beef, 100% beef	lb	1.58	4/93	16r
Ground beef, lean and extra lean	lb	2.09	4/93	16r
Ground beef or hamburger	lb	1.44	4Q 92	4c
Ground chuck, 100% beef	lb	1.98	4/93	16r
Ham, boneless, excluding canned	lb	2.89	4/93	16r
Ham, picnic, shoulder, bone-in, smoked	lb	1.02	4/93	16r
Ham, rump or steak half, bone-in, smoked	lb	1.48	4/93	16r
Honey, jar	8 oz	0.73-1.19	92	5r
Honey, jar	lb	1.10-1.79	92	5r
Honey, squeeze bear	12-oz	1.19-1.50	92	5r
Ice cream, prepackaged, bulk, regular	1/2 gal	2.41	4/93	16r
Lemons	lb	1.05	4/93	16r
Lettuce, iceberg	head	1.04	4Q 92	4c
Lettuce, iceberg	lb	0.81	4/93	16r
Margarine, Blue Bonnet or Parkay cubes	lb	0.68	4Q 92	4c
Margarine, stick	lb	0.88	4/93	16r
Milk, whole	1/2 gal	1.49	4Q 92	4c
Orange juice, Minute Maid frozen	12-oz can	1.40	4Q 92	4c
Oranges, navel	lb	0.55	4/93	16r
Peaches	29-oz can	1.49	4Q 92	4c
Pears, Anjou	lb	0.92	4/93	16r
Peas Sweet, Del Monte or Green Giant	15-17 oz can	0.63	4Q 92	4c
Pork chops, center cut, bone-in	lb	3.13	4/93	16r
Potato chips	16 oz	2.94	4/93	16r
Potatoes, white	lb	0.43	4/93	16r
Potatoes, white or red	10-lb sack	2.57	4Q 92	4c
Rib roast, USDA choice, bone-in	lb	4.63	4/93	16r
Rice, white, long grain, uncooked	lb	0.45	4/93	16r
Round roast, graded & ungraded, ex USDA prime & choice	lb	3.03	4/93	16r
Round roast, USDA choice, boneless	lb	3.09	4/93	16r
Sausage, fresh, loose	lb	2.08	4/93	16r
Sausage, Jimmy Dean, 100% pork	lb	2.14	4Q 92	4c
Short ribs, bone-in	lb	2.66	4/93	16r
Shortening, vegetable oil blends	lb	0.69	4/93	16r
Shortening, vegetable, Crisco	3-lb can	2.15	4Q 92	4c
Soft drink, Coca Cola	2 liter	0.98	4Q 92	4c
Spaghetti and macaroni	lb	0.81	4/93	16r
Steak, rib eye, USDA choice, boneless	lb	6.24	4/93	16r
Steak, round, graded & ungraded, ex USDA prime & choice	lb	3.31	4/93	16r
Steak, round, USDA choice, boneless	lb	3.34	4/93	16r
Steak, sirloin, graded & ungraded, ex USDA prime & choice	lb	4.19	4/93	16r
Steak, sirloin, USDA choice, boneless	lb	4.46	4/93	16r
Steak, T-bone	lb	4.84	4Q 92	4c
Steak, T-bone, USDA choice, bone-in	lb	5.25	4/93	16r
Strawberries, dry pint	12 oz	0.92	4/93	16r
Sugar, cane or beet	4 lb	1.70	4Q 92	4c
Sugar, white	lb	0.39	4/93	16r

Wichita Falls, TX - continued

Item	Per	Value	Date	Ref.
Groceries - continued				
Sugar, white, 33-80 oz pk	lb	0.38	4/93	16r
Tomatoes, field grown	lb	0.88	4/93	16r
Tomatoes, Hunt's or Del Monte	14.5-oz can	0.70	4Q 92	4c
Tuna, chunk, light	6.125-6.5 oz can	0.65	4Q 92	4c
Tuna, chunk, light	lb	1.79	4/93	16r
Turkey, frozen, whole	lb	1.04	4/93	16r
Yogurt, natural, fruit flavored	1/2 pint	0.57	4/93	16r
Health Care				
ACCRA Index, Health Care		91.70	4Q 92	4c
Analgesic, Aspirin, Bayer, 325 mg tablets	100	5.32	4Q 92	4c
Childbirth, cesarean, hospital		5034	91	62r
Childbirth, cesarean, physician's fee		2053	91	62r
Childbirth, normal, hospital		2712	91	62r
Childbirth, normal, physician's fee		1492	91	62r
Dentist's fee, adult teeth cleaning and periodic oral exam	visit	38.67	4Q 92	4c
Doctor's fee, routine exam, established patient	visit	35.48	4Q 92	4c
Health care spending, state	capita	2192	3/93	84s
Hospital care, semiprivate room	day	292.50	4Q 92	4c
Medical insurance premium, per employee, small group comprehensive	month	335.80	10/91	25c
Mental health care, exp	capita	20.37-28.83	90	38s
Mental health care, exp, state mental health agency	capita	22.72	90	38s
Mental health care, hospital psychiatric services, non-Federal, exp	capita	7.95	88	38s
Mental health care, mental health organization, multiservice, exp	capita	12.05	88	38s
Mental health care, psychiatric hospitals, private, exp	capita	37.78	88	38s
Mental health care, psychiatric out-patient clinics, freestanding, exp	capita	0.43	88	38s
Mental health care, state and county mental hospitals, exp	capita	12.54	88	38s
Mental health care, VA medical centers, exp	capita	5.35	88	38s
Physician fee, family practice, first-visit		75.00	91	62r
Physician fee, family practice, revisit		34.00	91	62r
Physician fee, general practice, first-visit		61.00	91	62r
Physician fee, general practice, revisit		32.00	91	62r
Physician fee, general surgeon, first-visit		64.00	91	62r
Physician fee, general surgeon, revisit		40.00	91	62r
Physician fee, internal medicine, first-visit		98.00	91	62r
Physician fee, internal medicine, revisit		40.00	91	62r
Physician fee, median, neurosurgeon, first-visit		130.00	91	62r
Physician fee, median, nonsurgical specialist, first-visit		95.00	91	62r
Physician fee, median, orthopedic surgeon, first-visit		91.00	91	62r
Physician fee, median, plastic surgeon, first-visit		66.00	91	62r
Physician fee, median, surgical specialist, first-visit		62.00	91	62r
Physician fee, neurosurgeon, revisit		50.00	91	62r
Physician fee, nonsurgical specialist, revisit		40.00	91	62r
Physician fee, obstetrics/gynecology, first-visit		64.00	91	62r
Physician fee, obstetrics/gynecology, revisit		41.00	91	62r
Physician fee, orthopedic surgeon, revisit		40.00	91	62r
Physician fee, pediatrician, first-visit		49.00	91	62r
Physician fee, pediatrician, revisit		33.00	91	62r
Physician fee, plastic surgeon, revisit		43.00	91	62r
Physician fee, surgical specialist, revisit		37.00	91	62r
Substance abuse, hospital ancillary charge	incident	3750	90	70s

Values are in dollars or fractions of dollars. In the column headed *Ref*, references are shown to sources. Each reference is followed by a letter. These refer to the geographical level for which data were reported: s=State, r=Region, and c=City or metro. The abbreviation *ex* is used to mean *except* or *excluding*; *exp* stands for *expenditures*. For other abbreviations and further explanations, please see the Introduction.

Wichita Falls, TX - continued

Item	Per	Value	Date	Ref.
Health Care				
Substance abuse, hospital physician charge	incident	1080	90	70s
Substance abuse, hospital room and board	incident	5320	90	70s
Household Goods				
Appliance repair, home, service call, washing machine	min labor charge	30.75	4Q 92	4c
Laundry detergent, Tide Ultra, Bold, or Cheer	42 oz	3.06	4Q 92	4c
Tissues, facial, Kleenex brand	175-count box	1.07	4Q 92	4c
Housing				
ACCRA Index, Housing		87.10	4Q 92	4c
House, 1,800 sq ft, 8,000 sq ft lot, new, urban	total	100260	4Q 92	4c
House payment, principal and interest, 25% down payment	month	557	4Q 92	4c
Mortgage rate, incl. points & origination fee, 30-year fixed or adjustable rate	percent	8.10	4Q 92	4c
Rent, apartment, 2 bedrooms - 1-1/2 to 2 baths, unfurnished, 950 sq ft, water	month	379	4Q 92	4c
Rental unit, 1 bedroom	month	372	93	23c
Rental unit, 2 bedroom	month	438	93	23c
Rental unit, 3 bedroom	month	547	93	23c
Rental unit, 4 bedroom	month	614	93	23c
Rental unit, efficiency	month	306	93	23c
Insurance and Pensions				
Auto insurance, private passenger	year	709.79	91	63s
Personal Goods				
Shampoo, Alberto VO5	15 oz	0.96	4Q 92	4c
Toothpaste, Crest or Colgate	6-7 oz	1.81	4Q 92	4c
Personal Services				
Dry cleaning, man's 2-piece suit		5.27	4Q 92	4c
Haircare, woman's shampoo, trim and blow-dry		15.20	4Q 92	4c
Haircut, man's barbershop, no styling		5.67	4Q 92	4c
Restaurant Food				
Chicken, fried, thigh and drumstick		2.10	4Q 92	4c
Hamburger with cheese	1/4 lb	1.88	4Q 92	4c
Pizza, Pizza Hut or Pizza Inn, cheese, thin crust	12-13 in	8.60	4Q 92	4c
Taxes				
Tax, cigarette	pack	41	91	77s
Tax, gasoline	gal	20	91	77s
Taxes, state	capita	923	91	77s
Transportation				
ACCRA Index, Transportation		100.40	4Q 92	4c
Bus fare, up to 10 miles	one-way	0.75	4Q 92	4c
Driver's license fee		16.00	12/90	43s
Tire balance, computer or spin balance, front	wheel	6.83	4Q 92	4c
Travel				
Business travel	day	193.00	4/93	89r
Utilities				
ACCRA Index, Utilities		102.80	4Q 92	4c
Electricity	mil Btu	17.09	90	64s
Electricity, partial electric and other energy, 1,800 sq ft living area new home	month	77.24	4Q 92	4c
Electricity, residential	KWh	5.92	2/93	94s

Wilkes-Barre, PA

Item	Per	Value	Date	Ref.
Composite ACCRA index		105.80	4Q 92	4c
Alcoholic Beverages				
Beer, Miller Lite or Budweiser, 12-oz containers	6 pack	4.87	4Q 92	4c
Liquor, J & B Scotch	750 ml	16.39	4Q 92	4c
Wine, Gallo Chablis blanc, 1.5 liter	bottle	5.79	4Q 92	4c
Child Care				
Child care fee, average, center	hour	2.18	90	65r
Child care fee, average, nonregulated family day care	hour	1.83	90	65r
Child care fee, average, regulated family day care	hour	2.02	90	65r
Clothing				
Jeans, man's denim		33.62	4Q 92	4c
Shirt, man's dress shirt		21.22	4Q 92	4c
Undervest, boy's size 10-14, cotton	3	3.77	4Q 92	4c
Communications				
Long-distance telephone service, day, initial minute, 0-100 miles	min	0.15-0.29	91	12s
Long-distance telephone service, day, additional minute, 0-100 miles	min	0.06-0.22	91	12s
Long-distance telephone service, evenings/weekends, 0-100 mi, initial minute	min	0.06-0.14	91	12s
Long-distance telephone service, evenings/weekends, 0-100 mi, additional minute	min	0.03-0.11	91	12s
Newspaper subscription, daily and Sunday home delivery, large-city	month	7.83	4Q 92	4c
Telephone bill, family of four	month	14.59	4Q 92	4c
Education				
Board, 4-yr private college/university	year	2019	91	22s
Board, 4-yr public college/university	year	1656	91	22s
Expenditures, local gov't, public elementary/secondary	pupil	6980	92	20s
Room, 4-year private college/university	year	2179	91	22s
Room, 4-year public college/university	year	1719	91	22s
Tuition, 2-year private college/university	year	6314	91	22s
Tuition, 2-year public college/university	year	1505	91	22s
Tuition, 4-year private college/university	year	9848	91	22s
Tuition, 4-year public college/university, in-state	year	3401	91	22s
Energy and Fuels				
Coal	mil Btu	1.57	90	64s
Energy	mil Btu	8.63	90	64s
Energy, combined forms, 1,800 sq ft heating area	month	171.15	4Q 92	4c
Energy exp/householder, 1-family unit	year	588	90	28r
Energy exp/householder, <1,000 sq ft heating area	year	477	90	28r
Energy exp/householder, 1,000-1,999 sq ft heating area	year	517	90	28r
Energy exp/householder, 2,000+ sq ft heating area	year	630	90	28r
Energy exp/householder, mobile home	year	412	90	28r
Energy exp/householder, multifamily	year	498	90	28r
Gas, natural	mil Btu	5.24	90	64s
Gas, natural	000 cu ft	6.76	91	46s
Gas, natural, exp	year	703	91	46s
Gasoline, motor	gal	1.15	4Q 92	4c
Gasoline, unleaded regular	mil Btu	9.35	90	64s
Entertainment				
Bowling, evening rate	game	1.85	4Q 92	4c
Monopoly game, Parker Brothers', No. 9		10.01	4Q 92	4c
Movie	admission	5.50	4Q 92	4c
Tennis balls, yellow, Wilson or Penn, 3	can	2.21	4Q 92	4c
Funerals				
Casket, 18-gauge steel, velvet interior		1811.58	91	24r
Cosmetology, hair care, etc.		111.08	91	24r

Values are in dollars or fractions of dollars. In the column headed *Ref*, references are shown to sources. Each reference is followed by a letter. These refer to the geographical level for which data were reported: s=State, r=Region, and c=City or metro. The abbreviation *ex* is used to mean *except* or *excluding*; *exp* stands for *expenditures*. For other abbreviations and further explanations, please see the Introduction.

Wilkes-Barre, PA - continued

Item	Per	Value	Date	Ref.
Funerals				
Embalming		329.42	91	24r
Facility use for ceremony		201.29	91	24r
Hearse, local		135.27	91	24r
Limousine, local		127.24	91	24r
Remains to funeral home, transfer		103.98	91	24r
Service charge, professional		724.98	91	24r
Vault, concrete, non-metallic liner		766.71	91	24r
Viewing facilities, use		260.60	91	24r
Goods and Services				
ACCRA Index, Miscellaneous Goods and Services		96.60	4Q 92	4c
Groceries				
ACCRA Index, Groceries		109.20	4Q 92	4c
Apples, Red Delicious	lb	0.85	4/93	16r
Babyfood, strained vegetables, lowest price	4-4.5 oz jar	0.39	4Q 92	4c
Bacon	lb	2.12	4/93	16r
Bananas	lb	0.44	4Q 92	4c
Bananas	lb	0.54	4/93	16r
Bread, white	24 oz	0.87	4Q 92	4c
Bread, white, pan	lb	0.81	4/93	16r
Butter	lb	2.02	4/93	16r
Carrots, short trimmed and topped	lb	0.51	4/93	16r
Cheese, Kraft grated Parmesan	8-oz canister	3.20	4Q 92	4c
Chicken, fresh, whole	lb	1.04	4/93	16r
Chicken, fryer, whole	lb	1.06	4Q 92	4c
Chicken breast, bone-in	lb	2.21	4/93	16r
Chicken legs, bone-in	lb	1.16	4/93	16r
Chuck roast, USDA choice, boneless	lb	2.82	4/93	16r
Cigarettes, Winston	carton	17.86	4Q 92	4c
Coffee, 100% ground roast, all sizes	lb	2.66	4/93	16r
Coffee, vacuum-packed	13-oz can	2.06	4Q 92	4c
Corn, frozen	10 oz	0.68	4Q 92	4c
Corn Flakes, Kellogg's or Post Toasties	18 oz	2.02	4Q 92	4c
Cucumbers	lb	0.85	4/93	16r
Eggs, Grade A large	doz	0.93	4Q 92	4c
Eggs, Grade A large	doz	1.15	4/93	16r
Grapefruit	lb	0.45	4/93	16r
Grapes, Thompson Seedless	lb	1.52	4/93	16r
Ground beef, lean and extra lean	lb	2.36	4/93	16r
Ground beef or hamburger	lb	1.65	4Q 92	4c
Ground chuck, 100% beef	lb	2.02	4/93	16r
Honey, jar	8 oz	0.96-1.75	92	5r
Honey, jar	lb	1.50-3.00	92	5r
Honey, squeeze bear	12-oz	1.50-1.99	92	5r
Ice cream, prepackaged, bulk, regular	1/2 gal	2.80	4/93	16r
Lemons	lb	0.96	4/93	16r
Lettuce, iceberg	head	1.16	4Q 92	4c
Lettuce, iceberg	lb	0.95	4/93	16r
Margarine, Blue Bonnet or Parkay cubes	lb	0.71	4Q 92	4c
Margarine, stick	lb	0.81	4/93	16r
Milk, fresh, whole, fortified	1/2 gal	1.30	4/93	16r
Milk, whole	1/2 gal	1.20	4Q 92	4c
Orange juice, Minute Maid frozen	12-oz can	1.69	4Q 92	4c
Oranges, navel	lb	0.56	4/93	16r
Peaches	29-oz can	1.34	4Q 92	4c
Peanut butter, creamy, all sizes	lb	1.88	4/93	16r
Peas Sweet, Del Monte or Green Giant	15-17 oz can	0.67	4Q 92	4c
Pork chops, center cut, bone-in	lb	3.34	4/93	16r
Potato chips	16 oz	2.88	4/93	16r
Potatoes, white	lb	0.37	4/93	16r
Potatoes, white or red	10-lb sack	1.91	4Q 92	4c
Rib roast, USDA choice, bone-in	lb	4.94	4/93	16r
Round roast, USDA choice, boneless	lb	3.17	4/93	16r

Item	Per	Value	Date	Ref.
Groceries - continued				
Sausage, Jimmy Dean, 100% pork	lb	2.54	4Q 92	4c
Shortening, vegetable oil blends	lb	0.98	4/93	16r
Shortening, vegetable, Crisco	3-lb can	2.53	4Q 92	4c
Soft drink, Coca Cola	2 liter	1.21	4Q 92	4c
Spaghetti and macaroni	lb	0.82	4/93	16r
Steak, round, graded & ungraded, ex USDA prime & choice	lb	4.04	4/93	16r
Steak, round, USDA choice, boneless	lb	3.90	4/93	16r
Steak, sirloin, USDA choice, boneless	lb	4.97	4/93	16r
Steak, T-bone	lb	6.12	4Q 92	4c
Strawberries, dry pint	12 oz	0.90	4/93	16r
Sugar, cane or beet	4 lb	1.80	4Q 92	4c
Sugar, white	lb	0.50	4/93	16r
Sugar, white, 33-80 oz pk	lb	0.41	4/93	16r
Tomatoes, field grown	lb	1.23	4/93	16r
Tomatoes, Hunt's or Del Monte	14.5-oz can	0.78	4Q 92	4c
Tuna, chunk, light	6.125-6.5 oz can	0.71	4Q 92	4c
Tuna, chunk, light	lb	2.22	4/93	16r
Turkey, frozen, whole	lb	1.04	4/93	16r
Health Care				
ACCRA Index, Health Care		91.80	4Q 92	4c
Analgesic, Aspirin, Bayer, 325 mg tablets	100	4.91	4Q 92	4c
Childbirth, cesarean, hospital		5826	91	62r
Childbirth, cesarean, physician's fee		2053	91	62r
Childbirth, normal, hospital		2964	91	62r
Childbirth, normal, physician's fee		1492	91	62r
Dentist's fee, adult teeth cleaning and periodic oral exam	visit	40.25	4Q 92	4c
Doctor's fee, routine exam, established patient	visit	34.40	4Q 92	4c
Hospital care, semiprivate room	day	257.88	90	27c
Hospital care, semiprivate room	day	307.50	4Q 92	4c
Medical plan per employee	year	3942	91	45r
Mental health care, exp	capita	53.68-118.35	90	38s
Mental health care, exp, state mental health agency	capita	56.85	90	38s
Mental health care, hospital psychiatric services, non-Federal, exp	capita	22.11	88	38s
Mental health care, mental health organization, multiservice, exp	capita	21.01	88	38s
Mental health care, psychiatric hospitals, private, exp	capita	26.48	88	38s
Mental health care, psychiatric out-patient clinics, freestanding, exp	capita	4.17	88	38s
Mental health care, psychiatric partial-care organizations, freestanding, exp	capita	0.94	88	38s
Mental health care, state and county mental hospitals, exp	capita	37.11	88	38s
Mental health care, VA medical centers, exp	capita	9.77	88	38s
Prescription drug co-pay, Medicaid	month	6.00	91	21s
Substance abuse, hospital ancillary charge	incident	720	90	70s
Substance abuse, hospital physician charge	incident	210	90	70s
Substance abuse, hospital room and board	incident	5400	90	70s
Household Goods				
Appliance repair, home, service call, washing machine	min labor charge	21.16	4Q 92	4c
Laundry detergent, Tide Ultra, Bold, or Cheer	42 oz	3.66	4Q 92	4c
Tissues, facial, Kleenex brand	175-count box	1.18	4Q 92	4c

Values are in dollars or fractions of dollars. In the column headed *Ref*, references are shown to sources. Each reference is followed by a letter. These refer to the geographical level for which data were reported: s=State, r=Region, and c=City or metro. The abbreviation *ex* is used to mean *except* or *excluding*; *exp* stands for expenditures. For other abbreviations and further explanations, please see the Introduction.

Wilkes-Barre, PA - continued

Item	Per	Value	Date	Ref.
Housing				
ACCRA Index, Housing		110.90	4Q 92	4c
House, 1,800 sq ft, 8,000 sq ft lot, new, urban	total	120033	4Q 92	4c
House payment, principal and interest, 25% down payment	month	681	4Q 92	4c
Mortgage rate, incl. points & origination fee, 30-year fixed or adjustable rate	percent	8.32	4Q 92	4c
Rent, apartment, 2 bedrooms - 1-1/2 to 2 baths, unfurnished, 950 sq ft, water	month	548	4Q 92	4c
Insurance and Pensions				
Auto insurance, private passenger	year	683.57	91	63s
Personal Goods				
Shampoo, Alberto VO5	15 oz	1.21	4Q 92	4c
Toothpaste, Crest or Colgate	6-7 oz	2.16	4Q 92	4c
Personal Services				
Dry cleaning, man's 2-piece suit		6.20	4Q 92	4c
Haircare, woman's shampoo, trim and blow-dry		15.49	4Q 92	4c
Haircut, man's barbershop, no styling		6.25	4Q 92	4c
Restaurant Food				
Chicken, fried, thigh and drumstick		3.00	4Q 92	4c
Hamburger with cheese	1/4 lb	1.93	4Q 92	4c
Pizza, Pizza Hut or Pizza Inn, cheese, thin crust	12-13 in	7.69	4Q 92	4c
Taxes				
Tax, cigarette	pack	31	91	77s
Tax, gasoline	gal	12	91	77s
Taxes, state	capita	1089	91	77s
Transportation				
ACCRA Index, Transportation		87.90	4Q 92	4c
Bus fare, up to 10 miles	one-way	1.00	4Q 92	4c
Driver's license fee		22.00	12/90	43s
Tire balance, computer or spin balance, front	wheel	4.44	4Q 92	4c
Travel				
Business travel	day	165.00	4/93	89r
Utilities				
ACCRA Index, Utilities		148.60	4Q 92	4c
Electricity	mil Btu	22.46	90	64s
Electricity, all electric, 1,800 sq ft living area new home	month	171.15	4Q 92	4c

Williamsport, PA

Item	Per	Value	Date	Ref.
Composite ACCRA index		102.60	4Q 92	4c
Alcoholic Beverages				
Beer, Miller Lite or Budweiser, 12-oz containers	6 pack	4.44	4Q 92	4c
Liquor, J & B Scotch	750 ml	16.39	4Q 92	4c
Wine, Gallo Chablis blanc, 1.5 liter	bottle	5.79	4Q 92	4c
Child Care				
Child care fee, average, center	hour	2.18	90	65r
Child care fee, average, nonregulated family day care	hour	1.83	90	65r
Child care fee, average, regulated family day care	hour	2.02	90	65r
Clothing				
Jeans, man's denim		33.99	4Q 92	4c
Shirt, man's dress shirt		26.62	4Q 92	4c
Undervest, boy's size 10-14, cotton	3	3.99	4Q 92	4c
Communications				
Long-distance telephone service, day, initial minute, 0-100 miles	min	0.15-0.29	91	12s

Williamsport, PA - continued

Item	Per	Value	Date	Ref.
Communications - continued				
Long-distance telephone service, day, additional minute, 0-100 miles	min	0.06-0.22	91	12s
Long-distance telephone service, evenings/weekends, 0-100 mi, initial minute	min	0.06-0.14	91	12s
Long-distance telephone service, evenings/weekends, 0-100 mi, additional minute	min	0.03-0.11	91	12s
Newspaper subscription, daily and Sunday home delivery, large-city	month	7.61	4Q 92	4c
Telephone bill, family of four	month	14.55	4Q 92	4c
Education				
Board, 4-yr private college/university	year	2019	91	22s
Board, 4-yr public college/university	year	1656	91	22s
Expenditures, local gov't, public elementary/secondary	pupil	6980	92	20s
Room, 4-year private college/university	year	2179	91	22s
Room, 4-year public college/university	year	1719	91	22s
Tuition, 2-year private college/university	year	6314	91	22s
Tuition, 2-year public college/university	year	1505	91	22s
Tuition, 4-year private college/university	year	9848	91	22s
Tuition, 4-year public college/university, in-state	year	3401	91	22s
Energy and Fuels				
Coal	mil Btu	1.57	90	64s
Energy	mil Btu	8.63	90	64s
Energy, combined forms, 1,800 sq ft heating area	month	57.66	4Q 92	4c
Energy exp/householder, 1-family unit	year	588	90	28r
Energy exp/householder, <1,000 sq ft heating area	year	477	90	28r
Energy exp/householder, 1,000-1,999 sq ft heating area	year	517	90	28r
Energy exp/householder, 2,000+ sq ft heating area	year	630	90	28r
Energy exp/householder, mobile home	year	412	90	28r
Energy exp/householder, multifamily	year	498	90	28r
Gas, natural	mil Btu	5.24	90	64s
Gas, natural	000 cu ft	6.76	91	46s
Gas, natural, exp	year	703	91	46s
Gasoline, motor	gal	1.13	4Q 92	4c
Gasoline, unleaded regular	mil Btu	9.35	90	64s
Entertainment				
Bowling, evening rate	game	1.78	4Q 92	4c
Monopoly game, Parker Brothers', No. 9		11.58	4Q 92	4c
Movie	admission	5.50	4Q 92	4c
Tennis balls, yellow, Wilson or Penn, 3	can	2.88	4Q 92	4c
Funerals				
Casket, 18-gauge steel, velvet interior		1811.58	91	24r
Cosmetology, hair care, etc.		111.08	91	24r
Embalming		329.42	91	24r
Facility use for ceremony		201.29	91	24r
Hearse, local		135.27	91	24r
Limousine, local		127.24	91	24r
Remains to funeral home, transfer		103.98	91	24r
Service charge, professional		724.98	91	24r
Vault, concrete, non-metallic liner		766.71	91	24r
Viewing facilities, use		260.60	91	24r
Goods and Services				
ACCRA Index, Miscellaneous Goods and Services		102.30	4Q 92	4c
Groceries				
ACCRA Index, Groceries		99.60	4Q 92	4c
Apples, Red Delicious	lb	0.85	4/93	16r
Babyfood, strained vegetables, lowest price	4-4.5 oz jar	0.39	4Q 92	4c
Bacon	lb	2.12	4/93	16r
Bananas	lb	0.50	4Q 92	4c
Bananas	lb	0.54	4/93	16r

Values are in dollars or fractions of dollars. In the column headed *Ref*, references are shown to sources. Each reference is followed by a letter. These refer to the geographical level for which data were reported: s=State, r=Region, and c=City or metro. The abbreviation *ex* is used to mean *except* or *excluding*; *exp* stands for expenditures. For other abbreviations and further explanations, please see the Introduction.

Williamsport, PA - continued

Item	Per	Value	Date	Ref.
Groceries				
Bread, white	24 oz	0.78	4Q 92	4c
Bread, white, pan	lb	0.81	4/93	16r
Butter	lb	2.02	4/93	16r
Carrots, short trimmed and topped	lb	0.51	4/93	16r
Cheese, Kraft grated Parmesan	8-oz canister	3.29	4Q 92	4c
Chicken, fresh, whole	lb	1.04	4/93	16r
Chicken, fryer, whole	lb	0.63	4Q 92	4c
Chicken breast, bone-in	lb	2.21	4/93	16r
Chicken legs, bone-in	lb	1.16	4/93	16r
Chuck roast, USDA choice, boneless	lb	2.82	4/93	16r
Cigarettes, Winston	carton	17.86	4Q 92	4c
Coffee, 100% ground roast, all sizes	lb	2.66	4/93	16r
Coffee, vacuum-packed	13-oz can	1.98	4Q 92	4c
Corn, frozen	10 oz	0.63	4Q 92	4c
Corn Flakes, Kellogg's or Post Toasties	18 oz	2.10	4Q 92	4c
Cucumbers	lb	0.85	4/93	16r
Eggs, Grade A large	doz	0.78	4Q 92	4c
Eggs, Grade A large	doz	1.15	4/93	16r
Grapefruit	lb	0.45	4/93	16r
Grapes, Thompson Seedless	lb	1.52	4/93	16r
Ground beef, lean and extra lean	lb	2.36	4/93	16r
Ground beef or hamburger	lb	1.38	4Q 92	4c
Ground chuck, 100% beef	lb	2.02	4/93	16r
Honey, jar	8 oz	0.96-1.75	92	5r
Honey, jar	lb	1.50-3.00	92	5r
Honey, squeeze bear	12-oz	1.50-1.99	92	5r
Ice cream, prepackaged, bulk, regular	1/2 gal	2.80	4/93	16r
Lemons	lb	0.96	4/93	16r
Lettuce, iceberg	head	0.99	4Q 92	4c
Lettuce, iceberg	lb	0.95	4/93	16r
Margarine, Blue Bonnet or Parkay cubes	lb	0.71	4Q 92	4c
Margarine, stick	lb	0.81	4/93	16r
Milk, fresh, whole, fortified	1/2 gal	1.30	4/93	16r
Milk, whole	1/2 gal	1.19	4Q 92	4c
Orange juice, Minute Maid frozen	12-oz can	1.31	4Q 92	4c
Oranges, navel	lb	0.56	4/93	16r
Peaches	29-oz can	1.32	4Q 92	4c
Peanut butter, creamy, all sizes	lb	1.88	4/93	16r
Peas Sweet, Del Monte or Green Giant	15-17 oz can	0.62	4Q 92	4c
Pork chops, center cut, bone-in	lb	3.34	4/93	16r
Potato chips	16 oz	2.88	4/93	16r
Potatoes, white	lb	0.37	4/93	16r
Potatoes, white or red	10-lb sack	1.99	4Q 92	4c
Rib roast, USDA choice, bone-in	lb	4.94	4/93	16r
Round roast, USDA choice, boneless	lb	3.17	4/93	16r
Sausage, Jimmy Dean, 100% pork	lb	2.59	4Q 92	4c
Shortening, vegetable oil blends	lb	0.98	4/93	16r
Shortening, vegetable, Crisco	3-lb can	2.37	4Q 92	4c
Soft drink, Coca Cola	2 liter	1.18	4Q 92	4c
Spaghetti and macaroni	lb	0.82	4/93	16r
Steak, round, graded & ungraded, ex USDA prime & choice	lb	4.04	4/93	16r
Steak, round, USDA choice, boneless	lb	3.90	4/93	16r
Steak, sirloin, USDA choice, boneless	lb	4.97	4/93	16r
Steak, T-bone	lb	4.40	4Q 92	4c
Strawberries, dry pint	12 oz	0.90	4/93	16r
Sugar, cane or beet	4 lb	1.70	4Q 92	4c
Sugar, white	lb	0.50	4/93	16r
Sugar, white, 33-80 oz pk	lb	0.41	4/93	16r
Tomatoes, field grown	lb	1.23	4/93	16r
Tomatoes, Hunt's or Del Monte	14.5-oz can	0.73	4Q 92	4c

Williamsport, PA - continued

Item	Per	Value	Date	Ref.
Groceries - continued				
Tuna, chunk, light	6.125-6.5 oz can	0.70	4Q 92	4c
Tuna, chunk, light	lb	2.22	4/93	16r
Turkey, frozen, whole	lb	1.04	4/93	16r
Health Care				
ACCRA Index, Health Care		96.10	4Q 92	4c
Analgesic, Aspirin, Bayer, 325 mg tablets	100	5.67	4Q 92	4c
Childbirth, cesarean, hospital		5826	91	62r
Childbirth, cesarean, physician's fee		2053	91	62r
Childbirth, normal, hospital		2964	91	62r
Childbirth, normal, physician's fee		1492	91	62r
Dentist's fee, adult teeth cleaning and periodic oral exam	visit	46.00	4Q 92	4c
Doctor's fee, routine exam, established patient	visit	31.20	4Q 92	4c
Hospital care, semiprivate room	day	247.68	90	27c
Hospital care, semiprivate room	day	330.25	4Q 92	4c
Medical insurance premium, per employee, small group comprehensive	month	222.20	10/91	25c
Medical plan per employee	year	3942	91	45r
Mental health care, exp	capita	53.68-118.35	90	38s
Mental health care, exp, state mental health agency	capita	56.85	90	38s
Mental health care, hospital psychiatric services, non-Federal, exp	capita	22.11	88	38s
Mental health care, mental health organization, multiservice, exp	capita	21.01	88	38s
Mental health care, psychiatric hospitals, private, exp	capita	26.48	88	38s
Mental health care, psychiatric out-patient clinics, freestanding, exp	capita	4.17	88	38s
Mental health care, psychiatric partial-care organizations, freestanding, exp	capita	0.94	88	38s
Mental health care, state and county mental hospitals, exp	capita	37.11	88	38s
Mental health care, VA medical centers, exp	capita	9.77	88	38s
Prescription drug co-pay, Medicaid	month	6.00	91	21s
Substance abuse, hospital ancillary charge	incident	720	90	70s
Substance abuse, hospital physician charge	incident	210	90	70s
Substance abuse, hospital room and board	incident	5400	90	70s
Household Goods				
Appliance repair, home, service call, washing machine	min labor charge	31.65	4Q 92	4c
Laundry detergent, Tide Ultra, Bold, or Cheer	42 oz	2.99	4Q 92	4c
Tissues, facial, Kleenex brand	175-count box	1.02	4Q 92	4c
Housing				
ACCRA Index, Housing		125.10	4Q 92	4c
House, 1,800 sq ft, 8,000 sq ft lot, new, urban	total	146000	4Q 92	4c
House payment, principal and interest, 25% down payment	month	829	4Q 92	4c
Mortgage rate, incl. points & origination fee, 30-year fixed or adjustable rate	percent	8.34	4Q 92	4c
Rent, apartment, 2 bedrooms - 1-1/2 to 2 baths, unfurnished, 950 sq ft, water	month	479	4Q 92	4c
Insurance and Pensions				
Auto insurance, private passenger	year	683.57	91	63s
Personal Goods				
Shampoo, Alberto VO5	15 oz	1.48	4Q 92	4c
Toothpaste, Crest or Colgate	6-7 oz	2.42	4Q 92	4c

Values are in dollars or fractions of dollars. In the column headed *Ref*, references are shown to sources. Each reference is followed by a letter. These refer to the geographical level for which data were reported: s=State, r=Region, and c=City or metro. The abbreviation *ex* is used to mean *except* or *excluding*; *exp* stands for expenditures. For other abbreviations and further explanations, please see the Introduction.

Williamsport, PA - continued

Item	Per	Value	Date	Ref.
Personal Services				
Dry cleaning, man's 2-piece suit		6.69	4Q 92	4c
Haircare, woman's shampoo, trim and blow-dry		14.40	4Q 92	4c
Haircut, man's barbershop, no styling		4.80	4Q 92	4c
Restaurant Food				
Chicken, fried, thigh and drumstick		2.43	4Q 92	4c
Hamburger with cheese	1/4 lb	1.85	4Q 92	4c
Pizza, Pizza Hut or Pizza Inn, cheese, thin crust	12-13 in	7.69	4Q 92	4c
Taxes				
Tax, cigarette	pack	31	91	77s
Tax, gasoline	gal	12	91	77s
Taxes, state	capita	1089	91	77s
Transportation				
ACCRA Index, Transportation		90.30	4Q 92	4c
Bus fare	one-way	1.00	3/93	2c
Driver's license fee		22.00	12/90	43s
Tire balance, computer or spin balance, front	wheel	5.25	4Q 92	4c
Travel				
Business travel	day	165.00	4/93	89r
Utilities				
ACCRA Index, Utilities		55.00	4Q 92	4c
Electricity	mil Btu	22.46	90	64s
Electricity, all electric, 1,800 sq ft living area new home	month	57.66	4Q 92	4c

Wilmington, DE

Item	Per	Value	Date	Ref.
Composite ACCRA index		114.40	4Q 92	4c
Alcoholic Beverages				
Beer, Miller Lite or Budweiser, 12-oz containers	6 pack	4.16	4Q 92	4c
Liquor, J & B Scotch	750 ml	15.34	4Q 92	4c
Wine, Gallo Chablis blanc, 1.5 liter	bottle	5.49	4Q 92	4c
Child Care				
Child care fee, average, center	hour	1.29	90	65r
Child care fee, average, nonregulated family day care	hour	0.89	90	65r
Child care fee, average, regulated family day care	hour	1.32	90	65r
Clothing				
Jeans, man's denim		35.98	4Q 92	4c
Shirt, man's dress shirt		25.40	4Q 92	4c
Undervest, boy's size 10-14, cotton	3	4.65	4Q 92	4c
Communications				
Long-distance telephone service, day, initial minute, 0-100 miles	min	0.09	91	12s
Long-distance telephone service, day, additional minute, 0-100 miles	min	0.07	91	12s
Long-distance telephone service, evenings/weekends, 0-100 mi, initial minute	min	0.06	91	12s
Long-distance telephone service, evenings/weekends, 0-100 mi, additional minute	min	0.04	91	12s
Newspaper subscription, daily and Sunday home delivery, large-city	month	14.35	4Q 92	4c
Telephone, flat rate	month	2.25	91	11c
Telephone bill, family of four	month	15.01	4Q 92	4c
Education				
Board, 4-yr private college/university	year	1660	91	22s
Board, 4-yr public college/university	year	1528	91	22s
Expenditures, local gov't, public elementary/secondary	pupil	6080	92	20s
Room, 4-year private college/university	year	1972	91	22s
Room, 4-year public college/university	year	1770	91	22s

Wilmington, DE - continued

Item	Per	Value	Date	Ref.
Education - continued				
Tuition, 2-year public college/university	year	936	91	22s
Tuition, 4-year private college/university	year	5831	91	22s
Tuition, 4-year public college/university, in-state	year	2910	91	22s
Energy and Fuels				
Coal	mil Btu	1.76	90	64s
Energy	mil Btu	9.14	90	64s
Energy, combined forms, 1,800 sq ft heating area	month	126.67	4Q 92	4c
Energy exp/householder, 1-family unit	year	487	90	28r
Energy exp/householder, <1,000 sq ft heating area	year	393	90	28r
Energy exp/householder, 1,000-1,999 sq ft heating area	year	442	90	28r
Energy exp/householder, 2,000+ sq ft heating area	year	577	90	28r
Energy exp/householder, mobile home	year	366	90	28r
Energy exp/householder, multifamily	year	382	90	28r
Gas, cooking, 10 therms	month	9.16	92	56c
Gas, cooking, 30 therms	month	21.53	92	56c
Gas, cooking, 50 therms	month	33.91	92	56c
Gas, heating, winter, 100 therms	month	59.34	92	56c
Gas, heating, winter, average use	month	69.52	92	56c
Gas, natural	mil Btu	3.82	90	64s
Gas, natural	000 cu ft	5.86	91	46s
Gas, natural, exp	year	460	91	46s
Gasoline, motor	gal	1.12	4Q 92	4c
Gasoline, unleaded regular	mil Btu	10.26	90	64s
Entertainment				
Bowling, evening rate	game	2.51	4Q 92	4c
Miniature golf admission	adult	6.18	92	1r
Miniature golf admission	child	5.14	92	1r
Monopoly game, Parker Brothers', No. 9		13.57	4Q 92	4c
Movie	admission	5.75	4Q 92	4c
Tennis balls, yellow, Wilson or Penn, 3	can	2.58	4Q 92	4c
Waterpark admission	adult	11.00	92	1r
Waterpark admission	child	8.55	92	1r
Funerals				
Casket, 18-gauge steel, velvet interior		2029.08	91	24r
Cosmetology, hair care, etc.		75.10	91	24r
Embalming		249.24	91	24r
Facility use for ceremony		162.27	91	24r
Hearse, local		114.04	91	24r
Limousine, local		88.57	91	24r
Remains to funeral home, transfer		92.61	91	24r
Service charge, professional		682.42	91	24r
Vault, concrete, non-metallic liner		798.70	91	24r
Viewing facilities, use		163.86	91	24r
Goods and Services				
ACCRA Index, Miscellaneous Goods and Services		110.30	4Q 92	4c
Groceries				
ACCRA Index, Groceries		117.70	4Q 92	4c
Apples, Red Delicious	lb	0.79	4/93	16r
Babyfood, strained vegetables, lowest price	4-4.5 oz jar	0.42	4Q 92	4c
Bacon	lb	1.75	4/93	16r
Bananas	lb	0.46	4Q 92	4c
Bananas	lb	0.42	4/93	16r
Beef, stew, boneless	lb	2.61	4/93	16r
Bologna, all beef or mixed	lb	2.24	4/93	16r
Bread, white	24 oz	0.93	4Q 92	4c
Bread, white, pan	lb	0.64	4/93	16r
Bread, whole wheat, pan	lb	0.96	4/93	16r
Cabbage	lb	0.37	4/93	16r
Carrots, short trimmed and topped	lb	0.47	4/93	16r
Celery	lb	0.64	4/93	16r

Values are in dollars or fractions of dollars. In the column headed *Ref*, references are shown to sources. Each reference is followed by a letter. These refer to the geographical level for which data were reported: s=State, r=Region, and c=City or metro. The abbreviation *ex* is used to mean *except* or *excluding*; *exp* stands for expenditures. For other abbreviations and further explanations, please see the Introduction.

Wilmington, DE - continued

Item	Per	Value	Date	Ref.
Groceries				
Cheese, American	lb	2.98	4/93	16r
Cheese, Cheddar	lb	3.28	4/93	16r
Cheese, Kraft grated Parmesan	8-oz canister	3.59	4Q 92	4c
Chicken, fresh, whole	lb	0.77	4/93	16r
Chicken, fryer, whole	lb	0.88	4Q 92	4c
Chicken breast, bone-in	lb	1.92	4/93	16r
Chicken legs, bone-in	lb	1.06	4/93	16r
Chuck roast, graded and ungraded, ex USDA prime and choice	lb	2.40	4/93	16r
Chuck roast, USDA choice, bone-in	lb	2.19	4/93	16r
Chuck roast, USDA choice, boneless	lb	2.38	4/93	16r
Cigarettes, Winston	carton	17.26	4Q 92	4c
Coffee, 100% ground roast, all sizes	lb	2.48	4/93	16r
Coffee, vacuum-packed	13-oz can	2.27	4Q 92	4c
Corn, frozen	10 oz	0.63	4Q 92	4c
Corn Flakes, Kellogg's or Post Toasties	18 oz	2.01	4Q 92	4c
Crackers, soda, salted	lb	1.15	4/93	16r
Eggs, Grade A large	doz	1.19	4Q 92	4c
Eggs, Grade A large	doz	0.96	4/93	16r
Flour, white, all purpose	lb	0.24	4/93	16r
Frankfurters, all meat or all beef	lb	2.01	4/93	16r
Grapefruit	lb	0.44	4/93	16r
Grapes, Thompson Seedless	lb	1.40	4/93	16r
Ground beef, 100% beef	lb	1.58	4/93	16r
Ground beef, lean and extra lean	lb	2.09	4/93	16r
Ground beef or hamburger	lb	1.71	4Q 92	4c
Ground chuck, 100% beef	lb	1.98	4/93	16r
Ham, boneless, excluding canned	lb	2.89	4/93	16r
Ham, picnic, shoulder, bone-in, smoked	lb	1.02	4/93	16r
Ham, rump or steak half, bone-in, smoked	lb	1.48	4/93	16r
Ice cream, prepackaged, bulk, regular	1/2 gal	2.41	4/93	16r
Lemons	lb	1.05	4/93	16r
Lettuce, iceberg	head	1.25	4Q 92	4c
Lettuce, iceberg	lb	0.81	4/93	16r
Margarine, Blue Bonnet or Parkay cubes	lb	0.87	4Q 92	4c
Margarine, stick	lb	0.88	4/93	16r
Milk, whole	1/2 gal	1.39	4Q 92	4c
Orange juice, Minute Maid frozen	12-oz can	1.93	4Q 92	4c
Oranges, navel	lb	0.55	4/93	16r
Peaches	29-oz can	1.61	4Q 92	4c
Pears, Anjou	lb	0.92	4/93	16r
Peas Sweet, Del Monte or Green Giant	15-17 oz can	0.67	4Q 92	4c
Pork chops, center cut, bone-in	lb	3.13	4/93	16r
Potato chips	16 oz	2.94	4/93	16r
Potatoes, white	lb	0.43	4/93	16r
Potatoes, white or red	10-lb sack	2.37	4Q 92	4c
Rib roast, USDA choice, bone-in	lb	4.63	4/93	16r
Rice, white, long grain, uncooked	lb	0.45	4/93	16r
Round roast, graded & ungraded, ex USDA prime & choice	lb	3.03	4/93	16r
Round roast, USDA choice, boneless	lb	3.09	4/93	16r
Sausage, fresh, loose	lb	2.08	4/93	16r
Sausage, Jimmy Dean, 100% pork	lb	3.52	4Q 92	4c
Short ribs, bone-in	lb	2.66	4/93	16r
Shortening, vegetable oil blends	lb	0.69	4/93	16r
Shortening, vegetable, Crisco	3-lb can	2.99	4Q 92	4c
Soft drink, Coca Cola	2 liter	1.03	4Q 92	4c
Spaghetti and macaroni	lb	0.81	4/93	16r
Steak, rib eye, USDA choice, boneless	lb	6.24	4/93	16r
Steak, round, graded & ungraded, ex USDA prime & choice	lb	3.31	4/93	16r
Steak, round, USDA choice, boneless	lb	3.34	4/93	16r
Steak, sirloin, graded & ungraded, ex USDA prime & choice	lb	4.19	4/93	16r

Wilmington, DE - continued

Item	Per	Value	Date	Ref.
Groceries - continued				
Steak, sirloin, USDA choice, boneless	lb	4.46	4/93	16r
Steak, T-bone	lb	6.15	4Q 92	4c
Steak, T-bone, USDA choice, bone-in	lb	5.25	4/93	16r
Strawberries, dry pint	12 oz	0.92	4/93	16r
Sugar, cane or beet	4 lb	2.07	4Q 92	4c
Sugar, white	lb	0.39	4/93	16r
Sugar, white, 33-80 oz pk	lb	0.38	4/93	16r
Tomatoes, field grown	lb	0.88	4/93	16r
Tomatoes, Hunt's or Del Monte	14.5-oz can	0.79	4Q 92	4c
Tuna, chunk, light	6.125-6.5 oz can	0.87	4Q 92	4c
Tuna, chunk, light	lb	1.79	4/93	16r
Turkey, frozen, whole	lb	1.04	4/93	16r
Yogurt, natural, fruit flavored	1/2 pint	0.57	4/93	16r
Health Care				
ACCRA Index, Health Care		121.90	4Q 92	4c
Analgesic, Aspirin, Bayer, 325 mg tablets	100	5.31	4Q 92	4c
Childbirth, cesarean, hospital		5034	91	62r
Childbirth, cesarean, physician's fee		2053	91	62r
Childbirth, normal, hospital		2712	91	62r
Childbirth, normal, physician's fee		1492	91	62r
Dentist's fee, adult teeth cleaning and periodic oral exam	visit	67.20	4Q 92	4c
Doctor's fee, routine exam, established patient	visit	34.00	4Q 92	4c
Hospital care, semiprivate room	day	385.00	90	27c
Hospital care, semiprivate room	day	467.67	4Q 92	4c
Medical insurance premium, per employee, small group comprehensive	month	350.40	10/91	25c
Medical plan per employee	year	3495	91	45r
Mental health care, exp	capita	37.60-53.67	90	38s
Mental health care, exp, state mental health agency	capita	54.88	90	38s
Mental health care, hospital psychiatric services, non-Federal, exp	capita	13.64	88	38s
Mental health care, mental health organization, multiservice, exp	capita	10.16	88	38s
Mental health care, psychiatric hospitals, private, exp	capita	30.65	88	38s
Mental health care, psychiatric out-patient clinics, freestanding, exp	capita	6.20	88	38s
Mental health care, state and county mental hospitals, exp	capita	41.19	88	38s
Mental health care, VA medical centers, exp	capita	0.49	88	38s
Physician fee, family practice, first-visit		75.00	91	62r
Physician fee, family practice, revisit		34.00	91	62r
Physician fee, general practice, first-visit		61.00	91	62r
Physician fee, general practice, revisit		32.00	91	62r
Physician fee, general surgeon, first-visit		64.00	91	62r
Physician fee, general surgeon, revisit		40.00	91	62r
Physician fee, internal medicine, first-visit		98.00	91	62r
Physician fee, internal medicine, revisit		40.00	91	62r
Physician fee, median, neurosurgeon, first-visit		130.00	91	62r
Physician fee, median, nonsurgical specialist, first-visit		95.00	91	62r
Physician fee, median, orthopedic surgeon, first-visit		91.00	91	62r
Physician fee, median, plastic surgeon, first-visit		66.00	91	62r
Physician fee, median, surgical specialist, first-visit		62.00	91	62r
Physician fee, neurosurgeon, revisit		50.00	91	62r
Physician fee, nonsurgical specialist, revisit		40.00	91	62r
Physician fee, obstetrics/gynecology, first-visit		64.00	91	62r
Physician fee, obstetrics/gynecology, revisit		41.00	91	62r
Physician fee, orthopedic surgeon, revisit		40.00	91	62r

Values are in dollars or fractions of dollars. In the column headed *Ref*, references are shown to sources. Each reference is followed by a letter. These refer to the geographical level for which data were reported: s = State, r = Region, and c = City or metro. The abbreviation *ex* is used to mean *except* or *excluding*; *exp* stands for expenditures. For other abbreviations and further explanations, please see the Introduction.

Wilmington, DE - continued

Item	Per	Value	Date	Ref.
Health Care				
Physician fee, pediatrician, first-visit		49.00	91	62r
Physician fee, pediatrician, revisit		33.00	91	62r
Physician fee, plastic surgeon, revisit		43.00	91	62r
Physician fee, surgical specialist, revisit		37.00	91	62r
Household Goods				
Appliance repair, home, service call, washing machine	min labor charge	38.39	4Q 92	4c
Laundry detergent, Tide Ultra, Bold, or Cheer	42 oz	3.83	4Q 92	4c
Tissues, facial, Kleenex brand	175-count box	1.27	4Q 92	4c
Housing				
ACCRA Index, Housing		122.80	4Q 92	4c
Home, median price	unit	117.20		26c
House, 1,800 sq ft, 8,000 sq ft lot, new, urban	total	140400	4Q 92	4c
House payment, principal and interest, 25% down payment	month	787	4Q 92	4c
Mortgage rate, incl. points & origination fee, 30-year fixed or adjustable rate	per-cent	8.20	4Q 92	4c
Rent, apartment, 2 bedrooms - 1-1/2 to 2 baths, unfurnished, 950 sq ft, water	month	531	4Q 92	4c
Rental unit, 1 bedroom	month	542	93	23c
Rental unit, 2 bedroom	month	646	93	23c
Rental unit, 3 bedroom	month	808	93	23c
Rental unit, 4 bedroom	month	961	93	23c
Rental unit, efficiency	month	454	93	23c
Insurance and Pensions				
Auto insurance, private passenger	year	783.59	91	63s
Legal Assistance				
Living trust, 77-year-old, $80,000 estate		350	9/92	3c
Living trust, married couple with $150,000 home and $50,000 in stocks		565	9/92	3c
Will		143	9/92	3c
Will and probate, $80,000 estate		1501	9/92	3c
Will and probate, $80,000 estate, 77-year-old		1501	9/92	3c
Personal Goods				
Shampoo, Alberto VO5	15 oz	1.56	4Q 92	4c
Toothpaste, Crest or Colgate	6-7 oz	1.89	4Q 92	4c
Personal Services				
Dry cleaning, man's 2-piece suit		5.64	4Q 92	4c
Haircare, woman's shampoo, trim and blow-dry		18.66	4Q 92	4c
Haircut, man's barbershop, no styling		7.60	4Q 92	4c
Restaurant Food				
Chicken, fried, thigh and drumstick		2.19	4Q 92	4c
Hamburger with cheese	1/4 lb	1.88	4Q 92	4c
Pizza, Pizza Hut or Pizza Inn, cheese, thin crust	12-13 in	8.99	4Q 92	4c
Taxes				
Tax, cigarette	pack	24	91	77s
Tax, gasoline	gal	19	91	77s
Taxes, state	capita	1713	91	77s
Transportation				
ACCRA Index, Transportation		99.00	4Q 92	4c
Bus fare	one-way	1.15	3/93	2c
Driver's license fee		12.50	12/90	43s
Tire balance, computer or spin balance, front	wheel	6.41	4Q 92	4c
Travel				
Breakfast	day	6.80	6/91	60c
Business travel	day	193.00	4/93	89r
Dinner	day	20.46	6/91	60c
Lodging	day	98.00	91	60c

Wilmington, DE - continued

Item	Per	Value	Date	Ref.
Travel - continued				
Lunch	day	11.35	6/91	60c
Utilities				
ACCRA Index, Utilities		112.10	4Q 92	4c
Electricity	mil Btu	19.00	90	64s
Electricity, all electric, 1,800 sq ft living area new home	month	126.67	4Q 92	4c
Electricity, winter, 250 KWh	month	26.67	92	55c
Electricity, winter, 500 KWh	month	48.78	92	55c
Electricity, winter, 750 KWh	month	68.69	92	55c
Electricity, winter, 1000 KWh	month	88.60	92	55c

Winston-Salem, NC

Item	Per	Value	Date	Ref.
Composite ACCRA index		98.50	4Q 92	4c
Alcoholic Beverages				
Beer, Miller Lite or Budweiser, 12-oz containers	6 pack	3.72	4Q 92	4c
Liquor, J & B Scotch	750 ml	17.65	4Q 92	4c
Wine, Gallo Chablis blanc, 1.5 liter	bottle	4.37	4Q 92	4c
Child Care				
Child care fee, average, center	hour	1.29	90	65r
Child care fee, average, nonregulated family day care	hour	0.89	90	65r
Child care fee, average, regulated family day care	hour	1.32	90	65r
Clothing				
Jeans, man's denim		28.77	4Q 92	4c
Shirt, man's dress shirt		24.00	4Q 92	4c
Undervest, boy's size 10-14, cotton	3	3.88	4Q 92	4c
Communications				
Long-distance telephone service, day, initial minute, 0-100 miles	min	0.10-0.33	91	12s
Long-distance telephone service, day, additional minute, 0-100 miles	min	0.10-0.33	91	12s
Long-distance telephone service, evenings/weekends, 0-100 mi, initial minute	min	0.08-0.24	91	12s
Long-distance telephone service, evenings/weekends, 0-100 mi, additional minute	min	0.05-0.17	91	12s
Newspaper subscription, daily and Sunday home delivery, large-city	month	9.13	4Q 92	4c
Telephone, flat rate	month	12.19	91	11c
Telephone bill, family of four	month	17.76	4Q 92	4c
Education				
Board, 4-yr private college/university	year	1768	91	22s
Board, 4-yr public college/university	year	1568	91	22s
Expenditures, local gov't, public elementary/secondary	pupil	5078	92	20s
Room, 4-year private college/university	year	1467	91	22s
Room, 4-year public college/university	year	1386	91	22s
Tuition, 2-year private college/university	year	4964	91	22s
Tuition, 2-year public college/university	year	334	91	22s
Tuition, 4-year private college/university	year	7826	91	22s
Tuition, 4-year public college/university, in-state	year	1112	91	22s
Energy and Fuels				
Coal	mil Btu	1.79	90	64s
Energy	mil Btu	10.06	90	64s
Energy, combined forms, 1,800 sq ft heating area	month	119.35	4Q 92	4c
Energy exp/householder, 1-family unit	year	487	90	28r
Energy exp/householder, <1,000 sq ft heating area	year	393	90	28r
Energy exp/householder, 1,000-1,999 sq ft heating area	year	442	90	28r
Energy exp/householder, 2,000+ sq ft heating area	year	577	90	28r
Energy exp/householder, mobile home	year	366	90	28r
Energy exp/householder, multifamily	year	382	90	28r

Values are in dollars or fractions of dollars. In the column headed *Ref*, references are shown to sources. Each reference is followed by a letter. These refer to the geographical level for which data were reported: s=State, r=Region, and c=City or metro. The abbreviation *ex* is used to mean *except* or *excluding*; *exp* stands for expenditures. For other abbreviations and further explanations, please see the Introduction.

Winston-Salem, NC - continued

Item	Per	Value	Date	Ref.
Energy and Fuels				
Gas, natural	mil Btu	4.19	90	64s
Gas, natural	000 cu ft	6.24	91	46s
Gas, natural, exp	year	439	91	46s
Gasoline, motor	gal	1.07	4Q 92	4c
Gasoline, unleaded regular	mil Btu	9.44	90	64s
Entertainment				
Bowling, evening rate	game	2.72	4Q 92	4c
Miniature golf admission	adult	6.18	92	1r
Miniature golf admission	child	5.14	92	1r
Monopoly game, Parker Brothers', No. 9		10.39	4Q 92	4c
Movie	admission	5.40	4Q 92	4c
Tennis balls, yellow, Wilson or Penn, 3	can	2.53	4Q 92	4c
Waterpark admission	adult	11.00	92	1r
Waterpark admission	child	8.55	92	1r
Funerals				
Casket, 18-gauge steel, velvet interior		2029.08	91	24r
Cosmetology, hair care, etc.		75.10	91	24r
Embalming		249.24	91	24r
Facility use for ceremony		162.27	91	24r
Hearse, local		114.04	91	24r
Limousine, local		88.57	91	24r
Remains to funeral home, transfer		92.61	91	24r
Service charge, professional		682.42	91	24r
Vault, concrete, non-metallic liner		798.70	91	24r
Viewing facilities, use		163.86	91	24r
Goods and Services				
ACCRA Index, Miscellaneous Goods and Services		99.40	4Q 92	4c
Groceries				
ACCRA Index, Groceries		90.70	4Q 92	4c
Apples, Red Delicious	lb	0.79	4/93	16r
Babyfood, strained vegetables, lowest price	4-4.5 oz jar	0.31	4Q 92	4c
Bacon	lb	1.75	4/93	16r
Bananas	lb	0.43	4Q 92	4c
Bananas	lb	0.42	4/93	16r
Beef, stew, boneless	lb	2.61	4/93	16r
Bologna, all beef or mixed	lb	2.24	4/93	16r
Bread, white	24 oz	0.60	4Q 92	4c
Bread, white, pan	lb	0.64	4/93	16r
Bread, whole wheat, pan	lb	0.96	4/93	16r
Cabbage	lb	0.37	4/93	16r
Carrots, short trimmed and topped	lb	0.47	4/93	16r
Celery	lb	0.64	4/93	16r
Cheese, American	lb	2.98	4/93	16r
Cheese, Cheddar	lb	3.28	4/93	16r
Cheese, Kraft grated Parmesan	8-oz canister	3.25	4Q 92	4c
Chicken, fresh, whole	lb	0.77	4/93	16r
Chicken, fryer, whole	lb	0.83	4Q 92	4c
Chicken breast, bone-in	lb	1.92	4/93	16r
Chicken legs, bone-in	lb	1.06	4/93	16r
Chuck roast, graded and ungraded, ex USDA prime and choice	lb	2.40	4/93	16r
Chuck roast, USDA choice, bone-in	lb	2.19	4/93	16r
Chuck roast, USDA choice, boneless	lb	2.38	4/93	16r
Cigarettes, Winston	carton	15.25	4Q 92	4c
Coffee, 100% ground roast, all sizes	lb	2.48	4/93	16r
Coffee, vacuum-packed	13-oz can	1.94	4Q 92	4c
Corn, frozen	10 oz	0.54	4Q 92	4c
Corn Flakes, Kellogg's or Post Toasties	18 oz	1.70	4Q 92	4c
Crackers, soda, salted	lb	1.15	4/93	16r
Eggs, Grade A large	doz	0.90	4Q 92	4c
Eggs, Grade A large	doz	0.96	4/93	16r
Flour, white, all purpose	lb	0.24	4/93	16r
Frankfurters, all meat or all beef	lb	2.01	4/93	16r

Winston-Salem, NC - continued

Item	Per	Value	Date	Ref.
Groceries - continued				
Grapefruit	lb	0.44	4/93	16r
Grapes, Thompson Seedless	lb	1.40	4/93	16r
Ground beef, 100% beef	lb	1.58	4/93	16r
Ground beef, lean and extra lean	lb	2.09	4/93	16r
Ground beef or hamburger	lb	1.41	4Q 92	4c
Ground chuck, 100% beef	lb	1.98	4/93	16r
Ham, boneless, excluding canned	lb	2.89	4/93	16r
Ham, picnic, shoulder, bone-in, smoked	lb	1.02	4/93	16r
Ham, rump or steak half, bone-in, smoked	lb	1.48	4/93	16r
Ice cream, prepackaged, bulk, regular	1/2 gal	2.41	4/93	16r
Lemons	lb	1.05	4/93	16r
Lettuce, iceberg	head	0.75	4Q 92	4c
Lettuce, iceberg	lb	0.81	4/93	16r
Margarine, Blue Bonnet or Parkay cubes	lb	0.47	4Q 92	4c
Margarine, stick	lb	0.88	4/93	16r
Milk, whole	1/2 gal	1.38	4Q 92	4c
Orange juice, Minute Maid frozen	12-oz can	1.20	4Q 92	4c
Oranges, navel	lb	0.55	4/93	16r
Peaches	29-oz can	1.31	4Q 92	4c
Pears, Anjou	lb	0.92	4/93	16r
Peas Sweet, Del Monte or Green Giant	15-17 oz can	0.46	4Q 92	4c
Pork chops, center cut, bone-in	lb	3.13	4/93	16r
Potato chips	16 oz	2.94	4/93	16r
Potatoes, white	lb	0.43	4/93	16r
Potatoes, white or red	10-lb sack	1.57	4Q 92	4c
Rib roast, USDA choice, bone-in	lb	4.63	4/93	16r
Rice, white, long grain, uncooked	lb	0.45	4/93	16r
Round roast, graded & ungraded, ex USDA prime & choice	lb	3.03	4/93	16r
Round roast, USDA choice, boneless	lb	3.09	4/93	16r
Sausage, fresh, loose	lb	2.08	4/93	16r
Sausage, Jimmy Dean, 100% pork	lb	1.98	4Q 92	4c
Short ribs, bone-in	lb	2.66	4/93	16r
Shortening, vegetable oil blends	lb	0.69	4/93	16r
Shortening, vegetable, Crisco	3-lb can	2.03	4Q 92	4c
Soft drink, Coca Cola	2 liter	1.00	4Q 92	4c
Spaghetti and macaroni	lb	0.81	4/93	16r
Steak, rib eye, USDA choice, boneless	lb	6.24	4/93	16r
Steak, round, graded & ungraded, ex USDA prime & choice	lb	3.31	4/93	16r
Steak, round, USDA choice, boneless	lb	3.34	4/93	16r
Steak, sirloin, graded & ungraded, ex USDA prime & choice	lb	4.19	4/93	16r
Steak, sirloin, USDA choice, boneless	lb	4.46	4/93	16r
Steak, T-bone	lb	5.47	4Q 92	4c
Steak, T-bone, USDA choice, bone-in	lb	5.25	4/93	16r
Strawberries, dry pint	12 oz	0.92	4/93	16r
Sugar, cane or beet	4 lb	1.43	4Q 92	4c
Sugar, white	lb	0.39	4/93	16r
Sugar, white, 33-80 oz pk	lb	0.38	4/93	16r
Tomatoes, field grown	lb	0.88	4/93	16r
Tomatoes, Hunt's or Del Monte	14.5-oz can	0.55	4Q 92	4c
Tuna, chunk, light	6.125-6.5 oz can	0.53	4Q 92	4c
Tuna, chunk, light	lb	1.79	4/93	16r
Turkey, frozen, whole	lb	1.04	4/93	16r
Yogurt, natural, fruit flavored	1/2 pint	0.57	4/93	16r
Health Care				
ACCRA Index, Health Care		91.40	4Q 92	4c
Analgesic, Aspirin, Bayer, 325 mg tablets	100	4.39	4Q 92	4c
Childbirth, cesarean, hospital		5034	91	62r
Childbirth, cesarean, physician's fee		2053	91	62r
Childbirth, normal, hospital		2712	91	62r
Childbirth, normal, physician's fee		1492	91	62r

Values are in dollars or fractions of dollars. In the column headed *Ref*, references are shown to sources. Each reference is followed by a letter. These refer to the geographical level for which data were reported: s=State, r=Region, and c=City or metro. The abbreviation *ex* is used to mean *except* or *excluding*; *exp* stands for expenditures. For other abbreviations and further explanations, please see the Introduction.

Winston-Salem, NC - continued

Item	Per	Value	Date	Ref.
Health Care				
Dentist's fee, adult teeth cleaning and periodic oral exam	visit	45.60	4Q 92	4c
Doctor's fee, routine exam, established patient	visit	35.80	4Q 92	4c
Hospital care, semiprivate room	day	240.00	90	27c
Hospital care, semiprivate room	day	227.00	4Q 92	4c
Medical insurance premium, per employee, small group comprehensive	month	267.40	10/91	25c
Medical plan per employee	year	3495	91	45r
Mental health care, exp	capita	37.60-53.67	90	38s
Mental health care, exp, state mental health agency	capita	45.66	90	38s
Mental health care, hospital psychiatric services, non-Federal, exp	capita	12.05	88	38s
Mental health care, mental health organization, multiservice, exp	capita	29.54	88	38s
Mental health care, psychiatric hospitals, private, exp	capita	15.07	88	38s
Mental health care, psychiatric out-patient clinics, freestanding, exp	capita	0.11	88	38s
Mental health care, state and county mental hospitals, exp	capita	26.36	88	38s
Mental health care, VA medical centers, exp	capita	2.23	88	38s
Physician fee, family practice, first-visit		75.00	91	62r
Physician fee, family practice, revisit		34.00	91	62r
Physician fee, general practice, first-visit		61.00	91	62r
Physician fee, general practice, revisit		32.00	91	62r
Physician fee, general surgeon, first-visit		64.00	91	62r
Physician fee, general surgeon, revisit		40.00	91	62r
Physician fee, internal medicine, first-visit		98.00	91	62r
Physician fee, internal medicine, revisit		40.00	91	62r
Physician fee, median, neurosurgeon, first-visit		130.00	91	62r
Physician fee, median, nonsurgical specialist, first-visit		95.00	91	62r
Physician fee, median, orthopedic surgeon, first-visit		91.00	91	62r
Physician fee, median, plastic surgeon, first-visit		66.00	91	62r
Physician fee, median, surgical specialist, first-visit		62.00	91	62r
Physician fee, neurosurgeon, revisit		50.00	91	62r
Physician fee, nonsurgical specialist, revisit		40.00	91	62r
Physician fee, obstetrics/gynecology, first-visit		64.00	91	62r
Physician fee, obstetrics/gynecology, revisit		41.00	91	62r
Physician fee, orthopedic surgeon, revisit		40.00	91	62r
Physician fee, pediatrician, first-visit		49.00	91	62r
Physician fee, pediatrician, revisit		33.00	91	62r
Physician fee, plastic surgeon, revisit		43.00	91	62r
Physician fee, surgical specialist, revisit		37.00	91	62r
Substance abuse, hospital ancillary charge	incident	1090	90	70s
Substance abuse, hospital physician charge	incident	460	90	70s
Substance abuse, hospital room and board	incident	4880	90	70s
Household Goods				
Appliance repair, home, service call, washing machine	min labor charge	31.19	4Q 92	4c
Laundry detergent, Tide Ultra, Bold, or Cheer	42 oz	2.67	4Q 92	4c
Tissues, facial, Kleenex brand	175-count box	0.99	4Q 92	4c
Housing				
ACCRA Index, Housing		100.30	4Q 92	4c
House, 1,800 sq ft, 8,000 sq ft lot, new, urban	total	118600	4Q 92	4c

Winston-Salem, NC - continued

Item	Per	Value	Date	Ref.
Housing - continued				
House payment, principal and interest, 25% down payment	month	648	4Q 92	4c
Mortgage rate, incl. points & origination fee, 30-year fixed or adjustable rate	percent	7.92	4Q 92	4c
Rent, apartment, 2 bedrooms - 1-1/2 to 2 baths, unfurnished, 950 sq ft, water	month	422	4Q 92	4c
Insurance and Pensions				
Auto insurance, private passenger	year	522.39	91	63s
Personal Goods				
Shampoo, Alberto VO5	15 oz	1.05	4Q 92	4c
Toothpaste, Crest or Colgate	6-7 oz	1.87	4Q 92	4c
Personal Services				
Dry cleaning, man's 2-piece suit		6.56	4Q 92	4c
Haircare, woman's shampoo, trim and blow-dry		20.80	4Q 92	4c
Haircut, man's barbershop, no styling		7.60	4Q 92	4c
Restaurant Food				
Chicken, fried, thigh and drumstick		1.99	4Q 92	4c
Hamburger with cheese	1/4 lb	1.81	4Q 92	4c
Pizza, Pizza Hut or Pizza Inn, cheese, thin crust	12-13 in	7.99	4Q 92	4c
Taxes				
Tax, cigarette	pack	5	91	77s
Tax, gasoline	gal	21.90	91	77s
Taxes, state	capita	1165	91	77s
Transportation				
ACCRA Index, Transportation		95.90	4Q 92	4c
Bus fare	one-way	0.60	3/93	2c
Driver's license fee		15.00	12/90	43s
Tire balance, computer or spin balance, front	wheel	6.30	4Q 92	4c
Vehicle registration and license plate	year	35.00	93	50s
Travel				
Business travel	day	193.00	4/93	89r
Utilities				
ACCRA Index, Utilities		107.50	4Q 92	4c
Electricity	mil Btu	18.74	90	64s
Electricity, all electric, 1,800 sq ft living area new home	month	119.35	4Q 92	4c

Worcester, MA

Item	Per	Value	Date	Ref.
Child Care				
Child care fee, average, center	hour	2.18	90	65r
Child care fee, average, nonregulated family day care	hour	1.83	90	65r
Child care fee, average, regulated family day care	hour	2.02	90	65r
Communications				
Long-distance telephone service, day, initial minute, 0-100 miles	min	0.18-0.31	91	12s
Long-distance telephone service, day, additional minute, 0-100 miles	min	0.08-0.13	91	12s
Long-distance telephone service, evenings/weekends, 0-100 mi, initial minute	min	0.67-0.12	91	12s
Long-distance telephone service, evenings/weekends, 0-100 mi, additional minute	min	0.04-0.05	91	12s
Education				
Board, 4-yr private college/university	year	2698	91	22s
Board, 4-yr public college/university	year	1741	91	22s
Expenditures, local gov't, public elementary/secondary	pupil	6687	92	20s
Room, 4-year private college/university	year	2945	91	22s
Room, 4-year public college/university	year	2144	91	22s
Tuition, 2-year private college/university	year	7750	91	22s

Values are in dollars or fractions of dollars. In the column headed *Ref*, references are shown to sources. Each reference is followed by a letter. These refer to the geographical level for which data were reported: s = State, r = Region, and c = City or metro. The abbreviation *ex* is used to mean *except* or *excluding*; *exp* stands for *expenditures*. For other abbreviations and further explanations, please see the Introduction.

Worcester, MA - continued

Item	Per	Value	Date	Ref.
Education				
Tuition, 2-year public college/university	year	1528	91	22s
Tuition, 4-year private college/university	year	12446	91	22s
Tuition, 4-year public college/university, in-state	year	2580	91	22s
Energy and Fuels				
Coal	mil Btu	1.77	90	64s
Energy	mil Btu	10.57	90	64s
Energy exp/householder, 1-family unit	year	588	90	28r
Energy exp/householder, <1,000 sq ft heating area	year	477	90	28r
Energy exp/householder, 1,000-1,999 sq ft heating area	year	517	90	28r
Energy exp/householder, 2,000+ sq ft heating area	year	630	90	28r
Energy exp/householder, mobile home	year	412	90	28r
Energy exp/householder, multifamily	year	498	90	28r
Gas, natural	mil Btu	5.55	90	64s
Gas, natural	000 cu ft	8.11	91	46s
Gas, natural, exp	year	741	91	46s
Gasoline, unleaded regular	mil Btu	9.53	90	64s
Entertainment				
Miniature golf admission	adult	6.18	92	1r
Miniature golf admission	child	5.14	92	1r
Waterpark admission	adult	11.00	92	1r
Waterpark admission	child	8.55	92	1r
Funerals				
Casket, 18-gauge steel, velvet interior		1853.42	91	24r
Cosmetology, hair care, etc.		98.33	91	24r
Embalming		273.94	91	24r
Facility use for ceremony		196.06	91	24r
Hearse, local		145.67	91	24r
Limousine, local		131.07	91	24r
Remains to funeral home, transfer		135.24	91	24r
Service charge, professional		843.16	91	24r
Vault, concrete, non-metallic liner		709.14	91	24r
Viewing facilities, use		229.85	91	24r
Groceries				
Apples, Red Delicious	lb	0.85	4/93	16r
Bacon	lb	2.12	4/93	16r
Bananas	lb	0.54	4/93	16r
Bread, white, pan	lb	0.81	4/93	16r
Butter	lb	2.02	4/93	16r
Carrots, short trimmed and topped	lb	0.51	4/93	16r
Chicken, fresh, whole	lb	1.04	4/93	16r
Chicken breast, bone-in	lb	2.21	4/93	16r
Chicken legs, bone-in	lb	1.16	4/93	16r
Chuck roast, USDA choice, boneless	lb	2.82	4/93	16r
Coffee, 100% ground roast, all sizes	lb	2.66	4/93	16r
Cucumbers	lb	0.85	4/93	16r
Eggs, Grade A large	doz	1.15	4/93	16r
Grapefruit	lb	0.45	4/93	16r
Grapes, Thompson Seedless	lb	1.52	4/93	16r
Ground beef, lean and extra lean	lb	2.36	4/93	16r
Ground chuck, 100% beef	lb	2.02	4/93	16r
Honey, jar	8 oz	0.96-1.75	92	5r
Honey, jar	lb	1.50-3.00	92	5r
Honey, squeeze bear	12-oz	1.50-1.99	92	5r
Ice cream, prepackaged, bulk, regular	1/2 gal	2.80	4/93	16r
Lemons	lb	0.96	4/93	16r
Lettuce, iceberg	lb	0.95	4/93	16r
Margarine, stick	lb	0.81	4/93	16r
Milk, fresh, whole, fortified	1/2 gal	1.30	4/93	16r
Oranges, navel	lb	0.56	4/93	16r
Peanut butter, creamy, all sizes	lb	1.88	4/93	16r
Pork chops, center cut, bone-in	lb	3.34	4/93	16r
Potato chips	16 oz	2.88	4/93	16r
Potatoes, white	lb	0.37	4/93	16r
Rib roast, USDA choice, bone-in	lb	4.94	4/93	16r
Round roast, USDA choice, boneless	lb	3.17	4/93	16r

Worcester, MA - continued

Item	Per	Value	Date	Ref.
Groceries - continued				
Shortening, vegetable oil blends	lb	0.98	4/93	16r
Spaghetti and macaroni	lb	0.82	4/93	16r
Steak, round, graded & ungraded, ex USDA prime & choice	lb	4.04	4/93	16r
Steak, round, USDA choice, boneless	lb	3.90	4/93	16r
Steak, sirloin, USDA choice, boneless	lb	4.97	4/93	16r
Strawberries, dry pint	12 oz	0.90	4/93	16r
Sugar, white	lb	0.50	4/93	16r
Sugar, white, 33-80 oz pk	lb	0.41	4/93	16r
Tomatoes, field grown	lb	1.23	4/93	16r
Tuna, chunk, light	lb	2.22	4/93	16r
Turkey, frozen, whole	lb	1.04	4/93	16r
Health Care				
Childbirth, cesarean, hospital		5826	91	62r
Childbirth, cesarean, physician's fee		2053	91	62r
Childbirth, normal, hospital		2964	91	62r
Childbirth, normal, physician's fee		1492	91	62r
Health care spending, state	capita	3031	3/93	84s
Medical plan per employee	year	3958	91	45r
Mental health care, exp	capita	53.68-118.35	90	38s
Mental health care, exp, state mental health agency	capita	83.91	90	38s
Mental health care, hospital psychiatric services, non-Federal, exp	capita	22.67	88	38s
Mental health care, mental health organization, multiservice, exp	capita	36.07	88	38s
Mental health care, psychiatric hospitals, private, exp	capita	38.65	88	38s
Mental health care, psychiatric out-patient clinics, freestanding, exp	capita	4.41	88	38s
Mental health care, psychiatric partial-care organizations, freestanding, exp	capita	0.92	88	38s
Mental health care, state and county mental hospitals, exp	capita	30.59	88	38s
Mental health care, VA medical centers, exp	capita	21.14	88	38s
Substance abuse, hospital ancillary charge	incident	1310	90	70s
Substance abuse, hospital physician charge	incident	460	90	70s
Substance abuse, hospital room and board	incident	3450	90	70s
Insurance and Pensions				
Auto insurance, private passenger	year	912.83	91	63s
Taxes				
Tax, cigarette	pack	26	91	77s
Tax, gasoline	gal	21	91	77s
Taxes, state	capita	1615	91	77s
Transportation				
Driver's license fee		35.00	12/90	43s
Travel				
Business travel	day	165.00	4/93	89r
Utilities				
Electricity	mil Btu	25.93	90	64s

Yakima, WA

Item	Per	Value	Date	Ref.
Composite ACCRA index		100.50	4Q 92	4c
Alcoholic Beverages				
Beer, Miller Lite or Budweiser, 12-oz containers	6 pack	3.88	4Q 92	4c
Liquor, J & B Scotch	750 ml	17.95	4Q 92	4c
Wine, Gallo Chablis blanc, 1.5 liter	bottle	5.20	4Q 92	4c
Child Care				
Child care fee, average, center	hour	1.71	90	65r
Child care fee, average, nonregulated family day care	hour	1.32	90	65r

Values are in dollars or fractions of dollars. In the column headed *Ref*, references are shown to sources. Each reference is followed by a letter. These refer to the geographical level for which data were reported: s = State, r = Region, and c = City or metro. The abbreviation *ex* is used to mean *except* or *excluding*; *exp* stands for expenditures. For other abbreviations and further explanations, please see the Introduction.

Yakima, WA - continued

Item	Per	Value	Date	Ref.
Child Care				
Child care fee, average, regulated family day care	hour	1.86	90	65r
Clothing				
Jeans, man's denim		24.59	4Q 92	4c
Shirt, man's dress shirt		24.75	4Q 92	4c
Undervest, boy's size 10-14, cotton	3	4.45	4Q 92	4c
Communications				
Long-distance telephone service, day, initial minute, 0-100 miles	min	0.15-0.37	91	12s
Long-distance telephone service, day, additional minute, 0-100 miles	min	0.01-0.03	91	12s
Long-distance telephone service, evenings/weekends, 0-100 mi, initial minute	min	0.05-0.19	91	12s
Long-distance telephone service, evenings/weekends, 0-100 mi, additional minute	min	0.00-0.01	91	12s
Newspaper subscription, daily and Sunday home delivery, large-city	month	8.50	4Q 92	4c
Telephone, flat rate	month	9.75	91	11c
Telephone bill, family of four	month	14.58	4Q 92	4c
Education				
Board, 4-yr private college/university	year	1811	91	22s
Board, 4-yr public college/university	year	1539	91	22s
Expenditures, local gov't, public elementary/secondary	pupil	5317	92	20s
Room, 4-year private college/university	year	1885	91	22s
Room, 4-year public college/university	year	1698	91	22s
Tuition, 2-year private college/university	year	6743	91	22s
Tuition, 2-year public college/university	year	844	91	22s
Tuition, 4-year private college/university	year	9463	91	22s
Tuition, 4-year public college/university, in-state	year	1823	91	22s
Energy and Fuels				
Energy	mil Btu	7.39	90	64s
Energy, combined forms, 1,800 sq ft heating area	month	99.88	4Q 92	4c
Energy exp/householder, 1-family unit	year	362	90	28r
Energy exp/householder, <1,000 sq ft heating area	year	254	90	28r
Energy exp/householder, 1,000-1,999 sq ft heating area	year	358	90	28r
Energy exp/householder, 2,000+ sq ft heating area	year	467	90	28r
Energy exp/householder, mobile home	year	390	90	28r
Energy exp/householder, multifamily	year	252	90	28r
Gas, natural	mil Btu	3.60	90	64s
Gas, natural	000 cu ft	4.68	91	46s
Gas, natural, exp	year	440	91	46s
Gasoline, motor	gal	1.22	4Q 92	4c
Gasoline, unleaded regular	mil Btu	9.45	90	64s
Entertainment				
Bowling, evening rate	game	1.78	4Q 92	4c
Miniature golf admission	adult	6.18	92	1r
Miniature golf admission	child	5.14	92	1r
Monopoly game, Parker Brothers', No. 9		9.84	4Q 92	4c
Movie	admission	5.50	4Q 92	4c
Tennis balls, yellow, Wilson or Penn, 3	can	2.19	4Q 92	4c
Waterpark admission	adult	11.00	92	1r
Waterpark admission	child	8.55	92	1r
Funerals				
Casket, 18-gauge steel, velvet interior		1781.09	91	24r
Cosmetology, hair care, etc.		84.64	91	24r
Embalming		207.41	91	24r
Facility use for ceremony		205.76	91	24r
Hearse, local		105.14	91	24r
Limousine, local		83.21	91	24r
Remains to funeral home, transfer		113.82	91	24r
Service charge, professional		626.33	91	24r

Yakima, WA - continued

Item	Per	Value	Date	Ref.
Funerals - continued				
Vault, concrete, non-metallic liner		599.54	91	24r
Viewing facilities, use	.	85.81	91	24r
Goods and Services				
ACCRA Index, Miscellaneous Goods and Services		99.70	4Q 92	4c
Groceries				
ACCRA Index, Groceries		109.00	4Q 92	4c
Apples, Red Delicious	lb	0.80	4/93	16r
Babyfood, strained vegetables, lowest price	4-4.5 oz jar	0.33	4Q 92	4c
Bacon	lb	1.79	4/93	16r
Bananas	lb	0.43	4Q 92	4c
Bananas	lb	0.53	4/93	16r
Bologna, all beef or mixed	lb	2.67	4/93	16r
Bread, white	24 oz	0.68	4Q 92	4c
Bread, white, pan	lb	0.81	4/93	16r
Carrots, short trimmed and topped	lb	0.39	4/93	16r
Cheese, Kraft grated Parmesan	8-oz canister	3.75	4Q 92	4c
Chicken, fresh, whole	lb	0.94	4/93	16r
Chicken, fryer, whole	lb	0.91	4Q 92	4c
Chicken breast, bone-in	lb	2.19	4/93	16r
Chuck roast, graded and ungraded, ex USDA prime and choice	lb	2.26	4/93	16r
Cigarettes, Winston	carton	19.58	4Q 92	4c
Coffee, 100% ground roast, all sizes	lb	2.33	4/93	16r
Coffee, vacuum-packed	13-oz can	2.48	4Q 92	4c
Corn, frozen	10 oz	0.68	4Q 92	4c
Corn Flakes, Kellogg's or Post Toasties	18 oz	2.25	4Q 92	4c
Eggs, Grade A large	doz	0.89	4Q 92	4c
Eggs, Grade AA large	doz	1.18	4/93	16r
Flour, white, all purpose	lb	0.22	4/93	16r
Grapefruit	lb	0.52	4/93	16r
Grapes, Thompson Seedless	lb	1.50	4/93	16r
Ground beef, 100% beef	lb	1.44	4/93	16r
Ground beef, lean and extra lean	lb	2.34	4/93	16r
Ground beef or hamburger	lb	1.43	4Q 92	4c
Ham, boneless, excluding canned	lb	2.56	4/93	16r
Honey, jar	8 oz	0.89-1.00	92	5r
Honey, jar	lb	1.35-1.97	92	5r
Honey, squeeze bear	12-oz	1.19-1.50	92	5r
Ice cream, prepackaged, bulk, regular	1/2 gal	2.40	4/93	16r
Lemons	lb	0.81	4/93	16r
Lettuce, iceberg	head	0.88	4Q 92	4c
Lettuce, iceberg	lb	0.84	4/93	16r
Margarine, Blue Bonnet or Parkay cubes	lb	0.71	4Q 92	4c
Margarine, stick	lb	0.81	4/93	16r
Milk, whole	1/2 gal	1.42	4Q 92	4c
Orange juice, Minute Maid frozen	12-oz can	1.57	4Q 92	4c
Oranges, navel	lb	0.48	4/93	16r
Peaches	29-oz can	1.48	4Q 92	4c
Peas Sweet, Del Monte or Green Giant	15-17 oz can	0.71	4Q 92	4c
Pork chops, center cut, bone-in	lb	3.25	4/93	16r
Potato chips	16 oz	2.89	4/93	16r
Potatoes, white	lb	0.38	4/93	16r
Potatoes, white or red	10-lb sack	1.61	4Q 92	4c
Round roast, graded & ungraded, ex USDA prime & choice	lb	3.00	4/93	16r
Round roast, USDA choice, boneless	lb	3.16	4/93	16r
Sausage, Jimmy Dean, 100% pork	lb	3.28	4Q 92	4c
Shortening, vegetable oil blends	lb	0.86	4/93	16r
Shortening, vegetable, Crisco	3-lb can	2.73	4Q 92	4c
Soft drink, Coca Cola	2 liter	1.44	4Q 92	4c
Spaghetti and macaroni	lb	0.84	4/93	16r

Values are in dollars or fractions of dollars. In the column headed *Ref*, references are shown to sources. Each reference is followed by a letter. These refer to the geographical level for which data were reported: s=State, r=Region, and c=City or metro. The abbreviation *ex* is used to mean *except* or *excluding*; *exp* stands for expenditures. For other abbreviations and further explanations, please see the Introduction.

Yakima, WA - continued

Item	Per	Value	Date	Ref.
Groceries				
Steak, round, graded & ungraded, ex USDA prime & choice	lb	3.34	4/93	16r
Steak, round, USDA choice, boneless	lb	3.24	4/93	16r
Steak, sirloin, graded & ungraded, ex USDA prime & choice	lb	3.75	4/93	16r
Steak, sirloin, USDA choice, boneless	lb	4.49	4/93	16r
Steak, T-bone	lb	4.91	4Q 92	4c
Sugar, cane or beet	4 lb	1.14	4Q 92	4c
Sugar, white	lb	0.41	4/93	16r
Sugar, white, 33-80 oz pk	lb	0.38	4/93	16r
Tomatoes, field grown	lb	1.01	4/93	16r
Tomatoes, Hunt's or Del Monte	14.5-oz can	0.63	4Q 92	4c
Tuna, chunk, light	6.125-6.5 oz can	0.92	4Q 92	4c
Turkey, frozen, whole	lb	1.04	4/93	16r
Health Care				
ACCRA Index, Health Care		106.90	4Q 92	4c
Analgesic, Aspirin, Bayer, 325 mg tablets	100	5.28	4Q 92	4c
Childbirth, cesarean, hospital		5533	91	62r
Childbirth, cesarean, physician's fee		2053	91	62r
Childbirth, normal, hospital		2745	91	62r
Childbirth, normal, physician's fee		1492	91	62r
Dentist's fee, adult teeth cleaning and periodic oral exam	visit	57.80	4Q 92	4c
Doctor's fee, routine exam, established patient	visit	35.30	4Q 92	4c
Hospital care, semiprivate room	day	285.86	90	27c
Hospital care, semiprivate room	day	310.00	4Q 92	4c
Medical insurance premium, per employee, small group comprehensive	month	284.70	10/91	25c
Medical plan per employee	year	3421	91	45r
Mental health care, exp	capita	37.60-53.67	90	38s
Physician fee, family practice, first-visit		111.00	91	62r
Physician fee, family practice, revisit		45.00	91	62r
Physician fee, general practice, first-visit		100.00	91	62r
Physician fee, general practice, revisit		40.00	91	62r
Physician fee, internal medicine, first-visit		137.00	91	62r
Physician fee, internal medicine, revisit		48.00	91	62r
Physician fee, median, neurosurgeon, first-visit		157.00	91	62r
Physician fee, median, nonsurgical specialist, first-visit		131.00	91	62r
Physician fee, median, orthopedic surgeon, first-visit		124.00	91	62r
Physician fee, median, plastic surgeon, first-visit		88.00	91	62r
Physician fee, median, surgical specialist, first-visit		100.00	91	62r
Physician fee, neurosurgeon, revisit		51.00	91	62r
Physician fee, nonsurgical specialist, revisit		47.00	91	62r
Physician fee, obstetrics/gynecology, first-visit		95.00	91	62r
Physician fee, obstetrics/gynecology, revisit		50.00	91	62r
Physician fee, orthopedic surgeon, revisit		51.00	91	62r
Physician fee, pediatrician, first-visit		81.00	91	62r
Physician fee, pediatrician, revisit		42.00	91	62r
Physician fee, plastic surgeon, revisit		48.00	91	62r
Physician fee, surgical specialist, revisit		49.00	91	62r
Substance abuse, hospital ancillary charge	incident	1360	90	70s
Substance abuse, hospital physician charge	incident	150	90	70s
Substance abuse, hospital room and board	incident	4200	90	70s
Household Goods				
Appliance repair, home, service call, washing machine	min labor charge	34.28	4Q 92	4c

Yakima, WA - continued

Item	Per	Value	Date	Ref.
Household Goods - continued				
Laundry detergent, Tide Ultra, Bold, or Cheer	42 oz	3.88	4Q 92	4c
Tissues, facial, Kleenex brand	175-count box	1.43	4Q 92	4c
Housing				
ACCRA Index, Housing		101.00	4Q 92	4c
House, 1,800 sq ft, 8,000 sq ft lot, new, urban	total	113000	4Q 92	4c
House payment, principal and interest, 25% down payment	month	629	4Q 92	4c
Mortgage rate, incl. points & origination fee, 30-year fixed or adjustable rate	percent	8.12	4Q 92	4c
Rent, apartment, 2 bedrooms - 1-1/2 to 2 baths, unfurnished, 950 sq ft, water	month	480	4Q 92	4c
Rental unit, 1 bedroom	month	444	93	23c
Rental unit, 2 bedroom	month	523	93	23c
Rental unit, 3 bedroom	month	655	93	23c
Rental unit, 4 bedroom	month	735	93	23c
Rental unit, efficiency	month	366	93	23c
Insurance and Pensions				
Auto insurance, private passenger	year	627.71	91	63s
Personal Goods				
Shampoo, Alberto VO5	15 oz	1.04	4Q 92	4c
Toothpaste, Crest or Colgate	6-7 oz	1.64	4Q 92	4c
Personal Services				
Dry cleaning, man's 2-piece suit		6.43	4Q 92	4c
Haircare, woman's shampoo, trim and blow-dry		19.00	4Q 92	4c
Haircut, man's barbershop, no styling		8.10	4Q 92	4c
Restaurant Food				
Chicken, fried, thigh and drumstick		2.10	4Q 92	4c
Hamburger with cheese	1/4 lb	2.20	4Q 92	4c
Pizza, Pizza Hut or Pizza Inn, cheese, thin crust	12-13 in	9.37	4Q 92	4c
Taxes				
Tax, cigarette	pack	34	91	77s
Tax, gasoline	gal	23	91	77s
Taxes, state	capita	1592	91	77s
Transportation				
ACCRA Index, Transportation		97.00	4Q 92	4c
Bus fare	one-way	0.35	3/93	2c
Bus fare, up to 10 miles	one-way	0.35	4Q 92	4c
Driver's license fee		14.00	12/90	43s
Tire balance, computer or spin balance, front	wheel	6.45	4Q 92	4c
Travel				
Business travel	day	178.00	4/93	89r
Utilities				
ACCRA Index, Utilities		89.80	4Q 92	4c
Electricity	mil Btu	10.03	90	64s
Electricity, all electric, 1,800 sq ft living area new home	month	99.88	4Q 92	4c
Electricity, winter, 250 KWh	month	12.74	92	55c
Electricity, winter, 500 KWh	month	21.73	92	55c
Electricity, winter, 750 KWh	month	32.48	92	55c
Electricity, winter, 1000 KWh	month	44.41	92	55c

York, PA

Item	Per	Value	Date	Ref.
Child Care				
Child care fee, average, center	hour	2.18	90	65r

Values are in dollars or fractions of dollars. In the column headed *Ref*, references are shown to sources. Each reference is followed by a letter. These refer to the geographical level for which data were reported: s = State, r = Region, and c = City or metro. The abbreviation *ex* is used to mean *except* or *excluding*; *exp* stands for *expenditures*. For other abbreviations and further explanations, please see the Introduction.

York, PA - continued

Item	Per	Value	Date	Ref.
Child Care				
Child care fee, average, nonregulated family day care	hour	1.83	90	65r
Child care fee, average, regulated family day care	hour	2.02	90	65r
Communications				
Long-distance telephone service, day, initial minute, 0-100 miles	min	0.15-0.29	91	12s
Long-distance telephone service, day, additional minute, 0-100 miles	min	0.06-0.22	91	12s
Long-distance telephone service, evenings/weekends, 0-100 mi, initial minute	min	0.06-0.14	91	12s
Long-distance telephone service, evenings/weekends, 0-100 mi, additional minute	min	0.03-0.11	91	12s
Education				
Board, 4-yr private college/university	year	2019	91	22s
Board, 4-yr public college/university	year	1656	91	22s
Expenditures, local gov't, public elementary/secondary	pupil	6980	92	20s
Room, 4-year private college/university	year	2179	91	22s
Room, 4-year public college/university	year	1719	91	22s
Tuition, 2-year private college/university	year	6314	91	22s
Tuition, 2-year public college/university	year	1505	91	22s
Tuition, 4-year private college/university	year	9848	91	22s
Tuition, 4-year public college/university, in-state	year	3401	91	22s
Energy and Fuels				
Coal	mil Btu	1.57	90	64s
Energy	mil Btu	8.63	90	64s
Energy exp/householder, 1-family unit	year	588	90	28r
Energy exp/householder, <1,000 sq ft heating area	year	477	90	28r
Energy exp/householder, 1,000-1,999 sq ft heating area	year	517	90	28r
Energy exp/householder, 2,000+ sq ft heating area	year	630	90	28r
Energy exp/householder, mobile home	year	412	90	28r
Energy exp/householder, multifamily	year	498	90	28r
Gas, natural	mil Btu	5.24	90	64s
Gas, natural	000 cu ft	6.76	91	46s
Gas, natural, exp	year	703	91	46s
Gasoline, unleaded regular	mil Btu	9.35	90	64s
Funerals				
Casket, 18-gauge steel, velvet interior		1811.58	91	24r
Cosmetology, hair care, etc.		111.08	91	24r
Embalming		329.42	91	24r
Facility use for ceremony		201.29	91	24r
Hearse, local		135.27	91	24r
Limousine, local		127.24	91	24r
Remains to funeral home, transfer		103.98	91	24r
Service charge, professional		724.98	91	24r
Vault, concrete, non-metallic liner		766.71	91	24r
Viewing facilities, use		260.60	91	24r
Groceries				
Apples, Red Delicious	lb	0.85	4/93	16r
Bacon	lb	2.12	4/93	16r
Bananas	lb	0.54	4/93	16r
Bread, white, pan	lb	0.81	4/93	16r
Butter	lb	2.02	4/93	16r
Carrots, short trimmed and topped	lb	0.51	4/93	16r
Chicken, fresh, whole	lb	1.04	4/93	16r
Chicken breast, bone-in	lb	2.21	4/93	16r
Chicken legs, bone-in	lb	1.16	4/93	16r
Chuck roast, USDA choice, boneless	lb	2.82	4/93	16r
Coffee, 100% ground roast, all sizes	lb	2.66	4/93	16r
Cucumbers	lb	0.85	4/93	16r
Eggs, Grade A large	doz	1.15	4/93	16r
Grapefruit	lb	0.45	4/93	16r
Grapes, Thompson Seedless	lb	1.52	4/93	16r

York, PA - continued

Item	Per	Value	Date	Ref.
Groceries - continued				
Ground beef, lean and extra lean	lb	2.36	4/93	16r
Ground chuck, 100% beef	lb	2.02	4/93	16r
Honey, jar	8 oz	0.96-1.75	92	5r
Honey, jar	lb	1.50-3.00	92	5r
Honey, squeeze bear	12-oz	1.50-1.99	92	5r
Ice cream, prepackaged, bulk, regular	1/2 gal	2.80	4/93	16r
Lemons	lb	0.96	4/93	16r
Lettuce, iceberg	lb	0.95	4/93	16r
Margarine, stick	lb	0.81	4/93	16r
Milk, fresh, whole, fortified	1/2 gal	1.30	4/93	16r
Oranges, navel	lb	0.56	4/93	16r
Peanut butter, creamy, all sizes	lb	1.88	4/93	16r
Pork chops, center cut, bone-in	lb	3.34	4/93	16r
Potato chips	16 oz	2.88	4/93	16r
Potatoes, white	lb	0.37	4/93	16r
Rib roast, USDA choice, bone-in	lb	4.94	4/93	16r
Round roast, USDA choice, boneless	lb	3.17	4/93	16r
Shortening, vegetable oil blends	lb	0.98	4/93	16r
Spaghetti and macaroni	lb	0.82	4/93	16r
Steak, round, graded & ungraded, ex USDA prime & choice	lb	4.04	4/93	16r
Steak, round, USDA choice, boneless	lb	3.90	4/93	16r
Steak, sirloin, USDA choice, boneless	lb	4.97	4/93	16r
Strawberries, dry pint	12 oz	0.90	4/93	16r
Sugar, white	lb	0.50	4/93	16r
Sugar, white, 33-80 oz pk	lb	0.41	4/93	16r
Tomatoes, field grown	lb	1.23	4/93	16r
Tuna, chunk, light	lb	2.22	4/93	16r
Turkey, frozen, whole	lb	1.04	4/93	16r
Health Care				
Childbirth, cesarean, hospital		5826	91	62r
Childbirth, cesarean, physician's fee		2053	91	62r
Childbirth, normal, hospital		2964	91	62r
Childbirth, normal, physician's fee		1492	91	62r
Medical plan per employee	year	3942	91	45r
Mental health care, exp	capita	53.68-118.35	90	38s
Mental health care, exp, state mental health agency	capita	56.85	90	38s
Mental health care, hospital psychiatric services, non-Federal, exp	capita	22.11	88	38s
Mental health care, mental health organization, multiservice, exp	capita	21.01	88	38s
Mental health care, psychiatric hospitals, private, exp	capita	26.48	88	38s
Mental health care, psychiatric out-patient clinics, freestanding, exp	capita	4.17	88	38s
Mental health care, psychiatric partial-care organizations, freestanding, exp	capita	0.94	88	38s
Mental health care, state and county mental hospitals, exp	capita	37.11	88	38s
Mental health care, VA medical centers, exp	capita	9.77	88	38s
Prescription drug co-pay, Medicaid	month	6.00	91	21s
Substance abuse, hospital ancillary charge	incident	720	90	70s
Substance abuse, hospital physician charge	incident	210	90	70s
Substance abuse, hospital room and board	incident	5400	90	70s
Insurance and Pensions				
Auto insurance, private passenger	year	683.57	91	63s
Taxes				
Tax, cigarette	pack	31	91	77s
Tax, gasoline	gal	12	91	77s
Taxes, state	capita	1089	91	77s
Transportation				
Driver's license fee		22.00	12/90	43s
Travel				
Business travel	day	165.00	4/93	89r

Values are in dollars or fractions of dollars. In the column headed *Ref*, references are shown to sources. Each reference is followed by a letter. These refer to the geographical level for which data were reported: s = State, r = Region, and c = City or metro. The abbreviation *ex* is used to mean *except* or *excluding*; *exp* stands for expenditures. For other abbreviations and further explanations, please see the Introduction.

York, PA - continued

Item	Per	Value	Date	Ref.
Utilities				
Electricity	mil Btu	22.46	90	64s

Youngstown, OH

Item	Per	Value	Date	Ref.
Composite ACCRA index		95.20	4Q 92	4c
Alcoholic Beverages				
Beer, Miller Lite or Budweiser, 12-oz containers	6 pack	3.99	4Q 92	4c
Liquor, J & B Scotch	750 ml	18.30	4Q 92	4c
Wine, Gallo Chablis blanc, 1.5 liter	bottle	5.49	4Q 92	4c
Child Care				
Child care fee, average, center	hour	1.63	90	65r
Child care fee, average, nonregulated family day care	hour	1.83	90	65r
Child care fee, average, regulated family day care	hour	1.42	90	65r
Clothing				
Jeans, man's denim		24.99	4Q 92	4c
Shirt, man's dress shirt		23.40	4Q 92	4c
Undervest, boy's size 10-14, cotton	3	3.52	4Q 92	4c
Communications				
Long-distance telephone service, day, initial minute, 0-100 miles	min	0.26-0.43	91	12s
Long-distance telephone service, day, additional minute, 0-100 miles	min	0.14-0.24	91	12s
Long-distance telephone service, evenings/weekends, 0-100 mi, initial minute	min	0.11-0.17	91	12s
Long-distance telephone service, evenings/weekends, 0-100 mi, additional minute	min	0.06-0.10	91	12s
Newspaper subscription, daily and Sunday home delivery, large-city	month	8.70	4Q 92	4c
Telephone bill, family of four	month	20.55	4Q 92	4c
Education				
Board, 4-yr private college/university	year	1872	91	22s
Board, 4-yr public college/university	year	1742	91	22s
Expenditures, local gov't, public elementary/secondary	pupil	5451	92	20s
Room, 4-year private college/university	year	1695	91	22s
Room, 4-year public college/university	year	2259	91	22s
Tuition, 2-year private college/university	year	6093	91	22s
Tuition, 2-year public college/university	year	1768	91	22s
Tuition, 4-year private college/university	year	8729	91	22s
Tuition, 4-year public college/university, in-state	year	2622	91	22s
Energy and Fuels				
Coal	mil Btu	1.54	90	64s
Energy	mil Btu	8.32	90	64s
Energy, combined forms, 1,800 sq ft heating area	month	123.40	4Q 92	4c
Energy, exc electricity, 1,800 sq ft heating area	month	39.17	4Q 92	4c
Energy exp/householder, 1-family unit	year	471	90	28r
Energy exp/householder, <1,000 sq ft heating area	year	430	90	28r
Energy exp/householder, 1,000-1,999 sq ft heating area	year	481	90	28r
Energy exp/householder, 2,000+ sq ft heating area	year	473	90	28r
Energy exp/householder, mobile home	year	430	90	28r
Energy exp/householder, multifamily	year	461	90	28r
Gas, natural	mil Btu	4.54	90	64s
Gas, natural	000 cu ft	5.28	91	46s
Gas, natural, exp	year	606	91	46s
Gasoline, motor	gal	1.11	4Q 92	4c
Gasoline, unleaded regular	mil Btu	9.35	90	64s

Youngstown, OH - continued

Item	Per	Value	Date	Ref.
Entertainment				
Bowling, evening rate	game	1.80	4Q 92	4c
Miniature golf admission	adult	6.18	92	1r
Miniature golf admission	child	5.14	92	1r
Monopoly game, Parker Brothers', No. 9		10.17	4Q 92	4c
Movie	admission	5.50	4Q 92	4c
Tennis balls, yellow, Wilson or Penn, 3	can	2.56	4Q 92	4c
Waterpark admission	adult	11.00	92	1r
Waterpark admission	child	8.55	92	1r
Funerals				
Casket, 18-gauge steel, velvet interior		1926.72	91	24r
Cosmetology, hair care, etc.		97.64	91	24r
Embalming		249.14	91	24r
Facility use for ceremony		208.59	91	24r
Hearse, local		130.12	91	24r
Limousine, local		104.66	91	24r
Remains to funeral home, transfer		93.61	91	24r
Service charge, professional		724.62	91	24r
Vault, concrete, non-metallic liner		734.53	91	24r
Viewing facilities, use		236.06	91	24r
Goods and Services				
ACCRA Index, Miscellaneous Goods and Services		94.80	4Q 92	4c
Groceries				
ACCRA Index, Groceries		99.20	4Q 92	4c
Apples, Red Delicious	lb	0.77	4/93	16r
Babyfood, strained vegetables, lowest price	4-4.5 oz jar	0.30	4Q 92	4c
Bacon	lb	1.85	4/93	16r
Bananas	lb	0.36	4Q 92	4c
Bananas	lb	0.46	4/93	16r
Beef, stew, boneless	lb	2.53	4/93	16r
Bologna, all beef or mixed	lb	2.19	4/93	16r
Bread, white	24 oz	0.76	4Q 92	4c
Bread, white, pan	lb	0.78	4/93	16r
Butter	lb	1.50	4/93	16r
Cabbage	lb	0.40	4/93	16r
Carrots, short trimmed and topped	lb	0.45	4/93	16r
Cheese, Cheddar	lb	3.47	4/93	16r
Cheese, Kraft grated Parmesan	8-oz canister	3.18	4Q 92	4c
Chicken, fresh, whole	lb	0.84	4/93	16r
Chicken, fryer, whole	lb	0.84	4Q 92	4c
Chicken breast, bone-in	lb	1.94	4/93	16r
Chicken legs, bone-in	lb	1.02	4/93	16r
Chuck roast, graded and ungraded, ex USDA prime and choice	lb	2.43	4/93	16r
Chuck roast, USDA choice, bone-in	lb	2.11	4/93	16r
Chuck roast, USDA choice, boneless	lb	2.44	4/93	16r
Cigarettes, Winston	carton	16.29	4Q 92	4c
Coffee, 100% ground roast, all sizes	lb	2.47	4/93	16r
Coffee, vacuum-packed	13-oz can	2.40	4Q 92	4c
Cookies, chocolate chip	lb	2.73	4/93	16r
Corn, frozen	10 oz	0.73	4Q 92	4c
Corn Flakes, Kellogg's or Post Toasties	18 oz	2.02	4Q 92	4c
Eggs, Grade A large	doz	0.76	4Q 92	4c
Eggs, Grade A large	doz	0.93	4/93	16r
Flour, white, all purpose	lb	0.21	4/93	16r
Grapefruit	lb	0.45	4/93	16r
Grapes, Thompson Seedless	lb	1.46	4/93	16r
Ground beef, 100% beef	lb	1.63	4/93	16r
Ground beef, lean and extra lean	lb	2.08	4/93	16r
Ground beef or hamburger	lb	1.39	4Q 92	4c
Ground chuck, 100% beef	lb	1.94	4/93	16r
Ham, boneless, excluding canned	lb	2.21	4/93	16r
Honey, jar	8 oz	0.97-1.25	92	5r
Honey, jar	lb	1.25-2.25	92	5r
Honey, squeeze bear	12-oz	1.25-1.99	92	5r
Ice cream, prepackaged, bulk, regular	1/2 gal	2.41	4/93	16r

Values are in dollars or fractions of dollars. In the column headed *Ref*, references are shown to sources. Each reference is followed by a letter. These refer to the geographical level for which data were reported: s=State, r=Region, and c=City or metro. The abbreviation *ex* is used to mean *except* or *excluding*; *exp* stands for expenditures. For other abbreviations and further explanations, please see the Introduction.

702

Youngstown, OH - continued

Item	Per	Value	Date	Ref.
Groceries				
Lemons	lb	0.82	4/93	16r
Lettuce, iceberg	head	1.01	4Q 92	4c
Lettuce, iceberg	lb	0.83	4/93	16r
Margarine, Blue Bonnet or Parkay cubes	lb	0.55	4Q 92	4c
Margarine, stick	lb	0.77	4/93	16r
Milk, whole	1/2 gal	1.35	4Q 92	4c
Orange juice, Minute Maid frozen	12-oz can	1.37	4Q 92	4c
Oranges, navel	lb	0.50	4/93	16r
Peaches	29-oz can	1.48	4Q 92	4c
Peanut butter, creamy, all sizes	lb	1.82	4/93	16r
Pears, Anjou	lb	0.85	4/93	16r
Peas Sweet, Del Monte or Green Giant	15-17 oz can	0.61	4Q 92	4c
Pork chops, center cut, bone-in	lb	3.17	4/93	16r
Potato chips	16 oz	2.68	4/93	16r
Potatoes, white	lb	0.26	4/93	16r
Potatoes, white or red	10-lb sack	1.54	4Q 92	4c
Round roast, graded & ungraded, ex USDA prime & choice	lb	2.88	4/93	16r
Round roast, USDA choice, boneless	lb	2.96	4/93	16r
Sausage, Jimmy Dean, 100% pork	lb	2.61	4Q 92	4c
Shortening, vegetable oil blends	lb	0.79	4/93	16r
Shortening, vegetable, Crisco	3-lb can	2.23	4Q 92	4c
Soft drink, Coca Cola	2 liter	0.98	4Q 92	4c
Spaghetti and macaroni	lb	0.76	4/93	16r
Steak, rib eye, USDA choice, boneless	lb	6.29	4/93	16r
Steak, round, USDA choice, boneless	lb	3.24	4/93	16r
Steak, sirloin, graded & ungraded, ex USDA prime & choice	lb	4.00	4/93	16r
Steak, sirloin, USDA choice, bone-in	lb	3.57	4/93	16r
Steak, sirloin, USDA choice, boneless	lb	4.17	4/93	16r
Steak, T-bone	lb	5.81	4Q 92	4c
Steak, T-bone, USDA choice, bone-in	lb	5.60	4/93	16r
Strawberries, dry pint	12 oz	0.90	4/93	16r
Sugar, cane or beet	4 lb	1.43	4Q 92	4c
Sugar, white	lb	0.36	4/93	16r
Sugar, white, 33-80 oz pk	lb	0.35	4/93	16r
Tomatoes, field grown	lb	0.99	4/93	16r
Tomatoes, Hunt's or Del Monte	14.5-oz can	0.71	4Q 92	4c
Tuna, chunk, light	6.125-6.5 oz can	0.71	4Q 92	4c
Tuna, chunk, light	lb	1.76	4/93	16r
Turkey, frozen, whole	lb	0.91	4/93	16r
Health Care				
ACCRA Index, Health Care		84.70	4Q 92	4c
Analgesic, Aspirin, Bayer, 325 mg tablets	100	5.10	4Q 92	4c
Childbirth, cesarean, hospital		4688	91	62r
Childbirth, cesarean, physician's fee		2053	91	62r
Childbirth, normal, hospital		2657	91	62r
Childbirth, normal, physician's fee		1492	91	62r
Dentist's fee, adult teeth cleaning and periodic oral exam	visit	33.40	4Q 92	4c
Doctor's fee, routine exam, established patient	visit	32.00	4Q 92	4c
Hospital care, semiprivate room	day	244.00	90	27c
Hospital care, semiprivate room	day	306.60	4Q 92	4c
Medical insurance premium, per employee, small group comprehensive	month	328.50	10/91	25c
Medical plan per employee	year	3443	91	45r
Mental health care, exp	capita	37.60-53.67	90	38s
Mental health care, exp, state mental health agency	capita	40.93	90	38s
Mental health care, hospital psychiatric services, non-Federal, exp	capita	15.03	88	38s

Youngstown, OH - continued

Item	Per	Value	Date	Ref.
Health Care - continued				
Mental health care, mental health organization, multiservice, exp	capita	14.46	88	38s
Mental health care, psychiatric hospitals, private, exp	capita	7.93	88	38s
Mental health care, psychiatric out-patient clinics, freestanding, exp	capita	2.93	88	38s
Mental health care, psychiatric partial-care organizations, freestanding, exp	capita	0.32	88	38s
Mental health care, state and county mental hospitals, exp	capita	23.79	88	38s
Mental health care, VA medical centers, exp	capita	7.76	88	38s
Physician fee, family practice, first-visit		76.00	91	62r
Physician fee, family practice, revisit		33.00	91	62r
Physician fee, general practice, first-visit		61.00	91	62r
Physician fee, general practice, revisit		31.00	91	62r
Physician fee, general surgeon, first-visit		65.00	91	62r
Physician fee, general surgeon, revisit		35.00	91	62r
Physician fee, internal medicine, first-visit		91.00	91	62r
Physician fee, internal medicine, revisit		40.00	91	62r
Physician fee, median, neurosurgeon, first-visit		106.00	91	62r
Physician fee, median, nonsurgical specialist, first-visit		90.00	91	62r
Physician fee, median, orthopedic surgeon, first-visit		83.00	91	62r
Physician fee, median, surgical specialist, first-visit		61.00	91	62r
Physician fee, neurosurgeon, revisit		41.00	91	62r
Physician fee, nonsurgical specialist, revisit		40.00	91	62r
Physician fee, obstetrics/gynecology, first-visit		61.00	91	62r
Physician fee, obstetrics/gynecology, revisit		40.00	91	62r
Physician fee, orthopedic surgeon, revisit		41.00	91	62r
Physician fee, pediatrician, first-visit		46.00	91	62r
Physician fee, pediatrician, revisit		33.00	91	62r
Physician fee, surgical specialist, revisit		36.00	91	62r
Substance abuse, hospital ancillary charge	incident	940	90	70s
Substance abuse, hospital physician charge	incident	380	90	70s
Substance abuse, hospital room and board	incident	5410	90	70s
Household Goods				
Appliance repair, home, service call, washing machine	min labor charge	29.23	4Q 92	4c
Laundry detergent, Tide Ultra, Bold, or Cheer	42 oz	3.19	4Q 92	4c
Tissues, facial, Kleenex brand	175-count box	1.05	4Q 92	4c
Housing				
ACCRA Index, Housing		88.40	4Q 92	4c
Home, median price	unit	57.50		26c
House, 1,800 sq ft, 8,000 sq ft lot, new, urban	total	98500	4Q 92	4c
House payment, principal and interest, 25% down payment	month	563	4Q 92	4c
Mortgage rate, incl. points & origination fee, 30-year fixed or adjustable rate	percent	8.40	4Q 92	4c
Rent, apartment, 2 bedrooms - 1-1/2 to 2 baths, unfurnished, 950 sq ft, water	month	390	4Q 92	4c
Rental unit, 1 bedroom	month	370	93	23c
Rental unit, 2 bedroom	month	435	93	23c
Rental unit, 3 bedroom	month	546	93	23c
Rental unit, 4 bedroom	month	613	93	23c
Rental unit, efficiency	month	304	93	23c
Insurance and Pensions				
Auto insurance, private passenger	year	547.38	91	63s

Youngstown, OH - continued

Item	Per	Value	Date	Ref.
Personal Goods				
Shampoo, Alberto VO5	15 oz	1.31	4Q 92	4c
Toothpaste, Crest or Colgate	6-7 oz	1.74	4Q 92	4c
Personal Services				
Dry cleaning, man's 2-piece suit		5.87	4Q 92	4c
Haircare, woman's shampoo, trim and blow-dry		21.80	4Q 92	4c
Haircut, man's barbershop, no styling		7.50	4Q 92	4c
Restaurant Food				
Chicken, fried, thigh and drumstick		2.10	4Q 92	4c
Hamburger with cheese	1/4 lb	1.87	4Q 92	4c
Pizza, Pizza Hut or Pizza Inn, cheese, thin crust	12-13 in	7.50	4Q 92	4c
Taxes				
Tax, cigarette	pack	18	91	77s
Tax, gasoline	gal	21	91	77s
Taxes, state	capita	1056	91	77s
Transportation				
ACCRA Index, Transportation		99.90	4Q 92	4c
Bus fare	one-way	0.70	3/93	2c
Bus fare, up to 10 miles	one-way	0.70	4Q 92	4c
Driver's license fee		5.00	12/90	43s
Tire balance, computer or spin balance, front	wheel	6.88	4Q 92	4c
Utilities				
ACCRA Index, Utilities		112.30	4Q 92	4c
Electricity	mil Btu	17.33	90	64s
Electricity, partial electric and other energy, 1,800 sq ft living area new home	month	84.23	4Q 92	4c

Yuba City, CA

Item	Per	Value	Date	Ref.
Child Care				
Child care fee, average, center	hour	1.71	90	65r
Child care fee, average, nonregulated family day care	hour	1.32	90	65r
Child care fee, average, regulated family day care	hour	1.86	90	65r
Communications				
Long-distance telephone service, day, initial minute, 0-100 miles	min	0.17-0.40	91	12s
Long-distance telephone service, day, additional minute, 0-100 miles	min	0.07-0.31	91	12s
Long-distance telephone service, evenings/weekends, 0-100 mi, initial minute	min	0.07-0.16	91	12s
Long-distance telephone service, evenings/weekends, 0-100 mi, additional minute	min	0.03-0.12	91	12s
Education				
Board, 4-yr private college/university	year	2515	91	22s
Board, 4-yr public college/university	year	2268	91	22s
Expenditures, local gov't, public elementary/secondary	pupil	4866	92	20s
Room, 4-year private college/university	year	2622	91	22s
Room, 4-year public college/university	year	2406	91	22s
Tuition, 2-year private college/university	year	7942	91	22s
Tuition, 2-year public college/university	year	114	91	22s
Tuition, 4-year private college/university	year	10863	91	22s
Tuition, 4-year public college/university, in-state	year	1220	91	22s
Energy and Fuels				
Coal	mil Btu	2.01	90	64s
Energy	mil Btu	9.08	90	64s
Energy exp/householder, 1-family unit	year	362	90	28r
Energy exp/householder, <1,000 sq ft heating area	year	254	90	28r

Yuba City, CA - continued

Item	Per	Value	Date	Ref.
Energy and Fuels - continued				
Energy exp/householder, 1,000-1,999 sq ft heating area	year	358	90	28r
Energy exp/householder, 2,000+ sq ft heating area	year	467	90	28r
Energy exp/householder, mobile home	year	390	90	28r
Energy exp/householder, multifamily	year	252	90	28r
Gas, natural	mil Btu	4.31	90	64s
Gas, natural	000 cu ft	6.27	91	46s
Gas, natural, exp	year	369	91	46s
Gasoline, unleaded regular	mil Btu	8.57	90	64s
Entertainment				
Miniature golf admission	adult	6.18	92	1r
Miniature golf admission	child	5.14	92	1r
Waterpark admission	adult	11.00	92	1r
Waterpark admission	child	8.55	92	1r
Funerals				
Casket, 18-gauge steel, velvet interior		1781.09	91	24r
Cosmetology, hair care, etc.		84.64	91	24r
Embalming		207.41	91	24r
Facility use for ceremony		205.76	91	24r
Hearse, local		105.14	91	24r
Limousine, local		83.21	91	24r
Remains to funeral home, transfer		113.82	91	24r
Service charge, professional		626.33	91	24r
Vault, concrete, non-metallic liner		599.54	91	24r
Viewing facilities, use		85.81	91	24r
Groceries				
Apples, Red Delicious	lb	0.80	4/93	16r
Bacon	lb	1.79	4/93	16r
Bananas	lb	0.53	4/93	16r
Bologna, all beef or mixed	lb	2.67	4/93	16r
Bread, white, pan	lb	0.81	4/93	16r
Carrots, short trimmed and topped	lb	0.39	4/93	16r
Chicken, fresh, whole	lb	0.94	4/93	16r
Chicken breast, bone-in	lb	2.19	4/93	16r
Chuck roast, graded and ungraded, ex USDA prime and choice	lb	2.26	4/93	16r
Coffee, 100% ground roast, all sizes	lb	2.33	4/93	16r
Eggs, Grade AA large	doz	1.18	4/93	16r
Flour, white, all purpose	lb	0.22	4/93	16r
Grapefruit	lb	0.52	4/93	16r
Grapes, Thompson Seedless	lb	1.50	4/93	16r
Ground beef, 100% beef	lb	1.44	4/93	16r
Ground beef, lean and extra lean	lb	2.34	4/93	16r
Ham, boneless, excluding canned	lb	2.56	4/93	16r
Honey, jar	8 oz	0.89-1.00	92	5r
Honey, jar	lb	1.35-1.97	92	5r
Honey, squeeze bear	12-oz	1.19-1.50	92	5r
Ice cream, prepackaged, bulk, regular	1/2 gal	2.40	4/93	16r
Lemons	lb	0.81	4/93	16r
Lettuce, iceberg	lb	0.84	4/93	16r
Margarine, stick	lb	0.81	4/93	16r
Oranges, navel	lb	0.48	4/93	16r
Pork chops, center cut, bone-in	lb	3.25	4/93	16r
Potato chips	16 oz	2.89	4/93	16r
Potatoes, white	lb	0.38	4/93	16r
Round roast, graded & ungraded, ex USDA prime & choice	lb	3.00	4/93	16r
Round roast, USDA choice, boneless	lb	3.16	4/93	16r
Shortening, vegetable oil blends	lb	0.86	4/93	16r
Spaghetti and macaroni	lb	0.84	4/93	16r
Steak, round, graded & ungraded, ex USDA prime & choice	lb	3.34	4/93	16r
Steak, round, USDA choice, boneless	lb	3.24	4/93	16r
Steak, sirloin, graded & ungraded, ex USDA prime & choice	lb	3.75	4/93	16r
Steak, sirloin, USDA choice, boneless	lb	4.49	4/93	16r
Sugar, white	lb	0.41	4/93	16r
Sugar, white, 33-80 oz pk	lb	0.38	4/93	16r
Tomatoes, field grown	lb	1.01	4/93	16r

Values are in dollars or fractions of dollars. In the column headed *Ref*, references are shown to sources. Each reference is followed by a letter. These refer to the geographical level for which data were reported: s=State, r=Region, and c=City or metro. The abbreviation *ex* is used to mean *except* or *excluding*; *exp* stands for expenditures. For other abbreviations and further explanations, please see the Introduction.

Yuba City, CA - continued

Item	Per	Value	Date	Ref.
Groceries				
Turkey, frozen, whole	lb	1.04	4/93	16r
Health Care				
Cardizem 60 mg tablets	30	24.04	92	49s
Cector 250 mg tablets	15	35.87	92	49s
Childbirth, cesarean, hospital		5533	91	62r
Childbirth, cesarean, physician's fee		2053	91	62r
Childbirth, normal, hospital		2745	91	62r
Childbirth, normal, physician's fee		1492	91	62r
Health care spending, state	capita	2894	3/93	84s
Medical plan per employee	year	3421	91	45r
Mental health care, exp	capita	37.60-53.67	90	38s
Mental health care, exp, state mental health agency	capita	42.32	90	38s
Mental health care, hospital psychiatric services, non-Federal, exp	capita	10.64	88	38s
Mental health care, mental health organization, multiservice, exp	capita	28.56	88	38s
Mental health care, psychiatric hospitals, private, exp	capita	18.60	88	38s
Mental health care, psychiatric out-patient clinics, freestanding, exp	capita	2.28	88	38s
Mental health care, psychiatric partial-care organizations, freestanding, exp	capita	0.24	88	38s
Mental health care, state and county mental hospitals, exp	capita	13.60	88	38s
Mental health care, VA medical centers, exp	capita	2.33	88	38s
Mevacor 20 mg tablets	30	67.62	92	49s
Physician fee, family practice, first-visit		111.00	91	62r
Physician fee, family practice, revisit		45.00	91	62r
Physician fee, general practice, first-visit		100.00	91	62r
Physician fee, general practice, revisit		40.00	91	62r
Physician fee, internal medicine, first-visit		137.00	91	62r
Physician fee, internal medicine, revisit		48.00	91	62r
Physician fee, median, neurosurgeon, first-visit		157.00	91	62r
Physician fee, median, nonsurgical specialist, first-visit		131.00	91	62r
Physician fee, median, orthopedic surgeon, first-visit		124.00	91	62r
Physician fee, median, plastic surgeon, first-visit		88.00	91	62r
Physician fee, median, surgical specialist, first-visit		100.00	91	62r
Physician fee, neurosurgeon, revisit		51.00	91	62r
Physician fee, nonsurgical specialist, revisit		47.00	91	62r
Physician fee, obstetrics/gynecology, first-visit		95.00	91	62r
Physician fee, obstetrics/gynecology, revisit		50.00	91	62r
Physician fee, orthopedic surgeon, revisit		51.00	91	62r
Physician fee, pediatrician, first-visit		81.00	91	62r
Physician fee, pediatrician, revisit		42.00	91	62r
Physician fee, plastic surgeon, revisit		48.00	91	62r
Physician fee, surgical specialist, revisit		49.00	91	62r
Prozac 20 mg tablets	14	33.22	92	49s
Substance abuse, hospital ancillary charge	incident	1760	90	70s
Substance abuse, hospital physician charge	incident	750	90	70s
Substance abuse, hospital room and board	incident	6390	90	70s
Tagamet 300 mg tablets	100	77.08	92	49s
Xanax 0.25 mg tablets	90	64.08	92	49s
Zantac 160 mg tablets	60	92.31	92	49s
Housing				
Home, median price	unit	131,200	92	58s
Insurance and Pensions				
Auto insurance, private passenger	year	904.37	91	63s

Yuba City, CA - continued

Item	Per	Value	Date	Ref.
Taxes				
Tax, cigarette	pack	35	91	77s
Tax, gasoline	gal	16	91	77s
Taxes, state	capita	1477	91	77s
Transportation				
Driver's license fee		10.00	12/90	43s
Travel				
Business travel	day	178.00	4/93	89r
Utilities				
Electricity	mil Btu	25.98	90	64s

Yuma, AZ

Item	Per	Value	Date	Ref.
Composite ACCRA index		98.20	4Q 92	4c
Alcoholic Beverages				
Beer, Miller Lite or Budweiser, 12-oz containers	6 pack	3.77	4Q 92	4c
Liquor, J & B Scotch	750 ml	16.17	4Q 92	4c
Wine, Gallo Chablis blanc, 1.5 liter	bottle	4.67	4Q 92	4c
Child Care				
Child care fee, average, center	hour	1.71	90	65r
Child care fee, average, nonregulated family day care	hour	1.32	90	65r
Child care fee, average, regulated family day care	hour	1.86	90	65r
Clothing				
Jeans, man's denim		30.25	4Q 92	4c
Shirt, man's dress shirt		22.66	4Q 92	4c
Undervest, boy's size 10-14, cotton	3	4.47	4Q 92	4c
Communications				
Long-distance telephone service, day, initial minute, 0-100 miles	min	0.24-0.42	91	12s
Long-distance telephone service, day, additional minute, 0-100 miles	min	0.10-0.26	91	12s
Long-distance telephone service, evenings/weekends, 0-100 mi, initial minute	min	0.14-0.25	91	12s
Long-distance telephone service, evenings/weekends, 0-100 mi, additional minute	min	0.06-0.17	91	12s
Newspaper subscription, daily and Sunday home delivery, large-city	month	8.00	4Q 92	4c
Telephone, flat rate	month	12.40	91	11c
Telephone bill, family of four	month	16.75	4Q 92	4c
Education				
Board, 4-yr private college/university	year	1460	91	22s
Board, 4-yr public college/university	year	1697	91	22s
Expenditures, local gov't, public elementary/secondary	pupil	4489	92	20s
Room, 4-year private college/university	year	1350	91	22s
Room, 4-year public college/university	year	1556	91	22s
Tuition, 2-year private college/university	year	8977	91	22s
Tuition, 2-year public college/university	year	579	91	22s
Tuition, 4-year private college/university	year	4660	91	22s
Tuition, 4-year public college/university, in-state	year	1478	91	22s
Energy and Fuels				
Coal	mil Btu	1.45	90	64s
Energy	mil Btu	11.37	90	64s
Energy, combined forms, 1,800 sq ft heating area	month	129.45	4Q 92	4c
Energy, exc electricity, 1,800 sq ft heating area	month	26.09	4Q 92	4c
Energy exp/householder, 1-family unit	year	372	90	28r
Energy exp/householder, <1,000 sq ft heating area	year	335	90	28r
Energy exp/householder, 1,000-1,999 sq ft heating area	year	365	90	28r
Energy exp/householder, 2,000+ sq ft heating area	year	411	90	28r

Values are in dollars or fractions of dollars. In the column headed *Ref*, references are shown to sources. Each reference is followed by a letter. These refer to the geographical level for which data were reported: s = State, r = Region, and c = City or metro. The abbreviation *ex* is used to mean *except* or *excluding*; *exp* stands for expenditures. For other abbreviations and further explanations, please see the Introduction.

Yuma, AZ - continued

Item	Per	Value	Date	Ref.
Energy and Fuels				
Energy exp/householder, mobile home	year	305	90	28r
Energy exp/householder, multifamily	year	372	90	28r
Gas, natural	mil Btu	4.48	90	64s
Gas, natural	000 cu ft	6.99	91	46s
Gas, natural, exp	year	341	91	46s
Gasoline, motor	gal	1.27	4Q 92	4c
Gasoline, unleaded regular	mil Btu	9.22	90	64s
Entertainment				
Bowling, evening rate	game	2.07	4Q 92	4c
Miniature golf admission	adult	6.18	92	1r
Miniature golf admission	child	5.14	92	1r
Monopoly game, Parker Brothers', No. 9		12.29	4Q 92	4c
Movie	admission	5.00	4Q 92	4c
Tennis balls, yellow, Wilson or Penn, 3	can	2.27	4Q 92	4c
Waterpark admission	adult	11.00	92	1r
Waterpark admission	child	8.55	92	1r
Funerals				
Casket, 18-gauge steel, velvet interior		1929.04	91	24r
Cosmetology, hair care, etc.		88.52	91	24r
Embalming		249.33	91	24r
Facility use for ceremony		182.75	91	24r
Hearse, local		110.04	91	24r
Limousine, local		66.67	91	24r
Remains to funeral home, transfer		84.58	91	24r
Service charge, professional		593.00	91	24r
Vault, concrete, non-metallic liner		647.38	91	24r
Viewing facilities, use		99.87	91	24r
Goods and Services				
ACCRA Index, Miscellaneous Goods and Services		99.20	4Q 92	4c
Groceries				
ACCRA Index, Groceries		98.80	4Q 92	4c
Apples, Red Delicious	lb	0.80	4/93	16r
Babyfood, strained vegetables, lowest price	4-4.5 oz jar	0.29	4Q 92	4c
Bacon	lb	1.79	4/93	16r
Bananas	lb	0.42	4Q 92	4c
Bananas	lb	0.53	4/93	16r
Bologna, all beef or mixed	lb	2.67	4/93	16r
Bread, white	24 oz	0.78	4Q 92	4c
Bread, white, pan	lb	0.81	4/93	16r
Carrots, short trimmed and topped	lb	0.39	4/93	16r
Cheese, Kraft grated Parmesan	8-oz canister	3.41	4Q 92	4c
Chicken, fresh, whole	lb	0.94	4/93	16r
Chicken, fryer, whole	lb	0.74	4Q 92	4c
Chicken breast, bone-in	lb	2.19	4/93	16r
Chuck roast, graded and ungraded, ex USDA prime and choice	lb	2.26	4/93	16r
Cigarettes, Winston	carton	16.64	4Q 92	4c
Coffee, 100% ground roast, all sizes	lb	2.33	4/93	16r
Coffee, vacuum-packed	13-oz can	1.96	4Q 92	4c
Corn, frozen	10 oz	0.64	4Q 92	4c
Corn Flakes, Kellogg's or Post Toasties	18 oz	2.24	4Q 92	4c
Eggs, Grade A large	doz	0.75	4Q 92	4c
Eggs, Grade AA large	doz	1.18	4/93	16r
Flour, white, all purpose	lb	0.22	4/93	16r
Grapefruit	lb	0.52	4/93	16r
Grapes, Thompson Seedless	lb	1.50	4/93	16r
Ground beef, 100% beef	lb	1.44	4/93	16r
Ground beef, lean and extra lean	lb	2.34	4/93	16r
Ground beef or hamburger	lb	1.09	4Q 92	4c
Ham, boneless, excluding canned	lb	2.56	4/93	16r
Honey, jar	8 oz	0.89-1.00	92	5r
Honey, jar	lb	1.35-1.97	92	5r
Honey, squeeze bear	12-oz	1.19-1.50	92	5r

Yuma, AZ - continued

Item	Per	Value	Date	Ref.
Groceries - continued				
Ice cream, prepackaged, bulk, regular	1/2 gal	2.40	4/93	16r
Lemons	lb	0.81	4/93	16r
Lettuce, iceberg	head	0.81	4Q 92	4c
Lettuce, iceberg	lb	0.84	4/93	16r
Margarine, Blue Bonnet or Parkay cubes	lb	0.66	4Q 92	4c
Margarine, stick	lb	0.81	4/93	16r
Milk, whole	1/2 gal	1.33	4Q 92	4c
Orange juice, Minute Maid frozen	12-oz can	1.44	4Q 92	4c
Oranges, navel	lb	0.48	4/93	16r
Peaches	29-oz can	1.35	4Q 92	4c
Peas Sweet, Del Monte or Green Giant	15-17 oz can	0.59	4Q 92	4c
Pork chops, center cut, bone-in	lb	3.25	4/93	16r
Potato chips	16 oz	2.89	4/93	16r
Potatoes, white	lb	0.38	4/93	16r
Potatoes, white or red	10-lb sack	1.61	4Q 92	4c
Round roast, graded & ungraded, ex USDA prime & choice	lb	3.00	4/93	16r
Round roast, USDA choice, boneless	lb	3.16	4/93	16r
Sausage, Jimmy Dean, 100% pork	lb	3.00	4Q 92	4c
Shortening, vegetable oil blends	lb	0.86	4/93	16r
Shortening, vegetable, Crisco	3-lb can	2.59	4Q 92	4c
Soft drink, Coca Cola	2 liter	1.22	4Q 92	4c
Spaghetti and macaroni	lb	0.84	4/93	16r
Steak, round, graded & ungraded, ex USDA prime & choice	lb	3.34	4/93	16r
Steak, round, USDA choice, boneless	lb	3.24	4/93	16r
Steak, sirloin, graded & ungraded, ex USDA prime & choice	lb	3.75	4/93	16r
Steak, sirloin, USDA choice, boneless	lb	4.49	4/93	16r
Steak, T-bone	lb	4.73	4Q 92	4c
Sugar, cane or beet	4 lb	1.73	4Q 92	4c
Sugar, white	lb	0.41	4/93	16r
Sugar, white, 33-80 oz pk	lb	0.38	4/93	16r
Tomatoes, field grown	lb	1.01	4/93	16r
Tomatoes, Hunt's or Del Monte	14.5-oz can	0.71	4Q 92	4c
Tuna, chunk, light	6.125-6.5 oz can	0.65	4Q 92	4c
Turkey, frozen, whole	lb	1.04	4/93	16r
Health Care				
ACCRA Index, Health Care		104.10	4Q 92	4c
Analgesic, Aspirin, Bayer, 325 mg tablets	100	5.33	4Q 92	4c
Childbirth, cesarean, hospital		5533	91	62r
Childbirth, cesarean, physician's fee		2053	91	62r
Childbirth, normal, hospital		2745	91	62r
Childbirth, normal, physician's fee		1492	91	62r
Dentist's fee, adult teeth cleaning and periodic oral exam	visit	37.80	4Q 92	4c
Doctor's fee, routine exam, established patient	visit	37.00	4Q 92	4c
Hospital care, semiprivate room	day	495.00	4Q 92	4c
Medical plan per employee	year	3218	91	45r
Mental health care, exp	capita	20.37-28.83	90	38s
Mental health care, exp, state mental health agency	capita	27.27	90	38s
Mental health care, hospital psychiatric services, non-Federal, exp	capita	8.91	88	38s
Mental health care, mental health organization, multiservice, exp	capita	11.35	88	38s
Mental health care, psychiatric hospitals, private, exp	capita	36.59	88	38s
Mental health care, psychiatric out-patient clinics, freestanding, exp	capita	1.11	88	38s
Mental health care, state and county mental hospitals, exp	capita	8.18	88	38s

Values are in dollars or fractions of dollars. In the column headed *Ref*, references are shown to sources. Each reference is followed by a letter. These refer to the geographical level for which data were reported: s=State, r=Region, and c=City or metro. The abbreviation *ex* is used to mean *except* or *excluding*; *exp* stands for expenditures. For other abbreviations and further explanations, please see the Introduction.

Yuma, AZ - continued

Item	Per	Value	Date	Ref.
Health Care				
Mental health care, VA medical centers, exp	capita	2.60	88	38s
Physician fee, family practice, first-visit		111.00	91	62r
Physician fee, family practice, revisit		45.00	91	62r
Physician fee, general practice, first-visit		100.00	91	62r
Physician fee, general practice, revisit		40.00	91	62r
Physician fee, internal medicine, first-visit		137.00	91	62r
Physician fee, internal medicine, revisit		48.00	91	62r
Physician fee, median, neurosurgeon, first-visit		157.00	91	62r
Physician fee, median, nonsurgical specialist, first-visit		131.00	91	62r
Physician fee, median, orthopedic surgeon, first-visit		124.00	91	62r
Physician fee, median, plastic surgeon, first-visit		88.00	91	62r
Physician fee, median, surgical specialist, first-visit		100.00	91	62r
Physician fee, neurosurgeon, revisit		51.00	91	62r
Physician fee, nonsurgical specialist, revisit		47.00	91	62r
Physician fee, obstetrics/gynecology, first-visit		95.00	91	62r
Physician fee, obstetrics/gynecology, revisit		50.00	91	62r
Physician fee, orthopedic surgeon, revisit		51.00	91	62r
Physician fee, pediatrician, first-visit		81.00	91	62r
Physician fee, pediatrician, revisit		42.00	91	62r
Physician fee, plastic surgeon, revisit		48.00	91	62r
Physician fee, surgical specialist, revisit		49.00	91	62r
Substance abuse, hospital ancillary charge	incident	1800	90	70s
Substance abuse, hospital physician charge	incident	800	90	70s
Substance abuse, hospital room and board	incident	6480	90	70s
Household Goods				
Appliance repair, home, service call, washing machine	min labor charge	35.00	4Q 92	4c
Laundry detergent, Tide Ultra, Bold, or Cheer	42 oz	3.79	4Q 92	4c
Tissues, facial, Kleenex brand	175-count box	1.23	4Q 92	4c
Housing				
ACCRA Index, Housing		85.00	4Q 92	4c
House, 1,800 sq ft, 8,000 sq ft lot, new, urban	total	88375	4Q 92	4c
House payment, principal and interest, 25% down payment	month	493	4Q 92	4c
Mortgage rate, incl. points & origination fee, 30-year fixed or adjustable rate	percent	8.14	4Q 92	4c
Rent, apartment, 2 bedrooms - 1-1/2 to 2 baths, unfurnished, 950 sq ft, water	month	489	4Q 92	4c
Rental unit, 1 bedroom	month	482	93	23c
Rental unit, 2 bedroom	month	570	93	23c
Rental unit, 3 bedroom	month	712	93	23c
Rental unit, 4 bedroom	month	798	93	23c
Rental unit, efficiency	month	397	93	23c
Insurance and Pensions				
Auto insurance, private passenger	year	704.41	91	63s
Personal Goods				
Shampoo, Alberto VO5	15 oz	1.24	4Q 92	4c
Toothpaste, Crest or Colgate	6-7 oz	1.99	4Q 92	4c
Personal Services				
Dry cleaning, man's 2-piece suit		7.01	4Q 92	4c
Haircare, woman's shampoo, trim and blow-dry		16.00	4Q 92	4c
Haircut, man's barbershop, no styling		5.30	4Q 92	4c

Yuma, AZ - continued

Item	Per	Value	Date	Ref.
Restaurant Food				
Chicken, fried, thigh and drumstick		2.05	4Q 92	4c
Hamburger with cheese	1/4 lb	1.99	4Q 92	4c
Pizza, Pizza Hut or Pizza Inn, cheese, thin crust	12-13 in	8.19	4Q 92	4c
Taxes				
Tax, cigarette	pack	18	91	77s
Tax, gasoline	gal	18	91	77s
Taxes, state	capita	1256	91	77s
Transportation				
ACCRA Index, Transportation		112.70	4Q 92	4c
Driver's license fee		7.00	12/90	43s
Tire balance, computer or spin balance, front	wheel	7.34	4Q 92	4c
Travel				
Business travel	day	178.00	4/93	89r
Utilities				
ACCRA Index, Utilities		115.30	4Q 92	4c
Electricity	mil Btu	22.82	90	64s

Values are in dollars or fractions of dollars. In the column headed *Ref*, references are shown to sources. Each reference is followed by a letter. These refer to the geographical level for which data were reported: s=State, r=Region, and c=City or metro. The abbreviation *ex* is used to mean *except* or *excluding*; *exp* stands for expenditures. For other abbreviations and further explanations, please see the Introduction.

707

LIST OF SOURCES

This section shows all sources used in *American Cost of Living Survey*. Numerals in bold on the left are those found in the data tables in the column marked *Ref.*. Notes to the data are also provided as shown in the source.

1   **1992 IAAPA BUSINESS MANAGERS SURVEY**

IAAPA 1992 Amusement Industry Abstract. For additional information contact: International Association of Amusement Parks and Attractions, 1448 Duke Street, Alexandria, VA 22314 (703) 836-4800.

Date: 1992

Page reference: 11, 14

2   **1993 APTA TRANSIT FARE SUMMARY**

1993 APTA Transit Fare Summary, April 1993. American Public Transit Association (APTA). For additional information contact: American Public Transit Association, 1201 New York Ave. N.W., Suite 400, Washington, DC 20005 (202) 898-4000.

3   **AARP PRODUCT REPORT**

AARP Product Report, as cited in *Consumer Fraud and the Elderly: Easy Prey?*. Hearing before the Special Committee on Aging. United States Senate. 102d Congress, 2d Session, September 24, 1992. Washington, DC: U.S. Government Printing Office, 1993. For additional information contact: American Association of Retired Persons (AARP), 601 E Street NW, Washington, DC 20049.

Date: 1992

4   **ACCRA COST OF LIVING INDEX**

ACCRA Cost of Living Index, Fourth Quarter 1992, Volume 25, No. 4.: Price Reports. Copyright 1993, ACCRA. Reproduced by permission. ACCRA is a nonprofit organization promoting excellence in research for community and economic development. *ACCRA Cost of Living Index* has been published quarterly without interruption since 1968. For additional information contact: ACCRA, P.O. Box 6749, Louisville, KY 40206-6749. The quarterly report is available by subscription for $100 per year. Single copies may be purchased for $50 each.

Date: October 1992 - December 1992

Page reference: 2.1

5   **AMERICAN BEE JOURNAL**

American Bee Journal. Copyright, American Bee Journal. Reprinted by permission. For additional information contact: Dadant & Sons, Inc., Hamilton, IL 62341 (217) 847-3324. *Note:* Prices for honey are not intended to provide a realistic reflection of prices in all states or in a particular region. Prices may vary between and among states and within an individual state.

Date: December 1992

Page reference: 762

6 AMERICAN DEMOGRAPHICS

American Demographics. For additional information contact: American Demographics, P.O. Box 68, Ithaca, NY 14851-0068.

Date: September 1992

Page reference: 52

7 AMERICAN DEMOGRAPHICS

Date: October 1992

Page reference: 26

8 ANAHEIM CHAMBER OF COMMERCE/BTA RESEARCH INSTITUTE.

Anaheim Chamber of Commerce/BTA Research Institute. For additional information contact: Anaheim Chamber of Commerce, 100 S. Anaheim Blvd., #300, Anaheim, CA 92805 (714) 758-0222.

Date: 1993

9 ANCHORAGE STAR OF THE NORTH CHAMBER OF COMMERCE

Anchorage Star of the North Chamber of Commerce. 441 W. Fifth Ave., #300, Anchorage, AK 99501-2309.

Date: 1993

10 ARKANSAS DEPARTMENT OF FINANCE AND ADMINISTRATION

Arkansas Department of Finance and Administration, Revenue Division, Office of Motor Vehicles, Little Rock, AR 72203 (501) 682-4702. Note: Vehicle registration fee varies according to vehicle weight. The fee for vehicle weight of up to and including 3000 lbs. is $17.00; for vehicle weight of 3001 lbs. to 4500 lbs., $25.00; and for vehicle weight of 4501 lbs. and over, $30.00.

Date: 1993

11 BELL OPERATING COMPANIES EXCHANGE SERVICE TELEPHONE RATES

Bell Operating Companies Exchange Service Telephone Rates. National Association of Regulatory Utility Commissioners (NARUC). Compiled by Bellcore, Inc. Copyright, Bellcore, Inc. Reprinted by permission from Bell Operating Companies Exchange Service Telephone Rates. This material can be ordered from NARUC for $47.50 plus a $4.75 shipping and handling fee. Orders can be sent to: NARUC, 1102 ICC Building, P.O. Box 684, Washington, DC 20044-0684 (202) 898-2200.

Date: December 31, 1991

Page reference: 8

12 BELL OPERATING COMPANIES LONG DISTANCE MESSAGE TELEPHONE RATES

Bell Operating Companies Long Distance Message Telephone Rates. National Association of Regulatory Utility Commissioners (NARUC). Compiled by Bellcore, Inc. Copyright, Bellcore, Inc. Reprinted by permission from Bell Operating Companies Long Distance Message Telephone Rates.

This material can be ordered from NARUC for $35.00 plus a $3.50 shipping and handling fee. Orders can be sent to NARUC, 1102 ICC Building, P.O. Box 684, Washington, DC 20044-0684 (202) 898-2200. *Note:* Day rates typically apply from 8:00 to 5:00 p.m. Monday through Friday in most states.

Date: December 31, 1991

Page reference: 8

13 BUILDER

Builder.

Date: November 1992

Page reference: 28

14 COLORADO SPRINGS FACT SHEET

Colorado Springs Fact Sheet. For additional information contact: The Greater Colorado Springs Economic Development Corporation, Box B, Colorado Springs, CO 80901 (719) 471-8183.

Date: May 1992

15 CONSUMER EXPENDITURE SURVEY 1988-89

Consumer Expenditure Survey 1988-89. U.S. Department of Labor. Bureau of Labor Statistics.

Date: August 1993

Page reference: 83

16 CPI DETAILED REPORT

CPI Detailed Report, Data for April 1993, p. 90. U.S. Department of Labor. Bureau of Labor Statistics. To order a 1-2 yr. subscription to this monthly report contact: New Orders, Superintendent of Documents, P.O. Box 371954. Pittsburgh, PA 15250-7954. Subscription price per year is $26 domestic, $32.50 foreign. The price for a single copy is $7 domestic, $8.75 foreign. Prices are subject to change by the U.S. Government Printing Office.

Date: April 1993

17 DETROIT NEWS

Detroit News. For additional information contact: Gannett Newspaper Group, 615 W. Lafayette Blvd., Detroit, MI 48231 (313) 222-6400. *Note:* The national average for day care for a three-year-old child is $4,160 a year.

Date: February 15, 1993

Page reference: F4

18 DETROIT NEWS

Date: March 14, 1993

Page reference: H1

19 DETROIT NEWS

Note: An additional .25 is added to the fares for Park & Ride and SMART limited.

Date: April 1, 1993

Page reference: B1

20 DIGEST OF EDUCATION STATISTICS 1991-1992

Digest of Education Statistics 1991-1992. U.S. Department of Education. National Center for Education Statistics. *Note:* The figures are in constant 1989-90 dollars, based on the Consumer Price Index, U.S. Department of Labor, Bureau of Labor Statistics, and do not reflect differences in inflation rates from state to state.

Page reference: 45

21 DRUG TOPICS

Drug Topics. For additional information contact: Medical Economics Publishing, 680 Kinderkamack Road, Oradell, NJ 07649 (201) 262-3030.

Date: December 9, 1992

Page reference: 96

22 FALL ENROLLMENT

Fall Enrollment and *Institutional Characteristics* surveys, 1991-1992, p. 45. U.S. Department of Education. National Center for Education Statistics. Integrated Postsecondary Education Data System (IPEDS). *Note:* Data reflect average charges. Tuition and fees were weighted by the number of full-time-equivalent undergraduate students but are not adjusted to reflect student residency. Room and board rates are based on full-time students.

23 FEDERAL REGISTER

Federal Register, Department of Housing and Urban Development, *24 CFR Part 888, Section 8 Housing Assistance Payments Program, Fair Market Rent Schedules; Final Rule,* October 1, 1992. *Note:* The Fair Market Rent Schedule for unit sizes larger than four bedrooms is calculated by adding 15% to the four bedroom Fair Market Rental for each extra bedroom.

Date: October 1, 1992

Page reference: 45471

24 FTC MANDATED GENERAL PRICE LIST

FTC Mandated General Price List, 1993. National Funeral Directors Association. Reprinted by permission. For additional information, contact: National Funeral Directors Association, 11121 W. Oklahoma Ave., Milwaukee, WI 53227 (414) 541-2500.

25 GROUP COMPREHENSIVE MAJOR MEDICAL NET CLAIM COST RELATIONSHIPS BY AREA

Group Comprehensive Major Medical Net Claim Cost Relationships by Area, by Mark Alan Chesner, FSA, MAAA, FCA, *The Proceedings,* Conference of Consulting Actuaries, Volume XXXXI, 1991.

Reprinted by permission. For additional information contact: Mark Alan Chesner, Milliman & Robertson Inc., Two Pennsylvania Plaza, Suite 1552, New York, NY 10121-0088 (212) 629-5657.

Date: 1991

Page reference: 593-602

26 HOME SALES

Home Sales: Existing and New Single-Family Apartment Condos and Co-ops. Vol. 7, No. 2. Copyright, National Association of Realtors. Reprinted by permission. Correspondence should be addressed to: Research Division, National Association of Realtors, 777 14th Street NW, Washington, DC 20005 (202) 383-1110. The price of an annual subscription to *Home Sales* is $75 to members, $100 to non-members. *Note:* California values courtesy of California Association of Realtors.

Date: February 1993

Page reference: 9, 14

27 HOSPITAL SEMI-PRIVATE ROOM CHARGES SURVEY

Hospital Semi-Private Room Charges Survey, 1990 Survey, p. 1. Copyright, 1976, 1990, Health Insurance Association of America (HIAA). Reprinted by permission. For a catalog of HIAA publications, contact: HIAA Fulfillment, P.O. Box 41455, Washington, DC 20018, (202) 223-7808. *Note:* Some rates are an average of two or more rates charged by different hospitals in the same city.

28 HOUSEHOLD ENERGY CONSUMPTION AND EXPENDITURES 1990 SUPPLEMENT: REGIONAL DATA

Household Energy Consumption and Expenditures 1990 Supplement: Regional Data, U.S. Department of Energy. Energy Information Administration.

Date: 1991

Page reference: 10

29 IDAHO TRANSPORTATION DEPARTMENT, MOTOR VEHICLE BUREAU

Idaho Transportation Department, Motor Vehicle Bureau, P.O. Box 7129, Boise, ID 83707 (208) 334-8742. *Note:* Vehicle registration fee varies according to age of vehicle and month in which the vehicle is registered. Registration renewals require payment of a 12-month fee.

Date: 1993

30 IOWA UTILITIES BOARD

Iowa Utilities Board. *Note:* Rates are calculated for the largest area in each utility's service territory. Figures include all charges except sales tax.

Date: 1993

31 JOURNAL OF COMMERCE

Journal of Commerce. For additional information contact: The Journal of Commerce, 110 Wall Street, New York, NY 10005 (212) 425-1616. *Note:* State gross receipts tax not included in Connecticut or

New Jersey. Unless indicated, superfund tax is not included.

Date: December 15, 1992

Page reference: 6B

32 KANSAS DEPARTMENT OF REVENUE

Kansas Department of Revenue, Vehicles Division, Topeka, KS 66612-1588 (913) 296-7074. *Note:*Vehicle registration fees vary according to the vehicle's weight, from $27.25 for a vehicle weight up to 4500 lbs. to $37.25 for a vehicle weight of 4501 lbs. and over. Registration fee for a special interest vehicle is $28.25.

Date: 1993

33 LODGING HOSPITALITY

Lodging Hospitality. For additional information contact: Penton Publishing, 100 Superior Avenue, Cleveland, OH 44114 (216) 696-7000.

Date: February 1993

Page reference: 35

34 LOS ANGELES TIMES

Los Angeles Times. For additional information contact: Times Mirror Square, Los Angeles, CA 90053 (213) 237-3000. *Note:* The counties of San Francisco, Los Angeles, and Orange had the most expensive preferred provider plans in the nation. New York's indemnity plans are among the most expensive; and Cleveland has the most expensive health maintenance organization plans. The cities of Minneapolis-St. Paul and Seattle had the least expensive plans.

Date: March 8, 1993

Page reference: D2

35 LOS ANGELES TIMES

Note: Figures are an average of the price of premiums of five insurance companies in different cities in California. Price to driver aged 30 who has held a driver's license for 14 years and who has no driving violations on record. The vehicle is driven 15 miles each way to work. Annual mileage is 12,000. Price covers liability insurance only.

Date: April 12, 1993

Page reference: A-4

36 MANAGEMENT REVIEW

Management Review. Note: Figures are based on a family of four with an annual family income of $60,000.

Date: February 1993

Page reference: 8

37 MEMPHIS BUSINESS JOURNAL

Memphis Business Journal. For additional information contact: Mid-South Communications Inc., 88 Union, Suite 102, Memphis, TN 38103-5195 (901) 523-1000.

Date: June 22, 1992 - June 26, 1992

Page reference: 3

38 MENTAL HEALTH, UNITED STATES, 1992

Mental Health, United States, 1992. By R. W. Manderscheid and M. A. Sonnenschein, eds. DHHS Pub. No. (SMA) 92-1942, Washington, D.C.: Superintendent of Documents, U.S. Government Printing Office. *Note:* The populations used in the calculation of these rates are the civilian population by state as of July 1988, provided by the U.S. Bureau of the Census. VA medical centers include the Department of Veterans Affairs; neuropsychiatric hospitals, general hospital psychiatric services, and psychiatric outpatient clinics.

Date: 1992

Page reference: 64, 184

39 MIAMI HERALD

Miami Herald. For additional information contact: The Miami Herald, One Herald Plaza, Miami, FL 33132-1693 (305)350-2111.

Date: March 2, 1993

Page reference: C-1

40 MICHIGAN SECRETARY OF STATE

Michigan Secretary of State, Lansing, Michigan 48918 (517) 322-1583. *Note:*Vehicle registration fee varies according to vehicle's weight, age and base price; most original license plate fees are prorated for the number of months of issuance.

Date: 1993

41 MISSOURI DEPARTMENT OF REVENUE

Missouri Department of Revenue, Motor Vehicle Bureau, Box 311, Jefferson City, MO 65105 (314) 751-5486. *Note:* Registration fee varies according to vehicle's horsepower; most original license fees are for the number of months of issuance.

Date: 1993

42 MODERN HEALTHCARE

Modern Healthcare. For additional information contact: Crain Communications Inc., 740 N. Rush Street, Chicago, IL 60611-2590.

Date: March 8, 1993

Page reference: 12

43 MOTOR VEHICLE OPERATORS AND CHAUFFEURS LICENSES: 1990

Motor Vehicle Operators and Chauffeurs Licenses: 1990, Table 8.16, *The Book of the States*. Copyright, 1993 The Council of State Governments. Reprinted by permission from The Book of the States. For additional information, contact: The Council of State Governments, P.O. Box 11910, Iron Works Pike, Lexington, KY 40578-1910 (606) 231-1939. *Notes:* Examination fees are in addition to the fee shown for a license. In Alabama, Rhode Island, and Wisconsin, the fee is $5; in Connecticut, $23; in Kansas, $3; in Massachusetts, $20; in South Carolina, $2; in Vermont, the written examination fee for the first examination is $15, with $10 charged for each additional examination; in Washington, $7.

Date: 1993

Page reference: 537

44 MOTOR VEHICLE SERVICES, STATE OF NEW JERSEY

Motor Vehicle Services, State of New Jersey, Department of Law and Public Safety, Division of Motor Vehicles, Trenton, NJ 08660 (609) 292-6500. *Note:*Prices vary according to age and weight of the vehicle.

Date: 1993

45 NATION'S BUSINESS

Nation's Business. For additional information contact: U.S. Chamber of Commerce, 1615 H Street NW, Washington, DC 20062 (202) 463-5650.

Date: May 1992

Page reference: 62

46 NATURAL GAS ANNUAL 1991

Natural Gas Annual 1991. Energy Information Administration. Office of Oil and Gas. U.S. Department of Energy.

Page reference: 69

47 NEBRASKA VEHICLE SERVICES DIVISION

Nebraska Vehicle Services Division, Lincoln, NE 68509 (402) 471-3909. *Note:* An additional $2.50 is added to the registration fee, and a $1.50 fee per plate is charged for new plate issuance.

Date: 1993

48 NEW YORK TIMES

New York Times. For additional information contact: The New York Times Company, 229 W. 43rd Street, New York, NY 10036 (212) 556-1234. *Note:* These are comparative costs of cooking lessons at schools for nonprofessionals. Selected schools represent the range of instruction available, from basic kitchen skills to lessons in specialized gourmet cuisine. The cost of food and supplies is included.

Date: August 22, 1992

Page reference: 16

49 NEW YORK TIMES

Date: November 23, 1992

Page reference: A8

50 NORTH CAROLINA DIVISION OF MOTOR VEHICLES

North Carolina Division of Motor Vehicles, Raleigh, NC 27609. *Note:* A 3% Highway Use Tax also is due on new and used vehicles. The minimum tax is $40.00. As of July 1, 1993, the maximum tax will be $1500.00.

Date: 1993

51 NORTH DAKOTA DEPARTMENT OF TRANSPORTATION

North Dakota Department of Transportation, Driver and Vehicle Services Division, Bismark, ND 58505 (710) 224-2601. *Note:* Vehicle registration fee varies according to vehicle weight and the year in which the vehicle is first registered.

Date: 1993

52 OFFICE OF THE SECRETARY OF STATE, ILLINOIS

Office of the Secretary of State, Springfield, IL 62723. *Note:* The registration for multiyears in Illinois has a staggered expiration date and applies to vehicles of up to 8,000 lbs.

Date: 1993

53 OREGON MOTOR VEHICLES DIVISION

Oregon Motor Vehicles Division, Salem, OR 97314. *Note:* The registration renewal fee in the state of Oregon is $16.25.

Date: 1993

54 PROGRESSIVE GROCER

Progressive Grocer, 59th Annual Report. For additional information contact: Maclean Hunter Media Inc., Four Stamford Forum, Stamford, CT 06904 (203) 325-3500.

Date: April 1992

Page reference: 52

55 RESIDENTIAL ELECTRIC BILLS, WINTER 1991-92

Residential Electric Bills, Winter 1991-92, p. 2. National Association of Regulatory Utility Commissioners (NARUC). This material can be ordered for $27.50 plus a $2.75 shipping and handling fee from: NARUC, 1102 ICC Building, P.O. Box 684, Washington, DC 20044-0684, (202) 898-2200. *Note:* Rates are calculated for the largest area in each utility's service area and are for non-space heating customers only. The state of Nebraska does not regulate retail electric rates. Customers using electric heat can expect to receive a higher bill.

56 RESIDENTIAL GAS BILLS, WINTER 1991-92

Residential Gas Bills, Winter 1991-92, p. 2. National Association of Regulatory Utility Commissioners (NARUC). This material can be ordered for $30.00 plus a $3.00 shipping and handling fee from: NARUC, 1102 ICC Building, P.O.Box 684, Washington, DC 20044-0684 (202) 898-2200. *Note:* Rates are calculated for the largest area in each utility's service area. Bill computations are based on the rate schedule applicable to the majority of a utility's space heating and non-space heating customers within each state. The total bill includes the base rate, the purchased gas adjustment charge, and all taxes except sales taxes not covered by the utility for the tax imposing authority. The state of Nebraska does not regulate natural gas rates.

57 RHODE ISLAND DEPARTMENT OF TRANSPORTATION

Rhode Island Department of Transportation, Division of Motor Vehicles, Office of the Deputy Director, Providence, RI 02903.

Date: 1993

58 SACRAMENTO RELOCATION GUIDE

Sacramento Relocation Guide. For additional information contact: Sacramento Metropolitan Chamber of Commerce, 917 Seventh Street, P.O. Box 1017, Sacramento, CA 95812-1017 (916) 552-6800.

Date: 1992

59 ST. LOUIS BUSINESS JOURNAL

St. Louis Business Journal. For additional information contact: American City Business Journals, 612 N. Second Street, P.O. Box 647, St. Louis, MO 63188 (314) 421-6200. *Note:* Based on nursing homes with a minimum of 150 beds. Average is based on prices in 20 institutions.

Date: June 22, 1992 - July 5, 1992

Page reference: 20

60 SALES & MARKETING MANAGEMENT

Sales & Marketing Management. Copyright, Sales & Marketing Management. Reprinted by permission. For additional information contact: Sales & Marketing Management, 633 Third Ave., New York, NY 10017 (212) 592-6200. *Notes:* Operating costs include fuel, oil, tires, and maintenance. Fixed costs includes financing, insurance, depreciation, taxes, and licensing fees. Figures are based on expenses for a 1991 model mid-sized 4-door automobile equipped with automatic transmission, power steering, power disc brakes, tinted glass, AM-FM stereo, cruise control, and air conditioning with an assumed retention cycle of 4 years and 60,000 miles.

Date: June 17, 1991

Page reference: 16, 96, 98

61 SECRETARY OF STATE, MAINE

Secretary of State, Bureau of Motor Vehicles, Augusta, ME 04333.

Date: 1993

62 SOURCE BOOK OF HEALTH INSURANCE DATA 1991

Source Book of Health Insurance Data 1991. Copyright, Health Insurance Association of America (HIAA). Reprinted by permission. For a catalog of HIAA publications, contact: HIAA Fulfillment, P.O. Box 41455, Washington, DC 20018 (202) 223-7808. *Note:* Physicians' fees include prenatal charges and delivery fees.

Date: 1992

Page reference: 55, 72, 74

63 STATE AVERAGE EXPENDITURES AND PREMIUMS FOR PERSONAL AUTOMOBILE IN-SURANCE

State Average Expenditures and Premiums for Personal Automobile Insurance in 1991. Copyright 1993, National Association of Insurance Commissioners (NAIC). Reprinted by permission. This material can be ordered for $25.00 plus a $5.00 freight fee from: NAIC, P.O. Box 263, Dept. 42, Kansas City, MO 64193-0042 (816) 374-7259. *Note:* Price covers liability, collision, and comprehensive insurance.

Date: January 1993

64 STATE ENERGY EXPENDITURE REPORT 1990

State Energy Expenditure Report 1990. Energy Information Administration. Office of Energy Markets and End Use. U.S. Department of Energy.

Date: September 1992

Page reference: 10-16

65 STATE GOVERNMENT NEWS

State Government News, Volume 35, No. 8. For additional information contact: The Council of State Governments, Iron Works Pike, P.O. Box 11910, Lexington, KY 40578-1910 (606) 231-1812.

Date: August 1992

Page reference: 29

66 STATE OF MINNESOTA, DEPARTMENT OF PUBLIC SAFETY

State of Minnesota, Department of Public Safety, St. Paul, MN 55155. *Note:* Passenger vehicle registration in Minnesota consists of an ad valorem tax of 1.25% of the base value of the vehicle plus $10. The minimum tax is $35.00.

Date: 1993

67 STATE OF NEW YORK, DEPARTMENT OF MOTOR VEHICLES

State of New York, Department of Motor Vehicles, Albany, NY 12228. *Note:* Registration fee varies according to vehicle weight. Vehicle weight of up to and including 1350 lbs. is $27.50; vehicle weight of 6951 lbs. and over is $149.50.

Date: 1993

68 STATE OF VERMONT, AGENCY OF TRANSPORTATION

State of Vermont, Agency of Transportation, Department of Motor Vehicles, Montpelier, VT 05602. *Note:* The vehicle registration fee for vehicles that use fuels other than gas or diesel is $73.50.

Date: 1993

69 STATE OF WEST VIRGINIA, DEPARTMENT OF TRANSPORTATION

State of West Virginia, Department of Transportation, Division of Motor Vehicles, Charleston, WV 25317. *Note:* Vehicle registration fee varies according to weight of vehicle. The fee for a vehicle weight of up to and including 3001 lbs. is $26.50; vehicle weight of 3001 lbs. up to and including 4000 lbs. is $31.50; vehicle weight of 4000 lbs. and over is $37.50. Prices include an insurance recording fee for all plates.

Date: 1993

70 STATISTICAL BULLETIN

Statistical Bulletin. Reprinted by permission of Metropolitan Life Insurance Company. For additional information contact: Metropolitan Life Insurance Company, Health and Safety, Room 16UV, One Madison Avenue, New York, NY 10010 (212) 578-2211.

Date: October 1991 - December 1991

Page reference: 31

71 SUPERMARKET BUSINESS

Supermarket Business. Copyright, Supermarket Business. Reprinted by permission. For additional information contact: Rick De Santa, Supermarket Business, 1086 Teaneck Road, Teaneck, NJ 07666 (201) 833-1900. *Note:* Price is an average for the same product sold in six different stores.

Date: April 1991

Page reference: 26

72 SUPERMARKET BUSINESS

Note: Price is an average for the same product sold in three different stores.

Date: January 1992

Page reference: 30

73 SUPERMARKET BUSINESS

Note: Price is an average for the same product sold in five different stores.

Date: May 1992

Page reference: 42

74 SUPERMARKET BUSINESS

Note: Price is an average for the same product sold in five different stores.

Date: May 1992

Page reference: 41

75 SUPERMARKET BUSINESS

Note: Price is an average for the same product sold in five different stores.

Date: June 1992

Page reference: 26

76 SUPERMARKET BUSINESS

Note: Price is an average for the same product sold in seven different stores.

Date: July 1992

Page reference: 22

77 SURVEY OF STATE TAX RATES AND COLLECTIONS

Survey of State Tax Rates and Collections. Special Report. Tax Foundation. For additional information, contact: Tax Foundation, 470 L'Enfant Plaza SW, Suite 7400, Washington, DC 20024 (202) 863-5454. *Note:* Rankings include only state-level taxes. In Washington and other states, combining state with local taxes would yield significantly different results.

Date: November 1992

Page reference: 2, 7

78 TELEPHONE RATES UPDATE

Telephone Rates Update. Prepared by James L. Lande, Industry Analysis Division, Common Carrier Bureau, Federal Communications Commission, Washington, DC 20554. *Note:* Prices include surcharges and taxes.

Date: October 1991

79 TUCSON HAS IT!

Tucson Has It!. The Economic Development Department, Tucson Metropolitan Chamber of Commerce. For additional information contact: Tucson Metropolitan Chamber of Commerce, 465 W. St.

Mary's Road, P.O. Box 991, Tucson, AZ 85702 (602) 792-1212.

Date: 1993

80   U. S. NEWS & WORLD REPORT

U.S. News & World Report. For additional information contact: U.S. News & World Report, 2400 N Street NW, Washington, DC 20037 (202) 955-2000. *Note:* Price is for a family of four, and covers tickets, parking, food, and mementos.

Date: September 16, 1991

Page reference: 69

81   U. S. NEWS & WORLD REPORT

Date: October 19, 1992

Page reference: 18

82   USA TODAY

USA TODAY. For additional information contact: USA TODAY, 99 W. Hawthorne Ave., Valley Stream, NY 11580-6101 (516) 568-9191. *Note:* Price includes lodging, rental car, and food.

Date: August 10, 1992

Page reference: 1B

83   USA TODAY

Note: Taxes and tips are not included in price.

Date: October 8, 1992

Page reference: 6D

84   USA TODAY

Date: November 12, 1992

Page reference: 6D

85   USA TODAY

Date: December 10, 1992

Page reference: 6D

86   USA TODAY

Note: Price includes three meals and one night's stay in a business-class hotel.

Date: February 11, 1993

Page reference: 4D

87 USA TODAY

Date: March 31, 1993

Page reference: 1B

88 USA TODAY

Note: Figures represent the average cost of a hotel room, three full meals a day, and a mid-size rental car.

Date: April 9, 1993

Page reference: 2B

89 USA TODAY

Note: Price covers hotel, car, and food.

Date: April 28, 1993

Page reference: B-1

90 VIRGINIA DEPARTMENT OF MOTOR VEHICLES

Virginia Department of Motor Vehicles, Richmond, VA 23220. *Note:* Vehicle registration fee varies according to vehicle weight. Fee for vehicle of up to and including 4000 lbs. is $26.50; for vehicle weight of 4001 lbs. to 6500 lbs., $31.50; for vehicle weight of 6501 to 7500 lbs., $37.50.

Date: 1993

91 WALL STREET JOURNAL

The Wall Street Journal. For additional information contact: Dow Jones & Co. Inc., 200 Liberty Street, New York, NY 10281 (212) 416-2000. *Note:* Rates shown are an average of the prices charged by the four largest rental car companies.

Date: November 4, 1992

Page reference: B-1

92 WALL STREET JOURNAL

Date: December 14, 1992

Page reference: B1

93 WALL STREET JOURNAL

Date: February 9, 1993

Page reference: B6

94 WALL STREET JOURNAL

Date: February 12, 1993

Page reference: B4

SECONDARY SOURCES

The following 25 sources were cited in the original source materials used to compile *American Cost of Living Survey*. The list is provided to aid users interested in additional research.

1990 Census

84 Lumber Company

American Economics Group, Inc.

Automobile Premium Survey, California 1993

Bon Vivant School of Cooking

California Department of Insurance

Coldwell Banker Home Price Comparison Index Spring 1992

Corporate Travel/RIT

Denver Advisory Group

Families USA Foundation

A. Foster Higgins & Co. Inc.

Foster Higgins 1992 Health Care Benefits Survey

Foster Higgins Survey of 2,448 employers

The Guide to Cooking Schools (Show Guides)

International Paper Company

Joint Commission on Accreditation of Healthcare Organizations

Paul Kagan & Associates, Inc.

LaVarenne Cooking School

National Child Care Survey 1990

National Pharmaceutical Council

New School for Social Research

A Profile of Child Care Settings

Runzheimer International

Runzheimer Meal-Lodging Cost Index

Texas Transportation Institute at Texas A & M